Western Europe

THIS EDITION WRITTEN AND RESEARCHED BY

Ryan Ver Berkmoes,
Alexis Averbuck, Oliver Berry, Kerry Christiani, Mark Elliott,
Duncan Garwood, Anthony Ham, Virginia Maxwell, Craig McLachlan,
Andrea Schulte-Peevers, Regis St Louis, Nicola Williams, Neil Wilson

PLAN YOUR TRIP

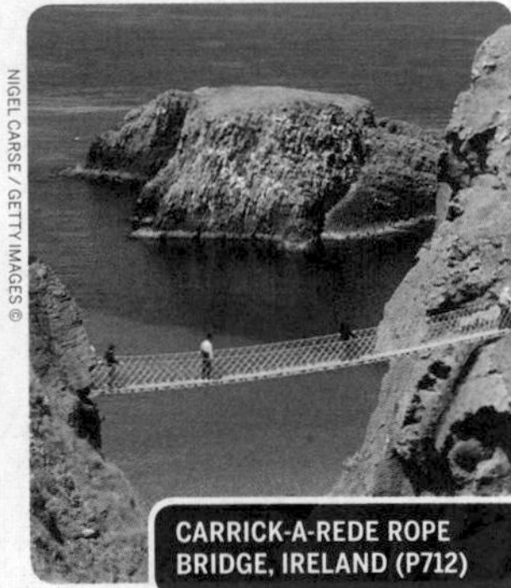

CARRICK-A-REDE ROPE BRIDGE, IRELAND (P712)

BIG BEN, BRITAIN (P167)

ON THE ROAD

Contents

ON THE ROAD

Contents

welcome to Western Europe

Perfect First Big Trip

You haven't been anywhere until you've been to Europe – and this means the countries at its core: Western Europe. There is no other place on Earth with so many different nations so close together, with so much history connecting them all – touring this patchwork quilt of tiny dots has enthralled travellers for generations.

Europe is easy; it's as simple as that. It's the perfect reason to get your passport, book your flight and go. Paris, Rome and London are just the start. You could wash up on a rocky Mediterranean beach with little more than a credit card and some cash and enjoy yourself quite nicely. Yes, it can be expensive, but probably not much more than you're used to paying at home. And home was never like this.

Perfect First Dream

Think back to your first thoughts of Europe. Was it building the Leaning Tower of Pisa out of Lego blocks? Or wondering why the best toast was called French? Or quaffing a Heineken behind the neighbour's shed? Try to remember all the impressions and thoughts you had about Europe before you ever set foot on the continent... Good luck!

For a place that's not very big, the range and breadth of Europe's impact is extraordinary. Western Europe occupies less than

Charm, fascination, pleasure, wonderment – just a few of the emotions you'll feel in Europe, the continent with the most of everything travellers want.

(left) Grand Place (p101), Brussels
(below) Market shopping in Provence (p396)

one-third the space of the US or Australia and yet has still managed to produce Plato, da Vinci and Churchill.

Nowhere else has Europe's variety of cultures, places and experiences all crammed together in such a tight space. Fast trains mean you can wake up on the Mediterranean coast, have lunch in Paris and see a show that night in London. Have a dab of this and a dab of that as it suits your mood.

Perfect Every Time

Whether this is your fifth trip to Western Europe or a first-time dream come true – or even if you live there – surprises await. Feel the chill on your spine when you see that iconic work of art. Find yourself standing right on the spot where *that* happened. Or catch yourself on a beach or on a glacier, at a cafe or in a club thinking, 'These people really know how to live'.

Sure, the continent is experiencing challenges to the monumental effort of coexistence called the EU. But compared to the events of the 20th century, the Western Europe of today couldn't be more peaceful and prosperous, with old-world manners that visitors are always charmed to discover – and which will charm you long after your trip.

So grab that passport. Go. Enjoy. Love every minute.

› Western Europe

Berlin
Find memories of the Wall (p441)
Munich
Beer halls to beer gardens (p489)
Vienna
Live a Baroque fantasy (p48)
Venice
Impossibly beautiful yet easily loved (p772)
Rome
Start with the Palatino (p730)
Tuscany
Get bathed in golden light (p787)
Santorini
Island-hoppers' delight (p614)
FINLAND
Helsinki
St Petersburg
NORWAY
Oslo
Stockholm
Tallinn
ESTONIA
Saaremaa
Moscow
SWEDEN
LATVIA
Riga
RUSSIA
Skagerrak
Gotland
Baltic Sea
Öland
DENMARK
LITHUANIA
Vilnius
BELARUS
Copenhagen
Zealand
Bornholm
RUSSIA
Kaliningrad
Minsk
Stralsund
Hamburg
Schwerin
POLAND
Odra
Elbe
Bremen
Berlin
Warsaw
GERMANY
UKRAINE
Kiev
Dnieper
Dresden
Erfurt
Frankfurt-am-Main
Prague
CZECH REPUBLIC
SLOVAKIA
CARPATHIAN MOUNTAINS
MOLDOVA
Chisinau
Stuttgart
Munich
Vienna
Bratislava
Budapest
Salzburg
Zurich
LIECHTENSTEIN
HUNGARY
Vaduz
AUSTRIA
SWITZERLAND
ALPS
SLOVENIA
Ljubljana
CROATIA
Zagreb
ROMANIA
Bucharest
Black Sea
Milan
Venice
Po
ITALY
Genoa
Bologna
San Marino
SAN MARINO
BOSNIA & HERZEGOVINA
Sarajevo
SERBIA
BULGARIA
Pisa
TUSCANY
Ligurian Sea
KOSOVO
Sofiya
MONTENEGRO
Priština
Perugia
Corsica (Fr)
Elba
Podgorica
Skopje
Istanbul
Sea of Marmara
APPENINES
MACEDONIA
Ajaccio
Rome
Adriatic Sea
Tirana
Thessaloniki
Bari
ALBANIA
Sassari
Naples
Salerno
Tyrrhenian Sea
TURKEY
Aegean Sea
Lesvos
Ioannina
Sardinia (It)
Corfu
Evia
Cagliari
Aeolian Islands
Ionian Sea
Ionian Islands
Athens
Palermo
Tripoli
Sicily
GREECE
Cyclades Islands
Syracuse
Dodecanese Islands
Tunis
Pantelleria
TUNISIA
MALTA
Valletta
Crete
60°N
55°N
45°N
20°E
15°E
10°E
30°E
25°E

26 TOP EXPERIENCES

Eiffel Tower, Paris

1 Seven million people visit the Eiffel Tower (p301) annually, but few disagree that each visit is unique. From an evening ascent amid twinkling lights to lunch in the company of a staggering city panorama, there are 101 ways to 'do' it. Pedal beneath it, skip the lift and hike up, buy a crêpe from a stand or a key ring from the street, snap yourself in front of it, visit at night or even – our favourite – experience the lucky chance to see all 324m of it glow in a different colour for a light show on a special occasion.

London

2 Can you hear that, music lovers? That's London (p159) calling – from the theatres, concert halls, nightclubs, pubs and even tube stations, where on any given night hundreds, if not thousands, of performers take to the stage. Search for your own iconic London experience, whether it's the Proms at the Royal Albert Hall (p196), an East End singalong around a pub piano, a classic musical in the West End, a superstar DJ set at Fabric or a floppy-fringed guitar band at a Hoxton boozer. BBC Proms at the Royal Albert Hall

1

LOIC LAGARDE/GETTY IMAGES ©

3

SYLVAIN SONNET / GETTY IMAGES ©

Ancient Rome

3 Rome's famous seven hills (there are really nine) offer superb vantage points. The Palatino (p731) is a gorgeous green expanse of evocative ruins, towering pines and unforgettable views over the Roman Forum. This is where Romulus supposedly founded the city, where ancient Roman emperors lived in unimaginable luxury. As you walk the gravel paths you can almost sense the ghosts in the air.

Roman Forum

Gaping at the Matterhorn

4 Sure, it graces Toblerone packages and evokes stereotypical 'Heidi' scenes, but nothing prepares you for the allure of the Matterhorn (p1065). As soon as you step into the timber-chalet-filled village of Zermatt in the Swiss Alps, this loner looms above you, mesmerising you with its chiselled, majestic peak. Gaze at it from a tranquil sidewalk cafe, hike in its shadow along the tangle of alpine paths above town with cowbells clinking in the distance, or pause on a ski slope and admire its magnetic stance.

Venice

5 There's something magical about Venice (p772) on a sunny winter's day. With far fewer tourists around and the light sharp and clear, it's the perfect time to lap up the city's unique and magical atmosphere. Ditch your map and wander Dorsoduro's shadowy backlines while imagining secret assignations and whispered conspiracies at every turn. Then visit two of Venice's top galleries, the Gallerie dell'Accademia and the Collezione Peggy Guggenheim (p774), the latter of which houses works by many of the giants of 20th-century art.

4

RICHARD ELLIOTT / GETTY IMAGES ©

5

BLEND IMAGES/PBNJ PRODUCTIONS / GETTY IMAGES ©

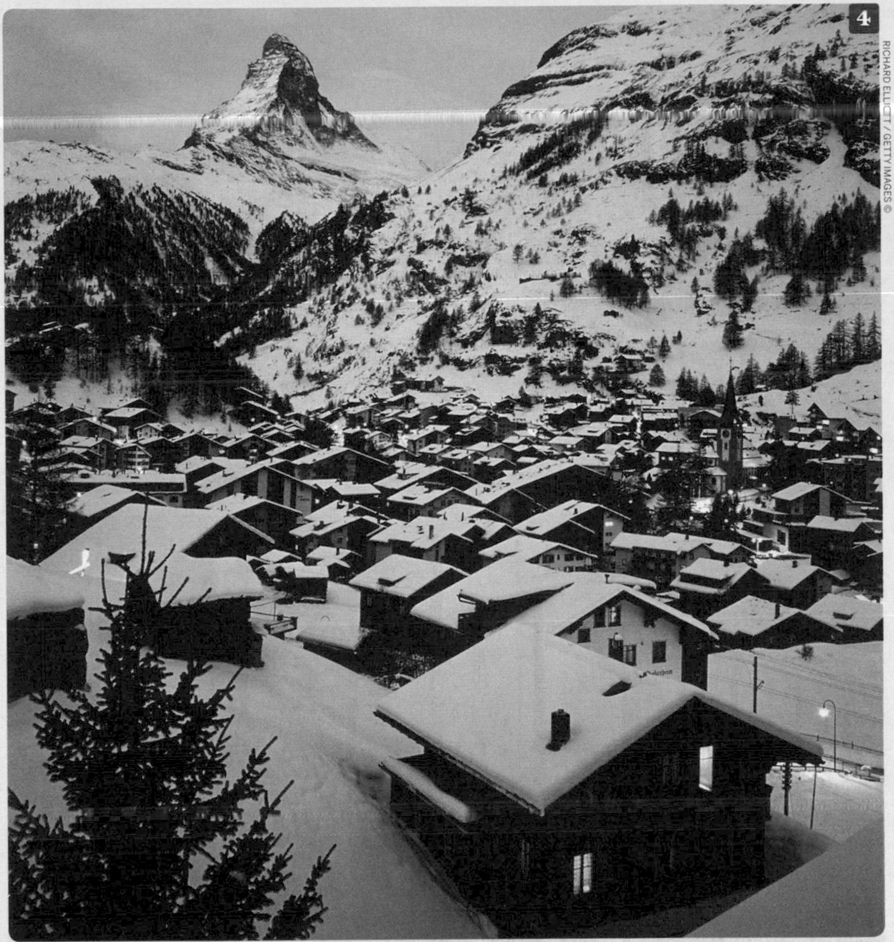

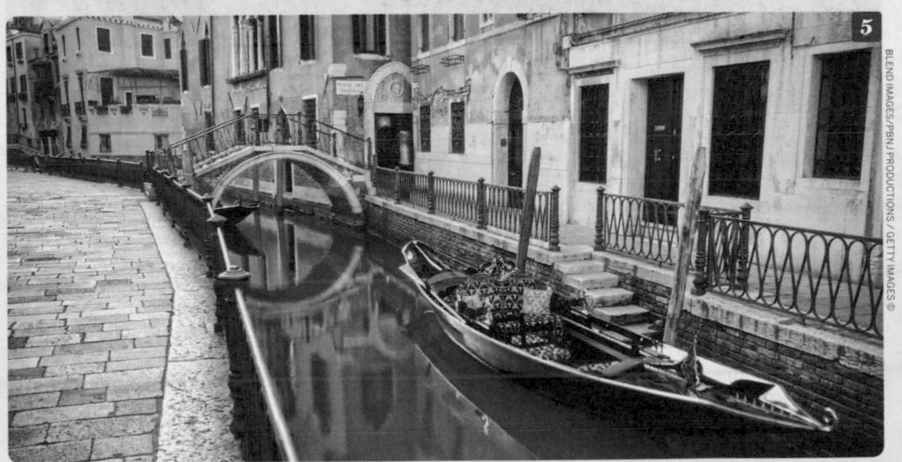

ROBERT HARDING / GETTY IMAGES ©

JEFF HUNTER / GETTY IMAGES ©

Tuscany

6 Don't dismiss a travel cliché out of hand without investigating fully; for example, the gently rolling hills of Tuscany (p787), bathed in golden light and dotted with ancient vineyards. Battalions of books, postcards and lifestyle TV shows try to do this magical region justice, but nothing really succeeds like a visit. Here, picture-perfect towns full of Renaissance treasures vie with magnificent scenery and Italy's best food and wine. Once you've had a taste of Tuscany, every cliché will ring absolutely true.

Remembering the Wall, Berlin

7 Even after 20 years, the sheer magnitude and disbelief that the Berlin Wall really cut through this city doesn't sink in. But the best way to examine its role in Berlin is to make your way – on foot or by bike – along the Berlin Wall Trail. Passing the Brandenburg Gate (p445), analysing graffiti at the East Side Gallery (p452) or visiting Checkpoint Charlie (p446): the path brings it all into context. It's heartbreaking and hopeful and sombre, but integral to trying to understand Germany's capital.

8
GARETH MCCORMACK / GETTY IMAGES ©

9
JON BOYES / GETTY IMAGES ©

Coastal Exploring, Northern Ireland

8 Hiking the Causeway Coast (p712) between Ballycastle and Bushmills will take you through some of Northern Ireland's most inspiring and impressive coastal scenery. Its geological centrepiece is the Giant's Causeway, a strange and beautiful natural wonder that has been pulling in international visitors for a couple of centuries. But there's also the nerve-testing challenge of the spectacular Carrick-a-Rede rope bridge – and, waiting at journey's end, a well-deserved dram at Bushmills' whiskey distillery. Giant's Causeway

Slow-boating the Rhine

9 It sounds staid: sitting on a boat bobbing along looking at the sights. Well, we dare anyone to take a cruise on the Rhine from Koblenz to Mainz (p526) and not be utterly ready to do it again. Sitting on deck, you'll see the busy river is framed by vineyard-clad hills on either side, studded with castle ruins. (Who doesn't like a castle?) And in between are cute little towns with half-timbered buildings; don't be fooled by fakes elsewhere – these are the real thing. Boppard, Rhine Valley

Beer drinking in Munich

10 It's not so much the idea that you can drink beer in Munich (p489) – everybody knows you can – it's the variety of places where you can drink that astounds and makes this a must-stop. There's Oktoberfest, of course, and then there are the famous beer halls, from the huge and infamous (Hofbräuhaus) to the huge and merely wonderful (Augustiner Bräustuben). And why stay inside for your frothy, refreshing litre of lager? You can drink it in a park (Chinesischer Turm) or in the city centre (Viktualienmarkt) – or really just about anywhere. Oktoberfest beer hall

Alhambra, Granada

11 The Alhambra (p1022), one of the world's most refined examples of Islamic art, is the most enduring symbol of the 800 years of Moorish rule in Al-Andalus. The Alhambra's red fortress towers dominate the Granada skyline against the Sierra Nevada's snow-capped peaks, while its perfectly proportioned Generalife gardens complement the exquisite detail of the Palacio Nazariés. Put simply, this is Spain's most beautiful monument.

EURASIA / GETTY IMAGES ©

IMAGNO / GETTY IMAGES ©

KRZYSZTOF DYDYNSKI / GETTY IMAGES ©

Champagne

12 Name-brand Champagne houses such as Mumm, Mercier and Moët & Chandon, in the main towns of Reims (p350) and Épernay (p352), are known the world over. Our secret tip? Much of Champagne's best liquid gold is made by thousands of small-scale vignerons (wine makers) in hundreds of villages. Dozens welcome visitors for a taste, tipple and shop at producers' prices, rendering the region's scenic driving routes the best way to taste fine bubbly amid rolling vineyards and drop-dead-gorgeous villages. Vineyards near Reims

Imperial Vienna

13 Imagine what you could do with unlimited riches and Austria's top architects at your disposal and you have the Vienna of the Habsburgs. The monumentally graceful Hofburg (p48) whisks you back to the age of empires as you marvel at the treasury's imperial crowns, the equine ballet of the Spanish Riding School and the chandelier-lit apartments fit for an empress. The palace is rivalled in grandeur only by the 1441-room Schloss Schönbrunn (p49), a Unesco World Heritage site, and the baroque Schloss Belvedere (p53), both set in exquisite landscaped gardens. Schloss Belvedere

Beer & Chocolate, Belgium

14 Belgium has a brew for all seasons, and then some. From tangy lambics to full-flavoured Trappists, the range of beer styles is quite exceptional and each is served in its own special glass. Best of all, you can sip a selection in timeless cafes, hidden away in the atmospheric cores of Belgium's great 'art cities' – Ghent, Bruges, Antwerp and Brussels – with their appealing mixtures of medieval and art-nouveau architecture. For nondrinkers, there's an unparalleled range of chocolate shops selling melt-in-the-mouth pralines incorporating ever-more-intriguing flavour combinations.

The Netherlands by Bike

15 The Netherlands (p849) equals nirvana for bike riders. The nation where everyone rides bikes to commute, to visit friends, to shop or just to have fun is perfectly designed for cyclists. Consider: it's flat (mostly); you can glide alongside canals while spotting windmills; there are over 20,000km of dedicated bike paths; and except for motorways there's virtually nowhere bicycles can't go. Whether you spend an entire trip cycling Holland or even just the occasional jaunt, it'll be a highlight of your trip.

Bath

16 Britain can boast many great cities, but Bath (p210) stands out as the belle of the ball. The Romans built a health resort to take advantage of the hot water bubbling to the surface here. These springs were rediscovered in the 18th century and Bath became the place to see and be seen in British high society. Today, the stunning Georgian architecture of grand townhouses, sweeping crescents and Palladian mansions (not to mention Roman remains, a beautiful cathedral and a 21st-century spa) means Bath demands your undivided attention. Roman Baths

15

FRANS LEMMENS / GETTY IMAGES ©

16

ED PRITCHARD / GETTY IMAGES ©

17

DAVID JOYNER / GETTY IMAGES ©

18

HANS GEORG EIBEN / GETTY IMAGES ©

Navigating Amsterdam's Canals

17 To say Amsterdammers love the water is an understatement. Sure, the city (p852) made its first fortune in maritime trade, but that's ancient history. You can stroll next to the canals and check out some of the city's 3300 houseboats. Or, better still, go for a ride. From boat level you'll get to see a whole new set of architectural details, like the ornamentation bedecking the bridges. And when you pass the canalside cafe terraces, you can just look up and wave.

Luxembourg's Capital Castles

18 Beyond the banks that help make Luxembourg Europe's wealthiest country, the little Grand Duchy is an unexpectedly attractive rural patchwork of undulating fields, wooded hills and deep-cut river valleys. The extraordinary fortifications of Luxembourg City (p140), the fascinating Unesco-listed capital, still astound. And many of the nation's neat little country villages retain highly impressive castle ruins. None are more dramatic than those at Bourscheid or Vianden. Larochette village

19
RAINER MARTINI / GETTY IMAGES ©

20
LONELY PLANET / GETTY IMAGES ©

21
LONELY PLANET / GETTY IMAGES ©

Alfama, Lisbon

19 The Alfama (p892), with its labyrinthine alleyways, hidden courtyards and curving, shadow-filled lanes, is a magical place to lose all sense of direction and delve into the soul of the city. On the journey, you'll pass breadbox-sized grocers, brilliantly tiled buildings and cosy taverns filled with easy-going chatter, with the scent of chargrilled sardines and the mournful rhythms of fado drifting in the breeze. Then you round a bend and catch sight of steeply pitched rooftops leading down to the glittering Rio Tejo and you know you're hooked...

Ancient Landmarks, Greece

20 From Athens' renowned Acropolis to the monastery-crowned rock spires of Meteora, Greece (p569) offers some of Europe's most impressive historical sights, such as the oracular Temple of Apollo, in Delphi; Olympia, home to the first Olympic Games; Epidavros' acoustically perfect theatre; and the mystical Sanctuary of Asclepius, an ancient healing centre. Olive and orange groves surround the vast ruins of Mystras, a one-time part of the Byzantine Empire. Start with the Acropolis and follow the path of history over Greece's landscape. Acropolis, Athens

Dublin

21 Ireland's capital city (p662) boasts all the attractions and distractions of a major international metropolis, but manages to retain the friendliness, intimacy and atmosphere of a small town. Whether wandering the leafy Georgian terraces of St Stephen's Green or getting up close and personal with the past at Kilmainham Gaol, you're never far from a friendly pub where the beer is grand and the craic is flowing. And, of course, there's the chance to sink a pint of the black stuff at that fountainhead of froth, the original Guinness brewery. Traditional music at an Irish pub

Skiing in Chamonix

22 Sure, 007 did it, but so can you: the Vallée Blanche is a once-in-a-lifetime experience. You won't regret the €70-odd it costs to do the 20km off-piste descent from the spike of the Aiguille du Midi (p375) to mountaineering mecca Chamonix (p374) – every minute of the five hours it takes to get down will pump more adrenalin in your body than anything you've ever done.

Baroque Salzburg

23 A fortress on a hill, 17th-century cobbled streets, Mozart, and the ultimate singalong: if Salzburg (p69) didn't exist, someone would have to invent it just to keep all the acolytes who visit each year happy. It's hard to say what's more popular, but you just have to see all the DVDs for sale to know that this is *Sound of Music* country, and faster than you can say 'Do-Re-Mi' you can be whisked into the gorgeous steep hills that are alive with tour groups year-round. Salzburg Cathedral

22

JULIAN LOVE/ GETTY IMAGES ©

23

DAVE LONG / GETTY IMAGES ©

Santorini

24 On first view, startling Santorini (p614) grabs your attention and doesn't let go. The submerged caldera, surrounded by lava-layered cliffs topped by villages that look like a sprinkling of icing sugar, is one of nature's great wonders, best experienced by a walk along the clifftops from the main town of Fira to the northern village of Oia. The precariousness and impermanence of the place is breathtaking. Recover from your efforts with an ice-cold Mythos beer in Oia as you wait for its famed picture-perfect sunset. Sunset over Oia

Edinburgh

25 Edinburgh (p263) is a city of many moods, famous for its amazing range of festivals and especially lively in the summer. The Scottish capital is also well worth visiting out of season, for sights like the castle silhouetted against the blue spring sky with a yellow haze of daffodils decorating the slopes below; or for the fog snagging the spires of the Old Town, with rain on the cobblestones and a warm glow beckoning from the window of a pub on a chilly December day. Artists at the Edinburgh Festival

CHRIS HEPBURN / GETTY IMAGES ©

25

BRIAN FAIRBROTHER / GETTY IMAGES ©

JOSE FUSTE RAGA / GETTY IMAGES ©

Barcelona's La Sagrada Família

26 One of Spain's top sights, the Modernista brainchild of Antoni Gaudí remains a work in progress more than 80 years after the architect's death. Fanciful and profound, inspired by nature and barely restrained by a Gothic style, Barcelona's quirky La Sagrada Família (p976) soars skyward with an almost playful majesty. The improbable angles and departures from architectural convention will have you shaking your head in disbelief, but the detail of the decorative flourishes on the Passion and Nativity facades are worth studying for hours.

need to know

Buses

» There are some long-distance buses; most useful for day trips to small places outside cities.

Trains

» Trains go almost everywhere; often fast and usually frequent.

When to Go

High Season

(Jun–Aug)

» Everybody comes to Europe and all of Europe hits the road.

» With all and sundry needing a bed, prices peak.

» Beautiful weather means that everybody is outside in cafes.

Shoulder

(Apr–May & Sep–Oct)

» Moderate weather means days can be bright and clear.

» Europe is popular but not overrun and prices are moderate: Europeans are sleeping at home.

» Almost everything is open.

Low Season

(Nov–Mar)

» Outside of ski resorts and Christmas markets, most regions are quiet; much is closed.

» Prices reflect hope more than greed.

» Secret time to enjoy major cities where the pleasures indoors don't close.

Your Daily Budget

Budget less than

€70

» Dorm beds: €20–€35

» Excellent markets and local quick eats hold costs down

» Look for museum free days, walk and absorb city culture

Midrange

€70–€220

» Double room in a nice midrange hotel: €80–€160

» Stay at small hotels for a special experience

» Lunch at top restaurants can be great value

Top End over

€220

» Stays at iconic hotels: €200 and up

» Look for tastings menus at hot restaurants

» Enjoy the duty-free refund from an afternoon's stylish shopping

Driving

» Car hire readily available throughout Europe.

Ferries

» Relax at sea between Ireland and Britain, Britain and the Continent, Italy and Greece.

Bicycles

» From the two-wheel heaven of the Netherlands to the mountainous thrills of Italy, Western Europe is pure cycling joy.

Planes

» Cheap airfares take you from one end of the continent to the other.

Websites

» **Lonely Planet** (www.lonelyplanet.com/europe) Destination information, hotel bookings, traveller forums and more.

» **The Man in Seat 61** (www.seat61.com) All about getting around Europe by train.

» **Michelin** (www.viamichelin.com) Calculates the best route from A to B by car.

» **BBC News** (www.bbc.co.uk/news) Find out what's happening before you arrive.

» **Tourist Office Directory** (www.towd.com) Links to tourist offices everywhere.

Money

Credit cards are widely accepted, with a few exceptions. See individual country chapters for more information on money and current exchange rates.

» **Euro (€)** Andorra, Austria, Belgium, France, Germany, Greece, Ireland, Italy, Liechtenstein, Luxembourg, The Netherlands, Portugal, Spain

» **Pound (£)** Britain

» **Swiss franc (Sfr)** Switzerland

Visas

Generally not required for stays of up to 90 days for citizens of most Western countries (Australia, Canada, Japan, New Zealand, USA etc). The Schengen Agreement (no passport controls at borders between member countries) applies to some areas, with the UK being a notable exception. Other nationals (eg China and India) will need a Schengen visa, which is good for a maximum stay of 90 days in a six-month period.

Arriving in Europe

» **Schiphol Airport, Amsterdam**
Trains to the centre (20min).

» **Heathrow Airport, London**
Trains (15min) and Tube (1hr) to the centre.

» **Aéroport Roissy Charles de Gaulle, Paris**
Buses (1hr) and trains (30min) to the centre.

» **Frankfurt Airport**
Trains (15min) to the centre.

» **Leonardo da Vinci Airport, Rome**
Buses (1hr) and trains (30min) to the centre.

What to Take

» **Sandals or thongs (flip-flops)** for that rocky yet alluring Mediterranean beach

» **Raincoat, waterproof jacket or umbrella** for the weather that keeps Europe green

» **A good pair of earplugs** for sleeping in the heart of boisterous culture

» **Menu phrasebook** so you don't just order boring stuff or get an offal surprise

» **Map** so you can show new friends where you come from

» **Extra duffel bag** for the booty from your Paris shopping spree

» **Sunglasses** to protect your eyes and to look so, so cool while lounging at a sidewalk cafe

» **Bottle-opener** for when the perfect bottle of wine calls your name

» **Data plan** so you can roam with your smartphone and use all the great apps

» **Smart set of clothes** for blowing the budget

if you like...

Castles & Palaces

First there were castles, the A-bombs of their day, designed to frustrate enemies and make their owners impervious. Later there were armies, and royalty could define flamboyance through vast palaces and grounds that continue to astound.

Versailles The palace against which all others are measured, from the Hall of Mirrors to Marie Antoinette's refuge (p333)

Neuschwanstein So what if it's not even 200 years old? In the heart of the Bavarian Alps, this is everybody's (including Disney's) castle fantasy (p504)

Conwy Castle What a serious castle should look like, right down to the eight defensive towers. No frippery here, just grim walls, a whiff of boiling oil and the echo of a catapult (p262)

Vienna's palaces At imperial spectacles like the Hofburg, you can see the royal excess that impoverished a continent and fuelled revolutions (p48)

Beer & Wine

Europe packs a large variety of beer and wine into a small space: every region seems to have at least one liquid creation it's known for.

Belgian beer As varied and diverse as it gets, with over 400 breweries and zillions of beers; some brewed by monks, others flavoured with fruit, all worth trying (p151)

Burgundy The centre of Burgundy might as well be the centre of the wine universe – at least the red one (p367)

English ales Not warm, just not ice cold, which means that the flavours – from fruity to bitter – come through. Best enjoyed in a country pub (p291)

Tuscany's best chianti You can almost taste the warm burnt-umber colours of the iconic Italian region in every glass. Don't skimp: go for the Classico (p787)

German riesling No longer the plonk of old, this classic white wine is now renowned for its quality (p562)

Historic Places

When you were 13 you learned more about Western European history than you hoped to know, but now that you're on the ultimate field trip, you'll want to see more history than you'll have time to find.

Pompeii Rome's elite literally frozen in time. Wander the streets and alleys of this great ancient city, buried by a volcanic eruption two millennia ago (p816)

Athens Acropolis, Ancient Agora, Roman Agora, Temple of Olympian Zeus, Hadrian's Arch... The list of historic plums just goes on and on (p571)

Bruges Beautiful Renaissance town in Belgium with gables, canals, bell towers and an overall harmony that's still beguiling (p128)

Dachau The first WWII concentration camp is close to Munich, and a harrowing introduction to one of the 20th century's worst horrors (p500)

DE AGOSTINI / GETTY IMAGES ©

» Ruins of Pompeii (p816)

Cultural Cuisine

Europeans love their food and you'll love it too, in all its tasty variations. Saving room for dessert is mandatory, despite all the temptations day in and day out.

Spanish tapas Little plates of treats of every description; savoury Iberian ham or a perfect stuffed olive or a little deep-fried... (p952)

British fish and chips Cod battered, fried and served with a scoop of fresh chips may seem humdrum, but in the right hands – and with the right vinegar – the results are sublime (p291)

German Würste The long and the short of it is simple: sausages are delicious and Germany has hundreds of varieties – often the source of great local pride (p440)

Belgian chocolate The only thing that might melt quicker is your heart when you ponder a box of these extravagant confections: a dose of perfection in your mouth (p152)

Cafes & Bars

Whether it's a coffee savoured for an hour or a drink with a roomful of new friends, you'll find plenty of places for liquid joy.

Vienna's coffee houses Unchanged in decades and redolent with the air of refinement; pause for a cup served just so (p59)

Irish pubs Guinness would have you believe otherwise, but their iconic stout tastes best at home when served in the most gregarious places on the planet (p670)

Parisian cafes What's more clichéd? The practised curtness of the waiter or the studied boredom of the customer? Probably both, and we wouldn't miss the show for anything (p320)

Dutch brown cafes So called for the stains on the walls from legions of smokers, they should just be called cosy, for the warm and friendly atmosphere (p884)

Brussels bars You'll find excellent ones hidden in alleys around the Bourse (p112)

Beaches

They rim the Mediterranean: lovely strands of blindingly white sand moistened by lapping waves of azure. You can find solitude or join an entire community, and seldom will you need much fabric or coin for what you wear.

St-Tropez The name means beach, and at the Plage de Pampelonne the beautiful people are really the extra-beautiful people (p415)

Lefkada Cliffs drop to broad swaths of white sand and turquoise waters on the west coast of this untrammelled Greek island (p642)

Karpathos Apella and Ammoöpi beaches on this snug island avoid cliché and deliver the goods in a package that includes white sand backed by tidy ancient villages (p628)

Menorca Beaches, so beautiful you'll think they may merely be dreams, are tucked away in little coves like pearls in oysters. In fact, dig a little and you may find an archaeological treasure (p1012)

If you like... fabulous free food
From Madrid to the Basque country, Spanish bars are renowned for *tapas*, the complimentary treats served in the early evening (p952)

If you like... Roman ruins
The Forum in Rome is the ultimate seven hills of fantasy (p731)

If you like... gardens
The magnificent Alhambra will spoil you for any other garden you'll ever see (p1022)

Outdoor Fun

Don't just stare at the beautiful scenery, dive right into it. Legendary places across the continent come alive when you get active and take that hill or surmount that wave. There's something to do no matter the season.

An English stroll The entire countryside seems to have been made for beautiful, memorable walking (p293)

Biking the Loire Valley There's a gorgeous chateau around every bend in the river in this beautiful valley (p358)

Ski year-round Experience Olympic-sized skiing in Innsbruck, the Austrian alpine city ringed by famous pistes. Head to the glaciers in August for downhill action (p80)

Big blow The wind is always howling in Tarifa, which windsurfers have proclaimed to be the best spot on the Mediterranean (p1031)

Hiking the Alps Hundreds of kilometres of trails web Switzerland's Jungfrau region, where the views always astound (p1075)

Great Dining

Europe is where the sly concept of 'slow food' was invented: we love to eat well, so why rush it? And eat well you can!

Paris dining The city and culture that taught the rest of the world about refined food (p320)

Pizza in Naples The peasant dish that ate the world – or vice versa – is most vibrant in the city of its birth (p808)

San Sebastián Spain's Basque powerhouse boasts more Michelin stars per capita than anywhere else in the world (p992)

Provence glory It has been known to cause people to swoon: the market at Carpentras bursts with hundreds of stalls laden with the produce of Provence, the province of food (p407)

Nightlife

The best clubs in the world, the stars on stage and moody haunts of night owls are all part of the scene after dark.

Berlin More cutting-edge clubs than seems possible, where DJs experiment with the sounds of tomorrow (p441)

London The stages of London have been graced by some famous types through the years; remember that Shakespeare guy? On any given night – or afternoon – there are dozens of theatre productions, from crowd-pleasing musicals to edgy drama (p159)

Rotterdam Holland's second city doesn't play second fiddle (or synthesiser) after midnight, when its massive clubs draw the best tune talent of Europe (p871)

Paris The City of Light is just that after dark, when romantic strolls amid the lit-up splendour can end in jazz clubs, idiosyncratic cafes, cabarets and much more (p301)

Madrid Night-time energy never abates in a city where life is lived on the streets 24/7 (p937)

SYLVAIN GRANDADAM / GETTY IMAGES ©

» Opera in Vienna (p48)

Art

From Greek statues to works that defy description or even understanding, Europe's art is ever-evolving. Great art museums – and artfully great cities – are reason enough for a trip.

Louvre It's not really France's museum, it's the world's; treasures from everywhere in exhaustive quantity (p312)

Tate Modern London's modern art museum barely fits into a huge old power station on the banks of the Thames; its works always stir imaginations and controversy (p174)

Florence It starts with the Duomo, continues through the Uffizi Gallery and crosses the Ponte Vecchio – the entire Renaissance embodied in one city (p789)

Rijksmuseum After years of renovations, one of Europe's great museums has reopened in Amsterdam. The assorted old masters have never looked so grand (p855)

Madrid The golden mile – the Prado, Reina Sofía and Thyssen galleries – could just be Europe's richest concentration of art (p937)

Music

Classical music of royalty, soulful songs of the masses, pop culture that changed the world: just some of the ways the European love of music will swirl through your senses.

Vienna's state opera The Staatsoper is the premier venue in a city synonymous with opera and classical music. Wait! Is that Mozart I hear? (p59)

The Beatles They sprang – and sang – from Liverpool and now the city does them proud at the Beatles Story (p253)

Irish music The Irish love their music and it takes little – sometimes just the pull of a pint – to get them singing. The west coast hums with music pubs, especially in Galway (p697)

Fado Portuguese love the melancholy, nostalgic songs of fado. Hear it in Lisbon's Alfama district (p892)

Berlin Myriad clubs in venues big and small throb to the ever-inventive cuts of the world's best DJs (p461)

Scenic Journeys

There are beautiful journeys aplenty in Europe, from the Highlands of Scotland to the high lands of the Swiss Alps.

Cinque Terre Five picture-perfect seaside villages are linked by a trail along beaches, hillside vineyards and olive groves; much-restored after huge floods (p762)

Rugged Scotland The route between Inverness and remote Kyle of Lochalsh is one of Britain's great scenic train journeys (p282)

Rhine by rail The slow train between Mainz and Koblenz has stunning views and lets you hopscotch through every quaint little half-timbered village (p526)

Bernina Express Two of Switzerland's most fabled resorts, Lugano and St Moritz, are linked by a journey that includes the spectacular Unesco–recognised rail line south of St Moritz (p1091)

month by month

Top Events

1 **Christmas Markets** December

2 **Oktoberfest** September

3 **Carnevale** February

4 **Edinburgh International Festival** August

5 **Notting Hill Carnival** August

January

A Hot Cold New Year

An enormous, raucous Edinburgh street party (Hogmanay) sees in the New Year in Scotland. It's replicated Europe-wide as main squares resonate with champagne corks and fireworks.

February

Carnival in all its manic glory sweeps through the Catholic regions of Continental Europe. Cold temperatures – even in Venice – are forgotten amid masquerades, street festivals and general bacchanalia. Expect to be kissed by a stranger.

Carnaval

Pre-Lent is celebrated with greater vigour in Maastricht than anywhere else in Northern Europe. While the rest of the Netherlands hopes the canals will freeze for ice-skating, this Dutch corner cuts loose with a celebration that would have done its former Roman residents proud.

Carnevale

In the period before Ash Wednesday, Venice goes mad for masks. Costume balls, many with traditions centuries old, enliven the social calendar in this storied old city like no other event. Even those without a coveted invite are swept up in the pageantry.

Karneval/ Fasching

Germany doesn't leave the pre-Lent season solely to its neighbours. Karneval is celebrated with abandon in the traditional Catholic regions of the country including Bavaria, along the Rhine and deep in the Black Forest. It's the wild bookend to Oktoberfest in Munich.

March

Let's hear it for the crocus, the tiny bulb whose purple flower breaks through the ice-crusted soil to let Europe know that there's a thaw in the air and spring will soon come.

St Patrick's Day

Parades and celebrations are held on March 17 in Irish towns big and small to honour their beloved St Patrick. While elsewhere the day is a commercialised romp of green beer, in his home country it's a time to celebrate with friends and family.

April

Spring arrives with a burst of colour, from the glorious bulb fields of the Netherlands to the blooming orchards of Spain. On the southernmost beaches it's time to shake the sand out of the umbrellas.

Semana Santa

Procession of penitents and holy icons in Spain, notably in Seville, during Easter week. Throughout the week thousands of members of religious brotherhoods parade in traditional garb. Look for the pointed *capirotes* (hoods).

Settimana Santa

Italy celebrates Holy Week with processions and passion plays. By Holy Thursday, Rome is thronged with the faithful and even non-believers are swept up in the emotion and piety of hundreds of thousands of faithful flocking to the Vatican and St Peter's Basilica.

Greek Easter

The most important festival in the Greek Orthodox calendar. The emphasis is on the Resurrection so it's a celebratory event – the most significant part is midnight on Easter Saturday when fireworks explode. The night before, candlelit processions hit the streets.

Feria de Abril

Hoods off! A week-long party held in Seville, Spain in late April to counterbalance the religious peak of Easter. The many beautiful old squares of this gorgeous city come alive during the long, warm nights the nation is known for.

Koninginnedag (Queen's Day)

Nationwide celebration in the Netherlands on 30 April, but especially in Amsterdam, which becomes awash with orange costumes and fake afros, beer, balloon animals, beer, dope, Red Bull, beer, leather boys, skater grrrls, temporary roller coasters, clogs, beer, fashion victims, grannies…

May

Expect nice weather anywhere but especially in the south where the Mediterranean summer is already full steam ahead. Yachts prowl the harbours while beautiful people ply the sands.

Cannes Film Festival

The famous, not-so-famous and the merely topless converge for a year's worth of movies in little more than one week in Cannes. Join the sun-drenched crowds strolling the strand and soaking up the glitz.

Brussels Jazz Marathon

Around-the-clock jazz performances hit Brussels during the second-last weekend in May (www.brusselsjazzmarathon.be), encompassing everything from zydeco to boogie-blues. Performances are everywhere from open stages in city squares to tight-packed cafes and pubs.

Queima das Fitas

Coimbra's annual highlight is this boozy week of fado music and revelry that begins on the first Thursday in May when students celebrate the end of the academic year. These are clearly honour students as they do it in this Portuguese town better than anywhere.

June

The huge summer travel season hasn't started yet but the sun has busted through the clouds and the weather is gorgeous, from the hot shores in the south to the cool climes of the north.

Festa de Santo António

In Portugal there's feasting, drinking and dancing in Lisbon's Alfama in honour of St Anthony (12 to 13 June). This caps off the even grander three-week-long Festas de Lisboa, which features processions and dozens of street parties.

Festa de São João

Elaborate processions, live music on Porto's plazas and merry-making all across Portugal's second city. Squeaky plastic hammers (available for sale everywhere) come out for the unusual custom of whacking one another. Everyone is fair game – expect no mercy.

Luxembourg National Day

Held on 23 June, this is the Grand Duchy's biggest event – a celebration of the birth of the Grand Duke (though it doesn't actually fall on a Grand Ducal birthday). Fireworks in Luxembourg City kick it off on the evening of 22 June.

Glastonbury Festival

The town's youthful summer vibe peaks during a long weekend of music, theatre and New Age shenanigans (www.glastonburyfestivals.co.uk); one of England's favourite outdoor events. More than 100,000 turn up to writhe in Pilton Farm's grassy fields (or deep mud).

Christopher Street Day

The annual pan-European celebration of Gay Pride happens on a summer weekend usually in late June but at times as late as August.

July

Visitors have arrived from around the world and outdoor cafes, beer gardens and beach clubs are hopping. Expect beautiful – even steamy – weather anywhere you go.

Il Palio

Siena's great annual event is the Palio (2 July and 16 August), a pageant culminating in a bareback horse race round Il Campo. The city is divided into 17 *contrade* (districts), of which 10 compete for the *palio* (silk banner) and emotions explode.

Montreux Jazz Festival

It's not just all that jazz as big-name rock acts also hit town for this famous festival held during the first two weeks of July (www.montreuxjazz.com). Glitterati from across the globe gather for a top-end celebration of top-flight music on the shores of Lake Geneva.

Sanfermines (aka 'Running of the Bulls')

Huge male bovines and people who want to be close to them invade Pamplona, Spain for the famous Sanfermines festival from 6 to 14 July, when the city is overrun with thrill-seekers, curious onlookers and, oh yeah, bulls. Its most famous event, the Encierro (Running of the Bulls), begins at 8am daily.

Bastille Day

Fireworks, balls, processions and more for France's national day, 14 July. Celebrated in every French town and city: go to the heart of town and get caught up in this patriotic festival that, of course, has wonderful food and wine.

De Gentse Feesten

Belgium's Ghent is transformed into a 10-day party of music and theatre; a highlight is a vast techno celebration called 10 Days Off (www.gentsfeesten.be). This under-appreciated gem of the low country is high on fine bars serving countless kinds of beer.

August

Everybody's going someplace as half of Europe shuts down to go and enjoy the traditional month of holiday with the other half. If it's near the beach, from Germany's Baltic to Spain's Balearic, it's mobbed.

Salzburg Festival

Austria's most renowned classical music festival, the Salzburg Festival (www.salzburgfestival.at) attracts international stars from late July to the end of August. That urbane person who looks like a famous cellist sitting by you having a glass of wine probably is.

Street Parade

In Switzerland, it's Zürich's turn to let its hair down with an enormous techno parade (www.street-parade.ch). All thoughts of numbered accounts are forgotten as bankers and everybody else in this otherwise staid burg parties to orgasmic deep-base thump, thump, thump.

Notting Hill Carnival

Held over two days in August, this is Europe's largest and London's most vibrant outdoor carnival, where the local Caribbean community shows the city how to party. Food, frolic and fun are just a part of a vast multicultural celebration.

Edinburgh International Festival

Three weeks of innovative drama, comedy, dance, music and more, held in Edinburgh (www.eif.co.uk). Two weeks overlap with the celebrated Fringe Festival (www.edfringe.com), which draws innovative acts from around the globe. Expect cutting-edge comedy, drama and productions that defy description.

September

It's cooling off in every sense, from the northern countries to the romance started on a dance floor in Ibiza. It's maybe the best time to visit: the weather's still good and the crowds have thinned.

Venice International Film Festival

The Mostra del Cinema di Venezia (www.labiennale.org) is Italy's top film festival and one of the world's top indie film fests. The judging here is seen as an early indication of what to look for at the next year's Oscars.

Oktoberfest

Germany's legendary beer-swilling party (www.oktoberfest.de) starts mid-September in Munich (don't ever tell anyone you turned up for it in October, even if you did). Millions descend for litres of beer and carousing that has no equal. If you don't plan ahead, you'll sleep in Austria.

Festes de la Mercè

Barcelona knows how to party until dawn and it outdoes itself for the Festes de la Mercè (around 24 September), the city's biggest celebration, with four days of concerts, dancing, *castellers* (human-castle builders), fireworks and *correfocs* – a parade of firework-spitting dragons and devils.

October

Although your beach fantasies may go unfulfilled, this is another good month to visit. Almost everything is still open and prices and visitor numbers are way down. Look for sales on rain coats, you'll need them.

Festival at Queen's

Belfast hosts the second-largest arts festival (www.belfastfestival.com) in the UK for three weeks in late October/early November in and around Queen's University. It's a time for the city to shed its gritty legacy and celebrate the intellectual and the creative without excessive hype.

November

Leaves have fallen and snow is about to in much of Europe. Even in the temperate zones around the Mediterranean it can get chilly, rainy and blustery. Most seasonal attractions have closed for the year.

Guy Fawkes Night

Bonfires and fireworks flare up across Britain on 5 November recalling a failed antigovernment plot from the 1600s. Go to high ground in London to see glowing explosions erupt everywhere.

December

Christmas is a good excuse for warm cheer despite the cold weather in virtually every city and town. Decorations transform even the drabbest shopping street and every region has its own traditions.

Christmas Markets

Christkindlmarkts are held across Germany and Austria. The most famous are in Nuremberg and Vienna, but every town has one. Warm your hands through your mittens holding a hot mug of mulled wine and find that special (or kitsch) present.

Natale

Italian churches set up intricate cribs or *presepi* (nativity scenes) in the lead-up to celebrating Christmas. Some are quite famous, most are works of art and many date back hundreds of years and are venerated for their spiritual ties.

itineraries

Whether you've got six days or 60, these itineraries provide a starting point for the trip of a lifetime. Want more inspiration? Head online to lonelyplanet.com/thorntree to chat with other travellers.

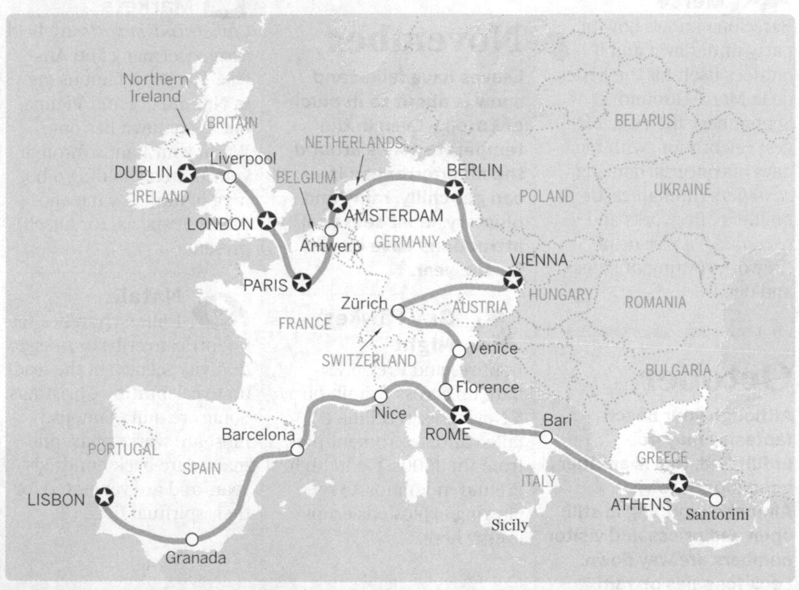

One to Two Months
Ultimate Europe

Have limited time but want to see a bit of everything? Start in **Dublin**, sampling the vibrant pubs and traditional Irish craic. From Ireland, take a ferry to **Liverpool** or fly to **London** for some great theatre. From London, catch the Eurostar train to unmissable **Paris**.

Head north from Paris to **Antwerp** for amazing beer, and then further north to **Amsterdam**, not forgetting to ride a canal boat. Go east, stopping for a cruise on the Rhine, and spend a few days exploring (and surviving) the nightlife in **Berlin**. Next, **Vienna** beckons with classical-music riches. Step west to **Zürich** and the Alps for awe-inspiring ski slopes and vistas.

Head to the canals of **Venice** and through **Florence** to historic **Rome**. Train it to **Bari** and take a ferry to **Athens**, then explore island beaches, starting with the stunning **Santorini**. Connect by air or go by ferry and train to the French Riviera, to check out quintessential Mediterranean towns such as **Nice**. Continue to **Barcelona** before heading to the Moorish towns of southern Spain, perhaps **Granada**. End your trip in laid-back **Lisbon**, enjoying local port wine to celebrate completing your grand journey!

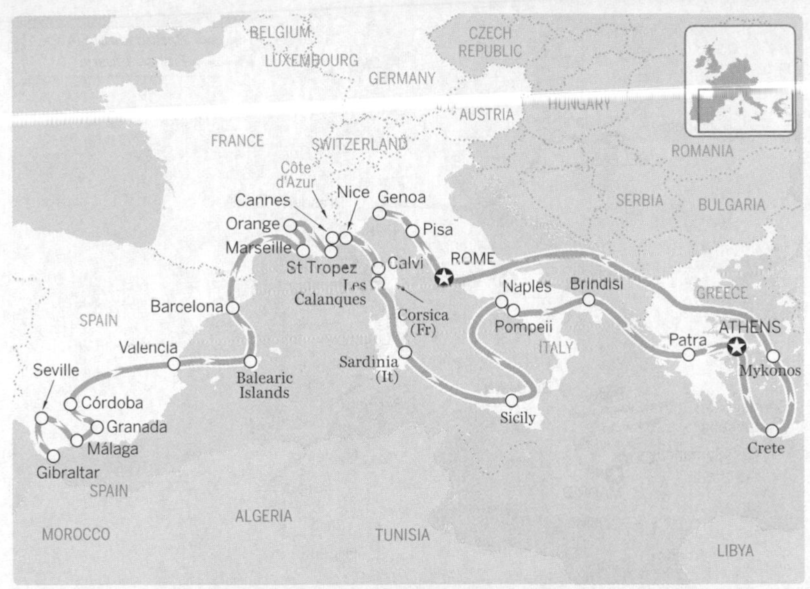

One to Two Months
Mediterranean Europe

Beautiful weather and scenery are the draw of this comprehensive tour that follows famous towns and cities from antiquity to the present.

Start in southern Spain with some British flavour in **Gibraltar**, where you can view the only wild primates in Europe. Go north to the city that defines lovely: **Seville**. Make your way up the eastern coast past the Moorish town of **Málaga** and on to the ever-beautiful **Granada** and **Córdoba**. Then it's back to the coast at **Valencia**, for a ferry hop to the parties and beaches of the **Balearic Islands**.

Back on the mainland, **Barcelona** is filled with the architecture of Gaudí. From here, head into France's Provence region, where in **Marseille** you can see the fortress that was inspiration for the novel *The Count of Monte Cristo*. Leave the sea for the hills and lavender-scented towns like **Orange**. On to the **Côte d'Azur** and its playground for the rich and famous, **St-Tropez**. A quick stop in the capital of the French Riviera, **Nice**, makes a good jumping-off point for other nearby hot spots such as **Cannes**.

Take a ferry to **Corsica** and experience the traditional lifestyle of quiet fishing villages. Hit the snowy peaks at **Calvi** and the groves of **Les Calanques** before hopping down to **Sardinia**. From here, take a long ferry ride or a quick flight to **Sicily** to visit colossal Greek temples and its famous volcano, Mt Etna.

Catch a ferry to **Naples**, on the Italian mainland, and take a trip to **Pompeii**. Move east to **Brindisi** for a ferry to Greece that passes rocky coasts seen by mariners for millennia, landing in **Patra**. Head to **Athens** to wonder at ancient treasures before getting a plane or ferry to islands such as **Crete** and **Mykonos**. Retrace your steps to Italy. Head north to **Rome**, taking time to wander amid its ruins and piazzas. Continue through Tuscany, stopping at **Pisa** to see its famous 'leaning tower'. Finish up along the Ligurian coast in the port city of **Genoa** via the coastal towns of the Cinque Terre, where you can stroll along the Via dell'Amore.

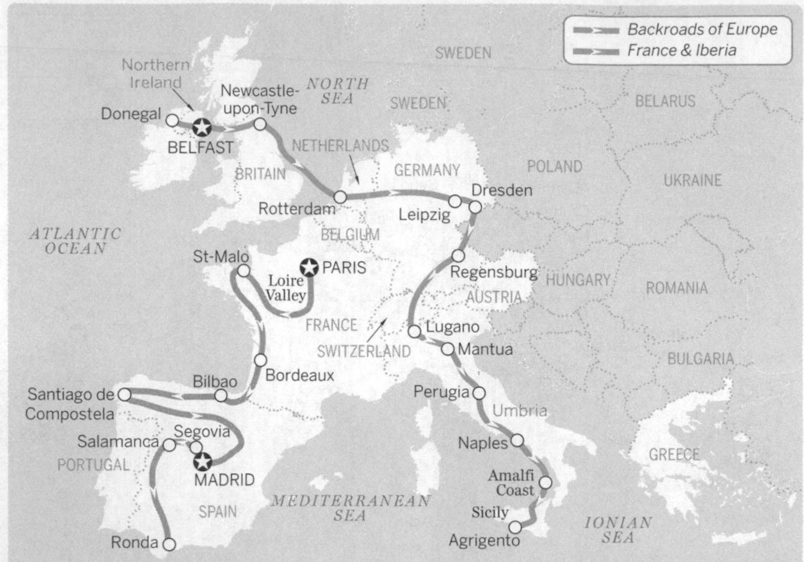

Two Weeks
France & Iberia

Get a feel for two of Europe's most distinct countries on this relatively compact jaunt. Start in **Paris**, of course. Sample the chateaux of the **Loire Valley**, then take the fast TGV train to Brittany, where the battlements of **St-Malo** always astound. Although the apple ciders of the region delight, you'll want to continue south to Burgundy, where red wine reaches its pinnacle in the region around **Bordeaux**. Head across the border to the Basque city of **Bilbao** before continuing to the pilgrimage shrine of **Santiago de Compostela**.

If you think you eat late at home, you've got nothing on **Madrid**, where an evening of tapas and drinks in tiny bars can postpone dinner until midnight. Find your favourite square and become a regular. Spend a day inside the walls of the beautiful hill town of **Segovia**. And don't let the sandstone splendour of **Salamanca** pass without a stop. Go south and plan on using a car to explore the many hill towns of Andalucía. Little winding roads traverse stark landscapes and olive orchards before reaching places like **Ronda**, where whitewashed buildings gleam in the distance. End at the coast or return to Paris.

Three Weeks
Backroads of Europe

You've already done the major capitals and ticked every must-see box. Now start seeing the rest of Europe. The far north of Ireland is rugged and uncrowded; start yourself in **Donegal**, then head to the very welcoming Northern Ireland – **Belfast** in particular. Head southeast to the gritty yet charming town of **Newcastle-upon-Tyne** in England, then catch the ferry to the Netherlands, where **Rotterdam** combines edgy modern architecture with rocking charm.

Go east to the former East German cities of **Leipzig** and **Dresden**, each of which are creating a new future from their historic pasts. Turn south via the amazing **Regensburg** to the temperate Swiss town of **Lugano**. Traverse Italy and the hidden gem of **Mantua**, followed by beautiful Umbria and towns such as **Perugia**. In the far south, take time to wander frenetic **Naples** and the ruin-filled **Amalfi Coast** before pressing on to **Sicily** and its ancient and colourful culture. Marvel at the Grecian Valley of Temples in **Agrigento**, which rival anything in Greece itself.

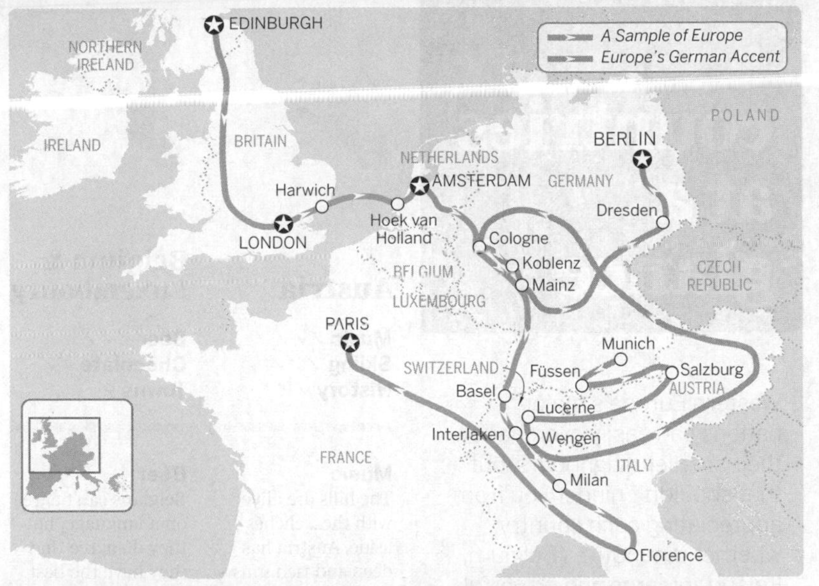

Two Weeks
A Sample of Europe

Watching Europe from the window of a train, gazing at the sea rolling past the handrail of a ferry – that's the way generations of travellers have explored the continent, and you can, too. To stick to tradition you might even grab a kiss on a misty station platform or share a hug on deck as the land slips away behind you. Start in the Scottish castle-town of **Edinburgh**, then take the train to **London** and on to **Harwich** for a ferry crossing to **Hoek van Holland**. From here, trains connect to fabled, gabled **Amsterdam**.

Take a fast train to **Cologne** and then mellow out on a river cruise down the alluring Rhine River. Alight at **Mainz** and connect by train through **Basel** to **Interlaken** for the slow-moving trains and trams that wend through glaciers of the Alps. Next take a train past rugged scenery to connect with stylish **Milan**, where a fast Italian Eurostar train zips to **Florence**, the heart of the Slow Food Movement. Reserve a sleeping compartment and snuggle up tight on the night train to **Paris**, feeling the romance in the rhythm of the rails.

Two Weeks
Europe's German Accent

Fly into **Munich**, where beer halls are a short hop away. This is a good spot to spend a couple of days – when it's clear, you can see the Alps. Head for the hills and behold the cutest castle on a hilltop you'll ever find: the wildly popular Neuschwanstein, in **Füssen**. A short jaunt east brings you to Austria's perfect combination of hills and music: **Salzburg**. Move west into Switzerland's lakeside city of **Lucerne**, where iconic half-timbered bridges cross glacier-cold waters. Start your ascent by setting up in one of the cosy chalets of **Wengen**, where an imposing wall of Alps looms before you. Now head north into Germany and catch one of the country's renowned high-speed trains to **Cologne**, with its stunning cathedral. Set aside a day for a cruise up the Rhine River from **Koblenz** to **Mainz**. Steep hillsides are covered in vineyards and crowned by castles. Get another high-speed train east to **Dresden**, which drips in history both glorious and tragic, plus nightlife that's edgy and endless. Finish in **Berlin**, the ever-surprising capital that has more stories and drama than a week's worth of TV shows.

countries at a glance

Western Europe's major nations can easily overshadow their smaller neighbours, but that shouldn't hinder you from appreciating each country, whether diminutive (Belgium, Ireland) or large and powerful (Britain, France, Germany and Spain). In the middle, you need only think about, say, the Netherlands and Switzerland to realise that size doesn't always matter. In fact, each Western European nation has a distinct and tangible culture (often more than one) and differs from its neighbours in myriad ways. And that's the real joy of a vacation to the continent: so much in such a small space.

Austria

Music ✓✓✓
Skiing ✓✓✓
History ✓✓

Music
The hills are alive with the... clichés aside, Austria has deep and rich musical traditions that extend beyond Mozart (and iconic Hollywood musicals).

Skiing
The Olympic-sized skiing pleasures of Innsbruck and the Alps draw people to the pistes from all over the world. Kitzbühel is another premier ski resort that enjoys world-class races and competitions that thrill millions of viewers worldwide.

History
Regal and elegant, Vienna is a grand capital for a grand empire that no longer exists. Enjoy its faded elegance amid beautiful boulevards. On a smaller scale but equally evocative are the baroque wonders of Salzburg.

p44

Belgium & Luxembourg

Beer ✓✓✓
Chocolate ✓✓
Towns ✓

Beer
Belgians can't agree on a language, but they do agree that they have the best beer varieties in the world. From the lightest lagers to the darkest stouts, the fruitiest framboise to the toughest Trappist, the beers are fantastic.

Chocolate
Famous names abound in the galleries of Brussels, where gilt-covered boxes are filled with delights.

Towns
Luxembourg surprises by having more than you'd think. The deep Ardennes forests hide old fortified towns like Echternach, while the namesake capital was once the toughest fortress in Europe. In Belgium few can resist Bruges.

p99

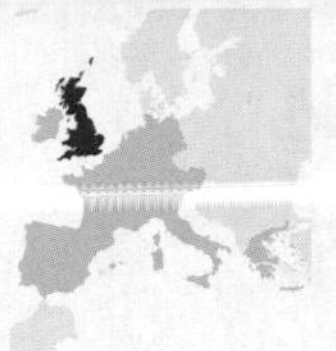

Britain

History ✓✓✓
Culture ✓✓✓
Nature ✓

History

British history reads like the history of the world, from Roman times on. The wives of Henry VIII, the Battle of Britain and the War of the Roses are just a few of the iconic events from these islands.

Culture

The UK has given English-speakers their language and much of their literature and music. Who can't think up a quote from Shakespeare on demand? Today you can continue to enjoy the best in performing arts.

Nature

Corners of Great Britain are as beautiful as anywhere. From the Lake District to the Cotswalds and a thousand points in between you'll find classic beauty.

p157

France

Cities ✓✓✓
Food ✓✓✓
Wine ✓✓✓

Cities

There's Paris and then there's Paris and that's enough reason to visit France. But consider all the other extraordinary towns and regions, such as Lyon and Provence. In fact, you can just board a French train and almost get off at random to discover a great town or city.

Food

Enjoy fabulous French food through, well, France! Another Gallic gift to the world, you can find a delicious meal in a simple cafe or in a legendary restaurant where there's a star for almost every course.

Wine

Bordeaux. Burgundy. Champagne. What more need we say about a country where the unveiling of the Beaujolais is a national day of celebration?

p299

Germany

History ✓✓✓
Beer ✓✓
Festivals ✓

History

Germany has been at the heart of critical moments in history for more than 100 years. Just walking Berlin has the full panoply on display from Hitler to WWII to the Cold War to Reunification.

Beer

Germany's purity laws are models for brewers worldwide, but that doesn't stop hops-lovers from flocking to the country for its myriad styles of beer from hundreds of breweries.

Festivals

Germany's love of festivals and beer combine at Munich's Oktoberfest. And there are hundreds of other special events around the country, including the Christmas markets that make December merry in almost every town.

p439

Greece

Monuments ✓✓✓
Islands ✓✓✓
Food ✓

Monuments

The Acropolis is the iconic symbol of an ancient civilisation that is the basis for so much of Western culture. Ancient treasures abound across the islands; sometimes it seems like there's a temple on every hill.

Islands

For many, Greece means scores of beguiling islands. Some, like Mykonos, are havens for sun-seekers desperate for warmth and fun. Others, like Hydra, are cultured centres of respite from daily cares. Best of all, many combine both.

Food

Ultra-fresh seafood like calamari can be found at family-run tavernas big and small across Greece. The eating joys continue with grilled octopus, souvlaki, famous salads and desserts oozing with honey.

p569

Ireland

People ✓✓✓
Culture ✓✓✓
Nature ✓✓

People
Ireland may be known for its pubs, but it's not the buildings or the beer but rather the people that make them unique in the world. And whether it's a spontaneous conversation at the bar or any place else, the hours will fly by gabbing about matters great and small.

Culture
The Irish gift of language isn't limited to spontaneous displays. Whether it's plays, novels or music, they've created cultural poetry.

Scenery
Known as the Emerald Isle, Ireland is green and offers both gentle landscapes and brutally rugged coasts.

p659

Italy

History ✓✓✓
Culture ✓✓✓
Food ✓✓✓

History
The Roman Empire. Is more needed after you think of the Forum, the Pantheon and the Coliseum? Perhaps 2000 years of Christianity as you'll find at the Vatican? Still need more? There's always Pompeii, Florence and the Medicis, Pisa...

Culture
There's a reason it's called the 'Italian Renaissance'. Michelangelo, da Vinci and Raphael are just the beginning.

Food
Is there a more beloved food worldwide? Pasta seems to be on everybody's menu, so why not savour the multitude of variations of this signature food in the country where it was invented?

p727

Netherlands

Biking ✓✓✓
Art ✓✓
Towns ✓✓

Cycling
There are more places to ride your bike than drive a car in the Netherlands, which is only one of the reasons it's the best place in the world to cycle. There's the trademark flatness for one, and a whole nationwide bike infrastructure for another. Then there's simply the joy of riding along beautiful canals past windmills and tulip fields.

Art
The Golden Age in the Netherlands gave us Rembrandt, Vermeer and more. Two centuries later came Van Gogh.

Towns
The quaint towns begin with frolicsome Amsterdam and continue to gems like Haarlem, Delft, Leiden, Utrecht and more.

p849

Portugal

Towns ✓✓
Culture ✓✓
Beaches ✓

Towns
You can wander the atmospheric lanes of Unesco-recognised Porto, try to escape the pull of Coimbra with its medieval backstreets or just succumb to the heart of it all: Lisbon.

Culture
Portugal may be tiny but it's packed with treasures like the ones you'll find in places like Sintra, where you can gaze on architectural wonders from the Middle Ages. And keep your ears open for fado music playing in tiny backstreet clubs.

Beaches
Explore the island beaches of the Algarve or just let yourself wash ashore at Lagos with it's Atlantic-driven surf and night-time high jinks.

p889

Spain

Cities ✓✓✓
Food ✓✓
Beaches ✓

Cities

You really can smell the orange blossoms in Seville, which has architecture that will beguile as you stroll from one street to the next. The pleasures continue in Granada with its Alhambra, Barcelona with its unbeatable culture and Madrid with its all-night pleasures. The list goes on.

Food

Basque tapas bars are one of Spain's great contributions to the world. Other culinary treasures include paella, ham in endless variety, the natural elixir of olive oil and more.

Beaches

Ever sunny, Spain works its spell from the famous beaches of Andalucía, the endless partying of Mallorca and the less trod corners of Valencia.

p935

Switzerland

Mountains ✓✓✓
Train Rides ✓✓✓
Skiing ✓✓

Mountains

Even if Switzerland were flat, it would still have chocolate. But add in the Alps and you might forget your sweet tooth. Traversing, climbing, hiking, skiing or contemplating spectacles like the Jungfrau are sublime.

Train Rides

Just boarding a Swiss train offers the promise of something special. But some routes are more special than others. At an amusement park you'd line up for hours to enjoy the thrills of the Bernina Pass or even the run from Lucerne to Interlaken.

Skiing

With all those Alps, if you're going to go up them you might as well come down – and why not do so on skies or a board. The thrills are endless.

p1049

❯ **Every listing is recommended by our authors, and their favourite places are listed first**

❯ **Look out for these icons:**

Our author's top recommendation

A green or sustainable option

No payment required

See the Index for a full list of destinations covered in this book.

On the Road

Austria

Includes »

Best Places to Eat

» Mill (p56)

» Magazin (p74)

» Chez Nico (p84)

» Der Steirer (p67)

» Restaurant Maria Loretto (p68)

Best Places to Stay

» Hotel Rathaus Wein & Design (p55)

» Haus Ballwein (p73)

» Hotel Weisses Kreuz (p83)

» Hotel Schloss Dürnstein (p64)

» Himmlhof (p88)

Why Go?

For such a small country, Austria has made it big. This is, after all, the land where Mozart was born, Strauss taught the world to waltz and Julie Andrews grabbed the spotlight with her twirling entrance in *The Sound of Music*. This is where the Habsburgs built their 600-year empire, and where past glories still shine in the resplendent baroque palaces and chandelier-lit coffee houses of Vienna, Innsbruck and Salzburg. This is a perfectionist of a country and whatever it does – mountains, classical music, new media, castles, cake, you name it – it does exceedingly well.

Beyond its grandiose cities, Austria's allure lies outdoors. And whether you're schussing down the legendary slopes of Kitzbühel, climbing high in the Alps of Tirol or pedalling along the banks of the sprightly Danube (Donau), you'll find the kind of inspiring landscapes that no well-orchestrated symphony, camera lens or singing nun could ever quite do justice.

When to Go

Vienna

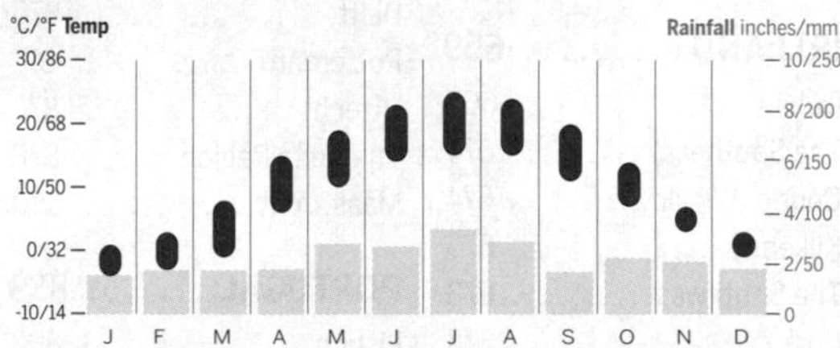

Jul–Aug Alpine hiking in Tirol, lake swimming in Salzkammergut and lots of summer festivals.

Sep–Oct New wine in vineyards near Vienna, golden forest strolls and few crowds.

Dec–Jan Christmas markets, skiing in the Alps and Vienna waltzing into the New Year.

Connections

Bang in the heart of Europe, Austria has speedy connections to its eight neighbouring countries. Trains from Vienna run to many Eastern European destinations, including Bratislava, Budapest, Prague and Warsaw; there are also connections south to Italy via Klagenfurt and north to Berlin. Salzburg is within sight of the Bavarian border, and there are many trains Munich-bound and beyond from the baroque city. Innsbruck is on the main rail line from Vienna to Switzerland, and two routes also lead to Munich. Look out for the fast, comfortable RailJet services to Germany and Switzerland.

ITINERARIES

Two Days

Spend this entire time in Vienna, making sure to visit the Habsburg palaces and Stephansdom before cosying up in a *Kaffeehäus* (coffee house). At night, check out the pumping bar scene.

One Week

Spend two days in Vienna, plus another day exploring the Wachau wine region, a day each in Salzburg and Innsbruck, one day exploring the Salzkammergut lakes, and finally one day in St Anton am Arlberg or Kitzbühel hiking or skiing (depending on the season).

Essential Food & Drink

» **Make it meaty** Go for a classic Wiener schnitzel, *Tafelspitz* (boiled beef with horseradish sauce) or *Schweinebraten* (pork roast). The humble wurst (sausage) comes in various guises.

» **On the side** Lashings of potatoes, either fried (*Pommes*), roasted (*Bratkartoffeln*), in a salad (*Erdapfelsalat*) or boiled in their skins *(Quellmänner)*; *Knödel* (dumplings) and *Nudeln* (flat egg noodles).

» **Kaffee und Kuchen** Coffee and cake is Austria's sweetest tradition. Must-tries: flaky apple strudel, rich, chocolatey *Sacher Torte* and *Kaiserschmarrn* (sweet pancakes with raisins).

» **Wine at the source** Jovial locals gather in rustic *Heurigen* (wine taverns) in the wine-producing east, identified by an evergreen branch above the door. Sip crisp grüner veltliner whites and spicy blaufränkisch wines.

» **Cheese fest** Dig into gooey *Käsnudeln* (cheese noodles) in Carinthia, *Kaspressknodel* (fried cheese dumplings) in Tirol and *Käsekrainer* (cheesy sausages) in Vienna. The hilly Bregenzerwald is studded with dairies.

AT A GLANCE

» **Currency** euro (€)

» **Language** German

» **Money** ATMs widely available; banks open Mon-Fri

» **Visas** Schengen rules apply

Fast Facts

» **Area** 83,871 sq km

» **Capital** Vienna

» **Country code** ☎43

» **Emergency** ☎112

Exchange Rates

Australia	A$1	€0.82
Canada	C$1	€0.77
Japan	¥100	€0.83
New Zealand	NZ$1	€0.65
UK	UK£1	€1.18
USA	US$1	€0.78

Set Your Budget

» **Budget hotel room** €50

» **Two-course meal** €15

» **Museum entrance** €8

» **Beer** €3

» **City transport ticket** €2

Resources

» **ÖAV** (www.alpenverein.at) Austrian Alpine Club

» **ÖBB** (☎05 17 17; www.oebb.at) Austrian Federal Railways

» **Österreich Werbung** (www.austria.info) National tourism authority

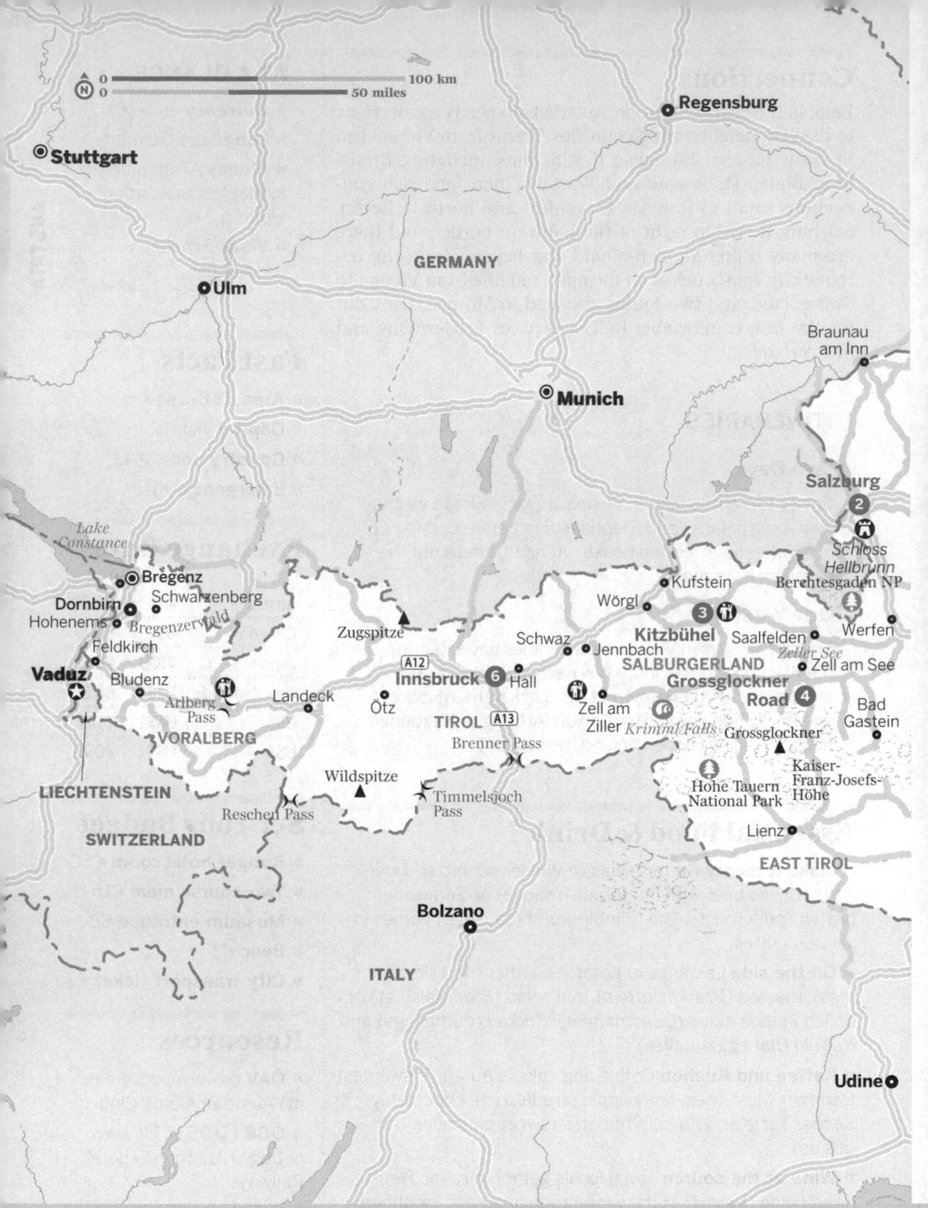

Austria Highlights

1. Discover the opulent Habsburg palaces, coffee houses and cutting-edge galleries of **Vienna** (p48)
2. Survey the baroque cityscape of **Salzburg** (p69) from the giddy height of 900-year-old Festung Hohensalzburg
3. Send your spirits soaring from peak to peak hiking and skiing in **Kitzbühel** (p86)
4. Buckle up for a roller-coaster ride of Alps and glaciers on the **Grossglockner Road** (p89), one of Austria's greatest drives

5 Dive into the crystal-clear lakes of **Salzkammergut** (p77), Austria's summer playground

6 Whiz up to the Tyrolean Alps in Zaha Hadid's space-age funicular from picture-perfect **Innsbruck** (p80)

7 Explore the romantic Wachau and technology trailblazer Linz in the **Danube Valley** (p63)

VIENNA

☎01 / POP 1.72 MILLION

Few cities in the world waltz so effortlessly between the present and the past like Vienna. Its splendid historical face is easily recognised: grand imperial palaces and bombastic baroque interiors, revered opera houses and magnificent squares.

But Vienna is also one of Europe's most dynamic urban spaces. A stone's throw from Hofburg (the Imperial Palace), the MuseumsQuartier houses some of the world's most provocative contemporary art behind a striking basalt facade. In the Innere Stadt (inner city), up-to-the-minute design stores sidle up to old-world confectioners, and Austro-Asian fusion restaurants stand alongside traditional *Beisl* (small taverns). In this Vienna, it's OK to mention poetry slam and Stephansdom in one breath.

Throw in the mass of green space within the confines of the city limits and the 'blue' Danube cutting a path east of the historical centre, and this is a capital that is distinctly Austrian.

History

Vienna was probably an important trading post for the Celts when the Romans arrived around 15 BC. They set up camp and named it Vindobona, after the Celtic tribe Vinid, and by the 3rd century it had developed into a town and vineyards were introduced to the area. It was first officially recorded as 'Wenia' in 881 and became a Babenberg stronghold in the 11th century. The Babenbergs ruled for 200 years, until the Habsburgs took control of the city's reins and held them firm until the end of WWI.

Over the centuries Vienna suffered Ottoman sieges in 1529 and 1683, and occupation in 1805 and 1809 by Napoleon and his armies. In the years in between, it received a major baroque makeover, the remnants of which can be seen in many buildings throughout the city. The mid-19th century saw Vienna blossom again, and the royal coffers were emptied to build the celebrated Ringstrasse and accompanying buildings.

Between the two world wars Vienna's political pendulum swung from one extreme to the other – the 1920s saw the influx of socialism and the 1930s the rise of fascism. Vienna suffered heavily under Allied bombing, and on 11 April 1945 advancing Russian troops liberated the city. The Allies joined them until Austria became independent in 1955, and since then it has gone from the razor's edge of Cold War to the focal point between new and old EU member nations.

Sights

Vienna's stately buildings and beautifully tended parks are made for the aimless ambler. Humming with street entertainers, pedestrian-only shopping lanes in the Innere Stadt such as Kärntner Strasse and Graben are great for a shop 'n' stroll.

Some former homes of the great composers, including those of Mozart and Beethoven, are open to the public; ask at the tourist office.

Many sights and attractions open slightly later in July and August, and close earlier from November to March.

Hofburg PALACE

(Imperial Palace; www.hofburg-wien.at; Michaelerkuppel; 🚌1A, 2A Michaelerplatz, Ⓜ Herrengasse, 🚋1, 2, D, 71, 46, 49 Burgring) Nothing symbolises the culture and heritage of Austria more than its Hofburg, home base of the Habsburgs for six centuries, from the first emperor (Rudolf I in 1273) to the last (Karl I in 1918). The Hofburg owes its size and architectural diversity to plain old one-upmanship; the oldest section is the 13th-century **Schweizerhof** (Swiss Courtyard).

The **Kaiserappartements** (Imperial Apartments; www.hofburg-wien.at; adult/child with audio guide €10.50/6.50, with guided tour €13/7.50; ⏲9am-5.30pm; Ⓜ Herrengasse), once occupied by Franz Josef I and Empress Elisabeth, are extraordinary for their chandelier-lit opulence. Included in the entry price, the **Sisi Museum** is devoted to the life of Austria's beauty-obsessed Empress Elisabeth, nicknamed 'Sisi'. Highlights include a reconstruction of her luxurious coach and the dress she wore on the eve of her wedding. A ticket to the Kaiserappartements also includes entry to the **Silberkammer** (Silver Chamber), showcasing fine silverware and porcelain.

Among several other points of interest within the Hofburg you'll find the Burgkapelle (Royal Chapel), where the Vienna Boys' Choir performs (p60); the Spanische Hofreitschule (p60); and the **Schatzkammer** (Imperial Treasury; www.kaiserliche-schatzkammer.at; 01, Schweizerhof; adult/under 19yr €12/free; ⏲9am-5.30pm Wed-Mon), which holds all manner of wonders including the 10th-century Imperial Crown, a 2860-carat Columbian emerald and even a thorn from Christ's crown.

Stephansdom CHURCH

(www.stephanskirche.at; 01, Stephansplatz; side aisle free, main nave adult/child €3.50/free; cathedral, catacombs & towers with audioguide adult plus child €16; ⌚6am-10pm Mon-Sat, 7am-10pm Sun, main nave & Domschatz audio tours 9-11.30am & 1-5.30pm Mon-Sat, 1-5.30pm Sun ; Ⓜ Stephansplatz) Rising high and mighty above Vienna with its dazzling mosaic tiled roof is Stephansdom, or Steffl (little Stephen) as the Viennese call it. The cathedral was built on the site of a 12th-century church but its most distinctive features are Gothic. Only limited areas can be visited without a ticket. Entry is free for worshippers.

Taking centre stage inside is the magnificent Gothic **stone pulpit**, fashioned in 1515 by Anton Pilgram. The baroque **high altar** in the main chancel depicts the stoning of St Stephen; the left chancel contains a winged altarpiece from Wiener Neustadt, dating from 1447; the right chancel houses the Renaissance-style red marble tomb of Friedrich III.

Dominating the cathedral is the skeletal, 136.7m-high **Südturm** (adult/child €3.50/1; ⌚9am-5.30pm). Negotiating 343 steps brings you to a cramped viewing platform for a stunning panorama of Vienna. You can also explore the cathedral's **Katakomben** (tours adult/child €5/2.50; ⌚10-11.30am & 1.30-4.30pm Mon-Sat, 1.30-4.30pm Sun), housing the remains of plague victims in a bone house, plus urns containing some of the organs of Habsburg rulers – gripping stuff.

TOP CHOICE **Albertina** GALLERY

(www.albertina.at; 01, Albertinaplatz 3; adult/child €11/free; ⌚10am-6pm Thu-Tue, 10am-9pm Wed; Ⓜ Karlsplatz, Stephansplatz, 🚋D, 1, 2, 71 Kärntner Ring/Oper) Simply reading the highlights should have any art fan lining up for entry into this gallery. Among its enormous collection (1.5 million prints and 50,000 drawings) are 70 Rembrandts, 145 Dürers (including the famous *Hare*) and 43 Raphaels, as well as works by da Vinci, Michelangelo, Rubens, Cézanne, Picasso, Klimt and Kokoschka.

In addition to the mostly temporary exhibitions, a series of Habsburg staterooms are always open.

Schloss Schönbrunn PALACE, MUSEUM

(www.schoenbrunn.at; 13, Schönbrunner Schlossstrasse 47; Imperial Tour with audioguide adult/child €10.50/7.50, gardens admission free, maze adult/child €3.50/2.20; ⌚8.30am-5.30pm, gardens 6am-dusk, maze 9am-6pm) The Habsburgs' opulent summer palace is now a Unesco World Heritage site. Of the palace's 1441 rooms, 40 are open to the public; the Imperial Tour takes you into 26 of these. Because of the popularity of the palace, tickets are stamped with a departure time and there may be a time lag before you can enter, so buy your ticket straight away and then explore the gardens.

Fountains dance in the French-style formal **gardens**. The gardens harbour the world's oldest zoo, the **Tiergarten** (www.zoovienna.at; adult/child €15/7; ⌚9am-6.30pm), founded in 1752; a 630m-long hedge **maze**; and the **Gloriette** (adult/child €3/2.20; ⌚9am-btwn 4pm & 7pm, closed early Nov-late Mar), whose roof offers a wonderful view over the palace grounds and beyond.

TOP CHOICE **Kaisergruft** CHURCH

(Imperial Burial Vault; www.kaisergruft.at; 01, Neuer Markt; adult/child €5/2; ⌚10am-6pm; Ⓜ Stephansplatz, Karlsplatz, 🚋D, 1, 2, 71 Kärntner Ring/Oper) Beneath the Kapuzinerkirche (Church of the Capuchin Friars), the high-peaked Kaisergruft is the final resting place of most of the Habsburg elite. The tombs range from simple to elaborate, such as the 18th-century baroque double casket of Maria Theresia and Franz Stephan. Empress Elisabeth's ('Sisi') coffin receives the most attention, however: lying alongside that of her husband, Franz Josef, it is often strewn with fresh flowers.

Kunsthistorisches Museum GALLERY

(Museum of Fine Arts; www.khm.at; Maria-Theresien-Plaz, 01; adult/under 19yr €14/free; ⌚10am-6pm Tue-Sun, to 9pm Thu; Ⓜ MuseumsQuartier, 🚋1, 2, D) When it comes to classical works of art, nothing comes close to the Kunsthistorisches Museum. It houses a huge range of art amassed by the Habsburgs and includes works by Rubens, Van Dyck, Holbein and Caravaggio. Paintings by Pieter Bruegel the Elder, including *Hunters in the Snow,* also feature. There is an entire wing of ornaments, clocks and glassware, and Greek, Roman and Egyptian antiquities.

MuseumsQuartier MUSEUM COMPLEX

(Museum Quarter; www.mqw.at; combi ticket €25; ⌚information & ticket centre 10am-7pm) Small books have been written on this popular site, so only a taste can be given here. This remarkable ensemble of museums, cafes, restaurants and bars occupies the former imperial stables designed by Fischer von Erlach. Spanning 60,000 sq metres, it's one of the world's most ambitious cultural spaces.

Central Vienna

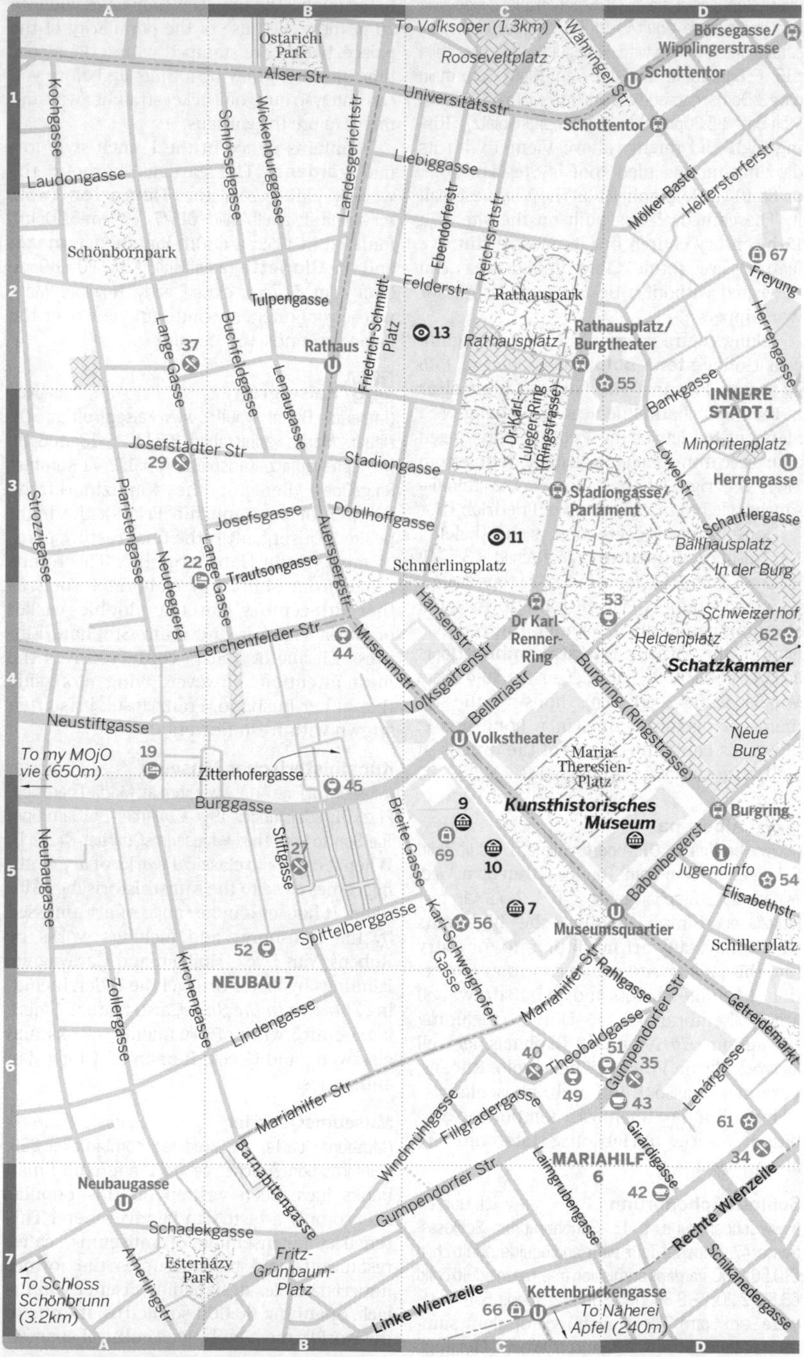

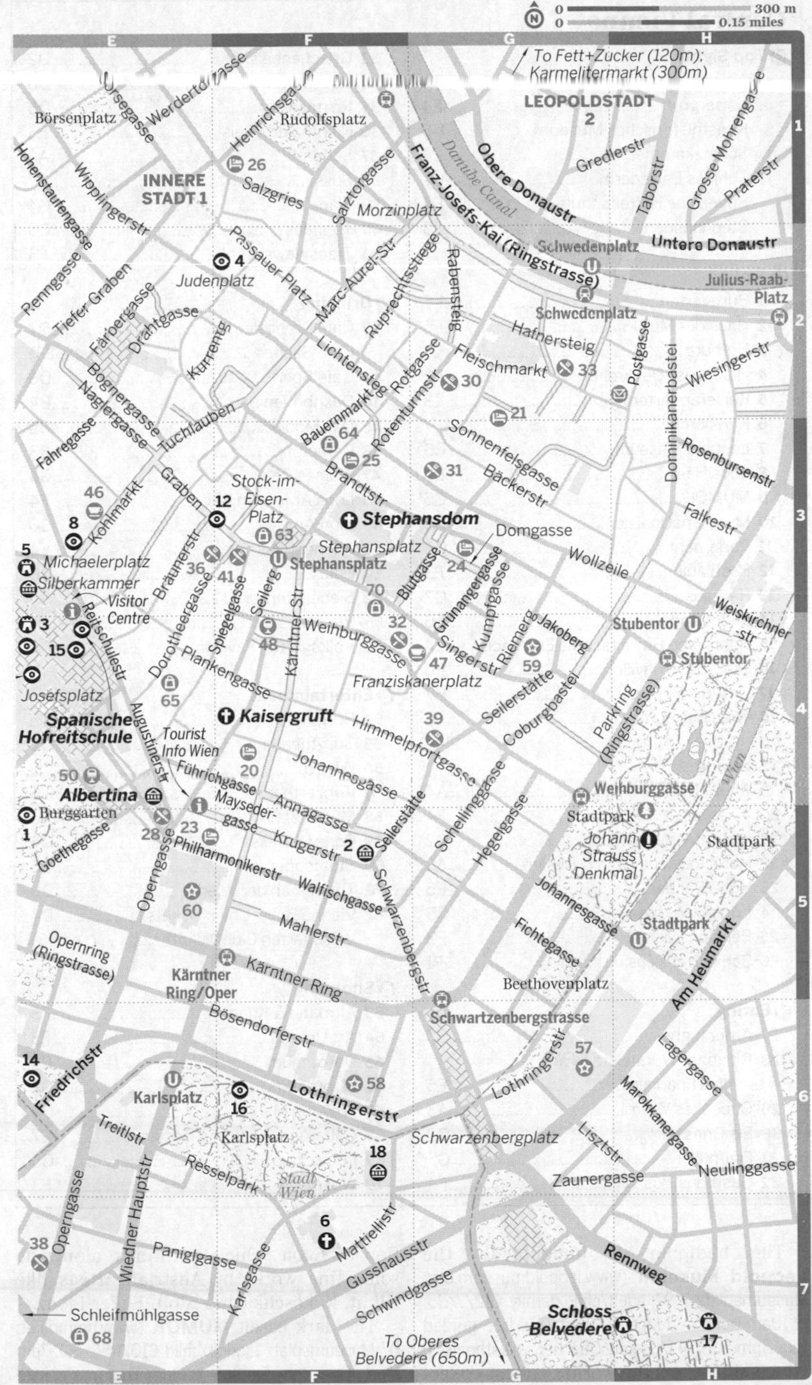

0 300 m
0 0.15 miles
E
F
G
H
1
2
3
4
5
6
7
To Fett+Zucker (120m); Karmelitermarkt (300m)
LEOPOLDSTADT 2
Börsenplatz
Werdertorgasse
Ursegasse
Rudolfsplatz
Heinrichsgasse
26
Hohenstaufengasse
Wipplingerstr
INNERE STADT 1
Salzgries
Salztorgasse
Morzinplatz
Franz-Josefs-Kai (Ringstrasse)
Danube Canal
Obere Donaustr
Gredlerstr
Taborstr
Grosse Mohrengasse
Praterstr
Untere Donaustr
Schwedenplatz
Julius-Raab-Platz
4
Judenplatz
Passauer Platz
Marc-Aurel-Str
Ruprechtsstiege
Rabensteig
Renngasse
Tiefer Graben
Färbergasse
Drahtgasse
Kurrentg
Lichtensteg
Rotgasse
Hafnersteig
Fleischmarkt
33
Postgasse
Dominikanerbastei
Wiesingerstr
30
Bognergasse
Naglergasse
Tuchlauben
Bauernmarkt
Rotenturmstr
21
64
25
Sonnenfelsgasse
Rosenbursenstr
Fahregasse
Kohlmarkt
46
8
Graben
12
Stock-im-Eisen-Platz
Brandtstr
31
Bäckerstr
Falkestr
Stephansdom
Domgasse
5
Michaelerplatz
Silberkammer
Bräunerstr
36
41
63
Stephansplatz
24
Wollzeile
Visitor Centre
3
15
Reitschulestr
Dorotheergasse
Spiegelgasse
Seilerg
Kärntner Str
48
70
Blutgasse
Grünangergasse
Kumpfgasse
32
Weihburggasse
47
Singerstr
Riemerg
Jakoberg
59
Stubentor
Weiskirchnerstr
Plankengasse
65
Josefsplatz
Franziskanerplatz
Seilerstätte
Coburgbastei
Parkring (Ringstrasse)
Spanische Hofreitschule
Augustinerstr
Kaisergruft
39
Himmelpfortgasse
Tourist Info Wien
20
Johannesgasse
50
Führichgasse
Albertina
Mayseder-gasse
Annagasse
Weihburggasse
Stadtpark
Burggarten
1
23
28
Goethegasse
Krugerstr
2
Seilerstätte
Schellinggasse
Hegelgasse
Johann Strauss Denkmal
Stadtpark
Philharmonikerstr
Walfischgasse
Operngasse
60
Schwarzenbergstr
Johannesgasse
Mahlerstr
Fichtegasse
Stadtpark
Am Heumarkt
Opernring (Ringstrasse)
Kärntner Ring/Oper
Kärntner Ring
Beethovenplatz
Schwartzenbergstrasse
Bösendorferstr
57
Lagergasse
14
Friedrichstr
Karlsplatz
16
58
Lothringerstr
Lothringerstr
Marokkanergasse
Treitlstr
Karlsplatz
18
Schwarzenbergplatz
Lisztstr
Neulinggasse
Resselpark
Stadt Wien
Zaunergasse
Operngasse
Wiedner Hauptstr
6
Mattiellistr
38
Paniglgasse
Karlsgasse
Gusshausstr
Rennweg
Schwindgasse
Schleifmühlgasse
68
To Oberes Belvedere (650m)
Schloss Belvedere
17

Central Vienna

Top Sights

Albertina ... E4
Kaisergruft ... F4
Kunsthistorisches Museum ... D5
Schatzkammer ... E4
Schloss Belvedere ... H7
Spanische Hofreitschule ... E4
Stephansdom ... F3

Sights

1 Burggarten ... E5
2 Haus der Musik ... F5
3 Hofburg ... E4
4 Holocaust-Denkmal ... F2
5 Kaiserappartements ... E3
6 Karlskirche ... F7
7 Leopold Museum ... C5
8 Loos Haus ... E3
9 MUMOK ... C5
10 MuseumsQuartier ... C5
11 Parlament ... C3
12 Pestsäule ... F3
13 Rathaus ... C2
14 Secession ... E6
15 Spanische Hofreitschule Entrance ... E4
16 Stadtbahn Pavillons ... F6
17 Unteres Belvedere ... H7
18 Wien Museum ... F6

Sleeping

19 Altstadt ... A4
20 Aviano ... F4
21 Hotel Kärtnerhof ... G2
22 Hotel Rathaus Wein & Design ... A3
23 Hotel Sacher ... E5
24 König von Ungarn ... G3
25 Pension Sacher ... F3
26 Schweizer Pension ... F1

Eating

27 Amerlingbeisl ... B5
28 Bitzinger Würstelstand am Albertinaplatz ... E5
29 Cupcakes Wien ... A3
30 Eis Griessler ... G2
31 Figlmüller ... G3
32 Gasthaus Pöschl ... F4
33 Griechenbeisl ... G2
34 Naschmarkt ... D6
35 Ra'mien ... D6
36 Reinthaler's Beisl ... E3
37 Schnattl ... A2
38 Süssi ... E7
39 Tian ... G4
40 Tongues ... C6
41 Trzesniewski ... F3

Drinking

42 Café Drechsler ... D7
Café Sacher ... (see 23)
43 Café Sperl ... D6
44 Dachboden ... B4
45 Das Möbel ... B5
46 Demel ... E3
47 Kleines Café ... G4
48 Loos American Bar ... F4
49 Mon Ami ... C6
50 Palmenhaus ... E4
51 Phil ... D6
52 Siebensternbräu ... B5
Vis-à-vis ... (see 31)
53 Volksgarten Pavillon ... D4

Entertainment

54 Burg Kino ... D5
55 Burgtheater ... D2
56 Donau ... C5
57 Konzerthaus ... G6
58 Musikverein ... F6
59 Porgy & Bess ... G4
60 Staatsoper ... E5
61 Theater an der Wien ... D6
62 Vienna Boys' Choir Tickets ... D4
Volksgarten ClubDiskothek ... (see 53)

Shopping

63 Altmann & Kühne ... F3
64 Art Up ... F3
65 Dorotheum ... E4
66 Flohmarkt ... C7
67 Freyung Market ... D2
68 Gabarage Upcycling Design ... E7
69 Lomoshop ... C5
70 Woka ... F3

The highpoint is undoubtedly the **Leopold Museum** (www.leopoldmuseum.org; Museumsplatz 1, 07; adult/child/family €12/7/25; ⏲10am-6pm Wed-Mon, to 9pm Thu, free guided tour 3pm Sun; Ⓜ MuseumsQuartier, Volkstheater), which showcases the world's largest collection of Egon Schiele paintings, alongside some fine works by Austrian artists like Klimt, Kokoschka and Albin Egger-Lienz.

The dark basalt **MUMOK** (www.mumok.at; 07, Museumsplatz 1; adult/child €10/free; ⏲2-7pm Mon, 10am-7pm Tue-Sun, to 9pm Thu, free guided tour 2pm Sat & Sun, 7pm Thu; MuseumsQuartier, Volkstheater, 49 Volkstheater) is alive with Vienna's premier collection of 20th-century art, centred on fluxus, nouveau réalism, pop art and photo-realism.

Schloss Belvedere PALACE, GALLERY
(www.belvedere.at; combined ticket adult/child €16/free; D) Belvedere is a masterpiece of total art and one of the world's finest baroque palaces, designed by Johann Lukas von Hildebrandt (1668–1745).

The first of the palace's two main buildings is the **Oberes Belvedere** (Upper Belvedere; 03, Prinz-Eugen-Strasse 27; adult/child €11/free; 10am-6pm ; D). Pride and joy of the gallery is Gustav Klimt's rich gold *The Kiss* (1908), which perfectly embodies Viennese art nouveau, accompanied by other late-19th- to early-20th-century Austrian works. The second is the grandiose **Unteres Belvedere** (Lower Belvedere; 03, Rennweg 6; adult/child €11/free; 10am-6pm Thu-Tue, to 9pm Wed; D), which contains a baroque museum. The buildings sit at opposite ends of a manicured garden.

KunstHausWien MUSEUM
(www.kunsthauswien.com; 03, Untere Weissgerberstrasse 13; adult/child €10/5, audioguide €3; 10am-7pm; 1, O Radetzkyplatz) Like something out of a toy shop, this gallery was designed by eccentric Viennese artist and architect Friedensreich Hundertwasser (1928–2000), whose love of uneven floors, colourful mosaic ceramics, irregular corners and rooftop greenery shines through. The permanent collection is a tribute to Hundertwasser, showcasing his paintings, graphics and philosophy on ecology and architecture.

Down the road there's a block of residential flats by Hundertwasser, the **Hundertwassershaus** (cnr Löwengasse & Kegelgasse; 1). It's not possible to see inside, but you can visit the **Kalke Village** (www.kalke-village.at; Kegelgasse 37-39; 9am-6pm), also the handiwork of Hundertwasser, created from an old Michelin factory, in typical fashion with a distinct absence of straight lines.

Trams trams 1 and O to Radetzkyplatz stop close by.

Prater AMUSEMENT PARK
(www.wiener-prater.at; U1 Praterstern, 5, O) This large park encompasses grassy meadows, woodlands, an amusement park known as the **Würstelprater** and one of the city's icons, the **Riesenrad** (www.wienerriesenrad.com; 02, Prater 90; adult/child €9/4; 9am-11.45pm, shorter hrs in winter). Built in 1897, this 65m-high Ferris wheel takes about 20 minutes to rotate its 430-tonne weight, offering far-reaching views of Vienna. It achieved celluloid fame in *The Third Man*. Take U1 to Praterstern.

Secession LANDMARK, MUSEUM
(www.secession.at; 01, Friedrichstrasse 12; adult/child €8.50/5, audioguide €3; 10am-6pm Tue-Sun; U1, U2, U4 Karlsplatz) This popular art nouveau 'temple of art' building was built in 1898 and bears an intricately woven gilt dome that the Viennese nickname the 'golden cabbage'. The highlight inside is the 34m-long *Beethoven Frieze* by Klimt.

Haus der Musik MUSIC MUSEUM
(513 4850; www.hdm.at; 01, Seilerstätte 30; adult/child €12/5.50, with Mozarthaus €17/7; 10am-10pm; Karlsplatz, D, 1, 2 Kärntner Ring/Oper) Delving into the physics of sounds and paying tribute to Austria's great composers, this interactive museum is a fascinating journey through music. Most fun of all is the room where you can virtually conduct the Vienna Philharmonic.

Pestsäule MEMORIAL
Graben is dominated by the knobbly outline of this memorial, designed by Fischer von Erlach in 1693 to commemorate the 75,000 victims of the Black Death.

Holocaust-Denkmal MEMORIAL
(01, Judenplatz; Stephansplatz) This is Austria's first Holocaust memorial, the 'Nameless Library'. The squat, boxlike structure pays homage to the 65,000 Austrian Jews who were killed during the Holocaust.

FREE **Zentralfriedhof** CEMETERY
(www.friedhoefewien.at; 11, Simmeringer Hauptstrasse 232-244; 7am-8pm, shorter hours in winter; 6, 71) Situated about 4km south of the centre, this is one of Europe's largest cemeteries. With two and a half million graves, it

WANT MORE?

For in-depth information, reviews and recommendations at your fingertips, head to the Apple App Store to purchase Lonely Planet's *Vienna City Guide* iPhone app.

Alternatively, head to **Lonely Planet** (www.lonelyplanet.com/austria/vienna) for planning advice, author recommendations, traveller reviews and insider tips.

VIENNA IN...

One Day

Jump on tram 1 or 2 and circle the **Ringstrasse** (Ring road) for a brief but rewarding tour of the boulevard's monumental buildings. Get out at Kärntner Strasse and wander towards the Gothic **Stephansdom** before heading to the **Hofburg** and the breathtaking art collection of the **Kunsthistorisches Museum**. Dine at an **Innere Stadt restaurant** before a night at the **Staatsoper**.

Two Days

On day two, visit imperial palace **Schönbrunn** before a feast of Austrian art at the **Leopold Museum**. Eat at Vienna's celebrated **Naschmarkt**, then cross the city for a twilight ride on the **Riesenrad**. Finish the day with local wine and food at a **Heuriger**.

has more 'residents' than Vienna. Beethoven, Schubert and Brahms have memorials here. Take tram 6 or 71 to Zentralfriedhof.

Sigmund Freud Museum MUSEUM
(www.freud-museum.at; 09, Berggasse 19; adult/child €8/3.50; 9am-6pm; U2 Schottentor, U4 Schottenring, 1, D) Former house of the famous psychologist, now housing a small museum featuring some of his personal belongings. The museum is 600m north of Schottentor.

Wien Museum MUSEUM
(www.wienmuseum.at; 04, Karlsplatz 8; adult/under 19yr €8/free, free first Sun of month; 10am-6pm Tue-Sun; U1, U2, U4 Karlsplatz) Provides a snapshot of the city's history, and contains a handsome art collection with paintings by Klimt and Schiele.

Loos Haus ARCHITECTURE
(01, Michaelerplatz; 9am-5pm Mon-Fri, to 5.30pm Thu; 2A, Herrengasse) A perfect example of the clean lines of Loos' work. Franz Josef hated it and described the windows, which lack lintels, as 'windows without eyebrows'.

Stadtbahn Pavillons LANDMARK
(www.wienmuseum.at; 04, Karlsplatz; adult/under 19yr €4/free; 10am-6pm Tue-Sun Apr-Oct; U1, U2, U4 Karlsplatz) Jugendstil pavilions designed by Otto Wagner for Vienna's first public transport system.

Activities

Dividing the Danube from the Neue Donau is the svelte Donauinsel (Danube Island), which stretches some 21.5km from opposite Klosterneuburg in the north to the Nationalpark Donau-Auen in the south. The island features long sections of **swimming** areas, concrete paths for **walking** and **cycling**, and restaurants and snack bars. The Alte Donau is a landlocked arm of the Danube, a favourite of **sailing** and boating enthusiasts, swimmers, walkers, fisherfolk and, in winter (when it's cold enough), **ice skaters**.

Tours

The tourist office publishes a monthly list of guided walks, *Wiener Spaziergänge,* and can advise on bus tours and river cruises.

Vienna Tour Guides WALKING TOUR
(774 89 01; www.wienguide.at; adult/child €14/7) Conducts 60 different guided walking tours, some of which are in English, from art nouveau architecture to Jewish traditions and the ever-popular *Third Man* tour.

Festivals & Events

Pick up a copy of the monthly booklet of events from the tourist office. Tickets for many events are available at **Wien-Ticket Pavillon** in the hut by the Staatsoper.

Opernball BALL
(01, Staatsoper) Of the 300 or so balls held in January and February, the Opernball (Opera Ball) is the ultimate. It's a supremely lavish affair, with the men in tails and women in shining white gowns.

Wiener Festwochen ARTS FESTIVAL
(www.festwochen.at) Wide-ranging program of arts from around the world, from May to mid-June.

Donauinselfest MUSIC FESTIVAL
(https://donauinselfest.at) Free three-day festival of rock, pop, hardcore, folk and country music on the Donauinsel in June.

Musikfilm Festival FILM FESTIVAL
(01, Rathausplatz) Screenings of operas, operettas and concerts outside the Rathaus in July and August.

Viennale Film Festival FILM FESTIVAL
(01 526 59 47; www.viennale.at) The country's biggest and best film festival, featuring fringe and independent films from around the world in October.

Christkindlmärkte CHRISTMAS MARKET
(www.christkindlmarkt.at) Vienna's much-loved Christmas market season runs from mid-November to Christmas Eve.

Sleeping

Hotel Rathaus Wein & Design BOUTIQUE HOTEL €€€
(400 11 22; www.hotel-rathaus-wien.at; 08, Lange Gasse 13; s/d/tr €150/210/240 ; ; U2 Rathaus, U3 Volkstheater, 46) Each stylish room in this boutique hotel is dedicated to an Austrian winemaker and the chandelier-lit wine bar zooms in on a different winery every month. The open-plan, minimalist-chic rooms reveal a razor-sharp eye for design, especially the opalescent ones with hybrid beds and bathtubs.

Pension Sacher PENSION €€
(533 32 38; www.pension-sacher.at; 01, Rothenturmstrasse 1; apt €90-136;) Filled with chintzy knick-knacks, florals and solid wood furnishings, these super-central, spacious apartments are lovingly kept by the Sacher family of chocolate cake fame. There's everything you need to feel right at home and the views of Stephansdom are phenomenal.

Boutiquehotel Stadthalle HOTEL €€
(982 42 72; www.hotelstadthalle.at; Hackengasse 20, 15; s €78-138, d €118-198; ; U3 Schweglerstrasse, 9, 49) Welcome to Vienna's most sustainable hotel, which makes the most of solar power, rainwater collection and LED lighting, and has a roof planted with fragrant lavender. Rooms are a blend of modern with polished antiques. An organic breakfast is served in the leafy garden in summer. Arrive by bike or train for a 10% discount. The hotel is located 650m northwest of Westbahnhof.

TOP CHOICE Altstadt PENSION €€
(522 66 66; www.altstadt.at; 07, Kirchengasse 41; s €125-175, d €145-215, ste €195-350; ; U2, U3 Volkstheater, 46) One of Vienna's finest pensions, Altstadt has charming, individually decorated rooms, with high ceilings, plenty of space and a cosy lounge with free afternoon tea and cakes. Staff are genuinely affable and artworks are from the owner's personal collection.

my MOjO vie HOSTEL €
(0676-551 11 55; http://mymojovie.at; 07, Kaiserstrasse 77; dm/d/tr/q €26/58/84/108; ; U6 Burggasse, 5) An old-fashioned cage lift rattles up to these incredible backpacker digs. Everything you could wish for is here: design-focused dorms complete with dressing tables and snug-as-a-bug rugs, a kitchen with free

MORE FOR YOUR MONEY

If you're planning on doing a lot of sightseeing, consider purchasing the **Wien-Karte** (Vienna Card; €19.90) for 72 hours of unlimited travel plus discounts at selected museums, attractions, cafes and shops. It's available from hotels and ticket offices.

The City of Vienna runs some 20 **municipal museums** (www.museum.vienna.at), which are included in a free booklet available at the Rathaus. Permanent exhibitions in all are free on the first Sunday of the month.

SPIN OF THE RING

The Ringstrasse, often just called the Ring, is a wide, tree-lined boulevard encircling much of the Innere Stadt. The best way to see its monumental buildings is by jumping on tram 1 or 2 for a brief but rewarding self-guided tour. For the price of a single ticket you'll take in the neo-Gothic **Rathaus** (City Hall; 525 50; www.wien.gv.at; 01, Rathausplatz 1; guided tours 1pm Mon, Wed & Fri; Rathaus), the Greek Revival–style **Parlament** (www.parlament.gv.at; 01, Dr-Karl-Renner-Ring 3; tours adult/child €5/2.50, visitor centre admission free; guided tours hourly 11am-4pm Mon-Sat, visitor centre 8.30am-6.30pm Mon-Fri, 9.30am-4.30pm Sat), the 19th-century **Burgtheater** (National Theatre; 514 44 4440; www.burgtheater.at; 01, Universitätsring 2; box office 9am-5pm Mon-Fri; Rathaus) and the baroque **Karlskirche** (St Charles' Church; www.karlskirche.at; Karlsplatz; adult/child €8/4, audioguide €2; 9am-5.30pm Mon-Sat, 11.30am-5.30pm Sun; U1, U2, U4 Karlsplatz), among others.

Or hop off to relax in one of the Ring's three parks: flower-strewn **Burggarten** (www.bundesgaerten.at; 01, Burgring; 6am-10pm Apr-Oct, 6.30am-7pm Nov-Mar; Museumsquartier), **Volksgarten** or **Stadtpark**, with its gold **statue of Johann Strauss**.

supplies, netbooks for surfing, books for browsing and even musical instruments for your own jam session. Tram 5 stops close by.

Aviano PENSION €€
(☎512 83 30; www.secrethomes.at; 01, Marco-d'Aviano-Gasse 1; s €87-112, d €127-187; 📶; MStephansplatz) Aviano is a supremely central, good-value choice. The small high-ceilinged rooms feature whitewashed antique furnishings and decorative moulding. In summer, the sunny breakfast room opens onto a small balcony.

Believe It Or Not HOSTEL €
(☎0676-550 00 55; www.believe-it-or-not-vienna.at; 07, Myrthengasse 10; dm €25-30; @📶; 🚌48A, SU2, U3 Volkstheater) It may seem nondescript on the face of things, but you really won't believe what a cosy, homely hostel this is. We love the dorms with mezzanine-style beds, laid-back lounge, kitchen with free basics, and laptops for guest use. Lily, your South African host, puts on a great spread at breakfast.

König von Ungarn HOTEL €€€
(☎51 584; www.kvu.at; 01, Schulerstrasse 10; s/d €155/220, ste €350; 📶; MStephansplatz) Vienna's oldest hotel (1746) balances class and informality. Rooms are individually furnished with antiques (the best face Domgasse) and the inner courtyard is wonderful.

Hotel Sacher LUXURY HOTEL €€€
(☎514 560; www.sacher.com; 01, Philharmonikerstrasse 4; r €480-1350, ste €1600-2900; ❄@📶; MKarlsplatz, 🚋D, 1, 2, 71 Kärntner Ring/Oper) Walking into the Sacher is like turning back the clock a hundred years. All of the lavishly decorated rooms boast baroque furnishings and 19th-century oil paintings, and the top-floor spa pampers with chocolate treatments.

Pension Kraml PENSION €
(☎587 85 88; 06, www.pensionkraml.at; Brauergasse 5; s €35, d €56-76, tr €78-87, q €120; @📶; SU3 Zieglergasse) A quiet and cosy family-run pension, where old-school politeness and comfort are paramount. Rooms are large (if a little dated).

Hotel Kärntnerhof HOTEL €€
(☎512 19 23; www.karntnerhof.com; 01, Grashofgasse 4; s €99-129, d €135-195, tr €199-235, ste €279-299; @📶; MStephansplatz) Tucked away from the bustle, this treasure oozes old Vienna charm, from the period paintings to the wood- and frosted-glass-panelled lift to the roof terrace. Rooms mix a few plain pieces with antiques, chandeliers and elegant curtains.

Schweizer Pension PENSION €
(☎533 81 56; www.schweizerpension.com; 01, Heinrichsgasse 2; s €56-75, d €75-98; MSchottentor, 🚋1 Salztorbrücke) This small, family-run pension is a superb deal, with homely touches and eco credentials. Book in advance, though, as it has only 11 rooms and is popular among those on squeezed budgets.

Altwienerhof HOTEL €€
(☎892 60 00; www.altwienerhof.at; 15, Herklotzgasse 6; s €50-65, d €89-99, q €125; @; SU6 Gumpendorfer Strasse) This pseudo-plush family-run hotel, just outside the Gürtel ring, offers ridiculously romantic abodes – think miniature chandeliers, antique pieces, floral bedding and lace tablecloths. Breakfast is taken in the conservatory or large inner courtyard. The hotel is a minute's walk west of U6 station Gumpendorfer Strasse.

Eating

Vienna has thousands of restaurants covering all budgets and styles of cuisine, but dining doesn't stop there. *Kaffeehäuser* (coffee houses), *Beisl* (small taverns) and *Heurigen* (wine taverns) are just as fine for a good meal. *Würstel Stande* (sausage stands) are conveniently located on street corners and squares.

Mill AUSTRIAN €€
(☎966 40 73; www.mill32.at; 06, Millergasse 32; mains €8-17.50; ⏰11.30am-3pm & 5pm-midnight Mon-Fri, 11am-4pm Sun; SU3, U6 Westbahnhof, 🚋9, 18, 52, 58) This art-slung bistro, with a hidden courtyard for summer days, still feels like a local secret. Scarlet brick walls and wood floors create a warm backdrop for spot-on seasonal food like chanterelle cannelloni and Styrian chicken salad drizzled with pumpkin-seed oil. The two-course lunch is a snip at €6.90. Mill is 400m south of the U3 Westbahnhof station on Mariahilfer Strasse.

TOP CHOICE **Tian** VEGETARIAN €€
(☎890 4665; www.tian-vienna.com; 01, Himmelpfortgasse 23; 3-course lunch €12.50-16, 3–6-course evening menu €39-69, mains €18; ⏰noon-4pm, 6pm-midnight Mon-Fri, from 9am Sat; 🖉; MStephansplatz, 🚋2 Weihburggasse) Vaulted charm meets urban attitude at this sleek lounge-style restaurant which takes vegetarian cuisine to delicious heights. Lunch menus offer the best value; you can also enjoy a drink at the cocktail bar.

Schnattl INTERNATIONAL €€€
(☎405 34 00; www.schnattl.com; 08, Lange Gasse 40; mains €21-26, 3-course menus €33-38; ⏰6pm-

midnight Mon-Fri; ; 13A, 2) Wilhelm Schnattl gives flight to culinary fantasy at this wood-panelled bistro, centred on an inner courtyard and attracting a food-loving crowd of artists and actors. The menu puts a creative spin on whatever is seasonal, be it mushrooms, shellfish, asparagus or game.

Gasthaus Pöschl AUSTRIAN €€
(513 52 88; 01, Weihburggasse 17; mains €9-18; lunch & dinner) Close to pretty Franziskanerplatz, this small, wood-panelled *Beisl* brims with Viennese warmth and bonhomie. Austrian classics like *Tafelspitz* (boiled beef) and schnitzel are cooked to a T.

Tongues DELI, CAFE €
(www.tongues.at; 06, Theobaldgasse 16; lunch mains €3.60; 11am-9pm Mon-Fri, 11am-6pm Sat;) DJs can sometimes be found on the decks at this record shop and rustic deli, where you can pop in for a healthy lunch, electro on vinyl or some locally sourced cheese, salami, honey and wood-oven bread.

Reinthaler's Beisl AUSTRIAN €
(513 12 49; 01, Dorotheergasse 2-4; mains €9-13) This warm, woody *Beisl* has got everything going for it: a cracking location just off Graben, a buzzy pavement terrace and a menu championing Viennese home cooking from brothy goulash with dumplings to perfectly crisp schnitzel.

Ra'mien ASIAN €€
(585 47 98; www.ramien.at; 06, Gumpendorfer Strasse 9; mains €7-16; Tue-Sun;) Bright young things gravitate towards this minimalist-chic noodle bar, with a choice of Thai, Japanese, Chinese and Vietnamese noodle soups and rice dishes. The lounge bar downstairs has regular DJs and stays open until at least 2am.

Bitzinger Würstelstand am Albertinaplatz SAUSAGE STAND €
(01, Albertinaplatz; sausages €3.70-4.10; 9.30-5am, drinks from 8am) Located behind the Staatsoper, this is one of Vienna's best sausage stands. Watch ladies and gents dressed to the nines while enjoying your wurst and a beer.

Amerlingbeisl AUSTRIAN €
(526 16 60; www.amerlingbeisl.at; Stiftgasse 8, 07; mains €7-14; 9am-2am; ; M Volkstheater, 49 Stiftgasse) The cobbled inner courtyard of this Spittelberg *Beisl*, with tables set up under the trees, is a summer evening magnet. The chef cooks Austro-Italian, hitting the mark with homemade pasta and dishes like pike perch with saffron noodles.

DON'T MISS

SWEETNESS & LIGHT

Indulge your sweet tooth at these three Viennese favourites.

Cupcakes Wien (www.cupcakes-wien.at; 08, Josefstädter Strasse 17 ; cupcakes €3.90; 10am-7.30pm Mon-Fri, 10am-6pm Sat; ; S U2 Rathaus, 2) A pretty pink wonderland of cupcakes, with mascarpone toppings in flavours like lime, peanut and mint.

Süssi (943 13 24; www.suessi.at; 04, Operngasse 30; desserts €3.50-6, afternoon tea €17; 11am-9pm Tue-Sat, 1-9pm Sun; S U1, U2, U4 Karlsplatz) This tiny and fabulously OTT French tea room serves Mariage Frères brews with delectable nut tarts, cream cakes and macarons.

Fett+Zucker (www.fettundzucker.at; 02, Hollandstrasse 16; cakes & snacks €2.50-6; 1-9pm Wed-Fri, 11am-9pm Sat & Sun; ; S U2 Taborstrasse, 2) As the name suggests, the cheesecakes, strudels and brownies at this retro cafe don't skimp on the fat and sugar.

Figlmüller BISTRO, PUB €€
(512 61 77; www.figlmueller.at; 01, Wollzeile 5; mains €12.90-22.90; 11am-10.30pm; ; M Stephansplatz) This famous *Beisl* has been sizzling up some of the biggest (and best) schnitzels in town since 1905. Sure, the rural decor is contrived, but it doesn't get more Viennese than this.

Trzesniewski SANDWICHES €
(01, Dorotheergasse 1; sandwiches from €1.10; 8.30am-7.30pm Mon-Fri, 9am-5pm Sat; M Stephansplatz) Possibly Austria's finest open-sandwich shop, with delectably thick spreads, from tuna with egg to Swedish herring. Two bites and they're gone. Wash them down with a tiny *Pfiff* beer.

Eis Griessler ICE CREAM €
(01, Rotenturmstrasse 14; scoop €1.30; 10.30am-11pm) Organic milk and fresh fruit go into dreamily smooth ice creams like Alpine caramel and Wachau apricot at this hole-in-the-wall parlour.

DON'T MISS

FOOD MARKET FINDS

Foodies gravitate towards the sprawling **Naschmarkt** (06, Linke & Rechte Wienzeile; 6am-7.30pm Mon-Fri, to 6pm Sat; U1, U2, U4 Karlsplatz, U4 Kettenbrückengasse), the place to *nasch* (snack) in Vienna. Assemble your own picnic from stalls piled high with meats, fruits, vegetables, cheeses, olives, spices and wine. There are also plenty of people-watching cafes dishing up good-value lunches, and delis and takeaway stands where you can grab a falafel or kebab.

Freyung Market (www.biobauernmarkt-freyung.at; 01, Freyung; 9am-6pm Fri & Sat ; 1A, U2 Schottentor) sells farm-fresh produce, as does the bustling **Karmelitermarkt** (02, Karmelitermarkt; 6am-7.30pm Mon-Fri, 6am-5pm Sat; 5A, U2 Taborstrasse, 2). Head to the Saturday farmers market at the latter for brunch at one of the excellent deli-cafes, followed by a mooch around stalls selling top-quality local goodies.

TOP CHOICE **Griechenbeisl** BISTRO, PUB €€
(533 19 77; 01, Fleischmarkt 11; mains €11.60-24.90; 11am-1am; Schwedenplatz, 1, 2) This is Vienna's oldest *Beisl* (dating from 1447), once frequented by the likes of Beethoven, Schubert and Brahms. The vaulted, wood-panelled rooms are a cosy setting for classic Viennese dishes.

Drinking

Pulsating bars cluster north and south of the Naschmarkt, around Spittelberg and along the Gürtel (mainly around the U6 stops of Josefstädter Strasse and Nussdorfer Strasse). The Bermuda Dreieck (Bermuda Triangle), near the Danube Canal in the Innere Stadt, also has many bars, but they are more touristy.

Vienna's *Heurigen* cluster in the wine-growing suburbs to the north, southwest, west and northwest of the city. They are identified by a *Busch'n* (a green wreath or branch) hanging over the door. Opening times are approximately from 4pm to 11pm, and wine costs around €3 per *Viertel* (250mL).

Palmenhaus BAR, CAFE
(www.palmenhaus.at; 01, Burggarten; 10am-2am) Housed in a beautifully restored Jugendstil palm house, the Palmenhaus has a relaxed vibe. In summer, tables spill out onto the terrace overlooking the Burggarten, and DJs spin here on Friday nights.

Phil BAR, CAFE
(www.phil.info; 06, Gumpendorfer Strasse 10-12; 5pm-1am Mon, 9am-1am Tue-Sun) A retro bar, book and record store, Phil attracts a bohemian crowd happy to squat on kitsch furniture your grandma used to own. Staff are super-friendly and the vibe is as relaxed as can be.

Volksgarten Pavillon BAR
(www.volksgarten-pavillon.at; 01, Burgring 1; 11am-2am Apr–mid-Sep; Volkstheater, 1, 2, D, 71 Dr-Karl-Renner-Ring) A lovely 1950s-style pavilion with views of Heldenplatz and an ever-popular garden.

Das Möbel BAR, CAFE
(http://dasmoebel.at; 07, Burggasse 10; 10am-midnight; Volkstheater) The interior is never dull at this bar near the MuseumsQuartier. It's remarkable for its funky decor and furniture – cube stools, assorted moulded lamps – and everything is up for sale.

Mon Ami BAR
(www.monami.at; 06, Theobaldgasse 9; 6pm-1am Wed-Sat; U2 MuseumsQuartier) This former pet-grooming salon morphed into a lovely '60s-style bar mixes excellent cocktails, has DJ and jam session nights, and attracts a laid-back, unpretentious crowd.

TOP CHOICE **Dachboden** BAR
(25hours Hotel, 07, Lerchenfelder Strasse 1-3; 2pm-1am Tue-Sat, 2-10pm Sun; Volkstheater, 2) The terrace with knockout views of Vienna is the big deal, but even in winter this arty attic bar is wonderfully relaxed, with low cushion seating and the occasional DJ night.

Vis-à-vis WINE BAR
(512 93 50; www.weibel.at; 01, Wollzeile 5; 4.30-10.30pm Tue-Sat; Stephansplatz) Hidden down a narrow, atmospheric passage is this wee wine bar. It may only seat close to 10 but it makes up for it with over 350 wines on offer (with a strong emphasis on Austrian faves) and great antipasti.

TOP CHOICE **Strandbar Herrmann** BAR
(www.strandbarherrmann.at; 03, Herrmannpark; 10am-2am Apr–early Oct; 1, O) You'd swear you're by the sea at this hopping canalside beach bar, with beach chairs, sand

and hordes of Viennese livin' it up on hot summer evenings.

TOP CHOICE Loos American Bar COCKTAIL BAR

(www.loosbar.at; 01, Kärntner Durchgang 10; ⊙noon-5am Thu-Sat, to 4am Sun-Wed; MStephansplatz) Designed by Adolf Loos in 1908, this tiny box decked head-to-toe in onyx is *the* spot for a classic cocktail in the Innere Stadt, expertly whipped up by talented mixologists.

10er Marie WINE BAR

(16, Ottakringerstrasse 222-224; ⊙3pm-midnight Mon-Sat; MU3) Vienna's oldest *Heuriger* has been going strong since 1740 – Schubert, Strauss and Crown Prince Rudolf all kicked back a glass or three here. The usual buffet is available. The *Heuriger* is 400m northwest of U3 Ottakring station.

FREE Siebensternbräu MICROBREWERY

(www.7stern.at; 07, Siebensterngasse 19; ⊙11am-midnight; MNeubaugasse, 49) Large brewery with all the main varieties, plus hemp beer, chilli beer and smoky beer. The hidden back garden is sublime in summer.

☆ Entertainment

Vienna is, and probably will be till the end of time, the European capital of opera and classical music. The line-up of music events is never-ending and even the city's buskers are often classically trained musicians.

Box offices are generally open from Monday to Saturday.

TOP CHOICE Staatsoper OPERA

(☎514 44 7880; www.wiener-staatsoper.at; 01, Opernring 2) Performances at Vienna's premier opera and classical music venue are lavish, formal affairs, where people dress up. Standing-room tickets (€3 to €4) are sold 80 minutes before performances begin.

Musikverein CONCERT VENUE

(☎505 81 90; www.musikverein.at; 01, Bösendorferstrasse 12) The opulent Musikverein, home to the Vienna Philharmonic Orchestra, is celebrated for its acoustics. Standing-room tickets in the main hall cost €5 to €6.

Pratersauna CLUB

(www.pratersauna.tv; Waldsteingartenstrasse 135; ⊙club 9pm-6am Wed-Sun, pool 1-9pm Fri & Sat Jun-Sep; SU2 Messe-Prater) Pool, cafe, bistro and club converge in a former sauna. These days, you'll sweat it up on the dance floor any given night, with DJs playing mostly techno and electro. Take U2 to Messe-Prater and walk south 600m.

Porgy & Bess JAZZ

(☎512 88 11; www.porgy.at; 01, Riemergasse 11; €18 most nights; ⊙concerts from 7pm or 8pm; MStubentor, 2) Quality is the cornerstone of Porgy & Bess' popularity. The sophisticated

COFFEE HOUSE CULTURE

Vienna's legendary *Kaffeehäuser* (coffee houses) are wonderful places for people-watching, daydreaming and catching up on gossip or world news. Most serve light meals alongside mouth-watering cakes and tortes. Expect to pay around €8 for a coffee with a slice of cake. These are just five of our favourites.

Café Sperl (www.cafesperl.at; 06, Gumpendorfer Strasse 11; ⊙7am-11pm Mon-Sat, 11am-8pm Sun; ; 57A, SU2 Museumsquartier) Gorgeous Jugendstil fittings, grand dimensions, cosy booths and an unhurried air. The must-try is *Sperl Torte* – an almond and chocolate cream dream.

Kleines Café (01, Franziskanerplatz 3; ⊙10am-2am) Tiny bohemian cafe with wonderful summer seating on Franziskanerplatz.

Café Sacher (01, Philharmonikerstrasse 4; ⊙8am-midnight) This opulent coffee house is celebrated for its *Sacher Torte* (€4.90), a rich chocolate cake with apricot jam once favoured by Emperor Franz Josef.

Demel (01, Kohlmarkt 14; ⊙9am-7pm; 1A, 2A Michaelerplatz, MHerrengasse, Stephansplatz) An elegant, regal cafe near the Hofburg. Demel's speciality is the *Anna Torte*, a chocolate and nougat calorie-bomb.

Café Drechsler (www.cafedrechsler.at; 06, Linke Wienzeile 22; ⊙open 23hr, closed 2-3am; ; SKettenbrückengasse) Sir Terence Conran revamped this stylish yet distinctly Viennese cafe. Its goulash is legendary, as are the DJ tunes that keep the vibe hip and upbeat.

club presents a top-drawer line-up of modern jazz acts, and DJs fill spots on weekends.

Volksoper CONCERT VENUE
(People's Opera; 514 44 36 70; www.volksoper.at; 09, Währinger Strasse 78) Vienna's second opera house features operettas, dance and musicals. Standing tickets go for as little as €2 to €6.

Donau CLUB
(www.donautechno.com; 07, Karl-Schweighofer-Gasse 10; 8pm-btwn 2am & 6am) DJs spin techno to a friendly, cocktail-sipping crowd at this columned, strikingly illuminated club. It's easily missed – look for the grey metal door.

Konzerthaus CONCERT VENUE
(242 002; www.konzerthaus.at; 03, Lothringerstrasse 20; box office 9am-7.45pm Mon-Fri, 9am-1pm Sat, plus 45 mins before performance; M Stadtpark, 71, D) This is a major venue in classical music circles, but throughout the year ethnic music, rock, pop or jazz can also be heard in its hallowed halls.

Volksgarten ClubDiskothek CLUB
(www.volksgarten.at; 01, Burgring 1; admission from €6; 10pm-4am Tue & Thu-Sat ; M MuseumsQuartier, Volkstheater, 1, 2, D, 71 Dr-Karl-Renner-Ring) This club attracts a well-dressed crowd keen to strut their stuff and scan for talent from the long bar. The quality sound system pumps out an array of music styles.

Theater an der Wien THEATRE
(588 85; www.theater-wien.at; 06, Linke Wienzeile 6; 59A, S U1, U2, U4 Karlsplatz) Once the host of monumental premieres such as Mozart's *Die Zauberflöte (The Magic Flute),* this theatre now showcases opera, dance and concerts.

Burg Kino CINEMA
(587 84 06; www.burgkino.at; 01, Opernring 19; S U2 MuseumsQuartier, 1, 2, D) English films; has regular screenings of *The Third Man.*

Shopping

In the alley-woven Innere Stadt, go to Kohlmarkt for designer chic, Herrengasse for antiques and Kärntnerstrasse for high-street brands. Naglergasse's old-world speciality stores are pure nostalgia. Tune into Vienna's creative pulse in the idiosyncratic boutiques and concept stores in Neubau, especially along Kirchengasse and Lindengasse.

Dorotheum ANTIQUES
(www.dorotheum.com; 01, Dorotheergasse 17; 10am-6pm Mon-Fri, 9am-5pm Sat; M Stephansplatz) One of Europe's largest auction houses, where surprisingly not every item is priced out of this world. Stop by and simply browse – it's as entertaining as visiting many of Vienna's museums.

TOP CHOICE **Blühendes Konfekt** FOOD
(www.bluehendes-konfekt.com; 06, Schmalzhofgasse 19; 10am-6.30pm Wed-Fri; S U3 Zieglergasse, Westbahnhof, 5) Violets, forest strawberries and cherry blossom, wild mint and oregano – Michael Diewald makes the most of the seasons and what grows in his garden to create one-of-a-kind candied bouquets and confectionery. The shop is 350m southwest of U3 Zieglergasse station on Mariahilfer Strasse.

Näherei Apfel FOOD, FASHION
(www.naeherei-apfel.at; Kettenbrückengasse 8; 11am-7pm Tue-Fri, 10am-4pm Sat; S U4 Kettenbrückengasse) At this little workshop-store

IMPERIAL ENTERTAINMENT

Founded over five centuries ago by Maximilian I, the world-famous **Vienna Boys' Choir** (www.wsk.at) is the original boy band. These cherubic angels in sailor suits still hold a fond place in Austrian hearts. **Tickets** (533 99 27; www.hofburgkapelle.at; 01, Hofburg, Schweizerhof; Sunday in Burgkapelle €5-29) for their Sunday performances at 9.15am (September to June) in the Burgkapelle (Royal Chapel) in the Hofburg should be booked around six weeks in advance. The group also performs regularly in the Musikverein.

Another throwback to the Habsburg glory days is the **Spanische Hofreitschule** (Spanish Riding School; 533 90 31; www.srs.at; 01, Michaelerplatz 1; performances 11am Sat & Sun mid-Feb–Jun & late Aug-Dec). White Lipizzaner stallions gracefully perform equine ballet to classical music, while chandeliers shimmer from above and the audience cranes to see from pillared balconies. Tickets, costing between €23 and €158, are ordered through the website, but be warned that performances usually sell out months in advance. Unclaimed tickets are sold about two hours before performances. **Morning Training** (adult/child/family €14/7/28; 10am-noon Tue-Fri Feb-Jun & mid-Aug–Dec) same-day tickets are available at the **visitor centre** (9am-4pm Tue-Sun) on Michaelerplatz.

you can learn to sew (a two-hour intro course costs €23), browse Ursula's hand-crafted clothing and bags, and buy Burgenland apples dried, preserved, juiced and by the kilo.

Gabarage Upcycling Design DESIGN
(www.gabarage.at; 06, Schleifmühlgasse 6; ⏲10am-6pm Mon-Thu, 10am-7pm Fri, 11am-5pm Sat; Ⓢ U1 Taubstummengasse, 🚊1, 62) Upcycling is the word at this innovative design store, turning waste into wonders, from rubbish bin couches to bowling pin vases.

TOP CHOICE **Art Up** FASHION, ACCESSORIES
(www.artup.at; 01, Bauernmarkt 8; ⏲11am-6.30pm Mon-Fri, 11am-5pm Sat; Ⓜ Stephansplatz) Take the temperature of Vienna's contemporary design scene at Art Up, showcasing the latest designs of around 80 Austrian creatives.

Woka HOMEWARES
(www.woka.at; 01, Singerstrasse 16; ⏲10am-6pm Mon-Fri, 10am-5pm Sat; 🚊Stephansplatz) Accurate re-creations of Wiener Werkstätte lamps are the hallmark of Woka.

Altmann & Kühne FOOD
(www.altmann-kuehne.at; Graben 30; ⏲9am-6.30pm Mon-Fri, 10am-5pm Sat) Altmann & Kühne has been producing, and beautifully packaging, handmade bonbons for over 100 years. Stop by for a box of its famous *Liliputkonfekt* (miniature pralines).

Lomoshop PHOTOGRAPHY
(07, Museumsplatz 1; ⏲11am-7pm; Ⓢ U2 Museums-Quartier) Cult Lomo cameras, gadgets and accessories in the MuseumsQuartier.

TO MARKET

Vienna's atmospheric **Flohmarkt** (Flea Market; 05, Kettenbrückengasse; ⏲dawn-4pm Sat; Ⓢ U4 Kettenbrückengasse) shouldn't be missed, with goods piled up in apparent chaos on the walkway. Books, clothes, records, ancient electrical goods, old postcards, ornaments, carpets…you name it, it's all here. Come prepared to haggle.

From mid-November, *Christkindlmärkte* (Christmas markets) bring festive sparkle to Vienna, their stalls laden with gifts, *glühwein* (mulled wine) and *Maroni* (roasted chestnuts). Some of the best include the pretty but touristy **Rathausplatz market** (🚊1, 2), the traditional **Spittelberg market** (🚌48A, Ⓢ U2, U3 Volkstheater, 🚊49) in Spittelberg's cobbled streets, where you can pick up quality crafts, and the authentic, oft-forgotten **Heiligenkreuzerhof market** (Ⓜ Schwedenplatz, 🚊2 Stubentor).

Information

Many cafes and bars offer free wi-fi for their customers. Free public hotspots include Rathausplatz, Naschmarkt and Prater.

Airport Information Office (⏲6am-11pm) Located in the arrivals hall.

Allgemeines Krankenhaus (☎404 000; www.akhwien.at; 09, Währinger Gürtel 18-20) Hospital with a 24-hour casualty ward.

Jugendinfo (Vienna Youth Information; ☎4000-84 100; www.jugendinfowien.at; 01, Babenbergerstrasse 1; ⏲2-7pm Mon-Wed, 1-6pm Thu-Sat) Offers various reduced-price tickets for people aged 13 to 26.

Main Post Office (01, Fleischmarkt 19; ⏲7am-10pm Mon-Fri, 9am-10pm Sat & Sun)

Police Station (☎31 310; 01, Schottenring 7-9)

Tourist Info Wien (☎245 55; www.wien.info; 01, Albertinaplatz; ⏲9am-7pm; 📶; Ⓜ Stephansplatz, 🚊1, 2, D, 71 Kärntner Ring/Oper) Vienna's main tourist office, with a ticket agency, hotel booking service, free maps and every brochure you could ever wish for.

Getting There & Away

Air

For details on flying to Vienna, see p96.

Boat

Fast hydrofoils travel eastwards to Bratislava (one way €19 to €33, return €38 to €66, 1¼ hours) daily from April to October. From May to September, they also travel twice weekly to Budapest (one way/return €109/125, 5½ hours). Bookings can be made through **DDSG Blue Danube** (☎58 880; www.ddsg-blue-danube.at; Handelskai 265).

Heading west, a series of boats ply the Danube between Krems and Melk, with a handful of services originating in Vienna. Two respectable operators include DDSG Blue Danube and **Brandner** (☎07433-25 90 21; www.brandner.at; Ufer 50, Wallsee), the latter located in Wallsee. Both run trips from April through October that start at around €15 one way. For trips into Germany, contact **Donauschiffahrt Wurm + Köck** (☎0732-783 607; www.donauschiffahrt.de; Untere Donaulände 1, Linz).

Bus

Vienna currently has no central bus station. National Bundesbuses arrive and depart from several different locations, depending on the

MEDIA

Tune into Vienna's cultural scene on the following websites:

About Vienna (www.aboutvienna.org) General website with cultural and sightseeing information.

City of Vienna (www.wien.gv.at) Comprehensive government-run website.

Falter (www.falter.at, in German) Online version of the ever-popular *Falter* magazine.

Vienna Online (www.vienna.at, in German) Site with info on parties, festivals and news.

destination. Bus lines serving Vienna include **Eurolines** (☎798 29 00; www.eurolines.com; Erdbergstrasse 200; ⏱6.30am-9pm).

Car & Motorcycle

The Gürtel is an outer ring road that joins up with the A22 on the north bank of the Danube and the A23 southeast of town. All the main road routes intersect with this system, including the A1 from Linz and Salzburg, and the A2 from Graz.

Train

Vienna is one of central Europe's main rail hubs. **Österreichische Bundesbahn** (ÖBB; www.oebb.at; Austrian Federal Railway) is the main operator. There are direct services and connections to many European cities. Sample destinations include Budapest (2½ to three hours, €37.40), Munich (four to five hours, €88), Paris (11½ to 15 hours, €88), Prague (4½ hours, €64.40) and Venice (seven to 11 hours, €63 to €99).

Vienna has multiple train stations. At press time, a massive construction project was in progress at Vienna's former Südbahnhof: an eastern section had been set up as a temporary station to serve some trains to/from the east, including Bratislava. The complex is due to reopen as Hauptbahnhof Wien (Vienna Central Station) in 2013, and as the main station it will receive international trains. As a result, all long-distance trains are being rerouted among the rest of Vienna's train stations, including the recently revamped Westbahnhof. Further train stations include Franz-Josefs-Bahnhof (which handles trains to/from the Danube Valley), Wien Mitte, Wien Nord and Meidling.

Vienna's shiny new **Hauptbahnhof** (Vienna Central Station; www.hauptbahnhof-wien.at; 🚌13A, 69A, Ⓜ U1, 🚋D, 0, 18) partially reopened in December 2012, with an eastern section set up to serve some trains to/from the east, including Bratislava. The rail project is a massive €987 million undertaking and operations are expected to fully resume in 2015, with the main station receiving international trains. Currently, most long-distance trains are being rerouted among the rest of Vienna's train stations, including the recently revamped Westbahnhof. Further train stations include Franz-Josefs-Bahnhof (which handles trains to/from the Danube Valley), Wien Mitte, Wien Nord and Meidling.

Getting Around

To/From the Airport

It is 19km from the city centre to **Vienna International Airport** (VIE; www.viennaairport.com) in Schwechat. The **City Airport Train** (CAT; www.cityairporttrain.com; return adult/child under 15 yrs €19/free; ⏱5.36am-11.06pm from airport) runs every 30 minutes and takes 16 minutes between the airport and Wien Mitte; book online for a €2 discount. The S-Bahn (S7) does the same journey (single €4), but in 25 minutes.

Buses run every 20 or 30 minutes, between 5am and 11pm, from the airport (one way/return €8/13). Services run to Meidling, Westbahnhof and Schwedenplatz.

Taxis cost about €35. **C&K Airport Service** (☎444 44; www.cundk.at) charges €32 one way for shared vans.

Bicycle

Cycling is an excellent way to get around and explore the city – over 800km of cycle tracks criss-cross the capital. Popular cycling areas include the 7km path around the Ringstrasse, the Donauinsel, the Prater and along the Danube Canal (Donaukanal).

Vienna's city bike scheme is called **Vienna City Bike** (www.citybikewien.at; 1st hr free, 2nd/3rd hr €1/2, per hr thereafter €4), with more than 60 bicycle stands across the city. A credit card is required to rent bikes – just swipe your card in the machine and follow the instructions (in a number of languages).

Car & Motorcycle

Due to a system of one-way streets and expensive parking, you're better off using the excellent public transport system. If you do plan to drive in the city, take special care of the trams: they always have priority and vehicles must wait behind trams when they stop to pick up or set down passengers.

Fiakers

More of a tourist novelty than anything else, a *Fiaker* is a traditional-style horse-drawn carriage. Bowler-hatted drivers generally speak English and point out places of interest en route. Expect to pay a cool €80/105 for a

40-/60-minute ride from Stephansplatz, Albertinaplatz or Heldenplatz.

Public Transport

Vienna's unified public transport network encompasses trains, trams, buses, and underground (U-Bahn) and suburban (S-Bahn) trains. Free maps and information pamphlets are available from **Wiener Linien** (7909-100; www.wienerlinien.at).

Before use, all tickets must be validated at the entrance to U-Bahn stations and on buses and trams (except for weekly and monthly tickets). Tickets are cheaper to buy from ticket machines in U-Bahn stations and in *Tabak* (tobacconist) shops, where singles cost €2. On board, they cost €2.20. Singles are valid for an hour, and you may change lines on the same trip.

A 24-hour ticket costs €6.70, a 48-hour ticket €11.70 and a 72-hour ticket €14.50. Weekly tickets (valid Monday to Sunday) cost €15; the Vienna Card (€19.90) includes travel on public transport for up to three days. The Strip Ticket (*Streifenkarte*) costs €8 and gives you four single tickets.

Taxi

Taxis are metered for city journeys and cost €2.60 flag fall during the day and €2.70 at night, plus a small per kilometre fee. It's safe to hail taxis from the street.

THE DANUBE VALLEY

The stretch of Danube between Krems and Melk, known locally as the Wachau, is arguably the loveliest along the entire length of the mighty river. Both banks are dotted with ruined castles and medieval towns, and lined with terraced vineyards. Further upstream is the industrial city of Linz, Austria's avant-garde art and new technology trailblazer.

Krems an der Donau

02732 / POP 24,100

Sitting on the northern bank of the Danube against a backdrop of terraced vineyards, Krems marks the beginning of the Wachau. It has an attractive cobbled centre, a small university, some good restaurants and the gallery-dotted Kunstmeile (Art Mile).

Sights & Activities

It's a pleasure to wander the cobblestone streets of Krems, especially at night. Don't miss the baroque treasures of Schürerplatz.

Kunsthalle GALLERY
(www.kunsthalle.at; Franz-Zeller-Platz 3; adult/concessions €10/9; 10am-6pm) The flagship of Krems' **Kunstmeile** (www.kunstmeile-krems.at), an eclectic collection of galleries and museums, the Kunsthalle has a program of small but excellent changing exhibitions.

Sleeping & Eating

Arte Hotel Krems HOTEL €€
(71 123; www.arte hotel.at; Dr-Karl-Dorrek-Strasse 23; s €85-105, d €128-162; P) This comfortable new art hotel close to the university has large, well-styled rooms in bright colours and with open-plan bathrooms.

Hotel Unter den Linden HOTEL €€
(82 115; www.udl.at; Schillerstrasse 5; s €50, d €74-98) This big, yellow, family-run hotel has knowledgeable and helpful owners, bright comfortable rooms and a convenient location in Krems itself.

Mörwald Kloster Und AUSTRIAN €€€
(70 493; www.moerwald.at; Undstrasse 6; mains €35-39, 5-course menu €75, 3-course lunch €29; lunch & dinner Tue-Sat) Run by celebrity chef and winemaker Toni Mörwald, this is one of the Wachau's best restaurants. Delicacies from roast pigeon breast to fish dishes with French touches are married with top wines. There's a lovely garden.

Information

Krems Tourismus (82 676; www.krems.info; Utzstrasse 1; 9am-6pm Mon-Fri) Has excellent city walk and vineyard maps, and stocks a *Heurigen* calendar.

Getting There & Away

Frequent daily trains connect Krems with Vienna's Franz-Josefs-Bahnhof (€15.20, one hour) and Melk (€11.90, 1¼ hours). It is slightly quicker to take a bus to Melk (€10.20, one hour) rather than a train. The boat station is near Donaustrasse, about 2km west of the train station.

ON YOUR BIKE

Many towns in the Danube Valley are part of a bike-hire network called **Nextbike** (02742-229 901; www.nextbike.at; per hour/24 hours €1/8). After registering using a credit card (either by calling the hotline or on the website), a refunded €1 is deducted and you can begin renting bicycles.

Dürnstein

02711 / POP 870

The pretty town of Dürnstein, on a supple curve in the Danube, is known for its hilltop castle, **Kuenringerburg castle**, where Richard I (the Lionheart) of England was imprisoned in 1192. His unscheduled stopover on the way home from the Crusades came courtesy of Austrian archduke Leopold V, whom he had insulted.

There's not much left of the castle today. It's basically just a pile of rubble. Still, it's worth snapping a picture and the views from the top are breathtaking.

Sleeping & Eating

The tourist office has a list of private rooms and *Gasthöfe* (guesthouses) in Dürnstein.

Hotel Schloss Dürnstein HOTEL €€
(212; www.schloss.at; Dürnstein 2; s €139-169, d €185-225; P@) This castle is the last word in luxury in town, with antique-furnished rooms, a spa, two pools and a high-end restaurant (mains €16 to €30) with staggering views over the river.

Hotel Sänger Blondel HOTEL €€
(253; www.saengerblondel.at; Klosterplatz/Dürnstein 64; s €72, d €98-118; P@) Expect a warm welcome from the Schendl family at this hotel, with good-sized rooms facing the Danube, castle or tree-shaded garden. Breakfast is jazzed up with regional produce like Wachau apricot jam.

Restaurant Loibnerhof AUSTRIAN €€
(82 890; www.loibnerhof.at; Unterloiben 7; mains €15-26; Wed-Sun) Situated 1.5km east of Dürnstein in Unterloiben, this family-run restaurant inside a 400-year-old building has a leafy garden for enjoying local specialities and homegrown wines.

Information

For more about Dürnstein, contact the **tourist office** (200; www.duernstein.at; 9am-noon daily, plus 4-6pm Fri & Sat, closed mid-Oct–Mar), a two-minute walk south of the centre.

Getting There & Away

Dürnstein can be reached from Krems by train (€2.50, 18 minutes, hourly).

Melk

02752 / POP 5260

With its sparkling and majestic abbey-fortress, Melk is a highlight of any visit to the Danube Valley. Many visitors cycle here for the day – wearily pushing their bikes through the cobblestone streets.

Sights

TOP CHOICE **Stift Melk** ABBEY
(Benedictine Abbey of Melk; 5550; www.stift-melk.at; Abt Berthold Dietmayr Strasse 1; adult/child €9.50/5, with guided tour €11.50/7; 9am-5.30pm) Rising like a vision on a hill overlooking the town, Stift Melk is Austria's most famous abbey. It has been home to Benedictine monks since the 11th century, though it owes its current good looks to 18th-century mastermind Jakob Prandtauer.

The interior of the twin-spired monastery church is baroque gone barmy, with endless prancing angels and gold twirls. Other highlights include the **Bibliothek** (Library) and the **Marmorsaal** (Marble Hall); the trompe l'oeil on the ceiling (by Paul Troger) gives the illusion of greater height. Eleven of the imperial rooms, where dignitaries (including Napoleon) stayed, now house a **museum**.

From around November to March, the monastery can only be visited by guided tour (11am and 2pm daily). Always phone ahead to ensure you get an English-language tour.

Sleeping & Eating

Restaurants and cafes with alfresco seating line the Rathausplatz.

Hotel Restaurant zur Post HOTEL €€
(523 45; www.post-melk.at; Linzer Strasse 1; s €62-74, d €102-117, tr €125-145, q €150; P@) This bright hotel in the heart of town has large, comfortable rooms. There's a sauna, free bike use for guests and a decent restaurant serving Austrian classics.

Hotel Wachau HOTEL €€
(525 31; www.hotel-wachau.at; Am Wachberg 3; s €58-88, d €96-126; P@) For comfortable, modern rooms, try this hotel 2km southeast of the train station. The restaurant (mains €12 to €20, gourmet menu €45) is open for dinner Monday to Saturday and specialises in well-prepared regional cuisine.

Information

The centrally located **tourist office** (☎51 160; www.niederoesterreich.at/melk; Kremser Strasse 5; ⊙9.30am-6pm Mon-Sat, 9.30am-4pm Sun) has maps and plenty of useful information.

Getting There & Away

Boats leave from the canal by Pionierstrasse, 400m north of the abbey. There are hourly trains to Vienna (€17.10, 1¼ hours).

Linz

☎0732 / POP 191,100

In Linz beginnt's (It begins in Linz) goes the Austrian saying, and it's spot on. The technology trailblazer and European Capital of Culture 2009 is blessed with a leading-edge cyber centre and world-class contemporary art gallery.

LINZ CARD

The **Linz Card** (€15/25 for one/three days) gives entry to major sights and unlimited use of public transport.

Sights & Activities

Linz' baroque Hauptplatz and sculpture-strewn Danube Park are made for aimless ambling.

Ars Electronica Center MUSEUM
(www.aec.at; Ars Electronica Strasse 1; adult/child €8/5; ⊙9am-5pm Wed-Fri, to 9pm Thu, 10am-6pm Sat & Sun) Ars Electronica Center zooms in on tomorrow's technology, science and digital media. In themed labs you can interact with robots, animate digital objects and (virtually) travel to outer space. The shipshape centre kaleidoscopically changes colour after dark.

Lentos GALLERY
(www.lentos.at; Ernst-Koref-Promenade 1; adult/child €6.50/4.50; ⊙10am-6pm Wed-Mon, to 9pm Thu) Ars Electronica's rival icon across the Danube is the rectangular glass-and-steel Lentos, also strikingly illuminated by night. The gallery guards one of Austria's finest modern art collections, including works by Warhol, Schiele and Klimt, which sometimes feature in the large-scale exhibitions.

Neuer Dom CHURCH
(New Cathedral; Herrenstrasse 26; ⊙7.30am-7pm Mon-Sat, 8am-7pm Sun) This neo-Gothic giant of a cathedral was designed in the mid-19th century by Vinzenz Statz of Cologne Dom fame. The tower's height was restricted to 134m, so as not to outshine Stephansdom in Vienna.

Schlossmuseum MUSEUM
(Castle Museum; www.schlossmuseum.at; Schlossberg 1; adult/child €6.50/4.50; ⊙9am-6pm Tue-Fri, to 9pm Thu, 10am-5pm Sat & Sun) Linz' hilltop castle is a treasure trove of art and history. The Gothic ecclesiastical paintings are a highlight.

Pöstlingbergbahn VIEWPOINT
(adult/child €5.60/2.80; ⊙6am-10.30pm Mon-Sat, 7.30am-10.30pm Sun) This gondola features in the *Guinness Book of Records* as the world's steepest mountain railway – quite some feat for such a low-lying city! Far-reaching city and Danube views await at the summit.

Sleeping & Eating

Spitz Hotel HOTEL €€
(☎73 37 33; www.spitzhotel.at; Fiedlerstrasse 6; r €99-250; P❄@☜) Much-lauded Austrian architect Isa Stein has left her avant-garde imprint on the Spitz. Each of the hotel's rooms has unique artworks. Minimalism rules here, with clean lines, open-plan bathrooms and hardwood floors.

Hotel am Domplatz HOTEL €€
(☎77 30 00; www.hotelamdomplatz.at; Stifterstrasse 4; s €125-145, d €154-184; P❄@☜) Sidling up to the Neuer Dom, this glass-and-concrete design hotel reveals light, streamlined interiors. Wind down with a view at the rooftop spa.

k.u.k. Hofbäckerei CAFE €
(Pfarrgasse 17; coffee & cake €3-6; ⊙6.30am-6pm Mon-Fri, 7am-12.30pm Sat) The empire lives on at this gloriously stuck-in-time cafe. Here Fritz Rath bakes *the* best *Linzer Torte* in town – rich, spicy and with lattice pastry that crumbles just so.

Cubus FUSION €€
(Ars-Electronica-Strasse 1; mains €10.50-23.50; ⊙9am-1am Mon-Sat, 9am-6pm Sun; ☜) On the 3rd floor of the Ars Electronica Center, this glass cube has stellar Danube views. The menu is strictly fusion and the two-course lunch a snip at €7.20.

Information

Hotspot Linz (www.hotspotlinz.at) Free wi-fi at 120 hotspots in the city, including the Ars Electronica Center and Lentos.

Post Office (Domgasse 1; ⊙8am-6pm Mon-Fri, 9am-noon Sat) Handy to the centre.

Tourist Information Linz (7070 2009; www.linz.at; Hauptplatz 1; 9am-7pm Mon-Sat, 10am-7pm Sun, shorter hours winter) Free city maps and room reservation service.

Getting There & Around

AIR Austrian Airlines, Lufthansa, Ryanair and Air Berlin fly to the **Blue Danube Airport** (www.linz-airport.at), 13km southwest of Linz. An hourly shuttle bus (€2.70, 20 minutes) links the airport to the main train station.

PUBLIC TRANSPORT Bus and tram tickets are bought before you board from pavement dispensers or *Tabak* (tobacconist) shops. Single tickets cost €2 and day passes €4.

TRANSPORT Linz is halfway between Salzburg and Vienna on the main road and rail routes. Trains to Salzburg (€23.70, 1¼ hours) and Vienna (€34.30, 1½ hours) leave approximately twice hourly.

THE SOUTH

Austria's two main southern states, Styria (Steiermark) and Carinthia (Kärnten), often feel worlds apart from the rest of the country, both in climate and attitude. Styria is a blissful amalgamation of genteel architecture, rolling green hills, vine-covered slopes and soaring mountains. Its capital, Graz, is one of Austria's most attractive cities.

A fashion-conscious crowd heads to sun-drenched Carinthia in summer. Sidling up to Italy, the region exudes an atmosphere that's as close to Mediterranean as this staunch country gets.

Graz

0316 / POP 265,300

Austria's second-largest city is probably its most relaxed and, after Vienna, its liveliest for after-hours pursuits. It's an attractive place with bristling green parkland, red rooftops and a small, fast-flowing river gushing through its centre. Architecturally, it has Renaissance courtyards and provincial baroque palaces complemented by innovative modern designs.

The surrounding countryside, a mixture of vineyards, mountains, forested hills and thermal springs, is within easy striking distance.

Sights & Activities

Graz is a city easily enjoyed by simply wandering aimlessly. Admission to all of the major museums with a 24-hour ticket costs €11/4 for adults/children.

TOP CHOICE **Universalmuseum Joanneum** MUSEUM COMPLEX
(www.museum-joanneum.at; Raubergasse 10) The crowning glory of this Styria-wide ensemble of museums and palaces is the new **Joanneumsviertel** (www.joanneumsviertel.at; Kalchberggasse ; visitor centre 10am-5pm) quarter, gathered around squares and courtyards and seamlessly bringing together baroque and contemporary architecture. Besides the state library and multimedia collections, the complex is home to the **Neue Galerie Graz** (Joanneumsviertel, Kalchberggasse; adult/child €8/3; 10am-5pm Tue-Sun), with an outstanding collection of 19th- and 20th-century art, placing the emphasis on Austrian masters from Klimt to Otto Wagner.

Kunsthaus Graz GALLERY
(www.kunsthausgraz.at; Lendkai 1; adult/child €8/3; 10am-5pm Tue-Sun) Designed by British architects Peter Cook and Colin Fournier, this world-class contemporary art space looks something like a space-age sea slug. Exhibitions change every three to four months.

Schloss Eggenberg PALACE
(Eggenberger Allee 90; adult/child €8/3; palace tours 10am-4pm Tue-Sun Apr-Oct) A blend of gothic, Renaissance and baroque styles, this beautiful Unesco World Heritage palace can be reached by tram 1 from Hauptplatz. Admission includes a guided tour (on the hour except at 1pm), taking in 24 *Prunkräume* (staterooms), which are based around astronomy, the zodiac and classical or religious mythology.

FREE **Murinsel** BRIDGE
This artificial island-cum-bridge in the Mur River is an open seashell of glass, concrete and steel by New York artist Vito Acconci. It houses a trendy cafe-bar in aqua blue and a small stage.

Schlossberg VIEWPOINT
The wooded slopes of Schlossberg (473m) can be reached on foot, with the funicular **Schlossbergbahn** (Castle Hill Railway; 1hr ticket adult/child €2/1) from Kaiser-Franz-Josef-Kai, or by **Glass Lift** (Glass Lift 1hr ticket €1.90) from Schlossbergplatz. Napoleon was hard-pressed to raze this fortress, but raze it he did. Today the medieval **Uhrturm** (Clock Tower) is the legacy. The townsfolk paid Napoleon a ransom of 2987 florins and 11 farthings to spare the tower during the 1809 invasion.

Landeszeughaus MUSEUM
(www.zeughaus.at; Herrengasse 16; adult/child €8/3; ⏲10am-5pm Mon & Wed-Sun) A must-see for fans of armour and weapons, housing an astounding array of 30,000 gleaming exhibits.

FREE **Burg** CASTLE, PARK
(Hofgasse) At the far end of Graz' 15th-century castle is an ingenious **double staircase** (1499). Adjoining it is the **Stadtpark**, the city's largest green space.

Sleeping

Hotel zum Dom HOTEL €€
(☎82 48 00; www.domhotel.co.at; Bürgergasse 14; s €84-99, d €124-219, ste €194-239; P❄☎) Hotel zum Dom's individually furnished rooms come with power showers or whirlpools, and one suite even has a terrace whirlpool.

Hotel Daniel HOTEL €
(☎711 080; www.hoteldaniel.com; Europaplatz 1; r €59-79, breakfast per person €9 ; P❄@) Perched at the top of Annenstrasse, the Daniel is an exclusive design hotel. All rooms are tastefully furnished in minimalist designs. You can rent a Vespa (€15 per day) and there's a 24-hour espresso bar.

Augarten Hotel HOTEL €€
(☎20 800; www.augartenhotel.at; Schönaugasse 53; s €89-169, d €114-194; P❄☎≋) The arty Augarten is decorated with the owner's private collection. All rooms are bright and modern, and the pool and sauna round off an excellent option.

Gasthof-Pension zur Steirer-Stub'n GUESTHOUSE €€
(☎71 68 55; www.pension-graz.at; Lendplatz 8; s/d €43/86, apt €120-180; P☎) A bright and breezy guesthouse where many of the good-sized rooms have patios overlooking Lendplatz.

Eating

With leafy salads dressed in pumpkin-seed oil, fish specialities and *Pfand'l* (pan-grilled) dishes, Styrian cuisine is Austrian cooking at its light and healthy best.

Stock up for a picnic at the **farmers markets** (⏲4.30am-1pm, closed Sun) on Kaiser-Josef-Platz and Lendplatz. For **fast-food stands**, head for Hauptplatz and Jakominiplatz.

TOP CHOICE **Der Steirer** TAVERNA €€
(www.dersteirer.at; Belgiergasse 1; mains €10-19.50, tapas €2, lunch menu from €7.90; ⏲11am-midnight) This Styrian neo-*Beisl* and wine bar has a small but excellent selection of local dishes and a large choice of wines. The goulash with fried polenta is easily one of the best in the country. Or go for Styrian tapas like chanterelle tartar with speck.

Magnolia AUSTRIAN €€
(☎823 835; Schöngaugasse 53; 3-course menu €55-59, mains €15-20; ⏲lunch & dinner Mon-Fri) Alongside Augarten Hotel, with outdoor seating, this stylish restaurant with a seasonal menu and Austro-international cuisine is highly rated.

Landhauskeller AUSTRIAN €€
(☎83 02 76; Schmiedgasse 9; mains €11.50-26.50; ⏲11.30am-midnight Mon-Sat) What started as a spit-and-sawdust pub in the 16th century evolved into an atmospheric, medieval-style restaurant serving specialities like its four different sorts of *Tafelspitz* (prime boiled beef).

HUNDERTWASSER SPA

East Styria is famed for its thermal springs. Fans of Friedensreich Hundertwasser's playful architectural style won't want to miss the surreal **Rogner-Bad Blumau** (☎03383-51 00; www.blumau.com; adult/child €40/22; ⏲9am-11pm), 50km east of Graz. The spa has all the characteristics of his art, including uneven floors, grass on the roof, colourful ceramics and golden spires. Overnight accommodation includes entry to the spa. Call ahead to book treatments from sound meditation to invigorating Styrian elderberry wraps.

Drinking & Entertainment

The bar scene in Graz is split between three main areas: around the university; adjacent to the Kunsthaus; and on Mehlplatz and Prokopigasse (dubbed the 'Bermuda Triangle').

Orange BAR, CLUB
(www.cbo.at; Elisabethstrasse 30; ⏲8am-3am) A student crowd flocks to this modern cafe, bar and club, with a patio for summer evenings. DJs spin regularly here.

Kulturhauskeller BAR,
(Elisabethstrasse 30; ⏲9pm-5am Wed-Sat) Next to Orange, the Kulturhauskeller is a cavernous cellar bar that heaves with raunchy students on weekends.

Information

Graz Tourismus (☎80 75; www.graztourismus.at; Herrengasse 16; ⏲10am-6pm) Graz' main tourist office, with loads of free information on the city. Inside the train station is an information stand and terminal, and a free hotline to the tourist office.

Main Post Office (Neutorgasse 46; ⏲8am-7pm Mon-Fri, 9am-noon Sat).

Getting There & Away

AIR **Ryanair** (www.ryanair.com) has regular flights from London Stansted to **Graz Airport**, 10km south of the centre, while **Air Berlin** (www.airberlin.com) connects the city with Berlin.

BICYCLE Bicycle rental is available from **Bicycle** (☎688 645; Körösistrasse 5; per 24hr €15; ⏲7am-1pm & 2-6pm Mon-Fri).

PUBLIC TRANSPORT Single tickets (€2) for buses, trams and the Schlossbergbahn are valid for one hour, but you're usually better off buying a 24-hour pass (€4.50).

TRAIN Trains to Vienna (€37, 2½ hours) depart hourly, and six daily go to Salzburg (€48.60, four hours). International train connections from Graz include Ljubljana (€37.60, 3½ hours) and Budapest (€64, 5½ hours).

Klagenfurt

☎0463 / POP 94,800

With its dreamy location on Wörthersee and more Renaissance than baroque beauty, Carinthia's capital Klagenfurt has a distinct Mediterranean feel. While there isn't a huge amount here to see, it makes a handy base for exploring Wörthersee's lakeside villages and elegant medieval towns to the north.

Sights & Activities

Boating and swimming are usually possible from May to September. Free guided tours depart from the tourist office at 10am every Friday and Saturday during July and August.

TOP CHOICE Wörthersee LAKE

Owing to its thermal springs, the Wörthersee is one of the region's warmer lakes (an average 21°C in summer) and is great for swimming, lakeshore frolicking and water sports. The 40km **cycle path** circumnavigating the lake is one of Austria's best. In summer the tourist office cooperates with a hire company for bicycles (per 24 hours €10).

Europapark PARK

Europapark's green expanse and *Strandbad* (beach) on the shores of the Wörthersee are especially good for kids. The park's biggest draw is **Minimundus** (www.minimundus.at; Villacher Strasse 241; adult/child €13/8; ⏲9am-btwn 6pm & 8pm Mar-Oct), a 'miniature world' with 150 replicas of the world's architectural icons, downsized to a scale of 1:25. To get there, take bus 10 or 20 from Heiligengeistplatz.

Sleeping & Eating

When you check into accommodation in Klagenfurt, ask for a *Gästekarte* (guest card), which entitles you to discounts.

Hotel Geyer HOTEL €€

(☎578 86; www.hotelgeyer.com; Priesterhausgasse 5; s €70-88, d €102-135, q €155-170; P @) Colourful fabrics, paintings and objets d'art lend a personal feel to this central pick. Rooms are bright and contemporary, there is a little spa area for relaxing moments, and breakfast is served on a pretty patio in summer.

Arcotel Moser Verdino HOTEL €€

(☎578 78; www.arcotel.at/moserverdino; Domgasse 2; s €80-144, d €104-256, ste €128-180, apt €148-1920; @) This excellent pick has high-quality modern rooms with flair, very helpful staff and often discounted rates.

Restaurant Maria Loretto AUSTRIAN €€

(☎24 465; Lorettoweg 54; mains €15-25; ⏲lunch & dinner) A wonderful restaurant situated on a headland above Wörthersee near the *Strandbad*, serving fresh lake fish and dishes prepared with home-grown herbs. Reserve for an outside table.

Dolce Vita ITALIAN €€€

(☎554 99; Heuplatz 2; lunch menu €29-49, dinner mains €28, 4-6 course menu €59-79; ⏲Mon-Fri) In a region strongly influenced by northern Italian cuisine, this restaurant is something of a local flagship, building a seasonal menu mostly around fresh local produce and game.

Information

Tourist Office (☎53 722 23; www.info.klagenfurt.at; Neuer Platz 1, Rathaus; ⏲8am-6pm Mon-Fri, 10am-5pm Sat, 10am-3pm Sun) Books accommodation and sells Kärnten cards (www.kaerntencard.at, adult/child €36/15.50) which give free entry to 100 sights in the region over a one-week period.

Getting There & Around

AIR Klagenfurt's **airport** (www.klagenfurt-airport.com; Flughafenstrasse 60-66) is served by Ryanair from London Stansted and **TUIfly** (www.tuifly.com) from major German cities.

BUS Bus drivers sell single tickets (€2) and 24-hour passes (€4.40). Bus 42 shuttles between the Hauptbahnhof and the airport.

TRAIN Two hourly direct trains run from Klagenfurt to Vienna (€50, 3¾ hours) and Salzburg (€38.70, three hours). Trains to Graz depart every two to three hours (€38.70, 2¾ hours). Trains to western Austria, Italy, Slovenia and Germany go via Villach (€7.80, 30 to 40 minutes, two to four per hour).

SALZBURG

0662 / POP 149,500

The joke 'If it's baroque, don't fix it' is a perfect maxim for Salzburg; the tranquil Old Town burrowed below steep hills looks much as it did when Mozart lived here 250 years ago. Second only to Vienna in numbers of visitors, this compact city is centred on a tight grouping of narrow, cobbled streets overshadowed by ornate 17th-century buildings, which are in turn dominated by the medieval Hohensalzburg fortress from high above. Across the fast-flowing Salzach River rests the baroque Schloss Mirabell, surrounded by gorgeous manicured gardens.

If this doesn't whet your appetite, then bypass the grandeur and head straight for kitsch-country by joining a tour of *The Sound of Music* film locations.

Sights

Old Town HISTORIC AREA

A Unesco World Heritage site, Salzburg's Old Town centre is equally entrancing whether viewed from ground level or the hills above.

The grand **Residenzplatz**, with its horse-drawn carriages and mythical fountain, is a good starting point for a wander. The overwhelmingly baroque **Dom** (Cathedral; Domplatz; 8am-7pm Mon-Sat, from 1pm Sun), slightly south, is entered via bronze doors symbolising faith, hope and charity. The adjacent **Dommuseum** (adult/concession €5/1.50; 10am-5pm Mon-Sat, 11am-6pm Sun May-Oct) is a treasure-trove of ecclesiastical art.

From here, head west along Franziskanergasse and turn left into a courtyard for **Stiftskirche St Peter** (St Peter's Abbey Church; St Peter Bezirk 1-2; church 8.30am-noon & 2.30-6.30pm, cemetery 6.30am-7pm), an abbey church founded around 700. Among the lovingly tended graves in the grounds you'll find the **Katakomben** (adult/student €1.50/1; 10.30am-5pm Tue-Sun), or catacombs, cavelike chapels and crypts hewn out of the Mönchsberg cliff face.

The western end of Franziskanergasse opens out into Max Reinhardt Platz, where you'll see the back of Fisher von Erlach's **Kollegienkirche** (Universitätsplatz; 8am-6pm), another outstanding example of baroque architecture. The **Stift Nonnberg** (Nonnberg Convent; Nonnberggasse 2; 7am-dusk), where Maria first appears in *The Sound of Music*, is back in the other direction, a short climb up the hill to the east of the Festung Hohensalzburg.

SALZBURG CARD

The money-saving **Salzburg Card** (1-/2-/3-day card €26/35/41) gets you entry to all of the major sights and attractions, a free river cruise, unlimited use of public transport (including cable cars) plus numerous discounts on tours and events. The card is half-price for children and €3 cheaper in the low season.

WANT MORE?

Head to **Lonely Planet** (www.lonelyplanet.com/austria/salzburg) for planning advice, author recommendations, traveller reviews and insider tips.

Festung Hohensalzburg FORT

(www.salzburg-burgen.at; Mönchsberg 34; adult/child/family €7.80/4.40/17.70, with Festungsbahn funicular €11/6.30/25.50; 9am-7pm) Salzburg's most visible icon is this mighty clifftop fortress, one of the best preserved in Europe. Built in 1077, it was home to many prince-archbishops who ruled Salzburg from 798. Inside are the impressively ornate staterooms, torture chambers and two museums.

It takes 15 minutes to walk up the hill to the fortress, or you can catch the **Festungsbahn funicular** (Festungsgasse 4).

Salzburg Museum MUSEUM

(www.salzburgmuseum.at; Mozartplatz 1; adult/child/family €7/3/14; 9am-5pm Tue-Sun, to 8pm Thu) Housed in the baroque Neue Residenz palace, this flagship museum takes you on a romp through Salzburg past and present. Ornate rooms showcase medieval sacred art, prince-archbishop portraits and highlights such as Carl Spitzweg's renowned *Sonntagsspaziergang* (Sunday Stroll; 1841) painting.

Salzburg's famous 35-bell glockenspiel, which chimes daily at 7am, 11am and 6pm, is on the palace's western flank.

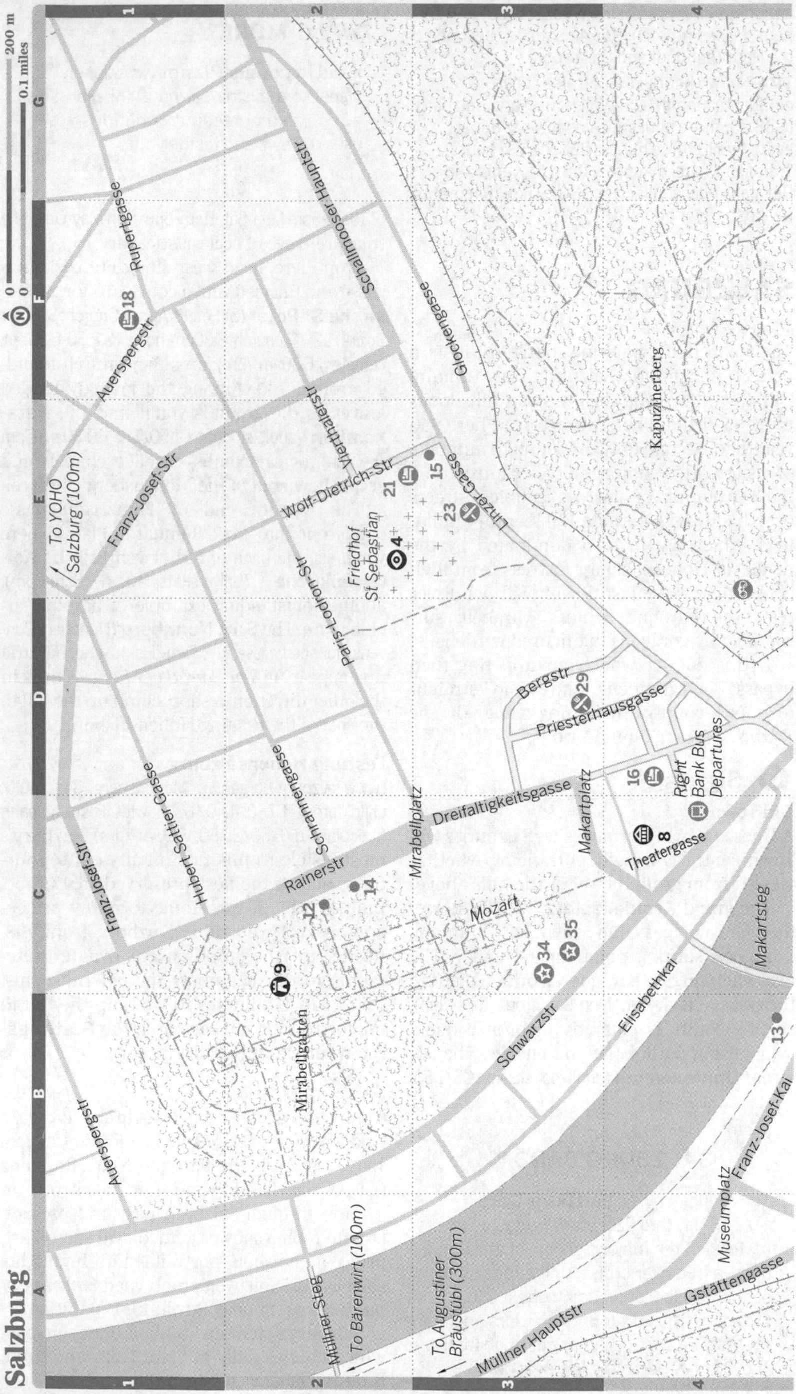

Salzburg

0 200 m
0 0.1 miles
A
B
C
D
E
F
G
1
2
3
4
To YOHO Salzburg (100m)
Auerspergstr
Franz-Josef-Str
Hubert Sattier Gasse
Franz-Josef-Str
Auerspergstr
18
Rupertgasse
9
Mirabellgarten
12
Rainerstr
Schrannengasse
Paris-Lodron-Str
Wolf-Dietrich-Str
Vierthalerstr
Schallmooser Hauptstr
Müllner Steg
To Bärenwirt (100m)
14
Friedhof St Sebastian
4
21
Mirabellplatz
15
To Augustiner Bräustübl (300m)
23
Glockengasse
Linzer Gasse
Mozart
Dreifaltigkeitsgasse
Priesterhausgasse
Bergstr
Müllner Hauptstr
Schwarzstr
34
35
29
Makartplatz
16
Elisabethkai
8
Theatergasse
Kapuzinerberg
Right Bank Bus Departures
Gstättengasse
Museumplatz
Franz-Josef-Kai
13
Makartsteg

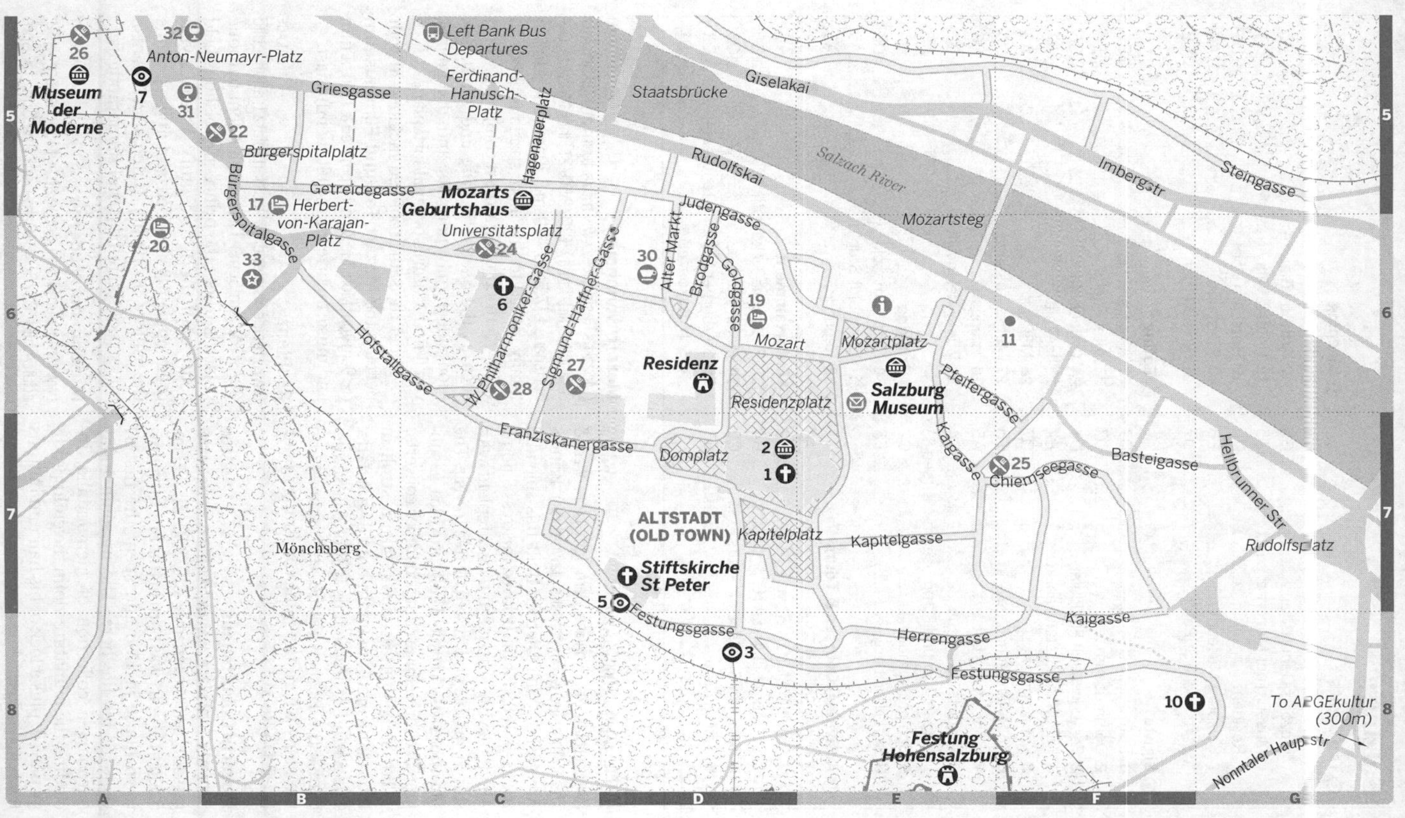
Museum der Moderne
26
7
Anton-Neumayr-Platz
32
31
22
Left Bank Bus Departures
Griesgasse
Ferdinand-Hanusch-Platz
Hagenauerplatz
Staatsbrücke
Giselakai
Salzach River
Rudolfskai
Imbergstr
Steingasse
Bürgerspitalplatz
Bürgerspitalgasse
Getreidegasse
Mozarts Geburtshaus
17
Herbert-von-Karajan-Platz
20
33
Universitätsplatz
24
6
W Philharmoniker-Gasse
Sigmund-Haffner-Gasse
27
28
Hofstallgasse
Judengasse
Alter Markt
30
Brodgasse
Goldgasse
19
Mozart
Mozartplatz
Mozartsteg
11
Residenz
Residenzplatz
Salzburg Museum
Pfeifergasse
Kaigasse
25
Chiemseegasse
Basteigasse
Hellbrunner Str
Rudolfsplatz
Franziskanergasse
Domplatz
2
1
ALTSTADT (OLD TOWN)
Kapitelplatz
Kapitelgasse
Mönchsberg
Stiftskirche St Peter
5
Festungsgasse
3
Herrengasse
Kaigasse
Festungsgasse
10
Festung Hohensalzburg
To ARGEkultur (300m)
Nonntaler Haupstr
A
B
C
D
E
F
G
5
6
7
8

Salzburg

Top Sights

- Festung Hohensalzburg ... E8
- Mozarts Geburtshaus ... C5
- Museum der Moderne ... A5
- Residenz ... D6
- Salzburg Museum ... E6
- Stiftskirche St Peter ... D7

Sights

1 Dom ... D7
2 Dommuseum ... D7
3 Festungsbahn Funicular ... D8
4 Friedhof St Sebastian ... E2
5 Katakomben ... D7
6 Kollegienkirche ... C6
7 Mönchsberg Lift ... A5
8 Mozart-Wohnhaus ... C4
Mozart Ton-und Filmmuseum ... (see 8)
9 Schloss Mirabell ... C2
10 Stift Nonnberg ... F8

Activities, Courses & Tours

11 Bob's Special Tours ... F6
12 Fräulein Maria's Bicycle Tours ... C2
13 Salzburg Schiffsfahrt ... B4
14 Salzburg Sightseeing Tours ... C2
15 Segway Tours ... E3

Sleeping

16 Arte Vida ... D4
17 Arthotel Blaue Gans ... B5
18 Hotel & Villa Auersperg ... F1
19 Hotel Am Dom ... D6
20 Stadtalm ... A6
21 Wolf Dietrich ... E2

Eating

22 Afro Café ... B5
23 Alter Fuchs ... E3
24 Grüner Markt ... C6
25 IceZeit ... F7
26 M32 ... A5
27 Mensa Toskana ... C6
28 Triangel ... C6
29 Zum Fidelen Affen ... D3

Drinking

30 Café Tomaselli ... D6
31 Humboldt Stub'n ... A5
32 Republic ... A5

Entertainment

33 Festspiele Ticket Office ... B6
34 Mozarteum ... C3
35 Salzburger Marionettentheater ... C3
Schlosskonzerte ... (see 9)

FREE Schloss Mirabell PALACE

(Mirabellplatz 4; palace 8am-4pm Mon, Wed & Thu, 1-4pm Tue & Fri, gardens dawn-dusk) Prince-Archbishop Wolf Dietrich built this splendid palace in 1606 for his beloved mistress Salome Alt. Its lavish baroque interior, replete with stucco, marble and frescos, is free to visit. The **Marmorsaal** (Marble Hall) provides a sublime backdrop for evening chamber concerts.

For stellar fortess views, take a stroll in the manicured, fountain-dotted **gardens**. *The Sound of Music* fans will of course recognise the Pegasus statue, the gnomes and the steps where the mini von Trapps practised 'Do-Re-Mi'.

Mozarts Geburtshaus MUSEUM

(Mozart's Birthplace; www.mozarteum.at; Getreidegasse 9; adult/child/family €10/3.50/21; 9am-5.30pm) Mozart was born in this bright-yellow town house in 1756 and spent the first 17 years of his life here. The museum today harbours a collection of memorabilia, including the miniature violin the child prodigy played, plus a lock of his hair and buttons from his jacket.

Mozart-Wohnhaus MUSEUM

(Mozart's Residence; www.mozarteum.at; Makartplatz 8; adult/child/family €10/3.50/21, incl Mozarts Geburtshaus €17/5/36; 9am-5.30pm) The Mozart family moved to this more spacious abode in 1773, where a prolific Mozart composed works such as the *Shepherd King* and *Idomeneo*. Alongside family portraits and documents, you'll find Mozart's original fortepiano.

Under the same roof and included in your ticket is the **Mozart Ton-und Filmmuseum** (9am-1pm Mon, Tue & Fri, 1-5pm Wed & Thu), a film and music archive for the ultra-enthusiast.

Residenz PALACE

(www.residenzgalerie.at; Residenzplatz 1; adult/child €9/3; 10am-5pm) This resplendent baroque palace is where the prince-archbishops held court until the 19th century. You can visit their opulently frescoed staterooms, while the gallery spotlights Dutch and Flemish masters of the Rubens and Rembrandt ilk.

Museum der Moderne GALLERY

(www.museumdermoderne.at; Mönchsberg 32; adult/child €8/6; 10am-6pm Tue-Sun, to 8pm

Wed) Straddling Mönchsberg's cliffs, this contemporary gallery shows first-rate exhibitions of 20th- and 21st-century art. The works of Alberto Giacometti, Emil Nolde and John Cage have previously featured. There's a free guided tour of the gallery at 6.30pm every Wednesday.

The **Mönchsberg Lift** (Gstättengasse 13; one-way/return €2.10/3.40, incl gallery ticket €9.70/6.80; ⏲8am-7pm Thu-Tue, to 9pm Wed) whizzes up to the gallery year-round.

Friedhof St Sebastian CEMETERY
(Linzer Gasse 41; ⏲9am-7pm) Tucked away behind the baroque St Sebastian's Church, this peaceful cemetery is the final resting place of Mozart family members and 16th-century physician Paracelsus. Outpomping them all, though, is Prince-Archbishop Wolf Dietrich von Raitenau's mosaic-tiled **mausoleum**, an elaborate memorial to himself.

Tours

If you would rather go it alone, the tourist office has four-hour iTour audioguides (€9), which take in big-hitters like the Residenz, Mirabellgarten and Mozartplatz.

Fräulein Maria's Bicycle Tours BICYCLE TOUR
(www.mariasbicycletours.com; Mirabellplatz 4; adult/child €26/18; ⏲9.30am & 4.30pm May-Sep) Belt out *The Sound of Music* faves as you pedal on one of these 3½-hour bike tours of the film locations. No booking is required; just turn up at the Mirabellplatz meeting point.

Segway Tours SEGWAY TOUR
(www.segway-salzburg.at; Wolf-Dietrich-Strasse 3; city/Sound of Music tour €33/65 ; ⏲tours 9am, noon, 3pm & 5pm Mar-Oct) These guided Segway tours take in the big sights by zippy battery-powered scooter.

Bob's Special Tours BUS TOUR
(☎84 95 11; www.bobstours.com; Rudolfskai 38; ⏲office 10am-3pm Mon-Fri, noon-2pm Sat & Sun) Minibus tours to *The Sound of Music* locations (€45), the Bavarian Alps (€45) and Grossglockner (€90). Reservations essential.

Salzburg Sightseeing Tours BUS TOUR
(www.salzburg-sightseeingtours.at; Mirabellplatz 2; adult/child €16/8; ⏲office 8am-6pm) Sells a 24-hour ticket for a multilingual hop-on, hop-off bus tour of the city and *The Sound of Music* locations.

Salzburg Schiffsfahrt BOAT TOUR
(www.salzburghighlights.at; Makartsteg ; adult/child €14/7; ⏲Apr-Oct) Hour-long cruises depart from Makartsteg bridge, with some chugging on to Schloss Hellbrunn (the ticket price does not cover entry to the palace).

Festivals & Events

Austria's most renowned classical music festival, the **Salzburg Festival** (www.salzburgerfestspiele.at) attracts international stars from late July to late August. Book on its website before January, or ask the **ticket office** (☎80 45-500; info@salzburgfestival.at; Herbert-von-Karajan-Platz 11; ⏲9.30am-1pm & 2-5pm Mon-Sat) about cancellations during the festival.

Sleeping

Ask for the tourist office's hotel brochure, which gives prices for hotels, pensions, hostels and camping grounds. Accommodation is at a premium during festivals.

TOP CHOICE **Haus Ballwein** GUESTHOUSE €
(☎82 40 29; www.haus-ballwein.at; Moosstrasse 69a; s €35-45, d €58-68, apt €100-115; P) Country or city? Why not both at this farmhouse guesthouse, a 10-minute trundle from the Altstadt on bus 21. With its bright, pine-filled rooms, mountain views, free bike hire and garden patrolled by duck duo, Rosalee and Clementine, this place is big on charm. Breakfast is a wholesome spread of fresh rolls, eggs, fruit, muesli and cold cuts.

TOP CHOICE **Arte Vida** GUESTHOUSE €€
(☎87 31 85; www.artevida.at; Dreifaltigkeitsgasse 9; s €55-140, d €80-152;) Arte Vida has the boho-chic feel of a Marrakesh *riad*, with its lantern-lit salon, communal kitchen and individually designed rooms done out in rich colours and fabrics. Your affable host Reinhold arranges yoga sessions in the quiet garden, and outdoor activities.

Hotel Am Dom BOUTIQUE HOTEL €€
(☎84 27 65; www.hotelamdom.at; Goldgasse 17; s €90-160, d €130-280;) Antique meets boutique at this Altstadt hotel, where the original vaults and beams of the 800-year-old building contrast with razor-sharp design features. Artworks inspired by the Salzburg Festival grace the strikingly lit rooms.

Hotel & Villa Auersperg BOUTIQUE HOTEL €€
(☎88 94 40; www.auersperg.at; Auerspergstrasse 61; s €129-155, d €165-205, ste 235-310; P@) This charismatic villa-hotel hybrid fuses late-19th-century flair with contemporary design. Relax by the lily pond in the garden

or in the rooftop wellness area with mountain views. Free bike hire is a bonus.

Haus Steiner GUESTHOUSE €
(☎83 00 31; www.haussteiner.com; Moosstrasse 156; s/d/tr €34/56/78; P 📶) Kind-natured Rosemarie runs a tight ship at this chalet-style guesthouse. The pick of the petite rooms, furnished in natural wood, come with fridges and balconies with mood-lifting mountain views. The Altstadt is a 15-minute ride away on bus 21.

Haus Wartenberg GUESTHOUSE €€
(☎84 84 00; www.hauswartenberg.com; Riedenburgerstrasse 2; d €128; P @ 📶) Set in vine-strewn gardens, this 17th-century chalet guesthouse is a 10-minute stroll west of the Altstadt. Country-style rooms done out in chunky pinewood and florals are in keeping with the character of the place.

Wolf Dietrich HISTORIC HOTEL €€
(☎87 12 75; www.salzburg-hotel.at; Wolf-Dietrich-Strasse 7; s €90-130, d €152-222, ste €197-277; P 📶 🏊) For old-fashioned elegance you can't beat this central hotel, where rooms are dressed in polished wood furnishings and floral fabrics. In contrast, the spa and pool are ultramodern. Organic produce is served at breakfast.

Arthotel Blaue Gans BOUTIQUE HOTEL €€€
(☎84 24 91; www.hotel-blaue-gans-salzburg.at; Getreidegasse 41-43; s €125-175, d €159-320; ❄ 📶) Contemporary design blends harmoniously with the original vaulting and beams of this 660-year-old hotel, with sleek yet comfortable rooms.

YOHO Salzburg HOSTEL €
(☎879 649; www.yoho.at; Paracelsusstrasse 9; dm €19-23, d €65-75; @ 📶) Comfy bunks, free wi-fi, plenty of cheap beer – what more could a backpacker ask for? Except, perhaps, a merry sing-along: *The Sound of Music* is screened daily (yes, *every* day). The friendly crew can arrange tours, adventure sports and bike hire.

Stadtalm HOSTEL €
(☎84 17 29; www.diestadtalm.com; Mönchsberg 19C; dm €19) This turreted hostel plopped on top of Mönchsberg takes in the entire Salzburg panorama, from the city's spires and fortress to Kapuzinerberg.

Eating

Self-caterers can find picnic fixings at the **Grüner Markt** (Green Market; Universitätsplatz; ⏲Mon-Sat).

TOP CHOICE **Magazin** MODERN EUROPEAN €€€
(☎84 15 84; www.magazin.co.at; Augustinergasse 13a; mains €25-31, tasting menus €57-79, cookery classes €130-150; ⏲Mon-Sat) Gathered around a courtyard below Mönchsberg's sheer rock wall, Magazin shelters a deli, wine store, cookery school and restaurant. Chef Richard Brunnauer's menus, fizzing with seasonal flavours like scallops with vine-ripened peaches and venison medallions in porcini sauce, are matched with wines from the 850-bottle cellar. Buses 4 and 21 stop at Augustinergasse.

TOP CHOICE **Bärenwirt** AUSTRIAN €€
(☎42 24 04; www.baerenwirt-salzburg.at; Müllner Hauptstrasse 8; mains €9-18; ⏲11am-11pm) Sizzling and stirring since 1663, Bärenwirt combines a woody, hunting-lodge-style interior with a river-facing terrace. Go for hearty *Bierbraten* (beer roast) with dumplings, locally caught trout or organic wild boar bratwurst.

Alter Fuchs AUSTRIAN €€
(☎88 20 22; Linzer Gasse 47-49; mains €10-17; ⏲noon-midnight Mon-Sat; 🌶 👪) This old fox prides itself on serving up old-fashioned Austrian fare, such as schnitzels fried to golden perfection. Foxes clad in bandanas guard the bar in the vaulted interior and there's a courtyard for good-weather dining.

Zum Fidelen Affen AUSTRIAN €€
(☎87 73 61; www.fideleraffe.at; Priesterhausgasse 8; mains €10.50-16.50; ⏲5pm-midnight Mon-Sat) At the jovial monkey you'll dine heartily on Austrian classics like goulash and sweet curd dumplings in the vaulted interior or on the pavement terrace. Reservations are recommended.

Afro Café AFRICAN €
(☎84 48 88; www.afrocoffee.com; Bürgerspitalplatz 5; lunch €6.70, mains €10-15; ⏲9am-midnight Mon-Sat) Hot-pink walls, beach-junk art and *big* hair...this afro-chic cafe keeps the good vibes coming. Fruity cocktails wash down dishes like springbok in a sesame-coriander crust and lemongrass-zucchini cake.

Riedenburg MODERN EUROPEAN €€€
(☎83 08 15; www.riedenburg.at; Neutorstrasse 31; lunch €18, mains €26-35; ⏲Tue-Sat) At this romantic Michelin-starred pick, creative Austrian signatures such as venison and guinea fowl crêpes with wild herbs are expertly matched with top wines. Take bus 1, 4 or 5 to Moosstrasse.

NO TOURIST TRAPP

Did you know that there were 10 (not seven) von Trapp children? Or that Rupert was the eldest (so long Liesl) and the captain a gentle-natured man? For the truth behind the Hollywood legend, stay at **Villa Trapp** (☎630 860; www.villa-trapp.com; Traunstrasse 34; d €109-500) in Aigen district, 3km southeast of the Altstadt. Marianne and Christopher have transformed the von Trapp's elegant 19th-century villa into a beautiful guesthouse, brimming with family heirlooms and snapshots. The villa sits in Salzburg's biggest private park.

M32 FUSION €€
(☎84 10 00; www.m32.at; Mönchsberg 32; 3-course lunch €27, 5-course dinner €68-70, mains €14-23; ⌚9am-1am Tue-Sun;) Bold colours and a forest of stag antlers reveal architect Matteo Thun's imprint at Museum der Moderne's glass-walled restaurant. The seasonal food and views are fantastic.

Triangel AUSTRIAN €€
(☎84 22 29; Wiener-Philharmoniker-Gasse 7; lunch from €4.90, mains €9-29; ⌚noon-midnight Mon-Sat) Arty bistro near the Festspielhaus, with a market-fresh menu.

Mensa Toskana CAFE €
(Sigmund-Haffner-Gasse 11; lunch €4.50-5.40; ⌚lunch Mon-Fri) Atmospheric university cafe in the Altstadt, with a sunny terrace and decent lunches.

IceZeit ICE CREAM €
(Chiemseegasse 1; scoop €1.20; ⌚11am-8pm) Grab a cone at Salzburg's best ice-cream parlour.

Drinking

You'll find the biggest concentration of bars along both banks of the Salzach and the hippest around Gstättengasse and Anton-Neumayr-Platz.

TOP CHOICE **Augustiner Bräustübl** BREWERY
(www.augustinerbier.at; Augustinergasse 4-6; ⌚3-11pm Mon-Fri, 2.30-11pm Sat & Sun) Who says monks can't enjoy themselves? Since 1621, this cheery monastery-run brewery has been serving potent home brews in the vaulted hall and beneath the chestnut trees in the 1000-seat beer garden.

Republic BAR
(www.republic-cafe.at; Anton-Neumayr-Platz 2; ⌚8am-1am Sun-Thu, to 4am Fri & Sat) One of Salzburg's most happening haunts, with regular DJs and free events from jazz breakfasts to Tuesday salsa nights.

Unikum Sky CAFE
(Unipark Nonntal; ⌚10am-7pm Mon-Fri, 9.30am-6pm Sat) For knockout fortress views, drinks and inexpensive snacks, head up to this sun kissed terrace atop the new Unipark Nonntal campus.

Humboldt Stub'n BAR
(Gstättengasse 4-6; ⌚10am-2am, to 4am Fri & Sat) A nail-studded Mozart punk guards this upbeat bar opposite Republic. Try a sickly Mozart cocktail (liqueur, cherry juice, cream and chocolate). Beers are €2.50 at Wednesday's student night.

Café Tomaselli CAFE
(www.tomaselli.at; Alter Markt 9; ⌚7am-9pm Mon-Sat, 8am-9pm Sun) If you like your service with a dollop of Viennese grumpiness and strudel with a dollop of cream, this grand, wood-panelled coffee house in the city centre is just the ticket.

Entertainment

Some of the high-brow venues include the **Schlosskonzerte** (☎84 85 86; www.salzburger-schlosskonzerte.at; Theatergasse 2; ⌚8pm), in Schloss Mirabell's sublime baroque Marble Hall, and the **Mozarteum** (☎889 40; www.mozarteum.at; Schwarzstrasse 26-28). Marionettes bring *The Sound of Music* and Mozart's operas magically to life at **Salzburger Marionettentheater** (☎87 24 06; www.marionetten.at; Schwarzstrasse 24; ⌚May-Sep, Christmas, Easter;).

Most bands with a modern bent will invariably play at either the **Rockhouse** (www.rockhouse.at; Schallmooser Hauptstrasse 46) or **ARGEkultur** (www.argekultur.at; Ulrike-Gschwandtner-Strasse 5); both double as popular bars.

Information

Many hotels and bars offer free wi-fi, and there are several cheap internet cafes near the train station. *Bankomaten* (ATMs) are all over the place.

City Net Café (Gstättengasse 11; per hr €2; ⌚10am-10pm) Central internet cafe also offering discount calls.

Hospital (☎44 82; Müllner Hauptstrasse 48) Just north of Mönchsberg.

Main Post Office (Residenzplatz 9; ⏲8am-6pm Mon-Fri, 9am-noon Sat)

Police Headquarters (☎63 83; Alpenstrasse 90)

STA Travel (www.statravel.at; Rainerstrasse 2) Student and budget travel agency.

Tourist Office (☎889 87-330; www.salzburg.info; Mozartplatz 5; ⏲9am-6pm, closed Sun Sep-Mar) Has plenty of information about the city and its immediate surrounds; there's a ticket booking agency in the same building. For information on the rest of the province, visit the **Salzburgerland Tourismus** (www.salzburgerland.com) website.

 Getting There & Away

Air

Salzburg airport (www.salzburg-airport.com) has regular scheduled flights to destinations all over Austria and Europe. Low-cost flights from the UK are provided by **Ryanair** (www.ryanair.com) and **easyJet** (www.easyjet.com). Other airlines include **British Airways** (www.britishairways.com) and **Jet2** (www.jet2.com).

Bus

Buses depart from just outside the Hauptbahnhof on Südtiroler Platz. For more information on buses in and around Salzburg and an online timetable, see www.svv-info.at and www.postbus.at.

Car & Motorcycle

Three motorways converge on Salzburg to form a loop around the city: the A1/E60 from Linz, Vienna and the east; the A8/E52 from Munich and the west; and the A10/E55 from Villach and the south. The quickest way to Tirol is to take the road to Bad Reichenhall in Germany and continue to Lofer (B178) and St Johann in Tirol.

Train

Salzburg has excellent rail connections with the rest of Austria, though its Hauptbahnhof is undergoing extensive renovation until 2014.

Fast trains leave hourly for Vienna (€49.90, three hours) via Linz (€23.70, 1¼ hours). There is a two-hourly express service to Klagenfurt (€38.70, three hours). The quickest way to Innsbruck (€41.30, two hours) is by the 'corridor' train through Germany via Kufstein; trains depart at least every two hours. There are trains every hour or so to Munich (€34, 1¾ hours).

 Getting Around

TO/FROM THE AIRPORT **Salzburg airport** (www.salzburg-airport.com) is located 5.5km west of the city centre. Bus 2 goes there from the Hauptbahnhof (€2.30, 19 minutes). A taxi costs about €20.

BICYCLE **Top Bike** (www.topbike.at; Staatsbrücke; ⏲10am-5pm) rents bikes for around €15 per day (half-price for kids). The Salzburg Card yields a 20% discount.

BUS Bus drivers sell single (€2.30) and 24-hour (€5.20) tickets. Weekly tickets (€13.60) can be purchased from machines and *Tabak* shops.

Bus 1 starts from the Hauptbahnhof and skirts the pedestrian-only Altstadt. Another central stop is Hanuschplatz.

CAR & MOTORCYCLE Parking places are limited and much of the Altstadt is pedestrian-only, so it's easier to leave your car at one of three park-and-ride points to the west, north and south of the city. The largest car park in the centre is the Altstadt Garage under Mönchsberg (€14 per day).

FIAKER A *Fiaker* (horse-drawn carriage) for up to four people costs €40 for 25 minutes. The drivers line up on Residenzplatz.

AROUND SALZBURG

Schloss Hellbrunn

A prince-archbishop with a wicked sense of humour, Markus Sittikus built Italianate **Schloss Hellbrunn** (www.hellbrunn.at; Fürstenweg 37; adult/concession/family €9.50/6.50/24; ⏲9am-5.30pm, to 9pm Jul & Aug; 👪) as a 17th-century summer palace and an escape from his Residenz functions.

The ingenious trick fountains and water-powered figures are the big draw. When the tour guides set them off, expect to get wet! Admission includes entry to the baroque palace. The rest of the sculpture-dotted gardens are free to visit. Look out for *The Sound of Music* pavilion of 'Sixteen Going on Seventeen' fame.

Bus 25 runs to Hellbrunn, 4.5km south of Salzburg, every 20 minutes from Rudolfskai in the Altstadt.

Werfen

☎06468 / POP 3000

Framed by the limestone turrets of the Tennengebirge, Werfen's Alpine beauty hasn't escaped Hollywood producers – it stars in WWII action film *Where Eagles Dare* (1968) and makes a cameo appearance in the picnic scene of *The Sound of Music*.

Both its ice caves and fortress can be visited as a day trip from Salzburg if you start early (tour the caves first and be at the fortress for the last falconry show), otherwise consult the **tourist office** (☎53 88; www.werfen.at; Markt 24;

9am-12.30pm & 1-6pm Mon-Fri year-round, 2-4pm Sat May-Sep) for accommodation options.

Sights & Activities

TOP CHOICE **Eisriesenwelt** ICE CAVE
(www.eisriesenwelt.at; adult/concession €9/8, with cable car €20/18; 9am-3.30pm May-Oct;) Billed as the world's largest accessible ice caves, more than 1000m above Werfen in the Tennengebirge mountains, this glittering ice empire is a once seen, never forgotten experience. The 1¼-hour tour takes you through twinkling passageways and chambers, the carbide lamps picking out otherworldly ice sculptures. Dress for subzero temperatures.

Burg Hohenwerfen CASTLE
(adult/concession/family €14/12/33; 9am-5pm Apr-Oct;) High on a wooded clifftop, Burg Hohenwerfen has kept watch over the Salzach Valley since 1077, although its current appearance dates from the 16th century. Highlights include far-reaching views over Werfen from the belfry, dungeons containing some pretty nasty torture instruments, and a dramatic **falconry show** (11.15am and 2.15pm or 3.15pm). The walk up from the village takes 20 minutes.

Getting There & Around

Werfen is 45km south of Salzburg on the A10/E55 motorway. Trains run frequently to Salzburg (€10, 40 minutes). In summer, minibuses (single/return €3.10/6.10) run every 25 minutes between Eisriesenstrasse in Werfen and the car park, a 20-minute walk from the cable car to Eisriesenwelt.

SALZKAMMERGUT

A wonderland of glassy blue lakes and tall craggy peaks, Austria's Lake District is a long-time favourite holiday destination. The peaceful lakes attract visitors in droves from Salzburg and beyond, with limitless opportunities for boating, fishing, swimming or just lazing on the shore.

Bad Ischl

06132 / POP 13,900

During the last century of the Habsburg reign, Bad Ischl became the favourite summertime retreat for the imperial family and its entourage. Today the town and many of its dignified buildings still have a stately aura, and a perhaps surprisingly high proportion of the local women still go about their daily business in *Dirndl* (Austria's traditional full pleated skirt). It makes a good base for exploring the entire Salzkammergut region.

Sights & Activities

Kaiservilla PALACE
(www.kaiservilla.com; Jainzen 38; adult/child €13/7.50, grounds only €4.50/3.50; 9.30am-4.45pm, closed Thu-Tue Jan-Mar, closed Nov) This Italianate building was Franz Josef's summer residence and shows that he loved huntin', shootin' and fishin' – it's decorated with an obscene number of animal trophies. It can be visited only by guided tour, during which you'll pick up little gems, like the fact that it was here that the Kaiser signed the letter declaring war on Serbia, which led to WWI.

What was once the teahouse of Franz Josef's wife, Elisabeth, now contains a small **Photomuseum** (adult/child €2/1.50; 9.30am-5pm, closed Nov-Mar).

Cable Car CABLE CAR
(www.katrinseilbahn.com; return adult/child €18.50/12; 9am-5pm May-early Nov) The local mountain (1542m) with walking trails and limited skiing in winter is served by a cable car.

Salzkammergut Therme SPA
(www.eurothermen.at; Voglhuberstrasse 10; adult/child €14.50/10.50; 9am-midnight) If you'd like to follow in Princess Sophie's (mother of Franz Josef) footprints, take the thermal waters at this effervescent spa.

Festivals & Events

Bad Ischl stages the works of operetta composer Franz Lehár at the **Lehár Festival** (www.leharfestival.at) in July and August.

Sleeping & Eating

Staff at both the tourist offices can help find rooms.

Hotel Garni Sonnhof HOTEL €€
(230 78; www.sonnhof.at; Bahnhofstrasse 4; s €65-95, d €90-150; P) Nestled in a leafy glade of maple trees next to the station, this hotel has cosy, traditional decor, a beautiful garden, chickens that deliver breakfast eggs, and a sunny conservatory. There's a sauna and a steam bath on site.

Goldenes Schiff HOTEL €€
(242 41; www.goldenes-schiff.at; Adalbert-Stifter-Kai 3; s €95-112, d €134-180, apt €180-196; P@)

The best rooms at this comfortable pick have large windows overlooking the river. There's also a spa area and an excellent restaurant (mains €14 to €21) serving regional cuisine from game to Wolfgangsee fish.

Weinhaus Attwenger AUSTRIAN €€
(☎248 10; www.weinhaus-attwenger.com; Lehárkai 12; mains €14-22; ⏰closed Mon, also closed Tue Sep-early May) This quaint chalet with a riverside garden serves prime-quality Austrian cuisine from a seasonal menu, with wines to match.

Grand Café & Restaurant Zauner Esplanade AUSTRIAN €€
(Hasner Allee 2; mains €10-18.50; ⏰10am-10pm) This offshoot of Café Zauner, the famous pastry shop at Pfarrgasse 7, serves Austrian staples, some using organic local meats, in a pleasant location beside the river.

Information

Post Office (Auböckplatz 4; ⏰8am-6pm Mon-Fri, 9am-noon Sat)

Salzkammergut Touristik (☎0613 224 000; www.salzkammergut.co.at; Götzstrasse 12; ⏰9am-7pm, closed Sun Oct-Mar) Has bike rental (per 24 hours €13) and internet (per 10 minutes €1.10).

Tourist Office (☎277 57; www.badischl.at; Auböckplatz 5; ⏰9am-6pm Mon-Sat, 10am-6pm Sun) Has a telephone service (8am to 10pm) for rooms and information.

Getting There & Around

BUS Buses depart from outside the train station, with hourly buses to St Gilgen (€5.10, 40 minutes). Buses to St Wolfgang (€3.80, 32 minutes) go via Strobl.

CAR & MOTORCYCLE Most major roads in the Salzkammergut go to or near Bad Ischl; Hwy 158 from Salzburg and the north–south Hwy 145 intersect just north of the town centre.

TRAIN Hourly trains to Hallstatt (€3.80, 25 minutes) go via Steeg/Hallstätter See, at the northern end of the lake, and continue on the eastern side via Hallstatt station to Obertraun (€5.70, 30 minutes). A boat from Hallstatt station (€2.40) takes you to the township. There are also frequent trains to Gmunden (€7.80, 40 minutes) and Salzburg (€22.70, two hours) via Attnang-Puchheim.

Hallstatt

☎06134 / POP 790

With pastel-hued homes, swans and towering mountains on either side of a glassy green lake, Hallstatt looks like some kind of greeting card for tranquillity. Boats chug lazily across the water from the train station to the village itself, which clings precariously to a tiny bit of land between mountain and shore. So small is the patch of land occupied by the village that its annual Corpus Christi procession takes place largely in small boats on the lake.

Sights & Activities

Hallstatt has been classified a Unesco World Heritage site for its natural beauty and for evidence of human settlement dating back 4500 years. Over 2000 graves have been discovered in and around the village, most dating from 1000 to 500 BC.

Salzbergwerk SALT MINE
(funicular return plus tour adult/child €24/12, tour only €12/6; ⏰9.30am-4.30pm, closed early Nov–late Apr) The region's major cultural attraction is situated high above Hallstatt on Salzberg (Salt Mountain). In 1734 the fully preserved body of a prehistoric miner was found and today he is known as the 'Man in Salt'. The standard tour revolves around his fate, with visitors travelling down an underground railway and miners' slides (a photo is taken of you while sliding) to an illuminated subterranean salt lake.

The mine can be reached on foot or with the funicular.

Beinhaus CHURCH
(Bone House; Kirchenweg 40; admission €1.50; ⏰10am-6pm, closed Nov-Apr) Don't miss the macabre yet beautiful Beinhaus behind Hallstatt's parish church. It contains rows of stacked skulls painted with flowery designs and the names of the deceased. The old Celtic pagan custom of mass burial has been practised here since 1600 (mainly due to the lack of graveyard space), and the last skull in the collection was added in 1995.

Hallstätter See LAKE
(boat hire per hr from €11) If you don't fancy a chilly dip in the crystal-clear waters, hire a rowboat, kayak or pedalo for a scenic spin of the lake.

Sleeping & Eating

Rooms fill quickly in summer, so book ahead, arrive early, or go straight for the tourist office and the staff will help you find something.

Pension Sarstein GUESTHOUSE €
(☎82 17; Gosaumühlstrasse 83; d €55-70, apt €65-100; 📶) The affable Fischer family take

OBERTRAUN

At nearby Obertraun you'll find the intriguing **Dachstein Rieseneishöhle** (www.dachstein-salzkammergut.com; cable car return plus one cave adult/child €27/15, all-inclusive ticket adult/child €39/23). The caves are millions of years old and extend into the mountain for almost 80km in places. The ice itself is around 500 years old, and is increasing in thickness each year – the 'ice mountain' is 8m high, twice as high now as it was when the caves were first explored in 1910.

From Obertraun it's also possible to catch a cable car to **Krippenstein** (return adult/child €23/14; closed mid-Oct–Nov & Easter–mid-May), where you'll find the freaky **5 Fingers viewing platform**, which protrudes over a sheer cliff face. Not for sufferers of vertigo.

pride in their little guesthouse, a few minutes' walk along the lakefront from central Hallstatt. The old-fashioned rooms are nothing flash, but they are neat, cosy and have balconies with dreamy lake and mountain views. Family-sized apartments come with kitchenettes.

Pension Hallberg GUESTHOUSE **€€**
(87 09; www.pension-hallberg.at.tf; Seestrasse 113; s €60-80, d €70-130) Interesting artefacts rescued from the lake line the staircase leading up to the rooms, the best of which are light and airy, furnished with pale wood and have superb views over the lake.

Gasthof Simony AUSTRIAN **€€**
(206 46; www.gasthof-simony.at; Wolfengasse 105 ; mains €9-17; lunch Thu-Sun, dinner Thu-Tue) What a view! With a garden right on the lakeshore, this is a prime setting for a panoramic lunch or dinner. Tuck into good old-fashioned home cooking: smoked trout with horseradish, goulash, strudel and the like.

Information

Tourist Office (82 08; www.dachstein-salzkammergut.at; Seestrasse 169; 9am-6pm Mon-Fri, 9am-4pm Sat & Sun, closed Sat & Sun Sep-Jun) Turn left from the ferry to reach the office. It stocks the free leisure map of lakeside towns, and hiking and cycling trail maps.

Getting There & Away

BOAT The last ferry connection leaves Hallstatt train station at 6.50pm (€2.40, 10 minutes). Ferry excursions do the circuit Hallstatt Lahn via Hallstatt Markt, Obersee, Untersee and Steeg return (€10, 90 minutes) three times daily from July to early September.

BUS Eight to 10 buses connect Hallstatt (Lahn) town with Obertraun (€2.20, eight minutes) daily.

TRAIN Hallstatt train station is across the lake. The boat service from there to the village coincides with train arrivals. About a dozen trains daily connect Hallstatt and Bad Ischl (€3.80, 22 minutes) and Hallstatt with Bad Aussee (€3.80, 15 minutes).

Wolfgangsee

Wolfgangsee is a hugely popular place to spend the summer swimming, boating, walking or simply lazing by its soothing waters. Its two main resorts are St Wolfgang and St Gilgen, the first of which takes first prize in the beauty stakes.

Coming from Salzburg, the first town you come across is **St Gilgen**. It's a fine point from which to explore the surrounding region, and its **tourist office** (06227-23 48; www.wolfgangsee.at; Mondsee Bundesstrasse 1a; 9am-7pm) can help with accommodation and activities.

St Wolfgang, towards the southern end of Wolfgangsee, is squeezed between the northern shoreline of the lake and the towering peak of Schafberg (1783m). Its **tourist office** (06138-80 03; www.wolfgangsee.at; Au 140; 9am-7pm Mon-Fri, 9am-6pm Sat, 10am-5pm Sun) has plenty of information for travellers.

In the heart of the village you'll find the 14th-century **Pilgrimage Church** (donation €1; 9am-6pm), a highly ornate example that still attracts pilgrims. Reaching the top of **Schafberg** is an easy exercise – from May to October, a cogwheel railway climbs to its summit in 40 minutes (one way/return €20.40/29.80). Otherwise it's a three- to four-hour walk.

Both St Wolfgang and St Gilgen have numerous pensions, starting from about €25 per person; the local tourist offices have details.

On the lakefront, 1km east of St Wolfgang, **Camping Appesbach** (06138 22 06; www.appesbach.at; Au 99; campsite per adult/child/tent €7/4.20/10; P) is a favourite with Austrian holidaymakers. A plusher option with lake views, a wellness area and two pools is **Im Weissen Rössl** (06138-23 06; www.weissesroessl.at; Markt 74; s €128-184, d €156-318;), the setting for Ralph Benatzky's operetta *The White Horse*.

A ferry operates May to October between Strobl and St Gilgen (one way €9, 75 minutes), stopping at points en route. Services are most frequent from June to early September. Boats run from St Wolfgang to St Gilgen almost hourly during the day (one way €6.80, 50 minutes); the free *Eintauchen & Aufsteigen* timetable from local tourist offices gives exact times.

A Postbus service from St Wolfgang via Strobl to St Gilgen (€4.20, 30 minutes) is frequent out of season, but tails off somewhat in summer when the ships run. For Salzburg you need to connect in Strobl (€2.20, 12 minutes).

Northern Salzkammergut

Mondsee is popular for two reasons – its close proximity to Salzburg (only 30km) and its warm water. The main village on the lake, also called Mondsee, is home to an attractive 15th-century church that was used in the wedding scene of *The Sound of Music* and a small and helpful **tourist office** (06232-22 70; www.mondsee.at; Dr Franz Müller Strasse 3; 8am-6pm Mon-Fri, 9am-6pm Sat & Sun, closed Sat & Sun Oct-May).

Lying to the east of Mondsee is **Attersee**, Salzkammergut's largest lake and a favourite with sailors. East again from Attersee you'll find **Traunsee** and its three main resorts: Gmunden, Traunkirchen and Ebensee. **Gmunden** is famous for its twin castles, linked by a causeway on the lake, and its green and white ceramics. Contact the local **tourist office** (07612-64 305; www.traunsee.at; Toscanapark 1; 8am-8pm Mon-Fri, 10am-7pm Sat & Sun) for information on accommodation and activities on and around the lake.

Buses run every hour to Mondsee from Salzburg (€9.10, 55 minutes). Gmunden is connected to Salzburg by train (€17, 1¼ hours), via Attnang-Puchheim.

TIROL

With converging mountain ranges behind lofty pastures and tranquil meadows, Tirol (also Tyrol) captures a quintessential Alpine panoramic view. Occupying a central position is Innsbruck, the region's jewel, while in the northeast and southwest are superb ski resorts. In the southeast, separated somewhat from the main state since part of South Tirol was ceded to Italy at the end of WWI, lies the protected natural landscape of the Hohe Tauern National Park, an Alpine wonderland of 3000m peaks, including the country's highest, the Grossglockner (3798m).

Innsbruck

0512 / POP 121,300

Tirol's capital is a sight to behold. The mountains are so close that within 25 minutes it's possible to travel from the heart of the city to over 2000m above sea level. Summer and winter outdoor activities abound, and it's understandable why some visitors only take a peek at Innsbruck proper before heading for the hills. But to do so is a shame, for Innsbruck has its own share of gems, including an authentic medieval Altstadt (Old Town), inventive architecture and vibrant student-driven nightlife.

Sights

Innsbruck's atmospheric, Altstadt is ideal for a lazy stroll. Many of the following sights listed close an hour or two earlier in winter.

TOP CHOICE **Goldenes Dachl & Museum** MUSEUM
(Golden Roof; Herzog-Friedrich-Strasse 15; adult/child €4/2; 10am-5pm, closed Mon Oct-Apr) Innsbruck's golden wonder is this Gothic oriel, built for Emperor Maximilian I in 1500 and glittering with 2657 fire-gilt copper tiles. An audioguide whizzes you through the history in the museum; look for the grotesque tournament helmets designed to resemble the Turks of the rival Ottoman Empire.

Hofkirche CHURCH
(www.tiroler-landesmuseum.at; Universitätstrasse; adult/child €5/4, combined Volkskunstmuseum ticket adult/child €10/6; 9am-5pm Mon-Sat, 12.30-5pm Sun) The 16th-century Hofkirche is one of Europe's finest royal court churches. Top billing goes to the empty **sarcophagus** of Emperor Maximilian I (1459–1519), a masterpiece of German Renaissance sculpture, guarded by 28 giant bronze figures including Dürer's legendary King Arthur. You're now forbidden to touch the statues, but

CITY SAVERS

The **Innsbruck Card** gives one visit to Innsbruck's main sights and attractions, a return journey on seven cable cars, unlimited use of public transport including the Sightseer bus, and five-hour bike rental. It's available at the tourist office and costs €31/39/45 for 24/48/72 hours (half-price for children).

Stay overnight in Innsbruck and you'll automatically receive a **Club Innsbruck Card**, which gives discounts on transport and activities, and allows you to join the tourist office's free guided hikes in summer.

numerous inquisitive hands have already polished parts of the dull bronze, including Kaiser Rudolf's codpiece!

Volkskunstmuseum MUSEUM

(Folk Art Museum; www.tiroler-landesmuseum.at; Universitätstrasse; combined Hofkirche ticket adult/child €10/6; ⌚9am-5pm) Next door to the Hofkirche, the Volkskunstmuseum houses Tyrolean folk art from handcarved sleighs and Christmas cribs to carnival masks and cow bells.

Hofburg PALACE

(Imperial Palace; www.hofburg-innsbruck.at; Rennweg 1; adult/child €8/free, Hofgarten admission free; ⌚palace 9am-5pm, garden 6am-dusk) Empress Maria Theresia gave this Habsburg palace a total baroque makeover in the 16th century. The highlight of the state apartments is the Riesensaal (Giant's Hall), lavishly adorned with frescos and paintings of Maria Theresia and her 16 children, including Marie Antoinette.

Tucked behind the palace is the Hofgarten, an attractive garden for a botanical stroll.

Bergisel SKI JUMP

(www.bergisel.info; adult/child €9/4; ⌚9am-6pm) Rising above Innsbruck like a celestial staircase, this glass-and-steel ski jump was designed by much-lauded Iraqi architect Zaha Hadid. From May to July, fans pile in to see athletes train, while preparations step up a gear in January for the World Cup Four Hills Tournament.

It's 455 steps or a two-minute funicular ride to the 50m-high **viewing platform**. Here, the panorama of the Nordkette range, Inn Valley and Innsbruck is breathtaking, though the cemetery at the bottom has undoubtedly made a few ski jumping pros quiver in their boots.

Tram 1 trundles from central Innsbruck to Bergisel.

Tiroler Landesmuseum Ferdinandeum GALLERY

(www.tiroler-landesmuseum.at; Art Museum; adult/child €10/6; ⌚9am-5pm Tue-Sun) This treasure-trove of Tyrolean history and art contains the original reliefs used to design the Goldenes Dachl. In the gallery you'll find old master paintings, Gothic altarpieces, a handful of Kokoschka and Klimt originals, and Viennese actionism works with shock factor.

Schloss Ambras CASTLE

(www.khm.at/ambras; Schlossstrasse 20; adult/child €10/free; ⌚10am-5pm) Archduke Ferdinand II transformed Schloss Ambras from a fortress into a Renaissance palace in 1564. A visit takes in the ever-so-grand banquet hall, shining armour (look out for the 2.6m suit created for giant Bartlmä Bon) and room upon room of Habsburg portraits, with Titian, Velázquez and van Dyck originals. It's free to stroll or picnic in the expansive **gardens**.

Schloss Ambras is 4.5km southeast of the centre. Take bus 4134 from the Hauptbahnhof for discounted entry and a free return journey. The Sightseer bus also stops here.

FREE **Dom St Jakob** CHURCH

(St James' Cathedral; Domplatz; ⌚10.15am-7.30pm Mon-Sat, 12.30-7.30pm Sun) Innsbruck's 18th-century cathedral is a feast of over-the-top baroque. The Madonna above the high altar is by the German Renaissance painter Lucas Cranach the Elder.

DON'T MISS

FREE GUIDED HIKES

From late May to October, Innsbruck Information arranges daily guided hikes – from sunrise walks to lantern-lit strolls and half-day mountain jaunts – which are, incredibly, free to guests with a Club Innsbruck Card. Pop into the tourist office to register and browse the program.

Innsbruck Altstadt

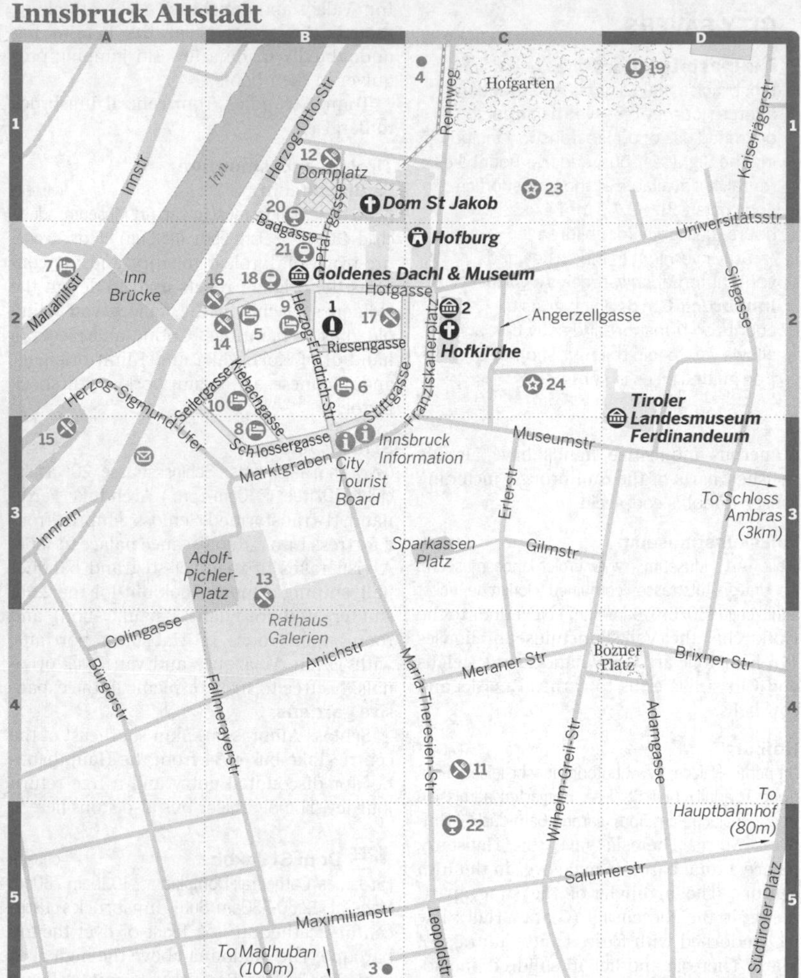

Alpenzoo ZOO
(www.alpenzoo.at; Weiherburggasse 37; adult/child €8/4; ⊙9am-6pm) Home to Alpine wildlife like golden eagles, chamois and ibexes. To get there, walk up the hill from Rennweg or take bus W from Marktplatz.

Stadtturm TOWER
(Herzog-Friedrich-Strasse 21, City Tower; adult/child €3/1.50; ⊙10am-8pm) Climb this tower's 148 steps for 360-degree views of the city's rooftops, spires and surrounding mountains.

Activities

Anyone who loves playing in the great outdoors will be itching to head up into the Alps in Innsbruck.

Nordkettenbahnen FUNICULAR
(www.nordkette.com; one way/return to Hungerburg €4/6.80, Seegrube €14.60/23.40, Hafelekar €16.20/27; ⊙Hungerburgbahn 7am-7.15pm Mon-Fri, 8am-7.15pm Sat, Seegrubenbahn 8.30am-5.30pm, Hafelekarbahn 9am-5pm) Zaha Hadid's space-age funicular runs every 15 minutes, whizzing you from the Congress Centre to the slopes in no time. Walking trails head

Innsbruck Altstadt

Top Sights
- Dom St Jakob ... B1
- Goldenes Dachl & Museum ... B2
- Hofburg ... C2
- Hofkirche ... C2
- Tiroler Landesmuseum Ferdinandeum ... D3

Sights
- 1 Stadtturm ... B2
- 2 Volkskunstmuseum ... C2

Activities, Courses & Tours
- 3 Inntour ... B5
- 4 Nordkettenbahnen ... C1

Sleeping
- 5 Goldener Adler ... B2
- 6 Hotel Weisses Kreuz ... B2
- 7 Mondschein ... A2
- 8 Nepomuks ... B3
- 9 Weinhaus Happ ... B2
- 10 Weisses Rössl ... B2

Eating
- Cafe Munding ... (see 8)
- 11 Chez Nico ... C4
- 12 Fischerhäusl ... B1
- 13 Lichtblick ... B3
- 14 Mamma Mia ... B2
- 15 Markthalle ... A3
- 16 Ottoburg ... B2
- 17 s'Speckladele ... B2

Drinking
- 360° ... (see 13)
- 18 Elferhaus ... B2
- 19 Hofgarten Café ... D1
- 20 Moustache ... B1
- 21 s'Culinarium ... B2
- 22 Theresienbräu ... C5

Entertainment
- 23 Tiroler Landestheater ... C1
- 24 Treibhaus ... C2

off in all directions from **Hungerburg** and **Seegrube**. For more of a challenge, there is a downhill track for mountain bikers and two fixed-rope routes (*Klettersteige*) for climbers.

Patrolled by inquisitive Alpine sheep, the 2334m summit of **Hafelekar** affords tremendous views over Innsbruck to the snow-capped giants of the Austrian Alps, including 3798m Grossglockner.

Inntour ADVENTURE SPORTS
(☎214 466; www.inntour.com; Leopoldstrasse 4; ⏲9am-6.30pm Mon-Fri, to 5pm Sat) A one-stop adrenalin shop taking you canyoning (€75), tandem paragliding (€95), white-water rafting (€45) and bungee jumping (€140) from the 192m Europabrücke.

Olympia SkiWorld Innsbruck SKIING
Innsbruck is the gateway to this massive ski arena, covering nine surrounding resorts and 300km of slopes to test all abilities. The most central place to pound powder is the **Nordkette/Seegrube**, accessed by the Nordkettenbahnen. A three-/seven-day OlympiaWorld Ski Pass covering all areas costs €117/218; ski buses are free to anyone with a Club Innsbruck Card.

Sleeping

The tourist office has lists of private rooms costing between €20 and €40 per person.

Hotel Weisses Kreuz HISTORIC HOTEL €€
(☎594 79; www.weisseskreuz.at; Herzog-Friedrich-Strasse 31; s €38-78, d €78-142; P@🛜) Beneath the Altstadt's arcades, this atmospheric 500-year-old pile has played host to famous guests including a 13-year-old Mozart. With its wood-panelled parlours and twisting staircase, the hotel oozes history with every creaking beam. Rooms are supremely comfortable, staff charming and breakfast is a lavish spread.

TOP CHOICE **Nepomuks** HOSTEL €
(☎584 118; www.nepomuks.at; Kiebachgasse 16; dm €23-25, d €56; 🛜) Could this be backpacker heaven? Nepomuks sure comes close, with its Altstadt location, well-stocked kitchen and high-ceilinged dorms with homely touches like CD players. The delicious breakfast in attached Café Munding, with homemade pastries, jam and fresh-roasted coffee, gets your day off to a grand start.

Goldener Adler HISTORIC HOTEL €€
(☎571 111; www.goldeneradler.com; Herzog-Friedrich-Strasse 6; s €85-125, d €126-240; P❄🛜)

Since opening in 1390, the grand Goldener Adler has welcomed kings, queens and Salzburg's two biggest exports: Mozart and Mrs von Trapp. Rooms are elegant with gold drapes and squeaky-clean marble bathrooms.

Weisses Rössl GUESTHOUSE €€
(☎583 057; www.roessl.at; Kiebachgasse 8; s €70-110, d €100-160; P@) An antique rocking horse greets you at this late-16th-century guesthouse, with vaulted interiors and bright, spacious rooms. Host Mr Plank is a keen hunter and the restaurant (mains €10 to €26) has a meaty menu.

Mondschein HOTEL €€
(☎227 84; www.mondschein.at; Mariahilfstrasse 6; s €87-105, d €105-180; P❄@) As the name suggests, the moon lights the way to this riverside hotel. Done up in midnight blue and cream tones, rooms are light, spacious and classically elegant. Most have Altstadt views and the best sport Swarovski–crystal studded bathrooms.

Weinhaus Happ GUESTHOUSE €€
(☎582 980; www.weinhaus-happ.at; Herzog-Friedrich-Strasse 14; s/d €75/110) Happ exudes old-world atmosphere. The '70s-style rooms could do with a lick of paint, but its plus points are many: prime views of the Goldenes Dachl, a cavernous wine cellar and a rustic restaurant (mains €7 to €21).

Pension Paula GUESTHOUSE €
(☎292 262; www.pensionpaula.at; Weiherburggasse 15; s/d €41/65; P) Nestled in the hills above Innsbruck and with great city views, this family-run pension has super-clean, homely rooms (most with balcony). It's 1km north of the Altstadt, near the Alpenzoo.

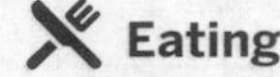

Eating

TOP CHOICE **Chez Nico** VEGETARIAN €€
(☎0650-451 06 24; www.chez-nico.at; Maria-Theresien-Strasse 49; lunch from €12.50, 6-course menu €51; ⊙lunch & dinner Tue-Fri, dinner Sat; ✎) Take a creative Parisian chef with an artistic eye and a passion for herbs, *et voilà,* you get Chez Nico. Nicolas Curtil (Nico) cooks seasonal vegetarian delights like porcini-sage ravioli and baked figs with rose sorbet at this intimate bistro.

Lichtblick FUSION €€€
(☎566 550; www.restaurant-lichtblick.at; Rathaus Galerien; lunch €9.50-13, set menus €40-50; ⊙10am-1am Mon-Sat) On the 7th floor of the Rathaus Galerien, this glass-walled restaurant has knockout views over Innsbruck to the mountains beyond. Season-driven specialities like homemade leek-truffle ravioli and schnitzel with chanterelles are all beautifully cooked and presented.

Cafe Munding CAFE €
(www.munding.at; Kiebachgasse 16; cake €2-4; ⊙8am-8pm) Scrumptious fruit tortes, cheesecakes, chocolate cake and home-roasted coffee.

Fischerhäusl AUSTRIAN €€
(☎583 535; www.fischerhaeusl.com; Herrengasse 8; mains €9-21; ⊙10.30am-1am Mon-Sat) The lemon-fronted Fischerhäusl has stood in this hidden spot between Domplatz and the Hofburg since 1758. On the menu is Tyrolean grub such as *Kaspressknödelsuppe*, cheesy dumplings swimming in broth, and *Gröstl*, a

DON'T MISS

AROUND INNSBRUCK

Just 9km east of Innsbruck is the town of Hall in Tirol. The labyrinth of pretty cobbled streets at its medieval heart pays testament to the massive wealth it accumulated from silver mines over the centuries. You can learn more about this legacy at **Burg Hasegg** (Burg Hasegg 6; adult/child €8/6; ⊙10am-5pm Tue-Sun), a 14th-century castle that had a 300-year career as a mint for silver *Thalers* (coins, the root of the modern word 'dollar').

Another 9km east along the valley in Wattens is **Swarovski Kristallwelten** (Swarovski Crystal Worlds; http://kristallwelten.swarovski.com; Kristallweltenstrasse 1; adult/child €11/free; ⊙9am-6.30pm), one of Austria's most-visited attractions. A crystal winterscape by Alexander McQueen, a kaleidoscopic crystal dome and a striking Terence Conran–designed shop are part of the fabulously glittering experience.

From Innsbruck, trains run frequently to Hall in Tirol (€2, eight minutes) and Fritzens-Wattens (€3.60, 16 minutes), 3km north of Swarovski Kristallwelten.

PICNIC GOODIES

s'Speckladele (Stiftgasse 4; ⌚9am-1pm & 2-6pm Mon-Fri, 9am-3pm Sat) This hole-in-the-wall shop has been doing a brisk trade in regional sausages, hams and speck made from 'happy pigs' for the past 60 years. Mini *Teufel* sausages with a chilli kick are the must-try.

s'Culinarium (Pfarrgasse 1; ⌚10am-6pm Mon-Sat) Herby Signor will help you pick an excellent bottle of Austrian wine at his shop-cum-bar.

Markthalle (www.markthalle-innsbruck.at; Innrain; ⌚7am-6.30pm Mon-Fri, to 1pm Sat) Freshly baked bread, Tyrolean cheese, organic fruit, smoked ham and salami – it's all under one roof at this riverside covered market.

potato, bacon and onion fry-up. The terrace fills quickly on warm days.

Ottoburg AUSTRIAN €€
(☎584 338; www.ottoburg.at; Herzog-Friedrich-Strasse 1; mains €16.50-28; ⌚lunch & dinner Tue-Sun; 👪) This medieval castle hides a warren of wood-panelled *Stuben* (parlours). Dig into tournedos of venison, *Topfenknödel* (cottage-cheese dumplings) and other hearty fare.

Madhuban INDIAN €
(☎589 157; www.madhuban.at; Templstrasse 2; mains €7-12; ⌚lunch & dinner Mon-Fri, dinner Sat & Sun) If you've had your fill of schnitzel and strudel and fancy a little spice, Madhuban does a spot-on curry. The two-course lunch is a snip at €7.50.

Mamma Mia PIZZERIA €
(☎562 902; Kiebachgasse 2; mains €7-9; ⌚lunch & dinner) No-frills Italian bistro with a great buzz, huge pizzas and a shady terrace.

Drinking

Moustache BAR
(www.cafe-moustache.at; Herzog-Otto-Strasse 8; ⌚11am-2am Tue-Sun) You too can try your hand at playing Spot-the-Moustache (Einstein, Charlie Chaplin and others), the preferred pastime at this retro newcomer. It has a terrace overlooking pretty Domplatz, as well as Club Aftershave in the basement.

Hofgarten Café BAR
(Rennweg 6a; ⌚11am-2am Tue-Thu, to 4am Fri-Sun) DJs spin at this tree-shaded beer garden and star-studded pavilion. The happening events line-up skips from summer festivals to weekend house parties.

360° BAR
(Rathaus Galerien; ⌚10am-1am Mon-Sat) There's no better place to see Innsbruck start to twinkle. Grab a cushion and drink in 360-degree views of the city and Alps from the balcony skirting the circular bar.

Theresienbräu PUB
(Maria-Theresien-Strasse 53; ⌚11am-1am Mon-Wed, to 2am Thu-Sat, noon-9pm Sun) A lively microbrewery with a big beer garden for quaffing a cold one.

Elferhaus PUB
(Herzog-Friedrich-Strasse 11; ⌚10am-2am) Nurse a beer beside gothic gargoyles at the bar or take a church-like pew to hear live rock bands play.

☆ Entertainment

For up-to-date entertainment listings, visit www.innsider.at (in German).

Tiroler Landestheater COMEDY
(☎0512-520 744; www.landestheater.at; Rennweg 2; tickets €3-38; ⌚ticket office 8.30am-8.30pm Mon-Sat, 5.30-8.30pm Sun) This neoclassical theatre is the city's main stage for opera, dance and drama.

Treibhaus CULTURAL CENTRE
(www.treibhaus.at; Angerzellgasse 8; ⌚10am-1am) Young Innsbruckers flock to this cultural complex to enjoy the big garden terrace, the chilled atmosphere and regular DJs. There's free live music on Friday evenings.

ℹ Information

Bubble Point (Innstrasse 11; ⌚7.30am-10.30pm Mon-Fri, 7.30am-10pm Sat & Sun) A laundry with high-speed internet for €2 per hour.

Innsbruck Information (☎535 60; www.innsbruck.info; Burggraben 3; ⌚9am-6pm) Main tourist office with truckloads of info on the city and surrounds, including skiing and walking. Sells ski passes, public-transport tickets and city maps (€1); will book accommodation (€3 commission) and has an attached ticketing service.

Getting There & Away

AIR **Innsbruck Airport**, 4km to the west of the city centre, caters to national and international flights, handled mostly by Austrian Airlines, BA, easyJet and Welcome Air.

CAR & MOTORCYCLE The A12 and the parallel Hwy 171 are the main roads heading west and east. The B177, to the west of Innsbruck, continues north to Munich (Germany). The A13 is a toll road (€8) running south through the Brenner Pass to Italy and crossing the 192m Europabrücke, spanning the Sill River. Toll-free Hwy 182 follows the same route, passing under the bridge.

TRAIN Fast trains depart at least every two hours for Bregenz (€34.40, 2½ hours), Salzburg (€41.30, two hours), Kitzbühel (€19.20, 1½ hours) and Munich (€39.60, two hours). There are several daily services to Lienz (€19.20 to €35.20, 3¼ to 4½ hours).

Getting Around

To/From the Airport The airport is 4km west of the centre and served by bus F. Buses depart every 15 or 20 minutes from Maria-Theresien-Strasse (€1.90); taxis charge about €10 for the same trip.

Car & Bicycle Street parking is very limited in the city centre. Parking garages (eg under the Altstadt) cost around €17 per day. At the same address as Inntour (p83) Die Börse rents city, mountain, electric and children's bikes for €18/25/25/13 per day respectively.

Public Transport Single tickets on buses and trams cost €1.90 (from the driver; valid upon issue). A 24-hour ticket is €4.30.

SUMMER IN THE ZILLERTAL

The Zillertal is one of Austria's greatest outdoor playgrounds. Come summer the valley buzzes with cyclists, with 1000km of well-marked trails reaching from easygoing valley jaunts to gruelling mountain passes. Bicycles are available for hire at train stations throughout the Zillertal for €8/12 per half/full day; www.zillertal.at has interactive maps and route descriptions.

Hikers head for the pristine Alpine landscapes of **Naturpark Zillertaler Alpen** (www.naturpark-zillertal.at). From May to October, the nature reserve runs 250 guided walks, from llama trekking to sunrise photo excursions, most costing around €5. For adrenalin-fuelled pursuits like rock climbing, rafting and paragliding, try **Action Club Zillertal** (☎62 977; www.actionclub-zillertal.com; Hauptstrasse 458 ; ⊙9am-noon & 3-6pm) in Mayrhofen.

Mayrhofen

☎05285 / POP 3820

Tirol is ribbed by beautiful valleys, but the Zillertal is among the best, its soaring peaks begging outdoor escapades. A central place to base yourself is Mayrhofen, a mecca for skiers and après-skiers in winter, and mountain bikers, hikers and lederhosen-clad *Volksmusik* (folk music) fans in summer.

Snow-sure Mayrhofen has varied skiing on 159km of slopes, one of Europe's best terrain parks for snowboarders and the infamous Harakiri, Austria's steepest piste with a 78% gradient. A one-day ski pass, valid for all cable cars and lifts, costs €45.

The **tourist office** (☎67 600; www.mayrhofen.at; Dursterstrasse 225; ⊙9am-6pm Mon-Fri, 2-6pm Sat, 10am-2pm Sun) should be your first port of call for a handy accommodation booklet and the lowdown on activities.

Right in the centre, 500-year-old **Hotel Kramerwirt** (☎67 00; www.kramerwirt.at; Am Marienbrunnen 346; s incl half-board €91-117, d €158-210, mains €8-21; P ⊗) has spacious rooms, a whirlpool for relaxing moments and a traditional restaurant.

To gorge on *Schlutzkropf'n* (fresh pasta filled with cheese) and the like in the cosiest of surrounds, head to woodsy chalet **Wirtshaus zum Griena** (☎62 778; www.wirtshaus-griena.at; Dorfhaus 768; mains €8-16; ⊙Tue-Sun). Or assemble your own meaty snack at **Metzgerei Kröll** (Scheulingstrasse 382; snacks €3-8; ⊙7.30am-12.30pm & 2.30-6pm Mon-Fri, 7am-noon Sat), famous for its aromatic *Schlegeis-Speck* ham cured at 1800m. Pizza and pasta dominate the menu at **Mamma Mia** (☎67 68; Einfahrt Mitte 432; mains €7-9; ⊙11am-midnight).

Trains run regularly to Jenbach (€6.90, 55 minutes), where they connect with services to Innsbruck (€7.80, 20 minutes).

Kitzbühel

☎05356 / POP 8450

Kitzbühel began life in the 16th century as a silver- and copper-mining town, and today preserves a charming medieval centre despite its other persona – as a fashionable

KRIMML FALLS

The thunderous, three-tier **Krimml Falls** (www.wasserfaelle-krimml.at; adult/child €2.50/0.50, free Dec-Apr; ⏲ticket office 8am-6pm mid-Apr–late Oct) is Europe's highest waterfall at 380m, and one of Austria's most unforgettable sights. The pretty Alpine village of Krimml has a handful of places to sleep and eat; contact the **tourist office** (☎72 39; www.krimml.at; Oberkrimml 37; ⏲8am-noon & 2-6pm Mon-Fri, 8.30-10.30am & 4.30-6pm Sat) for more information.

Krimml is on Hwy 168 (which becomes Hwy 165). Buses run year-round from Krimml to Zell am See (€9.90, 1¼ hours, hourly), with frequent onward train connections to Salzburg (€21.50, 1½ hours) .

and prosperous winter resort. It's renowned for the white-knuckled Hahnenkamm downhill ski race in January and the excellence of its slopes.

Activities

There's an Alpine **flower garden** (free) on Kitzbüheler Horn (note there's a toll road for drivers). The forest-fringed Schwarzsee, 3km to the northwest, is a fine location for summer **swimming**.

Skiing — SKIING

In winter there's first-rate intermediate skiing and freeriding on 170km of well-groomed slopes. A one-day AllStarCard ski pass covering Kitzbühel and the surrounding region costs €46.50.

Hiking — HIKING

Dozens of summer hiking trails thread through the Kitzbühel Alps; the tourist office gives walking maps and runs free guided hikes for guests staying in town. The Flex-Ticket covering all cable cars costs €43.50/36 with/without bus for three out of seven days.

Sleeping & Eating

The tourist office can help with accommodation, but it's best to book well ahead. Rates leap up by 50% in the high winter season.

For self-caterers, there's a **Spar supermarket** (Bichlstrasse 22) and **Metzgerei Huber** (Bichlstrasse 14; snacks €3.50-7; ⏲8am-6pm Mon-Fri, 8am-12.30pm Sat) for carnivorous snacks.

Villa Licht — HOTEL €€

(☎62 293; www.villa-licht.at; Franz-Reich-Strasse 8; d €150-230; P 📶 🏊) Pretty gardens, warm-hued rooms with pine trappings, mountain views – this charming Tyrolean chalet has the lot. Kids love the tree house and outdoor pool.

Snowbunny's Hostel — HOSTEL €

(☎067-6794 0233; www.snowbunnys.co.uk; Bichlstrasse 30; dm €25-40, d €74-100; @ 📶) Friendly, laid-back hostel, a bunny-hop from the slopes. Breakfast is DIY-style in the kitchen, and there's a TV lounge, ski storage and shop for backpacker staples (Vegemite, Jägermeister etc).

Pension Kometer — PENSION €€

(☎622 89; www.pension-kometer.com; Gerbergasse 7; s €65-90, d €110-160; P) Make yourself at home in the bright, sparkling clean rooms at this family run guesthouse. There's a relaxed lounge with games and DVDs. Breakfast is a treat with fresh breads, fruit and eggs.

Huberbräu Stüberl — AUSTRIAN €

(☎656 77; Vorderstadt 18; mains €7-13) This vaulted tavern serves hearty portions of Austrian classics, such as schnitzel and liver dumplings, cooked to perfection.

Hosteria — ITALIAN €

(☎733 02; Alf Petzoldweg 2; mains €8-16; ⏲lunch Thu-Mon, dinner Wed-Mon) Authentic antipasti and wood-fired pizzas are matched with fine wines and genuine smiles at this stylish little Italian.

Information

The **tourist office** (☎66 660; www.kitzbuehel.com; Hinterstadt 18; ⏲8.30am-6pm Mon-Fri, 9am-6pm Sat, 10am-noon & 4-6pm Sun) has loads of info in English and a 24-hour accommodation board.

Getting There & Away

BUS It's quicker and cheaper to get from Kitzbühel to Lienz by bus (€14.70, two hours, twice daily) than by train.

CAR & MOTORCYCLE Kitzbühel is on the B170, 30km east of Wörgl and the A12/E45 motorway. Heading south to Lienz, you pass through some marvellous scenery. Hwy 108 (Felber Tauern Tunnel) and Hwy 107 (Grossglockner Rd; closed in winter) both have toll sections.

TRAIN Trains run frequently from Kitzbühel to Innsbruck (€19.20, 1¾ hours) and Salzburg (€28, 2½ hours). For Kufstein (€10, one hour), change at Wörgl.

St Anton am Arlberg

☎05446 / POP 2564

At the heart of the wild and austerely beautiful Arlberg region lies St Anton am Arlberg. In 1901 the first ski club in the Alps was founded here, downhill skiing was born and the village never looked back. Today the resort has legendary slopes and is Austria's unrivalled king of après ski.

Activities

Skiing SKIING

St Anton attracts both intermediate and advanced skiers and boarders, with challenging slopes, fantastic backcountry opportunities and a freestyle park on Rendl. A ski pass covering the whole Arlberg region and valid for all 85 ski lifts costs €47/257 for one/seven days in the high season.

Hiking HIKING

(Wanderpass €31/36 for three/seven days) Naturally, hiking is the number-one summer pastime: the Wanderpass gives you a head start with access to all lifts.

H2O Adventure ADVENTURE SPORTS

(☎05472-66 99; www.h2o-adventure.at; Bahnhofstrasse 1, Arlrock; ⏲May–mid-Oct) H2O Adventures gets adrenalin pumping, with activities from rafting to canyoning and mountain biking.

Sleeping & Eating

Rates can be almost double in the high winter season, when you'll need to book well ahead. Hit Dorfstrasse for snack bars and restaurants serving everything from tapas to Tex-Mex with a side order of après-ski. Most restaurants and bars close in summer.

Himmlhof GUESTHOUSE €€

(☎232 20; www.himmlhof.com; Im Gries 9; d €164-304; P@📶) This *himmlisch* (heavenly) Tyrolean chalet has wood-clad rooms brimming with original features (tiled ovens, four-poster beds and the like). An open fire and spa beckon after a day's skiing.

Altes Thönihaus GUESTHOUSE €€

(☎28 10; www.altes-thoenihaus.at; Im Gries 1; s €60-64, d €116-124; P📶) Dating to 1465, this listed wooden chalet oozes Alpine charm from every last beam. Fleecy rugs and pine keep the mood cosy in rooms with mountain-facing balconies. Downstairs there's a superb little spa and restored *Stube* (parlour).

Museum Restaurant AUSTRIAN €€

(☎24 75; Rudi-Matt-Weg 10; mains €17.50-32.50; ⏲dinner) Arlberger hay soup, succulent Tyrolean beef and fresh-from-the-pond trout land on your plate at this wood-panelled restaurant, picturesquely housed in the village museum.

Information

The **tourist office** (☎22 690; www.stantonamarlberg.com; Dorfstrasse 8; ⏲8am-6pm Mon-Fri, 9am-6pm Sat, 9am-noon & 3-6pm Sun) has maps and information on accommodation and activities, and an accommodation board with free telephone outside.

Getting There & Away

St Anton is on the main railway route between Bregenz (€19.20, 1½ hours) and Innsbruck (€21.50, 1¼ hours). The town is close to the eastern entrance of the Arlberg Tunnel, the toll road connecting Vorarlberg and Tirol. The tunnel toll is €8.50 one way. You can avoid the toll by taking the B197, but no vehicles with trailers are allowed on this winding road.

Lienz

☎04852 / POP 11,800

The Dolomites rise like an amphitheatre around Lienz, straddling the Isel and Drau rivers, and just 40km north of Italy. Those same arresting river and mountain views welcomed the Romans, who settled here some 2000 years ago. Lienz is also a stopover for skiers and hikers passing through or on the way to the Hohe Tauern National Park.

Sights & Activities

Schloss Bruck CASTLE

(Schlossberg 1; adult/child €7.50/2.50; ⏲10am-6pm mid-May–late Oct) Lienz' biggest crowd-puller is its medieval fortress. The museum displays everything from Tyrolean costumes to emotive paintings by famous local son Albin Egger-Lienz.

Stadtpfarrkirche St Andrä CHURCH
(Pfarrgasse 4; daylight hours) More of Albin Egger-Lienz' sombre works can be seen at the Gothic St Andrew's Church.

Aguntum ARCHAEOLOGICAL SITE
(www.aguntum.info; Stribach 97; adult/child €6/4; 9.30am-5pm, closed Nov-Apr) For an insight into Lienz' Roman past, visit the Aguntum archaeological site.

Skiing SKIING
A €36 day pass covers skiing on the nearby **Zettersfeld** and **Hochstein** peaks. However, the area is more renowned for its 100km of cross-country trails; the town fills up for the annual **Dolomitenlauf** cross-country skiing race in mid-January.

Dolomiten Lamatrekking HIKING
(68 087; www.dolomitenlama.at) The Dolomites make for highly scenic hiking, with cable cars rising to Hochstein (return €13) and Zettersfeld (€10). From this outfitter you can enlist a gentle-natured llama to accompany you.

Sleeping & Eating

The tourist office can point you in the direction of good-value guesthouses and camping grounds.

Hotel Haidenhof HOTEL €€
(624 40; www.haidenhof.at; Grafendorferstrasse 12; s €89-101, d €140-186; P) High above Lienz, this country retreat has a dress-circle view of the Dolomites. The spacious rooms and roof terrace maximise those views. Home-grown produce features in the restaurant (mains €16.50 to €26).

Romantik Hotel Traube HOTEL €€
(644 44; www.hoteltraube.at; Hauptplatz 14; s €65-99, d €134-190; P@) Right on the main square, Traube races you back to the Biedermeier era with its high ceilings and antique-meets-boutique rooms. The 6th-floor pool affords views over Lienz to the Dolomites.

Kirchenwirt AUSTRIAN €€
(625 00; www.kirchenwirt-lienz.at; Pfarrgasse 7; mains €9-18; 9am-midnight) Up on a hill opposite Stadtpfarrkirche St Andrä, this is Lienz' most atmospheric restaurant. Dine under the vaults or on the streamside terrace on local dishes like East Tyrolean milk-fed lamb.

Information

The **tourist office** (050-212 400; www.lienzerdolomiten.info; Europaplatz 1; 8am-6pm Mon-Fri, 9am-noon & 4-6pm Sat) will find rooms free of charge, or you can use the hotel board (free telephone) outside. Free internet access is available at the local **library** (Muchargasse 4; 9am-noon & 3-6pm Tue-Fri, 9am-noon Sat).

Getting There & Away

There are several daily services to Innsbruck (€19.20 to €35.20, 3¼ to 4½ hours). Trains run every two hours to Salzburg (€37, 3½ hours). To head south by car, you must first divert west or east along Hwy 100.

Hohe Tauern National Park

If you thought Mother Nature pulled out all the stops in the Austrian Alps, Hohe Tauern National Park was her magnum opus. Straddling Tirol, Salzburg and Carinthia, this national park is the largest in the Alps; a 1786-sq-km wilderness of 3000m peaks, Alpine meadows and waterfalls. At its heart lies **Grossglockner** (3798m), Austria's highest mountain, which towers over the 8km-long **Pasterze Glacier**, best seen from the outlook at **Kaiser-Franz-Josefs-Höhe** (2369m).

The 48km **Grossglockner Road** (www.grossglockner.at; Hwy 107; car/motorcycle €32/22; May-early Nov) from Bruck in Salzburgerland to Heiligenblut in Carinthia is one of Europe's greatest Alpine drives. A feat of 1930s engineering, the road swings giddily around 36 switchbacks, passing jewel-coloured lakes, forested slopes and wondrous glaciers.

If you have wheels, you'll have more flexibility, although the road is open only between May and early November, and you must pay tolls.

The major village on the Grossglockner Road is **Heiligenblut**, dominated by mountain peaks and the needle-thin spire of its 15th-century pilgrimage church. Here you'll find a **tourist office** (04824-27 00; www.heiligenblut.at; Hof 4; 9am-6pm), which can advise on guided ranger hikes, mountain hiking and skiing. The village also has a campsite, a few restaurants and a spick-and-span **Jugendherberge** (hostel; 22 59; www.oejhv.or.at; Hof 36; dm/s/d €20.50/28.50/49; P@).

Bus 5002 runs frequently between Lienz and Heiligenblut on weekdays (€15.80, one

BREGENZERWALD

Only a few kilometres southeast of Bregenz, the forest-cloaked slopes, velvet-green pastures and limestone peaks of the Bregenzerwald unfold. In summer it's a glorious place to spend a few days hiking the hills and filling up on home-made cheeses in Alpine dairies. Winter brings plenty of snow, and the area is noted for its downhill and cross-country skiing. The **Bregenzerwald tourist office** (☎05512-23 65; www.bregenzerwald.at; Impulszentrum 1135, Egg; ⏰9am-5pm Mon-Fri, 8am-1pm Sat) has information on the region.

hour), less frequently at weekends. From late June to mid-September, three buses run from Monday to Friday and Sunday, plus one on Saturday between Heiligenblut and Kaiser-Franz-Josefs-Höhe (€7.90, 30 minutes). Check the timetables with the tourist office in Lienz before setting off.

VORARLBERG

Vorarlberg has always been a little different. Cut off from the rest of Austria by the snow-capped Arlberg massif, this westerly region has often associated itself more with Switzerland than Vienna far to the east, and its citizens have developed a strong dialect even Tyroleans find hard to decipher.

Trickling down from the Alps to the shores of Bodensee (Lake Constance), Vorarlberg is an alluringly beautiful destination in its own right, attracting everyone from classical-music buffs to skiers. It's also a gateway, by rail or water, to Germany, Liechtenstein and Switzerland.

Bregenz

☎05574 / POP 28,000

Clichéd though it sounds, Vorarlberg's pocket-sized capital really does seem to have it all, with its mountains-meets-lake location, avant-garde art and monster of an opera festival. Every sunray is used to the max in summer for boating, cycling, swimming and lounging on the shores of Bodensee.

Sights

Kunsthaus GALLERY

(www.kunsthaus-bregenz.at; Karl-Tizian-Platz; adult/child €9/free; ⏰10am-6pm Tue-Sun, to 9pm Thu) The architecturally eye-catching Kunsthaus, by award-winning Swiss architect Peter Zumthor, hosts first-rate contemporary art exhibitions.

Oberstadt HISTORIC AREA

Set high above the modern centre is the Oberstadt, the storybook old town; look for the enormous onion dome of the **Martinsturm** (St Martin's Tower; www.martinsturm.at; Martinsgasse; adult/child €3.50/1; ⏰10am-5pm Tue-Sun Apr-Oct), reputedly the largest in central Europe.

Pfänder Cable Car CABLE CAR

(www.pfaenderbahn.at; Steinbruchgasse 4; one-way adult/child €6.50/3.20, return €11.20/5.60; ⏰8am-7pm) For spectacular views of the lake, town and not-so-distant Alps, catch the cable car, which rises to 1064m.

Activities

Bregenz' shimmering centrepiece is the **Bodensee**, Europe's third-largest lake, straddling Austria, Switzerland and Germany. Lakeside activities include **sailing** and **diving** at Lochau, 5km north of town, and **swimming**.

Bodensee Radweg CYCLING

(www.bodensee-radweg.com) In summer, the well-marked Bodensee Radweg that circumnavigates the Bodensee becomes an autobahn for lycra-clad *Radfahrer* (cyclists). Hire your own set of wheels at **Fahrradverleih Bregenz** (Seepromenade; per day city bike €15-18, e-bike €25; ⏰9am-7pm Apr-Oct).

Festivals & Events

The **Bregenzer Festspiele** (Bregenz Festival; ☎407-6; www.bregenzerfestspiele.com), running from mid-July to mid-August, is the city's premier cultural festival. World-class operas and orchestral works are staged on the Seebühne, a floating stage on the lake, in the Festspielhaus and at the Vorarlberger Landestheater. Tickets are up for grabs about nine months before the festival.

Sleeping & Eating

Prices soar and beds are at a premium during the Bregenzer Festspiele – book ahead.

TOP CHOICE **Deuring-Schlössle** HISTORIC HOTEL €€€
(☎478 00; www.deuring-schloessle.at; Ehre-Guta-Platz 4; d €212-240, ste €314-420; P@) Bregenz' best rooms are found in this fabulously renovated old castle. Each one is decorated differently, but all have loads of medieval charm and grace. Its restaurant (mains around €30) is also Bregenz' best, with a sophisticated look and a market-fresh menu.

JUFA Gästehaus Bregenz HOSTEL €
(☎05708-35 40; www.jufa.at/bregenz; Mehrerauerstrasse 5; dm €28.20; P@) Housed in a former needle factory near the lake, this HI hostel now reels backpackers in with its super-clean dorms and excellent facilities including a common room and restaurant.

Hotel Weisses Kreuz HOTEL €€
(☎498 80; www.hotelweisseskreuz.at; Römerstrasse 5; s €109-119, d €126-186, mains €14-29; P@) Service is attentive at this central pick, with a restaurant rolling out seasonal Austrian fare. The smart rooms sport cherry wood furnishings, flat-screen TVs and organic bedding.

Wirtshaus am See AUSTRIAN €€
(☎422 10; www.wirtshausamsee.at; Seepromenade 2; mains €11-18; 9am-midnight) Snag a table on the lakefront terrace at this mock half-timbered villa, dishing up local specialities like buttery Bodensee whitefish and venison ragout. It's also a relaxed spot for quaffing a cold one.

Cafesito CAFE €
(Maurachgasse 6; bagels €3-4; 7.45am-6.30pm Mon-Fri, 9am-2.30pm Sat) Tiny Cafesito does the best create-your-own bagels, smoothies and fair-trade coffee in town.

Information

Bregenz' **tourist office** (☎49 59; www.bregenz.travel; Rathausstrasse 35a; 9am-6pm Mon-Fri, to noon Sat) has information on the city and the surrounding area, and can help with accommodation.

Getting There & Away

BOAT From April to mid-October, there's a frequent boat service between Bregenz and a number of towns and cities on the Bodensee, including Konstanz (one way €16.40, 4¼ hours), Lindau (€5.30, 22 minutes) and Friedrichshafen (€13.50, two hours) in Germany. For information, consult www.bodenseeschifffahrt.at.

TRAIN Trains to Munich (€45.40, three hours) often go via Lindau (€2.20, nine minutes), and Zürich (€34, 2¼ hours) via St Gallen (€14, 50 minutes). Twelve trains depart daily for Innsbruck (€34.40, 2½ hours). Trains to Konstanz (€32.40, 1¾ to 2½ hours) may be frequent, but require between one and four changes.

UNDERSTAND AUSTRIA

History

Austria has been a galvanic force in shaping Europe's history. This landlocked little country was once the epicentre of the mighty Habsburg empire and, in the 20th century, a pivotal player in the outbreak of WWI.

Civilisation & Empire

Like so many European countries, Austria has experienced invasions and struggles since time immemorial. There are traces of human occupation since the ice age, but it was the Celts who made the first substantial mark on Austria around 450 BC. The Romans followed 400 years later, and in turn were followed by Bavarians and, in 1278, the House of Habsburg, which took control of the country by defeating the head of the Bavarian royalty.

The Habsburg Monarchy

For six centuries the Habsburgs used strategic marriages to maintain their hold over a territory that encompassed much of central and Eastern Europe and, for a period, even Germany. But defeat in WWI brought that to an end, when the Republic of Austria was formed in 1918.

The 16th and 17th centuries saw the Ottoman threat reach the gates of Vienna, and in 1805 Napoleon defeated Austria at Austerlitz. Austrian Chancellor Metternich cleverly reconsolidated Austria's power in 1815 after Waterloo, but the loss of the 1866 Austro-Prussian War, and creation of the Austro-Hungarian empire in 1867, diminished the Habsburg's influence in Europe.

However, these setbacks pale beside Archduke Franz Ferdinand's assassination by Slavic separatists in Sarajevo on 28 June 1914. When his uncle, the Austro-Hungarian emperor Franz Josef, declared war on Serbia in response, the ensuing 'Great War' (WWI) would prove the Habsburgs' downfall.

WWII & Postwar Austria

During the 1930s the Nazis began to influence Austrian politics, and by 1938 the recession-hit country was ripe for picking. Invading German troops met little resistance and Hitler was greeted on Heldenplatz as a hero by 200,000 Viennese.

Austria was heavily bombed during WWII, but the country recovered well, largely through the Marshall Plan and sound political and economic decisions (excluding its foray with the far-right Freedom Party and its controversial leader, Jörg Haider, in the 1990s). Austria has maintained a neutral stance since 1955, been home to a number of international organisations, including the UN, since 1979, and joined the EU in 1995.

Austria today enjoys the kind of economic, social and political stability that many other nations would dream of. Cities forging ahead include Linz, which seized the reins as European Capital of Culture in 2009, and Innsbruck, which hosted the first Winter Youth Olympics in 2012. Vienna, too, has plenty to look pleased about, topping the Mercer Quality of Living List in 2011 and with a shiny new Hauptbahnhof in the making.

Arts & Architecture

Classical Music

What other country can match the musical heritage of Austria? Great composers were drawn to Vienna by the Habsburgs' generous patronage during the 18th and 19th centuries. The era most strongly associated with Austrian music is *Wiener Klassik* (Vienna Classic), which dates back to the mid- and late 18th century and has defined the way we perceive classical music today. It began life as a step down from the celestial baroque music of the royal court and church, and shifted the focus of performance onto the salons and theatres of upper middle-class society.

Joseph Haydn (1732–1809) is considered to be the first of the great composers of the *Wiener Klassik* era, followed by Salzburg wunderkind Wolfgang Amadeus Mozart (1756–91). Beethoven's musical genius reached its zenith in Vienna. *Lieder* (song) master Franz Schubert (1797–1828) was the last of the heavyweight *Wiener Klassik* composers.

Vienna Secession & Expressionism

In 1897, 19 progressive artists broke away from the conservative artistic establishment and formed the Vienna Secession (*Sezession*) movement, synonymous with art nouveau. Vienna turned out such talents as the painter Gustav Klimt (1862–1918); Schloss Belvedere showcases one of his finest works, *The Kiss*. Vienna-born architect Otto Wagner (1841–1918) ushered in a new, functional direction around the turn of the 20th century and gave the capital a metro system replete with attractive art nouveau stations.

Gustav Klimt strongly influenced the work of well-known Austrian expressionists like Egon Schiele (1890–1918), who was obsessed with capturing the erotic on canvas, and Oskar Kokoschka (1886–1980). The paintings of these three Austrian greats hang out in the Leopold Museum in Vienna's MuseumsQuartier.

Baroque Heyday

Thanks to the Habsburg monarchy and its obsession with pomp and splendour, Austria is packed with high-calibre architecture, which reached giddy heights of opulence during the baroque era of the late 17th and early 18th century. It took the graceful column and symmetry of the Renaissance and added elements of the grotesque, burlesque and the saccharin.

Johann Bernhard Fischer von Erlach (1656–1723), the mastermind behind Schloss Schönbrunn, was the country's greatest baroque architect. Like Fischer von Erlach, Austria's second architect of the era, Johann Lukas von Hildebrandt (1668–1745), was famous for his interior decorative work of palaces for the aristocracy, such as Schloss Belvedere. Paul Troger (1698–1762) is Austria's master of the baroque fresco and his work is best appreciated at Stift Melk. Other baroque highlights include Karlskirche in Vienna, Salzburg's Dom and the Hofburg in Innsbruck.

Food & Drink

Staples & Specialities

Austria is famous for its Wiener schnitzel, goulash and desserts like *Sacher Torte*

(Sacher cake) and *Kaiserschmarrn* (sweet pancakes with raisins). Certainly, these classics are not to be missed, but the Austrian table offers a host of other regional and seasonal delights. Throw in excellent red wines from Burgenland and quality whites and reds from Lower Austria, Styria and elsewhere, and you have the makings of an exciting and unexpected culinary experience.

In Lower Austria try Waldviertel game, beef and poppy dishes, tangy cider from the Mostviertel, and pike and carp from Burgenland. The Wachau goes mad for *Marillen* (apricots) around mid-July. Styria is renowned for its *Almochsen* (meadow beef) and healthy, nutty pumpkin oil. Upper Austria is *Knödel* (dumpling) country, while the must-eat in neighbouring Salzburgerland is *Salzburger Nockerln*, a sweet soufflé. Freshwater fish in Carinthia, *Heumilchkäse* (hay milk cheese) from Vorarlberg and Tirol's hearty *Gröstl* (a fry-up from leftover potatoes, pork and onions) are other regional specialities.

Where to Eat & Drink

Solid Austrian fare is on the menu in Vienna's homely, good-value inns called *Beisl* (small taverns; from the Yiddish word for 'little houses'). Besides cake, most coffee houses serve light or classic dishes like goulash. In the winegrowing regions, rustic *Heurigen* (wine taverns) sell their wine directly from their own premises and food is available buffet-style. They open on a roster so pick up the local *Heurigenkalendar* (*Heurigen* calendar) from the tourist offices.

For cheap food, try *Mensen* (university canteens). Another money-saving trick is to make lunch the main meal of the day, as many Austrians do; most restaurants provide a good-value *Tagesteller* or *Tagesmenü* (fixed-price menu). You can assemble your own picnic at local farmers markets.

THROUGH THE GRAPEVINE

The 830km **Weinstrasse Niederösterreich** (www.weinstrassen.at; Lower Austria Wine Rd) wends through eight wine-producing regions in Lower Austria, including the Kremstal, Kamptal and Weinviertel, passing beautiful terraced vineyards, bucolic villages, castles and abbeys. Visit the website for the low-down on local wineries (some with accommodation), wine shops and rustic *Heurigen* (wine taverns), where you can taste the region's pinot blanc (Weissburgunder), grüner veltliner, Riesling and red wines. Autumn is the time for semifermented *Sturm* (new wine).

SURVIVAL GUIDE

Directory A–Z

Accommodation

From simple mountain huts to five-star hotels fit for kings – you'll find the lot in Austria. Tourist offices invariably keep lists and details, and some arrange bookings for free or for a nominal fee. Some useful points:

» It's wise to book ahead at all times, particularly during the high seasons: July and August and December to April (in ski resorts).

» Be aware that confirmed reservations in writing are considered binding, and cancellations within several days of arrival often involve a fee or full payment.

» Some hostels and some rock-bottom digs have an *Etagendusche* (communal shower).

» Very often a hotel won't have lifts; if this is important, always check ahead.

» In mountain resorts, high-season prices can be up to double the prices charged in the low season (May to June and October to November).

» In some resorts (not often in cities), a *Gästekarte* (guest card) is issued if you stay overnight, which offers discounts on things such as cable cars and admission.

» Locally, always check the city or region website, as many (such as in Vienna, Salzburg and Graz) have an excellent booking function.

Some useful websites:

Austrian Hotelreservation (www.austrian-hotelreservation.at)

Austrian National Tourist Office (www.austria.info)

Booking.com (www.booking.com)

Hostelling International (HI; www.hihostels.com)

Hostelworld (www.hostelworld.com)

PRACTICALITIES

» **Opening Hours** Most sights and tourist offices operate on reduced hours from November to March. Opening hours we provide are for the high season, so outside those months it can be useful to check ahead.

» **Seasonal Closures** In the Alps, many hotels, restaurants and sometimes tourist offices close between seasons, from around May to mid-June and mid-September to early December.

» **Concessions** Museums and sights have concessions for families, children (generally under 16 year olds), students and senior citizens; you may need to show proof of age. Children under 12 years usually receive a substantial discount on rooms they share with parents.

» **Smoking** Unless a separate room has been set aside, smoking is not allowed in restaurants. It's legal to smoke anywhere on outdoor terraces.

PRICE RANGES

Our reviews refer to double rooms with private bathrooms, except in hostels or where otherwise specified. Quoted rates are for the high season: December to April in the Alps, June and August everywhere else.

€€€ more than €200

€€ €80 to €200

€ less than €80

Activities

Austria is a wonderland for outdoorsy types, with much of the west given over to towering Alpine peaks. Opportunities for hiking and mountaineering are boundless in Tirol, Salzburgerland and the Hohe Tauern National Park, all of which have extensive Alpine hut networks (see www.alpenverein.at). Names like St Anton, Kitzbühel and Mayrhofen fire the imagination of serious skiers, but you may find cheaper accommodation and lift passes in little-known resorts; visit www.austria.info for the lowdown.

Business Hours

Banks 8am-3pm Mon-Fri, to 5.30pm Thu

Clubs 10pm to late

Post offices 8am-noon & 2-6pm Mon-Fri, 8am-noon Sat

Pubs 6pm-1am

Cafes 7.30am-8pm; hours vary widely

Restaurants noon-3pm, 7-11pm

Shops 9am-6.30pm Mon-Fri, 9am-5pm Sat

Supermarkets 9am-8pm Mon-Sat

Discount Cards

Regional Various discount cards are available, many of them covering a whole region or province. Some are free with an overnight stay.

Student & Youth Cards International Student Identity Cards (ISIC) and the European Youth Card (Euro<26; check www.euro26.org for discounts) will get you discounts at most museums, galleries and theatres. Admission is generally a little higher than the price for children.

Discount Rail Cards See p98.

Embassies & Consulates

All of the embassies and consulates listed following are located in Vienna (telephone prefix ☎01).

Australian Embassy (☎506 740; www.australian-embassy.at; Mattiellistrasse 2-4, Vienna)

Canadian Embassy (☎5313 83 000; www.canadainternational.gc.ca; Laurenzerberg 2, Vienna)

New Zealand Embassy (☎505 30 21; www.nzembassy.com/austria; Mattiellistrasse 2-4, Vienna)

UK Embassy (☎716 130; http://ukinaustria.fco.gov.uk; Jaurèsgasse 12, Vienna)

US Embassy (☎313 390; http://austria.usembassy.gov; Boltzmanngasse 16, Vienna)

Food

Price ranges in this chapter are for a two-course meal excluding drinks:

€€€ more than €30

€€ €15 to €30

€ less than €15

Money

ATMs Some *Bankomaten* (ATMs) are 24 hours. Most accept at the very least Maestro debit cards and Visa and MasterCard credit cards.

Credit Cards Visa and MasterCard (Eurocard) are accepted a little more widely than American Express (Amex) and Diners Club.

Taxes *Mehrwertsteuer* (MWST; value-added tax) is set at 20% for most goods.

Tipping It's customary to tip about 10% in restaurants, bars and cafes, and in taxis.

Transfers For emergency transfers, Western Union (www.westernunion.com) offices are available in larger towns.

Public Holidays

New Year's Day (Neujahr) 1 January

Epiphany (Heilige Drei Könige) 6 January

Easter Monday (Ostermontag) March/April

Labour Day (Tag der Arbeit) 1 May

Whit Monday (Pfingstmontag) Sixth Monday after Easter

Ascension Day (Christi Himmelfahrt) Sixth Thursday after Easter

Corpus Christi (Fronleichnam) Second Thursday after Whitsunday

Assumption (Maria Himmelfahrt) 15 August

National Day (Nationalfeiertag) 26 October

All Saints' Day (Allerheiligen) 1 November

Immaculate Conception (Mariä Empfängnis) 8 December

Christmas Day (Christfest) 25 December

St Stephen's Day (Stephanitag) 26 December

Telephone

Austrian telephone numbers consist of an area code followed by the local number.

Country code 43

International access code 00

Mobile Phones The network works on GSM 1800 and is compatible with GSM 900 phones. Phone shops sell prepaid SIM cards for about €10.

Public Telephones Phonecards in different denominations are sold at post offices and *Tabak* (tobacconist) shops. Call centres are widespread in cities, and many internet cafes are geared for Skype calls.

WHERE TO STAY

Hotels & Pensions Hotels and pensions (B&Bs) are rated by the same criteria from one to five stars.

Hostels In Austria over 100 hostels *(Jugendherberge)* are affiliated with Hostelling International (HI). Facilities are often excellent. Four- to six-bed dorms with shower/toilet are the norm, though some places also have doubles and family rooms. See www.oejhv.or.at or www.oejhw.at for details.

Private Rooms *Privatzimmer* (private rooms) are cheap (often about €50 per double). On top of this, you will find *Bauernhof* (farmhouses) in rural areas, and some *Öko-Bauernhöfe* (organic farms).

Alpine Huts There are over 530 of these huts in the Austrian Alps; most are maintained by the Österreichischer Alpenverein (ÖAV; Austrian Alpine Club; www.alpenverein.at, in German). Meals are often available. Bed prices for nonmembers are around €26 to €44 in a dorm; ÖAV members pay half-price.

Rental Accommodation *Ferienwohnungen* (self-catering apartments) are ubiquitous in Austrian mountain resorts; advance booking is recommended. Contact a local tourist office for lists and prices.

Camping Austria has over 490 camping grounds, many well equipped and scenically located. Prices can be as low as €4 per person or small tent and as high as €10. Many close in winter, so phone ahead to check. Search for camping grounds by region at www.camping-club.at (in German).

Eco-Hotels To search *Bio-* or *Öko-* ('eco') hotels by region, see www.biohotels.info.

Tourist Information

Tourist offices, which are dispersed far and wide in Austria, tend to adjust their hours from one year to the next, so business hours may have changed slightly by the time you arrive.

The **Austrian National Tourist Office** (www.austria.info) has a number of overseas offices. There is a comprehensive listing on the ANTO website.

Visas

Schengen visa rules apply. See p1114 for further details. The Austrian Foreign Ministry website, www.bmeia.gv.at, lists embassies.

Getting There & Away

Air

Vienna is the main transport hub for Austria, but Graz, Linz, Klagenfurt, Salzburg and Innsbruck all receive international flights. Flights to these cities are often a cheaper option than those to the capital, as are flights to Airport Letisko (Bratislava Airport), 85km east of Vienna in Slovakia.

Among the low-cost airlines, Ryanair and Air Berlin fly to Graz, Innsbruck, Klagenfurt, Linz, Salzburg and Vienna (Ryanair to Bratislava for Vienna).

Following are the key international airports in Austria:

Graz Airport (☎29 020; www.flughafen-graz.at)

Innsbruck Airport (INN; ☎0512-22 525; www.innsbruck-airport.com)

Klagenfurt Airport (KLU; ☎0463-41 500; www.klagenfurt-airport.com)

Blue Danube Airport (LNZ; ☎0722-16 00; www.flughafen-linz.at)

Salzburg Airport (SZG; ☎0662-85 800; www.salzburg-airport.com)

Vienna Airport (VIE; ☎01-7007 22 233; www.viennaairport.com)

Airport Bratislava (BTS; ☎421 2 3303 33 53; www.airportbratislava.sk) Serves Bratislava and has good transport connections to Vienna. Used by Ryanair.

Land

BUS

Buses depart from Austria for as far afield as England, the Baltic countries, the Netherlands, Germany and Switzerland. But most significantly, they provide access to Eastern European cities small and large – from the likes of Sofia and Warsaw, to Banja Luka, Mostar and Sarajevo.

Services operated by **Eurolines** (www.eurolines.at) leave from Vienna and from several regional cities.

CAR & MOTORCYCLE

There are numerous entry points into Austria by road from Germany, the Czech Republic, Slovakia, Hungary, Slovenia, Italy and Switzerland. All border-crossing points are open 24 hours.

Standard European insurance and paperwork rules apply.

TRAIN

Austria has excellent rail connections. The main services in and out of the country from the west normally pass through Bregenz, Innsbruck or Salzburg en route to Vienna. Trains to Eastern Europe leave from Vienna. Express services to Italy go via Innsbruck or Villach; trains to Slovenia are routed through Graz.

Express & High-Speed Trains Express trains are identified by the symbols EC (EuroCity; serving international routes) or IC (InterCity; serving national routes).

Online Timetables **ÖBB** (☎05 17 17; www.oebb.at) Austrian National Railways, with national and international connections. Only national connections have prices online.

Reservations Extra charges can apply on fast trains and international trains, and it is a good idea (sometimes obligatory) to make seat reservations for peak times.

SparSchiene (discounted ÖBB tickets) These are often available when you book online in advance and can cost as little as a third of the standard train fare.

River & Lake

Hydrofoils run to Bratislava and Budapest from Vienna; slower boats cruise the Danube between the capital and Passau. The **Danube Tourist Commission** (www.danube-river.org) has a country-by-country list of operators and agents who can book tours. Germany and Switzerland can be reached from Bregenz.

Getting Around

Air

Flying within a country the size of Austria is not usually necessary. The main airline serving longer routes is **Austrian Airlines** (www.austrian.com) The national carrier and its joint flight operator Tyrolean offer several flights daily between Vienna and Graz, Innsbruck, Klagenfurt, Linz and Salzburg.

Bicycle

Bike Hire All cities have at least one bike shop that doubles as a rental centre; expect to pay around €10 to €15 per day.

Bike Touring Most tourist boards have brochures on cycling facilities and plenty of designated cycling routes within their region. Separate bike tracks are common in cities, and long-distance tracks and routes also run along major rivers such as the Danube and lakes such as Wörthersee in Carinthia and Bodensee (Lake Constance) in Vorarlberg.

Bike Transport You can take bicycles on any train with a bicycle symbol at the top of its timetable. A day ticket costs €5 for regional, €10 for national (InterCity) and €12 for international trains. You can't take bicycles on buses.

Boat

The Danube serves as a thoroughfare between Vienna and Lower and Upper Austria. Services are generally slow, scenic excursions rather than functional means of transport.

Bus

Postbus services usually depart from outside train stations. In remote regions, there are fewer services on Saturday and often none on Sunday. Generally, you can only buy tickets from the drivers. For information inside Austria, call ☎0810 222 333 (6am to 8pm); from outside Austria, call ☎+43 1 71101, or visit the website, www.postbus.at.

Car & Motorcycle

Autobahns ('A') and *Bundesstrassen* ('B') are major roads, while *Landstrassen* ('L') let you enjoy the ride and are usually good for cyclists. A daily motorail service links Vienna to Innsbruck, Salzburg and Villach.

AUTOMOBILE ASSOCIATIONS

Annual membership for Austria's two automobile associations costs €75.60 and includes a free 24-hour breakdown service. The two associations:

ARBÖ (☎24hr emergency assistance 123, office 123 123; www.arboe.at; Mariahilfer Strasse 180, Vienna; ⊙office telephone 6am-7pm daily, office premises 8am-5.30pm Mon-Fri)

ÖAMTC (☎24hr emergency assistance 120, office 01-711 99-0; www.oeamtc.at; Schubertring 1-3, Vienna; ⊙8am-6pm Mon-Fri, 9am-1pm Sat)

HIRE

Multinational car-hire firms **Avis** (www.avis.at), **Budget** (www.budget.at), **Europcar** (www.europcar.co.at) and **Hertz** (www.hertz.at) all have offices in major cities; ask at tourist offices for details. The minimum age for hiring small cars is 19 years, or 25 years for larger, 'prestige' cars. Customers must have held a driving licence for at least a year. Many contracts forbid customers to take cars outside Austria, particularly into Eastern Europe.

MOTORWAY & TUNNEL TOLLS

A *Vignette* (toll sticker) is imposed on all motorways; charges for cars/motorbikes are €8.30/4.80 for 10 days and €24.20/12.10 for two months. *Vignette* can be purchased at border crossings, petrol stations and *Tabak* shops. There are additional tolls (usually €2.50 to €10) for some mountain tunnels.

ROAD RULES

» The minimum driving age is 18.

» Drive on the right, overtake on the left.

» Give way to the right at all times except when a priority road sign indicates otherwise. Trams always have priority.

» An international driving licence should always be carried.

» Seat belts are compulsory.

» The speed limit is 50km/h in built-up areas, 130km/h on motorways and 100km/h on other roads. Except for the A1 (Vienna–Salzburg) and the A2 (Vienna–Villach), the speed limit is 110km/h on the autobahn from 10pm to 5am.

» The penalty for drink-driving – over 0.05% – is a hefty on-the-spot fine and confiscation of your driving licence.

» Crash helmets are compulsory for motorcyclists and their passengers, not for cyclists.
» Children under the age of 14 who are shorter than 1.5m must have a special seat or restraint.
» Carrying a warning triangle, safety vest and first-aid kit in your vehicle is compulsory.
» Winter tyres and/or snow chains are compulsory from November to mid-April.
» It's illegal to hitchhike on Austrian motorways.

Train

Austria has a clean, efficient rail system, and if you use a discount card it's very inexpensive.

Disabled Passengers Use the 24-hour ☎05-17 17 customer number for special travel assistance; do this at least 24 hours ahead of travel (48 hours ahead for international services). Staff at stations will help with boarding and alighting.

Fares Fares quoted here are for 2nd-class tickets.

Information ÖBB (www.oebb.at) is the main operator, supplemented with a handful of private lines. Tickets and timetables are available online.

RailJet It's worth seeking out RailJet train services connecting Vienna, Graz, Villach, Salzburg, Innsbruck, Linz and Klagenfurt, as they travel up to 200km/h.

Reservations In 2nd class within Austria this costs €3.50 for most express services; recommended for travel on weekends.

RAIL PASSES

Depending on the amount of travelling you intend to do in Austria, rail passes can be a good deal.

Eurail Austria Pass This handy pass is available to non-EU residents; prices start at €123 for three days' unlimited 2nd-class travel within one month, and youths under 26 receive substantial discounts. See the website at www.eurail.com for all options.

InterRail Passes are for European citizens and include One Country Pass Austria (three/four/six/eight days €181/205/267/311). Youths under 26 receive substantial discounts. See www.interrailnet.com for all options.

Vorteilscard Reduces fares by at least 45% and is valid for a year, but not on buses. Bring a photo and your passport or ID. It costs adult/under 26 years/senior €100/20/27.

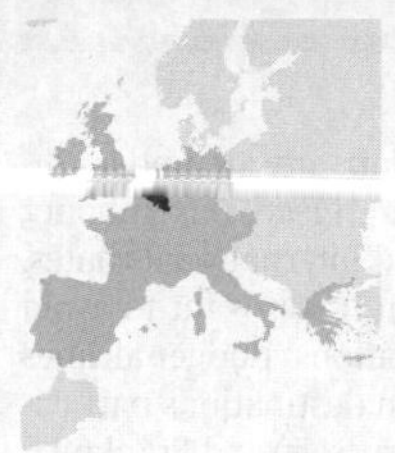

Belgium & Luxembourg

Includes »

Best Places to Eat

» De Stove (p132)

» Salon des Lumières (p139)

» House of Eliott (p126)

» L'Ogenblik (p110)

» In 't Nieuwe Museum (p132)

Best Places to Stay

» Guesthouse Nuit Blanche (p130)

» Chambres d'Hôtes Verhaegen (p125)

» Hotel Julien (p117)

» Hôtel Parc Beaux-Arts (p141)

Why Go?

Stereotypes of comic books, chips and sublime chocolates are just the start in eccentric little Belgium; its self-deprecating people have quietly spent centuries producing some of Europe's finest art and architecture. Bilingual Brussels is the dynamic yet personable EU capital, but also sports what's arguably the world's most beautiful city square. Flat, Dutch-speaking Flanders has many other alluring medieval cities, all easily linked by regular train hops. In hilly, French-speaking Wallonia, the attractions are contrastingly rural – castle villages, outdoor activities and extensive cave systems. Independent Luxembourg, the EU's richest country, is compact and hilly with its own wealth of castle villages. The grand duchy's capital city is famed for banking but also sports a fairy-tale Unesco-listed old town. And from the brilliant beers of Belgium to the sparkling wines of Luxembourg's Moselle Valley, there's plenty to lubricate some of Europe's best dining. Welcome to the good life.

When to Go

Brussels

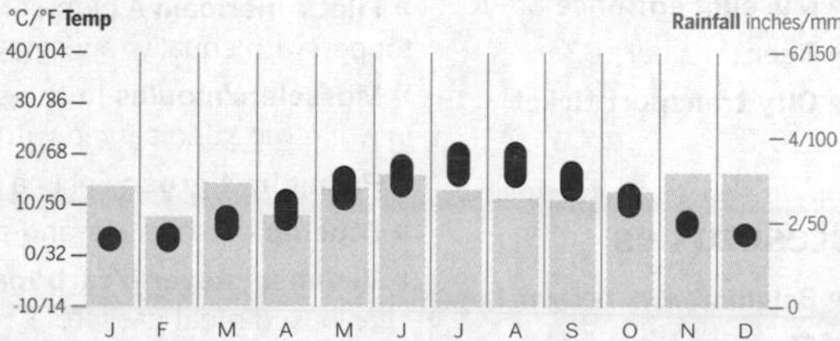

Pre-Easter weekends Belgium hosts many of Europe's weirdest carnivals.

Feb–Mar Both countries symbolically burn the spirit of winter on the first weekend after Carnival.

Jul–Aug Countless festivals, hotels packed at the coast but cheaper in Brussels and Luxembourg City.

AT A GLANCE

- **Currency** euro (€)
- **Languages** Dutch, French, German, Lëtzebuergesch
- **Money** ATMs common; credit cards widely accepted
- **Visas** Schengen rules apply

Fast Facts (Bel/Lux)

- **Area** 30,278/2586 sq km
- **Capitals** Brussels/ Luxembourg City
- **Country code** ☎32/352
- **Emergency** ☎112

Exchange Rates

Australia	A$1	€0.82
Canada	C$1	€0.77
Japan	¥100	€0.83
New Zealand	NZ$1	€0.65
UK	UK£1	€1.18
USA	US$1	€0.78

Set Your Budget

- **Budget hotel room** under €60
- **Two-course meal** €25
- **Museum entrance** €5–10
- **Beer** (in a bar) €2
- **City transport ticket** €1.20-2

Resources

- **Belgium** (www.belgium.be)
- **Flanders** (www.visitflanders.com)
- **Wallonia** (www.visitwallonia.be)
- **Luxembourg** (www.ont.lu)
- **Lonely Planet** (www.lonelyplanet.com/belgium)

Connections

Amsterdam, Paris, Cologne and London are all under 2½ hours from Brussels by high-speed train. Liège, Luxembourg City and Antwerp are also on high-speed international routes. Go via Tournai to reach France by train if you want to avoid such lines and their compulsory reservations. Budget airlines offer cheap deals to numerous European destinations particularly from Charleroi (an hour south of Brussels) and Frankfurt-Hahn airport in Germany (two hours from Luxembourg City).

ITINERARIES

Four Days

Just long enough to get a first taste of Belgium's four finest 'art cities': Bruges, Ghent, Brussels and Antwerp, all easy jump-offs or short excursions while you're train-hopping between Paris and Amsterdam. Bruges is the fairy-tale 'Venice of the north', Ghent has similar canal-side charms without the tourist hordes, and Brussels' incomparable Grand Place is worth jumping off any train for, even if you have only a few hours to spare. Cosmopolitan Antwerp goes one further, adding in fashion and diamonds. If you're overnighting make sure to hit Brussels on a weekend and Bruges on a weekday to get the best deals on accommodation.

Ten Days

Add an extra night in each of the above and consider stops in the moving WWI sites of historic Ypres, hopping to Antwerp via Leuven, Mechelen and Lier, or possibly adding a day or two in Luxembourg en route to Koblenz, Germany.

Essential Food & Drink

Classic, home-style dishes include the following:

- **Chicons au gratin** Endive rolled in ham and cooked in cheese/béchamel sauce.
- **Filet Américain** A blob of raw minced beef, typically topped with equally raw egg yolk.
- **Mosselen/moules** In-the-shell mussels, typically cooked in white wine and served with a mountain of *frites* (chips).
- **Paling in 't groen** Eel in a sorrel or spinach sauce.
- **Stoemp** Mashed veg-and-potato dish.
- **Vlaamse stoverij/carbonade flamande** Semi-sweet beer-based meat casserole.
- **Waterzooi** A cream-based chicken or fish stew.
- **Judd mat gaardebounen** Luxembourg's national dish; smoked pork-neck in a cream-based sauce with chunks of potato and broad beans.
- **Kniddelen** 'Dumplings'; often gnocchi-style balls served in various sauces, but the term can also refer to meatballs, which are known as ballekes/bouletten in Belgium.

BRUSSELS

POP 1.12 MILLION

Like the country it represents, Brussels (Bruxelles in French, Brussel in Dutch) is a surreal, multilayered place pulling several disparate identities into one enigmatic core. It subtly seduces with great art, tempting chocolate shops and classic cafes. Meanwhile a confusing architectural smorgasbord pits awesome art nouveau and 17th-century masterpieces against shabby suburbanism and the disappointingly soulless glass-faced anonymity of the EU area. Note that Brussels is officially bilingual, so all names – from streets to train stations – have both Dutch and French versions, but for simplicity we use only the French versions.

Sights

CENTRAL BRUSSELS

Although Brussels is very spread out, most key sights and numerous unmissable cafes are within leisurely walking distance of the fabulous Grand Place.

TOP CHOICE Grand Place SQUARE

(Ⓜ Gare Centrale) Brussels' incomparable central square tops any itinerary. Its splendidly spired Gothic **Hôtel de Ville** was the only building to escape bombardment by the French in 1695, quite ironic considering that it was their main target. Today the pedestrianised square's splendour is due largely to its intact collection of **guildhalls**, rebuilt by merchant guilds after 1695 and fancifully adorned with gilded statues. If you're using a BrusselsCard (see p107) don't miss your free beer at the two-room **Brewery Museum** (www.beerparadise.be; Grand Place 10; adult/BrusselsCard €6/free; ⏲10am-5pm daily Easter-Nov, noon-5pm Sat & Sun Dec-Easter; Ⓜ Gare Centrale).

TOP CHOICE Galeries St-Hubert COVERED ARCADE

(www.galeries-saint-hubert.com; off Rue du Marché aux Herbes; Ⓜ Gare Centrale) Europe's very first shopping arcade opened in 1847 with neoclassical glassed-in arches flanked by marble pilasters. Directly west are two enchantingly colourful lanes of close-packed fish restaurants (Rue/Petit Rue des Bouchers) but beware that (with some exceptions) many of those are notorious tourist traps.

Bourse STOCK EXCHANGE

(Place de la Bourse) You can't enter Belgium's 1873 stock exchange building, but its grandiose neoclassical facade is brilliantly festooned with friezes, reclining nudes, lunging horses and a multitude of allegorical figures. Some of the work was by Rodin when he was a young apprentice sculptor.

Manneken Pis MONUMENT

(Cnr Rue de l'Étuve & Rue du Chêne; Ⓜ Gare Centrale) This tiny fountain-statue of a little boy cheerfully taking a leak is a perversely perfect national symbol for surreal Belgium. More often than not the tiny statue's nakedness is largely hidden beneath a costume relevant to an anniversary, national day or local event: his ever-growing wardrobe is partly displayed at the **Maison du Roi** (Musée de la Ville de Bruxelles; Grand Place).

TOP CHOICE Musées Royaux des Beaux-Arts ART MUSEUM

(☎02-508 32 11; www.fine-arts-museum.be; Rue de la Régence 3; adult/student/BrusselsCard €8/5/free, €13 combined with Musée Magritte; ⏲10am-5pm Tue-Sun; Ⓜ Gare Centrale, Parc) Belgium's national gallery has a superb collection ranging from 15th-century Flemish Primitives via the fleshy religious works of Rubens to a top quality selection of 20th-century works. Highlights include Rogier Van der Weyden's *Pietà* with its hallucinatory dawn sky, Hans Memling's refined portraits and the world-famous *Fall of Icarus*, long attributed to Bruegel, though possibly a copy.

TOP CHOICE Musée Magritte ART MUSEUM

(www.musee-magritte-museum.be; Place Royale; adult/under 26yr/BrusselsCard €8/2/free; ⏲10am-5pm Tue-Sun; Ⓜ Gare Centrale, Parc) Opened in 2009, this beautifully presented museum traces the stylistic development of Belgium's foremost surrealist artist René Magritte, from colourful Braque-style cubism in 1920 through a Dalí-esque phase and a late-1940s period of Kandinsky-like brushwork. Regular screenings of a 52-minute documentary provide insights into Magritte's unconventionally conventional life. Discounted entrance fees apply if you also visit the Musées Royaux des Beaux-Arts next door.

MIM MUSEUM

(Musée des Instruments de Musique; ☎02-545 01 30; www.mim.fgov.be; Rue Montagne de la Cour 2; adult/concession €5/4; ⏲9.30am-5pm Tue-Fri, 10am-5pm Sat & Sun; Ⓜ Gare Centrale, Parc) An incredible collection of musical

Belgium & Luxembourg Highlights

1 Come on weekdays off-season to appreciate the picture-perfect canal scenes of medieval **Bruges** (p128), without the tourist overload

2 Be wooed by underappreciated **Ghent** (p123), one of Europe's greatest all-round discoveries

3 Savour the 'world's most beautiful square', then seek out the remarkable cafes, chocolate shops and art nouveau facades in **Brussels** (p101)

4 Follow fashion to hip yet historic **Antwerp** (p115)

5 Spend the weekend in Unesco-listed **Luxembourg City** (p140) then head out to the grand duchy's evocative castle villages

6 Drive Flanders' back lanes to St-Sixtus Abbey in **Westvleteren** (p137) in search of Westvleteren 12, the holy grail of beer lovers

7 Ponder the heartbreaking futility of WWI in Flanders' fields around meticulously rebuilt **Ypres** (p135)

8 Explore the caves and castles of rural Wallonia around **Rochefort** (p138)

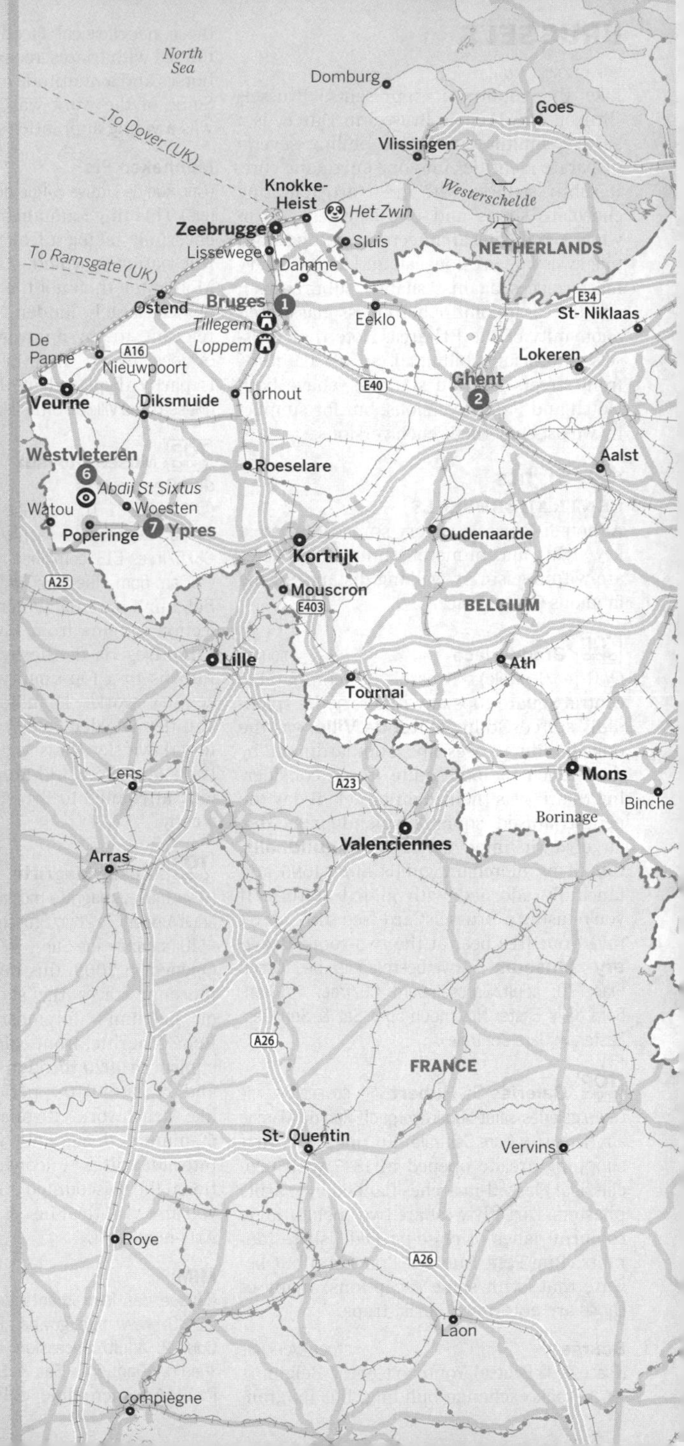

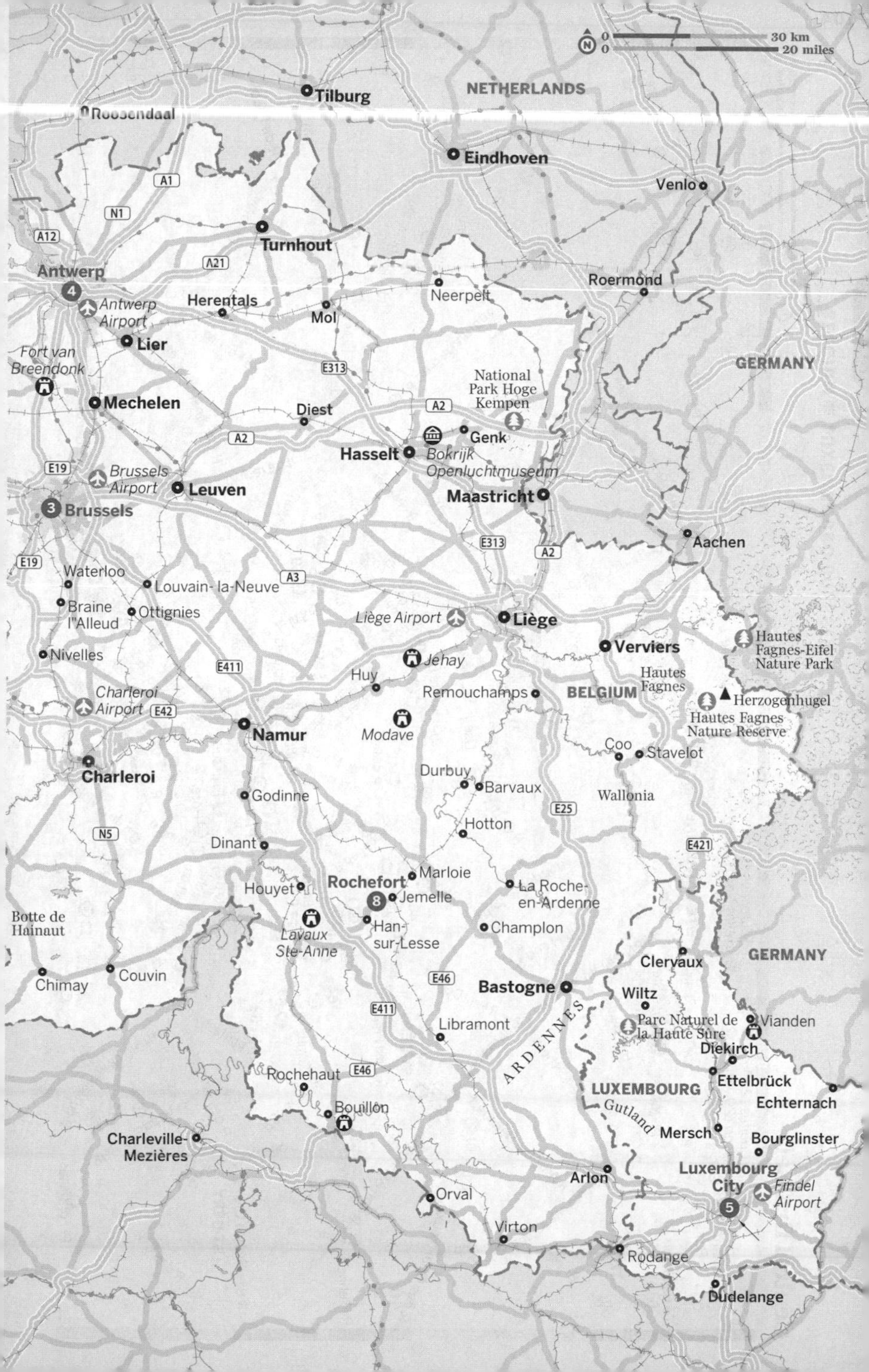

0 30 km
0 20 miles
NETHERLANDS
Tilburg
Roosendaal
Eindhoven
Venlo
A1
N1
A12
Turnhout
A21
Antwerp
4
Antwerp Airport
Herentals
Mol
Neerpelt
Roermond
Lier
Fort van Breendonk
GERMANY
E313
National Park Hoge Kempen
Mechelen
Diest
A2
Genk
Hasselt
Bokrijk Openluchtmuseum
E19
Brussels Airport
Leuven
Maastricht
3
Brussels
E313
A2
Aachen
E19
Waterloo
Louvain-la-Neuve
A3
Braine l''Alleud
Ottignies
Liège Airport
Liège
Verviers
Hautes Fagnes-Eifel Nature Park
Nivelles
E411
Jehay
Huy
Hautes Fagnes
Remouchamps
BELGIUM
Herzogenhugel
Charleroi Airport
E42
Hautes Fagnes Nature Reserve
Namur
Modave
Coo
Stavelot
Charleroi
Durbuy
Barvaux
Godinne
Wallonia
E25
Hotton
N5
Dinant
E421
Marloie
Rochefort
Houyet
8
Jemelle
La Roche-en-Ardenne
Botte de Hainaut
Lavaux Ste-Anne
Han-sur-Lesse
Champlon
GERMANY
Clervaux
Chimay
Couvin
E46
Bastogne
Wiltz
E411
Parc Naturel de la Haute Sûre
Vianden
Libramont
ARDENNES
Diekirch
Rochehaut
E46
Ettelbrück
LUXEMBOURG
Echternach
Bouillon
Gutland
Mersch
Charleville-Mezières
Bourglinster
Luxembourg City
Arlon
Findel Airport
Orval
5
Virton
Rodange
Dudelange

Central Brussels

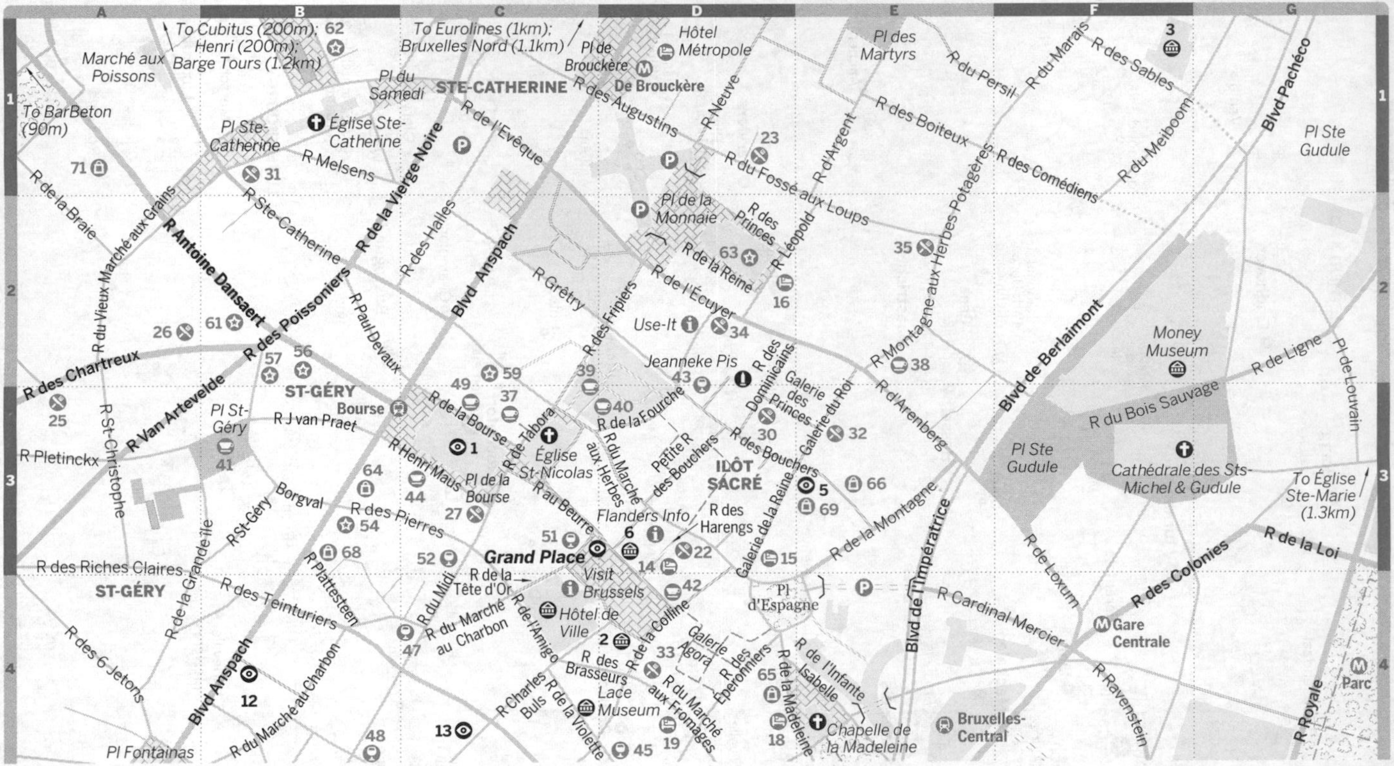

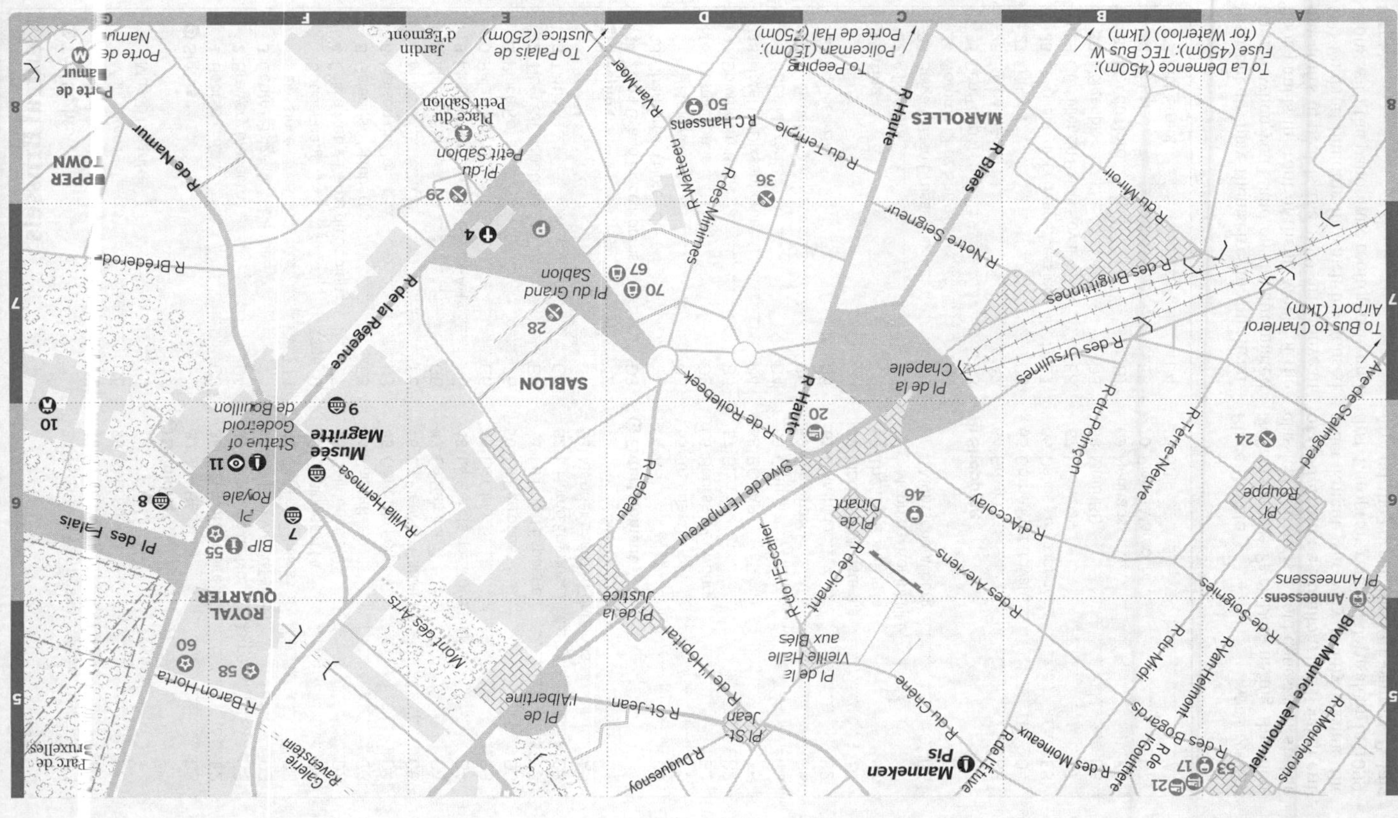
Parc de Bruxelles
Galerie Ravenstein
R Baron Horta
ROYAL QUARTER
Pl des Palais
BIP
Pl Royale
Statue of Godefroid de Bouillon
Musée Magritte
R Villa Hermosa
Mont des Arts
Pl de l'Albertine
R St-Jean
R Duquesnoy
Pl St-Jean
R de l'Hôpital
Pl de la Justice
R Lebeau
R de la Régence
R Bréderode
UPPER TOWN
R de Namur
Porte de Namur
Jardin d'Egmont
Place du Petit Sablon
Pl du Petit Sablon
SABLON
Pl du Grand Sablon
R de Rollebeek
R Watteeu
R Van Moer
R des Minimes
R C Hanssens
To Palais de Justice (250m)
To Peeping Policeman (150m); Porte de Hal (750m)
R du Temple
R Haute
MAROLLES
R Blaes
R Notre Seigneur
Pl de la Chapelle
Blvd de l'Empereur
R de l'Escalier
R de Dinant
Pl de Dinant
Pl de la Vieille Halle aux Blés
Manneken Pis
R du Chêne
R de l'Etuve
R des Moineaux
R des Alexiens
R d'Accolay
R du Poinçon
R des Ursulines
R des Brigittines
R du Miroir
R Terre-Neuve
To La Démence (450m); Fuse (450m); TEC Bus W (for Waterloo) (1km)
To Bus to Charleroi Airport (1km)
Ave de Stalingrad
Pl Rouppe
R de l'Gouttière
R des Bogards
R du Midi
R Van Helmont
R de Soignies
Blvd Maurice Lemonnier
R d Moucherons
Anneessens
Pl Anneessens

Central Brussels

Top Sights

Grand Place C3
Manneken Pis C5
Musée Magritte F6

Sights

1 Bourse C3
2 Brewery Museum D4
3 Centre Belge de la Bande Dessinée F1
Coudenberg .... (see 8)
4 Église Notre-Dame du Sablon E7
5 Galeries St-Hubert E3
6 Maison du Roi D3
7 MIM F6
8 Musée BELvue G6
9 Musées Royaux des Beaux-Arts F6
10 Palais Royal G6
11 Place Royale F6
12 Tibet & Duchâteau B4
13 Tintin C4

Sleeping

14 2Go4 Grand Place Rooms D3
15 Chambres d'Hôtes du Vaudeville D3
16 Dominican D2
17 Downtown-BXL B5
18 Hôtel Le Dixseptième D4
19 Hotel Mozart D4
20 JH Bruegel C6
21 La Casa-BXL B5

Eating

22 A l'Ombra D3
23 Belga Queen Brussels D1
24 Comme Chez Soi A6
25 Den Teepot A3
26 Fin de Siècle A2
27 Fritland C3
28 Le Village de la Bande Dessinée E7
29 L'Ecailler du Palais Royal E8
30 L'Ogenblik D3
31 Mer du Nord B1
32 Mokafé E3
33 Pita Street D4
34 Ricotta & Parmesan D2
35 Sea Grill E2
36 Soul Food D8

Drinking

37 À la Bécasse C3
38 À la Mort Subite E2
39 A l'Image de Nostre-Dame C3
40 Au Bon Vieux Temps D3
41 Café des Halles B3
42 Chaloupe d'Or D4
43 Délirium Café D2
44 Falstaff C3
45 Goupil le Fol D4
46 La Fleur en Papier Doré C6
47 Le Belgica C4
48 Le Cercle des Voyageurs B4
49 Le Cirio C3
50 Le Perroquet D8
51 Le Roy d'Espagne C3
52 L'Homo Erectus C3
53 Moeder Lambic Fontainas A5

Entertainment

54 AB B3
55 Arsène50 .... F6
56 Beursschouwburg B2
57 Bizon B2
58 BOZAR F5
59 Celtica C2
60 Cinematek G5
61 L'Archiduc B2
62 Madame Moustache B1
63 Théâtre Royal de la Monnaie/Koninklijke Muntschouwburg D2

Shopping

64 Brüsel B3
65 Corné Port Royal D4
66 Délices et Caprices E3
67 Leonidas D7
68 Multi-BD B3
69 Neuhaus E3
70 Pierre Marcolini D7
71 Stijl A1

instruments 'play' themselves in your headphones when you stand on the automated floor panels in front of them. Much of the museum's appeal is the 1899 art nouveau Old England building in which it's housed ,along with the panoramic rooftop cafe and terrace.

Place Royale NEIGHBOURHOOD

(MGare Centrale, Parc) Dominating this neoclassical square is a bold equestrian **statue of Godefroid de Bouillon**, the Belgian crusader knight who very briefly became the first European ruler of Jerusalem in 1099. Around the corner, the 19th-century **Palais**

Royal (☎02-551 20 20; www.monarchy.be; Place des Palais; admission free; ⊙10.30am-4.30pm Tue-Sun late Jul-early Sep) is Belgium's slightly less-inspired cousin to Buckingham Palace. It's the Belgian king's office, but the royals no longer live here.

If you've bought a BrusselsCard, peep into **Musée BELvue** (☎07-022 04 92; www.belvue.be; Place des Palais 7; adult/concession €5/4; ⊙10am-5pm Tue-Fri, to 6pm Sat & Sun), which introduces Belgian history through a fascinating overload of documents, images and videos. Then descend into the attached **Coudenberg** (www.coudenberg.com; adult/under 26yr/BrusselsCard €5/3/free, with Musée BELvue €8/4/free), the subterranean archaeological site of Charles Quint's 16th-century palace complex. You'll emerge eventually near MIM.

MARROLES & SABLON

Dominated by the flamboyantly Gothic church, **Église Notre-Dame du Sablon** (www.ebru.be/Other/Kerken/krkzavel.html; Rue de la Régence; ⊙9am-6pm Mon-Fri, 10am-6pm Sat & Sun; Ⓜ Porte de Namur), the cobbled **Grand Place du Sablon** is lined with upmarket cafes and chocolate boutiques, with antique shops filling nearby streets. Pretty **Place du Petit Sablon** features a garden of 48 bronze statuettes representing the medieval guilds.

Palais de Justice LAW COURTS

(Ⓜ Louise, 🚌92, 94) When constructed in 1883, this gigantic domed law court was Europe's biggest building. Outside there's a panoramic viewpoint looking across rooftops towards the distant Atomium (p108) and **Koekelberg Basilica**, one of the world's biggest churches. A glass **elevator** (admission free, ⊙7.30am-11.45pm) leads down into the quirky, downmarket but slowly gentrifying **Marolles quarter**.

IXELLES

Southwest of the pentagonal Inner Ring highway, this sizeable inner suburb sports numerous elegant, century-old houses, upmarket boutiques on Ave Louise but also the contrastingly multicultural, downmarket Matonge district.

TOP CHOICE **Musée Horta** MUSEUM

(☎02-543 04 90; www.hortamuseum.be; Rue Américaine 25; adult/child €7/3.50; ⊙2-5.30pm Tue-Sun; Ⓜ Horta, 🚌91, 92) Behind a typically austere exterior, the former home (built 1898–1901) of superstar architect Victor Horta has an outstanding art nouveau interior.

> **BRUSSELS DISCOUNTS & FREEBIES**
>
> The **BrusselsCard** (www.brusselscard.be; 24/48/72hr €24/34/40) allows free visits to over 30 Brussels-area museums, various other discounts, plus unlimited free use of city public transport. You'll need to be a seriously hyperactive museum fan to save much money, but it's fun trying. Remember that most museums close Mondays. On the first Wednesday afternoon of each month many museums are free.

Floor mosaics, glittering stained glass and ceramic brick walls are all memorable but the structural triumph is the stairway, which becomes more exuberant as you ascend.

Matonge NEIGHBOURHOOD

Nicknamed for a square in Kinshasa, Congo, **Matonge** is home to much of Brussels' African community. The architecture includes its fair share of tired old 1960s concrete but **Chaussée de Wavre** and the dreary **Galerie d'Ixelles** come to life with African hairstylists, grocers, music outlets and inexpensive eateries to sample African foods.

PARC DU CINQUANTENAIRE

Hop off metro line 1 or 5 at Mérode to see Leopold II's triumphal arch and associated grand museums.

Cinquantenaire ARCHITECTURE

(Ⓜ Mérode) Designed to celebrate Belgium's 50th anniversary in 1880, Brussels' version of the Arc de Triomphe was only finally completed in 1905, 25 years late. To climb it use stairs within the impressive **military museum** (Royal Museum of the Armed Forces and of Military History; ☎02-737 78 11; www.klm-mra.be; Parc du Cinquantenaire 3; admission/audioguide free/€3; ⊙9am-noon & 1-4.45pm Tue-Sun; Ⓜ Mérode) next door.

TOP CHOICE **Musées Royaux d'Art et d'Histoire** MUSEUM

(☎02-741 72 11; www.kmkg-mrah.be; Parc du Cinquantenaire 10; adult/child/BrusselsCard €5/free/free; ⊙9.30am-5pm Tue-Fri, 10am-5pm Sat & Sun; Ⓜ Mérode) Belgium's most underestimated museum has an astonishingly rich collection ranging from ancient Egyptian sarcophagi to Meso-American masks, icons to wooden bicycles. You'd need days to appreciate it all.

COMIC-STRIP CULTURE

In Belgium, comic strips (*bande dessinée*) are revered as the 'ninth art'. Over 40 cartoon murals enliven Brussels buildings, most mapped on www.brusselscomics.com/en/route_bd.cfm with a more detailed free brochure available from tourist offices. Strolling past a few of these makes a great excuse to explore less-visited neighbourhoods. Some favourites include the following:

Tibet & Duchâteau (Rue du Bon Secours 9)

Josephine Baker (Rue des Capucins 9)

Tintin (Rue de l'Étuve)

Peeping Policeman (Rue Haute)

Cubitus (Rue de Flandre)

Each September Brussels hosts a major **Comic-Strip Festival** (www.fetedelabd.be) at the splendid St-Gilles town hall. Serious comic fans might also enjoy Brussels' comprehensive **Centre Belge de la Bande Dessinée** (☎02-219 19 80; www.comicscenter.net; Rue des Sables 20; adult/concession €8/6; ⌚10am-6pm Tue-Sun; Ⓜ Rogier) in a distinctive Horta-designed art nouveau building, though relatively little is in English. Comic shops include **Brüsel** (www.brusel.com; Blvd Anspach 100; ⌚10.30am-6.30pm Mon-Sat, noon-6.30pm Sun) and **Multi-BD** (www.multibd.com; Blvd Anspach 122-124; ⌚10.30am-7pm Mon-Sat, 12.30-6.30pm Sun). There's even a cartoon-based cafe-restaurant, **Le Village de la Bande Dessinée** (☎02-523 13 23; comicscafe.be; Place du Grand Sablon 8; snacks from €6), complete with Tintin statue and original Hergé sketches.

The English-language audioguide (€3 extra) is worth considering.

Autoworld MUSEUM
(www.autoworld.be; adult/BrusselsCard €9/free; ⌚10am-6pm Apr-Sep, to 5pm Oct-Mar; Ⓜ Mérode) One of Europe's biggest ensembles of vintage and 20th-century cars.

ANDERLECHT

Internationally best known for its **football team** (www.rsca.be/go/en; Ave Théo Verbeeck 2, Van den Stock Stadium; Ⓜ St-Guidon), this sprawling western suburb now has a grimy, rundown reputation. But back in 1521 it was still a country village when the world-famous humanist Erasmus came to 'play at farming'.

Erasmus House MUSEUM
(www.erasmushouse.museum; Rue du Chapitre 31; admission €1.50; ⌚10am-6pm Tue-Sun, begijnhof closed noon-2pm; Ⓜ St-Guidon) This unexpected little gem is furnished with fine artworks and priceless manuscripts. The very modest entry fee also allows access to Belgium's smallest *begijnhof*, now an appealing something-of-everything museum housed in two historic buildings.

Cantillon Brewery BREWERY
(Musée Bruxellois de la Gueuze; ☎02-521 49 28; www.cantillon.be; Rue Gheude 56; admission €6; ⌚9am-5pm Mon-Fri, 10am-5pm Sat; Ⓜ Clemenceau) Self-guided tours of this atmospheric, family-run brewery introduce the odd concept of lambic beers, show off the ageing barrel rooms and a vast, shallow copper tub in which the miraculous spontaneous fermentation occurs. Expect plenty of cobwebs as spiders are considered friends of the winter fermentation process. The entry fee includes two taster-glasses of Cantillon's startlingly acidic brews.

HEYSEL

A 15-minute metro ride to Brussels' northern edge brings you to an area of trade fairs, the national stadium and curious **Mini Europe** (www.minieurope.com; adult/child €14/10.50, with Atomium €23.25/15.25; ⌚10am-5pm Apr-Jun & Sep-Dec, 9.30am-8pm Jul-Aug; Ⓜ Heysel), featuring walk-through recreations of the continent's top tourist sights at 1:25 scale.

TOP CHOICE **Atomium** MONUMENT, MUSEUM
(www.atomium.be; Sq de l'Atomium; adult/Brussels Card €11/9; ⌚10am-7pm May-Sep, to 6pm Oct-Apr; Ⓟ; Ⓜ Heysel, 🚊51) This space-age leftover from the 1958 World Fair consists of nine house-sized metallic balls linked by steel tube-columns containing escalators and lifts. Like an alien schoolchild's chemistry

set, it represents an iron crystal lattice enlarged 165 billion times. It's an unforgettable sight and the top sphere offers wide views but inside exhibits aren't enormously compelling.

Tours

On the last Saturday of most months, **ARAU** (☎02-219 33 45; www.arau.org; Blvd Adolphe Max 55; ⏲Apr–mid-Dec) tours visit some of Brussels' otherwise private art nouveau showpieces.

Sleeping

With much of Brussels' accommodation scene aimed squarely at Eurocrats and business travellers, many business hotels drop their rates dramatically at weekends and in summer. Double rooms with September midweek rates of €240 might cost as little as €69 in August – so why use a hostel? Shop around and check carefully for internet deals, especially on chain hotels.

Beware that several otherwise decent hotels around Rogier and Bruxelles-Nord lie uncomfortably close to a seedy red-light district. The nicer Ste-Catherine area is central but calm, while St-Gilles offers a more 'local' experience.

Brussels has a reasonable network of B&Bs, many bookable through Bed & Brussels (www.bnb-brussels.be) and Airbnb (www.airbnb.com).

TOP CHOICE Maison Noble B&B €€
(☎02-219 23 39; www.maison-noble.eu; Rue du Marcq 10; from €129; ❄@📶) This splendidly refined four-room guesthouse includes a neo-Renaissance piano room where, once in a while, recitals feature up-and-coming concert pianists. Hotel-standard rooms have rainforest showers, fine linens, and framed Breugel prints over the beds. The target market is married gay couples but it's very much hetero-friendly.

Hôtel Le Dixseptième BOUTIQUE HOTEL €€€
(☎02-502 57 44; www.ledixseptieme.be; Rue de la Madeleine 25; s/d/ste from €180/200/270, weekend from €100/100/200; ❄📶) A hushed magnificence greets you in this alluring boutique hotel, partly occupying the former 17th-century residence of the Spanish ambassador. Spacious executive suites come with four-poster beds; some of the less expensive rooms are a big step down in opulence.

Chambres d'Hôtes du Vaudeville B&B €€
(☎0471 47 38 37; www.chambresdhotesduvaudeville.be; Galerie de la Reine 11; d from €115; 📶) This classy B&B has an incredible location right within the gorgeous (if reverberant) Galeries St-Hubert. Delectable decor styles include African, modernist and 'Madame Loulou' (with 1920s nude sketches). Larger front rooms have claw-foot bathtubs and *galerie* views, but can be noisy with clatter that continues all night. Get keys via the art deco–influenced Café du Vaudeville, where breakfast is included.

Dominican BUSINESS HOTEL €€€
(☎02-203 08 08; www.thedominican.be; Rue Léopold 9; r weekday/weekend from €180/115; ❄@📶) Combining classic elegance with understated modern chic, this excellent top-range palace occupies the site of a former abbey right behind La Monnaie. It's hard to beat for style and the location is wonderfully central, albeit in an area suffering from rather patchy architecture and atmosphere.

Pantone HOTEL €€
(☎02-541 48 98; pantonehotel.com; Place Loix 1; r €99-129) Modern, stylishly functional and surprisingly affordable the Pantone greets you with an eye-popping array of colours, from the turquoise pushbike at reception to the moulded plastic chairs to the lime green bedrooms – all with refreshing swathes of white too.

Downtown-BXL B&B €€
(☎0475 29 07 21; www.downtownbxl.com; Rue du Marché au Charbon 118-120; r €77-109; 📶) Near the capital's gay district, this B&B is superbly located for those wanting to dance the night away. From the communal breakfast table and help-yourself coffee bar, a classic staircase winds up to good-value rooms featuring zebra striped cushions and Warhol Marilyn prints. Adjacent **Casa-BXL** (☎0475 29 07 21; http://www.lacasabxl.com/; Rue du Marché au Charbon 16; €89 per room) offers three rooms in a Moroccan-Asian style.

Hôtel Noga FAMILY HOTEL €€
(☎02-218 67 63; www.nogahotel.com; Rue du Béguinage 38; weekday/weekend from s €95/70, d €110/85; ❄@📶) This very welcoming family hotel established in 1958 uses model yachts to give the lobby and piano room a certain nautical feel. Sepia photos of Belgian royalty, along with historic bellows, top hats and assorted random kitsch, lead up to variously

decorated rooms that are neat and clean without particular luxury. Wi-fi is free for the first hour.

Hotel Mozart HOTEL €€
(☎02-502 66 61; www.hotel-mozart.be; Rue du Marché aux Fromages 23; s/d €80/100;) Mozart? Think Sultanahmet rather than Salzburg when imagining the sensory overload of this place – lashings of Turkish mosaic-work plus wall fountains, gilt rococo-styled chairs and an incredible crush of imitation antiques, paintings and 'art nouveau' lamps. Garish, fun and very central, but mattresses are saggy, bathrooms have their defects and you'll need good earplugs in the front rooms, which overlook never-sleeping 'Pita' street.

Hostel Jacques Brel HOSTEL €
(☎02-218 01 87; www.laj.be; Rue de la Sablonnière 30; HI members dm/s/tw €23/36/53.75; @) Neat, presentable and reasonably spacious hostel in a pleasant, nearly central area. The bar has occasional live music (sometimes guests play for their bed!), there's a 2nd-floor terrace, free wi-fi, laundry for €4, no lockout and a partly *'bio'* (organic) breakfast is included.

JH Bruegel HI HOSTEL €
(☎02-511 04 36; www.jeugdherbergen.be; Rue du St-Esprit 2; HI members dm/s/d €21.50/35.50/51.50; @) Brussels' most central hostel has a cellar bar, several sitting areas and decent, gender-segregated dorms with showers (toilets shared). The 10am to 2pm lockout is infuriating; read the regulations carefully and ask for a night key (deposit €20) if staying out beyond 1am.

Centre Vincent van Gogh HOSTEL €
(☎02-217 01 58; www.chab.be; Rue Traversière 8; dm €19.50-23, s/d €35/54; @) The lobby bar and pool-table verandah are unusually hip for a hostel, but rooms are less glamorous and, from some, reaching the toilets means crossing the garden courtyard. No membership required but you have to be under 35 unless in a group.

2GO4 HOSTEL €
(☎02-219 30 19; www.2go4.be; Blvd Émile Jacqmain 99; dm €24-27, s/d €50/65; reception 7am-1pm & 4-11pm;) A well-equipped if somewhat claustrophobic hostel in a slightly sleazy part of town. Check in here even if you are booked into its other accommodation, the fabulously central **Grand Place Rooms** (Rue des Harengs; d €59-70, tr €90-105), which features low ceilings and hefty beams. There's an age limit of 45 for dorm rooms.

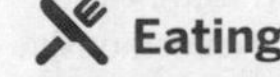

Eating

CENTRAL BRUSSELS

Several interesting options are dotted along Rue de Flandre, with reliable seafood restaurants around nearby Place Ste-Catherine and Marché aux Poissons. Inexpensive, if rarely authentic, Asian restaurants line Rue J van Praet between the Bourse and Place St-Géry. Restaurants reviewed here focus on value for money, but with formal attire, advance bookings and a plutonium credit card, central gourmet options include **Comme Chez Soi** (www.commechezsoi.be; Place Rouppe 23), **Sea Grill** (☎02-212 08 00; www.seagrill.be; Radisson SAS Royal Hotel Brussels, Rue du Fossé aux Loups 47; noon-2pm & 7-10pm, closed mid-July–mid-Aug; MDe Brouckère) and **L'Ecailler du Palais Royal** (www.lecaillerdupalaisroyal.be). Beware of unscrupulous 'deals' at the very attractive tourist-trap seafood restaurants of Rue/Petite Rue des Bouchers.

TOP CHOICE **L'Ogenblik** FRENCH €€€
(☎02-511 61 51; www.ogenblik.be; Galerie des Princes 1; mains €23-28, lunch €11; noon-2.30pm & 7pm-midnight) This archetypal bistro-restaurant is more convivially casual than most top-notch Brussels restaurants, with its lace curtains, resident cat and marble-topped tables. But the classic French dishes and fish specialities show a deft culinary expertise, and the saucy humour of the waiters adds to the fun of a special dining experience.

Henri FUSION €€
(☎02-218 00 08; www.restohenri.be; Rue de Flandre 113; mains €15-20; noon-2pm Tue-Fri & 6pm-10pm Tue-Sat; MSte-Catherine) On an inspiring street that's always worth checking for quirky new dining and drinking options, Henri concocts tangy fusion dishes. Astute wine list, well-briefed staff.

TOP CHOICE **Fin de Siècle** BELGIAN €
(Rue des Chartreux 9; mains €11.25-20; bar 4.30pm-1am, kitchen 6pm-12.30am) From *carbonade* (beer-based hot-pot) and chicken in cherry beer, to mezzes and tandoori dishes, the food selection is as eclectic as the decor in this low-lit cult place. Tables are rough, music constant, ceilings purple and prices still converted to the nearest centime from Belgian francs. To quote the barman 'there's no phone, no bookings, no sign on the door...

we do everything to put people off but they still keep coming'. Queues are common.

Belga Queen Brussels BELGIAN €€
(☎02-217 21 87; www.belgaqueen.be; Rue du Fossé aux Loups 32; mains €16-25, weekday lunch €16; ⏲noon-2.30pm & 7pm-midnight) Belgian cuisine is given a chic, modern twist within a magnificent if reverberant 19th-century bank building. Classical stained-glass ceilings and marble columns are hidden behind an indecently hip oyster counter and bar (open noon till late) offering wide-ranging beers and cocktails. In the former bank vaults beneath there's a cigar lounge that morphs into a nightclub after 10pm Wednesday to Saturday.

A l'Ombra ITALIAN €
(Rue des Harengs 2; pastas €8.50-13, mains €10.50-16; ⏲noon-2.30pm & 6.30pm-11.30pm Mon-Sat) Take a tiny, tile-walled 1920s shophouse. Keep the classic decor, wooden shelf-holders and cashier booth. Insert stools and a narrow communal table. Serve great fresh pasta and see if the customers finally communicate. Perhaps… at least with the farewell grappa.

Ricotta & Parmesan ITALIAN €
(www.ricottaparmesan.com; Rue de l'Écuyer 31; mains €9-15; ⏲noon-2.30pm & 6.30pm-11pm Mon-Sat) Excellent-value Italian food enjoyed in a pair of antique buildings that are decorated with olive-oil bottles and antique cooking implements, some fancifully framed.

Mer du Nord SEAFOOD €
(www.vishandelnoordzee.be; Rue Ste-Catherine 1; ⏲8am-6pm Tue-Sun; Ⓜ Ste-Catherine) Well-reputed fishmonger's window catering to a queue of stand-and-snack lunch-grabbers around bare metal outdoor tables.

Den Teepot VEGAN €
(Rue des Chartreux 66; ⏲noon-2pm Mon-Sat; 🖉) Macrobiotic, vegie lunch place located above a mustard-yellow organic grocery shop. Bright decor with murals adorning the walls.

Pita Street KEBABS €
(Rue du Marché aux Fromages; ⏲11am-3am) Falafels and döner kebab snacks from €3 in a bustling pedestrian street just behind the Grand Place.

Mokafé WAFFLES €
(☎02-511 78 70; Galerie du Roi; waffles from €3; ⏲7.30am-11.30pm; Ⓜ De Brouckère) Locals get their waffles in this old-fashioned cafe under the glass arch of the Galeries-St Hubert. It's a little timeworn inside but wicker chairs in the beautiful arcade provide you with a *m'as-tu-vu* view of passing shoppers.

Fritland CHIPS €
(Rue Henri Maus 49; ⏲11am-1am Sun-Thu, 10am-3am Fri & Sat) Sit-down or takeaway *frites* (fries).

MARROLES & SABLON

The Sablon has many interesting, relatively upmarket eateries. Dotted along Rue Haute are several more idiosyncratic choices.

TOP CHOICE **Le Perroquet** BAR €
(Rue Watteeu 31; light meals €6.50-11; ⏲noon-1am; Ⓜ Porte de Namur) One of Brussels' most perfecty preserved art nouveau cafes, the Perroquet retains its stained glass, marble tables and timber panelling yet is comparatively inexpensive for a drink or an imaginatively filled pitta snack.

Restobières BELGIAN €€
(☎02-502 72 51; www.restobieres.eu; Rue des Renards 9; mains €12-22, menus €18-38; ⏲noon-3pm daily, 6.30pm-11pm Wed-Sun) Beer-based twists on typical Belgian meals served in a delightful if slightly cramped restaurant. The walls are plastered with bottles, grinders and countless antique souvenir biscuit tins featuring Belgian royalty

Soul Food ORGANIC €€
(☎02-513 52 13; www.soulresto.com; Rue de la Samaritaine 20; mains €15-22; ⏲7-10pm Wed-Sun; 🖉; Ⓜ Louise) Informal fusion food restaurant where organic, additive-free meals steer clear of butter and cream in favour of interesting oils, grains and seeds.

Het Warmwater CAFE €
(www.hetwarmwater.be; Rue des Renards 25; 🖉; Ⓜ Porte de Hal) Simple, satisfying food in an endearing little daytime cafe with stencilled teapots and art collages on the walls.

IXELLES

Many ever-buzzing options line Rue St-Boniface while numerous inexpensive world cuisines can be found in the neighbouring streets of Matonge. There are many fashion-conscious restaurants further south around Flagey and Place du Châtelain.

L'Horloge du Sud AFRICAN €
(www.horlogedusud.be; Rue du Trône 141; mains from €12; Ⓜ Porte de Namur) This Senegalese-owned

BOURSE AREA CAFES

Many of Brussels' most iconic cafes are within stumbling distance of the Bourse. Don't miss century-old **Falstaff** (www.lefalstaff.be/; Rue Henri Maus 17; ⌚10am-1am; 🚊Bourse) with its festival of stained glass ceilings, or **Le Cirio** (Rue de la Bourse 18; ⌚10am-midnight), a sumptuous yet affordable 1866 marvel full of polished brasswork serving great-value pub meals. Three more classics are hidden up shoulder-wide alleys: the medieval yet unpretentious **A l'Image de Nostre-Dame** (off Rue du Marché aux Herbes 5; ⌚noon-midnight Mon-Fri, 3pm-1am Sat, 4-10.30pm Sun); the 1695 Rubenseque **Au Bon Vieux Temps** (Impasse Saint Michel; ⌚11am-midnight), which sometimes stocks ultrarare Westvleteren beers (€10!); and lambic specialist **À la Bécasse** (www.alabecasse.com; Rue de Tabora 11; ⌚11am-midnight, to 1am Fri & Sat ; Ⓜ Gare Centrale), with its vaguely puritanical rows of wooden tables.

If those classics seem a little staid for your taste, head a block west of the Bourse to Place Saint-Géry where a whole series of characterful but youthfully fashion-conscious cafes surround the **Café des Halles** (www.cafedeshalles.be), an 1881 market hall that's now part bar, part exhibition hall and hosts a free weekend nightclub in its cellars. There are many great options for sipping a quiet coffee by day or being buffeted by music at night.

Matonge institution is easily distinguished by the large clock out front and is a fine place to sample many types of African food.

L'Ultime Atome BELGIAN €€
(☎02-513 13 67; Rue St-Boniface 14; mains €11-17; ⌚8.30am-1am Mon-Fri, 10am-1am Sat & Sun; Ⓜ Porte de Namur) This cavernous brasserie has curious train-wheel decor enlivening the pale wooden panelling of an otherwise classic cafe. A youthful crowd keeps things buzzing day and night and the nonstop kitchen turns out great-value meals including cheesy endives, tajines and mussels.

Imagin'Air ORGANIC €
(☎02-511 33 31; Place Fernand Cocq 6; mains €9-17; ⌚10am-10pm Mon-Sat, to 6pm Sun, closed Wed in winter; ✎) Adorable, organic-food 'Art Café' with exposed brick walls and one of Brussels' prettiest patio terraces decked with plants and bonsai-sized trees. Short, handwritten menus change frequently.

Drinking

Cafe culture is one of Brussels' greatest attractions. On the Grand Place itself, 300-year-old gems, like **Le Roy d'Espagne** (www.roydespagne.be/; Grand Place 1) and **Chaloupe d'Or** (Grand Place 24) are magnificent but predictably pricey. Somewhat cheaper classics lie around the Bourse, with livelier pubs located around Place St-Géry and further south around fashion-conscious Flagey.

TOP CHOICE **Moeder Lambic Fontainas** BEER HALL
(www.moederlambic.eu; Place Fontainas 8; ⌚11am-1am Mon-Thu & Sun, to 2am Fri & Sat; 🚊Annessens, Bourse) Dozens of artisanal draft beers served in a contemporary rather than old world setting with a mood that's upbeat and set to music.

Délirium Café PUB
(www.deliriumcafe.be; Impasse de la Fidélité 4A; ⌚10am-4am Mon-Sat, to 2am Sun) The main bar has barrel tables, beer-tray ceilings and over 2000 world beers and the tap house has 25 more on draft. There's also an associated rum garden and Floris Bar (from 8pm) serving hundreds of *jenevers* (Dutch gin), vodkas and absinthes. No wonder it's lively. Live music after 10pm.

À la Mort Subite CAFE
(☎02-513 13 18; www.alamortsubite.com; Rue Montagne aux Herbes Potagères 7; ⌚11am-1am Mon-Sat, noon-midnight Sun; Ⓜ Gare Centrale) An absolute classic – unchanged since 1928, with lined-up wooden tables, arched mirror-panels and entertainingly brusque service.

Le Cercle des Voyageurs BRASSERIE
(☎02-514 39 49; www.lecercledesvoyageurs.com; Rue des Grands Carmes 18, ⌚8am-11pm Wed-Mon; 📶; Ⓜ Annessens, Bourse) Invite Phileas Fogg for coffee to this delightful bistro featuring globes, an antique-map ceiling and a travel library. If he's late, flick through old National Geographics in your colonial leather chair. The global brasserie food is pretty good, and

there's free live music, piano jazz Tuesdays, and experimental music Thursdays.

Goupil le Fol BAR
(☎02-511 13 96; Rue de la Violette 22; ⏲9pm-5am; Ⓜ Gare Centrale) Enter an acid-trip sensory overload of rambling passageways, ragged old sofas and inexplicable beverages mostly based on madly fruit-flavoured wines. Unmissable.

La Fleur en Papier Doré BROWN CAFE
(www.goudblommekeinpapier.be; Rue des Alexiens 53; ⏲11am-midnight Tue-Sat, to 7pm Sun) Once popular with Magritte and his surrealist pals, this tiny cafe has its nicotine-stained walls covered with writings, art and scribbles, some reputedly traded for free drinks. '*Ceci n'est pas un musée*', quips a sign on the door, reminding visitors to buy a drink and not just look around.

BarBeton BAR
(www.barbeton.be; Rue Antoine Dansaert 114; ⏲8am-late; 📶; Ⓜ Ste-Catherine) Typical of the new array of hip but relaxed Brussels bars, BarBeton has a cocktail happy hour 7pm to 8pm Thursdays, *aperitivo* buffet 6pm to 8pm Fridays and DJs from 10pm Saturdays.

☆ Entertainment

AB LIVE MUSIC
(Ancienne Belgique; ☎02-548 24 00; www.abconcerts.be; Blvd Anspach 110; 🚋Bourse) The AB's two auditoriums are favourite venues for midlevel international rock bands and plenty of home-grown talent. The ticket office is located on Rue des Pierres.

Théâtre Royal de la Monnaie/ Koninklijke Muntschouwburg OPERA, DANCE
(☎02-229 13 72; www.lamonnaie.be; Place de la Monnaie; Ⓜ De Brouckère) Belgium was born when an opera at this grand venue inspired the 1830 revolution. It primarily mounts contemporary dance and operas new and old.

Beursschouwburg LIVE MUSIC
(☎02-513 82 90; www.beursschouwburg.be; Rue Auguste Orts 22; ⏲exhibition area 10am-6pm Mon-Sat, cafe 7.30pm-late Thu-Sun; 🚋Bourse) Diverse mix of contemporary music including rock, jazz, rap and disco. The cafe turns into a free nightclub late on weekend nights.

BOZAR LIVE MUSIC
(www.bozar.be; Palais des Beaux-Arts, Rue Ravenstein 23; Ⓜ Gare Centrale) Celebrated classical-music venue, home to the National Orchestra and Philharmonic Society. From outside, the Horta-designed 1928 art deco building lacks much charm but its Henri Le Bœuf Hall is considered to be one of the five best in the world for acoustic quality.

Cinematek CINEMA
(☎02-507 83 70; www.cinematheque.be; Rue Baron Horta 9; Ⓜ Gare Centrale) Includes a museum of cinema archives and memorabilia, screens arthouse movies and has a wonderful program of silent films screened with live piano accompaniment.

L'Archiduc JAZZ
(☎02-512 06 52; www.archiduc.net; Rue Antoine Dansaert 6; ⏲4pm-late) Intimate, split-level art deco jazz bar that can get incredibly packed but remains convivial. You might need to ring the doorbell. Saturday concerts are free (5pm), Sundays bring in international talent and admission charges vary.

Bizon BLUES
(☎02-502 46 99; www.cafebizon.com; Rue du Pont de la Carpe 7; admission free; ⏲6pm-late) Happening little grunge bar in St-Géry featuring home-grown live blues, a range of beers and a selection of *jenever*. Located on a street of lively cafe-bars.

Nightclubs

Fuse CLUB
(www.fuse.be; Rue Blaes 208; admission €5-12; ⏲11pm-7am Sat; Ⓜ Porte de Hal) The Marolles club that 'invented' European techno still crams up to 2000 people onto its two dance

GAY & LESBIAN BRUSSELS

Brussels' compact, thriving Rainbow Quarter is clustered around Rue du Marché au Charbon, where you'll find two LGBT information centres (www.rainbowhouse.be, www.telsquels.be) and a dozen gay-oriented bars including **L'Homo Erectus** (www.lhomoerectus.com; Rue des Pierres 57; ⏲4pm-dawn) and **Le Belgica** (www.lebelgica.be; Rue du Marché au Charbon 32; ⏲10pm-3am Thu-Sun). The **Belgian Gay & Lesbian Pride** (www.blgp.be; ⏲1st Sat in May) culminates in this area with a vast-scale all-night party. Once a month, **La Démence** (www.lademence.com) at Fuse is one of Europe's major raves for gay men.

floors. Once a month it also hosts epic gay night La Démence (p113).

Celtica BAR
(www.celticpubs.com/celtica; Rue de Marche aux Poulets 55; MBourse) Lairy, loud, central and cheap – just €1 for a beer in the early evening. Later there's boozy dancing with different musical styles on different floors.

Madame Moustache CLUB
(www.madamemoustache.be; Quai au Bois à Brûler 5-7; 9pm-4am Tues-Sun ; MSte-Catherine) Cute Ste-Catherine club with a retro, burlesque feel. It hosts funk all-nighters, swing nights and DJ sets.

Shopping

Tourist-oriented shops selling chocolate, beer, lace and Atomium baubles stretch between the Grand Place and Manneken Pis. For better **chocolate shops** in calmer, grander settings, peruse the resplendent **Galeries St-Hubert** or the upmarket Sablon area. In the Marolles, Rue Haute and Rue Blaes are full of quirky **interior design shops** while Place du Jeu-de-Balle has a daily **flea market** (6am-2pm). Rue Antoine Dansaert has most of Brussels' **high-fashion boutiques**, with **Stijl** (www.stijl.be; Rue Antoine Dansaert 74) hosting many cutting-edge collections.

Supermarkets sell a range of Belgian beers relatively cheaply. For wider selections and the relevant glasses, try **Beermania** (www.beermania.be; Chaussée de Wavre 174; 11am-9pm Mon-Sat) or the very personal little **Délices et Caprices** (www.the-belgian-beer-tasting-shop.be; Rue des Bouchers 68; 2-8pm Thu-Mon).

Information

Money

ATMs are widespread. Exchange agency rates are usually best around the Bourse.

Tourist Information

In addition to places listed here there are also information counters at Brussels Airport and Bruxelles-Midi station.

Visit Brussels (02-513 89 40; visitbrussels.be; Hôtel de Ville; 9am-6pm; MBourse) Stacks of city-specific information. A second branch (02-548 04 58; www.biponline.be; Rue Royale 2-4; 10am-6pm) at 2 Rue Royale is much less crowded and its Arsène50 (02-512 57 45; www.arsene50.be; Rue Royale 2; 12.30-5.30pm Tue-Sat) ticketing desk provides discounts for cultural events.

Flanders Info (02-504 03 90; www.visitflanders.com; Rue du Marché aux Herbes 61; 9am-6pm Mon-Sat, 10am-5pm Sun;) For Flanders information, obviously. Free wi-fi.

Use-It (02-218 39 06; www.use-it.be; Quai à la Houille 9B; 10am-1pm & 2-6pm Mon-Sat; ; MSte-Catherine) Meeting place for young travellers with free coffee and tea, sofas, internet, info map-guides and an invaluable list of live-music events. At 2pm on Mondays a free city tour emphasises social history and nightlife over conventional sights.

Getting There & Away

BUS International bus service **Eurolines** (02-274 13 50; www.eurolines.be; Rue du Progrès 80; 5.45am-8.45pm; Gare du Nord) has buses departing from Bruxelles-Nord train station.

TRAIN Eurostar, TGV and Thalys high-speed trains stop only at Bruxelles-Midi (Brussel-Zuid). Jump on any local service for the four-minute hop to conveniently central Bruxelles-Central. All domestic trains, plus some Amsterdam services, stop there. Consult www.belgianrail.be for timetable information.

Getting Around

To/From the Airports

BRUSSELS AIRPORT

TAXI Fares start around €35. Very bad idea in rush-hour traffic.

TRAIN Four per hour (5.30am to 11.50pm), €7.60. Takes 20 minutes to Bruxelles-Central, 24 minutes to Bruxelles-Midi.

CHARLEROI ('BRUSSELS-SOUTH') AIRPORT

BUS Direct services operated by **L'Elan** (www.voyages-lelan.be) run to/from a stop behind Bruxelles-Midi station roughly every half hour (single/return €13/22); last services to/from the airport are 8.30pm/11.45pm. Should take around an hour but allow far more at rush hour.

TRAIN The nearest mainline train station, Charleroi-Sud, is linked to Charleroi Airport by TEC bus A (€3, 18 minutes) twice hourly on weekdays, hourly at weekends. A combined bus-and-rail ticket never costs more than €12 to anywhere in Belgium if pre-purchased. Brussels-Charleroi-Sud trains take around 50 minutes.

Bicycle

LONG-TERM HIRE As you leave Bruxelles-Central station by the Madeleine exit, **Fiets Punt/PointVelo** (www.recyclo.org; per 1/3 days €7.50/15; 7am-7pm Mon-Fri) is on the left. You'll need ID, plus a credit card or a €150 cash deposit.

SHORT-TERM HIRE There are 180 automated rental stands operated by **Villo!** (07-805 11 10; http://en.villo.be; subscription day/week €1.60/7.50). Only some of them are equipped with the credit-card reader needed to pay the initial membership subscription. As usual with such schemes, the idea is never to keep one bike more than 30 minutes (or else you pay rapidly escalating fees). Drop it off then take another as required.

TOURS Starting from the Grand Place, **Brussels Bike Tours** (☎0484 89 89 36; www.brusselsbiketours.com; tour incl bicycle rental adult/student €22/25; ⏰10am Feb-Nov, 10am & 3pm Apr-Sep) take around 3½ hours, including stops for beer and *frites*. Maximum group size 12.

Public Transport

Costs Tickets valid for one hour are sold at metro stations, STIB/MIVB kiosks, newsagents and on buses and trams. Single-/five-/10-journey STIB/MIVB tickets cost €1.80/7.50/12 including transfers. Unlimited one/two/three-day passes cost €6/10/13. Airport buses are excluded. Children under six travel free. Tickets must be machine-validated before travel or you could face a €55 fine.

Information For fare/route information see www.stib.be.

Operating hours 6am to midnight daily. Limited 'Noctis' buses (€3) run from midnight to 3am Friday and Saturday.

Taxi

Taxis (www.autolux.be) cost €2.40 flagfall plus €1.35 per km in Brussels, €2.70 per km beyond city limits. There are taxis ranks at Bruxelles-Midi and Madeleine, or prebook on ☎02-268 00 00 or ☎02-349 49 49. Flagging down cabs London-style doesn't work.

Around Brussels

WATERLOO BATTLEFIELD

European history changed course in June 1815 when Napoleon was definitively defeated at the Battle of Waterloo, 20km south of Brussels. The battlefield, a vast patchwork of rolling fields, has a hamlet of visitor attractions. Most striking is a grassy hill topped with a great bronze **lion** (www.waterloo-tourisme.be; adult/child €6/4), which you can climb to survey the scene. Enter through the large **visitor centre** (www.waterloo1815.be; ⏰10am-5pm), which offers a range of passes incorporating other Napoleon-related attractions, such as a guided truck tour to key battle sites (adult/concession €12/9).

The lion/battlefield is 5km south of Waterloo town. TEC bus W gets you within 800m, starting from either Ave Fonsny (outside Bruxelles-Midi in Brussels) or from Braine l'Alleud train station on the Brussels-Charleroi line (not from Waterloo station).

FLANDERS

Antwerp

POP 511,700

Cosmopolitan, confident and full of contrasts, Antwerp (Antwerpen in Dutch, Anvers in French) was one of northern Europe's foremost cities in the 17th century when it was home to Pieter Paul Rubens, diplomat, philosopher and northern Europe's greatest baroque artist. Today it once again revels in fame and fortune attracting art lovers and mode moguls, club queens and diamond dealers.

Sights

CITY CENTRE

Brabo Fountain STATUE

(Grote Markt) As with every great Flemish city, Antwerp's medieval heart is a classic **Grote Markt** (Market Sq). It's flanked on two sides by very photogenic **guildhalls** and dominated by an impressive Italo-Flemish Renaissance-style **stadhuis** (town hall), completed in 1565. The central feature is a voluptuous, baroque fountain depicting the Roman hero Brabo who, having slain the giant that terrorised the city, cut off his forearm and flung it into the air. This unlikely Hand Werpen (hand throwing) is popularly cited as the source of the settlement's name Antwerpen.

TOP CHOICE **Onze-Lieve-Vrouwekathedraal** CATHEDRAL

(www.dekathedraal.be; Handschoenmarkt; adult/concession €5/3; ⏰10am-5pm Mon-Fri, to 3pm Sat, to 4pm Sun) Belgium's finest Gothic cathedral was 169 years in the making (1352–1521). Wherever you wander in Antwerp, its gracious, 123m-high spire has a habit of popping unexpectedly into view and rarely fails to jolt a gasp of awe. The sight is particularly well framed looking up Pelgrimstraat in afternoon light. The cathedral's imposing interior sports later-baroque decorations, including four early Rubens canvases. While the city's Museum of Fine Arts (KMSKA) is closed, some of that collection's religious masterpieces are displayed here, too. For a free glimpse down the nave turn left on entry to the 'prayer' area, but remain quiet. Guided tours at 11am.

WORTH A TRIP

BRUSSELS TO ANTWERP

Between Brussels and Antwerp it's easy to make a multihop trip with minor detours via Leuven (30 minutes), Mechelen (22 minutes) and Lier (15 minutes). All have imaginative accommodation and in each town the station is only around 15 minutes' walk from the centre. Mechelen and Leuven have hostels.

Leuven

Home to the vast **Stella Artois brewery** (www.breweryvisits.com; Vuurkruisenlaan), lively, self-confident Leuven (Louvain in French; www.leuven.be) is Flanders' oldest university town. The town's greatest attraction is a flamboyant 15th-century **stadhuis** (Grote Markt 9; tour €2; ⌚tour 3pm) lavished with exterior statuary. Other architectural attractions are patchy due to heavy damage sustained in 20th-century wars, but the iconic university library has been rebuilt, twice. Muntstraat is a loveable medieval alley full of restaurants and Oude Markt is a square of wall-to-wall bars that hums till the wee hours. Behind the train station, an HI Hostel and Ibis Budget hotel offer the best low-cost options for those wanting to sleep near Brussels Airport, a mere 16 minutes away by train. Homely **Leuven City Hostel** (☎016 84 30 33; www.leuvencityhostel.com; Ravenstraat 37; dm/d €22/52; ⌚reception 4-8pm; @ 📶) and stylish B&B **Casa Bollicine** (☎0497 83 97 17; www.casabollicine.be; Parijsstraat 7; s/d €120/150; 📶) are more central.

Mechelen

Belgium's religious capital, Mechelen (Malines in French) has a cathedral whose 97m, 15th-century tower soars above a particularly memorable central market square. There are other splendid churches on Keizerstraat, where the courthouse and theatre were both once royal palaces in the days when the Low Countries were effectively run from Mechelen. Other top sights include a brilliant Toy Museum and the Schepenhuis gallery tower on IJzerenleen, a street of fine baroque facades that leads towards the main station. It passes close to Vismarkt, the compact bar-cafe zone where you'll also find the recommended **Hotel Vé** (☎015 20 07 55; www.hotelve.com; Vismarkt 14; s/d from €158/184, weekends & holidays from €79/98; ❄📶). Across the canal, **Martins' Patershof** (☎015 46 46 46; www.martins-hotels.com; Karmelietenstraat 4; d weekend/weekday from €89/125; ❄📶) offers stylish hotel accommodation in a tastefully converted church.

Lier

Another of Flanders' overlooked historical gem towns, compact Lier is ringed by a circular waterway. It has a delightful *begijnhof* (founded 1258), a fanciful **clocktower** (www.zimmertoren.be) that's eccentrically over-endowed with dials, and a small but excellent art gallery. On the market square the stadhuis (city hall) has an elfin-spired 1369 belfry and hosts the **tourist office** (www.toerismelier.be; Grote Markt 57) in its basement. The **Hof van Aragon** (☎03-491 08 00; www.hofvanaragon.be; Mosdijk 1-6; r €87-119; 📶) offers appealing canalside accommodation in a converted medieval building.

TOP CHOICE Museum Plantin-Moretus HISTORIC BUILDING
(www.museumplantinmoretus.be; Vrijdag Markt 22; adult/child €8/1; ⌚10am-5pm Tue-Sun) Once home to the world's first industrial printing works, this impressive medieval courtyard mansion has been a museum since 1876. Highlights include the preserved 1640 library, the historic bookshop, a roomful of antique printing presses and a priceless collection of manuscripts, painting and tapestries.

Rubenshuis MUSEUM
(www.rubenshuis.be; Wapper 9-11; adult/child €8/1, audio guide €2; ⌚10am-5pm Tue-Sun) Restored and furnished along original lines, the 1611 building was built as a home and studio by celebrated painter Pieter Paul Rubens. Rescued from ruins in 1937, the building is architecturally indulgent with baroque portico, rear facade and formal garden. The splendid art collection includes 10 Rubens canvases, including one where

Eve appears to glance lustfully at Adam's fig-leaf (guide-ref 50).

Het Steen CASTLE

(Steenplein) On a riverside knoll, Het Steen is a dinky but photogenic castle from AD 1200 occupying the site of Antwerp's original Gallo-Roman settlement. Outside is a humorous statue of **Lange Wapper**, a tall folkloric 'peeping Tom' figure showing off his codpiece to two diminutive onlookers.

FREE **St-Annatunnel** TUNNEL

On the tree-shaded square called St-Jansvliet, a lift descends to this 1930s tunnel, allowing pedestrians and cyclists to cross beneath the river to the Linkeroever (Left Bank). It's worth the stroll for the novel city skyline view back from the other side.

MEIR

If walking from the main train station to Groenplaats, revel in the grand, statue-draped architecture of pedestrianised Meir and Leysstraat. The gilt-overloaded **Stadsfeestzaal** (www.stadsfeestzaal.com; Meir 76; ⌚9.30am-7pm Mon-Sat) is one of the world's most indulgently decorated shopping malls. Watch top-quality chocolates being made behind **Chocolate Line** (www.thechocolateline.be; ⌚10.30am-6.30pm), a shop that occupies a mural-filled room of the 1745 **Paleis op de Meir** (www.paleisopdemeir.be; Meir 50; tour €8; ⌚tour 2pm Tue-Sat).

STATION AREA

Antwerpen-Centraal train station is an attraction in itself and the famous **Antwerp zoo** (www.zooantwerpen.be) is just outside.

Diamond Quarter NEIGHBOURHOOD

(www.awdc.be) An astounding 80% of the world's uncut diamonds are traded in Antwerp. But there's little glitz to the four dour exchange buildings on Hoveniersstraat and Schapstraat, heavily guarded streets that are also home to Indian banks, specialist transportation companies, diamond 'boilers' and the industry's governing body HRD Antwerp. Though now Indian dominated, historically the diamond business was mainly the domain of Orthodox Jews, whose black coats, broad-rimmed hats and long hair-curls remain a distinctive sight here.

'T ZUID

Around 1km south of the fashion district, 't Zuid is a conspicuously prosperous area dotted with century-old architecture, hip bars, fine restaurants and interesting museums, though centrepiece art gallery, **KMSKA** (www.kmska.be; Leopold De Waelplaats), is closed for renovation until 2017.

FoMu MUSEUM

(FotoMuseum; ☎03-242 93 00; www.fotomuseum.be; Waalsekaai 47; adult/child €7/1; ⌚10am-5pm Tue-Sun) The permanent collection gives a splendid potted history of photography (albeit mostly in Dutch) but there are also regularly changing exhibitions of no-holds-barred work by contemporary photo-artists.

MHKA ART GALLERY

(☎03-238 59 60; www.muhka.be; Leuvenstraat 32; adult/child €8/1; ⌚11am-6pm Tue-Sun, to 9pm Thu) Madness or inspiration? Whatever your thoughts on installation-style art, few contemporary galleries beat MHKA for provocation.

T'EILANDJE

Around 600m north of the old centre, t'Eilandje is Antwerp's regenerated dockland area, whose yacht harbour is now dominated by **MAS** (Museum aan de Stroom; www.mas.be; Hanzestedenplaats; adult/senior/youth €5/3/1; ⌚10am-5pm), the city's state-of-the-art 10-storey museum gallery complex. Borrow one of their iPods (free with passport deposit) or use your own smart phone to read the QR-coded labels.

Sleeping

Over 40 B&Bs can be sorted by price or map location on www.bedandbreakfast-antwerp.com, but relatively few are central.

TOP CHOICE **Hotel Julien** BOUTIQUE HOTEL **€€€**

(☎03-229 06 00; www.hotel-julien.com; Korte Nieuwstraat 24; r €195-295; ❄@📶) This very discreet boutique mansion-hotel exudes an exquisitely tasteful understated elegance. Rooms feature underfloor heating, Moroccan

ANTWERP MONEYSAVERS

Check out www.antwerpforfree.be. a daily calendar of free concerts and events. Most major city-run museums are free on the last Wednesday of each month. At other times a 48-hour **Antwerp Card** (€28) will save you money if you visit four of the city's splendid museums.

Antwerp Centre

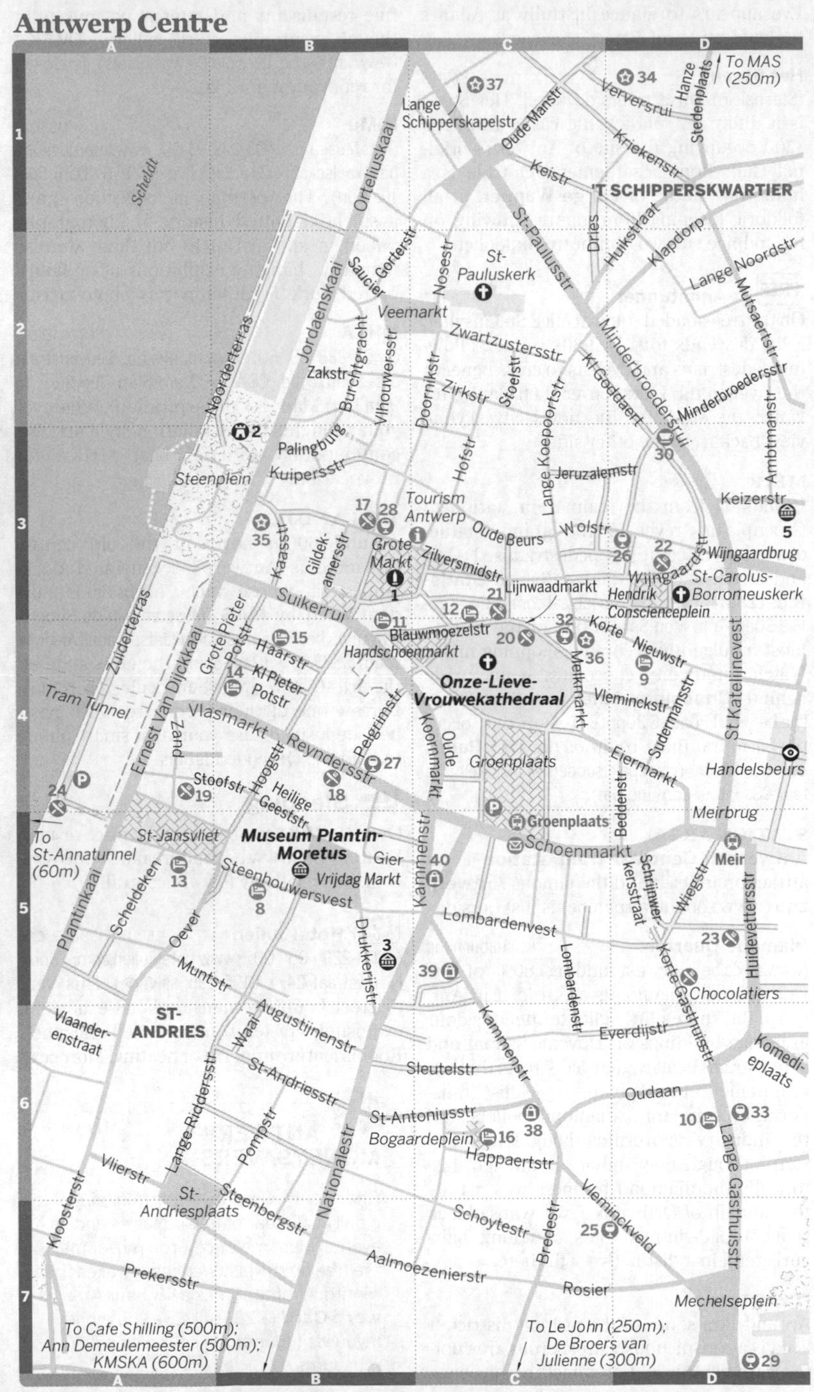

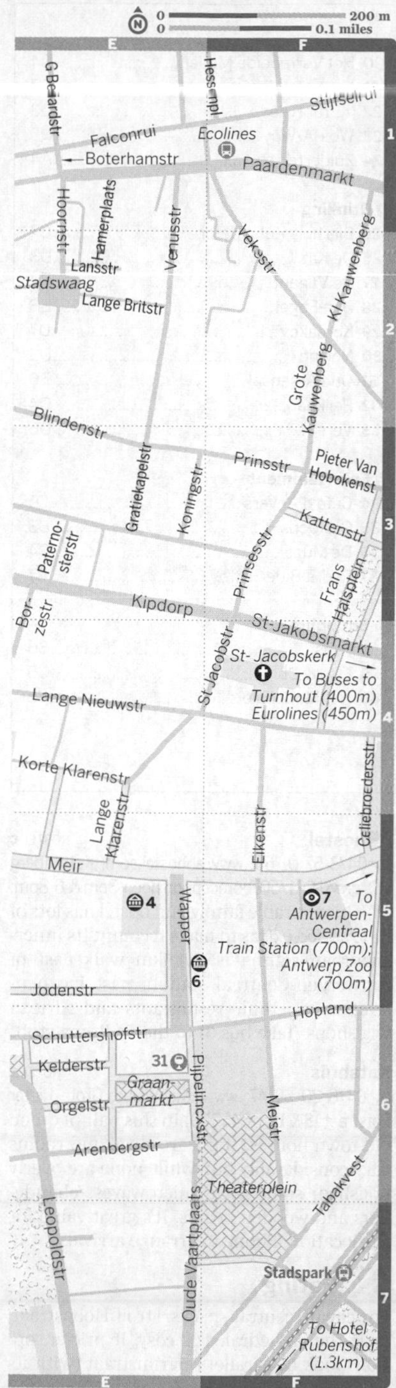

plaster, DVD players and fresh orchids. Some have exposed beams or old brick-tile floors. A swish new wellness centre hides in the subterranean caverns and the rooftop view is a well kept secret.

Hotel Les Nuits DESIGNER HOTEL €€€
(☎03-225 02 04; www.hotellesnuits.be; Lange Gasthuisstraat 12; d/ste from €149/179; 📶) Black-on-black corridors that are fashionable fantasies more than Halloween howlers lead to 24 designer-modernist rooms, each with its own special touches, supercomfy bed and rainforest shower. Sauna use is free. Breakfast (€16) is taken in the casually suave restaurant where you check in; there's no reception.

Matelote Hotel BOUTIQUE HOTEL €€
(☎03-201 88 00; www.hotel-matelote.be; Haarstraat 11; r €90-190; ❄@📶) In a 16th-century building on a pedestrianised old-city backstreet, the Matelote has 10 contemporary styled rooms in five different types, some rather small, others with original beams and pebble-floored bathrooms. Air conditioning in upper rooms.

B&B Siddartha APARTMENTS €€
(☎03-232 97 44; www.bazarbizar.be; Steenhouwersvest 18; d/tr/f €129/172/226) Two apartment-sized rooms entrancingly furnished with Moroccan or Balinese themes sit above an oriental gift shop in the heart of the city.

Hotel O HOTEL €€
(☎03-500 89 50; www.hotelhotelo.com; Handschoenmarkt 3; r €89-129) In an unbeatable location staring right at the cathedral frontage, the O has an intriguing little foyer of 1950s radios and big low-wattage lamp-bulbs. All-black interior decor is relieved in midsized rooms by giant Rubens prints spilling over onto the ceilings. Some rooms are very small.

Hotel Rubenshof HOTEL €€
(☎03-237 07 89; www.rubenshof.be; Amerikalei 115-117; s/d €55/76, without bathroom €33/52; 🚌12) Unrenovated rooms on lower floors are tired but mostly fair sized and very reasonably priced. Those above have been florally redecorated while the top floor (no lift) are fresh and neat if you don't mind skylights instead of windows. The big selling point is the fabulous art nouveau breakfast room.

Hotel Postiljon PENSION €€
(☎03-231 75 75; www.hotelpostiljon.be; Blauwmoezelstraat 6-7; s/d from €70/80, with shared toilet €57/72; 📶) This relatively simple, neat

Antwerp Centre

Top Sights

Museum Plantin-Moretus B5
Onze-Lieve-Vrouwekathedraal C4

Sights

1 Brabo Fountain B3
Chocolate Line .... (see 4)
2 Het Steen B3
3 MoMu B5
4 Paleis op de Meir E5
5 Rockoxhuis D3
6 Rubenshuis E5
7 Stadsfeestzaal F5

Sleeping

8 B&B Siddartha B5
9 Hotel Julien D4
10 Hotel Les Nuits D6
11 Hotel O B4
12 Hotel Postiljon C3
13 Hotel Scheldezicht A5
14 Katshuis B4
Maison d'Anvers .... (see 12)
15 Matelote Hotel B4
16 Pulcinella C6

Eating

17 De 7 Schaken B3
18 De Groote Witte Arend B4
19 De Kleine Zavel A4
20 Het Vermoeide Model C4
21 Kathedraalcafe C3
22 't Brantyser D3
23 Wok-A-Way D5
24 Zuiderterras A4

Drinking

25 Bierhuis Kulminator C7
26 De Kat D3
27 De Vagant B4
28 Den Engel B3
29 Korsåkov D7
30 Normo D3
31 Oud Arsenaal E6
32 Pelikaan C4
33 Verso D6

Entertainment

34 Café d'Anvers D1
35 Cartoons B3
36 De Muze C4
37 Red & Blue C1

Shopping

38 Fans C6
39 Fish & Chips C5
40 Het Modepaleis C5

family hotel is tucked right beside the cathedral's right flank. Some rooms are hidden up steep stairs. The newest six rooms, decidedly more elegant and well equipped, are sometimes marketed under the name **Maison d'Anvers** (www.maisondanvers.be; s/d €97/112). Breakfast costs €11.

Hotel Scheldezicht HOTEL €
(☎03-231 66 02; www.hotelscheldezicht.be; St-Jansvliet 12; s/d with shared bathroom from €50/70; ⏲reception 7am-10pm; 📶) This sweetly old-fashioned hotel has irregular floors and most rooms share toilets, but many are spacious, the decor has been recently spruced up and the location is delightful on a small, central tree-lined square.

Pulcinella HHOSTEL €
(☎03-234 03 14; www.vjh.be/antwerpen.htm; Bogaardeplein 1; dm/d €26/59, HI members save €3; @📶) This giant, tailor-made HI Hostel is hard to beat for its fashion district location and brand new facilities.

ABhostel HOSTEL €
(☎0473 57 01 66; www.abhostel.com; Kattenberg 110; dm/d €21/50; ⏲reception noon-3pm & 6-8pm; 📶) This adorable family-run hostel has lots of little added extras to make it comfy. Its inner-suburban setting is a 1.5km walk east of Antwerpen-Centraal station, past inexpensive shops, ethnic restaurants and African wig shops. Take bus 31 to the de Roma stop.

Katshuis HOTEL €
(☎0476 20 69 47; www.katshuis.be; Grote Pieter Potstraat 18 & 19; r €45-120) In this pair of quiet, old-town houses, stairs are steep and rooms vary considerably but, while none are overly polished, some have microwaves, chandeliers and wooden beams. It's great value for the location. Phone to arrange arrivals.

Eating

For cheap, central snacks, stroll Hoogstraat, near the cathedral. For cosy, if pricier, options look in parallel Pelgrimstraat (with its 'secret' medieval alley, Vlaaikeusgang) or the picturesque lanes leading to Rubens' wonderful St-Carolus-Borromeuskerk. There are many more excellent options in 't Zuid, north and west of KMSKA.

TOP CHOICE De Groote Witte Arend BELGIAN €€
(☎03-233 50 33; www.degrootewittearend.be; Reyndersstraat 18; mains €13-22; ⏰10.30am-midnight, kitchen 11.30am-3pm & 5-10pm; 📶) Retaining the Tuscan stone arcade of a 15th–17th century convent building, this relaxed central gem combines the joys of a good beer bar with the satisfaction of well-cooked, sensibly priced Flemish home cuisine.

Het Vermoeide Model BELGIAN €€
(☎03-233 52 61; www.hetvermoeidemodel.be; Lijnwaadmarkt 2; mains €16.50-25, set menu €26; ⏰4-10pm Tue-Sun) This very atmospheric, if somewhat touristy, medieval house-restaurant has rooms full of exposed brickwork, and there's live piano music on some winter weekends. But the 'secret' surprise is a steep, creaky staircase leading up to a little roof terrace for which reservations are essential in summer. The menu includes steaks, ribs, *waterzooi* (Belgian stew) and seasonal mussels in calvados.

De Kleine Zavel MEDITERRANEAN €€€
(☎03-231 96 91; www.kleinezavel.be; Stoofstraat 2; mains €25-38, lunch/dinner menu €35/53; ⏰noon-2.30pm & 6-10.30pm Tue-Sun) The rough floorboards and wrought-iron chandeliers might suggest the informality of a bistro–cafe but this is in fact a restaurant with high gastronomic standing for fusion cuisine, with an accent on fish and Mediterranean flavours.

't Brantyser EUROPEAN €€
(☎03-233 18 33; www.brantyser.be; Hendrik Conscienceplein 7; snacks €6-12.50, mains €16.50-26.50; ⏰11.15am-10pm) The cosy, double-level Brantyser gets the antique clutter effect just right while its enviable terrace surveys one of Old Antwerp's most appealing pedestrian squares. Other restaurants nearby might be more refined, but the food here is tasty and portions generous.

Le John INTERNATIONAL €€
(☎03-289 92 25; www.lejohn.be; Kasteelpleinstraat 21; mains €13-26; ⏰6pm-10.30pm Mon-Sat) Sitting on 1960s-style school chairs in roughly whitewashed cube-rooms gives the impression of being part of some piece of conceptual art. The short, monthly changing menu presents an unpredictable mixture of styles, attractively presented and prepared at a glass-fronted show kitchen.

Zuiderterras EUROPEAN €€
(☎03-234 12 75; www.zuiderterras.be; Ernest van Dijckkaai 37; mains €17.50-28.50; ⏰9am-10pm) This landmark retro-'50s building provides river views through enormous plate-glass windows, and from summer tables that fan out along the walkway. It's a superb place to be dazzled by sunset rays over respected contemporary cuisine. Bookings advised.

De 7 Schaken BISTRO €€
(www.de7schaken.be; Braderijstraat 24; snacks €7-10, mains €12-22; ⏰11am-11pm) Entered through a wood-panelled pub just off Grote Markt, this traditionally styled bistro serves sensibly priced Belgian classics and stays open all day. Multilingual menus.

De Broers van Julienne VEGETARIAN €
(☎03-232 02 03; www.debroersvanjulienne.be; Kasteelpleinstraat 45; mains €9.50-18; ⏰noon-7pm Mon-Thu, to 10pm Fri-Sat; 🌿) Antwerp's best vegie outlet has superb takeaway quiches in its

FASHION FRENZY

Antwerp has emerged as an avant-garde fashion capital, thanks to talented alumni of the Flanders Fashion Institute. Its style museum, **MoMu** (www.momu.be; Nationalestraat 28; adult/concession €8/6; ⏰10am-6pm Tue-Sun), features regularly changing exhibitions and marks the epicentre of Antwerp's 'fashion district'. Boutique lovers will swoon at the incredible choice of designer outlets along Schuttershofstraat, Huidevettersstraat and Nationalestraat, where **Het Modepaleis** (www.driesvannoten.be; Nationalestraat 16; ⏰10am-6.30pm Mon-Sat) is the elegant flat-iron shaped flagship outlet of Dries Van Noten. Kammenstraat focuses more on street wear; see (**Fans** (☎03-232 31 72; www.fanssite.be; Kammenstraat 80) and **Fish & Chips** (☎03-227 08 24; www.fishandchips.be; Kammenstraat 36-38). There's also plenty of choice scattered around 't Zuid, including **Ann Demeulemeester** (www.anndemeulemeester.be; Leopold de Waelplaats) and the cutting-edge multidesigner outlet **Hospital** (www.hospital-antwerp.com; De Burburestraat 4a; ⏰1-6.30pm Tue-Sun).

deli section and a restaurant stretching back through a vine-draped verandah into a narrow, sunny garden with bench chairs.

Kathedraalcafe BELGIAN €€
(www.kathedraalcafe.be; Torfbrug 10; mains €14-24.50, sandwiches €8.50; ⏲noon-11pm) This ivy-clad medieval masterpiece has an astounding interior decked with angels, saints, pulpits and several deliciously sacrilegious visual jokes.

Wok-A-Way ASIAN, FAST FOOD €
(www.wokaway.com; Groendalstraat 14; mains €8-14; ⏲11.30am-8pm Mon-Sat; 📶) Brash, bright-coloured new diner where you pick your ingredients and have them 'woked' into an 'ecofriendly, sustainable' meal. Dim sum also available.

Aahaar INDIAN, VEGAN €
(www.aahaar.com; Lange Herentalsestraat 23; buffet €9; ⏲noon-3pm & 5.30-9.30pm Mon-Fri, 1-9.30pm Sat & Sun; 🥬) Inexpensive, 100% vegetarian Jain-Indian buffets. From Antwerpen-Centraal walk a block west along De Keyserlei then a block south on Appelmansstraat.

Kubus Permeke CAFETERIA €
(www.casvzw.eu; De Coninckplein 25; sandwiches/mains/set menu from €2.40/8.70/10.50; ⏲10am-8.30pm Mon-Thu, to 5.30pm Fri & Sat, to 2.30pm Sun) Architecturally interesting glass cube where a city-run project provides inexpensive food and drinks. It's aimed at low-income families but anyone can go.

Drinking

To sound like a local, stride into a pub and ask for a *bolleke*. Don't worry, that means a 'little bowl' (ie glass) of De Koninck, the city's favourite ale. Cheap places to try it include classic cafes **Oud Arsenaal** (Pijpelincxstraat 4; ⏲10am-10pm Wed-Fri, 7.30am-7.30pm Sat & Sun), **De Kat** (Wolstraat 22) and the livelier **Pelikaan** (www.facebook.com/cafepelikaan; Melkmarkt 14; ⏲8.30am-3am). Countless other great bars lie around KMSKA in the Zuid area.

Den Engel PUB
(www.cafedenengel.be; Grote Markt 5; ⏲9am-2am) Historic guildhall pub with cathedral views from the terrace.

De Vagant PUB
(www.devagant.be; Reyndersstraat 25; ⏲noon-late) More than 200 *jenever* (€2.20 to €7.50) are served in this bare-boards local cafe or sold by the bottle across the road from its *slijterij* (bottleshop), which resembles an old-style pharmacy.

Bierhuis Kulminator BEER PUB
(Vleminckveld 32; ⏲4pm-midnight Tue-Sat, 8pm-midnight Mon) Classic beer-pub boasting 700 mostly Belgian brews, including notably rare 'vintage' bottles laid down to mature for several years like fine wine.

Korsåkov BAR
(Mechelseplein 21; snacks €3.50-5.50, Primus/Chouffe €2/2.50; ⏲10am-4am) One of Mechelseplein's trio of super-late bars, Korsåkov has star-tiled floors, blue formica tables and a few games to play.

Normo CAFE
(www.normocoffee.com; Minderbroedersrui 30; coffees €2-3.50, muffins €2; ⏲10am-7pm Mon-Fri, to 6pm Sat) Coffee is art at Normo, from the science-project dripping station to the rough walled room full of roasting ovens and the mismatched furniture. Student vibe.

Verso BAR
(Lange Gasthuisstraat 11; ⏲10am-7pm Mon-Sat) The fashion district's place to see and be seen. Drink prices are high but accompanying finger snacks amply compensate.

Cafe Shilling CAFE
(www.cafeshilling.be; Graaf van Egmontstraat 60; ⏲8am-1am; 📶) Comfy but not over-exclusive lounge with Chesterfield leather chairs hides above an equally appealing downstairs bar with mismatching wooden carved panels, silvered ceilings and soft jazzy music.

Chatleroi BAR
(Graaf van Hoornsestraat 2; ⏲noon-3am Sun-Wed, to 5am Thu-Sat; 📶) Grungier than most Zuid cafes; wildly swerving musical styles create an atmosphere for those left standing very late.

GAY & LESBIAN ANTWERP

Antwerp's vibrant LGBT scene is widely diffused around town, with relevant places usually flying rainbow flags. Tourism Antwerp produces a useful multilingual map-guide *Gay Antwerpen,* with more information available from gay-and-lesbian bookshop-cafe **Boekhandel 't Verschil** (www.verschil.be; Minderbroedersrui 33; ⏲11am-6pm Wed-Sat, 1-6pm Sun).

TRAINS FROM ANTWERPEN-CENTRAAL

DESTINATION	FARE (€)	DURATION (MIN)	FREQUENCY (PER HR)
Amsterdam	34.50/77	135/74	1
Bruges	14.25	75	2
Brussels	6.90	35-49	5
Ghent-Dampoort	9	46	3
Leuven	6.90	42-63	4
Lier	2.70	17	5
Mechelen-Nekkerspoel	3.70	15	2
Paris	106	138	seven daily

☆ Entertainment

For listings consult www.weekup.be/antwerpen/week; www.zva.be in summer; and www.gratisinantwerpen.be for free events.

Café Local CLUB
(www.cafelocal.be; Waalsekaai 25; cover €7-15; 10pm-late Wed-Sun; 4) Popular 't Zuid nightclub with a Mexican trading-post themed bar-island. Wednesdays are formal (collared shirts required), Thursday student nights are free (18 to 25 year olds), Fridays are for over 40s while Paradise Saturdays see deckchairs and palm fronds appear. On the first Sunday of each month the music is salsa-merengue.

De Muze JAZZ
(03-226 01 26; jazzmuze.be; Melkmarkt 15; noon 4am) Very appealing triple-level cafe with an Escher-like interior hosting great live jazz from 10pm Monday to Saturday (but not Wednesday or Thursday in summer).

Cartoons CINEMA
(www.cartoons-cinema.be; Kaasstraat 4-6) Art-house and quality foreign movies.

Café d'Anvers DISCO, CLUB
(www.cafe-d-anvers.com; Verversrui 15; €10; 11pm-7.30am Thu-Sat; 7) Lurid scarlet interiors reflect the red-light-district setting.

Red & Blue CLUB
(www.redandblue.be; Lange Schipperskapelstraat 11; 11pm-7am Thu-Sat; 7) Great dance venue with decent sized yet still intimate dance floor. It's most famous for its Saturday gay night. There's also a Thursday student night, TGIT (www.thankgoditsthursday.be), Fridays see a mixed crowd groove to house music, and some Sundays there are classic '70s-style discos.

Information

Tourism Antwerp (03-232 01 03; www.visitantwerpen.be; Grote Markt 13; 9am-5.45pm Mon-Sat, to 4.45pm Sun & holidays) is a central tourist office with a branch on level zero of Antwerpen-Centraal train station.

Getting There & Away

BUS International **Eurolines** (03-233 86 62; www.eurolines.com; Van Stralenstraat 8; 9am-5.45pm Mon-Fri, to 3.15pm Sat) buses depart from points near Franklin Rooseveltplaats. Many regional buses (eg to Lier) and **Ecolines** (www.ecolines.net; Paardenmarkt 65, Ticket agent Euro-Maror) services for Eastern Europe depart from near Antwerpen-Berchem train station, 2km southeast of Antwerpen-Centraal.

TRAIN Located 1.5km east of the historic centre, **Antwerpen-Centraal Station** (Diamant) is a veritable cathedral of a building, considered by many to be among the world's most handsome stations.

Getting Around

Franklin Rooseveltplaats and Koningin Astridplein are hubs for the integrated network of **De Lijn** (www.delijn.be) buses and trams (some running underground-metro-style).

Ghent

POP 248,200

Known as Gent in Dutch and Gand in French, Ghent is Flanders' unsung historic city. Like a grittier Bruges without the crush of tourists, it sports photogenic canals, medieval towers, great cafes and some of Belgium's most inspired museums. Always a lively student city, things go crazy in mid-July during the 10-day **Gentse Feesten** (www.gentsefeesten.be; ⏲Jul), a city-wide party of music and theatre.

Sights

CITY CENTRE

The main sights are strolling distance from Korenmarkt, the westernmost of three interlinked squares that form the heart of Ghent's historic core.

TOP CHOICE St-Baafskathedraal CHURCH

(www.users.skynet.be/sintbaafskathedraal-gent; St-Baafsplein; ⏲8.30am-6pm Apr-Oct, to 5pm Nov-Mar) The cathedral's towering interior has some fine stained glass and an unusual combination of brick vaulting with stone tracery. A €0.20 leaflet guides you round the cathedral's numerous art treasures, including a big original Rubens opposite the stairway that leads down into the partly muralled crypts. But most visitors come to see just one magnificent work – Van Eyck's 1432 'Flemish Primitive' altarpiece, **The Adoration of the Mystic Lamb** (Het Lam Gods; http://vaneyck.kikirpa.be; St- Baafskathedraal; adult/child €4/1.50, audio guide €1; ⏲9.30am-4.45pm Mon-Sat, 1-4.30pm Sun, closes 4pm Nov-Mar), kept in a specially temperature-controlled, half-darkened chapel near the west entrance. Some panels have been temporarily removed to the MSK gallery for restoration. If you want to see the whole display or simply don't want to queue to see the original, a photographic copy is displayed for free in side-chapel 30, the sixth on the right beside the altar.

Belfort BELFRY

(Botermarkt; adult/concession €5/3.75; ⏲10am-5.30pm) Ghent's soaring Unesco-listed 14th-century belfry is topped by a large dragon. That's a weathervane not a fire breather and it's become something of a city mascot. You'll meet two previous dragon incarnations on the climb to the top (mostly by lift) but other than some bell-making exhibits the real attraction is the view. Enter through the **Lakenhalle**, Ghent's cloth hall that was left half-built in 1445 and only completed in 1903. The Belfort bells are played at carillon concerts at 11.30am Fridays and 11am summer Sundays.

Gravensteen CASTLE

(St-Veerleplein; adult/child €8/4; ⏲10am-6pm Apr-Oct, 9am-5pm Nov-Mar) The Counts of Flanders' quintessential 12th-century stone castle comes complete with moat, turrets and arrow slits. The relative lack of interior furnishings is compensated with a hand-held 45-minute movie-guide, which sets a somewhat tongue-in-cheek historical costumed drama in the rooms, prison pit and battlements that you visit. If you just wish to photograph the castle's exterior there's a great **viewpoint** on St-Widostraat.

Grasbrug VIEWPOINT

To admire Ghent's towers and gables at their most photogenic, stand just west of the little Grasbrug bridge at dusk. Canal boat trips depart from either end of the Grasbrug and nearby Vleeshuisbrug bridges.

Patershol NEIGHBOURHOOD

(www.patershol.be) Dotted with half-hidden restaurants, enchanting Patershol is a web of twisting cobbled lanes with old-world houses that were once home to leather tradespeople and to the Carmelite Fathers (Paters), hence the name.

Huis van Alijn MUSEUM

(www.huisvanalijn.be; Kraanlei 65; adult/child €5/1; ⏲11am-5pm Tue-Sat, 10am-5pm Sun) If you have a Museumpass, don't miss this restored 1363 children's hospice hosting a museum about life in the 20th century. Although little is in English, the engrossing exhibits are self explanatory and family home videos prove unexpectedly moving.

MIAT MUSEUM

(Museum voor Industriële Archeologie en Textiel; www.miat.gent.be; Minnemeers 9; adult/child €5/1; ⏲10am-6pm Tue-Sun) In a five-floor, 19th-century mill-factory building, this thought provoking museum celebrates Ghent's history of textile production and examines the social effects of 250 years of industrialisation. A very extensive collection of heavy mechanical weaving equipment comes deafeningly alive on Tuesday and Thursday mornings around 10am. There are great city-skyline views from the top floor.

Design Museum MUSEUM

(www.designmuseumgent.be; J Breydelstraat 5; adult/child €5/free; ⏲10am-6pm Tue-Sun) A vast toilet-roll 'sculpture' humorously marks the back side of this museum, which specialises in displays of home furnishings through the ages, especially the 20th century.

Werregarensteeg STREET

(www.ghentizm.be) Graffiti is positively encouraged as an art form in this tiny central alley.

OUT OF THE CENTRE

Museum Dr Guislain MUSEUM
(www.museumdrguislain.be; Jozef Guislainstraat 43; adult/child €6/1; 9am-5pm Tue-Fri, 1-5pm Sat & Sun; 1) Hidden away an 1857 neo-Gothic lunatic asylum, this enthralling mental-health museum takes visitors on a trilingual, multicultural journey through the history of psychiatry. Dr D'Arsonval's extraordinary 1909 radiographic apparatus looks like a Frankenstein creation. Tram 1 stops outside.

STAM MUSEUM
(www.stamgent.be; Bijloke Complex; adult/concession €6/4.50; 10am-6pm Tue-Sun; 4) Shoehorned into a 17th-century former nunnery-hospital complex, this satisfying 21st-century museum examines Ghent's city history with treaties and treasures interspersed with choose-your-own film clips and a chance to peer into the future. You'll need hours to see everything.

TOP CHOICE **MSK** ART GALLERY
(Museum voor Schone Kunsten; 09-240 07 00; www.mskgent.be; Citadelpark; adult/child €5/1; 10am-6pm) Styled like a Greek temple, this superb 1903 fine-art gallery introduces a veritable A–Z of great Belgian and Low Countries' painters from the 14th to mid-20th centuries. Highlights include a happy family of coffins by Magritte, Luminist canvases by Emile Claus, and Pieter Breughel the Younger's 1621 *Dorpsadvocaat* – a brilliant portrait of a village lawyer oozing with arrogance.

SMAK ART GALLERY
(www.smak.be; Citadelpark; adult/child €6/free, 10am-1pm Sun free; 10am-6pm Tue-Sun; 5) Ghent's highly regarded Museum of Contemporary Art features regularly changing exhibitions of provocative, cutting-edge installations.

Sleeping

Ghent offers innovative accommodation in all budget ranges. Websites www.gent-accommodations.be and www.bedandbreakfast-gent.be help you judge availability in the city's numerous appealing B&Bs.

TOP CHOICE **Chambres d'Hôtes Verhaegen** BOUTIQUE B&B €€€
(09-265 07 60; www.hotelverhaegen.be; Oude Houtlei 110; d €195-265; reception 2-6pm) This sumptuous 1770s urban palace retains original sections of 18th-century Chinese wallpaper, a dining room with romantic Austrian-era murals, dazzling salon and neatly manicured parterre garden. The five exclusive guest rooms combine well-placed modernist and retro touches. Breakfast costs €18.

Hotel Harmony BOUTIQUE HOTEL €€€
(09-324 26 80; www.hotel-harmony.be; Kraanlei 37; s €139-209, d €154-229;) Luxuriously heaped pillows, fine linens, Miro-esque art and swish modern colours lie beneath the 18th-century beams of this old-meets-new beauty. Each of the 25 rooms has a coffee maker and even the smallest is amply sized, but shapes and views vary. Check Facebook for promotional deals.

Atlas B&B B&B €€
(09-233 49 91; www.atlasbenb.be; Rabotstraat 40; s €57-72, d €73-93; P@) This fine 1863 townhouse has gorgeous belle époque, art deco and art nouveau touches in a lounge featuring maps, globes and an honesty bar. Four very distinctive guest rooms are themed by continent.

Hostel 47 HOSTEL €€
(0478 71 28 27; www.hostel47.com; Blekerijstraat 47-51; dm €26.50-29.50, d €71;) Unusually calm yet pretty central, this inviting hostel has revamped a high-ceilinged historic house with virginal white walls, spacious bunk rooms and designer fittings. Free lockers and cursory breakfast with Nespresso coffee; no bar.

Bon Vivant BOATHOUSE €€
(0496 70 35 41; www.bed-on-boat.be; Stapelplein 84E; d €60, breakfast €7;) This converted river barge has four rooms that are unexpectedly spacious (for a boat) and better value than many lower-range hotels.

Uppelink HOSTEL €€
(09-279 44 77; www.hosteluppelink.com; Sint-Michielsplein 21; dm €27.50-37.50 d without bathroom €71) The show-stopping attraction

GHENT MONEYSAVERS

The good value **Museumpass** (www.visitgent.be; 3-day ticket €20) provides three days' free entrance to a number of sights and attractions (except for boat tours), and all city transport. It's sold at museums, De Lijn booths and the tourist office.

at this brand new hostel is the unbeatable view of Ghent's main towers as seen from the breakfast room and from the biggest, least expensive dorms.

Hotel Flandria HOTEL €€

(☎09-223 06 26; www.hotelflandria-gent.be; Barrestraat 3; s/d €60/70, without bathroom €45/55; @📶) Map-plastered walls beckon you into this helpfully central hotel. Rooms are mostly cramped and simple, some better appointed than others. Good beds.

De Draecke HOSTEL €€

(☎09-233 70 50; www.vjh.be; St-Widostraat 11; dm/s/tw €24/52.75/76, HI members save €3; @📶) Behind a pseudo-medieval facade facing a picturesque willow-lined central canal lies this slightly institutional modern hostel. Lockers cost €2 but the luggage room is free. No lockout.

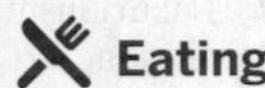

Eating

Cosy, upper-market restaurants in the delightful cobbled alleyways of Patershol cover many cuisines. Several eateries jostle for summer terrace space on Graslei's gorgeous canalside terrace. There's fast food around Korenmarkt and great-value Turkish options along Sleepstraat. Numerous vegetarian and organic choices feature on the tourist office's free Veggieplan Gent guide map. Thursday is Veggieday.

House of Eliott LOBSTER €€€

(☎09-225 21 28; www.thehouseofeliott.be; J Breydelstraat 36; mains €25-45, menus €46-59; ⊗noon-2pm & 6-11pm Thu-Mon, closed Sep) Oozing pseudo-1920s charm, this gently camp, canalside gem is full of flapper mannequins and sepia photos inspired by an old British TV series. Its little balcony terrace perches just above the canal waters. Gastronomically, lobster dominates.

Brasserie Pakhuis EUROPEAN, OYSTERS €€

(☎09-223 55 55; www.pakhuis.be; Schuurkenstraat 4; mains €17-29, weekday lunch €13.50, menus €27-43; ⊗lunch & dinner Mon-Sat, bar 11am-1am) This hip, if mildly ostentatious, modern brasserie-bar-restaurant is set in a magnificently restored former textile warehouse. It retains the original century-old wrought ironwork and an incredible roof. It's well worth popping inside, even if you only stop for a drink.

Panda VEGETARIAN €€

(☎09-225 07 86; Oudburg 38; mains €16.50-20.50, lunch €13-22.50; ⊗noon-2pm & 6.15-8.45pm Mon-Sat; 🖉) Excellent vegie food set to classical music and served on pressed linens at tables with fresh orchids. The daily-changing lunch plate presents a truly artistic palate of flavours. It's hidden away at the back of an organic grocery shop.

Amadeus RIBS €€

(☎09-225 13 85; www.amadeusspareribrestaurant.be; Plotersgracht 8/10; mains €13.75-19; ⊗6.30-11pm) All-you-can-eat spare ribs at four Ghent addresses, all within ancient buildings that are full of atmosphere, bustle and cheerful conversation.

Soup Lounge SOUP €

(www.souplounge.be; Zuivelbrug 4; small/large soup €4/5, sandwiches 2.80; ⊗10am-6pm) At this bright, central, retro-'70s soup kitchen, each bowlful comes with add-your-own cheese and croutons, two rolls and a piece of fruit. Canal views are free.

't Oud Clooster TAVERN €

(☎09-233 78 02; Zwartezusterstraat 5; mains €9-17; ⊗6pm-late Mon-Sat, kitchen till midnight) Mostly candlelit at night, this atmospheric double level 'pratcafe' is built into sections of what was long ago a nunnery, hence the sprinkling of religious statues and cherub lamp-holders. Well-priced cafe food is presented with unexpected style.

Avalon VEGETARIAN €

(☎09-224 37 24; www.restaurantavalon.be; Geldmunt 32; mains €11-15; ⊗lunch Mon-Sat; 🖉) 'Live well and laugh often' is the Avalon's sage suggestion, backed up with copious, reliably delicious vegetarian and vegan lunches. Eat in its intriguing warren of little rooms or on a delightful tree-shaded rear terrace.

Pizza Gülhan TURKISH €

(Sleepstraat 70; pide €4-6.50, grills €9-13.50, beer/cava/tea €1.80/3.20/1.25; ⊗11.30am-midnight Wed-Mon) Fill up for around €5 with groaning plate-loads of excellent, garnished fresh pide.

Drinking

Hotsy Totsy JAZZ BAR

(www.hotsytotsy.be; Hoogstraat 1; ⊗6pm-1am Mon-Fri, 8pm-2am Sat & Sun) A 1930s vamp pouts above the zinc of this classic artist's cafe with silver-floral wallpaper, black-and-white film photos and free live jazz at 9pm most Thursdays (October to April).

Het Waterhuis aan de Bierkant BEER PUB
(www.waterhuisaandebierkant.be; Groentenmarkt 12; ⏲11am-1am) Sharing an enticing waterfront terrace with atmospherically austere *jenever* bar **'t Dreupelkot** (⏲4pm-late), this photogenic, classic beer-pub has an interior draped in dried hops and three exclusive house beers amid the wide selection.

Rococo BAR
(Corduwaniersstraat 5; ⏲from 10pm) Lit only by candles, this classic late night cafe-bar with carved wooden ceilings is an ideal place for cosy midnight conversations.

Pink Flamingo's CAFE-BAR
(www.pinkflamingos.be; Onderstraat 55; ⏲noon-midnight Mon-Wed, noon-3am Thu-Sat, 2pm-midnight Sun) Lively kitsch-overloaded cafe-bar with Barbie lamps, 1970s wallpaper and ample plastic fruit.

Hot Club de Gand BAR
(www.hotclubdegand.be; Schuddevisstraatje; ⏲3pm-late) Hidden down the tiny alley behind 't Dreupelkot *jenever* bar, this is a great place to seek out live acoustic music. Be it jazz, gypsy, blues or flamenco, there's likely to be a concert most term-time nights, sometimes until very late.

Herberg de Dulle Griet BEER PUB
(www.dullegriet.be; Vrijdagmarkt 50; ⏲noon-1am Tue-Sat, to 7pm Sun, 4.30pm-1am Mon) Heavy beams, a heraldic ceiling, barrel tables, lacy lampshades and the odd boar's head all add character to one of Ghent's best-known beer pubs.

Limonada LOUNGE
(www.facebook.com/limonada.gent; Heilige Geeststraat 7; ⏲10pm-3am Mon-Sat) *Clockwork Orange*-style, '70s-retro lounge with bean-bag seats around low luminous tables.

Charlatan BAR
(www.charlatan.be; Vlasmarkt 9; ⏲7pm-late Tue-Sun during term) At this boisterous late-night drinking spot you might find live music in virtually any genre (from 10pm, see website), sometimes with cover charge. It generally opens long enough to leave you ready for breakfast. If not, others next door will.

☆ Entertainment

For listings of what's on, see *Week-Up* (www.weekup.be/gent/week), *Zone 09* magazine (free), which can be found in distribution boxes around town, or www.democrazy.be. All are in Dutch.

Vooruit THEATRE
(www.vooruit.be; St-Pietersnieuwstraat 23; 🚍5) A visionary architectural premonition of art deco, the 1912 Vooruit building is a prominent venue for dance, rock concerts, film and visiting theatre companies.

Culture Club CLUB
(☎09-233 09 46; www.cultureclub.be; Afrikalaan 174; ⏲Thu-Sat Oct-May) Once dubbed the 'world's hippest club', Culture Club's themes and cover charges vary. It's roughly 1.5km north of Gent-Dampoort station via Koopvaardijlaan.

De Bijloke CLASSICAL MUSIC
(www.debijloke.be; Jozef Kluyskensstraat 2) Good selection of classical-music concerts on a site recycled from a historic abbey and hospital.

De Vlaamse Opera OPERA
(www.vlaamseopera.be; Schouwburgstraat 3) Ghent's 1840 opera hall boasts horseshoe-shaped tiered balconies and elegant salons.

Handelsbeurs CONCERT VENUE
(www.handelsbeurs.be; Kouter 29) Central concert-hall for anything from classical music to Latin to blues.

ℹ Information

Ghent Tourist Office (☎09-266 56 60; www.visitgent.be; Oude Vismijn, St-Veerleplein 5; ⏲9.30am-6.30pm mid-Mar–mid-Oct, to 4.30pm winter) Very helpful for free maps and accommodation bookings.

ℹ Getting There & Away

Bus

INTERNATIONAL There's a **Eurolines Office** (☎09-220 90 24; www.eurolines.be; Koningin Elisabethlaan 73; ⏲8.30am-noon & 1.30-5.30pm Mon-Fri, 8.30am-noon Sat) near Gent-St-Pieters, but their international buses (eg to London at 11.35pm) currently depart from Gent-Dampoort.

REGIONAL Some **De Lijn** (www.delijn.be; Cataloniestraat 4; ⏲10.15am-5pm Mon-Sat) services depart from **Gent-Zuid bus station** (Woodrow Wilsonplein), others from various points around Gent-St-Pieters train station.

Train

Gent-Dampoort, 1km west of the old city, is the handiest station with useful trains to Antwerp (€8.50, fast/slow 42/64 minutes, three per hour), Bruges (€6.20, 36 minutes, hourly) and Kortrijk (€6.60, 35 minutes, hourly).

The main station, **Gent-St-Pieters** (2.5km south of centre), has more choice, including Brussels (€9, 36 minutes, twice hourly), Bruges (fast/slow 24/42 minutes, five per hour), Kortrijk (€6.60, fast/slow 26/33 minutes) and Ostend (€9, fast/slow 38/55 minutes).

Getting Around

Driving a car in Ghent is purgatory. Park it and walk or ride.

Bicycle

HIRE Biker (Steendam 16; per half-/full day €6.50/9; 9am-12.30pm & 1.30-6pm Tue-Sat)

Max Mobiel (www.max-mobiel.be; Vokselslaan 27; per day/week/month €9/25/30) Two minutes' walk south of Gent-St-Pieters station. Branch kiosk at Gent-Dampoort station.

Be warned that police confiscate illegally parked bikes.

Bus & Tram

TICKETS One-hour/all-day tickets cost €1.20/5 if purchased ahead of time from ticket machines or De Lijn offices beside **Gent-St-Pieters** (7am-1.30pm & 2-7pm Mon-Fri) or in the centre. Handy tram 1 runs from Gent-St-Pieters to and through the centre passing walkably close to most major sites.

Bruges

POP 117,000

Cobblestone lanes, dreamy canals, soaring spires and whitewashed old almshouses combine to make central Bruges (Brugge in Dutch) one of Europe's most picture-perfect historic cities. The only problem is that everyone knows.

Sights

Beyond the sights listed, the real joy of Bruges is simply wandering alongside the canals, soaking up the atmosphere. To avoid the worst crowds, explore east of pretty Jan van Eyckplein, or maybe seek out the windmills beside the city's eastern 'moat', heading north of the fortified Kruispoort gate-tower at Langestraat's eastern end.

TOP CHOICE Groeningemuseum ART GALLERY

(www.brugge.be; Dijver 12; adult/concession €8/6; 9.30am-5pm Tue-Sun) Bruges' most celebrated art gallery packs 11 rooms with an astonishingly rich collection. Superb Flemish Primitive works, including Jan van Eyck's radiant, if rather odd, masterpiece *Madonna with Canon George Van der Paele* (1436), are the main drawcard but later artistic genres also get a look in. There's a typically androgynous figure by superstar symbolist Fernand Khnopff, and a surrealist canvas each from Magritte and Delvaux.

BRUGES MONEYSAVERS

A **Bruges City Card** (www.bruggecity card.be; 48/72 hours €35/€40) gives entry to all the main city museums, plus private attractions including Choco-Story and De Halve Maan brewery. You'll also score a canal boat ride and discounts on bicycle rental, concerts, films and theatre.

Markt SQUARE

The heart of ancient Bruges, the old market square is lined with pavement cafes beneath step-gabled facades. The buildings aren't always quite as medieval as they look, but together they create a fabulous scene and even the neo-Gothic **post office** is architecturally magnificent. The scene is dominated by the **Belfort** (Belfry; adult/child €8/5; 9.30am-5pm, last tickets 4.15pm), Belgium's most famous belfry – its iconic octagonal tower is arguably better appreciated from afar than by climbing 366 claustrophobic steps to the top.

Burg SQUARE

Bruges' 1420 **Stadhuis** (City Hall; Burg 12) is smothered in statuettes and contains a breathtaking **Gotishe Zaal** (Gothic Hall; Burg; adult/concession €4/3; 9.30am-5pm), featuring dazzling polychromatic ceilings, hanging vaults and historicist murals. Tickets include entry to part of the early baroque **Brugse Vrije** (Burg 11a; 9.30am-noon & 1.30-4.30pm) next door. With its gilt highlights and golden statuettes, this palace was once the administrative centre for a large autonomous territory ruled from Bruges between 1121 and 1794.

Heilig-Bloedbasiliek CHURCH

(Basilica of the Holy Blood; Burg 5; 9.30-11.50am & 2-5.50pm Apr-Sep, 10-11.50am & 2-3.50pm Thu-Tue, 10-11.50am Wed Oct-Mar) The Stadhuis' western end morphs into the Heilig-Bloedbasiliek. The basilica takes its name from a phial supposedly containing a few drops of Christ's blood that was brought here after the 12th-century Crusades. The right-hand door leads upstairs to a colourfully adorned chapel where the relic is hidden behind a flamboyant silver tabernacle and brought out for pious veneration at 2pm daily. Also upstairs is the basilica's one-room **treasury** (adult/child €1.50/free), where you'll see the jewel-studded reliquary in which the phial is mounted on Ascension Day for Bruges' biggest annual parade, the Heilig-Bloed-processie.

Downstairs, entered via a different door, is the basilica's contrasting bare stone 12th-century Romanesque chapel.

Historium MUSEUM

(www.historium.be; Markt 1; adult/child €11/5.50; ⏲10am-9pm) Taking visitors back to 1435, this immersive multimedia experience was due to open as we went to press. Claiming to be more medieval movie than museum, the site features a fictional love story to provide narrative structure, and you can nose around Van Eyck's studio.

Onze-Lieve-Vrouwekerk CHURCH

(Church of Our Lady; Mariastraat; ⏲9.30am-4.50pm Mon-Sat, 1.30-4.50pm Sun) This large, somewhat sober 13th-century church sports an enormous tower that's currently 'wrapped' for extensive renovation. Inside it's best known for Michelangelo's serenely contemplative *Madonna and Child* (1504) statue, the only such work by Michelangelo to leave Italy during the artist's lifetime. In the church's apse, the **treasury section** (adult/concession €2.50/2) displays some splendid 15th- and 16th-century artworks plus the fine stone-and-bronze tombs of Charles the Bold (Karel de Stoute) and his daughter, Mary of Burgundy, whose pivotal marriage dragged the Low Countries into the Hapsburg empire, with far-reaching consequences.

Museum St-Janshospitaal MUSEUM

(Memlingmuseum; Mariastraat 38; adult/child €8/free; ⏲9.30am-5pm Tue-Sun) In the restored chapel of a 12th-century hospital building with superb timber beamwork, this museum displays nightmarish historical medical implements, hospital sedan chairs and a gruesome 1679 painting of an anatomy class. But it's best known for displaying six masterpieces by 15th-century artist Hans Memling, including the gilded oak reliquary of St-Ursula, shaped like a mini Gothic cathedral. Your ticket also allows visits to the hospital's restored 17th-century **apotheek** (pharmacy; Mariastraat; ⏲9.30-11.45am & 2-5pm Tue-Sun), accessed by an easily missed rear door.

TOP CHOICE Begijnhof BEGIJNHOF

(admission free; ⏲6.30am-6.30pm) Bruges' delightful *begijnhof* originally dates from the 13th century. Although the last *begijn* has long since passed away, today residents of the pretty, whitewashed garden complex include a convent of Benedictine nuns. Despite the hoards of summer tourists, the *begijnhof* remains a remarkably tranquil haven. In spring a carpet of daffodils adds to the quaintness of the scene. Outside the *begijnhof*'s 1776 gateway bridge lies a tempting, if predictably tourist-priced, array of terraced restaurants, lace shops and waffle peddlers.

Choco-Story MUSEUM

(www.choco-story.be; Wijnzakstraat 2, on Sint-Jansplein; adult/child €7/4; ⏲10am-5pm) This highly absorbing chocolate museum traces the cocoa bean back to its role as an Aztec currency, shows videos on cocoa production and provides samples of pralines that are made as you watch (last demonstration 4.45pm).

Brouwerij De Halve Maan BREWERY

(☎050 33 26 97; www.halvemaan.be; Walplein 26; ⏲10.30am-6pm, closed 2 weeks mid-Jan) Founded in 1856, this is the last family *brouwerij* (brewhouse) in central Bruges. Multilingual **guided visits** (tours €6.50; ⏲11am-4pm Apr-Sep, 11am & 3pm Oct-Mar), lasting 45 minutes, depart on each hour and include a tasting. Alternatively simply sip one of its excellent *Brugse Zot* beers in the appealing brewery cafe.

Museum voor Volkskunde MUSEUM

(Museum of Folklore; Balstraat 43; adult/concession €4/3; ⏲9.30am-5pm Tue-Sun) Flemish life in times gone by is illustrated by 18 themed tableaux, including a 1930s sweetshop, a hatter's workshop and a traditional kitchen. It's a static affair, but the setting is an attractive *godshuis* (historic almshouse complex), and the time-warp museum cafe, **De Zwarte Kat** (Balstraat 43; ⏲closed 11.45am-2pm), charges just €1.25 for a beer. Temporary exhibits upstairs are often worth a look.

Sleeping

Although there are well over 250 hotels and B&Bs, accommodation can still prove oppressively overbooked from Easter to September, over Christmas and, especially, at weekends, when two-night minimum stays are commonly required. In the lowest seasons (early November, late January), midrange options sometimes give big

Bruges

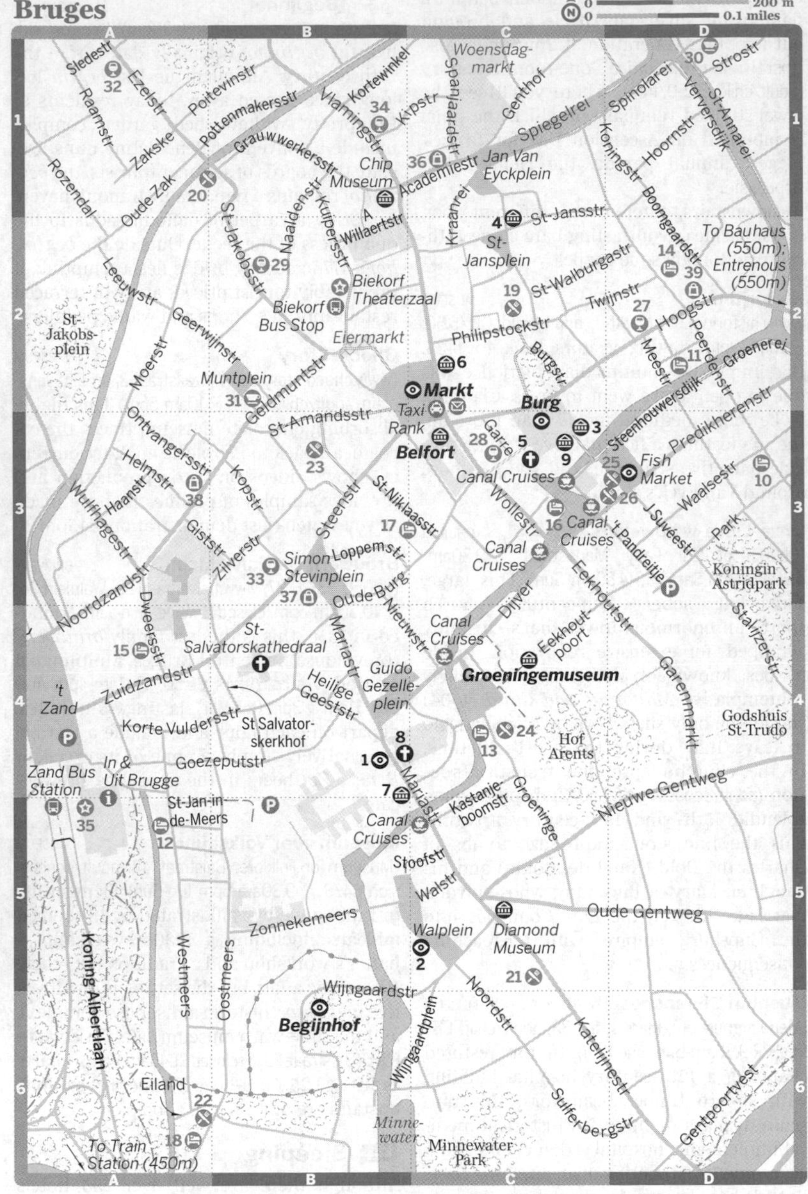

last-minute discounts. An all-night touchscreen computer outside the main tourist office displays hotel availability and contact information, and www.brugge.be has a booking engine.

TOP CHOICE **Guesthouse Nuit Blanche** B&B €€€
(☎0494 40 04 47; www.bruges-bb.com; Groeninge 2; d €175-195) Step into a Van Eyck painting where original Gothic fireplaces and period furniture cunningly hide an array of modern fittngs. The historic house once hosted

Bruges

Top Sights	
Begijnhof	B6
Belfort	C3
Burg	C3
Groeningemuseum	C4
Markt	C2

Sights	
1 Apotheek	B4
2 Brouwerij De Halve Maan	C5
3 Brugse Vrije	C3
4 Choco-Story	C2
Gotische Zaal	(see 9)
5 Heilig-Bloedbasiliek	C3
6 Historium	C2
7 Museum St-Janshospitaal	B4
8 Onze-Lieve-Vrouwekerk	B4
9 Stadhuis	C3

Sleeping	
10 B&B Dieltiens	D3
11 B&B Huyze Hertsberge	D2
12 Baert B&B	A5
13 Guesthouse Nuit Blanche	C4
14 Hotel Patritius	D2
15 Passage Bruges	A4
16 Relais Bourgondisch Cruyce	C3
17 St-Niklaas B&B	B3
18 't Keizershof	A6

Eating	
19 Cambrinus	C2
20 De Bottelier	A1
21 De Bron	C5
22 De Stoepa	A6
23 De Stove	B3
24 Den Gouden Harynck	C4
25 Den Gouden Karpel	D3
26 Est Wijnbar	D3

Drinking	
27 Charlie Rockets	D2
28 De Garre	C3
29 De Republiek	B2
30 Herberg Vlissinghe	D1
31 Merveilleux Tearoom	B2
32 Snuffel Hostel	A1
33 't Brugs Beertje	B3
34 't Poatersgat	B1

Entertainment	
35 Concertgebouw	A5

Shopping	
2-Be	(see 16)
36 Bacchus Cornelius	C1
37 Chocolate Line	B3
38 L'Héroïne	A3
39 Madam Mim	D2

Churchill as well as Belgian royalty. Room rates cover the bottle of bubbly in your minibar. Drink it in the fabulous canalside garden or on 'Lovers' Bridge' to which the guesthouse has a unique private entrance.

B&B Huyze Hertsberge B&B €€€
(☎050 33 35 42; www.bruges-bedandbreakfast.be; Hertsbergestraat 8; r €150-165) Very spacious and oozing with good taste, this late-17th-century house has a gorgeous period salon decked with antiques and sepia photos of the charming owner's great-great-grandparents (who first moved in here in 1901). The four guest rooms are comfortably grand, each with at least partial views of the tranquil little canalside garden.

Relais Bourgondisch Cruyce BOUTIQUE HOTEL €€€
(☎050 33 79 26; www.relaisbourgondischcruyce.be; Wollestraat 41-47; d €185-375) This luxurious little boutique hotel occupies a unique part-timbered medieval house graced with art, antiques, Persian carpets and fresh orchids. Relax in the canalside lounge while tourists cruise past on barge tours. Most rooms are somewhat small but full of designer fittings, including top-quality Vispring beds, Ralph Lauren fabrics and (in some) Philippe Starck bathrooms.

B&B Dieltiens B&B €€
(☎050 33 42 94; www.bedandbreakfastbruges.be; Waalsestraat 40; s €60-80, d €70-90) Old and new art fills this lovingly restored classical mansion, which remains an appealingly real home run by charming musician hosts. Superbly central yet quiet.

Baert B&B B&B €€
(☎050 33 05 30; www.bedandbreakfastbrugge.be; Westmeers 28; s/d €75/85) In a 1613 former stable this is one of very few places in Bruges that you'll get a private canalside terrace -- adorably flower-decked, though not on the loveliest canal section. Floral rooms have bathrooms across the landing; bathrobes are provided. A big breakfast spread is served in

a glass verandah, and extras include a welcome drink and a pack of chocolates.

St-Niklaas B&B B&B €€
(050 61 03 08; www.sintnik.be; St-Niklaasstraat 18; s €95-115, d €120-145;) Room 1 has a clawfoot bath and antique glass panel, but it's the other two rooms' remarkable Pisa-like belfry views that make this welcoming B&B so special and popular.

Hotel Patritius HOTEL €€
(050 33 84 54; www.hotelpatritius.be; Riddersstraat 11; d €70-130, tr €134-155, q €160-180;) Enter this proud 1830s townhouse through the tall carriageway and past a little bar-lounge. Up the historic spiral staircase, 16 guest rooms vary quite radically in size and style, some with exposed beams, others mildly chintzy and some renovated in bolder style (albeit with oddly kitschy dog portraiture). Pretty garden.

Hobo B&B B&B €€
(050 34 14 65; www.hobo-bedandbreakfast.be; Ganzenstraat 54; s/d €65/70;) Unpretentiously charming, real-home B&B where the Laura Ashley–esque 'Romantic Room' (up some steep stairs) has a private bathroom. The smarter 'B&W' and mildly nautical 'Blue' rooms have their own showers but share a toilet. Generous breakfasts served amid a decor of danging cutlery.

't Keizershof HOTEL €
(050 33 87 28; www.hotelkeizershof.be; Oostermeers 126; s €25-44, d €45;) Remarkably tasteful and well kept for this price, the seven simple rooms with shared bathrooms are above a former brasserie-cafe decorated with old radios (now used as the breakfast room). Free parking.

Bauhaus HOSTEL €
(050 34 10 93; www.bauhaus.be; Langestraat 145; hostel dm/tw €16/50, hotel s/d €16/50, 2-4 person apt per weekend from €240;) Almost a backpacker 'village', Bauhaus incorporates a bustling hostel, apartments, a nightclub, internet cafe, bike rental and laundrette. There are simple and slightly cramped dorms; hotel-section double rooms have private shower cubicles. The bar-restaurant (Sacré Coeur) is excellent except when you're trying to sleep above it. Take bus 6 or 16 from the train station.

Passage Bruges HOSTEL €€
(050 34 02 32; www.passagebruges.com; Dweersstraat 26-28; dm €16, d €67, without bathroom €52) This recently renovated hostel has dorms above an invitingly old-fashioned cafe-restaurant. The next-door building houses spartan but large and well-priced hotel rooms.

Ibis Budget CHAIN HOTEL €
(050-40 51 20; Marie Popelinplantsoen 4, Bruges Station; r €46-70;) This new, 184-room hotel has retro fittings that are unexpectedly hip for a budget chain. Reception is attended 24 hours. Wi-fi extra.

Eating

Touristy terraces crowd the Markt and line pedestrianised St-Amandsstraat where there are many cheaper eateries. Along eclectic Langestraat (the eastward extension of Hoogstraat), you'll find everything from kebabs to Michelin stars. About town, numerous taverns and bakeries serve snacks and several hostels offer great meal deals.

TOP CHOICE **De Stove** GASTRONOMIC €€
(050 33 78 35; www.restaurantdestove.be; Kleine St-Amandsstraat 4; mains €19-33, menu without/with wine €48/64; noon-1.30pm Sat & Sun, 7-9pm Fri-Tue) Despite perennial rave reviews, this calm, one-room family restaurant remains friendly, reliable and inventive, without a hint of tourist-twee-ness. The monthly changing menu often favours fresh fish. Almost everything is homemade, from the bread to the ice cream.

Den Gouden Harynck GASTRONOMIC €€€
(050 33 76 37; www.dengoudenharynck.be; Groeninge 25; mains €38-45, set lunch menu €39, 4-/5-course menu €75/89; lunch & dinner Tue-Sat) Behind an ivy-clad facade, this uncluttered Michelin-starred restaurant garners consistent praise and won't hurt the purse quite as severely as certain better-known competitors. A lovely location: both central and secluded.

TOP CHOICE **In 't Nieuwe Museum** BROWN CAFE €€
(050 33 12 22; Hooistraat 42; mains €16-22; noon-2pm & 6-10pm Thu-Tue, closed lunch Sat) This family-owned local favourite is so-called because of the museum-like collection of brewery plaques and money boxes. It serves great value lunches (€7 to €12.50) and dinners of succulent meat cooked at a 17th-century open fireplace along with vegie burgers, eel dishes and creamy *vispannetje* (fish casserole).

To find it follow Hoogstraat/Langestraat west past the famous **de Karmeliet**, then turn right and walk one block down Ganzenstraat.

De Bottelier MEDITERRANEAN €€
(☎050 33 18 60; www.debottelier.com; St-Jakobsstraat 63; pasta/veg dishes from €9/13.50, mains from €16; ⏲lunch & dinner Tue-Fri, dinner Sat) Decorated with hats and old clocks, this adorable little restaurant sits above a wine shop overlooking a delightful handkerchief of canalside garden. Local diners predominate; reservations recommended.

De Stoepa BISTRO €€
(☎050 33 04 54; www.stoepa.be; Oostmeers 124; ⏲noon-2pm & 6pm-midnight Tues-Sat, noon-3pm & 6pm-11pm Sun) A gem of a place in a peaceful residential setting with a slightly hippy/Buddhist feel. Oriental statues, terracotta-coloured walls, a metal stove and wooden floors and furniture give a homely but chic feel. Best of all, though, is the leafy terrace garden and the upmarket bistro-style food.

Est Wijnbar TAPAS €
(☎050 33 38 39; www.wijnbarest.be; Braambergstraat 7; mains €9.50-12.50, tapas €3.50-9.50; ⏲4pm-midnight Wed-Sun; ☑) In a 1637 building, this attractive little wine bar is especially convivial on Sunday's acoustic music nights but it's a pleasantly informal supper spot any evening with raclette, pasta, snacks and salads dominating the menu.

Den Gouden Karpel SEAFOOD €
(☎050 33 33 89; www.dengoudenkarpel.be; Vismarkt 9-11; ⏲11am-6pm Tues-Sat) Takeaway or eat in, this sleek little cafe-bar is a great location for a jumpingly fresh seafood lunch, right by the fish market.

Cambrinus BEER PUB €€
(☎050 33 23 28; www.cambrinus.eu; Philipstockstraat 19; ⏲11am-11pm Sun-Thu, to late Fri & Sat) This 17th-century sculpture-adorned brasserie/pub is a tourist favourite for traditional Belgian- and Italian-inspired snacks as well as good-value menus that help soak up the hundreds of varieties of beer.

De Bron VEGETARIAN €
(☎050 33 45 26; Katelijnestraat 82; ⏲11.45am-2pm Mon-Fri; ☑) Neat, tidy, glass-roofed place for vegetarian soups and lunch-of-the-day. Vegan options on request.

Drinking

Hostels Bauhaus, Passage Bruges, **Charlie Rockets** (☎050 33 06 60; www.charlierockets.com; Hoogstraat 19; ⏲8am-4am) and **Snuffel** (www.snuffel.be) all have congenial backpacker-oriented pubs, most serving decent yet inexpensive food. Eiermarkt, just north of Markt, has many plain but lively bars, with DJs and seemingly endless happy hours.

TOP CHOICE **'t Brugs Beertje** BEER PUB
(www.brugsbeertje.be; Kemelstraat 5; ⏲4pm-1am Thu-Tue) Legendary for its hundreds of Belgian brews, this cosy brown cafe is one of those perfect beer bars with smoke-yellowed walls, enamel signs, hop-sprig ceilings and knowledgeable staff to help you choose from a book full of brews.

TOP CHOICE **Herberg Vlissinghe** HISTORIC CAFE
(☎050 34 37 37; www.cafevlissinghe.be; Blekerstraat 2; ⏲11am-10pm Wed-Sat, to 7pm Sun) First opened in 1515, this is where, according to local legend, Rubens once painted an imitation coin on the table then did a runner. The interior is gorgeously preserved.

De Garre BEER PUB
(☎050 34 10 29; www.degarre.be; Garre 1; ⏲noon-midnight) This hidden two-floor *estaminet* (tavern) stocks dozens of fine Belgian brews, including remarkable Struise Pannepot (€3.50), but don't miss the pub's fabulous 11% Garre house beer, which comes with a thick floral head in a glass that's almost a brandy balloon.

't Poatersgat PUB
(www.poatersgat.com; Vlaamingstraat 82; ⏲5pm-late) Look carefully for the concealed 'Monk's hole' in the wall and follow the staircase down into this cross-vaulted cellar glowing with ethereal white lights and flickering candles.

Merveilleux Tearoom TEAROOM
(☎050 61 02 09; www.merveilleux.eu; Muntpoort 8; high tea €10, mains €15-22; ⏲10am-6pm) Elegant marble-floored tearoom on a cobbled passage near the Markt.

De Republiek PUB
(www.derepubliek.be; St-Jakobsstraat 36; ⏲11am-late) Set around a courtyard of characterful brick buildings, this big, buzzing space is superpopular with locals. DJs hit the decks

on weekend nights and there's food available till midnight. Long cocktail list.

☆ Entertainment

Cultuurcentrum Brugge THEATRE
(☎info 050 44 30 40, tickets 050 44 30 60; www.ccbrugge.be) Coordinates theatrical and concert events at several venues.

Concertgebouw CONCERT HALL
(☎050 47 69 99; www.concertgebouw.be; 't Zand 34; tickets from €10) Theatre, classical music and dance are regularly staged in this very conspicuous 21st-century concert hall. Its architectural design cues supposedly come from the city's famous towers and red bricks.

Cactus Muziekcentrum LIVE MUSIC
(☎050 33 20 14; www.cactusmusic.be; Magdalenastraat 27) Venue for contemporary and world music, live bands and DJs. It also organises festivals including July's **Cactus Music Festival** (www.cactusfestival.be), held in Minnewater park.

Entrenous CLUB
(☎050 34 10 93; www.bauhauszaal.be; Langestraat 145; ⏲10pm-late Fri & Sat) Nightclub catering to a very youthful crowd, with DJ nights, gigs and afterparties.

Shopping

TOP CHOICE **'t Apostelientje** LACE
(www.apostelientje.be; Balstraat 11; ⏲1-5pm Tue, 9.30am-12.15pm & 1.15-5pm Wed-Sat, 10am-1pm Sun) Bruges overflows with lace vendors, but this sweet little 'museum shop' is authentic and well off the normal tourist trail.

TOP CHOICE **Chocolate Line** CHOCOLATE
(www.thechocolateline.be; Simon Stevinplein 19; per kg €50; ⏲10am-6pm) 'Shock-o-latier' Dominique Persoone is famous for using wildly experimental flavours and creating novel new products, from chocolate body paint to nasal choco-shots.

2-Be FOOD, DRINK
(www.2-be.biz; Wollestraat 53; ⏲10am-7pm) Vast range of Belgian products, from beers to biscuits. Prices can be steep but its 'beer wall' is worth a look, and the canalside bar terrace serves 'monster' 3L draught beers that are surely Belgium's biggest.

Bacchus Cornelius BEER
(www.bacchuscornelius.com; Academiestraat 17; ⏲1-6.30pm) Around 450 beers, plus flavoured *jenevers* and liqueurs to take home. Two pianos to play and a winter fireplace make things cosy for shoppers.

Madam Mim FASHION, ANTIQUES
(www.madammim.be; Hoogstraat 29; ⏲11am-6pm Wed-Mon) Joys here include quirky clothes handmade from vintage fabrics, '60s crockery, glorious hats and well-priced vintage lace.

L'Héroïne DESIGNER FASHION
(www.lheroine.be; Noordzandstraat 32; ⏲Mon-Sat) Discreet little high-fashion boutique representing a handful of Belgium's top designers.

Information

The tourist office, **In & Uit Brugge** (☎050 44 46 46; www.brugge.be; 't Zand 34; ⏲10am-6pm Mon-Sun), is situated at street level of the Concertgebouw with a branch at the train station. Standard city maps cost €0.50, comprehensive guide pamphlets €2. Excellent *Use-It* guide-maps (www.use-it.be) are free if you ask for one.

Bruggecentraal (www.bruggecentraal.be) has events listings.

Getting There & Away

Bruges' train station is about 1.5km south of the Markt, a lovely walk via the Begijnhof. It offers the following services:

Antwerp (€14.25, 75 minutes) Twice hourly.

Brussels (€14, one hour) Twice hourly.

Ghent (€6.20, fast/slow 24/42 minutes) Five hourly to Ghent-St-Peters, two continue to more central Gent-Dampoort.

Ypres (Ieper in Dutch) Take a train to Roeselare (€4.50, fast/slow 22/33 minutes), then bus 94 or 95: both buses pass key WWI sites en route.

Getting Around

BICYCLE B-Bike (☎0499 70 50 99; Zand Parking 26; per hr/day €4/12; ⏲10am-7pm Apr-Oct)

Quasimundo (☎050 33 07 75; www.quasimundo.eu; adult/student €25/23; ⏲approx Mar-Oct) Guided bicycle tours around Bruges (2½ hours, morning) or via Damme to the Dutch border (four hours, afternoons). Bike rental included. Book ahead.

Rijwielhandel Erik Popelier (☎050 34 32 62; www.fietsenpopelier.be; Mariastraat 26; per hr/half-/full day €4/8/12, tandem per hr/half-/full day €10/17/25; ⏲10am-6pm) Good bicycles for adults and kids; helmets for hire, free map, no deposit.

BOAT A classic way to see and 'feel' Bruges from new angles, **Canal Tours** (adult/child €7.60/3.40; ⏲10am-6pm Mar–mid-Nov) are a must for many visitors. Boats depart roughly every 20 minutes from various jetties, taking 30 minutes.

BUS To get from the train station to Markt, take any bus marked 'Centrum'. For the way back, buses stop at Biekorf, just northwest of Markt on Kuiperstraat.

HORSE-DRAWN CARRIAGE Up to five people per carriage (€39) on a well-trodden, 35-minute route from the Markt. Includes a five-minute nosebag stop near the Begijnhof.

Around Bruges

Historic, quaint but often tourist-jammed, the inland port-village of **Damme** (www.toerismedamme.be) makes a popular summer excursion by canal **paddle steamer** (adult/child one way €7.50/5.50, return €10/8; ⏲10am-5pm Easter–mid-Oct), departing every two hours from Bruges' Noorweegse Kaai (bus 4 from Markt). Consider cycling instead: it's only 5km and, by continuing 2km further along the idyllic canal, you'll escape from the worst of the visitor overload. If you're still energetic, consider then heading 10km northwest via Dudzele and **Hof Ter Doest** (www.terdoest.be) to sweet little **Lissewege** (www.lissewege.be), an artists' village from which hourly trains return to Bruges.

Quasimodo (☎050 37 04 70; www.quasimodo.be; adult/under-26 €62.50/52.50) visits most of these by minibus on its **Triple Treat tours** (under/over 26yr €45/55; ⏲9am Mon, Wed & Fri Feb–mid-Dec), adding castles at **Loppem** and **Tillegem** and fascinating **WWII coastal defences** near Ostend. The same company's **Flanders Fields tours** (under/over 26yr €45/55; ⏲9am Tue-Sun Apr-Oct) visit Ypres Salient.

Ypres

POP 35,100

Especially when viewed from the southeast, the Grote Markt of Ypres (Ieper in Dutch, pronounced 'eepr' in French and English) is one of the most breathtaking market squares in Flanders. It's all the more astonishing once you discover that virtually all of its convincingly 'medieval' buildings are in fact 20th-century copies. The originals had been brutally bombarded into oblivion between 1914 and 1918 when the historic city failed to capitulate to German WWI advances. WWI battles in the surrounding poppy fields, known as the Ypres Salient, killed hundreds of thousands of soldiers. A century later, countless lovingly tended cemeteries remain, along with numerous widely spread WWI-based museums and trench remnants. Together they present a thoroughly moving introduction to the horrors and futility of war.

WWI GRAVESITE SEARCHES

If your relative died in the region's WWI battles, Ypres bookshops offer a grave finding service or you can look for yourself online:

American www.abmc.gov

British & Commonwealth www.cwgc.org

French www.memoiredeshommes.sga.defense.gouv.fr

German www.volksbund.de

Sights

CENTRAL YPRES

Grote Markt SQUARE

The brilliantly rebuilt **Lakenhallen**, a vast Gothic edifice originally serving as the 13th-century cloth market, dominates this very photogenic central square. It sports a 70m-high belfry, reminiscent of London's Big Ben, and hosts the gripping museum **In Flanders Fields** (www.inflandersfields.be; Lakenhalle, Grote Markt 34; adult/child €8/1; ⏲10am-6pm Apr–mid-Nov, 10am-5pm Tue-Sun mid-Nov–Mar), a highly recommended multimedia WWI experience honouring ordinary people's experiences of wartime horrors. The ticket allows free entry to three other minor city museums.

Menin Gate MEMORIAL

(Menenpoort) A block east of Grote Markt, this huge stone gateway straddles the main road at the city moat. It's inscribed with the names of 54,896 'lost' British and other Commonwealth WWI troops whose bodies were never found.

Last Post CEREMONY

(www.lastpost.be; ⏲8pm daily) At 8pm, traffic through the Menin Gate is halted while buglers sound the *Last Post* in remembrance of the WWI dead, a moving tradition started in 1928. Every evening the scene is different, possibly accompanied by pipers, troops of cadets or maybe a military band.

YPRES SALIENT

Many Salient sites are awkward to reach without a car or tour bus, but the following are all within 600m of Ypres–Roeselare bus routes 94 and 95 (once or twice hourly on weekdays, five daily on weekends), so could be visited en route to or from Bruges.

Memorial Museum Passchendaele 1917 MUSEUM
(www.passchendaele.be; Ieperstraat 5; admission €5; ⌚10am-6pm Feb-Nov; 🚌94) In central **Zonnebeke village** (www.zonnebeke.be), a lake-fronted Normandy chalet-style mansion (built 1922) now hosts an impressive WWI museum charting local battle progressions with plenty of multilingual commentaries. The big attraction here is descending into its multiroom 'trench experience' with low-lit wooden-clad subterranean bunk rooms and a soundtrack to add wartime atmosphere. Entirely indoors, explanations are much more helpful here than in 'real' trenches elsewhere.

FREE **Tyne Cot** CEMETERY
(⌚24hr, visitor centre 9am-6pm Feb-Nov; 🚌94) With 11,956 graves, this is the world's biggest British Commonwealth war cemetery, and a huge semicircular wall commemorates another 34,857 lost-in-action soldiers whose names wouldn't fit on Ypres' Menin Gate. The name Tyne Cot was coined by Northumberland Fusiliers who fancied that German bunkers on the hillside here looked like Tyneside cottages. Three such dumpy concrete bunkers still sit amid the graves here. Bus 94 stops 600m away.

FREE **Deutscher Soldatenfriedhof** CEMETERY
The area's main German WWI cemetery is smaller than Tyne Cot but arguably more memorable, amid oak trees and trios of squat, mossy crosses. Some 44,000 corpses were grouped together here, up to 10 per granite grave slab and four eerie silhouette statues survey the site. Entering takes you through a black concrete 'tunnel' that clanks and hisses with distant war sounds, while four short video-montages commemorate the tragedy of war. It's beyond the northern edge of Langemark on bus route 95.

Tours

There are dozens more WWI sites to seek out. Two bookshops towards Menin Gate sell a range of useful guidebooks and specialist publications and each offer twice-daily, half-day guided minibus tours of selected war sites (advance booking suggested):

Over the Top BOOKSHOP, TOURS
(☎0472 34 87 47; www.overthetoptours.be; Meensestraat 41; ⌚9am-12.30pm, 1.30-5.30pm & 7.30-8.30pm)

British Grenadier BOOKSHOP, TOURS
(☎057 21 46 57; www.salienttours.be; Meensestraat 5; ⌚9.30am-1pm, 2-6pm & 7.30-8.30pm)

Sleeping

The nearest youth hostel is located in Kortrijk, 30 minutes away by train.

TOP CHOICE **Main Street Hotel** GUESTHOUSE €€€
(☎057 46 96 33; www.mainstreet-hotel.be; Rijselsestraat 136; d €140-200; 📶) Combining funky eccentricity with historical twists and luxurious comfort, this is a one-off that simply oozes character. The smallest room is designed like a mad professor's experiment, the breakfast room has a Tiffany glass ceiling... and so it goes on!

Ariane Hotel HOTEL €€
(☎057 21 82 18; www.ariane.be; Slachthuisstraat 58; s/d from €94/120; P📶) This peaceful, professionally managed larger hotel has a designer feel to the rooms and popular restaurant. Wartime memorabilia dots the spacious common areas.

Yoaké B&B B&B €€
(☎057 20 35 14; www.yoake-ieper.be/bedhome.htm; Tempelstraat 35; d from €80; ❄📶) Smart two-room B&B attached to a hip wellness centre.

B&B Ter Thuyne B&B €€
(☎057 36 00 42; www.terthuyne.be; Gustave de Stuersstraat 19; d €85; @) Three comfortable rooms that are luminously bright and scrupulously clean but not overly fashion conscious.

Hotel Regina HOTEL €€
(☎057 21 88 88; www.hotelregina.be; Grote Markt 45; s/d from €70/85; 📶) Location, location, location. You can forgive the sometimes dated decor to be right on the central square overlooking the Lakenhalle. Friendly staff, decent food.

Eating & Drinking

De Ruyffelaer FLEMISH €€
(☎057 36 60 06; www.deruyffelaer.be; Gustave de Stuersstraat 9; mains €13-19, menus €24-33;

WORTH A TRIP

BEER COUNTRY

Dotted with windmills, the almost pan-flat hop fields north and west of Ypres produce many of Belgium's most sought-after beers, and Poperinge has a **Hop Museum** (☎057 33 79 22; www.hopmuseum.be; Gasthuisstraat 71; adult/under 26yr €5/2.50; ⏲10am-6pm Tue-Fri, 2pm-6pm Sat, 10am-noon & 2-6pm Sun, closed Dec-Feb). **De Dolle** (www.dedollebrouwers.be; ⏲brewery visits 2pm Sun) creates Oerbier at Esen near attractive Diksmuide, which, like Ypres, had its historic core totally rebuilt after WWI. Watou is known for the full-flavoured **St-Bernardus** (www.sintbernardus.be). Like liquid alcoholic chocolate, extraordinary **Pannepot** (www.struise.noordhoek.com/eng) is often available to take-away from the dreary-looking Deca Brewery in Woesten on the windmill-dotted road between Ypres and the gorgeous medieval town of Veurne. The 'holy grail' of Trappist beers, Westvleteren 12°, is often cited as the world's best brew but the only place you can reliably taste its fruity complexity is at the isolated bar **In de Vrede** (www.indevrede.be; Donkerstraat 13; ⏲10am-8pm Sat-Wed) opposite **Abdij St-Sixtus** (www.sintsixtus.be; St Sixtus Abbey; ⏲closed to visitors) where it's brewed. It's not available for takeaway without (very awkward) prebooking.

⏲11.30am-3.30pm Sun, 5.30-9.30pm Thu-Sun) Traditional local dishes are served in an adorable, wood-panelled interior with old checkerboard floors and a *brocante* decor, including dried flowers, old radios and antique biscuit tins.

In 't Klein Stadhuis PUB, RESTAURANT €€
(www.inketkleinstadhuis.be; Grote Markt 32; snacks €8.50-14, mains €16-27; ⏲11am-midnight, kitchen until 10.30pm) Tucked away in a quirkily decorated historic guildhall beside the Stadhuis, this split-level cafe serves gigantic, good-value meals, including some beer-based recipes.

De Vage Belofte PUB
(www.facebook.com/devagebelofte; Vismarkt 3; ⏲4pm-late Tue-Sun) A piano hangs on the two-storey inner wall above a row of champagne bottles, summer tables spill out across appealing Vismarkt, and DJs turn the tables on weekend nights.

ℹ Information

The well-equipped tourist office **Tourist Office** (☎057 23 92 20; www.ieper.be; Grote Markt 34; ⏲9am-6pm) is within the Lakenhallen.

ℹ Getting There & Around

BICYCLE Rent bicycles from **Hotel Ambrosia** (☎057 36 63 66; www.ambrosiahotel.be; D'Hondtstraat 54; standard/electric bike per day €12/35; ⏲7.30am-7pm).

BUS Services pick up passengers in Grote Markt's northeast corner (check the direction carefully!). For Bruges take Roeselare-bound routes 94 or 95 then change to train.

TRAIN Services run hourly to Ghent (€11, one hour) and Brussels (€16.75, 1¾ hours) via Kortrijk (€5, 30 minutes), where you could change for Bruges or Antwerp.

WALLONIA

Tournai

POP 68,000

Pleasant Tournai (Doornik in Dutch) is Wallonia's oldest city. It was battered by WWII bombs, but the very photogenic **Grand Place** has since been convincingly rebuilt. Tournai's skyline is dominated by the five iconic spires of the sober **Cathédrale Notre Dame** (Pl de l'Évêché; admission free; ⏲9.30am-noon & 2-6pm Apr-Oct, to 5pm Nov-Mar). Despite all the scaffolding, its interior remains a fascinating textbook example of evolving architectural styles, from the magnificent Romanesque nave through a curious bridging transept into an early Gothic choir. It's a Unesco World Heritage site, as is the 72m-high **belfry** (adult/concession €2/1; ⏲9.30am-12.15pm & 2-4.15pm Tue-Sun), Belgium's oldest. Facing the belfry, the **Tourist Office** (☎069 22 20 45; www.tournai.be; Vieux Marché aux Poteries 14; ⏲8.30am-5.30pm Mon-Fri, 10am-noon & 2-5pm Sat & Sun) can point you towards a cache of enjoyable museums (free first Sunday of each month), several of which are clustered near the friendly HI Hostel **Auberge de Jeunesse** (☎069 21 61 36; www.laj.be; Rue St-Martin 64; dm/s/d €23/36.50/54.75, HI members save €3; ⏲check-in 5-10pm), 400m

ON THE ROAD IN WALLONIA

If you take public transport you'll spend longer reaching most of the Wallonia's rural sites than actually enjoying them. But by car, combining a handful of destinations can make for a very enjoyable day out. For in-depth coverage, see Lonely Planet's *Belgium & Luxembourg*.

Kayaking & Outdoor Activities

Durbuy (www.durbuyinfo.be) The 'world's smallest town' is quaint, if touristy, and is well set up for all manner of sporting fun. Plenty of hotels.

La Roche-en-Ardenne (www.ardenne-aventures.be) Water sports and mountain biking from a charmingly compact town nestled around a medieval castle ruin.

Coo (www.coo-adventure.com) The hamlet's famous 15m 'waterfall' is underwhelming but outdoor options are numerous and there's a family **amusement park** (www.plopsa.be). Accommodation is limited in Coo but is more plentiful in nearby Stavelot.

Caves

Belgium's publicly accessible cave systems each have their own character. Visits take over an hour with set departure times that vary seasonally (check websites). There's no 'escape' once you've started so don't forget appropriate footwear, warm clothes and a pre-emptive bathroom stop.

Han-sur-Lesse (www.grotte-de-han.be) Belgium's foremost stalactite-rich caves are accessed by a little train ride then guided walk. Gets very busy in summer.

Rochefort (www.valdelesse.be) The Grotte de Lorette, remarkable for its depth more than its stalagmites, is walking distance from attractive Rochefort, famous for its Trappist beers and offering a good choice of accommodation.

Hotton (www.grottesdehotton.com) Great grottoes and a jaw-dropping vertical subterranean chasm, yet relatively uncommercial.

Remouchamps (www.grottes.be) Lacks the drama of the three 'greats' above, but you get to ride an underground river in a boat.

Castles

Wallonia's capital **Namur** (www.namurtourisme.be) is dominated by a massive, sober fortified **citadel** (www.citadelle.namur.be; admission free), but the region has many more romantic castles, including the following:

Château de Jehay (www.chateaujehay.be; adult/student €5/2.50, audio guide €1; ⌚2-6pm Tue-Fri, 11am-6pm Sat & Sun Apr-Sep) A gingerbread fantasy (dating from 1550) of alternating brick and stone layers rising from a tree-ringed moat. The interior is under reconstruction.

Château de Modave (www.modave-castle.be; adult/child €7.50/free; ⌚10am-5pm Tue-Sun Apr–mid-Nov) Palatial chateau with 20 majestically furnished rooms and 17th-century stucco ceilings.

Château de Lavaux-Sainte-Anne (www.chateau-lavaux.com; adult/child €7/5; ⌚9am-5.30pm Wed-Sun, last entry 4.15pm) Partly furnished moated fortress (dating from 1450) visible west of the E411 motorway as you pass junction 22a just 10km from Han-sur-Lesse.

Bouillon (☎061 46 42 02; www.bouillon-initiative.be; Rue du Château; adult/child €6.50/4.50; ⌚10am-7pm Jul & Aug, to 5pm Mar-Jun & Sep-Nov, shorter hs in winte ; Ⓟ👪) Attractive town dominated by a central crusader castle ruin that once belonged to the 'Belgian' conqueror of Jerusalem. While there do drive or kayak the lovely Semois Valley overlooked by panoramic viewpoints at **Rochehaut** and **Tombeau du Géant**.

southwest. Central, though hidden, the likeable **Hôtel d'Alcantara** (069 21 26 48; www.hotelalcantara.be; Rue des Bouchers St-Jacques 2; s €88-108, d €98-118;) experiments semi-successfully with '70s-retro design within a regal old townhouse.

The train station is 1km northeast of the centre. Connections include Brussels (€12.25, fast/slow 61/73 minutes), Mons (€6.90, fast/slow 23/43 minutes) and Lille-Flandres (€6.50, 25 minutes). The latter connection makes Tournai a useful staging point if you're trying to reach Lille (France) from Brussels without high-speed train supplements/bookings.

Mons

POP 93,100

Historic Mons (Bergen in Dutch) is being smartened up for its role as European City of Culture in 2015, and its new **gallery** (www.bam.mons.be) is planning to host a major Van Gogh exhibition. Till then, highlights include the 80m baroque belfry (Beffroi), the oversized 15th-century church of **Ste-Waudru** (www.waudru.be; Place du Chapitre; 9am-6pm) and the attractive Grand Place. This great square comes to life on Trinity Sunday when the festivities of the Ducasse (www.ducasse demons), reach a raucous culmination with a George-versus-the-dragon battle.

The **Hôtel St James** (065 72 48 24; www.hotelstjames.be; Place de Flandre 8; r €73-83;) offers good-value accommodation, and for an unforgettable dinner in 17th-century style don't miss the **Salon des Lumières** (0474 29 25 84; www.salondeslumieres.com; Rue du Mirroir 23; mains €16.50-20; 7-10pm Wed-Sun, from 6pm winter).

Liège

POP 195,600

Beneath its brutally disfigured, post-industrial surface, sprawling Liège (Luik in Dutch) is a living architectural onion concealing layer upon layer of history. Fine churches abound, as befits a city that spent 800 years as the capital of an independent principality run by bishops. Proudly free-spirited citizens are disarmingly friendly and no Belgian city bubbles with more joie de vivre.

The somewhat grimy historic zone has several excellent museums. The **Grand Curtius** (www.grandcurtiusliege.be; Féronstrée 136; adult/child €9/free; 10am-6pm Wed-Mon) presents a millennium's development of decorative arts. Art gallery **Musée de l'Art Wallon** (Rue St-Georges; adult/child €5/free; 11am-6pm Tue-Sat, 11am-6pm Sun) is richly endowed, if architecturally hideous.

Love it or loathe it, Liège is quirky and oddly compulsive, especially during its chaotic August 15th festival, held just across the river in the self-declared 'republic' of Outremeuse, where there's a handy HI Hostel. The most appealing central accommodation options are the cosy little **Hôtel Hors Château** (04-250 60 68; www.hors-chateau.be; Rue Hors Château 62; s/d/ste €78/95/125;) and the awesome new **Crowne Plaza** (04-222 94 94; www.crowneplazaliege.be; Mont St-Martin 9; €109-690). For real Liègois food, dine at **Amon Nanesse** (www.maisondupeket.be; Rue de l'Epée 4; meals €10.50-18.50; 10am-2am, kitchen noon-2.30pm & 6-10.30pm).

Liège's great archtectural masterpiece is its 21st-century Guillermins train station, shaped vaguely like a giant concrete manta-ray. That's on the Brussels–Frankfurt mainline, though Liège-Palais station is far more central.

Bastogne

POP 15,100

In late 1944 Allied forces were sweeping east across Europe. But WWII wasn't yet over. Hitler's last gasp was a midwinter counter-attack that devastated the Ardennes and nearby Luxembourg, creating a 'bulge' in the Allied frontline. During this pivotal 'Battle of the Bulge', plucky Bastogne (www.paysdebastogne.be) was surrounded but refused to capitulate, the defending US commander McAuliffe responding to German surrender demands with a single word: 'Nuts!' Today the town isn't lovely, but it's a must-see for WWII buffs. Of numerous WWII museums, Bastogne's best is **J'avais 20 ans en '45** (061 50 20 02; www.bastogne.be/20ansen45; adult/child €6.50/5; 10am-6pm, closed Fri Oct-Apr, last entry 5pm), an imaginative exhibition giving movingly balanced insights into the conflict through dozens of eyewitness video accounts. A big new **war museum** (www.bastognewarmuseum.be) is under construction on a gentle hilltop 1.5km further northeast at Mardasson, beside a big star-shaped **American War Memorial**.

Right on Bastogne's main square, the warm and friendly **Hôtel Collin** (☎061 21 48 88; www.hotel-collin.com; Place McAuliffe 8; s/d/€70/90) is a pleasant family hotel with a pseudo-art-nouveau cafe and a Mediterranean-styled restaurant.

Bus 163b (45 minutes) runs every two hours to Libramont on the Brussels–Luxembourg train line. Buses also run hourly (except Sundays) to Ettelbrück (one hour) in Luxembourg.

LUXEMBOURG

Ruled by its own monarchy, the Grand Duchy of Luxembourg is famed for its banks but visually is mostly an undulating series of pretty wooded hills dotted with castle villages. These are made easily accessible from the highly attractive capital city by excellent roads and a very-well-organised single-price public transport system (p146).

Luxembourg City

POP 100,000

World Heritage–listed Luxembourg City sits high on a promontory overlooking the deep-cut valleys of the Pétrusse and Alzette Rivers. For a thousand years these gorges were the key to the city's defence. Originating in AD 963 when Count Sigefroi (or Siegfried) of Ardennes built a castle here, Luxembourg grew to become one of Europe's strongest fortresses, earning the nickname 'Gibraltar of the North'. In 1867 the majority of the fortifications were removed as part of a treaty to reduce tensions between France and Germany, though a remarkable mass of bastion remnants and tunnels survive, providing visitors with spectacular viewpoints overlooking the interesting old quarters of Clausen, Pfaffenthal and the Grund.

Sights

OLD TOWN

Within the compact, mostly pedestrianised Old Town all sights are walking distance from each other. Access to the Grund area is easiest using a public elevator on Plateau du St-Esprit.

TOP CHOICE Chemin de la Corniche PROMENADE

This pedestrian promenade has been hailed as 'Europe's most beautiful balcony'. It winds along the course of the 17th-century city ramparts with views across the river canyon towards the hefty fortifications of the **Wenzelsmauer** (Wenceslas Wall). Across Rue Sigefroi, the rampart-top walk continues along Blvd Victor Thorn to the **Dräi Tier** (Triple Gate) tower.

LUXEMBOURG CARD

The brilliant value **Luxembourg Card** (www.ont.lu/en/luxembourg-card; 1-/2-/3-day adult €11/19/27, family €22/38/54), marked LC in reviews, allows free admission to most of the grand duchy's main attractions and unlimited use of public transport nationwide. You can buy it from tourist offices, museums or certain hotels.

Royal Palace PALACE

(17 Rue du Marché-aux-Herbes; with guided tour €7; ⏲guided tours 4pm, Mon-Sat mid-Jul & Aug) Photogenic with little pointy turrets, this palace (1573) has been much extended over the years. It now houses the Grand Duke's office with parliament using its 1859 annex. For a brief period in summer the palace opens for gently humorous 45-minute guided tours, which deal mostly with the Duke's family history. From the medieval dining room, the palace's interior style morphs into sumptuous gilded romanticism upstairs. Prebook tours via the tourist office at least a few hours ahead.

Bock Casemates SUBTERRANEAN FORTIFICATIONS

(Montée de Clausen; adult/child €3/2.50; ⏲10am-5pm Mar-Oct) At the top of the Chemin de la Corniche, there are lovely views to both north and south from the Montée de Clausen, the clifftop site of Count Sigefroi's once-mighty fort. Beneath is the entrance to the Bock Casemates, a mildly interesting honeycomb of rock galleries and passages initially carved by the Spaniards between 1737 and 1746. Over the years the casemates have housed everything from bakeries to slaughterhouses and garrisons of soldiers; during WWI and WWII they sheltered 35,000 locals.

TOP CHOICE Musée d'Histoire de la Ville de Luxembourg MUSEUM

(www.mhvl.lu; 14 Rue du St-Esprit; adult/LC €5/free; ⏲10am-6pm Tue-Sun, to 8pm Thu) This remarkably engrossing and interactive city history museum hides within a series of 17th-century houses, including a former 'holiday home' of the Bishop of Orval. A lovely garden and open terrace offers great views.

MNHA MUSEUM
(Musée National d'Histoire et d'Art; www.mnha.lu; Marché-aux-Poissons; adult/LC €5/free; ⏲10am-6pm Tue-Sun, to 8pm Thu) Startlingly modern for its Old Town setting, this unusual museum offers a fascinating if uneven coverage of art and history. It starts deep in an excavated rocky basement with exhibits of neolithic flints then sweeps you somewhat unevenly through Gallic tomb chambers, Roman mosaics and Napoleonic medals to an excellent if relatively small art gallery. Cézanne and Picasso get a look in while Luxembourg's expressionist artist Joseph Kutter (1894–1941) gets a whole floor.

Cathédrale Notre Dame CHURCH
(Blvd Roosevelt; ⏲10am-noon & 2-5.30pm) Most memorable for its distinctively elongated black spires, the cathedral contains a tiny but highly revered Madonna-and-child idol (above the altar) and the graves of the royal family (in the crypt).

SOUTH OF THE PÉTRUSSE

FREE **Spuerkeess** MUSEUM, ARCHITECTURE
(www.spuerkeess.lu; 1 Place de Metz) In a dramatic, century-old, castle-style building, Spuerkeess, the state savings bank, hosts an intriguing **Bank Museum** (⏲9am-5.30pm Mon-Fri) tracing 1½ centuries of tradition and innovation in banking, from piggy banks to ATMs and bank robbers.

KIRCHBERG

Home to numerous EU institutions, Kirchberg is a fascinatingly stark new business district of gleaming glass-and-concrete buildings, about 2km northeast of the centre.

TOP CHOICE **Mudam** ART MUSEUM
(www.mudam.lu; 3 Parc Dräi Eechelen; adult/LC €5/free; ⏲11am-8pm Wed-Fri, to 6pm Sat-Mon) Groundbreaking exhibitions of modern, installation and experiential art are hosted in this 2006 architectural icon designed by IM Pei, better known for the Louvre pyramid in Paris. The museum's collection includes everything from photography to fashion, design and multimedia.

Access is by buses 1, 13 or 16 to 'Philharmonie'. To return to town on foot descend past Fort Thüngen and through Fort Obergrünwald, then turn left (easily missed) and descend a long zigzag stairway. You'll emerge on Rue Vauban/Allée Pierre De Mansfeld, the road leading beneath the viaduct close to the youth hostel.

HAMM

US Military Cemetery CEMETERY
(⏲9am-5pm) Lying in a beautifully maintained graveyard near Hamm are more than 5000 US WWII war casualties, including George S Patton Jr, the audacious general of the US Third Army who played a large part in Luxembourg's 1944 liberation. Take bus 15 from Grand Hotel Alfa (which was a WWII HQ) to Käschtewee then walk 10 minutes.

Sleeping

Luxembourg City's accommodation scene is heavy with business options but at weekends and during July and August many places slash their rates, so look for online bargains at these times.

CITY CENTRE

TOP CHOICE **Hôtel Parc Beaux-Arts** BOUTIQUE HOTEL €€€
(☎26 86 76 1; www.parcbeauxarts.lu; 1 Rue Sigefroi; ste Mon-Thu advance/rack rates €183/400, Fri-Sun from €135; @📶) Exuding understated luxury, this charming little hotel comprises a trio of 18th-century houses containing 10 gorgeous suites. Each features original artworks by contemporary artists, oak floors, Murano crystal lamps and a fresh rose daily. Seek out the 'secret' lounge hidden away in the original timber eaves.

TOP CHOICE **Le Place d'Armes** BOUTIQUE HOTEL €€€
(☎27 47 37; www.hotel-leplacedarmes.com; 18 Place d'Armes; rack rates €320-758, online rates from €149; 📶) History, art and style meld perfectly in this gorgeous five-star hotel. Seven antique buildings have been

OTHER HOSTELS

If you don't mind the bus ride there are HI hostels in the pretty castle villages of **Bourglinster** (17km) and **Larochette** (28km), both on Luxembourg City–Diekirch bus route 100. There's also an excellent HI hostel in **Remerschen** (3km north of Schengen on bus route 185), that's handily across the road from an inexpensive wine-tasting bar.

Luxembourg City

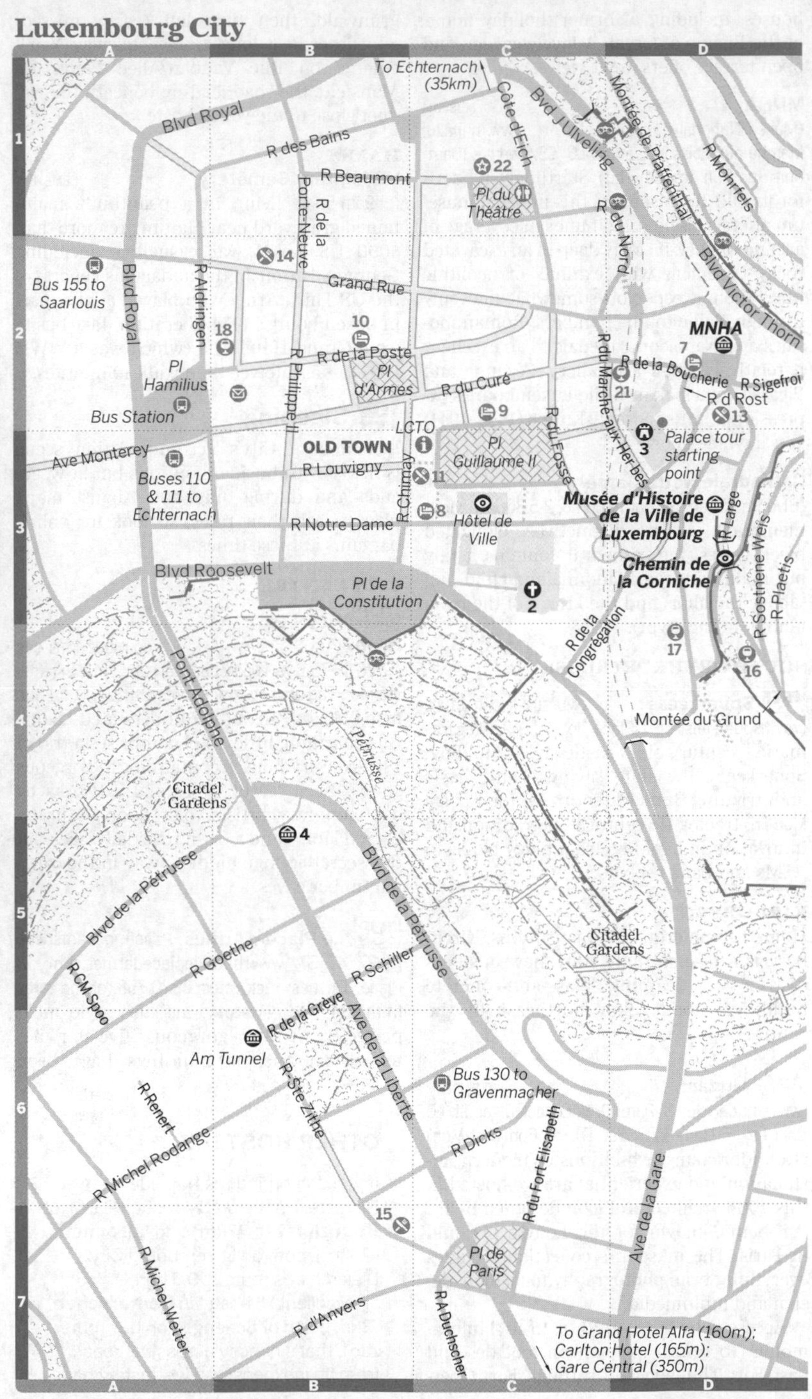

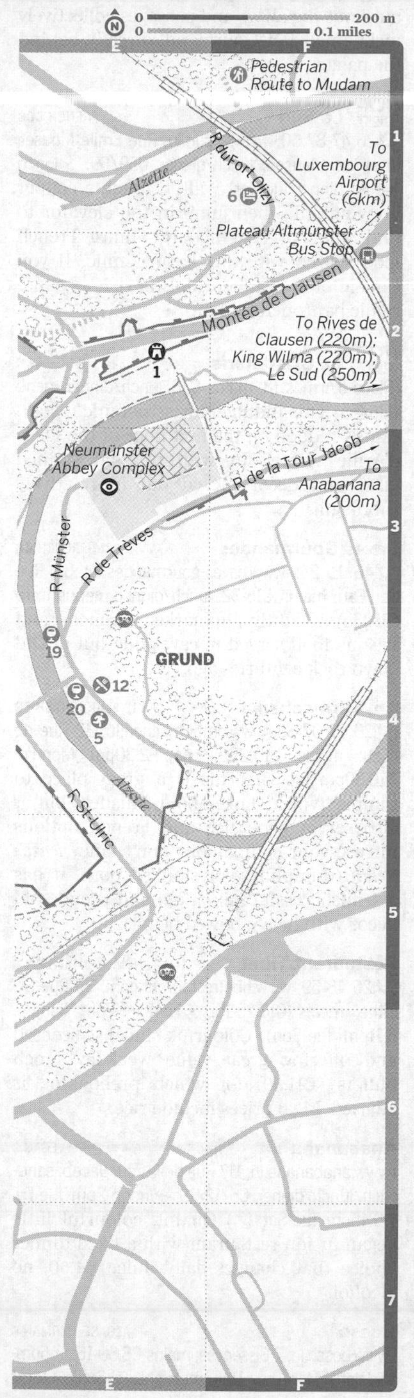

Luxembourg City

Top Sights

Sights

Activities, Courses & Tours

Sleeping

Eating

Drinking

Entertainment

combined into an enchanting labyrinth incorporating part-cave stone-walled meeting rooms, light-touch modern lounges and inner courtyards.

Hôtel Simoncini HOTEL €€
(☎22 28 44; www.hotelsimoncini.lu; 6 Rue Notre Dame; s/d midweek from €140/165, weekend €115/125; @📶) A delightful contemporary option in the city centre, the Simoncini's foyer is a modern-art gallery and the smart, bright rooms have slight touches of retro-cool. There's free wi-fi in lobby, plug-in internet in rooms.

Hôtel Vauban HOTEL €€

(☎22 04 93; www.hotelvauban.lu; 10 Place Guillaume II; s/d €95/130) The location is fabulously central and the 16 rooms were pleasantly spruced up in 2011, though smaller singles are rather claustrophobic.

CLAUSEN

Auberge de Jeunesse HOSTEL €

(☎22 68 89; luxembourg@youthhostels.lu; 2 Rue du Fort Olizy; dm/s/d €20.75/32.75/51.25, HI members €17.75/29.75/45.50; P; 9) This state-of-the-art hostel has very comfortably appointed, sex-segregated dorms with magnetic-key entry systems. There are good sized lockers (bring padlock), laundry facilities and masses of relaxing space including a great terrace area from which to admire views towards an arc of the Old town. It's a short but steep walking descent from the Casemates area using a stairway from near the 'Clausen Plateau Altmünster' bus stop.

STATION AREA

Towards the unexotic Gare Centrale area hotels are generally less expensive, though the cheapest are, not coincidentally, clustered around the tiny red-light district.

Carlton Hôtel HOTEL €€

(☎29 96 60; www.carlton.lu; 9 Rue de Strasbourg; s/d Mon-Thu €120/135, Fri-Sun €90/105;) Despite attempts to disfigure its grand facade with new red signage, this remains an atmospheric 1920 building with original staircases and floral stained-glass in the old fashioned foyer. Rooms have been upgraded and corridors are given a special touch with conical torch-style lamps. Breakfast included.

Grand Hotel Alfa HOTEL €€€

(☎49 00 11 1; www.mercure.com; 16 Place de la Gare; d €240;) Behind the imposing 1936 facade, rooms are blandly international but undergoing major renovation. While over-priced at rack rates, this hotel is an incredible bargain if you score a summer weekend package (two nights for two people €176) including free Luxembourg Card and excellent breakfast buffet served in the splendid art deco brasserie.

Eating

Tree-shaded Place d'Armes overflows with terrace seating in summer and covers all bases from fast food to ritzy resto. Cheaper terraced places can be found on or near relatively unexotic Place de Paris while for intimate and more original dining options hunt out the alleys and passages collectively nicknamed Ilôt Gourmand, directly behind the palace.

TOP CHOICE **Le Sud** FRENCH €€€

(☎26 47 87 50; www.le-sud.lu; Rue Émile Mousel, Rives de Clausen; lunch/dinner €59/69; lunch Tue-Fri, dinner Tue-Sat) Walk through a copper brewing still, then jump in the elevator to find some of Luxembourg's finest French food served with an elegant smile. If you can't afford to eat here, do still visit its panoramic bar (open till 1am).

TOP CHOICE **La Cristallerie** FRENCH €€€

(Place d'Armes 18; mains €36, lunch/dinner menu €36/55) This indulgent gastronomic restaurant is hidden on the first floor of the Place d'Armes Hotel, lit with original stained glass and decor picked out in relatively subtle gilt.

Caves Gourmandes FRENCH €€

(☎46 11 24; www.caves-gourmandes.lu; 32 Rue de l'Eau; mains €15-32, lunch/dinner menus from €15/35) Slightly upmarket French and Basque food served in caves dug out of Old Town rock centuries ago.

Am Tiirmschen LUXEMBOURGISH €€

(☎26 27 07 33; www.amtiirmschen.lu; 32 Rue de l'Eau; mains €10-25; noon-2.30pm Mon-Fri, 7-10.30pm Tue-Sat) This is a great place to sample typical Luxembourg dishes, but it also serves good fish and French options in case your companions don't fancy *kniddelen* (dumplings) or smoked pork. It has a semisuccessful mix of old and pseudo-old decor with heavy, bowed beams.

Restaurant Tibet INDIAN, HIMALAYAN €

(☎26 48 59; www.tibetrestaurant.com; 39 Rue St-Zithe; meals €10.25-15; 11.45am-2pm Sun-Fri, 6-11pm Tue-Sun) Colourful, incense-scented and offering great value weekday lunch buffets (€11.50) for which prebooking is advised. Meal prices include rice.

Anabanana VEGAN €

(www.anabanana.lu; 117 Rue de la Tour Jacob; sandwich/lunch/dinner €5/12/19; noon-2pm Tue-Fri, 7-9.45pm Tue-Sat;) Quaint, colourful little vegan-fusion restaurant with a fixed dinner choice that changes daily. Juice €4.50, no alcohol.

Bosso ALSACE, GERMAN €

(www.bosso.lu; 7 Bisserwée; mains €8.50-16; 5pm-midnight Mon-Thu, 11am-midnight Fri-Sun) Good value, tourist-centric restaurant with a hidden courtyard garden and a speciality of *flammeküeche*, wafer-thin Alsatian 'pizzas' made with sour cream instead of tomato sauce.

Á la Soupe SOUP €
(www.alasoupe.net; Rue Chimay; breakfast €3.50-7, soup €4.50-6.50; ⌚7.30am-7.30pm Mon-Sat) Central soup station.

Exki ORGANIC, FAST FOOD €
(www.exki.lu; 72 Grand Rue; snacks & light meals €4-7; ⌚7am-7pm Mon-Fri, 8am-6.30pm Sat; wi-fi) Modern self-service cafe offering wholesome organic food and free wi-fi. Before 11am coffee costs €1.

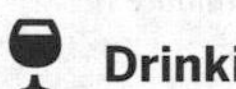

Drinking

Watering holes compete for wealthy young clientele and ratchet up the music's volume as the evening progresses.

Rives de Clausen NIGHTLIFE AREA
(www.rivesdeclausen.com) Nearly a dozen themed bar-restaurant clubs form the city's liveliest youth scene in the recently repurposed former Mousel brewery complex. Options include **Verso** (www.verso.lu), **Rock Box** (www.rockbox.lu) and curious, safari-themed **King Wilma** (www.kingwilma.lu), with its skeletal wooden centrepiece. On Friday and Saturday nights, shuttle buses running until 3.30am bring revellers back to the Glacis car park (800m northwest of Place d'Armes) and to Rue des Bains.

Urban Bar BAR
(www.urban.lu/urbancity.html; 2 Rue de la Boucherie; ⌚noon-late, kitchen 1-6pm) One of several closely huddled hip bar-cafes in the Old Town drawing cosmopolitan crowds with lots of English spoken. The waves of '70s-retro foam panelling look like ceilings for a *Star Trek* space-pod.

Liquid Café PUB, LIVE MUSIC
(www.liquid.lu; 17 Rue Münster; ⌚5pm-1am Mon-Fri, 8pm-1am Sat & Sun) Atmospheric Grund pub-cafe where two rough-walled antique houses have been knocked together and straddled by a central horseshoe of bar. Live jazz Tuesdays, blues gigs Thursdays.

D:qliq BAR, CLUB
(www.dqliq.com; 17 Rue du St-Esprit; ⌚5pm-1am Tue-Thu, 6pm-3am Fri & Sat) This small, graffiti-chic, Old Town bar has a varying program of DJ-nights, parties and concerts (predominantly electro), usually without cover charge.

Café des Artistes PUB, BAR
(22 Montée du Grund; ⌚evenings Tue-Sun) In this lovable, atmospheric cafe, every inch of wall and ceiling is covered with posters old and new. The old candlelit piano usually bursts into life with folk tunes Wednesday to Saturday nights.

L'Interview PUB
(Rue Aldringen; ⌚7.30am-1am) Mirrors and wood panelling make this wonderfully unpretentious cafe look like an old-timers' hang-out. But the evening's pumping, well-chosen music caters predominantly for a preparty student-age crowd.

Scott's PUB
(www.scotts.lu; 4 Bisserwée; ⌚11am-1am) Inside it's a British-style pub, outside seating is perched right above the river.

Entertainment

For entertainment listings see www.agendalux.lu, www.luxembourgticket.lu, www.nightlife-mag.lu or www.rave.lu. Note that the country's two biggest rock/pop music venues, **Rockhal** (www.rockhal.lu) and **Kulturfabrik** (www.kulturfabrik.lu), are both a 20-minute train ride away in Esch-sur-Alzette.

Philharmonie CONCERT HALL
(☎26 32 26 32; www.philharmonie.lu; 1 Place de l'Europe) Stunning modernist glass oval across the Red Bridge in Kirchberg that hosts jazz, classical and opera. Bus access as for Mudam Art Museum.

Cinémathèque Municipal CINEMA
(☎29 12 59; www.vdl.lu; 17 Place du Théâtre; adult/concession €3.70/2.40) Art-house offerings with some summer open-air screenings in the courtyard of nearby Théâtre des Capucins.

Den Atelier LIVE MUSIC
(☎49 54 66; www.atelier.lu; 56 Rue de Hollerich) Looking like a glum factory, this venue for local groups and visiting alternative-music stars is on an unpromising-looking main road about 500m west of Gare Centrale. A gaggle of bar-clubs lies 200m further east with more hidden behind no 42.

Information

Internet Access

Bibliothèque Municipale (3 Rue Génistre; ⌚10am-7pm Tue-Fri, to 6pm Sat) Sign up (with ID) for one hour's free internet. No printing.

Cyber (3 Rue du Curé; per 10min/hr €1/3.90; ⌚9am-10pm Mon-Fri, 2-8pm Sat) Internet with

LUXEMBOURG'S TRANSPORT SYSTEM

One ticket fits all Luxembourg has an integrated transport system. Using bus, train or any combination, travel anywhere within the city or entire country (except border stations) costs €2 provided you finish the trip within two hours of time-stamping your ticket (called a *kuurzzäitbilljee* or *billet courte durée*).

Day pass For €4 a *dagesbilljee* (day ticket; *billet longue durée*) is valid all day and until 8am the next morning.

Buying tickets Sold aboard buses. If using trains prepurchase from station to avoid a supplement. Books of ten tickets cost €16 from stations and post offices.

Luxembourg Card (p140) Includes unlimited public travel.

Timetables See www.autobus.lu and www.cfl.lu.

printing possible, upstairs above Brasserie Curé.

Left Luggage

There are **lockers** (Gare Centrale; per day €2-4; ⏲6am-9.30pm) at the far north end of platform 3; inaccessible at night.

Medical

A central clinc, **Zitha Klinik** (☎49 77 61; www.zitha.lu; 36 Rue Ste-Zithe; ⏲7am-7pm Mon-Fri) is where you can see a doctor without appointment. When it's closed go around the corner to **Maison Médicale** (Rue Michel Welter).

Tourist Information

LCTO (☎22 28 09; www.lcto.lu; Place Guillaume II; ⏲9am-6pm Mon-Sat, 10am-6pm Sun) Free city maps, walking-tour pamphlets and event guides.

Getting There & Away

Bus

Long distance buses pick up from a variety of central points, often starting from beside the train station. A thrice-daily bus to Frankfurt (4½ hours, €36) goes via Mainz (3½ hours). Some Flibco airport buses also continue to Frankfurt.

Train

The following services operate from Gare Centrale, 1km south of the old city:

Basel, Switzerland (€54, 3½ hours), via Strasbourg (two hours), twice daily.

Brussels (€36.25, three hours) hourly via Arlon (€11.25, 20 minutes) and Namur (€32.25, two hours).

Diekirch (30 minutes) hourly via Ettelbrück.

Liège (from €35, 2½ hours) every two hours via Clervaux (one hour) and Coo (1¾ hours).

Nancy (€25.40, 1½ hours) CRE trains also go via Thionville (25 minutes) and Metz (46 minutes).

Paris (from €56, 145 minutes) by TGV five times daily via Thionville (19 minutes), more often if changing in Metz (40 minutes).

Trier (€10-16, 50 minutes) hourly, several continuing to Koblenz (€34, 130 minutes).

Getting Around

To/From Luxembourg Airport

Luxembourg Airport (www.lux-airport.lu) is 6km east of Place d'Armes. Bus 16 takes 20 minutes from Gare Centrale via Place Hamilius and Philharmonie. Bus 9 takes 30 minutes via Plateau Altmünster (handy for the youth hostel) and Clausen. Both cost €1.50, and run four times hourly weekdays, and twice hourly Sundays until 9pm. A taxi costs around €30.

To/From Other Airports

Flibco (www.flibco.com) shuttlebuses from Gare Centrale run to budget airports Frankfurt-Hahn (€17, two hours) in Germany and Charleroi (€22, 2¼ hours) in Belgium.

Bicycle

LONG-TERM HIRE **Vélo en Ville** (☎47 96 23 83; 8 Bisserwée; per half-/full day/weekend/week €12.50/20/37.50/75; ⏲10am-noon & 1-8pm Apr-Sep, 7am-3pm Mar & Oct) Mountain bikes and free cycle-routes pamphlet available, tandems cost double. Renters under 26 get 20% discounts.

SHORT-TERM HIRE **Velóh** (☎800 611 00; www.en.veloh.lu; subscription per week/year €1/15; ⏲24hr) Luxembourg City's short-hop bicycle rental scheme works much like Brussels' Villo!, ie return the bicycle within 30 minutes to any of 72 stations and it's free, apart from the initial subscription payable by bank-card at one of 25 special stands.

Bus

The main bus stand for the Old Town is at Place Hamilius. Frequent buses shuttle to Gare Centrale (the train station); its ticket office has detailed route maps and timetables. Buses usually operate from 5.30am to 10pm. Frequency is low on Sundays.

Car & Motorcycle

Much of the Old Town is pedestrianised. The cheapest open-air car park is Glacis, 800m northwest of Place d'Armes. Street parking is free after 6pm and on Sundays.

Around Luxembourg

VIANDEN

POP 1600

Palace, citadel or fortified cathedral? At first glance it's hard to tell just what it is that towers so grandly above magical little Vianden. In fact it's a vast slate-roofed **castle** (☎83 41 08 1; www.castle-vianden.lu; adult/child/LC €6/2/free; ⏲10am-4pm Nov-Feb, to 5pm Mar & Oct, to 6pm Apr-Sep) and its impregnable stone walls glow golden in the evening's floodlights to create one of Luxembourg's most photogenic scenes. The partly furnished interior includes a vaulted hall full of pikes and armour, an unusual 13th-century chapel, impressive kitchen and photos of celebrity visitors from Mikhail Gorbachev to John Malkovich.

Vianden's appealing Old Town is essentially one road, the cobbled Grand Rue, which descends 700m from the castle to the riverside **tourist office** (☎83 42 57 1; www.vianden-info.lu; 1a Rue du Vieux Marché; ⏲9am-noon & 1-5pm Mon-Fri, 10am-2pm Sat & Sun summer weekends) passing several other minor sights including the cute little bakery museum, **Musée Veiner** (☎83 45 91; 96-98 Grand Rue; adult/child/LC €3/1.50/free; ⏲11am-5pm Tue-Sun Easter-Oct). If you have a Luxembourg Card it's well worth using your free ride on the **Télésiège** (39 Rue du Sanatorium; adult/child return €4.90/2.60, one way €3.60/2.10, with LC free; ⏲10am-5pm Easter-Oct, closed Mon Easter-May & Oct) to swing across the river and be whisked up the wooded hillside to a viewpoint cafeteria 15 minutes' walk above the castle.

Vianden can get overcrowded on summer weekends, but get up early and you'll have the delightful place largely to yourself.

Sleeping & Eating

There's ample choice along both Grand Rue and the river banks.

TOP CHOICE **Auberge Aal Veinen** HOTEL €€
(☎83 43 68; www.hotel-aal-veinen.lu; 114 Grand Rue; d €80; ⏲closed mid-Dec–mid-Jan; 📶) Eight refitted guest rooms (plus a simple €60 single) manage to feel remarkably stylish and well appointed considering they've been seamlessly inserted into an ultraquaint barrage of ancient dark-wooden beamwork. This is most apparent in the ground floor restaurant, which is partly built into the living rock.

Hôtel Heintz HISTORIC INN €€
(☎83 41 55; www.hotel-heintz.lu; 55 Grand Rue; s €55-70, d €61-86; ⏲closed Oct-Easter; 📶) The Heintz was once the brewery-inn of the Trinitarian monks. Grandfather clocks, a rack of top-hats and other historical knick-knacks decorate landings flanking a fine old staircase. Guestrooms are fresh, sometimes brightly coloured, and sport watercolours or paintings of Vianden.

Auberge de Jeunesse HOSTEL €
(☎83 41 77; www.youthhostels.lu; 3 Montée du Château; members dm/s/d €16.25/28.25/42.50, nonmembers €19.25/31.50/48.50; 🚭📶) Located within an archetypal shutter-fronted Vianden mansion close to the château, this standard, well-kept hostel is up near the castle gates. Before lugging your bags up the hill be aware that reception is closed between 10am and 5pm.

Lajolla Lounge CAFE, RESTAURANT €
(35 Rue de la Gare; beer/snacks/mains from €2.80/11/14; ⏲10am-last customer) This outdoor terrace has about the best view of the castle you can hope for from a cafe. It serves anything from drinks to ducks liver, bready pizza to grey shrimp croquettes, but it closes in bad weather or when custom is poor. It's beneath the recently revamped, if still slightly musty **Auberge de l'Our** (www.aubergevianden.lu).

ℹ Getting There & Away

If arriving by bus, hop out at the convenient Vianden–Bréck stop, which is right outside the tourist office.

Clervaux Bus 663 (32 minutes) picks up at 9.16am, 10.46am, 2.46pm and 6.16pm daily.

Diekirch Bus 570 (18 minutes) runs twice hourly weekdays; less frequent at weekends.

ECHTERNACH

POP 5600

Useful as a hiking base, the ancient town of Echternach has some modest Roman remains, a pretty central square and a gigantic **basilica** (⏲9.30am-6.30pm) that was rebuilt in sombre neo-Romanesque style after suffering merciless WWII bombing. This is Luxembourg's most important religious building, its crypt housing the sacred relics of its founder, the Northumbrian

CASTLES & CASTLE VILLAGES

Vianden is just the start for castle lovers. The isolated, rural **Château de Bourscheid** (www.bourscheid.lu; adult/senior/LC €5/4/free; ⌚9.30am-5.30pm Apr–mid-Oct, 11am-4pm mid-Oct–Mar) is Luxembourg's most evocative ruin, its squat 12th-century keep framing classic views of a river bend far below. Bus 545 from Ettelbrück stops in Bourscheid village 1.8km away; descend the winding lane past **Camping Bourscheid** where there's a panoramic viewpoint.

Almost as dramatic are the medieval ruins perched on a cliff above little **Larochette** (www.larochette.eu) village which has several hotels and an HI hostel. Hourly bus 100 stops in Larochette between Diekirch (20 minutes) and Luxembourg City (one hour). Bus 414 continues to Echternach via **Beaufort Village** (www.beaufort.lu), whose ruined fortress is far less conspicuous.

The distinctive, whitewashed castle at the centre of **Clervaux** (www.tourisme-clervaux.lu) is a total reconstruction of a 12th-century original that was razed in WWII. It hosts the world-famous **Family of Man photography exhibition** (www.steichencollections.lu). The station, 1km north, has hourly trains to Luxembourg City (52 minutes) via Ettelbrück (26 minutes) and every two hours to Liège (Belgium, 1½ hours). For Vianden (45 minutes) bus 663 departs at 8.30am, 10am, 2pm and 5pm.

missionary St-Willibrord (AD 658–739). The church is enclosed by reconstructed 18th-century abbey buildings within which you'll find the **tourist office** (☎72 02 30; www.echternach-tourist.lu; Parvis de la Basilique; ⌚9.30am-5.30pm Mon-Fri Sep-Jun, daily Jul & Aug) and the poorly marked **Musée de l'Abbaye** (www.willibrord.lu/1/Abteimuseum; adult/LC €3/free; ⌚10am-noon & 2-5pm Apr-Oct, 10am-6pm Jul & Aug). The latter displays ancient codex copies in vaulted subterranean cellars that once housed Europe's foremost medieval scriptorium. It also shows a video about Echternach's unique annual dancing procession, **Sprinprozession**, held on the Tuesday after Whitsun (which is the seventh Sunday after Easter).

Hotels and fair-priced street cafes line Rue de la Gare, the pedestrianised street that links the bus station to the main square, Place du Marché, where there's further choice, including the appealing **Hostellerie de la Basilique** (☎72 94 83; www.hotel-basilique.lu; 7 Place du Marché; s/d/tr €92/118/162; ⌚Apr–early Nov; ❄@📶).

Echternach's modern **HI Hostel** (Auberge de Jeunesse; ☎72 01 58; echternach@youthhostels.lu; dm/s €18.25/29, nonmembers €21.25/32; ⌚reception 8am-10am & 5-10pm; P🚭📶) is set in a lakeside country park and features a popular **climbing wall** (guest/nonguest €3.50/6; ⌚7-10pm Tue, Wed, Fri & Sat). To get there from Echternach's main square head 800m southwest to the fire station (facing the Q8 petrol station), bus stop Centre de Secours on route 110 Luxembourg City–Echternach. Then walk 1.2km southeast in the direction of Rodenhof (Roudenhaff).

ℹ Getting There & Around

BUS Echternach–Luxembourg City Bus 110 (50 minutes, hourly) direct. Bus 111 (55 minutes, hourly) via Berdorf.

Echternach–Diekirch Bus 500 (35 minutes, hourly) direct, or take bus 414 and change in Beaufort.

Echternach-Grevenmacher Bus 485 (40 minutes hourly, six times on Sundays) passes Wasserbillig train station on the Luxembourg City–Trier–Cologne line.

BICYCLE Rental mountain bikes cost half-/full day €8/15 from the youth hostel.

DIEKIRCH & ETTELBRÜCK

Of many museums commemorating 1944's Battle of the Ardennes, Diekirch's **Musée National d'Histoire Militaire** (www.mnhm.lu; 110 Rue Bamertal; adult/LC €5/free, WWII veterans free; ⌚10am-6pm Apr–mid-Nov, 2-6pm mid-Nov–Mar) is Luxembourg's most comprehensive and visual. Packed full of WWII weaponry, vehicles and memorabilia, numerous well-executed mannequin scenes illustrate the suffering and hardships of that far-from-festive snowy Christmas. It's 800m north of Diekirch's train station. Twice-hourly trains take 40 minutes to Luxembourg City via Ettelbrück (10 minutes), a useful transport hub with bus connections to Bastogne (in Belgium) for other major WWII sites.

MOSELLE VALLEY

Welcome to wine country. Smothering the Moselle River's steeply rising banks are the neatly clipped vineyards that produce Luxembourg's balanced rieslings, fruity *rivaners* and excellent *crémants* (sparkling *méthode traditionelle* wines). The region's various wine towns aren't architecturally memorable but **Ahn** and hillside **Wellenstein** are gently picturesque villages, while bigger **Remich** offers one-hour summer **river cruises** (www.navitours.lu; adult/child/dog €7/4/1). About 1.5km north of Remich's bus terminal (bus 175 from Luxembourg City), **St-Martin** (23 69 97 74; www.cavesstmartin.lu; 53 Route de Stadtbredimus; tour with one taster €4.75, free with LC; 10am, 1.30pm & 3pm Tue-Sun Apr-Oct) has wine *caves* that really are caves – cool, damp tunnels hewn deep into the rock face. To join its hour-long **tours** (€3.50; 11am, 1pm & 3pm Tue-Sun Apr-Oct) it's worth reserving. In contrast, bookings are unnecessary if you continue to the grand **Caves Bernard-Massard** (75 05 45 1; www.bernard-massard.lu; 8 Rue du Pont; tour adult/child/LC from €4/2.50/free; 9.30am-6pm Apr-Oct) in central **Grevenmacher**, where frequent 20-minute **winery tours** (adult/child from €4/2.50) are multilingual, spiced with humour and culminate in a genteel sampling cafe. The Enner der Bréck bus stop outside is on bus routes 130 (to Rue Heine in Luxembourg City) and 450 to Remich.

Bicycles from **Rentabike Miselerland** (www.visitmoselle.lu/rentabike-miselerland; per day €7, LC free) can be picked up at Remich bus station and returned at Grevenmacker's Butterfly Garden (among various other points) allowing visits en route to Ehnen's **wine museum** (76 00 26; 115 Route du Vin; adult/child/LC €3.50/1.50/free; 9.30-11.30am & 2-5pm Tue-Sun Apr-Oct) and winery **Poll-Fabaire** (76 82 11; www.pollfabaire.lu; 115 Route du Vin; tours €4; tours 1pm-5.30pm, tasting room 10.30am-8pm May-Oct, 10.30am-6pm Nov-Apr).

UNDERSTAND BELGIUM & LUXEMBOURG

History

Bruges, Ghent and Ypres boomed in the 13th and 14th centuries as northern Europe's foremost cloth trading cities. Craftspeople established powerful guilds that built elaborate guildhouses around fine market squares, typically adorned with a belfry as a symbol of civic pride.

When Protestantism swept across Europe in the 16th century, the Low Countries (present-day Belgium, the Netherlands and Luxembourg) embraced it, much to the chagrin of their ruler, the fanatically Catholic Philip II of Spain. The result, from 1568, was a war that lasted 80 years and, in the end, roughly laid the region's present-day borders. Holland and its allied provinces victoriously expelled the Spaniards, while Belgium and Luxembourg stayed under their strict Catholic rule.

For the next 200 years Belgium remained a battlefield for successive foreign powers. After the Spaniards came the Austrians, and, in turn, the French. After Napoleon was trounced in 1815 at Waterloo, near Brussels, the Dutch took over for 15 years. In 1830, the Catholic Belgians split from protestant Holland and finally formed their own kingdom initially trying to take Luxembourg with them. As a Belgo-Dutch compromise the grand duchy was eventually split in 1839, with strategically important Luxembourg

MÜLLERTHAL TRAILS

West of Echternach, well-signposted **forest trails** (www.mullerthal-trail.lu) take hikers through shoulder-wide microgorges, across trickling streams with mossy banks and past distinctively eroded sandstone formations. This is hardly Bryce Canyon but quaintness trumps grandeur and one almost expects to meet Asterix and his band around the next rocky pinnacle. If you're driving, there are handily accessible tasters right beside the main road either side of Berdorf village (itself uninteresting). Alternatively, try hiking the **E1** (11.7km, four hours), a well-marked circular path that starts up Rue Charly from Echternach bus station and winds through the intriguing **Gorge du Loup**. If this whets your appetite, other Müllerthal trails offer longer alternatives exploring Luxembourg's 'Little Switzerland', so named for the patchwork of forests and grassy fields – don't imagine even the vaguest hint of an Alpine peak.

City remaining as capital of the Dutch part with the Dutch King as Grand Duke. When the Dutch King William III died in 1890 his daughter Wilhelmina became Queen of the Netherlands. But the rules of succession for Luxembourg's grand dukes demanded, in those days, a male ruler. This odd quirk resulted in Luxembourg's previously nominal independence becoming an actual reality.

From the late 19th century, Belgium rapidly grew wealthy, both through industrialisation and through King Léopold II's profiting from the Congo, which was brutal even by the colonial standards of that era.

When WWI kicked off in 1914 Belgium was officially neutral, but the Germans invaded anyway. Western Flanders became a blood-soaked killing field and whole towns, including historic Ypres, were bombarded into the mud. Incredibly, Ypres' ancient heart has since been meticulously rebuilt and tours of the Ypres Salient offer poignant WWI reminders.

During WWII, Belgium was taken over within three weeks of a surprise German attack in May 1940 and, during Nazi occupation, most of the Jewish population was deported to death camps. After an initial 1944 liberation, both Luxembourg and eastern Belgium suffered a second devastation during Hitler's last-gasp counter-attack in the Ardennes. Despite the wars, for much of the 20th century Wallonia's mining, glassware, steel and other heavy industries made Belgium one of Europe's strongest economies, but since the 1970s, the old economic balance has reversed, with a serious post-industrial decline affecting much of Wallonia, while formerly agricultural Flanders has boomed with new higher-tech industries. A parallel series of political changes have increasingly emphasised the north–south linguistic divide. With ever less communication between the regions, forming a national consensus has proved ever more difficult in recent years. After the 2010 elections Belgium proved unable to agree a new government coalition for well over a year, a deadlock only eventually broken with the institution of constiturtional reforms that took the country one stage closer to separation. But the risk of Flanders rapidly declaring unilateral independence is probably overstated, since nobody quite knows what would then become of Brussels; plus it would all be very expensive.

Meanwhile postwar Luxembourg's governments diversified the economy such that the little country rode out a depression in the iron and steel industries during the 1970s to become a noted financial centre and tax haven. Luxembourg also became home to several key EU institutions. Today the country has the highest per capita GDP in the EU and its Grand Ducal family's considerable popularity was on display in 2012 for the wedding of the heir apparent.

People

Belgium's population is split north–south by language. In Flanders (Vlaanderen) the language is the Flemish dialect of Dutch. South of the divide in Wallonia (La Wallonie), people speak French with some Belgian peculiarities, though a small area of the eastern Ardennes is German speaking. Brussels is officially bilingual but, in day-to-day reality, spoken French (and English) predominates. Luxembourg has its own language, Lëtzebuergesch, in which *moien* is the standard greeting. Most locals also speak French and German, handy for communicating with the roughly 30% of the population who are immigrants (predominantly Portuguese, Italian and Francophones). Many Belgian cities have large immigrant communities, too, notably from Italy and France, but also from Turkey, north Africa and Congo.

Religiously, both countries follow a low-key form of tolerant Roman Catholicism. Religious-based traditions remain strong but, to a great extent, being Catholic is more a badge of social status than a spiritual dogma. The vast majority of Belgium's roughly 600,000 Muslims are of immigrant background. The small Jewish community is most visible in Antwerp's diamond district.

Arts

Literature

One of Belgium's foremost novelists was Hugo Claus, whose masterpiece, *The Sorrow of Belgium,* weaves a beautifully nuanced examination of Nazi collaboration during WWII. Georges Simenon, the creator of Inspector Maigret, was born in Liège.

Music & Dance

Belgium owes its independence to an 1830 revolution that started with an opera at La Monnaie/De Munt, still Brussels' foremost classical venue. Jazz owes much to Belgium's Adolphe Sax who invented the saxophone.

Brussels' three-day **Jazz Marathon** (www.brusselsjazzmarathon.be; ⏲late May) remains one of the capital's most joyous events.

In the 1950s Flemish-born *chanson* star Jacques Brel took the French-speaking world by storm and remains widely revered. Among more contemporary names, keep an ear out for Puggy, Arid, Ghinzu and dEUS (alternative rock), Soulwax/2manyDJs (electro/mash-up), Axelle Red (pop-chanson) and Hooverphonic (trip hop).

Foremost in Belgian dance are the **Royal Flanders Ballet** (www.kbvv.be) and dynamic contemporary groups **Rosas** (www.rosas.be) and **Danses/Plan K** (www.charleroi-danses.be).

Architecture

Dozens of Belgium's earliest buildings feature on Unesco's World Heritage list, including many a great belfry *(belfort, beffroi)* and *begijnhof* (*beguinage*, a walled urban village of historic dwellings originally built to house lay-sisters). Belgium was at the forefront of sinuously beautiful art nouveau, the design wave that swept across Europe at the end of the 19th century. Although later 20th-century neglect put much of this heritage under the demolition ball, there are still some fine examples in Brussels (Musée Horta, MIM) and Antwerp ('t Zuid and Zurenborg areas).

Apart from the mind-boggling 1958 Atomium, later 20th-century architecture proved far less inspired. Brussels' glass-tower EU quarter tragically wasted a great opportunity for city reinvention, but the last decade has seen a few contemporary masterpieces, such as Santiago Calatrava's Guillemins train station in Liège.

Visual Arts

In the late Middle Ages, sophisticated artists known quite misleadingly as the Flemish Primitives were at the forefront of a secularisation of painting. Key players included Jan van Eyck and Hans Memling, whose works are prominent in Belgian art galleries. Brussels' Breugel (Breughel) family created some of the 16th century's most memorable art, from peasant scenes to terrifying Bosch-like allegories of hell and damnation. But styles changed radically with the 17th-century Counter-Reformation. To remind upstart citizens of the Catholic God's mystical power, baroque altarpieces and giant paintings burst forth with chubby cherubs and angelic awe. That era's foremost artist was Antwerp-based Pieter Paul Rubens, whose works are still an essential feature of numerous Antwerp museums and churches.

In the 19th and early 20th centuries, Belgian art greats included sculptor and social realist painter Constantin Meunier, expressionist pioneer James Ensor, fauvist Rik Wouters and multitalented Jean Brusselmans. Symbolist Fernand Khnopff produced beguiling work echoing the contemporary pre-Raphaelites and giving a foretaste of surrealism, prior to surrealism's foremost Belgian star René Magritte, now celebrated in an excellent new Brussels museum.

Amongst Belgium's best-known contemporary artists are Panamarenko, Luc Tuymans and Jan Fabre, notable for covering a ceiling in Brussels' Palais Royal with 1.4 million iridescent beetle wing cases.

Food & Drink

Dining is a treat in Belgium and Luxembourg, where meals are often described as being French in quality, German in quantity. Though heavier home-cooking is making a commercial resurgence, many upper-range restaurants still prefer French-influenced cuisine. Here starters regularly include pâtés, garlic snails and possibly scallops. Main courses typically offer relatively unfussy fresh-fish dishes (monkfish, sole or perhaps cod) and quality meats. Steaks are generally served bloodier than English speaking visitors anticipate: *à point* translates in phrase books as 'medium' but tends to approach what many Anglophones consider as rare. 'Blue' steaks have barely bounced off the grill.

Although restaurants (www.resto.be, www.gastronomie.lu) can be pricey, you can save money by taking a weekday lunchtime *dagschotel*/plat du jour (dish of the day) or *dagmenu*/*menu du jour* (multicourse meal of the day), or by eating in cafes or Asian places (where rice is generally included in menu prices). A *belegd broodje*/*sandwich garni* (half a baguette with filling) makes a great, inexpensive, quick lunch.

If you want to hear the hiss of a cappuccino steamer head to one of the new breed of coffee houses. Cafes also serve good coffee but are more like pubs and convivial places to sample Belgium's amazing range of beers. While famous lagers (eg Stella Artois) and white beers (Hoegaarden) are now global brands, what has connoisseurs really drooling are the robust, rich 'abbey' beers (which were originally

BUYING BELGIAN CHOCOLATES

Mouth-watering Belgian chocolate is some of the world's best as it always uses 100% pure cocoa butter and involves lengthy 'conching' (stirring) to create a silky smooth texture. Within any specialist chocolatier shop, archetypal pralines (filled, bite-size chocolates) and creamy manons cost the same whether you select piece-by-piece or take a pre-mixed ballotin selection pack, but prices vary radically between brands. Although maligned by Belgian choco snobs, ubiquitous **Leonidas** (www.leonidas.com; per kg €24.30) has a price-quality ratio that's hard to beat. You'll pay around double at **Corné Port Royal** (www.corneportroyal.be), **Galler** (www.galler.com), **Chocolate Line** (www.thechocolateline.be) and **Neuhaus** (www.neuhaus.be), creator of Belgium's original pralines, or three times at exclusive **Pierre Marcolini** (www.marcolini.be), famed for using rare chocolate beans, experimental flavours and fashion-conscious black-box packaging.

brewed in monasteries), and the 'Trappist beers' (that still are). Chimay, Rochefort, Westmalle and Orval are the best known, but, for beer maniacs, the one that really counts is Westvleteren 12° (see p137). A Belgian beer oddity is spontaneously fermented *lambic*, a startlingly acidic brew made more palatable by ageing then blending into *gueuze* or macerating with cherries to produce *kriek*.

Although tap water is always drinkable, in restaurants it's never served. Buy the bottled stuff – or beer, which could be cheaper.

Note that smoking is banned in restaurants and in Belgian cafes, but not in bars in Luxembourg.

SURVIVAL GUIDE

Directory A–Z

Accommodation

Tourist offices are superb sources of accommodation assistance, usually free.

B&Bs Rooms rented in local homes *(gastenkamers/chambres d'hôtes)* can be cheap and cheerful and some offer standards equivalent to a boutique hotel (up to €160 per double). Discounts of around €10 per room are common if you stay at least a second night.

Holiday houses *Gîtes* are easily rented in Wallonia (www.gitesdewallonie.be) and Luxembourg (www.gites.lu), but minimum stays apply and there's a hefty 'cleaning fee' on top of quoted rates.

Short term apartments Bookable through sites including www.airbnb.com and www.wimdu.com.

Hostels Typically charge around €20 to €26 for dormitory beds, somewhat less in Bruges. HI hostels (*jeugdherbergen* in Dutch, *auberges de jeunesse* in French) affiliated with **Hostelling International** (www.youthhostels.be), charge €3 less for members, and some take off €2 for under-26-year-olds. Prices usually include sheets and a basic breakfast. Always read the conditions.

Camping Opportunities are plentiful, especially in the Ardennes. For extensive listings see www.campingbelgique.be (Wallonia), www.camping.be (Flanders) and www.camping.lu (Luxembourg).

PRICE RANGES

Our sleeping reviews refer to double rooms with a private bathroom, except in hostels or where otherwise specified. The rates quoted are for high season, which is May to September in Bruges, Ypres and the Ardennes, but September to June in business cities.

€ under €60; expect shared bathrooms and only basic facilities.

€€ €60 to €140; good B&B or relatively functional hotel.

€€€ over €140; note that top-end business establishments in Brussels and Luxembourg City often cut prices radically at weekends and in summer.

Activities

In **Flanders** (www.fietsroute.org), **bicycles** are a popular means of everyday travel and many roads have dedicated cycle lanes. In **Wallonia** (www.ravel.wallonie.be), the hilly terrain favours mountain bikes (*VTT*).

Canoeing and **kayaking** are best in the Ardennes, but don't expect rapids of any magnitude.

Local tourist offices have copious information about footpaths and sell regional **hiking** maps. Hilly Wallonia is more inspiring than flat Flanders.

Business Hours

Opening hours given in the text are for high season. Many tourism-based businesses reduce their hours off season.

Banks 9am to 3.30pm Monday to Friday; Saturday mornings too in Luxembourg.

Brasseries 11am to midnight

Clubs 11pm to 6am Friday to Sunday

Pubs & cafes till 1am or later

Restaurants 11.30am to 2.30pm and 6.30 to 10.30pm

Shops 10am to 6pm Monday to Saturday, some close for lunch. Limited opening on Sundays in Belgium.

Supermarkets 9am to 8pm Monday to Saturday, some open Sundays.

Embassies

The following are located in Brussels:

Australian Embassy (www.eu.mission.gov.au)

Canadian Embassy (www.ambassade-canada.be)

New Zealand Embassy (www.nzembassy.com)

UK Embassy (www.ukinbelgium.fco.gov.uk)

US Embassy (http://belgium.usembassy.gov)

Food

Price ranges for average main courses are as follows:

€€€ more than €25

€€ €15 to €25

€ less than €15

Money

Banks usually offer better exchange rates than **exchange bureaux** (*wisselkantoren* in Dutch, *bureaux de change* in French), though often only for their banking clients, especially in Luxembourg.

ATMs Widespread, but often hidden within bank buildings.

Tipping Not expected in restaurants or cabs; service and VAT are always included.

Public Holidays

School holidays are July and August (slightly later in Luxembourg), one week in early November; two weeks at Christmas; one week around Carnival; two weeks at Easter (February); one week in May (Ascension).

Public holidays are as follows:

New Year's Day 1 January

Easter Monday March/April

Labour Day 1 May

Ascension Day Fortieth day after Easter

Whit Monday Seventh Monday after Easter

National Day (Luxembourg) 23 June

Flemish Community Festival 11 July (Flanders only)

National Day (Belgium) 21 July

Assumption 15 August

Francophone Community Festival 27 September (Wallonia only)

All Saints' Day 1 November

Armistice Day 11 November (Belgium only)

German-Speaking Community Festival 15 November (eastern cantons only)

Christmas Day 25 December

Telephone

Dial full numbers; there's no optional area code.

International operator Belgium/Luxembourg ☎1324/☎12410

Directory Enquiries Belgium www.whitepages.be, Luxembourg www.editus.lu/ed/en.

Visas

Schengen visa rules apply. Embassies are listed at www.diplomatie.belgium.be/en and www.mae.lu.

Getting There & Away

Air

Antwerp airport (ANR; www.antwerpairport.be) is tiny with just a few flights to the UK on **CityJet** (WX; www.cityjet.com).

Brussels airport (BRU; www.brusselsairport.be) is Belgium's main long-haul gateway. Domestic airline **Brussels Airlines** (SN; www.brusselsairlines.com) flies from here to numerous

EUROLINES SERVICES

LINE	STANDARD PRICE (€)	SUPER-PROMO PRICE (€)	DURATION (HR)	FREQUENCY
Brussels–Amsterdam	20	9	3½-4½	up to 9 daily
Brussels–Frankfurt	46	23	6	2 daily
Brussels–London	51	9	6 (day), 8½ (night)	2 daily
Bruges–London	48	9	4¼	4 weekly, daily in holidays
Brussels–Paris	34	19	4	10 daily

European and African destinations. Brussels is also a European hub for Chinese airline **Hainan Airlines** (HU; www.global.hnair.com), Gulf-based **Etihad** (EY; www.etihadairways.com) and **Qatar Airways** (QR; www.qatarairways.com), and Indian airline **Jet Airways** (QJ; www.jetairways.com), with useful connections to North America and throughout Asia.

Budget airlines **Ryanair** (www.ryanair.com), **JetAirFly** (www.jetairfly.com) and **WizzAir** (www.wizzair.com) use the misleadingly named **Brussels-South Charleroi Airport** (CRL; ☎07 125 12 11; www.charleroi-airport.com), which is actually 55km south of Brussels, 6km north of the ragged, post-industrial city of Charleroi.

Luxembourg Airport, 6km east of Luxembourg City, has flights to many European cities notably on **Luxair** (LG; www.luxair.lu). Budget carrier **easyJet** (U2; www.easyjet.com) flies to London Gatwick. Other budget flights on Ryanair arrive at **Frankfurt Hahn** (HHN; www.hahn-airport.de), two hours from Luxembourg City by regular **Flibco** (www.flibco.com) buses.

Land

BUS

Ecolines (www.ecolines.net) and **Eurobus** (☎02 527 50 12; www.eurobus.pl) operate from Brussels and Antwerp to various destinations in eastern Europe.

Eurolines (www.eurolines.be) is part of the Europe-wide network. Prebookings are compulsory but, although nine Belgian cities are served, only Brussels, Antwerp, Ghent and Liège have ticket offices.

Useful local cross-border buses include De Panne–Dunkerque (France) and Luxembourg City–Trier (Germany).

CAR & MOTORCYCLE

Border crossings are not usually controlled.

Petrol Diesel is cheaper than unleaded. Both are cheaper in Luxembourg than almost anywhere else in western Europe.

Car-share **EuroStop** (www.eurostop.be; €4 per 100km) matches paying hitchhikers with drivers for long-distance international rides.

A driving licence from your home country will usually suffice for foreign drivers.

Priorité à droite As in France, give way to the right.

Motorway speed limit 120/130km/h in Belgium/Luxembourg

TRAIN

For comprehensive timetables and international bookings, see www.belgianrail.be or www.cfl.lu.

International high-speed trains have compulsory pre-booking requirements and charge radically different prices according to availability, so advance booking can save a packet.

Thalys (www.thalys.com) operates on the following routes:

» Brussels Midi–Liege–Aachen–Cologne (2¾ hours, 5 daily)

» Brussels Midi–Paris-Nord (82 minutes, 12 daily)

» Brussels Midi–Antwerp–Rotterdam–Schiphol–Amsterdam (109 minutes).

Fyra (www.fyra.com) runs trains from both Brussels Midi and Brussels Central to Amsterdam (€25 to €54, two hours) 10 times daily via Antwerp, Rotterdam and Schipol airport.

Eurostar (www.eurostar.com) runs Brussels Midi–Lille–London St Pancras (two hours) up to 10 times daily.

ICE (www.db.de) runs Brussels Midi–Liège–Aachen–Frankfurt (3¼ hours, three daily) via Cologne (2¼ hours) and Frankfurt airport (three hours).

TGV (www.sncf.com) runs Brussels Aéroport–Paris CDG Airport-Marne-la-Vallée (for Disneyland Paris, 1¾ hours) continuing to various southern French cities. TGVs from Brussels don't stop in central Paris, but those from Luxembourg reach Paris-Est in 2¼ hours.

Other International Trains

With European railcards high-speed trains incur a surcharge. To avoid this or to travel when high-speed trains are fully booked there are alternative slower trains:

Aachen Hourly local trains from Liège take an hour, compared with 22 minutes by high speed service.

Amsterdam To reach the Netherlands' main cities without a reservation you'll need to use Antwerp–Rosendaal local trains (48 minutes, hourly) and change.

Frankfurt Can be reached from Luxembourg in around four hours changing at Koblenz (2¼ hours).

Lille Hourly local trains run from Kortrijk and Tournai.

London: There are no sensible 'ordinary' options. Your best bet is Eurostar.

Maastricht Hourly local trains take 33 minutes from Liège-Guillemins.

Paris There's no easy nonreserved option but if you're desperate (eg all Lille–Paris trains are already booked up) you could take one of eight weekday trains from Charleroi to Jeumont, then head for Paris-Nord (2¼ hours) connecting at Aulnoye-Aymeries or Mauberge.

Trier Served regularly from Luxembourg City (50 minutes).

Basel Every morning from Brussels Midi (6¾ hours).

Sea

Most UK-bound motorists drive a couple of hours west to Calais in France. However, there are two direct options from Belgium:

Zeebrugge–Hull P&O (www.poferries.com) A 14-hour overnight service costs from £106 one-way for pedestrians. A very useful connecting bus to/from Bruges train station (£6.75) can be prebooked through P&O.

Ostend–Ramsgate TransEuropa Ferries (www.transeuropaferries.com) One-way charge is €59/60 for cars/motorbikes one-way, but from just €30 for a 72-hour return ticket. The crossing takes 4½ hours, three times daily. No pedestrians are carried.

Getting Around

For Luxembourg, see p146.

Bicycle

Cycling is a great way to get around in flat Flanders, less so in chaotic Brussels or undulating Wallonia. The Belgian countryside is riddled with cycling routes and most tourist offices sell helpful regional cycling maps.

Bikes on the train Free in Luxembourg. In Belgium bikes cost €5 one-way (or €8 all day) on top of the rail fare. A few busy city-centre train stations don't allow bicycle transportation.

Bike hire is available at or near most major train stations. Short-hop hire schemes are available in Brussels, Antwerp, Namur and Luxembourg City.

Bus & Tram

Regional buses are well coordinated with Belgium's rail network, but in rural regions you can still find that relatively short distances can involve long waits. In Brussels and Antwerp, trams that run underground are called '*premetro*'. Bus companies:

De Lijn (www.delijn.be) In Flanders.

STIB (www.stib.be) In Brussels.

TEC (www.infotec.be) In Wallonia.

Car & Motorcycle

Motorways are toll free. Speed limits are 50km/h in most towns (30km/h near schools), 70km/h to 90km/h on intertown roads, and 120/130km/h on motorways in Belgium/Luxembourg. The maximum legal blood alcohol limit is 0.05%. Car hire is available at airports and major train stations, but is usually cheaper from city-centre offices.

Taxi

Taxis must usually be prebooked but there are ranks near main stations. Tips and taxes are always included in metered fares.

Train

NMBS/SNCB (Belgian Railways; ☎02 528 28 28; www.b-rail.be) trains are completely non-smoking. Special fare categories:

» After 9am, kids under 12 travel for free if accompanied by an adult.

» People over 65 pay only €5 for a return 2nd-class trip anywhere in Belgium (some exclusions apply).

» B-Excursions offer a good-value one-day excursion fares including return rail ticket plus selected entry fees.

» Go Pass/Rail Pass allows 10 one-way 2nd-class trips to anywhere in Belgium (except frontier points) costing €50/76 for people under/over 26 years.

» Weekend return tickets are valid from 7pm Friday to Sunday night, for just 20% more than a single.

Britain

Includes »

Best Places to Eat

» Modern Pantry (p192)

» Muset by Ronnie (p215)

» Australasia (p249)

» J Baker's Bistro Moderne (p242)

» Ondine (p269)

Best Places to Stay

» Hoxton Hotel (p189)

» Halcyon (p212)

» Hotel Indigo (p245)

» Hotel Missoni (p268)

» Clachaig Inn (p282)

Why Go?

Few places cram so much history, heritage and scenery into such a compact space as Britain. Twelve hours is all you'll need to travel from tip-to-tip, but you could spend a lifetime exploring – from the ancient relics of Stonehenge and Hadrian's Wall, to the great medieval cathedrals of Westminster, Ely and Canterbury, and the magnificent country houses of Chatsworth and Castle Howard.

In fact, Britain isn't really one country at all, it's three. While they haven't always been easy bedfellows, the contrast between Britain's nations is one of the things that makes this such a rewarding place to visit. And with a wealth of glorious coastline, rolling countryside, stately cities, world-class museums and national parks to explore, Britain really is one of Europe's most unmissable destinations. And despite what you may have heard, it doesn't rain *all* the time – but even so, a brolly and a raincoat will certainly come in handy...

When to Go

London

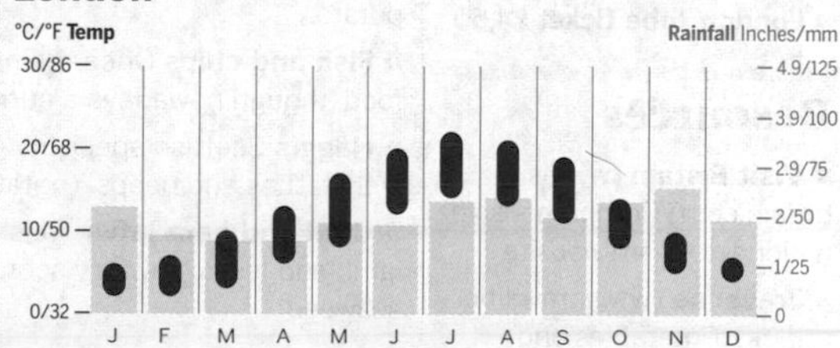

Easter–May Fewer crowds, especially in popular spots like Bath, York and Edinburgh.

Jun–Aug The weather is at its best but the coast and national parks are busy.

Mid-Sep–Oct Prices drop and the weather is often surprisingly good.

AT A GLANCE

» **Currency** pound sterling (£)

» **Languages** English, Welsh, Scottish Gaelic

» **Money** Change bureaus and ATMs widely available

» **Visas** Schengen rules do not apply

Fast Facts

» **Area** 88,500 sq miles

» **Capital** London

» **Country code** ☎44

» **Emergency** ☎999 or 112

Exchange Rates

Australia	A$1	UK £0.68
Canada	C$1	UK £0.64
Euro Zone	€1	UK £0.84
Japan	¥100	UK £0.70
New Zealand	NZ$1	UK £0.55
USA	US$1	UK £0.65

Set Your Budget

» **Budget hotel room** £60-80

» **Two-course meal** £10–15

» **Pint of beer** £3-4

» **London Tube ticket** £4.50

Resources

» **Visit Britain** (ww.visit britain.com) Comprehensive national tourism website.

» **Traveline** (www.traveline.org.uk) Timetables and travel advice for public transport across Britain.

» **Lonely Planet** (www.lonelyplanet.com/england/london) Planning advice, traveller reviews and insider tips.

Connections

The opening of the Channel Tunnel in 1994 introduced direct Eurostar rail services to Britain from Paris and Brussels. Ferries sail from southern England to France in a couple of hours, from eastern England to the Netherlands, Germany or northern Spain, from northern England to Scandinavia, from southwest Scotland to Northern Ireland, and from Wales to the Republic of Ireland.

ITINERARIES

One Week

With just seven days, you're pretty much limited to sights in England. Start in London, then branch out to Canterbury and Brighton, or Salisbury and Stonehenge (or all four). Sample the delights of historic Bath, tootle up to Oxford and Stratford-upon-Avon, then head east to Cambridge before returning to London.

Two Weeks

Start in London, then do a southeast–southwest loop via the grand cathedral cities of Canterbury, Winchester and Salisbury. Marvel at the iconic menhirs of Stonehenge and nearby Avebury, and enjoy more history in beautiful Bath. Head over to Cardiff for a taste of Wales, then cruise across the classic English countryside of the Cotswolds to reach Oxford. Not far away is Stratford-upon-Avon, for everything Shakespeare. Strike out north to Scotland's capital Edinburgh, before recrossing the border down to Durham and York, followed by Cambridge and back to London.

Essential Food & Drink

» **Roast beef with Yorkshire pudding** Iconic English dish: beef with baked-batter pudding.

» **Bangers and mash** Another icon: sausages and mashed potato.

» **Fish and chips** Once the nation's most popular takeaway food, though nowadays a curry is the favourite.

» **Haggis** Scottish speciality of sheep-offal pudding served with 'tatties and neeps' (potatoes and turnips).

» **Cawl and bara lafwr** Welsh treats: a broth made with lamb and leeks; savoury scones made with oatmeal and seaweed.

LONDON

POP 7.51 MILLION

One of the world's greatest cities, London has enough history, vitality and cultural drive to keep you occupied for weeks. This cosmopolitan capital is at the forefront of international trends in music, fashion and the arts, riding a wave of 21st-century British confidence, breathing new life into established neighbourhoods like Westminster and Knightsbridge, and reinventing areas like Clerkenwell and Southwark that were formerly off the tourist track. And fresh from its stint as host for the Queen's Golden Jubilee celebrations and the 2012 Olympics, London's riding the crest of a creative wave – there's never been a better time to visit.

The downside of this renaissance is increasing cost: London is now Europe's most expensive city for visitors, whatever their budget. But with some careful planning and a bit of common sense, you can find great bargains and freebies among the popular attractions.

And don't forget that many of London's greatest assets – its wonderful parks, bridges, squares and boulevards, not to mention many of its landmark museums – come completely free.

History

London first came into being as a Celtic village near a ford across the River Thames, but the city only really took off after the Roman invasion in AD 43. The Romans enclosed their Londinium in walls that still find refrain in the shape of the City of London today.

Then came the Saxons, and the town, which was by now called Lundenwic, prospered. Perhaps too much so, for it caught the eye of Danish Vikings, who launched many invasions and razed the city in the 9th century. The Saxons held on to power until 1016, when they finally accepted the Danish ruler Knut (Canute) as King of England, and London became the capital (replacing Winchester).

The Norman Conquest saw William the Conqueror marching into London, where he was crowned king. He built the White Tower (the core of the Tower of London), negotiated taxes with the merchants, and affirmed the city's independence and right to self-government.

London grew prosperous and increased in global importance throughout the medieval period, surviving devastating challenges like the 1665 Plague and 1666 Great Fire. Many of its great landmarks such as St Paul's Cathedral were built at this time by visionary architect Christopher Wren.

By the early 1700s Georgian London had become one of Europe's largest and richest cities, but it was during the Victorian era that London really hit its stride, fuelled by vast mercantile wealth and an empire that covered over a quarter of the earth's surface.

LONDON IN...

Two Days

Only two days? Focus your attention on the attractions around Trafalgar Square – including the Houses of Parliament, Westminster Abbey, Buckingham Palace, the National Gallery and Hyde Park. Spend the evening exploring the nightlife of Soho.

On day two, head for the river and visit St Paul's Cathedral and the Tower of London, then while away the afternoon at the Tate Modern. If you have time, catch a bit of Shakespeare at the Globe, or treat yourself to a slap-up meal and a show in the West End.

Four Days

On day three, head for the British Museum, or focus on South Kensington, with the Natural History Museum and the Victoria & Albert. Spend the rest of the day shopping and dining in Knightsbridge, Notting Hill or Marylebone.

On day four, head for the East End and explore the multicultural area around Brick Lane, followed by a visit to the Olympic Park or one of the area's quirky museums. In the evening, check out the bars and pubs around Clerkenwell or Hoxton.

One Week

With a week, you'll have enough time for Greenwich, the Royal Botanic Gardens at Kew and a river cruise to Hampton Court Palace.

Britain Highlights

1 Explore the streets of one of the world's greatest capital cities, **London** (p159)

2 Visit Roman baths and admire grand Georgian architecture in **Bath** (p210)

3 Explore the Romans' engineering ingenuity along **Hadrian's Wall** (p246)

4 Head for the coast and discover Britain's quirkiest seaside city, **Brighton** (p203)

5 Delve into the history – Roman, Viking and medieval – of **York** (p238)

6 Enjoy some classic English countryside in the villages of the **Cotswolds** (p226)

7 Step back in time among the great trilithons of **Stonehenge** (p209)

8 Join the party in Scotland's festival city, **Edinburgh** (p263)

9 Head north to experience the epic grandeur of the **Scottish Highlands** (p281)

10 Marvel at the mountainous scenery of Wales' **Snowdonia National Park** (p260)

The death of Queen Victoria marked a seachange for London, as for the rest of Britain. The ravages of the Great War were followed by the economic troubles of the 1920s and 1930s, but it was WWII that wrought the greatest damage: huge swathes of the city were reduced to rubble during a series of devastating bombings known as the Blitz. The rush to rebuild in the 1950s led to groundbreaking developments such as the National Theatre and the Festival Hall, but also resulted in a host of concrete carbuncles that still divide opinion to this day.

During the 1960s, Swinging London became the world's undisputed cultural capital, with an explosion of innovative new art, music, writing, theatre and fashion. The 1970s proved even more turbulent, with widespread unrest and economic discontent, while the 1980s was marked by an economic boom in London's financial district (known as the City), which brought a forest of new skyscrapers to the city's skyline.

In 2000 London gained its first elected Mayor, the avowedly left-wing Ken Livingstone, whose controversial decisions included the introduction of a new congestion charge and the scrapping of many of London's double-decker 'Routemaster' buses. Livingstone also worked tirelessly on London's bid to win the 2012 Olympics, a moment of elation that was abruptly shattered by the bombings on 7 July 2005 (now known as 7/7), when four British-born terrorists detonated bombs on the tube, killing 52 people and injuring many more.

Livingstone served two terms as mayor before being ousted by his Eton-educated, blonde-mopped Conservative rival, Boris Johnson, in 2008. During his first term, populist Boris commissioned new Routemaster buses, introduced London's first city-wide bike-hire scheme, and oversaw the redevelopment of a large area of the East End in preparation for the 2012 Olympic and Paralympic Games. Johnson was also in charge during the troubling riots that rocked the city in August 2011, when gangs took to the city's streets, looting and plundering at will and causing millions of pounds' worth of damage.

Johnson was re-elected in 2012 and oversaw the celebrations to mark the Queen's Golden Jubilee, followed by London's stint as Olympics host, an event that was deemed a great success. Johnson's very public presence during the Games even has many pundits tipping him as a future prime minister.

BEST FOR HISTORY

» Tower of London (p172)
» Buckingham Palace (p169)
» Westminster Abbey (p166)
» St Paul's Cathedral (p169)

Sights

London is teeming with magnificent buildings, world-leading museums (many of which offer free admission) and cutting-edge attractions. With so much to see and do, it can be hard to know where to start. Weather will be a determining factor: if it's raining, it's a day for museums and galleries; if the sun shines, make like a Londoner and include the parks on your itinerary.

WEST END

If anywhere is the beating heart of London, it's the West End – a strident mix of culture and consumerism.

Trafalgar Square SQUARE

(Map p164; ⊖Charing Cross) Trafalgar Square is the public heart of London. It hosts rallies, marches and feverish New Year's festivities, and Londoners congregate here to celebrate anything from football victories to the ousting of political leaders.

The square is one of the world's grandest public places, with Admiral Nelson surveying his fleet from the 43.5m-high **Nelson's Column** (Map p164) at its heart, erected in 1843 to commemorate his 1805 victory over Napoleon off Spain's Cape Trafalgar. The square is flanked by splendid buildings: Canada House to the west, the National Gallery and National Portrait Gallery to the north, South Africa House and the church of St Martin-in-the-Fields to the east. Further south stands **Admiralty Arch** (Map p164; leading out of Trafalgar Square; ⊖Charing Cross), built in honour of Queen Victoria in 1910 (and with a mysterious stone nose around seven foot up from the ground on one of the northernmost arches). Beyond that, The Mall (rhymes with 'shall', not 'shawl') is the ceremonial route leading to Buckingham Palace.

FREE **National Gallery** GALLERY

(Map p164; www.nationalgallery.org.uk; Trafalgar Square; ⏲10am-6pm Sat-Thu, to 9pm Fri; ⊖Charing Cross) Gazing grandly over Trafalgar Square through its Corinthian columns, the

London

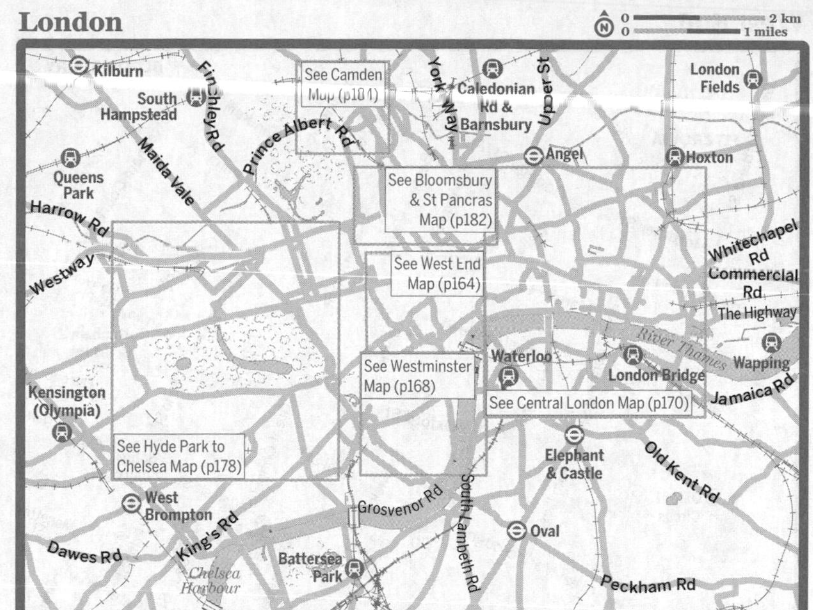

National Gallery is the nation's most important repository of art. Four million visitors come annually to admire its 2300-plus Western European paintings, spanning the years 1250 to 1900. Highlights include Turner's *The Fighting Temeraire,* Botticelli's *Venus and Mars* and van Gogh's *Sunflowers.* The medieval religious paintings in the Sainsbury Wing are fascinating, but for a short, sharp blast of brilliance, you can't beat the truckloads of Monets, Cézannes and Renoirs.

FREE **National Portrait Gallery** GALLERY
(Map p164; www.npg.org.uk; St Martin's Pl; ⏲10am-6pm Sat-Wed, to 9pm Thu & Fri; ⊖Charing Cross) The fascinating National Portrait Gallery is like stepping into a picture book of English history. Founded in 1856, the permanent collection (around 11,000 works) starts with the Tudors on the 2nd floor and descends to contemporary figures (from pop stars to scientists), including Marc Quinn's *Self,* a frozen self-portrait of the artist's head cast in blood and recreated every five years. An audiovisual guide (£3) will lead you through the gallery's most famous pictures.

Piccadilly Circus SQUARE
(Map p164; Piccadilly Circus; ⊖Piccadilly Circus) John Nash had originally designed Regent St and Piccadilly to be the two most elegant streets in town but, curbed by city planners, couldn't realise his dream to the full. He would certainly be disappointed with what Piccadilly Circus has become: swamped with visitors, flanked by flashing advertisement panels and surrounded by shops flogging tourist tat.

Despite the crowds and traffic, Piccadilly Circus has become a postcard for the city, buzzing with the liveliness that makes it exciting to be in London. At the centre of the circus is the famous aluminium statue, **Anteros** (Map p164; Piccadilly Circus), twin brother of Eros, dedicated to the philanthropist and child-labour abolitionist Lord Shaftesbury.

Covent Garden Piazza SQUARE
(Map p164; ⊖Covent Garden) Hallowed turf – or cobbles – for opera fans descending on the esteemed Royal Opera House (p197), Covent Garden is one of London's biggest tourist hot spots. London's first planned square, Covent Garden Piazza now hosts bands of tourists shopping in quaint old arcades and ringing street entertainers and buskers. On its western flank rises **St Paul's Church** (Map p164; www.actorschurch.org; Bedford St; ⏲8.30am-5.30pm Mon-Fri, 9am-1pm Sun), with a lovely courtyard at the back, ideal for a picnic in the sun.

West End

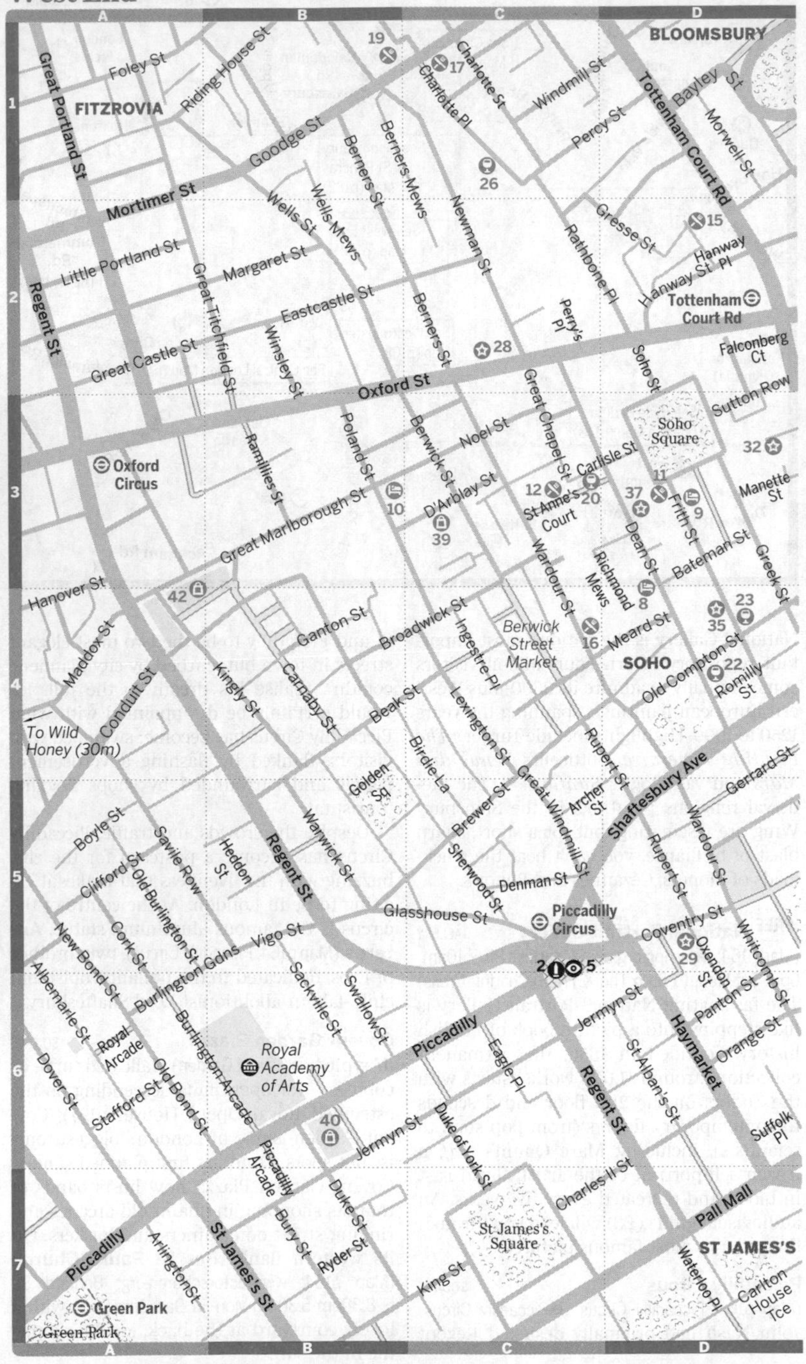

BRITAIN LONDON

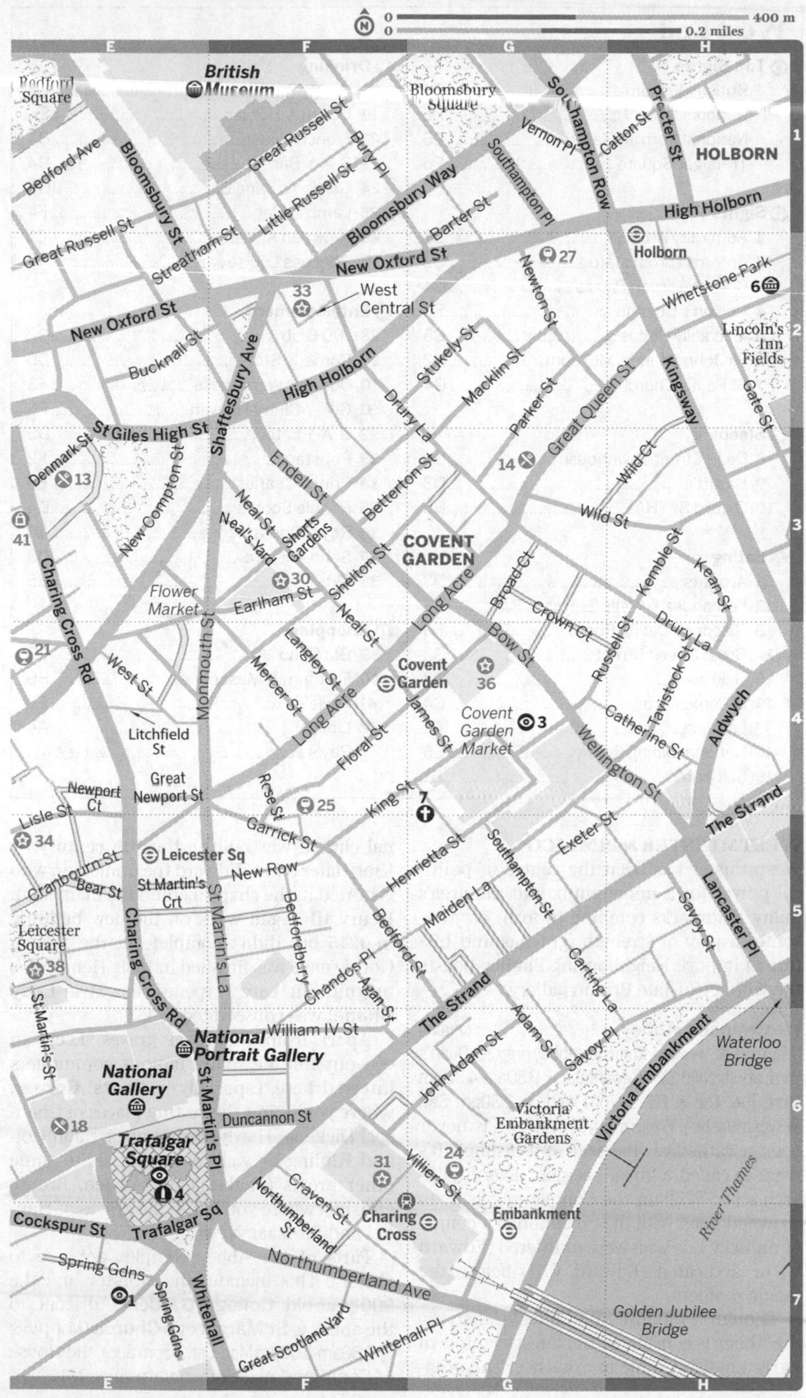
0 400 m
0 0.2 miles
British Museum
Bedford Square
Bloomsbury Square
HOLBORN
Holborn
High Holborn
New Oxford St
Bloomsbury Way
Southampton Row
Great Russell St
Bloomsbury St
Shaftesbury Ave
St Giles High St
Charing Cross Rd
COVENT GARDEN
Covent Garden
Covent Garden Market
Long Acre
Endell St
Drury La
Great Queen St
Kingsway
Lincoln's Inn Fields
Aldwych
The Strand
Lancaster Pl
Wellington St
Leicester Sq
Leicester Square
St Martin's La
Monmouth St
National Portrait Gallery
National Gallery
Trafalgar Square
Trafalgar Sq
Cockspur St
Whitehall
Northumberland Ave
Charing Cross
Embankment
Victoria Embankment
Victoria Embankment Gardens
Waterloo Bridge
Golden Jubilee Bridge
River Thames
Flower Market
West Central St
Litchfield St
BRITAIN LONDON

West End

Top Sights

	British Museum	E1
	National Gallery	E6
	National Portrait Gallery	E6
	Trafalgar Square	E6

Sights

1	Admiralty Arch	E7
2	Anteros (Eros) statue	C5
3	Covent Garden Piazza	G4
4	Nelson's Column	E6
5	Piccadilly Circus	C5
6	Sir John Soane's Museum	H2
7	St Paul's Church	G4

Sleeping

8	Dean Street Townhouse	D4
9	Hazlitt's	D3
10	Oxford St YHA	B3

Eating

11	Arbutus	D3
12	Fernandez & Wells Espresso Bar	C3
13	Giaconda Dining Room	E3
14	Great Queen Street	G3
15	Hakkasan	D2
16	Hummus Bros	C4
17	Lantana	C1
18	National Dining Rooms	E6
19	Salt Yard	B1

Drinking

20	Candy Bar	C3
21	Coach & Horses	E4
22	French House	D4
23	G-A-Y Bar	D4
24	Gordon's Wine Bar	G6
25	Lamb & Flag	F4
26	Newman Arms	C1
27	Princess Louise	G2

Entertainment

28	100 Club	C2
29	Comedy Store	D5
30	Donmar Warehouse	F3
31	G-A-Y Club@Heaven	F6
32	G-A-Y Late	D3
33	Popstarz	F2
34	Prince Charles	E5
35	Ronnie Scott's	D4
36	Royal Opera House	G4
37	Soho Theatre	D3
38	Tkts	E5

Shopping

39	BM Soho	C3
40	Fortnum & Mason	B6
41	Foyle's	E3
42	Liberty	A4
	Ray's Jazz	(see 41)

WESTMINSTER & PIMLICO

Westminster has been the centre of political power for a millennium, and the area's many landmarks combine to form an awesome display of strength, gravitas and historical import. Neighbouring Pimlico boasts the wonderful Tate Britain gallery.

Westminster Abbey CHURCH

(Map p168; www.westminster-abbey.org; 20 Dean's Yard; adult/child £15/6, tours £3; 9.30am-4.30pm Mon, Tue, Thu & Fri, to 7pm Wed, to 2.30pm Sat; Westminster) Westminster Abbey has never been a cathedral (the seat of a bishop). It's what is called a 'royal peculiar'. Every monarch since William the Conqueror has been crowned here, with the exception of a couple of unlucky Eds who were murdered (Edward V) or abdicated (Edward VIII) before the magic moment.

Though a mixture of architectural styles, the Abbey is considered the finest example of Early English Gothic in existence. The original church was built in the 11th century by King (later Saint) Edward the Confessor, who is buried in the chapel behind the main altar. Henry III began work on the new building in 1245 but didn't complete it; the French Gothic nave was finished in 1388. Henry VII's magnificent Late Perpendicular–style **Lady Chapel** was consecrated in 1519.

Apart from the royal graves, keep an eye out for the many famous commoners interred here, especially in **Poets' Corner**, where you'll find the resting places of Chaucer, Dickens, Hardy, Tennyson, Dr Johnson and Kipling as well as memorials to some other greats (Shakespeare, Austen, Brontë etc). Elsewhere you'll find the graves of Handel and Sir Isaac Newton.

Parts of the Abbey complex are free to visitors. This includes the **cloister** and the 900-year-old **College Garden**. Adjacent to the abbey is **St Margaret's Church** (Map p168; 9.30am-3.30pm Mon-Sat, 2-5pm Sun), the House of Commons' place of worship since 1614.

Verger-led tours are held several times a day (except Sundays) and are limited to 25 people per tour; call ahead to secure your place. Admission to the Abbey is free if you wish to attend a service. On weekdays, Matins is at 7.30am, Holy Communion at 8am and 12.30pm, and Choral Evensong at 5pm. There are services throughout the day on Sundays.

Westminster Cathedral CHURCH

(Map p168; www.westminstercathedral.org.uk; Victoria St; tower adult/child £5/2.50; 7am-7pm; Victoria) With its distinctive candy-striped red-brick and white-stone tower features, John Francis Bentley's 19th-century cathedral, the mother church of Roman Catholicism in England and Wales, is a splendid example of neo-Byzantine architecture. Although construction started here in 1896 and worshippers began attending services seven years later, the church ran out of money and the gaunt interior remains largely unfinished.

The **Chapel of the Blessed Sacrament** and other parts of the interior are ablaze with Eastern Roman mosaics and ornamented with 100 types of marble; other areas are just bare brick. The work is also expensive, with £500,000 needed to decorate the exposed bricks of St George's Chapel alone.

The views from the 83m-tall **bell tower** – thankfully, accessible by lift – are unsurprisingly impressive. Six Masses are said daily from Sunday to Friday and five on Saturday.

Houses of Parliament HISTORIC BUILDING

(Map p168; www.parliament.uk; Parliament Sq; Westminster) Coming face to face with one of the world's most recognisable landmarks is always surreal, but in the case of the Houses of Parliament it's a revelation. Photos just don't do justice to the ornate stonework and golden filigree of Charles Barry and Augustus Pugin's neo-Gothic masterpiece.

Officially called the **Palace of Westminster**, the oldest part is **Westminster Hall** (1097), which is one of only a few sections that survived a catastrophic fire in 1834. Its roof, added between 1394 and 1401, is the earliest known example of a medieval hammerbeam roof.

The palace's most famous feature is its clock tower, aka **Big Ben** (Map p168). Ben is actually the 13-ton bell, named after Benjamin Hall, who was commissioner of works when the tower was completed in 1858.

At the business end, parliament is split into two houses. The green-hued **House of Commons** is the lower house, where the 650 elected Members of Parliament sit. Traditionally the home of hereditary blue-bloods, the scarlet-decorated **House of Lords** now has peers appointed through various means.

When parliament is in session, visitors are admitted to the **House of Commons Visitors' Gallery**. Expect to queue for at least an hour and possibly longer during Question Time (at the beginning of each day). The **House of Lords Visitors' Gallery** can also be visited.

Parliamentary recesses (ie MP holidays) last for three months over summer and a couple of weeks over Easter and Christmas. When parliament is in recess there are guided **tours** (0844 847 1672; www.ticketmaster.co.uk/housesofparliament; 75min tours adult/child £15/6) of both chambers and other historic areas.

FREE **Tate Britain** MUSEUM

(Map p168; www.tate.org.uk; Millbank; 10am-5.40pm; Pimlico) The more elderly and venerable of the two Tate siblings, this riverside edifice celebrates paintings from 1500 to the present, with works from Blake, Hogarth, Gainsborough, Barbara Hepworth, Whistler, Constable and Turner, whose light-infused visions dominate the **Clore Gallery**.

The gallery also has more modern pieces by luminaries such as Lucian Freud, Francis Bacon and Tracey Emin, while the controversial Turner Prize for contemporary art is held here every year between October and January.

Free one-hour thematic tours are held at 11am, noon, 2pm and 3pm from Monday to Friday (noon and 3pm on Saturday and Sunday) are eye-opening but don't overlook **Late at Tate** night (first Friday of the month), when the gallery stays open till 10pm.

Churchill Museum & Cabinet War Rooms MUSEUM

(Map p168; www.iwm.org.uk/cabinet; Clive Steps, King Charles St; adult/child £15/free; 9.30am-6pm; Westminster) Winston Churchill

TATE-A-TATE

To get between London's Tate galleries in style, the **Tate Boat** (Map p170; www.thamesclippers.com) will whisk you from one to the other, stopping en route at the London Eye (p175). Services run from 10.10am to 5.28pm daily at 40-minute intervals. A River Roamer hop-on hop-off ticket (purchased on board) costs £12, single tickets £5.

Westminster

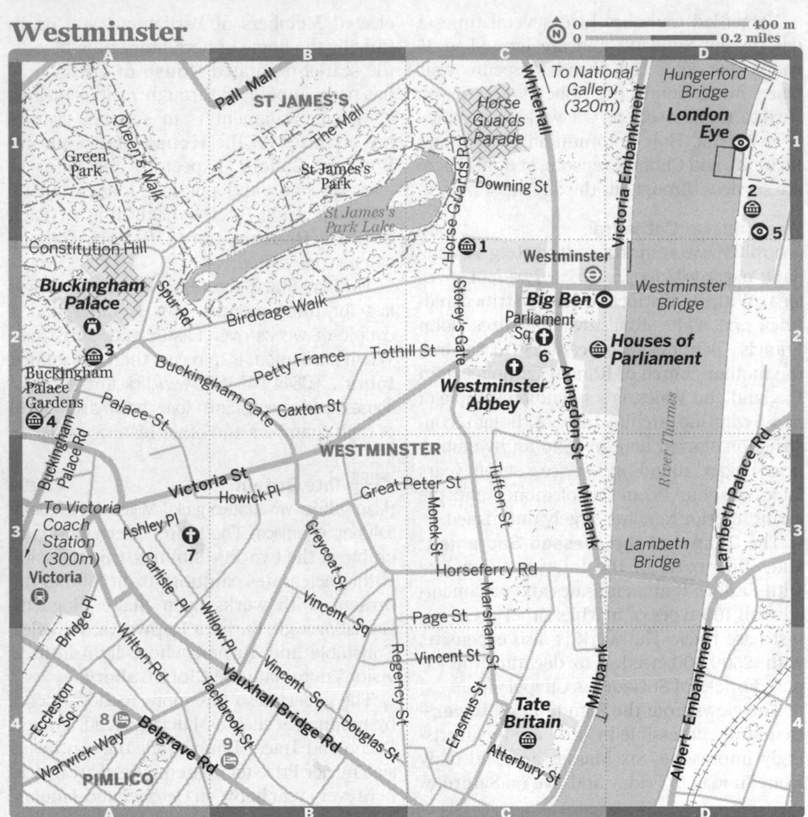

Westminster

Top Sights

Big Ben	C2
Buckingham Palace	A2
Houses of Parliament	C2
London Eye	D1
Tate Britain	C4
Westminster Abbey	C2

Sights

1 Churchill Museum & Cabinet War Rooms	C2
2 London Dungeon	D1
3 Queen's Gallery	A2
4 Royal Mews	A2
5 Sea Life	D1
6 St Margaret's Church	C2
7 Westminster Cathedral	A3

Sleeping

8 easyHotel	A4
9 Luna Simone Hotel	B4

coordinated the Allied resistance against Nazi Germany on a Bakelite telephone from this underground military HQ during WWII. The Cabinet War Rooms remain much as they were when the lights were flicked off in 1945, capturing the drama and dogged spirit of the time, while the museum affords intriguing insights into the resolute, cigar-smoking wartime leader.

ST JAMES'S & MAYFAIR

Put on your best rah-rah voice to wander this aristocratic enclave of palaces, gentlemen's clubs, famous hotels, historic shops and elegant buildings.

Buckingham Palace PALACE
(Map p168; ☎020-7766 7300; www.royalcollection.org.uk; Buckingham Palace Rd; adult/child £17/9.75; ⊙late Jul-Sep, changing of the guard 11.30am May-Jul, alternate days rest of year; ⊖Victoria) Built in 1703 for the Duke of Buckingham, Buckingham Palace replaced St James's Palace as the monarch's official London residence in 1837. When she's not giving her famous wave to far-flung parts of the Commonwealth, Queen Elizabeth II divides her time between here, Windsor and Balmoral. To know if she's at home, check whether the yellow, red and blue standard is flying.

Nineteen lavishly furnished State Rooms – hung with artworks by the likes of Rembrandt, van Dyck, Canaletto, Poussin and Vermeer – are open to visitors when Her Majesty takes her holidays. The two-hour tour includes the **Throne Room**, with his-and-hers pink chairs initialled 'ER' and 'P'. Access is by timed tickets with admission every 15 minutes (audioguide included).

Your ticket to Buckingham Palace is good for a return trip if bought direct from the palace ticket office (ask to have it stamped). *A Royal Day Out* is a combined ticket including the State Rooms, Queen's Gallery and Royal Mews (adult/child £31.95/18.20).

Queens Gallery

Originally designed by John Nash as a conservatory, the **gallery** (Map p168; www.royalcollection.org.uk; southern wing, Buckingham Palace, Buckingham Palace Rd; adult/child £9/4.50; ⊙10am-5.30pm) showcases some of the palace's treasures on a rotating basis, through temporary exhibitions.

Royal Mews

Indulge your Cinderella fantasies while inspecting the exquisite state coaches in the **Royal Mews** (Map p168; www.royalcollection.org.uk; Buckingham Palace Rd; adult/child £8/5; ⊙10am-5pm Apr-Oct, to 4pm Mon-Sat Nov-Dec), a working stable looking after the royals' horses and carriages. Highlights include the magnificent gold coach of 1762 and the 1910 Glass Coach (Prince William and Catherine Middleton used the 1902 State Landau for their wedding in 2011).

St James's Park & Green Park PARK
With its manicured flowerbeds and ornamental lake, St James's Park is a wonderful place to stroll and take in the views of Westminster, Buckingham Palace and St James's Palace. The expanse of Green Park links St James's Park to Hyde Park and Kensington Gardens, creating a green corridor from Westminster all the way to Kensington.

CHANGING OF THE GUARD

At 11.30am daily from May to July (on alternate days, weather permitting for the rest of the year), the old guard (Foot Guards of the Household Regiment) comes off duty to be replaced by the new guard on the forecourt of Buckingham Palace. The highly popular show lasts about half an hour (brace for crowds).

THE CITY

For centuries, the City (note the capital C) *was* London. Its boundaries have changed little from the Roman walls built in this area two millennia ago, and today it's London's central business district (also known as the 'square mile').

TOP CHOICE **St Paul's Cathedral** CHURCH
(Map p170; www.stpauls.co.uk; St Paul's Churchyard EC4; adult/child £15/6; ⊙8.30am-4.30pm Mon-Sat, last entry at 4pm; ⊖St Paul's) Dominating the City with one of the world's largest church domes (around 65,000 tonnes worth), St Paul's Cathedral was designed by Christopher Wren after the Great Fire and built between 1675 and 1710. The site is ancient hallowed ground with four other cathedrals preceding Wren's masterpiece here, the first dating from 604. As part of the 300th anniversary celebrations, St Paul's underwent a £40 million renovation project that gave the church a deep clean.

Inside, some 30m above the main paved area, is the first of three domes (actually a dome inside a cone inside a dome) supported by eight huge columns. The walkway around its base, 257 steps up a staircase on the western side of the southern transept, is called the **Whispering Gallery**, because if you talk close to the wall, your words will carry to the opposite side 32m away. A further 119 steps brings you to the **Stone Gallery**, 152 iron steps above which is the **Golden Gallery** at the very top, rewarded with unforgettable views of London.

The **Crypt** has memorials to up to 300 military demigods, including Wellington, Kitchener and Nelson, whose body lies below the dome. But the most poignant memorial is to Wren himself. On a simple

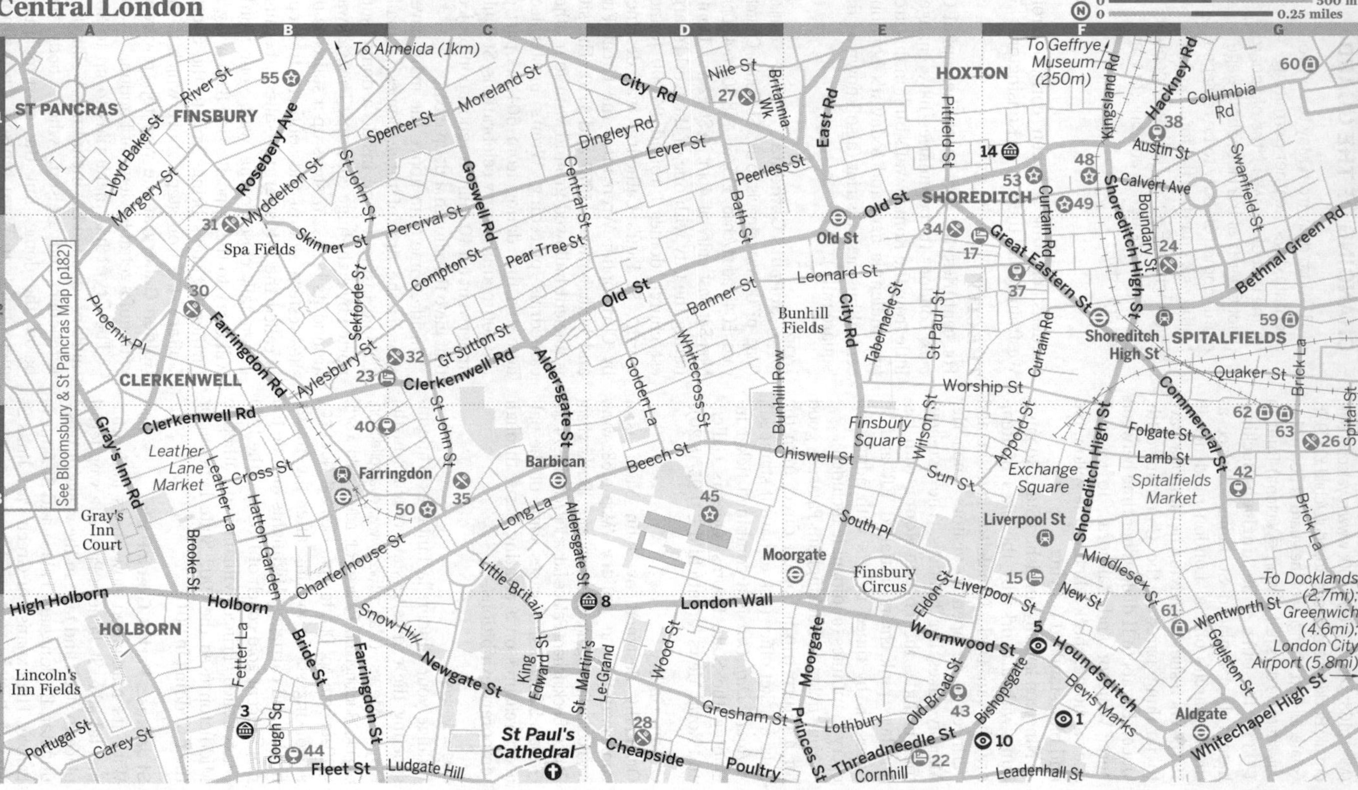
Central London
500 m
0.25 miles
See Bloomsbury & St Pancras Map (p182)
To Almeida (1km)
To Geffrye Museum (250m)
To Docklands (2.7mi); Greenwich (4.6mi); London City Airport (5.8mi)
ST PANCRAS
FINSBURY
CLERKENWELL
HOLBORN
HOXTON
SHOREDITCH
SPITALFIELDS
Gray's Inn Rd
Clerkenwell Rd
Farringdon Rd
Rosebery Ave
St John St
Goswell Rd
Aldersgate St
Old St
City Rd
East Rd
Great Eastern St
Shoreditch High St
Commercial St
Bethnal Green Rd
Hackney Rd
Kingsland Rd
Curtain Rd
Pitfield St
Moorgate
London Wall
Wormwood St
Houndsditch
Bishopsgate
Threadneedle St
Princes St
Poultry
Cheapside
Newgate St
Holborn
High Holborn
Farringdon St
Fleet St
Bride St
Hatton Garden
Leather La
Charterhouse St
Long La
Barbican
Farringdon
Liverpool St
Aldgate
Whitechapel High St
St Paul's Cathedral
Finsbury Square
Finsbury Circus
Bunhill Fields
Spitalfields Market
Exchange Square
Leather Lane Market
Gray's Inn Court
Lincoln's Inn Fields
Brick La
Spital St
Bevis Marks
Leadenhall St
Cornhill
Lothbury
Gresham St
Wood St
Whitecross St
Golden La
Beech St
Chiswell St
Bunhill Row
Bath St
Central St
Lever St
Dingley Rd
Moreland St
Spencer St
Percival St
Compton St
Gt Sutton St
Sekforde St
Aylesbury St
Skinner St
Spa Fields
Myddelton St
Margery St
Lloyd Baker St
River St
Phoenix Pl
Brooke St
Cross St
Snow Hill
Ludgate Hill
Fetter La
Gough Sq
Carey St
Portugal St
Little Britain
King Edward St
St Martin's Le-Grand
Old Broad St
Eldon St
South Pl
Sun St
Wilson St
Worship St
Appold St
Tabernacle St
St Paul St
Leonard St
Banner St
Pear Tree St
Nile St
Britannia Wk
Peerless St
Calvert Ave
Austin St
Boundary St
Columbia Rd
Swanfield St
Quaker St
Folgate St
Lamb St
Middlesex St
New St
Wentworth St
Goulston St

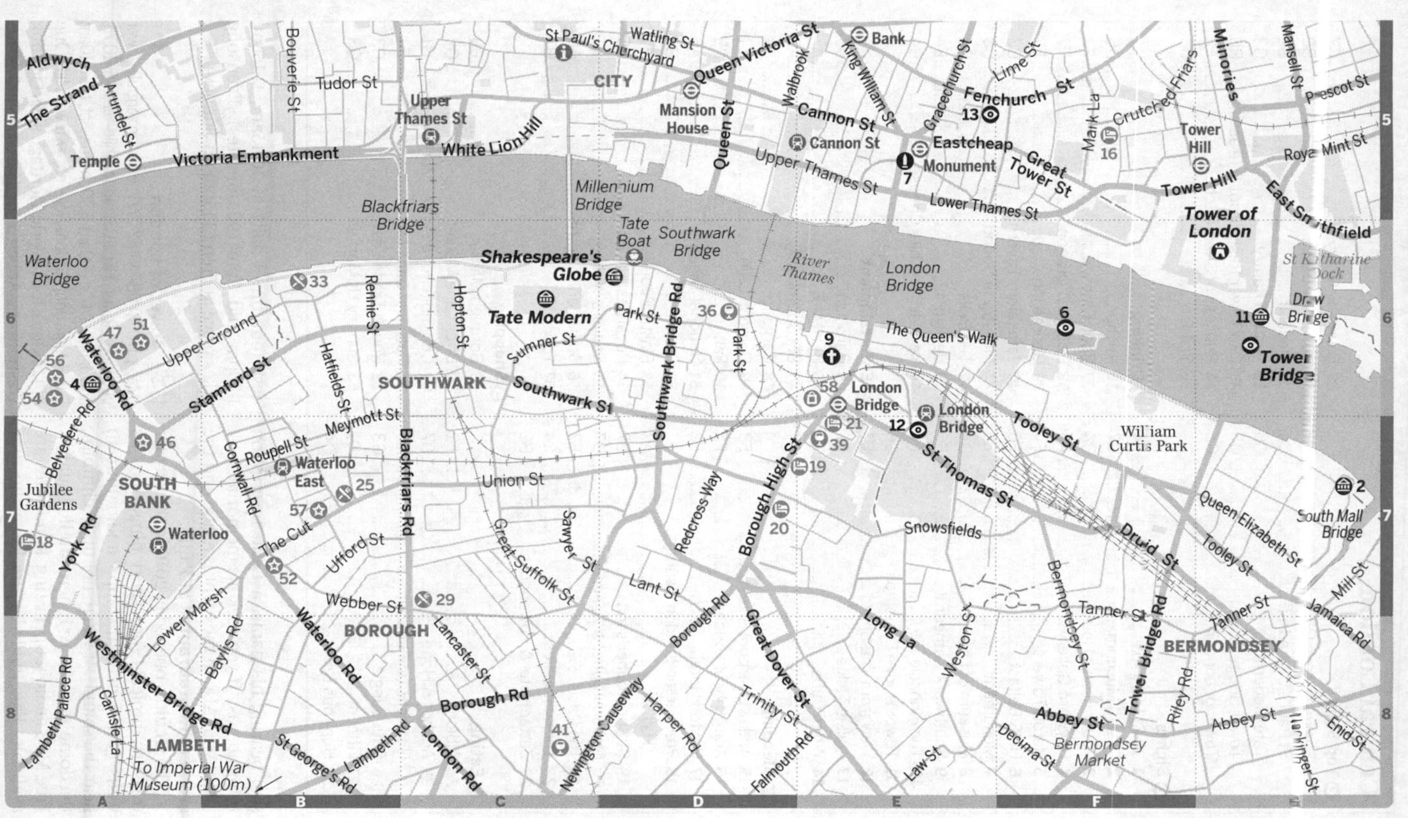
Aldwych
The Strand
Arundel St
Temple
Bouverie St
Tudor St
Victoria Embankment
Upper Thames St
White Lion Hill
St Paul's Churchyard
Watling St
CITY
Queen Victoria St
Mansion House
Queen St
Walbrook
Bank
King William St
Cannon St
Cannon St
Upper Thames St
Gracechurch St
Lime St
Fenchurch St
Eastcheap
Monument
Great Tower St
Lower Thames St
Mark La
Crutched Friars
Tower Hill
Tower Hill
Minories
Mansell St
Prescot St
Royal Mint St
East Smithfield
Tower of London
St Katharine Dock
Draw Bridge
Tower Bridge
Blackfriars Bridge
Millennium Bridge
Tate Boat
Southwark Bridge
River Thames
London Bridge
Waterloo Bridge
Shakespeare's Globe
Tate Modern
Park St
Park St
The Queen's Walk
Upper Ground
Waterloo Rd
Stamford St
Rennie St
Hopton St
Sumner St
Southwark Bridge Rd
SOUTHWARK
Southwark St
Hatfields St
Meymott St
London Bridge
London Bridge
Tooley St
St Thomas St
William Curtis Park
Belvedere Rd
Roupell St
Waterloo East
Cornwall Rd
Blackfriars Rd
Union St
Borough High St
Redcross Way
Jubilee Gardens
SOUTH BANK
Waterloo
York Rd
The Cut
Ufford St
Great Suffolk St
Sawyer St
Snowsfields
Druid St
Queen Elizabeth St
Tooley St
South Mall Bridge
Mill St
Jamaica Rd
Tanner St
Webber St
Lower Marsh
Baylis Rd
BOROUGH
Waterloo Rd
Lancaster St
Lant St
Borough Rd
Great Dover St
Long La
Weston St
Bermondsey St
Tanner St
Tower Bridge Rd
BERMONDSEY
Westminster Bridge Rd
Lambeth Palace Rd
Carlisle La
LAMBETH
To Imperial War Museum (100m)
St George's Rd
Lambeth Rd
London Rd
Borough Rd
Newington Causeway
Harper Rd
Trinity St
Falmouth Rd
Law St
Abbey St
Decima St
Bermondsey Market
Riley Rd
Abbey St
Enid St

Central London

Top Sights

Shakespeare's Globe ... D6
St Paul's Cathedral ... C4
Tate Modern ... C6
Tower Bridge ... G6
Tower of London ... G6

Sights

1 30 St Mary Axe ... F4
2 Design Museum ... G7
3 Dr Johnson's House ... B4
4 Hayward Gallery ... A6
5 Heron Tower ... F4
6 HMS Belfast ... F6
7 Monument ... E5
8 Museum of London ... D4
9 Southwark Cathedral ... E6
10 The Pinnacle ... F4
11 Tower Bridge Exhibition ... G6
12 View from The Shard ... E7
13 Walkie Talkie ... E5
14 White Cube ... F1

Sleeping

15 Andaz Liverpool Street ... F3
16 Apex City of London ... F5
17 Hoxton Hotel ... E2
18 Premier Inn London County Hall ... A7
19 St Christopher's Inn ... E7
20 St Christopher's Village ... D7
21 The Oasis ... E7
22 Threadneedles ... E4
23 Zetter Hotel & Townhouse ... B2

Eating

24 Albion ... F2
25 Anchor & Hope ... B7
Bistrot Bruno Loubet ... (see 23)
26 Cafe Bangla ... G3
27 Fifteen ... D1
28 Hummus Bros ... D4
29 Laughing Gravy ... C7
30 Little Bay ... B2
31 Medcalf ... B2
32 Modern Pantry ... C2
33 Oxo Tower Restaurant & Brasserie ... B6
34 Princess of Shoreditch ... E2
35 St John ... C3

Drinking

36 Anchor ... D6
37 Book Club ... F2
38 George & Dragon ... F1
39 George Inn ... E7
40 Jerusalem Tavern ... B3
41 Ministry of Sound ... C8
42 Ten Bells ... G3
43 Vertigo 42 ... E4
44 Ye Olde Cheshire Cheese ... B4

Entertainment

45 Barbican ... D3
46 BFI IMAX ... A7
47 BFI Southbank ... A6
48 Cargo ... F1
49 Comedy Café ... F1
50 Fabric ... C3
51 National Theatre ... A6
52 Old Vic ... B7
53 Plastic People ... F1
54 Royal Festival Hall ... A6
55 Sadler's Wells ... B1
56 Southbank Centre ... A6
57 Young Vic ... B7

Shopping

58 Borough Market ... E6
59 Brick Lane Market ... G2
60 Columbia Road Flower Market ... G1
61 Petticoat Lane Market ... F4
62 Rough Trade East ... G3
63 Sunday UpMarket ... G3

slab bearing his name, a Latin inscription translates as: 'If you seek his memorial, look about you'. Also in the crypt is a cafe and the excellent **Restaurant** at St Paul's.

The **Oculus**, opened in 2010 in the former treasury, projects four short films onto its walls (you'll need the mp3 audio tour to hear the sound). If you're not up to climbing the dome, experience it here (audiovisually). Free MP3 audio tours lasting 45 minutes are available. Free guided tours leave the tour desk four times daily at 10.45am, 11.15am, 1.30pm and 2pm (90 minutes). Evensong takes place at 5pm (3.15pm on Sunday).

TOP CHOICE **Tower of London** CASTLE

(Map p170; ☎0844 482 7777; www.hrp.org.uk/toweroflondon; Tower Hill EC3; adult/child £21.45/10.75, audioguide £4/3; ⏰9am-5.30pm Tue-Sat, from 10am Sun & Mon, until 4.30pm Nov-Feb; ⊖Tower Hill) One of London's four World Heritage sites (joining Westminster Abbey, Kew Gardens and Maritime Greenwich), the Tower offers a window on to a gruesome and compelling history.

In the 1070s, William the Conqueror started work on the White Tower to replace the castle he'd previously had built here. By 1285, two walls with towers and a moat were built around it and the defences have barely been altered since. A former royal residence, treasury, mint and arsenal, it became most famous as a prison when Henry VIII moved to Whitehall Palace in 1529 and started meting out his preferred brand of punishment.

The most striking building is the central **White Tower**, with its solid Romanesque architecture and four turrets. Today it houses a collection from the Royal Armouries, including Henry VIII's commodious suit of armour. On the 2nd floor is **St John's Chapel**, dating from 1080 and therefore the oldest church in London. To the north stands **Waterloo Barracks**, which now contains the spectacular and newly redisplayed **Crown Jewels**, including the platinum crown of the late Queen Mother, set with the 105-carat **Koh-i-Noor** (Mountain of Light) diamond and the **Imperial State Crown**. Slow-moving travelators shunt wide-eyed visitors past the collection. On the far side of the White Tower rises the **Bloody Tower**, where the 12-year-old Edward V and his little brother were held 'for their own safety' and later murdered, probably by their uncle, the future Richard III. Sir Walter Raleigh did a 13-year stretch here, when he wrote his *History of the World*.

On the small green in front of the **Chapel Royal of St Peter ad Vincula** stood Henry VIII's **scaffold**, where seven people, including Anne Boleyn and her cousin Catherine Howard (Henry's second and fifth wives) were beheaded.

Look out for the latest in the Tower's long line of famous ravens, which legend says could cause the White Tower to collapse should they leave (their wings are clipped in case they get any ideas).

To get your bearings, take the hugely entertaining free guided tour with any of the Beefeaters (Yeoman Warders). Hour-long tours leave every 30 minutes from the bridge near the main entrance; the last tour is an hour before closing. Book online for cheaper rates for the Tower.

Tower Bridge BRIDGE

(Map p170; ⊖Tower Hill) London was still a thriving port in 1894 when Tower Bridge was built. Designed to be raised to allow ships to pass, electricity has now taken over from the original steam engines. A lift leads up from the northern tower to the overpriced **Tower Bridge Exhibition** (Map p170; www.towerbridge.org.uk; adult/child £8/3.40; ⏲10am-6pm Apr-Sep, 9.30am-5.30pm Oct-Mar, last admission 30min before closing; ⊖Tower Hill), where the story of its building is recounted within the upper walkway. The same ticket allows entry into the engine rooms below the southern tower. Below the bridge on the City side is **Dead Man's Hole**, where corpses that had made their way into the Thames (through suicide, murder or accident) were regularly retrieved.

MAPS

No Londoner would be without a pocket-sized *London A–Z* map-book – you can buy them at news stands and shops everywhere. For getting around the London Underground ('the tube'), maps are free at underground stations.

FREE **Museum of London** MUSEUM

(Map p170; www.museumoflondon.org.uk; 150 London Wall EC2; ⏲10am-6pm; ⊖Barbican) Catching this riveting museum early on in your stay helps peel back the layers of historical London for valuable perspectives on this great city.

The first gallery, **London before London**, illustrates the settlements predating the capital prior to the Roman era. The Roman section explores the ancient roots of the modern city as we know it while Saxon, medieval, Tudor and Stuart London are intriguingly brought to life. The museum's new £20 million **Galleries of Modern London** encompasses everything from 1666 (the devastating Great Fire of London) to the present day.

Dr Johnson's House MUSEUM

(Map p170; www.drjohnsonshouse.org; 17 Gough Sq EC4; adult/child £4.50/1.50, audioguide £2; ⏲11am-5.30pm Mon-Sat May-Sep, to 5pm Mon-Sat Oct-Apr; ⊖Chancery Lane) The Georgian house where Samuel Johnson and his assistants compiled the first English dictionary (between 1748 and 1759) is full of prints and portraits of friends and intimates, including the good doctor's Jamaican servant to whom he bequeathed this grand residence.

Monument TOWER

(Map p170; www.themonument.info; Fish Street Hill EC3; adult/child £3/1; ⏲9.30am-5.30pm; ⊖Monument) Designed by Wren to commemorate the Great Fire, the towering Monument is 60.6m high, the exact distance from its base to the bakery on Pudding Lane where the blaze began. Corkscrew your way up the 311 tight spiral steps (claustrophobes beware) for some of London's best wraparound views and twist down again to collect a certificate commemorating your climb.

CLERKENWELL & HOLBORN

In these now fashionable streets it's hard to find an echo of the notorious 'rookeries' of the 19th century, where families lived in probably the worst conditions in the city's long history, as documented so vividly in the novels of Charles Dickens.

Charles Dickens Museum — MUSEUM

(Map p182; www.dickensmuseum.com; 48 Doughty St; adult/child £6/3; ⏲10am-5pm Mon-Sat, 11am-5pm Sun; ⊖Russell Sq) Dickens' sole surviving London residence is where his work really flourished – *The Pickwick Papers, Nicholas Nickleby* and *Oliver Twist* were all written here. The handsome four-storey house opened as a museum in 1925, and visitors can stroll through rooms choc-a-bloc with fascinating memorabilia.

Sir John Soane's Museum — MUSEUM

(Map p164; www.soane.org; 13 Lincoln's Inn Fields; tours £5; ⏲10am-5pm Tue-Sat, 6-9pm 1st Tue of month; P; ⊖Holborn) This little museum is one of the most atmospheric and fascinating sights in London. The building is housed in the beautiful home of architect Sir John Soane (1753–1837), and it's full of his fascinating possessions and personal effects. It has a glass dome that brings light right down to the basement, a lantern room filled with statuary, rooms within rooms, and a picture gallery where paintings are stowed behind each other on folding wooden panes. This is where Soane's choice paintings are displayed, including *Riva degli Schiavoni, Looking West* by Canaletto, drawings by Christopher Wren and Robert Adam, and the original *Rake's Progress,* William Hogarth's set of cartoon caricatures of late-18th-century London lowlife.

The first Tuesday evening of each month is the best time to visit as the house is lit by candles and the atmosphere is even more magical (it is very popular and there are always long queues).

SOUTH BANK

Londoners once crossed the river to the area controlled by the licentious Bishops of Southwark for all manner of bawdy frolicking frowned upon in the City. It's a much more seemly area now, but the frisson of theatre and entertainment remains.

FREE Tate Modern — MUSEUM

(Map p170; www.tate.org.uk; Queen's Walk; ⏲10am-6pm Sun-Thu, to 10pm Fri & Sat; ⊖Southwark) One of London's most popular attractions, this outstanding modern and contemporary art gallery is housed in the creatively revamped **Bankside Power Station** south of the Millennium Bridge. A spellbinding synthesis of funky modern art and capacious industrial brick design, the eye-catching result is one of London's must-see sights. An extension is under construction, aiming for a 2016 completion date.

The multimedia guides (£3.50) are worthwhile and there are free 45-minute guided tours of the collection's highlights (Level 3 at 11am and noon; Level 5 at 2pm and 3pm). Note the late-night opening hours on Friday and Saturday.

Shakespeare's Globe — HISTORIC BUILDING

(Map p170; ☎020-7401 9919; www.shakespeares-globe.org; 21 New Globe Walk SE1; adult/child £11/7; ⏲10am-5pm; ⊖London Bridge) Today's Londoners may flock to Amsterdam to misbehave but back in the Bard's day they'd cross London Bridge to Southwark. Free from the city's constraints, men could settle down to a diet of whoring, bear-baiting and heckling of actors. The most famous theatre was the Globe, where a genius playwright was penning box-office hits such as *Macbeth* and *Hamlet.*

The original Globe – known as the 'Wooden O' after its circular shape and roofless centre – was erected in 1599, but burned down within two hours during a performance in 1613 (a stage cannon ignited the thatched roof). Its present-day incarnation is the vision of American actor and director Sam Wanamaker, who sadly died before the opening night in 1997. Admission includes the **exhibition hall** and **guided tour** of the theatre (departing every 15 to 30 minutes), faithfully reconstructed from oak beams, handmade bricks, lime plaster and thatch. Tours shift to the nearby Rose Theatre instead when matinees are being staged in season.

From April to October plays are performed, and while Shakespeare and his contemporaries dominate, modern plays are also staged (see the website for upcoming performances). As in Elizabethan times, seatless 'groundlings' can watch in all-weather conditions (£5; seats are £15 to £39) for the best views. There's no protection from the elements and you'll have to stand, but it's an unforgettable experience.

London Eye VIEWPOINT
(Map p168; ☎0871 781 3000; www.londoneye.com; adult/child £19.20/12.30; ⊙10am-8pm; ⊖Waterloo) This 135m-tall, slow-moving Ferris-wheel-like attraction is the tallest in the western hemisphere. Passengers ride in enclosed egg-shaped pods; the wheel takes 30 minutes to rotate completely, offering 25-mile views on clear days. Drawing 3.5 million visitors annually, at peak times (in July and August and school holidays), it can seem like they are all in the queue with you. Save money and shorten queues by buying tickets online, or cough up an extra £10 to show off your fast-track swagger.

FREE **Imperial War Museum** MUSEUM
(www.iwm.org.uk; Lambeth Rd; ⊙10am-6pm; ⊖Lambeth North) Fronted by a pair of intimidating 15in naval guns that could lob a 1938lb shell over 16 miles, this riveting museum is housed in what was once Bethlehem Royal Hospital, known as Bedlam. There's not just Lawrence of Arabia's 1000cc motorbike here, but a German V-2 rocket, a Sherman tank, a lifelike replica of Little Boy (the atom bomb dropped on Hiroshima), a P-51 Mustang, a Focke-Wulf Fw 190 and other classic fighter planes dangling from the ceiling, plus a recreated WWI trench, WWII bomb shelter, and a Holocaust exhibition.

FREE **Southwark Cathedral** CHURCH
(Map p170; ☎020-7367 6700; http://cathedral.southwark.anglican.org; Montague Close; donations welcome; ⊙8am-6pm Mon-Fri, from 9am Sat & Sun; ⊖London Bridge) Although the central tower dates from 1520 and the choir from the 13th century, Southwark Cathedral is largely Victorian. Inside are monuments galore, including a Shakespeare Memorial.

View from The Shard BUILDING
(Map p170; www.the-shard.com; The Shard, 32 London Bridge St; adult/child £29.95/23.95; ⊙9am-10pm; ⊖London Bridge) Puncturing the skies above London, the dramatic splinterlike form of The Shard – the tallest building in Western Europe – has rapidly become an icon. Approaching completion at the time of writing, the tower will boast the rooms-with-a-view, five-star Shangri-La Hotel, restaurants and a 360-degree viewing gallery in the clouds, accessible via high-speed lifts.

Design Museum MUSEUM
(Map p170; www.designmuseum.org; 28 Shad Thames; adult/child £8.50/5; ⊙10am-5.45pm; ⊖Tower Hill) Housed in a 1930s-era warehouse, the rectangular galleries of the Design Museum stage a revolving program of special exhibitions devoted to contemporary design. Both populist and popular, past shows have ranged from Manolo Blahnik shoes to Formula One racing cars, the output of Dutch graphic designer Wim Crouwel and that miracle material, Velcro.

The **Blueprint Cafe** (⊙noon-3pm and 6pm-11pm Mon-Sat, until 4pm Sun) has delicious views over Tower Bridge. The museum plans to move to a new site in the former **Commonwealth Institute** (Kensington High St W8; ⊖High St Kensington) in 2014.

HMS Belfast SHIP
(Map p170; http://hmsbelfast.iwm.org.uk; Queen's Walk; adult/child £14.50/free; ⊙10am-5pm; ⊖London Bridge) White Ensign flapping on the Thames breeze, HMS *Belfast* is a magnet for naval-gazers. This large, light cruiser served in WWII, helping sink the German battleship *Scharnhorst* and shelling the Normandy coast on D-Day. Explore the nine decks and see the engine room, gun decks, galley, chapel, punishment cells, canteen and dental surgery. An audioguide is available.

London Dungeon HISTORIC BUILDING
(Map p168; www.thedungeons.com/london; County Hall, Westminster Bridge Rd, SE1; adult/child £24.60/19.20; ⊙10am-5pm, extended hours during holidays; ⊖Westminster or Waterloo) Older kids tend to love the London Dungeon, as the terrifying queues during school holidays and weekends testify. It's all spooky music, ghostly boat rides, macabre hangman's drop-rides, fake blood and actors dressed up as torturers and gory criminals (including Jack the Ripper and Sweeney Todd). Beware the interactive bits.

Sea Life AQUARIUM
(Map p168; ☎0871 663 1678; www.sealife.co.uk/london; County Hall; adult/child £18/13; ⊙10am-6pm; ⊖Waterloo) One of the largest aquariums in Europe, Sea Life has all sorts of aquatic creatures organised into different zones (coral cave, rainforest, River Thames), culminating with the shark walkway. Check the website

LONDON'S NEW SKYSCRAPERS

The Olympic effect saw a sudden scramble for high-altitude towers to shake up the otherwise low-lying London skyline. Most famous is The Shard (p175), rising over London Bridge like a vast glass splinter. The City of London's tallest building, the straight-edged **Heron Tower** (Map p170; 110 Bishopsgate EC2; ⊖Aldgate or Bank), was completed just up the road from **30 St Mary Axe** (The Gherkin; Map p170; www.30stmaryaxe.co.uk; 30 St Mary Axe EC3; ⊖Aldgate) in 2011. Aiming for a 2014 completion date, the top-heavy **Walkie Talkie** (20 Fenchuch St; Map p170; 20 Fenchurch St EC3) will be topped with a vast sky garden boasting magnificent views over town. Further construction on the concrete stub of the radical looking **Pinnacle** (Helter Skelter; Map p170; 22-24 Bishopgate; ⊖Aldgate or Bank) – nicknamed the Helter Skelter due to its cork-screwing top – was on hold at the the time of writing.

for shark-feeding times and book online for a 10% discount.

Hayward Gallery GALLERY
(Map p170; www.southbankcentre.co.uk; Belvedere Rd; ⏲10am-6pm Sat-Wed, to 8pm Thu & Fri; ⊖Waterloo) Part of the Southbank Centre, the Hayward hosts a changing roster of contemporary art (video, installations, photography, collage, painting etc) in a 1960s Brutalist building.

CHELSEA, KENSINGTON & KNIGHTSBRIDGE

It's called the Royal Borough of Kensington and Chelsea, and residents are certainly paid royally, earning the highest incomes in the UK (shops and restaurants will presume you do too). Knightsbridge has some of London's best-known department stores, while Kensington High St has a lively mix of chains and boutiques. Away from Mammon, South Kensington boasts some of London's most interesting museums.

FREE **Natural History Museum** MUSEUM
(Map p178; www.nhm.ac.uk; Cromwell Rd; ⏲10am-5.50pm; ⊖South Kensington) This ornate building itself is one of London's finest and a work of art. A sure-fire hit with kids of all ages, this splendid museum is crammed with fascinating discoveries, starting with the giant **Diplodocus** skeleton that greets you in the main hall. In the **dinosaur gallery**, the fleshless fossils are brought to robotic life with the roaring 4m-high animatronic **Tyrannosaurus Rex**.

An escalator slithers up and into a hollowed-out globe where two exhibits – The Power Within and Restless Surface – explain how wind, water, ice, gravity and life itself impact on the earth. The **mock-up of the Kobe earthquake** is a bone-rattling lesson in plate tectonics.

The **Darwin Centre** houses a team of biologists and a staggering 20-million-plus species of animal and plant specimens. Take a lift to the top of the Cocoon, a seven-storey egg-shaped structure encased within a glass pavilion, and make your way down through the floors of interactive displays. Windows allow you to watch the scientists at work.

Finally, don't overlook **Sensational Butterflies** by the East Lawn and the charming **Wildlife Garden**, a slice of English countryside in SW7.

FREE **Victoria & Albert Museum** MUSEUM
(V&A; Map p178; www.vam.ac.uk; Cromwell Rd; ⏲10am-5.45pm Sat-Thu, to 10pm Fri; ⊖South Kensington) This outstanding museum boasts an unparalleled collection specialising in decorative art and design with some 4.5 million objects from Britain and around the globe.

Part of Albert's legacy to Londoners in the wake of the Great Exhibition of 1851, the museum is a bit like the nation's attic, spread generously through nearly 150 galleries. Highlights of the world's greatest collection of decorative arts include the **Ardabil Carpet** (Room 42, Level 1), the sumptuous **China Collection** and **Japan Gallery** (Rooms 44 and 47e, Level 1), **Tipu's Tiger** (Room 41, Level 1), the astonishing **Cast Courts** (Room 46a, Level 1), the **Raphael Cartoons** (Rooms 48a, Level 1), the hefty **Great Bed of Ware** (Room 57, Level 2) and the stunning **Jewellery Gallery** (Rooms 91–93, Level 3).

You'll need to plan as the museum is epic, but it's open late on Friday evenings.

FREE **Science Museum** MUSEUM
(Map p178; www.sciencemuseum.org.uk; Exhibition Rd; ⏲10am-6pm; ⊖South Kensington) With seven floors of interactive and educational exhibits, this scientifically spellbinding museum

will mesmerise even the most precocious of young Einsteins. Some children head straight for voice warpers, lava lamps, boomerangs, bouncy globes and alien babies in the ground-floor shop, and stay put. Highlights include the Energy Hall on the ground floor, the riveting Flight Gallery on the 3rd floor and the flight simulator. There's also a 450-seat Imax cinema. If you've kids under the age of five, pop down to the basement The Garden, where there's a fun-filled play zone, including a water-play area, besieged by tots in red waterproof smocks.

Hyde Park PARK

(Map p178; ⏲5.30am-midnight; ⊖Marble Arch, Hyde Park Corner or Queensway) At 145 hectares, Hyde Park is central London's largest open space. Henry VIII expropriated it from the Church in 1536, when it became a hunting ground and later a venue for duels, executions and horse racing. The 1851 Great Exhibition was held here, and during WWII the park became an enormous potato field.

There's boating on the **Serpentine** (Map p178; Kensington Gardens; ⊖Knightsbridge or South Kensington) for the energetic, while **Speakers Corner** (Map p178; Park Lane; ⊖Marble Arch) is for oratorical acrobats. Nearby **Marble Arch** (Map p178; ⊖Marble Arch) was designed by John Nash in 1828 as the entrance to Buckingham Palace. It was moved here in 1851. The infamous **Tyburn Tree** (Map p178; ⊖Marble Arch), a three-legged gallows, once stood nearby. It is estimated that up to 50,000 people were executed here between 1196 and 1783.

A soothing structure, the **Diana, Princess of Wales Memorial Fountain** (Map p178; Kensington Gardens; ⊖Knightsbridge) was unveiled in mid-2004, instigating an inevitable debate over matters of taste and gravitas.

Kensington Palace PALACE

(Map p178; www.hrp.org.uk/kensingtonpalace; Kensington Gardens; adult/child £14.50/free; ⏲10am-6pm; ⊖High St Kensington) Kensington Palace became the favourite royal residence under the joint reign of William and Mary and remained so until George III became king and moved to Buckingham Palace. It still has private apartments where various members of the royal extended family live. In popular imagination it's most associated with three intriguing princesses: Victoria (who was born here in 1819 and lived here with her domineering mother until her accession to the throne), Margaret (sister of the current queen, who lived here until her 2002 death) and, of course, Diana. More than a million bouquets were left outside the gates following her death in 1997. The building underwent magnificent restoration work totalling £12 million and was reopened in early 2012.

Kensington Gardens GARDENS

(Map p178; ⏲dawn-dusk; ⊖High St Kensington) Immediately west of Hyde Park and across the Serpentine, these gardens are technically part of Kensington Palace. If you have kids, the **Diana, Princess of Wales Memorial Playground** (Map p178; Kensington Gardens; ⊖Queensway), in the northwest corner of the gardens, has some pretty ambitious attractions for children. Next to the playground is the delightful **Elfin Oak** (Map p178), an ancient tree stump carved with elves, gnomes, witches and small animals.

George Frampton's celebrated **Peter Pan statue** (Map p178; Kensington Gardens; ⊖Lancaster Gate) is close to the lake. On the opposite side is a statue of Edward Jenner, who developed a vaccine for smallpox.

MARYLEBONE

With one of London's best high streets and plenty of green space, increasingly hip Marylebone is a great area to wander.

Regent's Park PARK

(Map p184; ⊖Regent's Park) A former royal hunting ground, Regent's Park was designed by John Nash early in the 19th century, although what was actually laid out is only a fraction of the celebrated architect's grand plan. Nevertheless, it's one of London's most lovely open spaces – at once serene and lively, cosmopolitan and local – with football pitches, tennis courts, a boating lake, London Zoo, and Regent's Canal along its northern side. Queen Mary's Gardens, towards the south of the park, are particularly pretty, with spectacular roses in summer. **Open Air Theatre** (☎020-7935 5756; www.openairtheatre.org) hosts performances of Shakespeare and other classics here on summer evenings, along with comedy and concerts.

BEST FOR CULTURE

- » British Museum (p181)
- » Tate Modern (p174)
- » Victoria & Albert Museum (p176)
- » National Gallery (p162)
- » Shakespeare's Globe (p174)

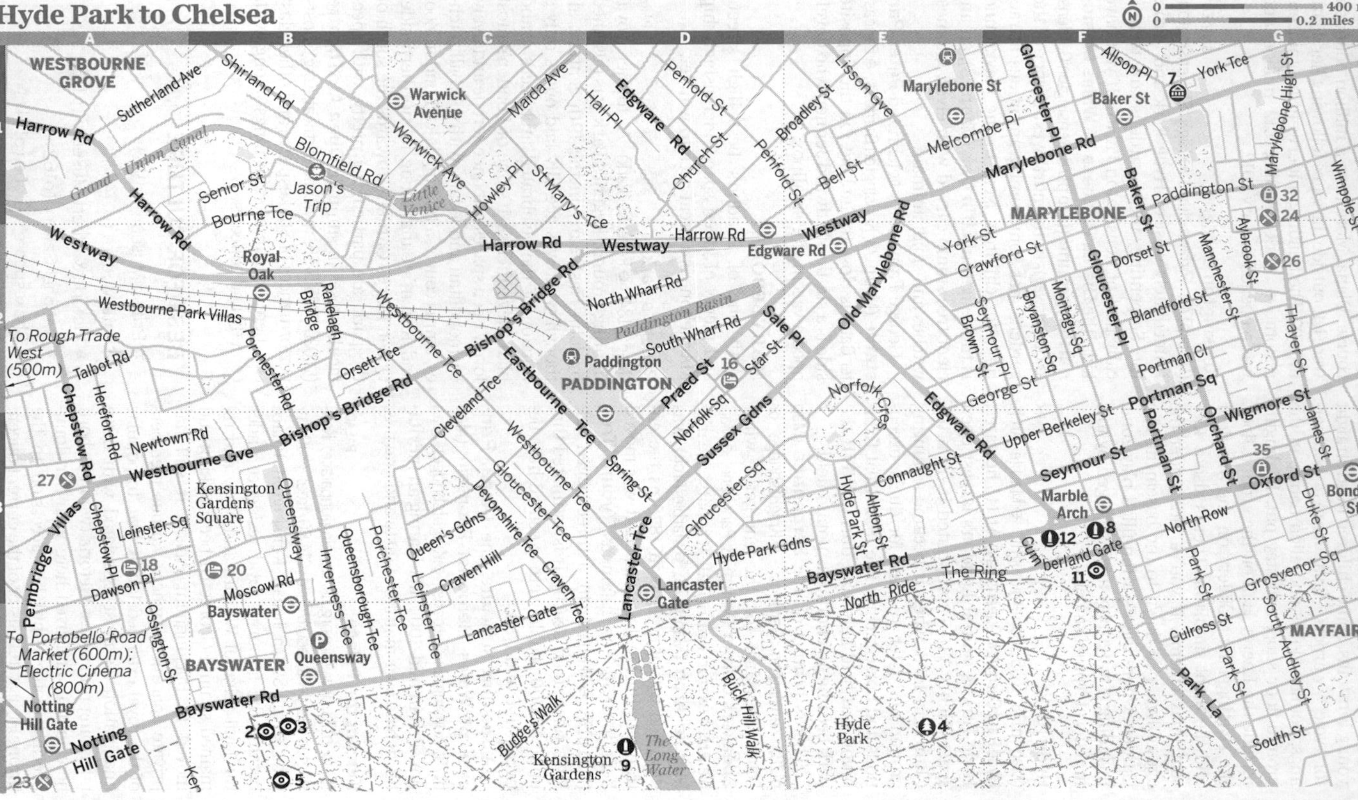
Hyde Park to Chelsea
0 400 m
0 0.2 miles
WESTBOURNE GROVE
Sutherland Ave
Shirland Rd
Warwick Avenue
Maida Ave
Hall Pl
Edgware Rd
Penfold St
Broadley St
Lisson Gve
Marylebone St
Gloucester Pl
Allsop Pl
York Tce
Baker St
Marylebone High St
Wimpole St
Harrow Rd
Grand Union Canal
Blomfield Rd
Warwick Ave
Little Venice
Howley Pl
St Mary's Tce
Church St
Penfold St
Bell St
Melcombe Pl
Marylebone Rd
Paddington St
MARYLEBONE
Senior St
Jason's Trip
Bourne Tce
Harrow Rd
Westway
Royal Oak
Harrow Rd
Westway
Harrow Rd
Edgware Rd
Westway
Old Marylebone Rd
York St
Crawford St
Dorset St
Manchester St
Aybrook St
Westbourne Park Villas
Ranelagh Bridge
Porchester Rd
Westbourne Tce
Bishop's Bridge Rd
North Wharf Rd
Paddington Basin
South Wharf Rd
Sale Pl
Seymour Pl
Brown St
Bryanston Sq
Montagu Sq
Blandford St
Thayer St
To Rough Trade West (500m)
Talbot Rd
Orsett Tce
Eastbourne Tce
Paddington
PADDINGTON
Praed St
Star St
Norfolk Cres
Portman Cl
Chepstow Rd
Hereford Rd
Bishop's Bridge Rd
Cleveland Tce
Norfolk Sq
George St
Portman Sq
Newtown Rd
Westbourne Gve
Westbourne Tce
Sussex Gdns
Edgware Rd
Upper Berkeley St
Wigmore St
James St
Spring St
Seymour St
Portman St
Orchard St
Oxford St
Bond St
Kensington Gardens Square
Queensway
Gloucester Tce
Devonshire Tce
Gloucester Sq
Connaught St
Marble Arch
Pembridge Villas
Chepstow Pl
Leinster Sq
Dawson Pl
Queen's Gdns
Queensborough Tce
Inverness Tce
Porchester Tce
Leinster Tce
Craven Hill
Craven Tce
Lancaster Tce
Hyde Park Gdns
Hyde Park St
Albion St
Cumberland Gate
North Row
Duke St
Grosvenor Sq
Moscow Rd
Bayswater
Lancaster Gate
Lancaster Gate
Bayswater Rd
The Ring
North Ride
Park St
Culross St
South Audley St
MAYFAIR
To Portobello Road Market (600m); Electric Cinema (800m)
Ossington St
BAYSWATER
Queensway
Notting Hill Gate
Bayswater Rd
Budge's Walk
Buck Hill Walk
Hyde Park
Park La
Park St
South St
Notting Hill Gate
Kensington Gardens
The Long Water
Ken

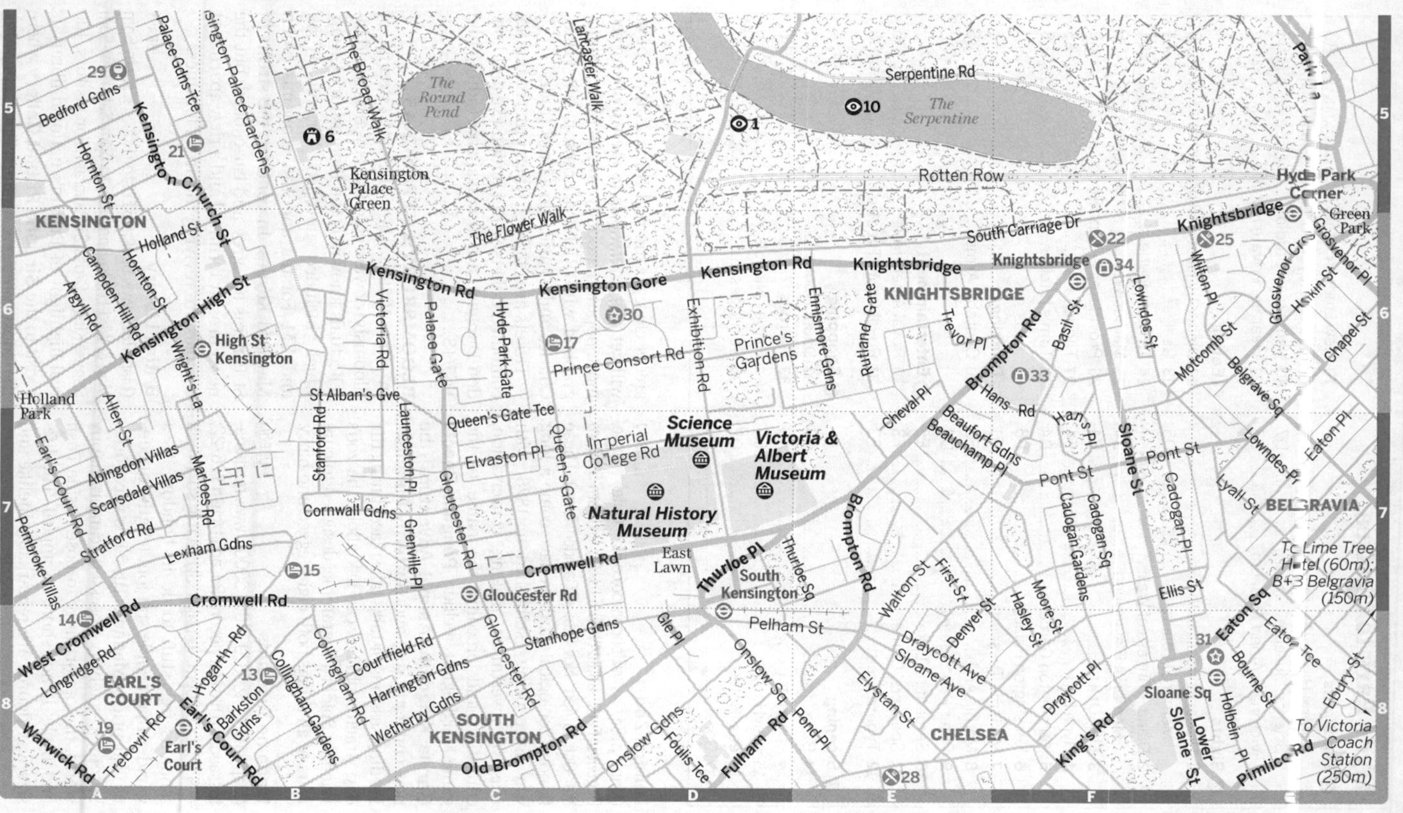
A
B
C
D
E
F
G
5
6
7
8
Bedford Gdns
29
Palace Gdns Tce
Kensington Palace Gardens
Kensington Church St
21
Hornton St
KENSINGTON
Holland St
Campden Hill Rd
Argyll Rd
Hornton St
Kensington High St
High St Kensington
Wright's La
Holland Park
Allen St
Earl's Court Rd
Abingdon Villas
Scarsdale Villas
Marloes Rd
Stratford Rd
Pembroke Villas
Lexham Gdns
15
14
West Cromwell Rd
Longridge Rd
EARL'S COURT
Hogarth Rd
13
Barkston Gdns
Collingham Gardens
Collingham Rd
19
Trebovir Rd
Earl's Court
Earl's Court Rd
Warwick Rd
The Broad Walk
The Round Pond
6
Kensington Palace Green
The Flower Walk
Lancaster Walk
Kensington Rd
Kensington Gore
30
Victoria Rd
Palace Gate
Hyde Park Gate
17
Prince Consort Rd
St Alban's Gve
Launceston Pl
Queen's Gate Tce
Stanford Rd
Elvaston Pl
Queen's Gate
Imperial College Rd
Cornwall Gdns
Grenville Pl
Gloucester Rd
Cromwell Rd
Gloucester Rd
Courtfield Rd
Harrington Gdns
Wetherby Gdns
SOUTH KENSINGTON
Old Brompton Rd
Stanhope Gdns
Gloucester Rd
Serpentine Rd
10
The Serpentine
1
Rotten Row
South Carriage Dr
Exhibition Rd
Kensington Rd
Prince's Gardens
Ennismore Gdns
Rutland Gate
Knightsbridge
KNIGHTSBRIDGE
Science Museum
Victoria & Albert Museum
Natural History Museum
East Lawn
Thurloe Pl
South Kensington
Thurloe Sq
Pelham St
Gle Pl
Onslow Sq
Onslow Gdns
Foulis Tce
Fulham Rd
Pond Pl
Brompton Rd
Walton St
First St
Denyer St
Draycott Ave
Sloane Ave
Elystan St
CHELSEA
28
Trevor Pl
Brompton Rd
Cheval Pl
33
Hans Rd
Beaufort Gdns
Beauchamp Pl
Hans Pl
Basil St
Knightsbridge
34
22
Lowndes St
Sloane St
Pont St
Cadogan Sq
Cadogan Gardens
Hasley St
Moore St
Draycott Pl
Cadogan Pl
Ellis St
Hyde Park Corner
Knightsbridge
Green Park
25
Wilton Pl
Grosvenor Cres
Grosvenor Pl
Halkin St
Chapel St
Motcomb St
Belgrave Sq
Lowndes Pl
Eaton Pl
Lyall St
BELGRAVIA
To Lime Tree Hotel (60m); B+B Belgravia (150m)
Eaton Sq
31
Eaton Tce
Bourne St
Holbein Pl
Ebury St
Sloane Sq
Lower Sloane St
King's Rd
Pimlico Rd
To Victoria Coach Station (250m)

Hyde Park to Chelsea

Top Sights
- Natural History Museum D7
- Science Museum D7
- Victoria & Albert Museum D7

Sights
- 1 Diana, Princess of Wales Memorial Fountain D5
- 2 Diana, Princess of Wales Memorial Playground B4
- 3 Elfin Oak B4
- 4 Hyde Park E4
- 5 Kensington Gardens B4
- 6 Kensington Palace B5
- 7 Madame Tussauds F1
- 8 Marble Arch F3
- 9 Peter Pan Statue D4
- 10 Serpentine Lake E5
- 11 Speakers' Corner F3
- 12 Tyburn Tree F3

Sleeping
- 13 Base2stay B8
- 14 easyHotel A8
- 15 easyHotel B7
- 16 easyHotel D2
- 17 Gore C6
- 18 New Linden Hotel A3
- 19 Twenty Nevern Square A8
- 20 Vancouver Studios B3
- 21 Vicarage Private Hotel A5

Eating
- 22 Dinner by Heston Blumenthal F6
- 23 Geales A4
- 24 La Fromagerie G1
- 25 Marcus Wareing at the Berkeley G6
- 26 Providores & Tapa Room G2
- 27 Taquería A3
- 28 Tom's Kitchen E8

Drinking
- 29 Churchill Arms A5

Entertainment
- 30 Royal Albert Hall D6
- 31 Royal Court Theatre G8

Shopping
- 32 Daunt Books G1
- 33 Harrods F6
- 34 Harvey Nichols F6
- 35 Selfridges G3

London Zoo ZOO

(Map p184; www.londonzoo.co.uk; Outer Circle, Regent's Park; adult/child £18/14; ⌚10am-5.30pm Mar-Oct, to 4pm Nov-Feb; ⊖Camden Town) These famous zoological gardens have come a long way since being established in 1828, with massive investment making conservation, education and breeding the name of the game. Highlights include **Penguin Beach**, **Gorilla Kingdom**, **Animal Adventure** (the new children's zoo) and **Butterfly Paradise**. Feeding sessions or talks take place during the day. Arachnophobes can ask about the zoo's Friendly Spider Programme, designed to cure fears of all things both eight-legged and hairy.

Madame Tussauds MUSEUM

(Map p178; ☎0870 400 3000; www.madame-tussauds.co.uk; Marylebone Rd; adult/child £26/22; ⌚9.30am-5.30pm; ⊖Baker St) With so much fabulous free stuff to do in London, it's a wonder that people still join lengthy queues to visit pricey Madame Tussauds waxworks, but in a celebrity-obsessed, camera-happy world, the opportunity to pose beside Posh and Becks is not short on appeal. The life-size wax figures are remarkably lifelike and are as close to the real thing as most of us will get. It's interesting to see which are the most popular; nobody wants to be photographed with Richard Branson, but Prince Charles and Camilla do a brisk trade.

Tickets are cheaper when ordered online; combined tickets with London Eye and London Dungeon are also available (adult/child £65/48).

BLOOMSBURY & ST PANCRAS

In the 1930s, the pleasant streets of Bloomsbury were colonised by artists and intellectuals known as the Bloomsbury Group, which included novelists Virginia Woolf and EM Forster and the economist John Maynard Keynes. In contrast, the streets of St Pancras are grey and car-choked, but the new Eurostar terminal and a ritzy apartment complex are reviving the area's fortunes.

British Library LIBRARY

(Map p182; www.bl.uk; 96 Euston Rd; ⌚9.30am-6pm Mon & Wed-Fri, to 8pm Tue, to 5pm Sat, 11am-5pm Sun; ⊖King's Cross St Pancras) For visitors, the real highlight of Britain's national library is a visit to the **Sir John Ritblat Gallery** where the most precious manuscripts, spanning almost three millennia, are held. Here you'll find the *Codex Sinaiticus* (the first complete text of the New Testament), a Gutenberg Bible (1455), the stunningly illustrated Jain sacred texts, Leonardo da Vinci's notebooks, a copy of the *Magna Carta* (1215), explorer Captain Scott's final diary, Shakespeare's First Folio (1623) and the lyrics to 'A Hard Day's Night' (scribbled on the back of Julian Lennon's birthday card) plus original scores by Handel, Mozart and Beethoven.

FREE British Museum MUSEUM
(Map p164; 020-7323 8000; www.britishmuseum.org; Great Russell St; 10am-5.30pm Sat-Wed, to 8.30pm Thu & Fri; Russell Sq) The country's largest museum and one of the oldest and finest in the world, this famous repository boasts vast Egyptian, Etruscan, Greek, Roman, European and Middle Eastern galleries, among many others.

Begun in 1753 with a 'cabinet of curiosities' bequeathed by Sir Hans Sloane to the nation on his death, the collection mushroomed over the ensuing years partly through plundering the empire. The grand **Enlightenment Gallery** was the first section of the redesigned museum to be built (in 1820).

Among the must-sees are the **Rosetta Stone**, the key to deciphering Egyptian hieroglyphics, discovered in 1799; the controversial **Parthenon Sculptures**, stripped from the walls of the Parthenon in Athens by Lord Elgin (the British ambassador to the Ottoman Empire), and which Greece wants returned; the stunning **Oxus Treasure** of 7th- to 4th-century BC Persian gold; and the Anglo-Saxon **Sutton Hoo** burial relics.

The **Great Court** was restored and augmented by Norman Foster in 2000 and now has a spectacular glass-and-steel roof, making it one of the most impressive architectural spaces in the capital. In the centre is the Reading Room, with its stunning blue-and-gold domed ceiling, where Karl Marx wrote *Manifesto of the Communist Party.*

You'll need multiple visits to savour even the highlights here; happily there are 15 free half-hour 'Eye Opener' tours between 11am and 3.45pm daily, focusing on different parts of the collection. Other tours include the 90-minute highlights tour at 10.30am, 1pm and 3pm daily (adult/child £8/5), and audioguides are available (£4.50).

CAMDEN TOWN

Once well outside the city limits, the former hamlets of North London have long since been gobbled up by the metropolis, and yet still maintain a semblance of a village atmosphere and distinct local identity. Of these, the enclave of Camden Town is a lively neighbourhood of pubs, live-music venues, boutiques, technicolour hairstyles, facial furniture, intricate tattoos, ambitious platform shoes and, most famously, Camden Market (p198).

HOXTON, SHOREDITCH & SPITALFIELDS

The East End suburbs of Hoxton, Shoreditch and Spitalfields are traditionally working class but increasingly trendy these days. They're a great place for diverse ethnic cuisine, thanks to the waves of immigrants that have arrived here over the centuries.

FREE Geffrye Museum MUSEUM
(www.geffrye-museum.org.uk; 136 Kingsland Rd; 10am-5pm Tue-Sat, noon-5pm Sun; Hoxton or Old St) If you like nosing around other people's homes, you'll love this museum. Devoted to middle-class domestic interiors, these former almshouses (1714) have been converted into a series of living rooms dating from 1630 to the current Ikea generation. On top of the interiors, the back garden has been transformed into period garden 'rooms' and a lovely walled herb garden (April to October only).

FREE White Cube GALLERY
(Map p170; www.whitecube.com; 48 Hoxton Sq; 10am-6pm Tue-Sat; Old St) In an industrial building with an impressive glazed-roof extension, White Cube offers contemporary art exhibitions from sculptures to video, installations and painting.

DOCKLANDS

East of the centre, London's port was once the global trade hub of the enormous British Empire. In the 40 years following WWII, the port and surrounding Docklands area went downhill, but massive redevelopment, spearheaded by the towers of Canary Wharf, means crusty seadogs have been replaced with battalions of dark-suited office workers.

Queen Elizabeth Olympic Park PARK
(www.london2012.com/olympic-park; Stratford) From 2008, a huge, once-contaminated and largely neglected swathe of industrial East London was ambitiously regenerated and transformed into London's Olympic Park for the 2012 Games. Complementing its iconic architecture, the Olympic Park was thoughtfully designed with a diverse mix of

Bloomsbury & St Pancras

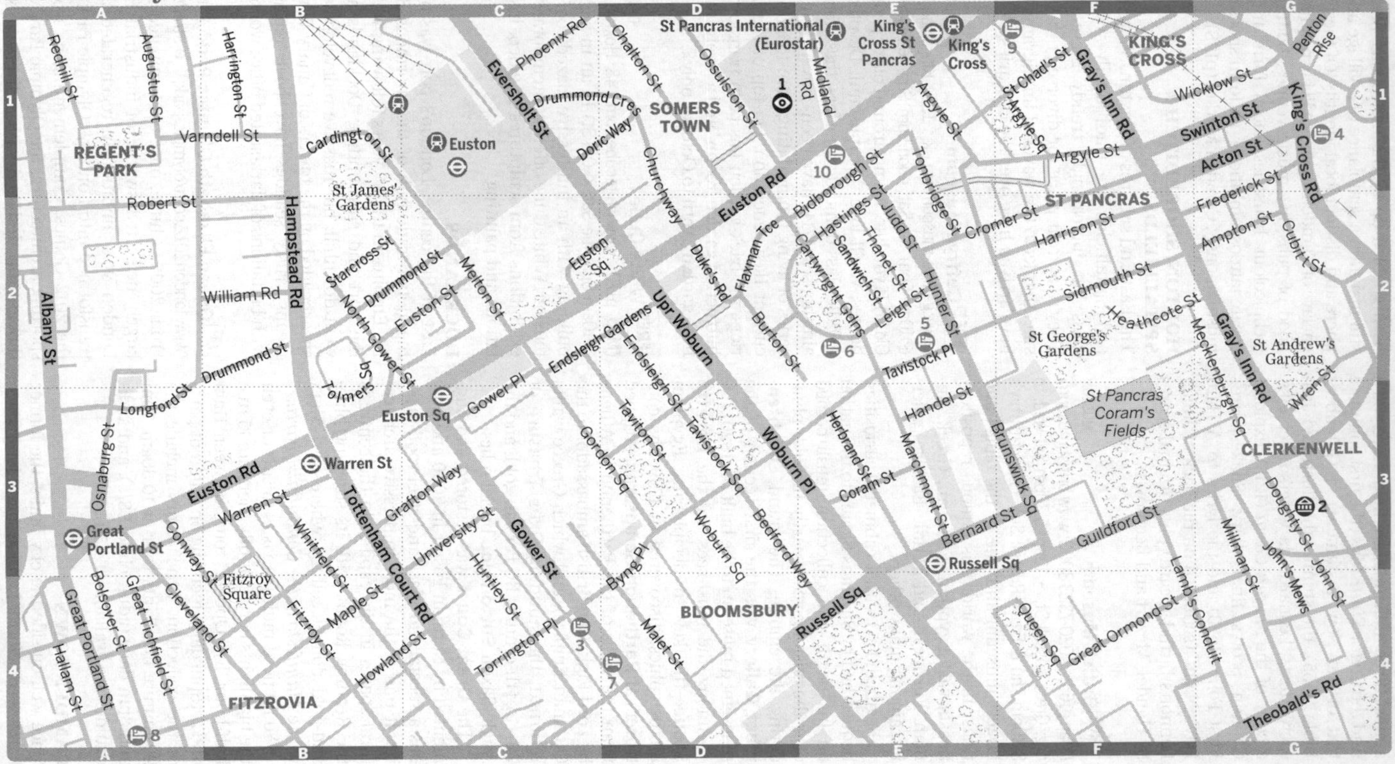

Bloomsbury & St Pancras

Sights
1 British Library ... D1
2 Charles Dickens Museum ... G3

Sleeping
3 Arosfa Hotel ... C4
Arran House Hotel ... (see 3)
4 Clink78 ... G1
5 Generator ... E2
6 Harlingford Hotel ... E2
7 Jesmond Hotel ... D4
8 London Central YHA ... A4
9 Rough Luxe ... F1
10 YHA London St Pancras ... E1

wetland, woodland, meadow and other wildlife habitats as an environmentally fertile legacy for the future. The twisted, abstract tangle of metal overlooking everything is the ArcelorMittal Orbit, aka the 'Hubble Bubble Pipe', a 115m-high observation tower. Panoramic views of the Olympic Park can also be had from the **View Tube** (www.theviewtube.co.uk; The Greenway; 9am-5pm; DLR Pudding Mill Lane) on the Greenway, next to the park.

FREE Museum of London Docklands MUSEUM

(www.museumoflondon.org.uk/docklands; Hertsmere Rd, West India Quay; 10am-6pm; DLR West India Quay) Housed in a heritage-listed warehouse, this museum uses a combination of artefacts and multimedia to chart the history of the city through its river and docks. There's a lot to see here, including an affecting section on the slave trade.

GREENWICH

An extraordinary cluster of buildings have earned 'Maritime Greenwich' its place on Unesco's World Heritage list. It's also famous for straddling the hemispheres; this is degree zero, the home of Greenwich Mean Time.

Greenwich is easily reached on the DLR train. Or go by boat: **Thames River Services** (www.thamesriverservices.co.uk; adult/child single £12/6, return £15.50/7.75) depart half-hourly from Westminster Pier (one hour, every 40 minutes). **Thames Clippers** (www.thamesclippers.com; adult/child £5.30/2.65) are cheaper.

FREE Old Royal Naval College HISTORIC BUILDING

(www.oldroyalnavalcollege.org; 2 Cutty Sark Gardens; 10am-5pm; DLR Cutty Sark) Designed by Wren, the Old Royal Naval College is a magnificent example of classical architecture. Parts are now used by the University of Greenwich and Trinity College of Music, but you can visit the **chapel** and the extraordinary **Painted Hall**, which took artist Sir James Thornhill 19 years to complete. Yeomen-led tours of the complex leave at 2pm daily, taking in areas not otherwise open to the public (£6, 90 minutes).

FREE National Maritime Museum MUSEUM

(020-8858 4422; www.nmm.ac.uk; Romney Rd; 10am-5pm; DLR Cutty Sark) With its newly opened Sammy Ofer Wing, the National Maritime Museum houses a splendid collection of nautical paraphernalia recounting Britain's brine-soaked seafaring history. Exhibits range from *Miss Britain III* (the first boat to top 100mph on open water) from 1933, the 19m-long golden state barge built in 1732 for Frederick, Prince of Wales, humdingers such as Cook's journals and Nelson's uniform, complete with bullet hole, and interactive plus educational displays.

O2 STADIUM

(www.theo2.co.uk; Peninsula Sq; North Greenwich) The world's largest dome (365m in diameter) opened on 1 January 2000, at a cost of £789 million, as the Millennium Dome. Renamed the O2, it's now a 20,000-seat sports and entertainment arena. O2 conducts regular guided climbs of the dome's exterior (£22 to £28). There are ferry services from central London on concert nights.

WEST LONDON

Kew Gardens GARDENS

(www.kew.org.uk; Kew Rd; adult/child £16/free, Kew Explorer adult/child £4/2; 9.30am-6.30pm Apr-Aug, earlier closing other months; Kew Bridge, Kew Gardens, ferry Kew Pier) In 1759 botanists began rummaging around the world for specimens they could plant in the 3-hectare plot known as the Royal Botanic Gardens. They never stopped collecting, and the gardens, which have bloomed to 120 hectares, provide the most comprehensive botanical collection on earth (including the world's largest collection of orchids). The gardens are now a Unesco World Heritage site.

Camden

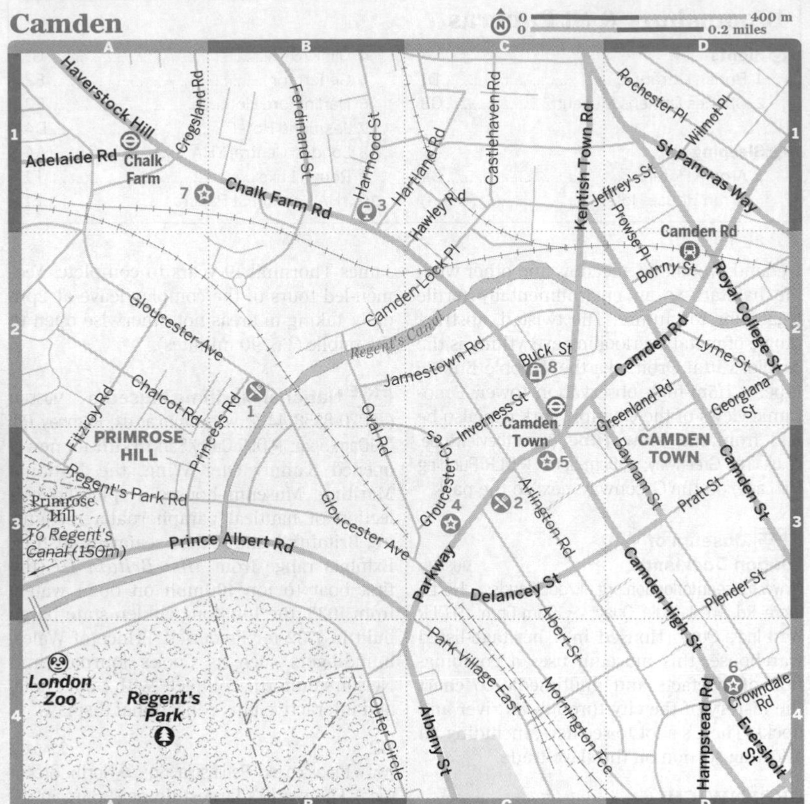

Camden

Top Sights

London Zoo	A4
Regent's Park	A4

Eating

1 Engineer	B2
2 Market	C3

Drinking

3 Lock Tavern	B1

Entertainment

4 Dublin Castle	C3
5 Jazz Café	C3
6 KOKO	D4
7 Roundhouse	A1

Shopping

8 Camden Market	C2

You can easily spend a whole day wandering around, but if you're pressed for time, the Kew Explorer (adult/child £4/1) is a hop-on, hop-off road train that leaves from Victoria Gate and takes in the gardens' main sights.

Highlights include the enormous early Victorian **Palm House**, a hothouse of metal and curved sheets of glass; the impressive **Princess of Wales Conservatory**; the red-brick, 1631 **Kew Palace** (www.hrp.org.uk/kewpalace; ⌚9.30am-5.30pm Apr-Sep), formerly King George III's country retreat; the celebrated **Great Pagoda** designed by William Chambers in 1762; the **Temperate House**, the world's largest ornamental glasshouse; and the very enjoyable **Rhizotron and Xstrata Treetop Walkway**, where you can survey the tree canopy from 18m up in the air.

The gardens are easily reached by tube, but you might prefer to take a cruise on a riverboat from the **Westminster Passenger Services Association** (☎020-7930 2062; www.wpsa.co.uk; adult/child return to Kew Gardens £18/9), which runs several daily boats from April to October, departing from Westminster Pier (return adult/child £18/9, 90 minutes).

Hampton Court Palace PALACE
(www.hrp.org.uk/HamptonCourtPalace; adult/child £14/7; ⊙10am-6pm Apr-Oct, to 4.30pm Nov-Mar; Hampton Court) Built by Cardinal Thomas Wolsey in 1514 but coaxed from him by Henry VIII just before Wolsey (as chancellor) fell from favour, Hampton Court Palace is England's largest and grandest Tudor structure.

Take a themed tour led by costumed historians or, if you're in a rush, visit the highlights: **Henry VIII's State Apartments**, including the Great Hall with its spectacular hammer-beamed roof; the **Tudor Kitchens**, staffed by 'servants'; and the **Wolsey Rooms**. You could easily spend a day exploring the palace and its 24 hectares of riverside gardens, especially if you get lost in the 300-year-old **maze**.

Hampton Court is 13 miles southwest of central London and is easily reached by train from Waterloo. Alternatively, the riverboats that head from Westminster to Kew continue here (return adult/child £22.50/11.25, three hours).

Richmond Park PARK
(⊙7am-dusk Mar-Sep, from 7.30am Oct-Feb; Richmond) London's wildest park and the largest urban parkland in Europe – spans more than 1000 hectares and is home to all sorts of wildlife, most notably herds of red and fallow deer. It's a terrific place for bird-watching, rambling and cycling.

To get there from Richmond tube station, turn left along George St then left at the fork that leads up Richmond Hill.

Activities

Emirates Air Line CABLE CAR
(www.emiratesairline.co.uk; adult/child single £4.30/2.20, return £8.60/4.40 with Oyster or Travelcard single £3.20/1.60, return £6.40/3.20; ⊙7am-9pm Mon-Fri, from 8am Sat, from 9am Sun Apr-Sep, closes one hour earlier rest of year; DLR Royal Victoria, North Greenwich) Destined to become a sight in its own right and capable of ferrying 2400 people per hour across the Thames in either direction, the new Emirates Air Line Cable Car links the Greenwich Peninsula and the Royal Docks in a five- to 10-minute journey. Oyster Card and Travelcard holders get a discount for journeys, which are bike-friendly too.

LOO STOP

While facilities are available at most museums and sights, many foreign visitors are surprised at London's lack of public toilets (also coyly called 'public conveniences' on signs) out on the street.

Very few tube stations have facilities but bigger rail stations usually do (although they're often coin-operated, so yes it's 20p to pee). Department stores are a good bet, if you can face five floors on an escalator, as are fast-food outlets. In a pub, you might be able to sneak in to use the loo, but it's polite to order a drink afterwards – which kinda defeats the purpose.

Tours

One of the best ways to orientate yourself when you first arrive in London is with a 24-hour hop-on/hop-off pass for the double-decker bus tours. The buses loop around interconnecting routes throughout the day, providing a commentary as they go, and the price includes a river cruise and three walking tours. You'll save a couple of pounds by booking online.

Original Tour BUS TOUR
(www.theoriginaltour.com; adult/child/family £26/13/91; ⊙every 20min 8.30am-5.30pm)

Big Bus Tours BUS TOUR
(www.bigbustours.com; adult/child £29/12/70; ⊙every 20min 8.30am-6pm Apr-Sept, to 5pm Oct & Mar, to 4.30pm Nov Feb) Informative commentaries in eight languages. The ticket includes a free river cruise with City Cruise and four thematic walking tours (Royal London, Harry Potter film locations, the Beatles, and the Ghosts by Gaslight).

London Walks WALKING TOUR
(☎020-7624 3978; www.walks.com; adult £9) Harry Potter tours, ghost walks and the ever-popular Jack the Ripper tours.

London Mystery Walks WALKING TOUR
(☎07957-388280; www.tourguides.org.uk; adult/child £10/9) Tour Jack the Ripper's old haunts at 7pm on Monday, Wednesday and Friday. You must book in advance.

Capital Taxi Tours TAXI TOUR
(☎020-8590 3621; www.capitaltaxitours.co.uk; 2hr day tour per taxi £165, by night 2½hr tour per taxi £235) Takes up to five people on a variety of tours with Blue Badge, City of London and City of Westminster registered guides/drivers; cheeky Cockney Cabbie option and foreign language availability.

Festivals & Events

University Boat Race BOAT RACE
(www.theboatrace.org) A posh-boy grudge match held annually since 1829 between the rowing crews of Oxford and Cambridge universities (late March).

London Marathon RUNNING RACE
(www.london-marathon.co.uk) Up to half a million spectators watch the whippet-thin champions and bizarrely clad amateurs take to the streets in late April.

Trooping the Colour ROYAL PARADE
Celebrating the Queen's official birthday (in June), this ceremonial procession of troops, marching along the Mall for their monarch's inspection, is a pageantry overload.

Meltdown Festival MUSIC
(www.southbankcentre.co.uk) The Southbank Centre hands over the curatorial reigns to a legend of contemporary music (such as David Bowie, Morrissey or Patti Smith) to pull together a full program of concerts, talks and films in late June.

Wimbledon Lawn Tennis Championships TENNIS
(www.wimbledon.org) The world's most splendid tennis event takes place in late June.

Pride GAY & LESBIAN
(www.pridelondon.org) The big event on the gay and lesbian calendar, a technicolour street parade heads through the West End in late June or early July, culminating in a concert in Trafalgar Square.

Notting Hill Carnival STREET PARADES
(www.thenottinghillcarnival.com) Held over two days in August, this is Europe's largest and London's most vibrant outdoor carnival, where the Caribbean community shows the city how to party. Unmissable and truly crazy.

Sleeping

When it comes to accommodation, London is one of the most expensive places in the world. 'Budget' is pretty much anything below £90 per night for a double; at the top end, how does a £14,000-per-night suite on Hyde Park Corner sound? Double rooms ranging between £90 and £180 per night are considered midrange; more expensive options fall into the top-end category. Public transport is good, so you don't need to be sleeping at Buckingham Palace to be at the heart of things.

WEST END

Like in Monopoly, land on a Mayfair hotel and you may have to sell your house, or at least remortgage.

TOP CHOICE **Hazlitt's** HISTORIC HOTEL £££
(Map p164; ☎020-7434 1771; www.hazlittshotel.com; 6 Frith St; s £206, d/ste from £259/646; ❄📶; ⊖Tottenham Court Rd) Staying in this charming Georgian house (1718) is a trip back into a time when four-poster beds and claw-foot baths were the norm for gentlefolk. Each of the individually decorated 30 rooms is packed with antiques and named after a personage connected with the house.

Dean Street Townhouse BOUTIQUE HOTEL £££
(Map p164; ☎020-7434 1775; www.deanstreettownhouse.com; 69-71 Dean St; r £160-310; ❄📶; ⊖Tottenham Court Rd) This Soho gem enjoys a delightful boudoir atmosphere with choice rooms. Afternoon tea (£16.75) in the parlour hardly gets better; it's old-world cosy, with its upholstered furniture and roaring fireplace, and the pastries are divine.

Oxford St YHA HOSTEL £
(Map p164; ☎0845 371 9133; www.yha.org.uk; 14 Noel St; dm/tw from £18/44; @📶; ⊖Oxford Circus) In most respects, this is a bog-standard YHA hostel, with tidy rooms and all the usual facilities (kitchen, TV room, laundry). What it's got going for it are a terrific (albeit noisy) location and decent views over London's rooftops from some of the rooms.

WESTMINSTER & PIMLICO

Handy for the major sights; these areas have some good-value options.

TOP CHOICE **B+B Belgravia** B&B £
(☎020-7259 8570; www.bb-belgravia.com; 64-66 Ebury St; d/apt from £84/225, studio £89-140; @📶; ⊖Victoria) This lovely place marries contemporary chic with Georgian elegance; rooms are neat and, although not very spacious, fine studio rooms with compact kitchens are along the road at No 82.

Lime Tree Hotel B&B ££
(☎020-7730 8191; www.limetreehotel.co.uk; 135-137 Ebury St; s £99, d £150-175; @; ⊖Victoria) A smartly renovated Georgian townhouse hotel with a beautiful back garden to catch the late-afternoon rays. Contemporary renovations make it the best of the Belgravia crop.

Luna Simone Hotel B&B ££
(Map p168; ☎020-7834 5897; www.lunasimonehotel.com; 47-49 Belgrave Rd; s £70-75, d £95-120; @; ⊖Pimlico) Rooms are quite compact but clean and calming at this central, welcoming hotel; the ones at the back are quieter. Belgrave Rd follows on from Eccleston Bridge, directly behind Victoria Station.

THE CITY

Bristling with bankers during the week; you can often pick up a considerable bargain at weekends.

Apex City of London HOTEL ££
(Map p170; ☎020-7702 2020; www.apexhotels.co.uk; 1 Seething Ln; r from £100; ; ⊖Tower Hill) Business-focused but close enough to the Tower to hear the heads roll, the Apex offers enticing weekend rates, a gym, huge TVs, free wi-fi and a rubber ducky in every room.

Threadneedles HOTEL ££
(Map p170; ☎7657 8080; www.hotelthreadneedles.co.uk; 5 Threadneedle St EC2; r weekend/weekday from £150/250; ; ⊖Bank) The incredible stained-glass dome in the lobby points to Threedneedles' former status as a bank HQ. Today it's still popular with suits, but the atmosphere is chic rather than stuffy. Request one of the two deluxe rooms with balconies.

SOUTH BANK

Immediately south of the river is good if you want to immerse yourself in workaday London and still be central.

Kennington B&B B&B ££
(☎020-7735 7669; www.kenningtonbandb.com; 103 Kennington Park Rd, SE11; d £120-150; ; ⊖Kennington) With gorgeous bed linen and well-preserved Georgian features, this lovely B&B is very tasteful in virtually every regard, from the shining, tiled shower rooms and Georgian shutters to the fireplaces and cast-iron radiators. It's a short walk from Kennington underground station.

Premier Inn London County Hall HOTEL ££
(Map p170; ☎0871 527 8648; www.premierinn.com; County Hall, Belvedere Rd; r £112-160; ; ⊖Waterloo) Location, location, location is what this chain hotel is all about, with a choice positioning within a landmark historic building and a few steps from the London Eye, Westminster and Big Ben.

St Christopher's Village HOSTEL £
(Map p170; ☎020-7939 9710; www.st-christophers.co.uk; 163 Borough High St; dm/r from £14/62; @; ⊖London Bridge) The Village – a huge, up-for-it party hostel, with a club that hops till 4am at weekends and a roof terrace bar – is the main hub of three locations on the same street. **St Christopher's Inn** (Map p170; 121 Borough High St) is above a very nice pub, while **Oasis** (Map p170; 59 Borough High St) is women-only.

CHELSEA, KENSINGTON & KNIGHTSBRIDGE

These classy zones offer easy access to the museums and big-name fashion stores. It's all a bit sweetie-darling, along with the prices.

Gore HOTEL £££
(Map p178; ☎020-7584 6601; www.gorehotel.com; 190 Queen's Gate; r from £205; @; ⊖Gloucester Rd) A short stroll from the Royal Albert Hall, the Gore serves up British grandiosity (antiques, carved four-posters, polished mahogany, a secret bathroom in the Tudor room) in 50 individually furnished, magnificent rooms.

Vicarage Hotel B&B ££
(Map p178; ☎020-7229 4030; www.londonvicaragehotel.com; 10 Vicarage Gate; s/d £110/138, without bathroom £65/110; @; ⊖High St Kensington or Notting Hill Gate) On the corner with Palace Gardens Terrace (with its astonishing cherry trees in spring), this place is all about location (between Notting Hill Gate and Kensington High St) and value for money. Breakfast is included and rates fall in winter.

BLOOMSBURY & ST PANCRAS

One step from the West End and crammed with Georgian townhouse conversions, these are more affordable neighbourhoods. A stretch of lower-priced hotels runs along Gower St and on the pretty Cartwright Gardens crescent. While hardly a salubrious location, St Pancras is handy, with some excellent budget options.

TOP CHOICE **Clink78** HOSTEL £
(Map p182; ☎020-7183 9400; www.clinkhostels.com; 78 King's Cross Rd; dm/r from £9/40; @; ⊖King's Cross St Pancras) If anyone can think of a more right-on London place to stay than the courthouse where The Clash went on trial, please let us know. You can watch

TV from the witness box or sleep in the converted cells, but the majority of the rooms are custom-built and quite comfortable.

Rough Luxe BOUTIQUE HOTEL £££

(Map p182; ☎020-7837 5338; www.roughluxe.co.uk; 1 Birkenhead St, WC1; r £229-289; ; King's Cross St Pancras) Half rough, half luxury goes the blurb; the blend of shabby and chic at this Grade-II listed property is a compelling formula. Rooms treat you to the finest-quality bed linen, eclectic art works cling to walls, you may get a free-standing copper bath, and service is top-notch, but the wallpaper is fetchingly distressed and the 1970s TV doesn't quite work.

Arran House Hotel B&B ££

(Map p182; ☎020-7636 2186; www.arranhotel-london.com; 77-79 Gower St; s/d/tr/q £70/110/128/132, without bathroom £60/80/105/111; @; Goodge St) Period features such as cornicing and fireplaces, gorgeous gardens out back for a summer drink and a cosy lounge with two computers pushes this welcoming hotel from the average to the appealing. Squashed ensuites or shared bathrooms are the trade-off for these reasonable rates.

Arosfa Hotel B&B ££

(Map p182; ☎020-7636 2115; www.arosfalondon.com; 83 Gower St; s £60-65, d/tr/q £90/102/110; Goodge St) While the decor of the immaculately presented rooms is more unnoticeable, Arosfa's guest lounge is blinged up with chandeliers and clear plastic chairs. Recent refurbishments have added ensuites to all 15 bedrooms, but they're tiny (putting the 'closet' back into water closet).

Jesmond Hotel B&B ££

(Map p182; ☎020-7636 3199; www.jesmondhotel.org.uk; 63 Gower St; s/d/tr/q £60/100/130/145, without bathroom £50/80/105/135; @; Goodge St) This family-run B&B in Bloomsbury is a charmer of a place with a very handy location and fab breakfasts. Rooms may be basic and rather small but are clean and everyone is made to feel welcome. Quieter rooms face the pretty garden.

Harlingford Hotel B&B ££

(Map p182; ☎020-7387 1551; www.harlingfordhotel.com; 61-63 Cartwright Gardens; s/d/tr £86/115/130; ; Russell Sq) This family-run Georgian 43-room hotel sports refreshing, upbeat decor: bright-green mosaic-tiled bathrooms (with trendy sinks), fuchsia bedspreads and colourful paintings in a neighbourhood of stiff competition. It's all stairs and no lift; request a 1st-floor room.

London Central YHA HOSTEL £

(Map p182; ☎0845 371 9154; www.yha.org.uk; 104-108 Bolsover St; dm £21-32, q from £70; @; Great Portland St) One of London's new breed of YHA hostels, most of the four- to six-bed rooms have ensuites. There's a flash cafe-bar attached to reception and a wheelchair-accessible kitchen downstairs.

YHA London St Pancras HOSTEL £

(Map p182; ☎020-7388 9998; www.yha.org.uk; 79 Euston Rd; dm/r from £20/61; @; King's Cross St Pancras) Recent renovations have made this 185-bed hostel a dependable central London choice – despite the busy road. Rooms range from private doubles to six-bed dorms; most have bathrooms. There's a good bar and cafe, but no kitchen.

Generator HOSTEL £

(Map p182; ☎020-7388 7666; www.generatorhostels.com/london; 37 Tavistock Pl; dm/r from £18/55; @; Russell Sq) Lashings of primary colours and shiny metal are the hallmarks of this huge hostel. This former police barracks has 820 beds; a bar that stays open until 2am and hosts quizzes, pool competitions, karaoke and DJs; safe-deposit boxes; and a large eating area (but no kitchen). Come to party.

EARL'S COURT & FULHAM

Earl's Court is lively, cosmopolitan and so popular with travelling antipodeans that it's been nicknamed Kangaroo Valley. There are no real sights as such, but it does have inexpensive digs and an infectious holiday atmosphere.

Barclay House B&B ££

(☎020-7384 3390; www.barclayhouselondon.com; 21 Barclay Rd; r £110-125; @; Fulham Broadway) A proper homestay B&B with a handful of rooms with ensuite in a charming Victorian townhouse. It's so popular there's now a four-night minimum stay requirement, unless they can shoehorn you in between slots. From the tube station head west on Fulham Broadway and then look out for Barclay Rd on your left.

Twenty Nevern Square HOTEL ££

(Map p178; ☎020-7565 9555; www.20nevernsquare.com; 20 Nevern Sq; r from £115; ; Earl's Court) An Ottoman theme runs through this Victorian townhouse hotel, where a mix of wooden furniture, luxurious fabrics and natural light helps maximise space – even in the excellent-value cheaper rooms.

Base2stay HOTEL ££

(Map p178; ☎020-7244 2255; www.base2stay.com; 25 Courtfield Gardens; s/d from £93/99; ; Earl's Court) With comfort, smart decor, power showers, flatscreen TVs with internet access, artfully concealed kitchenettes, neat rooms and a sustainable credo, this boutique establishment feels like a four-star hotel without the wallet-emptying price tag.

easyHotel HOTEL £

(www.easyhotel.com; r from £25) Earl's Court (Map p178; 44 West Cromwell Rd; Earl's Court) Paddington (Map p178; 10 Norfolk Pl; Paddington) South Kensington (Map p178; 14 Lexham Gardens; Gloucester Rd) Victoria (Map p168; 36 Belgrave Rd; Victoria) Run along the same principles as its sibling business easyJet, this no-frills chain has tiny rooms with even tinier bathrooms.

NOTTING HILL, BAYSWATER & PADDINGTON

Don't be fooled by the movie. Notting Hill and the areas immediately north of Hyde Park are as shabby as they are chic, while scruffy Paddington has lots of cheap hotels, with a major strip along Sussex Gardens, worth checking if you're short on options.

New Linden Hotel BOUTIQUE HOTEL ££

(Map p178; ☎020-7221 4321; www.newlinden.co.uk; Hereford Rd, 59 Leinster Sq; s/d from £79/105; ; Bayswater) Cramming in a fair amount of style for little whack, this terrace house hotel exudes a modern and cool feel. The quiet location, helpful staff and monsoon shower heads in the deluxe rooms make this an excellent proposition.

Vancouver Studios APARTMENT ££

(Map p178; ☎020-7243 1270; www.vancouverstudios.co.uk; 30 Prince's Sq; apt £97-350; ; Bayswater) It's the addition of kitchenettes and a self-service laundry that differentiate these smart, reasonably priced studios and three bedroom apartment (sleeping one to six people) from a regular Victorian townhouse hotel.

HOXTON, SHOREDITCH & SPITALFIELDS

It's always had a rough-edged reputation, but London's East End is being speedily gentrified, with some good options close to the nightlife.

TOP CHOICE **Hoxton Hotel** HOTEL ££

(Map p170; ☎020-7550 1000; www.hoxtonhotels.com; 81 Great Eastern St; d & tw £59-199; ; Old St) A revolutionary pricing structure means that while all the rooms are identical, the hotel aims at constantly full occupancy. Book a couple of months ahead (sign up on the website) and you can nab £49 to £69 deals. The reasonably sized rooms all have comfy beds, quality linen and TVs that double as computers.

Zetter Hotel & Townhouse BOUTIQUE HOTEL £££

(Map p170; ☎020-7324 4444; www.thezetter.com; 86-88 Clerkenwell Rd; d from £222, studio £294-438; ; Farringdon) A slick 21st-century conversion of a Victorian warehouse. The furnishings and facilities are cutting edge. You can even choose the colour of your room's lighting.

Andaz Liverpool Street HOTEL ££

(Map p170; ☎7961 1234; www.london.liverpoolstreet.andaz.com; 40 Liverpool St EC2; r weekend/weekday from £145/290; ; Liverpool St) The former Great Eastern Hotel is now the London flagship for Hyatt's youth-focused Andaz chain. There's no reception here, just black-clad staff who check you in on laptops. Rooms are a little generic but have free juice, snacks and wi-fi.

GREENWICH

Number 16 St Alfege's B&B ££

(☎020-8853 4337; www.st-alfeges.co.uk; 16 St Alfege Passage; s/d £75/125; DLR Greenwich) This one-time sweet (candy) shop has two well-appointed doubles and a single, individually decorated in shades of blue, green or yellow and all with bathroom or shower room. From the DLR station head up Greenwich High St and look for St Alfege Passage on your left – it's the lane that skirts the church.

AIRPORTS

Yotel HOTEL £

(☎020-7100 1100; www.yotel.com; s/d £69/85, or per 4hr £29/45 then per additional hour £8;) Gatwick (South Terminal) Heathrow (Terminal 4) The best news for early morning flyers since coffee-vending machines, Yotel's smart

> **WANT MORE?**
>
> For in-depth information, reviews and recommendations at your fingertips, head to the Apple App Store to purchase Lonely Planet's *London City Guide* app.

'cabins' offer pint-sized luxury: comfy beds, soft lights, internet-connected TVs, monsoon showers and fluffy towels. Swinging cats isn't recommended, but when is it ever?

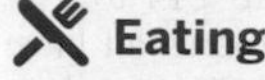

Eating

Dining out in London has become so fashionable that you can hardly open a menu without banging into a celebrity chef, while the range and quality of eating options has increased massively over the last few decades.

WEST END

Between them, Mayfair, Soho and Covent Garden are the gastronomic heart of London, with stacks of restaurants and cuisines at a wide range of budgets.

National Dining Rooms BRITISH ££
(Map p164; ☎020-7747 2525; www.peytonandbyrne.co.uk; Sainsbury Wing, National Gallery; mains £14.50-19.50; ⏰10am-5pm Sat-Thu, 10am-8.30pm Fri; ⊖Charing Cross) It's fitting that this acclaimed restaurant should celebrate British food, being in the National Gallery and overlooking Trafalgar Square. For a much cheaper option with the same views, ambience, quality produce and excellent service, try a salad, pie or tart at the adjoining bakery.

Great Queen Street BRITISH ££
(Map p164; ☎7242 0622; 32 Great Queen St WC2; mains £12-16; ⏰lunch daily, dinner till 10.30 Mon-Sat; ⊖Holborn) The claret-coloured walls and mismatched wooden chairs convey cosiness and tie-loosening informality, but the daily changing seasonal menu is still the very best of British, and booking is a must.

Wild Honey MODERN EUROPEAN £££
(☎7758 9160; www.wildhoneyrestaurant.co.uk; 12 St George St W1; mains £24-30; ⏰lunch & dinner till 11pm Mon-Thu, 11.30 Fri & Sat, till 10.30pm Sun; ⊖Oxford Circus) If you fancy a relatively affordable meal within the oak-panelled ambience of a top Mayfair restaurant, Wild Honey offers excellent lunch and pre-theatre set menus (respectively £21.95 and £22.95 for three courses).

Giaconda Dining Room MODERN EUROPEAN ££
(Map p164; ☎7240 3334; www.giacondadining.com; 9 Denmark St WC2; mains £15-19.50; ⏰lunch Tue-Fri, dinner till 9.30pm Mon-Sat; ⊖Tottenham Court Rd) Blink and you'll miss this 10-table restaurant (we did at first). It's well worth hunting down for quality British, French and Italian dishes and attentive service. Pig trotters are a speciality but for those less au fait with offal, there's always a choice of fish dishes.

Arbutus MODERN EUROPEAN ££
(Map p164; ☎7734 4545; www.arbutusrestaurant.co.uk; 63-64 Frith St W1; mains £18-20; ⏰lunch & dinner till 11pm Mon-Thu, till 11.30pm Fri & Sat, till 10.30pm Sun; ⊖Tottenham Court Rd) Focusing on seasonal produce, inventive dishes and value-for-money set meals, Anthony Demetre's Michelin-starred brainchild just keeps getting better.

Tamarind INDIAN ££
(☎020-7629 3561; www.tamarindrestaurant.com; 20 Queen St; mains £6.95-28; ⏰lunch Sun-Fri, dinner daily; ⊖Green Park) A mix of spicy Moghul classics and new creations have earned this northwest Indian restaurant a Michelin star. The set lunches are a good deal (two/three-courses £17/19).

Fernandez & Wells Espresso Bar CAFE £
(Map p164; ☎020-7494 4242; 16a St Anne's Ct; ⊖Oxford Circus) A wonderful Soho mini-chain, this is one of the three branches of Fernandez & Wells, each located within 200m of each other in small, friendly and elegant spaces. The Café and the Espresso Bar both do sandwiches and incredibly good coffee.

Hummus Bros CAFE £
(www.hbros.co.uk; mains £4-8;) Soho (Map p164; 88 Wardour St; ⊖Piccadilly Circus) Holborn (37-63 Southampton Row; ⊖Holborn) Cheapside (Map p170; 128 Cheapside; ⊖St Paul's) Don't come here if you're chickpea-challenged, because this informal place is hummus heaven. It comes in small or regular bowls with a choice of meat or vegie toppings and a side of pita bread.

SOUTH BANK

Popular restaurants make the most of the iconic riverside views but scouting around turns up gems all over the place. For a feed with a local feel, head to Borough Market (p198) or Bermondsey St.

Laughing Gravy BRITISH ££
(Map p170; ☎020-7998 1707; www.thelaughinggravy.co.uk; 154 Blackfriars Rd; mains £8.50-17.50; ⏰11am-late Mon-Fri, 5.30pm-late Sat, noon-6pm Sun; ⊖Southwark) Recently steered in a lucrative fresh direction by new owners, this restaurant is a Southwark gem, with a sure-fire menu combining locally sourced food and culinary talent, plus splendid roasts on Sunday and attentive service all round.

Oxo Tower Restaurant & Brasserie FUSION £££
(Map p170; ☎020-7803 3888; www.harveynichols.com/restaurants/oxo-tower-london; Barge House St; mains £18-26; ⊙lunch & dinner; ⊖Waterloo) The extravagant views are the big draw-card, so skip the restaurant and head for the slightly less extravagantly priced brasserie, or, if you're not hungry, the bar. The food is excellent, combining European and East Asian flavours. Set price menus (two/three courses £22.50/26.50) are offered at lunch-time, before 6.15pm and after 10pm.

Anchor & Hope PUB ££
(Map p170; 36 The Cut; mains £12-20; ⊙noon-2.30pm Tue-Sat, 6-10.30pm Mon-Sat, Sunday lunch at 2pm; ⊖Southwark) The hope is that you'll get a table without waiting hours because you can't book at this quintessential gastro-pub, except for Sunday lunch at 2pm. The anchor is gutsy, unashamedly carnivorous British food.

CHELSEA, KENSINGTON & KNIGHTSBRIDGE

These highbrow neighbourhoods have some of London's very best (and priciest) restaurants.

TOP CHOICE **Dinner by Heston Blumenthal** MODERN BRITISH £££
(Map p178; ☎020-7201 3833; www.dinnerbyheston.com; Mandarin Oriental Hyde Park, 66 Knightsbridge; set lunch £28, mains £32-72; ⊖Knightsbridge) The eagerly awaited opening of sumptuously presented Dinner is a gastronomic *tour-de-force,* ushering diners on a tour of British culinary history (with inventive modern inflections).

Tom's Kitchen MODERN EUROPEAN ££
(Map p178; ☎020-7349 0202; www.tomskitchen.co.uk; 27 Cale St; breakfast £4-15, mains £13.90-30; ⊙breakfast Mon-Fri, lunch & dinner daily; ⊖South Kensington) Celebrity chef Tom Aikens' restaurant keeps the magic flowing through the day, with award-winning breakfasts and pancakes drawing acclaim and crowds to its informal, but engaging, dining setting.

Marcus Wareing at the Berkeley FRENCH £££
(Map p178; ☎020-7235 1200; www.marcus-wareing.com; Berkeley Hotel, Wilton Pl; 3-course lunch/dinner £38/80; ⊖Knightsbridge) Wareing runs this one-time Gordon Ramsay restaurant under his own name, and its reputation for exquisite food and exemplary service has only been enhanced.

MARYLEBONE

Marylebone's charming High St has a huge range of eateries. You won't go too far wrong planting yourself at a table anywhere.

TOP CHOICE **Providores & Tapa Room** FUSION £££
(Map p178; ☎7935 6175; www.theprovidores.co.uk; 109 Marylebone High St W1; 2/3/4/5 courses £33/47/57/63; ⊙lunch & dinner till 10.30pm Mon-Sat, till 10pm Sun; ⊖Baker St) New Zealand's most distinctive culinary export since kiwi fruit, chef Peter Gordon works his fusion magic here, matching his creations with NZ wines. Downstairs, in a cute play on words, the Tapa Room (as in the Polynesian bark-cloth) serves sophisticated tapas, along with excellent breakfasts.

La Fromagerie CAFE ££
(Map p178; www.lafromagerie.co.uk; 2-6 Moxon St W1; mains £7-16.50; ⊙8am-7.30pm Mon-Fri, 9am-7pm Sat, 10am-6pm Sun; ⊖Baker St) This deli-cafe has bowls of delectable salads, antipasto, peppers and beans scattered about the long communal table.

FITZROVIA

Tucked away behind busy Tottenham Court Rd, Fitzrovia's Charlotte and Goodge Sts form one of central London's most vibrant eating precincts.

Hakkasan CHINESE £££
(Map p164; ☎7927 7000; www.hakkasan.com; 8 Hanway Pl W1; mains £11-61; ⊙noon-12.30am Mon-Wed, till 1.30am Thu-Sat, till midnight Sun; ⊖Tottenham Court Rd) Michelin-starred Hakkasan – hidden down a lane like all fashionable haunts should be – elegantly pairs fine Chinese dining with stunning design and some persuasive cocktail chemistry. The menu embraces everything from Sichuan *ma po doufu* to grilled Shanghai dumplings, Peking duck and beyond.

Salt Yard TAPAS ££
(Map p164; ☎020-7637 0657; www.saltyard.co.uk; 54 Goodge St; tapas £4-8; ⊖Goodge St) Named after the place where cold meats are cured, this softly lit joint serves delicious Spanish and Italian tapas.

Lantana CAFE £
(Map p164; www.lantanacafe.co.uk; 13 Charlotte Pl; mains £4-10; ⊙breakfast & lunch Mon-Sat; ⊖Goodge St) Excellent coffee and inventive brunches induce queues on Saturday mornings outside this Australian-style cafe.

NOTTING HILL, BAYSWATER & PADDINGTON

Notting Hill teems with good places to eat, from cheap takeaways to atmospheric pubs and restaurants worthy of the fine-dining tag. Queensway has the best strip of Asian restaurants this side of Soho.

Taquería MEXICAN £

(Map p178; www.taqueria.co.uk; 139-143 Westbourne Gr; tacos from £4.10; ⏲noon-11pm Mon-Fri, 10am-11.30pm Sat, noon-10.30pm Sun; ⊖Notting Hill Gate) Its sustainable credentials are as appealing as its authentic, freshly made tortillas – this place instantly elbows other Mexican restaurants into the Tex-Mex shade.

Geales SEAFOOD ££

(Map p178; ☎7727 7528; www.geales.com; 2 Farmer St; 2/3-course lunch £11.95/14.95, mains £10.95-22.95; ⏲closed lunch Mon; ⊖Notting Hill Gate) Frying fish since 1939, Geales' fish is highly succulent, although chips disappointingly cost extra (outside of the set lunch) in what should be a classic combination.

CLERKENWELL & FARRINGDON

Clerkenwell's hidden gems are worth digging for; Exmouth Market is a good place to start.

TOP CHOICE **Modern Pantry** FUSION ££

(Map p170; ☎020-7553 9210; www.themodernpantry.co.uk; 47-48 St John's Sq; mains £15-22; ; ⊖Farringdon) This Georgian townhouse in the heart of Clerkenwell has a cracking fusion menu, which gives almost as much pleasure to read as to eat from. Ingredients are combined sublimely into unusual dishes such as tamarind miso marinated onglet steak, or panko and Parmesan crusted veal escalope. Reservations recommended for dinner.

Bistrot Bruno Loubet FRENCH ££

(Map p170; ☎020-7324 4455; www.bistrotbrunoloubet.com; 86-88 Clerkenwell Rd; mains £12-17; ; ⊖Farringdon) Facing onto St John's Sq, this elegant restaurant from Bruno Loubet at the Zetter matches top-quality ingredients and inventive taste combinations with impeccable execution.

St John BRITISH ££

(Map p170; ☎020-7251 0848; www.stjohnrestaurant.com; 26 St John St; mains £17-23; ⊖Farringdon) Whitewashed brick walls, high ceilings and simple wooden furniture keep diners free to concentrate on nose-to-tail offerings such as chitterlings and ox tongue at this modern London classic.

Little Bay EUROPEAN £

(Map p170; ☎020-7278 1234; www.little-bay.co.uk; 171 Farringdon Rd; mains before/after 7pm £6.45/8.45; ⊖Farringdon) The crushed-velvet ceiling, handmade twisted lamps that improve around the room (as the artist got better) and elaborately painted bar and tables showing nymphs frolicking are weird but fun. The hearty food is very good value.

Medcalf BRITISH ££

(Map p170; ☎020-7833 3533; www.medcalfbar.co.uk; 40 Exmouth Market; mains £10-16; ⏲closed dinner Sun; ⊖Farringdon) Medcalf is one of the best-value hang-outs on Exmouth Market. Housed in a beautifully converted 1912 butcher's shop, it serves up interesting and well-realised British fare.

CAMDEN TOWN

Camden's great for cheap eats, while neighbouring Chalk Farm and Primrose Hill are salted with gastropubs and upmarket restaurants.

Market MODERN BRITISH ££

(Map p184; ☎020-7267 9700; www.marketrestaurant.co.uk; 43 Parkway; 2-course lunch £10, mains £10-14; ⏲lunch & dinner Mon-Sat, lunch Sun; ⊖Camden Town) This fabulous restaurant is an ode to great, simple British food with a hint of European thrown in. The light and airy space with bare brick walls, steel tables and basic wooden chairs reflects this simplicity.

Engineer PUB ££

(Map p184; ☎020-7722 0950; 65 Gloucester Ave; mains £13-21; ⊖Chalk Farm) One of London's original gastropubs, the Engineer has been serving up consistently good international cuisine to hip north Londoners for a fair while now. The courtyard garden is a real treat on balmy summer nights.

HOXTON, SHOREDITCH & SPITALFIELDS

From the hit-and-miss Bangladeshi restaurants of Brick Lane to the Vietnamese strip on Kingsland Rd, via the Jewish, Spanish, French, Italian and Greek eateries in between, the East End's cuisine is as multicultural as its residents.

Fifteen ITALIAN ££

(Map p170; ☎0871 330 1515; www.fifteen.net; 15 Westland Pl; breakfast £2-8.50, trattoria £6-11, restaurant £11-25; ; ⊖Old St) Jamie Oliver's culinary philanthropy started at Fifteen, set up to give unemployed young people a shot at a career.

The Italian food is beyond excellent, and even those on limited budgets can afford a visit.

Albion BRITISH £
(Map p170; www.albionoaff.oo.uk; 2 4 Boundary St; mains £9-13; ⊙8am-11pm; ; ⊖Old St) For those wanting to be taken back to Dear Old Blighty's cuisine but with rather less grease and stodge, this self-consciously retro 'caff' serves up top-quality bangers and mash, steak-and-kidney pies, devilled kidneys and, of course, fish and chips.

Sông Quê VIETNAMESE £
(www.songque.co.uk; 134 Kingsland Rd; mains £6-9; ⊖Hoxton) Arrive after 7.30pm and you can expect to queue: this humble eatery is one of the best Vietnamese restaurants in London and you'll be shunted out shortly after your last bite. Sông Quê is 300m along Kingsland Rd, the continuation of Shoreditch High St.

Princess of Shoreditch PUB ££
(Map p170; 020-7729 9270; www.theprincessofshoreditch.com; 76 Paul St; pub mains £10-18.50; ; ⊖Old St) Perfect for a drink or a meal, the Princess gets busy thanks to its excellent gastropub menu, fine wine list, choice ales and particularly good-looking interior. Upstairs is the slightly more expensive dining room.

Cafe Bangla BANGLADESHI £
(Map p170; 128 Brick Lane; mains £5-15; ⊖Liverpool St) Dining in the famous curry houses of Brick Lane is inevitably more about the experience than the food. Among the hordes of practically interchangeable restaurants, this one stands out for its murals of scantily clad women riding dragons, alongside a tribute to Princess Di.

Drinking

As long as there's been a city, Londoners have loved to drink – and, as history shows, often immoderately.

WEST END

TOP CHOICE Gordon's Wine Bar BAR
(Map p164; www.gordonswinebar.com; 47 Villiers St; ⊖Embankment) What's not to love about this cavernous, candlelit wine cellar that's practically unchanged for the last 120 years? Get here before the office crowd (generally around 6pm) or forget about getting a table.

French House BAR
(Map p164; http://frenchhousesoho.com; 49 Dean St W1; ⊙noon-11.30pm Mon-Sat, to 10.30pm Sun; ⊖Leicester Sq) French House is Soho's legendary boho boozer with a history to match: this was the meeting place of the Free French Forces during WWII, and de Gaulle is said to have drunk here often, while Dylan Thomas, Peter O'Toole and Francis Bacon all frequently ended up on the wooden floors.

Princess Louise PUB
(Map p164; 208 High Holborn; ⊖Holborn) This late-19th-century Victorian boozer is arguably London's most beautiful pub. Spectacularly decorated with fine tiles, etched mirrors, plasterwork and a gorgeous central horseshoe bar, it gets packed with the after-work crowd.

Coach & Horses PUB
(Map p164; www.coachandhorsessoho.co.uk; 29 Greek St; ⊖Leicester Sq) Regulars at this no-nonsense Soho institution have included Francis Bacon, Peter O'Toole and Lucian Freud. The Wednesday and Saturday night singalongs are tops.

Lamb & Flag PUB
(Map p164; 33 Rose St; ⊖Covent Garden) Everyone's Covent Garden 'find', this historic pub is often as jammed with punters as it is packed with history. Built in 1623 and formerly called the 'Bucket of Blood', inside it's all brass fittings and creaky wooden floors.

THE CITY

Vertigo 42 BAR
(Map p170; www.vertigo42.co.uk; Tower 42, 25 Old Broad St EC2; ⊙noon 4pm & 5 11pm Mon Fri, 5-11pm Sat; ⊖Liverpool St) On the 42nd floor of a 183m-high tower, this circular bar has expansive views over the city that stretch for miles on a clear day.

Ye Olde Cheshire Cheese PUB
(Map p170; Wine Office Ct, 145 Fleet St; ⊙11am-11pm Mon-Fri, from noon Sat; ⊖Chancery Lane) Rebuilt six years after the Great Fire, this hoary pub was popular with Dr Johnson, Thackeray, Dickens and the visiting Mark Twain. Touristy but always atmospheric and enjoyable.

SOUTH BANK

George Inn PUB
(Map p170; www.nationaltrust.org.uk/main/w-georgeinn; 77 Borough High St SE1; ⊙11am-11pm; ⊖London Bridge) This glorious old boozer is London's last surviving galleried coaching inn, dating from 1676 and now a National Trust property. Getting a mention in Dickens' *Little Dorrit*, it also stands on the site of the Tabard Inn, where the pilgrims in Chaucer's *Canterbury Tales* gathered before hitting the road to Canterbury.

Anchor PUB
(Map p170; 34 Park St; ⌚11am-11pm Sun-Wed, to midnight Thu-Sat; ⊖London Bridge) This 18th-century riverside boozer replaced the 1615 original where Samuel Pepys witnessed the Great Fire. Trips to the terrace are rewarded with fine views, but brace for a constant deluge of drinkers.

BLOOMSBURY & ST PANCRAS

TOP CHOICE **Newman Arms** PUB
(Map p164; www.newmanarms.co.uk; 23 Rathbone St W1; ⌚noon-11pm Mon & Tue, to 11.30pm Wed-Fri; ⊖Goodge St) One of the few family-run pubs in central London, this tiny one-room affair with upstairs pie room has a big history; George Orwell and Dylan Thomas drank here and a scene from Michael Powell's *Peeping Tom* was filmed in the passageway alongside the pub in 1960.

NOTTING HILL, BAYSWATER & PADDINGTON

Churchill Arms PUB
(Map p178; www.churchillarmskensington.co.uk; 119 Kensington Church St; ⌚11am-11pm Mon-Wed, 11am-midnight Thu-Sat, noon-10.30pm Sun; 📶; ⊖Notting Hill Gate) Adorned with a gob-smacking array of flower baskets and Union Jacks, this magnificent old boozer on Kensington Church St is a London classic, famed for its atmosphere, Winston memorabilia, knick-knacks and attached conservatory serving fine Thai food.

CAMDEN TOWN

Lock Tavern PUB
(Map p184; www.lock-tavern.co.uk; 35 Chalk Farm Rd; ⊖Camden Town) The archetypal Camden pub, the Lock has both a rooftop terrace and a beer garden and attracts an interesting crowd with its mix of ready conviviality and regular live music.

CLERKENWELL & FARRINGDON

TOP CHOICE **Jerusalem Tavern** PUB
(Map p170; www.stpetersbrewery.co.uk; 55 Britton St; 📶; ⊖Farringdon) Pick a wood-panelled cubbyhole to park yourself in at this tiny 1720 coffee-shop-turned-inn (named after the Priory of St John of Jerusalem) and choose from a selection of St Peter's fantastic beers and ales, brewed in North Suffolk.

HOXTON, SHOREDITCH & SPITALFIELDS

TOP CHOICE **Book Club** BAR
(Map p170; ☎020-7684 8618; www.wearetbc.com; 100 Leonard St; ⌚8am-midnight Mon-Wed, 8am-2am Thu & Fri, 10am-2am Sat & Sun; 📶; ⊖Old St) A creative vibe animates this fantastic Victorian warehouse in Shoreditch that hosts cultural events and DJ nights to complement the drinking, ping-pong and pool-playing.

Ten Bells PUB
(Map p170; cnr Commercial & Fournier Sts; ⊖Liverpool St) This landmark Victorian pub, with its large windows and beautiful tiles, is perfect for a pint after a wander round Spitalfields Market. It's famous for being one of Jack the Ripper's pick-up joints, although these days it attracts a rather more salubrious and trendy clientele.

☆ Entertainment

Theatre

London is a world capital for theatre and there's a lot more than mammoth musicals to tempt you into the West End. On performance days, you can buy half-price tickets for West End productions (cash only) from the official agency **tkts** (Map p164; www.tkts.co.uk; Leicester Sq; ⌚10am-7pm Mon-Sat, noon-4pm Sun). The booth is the one with the clock tower; beware of touts selling dodgy tickets. For more, see www.officiallondontheatre.co.uk or www.theatremonkey.com.

Royal Court Theatre THEATRE
(Map p178; ☎020-7565 5000; www.royalcourttheatre.com; Sloane Sq; ⊖Sloane Sq) Progressive theatre and champion of new talent.

National Theatre THEATRE
(Map p170; ☎020-7452 3000; www.nationaltheatre.org.uk; South Bank; ⊖Waterloo) Cheaper tickets for classics and new plays from some of the world's best companies.

Royal Shakespeare Company THEATRE
(☎0844 800 1110; www.rsc.org.uk) Productions of the Bard's classics and other quality stuff.

Old Vic THEATRE
(Map p170; ☎0844 871 7628; www.oldvictheatre.com; The Cut; ⊖Waterloo) Kevin Spacey continues his run as artistic director (and occasional performer) at this venue, which features classic, highbrow drama.

GAY & LESBIAN LONDON

The West End, particularly Soho, is the visible centre of gay and lesbian London, with numerous venues clustered around Old Compton St; and many other areas have their own mini-scenes.

The easiest way to find out what's going on is to pick up the free press from a venue (Pink Paper, Boyz, QX). The gay section of *Time Out* is useful, as are www.gaydarnation.com (for men) and www.gingerbeer.co.uk (for women). Some venues to get you started:

Candy Bar (Map p164; www.candybarsoho.com; 4 Carlisle St; ⊖Tottenham Court Rd) Long-running lesbian hang-out.

G-A-Y (www.g-a-y.co.uk) G-A-Y Bar (Map p164; 30 Old Compton St; ⊖Leicester Sq) G-A-Y Late (Map p164; 5 Goslett Yard; ⏲11pm-3am; ⊖Tottenham Court Road) G-A-Y Club@Heaven (Map p164; The Arches, Villiers St; ⏲11pm-4am Thu-Sat; ⊖Charing Cross) G-A-Y now operates bars and club nights at one of gaydom's most internationally famous venues, Heaven.

George & Dragon (Map p170; 2 Hackney Rd ; ⊖Old Street) Appealing corner pub where the crowd is often as eclectically furnished as the venue.

Popstarz (Map p164; www.popstarz.org; The Den, 18 West Central St; ⏲10pm-4am Fri; ⊖Tottenham Court Rd) London's legendary indie pop club night. The online flyer gets you in free.

Royal Vauxhall Tavern (RVT; www.rvt.org.uk; 372 Kennington Lane; admission free-£9; ⊖Vauxhall) Much-loved pub with crazy cabaret and drag acts.

Donmar Warehouse THEATRE
(Map p164; ☎0844 871 7624; www.donmarwarehouse.com; 41 Earlham St; ⊖Covent Garden) A not-for-profit company that has forged itself a West End reputation.

Almeida THEATRE
(☎020-7359 4404; www.almeida.co.uk; Almeida St; ⊖Highbury & Islington) A plush Islington venue that can be relied on to provide the city with an essential program of imaginative theatre, under its creative artistic director, Michael Attenborough.

Young Vic THEATRE
(Map p170; ☎020-7922 2922; www.youngvic.org; 66 The Cut; ⊖Waterloo) One of the capital's most respected theatre troupes – bold, brave and talented – the Young Vic stages winning performances.

Nightclubs

Clubland is no longer confined to the West End, with megaclubs scattered throughout the city wherever there's a venue big enough, cheap enough or quirky enough to hold them. The big nights are Friday and Saturday, although some of the most cutting-edge sessions are midweek. Admission prices vary widely; it's often cheaper to arrive early or prebook tickets.

Fabric CLUB
(Map p170; www.fabriclondon.com; 77a Charterhouse St; admission £8-18; ⏲10pm-6am Fri, 11pm-8am Sat, 11pm-6am Sun; ⊖Farringdon) Consistently rated by DJs as one of the world's greatest, Fabric's three dance floors occupy a converted meat cold-store opposite the Smithfield meat market.

Plastic People CLUB
(Map p170; www.plasticpeople.co.uk; 147-149 Curtain Rd; admission £5-10; ⏲10pm-3.30am Fri & Sat, to 2am Sun; ⊖Old St) Taking the directive 'underground club' literally, Plastic People provides a low-ceilinged subterranean den of dubsteppy, wonky, funky, no-frills fun times.

Ministry of Sound CLUB
(Map p170; ☎020-7740 8600; www.ministryofsound.com; 103 Gaunt St; admission £13-22; ⏲11pm-6.30am Fri & Sat; ⊖Elephant & Castle) Where the global brand started, it's London's most famous club and still packs in a diverse crew with big local and international names.

Cargo CLUB
(Map p170; www.cargo-london.com; 83 Rivington St; admission free-£16; ⊖Old St) Cargo is one of London's most eclectic clubs. Under its brick railway arches you'll find a dance-floor room, bar and outside terrace.

Rock, Pop & Jazz

KOKO CONCERT VENUE
(Map p184; www.koko.uk.com; 1a Camden High St; ⏲7-11pm Sun-Thu, to 4am Fri & Sat; ⊖Mornington Cres) Occupying the grand Camden Palace

theatre, Koko hosts live bands most nights and the regular Club NME (New Musical Express; £5) on Friday.

O2 Academy Brixton LIVE MUSIC
(☎box office 0844 477 2000; www.o2academy brixton.co.uk; 211 Stockwell Rd; ⊖Brixton) This Grade II–listed art deco venue hosts big-name acts in a relatively intimate setting (5000 capacity).

Jazz Café LIVE MUSIC
(Map p184; www.jazzcafe.co.uk; 5 Parkway; ⊖Camden Town) Jazz is just one part of the picture at this intimate club that stages a full roster of rock, pop, hip hop and dance, including famous names.

Ronnie Scott's JAZZ
(Map p164; ☎020-7439 0747; www.ronniescotts.co.uk; 47 Frith St; ⊖Leicester Sq) London's legendary jazz club has been pulling in the hep cats since 1959.

100 Club LIVE MUSIC
(Map p164; ☎020-7636 0933; www.the100club.co.uk; 100 Oxford St; ⊖Oxford Circus) Hosting live music for 70 years, this legendary London venue once showcased the Stones and was at the centre of the punk revolution. It now divides its time between jazz, rock and even a little swing.

Roundhouse LIVE MUSIC
(Map p184; ☎0844 482 8008; www.roundhouse.org.uk; Chalk Farm Rd; ⊖Chalk Farm) Built in 1847 as a railway shed, Camden's Roundhouse has been an iconic concert venue since the 1960s (capacity 3300), hosting the likes of the Rolling Stones, Led Zeppelin and The Clash. Theatre and comedy are also staged.

Dublin Castle LIVE MUSIC
(Map p184; ☎020-7485 1773; www.thedublincastle.com; 94 Parkway; ⊖Camden Town) There's live punk or alternative music most nights in this pub's back room (cover usually £6).

Comedy

TOP CHOICE **Comedy Store** COMEDY
(Map p164; ☎0844 847 1728; www.thecomedy store.co.uk; 1A Oxendon St; admission from £20; ⊖Piccadilly Circus) One of London's first comedy clubs, featuring the capital's most famous improvisers, the Comedy Store Players, on Wednesdays (8pm) and Sundays (7.30pm).

Comedy Café COMEDY
(Map p170; ☎020-7739 5706; www.comedycafe.co.uk; 68 Rivington St; admission free-£15; ⏲Wed-Sat; ⊖Old St) This major venue can be a little too try-hard and wacky, but it's worth seeing the Wednesday night try-out spots.

Soho Theatre COMEDY
(Map p164; ☎020-7478 0100; www.sohotheatre.com; 21 Dean St; tickets around £10-20; ⊖Tottenham Court Rd) This is where grown-up comedians graduate to, once crowds start paying attention.

Cinemas

Electric Cinema CINEMA
(☎020-7908 9696; www.electriccinema.co.uk; 191 Portobello Rd; tickets £8-18; ⊖Ladbroke Grove) The UK's oldest cinema, updated with leather armchairs, footstools, tables in the auditorium and an excellent brasserie next door.

BFI Southbank CINEMA
(Map p170; ☎020-7928 3232; www.bfi.org.uk; Belvedere Rd; tickets £9; ⏲11am-11pm; ⊖Waterloo) The city's famous temple to film screens some 2000 flicks a year, from old classics to foreign arthouse.

BFI IMAX CINEMA
(Map p170; ☎020-7199 6000; www.bfi.org.uk/imax; Waterloo Rd; tickets £9-16; ⊖Waterloo) Watch 3D movies on the UK's biggest screen: 20m high (nearly five double-decker buses) and 26m wide.

Prince Charles CINEMA
(Map p164; www.princecharlescinema.com; Leicester Pl; ⊖Leicester Sq) Dodge eye-watering West End ticket prices at this brilliant budget cinema off Leicester Sq, which also hosts mini-festivals and late-night singalongs.

Classical Music, Opera & Dance

Royal Albert Hall CONCERT HALL
(Map p178; ☎020-7589 8212; www.royalalberthall.com; Kensington Gore; ⊖South Kensington) This landmark elliptical Victorian arena – classically based on a Roman amphitheatre – hosts classical concerts and contemporary artists, but is best known as the venue for the annual classical music festival, the Proms.

Barbican PERFORMING ARTS
(Map p170; ☎0845 121 6823; www.barbican.org.uk; Silk St EC2; ⊖Barbican) Home to the London Symphony Orchestra, this famously hulking complex (named after a Roman fortification) has a rich program of film, music, theatre, art and dance, including concerts.

Southbank Centre CONCERT HALL
(Map p170; ☎020-7960 4200; www.southbank centre.co.uk; Belvedere Rd; ⊖Waterloo) Home to

the **London Philharmonic Orchestra** (www.lpo.co.uk), **Sinfonietta** (www.londonsinfonietta.org.uk) and the **Philharmonia Orchestra** (www.philharmonia.co.uk), among others, this centre hosts classical, opera, jazz and choral music in three premier venues: the **Royal Festival Hall** (Map p170; ☎7960 4242; admission £6-60), the smaller **Queen Elizabeth Hall** and the **Purcell Room**.

Royal Opera House OPERA, DANCE
(Map p164; ☎020-7304 4000; www.roh.org.uk; Bow St; tickets £5-195; ⊖Covent Garden) Covent Garden is synonymous with opera thanks to this world-famous venue, which is also the home of the Royal Ballet, Britain's premier classical ballet company. Backstage tours take place three times a day on weekdays and four times on Saturdays (£10.50; book ahead).

Sadler's Wells DANCE
(Map p170; ☎0844 412 4300; www.sadlerswells.com; Rosebery Ave; tickets £10-49; ⊖Angel) A glittering modern venue that was, in fact, first established in the 17th century, Sadler's Wells has been given much credit for bringing modern dance to the mainstream.

Shopping

From world-famous department stores to quirky backstreet retail revelations, London is a mecca for shoppers with an eye for style and a card to exercise.

Department Stores

London's famous department stores are an attraction in themselves, even if you're not interested in buying.

Selfridges DEPARTMENT STORE
(Map p178; www.selfridges.com; 400 Oxford St; ⊖Bond St) Famed for its innovative window displays – especially at Yuletide – the funkiest of London's one-stop shops bursts with fashion labels, an unparalleled food hall and Europe's largest cosmetics department.

Fortnum & Mason DEPARTMENT STORE
(Map p164; www.fortnumandmason.com; 181 Piccadilly; ⊖Piccadilly Circus) It's the byword for quality and service from a bygone era, steeped in 300 years of tradition. The old-world basement food hall is where Britain's elite come for their pantry provisions.

Liberty DEPARTMENT STORE
(Map p164; www.liberty.co.uk; Great Marlborough St; ⊖Oxford Circus) An irresistible blend of contemporary styles and indulgent pampering in a mock-Tudor fantasyland of carved dark wood.

TOP CHOICE **Harrods** DEPARTMENT STORE
(Map p178; www.harrods.com; 87 Brompton Rd; ⊖Knightsbridge) Garish, stylish, kitsch, yet perennially popular department store.

Harvey Nichols DEPARTMENT STORE
(Map p178; www.harveynichols.com; 109-125 Knightsbridge; ⊖Knightsbridge) London's temple of high fashion, jewellery and perfume.

Music

As befitting a global music capital, London has a wide range of music stores.

Ray's Jazz MUSIC
(Map p164; www.foyles.co.uk; Foyles, 113-119 Charing Cross Rd; ⊖Tottenham Court Rd) Where aficionados find those elusive back catalogues from their favourite jazz and blues artists.

BM Soho MUSIC
(Map p164; www.bm-soho.com; 25 D'Arblay St; ⊖Oxford Circus) Your best bet for dance – if they haven't got what you're after, they'll know who has.

Rough Trade MUSIC
(www.roughtrade.com) East (Map p170; Dray Walk, Old Truman Brewery, 91 Brick Lane; ⌚8am-8pm Mon-Fri, 11am-7pm Sat & Sun; ⊖Liverpool St) West (130 Talbot Rd; ⌚10am-6.30pm Mon-Sat, 11am-5pm Sun; ⊖Ladbroke Grove) The best place to come for anything of an indie or alternative bent.

Bookshops

Foyle's BOOKS
(Map p164; www.foyles.co.uk; 113-119 Charing Cross Rd WC2; ⊖Tottenham Court Rd) London's most legendary bookshop.

Daunt Books BOOKS
(Map p178; 83 Marylebone High St; ⊖Baker St) Famous travel bookshop, with guidebooks, travel literature, fiction and reference books, all sorted by country.

Information

City of London Information Centre (Map p170; www.visitthecity.co.uk; St Paul's Churchyard EC4; ⌚9.30am-5.30pm Mon-Sat, 10am-4pm Sun; ⊖St Paul's) Tourist information, fast-track tickets to City attractions and guided walks (adult/child £6/4).

ROLL OUT THE BARROW

London has more than 350 markets selling everything from antiques and curios to flowers and fish. Some, such as Camden and Portobello Road, are full of tourists, while others exist just for the locals.

Columbia Road Flower Market (Map p170; Columbia Rd; ⏲8am-3pm Sun; ⊖Old St) The best place for East End barrow boy banter ('We got flowers cheap enough for ya muvver-in-law's grave'). Unmissable.

Borough Market (Map p170; Southwark St; ⊖London Bridge) A farmers market sometimes called London's Larder.

Camden Market (Map p184; www.camdenmarkets.org; Camden High St; ⏲10am-5.30pm; ⊖Camden Town) Actually a series of markets spread along Camden High St; the Lock and Stables markets are the place for punk fashion, cheap food, bongs and hippy-dippy stuff.

Portobello Road Market (www.portobellomarket.org; Portobello Rd; ⏲8am-6.30pm Mon-Sat, to 1pm Thu; ⊖Notting Hill Gate or Ladbroke Grove) One of London's most famous (and crowded) street markets; new and vintage clothes, antiques and food.

Broadway Market (www.broadwaymarket.co.uk; London Fields; ⏲9am-5pm Sat; ⊖Bethnal Green) Graze from the organic food stalls or choose a cooked meal.

Brixton Market (www.brixtonmarket.net; Electric Ave & Granville Arcade; ⏲8am-6pm Mon-Sat, 8am-3pm Wed; ⊖Brixton) Immortalised in the Eddie Grant song, Electric Ave is a cosmopolitan treat that mixes everything from reggae music to exotic spices.

Sunday (Up)market (Map p170; www.sundayupmarket.co.uk; The Old Truman Brewery, Brick Lane; ⏲10am-5pm Sun; ⊖Liverpool St) Handmade handbags, jewellery, new and vintage clothes and shoes.

Brick Lane Market (Map p170; www.visitbricklane.org; Brick Lane; ⏲8am-2pm Sun; ⊖Liverpool St) A sprawling East End bazaar featuring everything from fruit to paintings and bric-a-brac.

Petticoat Lane Market (Map p170; Wentworth St & Middlesex St; ⏲9am-2pm Sun-Fri; ⊖Aldgate) A cherished East End institution overflowing with cheap consumer durables and jumble-sale ware.

ℹ Getting There & Away

Bus & Coach

The London terminus for long-distance buses (called 'coaches' in Britain) is **Victoria Coach Station** (164 Buckingham Palace Rd SW1; ⊖Victoria).

Train

Most of London's main-line rail terminals are linked by the Circle line on the tube.

Charing Cross Canterbury
Euston Manchester, Liverpool, Carlisle, Glasgow
King's Cross Cambridge, Hull, York, Newcastle, Scotland
Liverpool Street Stansted airport (Stanstead Express), Cambridge
London Bridge Gatwick airport, Brighton
Marylebone Birmingham
Paddington Heathrow airport (Heathrow Express), Oxford, Bath, Bristol, Exeter, Plymouth, Cardiff
St Pancras Gatwick and Luton airports, Brighton, Nottingham, Sheffield, Leicester, Leeds, Paris (Eurostar)
Victoria Gatwick airport (Gatwick Express), Brighton, Canterbury
Waterloo Windsor, Winchester, Exeter, Plymouth

ℹ Getting Around

To/From the Airports

GATWICK Mainline trains run every 15 minutes between Gatwick's South Terminal and Victoria (from £12, 37 minutes), hourly at night, or to/from St Pancras (from £12, 66 minutes) via London Bridge, City Thameslink, Blackfriars and Farringdon.

Gatwick Express (www.gatwickexpress.com; one way/return £19.90/34.90) trains run to/from Victoria 5am to 11.45pm (one way/return £16/26, 30 minutes, first/last train 3.30am/12.32am).

The **easyBus** (www.easybus.co.uk; one way £10, return from £12) minibus service between Gatwick and Earl's Court (every 30 minutes from 4.25am to 1am, about 1¼ hours) costs from £2 to £10, depending on when you book. You're charged extra if you have more than one carry-on and one check-in bag.

HEATHROW The cheapest option from Heathrow is to take the underground (tube). The Piccadilly line is accessible from every terminal (£5.30, one hour to central London, departing from Heathrow every five minutes from around 5am to 11.30pm).

Faster, and much more expensive, is the **Heathrow Express** (www.heathrowexpress.com; one way/return £20/34) train to Paddington station (one way/return £18/34, 15 minutes, every 15 minutes 5.12am to 11.48pm). You can purchase tickets on board (£5 extra), from self-service machines (cash and credit cards accepted) at both stations, or online.

A taxi to the centre of London will cost between £50 and £85.

LONDON CITY The Docklands Light Railway (DLR) connects London City Airport to the tube network, taking 22 minutes to reach Bank station (£4.30). A black taxi costs around £25 to/from central London.

LUTON There are regular National Rail services from St Pancras (£13, 29 to 39 minutes) to Luton Airport Parkway station, where a shuttle bus (£1.50) will get you to the airport within 10 minutes. **easyBus** (www.easybus.co.uk) minibuses head from Victoria, Earl's Court and Baker St to Luton (from £2, walk-on £10, allow 1½ hours, every 30 minutes). A taxi costs around £65.

STANSTED The **Stansted Express** (☎0845 850 0150; www.stanstedexpress.com) connects with Liverpool Street station (one way/return £21.50/29.50, 46 minutes, every 15 minutes 6am to 12.30am).

easyBus also has services between Stansted and Baker St (from £2, £10 walk-on, 1¼ hours, every 20 minutes). The Airbus A6 links with Victoria Coach tation (£11, allow 1¾ hours, at least every 30 minutes).

National Express (www.nationalexpress.com) also runs buses to Stansted from Liverpool Street station (£9 one way, 80 minutes, every 30 minutes).

A taxi to/from central London costs about £100.

Bus

Travelling around London by double-decker bus is a great way to get a feel for the city, but it's usually slower than the tube. Buses run regularly during the day, while less frequent night buses (prefixed with the letter 'N') wheel into action when the tube stops.

Heritage 'Routemaster' buses with conductors operate on route 9 (from Aldwych to Royal Albert Hall) and 15 (between Trafalgar Square and Tower Hill); these are the only buses without wheelchair access. In 2012 a brand new fleet of freshly designed hybrid diesel/electric hop-on/hop-off (and wheelchair-accessible) Routemasters began running on route 38 between Victoria and Hackney.

Single-journey bus tickets (valid for two hours) cost £2.30 (£1.35 on Oyster, capped at £4.20 per day); a weekly pass is £18.80. Children ride for free. At stops with yellow signs, you must buy your ticket from the automatic machine (or use an Oyster) before boarding.

Buses stop on request, so clearly signal the driver with an outstretched arm.

Bicycle

Central London is mostly flat, relatively compact and the traffic moves slowly – all of which make it surprisingly good for cyclists. It can get terribly congested though, so you'll need to keep your wits about you – and lock your bike (including both wheels) securely.

Bikes can be hired from numerous self-service docking stations through London's **Cycle Hire** (www.tfl.gov.uk; free 1st 30min, then 1/2/3/6/24hr £1/6/15/35/50) scheme.

Car

Don't. London was recently rated western Europe's second-most congested city (congratulations Brussels). In addition, you'll pay £8 per day simply to drive into central London from 7am to 6pm on a weekday. If you're hiring a car to continue your trip around Britain, take the tube or train to a major airport and pick it up from there.

Taxi

London's famous black cabs are available for hire when the yellow light above the windscreen is lit. Fares are metered, with flag fall of £2.20 and the additional rate dependent on time of day, distance travelled and taxi speed. A 1-mile trip will cost between £5.20 and £8.40.

Licensed minicabs operate via agencies (most busy areas have a walk-in office with drivers waiting). They're a cheaper alternative to black cabs and quote trip fares in advance. Only use drivers from proper agencies; licensed minicabs aren't allowed to tout for business or pick you up off the street without a booking.

Underground & DLR

'The tube', as it's universally known, extends its subterranean tentacles throughout London and into the surrounding counties, with services running every few minutes from roughly 5.30am to 12.30am (from 7am to 11.30pm Sunday). Tickets (or Oyster card top-ups) can be purchased from counters or machines at the entrance to each station using either cash or credit card.

Lines are colour-coded (red for the Central Line, yellow for the Circle Line, black for the Northern Line and so on). It helps to know the direction you're travelling in (ie northbound or southbound, eastbound or westbound) as well as the terminus of the line you're travelling on.

LONDON'S YOUR OYSTER

The best-value way to get around London is with an **Oyster Card**, a reusable travel card which covers most of the city's public transport system. The card itself costs £5 (refundable when you leave).

London is divided into five travel zones; most sights are in Zones 1 and 2. A weekly/monthly season ticket covering all tube, bus and rail services within these zones currently costs £29/112. All you need to do is touch your card to the sensors on the station turnstiles or at the front of the bus.

Alternatively, you can load the card with credit, and have fares deducted each time you use a train or bus. Fares are much cheaper compared to standard paper tickets (a Zone 1 tube journey on an Oyster Card is £2.10, compared to £4.50 for a paper ticket). Even better, in any single day your fares will be capped at the Oyster day-pass rate for the zones you've travelled in (Zones 1-2 peak/off-peak £8.40/7).

Oyster Cards can be bought at any London tube or train station, as well as some newsagents, garages and off-licences. Alternatively, you can buy Oyster Cards in advance online from the Transport for London website (http://visitorshop.tfl.gov.uk).

If you get confused, don't worry, as copies of the tube's famous map are posted everywhere, showing how the 14 different routes intersect. Be warned: the distances between stations on the tube map aren't remotely to scale.

The Docklands Light Railway (DLR) links the City to Docklands, Greenwich and London City Airport.

Boat

The myriad boats that ply the Thames are a great way to travel, avoiding traffic jams and giving great views. Passengers with Travelcards (including Oyster) get a third off all fares.

Thames Clippers (www.thamesclippers.com) runs regular commuter services between Embankment, Waterloo, Blackfriars, Bankside, London Bridge, Tower, Canary Wharf, Greenwich, North Greenwich and Woolwich piers (adult/child £5.30/2.65) from 7am to midnight (from 9.30am weekends).

London Waterbus Company (☎020-7482 2660; www.londonwaterbus.com; single/return £7.20/10.30) and **Jason's Trip** (www.jasons.co.uk; opposite 42 Blomfield Rd; single/return £8/9) both run canal boat journeys between Camden Lock and Little Venice; see websites for times.

Leisure services include the Tate-to-Tate boat (see box p167) and Westminster–Greenwich services. There are also boats to Kew Gardens and Hampton Court Palace.

AROUND LONDON

'When you're tired of London, you're tired of life' opined 18th-century Londoner Samuel Johnson. But he wasn't living in an age when too many days on the tube can leave you exhausted and grouchy. Luckily, the capital is surprisingly close to some excellent day escapes. Brighton and Oxford are well-known day-trip haunts, while Windsor and Eton are two gems that are an easy train ride from the capital.

Windsor & Eton

POP 31,000

Dominated by the massive bulk and heavy influence of Windsor Castle, these twin towns have a rather surreal atmosphere, with the morning pomp and ceremony of the changing of the guards in Windsor and the sight of school boys dressed in formal tail coats wandering the streets of Eton.

Sights

Windsor Castle CASTLE
(www.royalcollection.org.uk; adult/child £17/10; ⏲9.45am-5.15pm) The largest and oldest occupied fortress in the world, Windsor Castle is a majestic vision of battlements and towers used for state occasions and as the Queen's weekend retreat.

William the Conqueror first established a royal residence in Windsor in 1070; since then successive monarchs have rebuilt, remodelled and refurbished the castle complex to create the massive and sumptuous palace that stands here today. You can join a free guided tour (every half-hour) or take a multilingual audio tour.

The castle's highlights are undoubtedly the lavish **State Apartments**, including the magnificent St George's Hall: the **Waterloo Chamber**, with its paintings commemorating the victory over Napoleon; and the **King's Dressing Room**, with Renaissance masterpieces by Van Dyck, Hans Holbein, Rembrandt and Rubens.

Equally impressive are the castle's chapels, especially **St George's Chapel**, one of Britain's finest examples of Perpendicular Gothic architecture. The nave and fan-vaulted roof were completed under Henry VII, but the final nail was struck under Henry VIII in 1528. Many notable royals are buried here, most recently the Queen Mother (1900–2002). The **Albert Chapel** was originally built in 1240, but was redecorated by Queen Victoria following the death of her husband Prince Albert in 1861.

While you're here, don't miss a picnic in the groomed grounds of Windsor Great Park, and the chance to watch the ceremonial **Changing of the Guard** (⏲11am Mon-Sat Apr-Jul, alternate days Aug-Mar).

Eton College NOTABLE BUILDING
(www.etoncollege.com; adult/child £7/5.50; ⏲guided tours 2pm & 3.15pm daily school holidays, Wed, Fri, Sat & Sun term time) Founded in 1440, England's oldest and most prestigious public school, Eton College, has been educating the great and good of English society for over five centuries. Among its famous alumni are 18 prime ministers, as well as the Duke of Wellington, Princes William and Harry, George Orwell, Ian Fleming, Aldous Huxley, Sir Ranulph Fiennes, John Maynard Keynes and Bear Grylls.

All the boys are boarders and must wear formal tailcoats, waistcoats and white collars to lessons (though the top hats went out in 1948); fencing, shooting, polo and beagling all feature on the curriculum.

Tours take in the **chapel**, the **cloisters**, the **lower school**, with names etched into its ancient desks by bored students, and the **school yard**, with a memorial to Etonians who died in the two world wars. You may recognise some of the buildings, as *Chariots of Fire*, *The Madness of King George*, *Mrs Brown* and *Shakespeare in Love* are just some of the movies that have been filmed here.

Tickets must be purchased in advance at the tourist office.

ℹ Information

Royal Windsor Information Centre (www.windsor.gov.uk; Old Booking Hall, Windsor Royal Shopping Arcade; ⏲9.30am-5pm Mon-Sat, 10am-4pm Sun)

ℹ Getting There & Away

Trains from Windsor Central station on Thames St go to London Paddington (27 to 43 minutes). Trains from Windsor Riverside station go to London Waterloo (56 minutes). Services run half-hourly from both stations and tickets cost £9.40.

SOUTHEAST ENGLAND

Rolling chalk downs, venerable Victorian resorts, seaside towns – England's southeast makes a bracing change from London's traffic-clogged streets. The region makes a great day-trip from the capital, with England's stateliest cathedral in Canterbury, the mighty Dover Castle, and the laid-back charm of Brighton all within easy reach.

For general information, see www.visitsoutheastengland.com.

Canterbury

POP 43,432

With its jaw-dropping cathedral, surrounded by medieval cobbled streets, this World Heritage city has been a Christian pilgrimage site for several centuries, and a tourist attraction for almost as long. Today's visitors come to immerse themselves in religious and secular history, including Thomas Becket's murder and the bawdy works of Geoffrey Chaucer, but this is no mothballed outdoor museum: Canterbury is surprisingly vibrant, and a good base for exploring the wider region.

👁 Sights

Canterbury Cathedral CHURCH
(www.canterbury-cathedral.org; adult/child £8/7, tour adult/child £5/3, audio tour adult/child £3.50/2.50; ⏲9am-5pm Mon-Sat, 12.30-2.30pm Sun) A rich repository of more than 1400 years of Christian history, the Church of England's mother ship is an truly extraordinary place with an absorbing history. This Gothic cathedral, the highlight of the city's World Heritage sites, is the southeast's top tourist attraction as well as a pious place of worship. Allow at least two hours to do it justice. This ancient structure is packed with monuments commemorating the nation's battles. Also here are the grave and heraldic tunic of one of the nation's most famous warmongers, Edward the Black Prince (1330–76). The spot in the northwest transept where Archbishop Thomas

Becket met his grisly end has been drawing pilgrims for more than 800 years and is marked by a flickering candle and striking modern altar.

Canterbury Heritage Museum MUSEUM
(www.canterbury-museums.co.uk; Stour St; adult/child £8/free; ⏲10am-5pm) A fine 14th-century building, once the Poor Priests' Hospital, now houses the city's absorbing museum, which has a jumble of exhibits from pre-Roman times to the assassination of Becket, and from Joseph Conrad to locally born celebs. The building also houses the fun **Rupert Bear Museum** – Rupert's creator, Mary Tourtel, was born in Canterbury – and a gallery celebrating another children's favourite of old, Bagpuss.

Canterbury Tales INTERPRETATION CENTRE
(www.canterburytales.org.uk; St Margaret's St; adult/child £7.75/5.75; ⏲10am-5pm Mar-Oct) A three-dimensional interpretation of Chaucer's classic tales through jerky animatronics and audioguides, the ambitious Canterbury Tales show is certainly entertaining but could never do full justice to the original tales. However, it does serve as a light-hearted introduction for the young or uninitiated.

Sleeping

TOP CHOICE **Abode Canterbury** BOUTIQUE HOTEL £££
(☎01227-766266; www.abodehotels.co.uk; 30-33 High St; r from £135;) The only boutique hotel in town, the 72 rooms at this super-central option are graded from 'comfortable' to 'fabulous' and, for the most part, live up to their tags. There's a splendid Champagne bar, restaurant and tavern here, too.

House of Agnes HOTEL ££
(☎01227-472185; www.houseofagnes.co.uk; 71 St Dunstan's St; r from £83; @) Situated near the West Gate, this rather wonky 13th-century beamed inn, mentioned in Dickens' *David Copperfield,* has eight themed rooms bearing such names as 'Marrakesh' (Moorish), 'Venice' (inevitable carnival masks), 'Boston' (light and airy) and 'Canterbury' (antiques and heavy fabrics).

Arthouse B&B B&B ££
(☎01227-453032; www.arthousebandb.com; 24 London Rd; r £60-65; P) A night at Canterbury's newest and most laid-back digs, housed in a 19th-century fire station, is a bit like kipping over at a really cool art student's pad. The theme is funky and eclectic, with furniture by local designers and artwork on the walls by the instantly likeable artist owners. Shame only one of the three rooms is ensuite.

Kipp's Independent Hostel HOSTEL £
(☎01227-786121; www.kipps-hostel.com; 40 Nunnery Fields; dm/s/d £16/22/36; @) Occupying a red-brick townhouse in a quietish residential area less than a mile from the city centre, these superb backpacker digs enjoy a homely atmosphere and clean though cramped dorms.

Eating & Drinking

TOP CHOICE **Deeson's** BRITISH ££
(☎01227-767854; 25-27 Sun St; mains £4.50-16) Local fruit and veg, award-winning wines, beers and ciders, fish from Kent's coastal waters and the odd ingredient from the proprietor's very own allotment, all served in a straightforward, contemporary setting, a Kentish apple's throw from the cathedral gates. What more do you want? Bookings recommended.

Boho INTERNATIONAL £
(43 St Peter's St; snacks £3-10; ⏲9am-6pm Mon-Sat, 10am-5pm Sun) In a prime spot on the main drag, next to the Eastbridge Hospital, this hip eatery is extraordinarily popular and you'd be lucky to get a table on busy shopping days. Tuck into humungous burgers, full-monty breakfasts and imaginative, owner-cooked international mains. No bookings, so be prepared to queue.

Tiny Tim's Tearoom CAFE £
(☎01227-450793; 34 St Margaret's St; mains £7-9; ⏲9.30am-5pm Tue-Sat, 10.30am-4pm Sun) Swish 1930s English tearoom offering hungry shoppers big breakfasts bursting with Kentish ingredients and tiers of cakes, crumpets and scones plastered in clotted cream.

Goods Shed MARKET ££
(☎01227-459153; Station Rd West; mains £12-20; ⏲market 9am-7pm Tue-Sat, 10am-4pm Sun, restaurant breakfast, lunch & dinner Tue-Sat, lunch Sun) Farmers market, food hall and fabulous restaurant all rolled into one, this converted station warehouse by the Canterbury West train station is a hit with everyone from self-caterers to sit-down gourmands.

Information

Tourist Office (☎01227-378100; www.canterbury.co.uk; 18 High St; ⏲9am-5pm Mon-Wed, Fri & Sat, to 7pm Thu, 10am-5pm Sun)

Recently moved to the Royal Museum & Art Gallery; staff can help book accommodation, excursions and theatre tickets.

Getting There & Away

There are two train stations: Canterbury East for London Victoria and Dover; and Canterbury West for London's Charing Cross and St Pancras stations. Connections:

Dover Priory (£7.50, 25 minutes, every 30 minutes)

London St Pancras (£31.80, one hour, hourly)

London Victoria/Charing Cross (£26.80, 1¾ hours, two to three hourly)

CANTERBURY ATTRACTIONS PASSPORT

The **Canterbury Attractions Passport** (adult/child £19/15.25) gives entry to the cathedral and the Canterbury Tales, plus St Augustine's Abbey and one of the city's museums. It's available from the tourist office.

Dover

POP 39,078

Dover's shabby town centre is a sad introduction to Britain for travellers arriving by boat, but the town has a couple of stellar attractions to redeem it.

Sights

Dover Castle CASTLE

(EH; www.english-heritage.org.uk; adult/child £16.50/9.90; 10am-6pm Apr-Jul & Sep, from 9.30am Aug, to 5pm Oct, 10am-4pm Sat & Sun Nov-Mar; P) Occupying top spot, literally and figuratively, on the Dovorian townscape, this most impressive of castles was built to bolster the country's weakest point at this, the shortest sea-crossing to mainland Europe.

The robust 12th-century **Great Tower**, with walls up to 7m thick, is a medieval warren filled with interactive exhibits and light-and-sound shows that take visitors back to the times of Henry II. But the biggest draw here is the network of claustrophobic **secret wartime tunnels**, first excavated during the Napoleonic Wars and then expanded to house a command post and hospital in WWII.

The new and highly enjoyable 50-minute guided tour (every 20 minutes) tells the story of one of Britain's most famous wartime operations, code-named Dynamo, which was directed from here in 1940 and saw hundreds of thousands of men evacuated from the beaches at Dunkirk.

White Cliffs of Dover LANDMARK

Immortalised in song, film and literature, these iconic cliffs are embedded in the national consciousness, a big 'Welcome Home' sign to generations of travellers and soldiers. The cliffs rise to 100m high and extend on either side of Dover, but the best bit is the 6-mile stretch that starts about 2 miles east of town, properly known as the Langdon Cliffs.

The area is managed by the National Trust and there's a small information office, from where you can take the stony path east along the clifftops for a bracing 2-mile walk to the **South Foreland Lighthouse** (NT; www.nationaltrust.org.uk; adult/child £4/2; guided tours 11am-5.30pm Fri-Mon mid-Mar–Oct).

Information

Tourist Office (01304-205108; www.whitecliffscountry.org.uk; Market Sq; 9.30am-5pm Mon-Sat year-round, 10am-3pm Sun Apr-Sep) Located in Dover Museum, this friendly office can book accommodation and ferries for a small fee.

Getting There & Away

BUS **Canterbury** (45 minutes, twice hourly) Bus 15.

London Victoria (£13.50, 2¾ hours, 19 daily) Coach 007.

TRAIN **London Charing Cross** (£21.10, two hours, twice hourly)

London St Pancras (£36.20, one hour, hourly) High-speed service.

Getting Around

The ferry companies run regular shuttle buses between the docks and the train station (five minutes) as they're a long walk apart.

Taxis offering 24-hour services include **Heritage** (01304-204420) and **Star Taxis** (01304-228822).

Brighton & Hove

POP 247, 817

Brighton is the UK's most colourful and outrageous seaside city. It's also home to the UK's biggest gay community, and has a fantastic cultural and clubbing scene to boot. Brighton rocks all year round, but really comes to life during the summer months.

Sights

Royal Pavilion PALACE
(www.royalpavilion.org.uk; Royal Pavilion Gardens; adult/child £9.80/5.60; ⏲9.30am-5.45pm Apr-Sep, 10am-5.15pm Oct-Mar) The city's must-see attraction is the Royal Pavilion, the glittering party pad and palace of Prince George, who later became the Prince Regent and then King George IV. It's one of the most opulent buildings in England, certainly the finest example of early-19th-century Chinoiserie anywhere in Europe, and is an apt symbol of Brighton's reputation for decadence and high living.

Brighton Pier AMUSEMENT PARK
(www.brightonpier.co.uk; Madeira Dr) This grand old centenarian pier is the place to experience Brighton's tackier side. There are plenty of stomach-churning fairground rides and dingy amusement arcades to keep you amused, plus candy floss and Brighton rock to chomp on while you're doing so. Look west and you'll see the sad remains of the **West Pier**, a skeletal iron hulk that attracts flocks of starlings at sunset. It's a sad end for a Victorian marvel, upon which the likes of Charlie Chaplin and Stan Laurel once performed.

FREE **Brighton Museum & Art Gallery** MUSEUM
(www.brighton-hove-museums.org.uk; Royal Pavilion Gardens; ⏲10am-5pm Tue-Sun) Set in the Royal Pavilion's renovated stable block, this museum and art gallery has a glittering collection of 20th-century art and design, including a crimson Salvador Dalí sofa modelled on Mae West's lips.

The Lanes NEIGHBOURHOOD
Brighton's original fishing-village heart is the Lanes, a cobblestone web of 17th-century cottages housing a gentrified cornucopia of independent shops, pubs and one-of-a-kind eateries. The adjacent **North Laine** has a funkier vibe with streets of multicoloured shops, secondhand record stores and vegetarian cafes for local hipsters.

Festivals & Events

There's always something fun going on in Brighton, but the main events include **Gay Pride** (www.brightonpride.org) in early August and the **Brighton Festival** (☎01273-709709; www.brightonfestival.org) in May, the biggest in Britain after Edinburgh, drawing theatre, dance, music and comedy performers from around the globe.

WORTH A TRIP

LEEDS CASTLE

Leeds Castle (www.leeds-castle.com; adult/child £19.75/12.50; ⏲10am-6pm Apr-Sep, to 5pm Oct-Mar) is one of the most visited attractions in Britain. It's not in Leeds, despite the rather confusing name – it's actually just east of Maidstone. This impressive structure balancing on two islands amid a large lake has been transformed from fortress to lavish palace over the centuries, and the vast estate is ideal for peaceful walks.

Trains run from London Victoria to Bearsted (£19.60, one hour) where you catch a special shuttle coach to the castle (£5 return, daily March to October, weekends only in winter).

Sleeping

Despite a glut of hotels in Brighton, prices are high and you'd be wise to book well ahead for summer weekends and for the Brighton Festival in May. Expect to pay up to a third more at weekends across the board.

Brighton's hostels are a varied bunch. Several cater to stag and hen nights; others are more homely. Choose wisely!

TOP CHOICE **Hotel Una** BOUTIQUE HOTEL ££
(☎01723-820464; www.hotel-una.co.uk; 55-56 Regency Sq; s £55-75, d £115-150; ❄📶) All the 19 rooms here wow guests with their bold-patterned fabrics, supersize leather sofas, in-room free-standing baths and vegan/vegie/carnivorous breakfast in bed.

Neo Hotel BOUTIQUE HOTEL ££
(☎01273-711104; www.neohotel.com; 19 Oriental Pl; d from £100; 📶) You won't be surprised to learn that the owner of this gorgeous hotel is an interior stylist; the nine rooms could have dropped straight out of the pages of a design magazine, each finished in rich colours and tactile fabrics, with bold floral and Asian motifs and black-tiled bathrooms.

Baggies Backpackers HOSTEL £
(☎01273-733740; www.baggiesbackpackers.com; 33 Oriental Pl; dm/d £13/35; 📶) A warm atmosphere, worn-in charm and clean, snug dorms have made this hostel an institution. It's also blessed with a homely kitchen, an inexpensive laundry and a cosy basement

chill-out room. The hostel only takes phone bookings. Cash only.

TOP CHOICE Kipps Brighton HOSTEL £

(☎01273-604182; www.kipps-brighton.com; 76 Grand Pde; dm/d from £15/40; @ 📶) Owners of Canterbury's award-winning hostel have created equally commendable budget digs here in Brighton. There's a real cafe vibe around reception and facilities include a communal kitchen.

myhotel HOTEL ££

(☎01273-900300; www.myhotels.com; 17 Jubilee St; r from £89; P @ 📶) With trend-setting rooms looking like space-age pods, full of curved white walls, floor-to-ceiling observation windows and suspended flatscreen TVs, there's nothing square about this place, daddy-o.

Snooze HOTEL ££

(☎01273-605797; www.snoozebrighton.com; 25 St George's Tce; s/d from £55/65; @ 📶) This eccentric Kemptown pad is fond of retro styling. Rooms feature vintage posters, bright '60s and '70s patterned wallpaper, flying wooden ducks, floral sinks and mad clashes of colour. You'll find it just off St James' St about 500m east of New Steine.

Eating

Brighton easily has the best choice on the south coast, with cafes, restaurants, pubs and bars to fulfil every whim.

Terre à Terre VEGETARIAN ££

(☎01273-729051; www.terreaterre.co.uk; 71 East St; mains £14; ⊙lunch & dinner Tue-Sun; ✎) Even staunch meat eaters will come out raving about this legendary vegetarian restaurant. A sublime dining experience, from the vibrant, modern space and the entertaining menus, to the delicious, inventive dishes full of rich robust flavours.

The Gingerman MODERN EUROPEAN £££

(☎01273-326688; 21a Norfolk Sq; 3-course menu £18; ⊙lunch & dinner Tue-Sun) Seafood from Hastings, Sussex beef, Romney Marsh lamb, local sparkling wines and countless other seasonal, local and British treats go into the adroitly flash-fried and slow-cooked dishes at this snug eatery. Reservations advised.

Iydea VEGETARIAN £

(www.iydea.co.uk; 17 Kensington Gardens; mains £5.50-7; ⊙9am-5.30pm Mon-Sat, from 9.30am Sun; 📶✎) The food at this new vegetarian cafe is a treat. All of the daily changing menus of curries, lasagnes, falafel, enchiladas and quiches can be eaten in or taken away in environmentally friendly packaging, and the award-winning vegie breakfast is one of the UK's best.

JB's American Diner BISTRO £

(31 King's Rd; burgers £7, mains £6.50-12) A hefty slab of authentic Americana teleported to the Brighton seafront, complete with shiny leather booths, 1950s soundtrack and colossal burgers, fries and milkshakes.

Al Fresco ITALIAN ££

(www.alfresco-brighton.co.uk; Kings Rd Arches; mains £10-23; ⊙noon-midnight) The showstopping feature here is the widescreen vista out across the Channel and along the seafront. The pizzas, pastas and Italian meat dishes make a tasty accompaniment to the views.

English's Oyster Bar SEAFOOD ££

(www.englishs.co.uk; 29-31 East St; mains £11-25) An almost 70-year-old institution and celebrity haunt, this Brightonian seafood paradise dishes up everything from Essex oysters to locally caught lobster to Dover sole. It's converted from fishermen's cottages, with echoes of the elegant Edwardian era inside.

Drinking

Drunken stag parties and tacky nightclubs rule on West St, but there are many other options, including the unique mix of seafront clubs and bars. For pointers, visit www.drinkinbrighton.co.uk

Dorset PUB

(www.thedorset.co.uk; 28 North Rd; 📶) This laidback Brighton institution throws open its doors and windows in fine weather and spills tables onto the pavement. There's also a decent gastropub menu.

Evening Star PUB

(www.eveningstarbrighton.co.uk; 55-56 Surrey St) This cosy, unpretentious pub is a beer drinker's nirvana, with a wonderful selection of award-winning real ales, Belgian beers, organic lagers and seasonal brews.

Coalition BAR

(171-181 Kings Rd Arches) On a summer's day, there's nowhere better to sit and watch the world go by than at this popular beach bar, diner and club. All sorts of events happen here, from comedy to live music and club nights.

Entertainment

Brighton offers the best entertainment line-up on the south coast. When Britain's top DJs aren't plying their trade in London, Ibiza or Aya Napia, chances are you'll spy them here.

Audio CLUB
(www.audiobrighton.com; 10 Marine Pde) Some of the city's top club nights can be found at this ear-numbing venue where the music is top priority, attracting a young, up-for-it crowd.

Tube CLUB
(Kings Rd Arches) Twin giant, brick, subterranean tunnels have bars at the front and back, playing funky house, '70s, R&B and disco to a stylish and attitude-free crowd.

Funky Fish Club CLUB
(www.funkyfishclub.co.uk; 19-23 Marine Pde) Fun, friendly and unpretentious little club playing soul, funk, jazz, Motown and old-school breaks. No big-name DJs or stringent door policies, just cheap drinks and a rocking atmosphere.

Concorde 2 CLUB
(www.concorde2.co.uk; Madeira Dr) Brighton's best-known and best-loved club is a disarmingly unpretentious den, where DJ Fatboy Slim pioneered the Big Beat Boutique and still occasionally graces the decks.

Information

Tourist Office (☎01273-290337; www.visitbrighton.com; Royal Pavilion Shop; ⏰9.30am-5.30pm) Superbly run office with an accommodation booking service (£1.50), train and bus ticketing and a highly recommended (free) greeter scheme.

GAY & LESBIAN BRIGHTON

For more than a century, Brighton has been a gay haven. With more than 25,000 gay men and around 15,000 lesbians living here, it is the most vibrant queer community in the country outside London. Kemptown (aka Camptown), on and off St James' St, is where it's all at. The old Brunswick Town area of Hove is a quieter alternative.

For up-to-date information on gay Brighton, check out www.gay.brighton.co.uk and www.realbrighton.com, or pick up the free monthly magazine *Gscene* (www.gscene.com) from the tourist office.

Getting There & Away

All London-bound services pass through Gatwick Airport (£9.50, 30 to 40 minutes, up to five hourly).

Eastbourne (£9.50, 30 to 40 minutes, half-hourly)

London St Pancras (£15.40, 1¼ hours, half-hourly)

London Victoria (£16, 50 minutes, three hourly)

Winchester

POP 41,420

Calm, collegiate Winchester is a mellow must-see for all visitors. The past still echoes around the flint-flecked walls of this ancient cathedral city. It was the capital of Saxon kings, and its statues and sights evoke two of England's mightiest myth-makers: Alfred the Great and King Arthur (yes, he of the round table).

Sights

Winchester Cathedral CHURCH
(☎01962-857275; www.winchester-cathedral.org.uk; adult/child £6/free, incl tower tour £9/free; ⏰9am-5pm Sat, 12.30-3pm Sun) Winchester Cathedral is one of southern England's most awe-inspiring buildings. Its walls contain evidence of almost 1000 years of history, best experienced on one of the memorable tours of its sturdy tower. The Cathedral's exterior features a fine Gothic facade, but it's the inside that steals the show, with one of the longest **medieval naves** (164m) in Europe, and a fascinating jumble of features from all eras. Jane Austen, who spent her last weeks at a nearby house, is buried near the entrance in the cathedral's northern aisle.

Cathedral tours (⏰hourly 10am-3pm Mon-Sat) last one hour. **Tower and roof tours** (tickets £6; ⏰11.30am Sat & 2.15pm Mon, Wed, Fri & Sat Jun-Aug, 11.30am Sat & 2.15pm Wed & Sat Sep-May) venture onto the roof for views as far as the Isle of Wight. For safety reasons these tours are only open to those aged 12 to 70. They're popular, so book well in advance. **Crypt tours** (tour free; ⏰10.30am, 12.30pm & 2.30pm Mon-Sat Apr-Oct) aren't always available because of flooding.

FREE **Great Hall & Round Table** HISTORIC BUILDING
(Castle Ave; suggested donation adult/child £1/50p; ⏰10am-5pm) The cavernous Great Hall is the only part of 11th-century Winchester Castle that Oliver Cromwell spared from destruction. Crowning the wall is what centuries of mythology have dubbed King Arthur's Round Table. It's actually a 700-year-old copy, but is fascinating nonetheless.

Hospital of St Cross HISTORIC BUILDING
(☎01962-853525; www.stcrosshospital.co.uk; St Cross Rd; adult/child £3/1; ⏰9.30am-5pm Mon-Sat, 1-5pm Sun) Monk, bishop, knight, politician and grandson of William the Conqueror, Henry de Blois, founded this hospital in 1132 to house pilgrims and crusaders en route to the Holy Land. It's the oldest charitable institution in the country, and is still roamed by 25 elderly black- or red-gowned brothers in pie-shaped trencher hats, who continue to hand out alms.

WORTH A TRIP

JANE AUSTEN'S HOUSE

There's more than a touch of period drama at the former home of Jane Austen (1775–1817), where she wrote *Mansfield Park, Emma* and *Persuasion*, and revised *Sense and Sensibility, Pride and Prejudice* and *Northanger Abbey*. This appealing red brick house, where the celebrated English novelist lived from 1809 to 1817, is now a **museum** (☎01420-83262; www.jane austens-house-museum.org.uk; Chawton; adult/child £7/2; ⏰10.30am-4.30pm mid-Feb–Dec).

The museum is 18 miles east of Winchester; take bus 64 from Winchester to Chawton roundabout (50 minutes, hourly Monday to Saturday, six on Sunday) then walk the 500m to Chawton village.

Sleeping

Wykeham Arms INN ££
(☎01962-853834; www.fullershotels.com; 75 Kingsgate St; s/d/ste £70/119/150; P 📶) At 250-odd years old, the Wykeham bursts with history – it used to be a brothel and also put Nelson up for a night. Creaking stairs lead to plush bedrooms with brass bedsteads, jazzy throws, oak dressers and teddy bears.

Dolphin House B&B ££
(☎01962-853284; www.dolphinhousestudios.co.uk; 3 Compton Rd; s/d £55/70; P 📶) At this kind-of B&B your continental breakfast is delivered to a compact kitchen – perfect for lazy lie-ins. The terrace, complete with cast-iron tables and chairs, overlooks a gently sloping lawn.

Eating & Drinking

TOP CHOICE **Black Rat** MODERN BRITISH ££
(☎01962-844465; www.theblackrat.co.uk; 88 Chesil St; mains £17-20; ⏰dinner daily, lunch Sat & Sun) The decor here is casually countrified, but the food is something else. Accomplished cooking has won it a Michelin star – expect hearty cuts of braised beef cheek, lamb rump and oxtail. Bookings required.

Chesil Rectory BRITISH ££
(☎01962-851555; www.chesilrectory.co.uk; 1 Chesil St; mains £16) Flickering candles and low beams lend this 15th-century restaurant a romantic feel. Locally sourced delicacies include carpaccio of Hampshire venison with mushrooms, and smoked trout with watercress. The two-course lunch and early evening menu (£16; served 6pm to 7pm) is a steal. Bookings recommended.

Black Boy PUB
(www.theblackboypub.com; 1 Wharf Hill) This adorable old boozer is filled with a happy band of drinkers and sometimes-obsessive collections, from pocket watches to wax facial features; bear traps to sawn-in-half paperbacks. The pumps produce five locally brewed real ales.

Information

Tourist Office (☎01962-840500; www.visitwinchester.co.uk; High St; ⏰10am-5pm Mon-Sat, plus 11am-4pm Sun May-Sep)

Getting There & Away

BUS Regular, direct National Express buses shuttle to London Victoria (£12, 1¾ hours) and Southampton (one hour).

TRAIN There are fast links to the Midlands. Other train services:

London Waterloo (£30, 1¼ hours, every 30 minutes)

Portsmouth (£10.20, one hour, hourly)

Southampton (£5.80, 20 minutes, every 30 minutes)

SOUTHWEST ENGLAND

England's southwest is simply spectacular. Here the past is ever present – prepare for close encounters with iconic stone circles, Iron Age hill forts and Roman baths. The landscape immerses you in the myths of Kings Arthur and Alfred the Great, and the writings of Thomas Hardy, Jane Austen and Daphne du Maurier.

Then there are three wildlife-rich national parks, fossil-studded shores, England's best surf spots and a coastline flecked with exquisite bays and tranquil sweeps of sandy beach. With the southwest it's not so much why go, as what to do first.

For general information, see www.visitsouthwest.com.

DON'T MISS

AVEBURY

While the tour buses usually head straight to Stonehenge, prehistoric purists make for **Avebury Stone Circle**. Though it lacks the dramatic trilithons ('gateways') of its sister site across the plain, Avebury is the largest stone circle in the world and a more rewarding place to visit simply because you can get closer to the giant boulders.

A large section of Avebury village is actually inside the circle, meaning you can sleep, or at least have lunch and a pint, inside the mystic ring.

To get here, bus 5/6/96 runs from Salisbury (1¾ hours, hourly Monday to Saturday, five on Sunday).

Salisbury

POP 43,335

Centred on a majestic cathedral topped by the tallest spire in England, Salisbury has been an important provincial city for more than 1000 years. Its streets form an architectural timeline ranging from medieval walls and half-timbered Tudor townhouses to Georgian mansions and Victorian villas. It's also a lively modern town with plenty of bars, restaurants and terraced cafes, as well as a concentrated cluster of excellent museums.

Sights

FREE **Salisbury Cathedral** CHURCH

(01722-555120; www.salisburycathedral.org.uk; requested donation adult/child £5/3; 7.15am-6.15pm) England is endowed with countless stunning churches, but few can match the sheer spectacle of Salisbury Cathedral. Built between 1220 and 1258, the structure bears all the hallmarks of the early English Gothic style, with an elaborate exterior decorated with pointed arches and flying buttresses, and a sombre, austere interior designed to keep its congregation suitably pious.

Beyond the highly decorative **West Front**, a small passageway leads into the 70m-long nave, lined with handsome pillars of Purbeck stone. In the north aisle look out for a fascinating **medieval clock** dating from 1386, probably the oldest working timepiece in the world. The cathedral's 123m crowning glory, its **spire**, was added in the mid-14th century, and is the tallest in Britain. Look closely and you'll see that the additional weight has buckled the four central piers of the nave.

Ninety-minute **tower tours** (01722-555156; adult/child £8.50/6.50; 11am-2.30pm Apr-Sep, 1 per day Mon-Sat Nov-Mar) allow you to climb 332 vertigo-inducing steps to the base of the spire for jaw-dropping views. Bookings are required.

The remains of Salisbury's first cathedral, known as **Old Sarum** (EH; 01722-335398; www.english-heritage.org.uk; adult/child £3.50/1.80; 10am-5pm; P), sit on a hill 2 miles north of Salisbury. Buses 5 and 8 run twice an hour from Salisbury to Old Sarum (hourly on Sundays).

Sleeping

TOP CHOICE **St Ann's House** B&B ££

(01722-335657; www.stannshouse.co.uk; 32 St Ann St; s/d £60/110) For some perfectly priced indulgence head to this sumptuous Georgian terrace, which overflows with antiques, fine silk and linen direct from Istanbul. The gourmet breakfast buffet includes *ashera* (a cinnamon-scented Turkish pudding), roll mops and baked goat's cheese.

Spire House B&B ££

(01722-339213; www.salisbury-bedandbreakfast.com; 84 Exeter St; s £65-75, d £80, f £95-100; P) Breakfast tables here groan with homemade goodies: Dorset apple cakes, muffins, bread and jam. The comfy rooms have four-poster beds, Georgian-themed wallpaper and, at the front, cathedral views.

Salisbury YHA HOSTEL £
(☎0845-371 9537; www.yha.org.uk; Milford Hill; dm £18; P@) A real gem: neat rooms in a rambling, listed Victorian building. Choose from doubles or dorms; a cafe-bar, laundry and dappled gardens add to the appeal.

Eating & Drinking

Anokaa INDIAN ££
(☎01722-414142; www.anokaa.com; 60 Fisherton St; mains £11-32;) Sophisticated, contemporary Indian cuisine makes this the top table in town. Expect chargrilled halibut to be flavoured with curry leaves, and asparagus to come with cheese and roast strawberries. Wise locals head for the bargain buffet lunches (£9 per person).

Pheasant PUB ££
(☎01722-322866; www.restaurant-salisbury.com; 19 Salt Lane; mains £7-15; food noon-9.30pm) Flying the flag for great British bar food, this chilled-out gastropub does the basics well; try the pheasant stuffed with bacon and leeks, and the gooey, crumbly Eton mess. To drink? Perhaps a pint of Pigswill (honestly – it's a local ale).

Information

Tourist Office (☎01722-334956; www.visitwiltshire.co.uk/salisbury; Fish Row, Market Sq; 9.30am-6pm Mon-Sat, 10am-4pm Sun Jun-Sep, 9.30am-5pm Mon-Sat Oct-Apr)

Getting There & Away

BUS National Express services include:

Bath (£11, 1¼ hours, one daily)

Bristol (£10, 2¼ hours, daily)

London (£10, three hours, three daily) Via Heathrow.

Tour buses regularly leave Salisbury for Stonehenge.

TRAIN Trains run half-hourly from London Waterloo (£35, 1½ hours). Hourly connections include:

Bath (£9, one hour)

Bristol (£11, 1¼ hours)

Exeter (£30, two hours)

Stonehenge

This compelling ring of monolithic stones has been attracting a steady stream of pilgrims, poets and philosophers for the last 5000 years and is easily Britain's most iconic archaeological site.

STONE CIRCLE ACCESS

Visitors normally have to stay outside the stone circle itself. But on **Stone Circle Access Visits** (☎01722 343830; www.english-heritage.org.uk; adult/child £14.50/7.50) you get to wander round the core of the site, getting up-close views of the iconic bluestones and trilithons. The walks take place in the evening or early morning, so the quieter atmosphere and the slanting sunlight add to the effect. Each visit only takes 26 people; to secure a place book at least two months in advance.

The landscape around **Stonehenge** (EH; ☎0870-333 1181; www.english-heritage.org.uk; adult/child £6.90/3.50; 9am-7pm) is undergoing a long-overdue revamp which, when completed, should dramatically improve the experience of those visiting. But even before the changes, and despite the huge numbers of tourists who traipse around the perimeter, Stonehenge still manages to be a mystical, ethereal place – a haunting echo from Britain's forgotten past, and a reminder of the people who once walked the many ceremonial avenues across Salisbury Plain.

Even more intriguingly, it's still one of Britain's great archaeological mysteries: despite countless theories about what the site was used for, ranging from a sacrificial centre to a celestial timepiece, in truth, no one knows for sure what drove prehistoric Britons to expend so much time and effort on its construction.

Admission to Stonehenge is free for both English Heritage (EH) and National Trust (NT) members.

Getting There & Around

BUS No regular buses go to the site. The **Stonehenge Tour** (☎01722-336855; www.thestonehengetour.info; return adult/child £11/5) leaves Salisbury's railway and bus stations half-hourly in June and August, and hourly between September and May. Tickets last all day, so you can hop off at Old Sarum on the way back.

TAXI Taxis charge £40 to go to Stonehenge from Salisbury, wait for an hour and come back.

Bath

POP 90,144

Britain is littered with beautiful cities, but precious few can hold a candle to Bath. Home to some of the nation's grandest Georgian architecture and stateliest streets – not to mention one of the world's best-preserved Roman bathhouses – this slinky, sophisticated city has been a tourist draw for nigh-on 2000 years.

Founded on the site of a network of natural hot springs, Bath's heyday really began during the 18th century, when local

Bath

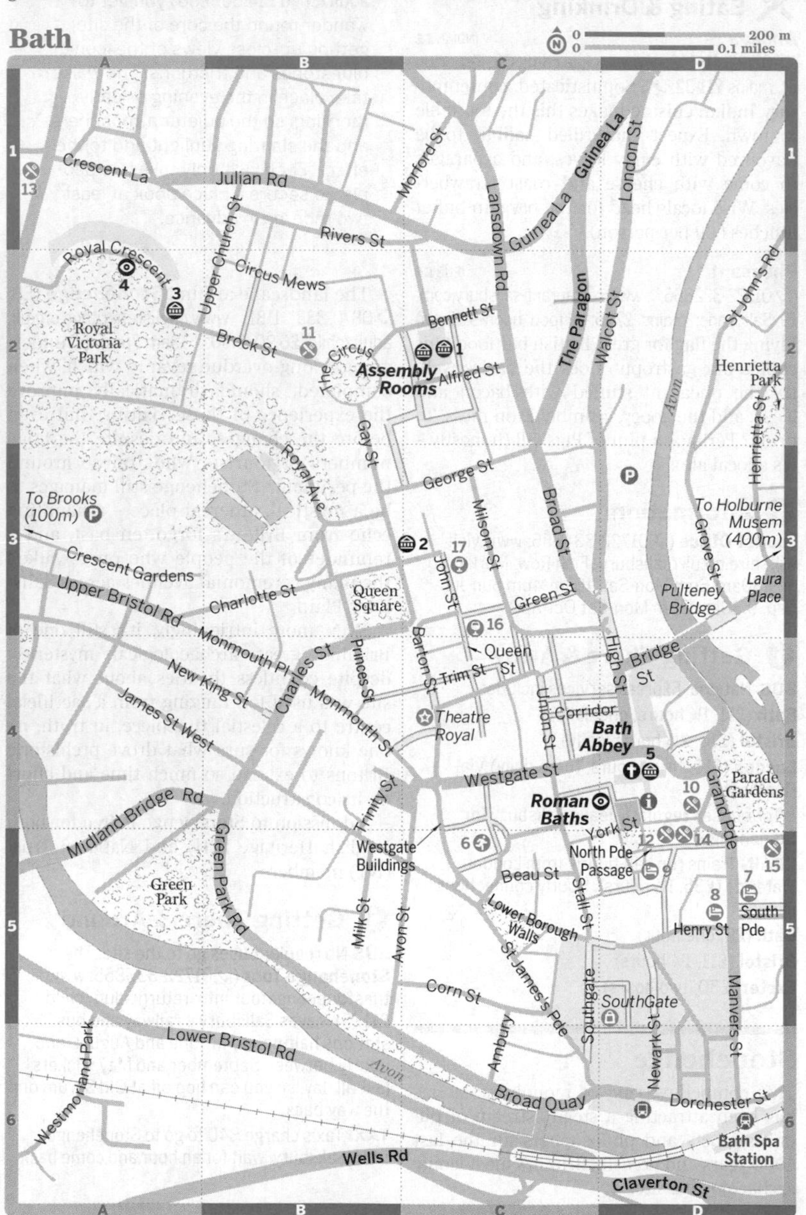

entrepreneur Ralph Allen and his team of father-and-son architects, John Wood the Elder and Younger, turned this sleepy backwater into the toast of Georgian society and constructed fabulous landmarks such as the Circus and Royal Crescent.

But while its architecture seems to have been pickled in time, Bath is very much a cosmopolitan, 21st-century city, with a wealth of modern cafes, bistros and boutiques dotted along its streets, as well as the huge new shopping SouthGate, seamlessly designed to blend in with the rest of Bath's period buildings.

Sights

TOP CHOICE **Roman Baths** HISTORIC SITE
(www.romanbaths.co.uk; Abbey Churchyard; adult/child/family £12.75/8.50/36; 9am-10pm July & Aug, 9am-6pm Mar-Jun, Sept & Oct, 9.30am-5.30pm Nov-Feb) Ever since the Romans arrived in Bath, life in the city has revolved around the three geothermal springs that bubble up near the abbey. The Romans constructed a glorious complex of bathhouses above these thermal waters to take advantage of their natural temperature, which emerges at a constant 46°C. Situated alongside an important temple dedicated to the healing goddess Sulis Minerva, the baths are believed to have attracted tourists from right across the Empire, and now form one of the best-preserved ancient Roman spas in the world.

The heart of the complex is the **Great Bath**, a large lead-lined pool filled with steaming, geothermally heated water from the so-called 'Sacred Spring' to a depth of 1.6m. Though it's now open to the air, the bath would originally have been covered by a 45m-high barrel-vaulted roof. Further bathing pools are situated to the east and west, with excavated sections revealing the hypocaust system that would have kept the bathing rooms balmy.

One of the most picturesque corners of the complex is the 12th-century **King's Bath**, built around the original sacred spring; 1.5 million litres of hot water still pour into the pool every day. Beneath the Pump Room are the remains of the **Temple of Sulis-Minerva**; look out for the famous gilded head of Minerva herself and the engraved Haruspex stone on which the statue would originally have stood.

The baths get unbelievably busy; you can usually avoid the worst crowds by buying tickets online, visiting early on a midweek morning, and by avoiding July and August. Admission includes an audioguide in eight languages, featuring a special commentary by the bestselling author Bill Bryson.

Royal Crescent STREET
(Royal Crescent) Bath's grandest street is the Royal Crescent, a semicircular terrace of majestic townhouses overlooking the green sweep of Royal Victoria Park. Designed by John Wood the Younger (1728–82) and built between 1767 and 1775, the houses were designed to appear perfectly symmetrical from the outside, but inside no two houses on the Crescent are quite the same.

For a glimpse into the splendour and razzle-dazzle of Georgian life, head for **No 1 Royal Crescent** (www.bath-preservation-trust.org.uk; 1 Royal Cres; adult/child £6.50/2.50; 10.30am-5pm Tue-Sun late Feb–mid-Dec), which has been restored using only 18th-century materials. Among the rooms on display are the drawing room, several bedrooms and the huge kitchen, complete with massive hearth, roasting spit and mousetraps.

Bath

Top Sights

Assembly Rooms	C2
Bath Abbey	D4
Roman Baths	D4

Sights

1 Fashion Museum	C2
2 Jane Austen Centre	C3
3 No 1 Royal Crescent	A2
4 Royal Crescent	A2
5 Vaults Heritage Museum	D4

Activities, Courses & Tours

6 Thermae Bath Spa	C5

Sleeping

7 Halcyon	D5
8 Henry	D5
9 Three Abbey Green	D5

Eating

10 Café Retro	D4
11 Circus	B2
12 Demuth's	D5
13 Marlborough Tavern	A1
14 Sally Lunn's	D5
15 Sotto Sotto	D5

Drinking

16 Raven	C3
17 Salamander	C3

Bath Abbey CHURCH
(www.bathabbey.org; requested donation £2.50; ⌚9am-6pm Mon-Sat, 1-2.30pm & 4.30-5.30pm Sun) Looming above the centre of the city, Bath's huge abbey church was built between 1499 and 1616, making it the last great medieval church raised in England. Its most striking feature is the west facade, where angels climb up and down stone ladders, commemorating a dream of the founder, Bishop Oliver King. Among those buried here are Sir Isaac Pitman (who devised the Pitman method of shorthand) and the celebrated Bath bon viveur Beau Nash.

On the abbey's southern side, the small **Vaults Heritage Museum** (⌚10am-4pm Mon-Sat) explores the abbey's history and its links with the nearby baths.

FREE **Holburne Museum** GALLERY
(www.holburne.org; Great Pulteney St; temporary exhibitions incur fee; ⌚10am-5pm) Sir William Holburne, the 18th-century aristocrat, aesthete and art fanatic, amassed a huge collection which now forms the core of the Holburne Museum, in a lavish mansion at the end of Great Pulteney St. Fresh from a three-year refit, the museum houses an impressive roll call of works by artists including Turner, Stubbs, William Hoare and Thomas Gainsborough, as well as a fine collection of 18th-century majollica and porcelain.

Assembly Rooms HISTORIC BUILDING
(NT; www.nationaltrust.org.uk/bath-assembly-rooms; 19 Bennett St; adult/child £2/free; ⌚10.30am-6pm) Opened in 1771, the city's glorious Assembly Rooms were where fashionable Bath socialites once gathered to waltz, play cards and listen to the latest chamber music. You're free to wander around the rooms, as long as they haven't been reserved for a special function; all are lit by their original 18th-century chandeliers.

THE THERMAE BATH SPA

Larking about in the Roman Baths might be off the agenda, but you can still sample the city's curative waters at **Thermae Bath Spa** (☎0844-888 0844; www.thermaebathspa.com; Bath St; ⌚9am-10pm, last entry 7.30pm), where the old Cross Bath is now incorporated into an ultramodern shell of local stone and plate glass. The New Royal Bath ticket includes steam rooms, waterfall shower and a choice of bathing venues – including the open-air rooftop pool, where you can swim in the thermal waters with a backdrop of Bath's stunning cityscape.

Fashion Museum MUSEUM
(www.fashionmuseum.co.uk; Assembly Rooms, Bennett St; adult/child £7.25/5.25; ⌚10.30am-5pm) In the basement of the Assembly Rooms, this museum contains a wonderful collection of costumes worn from the 16th to late 20th centuries. Exhibitions are changed annually, so check the website for the latest shows.

Jane Austen Centre MUSEUM
(www.janeausten.co.uk; 40 Gay St; adult/child £7.45/4.25; ⌚9.45am-5.30pm) Bath is known to many as a location in Jane Austen's novels, including *Persuasion* and *Northanger Abbey*. Though Austen only lived in Bath for five years from 1801 to 1806, she remained a regular visitor throughout her life. This museum houses a small collection of memorabilia relating to the writer's life in Bath, and costumed guides bring the era to life. There's also a Regency tearoom that serves crumpets and cream teas in suitably frilly surrounds.

Sleeping

TOP CHOICE **Halcyon** HOTEL ££
(☎01225-444100; www.thehalcyon.com; 2/3 South Pde; d £125-145; 📶) Just what Bath needed: a smart, stylish city-centre hotel that doesn't break the bank. Situated in a listed terrace off Manvers St, the Halcyon offers style on a budget, along with a smart basement breakfast room and the brand-new Circo cocktail bar. The drawbacks? Rooms are spread out over three floors and there's no lift.

Henry B&B ££
(☎01225-424052; www.thehenry.com; 6 Henry St; d £80-120, f £145-165) This tall, slim townhouse offers a good choice of clean, uncluttered rooms finished in crisp whites and smooth beiges. It's decent value considering the location, but there's no parking and it can feel very cramped when it's full. Two-night minimum stay at weekends.

Brooks HOTEL ££
(☎01225-425543; www.brooksguesthouse.com; 1 & 1a Crescent Gardens; s £59-89, d £80-150, f £120-160; 📶) On the west side of Bath, this townhouse blends heritage fixtures attractively with snazzy finishes. The owners have

focused on the details: goosedown duvets, pocket-sprung mattresses, DAB radios and breakfast choices including smoked salmon brioche and homemade muesli. Parking's problematic.

Three Abbey Green B&B ££
(☎01225-428558; www.threeabbeygreen.com; 3 Abbey Green; d £90-140, f £140-220;) Considering the location, this place is a steal – tumble out of the front door and you'll find yourself practically on the abbey's doorstep. It's on a leafy square, and though the rooms lack sparkle, the suites have adjoining singles – ideal for family travellers.

Bath YHA HOSTEL £
(www.yha.org.uk; Bathwick Hill; dm £20.40, d from £59; P@) Lodged inside an Italianate mansion and a more modern annexe, a steep climb (or a short hop on bus 18) from the city centre, this hostel offers decent rooms, spacious kitchens and lovely grounds.

Eating & Drinking

Bath is full of eating and drinking options. The narrow lanes off Milsom St, the quieter streets around the Theatre Royal and the area around Walcot St are good places to start exploring.

Circus MODERN BRITISH ££
(☎01225-466020; www.thecircuscafeandrestaurant.co.uk; 34 Brock St; mains lunch £5.50-10, dinner £11-14; ⊙10am-midnight Mon-Sat) Installed in a converted townhouse between the Circus and Royal Crescent, this is the model of a modern Brit bistro: chef Ali Golden has a taste for hearty dishes such as rabbit pie and roast guinea-fowl. Reserve ahead.

Marlborough Tavern PUB ££
(☎01225-423731; www.marlborough-tavern.com; 35 Marlborough Buildings; mains £12-17) Bath isn't short on gastropubs, but the Marlborough is still very much top of the class. It's half cosy boozer, half contemporary bistro, with big wooden tables, deep seats, and a crackling fire on winter nights. Chef Richard Knighting previously worked in Michelin-starred restaurants, and it shows.

Demuth's VEGETARIAN ££
(☎01225-446059; www.demuths.co.uk; 2 North Pde Passage; lunch £4.95-11, dinner £14.50-17;) Even the most committed of carnivores can't fail to fall for this long-established vegie restaurant, which consistently turns out some of the city's most creative food – from cheddar soufflé served with figs, walnut purée and spring greens, to a port-poached pear baked with fennel seeds and sheep's cheese.

Sotto Sotto ITALIAN ££
(☎01225-330236; 10a North Pde; pasta £9, mains £13-17) Authentic Italian food served in a lovely cellar setting complete with barrel-brick roof. Ingredients are shipped in directly and everything's just like mama made, from the osso bucco (veal shank) to the *orecchiette mare e monti* (top-hat pasta with seafood, beans and pancetta).

Café Retro CAFE £
(18 York St; mains £5-11; ⊙breakfast, lunch & dinner Tue-Sat, breakfast & lunch Mon) The paint job's scruffy, the crockery's ancient and none of the furniture matches, but that's all part of the charm: this is a cafe from the old school, and there's nowhere better for a burger, cake or hot mug of tea. Takeaways available from Retro to Go next door.

Sally Lunn's CAFE £
(4 North Pde Passage; lunch mains £5-6, dinner mains from £8) This fabulously frilly tearoom occupies one of Bath's oldest houses, and makes the perfect venue for classic cream tea (served in proper bone china), accompanied by finger sandwiches, dainty cakes and the trademark Sally Lunn's Bun.

Raven PUB
(Queen St) This traditional pub commands a devoted following for its well-kept real ales and trad atmosphere, complete with beer mats, bar and brass trinkets.

Salamander PUB
(3 John St) Run by local brewer Bath Ales, this modern pub offers a range of bespoke ales. At the lighter end are amber-coloured Gem and Golden Hare, while the strongest is dark Rare Hare at a punchy 5.2%.

Information

Bath Visitor Centre (www.visitbath.co.uk; Abbey Churchyard; ⊙9.30am-5pm Mon-Sat, 10am-4pm Sun) Sells the Bath City Card (£3), which is valid for three weeks and offers discounts at many local shops, restaurants and attractions.

Getting There & Away

BUS Bath's **bus and coach station** (Dorchester St; ⊙9am-5pm Mon-Sat) is near the train station.

National Express coaches run directly to London (£20.70, 3½ hours, eight to 10 daily) via Heathrow (£20.70, 2¾ hours).

TRAIN Bath Spa station is at the end of Manvers St. Many services connect through Bristol (£9.90, 20 minutes, two or three per hour), especially to the north of England. Direct services:

Cardiff Central (£18, one hour, hourly)
Exeter (£27.50, 1¼ hours, hourly)
London Paddington or **Waterloo** (£39, 1½ hours, half-hourly)
Salisbury (£15.70, one hour, hourly)

Bristol

POP 393,300

Bristol might just be Britain's most overlooked city. While most visitors speed past en route to Bath without giving the southwest's biggest metropolis so much as a second glance, they're missing out on one of Britain's quirkiest and coolest cities. Once dominated by heavy industry and badly damaged during WWII, Bristol has reinvented itself over the last decade or so as a hub of culture and creativity, with a wealth of art galleries, theatres, design studios and media companies dotted around the much-revitalised centre.

Sights

TOP CHOICE SS Great Britain SHIP
(www.ssgreatbritain.org; Great Western Dock, Gas Ferry Rd; adult/child/family £12.50/6.25/33.50; ⌚10am-5.30pm Apr-Oct) Bristol's pride and joy is the mighty steamship SS *Great Britain,* designed by the genius engineer Isambard Kingdom Brunel in 1843. Built from iron and driven by a revolutionary screw propeller, this massive vessel was one of the largest and most technologically advanced steamships ever built, measuring a mighty 322ft (98m) from stern to tip, and capable of completing the transatlantic crossing between Bristol and New York in just 14 days. A painstaking 30-year restoration program has since brought her back to stunning life. You can wander around the ship's impeccably refurbished interior, including the galley, surgeon's quarters, dining saloon and the great engine room, but the highlight is the amazing 'glass sea' on which the ship sits, enclosing an airtight dry dock that preserves the delicate hull.

Tickets also allow admission to the neighbouring **Maritime Heritage Centre** (☎0117-927 9856; Great Western Dockyard, Gas Ferry Rd; ⌚10am-5.30pm Apr-Oct, 10am-4.30pm Nov-Mar), which has exhibits relating to the ship's illustrious past and the city's boat-building heritage. During autumn and winter, a replica of John Cabot's ship, the **Matthew** (☎0117-927 6868; www.matthew.co.uk), is moored nearby, the same design of ship in which the explorer made his landmark voyage from Bristol to Newfoundland in 1497. When the ship's docked in Bristol, it runs cruises around the harbour (adult/child £10/8); see the website for the next sailing dates.

FREE M Shed MUSEUM
(www.mshed.org; Princes Wharf; ⌚10am-5pm Tue-Fri, 10am-6pm Sat & Sun) It's taken four years and £27m to build, but Bristol's brand-new museum is finally open – and it's really rather brilliant. Lodged in a massive old warehouse overlooking the docks, it's a treasure trove of weird-and-wonderful memorabilia tracing the city's past. The 3000-odd exhibits are divided into three sections (People, Place and Life), and provide a panoramic overview of Bristol's history – from slaves' possessions and vintage double-decker buses to *Wallace*

BANKSY

Bristol brings you closer to the guerrilla graffiti artist Banksy. Acknowledged as a local boy, his true identity is a secret, though his work is well known. Headline-grabbing works include issuing spoof British £10 notes (with Princess Diana's head instead of the Queen's); replacing 500 copies of Paris Hilton's debut album in record shops with remixes (featuring tracks titled 'Why Am I Famous?' and 'What Have I Done?'); painting an image of a ladder going up and over the Israeli West Bank Barrier; and covertly inserting his own version of a primitive cave painting (with a human hunter-gatherer pushing a shopping trolley) into the British Museum in London.

Around Bristol, a few of his early works survive. Look out for his *Love Triangle* (featuring an angry husband, a two-timing wife, and a naked man dangling from a window) at the bottom of Park St, and the large mural called *Mild Mild West* featuring a Molotov cocktail–wielding teddy bear on Cheltenham Rd, opposite the junction with Jamaica St.

For more, see www.banksy.co.uk.

& Gromit figurines and a set of bright-pink decks once used by Massive Attack. Best of all, it's free – although well worth the £2 suggested donation.

Clifton Village NEIGHBOURHOOD

During the 18th and 19th centuries, wealthy Bristol merchants transformed the former spa resort of Clifton into an elegant hilltop suburb packed with impressive Georgian mansions. Some of the finest examples can be seen along **Cornwallis Crescent** and **Royal York Crescent**. These days, Clifton is still the poshest postcode in Bristol, with a wealth of streetside cafes and designer shops, and a village atmosphere that's far removed from the rest of the city.

Clifton Suspension Bridge BRIDGE

(www.cliftonbridge.org.uk) Clifton's most famous (and photographed) landmark is a Brunel masterpiece, the 76m-high Clifton Suspension Bridge, which spans the Avon Gorge from Clifton over to Leigh Woods in northern Somerset. Construction began in 1836, but Brunel died before the bridge's completion in 1864.

It's free to walk or cycle across the bridge; car drivers pay a 50p toll. There's a **visitor information point** (visitinfo@clifton-suspension-bridge.org; ⏲10am-5pm) near the tower on the Leigh Woods side. Free guided tours (£3) of the bridge take place at 3pm on Saturdays and Sundays from Easter to October.

At-Bristol MUSEUM

(www.at-bristol.org.uk; Anchor Rd; adult/child/family £12.50/8/35.50; ⏲10am-5pm Mon-Fri, to 6pm Sat & Sun) Bristol's interactive science museum has several zones spanning space, technology and the human brain. In the Curiosity Zone you get to walk through a tornado, spin on a human gyroscope and strum the strings of a virtual harp.

Arnolfini GALLERY

(www.arnolfini.org.uk; 16 Narrow Quay; ⏲10am-6pm Tue-Sun) The city's avantgarde art gallery occupies a hulking red-brick warehouse by the river, and remains the top venue in town for modern art, as well as occasional exhibitions of dance, film and photography.

Sleeping

Brooks Guest House B&B ££

(☎0117-930 0066; www.brooksguesthousebristol.com; Exchange Ave; d £70-99; 📶) Bristol has been crying out for a smart, modern B&B near the city centre for years – and at long last it has one, and in a fantastic spot right next door to St Nick's Market too. Parking is available for £9.50 at the nearby Queen Charlotte St car park.

Bristol YHA HOSTEL ££

(bristol@yha.org.uk; 14 Narrow Quay; dm/s/d £22/37/74; @) Few hostels can boast a position as good as this one, right beside the river in a red-brick warehouse. Facilities are great, including kitchens, cycle store, games room and the excellent Grainshed coffee lounge; the dorms are pretty functional, and the doubles are expensive.

Premier Inn, King St HOTEL ££

(☎0871 527 8158; www.premiertravelinn.com; King St; r £59-89; ❄📶) Yes, we realise this is a Premier Inn, but stop being snobby and just appreciate the cheap rates and riverside spot. Rooms have big beds, desk and wi-fi, and some even have glimpses of the harbour. Worth considering – although the Llangoger Trow pub next door gets rowdy at weekends.

Future Inn Cabot Circus HOTEL ££

(☎0845 094 5588; www.futureinns.co.uk/bristol-hotels; Bond St South; d £59-99; P📶) This hotel mini-chain has outlets in Plymouth, Cardiff and Bristol. It's modern and businessy, but the rooms are clean in beige, white and pine, and the rates are fantastic this close to the centre. Room prices include parking at the Cabot Circus car park.

Eating

Eating and drinking in Bristol is a real highlight – the city is jammed with restaurants, bars and pubs of every description. The areas around Park St and the waterfront are good options if you want to stroll and see what takes your fancy.

TOP CHOICE **Muset by Ronnie** BRITISH ££

(☎0117-973 7248; www.ronnies-restaurant.co.uk; 12-16 Clifton Rd; 2-/3-course lunch menu £13/16, dinner menu £19/22, mains £13-21) Chef Ron Faulkner has a new Clifton establishment, in addition to his original, much-vaunted address in Thornbury. Expect rich, hearty fare such as smoked eel, lamb shank and roast duck, served with a contemporary side of steamed kohlrabi or brown shrimp butter.

Riverstation BRITISH ££

(☎0117-914 4434; www.riverstation.co.uk; 2-/3-course lunch £12.75/15.50, mains £14.50-19.75)

LOCAL KNOWLEDGE

BRISTOL FERRY

A fun way to get around is on the boat run by **Bristol Ferry Boat Co** (☎0117-927 3416; www.bristolferry.com; adult/child return £3.80/3.20, day pass £7/5). Two routes go from the city centre dock, near the tourist office. The blue route goes east to Temple Meads via Millennium Sq, Welsh Back and Castle Park (for Broadmead and Cabot Circus); the red route goes west to Hotwells via Millennium Sq and the SS *Great Britain*.

It's been around for many years now, but this riverside bistro is as reliable as ever, turning out some of the city's best European cuisine. Head upstairs for dining, downstairs for coffee – and ask for a window table to make the most of the harbour views.

Thali Café INDIAN £
(☎0117-974 3793; www.thethalicafe.co.uk; 1 Regent St; meals £7.95-10.50) Bristol has some great Indian restaurants, but few are as beloved as this mini-chain of canteens, which now has four outlets, including this one in Clifton. It specialises in fresh, authentic thalis (multicourse Indian meals), as well as regional dishes ranging from Goan fish fries to Chompatti beach snacks.

Cowshed BRITISH ££
(☎0117-973 3550; www.thecowshedbristol.com; 46 Whiteladies Rd; 3-course lunch £10, dinner mains £12.95-21.50) Country dining in a city setting: lamb shoulder with root veg mash, or roast quail and pigeon with bubble-and-squeak. The Sunday roast is an institution.

Primrose Café BISTRO ££
(☎0117-946 6577; www.primrosecafe.co.uk; 1-2 Boyce's Ave; dinner mains £13.50-17.50; ⏲breakfast & lunch Mon-Sat, dinner Tue-Sat) A Clifton classic, perfect for morning coffee spent with the papers, a quick lunchtime snack or a proper sit-down dinner. It's right next door to one of Bristol's oldest shopping arcades.

Pieminister BAKERY £
(24 Stokes Croft; pies around £4.50; ⏲10am-7pm Sat, 11am-4pm Sun) Bristol's beloved pie shop turns out imaginative creations such as Thai Chook (chicken with green curry sauce) and Chicken of Aragon (chicken, bacon, garlic and vermouth), all drowned in lashings of gravy (meat-free if you wish). The main shop is on Stokes Croft, but there's an outlet in St Nick's market.

Drinking

Apple THEME BAR
(Welsh Back) Cider lovers won't want to miss this converted barge on Welsh Back, which offers over 40 varieties, including raspberry and strawberry, and six different perries (pear ciders).

Grain Barge PUB
(www.grainbarge.com; Mardyke Wharf, Hotwell Rd) Built in 1936, overhauled in 2007, this barge near SS *Great Britain* is owned by the city's renowned microbrewery, the Bristol Beer Factory. Gaze across the harbour while downing a pint of traditional No. 7 Bitter or dark Exhibition ale.

Entertainment

Bristol's nightclub scene moves fast, so check the latest listings at **Venue** (www.venue.co.uk).

Thekla CLUB
(www.thekla.co.uk; The Grove) Bristol's venerable club-boat has nights for all moods: electropunk, indie, disco and new wave, plus regular live gigs.

Colston Hall LIVE MUSIC
(www.colstonhall.org; Colston St) Bristol's historic concert hall tends to attract the best bands and big-name comedy acts.

Information

Bristol Tourist Information Centre (☎0333-321 0101; www.visitbristol.co.uk; E-Shed, 1 Canons Rd; ⏲10am-6pm)

Getting There & Away

BUS Bristol has excellent bus and coach connections. National Express destinations:

Birmingham (£21.30, two hours, six to eight daily)

Cardiff (£8.70, 1¼ hours, every two hours)

Exeter (£15, two hours, four daily)

London (£21, 2½ hours, hourly)

Useful local buses:

Bath (50 minutes, several per hour) Express bus X39/339.

Wells (one hour, half-hourly Monday to Saturday, hourly on Sunday, with onward connections to Glastonbury, 1¼ hours) Bus 376.

TRAIN Bristol is an important rail hub. Destinations include the following:

DESTINATION	DETAILS
Penzance	£42, 5½hr, hourly
Truro	£42, 5hr, hourly
Exeter	£25, 1hr, hourly
London Paddington	£39, 1¾hr, hourly
Birmingham	£47, 1½hr, hourly
Glasgow	£136.50, 6½hr, hourly
Edinburgh	£136.50, 6½hr, hourly

Wells

POP 10,406

With Wells, small is beautiful. This tiny, picturesque metropolis is England's smallest city, and only qualifies for the 'city' title thanks to a magnificent medieval cathedral. Wells has been the main seat of ecclesiastical power in this part of Britain since the 12th century, and is still the official residence of the Bishop of Bath and Wells. Medieval buildings and cobbled streets radiate from the cathedral green to a marketplace that has been the bustling heart of Wells for some nine centuries (Wednesday and Saturday are market days).

Sights

Wells Cathedral CHURCH
(www.wellscathedral.org.uk; Cathedral Green; requested donation adult/child £6/3; 7am-7pm) Wells' gargantuan Gothic cathedral (officially called the Cathedral Church of St Andrew) sits in the centre of the city, surrounded by one of the largest cathedral closes anywhere in England. It was built in several stages between 1180 and 1508, and consequently showcases a range of different Gothic styles.

Dominated by its squat towers, the cathedral's most famous asset is its **west front**, an immense sculpture gallery decorated with more than 300 figures, built in the 13th century and restored in 1986. The facade would once have been painted in vivid colours, but has long since reverted to its original sandy hue. Apart from the figure of Christ, installed in 1985 in the uppermost niche, all the figures are original.

Inside, the cathedral's famous **scissor arches** separate the nave from the choir. Though they appear purely decorative, they were actually built to counter the subsidence of the central tower. High up in the north transept is a **mechanical clock** dating from 1392 – the second-oldest in England after the one at Salisbury Cathedral – which shows the position of the planets and the phases of the moon.

Free guided tours usually run every hour from Monday to Saturday, but you'll need a photography permit (£3) to take pictures.

Bishop's Palace PALACE
(www.bishopspalacewells.co.uk; adult/child £6.35/2.70; palace 10am-6pm Apr-Dec, gardens Feb-Dec) Built for the bishop in the 13th century, this moat-ringed palace is purportedly the oldest inhabited building in England. The natural springs after which Wells is named bubble up in the palace's grounds. The swans in the moat have been trained to ring a bell outside one of the windows when they want to be fed.

Sleeping & Eating

Beryl B&B **££**
(01749-678738; www.beryl-wells.co.uk; Hawkers Lane; d £100-150; P) This grand gabled mansion offers a delicious taste of English eccentricity. Every inch of the house is crammed with antique atmosphere, and the rooms boast grandfather clocks, chaises longues and four-posters galore. It's about a mile from Wells.

Stoberry House B&B **££**
(01749-672906; www.stoberry-park.co.uk; Stoberry Park; d £75-115; P) Just outside the city outskirts, this refined B&B offers four fancy rooms equipped with plush throws and silky cushions. One-night stays incur a £10 to £20 surcharge.

Old Spot BRITISH **££**
(01749-689099; www.theoldspot.co.uk; 12 Sadler St; 2-/3-course lunch £15.50/18.50, dinner mains £14-18.50; lunch Wed-Sun, dinner Tue-Sat) Hale and hearty classics form the core of Ian Bates' bistro. It's heavy on rich, meaty dishes such as duck terrine, pork fillet with lentils and black pudding, or guinea-fowl with mushroom pithivier.

Goodfellows BISTRO, CAFE **££**
(01749-673866; www.goodfellows.co.uk; 5 Sadler St; 3-course bistro dinner £39) Two eateries in one, both excellent. The continental-style **cafe** (menus £10-17; 8.30am-4pm Mon & Tue, 8.30am-5pm & 6-10pm Wed-Sat) serves quick lunch food and pastries made by the in-house pastry chef. For something more sophisticated, the seafood **bistro** (mains £11.50-23; noon-2pm Tue-Sat, 6.30-9.30pm Wed-Sat)

offers a full line-up of fishy delights plus a choice of settings (downstairs for open-plan dining, upstairs for intimacy).

Information

Tourist Office (01749-672552; www.wellstourism.com; Market Pl; 9.30am-5.30pm Apr-Oct, 10am-4pm Nov-Mar)

Getting There & Away

The bus station is south of Cuthbert St, on Princes Rd. Bus 173 goes to Bath (one hour, hourly); bus 376/377 runs between Bristol (one hour, hourly) and Glastonbury (15 minutes) via Wells.

Exeter

POP 116,393

Well heeled and comfortable, Exeter exudes evidence of its centuries-old role as the spiritual and administrative heart of Devon. The city's gloriously Gothic cathedral presides over stretches of cobbled streets, fragments of the terracotta Roman city wall, and a tumbling of medieval and Georgian buildings. A snazzy new shopping centre brings bursts of the modern, while thousands of university students ensure a buzzing nightlife.

Sights

Exeter Cathedral CHURCH

(01392-285983; www.exeter-cathedral.org.uk; The Close; adult/child £6/free; 9am-4.45pm Mon-Sat) Magnificent in warm, honey-coloured stone, Exeter's Cathedral Church of St Peter is framed by lawns and wonky half-timbered buildings – a quintessentially English scene peopled by picnickers snacking to the sound of the bells. The site has been a religious one since at least the 5th century but the Normans started the current building in 1114; the towers of today's cathedral date from that period. In 1270 a 90-year remodelling process began, introducing a mix of Early English and Decorated Gothic styles.

Above the **Great West Front** scores of weather-worn figures line a once brightly painted screen that now forms England's largest collection of 14th-century sculpture. Inside, the ceiling is mesmerising – the longest unbroken Gothic vaulting in the world, it sweeps up to meet ornate ceiling bosses in gilt and vibrant colours. Look out for the 15th-century **Exeter Clock** in the north transept: in keeping with medieval astronomy it shows the earth as a golden ball at the centre of the universe with the sun, a fleur-de-lis, travelling round. Still ticking and whirring, it chimes on the hour.

For a sensational view, book a **roof tour** (01392-285983; www.exeter-cathedral.org.uk; adult/child £10/5; 2pm Tue-Thu, 11am Sat Apr-Sep) to the top of the North Tower. They're popular so book two weeks ahead.

Underground Passages HISTORIC SITE

(01392-665887; www.exeter.gov.uk/passages; Paris St; adult/child £5.50/4; 9.30am-5.30pm Mon-Sat, 10am-4pm Sun Jun-Sep, 11.30am-4pm Tue-Sun Oct-May) Prepare to crouch down, don a hard hat and possibly get spooked in what is the only publically accessible system of its kind in England. These medieval vaulted passages were built to house pipes bringing fresh water to the city. Guides lead you on a scramble through the network, telling tales of ghosts, escape routes and cholera. The last tour is an hour before closing; they're popular – book ahead.

Sleeping

ABode, Royal Clarence HOTEL ££

(01392-319955; www.abodehotels.co.uk/exeter; Cathedral Yard; r £150-330; @) The epitome of sink-into-it luxury. Exquisite rooms are categorised as Comfortable, Desirable, Enviable or Fabulous – either way they're a drop-dead gorgeous blend of Georgian grandeur and minimalist chic.

Raffles B&B ££

(01392-270200; www.raffles-exeter.co.uk; 11 Blackall Rd; s/d/f £48/78/96; P) The antique-dealer owner has peppered each room of this late-Victorian townhouse with heritage features – look out for Bakelite radios, wooden plant stands and creaking trunks. Largely organic breakfasts and a walled garden add to the appeal.

White Hart INN ££

(01392-279897; www.whitehartpubexeter.co.uk; 66 South St; s/d £50/70; P) They've been putting people up here since the 14th century. Rooms are either traditional (dark woods and rich drapes) or contemporary (laminate floors and light fabrics).

Globe Backpackers HOSTEL £

(01392-215521; www.exeterbackpackers.co.uk; 71 Holloway St; dm/d £17.50/43;) Rightly a firm favourite among budget travellers, this spotlessly clean, relaxed, rambling house boasts three doubles, roomy dorms and wet room showers that are positively luxurious.

WORTH A TRIP

GLASTONBURY

A long time bohemian haven and still a favourite hang-out for mystics and countercultural types of all descriptions, Glastonbury is best known for its massive music **festival** (www.glastonburyfestivals.co.uk), held (nearly) every year on Michael Eavis' farm in nearby Pilton.

The town owes much of its spirtual notoriety to nearby **Glastonbury Tor** (NT; www.nationaltrust.org.uk), a grassy hump about a mile from town, topped by the ruins of St Michael's Church. According to local legend, the tor is said to be the mythical Isle of Avalon, King Arthur's last resting place. It's also allegedly one of the world's great spiritual nodes, marking the meeting point of many mystical lines of power known as ley-lines.

There is no train station in Glastonbury, but bus 376/377 runs to Wells (30 minutes, hourly Monday to Saturday, seven on Sunday) and Bristol (1¼ hours), and south to Street (15 minutes).

Eating

MC Cafe, Bar & Grill BISTRO ££
(www.michaelcaines.com; Cathedral Yard; mains £10-20, 2/3 course lunch £11/16; 9am-10pm) The MC in the title stands for TV chef Michael Caines, so prepare for bistro classics with creative twists: beef burgers with onion confit; fish encased in a local Otter Ale batter.

Herbies VEGETARIAN £
(15 North St; mains £6-10; 11am-2.30pm Mon-Sat, 6-9.30pm Tue-Sat;) Cosy and gently groovy, Herbies has been cheerfully feeding Exeter's vegies for more than 20 years. It's *the* place in town to tuck into delicious sun-dried tomato and mushroom risotto or a hearty Greek vegetable pie. They're strong on vegan dishes too.

@Angela's MODERN BRITISH £££
(01392-499038; www.angelasrestaurant.co.uk; 38 New Bridge St; dinner mains £21; 6-9.30pm Mon-Sat, lunch Fri & Sat by reservation only) The chef here has a passion for local ingredients; his steamed John Dory with seared scallops is worth the trip alone. The beef has grazed Devon fields, while local duck is made memorable by a rich Grand Marnier sauce. Wise foodies opt for the prebooked lunch (2/3 courses £19/23).

Harry's BISTRO ££
(01392-202234; www.harrys-exeter.co.uk; 86 Longbrook St; mains £10; noon-2pm & 6-11pm) Harry's is the kind of welcoming neighbourhood eatery you wish was on your own doorstep but rarely is. The decor is all wooden chairs, blackboard menus and gilt mirrors; the food includes seared tuna, Spanish ham with marinated figs, and a hearty three-bean chilli.

Information

Tourist Office (01392-665700; www.exeterandessentialdevon.com; Paris St; 9am-5pm Mon-Sat, 10am-4pm Sun Jul & Aug)

Getting There & Away

BUS On Sundays between June and mid-September Bus 82, the Transmoor Link, makes five trips from Exeter to Plymouth via Moretonhampstead, Postbridge, Princetown and Yelverton.

Jurassic Coastlinx (bus X53) runs three to seven services daily to Lyme Regis, Weymouth and Poole.

Plymouth (£6.50, 1¼ hours, two-hourly Monday to Saturday, three on Sunday) Bus X38.

Totnes (50 minutes, seven daily Monday to Saturday, two on Sunday) Bus X64.

TRAIN Main-line and branch-line trains run from Exeter St David's and Exeter Central stations:

Bristol (£15, 1¼ hours, half-hourly)

London Paddington (£35, 2½ hours, half-hourly)

Penzance (£15, three hours, hourly)

Plymouth

TRANSPORT HUB

Devon's biggest city is an important Royal Navy port, thanks to its location beside a vast, sheltered bay. The city was practically flattened during WWII, and these days it's a little short on charm; still, it's very useful as a gateway for the southwest, especially Devon and Cornwall.

Sleeping

Fertile B&B hunting grounds are just back from the Hoe, especially around Citadel Rd: try **Sea Breezes** (01752-667205; www.plymouth-bedandbreakfast.co.uk; 28 Grand Pde;

s/d/f £40/70/95) or **Bowling Green** (☎01752-209090; www.thebowlinggreenplymouth.com; 10 Osborne Pl; s/d/f £50/70/80; P 📶).

Getting There & Away

BUS Services include:

Birmingham (£53, 5½ hours, four daily)

Bristol (£31, three hours, four daily)

Exeter (£6.50, 1¼ hours, two-hourly Monday to Saturday, three on Sunday) Bus X38.

London (£33, five to six hours, four daily)

Penzance (£9, 3½ hours, four daily)

TRAIN Services include:

Bristol (£25, two hours, two or three per hour)

Exeter (£8, one hour, two or three per hour)

London Paddington (£45, 3¼ hours, half-hourly)

Penzance (£8, two hours, half-hourly)

Dartmoor National Park

Dartmoor is a compelling landscape, very different from the rest of Devon. Exposed granite hills (called 'tors') crest the horizon, linked by swathes of moorland. On the fringes, streams tumble over boulders in woods of twisted trees. The centre of this 368-sq-mile wilderness is the higher moor; vast, treeless, moody and utterly empty. Naturally, Dartmoor's charms include superb walking and cycling, rustic pubs and country-house hotels – perfect boltholes when the mist rolls in.

For information, see www.dartmoor.co.uk.

Newquay

POP 19,423

Bright, breezy and unashamedly brash, Newquay in Cornwall is the undisputed capital of British surfing. All summer, a nonstop parade of beach lovers and boozed-up clubbers create a drink-till-dawn party atmosphere that's more Costa del Sol than Cornwall. If you've come to catch the waves, the best-known beach is **Fistral** – the venue for the annual Boardmasters surfing festival. Below town are **Great Western** and **Towan**; a little further up the coast you'll find **Tolcarne**, **Lusty Glaze**, **Porth** and **Watergate Bay**. All these beaches are good for swimming and supervised by lifeguards in summer.

Sleeping

The Hotel, Watergate Bay HOTEL ££
(☎01637-860543; www.watergatebay.co.uk; Watergate Bay; d £95-295, ste £205-400; P) Fresh from a multi-million-pound refit, the old Watergate has been reinvented as a beach-side beauty. It's pricey, but for this kind of location that's hardly surprising.

Newquay Townhouse B&B £
(☎01637-620009; www.newquaytownhouse.co.uk; 6 Tower Rd; d £50-70; P 📶) Near the town centre, with bright rooms livened up by stripy cushions and wicker furniture. Some have window seats, but only one has bay views.

Eating & Drinking

Beach Hut BISTRO ££
(☎01637-860877; Watergate Bay; mains £9.75-19.95; ⏰breakfast, lunch & dinner) This bistro by the sand has a beachy feel, and the menu's simple surf 'n' turf: sticky pork ribs, 'extreme' burgers and a different fish every day.

Café Irie CAFE £
(☎01637-859200; www.cafeirie.co.uk; 38 Fore St; lunch £3-8; ⏰breakfast & lunch Mon-Sat) A surfer's favourite in the centre of Newquay, perfect for hot chocolate, sticky cakes and jacket spuds before hitting the waves.

Chy BAR
(www.thekoola.com/the-chy-bar; 12 Beach Rd) Chrome, wood and leather dominate this cafe-bar overlooking Towan Beach. The action continues till late at the Koola nightclub downstairs.

Information

Tourist Office (☎01637-854020; www.newquay.co.uk; Marcus Hill; ⏰9.30am-5.30pm Mon-Sat, to 12.30pm Sun)

Getting There & Away

BUS The 585/586 is the fastest service to Truro (50 minutes, twice hourly Monday to Saturday).

TRAIN There are trains every couple of hours on the branch line between Newquay and Par (£4.30, 45 minutes) on the main London–Penzance line.

St Ives

POP 9870

Even if you've seen St Ives many times before, it's still hard not to be dazzled as you gaze across its jumble of slate roofs, church towers and turquoise bays. Once a busy pilchard harbour, St Ives later became the centre of Cornwall's arts scene in the 1920s and 1930s, and the town's cobbled streets are crammed with quirky galleries, cafes and restaurants.

Nearby, receding tides reveal 3 miles of golden beach at **Gwithian** and **Godrevy Towans**, both popular spots for kiteboarders and surfers.

Sights

Tate St Ives MUSEUM
(☎01736-796226; www.tate.org.uk/stives; Porthmeor Beach; adult/child £5.75/3.25; ⏲10am-5pm Mar-Oct, to 4pm Tue-Sun Nov-Feb) This far-westerly outpost of the Tate focuses mainly on the work of the artists of the so-called 'St Ives School'. Key works by Terry Frost, Patrick Heron, Naum Gabo, Ben Nicholson and Barbara Hepworth are all on show, as well as the naive paintings of fisherman-turned-artist Alfred Wallis, who didn't start painting until the ripe old age of 67. On the top floor there's a stylish cafe-bar which has a great panorama across St Ives.

A joint ticket with the Barbara Hepworth Museum costs adult/child £10/5.50.

Barbara Hepworth Museum MUSEUM
(☎01736-796226; Barnoon Hill; adult/child £5.50/3.25; ⏲10am-5pm Mar-Oct, 10am-4pm Tue-Sun Nov-Feb) Barbara Hepworth (1903–75) was one of the leading abstract sculptors of the 20th century, and a key figure in the St Ives art scene. Her studio on Barnoon Hill has remained almost untouched since her death, and the adjoining garden contains several of her most notable sculptures. Hepworth's work is scattered throughout St Ives; look for works outside the Guildhall and inside the 15th-century parish church of St Ia.

Sleeping

No 1 St Ives B&B ££
(☎01736-799047; www.no1stives.co.uk; 1 Fern Glen; d £85-125; P 📶) This renovated granite cottage bills itself as 'shabby chic', but it's nothing of the sort. It's a model of a modern B&B, and full of spoils – filtered water, goose-down duvets, iPod docks and White Company bathstuffs. Rooms vary in size, but all sport the same palette of white, cream and cappuccino.

Little Leaf Guest House B&B ££
(☎01736-795427; www.littleleafguesthouse.co.uk; Park Ave; r £80-115; 📶) This five-room B&B is uphill from town. Rooms are sweet and simple, finished in creamy colours and pine furniture. Ask for Room 2 or 5 if you're a sucker for a sea view.

DON'T MISS

EDEN PROJECT

If any one thing is emblematic of Cornwall's regeneration, it's the **Eden Project** (☎01726-811911; www.edenproject.com; adult/child £23/9.50; ⏲10am-6pm Apr-Oct, to 4.30pm Nov-Mar). Ten years ago the site was an exhausted clay pit; a symbol of the county's industrial decline. Now it's home to the largest plant-filled greenhouses on the planet – a monumental education project about the natural world. Tropical, temperate and desert environments have been recreated inside the massive biomes, so a single visit carries you from the steaming rainforests of South America to the dry deserts of northern Africa.

Eating & Drinking

TOP CHOICE **Porthminster Beach Café** BISTRO £££
(☎01736-795352; www.porthminstercafe.co.uk; Porthminster Beach; lunch £10.50-16.50, dinner £10-22; ⏲9am-10pm) For a seaside lunch there's nowhere better than this designer beach cafe, with its gorgeous suntrap terrace and Mediterranean-influenced menu. Tuck into rich bouillabaisse or Provençal fish soup, accompanied by beachy vistas.

Seagrass MODERN BRITISH ££
(☎01736-793763; www.seagrass-stives.com; Fish St; dinner mains £13.25-19.95; ⏲Tue-Fri) This vaunted restaurant on the waterfront is overseen by Lee Groves, who was a semifinalist on *Masterchef: The Professionals*. His elegant food and flavours have earned him plenty of plaudits: seafood and Cornish game figure heavily, often with an adventurous twist.

Blas Burgerworks CAFE ££
(The Warren; burgers £5-10; ⏲dinner Tue-Sun) Imaginative burger-joint with an ecofriendly, fair-trade manifesto. Traditionalists go for the 6oz, 100%-beef Blasburger, while vegies could plump for a halloumi stack or a ginger, coriander and chilli tofuburger.

The Hub CAFE, BAR
(www.hub-stives.co.uk; The Wharf) The open-plan Hub is the heart of St Ives' (limited) nightlife: frothy lattes by day, cocktails after dark, concertina doors onto the harbour.

Sloop Inn PUB

(The Wharf) A classic fishermen's boozer, complete with tankards behind the bar and a comprehensive selection of Cornish ales. The quayside tables go fast, so arrive early if it's sunny.

Information

St Ives Tourist Office (☎01736-796297; www.stivestic.co.uk; Street-an-Pol; ⊙9am-5.30pm Mon-Fri, 9am-5pm Sat, 10am-4pm Sun) Inside the Guildhall.

Getting There & Away

BUS The quickest bus to Penzance is bus 17 (30 minutes, twice hourly Monday to Saturday, hourly on Sunday). In summer the open-top bus 300 takes the scenic route via Zennor, Land's End and St Just.

TRAIN The gorgeous branch line from St Ives is worth taking just for the coastal views: trains terminate at St Erth (£3, 14 minutes, half-hourly), where you can catch connections along the Penzance–London Paddington main line.

Penzance

POP 21,168

The historic harbour town of Penzance is a hotchpotch of winding streets, old shopping arcades and a grand seafront promenade. It feels more authentic than prettified St Ives, and makes an excellent base for exploring the rest of west Cornwall.

Sights

TOP CHOICE **St Michael's Mount** MONASTERY

(NT; ☎01736-710507; www.stmichaelsmount.co.uk; castle & gardens adult/child £8.75/4.25; ⊙house 10.30am-5.30pm Sun-Fri late Mar-Oct, gardens Mon-Fri Apr-Jun, Thu & Fri Jul-Sep) Looming from the waters of Mount's Bay is the unmistakeable silhouette of St Michael's Mount, a dreamy abbey set on a rocky island that's connected to the small seaside town of Marazion by a cobbled causeway. There's been a monastery on the island since at least the 5th century, but the present abbey was mostly built during the 12th century by the Benedictine monks of Mont St Michel. It's now owned by the National Trust.

Highlights include the rococo drawing room, the original armoury, the 14th-century priory church and the abbey's subtropical cliff gardens.

You can catch a ferry (adult/child £2/1) at high tide from Marazion, about 3 miles from Penzance. At low tide you can walk across on the causeway, just as the monks and pilgrims did centuries ago.

The 513 bus runs three times daily from Penzance.

Sleeping

TOP CHOICE **Artist Residence Penzance** B&B ££

(☎01736-365664; www.arthotelcornwall.co.uk; Chapel St; d £80-120; 📶) This deliciously different new hotel on Chapel St is like sleeping inside an art gallery. All the rooms have their own bespoke design courtesy of a local artist. They're furnished with hand-picked bits of retro furniture, and most peep across Penzance's rooftops.

Penzance YHA HOSTEL £

(☎0845-371 9653; penzance@yha.org.uk; Castle Horneck, Alverton; dm from £14; P@) Penzance's YHA is inside an 18th-century house on the edge of town. It's a rambling place, with a cafe, laundry and four- to 10-bed dorms. It's a 15-minute walk from the front; buses 5 and 6 stop nearby.

Eating & Drinking

Bakehouse MEDITERRANEAN ££

(☎01736-331331; www.bakehouserestaurant.co.uk; Chapel St; mains £8.95-19.50; ⊙lunch Wed-Sat, dinner daily) This attractive double-floored diner is tucked down an alley off Chapel St. Food is filling and unpretentious: fish served with Med-style marinades, or steaks with a choice of sauces or spicy rubs. The dining room has A-frame beams and art, or there's a small palm-filled courtyard.

Archie Brown's CAFE £

(☎01736-362828; Bread St; mains £4-10; ⊙breakfast & lunch Mon-Sat) Archie Brown's has long been a favourite lunch spot for Penzance's artists and earth-mothers: it's perched above a health shop, and serves quiches, salads and home-baked cakes with a whole-food ethos.

Turk's Head PUB

(Chapel St) They pull a fine pint of ale at Penzance's oldest boozer. The bar's covered in maritime memorabilia, and it's said a secret smugglers' tunnel still links the pub to the harbour.

Zero Lounge BAR

(Chapel St) More urban chic than olde worlde, this open-plan bar also boasts the town's best beer garden.

Getting There & Away

BUS Services include:

St Ives (30 minutes, half-hourly Monday to Saturday, hourly on Sunday) Buses 17/17A/17B

Truro (one hour, three or four daily Monday to Saturday) Bus X18.

TRAIN Penzance is the last stop on the line from London Paddington. Trains run roughly hourly. Sample fares:

Exeter (£39.50, three hours)

London Paddington (£56, hourly, 5½ hours)

St Ives (£3.80, 30 minutes)

Truro (£9.50, 30 minutes)

Land's End

Just 9 miles from Penzance, Land's End is the most westerly point of mainland England, where cliffs plunge dramatically into the pounding Atlantic surf. The **Legendary Land's End** (www.landsend-landmark.co.uk; adult/child £10/7; ⏲10am-5pm Mar-Oct) theme park hasn't done much to enhance the view. Take our advice: skip the tacky multimedia shows and opt for an exhilarating clifftop stroll instead.

Bus 1/1A travels from Penzance (one hour, eight daily, five on Saturday) to Land's End; half the buses go via Sennen, the other half via Treen and Porthcurno.

CENTRAL ENGLAND

The geographic heartland of England is a mix of wildly differing scenes, with historic towns like Oxford and Stratford-upon-Avon, flower-decked villages in the Cotswolds, and rejuvenated former industrial cities like Birmingham.

For more information, see www.visitheartofengland.com (covering Birmingham and around, Warwickshire and Shropshire), www.oxfordshirecotswolds.org and www.visitpeakdistrict.com.

Oxford

POP 134,300

Oxford is a privileged place, one of the world's most famous university towns. It's steeped in history, studded with august buildings and yet maintains the feel of a young town, thanks to its large student population.

The city is a wonderful place to ramble: the oldest of its 39 separate colleges date back almost 750 years, and little has changed inside the hallowed walls since then (with the notable exception of female admissions, which only began in 1878). But along with the rich history, tradition and lively academic life, there is a whole other world beyond the college walls.

Sights

Much of the centre of Oxford is taken up by graceful university buildings, each one individual in its appearance and academic specialities. Not all are open to the public. For those that are, visiting hours change with the term and exam schedule. Check www.ox.ac.uk/colleges for full details.

TOP CHOICE Christ Church College NOTABLE BUILDING
(www.chch.ox.ac.uk; St Aldate's; adult/child £7.50/6; ⏲9am-5.30pm Mon-Sat, 2-5.30pm Sun) The largest and grandest of all of Oxford's colleges, Christ Church is also its most popular. The magnificent buildings, illustrious history and latter-day fame as a location for the *Harry Potter* films have tourists coming in droves.

The college was founded in 1525 by Cardinal Thomas Wolsey. Over the years numerous luminaries have been educated here, including Albert Einstein, philosopher John Locke, poet WH Auden, Charles Dodgson (Lewis Carroll) and 13 British prime ministers. The main entrance is below the imposing **Tom Tower**, the upper part of which was designed by former student Sir Christopher Wren. Mere visitors, however, are not allowed to enter the college this way and must go further down St Aldate's to the side entrance. Immediately on entering is the 15th-century cloister, a relic of the ancient Priory of St Frideswide, whose shrine was once a focus of pilgrimage. From here, you go up to the **Great Hall**, the college's magnificent dining room, with its hammerbeam roof and imposing portraits of past scholars. Coming down the grand staircase, you'll enter **Tom Quad**, Oxford's largest quadrangle, and from here, **Christ Church Cathedral**, the smallest cathedral in the country.

Christ Church is a working college, and the hall often closes between noon and 2pm and the cathedral in late afternoon.

Magdalen College NOTABLE BUILDING
(www.magd.ox.ac.uk; High St; adult/child £5/4; ⏲noon-7pm) Set amid 40 hectares of lawns, woodlands, river walks and deer park, Magdalen (*mawd*-len), founded in 1458, is

one of the wealthiest and most beautiful of Oxford's colleges.

An elegant Victorian gateway leads into a medieval chapel, with its glorious 15th-century tower, and on to the remarkable cloisters – with strange animals perching on the buttresses – some of the finest in Oxford. The fantastic gargoyles and grotesques along the frontage here are said to have inspired CS Lewis' stone statues in *The Chronicles of Narnia*. Behind the cloisters, the lovely **Addison's Walk** leads through the grounds and along the banks of the River Cherwell for just under a mile. Were you here in the mid-1870s, you would have encountered Oscar Wilde taking his pet lobster for a walk.

Magdalen has a reputation as an artistic college, and some of its other famous students and fellows have included TE Lawrence 'of Arabia', Poet Laureate Sir John Betjeman, Nobel Laureate Seamus Heaney and explorer Wilfred Thesiger, not to mention seven other Nobel Prize winners.

Merton College NOTABLE BUILDING

(www.merton.ox.ac.uk; Merton St; admission £2, guided tour £2; ⏲2-5pm Mon-Fri, 10am-5pm Sat & Sun, guided tour 45min) Founded in 1264, Merton is the oldest college and was the first to adopt collegiate planning, bringing scholars and tutors together into a formal community and providing a planned residence for them. Its distinguishing architectural features include the large gargoyles whose expressions suggest that they're about to throw up, and the charming 14th-century **Mob Quad** – the first of the college quads.

Just off the quad is a 13th-century **chapel** and the **Old Library** (admission on guided tour only), the oldest medieval library in use (look for the chained books). It is said that Tolkien spent many hours here writing *The Lord of the Rings* and that the trees in the Fellows' Garden inspired the walking trees of Middle Earth. Other literary giants associated with the college include TS Eliot and Louis MacNeice.

Bodleian Library LIBRARY

(www.bodley.ox.ac.uk; Broad St; Divinity School adult/child £1/free, audioguide £2.50, library tours £6.50; ⏲9am-5pm Mon-Fri, to 4.30pm Sat, 11am-5pm Sun, library tours 10.30am, 11.30am, 1pm & 2pm Mon-Sat, 11.30am, 2pm & 3pm Sun) Oxford's Bodleian Library is one of the oldest public libraries in the world. It currently holds over 11 million items, 117 miles of shelving and has seating space for up to 2500 readers, with a staggering 4000 books and articles arriving *every week* – all of which need to be catalogued and stored.

Most of the rest of the library is closed to visitors, but **library tours** allow access to the medieval Duke Humfrey's library. The tour takes about an hour and it's not suitable for children under 11 years old for fear that they will run amok.

Radcliffe Camera LIBRARY

(Radcliffe Sq; extended tours £13) The Radcliffe Camera is the quintessential Oxford landmark and one of the city's most photographed buildings. The spectacular circular library/reading room, filled with natural light, was built between 1737 and 1749 in grand Palladian style, and has Britain's third-largest dome. Tours from the Bodleian Library take place on Wednesdays and Saturdays at 9.15am and most Sundays at 11.15am and 1.15pm, and last about an hour and a half.

FREE **Ashmolean Museum** MUSEUM

(www.ashmolean.org; Beaumont St; ⏲10am-6pm Tue-Sun) This is Britain's oldest public museum, and second in repute only to London's British Museum. Its collections, displayed in bright, spacious galleries within one of Britain's best examples of neo-Grecian architecture, span the world and include everything from Egyptian mummies and sarcophagi, Islamic and Chinese art, Japan's 'floating world' and examples of the earliest written languages, to rare porcelain, tapestries and silverware, priceless musical instruments and extensive displays of European art (including works by Raphael and Michelangelo).

The Ashmolean has recently undergone a makeover, leaving it with new interactive features, a giant atrium, glass walls revealing galleries on different levels, and a beautiful rooftop restaurant.

Oxford Covered Market MARKET

(www.oxford-covered-market.co.uk; Market St; ⏲9am-5.30pm) A haven of traditional butchers, fishmongers, cobblers, barbers, delis, little eateries and independent shops; this lively market makes a good spot for lunch.

Sleeping

TOP CHOICE **Bath Place Hotel** BOUTIQUE HOTEL ££

(☎01865-791812; www.bathplace.co.uk; 4-5 Bath Pl, Holywell St; s/d from £95/120) Comprising several 17th-century weavers' cottages surrounding a tiny, plant-filled courtyard right in the shadow of New College, this is one of Oxford's more unusual hotels. Inside it's all creaky floors, exposed beams, canopied beds and soothing cream walls.

Ethos Hotel BOUTIQUE HOTEL ££
(☎01865-245800; www.ethoshotels.co.uk; 59 Western Rd; d from £125; @📶) Hidden away off Abingdon Rd, this funky new hotel has spacious rooms with bold, patterned wallpaper, enormous beds and marble bathrooms. It's aimed at independent travellers: you get a minikitchen with a microwave, and breakfast is delivered to your room in a basket. To get here, cross Folly Bridge to Abingdon Rd and take the first right onto Western Rd.

Oxford Rooms STUDENT ROOMS ££
(www.oxfordrooms.co.uk; s/d from £50/90; @) Didn't quite make the cut for a place at Oxford? During university holidays, you can sleep inside the hallowed college grounds. Most rooms are functional singles with basic furnishings and shared bathrooms, though there are some ensuite; twin and family rooms available.

Oxford YHA HOSTEL £
(☎0845-371 9131; www.yha.org.uk; 2a Botley Rd; dm/d from £23/50; @📶) Particularly convenient for budget travellers ridin' the rails, this is Oxford's best budget option, with simple but comfortable four- and six-bed ensuite dorms, private rooms and loads of facilities, including a restaurant, library, garden, laundry and a choice of lounges (though internet is not free).

Central Backpackers HOSTEL £
(☎01865-242288; www.centralbackpackers.co.uk; 13 Park End St; dm £19-22; @📶) A friendly budget option right in the centre of town. This small hostel has basic, bright and simple rooms that sleep four to 12 people, a rooftop terrace and a small lounge with satellite TV – all in a right-on-top-of-a-nightclub location.

Eating

Gee's MODERN BRITISH ££
(☎01865-553540; www.gees-restaurant.co.uk; 61 Banbury Rd; mains £12-19) Set in a Victorian conservatory, this top-notch restaurant is popular with the visiting parents of university students, thanks to its creative menu of British and European dishes. Book ahead.

PUNTING

Punting is a quintessential Oxford experience. A punt is a flat-bottomed boat, propelled (if that's the word) with a pole instead of oars. Punts are available to rent (£13/15 per hour weekdays/weekends, £65 deposit, mid-March to mid-October, 10am to dusk), and hold five people including the punter. The most central location is **Magdalen Bridge Boathouse** (www.oxfordpunting.co.uk; High St). From here, you can punt downstream around the Botanic Gardens and Christ Church Meadow or upstream around Magdalen Deer Park.

Door 74 MODERN BRITISH ££
(☎01865-203374; www.door74.co.uk; 74 Cowley Rd; mains £9-15; ⊙closed Mon & Sun dinner) This cosy little place woos its fans with a rich mix of British and Mediterranean flavours and friendly service. The menu is limited and the tables tightly packed, but the food is consistently good and weekend brunches (full English breakfast, pancakes) supremely filling.

Atomic Burger AMERICAN £
(www.atomicburger.co.uk; 96 Cowley Rd; mains £7-11; ⊙closed breakfast Mon-Fri) Atomic comes with the Fallout Challenge, which involves consuming a triple burger stack complete with fear-inducing ghost chilli hot sauce. Try the inventive Messy Jessie, Dead Elvis, the BBQ ribs and nachos and curly fries, all washed down with mega shakes.

Quod MODERN BRITISH ££
(www.quod.co.uk; 92 High St; mains £13-17) Bright, buzzing and decked out with modern art and beautiful people, this joint dishes up modern brasserie-style food to the masses. The two-course set lunch (£12.95) is great value.

Café Coco MEDITERRANEAN £
(www.cafe-coco.co.uk; 23 Cowley Rd; mains £6-10.50) This Cowley Rd institution is a hip hang-out, with classic posters on the walls and a bald plaster-cast clown in an ice bath. The food combines Mediterranean mains with waffles and pecan pie, and most people come for the atmosphere.

DON'T MISS

BLENHEIM PALACE

One of the country's greatest stately homes, **Blenheim Palace** (www.blenheimpalace.com; adult/child £20/10; ⊙10.30am-5.30pm mid-Feb–Oct) is a monumental baroque fantasy designed by Sir John Vanbrugh and Nicholas Hawksmoor between 1705 and 1722. Now a Unesco World Heritage site, it's home to the 11th Duke of Marlborough. Inside, Blenheim (*blen*-um) is stuffed with statues, tapestries, ostentatious furniture and giant oil paintings in elaborate gilt frames. Highlights include the **Great Hall**, a vast space topped by 20m-high ceilings adorned with images of the first duke in battle; the opulent **Saloon**, the most important public room; the three **state rooms** with their plush decor and priceless china cabinets; and the magnificent 55m **Long Library**. You can also visit the **Churchill Exhibition**, dedicated to the life, work and writings of Sir Winston, who was born at Blenheim in 1874. Outside, you can stroll through the lavish **gardens** and vast **parklands**, parts of which were landscaped by Lancelot 'Capability' Brown.

Blenheim Place is near the town of Woodstock, a few miles northwest of Oxford. To get there, Stagecoach bus S3 runs every half-hour (hourly on Sunday) from George St in Oxford.

Drinking

Turf Tavern PUB

(4 Bath Pl) Hidden away down a narrow alleyway, this tiny medieval pub is one of the town's best loved and bills itself as 'an education in intoxication' (this is also where president Bill Clinton 'did not inhale'). Home to 11 real ales, it's always packed with a mix of students, professionals and the lucky tourists who manage to find it. One of the few pubs in town with plenty of outdoor seating.

Bear PUB

(6 Alfred St) Arguably the oldest pub in Oxford (there's been a pub on this site since 1242). There's a great tie collection on the walls and ceiling (though you can no longer exchange yours for a pint).

Eagle & Child PUB

(49 St Giles) Affectionately known as the 'Bird & Baby', this atmospheric place, dating from 1650, was once the favourite haunt of Tolkien and CS Lewis. Its wood-panelled rooms and good selection of real ales still attract a mellow crowd.

Information

Tourist Office (☎01865-252200; www.visitoxford.org; 15-16 Broad St; ⊙9.30am-5pm Mon-Sat, 10am-4pm Sun)

Getting There & Away

BUS Oxford's main bus/coach station is at Gloucester Green. Services to London (£18 return) run up to every 15 minutes, day and night, and take about 90 minutes. There are also regular buses to/from Heathrow and Gatwick airports.

TRAIN Oxford's train station is conveniently placed at the western end of Park End St. There are half-hourly services to London Paddington (£23, one hour) and roughly hourly trains to Birmingham (£16, 1¼ hours). Hourly services also run to Bath (£16, 1¼ hours) and Bristol (£22, one to two hours), but require a change at Didcot Parkway.

The Cotswolds

A soft rural landscape, filled with glorious honey-coloured villages, old mansions, thatched cottages and atmospheric churches – welcome to the Cotswolds. If you've ever dreamed of falling asleep under English-rose wallpaper or lusted after a cream tea in the mid-afternoon, there's no finer place to fulfil your fantasies.

This is prime tourist territory, however, and the most popular villages can be besieged by traffic in summer. So visit the main centres early morning or late evening, focus your attention on the southern parts of the region, or take to the hills on foot or by bike.

A handy gateway town is **Moreton-in-Marsh**: a bus service runs to/from Cheltenham (seven times daily, one hour, Monday to Saturday) via Stow-on-the-Wold (15 minutes), with two Sunday services from May to September; there are trains roughly every two hours to/from London Paddington (£26.90, one hour 40 minutes) via Oxford (£7.90, 40 minutes).

CHIPPING CAMPDEN

POP 2206

An unspoiled gem in an area full of pretty villages, Chipping Campden is a glorious reminder of life in the Cotswolds in medieval times. The graceful curving main street is flanked by a picturesque array of wayward stone cottages, fine terraced houses, ancient inns and historic homes, many made of that honey-coloured stone that the Cotswolds are so famous for. Despite its obvious allure, the town remains relatively unspoiled by tourist crowds.

Sleeping & Eating

Eight Bells Inn B&B ££

(☎01386-840371; www.eightbellsinn.co.uk; Church St; s/d from £65/85) This 14th-century inn is an atmospheric B&B featuring bright, modern rooms with iron bedsteads, soothing neutral decor and warm accents. The pub downstairs wins points for its flagstone floors and good, no-nonsense pub grub (two-/three-course menu £18/22).

Volunteer Inn B&B £

(☎01386-840688; www.thevolunteerinn.net; Lower High St; s/d from £35/50) This is the favourite haunt of walkers and cyclists travelling along the Cotswold Way – a clutch of simple rooms atop a friendly, busy pub.

Getting There & Away

Between them, buses 21 and 22 run almost hourly to Stratford-upon-Avon or Moreton-in-Marsh. Bus 21 also stops in Broadway. No Sunday services.

You can hire a bike from **Cotswold Country Cycles** (www.cotswoldcountrycycles.com; Longlands Farm Cottage; per day £15).

BROADWAY

POP 2496

Yet another pretty Cotswold village, set at the foot of a steep escarpment. Its main street is lined with antiques shops, tearooms and art galleries, and is justifiably popular in the summer months. Take the time to wander, and you'll be rewarded with quiet back roads lined with stunning cottages, flower-filled gardens and picturesque churches.

For modern comfort within a 300-year-old exterior, complete with sloped floors, exposed beams and low ceilings, try the wonderfully friendly **Crown & Trumpet** (☎01386-853202; www.cotswoldholidays.co.uk; Station Rd; d £60; P, wi-fi), the Broadway 'local' with five rooms with ensuite above the lively pub.

STOW-ON-THE-WOLD

POP 2794

The highest town in the Cotswolds (244m), Stow is anchored by a large market square surrounded by handsome buildings and steep-walled alleyways, originally used to funnel the sheep into the fair; it is still an important market town. Today, it's famous for its twice-yearly Stow Horse Fair (May and October) and attracting a disproportionate number of people from passing coach tours.

Sleeping & Eating

Number 9 B&B ££

(☎01451-870333; www.number-nine.info; 9 Park St; s/d from £45/65; wi-fi) Centrally located and wonderfully atmospheric, this friendly B&B is all wonderfully sloping floors and exposed beams.

Stow-on-the-Wold YHA HOSTEL £

(☎0845-371 9540; www.yha.org.uk; The Square; dm £18; P @ wi-fi) In a you-can't-get-more-central-than-this location on the market square, the Cotswolds' only hostel is in a wonderful 16th-century townhouse, with compact dorms, a children's play area and its own on-site cafe, offering inexpensive hot meals.

Old Butchers MODERN EUROPEAN ££

(☎01451-831700; www.theoldbutchers.com; 7 Park St; mains £15-26; closed Mon & Sun dinner) Simple, smart and sophisticated, this is Stow's top spot for dining. It serves robust, local ingredients whipped up into sublime dishes with big flavours.

WINCHCOMBE

POP 4379

Winchcombe is a sleepy Cotswolds town, with butchers, bakers and small independent shops giving it a very authentic feel. It was capital of the Saxon kingdom of Mercia and important until the Middle Ages, and today the remnants of its illustrious past can still be seen.

Among the sleeping and eating options, the **White Hart Inn** (☎01242-602359; www.whitehartwinchcombe.co.uk; r £79-119) is excellent.

THE SLAUGHTERS

The picture-postcard villages of Upper and Lower Slaughter manage to maintain their unhurried medieval charm in spite of receiving a multitude of visitors. The village names have nothing to do with abattoirs; they are derived from the Old English 'sloughtre', meaning slough or muddy place.

Upper Slaughter is less visited than Lower Slaughter, and it's a pleasant stroll between the two villages.

For eating or sleeping, you can do no better than the elegant 17th-century mansion of **Lords of the Manor** (☎01451-820243; www.lordsofthemanor.com; Upper Slaughter; d £199-495; P) and its Michelin-starred restaurant (three-course menu £69).

To see the Slaughters at their best, arrive on foot from Bourton (a 1-mile walk) across the fields. From here you can continue for another mile across the fields to Upper Slaughter, with its own fine manor house and glorious cottages.

Shrewsbury

POP 67,126

On the western side of England, close to the border with Wales, Shrewsbury (*shroozbree*) is a delightful jumble of winding medieval streets and timbered Tudor houses leaning at precarious angles. It's also an excellent gateway to exploration in this quiet and scenic region, known as The Marches.

Sights

Shrewsbury Abbey CHURCH

(☎01743-232723; www.shrewsburyabbey.com; Abbey Foregate; entry by £2 donation; ⏲10.30am-3pm Mon-Sat, 11.30am-2.30pm Sun) Famous as the setting for Ellis Peters' *Chronicles of Brother Cadfael*, the lovely red-sandstone Shrewsbury Abbey is all that remains of a vast, cruciform Benedictine monastery founded in 1083. Twice the setting for meetings of the English parliament, the Abbey church lost its spire and two wings when the monastery was dissolved in 1540. It sustained further damage in 1826 when engineer Thomas Telford ran the London-Holyhead road right through the grounds. Nevertheless, you can still see some impressive Norman, Early English and Victorian features, including an exceptional 14th-century west window.

Shrewsbury Castle CASTLE

(☎01743-358516; adult/child £2.50/1.50; ⏲10am-5pm Mon-Sat, to 4pm Sun May-Sep, 10am-4pm Tue-Sat Feb-Apr) Hewn from flaking red Shropshire sandstone, the town castle contains the **Shropshire Regimental Museum**, plus fine views from **Laura's Tower** and the battlements. The lower level of the **Great Hall** dates from 1150.

Sleeping & Eating

Lion Hotel HOTEL ££

(☎01753-353107; www.thelionhotelshrewsbury.co.uk; Wyle Cop; s/d from £80/98; P) A gilded wooden lion crowns the doorway of this famous 16th-century coaching inn, decked out inside with portraits of lords and ladies in powdered wigs. Rooms are lovely, down to the period-pattern fabrics and ceramic water jugs. Breakfast included.

Tudor House B&B ££

(☎01743-351735; www.tudorhouseshrewsbury.com; 2 Fish St; s/d from £69/79; @) A bowing frontage festooned with hanging baskets and window boxes sets the scene at this delightful Tudor cottage. It's handy for everything in the centre, and rooms are adorned with shimmery fabrics and flowery trim. Not all rooms have an ensuite.

No 4 Butcher Row CAFE £

(☎01743-366691; www.number-four.com; 4 Butcher Row; mains £4-8.50; ⏲8.30am-4pm Mon-Fri, 8.30am-5pm Sat, dinner from 6.30pm Fri) Tucked away next to the Bull Inn near St Alkmond's Church, this neat, modern and very popular outfit is just the ticket for fantastic breakfasts, from eggs Benedict to bacon baguettes or a full English; lunch mains are excellent and affordable.

Good Life Wholefood Restaurant VEGETARIAN £

(☎01743-350455; Barracks Passage; mains £3.50-7; ⏲lunch Mon-Sat;) Wholesome, freshly prepared vegetarian food is on the cards at this healthy refuge off Wyle Cop. Favourites include quiches, nut loaf, salads, soups, vegie lasagne and the lovely spinach moussaka.

Getting There & Away

BUS Useful services:

Birmingham (£6.70, 1½ hours, twice daily) National Express.

Ironbridge (35 minutes, every two hours Monday to Saturday) Bus 96.

London (£19.80, 4½ hours, twice daily) National Express.

TRAIN From the station at the bottom of Castle Foregate, trains run half-hourly to Ludlow (£12.90, 30 minutes, hourly at weekends). For London Euston (£52, 2¾ hours) take one of the regular trains to Birmingham or Crewe and change.

If you're bound for Wales, **Arriva Trains Wales** (☎0845 900 0773; www.arrivatrainswales.co.uk) runs to Swansea (£33.80, 3¾ hours, hourly) and Holyhead (£39.80, three hours, hourly).

Stratford-upon-Avon

POP 22,187

The author of some of the most quoted lines in the English language, William Shakespeare, was born in Stratford in 1564 and died here in 1616. The five houses linked to his life form the centrepiece of a tourist attraction that verges on a cult of personality. Experiences range from the tacky (Bard-themed tearooms) to the humbling (Shakespeare's modest grave in Holy Trinity Church) and the sublime (a play by the world-famous Royal Shakespeare Company). If you can leave without buying at least a Shakespeare novelty pencil, you'll have resisted one of the most keenly honed marketing machines in the nation.

Sights

Shakespeare Houses MUSEUM
(☎01789-204016; www.shakespeare.org.uk; 5 properties adult/child £21.50/13.50, 3 in townhouses £14/9; ⊙9am-5pm Apr-Oct, hours vary Nov-Mar) Five of the most important buildings associated with Shakespeare, all run by the Shakespeare Birthplace Trust, contain museums that form the core of the visitor experience at Stratford. You can buy individual tickets, but it's more cost-effective to buy a combination ticket, either covering the three houses in town, or all five properties. Expect long queues throughout the summer.

Holy Trinity Church CHURCH
(☎01789-266316; www.stratford-upon-avon.org; Old Town; Shakespeare's grave adult/child £1.50/50p; ⊙8.30am-6pm Mon-Sat, 12.30-5pm Sun Apr-Sep, shorter hours Oct-Mar) The final resting place of the Bard is said to be the most visited parish church in England. Inside are handsome 16th- and 17th-century tombs (particularly in the Clopton Chapel), some fabulous carvings on the choir stalls and, of course, the grave of William Shakespeare, with its ominous epitaph: 'cursed be he that moves my bones'.

Sleeping

Church Street Townhouse BOUTIQUE HOTEL £££
(☎01789-262222; www.churchstreettownhouse.com; 16 Church St; r £110-180;) The 12 rather decadent rooms at this exquisite boutique hotel are divine and very plush, some with free-standing bath and all with iPod dock, flatscreen TVs and luxurious furnishings. Rooms are pricier at weekends.

ROYAL SHAKESPEARE COMPANY

You just can't come to Stratford without seeing one of the Bard's plays performed by the **Royal Shakespeare Company** (RSC; ☎0844 800 1110; www.rsc.org.uk; Waterside; tickets £8-38), especially since the multi-million-pound redevelopment of its two main theatres, the **Royal Shakespeare Theatre** and **Swan Theatre** on Waterside.

There are often special deals for under 25-year-olds, students and seniors, and a few tickets are held back for sale on the day of performance.

White Sails GUESTHOUSE ££
(☎01789-264326; www.white-sails.co.uk; 85 Evesham Rd; r from £95) Plush fabrics, framed prints, brass bedsteads and shabby-chic tables and lamps set the scene at this gorgeous, intimate guesthouse on the edge of the countryside.

Stratford-upon-Avon YHA HOSTEL £
(☎0845 371 9661; www.yha.org.uk; Hemmingford House, Alveston; dm from £16; P@) Set in a large, 200-year-old mansion 1.5 miles east of the town centre along Tiddington Rd, this superior hostel attracts travellers of all ages. There's a canteen, bar and kitchen, and buses 18 and 18a run here from Bridge St.

Eating & Drinking

Sheep St is clustered with eating options, mostly aimed at theatregoers (look out for good-value pretheatre menus).

Lambs MODERN EUROPEAN ££
(☎01789-292554; www.lambsrestaurant.co.uk; 12 Sheep St; mains £10.25-18.75; ⊙lunch Wed-Sun, dinner daily) Lambs swaps Shakespeare chintz in favour of Venetian blinds and modern elegance, but throws in authentic 16th-century ceiling beams for good measure. The food is quality European fare, underpinned by topnotch British ingredients.

Edward Moon's MODERN BRITISH ££
(☎01789-267069; www.edwardmoon.com; 9 Chapel St; mains £10-15) Named after a famous travelling chef who cooked up the flavours of home for the British colonial service, this snug and just-refurbished eatery serves delicious, hearty English dishes, many livened up with herbs and spices from the East.

Dirty Duck PUB
(Waterside) Officially called the 'Black Swan', this enchanting riverside alehouse is a favourite thespian watering hole, boasting a roll-call of former regulars (Olivier, Attenborough etc) that reads like a *Who's Who* of actors.

Windmill Inn PUB
(Church St) Ale was flowing here at the same time as rhyming couplets gushed from Shakespeare's quill – this pub with low ceilings has been around a while.

Information

Tourist Office (☎01789-264293; www.shakespeare-country.co.uk; 62 Henley St; ⊙10am-5pm, to 4pm winter)

Getting There & Away

BUS National Express coaches and other bus companies run from Stratford's Riverside bus station (behind the Stratford Leisure Centre on Bridgeway). Destinations:

Birmingham (£8.80, one hour, twice daily)

London Victoria (£17.60, three to four hours, five daily)

Oxford (£11.20, one hour, twice daily)

Warwick (40 minutes, hourly) Bus 16.

TRAIN From Stratford train station, London Midland runs to Birmingham (£6.80, one hour, hourly), Chiltern Railways runs to London Marylebone (£25, 2¼ hours, four daily).

Getting Around

A bicycle offers a handy means of transport for visiting the outlying Shakespeare properties, and **Stratford Bike Hire** (☎07711-776340; www.stratfordbikehire.com; 7 Seven Meadows Rd; per half-day/day from £7/13) will deliver to your accommodation.

Birmingham

TRANSPORT HUB

Once a byword for bad town planning, England's second-largest city – known to locals as 'Brum' – is shaking off the legacy of industrial decline, and spending some serious money replacing its drab 1960s concrete architecture with gleaming glass and steel. It's certainly looking better than it has in decades, but chances are you'll probably be passing through en route to somewhere else, although the city has lots of good museums and shops should you decide to linger longer.

Sleeping & Eating

Most Birmingham hotels target business travellers, B&Bs are concentrated outside the centre in Acocks Green (to the southeast) and Edgbaston and Selly Oak (to the southwest).

If you need somewhere to crash overnight, boutique **Bloc** (☎0121-212 1223; www.blochotels.com; St Paul's, Caroline St; r from £45; wi-fi) and **Birmingham Central Backpackers** (☎0121-643 0033; www.birminghamcentralbackpackers.com; 58 Coventry St; dm from £13; @ wi-fi) are both good options.

Birmingham is best known for its brilliant baltis, but the city has a flourishing reputation for fine dining. For cheap eats, look to the myriad Asian eateries in Chinatown, just south of the centre.

Getting There & Away

BUS Most intercity buses run from the **Birmingham Coach Station** (Digbeth High St), but the X20 to Stratford-upon-Avon (1¼ hours, hourly Monday to Friday, every two hours at weekends) leaves from a stop on Moor St, just north of the Pavilions mall. **National Express** (☎08718 81 81 81; www.nationalexpress.com) runs coaches between Birmingham and major cities across the country:

London (£15.70, 2¾ hours, every 30 minutes)

Manchester (£12.60, 2½ hours, 12 daily)

Oxford (£11.60, 1½ to two hours, five daily)

TRAIN Most long-distance trains leave from New St station, beneath the Pallasades shopping centre, but Chiltern Railways runs to London Marylebone (£31.90, 2½ hours, half-hourly) from Birmingham Snow Hill, and London Midland runs to Stratford-upon-Avon (£6.30, one hour, hourly) from Snow Hill and Moor St stations.

Useful services from New St:

Leicester (£13.10, one hour, half-hourly)

London Euston (£40.90, 1½ hours, half-hourly)

Manchester (£30.50, 1¾ hours, every 15 minutes)

Shrewsbury (£11.70, one hour, half-hourly)

Warwick

POP 25,434

Regularly name-checked by Shakespeare, Warwick is a treasure-house of medieval architecture, dominated by the soaring turrets of **Warwick Castle** (☎0870 442 2000; www.warwick-castle.co.uk; castle adult/child £19.95/11.95, castle & dungeon £27.45/19.45; ⊙10am-6pm Apr-Sep, to 5pm Oct-Mar; P), founded in 1068 by William the Conqueror, and later the ancestral home of the Earls of Warwick. It's now been transformed into a major tourist attraction by the owners of Madame Tussauds, with kid-centred activities and waxworks populating the private apartments.

Stagecoach bus 16 goes to Stratford-upon-Avon (40 minutes, hourly). Trains run to Birmingham (£7.40, 45 minutes, every half-hour), Stratford-upon-Avon (£5.20, 30 minutes, hourly) and London (£30, 1¾ hours, every 20 minutes).

Peak District National Park

Squeezed between the industrial Midlands to the south and the cities of Manchester and Sheffield to the west and east, the surprisingly rural **Peak District** (☎01629-816200; www.peakdistrict.gov.uk) is one of the finest areas in England for walking, cycling and other outdoor activities. Don't be misled by the name; there are few peaks, but plenty of wild moors, rolling farmland and deep valleys – plus hardy villages, prehistoric sites and limestone caves.

It's also one of England's best-loved national parks. The towns of Buxton to the west or Matlock to the east are good gateways, or you can stay right in the centre at Edale, Bakewell or Castleton.

The park's best-known attraction is **Chatsworth House** (☎01246-582204; www.chatsworth.org; house & gardens adult/child £15/9, gardens only £10/6, playground £5, park free; ⊙11am-5.30pm mid-Mar–late Dec, closed late Dec–mid-Mar), locally known as the 'Palace of the Peak'. This vast edifice has been occupied by the earls and dukes of Devonshire for centuries. While the core of the house dates from the 16th century, Chatsworth was altered and enlarged over the centuries. The current building has a Georgian feel, dating back to the last overhaul in 1820. Inside, the lavish apartments and mural-painted staterooms are packed with priceless paintings and period furniture, and outside there are 25 sq miles of grounds and ornamental gardens, some landscaped by Lancelot 'Capability' Brown.

Getting There & Around

National Express coaches run from London Victoria to Manchester and Buxton, from where you can switch to a local bus. Derby, south of the park, is another good gateway, easily reached by coach and train, and from there trains run to Matlock. Trains also run between Sheffield and Manchester via Edale and several other Peak villages.

By far the handiest local bus is the hourly **Transpeak** (www.transpeak.co.uk) service that cuts across the Peak District from Nottingham and Derby to Manchester, via Matlock, Bakewell and Buxton.

EASTERN ENGLAND

The vast flatland of eastern England (or East Anglia, as it's usually called) is a mix of lush farms, melancholy fens, big skies and the bucolic scenery that once inspired Constable and Gainsborough. Meanwhile, the meandering coast is lined with pretty fishing villages and bucket-and-spade resorts, while inland sit the watery charms of the Norfolk Broads.

Cambridge

POP 119,100

Drowning in exquisite architecture, steeped in history and tradition, and renowned for its quirky rituals, Cambridge is a university town extraordinaire. The tightly packed core of ancient colleges, the picturesque riversides and the leafy green meadows that surround the city give it a far more tranquil appeal than rival Oxford.

Sights

Cambridge University comprises 31 colleges, though not all are open to the public. Most close to visitors for the Easter term and all are closed for exams from mid-May to mid-June. Opening hours vary from day to day, and the hours given below are only a rough guide, so contact the colleges or the tourist office for information.

TOP CHOICE **Trinity College** NOTABLE BUILDING

(www.trin.cam.ac.uk; Trinity St; adult/child £1.50/1; ⊙10.30am-4.30pm) The largest of Cambridge's colleges, Trinity is entered through an impressive Tudor gateway first created in 1546. The **Great Court** is the largest of its kind in the world; to the right of the entrance is a small tree, planted in the 1950s and reputed to be a descendant of the apple tree made famous by Trinity alumnus Sir Isaac Newton. Other alumni include Alfred Tennyson, Francis Bacon, Lord Byron, HRH Prince Charles and at least nine prime ministers, British and international.

The college's vast hall has a dramatic hammerbeam roof and lantern, and beyond this are the dignified cloisters of Nevile's Court and the renowned **Wren Library** (⏲noon-2pm Mon-Fri).

King's College Chapel CHURCH

(www.kings.cam.ac.uk/chapel; King's Pde; adult/child £7.50/free, Evensong free; ⏲9.45am-4.30pm Mon, from 9.30am Tue-Sun, Evensong 5.30pm Mon-Sat, 10.30am & 3.30pm Sun, term time only) Chances are you will already have seen it on a thousand postcards, tea towels and choral CDs before you catch your first glimpse of the grandiose King's College Chapel, but still it inspires awe. It's one of the most extraordinary examples of Gothic architecture in England, begun in 1446 as an act of piety by Henry VI and finished by Henry VIII around 1516. The vast 80m-long **fan-vaulted canopy** is the work of John Wastell and is the largest expanse of fan vaulting in the world. The chapel is also remarkably light, its sides flanked by lofty **stained-glass windows** that retain their original glass – rare survivors of the excesses of the Civil War in this region. It's said that these windows were ordered to be spared by Cromwell himself, who knew of their beauty from his own studies in Cambridge.

The thickly carved wooden stalls are a stage for the chapel's world-famous **choir**. You can hear them in full voice during the magnificent **Evensong**. If you happen to be visiting at Christmas, it is also worth queuing for admission to the incredibly popular **Festival of Nine Lessons and Carols** on Christmas Eve.

The chapel is open for reduced hours during term time, and charges an entry fee for nonmembers of the University.

The Backs PARK

Behind the grandiose facades, stately courts and manicured lawns of the city's central colleges lies a series of gardens and parklands butting up against the river. Collectively known as the Backs, these tranquil green spaces and shimmering waters offer unparalleled views of the colleges.

The fanciful **Bridge of Sighs** (built in 1831) at St John's is best observed from the stylish bridge designed by Christopher Wren just to the south. The oldest crossing is at **Clare College**, built in 1639 and ornamented with decorative balls. Most curious of all is the flimsy-looking wooden construction joining the two halves of Queen's College, known as the **Mathematical Bridge**, first built in 1749. Despite what unscrupulous guides may tell you, it wasn't the handiwork of Sir Isaac Newton (he died in 1727), originally built without nails, or taken apart by academics who then couldn't figure how to put it back together.

TOP CHOICE **Fitzwilliam Museum** MUSEUM

(www.fitzmuseum.cam.ac.uk; Trumpington St; admission by donation, guided tour £5; ⏲10am-5pm Tue-Sat, noon-5pm Sun) Fondly dubbed 'the Fitz' by locals, this colossal neoclassical pile was one of the first public art museums in Britain, built to house the fabulous treasures that the seventh Viscount Fitzwilliam had bequeathed to his old university.

The lower galleries are filled with priceless treasures spanning the ancient world; look out for a Roman funerary couch, an inscribed copper votive plaque from Yemen (c 150 AD), a figurine of the Egyptian cat goddess Bastet, some splendid Egyptian sarcophagi and mummified animals – a cat, and an ibis – and some dazzling illuminated manuscripts. The Chinese ceramics section was closed at the time of writing due to a robbery. The upper galleries showcase works by Leonardo da Vinci, Titian, Rubens, the Impressionists, Gainsborough and Constable, right through to Rembrandt and Picasso; standout works include the tender *Pietà* by Giovanni del Ponte and Salvator Rosa's dark and intensely personal *L'Umana Fragilita*.

You can join a one-hour **guided tour** of the museum on Saturdays at 2.30pm.

Corpus Christi College NOTABLE BUILDING

(www.corpus.cam.ac.uk; King's Pde; admission £2.50; ⏲10am-4.30pm) Entry to this illustrious college is via the so-called **New Court**, which dates back a mere 200 years. To your right is the door to the Parker Library, which holds the finest collection of Anglo-Saxon manuscripts in the world. Look out for the fascinating sundial and plaque to playwright and past student Christopher Marlowe (1564–93), author of *Dr Faustus* and *Tamburlaine*.

On the corner of Bene't St you'll find the college's new **Corpus Clock**. Made from 24-carat gold, it displays the time through a series of concentric LED lights. A hideous-looking insect 'time-eater' crawls across the top. The clock is only accurate once every five minutes. At other times it slows or stops and then speeds up, which, according to its creator, JC Taylor, reflects life's irregularity.

Sleeping

Some of Cambridge's most central B&Bs use their convenient location as an excuse not to upgrade. Some of the better places are a bit of a hike from town but well worth the effort.

Hotel Felix BOUTIQUE HOTEL £££
(01223-277977; www.hotelfelix.co.uk; Whitehouse Lane, Huntingdon Rd; s/d from £165/200; P@) This luxurious boutique hotel occupies a lovely grey-brick Victorian villa in landscaped grounds a mile from the city centre. Its 52 rooms embody designer chic with minimalist style and wonderful touches such as Egyptian cotton bedding and rain showers in many rooms. Follow Castle St and then Huntingdon Rd out of the city for about 1.5 miles.

Benson House B&B ££
(01223-311594; www.bensonhouse.co.uk; 24 Huntingdon Rd; d from £90; P) Just a 15-minute walk from the city centre, the rooms at this B&B range from monochrome minimalism to muted classical elegance, and breakfast includes the less usual addition of kippers. To get here follow Castle St north of the city centre into Huntingdon Rd.

Cambridge Rooms COLLEGE ROOMS ££
(www.cambridgerooms.co.uk; s/d from £41/78) If you wish to experience life inside the hallowed college grounds, you can stay in a student room in one of several colleges. There's a good choice of rooms during university holidays.

Cambridge YHA HOSTEL £
(0845 371 9728; www.yha.org.uk; 97 Tenison Rd; dm/tw £19/45; @) Busy, popular hostel with compact dorms and good facilities near the train station.

Eating

Oak Bistro MODERN BRITISH ££
(01223-323361; www.theoakbistro.co.uk; 6 Lensfield Rd; mains £12-20, 2-/3-course set lunch £12/15; Mon-Sat) This great local favourite serves up simple, classic dishes with modern flair, such as tuna nicoise salad and slow-roasted lamb. Reservations are essential even for lunch due to its size and popularity.

Hakka CHINESE ££
(01223-568988; www.hak-ka.co.uk; 24 Milton Rd; mains £7.50-11.50; closed lunch;) Chef Daniel's mother has taught him the secrets of Hakka cooking and once you've tasted his signature salt and chilli chicken, you'll be inclined to give her a hug and a kiss. Service can be slow on busy nights.

Chop House TRADITIONAL BRITISH ££
(www.cambscuisine.com/cambridge-chop-house; 1 Kings Pde; mains £9.50-24) If you're craving sausage and mash, a sizzling steak, suet pudding, fish pie or potted ham, look no further. Sister restaurant **St John's Chop House** (www.cambscuisine.com/st-johns-chop-house; 21-24 Northampton St) has the same menu and is located near the rear entrance to St John's College.

Stickybeaks CAFE £
(www.stickybeakscafe.co.uk; 42 Hobson St; mains £3-7; 8am-5.30pm Mon-Fri, 9am-5.30pm Sat, 10am-5pm Sun;) Sip creamy hot chocolate, nibble on a wide array of cakes or tuck into some imaginative salads (couscous with pomegranate, puy lentils with goat's cheese) at this popular new cafe.

Drinking & Entertainment

Cambridge is awash with historic pubs that echo with intellectual banter and rowdy merrymaking – just as they have for centuries past.

Eagle PUB
(Bene't St) Cambridge's most famous pub has loosened the tongues and pickled the grey cells of many an illustrious academic in its day; among them were Nobel Prize–winning scientists Crick and Watson, who discussed their research into DNA here. It's a traditional 17th-century pub with five cluttered, cosy rooms and good pub grub, the back one once popular with WWII airmen, who left their signatures on the ceiling.

Maypole PUB
(www.maypolefreehouse.co.uk; 20a Portugal Pl) This friendly, popular pub has hit a winning formula: serve a good selection of real ales, throw in some great cocktails, and host a successful beer festival in 2012 (set to become an annual event).

Corn Exchange THEATRE
(www.cornex.co.uk; Wheeler St) The city's main centre for arts and entertainment, attracting the top names in pop and rock to ballet.

Information

Tourist Office (0871-266 8006; www.visitcambridge.org; Old Library, Wheeler St; 10am-5.30pm Mon-Fri, to 5pm Sat, 11am-3pm Sun) Pick up a guide to the Cambridge colleges (£4.99) in the gift shop or a leaflet (£1.20) outlining two city walks. Download audio tours from the website or book slots on a plethora of tours.

Getting There & Away

BUS From Parkside there are regular National Express (www.nationalexpress.co.uk) buses to the following destinations:

Gatwick (£37, 3½ to four hours)

Heathrow (£31, 2½ to three hours)

Oxford (£11, 3¼ to 3½ hours, twice-hourly)

Stansted (£13, 50 minutes)

TRAIN The train station is off Station Rd, which is off Hills Rd. Destinations:

Birmingham New Street (£30, three hours, hourly)

Ely (£4,15 minutes, three hourly)

London King's Cross (£19, 50 minutes to 1¼ hours)

Ely

POP 15,102

A small but charming city steeped in history and dominated by a jaw-dropping cathedral, Ely (*ee*-lee) makes an excellent day trip from Cambridge. Beyond the dizzying heights of the cathedral towers lie medieval streets, pretty Georgian houses and riverside walks reaching out into the eerie fens that surround the town.

Sights

Ely Cathedral — CHURCH

(www.elycathedral.org; tower tour £6 Mon-Sat, £8.50 Sun; ⏲7am-6.30pm, Evensong 5.30pm Mon-Sat, 4pm Sun, choral service 10.30am Sun) Dominating the town, the stunning silhouette of Ely Cathedral is locally dubbed the 'Ship of the Fens' due to its visibility across the flat fenland for vast distances. Walking into the early-12th-century Romanesque nave (with some Gothic arches added later to support the weight of the mighty walls) you're immediately struck by its clean, uncluttered lines and lofty sense of space. The cathedral is renowned for its entrancing ceiling, painted by two artists, Henry Le Strange and Thomas Gambier (can you spot the difference in style?), the masterly 14th-century Octagon – the most impressive of all of England's churches – and lantern towers, which soar upwards in shimmering colours. The cathedral's incredible architecture and light have made it a popular film location: you may recognise some of its fine details from scenes in *Elizabeth: The Golden Age* and *The Other Boleyn Girl*.

For more insight into the fascinating history of the cathedral join a free **guided tour**, or a **tower tour** of the Octagon Tower or the West Tower. Near the entrance a **stained-glass museum** (www.stainedglassmuseum.com; adult/child £4/3; ⏲10.30am-5pm Mon-Fri, to 5.30pm Sat, noon-6pm Sun Easter-Oct) tells the history of decorated glasswork from the 14th century onwards.

Oliver Cromwell's House — MUSEUM

(www.olivercromwellshouse.co.uk; adult/child £4.50/4, joint ticket with Ely Museum £6.80; ⏲10am-5pm) By St Mary's Green is the attractive half-timbered house where England's only dictator lived with his family from 1636 to 1647, when he was the local tithe collector. From the introductory video, and the audio-guided tour of the living quarters to exhibits on the Civil War, and Cromwell's posthumous execution, this entertaining museum challenges you to answer one question: was this complex character (who executed a king and fought a bloody Civil War that killed 185,000 people) a hero or a villain? The interactive exhibits keep children (and your inner child) happily occupied throughout.

Getting There & Away

TRAIN Services include:

Cambridge (£4, 20 minutes, every 20 minutes)

King's Lynn (£6, 30 minutes, hourly)

Norwich (£18, one hour, every 20 minutes)

Following the Fen Rivers Way (map available from tourist offices), it's a lovely 17-mile towpath walk from Cambridge to Ely.

NORTHEAST ENGLAND

By turns wild and pretty, rural and urban, modern and historic, northeast England contains the large and varied counties of Yorkshire and Northumberland, and three of Britain's great cities: historic York, Durham and resurgent Newcastle.

For general information, see www.yorkshirevisitor.com and www.visitnortheastengland.com.

Leeds

POP 750,200

One of the fastest-growing cities in the UK, Leeds is the glitzy, glamorous embodiment of newly rediscovered northern self-confidence. More than a decade of redevelopment has seen a transformation from near-derelict mill town into a vision of 21st-century urban chic, with skyscraping office blocks, waterfront apartments and renovated Victorian shopping arcades earning the city its much-hyped moniker: 'Knightsbridge of the North'. For visitors, it's also an excellent gateway to several major attractions.

Sights

FREE Royal Armouries MUSEUM
(www.royalarmouries.org; Armouries Dr; 10am-5pm) Leeds' most interesting museum is undoubtedly the Royal Armouries, beside the snazzy Clarence Dock residential development. It was originally built to house the armour and weapons from the Tower of London but was subsequently expanded to cover 3000 years' worth of fighting and self-defence. To get here, walk east along the river from Centenary Footbridge (10 minutes), or take bus 28 from Albion St.

FREE Leeds Art Gallery GALLERY
(www.leeds.gov.uk/artgallery; The Headrow; 10am-5pm Mon, Tue & Thu-Sat, noon-5pm Wed, 1-5pm Sun) The municipal gallery is packed with 19th- and 20th-century British heavyweights – Turner, Constable, Stanley Spencer, Wyndham Lewis et al – along with contemporary pieces by more recent arrivals such as Antony Gormley, sculptor of the *Angel of the North*.

Leeds Industrial Museum MUSEUM
(www.leeds.gov.uk/armleymills; Canal Rd; adult/child £3.30/1.20; 10am-5pm Tue-Sat, 1-5pm Sun) One of the world's largest textile mills has been transformed into a museum telling the story of Leeds' industrial past, both glorious and ignominious. The city became rich off the sheep's back, but at a cost – working conditions were, well, Dickensian. Take bus 5 from the train station to get here.

Sleeping

TOP CHOICE Quebecs BOUTIQUE HOTEL £££
(0113-244 8989; www.quebecshotel.co.uk; 9 Quebec St; d/ste from £180/300;) Victorian grace at its opulent best is the theme of our favourite hotel in town, a conversion of the former Leeds & County Liberal Club. Heavy discounts for online booking.

Roomzzz APARTMENT ££
(0844 499 4888; www.roomzzz.co.uk; 10 Swinegate & 2 Burley Rd; 2-person apt from £79;) This outfit offers bright and modern luxury apartments complete with fitted kitchen. Roomzzz Leeds City is at 10 Swinegate, right in the city centre; Roomzzz Leeds City West is half a mile west on Burley Rd.

Bewleys Hotel HOTEL ££
(0113-234 2340; www.bewleyshotels.com/leeds; City Walk, Sweet St; r from £64;) Bewleys is super-convenient for motorists, just off Junction 3 on the M621 but also just 10 minutes' walk from the city centre, and with secure basement parking.

Eating

Brasserie Blanc FRENCH ££
(0113-220 6060; www.brasserieblanc.com; Victoria Mill, Sovereign St; mains £10-18; lunch & dinner Mon-Fri, noon-10.30pm Sat, noon-9pm Sun;) Raymond Blanc manages to create a surprisingly intimate and romantic space amid the cast-iron pillars and red brick of an old Victorian warehouse. The menu is unerringly French, from escargots (edible snails) to Toulouse sausage.

Hansa's Gujarati INDIAN £
(www.hansasrestaurant.com; 72-74 North St; mains £6-8; lunch Sun, dinner Mon-Sat;) A Leeds institution, Hansa's has been dishing up wholesome Gujarati vegetarian cuisine for 20 years. The restaurant is plain and unassuming (save for a Hindu shrine), but the food is exquisite.

Pickles & Potter CAFE £
(www.picklesandpotter.co.uk; 18-20 Queens Arcade; mains £4-5; 9am-5pm Mon-Fri, to 6pm Sat, 10.30am-5pm Sun) This rustic cafe is famous for its superb sandwiches, especially the sumptuous roast-beef version complete with mustard, onion marmalade and fresh salad.

Information

Gateway Yorkshire & Leeds Visitor Centre
(0113-242 5242; www.visitleeds.co.uk; The Arcade, Leeds City Train Station; 9am-5.30pm Mon-Sat, 10am-4pm Sun)

Getting There & Away

BUS National Express serves most major cities, including London (from £12, 4½ hours, hourly) and Manchester (from £5, 1¼ hours, every 30 minutes).

Yorkshire Coastliner (www.coastliner.co.uk) has useful services from Leeds to York, Pickering, Goathland and Whitby (840); to York and Scarborough (843); and to Bridlington (845 and X45). A Freedom Ticket (£15) gives unlimited bus travel on this service for a day.

TRAIN Leeds City Station has hourly services from London King's Cross (£50, 2½ hours),

WORTH A TRIP

NORFOLK BROADS

A watery mesh of navigable slow-moving rivers, freshwater lakes, wild meadows, fens, bogs and saltwater marshes make up the Norfolk and Suffolk Broads – the region's most beautiful natural attraction. Home to some of the UK's rarest plants and animals and protected as a national park, with flourishing nature reserves and bird sanctuaries, it's also very popular with boaters. Walkers and cyclists will also find a web of lanes and riverside paths, as well as the Broads' highest point, How Hill, all of a dizzying 12m above sea level.

Sheffield (£13, one hour), Manchester (£15, one hour) and York (£12, 30 minutes).

Leeds is also the starting point for services on the famous Settle-Carlisle railway line.

Around Leeds

HAREWOOD HOUSE

The great park, sumptuous gardens and mighty stately home of **Harewood House** (www.harewood.org; adult/child £14/7; ⏲grounds 10am-6pm, house noon-3pm Apr-Oct) could easily fill an entire day trip from Leeds, and also makes a good port of call on the way to Harrogate. The house and grounds were built between 1759 and 1772 by the era's superstar designers: John Carr designed the exterior, Lancelot 'Capability' Brown laid out the park, Thomas Chippendale supplied the furniture, Robert Adams designed the interior, and Italy was raided to create an appropriate art collection.

Harewood is about 7 miles north of Leeds. Take bus 36 (half-hourly Monday to Saturday, hourly on Sunday), which continues to Harrogate. Visitors coming by bus get half-price admission, so hang on to your ticket.

NATIONAL COAL MINING MUSEUM FOR ENGLAND

For three centuries, West and South Yorkshire were synonymous with coal production, until the industry came to a shuddering halt in the 1980s. This era is now remembered by the **National Coal Mining Museum for England** (www.ncm.org.uk; Overton, near Wakefield; ⏲10am-5pm, last tour 3.15pm). The highlight of a visit is the underground tour (departing every 10 minutes) – equipped with helmet and head-torch – of the coal seam where massive drilling machines now stand idle. Former miners work as guides, and explain details, sometimes with a suitably authentic and almost impenetrable mix of local dialect and technical terminology.

The museum is about 10 miles south of Leeds, near Junction 40 on the M1. By public transport, take a train from Leeds to Wakefield (15 minutes, at least hourly), and then bus 232 towards Huddersfield (25 minutes, hourly).

YORKSHIRE SCULPTURE PARK

One of England's most impressive collections of sculpture is scattered across the formidable 18th-century estate of **Bretton Park**, 200-odd hectares of lawns, fields and trees, a bit like the art world's equivalent of a safari park. The **Yorkshire Sculpture Park** (www.ysp.co.uk; Bretton Park, near Wakefield; admission free, parking £4; ⏲10am-6pm Apr-Oct, to 5pm Nov-Mar) showcases the work of dozens of sculptors both national and international, but the main focus is the work of Barbara Hepworth and Henry Moore. Other highlights include pieces by Andy Goldsworthy and Eduardo Paolozzi.

The park is 12 miles south of Leeds, just off Junction 38 on the M1. By public transport, take a train from Leeds to Wakefield (15 minutes, at least hourly), then bus 444 which runs between Wakefield and Barnsley via Bretton Park (30 minutes, hourly Monday to Saturday).

Haworth

POP 6100

In the canon of English literature, it seems that only Shakespeare himself is held in higher esteem than the beloved Brontë sisters, judging by the eight million visitors a year who come to this hardy northern town where the classics *Jane Eyre* and *Wuthering Heights* were born.

Sights

Brontë Parsonage Museum MUSEUM
(www.bronte.info; Church St; adult/child £7/3.60; ⏲10am-5.30pm Apr-Sep, 11am-5pm Oct-Mar) Set in a pretty garden overlooking the church and graveyard, the house where the Brontë family lived from 1820 till 1861 is now a museum. The rooms are meticulously furnished and decorated exactly as they were in the

Brontë era, including Charlotte's bedroom, her clothes and her writing paraphernalia. There's also an informative exhibition, which includes the fascinating miniature books the Brontës wrote as children.

Sleeping

Old Registry B&B ££
(☎01535-646503; www.theoldregistryhaworth.co.uk; 2-4 Main St; r £75-120; 📶) This place is a bit special. It's an elegantly rustic guesthouse where each of the carefully themed rooms has a four-poster bed, whirlpool bath or valley view. The Blue Heaven room is just that – at least for fans of Laura Ashley's delphinium blue.

Ye Sleeping House B&B ££
(☎01535-546992; www.yesleepinghouse.co.uk; 8 Main St; s/d from £29/58) There's a cosy, country cottage atmosphere at this welcoming B&B, with just three small rooms and two friendly resident cats. Try to get the one ensuite room, which can sleep a family of four and has great views over the valley.

Aitches B&B ££
(☎01535-642501; www.aitches.co.uk; 11 West Lane; s/d from £40/60) A classy, stone-built Victorian house with four ensuite rooms, each differently decorated with a pleasantly olde-worlde atmosphere. There's a residents' dining room where a three-course meal will cost £16 (prebooked, minimum four persons).

Haworth YHA HOSTEL £
(☎0845 371 9520; www.yha.org.uk; Longlands Dr; dm £19.40; P@) A big old house with a games room, lounge, cycle store and laundry. It's on the northeastern edge of town, off Lees Lane.

Eating

Weaver's BRITISH ££
(☎01535-643822; www.weaversmallhotel.co.uk; 15 West Lane; mains £15-20; ⊙lunch Wed-Fri, dinner Tue-Sat) A stylish and atmospheric restaurant, Weaver's offers a menu featuring local produce (such as slow-cooked shoulder of Pennine lamb with fennel seed and coriander stuffing), or simple lunches like an Ellison's pork pie with mushy peas and mint sauce (two-course lunch £16).

Information

Tourist Office (☎01535-642329; www.haworth-village.org.uk; 2-4 West Lane; ⊙9am-5.30pm Apr-Sep, to 5pm Oct-Mar)

STEAM ENGINES & RAILWAY CHILDREN

Haworth is on the **Keighley & Worth Valley Railway** (www.kwvr.co.uk; adult/child return £10/5, Day Rover £15/7.50), where steam and classic diesel engines chug between Keighley and Oxenhope. It was here, in 1969, that the classic movie *The Railway Children* was shot; Mr Perks was stationmaster at Oakworth, where the Edwardian look has been meticulously maintained. Trains operate about hourly at weekends all year; daily in holiday periods.

Getting There & Away

From Leeds, the easiest approach is via Keighley, which is on the Metro rail network. Bus 500 runs from Keighley bus station to Haworth (15 minutes, hourly). However, the most interesting way to get from Keighley to Haworth is via the Keighley & Worth Valley Railway.

Skipton

POP 14,300

This busy town has long been dubbed the gateway to the Yorkshire Dales. There's been a market here for centuries; Monday, Wednesday, Friday and Saturday are market days, bringing crowds to the High St and giving the town something of a festive atmosphere.

A pleasant stroll from the tourist office along the canal path leads to **Skipton Castle** (www.skiptoncastle.co.uk; High St; adult/child £6.70/4.10; ⊙10am-6pm Mon-Sat, from noon Sun Mar-Sep, to 4pm Oct-Feb), one of the best-preserved medieval castles in England – a fascinating contrast to the ruins you'll see elsewhere.

The town has a good selection of B&Bs, cafes and pubs, and is easy to reach by Metro rail from Leeds (£8.40, 45 minutes, half-hourly, hourly on Sunday).

Yorkshire Dales National Park

From well-known names such as Wensleydale and Ribblesdale, to obscure Langstrothdale and Arkengarthdale, the Yorkshire Dales is one of the most beautiful parts of northern England. It's been protected as a national park since the 1950s, assuring its status as a walker's and cyclist's paradise.

For more details, see www.yorkshiredales.org.uk.

MALHAM

The pretty village of Malham is the jumping-off point for two of the national park's most spectacular features: **Malham Cove**, a huge rock amphitheatre lined with 80m-high vertical cliffs, and **Gordale Scar**, a deep limestone canyon with scenic cascades and the remains of an Iron Age settlement.

Sleeping

Beck Hall HOTEL ££
(01729-830332; www.beckhallmalham.com; s/d from £45/65; P) This rambling 17th-century country house on the edge of the village has 15 individually decorated rooms – we recommend the Green Room, with its old-style furnishings and four-poster bed.

Malham YHA HOSTEL £
(0845 371 9529; www.yha.org.uk; dm £19.50; P) In the village centre you will find this purpose-built hostel; the facilities are top-notch and young children are well catered for.

HORTON-IN-RIBBLESDALE

At the heart of the park, the little village of Horton is a firm favourite with outdoor enthusiasts. Despite its remote location, access is easy thanks to the Settle–Carlisle train line. Everything centres on the excellent **Pen-y-ghent Cafe** (mains £3-6; 9am-5.30pm Mon & Wed-Fri, 8.30am-5pm Sat & Sun), which acts as the village tourist office as well as filling walkers' fuel tanks with hearty grub and pint mugs of tea. It also sells maps, guidebooks and walking gear.

The best place for accommodation is the **Golden Lion** (01729-860206; www.goldenlionhotel.co.uk; dm £12, s/d from £40/65), a lively pub that offers comfortable B&B bedrooms, a 40-bed bunkhouse, and three public bars for grub and ale.

YORKSHIRE'S THREE PEAKS

Since 1968 more than 200,000 hikers have taken up the challenge of climbing Yorkshire's three highest peaks (Pen-y-Ghent, Whernside and Ingleborough) in less than 12 hours. The circular 25-mile route begins and ends at the Pen-y-ghent Cafe in Horton-in-Ribblesdale – where you clock-in and clock-out to verify your time. Succeed, and you're a member of the cafe's Three Peaks of Yorkshire Club.

During the annual **Three Peaks Race** (www.threepeaksrace.org.uk) on the last Saturday in April, competitors run the route instead of walking it. First held in 1954, it now attracts around 900 entries; the course record is a frankly astonishing 2 hours, 43 minutes and 3 seconds.

York

POP 181,100

Nowhere in northern England says 'medieval' quite like York, a city of extraordinary historical wealth that has lost little of its preindustrial lustre. Its spider's web of narrow streets is enclosed by a magnificent circuit of 13th-century walls and the city's rich heritage is woven into virtually every brick and beam. Modern, tourist-oriented York – with its myriad museums, restaurants, cafes and traditional pubs – is a carefully maintained heir to that heritage.

Sights

TOP CHOICE **York Minster** CHURCH
(www.yorkminster.org; Deangate; adult/child £9/free, combined ticket incl tower £14/3.50; 9am-5.30pm Mon-Sat Apr-Oct, 9.30am-5.30pm Mon-Sat Nov-Mar, noon-5.30pm Sun year-round) Not content with being Yorkshire's most important historic building, the awe-inspiring York Minster is also the largest medieval cathedral in all of northern Europe. Seat of the archbishop of York, primate of England, it is second in importance only to Canterbury, home of the primate of *all* England – the separate titles were created to settle a debate over whether York or Canterbury was the true centre of the English church.

The first church on this spot was a wooden chapel built for the baptism of King Edwin of Northumbria on Easter Day 627; its location is marked in the crypt. It was replaced with a stone church that was built on the site of a Roman basilica, parts of which can be seen in the foundations. The first Norman minster was built in the 11th century; again, you can see surviving fragments in the foundations and crypt.

Jorvik Viking Centre MUSEUM

(www.jorvik-viking-centre.co.uk; Coppergate; adult/child £9.25/6.25; ⏲10am-5pm Apr-Oct, to 4pm Nov-Mar) This is a smells-and-all reconstruction of the Viking settlement that was unearthed here during excavations in the late 1970s, brought to you courtesy of a 'time-car' monorail that transports you through 9th-century Jorvik (the Viking name for York). In the exhibition at the end of the monorail, look out for the **Lloyds Bank Turd** – a fossilised human stool that measures an eye-watering nine inches long and half a pound in weight, and must be the only jobbie in the world to have its own Wikipedia entry.

You can cut time spent waiting in the queue by booking your tickets online and choosing the time you want to visit – it costs £1 extra.

FREE **City Walls** ARCHAEOLOGICAL SITE

(⏲8am-dusk) If the weather's good, don't miss the chance to walk the city walls, which follow the line of the original Roman walls – it gives a whole new perspective on the city. The full circuit is 4.5 miles (allow 1½ to two hours); if you're pushed for time, the short stretch from Bootham Bar to Monk Bar is worth doing for the views of the minster.

At Monk Bar you'll find the **Richard III Museum** (www.richardiiimuseum.co.uk; adult/child £2.50/free; ⏲9am-5pm Mar-Oct, 9.30am-4pm Nov-Feb), which sets out the case of the murdered 'Princes in the Tower' and invites visitors to judge whether their uncle, Richard III, killed them. **Micklegate Bar Museum** (www.micklegatebar.com; Micklegate; adult/child £3.50/free; ⏲10am-4.30pm May-Sep, 11am-3.30pm Feb-Apr, Oct & Nov) charts the history of the city walls and the Battle of Towton, chief conflict in the Wars of the Roses.

FREE **National Railway Museum** MUSEUM

(www.nrm.org.uk; Leeman Rd; ⏲10am-6pm) York's National Railway Museum – the biggest in the world, with more than 100 locomotives – is so well presented and full of fascinating stuff that it's interesting even to folk whose eyes don't mist over at the thought of a 4-6-2 A1 Pacific class chuffing into a tunnel. Highlights for the trainspotters among us include a replica of George Stephenson's *Rocket* (1829), the world's first 'modern' steam locomotive; the sleek and streamlined *Mallard,* which set the world speed record for a steam locomotive in 1938 (126mph); a 1960s Japanese *shinkansen* bullet train; and the world-famous *Flying Scotsman,* the first steam engine to break the 100mph barrier (currently being restored to its former glory, and scheduled to return to the tracks in 2013).

Yorkshire Museum MUSEUM

(www.yorkshiremuseum.org.uk; Museum St; adult/child £7.50/free; ⏲10am-5pm) Most of York's Roman archaeology is hidden beneath the medieval city, so the recently revamped displays in the Yorkshire Museum are invaluable if you want to get an idea of what Eboracum was like. There are maps and models of Roman York, funerary monuments, mosaic floors, wall paintings, and a 4th-century bust of Emperor Constantine. There are excellent exhibits on Viking and medieval York too, including priceless artefacts such as the beautifully decorated 9th-century **York helmet**, and the exquisite 15th-century **Middleham Jewel**, an engraved gold pendant adorned with a giant sapphire. Kids will enjoy the **dinosaur exhibit**, centred around ichthyosaur fossils from Yorkshire's Jurassic coast.

In the grounds of the peaceful **Museum Gardens** (entrances on Museum St & Marygate; ⏲dawn-dusk) you can see the **Multangular Tower**, a part of the city walls that was once the western tower of the Roman garrison's defensive ramparts.

On the other side of the gardens are the ruins of **St Mary's Abbey** (founded 1089), dating from 1270–94. The ruined **Gatehall** was its main entrance, providing access from the abbey to the river. The adjacent **Hospitium** dates from the 14th century, although the timber-framed upper storey is a much-restored survivor from the 15th century; it was used as the abbey guesthouse. **St Mary's Lodge** was built around 1470 to provide VIP accommodation.

Shambles STREET

(www.yorkshambles.com) The narrow, cobbled lane known as the Shambles, lined with 15th-century Tudor buildings that overhang so much they seem to meet above your head, is the most visited street in Europe. It takes its name from the Saxon word *shamel,* meaning 'slaughterhouse' – in 1862 there were 26 butcher shops on this one street.

Clifford's Tower CASTLE

(EH; www.english-heritage.org.uk; Tower St; adult/child £4/2.40; ⏲10am-6pm Apr-Sep, to 5pm Oct) There's precious little left of York Castle except for this evocative stone tower, a highly unusual figure-of-eight design built into the castle's keep after the original one was

York

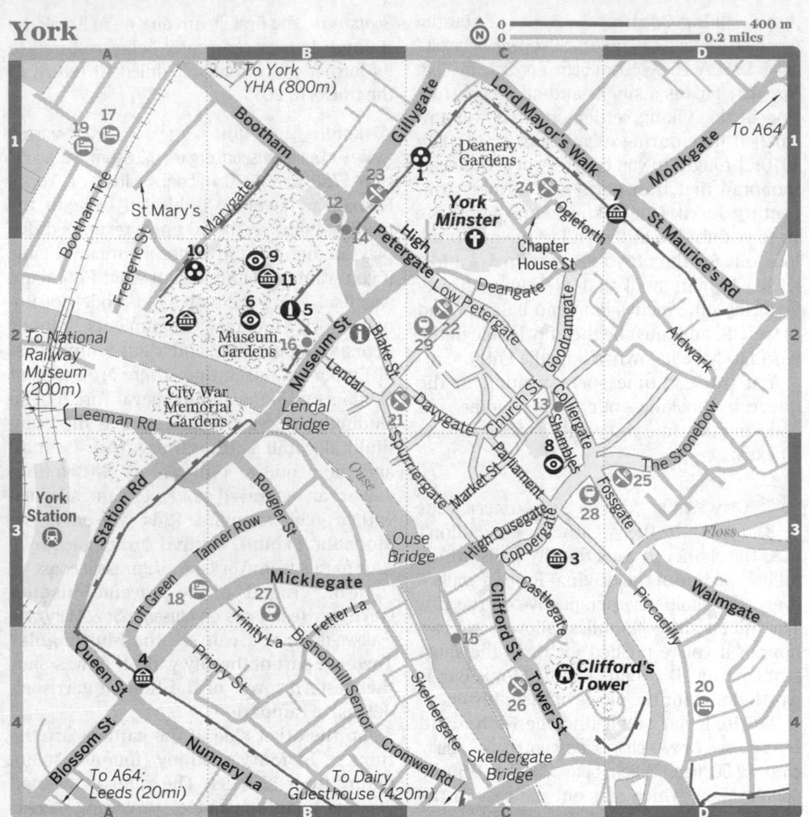

destroyed in 1190 during anti-Jewish riots. There's not much to see inside but the views over the city are excellent.

Tours

Ghost Hunt of York WALKING TOUR
(www.ghosthunt.co.uk; adult/child £5/3; tours 7.30pm) Award-winning and highly entertaining 75-minute tour laced with authentic ghost stories; the kids will just love this one. Begins at the Shambles, whatever the weather (they never cancel). No need to book.

Yorkwalk WALKING TOUR
(www.yorkwalk.co.uk; adult/child £5.50/3.50; tours 10.30am & 2.15pm Feb-Nov) Offers a series of two-hour themed walks on an ever-growing list of themes, from the classics – Roman York, the snickelways (alleys) and city walls – to specialised walks on chocolates and sweets, women in York, secret York and the inevitable graveyard, coffin and plague tour. Walks depart from Museum Gardens Gate on Museum St; no need to book.

YorkBoat BOAT TOUR
(www.yorkboat.co.uk; King's Staith; adult/child £7.50/3.50; tours 10.30am, noon, 1.30pm & 3pm) Runs one-hour cruises on the Ouse River departing from King's Staith (and Lendal Bridge 10 minutes later). Also special lunch, dinner and evening cruises.

York Citysightseeing BUS TOUR
(www.city-sightseeing.com; day ticket adult/child £10/4; 9am-5pm) Hop-on/hop-off route with 16 stops, calling at all the main sights. Buses leave every 10 minutes from Exhibition Sq near York Minster.

FREE **Association of Voluntary Guides** WALKING TOUR
(http://avgyork.co.uk; tours 10.15am & 2.15pm Apr-Oct, also 6.45pm Jun-Aug, 10.15am Nov-Mar) Two-

York

Top Sights

	Clifford's Tower	C4
	York Minster	C1

Sights

1	City Walls	C1
2	Gatehall	A2
	Hospitium	(see 2)
3	Jorvik Viking Centre	C3
4	Micklegate Bar Museum	A4
5	Multangular Tower	B2
6	Museum Gardens	B2
7	Richard III Museum	D1
8	Shambles	C3
9	St Mary's Abbey	B2
10	St Mary's Lodge	A2
11	Yorkshire Museum	B2

Activities, Courses & Tours

12	Association of Voluntary Guides	B1
13	Ghost Hunt of York	C2
14	York Citysightseeing	B1
15	YorkBoat	C4
16	Yorkwalk	B2

Sleeping

17	Abbeyfields	A1
18	Ace Hotel	A3
19	Elliotts B&B	A1
20	Hotel 53	D4

Eating

21	Bettys	B2
22	Betty's Stonegate	C2
23	Cafe No 8	B1
24	Grays Court	C1
25	J Baker's Bistro Moderne	D3
26	Olive Tree	C4

Drinking

27	Ackhorne	B3
28	Blue Bell	C3
29	Ye Olde Starre	C2

hour walking tours of the city starting from Exhibition Sq in front of York City Art Gallery.

Sleeping

Beds are tough to find in midsummer, even with the inflated prices of the high season. The tourist office's accommodation booking service charges £4.

Abbeyfields B&B ££
(☎01904-636471; www.abbeyfields.co.uk; 19 Bootham Tce; s/d from £49/79; wi-fi) Expect a warm welcome and thoughtfully arranged bedrooms here, with chairs and bedside lamps for comfortable reading.

Elliotts B&B B&B ££
(☎01904-623333; www.elliottshotel.co.uk; 2 Sycamore Pl; s/d from £55/80; P @ wi-fi) A beautifully converted 'gentleman's residence', Elliotts leans towards the boutique end of the guesthouse market with stylish and elegant rooms, and high-tech touches such as flatscreen TVs and free wi-fi. Excellent location, both quiet and central.

Dairy Guesthouse B&B ££
(☎01904-639367; www.dairyguesthouse.co.uk; 3 Scarcroft Rd; s/d from £55/75; wi-fi) A lovely Victorian home that has retained many of its original features, including pine doors, stained glass and cast-iron fireplaces. Minimum two-night stay at weekends.

Hotel 53 HOTEL ££
(☎01904-559000; www.hotel53.com; 53 Piccadilly; r from £95; P wi-fi) Modern and minimalist, but very central with secure parking just across the street.

York YHA HOSTEL £
(☎0845 371 9051; www.yha.org.uk; 42 Water End, Clifton; dm £18-23; P @ wi-fi) Originally the Rowntree (Quaker confectioners) mansion, this handsome Victorian house makes a spacious and child-friendly youth hostel, with most of the rooms being four-bed dorms. It's about a mile northwest of the city centre; take bus 2 from Station Ave or Museum St.

Ace Hotel HOSTEL £
(☎01904-627720; www.acehotelyork.co.uk; 88-90 Micklegate; dm £18-30, tw £68; @ wi-fi) Housed in a Grade I Georgian building that was once home to the High Sheriff of Yorkshire, this is a large and well-equipped hostel that is popular with school groups and stag and hen parties – don't come here looking for peace and quiet!

YORK PASS

If you plan on visiting a lot of sights, you can save yourself some money by using a **York Pass** (www.yorkpass.com; 1/2/3 days adult £34/48/58, child £18/22/26). It grants you free access to more than 70 pay-to-visit sights in Yorkshire, including all the major attractions in York. Available at York tourist office, or you can buy online.

Eating

TOP CHOICE J Baker's Bistro Moderne MODERN BRITISH ££
(01904-622688; www.jbakers.co.uk; 7 Fossgate; 2-/3-course lunch £20/25, dinner £25/30; lunch & dinner Tue-Sat) Superstar chef Jeff Baker left a Michelin star in Leeds to pursue his own vision of Modern British cuisine here. The ironic '70s-style decor matches his gourmet interpretations of retro classics – try Olde York cheese and spinach pasties with dried grapes, capers and aged balsamic vinegar, or a Whitby crab cocktail with apple 'textures' and curry-spiced granola.

Cafe No 8 BISTRO £
(01904-653074; www.cafeno8.co.uk; 8 Gillygate; mains £7-10, 2-course lunch £14; 11am-10pm Mon-Fri, 10am-10pm Sat & Sun;) A cool little bistro with modern artwork mimicking the Edwardian stained glass at the front, No 8 offers a day-long menu of classic bistro dishes using fresh local produce, including smoked duck breast salad, and cassoulet of Yorkshire pork and chorizo. Booking recommended.

Grays Court CAFE £
(www.grayscourtyork.com; Chapter House St; mains £6-10; lunch) An unexpected find right in the very heart of York, this 16th-century house has more of a country atmosphere. Enjoy gourmet coffee and cake in the sunny garden, or indulge in a light lunch in the historic setting of the oak-panelled Jacobean gallery.

Bettys CAFE ££
(www.bettys.co.uk; St Helen's Sq; mains £6-13, afternoon tea £18; 9am-9pm;) Afternoon tea, old-school style, with white-aproned waitresses, linen tablecloths and a teapot collection ranged along the walls. Betty's younger sister, **Bettys Stonegate** (www.bettys.co.uk; 46 Stonegate; mains £6-13; 10am-5.30pm Sun-Fri, 9am-5.30pm Sat;), is more demure and less crowded, and just as good.

Olive Tree MEDITERRANEAN ££
(01904-624433; www.theolivetreeyork.co.uk; 10 Tower St; mains £10-17; lunch & dinner) Local produce gets a Mediterranean makeover at this bright and breezy bistro with a view across the street to Clifford's Tower. The lunchtime and early evening menu offers two courses for £13.

Drinking

With only a couple of exceptions, the best drinking holes in town are the older, traditional pubs.

TOP CHOICE Blue Bell PUB
(53 Fossgate) This is what a real English pub looks like – a tiny, wood-panelled room with a smouldering fireplace, decor (and beer and smoke stains) dating from c 1798, a pile of ancient board games in the corner, friendly and efficient bar staff, and Timothy Taylor and Black Sheep ales on tap.

Ye Olde Starre PUB
(40 Stonegate) Licensed since 1644, this is York's oldest pub – a warren of small rooms and a small beer garden, with a half-dozen real ales on tap.

Ackhorne PUB
(9 St Martin's Lane) Tucked away off beery, sloppy Micklegate, this locals' inn is as comfortable as old slippers – some of the guys here look like they've merged with the furniture.

Information

York Visitor Centre (01904-550099; www.visityork.org; 1 Museum St; 9am-6pm Mon-Sat, 10am-5pm Sun Apr-Sep, shorter hours Oct-Mar)

Getting There & Away

BUS For timetable information call **Traveline Yorkshire** (0871 200 2233; www.yorkshiretravel.net), or check the computerised 24-hour information points at the train station and Rougier St. All local and regional buses stop on Rougier St, about 200m northeast of the train station.

There are **National Express** (08717 81 81 78; www.nationalexpress.com) coaches to London (£28, 5½ hours, four daily), Birmingham (£28, 3¼ hours, one daily) and Newcastle (£15, 2¾ hours, four daily).

TRAIN York is a major railway hub with frequent direct services to Birmingham (£45, 2¼ hours), Newcastle (£15, one hour), Leeds

(£11, 30 minutes), London's King's Cross (£80, two hours), Manchester (£15, 1½ hours) and Scarborough (£10, 50 minutes). There are also trains to Cambridge (£60, 2¾ hours), changing at Peterborough.

Around York

CASTLE HOWARD

Stately homes may be two a penny in England, but you'll have to try hard to find one as breathtakingly stately as **Castle Howard** (www.castlehoward.co.uk; adult/child house & grounds £13/7.50, grounds only £8.50/6; ⏲house 11am-4.30pm Apr-Oct, grounds 10am-5.30pm Mar-Oct & 1st 3 weeks Dec, 10am-4pm Nov-Feb), a work of theatrical grandeur and audacity, and one of the world's most beautiful buildings. It's instantly recognisable from its starring role in the 1980s TV series *Brideshead Revisited* and more recently in the 2008 film of the same name.

Inside, the great house is full of treasures – the breathtaking **Great Hall** with its soaring Corinthian pilasters, Pre-Raphaelite **stained glass** in the chapel, and corridors lined with classical antiquities. Outside, as you wander the grounds (populated by peacocks, naturally), views reveal Vanbrugh's playful **Temple of the Four Winds** and Hawksmoor's stately **mausoleum**, or wider vistas over the surrounding hills.

Castle Howard is 15 miles northeast of York. There are several organised tours from York – check with the tourist office. By public transport, Yorkshire Coastliner bus 840 (40 minutes from York, one daily) links Leeds, York, Castle Howard and Whitby.

RIEVAULX ABBEY

In a secluded valley, amid fields and woods loud with birdsong, stand the magnificent ruins of **Rievaulx Abbey** (www.english-heritage.org.uk; adult/child £5.80/3.50; ⏲10am-6pm Apr-Sep, reduced hours at other times). This idyllic spot was chosen by Cistercian monks in 1132 as a base for missionary activity in northern Britain. St Aelred, the third abbot, famously described the abbey's setting as 'everywhere peace, everywhere serenity, and a marvellous freedom from the tumult of the world'. But the monks of Rievaulx (ree-voe) were far from unworldly, and soon created a network of commercial interests ranging from sheep farms to lead mines. And with the money, they built this amazing structure.

> **THE SETTLE–CARLISLE RAILWAY**
>
> The 72-mile **Settle–Carlisle Railway** (www.settle-carlisle.co.uk), built between 1869 and 1875, was one of the greatest engineering projects of the Victorian era and today offers one of England's most scenic railway journeys, travelling over a breathtaking assortment of hills, valleys, tunnels, embankments and viaducts, including the famous 400m-long Ribblehead Viaduct.
>
> The entire journey from Leeds to Carlisle takes just under three hours. Various hop-on-hop-off passes for one or three days are also available. For more information, see www.settle-carlisle.co.uk.

Near the abbey is an attraction from a different era: **Rievaulx Terrace & Temples** (www.nationaltrust.org.uk; adult/child £5.50/3.10; ⏲11am-5pm Mar-Oct), a magnificent 18th-century landscaped park established by the aristocratic Duncombe family.

Rievaulx is about 3 miles west of Helmsley. Note that there's no direct access between the abbey and the terrace – their entrance gates are about a mile apart, though easily reached along a lane, steeply uphill if you're going from the abbey to the terrace.

Durham

POP 42,940

The grand city of Durham is crowned by a magnificent castle and Britain's finest Norman cathedral, together a Unesco World Heritage site. Surrounding them both is a maze of cobbled streets usually full of upper-crust students attending Durham's prestigious university.

Sights

Durham Cathedral CHURCH

(www.durhamcathedral.co.uk; donation requested, guided tours adult/child £4/free; ⏲7.30am-6pm, tours 10.30am, 11am & 2pm Mon-Sat, Evensong 5.15pm Mon-Sat, 3.30pm Sun) This exquisite cathedral is the definitive structure of the Anglo-Norman Romanesque style, one of the world's greatest places of worship and, since 1986, a Unesco World Heritage site. This is the first European cathedral to use stone-ribbed vaulting, which holds up the heavy stone roof and made it possible to build pointed transverse arches – the first in England, and a great architectural achievement. The central tower dates from 1262, but was damaged in a fire caused by lightning in 1429, and was unsatisfactorily patched up until it was entirely rebuilt in 1470. The western towers were added in 1217–26.

One of the cathedral's most beautiful parts is the **Galilee Chapel**, which dates from 1175 and whose northern side features rare examples of 12th-century wall painting (thought to feature portraits of Sts Cuthbert and Oswald). The chapel also contains the **tomb of the Venerable Bede**, the 8th-century Northumbrian monk turned historian: his *Ecclesiastical History of the English People* is still the prime source of information on the development of early Christian Britain.

The **tower** (£5) provides show-stopping vistas, but you have to climb 325 steps to enjoy them.

Durham Castle CASTLE
(www.dur.ac.uk; admission by guided tour only, adult/child £5/3.50; ⌚tours 2pm, 3pm & 4pm term time, 10am, 11am & noon during university vacations) Built as a standard motte-and-bailey fort in 1072, Durham Castle was the prince bishops' home until 1837, when it became the first college of the new university. It remains a university hall, and you can stay here. The castle has been much altered over the centuries, as each successive prince bishop sought to put his particular imprint on the place, but heavy restoration and reconstruction were necessary anyway as the castle is built of soft stone on soft ground. Highlights of the 45-minute tour include the groaning 17th-century **Black Staircase**, the 16th-century **chapel** and the beautifully preserved **Norman chapel** (1080).

Sleeping

TOP CHOICE **Gadds Townhouse** BOUTIQUE HOTEL ££
(☎0191-384 1037; www.gaddstownhouse.com; 34 Old Elvet; d from £99) Each room has a theme with the 'Le Jardin' featuring a shed and garden furniture, the 'Premiere' boasting a huge projection screen and popcorn machine, while the 'Edwardian Express' recreates a night in a yesteryear sleeper compartment.

Farnley Tower B&B ££
(☎0191-375 0011; www.farnley-tower.co.uk; The Ave; s/d from £65/75; P) A beautiful Victorian stone building that looks more like a small manor house than a family-run B&B, this place has 13 large rooms, none better than the superior class. It's situated around 1km southwest of the train station.

Eating

Oldfields BRITISH ££
(www.oldfieldsrealfood.co.uk; 18 Claypath; mains £12-19) With its strictly seasonal menus that use only local or organic ingredients sourced within a 60-mile radius of Durham, this award-winning restaurant is one of the county's finest, though it's not quite as good as its Newcastle sister.

Cottons CAFE £
(32 Silver St; snacks £2.50-5; ⌚9.30am-5.30pm Mon-Sat, 11am-4.30pm Sun) Down an inconspicuous flight of steps two doors along from the post office, this junk shop/art gallery/tearoom hides in a brick-and-stone cellar where a range of teas plus sandwiches, jacket potatoes and cakes are served.

Getting There & Away

BUS **Leeds** (£18.20, 2½ hours, four daily) National Express.
London (£36.90, 6½ hours, four daily) National Express.
Newcastle (one hour to 1¾ hours, several per hour) Buses 21, 44, X41, X2.

TRAIN **Edinburgh** (£54.50, two hours, hourly)
London King's Cross (£150.50, three hours, hourly)
Newcastle (£4.70, 15 minutes, five hourly)
York (£25, one hour, four hourly)

Newcastle-upon-Tyne

POP 189,863

Once synonymous with postindustrial decline, today's Newcastle is reborn and brimming with confidence. All of a sudden, this unfailingly friendly city, with its Geordie accent thicker than molasses, has kick-started a brand-new arts and entertainment scene, while riotous nightlife remains an established tradition.

Sights

CITY CENTRE

FREE **Great North Museum** MUSEUM
(www.greatnorthmuseum.org; Barras Bridge; ⌚10am-5pm Mon-Sat, 1-5pm Sun) This outstanding museum has been created by bringing to-

gether the contents of Newcastle University's museums and adding them to the natural history exhibits of the prestigious Hancock Museum, in the latter's renovated neoclassical building. The result is a fascinating jumble of dinosaurs, Roman altar stones, Egyptian mummies, samurai warriors and some impressive taxidermy, all presented in an engaging and easily digestible way.

Life Science Centre MUSEUM
(www.life.org.uk; Times Sq; adult/child £9.95/6.95; ⏲10am-6pm Mon-Sat, 11am-6pm Sun) This excellent science village, part of the sober-minded complex of institutes devoted to the study of genetic science, is one of the more interesting attractions in town. Through a series of hands-on exhibits and the latest technology you (or your kids) can discover the incredible secrets of life. The highlight is the Motion Ride, a motion simulator that lets you 'feel' what it's like to experience things like bungee jumping and other extreme sports (the 3D film changes every year).

FREE **Discovery Museum** MUSEUM
(www.twmuseums.org.uk; Blandford Sq; ⏲10am-5pm Mon-Sat, 2-5pm Sun) Tyneside's rich history is uncovered through a fascinating series of exhibits at this unmissable museum. The exhibitions, spread across three floors of the former Co-operative Wholesale Society building, surround the mightily impressive 30m-long *Turbinia,* the fastest ship in the world in 1897. There's an absorbing section dedicated to shipbuilding on the Tyne including a scale model of the river in 1929; a buzzers-and-bells science maze for the kids; and a 'Story of Newcastle' section, giving the lowdown on the city's history from Pons Aelius (Newcastle's Roman name) to Cheryl Cole.

GATESHEAD

As you cross the Tyne to its southern side you've technically left Newcastle and entered the town of Gateshead.

FREE **BALTIC – Centre for Contemporary Art** MUSEUM
(www.balticmill.com; Gateshead Quays; ⏲10am-6pm Wed-Mon, from 10.30am Tue) Once a huge, dirty, yellow grain store overlooking the Tyne, BALTIC is now a huge, dirty, yellow art gallery to rival London's Tate Modern. Unlike the Tate, there are no permanent exhibitions here, but the constantly rotating shows feature the work and installations of some of contemporary art's biggest show-stoppers. The complex has artists in residence, a performance space, a cinema, a bar, a spectacular rooftop restaurant (you'll need to book) and a ground-floor restaurant with riverside tables. There's also a viewing box for a fine Tyne vista.

BRIDGING THE TYNE

The classic view of Newcastle is along the River Tyne to the city's iconic cluster of bridges. Most famous is the **Tyne Bridge**; its resemblance to Australia's Sydney Harbour Bridge is no coincidence as both were built by the same company, at around the same time. The quaint little **Swing Bridge** pivots in the middle to let ships through. The **High Level Bridge**, designed by Robert Stephenson, was the world's first combined road and railway bridge (1849). The most recent addition is the multiple-award-winning **Millennium Bridge** (2002), which lifts like an eyelid to let ships pass.

Sleeping

The majority of city-centre options cater to party people and business folk. Most other accommodation is in the handsome northern suburb of Jesmond.

CITY CENTRE

TOP CHOICE **Hotel Indigo** HOTEL ££
(☎0191-300 9222; www.hotelindigonewcastle.co.uk; 2-8 Fenkle St; r from £99) This brand-new edition of the excellent boutique chain offers clean lines and pristine rooms equipped with all mod cons, including rainfall showers and iPod docks. Downstairs is the chain's partner restaurant, Marco Pierre White Steakhouse & Grill.

Greystreethotel HOTEL ££
(☎0191-230 6777; www.greystreethotel.com; 2-12 Grey St; r from £99; P) A bit of designer class along the classiest street in the city centre has been long overdue: the rooms are gorgeous if a touch poky, all cluttered up with flatscreen TVs, big beds and handsome modern furnishings.

Backpackers Newcastle HOSTEL £
(☎0191-340 7334; www.backpackersnewcastle.com; 262 Westgate Rd; dm from £17.95; wi-fi) This clean, well-run budget flophouse has just 26 beds, lending it a bit more of a backpacker

vibe than its competitors in the city. Bike storage, a kitchen, a big games room, power-showers and a mildly designer feel make this a great option on the Tyne.

JESMOND

Newcastle YHA HOSTEL £
(☎0845 371 9335; www.yha.org.uk; 107 Jesmond Rd; dm from £18.50) This nice, rambling place has small dorms that are generally full, so book in advance. It's close to the Jesmond Metro stop.

Eating

TOP CHOICE **Blackfriars** BRITISH ££
(☎0191-261 5945; www.blackfriarsrestaurant.co.uk; Friars St; mains £12-21; ⏲lunch & dinner Mon-Sat, lunch Sun) The city centre's top eatery is housed in a 12th-century friary, where chef Troy Terrington serves up a cuisine described as 'modern medieval' (check the tablemat map for the provenance of your bream, woodpigeon or roast suckling pygge). Bookings are recommended.

TOP CHOICE **The Broad Chare** PUB ££
(☎0191-211 2144; www.thebroadchare.co.uk; 25 Broad Chare; mains £11; ⏲lunch & dinner Mon-Sat, lunch Sun) Classic English pub grub – the grilled pork chop with black pudding and cider sauce is divine – and superb cask ales make this gastropub one of the best spots in town for a bite to eat. The Michelin people agreed, and stuck it into their Good Pub Guide. Recommended.

Scrumpy Willow & the Singing Kettle ORGANIC ££
(☎0191-221 2323; www.scrumpywillowandthesingingkettle.co.uk; 89 Clayton St; mains £5-11; ⏲Mon-Sat, lunch Sun; ✎) Voted one of the UK's top organic eateries by *Guardian* readers, this incredibly popular place bursts at the seams at mealtimes, and one mouthful is enough to understand why.

Drinking

It's no secret that Geordies like a good night out, epitomised by the cheap and colourful cocktails of the Bigg Market. The Ouseburn area attracts a mellower crowd; the western end of Neville St has a decent mix of great bars and is home to the best of the gay scene.

Centurion Bar BAR
(Central Station) Voted Newcastle's best bar in 2008, the former first-class waiting room at Central Station is ideal for a pre-club drink in style or a pre-train brew on the hop.

Blackie Boy PUB
(11 Groat Market) Locals grumble that this darkened boozer, one of the city's original taverns, has become too upmarket but it's still a popular place to drink even if the decor has gone all weird. Visitors from the US may have trouble deciphering the novel toilet door signage.

Cumberland Arms PUB
(off Byker Bank, Ouseburn) Sitting on a hill at the top of the Ouseburn, this 19th-century bar has a sensational selection of ales and ciders as well as a range of Northumberland meads. There's a terrace outside, where you can read a book from the Bring One, Borrow One library inside.

Information

Tourist Office (www.visitnewcastlegateshead.com) Main branch (☎0191-277 8000; www.visitnewcastlegateshead.com; Central Arcade, Market St; ⏲9.30am-5.30pm Mon-Sat, 10am-4pm Sun) Guildhall (☎0191-277 8000; www.visitnewcastlegateshead.com; Guildhall; ⏲10am-5pm Mon-Fri, 9am-5pm Sat, 9am-4pm Sun) Sage Gateshead (☎0191-478 4222; www.visitnewcastlegateshead.com; Sage Gateshead; ⏲10am-5pm)

Getting There & Away

BUS Local and regional buses leave from Haymarket or Eldon Sq bus stations. National Express buses arrive and depart from the coach station on St James Blvd.

Edinburgh (£17.50, three hours, two daily) National Express.

London (£12 to £35, seven hours, nine daily) National Express/Megabus.

Manchester (£21, five hours, five daily) National Express.

TRAIN Newcastle is on the main rail line between London and Edinburgh and is the starting point of the scenic Tyne Valley Line west to Carlisle.

Berwick (£23.50, 45 minutes, hourly)

Carlisle (£14.40, 1½ hours, hourly)

London King's Cross (£116.20, three hours, half-hourly)

York (£33.50, one hour, every 20 minutes)

Hadrian's Wall

Built in AD 122 to mark the edge of the Roman Empire, this 73-mile coast-to-coast barrier across England remains a major feature on the landscape nearly 2000 years later. Named in honour of the emperor who

ANGEL OF THE NORTH

This extraordinary, gigantic statue of a human frame with wings looms over the main A1 highway about 5 miles south of Newcastle. At 20m high, 200 tonnes in weight and with a wingspan wider than a Boeing 767, it's Antony Gormley's best-known sculpture and – thanks to all those passing cars – the most viewed piece of public art in the country.

You can walk right up to the base of the statue, and feel absolutely dwarfed. Buses 21 and 22 from Eldon Sq will take you there.

ordered it built, Hadrian's Wall is one of the Roman Empire's greatest engineering projects, a spectacular testament to ambition and the practical Roman mind. It was built to to protect Roman-occupied Britain from the unruly Pictish tribes to the north, in the area we know now as Scotland. When completed, the mammoth structure ran from the Solway Firth (west of Carlisle) to the mouth of the Tyne (east of Newcastle).

Although some parts of the wall have virtually disappeared, other stretches are remarkably well preserved and utterly spectacular. Several of the original forts which once guarded the wall are still in fairly good repair, including the ones at **Chesters** (EH; 01434-681379; Chollerford; adult/child £4.80/2.40; 10am-6pm Apr-Sep) near Chollerford, Vindolanda near Bardon Mill and Houseteads, between Bardon Mill and Haltwhistle.

Most local tourist offices have reams of information on the wall and the **Hadrian's Wall Path** (www.nationaltrail.co.uk/hadrianswall) which runs along almost the entire length of the wall. For general information, see the informative website at www.hadrians-wall.org.

Getting There & Away

Reaching Hadrian's Wall is straightforward. The Newcastle–Carlisle train line runs parallel to the wall a mile or two to the south, with stations at Hexham, Haydon Bridge, Bardon Mill, Haltwhistle and Brampton. There are hourly buses between Carlisle and Newcastle, via most of the same towns.

From June to September the hail-and-ride Hadrian's Wall Bus (number AD 122 – geddit?) shuttles between all the major sites, towns and villages along the way.

NORTHWEST ENGLAND

A place of two halves, northwest England offers two very contrasting experiences: culture, music and big nights out in the world-famous cities of Manchester and Liverpool; peace, quiet, fresh air and high peaks in the mountainous Lake District. So pack your dancing shoes and your hiking boots, and come on over.

Manchester

POP 394,270

Raised on lofty ambition and not afraid to declare its considerable bona fides, Manchester is – by dint of geography and history – England's second city (apologies to Birmingham), although if you were to ask a Mancunian what it's like to be second they might reply: 'Don't know; ask a Londoner.'

Even accounting for northern bluster, the uncrowned capital of the north is well deserving of the title. It has a rich history and culture, easily explored in its myriad museums and galleries. And while history and heritage make the city interesting, its distractions make Manchester fun: you can dine, drink and dance yourself into happy oblivion in the swirl of hedonism that is one of Manchester's most cherished characteristics.

Sights

CITY CENTRE

FREE **Museum of Science & Industry** MUSEUM
(MOSI; 0161-832 2244; www.msim.org.uk; Liverpool Rd; charges vary for special exhibitions; 10am-5pm) The city's largest museum comprises 2.8 hectares in the heart of 19th-century industrial Manchester. If there's anything you want to know about the Industrial (and postindustrial) Revolution and Manchester's key role in it, you'll find the answers among the collection of steam engines and locomotives, factory machinery from the mills, and the excellent exhibition telling the story of Manchester from the sewers up. It's an all-ages kind of museum, but the emphasis is on making sure the young 'uns don't get bored.

FREE **People's History Museum** MUSEUM
(0161-838 9190; www.phm.org.uk; Left Bank, Bridge St; 10am-5pm) The story of Britain's 200-year march to democracy is told in all its pain and pathos at this superb museum, housed in a refurbished Edwardian pumping

station. Clock in on the 1st floor (you literally punch your card in an old mill clock, which managers would infamously fiddle so as to make employees work longer) and plunge into the heart of Britain's struggle for basic democratic rights, labour reform and fair pay.

National Football Museum MUSEUM

(☎0161-605 8200; www.nationalfootballmuseum.com; Corporation St, Urbis, Cathedral Gardens; ⊙10am-5pm Mon-Sat, 11am-5pm Sun) It's the world's most popular game and Manchester is home to both the world's most popular and the world's richest teams, so it makes sense that a museum dedicated to the global charms of football should find its home here. The most interesting bit is Football Plus, a series of interactive stations spread throughout the museum that allow you to test your skills in simulated conditions; buy a token (£2.50) and try your luck – it's recommended for over-7s.

FREE **Manchester Art Gallery** GALLERY

(☎0161-235 8888; www.manchestergalleries.org; Mosley St; ⊙10am-5pm Tue-Sun) A superb collection of British art and a hefty number of European masters are on display at the city's top gallery.

SALFORD QUAYS

It's a cinch to get here from the city centre via Metrolink (£2). For the Imperial War Museum North and the Lowry, look for the Harbour City stop; get off at Old Trafford for the eponymous stadium.

TOP CHOICE **Imperial War Museum North** MUSEUM

(☎0161-836 4000; www.iwm.org.uk/north; Trafford Wharf Rd; admission free; ⊙10am-5pm) War museums generally appeal to those with a fascination for military hardware and battle strategy (toy soldiers optional), but Daniel Libeskind's stunning Imperial War Museum North takes a radically different approach. The exhibits cover the main conflicts of the 20th century through a selection of displays, but the really effective bit comes every half-hour when the entire exhibition hall goes dark and one of three 15-minute films (*Children and War, The War at Home* or *Weapons of War*) is projected throughout. Take the Metrolink to Harbour City or MediaCityUK.

The Lowry ARTS CENTRE

(☎0161-876 2020; www.thelowry.com; Pier 8, Salford Quays; ⊙11am-8pm Tue-Fri, 10am-8pm Sat, 11am-6pm Sun & Mon) Looking more like a shiny steel ship than an arts centre, the Lowry is the quays' most notable success. The complex is home to more than 300 paintings and drawings by northern England's favourite artist, LS Lowry (1887–1976), who was born in nearby Stretford. He became famous for his humanistic depictions of industrial landscapes and northern towns, and gave his name to the complex.

Old Trafford STADIUM

(☎0870 442 1994; www.manutd.com; Sir Matt Busby Way; ⊙9.30am-5pm) Home of the world's most famous club, the Old Trafford stadium is both a theatre and a temple for its millions of fans worldwide. The **tour** (adult/child £12.50/8.50; ⊙every 10min except match days 9.40am-4.30pm) includes a seat in the stands, a peek at the players' lounge and a walk down the tunnel to the pitchside dugout. The **museum** (adult/child £9/7; ⊙9.30am-5pm) has a comprehensive history of the club.

Sleeping

Velvet Hotel BOUTIQUE HOTEL ££

(☎0161-236 9003; www.velvetmanchester.com; 2 Canal St; r from £99; 📶) Nineteen beautiful bespoke rooms, each oozing style: there's the sleigh bed in Room 24, the double bath of Room 34, and the saucy framed photographs of a stripped-down David Beckham (this is Gay Village, after all!).

Abode HOTEL ££

(☎0161-247 7744; www.abodehotels.co.uk; 107 Piccadilly St; r from £75; @📶) Modern British style is the catchphrase at this converted textile factory. The original fittings have been combined successfully with 61 bedrooms divided into four categories of ever-increasing luxury: Comfortable, Desirable, Enviable and Fabulous.

Roomzzz APARTMENT ££

(☎0161-236 2121; www.roomzzz.co.uk; 36 Princess St; r £59-169; @📶) The inelegant name belies the designer digs inside this beautifully restored Grade II building, which features serviced apartments equipped with a kitchen and the latest connectivity gadgetry, including sleek iMac computers and free wi-fi throughout. There's a small pantry with food for sale downstairs.

Hatters HOSTEL £

(☎0161-236 9500; www.hattersgroup.com; 50 Newton St; dm/s/d/tr from £15.50/28/52/65; P@📶)

The old-style lift and porcelain sinks are the only leftovers of this former milliner's factory, now one of the best hostels in town, with location to boot – smack in the heart of the Northern Quarter, you won't have to go far to get the best of alternative Manchester.

TOP CHOICE **Manchester YHA** HOSTEL £
(☎0845 371 9647; www.yha.org.uk; Potato Wharf; dm incl breakfast from £16; P@) This purpose-built canalside hostel in the Castlefield area is one of the best in the country. It's a top-class option with four- and six-bed dorms, all with bathroom, as well as three doubles and a host of good facilities. Potato Wharf is just left off Liverpool Rd.

Eating

Manchester has something for every palate and every budget. To dine like an in-the-know Mancunian, go to suburbs like Didsbury, about 5 miles south of the city centre (take bus 43 or 143 from Oxford St).

TOP CHOICE **Australasia** MODERN AUSTRALIAN ££
(☎0161-831 0288; www.australasia.uk.com; 1 The Avenue, Spinningfields; mains £13-30, 2-/3-/4-course lunch £11/15/20) What should you do with the dusty old basement archive of the *Manchester Evening News?* Convert it into the city centre's best new restaurant, of course. Descend through an IM-Pei-inspired glass triangle into a stunning, beautifully lit space lined with comfortable booths. The menu combines Pacific Rim cuisine with flavours of Southeast Asia.

The Oast House INTERNATIONAL ££
(☎0161-829 3830; www.theoasthouse.uk.com; Crown Sq, Spinningfields; mains £9-15) An oast house is a 16th-century kiln used to dry out hops as part of the beer-making process, but in Manchester, it means Tim Bacon's exciting new BBQ restaurant. The kitchen is an outdoor covered grill, so staff have to shuttle the grilled delights (nothing fancy: burgers, kebabs, steaks and rotisserie chickens) to diners inside, but it works brilliantly.

TOP CHOICE **Sam's Chop House** BRITISH £
(☎0161-834 3210; www.samschophouse.co.uk; Back Pool Fold, Chapel Walks, off Cross St; mains £6-8) Arguably the city's top gastropub, Sam's is a Victorian classic that serves dishes straight out of a Dickens novel: the highlight is the crispy corned-beef hash cake, which is salt-cured for 10 days on the premises. The owners also run **Mr Thomas' Chop House** (52 Cross St; mains £10).

Richmond Tea Rooms CAFE £
(☎0161-237 9667; www.richmondtearooms.com; Richmond St; mains £5-8) Sandwiches, salads, rarebits and quiches are the mainstay at this retro tearoom. Afternoon tea includes finger sandwiches, cakes, scones and, of course, your choice of teas.

Mark Addy MODERN BRITISH ££
(☎0161-832 4080; www.markaddy.co.uk; Stanley St; mains £8.90-12.50; ⊙lunch & dinner Wed-Fri, dinner Sat) Another contender for best pub grub in town, the Mark Addy owes its culinary success to Robert Owen Brown, whose loving interpretations of standard British classics has them queuing at the door for a taste. It recently opened a riverside deck.

Drinking

Bluu BAR
(☎0161-839 7740; www.bluu.co.uk; Smithfield Market Buildings, Thomas St; ⊙noon-midnight Sun-Mon, to 1am Tue-Thu, to 2am Fri & Sat) Our favourite of the Northern Quarter's collection of great bars. Bluu is cool, comfortable and comes with a great terrace on which to enjoy a pint and listen to music selected by folks with really good taste.

Britons Protection PUB
(☎0161 236 5895; 50 Great Bridgewater St; mains £8) Whisky – 200 different kinds of it – is the beverage of choice at this liver-threatening, proper English pub that also does Tudor-style meals (boar, venison and the like; mains £8).

Lass O'Gowrie PUB
(☎0161-273 6932; 36 Charles St; meals £6) A Victorian classic, off Princess St, that brews its own beer in the basement. It's a favourite with students, old-timers and a clique of BBC employees who work just across the street in the Beeb's Manchester HQ. It also does good-value bar meals (£6).

Odd BAR
(☎0161-833 0070; www.oddbar.co.uk; 30-32 Thomas St; ⊙11am-11pm Mon-Sat, to 10.30pm Sun) This eclectic little bar – with its oddball furnishings, wacky tunes and anti-establishment crew of customers – is the perfect antidote to the increasingly similar look of so many modern bars. A slice of Mancuniana to be treasured.

Entertainment

With a terrific club scene, Manchester remains at the vanguard of dance-floor culture. Before going out, here's a handy tip: drop all mention of 'Madchester' and keep talk of being 'up for it' to strict irony.

Sankey's CLUB
(☎0161-950 4201; www.sankeys.info; Radium St, Ancoats; admission free-£12; ⏲10pm-3am Thu & Fri, to 4am Sat) If you're a fan of techno, electro or any kind of non-mainstream house music, then a pilgrimage to Manchester's best nightclub should on no account be missed.

Fac251 CLUB
(☎0161-272 7251; www.factorymanchester.com; 112-118 Princess St; admission £1-6; ⏲9.30pm-3am Mon-Sat) It might be a paeon to days of yore, but Fac251, located in Tony Wilson's former Factory Records HQ, stands on its own two feet as one of the best venues in town.

Information

Tourist Office (www.visitmanchester.com; Piccadilly Plaza, Portland St; guided tours £6/5 per adult/child daily; ⏲10am-5.15pm Mon-Sat, 10am-4.30pm Sun)

Getting There & Away

Air

Manchester Airport (p296), south of the city, is the UK's largest airport outside London and is served by 13 locations throughout Britain as well as over 50 international destinations.

Bus

National Express (☎08717 81 81 81; www.nationalexpress.com) serves most major cities almost hourly from Chorlton St coach station in the city centre. Sample destinations:

Leeds (£8.40, one hour, hourly)

Liverpool (£6.80, 1¼ hours, hourly)

London (£25, 3¾ hours, hourly)

Train

Manchester Piccadilly is the main station for trains to and from the rest of the country.

Liverpool Lime Street (£11, 45 minutes, half-hourly)

London Euston (£73.20, three hours, seven daily)

Newcastle (£54.20, three hours, six daily)

Chester

Marvellous Chester is one of English history's greatest gifts to the contemporary visitor. Its red-sandstone wall, which today gift-wraps a tidy collection of Tudor and Victorian buildings, was built during Roman times, and during the Middle Ages Chester grew into the most important port in the northwest. However, the River Dee silted up over time and Chester fell behind Liverpool in importance.

Sights

FREE **City Walls** LANDMARK
A good way to get a sense of Chester's unique character is to walk the 2-mile circuit along the walls that surround the historic centre. The tourist office's *Walk Around Chester Walls* leaflet is an excellent guide.

At **Eastgate**, you can see the most famous **clock** in England after London's Big Ben, built for Queen Victoria's Diamond Jubilee in 1897. At the southeastern corner of the walls are the **wishing steps**, added in 1785; local legend claims that if you can run up and down these uneven steps while holding your breath your wish will come true.

Just inside Southgate is the 1664 **Bear & Billet** (http://bearandbillet.com; Southgate) pub, Chester's oldest timber-framed building and once a tollgate into the city.

Rows ARCHITECTURE
Chester's other great draw is the Rows, a series of two-level galleried arcades along the four streets that fan out in each direction from the **Central Cross**. The architecture is a handsome mix of Victorian and Tudor (original and mock) buildings that house a fantastic collection of individually owned shops.

Chester Cathedral CHURCH
(☎01244-324756; www.chestercathedral.com; 12 Abbey Sq; adult/child £6/2.50; ⏲9am-5pm Mon-Sat, 1-4pm Sun) Originally a Benedictine abbey built on the remains of an earlier Saxon church dedicated to St Werburgh (the city's patron saint), it was shut down in 1540 as part of Henry VIII's dissolution frenzy but reconsecrated as a cathedral the following year.

Dewa Roman Experience MUSEUM
(☎01244-343 407; www.dewaromanexperience.co.uk; Pierpoint Lane; adult/child £4.95/3.25; ⏲9am-5pm Mon-Sat, 10am-5pm Sun) Walk through a reconstructed Roman street to reveal what Roman life was like. It's just off Bridge St.

FREE **Roman Amphitheatre** RUIN

(Little St John St) Just outside the city walls is what was once an arena that seated 7000 spectators (making it the country's largest).

Sleeping

TOP CHOICE **Stone Villa** B&B ££

(☎01244-345014; www.stonevillachester.co.uk; 3 Stone Pl, Hoole Rd; s/d from £45/75; P) Twice winner of Chester's B&B of the Year in the last 10 years, this beautiful villa has elegant bedrooms, a fabulous breakfast and welcoming owners – all adding up to one of the best lodgings in town.

Chester Townhouse B&B ££

(☎01244-350021; www.chestertownhouse.co.uk; 23 King St; s/d £45/75; P) Five beautifully decorated rooms in a handsome 17th-century house within the city walls make Chester Townhouse a terrific option.

Chester Backpackers HOSTEL £

(☎01244-400185; www.chesterbackpackers.co.uk; 67 Boughton; dm from £15.50;) Comfortable dorm rooms with nice pine beds in a typically Tudor white-and-black building. It's just a short walk from the city walls.

Eating

Chester has great food – it's just not in any of the tourist-oriented restaurants that line the Rows.

Joseph Benjamin MODERN BRITISH ££

(☎01244-344295; www.josephbenjamin.co.uk; 134-140 Northgate St; mains £13-17; ⊙9am-5pm Tue-Wed, 9am-midnight Thu-Fri, 10am-5pm Sun) This combo restaurant, bar and deli is great for take out or sit-in. Excellent sandwiches and gorgeous salads are the mainstay of the take-out menu, while the more formal dinner menu features fine modern British cuisine.

Old Harker's Arms PUB ££

(☎01244-344525; www.harkersarms-chester.co.uk; 1 Russell St; mains £9-14; ⊙lunch & dinner) An old-style boozer with a gourmet kitchen, this is the perfect place to tuck into Cumberland sausages or a Creole rice salad with sweet potatoes, and then rinse your palate with a pint of local ale, such as Cheshire Cat.

Information

Tourist Office (☎01244-402111; www.visitchester.com; Town Hall, Northgate St; ⊙9am-5.30pm Mon-Sat, 10am-4pm Sun May-Oct, 10am-5pm Mon-Sat Nov-Apr)

Getting There & Away

BUS National Express (☎08717 81 81 81; www.nationalexpress.com) coaches stop on Vicar's Lane, just opposite the tourist office by the Roman amphitheatre.

Birmingham (£14, 2¼ hours, four daily)

Liverpool (£7.90, one hour, four daily)

London (£23, 5½ hours, three daily)

Manchester (£7.40, 1¼ hours, three daily)

TRAIN The train station is about a mile from the city centre via Foregate St and City Rd, or Brook St.

Liverpool (£6.20, 45 minutes, hourly)

London Euston (£73.20, 2½ hours, hourly)

Manchester (£11.30, one hour, hourly)

Liverpool

POP 469,020

Few English cities are as shackled by reputation as Liverpool, and none has worked so hard to outgrow the cliches that for so long have been used to define it. A hardscrabble town with a reputation for wit and an obsessive love of football, Liverpool also has an impressive cultural heritage: it has more listed museums than any other city outside London, has recently undergone an impressive program of urban regeneration, and its collection of museums and galleries is easily among the best in the country. And then, of course, there's the Beatles...

The main attractions are Albert Dock (west of the city centre), and the trendy Ropewalks area (south of Hanover St and west of the two cathedrals). Lime St station, the bus station and the Cavern Quarter – a mecca for Beatles fans – lie just to the north.

Sights

CITY CENTRE

FREE **World Museum** MUSEUM

(☎0151-478 4399; www.liverpoolmuseums.org.uk/wml; William Brown St; ⊙10am-5pm) Natural history, science and technology are the themes of this sprawling museum, whose exhibits range from birds of prey to space exploration. It also includes the country's only free planetarium. This vastly entertaining and educational museum is divided into four major sections: the Human World, one of the top anthropological collections in the country; the Natural World, which includes a new aquarium as well as live insect colonies; Earth, a geological treasure trove; and Space & Time, which includes the planetarium.

DOING THE BEATLES TO DEATH

It doesn't matter that half of the band are gone or that the much-visited Cavern Club is an unfaithful reconstruction of the original, nor that, if he were alive, John Lennon might have devoted much of his cynical energy to mocking the 'Cavern Quarter' that has grown up around Mathew St. No, it doesn't matter at all, because the Beatles phenomenon lives on, and a huge chunk of the city's visitors come to visit, see and touch anything – and we mean anything – even vaguely associated with the Fab Four. Which isn't to say that a wander around Mathew St isn't fun: from shucking oysters in the Rubber Soul Oyster Bar to buying a Ringo pillowcase in the From Me to You shop, virtually all of your Beatles needs can be taken care of.

True fans will also undoubtedly want to visit the National Trust–owned **Mendips**, the home where John lived with his Aunt Mimi from 1945 to 1963, and **20 Forthlin Road**, where Paul grew up. You can only do so by prebooked **tour** (☎0151-427 7231; adult/child £16.80/3.15; ⏱10.30am & 11.20am Wed-Sun Easter-Oct), from outside the National Conservation Centre.

TOP CHOICE Walker Art Gallery GALLERY
(☎0151-478 4199; www.liverpoolmuseums.org.uk/walker; William Brown St; admission free; ⏱10am-5pm) The city's foremost gallery is the national gallery for northern England, housing an outstanding collection of art from the 14th to the 21st centuries. Its strong suits are Pre-Raphaelite art, modern British art and sculpture, not to mention the rotating exhibits of contemporary expression.

FREE St George's Hall CULTURAL CENTRE
(☎0151-707 2391; www.stgeorgesliverpool.co.uk; William Brown St; ⏱10am-5pm Tue-Sat, 1-5pm Sun) Arguably Liverpool's most impressive building is the Grade I–listed St George's Hall, a magnificent example of neoclassical architecture that is as imposing today as it was when it was completed in 1854. Curiously, it was built as law courts *and* a concert hall – presumably a judge could pass sentence and then relax to a string quartet. **Tours** (☎0151-225 6909; £3.50; ⏱2pm Wed, 11am & 2pm Sat & Sun) of the hall are run in conjunction with the tourist office.

Liverpool Cathedral CHURCH
(☎0151-709 6271; www.liverpoolcathedral.org.uk; Upper Duke St; visitor centre & tower admission £5; ⏱8am-6pm) Liverpool's Anglican cathedral is a building of superlatives. Not only is it Britain's largest church, it's also the world's largest Anglican cathedral, and that's all thanks to Sir Giles Gilbert Scott, who made its construction his life's work. (Sir Giles also gave us the red telephone box and the Southwark Power Station in London, now Tate Modern.) The central bell is the world's third-largest (with the world's highest and heaviest peal), while the organ, with its 9765 pipes, is likely the world's largest operational model.

The **visitor centre** (admission £5; ⏱8am-6pm) features the **Great Space**, a 10-minute, panoramic high-definition movie about the history of the cathedral. Your ticket also gives you access to the cathedral's 101m tower, from which there are terrific views of the city and beyond – on a clear day you can see Blackpool Tower.

Metropolitan Cathedral of Christ the King CHURCH
(☎0151-709 9222; www.liverpoolmetrocathedral.org.uk; Brownlow Hill; ⏱8am-6pm Mon-Sat, to 5pm Sun Oct-Mar) Known colloquially as Paddy's Wigwam, Liverpool's Catholic cathedral is a mightily impressive modern building that looks like a soaring concrete teepee, hence its nickname. It was completed in 1967 according to the design of Sir Frederick Gibberd, after the original plans by Sir Edwin Lutyens, whose crypt is inside. The central tower frames the world's largest stained-glass window, created by John Piper and Patrick Reyntiens.

ALBERT DOCK

Liverpool's biggest tourist attraction is **Albert Dock** (☎0151-708 8854; www.albertdock.com; admission free). This former port and its surrounding buildings is now a Unesco World Heritage site.

FREE International Slavery Museum MUSEUM
(☎0151-478 4499; www.liverpoolmuseums.org.uk/ism; Albert Dock; ⏱10am-5pm) Museums are, by their very nature, like a still of the past, but

the extraordinary International Slavery Museum resonates very much in the present. It reveals slavery's unimaginable horrors – including Liverpool's own role in the triangular slave trade – in a clear and uncompromising manner.

Beatles Story MUSEUM
(☎0151-709 1963; www.beatlesstory.com; Albert Dock; adult/student/child £12.95/9/7, incl Elvis & Us £15.95/12/7; ⏲9am-7pm, last admission 5pm) Liverpool's most popular museum won't illuminate any dark, juicy corners in the turbulent history of the world's most famous foursome – there's ne'er a mention of internal discord, drugs or Yoko Ono – but there's plenty of genuine memorabilia to keep a Beatles fan happy. Particularly impressive is the full-size replica Cavern Club (which was actually tiny) and the Abbey Rd studio where the lads recorded their first singles. You can also get a combo ticket for the **Elvis & Us** (☎0151-709 1963; www.elvisandus.com; Mersey Ferries Terminal, Pier Head; admission £6; ⏲9am-7pm Apr-Sep, 10am-6pm Oct-Mar) exhibit at the new Beatles Story extension on Pier Head.

FREE **Tate Liverpool** MUSEUM
(☎0151-702 7400; www.tate.org.uk/liverpool; Albert Dock; special exhibitions adult/child from £5/4; ⏲10am-5.50pm Jun-Aug, 10am-5.50pm Tue-Sun Sep-May) Touted as the home of modern art in the north, this gallery features a substantial checklist of 20th-century artists across its four floors, as well as touring exhibitions from the mother ship on London's Southbank. But it's all a little sparse, with none of the energy we'd expect from the world-famous Tate.

NORTH OF ALBERT DOCK

The area to the north of Albert Dock is known as **Pier Head**, after a stone pier built in the 1760s. This is still the departure point for ferries across the River Mersey, and was, for millions of migrants, their final contact with European soil.

It's home to the city's most famous trio of Edwardian buildings known as the 'Three Graces', dating from the days when Liverpool's star was still ascending. The southernmost, with the dome mimicking St Paul's Cathedral, is the **Port of Liverpool Building**, completed in 1907. Next to it is the **Cunard Building**, in the style of an Italian *palazzo*, once HQ to the Cunard Steamship Line. Finally, the **Royal Liver Building** (pronounced *lie*-ver) was opened in 1911 as the head office of the Royal Liver Friendly Society. It's crowned by Liverpool's symbol, the famous 5.5m copper Liver Bird.

FREE **Museum of Liverpool** MUSEUM
(☎0151-478 4545; www.liverpoolmuseums.org.uk; Pier Head; ⏲10am-5pm) Liverpool's storied past is explored within the confines of an eye-catching futuristic building designed in typical Scandinavian verve by Danish firm 3XN. Inside, it's all fizz-bang-wallop as you wend your way through an interactive exploration of the cultural and historical milestones of Liverpool – the railroad, poverty, wealth, *Brookside* (a popular '80s TV soap opera set in the city), the Beatles and football (the film on the meaning of the game to the city is worth the 15 minutes).

Tours

Beatles Fab Four Taxi Tour GUIDED TOUR
(☎0151-601 2111; www.thebeatlesfabfourtaxitour.co.uk; 2-/3-hour £40/50) Themed tours of the city's mop-top landmarks – there's the three-hour original Lennon tour or the two-hour Epstein express tour. Pick-ups arranged when booking. Up to five people per tour.

Magical Mystery Tour GUIDED TOUR
(☎0151-709 3285; www.beatlestour.org; per person £15.95; ⏲2.30pm year-round, plus noon Sat Jul & Aug) Two-hour tour that takes in all Beatles-related landmarks – their birthplaces, childhood homes, schools and places such as Penny Lane and Strawberry Field – before finishing up in the Cavern Club (which isn't the original). Departs from outside the tourist office on Albert Dock.

Yellow Duckmarine Tour WATER TOUR
(☎0151-708 7799; www.theyellowduckmarine.co.uk; adult/child £14.95/9.95; ⏲from 11am) Take to the dock waters in a WWII amphibious vehicle after a quickie tour of the city centre's main points of interest. It's not especially educational, but it is a bit of fun. Departs from Albert Dock, near the Beatles Story.

Sleeping

CITY CENTRE

Hotel Indigo HOTEL ££
(☎0151-559 0111; www.hotelindigoliverpool.co.uk; 10 Chapel St; r from £65; @📶) It's labelled a boutique hotel, but the 151-room Indigo is just too big and part of a franchise, so the feel is more corporate swish than bespoke boutique. An excellent midrange choice.

62 Castle St BOUTIQUE HOTEL ££
(☎0151-702 7898; www.62castlest.com; 62 Castle St; r from £69; P@) This elegant property on (arguably) the city's most handsome street successfully blends the traditional Victorian features of the neoclassical building with a sleek, contemporary style.

Roscoe House BOUTIQUE HOTEL ££
(☎0151-709 0286; www.hotelliverpool.net; 27 Rodney St; r from £50;) A handsome Georgian home once owned by Liverpool-born writer and historian William Roscoe (1753–1831) has been given the once-over and is now a chic boutique hotel. The elegant rooms combine period touches (original coving, fireplaces and furnishings) with contemporary comforts such as flatscreen TVs and fancy Egyptian cotton linen.

International Inn HOSTEL £
(☎0151-709 8135; www.internationalinn.co. uk; 4 South Hunter St; dm/d from £15/36;) A superb converted warehouse in the middle of uniland: heated rooms with tidy wooden beds and bunks accommodate from two to 10 people. Facilities include a lounge, baggage storage, laundry and 24-hour front desk. The staff is terrific and CafeLatte.net internet cafe is next door.

Around Albert Dock

Liverpool YHA HOSTEL £
(☎0845 371 9527; www.yha.org.uk; 25 Tabley St; dm from £16; P) It may have the look of an eastern European apartment complex, but this award-winning hostel, adorned with plenty of Beatles memorabilia, is one of the most comfortable you'll find anywhere in the country.

Eating

Liverpool has plenty of choices to satisfy every taste. The best areas include Ropewalks, along Hardman St and Hope St, or along Nelson St in the heart of Chinatown.

Monro PUB ££
(☎0151-707 9933; www.themonro.com; 92 Duke St; 2-course lunch £11.95, dinner mains £14-20; lunch & dinner) The constantly changing menu of classic British dishes made with ingredients sourced as locally as possible has transformed this handsome old pub into a superb dining experience. It's tough to find pub grub this good elsewhere, unless you go to its sister pub, the **James Monro** (☎0151-236 9700; www.thejamesmonro.com; 69 Tithebarn St; lunch & dinner Tue-Sun).

Italian Club ITALIAN £
(☎0151-708 5508; www.theitalianclubliverpool.co.uk; 85 Bold St; mains £6-11; 10am-7pm Mon-Sat) The Crolla family must have been homesick for southern Italy, so they opened this fabulous spot, adorned it with family pictures and began serving the kind of food relatives visiting from the home country would be glad to tuck into. They've been so successful that they recently opened **Italian Club Fish** (☎0151-707 2110; 128 Bold St; mains £8-14; Tue-Sun) just down the street, specialising in, erm, fish.

The Noble House INTERNATIONAL ££
(☎0151-236 5346; www.thenoblehouse.co.uk; Heywood Bldg, 5 Brunswick St; mains £10-16) The handsome Heywood Building (1799) was once the city's oldest bank – now it's a classy restaurant with a vaguely Manhattanite feel. It's owned by the same crowd that run the **Alma de Cuba** (☎0151-709 7097; www.alma-de-cuba.com; St Peter's Church, Seel St; mains £13-25; lunch & dinner).

Drinking

Philharmonic PUB
(36 Hope St; to 11.30pm) This extraordinary bar, designed by the shipwrights who built the *Lusitania,* is one of the most beautiful bars in all of England. The interior is resplendent with etched and stained glass, wrought iron, mosaics and ceramic tiling – and if you think that's good, just wait until you see inside the marble men's toilets, the only heritage-listed lav in the country.

Magnet BAR
(www.magnetliverpool.co.uk; 39 Hardman St) Red leather booths, plenty of velvet and a suitably seedy New York–dive atmosphere where Iggy Pop or Tom Waits would feel right at home.

Rigby's PUB
(21 Dale St) A traditional boozer that serves 'real ale' (ie a traditional brew with no extraneous carbon dioxide), Rigby's looks, feels and smells like an old-school pub. The perfect antidote to the high-octane noise of the city's newer bars.

Entertainment

Most of the city's clubs and late-night bars are concentrated in the area of Ropewalks.

Masque CLUB
(☎0151-707 6171; www.chibuku.com; 90 Seel St; admission £4-11; Mon-Sat) This converted theatre is home to our favourite club in town. The fortnightly Saturday Chibuku is one of the best club nights in all of England, led by a

mix of superb DJs including Yousef (formerly of Cream nightclub) and superstars such as Dmitri from Paris and Gilles Peterson.

Nation CLUB
(☎0151-709 1693; 40 Slater St, Wolstenholme Sq; admission £4-13) It looks like an air-raid shelter, but it's the big-name DJs dropping the bombs at the city's premier dance club, formerly the home of Cream.

Academy LIVE MUSIC
(☎0151-794 6868; Liverpool University, 11-13 Hotham St) Good spot to see midsize bands on tour.

Cavern Club LIVE MUSIC
(☎0151-236 1965; www.cavernclub.org; 8-10 Mathew St) It's a reconstruction, and not even on the same spot, but the 'world's most famous club' is still a great spot to see local bands.

Information

Most of Liverpool's tourist business is done online, including an **accommodation hotline** (☎0845 601 1125; ⏲9am-5.30pm Mon-Fri, 10am-4pm Sat). There is a small tourist office in Albert Dock.

Getting There & Away

BUS The **National Express Coach Station** (www.nationalexpress.com; Norton St) is 300m north of Lime St station. There are services to/from most major towns:

Birmingham (£13.80, 2¾ hours, five daily)
London (£28, five to six hours, six daily)
Manchester (£6.80, 1¼ hours, hourly)
Newcastle (£24.50, 6½ hours, three daily)

TRAIN Liverpool's main station is Lime St. It has hourly services to almost everywhere, including the following:

Chester (£6.20, 45 minutes)
London Euston (£73.20, 3¼ hours)
Manchester (£11, 45 minutes)

Lake District National Park

A dramatic landscape of high peaks, dizzying ridges and huge lakes gouged by the march of ice age glaciers, the Lake District in Cumbria is a beautiful corner of Britain. It may not be the wildest place on earth, and there are much bigger mountains in Wales and Scotland, but for England it's as extreme as it gets. Not surprisingly, the awe-inspiring geography here shaped the literary persona of some of Britain's best-known poets, including William Wordsworth.

Often called simply the Lakes, the national park and surrounding area attract around 15 million visitors annually. But if you avoid summer weekends, and especially if you do a bit of hiking, it's easy enough to miss the crush.

The key valleys of the Lake District radiate from a central high point like spokes of a wheel, with most of the larger towns at the outer edge. Principal gateways include the twin towns of Windermere and Bowness in the south, Ambleside slightly nearer the centre, and Keswick in the north. All have hostels, B&Bs, places to eat and shops selling maps and outdoor equipment.

There's a host of B&Bs and country-house hotels in the Lakes, plus over 20 YHA hostels, many of which can be linked by foot.

Information

The Lake District's tourist offices are crammed with information on local hikes, activities and accommodation, and stocked with guidebooks, maps and hiking supplies.

Brockhole National Park Visitor Centre (☎015394-46601; www.lake-district.gov.uk; ⏲10am-5pm Easter-Oct) Installed inside a 19th-century mansion 3 miles north of Windermere on the A591, this is the Lake District's flagship visitor centre, and also has a teashop, adventure playground and gardens.

Getting There & Away

BUS There's one daily National Express coach from London (£30, eight hours) via Lancaster and Kendal. Local buses:

555/556 Lakeslink Half-hourly Monday to Saturday, hourly at weekends; Windermere, Brockhole Visitor Centre (seven minutes), Ambleside (15 minutes), Grasmere (30 minutes), Keswick (one hour).

505 Coniston Rambler Eight daily Monday to Saturday, six on Sunday; Windermere to Coniston (50 minutes).

599 Lakes Rider Runs three times hourly Monday to Saturday, hourly on Sunday in summer; open-top bus between Bowness, Dove Cottage and Grasmere.

TRAIN Windermere is the only town in the national park accessible by train. It's on the branch line to Kendal (£4.20, 15 minutes) and on to Oxenholme (£4.90, 20 minutes), which has frequent connections north and south:

Edinburgh (£55, 2½ hours)
Glasgow (£43.40, 2¾ hours)
London Euston (£92.10, 3¼ hours)
Manchester Piccadilly (£32.40, 1½ to two hours via Lancaster £12.60, 45 minutes)

DON'T MISS

HILL TOP

The button-cute farmhouse of **Hill Top** (NT; 015394-36269; www.nationaltrust.org.uk/hill-top; adult/child £8/4; 10am-5pm Sat-Thu mid-Feb–Oct, shorter hours outside summer) is a must for Beatrix Potter buffs: it was her first house in the Lake District, and is also where she wrote and illustrated several of her famous tales. The house still contains much of Potter's own furniture and belongings, including her writing desk, kitchen dresser and doll collection. Entry is by timed ticket to avoid overcrowding, but the queues can still be daunting.

The cottage is in Near Sawrey, 2 miles from Hawkshead and Ferry House. The **Cross Lakes Experience** (http://www.lakedistrict.gov.uk/visiting/planningyourvisit/travelandtransport/crosslakes; Mar-Oct) stops en route from Ferry House to Hawkshead.

WINDERMERE & BOWNESS

POP 8432

Windermere – the lake and the town of the same name – has been a centre for Lakeland tourism since the first steam trains arrived in 1847. The station is still there, making this an excellent gateway. The town of Windermere is 1.5 miles uphill from the lake, and bustling Bowness (officially Bowness-on-Windermere) is on the lakeshore, where a bevy of boat trips, ice-cream booths and frilly teashops jostle for space.

Windermere Lake Cruises (015395-31188; www.windermere-lakecruises.co.uk) offers scheduled boat trips across the lake.

Sleeping

Wheatlands Lodge B&B ££
(015394-43789; www.wheatlandslodge-windermere.co.uk; Old College Lane; d £80-150; P) Between Bowness and Windermere, this detached house looks venerably Victorian, but inside you'll find eight elegant, contemporary rooms with either power shower or sit-down jacuzzi. It's set back from the road so it feels serene, and owner Sarah knows how to spoil her guests – from the welcome coffee-and-cake to the slap-up, locally sourced breakfast.

Lake District Backpackers Lodge HOSTEL £
(015394-46374; www.lakedistrictbackpackers.co.uk; High St; dm £15; @) Windermere's indie hostel is handy for the station, but it's cramped and showing its age. Dorms and kitchen are small, but rates include bed linen and breakfast.

Number 80 Bed Then Breakfast B&B ££
(015394-43584; www.number80bed.co.uk; 80 Craig Walk; d £80-90;) This cute Bowness refuge is still off the radar, so keep it under your hats. Just four rooms, but all are up-to-date: Room 1 has a pine four-poster, the other three feel more modern.

AMBLESIDE

POP 3382

Windermere and Bowness are tourist towns, but Ambleside is 100% for walkers and other outdoor types, with plenty of gear shops and the start point of several classic hikes on the surrounding high fells.

Sleeping

Lakes Lodge B&B ££
(015394-33240; www.lakeslodge.co.uk; Lake Rd; r £79-129; P) This modish minihotel offers a touch more luxury than Ambleside's other guesthouses. The 16 rooms are all clean lines, stark walls and zero clutter, and most feature a full-size wall mural depicting a local beauty spot. Some rooms are in an annexe next to the main building. Breakfast is self serve.

Ambleside YHA HOSTEL £
(0845 371 9620; ambleside@yha.org.uk; Windermere Rd; dm/d £23/40, f £99-149; P) One of the YHA's flagship Lake District hostels, this huge lakeside house organises activity holidays (everything from kayaking to ghyll-scrambling). Great facilities (kitchen, bike rental, boat jetty and bar) mean it's heavily subscribed, so book well ahead.

Ambleside Backpackers HOSTEL £
(015394-32340; www.englishlakesbackpackers.co.uk; Old Lake Rd; dm £16; P@) Cottage hostel a short walk south from Ambleside's centre.

GRASMERE

Grasmere is a gorgeous little Lakeland village, all the more famous because of its links with Britain's leading Romantic poet, William Wordsworth. Literary pilgrims come to **Dove Cottage** (015394-35544; www.wordsworth.org.uk; adult/child £7.50/4.50; 9.30am-5.30pm), his former home, where highlights include some fine portraits of the man himself, a cabinet containing his spectacles, and a set of scales used by his pal de Quincey to weigh out opium. At **St Oswald's Church** you'll see a memorial to the poet, and in the churchyard you'll find his grave.

To cure any sombre thoughts, head for **Sarah Nelson's Gingerbread Shop** (www.grasmeregingerbread.co.uk; Church Stile; 12 pieces of gingerbread £4.95; 9.15am-5.30pm Mon-Sat, 12.30-5pm Sun) and stock up on Grasmere's famous confectionery.

KESWICK

POP 5257

The main town of the north Lakes, Keswick sits beside lovely Derwent Water, a silvery curve studded by wooded islands and criss-crossed by puttering cruise boats, operated by the **Keswick Launch** (017687-72263; www.keswick-launch.co.uk; round-the-lake ticket adult/child £9.25/4.50).

Sleeping

TOP CHOICE **Howe Keld** B&B ££

(017687-72417; www.howekeld.co.uk; 5-7 The Heads; s £55-58, d £90-130;) This gold-standard B&B pulls out all the stops – goose-down duvets, slate-floored bathrooms, chic colours and furniture made by a local carpenter. Breakfast is a pick-and-mix delight: fresh smoothies, vegetarian rissoles, French pancakes and make-your-own muesli.

Oakthwaite House B&B ££

(017687-72398; www.oakthwaite-keswick.co.uk; 35 Helvellyn St; d £66-80) One of the top choices in the B&B-heavy neighbourhood round Helvellyn St. There are just four rooms (so not too crowded), all with power showers, white linen and soothingly neutral tones.

Keswick YHA HOSTEL £

(0845-371 9746; keswick@yha.org.uk; Station Rd; dm £23.40; @) Keswick's YHA is a beauty, lodged inside a converted woollen mill by the clattering River Rothay. Dorms are cosy, there's an excellent cafe and some rooms even have balconies over Fitz Park.

WALES

Lying to the west of England, the nation of Wales is a separate country within the state of Great Britain. It's a nation with Celtic roots, its own language and a rich historic legacy. While some areas in the south are undeniably scarred by coal mining and heavy industry, overall Wales boasts a landscape of wild mountains, rolling hills, rich farmland and some of the most beautiful beaches in all of Britain. If you're on a long tour, South Wales is most easily reached from southern or central England, and is well worth the diversion.

Cardiff

POP 324,800

The capital of Wales since only 1955, Cardiff has embraced its new role with vigour, emerging as one of Britain's leading urban centres in the 21st century. Caught between an ancient fort and an ultramodern waterfront, this compact city seems to have surprised even itself with how interesting it has become. This new-found confidence is infectious; people now travel to Cardiff for a good night out, bringing with them a buzz that reverberates through the streets.

Sights

CENTRAL CARDIFF

TOP CHOICE **Cardiff Castle** CASTLE

(www.cardiffcastle.com; Castle St; adult/child £11/8.50, incl guided tour £14/11; 9am-5pm) The grafting of Victorian mock-Gothic extravagance onto Cardiff's most important historical relics makes Cardiff Castle the city's leading attraction. The most conventional castle-y bits are the 12th-century motte-and-bailey **Norman keep** at its centre and the 13th-century **Black Tower**, which forms the entrance gate. A 50-minute guided tour takes you through the interiors of this flamboyant fantasy world.

FREE **National Museum Cardiff** MUSEUM

(www.museumwales.ac.uk; Gorsedd Gardens Rd; 10am-5pm Tue-Sun) Set around the green lawns and colourful flowerbeds of **Alexandra Gardens** is the Civic Centre, an early-20th-century complex of neo-Baroque buildings in gleaming white Portland stone. They include the **City Hall**, police headquarters, law courts, crown offices, Cardiff University and this excellent **museum**, one of Britain's best, covering natural history, archaeology and art. The **art gallery** houses an excellent collection, including many Impressionist and post-Impressionist pieces. Welsh artists such as Richard Wilson, Thomas Jones, David Jones, Gwen John and Augustus John are well represented.

Millennium Stadium STADIUM

(029-2082 2228; www.millenniumstadium.com; Westgate St; tours adult/child £7.50/4.95; 10am-5pm) The spectacular Millennium Stadium

TONGUE-TWISTING

At first sight, Welsh seems impossibly difficult to get your tongue around. But once you know that 'dd' is pronounced 'th', and 'w' can also be a vowel pronounced 'oo', and 'f' is 'v', while 'ff' is 'f', and 'll' is roughly 'cl', you might just about be able to ask the way to Llanfairpwllgwyngyllgogerychwyrndrobwllllantysiliogogogoch – a village in Anglesey with Britain's longest place name.

squats like a stranded spaceship on the River Taff's east bank. Attendance at international rugby and football matches has increased dramatically since this 72,500-seat, three-tiered stadium with sliding roof was completed in time to host the 1999 Rugby World Cup. The entrance for guided tours is at Gate 3 on Westgate St.

CARDIFF BAY

The redeveloped waterfront of Cardiff Bay is about 2 miles from the city centre, lined with bars, restaurants and shops, and a collection of stunning buildings.

Doctor Who Up Close EXHIBITION

(☎0844 801 3663; www.doctorwhoexhibitions.com; Porth Teigr; adult/child £15/11; ⊙10am-5pm Wed-Mon, daily school holidays) The huge success of the reinvented classic TV series *Doctor Who,* produced by BBC Wales, has brought Cardiff to the attention of sci-fi fans worldwide. Capitalising on Timelord tourism, this permanent exhibition has opened in the Red Dragon Centre, with props and costumes from both shows displayed alongside video clips from the episodes they feature in. Fans can pick up a locations guide (30p) from the nerdalicious shop.

FREE **Wales Millennium Centre** ARTS CENTRE

(☎029-2063 6464; www.wmc.org.uk; Bute Pl; guided tour adult/child £5.50/4.50; ⊙11am & 2.30pm) Designed by Welsh architect Jonathan Adams, this landmark building opened in 2004 as Wales' premier arts complex, housing the Welsh National Opera, National Dance Company, National Orchestra, Academi (Welsh National Literature Promotion Agency), Hi-Jinx Theatre and Ty Cerdd (Music Centre of Wales). You can wander through the public areas at will, or take an official **guided tour** that leads behind the giant letters, onto the main stage and into the dressing rooms, depending on what shows are on.

FREE **Senedd (National Assembly Building)** NOTABLE BUILDING

(☎0845 010 5500; www.assemblywales.org; ⊙10.30am-4.30pm Fri-Mon, 8am-end of business Tue-Thu) Designed by Lord Richard Rogers (the architect behind London's Lloyd's Building and Paris' Pompidou Centre), the Senedd houses Wales' National Assembly. It's won awards for an environmentally friendly design, which includes a huge rotating cowl on the roof for power-free ventilation and a gutter system that collects rainwater for flushing the toilets.

Sleeping

River House Backpackers HOSTEL £

(☎029-2039 9810; www.riverhousebackpackers.com; 59 Fitzhamon Embankment; dm/r from £18/35; @ 📶) Professionally run by a young brother-and-sister team, the River House has a well-equipped kitchen, a small garden and a TV lounge. Free breakfast (cereal and toast) and pizza nights are a nice touch, but the private rooms are very dormlike.

Parc Hotel HOTEL ££

(☎0871 376 9011; www.thistle.com/theparchotel; Park Pl; s/d from £74/79; @ 📶) A smart contemporary hotel located right at the heart of the main shopping area, with tasteful rooms, good facilities and helpful staff.

Jolyons Boutique Hotel HOTEL ££

(☎029-2048 8775; www.jolyons.co.uk; 5 Bute Cres; r from £76; 📶) A touch of Georgian elegance in the heart of Cardiff Bay. Jolyon's has six individually designed rooms combining antique furniture with contemporary colours and crisp cotton sheets.

Eating

Riverside Real Foodmarket MARKET £

(www.riversidemarket.org.uk; Fitzhamon Embankment; ⊙10am-2pm Sun) What it lacks in size it makes up for in sheer yumminess. This riverside market has stalls heaving with cooked meals, cakes, cheese, organic meat, charcuterie, apple juice and real ale.

Cafe Minuet ITALIAN £

(42 Castle Arcade; mains £5-8; ⊙lunch Mon-Sat) It may look a bit greasy spoon from the outside, but this unassuming eatery produces

excellent cheap and cheerful Italian food. Get in early at lunchtime or expect to wait for a table.

Goat Major PUB

(www.sabrain.com/goatmajor; 33 High St; pies £7.50; lunch) A solidly traditional pub with armchairs, a fireplace and lip-smacking Brains Dark real ale on tap. Its Wye Valley pie (a mixture of buttered chicken, leek, asparagus and Tintern Abbey cheese) was named Britain's best in 2010.

Zerodegrees ITALIAN ££

(www.zerodegrees.co.uk; 27 Westgate St; mains £8-16) Within a big factorylike space this microbrewery and restaurant combines all-day food with lip-smacking artisan-crafted beers. The excellent dining options include a UN of pizza toppings (Thai, Mexican, Indian, Portuguese), pasta, risotto and kilo pots of mussels, the house speciality.

Woods Bar & Brasserie MODERN EUROPEAN ££

(029-2049 2400; www.knifeandforkfood.co.uk; Stuart St; mains £11-16; lunch daily, dinner Mon-Sat) The historic Pilotage Building has been given a modern makeover – zany wallpaper, exposed stone walls and a floor-to-ceiling glass extension – to accommodate Cardiff Bay's best restaurant. The cuisine is modern European, light and flavoursome, with an emphasis on local ingredients.

Drinking & Entertainment

TOP CHOICE **Gwdihw** BAR

(www.gwdihw.co.uk; 6 Guildford Cres) The last word in Cardiff hipsterdom, this cute little bar has an eclectic lineup of entertainment; ukelele jams, comedy nights, cake and craft markets, and lots of live music (including microfestivals that spill over into the car park).

Buffalo Bar BAR

(www.myspace.com/wearebuffalobar; 11 Windsor Pl) A haven for cool kids about town, the laid-back Buffalo features retro furniture, tasty daytime food, life-affirming cocktails and cool tunes with DJ sets. Upstairs a roster of cutting-edge indie bands take to the stage.

Clwb Ifor Bach CLUB

(029-2023 2199; www.clwb.net; 11 Womanby St) Truly an independent music great, *Y Clwb* has broken many a Welsh band since the early 1980s.

Information

Cardiff Tourist Office (029-2087 3573; www.visitcardiff.com; The Hayes, Old Library; 9.30am-5.30pm Mon-Sat, 10am-4pm Sun) Piles of information, an accommodation-booking service and a good stock of OS maps, plus Welsh literature and internet access.

Getting There & Away

BUS National Express coach destinations include:

Bristol (£9, 1¼ hours)
Birmingham (£11, three hours)
Chepstow (£5.40, 45 minutes)
London (£11, 3½ hours)
Monmouth (£11, 1¼ hours)

The First Greyhound service travels regularly between Cardiff and Swansea (peak/off-peak £7/5 return, one hour).

TRAIN **Arriva Trains Wales** (www.arrivatrainswales.co.uk) operates all train services in Wales. Direct services from Cardiff include:

Abergavenny (£12, 40 minutes)
Bangor (£75, 4¼ hours)
Fishguard Harbour (£22, three hours)
London Paddington (£39, 2¼ hours)
Swansea (£7.70, 50 minutes)

Around Cardiff

CAERPHILLY CASTLE

The town of Caerphilly – now almost a suburb of Cardiff – is synonymous with a hard, slightly crumbly white cheese that originated in the surrounding area. However, the main attraction is **Caerphilly Castle** (Cadw; 029 2088 3143; www.cadw.wales.gov.uk; adult/child £3.60/3.20; 9am-5pm Apr-Oct, 9.30am-4pm Mon-Sat, 11am-4pm Sun Nov-Mar), one of the earliest castles to use lakes, bridges and a series of concentric fortifications for defence. To reach the inner court you had to overcome no fewer than three drawbridges, six portcullises and five sets of double gates.

Most of the construction was completed between 1268 and 1271 by the powerful English baron Gilbert de Clare, Lord Marcher of Glamorgan (1243–95), in response to the threat of Prince Llywelyn ap Gruffydd (the last Welsh Prince of Wales). Much of what you see today is the result of restoration from 1928 to 1939 by the fourth marquess of Bute.

The easiest way to reach Caerphilly from Cardiff is by train (£3.80, 19 minutes), or you can catch Stagecoach buses A, B and 26 (45 minutes).

CASTELL COCH

Perched atop a thickly wooded crag on the northern fringes of the city, **Castell Coch** (Cadw; ☎029-2081 0101; www.cadw.wales.gov.uk; adult/child £3.80/3.40; ⊙10am-4pm) was the summer retreat of the third marquess of Bute and, like Cardiff Castle, was designed by William Burges in gaudy Victorian Gothic style.

Raised on the ruins of Gilbert de Clare's 13th-century Castell Coch (Red Castle), the Butes' Disneyesque holiday home is a monument to high camp: Lady Bute's bedroom is festooned with extravagant murals and a mirrored cupola, while the octagonal drawing room is painted with scenes from Aesop's fables.

Stagecoach buses 26 and 132 (30 minutes) stop at Tongwynlais, a 10-minute walk to the castle. Bus 26 continues to Caerphilly Castle, and the two can be combined in a day trip. Bus 26A (four daily Monday to Friday) stops right at the castle gates.

Pembrokeshire Coast National Park

Established in 1952, **Pembrokeshire Coast National Park** (Parc Cenedlaethol Arfordir Sir Benfro; www.pembrokeshirecoast.org.uk) takes in almost the entire coast and its offshore islands, as well as the Preseli Hills in the north and the inland waters of the Cleddau rivers near Milford Haven. Pembrokeshire's sea cliffs and islands support huge breeding populations of seabirds, while seals, dolphins, porpoises and whales are frequently spotted in coastal waters.

There are three national park information centres – in Tenby, St Davids and Newport – and the local tourist offices scattered across Pembrokeshire are well stocked with park paraphernalia.

Brecon Beacons National Park

Rippling dramatically for 45 miles from Llandeilo in the west, all the way to the English border, **Brecon Beacons National Park** (Parc Cenedlaethol Bannau Brycheiniog; www.breconbeacons.org) encompasses some of the finest scenery in Mid-Wales. High mountain plateaux of grass and heather, their northern rims scalloped with glacier-scoured hollows, rise above wooded, waterfall-splashed valleys, and green, rural landscapes. It couldn't be more different than rock-strewn Snowdonia to the north, but it offers comparable thrills.

There are four distinct regions within the park, neatly bounded by main roads: the wild, lonely Black Mountain in the west, with its high moors and glacial lakes; Fforest Fawr, whose rushing streams and spectacular waterfalls form the headwaters of the Tawe and Neath Rivers; the Brecon Beacons proper, a group of very distinctive, flat-topped hills that includes Pen-y-Fan (886m), the park's highest peak; and, from the A40 northeast to the English border, the rolling heathland ridges of the Black Mountains.

There are hundreds of walking routes in the park, and the park's staff organise guided walks and other events throughout the summer. Maps and walk cards are available from local tourist offices, as well as the main visitor centre near Libanus.

Hay-on-Wye

This pretty little town on the banks of the River Wye, just inside the Welsh border, has become famous as one of Wales' literary landmarks. First came the explosion in secondhand bookshops, a charge led by local maverick Richard Booth, who opened his eponymous bookshop in the 1960s and went on to proclaim himself the King of Hay. Then came the town's famous literary knees-up, the **Hay Festival** (☎01497-822629; www.hayfestival.com) – dubbed 'the Woodstock of the mind' by Bill Clinton – which was established in 1988 and now attracts bookworms from all over the world, not to mention a host of heavyweight authors.

The 10-day festival is held in late May, when accommodation is almost impossible to find unless you've booked in advance.

Snowdonia National Park

Snowdonia National Park (Parc Cenedlaethol Eryri; www.eryri-npa.gov.uk) was founded in 1951 (making it Wales' first national park), primarily to keep the area from being loved to death. This is, after all, Wales' best known and most heavily used slice of nature, with the busiest part around Snowdon (1085m) itself. Around 350,000 people climb, walk or take the train to the summit each year, and all those sturdy shoes make trail maintenance a never-ending task for park staff.

Yet the park is so much more than just Snowdon, stretching some 35 miles east to west and over 50 miles north to south and incorporating coastal areas, rivers and Wales' biggest natural lake. The Welsh name for Snowdonia is Eryri (eh-ruh-ree), meaning highlands. The Welsh call Snowdon itself Yr Wyddfa (uhr-with-vuh), meaning Great Tomb – according to legend a giant called Rita Gawr was slain here by King Arthur and is buried at the summit.

BETWS-Y-COED

If you're looking for a base with an Alpine feel from which to explore Snowdonia National Park, the bustling little stone village of Betws-y-Coed (bet-us-ee-koyd) stands out as a natural option. It boasts a postcard-perfect setting above an inky river, engulfed in the verdant leafiness of the Gwydyr Forest and near the junction of three river valleys: the Llugwy, the Conwy and the Lledr.

Sleeping & Eating

Ty Gwyn Hotel HOTEL ££
(☎01690-710383; www.tygwynhotel.co.uk; r £56-130; P 📶) This ex-coaching inn has been welcoming guests since 1636, its venerable age borne out by misshapen rooms, low ceilings and exposed beams. Predictably, not all rooms have ensuites. The menu focuses on hearty, meaty mains (£13 to £18). It's located on the A5, just across Waterloo Bridge.

Betws-y-Coed Youth Hostel HOSTEL £
(☎01690-710796; www.yha.org.uk; Swallow Falls; dm from £18) A functional hostel that's part of a bustling traveller hub with camping and a pub.

Information

National Park Information Centre (☎01690-710426; www.betws-y-coed.co.uk; Royal Oak Stables; ⊙9.30am-4.30pm, to 5.30pm Easter-Oct)

Getting There & Away

BUS Snowdon Sherpa buses S2 and S6 stop outside the train station, with services to Swallow Falls (five minutes), Capel Curig (10 minutes), Pen-y-Pass (20 minutes) and Llanberis (30 minutes).

TRAIN Betws-y-Coed is on the **Conwy Valley Line** (www.conwyvalleyrailway.co.uk), with six daily services (three on Sunday) to Llandudno (£5.60, 52 minutes) and Blaenau Ffestiniog (£4.50, 27 minutes).

BEDDGELERT

Charming little Beddgelert is a conservation village of rough grey stone buildings overlooking the trickling River Glaslyn with its ivy-covered bridge. Flowers festoon the village in spring and the surrounding hills are covered in a purple blaze of heather in summer, reminiscent of a Scottish glen.

Sleeping & Eating

Plas Tan Y Graig B&B ££
(☎01766-890310; www.plastanygraig.co.uk; d £82; 📶) This bright, friendly place is the best B&B in the heart of the village. It has seven uncluttered rooms, five with bathrooms, and a lounge full of maps and books.

Information

Tourist Office & National Park Information Centre (☎01766-890615; Canolfan Hebog; ⊙9.30am-5.30pm daily Easter-Oct, to 4.30pm Fri-Sun Nov-Easter)

Getting There & Away

Beddgelert is a stop on the historic Welsh Highland Railway, which runs between Caernarfon (£25.20 return, 1½ hours) and Porthmadog (£18 return, 50 minutes). Snowdon Sherpa bus S4 heads from here to Caernarfon (30 minutes), while S97 heads to Porthmadog (25 minutes) in one direction and Pen-y-Pass (20 minutes) in the other.

CAPEL CURIG

Tiny Capel Curig, 5 miles west of Betws-y-Coed, is one of Snowdonia's oldest hill stations, and has long been a magnet for walkers, climbers and other outdoor junkies. At the western edge of the village, the **Plas y Brenin Nation Mountain Centre** (☎01690-720214; www.pyb.co.uk) offers an array of residential courses including rock climbing, mountaineering, kayaking and canoeing. Taster days run throughout the school holidays with an introduction to two activities for £35.

The superb five-star **Plas Curig Hostel** (☎01690-720225; www.snowdoniahostel.co.uk; dm/d/f from £22.50/50/90; P 📶), opened in 2011, offers great views across to the Snowdon Horseshoe.

Snowdon Sherpa buses S2 and S6 stop here.

SNOWDON

No Snowdonia experience is complete without coming face-to-face with Snowdon (1085m), Wales' highest mountain. On a clear day the views stretch to Ireland and the Isle of Man over Snowdon's fine jagged ridges, which drop away in great swoops to sheltered *cwms* (valleys) and deep lakes. Even on a gloomy day you could find yourself above the clouds. At the top is the striking **Hafod Eryri** visitor centre, opened in 2009 by Prince Charles.

Six paths of varying length and difficulty lead to the summit, all taking around six hours return, or you can cheat and catch the **Snowdon Mountain Railway** (☎0844 493 8120; www.snowdonrailway.co.uk; return adult/child £25/18; ⏲9am-5pm mid-Mar–Oct), opened in 1896 and still the UK's only public rack-and-pinion railway.

However you get to the summit, take warm, waterproof clothing, wear sturdy footwear and check the weather forecast before setting out.

Sleeping & Eating

Pen-y-Gwyrd HOTEL £

(☎01286-870211; www.pyg.co.uk; Nant Gwynant; r with/without bathroom 50/42) Eccentric but full of atmosphere, Pen-y-Gwryd was used as a training base by the 1953 Everest team, and memorabilia from their stay includes their signatures on the dining-room ceiling. The hotel is usually open January to October. You'll find it below Pen-y-Pass, at the junction of the A498 and A4086.

Snowdon Ranger Youth Hostel HOSTEL £

(☎0845 371 9659; www.yha.org.uk; dm from £20) On the A4085, 5 miles north of Beddgelert, at the trailhead for the Snowdon Ranger Path, this former inn is full of character and has its own adjoining lakeside beach.

Bryn Gwynant YHA HOSTEL £

(☎0845 371 9108; www.yha.org.uk; Nantgwynant; dm from £15; ⏲closed weekdays in winter) Victorian mansion overlooking the lake, 4 miles east of Beddgelert.

Getting There & Away

The Welsh Highland Railway stops at the trailhead of the Rhyd Ddu path, and there is a request stop (Snowdon Ranger Halt) where you can alight for the Snowdon Ranger path.

Snowdon Sherpa buses (£1 on buses S1, S2, S6; adult/child day ticket £4/2) stop at all of the trailheads.

CONWY CASTLE

On the north coast of Wales, the historic town of Conwy is utterly dominated by the Unesco-designated cultural treasure of **Conwy Castle** (Cadw; adult/child £4.80/4.30; ⏲9.30am-6pm Jul & Aug, 9.30am-5pm Mar-Jun, Sep & Oct, 10am-4pm Mon-Sat, 11am-4pm Sun Nov-Feb), the most stunning of all Edward I's Welsh fortresses. Built between 1277 and 1307 on a rocky outcrop, it has commanding views across the estuary and Snowdonia National Park. Exploring the castle's nooks and crannies makes for a superb, living-history visit, but best of all, head to the **battlements** for panoramic views and an overview of Conwy's majestic complexity. The 1200m-long **town wall** was built with the castle to guard Conwy's residents at night. Today you can walk partway round the wall for more excellent views; the best are to be had from Upper Gate.

SOUTHERN SCOTLAND

North of the border with England, and below the Central Belt region of Edinburgh and Glasgow, sits the broad region of southern Scotland. The western side of this region offers some fine scenery – high hills, moors, forests and a craggy coastline – without the attendant tour buses and crowds you might find in the Highlands. Ayrshire is immediately southwest of Glasgow, with Dumfries & Galloway beyond. Warmed by Gulf Stream currents, it also enjoys the region's mildest climate (we're speaking relatively here). This was also the home of Robbie Burns, Scotland's national poet. The eastern side of this region is called the Scottish Borders – an area of historic towns, ancient abbeys and lush glens with a unique beauty and romance that's often missed by travellers rushing through on their way to Edinburgh.

Alloway

The pretty town of Alloway is best known as the birthplace of Robert Burns (1759–96), Scotland's most famous poet and a national hero whose birthday (25 January) is celebrated as Burns Night by Scots around the world. He's best-known for penning the words to 'Auld Lang Syne', but wrote hundreds of poems during his short 37 years, mostly in Lallans, the Scottish Lowland dialect of English. For further information on Burns' life and work, visit www.robertburns.org.

The **Robert Burns Birthplace Museum** (NTS; www.nts.org.uk; adult/child £8/6; ⏲10am-5pm Oct-Mar, to 5.30pm Apr-Sep) displays a solid collection of Burnsiana, including manuscripts and possessions of the poet, such as the pistols he packed in order to carry out his daily work as a taxman. A Burns jukebox allows you to select readings of your favourite verses, and there are other entertaining audio and visual performances.

To get here, aim for the town of Ayr (easily reached from Glasgow), then take bus 57 (Monday to Saturday, hourly, 10 minutes).

Melrose

POP 1656

On the eastern side of southern Scotland, and epitomising the ambience of the Borders, the charming town of Melrose sits at the feet of the three heather-covered Eildon Hills, featuring a classic market square and one of the finest ruined abbeys in the region.

Sights

Melrose Abbey RUIN

(HS; www.historic-scotland.gov.uk; adult/child £5.50/3.30; ⏲9.30am-5.30pm Apr-Sep, to 4.30pm Oct-Mar) Perhaps the most interesting of all the great Border abbeys, the red-sandstone Melrose Abbey was repeatedly destroyed by the English in the 14th century. The remaining broken shell is pure Gothic and the ruins are famous for their decorative stonework – see if you can glimpse the pig gargoyle playing the bagpipes on the roof. You can climb to the top for tremendous views.

The abbey was founded by David I in 1136 for Cistercian monks from Rievaulx Abbey in Yorkshire. It was rebuilt by Robert the Bruce, whose heart is buried here. The ruins date from the 14th and 15th centuries, and were repaired by Sir Walter Scott in the 19th century.

The adjoining **museum** has many fine examples of 12th- to 15th-century stonework and pottery found in the area. Note the impressive remains of the 'great drain' outside – a medieval sewerage system.

Sleeping

TOP CHOICE **Old Bank House** B&B £

(☎01896-823712; www.oldbankhousemelrose.co.uk; 27 Buccleuch St; s/d £45/60; 📶🐾) Right in the middle of town, this is a superb B&B in a charming old building. Art on the walls, spacious rooms, and a sumptuous breakfast room are complemented by a generous can-do attitude. A great Borders base.

Information

Tourist Office (☎01896-822283; melrose@visitscotland.com; Abbey St; ⏲10am-4.30pm Mon-Sat, noon-4pm Sun Apr-Oct, 10am-4pm Fri & Sat Nov-Mar) By the abbey.

Getting There & Away

First (www.firstgroup.com) buses run to/from Edinburgh (£6, 2¼ hours, hourly) via Peebles. Change in Galashiels (20 minutes, frequent) for more-frequent Edinburgh services and for other Borders destinations.

WORTH A TRIP

ISLE OF ARRAN

Enchanting Arran is a jewel in Scotland's scenic crown, with some of Scotland's most dramatic landscapes – best explored by pulling on the hiking boots or jumping on a bicycle.

The island is home to a host of cosy pubs, inns and B&Bs, as well as lots of intriguing villages such as seaside **Brodick**, with an excellent brewery, and **Lochranza**, with its ruined 13th-century castle and world-famous whisky distillery. Wildlife is another island highlight – red deer, seals and eagles can all be spotted as you make your way around the Arran's shores.

Calmac runs ferries between Ardrossan and Brodick (passenger/car return £9.70/59, 55 minutes, four to eight daily). From April to late October services also run between Claonaig and Lochranza (passenger/car return £8.75/39.10, 30 minutes, seven to nine daily).

Edinburgh

POP 440,000

Edinburgh is a city that begs to be explored. From the vaults and *wynds* (narrow lanes) that riddle the Old Town, to the urban villages of Stockbridge and Cramond, it's filled with quirky come-hither nooks that tempt you to walk just a little bit further. And every corner turned reveals sudden views and unexpected vistas – green sunlit hills, a glimpse of rust-red crags, a blue flash of distant sea.

But there's more to Edinburgh than sightseeing – there are top shops, world-class restaurants and a bacchanalia of bars to enjoy, and in August during festival time, it seems as if half the world descends on Edinburgh for one enormous party.

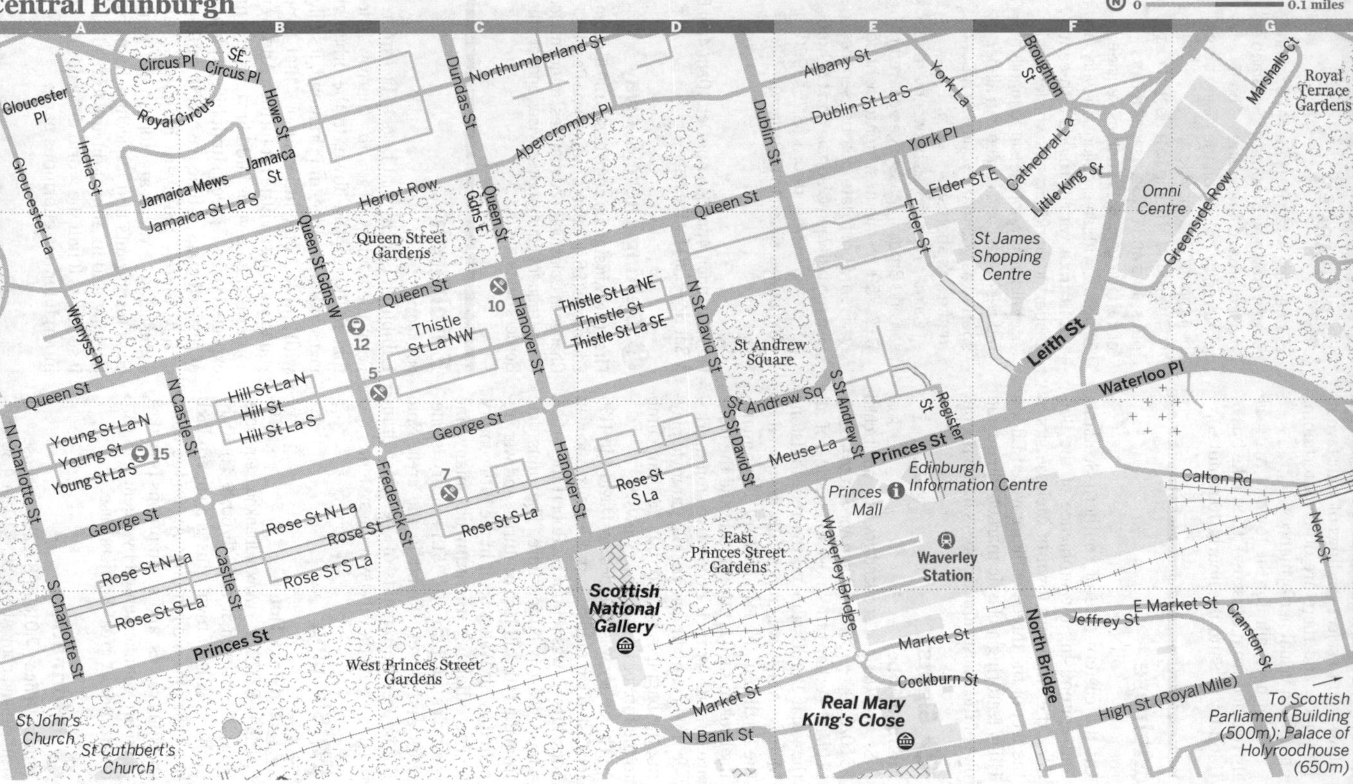
Central Edinburgh
0 200 m
0 0.1 miles
A
B
C
D
E
F
G
1
2
3
4
Circus Pl
SE
Circus Pl
Gloucester Pl
Royal Circus
India St
Gloucester La
Jamaica Mews
Jamaica St
Jamaica St La S
Howe St
Heriot Row
Queen Street Gardens
Queen St Gdns W
Queen St Gdns E
Dundas St
Northumberland St
Abercromby Pl
Albany St
Dublin St La S
Dublin St
York La
York Pl
Broughton St
Marshalls Ct
Royal Terrace Gardens
Cathedral La
Little King St
Elder St E
Elder St
Omni Centre
Greenside Row
St James Shopping Centre
Leith St
Waterloo Pl
Queen St
Wemyss Pl
12
Thistle St La NW
10
Hanover St
Thistle St La NE
Thistle St
Thistle St La SE
N St David St
St Andrew Square
S St Andrew St
St Andrew Sq
Register St
5
Hill St La N
Hill St
Hill St La S
N Castle St
Young St La N
Young St
Young St La S
15
N Charlotte St
George St
Frederick St
7
Rose St N La
Rose St
Rose St S La
Rose St S La
S St David St
Meuse La
Princes St
Edinburgh Information Centre
Princes Mall
Calton Rd
New St
Castle St
S Charlotte St
East Princes Street Gardens
Waverley Bridge
Waverley Station
Scottish National Gallery
E Market St
Jeffrey St
Cranston St
Market St
North Bridge
West Princes Street Gardens
Cockburn St
Market St
High St (Royal Mile)
Real Mary King's Close
N Bank St
To Scottish Parliament Building (500m); Palace of Holyroodhouse (650m)
St John's Church
St Cuthbert's Church

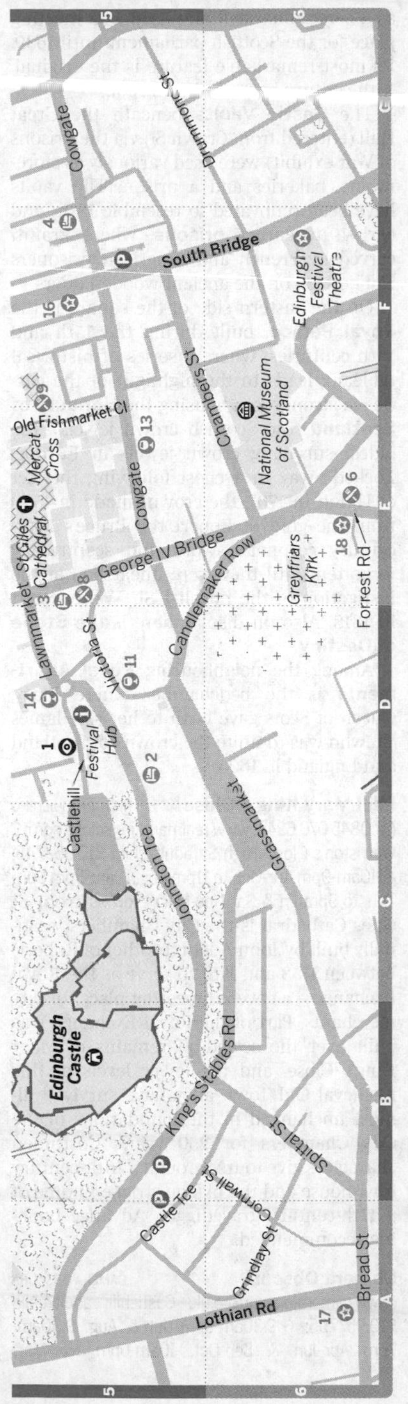

Central Edinburgh

Top Sights

Edinburgh Castle B5
Real Mary King's Close F4
Scottish National Gallery D4

Sights

1 Camera Obscura D5

Sleeping

2 Castle Rock Hostel D5
3 Hotel Missoni E5
4 Smart City Hostel F5

Eating

5 Café Marlayne B2
6 Mums E6
7 Mussel Inn C3
8 Ondine E5
9 Passepartout F5
10 The Dogs C2

Drinking

11 Bow Bar D5
12 Bramble B2
13 BrewDog E5
14 Jolly Judge D5
15 Oxford Bar A3

Entertainment

16 Cabaret Voltaire F5
17 Henry's Cellar A6
18 Sandy Bell's E6

Sights

Edinburgh's city centre is divided into two parts – Old Town and New Town – split by Princess Street Gardens. Most of the sights are here. A major exception is the Royal Yacht *Britannia,* in the redeveloped docklands district of Leith, 2 miles northeast of the centre.

OLD TOWN

Edinburgh's Old Town stretches along a ridge to the east of the castle, a jumbled maze of closes (alleys) and *wynds,* stairs and vaults, and cleft along its spine by the cobbled ravine of the Royal Mile, the name of the line of streets between the castle and the Palace of Holyroodhouse.

TOP CHOICE Edinburgh Castle CASTLE

(www.edinburghcastle.gov.uk; adult/child incl audioguide £16/9.60; ⌚9.30am-6pm Apr-Sep, to 5pm Oct-Mar, last admission 45min before closing) The brooding, black crags of Castle Rock, rising

WANT MORE?

For in-depth information, reviews and recommendations at your fingertips, head to the Apple App Store to purchase Lonely Planet's *Edinburgh City Guide* iPhone app.

Alternatively, head to **Lonely Planet** (www.lonelyplanet.com/scotland/edinburgh) for planning advice, author recommendations, traveller reviews and insider tips.

above the western end of Princes St, are the very reason for Edinburgh's existence. This rocky hill was the most easily defended hilltop on the invasion route between England and central Scotland, a route followed by countless armies from the Roman legions of the 1st and 2nd centuries AD to the Jacobite troops of Bonnie Prince Charlie in 1745.

Edinburgh Castle has played a pivotal role in Scottish history, both as a royal residence – King Malcolm Canmore (r 1058–93) and Queen Margaret first made their home here in the 11th century – and as a military stronghold. The castle last saw military action in 1745; from then until the 1920s it served as the British army's main base in Scotland. Today it is one of Scotland's most atmospheric, most popular – and most expensive – tourist attractions.

The **Entrance Gateway**, flanked by statues of Robert the Bruce and William Wallace, opens to a cobbled lane that leads up beneath the 16th-century **Portcullis Gate** to the cannons ranged along the Argyle and Mills Mount batteries. The battlements here have great views over New Town to the Firth of Forth. At the far end of Mills Mount Battery is the famous **One O'Clock Gun**, where crowds gather to watch a gleaming WWII 25-pounder fire an ear-splitting time signal at exactly 1pm (every day except Sunday, Christmas Day and Good Friday).

South of Mills Mount, the road curls up leftwards through **Foog's Gate** to the highest part of Castle Rock, crowned by the tiny, Romanesque **St Margaret's Chapel**, the oldest surviving building in Edinburgh. The main group of buildings on the summit of Castle Rock are ranged around Crown Sq, dominated by the shrine of the **Scottish National War Memorial**. Opposite is the **Great Hall**, built for James IV (r 1488–1513) as a ceremonial hall and used as a meeting place for the Scottish parliament until 1639. Its most remarkable feature is the original, 16th-century hammer-beam roof.

The **Castle Vaults** beneath the Great Hall (entered from Crown Sq via the Prisons of War exhibit) were used variously as storerooms, bakeries and a prison. The vaults have been renovated to resemble 18th- and early-19th-century **prisons**, where graffiti carved by French and American prisoners can be seen on the ancient wooden doors.

On the eastern side of the square is the **Royal Palace**, built during the 15th and 16th centuries, where a series of historical tableaux leads to the highlight of the castle – a strongroom housing the **Honours of Scotland** (the Scottish crown jewels), the oldest surviving crown jewels in Europe. Locked away in a chest following the Act of Union in 1707, the crown (made in 1540 from the gold of Robert the Bruce's 14th-century coronet), sword and sceptre lay forgotten until they were unearthed at the instigation of the novelist Sir Walter Scott in 1818. Also on display here is the **Stone of Destiny**.

Among the neighbouring **Royal Apartments** is the bedchamber where Mary, Queen of Scots gave birth to her son James VI, who was to unite the crowns of Scotland and England in 1603.

Real Mary King's Close HISTORIC BUILDING

(☎0845 070 6244; www.realmarykingsclose.com; 2 Warriston's Close, High St; adult/child £12.95/7.45; ⏲10am-9pm Apr-Oct, to 11pm Aug, 10am-5pm Sun-Thu, to 9pm Fri & Sat Nov-Mar) Across from St Giles Cathedral is the City Chambers, originally built by John Adam (brother of Robert) between 1753 and 1761 to serve as the Royal Exchange – a covered meeting place for city merchants. Part of the Royal Exchange was built over the sealed-off remains of Mary King's Close, and the lower levels of this medieval Old Town alley have survived almost unchanged in the foundations of the City Chambers for 250 years. Costumed characters give tours through a 16th-century townhouse and the plague-stricken home of a 17th-century gravedigger. Advance booking recommended.

Camera Obscura CAMERA OBSCURA

(www.camera-obscura.co.uk; Castlehill; adult/child £10.95/7.95; ⏲9.30am-9pm Jul & Aug, 9.30am-7pm Apr-Jun & Sep-Oct, 10am-6pm Nov-Mar)

Edinburgh's camera obscura is a curious 19th-century device – in constant use since 1853 – that uses lenses and mirrors to throw a live image of the city onto a large horizontal screen. Stairs lead up through various displays to the **Outlook Tower**, which offers great views over the city.

FREE Scottish Parliament Building NOTABLE BUILDING
(☎0131-348 5200; www.scottish.parliament.uk; ⏲9am-6.30pm Tue-Thu, 10am-5.30pm Mon & Fri in session, 10am-6pm Mon-Fri in recess Apr-Oct, 10am-4pm in recess Nov-Mar) The Scottish parliament building, built on the site of a former brewery close to the Palace of Holyroodhouse, was officially opened by HM the Queen in October 2005. The public areas of the parliament building – the Main Hall, where there is an exhibition, a shop and cafe, and the public gallery in the Debating Chamber – are open to visitors (tickets needed for public gallery – see website for details). You can also take a free, one-hour guided tour (advance booking recommended) that includes a visit to the Debating Chamber, a committee room, the Garden Lobby and, when possible, the office of an MSP (Member of the Scottish Parliament).

TOP CHOICE Palace of Holyroodhouse PALACE
(www.royalcollection.org.uk; adult/child £11/6.65; ⏲9.30am-6pm Apr-Oct, to 4.30pm Nov-Mar) This palace is the royal family's official residence in Scotland, but is more famous as the 16th-century home of the ill-fated Mary, Queen of Scots. The oldest surviving part of the building, the northwestern tower, was built in 1529 as a royal apartment for James V and his wife, Mary of Guise. Mary, Queen of Scots spent six turbulent years here, during which time she debated with John Knox, married both her first and second husbands, and witnessed the murder of her secretary David Rizzio. The palace is closed to the public when the royal family is visiting and during state functions (usually in mid-May, and mid-June to early July; check the website for exact dates).

Holyrood Park PARK
In Holyrood Park Edinburgh is blessed with a little bit of wilderness in the heart of the city. The former hunting ground of Scottish monarchs, the park covers 263 hectares of varied landscape, including crags, moorland and a loch. The highest point is the 251m summit of **Arthur's Seat**, the deeply eroded remnant of a long-extinct volcano. Holyrood Park can be circumnavigated by car or bike along Queen's Dr, and you can hike from Holyrood to the summit in around 45 minutes.

FREE Scottish National Gallery GALLERY
(www.nationalgalleries.org; The Mound; fee for special exhibitions; ⏲10am-5pm Fri-Wed, to 7pm Thu) Designed by William Playfair, this imposing classical building with its Ionic porticoes dates from the 1850s. Its octagonal rooms, lit by skylights, have been restored to their original Victorian decor of deep-green carpets and dark-red walls.

The gallery houses an important collection of **European art** from the Renaissance to post-Impressionism, with works by Verrocchio (Leonardo da Vinci's teacher), Tintoretto, Titian, Holbein, Rubens, Van Dyck, Vermeer, El Greco, Poussin, Rembrandt, Gainsborough, Turner, Constable, Monet, Pissarro, Gauguin and Cézanne. Each January the gallery exhibits its collection of **Turner watercolours**, bequeathed by Henry Vaughan in 1900. Room X is graced by Antonio Canova's white marble sculpture, **The Three Graces**; it is owned jointly with London's Victoria & Albert Museum.

The basement galleries dedicated to **Scottish art** include glowing portraits by Allan Ramsay and Sir Henry Raeburn, rural scenes by Sir David Wilkie and Impressionistic landscapes by William MacTaggart.

Royal Yacht Britannia SHIP
(www.royalyachtbritannia.co.uk; Ocean Terminal; adult/child £11.75/7.50; ⏲9.30am-4.30pm Jul-Sep, to 4pm Apr-Jun & Oct, 10am-3.30pm Nov-Mar, last admission 90min before closing) One of Scotland's biggest tourist attractions is the former Royal Yacht *Britannia*. She was the British royal family's floating home during their foreign travels from the time of her launch in 1953 until her decommissioning in 1997, and is now moored permanently in front of Ocean Terminal.

Britannia was joined in 2010 by the 1930s racing yacht *Bloodhound*, which was owned by the Queen in the 1960s. She is moored alongside *Britannia* (except in July and August, when she is away cruising) as part of an exhibition about the Royal Family's love of all things nautical.

The Majestic Tour bus runs from Waverley Bridge to *Britannia* during opening times. Alternatively, take Lothian Bus 11, 22 or 35 to Ocean Terminal.

Tours

Bus Tours

Open-topped bus tours leave from Waverley Bridge and offer hop-on, hop-off tours of the main sights. They're a good way to get your bearings, although with a bus map and a Day Saver bus ticket (£3) you could do much the same thing but without the commentary.

City Sightseeing BUS TOUR
(www.edinburghtour.com; adult/child £12/5) Bright-red, open-top buses depart every 20 minutes from Waverley Bridge.

Majestic Tour BUS TOUR
(www.edinburghtour.com; adult/child £12/5) Runs every 30 minutes (every 20 minutes in July and August) from Waverley Bridge to the Royal Yacht *Britannia* at Ocean Terminal via the New Town, Royal Botanic Garden and Newhaven, returning via Leith Walk, Holyrood and the Royal Mile.

Walking Tours

Black Hart Storytellers WALKING TOUR
(www.blackhart.uk.com; adult/concession £10/5) The 'City of the Dead' tour of Greyfriars Kirkyard is probably the scariest of Edinburgh's 'ghost' tours. Not suitable for young children.

Edinburgh Literary Pub Tour WALKING TOUR
(www.edinburghliterarypubtour.co.uk; adult/student £10/8) An enlightening two-hour trawl through Edinburgh's literary history – and its associated *howffs* (pubs) – in the entertaining company of Messrs Clart and McBrain. One of the city's best walking tours.

Rebus Tours WALKING TOUR
(www.rebustours.com; adult/student £10/9) Tours of the 'hidden Edinburgh' frequented by novelist Ian Rankin's fictional detective, John Rebus. Not recommended for children under 10.

Sleeping

OLD TOWN

TOP CHOICE **Hotel Missoni** BOUTIQUE HOTEL £££
(☎0131-220 6666; www.hotelmissoni.com; 1 George IV Bridge; r £90-225; wi-fi) The Italian fashion house has established a style icon in the heart of the medieval Old Town with this bold statement of a hotel – modernistic architecture, black-and-white decor with well-judged splashes of colour, impeccably mannered staff and, most importantly, very comfortable bedrooms and bathrooms with lots of nice little touches, from fresh milk in the minibar to plush bathrobes.

TOP CHOICE **Smart City Hostel** HOSTEL £
(☎0870 892 3000; www.smartcityhostels.com; 50 Blackfriars St; dm from £22, tr £107; @ wi-fi) A big (620 beds), bright, modern hostel that feels more like a hotel. Lockers in every room, a huge bar and a central location just off the Royal Mile make this a favourite place to stay for the young, party-mad crowd – don't expect a quiet night!

Castle Rock Hostel HOSTEL £
(☎0131-225 9666; www.scotlands-top-hostels.com; 15 Johnston Tce; dm/d £22/50; @ wi-fi) With its bright, spacious, single-sex dorms, superb views and friendly staff, the 200-bed Castle Rock has lots to like. It has a great location –

FESTIVAL CITY

Edinburgh boasts a frenzy of festivals, especially in August. See www.edinburghfestivals.co.uk for more.

Edinburgh Festival Fringe (☎0131-226 0026; www.edfringe.com; 180 High St) The biggest festival of the performing arts anywhere in the world, held over 3½ weeks in August; the last two weeks overlap with the first two weeks of the Edinburgh International Festival.

Edinburgh International Festival (☎0131-473 2099; www.eif.co.uk) Three weeks of inspirational music, opera, theatre and dance in August. Tickets can be purchased at the **Hub** (☎01131-473 2000; www.thehub-edinburgh.com; Castlehill; admission free; ⏲ticket centre 10am-5pm Mon-Sat).

Edinburgh Military Tattoo (☎0131-225 1188; www.edintattoo.co.uk; Tattoo Office, 32 Market St) A spectacular display of military marching bands, massed pipes and drums, acrobats, cheerleaders and motorcycle display teams, all played out in front of the magnificent backdrop of the floodlit castle during the first three weeks of August.

DON'T MISS

ROSSLYN CHAPEL

The success of Dan Brown's novel *The Da Vinci Code* and the subsequent Hollywood film has seen a flood of visitors descend on Scotland's most beautiful and enigmatic church: **Rosslyn Chapel** (Collegiate Church of St Matthew; www.rosslynchapel.org.uk; adult/child £9/free; ⌚9.30am-5pm Mon-Sat, noon-4.45pm Sun). The chapel was built in the mid-15th century for William St Clair, third earl of Orkney, and the ornate interior is a monument to the mason's art. As well as flowers, vines, angels and biblical figures, the carved stones include many examples of the pagan 'Green Man'; other figures are associated with Freemasonry and the Knights Templar. Intriguingly, there are also carvings of plants from the Americas that predate Columbus' voyage of discovery. The symbolism of these images has led some researchers to conclude that Rosslyn might be a secret Templar repository, concealing anything from the Holy Grail or the head of John the Baptist to the body of Christ himself.

The chapel is in Roslin, 7 miles south of Edinburgh's centre. Lothian Bus 15 (not 15A) runs from the west end of Princes St in Edinburgh to Roslin (£1.40, 30 minutes, every 30 minutes) via Penicuik (it may be faster to catch any bus to Penicuik, then the 15 to Roslin).

the only way to get closer to the castle would be to pitch a tent on the esplanade – a games room, reading lounge and big-screen video nights.

NEW TOWN & AROUND

B+B Edinburgh HOTEL ££

(☎0131-225 5084; www.bb-edinburgh.com; 3 Rothesay Tce; s/d £99/140; ⓦ) Built in 1883 as a grand home for the proprietor of the *Scotsman* newspaper, this Victorian extravaganza of carved oak, parquet floors, stained glass and elaborate fireplaces was given a designer makeover in 2011 to create a striking contemporary hotel.

Dene Guest House B&B ££

(☎0131-556 2700; www.deneguesthouse.com; 7 Eyre Pl; per person £25-50) The Dene is a friendly and informal place, set in a charming Georgian townhouse, with a welcoming owner and spacious bedrooms. The inexpensive single rooms make it ideal for solo travellers; children under 10 staying in their parents' room pay half price.

Eating

OLD TOWN

TOP CHOICE **Ondine** SEAFOOD £££

(☎0131-226 1888; www.ondinerestaurant.co.uk; 2 George IV Bridge; mains £15-25; ⌚lunch & dinner) Ondine is one of Edinburgh's finest seafood restaurants, with a menu based on sustainably sourced fish. Take an octopus-inspired seat at the curved Crustacean Bar and tuck into oysters Kilpatrick, lobster thermidor, a roast shellfish platter, or just good old haddock and chips (with minted pea purée, just to keep things posh). The two-course lunch (noon to 2.30pm) and pretheatre (5pm to 6.30pm) menu costs £17.

Passepartout INTERNATIONAL £

(☎0131-629 0252; 7 Old Fishmarket Close; platters for 2 £12-13) Hidden down a steep cobbled alley off the Royal Mile, with three indoor seating areas (including a 'cinema room' screening old movies) and a lovely little sun-trap of an outdoor terrace, this French-owned, Indian-inspired bistro offers an eclectic menu of dishes – from lobster with mussels to chickpea curry to kebabs – served as sharing platters for two, which you eat with your fingers.

Mums CAFE £

(www.monstermashcafe.co.uk; 4a Forrest Rd; mains £6-9; ⌚9am-10pm Mon-Sat, 10am-10pm Sun) This nostalgia-fuelled cafe serves up classic British comfort food that wouldn't look out of place on a 1950s menu – bacon and eggs, bangers and mash, shepherd's pie, fish and chips. But there's a twist – the food is all top-quality nosh freshly prepared from local produce, including Crombie's gourmet sausages.

NEW TOWN

TOP CHOICE **The Dogs** BRITISH ££

(☎0131-220 1208; www.thedogsonline.co.uk; 110 Hanover St; mains £9-13; ⌚noon-4pm & 5-10pm) One of the coolest tables in town, this bistro-style place uses cheaper cuts of meat and less-well-known, more-sustainable species of fish to create hearty, no-nonsense dishes such as lamb sweetbreads on toast, baked coley with *skirlie* (fried oatmeal and onion), and devilled liver with bacon and onions.

Mussel Inn SEAFOOD ££
(www.mussel-inn.com; 61-65 Rose St; mains £9-23; noon-10pm;) Owned by west-coast shellfish farmers, the Mussel Inn provides a direct outlet for fresh Scottish seafood. A 1kg pot of mussels with a choice of sauces – try leek, Dijon mustard and cream – costs £12.20.

Café Marlayne FRENCH ££
(0131-226 2230; www.cafemarlayne.com; 76 Thistle St; mains £12-15; noon-10pm) All weathered wood and candlelit tables, Café Marlayne is a cosy nook offering French farmhouse cooking – *brandade de morue* (salt cod) with green salad, slow-roast rack of lamb, *boudin noir* (black pudding) with scallops and sautéed potato – at very reasonable prices. Booking recommended.

Drinking

OLD TOWN

Bow Bar PUB
(80 West Bow) One of the city's best traditional-style pubs (it's not as old as it looks), serving a range of excellent real ales and a vast selection of malt whiskies, the Bow Bar often has standing-room only on Friday and Saturday evenings.

Jolly Judge PUB
(www.jollyjudge.co.uk; 7a James Ct;) A snug little *howff* tucked away down a close, the Judge exudes a cosy, 17th-century atmosphere (low, timber-beamed painted ceilings) and has the added attraction of a cheering open fire in cold weather.

BrewDog BAR
(www.brewdog.com; 143 Cowgate;) A new bar from Scotland's self-styled 'punk brewery', BrewDog stands out among the grimy, sticky-floored dives that line the Cowgate, with its cool, industrial-chic designer look.

NEW TOWN

Oxford Bar PUB
(www.oxfordbar.co.uk; 8 Young St) The Oxford is that rarest of things: a real pub for real people, with no 'theme', no music, no frills and no pretensions. 'The Ox' has been immortalised by Ian Rankin, author of the Inspector Rebus novels, whose fictional detective is a regular here.

Bramble COCKTAIL BAR
(www.bramblebar.co.uk; 16a Queen St) One of those places that easily earns the sobriquet 'best-kept secret', Bramble is an unmarked cellar bar where a maze of stone and brick hideaways conceals what is arguably the city's best cocktail bar.

Entertainment

The comprehensive source for what's on is *The List* (www.list.co.uk), an excellent magazine covering entertainment options in both Edinburgh and Glasgow.

Henry's Cellar LIVE MUSIC
(www.musicglue.com/theraft; 8a Morrison St) One of Edinburgh's most eclectic live-music venues, Henry's has something going on most nights of the week, from rock and indie to 'Balkan-inspired folk'. Open till 3am at weekends.

Sandy Bell's TRADITIONAL MUSIC
(25 Forrest Rd) This unassuming pub is a stalwart of the traditional music scene (the founder's wife sang with The Corries).

Cabaret Voltaire CLUB
(www.thecabaretvoltaire.com; 36 Blair St) An atmospheric warren of stone-lined vaults houses Edinburgh's most 'alternative' club.

Information

Edinburgh Information Centre (0131-473 3868; www.edinburgh.org; Princes Mall, 3 Princes St; 9am-9pm Mon-Sat, 10am-8pm Sun Jul & Aug, 9am-7pm Mon-Sat, 10am-7pm Sun May-Jun & Sep, 9am-5pm Mon-Wed, to 6pm Thu-Sun Oct-Apr) Includes an accommodation booking service, currency exchange, gift and bookshop, internet access and counters selling tickets for Edinburgh city tours and Scottish Citylink bus services.

Getting There & Away

Air

Edinburgh Airport (0131-333 1000; www.edinburghairport.com), 8 miles west of the city, has numerous flights to other parts of Scotland and the UK, Ireland and mainland Europe.

Bus

Edinburgh bus station is at the northeast corner of St Andrew Sq, with pedestrian entrances from the square and from Elder St.

Scottish Citylink (0871 266 3333; www.citylink.co.uk) buses connect Edinburgh with all of Scotland's cities and major towns. The following are sample one-way fares departing from Edinburgh.

DESTINATION	FARE
Aberdeen	£28
Dundee	£15
Fort William	£33
Glasgow	£6.80
Inverness	£28
Portree	£47
Stirling	£7.50

It's also worth checking with **Megabus** (☎0900 160 0900; www.megabus.com) for cheap intercity bus fares (from as little as £5) from Edinburgh to Aberdeen, Dundee, Glasgow, Inverness and Perth.

Train

The main terminus in Edinburgh is Waverley train station, located in the heart of the city. Trains arriving from, and departing for, the west also stop at Haymarket station, which is more convenient for the West End.

First ScotRail (☎08457 55 00 33; www.scotrail.co.uk) operates a regular shuttle service between Edinburgh and Glasgow (£12.90, 50 minutes, every 15 minutes), and frequent daily services to all Scottish cities, including Aberdeen (£45, 2½ hours), Dundee (£23, 1¼ hours) and Inverness (£40, 3½ hours).

Glasgow

POP 634,680

Displaying a disarming blend of sophistication and earthiness, Scotland's biggest city has evolved over the last couple of decades to become one of Britain's most intriguing metropolises. Its Victorian architectural legacy is now swamped with stylish bars, top-notch restaurants, and a hedonistic club culture that will bring out your nocturnal instincts. Glasgow's pounding live-music scene is one of the best in Britain, accessible through countless venues dedicated to home-grown beats.

Sights

CITY CENTRE

Glasgow's main square in the city centre is grand **George Square**, built in the Victorian era to show off the city's wealth, and dignified by statues of notable Scots, including Robert Burns, James Watt, John Moore and Sir Walter Scott. The prosperity of Glasgow's 18th-century 'tobacco lords', who made vast profits importing tobacco, rum and sugar via lucrative transatlantic trade routes, is reflected in the grand buildings they erected in the area east and southeast of George Sq, now known as the **Merchant City**; many have been renewed as stylish apartments, bars and restaurants.

THE GENIUS OF CHARLES RENNIE MACKINTOSH

Charles Rennie Mackintosh (1868–1928) is to Glasgow what Gaudí is to Barcelona. A designer, architect and master of the art nouveau style, his quirky, linear and geometric designs are seen all over Glasgow.

Many of the buildings are open to the public. If you're a fan, the **Mackintosh Trail** ticket (£16), available at the tourist office or any Mackintosh building, gives you a day's free admission to all his creations plus unlimited bus and subway travel.

Glasgow School of Art HISTORIC BUILDING
(☎0141-353 4526; www.gsa.ac.uk/tours; 167 Renfrew St; adult/child/family £8.75/7/24; ⏰9.30am-6.30pm Apr-Sep, 10.30am-5pm Oct-Mar) Mackintosh's greatest building, the Glasgow School of Art, still fulfils its original function, so just follow the steady stream of eclectically dressed students up the hill to find it. The interior is strikingly austere, with simple colour combinations (often just black and cream) and the uncomfortable-looking high-backed chairs for which Mackintosh is famous. The library, designed as an addition in 1907, is a masterpiece.

Excellent hour-long guided tours (roughly hourly in summer; 11am, 1pm and 3pm in winter) run by architecture students leave from here; this is the only way (apart from enrolling) you can visit the building's interior. They're worth booking by phone at busy times. Multilingual translations are available.

FREE **Willow Tearooms** HISTORIC BUILDING
(www.willowtearooms.co.uk; 217 Sauchiehall St; ⏰9am-5pm Mon-Sat, 11am-5pm Sun) Admirers of the great Mackintosh will love the Willow Tearooms, an authentic reconstruction of tearooms Mackintosh designed and furnished in the early 20th century for restaurateur Kate Cranston. Reconstruction took two years and the Willow reopened as a tearoom in 1980 (having been closed since 1926).

Glasgow

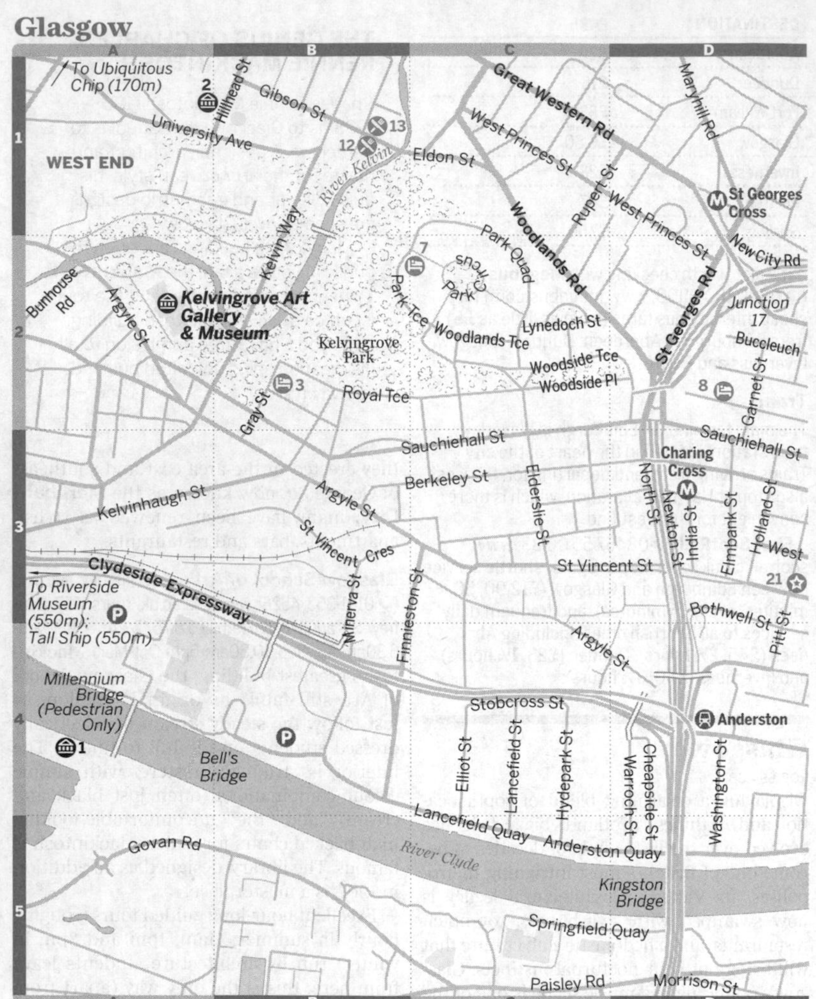

EAST END

Glasgow Cathedral CHURCH

(HS; www.historic-scotland.gov.uk; Cathedral Sq; ⌚9.30am-5.30pm Mon-Sat, 1-5pm Sun Apr-Sep, closes 4.30pm Oct-Mar) Glasgow Cathedral is a shining example of Gothic architecture, and, unlike nearly all Scotland's cathedrals, survived the turmoil of the Reformation mobs almost intact. Most of the current building dates from the 15th century. Many of the cathedral's stunning, narrow windows of stained glass are modern; to your left is Francis Spear's 1958 work *The Creation*, which fills the west window.

THE CLYDE

Once a thriving shipbuilding area, the Clyde sank into dereliction during the postwar era, but is being rejuvenated.

Glasgow Science Centre MUSEUM

(☎0141-420 5000; www.gsc.org.uk; 50 Pacific Quay; Science Mall adult/child £9.95/7.95, IMAX, tower or planetarium £2.50; ⌚10am-5pm Wed-Sun) Scotland's flagship millennium project, this superb museum will keep the kids entertained for hours (that's middle-aged kids, too!). It consists of an egg-shaped titanium-covered IMAX theatre (phone for current screenings) and

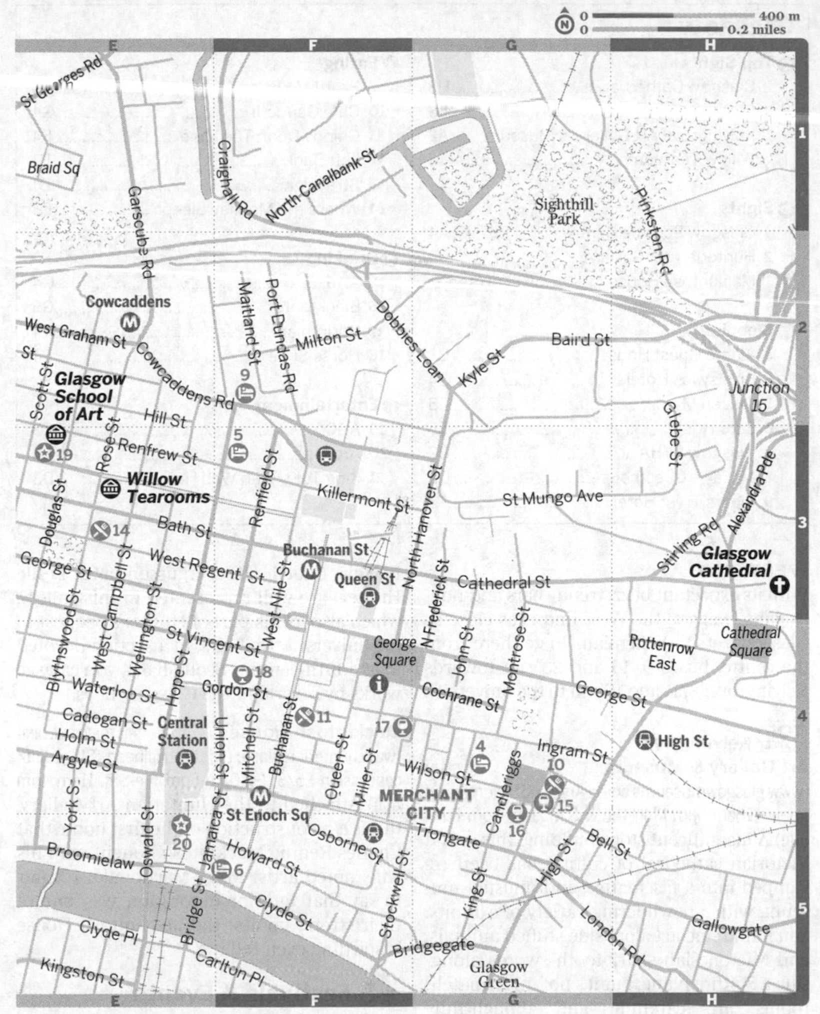

an interactive Science Mall. There's also a rotating observation tower, 127m high. To get here take bus 24 from Renfield St or bus 89 or 90 from Union St. It closes earlier in winter, and doesn't open Monday or Tuesday.

FREE **Riverside Museum** MUSEUM
(www.glasgowmuseums.com; 100 Pointhouse Pl; ⌚10am-5pm Mon-Thu & Sat, 11am-5pm Fri & Sun) The latest development along the Clyde is this visually impressive new transport museum, whose striking curved facades are the work of Iraqi architect Zaha Hadid. Inside, you'll find an excellent series of cars made in Scotland, plus assorted railway locos, trams, bikes and model Clyde-built ships. The magnificent **Tall Ship Glenlee** (www.thetallship.com; adult/child £5/3; ⌚10am-5pm Mar-Oct, till 4pm Nov-Feb), a beautiful three-master launched in 1896, is berthed alongside the museum.

The Riverside is west of the centre at Glasgow Harbour; you can reach it on bus 100 from the north side of George Sq, or via the Clyde Clippers boat service.

Glasgow

Top Sights
- Glasgow Cathedral H3
- Glasgow School of Art E3
- Kelvingrove Art Gallery & Museum A2
- Willow Tearooms E3

Sights
- 1 Glasgow Science Centre A4
- 2 Hunterian Art Gallery A1
- Mackintosh House .... (see 2)

Sleeping
- 3 Alamo Guest House B2
- 4 Brunswick Hotel G4
- 5 Citizen M F3
- 6 Euro Hostel F5
- 7 Glasgow SYHA C2
- 8 McLay's Guesthouse D2
- 9 Pipers Tryst Hotel F2

Eating
- Brutti Ma Buoni .... (see 4)
- 10 Café Gandolfi G4
- 11 Chippy Doon The Lane F4
- 12 Left Bank B1
- 13 Stravaigin B1
- 14 Where the Monkey Sleeps E3

Drinking
- 15 Artà G4
- 16 Blackfriars G5
- 17 Corinthian F4
- 18 Horse Shoe F4

Entertainment
- 19 ABC E3
- 20 Arches E5
- 21 King Tut's Wah Wah Hut D3

WEST END

With its expectant buzz, trendy bars and nonchalant swagger, the West End is as close as Glasgow gets to bohemian. To get here from the centre, buses 9, 16 and 23 run towards Kelvingrove; 8, 11 and 16 run to the university.

TOP CHOICE Kelvingrove Art Gallery & Museum MUSEUM
(www.glasgowmuseums.com; Argyle St; admission free; ⌚10am-5pm Mon-Thu & Sat, 11am-5pm Fri & Sun) A magnificent stone building, this grand Victorian cathedral of culture has been revamped into a fascinating and unusual museum, with a bewildering variety of exhibits. You'll find fine art alongside stuffed animals, and Micronesian shark-tooth swords alongside a Spitfire plane, but it's not mix'n'match: rooms are carefully and thoughtfully themed, and the collection is a manageable size. There's an excellent room of Scottish art, a room of fine French Impressionist works, and quality Renaissance paintings from Italy and Flanders. Salvador Dalí's superb *Christ of St John of the Cross* is also here.

There are free hour-long guided tours beginning at 11am and 2.30pm. Bus 17, among many others, runs here from Renfield St.

FREE Hunterian Art Gallery GALLERY
(www.hunterian.gla.ac.uk; 82 Hillhead St; ⌚10am-5pm Tue-Sat, 11am-4pm Sun) Across the road from the Hunterian Museum, the bold tones of the Scottish Colourists (Samuel Peploe, Francis Cadell, JD Fergusson and Leslie Hunter) are well represented in this gallery, which also forms part of Hunter's bequest to the university. Upstairs, in a section devoted to late-19th-century Scottish art, you can see works by several of the Glasgow Boys.

Mackintosh House HISTORIC BUILDING
(www.hunterian.gla.ac.uk; 82 Hillhead St; adult/concession £5/3; ⌚10am-5pm Tue-Sat, 11am-4pm Sun) Attached to the Hunterian Art Gallery, this is a reconstruction of the first home that Charles Rennie Mackintosh bought with his wife, noted artist Mary Macdonald. It's fair to say that interior decoration was one of their strong points; the Mackintosh House is startling even today.

Festivals & Events

Celtic Connections MUSIC
(☎0141-353 8000; www.celticconnections.com) Two-week music festival held in January.

West End Festival ARTS
(☎0141-341 0844; www.westendfestival.co.uk) This music and arts event is Glasgow's biggest festival, running for three weeks in June.

Sleeping

CITY CENTRE

TOP CHOICE Brunswick Hotel HOTEL ££
(☎0141-552 0001; www.brunswickhotel.co.uk; 106 Brunswick St; d £50-95; 📶🐾) You couldn't ask for a more relaxed and friendly Merchant

City base. The rooms are stylish with a mixture of minimalism and rich, sexy colours. There's an excellent restaurant downstairs and occasional nightclub in the basement.

Citizen M HOTEL ££

(☎0141-404 9485; www.citizenm.com; 60 Renfrew St; r £70-120; @📶) This modern chain does away with some of the accoutrements of the standard hotel in favour of self-check-in terminals and minimalist, plasticky modern rooms with just two features: a big, comfortable king-sized bed and a decent shower with mood lighting.

Pipers Tryst Hotel HOTEL ££

(☎0141-353 5551; www.thepipingcentre.co.uk; 30-34 McPhater St; s/d £50/65; 📶) The name is no strategy to lure tartan tourists; this intimate, cosy hotel is in a noble building actually run by the adjacent bagpiping centre, and all profits going towards maintaining it. Cheery staff, great value and a prime city centre location make this a cut above other places.

Euro Hostel HOSTEL £

(☎0141-222 2828; www.euro-hostels.co.uk; 318 Clyde St; dm £17-20, s £29-40, d £36-52; @📶) With hundreds of beds, this mammoth hostel is handily close to the station and centre. While it feels a bit institutional, it has excellent facilities, including ensuite dorms with lockers, internet access, a compact kitchen, breakfast and a laundry.

McLay's Guesthouse B&B £

(☎0141-332 4796; www.mclays.com; 260 Renfrew St; s/d £36/56, without bathroom £28/48; @📶) The string of cheapish guesthouses along the western end of Renfrew St are a mixed bag but offer a tempting location right by the Sauchiehall nightlife, and are a block or so from the College of Art. This is among the best of them; a solid choice with decent, warm rooms and fair prices.

WEST END

Glasgow SYHA HOSTEL £

(☎0141-332 3004; www.syha.org.uk; 8 Park Tce; dm/tw £23/62; @📶) Perched on a hill overlooking Kelvingrove Park in a charming townhouse, this place is one of Scotland's best official hostels. Dorms are mostly four to six beds, with padlock lockers and all have their own ensuite – very posh. There's no curfew, a good kitchen, and meals are available.

Alamo Guest House B&B ££

(☎0141-339 2395; www.alamoguesthouse.com; 46 Gray St; d/superior d £95/145, without bathroom s/d £55/74; @📶) Opposite Kelvingrove Park, this place feels miles from the hustle of the city. The decor is an enchanting mixture of antique furnishings and modern design, with excellent bathrooms, and the owners will make you very welcome. Breakfast is abundant but there's no full Scottish option.

Eating

Glasgow is the best place to eat in Scotland, with an excellent range of eateries. The West End is the culinary centre of the city; Merchant City also boasts an incredible concentration of quality restaurants and cafes.

CITY CENTRE

Café Gandolfi CAFE, BISTRO ££

(☎0141-552 6813; 64 Albion St; mains £11-15; ⏲9am-11.30pm) In the fashionable Merchant City, this cafe was once part of the old cheese market. It's an excellent, friendly bistro and upmarket coffee shop. Book a Tim Stead-designed, medieval-looking table in advance for well-prepared Scottish and Continental food. There's an expansion, specialising in fish, next door.

Brutti Ma Buoni MEDITERRANEAN £

(☎0141-552 0001; www.brunswickhotel.co.uk; 106 Brunswick St; mains £7-11; ⏲11am-10pm; 👪) If you like dining in a place that has a sense of fun, Brutti delivers – it's the antithesis of some of the pretentious places around the Merchant City. With dishes such as 'ugly but good' pizza and 'angry or peaceful' prawns, Brutti's menu draws a smile for its quirkiness and its prices.

Chippy Doon The Lane FISH & CHIPS £

(www.thechippyglasgow.com; McCormick Lane, 84 Buchanan St; meals £6-11; ⏲noon-9.30pm) Don't be put off by it's location in a down-at-heel alleyway off the shopping precinct: this is a cut above your average chip shop. Sustainable seafood is served in a chic space, all old-time brick, metal archways and jazz.

Where the Monkey Sleeps CAFE £

(www.monkeysleeps.com; 182 West Regent St; dishes £4-7; ⏲7am-5pm Mon-Fri) This funky little number in the middle of the business district is a perfect escape from the ubiquitous coffee chains. Laid-back and a little hippy, the bagels and paninis – with names like Burn the Witch or Meathammer – are highlights, as are some very inventive dishes, such as the 'nuclear' beans, dripping with cayenne and Tabasco.

West End

TOP CHOICE **Ubiquitous Chip** SCOTTISH £££
(☎0141-334 5007; www.ubiquitouschip.co.uk; 12 Ashton Lane; 2-/3-course dinner £35/40, brasserie mains lunch £7-12, dinner £12-15) The original champion of Scottish produce, The Ubiquitous Chip has won lots of awards for its unparalleled Scottish cuisine, and for its lengthy wine list. Named to poke fun at Scotland's perceived lack of finer cuisine, it offers a French touch but resolutely Scottish ingredients, carefully selected and following sustainable principles.

Stravaigin SCOTTISH ££
(☎0141-334 2665; www.stravaigin.co.uk; 28 Gibson St; mains £10-18; ⏲9am-11pm) Stravaigin is a serious foodie's delight, with a menu constantly pushing the boundaries of originality and offering creative culinary excellence. The cool contemporary dining space in the basement has booth seating, and helpful, laid-back waiting-staff to assist in deciphering the audacious menu.

Left Bank BISTRO ££
(☎0141-339 5969; www.theleftbank.co.uk; 33 Gibson St; mains £12-18; ⏲9am-10pm Mon-Fri, 10am-10pm Sat & Sun;) Huge windows fronting the street greet patrons to this outstanding eatery specialising in gastronomic delights and lazy afternoons. The large starter-menu can be treated like tapas, making it good for sharing. Locally sourced ingredients are used wherever possible.

Drinking

TOP CHOICE **Artà** BAR
(www.arta.co.uk; 62 Albion St; ⏲5pm-3am Thu-Sat) Set in a former cheese market, Artà's opulent, candle-lit interior features floor-to-ceiling velvet and red curtains that reveal a staircase to the tapas bar and restaurant. Despite the luxury, it has a relaxed, chilled vibe and a mixed crowd.

Horse Shoe PUB
(www.horseshoebar.co.uk; 17 Drury St) This legendary city pub and popular meeting place dates from the late 19th century and is largely unchanged. It's a picturesque spot, with the longest continuous bar in the UK, but its main attraction is what's served over it – real ale and good cheer.

Corinthian BAR
(www.thecorinthianclub.co.uk; 191 Ingram St;) Originally a bank and later Glasgow's High Court, this regal building's main bar has to be seen to be believed. Cosy wraparound seating and space to spare are complemented by a snug wine bar and a plush club downstairs in old court cells.

Blackfriars PUB
(www.blackfriarsglasgow.com; 36 Bell St) Merchant City's most relaxed and atmospheric pub, Blackfriars' friendly staff and chilled-out house make it special. They take their cask ales seriously here, and there's a seating area with large windows that are great for people-watching.

Entertainment

Arches CLUB
(www.thearches.co.uk; 253 Argyle St) R-e-s-p-e-c-t is the mantra at the Arches. The Godfather of Glaswegian clubs, it has a design based around hundreds of arches slammed together, and is a must for funk and hip-hop freaks. It's off Jamaica St.

King Tut's Wah Wah Hut LIVE MUSIC
(☎0141-221 5279; www.kingtuts.co.uk; 272a St Vincent St) One of the city's premier live-music pub venues, the excellent King Tut's Wah Wah Hut hosts bands every night of the week. Oasis were signed after playing here.

ABC CLUB
(O2 ABC; www.o2abcglasgow.co.uk; 300 Sauchiehall St) Both nightclub and venue, this star of Sauchiehall has two large concert spaces and several attractive bars.

Information

Glasgow Information Centre (☎0141-204 4400; www.seeglasgow.com; 11 George Sq; ⏲9am-5pm Mon-Sat) Excellent tourist office; makes local and national accommodation bookings (£4). Closes later and opens Sundays in summer.

Getting There & Away

Air

Ten miles west of the city, **Glasgow International Airport** (GLA; www.glasgowairport.com) handles domestic traffic and international flights. **Glasgow Prestwick Airport** (PIK; www.glasgowprestwick.com), 30 miles southwest of Glasgow, is used by budget airlines, with many connections to Britain and Europe.

Bus

All long-distance buses arrive at and depart from **Buchanan bus station** (☎0141-333 3708;

www.spt.co.uk; Killermont St), which has pricey lockers, ATMs, and a cafe with wi-fi.

Scottish Citylink (☎0871 266 3333; www.citylink.co.uk) has buses to most major towns in Scotland, including:

DESTINATION	COST	DURATION	FREQUENCY
Aberdeen	£28.80	2½ to three hours	hourly
Edinburgh	£6.80	1¼ hours	every 15 minutes
Fort William	£22	three hours	seven daily
Inverness	£27.50	3½ hours	eight daily
Stirling	£7.30	45 minutes	at least hourly

Train

As a general rule, Glasgow Central station serves southern Scotland, England and Wales, and Queen St station serves the north and east. Buses run between the two stations every 10 minutes. There are direct trains to London's Euston station; they're much quicker (advance purchase single £28 to £105, full fare £162, 4½ hours, more than hourly) and more comfortable than the bus.

Scotrail (☎08457 55 00 33; www.scotrail.co.uk) runs Scottish trains. Destinations include:

DESTINATION	COST	DURATION	FREQUENCY
Aberdeen	£45.20	2½ hours	hourly
Dundee	£25.30	1½ hours	hourly
Edinburgh	£12.90	50 minutes	every 15 minutes
Fort William	£26.30	3¾ hours	four to five daily
Inverness	£79	3½ hours	10 daily
Oban	£21.60	three hours	three to four daily

CENTRAL SCOTLAND

Central Scotland is less a geographical region and more a catch-all term for everything between the Glasgow–Edinburgh conurbation and the mountains of the northwestern Highlands. Anything you ever dreamed about Scotland you can find here: lochs, hills, castles, whisky distilleries and some truly beautiful islands.

Loch Lomond

The 'bonnie banks' and 'bonnie braes' of Loch Lomond have long been Glasgow's rural retreat, and today the loch's popularity shows no sign of decreasing. The main tourist focus is on the loch's western shore, along the A82. The southern end, around Balloch, is occasionally a nightmare of jet skis and motorboats. The eastern shore, followed by the West Highland Way long-distance footpath, is a little quieter. The region's importance was recognised when it became the heart of **Loch Lomond & the Trossachs National Park** (www.lochlomond-trossachs.org) – Scotland's first national park, created in 2002.

The main centre for boat trips is Balloch, where **Sweeney's Cruises** (☎01389-752376; www.sweeneyscruises.com; Balloch Rd, Balloch) offers a range of trips including a one-hour cruise to Inchmurrin and back (adult/child £8.50/5, departs hourly).

Sleeping & Eating

Loch Lomond Youth Hostel HOSTEL £
(SYHA; ☎01389-850226; Arden; dm £18; ⊙Mar-Oct; P@) Forget about roughing it, this is one of the most impressive hostels in the country – an imposing 19th-century country house set in beautiful grounds overlooking the loch. It's 2 miles north of Balloch and very popular, so book in advance in summer. And yes, it *is* haunted.

TOP CHOICE **Drover's Inn** PUB ££
(☎01301-704234; www.thedroversinn.co.uk; bar meals £7-12; ⊙lunch & dinner; P) This is one *howff* you shouldn't miss – a low-ceilinged place with smoke-blackened stone, bare wooden floors spotted with candle wax, barmen in kilts, and walls festooned with moth-eaten stags' heads and stuffed birds. There's even a stuffed bear and the desiccated husk of a basking shark.

Getting There & Away

BUS First Glasgow (☎0141-423 6600; www.firstglasgow.com) buses 204 and 215 run from Argyle St in central Glasgow to Balloch and Loch Lomond Shores (1½ hours, at least two per hour).

Scottish Citylink (www.citylink.co.uk) coaches from Glasgow to Oban and Fort William stop at Luss (£8.20, 55 minutes, six daily), Tarbet (£8.20, 65 minutes) and Ardlui (£14.30, 1¼ hours).

TRAIN Train services:

Glasgow to Balloch (£4.70, 45 minutes, every 30 minutes)

Glasgow to Ardlui (£14, 1½ hours, three or four daily) Continuing to Oban and Fort William.

Stirling

POP 32,673

With an utterly impregnable position atop a mighty wooded crag (the plug of an extinct volcano), Stirling's beautifully preserved Old Town is a treasure-trove of noble buildings and cobbled streets winding up to the ramparts of its dominant castle, which offers views for miles around. Clearly visible is the brooding Wallace Monument, a strange Victorian Gothic creation honouring the legendary freedom fighter of *Braveheart* fame. Nearby is Bannockburn, scene of Robert the Bruce's major triumph over the English.

Sights

TOP CHOICE Stirling Castle CASTLE

(HS; www.historic-scotland.gov.uk; adult/child £13/6.50; ⏲9.30am-6pm Apr-Sep, to 5pm Oct-Mar) Hold Stirling and you control Scotland, or so the saying goes. This impressive fortress has played a pivotal role in Scotland's fortunes down the centuries, and it's every bit as dramatic as Edinburgh Castle. It also draws a similar number of visitors, so it's advisable to visit in the afternoon; many tourists come on day trips, so you may have the castle to yourself by about 4pm.

The current castle dates from the late 14th to the 16th century, when it was a residence of the Stuart monarchs. The undisputed highlight of a visit is the fabulous, recently restored **Royal Palace**. The idea was that it should look brand new, just as when it was constructed by French masons under the orders of James V in the mid-16th century with the aim of impressing his new (also French) bride and other crowned heads of Europe. The suite of six rooms – three for the king, three for the queen – is a sumptuous riot of colour. Particularly notable are the fine fireplaces, the recreated painted oak discs in the ceiling of the king's audience chamber, and the fabulous series of **tapestries** that have been painstakingly woven over many years.

The other buildings surrounding the main castle courtyard are the vast **Great Hall**, built by James IV; the **Royal Chapel**, remodelled in the early 17th century by James VI and with the colourful original mural painting intact; and the King's **Old Building**. This is now home to the **Museum of the Argyll & Sutherland Highlanders** (donations appreciated), which traces the history of this famous regiment from 1794, including its famous defensive action in the Battle of Balaclava in 1854. Until the last tapestry is completed, probably in late 2013, you can watch the weavers at work in the **Tapestry Studio** at the far end of the castle. The magnificent vistas from the **ramparts** are also stirring.

Admission includes an audioguide, and free guided tours leave regularly from near the entrance. Tours (£2 extra, free for HS members) also run to **Argyll's Lodging**, at the top of Castle Wynd. Complete with turrets, this spectacular lodge is Scotland's most impressive 17th-century townhouse.

National Wallace Monument MONUMENT

(www.nationalwallacemonument.com; adult/child £8.25/5.25; ⏲10am-5pm Apr-Jun, Sep & Oct, to 6pm Jul & Aug, 10.30am-4pm Nov-Mar) Towering over Scotland's narrow waist, this nationalist memorial is so Victorian Gothic it deserves circling bats and ravens. It commemorates the bid for Scottish independence depicted in the film *Braveheart*. From the visitor centre below, walk or shuttle-bus up the hill to the building itself. Once there, break the climb up the narrow staircase inside to admire Wallace's 66 inches of broadsword and see the man himself recreated in a 3D audiovisual display.

Buses 62 and 63 run from Murray Pl in Stirling to the tourist office, otherwise it's a half-hour walk from central Stirling. There's a cafe here.

Bannockburn HISTORIC SITE

Though Wallace's heroics were significant, it was Robert the Bruce's defeat of the English on 24 June 1314 at Bannockburn, just outside Stirling, that eventually established lasting Scottish nationhood. The **Bannockburn Heritage Centre** (NTS; www.nts.org.uk) is due to reopen after a big refurbishment in spring 2014, in time for the 700th anniversary of the battle.

The battlefield itself (which never closes) will hopefully receive a bit of work too; at present, apart from a statue of the victor astride his horse and a misbegotten flag memorial, there's nothing to see. Bannockburn is 2 miles south of Stirling; you can reach it on bus 51 from Murray Pl in the centre.

Sleeping

Castlecroft Guest House B&B ££

(☎01786-474933; www.castlecroft-uk.com; Ballengeich Rd; s/d £50/65; P@📶) Nestling into the hillside under the back of the castle, this great hideaway feels like a rural retreat but is a short, spectacular walk from the heart of historic Stirling. The fabulous lounge and deck area boast extravagant views over green fields to the hills that gird the town.

Willy Wallace Backpackers Hostel HOSTEL £
(☎01786-446773; www.willywallacehostel.com; 77 Murray Pl; dm/tw £16/36; @☎) This central hostel is friendly, roomy and sociable. The colourful, spacious dormitories are clean and light, there's free tea and coffee, a good kitchen and a laissez-faire atmosphere. Other amenities include bicycle hire, laundry and free internet and wi-fi.

Sruighlea B&B ££
(☎01786-471082; www.sruighlea.com; 27 King St; s/d £40/60; ☎) This place feels like a secret hideaway – there's no sign – but it's conveniently located smack bang in the centre of town. You'll feel like a local staying here, and there are eating and drinking places practically on the doorstep.

Stirling SYHA HOSTEL £
(☎01786-473442; www.syha.org.uk; St John St; dm/tw £18.75/48; P@☎) Right in the Old Town, this hostel has an unbeatable location and great facilities. Though its facade is that of a former church, the interior is modern and efficient. The dorms are compact but comfortable with lockers and ensuite bathrooms; other highlights include a pool table, bike shed and, at busy times, cheap meals on offer.

Information

Tourist Office (☎01786-475019; stirling@visitscotland.com; 41 Dumbarton Rd; ⊙10am-5pm Mon-Sat, plus Sun Jun–mid-Sep)

Getting There & Away

BUS The **bus station** (☎01786-446474) is on Goosecroft Rd. **Citylink** (☎0871 266 33 33; www.citylink.co.uk) offers a number of services to/from Stirling:

Dundee (£13, 1½ hours, hourly)
Edinburgh (£7.50, one hour, hourly)
Glasgow (£7, 40 minutes, hourly)

Some buses continue to Aberdeen, Inverness and Fort William; more frequently a change will be required.

TRAIN First ScotRail (www.scotrail.co.uk) has services to/from a number of destinations, including the following:

Aberdeen (£43.30, 2¼ hours, hourly weekdays, every two hours Sunday)
Dundee (£17.70, one hour, hourly weekdays, every two hours Sunday)
Edinburgh (£7.70, 55 minutes, twice hourly Monday to Saturday, hourly Sunday)
Glasgow (£8, 40 minutes, twice hourly Monday to Saturday, hourly Sunday)

Aberdeen

POP 197,300

Aberdeen is the powerhouse of the northeast, fuelled by the North Sea petroleum industry. Oil money has made the city as expensive as London and Edinburgh, and there are hotels, restaurants and clubs with prices to match the depth of oil-wealthy pockets. Fortunately, most of the cultural attractions, such as the excellent Maritime Museum and the Aberdeen Art Gallery, are free.

Aberdeen is known throughout Scotland as 'the granite city'. On a sunny day the granite lends an attractive glitter, but when grey rain clouds scud in off the North Sea, it can be hard to tell where the buildings stop and the sky begins.

Sights

FREE **Marischal College & Museum** MUSEUM
(www.abdn.ac.uk/marischal_museum; Marischal College, Broad St; ⊙10am-5pm Mon-Fri, 2-5pm Sun) Marischal College, founded in 1593 by the 5th Earl Marischal, merged with King's College (founded 1495) in 1860 to create the modern University of Aberdeen.

Founded in 1786, the Marischal Museum houses a fascinating collection of material donated by graduates and friends of the university over the centuries. In one room, the history of northeastern Scotland is depicted through its myths, customs, famous people, architecture and trade. The other gallery gives an anthropological overview of the world, incorporating objects from vastly different cultures, arranged thematically (Polynesian wooden masks alongside gas masks and so on). There are the usual Victorian curios, an Inuit kayak found in the local river estuary in the 18th century, and Inuit objects collected by whalers. At the time of research the museum was still closed to the public following renovation work; check the website for notice of its reopening.

FREE **Aberdeen Art Gallery** GALLERY
(☎01224-523700; www.aagm.co.uk; Schoolhill; ⊙10am-5pm Tue-Sat, 2-5pm Sun) Behind the grand facade of Aberdeen Art Gallery is a

WORTH A TRIP

ST ANDREWS

This little Scottish city is famous across the globe as the spiritual home of golf. The sport's been played here since the 15th century, and for many golf aficionados the chance to tee off on the fabled Old Course is a lifelong ambition.

If you want to play, your best bet is to book a slot in advance via St Andrews Links Trust; otherwise you can enter a public ballot for a tee-off time a couple of days in advance. Be warned that applications by ballot are normally heavily oversubscribed, and green fees are £150 in summer. No advance bookings are taken for Saturdays or the month of September.

There's no train station in St Andrews; public buses run to Edinburgh (£9.40, two hours, hourly), Glasgow (£9.40, 2½ hours, hourly) and Stirling (£7.30, two hours, six to seven Monday to Saturday).

cool, marble-lined space exhibiting the work of contemporary Scottish and English painters, such as Gwen Hardie, Stephen Conroy, Trevor Sutton and Tim Ollivier. There are also several landscapes by Joan Eardley, who lived in a cottage on the cliffs near Stonehaven in the 1950s and '60s, and painted tempestuous oils of the North Sea and poignant portraits of slum children.

FREE Aberdeen Maritime Museum MUSEUM
(☎01224-337700; www.aagm.co.uk; Shiprow; ⊙10am-5pm Tue-Sat, noon-3pm Sun) Centred on a three-storey replica of a North Sea oil production platform, this museum explains all you ever wanted to know about the petroleum industry. Other galleries, some situated in **Provost Ross's House**, the oldest building in the city and part of the museum, cover the shipbuilding, whaling and fishing industries.

Sleeping

There are clusters of B&Bs on Bon Accord St and Springbank Tce (both 400m southwest of the train station), and along Great Western Rd (the A93, a 25-minute walk southwest of the city centre).

TOP CHOICE Globe Inn B&B ££
(☎01224-624258; www.the-globe-inn.co.uk; 13-15 North Silver St; s/d £70/75) This popular pub has seven appealing and comfortable guest bedrooms upstairs, done out in dark wood with burgundy bedspreads. There's live music in the pub on weekends so it's not a place for early-to-bed types, but the price vs location factor can't be beaten.

Butler's Guest House B&B ££
(☎01224-212411; www.butlersguesthouse.com; 122 Crown St; s/d from £58/65; @☎) Butler's is a cosy place with a big breakfast menu that includes fresh fruit salad, kippers and kedgeree as alternatives to the traditional fry-up (rates include a continental breakfast – cooked breakfast is £5 extra per person).

Aberdeen Youth Hostel HOSTEL £
(SYHA; ☎01224-646988; 8 Queen's Rd; dm £21; @☎) This hostel, set in a granite Victorian villa, is a mile west of the train station. Walk west along Union St and take the right fork along Albyn Pl until you reach a roundabout; Queen's Rd continues on the western side of the roundabout.

Eating & Drinking

TOP CHOICE Café 52 BISTRO ££
(☎01224-590094; www.cafe52.net; 52 The Green; mains £12; ⊙noon-midnight Mon-Sat, to 6pm Sun; ☎) This little haven of laid-back industrial chic – a high, narrow space lined with bare stonework, rough plaster and exposed ventilation ducts – serves some of the finest and most inventive cuisine in the northeast.

Sand Dollar Café CAFE £
(☎01224-572288; www.sanddollarcafe.com; 2 Beach Esplanade; mains £4-10; ⊙9am-9pm daily, closed 4-6pm Thu-Sat) A cut above your usual seaside cafe – there's a tempting menu that includes pancakes with maple syrup, homemade burgers and chocolate brownie with Orkney ice cream. An evening bistro menu (mains £12 to £24, served from 6pm Thursday to Saturday) offers steak and seafood dishes. The cafe is on the esplanade, 800m northeast of the city centre.

Prince of Wales PUB

(7 St Nicholas Lane) Tucked down an alley off Union St, Aberdeen's best-known pub boasts the longest bar in the city, a great range of real ales and good value pub grub. Quiet in the afternoons, but standing-room only in the evenings.

Information

Aberdeen Tourist Office (☎01224-288828; www.aberdeen-grampian.com; 23 Union St; ⊙9am-6.30pm Mon-Sat, 10am-4pm Sun Jul & Aug, 9.30am-5pm Mon-Sat Sep-Jun)

Getting There & Away

BUS The **bus station** (Guild St) is next to Jurys Inn, close to the train station.

Edinburgh (£28, 3¼ hour, hourly) Change at Perth.

Glasgow (£28, three hours, hourly)

Inverness (£9, 3¾ hours, hourly) Via Huntly, Keith, Fochabers, Elgin and Nairn.

TRAIN The train station is south of the city centre, next to the massive Union Square shopping mall.

Dundee (£27, 1¼ hours, twice an hour)

Edinburgh (£45, 2½ hours, hourly)

Glasgow (£45, 2¾ hours, hourly)

Inverness (£28, 2¼ hour, eight daily)

For London King's Cross (£140, eight hours, hourly) some trains are direct, but most change at Edinburgh.

NORTHERN & WESTERN SCOTLAND

This area is a long way north, and takes effort to reach, but it is by far the best bit of Scotland, and one of the best bits of the whole of Britain too. Some folks (well, those who love mountains and wild places) would even say that it's one of the finest parts of the whole of Europe.

The western part of this area includes deep lochs, misty glens and towering snow-covered mountains. Famous name-checks include Ben Nevis, Britain's highest peak. The northern area, often called the Northwest Highlands, is the land beyond the Great Glen – the geological fault running across Scotland from Fort William to Inverness, separating this remote and rugged region from the rest of the country.

It's easy to underestimate the scale of this part of Scotland, so give yourself extra time to explore. See www.visithighlands.com for transport and accommodation advice.

Inverness

POP 55,000

Inverness, the primary city and shopping centre of the Highlands, has a great location astride the River Ness at the northern end of the Great Glen. In summer it overflows with visitors intent on monster hunting at nearby Loch Ness, but it's worth a visit in its own right for a stroll along the picturesque river, a cruise on the loch, and a meal in one of the city's excellent restaurants.

Sleeping

Trafford Bank B&B ££

(☎01463-241414; www.traffordbankguesthouse.co.uk; 96 Fairfield Rd; d £110-125; P 🛜) Lots of word-of-mouth rave reviews for this elegant Victorian villa, which was once home to a bishop, just a mitre-toss from the Caledonian Canal and 10 minutes' walk west from the city centre. The luxurious rooms include fresh flowers and fruit, bathrobes and fluffy towels.

Ardconnel House B&B ££

(☎01463-240455; www.ardconnel-inverness.co.uk; 21 Ardconnel St; r per person £35-40; 🛜) The six-room Ardconnel is one of our favourites – a terraced Victorian house with comfortable ensuite rooms, a dining room with crisp white table linen, and a breakfast menu that includes Vegemite for homesick Antipodeans. Kids under 10 not allowed.

Bazpackers Backpackers Hotel HOSTEL £

(☎01463-717663; www.bazpackershostel.co.uk; 4 Culduthel Rd; dm/tw £17/44; @ 🛜) This may be Inverness' smallest hostel (30 beds), but it's hugely popular. It's a friendly, quiet place – the main building has a convivial lounge centred on a wood-burning stove, and a small garden and great views (some rooms are in a separate building with no garden).

Inverness Millburn SYHA HOSTEL £

(SYHA; ☎01463-231771; www.syha.org.uk; Victoria Dr; dm £18; ⊙Apr-Dec; P @ 🛜) Inverness' modern 166-bed hostel is 10 minutes' walk northeast of the city centre. With its comfy beds and flashy stainless-steel kitchen, some reckon it's the best hostel in the country. Booking is essential, especially at Easter, and in July and August.

Eating & Drinking

Café 1 BISTRO ££

(☎01463-226200; www.cafe1.net; 75 Castle St; mains £10-23; ⊙noon-9.30pm Mon-Fri, noon-2.30pm &

6-9.30pm Sat) Café 1 is a friendly and appealing bistro with candlelit tables amid elegant blonde-wood and wrought-iron decor. Early-bird menu (one/two courses for £9/12.50) is served noon to 6.45pm weekdays, and noon to 2.30pm Saturday.

Mustard Seed BISTRO ££
(☎01463-220220; www.mustardseedrestaurant.co.uk; 16 Fraser St; mains £11-16) The menu at this bright and bustling bistro changes weekly, but focuses on Scottish and French cuisine with a modern twist. And a two-course lunch for £7 – yes, that's right – is hard to beat.

Clachnaharry Inn PUB
(☎01463-239806; www.clachnaharryinn.co.uk; 17-19 High St) Just over a mile northwest of the city centre, on the bank of the Caledonian Canal just off the A862, this is a delightful old coaching inn (with beer garden out back) serving an excellent range of real ales and good pub grub.

Information

Inverness tourist office (☎01463-252401; www.visithighlands.com; Castle Wynd; internet access per 20min £1; ⌚9am-6pm Mon-Sat, 9.30am-5pm Sun Jul & Aug, 9am-5pm Mon-Sat, 10am-4pm Sun Jun, Sep & Oct, 9am-5pm Mon-Sat Apr & May) Bureau de change and accommodation booking service; also sells tickets for tours and cruises.

Getting There & Away

BUS Services depart from **Inverness bus station** (Margaret St).

London buses (£45, 13 hours, one daily) are operated by **National Express** (☎08717 81 81 78; www.gobycoach.com); more frequent services require a change at Glasgow.

DESTINATION	COST	DURATION	FREQUENCY
Aberdeen	£9	3¾ hours	hourly
Edinburgh	£28	3½ to 4½ hours	hourly
Glasgow	£28	3½ to 4½ hours	hourly
Fort William	£12	two hours	five daily
Portree	£23	3½ hours	four daily

TRAIN The Kyle of Lochalsh (£13, 2½ hours, four daily Monday to Saturday, two Sunday) trip is one of Britain's great scenic train journeys.

There is one daily direct train to London (£100, eight hours); others require a change at Edinburgh.

Aberdeen (£28, 2¼ hours, eight daily)
Edinburgh (£40, 3½ hours, eight daily)
Glasgow (£40, 3½ hours, eight daily)

Loch Ness

Deep, dark and narrow, Loch Ness stretches for 23 miles between Inverness and Fort Augustus. Its bitterly cold waters have been extensively explored in search of the elusive Loch Ness monster, but most visitors see her only in cardboard cut-out form at the monster exhibitions. The village of **Drumnadrochit** is a hotbed of beastie fever, with two monster exhibitions battling it out for the tourist dollar.

The **Loch Ness Exhibition Centre** (☎01456-450573; www.lochness.com; adult/child £6.95/4.95; ⌚9am-6pm Jul & Aug, to 5.30pm Jun, 9.30am-5pm Easter-May & Sep-Oct, 10am-3.30pm Nov-Easter) is the better of the two Nessie-themed attractions, with a scientific approach that allows you to weigh the evidence for yourself.

Scottish Citylink and Stagecoach buses from Inverness to Fort William run along the shores of Loch Ness (six to eight daily, five on Sunday); those headed for Skye turn off at Invermoriston. There are bus stops at Drumnadrochit (£6.20, 30 minutes) and Urquhart Castle (£6.60, 35 minutes).

Glen Coe

Scotland's most famous glen is also one of the grandest and, in bad weather, the grimmest. The southern side is dominated by three massive, brooding spurs, known as the **Three Sisters**, while the northern side is enclosed by the continuous steep wall of the knife-edged **Aonach Eagach** ridge. The main road threads its lonely way through the middle of all this mountain grandeur.

Glencoe village was written into the history books in 1692 when the resident MacDonalds were murdered by Campbell soldiers in what became known as the Glencoe Massacre.

The little village of Glencoe stands on the south shore of Loch Leven at the western end of the glen.

Sleeping & Eating

TOP CHOICE **Clachaig Inn** HOTEL ££
(☎01855-811252; www.clachaig.com; s/d from £70/92; P) The Clachaig has long been a favourite haunt of hill walkers and climbers. As well as comfortable ensuite accom-

LOCAL KNOWLEDGE

CLIMBING BEN NEVIS

Looming over Fort William is Ben Nevis (1344m). As the highest peak in the British Isles, it attracts thousands of people who would not normally go anywhere near the summit of a Scottish mountain. Many get to the top with no trouble, but every year a surprisingly large number of people have to be rescued. Even if you're climbing 'the Ben' on a fine summer's day, an ascent should not be undertaken lightly. You will need proper walking boots (the path is rough and stony, and there may be wet snowfields on the summit), warm clothing, waterproofs, a map and compass, and plenty of food and water. And don't forget to check the weather forecast (see www.bennevisweather.co.uk). In thick cloud, visibility at the summit can be 10m or less; in such conditions, the only safe way off the mountain requires careful use of a map and compass to avoid walking over 700m cliffs.

modation, there's a smart, wood-panelled lounge-bar with lots of sofas and armchairs, mountaineering photos, and climbing magazines to leaf through. Climbers usually head for the lively **Boots Bar**. It's 2 miles southeast of Glencoe village.

Glencoe Independent Hostel HOSTEL £
(☎01855-811906; www.glencoehostel.co.uk; dm £13-16.50, bunkhouse £11.50-13.50; P@) This handily located hostel, just 10 minutes' walk from the Clachaig Inn and 1.5 miles southeast of Glencoe village, is set in an old farmhouse with six- and eight-bed dorms, and a bunkhouse with another 16 bed spaces in communal, Alpine-style bunks. There's also a cute little wooden cabin that sleeps up to three (£20 to £24 per person per night).

Getting There & Away

Scottish Citylink (☎0871 266 3333; www.citylink.co.uk) buses run between Fort William and Glencoe (£7.50, 30 minutes, eight daily) and from Glencoe to Glasgow (£20, 2½ hours, eight daily). Buses stop at Glencoe village, Glencoe Visitor Centre and Glencoe Mountain Resort.

Stagecoach (www.stagecoachbus.com) bus 44 links Glencoe village with Fort William (35 minutes, hourly Monday to Saturday, three on Sunday) and Kinlochleven (25 minutes).

Fort William

POP 9910

Basking on the shores of Loch Linnhe amid magnificent mountain scenery, Fort William has one of the most enviable settings in the whole of Scotland. If it wasn't for the busy dual carriageway crammed between the town centre and the loch, and one of the highest rainfall records in the country, it would be almost idyllic. Even so, 'Fort Bill' has carved out a reputation as 'Outdoor Capital of the UK' (www.outdoorcapital.co.uk), and easy access by rail and bus makes it a good launch-pad for Highland exploration.

Sleeping

TOP CHOICE **Lime Tree** HOTEL ££
(☎01397-701806; www.limetreefortwilliam.co.uk; Achintore Rd; s/d from £80/110; P) Much more interesting than your average guesthouse, this former Victorian manse overlooking Loch Linnhe is an 'art gallery with rooms', decorated throughout with the artist-owner's atmospheric Highland landscapes.

Grange B&B ££
(☎01397-705516; www.grangefortwilliam.com; Grange Rd; r per person £58-63; P) An exceptional 19th-century villa set in its own landscaped grounds, the Grange is crammed with antiques and fitted with log fires, chaise longues and Victorian roll-top baths. It's 500m southwest of the town centre.

Fort William Backpackers HOSTEL £
(☎01397-700711; www.scotlands-top-hostels.com; Alma Rd; dm/tw £18/47; P@) A 10-minute walk from the bus and train stations, this lively and welcoming hostel is set in a grand Victorian villa, perched on a hillside with great views over Loch Linnhe.

Drinking

Grog & Gruel PUB
(☎01397-705078; www.grogandgruel.co.uk; 66 High St; ⏲bar meals noon-9pm) The Grog & Gruel is a traditional-style, wood-panelled pub with an excellent range of cask ales from regional Scottish and English microbreweries.

Information

Fort William tourist office (01397-703781; www.visithighlands.com; 15 High St; internet per 20min £1; 9am-6pm Mon-Sat, 10am-5pm Sun Apr-Sep, limited hours Oct-Mar)

Getting There & Away

BUS **Scottish Citylink** (www.citylink.co.uk) buses link Fort William with other major towns and cities.

To Edinburgh (£33, 4½ hours) there is one daily direct, seven with a change at Glasgow; via Glencoe and Crianlarich.

Glasgow (£22, three hours, eight daily)
Inverness (£12, two hours, five daily)
Oban (£9.40, 1½ hours, three daily)
Portree (£28.60, three hours, four daily)

TRAIN The spectacular West Highland line runs from Glasgow to Mallaig via Fort William. The overnight *Caledonian Sleeper* service connects Fort William and London Euston (£103 sharing a twin-berth cabin, 13 hours).

Isle of Skye

POP 9900

The Isle of Skye is the biggest of Scotland's islands, a 50-mile-long smorgasbord of velvet moors, jagged mountains, sparkling lochs and towering sea cliffs. It takes its name from the old Norse *sky-a*, meaning 'cloud island', a Viking reference to the often mist-enshrouded Cuillin Hills. The stunning scenery is the main attraction, but there are plenty of cosy pubs to retire to when the mist closes in.

Sleeping

Portree, the island's capital, has the largest selection of accommodation, eating places and other services. A small selection of favourites is listed here, but there are many more hostels and B&Bs dotted around the island.

Ben Tianavaig B&B B&B ££
(01478-612152; www.ben-tianavaig.co.uk; 5 Bosville Tce; r £70-80; P) A warm welcome awaits from the Irish-Welsh couple who run this appealing B&B bang in the centre of town.

Peinmore House B&B ££
(01478-612574; www.peinmorehouse.co.uk; r £130-140; P) Signposted off the main road about 2 miles south of Portree, this former manse has been cleverly converted into a guesthouse that is more stylish and luxurious than most hotels. The bedrooms and bathrooms are huge, and there are panoramic views to the Old Man of Storr.

Bayfield Backpackers HOSTEL £
(01478-612231; www.skyehostel.co.uk; Bayfield; dm £17; @) Clean, central and modern, this hostel provides the best backpacker accommodation in town. The owner really makes you feel welcome, and is a fount of advice on what to do and where to go in Skye.

Bayview House B&B £
(01478-613340; www.bayviewhouse.co.uk; Bayfield; r per person from £20; P) This is a modern house with Spartan but sparklingly clean rooms, some with sea and mountain views, and bathrooms with power showers. At this price and location, it's a bargain.

Eating

Café Arriba CAFE £
(01478-611830; www.cafearriba.co.uk; Quay Brae; mains £4-8; 7am-10pm May-Sep, 8am-5.30pm Oct-Apr;) Arriba is a funky little cafe, brightly decked out in primary colours and offering delicious flatbread melts (bacon, leek and cheese is our favourite) as well as the best choice of vegetarian grub on the island.

Sea Breezes SEAFOOD ££
(01478-612016; www.seabreezes-skye.co.uk; 2 Marine Buildings, Quay St; mains £12-19; lunch & dinner Apr-Oct) Sea Breezes is an informal, no-frills restaurant specialising in local fish and shellfish fresh from the boat – try the impressive seafood platter, a small mountain of langoustines, crab, oysters and lobster. Book early, as it's often hard to get a table.

Getting There & Away

BOAT The Isle of Skye became permanently tethered to the Scottish mainland when the Skye Bridge opened in 1995, but a number of ferries still serve the island.

CalMac (www.calmac.co.uk; per person/car £4.35/22.60) operates the Mallaig to Armadale ferry. It's very popular in July and August, so book ahead if you're travelling by car.

Skye Ferry (www.skyeferry.co.uk; car with up to four passengers £14) runs a tiny vessel (six cars only) on the short Glenelg to Kylerhea crossing. The ferry operates from 10am to 6pm daily from Easter to October only, till 7pm June to August.

BUS Services include:

Glasgow to Portree (£40, seven hours, four daily)
Glasgow to Uig (£40, 7½ hours, two daily) Via Crianlarich, Fort William and Kyle of Lochalsh.
Inverness to Portree (£23, 3½ hours, three daily)

JOHN O'GROATS & AROUND

Best known as the endpoint of the epic 874-mile trek from Land's End in Cornwall, **John O'Groats** is really nothing more than a car park surrounded by tourist shops, and offers little to the visitor beyond a means to get across to Orkney. Even the famous pub has been shut for a while now (although there are a couple of cafes).

Two miles east, **Duncansby Head** provides a more solemn end-of-Britain moment with a small lighthouse and 60m cliffs sheltering nesting fulmars. From here a 15-minute walk through a sheep paddock yields spectacular views of the sea-surrounded monoliths known as **Duncansby Stacks**.

The most northerly point on the British mainland is actually at **Dunnet Head**, 8 miles east of Thurso, which offers inspiring views of the Orkney Islands, flopping seals and nesting seabirds below, and a lighthouse built by Robert Louis Stevenson's grandad.

Orkney Islands

POP 19,300

Just 6 miles off the northern coast of Scotland, this archipelago is renowned for its dramatic coastal scenery – from soaring cliffs to sandy beaches – abundant bird life, Viking heritage and a plethora of prehistoric sites. There are about 70 islands in all (16 inhabited); the largest goes by the imaginative name of Mainland, with Kirkwall the capital and Stromness the major port.

Stenness, a short bus ride from Kirkwall or Stromness, is the most accessible spot for exploring prehistoric Orkney, including **Skara Brae**, a 5000-year-old village, the **Standing Stones of Stenness** and **Barnhouse Neolithic Village**.

Particularly recommended is **Maes Howe** (HS; ☎01856-761606; www.historic-scotland.gov.uk; adult/child £5.50/3.30; ⏲tours hourly 10am-4pm), an ancient – and atmospheric – Stone Age tomb. Creeping down the long stone passageway to the central chamber, you feel the indescribable gulf of years that separate us from the architects of this mysterious place. The long journey to Orkney is worth it for this alone.

There's a good selection of low-priced B&Bs and hostels across the Orkneys – especially on Mainland – and plenty of cafes, restaurants and pubs.

Tours

Wildabout Orkney GUIDED TOUR
(☎01856-877737; www.wildaboutorkney.com) Operates tours covering Orkney's history, ecology, folklore and wildlife. Day trips operate year-round and cost £49, with pick-ups in Stromness and Kirkwall.

John O'Groats Ferries BUS TOUR
(☎01955-611353; www.jogferry.co.uk; ⏲May-Sep) If you're in a hurry, this operator runs a one-day tour of the main sites for £52, including the ferry from John O'Groats. You can do the whole thing as a long day trip from Inverness.

Information

Tourist Office (☎01856-872856; www.visitorkney.com; 6 Broad St; ⏲9am-6pm summer, 9am-5pm Mon-Fri, 10am-4pm Sat winter)

Getting There & Away

AIR **Flybe/Loganair** (☎0871 700 0535; www.flybe.com) flies daily from Kirkwall to Aberdeen, Edinburgh, Glasgow, Inverness and Sumburgh (Shetland).

BOAT **NorthLink Ferries** (☎0845 6000 449; www.northlinkferries.co.uk) run to/from Aberdeen, while **John O'Groats Ferries** (☎01955-611353; www.jogferry.co.uk) operates a passenger shuttle to/from John O'Groats.

Pentland Ferries (☎01856-831226, 0800 688 8998; www.pentlandferries.co.uk) boats leave from Gills Bay, about 3 miles west of John O'Groats, and head to St Margaret's Hope on South Ronaldsay (passenger/car £14/33, one hour). There are three to four crossings daily.

Getting Around

BICYCLE Various locations on Mainland hire bikes, including **Cycle Orkney** (☎01856-875777; www.cycleorkney.com; Tankerness Lane, Kirkwall; per day £15; ⏲Mon-Sat) and **Orkney Cycle Hire** (☎01856-850255; www.orkneycyclehire.co.uk; 54 Dundas St, Stromness; per day £8.50-10).

BOAT **Orkney Ferries** (☎01856-872044; www.orkneyferries.co.uk) operates car ferries from Mainland to the islands.

BUS Buses run on Mainland. Dayrider (£7.75) and 7-Day Megarider (£17) tickets allow unlimited travel.

UNDERSTAND BRITAIN

History

It may be a small island on the edge of western Europe, but Britain was never on the sidelines of history. For thousands of years, invaders and incomers have arrived, settled and made their mark. The result is Britain's fascinating mix of landscape, culture and language – a dynamic pattern that shaped the nation and continues to evolve today.

Celts & Romans

Populated by bands of hunter-gatherers for centuries, the island now called Britain changed significantly around 4000 BC when a group of Neolithic migrants wielding newfangled stone tools arrived from the European mainland. These early settlers built many burial mounds and passage graves, as well as stone circles such as those at Avebury and Stonehenge in southern England. In their wake came the Celts, whose bronze- and iron-smelting skills transformed the British landscape and created a distinct new culture.

The Romans arrived on the island they called Britannia in AD 43, and stayed for the next 350 years. Their legacy still remains in the shape of many villas, forts and bath houses, best seen in Bath and the great northern barrier of Hadrian's Wall.

The Dark Ages

With its empire crumbling across Europe, the Romans abandoned Britain in AD 410, heralding the period now known as the Dark Ages. Towns were abandoned and rural areas became no-go zones as local warlords fought over fiefdoms.

By the late 6th century much of southern and central Britain had been colonised by Anglo-Saxons. The land was divided into separate kingdoms dominated by Wessex (in today's southern England), Mercia (today's central England) and Northumbria (today's northern England and southern Scotland), while the Celtic culture was slowly pushed to the island's western and northern edges (especially Cornwall, Wales and northern Scotland).

While the tribal kingdoms of Britain ebbed and flowed, marauding bands of Nordic Vikings had occupied much of large swathes of land across much of Scotland, and eastern and northern England, where York became their capital. After several decades of sporadic raids, they eventually settled, and traces of their language can still be heard across much of northern England in words such as *beck* (river), *force* (waterfall) and *thwaite* (village). Thus England was divided in two: north and east was Viking 'Danelaw', while south and west was Anglo-Saxon territory.

After leading great victories against the Vikings, King Alfred was hailed as king of the English – the first time the Anglo-Saxons regarded themselves as a truly united people. His son, Athelstan, was crowned the first King of England in 927.

1066 & All That

In 1066, the Norman duke, William of Normandy – who had a tenuous claim on the English throne thanks to his royal bloodline – decided to enforce his birthright following the death of Edward the Confessor. He won a decisive victory at the Battle of Hastings, when the English King Harold was killed (supposedly by an arrow in the eye). William became king of England, earning himself the prestigious epithet Conqueror.

The Normans had a great influence on England, importing French aristocrats to take charge, and building an imposing network of hulking castles and astonishing cathedrals. Many architectural landmarks in Britain date from this period, such as Windsor Castle near London and Durham Cathedral in northeast England. But while the French–Norman effect changed England and lowland Scotland over the following centuries, further north the Highland clans remained isolated in their glens – a law unto themselves for another 600 years.

Medieval Britain

The centuries after the Norman invasion saw England racked with intrigue and conspiracy as aristocratic families squared off against each other to influence the royal succession. The era also introduced an equally enduring tendency of bickering between royalty and the church – epitomised in 1170 when King Henry II had 'turbulent priest' Thomas Becket murdered in Canterbury Cathedral, still an important shrine and tourist attraction today.

The following century saw King Edward I come to the English throne. An ambitious general, he led a bloody invasion of Wales that lasted much of the 1270s, ending with the defeat of Welsh Prince Llewellyn. There were no more Welsh kings, and just to make it clear who was boss, Edward made his eldest son Prince of Wales, a tradition that continues to this day.

Edward had less luck in Scotland. In 1297, at the Battle of Stirling Bridge, the English were defeated by a Scots army under the leadership of the rebel William Wallace. The Scottish struggle for independence continued under Robert the Bruce, who scored another decisive victory against Edward II at the Battle of Bannockburn in 1314.

Great Dynasties

In 1399 Henry IV – the first monarch of the House of Lancaster – came to the throne, but his rule was disrupted by a final cry of resistance from the downtrodden Welsh, led by Owain Glyndŵr (Owen Glendower to the English). The rebellion was crushed, vast areas of farmland were destroyed, Glyndŵr died an outlaw and the Welsh elite were barred from public life for many years.

By 1485 King Henry VII had been crowned, the first of the Tudor dynasty – a period characterised by the timber-framed buildings of English towns like Chester and Stratford-upon-Avon. Henry diligently mended fences with his northern neighbours by marrying off his daughter to James IV of Scotland. He also withdrew many of the anti-Welsh restrictions imposed after the Glyndŵr uprising.

Matrimony may have been more useful than warfare for Henry VII, but the multiple marriages of his successor, Henry VIII, were a very different story. Fathering a male heir was his problem – hence the famous six wives – but the pope's disapproval of divorce led to a split with the Roman Catholic Church, and parliament made Henry the head of the Protestant Church of England. It was the beginning of a pivotal division between Catholics and Protestants that still exists in some areas of Britain.

In 1536 Henry's next step was the 'dissolution' of many abbeys and monasteries, and the romantic ruins of some of these – including Whitby Abbey and Glastonbury Abbey – can still be visited. At the same time, Henry signed the Acts of Union (1536–43), formally uniting England and Wales for the first time.

The Elizabethan Age

When Henry VIII died, he was succeeded by his son Edward VI, then by daughter Mary I, but their reigns were short. So, unexpectedly, the third child, Elizabeth, came to the throne. During her 45-year reign, Elizabeth I (sometimes called 'The Virgin Queen') oversaw a great cultural and economic renaissance in England, with seafarers such as Walter Raleigh and Francis Drake founding colonies across the New World, and playwrights including William Shakespeare and Christopher Marlowe reinventing the English stage. She also masterminded the defeat of the Spanish Armada, when King Philip II sought to invade England in a botched attempt to reconvert the country to Catholicism.

Meanwhile, Elizabeth's cousin Mary (daughter of Scottish King James V, and a Catholic) had become queen of Scotland. She'd spent her childhood in France and had married the French dauphin (crown prince), thereby becoming queen of France as well. Why stop at two? After her husband's death, Mary returned to Scotland, and from there ambitiously claimed the English throne as well – on the grounds that Elizabeth was illegitimate. Mary's plans failed; she was imprisoned and forced to abdicate. In an uncharacteristic display of indecision, Elizabeth held Mary under arrest before finally ordering her execution 19 years later.

Britain United

When Elizabeth died in 1603, despite a bountiful reign, one thing the Virgin Queen failed to provide was an heir. She was succeeded by her closest relative, the Scottish (and safely Protestant) King James, son of the executed Mary. He became James I of England and VI of Scotland, the first king of both nations, and the first monarch of the Stuart dynasty.

A century later, in 1707, the Act of Union was passed, bringing an end to the independent Scottish parliament, and finally linking the countries of England, Wales and Scotland under one unified parliament (based in London). The nation of Britain was now established as a single state for the first time in history.

The Empire Strikes Out

Unity in Britain was mirrored by expansion abroad. Vast swathes of territory in America, Canada and India became part of the British Empire, and the first claims were made to Australia after Captain James Cook's epic voyage in 1768.

The empire's first major setback came when the American colonies won the War of Independence (1776–83). This forced Britain to withdraw from the world stage for a while, a gap not missed by French ruler Napoléon. He threatened to invade Britain and hinder the power of the British overseas, before his ambitions were curtailed by naval hero Viscount Horatio Nelson and military hero the Duke of Wellington at the famous battles of Trafalgar (1805) and Waterloo (1815).

The Industrial Age

While the empire expanded abroad, at home Britain had become the crucible of the Industrial Revolution. Steam power (patented by James Watt in 1781) and steam trains (launched by George Stephenson in 1830) transformed methods of production and transport, and the towns of the English Midlands became the first industrial cities.

Across Britain, industrialisation meant people were on the move as never before. People left the land their families had occupied for generations; perhaps most notably in the Scottish Highlands, where landowners expelled entire farms and villages to make way for sheep farms, a seminal event in Scotland's history known as the Clearances.

By the time Queen Victoria took the throne in 1837, Britain's factories dominated world trade and Britain's fleets dominated the oceans. The rest of the 19th century was seen as Britain's golden age, a period of confidence not seen since the days of the last great queen, Elizabeth I.

The lasting cultural impact of the Victorian era is still evident throughout the country in the great red-brick factories, enormous glass-roofed train stations and magnificent public buildings in cities such as London, Newcastle, Manchester, Edinburgh and Glasgow.

The Modern Era

Most of Britain's 20th century was a period of conflict and decline. Two world wars brought the nation almost to its knees, although many still recall the 1940 Battle of Britain, when the country resisted a three-month air attack from Germany, as its finest hour.

In the 1950s and 1960s, the once-great manufacturing industries started to falter, and the 1970s and 1980s saw them pretty much die completely.

By the 1990s, though, Britain had bounced back and entered the new millennium with one of the world's strongest economies and a cultural scene dubbed (briefly) 'Cool Britannia'. In the general election of 1997, after nearly 18 years of Conservative rule, 'New' Labour swept to power under fresh-faced Tony Blair.

New Millennium

In the early part of the 21st century, Britain's role on the world stage was exemplified by its relationship with the USA and participation in military campaigns in Afghanistan and Iraq – not that everyone agreed with such moves; millions of people took to the streets of London and other major British cities to protest their nation's involvement.

June 2007 saw the resignation of Tony Blair, allowing Gordon Brown, the Chancellor of the Exchequer (the British term for Minister of Finance) and for so long the prime-minister-in-waiting, to finally get the top job.

History turned full circle as the state of Britain began to divide into its three constituent nations, with the Labour government announcing a referendum on Scottish devolution. The Scots voted overwhelmingly in favour, and representatives to the new Scottish parliament – which has limited but increasing law-making powers – were elected in 1999. Concurrently, in a step towards greater political autonomy, the people of Wales voted to be governed by a Welsh Assembly, which now meets in a landmark new building in Cardiff.

Britain Today

In 2010, a record 14 years of Labour rule came to an end, and a new coalition between the Conservative and Liberal-Democrat parties became the new government, with David Cameron as the prime minister.

Facing one of the largest public deficits and deepest recessions in a century, the coalition embarked on a tough program of cuts aimed at staving off the financial problems faced by many of Britain's European neighbours.

While events such as the 2012 London Olympics briefly lifted the nation's spirits, the road out of recession has been rocky, compounded by the economic problems of the Eurozone and the omnipresent tensions within the coalition. Even more important, perhaps, is Scotland's decision to hold a referendum on independence in 2014, a long-held dream for the Scottish National Party (SNP) and its ebullient leader, Alex Salmond. Controversially, only Scots will have the right to vote on independence, in what could be one of the most momentous events in British history since the Act of Union in 1707.

People

Britain's population is 58 million (England around 50 million, Wales around three million and Scotland around five million), making it one of the world's most densely populated countries.

Several big towns and cities in Britain – particularly London, Glasgow, Birmingham and Manchester – have large ethnic communities, mainly from Britain's former colonies in the Caribbean, India, Pakistan and parts of Africa. In recent years, large numbers of people from eastern Europe have also come to Britain for work.

Religion

In the 2001 national census, around 35 million people in Britain stated their religion as Christian, the majority of which are 'C of E' (Church of England, England's main Protestant church). Other Christian faiths include Roman Catholic (about 10%), plus sizeable groups of Methodists, Baptists and other nonconformists, especially in Wales and Scotland. Church attendance has declined rapidly over the last 50 years.

The most recent census also recorded around 1.5 million Muslims (about 3%), Hindus (1%), Sikhs (0.7%), Jews (0.5%) and Buddhists (0.3%).

Arts

Literature

Britain's landscape is a literary one, and you'll encounter the ghosts of great writers practically everywhere you travel. The Romantics sought inspiration and escape in the Lake District, Jane Austen documented the social strata of Georgian Bath, while the Scottish glens still summon the spirit of Robbie Burns.

Two of the great figures you'll definitely encounter are Shakespeare, whose hometown of Stratford-upon-Avon is a must for literary buffs; and Charles Dickens, who set many of his tales in the grimy streets of Victorian London's East End. More recent literary heavyweights include Edinburgh-based JK Rowling, author of the *Harry Potter* stories, and Philip Pullman, whose *His Dark Materials* trilogy made memorable use of Oxford's dreaming spires. Leading literary novelists such as Martin Amis, Zadie Smith, Ian McEwan, Will Self, Sarah Waters, David Mitchell and Salman Rushdie have all delved into Britain's complex character in their novels, along with their more populist counterparts such as Nick Hornby, David Nicholls and Sebastian Faulks.

Britain's most prestigious literary award, the Man Booker Prize, is held in October. In 2012, Hilary Mantel became the first woman to win the prize twice, the second time for her novel *Bring Up The Bodies,* set among the intrigue of Henry VIII's royal court.

Cinema & TV

Britain's home-grown film industry ebbs and flows, with most of its contemporary worldwide hits – including *Shakespeare in Love* and *Bend It Like Beckham* – occupying the heart-warming side of film narrative. For a more realistic take, directors such as Mike Leigh and Ken Loach are two of Britain's most successful directors, known for their careful character work and naturalistic style.

Comedy is another great British export, perhaps most notably thanks to the work of teams such as Ricky Gervais and Stephen Merchant (creators of *The Office* and *Extras*) and Edgar Wright, Nick Frost and Simon Pegg (who made *Shaun of the Dead* and *Hot Fuzz*).

Britain's national broadcaster is the BBC, a public-service operator paid for by a compulsory annual licence fee. The BBC operates several TV and radio channels, none of which are allowed to include adverts. Their commercial rivals include ITV, C4 and C5, as well as satellite-only Sky, all of which are funded mainly by advertising.

Music

Britain might no longer have an empire, but it still leads the world when it comes to music. From the Fab Four and the Rolling Stones through to world-beating modern bands such as Oasis and Radiohead, Britain has one of the world's richest music cultures.

Today British pop music is as fast-moving and varied as ever, divided into a host of different genres. Alongside the stalwarts of rock, indie and electronica such as Blur, Coldplay, PJ Harvey and Muse, there's been an increasing interest in British folk in recent years, spearheaded by the all-conquering Mumford & Sons, whose album *Babel* became one of the fastest-selling in music history. Names such as Dizzee Rascal, Tinie Tempah and Plan B have heralded a new wave of British hip-hop, grime and garage artists, while singer-songwriters including Adele and the late Amy Winehouse have helped promote a new style of British soul and R&B. One of the best introductions to the most exciting new British albums is the annual Mercury Prize (www.mercuryprize.com) held in November, which has a reputation for turning up exciting new artists from right across the musical spectrum.

Britain also hosts a huge number of annual outdoor festivals dedicated to its music scene. The most famous is the Glastonbury Festival of Performing Arts, held most years on a dairy farm in rural Somerset, but there are many more events to discover such as Green Man, Bestival, V Festival, Latitude and the new Festival Number 6 in Portmeirion, each with their own unique character.

Sport

If you want to take a shortcut into the heart of British culture, watch the British at play. They're fierce and passionate about their sport, whether participating or spectating. Sometimes it's the success of the nations that matters; Scotland, Wales and England all field their own football (soccer) and rugby sides, and little love is lost when the sides meet in international competitions. Sometimes, however, Britain comes together in support of the national team – something that was clearly displayed during the 2012 Olympics and Paralympics, when a glowing sense of collective pride (briefly) superseded national loyalties.

Key events in the British sporting calendar include the Wimbledon Lawn Tennis Championships (held in June/July), the FA Cup (the main football cup, held at the end of July), horse races including the Grand National (usually in April) and Royal Ascot (June), and the Six Nations rugby tournament (February/March), contested between England, Scotland, Wales, Ireland, France and Italy.

Environment

The island of Britain sits on the eastern edge of the North Atlantic and consists of three nations: England in the south, Scotland to the north and Wales to the west; together they make up the state of Great Britain.

The Land

When it comes to topology, Britain is not a place of extremes, but even a short journey can take you through a surprising mix of landscapes.

Southern England's countryside is gently undulating, with hilly areas such as the Cotswolds and a mix of cities, towns and farmland. East Anglia is mainly low and flat, while the southwest peninsula has a rugged coast with sheltered beaches, making it a favourite holiday destination.

In the north of England, the landscape is a mix of rural countryside interspersed with towns and cities. A line of large hills called the Pennines (fondly tagged 'the backbone of England'), runs from Derbyshire to the Scottish border, and includes the peaty plateaus of the Peak District, the wild moors around Haworth (immortalised in Brontë novels) and the delightful valleys of the Yorkshire Dales.

Perhaps England's best-known landscape is the Lake District, a small but spectacular cluster of mountains in the northwest, where Scafell Pike (a towering 978m) is England's highest peak.

The landscape of Wales is also defined by hills and mountains: notably the Brecon Beacons in the south, and the spiky peaks of Snowdonia in the north, with Snowdon (1085m) the highest peak in Wales. In between lie the wild Cambrian Mountains of Mid-Wales, rolling towards a west coast of spectacular cliffs and shimmering river estuaries.

For real mountains, though, you've got to go to Scotland. Ben Nevis (1344m) is Scotland's – and Britain's – highest mountain, but there are many more to choose from.

UK OK?

The nation of Great Britain consists of England, Wales and Scotland. So far, so good. So what's the UK? The United Kingdom (UK) consists of the three countries of Great Britain plus Northern Ireland. And just for the record, the island of Ireland consists of Northern Ireland and the Republic of Ireland (also called Eire), while the British Isles is a geographical term for the whole group of islands that make up the UK and the Republic of Ireland, plus some autonomous and semiautonomous islands such as the Isle of Man and Channel Islands.

NATIONAL PARKS & CONSERVATION AREAS

In 1810, poet and outdoors lover William Wordsworth suggested that the Lake District should be 'a sort of national property, in which every man has a right'. More than a century later, the Lake District became a national park (although quite different from Wordsworth's vision), alongside the national parks of Brecon Beacons, Cairngorms, Dartmoor, Exmoor, Loch Lomond & the Trossachs, New Forest, Norfolk & Suffolk Broads, Northumberland, North York Moors, Peak District, Pembrokeshire Coast, Snowdonia and the Yorkshire Dales, as well as the newly created South Downs National Park, established in 2011.

Britain's national parks now cover over 10% of the country, although the term 'national park' means something rather different here than in many other countries. First, these areas are not state owned: nearly all land is private, belonging to farmers, companies, estates and conservation organisations. Second, they aren't untouched wildernesses: although development is strictly controlled, many local industries such as quarrying, agriculture and cattle-farming are allowed to continue, albeit carefully supervised. Tourism also forms an important part of most of the parks' incomes, and they're a paradise for hikers, bikers, wildlife-spotters and other outdoor enthusiasts.

For more details on Britian's national parks, see www.nationalparks.gov.uk.

The Highlands are further enhanced by the vast cluster of beautiful islands that lie off the loch-indented west coast.

Food & Drink

Staples & Specialities

Britain's traditional meals include roast beef, fish and chips, bangers and mash, and steak and kidney pie, many of which have been given a modern twist by Britain's celeb chefs.

Another speciality – especially if you're staying at B&Bs – is the fry-up breakfast (also known as 'the full English') containing bacon, sausage, egg, beans, mushrooms, toast and more. In Scotland you may be offered haggis or black pudding, and oatcakes instead of toast.

Alongside the home-grown favourites, most Brits have also embraced many ethnic cuisines, with Chinese and Indian restaurants now more common than traditional chippies, and cities like Glasgow, Birmingham and Manchester vying to be the nation's curry capital.

Where to Eat & Drink

You'll find a good variety of eateries in most British towns and cities – whether you're vegetarian, vegan or carnivore.

As well as restaurants and cafes, in country areas you'll find teashops (essentially a smart cafe), and across Britain pubs are often a good option for good-value, nononsense food. Look out for the ploughman's lunch, a plate of bread, cheese and pickles, which goes down well with a pint of 'real ale' (traditional beer, served warm and flat).

Across Britain, smoking is banned in all enclosed public places, and that includes all bars, pubs, cafes and restaurants.

SURVIVAL GUIDE

Directory A–Z

Accommodation

Accommodation in Britain is as varied as the sights you visit. From hip hotels to basic barns, the wide choice is all part of the attraction. Accommodation in the big cities inevitably tends to be more expensive, with London in a class all of its own.

» Rates tend to drop in low season (October to April), and rocket during high season (July to September).

» Breakfast is usually included at most B&Bs and hotels, but may be an extra at many hostels and top-end hotels.

» Rates are often quoted per person, rather than per room, and include a private bathroom unless otherwise stated.

» Smoking is banned in all hotels, B&Bs and other accommodation.

» In summer, popular spots (York, Canterbury, Bath etc) get very crowded, so booking ahead is essential.

» Accommodation can be difficult to find during holidays (especially around Easter and New Year) and major events (such as the Edinburgh Fringe Festival).

» Local tourist offices often provide an accommodation booking service for a small fee.

PRICE RANGES

Our reviews refer to double rooms with a private bathroom, except in hostels or where otherwise specified. Quoted rates are for a double room in high season.

£ less than £60 (London less than £90)

££ £60-130 (London £90-180)

£££ more than £130 (London more than £180)

CAMPING

The opportunities for camping in Britain range from farmers' fields with a tap and a basic toilet, costing from £3 per person per night, to smarter affairs with hot showers and many other facilities, charging up to £10. You usually need your own gear.

HOSTELS

Britain has two national hostelling organisations: **Youth Hostels Association** (YHA; www.yha.org.uk), covering England and Wales, and **Scottish Youth Hostels Association** (SYHA; ☎0845-293 7373; www.syha.org.uk). Dorm beds range from £10 to £20 per night. Larger hostels with more facilities are £15 to £20. London's YHAs cost from £25. Advance bookings and payments with credit card are usually possible.

You don't have to be a member of the YHA/SYHA (or another Hostelling International organisation) to stay, but most hostels charge extra if you're not a member (£3 at YHA hostels; £1 at SYHA hostels), so it's usually worth joining.

Annual YHA membership costs £16; annual SYHA membership costs £10; younger people and families get discounts.

There's a growing array of independent hostels and backpackers across Britain, varying widely in quality, facilities and price (typically from £10 to £25 per night). Some are quiet and cosy, while others are for serious party travellers.

The print and online **Independent Hostel Guide** (www.independenthostelguide.co.uk) is the best listing. North of the English border, an excellent site is www.hostel-scotland.co.uk.

HOTELS

British hotels vary widely in style and quality, from farmhouse conversions to luxury country houses and stylish boutique hotels. At the bargain end, you might find rooms from £50 per night; move up the scale and you could pay £100/150 per night or more.

Hotel chains can be a good option for accommodation on a budget, especially in larger cities. They're often a bit short on character, but rates are generally cheap and they're often in great central locations.

Etap Hotels (www.etaphotel.com)

Premier Inn (www.premierinn.com)

Travelodge (www.travelodge.co.uk)

B&BS & GUESTHOUSES

The B&B ('bed and breakfast') is a great British institution. At smaller places it's pretty much a room in somebody's house; larger places may be called a 'guest house', ie halfway between a B&B and a full hotel. Prices start at around £30 per person for an ensuite room, up to £60 or more for really special places.

» B&B prices are usually quoted per person, based on two people sharing a room.

» Single rooms for solo travellers are harder to find, and attract a 20% to 50% premium.

» If you haven't booked, most towns have a main drag of B&Bs; look out for 'Vacancies' signs.

» Many B&Bs require a minimum two nights at weekends and during busy periods.

» When booking, check where your B&B actually is, as they are often some distance from the nearest town.

BOOKING SERVICES

At Home in London (☎020-8748 1943; www.athomeinlondon.co.uk) B&Bs.

British Hotel Reservation Centre (☎020-7592 3055; www.bhrconline.com) Apartments.

GKLets (☎020-7613 2805; www.gklets.co.uk) Apartments.

London Homestead Services (☎020-7286 5115; www.lhslondon.com) B&Bs.

LondonTown (☎020-7437 4370; www.londontown.com) Hotels and B&Bs.

Uptown Reservations (☎020-7937 2001; www.uptownres.co.uk) Upmarket B&Bs.

Visit London (☎per min 10p 0871 222 3118; www.visitlondonoffers.com) Hotels.

PUBS & INNS

As well as selling drinks, many pubs and inns offer lodging, particularly in country areas. For bed and breakfast, you'll pay around £20 per person for a basic room, around £35 for something better. An advantage for solo tourists is that pubs often have single rooms.

UNIVERSITY ACCOMMODATION

Many universities offer student accommodation to visitors during vacations. Prices range from £15 to £30 per person. A handy portal is www.universityrooms.co.uk.

Activities

Britain is a great destination for outdoor enthusiasts. Walking and cycling are the most popular activities – you can do them on a whim, and they're the perfect way to open up some beautiful corners of the country.

CYCLING

Compact Britain is an excellent destination to explore by bike. Popular regions to tour include southwest England, the Yorkshire Dales, Derbyshire's Peak District, Mid-Wales and the Scottish Borders. Bike hire outlets are widespread; rates range from £10 per day to £60 per week.

The 10,000-mile **National Cycle Network** (www.nationalcyclenetwork.org.uk) is a web of quiet roads and traffic-free tracks that pass through busy cities and remote rural areas.

Sustrans (www.sustrans.org.uk) is another useful organisation, and publishes a wide range of maps, guides and planning tools.

SURFING & KITESURFING

Surfing in Britain isn't for the faint-hearted: temperatures in summer rarely get much above 13°C, and can be just a few degrees above freezing in winter. But with a decent wetsuit you'll be able to discover some of Europe's best breaks, especially around southwest Wales, Cornwall and Devon. For info, see www.britsurf.co.uk.

Britain is great for kitesurfing too; once again, Cornwall and Pembrokeshire are favourite spots. See www.kitesurfing.org.

WALKING & HIKING

Hiking is a hugely popular pastime in Britain, especially in scenic areas such as Snowdonia, the Lake District, the Yorkshire Dales and the Scottish Highlands. Various long-distance routes cross the countryside, including the **Coast to Coast** (http://www.thecoasttocoastwalk.info), the **Cotswold Way** (www.nationaltrail.co.uk/cotswold), the **West Highland Way** (☎01389-722600; www.west-highland-way.co.uk) and the **South West Coast Path** (www.southwestcoastpath.com).

The **Ramblers Association** (☎020-7339 8500; www.ramblers.org.uk) is the country's leading walkers' organisation, and its website is a mine of background information.

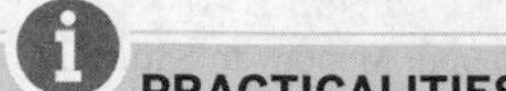

PRACTICALITIES

Newspapers & Magazines Leading tabloids include the *Sun* and *Mirror;* quality papers (from right to left, politically) include the *Telegraph, Times, Independent* and *Guardian*.

TV All TV in the UK is digital. Leading broadcasters include BBC, ITV and Channel 4. Satellite and cable TV providers include Sky and Virgin Media.

Weights & Measures Britain uses both metric and imperial measures. For example, petrol is sold by the litre but beer by the pint; mountain heights are in metres but road distances are in miles.

Radio BBC stations are Radio 1 (98-99.6MHz FM), Radio 2 (88-92MHz FM), Radio 3 (90-92.2 MHz FM), Radio 4 (92–94.4MHz FM) and Radio 5Live (909 or 693 AM). National commercial stations include Virgin Radio (1215Hz MW) and Classic FM (100–102MHz FM).

DVD PAL format, Region 2.

Business Hours

Standard business hours are as follows:

Banks 9.30am to 4pm or 5pm Monday to Friday, 9.30am to 1pm Saturday.

Museums Smaller museums may close Monday and/or Tuesday, and close on weekdays in the low season.

Nightclubs to 2am or beyond.

Post offices 9am to 5pm Monday to Friday, 9am to 12.30pm Saturday (main branches to 5pm).

Pubs 11am to 11pm Sunday to Thursday, sometimes to midnight or 1am Friday and Saturday; some pubs close between 3pm and 6pm; bars open to midnight or later.

Restaurants Lunch noon to 3pm, dinner 6pm to 11pm or later; some restaurants close on Sunday evenings or all day Monday; cafes open 7am to 6pm; teashops open for lunch until 5pm or later in summer.

Shops 9am to 5pm Monday to Saturday (to 5.30pm or 6pm in cities), 10am to 4pm Sunday; in smaller towns or country areas, shops may close for lunch from 1pm to 2pm and on Wednesday or Thursday afternoon.

Customs & Regulations

The UK has a two-tier customs system:

» Duty-free from outside the EU includes 200 cigarettes or equivalent in cigars, 4L of wine, 1L of spirits, 60c of perfume, and other goods worth up to £390.

» Tax and duty paid within the EU guidelines are 800 cigarettes, 200 cigars, 10L of spirits, 90L of wine and 110L of beer.

Embassies & Consulates

This is a selection of embassies, consulates and high commissions in London. For a complete list, see the website of the **Foreign & Commonwealth Office** (www.fco.gov.uk).

Australia (☎020-7379 4334; www.australia.org.uk; Australia House, The Strand)

Canada (☎020-7258 6600; www.canada.org.uk; 1 Grosvenor Sq)

New Zealand (☎020-7930 8422; www.nzembassy.com/uk; 80 Haymarket)

USA (☎020-7499 9000; www.usembassy.org.uk; 24 Grosvenor Sq)

Food

The prices we quote for eateries are for a main meal unless otherwise indicated. The symbols used in each review indicate the following prices:

£ less than £9

££ £9 to £18

£££ more than £18

Gay & Lesbian Travellers

Most major cities – especially London, Brighton, Manchester and Glasgow – have gay and lesbian scenes. Useful resources:

» **Diva** (www.divamag.co.uk)

» **Gay Times** (www.gaytimes.co.uk)

» **Pink Paper** (www.pinkpaper.com)

Heritage Organisations

Many of the UK's castles and stately homes, as well as large areas of countryside, are owned by national heritage organisations. If you're a member, you get free admission, free parking, information handbooks and so on. You can join at the first site you visit; if you join an English heritage organisation, it covers you for Wales and Scotland, and vice versa. We have included the relevant acronym (NT, NTS, EH etc) in the information for listed properties.

Annual **English Heritage** (www.english-heritage.org.uk) membership costs £47. An Overseas Visitors Pass allows free entry to most sites for seven/14 days for £23/27. In Wales and Scotland the equivalent organisations are **Cadw** (www.cadw.wales.gov.uk) and **Historic Scotland** (www.historic-scotland.gov.uk).

National Trust (NT; www.nationaltrust.org.uk) annual membership costs £53 (with discounts for under-26s). A Touring Pass allows free entry to NT properties for one/two weeks (£23/28 per person). The **National Trust for Scotland** (NTS; www.nts.org.uk) is similar.

Language

The dominant language of Britain is English. In Wales about 600,000 people (20% of the population) speak Welsh as a first language, while in Scotland, Gaelic – another Celtic language – is spoken by about 80,000 people, mainly in the Highlands and Islands.

Money

ATMs ATMs (often called 'cash machines') are easy to find in cities and even small towns.

Changing Money Most banks and some post offices offer currency exchange services. Check rates at bureaux de change; they may claim 'no commission' but often rates are poor.

Credit & Debit Cards Smaller businesses, such as pubs or B&Bs, prefer debit cards (or charge a fee for credit cards), and some take cash or cheque only. Nearly all credit and debit cards use a 'Chip and PIN' system (instead of signing).

Currency The currency of Britain is the pound sterling (£). Paper money ('notes') comes in £5, £10, £20 and £50 denomina-

SCOTTISH POUNDS

Scotland issues its own currency (including a £1 note), interchangeable with the money used in the rest of the UK. However, you'll find shops more readily accept Scottish money in the north of England than in the south. Banks will always change Scottish pounds.

tions, although some shops don't accept £50 notes because fakes circulate.

Tipping In Britain, you're not obliged to tip if service or food was unsatisfactory (even if it's been added to your bill as a 'service charge'). 10% is fine for restaurants, cafés, taxi drivers and pub meals; if you order drinks and food at the bar, there's no need to tip.

Travellers Cheques Travellers cheques are rarely used in Britain these days.

Public Holidays

In many areas of Britain, bank holidays are just for the banks – many larger businesses and some visitor attractions such as supermarkets stay open.

New Year's Day 1 January

Easter March/April (Good Friday to Easter Monday inclusive)

May Day First Monday in May

Spring Bank Holiday Last Monday in May

Summer Bank Holiday Last Monday in August

Christmas Day 25 December

Boxing Day 26 December

Safe Travel

Britain is a remarkably safe country, but crime does occur in London and other cities. When travelling by tube, tram or urban train service at night, choose a carriage containing other people.

HOLIDAY SEASONS

Roads get busy and hotel prices go up during school holidays. Exact dates vary from year to year and region to region, but are roughly:

Easter Holiday Week before and week after Easter.

Summer Holiday Third week of July to first week of September.

Christmas Holiday Mid-December to first week of January.

There are also three week-long 'half-term' school holidays – usually late February (or early March), late May and late October. These vary between Scotland, England and Wales.

Unlicensed minicabs – a bloke with a car earning money on the side – operate in large cities, and are usually worth avoiding. Use a metered taxi or phone a reputable minicab company and get an up-front quote for the fare.

Telephone

AREA CODES

Area codes and individual numbers have been listed together, separated by a hyphen. Other codes:

» 0500 or 0800 – free calls

» 0845 – calls at the local rate, wherever you're dialling from within the UK

» 087 – calls at the national rate

» 089 or 09 – premium rate

» 07 – mobile phones, more expensive than calling a landline

To call outside the UK, dial ☎00, then the country code (☎1 for USA, ☎61 for Australia etc), the area code (you usually drop the initial zero) and the number.

» operator ☎100

» international operator ☎155 – also for reverse-charge (collect) calls

For directory enquiries, a host of agencies compete for your business and charge from 10p to 40p; numbers include ☎118 192, ☎118 118, ☎118 500 and ☎118 811.

MOBILE PHONES

Phones from most other countries operate in England, but attract roaming charges. Local SIM cards cost from £10; SIM and basic handset around £30.

PUBLIC PAYPHONES

The famous red telephone boxes are a dying breed, surviving mainly in conservation areas. You'll mainly see two types of public payphones in Britain: one takes money (and doesn't give change), while the other uses prepaid phonecards and credit cards. Some phones accept both coins and cards. The minimum call price is 50p.

Time

In winter (late October to late March) Britain is on GMT/UTC 0.

In summer (late March to late October) Britain uses daylight saving so the time is GMT/UTC +1.

In summer, if it's noon in London, it's:

» 9pm in Melbourne, Australia

» 7am in New York, USA

Tourist Information

All British cities and towns, and some villages, have a tourist information centre (TIC) with helpful staff, books and maps, free leaflets and loads of advice on things to see or do. They can also assist with booking accommodation.

Most tourist offices keep regular business hours; in quiet areas they close from October to March, while in popular areas they open daily year-round. For a list see www.visitmap.info/tic.

Visas

European Economic Area (EEA) nationals don't need a visa to visit (or work in) Britain. Citizens of Australia, Canada, New Zealand, South Africa and the USA can visit for up to six months (three months for some nationalities), but are prohibited from working. For more info see www.ukvisas.gov.uk or www.ukba.homeoffice.gov.uk.

Getting There & Away

Air

You can easily fly to Britain from just about anywhere in the world. In recent years regional airports around Britain have massively increased their choice – especially on budget ('no-frills') airlines to/from mainland Europe.

LONDON AIRPORTS

London is served by five airports; Heathrow and Gatwick are the busiest.

London Heathrow (www.heathrowairport.com)

London Gatwick (www.gatwickairport.com)

London City Airport (www.londoncityairport.com)

Luton (LTN; www.london-luton.co.uk) Some 35 miles north of central London, well-known as a holiday-flight airport.

Stansted (STN; www.stanstedairport.com) About 35 miles northeast of central London, mainly handling charter and budget European flights.

REGIONAL AIRPORTS

Regional airports with international flights:

Bristol Airport (www.bristolairport.co.uk)

Cardiff Airport (www.tbicardiffairport.com)

Edinburgh Airport (www.edinburghairport.com)

Glasgow Airport (www.glasgowairport.com)

Liverpool Airport (www.liverpooljohnlennonairport.com)

Manchester Airport (www.manchesterairport.co.uk)

Newcastle Airport (www.newcastleairport.com)

Southampton Airport (www.southamptonairport.com)

Land

BUS & COACH

The international network **Eurolines** (www.eurolines.com) connects a huge number of European destinations; buy tickets online via one of the national operators.

Services to/from Britain are operated by **National Express** (www.nationalexpress.com). Some sample journey times to/from London:

Amsterdam 12 hours

Barcelona 24 hours

Dublin 12 hours

Paris Eight hours

TRAIN

Eurostar (www.eurostar.com) has high-speed passenger services that shuttle at least 10 times daily between London and Paris (2½ hours) or Brussels (two hours) via the Channel Tunnel. The normal single fare between London and Paris/Brussels is around £150, but if you buy in advance, deals drop to around £90 return or less.

Drivers use the **Eurotunnel** (www.eurotunnel.com) at Folkestone in England or Calais in France: you drive onto a train, get carried through the tunnel and drive off at the other end. The trains run four times an hour from 6am to 10pm, then hourly. Loading and unloading takes an hour; the journey through the tunneltakes 35 minutes. The one-way cost for a car and passengers is around £90 to £150 depending on the time of day (less busy times are cheaper); promotional fares bring it nearer to £50.

Travelling between Ireland and Britain, the main train–ferry–train route is Dublin to London, via Dun Laoghaire and Holyhead. Ferries also run between Rosslare and Fishguard or Pembroke, with connections on either side.

Sea

The main ferry routes between Britain and mainland Europe include Dover to Calais or Boulogne (France), Harwich to Hook of Holland (Netherlands), Hull to Zeebrugge (Belgium) or Rotterdam (Netherlands), Rosyth to Zeebrugge, Portsmouth to Santander or Bilbao (Spain), and Newcastle to Bergen (Norway) or Gothenberg (Sweden). Routes to/from Ireland include Holyhead to Dun Laoghaire.

Competition from the Eurotunnel and budget airlines means ferry operators discount heavily at certain times of year. The short cross-channel routes such as Dover to Calais or Boulogne can be as low as £20 for a car plus up to five passengers, although around £50 is more likely. If you're a foot passenger, or cycling, crossings can start from as little as £10 each way.

Broker sites covering all routes and options include www.ferrybooker.com and www.directferries.co.uk.

Brittany Ferries (www.brittany-ferries.com)

DFDS Seaways (www.dfds.co.uk)

Irish Ferries (www.irishferries.com)

P&O Ferries (www.poferries.com)

Stena Line (www.stenaline.com)

Getting Around

For getting around Britain, your first main choice is going by car or public transport. Having your own car makes the best use of time and helps reach remote places, but rental, fuel costs and parking can be expensive – so public transport is often the better way to go.

Cheapest but slowest are long-distance buses (called coaches in Britain). Trains are faster but much more expensive.

Air

Britain's domestic air companies include **British Airways** (www.britishairways.com), **easyJet** (www.easyjet.com) and **Ryanair** (www.ryanair.com). On most shorter routes (eg London to Newcastle, or Manchester to Bristol), it's often faster to take the train once airport downtime is factored in.

Bus

Long-distance buses (coaches) nearly always offer the cheapest way to get around. Many towns have separate bus and coach stations; make sure you're in the right place!

National Express (www.nationalexpress.com) is England's main coach operator. North of the border, **Scottish Citylink** (☎08705 505050; www.citylink.co.uk) is the leading coach company. Tickets are cheaper if you book in advance and travel at quieter times. As a rough guide, a 200-mile trip (eg London to York) will cost around £15 to £20 booked a few days in advance.

Also offering cheap fares (if you're lucky, from £1!) is **Megabus** (www.megabus.com), which serves about 30 destinations in Britain.

If train doesn't get you all the way to your destination, a PlusBus supplement (usually around £2) validates your train ticket for onwards travel by bus.

BUS PASSES

National Express offers discount passes to full-time students and under-26s, called Young Persons Coachcards. They cost £10 and get 30% off standard adult fares. Also available are coachcards for people over 60, families and disabled travellers.

For touring the country, National Express offers Brit Xplorer passes, allowing unlimited travel for seven days (£79), 14 days (£139) and 28 days (£219).

> **HOW MUCH TO...?**
>
> When travelling long-distance by train or bus/coach in Britain, it's important to realise that there's no such thing as a standard fare. Book long in advance and travel on Tuesday mid-morning, for example, and it's cheap. Buy your ticket on the spot late Friday afternoon, and it'll be a lot more expensive. Throughout this chapter, we have generally quoted sample fares somewhere in between the very cheapest and most expensive options.

Car & Motorcycle

Most overseas driving licences are valid in Britain for up to 12 months from the date of entry.

RENTAL

Compared to many countries (especially the USA), car rental is expensive in Britain; you'll pay from around £120 per week for the smallest model, or £250 per week for a medium-sized car (including insurance and unlimited mileage). All of the major players including Avis, Hertz and Budget operate here.

Using a rental-broker site such as **UK Car Hire** (www.ukcarhire.net) or **Auto Europe** (www.auto-europe.co.uk) can help find bargains.

TRAVELINE

Traveline (☎0871 200 2233; www.traveline.org.uk) is a very useful information service covering bus, coach, taxi and train services nationwide.

It's illegal to drive a car or motorbike in Britain without (at least) third-party insurance. This will be included with all rental cars. If you're bringing your own car, you will need to arrange this.

ROAD RULES

The *Highway Code,* available in bookshops (or at www.direct.gov.uk/en/TravelAndTransport/Highwaycode), contains everything you need to know about Britain's road rules. The main ones to remember:

» Always drive on the left

» Give way to your right at junctions and roundabouts

» Always use the left-hand lane on motorways and dual-carriageways, unless overtaking (passing)

» Wear seat belts in cars and crash helmets on motorcycles

» Don't use a mobile phone while driving

» Don't drink and drive; the maximum blood-alcohol level allowed is 0.08%

» Yellow lines (single or double) along the edge of the road indicate parking restrictions, red lines mean no stopping whatsoever

» Speed limits are 30mph in built-up areas, 60mph on main roads, and 70mph on motorways and most dual carriageways

Train

The British like to moan about their trains, but around 85% run on time.

Around 20 companies operate train services in Britain, including **First Great Western** (www.firstgreatwestern.co.uk), which runs from London to Bristol; **Crosscountry** (☎0844 811 0124; www.crosscountrytrains.co.uk), which runs services all the way from Glasgow to Penzance; and **Virgin Trains** (www.virgintrains.co.uk), which runs the 'west coast' route from London to Birmingham and Glasgow.

National Rail Enquiries (☎08457 48 49 50; www.nationalrail.co.uk) provides booking and timetable information for Britain's entire rail network.

CLASSES

Rail travel has two classes: 1st and standard. Travelling 1st class costs around 50% more than standard. At weekends some train operators offer 'upgrades' for an extra £10 to £15 on top of your standard-class fare.

COSTS & RESERVATIONS

For longer journeys, on-the-spot fares are always available, but tickets are much cheaper if bought in advance. The earlier you book, the cheaper it is. You can also save if you travel 'off-peak' (ie the days and times that aren't busy). Advance purchase usually gets a reserved seat, too.

If you buy online, you can have the ticket posted (UK addresses only), or collect it from station machines on the day of travel.

There are three main fare types:

Anytime Buy anytime, travel anytime – usually the most expensive option.

Off-peak Buy anytime, travel off-peak.

Advance Buy in advance, travel only on specific trains (usually the cheapest option).

TRAIN PASSES

If you're staying in Britain for a while, passes known as railcards (www.railcard.co.uk) are available:

16-25 Railcard For those aged 16 to 25, or a full-time UK student.

Senior Railcard For anyone over 60.

Family & Friends Railcard Covers up to four adults and four children travelling together.

Railcards cost around £28 (valid for one year, available from major stations or online) and get 33% discount on most train fares, except those already heavily discounted. With the Family card, adults receive 33% and children 60% discounts, so the fee is easily repaid in a couple of journeys.

REGIONAL PASSES

Various local train passes are available covering specific areas – ask at a local train station to gain an idea of what's available.

NATIONAL PASSES

For country-wide travel, **BritRail** (www.britrail.com) passes are available for visitors from overseas. They must be bought in your country of origin (not in Britain) from a specialist travel agency. They're available in three different versions (England only; all Britain; UK and Ireland) and for periods from four to 30 days. Eurail cards are not accepted in Britain, and InterRail cards are only valid if bought in another mainland European country.

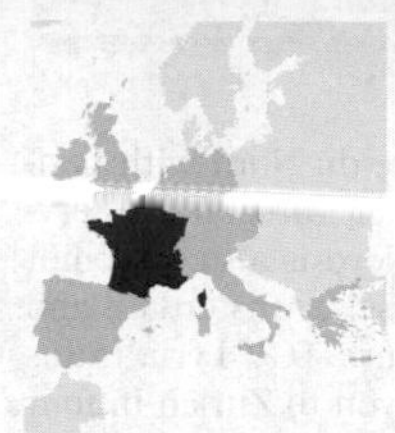

France

Includes »

Best Places to Eat

» Beef Club (p320)
» Frenchie (p320)
» Septime (p321)
» La Table de Ventabren (p402)
» Les Vieilles Luges (p377)

Best Places to Stay

» Hôtel Amour (p320)
» Hôtel Crayon (p317)
» L'Épicerie (p402)
» Hôtel 7e Art (p413)
» Nice Pebbles (p410)

Why Go?

Few countries provoke such passion as La Belle France. Love it or loathe it, everyone has their own opinion about this Gallic Goliath. Snooty, sexy, superior, chic, infuriating, arrogant, officious and inspired in equal measures, the French have long lived according to their own idiosyncratic rules, and if the rest of the world doesn't always see eye-to-eye with them, well, *tant pis* (too bad) – it's the price you pay for being a culinary trendsetter, artistic pioneer and cultural icon.

If ever there was a country of contradictions, this is it. France is a deeply traditional place: castles, chateaux and ancient churches litter the landscape, while centuries-old principles of rich food, fine wine and joie de vivre underpin everyday life. Yet it is also a country that has one of Western Europe's most multicultural make-ups, not to mention a well-deserved reputation for artistic experimentation and architectural invention. Enjoy!

When to Go

Paris

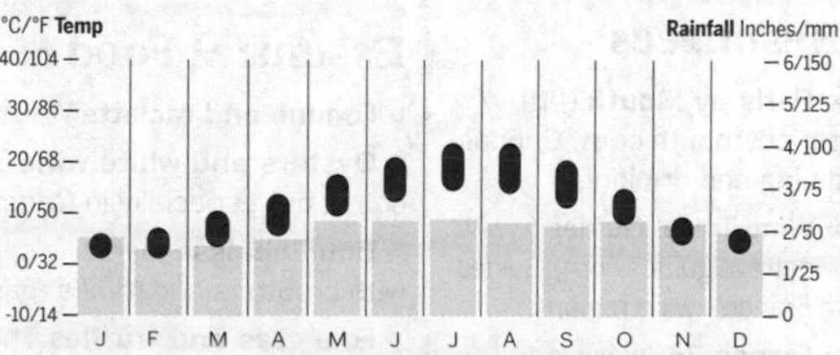

Dec–Mar Hit the French Alps, Jura or Pyrenees for some serious ski action. Eat truffles.

Apr–Jun France at its springtime best, *sans* crowds; June's Fête de la Musique gets you jigging.

Sep Cooling temperatures, abundant produce and the grape harvest; perfect for cycling through Provence.

AT A GLANCE

» **Currency** euro (€)

» **Language** French

» **Money** ATMs everywhere

» **Visas** Schengen rules apply

Fast Facts

» **Area** 551,000 sq km

» **Capital** Paris

» **Country code** ☎33

» **Emergency** ☎112

Exchange Rates

Australia	A$1	€0.82
Canada	C$1	€0.77
Japan	¥100	€0.83
New Zealand	NZ$1	€0.65
UK	UK£1	€1.18
USA	US$1	€0.78

Set Your Budget

» **Budget hotel room** €60–80

» **Two-course meal** €15–50

» **Museum entrance** €4–10

» **Glass of wine** €2–5

» **Paris metro ticket** €1.70

Resources

» **Paris by Mouth** (http://parisbymouth.com) Capital dining and drinking.

» **Wine Travel Guides** (www.winetravelguides.com) Guides to France's wine regions.

» **France 24** (www.france24.com/en/france) French news in English.

» **Lost in Cheeseland** (www.lostincheeseland.com) French life seen through the eyes of an American expat.

Connections

High-speed TGV trains link Paris' Gare du Nord with London's St Pancras (via the Channel Tunnel/Eurostar rail service) in just over two hours; Gare du Nord is also the point of departure for speedy trains to Brussels, Amsterdam and Cologne; and Gare de l'Est for Frankfurt. TGV Lyria trains whisk travellers from Paris' Gare de Lyon to Zurich in four hours. Many more trains make travelling between the French capital and pretty much any city in every neighbouring country a real pleasure. Ferry links from Cherbourg, St-Malo, Calais and other north-coast ports travel to England and Ireland; ferries from Marseille and Nice provide regular links with seaside towns in Corsica, Italy and North Africa.

Regular bus and rail links cross the French–Spanish border via the Pyrenees, and the French–Italian border via the Alps and the southern Mediterranean coast.

ITINERARIES

One Week

Start with a few days exploring Paris, taking in the Louvre, Eiffel Tower, Musée d'Orsay, Notre Dame, Montmartre and a boat trip along the Seine. Then head out to Normandy, Monet's garden at Giverny, and Versailles; or throw yourself into the Renaissance high life at chateaux in the Loire Valley.

Two Weeks

With Paris and surrounds having taken up much of the first week, concentrate on exploring one or two regions rather than trying to do too much in a whistlestop dash. High-speed TGV trains zip from Paris to every province: for prehistoric and gastronomic interest, head to the Dordogne; for architectural splendour, you can't top the Loire Valley; for typical French atmosphere, try the hilltop villages of Provence; and for sunshine and seafood, head to the French Riviera on the sparkling Med.

Essential Food & Drink

» **Fondue and raclette** Warming cheese dishes in the Alps.

» **Oysters and white wine** Everywhere on the Atlantic coast, but especially in Cancale and Bordeaux.

» **Bouillabaisse** Marseille's signature hearty fish stew, eaten with croutons and *rouille* (garlic-and-chilli mayonnaise).

» **Foie gras and truffles** The Dordogne features goose and 'black diamonds' from December to March. Provence is also good for indulging in the aphrodisiac-like fungi.

» **Piggy-part cuisine** Lyon is famous for its juicy *andouillette* (pig-intestine sausage); try it with a local Côtes du Rhône red.

» **Champagne** Tasting in century-old cellars is an essential part of Champagne's bubbly experience.

PARIS

POP 2.2 MILLION

What can be said about the sexy, sophisticated City of Lights that hasn't already been said a thousand times before? Quite simply, this is one of the world's great metropolises – a trendsetter, market leader and cultural capital for over a thousand years and still going strong. This is the place that gave the world the can-can and the cinematograph, a city that reinvented itself during the Renaissance, bopped to the beat of the jazz age, and positively glittered during the belle époque (literally, 'beautiful era').

As you might expect, Paris is strewn with historic architecture, glorious galleries and cultural treasures galore. But the modern-day city is much more than just a museum piece: it's a heady hodgepodge of cultures and ideas – a place to stroll the boulevards, shop till you drop, flop riverside, or simply do as the Parisians do and watch the world buzz by from a streetside cafe. Savour every moment.

History

The Parisii, a tribe of Celtic Gauls, settled the Île de la Cité in the 3rd century BC. Paris prospered during the Middle Ages and flourished during the Renaissance, when many of the city's most famous buildings were erected.

The excesses of Louis XVI and his queen, Marie Antoinette, led to an uprising of Parisians on 14 July 1789, and the storming of the Bastille prison – kick-starting the French Revolution.

In 1851 Emperor Napoléon III oversaw the construction of a more modern Paris, complete with wide boulevards, sculptured parks and a sewer system. Following the disastrous Franco-Prussian War and the establishment of the Third Republic, Paris entered its most resplendent period, the belle époque, famed for its art nouveau architecture and artistic and scientific advances. By the beginning of the 1930s, Paris had become a centre for the artistic avant-garde, and it remained so until the Nazi occupation of 1940–44.

After WWII, Paris regained its position as a creative centre and nurtured a revitalised liberalism that climaxed in student-led uprisings in 1968.

During the 1980s President François Mitterrand initiated several *grands projets*, building projects that garnered widespread approval even when the results were popular failures. In 2001 Bertrand Delanoë, a socialist with support from the Green Party, became Paris' – and a European capital's – first openly gay mayor. He returned to power for another term in the 2008 elections.

Sights

LEFT BANK

Eiffel Tower LANDMARK

(Map p304; ☎01 44 11 23 23; www.tour-eiffel.fr; lift to 3rd fl adult/12-24yr/4-12yr €14/12.50/9.50, lift to 2nd fl €8.50/7/4, stairs to 2nd fl €5/3.50/3; ⏲lifts & stairs 9am-midnight mid-Jun–Aug, lifts 9.30am-11pm, stairs 9.30am-6pm Sep–mid-Jun; Ⓜ Bir Hakeim or RER Champ de Mars-Tour Eiffel) Named after its designer, Gustave Eiffel, this Paris icon was built for the 1889 Exposition Universelle (World Fair), marking the centenary of the French Revolution. At the time it faced massive opposition

PARIS IN...

Two Days

Join a morning tour then focus on those Parisian icons: **Notre Dame**, the **Eiffel Tower** and the **Arc de Triomphe**. Late afternoon have a coffee or glass of wine on the **av des Champs-Élysées**, then mooch to Montmartre for dinner. On the second day enjoy the **Musée d'Orsay**, **Ste-Chapelle** and the **Musée Rodin**. Dine and revel in a night of mirth and gaiety in the dine-well, nightlife-buzzy Marais.

Four Days

With another two days, consider a cruise along the **Seine** or **Canal St-Martin** bookended by visits to the **Cimetière du Père Lachaise** and **Parc de la Villette**. By night take in a concert, opera or ballet at the **Palais Garnier** or **Opéra Bastille**, followed by a bar-club crawl along Ménilmontant's rue Oberkampf or through the Bastille area.

One Week

Seven days allows you to see a good many of the major sights and day-trip it out of Paris proper to surrounding areas such as **Versailles**.

France Highlights

1 Gorge on the iconic sights and sophistication of Europe's most hopelessly romantic city, **Paris** (p301)

2 Relive the French Renaissance with extraordinary chateaux built by kings and queens in the **Loire Valley** (p359)

3 Do a Bond and swoosh down slopes in the shadow of Mont Blanc in **Chamonix** (p374)

4 Dodge tides, stroll moonlit sand and immerse yourself in legend at island abbey **Mont St-Michel** (p345)

5 Savour ancient ruins, modern art, markets, lavender and hilltop villages in slow-paced **Provence** (p396)

6 Taste bubbly in ancient *caves* (cellars) in **Reims** (p350) and **Épernay** (p352), the heart of Champagne

7 Tuck into **Lyon's** piggy-driven cuisine in a traditional bouchon (p372)

8 Soak up the mystery of the world's best megaliths from the back of a Breton bicycle around **Carnac** (p345)

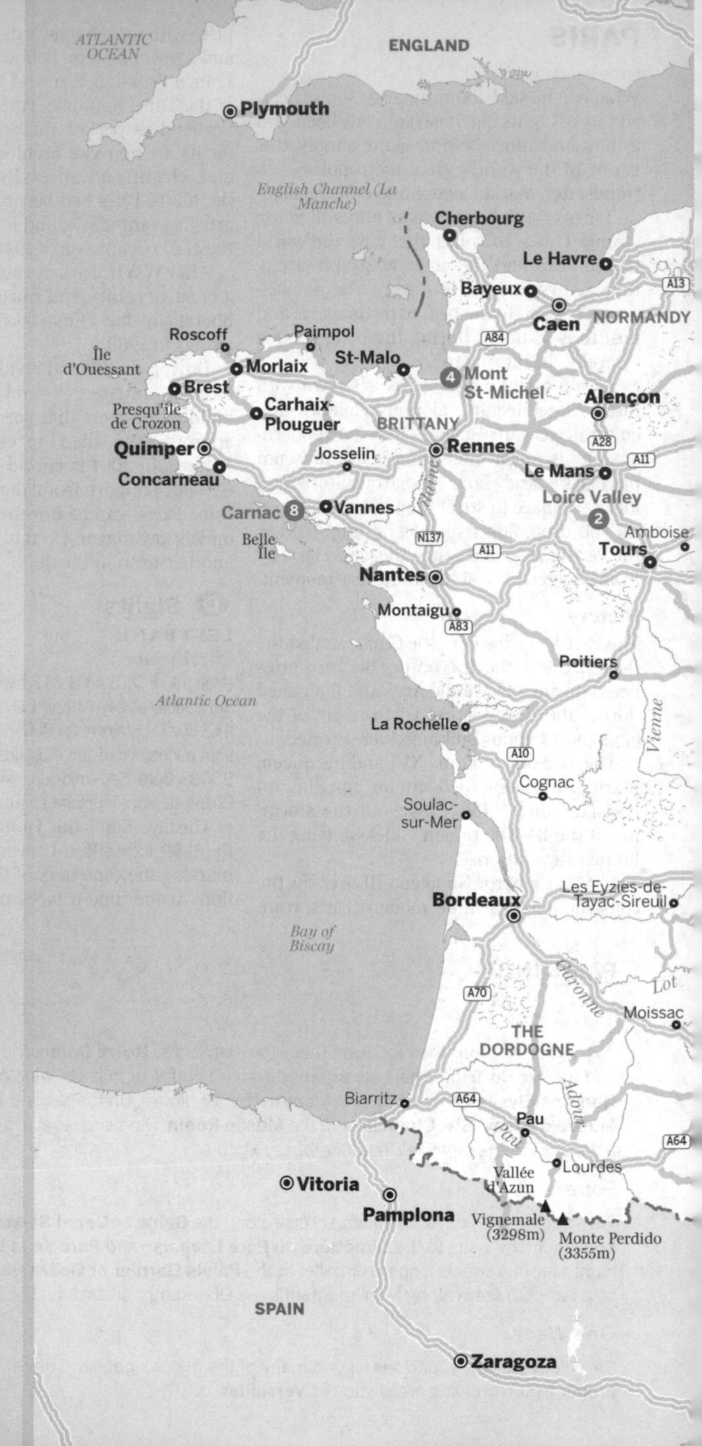

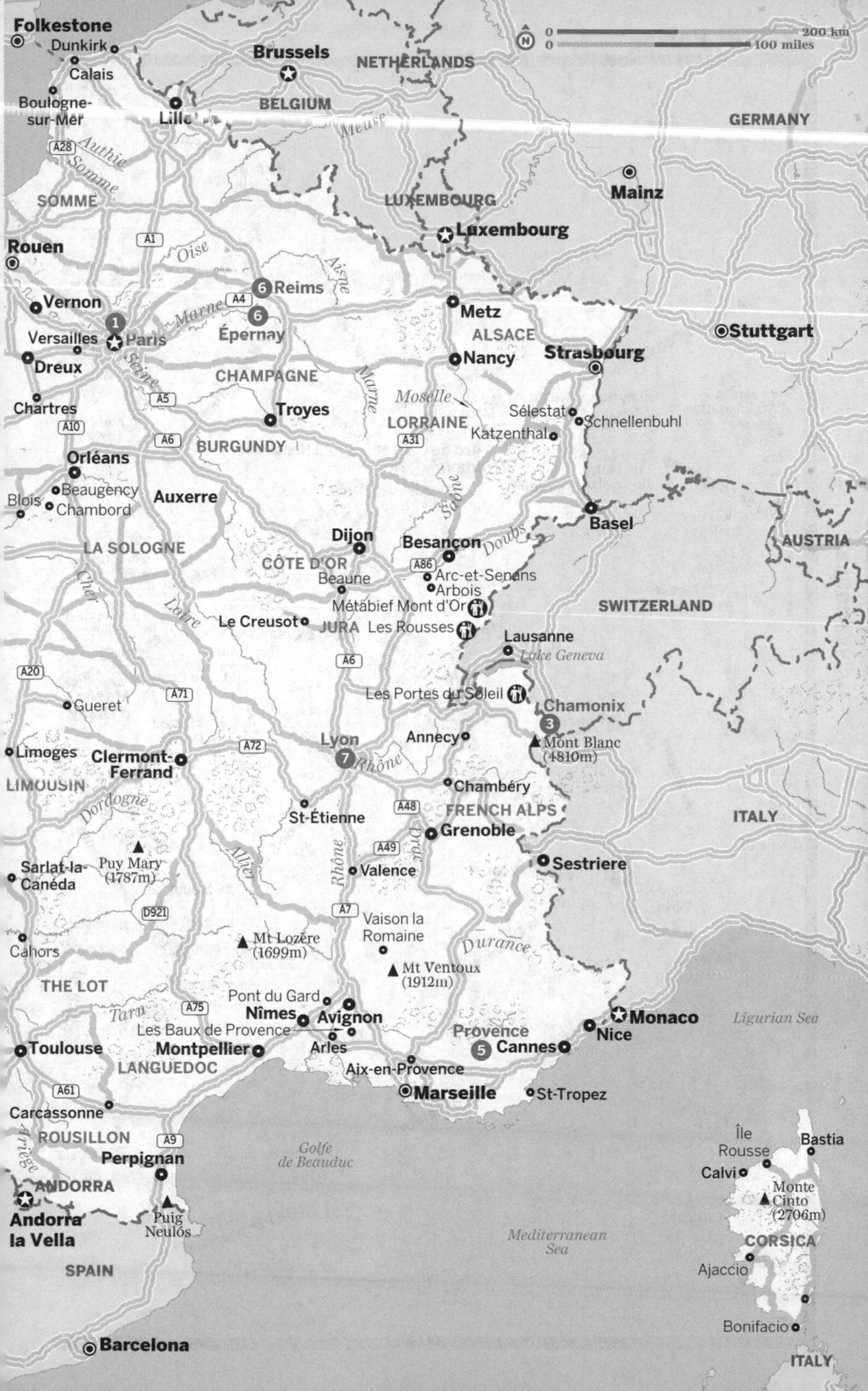

Folkestone
Dunkirk
Calais
Boulogne-sur-Mer
Lille
Brussels
NETHERLANDS
BELGIUM
GERMANY
0 200 km
0 100 miles
Meuse
Authie
Somme
SOMME
LUXEMBOURG
Mainz
Luxembourg
Rouen
Oise
Aisne
Reims
Vernon
Marne
Épernay
Metz
Paris
Versailles
ALSACE
Stuttgart
Dreux
Nancy
Strasbourg
CHAMPAGNE
Seine
Marne
Moselle
Chartres
Troyes
LORRAINE
Sélestat
Schnellenbuhl
Katzenthal
BURGUNDY
Orléans
Beaugency
Blois
Chambord
Auxerre
Saône
Basel
LA SOLOGNE
Dijon
Besançon
Doubs
AUSTRIA
CÔTE D'OR
Beaune
Arc-et-Senans
Arbois
Cher
Métabief Mont d'Or
SWITZERLAND
Loire
Le Creusot
JURA
Les Rousses
Lausanne
Lake Geneva
Les Portes du Soleil
Gueret
Chamonix
Lyon
Annecy
Mont Blanc (4810m)
Limoges
Clermont-Ferrand
Rhône
LIMOUSIN
Chambéry
Dordogne
St-Étienne
FRENCH ALPS
ITALY
Grenoble
Puy Mary (1787m)
Allier
Drac
Sarlat-la-Canéda
Rhône
Valence
Sestriere
Vaison la Romaine
Durance
Mt Lozère (1699m)
Cahors
Mt Ventoux (1912m)
THE LOT
Pont du Gard
Tarn
Nîmes
Avignon
Monaco
Ligurian Sea
Les Baux de Provence
Provence
Nice
Toulouse
Montpellier
Arles
Cannes
LANGUEDOC
Aix-en-Provence
Carcassonne
Marseille
St-Tropez
ROUSILLON
Île Rousse
Bastia
Ariège
Perpignan
Golfe de Beauduc
Calvi
ANDORRA
Monte Cinto (2706m)
Andorra la Vella
Puig Neulós
Mediterranean Sea
CORSICA
SPAIN
Ajaccio
Bonifacio
Barcelona
ITALY

Greater Paris

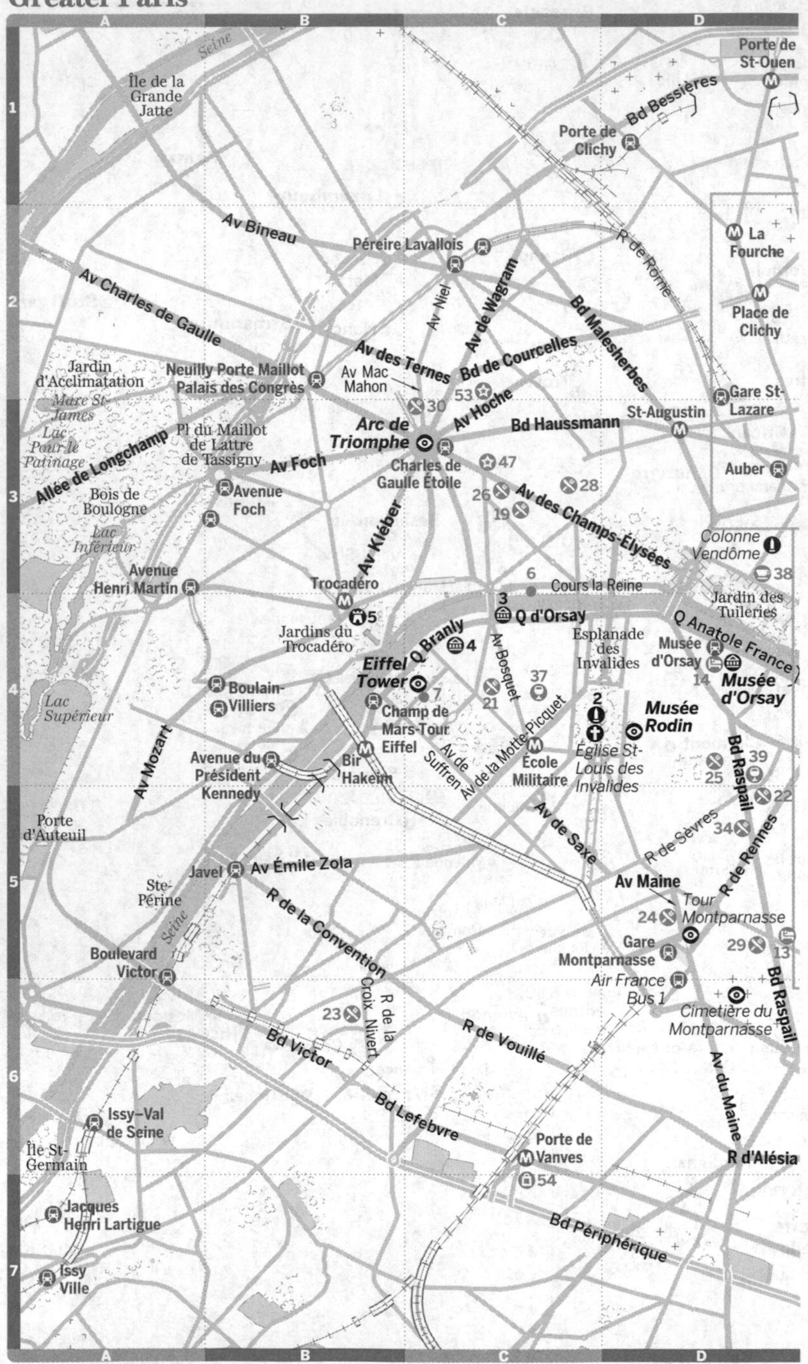

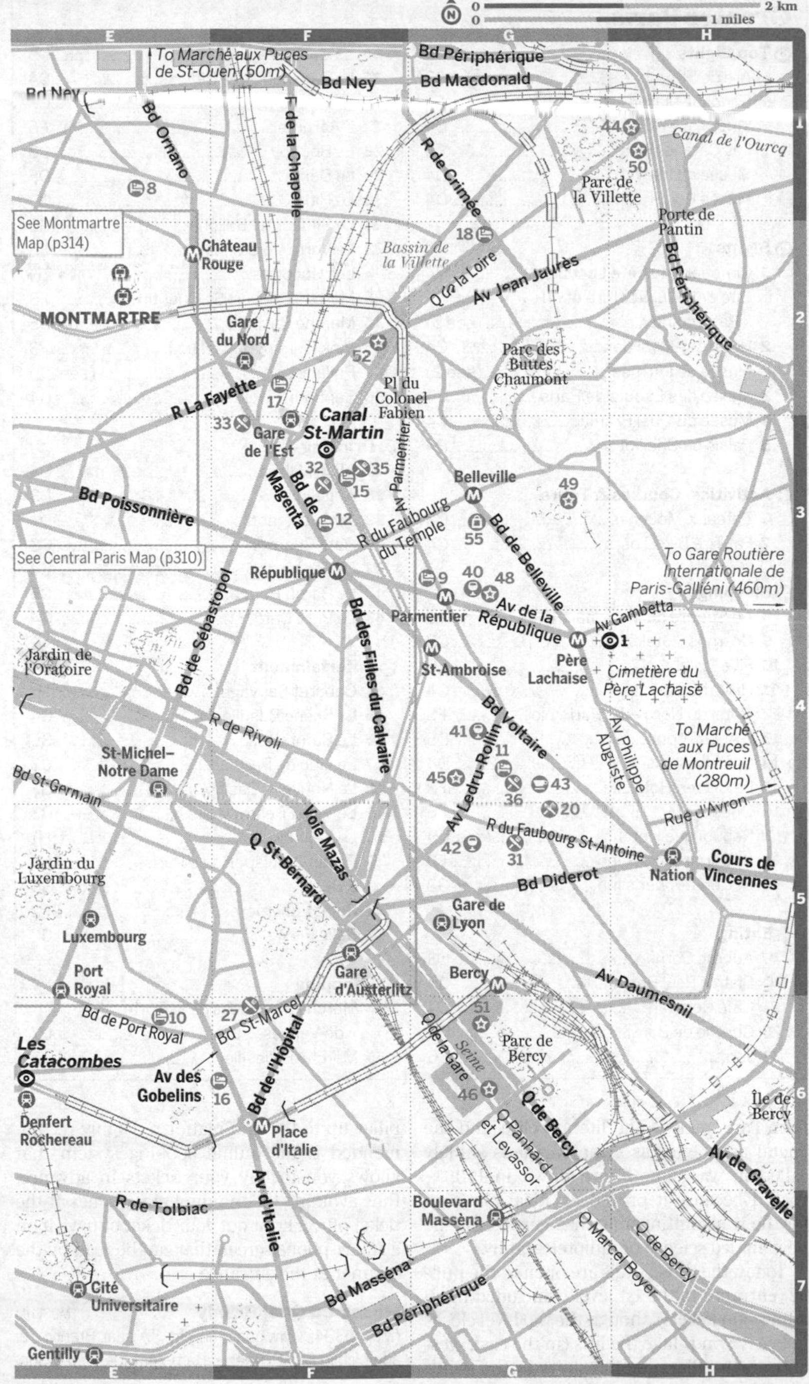
0 2 km
0 1 miles
E
F
G
H
To Marché aux Puces de St-Ouen (50m)
Bd Périphérique
Bd Ney
Bd Macdonald
Bd Ney
Bd Ornano
F de la Chapelle
R de Crimée
44
50
Canal de l'Ourcq
Parc de la Villette
8
See Montmartre Map (p314)
Château Rouge
18
Bassin de la Villette
Porte de Pantin
Bd Périphérique
Q de la Loire
Av Jean Jaurès
MONTMARTRE
Gare du Nord
52
Parc des Buttes Chaumont
R La Fayette
17
Pl du Colonel Fabien
33
Gare de l'Est
Canal St-Martin
32
35
15
Av Parmentier
Belleville
49
Bd Poissonnière
Bd de Magenta
12
R du Faubourg du Temple
55
Bd de Belleville
See Central Paris Map (p310)
To Gare Routière Internationale de Paris-Galliéni (460m)
République
9
40
48
Bd des Filles du Calvaire
Parmentier
Av de la République
Av Gambetta
1
Jardin de l'Oratoire
Bd de Sébastopol
St-Ambroise
Père Lachaise
Cimetière du Père Lachaise
R de Rivoli
Bd Voltaire
41
11
Av Philippe Auguste
To Marché aux Puces de Montreuil (280m)
St-Michel–Notre Dame
45
36
43
Bd St-Germain
20
Rue d'Avron
Av Ledru-Rollin
Voie Mazas
42
R du Faubourg St-Antoine
31
Q St-Bernard
Jardin du Luxembourg
Nation
Cours de Vincennes
Bd Diderot
Gare de Lyon
Luxembourg
Gare d'Austerlitz
Port Royal
Bercy
Av Daumesnil
27
10
51
Bd de Port Royal
Bd St-Marcel
Seine
Q de la Gare
Parc de Bercy
Les Catacombes
Av des Gobelins
16
Bd de l'Hôpital
46
Q de Bercy
Q Panhard et Levassor
Île de Bercy
Denfert Rochereau
Place d'Italie
Av de Gravelle
Av d'Italie
R de Tolbiac
Boulevard Masséna
Q Marcel Boyer
Q de Bercy
Bd Masséna
Cité Universitaire
Bd Périphérique
Gentilly
1
2
3
4
5
6
7

Greater Paris

Top Sights

Arc de Triomphe C3
Canal St-Martin F3
Eiffel Tower C4
Les Catacombes E6
Musée d'Orsay D4
Musée Rodin D4

Sights

1 Cimetière du Père Lachaise H4
Cité de l'Architecture et du Patrimoine .... (see 5)
2 Hôtel des Invalides C4
Musée de l'Armée .... (see 2)
3 Musée des Égouts de Paris C4
4 Musée du Quai Branly C4
5 Palais de Chaillot B4

Activities, Courses & Tours

6 Bateaux-Mouches C3
7 Fat Tire Bike Tours C4

Sleeping

8 Au Sourire de Montmartre E1
9 Cosmos Hôtel G3
10 Five Hotel E6
11 Hi Matic G4
12 Hôtel du Nord – Le Pari Vélo F3
13 L'Apostrophe D5
14 Le Bellechasse D4
15 Le Citizen Hotel F3
16 Oops F6
République Hôtel .... (see 12)
17 St Christopher's Inn F2
18 St Christopher's Inn G2

Eating

19 Aubrac Corner C3
20 Bistrot Paul Bert G5
21 Café Constant C4
22 Cuisine de Bar D5
23 Jadis B6
24 La Cabane à Huîtres D5
25 La Pâtisserie des Rêves D4
26 Ladurée C3
27 L'Agrume F6
28 Le Boudoir C3
29 Le Dôme D5
30 Le Hide C3
31 Le Siffleur de Ballons G5
32 Le Verre Volé F3
Les Cocottes .... (see 21)
33 Marché Couvert St-Quentin F3
34 Marché Raspail D5
35 Pink Flamingo F3
Poilâne .... (see 22)
36 Septime G4

Drinking

37 Alain Milliart C4
38 Angelina D3
39 Au Sauvignon D4
40 Café Charbon G3
41 La Fée Verte G4
42 Le Baron Rouge G5
43 Le Pure Café G4

Entertainment

44 Cabaret Sauvage H1
45 La Scène Bastille G4
46 Le Batofar G6
47 Le Lido de Paris C3
48 Le Nouveau Casino G3
49 Le Vieux Belleville G3
50 Le Zénith H1
51 Palais Omnisports de Paris-Bercy G6
52 Point Éphémère F2
53 Salle Pleyel C2

Shopping

54 Marché aux Puces de la Porte de Vanves C7
55 Marché Belleville G3

from Paris' artistic and literary elite, and the 'metal asparagus', as some Parisians snidely called it, was almost torn down in 1909 – spared because it proved an ideal platform for the transmitting antennas needed for the newfangled science of radiotelegraphy.

Today, the three levels are open to the public (entrance to the 1st level is included in all admission tickets), though the top level closes in heavy wind. Take the lifts (in the east, west and north pillars) or the stairs in the south pillar up to the 2nd platform. Highly recommended is the online booking system that allows you to buy your tickets in advance, thus avoiding the monumental queues at the ticket office. Print out your ticket or have it on a smart-phone screen that can be read by the scanner at the entrance.

Musée du Quai Branly MUSEUM

(Map p304; www.quaibranly.fr; 37 quai Branly, 7e; adult/child €8.50/free; 11am-7pm Tue, Wed & Sun,

11am-9pm Thu-Sat; Ⓜ Alma-Marceau or RER Pont de l'Alma) No other museum in Paris provides such inspiration to those who appreciate the beauty of traditional craftsmanship. A tribute to the incredible diversity of human culture, it presents an overview of indigenous and folk art from around the world. Divided into four main sections, the museum showcases an impressive array of masks, carvings, weapons, jewellery and more, all displayed in a refreshingly unique interior without rooms or high walls. Don't miss the views from the 5th-floor restaurant Les Ombres.

Musée d'Orsay MUSEUM

(Map p304; www.musee-orsay.fr; 62 rue de Lille, 7e; adult/18-25yr/under 18yr €9/6.50/free; ⊙9.30am-6pm Tue, Wed & Fri-Sun, to 9.45pm Thu; Ⓜ Assemblée Nationale or RER Musée d'Orsay) The home of France's national collection from the impressionist, postimpressionist and art nouveau movements spanning from the 1840s and 1914 is the glorious former Gare d'Orsay railway station – itself an art nouveau showpiece. Highlights include Manet's *On The Beach* and *Woman With Fans*; Monet's gardens at Giverny; Cézanne's card players and still lifes; Renoir's *Ball at the Moulin de la Galette* and *Girls at the Piano*; Degas' ballerinas; Toulouse-Lautrec's cabaret dancers; and Van Gogh's self-portraits, *Bedroom in Arles* and *Starry Night*. There are also some magnificent decorative arts, graphic arts and sculptures.

Save time by prepurchasing tickets online or at **Kiosque du Musée d'Orsay** (⊙9am-5pm Tue-Fri school holidays, Tue only rest of year), in front of the museum, and head to entrance C. Admission drops to €6.50 after 4.30pm (after 6pm on Thursday).

Jardin du Luxembourg PARK

(Map p310; numerous entrances; ⊙hrs vary; Ⓜ St-Sulpice, Rennes or Notre Dame des Champs, or RER Luxembourg) The voyeur's spot to peek on Parisians, this 23-hectare park is where Parisians of all ages flock to jog, practise t'ai chi, gossip with friends, read, romance, play tennis, stroll through terraced gardens and orchards heavy with apples, or chase 1920s sailboats around the octagonal **Grand Bassin**.

Palais du Luxembourg, at the northen end of the garden, was built in the 1620s for Marie de Médici, Henri IV's consort, to assuage her longing for the Pitti Palace in Florence, where she had spent her childhood. Since 1958 the palace has housed the **Sénat** (Senate; Map p310; ☎01 44 54 19 49; www.senat.fr; rue de Vaugirard; adult/18-25yr €8/6), occasionally visitable by guided tour. Top spot for sun-soaking – there are always loads of the garden's signature sage-green chairs here – is the southern side of the palace's 19th-century **Orangery**, where lemon and orange trees, palms, grenadiers and oleanders shelter from the cold.

WANT MORE?

For in-depth information, reviews and recommendations at your fingertips, head to the Apple App Store to purchase Lonely Planet's *Paris City Guide* iPhone app.

Alternatively, head to **Lonely Planet** (www.lonelyplanet.com/france/paris) for planning advice, author recommendations, traveller reviews and insider tips.

Musée Rodin GARDEN, MUSEUM

(Map p304; www.musee-rodin.fr; 79 rue de Varenne, 7e; adult/under 25yr permanent exhibition €7/5, garden €1/free; ⊙10am-5.45pm Tue-Sun; Ⓜ Varenne) One of the most relaxing spots in the city, with a garden bespeckled with sculptures, this lovely art museum inside 18th-century Hôtel Biron displays vital bronze and marble sculptures by sculptor, painter, sketcher, engraver and collector Auguste Rodin. Highlights include that perennial crowd-pleaser *The Thinker*, and the sublime, the incomparable, that romance-hewn-in-marble called *The Kiss*. Buy tickets online to avoid queuing.

Les Catacombes CEMETERY

(Map p304; www.catacombes.paris.fr; 1 av Colonel Henri Roi-Tanguy, 14e; adult/13-26yr/under 13yr €8/4/free; ⊙10am-5pm Tue-Sun; Ⓜ Denfert Rochereau) Paris' most gruesome and macabre sight is this series of underground tunnels lined with skulls and bones exhumed from the city's overflowing cemeteries.

Created in 1810, the Catacombes takes visitors along 2km of subterranean passages with a mind-boggling amount of bones and skulls of millions of Parisians neatly packed along each and every wall. During WWII these tunnels were used as a headquarters by the Resistance; thrill-seeking *cataphiles* are often caught (and fined) roaming the tunnels at night.

Renting an audioguide greatly enhances the impossibly spooky experience.

MUSEUM TIPS

» If you're visiting more than two or three museums and monuments, buy a **Paris Museum Pass** (www.parismuseumpass.fr; 2/4/6 days €39/54/69), valid for entry to some 38 venues including the Louvre, Centre Pompidou, Musée d'Orsay, Musée Rodin and Château de Versailles. Pass-holders also get to bypass *looong* ticket queues at major attractions. Buy it online, at participating museums, tourist desks at airports, Fnac outlets and major metro stations.

» Most Paris museums are closed on Mondays, but some, including the Louvre and Centre Pompidou, are closed on Tuesdays instead.

» Paris' national museums are something of a bargain: admission is reduced for those aged over 60 years, and between 18 and 25; and completely free for EU residents under 26 years of age, anyone under 18 years, and everyone on the first Sunday of each month. These include: the Louvre, Musée National d'Art Moderne in the Pompidou, Musée du Quai Branly, Musée d'Orsay, Musée Rodin and Cité de l'Architecture et du Patrimoine.

» The following are free the first Sunday of the month from November to March: Arc de Triomphe, Conciergerie, Panthéon, Ste-Chapelle and the Tours de Notre Dame.

Musée des Égouts de Paris MUSEUM

(Map p304; place de la Résistance, 7e; adult/child €4.20/3.40; ⌚11am-5pm Sat-Wed May-Sep, 11am-4pm Sat-Wed Oct-Dec & Feb-Apr; Ⓜ Alma Marceau or RER Pont de l'Alma) Raw sewage flows beneath your feet as you walk through 480m of odoriferous tunnels in this working sewer museum. Exhibitions cover the development of Paris' waste-water disposal system. Enter via a rectangular maintenance hole topped with a kiosk across the street from 93 quai d'Orsay, 7e.

Panthéon MAUSOLEUM

(Map p310; www.monum.fr; place du Panthéon; adult/under 18yr €8.50/free; ⌚10am-6.30pm Apr-Sep, to 6pm Oct-Mar; Ⓜ Maubert-Mutualité, Cardinal Lemoine or RER Luxembourg) A superb example of 18th-century neoclassicism, this domed landmark was commissioned by Louis XV around 1750 as an abbey but due to financial and structural problems it wasn't completed until 1789. Two years later, the Constituent Assembly turned it into a secular mausoleum – now the eternal home of some of France's greatest thinkers including Voltaire, Jean-Jacques Rousseau, Louis Braille, Émile Zola and Jean Moulin. The first woman to be interred in the Panthéon was the two-time Nobel Prize-winner Marie Curie (1867-1934).

Hôtel des Invalides MONUMENT, MUSEUM

(Map p304; www.invalides.org; 129 rue de Grenelle, 7e; adult/child €9/free; ⌚10am-6pm Mon & Wed-Sun, 10am-9pm Tue, to 5pm Oct-Mar, closed 1st Mon of month; Ⓜ Invalides) Hôtel des Invalides was built in the 1670s by Louis XIV to provide housing for 4000 *invalides* (disabled war veterans). On 14 July 1789, a mob forced its way into the building and, after fierce fighting, seized 32,000 rifles before heading on to the prison at Bastille and the start of the French Revolution.

North of the main courtyard is the **Musée de l'Armée** (Army Museum; Map p304; www.invalides.org; 129 rue de Grenelle, 7e; ⌚10am-6pm Mon & Wed-Sat, to 9pm Tue), home to the nation's largest collection on French military history.

South are the **Église St-Louis des Invalides** and **Église du Dôme**, the latter of which contains the tomb of Napoléon I, comprising six coffins fitting into one another like a Russian *matryoshka* doll.

Palais de Chaillot PALACE

(Map p304; 17 place du Trocadéro et du 11 Novembre, 16e; Ⓜ Trocadéro) The two curved, colonnaded wings of this palace and the terrace in between them afford an exceptional panorama of the **Jardins du Trocadéro**, the Seine and the Eiffel Tower. The palace's eastern wing houses the standout **Cité de l'Architecture et du Patrimoine** (Map p304; www.citechaillot.fr; 1 place du Trocadéro et du 11 Novembre, 16e; adult/18-25yr/under 18yr €8/5/free; ⌚11am-7pm Wed-Mon, to 9pm Thu; Ⓜ Trocadéro), devoted to French architecture and heritage.

Jardin des Plantes BOTANIC GARDEN

(Map p310; www.jardindesplantes.net; 57 rue Cuvier, 5e; adult/child €6/4; ⌚7.30am-7.45pm Apr–mid-Oct, 8.30am-5.30pm mid-Oct–Mar; Ⓜ Gare d'Austerlitz, Censier Daubenton or Jussieu) Paris' 24-hectare botanical gardens were created in 1626 as a medicinal herb garden for Louis XIII. On its southern fringe is the Musée National d'Histoire Naturelle, France's natural-history museum.

Église St-Germain des Prés CHURCH

(Map p310; www.eglise-sgp.org; 3 place St-Germain des Prés, 6e; ⏲8am-7pm Mon-Sat, 9am-8pm Sun; Ⓜ St-Germain des Prés) Paris' oldest standing church, the Romanesque St Germanus of the Fields, was built in the 11th century on the site of a 6th-century abbey and was the dominant place of worship in Paris until the arrival of Notre Dame.

Église St-Sulpice CHURCH

(Map p310; www.paroisse-saint-sulpice-paris.org; place St-Sulpice, 6e; ⏲7.30am-7.30pm; Ⓜ St-Sulpice) Lined inside with 21 side chapels, this striking twin-towered church took six architects 150 years to build. What draws most people is not its Italianate facade with two rows of superimposed columns, its Counter-Reformation-influenced neoclassical decor or even the frescoes by Delacroix, but its setting for a murderous scene in Dan Brown's *Da Vinci Code*.

THE ISLANDS

Paris' twin set of islands could not be more different. **Île de la Cité** is bigger, full of sights and very touristy (few people live here). The site of the first settlement in Paris, around the 3rd century BC, and later the Roman town of Lutèce (Lutetia), Île de la Cité remained the centre of royal and ecclesiastical power throughout the Middle Ages. The seven decorated arches of Paris' oldest bridge, **Pont Neuf**, have linked Île de la Cité with both banks of the River Seine since 1607.

Smaller **Île St-Louis** is residential and quieter, with just enough boutiques and restaurants – and a legendary ice-cream maker – to attract visitors. The area around **Pont St-Louis**, the bridge across to the Île de la Cité, and **Pont Louis Philippe**, the bridge to the Marais, is one of the most romantic spots in Paris.

Cathédrale de Notre Dame de Paris CATHEDRAL

(Map p310; www.cathedraledeparis.com; 6 place du Parvis Notre Dame, 4e; admission free; ⏲7.45am-7pm; Ⓜ Cité) This is the heart of Paris: distances from Paris to every part of metropolitan France are measured from **place du Parvis Notre Dame**, the square in front of this French Gothic masterpiece. The most visited unticketed site in Paris, with upwards of 14 million visitors a year, Notre Dame is famed for its three spectacular **rose windows** and forest of ornate **flying buttresses**, best viewed from **square Jean XXIII**, the little park behind the cathedral. Built on a site occupied by earlier churches, it was begun in 1163 according to the design of Bishop Maurice de Sully, and largely completed by the early 14th century. Eugène Emmanuel Viollet-le-Duc carried out extensive renovations between 1845 and 1864.

The entrance to its famous towers, the **Tours de Notre Dame** (Notre Dame Towers; rue du Cloître Notre Dame, 4e; adult/18-25yr/under 18yr €8.50/5.50/free; ⏲10am-6.30pm daily Apr-Jun & Sep, 10am-6.30pm Mon-Fri, 10am-11pm Sat & Sun Jul & Aug, 10.30am-5.30pm daily Oct-Mar), is from the **North Tower**. Climb 422 spiralling steps and find yourself face-to-face with the cathedral's most frightening gargoyles, the 13-tonne bell **Emmanuel** (all of the cathedral's bells are named) and, last but not least, a spectacular view of Paris.

Ste-Chapelle CHAPEL

(Map p310; 4 bd du Palais, 1er; adult/under 18yr €8.50/free; ⏲9.30am-5pm Nov-Feb, to 6pm Mar-Oct; Ⓜ Cité) Built in just under three years (compared with nearly 200 for Notre Dame), this gemlike Holy Chapel – the most exquisite of Paris' Gothic monuments – was consecrated in 1248 within the walls of the city's **Palais de Justice** (Law Courts). It was conceived by Louis IX to house his personal collection of holy relics (including the Holy Crown now kept in the treasury at Notre Dame), but is better known today for its dazzling, finely detailed stained glass.

A combined adult ticket with the **Conciergerie** costs €12.50.

Conciergerie MONUMENT

(Map p310; www.monuments-nationaux.fr; 2 bd du Palais, Île de la Cité, 1er; adult/under 18yr €8.50/free, 1st Sun of month Nov-Mar free; ⏲9.30am-6pm; Ⓜ Cité) Built as a royal palace in the 14th century, this was the main prison during the Reign of Terror (1793–94), used to incarcerate alleged enemies of the Revolution before they were brought before the Revolutionary Tribunal, next door in the Palais de Justice. Queen Marie Antoinette was among the almost 2800 prisoners held here before being sent in tumbrels to the guillotine. The 14th-century **Salle des Gens d'Armes** (Cavalrymen's Hall), a fine example of Rayonnant Gothic style, is Europe's largest surviving medieval hall.

A joint ticket with Ste-Chapelle costs €12.50.

Central Paris

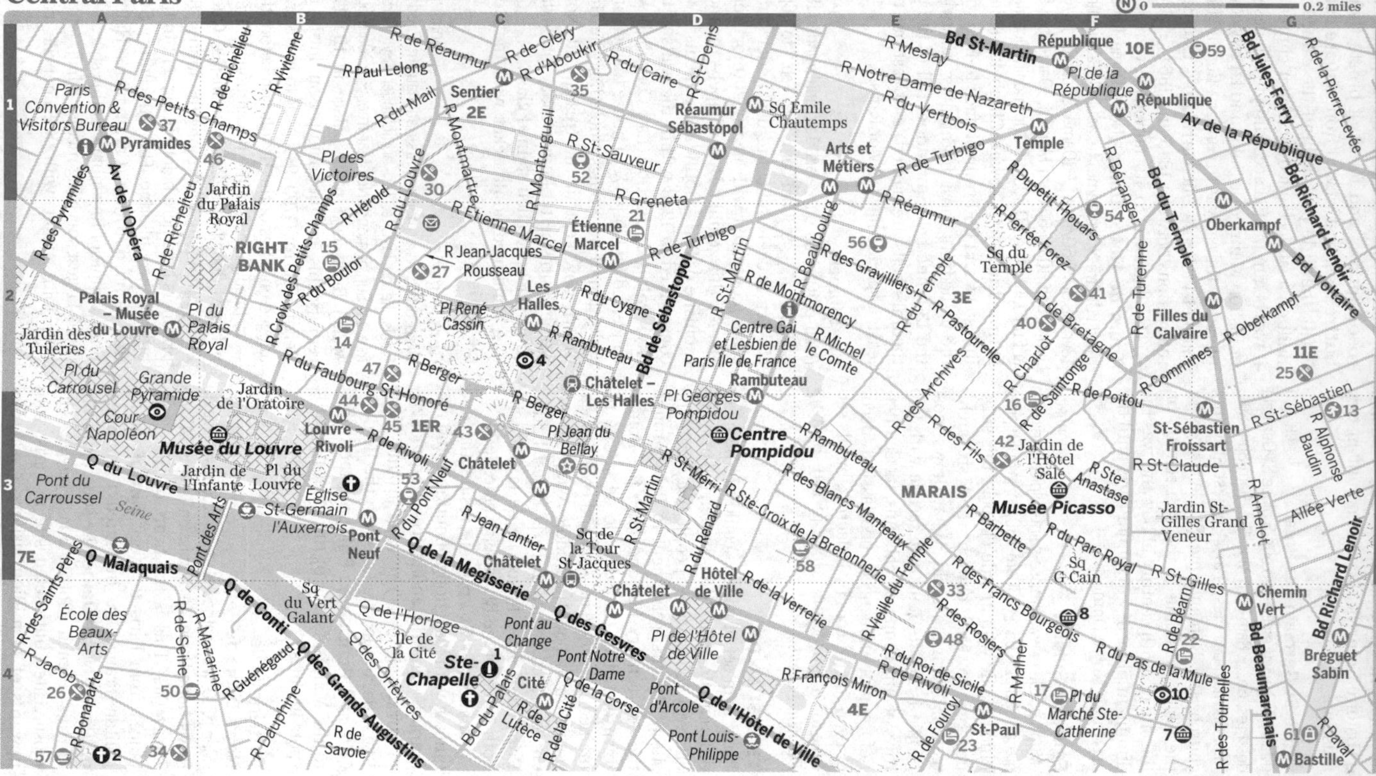

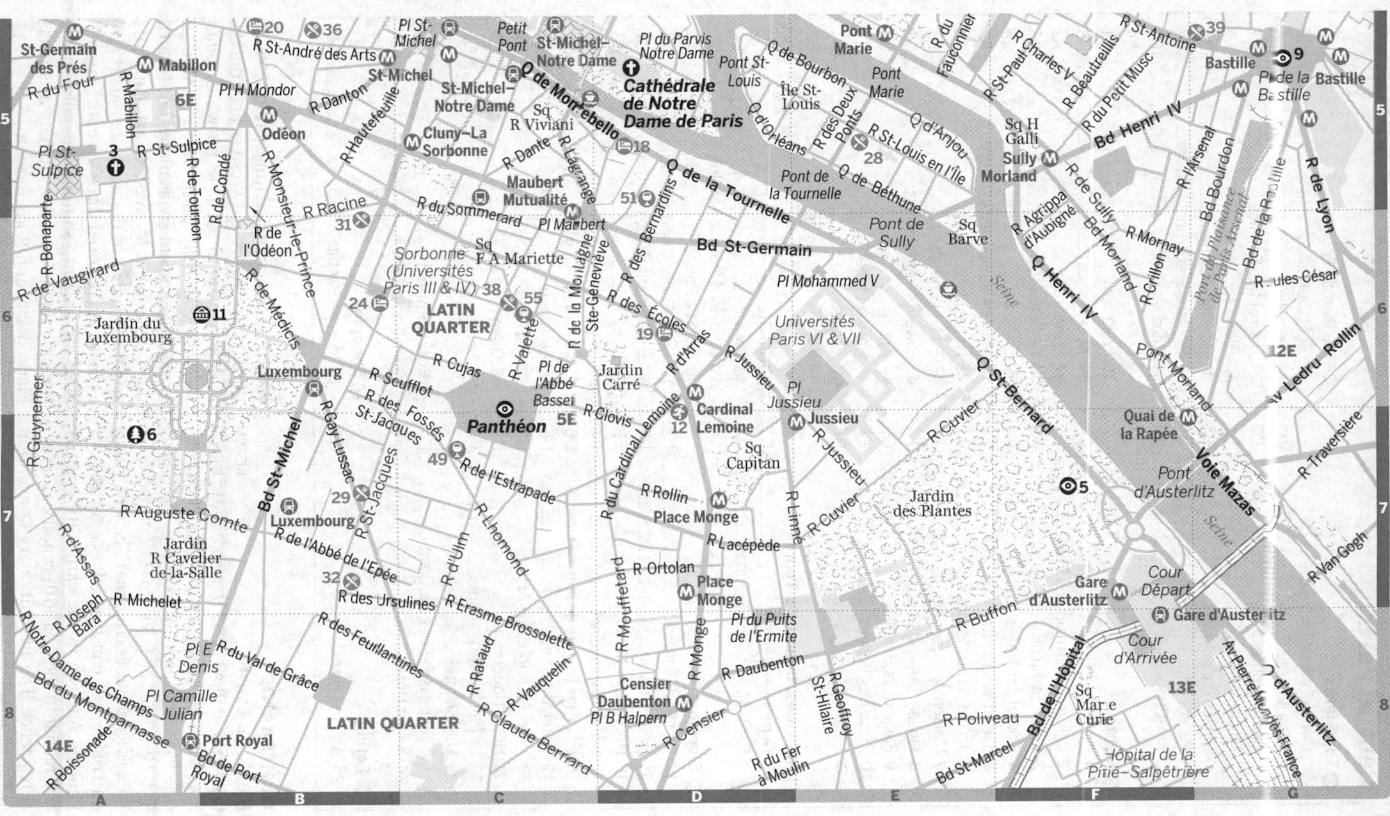

St-Germain des Prés
R du Four
Mabillon
R Mabillon
6E
Pl St-Sulpice
3
R St-Sulpice
R de Tournon
R de Condé
R Bonaparte
R de Vaugirard
Jardin du Luxembourg
11
6
R Guynemer
Pl H Mondor
Odéon
R Danton
R St-André des Arts
20
36
Pl St-Michel
St-Michel
R Hautefeuille
R Monsieur-le-Prince
R de l'Odéon
R Racine
31
R de Médicis
Luxembourg
Bd St-Michel
R Gay Lussac
29
R St-Jacques
R Auguste Comte
Jardin R Cavelier de-la-Salle
R d'Assas
R Joseph Bara
R Michelet
R Notre Dame des Champs
Bd du Montparnasse
Pl Camille Julian
Pl E Denis
R du Val de Grâce
Port Royal
Bd de Port Royal
14E
R Boissonade
Petit Pont
St-Michel–Notre Dame
Cluny–La Sorbonne
Sq R Viviani
R Dante
R du Sommerard
Maubert Mutualité
Pl Maubert
R Lagrange
Sorbonne (Universités Paris III & IV)
Sq F A Mariette
24
38
55
LATIN QUARTER
R Cujas
R Soufflot
R des Fossés St-Jacques
R Valette
Pl de l'Abbé Basset
Panthéon
5E
49
R de l'Estrapade
R de l'Abbé de l'Épée
32
R des Ursulines
R d'Ulm
R Lhomond
R Erasme Brossolette
R des Feuillantines
LATIN QUARTER
R Rataud
R Vauquelin
R Claude Berrard
Pl du Parvis Notre Dame
Cathédrale de Notre Dame de Paris
Q de Montebello
18
51
R des Bernardins
Q de la Tournelle
Pont de la Tournelle
Bd St-Germain
R de la Montagne Ste-Geneviève
R des Écoles
19
R d'Arras
Jardin Carré
R Clovis
R du Cardinal Lemoine
Cardinal Lemoine
12
R Rollin
Place Monge
R Lacépède
R Ortolan
R Mouffetard
Place Monge
R Monge
Censier Daubenton
Pl B Halpern
R Censier
R du Fer à Moulin
Pont St-Louis
Île St-Louis
Q de Bourbon
Q d'Orléans
R des Deux Ponts
R St-Louis en l'Île
28
Pont Marie
Q d'Anjou
Q de Béthune
Pont de Sully
Sq Barye
Pl Mohammed V
Universités Paris VI & VII
R Jussieu
Pl Jussieu
Jussieu
Sq Capitan
R Linné
R Cuvier
Q St-Bernard
Jardin des Plantes
5
Pl du Puits de l'Ermite
R Daubenton
R Geoffroy St-Hilaire
R Buffon
Gare d'Austerlitz
Cour Départ
Gare d'Austerlitz
Cour d'Arrivée
13E
Bd de l'Hôpital
Sq Marie Curie
Hôpital de la Pitié–Salpêtrière
R Poliveau
Bd St-Marcel
Av Pierre Mendès France
Pont d'Austerlitz
R du Fauconnier
R St-Paul
R Charles V
R Beautreillis
R du Petit Musc
R St-Antoine
39
Bastille
9
Pl de la Bastille
Sq H Galli
Sully Morland
Bd Henri IV
R de Sully
R Agrippa d'Aubigné
Bd Morland
Q Henri IV
Seine
R Mornay
R Crillon
R de l'Arsenal
Bd Bourdon
Port de Plaisance de Paris Arsenal
Bd de la Bastille
R de Lyon
R Jules César
12E
Av Ledru Rollin
Pont Morland
Quai de la Rapée
Voie Mazas
R Traversière
R Van Gogh
A
B
C
D
E
F
G
5
6
7
8

Central Paris

Top Sights
Cathédrale de Notre Dame de Paris ... D5
Centre Pompidou ... D3
Musée du Louvre ... B3
Musée Picasso ... F3
Panthéon ... C6
Ste-Chapelle ... C4

Sights
1 Conciergerie ... C4
2 Église St-Germain des Prés ... A4
3 Église St-Sulpice ... A5
4 Forum des Halles ... C2
5 Jardin des Plantes ... F7
6 Jardin du Luxembourg ... A7
7 Maison de Victor Hugo ... F4
8 Musée Carnavalet ... F4
9 Place de la Bastille ... G5
10 Place des Vosges ... F4
11 Sénat ... B6

Activities, Courses & Tours
12 Gepetto et Vélos ... D7
13 Paris à Vélo, C'est Sympa! ... G3

Sleeping
14 BVJ Paris-Louvre ... B2
15 Hôtel Crayon ... B2
16 Hôtel du Petit Moulin ... F3
17 Hôtel Jeanne d'Arc ... F4
18 Hôtel les Degrés de Notre Dame ... D5
19 Hôtel Minerve ... D6
20 Hôtel St-André des Arts ... B5
21 Hôtel Tiquetonne ... D2
22 Le Pavillon de la Reine ... F4
23 Maison Internationale de la Jeunesse et des Étudiants ... E4
24 Select Hôtel ... B6

Eating
25 Au Passage ... G2
26 Au Pied de Fouet ... A4
27 Beef Club ... C2
28 Berthillon ... E5
29 Bistrot Les Papilles ... B7
30 Blend ... C1
31 Bouillon Racine ... B6
32 Boulangerie Bruno Solques ... B7
33 Chez Marianne ... E4
34 Cosi ... A4
35 Frenchie ... C1
36 KGB ... B5
37 Kunitoraya ... A1
38 Le Coupe-Chou ... C6
39 Le Nôtre ... G5
40 Marché aux Enfants Rouges ... F2
41 Nanashi ... F2
42 Pink Flamingo ... F3
43 Saveurs Végét'Halles ... C3
44 Spring ... B3
45 Spring Épicerie ... B3
46 Verjus ... B1
47 Yam'Tcha ... B2

Drinking
48 3w Kafé ... E4
49 Café de la Nouvelle Mairie ... C7
50 Café La Palette ... A4
51 Curio Parlor Cocktail Club ... D5
52 Experimental Cocktail Club ... C1
53 Kong ... C3
54 Le Barav ... F2
55 Le Pub St-Hilaire ... C6
56 Le Tango ... E2
57 Les Deux Magots ... A4
58 Open Café ... E3
59 Scream Club ... G1

Entertainment
60 Le Baiser Salé ... C3

Shopping
61 Marché Bastille ... G4

RIGHT BANK

Musée du Louvre MUSEUM
(Map p310; ☎01 40 20 53 17; www.louvre.fr; rue de Rivoli & quai des Tuileries, 1er; permanent/temporary collection €11/12, both €15, under 18yr free; ⏱9am-6pm Mon, Thu, Sat & Sun, to 9.45pm Wed & Fri; Ⓜ Palais Royal–Musée du Louvre) The vast Palais du Louvre was constructed as a fortress by Philippe Auguste in the early 13th century and rebuilt in the mid-16th century as a royal residence. The Revolutionary Convention turned it into a national museum in 1793. Its raison d'être: to present Western art from the Middle Ages to about 1848 (at which point the Musée d'Orsay takes over), as well as works from ancient civilisations that formed the starting point for Western art. Late 2012 saw the opening of the new Islamic art galleries in the restored **Cour Visconti**, topped with an elegant, shimmering gold 'flying carpet' roof designed by Italian architects Mario Bellini and Rudy Ricciotti.

With some 35,000 paintings and objets d'art on display today, the sheer size and richness of the Louvre can be overwhelming; the south side facing the Seine is 700m long and it's said it would take nine months just to glance at every work. For many, the star attraction is Leonardo da Vinci's *La Joconde*, better known as the Mona Lisa (Room 6, 1st floor, Denon Wing). The most famous works from antiquity include the *Seated Scribe* (Room 22, 1st floor, Sully Wing), the *Code of Hammurabi* (Room 3, ground floor, Richelieu Wing), and that armless duo, the *Venus de Milo* (Room 16, ground floor, Sully Wing) and the *Winged Victory of Samothrace* (top of Daru staircase, 1st floor, Denon Wing). From the Renaissance, don't miss Michelangelo's *The Dying Slave* (Room 4, ground floor, Denon Wing) and works by Raphael, Botticelli and Titian (1st floor, Denon Wing). French masterpieces of the 19th century include Ingres' *The Turkish Bath* (off Room 60, 2nd floor, Sully Wing), Géricault's *The Raft of the Medusa* (Room 77, 1st floor, Denon Wing) and works by Corot, Delacroix and Fragonard (2nd floor, Sully Wing).

Arc de Triomphe LANDMARK

(Map p304; www.monuments-nationaux.fr; place Charles de Gaulle; adult/18-25yr €9.50/6; ⏲10am-10.30pm, to 11pm Apr-Sep; Ⓜ Charles de Gaulle–Étoile) If anything rivals the Eiffel Tower as the symbol of Paris, it's this magnificent 1836 monument to Napoléon's 1805 victory at Austerlitz. The intricately sculpted triumphal arch stands sentinel in the centre of **place de l'Étoile**. From the viewing platform on top of the arch (50m up via 284 steps; it's well worth the climb) you can see the dozen avenues that radiate from the arch.

Beneath the arch at ground level lies the **Tomb of the Unknown Soldier**, honouring the 1.3 million French soldiers who lost their lives in WWI; an eternal flame is rekindled daily at 6.30pm.

Centre Pompidou MUSEUM

(Map p310; ☎01 44 78 12 33; www.centrepompidou.fr; place Georges Pompidou, 1er; museum, exhibitions & panorama adult/child €13/free; ⏲11am-9pm Wed-Mon; Ⓜ Rambuteau) Paris' premier cultural centre – designed inside out with utilitarian features such as plumbing, pipes, air vents and electrical cables forming part of the external facade to free up the interior space for exhibitions and events – has amazed visitors since it was inaugurated in 1977. Temporary exhibitions fill the ground floor **Forum du Centre Pompidou** and 6th-floor galleries, while the 4th and 5th floors host the **Musée National d'Art Moderne**, France's national collection of art dating from 1905 onwards, which includes works by the surrealists and cubists, as well as pop art and contemporary works.

Sweeping views of Paris thrill diners over lunch at the chic, hyperindustrial restaurant, Georges, on the 6th floor, and also from the rooftop terrace; admission is included in museum and exhibition tickets or buy a panorama ticket just for the roof.

West of the centre, **Place Georges Pompidou** and the nearby pedestrian streets attract buskers, musicians, jugglers and mime artists. South of the centre on **place Igor Stravinsky** are fanciful mechanical fountains of skeletons, hearts, treble clefs and a big pair of ruby-red lips, created by Jean Tinguely and Niki de Saint Phalle.

Basilique du Sacré-Cœur BASILICA

(Map p314; www.sacre-coeur-montmartre.com; place du Parvis du Sacré-Cœur; Basilica dome admission €5, cash only; ⏲6am-10.30pm, dome 9am-7pm Apr-Sep, to 5.30pm Oct-Mar; Ⓜ Anvers) Crowning the **Butte de Montmartre** (Montmartre Hill), Sacred Heart Basilica was begun in 1876 but not consecrated until 1919. Some 234 spiralling

THE LOUVRE: TICKETS & TOURS

To best navigate the collection, opt for a self-guided **thematic trail** (1½ to three hours; download trail brochures in advance from the website) or a self-paced **multimedia guide** (€5). More formal, English-language **guided tours** depart from the Hall Napoléon, which also has free English-language maps.

The main entrance and ticket windows are covered by the 21m-high **Grande Pyramide**, a glass pyramid designed by the Chinese-born American architect IM Pei. Avoid the queues outside the pyramid or at the Porte des Lions entrance by entering the Louvre complex via the underground shopping centre **Carrousel du Louvre**, at 99 rue de Rivoli. Buy your tickets in advance – and enter the museum with little or no queue – from the ticket machines inside the latter, by phoning 08 92 68 46 94 or 01 41 57 32 28, or from *billeteries* (ticket offices) inside Fnac or Virgin Megastores.

Montmartre

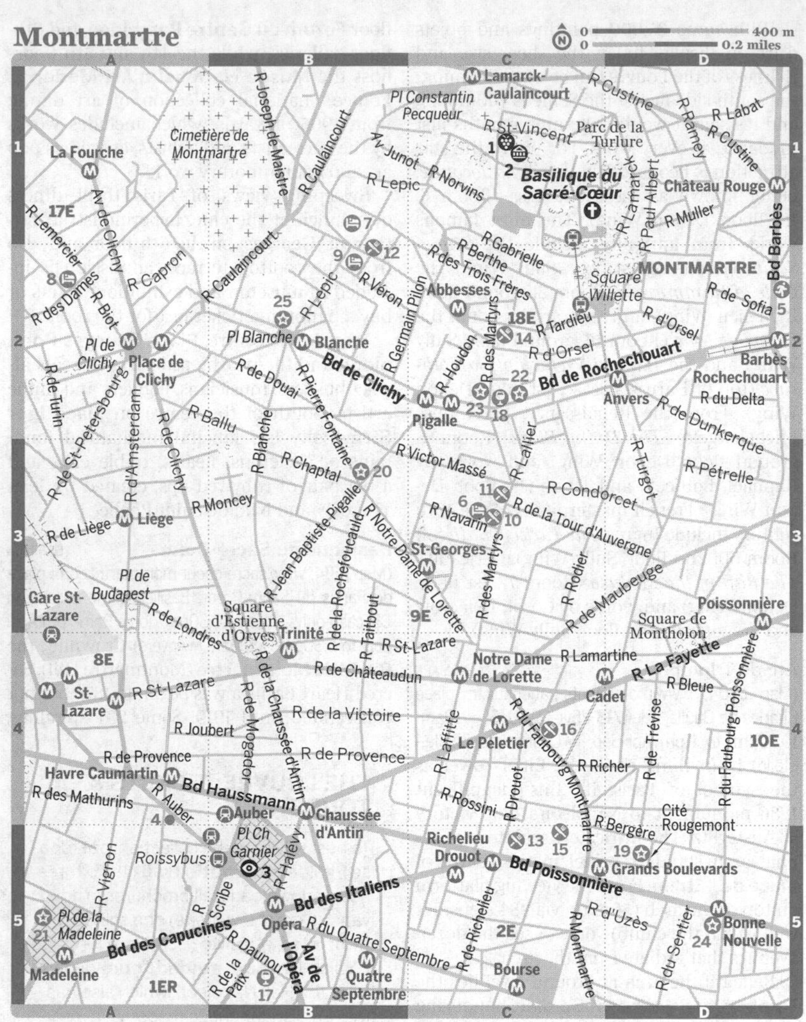

steps lead to its dome, which affords one of Paris' most spectacular panoramas – up to 30km on a clear day. The chapel-lined crypt, visited in conjunction with the dome, is huge.

Palais Garnier OPERA HOUSE

(Map p314; ☎08 25 05 44 05; www.operadeparis.fr; cnr rues Scribe & Auber; visit adult/10-25yr/under 10yr €9/6/free, guided tour adult/10-25yr/under 10yr €13.50/9.50/6.50; ⏰10am-4.30pm; MOpéra) From Degas' ballerinas to Gaston Leroux's phantom and Chagall's ceiling, the layers of myth painted on gradually over the decades have bestowed a particular air of mystery and drama to the Palais Garnier's ornate interior. Designed in 1860 by Charles Garnier – then an unknown 35-year-old architect – the opera house was part of Baron Haussmann's massive urban renovation project.

The opera is open for visits during the day; highlights include the opulent **Grand Staircase**, the **library-museum** (1st fl), where you'll find old show posters, costumes and original music scores, and the horseshoe-shaped **auditorium** (2nd fl), with its extravagant gilded interior and red velvet seats. Or reserve a spot on an English-language guided tour. Note that the

Montmartre

Top Sights

Basilique du Sacré-Cœur C1

Sights

1 Clos Montmartre C1
2 Musée de Montmartre C1
3 Palais Garnier B5

Activities, Courses & Tours

4 L'Open Tour A4
5 Vélib' D2

Sleeping

6 Hôtel Amour C3
7 Hôtel des Arts B1
8 Hôtel Eldorado A2
9 Plug-Inn Hostel B2

Eating

10 Arnaud Delmontel C3
11 Cul de Poule C3
12 La Mascotte B2
13 Le J'Go C5
14 Le Miroir C2
15 Le Zinc des Cavistes C5
16 Les Pâtes Vivantes C4

Drinking

17 Harry's New York Bar B5
18 La Fourmi C2

Entertainment

19 Au Limonaire D5
20 Bus Palladium B3
21 Kiosque Théâtre Madeleine A5
22 La Cigale C2
23 Le Divan du Monde C2
24 Le Rex Club D5
25 Moulin Rouge B2

auditorium cannot be visited when daytime rehearsals or matinees are scheduled; try to arrive before 1pm or check the website for the exact schedule.

Interestingly, a prop man at the opera house set up beehives on the roof a couple of decades ago – the honey, when available, is now sold at the gift shop.

Musée Picasso MUSEUM
(Map p310; ☎01 42 71 25 21; www.musee-picasso.fr; 5 rue de Thorigny; Ⓜ St-Paul or Chemin Vert) One of Paris' most beloved art collections opened its doors again after massive renovation works in summer 2013. Housed in the stunning, mid-17th-century Hôtel Salé, the Musée Picasso woos art lovers with more than 3500 drawings, engravings, paintings, ceramic works and sculptures by the *grand maître* (great master) Pablo Picasso (1881–1973). The extraordinary collection was donated to the French government by the artist's heirs in lieu of paying inheritance tax.

FREE **Musée Carnavalet** MUSEUM
(Map p310; www.carnavalet.paris.fr; 23 rue de Sévigné, 3e; ⏲10am-6pm Tue-Sun; Ⓜ St-Paul, Chemin Vert or Rambuteau) One of the city's best free sights, this enormous 100-room ode to the history of Paris is housed in two elegant *hôtels particuliers* (historic mansions) in the Marais. Displays chart the history of Paris from Gallo-Roman to modern times: some of the nation's most important documents, paintings and objects from the French Revolution are here, as is Marcel Proust's cork-lined bedroom from his apartment on bd Haussmann where he wrote most of *À la Recherche du Temps Perdu* (In Search of Lost Time).

Place des Vosges SQUARE
(Map p310; place des Vosges, 4e; Ⓜ St-Paul or Bastille) Paris' oldest square, place des Vosges is a strikingly elegant ensemble of 36 symmetrical houses with ground-floor arcades, steep slate roofs and large dormer windows arranged around a large and leafy square. The square was named in 1800 to honour the Vosges *département* for being the first in France to pay its taxes.

Between 1832 and 1848 writer Victor Hugo lived in an apartment on the 3rd floor of the square's **Hôtel de Rohan-Guéménée**, now the museum **Maison de Victor Hugo** (Map p310; www.musee-hugo.paris.fr; admission free; ⏲10am-6pm Tue-Sun; Ⓜ St-Paul or Bastille), devoted to his life and times.

Place de la Bastille SQUARE
(Map p310; Ⓜ Bastille) The Bastille, a 14th-century fortress built to protect the city gates, is the most famous Parisian monument that no longer exists. Transformed into a dreaded state prison under Cardinal Richelieu, it was demolished shortly after a mob stormed it on 14 July 1789. First impressions

DON'T MISS

CANAL ST-MARTIN

The shaded towpaths of the tranquil, 4.5km-long **Canal St-Martin** (Map p304; MRépublique, Jaurès, Jacques Bonsergent) are a wonderful place for a romantic stroll or a bike ride past nine locks, metal bridges and ordinary Parisian neighbourhoods. The canal's banks have undergone a real urban renaissance, and the southern stretch in particular is an ideal spot for cafe lounging, quayside summer picnics and late-night drinks. Hip new bistros have moved into the area (most are closed Sunday and often Monday) and if you're in Paris to tempt your taste buds, you'll wind up in these eastern suburbs sooner rather than later.

Linking the 10e arrondissement with **Parc de la Villette** in the 19e, the canal makes its famous dogleg turn in the 10e arrondissement. Parts of the waterway – which was built between 1806 and 1825 in order to link the Seine with the 108km-long **Canal de l'Ourcq** – are actually higher than the surrounding land. Take a **canal boat** cruise to savour the real flavour.

of today's busy traffic circle can be underwhelming. The bronze column topped with the gilded Spirit of Liberty commemorates victims of later revolutions in 1830 and 1848.

Cimetière du Père Lachaise CEMETERY
(Map p304; ☎01 43 70 70 33; www.pere-lachaise.com; 16 rue du Repos & bd de Ménilmontant, 20e; admission free; ⊙8am-6pm Mon-Fri, from 8.30am Sat, from 9am Sun; MPère Lachaise or Philippe Auguste) The world's most visited cemetery opened its one-way doors in 1804. Among the 800,000 people buried here are the composer Chopin; the playwright Molière; the poet Apollinaire; writers Balzac, Proust, Gertrude Stein and Colette; the actors Simone Signoret, Sarah Bernhardt and Yves Montand; the painters Pissarro, Seurat, Modigliani and Delacroix; the *chanteuse* Édith Piaf; the dancer Isadora Duncan; and even those immortal 12th-century lovers, Abélard and Héloïse, whose remains were disinterred and reburied here together in 1817 beneath a neo-Gothic tombstone. Particularly visited graves are those of Oscar Wilde (division 89) and 1960s rock star Jim Morrison (division 6).

Activities

Cycling

Paris is set to expand its 370km of cycling lanes to 700km by 2014. Many sections of road are shut to motorised traffic on Sundays and holidays. Pick up wheels with Vélib' (p332), join an organised bike tour or rent your own wheels and DIY with one of these outfits:

Gepetto et Vélos CYCLING
(Map p310; www.gepetto-et-velos.com; 59 rue du Cardinal Lemoine, 5e; bicycles per day €15; ⊙9am-1pm & 2-7.30pm Tue-Sat; MCardinal Lemoine)

Paris à Vélo, C'est Sympa! CYCLING
(Map p310; www.parisvelosympa.com; 22 rue Alphonse Baudin, 11e; bicycles per day €20; ⊙9.30am-1pm & 2-6pm Mon-Fri, 9am-1pm & 2-7pm Sat & Sun; MSt-Sébastien–Froissart)

Tours

Fat Tire Bike Tours CYCLING
(Map p304; ☎01 56 58 10 54; www.fattirebiketours.com) City bike tours, day and night, plus trips further afield to Versailles, Monet's garden in Giverny and the Normandy beaches. Tours generally meet opposite the Eiffel Tower's southern pillar at the start of the Champ de Mars; look for the yellow signs. Reserve in advance.

Bateaux-Mouches BOAT TOUR
(Map p304; ☎01 42 25 96 10; www.bateauxmouches.com; Port de la Conférence, 8e; adult/4-12yr €11/5.50; ⊙Apr-Dec; MAlma Marceau) River cruises (70 minutes) with commentary in French and English; set sail from the Right Bank, just east of Pont de l'Alma.

L'Open Tour BUS TOUR
(Map p314; www.pariscityrama.com; 2-day passes adult/child €32/15) Hop-on, hop-off bus tours aboard an open-deck bus.

Paris Walks WALKING TOUR
(www.paris-walks.com; adult/child €12/8) Highly rated by Lonely Planet readers, this long-established company runs thematic tours (fashion, chocolate, the French Revolution).

Festivals & Events

Fashion Week FASHION
(www.pretparis.com; MPorte de Versailles) Prêt-à-Porter, the ready-to-wear fashion salon that

is held twice a year in late January and again in September, is a must for fashion buffs; it's held at the Parc des Expositions at Porte de Versailles, 15e.

Paris Plages BEACH
(www.paris.fr) 'Paris Beaches' sees three waterfront areas transformed into sand-and-pebble 'beaches', complete with sun beds, beach umbrellas, atomisers, lounge chairs and palm trees; mid-July to mid-August.

Nuit Blanche ART
(www.paris.fr) Museums, bars, clubs and so on don't sleep during Paris' 'White Night' all-nighter; first Saturday and Sunday of October.

Fête des Vendanges de Montmartre HARVEST
(www.fetedesvendangesdemontmartre.com) This five-day festival during the second weekend in October celebrates Montmartre's grape harvest with costumes, speeches and a parade.

Sleeping

The Paris Convention & Visitors Bureau can find you a place to stay (no booking fee, but you need a credit card), though queues can be long in high season; it also has information on bed-and-breakfast accommodation.

LOUVRE & LES HALLES

The upside of this right-bank neighbourhood is its epicentral location, excellent transport links and proximity to many major sights and shops. However, the immediate area around the **Forum des Halles** (Map p310; www.forumdeshalles.com; 1 rue Pierre Lescot, 1er; shops 10am-8pm Mon-Sat; M Les Halles or RER Châtelet–Les Halles) may be noisy/inconvenient during construction works (not due for completion until 2016).

Hôtel Tiquetonne HOTEL €
(Map p310; 01 42 36 94 58; www.hoteltiquetonne; 6 rue Tiquetonne, 2e; d €65, with shared shower €45; ; M Étienne Marcel) What heart-warmingly good value this 45-room vintage cheapie is. This serious, well-tended address in the heart of party land has been in the hotel biz since the 1900s and is much-loved by a loyal clientele of all ages. Rooms straddle seven floors and sport an inoffensive mix of vintage decor – roughly 1930s to 1980s – with brand new bathrooms and parquet flooring in recently renovated rooms. Shared shower *jeton* (tokens) cost €5; ask at reception.

TOP CHOICE **Hôtel Crayon** BOUTIQUE HOTEL €€
(Map p310; 01 42 36 54 19; www.hotelcrayon.com; 25 rue du Bouloi, 1er; s €129-249, d €149-299; ; M Les Halles or Sentier) Line drawings by French artist Julie Gauthron bedeck walls and doors at this creative boutique hotel. The pencil *(le crayon)* is the theme, with rooms sporting a different shade of each floor's chosen colour – we love the coloured-glass shower doors and the books on the bedside table guests can swap and take home.

BVJ Paris-Louvre HOSTEL €
(Map p310; 01 53 00 90 90; www.bvjhotel.com; 20 rue Jean-Jacques Rousseau, 1er; dm/d incl breakfast €30/70; @; M Louvre Rivoli) This modern, 200-bed hostel has doubles and bunks in a single-sex room for four to 10 people with showers down the corridor. Guests must be aged 18 to 35. Rooms are accessible from 2.30pm on the day you arrive. No kitchen facilities.

MARAIS & BASTILLE

Buzzing nightlife, hip shopping and an inexhaustible range of eating options ensure the popularity of this trendy, right-bank neighbourhood. Nearby Bastille has fewer

BOHEMIAN SOULS IN MONTMARTRE

No address better captures the *quartier*'s rebellious, bohemian and artsy past than **Musée de Montmartre** (Map p314; www.museedemontmartre.fr; 12 rue Cortot, 18e; adult/18-25yr/10-17yr €8/6/4; 10am-6pm; M Lamarck–Caulaincourt), one-time home to painters Renoir, Utrillo and Raoul Dufy. The 17th-century manor house-museum displays paintings, lithographs and documents; hosts art exhibitions by contemporary artists currently living in Montmartre; and its excellent bookshop sells bottles of the wine produced from grapes grown in the *quartier*'s very own vineyard, **Clos Montmartre** (Map p314; 18 rue des Saules, 18e).

Later, pay your respects to bohemian souls – writers Émile Zola, Alexandre Dumas and Stendhal, composer Jacques Offenbach, artist Edgar Degas, film director François Truffaut and dancer Vaslav Nijinsky among others – laid to rest in the Cimetière de Montmartre. Around since 1798, the cemetery is Paris' most famous after Père Lachaise.

RENTING AN APARTMENT

Be it a night, a week or longer, apartment rental is increasingly the modish way to stay in Paris. **Haven in Paris** (www.haveninparis.com) is recommended – it has luxury apartments from €575 per week.

Paris Attitude (www.parisattitude.com) Thousands of apartment rentals, professional service, reasonable fees.

Guest Apartment Services (www.guestapartment.com) Romantic apartment rentals on and around Paris' islands.

Room Sélection (www.room-selection.com) Select apartment rentals centred on the Marais.

tourists, allowing you to better glimpse the daily grind of the 'real' Paris.

TOP CHOICE Hôtel Jeanne d'Arc HOTEL €€

(Map p310; ☎01 48 87 62 11; www.hoteljeannedarc.com; 3 rue de Jarente, 4e; s €65, d €81-96, tr €149, q €164; 📶; Ⓜ St-Paul) Book well in advance at this gorgeous address to snag one of its cosy, excellent-value rooms. Games to play, a painted rocking chair for tots in the bijou lounge, knick knacks everywhere, and the most extraordinary mirror in the breakfast room create a real 'family home' air to this 35-room house.

Le Pavillon de la Reine HISTORIC HOTEL €€€

(Map p310; ☎01 44 59 80 40; www.pavillondelareine.com; 28 place des Vosges, 3e; d from €330; Ⓜ Chemin Vert) Dreamily set on Paris' most beautiful and elegant square, place des Vosges, this sumptuous address loaded with history doesn't come cheap. But who cares when you can sleep like a queen (indeed the hotel is named after Anne of Austria, queen to Louis XIII from 1615, who stayed here).

Cosmos Hôtel HOTEL €

(Map p304; ☎01 43 57 25 88; www.cosmos-hotel-paris.com; 35 rue Jean-Pierre Timbaud, 11e; s/d/tr €55/62/78; 📶; Ⓜ République) Cheap, brilliant value and just footsteps from the fun and happening bars, cafes and music clubs of increasingly trendy rue JPT, Cosmos is a shiny star with retro style on the budget-hotel scene. It has been around for 30-odd years but, unlike most other hotels in the same price bracket, Cosmos has been treated to a thoroughly modern makeover this century. Enjoy.

Hôtel du Petit Moulin BOUTIQUE HOTEL €€€

(Map p310; ☎01 42 74 10 10; www.hoteldupetitmoulin.com; 29-31 rue du Poitou, 3e; d €190-350; Ⓜ Filles du Calvaire) This 17-room hotel, a bakery at the time of Henri IV, was designed by Christian Lacroix. Pick from medieval and rococo Marais (rooms sporting exposed beams and dressed in toile de Jouy wallpaper), to more modern surrounds with contemporary murals and heart-shaped mirrors just this side of kitsch.

Hi Matic HOTEL €€

(Map p304; ☎01 43 67 56 56; www.hi-matic.net; 71 rue de Charonne, 11e; r €110-160; ❄@📶; Ⓜ Bastille) This odd place has staked its claim as the 'urban hotel of the future'. The plus side is eco-friendly features (LED energy-saving lights, natural pigments instead of paint) and a colourful, imaginative space-saving design (mattresses are rolled out onto tatamis at night) that some will find fun. The downside is that service is kept to a minimum – check-in is via computer, and the organic breakfast comes out of a vending machine.

Maison Internationale de la Jeunesse et des Étudiants HOSTEL €

(MIJE; Map p310; ☎01 42 74 23 45; www.mije.com; 6 rue de Fourcy, 4e; dm incl breakfast €31, annual membership €2.50; Ⓜ St-Paul) Sweep through the elegant front door and congratulate yourself on finding such magnificent digs. The MIJE runs three hostels in attractively renovated 17th- and 18th-century *hôtels particuliers* in the Marais. Rooms are closed from noon to 3pm, and curfew is 1am to 7am.

LATIN QUARTER

Midrange hotels in this good-value Left Bank neighbourhood are particularly popular with visiting academics, making rooms hardest to find during conferences (March to June and October).

Five Hotel DESIGN HOTEL €€€

(Map p304; ☎01 43 31 74 21; www.thefivehotel-paris.com; 3 rue Flatters, 5e; d €202-342; ❄📶; Ⓜ Les Gobelins) Choose from one of five perfumes to fragrance your room at this contemporary romantic sanctum. Its private apartment, One by The Five, has a phenomenal 'suspended' bed.

Hôtel Minerve HOTEL €€

(Map p310; ☎01 43 26 26 04; www.parishotelminerve.com; 13 rue des Écoles, 5e; s €99, d €129-

165, tr €165; ❄@📶; Ⓜ Cardinal Lemoine) Oriental carpets, antique books, frescoes of French monuments and reproduction 18th-century wallpaper make this family-run hotel a charming place to stay. Some rooms have small balconies with views of Notre Dame; two have tiny romantic courtyards.

Select Hôtel BOUTIQUE HOTEL €€€

(Map p310; ☎01 46 34 14 80; www.selecthotel.fr; 1 place de la Sorbonne, 5e; s €165, d €215-299, tr €309-320; ❄@📶; Ⓜ Cluny–La Sorbonne) In the heart of the studenty Sorbonne area, the Select is a very Parisian art deco minipalace, with an atrium and cactus-strewn winter garden, an 18th-century vaulted breakfast room and 67 small but stylish bedrooms. The 1920s-style cocktail bar with 'library' is a delight.

Hôtel les Degrés de Notre Dame HOTEL €€

(Map p310; ☎01 55 42 88 88; www.lesdegreshotel.com; 10 rue des Grands Degrés, 5e; d incl breakfast €115-170; 📶; Ⓜ Maubert-Mutualité) Wonderfully old-school, with a winding timber staircase (no lift), and charming staff, the value is unbeatable at this hotel, a block from the Seine.

Oops HOSTEL €

(Map p304; ☎01 47 07 47 00; www.oops-paris.com; 50 av des Gobelins, 13e; dm/d €30/70; @📶; Ⓜ Gobelins) A lurid candyfloss-pink lift scales the six floors of Paris' first 'design hostel', each painted a different colour. Well-sized doubles and modern but locker-less four- to six-bed dorms all have ensuites and some have Eiffel Tower views. No kitchen. No credit cards and no alcohol allowed.

ST-GERMAIN, ODÉON & LUXEMBOURG

Staying in chic St-Germain des Prés (6e) is a delight. But beware – budget places just don't exist in this part of the Left Bank.

TOP CHOICE L'Apostrophe DESIGN HOTEL €€€

(Map p304; ☎01 56 54 31 31; www.apostrophe-hotel.com; 3 rue de Chevreuse, 6e; d €150-350; ❄@📶; Ⓜ Vavin) A street work-of-art with stencilled facade, this hotel's 16 rooms pay homage to the written word. Graffiti tags cover one wall of room U (for *'urbain'*) which has a ceiling shaped like a skateboard ramp. Room P (for 'Paris parody') sits in clouds overlooking Paris' rooftops.

Le Bellechasse DESIGN HOTEL €€

(Map p304; ☎01 45 50 22 31; www.lebellechasse.com; 8 rue de Bellechasse, 7e; d from €161; ❄📶; Ⓜ Solférino) Fashion designer Christian Lacroix's entrancing room themes make you feel like you've stepped into a larger-than-life oil painting. Mod cons include iPod docks and 200 TV channels.

Hotel St-André des Arts HOTEL €€

(Map p310; ☎01 43 26 96 16; 66 rue St-André des Arts, 6e; s/d/tr/q incl breakfast €75/95/119/132; 📶; Ⓜ Odéon) Snug on a lively, restaurant-lined thoroughfare, this 31-room hotel is a veritable bargain in the centre of the action. Rooms are basic, but public areas are evocative of *vieux Paris* (old Paris) with beamed ceilings and stone walls.

GARE DU NORD, GARE DE L'EST & RÉPUBLIQUE

The areas around the Gare du Nord and Gare de l'Est are far from the prettiest parts of Paris, but decent-value hotels are a dime a dozen.

TOP CHOICE Le Citizen Hotel BOUTIQUE HOTEL €€€

(Map p304; ☎01 83 62 55 50; www.lecitizenhotel.com; 96 quai de Jemmapes, 10e; d €177-275, q €450; 📶; Ⓜ Gare de l'Est, Jacques Bonsergent) A team of forward-thinking creative types put their heads together for this one, and the result is 12 alluring rooms equipped with iPads, filtered water and warm minimalist design.

Hôtel du Nord – Le Pari Vélo HOTEL €€

(Map p304; ☎01 42 01 66 00; www.hoteldunord-leparivelo.com; 47 rue Albert Thomas, 10e; s/d/q €71/85/110; 📶; Ⓜ République) Beyond the bric-a-brac charm (and the ever popular dog, Pluto), Hôtel du Nord's other winning attribute is its prized location near place République. Bikes are on loan for guests.

République Hôtel HOTEL €€

(Map p304; ☎01 42 39 19 03; www.republiquehotel.com; 31 rue Albert Thomas, 10e; s €82, d €95-120, tr €120, q €169; 📶; Ⓜ République) This hip spot is heavy on pop art – local street artists did some of the paintings here. Regardless of the garden gnomes in the breakfast room, you won't be able to fault the inexpensive rates and fantastic location off place République.

St Christopher's Inn HOSTEL €

(Map p304; ☎01 40 34 34 40; www.st-christophers.co.uk/paris-hostels; 68-74 quai de la Seine, 19e; dm €22-40, d from €70; @📶; Ⓜ Riquet or Jaurès) This is one of Paris' best, biggest and most up-to-date hostels with a modern design, four types of dorms (six- to 12-bed) and doubles with or without bathrooms. Other perks include a canal-side cafe, bar and a female-only floor. A new **branch** (Map p304; rue de Dunkerque) will open across from Gare du Nord.

MONTMARTRE & PIGALLE

What a charmer Montmartre is, with its varied accommodation scene embracing everything from boutique to bohemian, hostel to *hôtel particulier*.

TOP CHOICE Hôtel Amour BOUTIQUE HOTEL €€
(Map p314; ☎01 48 78 31 80; www.hotelamourparis.fr; 8 rue Navarin, 9e; s €105, d €155-215; 📶; MSt-Georges or Pigalle) The inimitable black-clad Amour (formerly a love hotel by the hour) features original design and artwork – you won't find a more original place to lay your head in Paris at these prices.

Au Sourire de Montmartre B&B €€
(Map p304; ☎06 64 64 72 86; www.sourire-de-montmartre.com; rue du Mont Cenis, 18e; r €125-170, apt per week €600; MJules Joffrin) This charming B&B on the backside of Montmartre has four rooms and a studio, each decorated with French antiques or Moroccan motifs. The surrounding neighbourhood is delightful, though slightly out of the way.

Hôtel Eldorado HOTEL €
(Map p314; ☎01 45 22 35 21; www.eldoradohotel.fr; 18 rue des Dames, 17e; s €39-65, d €58-85, tr €75-93; 📶; MPlace de Clichy) This bohemian place is one of Paris' greatest finds: a welcoming, reasonably well-run place with 23 colourful rooms and a private back garden. Cheaper-category singles have washbasin only.

Hôtel des Arts HOTEL €€
(Map p314; ☎01 46 06 30 52; www.arts-hotel-paris.com; 5 rue Tholozé, 18e; s €105, d €140-165; 📶; MAbbesses or Blanche) This attractive 50-room hotel, convenient to both place Pigalle and Montmartre, sports excellent-value midrange rooms; consider spending an extra €25 for the superior rooms, which have nicer views.

Plug-Inn Hostel HOSTEL €
(Map p314; ☎01 42 58 42 58; www.plug-inn.fr; 7 rue Aristide Bruant, 18e; dm/d/tr incl breakfast €25/60/90; @📶; MAbbesses or Blanche) This hostel is much-loved for its central Montmartre location, four to five-person rooms each with shower, the kitchen, free breakfast and no curfew at night.

Eating

LOUVRE & LES HALLES

Trendy restaurants are on the rise in this epicentral area.

TOP CHOICE Beef Club STEAK €€
(Map p310; ☎09 54 37 13 65; www.eccbeefclub.com; 58 rue Jean-Jacques Rousseau, 1er; mains €20-45; ⏲dinner; MLes Halles) No steak house is more chic or hip than this. Packed out ever since it threw its first T-bone on the grill in 2012, this beefy address is all about steak, prepared to sweet perfection by legendary Paris butcher Yves-Marie Le Bourdonnec. The vibe is hip New York and the downstairs cellar bar, Ballroom du Beef Club, shakes a mean cocktail (€12 to €15) courtesy of the Experimental Cocktail Club.

TOP CHOICE Frenchie BISTRO €€
(Map p310; ☎01 40 39 96 19; www.frenchie-restaurant.com; 5-6 rue du Nil, 2e; menus €34, €38 & €45; ⏲dinner Mon-Fri; MSentier) This bijou bistro with wooden tables and old stone walls is always packed and for good reason: excellent-value dishes are modern, market-driven (the menu changes daily with a choice of two dishes by course) and prepared with just the right dose of unpretentious creative flair by French chef Gregory Marchand.

Reserve for one of two sittings (7pm or 9.30pm) two months in advance, arrive at 7pm and pray for a cancellation, or – failing that – share tapas-style small plates with friends across the street at no-reservations **Frenchie Bar à Vin**.

Verjus INTERNATIONAL €€€
(Map p310; ☎01 42 97 54 40; www.verjusparis.com; 52 rue de Richelieu, 1er; 4-/6-course tasting menus €55/70, with wine pairings €85/110; ⏲dinner Mon-Fri; MBourse or Palais Royal–Musée du Louvre) Cuisine is contemporary and international at this hidden but hyped restaurant near Palais Royal that you really need to know about to find. Reservations are essential Thursday and Friday, but walk-ins Monday to Wednesday often end up with a table. And for diners who don't strike gold, there's the wine bar in the restaurant cellar famed in Parisian foodie circles for the best fried buttermilk chicken (€10) in town.

Yam'Tcha FUSION €€€
(Map p310; ☎01 40 26 08 07; www.yamtcha.com; 4 rue Sauval, 1er; lunch/dinner menus from €50/85; ⏲lunch Wed-Sun, dinner Wed-Sat; MLouvre-Rivoli)

TOP FIVE PATISSERIES

Ladurée (Map p304; www.laduree.fr; 75 av des Champs-Élysées, 8e; pastries from €1.50; 7.30am-11pm; George V) Paris' most historic and decadent; inventor of the *macaron*.

Le Nôtre (Map p310; www.lenotre.fr; 10 rue St-Antoine, 4e; Bastille) Delectable pastries and chocolate; 10-odd outlets around town.

La Pâtisserie des Rêves (Map p304; www.lapatisseriedesreves.com; 93 rue du Bac, 7e; 10am-8.30pm Tue-Sat, 8.30am-2pm Sun; Rue du Bac) Extraordinary cakes and tarts showcased beneath glass at the chic 'art' gallery of big-name *pâtissier* Philippe Conticini.

Boulangerie Bruno Solques (Map p310; 243 rue St-Jacques, 5e; 6.30am-8pm Mon-Fri; Place Monge or RER Luxembourg) Paris' most inventive *pâtissier*, Bruno Solques, excels at oddly shaped flat tarts and fruit-filled brioches.

Arnaud Delmontel (Map p314; 39 rue des Martyrs, 9e; 7am-8.30pm Wed-Mon; Pigalle) Award-winning baguettes, gorgeous cakes, pastries to die for.

Adeline Grattard's ingeniously fused French and Chinese flavours has earned her a Michelin star. Pair dishes on the frequently changing menu with wine or exotic teas.

Spring MODERN FRENCH €€

(Map p310; 01 45 96 05 72; www.springparis.fr; 6 rue Bailleul, 1er; lunch/dinner menus €44/76; lunch & dinner Wed-Fri, dinner Tue & Sat; Palais Royal–Musée du Louvre) One of the Right Bank's 'talk-of-the-town' addresses, with an American in the kitchen and stunning food. It has no printed menu, meaning hungry gourmets put their appetites in the hands of the chef and allow multilingual waiting staff to reveal what's cooking as each course is served. Advance reservations essential.

At lunchtime, nip to the **Spring Épicerie** (Map p310; www.springparis.fr; 52 rue de l'Arbre Sec, 1er; soup €12; noon-8pm Tue-Sat), a tiny wine shop which serves steaming bowls of chicken soup (€12) eaten at a bar stool or on the trot.

Kunitoraya JAPANESE €

(Map p310; www.kunitoraya.com; 39 rue Ste-Anne, 1er; mains €12-14; 11.30am-10pm; Pyramides) Grab a stool at the kitchen bar and watch hip young Japanese chefs strut their stuff over steaming bowls of soup, *grands bols de riz* (big bowls of rice) and some of the best udon (handmade Japanese noodles) in town. No credit cards and no reservations.

Blend BURGERS €

(Map p310; www.blendhamburger.com; 44 rue d'Argout, 2e; burgers €10, lunch menus €15 & €17; lunch & dinner Mon-Sat; Sentier) A burger cannot simply be a burger in gourmet Paris, where burger buffs dissolve into raptures of ecstacy at Blend. Think home-made brioche buns and ketchup, hand-cut meat and the most inventive of toppings that transform the humble burger into something really rather special.

Saveurs Végét'Halles VEGETARIAN €

(Map p310; 01 40 41 93 95; www.saveursvegethalles.fr; 41 rue des Bourdonnais, 1er; salads €11.90; lunch & dinner Mon-Sat; ; Châtelet) This vegan eatery offers quite a few mock-meat dishes like *poulet végétal aux champignons* ('chicken' with mushrooms). No alcohol.

MARAIS & BASTILLE

The Marais is one of Paris' premier dining neighbourhoods; book ahead for weekend dining. Traditional bistros and neobistros vie for supremacy in neighbouring Bastille.

TOP CHOICE **Septime** MODERN FRENCH €€€

(Map p304; 01 43 67 38 29; 80 rue de Charonne, 11e; lunch/5-course menus €26/55; lunch Tue-Fri, dinner Mon-Fri; Charonne) Reading the menu won't get you far given it more resembles a shopping list. But have no fear: alchemists in the kitchen produce truly beautiful creations, and the blue-smocked waitstaff go out of their way to ensure the culinary surprises are all pleasant ones.

Le Siffleur de Ballons WINE BAR €

(Map p304; www.lesiffleurdeballons.com; 34 rue de Citeaux, 12e; lunch menus €14, mains €7-15; 10.30am-3pm & 5.30-10pm Tue-Sat; Faidherbe Chaligny) With Tom Waits on the stereo and a few cactuses atop the register, this contemporary wine bar clearly has a dash of

TOP FIVE FOOD MARKETS

Marché Bastille (Map p310; bd Richard Lenoir; ⊙7am-2.30pm Thu & Sun; MBastille or Richard Lenoir) Paris' best outdoor food market.

Marché aux Enfants Rouges (Map p310; 39 rue de Bretagne, 3e; ⊙8.30am-1pm & 4-7.30pm Tue-Fri, 4-8pm Sat, 8.30am-2pm Sun; MFilles du Calvaire) The city's oldest food market, in the Marais, with food stalls and communal tables to lunch at.

Marché Belleville (Map p304; bd de Belleville, btwn rue Jean-Pierre Timbaud & rue du Faubourg du Temple, 11e & 20e; ⊙7am-2.30pm Tue & Fri; MBelleville or Couronnes) Fascinating entry into the large, vibrant communities of the eastern neighbourhoods, home to artists, students and immigrants from Africa, Asia and the Middle East.

Marché Couvert St-Quentin (Map p304; 85bis bd de Magenta, 10e) Iron-and-glass covered market built in 1866; lots of gourmet and upmarket food stalls.

Marché Raspail (Map p304; bd Raspail btwn rue de Rennes & rue du Cherche Midi, 6e; ⊙regular market 7am-2.30pm Tue & Fri, organic market 9am-3pm Sun; MRennes) Much-loved by foodies, particularly on Sunday for its organic produce.

California in its soul. The wines are French, natural, and paired to perfection with simple but delicious offerings: tartines, soups, lentil salad with truffle oil, cheeses and Iberian charcuterie plates. Look out for the weekly tastings with winemakers.

Bistrot Paul Bert BISTRO €€
(Map p304; ☎01 43 72 24 01; 18 rue Paul Bert, 11e; 3-course lunch/dinner menus €18/36; ⊙lunch & dinner Tue-Sat; MFaidherbe-Chaligny) An address that stars on every 'best Paris bistro' list, Paul Bert serves perfectly executed classic dishes in a timeless setting.

Au Passage BISTRO €€
(Map p310; ☎01 43 55 07 52; www.facebook.com/aupassage; 1bis passage de St-Sébastien, 11e; 2-/3-course lunch menus €13.50/19.50, dinners €20-35; ⊙lunch & dinner Mon-Fri, dinner Sat; MSt-Sébastien–Froissart) Have faith in talented Australian chef James Henry at this raved-about *petit bar de quartier* (neighbourhood bar) with vegetable crates piled scruffily in the window and a fridge filling one corner of the old-fashioned dining room.

The lunch menu – a good-value, uncomplicated choice of two starters and two mains – is chalked on the blackboard, while dinner sees waiting staff in jeans twirl in and out of the pocket-sized kitchen with tapas-style starters to share, followed by a feisty shoulder of lamb, side of beef or other meaty cut for the entire table.

Chez Marianne JEWISH €€
(Map p310; 2 rue des Hospitalières St-Gervais, 4e; mains €19-24; ⊙noon-midnight; MSt-Paul) Absolutely heaving at lunchtime, Chez Marianne translates as elbow-to-elbow eating beneath age-old beams on copious portions of falafel, hummus, purées of aubergine and chickpeas, and 25-odd other *zakouski* (hors d'œuvres; plate of 4/5/6 for €12/14/16). Fare is Sephardic and a hole-in-the-wall window sells falafel in pita (€6) to munch on the move.

Nanashi FUSION €
(Map p310; ☎09 60 00 25 59; www.nanashi.fr; 57 rue Charlot, 3e; bento €14-16; ⊙noon-midnight Mon-Fri, to 6pm Sat & Sun; MFilles du Calvaire) A fabulous lunch and after-dark address wedged between boutiques in the Haut Marais, this hip industrial space is uber-cool, ultra-healthy and great value. Pick from creative salads, soups and bento boxes, and don't miss the freshly squeezed fruit and veg cocktails. Weekend brunch €17.

LATIN QUARTER

From cheap student haunts to chandelier-lit palaces loaded with history, the 5e has something to suit every budget and culinary taste. Rue Mouffetard is famed for its food market and food shops; while its side streets, especially pedestrianised rue du Pot au Fer, cook up fine budget dining.

L'Agrume NEOBISTRO €€
(Map p304; ☎01 43 31 86 48; 15 rue des Fossés St-Marcel, 5e; 2-/3-course lunch menus €19/24, mains €26-39; ⊙lunch & dinner Tue-Sat; MCensier Daubenton) Snagging a table at 'Citrus Fruit' is tough, but the reward is watching chefs work with seasonal produce in the open kitchen while you dine. You have a choice of table, bar stool or *comptoir* (counter). Lunching is magnificent value,

while dinner is a no-choice *dégustation* (tasting) melody.

Bistrot Les Papilles BISTRO €€
(Map p310; ☎01 43 25 20 79; www.lespapillesparis.com; 30 rue Gay Lussac, 5e; lunch/dinner menus from €22/31; ⊙10.30am-midnight Mon-Sat; Ⓜ Raspail or RER Luxembourg) This hybrid bistro, wine cellar and *épicerie* (grocery) serves market-driven fare at simply dressed tables wedged beneath bottle-lined walls. Each weekday cooks up a different *marmite du marché* (market casserole). But what really sets it apart is its exceptional wine list.

Le Coupe-Chou FRENCH €€
(Map p310; ☎01 46 33 68 69; www.lecoupechou.com; 9 & 11 rue de Lanneau, 5e; 2-/3-course lunch menus €27, mains €18-25; ⊙Mon-Sat; Ⓜ Maubert-Mutualité) This maze of candlelit rooms inside a vine-clad 17th-century townhouse is overwhelmingly romantic. Ceilings are beamed, furnishings are antique, and background classical music mingles with the intimate chatter of diners. As in the days when Marlene Dietrich et al dined here, advance reservations are essential.

Le Coupe-Chou, incidentally, has nothing to do with cabbage *(chou)*; rather it's named after the barber's razor once wielded with a deft hand in one of its seven rooms.

ST-GERMAIN, ODÉON & LUXEMBOURG

There's far more to this fabled pocket of Paris than the literary cafes of Sartre or the picnicking turf of Jardin de Luxembourg. Rue St-André des Arts (Ⓜ St-Michel or Odéon) is lined with places to dine lightly or lavishly, as is the stretch between Église St-Sulpice and Église St-Germain des Prés (especially rue des Canettes, rue Princesse and rue Guisarde).

TOP CHOICE **Bouillon Racine** BRASSERIE €€
(Map p310; ☎01 44 32 15 60; www.bouillonracine.com; 3 rue Racine, 6e; lunch menu €14.50, menus €30-41; ⊙noon-11pm; Ⓜ Cluny–La Sorbonne) This heritage-listed 1906 art nouveau 'soup kitchen', with mirrored walls, floral motifs and ceramic tiling, was built in 1906 to feed market workers. Superbly executed dishes inspired by age-old recipes include stuffed, spit-roasted suckling pig, pork shank in Rodenbach red beer, and scallops and shrimp with lobster coulis. Finish off your foray into gastronomic history with an old-fashioned sherbet.

Café Constant NEOBISTRO €€
(Map p304; www.cafeconstant.com; 139 rue Ste-Dominique, 7e; 2-/3-course menus €16/23; ⊙lunch & dinner Tue-Sun; Ⓜ École Militaire or RER Port de l'Alma) Take a former Michelin-star chef and a simple corner cafe and what do you get? This jam-packed address with original mosaic floor, wooden tables and huge queues every meal time. The pride and joy of Christian and Catherine Constant, it cooks up creative bistro cuisine, mixing old-fashioned grandma staples like *purée de mon enfance* (mashed potato from my childhood) with Sunday treats like foie-gras-stuffed quail and herb-roasted chicken. **Les Cocottes** (Map p304; www.leviolondingres.com; 135 rue Ste-Dominique, 7e; 2-/3-course lunch menus €9/15, mains €14-28; ⊙lunch & dinner Mon-Sat; Ⓜ École Militaire or RER Port de l'Alma), a couple of doors down, is another Constant hit.

KGB FUSION €€
(Map p310; ☎01 46 33 00 85; http://zekitchengalerie.fr; 25 rue des Grands Augustins, 6e; 2-/3-course lunch menus €27/34, mains €27-32; ⊙lunch & dinner Tue-Sat; Ⓜ St-Michel) Overtly art gallery in feel, KGB draws a hip crowd for its casual platters of

CANAL ST-MARTIN: A PARISIAN-PERFECT PICNIC

Not just another pizza place! *Mais non, chérie!* Once the weather warms up, the **Pink Flamingo** (Map p304; ☎01 42 02 31 70; www.pinkflamingopizza.com; 67 rue Bichat, 10e; pizzas €10.50-16; ⊙lunch Tue-Sun, dinner daily; Ⓜ Jacques Bonsergent) unveils its secret weapon – pink helium balloons that the delivery guy uses to locate you and your perfect canalside picnic spot. Nip into the canalside pizzeria to order Paris' most inventive pizza (duck, apple and chèvre perhaps, or what about gorgonzola, figs and cured ham?), grab a balloon, and stroll off along the canal to your perfect picnic spot. There's also a **Marais branch** (Map p310; ☎01 42 71 28 20; 105 rue Vieille du Temple, 3e; pizzas €10.50-16; ⊙noon-3pm & 7-11.30pm; Ⓜ St-Sébastien–Froissart).

To make your picnic Parisian perfect, buy a bottle of wine from nearby **Le Verre Volé** (Map p304; ☎01 48 03 17 34; 67 rue de Lancry, 10e; mains €13-16; ⊙lunch & dinner; Ⓜ Jacques Bonsergent), a wine shop with a few tables, excellent wines (€5 to €60 per bottle, €4.50 per glass) and expert advice.

LOCAL KNOWLEDGE

PATRICIA WELLS, CULINARY SHOPPING SPREE

Cookery teacher and author of *The Food Lover's Guide to Paris*, American Patricia Wells (www.patriciawells.com) has lived, cooked and shopped in Paris since 1980, and is considered to have truly captured the soul of French cuisine.

What is it that makes Paris so wonderful for culinary shopping? The tradition, the quality, the quantity, the atmosphere and physical beauty!

Where do you shop? All over: the Sunday organic market at Rennes (Marché Raspail) – I love the dried fruits and nuts; Poilâne for bread; Quatrehomme for cheese; and Poissonnerie du Bac for fish. I shop regularly at Le Bon Marché's La Grande Épicerie de Paris; for special meals I order in advance and go from shop to shop – La Maison du Chocolat and Pierre Hermé for chocolate and cakes, and La Dernière Goutte for wine. That is the fun of Paris, and of France.

Your top food shopping tip? If you live in Paris, become a *client fidèle* so they reach in the back and give you the best stuff. If you only go once in a while, just smile and be friendly.

A perfect culinary souvenir from Paris? Fragonard, the perfume maker, has a great shop on bd St-Germain. They have a changing litany of *great* things for the home. Nothing is very expensive and the offerings change every few months. The gift wrapping alone is worth it!

Asian-influenced *hors d'œvres*, creative pastas, and mains spanning roast pigeon with ginger and cranberry condiment, suckling lamb, and grilled seabass with lemongrass and mandarin dressing.

Cuisine de Bar SANDWICHES €

(Map p304; 8 rue du Cherche Midi, 6e; dishes €7.50-13; ⏲8.30am-7pm Tue-Sat; Ⓜ Sèvres-Babylone) This is not any old sandwich bar, rather an ultrachic spot to lunch between designer boutiques on open sandwiches cut from celebrated **Poilâne** (Map p304; www.poilane.fr; 8 rue du Cherche Midi, 6e; ⏲7.15am-8.15pm Mon-Sat; Ⓜ Sèvres-Babylone) bread and fabulously topped with gourmet goodies such as foie gras, smoked duck, gooey St-Marcellin cheese and Bayonne ham.

Au Pied de Fouet BISTRO €

(Map p310; ☎01 43 54 87 83; www.aupieddefouet.com; 50 rue St-Benoît, 6e; mains €9-12.50; ⏲Mon-Sat; Ⓜ St-Germain des Prés) Wholly classic bistro dishes such as *entrecôte* (steak), *confit de canard* (duck cooked slowly its own fat) and *foie de volailles sauté* (pan-fried chicken livers) at this busy bistro are astonishingly good value. Round off your meal with a *tarte tatin*, wine-soaked prunes or a bowl of *fromage blanc* (a cross between yoghurt, sour cream and cream cheese).

Cosi SANDWICHES €

(Map p310; 54 rue de Seine, 6e; sandwich menus €10-15; ⏲noon-11pm; 👪; Ⓜ Odéon) This might just be Paris' most imaginative sandwich maker, with sandwich names like Stonker, Tom Dooley and Naked Willi chalked on the blackboard. Classical music plays in the background and homemade foccacia bread is still warm from the oven.

MONTPARNASSE

In the 1920s Montparnasse was one of Paris' premier avenues for cafe life and it still enjoys a clutch of worth-trying addresses.

Jadis NEOBISTRO €€

(Map p304; ☎01 45 57 73 20; www.bistrot-jadis.com; 202 rue de la Croix Nivert, 15e; lunch/dinner menus from €29/36; ⏲lunch & dinner Mon-Fri; Ⓜ Boucicaut) This upmarket neobistro on the corner of a very unassuming street packs a modern punch thanks to the daring of rising-star chef, Guillaume Delage, who braises pork cheeks in beer and uses black rice instead of white. The chocolate soufflé – order it at the start of your meal – is divine.

TOP CHOICE **La Cabane à Huîtres** SEAFOOD €

(Map p304; ☎01 45 49 47 27; 4 rue Antoine Bourdelle, 14e; dozen oysters €14.50, menus €19.50; ⏲lunch & dinner Wed-Sat; Ⓜ Montparnasse Bienvenüe) Wonderfully rustic, this wooden-styled *cabane* (cabin) with just nine tables is the pride and joy of fifth-generation oyster farmer Françis Dubourg, who splits his week between the capital and his oyster farm in Arcachon on the Atlantic Coast. The fixed menu includes a dozen oysters, foie gras, *magret de canard fumé* (smoked duck breast) or smoked salmon and scrumptious desserts.

Le Dôme BRASSERIE €€
(Map p304; ☎01 43 35 25 81; 108 bd du Montparnasse, 14e; mains €37-49, seafood platters €54; ⏱lunch & dinner; Ⓜ Vavin) A 1930s art deco extravaganza, Le Dôme is a monumental place for a meal service of the formal white-tablecloth and bow-tied-waiter variety. It's one of the swishest places around for shellfish platters piled high with fresh oysters, king prawns, crab claws and so on.

ÉTOILE & CHAMPS-ÉLYSÉES

The 8e arrondissement around the Champs-Élysées is known for its big-name chefs (Alain Ducasse, Pierre Gagnaire, Guy Savoy) and culinary icons (Taillevent), but there are all sorts of under-the-radar restaurants scattered in the backstreets where Parisians who live and work in the area dine. Gourmet food shops, some with attached eateries, garland **place Madeleine.**

Le Boudoir FRENCH €€
(Map p304; ☎01 43 59 25 29; www.boudoirparis.fr; 25 rue du Colisée, 8e; lunch menus €25, mains €25-29; ⏱lunch Mon-Fri, dinner Tue-Sat; Ⓜ St-Philippe du Roule or Franklin D Roosevelt) Spread across two floors, the quirky salons here are works of art. Expect classy bistro fare prepared by chef Arnaud Nicolas, a recipient of France's top culinary honour.

Le Hide FRENCH €€
(Map p304; ☎01 45 74 15 81; www.lehide.fr; 10 rue du Général Lanrezac, 17e; menus from €24; ⏱lunch Mon-Fri, dinner Mon-Sat; Ⓜ Charles de Gaulle–Étoile) This tiny neighbourhood bistro serves scrumptious traditional French fare: snails, baked shoulder of lamb with pumpkin purée or monkfish in lemon butter. Unsurprisingly, this place fills up faster than you can scamper down the steps at the nearby Arc de Triomphe. Reserve well in advance.

Aubrac Corner BURGERS €
(Map p304; www.aubrac-corner.com; 37 rue Marbeuf, 8e; sandwiches from €5, burgers from €9; ⏱7.30am-6.30pm Mon-Sat; Ⓜ Franklin D Roosevelt) Burgers? On the Champs-Élysées? It might not sound all that French, but rest assured, this isn't fast food – it's actually the gourmet deli of a famous steakhouse. The burgers come with bowls of fries or *aligot* (mashed potatoes with melted cheese); take it all downstairs into the hidden wine cellar, a welcome refuge from the nonstop commotion outside.

OPÉRA & GRANDS BOULEVARDS

The neon-lit area around bd Montmartre forms one of the Right Bank's most animated cafe and dining districts.

Le J'Go REGIONAL CUISINE €€
(Map p314; ☎01 40 22 09 09; www.lejgo.com; 4 rue Drouot, 9e; lunch/dinner menus €16/35; ⏱Mon-Sat; Ⓜ Richelieu Drouot) This contemporary Toulouse-style bistro whisks you away to southwestern France. Its bright yellow walls are decorated with bull-fighting posters and the flavourful regional cooking is based around the rotisserie – not to mention other Gascogne standards like cassoulet and foie gras. Roasting takes a minimum of 20 minutes.

Les Pâtes Vivantes CHINESE €
(Map p314; 46 rue du Faubourg Montmartre, 9e; noodles €9.50-12; ⏱Mon-Sat; Ⓜ Le Peletier) Feast on *là miàn* (hand-pulled noodles) made to order in the age-old northern Chinese tradition. It packs in a crowd, so arrive early to stake out a table and watch as the nimble noodle maker works his magic.

Le Zinc des Cavistes BAR, CAFE €
(Map p314; ☎01 47 70 88 64; 5 rue du Faubourg Montmartre, 9e; lunch menus €16, mains €11-19; ⏱8am-10.30pm; Ⓜ Grands Boulevards) Don't tell the masses standing dutifully in the Chartier queue that there's a much better restaurant right next door – your formerly friendly waiter will probably run off screaming. A local favourite, Le Zinc des Cavistes is as good for a full-blown meal (duck confit, salads) as it is for sampling new vintages.

MONTMARTRE & PIGALLE

Neobistros, wine bars and world cuisine all feature in this area – pick and choose carefully to avoid tourist traps.

THE GOURMET GLACIER

Berthillon (Map p310; 31 rue St-Louis en l'Île, 4e; ice cream from €2; ⏱10am-8pm Wed-Sun; Ⓜ Pont Marie) on Île St-Louis is the place to head to for Paris' finest ice cream. There are 70 flavours to choose from, ranging from fruity cassis to chocolate, coffee, *marrons glacés* (candied chestnuts), *Agenaise* (Armagnac and prunes), *noisette* (hazelnut) and *nougat au miel* (honey nougat). One scoop just won't be enough...

TOP CHOICE **Cul de Poule** MODERN FRENCH €€
(Map p314; ☎01 53 16 13 07; 53 rue des Martyrs, 9e; 2-/3-course menus lunch €15/18, dinner €23/28; ⏰closed Sun lunch; Ⓜ Pigalle) With plastic orange cafeteria seats outside, you probably wouldn't wander into the Cul de Poule by accident. But the light-hearted spirit (yes, there is a mounted chicken's derrière on the wall) is deceiving; this is one of the best and most affordable kitchens in the Pigalle neighbourhood, with excellent neobistro fare that emphasises quality ingredients from the French countryside.

Le Miroir BISTRO €€
(Map p314; ☎01 46 06 50 73; 94 rue des Martyrs, 18e; lunch menus €18, dinner menus €25-40; ⏰lunch Tue-Sun, dinner Tue-Sat; Ⓜ Abbesses) This unassuming modern bistro is smack in the middle of the Montmartre tourist trail, yet it remains a local favourite. There are lots of delightful pâtés and rillettes to start off with – guinea hen with dates, duck with mushrooms, haddock and lemon – followed by well-prepared standards like stuffed veal shoulder.

The lunch special includes a glass of wine, coffee and dessert; the Sunday brunch also gets the thumbs up. Afterwards, pop into its wine shop across the street.

La Mascotte SEAFOOD, CAFE €€
(Map p314; ☎01 46 06 28 15; www.la-mascotte-montmartre.com; 52 rue des Abbesses, 18e; lunch/dinner menus €25/41; ⏰7am-midnight; Ⓜ Abbesses) Founded in 1889, this unassuming bar is about as authentic as it gets in Montmartre. It specialises in quality seafood – oysters, lobster, scallops – and regional dishes (Auvergne sausage), but you can also pull up a seat at the bar for a simple glass of wine and a plate of charcuterie.

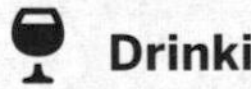

Drinking

The line between bars, cafes and bistros is blurred at best. Sitting at a table costs more than standing at the counter, more on a fancy square than a backstreet, more in the 8e than in the 18e. After 10pm many cafes charge a pricier *tarif de nuit* (night rate).

LOUVRE & LES HALLES

Angelina TEAHOUSE
(Map p304; 226 rue de Rivoli, 1er; ⏰daily; Ⓜ Tuileries) This beautiful, high-ceilinged tearoom has exquisite furnishings, mirrored walls, fabulous fluffy cakes, and the best, most wonderfully sickening 'African' hot chocolate (€7.20), served with a pot of whipped cream and carafe of water.

BAR-HOPPING STREETS

Prime Parisian drinking spots, perfect for evening meandering to soak up the scene:

Rue Vieille du Temple, 4e Marais cocktail of gay bars and chic cafes.

Rue Oberkampf & rue Jean-Pierre Timbaud, 11e Hip bars, bohemian hang-outs and atmospheric cafes.

Rue de Lappe, 11e Lively bars and clubs.

Rue Montmartre, 2e Atmospheric cafes.

Canal St-Martin, 10e Heady summer nights in casual canalside cafes.

Rue Princesse, 6e Student and sports bars.

Experimental Cocktail Club COCKTAIL BAR
(Map p310; www.experimentalcocktailclub.com; 37 rue St-Saveur, 2e; ⏰daily; Ⓜ Réaumur-Sebastopol) Called ECC by trendies, this fabulous speakeasy with grey facade and old-beamed ceiling is effortlessly hip. Oozing spirit and soul, the cocktail bar – with retro-chic decor by American interior designer Cuoco Black and sister bars in London and New York – is a sophisticated flashback to those *années folles* (crazy years) of prohibition New York.

Cocktails (€12 to €15) are individual and fabulous, and DJs set the space partying until dawn at weekends. The same guys are behind the equally hip Ballroom cocktail bar in the cellar of the New Yorker–style Beef Club (p320).

Kong BAR
(Map p310; www.kong.fr; 1 rue du Pont Neuf, 1er; ⏰daily; Ⓜ Pont Neuf) Late nights at this Philippe Starck–designed riot of iridescent champagne-coloured vinyl booths, Japanese cartoon cut-outs and garden gnome stools see Paris' glam young set guzzling Dom Pérignon, nibbling on tapas-style platters (mains €20 to €40) and shaking their designer-clad booty on the tables.

If you can, try to snag a table *à l'étage* (upstairs) in the part-glass-roofed terrace-gallery, where light floods across the giant geisha swooning horizontally across the ceiling, and stunning river views (particularly at sunset) will make you swoon. Smokers will appreciate the *fumoir* (a tiny heated room with no windows or ceiling) accessible from here.

MARAIS & BASTILLE

TOP CHOICE **Le Baron Rouge** WINE BAR
(Map p304; 1 rue Théophile Roussel, 12e; ⌚10am-2pm & 5-10pm Mon-Fri, 10am-10pm Sat, 10am-4pm Sun; Ⓜ Ledru-Rollin) Just about the ultimate Parisian wine-bar experience, this place has a dozen barrels of the stuff stacked up against the bottle-lined walls. As unpretentious as you'll find, it's a local meeting place where everyone is welcome and is especially busy on Sundays after the Marché d'Aligre wraps up. All the usual suspects – cheese, charcuterie and oysters – will keep your belly full.

For a small deposit, you can even fill up 1L bottles straight from the barrel for under €5.

Le Pure Café CAFE
(Map p304; 14 rue Jean Macé, 11e; ⌚daily; Ⓜ Charonne) A classic Parisian haunt, this rustic, cherry-red corner cafe was featured in the art-house film *Before Sunset* but it's still a refreshingly unpretentious spot for a drink or well-crafted fare like veal with chestnut purée.

La Fée Verte BAR
(Map p304; 108 rue de la Roquette, 11e; dishes €10-16; ⌚daily; 📶; Ⓜ Voltaire) Yes, the 'Green Fairy' specialises in absinthe (served traditionally with spoons and sugar cubes), but this old-fashioned neighbourhood cafe and bar also serves terrific food, including Green Fairy cheeseburgers.

Le Barav WINE BAR
(Map p310; ☎01 48 04 57 59; www.lebarav.fr; 6 rue Charles-François Dupuis, 3e; ⌚Tue-Sat; Ⓜ Temple) This hipster *bar à vin*, smart on one of the trendiest streets in the Haut Marais, oozes atmosphere – and one of the city's loveliest pavement terraces.

LATIN QUARTER

Café de la Nouvelle Mairie WINE BAR
(Map p310; 19 rue des Fossés St-Jacques, 5e; ⌚9am-8pm Mon-Fri; Ⓜ Cardinal-Lemoine) Shhhh... just around the corner from the Panthéon but hidden on a small, fountained square, this wine bar is a neighbourhood secret, serving blackboard-chalked wines by the glass or bottle. Tapas-style food is simple and delicious.

Curio Parlor Cocktail Club COCKTAIL BAR
(Map p310; www.curioparlor.com; 16 rue des Bernardins, 5e; ⌚7pm-2am Mon-Thu, to 4am Fri-Sun; Ⓜ Maubert-Mutualité) Run by the same switched-on team as the Experimental Cocktail Club, this hybrid bar-club looks to the interwar *années folles* (crazy years) of 1920s Paris, London and New York for inspiration. Its racing-green facade with a simple brass plaque on the door is the height of discretion.

Le Pub St-Hilaire PUB
(Map p310; www.pubsainthilaire.com; 2 rue Valette, 5e; ⌚3pm-2am Mon-Thu, 3pm-4am Fri, 4pm-4am Sat, 4pm-midnight Sun; Ⓜ Maubert-Mutualité) 'Buzzing' fails to do justice to the pulsating vibe inside this student-loved pub. Generous happy hours and a trio of pool tables, board games, music on two floors and hearty bar food pack out the place.

ST-GERMAIN, ODÉON & LUXEMBOURG

TOP CHOICE **Les Deux Magots** CAFE
(Map p310; www.lesdeuxmagots.fr; 170 bd St-Germain, 6e; ⌚7.30am-1am; Ⓜ St-Germain des Prés) If ever there were a cafe that summed up St-Germain des Prés' early-20th-century literary scene, it's this former hangout of anyone who was anyone. You will spend *beaucoup* to sip a coffee in a wicker chair on the terrace shaded by dark-green awnings and geraniums spilling from window boxes, but it's an undeniable piece of Parisian history.

Au Sauvignon WINE BAR
(Map p304; 80 rue des Saints Pères, 7e; ⌚8.30am-10pm; Ⓜ Sèvres-Babylone) There's no more authentic *bar à vin* than this. Grab a table in the evening sun or head to the quintessential bistro interior, with an original zinc bar, tightly packed tables and hand-painted ceiling celebrating French viticultural tradition. Order a plate of *casse-croûtes au pain Poilâne* – toast with ham, pâté, terrine, smoked salmon, foie gras and so on.

Alain Milliart JUICE BAR
(Map p304; ☎01 45 55 63 86; www.alain-milliat.com; 159 rue de Grenelle, 7e; ⌚10am-10pm Tue-Sat; Ⓜ La Tour Maubourg) Alain Milliart's fruit juices, all 33 varieties bottled in the south of France, star at his Parisian juice bistro. His jams and compotes are equally lush. Rosé grape, green tomato juice or white peach nectar anyone?

Café La Palette CAFE

(Map p310; www.cafelapaletteparis.com; 43 rue de Seine, 6e; ⏰6.30am-2am Mon-Sat; Ⓜ Mabillon) In the heart of gallery land, this *fin-de-siècle* cafe and erstwhile stomping ground of Paul Cézanne and Georges Braque attracts a grown-up set of fashion people and local art dealers. Its summer terrace is beautiful.

OPÉRA & GRANDS BOULEVARDS

Harry's New York Bar COCKTAIL BAR

(Map p314; www.harrysbar.fr; 5 rue Daunou, 2e; ⏰daily; Ⓜ Opéra) One of the most popular American-style bars in the prewar years, Harry's once welcomed writers like F Scott Fitzgerald and Ernest Hemingway, who no doubt sampled the bar's unique cocktail and creation: the Bloody Mary. The Cuban mahogany interior dates from the mid-19th century and was brought over from a Manhattan bar in 1911.

MONTMARTRE & PIGALLE

TOP CHOICE **La Fourmi** BAR, CAFE

(Map p314; 74 rue des Martyrs, 18e; ⏰8am-1am Mon-Thu, to 3am Fri & Sat, 10am-1am Sun; Ⓜ Pigalle) A Pigalle institution, La Fourmi hits the mark with its high ceilings, long zinc bar and unpretentious vibe. Get up to speed on live music and club nights or sit down for a reasonably priced meal and drinks.

☆ Entertainment

From jazz cellars to comic theatre, garage beats to go-go dancers, world-class art galleries to avant-garde artist squats, Paris is *the* capital of *savoir-vivre*, with spectacular entertainment to suit every budget, every taste. To find out what's on, buy *Pariscope* (€0.40) or *Officiel des Spectacles* (www.offi.fr, in French) at Parisian news kiosks. *Billeteries* (ticket offices) in **Fnac** (www.fnacspectacles.com) and **Virgin Megastores** sell tickets.

If you go on the day of a performance, you can snag a half-price ticket (plus €3 commission) for ballet, theatre, opera and other performances at the discount-ticket outlet **Kiosque Théâtre Madeleine** (Map p314; opp 15 place de la Madeleine, 8e; ⏰12.30-8pm Tue-Sat, to 4pm Sun; Ⓜ Madeleine).

French-language websites www.billetreduc.com, www.ticketac.com and www.webguichet.com all sell discounted tickets.

Cabaret

Whirling lines of feather boa-clad, high-kicking dancers at grand-scale cabarets like the can-can creator, the Moulin Rouge, are a quintessential fixture on Paris' entertainment scene – for everyone but Parisians. Still, the dazzling sets, costumes and dancing guarantee an entertaining evening (or matinee).

Tickets to these spectacles start from around €90 (from €130 with lunch, from €150 with dinner), and usually include a half-bottle of champagne. Advance reservations are essential.

Moulin Rouge CABARET

(Map p314; ☎01 53 09 82 82; www.moulinrouge.fr; 82 bd de Clichy, 18e; Ⓜ Blanche) Immortalised in the posters of Toulouse-Lautrec, the Moulin Rouge twinkles beneath a 1925 replica of its original red windmill. Yes, it's rife with bus-tour crowds. But it's a whirl of fantastical costumes, sets, choreography and champagne.

FREE SHOWS

Paris' eclectic gaggle of clowns, mime artists, living statues, acrobats, rollerbladers, buskers and other street entertainers can be bags of fun and cost substantially less than a theatre ticket (a few coins in the hat is a sweet gesture). Some excellent musicians perform in the long echo-filled corridors of the metro, a privilege that artists have to audition for. Outside, you can be sure of a good show at:

Place Georges Pompidou, 4e In front of the Centre Pompidou.

Pont St-Louis, 4e Bridge linking Paris' two islands (best enjoyed with Berthillon ice cream in hand; see box text p325).

Pont au Double, 4e Pedestrian bridge linking Notre Dame with the Left Bank.

Place Jean du Bellay, 1er Musicians and fire-eaters near the Fontaine des Innocents.

Parc de la Villette, 19e African drummers at the weekend.

Place du Tertre, Montmartre, 18e Montmartre's original main square wins hands down as Paris' busiest street-artist stage.

GAY & LESBIAN PARIS

The Marais (4e), especially the areas around the intersection of rue Ste-Croix de la Bretonnerie and rue des Archives, and eastwards to rue Vieille du Temple, has been Paris' main centre of gay nightlife for some three decades. There are also a few bars and clubs within walking distance of bd de Sébastopol. Other venues are scattered city-wide. The lesbian scene is less public than its gregarous male counterpart, and centres around a few Marais cafes and bars, particularly along rues des Écouffes.

The single best source of info on gay and lesbian Paris is the **Centre Gai et Lesbien de Paris** (CGL; ☎01 43 57 21 47; www.centrelgbtparis.org; 61-63 rue Beaubourg, 3e; ⏲6-8pm Mon, 3.30-8pm Tue-Thu, 1-8pm Fri & Sat; Ⓜ Rambuteau or Arts et Métiers), with a large library and happening bar.

Our top choices include:

Open Café (Map p310; www.opencafe.fr; 17 rue des Archives, 4e; ⏲daily; Ⓜ Hôtel de Ville) This wide, white-seated pavement terrace in the Marais is prime talent-watching.

Scream Club (Map p310; www.scream-paris.com; 18 rue du Faubourg du Temple, 11e; ⏲daily; Ⓜ Belleville or Goncourt) Saturday night's the night at 'Paris' biggest gay party'

3w Kafé (Map p310; 8 rue des Écouffes, 4e; ⏲Tue-Sat; Ⓜ St-Paul) For women.

Le Tango (Map p310; www.boite-a-frissons.fr; 13 rue au Maire, 3e; ⏲Fri-Sun; Ⓜ Arts et Métiers) Historic 1930s dance hosting legendary gay tea dances.

Le Lido de Paris CABARET
(Map p304; ☎01 40 76 56 10; www.lido.fr; 116bis av des Champs-Élysées, 8e; Ⓜ George V) Founded at the close of WWII, this gets top marks for its sets and the lavish costumes of its 70 artists, including the famed Bluebell Girls and now the Lido Boy Dancers.

Live Music

Palais Omnisports de Paris-Bercy (Map p304; www.bercy.fr; 8 bd de Bercy, 12e; Ⓜ Bercy); **Le Zénith** (Map p304; ☎01 55 80 09 38, 08 90 71 02 07; www.le-zenith.com; 211 av Jean Jaurès, 19e; Ⓜ Porte de Pantin) and **Stade de France** (☎08 92 39 01 00; www.stadefrance.com; rue Francis de Pressensé, ZAC du Cornillon Nord, St-Denis La Plaine; Ⓜ St-Denis-Porte de Paris) are Paris' big-name venues. But it's the smaller concert halls loaded with history and charm that most fans favour.

Salle Pleyel CLASSICAL
(Map p304; ☎01 42 56 13 13; www.sallepleyel.fr; 252 rue du Faubourg St-Honoré, 8e; ⏲box office noon-7pm Mon-Sat, to 8pm on day of performance; Ⓜ Ternes) This highly regarded hall dating from the 1920s hosts many of Paris' finest classical-music recitals and concerts, including those by the celebrated **Orchestre de Paris** (www.orchestredeparis.com).

Point Éphémère LIVE MUSIC
(Map p304; www.pointephemere.org; 200 quai de Valmy, 10e; ⏲noon-2am Mon-Sat, noon-10pm Sun; 📶; Ⓜ Louis Blanc) This arts and music venue by the Canal St-Martin attracts an underground crowd for drinks, meals, concerts, dance nights and even art exhibitions.

Le Nouveau Casino LIVE MUSIC
(Map p304; www.nouveaucasino.net; 109 rue Oberkampf, 11e; ⏲Tue-Sun; Ⓜ Parmentier) This club-concert annexe of **Café Charbon** (Map p304; www.lecafecharbon.com; 109 rue Oberkampf, 11e; ⏲daily; 📶; Ⓜ Parmentier) has made a name for itself amid the bars of Oberkampf with its live music concerts and lively weekend club nights. Electro, pop, deep house, rock – the program is eclectic, underground and always up to the minute.

La Cigale LIVE MUSIC
(Map p314; ☎01 49 25 81 75; www.lacigale.fr; 120 bd de Rochechouart, 18e; admission €25-60; Ⓜ Anvers or Pigalle) A historical monument, this music hall dates from 1887 but was redecorated 100 years later by Philippe Starck.

Le Vieux Belleville LIVE MUSIC
(Map p304; www.le-vieux-belleville.com; 12 rue des Envierges, 20e; Ⓜ Pyrénées) This old-fashioned bistro and *musette* at the top of Parc de Belleville is an atmospheric venue for performances of *chansons* featuring accordions and an organ grinder.

Cabaret Sauvage WORLD MUSIC
(Map p304; www.cabaretsauvage.com; 221 av Jean Jaurès, 19e; Ⓜ Porte de la Villette) This very cool

space in the Parc de la Villette (it looks like a gigantic yurt) hosts African, reggae and raï concerts, and DJ nights that last till dawn. Occasional hip-hop and indie acts pass through.

Le Baiser Salé LIVE MUSIC

(Map p310; www.lebaisersale.com; 58 rue des Lombards, 2e; ⌚daily; MChâtelet) One of several jazz clubs located on this street, this *salle de jazz* (jazz room) has concerts of jazz, Afro and Latin jazz and jazz fusion. Combining big names and unknown artists, it is known for its relaxed vibe and gift for discovering new talents. The Monday night *soirée bœuf* (jam session) is free.

Au Limonaire LIVE MUSIC

(Map p314; ☎01 45 23 33 33; http://limonaire.free.fr; 18 cité Bergère, 9e; ⌚7pm-midnight; MGrands Boulevards) This little wine bar is one of the best places to listen to traditional French *chansons* and local singer-songwriters. Entry is free, the wine is good and dinner is served (plat du jour €7). Reserve if you plan to dine.

Clubbing

Paris' residential make-up means nightclubs aren't ubiquitous. Lacking a mainstream scene, clubbing tends to be underground and mobile, making blogs, forums and websites the savviest means of keeping apace with what's happening. The best DJs and their followings have short stints in a certain venue before moving on, and the scene's hippest *soirées clubbing* (clubbing events) float between venues – including the city's many dance-driven bars.

La Scène Bastille NIGHTCLUB

(Map p304; www.scenebastille.com; 2bis rue des Taillandiers, 11e; ⌚Thu-Sun; MBastille or Ledru-Rollin) The 'Bastille Scene' puts on a mixed bag of concerts but focuses on electro, funk and hip hop.

Le Batofar NIGHTCLUB

(Map p304; www.batofar.org; opp 11 quai François Mauriac, 13e; ⌚9pm-midnight Mon & Tue, to 4am or later Wed-Sun; MQuai de la Gare or Bibliothèque) This much-loved, red-metal tugboat with rooftop bar and restaurant is known for its edgy, experimental music policy and live performances, mostly electro-oriented but also incorporating hiphop, new wave, rock, punk or jazz.

Le Divan du Monde LIVE MUSIC

(Map p314; www.divandumonde.com; 75 rue des Martyrs, 18e; ⌚Fri & Sat, open for events Mon-Fri; MPigalle) Inventive, open-minded, cross-cultural venue in Pigalle.

Le Rex Club NIGHTCLUB

(Map p314; www.rexclub.com; 5 bd Poissonnière, 2e; ⌚Wed-Sat; MBonne Nouvelle) Attached to the art deco Grand Rex cinema, this is Paris' premier house and techno venue where some of the world's hottest DJs strut their stuff on a 70-speaker, multidiffusion sound system.

Bus Palladium NIGHTCLUB

(Map p314; www.lebuspalladium.com; 6 rue Pierre Fontaine, 9e; ⌚11pm-5am Tue, Fri & Sat; MBlanche) Once the place to be back in the 1960s, the Bus is now back in business 50 years later, with funky DJs and a mixed bag of performances by indie and pop groups.

Shopping

As in most capital cities, shops are spread across different neighbourhoods, inspiring very different styles of shopping. Annual, month-long *soldes* (sales) see prices slashed by as much as 50%; they start up in mid-January and again in mid-June.

Key areas to mooch with no particular purchase in mind are the maze of backstreet lanes in the Marais (3e and 4e), around St-Germain des Prés (6e), and parts of Montmartre and Pigalle (9e and 18e). Or perhaps you have something specific to buy?

Designer haute couture The world's most famous designers stylishly jostle for window space on av Montaigne, av Georges V and rue du Faubourg St-Honoré, 8e.

Chain-store fashion Find Gap, H&M, Zara and other major, super-sized chain stores on rue de Rivoli in the 1er, Les Halles in the 2e, and av des Champs-Élysées, 8e.

Department stores On and around bd Haussmann, 9e, including Paris' famous Galeries Lafayette at No 40 and Printemps at No 64.

Factory outlets Cut-price fashion for men, women and kids the length of rue d'Alésia, 14e.

Hip fashion & art Young designers crowd rue Charlot, 3e, and beyond in the northern Haut Marais.

Fine art & antiques Right Bank place des Vosges, 4e, and Left Bank Carré Rive Gauche, 6e.

Design Eames, eat your heart out! Boutique galleries specialising in modern furniture, art and design (1950s to present) stud rue Mazarine and rue de Seine, 6e.

TOP THREE FLEA MARKETS

Marché aux Puces de Montreuil (av du Professeur André Lemière, 20e; ⏲8am-7.30pm Sat-Mon; Ⓜ Porte de Montreuil) Particularly known for its secondhand clothing, designer seconds, engravings, jewellery, linen, crockery and old furniture.

Marché aux Puces de St-Ouen (www.marchcauxpuces-saintouen.com; rue des Rosiers, av Michelet, rue Voltaire, rue Paul Bert & rue Jean-Henri Fabre; ⏲9am-6pm Sat, 10am-6pm Sun, 11am-5pm Mon; Ⓜ Porte de Clignancourt) Around since the late 19th century, and said to be Europe's largest.

Marché aux Puces de la Porte de Vanves (Map p304; http://pucesdevanves.typepad.com; av Georges Lafenestre & av Marc Sangnier, 14e; ⏲from 7am Sat & Sun; Ⓜ Porte de Vanves) The smallest and, some say, friendliest of the trio.

Information

Dangers & Annoyances

Paris is generally safe. Metro stations best avoided late at night include: Châtelet-Les Halles and its corridors; Château Rouge in Montmartre; Gare du Nord; Strasbourg St-Denis; Réaumur Sébastopol; and Montparnasse Bienvenüe.

Pickpocketing and thefts from handbags and packs is a problem wherever there are crowds (especially of tourists).

Medical Services

American Hospital of Paris (☎01 46 41 25 25; www.american-hospital.org; 63 bd Victor Hugo, Neuilly-sur-Seine; Ⓜ Pont de Levallois) Private hospital offering emergency 24-hour medical and dental care.

Hertford British Hospital (☎01 47 59 59 59; www.ihfb.org; 3 rue Barbès, Levallois; Ⓜ Anatole France) A less expensive, private, English-speaking option than the American Hospital.

Hôpital Hôtel Dieu (☎01 42 34 82 34; www.aphp.fr; 1 place du Parvis Notre Dame, 4e; Ⓜ Cité) One of the city's main government-run public hospitals; after 8pm use the emergency entrance on rue de la Cité.

Pharmacie Les Champs (☎01 45 62 02 41; Galerie des Champs, 84 av des Champs-Élysées, 8e; ⏲24hr; Ⓜ George V)

Tourist Information

Paris Convention & Visitors Bureau (Office de Tourisme et de Congrès de Paris; Map p304; ☎08 92 68 30 00; www.parisinfo.com; 25-27 rue des Pyramides, 1er; ⏲9am-7pm Jun-Oct, shorter hrs rest of year; Ⓜ Pyramides) Main tourist office with several branches around the city.

Getting There & Away

Air

Aéroport Roissy Charles de Gaulle (CDG; ☎01 70 36 39 50; www.aeroportsdeparis.fr) Three terminals, 30km northeast of Paris in the suburb of Roissy.

Aéroport d'Orly (ORY; ☎01 70 36 39 50; www.aeroportsdeparis.fr) Aéroport d'Orly is the older, smaller of Paris' two major airports, 19km south of the city.

Aéroport Beauvais (BVA; ☎08 92 68 20 66; www.aeroportbeauvais.com) Used by charter companies and budget airlines, 75km north of Paris.

Bus

Eurolines (☎01 43 54 11 99; www.eurolines.fr; 55 rue St-Jacques, 5e; ⏲9.30am-6.30pm Mon-Fri, 10am-1pm & 2-5pm Sat; Ⓜ Cluny–La Sorbonne)

Gare Routiére Internationale de Paris-Galliéni (☎08 92 89 90 91; 28 av du Général de Gaulle; Ⓜ Galliéni)

Train

Paris has six major train stations. For mainline train information contact **SNCF** (☎08 91 36 20 20, timetables 08 91 67 68 69; www.sncf.fr).

Gare d'Austerlitz (bd de l'Hôpital, 13e; Ⓜ Gare d'Austerlitz) Trains to/from Spain and Portugal, the Loire Valley and southwestern France.

Gare de l'Est (bd de Strasbourg, 10e; Ⓜ Gare de l'Est) Trains to/from Luxembourg, parts of Switzerland (Basel, Lucerne, Zurich), southern Germany (Frankfurt, Munich) and points further east; regular services to eastern France (Champagne, Alsace and Lorraine).

Gare de Lyon (bd Diderot, 12e; Ⓜ Gare de Lyon) Trains to/from parts of Switzerland (Bern, Geneva, Lausanne), Italy and points beyond; domestic services to areas southeast of Paris, including Dijon, Lyon, Provence, the Côte d'Azur and the Alps.

Gare Montparnasse (av du Maine & bd de Vaugirard, 15e; Ⓜ Montparnasse Bienvenüe) Trains to/from Brittany and places en route from Paris (eg Chartres, Angers, Nantes);

also to Tours, Nantes, Bordeaux and other destinations in southwestern France.

Gare du Nord (rue de Dunkerque, 10e; MGare du Nord) Terminus of high-speed Thalys trains to/from Amsterdam, Brussels, Cologne and Geneva, and Eurostar to London; domestic services to Paris' northern suburbs and northern France.

Gare St-Lazare (rue St-Lazare & rue d'Amsterdam, 8e; MSt-Lazare) Trains to Normandy.

Getting Around

To/From the Airports

Getting into town is straightforward and inexpensive thanks to a fleet of public-transport options. Bus drivers sell tickets. Children aged four to 11 years pay half-price on most services.

AÉROPORT ROISSY CHARLES DE GAULLE

RER B (32 46; www.ratp.fr; adult €9.10; 5am-11pm) Departs every 10 to 15 minutes, serving Gare du Nord, Châtalet-Les Halles and St-Michel–Notre Dame stations in the city centre. Journey time approximately 35 minutes.

Air France Bus 2 (08 92 35 08 20; http://videocdn.airfrance.com/cars-airfrance; adult €15; 6am-11pm) To/from the Arc de Triomphe and Porte Maillot metro station (35 to 50 minutes).

Air France Bus 4 (08 92 35 08 20; http://videocdn.airfrance.com/cars-airfrance; adult €16.50; 6am-10pm from Roissy Charles de Gaulle, 6am-9.30pm from Paris) Shuttles every 30 minutes to/from Gare de Lyon and Gare Montparnasse (50 to 55 minutes).

Noctilien Buses 140 & 143 (32 46; www.noctilien.fr; adult €7.60; 12.30am-5.30am) Hourly night buses to/from Gare de l'Est (140 & 143) and Gare de Nord (143).

RATP Bus 350 (32 46; www.ratp.fr; adult €5.10 or 3 metro tickets; 5.30am-11pm) Every 30 minutes to/from Gare de l'Est and Gare du Nord (both one hour).

Roissybus (32 46; www.ratp.fr; adult €10; 5.30am-11pm) Every 30 minutes to/from Opéra, 9e (45 minutes).

AÉROPORT D'ORLY

Air France Bus 1 (08 92 35 08 20; http://videocdn.airfrance.com/cars-airfrance; adult €11.50; 5am-10.20pm from Orly, 6am-11.20pm from Invalides) Shuttle bus to/from Gare Montparnasse (35 minutes), Invalides in the 7e, and the Arc de Triomphe.

Orlybus (32 46; www.ratp.fr; adult €6.90; 6am-11.20pm from Orly, 5.35am-11.05pm from Paris) RATP bus every 15 to 20 minutes to/from metro Denfert Rochereau (30 minutes) in the 14e.

Orlyval (32 46; www.ratp.fr; adult €10.75; 6am-11pm) Orlyval automatic metro from Orly to Antony station, then RER B to Gare du Nord, Châtalet-Les Halles and St-Michel–Notre Dame RER stations in the city centre.

BETWEEN ORLY & CHARLES DE GAULLE

Air France Shuttle Bus 3 (www.cars-airfrance.com; adult €20; 6am-10.30pm) Every 30 minutes; journey time 30 to 45 minutes.

AÉROPORT PARIS-BEAUVAIS

Navette Officielle (Official Shuttle Bus; 08 92 68 20 64, airport 08 92 68 20 66; adult €15) Links Beauvais airport with metro station Porte de Maillot; journey time 1¼ hours.

Bicycle

Vélib' (www.velib.paris.fr; day/week subscription €1/5, bike hire per 1st/2nd/additional 30min free/€2/4) With this self-service bike scheme pick up a bike from one roadside Vélib' station and drop it off at another. To get a bike, first purchase a 1-/7-day subscription (€1.70/8) online or at any bike terminal (by credit card with a microchip).

Boat

Batobus (www.batobus.com; 1-/2-/5-day pass €15/18/21; 10am-9.30pm Apr-Aug, to 7pm rest of year) Fleet of glassed-in trimarans dock at eight piers along the Seine; buy tickets at each stop or tourist offices and jump on and off as you like.

Public Transport

Paris' public transit system is operated by the **RATP** (www.ratp.fr). The same RATP tickets are valid on the metro, RER, buses, trams and Montmartre funicular. A single ticket is €1.70 while a *carnet* of 10 costs 12.70.

One ticket covers travel between any two metro stations (no return journeys) for 1½ hours; you can transfer between buses and between buses and trams, but not from metro to bus or vice versa.

Keep your ticket until you exit the station; ticket inspectors can fine you if you can't produce a valid ticket.

BUS Buses run from 5.30am to 8.30pm Monday to Saturday, with certain evening lines continuing until midnight or 12.30am, when hourly **Noctilien** (www.noctilien.fr) night buses kick in.

Short bus rides (ie rides in one or two bus zones) cost one metro/bus ticket (€1.70 or €1.90 direct from the driver); longer rides require two. Remember to punch single-journey tickets in the *composteur* (ticket machine) next to the driver.

METRO & RER Paris' underground network consists of the 14-line metro and the RER, a network of suburban train lines. Each metro train is known by the name of its terminus. The last metro train on each line begins sometime between 12.35am and 1.15am (2.15am Friday and Saturday), before starting up again around 5.30am.

TOURIST PASSES The **Mobilis Card** allows unlimited travel for one day in two to five zones (€6.40 to €14.20) on the metro, the RER, buses, trams and the Montmartre funicular; while the **Paris Visite** pass allows unlimited travel (including to/from airports) plus discounted entry to museums and activities and costs €9.75/15.85/21.60/31.15 for one to three zones for one/two/three/five days.

TRAVEL PASSES **Navigo** (www.navigo.fr), like London's Oyster or Hong Kong's Octopus cards, consists of a weekly, monthly or yearly unlimited pass that can be recharged at Navigo machines in most metro stations; swipe the card across the electronic panel to go through turnstiles. Standard Navigo passes, available to anyone with an address in Île de France, are free but take up to three weeks to be issued. Otherwise, pay €5 for a **Nagivo Découverte** (Navigo Discovery) card, issued on the spot. Both require a passport photo and can be recharged for periods of one week or more.

Otherwise, weekly tickets (*coupon hebdomadaire*) cost €19.15 for zones 1 and 2, valid Monday to Sunday.

Taxi

The flagfall is €2.40, plus €0.96 per km within the city limits from 10am and 5pm Monday to Saturday (Tarif A; white light on meter), and €1.21 per kilometre from 5pm to 10am, all day Sunday, and public holidays (Tarif B; orange light on meter).

Alpha Taxis (☎01 45 85 85 85; www.alphataxis.com)

Taxis Bleus (☎01 49 36 10 10; www.taxis-bleus.com)

Taxis G7 (☎01 41 27 66 99; www.taxisg7.fr)

AROUND PARIS

Bordered by five rivers – the Epte, Aisne, Eure, Yonne and Marne – the area around Paris looks rather like a giant island, and indeed is known as Île de France. Centuries ago this was where French kings retreated to extravagant chateaux in Versailles and Fontainebleau. These days such royal castles have been joined by a kingdom of an altogether different kind.

Disneyland Resort Paris

In 1992, Mickey Mouse, Snow White and chums set up shop on reclaimed sugar-beet fields 32km east of Paris at a cost of €4.6 billion. Though not quite as over-the-top as its American cousin, France's Disneyland packs in the crowds nonetheless.

The main **Disneyland Park** (⏰10am-8pm Mon-Fri, 9am-8pm Sat & Sun Sep-May, 9am-11pm Jun-Aug, hours can vary) comprises five *pays* (lands), including the 1900s idealised **Main St USA**, a recreation of the American Wild West in **Frontierland** with the legendary Big Thunder Mountain ride, futuristic **Discoveryland**, and the exotic-themed **Adventureland**, where you'll find the Pirates of the Caribbean and the spiralling 360-degrees roller coaster, Indiana Jones and the Temple of Peril. Pinocchio, Snow White and other fairy-tale characters come to life in the candy-coated heart of the park, **Fantasyland**.

Adjacent **Walt Disney Studios Park** (⏰9am-7pm late Jun-early Sep, 10am-7pm Mon-Fri & 9am-7pm Sat & Sun early Sep-late Jun) has a sound stage, backlot and animation studios illustrating how films, TV programs and cartoons are produced.

Standard admission fees at **Disneyland Resort Paris** (☎hotel booking 01 60 30 60 30, restaurant reservations 01 60 30 40 50; www.disneylandparis.com; one-day admission adult/child €59/53; ⏰hours vary; Ⓜ Marne-la-Vallée/Chessy) include admission to either Disneyland Park or Walt Disney, but there's always a multitude of different passes, special offers and accommodation/transport packages on offer.

Marne-la-Vallée/Chessy, Disneyland's RER station, is served by line A4; trains run every 15 minutes or so from central Paris (€7.10, 35 to 40 minutes).

Versailles

POP 88,930

Louis XIV transformed his father's hunting lodge into the monumental Château de Versailles in the mid-17th century, and it remains France's most famous, grandest palace. Situated in the prosperous, leafy and bourgeois suburb of Versailles, 28km southwest of Paris, the baroque palace was the kingdom's political capital and the seat of the royal court from 1682 up until 1789, when revolutionaries massacred the palace guard and dragged Louis XVI and Marie Antoinette back to Paris to be guillotined.

Sights

Château de Versailles PALACE
(☎01 30 83 78 00; www.chateauversailles.fr; admission passport (estate-wide access) €18, with

VERSAILLES TOP TIPS

» Don't go on Monday (closed); avoid Tuesday and Sunday (busiest days).

» Queues for tickets and entering the chateau spiral out of control by noon: arrive early morning.

» Pre-purchase tickets on the chateau's website and head straight to Entrance A.

» Access areas otherwise off limits with a **guided tour** (01 30 83 77 88; tours €16; English-language tours 9.30am & 2pm Tue-Sun) of the Private Apartments of Louis XV and Louis XVI and the Opera House or Royal Chapel. Tour tickets include access to the most famous parts of the palace, such as the Hall of Mirrors and the King's and Queen's State Apartments; prebook online.

» The estate is vast: rent an **electric car** (01 39 66 97 66; per hr €30), **bike** (01 39 66 97 66; per hr €6.50) or **boat** (01 39 66 97 66; per hr €15).

» Be dazzled by 17th-century **Bassin de Neptune** (Neptune's Fountain) dancing during the **Grandes Eaux Musicales** (adult/child €7.50/6.50; 11am-noon & 3.30-5pm Tue, Sat & Sun Apr-Sep) and after-dark **Grandes Eaux Nocturnes** (adult/child €23/19; 9-11.20pm Sat mid-Jun–Aug), magical, summertime water displays set to classical music.

musical events €25, palace €15; 8am-6pm Tue-Sat, 9am-6pm Sun Apr-Oct, 8.30am-5.30pm Tue-Sat, 9am-5.30pm Sun Nov-Mar) Built in the mid-17th century to project the absolute power of the French monarchy, Versailles reflects Louis XIV's taste for profligate luxury and his boundless appetite for grandstanding. In 1661 under the guidance of architect Louis Le Vau, painter and interior designer Charles Le Brun, and landscape artist André Le Nôtre, workers flattened hills, drained marshes and relocated forests to create the seemingly endless gardens, ponds and fountains. Inside, every moulding, cornice, ceiling and door was decorated with the most luxurious, ostentatious of appointments, peaking in opulence with the **Galerie des Glaces** (Hall of Mirrors), a 75m-long ballroom with 17 huge mirrors on one side and, on the other, an equal number of windows looking out over the gardens and the setting sun.

Until the current €400 million restoration program is completed in 2020 at least a part of the palace is likely to be clad in scaffolding when you visit.

Eating

Eateries within the estate include tearoom **Angelina** (www.angelina-versailles.fr; mains €10-24; 10am-6pm Tue-Sat Apr-Oct, to 5pm Tue-Sat Nov-Mar), famed for its decadent hot chocolate. In addition to the branch by the Petit Trianon, there's another inside the palace.

In the Louis XIV–created town of Versailles, rue de Satory is lined with restaurants serving cuisine from all over the globe.

For an enjoyable culinary experience, check out **La Cuisine de Bertrand** (www.lacuisinedebertrand.com), where you can learn traditional French cooking in Bertrand's Versailles home, followed by a meal with his family. Produce is from the chateau's Potager du Roi (royal veg patch).

À la Ferme REGIONAL CUISINE €€
(01 39 53 10 81; www.alaferme-versailles.com; 3 rue du Maréchal Joffre; lunch menus €13.80-23.90, dinner menus €19.50-23.90; Wed-Sun) Cowhide seats and rustic garlands strung from old wood beams add a country air to 'At the Farm', a temple to grilled meats and cuisine from southwest France.

Getting There & Away

The easiest way to get to/from Versailles is aboard RER line C5 (€4.20, 45 minutes, every 15 minutes) from Paris' Left Bank RER stations to Versailles-Rive Gauche, 700m southeast of the chateau.

Chartres

POP 45,600

The magnificent 13th-century cathedral of Chartres, crowned by two very different spires – one Gothic, the other Romanesque – rises from rich farmland 88km southwest of Paris and dominates the medieval town. With its astonishing blue stained glass and other treasures, France's best-preserved medieval basilica is a must-see.

Sights

Cathédrale Notre Dame CATHEDRAL

(www.diocese-chartres.com; place de la Cathédrale; 8.30am-7.30pm, to 10pm Tue, Fri & Sun Jun-Aug) One of the crowning architectural achievements of Western civilisation, this 130m-long Gothic cathedral was built during the first quarter of the 13th century to replace a Romanesque cathedral that had been devastated by fire – along with much of the town – in 1194. It is France's best-preserved medieval cathedral, having been spared postmedieval modifications, the ravages of war and the Reign of Terror.

The cathedral's west, north and south entrances have superbly ornamented triple portals, but the west entrance, known as the **Portail Royal**, is the only one that predates the fire. Carved from 1145 to 1155, its superb statues represent the glory of Christ in the centre, and the Nativity and the Ascension to the right and left, respectively. The structure's other main Romanesque feature is the 105m-high **Clocher Vieux** (Old Bell Tower; also called the Tour Sud or 'South Tower') - the tallest Romanesque steeple still standing. Superb views of three-tiered flying buttresses and the 19th-century copper roof, turned green by verdigris, reward the 350-step hike up the 112m-high **Clocher Neuf** (New Bell Tower, also known as North Tower).

Inside, 172 extraordinary **stained-glass windows**, mainly from the 13th century, form one of the most important ensembles of medieval stained glass in the world. The three most exquisite – renowned for the depth and intensity of their tones, famously known as 'Chartres blue' – are above the west entrance and below the rose window.

To study the extraordinary detail of the cathedral close up, rent binoculars (€2) from Chartres **tourist office** (02 37 18 26 26; www.chartres-tourisme.com; place de la Cathédrale; 9am-6pm Mon-Sat, 9.30am-5pm Sun), across the square from the cathedral's main entrance.

Eating

TOP CHOICE **Le Saint-Hilaire** REGIONAL CUISINE €€

(02 37 30 97 57; www.restaurant-saint-hilaire.fr; 11 rue du Pont Saint-Hilaire; 2-/3-course menus from €27/42; lunch & dinner Tue-Sat) Local products are transformed into to-die-for dishes – think stuffed mushrooms with lentils, snails in puff pastry with leek fondue, seasonal lobster, aromatic cheese platters – at this pistachio-painted, wood-beamed charmer.

La Chocolaterie PATISSERIE, TEAHOUSE €

(14 place du Cygne; 8am-7.30pm Tue-Sat, 10am-7.30pm Sun & Mon) Revel in local life at the open-air flower market are on place du Cygne. Its hot chocolate and macarons, flavoured with orange, apricot, peanut, pineapple, and so on are sublime, as are its crêpes and miniature madeleine sponge cakes.

Getting There & Away

Frequent SNCF trains link Paris' Gare Montparnasse (€14.40, 55 to 70 minutes) with Chartres via Versailles-Chantiers (€12.10, 45 minutes to one hour).

LILLE, FLANDERS & THE SOMME

When it comes to culture, cuisine, beer, shopping and dramatic views of land and sea, the friendly Ch'tis (residents of France's northern tip) and their region compete with the best France has to offer. Highlights include Flemish-style Lille, the cross-Channel shopping centre of Calais, and the moving battlefields and cemeteries of WWI.

Lille

POP 232,210

Lille (Rijsel in Flemish) may be the country's most underrated major city. In recent decades this once-grimy industrial metropolis has transformed itself – with generous government help – into a glittering and self-confident cultural and commercial hub. Highlights of the city include an attractive Old Town with a strong Flemish accent, three renowned art museums, stylish shopping and a cutting-edge, student-driven nightlife.

Sights

Vieux Lille OLD TOWN

Lille's Old Town, which begins just north of place du Général de Gaulle, is justly proud of its restored 17th- and 18th-century houses. Those along **rue de la Monnaie** house the city's chicest boutiques and the **Musée de l'Hospice Comtesse** (www.mairie-lille.fr; 32 rue de la Monnaie; adult/student/child €3.50/2.50/free; 10am-12.30pm & 2-6pm, closed Mon morning & Tue), featuring mainly religious art.

Palais des Beaux Arts MUSEUM
(Fine Arts Museum; www.pba-lille.fr; place de la République; adult/student/child €6.50/4/free; 2-6pm Mon, 10am-6pm Wed-Sun; République-Beaux Arts) Lille's world-renowned Fine Arts Museum displays a truly first-rate collection of 15th- to 20th-century paintings, including works by Rubens, Van Dyck and Manet.

Musée d'Art Moderne Lille-Métropole MUSEUM
(03 20 19 68 68; www.musee-lam.fr; 1 allée du Musée; adult/student/child €7/5/free; 10am-6pm Tue-Sun) Colourful, playful and just plain weird works of modern and contemporary art by masters such as Braque, Calder, Léger, Miró, Modigliani and Picasso are the big draw at this renowned, newly renovated museum and sculpture park in the Lille suburb of Villeneuve-d'Ascq, 9km east of Gare Lille-Europe. Take metro line 1 to Pont de Bois, then bus 41 (10 minutes) to Parc Urbain-Musée.

La Piscine Musée d'Art et d'Industrie MUSEUM
(www.roubaix-lapiscine.com; 23 rue de l'Espérance, Roubaix; adult/child €4.50/free; 11am-6pm Tue-Thu, 11am-8pm Fri, 1-6pm Sat & Sun; Gare Jean Lebas) Housed in an art deco municipal swimming pool (built 1927–32), this gallery, 12km northeast of Gare Lille-Europe, showcases fine arts, applied arts and sculpture in a delightfully watery environment.

Sleeping

TOP CHOICE **L'Hermitage Gantois** DESIGN HOTEL €€€
(03 20 85 30 30; www.hotelhermitagegantois.com; 224 rue de Paris; d €219-455; Mairie de Lille) This five-star hotel creates enchanting, harmonious spaces by complementing its rich architectural heritage – such as a Flemish-Gothic facade – with refined ultramodernism. The 67 rooms are huge and sumptuous, with Starck accessories next to Louis XV-style chairs and bathrooms that sparkle with Carrara marble. One of the four courtyards is home to a 220-year-old wisteria that's been declared a historic monument. The still-consecrated chapel was built in 1637.

Hotel Kanaï HOTEL €
(03 20 57 14 78; www.hotelkanai.com; 10 rue de Bethune; s €47-98, d €65-115; Rihour) In the heart of Lille's pedestrian zone, this newer hotel offers reasonably priced rooms with a clean modern design, ranging from a cozy single tucked away on the top floor to spacious doubles with queen beds and couches; all come with coffee makers, attractive tiled bathrooms and cable internet connections. Wi-fi only reaches the lounge and breakfast area.

Hôtel Brueghel HOTEL €€
(03 20 06 06 69; www.hotel-brueghel-lille.com; 5 parvis St-Maurice; s €79-95, d €89-105; Gare Lille-Flandres) At this dependable midrange hotel halfway between Gare Lille-Flandres and the Grande Place, the 65 rooms mix vaguely antique furnishings with modern styling (though none of them offers as much Flemish charm as the lobby). Some south-facing rooms have sunny views of the adjacent church.

Auberge de Jeunesse HOSTEL €
(03 20 57 08 94; www.fuaj.org; 12 rue Malpart; dm incl breakfast €21, d €42; Feb–mid-Dec; Mairie de Lille, République-Beaux Arts) This central former maternity hospital has 163 beds in rooms for two to eight, kitchen facilities and free parking. A few doubles have en-suite showers. Lockout 11am to 3pm (4pm Friday to Sunday).

Eating

Keep an eye out for *estaminets* (traditional eateries) serving Flemish specialities such as *carbonnade* (beef braised with Flemish beer, spice bread and brown sugar).

TOP CHOICE **Chez la Vieille** FLEMISH €
(03 28 36 40 06; 60 rue de Gand; mains €10-14; dinner Mon, lunch & dinner Tue-Sat) Old-time prints, antiques and fresh hops hanging from the rafters create the cozy ambience of a Flemish village c 1900 at this beloved *estaminet*. Its sister restaurant **Au Vieux de la Vieille** (www.

OLD TOWN EAT STREETS

Rue de Gand Small, moderately priced French and Flemish restaurants.

Rue de la Monnaie Quirky restaurants here and on neighbouring side streets.

Rue Royale Ethnic cuisine (couscous, Japanese etc).

Rue Solférino & rue Masséna Lively, student-dominated cheap eats near the Palais des Beaux Arts.

estaminetlille.fr; 2-4 rue des Vieux Murs; mains €10-14; ⊙lunch & dinner) serves an identical menu, with outdoor seating on picturesque cobblestoned Place de l'Oignon. The vibe at both is informal, but it's best to call ahead.

À l'Huîtrière SEAFOOD €€€
(☎03 20 55 43 41; www.huitriere.fr; 3 rue des Chats Bossus; lunch menus €45, dinner menus €110, oyster bar items from €15; ⊙lunch & dinner Mon-Sat, lunch Sun Sep-Jul) On the 'Street of the Hunchback Cats', this sophisticated restaurant is well known for its fabulous seafood and wine cellar. For a lighter meal with a lower price tag, sit at the oyster bar up front, where stunning art deco trappings – including sea-themed mosaics and stained glass – create a colorful, more relaxed atmosphere.

Crêperie Beaurepaire CREPERIE €
(www.creperiebeaurepaire.com; 1 rue St-Étienne; crêpes €5-9; ⊙lunch & dinner Mon-Sat; ⓂRihour) With its sunny beamed dining room, stone-walled cellar and sweet little outdoor courtyard, this hideaway just steps from place Charles de Gaulle is a lovely spot to enjoy crispy buckwheat galettes, salads and flaming dessert crêpes, accompanied by ceramic bowls full of cider.

La Source ORGANIC, VEGETARIAN €
(☎03 20 57 53 07; www.denislasource.com; 13 rue du Plat; menus €9.50-16; ⊙11.30am-2pm Mon-Sat, 7-9pm Fri; ⓂRépublique Beaux Arts) This Lille institution serves delicious vegetarian, fowl and fish plats du jour, each accompanied by five hot veggie side dishes. The light, airy ambience and the diners exude health, well-being and cheer.

Marché de Wazemmes MARKET €
(place de la Nouvelle Aventure; ⊙8am-2pm Tue Thu, 8am-8pm Fri & Sat, 8am-3pm Sun & holidays; ⓂGambetta) Beloved foodie space, 1.7km southwest of the tourist office in Lille's working-class quarter of Wazemmes.

Drinking

Think two key nightlife zones: Vieux Lille's small, chic bars, and the student-oriented bars around rue Masséna and rue Solférino. In summer, pavement cafe terraces render place de la Théâtre in front of the opera prime beer-sipping terrain.

Meert TEAHOUSE
(www.meert.fr; 27 rue Esquermoise; waffles €3; ⊙9.30am-7.30pm Tue-Sat, 9am-1pm & 3-7pm Sun; ⓂRihour) A delightful spot for morning coffee or mid-afternoon tea, this elegant tea-room dating to 1761 is beloved for its retro decor and its *gaufres* (waffles) filled with sweet Madagascan vanilla paste.

L'Illustration Café BAR, CAFE
(www.bar-illustration.com; 18 rue Royale; ⊙12.30pm-3am Mon-Sat, 3pm-3am Sun) Adorned with art nouveau woodwork and changing exhibits by local painters, this laid-back bar attracts artists, musicians, budding intellectuals and teachers in the mood to read, exchange weighty ideas – or just shoot the breeze. The mellow soundtrack mixes Western classical with jazz, French *chansons* and African beats.

NORTHERN BREWS

French Flanders brews some truly excellent *bière blonde* (lager) and *bière ambrée* (amber beer) with an alcohol content of up to 8.5%. Brands that give the Belgian brewers a run for their money include 3 Monts, Amadeus, Ambre des Flandres, Brasserie des 2 Caps, Ch'ti, Enfants de Gayant, Grain d'Orge, Hellemus, Jenlain, L'Angellus, La Wambrechies, Moulins d'Ascq, Raoul, Septante 5, St-Landelin, Triple Secret des Moines and Vieux Lille.

Information

Tourist Office (☎from abroad +33 359 57 94 00, in France 08 91 56 20 04; www.lilletourism.com; place Rihour; ⊙9am-6pm Mon-Sat, 10am-noon & 2-5pm Sun & holidays; ⓂRihour)

Getting There & Away

Lille has two train stations: Gare Lille-Flandres for regional services and trains to Paris' Gare du Nord (€42 to €58, one hour, 14 to 18 daily), and ultramodern Gare Lille-Europe for all other trains, including the Eurostar to London and TGV/Eurostar to Brussels-Nord (€18 to €25, 35 minutes, 12 daily).

Eurolines (☎08 92 89 90 91; www.eurolines.com; 23 parvis St-Maurice; ⓂGare Lille-Flandres) Serves cities such as Brussels (€18, 1½ hours), Amsterdam (€43, five hours) and London (€36, 5½ hours; by day via the Channel Tunnel, at night by ferry). Buses depart from blvd de Leeds near Gare Lille-Europe.

WORTH A TRIP

CÔTE D'OPALE

For a dramatic and beautiful intro to France, head to the 40km of majestic cliffs, sand dunes and beaches between Calais and Boulogne-sur-Mer. Known as the Côte d'Opale (Opal Coast) because of the ever-changing interplay of greys and blues in the sky and sea, it is a kaleidoscope of wind-buffeted coastal peaks, wide beaches and rolling farmland. The remains of Nazi Germany's Atlantic Wall, a chain of fortifications and gun emplacements built to prevent the Allied invasion that in the end took place in Normandy, stud the shore, which has been much loved by British beach-goers since Victorian times.

Protected by the **Parc Naturel Régional des Caps et Marais d'Opale** (www.parc-opale.fr), the area is criss-crossed by hiking paths, including the **GR120 Littoral trail** (with red-and-white trail markings) that snakes along the coast – except where the cliffs are in danger of collapse. Some trails are open to mountain bikers and horseriders. Each village along the Côte d'Opale has at least one camping ground, and most have places to eat.

By car, the D940 offers some truly spectacular vistas – or hop aboard Inglard's bus 44, which links the string of villages between Calais and Boulogne.

Getting Around

Lille's two metro lines, tramways and bus lines are run by **Transpole** (www.transpole.fr). Tickets (€1.40) are sold on buses but must be purchased (and validated in the orange posts) *before* boarding a metro or tram. A *Pass Journée* (all-day pass) costs €4.10.

Calais

POP 75,240

As Churchill might have put it, 'Never in the field of human tourism have so many travellers passed through a place and so few stopped to visit'. Over 15 million people pass through Calais en route to the cross-Channel ferries, but few explore the town itself – it's worth it, if only to see Rodin's famous sculpture, *Les Bourgeois de Calais* (The Burghers of Calais).

Sights

Beffroi de Calais BELL TOWER
(Town Hall Belfry; place du Soldat Inconnu; adult/child €5/3; 10am-noon & 2-5.30pm, closed Mon Oct-Apr) An elevator whisks you to the top of Calais' town hall belfry, a Unesco World Heritage site, from where you can admire 360-degree views.

Burghers of Calais SCULPTURE
(place du Soldat Inconnu) In front of Calais' Flemish Renaissance–style **Hôtel de Ville** (town hall) is Rodin's famous statue *Les Bourgeois de Calais* (The Burghers of Calais; 1895), honouring six local citizens who, in 1347, held off the besieging English forces for more than eight months. Edward III was so impressed he ultimately spared the Calaisiens and their six leaders.

TOP CHOICE **Cité Internationale de la Dentelle et de la Mode** MUSEUM
(International Centre of Lace & Fashion; 03 21 00 42 30; www.cite-dentelle.fr; 135 quai du Commerce; adult/child €5/2.50; 10am-6pm Wed-Mon) Enter the intricate world of lace-making, the industry that once made Calais a textile powerhouse, at this informative, cutting-edge exhibition on the history of lace. Situated 500m southeast of the *hôtel de ville.*

Sleeping

Hôtel Meurice HOTEL €€
(03 21 34 57 03; www.hotel-meurice.fr; 5-7 rue Edmond Roche; d €92-162; @) This veteran downtown hotel with 39 rooms offers plenty of atmosphere, thanks to its grand lobby staircase, antique furnishings and breakfast room with garden views.

Auberge de Jeunesse HOSTEL €
(03 21 34 70 20; www.auberge-jeunesse-calais.com; av Maréchal de Lattre de Tassigny; dm/s/tw incl breakfast €21/28/42; ; 3, 5, 9) Modern, well equipped and 200m from the beach.

Eating

Restaurants ring place d'Armes and are plentiful just south of there along rue Royale.

TOP CHOICE **Histoire Ancienne** BISTRO €€
(03 21 34 11 20; www.histoire-ancienne.com; 20 rue Royale; lunch menus €15, dinner menus €19-28; lunch & dinner Tue-Sat, lunch Mon) Specialising

in French and regional dishes, some grilled over an open wood fire, this 1930s Paris-style bistro offers excellent value lunch and dinner menus in a classy dining room at the heart of town.

Information

Tourist office (☎03 21 96 62 40; www.calais-cotedopale.com; 12 bd Georges Clemenceau; ⏰10am-6pm Mon-Sat, to 5pm Sun) Just across the bridge (north) from the train station.

Getting There & Around

Boat

Each day, over three dozen car ferries from Dover dock at Calais' bustling **car-ferry terminal**, 1.5km northeast of place d'Armes.

P&O Ferries (www.poferries.com; 41 place d'Armes) and **DFDS Seaways** (☎03 28 59 01 01; www.dfdsseaways.co.uk; ferry terminal) operate regular trans-Channel services. P&O accepts foot passengers; DFDS passengers with vehicles.

Shuttle buses (€2, roughly hourly from 11am to 6pm) link Gare Calais-Ville (train station) and place d'Armes (stop in front of Café de la Tour) with the car-ferry terminal. Departure times are posted at stops.

Bus

Ligne BCD (☎08 00 62 00 59; www.ligne-bcd.com) links Calais' train station (hours posted) with Dunkirk (€8.20, 50 minutes, six daily Monday to Friday, three Saturday).

Car & Motorcycle

To reach the Channel Tunnel's vehicle-loading area at Coquelles, 6km southwest of the town centre, follow the road signs on the A16 to 'Tunnel Sous La Manche' (exit 42).

Train

Calais has two train stations, linked by trains and a *navette* (shuttle bus; €2, free with train ticket).

Gare Calais-Ville (city centre) serves Amiens (€25.30, 2½ to 3½ hours, six daily), Boulogne (€7.70, 30 minutes, up to 19 daily), Dunkirk (€8.60, 50 minutes, two to six Monday to Saturday) and Lille-Flandres (€17.30, 1¼ hours, eight to 19 daily).

Gare Calais-Fréthun (TGV station 10km southwest of town near Channel Tunnel entrance) serves Paris' Gare du Nord (€44 to €61, 1¾ hours, three to six daily) and Eurostar to London's St Pancras (from €96, one hour, three daily).

Amiens

POP 137,030

One of France's most awe-inspiring Gothic cathedrals is reason enough to spend time in the former capital of Picardy, where Jules Verne spent the last two decades of his life. The mostly pedestrianised city centre, rebuilt after the war, is complemented by lovely green spaces along the Somme River. Some 25,000 students give the town a youthful feel.

Sights

TOP CHOICE **Cathédrale Notre Dame** CATHEDRAL
(place Notre Dame; audioguide 1st/2nd person €4/3, north tower adult/child €5.50/free; ⏰cathedral 8.30am-6.15pm daily, north tower afternoon only Wed-Mon) France's largest Gothic cathedral and a Unesco World Heritage Site, this magnificent structure was begun in 1220 to house the **skull of St John the Baptist**, framed in gold and jewels in the northern

WORTH A TRIP

KILLING FIELDS

The **Battle of the Somme**, a WWI Allied offensive waged northeast of Amiens, was planned with the goal of relieving the pressure on the beleaguered French troops at Verdun. On 1 July 1916, two-dozen divisions of British, Commonwealth and French troops went 'over the top' in a massive assault along a 34km front. But German positions proved virtually unbreachable, and on the first day alone 21,392 Allied troops were killed and another 35,492 were wounded.

By the time the offensive was called off in mid-November, some 1.2 million lives had been lost: the British had advanced just 12km, the French 8km. The Battle of the Somme has since become a symbol of the meaningless slaughter of war and its killing fields and cemeteries have since become a site of pilgrimage (see www.somme-battlefields.com). Amiens tourist office supplies maps, guides and minibus tours.

outer wall of the ambulatory. Connoisseurs rave about the soaring Gothic arches (42.3m high over the transept), unity of style and immense interior.

Weather permitting, it's possible to climb the **north tower**; tickets are sold in the boutique to the left as you approach the west facade.

A free 45-minute **light show** bathes the cathedral's facade in vivid medieval colours nightly from mid-June to mid-September and for the month of December.

Sleeping & Eating

Hôtel Victor Hugo HOTEL €

(☎03 22 91 57 91; www.hotel-a-amiens.com; 2 rue de l'Oratoire; r €46-70; 📶) Just a block from the cathedral, this friendly, family-run two-star hotel has 10 simple but comfortable rooms. Best value, if you don't mind a long stair climb, are the welcoming top-floor units (rooms 7 and 8) with rooftop views and lots of natural light.

Le T'chiot Zinc BISTRO €

(☎03 22 91 43 79; 18 rue de Noyon; menus €13-27; ⊙closed Sun, also closed Mon Jul & Aug) Inviting, bistro-style decor reminiscent of the belle époque provides a fine backdrop for the tasty French and Picard cuisine, including fish dishes and *caqhuse* (pork in a cream, wine vinegar and onion sauce). The proper Picard pronunciation of the restaurant's name is 'shtyoh-zang'.

Getting There & Away

Amiens is an important rail hub.

Calais-Ville €25.30, two to 2½ hours, six or seven daily.

Lille-Flandres €20.20, 1½ hours, six to 12 daily.

Paris' Gare du Nord €20.70, 1¼ to 1¾ hours, 14 to 30 daily.

Rouen €19.40, 1¼ hours, five daily.

DON'T MISS

THE CIDER ROAD

Normandy's signposted 40km **Route du Cidre**, about 20km east of Caen, wends its way through the **Pays d'Auge**, a rural area of orchards, pastures, hedgerows, half-timbered farmhouses and stud farms, through picturesque villages such as Cambremer and Beuvron-en-Auge. Along the way, signs reading 'Cru de Cambremer' indicate the way to about 20 small-scale, traditional producers who are happy to show you their facilities and sell you their home-grown cider (€3 a bottle) and Calvados (apple brandy).

NORMANDY

Famous for cows, cider and Camembert, this largely rural region (www.normandie-tourisme.fr) is one of France's most traditional – and most visited thanks to world-renowned sights such as the Bayeux Tapestry, historic D-Day beaches, Monet's garden at Giverny and spectacular Mont St-Michel.

Rouen

POP 119,927

With its elegant spires, beautifully restored medieval quarter and soaring Gothic cathedral, the ancient city of Rouen is a Normandy highlight. Devastated several times during the Middle Ages by fire and plague, the city was later badly damaged by WWII bombing raids, but has been meticulously rebuilt over the last six decades. The city makes an ideal base for exploring the northern Normandy coast.

Sights

Église Jeanne d'Arc CHURCH

(place du Vieux Marché; ⊙10am-noon & 2-6pm Apr-Oct) The old city's main thoroughfare, rue du Gros Horloge, runs from the cathedral west to **place du Vieux Marché**. Dedicated in 1979, the thrillingly bizarre Église Jeanne d'Arc, with its fish-scale exterior, marks the spot where 19-year-old Joan of Arc was burned at the stake in 1431.

Cathédrale Notre Dame CATHEDRAL

(place de la Cathédrale; ⊙2-6pm Mon, 7.30am-7pm Tue-Sat, 8am-6pm Sun) Rouen's stunning Gothic cathedral, with its polished, brilliant-white facade, is the famous subject of a series of paintings by Monet. Its 75m-tall **Tour de Beurre** (Butter Tower) was financed by locals who donated to the cathedral in return for being allowed to eat butter during Lent – or so the story goes.

Musée des Beaux-Arts MUSEUM

(☎02 35 71 28 40; www.rouen-musees.com; esplanade Marcel Duchamp; adult/child €5/free; ⊙10am-6pm Wed-Mon) Housed in a grand structure erected in 1870, Rouen's fine-arts museum features canvases by Caravaggio, Rubens,

DON'T MISS

LOUVRE-LENS

After years of anticipation, Europe's most ballyhooed new art museum has opened its doors. The innovative **Louvre Lens** (www.louvrelens.fr; 6 rue Charles Lecocq, Lens; Galerie du Temps & Pavillon de Verre free through 2013; ⊙10am-6pm Wed-Mon) showcases hundreds of treasures from Paris' venerable Musée du Louvre in a purpose-built, state-of-the-art new exhibition space in the former coal mining town of Lens. The futuristic ensemble of buildings and surrounding parkland was designed to look like five river boats drifting haphazardly together on the grassed-over site of a former coal mine.

Intended to give museumgoers a completely different experience than its Parisian cousin, the Louvre-Lens is all about making art accessible to everyone, while showing off the Louvre's remarkable holdings in exciting new ways. Visitors are invited behind the scenes to view the museum's storerooms and watch art restoration personnel at work. There is no permanent collection; rather, the central 120m-long exhibition space, **Galerie du Temps**, displays a limited but significant, ever-rotating collection of 200+ pieces from the original Louvre. The museum's grand opening featured European masterpieces such as Delacroix's *Liberty Leading the People* and Raphael's *Portrait of Baldassare Castiglione* alongside works as diverse as ancient Mesopotamian tablets, Persian glazed tiles, Greek statues, Pompeiian frescoes, Roman bronzes, Islamic art from Spain to Syria, and 11th-century Italian mosaics.

A second building, the glass-walled **Pavillon de Verre**, displays annually changing themed exhibits (such as the Renaissance in 2013).

To celebrate Louvre-Lens' grand opening, the main collections are free of charge during 2013 (temporary exhibits cost €9). Lens, 18km north of Arras and 40km southwest of Lille, is accessible by TGV trains from Paris' Gare du Nord (€28 to €46, 65 to 70 minutes) and regional trains from Lille (€7.60, 40 minutes) and Arras (€4.20, 15 minutes).

Modigliani, Pissarro, Renoir, Sisley (lots) and (of course) several works by Monet.

Sleeping

TOP CHOICE Hôtel de Bourgtheroulde HOTEL €€€
(☎02 35 14 50 50; www.hotelsparouen.com; 15 place de la Pucelle; r €240-380; P❄📶🏊) This stunning conversion of an old private mansion brings a dash of glamour and luxury to Rouen's hotel scene. Rooms are large, gorgeously designed and feature beautiful bathrooms.

La Boulangerie B&B €€
(☎06 12 94 53 15; www.laboulangerie.fr; 59 rue St-Nicaise; d €77-92, q €150; P📶) Tucked into a quiet side street slightly off the historic quarter, this adorable B&B occupying a former bakery offers three pleasingly decorated rooms. The largest 'Levain' room can sleep up to four people. Your charming hosts, Franck and Aminata, are a mine of local information.

Hôtel de la Cathédrale HOTEL €€
(☎02 35 71 57 95; www.hotel-de-la-cathedrale.fr; 12 rue St-Romain; s €66-86, d €76-104, q €143; @📶) Hiding behind a 17th-century half-timbered facade, this atmospheric hotel has 27 stylishly refitted rooms, mostly overlooking a quiet plant-filled courtyard.

Auberge de Jeunesse Robec HOSTEL €
(☎02 35 08 18 50; www.fuaj.org; 3 rue de la Tour; dm/s/d incl breakfast €22/33/56; 📶) The two- to eight-bed rooms at this modern hostel are comfortable and functional. Sadly, it's some way from the centre of town, off route de Darnétal – take bus T2 or T3 from Rouen's city centre and get off at the 'Auberge de Jeunesse' stop. Check in is from 5pm to 10pm only.

Eating

Little eateries crowd the north side of rue Martainville. For ethnic cuisine head two blocks south to rue des Augustins. More restaurants can be found along rue de Fontenelle (a block west of Église Jeanne d'Arc), and a few blocks east along rue Ecuyère.

TOP CHOICE Les Nymphéas FRENCH €€
(☎02 35 89 26 69; www.lesnympheas-rouen.com; 7-9 rue de la Pie; mains €29-37, menus €34-52; ⊙lunch & dinner Tue-Sat) Its formal table settings arrayed under 16th-century beams, this fine restaurant serves cuisine based on fresh ingredients.

DON'T MISS

MAISON DE CLAUDE MONET

Monet's home for the last 43 years of his life is now the delightful **Maison et Jardins de Claude Monet** (☎02 32 51 28 21; www.fondation-monet.com; adult/child €9/5; ⌚9.30am-5.30pm Apr-Oct), where you can view the Impressionist's pastel-pink house and famous gardens with lily pond, Japanese bridge draped in purple wisteria, and so on. Early to late spring, daffodils, tulips, rhododendrons, wisteria and irises bloom in the flowery gardens, followed by poppies and lilies. By June, nasturtiums, roses and sweet peas are in flower, while September is the month to see dahlias, sunflowers and hollyhocks.

The gardens are in Giverny, 66km southeast of Rouen. Several trains (€10.80, 40 minutes) leave Rouen before noon, with hourly return trains between 5pm and 8pm. From Paris' Gare St-Lazare up to 15 daily trains run to Vernon (€13.30, 50 minutes), 7km west of Giverny, from where shuttle buses (€6.50 return, three to six daily April to October) shunt passengers to Giverny.

Let chef Patrick Kukurudz and his team seduce you with meat and fish dishes accompanied with divinely inspired sauces. Even the cheaper lunch menu (€34) is exquisite.

Minute et Mijoté BISTRO **€€**
(58 rue de Fontenelle; mains €20, menus €13-30; ⌚lunch & dinner Mon-Sat) This smart bistro is one of our favourite finds in Rouen. The trademark here is freshness and great value for money, hence its fast-growing reputation. There's outdoor seating in summer.

L'Espiguette BISTRO **€**
(☎02 35 71 66 27; 25 place St-Amand; mains €13-19, lunch menu €11; ⌚lunch & dinner Tue-Sat) A growing number of local connoisseurs are enthusiastic about this place, which overlooks a picturesque square. No culinary acrobatics here, just pared-down classics such as *joue de bœuf* (ox cheek), beef sirloin and salads. Its fixed-priced menu, with loads of good choices, is a great deal.

Information

Tourist office (☎02 32 08 32 40; www.rouentourisme.com; 25 place de la Cathédrale; ⌚9am-7pm Mon-Sat, 9.30am-12.30pm & 2-6pm Sun & holidays)

Getting There & Away

TRAIN Direct services from Rouen train station, just north of the city centre.

Amiens from €19.40, 1¼ hours, four or five daily

Caen from €24.90, 1½ hours, eight to 10 daily

Dieppe from €11.10, 45 minutes, 14 to 16 daily Monday to Saturday, six Sunday

Le Havre €14.60, 50 minutes, 20 daily Monday to Saturday, 10 Sunday

Paris St-Lazare €21.90, 1¼ hours, at least hourly

Bayeux

POP 14,350

Bayeux has become famous throughout the English-speaking world thanks to a 68m-long piece of painstakingly embroidered cloth: the 11th-century Bayeux Tapestry, whose 58 scenes vividly tell the story of the Norman invasion of England in 1066. The town is also one of the few in Normandy to have survived WWII practically unscathed, with a centre crammed with 13th- to 18th-century buildings, wooden-framed Norman-style houses, and a spectacular Norman Gothic cathedral.

Sights

TOP CHOICE **Bayeux Tapestry** TAPESTRY
(☎02 31 51 25 50; www.tapisserie-bayeux.fr; rue de Nesmond; adult/child incl audioguide €7.80/3.80; ⌚9am-6.30pm mid-Mar–mid-Nov, to 7pm May-Aug, 9.30am-12.30pm & 2-6pm mid-Nov–mid-Mar) The world's most celebrated embroidery recounts the conquest of England from an unashamedly Norman perspective. Fifty-eight scenes fill the central canvas, and religious allegories and illustrations of everyday 11th-century life fill the borders. The final showdown at the Battle of Hastings is depicted in graphic fashion, complete with severed limbs and decapitated heads (along the bottom of scene 52); Halley's Comet, which blazed across the sky in 1066, appears in scene 32. Scholars believe the 68.3m-long tapestry was commissioned by Bishop Odo of Bayeux, William the Conqueror's half-brother, for the opening of Bayeux' cathedral in 1077.

Musée Mémorial de la Bataille de Normandie MUSEUM
(Battle of Normandy Memorial Museum; bd Fabien Ware; adult/child €7/3.80; 9.30am-6.30pm May-Sep, 10am-12.30pm & 2-6pm Oct-Apr) Using well-chosen photos, personal accounts, dioramas and wartime objects, this first-rate museum offers an excellent introduction to WWII in Normandy.

Sleeping

TOP CHOICE **Les Logis du Rempart** B&B €
(☎02 31 92 50 40; www.lecornu.fr; 4 rue Bourbesneur; d €60-80, q €130;) This *maison de famille* shelters three rooms oozing old-fashioned cosiness. The hosts run a tasting shop downstairs – the perfect place to stock up on top-quality, homemade Calvados and cider. Breakfast (€6) features organic apple juice and apple jelly.

Villa Lara BOUTIQUE HOTEL €€€
(☎02 31 92 00 55; www.hotel-villalara.com; 6 place de Québec; d €180-280, ste €290-450; P) Luxury and sophistication are the hallmarks of this 28-room boutique hotel, which opened in 2012. Clean lines, trendy colour schemes, top-quality fabrics and minimalist motifs distinguish the rooms, while other facilities include a bistro and a gym.

Hôtel Reine Mathilde HOTEL €€
(☎02 31 92 08 13; www.hotel-bayeux-reinemathilde.fr; 23 rue Larcher; d €70-105;) Above a bustling local cafe of the same name, this family-run hotel is an excellent bet, right in the centre of town, with smallish but comfortable rooms. The annexe sports six sleek, spacious and sparkling rooms in a converted barn by the river.

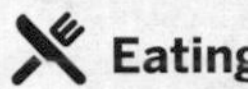

Eating

Local specialities to keep an eye out for include *cochon de Bayeux* (Bayeux-style pork). Rue St-Jean and rue St-Martin are home to a variety of cheap eateries and food shops.

La Rapière REGIONAL CUISINE €€
(☎02 31 21 05 45; 53 rue St-Jean; menus €15-33.50; lunch & dinner Fri-Tue) Housed in a late-1400s mansion composed of stone walls and big wooden beams, this atmospheric restaurant specialises in Normandy staples such as terrines, duck and veal with Camembert. Four fixed-price menus assure a splendid meal on any budget.

La Reine Mathilde CAKE SHOP €
(47 rue St-Martin; cakes from €2.50; 8.30am-7.30pm Tue-Sun) A sumptuous, c 1900-style patisserie and *salon de thé* (tearoom) that's ideal if you've got a hankering for something sweet. There's seating here, making it prime breakfast and afternoon-tea terrain.

Information

Tourist office (☎02 31 51 28 28; www.bessin-normandie.com; pont St-Jean; 9.30am-12.30pm & 2-6pm)

Getting There & Away

Trains link Bayeux with Caen (€6.20, 20 minutes, hourly), from where there are connections to Paris' Gare St-Lazare (€33.30, two hours) and Rouen (€24.90, 1½ hours).

D-Day Beaches

The D-Day landings, code-named 'Operation Overlord', were the largest military operation in history. Early on 6 June 1944,

WORTH A TRIP

RENOIR IN NORMANDY

Following the Seine valley west of Rouen, the D982 road winds through little towns, occasionally following the banks of the Seine as it climbs and descends. About 27km west of Rouen, in Jumièges, the **Abbaye de Jumièges** (☎02 35 37 24 02; Jumièges; adult/child €5/free; 9.30am-6.30pm Jul-Aug, 9.30am-1pm & 2.30-5.30pm Sep-Jun) is an absolute must-see, even if you're not a history buff. With its ghostly white stone set off by a backdrop of trees, it's one of the most evocative ruins in Normandy. The church was begun in 1020, and William the Conqueror attended its consecration in 1067. It declined during the Hundred Years War and then enjoyed a renaissance under Charles VII. It continued to flourish until the 18th-century revolutionaries booted out the monks and allowed the buildings to be mined for building materials. Should you be tempted to overnight in Jumièges, consider staying at **Le Clos Fleuri** (☎06 16 72 29 53, 02 35 81 49 00; www.closfleuri76.fr; 2196 rte du Mesnil; s/d €42/48), an economical B&B just 1km away from the abbey.

DON'T MISS

CAEN MÉMORIAL

Caen's hi-tech, hugely impressive **Mémorial – Un Musée pour la Paix** (Memorial – A Museum for Peace; ☎02 31 06 06 45; www.memorial-caen.fr; esplanade Général Eisenhower, Caen; adult/child €18.80/16.30; ⏲9am-6.30pm, closed Jan & Mon mid-Nov–mid-Dec) uses sound, lighting, film, animation and lots of exhibits to graphically explore and evoke the events of WWII, D-Day landings and the ensuing Cold War. Tickets remain valid for 24 hours. The museum also runs D-Day beach tours.

Allied troops stormed ashore along 80km of beaches north of Bayeux, code-named (from west to east) Utah, Omaha, Gold, Juno and Sword. The landings on D-Day – called 'Jour J' in French – were followed by the Battle of Normandy, which ultimately led to the liberation of Europe from Nazi occupation. Memorial museums in Caen and Bayeux provide a comprehensive overview, and there are many small D-Day museums dotted along the coast. For context, see www.normandiememoire.com and www.6juin1944.com.

The most brutal fighting on D-Day took place 15km northwest of Bayeux along the stretch of coastline now known as **Omaha Beach**, today a glorious stretch of fine golden sand partly lined with sand dunes and summer homes. **Circuit de la Plage d'Omaha**, trail-marked with a yellow stripe, is a self-guided tour along the beach, surveyed from a bluff above by the huge **Normandy American Cemetery & Memorial** (www.abmc.gov; Colleville-sur-Mer; ⏲9am-5pm). Featured in the opening scenes of Steven Spielberg's *Saving Private Ryan*, this is the largest American cemetery in Europe.

Tours

An organised minibus tour is an excellent way to get a sense of the D-Day beaches and their place in history. Bayeux tourist office (p343) handles reservations.

Mémorial MINIBUS TOURS
(www.memorial-caen.fr; adult/child €77/61) Excellent year-round minibus tours (four to five hours). Rates include entry to Mémorial. Book online.

Normandy Sightseeing Tours D-DAY TOUR
(☎02 31 51 70 52; www.normandywebguide.com) From May to October (and on request the rest of the year), this experienced outfit offers morning (adult/child €45/25) tours of various beaches and cemeteries. These can be combined into an all-day excursion (€90/50).

ℹ Getting There & Away

Bus Verts (www.busverts.fr) bus 70 (two or three daily Monday to Saturday, more in summer) goes northwest from Bayeux to Colleville-sur-Mer and Omaha Beach (€2.30, 35 minutes).

CAMEMBERT COUNTRY

Some of the most enduring names in the pungent world of French *fromage* come from Normandy, including Pont L'Évêque, Livarot and, most famous of all, Camembert, all named after towns south of Honfleur, on or near the D579.

It's thought that monks first began experimenting with cheesemaking in the Pays d'Auge sometime in the 11th century, but the present-day varieties didn't emerge until around the 17th century. The invention of Camembert is generally credited to Marie Harel, who was supposedly given the secret of soft cheesemaking by an abbot from Brie on the run from Revolutionary mobs in 1790. Whatever truth there is in the legend, the cheese was a huge success at the local market in Vimoutiers, and production of Camembert quickly grew from a cottage industry into an international operation. The distinctive round wooden boxes, in which Camembert is wrapped, have been around since 1890; they were designed by a local engineer to protect the soft disc during long-distance travel.

If you're interested in seeing how the cheese is made, you can take a guided tour of the **Président Farm** (☎02 33 36 06 60; www.fermepresident.com; adult/child €3/2; ⏲10am-6pm Jun-Aug, 10am-6pm Apr & Sep-Oct, 10am-5pm Mar, closed Nov-Feb), an early-19th-century farm restored by Président, one of the region's largest Camembert producers in the centre of the town of **Camembert**, 60km south of Honfleur.

DON'T MISS

THE MORBIHAN MEGALITHS

Pre-dating Stonehenge by about a hundred years, **Carnac** comprises the world's greatest concentration of megalithic sites. There are more than 3000 of these upright stones scattered across the countryside between **Carnac-Ville** and **Locmariaquer** village, most of which were erected between 5000 BC and 3500 BC. No one's quite sure what purpose these sites served, although theories abound. A sacred site? Phallic fertility cult? Or maybe a celestial calendar? Even more mysterious is the question of their construction – no one really has the foggiest idea how the builders hacked and hauled these vast granite blocks several millennia before the wheel arrived in Brittany, let alone mechanical diggers.

Because of severe erosion, the sites are usually fenced off to allow vegetation to regrow. **Guided tours** (€6) run in French year-round and in English from early July to late August. Sign up at the **Maison des Mégalithes** (☎02 97 52 29 81; rte des Alignements; tour adult/child €6/free; ⏰10am-8pm Jul & Aug, to 5.15pm Sep-Apr, to 7pm May & Jun). Opposite, the largest menhir field – with no fewer than 1099 stones – is the **Alignements du Ménec**, 1km north of Carnac-Ville. From here, the D196 heads northeast for about 1.5km to the **Alignements de Kermario**. Climb the stone observation tower midway along the site to see the alignment from above. Another 500m further on are the **Alignements de Kerlescan**, while the **Tumulus St-Michel**, 400m northeast of the Carnac-Ville tourist office, dates back to at least 5000 BC.

For background, Carnac's **Musée de Préhistoire** (☎02 97 52 22 04; www.museedecarnac.fr; 10 place de la Chapelle, Carnac-Ville; adult/child €5/2.50; ⏰10am-6pm) chronicles life in and around Carnac from the Palaeolithic and neolithic eras to the Middle Ages.

Mont St-Michel

On a rocky island opposite the coastal town of Pontorson, connected to the mainland by a narrow causeway, the sky-scraping turrets of the abbey of **Mont St-Michel** (☎02 33 89 80 00; www.monuments-nationaux.fr; adult/child incl guided tour €9/free; ⏰9am-7pm, last entry 1hr before closing) provide one of France's iconic sights. The surrounding bay is notorious for its fast-rising tides: at low tide the Mont is surrounded by bare sand for miles around; at high tide, just six hours later, the bay, causeway and nearby car parks can be submerged.

From the **tourist office** (☎02 33 60 14 30; www.ot-montsaintmichel.com; ⏰9am-12.30pm & 2-6.30pm Mon-Sat, 9am-noon & 2-6pm Sun), at the base of the mount, a cobbled street winds up to the **Église Abbatiale** (Abbey Church), incorporating elements of both Norman and Gothic architecture. Other notable sights include the arched **cloître** (cloister), the barrel-roofed **réfectoire** (dining hall), and the Gothic **Salle des Hôtes** (Guest Hall), dating from 1213. A one-hour tour is included with admission; English tours run hourly in summer, twice daily (11am and 3pm) in winter. In July and August, Monday to Saturday, there are illuminated *nocturnes* (night-time visits) with music from 7pm to 10pm.

Check the *horaire des marées* (tide table) at the tourist office. When the tide is out, you can walk all the way around Mont St-Michel, a distance of about 1km. Stray too far from the Mont and you risk getting stuck in wet sand – from which Norman soldiers are depicted being rescued in one scene of the Bayeux Tapestry – or being overtaken by the incoming tide, providing your next of kin with a great cocktail-party story.

Bus 6 (☎08 00 15 00 50; www.mobi50.com) links Mont St-Michel with Pontorson (€2.20, 13 minutes), from where there are two to three daily trains to/from Bayeux (€22.30, 1¾ hr) and Cherbourg (€28.10, three hours).

BRITTANY

Brittany is for explorers. Its wild, dramatic coastline, medieval towns, thick forests and the eeriest stone circles this side of Stonehenge make a trip here well worth the detour from the beaten track. This is a land of prehistoric mysticism, proud tradition and culinary wealth, where locals still remain fiercely independent, where Breton culture (and cider) is celebrated and where Paris feels a very long way away indeed.

BRETON MUSIC

Celtic culture is synonymous with music and Brittany is no exception. A wealth of indoor and outdoor festivals and concerts feature traditional instruments through to electronica, and everything in between, with some big-name international acts. Keep your finger on the pulse by picking up the free monthly 'zine *Ty Zicos* (www.tyzicos.com) in cafes and bars. In addition to an array of festivals and events, tune in to the region's top trio of music festivals each year.

Les Vieilles Charrues de Carhaix (www.vieillescharrues.asso.fr) Old-school crooners, electronic beats and more attract crowds of 300,000-plus to Carhaix in mid-July.

Astropolis (www.astropolis.org) Brest's electronic music fest in early August, with the main event atmospherically set in a castle.

Les Transmusicales de Rennes (www.lestrans.com) Groundbreaking indie bands in Rennes, in early December.

Quimper

POP 66,911

Small enough to feel like a village – with its slanted half-timbered houses and narrow cobbled streets – and large enough to buzz as the troubadour of Breton culture, Quimper (pronounced *kam-pair*) is the thriving capital of Finistère (meaning 'land's end'; in Breton *Penn ar Bed*, it means 'head of the world').

 Sights

Most of Quimper's historic architecture is concentrated in a tight triangle formed by place Médard, rue Kéréon, rue des Gentilhommes and its continuation, rue du Sallé, to place au Beurre.

Cathédrale St-Corentin CHURCH
(place Saint-Corentin; ⌚8.30am-noon & 1.30-6.30pm Mon-Sat, 8.30am-noon & 2-6.30 Sun) At the centre of the city is the cathedral with its distinctive kink, said to symbolise Christ's inclined head as he was dying on the cross. Construction began in 1239 but the cathedral's dramatic twin spires weren't added until the 19th century.

Musée Départemental Breton MUSEUM
(☎02 98 95 21 60; 1 rue du Roi Gradlon; adult/child €4/free; ⌚9am-6pm) Beside the cathedral, recessed behind a magnificent stone courtyard, this superb museum showcases Breton history, furniture, costumes, crafts and archaeology in a former bishop's palace.

Sleeping

Hôtel Manoir des Indes HOTEL €€
(☎02 98 55 48 40; www.manoir-hoteldesindes.com; 1 allée de Prad ar C'hras; s/d from €105/133; P 📶) This stunning hotel conversion, located in an old manor house just a short drive from the centre of Quimper, has been restored with the original world-traveller owner in mind. Decor is minimalist and modern with Asian objets d'art, lots of exposed wood and a couple of elephants outside.

Camping Municipal CAMPGROUND €
(☎02 98 55 61 09; av des Oiseaux; sites €0.79, person €3.70, car €1.85; ⌚Jun-Oct; 🚌1) This wooded park is 1km west of the old city and 3km from the train station. From quai de l'Odet, follow rue Pont l'Abbé northwestwards and continue straight ahead where it veers left. Alternatively, take bus 1 from the train station to the Chaptal stop.

 Eating

Crêperie du Quartier CREPERIE €
(☎02 98 64 29 30; 16 rue du Sallé; menus from €6, galettes €5-7.10) In a town where the humble crêpe is king, this cosy stone-lined place is one of the best. Its wide-ranging menu includes a *galette* of the week and, to follow up, you can go for the full monty: a crêpe stuffed with apple, caramel, ice cream, almonds and Chantilly. Wash it all down with a tipple from the range of local ciders.

L'Ambroisie GASTRONOMIC €€€
(☎02 98 95 00 02; www.ambroisie-quimper.com; 49 rue Elie Fréron; menus €25-62; ⌚lunch & dinner Tue-Sat, lunch Sun) Quimper's most celebrated gastronomic restaurant is sumptuously decorated with contemporary art and features elegant china on snow-white tablecloths. Regional produce provided by chef Gilbert Guyon's friends is used in the creation of house specials such as turbot with eschalots

as well as lots of those Breton favourites, scallops. Cooking classes on request.

Le Cosy Restaurant REGIONAL CUISINE € (☎02 98 95 23 65; 2 rue du Sallé; mains €10-14.50; ⊙closed Sun, lunch Mon & dinner Tue) Make your way through the *épicerie* crammed with locally canned sardines, ciders and other Breton specialities to this eclectic dining room where you can tuck into top-quality gratins and *tartines*.

Information

Tourist office (☎02 98 53 04 05; www.quimper-tourisme.com; place de la Résistance; ⊙9am-7pm Mon-Sat, 10am-12.45pm & 3-5.45pm Sun Jul-Aug, 9.30am-12.30pm & 1.30-6.30pm Mon-Sat, 10am-12.45pm Sun Jun & Sep)

Getting There & Away

CAT/Viaoo (www.viaoo29.fr) Bus destinations include Brest (€6, 1¼ hours).

Frequent trains serve Brest (€16.50, 1¼ hours), Rennes (€28 to €34, 2½ hours) and Paris' Gare Montparnasse (€70 to €86, 4¾ hours).

St-Malo

POP 48,800

The mast-filled port of fortified St-Malo is inextricably tied up with the deep briny blue: the town became a key harbour during the 17th and 18th centuries, functioning as a base for merchant ships and government-sanctioned privateers, and these days it's a busy cross-Channel ferry port and summertime getaway.

Sights

Walking on top of the city's sturdy 17th-century ramparts (1.8km) affords fine views of the old walled city known as **Intra-Muros** ('within the walls') or Ville Close – access the ramparts from any of the city gates.

Cathédrale St-Vincent CATHEDRAL (place Jean de Châtillon; ⊙9.30am-6pm) The city's centrepiece was constructed between the 12th and 18th centuries. The battle to liberate St-Malo destroyed around 80% of the old city during August 1944, and damage to the cathedral was particularly severe.

Fort National RUIN (www.fortnational.com; adult/child €5/3; ⊙Easter, school holidays & Jun–mid-Sep) From the city ramparts, spot the remains of St-Malo's former prison and the rocky islet of **Île du Grand Bé**, where the great St-Malo-born 18th-century writer Chateaubriand is buried. Walk at low tide, but check the tide times with the tourist office.

Musée du Château MUSEUM (☎02 99 40 71 57; adult/child €6/3; ⊙10am-noon & 2-6pm Apr-Sep, Tue-Sun Oct-Mar) Within **Château de St-Malo**, built by the dukes of Brittany in the 15th and 16th centuries, this museum looks at the life and history of the city.

Grand Aquarium AQUARIUM (☎02 99 21 19 00; www.aquarium-st-malo.com; av Général Patton; adult/child €16/11.50; ⊙9.30am-8pm; 👪; 🚌C1) Kids will adore the submarine ride and exhibits on local marine life at this excellent aquarium, about 4km south of the city centre. Bus C1 from the train station passes by every half-hour.

WORTH A TRIP

CULINARY CANCALE

No day trip from St-Malo is tastier than one to **Cancale** (www.cancale-tourisme.fr), an idyllic Breton fishing port 14km east, that's famed for its offshore *parcs à huîtres* (oyster beds).

Learn all about oyster farming at the **Ferme Marine** (☎02 99 89 69 99; www.ferme-marine.com; corniche de l'Aurore; adult/child €7/3.70; ⊙guided tours in French 11am, 3pm & 5pm Jul-Aug, in English 2pm, in German 4pm) and shop for oysters fresh from their beds at the **Marché aux Huîtres** (12 oysters from €3.50, lunch platters €20; ⊙9am-6pm), the local oyster market atmospherically clustered around the Pointe des Crolles lighthouse.

Le Coquillage (☎02 99 89 64 76; www.maisons-de-bricourt.com; 1 rue Duguesclin; menus €27-135; ⊙Mar-Dec), the sumptuous, Michelin-starred kitchen of superchef Olivier Roellinger, is housed in the gobsmackingly impressive Château Richeux, 4km south of Cancale. Crown the culinary experience with lunch or dinner here.

Keolis Emeraude (www.keolis-emeraude.com) runs buses from St-Malo (€2, 30 minutes) that stop in Cancale at Port de la Houle, next to the pungent fish market.

St-Malo

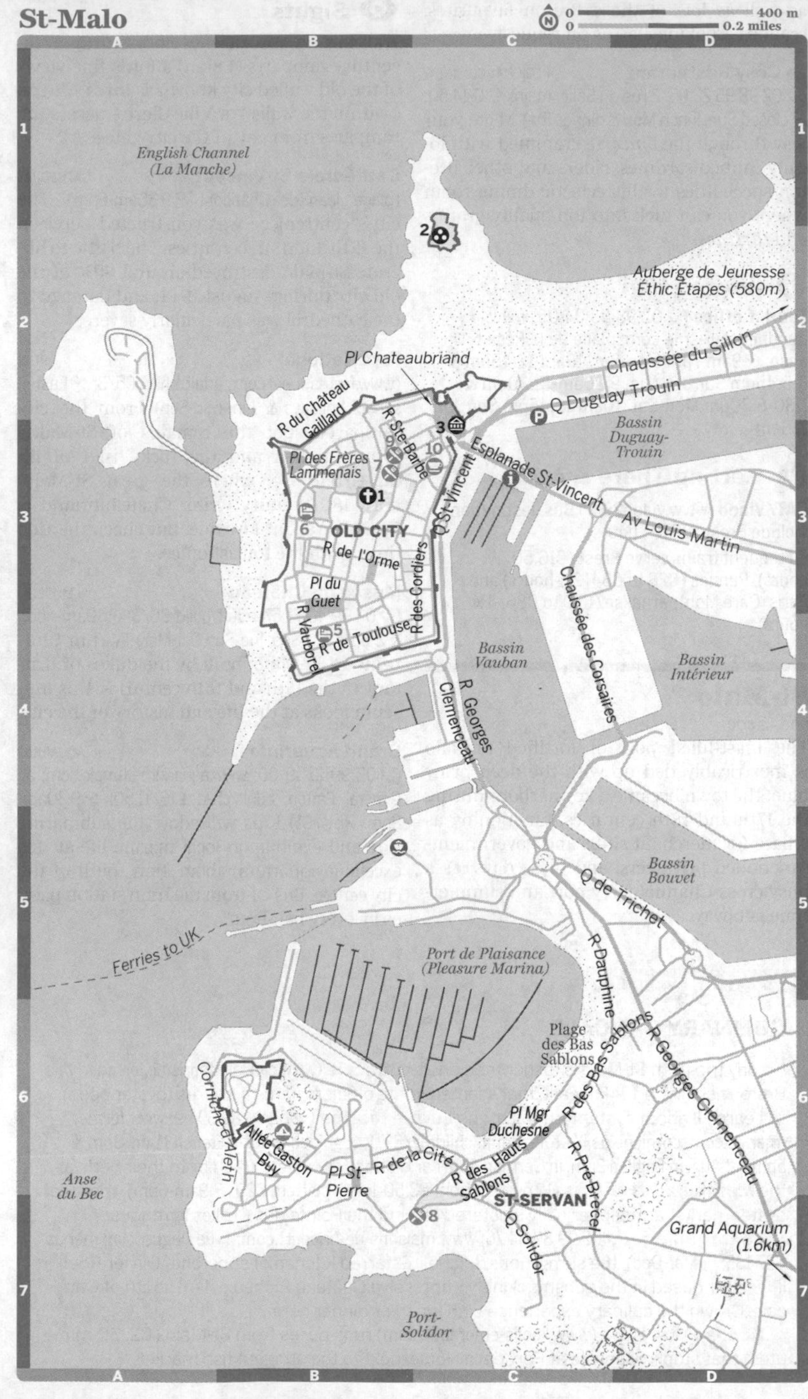

0 400 m
0 0.2 miles
English Channel (La Manche)
Auberge de Jeunesse Éthic Étapes (580m)
Pl Chateaubriand
Chaussée du Sillon
Q Duguay Trouin
R du Château Gaillard
R Ste-Barbe
Bassin Duguay-Trouin
Pl des Frères Lammenais
Esplanade St-Vincent
Q St-Vincent
Av Louis Martin
OLD CITY
R de l'Orme
Chaussée des Corsaires
Pl du Guet
R des Cordiers
R Vauborel
R de Toulouse
Bassin Vauban
Bassin Intérieur
R Georges Clemenceau
Bassin Bouvet
Q de Trichet
Ferries to UK
Port de Plaisance (Pleasure Marina)
R Dauphine
Plage des Bas Sablons
R des Bas Sablons
R Georges Clemenceau
Corniche d'Aleth
Pl Mgr Duchesne
Allée Gaston Buy
R de la Cité
R des Hauts Sablons
R Pré Brecel
Anse du Bec
Pl St-Pierre
ST-SERVAN
Q Solidor
Grand Aquarium (1.6km)
Port-Solidor

St-Malo

Sleeping

TOP CHOICE Hôtel Quic en Groigne BOUTIQUE HOTEL €€
(☎02 99 20 22 20; www.quic-en-groigne.com; 8 rue d'Estrées; s €64-72, d €79-102; ⊙closed mid-Nov–Feb; P 🛜) This exceptional hotel has 15 rooms that are the epitome of clean, simple style, and many a hotel twice the price should be envious of this place. If straight-out good value for money weren't enough then consider the staff who could hardly be more accommodating, an ideal location on a quiet old town street just a few metres from a (low-tide only) beach and secure lock-up parking.

Hôtel San Pedro HOTEL €€
(☎02 99 40 88 57; www.sanpedro-hotel.com; 1 rue Ste-Anne; s €58-60, d €69-79; P 🛜) Tucked at the back of the old city, the San Pedro has cool, crisp, neutral-toned decor with subtle splashes of colour, friendly service and superb sea views.

Camping Aleth CAMPGROUND €
(☎06 78 96 10 62; www.camping-aleth.com; allée Gaston Buy, St-Servan; per 2-person tent €14.40; 🛜) Perched on a peninsula, Camping Aleth has panoramic 360-degree views and is close to beaches and some lively bars.

Auberge de Jeunesse Éthic Étapes HOSTEL €
(☎02 99 40 29 80; www.centrevarangot.com; 37 av du Père Umbricht; dm incl breakfast €21; @; 🚌3) This efficient place has a self-catering kitchen and free sports facilities. Take bus 3 from the train station.

Eating

TOP CHOICE Le Bistro de Jean BISTRO €
(☎02 99 40 98 68; 6 rue de la Corne-de-Cerf; mains €15-19, menus from €12; ⊙closed Wed & Sat lunch, all day Sun) Want to know where the locals choose to eat inside the walls? Peer through the windows of this lively and authentic bistro and you'll get your answer.

Le Chalut SEAFOOD €€
(☎02 99 56 71 58; 8 rue de la Corne-du-Cerf; menus €26-70; ⊙Wed-Sun) This unremarkable-looking establishment is, in fact, St-Malo's most celebrated restaurant. Its kitchen overflows with the best the Breton coastline has to offer – buttered turbot, line-caught sea bass and scallops in champagne sauce.

Le Bulot BISTRO €
(☎02 99 81 07 11; www.lebulot.com; 13 quai Sébastopol; menus €10-15, mains €8-14; ⊙closed dinner Sun Oct-May) A laidback neighbourhood bistro with a modern feel and views over the Port-Solidor (best appreciated on sunny days from the restaurant's raised wooden

FANCY UN CAFÉ?

The word 'eccentric' must have been coined to describe the extraordinary and insanely named **La Cafe du Coin d'en Bas de la Rue du Bout de la Ville d'en Face du Port... La Java** (☎02 99 56 41 90; www.lajavacafe.com; 3 rue Sante-Barbe). Think part-museum, part-toyshop and the work of art of an ever-so-slightly-twisted mind. Traditional French accordion music plays in the background and the beady eyes of hundreds of dolls and puppets keep watch from shelves and alcoves in the walls. Customers sit on swings, not chairs, and fake elephant tusks reach down out of the lamp shades. Even the opening times are odd: it opens at 8.31am on the dot during the week and 8.33am on weekends. And the drinks? Ah, well they're actually quite sane – a hundred different kinds of coffee and a quality beer range.

terrace). There's a short menu of delicious fusion dishes at bargain prices and they'll even serve you lunch after 2pm (a rare occurrence in anything other than tourist-class restaurants).

Information

Tourist office (☎€0.15 per min 08 25 13 52 00; www.saint-malo-tourisme.com; esplanade St-Vincent; ⊙9am-7.30pm Mon-Sat, 10am-6pm Sun) Just outside the walls.

Getting There & Away

Brittany Ferries (www.brittany-ferries.com) sails between St-Malo and Portsmouth, UK; **Condor Ferries** (www.condorferries.co.uk) runs to/from Poole via Jersey or Guernsey.

TGV train services include to/from Rennes (€13.60, one hour) and Paris' Gare Montparnasse (€52 to €64, three hours, up to 10 daily).

CHAMPAGNE

Known in Roman times as Campania, meaning 'plain', the agricultural region of Champagne is synonymous these days with its world-famous bubbly. This multimillion-dollar industry is strictly protected under French law, ensuring that only grapes grown in designated Champagne vineyards can truly lay claim to the hallowed title. The town of Épernay, 30km south of the regional capital of Reims, is the best place to head for *dégustation* (tasting), and a self-drive **Champagne Route** wends its way through the region's most celebrated vineyards.

Reims

POP 184,984

Over the course of a millennium (816 to 1825), some 34 sovereigns – among them two dozen kings – began their reigns in Reims' famed cathedral. Meticulously reconstructed after WWI and again following WWII, the city – whose name is pronounced something like 'rance' and is often anglicised as Rheims – is endowed with handsome pedestrian zones, well-tended parks, lively nightlife and a state-of-the-art tramway.

Sights

TOP CHOICE Cathédrale Notre Dame CATHEDRAL
(www.cathedrale-reims.culture.fr; place du Cardinal Luçon; tower adult/child €7.50/free, incl Palais du Tau €11/free; ⊙7.30am-7.30pm, tower tours hourly 10am-5pm Tue-Sat, 2-5pm Sun Apr-Sep) The single most famous event to take place at this Gothic edifice, begun in 1211 and completed 100 years later, was the coronation of Charles VII, with Joan of Arc at his side, on 17 July 1429.

To get the most impressive first view of this Unesco World Heritage Site, approach the cathedral from the west, along rue Libergier. The finest stained-glass windows are the western facade's 12-petalled **great rose window**, its cobalt-blue neighbour below, and the **rose window** in the north transept (to the left as you walk from the entrance to the high altar), above the Flamboyant Gothic **organ case** (15th and 18th centuries). There are **windows by Chagall** (1974; a sign explains each panel) in the central axial chapel (directly behind the high altar) and, two chapels to the left, you'll find a **statue of Joan of Arc** in full body armour (1901).

End by climbing 250 steps up the **cathedral tower** on a one-hour tour. Book at Palais du Tau.

Palais du Tau MUSEUM
(http://palais-tau.monuments-nationaux.fr; 2 place du Cardinal Luçon; adult/child €7.50/free, incl cathedral tower €11/free; ⊙9.30am-6.30pm Tue-Sun) A Unesco World Heritage Site, this former archbishop's residence, constructed in 1690, was where French princes stayed before their coronations – and where they hosted sumptuous banquets afterwards. Now a museum, it displays truly exceptional statuary, liturgical objects and tapestries from the cathedral, some in the impressive Gothic-style **Salle de Tau** (Great Hall).

Basilique St-Rémi BASILICA
(place du Chanoine Ladame; ⊙8am-nightfall, to 7pm summer) This 121m-long former Benedictine abbey church, a Unesco World Heritage Site, mixes Romanesque elements from the mid-11th century (worn but stunning nave and transept) with early Gothic features from the latter half of the 12th century (choir). It is named in honour of Bishop Remigius, who baptised Clovis and 3000 Frankish warriors in 498. The 12th-century-style chandelier has 96 candles, one for each year of the life of St Rémi, whose tomb (in the choir) is marked by a mausoleum from the mid-1600s. The basilica is situated about 1.5km south-southeast of the tourist office; take the Citadine 1 or 2 or bus A or F to the St-Rémi stop.

Tours

The bottle-filled cellars (10°C to 12°C – bring a sweater!) of eight Reims-area champagne houses can be visited by guided tour which ends, *naturellement*, with a tasting session.

The **Reims City Card** (€16), available at the tourist office, entitles you to the champagne-house visit (including tasting) and two audioguide tours of your choice.

Mumm CHAMPAGNE HOUSE
(☎03 26 49 59 70; www.mumm.com; 34 rue du Champ de Mars; tours €11; ⏲tours begin 9am-11am & 2-5pm daily, closed Sun Nov-Feb) The only *maison* in central Reims was founded in 1827 and is now the world's third-largest producer (almost eight million bottles a year). Engaging and edifying one-hour tours take you through cellars filled with 25 million bottles of fine bubbly. Phone ahead if possible.

Taittinger CHAMPAGNE CELLAR
(☎03 26 85 84 33; www.taittinger.com; 9 place St-Niçaise; tours €16; ⏲tours begin 9.30-11.50am & 2pm-4.20pm, closed Sat & Sun Dec–mid-Mar) Parts of the cellars here occupy 4th-century Roman stone quarries; other bits were excavated by 13th-century Benedictine monks. Situated 1.5km southeast of Reims centre; take the Citadine 1 or 2 bus to the St-Niçaise or Salines stops.

Sleeping

TOP CHOICE **Les Telliers** D&D €€
(☎09 53 79 80 74; http://telliers.fr; 18 rue des Telliers; s €76, d €87-110, tr €123, q €142; 📶) Enticingly positioned down a quiet alley near the cathedral, this bijou B&B extends one of Reims' warmest *bienvenues*. The high-ceilinged rooms are big on art-deco character, and are handsomely decorated with ornamental fireplaces, polished oak floors and the odd antique.

La Parenthèse B&B €€€
(☎03 26 40 39 57; www.laparenthese.fr; 83 rue Clovis; min 2-night stay d €170-220; 📶) Tucked away in the backstreets of old Reims, this little B&B has tasteful rooms with wood floors and bursts of pastel colour, all with kitchenettes.

Hôtel de la Paix HOTEL €€€
(☎03 26 40 04 08; www.bestwestern-lapaix-reims.com; 9 rue Buirette; d €170-220; ❄@📶🏊) Outclassing most of Reims' midrange options, this contemporary, Best Western–affiliated hotel is the place to mellow in a pool, jacuzzi, hammam or Zen-like courtyard garden.

Eating

Place Drouet d'Erlon is lined with inexpensive restaurants and pub-cafes. More-discerning diners head to rue de Mars, adjacent to rue du Temple and place du Forum.

TOP CHOICE **Le Foch** GASTRONOMIC €€€
(☎03 26 47 48 22; www.lefoch.com; 37 bd Foch; lunch menus €31, dinner menus €48-80; ⏲lunch Tue-Fri & Sun, dinner Tue-Sat) Michelin-starred Le Foch serves up cuisine as beautiful as it is delicious. Specialities like scallops with Jerusalem artichokes, pistachios and truffle emulsion are expertly paired with wines and presented with panache.

La Table Anna TRADITIONAL FRENCH €€
(☎03 26 89 12 12; 6 rue Gambetta; lunch menus €17, dinner menus €25-42; ⏲lunch Tue-Sun, dinner Tue & Thu-Sun) So what if the decor is chintzy – there is a reason why this bistro is as busy as a beehive: friendly service and a menu packed with well-executed classics. The three-course, €17 lunch is a steal.

Brasserie Le Boulingrin BRASSERIE €€
(☎03 26 40 96 22; www.boulingrin.fr; 48 rue de Mars; menus €18.50-29; ⏲lunch & dinner Mon-Sat) A genuine, old-time brasserie – the decor and zinc bar date back to 1925 – whose ambience and cuisine make it an enduring favourite. September to June, the culinary focus is *fruits de mer* (seafood).

Drinking

Café du Palais CAFE
(www.cafedupalais.fr; 14 place Myron-Herrick; ⏲Tue-Sat) Run by the same family since 1930, this artdeco cafe is *the* place to sip a glass of champagne and see and be seen, at least if you're a *bon bourgeois* or a theatre type.

Information

Tourist office (☎08 92 70 13 51; www.reims-tourisme.com; 2 rue Guillaume de Machault; ⏲9am-7pm Mon-Sat, 10am-6pm Sun & holidays)

Getting There & Away

Direct trains link Reims with Épernay (€6.50, 21 to 50 minutes, seven to 18 daily) and Paris' Gare de l'Est (€26 to €34, 12 to 17 daily), half of which are speedy TGVs (45 minutes).

Épernay

POP 25,000

Prosperous Épernay, 25km south of Reims, is the self-proclaimed *capitale du champagne* and home to many of the world's most celebrated champagne houses. Beneath the town's streets, some 200 million of bottles of champagne are slowly being aged, just waiting around to be popped open for some fizz-fuelled celebration.

Sights & Activities

Many of Épernay's *maisons de champagne* (champagne houses) are based along the handsome and eminently strollable **av de Champagne**. Cellar tours end with a tasting and a visit to the factory-outlet bubbly shop.

Comtesse Lafond CHAMPAGNE HOUSE
(☎03 86 39 18 33; www.deladoucette.net; 79 av de Champagne; 3-glass tasting €9, incl cellar tour €14; ⊙10am-noon & 2-5.30pm daily) The whimsically turreted Comtesse Lafond is the most intimate and charming of the av de Champagne *maisons*. Tastings of three champagnes take place in the elegant salon or in manicured gardens overlooking vine-streaked hills.

Moët & Chandon CHAMPAGNE HOUSE
(☎03 26 51 20 20; www.moet.com; 20 av de Champagne; adult incl 1/2 glasses €16.50/23, 10-18yr €9.50; ⊙tours 9.30am-11.30am & 2-4.30pm, closed Sat & Sun mid-Nov–mid-Mar) Flying the Moët, French, European and Russian flags, this prestigious *maison* offers frequent one-hour tours that are among the region's most impressive. At the shop pick up a 15L bottle of Brut Impérial for €1500; a standard bottle costs €31.

Mercier CHAMPAGNE HOUSE
(☎03 26 51 22 22; www.champagnemercier.fr; 68-70 av de Champagne; adult incl 1/2/3 glasses €11/16/19, 12-17yr €5.50; ⊙tours 9.30-11.30am & 2-4.30pm, closed mid-Dec–mid-Feb) Everything here is flashy, including the 160,000L barrel that took two decades to build (for the Universal Exposition of 1889), the lift that transports you 30m underground, and the laser-guided touring train.

De Castellane CHAMPAGNE HOUSE
(☎03 26 51 19 11; www.castellane.com; 64 av de Champagne; adult incl 1 glass €10, under 12yr free; ⊙tours 10am-noon & 2-6pm, closed Christmas–mid-Mar) The 45-minute tours, in French and English, take in a museum dedicated to elucidating the *méthode champenoise* and its diverse technologies. The reward for climbing the 237 steps up the 66m-high tower (built 1905) is a fine panoramic view.

Sleeping

TOP CHOICE **Le Clos Raymi** HISTORIC HOTEL €€
(☎03 26 51 00 58; www.closraymi-hotel.com; 3 rue Joseph de Venoge; s €115, d €155-175; 📶) Staying here is like being a personal guest of Monsieur Chandon of Champagne fame, who occupied this luxurious townhouse over a century ago. The seven romantic rooms have giant beds, high ceilings and parquet floors. In winter there's often a fire in the cosy art deco living room.

La Villa St-Pierre HOTEL €
(☎03 26 54 40 80; www.villasaintpierre.fr; 14 av Paul Chandon; d €51-61; 📶) In an early-20th-century mansion, this homey place, with 11 simple rooms, retains some of the charm of yesteryear.

Eating & Drinking

La Grillade Gourmande REGIONAL CUISINE €€
(☎03 26 55 44 22; www.lagrilladegourmande.com; 16 rue de Reims; menus €19-55; ⊙lunch & dinner Tue-Sat) This chic, red-walled bistro is an inviting spot to try chargrilled meats and dishes rich in texture and flavour, such as crayfish pan-fried in champagne and lamb cooked in rosemary and honey until meltingly tender.

Chez Max TRADITIONAL FRENCH €€
(☎03 26 55 23 59; www.chez-max.com; 13 av AA Thevenet, Magenta; menus €13.50-38.50; ⊙lunch & dinner Tue-Sun, closed dinner Sun & Wed) No fuss, no frills, just good old-fashioned French cooking and a neighbourly vibe is what you'll get at Chez Max.

C. Comme CHAMPAGNE BAR
(8 rue Gambetta; light meals €7.50-12, 6-glass champagne tasting €33; ⊙10am-8.30pm Sun-Wed, 10am-11pm Thu, 10am-midnight Fri-Sat) The downstairs cellar has a stash of 300 different varieties of champagne; sample them (from €5.50 a glass) in the softly lit bar-bistro upstairs. Accompany your tipple with a tasting plate of regional cheese, charcuterie and *rillettes* (pork pâté).

Information

Tourist Office (☎03 26 53 33 00; www.ot-epernay.fr; 7 av de Champagne; ⊙9.30am-12.30pm & 1.30-7pm Mon-Sat, 11am-4pm Sun & holidays) Has excellent English brochures and maps on cellar visits, walking and cycling

FOODIE TRAILS

No matter whether you're planning to get behind the wheel for a morning, or pedal leisurely through the vineyards for a week, the picture-book **Route des Vins d'Alsace** (Alsace Wine Route) is a must. Swinging 170km from Marlenheim to Thann, the road is like a 'greatest hits' of Alsace, with its pastoral views, welcoming *caves* (cellars) and half-timbered villages. Go to www.alsace-route-des-vins.com to start planning.

Fancy cheese with your wine? Hit **Munster** to taste the pungent, creamy *fromage* first made by Benedictine monks. Munster tourist office (www.la-vallee-de-munster.com) arranges farmstays and dairy tours.

Having polished off the cheese and wine, it would be rude not to pass the chocolates, or gingerbread, or macarons, on the **Route du Chocolat et des Douceurs d'Alsace**. Pick up a map – 200km of sweet-toothed motoring – at Strasbourg tourist office.

options and car touring, and rents out a GPS unit (€7 per day) with self-guided vineyard driving tours in French, English and Dutch.

Getting There & Away

Direct trains link Épernay to Reims (€6.20, 20 to 36 minutes, 11 to 18 daily) and Paris' Gare de l'Est (€21, 1¼ hours, five to 10 daily).

ALSACE & LORRAINE

Alsace is a one-off cultural hybrid. With its Germanic dialect and French sense of fashion, love of foie gras and *choucroute* (sauerkraut), fine wine *and* beer, this distinctive region often leaves you wondering quite where you are. Where are you? In the land of living fairy tales, where vineyards fade into watercolour distance, and hilltop castles mingle with the region's emblematic storks and half-timbered villages.

Lorraine has high culture and effortless grace thanks to its historic roll-call of dukes and art nouveau pioneers, who had an eye for grand designs and good living. Its blessedly underrated cities, cathedrals and art collections leave first-timers spellbound, while its WWI battlefields render visitors speechless.

Strasbourg

POP 276,136

Strasbourg is the perfect overture to all that is idiosyncratic about Alsace – walking a fine tightrope between France and Germany and between a medieval past and a progressive future, it pulls off its act in inimitable Alsatian style.

Tear your gaze away from that mesmerising Gothic cathedral for just a minute and you'll be roaming the old town's twisting alleys lined with crooked half-timbered houses à la Grimm; feasting in cosy *winstubs* (Alsatian taverns) by the canalside in Petite France; and marvelling at how a city that does Christmas markets and gingerbread so well can also be home to the glittering EU Quarter and France's second-largest student population.

Sights

Grande Île HISTORIC QUARTER

(Langstross) History seeps through the twisting lanes and cafe-rimmed plazas of Grande Île, Strasbourg's Unesco World Heritage-listed old town, made for aimless ambling. It cowers beneath the soaring magnificence of the cathedral and its sidekick, the gingerbready 15th-century **Maison Kammerzell**, with its ornate carvings and leaded windows. The lantern-lit alleys are most atmospheric at night, while the half-timbered houses and flowery canals of **Petite France** on the Grande Île's southwestern corner are fairy-tale pretty.

STRASBOURG SAVER

The **Strasbourg Pass** (adult/child €14/7), a coupon book valid for three consecutive days, includes a visit to one museum, access to the cathedral platform, half a day's bicycle rental and a boat tour, plus hefty discounts on other tours.

Admission to all of Strasbourg's museums (www.musees-strasbourg.org), and to the cathedral's platform, is free on the first Sunday of the month.

TOP CHOICE **Cathédrale Notre-Dame** CATHEDRAL
(place de la Cathédrale; astronomical clock adult/child €2/1.50, platform adult/child €5/2.50; 7am-7pm, astronomical clock tickets sold from 11.45am, platform 9am-7.15pm; Langstross) At once immense and intricate, Strasbourg's centrepiece red-sandstone Gothic cathedral is a riot of filigree stonework and flying buttresses, leering gargoyles and lacy spires. The west facade was completed in 1284, but the 142m spire was not in place until 1439. The 30m-high Gothic-meets-Renaissance **astronomical clock** strikes solar noon at 12.30pm with a parade of carved wooden figures portraying the different stages of life and Jesus with his apostles.

A spiral staircase twists up to the 66m-high **platform** above the facade, from which the tower and its Gothic openwork spire soar another 76m.

Musée d'Art Moderne et Contemporain ART MUSEUM
(MAMCS; www.musees.strasbourg.eu; place Hans Jean Arp; adult/child €7/3.5; 10am-6pm Tue-Sun) This striking glass-and-steel cube showcases an outstanding collection of fine art, graphic art and photography. Kandinsky, Picasso, Magritte and Monet canvases hang out alongside curvaceous works by Strasbourg-born abstract artist Hans Jean Arp.

DON'T MISS

WHEN HELL WAS HELL

Hollywood gore seems tame compared with the tortures back when Hell really was hell. Sure to scare you into a life of chastity is *Les Amants Trépassés* (The Deceased Lovers), painted in 1470, showing a grotesque couple being punished for their illicit lust: both of their entrails are being devoured by dragon-headed snakes.

Track it down in Strasbourg's fabulous **Musée de l'Œuvre Notre Dame** (www.musees.strasbourg.org; 3 place du Château; adult/child €6/free; 10am-6pm Tue-Sun, to 8pm Thu; Langstross). Occupying a cluster of sublime 14th- and 16th-century buildings, the world-renowned ecclesiastical museum boasts one of Europe's premier collections of Romanesque, Gothic and Renaissance sculptures, 15th-century paintings, and stained glass.

Palais Rohan HISTORIC RESIDENCE
(2 place du Château; adult/child €6/free; noon-6pm Mon & Wed-Fri, 10am-6pm Sat & Sun; Langstross) Hailed a 'Versailles in miniature', this opulent 18th-century residence was built for the city's princely bishops. The basement **Musée Archéologique** spans the Palaeolithic period to AD 800. The ground floor **Musée des Arts Décoratifs** evokes the lavish lifestyle of 18th-century nobility, and the 1st-floor **Musée des Beaux-Arts** showcases 14th- to 19th-century art.

Tours

FREE **Cave des Hospices de Strasbourg** WINERY
(www.vins-des-hospices-de-strasbourg.fr; 1 place de l'Hôpital; 8.30am-noon & 1.30-5.30pm Mon-Fri, 9am-12.30pm Sat; Porte de l'Hôpital) Founded in 1395, this brick-vaulted wine cellar nestled deep in the bowels of Strasbourg's hospital has first-rate Alsatian wines.

Batorama BOAT TOUR
(www.batorama.fr; rue de Rohan; adult/child €9.20/4.80; tours half-hourly 9.30am-7pm, hourly 8-10pm; Langstross) Scenic 70-minute boat trips along the storybook canals of Petite France.

Brasseries Kronenbourg BREWERY
(03 88 27 41 59; www.brasseries-kronenbourg.com; 68 rte d'Oberhausbergen; adult/child €6/4.50; tours 1.30pm Tue-Sat; Ducs d'Alsace) Brewery tours in Cronenbourg, 2.5km northwest of Strasbourg's Grande Île; reserve in advance.

Festivals & Events

Vin chaud (mulled wine), spicy *bredele* and a Santa-loaded children's village feature in Strasbourg's festive **Marché de Noël** (Christmas Market; www.noel.strasbourg.eu), from the last Saturday in November to 24 December.

Raise a glass to Alsatian beer at October's **Mondial de la Bière** (www.mondialbierestrasbourg.com) or to wine at March's **Riesling du Monde** (www.portail-vins-du-monde.com).

Sleeping

Cour du Corbeau BOUTIQUE HOTEL €€€
(03 90 00 26 26; www.cour-corbeau.com; 6-8 rue des Couples; r €190-330; Porte de l'Hôpital) A 16th-century inn lovingly converted into a boutique hotel, Cour du Corbeau wins you over with its half-timbered charm and location steps from the river.

WORTH A TRIP

KATZENTHAL

Tiptoe off the tourist trail to Alsatian village **Katzenthal** (population 550), 9km west of Colmar and 80km south of Strasbourg. *Grand cru* vines ensnare the hillside, topped by the medieval ruins of Château du Wineck, from where walking trails into forest and vineyard begin.

Then there is the fabulous, family-run **Vignoble Klur** (☎03 89 80 94 29; www.klur.net; 105 rue des Trois Epis; apt €90-150, min 3-night stay), an organic winery and guest house that hosts wine tastings, Alsatian cookery classes and vineyard walks. Make yourself at home in a sunny apartment with kitchenette, read a book by an open fire in the salon, or unwind in the organic sauna. Oh, and don't miss Jean-Louis Frick's hilarious mural of hedonistic wine lovers above the entrance – it has raised a few local eyebrows, apparently.

Hôtel du Dragon HOTEL €€
(☎03 88 35 79 80; www.dragon.fr; 12 rue du Dragon; s €84-159, d €92-159; ; Porte de l'Hôpital) Step through a tree-shaded courtyard and into the blissful calm of this bijou hotel near Petite France.

Hôtel Régent Petite France DESIGN HOTEL €€€
(☎03 88 76 43 43; www.regent-hotels.com; 5 rue des Moulins; r €159-460; ; Alt Winmärik) Ice factory turned Strasbourg's hottest design hotel, this waterfront pile is quaint on the outside, ubercool inside. Work your relaxed look in the sauna, chic restaurant and champagne bar with dreamy River Ill views.

Eating

Appetising restaurants abound on Grande Île: try canalside Petite France for Alsatian fare and half-timbered romance; Grand Rue for curbside kebabs and *tarte flambée;* and rue des Veaux or rue des Pucelles for hole-in-the-wall eateries serving the world on a plate.

Le Gavroche MEDITERRANEAN €€
(☎03 88 36 82 89; www.restaurant-gavroche.com; 4 rue Klein; menu €38; Mon-Fri; ; Porte de l'Hôpital) Bistro food is given a pinch of creativity and southern sunshine at intimate, softly lit Le Gavroche. Mains like veal in a mint crust with crispy polenta and coriander-infused artichoke tagine are followed by zingy desserts like lime tart with lemon-thyme sorbet.

Kobus BISTRO €€
(☎03 88 32 59 71; www.restaurantkobus.com; 7 rue des Tonneliers; lunch/dinner menus €19.50/39.50; Tue-Sat; Langstross) Graphic artworks lend a contemporary feel to this stone-walled bistro with seasonal menu and a great €19.50 lunch deal.

Le Stras' INTERNATIONAL €€
(☎03 88 35 34 46; 9 rue des Dentelles; mains €19-24; Tue-Sat; Langstross) The chef puts an innovative spin on seasonal ingredients at this beamed, gallery-style bistro in Petite France – a terrific choice for an intimate dinner.

Bistrot et Chocolat CAFE €
(www.bistrotetchocolat.net; 8 rue de la Râpe; snacks €5-8, brunch €10-26; 11am-7pm Tue-Fri, 10am-7pm Sat & Sun; ; Langstross) This boho-flavoured bistro is hailed for its solid and liquid organic chocolate (ginger is superb). The terrace is a local hangout for light bites; also good for weekend brunches and children's cooking classes.

Information

Tourist office (☎03 88 52 28 28; www.otstrasbourg.fr; 17 place de la Cathédrale; 9am-7pm) Runs an annexe in the southern wing of Strasbourg train station, 400m west of Grande Île.

Getting There & Away

Air

Strasbourg's international **airport** (www.strasbourg.aeroport.fr) is 17km southwest of the city centre (towards Molsheim).

Ryanair links London Stansted with **Karlsruhe/Baden Baden airport** (www.badenairpark.de), 58km northeast of Strasbourg, across the Rhine in Germany.

Train

European cities with direct services include Basel SNCF (Bâle; €22, 1¼ hours, 25 daily), Brussels-Nord (€74, 5¼ hours, three daily), Karlsruhe (€25, 40 minutes, 16 daily) and Stuttgart (€47, 1¼ hours, four daily). Destinations within France include:

Paris Gare de l'Est €71, 2¼ hours, 19 daily
Lille €115, four hours, 17 daily
Lyon €71, 4½ hours, 14 daily
Marseille €161, 6¾ hours, 16 daily
Metz €24.50, two hours, 20 daily
Nancy €24, 1½ hours, 25 daily

Nancy

POP 108,597

Delightful Nancy has a refined air found nowhere else in Lorraine. With its resplendent central square, fine museums, medieval Old Town, formal gardens and shop windows sparkling with crystal, the former capital of the dukes of Lorraine catapults visitors back to the opulence of the 18th century (when much of the city centre was built).

Sights

TOP CHOICE Place Stanislas CITY SQUARE

Nancy's crowning glory is this neoclassical square, one of France's grandest public spaces and a Unesco World Heritage site. Your gaze will be drawn to an opulent ensemble of pale-stone buildings, gilded wrought-iron gateways and rococo fountains.

Musée de l'École de Nancy ART MUSEUM

(School of Nancy Museum; www.ecole-de-nancy.com; 36-38 rue du Sergent Blandan; adult/child €6/4; ⏲10am-6pm Wed-Sun) This museum brings together art nouveau interiors, curvaceous glass and landscaped gardens, all in a 19th-century villa 2km southwest of the centre; take bus 122 or 123 to the Nancy Thermal or Paul-Painlevé stop.

Musée des Beaux-Arts ART MUSEUM

(http://mban.nancy.fr; 3 place Stanislas; adult/child €6/free; ⏲10am-6pm Wed-Mon) Art nouveau glass creations by celebrated French glass maker Daum, and a rich selection of paintings from the 14th to 21st centuries, are among the star exhibits at this outstanding museum. Caravaggio, Rubens, Picasso and Monet masterpieces hang alongside works by Lorraine-born artists, such as Claude Lorrain's dreamlike baroque landscapes and the pared-down aesthetic of Nancy-born architect and designer Jean Prouvé (1901–1984)

Sleeping

TOP CHOICE Maison de Myon B&B €€

(☎03 83 46 56 56; www.maisondemyon.com; 7 rue Mably; s/d €110/130, apt €150-200; 📶) Slip behind the cathedral to reach this stately 17th-century house with wisteria-draped courtyard (is there a lovelier spot for breakfast?). Martine Quénot makes guests feel instantly at ease in her stylish home: wine tastings in the vaulted cellar, dinner alfresco, cookery classes – just say the word.

Hôtel des Prélats HISTORIC HOTEL €€

(☎03 83 30 20 20; www.hoteldesprelats.com; 56 place Monseigneur Ruch; s €75-95, d €105-115; ❄📶) Sleep in a former 17th-century bishop's palace right next to the cathedral. Service is as polished as the surrounds.

Hôtel de Guise BOUTIQUE HOTEL €€

(☎03 83 32 24 68; www.hoteldeguise.com; 18 rue de Guise; s/d/tr/q €68/80/92/98; 📶) Boutique chic meets 17th-century elegance at this hotel, with walled garden, down an old-town backstreet. Rooms are old-fashioned with antique furnishings, inlaid parquet and heavy drapes.

Eating

Eats street rue des Maréchaux dishes up everything from French to Italian, tapas, seafood, Indian and Japanese. Then there's Grande Rue, peppered with sweet bistros.

La Primatiale INTERNATIONAL €€

(☎03 83 30 44 03; www.la-primatiale.com; 14 rue de la Primatiale; menus €18-28; ⏲lunch Mon-Sat, dinner Mon & Wed-Sat) The food looks as good as it tastes at this upbeat, art-strewn bistro. Clean, bright flavours such as tartar of marinated salmon with dill and star anise and rack of lamb in a herb-olive crust reveal a definite Mediterranean slant.

Le V-Four BISTRO €€

(☎03 83 32 49 48; 10 rue St-Michel; menus €19-50; ⏲lunch & dinner Tue-Sat, lunch Sun) With just a handful of tables, this petit bistro is all about intimacy and understated sophistication. Mulberry chairs and crisp white tablecloths set the scene for original creations like grilled scallops with wasabi cream and tomato confit. Book ahead.

Chez Tanésy – Le Gastrolâtre BISTRO €€

(☎03 83 35 51 94; 23 Grande Rue; menus €27-45; ⏲Tue-Sat) A charmingly faded 16th-century townhouse is home to this cosy bistro with seasonal menu.

Information

Tourist office (☎03 83 35 22 41; www.ot-nancy.fr; place Stanislas; ⏲9am-7pm Mon-Sat, 10am-5pm Sun)

Getting There & Away

From the **train station** (place Thiers), 800m southwest of place Stanislas, destinations include:

Baccarat €10.50, 48 minutes, 15 daily

Metz €10, 38 minutes, 48 daily

DON'T MISS

CENTRE POMPIDOU-METZ

This architecturally innovative **museum** (www.centrepompidou-metz.fr; 1 parvis des Droits de l'Homme; adult/child €7/free; ⏲11am-6pm Mon, Wed & Sun, 11am-8pm Thu, Fri & Sat), dazzling white and sinuous, is the satellite branch of Paris' Centre Pompidou. Its gallery draws on Europe's largest collection of modern art to stage ambitious temporary exhibitions. The dynamic space also hosts top-drawer cultural events.

Paris Gare de l'Est €61, 1½ hours, 11 daily
Strasbourg €24, 1½ hours, 12 daily

Metz

POP 125,024

Straddling the confluence of the Moselle and Seille Rivers, Metz is Lorraine's graceful capital. Its Gothic marvel of a cathedral, Michelin star-studded dining scene, beautiful yellowstone Old Town and regal Quartier Impérial (up for Unesco World Heritage status) are a joy to discover, but nothing can beat the city's show-stopping Centre Pompidou-Metz.

Sights

FREE **Cathédrale St-Étienne** CATHEDRAL
(place St-Étienne; audioguide €7, treasury & crypt adult/child €4/2; ⏲8am-6pm, treasury & crypt 9.30am-12.30pm & 1.30-5.30pm Mon-Sat, 1.30-5.30pm Sun) Exquisitely lit by kaleidoscopic curtains of 13th- to 20th-century stained glass, this cathedral is nicknamed 'God's lantern' and its sense of height and light is indeed spiritually uplifting. Flamboyant **Chagall windows** in startling jewel-coloured shades of ruby, gold, sapphire, topaz and amethyst adorn the ambulatory, which also harbours the **treasury**. The sculpture of the **Graoully** ('*grau*-lee'), a dragon said to have terrified pre-Christian Metz, lurks in the 15th-century **crypt**.

Quartier Impérial HISTORIC QUARTER
The stately boulevards and bourgeois villas of the German Imperial Quarter, including rue Gambetta and av Foch, were the brainchild of Kaiser Wilhelm II. Built to trumpet the triumph of Metz' post-1871 status as part of the Second Reich, the architecture is a whimsical mix of art deco, neo-Romanesque and neo-Renaissance influences. Philippe Starck lamp posts juxtapose Teutonic sculptures, whose common theme is German imperial might, at the monumental Rhenish neo-Romanesque **train station**, completed in 1908.

Sleeping

TOP CHOICE **Hôtel de la Cathédrale** HISTORIC HOTEL €€
(☎03 87 75 00 02; www.hotelcathedrale-metz.fr; 25 place de Chambre; d €75-110; 📶) Expect a friendly welcome at this classy little hotel, occupying a 17th-century townhouse opposite the cathedral. Book well ahead for a cathedral view.

Péniche Alclair HOUSEBOAT €
(☎06 37 67 16 18; www.chambrespenichemetz.com; allée St-Symphorien; r incl breakfast €70; 📶) What a clever idea: this old barge has been revamped into a stylish blue houseboat, with two cheerful wood-floored rooms and watery views. Breakfast is served in your room or on the sundeck. It's a 15-minute stroll south of the centre along the river.

Eating

Metz has scores of appetising restaurants, many along and near the river. Place St-Jacques becomes one giant open-air cafe when the sun's out. Cobbled rue Taison and the arcades of place St-Louis shelter moderately priced bistros, pizzerias and cafes.

GO TO MARKET

If only every market were like Metz' grand **Marché Couvert** (Covered Market; place de la Cathédrale; ⏲8am-5.30pm Tue-Sat). Once a bishop's palace, now a temple to fresh local produce, this is the kind of place where you pop in for a baguette and struggle out an hour later with bags overflowing with charcuterie, ripe fruit and five different sorts of *fromage*.

Make a morning of it, stopping for an early, inexpensive lunch and a chat with the market's larger-than-life characters. **Chez Mauricette** (sandwiches €3-5, antipasti plate €5-7) tempts with Lorraine goodies from herby *saucisson* to local charcuterie and mirabelle pâté. Its neighbour, **Soupes á Soups** (soups €3.20), ladles out homemade soups, from mussel to creamy mushroom varieties.

CHÂTEAUX TOURS

Hard-core indie travellers might balk at the idea of a tour, but don't dismiss them out of hand, especially if you don't have your own transport.

Shuttlebus & Minibus

April to August, Blois tourist office and TLC offer a twice-daily shuttle (€6) from Blois to the chateaux at Chambord, Cheverny and Beauregard.

Many private companies offer a choice of well-organised itineraries, taking in various combinations of Azay-le-Rideau, Villandry, Cheverny, Chambord and Chenonceau (plus wine-tasting tours). Half-day trips cost between €20 and €35; full-day trips range from €45 to €52. Entry to the chateaux isn't included, although you'll likely get a discount on tickets. Reserve via the tourist offices in Tours or Amboise, from where most tours depart.

Bicycle

The Loire Valley is mostly flat – it's excellent cycling country. **Loire à Vélo** (www.loireavelo.fr) maintains 800km of signposted routes. Pick up a guide from tourist offices, or download route maps, audioguides and bike-hire details online.

Détours de Loire (☎02 47 61 22 23; www.locationdevelos.com) has bike-rental shops in Tours and Blois and can deliver bikes; they also allow you to collect/return bikes along the route for a small surcharge. Classic bikes cost €14/59 per day/week; tandems €45 per day.

Les Châteaux à Vélo (☎in Blois 02 54 78 62 52; www.chateauxavelo.com; per day €12-14) has a bike-rental circuit between Blois, Chambord and Cheverny, 300km of marked trails and can shuttle you by minibus. Free route maps and MP3 guides online.

Something Different

Alain Caillemer (☎02 47 95 87 59; dcaillemer@rand.com; half-day tour per couple €75) Personalised vineyard and tasting tours with a bilingual (French-English) guide near his native Chinon.

Cheval et Châteaux (www.cheval-et-chateaux.com; multiday tour per person €1062-2124) Four- to seven-day horseback excursions combining visits to several of the Loire's best known chateaux with overnights in castle-based B&Bs. Rates include gourmet meals, wine, B&B accommodation, horses, gear and guide.

Art Montgolfières (☎02 54 32 08 11; www.art-montgolfieres.fr; solo/duo €205/390) The Loire Valley by hot-air balloon: one hour in the air, two hours preparing the balloon, dismantling it and drinking a celebratory glass of champagne.

Le Bistro des Sommeliers BISTRO €€
(☎03 87 63 40 20; 10 rue Pasteur; mains €16-20; ⊙closed Sat lunch, Sun) This no-nonsense bistro near the station prides itself on its warm ambiance and consistently good French cooking. *Entrecôtes* (rib-eye steaks) are succulent, *frites* (chips) crisp, salads well dressed and wines perfectly matched to mains. The three-course *prix fixe* menu is a bargain at €15.

Restaurant Thierry FUSION €€
(☎03 87 74 01 23; www.restaurant-thierry.fr; 5 rue des Piques; menus €19.50-36.50; ⊙closed Wed & Sun) Combining the historic backdrop of a 16th-century townhouse with the subtly spiced cuisine, lighting and bohemian flair of Morocco, this is one of Metz' most coveted tables.

Information

Tourist office (☎03 87 55 53 76; http://tourisme.mairie-metz.fr; 2 place d'Armes; ⊙9am-7pm Mon-Sat, 10am-5pm Sun)

Getting There & Away

Train it from Metz' ornate early-20th-century **train station** (pl du Général de Gaulle) to Paris' Gare de l'Est (€61, 80 minutes, 13 daily), Nancy (€10, 37 minutes, 48 daily) and Strasbourg (€24.50, 1¾ hours, 14 daily).

THE LOIRE VALLEY

One step removed from the French capital, the Loire was historically the place where princes, dukes and notable nobles established their country getaways, and the countryside is littered with some of the most extravagant architecture outside Versailles. From sky-topping turrets and glittering banquet halls to slate-crowned cupolas and crenellated towers, the hundreds of chateaux dotted along this valley, a Unesco World Heritage site, comprise 1000 years of astonishingly rich architectural and artistic treasures.

Blois

POP 40,057

Blois' historic chateau was the feudal seat of the powerful counts of Blois, and its grand halls, spiral staircases and sweeping courtyards provide a whistlestop tour through the key periods of French architecture. Sadly for chocoholics, the town's historic chocolate factory, Poulain, is off-limits to visitors.

Sights

Blois' old city, heavily damaged by German attacks in 1940, retains its steep, twisting medieval streets.

Château Royal de Blois CHATEAU
(www.chateaudeblois.fr; place du Château; adult/child €9.50/4; 9am-6.30pm Apr-Sep, reduced hours rest of year) Blois' Royal Chateau makes an excellent introduction to the chateaux of the Loire Valley, with elements of Gothic (13th century), Flamboyant Gothic (1498–1503), early Renaissance (1515–24) and classical (1630s) architecture in its four grand wings.

Maison de la Magie MUSEUM
(www.maisondelamagie.fr; 1 place du Château; adult/child €8/5; 10am-12.30pm & 2-6.30pm Apr-Aug, 2-6.30pm Sep) Opposite Blois chateau is the former home of watchmaker, inventor and conjurer Jean Eugène Robert-Houdin (1805–71), after whom the great American magician Harry Houdini is named. Dragons emerge roaring from the windows on the hour, and the museum hosts magic shows and optical trickery.

Sleeping

TOP CHOICE **La Maison de Thomas** B&B €€
(02 54 46 12 10; www.lamaisondethomas.fr; 12 rue Beauvoir; s/d €75/85) Four spacious rooms and a friendly welcome await travelers at this homey bed and breakfast on a pedestrianised street. There's a wine cellar where you can sample local vintages.

Côté Loire HOTEL €
(02 54 78 07 86; www.coteloire.com; 2 place de la Grève; d €57-89;) If it's charm and colours you want, head for the "Loire Coast". Its rooms come in cheery checks, bright pastels and the odd bit of exposed brick.

Hôtel Anne de Bretagne HOTEL €
(02 54 78 05 38; www.hotelannedebretagne.com; 31 av du Dr Jean Laigret; s €45-54, d €56-80;) This creeper-covered hotel has friendly staff and a bar full of polished wood and vintage pictures. Modern rooms are finished in flowery wallpaper and stripy bedspreads.

Eating

L'Orangerie GASTRONOMIC €€€
(02 54 78 05 36; www.orangerie-du-chateau.fr; 1 av du Dr Jean Laigret; menus €35-80; lunch & dinner Tue-Sat) This acclaimed eatery is cloud nine for connoisseurs of haute cuisine. Plates are artfully stacked and the sparkling *salon* would make Louis XIV envious. On summer nights, dine in the courtyard.

Les Banquettes Rouges FRENCH €€
(02 54 78 74 92; www.lesbanquettesrouges.com; 16 rue des Trois Marchands; menus €17-32; lunch & dinner Tue-Sat) Handwritten slate menus and wholesome food, think rabbit with marmalade, duck with lentils and salmon with apple vinaigrette, all done with a spicy twist, distinguish the 'Red Benches'.

Le Castelet FRENCH €€
(02 54 74 66 09; 40 rue St-Lubin; lunch menu incl wine €18, dinner menus €19-34; lunch & dinner, closed Wed & Sun;) This country restaurant emphasises seasonal ingredients and hearty traditional dishes such as *fondant de porc au cidre* (pork stewed in cider, accompanied by baked apples and potatoes au gratin).

Information

Tourist office (02 54 90 41 41; www.bloischambord.com; 23 place du Château; 9am-7pm)

Getting There & Away

BUS TLC operates buses from Blois' train station (€2) to Chambord (Line 3; 25 to 40 minutes, two Monday to Saturday) and Cheverny (Line 4; 45 minutes, six to eight Monday to Friday, two Saturday, one Sunday).

DON'T MISS

DOMAINE NATIONAL DE CHAMBORD

Chambord is not just about its chateau: **Domaine National de Chambord**, the vast hunting reserve ensnaring it, is a must-explore. While most of its 54 sq km is reserved strictly for high-ranking French government officials (hard to imagine the French president astride a galloping stallion), 10 sq km of its **walking**, **cycling** and **equestrian trails** are open to anyone.

A real highlight is **wildlife-spotting**, especially in September and October during the rutting season, when you can watch stags, boars and red deer woo and mate. Observation towers dot the park; set out at dawn or dusk to spot.

Or pedal around: hire bikes at the **rental kiosk** (☎02 54 33 37 54; per hr/half-/full day €7/11/15; ⊙Apr-Oct) near the jetty on the Cosson River (where you can also rent boats). **Guided bike tours** (adult/child €10/6 plus bike hire) depart mid-August to September. Alternatively, join a **Land Rover Safari** (☎02 54 50 50 06; adult/child €20/12; ⊙Apr-Sep).

TRAIN The train station is 600m uphill from the chateau, on av Jean Laigret.

Amboise €6.60, 20 minutes, 10 daily
Orléans €10.50, 45 minutes, hourly
Paris Gares d'Austerlitz and **Montparnasse** from €26.70, 1½ to two hours, 26 daily
Tours €10.20, 40 minutes, 13 daily

Around Blois

CHÂTEAU DE CHAMBORD

For full-blown chateau splendour, you can't top **Chambord** (☎02 54 50 40 00; www.chambord.org; adult/child €11/free, parking €4; ⊙9am-6pm Apr–Sep, 10am-5pm Oct-Mar), constructed from 1519 by François I as a lavish base for hunting game in the Sologne forests, but eventually used for just 42 days during the king's 32-year reign (1515–47).

The chateau's most famous feature is its **double-helix staircase**, attributed by some to Leonardo da Vinci, who lived in Amboise (34km southwest) from 1516 until his death three years later. The Italianate **rooftop terrace**, surrounded by cupolas, domes, chimneys and slate roofs, was where the royal court assembled to watch military exercises and hunting parties returning at the end of the day.

Several times daily there are 1½-hour **guided tours** (€4) in English, and during school holidays **costumed tours** entertain kids.

Chambord is 16km east of Blois, 45km southwest of Orléans and 17km northeast of Cheverny.

CHÂTEAU DE CHEVERNY

Thought by many to be the most perfectly proportioned chateau of all, **Cheverny** (☎02 54 79 96 29; www.chateau-cheverny.fr; adult/child €8.70/5.70; ⊙9.15am-6.45pm Jul & Aug, 9.15am-6.15pm Apr-Jun & Sep, 9.45am-5.30pm Oct, 9.45am-5pm Nov-Mar) represents the zenith of French classical architecture, the perfect blend of symmetry, geometry and aesthetic order. It has hardly been altered since its construction between 1625 and 1634. Inside is a formal dining room, bridal chamber and children's playroom (complete with Napoléon III–era toys), as well as a guards' room full of pikestaffs, claymores and suits of armour.

Near the chateau's gateway, the kennels house pedigreed French pointer/English foxhound hunting dogs still used by the owners of Cheverny; feeding time is the **Soupe des Chiens** (⊙5pm Apr-Sep, 3pm Oct-Mar).

Behind the chateau is the 18th-century **Orangerie**, where many priceless art works (including the Mona Lisa) were stashed during WWII. Hergé used the castle as a model for Moulinsart (Marlinspike) Hall, the ancestral home of Tintin's sidekick, Captain Haddock. **Les Secrets de Moulinsart** (combined ticket with chateau adult/child €13.20/9.10) explores the Tintin connections.

STAYING OVER

Just 2km south of Cheverny amid grassland, 19th-century farmhouse **La Levraudière** (☎02 54 79 81 99; www.lalevraudiere.fr; 1 chemin de la Levraudière; s €62, d €66-69, tr €85-90) is a perfect blend of tradition and modernity. Breakfast is around a slablike wooden table laden with fabulous homemade jams, while rooms are all about crisp linens and meticulous presentation.

Cheverny is 16km southeast of Blois and 17km southwest of Chambord. For buses to/from Blois see p359.

CHÂTEAU DE CHAUMONT

Set on a defensible bluff behind the Loire, **Chaumont-sur-Loire** (www.domaine-chaumont.fr; adult/child €10/6, with gardens €15.50/11; ⌚10am-6.30pm Apr-Sep, to 5 or 6pm Oct-Mar) presents a resolutely medieval face, with its cylindrical corner turrets and sturdy drawbridge. The castle became a short-lived residence for Catherine de Medici following the death of Henry II in 1560, and later passed into the hands of Diane de Poitiers (Henry II's mistress). A collection of vintage carriages is displayed inside the truly sumptuous **écuries** (stables), built in 1877.

Chaumont's gorgeous English-style gardens are finest during the annual **Festival International des Jardins** (International Garden Festival; adult/child €11/7.50; ⌚9.30am-sunset late Apr–mid-Oct). The chateau is 17km southwest of Blois and 20km northeast of Amboise. Onzain, a 2.5km walk from Chaumont across the Loire, has trains to Blois (€3.40, 10 minutes, 13 daily) and Tours (€8, 30 minutes, 10 daily).

Tours

POP 138,590

Hovering somewhere between the style of Paris and the conservative sturdiness of central France, Tours is a key staging post for exploring chateaux country. It's a smart, vivacious kind of town, filled with wide 18th-century boulevards, parks and imposing public buildings, as well as a busy university of some 25,000 students.

Sights

Musée des Beaux-Arts MUSEUM

(18 place François Sicard; adult/child €4/2; ⌚9am-12.45pm & 2-6pm Wed-Mon) Arranged around the courtyard of the archbishop's gorgeous palace, this fine-arts museum flaunts grand rooms with works spanning several centuries, including paintings by Delacroix, Degas and Monet, as well as a rare Rembrandt miniature and a Rubens *Madonna and Child*.

Cathédrale St-Gatien CHURCH

(place de la Cathédrale; ⌚9am-7pm) With its twin towers, flying buttresses, stained glass and gargoyles, this cathedral is a showstopper. The interior dates from the 13th to 16th centuries, and the domed tops of the two 70m-high towers are Renaissance.

Musée du Compagnonnage MUSEUM

(www.museecompagnonnage.fr; 8 rue Nationale; adult/child €5.30/3.50; ⌚9am-12.30pm & 2-6pm, closed Tue mid-Sep–mid-Jun) France has long prided itself on its *compagnonnages*, guild organisations of skilled labourers who have been responsible for everything from medieval cathedrals to the Statue of Liberty. Dozens of professions – from pastry chefs to locksmiths – are celebrated here through displays of their handiwork.

Sleeping

Hôtel Ronsard BOUTIQUE HOTEL €

(☎02 47 05 25 36; www.hotel-ronsard.com; 2 rue Pimbert; s €58-72, d €66-78; ❄@📶) This recently renovated hotel offers comfort and good value. Halls are lined with colourful photographs, while the sleek, modern and immaculate rooms incorporate muted tones of grey with sparkling white linens.

Hôtel Colbert HOTEL €

(☎02 47 66 61 56; www.tours-hotel-colbert.fr; 78 rue Colbert; s €37-54, d €45-61; 📶) In the heart of Tours' pedestrianised restaurant row, this newly remodeled, family-run hotel offers a welcoming haven amid the surrounding street life.

Hôtel Val de Loire HOTEL €

(☎02 47 05 37 86; www.hotelvaldeloire.fr; 33 bd Heurteloup; s €45-58, d €55-78; 📶) A prime location near the train station, friendly management and bright remodeled rooms make this an excellent midtown choice. Period features are nicely complemented by modern touches including new showers, double glazing and sound-dampening doors. The nicer back rooms downstairs have high ceilings and pleasant garden views, while the less expensive top-floor rooms are tucked under the eaves.

Auberge de Jeunesse du Vieux Tours HOSTEL €

(☎02 47 37 81 58; www.fuaj.org/Tours; 5 rue Bretonneau; s/tw/tr incl breakfast €23/46/69; ⌚reception 8am-noon & 5-11pm; @📶) This friendly, bustling HI hostel attracts a large foreign-student and young-worker contingent. Most rooms have only one to three beds; all share communal bathrooms, small kitchens and lounges. Bike rental.

WORTH A TRIP

TOP THREE CHATEAUX TRIPS

From Tours, a trio of drop-dead gorgeous castles beg to be devoured:

Château de Chenonceau (☎02 47 23 90 07; www.chenonceau.com; adult/child €11/8.50, with audioguide €15/12; ⏰9am-7pm Apr-Sep, reduced hours rest of year) This 16th-century castle is one of the Loire's most architecturally attractive. Framed by a glassy moat and sweeping gardens, and topped by turrets and towers, it's straight out of a fairy tale. Don't miss the yew-tree labyrinth and the 60m-long Grande Gallerie spanning the Cher River.

Château d'Azay-le-Rideau (☎02 47 45 42 04; azay-le-rideau.monuments-nationaux.fr/en; adult/child €8.50/free; ⏰9.30am-6pm Apr-Sep, to 7pm Jul & Aug, 10am-5.15pm Oct-Mar) Built in the 1500s on an island in the Indre River, this romantic, moat-ringed wonder flouts geometric windows, ordered turrets and decorative stonework. Don't miss: its loggia staircase and summertime **Promenade Nocturne** (adult/child €5/free).

Château de Villandry (☎02 47 50 02 09; www.chateauvillandry.com; château & gardens adult/child €9.50/5.50, gardens only €6.50/4; ⏰9am-6pm Apr-Oct, earlier rest of year, closed mid-Nov–Dec) One of the last major Renaissance chateaux to be built in the Loire, this one is famous for its gardens, which are nothing short of glorious. Don't miss the Jardin d'Ornament depicting fickle, passionate, tender and tragic love.

Eating

In the old city, place Plumereau, rue du Grand Marché and rue de la Rôtisserie are crammed with cheap eats (quality variable).

TOP CHOICE Cap Sud BISTRO €€
(☎02 47 05 24 81; capsudrestaurant.fr; 88 rue Colbert; lunch menus €15.50-19, dinner menus €24-36; ⏰lunch & dinner Tue-Sat) The hot-mod red interior combines nicely with genial service and refined culinary creations made from the freshest ingredients. Expect stylishly presented dishes such as warm St-Maure cheese with a pistachio-herb crumble and baby vegetables, or mullet fillet with sweet peppers, squid risotto and a ginger-tomato emulsion. Reserve in advance.

Tartines & Co BISTRO €
(6 rue des Fusillés; sandwiches €9-13; ⏰lunch Mon-Sat, dinner Wed-Fri) This snazzy little bistro reinvents the *croque* (toasted sandwich) amidst jazz and friendly chatter. Choose your topping (chicken, roasted veg, beef carpaccio, foie gras with artichokes and honey vinaigrette) and it's served up quick-as-a-flash on toasted artisanal bread.

L'Atelier Gourmand BISTRO €€
(☎02 47 38 59 87; www.lateliergourmand.fr; 37 rue Étienne Marcel; lunch/dinner menus €12/23; ⏰lunch Tue-Fri, dinner Mon-Sat) Another foodie address, but bring dark glasses: the puce-and-silver colour scheme is straight out of a Brett Easton Ellis novel. Everything's delivered with a modern spin, and many dishes feature intriguing blends of the sweet and savory.

Le Zinc FRENCH €€
(☎02 47 20 29 00; 27 place du Grand Marché; menus €19.50-24.50; ⏰lunch Tue & Thu-Sat, dinner Thu-Tue) More concerned with market-fresh staples sourced from the nearby Les Halles than with Michelin stars or haute cuisine cachet, this bistro impresses with authentic, attractive country classics.

Information

Tourist office (☎02 47 70 37 37; www.tours-tourisme.fr; 78-82 rue Bernard Palissy; ⏰8.30am-7pm Mon-Sat, 10am-12.30pm & 2.30-5pm Sun) Sells chateau tickets at a slight reduction.

Getting There & Away

AIR Tours-Val de Loire Airport (www.tours.aeroport.fr), 5km northeast, is linked to London's Stansted, Manchester, Dublin, Marseille; Porto by Ryanair; and Southampton by Flybe.

BUS Touraine Fil Vert (☎02 47 31 14 00; www.tourainefilvert.com; single ticket €1.80) line C links Tours bus station, next to the train station, with Amboise (40 minutes, 10 daily Monday to Saturday) and Chenonceaux (1¼ hours, one daily).

TRAIN Tours' central train station is linked to TGV station St-Pierre-des-Corps, 4km east, by frequent shuttle trains.

Amboise €5.20, 20 minutes, 13 daily

Blois €10.20, 40 minutes, 13 daily

Chenonceau €6.40, 25 minutes, eight daily
Paris Gare d'Austerlitz €32.90, two to 2¾ hours, five daily (slow trains)
Paris Gare Montparnasse €44 to €82, 1¼ hours, eight daily (high-speed TGVs)
Saumur €11.20, 45 minutes, hourly
Bordeaux €50, 2¾ hours, at least hourly
Nantes €29, 1½ hours, at least hourly

Amboise

POP 12,860

The childhood home of Charles VIII and final resting place of Leonardo da Vinci, elegant Amboise, 23km northeast of Tours, is pleasantly perched along the southern bank of the Loire and overlooked by its fortified chateau. With some seriously posh hotels and a wonderful weekend market, Amboise is a very popular base for exploring nearby chateaux; coach tours arrive en masse to visit da Vinci's Clos Lucé.

Sights

Château Royal d'Amboise CASTLE
(www.chateau-amboise.com; place Michel Debré; adult/child €10.20/7, with audioguide €14.20/10; 9am-6pm Apr-Oct, earlier closing Nov-Mar) Sprawling across a rocky escarpment above town, this castle served as a weekend getaway from the official royal seat at nearby Blois. Charles VIII (r 1483–98), born and bred here, was responsible for the chateau's Italianate remodelling in 1492.

TOP CHOICE **Le Clos Lucé** HISTORIC BUILDING
(www.vinci-closluce.com; 2 rue du Clos Lucé; adult/child €13.50/8.50; 9am-7pm Feb-Oct, 10am-6pm Nov-Jan;) Leonardo da Vinci took up residence at this grand manor house in 1516 on the invitation of François I, who was greatly enamoured of the Italian Renaissance. Already 64 by the time he arrived, da Vinci spent his time sketching, tinkering and dreaming up new contraptions, scale models of which are now abundantly displayed throughout the home and its expansive gardens.

Pagode de Chanteloup HISTORIC SITE
(www.pagode-chanteloup.com; adult/child €8.90/6.90; 10am-7pm May-Sep, reduced hours Oct-Apr) Two kilometres south of Amboise, this curiosity was built between 1775 and 1778 when the odd blend of classical French architecture and Chinese motifs were all the rage. Clamber to the top for glorious views. In summer, picnic hampers (€6.50 to €26) are sold, you can rent rowing boats, and play free outdoor games.

Sleeping

Le Clos d'Amboise HISTORIC HOTEL €€€
(02 47 30 10 20; www.leclosamboise.com; 27 rue Rabelais; r €110-180, ste €210-310;) Backed by a grassy lawn with 200-year-old trees and heated pool, this posh pad is country living in the heart of town.

Villa Mary B&B €€
(02 47 23 03 31; www.villa-mary.fr; 14 rue de la Concorde; d €90-120, apt per week €1180) Sandwiched between the river and chateau, this spacious 18th-century townhouse includes four lovingly restored, old-fashioned rooms plus a 200-square-metre top-floor apartment. The owner, a former economics professor and inveterate world traveller with a passion for history, lives onsite.

Centre Charles Péguy-Auberge de Jeunesse HOSTEL €
(02 47 30 60 90; www.mjcamboise.fr; Île d'Or; per person incl breakfast €19; @) Efficient 72-bed boarding-school-style hostel on Île d'Or, an island in the middle of the Loire. Private rooms cost the same as dorms, making it an excellent budget option for solo travelers.

Hôtel Le Blason HOTEL €
(02 47 23 22 41; www.leblason.fr; 11 place Richelieu; s €50, d €53-63, q €83; @) Quirky, creaky budget hotel on a quiet square with 25 higgledy-piggledy rooms, wedged in around corridors: most are titchy, flowery

WORTH A TRIP

LUNCH IN THE COUNTRY

Renowned far and wide for its cosy atmosphere and superb food, country inn **Auberge de Launay** (02 47 30 16 82; www.aubergedelaunay.com; Le Haut Chantier, Limeray; menus €19.50-38; lunch Tue-Fri, dinner Mon-Sat), 8km east of Amboise, merits the detour for anyone with their own wheels. Herbs and vegetables from the garden out back find their way into classic French meat, fish and poultry dishes, accompanied by a superb wine list and finished off with a divine artisanal cheese platter or desserts like wine-poached pears and homemade macarons.

and timber-beamed. Upstairs units under the eaves come with airconditioning.

Eating

La Fourchette FRENCH €€
(☎06 11 78 16 98; 9 rue Malebranche; lunch/dinner menus €15/24; ⊙lunch Tue-Sat, dinner Fri & Sat) Tucked into a back alley behind the tourist office, this is Amboise's favourite address for straightforward home cooking. Chef Christine makes you feel like you've been invited to her house with daily specials like *travers de porc* (spare ribs), *poulet rôti* (roast chicken) and *blanquette de veau* (veal stew).

Chez Bruno REGIONAL CUISINE €€
(☎02 47 57 73 49; place Michel Debré; menus from €15; ⊙lunch & dinner Tue-Sat) Uncork a host of local vintages in a coolly contemporary setting, accompanied by honest, inexpensive regional cooking. If you're after Loire Valley wine tips, this is the place.

Bigot PATISSERIE €
(www.bigot-amboise.com; place du Château; ⊙noon-7.30pm Mon, 9am-7.30pm Tue-Fri, 8.30am-7.30pm Sat & Sun) Since 1913 this cake and chocolate shop has been whipping up some of the Loire's creamiest cakes and gooiest treats.

Information

Tourist office (☎02 47 57 09 28; www.amboise-valdeloire.com; ⊙9.30am-6pm Mon-Sat, 10am-1pm & 2-5pm Sun) In a riverside building opposite 7 quai du Général de Gaulle.

Getting There & Around

From the **train station** (bd Gambetta), 1.5km north of the chateau on the opposite side of the Loire, local trains run at least hourly to **Tours** (€5.20, 20 minutes) and **Blois** (€6.60, 20 minutes). Four daily express trains also serve **Paris Gare d'Austerlitz** (€30.10, 1¾ hours).

BURGUNDY & THE RHÔNE VALLEY

If there's one place in France where you're really going to find out what makes the nation tick, it's Burgundy. Two of the country's enduring passions – food and wine – come together in this gorgeously rural region, and if you're a sucker for hearty food and the fruits of the vine, you'll be in seventh heaven.

WORTH A TRIP

MUSEOPARC ALÉSIA

Opened in 2012, the sensational **MuseoParc Alésia** (www.alesia.fr; 1 rte des Trois Ormeaux, Alise-Ste-Reine; ⊙9am-9pm Jul-Aug, 9am-6pm Apr-Jun & Sep, 10am-5pm Oct-Dec & Feb-Mar, closed Jan), near the village of Alise-Ste-Reine in the Pays d'Auxois, is well worth the drive from Dijon (67km). This was the site of what was once Alésia, the camp where Vercingétorix, the chief of the Gaulish coalitions, was defeated by Julius Caesar after a long siege. The defeat marked the end of the Gallic/Celtic heritage in France. You can visit the well-organised interpretative centre as well as the vestiges of the Gallo-Roman city that developed after the battle. Entertaining workshops for kids.

Dijon

POP 250,000

Dijon is one of France's most appealing cities. Filled with elegant medieval and Renaissance buildings, dashing Dijon is Burgundy's capital, and spiritual home of French mustard. Its lively Old Town is wonderful for strolling, especially if you like to leaven your cultural enrichment with excellent food, fine wine and shopping.

Sights & Activities

Palais des Ducs et des États de Bourgogne PALACE
(Palace of the Dukes & States of Burgundy; place de la Libération) Once home to Burgundy's powerful dukes, this monumental palace with neoclassical facade overlooks **place de la Libération**, Old Dijon's magnificent central square dating from 1686. The palace's eastern wing houses the outstanding **Musée des Beaux-Arts**, whose entrance is next to the **Tour de Bar**, a squat 14th-century tower that once served as a prison.

Just off the **Cour d'Honneur**, the 46m-high, mid-15th-century **Tour Philippe le Bon** (adult/child €2.30/free; ⊙guided tours every 45min 9am-noon & 1.45-5.30pm late Nov–Easter, 1.30-3.30pm Wed, 9am-3.30pm Sat-Sun late Nov–Easter) affords fantastic views over the city. Spot Mont Blanc on a clear day.

Église Notre Dame CHURCH

(place Notre-Dame) A block north of the Palais des Ducs, this church was built between 1220 and 1240. Its extraordinary facade's three tiers are lined with leering gargoyles separated by two rows of pencil-thin columns. Atop the church, the 14th-century **Horloge à Jacquemart**, transported from Flanders in 1383 by Philip the Bold who claimed it as a trophy of war, chimes every quarter-hour.

Around the north side of the church, **Rue de la Chouette** is named after the small stone *chouette* (owl) carved into the exterior corner of the chapel, diagonally across from No 24. Said to grant happiness and wisdom to those who stroke it, it has been worn smooth by generations of fortune-seekers.

Cathédrale St-Bénigne CHURCH

(place St-Philibert) Built over the tomb of St Benignus (believed to have brought Christianity to Burgundy in the 2nd century), Dijon's Burgundian Gothic-style cathedral was built around 1300 as an abbey church.

FREE **Musée de la Vie Bourguignonne** MUSEUM

(☎03 80 48 80 90; 17 rue Ste-Anne; ⏱9am-noon & 2-6pm Wed-Mon) Housed in a 17th-century Cistercian convent, this museum explores village and town life in Burgundy in centuries past with evocative tableaux illustrating dress and traditional crafts. On the first floor, a whole street has been re-created.

Sleeping

Hôtel Le Jacquemart HOTEL €

(☎03 80 60 09 60; www.hotel-lejacquemart.fr; 32 rue Verrerie; s €52-58, d €60-70; [wi-fi]) In the heart of old Dijon, this two-star hotel is one of our favourite nests in town, with tidy, comfortable rooms and friendly staff. All the rooms are different; the best ones (Nos 5 and 6) are in a 17th-century annex just across the street; they're larger and better equipped than those within the hotel's original core, and combine vintage touches (stone walls, beamed ceiling) and modern conveniences.

Hôtel Le Sauvage HOTEL €

(☎03 80 41 31 21; www.hotellesauvage.com; 64 rue Monge; s €48-59, d €53-64, tr €85; [P][wi-fi]) Set in a 15th-century *relais de poste* (coaching inn) that ranges around a cobbled, vine-shaded courtyard, this little hotel is definitely good value. Rooms 10, 12, 14 and 17, with exposed beams, are the cosiest. It's in a lively area but the hotel is pleasingly quiet. Parking €5.

Hôtel Le Chambellan HOTEL €

(☎03 80 67 12 67; www.hotel-chambellan.com; 92 rue Vannerie; s/d/tr/q €48/53/68/72, s/d with shared bathroom €35/38; [wi-fi]) Built in 1730, this Old Town address has a vaguely medieval feel. Rooms come in cheerful tones of red, orange, pink and white; some have courtyard views.

Ethic Étapes Dijon HOSTEL €

(Centre De Recontres et de Séjour Internationales, CRISD; ☎03 80 72 95 20; www.cri-dijon.com; 1 av Champollion; dm/s/d incl breakfast €21/40/52; [P][@][wi-fi]) This institutional but friendly, 219-bed hostel, 2.5km northeast of the centre, has modern, two- to six-bed rooms with private bathrooms. Take bus line 3 to the Dallas CRI stop.

A ROOM WITH A VINE VIEW

For those with their own wheels, two or four, beautiful stone-laced vintner villages around Dijon and Beaune hide some of Burgundy's most sought-after sleeping addresses:

Villa Louise Hôtel (☎03 80 26 46 70; www.hotel-villa-louise.fr; 9 rue Franche, Aloxe-Corton; d €100-195; [P][@][wi-fi][pool]) Who needs city life when you can stow away in vineyard-side luxury? This tranquil mansion on the Côte de Beaune houses dreamy rooms, an expansive garden, sauna, pool and wine cellar.

Domaine Corgette (☎03 80 21 68 08; www.domainecorgette.com; rue de la Perrière, St-Romain; d €85-110; [P][wi-fi]) The sun-drenched terrace at this village winery faces dramatic cliffs. Rooms are light and airy with crisp linens, fireplaces and wooden floors.

Maison des Abeilles (☎03 80 62 95 42; www.chambres-beaune.fr; Magny-lès-Villers; d €63-68, q €112; [wi-fi]) Sweet and jolly Jocelyne maintains this impeccably clean *chambre d'hôte* (B&B) with flowery garden in a village off the Route des Grands Crus. Breakfast is a homemade feast.

MAD ABOUT MUSTARD

If there is one pilgrimage to be made in Dijon it is to **Moutarde Maille** (☎03 80 30 41 02; www.maille.com; 32 rue de la Liberté; ⏰10am-7pm Mon-Sat), the factory boutique of the company that makes Dijon's most famous mustard. The tangy odours of the sharp sauce assault your nostrils instantly upon entering and there are 36 different kinds to buy, including cassis-, truffle- or celery-flavoured; sample three on tap.

Or head to **Moutarderie Fallot** (Mustard Mill; www.fallot.com; 31 rue du Faubourg Bretonnière; adult/child €10/8; ⏰tours 10am & 11.30am Mon-Sat, also afternoons summer, closed Nov-Mar 15) in neighbouring **Beaune** where Burgundy's last family-run, stone-ground mustard company offers tours of its facilities and mustard museum. Demonstrations include hand-milling mustard seeds – young kids love it! Reserve ahead at Beaune tourist office.

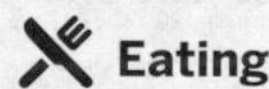

Eating

Eat streets loaded with restaurants include buzzy rue Berbisey, place Émile Zola, rue Amiral Roussin and around the perimeter of the covered market. Outdoor cafes fill place de la Libération.

DZ'Envies REGIONAL CUISINE €€
(☎03 80 50 09 26; www.dzenvies.com; 12 rue Odebert; mains €16-20, lunch menus €13-20, dinner menus €29-36; ⏰Mon-Sat) This zinging restaurant with cheery decorative touches is a good choice if you're tired of heavy Burgundian classics. The menu always involves seasonal, fresh ingredients, and dishes are imaginatively prepared and beautifully presented. At €18, the lunchtime *I love Dijon* (yes) menu is a steal.

Chez Nous BISTRO €
(impasse Quentin; mains €7-8, lunch menus €10-13; ⏰lunch noon-2pm Tue-Sat, bar 2pm-1am Mon, 11am-1am Tue-Sat) This quintessentially French *bar du coin* (neighbourhood bar), often crowded, hides down an alleyway near the covered market. At lunchtime join the flock and go for the fabulous-value *plat du jour* (daily special). Wash it all down with a glass of local wine (€2).

Chez Léon REGIONAL CUISINE €€
(☎03 80 50 01 07; www.restaurantchezleon.fr; 20 rue des Godrans; mains €11-29, lunch menus €15-21, dinner menus €22-27; ⏰Tue-Sat) From bœuf bourguignon (beef marinated in young red wine) to *andouillettes* (chitterling sausages), this is the perfect primer course in hearty regional fare celebrated in a cosy and joyful atmosphere. The dining room is cluttered but there's outdoor seating in warm months.

Information

Tourist office (☎08 92 70 05 58; www.visitdijon.com; 11 rue des Forges; ⏰9am-6.30pm Mon-Sat, 10am-6pm Sun) Rents bicycles.

Getting There & Away

BUS Transco (☎03 80 11 29 29; www.mobigo-bourgogne.com) Buses stop in front of the train station. Tickets sold on board (€1.50). Bus 44 goes to Nuits-St-Georges and Beaune. Bus 43 goes to Abbaye de Cîteaux.

TRAIN Trains leave the **train station** (www.voyages-sncf.com; rue du Dr Remy) for:

Lyon-Part Dieu from €22, 1½ hours, 25 daily

Marseille from €54, 3½ hours by TGV, six direct daily

Paris Gare de Lyon from €49, 1¾ hours by TGV, €42, three hours non-TGV, 25 daily

Beaune

POP 22,720

Beaune (pronounced 'bone'), 44km south of Dijon, is the unofficial capital of the Côte d'Or. This thriving town's raison d'être and the source of its joie de vivre is wine: making it, tasting it, selling it, but most of all, drinking it. Consequently, Beaune is one of the best places in all of France for wine tasting.

Sights & Activities

Beaune's amoeba-shaped old city is enclosed by **stone ramparts** sheltering wine cellars. Lined with overgrown gardens and ringed by a pathway, they make for a lovely stroll.

TOP CHOICE **Hôtel-Dieu des Hospices de Beaune** HISTORIC BUILDING
(www.hospices-de-beaune.com; rue de l'Hôtel-Dieu; adult/child €7/3; ⏰9am-5.30pm) Built in 1443, this magnificent Gothic hospital (in operation until 1971) is famously topped by stunning turrets and pitched rooftops covered in multicoloured tiles. Interior highlights include the barrel-vaulted **Grande Salle** (look

A TRIP BETWEEN VINES

Burgundy's most renowned vintages come from the **Côte d'Or** (Golden Hillside), a range of hills made of limestone, flint and clay that runs south from Dijon for about 60km. The northern section, the **Côte de Nuits**, stretches from Marsannay-la-Côte south to Corgoloin and produces reds known for their robust, full-bodied character. The southern section, the **Côte de Beaune**, lies between Ladoix-Serrigny and Santenay and produces great reds and whites.

Tourist offices provide brochures: *The Burgundy Wine Road* is an excellent free booklet published by the Burgundy Tourist Board (www.bourgogne-tourisme.com) and *Roadmap to the Wines of Burgundy* is a useful map. There's also the **Route des Grands Crus** (www.road-of-the-fine-burgundy-wines.com), a signposted road route of some of the most celebrated Côte de Nuits vineyards. Mandatory tasting stops for oenophiles after nirvana include 16th-century **Château du Clos de Vougeot** (☎03 80 62 86 09; www.closdevougeot.fr; Vougeot; adult/child €4/3.10; ⊙9am-5.30pm daily), with excellent guided tours, and **L'Imaginariim** (☎03 80 62 61 40; www.imaginarium-bourgogne.com; av du Jura, Nuits-St-Georges; adult/child €8/5; ⊙2-7pm Mon, 10am-7pm Tue-Sun) with an entertaining wine museum, in Nuits-St-Georges.

Wine & Voyages (☎03 80 61 15 15; www.wineandvoyages.com; tours from €53) and **Alter & Go** (☎06 23 37 92 04; www.alterandgo.fr; tours from €70), with an emphasis on history and winemaking methods, run minibus tours in English; reserve online or at the Dijon tourist office.

for the dragons and peasant heads up on the roof beams); an 18th-century **pharmacy** lined with flasks once filled with elixirs and powders; and the multipanelled masterpiece **Polyptych of the Last Judgement** by 15th-century Flemish painter Rogier van der Weyden, depicting Judgment Day in glorious technicolour.

Cellar Visits WINE TASTING

Millions of bottles of wine age to perfection in cool dark cellars beneath Beaune's buildings, streets and ramparts. Tasting opportunities abound and dozens of cellars can be visited by guided tour. Our favourites include the candlelit cellars of the former Église des Cordeliers, **Marché aux Vins** (www.marcheauxvins.com; 2 rue Nicolas Rolin; admission €10; ⊙9.30-11.30am & 2-5.30pm, no midday closure Jul-Aug), where 15 wines can be sampled; and **Cellier de la Vieille Grange** (www.bourgogne-cellier.com; 27 bd Georges Clemenceau; ⊙9am-noon & 2-7pm Wed-Sat, by appointment Sun-Tue), where locals flock to buy Burgundy wines *en vrac* (in bulk; bring your own jerrycan or buy a vinibag) for as little as €4.25 per litre for quality AOC wines. Tasting is done direct from barrels using a pipette. **Patriarche Père et Fils** (www.patriarche.com; 5 rue du Collège; audioguide tour €13; ⊙9.30-11.30am & 2-5.30pm), lined with about five million bottles of wine, has Burgundy's largest cellars.

Sleeping

Hôtel des Remparts HISTORIC HOTEL €€

(☎03 80 24 94 94; www.hotel-remparts-beaune.com; 48 rue Thiers; d €80-160; P❄🛜) Set around two delightful courtyards, this 17th-century townhouse has red-tiled or parquet floors and simple antique furniture. Some rooms come with exposed beams and a fireplace. Friendly staff rent bikes.

Abbaye de Maizières HISTORIC HOTEL €€

(☎03 80 24 74 64; www.beaune-abbaye-maizieres.com; 19 rue Maizières; d €118-190; ❄@) This is a character-laden establishment inside a 12th-century abbey with modern rooms and contemporary furnishings. Rooms on the top floor offer views over Beaune's famed multicolour tile roofs.

Chez Marie B&B €€

(☎06 64 63 48 20; www.chezmarieabeaune.com; 14 rue Poissonnerie; d €85-110; 🛜) Peace and calm five minutes from the centre of Beaune: Marie and her husband love having people to stay in their comfortable suburban house. Breakfast is served in a sweet garden. Bikes are available for rent.

Eating

Beaune harbours a host of excellent restaurants, many around place Carnot, place Félix Ziem and place Madeleine.

MONEY SAVER

If you'll be taking in a lot of sights and activities, including wine tasting, in the Beaune area, consider picking up the **Pass Pays Beaunois** at Beaune tourist offices. Ticket combos save 5% to 15% depending on the number of sights you plan to visit.

Loiseau des Vignes GASTRONOMIC €€€
(☎03 80 24 12 06; www.bernard-loiseau.com; 31 rue Maufoux; lunch menus €20-28, dinner menus €59-95; ⊙Tue-Sat) For that extra special meal, this culinary shrine is the place to go. Expect stunning concoctions ranging from caramelised pigeon to *quenelles de sandre* (dumplings made from pike fish), all exquisitely presented. And even the most budget-conscious can indulge – lunch menus are a bargain. In summer, the verdant garden is a plus.

Le Comptoir des Tontons REGIONAL CUISINE €€
(☎03 80 24 19 64; www.lecomptoirdestontons.com; 22 rue du Faubourg Madeleine; menus €25-36; ⊙Tue-Sat) Stylishly decorated in a hip bistro style, this local treasure entices with the passionate Burgundian cooking of chef Pepita. Most ingredients are organic and locally sourced.

Caves Madeleine FRENCH €€
(☎03 80 22 93 30; 8 rue du Faubourg Madeleine; mains €12-25, lunch menu €15; ⊙Mon-Wed & Sat, dinner Fri) This is a convivial restaurant where locals tuck into French classics such as *blanquette de veau* (veal stew) at long shared tables surrounded by wine racks.

Information

Tourist office (☎03 80 26 21 30; www.beaune-tourisme.fr; 6 bd Perpreuil; ⊙9am-7pm Mon-Sat, 9am-6pm Sun)

Getting There & Away

BUS Bus 44 links Beaune with Dijon (€1.50, 1½ hours, two to seven daily), stopping at Côte d'Or villages like Vougeot, Nuits-St-Georges and Aloxe-Corton.

Dijon €7.30, 25 minutes, 40 daily

Nuits-St-Georges from €4.50, 10 minutes, 40 daily

Paris Gare de Lyon from €41, 2¼ hours by TGV (non-TGV 3½ hours), 20 daily, two direct TGVs daily

Lyon-Part Dieu from €30, 1¾ hours, 16 daily

Lyon

POP 487,980

Gourmets, eat your heart out: Lyon is *the* gastronomic capital of France, with a lavish table of piggy-driven dishes and delicacies to savour. The city has been a commercial, industrial and banking powerhouse for the past 500 years, and is still France's second-largest conurbation, with outstanding art museums, a dynamic nightlife, green parks and a Unesco-listed Old Town.

Sights

VIEUX LYON

Old Lyon, with its cobblestone streets and medieval and Renaissance houses below Fourvière hill, is divided into three quarters: St-Paul at the northern end, St-Jean in the middle and St-Georges in the south. Lovely old buildings languish on **rue du Bœuf, rue St-Jean** and **rue des Trois Maries**.

The partly Romanesque **Cathédrale St-Jean** (place St-Jean, 5e; ⊙8am-noon & 2-7pm; ⓜVieux Lyon), seat of Lyon's 133rd bishop, was built from the late 11th to the early 16th centuries. Its **astronomical clock** chimes at noon, 2pm, 3pm and 4pm.

FOURVIÈRE

Over two millennia ago, the Romans built the city of Lugdunum on the slopes of Fourvière. Today, Lyon's 'hill of prayer' – topped by a basilica and the **Tour Métallique**, an Eiffel Tower–like structure built in 1893 and used as a TV transmitter – affords spectacular views of the city and its two rivers. Footpaths wind uphill, but the funicular is the least taxing way up.

Crowning Fourvière hill is the **Basilique Notre Dame de Fourvière** (www.fourviere.org; place de Fourvière, 5e; ⊙8am-7pm; funicular Fourvière funicular station), an iconic, 27m-high

WANT MORE?

For in-depth information, reviews and recommendations at your fingertips, head to the Apple App Store to purchase Lonely Planet's *Lyon City Guide* iPhone app.

Alternatively, head to **Lonely Planet** (www.lonelyplanet.com/france/burgundy-and-the-rhone/lyon) for planning advice, author recommendations, traveller reviews and insider tips.

basilica, a superb example of exaggerated 19th-century ecclesiastical architecture.

Around the corner, treasures from its interior enjoy pride of place in the **Musée d'Art Religieux** (8 place de Fourvière, 5e; adult/child €6/free; ⏲10am-12.30pm & 2-5.30pm; funicular Fourvière funicular station).

PRESQU'ÎLE

The centrepiece of **place des Terreaux** is a 19th-century fountain sculpted by Frédéric-Auguste Bartholdi, creator of the Statue of Liberty. The **Musée des Beaux-Arts** (www.mba-lyon.fr; 20 place des Terreaux, 1er; adult/child incl audioguide €7/free; ⏲10am-6pm Wed, Thu & Sat-Mon, 10.30am-6pm Fri; MHôtel de Ville) showcases France's finest collection of sculptures and paintings outside Paris.

Lyonnais silks are showcased at the **Musée des Tissus** (www.musee-des-tissus.com; 34 rue de la Charité, 2e; adult/child €10/7.50, after 4pm €8/5.50; ⏲10am-5.30pm Tue-Sun; MAmpère). Next door, the **Musée des Arts Décoratifs** (34 Rue de la Charité, 2e; free with Musée des Tissus ticket; ⏲10am-noon & 2-5.30pm Tue-Sun) displays 18th-century furniture, tapestries, wallpaper, ceramics and silver.

Laid out in the 17th century, **place Bellecour** – one of Europe's largest public squares – is pierced by an equestrian **statue of Louis XIV**. South of here, past **Gare de Perrache**, lies the once-downtrodden industrial area of **Lyon Confluence** (www.lyon-confluence.fr), where the Rhône and Saône meet. Trendy restaurants now line its quays, and the ambitious **Musée des Confluences** (www.museedesconfluences.fr; 28 Boulevard des Belges, 6e), a science-and-humanities museum inside a futuristic steel-and-glass transparent crystal, will open here in 2014.

North of place Bellecour, the charming hilltop quarter of **Croix Rousse** is famed for its lush outdoor food market and silk-weaving tradition, illustrated by the **Maison des Canuts** (www.maisondescanuts.com; 10-12 rue d'Ivry, 4e; adult/child €6.50/3.50; ⏲10am-6pm Mon-Sat, guided tours 11am & 3.30pm; MCroix Rousse).

RIVE GAUCHE

Parc de la Tête d'Or PARK

(www.loisirs-parcdelatetedor.com; bd des Belges, 6e; ⏲6am-11pm Apr-Sep, to 9pm Oct-Mar; 41, 47, MMasséna) France's largest urban park, landscaped in the 1860s, is graced by a lake (rent a rowing boat), botanic garden, rose garden, zoo, puppet theatre and tip-top **Musée d'Art Contemporain** (www.mac-lyon.com; 81 quai Charles de Gaulle, 6e; adult/child €8/free; ⏲11am-6pm Wed-Fri, 10am-7pm Sat & Sun). Buses 41 and 47 link the park with metro Part-Dieu.

LYON CITY CARD

The **Lyon City Card** (www.lyon-france.com; 1/2/3 days adult €21/31/41, child €12.50/17.50/22.50) covers admission to every Lyon museum and the roof of Basilique Notre Dame de Fourvière, as well as guided city tours, a river excursion (April to October) and discounts on other selected attractions.

The card also includes unlimited travel on buses, trams, the funicular and metro. Buy it online (www.en.lyon-france.com/Lyon-City-Card), from the tourist office, or at some hotels.

Musée Lumière MUSEUM

(www.institut-lumiere.org; 25 rue du Premier Film, 8e; adult/child €6.50/5.50; ⏲10am-6.30pm Tue-Sun; MMonplaisir-Lumière) Cinema's glorious beginnings are showcased at the art nouveau home of Antoine Lumière, who moved to Lyon with sons Auguste and Louis in 1870. The brothers shot the first reels of the world's first motion picture, *La Sortie des Usines Lumières* (Exit of the Lumières Factories) here in the grounds of one of their father's photographic factories on 19 March 1895. The former factory is the Hangar du Premier Film cinema today.

Centre d'Histoire de la Résistance et de la Déportation MUSEUM

(www.chrd.lyon.fr; 14 av Berthelot, 7e; adult/child €4/free; ⏲9am-5.30pm Wed-Sun; MPerrache or Jean Macé) The WWII headquarters of Gestapo commander Klaus Barbie evokes Lyon's role as the 'Capital of the Resistance' through moving multimedia exhibits. Reopened after extensive remodeling in 2012, the museum's new sections include sound recordings of 30 deportees and Resistance fighters, plus a varied collection of everyday objects associated with the Resistance (including the parachute Jean Moulin used to re-enter France in 1942).

Festivals & Events

Fête des Lumières WINTER FESTIVAL

(Festival of Lights; www.lumieres.lyon.fr) Over several days around the Feast of the Immaculate Conception (8 December), sound-and-light shows are projected onto key buildings, while locals illuminate window sills with candles.

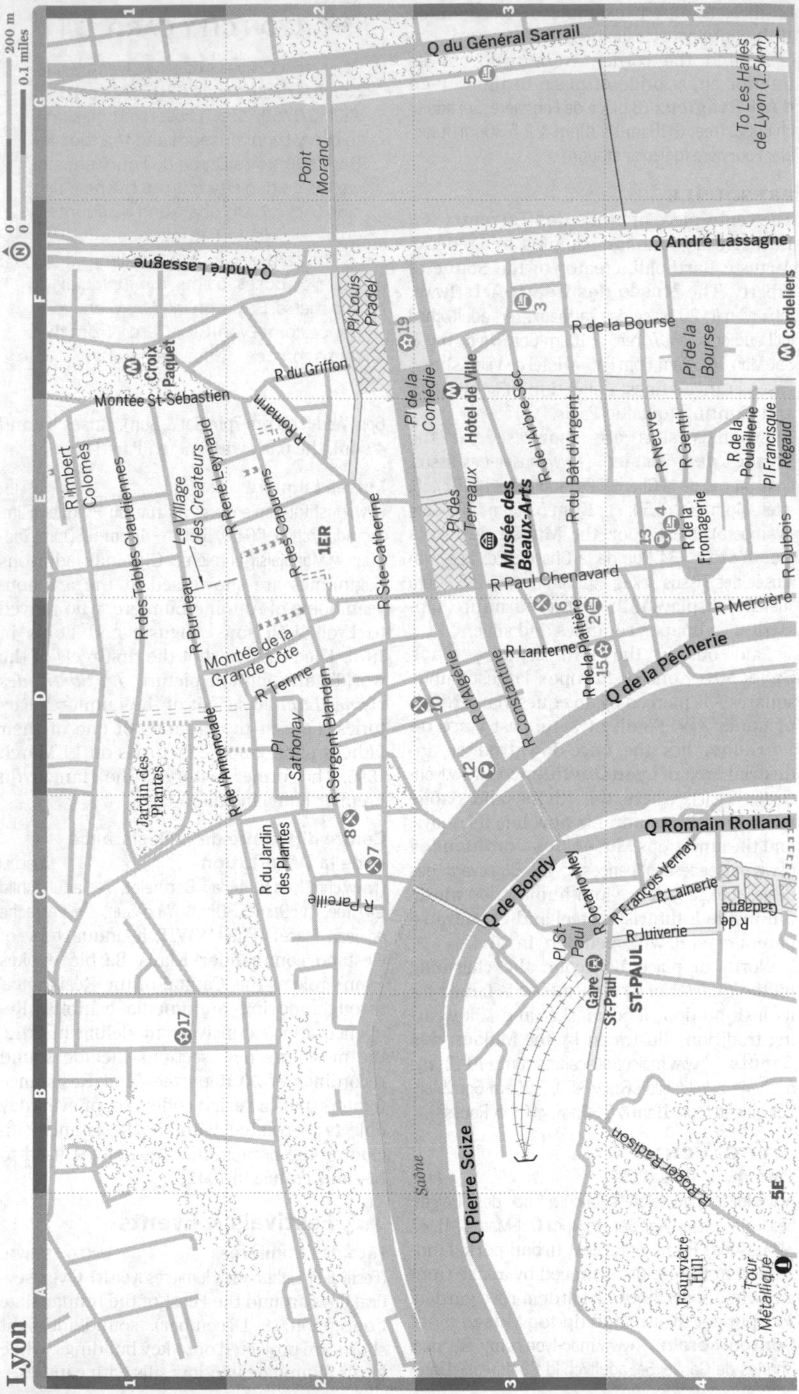

Lyon

0 — 200 m
0 — 0.1 miles

A B C D E F G
1 2 3 4

Q du Général Sarrail
To Les Halles de Lyon (1.5km)
Pont Morand
Q André Lassagne
Q André Lassagne
Pl Louis Pradel
Croix Paquet
R du Griffon
Montée St-Sébastien
R Romarin
Pl de la Comédie
Hôtel de Ville
R de la Bourse
Pl de la Bourse
Cordeliers
R de l'Arbre Sec
R du Bât d'Argent
R Neuve
R Gentil
R de la Poulaillerie
Pl Francisque Régaud
R Imbert Colomès
R des Tables Claudiennes
Le Village des Createurs
R René Leynaud
R des Capucins
1ER
R Ste-Catherine
Pl des Terreaux
Musée des Beaux-Arts
R de la Fromagerie
R Dubois
R Paul Chenavard
R Burdeau
Montée de la Grande Côte
R Terme
R Lanterne
R de la Platière
R Mercière
Q de la Pêcherie
R d'Algérie
R Constantine
Pl Sathonay
R Sergent Blandan
R de l'Annonciade
Jardin des Plantes
R du Jardin des Plantes
R Pareille
Q Romain Rolland
Q de Bondy
R Octavio Mey
R François Vernay
R Lainerie
R de Gadagne
R Juiverie
Pl St Paul
Gare St-Paul
ST-PAUL
Saône
Q Pierre Scize
R Roger Radisson
5E
Fourvière Hill
Tour Métallique

1 2 3 4 5 6 7 8 10 12 13 15 17 19

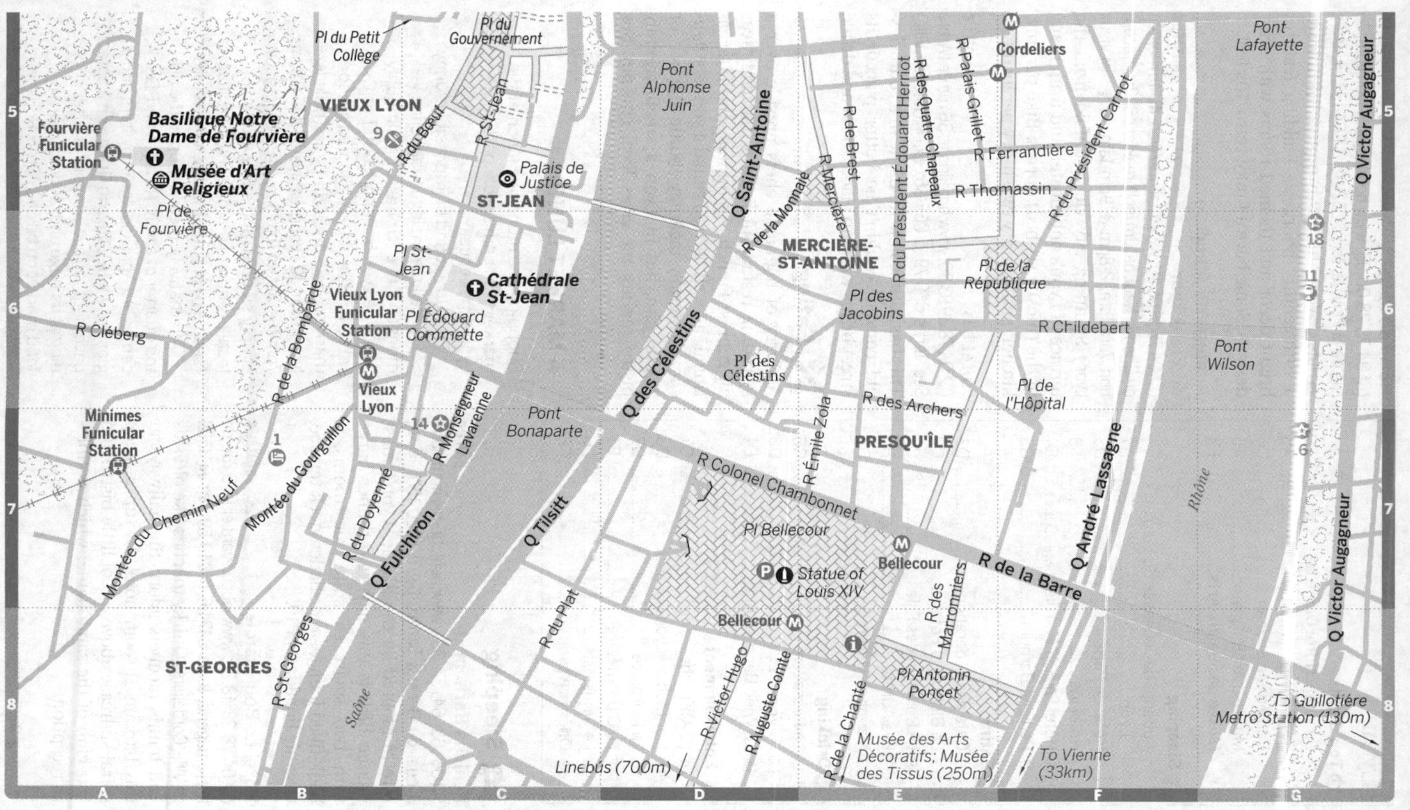

Fourvière Funicular Station
Basilique Notre Dame de Fourvière
Musée d'Art Religieux
Pl de Fourvière
VIEUX LYON
Pl du Petit Collège
Pl du Gouvernement
R du Bœuf
R St-Jean
Palais de Justice
ST-JEAN
Pl St-Jean
Cathédrale St-Jean
Vieux Lyon Funicular Station
Pl Édouard Commette
R Cléberg
R de la Bombarde
Vieux Lyon
Minimes Funicular Station
Montée du Gourguillon
Montée du Chemin Neuf
R Monseigneur Lavarenne
R du Doyenne
Q Fulchiron
ST-GEORGES
R St-Georges
Saône
Pont Alphonse Juin
Pont Bonaparte
Q Saint-Antoine
Q des Célestins
Q Tilsit
R du Plat
R de la Monnaie
R Mercière
R de Brest
R du Président Édouard Herriot
R des Quatre Chapeaux
R Palais Grillet
Cordeliers
R Ferrandière
R Thomassin
R du Président Carnot
MERCIÈRE-ST-ANTOINE
Pl des Jacobins
Pl de la République
R Childebert
Pl des Célestins
R Émile Zola
R des Archers
Pl de l'Hôpital
PRESQU'ÎLE
R Colonel Chambonnet
Pl Bellecour
Statue of Louis XIV
Bellecour
R des Marronniers
R de la Barre
Q André Lassagne
Pl Antonin Poncet
R Victor Hugo
R Auguste Comte
R de la Chanté
Linebus (700m)
Musée des Arts Décoratifs; Musée des Tissus (250m)
To Vienne (33km)
Rhône
Pont Wilson
Pont Lafayette
Q Victor Augagneur
To Guillotière Metro Station (130m)
9
14
1
18
11
6
A
B
C
D
E
F
G
5
6
7
8
FRANCE LYON

Lyon

Sleeping

Péniche Barnum B&B €€

(04 63 64 37 39; www.peniche-barnum.com; 3 quai du Général Sarrail, 6e; d €120-150; ; Foch) Moored on the Rhône, Lyon's most unique B&B is this navy-and-timber barge with two smart en suite guestrooms, a book-filled lounge, and shaded deck terrace. Organic breakfasts €10.

Hôtel Le Boulevardier HOTEL €

(04 78 28 48 22; www.leboulevardier.fr; 5 rue de la Fromagerie, 1er; s €47-56, d €49-59; ; Hôtel de Ville, Cordeliers) Quirky touches like old skis and tennis racquets adorn the hallways at this bargain 11-room hotel. It's up a steep spiral staircase above a cool little bistro and jazz club of the same name, which doubles as reception.

Hôtel de Paris HOTEL €€

(04 78 28 00 95; www.hoteldeparis-lyon.com; 16 rue de la Platière, 1er; s €52-92, d €64-135; ; Hôtel de Ville) This newly remodeled hotel in a 19th-century bourgeois building features bright decor and themed rooms with artsy designs. Some have a funky, retro '70s feel.

Auberge de Jeunesse du Vieux Lyon HOSTEL €

(04 78 15 05 50; www.fuaj.org/lyon; 41-45 montée du Chemin Neuf, 5e; dm incl breakfast €22; reception 7am-1pm, 2-8pm & 9pm-1am; ; Vieux Lyon) Stunning city views unfold from the terrace of Lyon's only hostel, and from many of the (mostly six-bed) dorms. Bike parking, kitchen and laundry (wash-dry per load €4).

Hôtel Iris HOTEL €

(04 78 39 93 80; www.hoteliris.fr; 36 rue de l'Arbre Sec, 1er; s €60-79, d €65-86; ; Hôtel de Ville) This basic but colourful dame in a centuries-old convent couldn't be better placed: its street brims with hip places to eat and drink.

Eating

A flurry of big-name chefs preside over a sparkling restaurant line-up that embraces all genres: French, fusion, fast and international, as well as traditional Lyonnais *bouchons* (literally meaning 'bottle stopper' or 'traffic jam', but in Lyon a small, friendly bistro serving the city's local cuisine). See

A MARKET LUNCH

Shopping and munching lunch at the market is an unmissable part of the Lyon experience.

Pick up a round of impossibly runny St Marcellin from legendary cheesemonger **Mère Richard**, or a knobbly Jésus de Lyon from pork butcher **Collette Sibilia** at Lyon's famed indoor market **Les Halles de Lyon** (hallede lyon.free.fr; 102 cours Lafayette, 3e; 8am-7pm Tue-Sat, to 1pm Sun; Part-Dieu). Or simply sit down and enjoy a lunch of local produce, lip-smacking *coquillages* (shellfish) included, at one of its stalls.

Alternatively, meander up to the hilltop quarter of **Croix Rousse** and, December to April, indulge in oysters and a glass of white Côtes du Rhône on a cafe pavement terrace – before or after shopping at its huge and glorious morning food market on bd de la Croix Rousse.

www.lyonresto.com (in French) for reviews, videos and ratings.

Les Adrets REGIONAL CUISINE €€
(☎04 78 38 24 30; 30 rue du Boeuf, 5e; lunch menu €15.50, dinner menus €23-45; ⏰lunch & dinner Mon-Fri; Ⓜ Vieux Lyon) This atmospheric spot serves some of Vieux Lyon's best food any time of day. The mix is half classic *bouchon* fare, half alternative choices like Parma ham and truffle risotto, or duck breast with roasted pears.

TOP CHOICE **Le Bouchon des Filles** REGIONAL CUISINE €€
(☎04 78 30 40 44; 20 rue Sergent Blandan, 1er; menus €25; ⏰dinner daily, lunch Sun; Ⓜ Hôtel de Ville) This contemporary ode to Lyon's legendary culinary *mères* (mothers) is run by an enterprising crew of young women with deep roots in the local *bouchon* scene. The light and fluffy *quenelles* (Lyonnaise dumplings) are among the best you'll find in Lyon, and the rustic atmosphere is warm and welcoming.

Le Bistrot du Potager TAPAS €
(☎04 78 29 61 59; www.lebistrotdupotager.com; 3 rue de la Martinière, 1er; tapas €5-12; ⏰lunch & dinner Tue-Sat; Ⓜ Hôtel de Ville) An offshoot of the renowned Potager des Halles restaurant next door, throngs of happy diners linger here over glasses of wine and Provençal duck carpaccio, grilled vegetables with pistou, stuffed artichokes, octopus salad, Tunisian-style chickpeas and platters of cheeses and charcuterie.

Magali et Martin REGIONAL CUISINE €€
(☎04 72 00 88 01; www.magalietmartin.fr; 11 rue Augustins, 1er; lunch menus €19.50-23, dinner menus €29-35; ⏰lunch & dinner Mon-Fri; Ⓜ Hôtel de Ville) Watch chefs turn out traditional but lighter, more varied *bouchon*-influenced cuisine, at this sharp dining address.

Café des Fédérations BOUCHON €€
(☎04 78 28 26 00; www.lesfedeslyon.com; 8-10 rue Major Martin, 1er; lunch/dinner menus from €19/25; ⏰lunch & dinner Mon-Sat; Ⓜ Hôtel de Ville) From the vast array of appetisers – lentils in mustardy sauce, slices of *rosette de Lyon* sausage, pickles, beets and more – clear through to a classic *baba au rhum* for dessert, this is *bouchon* dining at its finest.

Drinking & Entertainment

Cafe terraces on place des Terreaux buzz with all-hours drinkers, as do the British, Irish and other-styled pubs on nearby rue Ste-Catherine, 1er, and rue Lainerie and rue St-Jean, 5e, in Vieux Lyon.

Track new bars and nightclubs with *Le Petit Paumé* (www.petitpaume.com), a savvy city guide penned by local university students. Other what's on guides include **Lyon Poche** (www.lyonpoche.com) and **Le Petit Bulletin** (www.petit-bulletin.fr/lyon).

Tickets are sold at **Fnac Billetterie** (www.fnac.com/spectacles; 85 rue de la République, 2e; ⏰10am-7.30pm Mon-Sat; Ⓜ Bellecour).

Le Wine Bar d'à Côté WINE BAR
(www.cave-vin-lyon.com; 7 rue Pleney, 1er; ⏰Mon-Sat; Ⓜ Cordeliers) Hidden in a tiny alleyway, this cultured wine bar feels like a rustic English gentlemen's club with leather sofa seating and a library.

Le Voxx BAR
(1 rue d'Algérie, 1er; ⏰10am-3am daily; Ⓜ Hôtel de Ville) Minimalist but lively riverside bar packed with a mix of people, from students to city slickers.

Opéra de Lyon OPERA HOUSE
(www.opera-lyon.com; place de la Comédie, 1er; Ⓜ Hôtel de Ville) Premier venue for opera, ballet and classical music.

(L'A)Kroche LIVE MUSIC
(www.lakroche.fr; 8 rue Monseigneur Lavarenne, 5e; ⏰11am-1am Tue-Sat, 3-9pm Sun & Mon; Ⓜ Vieux Lyon) Hip concert cafe-bar with DJs spinning electro, soul, funk and disco; bands too.

Ninkasi Gerland LIVE MUSIC
(www.ninkasi.fr; 267 rue Marcel Mérieux, 7e; ⏰10am-late; Ⓜ Stade de Gerland) Spilling over with a fun, frenetic crowd, this microbrewery

EAT STREETS

Rue St-Jean (Ⓜ Vieux Lyon) A surfeit of restaurants jam Vieux Lyon's pedestrian main street.

Cobbled rue Mercière, rue des Marronniers & place Antonin Poncet, 2e (Ⓜ Bellecour) Buzzing streets, chock-a-block with eating options (of widely varying quality) and pavement terraces overflowing in summer.

Rue du Garet & Rue Verdi, 1er (Ⓜ Hôtel de Ville) Twinset of parallel streets snug by Lyon's opera house on the Presqu'île.

dishes up DJs, bands and film projections amid a backdrop of fish-and-chips, build-your-own burgers and other un-French food.

Le Club Théâtre PERFORMING ARTS
(www.thearte.fr; 4 impasse Flesselles, 1er; annual membership fee €2; Ⓜ Croix Rousse) Hip and unique, this hybrid bar-nightclub-cultural centre sits inside Croix Rousse's old neighbourhood wash-house, with the central wash basin doubling as stage and dance floor.

Hot Club de Lyon LIVE MUSIC
(www.hotclubjazz.com; 26 rue Lanterne, 1er; ⏲Tue-Sat; Ⓜ Hôtel de Ville) Lyon's leading jazz club, around since 1948.

Le Transbordeur LIVE MUSIC
(www.transbordeur.fr; 3 bd de Stalingrad, Villeurbanne; trolleybus Cité Internationale/Transbordeur) In an old industrial building near the northeastern corner of the Parc de la Tête d'Or, Lyon's prime concert venue draws international acts on the European concert-tour circuit.

Information

Tourist office (☎04 72 77 69 69; www.lyon-france.com; place Bellecour, 2e; ⏲9am-6pm; Ⓜ Bellecour)

Getting There & Away

Air

Lyon-St-Exupéry Airport (www.lyon.aeroport.fr), 25km east of the city, serves 120 direct destinations across Europe and beyond, including many budget carriers.

DRINKS AFLOAT

Floating bars with DJs and live bands rock until around 3am aboard the string of *péniches* (river barges) moored along the Rhône's left bank. Scout out the section of quai Victor Augagneur between Pont Lafayette (Ⓜ Cordeliers or Guichard) and Pont de la Guillotière (Ⓜ Guillotière).

Our favourites: laid-back **La Passagère** (21 quai Victor Augagneur, 3e; ⏲daily; Ⓜ Place Guichard - Bourse du Travail); party-hard **Le Sirius** (www.lesirius.com; 4 quai Victor Augagneur, 3e; ⏲daily; 📶; Ⓜ Place Guichard - Bourse du Travail); and electro-oriented **La Marquise** (www.marquise.net; 20 quai Victor Augagneur, 3e; ⏲Tue-Sun; Ⓜ Place Guichard - Bourse du Travail).

Bus

In the Perrache complex, **Eurolines** (☎04 72 56 95 30; www.eurolines.fr; Gare de Perrache) and Spain-oriented **Linebús** (☎04 72 41 72 27; www.linebus.com; Gare de Perrache) have offices on the bus-station level of the Centre d'Échange (follow the 'Lignes Internationales' signs).

Train

Lyon has two main-line train stations: **Gare de la Part-Dieu** (Ⓜ Part-Dieu), 1.5km east of the Rhône, and **Gare de Perrache** (Ⓜ Perrache).

Destinations by direct TGV include:

Dijon from €29, two hours, at least seven daily
Lille-Europe from €90, three hours, at least 11 daily
Marseille from €45, 1¾ hours, every 30 to 60 minutes
Paris Gare de Lyon from €69, two hours, every 30 to 60 minutes
Paris Charles de Gaulle Airport from €69, two hours, at least 11 daily
Strasbourg €88, 3¾ hours, five daily

Getting Around

Tramway **Rhonexpress** (www.rhonexpress.net) links the airport with Part-Dieu train station in under 30 minutes. A single ticket costs €14.

Buses, trams, a four-line metro and two funiculars linking Vieux Lyon to Fourvière are run by **TCL** (www.tcl.fr). Public transport runs from around 5am to midnight. Tickets cost €1.60 while a *carnet* of 10 is €13.70; bring coins as machines don't accept notes (or some international credit cards). Time-stamp tickets on all forms of public transport or risk a fine.

Bikes are available from 200-odd bike stations thanks to **vélo'v** (www.velov.grandlyon.com; first 30min free, first/subsequent hr €1/2).

THE FRENCH ALPS

Whether it's paragliding among the peaks, hiking the trails or hurtling down a mountainside strapped to a pair of glorified toothpicks, the French Alps is the undisputed centre of adventure sports in France. Under Mont Blanc's 4810m of raw wilderness lies the country's most spectacular outdoor playground

Chamonix

POP 9378 / ELEV 1037M

With the pearly white peaks of the Mont Blanc massif as a sensational backdrop, being an icon comes naturally to Chamonix.

LOCAL KNOWLEDGE

ERIC FAVRET: MOUNTAIN GUIDE

Eric Favret, guide with Compagnie des Guides de Chamonix, talked to Lonely Planet author Nicola Williams about his favourite local spots, views and thrills

Aiguille du Midi The Aiguille du Midi, with one of the highest cable cars in the world, cannot be missed. Beyond the summit ridge is a world of snow and ice offering some of the greatest intermediate off-piste terrain in the Alps.

Off-Piste Thrills The Vallée Blanche has to be seen. But the Aiguille du Midi also has amazing off-piste runs, such as Envers du Plan, a slightly steeper and more advanced version of Vallée Blanche, offering dramatic views in the heart of the Mont Blanc range There is also the less frequented run of the 'Virgin' or 'Black Needle' – a striking glacial run, it offers different views and a close-up look at the Giant's seracs.

Best-Ever Mont Blanc View No hesitation: the Traverse from Col des Montets to Lac Blanc. It's as popular as the Eiffel Tower for hikers in summer. I love swimming in mountain lakes, so I like to stop at Lac des Chéserys, just below, where it is quieter: what's better than a swim in pure mountain water, looking at Mont Blanc, the Grandes Jorasses and Aiguille Verte? This is what I call mountain landscape perfection!

First 'discovered' by Brits William Windham and Richard Pococke in 1741, this is the mecca of mountaineering. Its knife-edge peaks, plunging slopes and massive glaciers have enthralled generations of adventurers and thrill-seekers ever since. Its après-ski scene is equally pumping.

Sights

TOP CHOICE Aiguille du Midi VIEWPOINT

A jagged needle of rock rearing above glaciers, snowfields and rocky crags, 8km from the hump of Mont Blanc, the Aiguille du Midi (3842m) is one of Chamonix' most distinctive landmarks. If you can handle the height, the 360-degree views of the French, Swiss and Italian Alps from the summit are (quite literally) breathtaking.

Year-round, the vertiginous **Téléphérique de l'Aiguille de Midi** (place de l'Aiguille du Midi; adult/child return to Aiguille du Midi €46/39, Plan de l'Aiguille €26/22; ⌚8.30am-4.30pm) cable car links Chamonix with the Aiguille du Midi. Halfway, Plan de l'Aiguille (2317m) is a terrific place to start hikes or paraglide. In summer you will need to obtain a boarding card (marked with the number of your departing *and* returning cable car) in addition to a ticket. Ensure that you bring warm clothes as even in summer the temperature rarely rises above -10°C at the top.

From the Aiguille du Midi, between late June and early September, you can continue for a further 30 minutes of mind-blowing scenery – think suspended glaciers and spurs, seracs and shimmering ice fields – in the smaller bubbles of the **Télécabine Panoramic Mont Blanc** (adult/child return from Chamonix €70/59; ⌚8.30am-3.30pm) to Pointe Helbronner (3466m) on the French–Italian border. From here another cable car descends to the Italian ski resort of Courmayeur.

Le Brévent VIEWPOINT

The highest peak on the western side of the valley, Le Brévent (2525m) has tremendous views of the Mont Blanc massif, myriad hiking trails, ledges to paraglide from and summit restaurant Le Panoramic. Reach it with the **Télécabine du Brévent** (29 rte Henriette d'Angeville; adult/child return €26/22; ⌚8.50am-4.45pm).

Mer de Glace GLACIER

France's largest glacier, the glistening 200m-deep Mer de Glace (Sea of Ice) snakes 7km through mighty rock spires and turrets. The glacier moves up to 90m a year, and has become a popular attraction thanks to the rack-and-pinion railway line opened in 1908. The quaint red mountain train trundles up from **Gare du Montenvers** (35 place de la Mer de Glace; adult/child/family €26/22/79; ⌚10am-4.30pm) in Chamonix to Montenvers (1913m), from where a cable car takes you down to the glacier and cave. Besides covering the 20-minute journey, the cable car and the ice cave, your ticket gets you entry into the crystal-laced **Galerie des Cristaux** and the new **Glaciorium**, spotlighting the birth, life and future of glaciers.

DON'T MISS

ADVENTURE KNOW-HOW

These guide companies have got it. So go on and create your own adventure:

Compagnie des Guides de Chamonix (☎04 50 53 00 88; www.chamonix-guides.com; 190 place de l'Église) The crème de la crème of mountain guides, founded in 1821. Guides for skiing, mountaineering, ice climbing, hiking, mountain biking and every other Alpine pastime.

Association Internationale des Guides du Mont Blanc (☎04 50 53 27 05; www.guides-du-montblanc.com; 85 rue des Moulins) Extreme skiing, mountaineering, glacier trekking, ice and rock climbing, and paragliding.

Aventure en Tête (☎04 50 54 05 11; www.aventureentete.com; 420 rte du Chapeau, Le Lavancher) Ski touring and ski-alpinism expeditions; free-ride and off-piste courses; mountaineering and climbing in summer.

Chamonix Experience (☎09 77 48 58 69; www.chamex.com; 49 place Edmond Desailloud) Courses in off-piste skiing, avalanche awareness, ice climbing and ski touring; in summer, rock and Alpine climbing.

Wrap up warm to experience the **Grotte de la Mer de Glace** (late Dec-May & mid-Jun–Sep) ice cave, where frozen tunnels and ice sculptures change colour like mood rings.

The Mer de Glace can be reached on foot via the Grand Balcon Nord trail from Plan de l'Aiguille. The two-hour uphill trail from Chamonix starts near the summer luge track. Traversing the crevassed glacier requires proper equipment and an experienced guide.

Activities

Get the Mont Blanc lowdown on hiking, skiing and a zillion and one other adrenelin-pumping pursuits at the **Maison de la Montagne** (190 place de l'Église; 8.30am-noon & 3-7pm), opposite the tourist office.

Sleeping

TOP CHOICE **Auberge du Manoir** HOTEL €€
(☎04 50 53 10 77; http://aubergedumanoir.com; 8 rte du Bouchet; s €109-122, d €126-176, q €178;) This beautifully converted farmhouse ticks all the perfect alpine chalet boxes: pristine mountain views, pine-panelled rooms, outdoor hot tub, and a bar with open fire.

Hotel L'Oustalet HOTEL €€
(☎04 50 55 54 99; www.hotel-oustalet.com; 330 rue du Lyret; d/q €148/190;) You'll pray for snow at this alpine chalet near Aiguille du Midi cable car, just so you can curl up by the fire with a *chocolat chaud* (hot chocolate) and unwind in the sauna and whirlpool. The rooms, including family ones, are snugly decorated in solid pine and open onto balconies with Mont Blanc views.

Hôtel Faucigny BOUTIQUE HOTEL €€
(☎04 50 53 01 17; www.hotelfaucigny-chamonix.com; 118 place de l'Église; s/d/q €90/120/170;) This bijou hotel is a slice of minimalist alpine cool, with its charcoal-white rooms and slate-walled spa. Your hosts bend over backwards to please: free bike rental and afternoon tea, summer terrace with Mont Blanc views, open fire in winter, whirlpool and sauna.

Le Vert Hôtel HOTEL €€
(☎04 50 53 13 58; www.verthotel.com; 964 rte des Gaillands; s/d/tr/q € 80/103/129/151;) Self-proclaimed 'Chamonix' house of sports and creativity', this party house 1km south of town has no-frills rooms, some with microscopically small bathrooms. But what people really come for is the all-happening, ultrahip bar, a regular venue for top DJs and live music. Minimum four-night stay.

Camping Mer de Glace CAMPGROUND €
(☎04 50 53 44 03; http://chamonix-camping.com; 200 chemin de la Bagna; sites €23.50; late Apr–Sep;) Oh, what a beautiful morning! Draw back your tent flap and be dazzled by Mont Blanc and glaciated peaks at this campground, 2km northeast of Chamonix and an easy 20-minute stroll from the centre of town.

Eating

TOP CHOICE **Les Vieilles Luges** FRENCH €€
(☎06 84 42 37 00; www.lesvieillesluges.com; Les Houches, menus €20-35; ⊙lunch daily, dinner by reservation) This childhood dream of a 250-year-old farmhouse can only be reached by slipping on skis or taking a scenic 20-minute hike from Maison Neuve chairlift. Under low wood beams, Julie and Claude spoil you with their home cooking washed down with *vin chaud* (mulled wine) warmed over a wood fire. Magic.

La Crèmerie du Glacier FRENCH €€
(☎04 50 54 07 52; www.lacremerieduglacier.fr; 766 chemin de la Glacière; menus €12-22; ⊙lunch & dinner Thu-Tue) Crazy as it sounds for a piste restaurant, you might have to book to get a chance to bite into La Crèmerie du Glacier's world-famous *croûtes au fromage* (chunky slices of toasted bread topped with melted cheese). Ski to it on the red Pierre à Ric piste in Les Grands Montets.

La Petite Kitchen INTERNATIONAL €€
(80 place du Poilu; 2-course lunch menus €12.50, mains €18-28; ⊙lunch & dinner Wed-Mon) The Little Kitchen is just that: a handful of tables for the lucky few who get to indulge in its locally sourced feel-good food – filling English breakfasts, steaks with homemade *frites* (hot chips) and the stickiest of toffee puddings.

Le Bistrot GASTRONOMIC €€€
(☎04 50 53 57 64; www.lebistrotchamonix.com; 151 av de l'Aiguille du Midi; lunch menus €17-28, dinner menus €50-85; ⊙lunch & dinner daily; 👪) Michelin-starred chef Mickey experiments with textures and seasonal flavours to create taste sensations like pan-seared Arctic char with chestnuts, and divine warm chocolate macaroon with raspberry and red pepper coulis.

Le GouThé TEAHOUSE €
(95 rue des Moulins; snacks €3-10; ⊙9am-7pm daily; ✍) Welcome to the sweetest of tea rooms: hot chocolates, macarons, *galettes* (buckwheat crêpes) and crumbly homemade tarts.

Munchie FUSION €€
(☎04 50 53 45 41; www.munchie.eu; 87 rue des Moulins; mains €19-24; ⊙dinner daily) The style of this trendy Swedish-run hangout is pan-Asian fusion. Sittings go faster than musical chairs, so it's worth a try even if you haven't booked.

Drinking & Entertainment

Nightlife rocks. In the centre, riverside rue des Moulins boasts a line-up of après-ski joints serving food as well as booze.

Chambre Neuf BAR
(272 av Michel Croz; 📶) Cover bands and raucous drinking make Room 9 one of Chamonix' liveliest party haunts. Conversations about epic off-pistes and monster jumps that are, like, totally mental, man, dominate at every table.

MBC MICROBREWERY
(www.mbchx.com; 350 rte du Bouchet; ⊙4pm-2am) This trendy microbrewery run by four Canadians is fab. Be it with their burgers, cheesecake of the week, live music or amazing locally brewed and named beers (Blonde de Chamonix, Stout des Drus, Blanche des Guides etc), MBC delivers.

Elevation 1904 BAR
(259 av Michel Croz; ⊙7am-11pm or later) Alpine paraphernalia lines the walls of this merry bet by the train station with an all-day snack shack. The suntrap terrace is just right.

Information

Tourist office (☎04 50 53 00 24; www.chamonix.com; 85 place du Triangle de l'Amitié; ⊙8.30am-7pm)

Getting There & Away

BUS From **Chamonix bus station** (www.sat-montblanc.com; place de la Gare), next to the train station, five daily buses run to/from Geneva airport (one way/return €33/55, 1½ to two hours) and Courmayeur (one way/return €13/20, 45 minutes). Advanced booking only.

TRAIN The Mont Blanc Express narrow-gauge train trundles from St-Gervais-Le Fayet station, 23km west of Chamonix, to Martigny in Switzerland, stopping en route in Les Houches, Chamonix and Argentière. There are nine to 12 return trips daily between Chamonix and St-Gervais (€10, 45 minutes).

From St-Gervais-Le Fayet, there are trains to most major French cities.

Annecy

POP 52,161 / ELEV 447M

Lac d'Annecy is one of the world's purest lakes, receiving only rainwater, spring water and mountain streams. Swimming in its sapphire depths, surrounded by snowy mountains,

FREE WHEELER

Pick up a set of wheels to glide along the silky-smooth cycling path ensnaring Lake Annecy from **Vélonecy** (place de la Gare) at the train station for €15 per day (reduced to €5 with a valid train ticket). Or, in summer, simply head for the water and hire a bike lakeside from one of the many open-air stalls.

is a real Alpine highlight. Strolling the geranium-strewn streets of the historic Vieille Ville (Old Town) is not half bad either.

Sights & Activities

Vieille Ville & Lakefront HISTORIC QUARTER

It's a pleasure simply to wander aimlessly around Annecy's medieval old town, a photogenic jumble of narrow streets, turquoise canals and colonnaded passageways. Continue down to the tree-fringed lakefront and the flowery **Jardins de l'Europe**, linked to the popular picnic spot **Champ de Mars** by the poetic iron arch of the **Pont des Amours** (Lovers' Bridge).

Sleeping

Annecy Hostel HOSTEL €

(☎09 53 12 02 90; www.annecyhostel.fr; 32 av de Loverchy; dm/d €22/55; wi-fi) Run by two well-travelled brothers, this newcomer makes backpackers' hearts sing with its bright and funky four-bed dorms, shared kitchen, chilled TV lounge, cheap bike rental and garden. It's a five-minute walk southwest of the old town.

Hôtel Alexandra HOTEL €€

(☎04 50 52 84 33; www.hotelannecy-alexandra.fr; 19 rue Vaugelas; s/d/tr/q €55/75/95/110; wi-fi) Nice surprise: Annecy's most charming hotel is also one of its most affordable. The welcome is five-star, rooms are fresh and spotless – the best have balconies and canal views – and breakfast (€8) is a generous spread.

Splendid Hôtel BOUTIQUE HOTEL €€

(☎04 50 45 20 00; www.hotel-annecy-lac.fr; 4 quai Eustache Chappuis; s/d €109/121; air-con wi-fi) 'Splendid' sums up the lakefront position of this hotel, with breezy views from its boutique-chic, parquet-floor rooms.

Camping Les Rives du Lac CAMPGROUND €

(☎04 50 52 40 14; www.lesrivesdulac-annecy.com; 331 chemin des Communaux; sites €23; ⊙mid-Apr–Sep; ☺wi-fi) Pitch your tent near the lakefront at this shady campground, 5km south of town in Sévrier. A cycling track runs into central Annecy from here.

Eating

The old-town quays along Canal du Thiou are jam-packed with touristy cafes and pizzerias. Crêpes, kebabs, classic French cuisine – you'll find it all along pedestrianised rue Carnot, rue de l'Isle and rue Faubourg Ste-Claire.

TOP CHOICE **L'Esquisse** REGIONAL CUISINE €€

(☎04 50 44 80 59; www.esquisse-annecy.fr; 21 rue Royale; lunch menus €19-22, dinner menus €29-60; ⊙lunch & dinner Mon-Tue & Thu-Sat) A talented husband-and-wife team run the show at this intimate bistro, with just six tables that fill predictably quickly. Carefully composed menus sing with natural, integral flavours, from wild mushrooms to spider crab.

La Ciboulette GASTRONOMIC €€€

(☎04 50 45 74 57; www.laciboulette-annecy.com; 10 rue Vaugelas, cour du Pré Carré; menus €35-63; ⊙lunch & dinner Tue-Sat) Such class! Crisp white linen and gold-kissed walls set the scene at this Michelin-starred place, where chef Georges Paccard cooks fresh seasonal specialities. Reservations are essential.

L'Étage SAVOYARD €€

(☎04 50 51 03 28; 13 rue du Pâquier; menus €22-34; ⊙lunch & dinner) Cheese, glorious cheese... *Fromage* is given pride of place in spot-on fondues and *raclette* (melting cheese, boiled potatoes, charcuterie and baby gherkins), with mellow music and cheerful staff as backdrop.

La Cuisine des Amis BISTRO €€

(☎04 50 10 10 80; 9 rue du Pâquier; menus €15-31; ⊙lunch & dinner; child-friendly) Opening onto a great people-watching terrace, this charcoal-walled bistro welcomes its clientele like *amis* (friends). Dine well on dishes like *marmite du pêcheur* (seafood stew) and Moroccan-style *pastilla* (crisp puff pastry pie filled with goat's cheese, figs and honey).

Information

Tourist office (☎04 50 45 00 33; www.lac-annecy.com; Centre Bonlieu, 1 rue Jean Jaurès; ⊙9am-6.30pm Mon-Sat, 10am-1pm Sun)

Getting There & Away

BUS From the **bus station** (rue de l'Industrie), adjoining the train station, **Billetterie Crolard** (www.voyages-crolard.com) sells €1.50 tickets for roughly hourly buses to villages around the lake, local ski resorts and Lyon St-Exupéry airport (one-way/return €33/50, 2¼ hours). **Autocars Frossard** (www.frossard.eu) sells tickets for Geneva (€10.50, 1¾ hours, 16 daily).

TRAIN From Annecy's **train station** (place de la Gare), there are frequent trains to Lyon (€24.70, two hours) and Paris' Gare de Lyon (€76, four hours).

Grenoble

POP 158,221

With a dress-circle location overlooking the jagged mountains of the **Parc Naturel Régional de Chartreuse** and the **Parc Naturel Régional du Vercors**, Grenoble's backdrop is nothing short of extraordinary. At first glance the city iself is not quite so intoxicating, but taking a moment to linger rewards with fine museums, tasty dining and an effervescent nightlife buoyed by some 60,000 students.

Sights

Fort de la Bastille FORTRESS

(www.bastille-grenoble.com) Built high and mighty to withstand invasions by the dukes of Savoy, this 19th-century fort lures camera-toting crowds with its far-reaching views over Grenoble and the swiftly flowing River Isère to the peaks of the Vercors and, on cloud-free days, the snowy hump of Mont Blanc. Panels map out trails from gentle family walks to day hikes.

MOUNTAIN ACTION!

Get the scoop on mountain activities around Grenoble – skiing, snowboarding, ice climbing, walking, mountain biking, rock climbing and more – from knowledgeable staff at Grenoble's **Maison de la Montagne** (www.grenoble-montagne.com; 3 rue Raoul Blanchard; 9.30am-12.30pm & 1-6pm Mon-Fri, 10am-1pm & 2-5pm Sat).

If you're heading out for the day to one of the town's nearby ski resorts, jump lift-pass queues by buying your pass in advance from Grenoble's tourist office.

To reach the fort, hop aboard the riverside **Téléphérique Grenoble Bastille** (quai Stéphane Jay; adult/child one way €5/3, return €7/4.50; Feb-Dec). The ascent in glass bubbles, which climb 264m from the quay, is almost more fun than the fort itself.

TOP CHOICE **Musée de Grenoble** MUSEUM

(www.museedegrenoble.fr; 5 place de Lavalette; adult/child €5/free; 10am-6.30pm Wed-Mon) Also called the Musée des Beaux-Arts, Grenoble's boldest museum is renowned for its distinguished modern collection, including star pieces by Chagall, Matisse, Canaletto, Monet and Picasso.

Magasin Centre National d'Art Contemporain MUSEUM

(www.magasin-cnac.org; 155 cours Berriat; adult/child €3.50/2; 2-7pm Tue-Sun) Ensconced in a cavernous glass and steel warehouse built by Gustave Eiffel, this is one of Europe's leading centres of contemporary art. Take tram A to Berriat-Le Magasin stop, about 2km west of the town centre.

FREE **Musée Dauphinois** MUSEUM

(www.musee-dauphinois.fr; 30 rue Maurice Gignoux; 10am-6pm Wed-Mon) Atmospherically set in a 17th-century convent, this regional museum spells out alpine cultures, crafts and traditions, and the region's skiing history. Find it at the foot of the hill below Fort de la Bastille.

FREE **Musée de l'Ancien Évêché** MUSEUM

(www.ancien-eveche-isere.fr; 2 rue Très Cloîtres; 9am-6pm Mon, Tue, Thu & Fri, 1-6pm Wed, 11am-6pm Sat & Sun) On place Notre Dame, the Italianate **Cathédrale Notre Dame** and adjoining 13th-century **Bishops' Palace** – originally home to Grenoble's bishops – form this museum. The rich collection traces local history from prehistory to the 21st century, and takes visitors beneath the cathedral square to a crypt safeguarding old Roman walls and a baptistery dating from the 4th to 10th centuries.

FREE **Musée de la Résistance et de la Déportation de l'Isère** MUSEUM

(www.resistance-en-isere.fr; 14 rue Hébert; 9am-6pm Mon & Wed-Fri, 1.30-6pm Tue, 10am-6pm Sat & Sun) This emotive museum examines the deportation of Jews and other 'undesirables'

WORTH A TRIP

GREAT ESCAPES

Southwest of Grenoble, the gently rolling pastures and chiselled limestone peaks of the 1750-sq-km **Parc Natural Régional du Vercors** are the stuff of soft adventure. Quieter and cheaper than neighbouring Alpine resorts, the wildlife-rich park is a magnet for enthusiasts of fresh air, cross-country skiing, snowshoeing, caving and hiking. Its accommodation, moreover, is the stuff of Alpine dreams.

Les Allières (☎04 76 94 32 32; www.aubergedesallieres.com; Lans-en-Vercors; r with shared bathroom incl half board per person €47) This 1476m-high forest chalet offers no-frills digs (bunk beds, shared toilets) and wondrous mountain food (mains €18 to €30). The wood-fire *raclette* and *tarte aux myrtilles* (blueberry tart) are divine.

À la Crécia (☎04 76 95 46 98; www.gite-en-vercors.com; 436 Chemin des Cléments, Lans-en-Vercors; s/d/tr/q €58/63/78/93, dinner menus €19) Goats, pigs and poultry rule the roost at this 16th-century, solar-powered farm. Rooms are stylishly rustic with beams, earthy hues and mosaic bathrooms. Dinner is a farm-fresh feast.

Gîte La Verne (☎04 76 95 21 18; http://gite.laverne.free.fr; La Verne, Méaudre; apt per week for 4/8 people €500/750) Fitted with fully equipped kitchens, these beautiful apartments blend Alpine cosiness with mod cons. Whether you opt for self-catering or half-board, you'll luurv the *hammam* and outdoor Norwegian bath.

from Grenoble to Nazi camps during WWII in a cool-headed way. It also zooms in on the role of the Vercors region in the French Resistance.

Sleeping

Le Grand Hôtel HOTEL €€
(☎04 76 51 22 59; www.grand-hotel-grenoble.fr; 5 rue de la République; r €118-245; ❄@📶) Right in the thick of things, this newly revamped hotel raises the bar in Grenoble's style stakes with slick, monochromatic rooms, some with balconies looking out across the city to the Alps beyond.

Auberge de Jeunesse HOSTEL €
(☎04 76 09 33 52; www.fuaj.org; 10 av du Grésivaudan; dm incl breakfast €21.50; 📶) Grenoble's ultramodern, ecoconscious hostel is set in parkland, 5km from the centre. Take bus 1 to La Quinzaine stop, an easy two-minute walk from the hostel.

Eating & Drinking

Grenoble's most atmospheric bistros huddle on backstreets in the *quartier des Antiquaires* (Antiques Quarter). Don't miss local dish *gratin dauphinois* (finely sliced potatoes oven-baked in cream and a pinch of nutmeg).

La Petite Idée FRENCH €€
(☎04 76 47 52 95; www.la-petite-idee.fr; 7 cours Jean Jaurès; menus €15.50-28; ⊙lunch Sun-Fri, dinner Tue-Sun; 👪) This sweet bistro had *la petite idée* (the little idea) to drum up business with market-fresh, seasonal dishes, as simple as rosemary-rubbed lamb with creamy *gratin dauphinois*. The setting is convivial and the €9.50 *plat du jour* is great value.

Ciao a Te ITALIAN €€
(☎04 76 42 54 41; 2 rue de la Paix; mains €16.50-26; ⊙lunch & dinner Tue-Sat, closed Aug) Stylish yet relaxed, Ciao dishes up authentic Italian cuisine. Book ahead.

Chez Mémé Paulette CAFE €
(☎04 76 51 38 85; 2 rue St-Hugues; snacks €4-8; ⊙lunch & dinner Tue-Sat) This old curiosity shop of a cafe is crammed with antique books, milk jugs, cuckoo clocks and other knick-knacks. It draws a young crowd with its wallet-friendly grub – from soups to *tartines* and homemade tarts.

Le 365 WINE BAR
(3 rue Bayard; ⊙6pm-1am Tue-Sat) If Dionysus (god of wine) had a house, this is surely what it would look like: an irresistible clutter of bottles, oil paintings and candles that create an ultrarelaxed setting for quaffing one of the wines on offer.

Information

Tourist Office (☎04 76 42 41 41; www.grenoble-tourisme.com; 14 rue de la République; ⊙9am-6.30pm Mon-Sat, 9am-2pm Sun)

Getting There & Away

Air

Several budget airlines fly to/from **Grenoble-Isère airport** (www.grenoble-airport.com), 45km northwest and linked by **shuttle bus** (www.grenoble-altitude.com; single/return €12.50/22, 45 minutes, twice daily Tue-Sat).

Bus

From the **bus station** (rue Émile Gueymard), next to the train station, **VFD** (www.vfd.fr) and **Transisère** (www.transisere.fr) run buses to/from various destinations including Geneva (€46.50, two hours) and Lyon St-Exupéry (€22, one hour) airports.

Train

From the **train station** (rue Émile Gueymard), frequent trains run to/from Paris' Gare de Lyon (from €80, 3½ hours) and Lyon (€20.50, 1½ hours).

THE JURA

The dark wooded hills, rolling dairy country and limestone plateaux of the Jura Mountains, stretching in an arc for 360km along the Franco-Swiss border from the Rhine to the Rhône, comprise one of the least explored pockets in France. Rural, deeply traditional and *un petit peu* eccentric, the Jura is the place if you're seeking serenity, authentic farmstays and a taste of mountain life.

The Jura – from a Gaulish word meaning 'forest' – is France's premier cross-country skiing area. The range is dotted with ski stations, and every year the region hosts the **Transjurassienne**, one of the world's toughest cross-country skiing events.

Besançon

POP 121,391

Home to a monumental Vauban citadel, France's first public museum, and the birthplace of Victor Hugo and the Lumière Brothers, Besançon has an extraordinary background and yet, remarkably, remains something of a secret. Straddling seven hills and hugging the banks of the River Doubs, the cultured capital of Franche-Comté remains refreshingly modest and untouristy, despite charms such as its graceful 18th-century old town, first-rate restaurants and happening bars pepped up by the city's students.

The opening of a new TGV station in the village of Auxon, 12km north, in late 2011, put Besançon firmly back on the map.

Sights

TOP CHOICE **Citadelle de Besançon** CITADEL

(www.citadelle.com; rue des Fusillés de la Résistance; adult/child €9/6; ⏲9am-6pm) Besançon's crowning glory is this Unesco World Heritage-listed citadel designed by Vauban for Louis XIV in the late 17th century. It harbours three museums: the **Musée Comtois** covering local traditions, the **Musée d'Histoire Naturelle** on natural history, and the harrowing **Musée de la Résistance et de la Déportation** which look at the rise of Nazism and fascism, and the French Resistance movement. There's an **insectarium**, **aquarium**, pitch-black, ho-hum **noctarium** and an overly cramped **parc zoologique**.

TOP CHOICE **Musée des Beaux-Arts et d'Archéologie** MUSEUM

(www.musee-arts-besancon.org; 1 place de la Révolution; adult/child €5/free; ⏲9.30am-noon & 2-6pm Wed-Mon) This museum was founded in 1694 (when the Louvre was but a twinkle in Paris' eye). The stellar collection spans Egyptian mummies, Neolithic tools and Gallo-Roman mosaics; a cavernous drawing cabinet with 5500 works, including Dürer, Delacroix and Rodin masterpieces; and 14th- to 20th-century painting with standouts by Titian, Rubens, Goya and Matisse.

Tours

When the sun's out, a river cruise is a relaxed way to see Besançon. April to October, vessels dock beneath Pont de la République to take passengers on 1¼-hour cruises along the River Doubs, which include a glide

WORTH A TRIP

SALINE ROYALE

Envisaged by its designer, Claude-Nicolas Ledoux, as the 'ideal city', the 18th-century **Saline Royale** (Royal Saltworks; www.salineroyale.com; adult/child €7.50/3.50; ⏲9am-noon & 2-6pm) in Arc-et-Senans, 35km southwest of Besançon, is a showpiece of early Industrial Age town planning. Although his urban dream was never fully realised, Ledoux's semicircular saltworks is now listed as a Unesco World Heritage site.

Regular trains link Besançon and Arc-et-Senans (€7, 30 minutes, 10 daily).

WORTH A TRIP

A WINE LOVER'S TRIP

Corkscrewing through some 80km of well-tended vines, pretty countryside and stone villages is the **Route des Vins de Jura** (Jura Wine Road; www.laroutedesvinsdujura.com). Linger in **Arbois**, Jura wine capital, where the history of its *vin jaune* is told in the **Musée de la Vigne et du Vin** (www.juramusees.fr; adult/child €3.50/3; ⏲10am-noon & 2-6pm Wed-Mon), inside the whimsical **Château Pécauld**. Next to the chateau, pick up the **Chemin des Vignes** (2.5km) walking trail or **Circuit des Vignes** (8km) mountain-bike route through vines.

Later, lunch on local organic produce at **La Balance Mets et Vins** (☎03 84 37 45 00; 47 rue de Courcelles, Arbois; menus €16.50-37; ⏲lunch & dinner Thu-Mon, lunch Tue & Wed;). Its signature *coq au vin jaune et aux morilles* casserole, and crème brûlée doused in *vin jaune* are must-tastes, as are the wine *menus* with five glasses of Jurassienne wine (€17) or *vin jaune* (€25, including a vintage one). Kids can sniff, swirl and sip, too, with three kinds of organic grape juice (€7.80).

Above Arbois is **Pupillin**, a yellow-brick village famous for its wine production with several wine cellars to visit. Arbois' **tourist office** (☎03 84 66 55 50; www.arbois.com; 17 rue de l'Hôtel de Ville; ⏲9am-noon & 2-6pm Mon-Sat) has a list of many more. Trains links Arbois and Besançon (€9, 45 minutes, 10 daily).

along a 375m-long tunnel underneath the citadel.

Bateaux du Saut du Doubs BOAT TOUR
(www.sautdudoubs.fr; adult/child €13/9; ⏲10am, 2.30pm & 4.30pm Jul & Aug)

Sleeping & Eating

TOP CHOICE **Charles Quint Hôtel** HISTORIC HOTEL €€
(☎03 81 82 05 49; www.hotel-charlesquint.com; 3 rue du Chapître; d €89-145;) This grand 18th-century townhouse is sublime, with a pool-clad garden slumbering in the shade of the citadel, behind the cathedral.

Hôtel Granvelle HOTEL €
(☎03 81 81 33 92; www.hotel-granvelle.fr; 13 rue du Général Lecourbe; r €54-68;) You'll find 30 neat and tidy, if dated, rooms in this stone building below the citadel. 'Interactive' rooms have internet-linked computers and flatscreen TVs.

TOP CHOICE **Le Saint-Pierre** MODERN FRENCH €€€
(☎03 81 81 20 99; www.restaurant-saintpierre.com; 104 rue Battant; menus €38-70; ⏲lunch Mon-Fri, dinner Mon-Sat) White tablecloths, exposed stone and subtle lighting are the perfect backdrop for the intense flavours of lobster fricassee with spinach and herb ravioli, expertly paired with regional wines. The three-course *menu marché* is excellent value at €38. The restaurant is 500m north of Grande Rue on the opposite side of the river.

Getting There & Away

Besançon Gare Viotte is 800m uphill from the city centre. Useful routes:

Paris €60 to €85, 2¾ hours, 14 daily

Dijon €15, 70 minutes, 20 daily

Lyon €30 to €45, 2½ to three hours, 25 daily

Connections to major cities are quicker from the new **Gare de Besançon Franche-Comté TGV station**, 12km north of the centre and a 15-minute hop by train from Gare Viotte.

THE DORDOGNE

If it's French heart and soul you're after, look no further. Tucked in the country's south-western corner, the Dordogne fuses history, culture and culinary sophistication in one unforgettably scenic package. The region is best known for its sturdy *bastides* (fortified towns), clifftop chateaux and spectacular prehistoric cave paintings, neighboured to the southwest by the Mediterranean-tinged region of **the Lot**, with its endless vintage vineyards.

Sarlat-La-Canéda

POP 9943

A gorgeous tangle of honey-coloured buildings, alleyways and secret squares make up this unmissable Dordogne village – a natural, if touristy, launchpad into the Vézère Valley.

Part of the fun of Sarlat is getting lost in its twisting alleyways and backstreets. **Rue Jean-Jacques Rousseau** or **rue Landry** are good starting points, but for the grandest buildings and *hôtels particuliers,* explore **rue des Consuls**. Whichever street you take, sooner or later you'll hit the **Cathédrale St-Sacerdos** (place du Peyrou), a real mix of architectural styles and periods: the belfry and western facade are the oldest parts.

Nearby, the former **Église Ste-Marie** (place de la Liberté) houses Sarlat's mouthwatering **Marché Couvert** (covered market) and a state-of-the-art **panoramic lift** (elevator), designed by French architect Jean Nouvel, in its bell tower.

Sleeping

Villa des Consuls B&B €€
(05 53 31 90 05; www.villaconsuls.fr; 3 rue Jean-Jacques Rousseau; d €82-103, apt €124-184;) Despite its Renaissance exterior, the enormous rooms here are modern through and through, with shiny wood floors, sofas and original roof trusses.

La Maison des Peyrat HOTEL €€
(05 53 59 00 32; www.maisondespeyrat.com; Le Lac de la Plane; r €56-103) This beautiful 17th-century house with lovingly tended gardens sits on a hill about 1.5km from town. Its 11 generously sized rooms are fairly plain, but ooze country charisma.

Hôtel Les Récollets HOTEL €
(05 53 31 36 00; www.hotel-recollets-sarlat.com; 4 rue Jean-Jacques Rousseau; d €49-89;) Budget rooms with an old town location, set around a pretty hidden courtyard.

Eating

 **Le Grand Bleu** GASTRONOMIC €€€
(05 53 29 82 14; www.legrandbleu.eu; 43 av de la Gare; menus €36-65; lunch Thu-Sun, dinner Tue-Sat) For a proper supper, this Michelin-starred restaurant is the choice – think creative cuisine that makes maximum use of luxury produce: truffles, lobster, turbot and St-Jacques scallops. Cooking courses as well.

Le Bistrot REGIONAL CUISINE €€
(05 53 28 28 40; place du Peyrou; menus €18.50-28.50; Mon-Sat) This dinky diner is the best of the bunch on cafe-clad place du Peyrou. Gingham cloths and tiny tables create a cosy bistro feel, and the menu's heavy on Sarlat classics – especially walnuts, *magret de canard* (duck breast) and *pommes sarlardaises* (potatoes cooked in duck fat).

Information

Tourist Office (05 53 31 45 45; www.sarlat-tourisme.com; rue Tourny; 9am-7pm Mon-Sat, 10am-1pm & 2-6pm Sun Jul & Aug, shorter hours Sep-Jun)

TRUFFLE CAPITAL

For culinary connoisseurs there is just one reason to visit the Dordogne: black truffles *(truffes).* A subterranean fungi that thrives on the roots of oak trees, this mysterious little mushroom is notoriously capricious. The art of truffle-hunting is a closely guarded secret and vintage crops fetch as much as €1000 per kg. Truffles are sought after by top chefs for an infinite array of gourmet dishes, but black truffles are often best eaten quite simply in a plain egg omelette, shaved over buttered pasta or sliced on fresh crusty bread.

Truffles are hunted by dogs (and occasionally pigs) from December to March and sold at special truffle markets in the Dordogne, including in Périgueux, Sarlat and most notably, the 'world's truffle capital', **Sorges** (population 1234). This tiny village, 23km northeast of Périgueux on the N21, is the place to brush up on truffle culture; head to the **Ecomusée de la Truffe** (www.ecomusee-truffe-sorges.com; Le Bourg, Sorges; adult/child €5/2.50; 9.30am-12.30pm & 2.30-6.30pm daily Jun-Sep, closed Mon Oct-May) and hook yourself up with a truffle hunt. **La Truffe Noire de Sorges** (06 08 45 09 48; www.truffe-sorges.com; tours €15-25; by reservation Dec-Feb & Jun-Sep) runs tours of *truffiéres* (the areas where truffles are cultivated), followed by a tasting.

Then there is **Auberge de la Truffe** (05 53 05 02 05; www.auberge-de-la-truffe.com; Sorges; r €55-81, f €110-145;) in the centre of Sorges, with its stylish and renowned **restaurant** (menus €23-57) serving sensational seasonal cuisine. For culinary connoisseurs there is just one fixed menu to order, the *menu truffe* (€100).

Getting There & Away

The **train station** (ave de la Gare), 1.3km south of the old city, serves Périgueux (change at Le Buisson; €14.80, 1¾ hours, three daily) and Les Eyzies (change at Le Buisson; €9.80, 50 minutes to 2½ hours, three daily).

Les Eyzies-de-Tayac-Sireuil

POP 860

A hot base for touring the extraordinary cave collection of the **Vézère Valley**, this village is essentially a clutch of touristy shops strung along a central street. Its **Musée National de Préhistoire** (05 53 06 45 45; www.musee-prehistoire-eyzies.fr; 1 rue du Musée; adult/child €5/3, 1st Sun of month free; 9.30am-6pm Wed-Mon), rife with amazing prehistoric finds, makes a great introduction to the area.

About 250m north of the museum is the Cro-Magnon shelter of **Abri Pataud** (05 53 06 92 46; pataud@mnhn.fr; 20 rue du Moyen Âge; adult/child €5/3; 10am-noon & 2-6pm Sun-Thu), with an ibex carving dating from about 19,000 BC. Admission includes a guided tour (some in English).

Train services link Les Eyzies with Sarlat-la-Canéda.

THE ATLANTIC COAST

With quiet country roads winding through vine-striped hills and wild stretches of coastal sands interspersed with misty islands, the Atlantic coast is where France gets back to nature. Much more laid-back than the Med, this is the place to slow right down.

If you're a surf nut or a beach bum, then the sandy bays around Biarritz will be right up your alley, while oenophiles can sample the fruits of the vine in the high temple of French winemaking, Bordeaux. Towards the Pyrenees you'll find the Basque Country, which in many ways is closer to the culture of northern Spain than to the rest of France.

Nantes

POP 290,100

You can take Nantes out of Brittany (as happened when regional boundaries were redrawn during WWII), but you can't take Brittany out of its long-time capital, Nantes ('Naoned' in Breton). Spirited and innovative, this city has a long history of reinventing itself. Founded by Celts, the city later became France's foremost port, industrial cen-

DON'T MISS

PREHISTORIC PAINTINGS

Fantastic prehistoric **caves** with some of the world's finest **cave art** is what makes the Vézère Valley so very special. Most of the caves are closed in winter, and get very busy in summer. Visitor numbers are strictly limited, so you'll need to reserve well ahead.

Of the valley's 175 known sites, the most famous include **Grotte de Font de Gaume** (05 53 06 86 00; http://eyzies.monuments-nationaux.fr/; adult/child €7.50/free; 9.30am-5.30pm Sun-Fri mid-May–mid-Sep, 9.30am-12.30pm & 2-5.30pm Sun-Fri mid-Sep–mid-May), 1km northeast of Les Eyzies. About 14,000 years ago, prehistoric artists created the gallery of over 230 figures, including bison, reindeer, horses, mammoths, bears and wolves, of which 25 are on permanent display.

About 7km east of Les Eyzies, **Abri du Cap Blanc** (05 53 06 86 00; adult/child €7.50/free; 10am-6pm Sun-Fri mid-May–mid-Sep, 10am-noon & 2-6pm Sun-Fri mid-Sep–mid-May) showcases an unusual sculpture gallery of horses, bison and deer.

Then there is **Grotte de Rouffignac** (05 53 05 41 71; www.grottederouffignac.fr; adult/child €6.50/4.20; 9-11.30am & 2-6pm Jul & Aug, 10-11.30am & 2-5pm Sep-Jun), sometimes known as the 'Cave of 100 Mammoths' because of its painted mammoths. Access to the caves, hidden in woodland 15km north of Les Eyzies, is aboard a trundling electric train.

Star of the show goes hands down to **Grotte de Lascaux** (Lascaux II; 05 53 51 95 03; www.semitour.com; adult/child €8.80/6; 9.30am-6pm), 2km southeast of Montignac, featuring an astonishing menagerie including oxen, deer, horses, reindeer and mammoth, as well as an amazing 5.5m bull, the largest cave drawing ever found. The original cave was closed to the public in 1963 to prevent damage to the paintings, but the most famous sections have been meticulously recreated in a second cave nearby – a massive undertaking that required some 20 artists and took 11 years.

NANTES CITY PASS

Sold at the tourist office, the **Pass Nantes** (one-/two-/three day pass €25/35/45) gets you unlimited travel on buses and trams, entry into museums and monuments, a guided tour, shopping discounts and various other handy extras.

tre and shipbuilding hub, and has recently reinvented itself again as a cultural centre and youthful metropolis – one in two Nantais is under 40!

Sights

TOP CHOICE Les Machines de l'Île de Nantes THEME PARK
(www.lesmachines-nantes.fr; Parc des Chantiers, Blvd Léon Bureau; adult/child €7/5.50; ⊙10am-7pm Jul-Aug, hrs vary rest of year) Inside this fantasy world you can prance around on the back of a 45-tonne **mechanical elephant**, voyage on a boat through rough and dangerous oceans, or twirl through the sky aboard Le Carrousel des Mondes Marines; a 25m high funfair carousel like you've never seen before. Gallery tickets are good for the workshop, where you can watch these fantastical contraptions being built.

Château des Ducs de Bretagne CASTLE, MUSEUM
(www.chateau-nantes.fr; 4 place Marc Elder; adult/child €5/3; ⊙8am-7pm Apr-Oct, shorter hrs rest of year) Forget fusty furnishings – the stripped, light-filled interior of the restored Château des Ducs de Bretagne houses multimedia-rich exhibits detailing the city's history. Frequent temporary exhibitions (additional fee), too.

Musée Jules Verne MUSEUM
(www.julesverne.nantes.fr; 3 rue de l'Hermitage; adult/child €3/1.50; ⊙10am-7pm Tue-Sun) Overlooking the river, this is a magical museum with 1st-edition books, hand-edited manuscripts and cardboard theatre cut-outs. Child-friendly interactive displays introduce or reintroduce you to the work of Jules Verne, who was born in Nantes in 1828. The museum is a 2km walk down river from the town centre.

Musée des Beaux-Arts MUSEUM
(10 rue Georges Clemenceau; adult €3.50; ⊙10am-6pm Wed & Fri-Mon, to 8pm Thu) One of the finest collections of French paintings outside Paris hangs in the Musée des Beaux-Arts, with works by Georges de la Tour, Chagall, Monet, Picasso and Kandinsky among others. Due to reopen after renovations in late 2013.

Sleeping

TOP CHOICE Hôtel Pommeraye BOUTIQUE HOTEL €€
(☎02 40 48 78 79; www.hotel-pommeraye.com; 2 rue Boileau; s €54-139 d €59-144; ❄📶) Sleek and chic, this is more art gallery than hotel. Rooms have shimmering short-pile carpets and textured walls in shades of pale grey, gold, chocolate and violet.

Hötel Amiral HOTEL €€
(☎02 40 69 20 21; www.hotel-nantes.fr; 26bis rue Scribe; s/d from €84/89; 📶) The rooms at this excellent little hotel are fairly plain but the common areas are funky and the breakfast room a commotion of jungle plants. The family who run it are really helpful.

Hôtel Graslin HOTEL €€
(☎02 40 69 72 91; www.hotel-graslin.com; 1 rue Piron; r €59-109; 📶) The unlikely (but very Nantes) marriage of art deco and the '70s at this refurbished hotel includes details like eggplant-and-orange wing chairs in the lounge.

Auberge de Jeunesse La Manu HOSTEL €
(☎02 40 29 29 20; www.fuaj.org/Nantes; 2 place de la Manu; dm incl breakfast €20.10; ⊙closed Christmas; 📶) Housed in an old converted factory, this well-equipped 123-bed hostel is

DON'T MISS

INDUSTRIAL CHIC

Nantes has no shortage of edgy spots and there is no better place to start than the **Hangar à Bananes** (www.hangar-abananes.com; 21 quai des Antilles; ⊙daily till late), a rejuvenated banana-ripening warehouse on Île de Nantes with more than a dozen restaurants, bars and clubs (and combinations thereof), each hipper than the next. The front terraces of most face Daniel Buren's art installation **Anneaux de Buren** (quai des Antilles), illuminated at night.

Or try industrial-chic **Le Lieu Unique** (www.lelieuunique.com; 2 rue de la Biscuiterie), the one-time LU biscuit-factory-turned-performance-arts space where you can catch dance, theatre and contemporary art. Its restaurant, polished concrete bar buzzes and basement *hamman* (Turkish bath) buzzes.

WORTH A TRIP

GREEN VENICE

Floating along emerald waterways – tinted green in spring and summer by duckweed – in a kayak or rowing boat is a real Zen highlight. Dubbed *Venise Verte* (Green Venice), the **Parc Naturel Interrégional du Marais Poitevin** is a tranquil, bird-filled wetland covering some 800 sq km of wet and drained marshland, threaded with canals, cycling paths and the odd waterside village.

Boating and **cycling** are the only ways to explore and there is no shortage of bikes (per hour/half-day €6/13) and flat-bottomed boats (from €15/38) or kayaks (from €12/30) to rent from the Marais Poitevin's two main bases: tiny, honey-coloured **Coulon** and (our favourite, being a sucker for romance), the pretty village of **Arçais**. Try **Arçais Venise Verte** (www.veniseverteloisirs.fr), **Au Martin Pecheur** (www.aumartinpecheur.com) or **Bardet-Huttiers** (www.marais-arcais.com).

To ensure complete and utter head-over-the-heels love, stay overnight at the environmentally friendly **Maison Flore** (05 49 76 27 11; www.maisonflore.com; rue du Grand Port, Arçais; s/d €63/74; closed Christmas–mid-Feb; P@). Romantically set on Arçais' waterfront, the 10-room boutique hotel is painted the colours of local marsh plants such as the pale-green angelica and bright-purple iris. Books and board games in the lounge add a cosy touch and you can rent boats.

Getting to Green Venice is painful in anything other than your own car.

a 15-minute walk from the centre. Lock-out noon to 4pm. Take tram 1 to the Manufacture stop.

Eating

Nantes' most cosmopolitan dining is in the medieval Bouffay quarter around rue de la Juiverie, rue des Petites Écuries and rue de la Bâclerie. Rue Jean Jacques Rousseau and rue Santeuil are other busy eat streets.

In March and November, buy sardines at street stalls all over town.

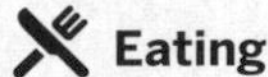

TOP CHOICE Le Bistrot de l'Écrivain MODERN FRENCH €€
(02 51 84 15 15; 15 rue Jean Jacques Rousseau; menus €14.50-18.50; Mon-Sat) Splashed in shades of red with wine bottles lining the walls, Le Bistrot de l'Écrivain is a relaxed place with all the Nantaise standards on the menu, plus dishes with an unexpected twist.

Les Pieds dans le Plat MODERN FRENCH €€
(02 40 69 25 15; 13 rue Jean-Jacques Rousseau; menus €13.50-25.50; 11.30am-midnight) This modern French bistro has exposed stone walls, colourful paint work and is the real flavour of the month; advance reservations strongly advised.

Un Coin en Ville MODERN FRENCH €
(02 40 20 05 97; 2 place de la Bourse; menus from €14.95; lunch & dinner Mon-Fri, dinner only Sat) Expect flickering tea-light candles, soulful jazz and blues, and cooking that combines local produce with exotic styles, such as red curry with prawns and scallops.

Information

Tourist office (www.nantes-tourisme.com; 2 place St-Pierre & cours Olivier de Clisson; 10am-6pm Mon-Sat, from 10.30am Thu)

Getting There & Away

AIR **Aéroport International Nantes-Atlantique** (www.nantes.aeroport.fr) is 12km southeast of town.

TRAIN Destinations from the **train station** (27 bd de Stalingrad) include Paris' Gare Montparnasse (from €58, two hours, 15 to 20 daily) and Bordeaux (€47, four hours, three or four daily).

Poitiers

POP 91,300

Inland from the coast, history-steeped Poitiers rose to prominence as the former capital of Poitou, the region governed by the Counts of Poitiers in the Middle Ages. Poitiers has one of the oldest universities in the country, first established in 1432 and today a lynchpin of this lively city.

Sights

Église Notre Dame la Grande CHURCH
(place Charles de Gaulle) The earliest parts of this church date from the 11th century; three of the five choir chapels were added in the 15th century, with the six chapels along the

northern wall of the nave added in the 16th century. The only original frescoes are the faint 12th- or 13th-century works that adorn the U-shaped dome above the choir. Every evening from 21 June to the third weekend in September, spectacular colours are cinematically projected onto the west facade of this church.

Baptistère St-Jean CHURCH
(rue Jean Jaurès; adult/child €2/1; ⌚10.30am-12.30pm & 3-6pm Wed-Mon Apr-Oct) Constructed in the 4th and 6th centuries on Roman foundations, Baptistère St-Jean, 100m south of Cathédrale St-Pierrel, was redecorated in the 10th century and used as a parish church. The octagonal hole under the frescos was used for total-immersion baptisms, practised until the 7th century. In July and August it's open daily.

Futuroscope THEME PARK
(www.futuroscope.com; adult/child €35/26; ⌚10am-11.15pm Jul-Aug, shorter hrs Sep-Dec & Feb-Jun) This cinematic theme park, 10km north of Poitiers in Jaunay-Clan, takes you whizzing through space, diving into the deep blue ocean depths and on a close encounter with futuristic creatures. To keep things cutting edge, one-third of the attractions change annually. Many are motion-seat setups requiring a minimum height of 120cm. From Poitiers' train station take bus 1 or E (€1.30, 30 minutes).

Sleeping & Eating

Hôtel de l'Europe HISTORIC HOTEL €
(☎05 49 88 12 00; www.hotel-europe-poitiers.com; 39 rue Carnot; s/d €59/65; 📶) The main building of this elegant, very un-two-star-like hotel dates from 1710, with a sweeping staircase, oversized rooms and refined furnishings. The annexe has modern rooms.

Hôtel Central HOTEL €
(☎05 49 01 79 79; www.hotel-central-poitiers.com; 35 place du Maréchal Leclerc; r from €52; 📶) At the southern edge of a charming pedestrian district of half-timbered houses, this two-star place is a terrific little bargain. Rooms are (very!) snug but sunlit.

La Serrurerie FRENCH €
(☎05 49 41 05 14; 28 rue des Grandes Écoles; menu €12.50, mains €10-17.50; ⌚8am-2am) Hecticly busy, this mosaic-and-steel bistro-bar is Poitiers' communal lounge-dining room. A chalked blackboard menu lists specialities like *tournedos* (thick slices) of salmon, pastas and a crème brûlée you'll be dreaming about until your next visit.

Information

Tourist office (☎05 49 41 21 24; www.ot-poitiers.fr; 45 place Charles de Gaulle; ⌚10am-11pm)

Getting There & Away

The **train station** (☎36 35; bd du Grand Cerf) has direct links to Bordeaux (€24, 1¾ hours), Nantes (from €30, 3¼ hours) and Paris' Gare Montparnasse (from €47, 1½ hours, 12 daily).

Bordeaux

POP 240,500

The new millennium was a turning point for the city long nicknamed La Belle au Bois Dormant (Sleeping Beauty), when the mayor, ex-Prime Minister Alain Juppé, roused Bordeaux, pedestrianising its boulevards, restoring its neoclassical architecture, and implementing a hi-tech public-transport system. Today the city is a Unesco World Heritage site and, with its merry student population and 2.5 million-odd annual tourists, scarcely sleeps at all.

Sights

Cathédrale St-André CATHEDRAL
This Unesco World Heritage site is almost overshadowed by the gargoyled, 50m-high Gothic belfry, **Tour Pey-Berland** (adult/child €5.50/free; ⌚10am-1.15pm & 2-6pm Jun-Sep, shorter hrs rest of year). Erected between 1440 and 1466, its spire was topped off in 1863 with the statue of Notre Dame de l'Aquitaine (Our Lady of Aquitaine). Scaling the tower's 231 narrow steps rewards you with a spectacular panorama of Bordeaux city.

Museums and Galleries MUSEUMS
Gallo-Roman statues and relics dating back 25,000 years are among the highlights at the impressive **Musée d'Aquitaine** (20 cours Pasteur), while an 1824 warehouse for French colonial produce (coffee, cocoa, peanuts, vanilla and the like) is the dramatic backdrop for cutting-edge modern art at the **CAPC Musée d'Art Contemporain** (rue Ferrére, Entrepôt 7; ⌚11am-6pm Tue & Thu-Sun, to 8pm Wed).

The evolution of Occidental art from the Renaissance to the mid-20th century fills the **Musée des Beaux-Arts** (20 cours d'Albret;

ON THE WINE TRAIL

Thirsty? The 1000-sq-km wine-growing area around the city of Bordeaux is, along with Burgundy, France's most important producer of top-quality wines. Whet your palate with Bordeaux tourist office's introduction wine-and-cheese courses (€24).

Serious students of the grape can enrol in a two-hour (€25) or two- to three-day course (€335 to €600) at the **École du Vin** (Wine School; ☎05 56 00 22 66; www.bordeaux.com) inside the **Maison du Vin de Bordeaux** (3 cours du 30 Juillet).

Bordeaux has over 5000 estates where grapes are grown, picked and turned into wine. Smaller chateaux often accept walk-in visitors, but at many places, especially better-known ones, you have to reserve in advance. If you have your own wheels, one of the easiest to visit is **Château Lanessan** (☎05 56 58 94 80; www.lanessan.com; Cussac-Fort-Medoc).

Favourite vine-framed villages brimming with charm and tasting/buying opportunities include medieval **St-Émilion** (www.saint-emilion-tourisme.com), port town **Pauillac** (www.pauillac-medoc.com) and **Listrac-Médoc**. In **Arsac-en-Médoc**, Philippe Raoux's vast glass-and-steel wine centre, **La Winery** (☎05 56 39 04 90; www.lawinery.fr; Rond-point des Vendangeurs, D1), stuns with concerts and contemporary art exhibitions alongside tastings to determine your *signe œnologique* ('wine sign'; booking required).

Many chateaux close during October's *vendange* (grape harvest).

⏲11am-6pm, closed Tue) inside the 1770s-built Hôtel de Ville.

Faience pottery, porcelain, gold, iron, glasswork and furniture are displayed at the **Musée des Arts Décoratifs** (39 rue Bouffard; ⏲2-6pm Wed-Mon).

Jardin Public GARDEN

(cours de Verdun) Landscaping is artistic as well as informative at the Jardin Public, established in 1755 and laid out in the English style a century later.

Sleeping

TOP CHOICE **Ecolodge des Chartrons** B&B €€

(☎05 56 81 49 13; www.ecolodgedeschartrons.com; 23 rue Raze; s €96-118, d €98-134; 📶) Hidden in a side street in Bordeaux' Chartrons wine merchant district, this *chambre d'hôte* is blazing a trail for ecofriendly sleeping with its solar-powered hot-water system, energy-efficient gas heating and hemp-based soundproofing. Each of the five rooms has a bathroom built from natural materials such as basalt. Organic breakfasts are served at a long timber table.

Les Chambres au Coeur de Bordeaux B&B €€

(☎05 56 52 43 58; www.aucoeurdebordeaux.fr; 28 rue Boulan; s/d from €85/95; 📶) This swish B&B has five charming rooms that are a very Bordeaux-appropriate mix of old and new; free *apéro* each evening at 7pm.

La Maison Bord'eaux BOUTIQUE HOTEL €€

(☎05 56 44 00 45; www.lamaisonbord-eaux.com; 113 rue du Docteur Albert Barraud; s/d from €145/165; P❄📶) You'd expect to find a sumptuous 18th-century chateau with conifer-flanked courtyard and stable in the countryside, but this stunning *maison d'hôte* is right in the middle of the city. *Table d'hôte* available by arrangement (€35 to €150 including wine).

Auberge de Jeunesse HOSTEL €

(☎05 56 33 00 70; www.auberge-jeunesse-bordeaux.com; 22 cours Barbey; dm incl sheets & breakfast €22.50; ⏲reception closed 11am-2pm; 📶) This ultra-modern building with kitchen reopened after renovation in 2013. From the train station, follow cours de la Marne northwest for 300m and turn left opposite the park; the hostel's about 250m ahead on your left.

Eating

Place du Parlement, rue du Pas St-Georges, rue des Faussets and place de la Victoire are loaded with dining addresses, as is the old waterfront warehouse district around quai des Marques – great for a sunset meal or drink.

TOP CHOICE **Le Cheverus Café** BISTRO €

(☎05 56 48 29 73; 81-83 rue du Loup; menus from €11.40; ⏲Mon-Sat) This neighbourhood bistro is friendly, cosy and chaotically busy (be prepared to wait for a table at lunchtime). The food dares to veer slightly away from the bistro standards of steak and chips; lunch *menus,* which include wine, are an all-out bargain. Come evening it morphs into something of a tapas bar.

TOP CHOICE **La Tupina** REGIONAL CUISINE €€
(☎05 56 91 56 37; www.latupina.com; 6 rue Porte de la Monnaie; menus €18-65, mains €27-45) Filled with the aroma of soup simmering inside an old *tupina* ('kettle' in Basque) over an open fire, this white-tableclothed place is feted far and wide for its seasonal southwestern French specialities. Find it a 10-minute walk upriver from the city centre, on a small side street. Any local can point you in the right direction.

La Boîte à Huîtres OYSTERS €€
(☎05 56 81 64 97; 36 cours du Chapeau Rouge; lunch menu €19, 6 oysters from €10) This rickety, wood-panelled place is the best place in Bordeaux to munch fresh Arcachon oysters. Traditionally they're served with sausage but you can have them in a number of different forms, including with foie gras.

Michels Bistrot BISTRO €
(15 rue du Pas-Saint-Georges; lunch menu €12) In Bordeaux's most bohemian quarter, this buzzing bistro is packed with students and those who wish they were still students. It's renowned for the quality of its beef – whether that be in hamburger form or a more classic steak. It's also a popular early evening *apéro* hangout.

ℹ Information

Main tourist office (☎05 56 00 66 00; www.bordeaux-tourisme.com; 12 cours du 30 Juillet; ⏲9am-7.30pm Mon-Sat, 9.30am-6.30pm Sun)

ℹ Getting There & Away

AIR Bordeaux airport (p434) is in Mérignac, 10km west of the city centre, with domestic and some international services.

BUS **Citram Aquitaine** (www.citram.fr) runs most buses to destinations in the Gironde.

International bus operator **Eurolines** (☎05 56 92 50 42; 32 rue Charles Domercq) faces the train station.

TRAIN From Gare St-Jean, 3km from the centre:

Paris Gare Montparnasse €73, three hours, at least 16 daily

Nantes €47.70, four hours

Poitiers €38, 1¾ hours

Toulouse from €35.30, 2¼ hours

DON'T MISS

SATURDAY-MORNING OYSTERS

A classic Bordeaux experience is a Saturday morning spent slurping oysters and white wine from one of the seafood stands to be found at **Marché des Capucins** (six oysters & glass of wine €6; ⏲7am-noon). Afterwards you can peruse the stalls while shopping for the freshest ingredients for a picnic in one of the city's parks. To get there, head south down cours Pasteur and once at place de la Victoire turn left onto rue Élie Gintrec.

Lourdes

In the heart of the Pyrenees, **Lourdes** has been one of the world's most important pilgrimage sites since 1858, when 14-year-old Bernadette Soubirous (1844–79) saw the Virgin Mary in a series of 18 visions that came to her in a grotto. The town now feels dangerously close to a religious theme park, with a roll-call of over six million miracle-seeking visitors and endless souvenir shops selling statues and Virgin Mary–shaped plastic bottles (just add holy water at the shrine). But the commercialism doesn't extend to the *sanctuaires* (sanctuaries) themselves, as they are mercifully souvenir free.

Grotte de Massabielle (Massabielle Cave) is the most revered site in the area. The Esplanade des Processions, which is lined with enormous flickering candles left by previous pilgrims, leads along a river to the grotto's entrance, where people queue up to enter the cave or to dip in one of the 19 holy baths. It's not for wallflowers: once you're behind the curtain, you're expected to strip off before being swaddled in a sheet and plunged backwards into the icy water.

The main 19th-century section of the sanctuaries is divided between the neo-Byzantine **Basilique du Rosaire**, the **crypt** and spire-topped **Basilique Supérieure** (Upper Basilica). From Palm Sunday to mid-October, nightly torchlight processions start from the Massabielle Grotto at 9pm, while at 5pm there's the **Procession Eucharistique** (Blessed Sacrament Procession) along Esplanade des Processions.

When the crowds of pilgrims get too much for you, seek refuge on the rocky 94m-high

DON'T MISS

DUNE DU PILAT

This colossal sand dune (sometimes referred to as the Dune de Pyla because of its location in the resort town of Pyla-sur-Mer), 65km west of Bordeaux, stretches from the mouth of the Bassin d'Arcachon southwards for almost 3km. Already the largest in Europe, it's spreading eastwards at 4.5m a year – it has swallowed trees, a road junction and even a hotel.

The view from the top – approximately 114m above sea level – is magnificent. To the west you can see the sandy shoals at the mouth of the **Bassin d'Arcachon**, including the **Banc d'Arguin bird reserve** and **Cap Ferret**. Dense dark-green pine forests stretch from the base of the dune eastwards almost as far as the eye can see.

Take care swimming in this area: powerful currents swirl out to sea from the deceptively tranquil *baïnes* (little bays).

Although an easy day trip from Bordeaux, the area around the dune is an enjoyable place to kick back for a while. Most people choose to camp in one of the swag of seasonal campgrounds. Lists and information on all of these (and more bricks-and-mortar-based accommodation) can be found at www.bassin-arcachon.com.

pinnacle of **Pic du Jer** – the panorama of Lourdes and the Pyrenees is inspiring. Walk three hours along a marked trail or ride six minutes in a century-old funicular. The summit is a superb picnic spot.

Lourdes is well connected by train; destinations include Bayonne (€22.40, 1¾ hours, up to four daily) and Paris' Gare Montparnasse (€75 to €107, 6½ hours, four daily).

Biarritz

POP 26,067

Edge your way south along the coast towards Spain and you arrive in stylish Biarritz, just as ritzy as its name suggests. The resort took off in the mid-19th century (Napoléon III had a rather soft spot for the place) and it still shimmers with architectural treasures from the belle époque and art deco eras. Big waves – some of Europe's best – and a beachy lifestyle are a magnet for Europe's hip surfing set.

Sights & Activities

Biarritz' raison d'être is its fashionable beaches, particularly central **Grande Plage** and **Plage Miramar**, lined end to end with sunbathing bodies on hot summer days. Stripy 1920s-style beach tents can be hired for €9.50 per day. North of Pointe St-Martin, the adrenaline-pumping surfing beaches of **Anglet** (the final 't' is pronounced) continue northwards for more than 4km. Take bus 10 or 13 from the bottom of av Verdun (just near av Édouard VII).

TOP CHOICE Cité de l'Océan MUSEUM
(☎05 59 22 75 40; www.citedelocean.com; 1 av de la Plage; adult/child €10.50/7; ⏲10am-10pm) Inside an eye-catching, wave-shaped building south of town, this museum will teach you everything about the ocean and, in between, get you to ride to the depths of the ocean in a submarine and watch giant squid and sperm whales do battle. A combined ticket with the Musée de la Mer costs €17.50/13 per adult/child.

Musée de la Mer MUSEUM
(☎05 59 22 75 40; www.museedelamer.com; Esplanade du Rocher de la Vierge; adult/child €13/9.50; ⏲9.30am-midnight Jul-Aug, shorter hrs rest of year) Housed in a wonderful art deco building, Biarritz' Sea Museum is seething with underwater life from the Bay of Biscay and beyond. Its tanks house sharks and tropical reef fish, but it's the seals that steal the show (feeding times 10.30am and 5pm).

Sleeping

TOP CHOICE Hôtel Mirano BOUTIQUE HOTEL €€
(☎05 59 23 11 63; www.hotelmirano.fr; 11 av Pasteur; d €68-130; P ⓦ) Squiggly purple, orange and black wallpaper and oversize orange perspex light fittings are some of the rad '70s touches at this retro boutique hotel, a 10-minute stroll from the town centre.

Hôtel de Silhouette DESIGNER HOTEL €€€
(☎05 59 24 93 82; www.hotel-silhouette-biarritz.com; 30 rue Gambetta; d from €220; ❄ ⓦ) This fabulous new addition to the Biarritz hotel scene has designer rooms with big-city

attitude that would feel quite at home in an upmarket Manhattan apartment. In order to remind you that the countryside is close at hand there are a couple of 'sheep' in the garden and frequently changing outdoor art and sculpture exhibitions.

Hôtel Edouard VII HISTORIC HOTEL €€
(05 59 22 39 80; www.hotel-edouardvii.com; 21 av Carnot; d €132-165;) From the ornate dining room full of gently tick-tocking clocks to the pots of lavender carefully colour coordinated to match the floral wallpaper, everything here screams 1920s Biarritz chic.

Auberge de Jeunesse de Biarritz HOSTEL €
(05 59 41 76 00; www.hihostels.com; 8 rue Chiquito de Cambo; dm incl sheets & breakfast €24.20; reception 8.30-11.30am & 6-9pm, to noon & 10pm May-Sep, closed mid-Dec–early Jan;) This popular place offers outdoor activities including surfing. From the train station, follow the railway westwards for 800m.

Eating

The area around covered market **Les Halles** (rue des Halles, rue du Centre, rue du Vieux Port) is the Biarritz hot spot for character-infused tapas bars loaded with tasty treats.

TOP CHOICE **Casa Juan Pedro** SEAFOOD €
(05 59 24 00 86; Port des Pêcheurs; mains €7-10) Down by the old port, this cute fishing-shack cooks up tuna, sardines and squid with plenty of friendly banter.

Le Crabe-Tambour SEAFOOD €€
(05 59 23 24 53; 49 rue d'Espagne; menus €13-18) Named after the famous 1977 film of the same name (the owner was the cook for the film set), this local hangout serves great seafood for a price that is hard to fault.

Bistrot des Halles BASQUE €€
(05 59 24 21 22; 1 rue du Centre; mains €15-17) One of a cluster of restaurants along rue du Centre that shop for their produce at the nearby covered market, this bustling place is known for its excellent fish and fresh modern French market fare.

Drinking

Great bars stud rue du Port Vieux, place Clemenceau and the central food-market area.

Ventilo Caffé BAR
(rue du Port Vieux; closed Tue Oct-Easter) Dressed up like a boudoir, this fun and funky place continues its domination of the Biarritz bar scene.

Arena Café Bar BAR
(Plage du Port Vieux; 9am-2am Apr-Sep, 10am-2am Wed-Sun Oct-Mar) Tucked into a tiny cove, this beachfront hang-out combines a style-conscious restaurant with a fashionista bar with DJs and sunset views.

Information

Tourist office (05 59 22 37 10; www.biarritz.fr; square d'Ixelles; 9am-7pm)

Getting There & Away

AIR **Biarritz-Anglet-Bayonne Airport** (www.biarritz.aeroport.fr), 3km southeast of Biarritz, is served by several low-cost carriers.

BUS **ATCRB buses** (www.transdev-atcrb.com) runs services down the coast to the Spanish border.

TRAIN Biarritz-La Négresse train station, 3km south of town, is linked to the centre by bus A1.

LANGUEDOC-ROUSSILLON

Languedoc-Roussillon comes in three distinct flavours: Bas-Languedoc (Lower Languedoc), land of bullfighting, rugby and robust red wines, where the region's major sights are found; sunbaked Nîmes with its fine Roman amphitheatre; and fairy-tale Carcassonne, crowned with a ring of witch-hat turrets.

Inland, Haut Languedoc (Upper Languedoc) is a mountainous, sparsely populated terrain made for lovers of the great outdoors; while to the south sits Roussillon, snug against the rugged Pyrenees and frontier to Spanish Catalonia. Meanwhile, Languedoc's traditional centre, Toulouse, was shaved off when regional boundaries were redrawn almost half a century ago, but we've chosen to include it in this section.

Nîmes

POP 146,500

This buzzy city boasts some of France's best-preserved classical buildings, including a famous Roman amphitheatre, although the city is most famous for its sartorial export, *serge de Nîmes* – better known to cowboys, clubbers and couturiers as denim.

FESTIVE NÎMES

Nîmes becomes more Spanish than French during its two *férias* (bullfighting festivals): the five-day **Féria de Pentecôte** (Whitsuntide Festival) in June, and the three-day **Féria des Vendanges** celebrating the grape harvest on the third weekend in September. Each is marked by daily *corridas* (bullfights). Buy tickets in situ or online at the **Billeterie des Arènes** (www.arenesdenimes.com; 2 rue de la Violette).

Sights

A **Pass Nîmes Romaine** (adult/child €10/7.70), valid for three days, covers all three sights; buy one at the first place you visit.

Les Arènes ROMAN SITES
(www.arenes-nimes.com; place des Arènes; adult/child €7.90/6; ⏲9am-8pm Jul-Aug, earlier closing at other times) Nîmes' twin-tiered amphitheatre, the best preserved in the Roman Empire, was built around AD 100 to stage gladiatorial contests and public executions – watched by an audience of 24,000 spectators. Public events of a less gory nature are held here today (although bullfights are still a regular fixture).

Maison Carrée ROMAN SITES
(place de la Maison Carrée; adult/child €4.60/3.80; ⏲10am-8pm Jul-Aug, earlier closing at other times) This gleaming limestone temple built around AD 5 to honour Emperor Augustus' two adopted sons is not actually square, despite its name, which means 'Square House' – to the Romans, 'square' simply meant a building with right angles.

Carré d'Art MUSEUM
(www.carreartmusee.com; place de la Maison Carrée; permanent collection free, exhibitions adult/child €5/3.70; ⏲10am-6pm Tue-Sun) The striking glass-and-steel art mseum facing the Maison Carrée was designed by British architect Sir Norman Foster. The rooftop restaurant makes a lovely lunch spot.

Sleeping

TOP CHOICE **Le Cheval Blanc** HOTEL €€
(☎04 66 76 05 22; www.lechevalblanc-nimes.com; 1 place des Arènes; d €115, f €180-210; 📶) A prime position overlooking Les Arènes and a spare, stripped-back style make this the swishest place to stay in central Nîmes. Bare wood, plaster and stone define the design, and there are several split-level apartments with galley kitchens. The building itself began life as a textile factory, but it feels deliciously modern now.

Hôtel Amphithéâtre HOTEL €€
(☎04 66 67 28 51; www.hoteldelamphitheatre.com; 4 rue des Arènes; s/d €65/85) Tucked away along a narrow backstreet, this tall townhouse hotel run by an ex-pat Cornishman and his wife has chic and stylish rooms; some have balconies overlooking place du Marché.

Auberge de Jeunesse HOSTEL €
(☎04 66 68 03 20; www.hinimes.com; 257 chemin de l'Auberge de Jeunesse, La Cigale; dm/d €15.55/36; ⏲reception 7.30am-1am) It's out in the sticks, 4km from the station, but there's lots in its favour: spacious dorms, family rooms, sweet garden with camping pitches, and a choice of self-catering kitchen or cafe. Take bus 1, direction Alès or Villeverte, to the Stade stop.

Eating

Look out for *cassoulet* (pork, sausage and white bean stew, sometimes served with duck), aïoli and *rouille* (a spicy chilli mayonnaise).

L'Imprévu MODERN FRENCH €€
(☎04 66 38 99 59; www.l-imprevu.com; 6 place d'Assas; mains €19.50-27.50; ⏲lunch & dinner) The simple, amber-stoned facade of this fine-dining French bistro looks homey, but the interior is light and contemporary, with swirly modern art, an open-plan kitchen and interior courtyard. There's a posh mix of *terre-et-mer* (surf-and-turf) dishes, mainly served à la carte.

Le Marché sur la Table MODERN FRENCH €€
(☎04 66 67 22 50; 10 rue Littré; mains €18-22; ⏲Wed-Sun) Husband-and-wife team Éric and Caroline Vidal focus on organic ingredients picked up from the market. The interior feels homespun and there's a quiet courtyard for alfresco dining.

Carré d'Art GASTRONOMIC €€
(☎04 66 67 52 40; www.restaurant-lecarredart.fr; 2 rue Gaston Boissier; 2-/3-course menu €24/29; ⏲Mon-Sat) Nîmes' top address for gourmet gastronomic dining.

DON'T MISS

PONT DU GARD

Southern France has some fine Roman sites, but for audacious engineering, nothing can top Unesco World Heritage site **Pont du Gard** (☎04 66 37 50 99; www.pontdugard.fr; car & up to 5 passengers €18, after 8pm €10, cyclists & walkers free; ⏰visitors centre & museum 9am-7pm Jun-Sep, 9am-6pm Mar-May & Sep, 9am-5pm Oct-Feb, car parks 9am-1am), 21km northeast of Nîmes. This three-tiered aqueduct was once part of a 50km-long system of water channels, built around 19 BC to transport water from Uzès to Nîmes. The scale is huge: 50m high, 275m long and graced with 35 precision-built arches, the bridge was sturdy enough to carry up to 20,000 cu metres of water per day. Each block was carved by hand and transported here from nearby quarries – no mean feat, considering the largest blocks weight over 5 tonnes.

The **Musée de la Romanité** provides background on the bridge's construction, while kids can try out educational activities in the **Ludo** play area. Nearby, the 1.4km **Mémoires de Garrigue** walking trail winds upstream through typically Mediterranean scrubland, and offers some of the best bridge views.

There are large car parks on both banks of the river, about 400m walk from the bridge. Parking costs a flat-rate €5.

Crowds can be a real problem in high summer; early evening is usually a great time to visit, especially since parking is free after 7pm and the bridge is stunningly lit after dark.

Information

Tourist office (☎04 66 58 38 00; www.ot-nimes.fr; 6 rue Auguste; ⏰8.30am-8pm Mon-Fri, 9am-7pm Sat, 10am-6pm Sun Jul & Aug, shorter hrs rest of year)

Getting There & Away

AIR Ryanair is the only airline to use Nîmes' **airport** (☎04 66 70 49 49; www.nimes-aeroport.fr), 10km southeast of the city on the A54.

BUS The **bus station** (☎04 66 38 59 43; rue Ste-Félicité) is next to the train station. Destinations include:

Pont du Gard 30 minutes, five to seven daily in summer

Uzès bus E52; 45 minutes, four to eight daily

TRAIN More than 12 TGVs daily run to/from Paris Gare de Lyon (€52 to €99.70, three hours). Local destinations include:

Arles €8 to €14, 30 minutes

Avignon €9, 30 minutes

Montpellier €9.20, 30 minutes

Toulouse

POP 446,200

Elegantly set at the confluence of the Canal du Midi and the River Garonne, this vibrant southern city – nicknamed *la ville rose* (the pink city) after the distinctive hot-pink stone used in many buildings – is one of France's liveliest metropolises. Busy, buzzy and bustling with students, this riverside dame has a history stretching back over 2000 years and has been a hub for the aerospace industry since the 1930s. With a thriving cafe and cultural scene, a wealth of impressive *hôtels particuliers* and an enormously atmospheric old quarter, France's fourth-largest city is one place you'll love to linger.

Sights

Place du Capitole PUBLIC SQUARE

(place du Capitole) Toulouse's magificent main square is the city's literal and metaphorical heart, where Toulousiens turn out en masse on sunny evenings to sip a coffee or an early aperitif at a pavement cafe. On the eastern side is the 128m-long facade of the **Capitole**, the city hall, built in the 1750s. To the south is the city's **Vieux Quartier** (Old Quarter), a tangle of lanes and leafy squares brimming with cafes, shops and eateries.

Basilique St-Sernin CHURCH

(place St-Sernin; ⏰8.30am-noon & 2-6pm Mon-Sat, 8.30am-12.30pm & 2-7.30pm Sun) This red-brick basilica is one of France's best-preserved Romanesque structures. Inside, the soaring nave and delicate pillars harbour the tomb of St-Sernin, a Toulouse bishop martyred in 250 AD.

Musée des Augustins MUSEUM

(www.augustins.org; 21 rue de Metz; adult/child €3/free; ⏰10am-6pm, to 9pm Wed) Toulouse's fabulous fine arts museum spans the centuries from the Roman era right through to the early 20th century. It's in a former

DON'T MISS

CARCASSONNE

Perched on a rocky hilltop and bristling with zig-zag battlements, stout walls and spiky turrets, the fortified city of Carcassonne looks like something out of a children's storybook from afar. It's most people's perfect idea of a medieval castle, and it's undoubtedly an impressive spectacle – not to mention one of the Languedoc's biggest tourist draws.

Unfortunately, the medieval magic's more than a tad tarnished by an annual influx of over four million visitors and it can be a tourist hell in high summer.

The old city, **La Cité**, is dramatically illuminated at night and enclosed by two rampart walls punctuated by 52 stone towers, Europe's largest city fortifications. Successive generations of Gauls, Romans, Visigoths, Moors, Franks and Cathars reinforced the walls, but only the lower sections are original; the rest, including the turrets, were stuck on by the 19th-century architect Viollet-le-Duc.

A drawbridge leads to the old gate of **Porte Narbonnaise** and rue Cros Mayrevieille en route to place Château and the 12th-century **Château Comtal** (adult/child €8.50/free; ⏲10am-6.30pm Apr-Sep). South is **Basilique St-Nazaire** (⏲9-11.45am & 1.45-5 or 5.30pm), illuminated by delicate medieval rose windows.

Carcassonne is on the main rail line to/from Toulouse (€14, 50 minutes).

Augustinian monastery, and its two 14th-century cloister gardens are postcard-pretty.

Les Abattoirs MUSEUM
(www.lesabattoirs.org; 76 allées Charles de Fitte; adult/student & child €7/free; ⏲11am-7pm Wed-Sun) As its name suggests, this red-brick structure was once the city's main abattoir; now it's a cutting-edge art gallery.

Tours

Toulouse is a river city, and you couldn't possibly leave without venturing out onto the water. March to November, several operators run scenic hour-long boat trips (adult/child €8/5) along the Garonne from quai de la Daurade; in summer, trips also pass through the St-Pierre lock onto the Canal du Midi and Canal de Brienne. Buy tickets on the boat, up to 10 minutes before departure, from **Les Bateaux Toulousains** (www.bateaux-toulousains.com), **Toulouses Croisières** (www.toulouse-croisieres.com) or **L'Occitania** (www.loccitania.fr).

Airbus Factory Tours AEROPLANES
(☎05 34 39 42 00; www.taxiway.fr) Dedicated plane-spotters can arrange a guided tour of Toulouse's massive J.L. Lagardère Airbus factory, 10km west in Colomiers. There are three options: the main tour of the A380 production line (adult/child €14.50/11.50), a 'Heritage Tour' of the factory's vintage planes (including Concorde, adult/child €11.50/10), and a 'Panoramic Tour' of the 700-hectare site by minibus (adult/child €10/8.50). Book in advance online or by phone; bring photo ID.

Sleeping

Les Loges de St-Sernin B&B €€
(☎05 61 24 44 44; www.leslogesdesaintsernin.com; 12 rue St-Bernard; r €125-150; 📶) Hidden behind an elegant rosy facade, Sylviane Tatin's lovely *chambre d'hôte* is a home away from home. The four rooms are huge, dolled up in shades of pink, lime and butter-yellow.

Hôtel St-Sernin BOUTIQUE HOTEL €€
(☎05 61 21 73 08; www.hotelstsernin.com; 2 rue St-Bernard; d from €130; 📶) This swish number opposite the Basilique St-Sernin has been stylishly renovated by a Parisian couple; the best rooms have floor-to-ceiling windows overlooking the basilica.

Hôtel La Chartreuse HOTEL €
(☎05 61 62 93 39; www.chartreusehotel.com; 4bis bd de Bonrepos; s/d/tr €45/51/63) Toulouse's station hotels are definitely on the scruffy side, but this family-run establishment is a welcome surprise: clean, friendly and quiet, with a lovely breakfast room and back garden patio.

Eating

Bd de Strasbourg, place St-Georges and place du Capitole are perfect spots for summer dining alfresco. Rue Pargaminières is the street for kebabs, burgers and other late-night student grub.

TOP CHOICE **Chez Navarre** REGIONAL CUISINE €€
(☎05 62 26 43 06; 49 Grande Rue Nazareth; menus €13-20; ⏲lunch & dinner Mon-Fri) Fancy rubbing shoulders with the locals? This *table d'hôte*

is the place, with honest Gascon cuisine served up beneath a creaky beamed ceiling at communal candlelit tables.

L'Air de Famille MODERN FRENCH €€
(☎05 61 29 85 89; www.lairdefamille-restaurant.com; 20 place Victor Hugo; mains from €13; ⊙lunch Tue & Wed, lunch & dinner Thu-Sat) Expect the freshest of ingredients at this intimate bistro where chef Georges turns out a small but perfectly formed menu concentrating on classic *saveurs Toulousiens* (flavours of Toulouse). It's tiny, so book.

Les Halles Victor Hugo BISTROS €
(place Victor Hugo; menus €10-20; ⊙lunch Tue-Sun) For a quintessentially Toulousien experience, join the punters at the string of tiny restaurants on the 1st floor of the Victor Hugo food market. They're lunchtime only, and the food is simple and unfussy, but they're full of character and the menus are brilliant value.

Drinking

Almost every square in the Vieux Quartier has at least one cafe-bar, busy day and night. After-dark streets include rue Castellane, rue Gabriel Péri and near the river around place St-Pierre.

Toulouse has a cracking live music and clubbing scene; see what's on at www.toulouse.sortir.eu.

Au Père Louis HISTORIC BAR
(45 rue des Tourneurs; ⊙8.30am-3pm & 5-10.30pm Mon-Sat) This antique bar has been quenching the city's thirst since 1889, and it's crammed with interesting nooks and crannies, not to mention its fair share of colourful characters. There's a huge selection of wines and beers, and it feels very cosy.

Connexion Café BAR, LIVE MUSIC
(www.connexion-cafe.com; 8 rue Gabriel Péri; ⊙from 5pm Mon-Sat) Housed in a converted carpark with old oil drums for tables, this lively bar hosts an eclectic line-up of events, from big-screen sports to live weekend gigs. When the weather's warm, they open up the plastic tarps and the action spills out onto the street.

La Maison BAR
(9 rue Gabriel Péri; ⊙5pm-2am Sun-Fri, to 5am Sat) 'The House' is a hip, shabby-chic hang-out for students and trendy types, with plenty of scruffy sofas and secondhand chairs dotted around the lounge-style bar.

Information

Tourist office (☎05 61 11 02 22; www.toulouse-tourisme.com; Square Charles de Gaulle; ⊙9am-7pm daily)

Getting There & Away

AIR **Toulouse-Blagnac Airport** (www.toulouse.aeroport.fr/en), 8km northwest of the centre, has frequent flights to Paris and other large French and European cities. A **Navette Aéroport Flybus** (Airport Shuttle; ☎05 61 41 70 70; www.tisseo.fr) links it with town.

TRAIN **Gare Matabiau** (blvd Pierre Sémard), 1km northeast of the centre, is served by frequent TGVs to Bordeaux (€38, two hours) and east to Carcassonne (€15, 45 minutes to one hour).

DON'T MISS

CITÉ DE L'ESPACE

This fantastic **space museum** (☎08 20 37 72 33; www.cite-espace.com/en; av Jean Gonord; adult €19.50-23, child €14-15; ⊙9.30am-5pm or 6pm, to 7pm mid-Jul–Aug, closed Jan) on the city's eastern outskirts explores Toulouse's illustrious aeronautical history.

The city's high-flying credentials stretch all the way back to WWI, when it was a hub for pioneering mail flights to Africa and South America. Since WWII, Toulouse has been the centre of France's aerospace industry, developing many important aircraft (including Concorde and the 555-seat Airbus A380) as well as components for many international space programs.

The museum brings this interstellar industry vividly to life through hands-on exhibits including a shuttle simulator, planetarium, 3D cinema and simulated observatory. There are even full-scale replicas of iconic spacecraft including the Mir Space Station and a 53m-high Ariane 5 space rocket. Multilingual audioguides allow you to explore at your own pace, but you'll need a full day to do it justice.

To get there, catch Bus 15 from allée Jean Jaurès to the last stop, from where it's a 500m walk. Dodge queues by buying your tickets online or at the tourist office.

PROVENCE

Provence conjures up images of rolling lavender fields, blue skies, gorgeous villages, wonderful food and superb wine. It certainly delivers on all those fronts, but it's not just worth visiting for its good looks – dig a little deeper and you'll also discover the multicultural metropolis of Marseille, the artistic haven of Aix-en-Provence and the old Roman city of Arles.

Marseille

POP 858,902

There was a time when Marseille was the butt of French jokes. No more. The *cité phocéenne* has made an unprecedented comeback, undergoing a vast makeover. Marseillais will tell you that the city's rough-and-tumble edginess is part of its charm and that, for all its flaws, it is a very endearing place. They're right: Marseille grows on you with its unique history, souklike markets, millennia-old port and spectacular *corniches* (coastal roads) – all good reasons indeed why Marseille was chosen European Capital of Culture in 2013.

Sights

Vieux Port HISTORIC QUARTER
(MVieux Port) Ships have docked for more than 26 centuries at Marseile's colourful Old Port. The main commercial docks were transferred to the Joliette area north of here in the 1840s, but the old port stil overflows with fishing boats, pleasure yachts and tourists.

Guarding the harbour are **Bas Fort St-Nicolas** and **Fort St-Jean**, founded in the 13th century by the Knights Hospitaller of St John of Jerusalem. The 40,000 sq metre state-of-the-art museum **Musée des Civilisations de l'Europe et de la Méditerranée** (MuCEM; Museum of European & Mediterranean Civilisations; ☎04 96 13 80 90; www.mucem.org; ⏲1pm-7pm Wed, Thu & Sat) will open inside in 2013.

Basilique Notre Dame de la Garde CHURCH
(Montée de la Bonne Mère; ⏲7am-8pm Apr-Sep, to 7pm Oct-Mar) Everywhere you go in Marseille, you can see the opulent, domed 19th-century Romano-Byzantine basilica, privy to dazzling 360-degree panoramas of the city's sea of terracotta roofs below.

The church's bell tower is crowned by a 9.7m-tall gilded statue of the Virgin Mary on a 12m-high pedestal. Walk or take bus 60 from the Vieux Port.

Château d'If ISLAND, CASTLE
(www.if.monuments-nationaux.fr; adult/child €5/free; ⏲9.30am-6.30pm May-Sep, to 4.45pm Tue-Sun Oct-

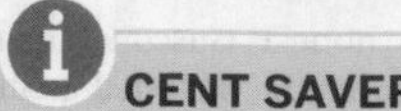

CENT SAVER

Buy a cent-saving **Marseille City Pass** (one-/two-day €22/29) at the tourist office. It covers admission to 15 museums, a city tour, unlimited public-transport travel, boat trips and so on.

LES CALANQUES

Marseille abuts the wild and spectacular Les Calanques, a protected 20km stretch of high, rocky promontories rising from the bright turquoise sea. Sheer cliffs are occasionally interrupted by idyllic beach-fringed coves, many only possible to reach with kayak. They've been protected since 1975 and became a national park in 2012.

Calanque de Sormiou is the largest rocky inlet, with two seasonal restaurants cooking up fabulous views: **Le Château** (☎04 91 25 08 69; mains €18-24; ⏲Apr–mid-Oct) – the better food – and **Le Lunch** (☎04 91 25 05 39, 04 91 25 05 37; http://wp.resto.fr/lelunch; mains €16-28; ⏲Apr–mid-Oct) – nearer the water; both require advance reservation. By bus, take No 23 from the Rond Point du Prado metro stop to La Cayolle, from where it's a 3km walk (note diners with a table reservation can drive through; otherwise, the road is open to cars weekdays only September to June).

Marseille's tourist office leads guided hikes in Les Calanques and has information on walking trails (shut July and August due to forest-fire risk). For great views from out at sea hop aboard a boat trip to the wine-producing port of **Cassis**, 30km east along the coast, with **Croisières Marseille Calanques** (www.croisieres-marseille-calanques.com; 74 quai du Port).

Apr) Immortalised in Alexandre Dumas' 1844 novel *Le Comte de Monte Cristo* (The Count of Monte Cristo), this 16th-century fortress-turned-prison sits on an island 3.5km west of the Vieux Port. Political prisoners were incarcerated here, along with hundreds of Protestants, the Revolutionary hero Mirabeau, and the Communards of 1871.

Frioul If Express (www.frioul-if-express.com; 1 quai des Belges) boats leave for Château d'If from the Vieux Port. Over 15 daily departures in summer, fewer in winter (€10 return, 20 minutes).

TOP CHOICE **Le Panier** HISTORIC QUARTER
(MVieux Port) From the Vieux Port, hike north up to this fantastic history-woven quarter, dubbed Marseille's Montmartre as much for its sloping streets as its artsy ambience. In Greek Massilia it was the site of the *agora* (marketplace), hence its name, which means 'the basket'. During WWII the quarter was dynamited and afterwards rebuilt. Today it's a mishmash of lanes hiding artisan shops, *ateliers* (workshops) and terraced houses strung with drying washing.

Its centerpiece is the fascinating **Centre de la Vieille Charité** (2 rue de la Charité, 2e; both museums adult/student €5/2.50; MJoliette).

La Friche La Belle de Mai CULTURAL CENTRE
(04 95 04 95 04; www.lafriche.org; 41 rue Jobin; 49 to Jobin) This former sugar-refining plant and subsequent tobacco factory is now host to artists' workshops, cinema studios, radio stations, multimedia displays, alfresco installation art, skateboard camps and electro/world-music parties – enter the gregarious 'voice' of contemporary Marseille. Check its program online, view art in the **Galerie de la Friche Belle de Mai** (admission free; 3-7pm Tue-Sat) and dine in its stylishly industrial **Les Grandes Tables de la Friche** (04 95 04 95 85; www.lesgrandestables.com; 12 rue François Simon; mains €10; 8.30am-8pm Mon-Fri).

FREE **Palais de Longchamp** PALACE, PARK
(Longchamp Palace; bd Philippon; ; MCinq Avenues–Longchamp, Longchamp) This colonnaded 1860s palace houses Marseille's oldest museum, the **Musée des Beaux-Arts**, slated to reopen after renovations in 2013. The shaded park is one of central Marseille's few green spaces.

Sleeping

TOP CHOICE **Casa Honoré** B&B €€€
(04 96 11 01 62; www.casahonore.com; 123 rue Sainte; d incl breakfast €150-200; ; MVieux Port) Los Angeles meets Marseille at this four-room *maison d'hôte*, built around a central courtyard with lap pool shaded by banana trees. One complaint: some bathrooms are partitioned by curtains, not doors.

Hôtel Vertigo HOSTEL €
(04 91 91 07 11; www.hotelvertigo.fr; 42 rue des Petites Maries; dm/d €25/60; @; MGare St-Charles) This snappy boutique hostel kisses goodbye to dodgy bunks and hospital-like decor and says 'hello' to vintage posters, designer chrome kitchen and groovy communal spaces. No curfew (or lift, alas).

Le Ryad BOUTIQUE HOTEL €€
(04 91 47 74 54; www.leryad.fr; 16 rue Sénac de Meilhan; s €80-105, d €95-125, family €170; ; MNoailles, Canebière Garibaldi) Le Ryad draws sumptuous influence from Morocco. Beautiful bathrooms, garden-view rooms and great service make up for the sometimes-sketchy neighbourhood. Book the top-floor room (Mogador) for its rooftop terrace.

Mama Shelter DESIGN HOTEL €€
(01 43 48 48 48; www.mamashelter.com; 64 rue de la Loubière; d €99-139, q €159, ste €209; ; MNotre Dame du Monte–Cours Julien) The brainchild of Serge Trigano, son of Gilbert (Club Med creator), this affordable-chic new kid on the block sports design by Philippe Starck.

Eating

The Vieux Port overflows with restaurants, but choose carefully. Head to Cours Julien and its surrounding streets for world cuisine.

TOP CHOICE **Le Café des Épices** MODERN FRENCH €€
(04 91 91 22 69; www.cafedesepices.com; 4 rue du Lacydon; 3-course lunch/dinner menu €25/40; lunch Tue-Sat, dinner Thu-Fri; ; MVieux Port) One of Marseille's best young chefs, Arnaud de Grammont, infuses his cooking with a panoply of flavours...think squid ink spaghetti with sesame and perfectly cooked scallops, or tender roasted potatoes with hints of coriander and citrus, topped by the catch of the day.

Marseille

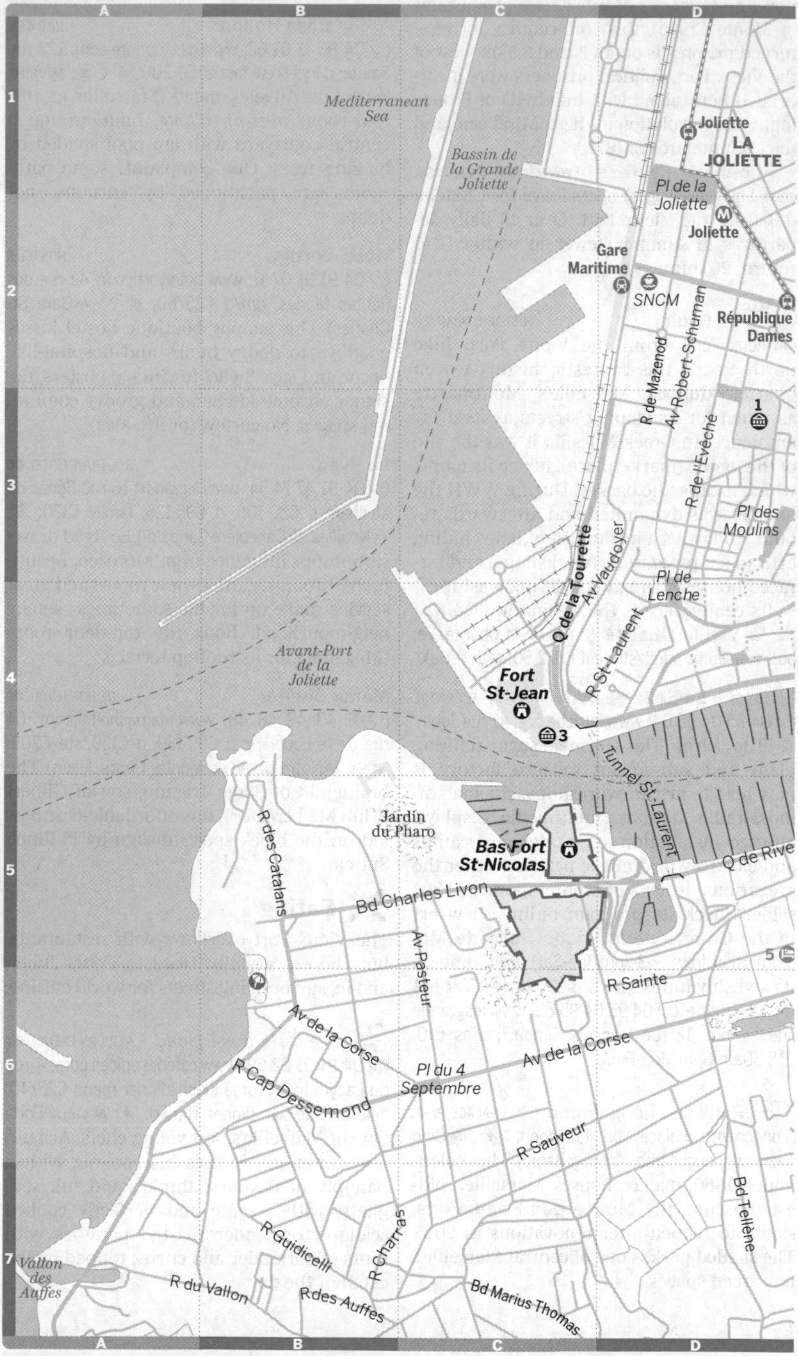

Mediterranean Sea
Bassin de la Grande Joliette
Joliette
LA JOLIETTE
Pl de la Joliette
Joliette
Gare Maritime
SNCM
République Dames
R de Mazenod
Av Robert Schuman
R de l'Evêché
1
Pl des Moulins
Av Vaudoyer
Q de la Tourette
Pl de Lenche
R St-Laurent
Avant-Port de la Joliette
Fort St-Jean
3
Tunnel St-Laurent
Jardin du Pharo
R des Catalans
Bas Fort St-Nicolas
Q de Rive
Bd Charles Livon
Av Pasteur
5
R Sainte
Av de la Corse
R Cap Dessemond
Pl du 4 Septembre
Av de la Corse
R Sauveur
Bd Tellène
R Guidicelli
R Charras
Vallon des Auffes
R du Vallon
R des Auffes
Bd Marius Thomas

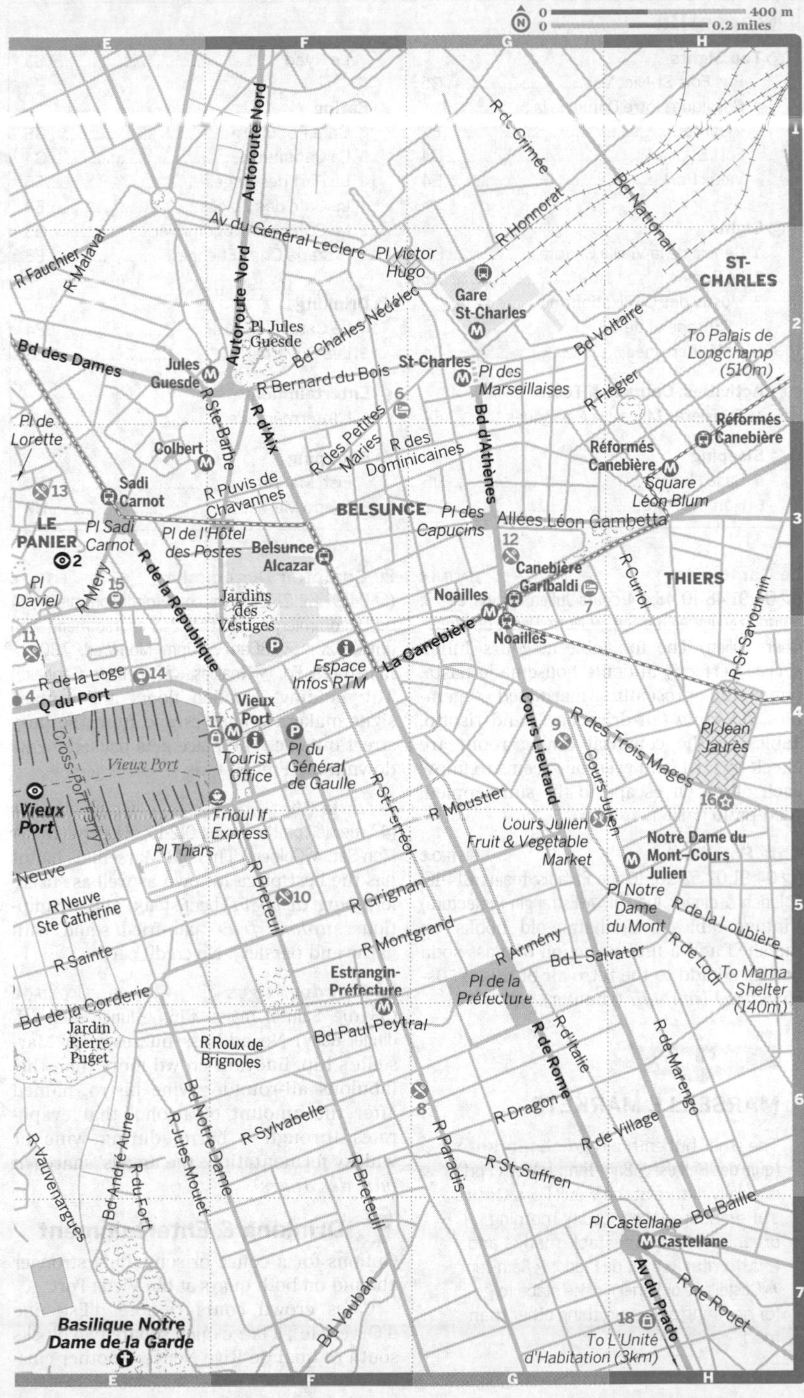

FRANCE MARSEILLE

Marseille

La Cantinetta ITALIAN €

(☎04 91 48 10 48; 24 cours Julien; mains €9-19; ⊙lunch & dinner Tue-Sat; Ⓜ Notre Dame du Mont–Cours Julien) The top table at cours Julien serves perfectly al dente housemade pasta, paper-thin prosciutto, marinated vegetables, *bresaola* (air-dried beef) and risotto. Tables in the convivial dining room are cheek by jowl, and everyone seems to know each other. Or escape to the sun-dappled, tiled patio garden.

Café Populaire BISTRO €

(☎04 91 02 53 96; 10 rue Paradis; mains €14-16; ⊙lunch & dinner Tue-Sat; Ⓜ Estrangin-Préfecture) Vintage tables and chairs, old books on the shelf and a fine collection of glass soda bottles all add to the retro air of this 1950s-styled jazz *comptoir* (counter).

DON'T MISS

MARSEILLE MARKETS

The small but enthralling **fish market** (quai des Belges; ⊙8am-1pm; Ⓜ Vieux Port) is a daily fixture at the Vieux Port. **Cours Julien** hosts a Wednesday-morning organic fruit and vegetable market and **Prado Market** (av du Prado; ⊙8am-1pm; Ⓜ Castellane or Périer) is the place to go for anything and everything other than food.

Le Comptoir Dugommier BISTRO €

(☎04 91 62 21 21; www.comptoirdugommier.fr; 14 bd Dugommier; mains €11-12, 3-course menu with drink €20; ⊙7.30am-3.30pm Mon-Wed, 7.30am-1am Thu & Fri; Ⓜ Noailles, 🚊 Canebière Garibaldi) Tin molding, wooden floors and vintage signs make a homey escape from the busy street outside. The place gets packed for its downhome French fare.

Pizzaria Chez Étienne REGIONAL CUISINE €

(43 rue de Lorette; mains €12-15; ⊙lunch & dinner Mon-Sat; Ⓜ Colbert) This old Marseillais haunt has the best pizza in town as well as succulent *pavé de boeuf* (beef steak) and scrumptious *supions frits* (pan-fried squid with garlic and parsley). No credit cards.

La Part des Anges BISTRO €

(33 rue Sainte; mains €15; ⊙lunch Mon-Sat, dinner daily) No address buzzes with Marseille's hip, buoyant crowd more than this fabulous all-rounder wine bistro, named after the amount of alcohol that evaporates through a barrel during wine or whisky fermentation: the angels' share *(la part des anges)*.

Drinking & Entertainment

Options for a coffee or something stronger abound on both quays at the Vieux Port.

Cafes crowd cours Honoré d'Estienne d'Orves (1e), a large open square two blocks south of quai de Rive Neuve. Another cluster overlooks place de la Préfecture, at the southern end of rue St-Ferréol (1er).

La Caravelle BAR
(34 quai du Port; ⏲7am-2am; Ⓜ Vieux Port) Look up or miss this upstairs hideaway with tiny but treasured portside terrace. Fridays have live jazz 9pm to midnight.

Les Buvards WINE BAR
(☎04 91 90 69 98; 34 Grand Rue; ⏲10am-1am; Ⓜ Vieux Port, Sadi Carnot) Grand selection of natural wines and munchies.

L'Intermédiaire NIGHTCLUB
(63 place Jean Jaurès; ⏲7pm-2am; Ⓜ Notre Dame du Mont–Cours Julien) This grungy venue with graffitied walls is one of the best for live bands or DJs (usually techno or alternative).

Information

Dangers & Annoyances

Petty crimes and muggings are common. Avoid the Belsunce area (southwest of the train station, bounded by La Canebière, cours Belsunce and rue d'Aix, rue Bernard du Bois and bd d'Athènes) at night. Walking La Canebiére is annoying, but generally not dangerous; expect to encounter kids peddling hash.

Tourist information

Tourist office (☎04 91 13 89 00; www.marseille-tourisme.com; 4 La Canebière; ⏲9am-7pm Mon-Sat, 10am-5pm Sun; Ⓜ Vieux Port)

Getting There & Away

Air

Aéroport Marseille-Provence (p434), 25km northwest in Marignane, has numerous budget flights to various European destinations. **Shuttle buses** (☎Marseille 04 91 50 59 34, airport 04 42 14 31 27; www.lepilote.com) link it with Marseille Gare St-Charles (€8; 25 minutes, every 20 minutes).

Boat

The **passenger ferry terminal** (www.marseille-port.fr; Ⓜ Joliette) is 250m south of Place de la Joliette (1er). **SNCM** (☎08 91 70 18 01; www.sncm.fr; 61 bd des Dames; Ⓜ Joliette) boats sail to Corsica, Sardinia and North Africa.

Train

From Marseille's Gare St-Charles, trains including TGVs go all over France and Europe.

Avignon €24, 35 minutes
Lyon €50, 1¾ hours
Nice €35, 2½ hours
Paris Gare de Lyon €103, three hours

Getting Around

Marseille has two metro lines, two tram lines and an extensive bus network, all run by **RTM** (☎04 91 91 92 10; www.rtm.fr; 6 rue des Fabres; ⏲8.30am-6pm Mon-Fri, 9am-12.30pm & 2-5.30pm Sat; Ⓜ Vieux Port), where you can obtain information and transport tickets (€1.50).

Pick up a bike from 100-plus stations across the city with **Le Vélo** (www.levelo-mpm.fr).

Aix-en-Provence

POP 141,895

Aix-en-Provence is to Provence what the Left Bank is to Paris: a pocket of bohemian chic crawling with students. It's hard to believe that 'Aix' (pronounced ex) is just 25km from chaotic, exotic Marseille. The city has been a cultural centre since the Middle Ages (two of the town's most famous sons are painter Paul Cézanne and novelist Émile Zola) but for all its polish, it's still a laid-back Provençal town at heart.

Sights

Cours Mirabeau HISTORIC QUARTER
No avenue better epitomises Provence's most graceful city than fountain-studded cours Mirabeau, sprinkled with elegant Renaissance *hôtels particuliers* and crowned with a summertime roof of leafy plane trees. Cézanne and Zola famously hung out at **Les Deux Garçons** (53 cours Mirabeau; ⏲7am-2am), a chic pavement cafe that buzzes with people-watchers despite its elevated prices and mediocre food.

Cézanne Sights ART
To see where local lad Paul Cézanne (1839–1906) ate, drank and painted, follow the **Circuit de Cézanne** (Cézanne Trail), marked by footpath-embedded bronze plaques. The informative English-language guide to the plaques, *Cézanne's Footsteps*, is free at the tourist office. A mobile app, *City of Cézanne in Aix-en-Provence* (€2), is available online.

Cézanne's last studio, **Atelier Paul Cézanne** (www.atelier-cezanne.com; 9 av Paul Cézanne; adult/child €5.50/2; ⏲10am-noon & 2-6pm, closed Sun winter), 1.5km north of the tourist office, has been preserved and recreated (not all the tools and still-life models strewn around the single room were his) as it was at the time of his death. Take bus 1 or 20 to the Atelier Cézanne stop, or walk 1.5km from the centre. A 10-minute walk uphill from the

WORTH A TRIP

A CULINARY DETOUR

Hilltop village **Ventabren** (population 5000), 16km west of Aix, provides the perfect lazy-day detour. Meander sun-dappled cobbled lanes; peep inside a 17th-century church; and get drunk on dizzying views of Provence from old chateau ruins before a superb lunch or dinner at **La Table de Ventabren** (04 42 28 79 33; www.latabledeventabren.com; 1 rue Cézanne; menus €41-50; lunch Wed-Sun, dinner Tue-Sun). Chef Dan Bessoudo, honoured with a coveted Michelin star, creates inventive wholly modern French dishes and knockout desserts – served in summer on a romantic terrace facing distant mountains and starry skies. Reservations essential.

bus stop is the **Terrain des Peintres** (opp 62 av Paul Cézanne), a wonderful terraced garden perfect for a picnic, from where Cézanne, among others, painted the Montagne Ste-Victoire.

Visits to the both the Cézanne family country manor **Le Jas de Bouffan** (04 42 16 10 91; adult/child €5.50/2; guided tours 10.30am-5.30pm daily summer, less frequent other times; 6 to Corsy) and **Les Carrières de Bibemus** (Bibémus Quarries; 04 42 16 10 91; adult/child €6.60/3.10; tours 9.45am daily Jun-Sep, 10.30am & 5pm Mon, Wed, Fri & Sun Apr, May & Oct, 3pm Wed & Sat Jan-Mar), the cabin the artist rented in 1895 on the edge of town, must be reserved in advance at the tourist office.

Cathédrale St-Sauveur CHURCH
(rue de la Roque; 8am-noon & 2-6pm) A potpourri of styles, Aix cathedral was begun in the 12th century and enlarged over the next century. Acoustics make Gregorian chants (4.30pm Sunday) unforgettable.

Musée Granet MUSEUM
(www.museegranet-aixenprovence.fr; place St-Jean de Malte; adult/child €4/free; 11am-7pm Tue-Sun) Housed in a 17th-century priory, this exceptional museum covers 16th- to 20th-century Italian, Flemish and French works. Modern art reads like a who's-who: Picasso, Léger, Matisse, Monet, Klee, Van Gogh, Giacometti and, of course, Cézanne.

Sleeping

L'Épicerie B&B €€
(06 08 85 38 68; www.unechambreenville.eu; 12 rue du Cancel; s incl breakfast €80-120, d incl breakfast €100-130;) This intimate B&B is the fabulous creation of born-and-bred Aixois lad, Luc. His breakfast room and *salon de thé* re-creates a 1950s grocery store, and the flowery garden out back is perfect for evening dining (book ahead).

Hôtel des Augustins HOTEL €€
(04 42 27 28 59; www.hotel-augustins.com; 3 rue de la Masse; r €99-250;) A heartbeat from the hub of Aixois life, this former 15th-century convent has volumes of history: for example, Martin Luther stayed here after his excommunication from Rome.

Hôtel les Quatre Dauphins BOUTIQUE HOTEL €
(04 42 38 16 39; www.lesquatredauphins.fr; 54 rue Roux Alphéran; s €55-60, d €70-85;) This sweet 13-room hotel is fresh and clean, with excellent new bathrooms. The tall terracotta-tiled staircase (no lift) leads to four attic rooms, with sloped beamed ceilings.

Hôtel Paul HOTEL €
(04 42 23 23 89; http://www.aix-en-provence.com/hotelpaul/; 10 av Pasteur; s/d/tr from €51/52/74; P) On the edge of Vieil Aix, this bright, cheery bargain has a sweet garden and a TV lounge. There are fans in summer, free motorcycle and bike parking, and Wi-fi at €1.50 per 30 minutes. No credit cards.

Eating

Aix' sweetest treat is the marzipan-like local speciality, *calisson d'Aix*, a small, diamond-shaped, chewy delicacy made with ground almonds and fruit syrup. The daily **produce market** (place Richelme; mornings) sells olives, goat's cheese, garlic, lavender, honey, peaches, melons and other sun-kissed products.

TOP CHOICE **Restaurant Pierre Reboul** GASTRONOMIC €€€
(04 42 20 58 26; www.restaurant-pierre-reboul.com; 11 Petite Rue St-Jean; 3-/7-/12-course menus €42/85/142; lunch Tue-Sat, dinner Wed-Sat, closed late Aug) Aix' newest culinary star invents playful, gorgeous creations in a relaxed dining room. The lunch special (€50), includes mineral water, coffee and a glass of perfectly paired wine.

Le Petit Verdot FRENCH €€
(☎04 42 27 30 12; www.lepetitverdot.fr; 7 rue d'Entrecasteaux; mains €15-25; ⏰dinner Mon-Sat, lunch Sat) Delicious menus are designed around what's in season and paired with excellent wines. Lively dining occurs around tabletops made of wine crates (expect to talk to your neighbour), and the gregarious owner speaks multiple languages.

Charlotte BISTRO €€
(☎04 42 26 77 56; 32 rue des Bernardines; 2-/3-course menus €15.50/19; ⏰lunch & dinner Tue-Sat; 👪) It's all very cosy at Charlotte, where everyone appears to know everyone. French classics like veal escalope and beef steak fill the handwritten menu, and there are always a couple of imaginative *plats du jour*. In summer everything moves into the garden.

La Mado MODERN FRENCH €€
(Chez Madeleine; ☎04 42 38 28 02; www.lamado-aix.com; 4 place des Prêcheurs; lunch/dinner menus €18/32; ⏰7am-2am) This smart daytime cafe and modern restaurant is an unbeatable spot for coffee and fashionable-people watching, or a delicious meal. It's been around for years, so the old guard dine while the hipsters shine.

Information

Tourist office (☎04 42 16 11 61; www.aixenprovencetourism.com; 37 av Giuseppi Verdi; ⏰8.30am-7pm Mon-Sat, 10am-1pm & 2-6pm Sun Oct-Jun, to 8pm Jul-Sep)

Getting There & Away

BUS From Aix' **bus station** (☎04 42 91 26 80, 08 91 02 40 25; av de l'Europe), a 10-minute walk southwest from La Rotonde, routes include Marseille (€5, 25 minutes), Arles (€9.20, 1½ hours) and Avignon (€17.40, 1¼ hours).

Half-hourly shuttle buses go to/from Aix TGV station and Aéroport Marseille-Provence.

TRAIN The only useful train from Aix' tiny **city centre train station** is to/from Marseille (€8, 45 minutes). **Aix TGV station**, 15km away, serves most of France; Marseille (€8, 20 daily) is a mere 12 minutes away.

Avignon

POP 92,454

Hooped by 4.3km of superbly preserved stone ramparts, this graceful city is the belle of Provence's ball. Famed for its annual performing arts festival and fabled bridge, Avignon is an ideal spot from which to step out into the surrounding region. Wrapping around the city, Avignon's defensive ramparts were built between 1359 and 1370, and are punctuated by a series of sturdy *portes* (gates).

CENT SAVER

The **Avignon Passion** discount card yields discounts of 10% to 50% on city museums, tours and monuments (pay full price at the first site, then discounts at each susbsequent site). The pass covers five people and is valid for 15 days. Available from the tourist office and tourist sites.

Sights

Palais des Papes PALACE
(Papal Palace; www.palais-des-papes.com; place du Palais; adult/child €6/3; ⏰9am-8pm Jul, 9am-9pm Aug, shorter hours Sep-Jun) This Unesco World Heritage site, the world's largest Gothic palace, was built when Pope Clement V abandoned Rome in 1309 to settle in Avignon, and it was the seat of papal power for 70-odd years. Today, it takes imagination to picture the former luxury of these vast, bare rooms, but PDA-style audio-video guides show 2- and 3D imagery of the once sumptuous furnishings.

Pont St-Bénézet BRIDGE
(adult/child €4.50/3.50; ⏰9am-8pm Jul, 9am-9pm Aug, shorter hours Sep-Jun) This fabled bridge, immortalised in the French nursery rhyme 'Sur le Pont d'Avignon', was completed in 1185 and rebuilt several times before all but four of its spans were washed away in the mid-1600s. See it free from the Rocher des Doms park, Pont Édouard Daladier or from across the river on Île de la Barhelasse's chemin des Berges.

Musée Calvet GALLERY
(☎04 90 86 33 84; 65 rue Joseph Vernet; adult/child €6/3; ⏰10am-1pm & 2-6pm Wed-Mon) The elegant Hôtel de Villeneuve-Martignan (1741–54) provides a fitting backdrop for Avignon's fine-arts museum.

Musée du Petit Palais MUSEUM
(www.petit-palais.org; place du Palais; adult/child €6/free; ⏰10am-1pm & 2-6pm Wed-Mon) The bishops' palace houses outstanding collections of primitive, pre-Rennaissance, 13th- to 16th-century Italian religious paintings.

Avignon

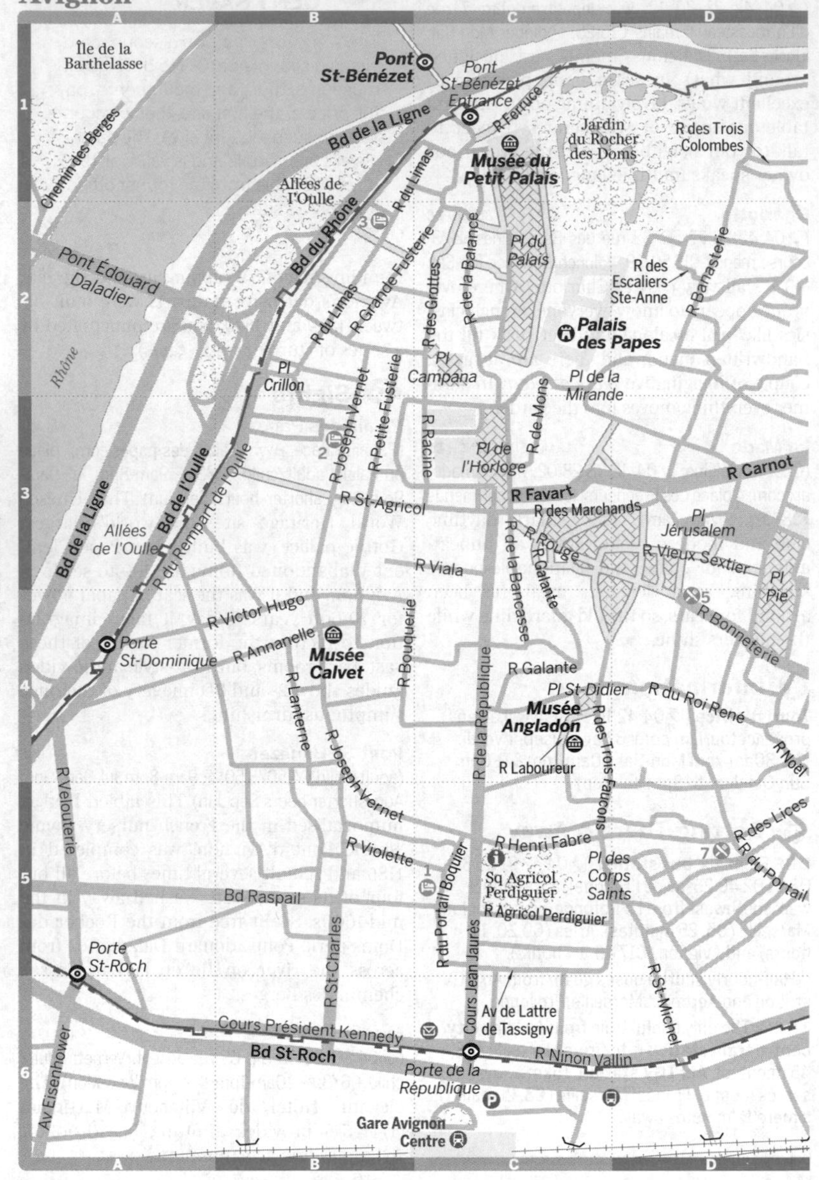

Musée Angladon GALLERY
(www.angladon.com; 5 rue Laboureur; adult/child €6/4; ⏲1-6pm Tue-Sun Apr-Nov, 1-6pm Wed-Sun Jan-Mar) This tiny museum harbours Impressionist treasures, including Van Gogh's *Railway Wagons* – look closely and notice the 'earth' isn't paint, but bare canvas. Also displayed are a handful of early Picasso sketches and artworks by Cézanne, Sisley, Manet and Degas; upstairs are antiques and 17th-century paintings.

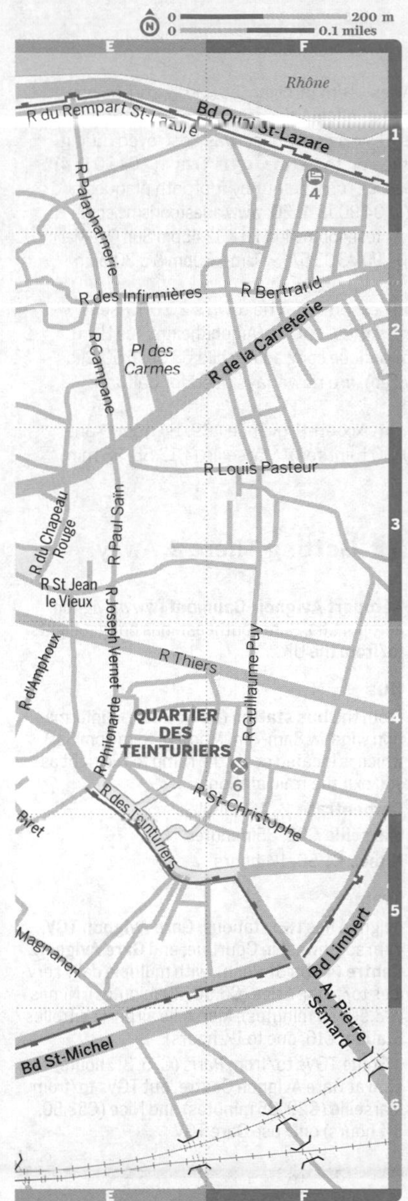

Festivals & Events

Hundreds of artists take to the stage and streets during the world-famous **Festival d'Avignon** (www.festival-avignon.com; ⏰Jul) and fringe **Festival Off** (www.avignonleoff.com; ⏰Jul), held early July to early August.

Avignon

Top Sights

- Musée Angladon C4
- Musée Calvet B4
- Musée du Petit Palais C1
- Palais des Papes C2
- Pont St-Bénézet C1

Sleeping

1 Hôtel Boquier C5
2 Hôtel Mignon B3
3 Le Limas B2
4 Lumani F1

Eating

5 Cuisine du Dimanche D4
6 L'Atelier de Damien F4
7 L'Epice and Love D5

Sleeping

Le Limas B&B €€
(☎04 90 14 67 19; www.le-limas-avignon.com; 51 rue du Limas; d/tr incl breakfast from €120/200; ❄@) This chic B&B in an 18th-century townhouse is like something out of *Vogue Living*. Breakfast on the sun-drenched terrace is a treat, as is bubbly owner Marion.

Lumani B&B €€
(☎04 90 82 94 11; www.avignon-lumani.com; 37 rue du Rempart St-Lazare; d incl breakfast €100-170; ❄📶) Art fills this fabulous *maison d'hôte*, a fount of inspiration for painters. Rooms include two suites and there's a fountained garden.

Hôtel Boquier HOTEL €
(☎04 90 82 34 43; www.hotel-boquier.com; 6 rue du Portail Boquier; d €50-70; ❄📶) The owners' infectious enthusiasm informs this upbeat, colorful, small central hotel; try for themed rooms Morocco or Lavender. Excellent value.

Hôtel Mignon HOTEL €
(☎04 90 82 17 30; www.hotel-mignon.com; 12 rue Joseph Vernet; r incl breakfast €62-84; ❄@📶) Cute and comfy, with 16 colorful rooms, this good-value hotel within the walled city is tops for no-frills budgeteers. Note: it has tiny baths and steep stairs.

Eating

Place de l'Horloge's touristy cafes have so-so food. *Papaline d'Avignon* is a pink, chocolate ball filled with potent Mont Ventoux herbal liqueur.

WORTH A TRIP

VAN GOGH'S ARLES

If the winding streets and colourful houses of Arles seem familiar, it's hardly surprising – Vincent van Gogh lived here for much of his life in a yellow house on place Lamartine, and the town regularly featured in his canvases. His original house was destroyed during WWII, but you can still follow in Vincent's footsteps on the **Van Gogh Trail** (☎04 90 18 41 20; www.arlestourism.com; esplanade Charles de Gaulle), marked out by footpath plaques and a brochure handed out by the **tourist office** (☎04 90 18 41 20; www.arlestourisme.com; esplanade Charles de Gaulle; ⊙9am-6.45pm Apr-Sep, to 4.45pm Mon-Fri & 12.45pm Sun Oct-Mar); there is also a branch at the **train station** (☎04 90 43 33 57; ⊙9am-1.30pm & 2.30-5pm Mon-Fri Apr-Sep).

Two millennia ago, Arles was a major Roman settlement. The town's 20,000-seat amphitheatre and 12,000-seat theatre, known as the **Arénes** (Amphitheatre; rue Henri Vadon) and the **Théâtre Antique** (www.theatre-antique.com; adult/child €8.50/6.50, 2nd child free; ⊙9am-6pm Mar-Oct, 9am-4.30pm Nov-Feb), are nowadays used for cultural events and bullfights.

Telleschi (☎04 42 28 40 22) buses go to/from Aix-en-Provence (€9, 1½ hours) and there are regular trains to/from Nîmes (€7.50, 30 minutes), Marseille (€13.55, 55 minutes) and Avignon (€6.50, 20 minutes).

TOP CHOICE Cuisine du Dimanche PROVENÇAL €€
(☎04 90 82 99 10; www.lacuisinedudimanche.com; 31 rue Bonneterie; mains €15-25; ⊙daily Jun-Sep, Tue-Sat Oct-May) Spitfire chef Marie shops every morning at Les Halles to find the freshest ingredients for her earthy flavour-packed cooking. The menu changes daily, but specialities include scallops and simple roast chicken with pan gravy.

L'Atelier de Damien MODERN FRENCH €€
(☎04 90 82 57 35; 54 rue Guillaume Puy; lunch/dinner menus €13.50/26; ⊙lunch Mon-Sat, dinner Wed-Sat) Unframed paintings and worn tile floors lend a rough-around-the-edges look to this off-the-tourist-radar restaurant on Avignon's less-glamorous side. Chef Damien Demazure draws inspiration from market-fresh ingredients, combining French with Asian – ginger, lemongrass and coriander are his favorites. Expect excellent fish, foie gras, and caramel-candy cake.

L'Epice and Love FRENCH €
(☎04 90 82 45 96; 30 rue des Lices; mains €11-12; ⊙dinner Mon-Sat) Tables are cheek by jowl at this tiny bohemian restaurantwith nothing fancy, just straightforward bistro fare, stews, roasts and other reliably good, home-style French dishes. Cash only.

ℹ Information

Tourist Office (Main) (41 cours Jean Jaurès; ⊙ 9am-6pm Mon-Fri, 9am-5pm Sat, 10am-noon Sun Nov-Mar, 9am-6pm Mon-Sat, 10am-5pm Sun Apr-Oct)

ℹ Getting There & Away

Air

Aéroport Avignon-Caumont (www.avignon.aeroport.fr), 8km southeast, has budget flights to/from the UK.

Bus

From the **bus station** (bd St-Roch; ⊙information window 8am-7pm Mon-Fri, 8am-1pm Sat), which is located down the ramp to the right as you exit the train station:

Carpentras €2, 45 minutes

Marseille €22, 35 minutes

Nîmes €1.50, 1¼ hours

Train

Avignon has two stations. **Gare Avignon TGV**, 4km southwest in Courtine; and **Gare Avignon Centre** (42 bd St-Roch), with multiple daily services to/from: Arles (€6.50, 20 minutes), Nîmes (€8.50, 30 minutes), Marseille airport (Vitrolles Station, €16, one to 1½ hours).

Some TGVs to/from Paris (€75, 3½ hours) stop at Gare Avignon Centre, but TGVs to/from Marseille (€29, 35 minutes) and Nice (€52.50, 3¼ hours) only use Gare TGV.

Around Avignon

LES BAUX DE PROVENCE

At the heart of the Alpilles, spectacularly perched above picture-perfect rolling hills of vineyards, olive groves and orchards, is the hilltop village of Les Baux de Provence. Van Gogh painted it and if you stroll around the deep dungeons, up crumbling towers and

DON'T MISS

CARPENTRAS MARKET

Don't miss **Carpentras**, 25km northeast of Avignon, on a Friday morning when its streets and squares spill over with hundreds of market stalls laden with breads, honeys, cheeses, olives, fruit and a rainbow of *berlingots* (the local striped, pillow-shaped hard-boiled sweet). Late November to March, pungent black-truffle stalls murmur with hushed-tones transactions.

around the maze-like ruins of **Château des Baux** (www.chateau-baux-provence.com; adult/child €7.60/5.70; 9am-6pm Sep-Jun, 9am-8pm Jul & Aug) you'll see why. Lunch afterwards at legendary **L'Oustau de Baumanière** (04 90 54 33 07; www.oustaudebaumaniere.com; menus €95-150;).

VAISON-LA-ROMAINE

This traditional market town 17km north of Avignon still has a thriving Tuesday-morning market, a delightful cobbled medieval quarter and a rich Roman legacy. It also makes a great base for hiking and cycling jaunts into the limestone ridge of the nearby **Dentelles de Montmirail** and also up the 'Giant of Provence', **Mont Ventoux** (1912m).

The **Gallo Roman ruins** (adult/child €8/3.50; closed Jan-early Feb) of Vasio Vocontiorum, the city that flourished here between the 6th and 2nd centuries BC, fill two central Vaison sites. Two neighbourhoods of this once-opulent city, Puymin (with the still-functioning 6000-seat **Théâtre Antique**) and La Villasse, lie on either side of the tourist office and av du Général-de-Gaulle. To make sense of the remains (and gather your audioguide), head for the **archaeological museum**, which revives Vaison's Roman past with incredible swag – superb mosaics, carved masks, and statues that include a 3rd-century silver bust and marble renderings of Hadrian and wife Sabina.

From the bus station, 400m east of the town centre on av des Choralies, there are services to/from Avignon (€4, 1½ hours via Orange).

THE FRENCH RIVIERA & MONACO

With its glistening seas, idyllic beaches and fabulous weather, the French Riviera (Côte d'Azur in French) screams exclusivity, extravagance and excess. It has been a favourite getaway for the European jet set since Victorian times and there is nowhere more chichi or glam in France than St-Tropez, Cannes and super-rich, sovereign Monaco.

But it's not just a high-roller's playground. Culture vultures will revel in the region's thriving art scene: the Riviera has fine art museums and rich Roman ruins to explore, while millions descend on this southern stripo of coast purely to bronze their bodies, smell the lavender and soak up the hip Mediterranean vibe.

Nice

POP 344,460

Riviera queen Nice is what good living is all about – shimmering shores, the very best of Mediterranean food, a unique historical heritage, free museums, a charming Old Town, exceptional art and Alpine wilderness within an hour's drive. To get stuck-in straight away, make a beeline upon arrival for **Promenade des Anglais**, Nice's curvaceous palm-lined seafront that follows its busy pebble beach for 6km from the city centre to the airport.

Sights

TOP CHOICE **Vieux Nice** HISTORIC QUARTER

(food markets 6am-1.30pm Tue-Sun) Ditch the map and get lost in this mellow-hued rabbit warren of 18th-century passages, alleyways, historic churches and hidden squares. **Cours Saleya**, running parallel to

DON'T MISS

THE CORNICHES

Some of the Riviera's most spectacular scenery stretches east between Nice and Monaco. A trio of *corniches* (coastal roads) hugs the cliffs between the two seaside cities, each higher up the hill than the last. The middle *corniche* ends in Monaco; the upper and lower continue to Menton near the French-Italian border.

Nice

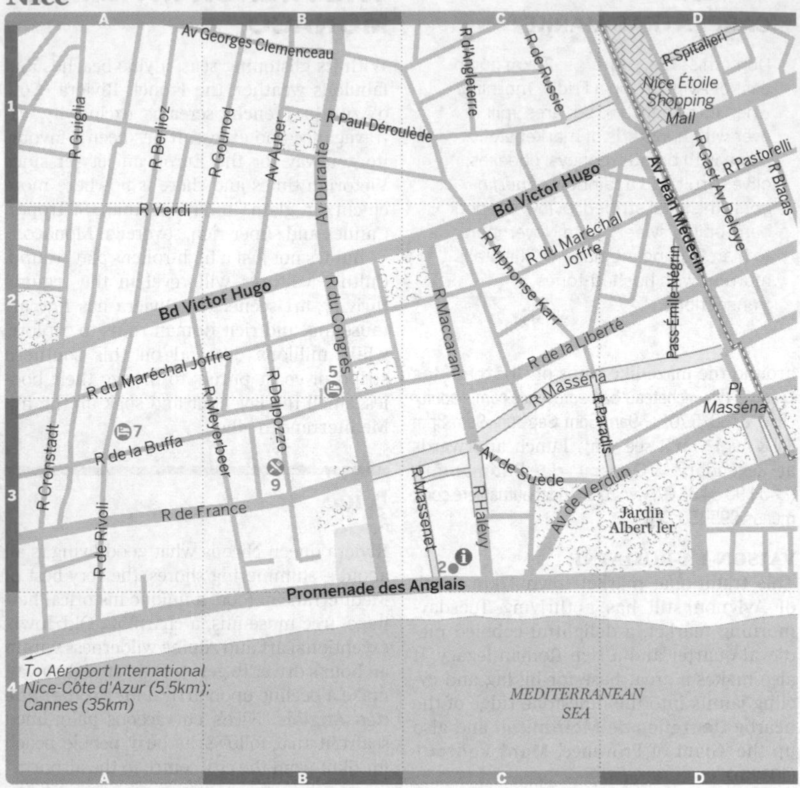

Nice

Top Sights

Cathédrale Ste-Réparate.....F3
Chapelle de la Miséricorde.....F3
MAMAC.....G1
Parc du Château.....G4
Vieux Nice.....F3

Activities, Courses & Tours

1 Centre du Patrimoine Walking Tours.....E3
2 Nice Guided Walking Tours.....C3
3 Trans Côte d'Azur.....H3

Sleeping

4 Hôtel Wilson.....E2
5 Nice Garden Hôtel.....B2
6 Nice Pebbles.....F1
7 Villa Rivoli.....A3

Eating

8 Fenocchio.....F3
9 La Cave de l'Origine.....B3
10 La Merenda.....E3
11 Le Bistrot d'Antoine.....F3
12 Le Comptoir du Marché.....F3
13 Luna Rossa.....E2
14 Zucca Magica.....H2

Drinking

15 L'Abat-Jour.....F3
16 Le Smarties.....F1
17 Les Distilleries Idéales.....F3

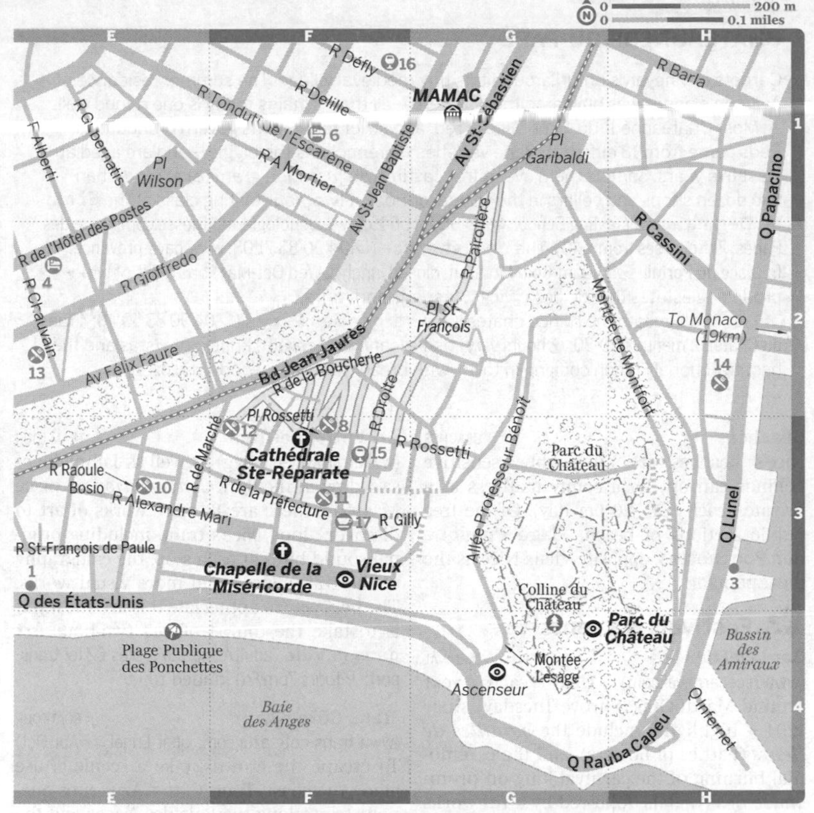

the seafront, remains a joyous, thriving market square with one of France's most vibrant food and flower markets. Rue de la Boucherie and rue Pairolièreare excellent for food shopping, a daily fish market fills place St François, and baroque aficionados will fall head over heels in love with architectural gems such as **Cathédrale Ste-Réparate** (place Rossetti) and the exuberant **Chapelle de la Miséricorde** (cours Saleya).

MAMAC MUSEUM

(Musée d'Art Moderne et d'Art Contemporain; www.mamac-nice.org; promenade des Arts; ⏲10am-6pm Tue-Sun) This ode to contemporary art houses some fantastic avant-garde art from the 1960s to the present, including iconic pop art from Roy Lichtenstein and Andy Warhol's 1965 *Campbell's Soup Can*. An awesome panorama of Vieux Nice unfolds from its rooftop garden-gallery.

FREE **Musée Matisse** GALLERY

(www.musee-matisse-nice.org; 164 av des Arènes de Cimiez; ⏲10am-6pm Wed-Mon) About 2km north in the leafy quarter of Cimiez, this museum houses a fascinating assortment of works by Matisse. Its permanent collection is displayed in a red-ochre 17th-century Genoese villa overlooking an olive-tree-studded park. Temporary exhibitions are hosted in the futuristic basement building. The artist is buried in the **Monastère de Cimiez** cemetery, across the park from the museum.

Musée National Marc Chagall GALLERY

(www.musee-chagall.fr; 4 av Dr Ménard; adult/child €7.50/5.50; ⏲10am-5pm Wed-Mon Oct-Jun, to 6pm Jul-Sep) Discover the largest public collection of works by Belarusian painter Marc Chagall (1887–1985) in this small museum, a 20-minute walk from the centre (signposted from av de l'Olivetto).

WORTH A TRIP

CHÂTEAUNEUF-DU-PAPE

Carpets of vineyards unfurl around this tiny medieval village. The summer residence of Avignon's popes was built atop the wall here – all that remains today is one ruined wall.

Most Châteauneuf-du-Pape wine is red, and strict regulations govern production. Reds come from 13 different grape varieties – grenache is the biggie – and are aged at least five years. Sample them over a free tasting *(dégustation gratuite)* at more than two dozen shops and cellars in the village, or book a two-hour tasting class at the **École de Dégustation** (Tasting School; ☎04 90 83 56 15; www.oenologie-mouriesse.com; 2 rue des Papes; 2hr courses from €40). The **tourist office** (☎04 90 83 71 08; www.pays-provence.fr; place du Portail; ⏲9.30am-6pm Mon-Sat, closed lunch & Wed Oct-May) has a list of wine-producing estates that do cellar visits, tastings and tours.

Perched beneath the ruined chateau, **Le Verger des Papes** (☎04 90 83 50 40; 4 rue du Château; menus €20-30; ⏲hours vary) has a leafy terrace with knockout vistas and the best traditional French cooking in town, with bread made in a wood-fired oven.

Beaches BEACHES

Nice's beaches are all pebbly; sensitive behinds can opt for a comfy mattress at a private beach (€15–20 per day). Of the free public sections of beach, **Plage Publique des Ponchettes**, opposite Vieux Nice, is the most popular.

Festivals & Events

Carnaval de Nice CARNIVAL

(www.nicecarnaval.com) Held each year around Mardi Gras (Shrove Tuesday) since 1294 – highlights include the *batailles de fleurs* (battles of flowers), and the ceremonial burning of the carnival king on promenade des Anglais, followed by a fireworks display.

Nice Jazz Festival MUSIC FESTIVAL

(www.nicejazzfestival.fr) France's original jazz festival has taken on a life of its own in its new promenade location, with fringe concerts popping up all around the venue, from Vieux Nice to Massena and the shopping streets around Rue de France.

Tours

Nice Guided Walking Tours WALKING TOUR

The best way to discover Nice's rich heritage is to take a guided walking tour. The **Centre du Patrimoine** (75 quai des Etats-Unis; ⏲8.30am-1pm & 2-5pm Mon-Thu, to 3.45pm) runs a two-hour Vieux Nice Baroque tour (Tuesday afternoon), as well as themed tours, including art deco, neoclassical and belle époque Nice. The tourist office runs a 2½-hour Vieux Nice tour in English (adult/child €12/6) at 9.30am on Saturday.

Art With The Tram TRAM TOUR

(www.tramway-nice.org) As well as Jaume Plensa's glow-in-the-dark *Conversation* on place Masséna, there are 13 more works of art to discover along Nice's tram, including original sound bites at each stop, the calligraphy of the tram's stops and more visual works. The best way to appreciate this artistic input is to take the tourist office's two-hour **Art dans la Ville** (adult/child €8/3, plus €2 for transport; ⏲tours 7pm Fri) guided tour.

Trans Côte d'Azur BOAT TOUR

(www.trans-cote-azur.com; quai Lunel; ⏲Apr-Oct) To escape the crowds, take a scenic cruise along the coast. Trans Côte d'Azur runs one-hour trips along the Baie des Anges and the Rade de Villefranche (adult/child €16/10) from April to October. From mid-June to mid-September it also runs regular excursions to Île Ste-Marguerite (€35/25, crossing one hour), St-Tropez (€58/44, crossing 2½ hours) and Monaco (€34/ 25, crossing 45 minutes). Reservations are essential.

Sleeping

Nice Garden Hôtel BOUTIQUE HOTEL €€

(☎04 93 87 35 63; www.nicegardenhotel.com; 11 rue du Congrès; s/d €75/100; ❄📶) Heavy iron gates hide this gem. Nine rooms are a subtle blend of old and new, and overlook a delightful garden with orange tree. Amazingly, all this charm and peacefulness is just two blocks from the promenade.

TOP CHOICE **Nice Pebbles** SELF-CONTAINED €€

(☎04 97 20 27 30; www.nicepebbles.com; 23 rue Gioffredo; 1-/3-bedroom apt from €105/320; 📶🏊) The concept is simple: the quality of a four-star boutique hotel in holiday flats. Apartments (one to three bedrooms) are equipped with flat-screen TV, kitchen, linen bedding and, in some cases, wi-fi, swimming pool, and balcony, and come with a useful starter pack (no need to rush to the supermarket). Nightly rates are significantly cheaper during low season.

Villa Saint-Exupéry HOSTEL €€
(☎04 93 84 42 83; www.villahostels.com; 22 av Gravier; dm/s/d incl breakfast €25-30/45/90; @📶) Set in a lovely converted monastery in the north of Nice, this is a great place. Chill out in the 24-hour common room housed in the old stained-glass chapel, sip a €1 beer on the barbecue terrace and stock up on travel tips.

Villa staff will pick you up from the nearby Comte de Falicon tram stop or St-Maurice stop for bus 23 (direct from the airport) when you first arrive. Rates include breakfast.

Villa Rivoli BOUTIQUE HOTEL €€
(☎04 93 88 80 25; www.villa-rivoli.com; 10 rue de Rivoli; s/d/q from 85/99/210; ❄📶) Built in 1890, this stately villa feels like your own pied-à-terre in the heart of Nice. Take breakfast in the garden's sun-dappled shade, or in the grand belle époque *salon*.

Hôtel Wilson BOUTIQUE HOTEL €
(☎04 93 85 47 79; www.hotel-wilson-nice.com; 39 rue de l'Hôtel des Postes; s/d €50/55; 📶) Many years of travelling, an experimental nature and exquisite taste have turned Jean-Marie's rambling flat into a compelling place to stay. The 16 rooms have individual, carefully crafted decor, and share the eclectic dining room.

Eating

Niçois nibbles include *socca* (a thin layer of chickpea flour and olive oil batter), *salade niçoise* and *farcis* (stuffed vegetables). Restaurants in Vieux Nice are a mixed bag, so choose carefully.

TOP CHOICE **Le Bistrot d'Antoine** MODERN FRENCH €€
(☎04 93 85 29 57; 27 rue de la Préfecture; mains €13-18; ⏲lunch & dinner Tue-Sat) This brasserie is full every night (booking essential), yet the 'bistro chic' cuisine never wavers, the staff are cool as cucumbers, the atmosphere is reliably jovial and the prices incredibly good value.

Luna Rossa ITALIAN €€
(☎04 93 85 55 66; www.lelunarossa.com; 3 rue Chauvain; mains €15-25; ⏲Tue-Fri, dinner Sat) Luna Rossa is like your dream Mediterranean dinner come true: fresh pasta, exquisitely cooked seafood, sun-kissed vegetables and divine meats.

Fenocchio ICE CREAM €
(2 place Rossetti; ice cream from €2; ⏲9am-midnight Feb-Oct) Dither too long over the 70-plus flavours of ice cream and sorbet at this unforgettable *glacier* (ice-cream shop) and you'll never make it to the front of the queue. Eschew predictable favourites and indulge in a new taste sensation: black olive, tomato-basil, avocado, rosemary or lavender.

La Cave de l'Origine MODERN FRENCH €€
(☎04 83 50 09 60; 3 rue Dalpozzo; mains €15-22; ⏲lunch & dinner Tue-Sat) This sleek new wine bar–restaurant has as much substance as style: great selection of wines by the glass, many local, and fantastic advice about what to pair with your food (well-executed, modern French fare with a touch of fusion).

Le Comptoir du Marché MODERN FRENCH €
(☎04 93 13 45 01; 8 rue du Marché; mains €13-15; ⏲lunch & dinner Tue-Sat) Vintage kitchen decor, recession-proof prices and a creative cuisine that gives a modern twist to French traditional recipes is the secret to the Counter's huge success.

La Merenda NIÇOIS €
(4 rue Raoul Bosio; mains €12-15; ⏲Mon-Fri) Simple, solid Niçois cuisine by former Michelin-starred chef Dominique Le Stanc draws the crowds to this pocket-sized bistro. No credit cards.

Zucca Magica VEGETARIAN €€
(☎04 93 56 25 27; www.lazuccamagica.com; 4bis quai Papacino; menus €30; ⏲Tue-Sat; ✎) The Magic Pumpkin serves a fixed five-course menu, dictated simply by the market and the chef's fancy. Seating is amid a fabulous collection of pumpkins and fairy lights.

Drinking & Entertainment

Vieux Nice's streets are stuffed with bars and cafes.

TOP CHOICE **Les Distilleries Idéales** CAFE
(24 rue de la Préfecture; ⏲9am-12.30am) Whether you're after an espresso on your way to the cours Saleya market or an *apéritif* (complete with cheese and charcuterie platters, €5.20) before trying out one of Nice's

fabulous restaurants, Les Distilleries is one of the most atmospheric bars in town.

Le Smarties BAR
(http://nicesmarties.free.fr; 10 rue Défly; ⌚6pm-2am Tue-Sat) We love Smarties' sexy '70s swirly orange style, which draws a hot-looking straight-gay crowd. On weekends, the tiny dance floor fills when DJs spin deep house, electro, techno and occasionally disco; weekdays are mellower. Free tapas with happy hour (nightly 6pm to 9pm).

L'Abat-Jour BAR
(25 rue Benoît Bunico) With its vintage furniture, rotating art exhibitions and alternative music, l'Abat-Jour is all the rage with Nice's young and trendy crowd. The basement has live music or DJ sessions.

Information

Tourist Office (☎08 92 70 74 07; www.nicetourisme.com; 5 promenade des Anglais; ⌚9am-6pm Mon-Sat) Also runs a branch at the train station.

Getting There & Away

Air

Nice-Côte d'Azur airport is 6km west of Nice, by the sea. A taxi to Nice centre costs around €25.

» Buses 98 and 99 link the airport terminal with Nice Gare Routière and Nice train station (€4, 35 minutes, every 20 minutes).

» Bus 110 (€18, hourly) links the airport with Monaco (40 minutes).

Boat

Nice is the main port for ferries to Corsica. **SNCM** (www.sncm.fr; quai du Commerce, ferry terminal) and **Corsica Ferries** (www.corsicaferries.com; quai Lunel) are the two main companies.

Bus

There are excellent intercity services around Nice. All journeys cost €1. The bus station was demolished in 2011 so bus stops are now scattered around the *coulée verte*. Smartphone users can also download the very useful Ligne d'Azur app or visit the company's office.

Train

From **Gare Nice Ville** (av Thiers), 1.2km north of the beach, there are frequent services to Cannes (€6.40, 40 minutes) and Monaco (€3.60, 20 minutes).

WORTH A TRIP

THE PINE CONE TRAIN

Chugging between mountains and the sea, narrow-gauge railway **Train des Pignes** (Pine Cone Train; www.trainprovence.com) is one of France's most picturesque train rides. Rising to 1000m, with breathtaking views, the 151km-long track between Nice and Digne-les-Bains passes through the scarcely populated back country of little-known Haute Provence.

Day-trip suggestion: a picnic and meander around the historical centre and citadel of the beautiful medieval village of **Entrevaux** (€20 return, 1½ hours).

Cannes

POP 74,445

Most have heard of Cannes and its celebrity film festival. The latter only lasts for two weeks in May, but the buzz and glitz linger all year thanks to regular visits from celebrities who come here to indulge in designer shopping, beaches and the palace hotels of the Riviera's glammest seafront, bd de la Croisette.

Offshore lie the idyllic islands, Îles de Lérins, the unexpected key to 2000-plus years of history – from Ligurian fishing communities (200 BC) to one of Europe's oldest religious communities (5th century AD) and the enigmatic Man in the Iron Mask.

Sights & Activities

La Croisette ARCHITECTURE
The multistarred hotels and couture shops that line the famous bd de la Croisette (aka La Croisette) may be the preserve of the rich and famous, but anyone can enjoy the palm-shaded promenade and take in the atmosphere. In fact, it's a favourite amongst Cannois (natives of Cannes), particularly at night when it's lit with bright colours.

There are great views of the bay and nearby Estérel mountains, and stunning art deco architecture among the seafront palaces, such as the **Martinez** or the legendary **Carlton InterContinental** – its twin cupolas were modelled on the breasts of the courtesan La Belle Otéro, infamous for her string of lovers.

Not so elegant but imposing nonetheless is the **Palais des Festivals** (Festival Palace; bd de la Croisette; guided tours adult/child €3/free; ⌚guided tours 2.30pm Jun-Apr), host to the world's most glamorous film festival. Climb the red carpet, walk down the auditorium, tread the stage and learn about cinema's most glamorous event and its numerous anecdotes on a **Palais des Festivals guided tour** (adult/child €3/free; ⌚1½ hr); tickets can only be booked in person at the tourist office.

Beaches BEACHES
Cannes is blessed with sandy beaches although much of bd de la Croisette is taken up by private beaches (open to all). This arrangement leaves only a small strip of free sand near the Palais des Festivals for the bathing hoi polloi; the much bigger **Plage du Midi** (bd Jean Hibert) and **Plage de la Bocca**, west from Vieux Port, are also free.

Le Suquet HISTORIC QUARTER
Cannes' historic quarter, pre-dating the glitz and glam of the town's festival days, retains a quaint village feel with its steep, meandering alleyways. There are wonderful views of the Baie de Cannes from the top of the hill.

Îles de Lérins ISLANDS
Although just 20 minutes away by boat, these tranquil islands feel far from the madding crowd. **Île Ste-Marguerite**, where the mysterious Man in the Iron Mask was incarcerated during the late 17th century, is known for its bone-white beaches, eucalyptus groves and small marine museum. Tiny **Île St-Honorat** has been a monastery since the 5th century. Boats leave Cannes from quai des Îles on the western side of the harbour.

Sleeping

TOP CHOICE **Hôtel Le Canberra** BOUTIQUE HOTEL €€€
(☎04 97 06 95 00; www.hotel-cannes-canberra.com; 120 rue d'Antibes; d from €255;) This boutique stunner, just a couple of blocks back from La Croisette, is the epitome of Cannes glamour: designer grey rooms with splashes of candy pink, sexy black-marble bathrooms with coloured lighting, heated pool (April to October) in a bamboo-filled garden, intimate atmosphere (there are just 35 rooms) and impeccable service. Rooms overlooking rue d'Antibes are cheaper.

Le Romanesque BOUTIQUE HOTEL €€
(☎04 93 68 04 20; 10 rue du Batéguier; s/d/tr €89/109/149;) Every room is individually decorated at this eight-room boutique charmer in the heart of the Carré d'Or nightlife district (book a back room if you're a light sleeper). Favourite rooms include Charlotte, with its sun-drenched bath; and Elizabeth, the former maid's quarters, with low, sloping beamed ceilings. Gay-friendly. Great service.

Hôtel 7e Art BOUTIQUE HOTEL €
(☎04 93 68 66 66; www.7arthotel.com; 23 rue Maréchal Joffre; s €68, d €60-98;) Hôtel 7e Art has put boutique style within reach of budgeters. The snappy design of putty-coloured walls, padded headboards and pop art, and perks like iPod docks in every room, far exceed what you'd expect at this price.

WORTH A TRIP

THE SCENT OF THE CÔTE D'AZUR

Mosey some 20km northwest of Cannes to inhale the sweet smell of lavender, jasmine, mimosa and orange-blossom fields. In **Grasse**, one of France's leading perfume producers, dozens of perfumeries create essences to sell to factories (for aromatically enhanced foodstuffs and soaps) as well as to prestigious couture houses – the highly trained noses of local perfume-makers can identify 3000 scents in a single whiff.

Learn about three millennia of perfume-making at the **Musée International de la Parfumerie** (MIP; www.museesdegrasse.com; 2 bd du Jeu de Ballon; adult/child €3/free; ⌚11am-6pm Wed-Mon;) and watch the process first-hand during a guided tour at **Fragonard** (www.fragonard.com; 20 bd Fragonard; ⌚9am-6pm Feb-Oct, 9am-12.30pm & 2-6pm Nov-Jan) perfumery, the easiest to reach by foot. The tourist office has information on other perfumeries and field trips to local flower farms, including the **Domaine de Manon** (☎06 12 18 02 69; www.le-domaine-de-manon.com; 36 chemin du Servan, Plascassier; admission €6). Roses are picked mid-May to mid-June, jasmine July to late October.

Hôtel Le Mistral BOUTIQUE HOTEL €€
(☎04 93 39 91 46; www.mistral-hotel.com; 13 rue des Belges; d from €89; ❄☜) This small boutique hotel wins the *palme d'or* for best value in town: rooms are decked out in flattering red and plum tones, bathrooms feature lovely designer fittings, there are seaviews from the top floor, and the hotel is a mere 50m from La Croisette.

Eating

TOP CHOICE **Sea Sens** FUSION €€
(☎04 63 36 05 06; www.five-hotel-cannes.com; Five Hotel & Spa, 1 rue Notre Dame; 2-/3-course lunch menu €29/39, mains €26-55; ☜) Run by the brilliant Pourcel brothers, Cannes' latest food sensation serves divine food blending French gastronomy and Asian elegance, with panoramic views of Le Suquet and Cannes' rooftops on the side. Come here for lunch to make the best of the great-value menus.

Mantel MODERN EUROPEAN €€
(☎04 93 39 13 10; www.restaurantmantel.com; 22 rue St-Antoine; menus €25-38; ⊙Fri-Mon, dinner Tue & Thu) Discover why Noël Mantel is the hotshot of the Cannois gastronomic scene at his refined old-town restaurant. Try the wonderfully tender glazed veal shank in balsamic vinegar or the original poached octopus *bourride*-style. Best of all though, you get not one but two desserts from pastry-chef wonder Christian Gonthier, who bakes the bread, and prepares the sweets served with coffee.

Aux Bons Enfants FRENCH €€
(80 rue Meynadier; menus €23; ⊙Tue-Sat) A people's-choice place since 1935, this informal restaurant cooks up regional dishes such as aïoli *garni* (aïoli with vegetables), *daube* (beef stew), and *rascasse meunière* (pan-fried rockfish), all in a convivial atmosphere. No credit cards and no booking.

PhilCat DELICATESSEN €
(La Pantiéro; sandwiches & salads €4-6.50; ⊙8.30am-5pm) Don't be put off by Phillipe and Catherine's unassuming prefab cabin on the Pantiéro: this is Cannes' best lunch house. Huge salads, made to order, are piled high with delicious fresh ingredients. Or if you're *really* hungry, try one of their phenomenal *pan bagna* (a moist sandwich bursting with Provençal flavours).

Information

Tourist office (☎04 92 99 84 22; www.cannes.travel; Palais des Festivals, bd de la Croisette; ⊙9am-7pm)

Getting There & Away

BUS From the **bus station** (place Cornut-Gentille), buses serve Nice (€1, 1½ hours) and Nice airport (€16, 50 minutes, half-hourly).

TRAIN From Cannes train station there are at least hourly services to/from:

Nice €6.40, 40 minutes
Antibes €2.70, 12 minutes
Monaco €8.70, one hour
Marseille €28.40, two hours

St-Tropez

POP 4986

In the soft autumn or winter light, it's hard to believe the pretty terracotta fishing village of St-Tropez is a stop on the Riviera celebrity circuit. It seems far removed from its glitzy siblings further up the coast, but come spring or summer, it's a different world: the population increases tenfold, prices triple and fun-seekers pile in to party till dawn, strut around the luxury-yacht-packed Vieux Port and enjoy the creature comforts of exclusive A-listers' beaches in the Baie de Pampelonne.

Sights & Activities

Musée de l'Annonciade MUSEUM
(place Grammont; adult/child €6/4; ⊙10am-noon & 2-6pm Wed-Mon Oct & Dec-May, 10am-noon & 3-7pm Wed-Mon Jun-Sep) In a gracefully converted 16th-century chapel, this famous art museum showcases an impressive collection of modern

DON'T MISS

THE MARKET

One of southern France's busiest and best, St-Tropez's **place des Lices market** (⊙mornings Tue & Sat) is a highlight of local life, with colourful stalls groaning under the weight of plump fruit and veg, mounds of olives, local cheeses, chestnut purée and fragrant herbs. Afterwards meander to the port and duck beneath the stone arch to the bijou **fish market** (⊙mornings Tue-Sun, daily summer), hidden between stone walls on place aux Herbes.

TOP FIVE BEACH EATS

Book lunch (well ahead) at the following, open May to September and around €15 to €40 for a main.

Club 55 (www.leclub55.fr; 43 bd Patch, Pampelonne) St-Tropez's oldest running beach club, this 1950s address was the crew canteen for the filming of *And God Created Woman* with Brigitte Bardot. The rich and famous flock here to be seen, although the food is nothing special.

Nikki Beach (www.nikkibeach.com/sttropez; rte de l'Epi, Epi Plage) Favoured by dance-on-the-bar celebs such as Paris Hilton and Pamela Anderson, the deafening scene ends at midnight.

Aqua Club (04 94 79 84 35; www.aqua-club-plage.fr; rte de l'Epi, Pampelonne; mains €22-29; Jan-Oct) Friendly mixed, gay-straight crowd, the most diverse by far.

Moorea Plage (04 94 97 18 17; www.moorea-plage-st-tropez.com; rte des Plages, Tahiti; mains €15-29) Ideal for conversation and backgammon (supplied); tops for steak.

Liberty Plage (04 94 79 80 62; www.plageleliberty.com; chemin des Tamaris, Pampelonne; mains €17-19; year-round) Clothing optional – eat naked.

art infused with that legendary Côte d'Azur light. Pointillist Paul Signac bought a house in St-Tropez in 1892 and introduced others to the area. The museum's collection includes his *St-Tropez, Le Quai* (1899) and *St-Tropez, Coucher de Soleil au Bois de Pins* (1896), which hangs juxtaposed with a window-view of contemporary St-Tropez.

Plage de Pampelonne BEACH

The golden sands of **Plage de Tahiti**, 4km southeast of town, morph into the 5km-long, celebrity-studded **Plage de Pampelonne**, which sports a line-up of exclusive beach restaurants and clubs in summer. The bus to Ramatuelle stops at various points along a road, 1km inland from the beach.

Citadelle de St-Tropez HISTORIC SITE

(admission €2.50; 10am-6.30pm) Built in 1602 to defend the coast against Spain, the citadel dominates the hillside overlooking St-Tropez to the east. The views (and peacocks!) are fantastic. Its dungeons shelter a **Musée Naval**, dedicated to the town's maritime history and the Allied landings in August 1944.

Sleeping

St-Tropez is no shoestring destination, but multistar camping grounds abound on the road to Plage de Pampelonne.

TOP CHOICE **Hôtel Lou Cagnard** PENSION €€

(04 94 97 04 24; www.hotel-lou-cagnard.com; 18 av Paul Roussel; d €75-156; Jan-Oct;) Book well ahead for this great-value courtyard charmer, shaded by lemon and fig trees. This pretty Provençal house with lavender shutters has its very own jasmine-scented garden, strung with fairy lights at night. The cheapest rooms have private washbasin and standup-bathtub but share a toilet; 15 of the 19 rooms have aircon.

Hôtel Le Colombier HOTEL €€

(04 94 97 05 31; http://lecolombierhotel.free.fr; impasse des Conquettes; r €84-158, without bathroom €76;) An immaculately clean converted house, five minutes' walk from place des Lices, the Colombier's fresh, summery decor is feminine and uncluttered, with pale pink bedrooms and vintage furniture.

Pastis HOTEL €€€

(04 98 12 56 50; www.pastis-st-tropez.com; 61 av du Général Leclerc; d from €200;) This stunning townhouse-turned-hotel is the brainchild of an English couple besotted with Provence and passionate about modern art. You'll die for the pop-art-inspired interior, and long for a swim in the emerald-green pool.

Eating

Quai Jean Jaurès at the Vieux Port is littered with restaurants and cafes.

TOP CHOICE **Auberge de l'Oumède** PROVENÇAL €€

(04 94 44 11 11; www.aubergedeloumede.com; Chemin de l'Oumède; mains €39-59, d from €225; dinner Tue-Sat May–mid-Sep, dinner daily Jul & Aug;) Epicureans come from far and wide to sample Jean-Pierre Frezia's Provençal cuisine served in a sea of vineyards. Dining at this isolated *bastide* down a

TRAFFIC-JAM DODGER

To skip the worst of July and August's high-season traffic, motorists get off the A8 at Le Muy (exit 35), take the D558 road through the Massif des Maures and via La Garde Freinet to **Port Grimaud**, park and hop aboard a **Les Bateaux Verts** (☎04 94 49 29 39; www.bateauxverts.com; quai Jean Jaurès) shuttle boat (15 minutes) to St-Tropez.

single-lane track is indeed a rare treat. It has seven rooms and a pool – handy should you really not want to leave.

Auberge des Maures PROVENÇAL €€
(☎04 94 97 01 50; 4 rue du Docteur Boutin; mains €31-39; ⏲dinner) The town's oldest restaurant remains the locals' choice for always-good, copious portions of earthy Provençal cooking, like *daube* (a Provençal beef stew) or tapenade-stuffed lamb shoulder. Book a table (essential) on the leafy courtyard.

Le Sporting BRASSERIE €€
(☎04 94 97 00 65; place des Lices; mains €14-24; ⏲8am-1am) There's a bit of everything on the menu at always-packed Le Sporting, but the speciality is a hamburger topped with *foie gras* and morel cream sauce. The Brittany-born owner also serves perfect buckwheat crêpes, honest lunch deals (€13), and a simple salad and *croque monsieur*.

Information

Tourist office (☎04 94 97 45 21; www.ot-saint-tropez.com; quai Jean Jaurès; ⏲9.30am-8pm Jul & Aug, 9.30am-12.30pm & 2-7pm Apr-Jun & Sep–mid-Oct, 9.30am-12.30pm & 2-6pm mid-Oct–Mar)

Getting There & Away

From the **bus station** (☎04 94 56 25 74; av du Général de Gaulle), buses run by **VarLib** (www.varlib.fr) serve Ramatuelle (€2, 35 minutes) and St-Raphaël train station (€2, 1¼ hours) via Grimaud, Port Grimaud and Fréjus. There are four daily buses to Toulon-Hyères airport (€15, 1½ hours).

Monaco

☎377 / POP 32,350

Your first glimpse of this pocket-sized principality will probably make your heart sink: after all the gorgeous medieval hilltop villages, glittering beaches and secluded peninsulas of the surrounding area, Monaco's concrete high-rises and astronomic prices come as a shock.

But Monaco is beguiling. The world's second-smallest state (a smidgen bigger than the Vatican), it is as famous for its tax-haven status as for its glittering casino, sports scene (Formula One, world-famous circus festival and tennis open) and a royal family on a par with British royals for best gossip fodder. For visitors, it just means an exciting trip: from an evening at the stunning casino, to a visit of the excellent Musée Océanographique to a spot of celebrity/royalty spotting, Monaco is a fun day out on the Riviera.

In terms of practicalities, Monaco is a sovereign state but has no border control. It has its own flag (red and white), national holiday (19 November) and telephone country code (377), but the official language is French and the country uses the euro even though it is not part of the European Union.

Most visit Monaco as a day trip from Nice, a 20-minute train ride away.

Sights & Activities

Casino de Monte Carlo CASINO
(www.casinomontecarlo.com; place du Casino; ⏲European Rooms from noon Sat & Sun, from 2pm Mon-Fri) Living out your James Bond fantasies just doesn't get any better than at Monte Carlo's monumental, richly decorated showpiece, the 1910-built casino. The European Rooms have poker/slot machines, French roulette and *trente et quarante* (a card game), while the Private Rooms offer

Monaco

Top Sights

Casino de Monte Carlo........C3
Cathédrale de Monaco........B6
Le Rocher........B6
Musée Océanographique de Monaco........C6
Palais du Prince........A6

Eating

1 Café Llorca........D1
2 La Montgolfière........B6
3 Zelo's........D1

Drinking

4 Brasserie de Monaco........B5

Monaco

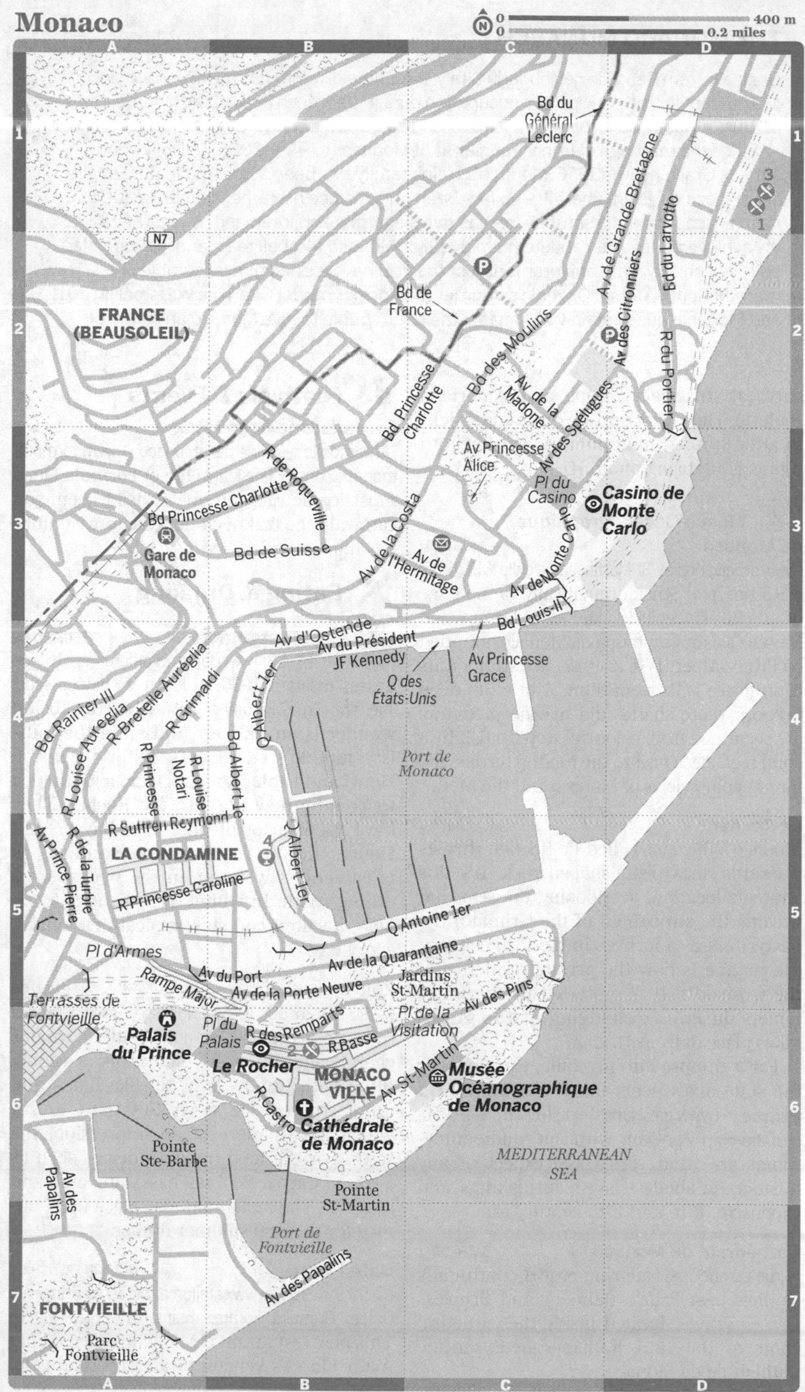
0
400 m
0
0.2 miles
Bd du Général Leclerc
N7
FRANCE (BEAUSOLEIL)
Bd de France
Av de Grande Bretagne
Av des Citronniers
Bd du Larvotto
R du Portier
Bd des Moulins
Bd Princesse Charlotte
Av de la Madone
Av des Spélugues
Av Princesse Alice
Pl du Casino
Casino de Monte Carlo
R de Roqueville
Bd Princesse Charlotte
Gare de Monaco
Bd de Suisse
Av de la Costa
Av de l'Hermitage
Av de Monte Carlo
Bd Louis-II
Av d'Ostende
Av du Président JF Kennedy
Q des États-Unis
Av Princesse Grace
Bd Rainier III
R Bretelle Auréglia
R Grimaldi
Q Albert 1er
R Louise Aureglia
R Princesse
R Louise Notari
Bd Albert 1e
Port de Monaco
R Suffren Reymond
LA CONDAMINE
Av Prince Pierre
R de la Turbie
R Princesse Caroline
Q Antoine 1er
Pl d'Armes
Av de la Quarantaine
Av du Port
Rampe Major
Av de la Porte Neuve
Jardins St-Martin
Av des Pins
Terrasses de Fontvieille
Pl du Palais
R des Remparts
Pl de la Visitation
Palais du Prince
R Basse
Le Rocher
MONACO VILLE
Av St-Martin
Musée Océanographique de Monaco
R Castro
Cathédrale de Monaco
Pointe Ste-Barbe
MEDITERRANEAN SEA
Av des Papalins
Pointe St-Martin
Port de Fontvieille
Av des Papalins
FONTVIEILLE
Parc Fontvieille

THE MONACO MONARCHY

Originally from Genoa in neighbouring Italy, the Grimaldi family has ruled Monaco since 1297, except for the principality's occupation during the French Revolution. Monaco's independence was again recognised by France in 1860, and it's been independent ever since.

Since the marriage of Prince Rainier III of Monaco (r 1949–2005) to Hollywood actress Grace Kelly in 1956, Monaco's ruling family has been a nonstop feature in gossip magazines. Even Albert II, who has been prince since his father's death in 2005, hasn't escaped media scrutiny: he has two illegitimate children and no legal heirs, but his achievements as an athlete (he played for Monaco football team and is a judo black belt), his charity work and promotion of the arts have earned him favourable press. He married South African Olympic swimmer and former model Charlene Wittstock in 2011, and Monégasques are now waiting for the royal couple to give Monaco an heir.

baccarat, blackjack, craps and American roulette. The jacket-and-tie dress code kicks in after 8pm. Minimum entry age for both rooms is 18; bring photo ID.

TOP CHOICE Musée Océanographique de Monaco AQUARIUM
(www.oceano.org; av St-Martin; adult/child €13/6.50; 9.30am-7pm) Stuck dramatically to the edge of a cliff since 1910, the world-renowned Musée Océanographique de Monaco, founded by Prince Albert I (1848-1922), is a stunner. Its centrepiece is its **aquarium**, with a 6m-deep **lagoon** where sharks and marine predators are separated from colourful tropical fish by a coral reef. Pay a visit to the rooftop terrace too for sweeping views of Monaco and the Med.

Le Rocher HISTORIC QUARTER
Monaco Ville, also called Le Rocher, thrusts skywards on a pistol-shaped rock. It's this strategic location, overlooking the sea, that became the stronghold of the Grimaldi dynasty. Built as a fortress in the 13th century, the **palace** is now the private residence of the Grimaldis. It is protected by the Carabiniers du Prince; **changing of the guard** takes place daily at 11.55am.

For a glimpse into royal life, you can tour the state apartments inside the **Palais du Prince** (www.palais.mc; adult/child €8/3.50; 10am-6pm Apr-Sep) with an audioguide; rooms are what you would expect of any aristocratic abode - lavish furnishings and expensive 18th- and 19th-century art.

Cathédrale de Monaco CATHEDRAL
(4 rue Colonel) An adoring crowd continually shuffles past Prince Rainier's and Princess Grace's graves, located inside the cathedral choir of the 1875 Romanesque-Byzantine Cathédrale de Monaco.

Festivals & Events

Formula One Grand Prix SPORTS
(Automobile Club de Monaco; www.formula1monaco.com; late May) One of Formula One's most iconic races. If you're dead keen, you can walk the 3.2km circuit; the tourist office has maps.

Eating & Drinking

TOP CHOICE La Montgolfière FUSION €€
(97 98 61 59; www.lamontgolfiere.mc; 16 rue Basse; mains €21-30; lunch & dinner Mon, Tue, Thu, Fri, Sun, dinner Sat) This tiny fusion wonder is an unlikely find amid the touristy jumble of Monaco's historic quarter. Henri and Fabienne Geraci had a great idea to breathe new life into the Rocher. They have spent a lot of time in Malaysia, and Henri's fusion cuisine is outstanding, as is Fabienne's welcome in the pocket-sized dining room. In winter, Henri cooks *bourride*, a salted cod stew typical of Monaco, every day.

Zelo's FUSION €€
(99 99 25 50; 10 av Princesse Grace, Grimaldi Forum; mains €25-30; dinner) With enormous chandeliers, intensely blue walls, a ceiling fitted with hundreds of starlike lights and uninterrupted sea views, it's hard to say which makes more of an impression, the setting or the food (modern dishes such as a trio of Carpaccio – sea bass, king crab and salmon). The restaurant also has a huge terrace for magical summer dining.

Café Llorca MODERN FRENCH €€
(99 99 29 29; www.cafellorca.mc; 10 av Princesse Grace, Grimaldi Forum; mains €15-26; lunch) This new restaurant is Michelin-starred-chef Alain Llorca's version of a traditional cafe:

the menu is classic French fare (pork loin with sautéed potatoes; *daube*, a local beef stew) but elevated to new heights in taste and presentation. In summer, tables are set out on the terrace overlooking the sea.

TOP CHOICE **Brasserie de Monaco** MICROBREWERY (www.brasseriedemonaco.com; 36 rte de la Piscine; 11am-1pm Sun-Thu, 11am-3am Fri & Sat) Tourists and locals rub shoulders at Monaco's only microbrewery, which crafts rich organic ales and lager, and serves tasty (if pricey) antipasti plates. Happy hour is 5pm to 8pm.

Information

Telephone

Calls between Monaco and France are international calls. Dial 00 followed by Monaco's country code (377) when calling Monaco from France or elsewhere abroad. To phone France from Monaco, dial 00 and France's country code (33).

Tourist information

Tourist office (www.visitmonaco.com; 2a bd des Moulins; 9am-7pm Mon-Sat, 11am-1pm Sun) From mid-June to late September additional tourist-info kiosks mushroom around the harbour and train station.

Getting There & Away

Monaco's **train station** (av Prince Pierre) has frequent trains to Nice (€3.60, 20 minutes), and east to Menton (€2, 10 minutes) and beyond into Italy.

One thing to note if planning a day trip to Monaco is that its sparkly, state-of-the-art train station has no lockers to stash your bags.

CORSICA

The rugged island of Corsica (Corse in French) is officially a part of France, but remains fiercely proud of its own culture, history and language. It's one of the Mediterranean's most dramatic islands, with a bevy of beautiful beaches, glitzy ports and a mountainous, maquis-covered interior to explore, as well as a wild, independent spirit all of its own.

The island has long had a love-hate relationship with the mother mainland – you'll see plenty of anti-French slogans and 'Corsicanised' road signs – but that doesn't seem to deter the millions of French tourists who descend on the island every summer. Prices skyrocket and accommodation is at a premium during the peak season between July and August, so you're much better off saving your visit for spring and autumn.

Bastia

POP 44,170

Filled with heart, soul and character, the bustling old port of Bastia is a good surprise. Sure, it might not measure up to Ajaccio's sexy style or the architectural appeal of Bonifacio, but it has an irresisible magnetism. Allow yourself at least a day to drink in the narrow old-town alleyways of Terra Vecchia, the seething Vieux Port (Old Port), dramatic 16th-century citadel perched up high, and the compelling history museum.

Sights & Activities

Even by Corsican standards, Bastia is a pocket-sized city. The 19th-century central square of **place St-Nicholas** sprawls along the seafront between the ferry port and harbour. Named after the patron saint of sailors – a nod to Corsica's seagoing heritage – the square is lined with plane trees, busy cafes and a **statue of Napoléon Bonaparte**, Corsica's famous son.

A network of narrow lanes leads south towards the neighbourhood of **Terra Vecchia**, a muddle of crumbling apartments and balconied blocks. Further south, the Vieux Port is ringed by pastel-coloured tenements and buzzy brasseries, as well as the twin-towered **Église St-Jean Baptiste**. The best views of the harbour are from the **Jetée du Dragon** (Dragon Jetty) or from the hillside park of **Jardin Romieu**, reached via a twisting staircase from the waterfront. Behind the garden looms Bastia's sunbaked **citadel**, built from the 15th to 17th centuries as a stronghold for the city's Genoese masters. Inside the citadel, the **Palais des Gouverneurs** (Governers Palace) houses Bastia's top-notch local history museum, **Musée d'Histoire de Bastia** (04 95 31 09 12; www.musee-bastia.com; place

MONEY MATTERS

Many restaurants and hotels in Corsica don't accept credit cards, and *chambres d'hôtes* (B&Bs) hardly ever: those that do quite frequently refuse card payments for amounts typically less than €15.

CORSICAN ICE

Wrapping your lips around a rich Corsican ice cream, flavoured with one of the island's distinctive edible products, is an essential part of the Bastia experience. And no address does it better than **Raugi** (2 rue du Chanoine Colombani; one/two/three scoops €1.30/2.60/3.90, cups €5-20), an ice-cream house dating to 1937, with its main cafe in town and a waterfront **takeaway parlour** (quai du 1er Bataillon de Choc) at the old port. Flavours range from bog-standard raspberry, lemon and so on to Corsican chestnut, mandarin, fig, aromatic *senteur de maquis* (scent of Corsican herbal scrubland) and sweet *myrte* (myrtle). Forget the chocolate flake; top it off with a *canistrelli* (local biscuit) stuck in the top.

du Donjon; admission €5; ⌚10am-7.30pm Tue-Sun Jul–mid-Sep, shorter hrs mid-Sep–Jun).

Sleeping

TOP CHOICE Hôtel Central HOTEL €€
(☎04 95 31 71 12; www.centralhotel.fr; 3 rue Miot; s €77, d €90; 📶) From the vintage, black-and-white-tiled floor in the entrance to the sweeping staircase and eclectic jumble of pot plants in the minscule interior courtyard, this family-run address oozes 1940s grace.

Hôtel Les Voyageurs HOTEL €€
(☎04 95 34 90 80; www.hotel-lesvoyageurs.com; 9 av Maréchal Sébastiani; s €60-85, d €75-100, q €110-150; P❄📶) In a city where parking can be tricky, the garage here is a big plus. Combine this with a gorgeous ginger facade, shabby-chic oyster-grey shutters and a modern three-star interior, and you'll be well pleased.

Eating

Tasty all-day options abound around the Vieux Port and along quai des Martyrs. Market stalls packed with local produce spill across **place de l'Hôtel de Ville** every Saturday and Sunday morning.

Le Lavezzi MODERN FRENCH €€
(☎04 95 31 05 73; 8 rue St-Jean; mains €20-35, lunch menus €19) A boutique address design-loving gourmets will love, Le Lavezzi is completely different. Its artsy interior is fabulous and funky, and the real heart stealer is the twinset of 1st-floor balconies with prime old-port views.

Petite Marie REGIONAL CUISINE €€
(☎04 95 32 47 83; 2 rue des Zéphyrs; mains €16-19; ⌚dinner Mon-Sat) Everything is home baked at Petite Marie, a bolt-hole hidden away in an alley a couple of blocks from the Vieux Port. Do as locals do and kick-start your feast with *friture de rougets* (battered, fried red mullet) followed by grilled crayfish. No frozen *frites* (fries) – only hand cut, home-made – and no credit cards.

Information

Tourist office (☎04 95 54 20 40; www.bastia-tourisme.com; place St-Nicolas; ⌚8am-6pm Mon-Sat, 8am-noon Sun)

Getting There & Away

Air

Aéroport Bastia-Poretta (www.bastia.aeroport.fr), 24km south, is linked by bus (€9, 30 minutes, 10 daily) with the Préfecture building in town.

Boat

Bastia Port (www.bastia.port.fr) has two ferry terminals; ferry companies have information

TRAMWAY DE LA BALAGNE

You may well tremble as the *trinighellu* (trembler) – as the **Tramway de la Balagne** (☎04 95 60 00 50, 04 95 65 00 61) is affectionately called – trundles periously close to the shore along sand-covered tracks between Calvi and Île Rousse. The dinky little train is the easiest way to access the numerous hidden coves and beaches sprinkled along the coast: you'll avoid traffic jams and experience an unforgettable trip alongside getaway beaches. The train runs four to eight times daily April to September, calling at 15 stations en route, all by request only. Out of season, regular trains run by **Chemins de Fer de la Corse** (☎04 95 32 80 57; http://train-corse.com) cover the same route. Hop off at an intermediate rocky cove or, for fine golden sand, leave the train at Algajola or Plage de Bodri, the last stop before Île Rousse. It costs €5.40 one-way.

offices in the **Southern Ferry Terminal** (www.port-de-bastia.net), usually open for same-day ticket sales a couple of hours before sailings. Ferries sail to/from Marseille, Toulon and Nice (mainland France), and Livorno, Savona, Piombino and Genoa (Italy).

Corsica Ferries (☎08 25 09 50 95; www.corsica-ferries.fr; 5bis rue Chanoine Leschi)

La Méridionale (☎08 10 20 13 20; www.lameridionale.fr; Port de Commerce)

Moby Lines (☎04 95 34 84 94; www.mobylines.com; 4 rue du Commandant Luce de Casabianca)

SNCM (☎32 60; www.sncm.fr)

Bus & Train

The **bus station** (1 rue du Nouveau Port) is north of place St-Nicolas and bus stops are scattered around town. Many buses depart from in front of Bastia **train station** (av Maréchal Sébastiani), the departure point for daily trains to Ajaccio (€25, 3¾ hours, four daily) via Corte (1¾ hours), and Calvi (three hours, three or four daily) via Île Rousse.

Transports Santini (☎04 95 37 02 98) Seasonal buses to Île Rousse (€15, 1¾ hrs, six weekly) leave from the train station.

Eurocorse Voyages (☎04 95 31 73 76; www.eurocorse.com; 1 rue Nouveau Port) Buses to Ajaccio (€21, three hours) via Corte (€11.50, two hours) twice daily except on Sunday from Bastia bus station.

Les Rapides Bleus (☎04 95 31 03 79; www.rapides-bleus.com; 1 av Maréchal Sébastiani) Buses leave from in front of the post office to Porto-Vecchio (€22, three hours) twice daily except Sunday.

Calvi

POP 5486

Basking between the fiery orange bastions of its 15th-century citadel and the glittering waters of a moon-shaped bay, Calvi feels closer to the chichi sophistication of a French Riviera resort than a historic Corsican port. Palatial yachts dock along its harbourside, while above the quay the watchtowers of the town's Genoese stronghold stand guard, proffering sweeping views inland to Monte Cinto (2706m).

Calvi's 15th-century **citadel** – also known as the Haute Ville (Upper City) – sits on a rocky promontory above the Basse Ville (Lower Town). Down below, its stellar 4km-long sandy **beach** begins at the marina and runs east around the Golfe de Calvi. Rent kayaks and windsurfs on the sand, and hook up with local diving schools by the **tourist office** (☎04 95 65 16 67; www.balagne-corsica.com; Port de Plaisance; ⌚9am-noon & 2-6pm daily Jul & Aug, Mon-Sat May, Jun, Sep & Oct, Mon-Fri Nov-Apr) at the marina.

DON'T MISS

CHEZ TAO

You won't find cooler (or more amazing sea views with cocktail in hand) than **Chez Tao**, (☎04 95 65 00 73; rue St-Antoine; ⌚Jun-Sep) a super-slick piano bar of mythical standing up high within the citadel. Founded in 1935 by White Russian émigré Tao Kanbey de Kerekoff, the lavishly decorated vaulted room still lures hedonistic hipsters seven decades on.

Sleeping & Eating

Hôtel Le Magnolia HOTEL €€
(☎04 95 65 19 16; www.hotel-le-magnolia.com; rue Alsace-Lorraine; d €70-150; ⌚Apr-Nov; ❄@📶) An oasis from the harbourside fizz, this attractive mansion sits behind a beautiful high-walled courtyard garden pierced by a handsome magnolia tree. Pretty much every room has a lovely outlook – Calvi rooftops, garden or sea – and connecting doubles makes it an instant hit with families.

Camping La Pinède CAMPGROUND €
(☎04 95 65 17 80; www.camping-calvi.com; rte de la Pinède; tent, car & 2 adults €34; ⌚Apr-Oct; P🏊) Handy for town and beach; mobile homes and chalets too.

A Candella TRADITIONAL CORSICAN €€
(☎04 95 65 42 13; 9 rue St-Antoine; mains €15-25) One of a handful of addresses to eat within the citadel, A Candella stands out for its romantic, golden-hued terrace of stone strung with pretty flowers in pots and olive trees. The food is Corsican hearty, and the sea view is the most marvellous you could hope for.

Getting There & Away

BOAT From Calvi's **ferry terminal** (quai Landry) regular ferries sail to/from Nice (France) and Savona (Italy).

BUS Les Beaux Voyages (☎04 95 65 15 02; place de la Porteuse d'Eau) runs daily buses to Bastia (2½ hours) via Île Rousse (15 minutes).

TRAIN Calvi's train station connects with Ajaccio (five hours, two daily) and Bastia (three hours) via Ponte Leccia.

DON'T MISS

LES CALANQUES

No amount of hyperbole can capture the astonishing beauty of **Les Calanques de Piana** (E Calanche in Corsican), sculpted cliffs teetering above the Golfe de Porto that rear up from the sea in staggering scarlet pillars, teetering columns, towers and irregularly shaped boulders of pink, ochre and ginger. Flaming red in the sunlight, this natural ensemble of gargantuan proportions is one of Corsica's most iconic, awe-inspiring sights. And as you sway around switchback after switchback along the rock-riddled 10km stretch of the D81 south of Porto towards the village of **Piana** (pop 500; www.otpiana.com), one mesmerising vista piggybacks another.

For the full technicolour experience, savour Les Calanques on foot. Trails start near **Pont de Mezzanu**, a road bridge on the D81 about 3km north of Piana. In the village itself, the **tourist office** (www.otpiana.com; place Mairie; ⌚9am-6pm Mon-Fri) stocks the leaflet *Piana: Sentiers de Randonnée*, detailing six walks. Afterwards, sand-flop on the idyllic beaches of **Ficajola** and **Arone**, 5km and 11km southwest respectively. Or splurge on lunch with a view at Corsica's original luxury hotel, **Les Roches Rouges** (☎04 95 27 81 81; www.lesrochesrouges.com; D81; s €102-123, d €114-136, tr €156-176, q €177-213; ⌚Apr-Oct; wi-fi), in business since 1912. Faded grandeur at its best, a meal in its superb gourmet restaurant (or, should you fancy staying over, a sea-view room) is worth every cent; at the very least partake in a drink on the romantic stone terrace to savour the truly extraordinary vista.

Ajaccio

POP 65,000

With its sweeping bay and buzzing centre replete with mellow-toned buildings, cafes and yacht-packed marina, Ajaccio, Corsica's main metropolis, is all class and seduction. Looming over this elegant port city is the spectre of Corsica's great general: Napoléon Bonaparte was born here in 1769 and the city is dotted with statues and museums relating to the diminutive dictator (starting with the main street in Ajaccio, cours Napoléon).

Sights & Activities

Palais Fesch – Musée des Beaux-Arts MUSEUM

(www.musee-fesch.com; 50-52 rue du Cardinal Fesch; adult/child €8/5; ⌚10.30am-6pm Mon, Wed & Sat, noon-6pm Thu, Fri & Sun year-round, to 8.30pm Fri Jul & Aug) This superb museum established by Napoléon's uncle has France's largest collection of Italian paintings outside the Louvre. Mostly the works of minor or anonymous 14th- to 19th-century artists, there are also canvases by Titian, Fra Bartolomeo, Veronese, Botticelli and Bellini.

Maison Bonaparte MUSEUM

(☎04 95 21 43 89; www.musee-maisonbonaparte.fr; rue St-Charles; adult/child €7/5.50; ⌚10.30am-12.30am & 1.15-6pm Tue-Sun Apr-Sep, 10am-noon & 2-4.45pm Oct-Mar) Napoléon spent his first nine years in this house, host to various memorabilia of the emperor and his siblings, including a glass medallion containing a lock of his hair. It's closed Monday mornings.

Boat Trips TOURS

Kiosks on the quayside opposite place du Maréchal Foch sell tickets for seasonal boat trips around the Golfe d'Ajaccio and Îles Sanguinaires (€27), and excursions to the **Réserve Naturelle de Scandola** (adult/child €50/35).

Sleeping

TOP CHOICE **Hôtel Kallisté** HOTEL €€

(☎04 95 51 34 45; www.hotel-kalliste-ajaccio.com; 51 cours Napoléon; s/d/tr €77/95/123; P ❄ @ wi-fi) Exposed brick, neutral tones, terracotta tiles and a funky glass lift conjure a neo-boutique feel at the Kallisté, which occupies a typical 19th-century Ajaccio townhouse. Facilities are fab – wi-fi, satellite TV, a copious buffet breakfast for a mere €4 extra, and the convenience of a hotel car park in a city where parking can be downright hellish.

Hôtel Marengo HOTEL €

(☎04 95 21 43 66; www.hotel-marengo.com; 2 rue Marengo; d €65-89, tr €95-115; ⌚Apr-Oct; ❄) For something nearer to the sand, try this charmingly eccentric small hotel near the beach. Rooms have a balcony, there's a quiet flower-filled courtyard and reception is an agreeable clutter of tasteful prints and personal objects. Find it down a cul de sac off bd Madame Mère.

Eating

TOP CHOICE Le 20123 TRADITIONAL CORSICAN €€

(☎04 95 21 50 05; www.20123.fr; 2 rue du Roi de Rome; menus €34.50; ⏰dinner Tue-Sun) This fabulous, one-of-a-kind place started life in the village of Pila Canale (postcode 20123 – get it?), and when the owner upped sticks to Ajaccio he decided to take the old village with him – water pump, washing line, life-sized dolls in traditional dress, central square et al. It all sounds a bit tacky, but you won't find many more character-filled places in Corsica. Needless to say, the food is 100% authentic, too - everyone feasts on the same four-course *menu*, presented orally, built solely from local produce and traditional recipes, and – amazingly – unchanged for 25 years.

L'Altru Versu GASTRONOMIC €€

(☎04 95 50 05 22; www.laltruversu.com; rte des Sanguinaires, Les Sept Chapelles; mains €20-30; ⏰lunch & dinner daily Jun-Sep, lunch & dinner Tue-Sun Oct-May; ❄) Ajaccio's top-notch restaurant belongs to the Mezzacqui brothers who are passionate gastronomes and excellent singers – they hitch on their guitars and serenade guests each Friday and Saturday night.

Da Mama TRADITIONAL CORSICAN €

(☎04 95 21 39 44; 3 passage de la Ghinghetta; lunch menus €12, dinner menus €17-25; ⏰dinner Mon, lunch & dinner Tue-Sat) Staunchly Corsican cuisine aside, the main draw of this unfussy eatery is its location in the shade of a magnificent rubber tree down a narrow alley.

Information

Tourist office (www.ajaccio-tourisme.com; 3 bd du Roi Jérôme; ⏰8am-7pm Mon-Sat, 9am-1pm Sun)

Getting There & Away

AIR Bus 8 (€4.50, 20 minutes) links **Aéroport d'Ajaccio-Campo dell'Oro** (☎04 95 23 56 56; www.ajaccio.aeroport.fr), 8km east, with Ajaccio's train and bus stations.

BOAT Boats to/from Toulon, Nice and Marseille depart from Ajaccio's **Terminal Maritime et Routier** (☎04 95 51 21 80; www.2a.cci.fr; quai L'Herminier).

BUS Local bus companies have ticket kiosks inside the ferry terminal building, the arrival/departure point for buses.

TRAIN From the **train station** (place de la Gare), services include Bastia (four hours, three to four daily), Corte (two hours, three to four daily) and Calvi (five hours, two daily; change at Ponte Leccia).

Bonifacio

POP 2973

With its glittering harbour, dramatic perch atop creamy white cliffs, and stout citadel teetering above the cornflower-blue waters of the Bouches de Bonifacio, this dazzling port is an essential stop. Just a short hop from Sardinia, Bonifacio has a distinctly Italianate feel: sun-bleached townhouses, dangling washing lines and murky chapels cram the web of alleyways of the old citadel while, down below on the harbourside, brasseries and boat kiosks tout their wares to the droves of day trippers.

Sights & Activities

Citadel (Haute Ville) HISTORIC NEIGHBOURHOOD

Much of Bonifacio's charm comes from strolling the citadel's shady streets, several spanned by arched aqueducts designed to collect rainwater to fill the communal cistern opposite **Église Ste-Marie Majeure**. From the marina, the paved **steps of montée du Rastello** and **montée St-Roch** bring you up to the citadel's old gateway, complete with an original 16th-century drawbridge. Inside the gateway is the 13th-century **Bastion de l'Étendard** (adult/child €2.50/free; ⏰9am-7pm Mon-Fri, 10am-6pm Sat & Sun Apr-Oct), home to a small history museum. Stroll the ramparts to **place du Marché** and **place de la Manichella** for jaw-dropping views over the Bouches de Bonifacio.

DON'T MISS

THE PERFECT PICTURE

If you're after that perfect snapshot, don't miss the fantastic, easy walk along the cliffs to the **Phare de Pertusato**, a lighthouse from where the seamless views of the cliffs, Îles Lavezzi, Bonifacio and Sardinia are memorable. Pick up the trail just to the left of the sharp bend on the hill up to Bonifacio's citadel. Count 1½ hours for the 5.6km round trip.

From the citadel, the **Escalier du Roi d'Aragon** (King of Aragon's stairway; adult/under 12yr €2.50/free; ⏲9am-7pm Mon-Fri, 10am-6pm Sat & Sun Apr-Oct) cuts down the southern cliffface. Legend says its 187 steep steps were carved in a single night by Aragonese troops during the siege of 1420, only for troops to be rebuffed by retaliating Bonifacio residents at the top. In reality, the steps served as an access path to an underground freshwater well.

Îles Lavezzi ARCHIPELAGO

Paradise! This protected clutch of uninhabited islets were made for those who love nothing better than splashing in tranquil lapis-lazuli waters. The 65-hectare Île Lavezzi, which gives its name to the whole archipelago, is the most accessible of the islands. Savage beauty aside, the island's superb natural pools and scenic stretches of sand beg for long-and-lazy sunbathing and swimming sessions. In summer, various companies organise **boat trips** here; buy tickets at the booths located on Bonifacio's marina and bring your own picnic lunch.

Sleeping & Eating

TOP CHOICE **Domaine de Licetto** HOTEL €€

(☎04 95 73 03 59; www.licetto.com; rte du Phare de Pertusato; s €55-85, d €70-105, q €115-175; ⏲Apr-Oct; P) Tucked in the maquis just a couple of kilometres east of Bonifacio, this motel-style address is a lovely surprise. Its seven minimalist rooms sport stylishly modern bathrooms, well-chosen furnishings and each has a terrace with table and chairs made for lounging alfresco in the surrounding peace and quiet. The restaurant on the estate is a feast in traditional dining and, best of all, Bonifacio town is a short idyllic walk away along the clifftop coastal path.

TOP CHOICE **Kissing Pigs** MODERN CORSICAN €

(☎04 95 73 56 09; quai Banda del Ferro; mains €9-15) Soothingly positioned by the harbour, this widely acclaimed restaurant and wine bar serves savoury fare in a seductively cosy interior, complete with wooden fixtures and swinging sausages. It's famed for its cheese and charcuterie platters; for the indecisive, the combination *moitié-moitié* (half-half) is perfect. The Corsican wine list is another hit.

Information

Tourist office (www.bonifacio.fr; 2 rue Fred Scamaroni; ⏲9am-8pm Jul & Aug, to 7pm May, Jun & Sep, 9am-noon & 2-6pm Oct-Apr)

Getting There & Away

AIR A taxi into town from **Aéroport de Figari** (www.figari.aeroport.fr), 21km north, costs about €40.

BOAT Saremar and Moby Lines sail between Bonifacio and Santa Teresa di Gallura (on the neighbouring island of Sardinia) in summer.

UNDERSTAND FRANCE

History

Prehistory

Neanderthals were the first to live in France (about 90,000 to 40,000 BC). Cro-Magnons followed 35,000 years ago and left behind cave paintings and engravings, especially around the Vézère Valley in the Dordogne. Neolithic people (about 7500 to 4000 years ago) created France's incredible menhirs (standing stones) and dolmens (megalithic tombs), especially in Brittany.

The Celtic Gauls arrived between 1500 and 500 BC, and were superseded by the Romans for around five centuries after Julius Caesar took control around 52 BC, until the Franks and Alemanii overran the country.

The Frankish Merovingian and Carolingian dynasties ruled from the 5th to the 10th century AD. In 732 Charles Martel defeated the Moors, preventing France from falling under Muslim rule. Martel's grandson, Charlemagne (742–814), extended the power and boundaries of the kingdom and was crowned Holy Roman Emperor in 800.

The Early French Kings

The tale of William the Conqueror's invasion of England in 1066 is recorded in the Bayeux Tapestry, sowing the seeds for a fierce rivalry between France and England that peaked with the Hundred Years War (1337–1453).

Following the occupation of Paris by the English-allied dukes of Burgundy, John Plantagenet was made regent of France on behalf of England's King Henry VI in 1422. Less than a decade later, he was crowned king at Paris' Notre Dame cathedral. Luckily for the French, a 17-year-old warrior called Jeanne d'Arc (Joan of Arc) came along in 1429. She persuaded Charles VII that she had a divine mission from God to expel the English from France. Following her capture by the Burgundians and subsequent sale to the English in 1430, Joan was convicted of witchcraft and heresy and burned at the stake in Rouen, on the site now marked by the city's cathedral.

Despite Charles' promised corination in July 1429, battles waged between the English and the French until 1453, when the English were driven out of France once and for all, marking the end of the war.

The arrival of Italian Renaissance culture during the reign of François I (r 1515–47) ushered in some of France's finest chateaux, especially in the Loire Valley.

The period from 1562 to 1598 was one of the bloodiest periods in French history. Ideological disagreement between the Huguenots (French Protestants) and the Catholic monarchy escalated into the French Wars of Religion.

The Sun King

Louis XIV, Le Roi Soleil (the Sun King), ascended the throne in 1643, and spent the next 60 years in a series of bloody wars. He also constructed the fabulous palace at Versailles.

Louis XV ascended to the throne in 1715 and shifted the royal court back to Paris. As the 18th century progressed, the ancient regime became increasingly out of step with the needs of the country. Antiestablishment and anticlerical ideas expressed by Voltaire, Rousseau and Montesquieu further threatened the royal reign.

Revolution to Republic

Social and economic crisis marked the 18th century. Discontent among the French populace turned violent when a Parisian mob stormed the prison at Bastille on the 14th of July 1789. France was declared a constitutional monarchy and Louis XVI was publicly guillotined in January 1793 on Paris' place de la Concorde.

The Reign of Terror between September 1793 and July 1794 saw religious freedoms revoked, churches closed, cathedrals turned into 'Temples of Reason' and thousands beheaded. In the chaos, a dashing young Corsican general named Napoléon Bonaparte (1769–1821) stepped from the shadows.

In 1799 Napoléon I assumed power and in 1804 he was crowned emperor of France at Notre Dame. Napoléon waged several wars in which France gained control over most of Europe. Two years later, Allied armies entered Paris, exiled Napoléon to Elba and restored the French throne at the Congress of Vienna (1814–15).

In 1815 Napoléon escaped, entering Paris on 20 May. His glorious 'Hundred Days' back in power ended with the Battle of Waterloo and his exile to the island of St Helena, where he died in 1821.

Second Republic to Second Empire

The subsequent years were marked by civil strife and political unrest, with monarchists and revolutionaries vying for power. Louis-Philippe (r 1830–48), a constitutional monarch, was chosen by parliament but ousted by the 1848 Revolution. The Second Republic was established and Napoléon's nephew, Louis Napoléon Bonaparte, was elected president. But in 1851 Louis Napoléon led a coup d'état and proclaimed himself Emperor Napoléon III of the Second Empire (1852–70).

France did enjoy significant economic growth during this period. Paris was transformed under urban planner Baron Haussmann (1809–91), who created the 12 huge boulevards radiating from the Arc de Triomphe. But Napoléon III embroiled France in various catastrophic conflicts, including the Crimean War (1853–56) and the Franco-Prussian War (1870–71), which ended with Prussia taking the emperor prisoner. Upon hearing the news, defiant Parisian masses took to the streets demanding a republic be declared – enter the Third Republic.

The World Wars

The 20th century was marked by two of the bloodiest conflicts in the nation's history, beginning with the Great War (WWI). The northeastern part of France bore the brunt of the devastating trench warfare between Allied and German forces: 1.3 million French soldiers were killed and almost one million injured, and the battlefields of the Somme have become powerful symbols of the unimaginable costs and ultimate futility of modern warfare.

After the war, the Treaty of Versailles imposed heavy reparations on the defeated nations, including the return of Alsace-Lorraine, which the French had lost to Germany in 1871. These punitive terms sowed the seeds for future unrest, when the fanatic leader Adolf Hitler rose to power and promised to restore the German nation's pride, power and territory. Despite constructing a lavish series of defences (the so-called Maginot Line) along its German border, France was rapidly overrun and surrendered in June 1940. The occupying Germans divided France into an Occupied Zone (in the north and west) and a puppet state in the south, centring on the spa town of Vichy.

The British Army was driven from France during the Battle of Dunkirk in 1940. Four years later, on 6 June 1944, Allied forces stormed the coastline of Normandy in the D-Day landings. The bloody Battle of Normandy followed and Paris was liberated on 25 August.

The Fourth Republic

In the first postwar election in 1945, the wartime leader of the Free French, Général Charles de Gaulle, was appointed head of the government,; he quickly sensed that the tide was turning against him and he resigned in 1946.

Progress rebuilding France's shattered economy and infrastructure was slow. By 1947 France was forced to turn to the USA for loans as part of the Marshall Plan to rebuild Europe. The economy gathered steam in the 1950s but the decade marked the end of French colonialism in Vietnam and in Algeria. The Algerian war of independence (1954–62) was particularly brutal, characterised by torture and massacre meted out to nationalist Algerians.

The Modern Era

De Gaulle assumed the presidency again in 1958, followed by his prime minister Georges Pompidou (in power 1969–74), Valéry Giscard d'Estaing (in power 1974–81), François Mitterrand (in power 1981–95), and the centre-right president Jacques Chirac, who (among other things) oversaw the country's adoption of the euro in 1999.

Presidential elections in 2007 ushered out Jacques Chirac (in his 70s with two terms under his belt) and brought in Nicolas Sarkozy. Dynamic, ambitious and media-savvy, the former interior minister and chairman of centre-right party UMP wooed voters with policies about job creation, lower taxes, crime crackdown and help for France's substantial immigrant population – issues that had particular pulling power coming from the son of a Hungarian immigrant father and Greek Jewish-French mother. Personal affairs dominated his first few months in office as he divorced his wife Cecilia and wed Italian multimillionaire singer Carla Bruni.

Unemployment soared during the 2008 global banking crisis that saw the French government inject €10.5 billion into France's six major banks. Sarkozy's party received a battering in the 2010 regional elections which saw the left scoop 54% of votes and take control of 21 out of 22 regions on mainland France and Corsica. Government popularity hit an all-time low.

France Today

Presidential elections in spring 2012 ushered in France's first socialist president since François Mitterand left office in 1995. The presidential campaign saw Sarkozy vie for a second term in office against left-wing candidate François Hollande (b 1954) of the Socialist party. Sarkozy promised to modernise the French economy, reduce the number of immigrants to France, and lower France's budget deficit; but with the electorate tired of the austerity policies of the Conservatives, it was Hollande's ambitious talk of reducing unemployment (at a 12-year high), clearing the country's debts (by 2017), upping tax on corporations and salaries over €1 million per annum, and increasing the minimum salary, that proved the more appealing platform. Parliamentary elections a month later sealed Hollande's grip on power with the Socialists winning a comfortable majority in France's 577-seat National Assembly, thus paving the way for Hollande to govern France during Europe's biggest economic crisis in decades.

Culturally, France is savouring a high. Art lovers are bursting with excitement over the reopening in Paris, after months of painstaking renovation, of both the Musée Picasso and the country's most prestigious theatre, the Comédie Française, where Molière trod the boards. At the 2012 Academy Awards, the French-made silent film *The Artist*, starring the quintessentially French Jean Dujardin, scooped five Oscars to effectively herald the renaissance of French cinema; while the grand opening of the striking new Louvre-Lens art museum in northern France promises to inject new creativity into the conventional French museum experience.

Arts

Literature

France has made huge contributions to European literature. The philosophical work of Voltaire (1694–1778) and Jean-Jacques Rousseau dominated the 18th century. A century later, the poems and novels of Victor Hugo – *Les Misérables* and *Notre Dame de Paris* (*The Hunchback of Notre Dame*)

MULTICULTURAL MUSINGS

No French writer better delves into the mind and politics of France's ethnic population than Faïza Guène (b 1985), writing in a notable 'urban slang' style, born and bred on a ghetto housing estate outside Paris. Her second semi-autobiographical novel, *Du Rêve pour les Oeufs* (2006), is published in English as *Dreams from the Endz* (2008). Another French writer to address ethnic issues so engagingly is JMG Le Clézio, born in Nice to a Niçois mother and Mauritian father. He grew up in Nigeria and won the 2008 Nobel Prize in Literature, confirming France's ranking as the country with the most literary Nobel Prize winners.

among them – became landmarks of French Romanticism.

In 1857 two literary landmarks were published: *Madame Bovary* by Gustave Flaubert (1821–80) and Charles Baudelaire's collection of poems, *Les Fleurs du Mal* (The Flowers of Evil). Émile Zola (1840–1902) meanwhile strove to convert novel-writing from an art to a science in his series *Les Rougon-Macquart*.

Symbolists Paul Verlaine (1844–96) and Stéphane Mallarmé (1842–98) aimed to express mental states through their poetry, while Verlaine's poems, along with those of Arthur Rimbaud (1854–91), are seen as French literature's first modern poems.

After WWII, the existentialist movement developed around the lively debates of Jean-Paul Sartre (1905–80), Simone de Beauvoir (1908–86) and Albert Camus (1913–60) over coffee and cigarettes in Paris' Left Bank cafes.

Contemporary authors include Françoise Sagan, Pascal Quignard, Anna Gavalda, Emmanuel Carrère and Yasmina Khadra (actually a man, a former colonel in the Algerian army, who adopted his wife's name as a nom de plume).

Marc Levy is France's best-selling writer, whose novels have been translated into 42 languages. *L'étrange voyage de Monsieur Daldry* (*The Strange Journey of Mr Daldry*; 2011) is his latest.

Cinema

Cinematographic pioneers the Lumière brothers shot the world's first-ever motion picture in March 1895 and French film flourished in the following decades. The post-WWII *nouvelle vague* (new wave) filmmakers, such as Claude Chabrol, Jean-Luc Godard and François Truffaut, pioneered the advent of modern cinema, using fractured narratives, documentary camerawork and highly personal subjects.

Big-name stars, slick production values and nostalgia were the dominant motifs in the 1980s, as filmmakers switched to costume dramas, comedies and 'heritage movies'. Claude Berri's depiction of prewar Provence in *Jean de Florette* (1986), Jean-Paul Rappeneau's *Cyrano de Bergerac* (1990) and *Bon Voyage* (2003), set in 1940s Paris – all starring France's best-known (and biggest-nosed) actor, Gérard Depardieu – found huge audiences in France and abroad.

Massive international box-office hit *Le Fabuleux Destin de Amélie Poulain* (*Amélie;* 2001) is a feel-good story about a Parisian do-gooder. *Bienvenue chez les Ch'tis* (2008) is another big film of recent years, which debunks grim stereotypes about the industrialised regions of the north of France with high jinks and hilarity.

'New French Extremity' is the tag given to the socially conscious, transgressive films of talented Paris-born, Africa-raised filmmaker Claire Denis. *Chocolat* (1988) and *Matériel Blanc* (*White Material*; 2009), scripted by Parisian novelist Marie NDiaye, both explore the legacy of French colonialism.

No French film has ever wooed the world at large quite like *The Artist* (2011), a silent B&W, romantic comedy set in 1920s Hollywood that scooped five Oscars heralding the renaissance of French film.

Music

French musical luminaries Charles Gounod (1818–93), César Franck (1822–90) and *Carmen* creator Georges Bizet (1838–75) among them were a dime a dozen in the 19th centu-

WORLD-CLASS WORLD MUSIC

No artist has cemented France's reputation in world music more than Paris-born, Franco-Congolese rapper, slam poet and three-time Victoire de la Musique-award winner, Abd al Malik. His albums, *Gibraltar* (2006), *Dante* (2008) and *Château Rouge* (2010) are classics.

ry. Claude Debussy (1862–1918) revolutionised classical music with *Prélude à l'Après-Midi d'un Faune* (Prelude to the Afternoon of a Faun); while Maurice Ravel (1875–1937) peppered his work, including *Boléro,* with sensuousness and tonal colour.

Jazz was the hot sound of 1920s Paris with the likes of Sidney Bechet, Kenny Clarke, Bud Powell and Dexter Gordon filling clubs in the capital.

The *chanson française,* a folkish tradition dating from medieval troubadours, was revived in the 1930s by Edith Piaf and Charles Trenet. In the 1950s, Paris' Left Bank cabarets nurtured *chansonniers* (cabaret singers) like Léo Ferré, Georges Brassens, Claude Nougaro, Jacques Brel and the much-loved crooner Serge Gainsbourg.

Frenc electronic music (think Daft Punk and Air) has a global following, while French rap never stops breaking new ground, pioneered in the 1990s by MC Solaar and continued by young French rappers such as Disiz La Peste, Monsieur R, the trio Malekal Morte, Marseille's home-grown IAM and five-piece band KDD from Toulouse. Cyprus-born Diam's (short for *'diamant'* meaning 'diamond'; www.diams-lesite.com), who arrived in Paris aged seven, is one of France's few female rappers, while Brittany's Manau trio engagingly fuses hip hop with traditional Celtic sounds.

French pop music has evolved massively since the 1960s *yéyé* (imitative rock) days of Johnny Hallyday. Particularly strong is world music, from Algerian raï and other North African music (artists include Natacha Atlas) to Senegalese *mbalax* (Youssou N'Dour) and West Indian zouk (Kassav, Zouk Machine). Musicians who combine many of these elements include Paris-born Manu Chao and Franco-Algerian Rachid Taja.

Architecture

Southern France is the place to find France's Gallo-Roman legacy, especially at the Pont du Gard (c 19 BC), and the amphitheatres in Nîmes and Arles (c 100 BC).

Several centuries later, architects adopted Gallo-Roman motifs in Romanesque masterpieces such as Poitier's Église Notre Dame la Grande, dating from the 11th to 16th centuries.

Impressive 12th-century Gothic structures include Avignon's pontifical palace, Chartres' cathedral and, of course, Notre Dame in Paris.

Art nouveau (1850–1910) combined iron, brick, glass and ceramics in new ways. See it for yourself at Paris' metro entrances and in the Musée d'Orsay.

Contemporary buildings to look out for include the once-reviled (now much-revered) Centre Pompidou and IM Pei's glass pyramid at the Louvre. In the provinces, notable buildings include Strasbourg's European Parliament, a 1920s art deco swimming pool-turned-art museum in Lille, the stunning new Centre Pompidou in Metz, and Louvre-Lens, in the former mining town of Lens.

Painting

An extraordinary flowering of artistic talent occurred in 19th- and 20th-century France. The Impressionists, who endeavoured to capture the ever-changing aspects of reflected light, included Edouard Manet, Claude Monet, Edgar Degas, Camille Pissarro, and Pierre-Auguste Renoir. They were followed by the likes of Paul Cézanne (who lived in Aix-en-Provence) and Paul Gauguin, as well as the fauvist Henri Matisse (a resident of Nice on the French Riviera) and Cubists including Spanish-born Pablo Picasso and Georges Braque.

Environment

The Land

Hexagon-shaped France is the largest country in Europe after Russia and Ukraine. The country's 3200km-long coastline ranges from chalk cliffs (Normandy) to fine sand (Atlantic coast) and pebbly beaches (Mediterranean coast).

Europe's highest peak, Mont Blanc (4810m), crowns the French Alps along France's eastern border, while the rugged Pyrenees define France's 450km-long border with Spain, peaking at 3404m. The country's major river systems include the Garonne, Rhône, Seine, and France's longest river, the Loire.

Wildlife

France has more mammals (around 110) than any other country in Europe. Couple this with 363 bird species, 30 types of amphibian, 36 varieties of reptile and 72 kinds of fish, and wildlife-watchers are in paradise. Several distinctive animals can still be found in the Alps and Pyrenees, including the marmot, *chamois* (mountain antelope), *bouquetin* (Alpine ibex) and *mouflon* (wild mountain sheep), introduced in the 1950s. The *loup* (wolf) disappeared from France in the 1930s, but was reintroduced to the Parc National du Mercantour in 1992. The *aigle royal* (golden eagle) is a rare but hugely rewarding sight in the French mountain parks.

National Parks

The proportion of protected land is low relative to the country's size: seven national parks (www.parcsnationaux-fr.com) fully protect around 0.8% of the country. Another 13% is protected by 45 regional parks (www.parcs-naturels-regionaux.tm.fr) and a further few percent by 320 smaller nature reserves (www.reserves-naturelles.org).

Environmental Issues

Summer forest fires are an annual hazard. Wetlands, essential for the survival of a great number of species, are shrinking. More than two million hectares – 3% of French territory – are considered important wetlands, but only 4% of this land is protected.

France generates around 80% of its electricity from nuclear power stations – the highest ratio in the world – with the rest coming from carbon-fuelled power stations and renewable resources (mainly wind farms and hydroelectric dams). Indeed, one of the last decisions Nicolas Sarkozy made as French president was to guarantee, in February 2012, the life of France's nuclear-power stations for another 40 years. Costing an extraordinary €6 billion, the country's most recent nuclear reactor, Flamanville 3, on Normandy's west coast near Cherbourg, is due for completion in 2016.

Europe's largest solar-powered electricity-generating farm sits 1000m-high on a south-facing slope near the tiny village of Curbans in Provence. Since its inauguration in 2011 the farm's 150-hectare array of photovoltaic cells – 145,000 panels in all – have removed 120,000 metric tonnes of carbon dioxide annually from the French energy bill.

Food & Drink

France means food. Every region has its distinctive cuisine, from the rich classic dishes of Burgundy, the Dordogne, Lyon and Normandy, to the sun-filled Mediterranean flavours of Provence, Languedoc and Corsica. Broadly speaking, the hot south tends to favour olive oil, garlic and tomatoes, while the cooler pastoral north favours cream and butter. Coastal areas overflow with mussels, oysters and saltwater fish.

A countrywide essential is *pain* (bread), typically eaten with every meal. Order in a restaurant and within minutes a basket should be on your table. Except in a handful of top-end gastronomic restaurants, butter (unsalted) is never an accompaniment. The long, thin *baguette* is the classic 'loaf', but there are countless others.

France *is* cheese land. There are nearly 500 varieties of *fromage* (cheese), ranging from world-known classics such as Brie, Camembert and Époisses de Bourgogne (France's smelliest cheese?) to local varieties available only in the regions where they're made. At meal times, cheese is always served after the main course and before dessert.

Charcuterie – hams, *saucissons* (salamis), sausages, black pudding and the fabulous *andouillette* (pig intestine sausage) – is the backbone of any self-respecting French picnic. Traditionally charcuterie is made only from pork, though other meats (beef, veal, chicken or goose) go into sausages, salamis, blood puddings and other cured and salted meats.

MONT ST-MICHEL

Environmental protection is rarely straightforward, as recent developments at the iconic, abbey-crowned mount of Mont St-Michel demonstrate. A €200 million project is designed to stop the mythical bay silting up by building a dam, ridding the mount of cars and motorised vehicles from its traffic-congested foot, and replacing the original tidal causeway trodden by pilgrims since 1879 with an ultralightweight bridge (by 2014). This would allow the 14m-high tidal waters for which this part of Normandy is famed to swirl without environmental consequence. Yet, just as the motorised vehicles go and the 2.5 million annual visitors embrace the final leg of one of France's top tourist pilgrimages on foot or by shuttle, Mont St-Michel risks losing its Unesco World Heritage status. The reason: the proposed construction of offshore turbine farms some 20km out to sea from the priceless mount.

The principal wine-producing regions are Alsace, Bordeaux, Burgundy, Champagne, Languedoc-Roussillon, the Loire region and the Rhône. Areas such as Burgundy comprise many well-known districts, including Chablis, Beaujolais and Mâcon, while Bordeaux encompasses Médoc, St-Émilion and Sauternes among many others. Northern France and Alsace produce excellent local beers; *bière à la pression* (draught beer) is served by the *demi* (about 33cL).

Coffee and mineral water are drunk by the gallon in France. In restaurants, save cents by asking for a jug of tap water *(une carafe d'eau)* rather than pricier bottled water. The most common coffee, simply called *un café* in French, is espresso – ordering anything other than this at the end of a meal is a real faux pas.

Where to Eat & Drink

Auberge Country inn serving traditional country fare, often attached to a rural B&B or small hotel.

Ferme auberge Working farm that cooks up meals built squarely from local farm products.

Bistro (also spelled *bistrot*) Anything from a pub or bar with snacks and light meals to a small, fully fledged restaurant.

Brasserie Like a cafe except it serves full meals, drinks and coffee from morning till 11pm or even later. Classic fare includes *choucroute* (sauerkraut) and *moules-frites* (mussels and fries).

Cafe Serves basic food as well as drinks, most commonly a chunk of baguette filled with Camembert or pâté and *cornichons* (mini gherkins), a *croque-monsieur* (grilled ham and toasted-cheese sandwich) or *croque-madame* (a toasted-cheese sandwich topped with a fried egg).

Creperie Casual address specialising in sweet crêpes and savoury galettes.

Restaurant Serves lunch and dinner five or six days; standard opening hours are noon-2.30 or 3pm, and 7-10 or 11pm.

Salon de thé Tearoom often serving light lunches (quiche, salads, pies and tarts) as well as cakes, pastries, tea and coffee.

THE MENU

In France a menu is not the card given to you in restaurants listing what's cooking (*la carte* in French). Rather, *un menu* is a preset, three-course meal at a fixed price – by far the best-value dining around and available in 99% of restaurants.

Lunch *menus* often include a glass of wine and/or coffee, and are a great way of dining at otherwise unaffordable gastronomic addresses.

All but top-end places often offer *une formule* too, a cheaper lunchtime option usually comprising the *plat du jour* (dish of the day) plus a starter or dessert.

SURVIVAL GUIDE

Directory A–Z

Accommodation

France has accommodation to suit every taste, budget and mood.

» Budget covers everything from bare-bones hostels to simple family-run places; midrange means a few extra creature comforts such as satellite TV, air-conditioning and free wi-fi; while top-end places stretch from luxury five-star chains with the mod cons and swimming pools to boutique-chic chalets in the Alps.

» Accommodation costs vary wildly between regions: what will buy you a night in a romantic *chambre d'hôte* (B&B) in the countryside may only get you a dorm bed in major cities and ski resorts.

» Many tourist offices make room reservations, often for a fee of €5, but many only do so if you stop by in person. In the French Alps, ski-resort tourist offices operate a central reservation service.

PRICE RANGES

Our reviews refer to the cost of a double room with private bathroom, except in hostels or where otherwise specified. Quoted rates are for high season, which is July and August in southern France (Provence and the French Riviera, Languedoc-Roussilon, Corsica) and December to March in the French Alps. Prices exclude breakfast unless otherwise noted.

€€€ more than €180 (€200 in Paris)

€€ €80 to €180 (€110 to €200 in Paris)

€ below €80 (€110 in Paris)

B&BS

For charm, a heartfelt *bienvenue* (welcome) and home cooking, it's hard to beat a *chambre d'hôte* (B&B). Pick up lists at local tourist offices or online:

Bienvenue à la Ferme (www.bienvenue-a-la-ferme.com)

Chambres d'Hôtes France (www.chambresdhotesfrance.com)

Fleurs de Soleil (www.fleursdesoleil.fr) Selective collection of 550 stylish *maisons d'hôte*, mainly in rural France.

Gîtes de France (www.gites-de-france.com) France's primary umbrella organisation for B&Bs and *gîtes* (self-catering houses and apartments).

Samedi Midi Éditions (www.samedimidi.com) Choose your *chambre d'hôte* by location or theme (romance, golf, design, cooking courses).

CAMPING

Camping has never been more *en vogue*. **Gîtes de France** (www.gites-de-france.com) and **Bienvenue à la Ferme** (www.bienvenue-a-la-ferme.com) coordinate camping on farms.

» Most camping grounds open March or April to October.

» Euro-economisers should look for good-value but no-frills *campings municipaux* (municipal camping grounds).

» Camping in nondesignated spots (*camping sauvage*) is illegal in France.

Easy-to-navigate websites with campsites searchable by location and facilities:

Camping en France (www.camping.fr)

Camping France (www.campingfrance.com)

Guide du Camping (www.guideducamping.com)

Cabanes de France (www.cabanes-de-france.com) Tree houses.

HOSTELS

Hostels range from funky to threadbare.

» A dorm bed in an *auberge de jeunesse* (youth hostel) costs about €25 in Paris, and anything from €10.50 to €28 in the provinces; sheets are always included and often breakfast too.

» To prevent outbreaks of bed bugs, sleeping bags are no longer permitted.

» All hostels are nonsmoking.

HOTELS

French hotels almost never include breakfast in their advertised nightly rates.

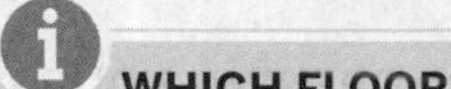

WHICH FLOOR?

In France, as elsewhere in Europe, 'ground floor' refers to the floor at street level, the 1st floor – what would be called the 2nd floor in the US – is the floor above that.

» Hotels in France are rated with one to five stars; ratings are based on objective criteria (eg size of entry hall), not service, decor or cleanliness.

» A double room has one double bed (or two singles pushed together); a room with twin beds is more expensive, as is a room with bathtub instead of shower.

Activities

From glaciers, rivers and canyons in the Alps to porcelain-smooth cycling trails in the Dordogne and Loire Valley – not to mention 3200km of coastline stretching from Italy to Spain and from the Basque country to the Straits of Dover – France's landscapes offer exhilarating outdoor escapes.

» The French countryside is criss-crossed by a staggering 120,000km of *sentiers balisés* (marked walking paths), which pass through every imaginable terrain in every region of the country. No permit is needed to hike.

» The best-known trails are the *sentiers de grande randonnée* (GR), long-distance paths marked by red-and-white-striped track indicators.

» For complete details on regional activities, courses, equipment rental, clubs, companies and organisations, contact local tourist offices.

Business Hours

» French business hours are regulated by a maze of government regulations, including the 35-hour working week.

» The midday break is uncommon in Paris but, in general, gets longer the further south you go.

» French law requires most businesses to close Sunday; exceptions include grocery stores, *boulangeries*, florists and businesses catering to the tourist trade.

» In many places shops close on Monday.

» Many service stations open 24 hours a day and stock basic groceries.

» Restaurants generally close one or two days of the week.

STANDARD OPENING HOURS

We've only listed business hours where they differ from the following standards:

BUSINESS	OPENING HOURS
Bank	9am-noon & 2-5pm Mon-Fri or Tue-Sat
Bar	7pm-1am Mon-Sat
Cafe	7am or 8am-10pm or 11pm Mon-Sat
Nightclub	10pm-3am, 4am or 5am Thu-Sat
Post office	8.30am or 9am-5pm or 6pm Mon-Fri, 8am-noon Sat
Restaurant	lunch noon-2.30pm (or 3pm in Paris), dinner 7-11pm (until 10pm to midnight in Paris) six days a week
Shop	9am or 10am-7pm Mon-Sat (often with lunch break noon-1.30pm)
Supermarket	8.30am-7pm Mon-Sat, 8.30am-12.30pm Sun

» Most (but not all) national museums are closed on Tuesday, while most local museums are closed on Monday, though in summer some open daily. Some museums close for lunch.

Embassies & Consulates

All foreign embassies are in Paris.

» Many countries – including Canada, Japan, the UK, USA and most European countries – also have consulates in other major cities such as Bordeaux, Lyon, Nice, Marseille and Strasbourg.

» To find a consulate or an embassy not listed here, visit www.embassiesabroad.com or look up '*ambassade*' in the super user-friendly **Pages Jaunes** (Yellow Pages; www.pagesjaunes.fr).

Australia (☎01 40 59 33 00; www.france.embassy.gov.au; 4 rue Jean Rey, 15e; Ⓜ Bir Hakeim)

Canada (☎01 44 43 29 00; www.amb-canada.fr; 35 av Montaigne, 8e; Ⓜ Franklin D Roosevelt)

Japan (☎01 48 88 62 00; www.amb-japon.fr; 7 av Hoche, 8e; Ⓜ Courcelles)

New Zealand (☎01 45 01 43 43; www.nzembassy.com; 7ter rue Léonard de Vinci, 16e; Ⓜ Victor Hugo)

UK (☎01 44 51 31 00; http://ukinfrance.fco.gov.uk; 35 rue du Faubourg St-Honoré, 8e; Ⓜ Concorde)

USA (☎01 43 12 22 22; http://france.usembassy.gov; 4 av Gabriel, 8e; Ⓜ Concorde)

Food

Price ranges refer to a two-course meal:

€€€ more than €50

€€ €15 to €50

€ below €15

Gay & Lesbian Travellers

Gay mayors (including Paris' very own Bertrand Delanoë), artists and film directors, camper-than-camp fashion designers…the rainbow flag flies high in France, one of Europe's most liberal countries when it comes to homosexuality.

» Major gay and lesbian organisations are based in Paris.

» Bordeaux, Lille, Lyon, Toulouse and many other towns have active communities.

» Attitudes towards homosexuality tend to be more conservative in the countryside and villages.

» Gay Pride marches are held in major French cities from mid-May to early July.

Online try:

French Government Tourist Office (www.us.franceguide.com/special-interests/gay-friendly) Information about 'the gay-friendly destination par excellence'.

France Queer Resources Directory (www.france.qrd.org) Gay and lesbian directory.

Language Courses

» The website www.studyabroadlinks.com can help you find specific courses and summer programs, while www.edufrance.fr/en has information about university study.

» All manner of French-language courses are available in Paris and provincial towns and cities; many arrange accommodation.

» Prices and courses vary greatly and the content can often be tailored to your specific needs (for a fee).

Some schools you might consider:

Centre de Linguistique Appliquée de Besançon (☎03 81 66 52 00; http://cla.univ

-fcomte.fr; 6 rue Gabriel Plançon, Besançon) One of France's largest language schools in a beautiful city.

Centre Méditerranéen d'Études Françaises (www.monte-carlo.mc/centremed; chemin des Oliviers, Cap d'Ail) Mythical French Riviera school around since 1952.

Eurocentres (www.eurocentres.com) Trio of small, affiliated schools in Amboise, La Rochelle and Paris.

Aix-Marseille Université (www.univ-provence.fr; 29 av Robert Schumann, Aix-en-Provence) A hot choice in Provence; semester-long courses as well as summer classes.

Legal Matters

French police have wide powers of stop-and-search and can demand proof of identity at any time. Foreigners must be able to prove their legal status in France (eg passport, visa, residency permit).

Money

Credit and debit cards are accepted almost everywhere in France.

» Some places (eg 24hr petrol stations and some *autoroute* toll machines) only take credit cards with chips and PINs.

» In Paris and major cities, *bureaux de change* (exchange bureaux) are fast, easy, open longer hours and offer competitive exchange rates.

For lost cards, call:

Amex (☎01 47 77 72 00)

Diners Club (☎08 10 31 41 59)

MasterCard (☎08 00 90 13 87)

Visa (Carte Bleue; ☎08 00 90 11 79)

Public Holidays

New Year's Day (Jour de l'An) 1 January

Easter Sunday & Monday (Pâques & lundi de Pâques) March or April

May Day (Fête du Travail) 1 May – traditional parades.

Victoire 1945 8 May – commemorates the Allied victory in Europe that ended WWII.

Ascension Thursday (Ascension) May – celebrated on the 40th day after Easter.

Pentecost/Whit Sunday & Whit Monday (Pentecôte & lundi de Pentecôte) Mid-May to mid-June – celebrated on the seventh Sunday after Easter.

Bastille Day/National Day (Fête Nationale) 14 July – *the* national holiday.

Assumption Day (Assomption) 15 August

All Saints' Day (Toussaint) 1 November

Remembrance Day (L'onze novembre) 11 November – marks the WWI armistice.

Christmas (Noël) 25 December

Telephone

MOBILE PHONES

French mobile phones numbers begin with 06 or 07.

» France uses GSM 900/1800, compatible with the rest of Europe and Australia but not with the North American GSM 1900 or the totally different system in Japan (though some North Americans have tri-band phones that work here).

» It's usually cheaper to buy your own French SIM card (€20 to €30) sold at ubiquitous outlets run by France's three mobile phone companies, **Bouygues** (www.bouyguestelecom.fr), France Telecom's **Orange** (www.orange.com) and **SFR** (www.sfr.com).

» Recharge cards are sold at *tabacs* (tobacconists) and newsagents; domestic prepaid calls cost about €0.50 per minute.

PHONE CODES

Calling France from abroad Dial your country's international access code, ☎33 (France's country code), and the 10-digit local number *without* the initial 0.

DRUGS & ALCOHOL

» French law does not distinguish between 'hard' and 'soft' drugs.

» The penalty for any personal use of *stupéfiants* (including cannabis, amphetamines, ecstasy and heroin) can be a one-year jail sentence and a €3750 fine but, depending on the circumstances, it might be anything from a stern word to a compulsory rehab program.

» Importing, possessing, selling or buying drugs can get you up to 10 years' prison and a fine of up to €500,000.

» *Ivresse* (drunkeness) in public is punishable by a monetary fine.

Calling internationally from France Dial ☎00 (the international access code), the country code, area code (without the initial zero if there is one) and local number.

Directory inquiries For France Telecom's *service des renseignements* (directory inquiries), dial ☎11 87 12 or use the online service for free www.118712.fr.

International directory inquiries For numbers outside France, dial ☎11 87 00.

Emergency number ☎112, can be dialled from public phones without a phonecard.

Toilets

» Public toilets, signposted WC or *toilettes*, are not always plentiful in France.

» Love them (sci-fi geek) or loathe them (claustrophobe), France has its fair share of 24hr self-cleaning toilets, €0.50 in Paris and free elsewhere.

» Some older cafes and restaurants still have the hole-in-the-floor squat toilets.

» The French are blasé about unisex toilets; save your blushes when tiptoeing past the urinals to reach the loo.

Visas

For up-to-date details on visa requirements, visit the **French Foreign Affairs Ministry** (www.diplomatie.gouv.fr).

Visa requirements:

» EU nationals and citizens of Iceland, Norway and Switzerland need only a passport or national identity card to enter France and stay in the country, even for stays of over 90 days. Citizens of new EU member states may be subject to various limitations on living and working in France.

» Citizens of Australia, the USA, Canada Israel, Hong Kong, Japan, Malaysia, New Zealand, Singapore, South Korea and many Latin American countries do not need visas to visit France as tourists for up to 90 days. For longer stays of over 90 days, contact your nearest French embassy or consulate.

» Other people wishing to come to France as tourists have to apply for a Schengen Visa.

» Tourist visas cannot be changed into student visas after arrival. However, short-term visas are available for students sitting university-entrance exams in France.

Getting There & Away

Entering the Country

Entering France from other parts of the continental EU should be a breeze – no border checkpoints or customs thanks to the Schengen Agreement signed by all of France's neighbours except the UK, the Channel Islands and Andorra. For these three entities, old-fashioned document and customs checks remain the norm, at least when exiting France (when entering France in the case of Andorra).

INTERNATIONAL AIRPORTS

Paris Charles de Gaulle (CDG; www.aeroportsdeparis.fr)

Paris Orly (ORY; www.aeroportsdeparis.fr)

Aéroport de Bordeaux (www.bordeaux.aeroport.fr)

Aéroport de Lille (www.lille.aeroport.fr)

Aéroport International Strasbourg (www.strasbourg.aeroport.fr)

Aéroport Lyon-Saint Exupéry (www.lyonaeroports.com)

Aéroport Marseille-Provence (www.marseille.aeroport.fr)

Aéroport Nantes Atlantique (www.nantes.aeroport.fr)

Aéroport Nice-Côte d'Azur (http://societe.nice.aeroport.fr)

Aéroport Toulouse-Blagnac (www.toulouse.aeroport.fr)

EuroAirport (Basel-Mulhouse-Freiburg; www.euroairport.com)

Land

BUS

Eurolines (☎in France 08 92 89 90 91; www.eurolines.eu), a grouping of 32 long-haul coach operators (including the UK's National Express), links France with cities all across Europe and in Morocco and Russia. Discounts are available to people under 26 and over 60. Make advance reservations, especially in July and August.

The standard Paris–London fare is between €45 and €59, but the trip – including a Channel crossing by ferry or the Chunnel (Channel tunnel) – can cost as little as €13 if you book 45 days ahead.

CAR & MOTORCYCLE

A right-hand-drive vehicle brought to France from the UK or Ireland must have deflectors affixed to the headlights to avoid dazzling oncoming traffic.

Departing from the UK, **Eurotunnel Le Shuttle** (www.eurotunnel.com) trains whisk bicycles, motorcycles, cars and coaches in 35 minutes from Folkestone through the Channel Tunnel to Coquelles, 5km southwest of Calais. Shuttles run 24 hours a day, with up to three departures an hour during peak periods. The earlier you book, the less you pay. Fares for a car, including up to nine passengers, start at £30.

TRAIN

Rail services – including a dwindling number of overnight services to/from Spain, Italy and Germany – link France with virtually every country in Europe. Book tickets and get train information from **Rail Europe** (www.raileurope.com). In France ticketing is handled by **SNCF** (from abroad +33 8 92 35 35 35, in France 36 35; www.sncf.com); internet bookings are possible but they won't post tickets outside France.

High-speed train travel between France and the UK, Belgium, the Netherlands, Germany and Austria is covered by **Railteam** (www.railteam.co.uk) and **TGV-Europe** (www.tgv-europe.com).

Certain rail services between France and its continental neighbours are marketed under a number of unique brand names:

Elipsos (www.elipsos.com) Luxurious 'train-hotel' services to Spain.

TGV Lyria (www.tgv-lyria.fr) To Switzerland.

Thalys (www.thalys.com) Thalys trains pull into Paris' Gare du Nord from Brussels, Amsterdam and Cologne.

Eurostar (France 08 92 35 35 39, UK 08432 186 186; www.eurostar.com) Runs from London St Pancras station to Paris Gare du Nord in 2¼ hours, with onward connections to destinations all over France. Ski trains connecting England with the French Alps run weekends mid-December to mid-April.

Sample Train Fares

ROUTE	FULL FARE (€)	DURATION (HR)
Amsterdam–Paris	89	3¼
Madrid–Blois	153	12½
Berlin–Paris	189	8
Brussels–Paris	69	1½
Dijon–Milan	80	7
Paris–Venice	100	11¾
Geneva–Marseille	50	3½
Vienna-Strasbourg	153	9¾

SEA

Regular ferries travel to France from Italy, the UK, Channel Islands and Ireland. Several ferry companies ply the waters between Corsica and Italy.

INTERNATIONAL FERRY ROUTES

COMPANY	ROUTES	WEBSITE
Brittany Ferries	England–Normandy, England–Brittany, Ireland-Brittany	www.brittany-ferries.co.uk; www.brittanyferries.ie
Celtic Link Ferries	Ireland–Normandy	www.celticlinkferries.com
Condor Ferries	England–Normandy, England–Brittany, Channel Islands–Brittany	www.condorferries.com
CTN	Tunisia–France	www.ctn.com.tn
Irish Ferries	Ireland–Normandy, Ireland–Brittany	www.irishferries.ie; www.shamrock-irlande.com, in French
LD Lines	England–Channel Ports, England–Normandy	www.ldlines.co.uk
Manche Îles Express	Channel Islands–Normandy	www.manche-iles-express.com
Norfolk Line (DFDS Seaways)	England–Channel Ports	www.norfolkline.com
P&O Ferries	England–Channel Ports	www.poferries.com
SNCM	Algeria–France, Sardinia–France, Tunisia–France	www.sncm.fr
Transmanche Ferries	England–Normandy	www.transmancheferries.com

Getting Around

Air

France's vaunted high-speed train network has made rail travel between some cities (eg from Paris to Lyon and Marseille) faster and easier than flying.

Air France (www.airfrance.com) and its subsidiaries **Brit Air** (www.britair.fr) and **Régional** (☎36 54; www.regional.com) control the lion's share of France's long-protected domestic airline industry. Good deals can be had if you buy your ticket well in advance (at least 42 days ahead for the very best deals), stay over a Saturday night and don't mind tickets that can't be changed or reimbursed.

Budget carriers offering flights within France include **easyJet** (www.easyjet.com), **Airlinair** (www.airlinair.com), **Twin Jet** (www.twinjet.net) and **Air Corsica** (www.aircorsica.com).

Bus

You're nearly always better off travelling by train in France if possible, as the SNCF domestic railway system is heavily subsidised by the government and is much more reliable than local bus companies. Nevertheless, buses are widely used for short-distance travel within *départements,* especially in rural areas with relatively few train lines (eg Brittany and Normandy).

Bicycle

France is a great place to cycle. Not only is much of the countryside drop-dead gorgeous, but the country has an extensive network of secondary and tertiary roads with relatively light traffic, and a growing number of urban and rural *pistes cyclables* (bike paths and lanes); see **Voie Vertes** (www.voiesvertes.com). French train company SNCF does its best to make travelling with a bicycle easy; see www.velo.sncf.com for full details.

Most French cities and towns have at least one bike shop that rents out mountain bikes (VTT; around €15 a day), road bikes (VTCs) and cheaper city bikes. You have to leave ID and/or a deposit (often a credit-card slip) that you forfeit if the bike is damaged or stolen. A growing number of cities have automatic bike rental systems.

Car & Motorcycle

A car gives you exceptional freedom and allows you to visit more-remote parts of France. But it can be expensive and, in cities, parking and traffic are frequently a major headache. Motorcyclists will find France great for touring, with winding roads of good quality and lots of stunning scenery.

> **PRIORITY TO THE RIGHT**
>
> Under the *priorité à droite* (priority to the right) rule, any car entering an intersection from a road on your right has the right of way, unless the intersection is marked *'vous n'avez pas la priorité'* (you do not have right of way) or *'cédez le passage'* (give way).

BRINGING YOUR OWN VEHICLE

All foreign motor vehicles entering France must display a sticker or licence plate identifying its country of registration. If you're bringing a right-hand-drive vehicle remember to fix deflectors on your headlights to avoid dazzling oncoming traffic.

DRIVING LICENCE & DOCUMENTS

All drivers must carry a national ID card or passport; a valid driving licence (*permis de conduire;* most foreign licences can be used in France for up to a year); car-ownership papers, known as a *carte grise* (grey card); and proof of third-party (liability) insurance.

FUEL & TOLLS

Essence (petrol), also known as *carburant* (fuel), costs around €1.45/L for 95 unleaded (Sans Plomb 95 or SP95, usually available from a green pump), and €1.30 for diesel (*diesel, gazole* or *gasoil,* usually available from a yellow pump). Filling up *(faire le plein)* is most expensive along *autoroutes* and cheapest at supermarkets on town outskirts.

Many French motorways (*autoroutes*) are fitted with toll *(péage)* stations that charge a fee based on the distance you've travelled; factor in these costs when driving.

HIRE

To hire a car you'll usually need to be over 21 and in possession of a valid driving licence and a credit card. Auto transmissions are *very* rare in France; you'll need to order one well in advance.

There are major car rental companies with offices across France and Europe.

INSURANCE

Unlimited third-party liability insurance is mandatory in France. Third-party liability insurance is provided by car-rental companies, but collision-damage waivers (CDW) vary between companies. When comparing rates check the *franchise* (excess). Your credit card may cover CDW if you use it to pay for the car rental.

ROAD RULES

Cars drive on the right in France. Speed limits on French roads are as follows:

» 50km/h in built-up areas

» 90km/h (80km/h if it's raining) on N and D highways

» 110km/h (100km/h if it's raining) on dual carriageways

» 130km/h (110km/h if it's raining) on *autoroutes*

Child-seat rules:

» Children under 10 are not permitted to ride in the front seat (unless the back is already occupied by other children under 10).

» A child under 13kg must travel in a backward-facing child seat (permitted in the front seat only for babies under 9kg and if the airbag is deactivated).

» Up to age 10 and/or a minimum height of 140cm, children must use a size-appropriate type of front-facing child seat or booster.

Other key rules of the road:

» Blood-alcohol limit is 0.05% (0.5g per litre of blood) – the equivalent of two glasses of wine for a 75kg adult. Police often conduct random breathalyser tests and penalties can be severe, including imprisonment.

» Mobile phones may be used only if they are equipped with a hands-free kit or speakerphone.

» All passengers must wear seatbelts.

» All vehicles must carry a reflective safety jacket (stored inside the car, not the trunk/boot), a reflective triangle, and a portable, single-use breathalyser kit. The fine for not carrying any of these items is €90.

» Riders of any type of two-wheeled vehicle with a motor (except motor-assisted bicycles) must wear a helmet.

» North American drivers, remember: turning right on a red light is illegal.

Train

France's superb rail network is operated by the state-owned **SNCF** (www.sncf.com); many rural towns not on the SNCF train network are served by SNCF buses.

The flagship trains on French railways are the superfast TGVs, which reach speeds in excess of 200mph and can whisk you from Paris to the Côte d'Azur in as little as three hours.

Many non-high-speed lines are also served by TGV trains; otherwise you'll find yourself aboard a non-TGV train, referred to as a *corail* or TER *(train express régional)*.

TGV lines and key stations:

TGV Nord, Thalys & Eurostar Link Paris Gare du Nord with Arras, Lille, Calais, Brussels (Bruxelles-Midi), Amsterdam, Cologne and, via the Channel Tunnel, Ashford, Ebbsfleet and London St Pancras.

TGV Est Européen Connects Paris Gare de l'Est with Reims, Nancy, Metz, Strasbourg, Zurich and Germany, including Frankfurt and Stuttgart. At present, the super-high-speed track stretches only as far east as Lorraine but it's supposed to reach Strasbourg in 2016.

TGV Sud-Est & TGV Midi-Méditerranée Link Paris Gare de Lyon with the southeast, including Dijon, Lyon, Geneva, the Alps, Avignon, Marseille, Nice and Montpellier.

TGV Atlantique Sud-Ouest & TGV Atlantique Ouest Link Paris Gare Montparnasse with western and southwestern France, including Brittany (Rennes, Brest, Quimper), Tours, Nantes, Poitiers, La Rochelle, Bordeaux, Biarritz and Toulouse.

TGV Rhin-Rhône France's most recent high-speed rail route – the first section of which opened in December 2011 – bypasses Paris altogether in its bid to better link the provinces. Six services a day speed between Strasbourg and Lyon, with most continuing south to Marseille or Montpellier on the Mediterranean.

VALIDATE YOURSELF

Before boarding any train, you must validate *(composter)* your ticket by time-stamping it in a *composteur*, one of those yellow posts located on the way to the platform. If you forget (or don't have a ticket for some other reason), find a conductor on the train before they find you – or risk an unwelcome fine.

SNCF TRAIN FARES & DISCOUNTS

The Basics

» Full-fare return travel costs twice as much as a one-way fare.

» 1st-class travel, where available, costs 20% to 30% extra.

» Ticket prices for some trains, including most TGVs, are pricier during peak periods.

» The further in advance you reserve, the lower the fares.

» Children under four travel for free (€8.50 to any destination if they need a seat).

» Children aged four to 11 travel for half price.

Discount Tickets

Prem's The SNCF's most heavily discounted, use-or-lose tickets, sold online, by phone and at ticket windows/machines a maximum of 90 days and minimum 14 days before you travel.

Bons Plans A grab-bag of cheap options for different routes/dates, advertised online under the tab '*Dernière Minute*' (Last Minute).

iDTGV Cheap tickets on advance-purchase TGV travel between about 30 cities; only sold at www.idtgv.com.

Discount Cards

Reductions of 25% to 60% are available with several discount cards (valid for one year):

Carte 12-25 (www.12-25-sncf.com; €50) For travellers aged 12 to 25 years.

Carte Enfant Plus (www.enfantplus-sncf.com; €71) For one to four adults travelling with a child aged four to 11 years.

Carte Escapades (www.escapades-sncf.com; €76) Discounts on return journeys of at least 200km that include a Saturday night away or only involve travel on a Saturday or Sunday; for 26- to 59-year-olds.

Carte Sénior (www.senior-sncf.com; €57) Travellers over 60 years.

TICKETS

Buying online at the various SNCF websites can reward with you some great reductions on fares, but be warned – these are generally intended for domestic travellers, and if you're buying abroad be aware of the pitfalls. Many tickets can't be posted outside France, and if you buy with a non-French credit card, you might not be able to use it in the automated ticket collection machines at many French stations. Buying from a ticket office may not secure you the cheapest fare, but at least you'll be sure of being able to pick up your ticket.

RAIL PASSES

The **InterRail One Country Pass** (www.interrailnet.com; 3/4/6/8 days €205/226/288/319, 12–25yr €139/149/190/211), valid in France, entitles residents of Europe who do not live in France to unlimited travel on SNCF trains for three to eight days over a month.

Germany

Includes »

Best Places to Eat

- » Cafe Jacques (p458)
- » Café Schäfer (p522)
- » Bratwursthäusle (p509)
- » Auerbachs Keller (p473)

Best Places to Stay

- » Circus Hotel (p455)
- » Romantik Hotel Theophano (p483)
- » Steigenberger Grandhotel Handelshof (p473)
- » Grüne Zitadelle (p479)
- » Hotel Elch (p509)

Why Go?

Beer or wine? That sums up the German conundrum. One is at the heart of a pilsner-swilling culture, is the very reason for one of the world's great parties (Oktoberfest) and is consumed with pleasure across the land. The other is responsible for gorgeous vine-covered valleys, comes in myriad forms and is enjoyed everywhere, often from cute little green-stemmed glasses.

And the questions about Germany continue. Berlin or Munich? Castle or club? Ski or hike? East or west? BMW or Mercedes? In fact, the answers are simple: both. Why decide? The beauty of Germany is that rather than choosing, you can revel in the contrasts.

Berlin, edgy and vibrant, is a grand capital in a constant state of reinvention. Munich rules Bavaria, the centre of national traditions. Half-timbered villages bring smiles as you wander the cobblestoned and castle-shadowed lanes. Exploring this country and all its facets keeps visitors happy for weeks.

When to Go

Berlin

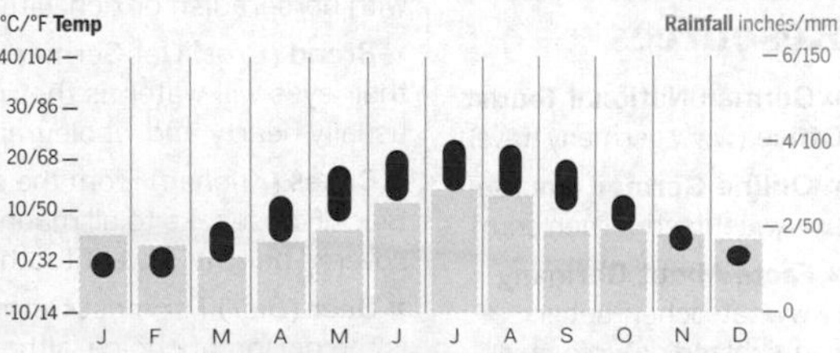

Jun–Aug Warm summers cause Germans to shed their clothes; night never seems to come.

Sep The real month of Oktober fest; autumn celebrations are found throughout Bavaria.

Dec It's icy, it's cold and you can drink hot wine at Christmas markets country-wide.

AT A GLANCE

» **Currency** euro (€)

» **Language** German

» **Money** ATMs common, cash preferred for most purchases

» **Visas** Schengen rules apply

Fast Facts

» **Area** 356,866 sq km

» **Capital** Berlin

» **Country code** ☎49

» **Emergency** ☎112

Exchange Rates

Australia	A$1	€0.82
Canada	C$1	€0.77
Japan	¥100	€0.83
New Zealand	NZ$1	€0.65
UK	UK£1	€1.18
USA	US$1	€0.78

Set Your Budget

» **Budget hotel room** €80

» **Two-course meal** €15-25

» **1L of beer** €6-8

» **Bottle of wine in shop** from €4

» **U-Bahn ticket** around €2

Resources

» **German National Tourist Office** (www.germany.travel)

» **Online German Course** (www.deutsch-lernen.com)

» **Facts About Germany** (www.tatsachen-ueber-deutschland.de) Info on all aspects of German society.

» **Deutschland Online** (www.magazine-deutschland.de) Insightful features on culture, business and politics.

Connections

At the heart of Europe, Germany has a superb railway network that's well linked to surrounding countries. Freiburg and Stuttgart have services south to Switzerland and Italy, Munich is close to the Czech Republic and Austria (including Salzburg and Innsbruck), Berlin is close to Poland, Hamburg has frequent services to Denmark, Cologne is good for fast trains to the Netherlands and Belgium (including Brussels for Eurostar to London), and Frankfurt is the base for high-speed trains to Paris, Strasbourg and other parts of France.

ITINERARIES

One Week

Spend three days in and around Berlin (eg Potsdam), then marvel at Dresden's rebirth and Nuremberg's historical pedigree before wrapping up your journey with a couple of days in Munich.

Two Weeks

Start in Munich for some Bavarian joy followed by an Alpine side trip to the top of Germany – the Zugspitze – aboard a spectacular train–cable-car combo. Admire the sugary confection of Schloss Neuschwanstein before dipping into medieval times along the Romantic Road and being enchanted by Heidelberg. The Romantic Rhine delivers fine wine and ancient castles galore. Climb the grand cathedral in charismatic Cologne and finish it all in Berlin.

Essential Food & Drink

» **Sausage** *(Wurst)* More than 1500 types are made countrywide. From sweet, smoky and tiny Nürnbergers, to crunchy Thüringers, to that fast-food remedy for the munchies, the sliced and tomato-sauce-drowned *currywurst*.

» **Mustard** *(Senf)* The perfect accompaniment to sausages, schnitzels and more, German mustards can be hot, laced with horseradish or rich with seeds – or all three.

» **Bread** *(Brot)* Get Germans talking about bread and often their eyes will water as they describe their favourite type – usually hearty and wholegrained in infinite variations.

» **Cakes** *(Kuchen)* From the confectionery fantasy of the Black Forest cake to all manner of apple-laden, crumb-covered delights, sweet tooths never feel ignored.

» **Beer** *(Bier)* For most Germans, intensely hoppy pilsner is the poison of choice, although wheat beer is popular in summer and regional varieties abound, such as Kölsch in Cologne and Rauchbier in Bamberg.

» **Wine** *(Wein)* Winning competitions and critics' praises, German wine in the 21st century is leagues removed from that cloyingly sweet stuff of yore. The country's crisp rieslings are the world's best.

BERLIN

030 / POP 3.5 MILLION

There's just no escaping history in Berlin. You might be distracted by the trendy, edgy, gentrified streets, by the bars bleeding a laid-back cool factor, by the galleries sprouting talent and pushing the envelope, but make no mistake – reminders of the German capital's past assault you while modernity sits around the corner. Norman Foster's Reichstag dome, Peter Eisenman's Holocaust Memorial and the iconic Brandenburg Gate are all contained within a few neighbouring blocks. Potsdamer Platz and its shiny Sony Center hosts Berlin's star-studded film festival each year, on the very site where only 25 years ago you could climb up a viewing platform in the West and peer over the Berlin Wall for a glimpse behind the Iron Curtain.

Renowned for its diversity and its tolerance, its alternative culture and its night-owl stamina, the best thing about Berlin is the way it reinvents itself and isn't shackled by its mind-numbing history. And the world knows this – a steady stream of Germans from other parts of the country and a league of global expatriates are flocking here to see what all the fuss is about.

History

By German standards, Berlin entered onto the stage rather late and puttered along in relative obscurity for centuries. Founded in the 13th century as a trading post, it achieved a modicum of prominence after coming under the rule of the powerful Hohenzollern from southern Germany in 1411. The clan managed to cling to power until the abolition of the monarchy in 1918.

In 1701, Elector Friedrich III was elevated to King Friedrich I, making Berlin a royal residence. The promotion significantly shaped the city, which blossomed under Friedrich I's grandson, Frederick the Great, who sought greatness as much on the battlefield as through building and embracing the ideals of the Enlightenment. The best bits of Unter den Linden date back to his reign, when Berlin blossomed into a cultural centre nicknamed 'Athens on the Spree'.

As throughout northern Europe, the Industrial Revolution began its march on Berlin in the 19th century, vastly expanding the city's population and spawning a new working class. Berlin boomed politically, economically and culturally, especially after becoming capital of the German Reich in 1871. By 1900 the population had reached two million.

World War I stifled Berlin's momentum, while the 1920s were marred by instability, corruption and inflation. Berliners responded like there was no tomorrow and made their city as much a den of decadence as a cauldron of creativity. Artists of all stripes flocked to this city of cabaret, Dada and jazz.

Hitler's rise to power put an instant dampener on the fun as the dark ages of the Third Reich descended upon the world. Berlin suffered heavy bombing in WWII and a crushing invasion of 1.5 million Soviet soldiers during the final Battle of Berlin in April 1945. Few original Nazi-era sights remain, but memorials and museums keep the horror in focus.

After WWII, Germany fell into the cross hairs of the Cold War; a country divided ideologically and literally by a fortified border and the infamous Berlin Wall, whose construction began in 1961. Just how differently

BERLIN IN ...

One Day

Book ahead for an early time slot on the lift to the **Reichstag** dome, then snap a picture of the **Brandenburger Tor** before stumbling around the **Holocaust Memorial** and admiring the contemporary architecture of **Potsdamer Platz**. Ponder Cold War madness at **Checkpoint Charlie**, then head to **Museumsinsel** to admire Queen Nefertiti and the Pergamonaltar. Finish up with a night of mirth and gaiety around **Hackescher Markt**.

Two Days

Kick off day two coming to grips with what life was like in divided Berlin at the **Gedenkstätte Berliner Mauer**. Intensify the experience at the **DDR Museum** and on a walk along the **East Side Gallery**. Spend the afternoon soaking up the urban spirit of Kreuzberg with its sassy shops and street art, grab dinner along the canal, drinks around Kottbusser Tor and finish up with a night of clubbing at **Watergate** or **Berghain**.

Germany Highlights

1 Party day and night in **Berlin** (p441); save sleep for somewhere else as there's no time here with the clubs, museums, bars and ever-changing Zeitgeist

2 Time your journey for **Oktoberfest** (p494). Munich's orgy of suds, or just hang out in a beer garden

3 Go slow in Germany's alluring small towns like **Bamberg** (p510), with winding lanes, smoked beer (!) and a lack of cliché

4 Compare the soaring peaks of the Dom in **Cologne** (p535) with the slinky glasses of the city's famous beer

5 Go cuckoo in the **Black Forest** (p519), discovering its chilly crags, misty peaks and endless trails

6 Get into the swing of **Dresden** (p466), with a creative culture beyond the restorations

7 Cycle around one of the world's great harbours in **Hamburg** (p548), then follow the trail of the Beatles

8 Discover **Regensburg** (p511), Germany's Unesco-recognised ancient gem, with traces of Rome and Tuscany (and great sausages!) around every corner

Berlin

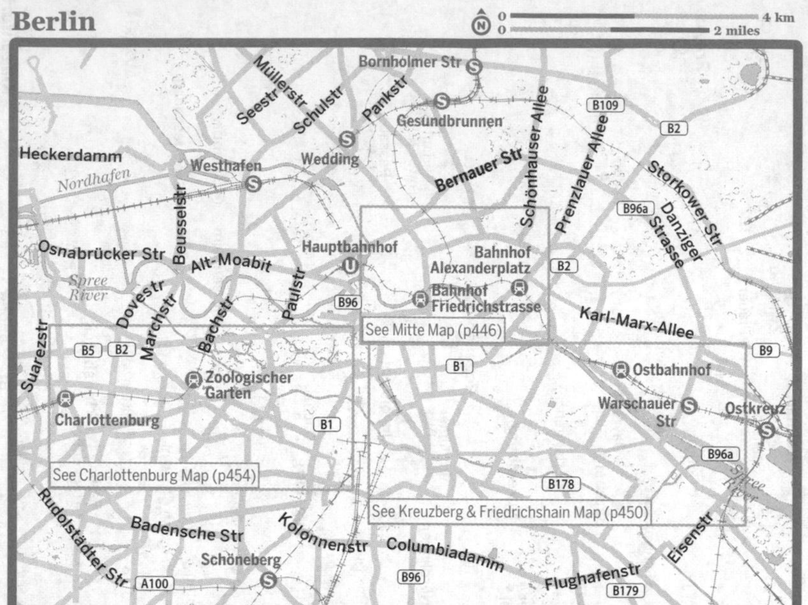

the two Germanys developed is still palpable in Berlin, expressed not only through Wall remnants but through vastly different urban planning and architectural styles.

Since reunification, Berlin has again become a hotbed of creativity, with unbridled nightlife, an explosive art scene and booming fashion and design industries. Sure, problems persist – empty city coffers, high unemployment, the delayed Berlin Brandenburg Airport, to name a few – but Berlin's allure to tourists and newcomers from around the world remains unabated. It's a city that dances to its own tune, where individualism triumphs over conformity and brilliant ideas are celebrated and welcome. Few people who live here don't love it. Few people who visit will ever forget it.

Sights

Key sights like the Reichstag, Brandenburger Tor, Checkpoint Charlie and Museumsinsel cluster in the historic city centre – Mitte – which is also home to a maze-like hipster quarter around Hackescher Markt. North of here, residential Prenzlauer Berg has a lively cafe and restaurant scene, while to the south loom the contemporary high-rises of Potsdamer Platz. Further south, gritty but cool Kreuzberg is party central, as is student-flavoured Friedrichshain east across the Spree River and home to the East Side Gallery stretch of the Berlin Wall. Western Berlin's hub is Charlottenburg, with great shopping and a famous royal palace.

REICHSTAG & UNTER DEN LINDEN

The Reichstag is the historic anchor of the federal government quarter, which also includes the postmodern chancellery and office buildings for the parliamentarians. Just south of here, chic Unter den Linden boulevard stretches 1.5km from the Brandenburger Tor to the giant treasure chest of the Museumsinsel, past a phalanx of grand old structures reflecting one-time Prussian grandeur.

TOP CHOICE **Reichstag** HISTORIC BUILDING

(Map p446; www.bundestag.de; Platz der Republik 1; lift ride 8am-midnight, last entry 11pm; 100, S Bundestag, Hauptbahnhof) One of Berlin's most iconic buildings, the Reichstag has been burned, bombed, rebuilt, buttressed by the Berlin Wall, wrapped in fabric and eventually turned into the modern home of Germany's parliament, the Bundestag.

The grand old structure was designed by Paul Wallot in 1894 and given a total post-reunification makeover by Norman Foster. The famous architect preserved only its historical shell while adding the glistening glass dome, which can be reached by lift (reservations mandatory). At the top, pick up a free auto-activated audioguide and learn about the building, city landmarks and the workings of the parliament while following the ramp spiralling up and around the dome's mirror-clad central funnel.

Brandenburger Tor & Pariser Platz HISTORIC SITE

(Map p446; S Brandenburger Tor, U Brandenburger Tor) A symbol of division during the Cold War, the landmark Brandenburg Gate now epitomises German reunification. Its architect Carl Gotthard Langhans found inspiration in Athen's Acropolis for this elegant triumphal arch, completed in 1791 as the royal city gate. It is crowned by the Quadriga sculpture of the winged goddess of victory piloting a chariot drawn by four horses. The Brandenburg Gate stands sentinel over Pariser Platz, a harmoniously proportioned square once again framed by banks as well as the US, British and French embassies, just as it was during its 19th-century heyday.

FREE **Holocaust Memorial** MEMORIAL

(Map p446; 2639 4336; www.stiftung-denkmal.de; Cora-Berliner-Strasse 1; audioguide €3; field 24hr, information centre 10am-8pm Tue-Sun, last entry 7.15pm Apr-Sep, 6.15pm Oct-Mar; S Brandenburger Tor, U Brandenburger Tor) The football-field-sized Memorial to the Murdered European Jews is Germany's central memorial to the Nazi-planned genocide and is colloquially known as the Holocaust Memorial. American architect Peter Eisenman created a maze of 2711 sarcophagi-like concrete columns rising in sombre silence from undulating ground. For context, visit the subterranean **Ort der Information** (information centre).

Hitler's Bunker HISTORIC SITE

(Map p450; cnr In den Ministergärten & Gertrud-Kolmar-Strasse; S Brandenburger Tor, U Brandenburger Tor) Berlin was burning and Soviet tanks advancing relentlessly when Adolf Hitler committed suicide on 30 April 1945 alongside Eva Braun, his long-time female companion, hours after their marriage. Today, a parking lot covers the site, revealing its dark history only via an information panel with a diagram of the vast bunker network, and information on its construction and post-WWII history.

WANT MORE?

For in-depth information, reviews and recommendations at your fingertips, head to the Apple App Store to purchase Lonely Planet's *Berlin City Guide* iPhone app.

Alternatively, head to **Lonely Planet** (www.lonelyplanet.com/germany/berlin) for planning advice, author recommendations, traveller reviews and insider tips.

Unter den Linden STREET

(Map p446; 100, 200, S Brandenburger Tor, U Brandenburger Tor) This chic boulevard stretches 1.5km from the Brandenburger Tor to the giant treasure chest of the Museumsinsel, past a phalanx of grand old structures built under various Prussian kings and reflecting the one-time grandeur of the royal family.

Bebelplatz MEMORIAL

(Map p446; Bebel Sq; 100, 200, S Französische Strasse, Hausvogteiplatz) Unter den Linden runs past this treeless square, where books by Brecht, Mann, Marx and other 'subversives' went up in flames during the first full-blown public book burning staged by Nazi students in 1933. Michael Ullmann's underground installation, *Empty Library*, beneath a glass pane at the square's centre, poignantly commemorates the event.

Bebelplatz was first laid out in the mid 18th century as part of the Forum Fridericianum, a cluster of cultural buildings envisioned by Frederick the Great. The **Staatsoper Unter den Linden**, the **Alte Königliche Bibliothek**, a palace for Fritz' brother Heinrich (now the Humboldt Universität), and the copper-domed **Sankt-Hedwigs-Kathedrale** all date from this time.

Deutsches Historisches Museum MUSEUM

(Map p446; 203 040; www.dhm.de; Unter den Linden 2; adult/concession €8/4; 10am-6pm; 100, 200, U Alexanderplatz, Hackescher Markt) This engaging museum zeroes in on two millennia of German history in all its gore and glory; not in a nutshell but on two floors of a Prussian-era armoury. Check out the Nazi globe, the pain-wrecked faces of dying warrior sculptures in the courtyard, and the temporary exhibits in the boldly modern annex designed by IM Pei.

Mitte

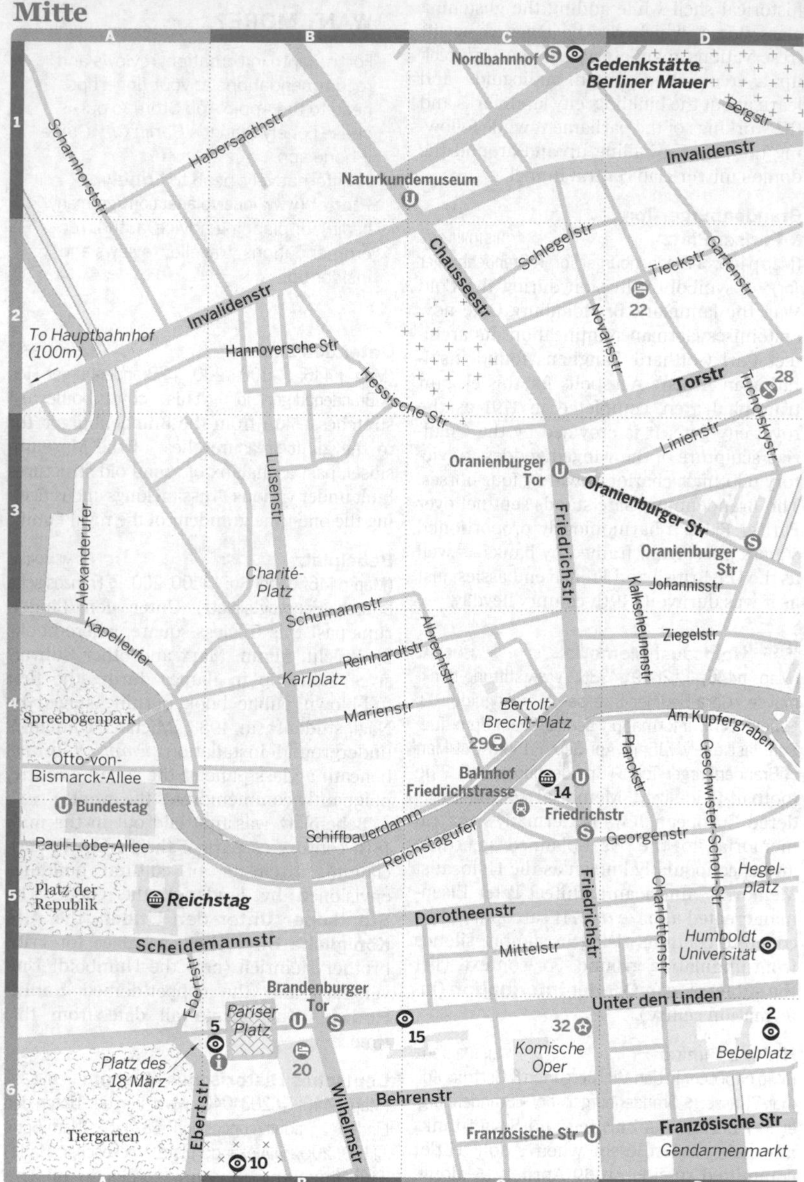

Checkpoint Charlie HISTORIC SITE

(Map p450; cnr Zimmerstrasse & Friedrichstrasse; ⏲24hr; S Kochstrasse, Stadtmitte) Checkpoint Charlie was the principal gateway for foreigners and diplomats between the two Berlins from 1961 to 1990. Unfortunately, this potent symbol of the Cold War has become a tacky tourist trap, although a free **open-air exhibit** that illustrates milestones in Cold War history is one redeeming aspect. New since September 2012 is Yadegar Asisi's **Berlin Wall Panorama** (Map

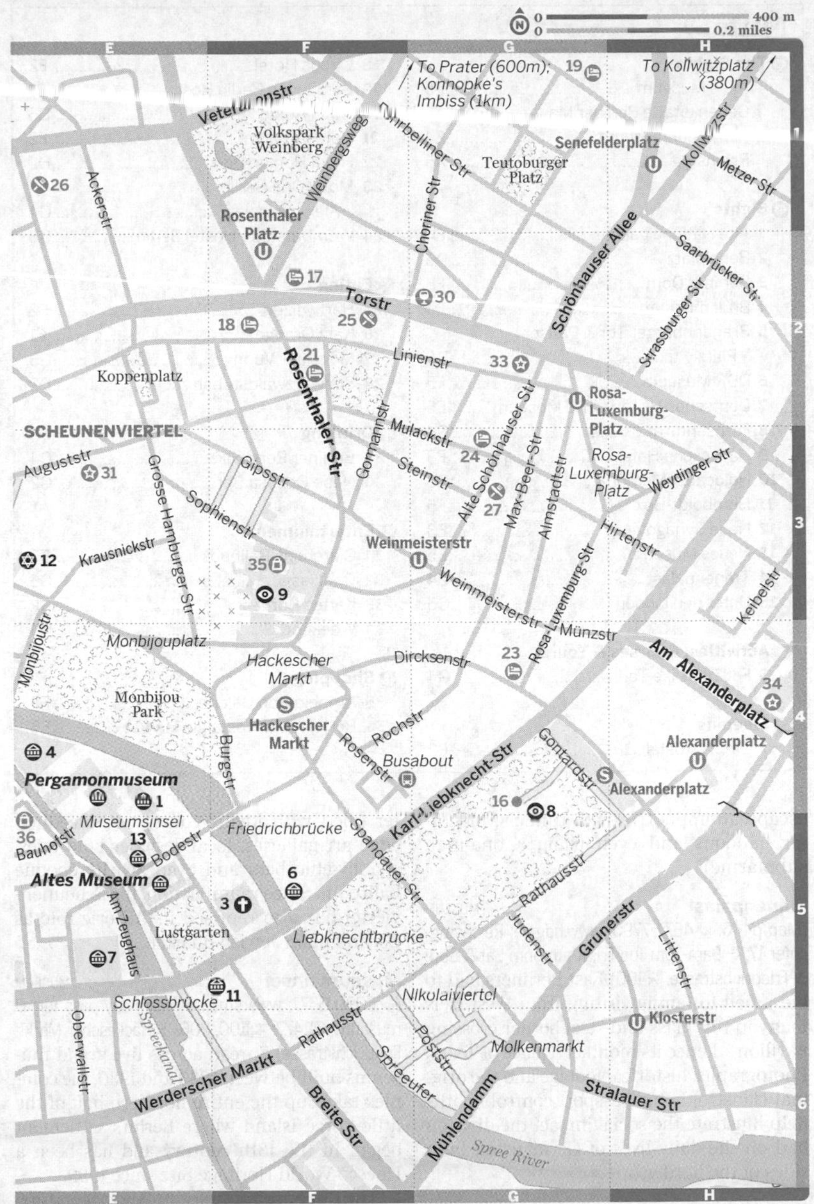

p450; www.asisi.de; cnr Friedrichstrasse & Zimmerstrasse; adult/concession €10/8.50; ⏲10am-6pm; Ⓢ Kochstrasse). An official Cold War Museum is in the planning stages and may open by 2015. Until then, a 'Blackbox' offers a preview.

Nearby, the privately run **Haus am Checkpoint Charlie** (Map p450; ☎253 7250; www.mauermuseum.de; Friedrichstrasse 43-45; adult/concession €12.50/9.50; ⏲9am-10pm; 👪; Ⓢ Kochstrasse, Stadtmitte) is especially strong when it comes to documenting spectacular

Mitte

Top Sights
- Altes Museum E5
- Gedenkstätte Berliner Mauer C1
- Pergamonmuseum E4
- Reichstag A5

Sights
- 1 Alte Nationalgalerie E4
- 2 Bebelplatz D6
- 3 Berliner Dom F5
- 4 Bodemuseum E4
- 5 Brandenburger Tor & Pariser Platz B6
- 6 DDR Museum F5
- 7 Deutsches Historisches Museum E5
- 8 Fernsehturm G4
- 9 Hackesche Höfe F3
- 10 Holocaust Memorial B6
- 11 Humboldt-Box F5
- 12 Neue Synagoge E3
- 13 Neues Museum E5
- 14 Tränenpalast C4
- 15 Unter den Linden C6

Activities, Courses & Tours
- 16 Fat Tire Bike Tours G4

Sleeping
- 17 Circus Hostel F2
- 18 Circus Hotel F2
- 19 EastSeven Berlin Hostel G1
- 20 Hotel Adlon Kempinski B6
- 21 Hotel Amano F2
- 22 Hotel Honigmond D2
- 23 Motel One Berlin-Alexanderplatz G4
- 24 Wombats City Hostel Berlin G3

Eating
- 25 Hartweizen F2
- 26 Katz Orange E1
- 27 Monsieur Vuong G3
- 28 Schwarzwaldstuben D2

Drinking
- 29 Berliner Republik C4
- 30 Neue Odessa Bar G2

Entertainment
- 31 Clärchens Ballhaus E3
- 32 Cookies C6
- 33 Kaffee Burger G2
- 34 Weekend H4

Shopping
- 35 Ampelmann Galerie F3
- 36 Berlin Art & Nostalgia Market E5

escape attempts (through tunnels, in hot-air balloons and even using a one-man submarine).

Tränenpalast MUSEUM
(Map p446; ☎4677 7790; www.hdg.de; Reichstagsufer 17; ⊙9am-7pm Tue-Fri, 10am-6pm Sat & Sun; Ⓢ Friedrichstrasse, 🚌100) East Berliners had to bid adieu to family visiting from West Germany in this glass-and-steel border crossing pavilion – hence its moniker 'Palace of Tears'. Photographs, historical footage and the original claustrophobic passport control booths help illustrate the social impact the division had on the daily lives of Germans on both sides of the border.

MUSEUMSINSEL & SCHEUNENVIERTEL

Museumsinsel (Museum Island) is Berlin's most important treasure trove, spanning 6000 years worth of art, artefacts, sculpture and architecture from Europe and beyond. It segues into the Scheunenviertel (Barn Quarter), a compact and charismatic quarter filled with idyllic courtyards, bleeding-edge art galleries, local-designer boutiques, shabby-chic bars and even a belle époque ballroom. Since reunification, the Scheunenviertel has also reprised its historic role as Berlin's main Jewish quarter.

Museumsinsel MUSEUM
(☎2090 5577; www.smb.museum; day pass for all museums €14/7; 🚌100, 200, Ⓢ Hackescher Markt, Friedrichstrasse) Spread across five grand museums built between 1830 and 1930, the complex takes up the entire northern half of the little Spree Island where Berlin's settlement began in the 13th century and has been a Unesco World Heritage Site since 1999.

The **Pergamonmuseum** (Map p446; ☎266 424 242; www.smb.museum; Am Kupfergraben 5; adult/concession €8/4; ⊙10am-6pm Fri-Wed, to 9pm Thu; 🚌Hackescher Markt, Friedrichstrasse, bus 100) is the island's top draw with monumental architecture from ancient worlds, including the namesake Pergamon Altar and the stunning Babylonian Ishtar Gate.

The **Altes Museum** (Old Museum; Map p446; ☎266 424 242; www.smb.museum; Am Lustgarten; adult/concession €8/4; ⊙10am-6pm Fri-Wed, to 8pm Thu; 🚌100, 200, 🚉Friedrichstrasse) was the first repository to open on the island, in 1830, and presents Greek, Etruscan and Roman antiquities. Note the *Praying Boy* bronze sculpture, Roman silver vessels and portraits of Caesar and Cleopatra.

The show-stopper of the Egyptian collection at the **Neues Museum** (New Museum; Map p446, ☎266 424 242; www.smb.museum; adult/concession €10/5, ⊙10am-6pm Sun Wed, to 8pm Thu-Sat; 🚌100, 200, 🚉Hackescher Markt) is the 3300-year-old bust of Queen Nefertiti; the equally enthralling Museum of Pre- and Early History has treasure from Troy.

Famous for its European sculpture from the Middle Ages to the 18th century (Riemenschneider, Donatello, Pisano, etc), the **Bodemuseum** (Map p446; ☎266 424 242; www.smb.museum; Monbijoubrücke; adult/concession €8/4; ⊙10am-6pm Tue, Wed & Fri-Sun, to 10pm Thu; 🚉Hackescher Markt) has a huge coin collection and Byzantine art.

The **Alte Nationalgalerie** (Old National Gallery; Map p446; ☎266 424 242; www.smb.museum; Bodestrasse 1-3; adult/concession €8/4; ⊙10am-6pm Fri-Wed, to 10pm Thu; 🚌100, 200, 🚉Hackescher Markt) trains its focus on 19th-century European art.

Berliner Dom CHURCH

(Berlin Cathedral; Map p446; ☎2026 9110; www.berlinerdom.de; Am Lustgarten; adult/concession €7/4; ⊙9am-8pm Mon-Sat, noon-8pm Sun Apr-Sep, to 7pm Oct-Mar; 🚌100, 200, 🚉Hackescher Markt) Pompous yet majestic, the Italian Renaissance-style former royal court church (1905) does triple duty as house of worship, museum and concert hall. Inside it's gilt to the hilt and outfitted with a lavish marble-and-onyx altar, a 7269-pipe Sauer organ and elaborate royal sarcophagi. Climb up the 267 steps to the gallery for glorious city views.

DDR Museum MUSEUM

(GDR Museum; Map p446; ☎847 123 731; www.ddr-museum.de; Karl-Liebknecht-Strasse 1; adult/concession €6/4; ⊙10am-8pm Sun-Fri, to 10pm Sat; 👪; 🚌100, 200, 🚉Hackescher Markt) The touchy-feely GDR Museum does a delightful job at pulling back the Iron Curtain on an extinct society. You'll learn that in East Germany, kids were put through collective potty training, engineers earned little more than farmers and everyone, it seems, went on nudist holidays. The more sinister sides of GDR life are also addressed, including the chronic supply shortages and Stasi surveillance.

Humboldt-Box MUSEUM

(Map p446; ☎0180-503 0707; www.humboldt-box.com; Schlossplatz; adult/concession €4/2.50; ⊙10am-8pm Apr-Oct, to 6pm Nov-Mar; 🚌100, 200, 🚉Alexanderplatz, Hackescher Markt) This oddly shaped structure offers a sneak preview of the planned reconstruction of the Berlin City Palace, to be known as Humboldtforum, on Schlossplatz, opposite the Museumsinsel museums. On display are teasers from each future resident – the Ethnological Museum, the Museum of Asian Art and a library – along with a fantastically detailed model of the historic city centre. Great views from the upstairs cafe terrace.

Fernsehturm LANDMARK

(Map p446; www.tv-turm.de; Panoramastrasse 1a; adult/child €12/7.50, VIP tickets €19.50/11.50; ⊙9am-midnight Mar-Oct, from 10am Nov-Feb; S Alexanderplatz, 🚉Alexanderplatz) Germany's tallest structure, the needle-like TV Tower is as iconic to Berlin as the Eiffel Tower is to Paris and has been soaring 368m high (including the antenna) since 1969. Come early to beat the queue for the lift to the panorama platform at 203m. There's also lovably stuffy cafe, which makes one revolution in 30 minutes.

FREE **Hackesche Höfe** HISTORIC SITE

(Map p446; ☎2809 8010; www.hackesche-hoefe.com; Rosenthaler Strasse 40/41, Sophienstrasse 6; 🚌M1, 🚉Hackescher Markt) The Hackesche Höfe is the largest and most famous of the interlinked courtyard complexes peppered throughout the Scheunenviertel. Take your sweet time pottering around this tangle of cafes, galleries, boutiques and entertainment venues. Court I, festooned with art nouveau tiles, is the prettiest.

Neue Synagoge SYNAGOGUE

(Map p446; ☎8802 8300; www.cjudaicum.de; Oranienburger Strasse 28-30; adult/concession €3/2; ⊙10am-8pm Sun & Mon, to 6pm Tue-Thu, to 5pm Fri, reduced hours Nov-Apr; S Oranienburger Tor, 🚉Oranienburger Strasse) The sparkling gilded dome of the New Synagogue is the most visible symbol of Berlin's revitalised Jewish community. The 1866 original was Germany's largest synagogue but its modern incarnation is more a place of remembrance called Centrum Judaicum.

Kreuzberg & Friedrichshain

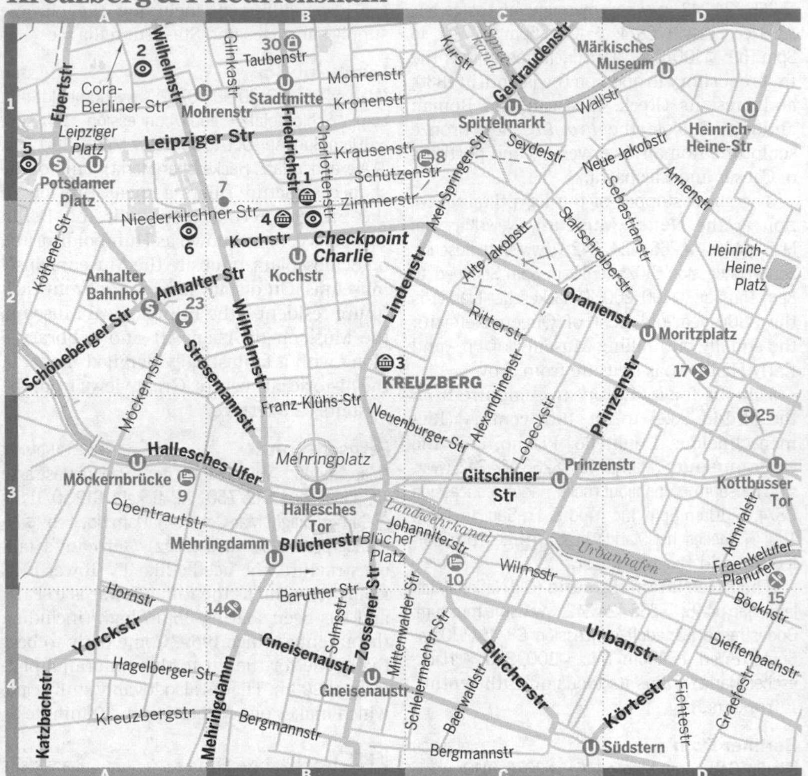

TOP CHOICE **Gedenkstätte Berliner Mauer** MEMORIAL

(☎467 986 666; www.berliner-mauer-gedenkstaette.de; Bernauer Strasse btwn Gartenstrasse & Brunnenstrasse; ⌚9.30am-7pm Apr-Oct, to 6pm Nov-Mar, open-air exhibit 24hr; Ⓡ Nordbahnhof) The central memorial site of German division incorporates a stretch of original Berlin Wall along with vestiges of the border installations, escape tunnels, a chapel and a monument. Multimedia stations, 'archaeological windows' and markers sprinkled throughout the memorial provide detailed background.

POTSDAMER PLATZ & TIERGARTEN

Berlin newest quarter, Potsdamer Platz, was forged in the 1990s from ground once bisected by the Berlin Wall. It's a showcase of contemporary architecture by such illustrious architects as Renzo Piano and Helmut Jahn whose flashy Sony Center – anchored by a plaza canopied by a tentlike glass roof – is the most eye-catching complex.

Just west of Potsdamer Platz, is the **Kulturforum**, a cluster of art museums of which the Gemäldegalerie and the Neue Nationalgalerie are standouts. Also here is the world-class Berliner Philharmonie. The leafy Tiergarten, meanwhile, with its rambling paths and hidden beer gardens, makes for a perfect sightseeing break.

Museum für Film und Fernsehen MUSEUM

(☎300 9030; www.deutsche-kinemathek.de; Potsdamer Strasse 2; adult/concession €6/4.50; ⌚10am-6pm Tue, Wed & Fri-Sun, to 8pm Thu; 🚌200, Ⓢ Potsdamer Platz, Ⓡ Potsdamer Platz) Every February, celluloid celebs sashay down the red carpet at Potsdamer Platz venues during the Berlin International Film Festival. Germany's film history, meanwhile, gets the star treatment year-round in this engaging museum. Skip through galleries dedicated to pioneers like Fritz Lang, groundbreaking

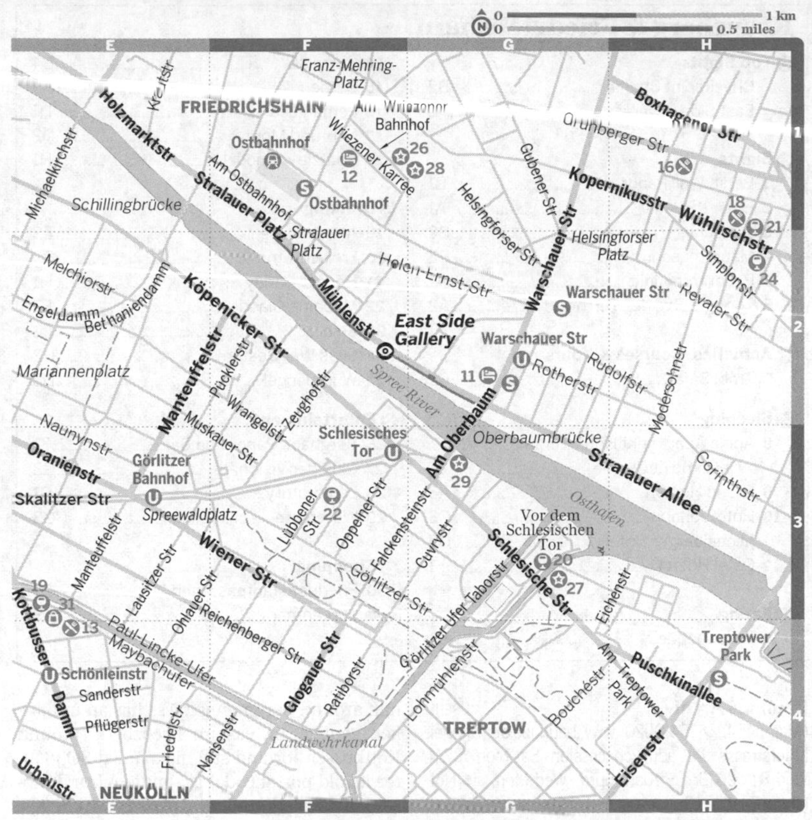

movies like Leni Riefenstahl's *Olympia* and legendary divas like Marlene Dietrich. The TV exhibit has more niche appeal but is still fun if you want to know what *Star Trek* sounds like in German.

Panoramapunkt VIEWPOINT
(Map p450; ☎2593 7080; www.panoramapunkt.de; Potsdamer Platz 1; adult/concession €5.50/4; ⏲10am-8pm, last ride 7.30pm, reduced hours in winter; 🚌M41, 200, Ⓢ Potsdamer Platz, Ⓤ Potsdamer Platz) A super-speedy lift yo-yos up and down the red-brick Kollhoff Building on Potsdamer Platz for fabulous 360-degree views from a lofty 100m. Information panels trace the square's history and there's a cafe to boot.

Neue Nationalgalerie GALLERY
(Map p454; ☎266 2951; www.neue-nationalgalerie.de; Potsdamer Strasse 50; adult/concession €10/5; ⏲10am-6pm Tue, Wed & Fri, to 10pm Thu, 11am-6pm Sat & Sun; Ⓢ Potzdamer Platz, Ⓤ Potsdamer Platz) The New National Gallery is a glass and steel temple designed in 1968 by Ludwig Mies van der Rohe. It presents changing exhibits of paintings and sculpture created by 20th-century European artists before 1960. Look for works by Picasso, Miró and Klee, along with German expressionists like Otto Dix, George Grosz and Ernst Ludwig Kirchner.

Gemäldegalerie GALLERY
(Map p454; ☎266 424 242; www.smb.museum/gg; Matthäikirchplatz 8; adult/concession €8/4; ⏲10am-6pm Tue, Wed & Fri-Sun, to 10pm Thu; 🚌M29, M41, 200, Ⓢ Potsdamer Platz, Ⓤ Potsdamer Platz) The principal Kulturforum museum boasts one of the world's finest and most comprehensive collections of European art from the 13th to the 18th centuries. Wear comfy shoes when exploring the 72 galleries: a walk past masterpieces by Rembrandt, Dürer, Vermeer, Gainsborough and many more Old Masters covers almost 2km.

Kreuzberg & Friedrichshain

Top Sights

Checkpoint Charlie ... B2
East Side Gallery ... F2

Sights

1 Berlin Wall Panorama ... B1
2 Hitler's Bunker ... A1
3 Jüdisches Museum ... B2
4 Mauermuseum ... B2
5 Panoramapunkt ... A1
6 Topographie des Terrors ... A2

Activities, Courses & Tours

7 Trabi Safari ... B2

Sleeping

8 Adina Apartment Hotel Berlin Checkpoint Charlie ... C1
9 Grand Hostel ... A3
10 Hotel Johann ... C3
11 Michelberger Hotel ... G2
12 Ostel Hostel ... F1

Eating

13 Cafe Jacques ... E4
14 Curry 36 ... B4
15 Defne ... D3
16 Lemon Leaf ... H1
17 Max und Moritz ... D2
18 Spätzle & Knödel ... H1

Drinking

19 Ankerklause ... E3
20 Freischwimmer ... G3
21 Hops & Barley ... H1
22 Madame Claude ... F3
23 Solar ... A2
24 Süss War Gestern ... H2
25 Würgeengel ... D3

Entertainment

26 Berghain/Panorama Bar ... F1
27 Club der Visionäre ... G3
28 Lab.oratory ... G1
29 Watergate ... G3

Shopping

30 Friedrichstadtpassagen ... B1
31 Türkenmarkt ... E3

Bauhaus Archiv MUSEUM

(Map p454; ☎254 0020; www.bauhaus.de; Klingelhöferstrasse 14; adult/concession Sat-Mon €7/4, Wed-Fri €6/3; ⏰10am-5pm Wed-Mon; S Nollendorfplatz) Changing exhibits using study notes, workshop pieces, photographs, blueprints, models and other objects and documents, illustrate the theories of this influential 20th-century design movement. Bauhaus founder Walter Gropius himself drafted the blueprints for the distinctive white shed-roofed building.

FREE **Topographie des Terrors** MEMORIAL

(Topography of Terror; Map p450; ☎2548 6703; www.topographie.de; Niederkirchner Strasse 8; ⏰10am-8pm May-Sep, to dusk Oct-Apr; 🚻; S Potsdamer Platz, R Potsdamer Platz) In the same spot where once stood the most feared institutions of Nazi Germany (including the Gestapo headquarters and the SS central command), this compelling exhibit dissects the anatomy of the Nazi state. A short stretch of the Berlin Wall runs along Niederkirchner Strasse.

KREUZBERG & FRIEDRICHSHAIN

Kreuzberg gets its street cred from being delightfully edgy and wacky. While the western half around Bergmannstrasse has an upmarket, genteel air, eastern Kreuzberg (around Kottbusser Tor and still nicknamed SO36 after its old postal code) is a multicultural mosaic of tousled students, aspiring creatives, shisha-smoking immigrants and international life artists. Spend a day searching for great street art, soaking up the multi-culti vibe, scarfing a shawarma, browsing vintage stores and hanging by the river or canal, then find out why Kreuzberg is also known as a night-crawler's paradise. Same goes for equally free-spirited Friedrichshain, across the Spree River in the former East Berlin.

FREE **East Side Gallery** HISTORIC SITE

(Map p450; www.eastsidegallery-berlin.de; Mühlenstrasse btwn Oberbaumbrücke & Ostbahnhof; ⏰24hr; S Warschauer Strasse, R Ostbahnhof, Warschauer Strasse) At 1.3km, the East Side Gallery is not only the longest surviving stretch of Berlin Wall, it is also the world's largest open-air mural collection. In 1989, dozens of international artists translated the era's global euphoria and optimism into more than 100 paintings that are a mix of political statements, drug-induced musings and truly artistic visions. It was restored in 2009.

Jüdisches Museum MUSEUM
(Jewish Museum; Map p450; ☎2599 3300; www.jmberlin.de; Lindenstrasse 9-14; adult/concession €5/2.50; ⏱10am-10pm Mon, to 8pm Tue-Sun, last admission 1hr before closing; Ⓢ Hallesches Tor, Kochstrasse) This engaging museum offers a chronicle of the trials and triumphs in 2000 years of Jewish history in Germany but it's Daniel Libeskind's landmark building that steals the show. A 3D metaphor for the tortured history of the Jewish people, its zigzag outline symbolises a broken Star of David, and its silvery titanium-zinc facade is sharply angled and pierced with small gashes.

Stasimuseum MUSEUM
(☎553 6854; www.stasimuseum.de; Haus 1, Ruschestrasse 103; adult/concession €5/4; ⏱11am-6pm Mon-Fri, noon-6pm Sat & Sun; Ⓢ Magdalenenstrasse) The former headquarters of East Germany's much-feared Ministry of State Security is now the Stasi Museum. Marvel at cunningly low-tech surveillance devices (hidden in watering cans, neckties, even rocks), a claustrophobic prisoner transport van and the obsessively neat offices of Stasi chief Erich Mielke. Other rooms introduce the ideology, rituals and institutions of GDR society. Panelling is partly in English.

Stasi Prison MEMORIAL SITE
(Gedenkstätte Hohenschönhausen; ☎9860 8230; www.stiftung-hsh.de; Genslerstrasse 66; tour adult/concession €5/2.50; ⏱tours hourly 11am-3pm Mon-Fri, 10am-4pm Sat & Sun, English tour 2.30pm daily; 🚊M5 to Freienwalder Strasse) Victims of Stasi persecution often ended up in this grim prison. Tours reveal the full extent of the terror and cruelty perpetrated upon thousands of suspected regime opponents, many utterly innocent. The prison is in the district of Lichtenberg, deep in the former East Berlin. Take tram M5 from Alexanderplatz to Freienwalder Strasse, then walk 10 minutes along Freienwalder Strasse.

CHARLOTTENBURG

The glittering heart of West Berlin during the Cold War, Charlottenburg has been eclipsed by historic Mitte and other eastern districts since reunification, but is now trying hard to stage a comeback with major construction and redevelopment around Zoo station. Its main artery is the 3.5km-long Kurfürstendamm (Ku'damm for short), Berlin's busiest shopping strip. Its main tourist attraction is the nicely restored Charlottenburg palace.

Schloss Charlottenburg PALACE
(☎320 911; www.spsg.de; Spandauer Damm 20-24; day pass adult/concession €15/11; 🚌145, 309, Ⓢ Richard-Wagner-Platz, Sophie-Charlotte-Platz) The grandest Prussian palace to survive in Berlin consists of the main building and three smaller structures scattered about the sprawling park. Each building charges separate admission; the day pass (*Tageskarte*) is good for one-day admission to every open building.

Charlottenburg palace started out as the summer residence of Sophie Charlotte, wife of King Friedrich I. The couple's baroque living quarters in the palace's oldest section, the **Altes Schloss** (☎320 911; www.spsg.de; Spandauer Damm; adult/concession €12/8; ⏱10am-6pm Tue-

TICKETS TO SAVINGS

If you're on a budget, various ticket deals and passes can help you stretch your euros further.

Bereichskarten The museum clusters on Museumsinsel and the Kulturforum offer area tickets good for same-day admission to all permanent collections in that particular area.

Berlin Museum Pass (www.visitberlin.de; adult/concession €19/9.50) Buys admission to the permanent exhibits of about 60 museums for three consecutive days, including top draws like the Pergamonmuseum. Sold at tourist offices and participating museums.

Berlin Welcome Card (www.visitberlin.de; 48-/72hr €17.90/23.90, 48hr incl Potsdam & up to 3 children under 15yr €19.90, 72hr incl Museumsinsel €34) Unlimited public transport and up to 50% discount to 200 sights, attractions and tours for periods of two, three or five days. It's also sold at tourist offices, U-Bahn and S-Bahn ticket vending machines and many hotels.

CityTourCard (www.citytourcard.com; 48hr/72hr/5 days €16.90/22.90/29.90) Similar to the Berlin Welcome Card, but a bit cheaper and with fewer discounts.

Charlottenburg

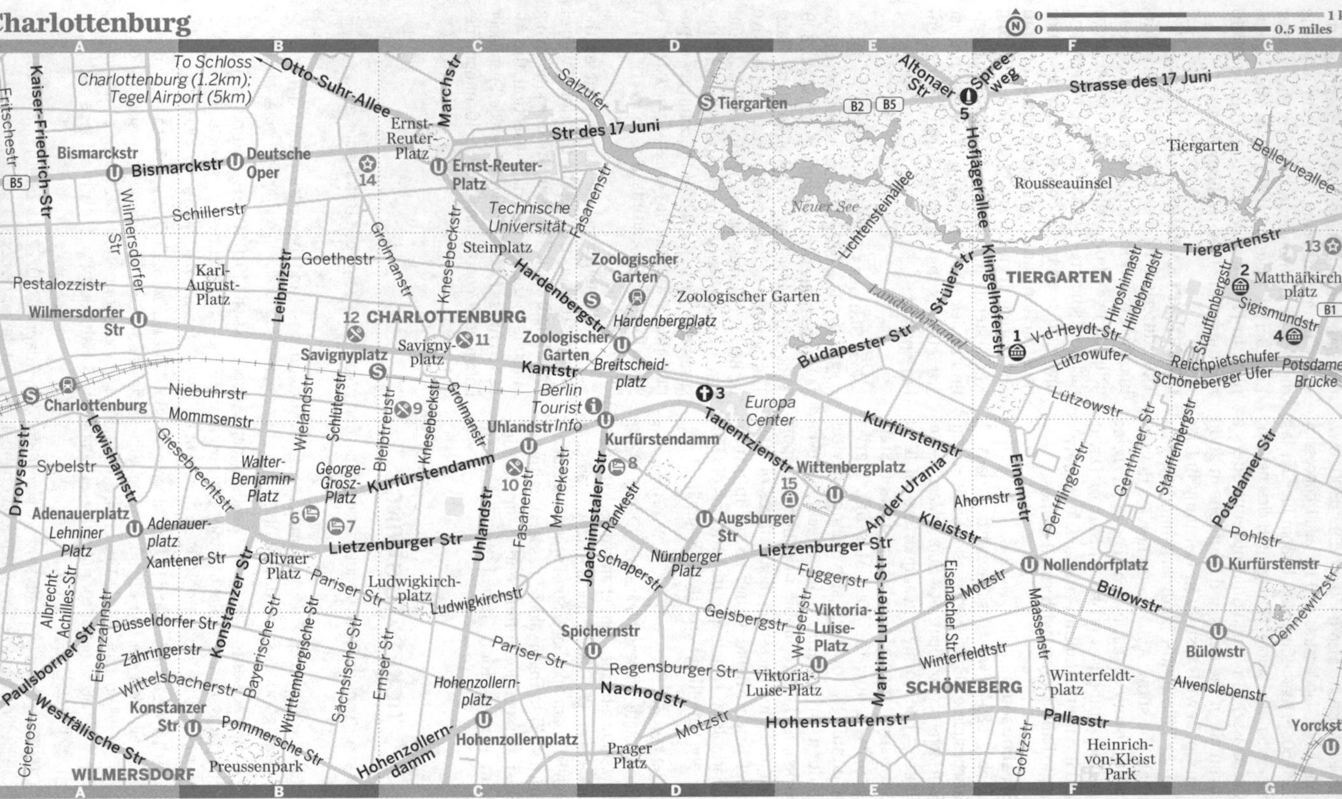

Charlottenburg

Sights

1 Bauhaus Archiv F2
2 Gemäldegalerie G2
3 Kaiser-Wilhelm-Gedächtniskirche D2
4 Neue Nationalgalerie G2
5 Siegessäule E1

Sleeping

6 Hotel Askanischer Hof B3
7 Hotel Bogota B3
8 Hotel Concorde Berlin D3

Eating

9 Ali Baba C2
10 Café-Restaurant Wintergarten im Literaturhaus C3
11 Dicke Wirtin C2
12 Good Friends B2

Entertainment

13 Berliner Philharmonie G2
14 Staatsoper unter den Linden @ Schillertheater B1

Shopping

15 KaDeWe E3

Sun Apr-Oct, to 5pm Tue-Sun Nov-Mar; 145, 309, S Richard-Wagner-Platz, Sophie-Charlotte-Platz), are an extravaganza in stucco, brocade and overall opulence, although the private chambers of Frederick the Great in the **Neuer Flügel** (New Wing; 320 911; www.spsg.de; Spandauer Damm 20-24; adult/concession incl audioguide €6/5; 10am-6pm Wed-Mon Apr-Oct, to 5pm Wed-Mon Nov-Mar; M45, 309, S Richard-Wagner-Platz, Sophie-Charlotte-Platz) – designed in flamboyant rococo style – are even more impressive.

Other buildings dotted around the park house 19th-century paintings (**Neuer Pavillon**), fancy porcelain (**Belvedere**) and dead royals (**Mausoleum**).

Kaiser-Wilhelm-Gedächtniskirche CHURCH
(Kaiser Wilhelm Memorial Church; Map p454; 218 5023; www.gedaechtniskirche.com; Breitscheidplatz; 9am-7pm; S Zoologischer Garten, Kurfürstendamm, Zoologischer Garten) The bombed-out tower of this landmark church in Charlottenburg serves as an antiwar memorial, standing quiet and dignified amid the roaring traffic. The 1895 original was a real beauty, as you can tell from the before and after pictures on the ground floor. The adjacent octagonal hall of worship, added in 1961, has amazing midnight-blue glass walls and a giant 'floating' Jesus.

Tours

Most of these English-language walking tours don't require reservations – just show up at one of the meeting points. Since these can change quite suddenly, we have not listed them here. Keep an eye out for flyers in hotel or hostel lobbies, or at tourist offices, or contact the companies directly.

Berlin Walks WALKING TOUR
(301 9194; www.berlinwalks.de; adult €12-15, concession €9-12) Get under the skin of Berlin's history and what makes the city tick today with the local expert guides of Berlin's longest-running English-language walking tour company.

New Berlin Tours WALKING TOUR
(www.newberlintours.com; adult €12-15, concession €10-15) Energetic and entertaining English-language walking tours by the pioneers of the donation-based 'free tour' and the pub crawl.

Fat Tire Bike Tours BICYCLE TOUR
(Map p446; 2404 7991; www.fattirebiketours.com/berlin; Panoramastrasse 1a; adult €24, concession €22; S Alexanderplatz, Alexanderplatz) Offers a huge range of tours, from standard city tours to themed tours along the former course of the Berlin Wall and/or a Cold War tour, historical tours and more.

Trabi Safari DRIVING TOUR
(Map p450; 2759 2273; www.trabi-safari.de; Zimmerstrasse 97; per person €30-90, Wall Ride €79-89, prices depending on group size; S Kochstrasse) Catch the *Good Bye, Lenin!* vibe on tours of Berlin's classic sights or the 'Wild East' with you driving or riding in convoy of a 'Trabi', East Germany's (now) cult car with live commentary (in English by prior arrangement) piped into your vehicle. Bring your drivers' license.

Sleeping

MITTE & PRENZLAUER BERG

TOP CHOICE **Circus Hotel** HOTEL €€
(Map p446; 2000 3939; www.circus-berlin.de; Rosenthaler Strasse 1; d €80-110; @; S Rosenthaler Platz) At our favourite budget boutique

DON'T MISS

BERLIN'S TIERGARTEN, A SWATH OF GREEN

Lolling about in the grass on a sunny afternoon is the quintessential Berlin pastime. Germans adore the outdoors and flock to urban green spaces whenever the weather is fine. They also dislike tan lines, so don't be surprised if you stumble upon locals sunbathing in the nude.

The Tiergarten is criss-crossed by a series of major roads and anchored by the Brandenburg Gate and the Reichstag on its northwestern edge. It's a tangle of curved walking and cycling paths, tiny ponds, open fields and thick woods. You'll probably get lost, but there are dozens of maps scattered about to help you find your way.

From the Reichstag, the Tiergarten's **carillon** (John-Foster-Dulles-Allee; 100 or 200) and the **Haus der Kulturen der Welt** (House of World Cultures; 397 870; www.hkw.de; John-Foster-Dulles-Allee 10; admission varies; exhibits 11am-7pm Wed-Mon; 100, S Bundestag) are clearly visible. The latter was the US contribution to the 1957 International Building Exposition and it's easy to see why locals call it the 'pregnant oyster'.

Further west, the wings of the **Siegessäule** (Victory Column; Map p454; Grosser Stern; 100, 200) were the *Wings of Desire* in that famous Wim Wenders film. This golden angel was built to commemorate Prussian military victories in the 19th century. However, there are better views than those at the column's peak.

hotel, none of the mod rooms are alike but all feature upbeat colours, thoughtful design details, sleek oak floors and quality beds. Unexpected perks include a well-stocked library and free iPod, netbook and DVD player rentals. Fabulous breakfast buffet to boot.

TOP CHOICE **EastSeven Berlin Hostel** HOSTEL €
(Map p446; 9362 2240; www.eastseven.de; Schwedter Strasse 7; dm €17-19, d €50; ; S Senefelderplatz) Friendly and fun, this small hostel is within strolling distance of hip hangouts and public transport. Cultural and language barriers melt quickly over a BBQ in the idyllic back garden, dinners in the modern kitchen (with dishwasher!) or chilling in the retro lounge. Come bedtime, retreat to comfy pine beds in brightly painted dorms or private rooms (baby beds are available).

Hotel Honigmond HOTEL €€
(Map p446; 284 4550; www.honigmond-berlin.de; Tieckstrasse 12; d €145-235; P; S Oranienburger Tor) This delightful hotel scores a perfect 10 on our 'charmometer', not for being particularly lavish but for its homey yet elegant ambience. The nicest rooms flaunt such historic features as ornate stucco ceilings, frescoes and parquet floors.

Hotel Amano HOTEL €€
(Map p446; 809 4150; www.amanogroup.de; Auguststrasse 43; d €80-160; P; S Rosenthaler Platz) This hit with designer-hotel devotees has inviting public areas dressed in brushed-copper walls and cocoa-hued banquettes. In the rather twee rooms, white furniture, oak floors and natural-toned fabrics create crisp cosiness. Great bar and fabulous summer rooftop terrace.

Motel One Berlin-Alexanderplatz HOTEL €
(Map p446; 2005 4080; www.motel-one.de; Dircksenstrasse 36; d from €69; P; S Alexanderplatz, Alexanderplatz) If you value location over luxury, this fast-growing budget designer chain makes for an excellent crash pad. Though small, rooms come with up-to-the-minute touches (flat-screen TVs, granite counters, massage showerheads, air-con) normally the staples of posher players. Check the website for other Motel One properties around town. Optional breakfast is €7.50.

Adina Apartment Hotel Berlin Checkpoint Charlie APARTMENT €€
(Map p450; 200 7670; www.adina.eu; Krausenstrasse 35-36; d €110-160, 1-bedroom apt from €140; P; S Stadtmitte, Spittelmarkt) Adina's contemporary and roomy one- and two-bedroom apartments with full kitchens are tailor-made for cost-conscious families, anyone in need of elbow room, and self-caterers (a supermarket is a minute away). Kitchenless rooms also available. See the website about other Berlin Adina properties. Optional breakfast is €15.

Hotel Adlon Kempinski LUXURY HOTEL €€€
(Map p446; 226 10; www.kempinski.com; Pariser Platz, Unter den Linden 77; r from €250; ; S Brandenburger Tor, Brandenburger Tor)

Opposite Brandenburger Tor, the Adlon has been Berlin's most high-profile defender of the grand tradition since 1907. The striking lobby is a mere overture to the full symphony of luxury awaiting in spacious, amenity-laden rooms and suites where the decor is old-fashioned in a regal sort of way. A ritzy day spa, gourmet restaurants and the swank Felix nightclub add 21st-century spice.

Wombats City Hostel Berlin HOSTEL €
(Map p446; ☎8471 0820; www.wombats-hostels.com; Alte Schönhauser Strasse 2; dm/d €25/70; @; Rosa-Luxemburg-Platz) Wombat's has a long track record at getting hostelling right. From backpack-sized in-room lockers to individual reading lamps and a guest kitchen with dishwasher, the attention to detail here is impressive. Spacious rooms with bathrooms are as de rigueur as freebie linen and a welcome drink, best enjoyed with fellow party pilgrims in the 7th-floor Wombar.

Circus Hostel HOSTEL €
(Map p446; ☎2000 3939; www.circus-hostel.de; Weinbergsweg 1a; dm €23-29, d from €80, with shared bathroom from €64, 2-/4-person apt €95/150; @; Rosenthaler Platz) Clean, cheerfully painted rooms, abundant showers and competent, helpful staff are among factors that keep Circus at the top of the hostel heap. Welcome tech touches include laptop and Skype phone rentals and laptop-sized in-room lockers with integrated electrical plug. To download its free self-guided MP3 city tour, go to www.circus-berlin.de/bustour.

KREUZBERG & FRIEDRICHSHAIN

Grand Hostel HOSTEL €
(Map p450; ☎209 5450; www.grandhostel-berlin.de; Tempelhofer Ufer 14; dm €12-15, d €58; @; Möckernbrücke) Afternoon tea in the library? Check. Rooms with stucco-ornamented ceilings? Got 'em. Canal views? Yup. OK, the Grand Hostel may be no five-star hotel, but it is one of Berlin's most comfortable and atmospheric hostels in an 1870s building. Dorms and private rooms have quality single beds (linen costs €3) and large lockers.

Ostel Hostel HOSTEL €
(Map p450; ☎2576 8660; www.ostel.eu; Wriezener Karree 5; dm/d/apt from €15/64/80; P@; Ostbahnhof) Fancy a stay with a *Good Bye, Lenin!* vibe? Book a bed in this unusual hostel, which resuscitates socialist GDR charm with original furnishings sourced from flea markets, grannies' attics and eBay. Rates include linen, towels and wi-fi. It's within stumbling distance to Berghain/Panorama Bar (p461).

TOP CHOICE Michelberger Hotel HOTEL €€
(Map p450; ☎2977 8590; www.michelbergerhotel.com; Warschauer Strasse 39; d 000 180; ; Warschauer Strasse, Warschauer Strasse) The pinnacle of creative crash pads, Michelberger perfectly encapsulates Berlin's offbeat DIY spirit. Rooms don't hide their factory pedigree but are comfortable and come in sizes suitable for lovebirds, families or rock bands. The bar-reception-lobby often doubles as a party venue. Great for the young and forever young.

Hotel Johann HOTEL €€
(Map p450; ☎225 0740; www.hotel-johann-berlin.de; Johanniterstrasse 8; d €95-120; P@; Prinzenstrasse, Hallesches Tor) This 33-room hotel consistently tops the popularity charts, thanks to its eager-to-please service and rooms pairing minimalist designer style with historic flourishes. Nice garden and within strolling distance of the Jüdisches Museum.

CHARLOTTENBURG

TOP CHOICE Hotel Askanischer Hof HOTEL €€
(Map p454; ☎881 8033; www.askanischer-hof.de; Kurfürstendamm 53; d €120-180; ; Adenauerplatz) If you're after character and vintage flair, you'll find heaps of both at this 17-room jewel with a Roaring Twenties pedigree. No two rooms are alike but all are filled with antiques, lace curtains, frilly chandeliers and time-worn oriental rugs; often used for fashion shoots.

Hotel Bogota HOTEL €€
(Map p454; ☎881 5001; www.bogota.de; Schlüterstrasse 45; d €90-150, with shared bathroom €64-77; ; Uhlandstrasse) Bogota has charmed travellers with charisma and vintage flair since 1964. Helmut Newton studied with

BUS TOUR ON THE CHEAP

Get a crash course in 'Berlinology' by hopping on the upper deck of bus 100 or 200 at Zoologischer Garten or Alexanderplatz and letting the landmarks whoosh by for the price of a standard bus ticket (€2.40, day pass €6.50). Bus 100 goes via the Tiergarten, 200 via Potsdamer Platz. Without traffic, trips take about 30 minutes. Watch out for pickpockets.

fashion photographer Yva here in the 1930s and to this day the retro landmark hosts glam-mag photo shoots. Room sizes and amenities vary greatly, so ask to see a few before settling in.

Hotel Concorde Berlin HOTEL €€€
(Map p454; ☎800 9990; www.concorde-hotels.com/concordeberlin; Augsburger Strasse 41; d €150-300; P ❄ @ 📶; S Kurfürstendamm) Designed by German architect Jan Kleihues, from the curved limestone facade to the door knobs, the Concorde channels New York efficiency, French lightness of being and Berlin-style unpretentiousness. Rooms and suites are supersized and accented with contemporary German art. Free wi-fi. Optional breakfast is €28.

Eating

If you crave traditional German comfort food, you'll certainly find plenty of places in Berlin to indulge in pork knuckles, smoked pork chops and calves liver. These days, though, 'typical' local fare is lighter, healthier, creative and more likely to come from organic eateries, a UN worth of ethnic restaurants and gourmet kitchens, including 13 that flaunt Michelin stars.

Berlin is a snacker's paradise, with Turkish (your best bet), *Wurst* (sausage), Greek, Italian and Chinese snack stalls throughout the city. Meat eaters should not leave the city without trying Berlin's famous *Currywurst*.

Excellent farmers markets include those at **Kollwitzplatz** (Kollwitzstrasse; ⏲noon-7pm Thu, 9am-4pm Sat; S Senefelderplatz) in Prenzlauer Berg and the **Türkenmarkt** (Turkish Market; Map p450; www.tuerkenmarkt.de; Maybachufer; ⏲11am-6.30pm Tue & Fri; S Schönleinstrasse, Kottbusser Tor) in Kreuzberg.

MITTE & PRENZLAUER BERG

TOP CHOICE **Katz Orange** INTERNATIONAL €€€
(Map p446; ☎983 208 430; www.katzorange.com; Bergstrasse 22; mains €13-22; ⏲dinner Tue-Sat year-round, lunch May-Sep; S Rosenthaler Platz) Wits its gourmet organic farm-to-table menu, feel-good country styling and swift and smiling servers, the 'Orange Cat' hits a gastro grand slam. The setting in a castle-like former brewery is stunning, especially in summer when the patio opens.

Oderquelle GERMAN €€
(☎4400 8080; Oderberger Strasse 27; mains €8-16; ⏲dinner; S Eberswalder Strasse) It's always fun to pop by this woodsy resto and see what's inspired the chef today. Most likely, it'll be a delicious well-crafted German meal, perhaps with a slight Mediterranean nuance. The generously topped and crispy *Flammekuche* (Alsatian pizza) are a reliable standby.

Hartweizen ITALIAN €€
(Map p446; ☎2849 3877; www.hartweizen.com; Torstrasse 96; mains €11-24; ⏲dinner Mon-Sat; S Rosenthaler Platz) This hipster favourite is eons away from Chianti-bottle kitsch. Instead, it is quite simply a top Italian restaurant focused on the feisty flavours of the Puglia region. The most creativity goes into the appetisers, but fish and meat are also first-rate, the pastas are homemade and the wines are fairly priced.

Konnopke's Imbiss GERMAN €
(Schönhauser Allee 44a; sausages €1.30-1.70; ⏲10am-8pm Mon-Fri, noon-8pm Sat; S Eberswalder Strasse) Brave the inevitable queue for great *Currywurst* from one of the city's cult sausage kitchens, now in shiny new glass digs but in the same historic spot since 1930.

Monsieur Vuong ASIAN €€
(Map p446; ☎9929 6924; www.monsieurvuong.de; Alte Schönhauser Strasse 46; mains around €8; ⏲noon-midnight; S Weinmeisterstrasse, Rosa-Luxemburg-Platz) At Berlin's 'godfather' of upbeat Indochina nosh-stops, the mini-menu features flavour-packed soups and two or three oft-changing mains. Come in the afternoon to avoid the feeding frenzy.

Schwarzwaldstuben GERMAN €€
(Map p446; ☎2809 8084; Tucholskystrasse 48; mains €7-14; 🚇Oranienburger Strasse) In the mood for a Hansel and Gretel moment? Then join the other 'lost kids' in this send-up of the Black Forest complete with plastic pines and baseball-capped Bambi heads. We can't get enough of the '*geschmelzte Maultaschen*' (sautéed ravioli-like pasta), the giant schnitzel and the Rothaus Tannenzäpfle beer.

Lucky Leek VEGAN €€
(☎6640 8710; www.lucky-leek.de; Kollwitzstrasse 46; mains around €12; ⏲dinner Tue & Thu-Sun; 🌿; S Senefelderplatz) At this popular vegan restaurant, quality ingredients, fearless flavour combinations, creative and colourful presentation and enthusiastic staff should make believers of even the most dedicated carnivores.

KREUZBERG & FRIEDRICHSHAIN

TOP CHOICE **Cafe Jacques** INTERNATIONAL €€€
(Map p450; ☎694 1048; Maybachufer 8; mains €12-20; ⏲dinner; S Schönleinstrasse) A favourite

with off-duty chefs and local foodies, Jacques infallibly charms with flattering candlelight, warm decor and fantastic wine. It's the perfect date spot but, quite frankly, you only have to be in love with good food to appreciate the French- and north African–inspired blackboard menu. Reservations essential.

TOP CHOICE Max und Moritz GERMAN €€
(Map p450; ☎6951 5911; www.maxundmoritzberlin.de; Oranienstrasse 162; mains €9-15; dinner; SMoritzplatz) This ode-to-old-school brewpub has lured hungry diners and drinkers with sudsy home brews and granny-style Berlin fare since 1902. A menu favourite is the *Kutschergulasch* (goulash cooked with beer).

Defne TURKISH €€
(Map p450; ☎8179 7111; www.defne-restaurant.de; Planufer 92c; mains €7.50-16; dinner; SKottbusser Tor, Schönleinstrasse) If you thought Turkish cuisine stopped at the doner kebab, canal-side Defne will teach you otherwise. The appetizer platter alone elicits intense food cravings (fabulous walnut-chilli paste!), but inventive mains such as *ali nacik* (sliced lamb with pureed eggplant and yoghurt) also warrant repeat visits.

Curry 36 GERMAN €
(Map p450; www.curry36.de; Mehringdamm 36; snacks €2-6; 9am-4pm Mon-Sat, to 3pm Sun; SMehringdamm) Top-ranked *Currywurst* purveyor that's been frying 'em up since the days when Madonna was singing about virgins.

Lemon Leaf ASIAN €
(Map p450; ☎2900 9471; Grünberger Strasse 69; mains €5-9; noon-midnight; ; SFrankfurter Tor) Cheap and cheerful, this place is always swarmed by local loyalists thanks to its light, inventive and fresh Indochina menu supplemented by daily specials. Raveworthy homemade mango lassi.

Spätzle & Knödel GERMAN €€
(Map p450; ☎2757 1151; Wühlischstrasse 20; mains €8-15; dinner; SSamariterstrasse) This elbows-on-the-table gastropub is a great place to get your southern German comfort food fix, with waist-expanding portions of roast pork, goulash and of course the eponymous *Spätzle* (German mac 'n' cheese) and *Knödel* (dumplings).

Schalander GERMAN €€
(☎8961 7073; www.schalander-berlin.de; Bänschstrasse 91; snacks €3.50-10, mains €8-14; 4pm-1am Mon-Fri, noon-1am Sat & Sun; ; SSamariterstrasse, Frankfurter Allee) See the pub action reflected in the very shiny steel vats that churn out the full-bodied pilsner, *dunkel* and *weizen* at this old-school gastropub far off the tourist track. The menu is big on southern German comfort food, along with *Flammkuche*.

CHARLOTTENBURG

Ali Baba ITALIAN €
(Map p454; ☎881 1350; www.alibaba-berlin.de; Bleibtreustrasse 45; dishes €3-9; 11am-2am Sun-Thu, to 3am Fri & Sat; Savignyplatz) Everybody feels like family at this been-here-forever port of call where the thin-crust pizza is delicious, the pasta piping hot and nothing costs more than €9.

Dicke Wirtin GERMAN €€
(Map p454; ☎312 4952; www.dicke-wirtin.de; Carmerstrasse 9; mains €6-15; noon-1am or later; Savignyplatz) Old Berlin charm oozes from every nook and cranny of this been-here-forever pub, which pours eight draught beers (including the superb Kloster Andechs) and nearly three dozen homemade schnapps varieties. Hearty local fare like roast pork, fried liver or breaded schnitzel keeps brains balanced.

Café-Restaurant Wintergarten im Literaturhaus INTERNATIONAL €€
(Map p454; ☎882 5414; www.literaturhaus-berlin.de; Fasanenstrasse 23; mains €8-16; 9.30am-1am; SUhlandstrasse) Tuck into dependably good seasonal bistro cuisine amid elegant Old Berlin flair in this graceful art nouveau villa or, if weather permits, in the idyllic garden. Breakfast is served until 2pm.

Good Friends CHINESE €€
(Map p454; ☎313 2659; www.goodfriends-berlin.de; Kantstrasse 30; mains €10-20; noon-2am; Savignyplatz) Sinophiles tired of the Kung Pao school of Chinese cooking will appreciate the real thing at this authentic Cantonese restaurant. The ducks dangling in the window are the overture to a menu long enough to confuse Confucius.

Drinking

Snug pubs, riverside beach bars, clubs, beer gardens, underground dives, DJ bars, snazzy hotel lounges, cocktail caverns – with such variety, finding a party pen to match your mood is not exactly a tall order. Kreuzberg and Friedrichshain are currently the edgiest bar-hopping grounds, with swanky Mitte and Charlottenburg being more suited for date nights than late nights. The line between cafe and bar is often blurred, with many places changing stripes as the hands move around the clock.

Madame Claude PUB

(Map p450; Lübbener Strasse 19; from 7pm; S Schlesisches Tor) Gravity is literally upended at Kreuzberg's David Lynch-ian booze burrow, where the furniture dangles from the ceiling and the moulding's on the floor. Don't worry, there are still comfy sofas for entertaining your posse, plus Wednesday's music quiz night, live music or DJs, and open-mike Sundays. Doesn't fill up until around 11pm.

Hops & Barley PUB

(Map p450; 2936 7534; Wühlischstrasse 40; S Warschauer Strasse, Warschauer Strasse) Conversation flows as freely as the unfiltered pilsner, malty *dunkel* (dark), fruity *weizen* (wheat) and potent cider produced right at this congenial Friedrichshain microbrewery inside a former butchers shop.

Würgeengel BAR

(Map p450; www.wuergeengel.de; Dresdener Strasse 122; from 7pm; S Kottbusser Tor) For a swish night out, point the compass to this '50s-style Kreuzberg cocktail cave, complete with glass ceiling, chandeliers and shiny black tables. The name, by the way, pays homage to the surreal 1962 Buñuel movie *Exterminating Angel*. Smoking allowed.

TOP CHOICE **Prater** BEER GARDEN

(448 5688; www.pratergarten.de; Kastanienallee 7-9; from noon Apr-Sep in good weather; S Eberswalder Strasse) In Prenzlauer Berg, Berlin's oldest beer garden (since 1837) has kept much of its traditional charm and is a fantastic place to hang and guzzle a cold one beneath the ancient chestnut trees (self-service). In foul weather or winter, the adjacent woodsy restaurant is a fine place to sample classic local fare (mains €8 to €19).

Neue Odessa Bar BAR

(Map p446; Torstrasse 89; S Rosenthaler Platz) Rub shoulders with a global mix of grown-ups with a hot fashion sense at this comfy-chic and always busy Mitte staple. The patterned wallpaper, velvet sofas and smart lamps create cosy ambience, no matter if your taste runs towards Krusovice or cocktails. Smoking allowed.

Ankerklause PUB

(Map p450; 693 5649; www.ankerklause.de; Kottbusser Damm 104; from 4pm Mon, from 10am Tue-Sun; S Kottbusser Tor) Ahoy there! This nautical kitsch tavern with an ass-kicking jukebox sets sail in an old harbour-master's shack, and is great for quaffing and waving to the boats puttering along the canal.

Süss War Gestern BAR

(Map p450; Wühlischstrasse 43; S Warschauer Strasse, Samariterstrasse, Warschauer Strasse, Ostkreuz) Chilled electro and well-mixed cocktails fuel the party spirit, and the low light makes everyone look good. Try the eponymous house cocktail made with real root ginger, ginger ale and whisky. Smoking ok. In Friedrichshain.

Berliner Republik PUB

(Map p446; www.die-berliner-republik.de; Schiffbauerdamm 8; 10am-6am; S Friedrichstrasse, Friedrichstrasse) Just as in a mini-stock exchange, the cost of drinks fluctuates with demand at this raucous riverside pub near Friedrichstrasse. Everyone goes Pavlovian when a heavy brass bell rings, signalling rock-bottom prices. Not too many locals but fun nonetheless.

Solar BAR

(Map p450; 0163-765-2700; www.solar-berlin.de; Stresemannstrasse 76; 6pm-2am Sun-Thu, to 4am Fri & Sat; Anhalter Bahnhof) Views of Potsdamer Platz and surrounds are truly impressive from this chic 17th-floor sky lounge above a posh restaurant (mains €18 to €29). Great for sunset drinks. Getting there aboard an exterior glass lift is half the fun. It's in a chunky high-rise behind the Pit Stop auto shop.

Freischwimmer BEER GARDEN

(Map p450; 6107 4309; www.freischwimmer-berlin.de; Vor dem Schlesischen Tor 2a; mains €7-15; from 4pm Tue-Fri, from 10am Sat & Sun; S Schlesisches Tor) In summertime, few places are more idyllic than this rustic ex-boathouse turned all-day, canal-side chill zone. Snacks and light meals are served, but they're more of an afterthought. It's sometimes open in winter – call ahead for hours.

☆ Entertainment

Sometimes it seems as though Berliners are the lotus eaters of Germany, people who love nothing better than a good time. Pack some stamina if you want to join them. With no curfew, this is a notoriously late city, where bars stay packed from dusk to dawn and beyond and some clubs don't hit their stride until 6am.

Zitty and *Tip* are the most widely read of the biweekly German-language listings magazines, available at news kiosks.

Nightclubs

Few clubs open before 11pm (and if you arrive before midnight you may be dancing solo) but they stay open well into the early hours – usually sunrise at least. With so many top electro DJs living in Berlin – and others happy to visit – the city is a virtual musical testing lab. Line-ups are often amazing and may include such DJ royalty as André Galluzzi, Ellen Allien, Ricardo Villalobos, Paul Kalkbrenner, Booka Shade and Richie Hawtin. To determine which clubs best match your style, go to www.clubmatcher.de.

Berghain/Panorama Bar CLUB

(Map p450; www.berghain.de; Wriezener Bahnhof; ⏲midnight Fri-Mon morning; Ⓡ Ostbahnhof) Still the holy grail of techno-electro clubs. Only world-class spinmasters heat up this hedonistic bass junkie hellhole inside a labyrinthine ex-power plant. The big factory floor (Berghain) is gay-leaning and pounds with minimal techno beats. One floor up, Panorama Bar is smaller, more mixed and pulsating with house and electro. Provocative art more than hints at the club's sexually libertine nature with its busy darkrooms, alcoves and toilets. Best time: after 4am. Strict door, no cameras.

Kaffee Burger CLUB

(Map p446; ☎2804 6495; www.kaffeeburger.de; Torstrasse 60; Ⓢ Rosa-Luxemburg-Platz) Nothing to do with either coffee or meat patties, this sweaty cult club with lovingly faded commie-era decor is the famous home of the twice-monthly Russendisko, fun-for-all concerts and parties with a sound policy that swings from indie and electro to klezmer punk without missing a beat.

Watergate CLUB

(Map p450; ☎6128 0394; www.water-gate.de; Falckensteinstrasse 49a; ⏲from 11pm Fri & Sat; Ⓢ Schlesisches Tor) Top DJs keep electro-hungry hipsters hot and sweaty till way past sunrise at this high-octane riverside club with two floors, panoramic windows and a floating terrace overlooking the Oberbaumbrücke. Long queues, tight door on weekends.

Cookies CLUB

(Map p446; www.cookies.ch; cnr Friedrichstrasse & Unter den Linden; ⏲from midnight Tue, Thu & Sat; Ⓢ Französische Strasse) This indoor playground complete with wicked little theme rooms (a mirror cabinet, a 'wedding' chapel) is still an essential after-dark player in Berlin. Top local and international electro DJs heat up the sexy crowd on the mosaic dance floor.

Clärchens Ballhaus CLUB

(Map p446; ☎282 9295; www.ballhaus.de; Auguststrasse 24; ⏲restaurant 12.30-11.30pm, dancing nightly; 🚊M1, Ⓡ Oranienburger Strasse) Yesteryear is now at this late, great 19th-century dance hall where groovers and grannies hoof it across the parquet without even a touch of irony. There are different sounds nightly – salsa to swing, tango to disco – and a live band on Saturday.

GAY & LESBIAN BERLIN

Berlin's legendary liberalism has spawned one of the world's biggest and most diverse GLBT playgrounds. The closest that Berlin comes to a 'gay village' is Schöneberg (Motzstrasse and Fuggerstrasse especially, get off at U-Bahn station Nollendorfplatz), where the rainbow flag has proudly flown since the 1920s. There's still plenty of (old-school) partying going on here.

Current hipster central is Kreuzberg, which teems with party pens along Mehringdamm and Oranienstrasse. Across the river, Friedrichshain has such key clubs as Berghain and the hardcore **Lab.oratory** (Map p450; www.lab-oratory.de; Am Wriezener Bahnhof; ⏲Thu-Mon; Ⓢ Ostbahnhof).

Mann-O-Meter (☎216 8008; www.mann-o-meter.de; Bülowstrasse 106; ⏲5-10pm Tue-Fri, 4-8pm Sat & Sun; Ⓢ Nollendorfplatz) is a one-stop information centre that also operates a hotline to report attacks on gays. **Siegessäule** (www.siegesaeule.de) is a weekly freebie mag that's the bible to all things gay and lesbian in town.

Weekend CLUB

(Map p446; www.week-end-berlin.de; Am Alexanderplatz 5; ⏲Thu-Sat; SAlexanderplatz, UAlexanderplatz) This house and electro den has an unbeatable location in a tower overlooking Alexanderplatz (in summer from the rooftop terrace) and is popular with suburban weekend warriors. Prices are hefty, door is middling.

Club der Visionäre CLUB

(Map p450; ☎6951 8942; www.clubdervisionaere.com; Am Flutgraben 1; ⏲from 2pm Mon-Fri, from noon Sat & Sun; SSchlesisches Tor, UTreptower Park) It's drinks, pizza and fine electro at this summertime chill and party playground in an old canalside boatshed. Hang out beneath the weeping willows or stake out some turf on the upstairs deck. On weekends party people invade 24/7.

Music & Opera

Berliner Philharmonie CLASSICAL MUSIC

(Map p454; ☎2548 8999; www.berliner-philharmoniker.de; Herbert-von-Karajan-Strasse 1; 🚌200, SPotsdamer Platz, UPotsdamer Platz) This landmark concert hall has supreme acoustics and, thanks to Hans Scharoun's clever terraced vineyard design, not a bad seat in the house. It's the home base of the world-famous Berliner Philharmoniker, currently led by Sir Simon Rattle.

Staatsoper unter den Linden @ Schillertheater OPERA

(Map p454; ☎information 203 540, tickets 2035 4555; www.staatsoper-berlin.de; Bismarckstrasse 110; SErnst-Reuter-Platz) Point your highbrow compass towards the Daniel Barenboim–led Staatsoper, Berlin's top opera company. While its historic digs on Unter den Linden are getting a facelift (probably until 2014), the high-calibre productions are staged at the Schiller Theater in Charlottenburg. All operas are sung in their original language.

Shopping

For high street shopping, head to Berlin's main shopping boulevard Kurfürstendamm and its extension Tauentzienstrasse, which are chock-a-bloc with the usual-suspect high-street chains. You'll find more of the same in malls such as Alexa near Alexanderplatz and Potsdamer Platz Arkaden at Potsdamer Platz. Indeed, getting the most out of shopping in Berlin means venturing off the high street and into the *Kieze* (neighbourhoods) for local flavour. Each comes with its own flair, identity and mix of stores calibrated to the needs, tastes and bank accounts of local residents.

Big shops in the centre are open from 10am to 8pm or 9pm. Local boutiques keep flexible hours, usually opening around 11am or noon and closing at 7pm.

Flea-market-hopping is a popular local pastime on the weekend, particularly Sundays. The **Berlin Art & Nostalgia Market** (Map p446; Georgenstrasse, Mitte; ⏲8am-5pm Sat & Sun; S Friedrichstrasse) is heavy on collectables, books, ethnic crafts and GDR memorabilia; the Flohmarkt am Mauerpark (p463) is known for its vintage wear and young-designer retro fashions; and the **Flohmarkt am Arkonaplatz** (www.mauerparkmarkt.de; Arkonaplatz; ⏲10am-4pm Sun; SBernauer Strasse) is the best spot to hit if you're looking for retro 1960s and 1970s furniture and accessories.

LOCAL KNOWLEDGE

SHOPPING BY NEIGHBOURHOOD

Unter den Linden Tacky souvenir shops meet big-label glamour haunts and top-flight galleries along Friedrichstrasse.

Scheunenviertel Boutique haven with Berlin-made fashions and accessories; also a high-end international designer and gallery quarter.

Charlottenburg Mainstream and couture on Kurfürstendamm, indie boutiques in the side streets, homewares on Kantstrasse.

Kreuzberg & Friedrichshain Vintage fashion, streetwear and music in indie boutiques, especially along Oranienstrasse and around Boxhagener Platz.

Prenzlauer Berg Berlin labels, niche boutiques around Kollwitzplatz, Helmholtzplatz and along Kastanienallee.

TOP CHOICE **KaDeWe** DEPARTMENT STORE

(Map p454; www.kadewe.de; Tauentzienstrasse 21-24; ⏲10am-8pm Mon-Thu, to 9pm Fri, 9.30am-8pm Sat; SWittenbergplatz) This venerable department store has an assortment so vast that a pirate-style campaign is the best way to plunder its bounty. Don't miss the legendary 6th-floor gourmet food hall.

Flohmarkt am Mauerpark MARKET
(www.mauerparkmarkt.de; Bernauer Strasse 63-64; ⏲10am-5pm Sun; S Eberwalder Strasse) On Sunday afternoons, join the throngs of thrifty trinket hunters, bleared-eyed clubbers and excited tourists sifting for treasure at this always busy flea market right where the Berlin Wall once ran.

Friedrichstadtpassagen SHOPPING CENTRE
(Map p450; Friedrichstrasse btwn Französische Strasse & Mohrenstrasse; ⏲10am-8pm Mon-Sat; S Französische Strasse, Stadtmitte) Even if you're not part of the Gucci and Prada brigade, the wow factor of this trio of indoor shopping arcades (called *Quartiere*) is undeniable.

Ampelmann Galerie SOUVENIRS
(Map p446; ☎4472 6438; www.ampelmann.de; Court V, Hackesche Höfe, Rosenthaler Strasse 40-41; ⏲9.30am-10pm Mon-Sat, 10am-7pm Sun; 🚋M1, 🚇Hackescher Markt) It took a vociferous grassroots campaign to save the little Ampelmann, the endearing fellow on East German pedestrian traffic lights. Now the beloved cult figure and global brand graces an entire store worth of T-shirts, fridge magnets and other knick-knacks.

Information

Berlin Tourismus (☎2500 2333; http://visitberlin.de; ⏲call centre 9am-7pm Mon-Fri, 10am-5pm Sat, 10am-2pm Sun) Berlin's tourist board operates three walk-in offices and a call centre with multilingual staff who field general questions and can make hotel and ticket bookings.

Hauptbahnhof (Europaplatz, ground fl, north entrance; ⏲8am-10pm; S Hauptbahnhof, 🚇Hauptbahnhof) Extended hours April to October.

Brandenburger Tor (Brandenburger Tor, Pariser Platz; ⏲9.30am-7pm daily; S Brandenburger Tor, 🚇Brandenburger Tor)

Kurfürstendamm (Neues Kranzler Eck, Kurfürstendamm 22; ⏲9.30am-8pm Mon-Sat, to 6pm Sun; S Kurfürstendamm) Extended hours April to October.

Getting There & Away

Air

Berlin's brand-new airport, Berlin Brandenburg Airport has been taking shape next to Schönefeld Airport, about 24km southeast of the city centre, since 2006. At the time of writing, construction problems and safety concerns have repeatedly delayed the original 2011 opening date; at press time, no new opening date had been announced. In the meantime, most major international airlines, as well as many discount carriers, including Ryanair, easyJet, Air Berlin and germanwings, continue to fly into Berlin's two other airports.

Tegel Airport (TXL; ☎01805 000 186; www.berlin-airport.de) About 8km northwest of the city centre.

Schönefeld Airport (SXF; ☎0180 5000 186; www.berlin-airport.de) About 22km southeast.

Bus

ZOB Berlin's 'central' bus station is in deepest western Berlin, next to the trade-fair grounds, about 4km west of Zoo Station.

BerlinLinienBus (☎861 9331; www.berlinlinienbus.de) The main operator; buy tickets online or at the ZOB Reisebüro ticket office at the bus station.

Deutsche Touring/Eurolines (☎069 790 3501; www.touring.de) Also has many domestic and international departures.

Busabout (www.busabout.com) Backpacker-oriented hop-on, hop-off service stops at the Citystay Hostel in Mitte.

Train

Berlin is well connected by train to other German cities, as well as to popular European destinations, including Prague, Warsaw and Amsterdam. All long-distance trains converge at the **Hauptbahnhof** (www.berlin-hauptbahnhof.de; Europaplatz, Washingtonplatz; S Hauptbahnhof, 🚇Hauptbahnhof).

The left-luggage office (€5 per piece per 24 hours) is behind the ReiseBank currency exchange on the first upper level, opposite the Reisezentrum. Self-service lockers are hidden on the lower level of the parking garage, accessible near the Kaiser's supermarket on the first lower floor.

Getting Around

To/From the Airport

TEGEL

The TXL bus connects Tegel with Alexanderplatz (40 minutes) every 10 minutes. For Kurfürstendamm and Zoo Station, take bus X9 (20 minutes). Tegel is not directly served by the U-Bahn, but both bus 109 and X9 stop at Jakob-Kaiser-Platz (U7), the station closest to the airport. Each of these trips costs €2.40. Taxi rides cost about €20 to Zoologischer Garten and €23 to Alexanderplatz and should take between 30 and 45 minutes.

SCHÖNEFELD

Airport-Express trains make the 30-minute trip to central Berlin twice hourly. Note: these are regular regional trains, identified as RE7 and RB14 in timetables. The S-Bahn S9 runs every 20 minutes and is slower but useful if you're headed to Friedrichshain or Prenzlauer Berg. For the Messe (trade-fair grounds), take the S45 to Südkreuz and change to the S41. Trains stop about 400m from

PUBLIC TRANSPORT TICKETS

Three tariff zones exist – A, B and C. Unless venturing to Potsdam or Schönefeld Airport, you'll only need an AB ticket.

TICKET	AB (€)	BC (€)	ABC (€)
Single	2.40	2.80	3.10
Day pass	6.50	6.80	7
Group day pass (up to 5 people)	15.50	15.80	16
7-day pass	28	28.90	34.60

the airport terminals. Free shuttle buses run every 10 minutes; walking takes about five minutes. You'll need a transport ticket covering zones ABC (€3.10). Taxi rides average €40 and take 35 minutes to an hour.

Bicycle

Many hostels and hotels have bikes for guest use, often for free or a nominal fee. Rental stations are everywhere – from convenience stores to clothing boutiques to petrol stations to bike shops. Keep an eye out for 'Rent-A-Bike' signs.

Bicycles may be taken aboard designated U-Bahn and S-Bahn carriages (usually the last car) as well as on trams and regional trains (RE, RB) and on night buses (Sunday to Thursday only). You need to get a separate ticket called a *Fahrradkarte* (bicycle ticket, €1.50).

Car & Motorcycle

Garage parking is expensive (about €2 per hour) and vehicles entering the environmental zone (within the S-Bahn rail ring) must display a special sticker (*Umweltplakette;* €5 to €15). Order it online at www.berlin.de/sen/umwelt/luftqualitaet/de/luftreinhalteplan/doku_umweltzone.shtml. The fine for getting caught without the sticker is €40. Rental cars automatically have this sticker.

Public Transport

One type of ticket is valid on all public transport, including the U-Bahn, buses, trams and ferries run by **BVG** (☎194 49; www.bvg.de), as well as the S-Bahn and regional RE, SE and RB trains operated by **Deutsche Bahn** (www.bahn.com).

Buy tickets from vending machines (English instructions available) in U-Bahn or S-Bahn stations and aboard trams, from bus drivers and at station offices and news kiosks sporting the yellow BVG logo.

Stamp all tickets, except those bought from bus drivers, before boarding or risk a €40 on-the-spot fine if caught without a validated ticket.

Services operate from 4am until just after midnight on weekdays, with half-hourly *Nachtbus* (night bus) services in between. At weekends, the U-Bahn and S-Bahn run all night long (except the U4 and U55).

Taxi

You can order a **taxi** (☎44 33 11, 20 20 20) by phone, flag one down or pick one up at a rank. Flagfall is €3.20, then it's €1.65 per km up to 7km and €1.28 for each km after that. Up to four passengers travel for the price of one. Tip about 10%. There is no surcharge for night trips.

AROUND BERLIN

Sachsenhausen Concentration Camp

In 1936 the Nazis opened a *Konzentrationslager* (concentration camp) for men in a disused brewery in Sachsenhausen, 35km north of Berlin. By 1945 about 200,000 prisoners had passed through the gates – cynically labelled, as at Auschwitz in Poland, *Arbeit Macht Frei* (Work Sets You Free). Tens of thousands died from hunger, exhaustion, illness, medical experiments and executions.

After the war the Soviets imprisoned some 60,000 German POWs in what was now Speziallager No 7 (Special Camp No 7); about 12,000 died of malnutrition and disease before it was dissolved in 1950.

Once you get to the **Sachsenhausen Memorial and Museum** (☎03301-200 200; www.stiftung-bg.de; admission free; ⏰8.30am-6pm mid-Mar–mid-Oct, to 4pm mid-Oct–mid-Mar), pick up a leaflet or, better yet, an audioguide at the visitor centre to get a better grasp of this huge site. Proceed to Tower A, the entrance gate, beyond which is the roll-call area and two restored barracks with exhibits illustrating the abysmal living conditions prisoners endured. Opposite, two original infirmary barracks have exhibits about the camp's poor medical care and on the horrid medical experiments performed on prisoners.

Further on, the Prisoners' Kitchen zeroes in on key moments in the camp's history during its various phases. Exhibits include instruments of torture, the original gallows and, in the cellar, heart-wrenching artwork scratched into the wall by prisoners. The most sickening displays, though, deal with the **Station Z extermination site**, a pit for shooting prisoners in the neck with a wooden 'catch' where bullets could be retrieved and recycled.

From Berlin take the frequent S1 train to Oranienburg station (€3.10, 45 minutes) from where it's a 2km signposted walk to the camp.

Potsdam

0331 / POP 150,000

Featuring ornate palaces and manicured parks, the Prussian royal seat of Potsdam is the most popular day trip from Berlin. Headlining the roll call of palaces is Schloss Sanssouci, the private retreat of King Friedrich II (Frederick the Great), who was also the visionary behind many of Potsdam's other fabulous pads and parks, which miraculously survived WWII with nary a shrapnel wound. When the shooting stopped, the Allies chose Schloss Cecilienhof for the Potsdam Conference of August 1945 to lay the groundwork for Germany's postwar fate.

Sights

Park Sanssouci GARDEN

(dawn-dusk) Park Sanssouci is the heart of Potsdam and what everyone comes to see. Its most celebrated palace is **Schloss Sanssouci** (www.spsg.de; adult/concession incl audioguide Apr-Oct €12/8, Nov-Mar €8/5; 10am-6pm Tue-Sun Apr-Oct, to 5pm Nov-Mar; 695, 606), a rococo extravaganza built by Frederick the Great in the 18th century. Admission is by timed ticket only; come early or, for guaranteed entry, join the city tour offered by the Potsdam tourist office. Standouts on the audio guided tours include the whimsically decorated Concert Hall, the intimate Library and the elegant Marble Room.

At the far western end of the park, the vast, domed **Neues Palais** (New Palace; 969 4200; Am Neuen Palais; adult/concession €6/5; 10am-6pm Wed-Mon Apr-Oct, to 5pm Nov-Mar; 695 or 605 to Neues Palais, to Potsdam, Park Sanssouci Bahnhof) was built for representational purposes and only used as a residence by the last German kaiser, Wilhelm II, until 1918. The interior is an opulent symphony of ceiling frescoes, gilded ornamentation and fanciful wall coverings.

Among the park's many other pearls, the **Chinesisches Haus** (Am Grünen Gitter; admission €2; 10am-6pm Tue-Sun May-Oct; 605 to Schloss Charlottenhof, 606 or 695 to Schloss Sanssouci, 91 to Schloss Charlottenhof) is a standout. It's a circular pavilion of gilded columns, palm trees and figures of Chinese musicians and animals that houses a porcelain collection.

Schloss Cecilienhof PALACE

(969 4244; www.spsg.de; Im Neuen Garten 11; tours adult/concession €6/5; 10am-6pm Tue-Sun Apr-Oct, to 5pm Nov-Mar; 603) This rustic English-style country palace was completed in 1917 for crown prince Wilhelm and his wife Cecilie but is most famous for hosting the 1945 Potsdam Conference where Stalin, Truman and Churchill (later Atlee) hammered out Germany's postwar fate. The conference room, with its giant round table, looks as though the delegates just left.

Altstadt HISTORIC AREA

Potsdam's historic town centre is east of Park Sanssouci. The baroque **Brandenburger Tor** (Brandenburg Gate) triumphal arch opens up to the Brandenburger Strasse shopping strip. Follow it to the pretty **Holländisches Viertel** (Dutch Quarter), a cluster of gabled red-brick houses filled with galleries, boutiques and restaurants.

Tours

Potsdam Sanssouci Tour GUIDED TOUR

(tours with/without Sanssouci Palace €27/16; Tue-Sun Apr-Oct) The local tourist office runs the 3½-hour Potsdam Sanssouci Tour, which checks off the highlights and guarantees admission to Schloss Sanssouci. Tours are in English and German and leave at 11.10am from the tourist office at the Hauptbahnhof.

Schiffahrt in Potsdam BOAT TOUR

(275 9210; www.schiffahrt-in-potsdam.de; Lange Brücke 6; 9.45am-7pm Apr-Oct) Boats cruise the Havel and the lakes around Potsdam. The most popular tour is the palace cruise (*Schlösserrundfahrt*; €13).

Information

Potsdam Tourist Office – Hauptbahnhof

(2755 8899; www.potsdamtourismus.com; inside the main train station; 9.30am-8pm

Mon-Sat, 10am-6pm Sun) There's another office at Brandenburger Tor.

Sanssouci Visitors Centre (☎969 4200; www.spsg.de; An der Orangerie 1, at the Historic Windmill; ⊙8.30am-6pm Apr-Oct, to 5pm Nov-Mar)

Getting There & Away

Regional trains leaving from Berlin-Hauptbahnhof and Zoologischer Garten take about half an hour to reach Potsdam Hauptbahnhof; some continue on to Potsdam-Charlottenhof and Potsdam-Sanssouci, which are actually closer to Park Sanssouci. The S7 from central Berlin makes the trip in about 40 minutes. You need a ticket covering zones A, B and C (€3) for either service.

DRESDEN & SAXONY

Saxony has everything you could want in a holiday: storybook castles peering down from craggy mountaintops, cobbled marketplaces serenaded by mighty churches, exuberant palaces, nostalgic steam trains and indigenous Sorb folk traditions. And through it all courses the broad-shouldered Elbe in its steady eternal flow out to the North Sea, past neatly arrayed vineyards, sculpted sandstone cliffs and villa-studded hillsides.

Many heavyweights have shaped Saxony's cultural landscape; Bach, Canaletto, Goethe and Wagner among them. Dresden and Leipzig grab top historical billing. The former became synonymous with the devastation of WWII, but has since resurrected its baroque heritage. And it was Leipzig that sparked the 'peaceful revolution' of 1989 that brought down the Berlin Wall and led to the momentous reunification of Germany.

Dresden

☎0351 / POP 512,000

Proof that there is life after death, Dresden has become one of Germany's most popular attractions, and for good reason. Restorations have returned the city to the glory days when it was famous throughout Europe as 'Florence on the Elbe', owing to the efforts of Italian artists, musicians, actors and master craftsmen who flocked to the court of Augustus the Strong, bestowing countless masterpieces upon the city.

The devastating bombing raids in 1945 levelled most of these treasures. But Dresden is a survivor and many of the most important landmarks have since been rebuilt, including the elegant Frauenkirche. Today, there's a constantly evolving arts and cultural scene and zinging pub and nightlife quarters, especially in the Outer Neustadt.

Sights

TOP CHOICE **Frauenkirche** CHURCH

(www.frauenkirche-dresden.de; Neumarkt; admission free, audioguide €2.50; ⊙usually 10am-noon & 1-6pm) The domed Frauenkirche – one of Dresden's most beloved symbols – has literally risen from the city's ashes. The original graced its skyline for two centuries before collapsing two days after the devastating February 1945 bombing. The East Germans left the rubble as a war memorial, but after reunification a grassroots movement helped raise the funds to rebuild the landmark. It was consecrated in November 2005.

A spitting image of the original, it may not bear the gravitas of age but that only slightly detracts from its festive beauty inside and out. The altar, reassembled from nearly 2000 fragments, is especially striking. You can also climb the **dome** (Neumarkt; adult/concession €8/5; ⊙10am-6pm Mon-Sat, 12.30-6pm Sun Mar-Oct, to 4pm Nov-Feb) for sweeping city views. The galleried interior is also a wonderful place for concerts, meditations and services. Check the website for the current schedule or stop by the **Frauenkirche Visitors Centre** (☎6560 6701; Weisse Gasse 8; movie €2; ⊙10am-7pm Mon-Fri, 10am-6pm Sat), which also screens a movie about the church's history and legacy.

Residenzschloss PALACE

(☎4914 2000; www.skd.museum; Schlossplatz; adult/concession €10/7.50; ⊙10am-6pm Wed-Mon) Dresden's fortresslike Renaissance city palace was home to the Saxon rulers from 1485 to 1918 and now shelters four precious collections, including the unmissable **Grünes Gewölbe** (Green Vault), a real-life Aladdin's Cave spilling over with precious objects wrought from gold, ivory, silver, diamonds and jewels. There's so much of it, two separate 'treasure chambers' – the Historisches Grünes Gewölbe and the Neues Grünes Gewölbe – are needed to display everything.

Another important collection in the palace is the **Kupferstich-Kabinett**, which counts around half a million prints and drawings by 20,000 artists (including Dürer, Rembrandt and Michelangelo) in its possession. Numismatists might want to drop by the **Münzkabinett** (Coin Cabinet) in the palace tower for a small array of historic coins and medals.

In 2013, the historic weapons and armour of the **Rüstkammer** (armoury), normally displayed in the Zwinger, also move into the Residenzschloss. Here, they join the exotic **Türckische Cammer** (Turkish Chamber), one of the richest collections of Ottoman art outside Turkey. A huge three-mast tent made of gold and silk is just one standout among many.

Tickets to the Residenzschloss are good for all these collections except for the **Historisches Grünes Gewölbe** (☎4914 2000; www.skd.museum; Residenzschloss, enter via Sophienstrasse or Kleiner Schlosshof; adult/under 16 incl audioguide €10/free; ⏲10am-7pm Wed-Mon). Admission here is by timed ticket only and you're strongly advised to order advance tickets online or by phone since only 40% are sold at the palace box office for same-day admission.

Zwinger MUSEUM
(☎4914 2000; www.skd.museum; Theaterplatz 1; adult/concession €10/7.50; ⏲10am-6pm Tue-Sun) A ravishing baroque complex, the sprawling Zwinger was primarily a royal party palace and now houses numerous precious collections. The most important is the **Gemäldegalerie Alte Meister**, which features a roll call of Old Masters including Botticelli, Titian, Rubens, Vermeer and Dürer. A key work is the 500-year-old *Sistine Madonna* by Raphael.

Admission also gives you access to the dazzling **Porzellansammlung** (Porcelain Collection) and the ancient scientific instruments, globes and timepieces of the **Mathematisch-Physikalischer Salon**.

Fürstenzug HISTORIC SITE
(Procession of Princes; Augustusstrasse) You'd need a really wide-angle lens to get a shot of Wulhelm Walther's amazing 102m-long tiled mural on the wall of the former Stendehaus (Royal Stables). The scene, a long row of royalty on horses, was painted in 1876 and then transferred to some 24,000 Meissen porcelain tiles in 1906.

Semperoper HISTORIC BUILDING
(☎320 7360; www.semperoper-erleben.de; Theaterplatz 2; tour adult/concession €8/4; ⏲varies) One of Germany's most famous opera houses, the original Semperoper burned down a mere three decades after its 1841 inauguration. Guided 45-minute tours operate almost daily (the 3pm tour is in English); exact times depend on the rehearsal and performance schedule. Buy advance tickets online to skip the queue.

NAVIGATING DRESDEN

The Elbe River splits Dresden in a rough V-shape, with the **Neustadt** (new city) to the north and the **Altstadt** (old city) to the south.

From the Hauptbahnhof, pedestrian-only **Prager Strasse** leads north into the Altstadt. Here there's a mix of communist-era triumphalism and modern-day commercialism. The lovely **Brühlsche Terrasse** runs along the Elbe between the Albertinum and the Zwinger, with boat docks below.

In the Neustadt, home to much of the city's nightlife, the main attractions for visitors are the **Albertplatz** and **Louisenstrasse** quarters. Here you'll find all manner of shops, galleries, funky boutiques and dozens of cafes, bars and clubs.

Albertinum GALLERY
(www.skd.museum; enter from Brühlsche Terrasse or Georg-Treu-Platz 2; adult/concession €8/6; ⏲10am-6pm; Ⓟ) After massive renovations following severe 2002 flood damage, the Renaissance-era former arsenal is now the stunning home of the **Galerie Neue Meister** (New Masters Gallery), an ark of paintings by leading artistic lights since the Romantic period – Caspar David Friedrich to Claude Monet and Gerhard Richter – in gorgeous rooms orbiting a light-filled central courtyard.

Militärhistorisches Museum Dresden MUSEUM
(☎823 2803; www.mhmbw.de; Olbrichtplatz 2; adult/concession €5/3; ⏲10am-6pm Tue-Sun, to 9pm Mon; 🚊7 or 8 to Stauffenbergallee) Even devout pacifists will be awed by this engaging museum which reopened in 2011 in a 19th-century arsenal bisected by a bold glass-and-steel wedge designed by Daniel Libeskind. Standouts among the countless intriguing objects are a 1975 Soyuz landing capsule, a V2 rocket and personal items of concentration-camp victims.

☞ Tours

Sächsische Dampfschiffahrt RIVER TOUR
(www.saechsische-dampfschiffahrt.de; adult/child from €16/8) Ninety-minute Elbe paddle-wheel steamer tours leave from the Terrassenufer

Dresden

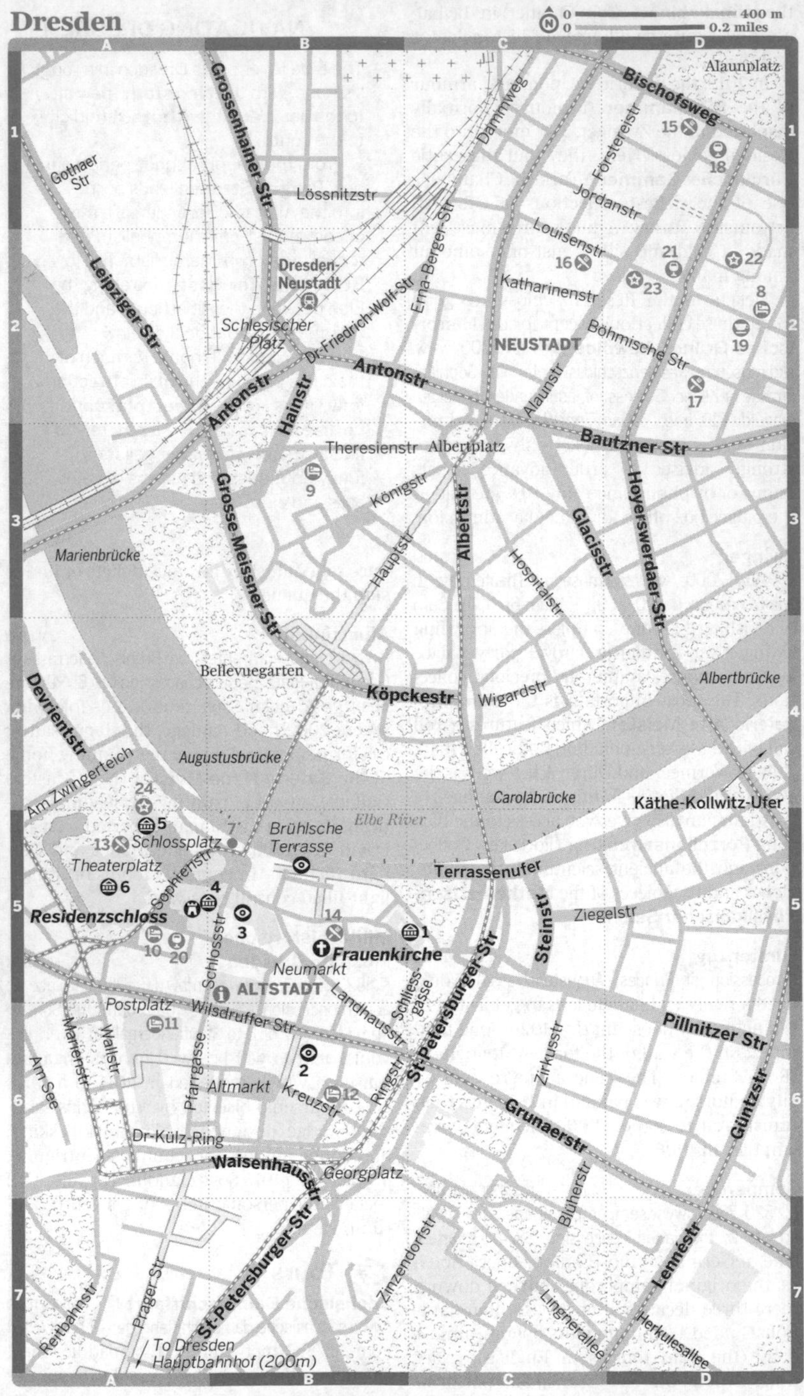

0 400 m
0 0.2 miles
Alaunplatz
Bischofsweg
Grossenhainer Str
Dammweg
Gothaer Str
Lössnitzstr
Förstereistr
Jordanstr
Louisenstr
Erna-Berger-Str
Dresden-Neustadt
Katharinenstr
Leipziger Str
Schlesischer Platz
Dr-Friedrich-Wolf-Str
Böhmische Str
NEUSTADT
Antonstr
Hainstr
Alaunstr
Bautzner Str
Theresienstr
Albertplatz
Königstr
Grosse Meissner Str
Albertstr
Glacisstr
Hoyerswerdaer Str
Hauptstr
Hospitalstr
Marienbrücke
Bellevuegärten
Köpckestr
Wigardstr
Albertbrücke
Devrientstr
Am Zwingerteich
Augustusbrücke
Carolabrücke
Käthe-Kollwitz-Ufer
Elbe River
Brühlsche Terrasse
Schlossplatz
Theaterplatz
Sophienstr
Terrassenufer
Residenzschloss
Steinstr
Ziegelstr
Frauenkirche
Neumarkt
Schlossstr
ALTSTADT
Landhausstr
Schliessgasse
St-Petersburger-Str
Postplatz
Wilsdruffer Str
Pillnitzer Str
Marienstr
Wallstr
Pfarrgasse
Ringstr
Zirkusstr
Am See
Altmarkt
Kreuzstr
Grunaerstr
Güntzstr
Dr-Külz-Ring
Waisenhausstr
Georgplatz
Blüherstr
Zinzendorfstr
Lennéstr
Reitbahnstr
Prager Str
Lingnerallee
Herkulesallee
To Dresden Hauptbahnhof (200m)

Dresden

Top Sights

Sights

Activities, Courses & Tours

Sleeping

Eating

Drinking

Entertainment

docks several times daily in summer along with services to Meissen and the villages of Saxon Switzerland.

Grosse Stadtrundfahrt BUS TOUR
(☎899 5650; www.stadtrundfahrt.com; day pass adult/concession €20/18; ⏲9.30am-5pm) This narrated hop-on, hop-off tour stops at 22 sights and also includes short walking tours of the Zwinger, Fürstenzug and Frauenkirche.

Sleeping

Hotel Martha Dresden HOTEL €€
(☎817 60; www.hotel-martha-hospiz.de; Nieritzstrasse 11; d €113-120; 📶) Fifty rooms with big windows, wooden floors and Biedermeier-inspired furnishings combine with an attractive winter garden and friendly staff into a pleasant place to hang your hat. The rustic restaurant serves local food and wine.

Radisson Blu Gewandhaus Hotel HOTEL €€
(☎494 90; www.radissonblu.com/gewandhaushotel-dresden; Ringstrasse 1; d from €133; P❄@📶≋) Public areas in this restored and converted 18th-century trading house are stunning and the Biedermeier-style rooms have marble-fitted bathrooms with whirlpool tubs. Tops for class and personal service.

Hostel Mondpalast HOSTEL €
(☎563 4050; www.mondpalast.de; Louisenstrasse 77; dm €14-19.50, d €48-56, linen €2, breakfast €6.50; @) Check in at the out-of-this-world bar-cafe (with cheap drinks) before being 'beamed up' to your room in the Moon Palace – each one dedicated to a sign of the zodiac or some other spacey theme. Bike rentals and large kitchen.

Hotel Taschenbergpalais Kempinski HOTEL €€€
(☎491 20; www.kempinski-dresden.de; Taschenberg 3; r €170-230; ❄@📶≋) Luxury is taken very seriously indeed at Dresden's grandest hotel. Checking in here buys views over the Zwinger from rakishly handsome rooms that beautifully bridge the traditional and the contemporary. In winter, the courtyard turns into an ice rink.

Pension am Zwinger PENSION €€
(☎8990 0100; www.pension-zwinger.de; Ostra-Allee 27; d €80-90; P@📶) Self-caterers, families and space-cravers will appreciate these bright, functional but stylish apartment-style rooms with basic kitchens. It's super-central and fairly quiet, despite being on a busy street. Note that the reception is at Maxstrasse 3 about 50m away.

Ibis Budget HOTEL €
(☎8339 3820; www.etaphotel.com; Wilsdruffer Strasse 25; r from €39; ❄@📶) The ship cabin-sized rooms have few frills but the key sights are just a hop, skip and jump away. With its upbeat ambience and friendly service, this is definitely a great budget base. It's part of the Altmarkt-Galerie shopping mall.

Eating

The Neustadt has oodles of cafes and restaurants, many found along Königstrasse and the streets north of Albertplatz. This is the most interesting part of town at night. Restaurants in the Altstadt are mostly tourist-geared.

TOP CHOICE La Casina Rosa ITALIAN €€
(☎801 4848; www.la-casina-rosa.de; Alaunstrasse 93; pizza & pasta €6.50-9.50; ⊙lunch Tue-Sat, dinner Mon-Sat) Everybody feels like family at this neighbourhood-adored trattoria with its warren of cosy rooms (plus idyllic summer garden) and feisty pasta and pizza, plus seasonally inspired specials. Menu stars include the 'piccola Capri' pizza topped with shrimp, zucchini and rucula. Reservations are key.

Raskolnikoff CAFE, BAR €€
(☎804 5706; www.raskolnikoff.de; Böhmische Strasse 34; mains €5-13; ⊙9am-2am) An artist squat in GDR times, Raskolnikoff still brims with artsy-bohemian flair. The menu is sorted by compass direction (borscht to fish soup and steak) and, in summer, the sweet little beer garden beckons. The beer itself comes from the Neustadt-based Schwingheuer brewery and is a steal at €2.40 per half litre. Upstairs are eight basic but handsomely done-up rooms (doubles €52 to €70).

Cafe Alte Meister INTERNATIONAL €€
(☎481 0426; www.altemeister.net; Theaterplatz 1a; mains €7-15; ⊙10am-1am) If you've worked up an appetite from museum-hopping, retreat to this elegant filling station between the Zwinger and the Semperoper for a smoked-trout sandwich, light salad, luscious cake or energy-restoring steak. A sculpture of composer Carl Maria von Weber guards the entrance.

PlanWirtschaft INTERNATIONAL €€
(☎801 3187; Louisenstrasse 20; mains €7-14; ⊙9am-1am) The winning formula at this long-time favourite: fresh ingredients sourced from local suppliers, a menu that dazzles with inventiveness and smiley staff that make even first-timers feel at home. Sit inside the cafe, the romantic garden or the cosy brick cellar.

Grand Café CAKES, SAXON €€
(☎496 2444; www.coselpalais-dresden.de; An der Frauenkirche 12; mains €10-15; ⊙10am-midnight) The cakes and imaginative mains are good, but, frankly, they almost play second fiddle to the gold-trimmed baroque setting of the Coselpalais. A stylish refuelling stop after climbing the Frauenkirche dome.

Drinking

If you're up for a night on the razzle, head out to the buzzing bars and cafes of the Neustadt, especially along Alaunstrasse, Louisenstrasse and Görlitzer Strasse.

Café 100 PUB
(☎273 5010; www.cafe100.de; Alaunstrasse 100; ⊙8pm-late) One of the first pubs in the Neustadt to open after reunification, Café 100 does double duty as a studenty pub on the ground floor and a candle-lit wine bar in the cavernous cellar.

Combo CAFE
(Louisenstrasse 66; ⊙9am-2am) Laid-back to the point of toppling, this '70s-retro cafe has enormous windows that fold back when the heat is on, 1960s airport furniture, and great coffee served with a side of water and two gummi bears.

Queens & Kings GAY BAR
(www.queens-dresden.de; Görlitzer Strasse 2b) The 'Queens' is dead, long live the 'Queens & Kings', across the street from the original gay fave party palace. The new version is more modern, a tad chicer and dressed in flamboyant colours.

Karl May Bar BAR
(☎491 20; www.kempinski.com; Taschenberg 3; ⊙6pm-2am) Cocktail connoisseurs gravitate to this sophisticated saloon inside the Taschenbergpalais hotel. Sink into a heavy burgundy-coloured leather chair to sip tried-and-true classics. Live music Friday and Saturday, happy hour 6pm to 8pm.

Entertainment

Semperoper Dresden OPERA
(☎491 1705; www.semperoper.de; Theaterplatz 2; ⊙ticket office 10am-6pm Mon-Fri, 10am-5pm Sat & Sun) Dresden's famous opera house is the home of the Sächsische Staatsoper Dresden, which puts on brilliant performances that usually sell out. Tickets are sold by phone, in person and online.

Blue Note JAZZ
(☎8014275; www.jazzdepartment.com; Görlitzer Strasse 2b; ⊙8pm-5am) Small, smoky and smooth, this converted smithy has concerts featuring regional talent almost nightly (usually jazz, but also rock and Latin), then turns into a night-owl magnet until the wee

hours. Many concerts are free. Global beers and awesome single malt whisky selection.

Katy's Garage LIVE MUSIC
(www.katysgarage.de; Alaunstrasse 48) As the name suggests, this cavernous party pit is set in a former tyre shop with matching decor and drinks named after car parts. You know the crowd skews young if one of their theme nights is the 'Älternabend' for people over 25.

Information

Tourist office - Hauptbahnhof (Hauptbahnhof; ⏲9am-7pm)

Tourist office Frauenkirche (Schlossstrasse 23; ⏲10am-7pm Mon-Fri, 10am-6pm Sat, 10am-3pm Sun, reduced hours Jan-Mar)

Getting There & Around

Dresden airport is about 9km north of the city centre. The S2 train links the airport with the city centre several times hourly (€2). Taxis are about €20.

By train, Dresden is linked to such major cities as Leipzig (€30, 70 minutes) and Berlin-Hauptbahnhof (€38, two hours) as well as to Meissen (€5.60, 40 minutes) by the local S1. Most trains stop at Hauptbahnhof (central train station) and at Dresden-Neustadt north of the river.

Buses and trams are run by **Dresdner Verkehrsbetriebe** (DVB; ☎857 1011). Fares within town cost €2, a day pass €5. Buy tickets from vending machines at stops or aboard trams. Trams 3, 7, 8 and 9 provide good links between the Hauptbahnhof, Altstadt and Neustadt.

Around Dresden

MEISSEN

☎03521 / POP 29,000

Straddling the Elbe around 25km upstream from Dresden, Meissen is the cradle of European porcelain manufacturing and still hitches its tourism appeal to the world-famous china first cooked up in its imposing 1710 castle. Adjacent to the soaring Gothic cathedral, it crowns a ridge above the Altstadt whose meandering cobbled lanes offer an escape from the porcelain pilgrims rolling in by tour bus.

Sights

TOP CHOICE Erlebniswelt Haus Meissen MUSEUM
(☎468 208; www.meissen.com; Talstrasse 9; adult/child €9/4.50; ⏲9am-6pm May-Oct, 9am-5pm Nov-Apr) There's no 'quiet time' to arrive at the popular and unmissable porcelain museum, where you can witness the astonishing artistry and craftsmanship that makes Meissen porcelain unique. It's next to the porcelain factory, about 1km south of the Altstadt. Visits start with a 30-minute tour (with English audioguide) of the **Schauwerkstätten**, where you can observe live demonstrations of vase throwing, plate painting, figure moulding and the glazing process. This helps you appreciate the fragile masterpieces displayed in the ensuing rooms.

Albrechtsburg CASTLE, MUSEUM
(☎352 147 070; www.albrechtsburg-meissen.de; Domplatz 1; adult/concession incl audioguide €8/4; ⏲10am-6pm Mar-Oct, 10am-5pm Nov-Feb) Lording it over Meissen, the 15th-century Albrechtsburg is famous as the birthplace of European porcelain. Production began in the castle in 1710 and only moved to a custom-built factory in 1863. An exhibit on the second floor chronicles how it all began.

The adjacent **cathedral** (☎452 490; adult/child €4/2; ⏲10am-6pm Mar-Oct, to 4pm Nov-Feb) contains an altarpiece by Lucas Cranach the Elder.

Information

Tourist office (www.touristinfo-meissen.de; Markt 3; ⏲10am-6pm Mon-Fri, to 4pm Sat & Sun Apr-Oct, 10am-5pm Mon-Fri, to 3pm Sat Nov-Mar)

Getting There & Away

Half-hourly S1 trains run from Dresden's Hauptbahnhof and Neustadt train stations (€5.80, 40 minutes). For the Erlebniswelt, get off at Meissen-Triebischtal.

Steam boats operated by **Sächsische Dampfschiffahrt** (☎0331-452 139; www.saechsische-dampfschiffahrt.de; one-way/return €14/19.50; ⏲May-Sep) depart from the Terrassenufer in Dresden. Consider going one way by boat and the other by train.

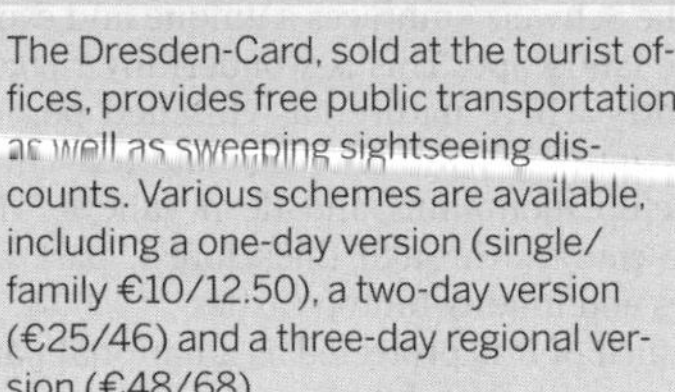

DRESDEN-CARD

The Dresden-Card, sold at the tourist offices, provides free public transportation as well as sweeping sightseeing discounts. Various schemes are available, including a one-day version (single/family €10/12.50), a two-day version (€25/46) and a three-day regional version (€48/68).

SAXON SWITZERLAND

About 40km south of Dresden, the Sächsische Schweiz embraces a unique and evocative landscape. This is wonderfully rugged country where nature has chiselled porous rock into bizarre columns, battered cliffs, tabletop mountains and deep valleys. The Elbe courses through thick forest, past villages and mighty hilltop castles.

Much of it is protected as a national park and popular with hikers and rock climbers. Even a short visit is rewarding, if you make your way to the **Bastei**, a stunning cluster of rock formations some 200m above the Elbe and the village of **Rathen**. It's a wonderland of fluted pinnacles and offers panoramic views of the surrounding forests, cliffs and mountains.

From April to October, steamers operated by Sächsische Dampfschiffahrt (p467) plough up the Elbe several times daily between Dresden and Bad Schandau, stopping in Rathen and other villages (5½ hours, adult/concession €23.90/19.10).

The region is also served frequently by the S1 train from Dresden. For the Bastei, get off at Rathen, catch the ferry across the Elbe, then follow a sweat-raising 30-minute trail to the top. Drivers can leave their car in the big car park near Rathen station.

Leipzig

0341 / POP 532,000

In Goethe's *Faust,* a character named Frosch calls Leipzig 'a little Paris'. He was wrong – Leipzig is more fun and infinitely less self-important than the Gallic capital. It's an important business and transport centre, a trade-fair mecca and – aside from Berlin – the most dynamic city in eastern Germany.

Culture has been big in Leipzig for centuries. After all, Bach's one-time backyard was also where Wagner was born and Mendelssohn-Bartholdy ran a music academy. Leipzig became known as the *Stadt der Helden* (City of Heroes) for its leading role in the 1989 'Peaceful Revolution' that led to the downfall of communist East Germany.

Sights

Leipzig's compact centre lies within a ring road along the town's medieval fortifications. Don't rush from sight to sight – wandering around Leipzig is a pleasure in itself, with many of the blocks around the central Markt criss-crossed by historic shopping arcades. Four good ones: **Steibs Hof** (100-year-old blue tiles and classic cafes), **Specks Hof** (soaring atrium, bookshops, cafes), **Jägerhofpassage** (galleries, theatre, antiques) and the classic **Mädlerpassage** (grand design, Auerbachs Keller restaurant).

TOP CHOICE **Nikolaikirche** CHURCH

(Church of St Nicholas; www.nikolaikirche-leipzig.de; Nikolaikirchhof 3; 10am-6pm Mon-Sat & during services 9.30am, 11.15am & 5pm Sun) The Church of St Nicholas has Romanesque and Gothic roots but since 1797 has sported a striking neoclassical interior with palmlike pillars and cream-coloured pews. It played a key role in the nonviolent movement that led to the collapse of East Germany by hosting 'peace prayers' every Monday at 5pm starting in 1982 (still held today).

FREE **Zeitgeschichtliches Forum** MUSEUM

(Forum of Contemporary History; 222 00; www.hdg.de/leipzig; Grimmaische Strasse 6; 9am-6pm Tue-Fri, 10am-6pm Sat & Sun) This fascinating exhibit tells the political history of the GDR from division and dictatorship to fall-of-the-Wall ecstasy and post-*Wende* blues. It's essential viewing for anyone seeking to understand the late country's inner workings.

FREE **Stasi Museum** MUSEUM

(961 2443; www.runde-ecke-leipzig.de; Dittrichring 24; 10am-6pm) In the GDR the walls had ears, as is chillingly documented in this exhibit in the former Leipzig headquarters of the East German secret police (the Stasi), a building known as the Runde Ecke (Round Corner). English-language audioguides aid in understanding the displays on propaganda, preposterous disguises, cunning surveillance devices, recruitment (even among children), scent storage and other chilling machinations that reveal the GDR's all-out zeal when it came to controlling, manipulating and repressing its own people.

Bach-Museum Leipzig MUSEUM

(913 7202; www.bach-leipzig.de; Thomaskirchhof 16; adult/concession €6/4, under 16yrs free; 10am-6pm Tue-Sun) Completely updated, this interactive museum does more than tell you about the life and accomplishments of heavyweight musician Johann Sebastian Bach. Learn how to date a Bach manuscript,

listen to baroque instruments or treat your ears to recordings of any of his compositions.

Thomaskirche CHURCH

(☎222 240; www.thomaskirche.org; Thomaskirchhof 18; tower €2; ⏲church 9am-6pm, tower 1pm, 2pm & 4.30pm Sat, 2pm & 3pm Sun) The composer Johann Sebastian Bach worked in the Thomaskirche as a cantor from 1723 until his death in 1750, and his remains lie buried beneath a bronze plate in front of the altar. The Thomanerchor (p474), once led by Bach, has been going strong since 1212. The tower can be climbed for sweeping city views.

Museum der Bildenden Künste MUSEUM

(☎216 990; www.mdbk.de; Katharinenstrasse 10; adult/concession €5/4; ⏲10am-6pm Tue & Thu-Sun, noon-8pm Wed) An edgy glass cube shelters Leipzig's well-respected collection of paintings from the 15th century to today, including works by native sons Max Beckmann and Neo Rauch, a chief representative of the post-reunification New Leipzig School.

Sleeping

TOP CHOICE **Steigenberger Grandhotel Handelshof** HOTEL €€€

(☎350 5810; www.steigenberger.com/Leipzig; Salzgässchen 6; r from €160; ❄@📶) Behind the imposing historic facade of a 1909 municipal trading hall, this luxe lodge outclasses most of Leipzig's hotels with its super-central location, charmingly efficient team and modern rooms dressed in crisp white-silver-purple colours. The stylish bi-level spa is the perfect bliss-out station.

Motel One HOTEL €

(☎337 4370; www.motel-one.de; Nikolaistrasse 23; d from €69, breakfast €7.50; P❄📶) The Leipzig outpost of this increasingly ubiquitous budget designer chain has a five-star location opposite the Nikolaikirche and also gets most other things right, from the Zeitgeist-capturing lobby-lounge to the snug but smartly designed rooms. No surprise it's often booked out.

arcona Living Bach 14 HOTEL, STUDIOS €€

(☎496 140; http://bach14.arcona.de; Thomaskirchhof 13/14; d from €90) In this musically themed marvel, within earshot of the Thomaskirche, you'll sleep sweetly in sleek rooms decorated with sound-sculpture lamps, Bach manuscript wallpaper and colours ranging from subdued olive to perky raspberry. The quietest ones are in the new garden wing but those in the historic front section have views of the church. Larger ones come with kitchenettes.

Quartier M APARTMENT €€

(☎2133 8800; www.apartment-leipzig.de; Markgrafenstrasse 10; apt €75-140; P) The building oozes old-world flair but the roomy apartments with full kitchens above an organic supermarket are state-of-the art and pack plenty of modern design cachet. Some units come with balcony or *terrasse*.

Hostel Sleepy Lion HOSTEL €

(☎993 9480; www.hostel-leipzig.de; Jacobstrasse 1; dm/d/apt from €12.50/42/55, linen €2.50, breakfast €3.50; @📶) Thumbs up for this clean and cheerfully painted hostel with a super-central location and clued-in staff. Every budget and privacy need can be accommodated in dorms sleeping four to 10, as well as in private rooms and apartments.

Eating

TOP CHOICE **Auerbachs Keller** GERMAN €€€

(☎216 100; www.auerbachs-keller-leipzig.de; Mädlerpassage; mains €14-22) Founded in 1525, cosy Auerbachs Keller is touristy, but the food's actually quite good and the setting memorable. In Goethe's *Faust - Part I*, Mephistopheles and Faust carouse here with students before riding off on a barrel. The scene is depicted on a carved tree trunk in what is now the Goethezimmer (Goethe Room), where the great writer allegedly came for 'inspiration'.

Zum Arabischen Coffe Baum CAFE €€

(☎961 0060; www.coffe-baum.de; Kleine Fleischergasse 4; mains €8-16; ⏲11am-midnight) One of Europe's oldest coffeehouses, this rambling outpost has hosted poets, politicians, professors and everyone else since 1720. The warren of rooms spread over several floors is an atmospheric spot to try a *Leipziger Lerche* (lark), a locally famous marzipan-filled shortcrust pastry. Other cakes, light meals and alcoholic drinks are also served.

Telegraph CAFE €€

(☎149 4990; www.cafe-telegraph.de; Dittrichring 18-20; mains €5-11; ⏲8am-midnight; 📶) Leipzig goes cosmopolitan at this high-ceilinged cafe with curved booths and wooden tables, a bilingual menu and a stack of international mags and dailies. It's a popular breakfast spot, available until a hangover-friendly 3pm. The menu is heavy on Austrian classics.

Gosenschenke 'Ohne Bedenken' BREWPUB €€
(☎566 2360; www.gosenschenke.de; Menckestrasse 5; mains €11-15; ⏰from noon daily Apr-Sep, from 4pm Mon-Fri & noon Sat & Sun Oct-Mar) This historic Leipzig institution, backed by the city's prettiest beer garden, is *the* place to sample *Gose*, a local top-fermented beer often served with a shot of liqueur. The menu requires that you surrender helplessly to your inner carnivore.

 Drinking & Entertainment

Party activity centres on three main areas: the boisterous Drallewatsch pub strip, the more upmarket theatre district around Gottschedstrasse, and the mix of trendy and alt-vibe joints along Karl-Liebknecht-Strasse (aka 'Südmeile').

Moritzbastei CAFE, BAR
(☎702 590; www.moritzbastei.de; Universitätsstrasse 9; dishes €2-5; ⏰cafe & Schwalbennest from 10am Mon-Fri, noon Sat, 9am Sun, Fuchsbau from 8pm; 📶) This time-honoured warren of historic cellars below the old city fortifications keeps an all-ages crowd happy with three locations in one: the sprawling **Cafe Barbarkane** for coffee, drinks or light meals; the intimate **Schwalbennest** for wine; and the cool **Fuchsbau** bar for cocktails. Bands or DJs often take over the space after dark. Summer terrace, too.

Noels Ballroom PUB
(☎303 2007; noels-ballroom.com; Kurt-Eisner-Strasse 43; ⏰5pm-late; 🚊10, 11 to Karl Liebknecht/Kurt-Eisner-Strasse) McCormacks has renamed itself but the high-octane vibe, foamy pints of Guinness and lovely flower-filled beer garden still make Noels one of the best Irish pubs in town.

naTo PUB
(☎391 5539; www.nato-leipzig.de; Karl-Liebknecht-Strasse 46) The mother of Leipzig's alternative-music pub-clubs, with jazz, experimental and indie sounds alongside films and theatre. Great outdoor seating in summer.

Thomanerchor CLASSICAL MUSIC
(☎984 4211; www.thomaskirche.org; Thomaskirchhof 18; tickets €2) This famous boys' choir performs Bach motets and cantatas at 6pm on Friday and 3pm on Saturday and also sings during Sunday services at 9.30am and 6pm at the Thomaskirche. To get a space, show up when doors open 45 minutes before concerts begin.

Gewandhausorchester CLASSICAL MUSIC
(☎127 0280; www.gewandhaus.de; Augustusplatz 8; tours €4.50; ⏰tours usually 12.30pm Thu) Once led by Felix Mendelssohn-Bartholdy, the Gewandhaus is one of Europe's finest and oldest civic orchestras (since 1743). Tickets are available by email, by phone and in person.

 Information

The Hauptbahnhof contains a large mall with shops open until 10pm Monday to Saturday and a few also on Sunday afternoon.

Tourist office (☎710 4260, room referral 710 4255; www.ltm-leipzig.de; Katharinenstrasse 8; ⏰9.30am-6pm Mon-Fri, to 4pm Sat, to 3pm Sun)

 Getting There & Away

Leipzig-Halle airport (LEJ; www.leipzig-halle-airport.de) is about 21km west of Leipzig and has domestic and international flights, including daily Ryanair service from London-Stansted, Rome, Milan and Malaga. It is linked to town by hourly RE train.

There are frequent trains to Frankfurt (€75, 3¾ hours), Dresden (€26, 1¼ hours) and Berlin (€45,1¼ hours), among others. Private Interconnex trains also go to Berlin twice daily (€19, 1¼ hours).

Getting Around

Buses and trams are run by **LVB** (☎194 49; www.lvb.de), which operates an information kiosk outside the Hauptbahnhof. The central tram station is here as well. Single tickets cost €1.50 for up to four stops and €2.10 for longer trips; day passes are €5.

WEIMAR & THURINGIA

Thuringia offers outstanding culture in its cities backed by the sprawling expanse of the Thuringian Forest. Top of the pops is Weimar, home to such seminal 18th-century poets and thinkers as Goethe and Schiller and the birthplace of the Bauhaus movement. Eisenach, where Bach was born, is dominated by the famous Wartburg castle, which is closely associated with the reformer Martin Luther, as is Erfurt, the state capital and a lively student town. It was the Nazis who put a dark stain on Thuringia's illustrious legacy when building Buchenwald concentration camp just outside Weimar.

Weimar

03643 / POP 65,500

Neither a monumental town nor a medieval one, Weimar appeals to those whose tastes run to cultural and intellectual pleasures. Over the centuries, it has been home to an entire pantheon of intellectual and creative giants, including Goethe, Schiller, Cranach, Bach, Herder, Liszt and Nietzsche. There are plenty of statues, plaques and museums to remind you of their legacy along with parks and gardens in which to take a break from the intellectual onslaught.

In the 20th century, Weimar won international name recognition as the place where the constitution of the Weimar Republic was drafted after WWI, though there are few reminders of this historical moment. Around the same time, Walter Gropius and other progressive architects founded the seminal Bauhaus design movement in town. The ghostly ruins of the nearby Buchenwald concentration camp, on the other hand, provide haunting evidence of the Nazi terror.

Sights

TOP CHOICE Goethe Haus & Nationalmuseum MUSEUM

(Frauenplan 1; combined ticket Goethe Haus & museum adult/concession €10.50/8.50, permanent museum exhibition only adult/concession €6.50/5.50; 9am-6pm Tue-Fri & Sun, to 7pm Sat) No other individual is as closely associated with Weimar as Johann Wolfgang von Goethe, who lived in this town from 1775 until his death in 1832, the last 50 years in what is now the **Goethe Haus**. This is where he worked, studied, researched and penned and other immortal works. His study and the bedroom where he died are both preserved in their original state. To get the most from your visit, use the audioguide (free). Visitors numbers are limited and tickets timed.

The adjacent museum, which zeroes in on Goethe's life and times, was being revamped at the time of research.

Schiller Haus MUSEUM

(Schillerstrasse 12; adult/concession €5/4; 9am-6pm Tue-Fri & Sun, to 7pm Sat) Dramatist (and Goethe's friend) Friedrich von Schiller lived in Weimar from 1799 until his early death in 1805. Study up on the man, his family and life before plunging on to the private quarters, including the study with his deathbed and the desk where he wrote *Wilhelm Tell* and other famous works.

Herzogin Anna Amalia Bibliothek LIBRARY

(www.klassik-stiftung.de; Platz der Demokratie 1; adult/concession incl audioguide €6.50/5.50; 9.30am-2.30pm Tue-Sun) Anna Amalia was an art-loving 18th-century duchess who had a penchant for collecting precious books that are now exhibited in a magnificent library which was beautifully restored after a disastrous 2004 fire. The magnificent Rokokosaal (Rococo Hall) is crammed with 40,000 tomes once used for research purposes by Goethe, Schiller and other Weimar hot shots. Entry is limited and by timed ticket, so book in advance or start queuing before the ticket office opens at 9.30am.

WORTH A TRIP

BUCHENWALD

The Buchenwald concentration camp **museum and memorial** (03643-4300; www.buchenwald.de; Ettersberg; buildings & exhibits 10am-6pm Tue-Sun Apr-Oct, to 4pm Tue-Sun Nov-Mar, grounds open until sunset) is 10km northwest of Weimar. Between 1937 and 1945, more than one-fifth of the 250,000 people incarcerated here died, among them such prominent German communists and social democrats as Ernst Thälmann and Rudolf Breitscheid. After 1943, prisoners were exploited in the production of weapons. Shortly before the end of the war, some 28,000 prisoners were sent on death marches.

After the war, the Soviet victors established Special Camp No 2, in which 7000 so-called anticommunists and ex-Nazis were literally worked to death.

Pamphlets and books in English are sold at the bookshop, where you can also rent an excellent multilanguage audioguide (€3 or €5 with images). Last admission is 30 minutes before closing but you really need at least an hour to do the site justice.

From Weimar, take bus 6 (direction Buchenwald) from Goetheplatz. By car, head north on Ettersburger Strasse from Weimar train station and turn left onto Blutstrasse.

Park an der Ilm PARK
This sprawling park, just east of the Altstadt, is as inspiring and romantic now as it was in Goethe's time. **Goethes Gartenhaus** (Goethe's Garden House; Park an der Ilm; adult/concession €4.50/3.50; ⏲10am-6pm Wed-Mon), where the writer lived from 1776 to 1782, is a highlight. A few decades later, the composer Franz Liszt resided – and wrote the *Faust Symphony* – in what is now the **Liszt-Haus** (Liszt House; Marienstrasse 17; adult/concession €4/3; ⏲10am-6pm Tue-Sun Apr-Sep, to 4pm Sat & Sun Oct-Mar).

Bauhaus Museum MUSEUM
(www.das-bauhaus-kommt.de; Theaterplatz; adult/concession €4.50/3.50; ⏲10am-6pm) Considering that Weimar is the birthplace of the influential Bauhaus school, this museum is a rather modest affair. Plans are to move to newer, larger premises, so check the situation again from 2013.

Sleeping

TOP CHOICE **Casa dei Colori** PENSION €€
(☎489 640; www.casa-colori.de; Eisfeld 1a; r €84-114; P ☎) This charming pension convincingly imports cheerfully exuberant Mediterranean flair to provincial Thuringia. The mostly good-sized rooms are dressed in bold colours and come with a small desk, a couple of comfy armchairs and a stylish bathroom.

Labyrinth Hostel HOSTEL €
(☎811 822; www.weimar-hostel.com; Goetheplatz 6; dm €14-21, s/d €35/46, linen €2.50, breakfast €3; @ ☎) Loads of imagination has gone into this professionally run hostel with artist-designed rooms where you sleep in a bed perched on stacks of books. Bathrooms are shared and so are the kitchen and the lovely rooftop terrace.

Hotel Amalienhof HOTEL €€
(☎5490; www.amalienhof-weimar.de; Amalienstrasse 2; s €67-75, d €97-105, ste €115-130; P ☎) The charms of this hotel are manifold: classy antique furnishings, richly styled rooms that point to history without burying you in it, and a late breakfast buffet for those who take their holidays seriously.

Hotel Elephant Weimar LUXURY HOTEL €€€
(☎8020; www.luxurycollection.com/elephant; Markt 19; r €109-221, ste €291; P @ ☎) The moment you enter this charmer's elegant art deco lobby, you sense that it's luxury all the way to the top. For over 300 years, this classic has wooed statesmen, artists, scholars and the merely rich with first-class service and amenities.

Eating

TOP CHOICE **Jo Hanns** GERMAN €€
(☎493 617; Scherfgasse 1; mains €11.50-17.50; ⏲11am-midnight) The food is satisfying but it's the 130 local wines that give Jo Hanns a leg up on the competition. No matter whether you order the classic steak, roast lamb or scallops and shrimp with mint-lime spaghetti, there's a bottle to suit.

Versilia ITALIAN €€
(☎770 359; www.versilia-weimar.de; Frauentorstrasse 17; mains €17.50-23.50, pasta €6-8.50; ⏲11am-midnight) This delightful wine bar and restaurant serves delicious antipasti, homemade pasta dishes and pan-Italian mains in a spacious setting.

ACC GERMAN €
(www.acc-cafe.de; Burgplatz 1; dishes €5-10; ⏲11-1am; ☎) Goethe's first pad upon arriving in Weimar is now an alt-vibe, artsy hang-out, where the food and wine are organic whenever possible and the upstairs gallery delivers a primer on the local art scene. The owners also rent out a room and a holiday flat (www.goethezimmer.de), both handsomely furnished.

Estragon HEALTH FOOD €
(Herderplatz 3; soups €3-5.50; ⏲10am-7pm Mon-Sat, noon-6pm Sun) There are days when a bowl of steamy soup feels as warm and embracing as a hug from a good friend. This little soup kitchen turns mostly organic ingredients into delicious flavour combos served in three sizes. It shares digs with a small organic supermarket.

Residenz-Café INTERNATIONAL €€
(Grüner Markt 4; mains €5-18; ⏲8am-1am; ✎) Everyone should find something to their taste at the 'Resi', one of Weimar's enduring favourites, no matter if it's time for breakfast, lunch, cake or dinner.

Information

Tourist office (☎7450; www.weimar.de; Markt 10; ⏲9.30am-7pm Mon-Sat, to 3pm Sun)

Getting There & Away

Weimar's Hauptbahnhof is a 20-minute walk from the centre. Frequent connections include

Erfurt (€8, 15 minutes), Eisenach (€14.40, one hour), Leipzig (€22, 1¼ hours), Dresden (€43, 2½ hours) and Berlin-Hauptbahnhof (€54, 2¼ hours).

Erfurt

0361 / POP 205,000

Thuringia's state capital is a scene-stealing combo of sweeping squares, time-worn alleyways, perky church towers, idyllic river scenery, and vintage inns and taverns. On the little Gera River, Erfurt was founded as a bishopric in 742 by the indefatigable missionary St Boniface. Rich merchants laid the foundation of the university in 1392, allowing students to study common law, rather than religious law. Its most famous graduate was the later Reformer Martin Luther, who studied philosophy here before becoming a monk at the local Augustinian monastery in 1505.

Sights

Mariendom CHURCH

(St Mary's Cathedral; Domplatz; 9am-6pm Mon-Sat, 1-6pm Sun) Erfurt's cathedral began life as a simple chapel founded by St Boniface, but the Gothic pile you see today has the hallmarks of the 14th century. Look for the superb stained-glass windows; the 12th-century Wolfram candelabrum in the shape of a man; the Gloriosa bell (1497); a Romanesque stucco Madonna; and the 14th-century choir stalls. The **Domstufen-Festspiele** (www.domstufen.de) classical music festival is held on the cathedral steps in July or August.

Severikirche CHURCH

(Domplatz; 9am-6pm Mon-Sat, 1-6pm Sun) This five-aisled hall church (1280) teems with such prized treasures as a stone Madonna (1345), a 15m-high baptismal font (1467), and the sarcophagus of St Severus.

WORTH A TRIP

EISENACH

On the edge of the Thuringian forest, Eisenach is the birthplace of Johann Sebastian Bach, but even the great composer plays second fiddle to the awe-inspiring hilltop **Wartburg castle** (www.wartburg-eisenach.de; tour adult/concession €9/5, museum & Luther study only €5/4; tours 8.30am-5pm, in English 1.30pm). Budget at least two hours: one for the guided tour, the rest for the museum and the grounds (views!).

When it comes to medieval castles and their importance in German history, the Wartburg is the mother lode. According to legend, the first buildings were put up in 1067 by the hilariously named local ruler Ludwig the Springer in an effort to protect his territory. In 1206, Europe's best minstrels met for the medieval version of *Pop Idol*, a song contest later immortalised in Richard Wagner's opera *Tannhäuser*. Shortly thereafter, Elisabeth, the most famous Wartburg woman, arrived. A Hungarian princess, she was married off to the local landgrave at age four and later chose to abandon court life for charitable work, earning canonisation quickly after her death in 1235.

The Wartburg's most famous resident, however, was Martin Luther, who went into hiding here in 1521 under the assumed name of Junker Jörg after being excommunicated and placed under papal ban. During this 10-month stay, he translated the New Testament from Greek into German, contributing enormously to the development of the written German language.

Bach fans, meanwhile, should head down into town where the **Bachhaus** (www.bachhaus.de; Frauenplan 21; adult/concession €7.50/4; 10am-6pm) has a modern exhibit about the great composer's life and work.

From April to October, bus 10 runs hourly from 9am to 5pm from the Hauptbahnhof (with stops at Karlsplatz and Mariental) to the Eselstation stop, from where it's a steep 10-minute walk up to the castle. In winter, buses are available on demand; call 228 822 for a pick-up.

Regional trains run frequently to Erfurt (€11.10, 45 minutes) and Weimar (€14.40, one hour). The **tourist office** (792 30; www.eisenach.de; Markt 24; 10am-6pm Mon-Fri, to 5pm Sat & Sun) can help you find accommodation if your day trip gets extended.

Krämerbrücke BRIDGE

Even if it were not the only bridge north of the Alps flanked by buildings, the medieval Merchant Bridge would still be a most charming spot. You can watch chocolate makers, potters, jewellers and other artisans at work in their teensy studios or pop into a cafe for refreshments. Of the two churches that once bookended the stone bridge only the **Ägidienkirche** remains. Its tower can sometimes be climbed.

Augustinerkloster CHURCH

(Augustinian Monastery; Augustinerstrasse 10, enter on Comthurgasse; tour adult/concession €6/4; ⏲tours hourly 10am-noon & 2-5pm Mon-Sat, 11am & noon Sun) Reformer Martin Luther lived at this monastery from 1505 to 1511 and was ordained a priest here in 1507. You're free to roam the grounds and visit the church, with its ethereal Gothic stained-glass windows but to get inside the monastery itself to see the cloister, a recreated Luther cell and an exhibit on the history of the Bible and Luther's life in Erfurt, you need to join a guided tour. Lodging is also available here.

Zitadelle Petersberg FORTRESS

(tour adult/concession €8/4; ⏲7pm Fri & Sat May-Oct) On the Petersberg hill northwest of Domplatz, this citadel ranks among Europe's largest and best-preserved baroque fortresses. It sits above a honeycomb of tunnels, which can be explored on two-hour guided tours run by the tourist office.

Alte Synagoge SYNAGOGUE

(Old Synagogue; http://alte-synagoge.erfurt.de; Waagegasse 8; adult/concession €5/3; ⏲10am-5pm Tue-Thu, 11am-5pm Fri-Sun) The Alte Synagoge in Erfurt is one of the oldest Jewish houses of worship in Europe, with roots in the 12th century. After the pogrom of 1349, it was converted into a storehouse and is now an exhibit space and museum.

Sleeping

TOP CHOICE **Re_4 Hostel** HOSTEL €

(☎600 0110; www.re4hostel.de; Puschkinstrasse 21; dm €13-16, s/d €26/52, without bathroom €20/40, linen €2; P@) This cool hostel in a former police station is run by an energetic, clued-in crew, happy to help you make the most out of your stay in Erfurt. Breakfast costs an extra €4.50. Room 13 has a 'chilling' surprise. The hostel's about 1.5km southwest from the Hauptbahnhof (tram 5 to Pushkinstrasse).

Opera Hostel HOSTEL €

(☎6013 1360; www.opera-hostel.de; Walkmühlstrasse 13; dm €13-18, s/d/tr €45/54/75, without bathroom €37/48/66, linen €2.50; @) Run with smiles and aplomb, this upmarket hostel in a historic building scores big with wallet-watching global nomads. Rooms are bright and spacious, many with an extra sofa for chilling. Make friends in the communal kitchen and on-site lounge-bar. Take bus 51 from Hauptbahnhof to Alte Oper.

Hotel am Kaisersaal HOTEL €€

(☎658 560; www.bachmann-hotels.de; Futterstrasse 8; s/d €89/104; P) Tip-top rooms are appointed with all expected mod cons in this highly rated hotel. Request a yard-facing one if you're bothered by street noise. Take tram 1 or 5 to Futterstrasse.

Eating

TOP CHOICE **Zwiesel** GERMAN €

(Michaelisstrasse 31; mains €6-9; ⏲6pm-late Mon-Thu, 3pm-late Fri-Sun) Been cut out of the family will? No problem at this reliable cheapie choice, which has 25 mains costing just €5.95 and drink prices to match. Even the rump steak is only €8.95. Any of the 350 cocktails cost €4.90.

Zum Goldenen Schwan GERMAN €€

(Michaelisstrasse 9; snacks €3-7, mains €8-17; ⏲11am-1am) This authentic inn serves Thuringian classics, including *Puffbohnenpfanne* (fried broad beans with roast bacon), an Erfurt speciality. Excellent house brews wash everything down well.

Steinhaus GERMAN €

(Allerheiligenstrasse 20-21; mains €4-8; ⏲11am-late, food till midnight) The ceiling beams may be ancient, but the crowd is intergenerational at this rambling gastro pub-cum-beer garden in the historic Engelsburg student centre.

Information

Tourist office (☎664 00; www.erfurt-tourismus.de; Benediktsplatz 1; ⏲10am-7pm Mon-Fri, to 6pm Sat, to 4pm Sun)

Getting There & Around

Fast trains leave frequently for Berlin (€60, 2½ hours, change in Leipzig), Dresden (€51, 2½ hours) and Frankfurt-am-Main (€54, 2¼ hours). Regional trains to Weimar (€5, 15 minutes) and Eisenach (€11.10, 45 minutes) run at least once hourly.

Trams 3, 4 and 6 run from Hauptbahnhof via Anger and Fischmarkt to Domplatz. Tickets cost €1.80, or €4.20 for a day pass.

SAXONY-ANHALT

Once the smog-filled heart of East Germany's chemical industry and open-pit coal mining, Saxony-Anhalt (Sachsen-Anhalt) has gone from humdrum to, well, not quite hip, but certainly more happening than its reputation would suggest. Open your eyes and you'll find deep wellsprings of beauty, ingenuity and historical magnitude. After all, Otto I, the first Holy Roman Emperor, is buried in Magdeburg; Martin Luther kick started the Reformation in Wittenberg; and, centuries later, the Bauhaus School revolutionised modern design and architecture from its base in Dessau.

Magdeburg

☎0391 / POP 231,500

Something old, something new: Magdeburg is constantly characterised by the juxtaposition of those two. Home to Germany's most ancient cathedral, the city also boasts the last of Austrian architect Friedensreich Hundertwasser's bonkers structures and teems with wide Cold War–era boulevards and enormous *Plattenbauten* (concrete tower blocks). Meanwhile, the historic cobbled streets around Hasselbachplatz are filled with cafes and bars.

Sights

Dom CHURCH

(www.magdeburgerdom.de; Am Dom 1; tour adult/concession €3/1.50; ⊙10am-6pm Mon-Sat, 11.30am-6pm Sun, tours 2pm Mon-Sat, 11.30am Sun) Magdeburg's main historical landmark traces its roots to 937 when Otto I (912–73) founded a Benedictine monastery and had it built up into a full-fledged cathedral within two decades. He and his English wife Editha are buried here amid stunning artistic treasures ranging from the delicate 13th-century **Magdeburg Virgins** sculptures to a haunting **antiwar memorial** by Ernst Barlach.

Grüne Zitadelle ARCHITECTURE

(Green Citadel; ☎620 8655; www.gruene-zitadelle.de; Breiter Weg 9; tour adult/concession €6/5; ⊙information office 10am-6pm, tours 11am, 3pm & 5pm Mon-Fri, hourly 10am-5pm Sat & Sun) Completed in 2005, Hundertwasser's piglet-pink final building sprouts trees from its roof and nicely reflects the architect's philosophy of creating highly unique spaces in harmony with nature. Inside are offices, flats and shops, as well as a small hotel and a cafe. Tours are in German only.

Sleeping & Eating

TOP CHOICE **Grüne Zitadelle** BOUTIQUE HOTEL €€

(☎620 780; www.hotel-zitadelle.de; Breiter Weg 9; s €105-135, d €125-145, breakfast €11; P❄🛜) Fans of Hundertwasser can ponder the architect's penchant for uneven, organic forms in these elegant rooms. The attached cafe (dishes €4 to €5, open 7am to 7pm) is open to the public, serving breakfast and light meals.

DJH Hostel HOSTEL €

(☎532 1010; www.jugendherberge.de/jh/magdeburg; Leiterstrasse 10; dm/s/tw €21/33/45, over 27yr extra €3; P@🛜) The smart, modern premises, generous space, good facilities and quiet but central location make this a winner.

Petriförder INTERNATIONAL €€

(☎597 9600; www.restaurant-petrifoerder-magdeburg.eu; Petriförder 1; mains €8-21; ⊙from 11.30am Mon-Fri, from 10am Sat & Sun) Right on the Elbe River, this resto-bar has a toe in all doors, with pasta, pizza, schnitzel and a good range of well-prepared poultry, fish and red-meat dishes. A beach bar sets up nearby in summer.

Information

Tourist office (☎194 33; www.magdeburg-tourist.de; Ernst-Reuter-Allee 12; ⊙10am-6.30pm Mon-Fri, to 4pm Sat)

Getting There & Away

Magdeburg is directly connected to Berlin Hauptbahnhof (€27, two hours), Leipzig (€27, 1¼ hours) and Dessau-Rosslau (€11.10, 50 minutes). For Lutherstadt Wittenberg (€16.40, 70 minutes), change in Rosslau. Magdeburg is just south of the A2 to Berlin or Hanover and also served by the A14 to Leipzig.

Dessau-Rosslau

☎0340 / POP 87,000

'Less is more' and 'form follows function' – both these dictums were taught in Dessau, home of the influential Bauhaus School. Between 1925 and 1932, some of the century's greatest artists and architects breathed life into the groundbreaking principles of modernism here, among them Walter Gropius, Paul Klee, Wassily Kandinsky and Ludwig Mies Van der Rohe. Their legacy still stands proud, in the immaculate Bauhaus School building, the lecturers' purpose-built homes and other pioneering constructions.

Sights

FREE Bauhausgebäude ARCHITECTURE

(Bauhaus Building; www.bauhaus-dessau.de; Gropiusallee 38; exhibition adult/concession €6/4, tour €4/3; ⏲10am-6pm, tours 11am & 2pm daily, also noon & 4pm Sat & Sun) Bauhaus founder Walter Gropius considered architecture the ultimate of all artistic endeavours, and this building was the first real-life example of his vision. It was revolutionary, bringing industrial construction techniques such as curtain walling and wide spans into the public domain and presaging untold buildings worldwide.

Today urban studies students use part of the building but much of it is open to the public. The gift shop sells cool trinkets, books, posters and postcards. Staff also rent English-language audioguides (adult/concession €4/3); note only the guided tours will get you inside the most interesting rooms.

Meisterhäuser ARCHITECTURE

(Masters' Houses; www.meisterhaeuser.de; Ebertallee 63, 65-67 & 69-71; admission to all 3 houses adult/concession €7.50/5.50, tours €11.50/8.50; ⏲11am-6pm Tue-Sun, tours 12.30pm & 3.30pm daily, also 1.30pm Sat & Sun) The leading lights of the Bauhaus movement – Gropius, Lyonel Feininger, Georg Muche, Wassily Kandisky and Paul Klee among them – lived together as neighbours in the so-called Meisterhäuser, white cubist structures that exemplify the Bauhaus aim of 'design for living' in a modern industrial world. They're on leafy Ebertallee, a 15-minute walk west of the Hauptbahnhof.

Sleeping & Eating

In Dessau-Rosslau, you really can eat, drink and sleep Bauhaus. For a different diet, investigate the main thoroughfare of Zerbster Strasse.

TOP CHOICE Hotel-Pension An den 7 Säulen HOTEL €

(☎619 620; www.pension7saeulen.de; Ebertallee 66; s €47-56, d €62-74; P) Rooms at this small pension are clean and nicely renovated; the owners are friendly, the garden is pleasant and the breakfast room overlooks the Meisterhäuser across the leafy street. Take bus 11 to Kornerhaus from Hauptbahnhof and walk back to Ebertallee.

NH Dessau HOTEL €€

(☎251 40; www.nh-hotels.com; Zerbsterstrasse 29; r €65-99, breakfast €16; P❄@📶) This modern hotel in white-grey tones is set in the pedestrianised strip leading to the Rathaus and tourist office. Nice touch: the rooftop sauna with attached terrace. Take bus 12 from the train station to Zerbsterstrasse.

Bauhaus Klub CAFE €

(Gropiusallee 38; light dishes €3.50-8.90; ⏲8am-midnight Mon-Fri, 9am-midnight Sat, 8am-6pm Sun; 📶) Breakfasts, salads, snacks and *Flammkuchen* are served downstairs in the congenial cafe and snack bar in the Bauhaus Building.

TOP CHOICE Pächterhaus GERMAN €€

(☎650 1447; www.paechterhaus-dessau.de; Kirchstrasse 1; mains €18-25; ⏲lunch & dinner Tue-Sun) Foodies on a mission won't mind making the small detour to this gorgeously restored half-timbered farm house where seasonal and locally sourced ingredients get the gourmet treatment. Take bus 11 to Kirchstrasse.

Information

Bauhaus Foundation (☎650 8251; www.bauhaus-dessau.de; Gropiusallee 38; ⏲10am-6pm) Offers educational info on, and tours of, Bauhaus buildings, sometimes in English.

Tourist office (☎204 1442, accommodation 220 3003; www.dessau-rosslau-tourismus.de; Zerbsterstrasse 2c; ⏲10am-6pm Mon-Fri, to 1pm Sat)

Getting There & Away

For Berlin (€36, 1½ hours), change in Lutherstadt Wittenberg (€7.50, 30 minutes). Direct regional services go to Leipzig (€11.10, 45 minutes), Halle (€11.10, 55 minutes) and Magdeburg (€11.10, 50 minutes).

Lutherstadt Wittenberg

☎03491 / POP 49,500

As its full name suggests, Wittenberg is first and foremost about Martin Luther (1483–1546), the monk who triggered the German Reformation by publishing his 95 theses against church corruption in 1517. Wittenberg back then was a hotbed of progressive thinking which also saw priests get married and educators like Luther's buddy Philipp Melanchthon argue for schools to accept female pupils. Today Wittenberg retains its significance for the world's 340 million Protestants, including 66 million Lutherans, as well as for those who simply admire Luther for his principled stand against authority. Sometimes called the 'Rome of the Protestants', its many Reformation-related sites garnered it the World Heritage Site nod from Unesco in 1996.

Sights

Lutherhaus MUSEUM

(www.martinluther.de; Collegienstrasse 54; adult/concession €5/3; ⊙9am-6pm) Even those with no previous interest in the Reformation will likely be fascinated by the state-of-the-art exhibits in the Lutherhaus, the former monastery turned Luther family home. Through an engaging mix of accessible narrative (in German and English), spotlit artefacts (eg his lectern from the Stadtkirche, indulgences chests, bibles, cloaks), famous oil paintings and interactive multimedia stations, you'll learn about the man, his times and his impact on world history. Highlights include Cranach's *Ten Commandments* in the refectory, and an original room furnished by Luther in 1535.

Schlosskirche CHURCH

(Castle Church; Schlossplatz; ⊙10am-6pm Mon-Sat, 11.30am-6pm Sun) Did or didn't he nail those 95 theses to the door of the Schlosskirche? We'll never know for sure, for the original portal was destroyed by fire in 1760 and replaced in 1858 with this massive bronze version inscribed with the theses in Latin. Luther himself is buried below the pulpit, opposite his friend and fellow reformer Philipp Melanchthon.

Stadtkirche St Marien CHURCH

(Jüdenstrasse 35; ⊙10am-6pm Mon-Sat, 11.30am-6pm Sun) This church was where Martin Luther's ecumenical revolution began, with the world's first Protestant worship services in 1521. It was also here that Luther preached his famous Lectern sermons in 1522, and where he married ex-nun Katharina von Bora three years later. The centrepiece is the large altar, designed jointly by Lucas Cranach the Elder and his son. The side facing the nave depicts Luther, Melanchthon and other Reformation figures, as well as Cranach himself, in biblical contexts.

Sleeping & Eating

TOP CHOICE **Alte Canzley** HOTEL €€

(☎429 190; www.alte-canzley.de; Schlossplatz 3-5; s €70-125, d €85-139; P@🛜) The nicest place in town for your money is in a 14th-century building opposite the Schlosskirche. Each of the eight spacious units are furnished in dark woods and natural hues, named for a major historical figure and equipped with a kitchenette. The vaulted downstairs harbours Saxony-Anhalt's first certified organic restaurant (dishes €7.20 to €23.90).

DJH Hostel HOSTEL €

(☎505 205; www.jugendherberge-wittenberg.de; Schlossstrasse 14/15; dm under/over 27yr €19/22, s/d €28.50/34, linen €3.50; P@🛜) Wittenberg's excellent youth hostel has 40 bright rooms sleeping up to six people and come with bathrooms, bedside reading lamps and private lockers.

Brauhaus Wittenberg GERMAN €€

(Markt 6, Im Beyerhof; mains €6.90-15.90; ⊙11am-11pm) This place – with a cobbled courtyard, indoor brewery and shiny copper vats – thrums with the noise of people having a good time. The menu is hearty but also features smaller dishes for waist-watchers. Upstairs are a few simple rooms with air-con (singles/doubles €57/79).

Information

Tourist office (☎498 610; www.wittenberg.de; Schlossplatz 2; ⊙9am-6pm Mon-Fri, 10am-4pm Sat & Sun)

Getting There & Away

Wittenberg is on the main train line to Halle and Leipzig (both €12.20, one hour). ICE (€30, 45 minutes) and RE trains (€21.50, 1¼ hours) travel to Berlin. Coming from Berlin, be sure to board for 'Lutherstadt Wittenberg', as there's also a Wittenberge west of the capital.

Harz Mountains

The Harz Mountains constitute a mini-Alpine region straddling Saxony-Anhalt and Lower Saxony. Here, medieval castles overlook fairy-tale historic towns, while there are caves, mines and numerous hiking trails to explore.

The region's highest – and most famous – mountain is the Brocken, where one-time visitor Johann Wolfgang von Goethe set the 'Walpurgisnacht' chapter of his play *Faust*. His inspiration came from folk tales depicting *Walpurgisnacht*, or *Hexennacht* (witches' night), as an annual witches' coven. Every 30 April to 1 May it's celebrated enthusiastically across the Harz region.

GOSLAR

05321 / POP 41,000

Goslar has a charming medieval Altstadt, which, together with its historic Rammelsberg mine, is a Unesco World Heritage Site. Founded by Heinrich I in 922, the town's early importance centred on silver and the Kaiserpfalz, the seat of the Saxon kings from 1005 to 1219. It fell into decline after a second period of prosperity in the 14th and 15th centuries, reflecting the fortunes of the Harz as a whole, and relinquished its mine to Braunschweig in 1552 and then its soul to Prussia in 1802.

Sights

Altstadt NEIGHBOURHOOD

One of the nicest things to do in Goslar is to wander through the historic streets around the Markt where the 1494 **Hotel Kaiserworth** is decorated with almost life-size figures. The **market fountain**, crowned by an ungainly eagle symbolising Goslar's status as a free imperial city, dates from the 13th century. Opposite the **Rathaus** (town hall), the **Glockenspiel** (carillon) depicts local mining scenes and plays at 9am, noon, 3pm and 6pm.

Kaiserpfalz CASTLE

(Kaiserbleek 6; adult/concession €4.50/2.50; 10am-5pm) Goslar's pride and joy is the reconstructed 11th-century Romanesque palace, Kaiserpfalz. The **St Ulrich Chapel** on the south side houses the heart of Heinrich III. Just below the palace, the **Domvorhalle** displays the 11th-century 'Kaiserstuhl' throne, used by German emperors.

Rammelsberg Museum & Besucherbergwerk MUSEUM

(Rammelsberg Museum & Visitors' Mine; www.rammelsberg.de; Bergtal 19; admission €12; 9am-6pm, last admission 4.30pm) About 1km south of town, the shafts and buildings of this 1000-year-old mine are now a museum and Unesco World Heritage Site. Admission includes a German-language tour and a pamphlet with English explanations of the 18th- and 19th-century Roeder Shafts, the mine railway and the ore processing section. Bus 803 stops here.

Sleeping & Eating

TOP CHOICE **Hotel Kaiserworth** HOTEL €€

(7090; www.kaiserworth.de; Markt 3; s €71-101, d €122-182, tr €172-207; P) This magnificent 500-year-old former merchant guild building has tasteful rooms, a good restaurant and a cafe that's open until 2am or the last customer.

Gästehaus Schmitz GUESTHOUSE €

(234 45; www.schmitz-goslar.de; Kornstrasse 1; s/d/tr €45/60/75; P) This slightly eccentric guesthouse is an excellent choice in the heart of town, especially for those on low budgets or looking for an apartment.

Die Butterhanne GERMAN €€

(www.butterhanne.de; Marktkirchhof 3; mains €8.50-14; from 8.30am) The fare is traditional and regular here and the outdoor seating is nice. The name refers to a famous local frieze showing a milkmaid churning butter while clutching her buttock to insult her employer.

Information

Tourist office (780 60; www.goslar.de; Markt 7; 9.15am-6pm Mon-Fri, 9.30am-4pm Sat, 9.30am-2pm Sun)

Getting There & Away

Bad Harzburg–Hanover trains stop here often, as do trains on the Braunschweig–Göttingen line. There are direct trains to Wernigerode (€9.10, 45 minutes, every two hours) and other services requiring a change at Vienenburg.

The B6 runs north to Hildesheim and east to Bad Harzburg, Wernigerode and Quedlinburg. The north–south A7 is reached via the B82.

QUEDLINBURG

03946 / POP 28,400

With over 1400 half-timbered houses dating from six centuries ago, Quedlinburg is a

LOCAL KNOWLEDGE

NARROW-GAUGE RAILWAYS

Fans of old-time trains or unusual journeys will be in their element on any of the three narrow-gauge railways crossing the Harz. This 140km integrated network – the largest in Europe – is served by 25 steam and 10 diesel locomotives, which tackle gradients of up to 1:25 (40%) and curves as tight as 60m in radius. There are three lines:

Harzquerbahn Runs 60km on a north–south route between Wernigerode and Nordhausen; the 14km between Wernigerode and Drei Annen Hohne includes 72 bends.

Brockenbahn From the junction at Drei Annen Hohne, this classic trains begins the steep climb up the Brocken, northern Germany's highest mountain. Direct trains also leave from Wernigerode and Nordhausen.

Selketalbahn Begins in Quedlinburg, crosses the plain to Gernrode and follows a creek through deciduous forest before joining the Selke Valley and climbing past Alexisbad to high plains around Friedrichshöhe and beyond.

For timetables and information, see **Harzer Schmalspurbahnen** (☎03943-5580; www.hsb-wr.de).

highlight of any trip to the Harz. In 1994 the city became a Unesco World Heritage Site; since then, work to save the crumbling treasures lining its romantic cobblestone streets has gradually progressed. You can also pick-up a narrow-gauge railway from here.

Sights

With so many historic buildings, Quedlinburg is perfect for just strolling around and soaking up the atmosphere.

Stiftskirche St Servatius CHURCH
(Schlossberg 1; adult/concession €4.50/3, combined ticket Dom, treasury, crypt & Schlossmuseum adult/concession €8.50/5.50; ⌚10am-6pm Tue-Sat) This 12th-century church is one of Germany's most significant from the Romanesque period. Its treasury contains reliquaries and early bibles, while the crypt features early frescoes and royal graves.

Schlossmuseum MUSEUM
(Schlossberg 1; adult/concession €4/2.50, combined ticket Dom, treasury, crypt & Schlossmuseum adult/concession €8.50/5.50; ⌚10am-6pm Tue-Sun) The present-day Renaissance palace, on a 25m-high plateau above Quedlinburg, contains the Schlossmuseum, with some fascinating Ottonian-period items dating from 919 to 1056.

Fachwerkmuseum Ständebau MUSEUM
(Wordgasse 3; adult/concession €3/2; ⌚10am-5pm Fri-Wed) Germany's earliest half-timbered houses were built using high perpendicular struts, a technique perfectly illustrated by this 1310 building, which also contains exhibits on the style and construction technique.

Sleeping

TOP CHOICE **Romantik Hotel Theophano** HOTEL €€
(☎963 00; www.hoteltheophano.de; Markt 13-14; s €69, d €99-140; P@) Each room is decorated in an individual style at this rambling, rustic hotel. Most are spacious and very comfortable, but the many staircases (no lift) and low thresholds might be a problem for some.

DJH Hostel HOSTEL €
(☎03946-811 703; www.jugendherberge.de; Neuendorf 28; dm €16.50-19.50, bedding €3) This excellent hostel offers four- and 10-bed dorms in a quiet and very central location. It's relatively small and fills quickly in summer.

Information

Tourist office (☎905 625; www.quedlinburg.de; Markt 2; ⌚9.30am-6pm Mon-Fri, to 3pm Sat, to 2pm Sun)

Getting There & Away

Frequent services to Thale (€2.20, 12 minutes). For trains to Wernigerode (€9.10, 45 minutes), change at Halberstadt. The narrow-gauge Selketalbahn runs to Gernrode (€3, 15 minutes) and beyond.

MECKLENBURG-WESTERN POMERANIA

Mecklenburg-Vorpommern combines historic Hanseatic-era towns like Schwerin, Wismar and Stralsund with holiday areas such as Warnemünde and Rügen Island. Often skipped by international travellers, in summer it seems like half of Germany is lolling on the sands and relaxing in a *Strandkorb* (basket-like beach wicker chairs). At other times of the year, intrepid visitors will be rewarded with discoveries far from the maddening crowds.

Schwerin

☎0385 / POP 95,200

State capital Schwerin has a modest dignity befitting its status. Picturesquely sited around seven lakes, the centrepiece of this engaging city is its Schloss (castle), built in the 14th century when the city was the seat of the Grand Duchy of Mecklenburg. It's small enough to explore on foot and, if you're on the move, as part of a half-day break on a train journey. But Schwerin's beauty and charm are invariably infectious, and few people regret spending extra time here.

Sights

Schloss Schwerin CASTLE

(☎525 2920; www.schloss-schwerin.de; adult/child €4/2.50; ⏰10am-6pm mid-Apr–mid-Oct, 10am-5pm Tue-Sun mid-Oct–mid-Apr) Gothic and Renaissance turrets, Slavic onion domes, Ottoman features and terracotta Hanseatic step gables are among the mishmash of architectural styles that make up Schwerin's inimitable Schloss, which is crowned by a gleaming golden dome. Nowadays the Schloss earns its keep as the state parliament building.

Inside the palace's opulently furnished rooms, highlights include a huge collection of Meissen porcelain and richly coloured stained glass windows in the **Schlosskirche**. Surrounding the palace, the **Burggarten** has a lovely orangerie with a restaurant and summer terrace cafe overlooking the water. Across the causeway south of here is the canal-laced, baroque **Schlossgarten** (Palace Garden).

Staatliches Museum MUSEUM

(☎595 80; www.museum-schwerin.de; Alter Garten 3; adult/concession €8/6; ⏰10am-6pm Tue-Sun & noon-8pm Thu Apr-Oct, 10am-5pm Tue-Sun & 1pm-8pm Thu Nov-Mar) An enormous neoclassical building, the state museum displays such old masters as Rembrandt, Rubens and Brueghel, as well as oils by Lucas Cranach the Elder and collections of more modern works by Marcel Duchamp and Ernst Barlach.

Dom CHURCH

(☎565 014; Am Dom 4; adult/child €2/1; ⏰11am-3pm Mon-Fri, 11am-4pm Sat, noon-3pm Sun) You don't get better examples of north German red-brick architecture than the 14th-century Gothic Dom, towering above the Markt. The tower was added in the 19th century and can be climbed (adult/child €1.50/0.50). Inside, check out the elaborately carved pews.

Sleeping

Zur guten Quelle HOTEL €

(☎565 985; www.zur-guten-quelle.m-vp.de; Schusterstrasse 12; s from €54, d from €78; P 📶) In a pretty half-timbered house, bang in the Altstadt, this hotel has half a dozen simple but comfortable rooms and is also known for its cosy traditional restaurant and beer garden.

Hotel Niederländischer Hof HOTEL €€

(☎591 100; www.niederlaendischer-hof.de; Karl-Marx-Strasse 12-13; s €84-124, d €125-170; P 📶) Overlooking the Pfaffenteich pond, this regal 1901-established hotel has 33 elegant rooms with black marble bathrooms, a library warmed by an open fire, and a lauded restaurant. Room decor ranges from trad luxe to whimsical seaside.

DJH Hostel HOSTEL €

(☎326 0006; www.jugendherberge.de; Waldschulweg 3; dm from €20) Though popular with school groups, this 91-bed/20-room hostel is in a peaceful, leafy location south of the city centre. Take bus 14.

Eating & Drinking

Zum Stadtkrug BREWERY €€

(☎593 6693; www.altstadtbrauhaus.de; Wismarsche Strasse 126; mains €10-20) The dark beer at this 1936-established microbrewery/pub consistently rates among the best in Germany. It's full of antique brewing equipment, and opens to a convivial beer garden. The menu features the usual assortment of schnitzels and porky mains but everything is well prepared. Sandwiches are excellent.

Weinhaus Wöhler GERMAN €€

(☎555 830; www.weinhaus-woehler.de; Puschkinstrasse 26; mains €9-22; 📶) In addition to wood-lined dining rooms, a large covered courtyard and a tapas/cocktail bar, this half-timbered inn also offers six rooms (€80 to €130). The seasonal regional menu is best enjoyed amidst the grape vines on the terrace.

Zum Freischütz PUB

(www.zum-freischuetz.de; Ziegenmarkt 11; ⌚11am-late Mon-Fri, 6pm-late Sat & Sun) A life-size bronze goat stands on the square near this characterful cafe overlooking Schwerin's old goat market. The storied pub has an old interior that features wooden chairs dating back decades. Sandwiches, soups and various cheap specials are served long into the night.

Information

Schwerin-Information (☎592 5212; www.schwerin.de; Markt 14; ⌚9am-7pm Mon-Fri, 10am-6pm Sat & Sun Apr-Oct, 9am-6pm Mon-Fri, 10am-4pm Sat & Sun Nov-Mar)

Getting There & Away

Train links include Hamburg (from €27, one hour), Rostock (from €20, one hour), Stralsund (from €33, two hours) and Wismar (€8, 30 minutes), with less frequent direct connections to/from Berlin (€35, 2¼ hours).

Wismar

☎03841 / POP 44,400

Wismar, a Hanseatic gem that's fast being discovered, joined the powerful trading league in the 13th century. For centuries it was in and out of Swedish control – hence the 'Swedish heads' dotted across town. The entire Altstadt was Unesco-listed in 2002. Quieter than Rostock or Stralsund, Wismar can fill up with visitors quickly in high season.

Sights & Activities

The old harbour, Alter Hafen, with old boats swaying in the breeze, evokes the trading days of yore. **Adler-Schiffe** (☎01805-123 344; www.adler-schiffe.de; adult/child €9.50/5.50; ⌚daily Apr-Oct, weekends Nov-Mar) operates hour-long harbour cruises.

Markt SQUARE

Dominating the central Markt is the landmark **Wasserkunst** (waterworks, 1602), an ornate, 12-sided well that supplied Wismar's drinking water until 1897. Behind it, the red-brick **Alter Schwede** (1380), with its striking step-gabled facade, houses a restaurant and guesthouse.

The 19th-century Rathaus (town hall) at the square's northern end houses the excellent **Rathaus Historical Exhibition** (adult/child €2/1; ⌚10am-6pm). Note the 15th-century murals, a glass-covered medieval well, and the elaborate coffin of a Swedish general named Wrangel.

St-Nikolai-Kirche CHURCH

(St-Nikolai-Kirchhof; www.kirchen-in-wismar.de; admission €2; ⌚8am-8pm May-Sep, 10am-6pm Apr & Oct, 11am-4pm Nov-Mar) Of the three great red-brick churches that once rose above Wismar before WWII, only the sober red-brick St-Nikolai-Kirche, the largest of its kind in Europe, was left intact. Today it contains a font from its older sister church, the St-Marien-Kirche.

Fürstenhof HISTORIC BUILDING

The restored Italian Renaissance Fürstenhof is now the city courthouse. The facades are slathered in terracotta reliefs depicting episodes from folklore and the town's history.

Sleeping & Eating

Boats along Alter Hafen sell fresh fish and seafood from 9am to 6pm daily.

TOP CHOICE **Hotel Reingard** HOTEL €€

(☎284 972; www.hotel-reingard.de; Weberstrasse 18; s €68-72, d €98-102; P) This charismatic boutique hotel has a dozen artistic rooms, a leafy little garden and wonderfully idiosyncratic touches such as a nightly classical music lightshow playing across the facade.

Pension Chez Fasan HOTEL €

(☎213 425; www.unterkunft-pension-wismar.de; Badestrasse 20a; s/d €25/47, s without bathroom €22) The 25 simple but perfectly comfortable rooms in these three linked houses, just one block north of the Markt, are fantastic value. Call ahead if you're not arriving during reception hours (normally 2pm to 8pm).

Alter Schwede SEAFOOD €

(☎283 552; mains €10-21; ⌚11.30am-late; ✎) Baltic eel with herbed potatoes, and catfish with mustard are among the specialities of this landmark spot. The facade alone is a tourist attraction, but the reproduction Swedish head over the door puts it over the top. Get a table out front and enjoy Markt action.

To'n Zägenkrog SEAFOOD €€

(☎282 716; www.ziegenkrug-wismar.de; Ziegenmarkt 10; mains €10-15; ⌚5-9pm) Excellent fish dishes are the mainstay of this cosy 1897-established pub. It's crammed with maritime mementoes and great harbour views.

SWEDISH HEADS

A 'Swedish head' isn't something you need to successfully assemble an IKEA bookcase. In Wismar, Swedish Heads refers to two baroque busts of Hercules that once graced mooring posts at the harbour entrance.

Semicomical, with great curling moustaches and wearing lions as hats, the statues are believed to have marked either the beginning of the harbour or the navigable channels within it. The originals were damaged when a Finnish barge rammed them in 1902, at which time replicas were made. One original is now in the **Schabbellhaus** (www.schabbellhaus.de; Schweinsbrücke 8), the town's historical museum (under renovation until at least 2014).

Information

Tourist office (☎251 3025; www.wismar.de; Am Markt 11; ⏲9am-6pm daily Apr-Oct, 9am-6pm Mon-Sat, 10am-4pm Sun Nov-Mar)

Getting There & Away

Trains travel every hour to/from Rostock (€12, 70 minutes) and Schwerin (€8, 40 minutes).

Rostock & Warnemünde

☎0381 / POP 202,700

Rostock is a major Baltic port and shipbuilding centre and was once an important Hanseatic trading city. Parts of the city centre, especially along Kröpeliner Strasse, retain the flavour of this period.

Its chief suburb – and chief attraction – is Warnemünde, 12km north of the centre. Among eastern Germany's most popular beach resorts, its broad, sandy beach is chock-a-block with bathers on hot summer days.

Sights

It takes just a couple of hours to see the city sights which cluster in the pedestrianised zone between Neuer Markt and Universitätsplatz.

TOP CHOICE **Marienkirche** CHURCH
(☎453 325; www.marienkirche-rostock.de; Am Ziegenmarkt; €1.50 donation requested; ⏲10am-6pm Mon-Sat, 11.15am-5pm Sun May-Sep, 10am-4pm Mon-Sat, 11.15am-noon Sun Oct-Apr) Rostock's pride and joy, the Marienkirche, built in 1290, was the only one of its four main churches to survive WWII unscathed. Notable features include the 12m-high astrological clock (1470–72) and the Gothic bronze baptismal font (1290).

Kröpeliner Strasse & Universitätsplatz SQUARE
Kröpeliner Strasse, a broad, shop-filled, cobblestone pedestrian mall lined with 15th- and 16th-century burghers' houses, runs from Neuer Markt west to the 55m-high Kröpeliner Tor (city gate).

At its centre is **Universitätsplatz**, a square lined with university buildings. At the southwestern end is the 13th-century convent **Kloster Zum Heiligen Kreuz**, which today houses the **Kulturhistorisches Museum Rostock** (☎203 590; www.kulturhistorisches-museum-rostock.de; Klosterhof 7; admission free; ⏲10am-6pm Tue-Sun), whose collection includes Victorian furniture and sculptures by Ernst Barlach.

Sleeping

Hanse Hostel HOSTEL €
(☎128 6006; www.hanse-hostel.de; Doberaner Strasse 136; dm €14-18, s/d without bathroom €24/44, breakfast €4;) On the edge of Rostock's trendy bar district, the KTV, is this family-run operation with great facilities spread over two buildings. Recently added rooms have private bathrooms (single/double €35/56). From the Hauptbahnhof, take tram 4 or 5 to the Volkstheater stop.

Hotel Kleine Sonne HOTEL €€
(☎497 3153; www.die-kleine-sonne.de; Steinstrasse 7; per person €52-102; @) This lovely place lives up to its name, the Little Sun, with sunny yellow and red detailing against otherwise starkly minimalist decor. Guests may use the wellness centre at the nearby Steigenberger Hotel Sonne.

Hotel-Pension Zum Kater GUESTHOUSE €€
(☎548 210; www.pension-zum-kater.de; Alexandrinenstrasse 115; s/d from €72/100; P) Less than 10 minutes' stroll from the beach in Warnemünde, and even closer to the harbour, this guesthouse is sweet and cosy. Get a room with a roof terrace. Short stays may incur slightly higher rates.

Eating

Excellent fish and *Wurst* stalls set up shop on Rostock's Neuer Markt and Warnemünde's harbour most mornings.

Café Central
CAFE €€

(☎490 4648; Leonhardstrasse 20; mains €6-15; ⏰from 10am) Café Central has cult status among Rostock's students, artists, hipsters and suits who loll around sipping long drinks on the banquettes or gabbing with friends at sidewalk tables. There are a lot of cheap ethnic restaurants nearby. It's 500m northwest of the Kröpeliner Tor.

Weineckck Krahnstöver
PUB €€

(Grosse Wasser Strasse 30; mains €10-18; ⏰closed Sun) One side is a wine bar with a pub feel, the other side a proper restaurant: both sides have a loyal local following and offer a lengthy list of wines that you sip in the warm, old-fashioned atmosphere between dark wood walls.

Zur Kogge
GERMAN €

(☎493 4493; www.zur-kogge.de; Wokrenterstrasse 27; mains €9-17; ⏰11am-9pm Mon-Sat; 👪) At this Rostock institution, cosy wooden booths are cradled by nautical decor and local fish dominate the menu. You can also stop by for coffee and cake between meal times, and there's an above-average kids' menu to boot.

Fischerklause
SEAFOOD €€

(☎525 16; www.fischer-klause.de; Am Strom 123; mains €9-15; 📶) One of Warnemünde's atmospheric old fishermen's cottages along Alter Strom crawls with tourists thanks to its fun ship's cabin decor and succulent fishy fare.

Information

Tourist office (☎381 2222; www.rostock.de; Neuer Markt 3; ⏰10am-6pm Mon-Fri, to 4pm Sat & Sun, shorter hours May-Sep)

Warnemünde-Information (☎548 000; www.warnemuende.de; Am Strom 59; ⏰9am-6pm Mon-Fri, 10am-4pm Sat & Sun, shorter hours Nov-Feb)

Getting There & Around

Ferries serving Denmark, Sweden, Latvia and Finland depart from Warnemünde's **Überseehafen** (Overseas Seaport; www.rostock-port.de).

There are frequent direct trains to Berlin (from €38, 2½ hours) and Hamburg (from €33, 2¼ hours), and hourly services to Stralsund (€15, one hour) and Schwerin (€20, one hour).

Rostock and Warnemünde are linked by frequent S-Bahn trains (single/day pass €2.70/5.40, 22 minutes).

Stralsund

☎03831 / POP 57,700

You instantly know you're next to the sea here. Possessing an unmistakable medieval profile, Stralsund was the second most powerful member of the medieval Hanseatic League, after Lübeck. An attractive town of imposing churches and elegant town houses, it brims with classic red-brick Gothic gabled architecture and is great for getting a feel for Baltic culture.

Sights

Alter Markt
SQUARE

Seven copper turrets and six triangular gables grace the red-brick Gothic facade of Stralsund's splendid **Rathaus** (1370). The upper portion of the northern facade, or *Schauwand* (show wall), has openings to prevent strong winds from knocking it over. Inside, the sky-lit colonnade boasts shiny black pillars on carved and painted bases; on the western side of the building is an ornate portal.

Through the Rathaus' eastern walkway you'll come to the main portal of the 1270 **Nikolaikirche** (☎299 799; www.nikolai-stralsund.de; adult/child €2/free; ⏰9am-7pm Mon-Sat, 1-5pm Sun May-Sep, 10am-6pm Mon-Sat, 1-5pm Sun Oct-Apr), which was modelled on Lübeck's Marienkirche and is filled with art treasures. The **main altar** (1708), designed by the baroque master Andreas Schlüter, shows the eye of God flanked by cherubs and capped by a depiction of the Last Supper. Also worth a closer look are the huge **high altar** (1470), showing scenes from Jesus' life, and, behind the altar, a 1394-built (but no longer operational) **astronomical clock**.

Opposite the Rathaus you'll find the **Wulflamhaus** (Alter Markt 5), a beautiful 15th-century town house named after an old mayor. Its turreted step gable imitates the Rathaus facade.

Marienkirche
CHURCH

(☎298 965; www.st-mariengemeinde-stralsund.de; ⏰9am-6pm Apr-Oct) The Neuer Markt is dominated by the massive 14th-century Marienkirche, another superb example of north German red-brick construction. You can climb the steep wooden steps up the tower for a sweeping view of the town, with its lovely red-tiled roofs, and over to Rügen Island. The ornate 17-century **organ** is a stunner.

WORTH A TRIP

RÜGEN ISLAND

Germany's largest island, Rügen is at times hectic, relaxed, windblown and naked – fitting, perhaps, since the resort tradition here reflects all aspects of Germany's recent past. In the 19th century, luminaries such as Einstein, Bismarck and Thomas Mann came to unwind in its fashionable coastal resorts. Later both Nazi and GDR regimes made Rügen the holiday choice for dedicated comrades.

The largest and most celebrated seaside resort is **Binz**, an alluring confection of ornate, white 19th-century villas, white sand and blue water. North of here, **Prora** was built by the Nazis as the 'world's largest holiday camp', a set of outside buildings hugging one of the island's most beautiful beaches.

The ruggedly beautiful area further north is protected as the **Jasmund National Park**. Its highlight is the **Stubbenkammer**, where jagged white-chalk cliffs plunge into the jade-coloured sea. Also here is Rügen's highest point – the 117m **Königsstuhl** – which offers views that inspired such artists as Caspar David Friedrich. The best view of the peak itself is from the **Viktoria-Sicht** some hundred metres to the east.

Other popular tourist destinations are **Jagdschloss Granitz** (1834), a castle surrounded by lush forest, and the twin lighthouses at **Kap Arkona** on the island's northern edge.

Tourismuszentrale Rügen (www.ruegen.de) and the **tourist office** (www.ostseebad-binz.de; Kurverwaltung, Heinrich-Heine-Strasse 7; ⌚9am-6pm Mon-Fri, 10am-6pm Sat & Sun Feb-Oct, 9am-4pm Mon-Fri, 10am-4pm Sat & Sun Nov-Jan) in Binz are your best bets for information.

Direct IC trains connect Binz with Hamburg (€58, four hours) and beyond and there is hourly service to Stralsund (€12, 50 minutes) as well. To get around the island and really appreciate it, a car is vital.

TOP CHOICE **Ozeaneum** AQUARIUM
(☎265 0610; www.ozeaneum.de; Hafeninsel Stralsund; adult/child €14/8, combination ticket with Meeresmuseum €18/11; ⌚9.30am-9pm Jun–mid-Sep, 9.30am-7pm mid-Sep–May) In an arctic-white wavelike building that leaps out from the surrounding red-brick warehouses, the state-of-the-art Ozeaneum takes you into an underwater world of creatures from the Baltic and North Seas and the Atlantic Ocean up to the polar latitudes.

Meeresmuseum AQUARIUM
(Maritime Museum; ☎265 010; www.meeresmuseum.de; Katharinenberg 14-20; adult/child €7.50/5, combination ticket with Ozeaneum €18/11; ⌚10am-6pm Jun-Sep, 10am-5pm Oct-May) Affiliated with the Ozeaneum, the Meeresmuseum aquarium is in a 13th-century ex-convent. Exhibits include a popular huge sea-turtle tank and polychromatic tropical fish.

Sleeping & Eating

TOP CHOICE **Altstadt Hotel Peiss** HOTEL €€
(☎303 580; www.altstadt-pension-peiss.de; Tribseer Strasse 15; s €50-85, d €55-115; P⊜☜) Thirteen spacious rooms with Paul Gauguin prints and sparkling bathrooms combine with cheery service at this bright and appealing guesthouse. With a terrace, small garden and bike rack, it's especially popular with cyclists.

Younior Hotel HOSTEL
(☎0800-233 388 234; www.younior-hotel.de; Tribseer Damm 78; dm €21-26; P⊜@) In an expanse of parkland near the train station, a grand old 1897 building that once housed Stralsund's railway offices now has a much more active life as a 300-bed hostel. Dorms have comfy, capsule-like triple-decker bunks, and fun facilities include a guest-only bar, a BBQ area and beach volleyball.

TOP CHOICE **Restaurant Esszimmer** MODERN EUROPEAN €€€
(www.esszimmer-stralsund.de; Am Querkanal 5; lunch mains from €12, set dinner menus from €40; ⌚noon-2.30pm, 5.30-10.30pm Thu-Tue) Esszimmer has a fresh and ever-changing menu that has a creative take on local seasonal foods and dishes. Service is excellent. Tables outside catch the clang of harbour bells in summer.

Hansekeller GERMAN €€
(www.hansekeller-stralsund.de; Mönchstrasse 48; mains €8-16) Entering an inconspicuous archway and descending a flight of steps brings you to this 16th-century cross-vaulted brick

cellar illuminated by glowing lamps and flickering candles. Taking a seat near the open kitchen lets you watch its chefs prepare regional specialities.

Nur Fisch SEAFOOD €€
(☎306 609; www.nurfisch.de; Heilgeiststrasse 92; mains €6-15; ⏰10am-6pm Mon-Fri, 11am-2pm Sat) Simple canteen-style bistro dedicated to marine delights – from fish sandwiches to sumptuous platters of seafood and even a fine seafood paella.

Information

Tourist office (☎246 90; www.stralsundtourismus.de; Alter Markt 9; ⏰10am-6pm Mon-Fri, to 4pm Sat & Sun May-Oct, 10am-5pm Mon-Fri, to 2pm Sat Nov-Apr)

Getting There & Away

Regional trains travel to/from Rostock (€15, one hour), Berlin Hauptbahnhof (from €40, 3½ hours) and other towns in the region at least every two hours.

BAVARIA

From the cloud-shredding Alps to the fertile Danube plain, Bavaria is a place that keeps its clichéd promises. Story-book castles bequeathed by an oddball king poke through dark forest, cowbells tinkle in flower-filled meadows, the thwack of palm on lederhosen accompanies the clump of frothy stein on timber benches, and medieval walled towns go about their time-warped business.

But diverse Bavaria offers much more than the chocolate-box idyll. Learn about Bavaria's state-of-the-art motor industry in Munich, discover its Nazi past in Nuremberg and Berchtesgaden, sip world-class wines in Würzburg, get on the Wagner trail in Bayreuth or seek out countless kiddy attractions across the state. Destinations are often described as possessing 'something for everyone', but in Bavaria's case this is no exaggeration.

Munich

☎089 / POP 1.38 MILLION

Munich is a flourishing success story that revels in its own contradictions. It's the natural habitat of well-heeled power dressers and lederhosen-clad thigh-slappers, Mediterranean-style street cafes and olde-worlde beer halls, high-brow art and high-tech industry. If you're looking for Alpine clichés, they're all here, but the Bavarian capital also has plenty of unexpected cards down its Dirndl.

Statistics show Munich is enticing more visitors than ever, especially in summer and during Oktoberfest. Munich's walkable centre retains a small-town air but holds some world-class sights, especially its art galleries and museums, along with a king's ransom of royal Bavarian heritage.

History

Munich derives its name from monks who first settled here in the 8th century, but the town itself was only first mentioned in an official document in 1158. In 1240 the city passed to the Wittelsbach dynasty who would rule over Munich (as well as Bavaria) until the 1918.

In the Middle Ages, Munich prospered as a salt trade hub but was hit hard by the outbreak of the plague in 1349. When the epidemic finally subsided 150 years later, the *Schäffler* (coopers) invented a ritualistic dance to remind residents of their good fortune. The *Schäfflertanz* is re-enacted daily by the little figures of the Glockenspiel (carillon) on Marienplatz.

By the early 19th century, furious monument-building gave Munich its spectacular architecture and wide Italianate avenues. Culture and the arts flourished, especially under King Ludwig I. His grandson, Ludwig II, took royal expenditure a bit too far; his grandiose projects, including numerous lavish palaces, bankrupted the royal house and threatened the government. Ironically, today they are the biggest money-spinners in Bavaria's booming tourism industry.

By 1901 Munich had a population of half a million souls but last century was a hard time for most of them. WWI practically starved the city; the Nazis first rose to prominence here and the next world war nearly wiped the city off the map. The 1972 Olympic Games ended in tragedy when 17 people were killed in a terrorist hostage-taking incident.

Today Munich is recognised for its high living standards, the most millionaires per capita in Germany after Hamburg, and for an appreciation of the good life.

Sights

ALTSTADT

Marienplatz SQUARE
(Ⓢ Marienplatz) The heart and soul of the Altstadt, Marienplatz is a popular gathering

Central Munich

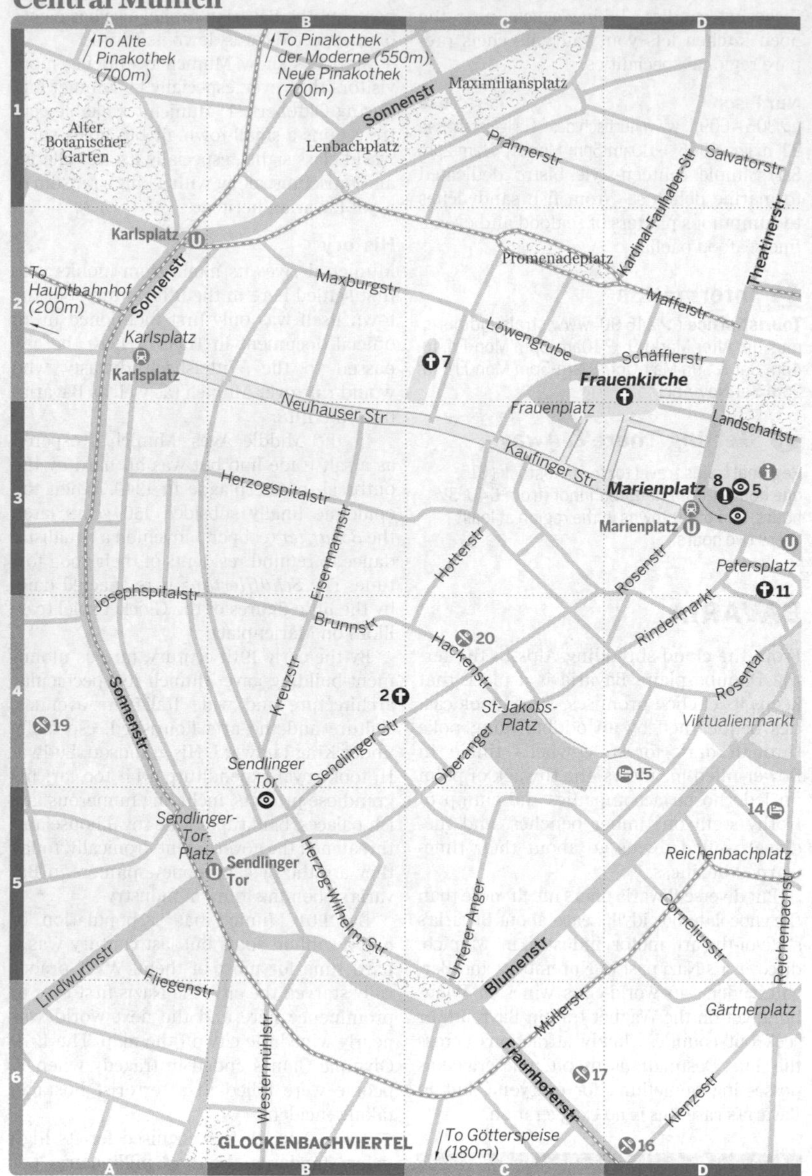

spot and packs a lot of personality into its relatively small frame. It's anchored by the **Mariensäule** (Mary's Column), built in 1638 to celebrate victory over Swedish forces during the Thirty Years' War; it's topped by a golden statue of the Virgin Mary balancing on a crescent moon.

The square is dominated by the heavily ornamented neo-Gothic **Neues Rathaus** (New Town Hall) whose highlight is the en-

Central Munich

Top Sights

Frauenkirche D2
Marienplatz D3
Residenzmuseum F2

Sights

1 Altes Rathaus E3
2 Asamkirche B4
3 Bier & Oktoberfestmuseum F4
4 Cuvilliés-Theater E1
5 Glockenspiel D3
6 Hofbräuhaus F3
7 Michaelskirche C2
8 Neues Rathaus Tower D3
9 Schatzkammer der Residenz E2
10 Spielzeugmuseum E3
11 St Peterskirche D3
12 Viktualienmarkt E4

Activities, Courses & Tours

13 Mike's Bike Tours E3

Sleeping

14 Hotel am Viktualienmarkt D5
15 Hotel Blauer Bock D4

Eating

16 Bergwolf D6
17 Fraunhofer C6
18 Königsquelle F5
19 La Vecchia Masseria A4
20 Prinz Myshkin C4
21 Weisses Brauhaus E3

Drinking

Hofbräuhaus .... (see 6)

Entertainment

22 Atomic Café F3

dearing **Glockenspiel** whose 43 bells and 32 figures perform two actual historic events. The top half tells the story of a knight's tournament held in 1568 to celebrate the marriage of Duke Wilhelm V to Renata of Lothringen, while the bottom half portrays the *Schäfflertanz*). For pinpointing Munich's landmarks without losing your breath, catch the lift up the 85m-tall **tower** (adult/child €2/€1; 9am-7pm Mon-Fri, 10am-7pm Sat & Sun).

Altes Rathaus HISTORICAL BUILDING

(Old Town Hall; Marienplatz; S Marienplatz, Marienplatz) The eastern side of Marienplatz is dominated by the Altes Rathaus (Old Town Hall). On 9 November 1938 Joseph Goebbels gave a hate-filled speech here that launched the nationwide *Kristallnacht* pogroms. Today it houses the adorable **Spielzeugmuseum** (Toy Museum;

DON'T MISS

RESIDENZ

The Residenz is a suitably grand palace that reflects the splendour and power of the Bavarian rulers who lived here from 1385 to 1918. Taking up half the compound is the treasure-packed **Residenzmuseum** (☎290 671; www.residenz-muenchen.de; adult/child €7/free, combination ticket for the museum, Schatzkammer & Cuvilliés-Theater €13/free; ⏲9am-6pm Apr–mid-Oct, 10am-5pm mid-Oct–Mar). Start at the **Grottenhof** (Grotto Court), home of the wonderful **Perseusbrunnen** (Perseus Fountain), with its namesake holding the dripping head of Medusa. Next door is the famous **Antiquarium**, a barrel-vaulted hall smothered in frescoes and built to house the Wittelsbach's enormous antique collection. It's widely regarded as the finest Renaissance interior north of the Alps.

Upstairs are the **Kurfürstenzimmer** (Electors Rooms), with some stunning Italian portraits and a passage lined with two dozen views of Italy. Also up here are François Cuvilliés' **Reiche Zimmer** (Rich Rooms), a six-room extravaganza of exuberant rococo. More rococo magic awaits in the **Ahnengallery** (Ancestors Gallery), a chronological roll call of 121 portraits of Bavarian rulers. The superb rococo **Steinzimmer** (Stone Rooms) are awash in intricately patterned and coloured marble.

The Residenzmuseum entrance also leads to the **Schatzkammer der Residenz** (Residence Treasury; adult/concession/under 18yr with parents €7/6/free; ⏲9am-6pm Apr–mid-Oct, 10am-5pm mid-Oct–Mar), a veritable banker's bonus worth of jewel-encrusted bling of yesteryear, from golden toothpicks to finely crafted swords, miniatures in ivory to gold entombed cosmetics trunks.

Another highlight is the **Cuvilliés-Theater** (adult/child €3.50/free; ⏲2-6pm Mon-Sat, from 9am Sun Apr-Jul & mid-Sep–mid-Oct, 9am-6pm daily Aug–mid-Sep, shorter hours mid-Oct–Mar), named for its architect and one of Europe's finest rococo theatres. Famous for hosting the premiere of Mozart's opera *Idomeneo*, restoration work in the mid-2000s revived the theatre's former glory, and its stage once again hosts high-brow musical and operatic performances.

www.toymuseum.de; Marienplatz 15; adult/child €4/1; ⏲10am-5.30pm) with its huge collection of rare and precious toys from Europe and the US.

St Peterskirche CHURCH
(Church of St Peter; Rindermarkt 1; church admission free, tower adult/child €1.50/1; ⏲tower 9am-5.30pm Mon-Fri, from 10am Sat & Sun; SMarienplatz, UMarienplatz) Some 306 steps divide you at ground level and the best view of central Munich from the 92m tower of St Peterskirche, Munich's oldest church (1150). Also known as Alter Peter (Old Peter), it's a virtual textbook of art through the centuries, with highlights including the Gothic St-Martin-Altar, Johann Baptist Zimmermann's baroque ceiling fresco, and Ignaz Günther's rococo sculptures.

Viktualienmarkt MARKET
(⏲Mon-Fri & Sat morning; SMarienplatz, UMarienplatz) Viktualienmarkt is a feast of flavours and one of Germany's finest gourmet markets where many of the stalls have been run by generations of the same family. Prices are predictably high, but so is the quality and many items sold here are hard to find elsewhere.

FREE **Hofbräuhaus** BEER HALL
(www.hofbraeuhaus.de; Am Platzl 9; SMarienplatz, UMarienplatz) Even teetotalling cliché-haters will at some point gravitate, out of simple curiosity, to the Hofbräuhaus, the world's most celebrated beer hall. The writhing hordes of tourists tend to overshadow the sterling interior, where dainty twirled flowers and Bavarian flags adorn the medieval vaults.

Frauenkirche CHURCH
(Church of Our Lady; Frauenplatz 1; tower €2; ⏲7am-7pm Sat-Wed, to 8.30pm Thu, to 6pm Fri) This 15th-century church is Munich's spiritual heart. No other building in the central city may stand taller than the 99m of its onion-domed twin towers. From April to October, you can enjoy panoramic city views from the **south tower**.

Michaelskirche CHURCH
(Church of St Michael; Kaufingerstrasse 52; crypt admission €2; ⏲crypt 9.30am-4.30pm Mon-Fri,

9.30am-2.30pm Sat & Sun; S Karlsplatz, Karlsplatz, Karlsplatz). Completed in 1597 as the then-largest Renaissance church north of the Alps, St Michaels boasts an impressive unsupported barrel-vaulted ceiling but is really most famous as the final resting place of King Ludwig II, whose humble tomb in the crypt is usually drowned in flowers. The building has been, and is set to be, under heavy renovation for years.

Bier & Oktoberfestmuseum MUSEUM

(Beer&OktoberfestMuseum; www.bier-und-oktoberfestmuseum.de; Sterneckerstrasse 2; adult/concession €4/2.50; 1-5pm Tue-Sat; Isartor, Isartor) If you can't be in town for the real thing, head to this popular museum to learn all about Bavarian suds and the world's most famous booze-up. The four floors heave with old brewing vats, historic photos and some of the earliest Oktoberfest regalia.

Asamkirche CHURCH

(Sendlinger Strasse 34; S Sendlinger Tor, Sendlinger Tor) Though pocket-sized, late baroque Asamkirche (1746) is as rich and epic as a giant's treasure chest. Its creators, the brothers Cosmas Damian and Egid Quirin, dipped deeply into their considerable talent box to swathe every inch of wall space with paintings, *Putti* (cherubs), gold leaf and stucco flourishes.

MAXVORSTADT, SCHWABING & ENGLISCHER GARTEN

North of the Altstadt, Maxvorstadt is home to Munich's *Kunstareal* (art district), a cluster of top-drawer art museums. It segues into cafe-filled Schwabing which rubs up against the vast Englischer Garten.

Alte Pinakothek ART MUSEUM

(www.pinakothek.de; Barer Strasse 27; adult/child €7/5, Sun €1, audioguide €4.50; 10am-8pm Tue, to 6pm Wed-Sun; Pinakotheken, Pinakotheken) Munich's main repository of Old European Masters is crammed with all the major players that decorated canvases between the 14th and 18th centuries.

The collection is world famous for its exceptional quality and depth, especially when it comes to German masters such as Lucas Cranach the Elder and Albrecht Dürer. Rubens fans also have reason to rejoice thanks, in part, to the 6m-high *Last Judgment* in its custom-designed hall. The Italians are represented by Botticelli, Raphael, Titian and many others, while the Spaniards field such heavy hitters as El Greco, Murillo and Velázquez.

Neue Pinakothek ART MUSEUM

(www.pinakothek.de; Barer Strasse 29; adult/child €7/5, Sun €1; 10am-6pm Thu-Mon, to 8pm Wed; Pinakotheken, Pinakotheken) Picking up where the Alte Pinakothek leaves off, the Neue Pinakothek harbours a well-respected collection of 19th- and early 20-century paintings and sculpture, from rococo to *Jugendstil* (art nouveau).

All the main household names get wall space here, including crowd-pleasing Impressionists such as Monet, Cézanne, Degas and Van Gogh. Memorable canvases also include the brooding landscapes of German Romantic painter Caspar David Friedrich and those of local artists Carl Spitzweg and Franz Lenbach.

Pinakothek der Moderne ART MUSEUM

(www.pinakothek.de; Barer Strasse 40; adult/child €10/7, Sun €1; 10am-6pm Tue, Wed & Fri-Sun, 10am-8pm Thu; Pinakotheken, Pinakotheken) This vast modern art museum has a spectacular four-storey interior centred on an eye-like dome which spreads soft natural light throughout white galleries.

The museum unites four significant collections under a single roof, most notably the **State Gallery of Modern Art**, which showcases exemplary modern classics by Picasso, Klee, Dalí, Kandinsky and more recent big shots like Andy Warhol, Cy Twombly and Joseph Beuys.

Retro fans gravitate to the **New Collection** which focuses on applied design from the industrial revolution via art nouveau

LOCAL KNOWLEDGE

NO WAVE GOODBYE

Munich is famous for beer, sausages and surfing. Yep, you read that right. Just go to the southern tip of the English Garden at Prinzregentenstrasse and you'll see scores of people leaning over a bridge to cheer on wetsuit-clad daredevils as they 'hang 10' on an artificially created wave in the Eisbach creek. It's only a single wave, but it's a damn fine one. In fact, the surfers are such an attraction, the tourist office even includes them in its brochures.

and Bauhaus to today. VW Beetles, Eames chairs and early Apple Macs stand alongside more obscure interwar items that wouldn't be out of place in a Kraftwerk video.

Also here is the **State Graphics Collection**, which boasts drawings, prints and engravings by such masters as Leonardo da Vinci and Paul Cézanne, and the **Architecture Museum**, which illustrates how such famous practioners as baroque architect Balthasar Neumann and Bauhaus maven Le Corbusier have influenced the genre.

TOP CHOICE Englischer Garten PARK
(Ⓢ Universität) The sprawling English Garden is among Europe's biggest city parks – bigger than even London's Hyde Park and New York's Central Park – and a favourite playground for locals and visitors alike.

Several historic follies lend the park a playful charm. The wholly unexpected **Chinesischer Turm** (Chinese Tower), now at the heart of Munich's oldest beer garden, was built in the 18th century during a pan-European craze for all things oriental. Further south, at the top of a gentle hill, stands the heavily photographed **Monopteros** (1838), a small Greek temple whose ledges are often knee-to-knee with dangling legs belonging to people admiring the view of the Munich skyline.

Further Afield

Schloss Nymphenburg PALACE
(www.schloss-nymphenburg.de; adult/child €6/5; ⌚9am-6pm Apr–mid-Oct, 10am-4pm mid-Oct–Mar; 🚋Schloss Nymphenburg) This commanding palace and its lavish gardens sprawl around 5km northwest of the Altstadt. Begun in 1664 as a villa for Electress Adelaide of Savoy, the stately pile was extended over the next century to create the royal family's summer residence.

The main palace building consists of a large villa and two wings of creaking parquet floors and sumptuous period rooms. Right at the beginning of the self-guided tour comes the highpoint of the entire Schloss, the **Schönheitengalerie** (Gallery of Beauties), housed in the former apartments of Queen Caroline. Some 38 portraits of attractive females chosen by an admiring King Ludwig I peer prettily from the walls.

Further along the tour route comes the **Queen's Bedroom**, which still contains the sleigh bed on which Ludwig II was born, and the **King's Chamber** resplendent with 3D ceiling frescoes.

Also in the main building is the **Marstall-Museum** (adult/concession €4.50/3.50; ⌚9am-6pm Apr–mid-Oct, 10am-4pm mid-Oct–Mar), displaying royal coaches and riding gear. This includes Ludwig II's fairy-tale-like rococo sleigh, ingeniously fitted with oil lamps for his crazed nocturnal outings.

BMW Museum MUSEUM
(www.bmw-welt.de; adult/child €12/6; ⌚10am-6pm Tue-Sun) The BMW Museum is like no other car museum on the planet. The seven themed 'houses' examine the development of BMW's product line and include sections on motorcycles and motor racing. However, the interior design of this truly unique building, with its curvy retro feel, futuristic bridg-

DON'T MISS

OKTOBERFEST

Hordes come to Munich for **Oktoberfest** (www.oktoberfest.de), running the 15 days before the first Sunday in October. Reserve accommodation well ahead and go early in the day so you can grab a seat in one of the hangar-sized beer 'tents'. The action takes place at the Theresienwiese grounds, about a 10-minute walk southwest of the Hauptbahnhof. While there is no entrance fee, those €9 1L steins of beer (called *Mass*) add up fast. Although its origins are in the marriage celebrations of Crown Prince Ludwig in 1810, there's nothing regal about this beery bacchanalia now: expect mobs, expect to meet new and drunken friends, expect decorum to vanish as night sets in and you'll have a blast.

A few tips:

» Locals call it *Wiesn* (meadow)

» The Hofbräu tent is big with tourists

» The Augustiner tent draws traditionalists

» Traditional Oktoberfest beer should be a rich copper colour; order it instead of the tourist-satisfying pale lager

es, squares and huge backlit wall screens, almost upstages the exhibits.

Deutsches Museum MUSEUM
(☎21 791; www.deutsches-museum.de; Museumsinsel 1; adult/child €8.50/3; ⊙9am-5pm; Deutsches Museum) Spending a few hours in this temple to technology is an eye-opening journey of discovery and a likely hit with young, sponge-like minds. There are tons of interactive displays (including glass blowing and papermaking), live demonstrations and experiments, model coal and salt mines, and engaging sections on cave paintings, geodesy, microelectronics and astronomy. In the fabulous **KinderReich** (Childrens Kingdom; ⊙9am-4.30pm), 1000 activities, from a kid-size mouse wheel to a fully explorable fire engine and heaps of colourful blocks, await.

Tours

Radius Tours GUIDED TOUR
(☎543 487 7720; www.radiustours.com; opp track 32, Hauptbahnhof; ⊙8.30am-6pm Apr-Oct, to 2pm Nov-Mar) Entertaining and informative English-language tours include the two-hour pay-what-you-like **Priceless Munich Walk** (⊙10am daily), the fascinating 2½-hour **Hitler & The Third Reich Tour** (adult/student €12/10; ⊙3pm Apr–mid-Oct, 11.30am Fri-Tue mid-Oct–Mar), and the three-hour **Prost! Beer & Food tour** (adult/student €29/27; ⊙6pm selected days). The company also runs popular excursions to Neuschwanstein, Salzburg and Dachau as well as a range of other themed tours.

Munich Walk Tours WALKING TOUR
(☎2423 1767; www.munichwalktours.de; Arnulfstrasse 2; tours from €12) In addition to running an almost identical roster of tours to Munich's other tour companies and acting as an agent for them (see website for times and prices), these guys also rent out bicycles (€15 per 24 hours) and offer internet access at Thomas-Wimmer-Ring 1 (€1 per 45 minutes).

Mike's Bike Tours BIKE TOURS
(☎2554 3987; www.mikesbiketours.com; departs Altes Rathaus, Marienplatz; tours from €24) This outfit runs guided bike tours of the city from the Altes Rathaus on Marienplatz. The standard tour is around four hours long (with a one-hour beer garden break; lunch not included); the extended tour goes for seven hours and covers 15km.

City Bus 100 BUS
Ordinary city bus that runs from the Hauptbahnhof to the Ostbahnhof via 21 of the city's museums and galleries.

Sleeping

Munich has no shortage of places to stay – except during Oktoberfest or some busy summer periods, when the wise (meaning those with a room) will have booked. Many budget and midrange places can be found in the cheerless streets around the train station. If you can, avoid this area as you'll find hotels with more charm and atmosphere elsewhere.

Hotel Blauer Bock HOTEL €€
(☎231 780; www.hotelblauerbock.de; Sebastiansplatz 9; s €55-99, d €90-153; ; SMarienplatz, Marienplatz) A stuffed olive's throw away from the Viktualienmarkt, this simple hotel has successfully slipped through the net of gentrification to become the Altstadt's best deal. The cheapest, unmodernised rooms have shared facilities, the updated ensuite chambers are of a 21st-century vintage and all are quiet, despite the location. Great restaurant to boot.

Hotel Cocoon DESIGN HOTEL €€
(☎5999 3907; www.hotel-cocoon.de; Lindwurmstrasse 35; s/d €79/99; SSendlinger Tor, Sendlinger Tor) If retro-design is your thing, you just struck gold. Things kick off in the reception with its faux '70s veneer and suspended '60s ball chairs, and continue in the rooms, all identical and decorated in cool retro oranges and greens.

The glass showers actually stand in the sleeping area, with only a kitschy Alpine meadow scene veiling life's vitals. Another branch, **Cocoon Stachus** (Adolf-Kolping-Strasse 11), opened in 2012.

Schiller 5 HOTEL €€
(☎515 040; www.schiller5.com; Schillerstrasse 5; s/d from €102/144; P; SHauptbahnhof, Hauptbahnhof, Hauptbahnhof) Not only are the pads at this semi-apartment hotel smartly trimmed, you also get a lot for your euro here in the shape of a well-equipped kitchenette, sound system, coffee machine and extra large bed. Street noise may be an issue.

Sofitel Munich Bayerpost HOTEL €€€
(☎599 480; www.sofitel.com; Bayerstrasse 12; s/d from €140/160; P@; SHauptbahnhof, Hauptbahnhof Süd, Hauptbahnhof) This high-concept jewel wraps all that's great about Munich – history, innovation, elegance, the

art of living – into one neat and appealing package. Be sure to make time for the luxurious spa whose grotto-like pool juts into the atrium lobby.

Hotel am Viktualienmarkt HOTEL €€
(☎231 1090; www.hotel-am-viktualienmarkt.de; Utzschneiderstrasse 14; d €50-120; ; Marienplatz, Marienplatz) Owners Elke and her daughter Stephanie run this good-value property with panache and a sunny attitude. The best of the up-to-date 26 rooms have wooden floors and framed poster art. All this, plus the city-centre location, makes it a superb deal.

Meininger's HOSTEL, HOTEL €
(☎5499 8023; www.meininger-hostels.de; Landsbergerstrasse 20; dm/s/d without breakfast from €15/45/80; @; Holzapfelstrasse.) About 800m west of the Hauptbahnhof, this hostel-hotel combo has basic, clean, bright rooms with big dorms divided into two for a bit of privacy. Room rates vary wildly depending on the date, special events and occupancy. Breakfast is an extra €4, bike hire €12 per day.

Hotelissimo Haberstock HOTEL €€
(☎557 855; www.hotelissimo.com; Schillerstrasse 4; s/d from €74/104; ; Hauptbahnhof, Hauptbahnhof, Hauptbahnhof) The cheery decor at this value-for-money pick reflects the vision of the owners, a husband-and-wife team with a knack for colour, fabrics and design.

Wombats City Hostel Munich HOSTEL €
(☎5998 9180; www.wombats-hostels.com; Senefelderstrasse 1; dm €12-24, d from €70; @; Hauptbahnhof, Hauptbahnhof) This professionally run affair near the train station has a whopping 300 dorm beds plus private rooms. Dorms come with ensuite facilities, sturdy lockers and comfy pine bunks. A free welcome drink awaits in the bar, but breakfast is €3.80 extra.

La Maison DESIGN HOTEL €€
(☎3303 5550; www.hotel-la-maison.com; Occamstrasse 24; s/d from €109/119; P@; Münchner Freiheit) Discerningly retro, this sassy number flaunts heated oak floors, jet-black basins and starkly contrasting design throughout. Cool bar on ground level.

Gästehaus Englischer Garten GUESTHOUSE €€
(☎383 9410; www.hotelenglischergarten.de; Liebergesellstrasse 8; s €68-177, d €79-177; P@; Münchner Freiheit) Cosily inserted into a 200-year-old ivy-clad mill, this small guesthouse on the edge of the English Garden offers a Bavarian version of the British B&B experience. Not all rooms are ensuite, but the breakfast is generous and there's cycle hire (€12 per day).

Hotel Mariandl HOTEL €€
(☎552 9100; www.mariandl.com; Goethestrasse 51; s €65-115, d €70-165; Sendlinger Tor, Sendlinger Tor) If you like your history laced with quirkiness, you'll find both aplenty in this rambling neo-Gothic mansion where rooms ooze art noveau flair with hand-selected antiques and ornamented ceilings. Breakfast is served until 4pm in the Vienna-style downstairs cafe, which also has live jazz or classical music nightly.

Hotel Uhland HOTEL €€
(☎543 350; www.hotel-uhland.de; Uhlandstrasse 1; s/d from €69/87; P; Theresienwiese) The Uhland is an enduring favourite with regulars who expect their hotel to feel like a home away from home. Three generations of family are constantly finding ways to improve their guests' experience, be it with wi-fi, bathroom phones, ice cubes, bike rentals or mix-your-own organic breakfast muesli.

Tent CAMPGROUND €
(☎141 4300; www.the-tent.com; In den Kirschen 30; tent bunk/floor space €10.50/7.50, tent pitch from €11; Jun-Nov; Botanischer Garten) A kilometre north of Schloss Nymphenburg, this youth-oriented camping ground has classic tent pitches, as well as a 160-bunk main tent with floor space and foam mats for shoestring nomads.

Eating

TOP CHOICE **Fraunhofer** BAVARIAN €€
(Fraunhoferstrasse 9; mains €7-17.50; 4pm-1am; ; Müllerstrasse) With its screechy parquet floors, stuccoed ceilings, wood panelling and virtually no trace that the last century even happened, this characterful brewpub is one of the city centre's best places to explore the region with a fork. The menu also features at least a dozen vegetarian dishes as well as local fish.

Prinz Myshkin VEGETARIAN €€
(☎265 596; www.prinzmyshkin.com; Hackenstrasse 2; mains €10-17; 11am-12.30am; ; Marienplatz, Marienplatz) Munich's premier meat-free dining spot fills out an open-plan, but strangely intimate vaulted dining space in a former brewery with health-conscious eaters. Join them in savouring such imagi-

native dishes as tofu stroganoff, 'Save the Tuna' pizza and succulent curries.

Wirtshaus in der Au BAVARIAN €€
(☎448 1400; Lilienstrasse 51; mains €8-19; ⏲5pm-midnight Mon-Fri, from 10am Sat & Sun; 🚋Deutsches Museum) Though this traditional Bavarian restaurant has a solid 21st-century vibe, it's that time-honoured staple, the dumpling, that's been declared top speciality here. Once a brewery, the space-rich indoor dining area has chunky tiled floors, a lofty ceiling and a crackling fireplace in winter. When spring springs, the beer garden fills.

Königsquelle ALPINE €€
(☎220 071; Baaderplatz 2; mains €9-18; ⏲dinner; 🚋Isartor, 🚆Isartor) This Munich institution is well loved for its attentive service, expertly prepared food, and dark, well-stocked hardwood bar (with a great selection of malt whiskys). The handwritten, Alpine-inflected menu hopscotches from schnitzel to linguine and goat's cheese to cannelloni.

Tantris FINE DINING €€€
(☎361 9590; www.tantris.de; Johann-Fichte-Strasse 7; menu from €75; ⏲lunch & dinner Tue-Sat; Ⓢ Dietlindenstrasse) Tantris means 'the search for perfection' and here, at one of Germany's most famous restaurants, they're not far off it. The interior design is full-bodied '70s – all postbox reds, truffle blacks and illuminated yellows – the food gourmet sublimity and the service sometimes as unintrusive as it is efficient. Great wine cellar to boot.

Weisses Brauhaus BAVARIAN €€
(Tal 7; mains €8-15; Ⓢ Marienplatz, 🚆Marienplatz) This brewpub's *Weisswurst* (veal sausage) sets the standard for the rest to aspire to; sluice down a pair with the unsurpassed Schneider Weissbier. At night, the dining halls are charged with red-faced, ale-infused hilarity where Alpine whoops accompany the rabble-rousing oompah band.

La Vecchia Masseria ITALIAN €€
(Mathildenstrasse 3; mains €6-15; ⏲11.30am-12.30am; Ⓢ Sendlinger Tor, 🚋Sendlinger Tor) One of Munich's more typically Italian *osterie*, this loud but still romantic place has earthy wood tables, antique tin buckets, baskets and clothing irons conjuring up the ambience of an Apennine farmhouse.

Bergwolf FAST FOOD €
(Fraunhoferstrasse 17; ⏲noon-2am Mon-Thu, noon-4am Fri & Sat, noon-10pm Sun, closed 3-6pm Sun-Fri; Ⓢ Fraunhoferstrasse) At this favourite pit

BEER HALLS & BEER GARDENS

Beer drinking is not just an integral part of Munich's entertainment scene, it's a reason to visit. Beer halls can be vast, boozy affairs seating thousands, or much more modest neighbourhood hang outs. The same goes for beer gardens. What's common is a certain camaraderie among strangers, huge 1L glasses of beer and lots of pretzels and sausages. In beer gardens you are usually allowed to bring your own picnic as long as you sit at tables without tablecloths and order something to drink.

Here are our top choices:

Augustiner Bräustuben (Landsberger Strasse 19; ⏲10am-midnight; 🚋Holzapfelstrasse) At this authentic beer hall inside the actual Augustiner brewery, the Bavarian grub here is superb, especially the *Schweinshaxe* (pork knuckles). Giant black draught horses are stabled behind glass on your way to the restroom. It's about 700m west of the Hauptbahnhof.

Hofbräuhaus (Am Platzl 9; ⏲9am-11.30pm; Ⓢ Marienplatz, 🚋Kammerspiele, 🚆Marienplatz) The ultimate cliché of Munich beer halls where tourists arrive by the busload but no one seems to mind. Wander upstairs for echoes of the past, a small museum and possibly a seat.

Hirschgarten (Hirschgartenallee 1; ⏲11am-11pm; 🚋Kriemhildenstrasse, 🚆Laim) The Everest of Munich beer gardens can accommodate up to 8000 Augustiner lovers, but still manages to feel airy and uncluttered. It's in a lovely spot in a former royal hunting preserve a short walk south of Schloss Nymphenburg.

Chinesischer Turm (Chinese Tower; ☎383 8730; Englischer Garten 3; ⏲10am-11pm; 🚌Chinesischer Turm, 🚋Tivolistrasse) This one's hard to ignore because of its English Garden location and pedigree as Munich's oldest beer garden (open since 1791). Join a motley crowd of fellow beer lovers around the wooden pagoda, showered by the strained sounds of possibly the world's drunkest oompah band.

stop for night owls, the poison of choice is *Currywurst,* a sliced spicy sausage provocatively dressed in a curried ketchup and best paired with a pile of crisp fries. Hangover prevention at its tastiest.

Götterspeise CAFE €
(Jahnstrasse 30; snacks from €3; ⏲8am-7pm Mon-Fri, 9am-6pm Sat; Müllerstrasse) The name of this place translates as 'food of the gods' and the edible in question is that most sinful of treats, chocolate. This comes in many forms, both liquid and solid, but there are also teas, coffees and cakes, and we love the little smokers' perches outside for puffing chocoholics.

Cafe an der Uni CAFE €
(Ludwigstrasse 24; snacks & mains €5-9; ⏲8am-1am Mon-Fri, from 9am Sat & Sun; ; S Universität) Anytime is a good time to be at charismatic CADU. Enjoy breakfast (served until a hangover-friendly 11.30pm!), a cuppa Java or a Helles in the lovely garden hidden by a wall from busy Ludwigstrasse.

Drinking

Apart from the beer halls and garden, Munich has no shortage of lively pubs. Schwabing and the Glockenbachviertel are good places to follow your ears. Many places serve food; most are open until 1am or later on weekends.

Alter Simpl PUB
(Türkenstrasse 57; ⏲11am-3am Mon-Fri, 11am-4am Sat & Sun; Schellingstrasse) Thomas Mann and Hermann Hesse used to knock 'em back at this well-scuffed and wood-panelled thirst parlour. A bookishly intellectual ambience still pervades and this is an apt spot to curl up with a weighty tome over a few Irish ales.

GAY & LESBIAN MUNICH

In Munich, the rainbow flag flies especially proudly along Müllerstrasse and the adjoining Glockenbachviertel. Keep an eye out for the freebie mags *Our Munich* and *Sergej*, which contain up-to-date listings and news about the community and gay-friendly establishments around town. Another source is www.gaymunich.de, which has a small section in English. For help with lodging, check out www.gaytouristoffice.com.

Baader Café CAFE
(Baaderstrasse 47; ⏲9.30am-1am; Fraunhoferstrasse) This literary think-and-drink institution lures all sorts, from short skirts to tweed jackets who linger over daytime coffees and night-hour cocktails. Popular Sunday brunch.

Trachtenvogl CAFE, LOUNGE
(Reichenbachstrasse 47; ⏲10am-1am Sun-Thu, to 2am Fri & Sat; Fraunhoferstrasse) At night you'll have to shoehorn your way into this buzzy lair favoured by a chatty, boozy crowd of scenesters, artists and students. Daytimes are mellower, all the better to slurp its hot-chocolate menu and check out the cuckoo clocks and antlers, left over from the days when this was a folkloric garment shop.

☆ Entertainment

Kultfabrik CLUB COMPLEX
(www.kultfabrik.de; Grafingerstrasse 6; Ostbahnhof) This former dumpling factory is party central with more than a dozen venues along with numerous fast-food eateries. Go to **11er** for electro and house, **Titty Twister** for hard rock and **Refugium** for metal. Nostalgic types can become dancing queens at **Noa**, **Rafael** and **Q Club** while rock-a-billies jive till the wee hours at **Eddy's**.

Münchner Philharmoniker CLASSICAL MUSIC
(☎480 980; www.mphil.de; Rosenheimer Strasse 5; Am Gasteig) Munich's premier orchestra regularly performs at the Gasteig Cultural Centre. Book tickets early as performances usually sell out.

Jazzclub Unterfahrt im Einstein BLUES, JAZZ
(☎448 2794; www.unterfahrt.de; Einsteinstrasse 42; S Max-Weber-Platz) Join a diverse crowd at this long-established, intimate club for a mixed bag of acts ranging from old bebop to edgy experimental. The Sunday open jam session is legendary.

Atomic Café CLUB
(www.atomic.de; Neuturmstrasse 5; ⏲from 10pm Tue-Sat; Kammerspiele) This bastion of indie sounds with funky '60s decor is known for bookers with a knack for catching upwardly hopeful bands before their big break. Otherwise it's party time; long-running Britwoch is the hottest Wednesday club night in town.

FC Bayern München SOCCER
(www.fcbayern.de; S Fröttmaning) Germany's most successful team plays at the impressive Allianz Arena, built for the 2006 World Cup. Tickets can be ordered online.

Shopping

Munich is a fun and sophisticated place to shop that goes far beyond chains and department stores. If you want those, head to Neuhauser Strasse and Kaufingerstrasse. Southeast of there, Sendlinger Strasse has smaller and somewhat more individualistic stores, including a few resale and vintage emporia.

To truly unchain yourself, though, you need to hit the Gärtnerplatzviertel and Glockenbachviertel, the bastion of well-edited indie stores and local designer boutiques. Hans-Sachs-Strasse and Reichenbachstrasse are especially promising.

Maxvorstadt, especially Türkenstrasse, also has an interesting line-up of stores with stuff you won't find on the high street back home.

Information

Tourist office (☎2339 6500; www.muenchen.de) There are two branches: Hauptbahnhof (Bahnhofplatz 2; ⏰9am-8pm Mon-Sat, 10am-6pm Sun) and Marienplatz (Marienplatz 8, Neues Rathaus; ⏰10am-7pm Mon-Fri, to 5pm Sat, to 2pm Sun).

City Tour Card (www.citytourcard-muenchen.com; 1/3 days €9.90/19.90) Includes public transport in the *Innenraum* (zones 1 to 4, marked white on transport maps) and discounts of between 10% and 50% for more than 50 attractions, tours, eateries and theatres. Available at some hotels, tourist offices, and U-Bahn, S-Bahn and DB vending machines.

Getting There & Away

Air

Munich Airport (MUC; www.munich-airport.de), aka Flughafen Franz-Josef Strauss, is second in importance only to Frankfurt's. It's linked to the Hauptbahnhof every 20 minutes by S-Bahn (S1 and S8, €10, 40 minutes) and by the Lufthansa Airport Bus (€10.50, 45 minutes, between 5am and 8pm). Budget between €50 and €70 for a taxi ride.

Note that Ryanair flies into Memmingen's **Allgäu Airport** (www.allgaeu-airport.de), 125km to the west. Seven buses daily shuttle between here and the Hauptbahnhof (€13, 1¾ hours).

Bus

Europabus links Munich to the Romantic Road. For times and fares for this service and all other national and international coaches contact **Sindbad** (☎5454 8989; Arnulfstrasse 20) near the Hauptbahnhof. Buses leave from **Zentraler Omnibusbahnhof** (Central Bus Station, ZOB; Arnulfstrasse 21) at S-Bahn station Hackerbrücke.

Car & Motorcycle

Munich has autobahns radiating in all directions. Take the A9 to Nuremberg, the A8 to Salzburg, the A95 to Garmisch-Partenkirchen and the A8 to Ulm or Stuttgart.

Train

Train connections from Munich to destinations within Bavaria, as well as to other German and European cities, are numerous. All services leave from the Hauptbahnhof, where **Euraide** (www.euraide.de; Desk 1, Reisezentrum, Hauptbahnhof; ⏰9.30am-8pm Mon-Fri May-Jul, 10am-7pm Mon-Fri Aug-Apr) is a friendly English-speaking agency that sells train tickets, makes reservations and can create personalised rail tours of Germany and beyond.

Useful connections from Munich include:

Baden-Baden (€81, five hours, hourly) Change in Mannheim.

Berlin (€121, six hours, every two hours)

Cologne (€134, 4½ hours, hourly)

Frankfurt (€95, 3¼ hours, hourly)

Nuremberg (€52, 1¼ hours, twice hourly)

Prague (€66, five hours 50 minutes, two daily)

Vienna (€85.80, 4½ hours, every two hours)

Würzburg (€67, two hours, twice hourly)

Getting Around

Car & Motorcycle

It's not worth driving in the city centre – many streets are pedestrian-only. The tourist office has a map that shows city-wide parking places (from €2 per hour).

Public Transport

Munich's efficient public transport system is run by **MVV** (www.mvv-muenchen.de) and is composed of buses, trams, the U-Bahn and the S-Bahn. The U-Bahn and S-Bahn run almost 24 hours a day, with a short gap between 2am and 4am.

The city is divided into four zones with most places of visitor interest (except Dachau and the airport) falling within the *Innenraum* (inner zone), which is marked white on public transport maps.

Short rides (*Kurzstrecke*; four bus or tram stops or two U-Bahn or S-Bahn stops) cost €1.20, longer trips cost €2.50. Children aged six to 14 pay a flat €1.20. Day passes are €5.60 for individuals and €10.20 for up to five people travelling together.

Bus drivers sell single tickets and day passes, but tickets for the U-/S-Bahn and other passes must be purchased from station vending machines. Tram tickets are available from vending machines aboard. Tickets must be stamped

WORTH A TRIP

DACHAU

Construction of the first Nazi concentration camp in **Dachau** (Dachau Memorial Site; www.kz-gedenkstaette-dachau.de; Alte Römerstrasse 75; admission free, tours €3; ⏲9am-5pm, tours 11am & 1pm Tue-Sun), some 16km northwest of central Munich, began in March 1933. More than 200,000 Jews, political prisoners, homosexuals and others deemed 'undesirable' were imprisoned here; more than 30,000 died. Pick up an audioguide (€3.50) at the visitors centre or join a 2½-hour tour (€3) offered at 11am and 1pm Tuesday to Sunday. A visit includes camp relics, memorials and a sobering museum that shows a 22-minute English-language documentary (10am, 11.30am, 12.30pm, 2pm and 3pm) that uses mostly post-liberation footage to outline what took place here.

The S2 makes the trip from Munich Hauptbahnhof (two-zone ticket, €5) to Dachau station in 21 minutes from where bus 726 (direction Saubachsiedlung) runs straight to the camp. Show your stamped ticket to the driver. By car, follow Dachauer Strasse straight out to Dachau and follow the 'KZ-Gedenkstätte' signs.

(validated) before use. The fine for getting caught without a valid ticket is €40.

Taxi

Taxis (☎216 10) are expensive and not much more convenient than public transport.

Bavarian Alps

Stretching west from Germany's remote southeastern corner to the Allgäu region near Lake Constance, the Bavarian Alps (Bayerische Alpen) form a stunningly beautiful natural divide along the Austrian border. Ranges further south may be higher, but these mountains shoot up from the foothills so abruptly that the impact is all the more dramatic.

The region is packed with cute villages, sprightly spas and plenty of possibilities for skiing, snowboarding, hiking, canoeing and paragliding. The ski season lasts from about late December until April.

GARMISCH-PARTENKIRCHEN

☎08821 / POP 26,000

An incredibly popular hangout for outdoorsy types and moneyed socialites, the double-barrelled resort of Garmisch-Partenkirchen is blessed with a fabled setting a snowball's throw from Germany's highest peak, the 2964m-high Zugspitze. Garmisch has a cosmopolitan feel, while Partenkirchen retains its old-world Alpine village vibe.

Sights & Activities

Zugspitze MOUNTAIN

(www.zugspitze.de) Views from Germany's rooftop are quite literally breathtaking and, on good days, extend into four countries. Skiing and hiking are the main activities here. The trip to the Zugspitze summit is as memorable as it is popular; beat the crowds by starting early in the day and, if possible, skip weekends altogether.

In Garmisch, board the **Zahnradbahn** (cogwheel train) at its own station behind the Hauptbahnhof. Trains first chug along the mountain base to the **Eibsee**, a forest lake, then wind their way through a mountain tunnel up to the **Schneeferner Glacier** (2600m). Here, you'll switch to the **Gletscherbahn** cable car for the final ascent to the summit. When you're done soaking in the panorama, board the **Eibsee-Seilbahn**, a steep cable car, that sways and swings its way back down to the Eibsee in about 10 minutes.

Most people come up on the train and take the cable car back down, but it works just as well the other way around. Either way, the entire trip costs €39/21.50 per adult/child in winter and €49.50/28 in summer. Winter rates include a day ski pass.

Partnachklamm GORGE

(www.partnachklamm.eu; adult/child €3/1.50; ⏲9am-5pm Oct-Easter, 8am-6pm Easter-Sep) One of the area's main attractions is the dramatically beautiful Partnachklamm, a narrow 700m-long gorge with walls rising up to 80m. A circular walk hewn from the rock takes you through the gorge, which is spectacular in winter when you can walk beneath curtains of icicles and frozen waterfalls.

Sleeping & Eating

Hotel Garmischer Hof HOTEL €€
(☎9110; www.garmischer-hof.de; Chamonixstrasse 10; s €59-94, d €94-130;) Property of the Seiwald family since 1928, many a climber, skier and Alpine adventurer has creased the sheets at this welcoming inn. Rooms are simply furnished but cosy, breakfast is served in the vaulted cafe-restaurant and there's a sauna providing *après-piste* relief.

Hostel 2962 HOSTEL €
(☎957 50; www.hostel2962.com; Partnachauenstrasse 3; dm/d from €20/60;) A bed in one of the four-bed dorms in this converted hotel is the cheapest sleep in town. For dorm dwellers breakfast costs €6.

Bräustüberl GERMAN €€
(☎2312; Fürstenstrasse 23; mains €6-17) A short walk from the centre, this quintessentially Bavarian tavern is the place to cosy up with some local nosh, served by *Dirndl*-trussed waitresses, while the enormous enamel coal-burning stove revives chilled extremities.

Information

Tourist office (☎180 700; www.gapa.de; Richard-Strauss-Platz 2; 8am-6pm Mon-Sat, 10am-noon Sun)

Getting There & Away

From Garmisch there is train service to Munich (€10, 80 minutes, hourly) and to Innsbruck, Austria (€15, 80 minutes, every two hours) via Mittenwald. **RVO bus 9606** (www.rvo-bus.de) runs to Füssen (€3, 2¼ hours, five to six daily), via Oberammergau and Wieskirche, from the train station.

The A95 from Munich is the direct road route. The most central parking is at the Kongresshaus (next to the tourist office) for €1 per hour.

Bus tickets cost €1.50 for journeys in town. For bike hire, try **Fahrrad Ostler** (☎3362; Kreuzstrasse 1; per day/week from €10/50).

OBERAMMERGAU

☎08822 / POP 5230

Quietly quaint Oberammergau occupies a wide valley surrounded by the dark forests and snow-dusted peaks of the Ammergauer Alps. The centre is packed with traditional painted houses, woodcarving shops and awe-struck tourists who come here to learn about the town's world-famous **Passion Play**, a blend of opera, ritual and Hollywood epic that's been performed since the late 17th century as a collective thank you from the villagers for being spared the plague. Half the village takes part, sewing amazing costumes and growing hair and beards for their roles (no wigs or false hair allowed). The next performances are in 2020 but, meanwhile, tours of the **Passionstheater** (☎945 8833; Passionswiese 1; combined tour & Oberammergau Museum entry adult/child/concession €8/3/6; tours 9.30am-5pm Apr-Oct) let you take a peek at the costumes and sets any time.

Oberammergau's other claim to fame is **Lüftmalerei**, the eye-popping house facades painted in an illusionist style. The pick of the crop is the amazing **Pilatushaus** (Ludwig-Thoma-Strasse 10; 3-5pm Tue-Sat May-Oct), whose painted columns snap into 3D as you approach. It contains a gallery and several craft workshops.

The town is also celebrated for its intricate **woodcarvings**. At workshops throughout town skilled craftspeople produce anything from an entire nativity scene in single walnut shell to a life-size Virgin Mary. Speciality shops and the **Oberammergau Museum** (☎941 36; www.oberammergaumuseum.de; Dorfstrasse 8; combined museum entry & Passiontheater tour adult/child/concession €8/3/6; 10am-5pm Tue-Sun Apr-Oct) display fine examples of the carvings.

Oberammergau has a **DJH hostel** (☎4114; www.oberammergau.jugendherberge.de; Malensteinweg 10; dm from €16.80) as well as several guesthouses, including the exceptionally good-value **Gästehaus Richter** (☎935 765; www.gaestehaus-richter.de; Welfengasse 2; s €28-35, d €56-70;) with immaculate ensuite rooms, a guest kitchen, free wi-fi and a filling Alpine breakfast. Recently updated **Hotel Turmwirt** (☎926 00; www.turmwirt.de; Ettalerstrasse 2; s/d from €75/99;) next to the church has pristine business-standard rooms, some with Alpine views from the balconies and bits of woodcarving art throughout.

ALP-HOPPING

While the public transport network is good, the mountain geography means there are few direct routes between the top Alpine draws; sometimes a shortcut via Austria is quicker (such as by road between Füssen and Garmisch-Partenkirchen). Bus rather than rail routes are often more practical. For those driving, the German Alpine Road (Deutsche Alpenstrasse) is a scenic way to go.

DON'T MISS

WIESKIRCHE

Known as 'Wies' for short, the **Wieskirche** (☎08862-932 930; www.wieskirche.de; ⊙8am-5pm) is one of Bavaria's best-known baroque churches and a Unesco-listed heritage site. About a million visitors a year flock to see this stuccoed wonder by the artist brothers Dominikus and Johann Baptist Zimmermann.

In 1730, a farmer in Steingaden, about 30km northeast of Füssen, witnessed the miracle of his Christ statue shedding tears. Pilgrims poured into the town in such numbers over the next decade that the local abbot commissioned a new church to house the weepy work. Inside the almost circular structure, eight snow-white pillars are topped by gold capital stones and swirling decorations. The unsupported dome must have seemed like God's work in the mid-17th century, its surface adorned with a pastel ceiling fresco celebrating Christ's resurrection.

From Füssen, regional RVO bus 73 (www.rvo-bus.de) makes the journey up to six times daily. The Europabus also stops here long enough in both directions to have a brief look round then get back on. By car, take the B17 northeast and turn right (east) at Steingaden.

The **tourist office** (☎922 740; www.ammergauer-alpen.de; Eugen-Papst-Strasse 9a; ⊙9am-6pm Mon-Fri, 9am-1pm Sat) can help find accommodation.

Hourly trains connect Munich with Oberammergau (change at Murnau; €18.10, 1¾ hours). **RVO bus 9606** (www.rvo-bus.de) travels hourly direct to Garmisch-Partenkirchen via Ettal; change at Echelsbacher Brücke for Füssen.

BERCHTESGADEN

☎08652 / POP 7600

Steeped in myth and legend, the Berchtesgadener Land is almost preternaturally beautiful. Framed by six formidable mountain ranges and home to Germany's second-highest mountain, the Watzmann (2713m), its dreamy, fir-lined valleys are filled with gurgling streams and peaceful Alpine villages.

Much of the terrain is protected as the Nationalpark Berchtesgaden, which embraces the pristine Königssee, one of Germany's most photogenic lakes. Yet, Berchtesgaden's history is also indelibly entwined with the Nazi period, as chronicled at the disturbing Dokumentation Obersalzberg. The Eagle's Nest, a mountaintop lodge built for Hitler, is now a major tourist attraction.

Sights & Activities

Königssee LAKE

Crossing the serenely picturesque, emerald-green Königssee makes for some unforgettable memories. Contained by steep mountain walls some 5km south of Berchtesgaden, it's Germany's highest lake (603m), with drinkable waters shimmering into fjordlike depths. Bus 841 makes the trip out here from the Berchtesgaden Hauptbahnhof roughly every hour.

Escape the hubbub of the bustling lakeside tourist village by taking an electric **boat tour** (www.seenschifffahrt.de; return adult/child €13.30/6.70) to **St Bartholomä**, a quaint onion-domed chapel on the western shore. At some point, the boat will stop while the captain plays a horn towards the Echo Wall – the sound will bounce seven times. Pure magic! The effect only fails during heavy fog. From the dock at St Bartholomä, an easy trail leads to the wondrous **Eiskapelle** in about one hour.

TOP CHOICE Dokumentation Obersalzberg MUSEUM

(www.obersalzberg.de; Salzbergstrasse 41, Obersalzberg; adult/child €3/free; ⊙9am-5pm daily Apr-Oct, 10am-3pm Tue-Sun Nov-Mar) In 1933 the quiet mountain retreat of **Obersalzberg** (3km from the town of Berchtesgaden) became the southern headquarters of Hitler's government, a dark period that's given the full historical treatment at the Dokumentation Obersalzberg. All facets of Nazi terror are dealt with, including Hitler's near-mythical appeal, his racial politics, the resistance movement, foreign policy and the death camps. Half-hourly bus 838 runs here from Berchtesgaden Hauptbahnhof.

Eagle's Nest HISTORIC SITE

(☎2969; www.kehlsteinhaus.de; ⊙mid-May–Oct) Berchtesgaden's most sinister draw is Mt Kehlstein (as the Eagle's Nest is known in

German), a sheer-sided peak at Obersalzberg where Martin Bormann, a key henchman of Hitler's, engaged 3000 workers to build a diplomatic meetinghouse for the Führer's 50th birthday. The Allies never regarded the site worth bombing, and so it survived WWII untouched and today houses a restaurant that donates profits to charity.

To get there, drive or take half-hourly bus 838 from the Hauptbahnhof to the Hotel InterContinental. From here the road is closed to private traffic and you must take a special **bus** (adult/child €15.50/9) up the mountain (35 minutes). The final 124m stretch to the summit is aboard a snazzy brass-clad lift (elevator).

You can also experience the sinister legacy of the Obersalzberg area, including the Eagle's Nest and the underground bunker system, on a four-hour guided English-language tour run by **Eagle's Nest Tours** (☎649 71; www.eagles-nest-tours.com; Königsseer Strasse 2; adult/child €50/35; ⏲1.15pm mid-May–Oct). Reservations are advised.

Salzbergwerk HISTORIC SITE
(www.salzzeitreise.de; Bergwerkstrasse 83; adult/child €15.50/9.50; ⏲9am-5pm May-Oct, 11am-3pm Nov-Apr) Once a major producer of 'white gold', Berchtesgaden has thrown open its salt mines for fun-filled 90-minute tours. Kids especially love donning miners' garb and whooshing down a wooden slide into the depth of the mine. Down below, highlights include mysteriously glowing salt grottoes and the crossing of a 100m-long subterranean salt lake on a wooden raft.

Sleeping & Eating

Hotel Bavaria HOTEL €€
(☎660 11; www.hotelbavaria.net; Sunklergässchen 11; r €50-130; P) In the same family for over a century, this well-run hotel offers a romantic vision of Alpine life with rooms bedecked in frilly curtains, canopied beds, heart-shaped mirrors and knotty wood galore. Five of the pricier rooms have their own whirlpools. Gourmet breakfasts include sparkling wine.

Holzkäfer CAFE, BAR €
(☎600 90; Buchenhöhe 40; dishes €4-9; ⏲11am-1am Wed-Mon) This funky log cabin in the Obersalzberg hills is a great spot for a night out with fun-loving locals. Cluttered with antlers, carvings and backwoods oddities, it's known for its tender pork roasts, dark beer and Franconian wines.

HITLER'S MOUNTAIN RETREAT

Of all the German towns tainted by the Third Reich, Berchtesgaden has a burden heavier than most. Hitler fell in love with nearby Obersalzberg in the 1920s and bought a small country home, later enlarged into the imposing Berghof.

After seizing power in 1933, Hitler established a part-time headquarters here and brought much of the party brass with him. They bought, or often confiscated, large tracts of land and tore down farmhouses to erect a 7ft-high barbed-wire fence. Obersalzberg was sealed off as the fortified southern headquarters of the NSDAP (National Socialist German Workers' Party).

In the final days of WWII, the Royal Air Force levelled much of Obersalzberg, though the Eagle's Nest, Hitler's mountaintop eyrie, was left unscathed.

Information

The **tourist office** (www.berchtesgaden.de; Königsseer Strasse 2; ⏲8.30am-6pm Mon-Fri, to 5pm Sat, 9am-3pm Sun Apr–mid-Oct, reduced hours mid-Oct–Mar) is just across the river from the train station.

Getting There & Away

Travelling from Munich by train involves a change at Freilassing (€30.90, three hours, five daily). The best option between Berchtesgaden and Salzburg is **RVO bus** (www.rvo-bus.de) 840 (45 minutes) which links both towns' train stations twice hourly. Berchtesgaden is south of the Munich–Salzburg A8 autobahn.

Romantic Road

From the vineyards of Würzburg to the foot of the Alps, the almost 400km-long Romantic Road (Romantische Strasse) draws two million visitors every year, making it by far the most popular of Germany's holiday routes. It passes through more than two dozen cities and towns, including Rothenburg ob der Tauber, Dinkelsbühl and Augsburg. Expect tourist coaches and kitsch galore, but also a fair wedge of *Gemütlichkeit* (cosiness) and genuine hospitality.

Getting There & Around

Though Frankfurt is the most popular gateway for the Romantic Road, Munich is a good launchpad as well, especially if you decide to take the bus.

It is possible to do this route using train connections and local buses, but the going is complicated, tedious and slow, especially at weekends. The ideal way to travel is by car, though Deutsche Touring's **Europabus** (☎0171-653 2340719 126 268; www.touring-travel.eu) is an alternative. Note that it gets incredibly crowded in summer. From April to October the special coach runs daily in each direction between Frankfurt and Füssen (for Neuschwanstein); the entire journey takes around 12 hours. There's no charge for breaking the journey and continuing the next day.

Tickets are available for short segments of the trip, and reservations are only necessary during peak-season weekends. Reservations can be made through travel agents, **Deutsche Touring** (www.touring.de), EurAide (p499) in Munich, and Deutsche Bahn's Reisezentrum offices in the train stations. Students, children, pensioners and rail-pass holders qualify for discounts of between 10% and 50%.

Füssen

☎08362 / POP 14,200

In the foothills of the Alps, the town of Füssen itself is often overlooked by the mobs swarming to Schloss Neuschwanstein and Hohenschwangau, the two fantasy castles associated with King Ludwig II. It has some baroque architecture and you can actually sense a certain Alpine serenity after dark while locals count the change from the day's day-tripper invasion.

VISITING THE CASTLES

Both Neuschwanstein and Hohenschwangau must be seen on guided tours (in German or English), which last about 35 minutes each. Timed tickets are only available from the **Ticket Centre** (☎930 40; www.hohenschwangau.de; Alpenseestrasse 12; ⊙tickets 8am-5pm Apr-Sep, 9am-3pm Oct-Mar) at the foot of the castles. In summer, come as early as 8am to ensure you get in that day.

All Munich's tour companies run day excursions out to the castles.

Sights

TOP CHOICE **Schloss Neuschwanstein** CASTLE
(☎930 830; www.hohenschwangau.de; adult/concession €12/11, with Hohenschwangau €23/21; ⊙8am-5pm Apr-Sep, 9am-3pm Oct-Mar) Appearing through the mountaintops like a misty mirage is the world's most famous castle, and the model for Disney's citadel, fairy-tale Schloss Neuschwanstein.

King Ludwig II planned this castle himself, with the help of a stage designer rather than an architect, and it provides a fascinating glimpse into the king's state of mind. Ludwig foresaw his showpiece palace as a giant stage on which to recreate the world of Germanic mythology in the operatic works of Richard Wagner. At its centre is the lavish **Sängersaal** (Minstrels' Hall), created to feed the king's obsession with Wagner and medieval knights. Wall frescos in the hall depict scenes from the opera *Tannhäuser*.

Other completed sections include Ludwig's *Tristan and Isolde*–themed **bedroom**, dominated by a huge Gothic-style bed crowned with intricately carved cathedral-like spires; a gaudy artificial grotto (another allusion to *Tannhäuser*); and the Byzantine **Thronsaal** (Throne Room) with an incredible mosaic floor containing over two million stones.

At the end of the tour visitors are treated to a 20-minute **film** on the castle and its creator, and there's a reasonably priced cafe and the inevitable gift shops.

For the postcard view of Neuschwanstein and the plains beyond, walk 10 minutes up to **Marienbrücke** (Mary's Bridge), which spans the spectacular Pöllat Gorge over a waterfall just above the castle. It's said Ludwig liked to come here after dark to watch the candlelight radiating from the Sängersaal.

Schloss Hohenschwangau CASTLE
(☎930 830; www.hohenschwangau.de; adult/concession €12/11, with Neuschwanstein €23/21; ⊙8am-5.30pm Apr-Sep, 9am-3.30pm Oct-Mar) Ludwig spent his formative years at the sun-yellow Schloss Hohenschwangau. Far less showy than Neuschwanstein, Hohenschwangau has a distinctly lived-in feel and every piece of furniture is original. After his father died, Ludwig's main alteration was having stars, illuminated with hidden oil lamps, painted on the ceiling of his bed-

room. Some rooms have frescos from German history and legend (including the story of the Swan Knight, *Lohengrin*). The swan theme runs throughout.

Museum der Bayerischen Könige MUSEUM
(Museum of the Bavarian Kings; www.museumderbayerischenkoenige.de; Alpseestrasse 27; adult/concession €8.50/7; ⌚8am-7pm Apr-Sep, 10am-6pm Oct-Mar) This architecturally stunning museum is packed with historical background on Bavaria's first family. The big-window lake views to the Alps are almost as stunning as the royal bling on show, which includes Ludwig II's famous blue and gold robe.

Sleeping & Eating

Altstadt Hotel zum Hechten HOTEL €€
(☎916 00; www.hotel-hechten.com; Ritterstrasse 6; s €59-65 d €90-99; 📶) This is one of Füssen's oldest hotels and a barrel of fun. Public areas are traditional in style but the bedrooms are mostly airy, light and brightly renovated. One of Füssen's better eateries awaits downstairs.

Franziskaner Stüberl BAVARIAN €€
(☎371 24; Kemptener Strasse 1; mains €5.50-15; ⌚lunch & dinner) This quaint restaurant specialises in *Schweinshaxe* (pork knuckle) and schnitzel, prepared in more varieties than you can shake a haunch at. Non-carnivores go for the scrumptious *Käsespätzle* (rolled cheese noodles) and the huge salads.

Information

Tourist Office (☎938 50; www.fuessen.de; Kaiser-Maximillian-Platz 1; ⌚9am-5pm Mon-Fri, 10am-2pm Sat, 10am-noon Sun)

Getting There & Away

Trains from/to Munich (€24, two hours) run every two hours. RVO buses 78 and 73 serve the castles from Füssen Bahnhof (€4 return).

The Europabus (p504) leaves from stop 3 outside Füssen train station at 8am. It arrives in Füssen after 8pm.

Augsburg

☎0821 / POP 264,700

The largest city on the Romantic Road, Augsburg is also one of Germany's oldest, founded over 2000 years ago by the stepchildren of Roman emperor Augustus. Today it's a lively provincial city, criss-crossed by little streams and imbued with an appealing ambience and vitality. It makes a good day trip from Munich or a stop on a Romantic Road foray.

Sights

Look for the very impressive onion-shaped towers on the 17th-century **Rathaus** and the adjacent **Perlachturm**, a former guard tower. North of here is the 10th-century **Dom Maria Heimsuchung** (Hoher Weg; ⌚7am-6pm), which has more 'modern' additions, such as the 14th-century doors showing scenes from the Old Testament.

The Fuggers – a 16th-century banking family – left their mark everywhere. They have lavish tombs inside **St Anna Kirche** (Im Annahof 2, off Annastrasse; ⌚10am-12.30pm & 3-6pm Tue-Sat, 10am-12.30pm & 3-4pm Sun), a place also known for being a Martin Luther bolt-hole. The 16th-century **Fuggerei** (www.fugger.de; Jakober Strasse; adult/concession €4/3; ⌚8am-8pm Apr-Sep, 9am-6pm Oct-Mar) was built with banking riches to house the poor, which, remarkably, it still does. The excellent **museum** (Mittlere Gasse 14; free with Fuggerei admission) shows how the family lived.

Sleeping & Eating

Hotel am Rathaus HOTEL €€
(☎346 490; www.hotel-am-rathaus-augsburg.de; Am Hinteren Perlachberg 1; s €79-98 d €98-125; 📶) Just steps from Rathausplatz and Maximilianstrasse, this super-central boutique hotel hires out 31 rooms with freshly neutral decor and a sunny little breakfast room.

Bauerntanz GERMAN €€
(Bauerntanzgässchen 1; mains €7-16; ⌚11am-11.30pm) Belly-satisfying helpings of creative Swabian and Bavarian food (*Spätzle*, veal medallions and more *Spätzle*) are plated up by friendly staff at this prim Alpine tavern with lace curtains, hefty timber interior and chequered fabrics.

Information

Tourist Office (☎502 0724; www.augsburg-tourismus.de; Maximilian Strasse 57; ⌚9am-6pm Mon-Fri, 10am-5pm Sat, 10am-2pm Sun Apr-Oct, 9am-5pm Mon-Fri, 10am-2pm Sat Nov-Mar)

Getting There & Away

Trains between Munich and Augsburg are frequent (€12 to €20, 40 minutes); it's on the main line to Frankfurt. The Romantic Road bus stops at the train station and the Rathaus.

Rothenburg ob der Tauber

☎09861 / POP 11,000

In the Middle Ages, Rothenburg's town fathers built strong walls to protect the town from siege; today they are the reason the town is under siege from tourists. The most stereotypical of all German walled towns, Rothenburg can't help being so cute. Granted 'free imperial city' status in 1274, it's a confection of twisting cobbled lanes and pretty architecture enclosed by towered stone walls. Swarmed during the day, the underlying charm oozes out after the last bus leaves.

Sights

Jakobskirche CHURCH
(Klingengasse 1; adult/child €2/0.50; ⏲9am-5pm) Rothenburg's most famous church sports wonderful stained-glass windows, but its real pièce de résistance is the **Heilig Blut Altar** (Sacred Blood Altar) carved with dizzying intricacy by medieval master Tilmann Riemenschneider.

Rathaus HISTORIC BUILDING
(Marktplatz; Rathausturm adult/concession €2/0.50; ⏲tower 9.30am-12.30pm & 1-5pm daily Apr-Oct, noon-3pm daily Dec, shorter hours Sat & Sun Nov & Jan-Mar) The highlight of Rothenburg's Renaissance town hall is the widescreen views of the city and surrounds from the tower's viewing platform (220 steps).

Mittelalterliches Kriminalmuseum MUSEUM
(☎5359; www.kriminalmuseum.rothenburg.de; Burggasse 3-5; adult/child €4.20/2.60; ⏲10am-6pm May-Oct, shorter hours Nov-Apr) Chastity belts, a cage for cheating bakers and a beer-barrel pen for drunks are among the medieval implements of torture and punishment at this gruesomely fascinating museum.

DRINK AND YE SHALL BE FREE

According to legend, Rothenburg was spared destruction during the Thirty Years' War when the mayor won a challenge by Catholic General Tilly and downed more than 3L of wine at a gulp. This 'Meistertrunk' scene is re-enacted several times daily by the clock figures on the tourist office building and at a festival during Whitsuntide.

Sleeping & Eating

Burg-Hotel HOTEL €€
(☎948 90; www.burghotel.eu; Klostergasse 1-3; s €100-135, d €100-170; P⊖☎) Each of the 15 elegantly furnished guest rooms at this boutique hotel built into the town walls has its own private sitting area. The lower floors shelter a decadent spa while phenomenal valley views unfurl from the breakfast room and stone terrace.

Altfränkische Weinstube HOTEL €
(☎6404; www.altfraenkische-weinstube-rothenburg.de; Klosterhof 7; r €59-89; ☎) In a quiet side street, this characterful inn has six atmosphere-laden rooms, most with four-poster or canopied beds. The restaurant (dinner only) serves up sound regional fare.

Zur Höll GERMAN €€
(☎4229; Burggasse 8; mains €6.50-18; ⏲dinner) This medieval wine tavern, with an appreciation for slow food, is in the town's oldest original building, dating back to the year 900. There's a small regional menu and some excellent wines from nearby Würzburg.

Getting There & Away

There are hourly trains to/from Steinach, a transfer point for service to Würzburg (€12.20, 1¼ hours). The Europabus pauses here for 35 minutes.

Würzburg

☎0931 / POP 133,500

Tucked in among river valleys lined with vineyards, Würzburg beguiles even before you reach the city centre, and is renowned for its art, architecture and delicate wines. For centuries the resident prince-bishops wielded enormous power and wealth, and the city grew in opulence under their rule. Its crowning glory is the Residenz, one of the finest baroque structures in Germany and a Unesco World Heritage site.

Sights

Residenz PALACE
(www.residenz-wuerzburg.de; Balthasar-Neumann-Promenade; adult/child €7.50/6.50; ⏲9am-6pm Apr-Oct, 10am-4.30pm Nov-Mar) The Unesco-listed Residenz is one of Germany's most important and beautiful baroque palaces. Its undisputed highlight is the **Grand Staircase** designed by Balthasar Neumann, a single set of steps that splits and

zigzags up to the 1st floor and is lidded by a humonguous Tiepolo fresco (667 sq metres). It allegorically depicts the four then-known continents (Europe, Africa, America and Asia).

Visits are by guided tour only and also take in the **Weisser Saal** (White Hall) with its ice-white stucco, the **Kaisersaal** (Imperial Hall) canopied by yet another impressive fresco by Tiepolo, and the gilded stucco **Spiegelkabinett** (Mirror Hall). German-language groups leave half-hourly; English tours leave at 11pm and 3pm year-round and, additionally, at 4.30pm April to October. The **Hofgarten** at the back is a beautiful relaxation spot.

Festung Marienberg FORTRESS

Panoramic views over the city's red rooftops and vine-covered hills extend from Marienberg Fortress. It has presided over Würzburg since the city's prince-bishops commenced its construction in 1201; they governed from here until 1719. Their pompous lifestyle is on show at the **Fürstenbaumuseum** (adult/child €4.50/3.50; ⏲9am-6pm Tue-Sun mid-Mar–Oct), while city history is laid out upstairs.

Also here is the **Mainfränkisches Museum** (www.mainfraenkisches-museum.de; adult/child €4/2; ⏲10am-5pm Tue-Sun) with a striking collection of Tilman Riemenschneider sculptures.

The fortress is a 30-minute walk up the hill from the Alte Mainbrücke via the **Tellsteige trail**, which is part of the 4km-long **Weinwanderweg** (wine hiking trail) through the vineyards around Marienberg.

Sleeping & Eating

Würzburg's many *Weinstuben* (wine taverns) are great for sampling the local vintages.

Babelfish HOSTEL €

(☎304 0430; www.babelfish-hostel.de; Haugerring 2; dm €17-23, s/d €45/70) This uncluttered and spotlessly clean hostel has 74 beds spread over two floors, a rooftop terrace, 24-hour reception and a well-equipped guest kitchen.

Hotel Rebstock HOTEL €€

(☎309 30; www.rebstock.com; Neubaustrasse 7; s/d from €101/120; ❄@☜) Don't be misled by the Best Western sign out front: Würzburg's top digs, in a squarely renovated rococo townhouse, has 70 unique, stylishly finished rooms, impeccable service and an Altstadt location.

Bürgerspital Weinstube WINE RESTAURANT €€

(☎352 880; Theaterstrasse 19; mains €7-23; ⏲lunch & dinner) The cosy nooks of this labyrinthine medieval place are among Würzburg's most popular eating and drinking spots. Choose from a broad selection of Franconian wines and wonderful regional dishes, including *Mostsuppe*, a tasty wine soup.

Alte Mainmühle FRANCONIAN €€

(☎167 77; Mainkai 1; mains €7-21; ⏲10am-midnight) Accessed straight from the old bridge, tourists and locals alike cram onto the double-decker terrace suspended above the Main River to savour modern twists on old Franconian favourites.

Information

Tourist Office (☎372 398; www.wuerzburg.de; Marktplatz; ⏲10am-6pm Mon-Fri, 10am-2pm Sat Apr-Dec, plus 10am-2pm Sun May-Oct, reduced hours Jan-Mar)

Getting There & Away

The Europabus stops next to the Hauptbahnhof and at the Residenzplatz.

Train connections from Würzburg:

Bamberg (€19, one hour, twice hourly)

Frankfurt (€33, one hour, hourly)

Nuremberg (€19.20 to €27, one hour, twice hourly)

Rothenburg ob der Tauber (€12.20, one hour, hourly) Change in Steinach.

Nuremberg

☎0911 / POP 503,000

Nuremberg (Nürnberg) woos visitors with its wonderfully restored medieval Altstadt, its grand castle and, in December, its magical *Christkindlmarkt* (Christmas market). Thriving culinary traditions include sizzling *Nürnberger Bratwürste* (finger-sized sausages) and *Lebkuchen* – large, soft gingerbread cookies, traditionally eaten at Christmas time but available here year-round. Both within and beyond the high stone wall encircling the Altstadt is a wealth of major museums that shed light on Nuremberg's significant history.

Nuremberg played a major role during the Nazi years. It was here that the fanatical party rallies were held, the boycott of Jewish businesses began and the infamous Nuremberg Laws outlawing Jewish citizenship were enacted. After WWII the city was chosen as the site of the War Crimes Tribunal, now known as the Nuremberg Trials.

CHRISTMAS MARKETS

Beginning in late November every year, central squares across Germany are transformed into Christmas markets or *Christkindlmärkte* (also known as *Weihnachtsmärkte*). Folks stamp about between the wooden stalls, perusing seasonal trinkets (from hand-carved ornaments to plastic angels) while warming themselves with *Glühwein* (mulled, spiced red wine) and grilled sausages. Locals love 'em and, not surprisingly, the markets are popular with tourists, so bundle up and carouse for hours. Markets in Nuremberg, Dresden, Cologne and Munich are especially famous.

Sights

Hauptmarkt SQUARE

This bustling square in the heart of the Altstadt is the site of daily markets as well as the famous *Christkindlesmarkt*. At the eastern end is the ornate Gothic **Pfarrkirche Unsere Liebe Frau** (Hauptmarkt 14), also known as the Frauenkirche. Daily at noon crowds crane their necks to witness the clock's figure enact a spectacle called *Männleinlaufen*. Rising from the square like a Gothic spire is the gargoyle-adorned, 19m-tall **Schöner Brunnen** (Beautiful Fountain). Touch the seamless golden ring in the ornate wrought-iron gate for good luck.

Kaiserburg CASTLE

(www.schloesser.bayern.de; adult/child incl museum €7/6; ⏲9am-6pm Apr-Sep, 10am-4pm Oct-Mar) Construction of Nuremberg's landmark, the immensely proportioned Kaiserburg, began in the 12th century and dragged on for about 400 years. The complex, for centuries the receptacle of the Holy Roman Empire's treasures, consists of three parts: the Kaiserburg and Stadtburg (the Emperor's Palace and City Fortress) and the Burggrafenburg (Count's Residence), which was largely destroyed in 1420.

The **Kaiserburg Museum** chronicles the history of the castle and provides a survey of medieval defence techniques. You can also visit the **royal living quarters**, the **Imperial and Knights' Halls**, and the **Romanesque Doppelkapelle** (Twin Chapel).

Enjoy panoramic city views from atop the **Sinwellturm** (Sinwell Tower; 113 steps) or peer into the amazing 48m-deep **Tiefer Brunnen** (Deep Well).

The grassy knoll at the southeast corner of the castle gardens (open seasonally) is called **Am Ölberg** and is a good spot to sit and gaze out over the city's rooftops.

Memorium Nuremberg Trials HISTORIC BUILDING

(☎3217 9372; www.memorium-nuremberg.de; Bärenschanzstrasse 72; adult/concession €5/3; ⏲10am-6pm Wed-Mon) Nazis were tried in 1945 and 1946 for crimes against peace and humanity in Schwurgerichtssaal 600 (Court Room 600) of what is still Nuremberg's regional courthouse. The proceedings became known as the Nuremberg Trials, and were held by the Allies in the city for obvious symbolic reasons. The initial and most famous trial, conducted by international prosecutors, saw 24 people accused, of whom 19 were convicted and sentenced, many to death by hanging. Hermann Göring, the Reich's field marshall, cheated the hangman by taking a cyanide capsule in his cell hours before his scheduled execution.

In addition to viewing the courtroom (if not in use), a new exhibition provides comprehensive background on the trials. The courthouse is about 2km from the Altstadt centre. To get here, take the U1 towards Bärenschanze and get off at 'Sielstrasse'.

Reichsparteitagsgelände HISTORIC SITE

(Luitpoldhain) If you've ever wondered where the infamous black-and-white images of ecstatic Nazi supporters hailing their Führer were filmed, it was here in Nuremberg. This orchestrated propaganda began as early as 1927 but, after 1933, Hitler opted for a purpose-built venue, the Reichsparteitagsgelände, about 4km southeast of the centre. Much of the outsize grounds were destroyed during Allied bombing raids, but 4 sq km remain, enough to get a sense of the megalomania behind it.

Exhibits at the **Dokumentationszentrum** (☎231 7538; Bayernstrasse 110; adult/concession €5/3; ⏲9am-6pm Mon-Fri, 10am-6pm Sat & Sun; 🚋) in the north wing of the Kongresshalle put the grounds into historical context by examining the rise of the NSDAP, the Hitler cult, the party rallies and the Nuremberg Trials. East of here, across an artificial pond, is the **Zeppelinfeld**, fronted by a 350m-long grandstand, where most of the big Nazi parades, rallies and events took place.

Take tram 9 from the Hauptbahnhof to 'Doku-Zentrum'.

Germanisches Nationalmuseum MUSEUM
(www.gnm.de; Kartäusergasse 1; adult/child €6/4; ⏲10am-6pm Tue & Thu-Sun, to 9pm Wed) Spanning prehistory to the early 20th century, the German National Museum is the country's most important museum of German culture. It features paintings and sculptures, an archaeological collection, arms and armour, musical and scientific instruments and toys. Among its many highlights is Dürer's anatomically detailed *Hercules Slaying the Stymphalian Birds*.

At the museum's entrance is the inspired **Way of Human Rights**, a symbolic row of 29 white concrete pillars (and one oak tree) bearing the 30 articles of the Universal Declaration of Human Rights.

Museums MUSEUMS
Nuremberg has a lot of toy companies and the **Spielzeugmuseum** (Toy Museum; Karlstrasse 13-15; adult/child €5/3; ⏲10am-5pm Tue-Fri, to 6pm Sat & Sun) presents their products in their infinite variety.

The **Deutsche Bahn Museum** (☎0180-444 22 33; www.db-museum.de; Lessingstrasse 6; adult/child €5/2.50, free with InterRail pass; ⏲9am-5pm Tue-Fri, 10am-6pm Sat & Sun) has a trainload of exhibits on the German railways.

Albrecht Dürer-Haus (Albrecht-Dürer-Strasse 39; adult/child €5/2.50; ⏲10am-5pm Fri-Wed, to 8pm Thu) is where Dürer, Germany's renowned Renaissance draughtsman, lived from 1509 to 1528. A digital version of his wife Agnes 'leads' tours.

Sleeping

Nuremberg hosts many a trade show through the year (including a huge toy fair in February). During these times – and Christmas market weekends – rates soar like a model rocket.

TOP CHOICE **Hotel Elch** HOTEL €€
(☎249 2980; www.hotel-elch.com; Irrerstrasse 9; s/d from €75/95; 📶) This 14th-century, half-timbered house is a snug and romantic 12-room gem. Rooms 2 and 7 have half-timbered walls and ceilings, but modern touches include contemporary art, glazed terracotta bathrooms and rainbow-glass chandeliers. Note the multicoloured elk heads throughout (the hotel's name means 'Elk').

Lette'm Sleep HOSTEL €
(☎992 8128; www.backpackers.de; Frauentormauer 42; dm €16-20, r from €50; @📶) A backpacker favourite, this indie hostel near the Hauptbahnhof has colourfully painted dorms and some groovy self-catering apartments. The retro-styled kitchen and common room are great chill areas; internet, tea and coffee are free, and staff are wired into what's happening around town.

Art & Business Hotel HOTEL €€
(☎232 10; www.art-business-hotel.com; Gleissbühlstrasse 15; s/d €89/115; 📶) You don't have to be an artist or a business person to stay at this up-to-the-minute place near the Hauptbahnhof. From the trendy bar to slate bathrooms, design here is bold, but not overpoweringly so. Small sculpture garden out back. Rates tumble at weekends.

Hotel Deutscher Kaiser HOTEL €€
(☎242 660; www.deutscher-kaiser-hotel.de; Königstrasse 55; s/d from €89/108; @📶) Super-central and with posh design and service, this treat of a historic hotel has been in the same family for over a century. Climb the castle-like granite stairs to find rooms of understated simplicity, flaunting oversize beds, Italian porcelain, silk lampshades and period furniture. Renovation work is ongoing.

Hotel Drei Raben HOTEL €€€
(☎274 380; www.hotel3raben.de; Königstrasse 63; s/d €130/150; 🚭📶) The design of this hotel builds upon the legend of the three ravens perched on the building's chimney stack, who tell stories from Nuremberg lore. Each of the 'mythology' rooms uses decor and art – including sandstone-sculpted bedheads and etched-glass bathroom doors – to reflect a particular tale.

Eating

Don't leave Nuremberg without trying its famous *Nürnberger Bratwürste*. Order 'em by the half dozen with *Meerrettich* (horseradish) on the side. Restaurants line the hilly lanes above the Burgstrasse.

TOP CHOICE **Bratwursthäusle** GERMAN €€
(http://die-nuernberger-bratwurst.de; Rathausplatz 2; meals €6-14; ⏲closed Sun) Seared over a flaming beech-wood grill, the little links sold at this rustic inn arguably set the standards for grilled sausages across the land. You can dine in the timbered restaurant or on the

terrace with views of the Hauptmarkt. Service can be flustered at busy times.

TOP CHOICE **Goldenes Posthorn** FRANCONIAN €€
(☎225 153; Glöckleinsgasse 2, cnr Sebalder Platz; mains €6-19; ⏰11am-11pm;) Push open the heavy copper door to find a real culinary treat that has been serving the folk of Nuremberg since 1498. The miniature local sausages are big here, but there's plenty else on the menu including many an obscure country dish and some vegie options. The choice of dining spaces ranges from formal to folksy, chunky wood to wood panelled.

Hütt'n GERMAN €€
(Bergstrasse 20; mains €5.50-15; ⏰4pm-midnight Mon-Fri, 11am-12.30am Sat, 11am-10.30pm Sun) This local haunt perpetually overflows with admirers of *Krustenschäufele* (roast pork with crackling, dumplings and sauerkraut salad) and the finest *Bratwurst* put to work in various dishes, though menus change daily (Friday is fish day). Also try a tankard of the Franconian *Landbier*.

Café am Trödelmarkt CAFE €
(Trödelmarkt 42; dishes €4-8.50; ⏰9am-6pm Mon-Sat, 11am-6pm Sun) A gorgeous place on a sunny day, this multilevel waterfront cafe overlooks the covered Henkersteg bridge. It's especially popular for its continental breakfasts, and has fantastic cakes as well as good blackboard lunchtime specials.

Information

Tourist Office (www.tourismus.nuernberg.de) Two branches: Künstlerhaus (☎233 60; Königstrasse 93; ⏰9am-7pm Mon-Sat, 10am-4pm Sun) and Hauptmarkt (Hauptmarkt 18; ⏰9am-6pm Mon-Sat, 10am-4pm Sun May-Oct).

Getting There & Around

Nuremberg **airport** (NUE; www.airport-nuernberg.de), 5km north of the centre, is served by regional and international carriers, including Lufthansa, Air Berlin and Air France. U-Bahn 2 runs every few minutes from the Hauptbahnhof to the airport (€2.40, 12 minutes). A taxi costs about €16.

Rail connections from Nuremberg include:

Berlin (€93, five hours, at least hourly)
Frankfurt (€51, two hours, at least hourly)
Munich (€52, one hour, twice hourly)
Vienna (€94.20, five hours, every two hours)

The best transport around the Altstadt is on foot. Public-transport day passes cost €4.80. Passes bought on Saturday are valid all weekend.

Bamberg

☎0951 / POP 70,000

Off the major tourist routes, Bamberg is revered by those in the know. It boasts a beautifully preserved collection of 17th- and 18th-century merchants' houses, palaces and churches. A canal and fast-flowing river spanned by cute little bridges run through the town, which even has its own local style of beer. No wonder it has been recognised by Unesco as a World Heritage site. Could it be the best small town in Germany?

Sights

Bamberger Dom CATHEDRAL
(www.erzbistum-bamberg.de; Domplatz; ⏰8am-6pm Apr-Oct, to 5pm Nov-Mar) The quartet of spires of Bamberg's Dom soars above the cityscape. Its star attraction is the statue of the chivalric knight-king, the **Bamberger Reiter**. Also note the **Lächelnde Engel** (Smiling Angel), who smirkingly hands the martyr's crown to the headless St Denis in the north aisle, and the **marble tomb** of Pope Clemens II, the only papal burial place north of the Alps, in the west choir.

Altes Rathaus HISTORIC BUILDING
(Obere Brücke) The best views of the Gothic 1462 Altes Rathaus (Old Town Hall), which perches on a tiny artificial island between two bridges like a ship in dry dock, are from the small Geyerswörthsteg footbridge across the Regnitz. See if you can spot the cherub's leg sticking out from the fresco on the east side.

Neue Residenz PALACE
(☎519 390; www.schloesser.bayern.de; Domplatz 8; adult/child €4.50/3.50; ⏰9am-6pm Apr-Sep, 10am-4pm Oct-Mar) The 45-minute guided tours of the former residence of Bamberg's prince-bishops take in some 40 stuccoed rooms crammed with furniture and tapestries from the 17th and 18th centuries. The palace also hosts a small branch of the **Bayerische Staatsgalerie** (Bavarian State Gallery) which has mostly medieval, Renaissance and baroque paintings

Sleeping

Hotel Sankt Nepomuk HOTEL €€
(☎984 20; www.hotel-nepomuk.de; Obere Mühlbrücke; r €95-145;) Named aptly after the patron saint of bridges, this is a classy establishment in a half-timbered former mill right on the Regnitz. It has a superb

restaurant (mains €15 to €30) with a terrace, along with 24 comfy rustic rooms.

Backpackers Bamberg HOSTEL €
(☎222 1718; www.backpackersbamberg.de; Heiliggrabstrasse 4; dm €15-18, s/d €27/40; 📶) This indie hostel is a well-kept old-school affair with clean dorms, a guest kitchen and a quiet, family-friendly atmosphere. It's left unstaffed for most of the day so let them know your arrival time. Located around 400m north along Luitpoldstrasse from the Luitpoldbrücke.

Hotel Europa HOTEL €€
(☎309 3020; www.hotel-europa-bamberg.de; Untere Königstrasse 6-8; r €89-119) The Europa is a spick-and-span but unfussy affair above a well-respected Italian restaurant just outside the Altstadt. Ask for a room with views of the Dom and the red-tiled roofs of the Altstadt.

Eating & Drinking

Bamberg's unique style of beer is called *Rauchbier,* which literally means smoked beer. With a bacon flavour at first, it is a smooth brew that goes down easily.

TOP CHOICE **Schlenkerla** GERMAN €€
(Dominikanerstrasse 6; mains €8-15; ⏰Wed-Mon) A warren of rooms decked out with antler lamps, this 16th-century restaurant is famous for tasty Franconian specialities and *Rauchbier,* served directly from oak barrels. This should be your one stop if you only have time for one (stop, not beers...).

Messerschmidt FRANCONIAN €€
(☎297 800; Lange Strasse 41; mains €12-25; ⏰lunch & dinner) This stylish gourmet eatery in the birth house of aviation engineer Willy Messerschmidt oozes old-world charm, with dark woods, white linens and formal service. Tuck into hearty local fare out on the park-facing terrace or in the attached wine tavern.

Klosterbräu BREWERY €
(☎522 65; Obere Mühlbrücke 1-3; mains €6-12; ⏰10.30am-11pm Mon-Fri, 10am-11pm Sat, 10am-10pm Sun) This beautiful half-timbered brewery is Bamberg's oldest. It draws *Stammgäste* (regulars) and tourists alike who wash down filling slabs of meat and dumplings with its excellent range of ales. English-language brewery tours on request.

Information

Tourist office (☎297 6200; www.bamberg.info; Geyerswörthstrasse 5; ⏰9.30am-6pm Mon-Fri, to 4pm Sat, to 2.30pm Sun)

Getting There & Away

Rail connections include:

Berlin (€76, 4¼ hours, every two hours)
Munich (€59, two to 2½ hours, every two hours)
Nuremberg (€12 to €21, 40 to 60 minutes, four hourly)
Würzburg (€19, one hour, twice hourly)

Regensburg

☎0941 / POP 135,500

On the wide Danube River, Regensburg has relics of historic periods reaching back to the Romans, yet doesn't have the tourist mobs you'll find in other equally attractive German cities. Oh well, their loss. At least Unesco noticed – it recognised that Regensburg has the only intact medieval centre in Germany. Amid the half-timbers, Renaissance towers that could be in Tuscany mix with Roman ruins. Meanwhile, some 25,000 students keep things lively.

Sights

Steinerne Brücke BRIDGE
A veritable miracle of engineering for its day, the Stone Bridge was cobbled together between 1135 and 1146 and for centuries remained the only solid crossing along the entire Danube.

Dom St Peter CHURCH
(Domplatz; ⏰6.30am-6pm Apr-Oct, to 5pm Nov-Mar) One of Bavaria's grandest Gothic cathedrals, St Peter's impressive features include kaleidoscopic stained-glass windows and the intricately gilded altar. The **Domschatzmuseum** (adult/child €2/1; ⏰10am-5pm Tue-Sat, noon-5pm Sun) brims with monstrances, tapestries and other church treasures.

Altes Rathaus HISTORIC BUILDING
(Rathausplatz; adult/concession €7.50/4; ⏰English tours 3pm Apr-Oct, 2pm Nov-Mar) The seat of the Reichstag for almost 150 years, the Altes Rathaus is now home to Regensburg's mayors and the **Reichstagsmuseum**. Tours take in not only the lavishly decorated **Reichssaal** (Imperial Hall), but also the original **torture chambers** in the basement.

Sleeping

Petit Hotel Orphée HOTEL €€
(☎596 020; www.hotel-orphee.de; Wahlenstrasse 1; s €35-125, d €70-135) Behind a humble door in the heart of the city lies a world of genuine charm, unexpected extras and real attention to detail. The wrought-iron beds, original sinks and cosy common rooms create the feel of a lovingly attended home. Another somewhat grander branch of the hotel is located above the **Café Orphée** (☎529 77; Untere Bachgasse 8; mains €7-18; ⏲9am-1am).

Brook Lane Hostel HOSTEL €
(☎696 5521; www.hostel-regensburg.de; Obere Bachgasse 21; dm/s/d from €16/40/50, apt per person €55;) Check-in at this small hostel is in the integrated convenience store; late landers should let staff know in advance. Dorms do the minimum required but the apartments and doubles here are applaudable deals. Access to kitchens and washing machines throughout.

Altstadthotel am Pach HOTEL €€
(☎298 610; www.regensburghotel.de; Untere Bachgasse 9; s €98-124, d €118-144; @) Those who have shaped Regensburg history, from Marcus Aurelius to Emperor Karl V, are commemorated in the 21 rooms of this sleek hotel. All are warmly furnished with thick carpets, comfy mattresses and a minifridge with complimentary beer and water.

Eating & Drinking

Historische Wurstkuchl GERMAN €
(Thundorfer Strasse 3; 6 sausages €7.80; ⏲8am-7pm) This titchy riverside eatery has been serving the city's traditional finger-size sausages, grilled over beech wood and dished up with sauerkraut and sweet grainy mustard, since 1135, giving cred to its claim of being the world's oldest sausage kitchen.

Dicker Mann BAVARIAN €€
(www.dicker-mann.de; Krebsgasse 6; mains €6.50-20; ⏲9am-11pm) Stylish, traditional and serving all the staples of Bavarian sustenance, the 'Chubby Chappy' is one of the oldest restaurants in town, allegedly dating back to the 14th century. On a balmy eve, be sure to bag a table in the lovely beer garden out back.

Spitalgarten BEER GARDEN
(St Katharinenplatz 1) A thicket of folding chairs and slatted tables by the Danube, this is one of the best places in town for some alfresco quaffing. It claims to have brewed beer (today's Spital) here since 1350, so it probably knows what it's doing by now.

Information

Tourist Office (www.regensburg.de; Altes Rathaus; ⏲9am-6pm Mon-Fri, to 4pm Sat & Sun)

Getting There & Away

Train connections include:

Munich (€25.20, 1½ hours, hourly)

Nuremberg (€19, one to two hours, hourly)

Passau (from €22 to €27, one to 1½ hours, hourly) Additional services via Plattling.

STUTTGART & THE BLACK FOREST

Germany's southwest is taken up by Baden-Württemberg, a prosperous, modern state created in 1951 out of three smaller regions: Baden, Württemberg and Hohenzollern (thank goodness the names stopped at two!). With the exception of cuckoo clocks in the Black Forest, it runs a distant second in the cliché race to Bavaria. But that's really all the better, as it leaves more for you to discover on your own.

This pretty land of misty hills, shadowy conifers and cute villages rewards exploration. If you want a big and quaint historical town, there's Heidelberg. Baden-Baden is the sybaritic playground for spa-goers, and Freiburg has youthful vibrancy in an intriguing historical package. Finally, Lake Constance is a lovely redoubt bordering Switzerland and has all the pleasures a large body of water can offer.

Stuttgart

☎0711 / POP 581,000

Hemmed in by vine-covered hills, comfortable Stuttgart enjoys a quality of life founded on its fabled car companies: Porsche and Mercedes. It's also Baden-Württemberg's state capital and the hub of its industries. At the forefront of Germany's economic recovery from the ravages of WWII, Stuttgart started life less auspiciously in 950 as a horse stud farm. About 80% of the city centre was destroyed in WWII, but there are a few historical buildings left and – no surprise – excellent car museums.

Stuttgart

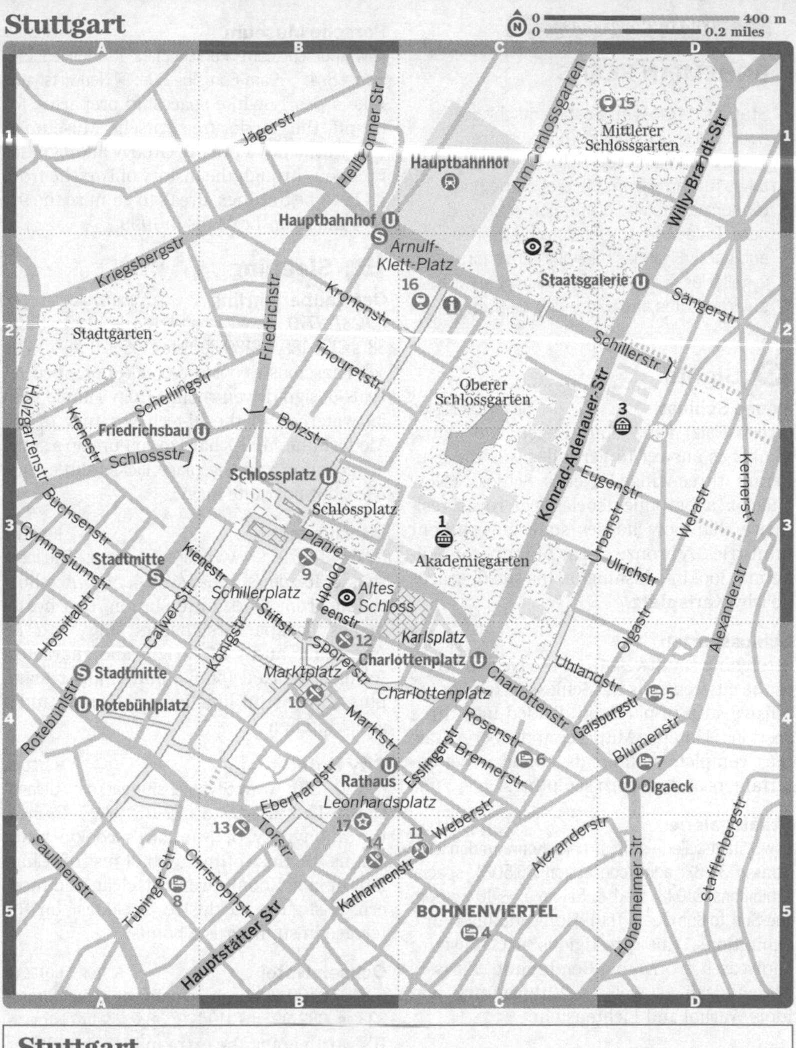

Stuttgart

Sights

1 Neues Schloss C3
2 Schlossgarten C2
3 Staatsgalerie D2

Sleeping

4 Abalon Hotel C5
5 City Hotel D4
6 Der Zauberlehrling C4
7 Hostel Alex 30 .... D4
8 Interhostel A5

Eating

9 Alte Kanzlei B3
10 Food Market B4
11 Irma la Douce C5
12 Markthalle B4
13 Reiskorn B5
14 Weinstube Fröhlich B5

Drinking

15 Biergarten im Schlossgarten D1
16 Sky Beach C2

Entertainment

17 Kiste B5

LOCAL KNOWLEDGE

BOHEMIAN BEANS

Stuttgart's most interesting neighbourhood is a short stroll from the centre. The **Bohnenviertel** (Bean District) takes its name from the diet of the poor tanners, dyers and craftsmen who lived here. Today the district's cobbled lanes and gabled houses harbour idiosyncratic galleries, workshops, bookstores, wine taverns, cafes and a red-light district.

Sights

Neues Schloss HISTORIC BUILDING

(Schlossplatz) Duke Karl Eugen von Württemberg's answer to Versailles was the exuberant three-winged Neues Schloss (New Palace), a baroque-neoclassical royal residence that now houses state government ministries. A bronze statue of Emperor Wilhelm I, looking dashing on his steed, graces nearby **Karlsplatz**.

Schlossgarten GARDEN

Stretching southwest from the Neckar River to the city centre is the Schlossgarten, an extensive strip of parkland divided into three sections (Unterer, Mittlerer and Oberer Garten), complete with ponds, swans, street entertainers and modern sculptures.

Staatsgalerie GALLERY

(www.staatsgalerie-stuttgart.de; Konrad-Adenauer-Strasse 30-32; adult/concession €5.50/4, special exhibitions €10/8, Wed & Sat free; ⏲10am-6pm Tue-Sun, to 8pm Tue & Thu) Alongside big-name exhibitions, this prestigious art museum showcases works by Rembrandt, Picasso, Monet, Dalí as well as 20th-century pop idols Warhol and Lichtenstein.

Mercedes-Benz Museum MUSEUM

(www.museum-mercedes-benz.com; Mercedesstrasse 100; adult/concession €8/4; ⏲9am-6pm Tue-Sun; Neckarpark) A futuristic swirl on the cityscape, the Mercedes-Benz Museum takes a chronological spin through the Mercedes empire. Look out for legends like the 1885 Daimler Riding Car, the world's first gasoline-powered vehicle, and the record-breaking Lightning Benz that hit 228km/h on Daytona Beach in 1909. Free English tour at 11am.

Porsche Museum MUSEUM

(www.porsche.com; Porscheplatz 1; adult/concession €8/4; ⏲9am-6pm Tue-Sun; Neuwirtshaus) Like a pearly white spaceship preparing for lift-off, the barrier-free Porsche Museum is every little boy's dream. Groovy audioguides race you through the history of Porsche from its 1948 beginnings. Break to glimpse the 911 GT1 that won Le Mans in 1998.

Sleeping

Der Zauberlehrling BOUTIQUE HOTEL €€€

(237 7770; www.zauberlehrling.de; Rosenstrasse 38; s €135-180, d €180-290, ste €195-320; P) The self-consciously cool 'sorcerer's apprentice' reveals design-driven rooms, from Titanic with its waterbed to the hi-tech wizardry of the Media Suite. Yet it's hard to conjure up a smile at reception and the place lacks a little soul. Nice, but not quite magic.

Interhostel HOSTEL €

(6648 2797; www.inter-hostel.com; Paulinenstrasse 16; dm/s/d €25/42/64;) A short toddle from Stadtmitte station, this hostel makes backpackers' hearts sing with its free coffee and wi-fi, bright and characterful digs, relaxed lounge and chipper team, plus handy stuff like luggage storage and a guest kitchen.

City Hotel HOTEL €€

(210 810; www.cityhotel-stuttgart.de; Uhlandstrasse 18; s €79-89, d €99-115; P) Eschew the anonymity of Stuttgart's cookie-cutter chains for this intimate hotel just off Charlottenplatz. Rooms are light, clean and modern, if slightly lacklustre. Breakfast on the terrace in summer is a bonus.

Ochsen Hotel HISTORIC HOTEL €€

(407 0500; www.ochsen-online.de; Ulmer Strasse 323; s €89-99, d €119-129; P; Inselstrasse) It's worth going the extra mile to this charismatic 18th-century hotel where some of the spacious, warm-hued rooms have whirlpool tubs perfect for a post-sightseeing bubble. The wood-panelled restaurant dishes up delicious local fare.

Abalon Hotel HOTEL €€

(217 10; www.abalon.de; Zimmermannstrasse 7-9; s €74-89, d €89-112; P) Affable staff, a top location and wallet-friendly rates make Abalon a great pick. The bright parquet-floored rooms are large and spotless.

Hostel Alex 30 HOSTEL €
(☎838 8950; www.alex30-hostel.de; Alexanderstrasse 30; dm/s/d/q €24/36/58/100, breakfast €8; P ☎) Backpackers find a relaxed base in these mellow digs with a bar, sun deck and communal kitchen. The spotless, citrus-bright rooms are light and contemporary.

Eating

Stuttgart is a great place to sample Swabian specialities such as *Spätzle* (noodles) and *Maultaschen* (a hearty ravioli in broth). Local wines edge out beer in popularity.

The **food market** (Marktplatz; ⏰7.30am-1pm Tue, Thu & Sat) and the **Markthalle** (Market Hall; Dorotheenstrasse 4; ⏰7am-6.30pm Mon-Fri, 7am-4pm Sat), with their bounty of local produce and gourmet items, are the best features of the otherwise humdrum Marktplatz.

TOP CHOICE **Irma la Douce** MEDITERRANEAN €€€
(☎470 4320; www.irmaladouce.de; Katharinenstrasse 21b; lunch €11-14, dinner €25-39.50; ⏰closed lunch Sat & Sun) An ornate fireplace and chandeliers cast flattering light across the polished wood, bookshelves and paintings at this 19th-century bistro where the food is inspired by the seasons and Mediterranean flavours.

Weinstube Fröhlich SWABIAN €€
(☎242 471; www.weinstube-froehlich.de; Leonhardstrasse 5; mains €12-23; ⏰5.30pm-12.30am) True, it's bang in the heart of the red-light district, but don't be put off. This softly lit, dark wood-panelled restaurant is an atmospheric choice for well-executed Swabian fare (cheese-rich *Käsespätzle*, *Maultaschen* with potato salad) and regional wines.

Alte Kanzlei GERMAN €€
(☎294 457; Schillerplatz 5a; mains €10.50-20.50) Empty tables are gold-dust rare at this convivial, high-ceilinged restaurant. Feast on Swabian favourites like *Spanferkel* (roast suckling pig) and *Flädlesuppe* (pancake soup), washed down with regional tipples.

Reiskorn INTERNATIONAL €
(☎664 7633; Torstrasse 27; mains €5.50-12.90; ⏰closed Sun lunch; ☑) With an easygoing vibe and bamboo-green retro interior, this culinary globetrotter serves everything from tangy Caribbean prawn salad to dim sum.

Drinking & Entertainment

Hans-im-Glück Platz is a hub of bars, while club- and lounge-lined Theodor-Heuss-Strasse is thronged with sashaying hipsters.

Biergarten im Schlossgarten BEER GARDEN
(www.biergarten-schlossgarten.de; ⏰10.30am-1am May-Oct; ☎) Toast summer with beer and pretzels at Stuttgart's best-loved, 2000-seat beer garden in the green heart of the Schlossgarten. Regular live music gets steins a-swinging.

Sky Beach BAR
(www.skybeach.de; Königstrasse 6, top floor Galeria Kaufhof; ⏰noon-12.30am Mon-Sat, 11am midnight Sun Easter-Sep) When the sun comes out, Stuttgarters live it up at this urban beach, complete with sand, cabana beds, DJs spinning mellow lounge beats and grandstand city views.

Kiste LIVE MUSIC
(www.kiste-stuttgart.de; Hauptstätter Strasse 35; ⏰6pm-1am Mon-Thu, to 2am Fri & Sat) Jam-packed at weekends, this hole-in-the-wall bar is Stuttgart's leading jazz venue, with nightly concerts starting at 9pm or 10pm.

Information

StuttCard (72hr with/without VVS ticket €18/9.70) Free entry to most museums, plus discounts on events, activities and guided tours. Sold at the tourist office and some hotels.

Tourist Office (www.stuttgart-tourist.de; Königstrasse 1a; ⏰9am-8pm Mon-Fri, 9am-6pm Sat, 11am-6pm Sun)

Getting There & Around

Stuttgart International Airport (www.stuttgart-airport.com), a major hub for germanwings, is 13km south of the city. S2 and S3 trains take about 30 minutes to get from the airport to the Hauptbahnhof (€3.50).

Trains head to all major German cities and many international ones, such as Zürich and Paris. Services include:

Frankfurt (€59, 1¼ hour)
Munich (€54, 2¼ hour)
Nuremberg (€39, 2¼ hour)

For travel within the city, single tickets are €2.10. A day pass, good for two zones (including the car museums), is better value at €6.10.

Tübingen

07071 / POP 84,000

Forty kilometres south of Stuttgart, Tübingen mixes all the charms of a late-medieval city – a hilltop fortress, cobbled alleys and half-timbered houses – with the erudition and mischief of a university town. Wander the winding alleys of old stone walls, then take a boat ride down the Neckar River.

The central **Marktplatz** is dominated by the 1435 **Rathaus**, which sports a baroque facade and astronomical clock. The nearby late-Gothic **Stiftkirche** (Am Holz-markt; 9am-5pm) houses the tombs of the Württemberg dukes and has excellent medieval stained-glass windows. Above town, the Renaissance **Schloss Hohentübingen** (Burgsteige 11; museum adult/concession €5/3; castle 7am-8pm daily, museum 10am-5pm Wed-Sun, to 7pm Thu) was where Friedrich Miescher discovered DNA in 1869. It has fine views over the town's steep, red-tiled rooftops and an archaeology museum whose starring attraction is the collection of 35,000-year-old Vogelherd figurines, the world's oldest figurative artworks.

Sleeping & Eating

TOP CHOICE **Hotel am Schloss** HISTORIC HOTEL €€
(929 40; www.hotelamschloss.de; Burgsteige 18; s €75, d €108-135; P, wi-fi) So close to the castle you can almost reach out and touch it, this flower-bedecked hotel has dapper rooms ensconced in a 16th-century building. Rumour has it Kepler was partial to the wine here.

Wurstküche GERMAN €€
(927 50; Am Lustnauer Tor 8; mains €9-17.50; 11am-midnight) The rustic, wood-panelled Wurstküche brims with locals quaffing wine and contentedly munching *Schupfnudeln* (potato noodles) and *Spanferkel* (roast suckling pig).

Weinhaus Beck BAR
(Am Markt 1; 9am-11pm) There's rarely an empty table at this wine tavern beside the Rathaus, a convivial place to enjoy a local tipple or coffee and cake.

Getting There & Away

The definition of a day trip: trains between Tübingen and Stuttgart run every 30 minutes (€12.20, one hour).

Heidelberg

06221 / POP 147,000

Germany's oldest and most famous university town is renowned for its baroque old town, lively university atmosphere, excellent pubs and evocative half-ruined castle, which draw 3.5 million visitors a year. They are following in the footsteps of the late 18th- and early 19th-century romantics, most notably Johann Wolfgang von Goethe. Mark Twain kicked off his European travels in 1878 with a three-month stay in Heidelberg, later recounting his bemused observations in *A Tramp Abroad*.

Sights

The tourist office runs English-language **walking tours** (adult/concession €7/5; 10.30am Fri & Sat Apr-Oct) of the Altstadt.

TOP CHOICE **Schloss** CASTLE
(www.schloss-heidelberg.de; adult/child incl Bergbahn €5/3, audioguide €4; 24hr, ticket required 8am-5.30pm) Sticking up above the Altstadt like a picture-book pop-up, Heidelberg's ruined Schloss is one of the most romantic spots in Germany. Palatinate princes, stampeding Swedes, rampaging French, Protestant Reformers and lightning strikes – this Renaissance castle has seen the lot. Its tumultuous history, lonely beauty and changing moods helped inspire the German Romantic movement two centuries ago. One of its biggest attractions is the **Grosses Fass**, a massive wine barrel capable of holding about 228,000L.

To reach the red-sandstone castle, perched above the Altstadt, either hoof it up the steep, cobbled Burgweg in about 10 minutes, or take the historic funicular called **Bergbahn** (Funicular Railway; www.bergbahn-heidelberg.de; every 10min 9am-about 5pm) from Kornmarkt. Schloss tickets include travel on the Bergbahn.

Studentenkarzer HISTORIC SITE
(Augustinergasse 2; adult/student incl Universitätsmuseum €3/2.50; 10am-6pm Tue-Sun Apr-Sep, 10am-4pm Tue-Sat Oct-Mar) Dominating Universitätsplatz are the 18th-century Alte Universität and the Neue Universität. On the back side, find the Studentenkarzer, the student jail from 1823 to 1914. Crimes that could get you locked up included public drunkenness, nocturnal singing and duelling.

Heiliggeistkirche CHURCH

(Marktplatz; spire adult/student €2/1; ⏲11am-5pm Mon-Sat, 12.30-5pm Sun & holidays mid-Mar–Oct, 11am-3pm Fri & Sat, 12.30-3pm Sun Nov–mid-Mar) Heidelberg's most famous church, the Gothic Church of the Holy Spirit, was built from 1398 to 1441. For a bird's-eye view of Heidelberg, you can climb 208 stairs to the top of the **spire**. Stop by at 12.30pm from Monday to Saturday (except in winter) for 10 minutes of exquisite **organ music**.

Philosophenweg TRAIL

Passing through steep fields and orchards on the slopes across the river from the Altstadt, the Philosophers' Way commands panoramic views of the Schloss as it wends its way through the forest to various monuments, towers, ruins, a beer garden and the **Thingstätte**, a Nazi-era amphitheatre.

Sleeping

Finding any accommodation during Heidelberg's high season can be difficult. Arrive early in the day or book ahead.

TOP CHOICE **Arthotel** BOUTIQUE HOTEL €€

(☎650 060; www.arthotel.de; Grabengasse 7; d without breakfast €115-198; P ❄ 📶) For 21st-century German style, head to this charmer. The red and black lobby, lit by a wall of windows, sets the tone, while the 24 rooms, equipped with huge bathrooms, are spacious and cleanly minimalist – except for three, which come with painted ceilings that date from 1790.

Hotel Goldener Hecht HOTEL €€

(☎166 025; www.hotel-goldener-hecht.de; Steingasse 2; d without breakfast €73-94; 📶) This atmospheric hotel, near the Alte Brücke, has just 13 rooms, six with bridge views; the three corner rooms are bright and gorgeous. It's very central but potentially noisy.

Hotel am Kornmarkt HOTEL €€

(☎905 830; www.hotelamkornmarkt.de; Kornmarkt 7; s/d from €65/85, without bathroom €40/70, breakfast €9; 📶) A block from the Marktplatz, this hotel is a beacon to euro-conscious travellers. The 20 rooms are no-frills but still comfortable and spotless; the priciest have Kornmarkt views.

Steffis Hostel HOSTEL €

(☎778 2772; www.hostelheidelberg.de; Alte Eppelheimer Strasse 50; dm from €18, d without bathroom €52; ⏲reception 8am-10pm; P @ 📶) Tucked into a 19th-century tobacco factory, Steffis offers bright, well-lit rooms (all with shared bathrooms), a colourful lounge, a spacious kitchen and an ineffable old-time hostel vibe. Perks include free wi-fi, tea, coffee and bicycles (deposit €20). It's just north of the Hauptbahnhof, above a Lidl supermarket, and reached by an industrial-size lift.

HEIDELBERG FAST TRACK

Heidelberg's captivating **old town** starts to reveal itself only after a charm-free 15-minute walk east from the main train station. Cut to the chase and go direct to the heart of town with bus 32 to Universitätsplatz or bus 33 to Bergbahn.

Eating

TOP CHOICE **Zur Herrenmühle** GERMAN €€€

(☎602 909; www.herrenmuehle-heidelberg.de; Hauptstrasse 237-239; mains €14.50-28.50; ⏲6-10pm Mon-Sat) A flour mill from 1690 has been turned into an elegant and highly cultured place to enjoy traditional 'country house' cuisine, including fish, under 300-year-old wood beams, a candle flickering romantically at each table. A five-course menu costs €36.50.

Schiller's Café CAFE €

(Heiliggeiststrasse 5; cakes €2.50; ⏲10am-8pm Sun-Wed, 10am-midnight Thu-Sat) Housed in one of Heidelberg's oldest residential buildings (the cellar and first floor date from the 1500s) this homey, wholesome cafe serves over 60 kinds of hot chocolate, homemade cakes, quiche and wines. Most dishes are organic and some are gluten-free.

KulturBrauerei CAFE €€

(☎502 980; Leyergasse 6; mains €10.50-26.50; ⏲7am-11pm or later) With its wood-plank floor, black iron chandeliers and time-faded ceiling frescoes, this microbrewery – in a hall that dates from 1903 – is an atmospheric spot to tuck into salad, soup or regional dishes such as *Schäufele* (pork shoulder) with sauerkraut (€10.50), or to quaff homebrews in the beer garden.

Café Burkardt CAFE €

(Untere Strasse 27; cake & snacks €3-8; ⏲9am-11pm Tue-Sat, 9am-6pm Sun) Full of doily-draped tables and dark-wood crannies, this friendly cafe serves salads, German dishes, pasta and some of Heidelberg's scrummiest tarts and cheesecakes. Also on offer are great breakfasts and local wines.

Drinking & Entertainment

Lots of the action centres on Untere Strasse. Two ancient pubs, **Zum Roten Ochsen** (☎209 77; Hauptstrasse 213) and **Zum Sepp'l** (☎230 85; Hauptstrasse 217), are now filled with tourists.

Kulturhaus Karlstorbahnhof LIVE MUSIC
(☎978 711; www.karlstorbahnhof.de; Am Karlstor 1; ⏲closed Aug) This edgy cultural centre shelters a concert venue, an art-house cinema and the popular **Klub K** (⏲10 or 11pm-5 or 6am Thu-Sat), whose DJs play everything from techno and dubstep to indie rock for a mixed crowd. It's train-track-adjacent, 100m east of the Karlstor.

Nachtschicht CLUB
(www.nachtschicht.com; Bergheimerstrasse 147; admission €3-6; ⏲10pm-4am Thu, 8pm-1am Fri, 11pm-5am Sat) Two blocks north of the Hauptbahnhof, this old tobacco factory has morphed into one of Heidelberg's most popular student clubs.

Information

Heidelberg Card (1/2/4 days €11/13/16, 2-day family pass €28) Includes public transport, admission to the Schloss (including the Bergbahn) and discounts at most museums, for bike and boat rental, and for tours. Available at the tourist offices.

Tourist Office (☎194 33, 584 4444; www.heidelberg-marketing.de) Branches include Hauptbahnhof (Willy-Brandt-Platz 1; ⏲9am-7pm Mon-Sat, 10am-6pm Sun & holidays Apr-Oct, 9am-6pm Mon-Sat Nov-Mar) and Marktplatz (Marktplatz 10; 8am-5pm Mon-Fri, 10am-5pm Sat).

Getting There & Away

There are hourly IC trains to/from Frankfurt (from €16.40, one hour) and Stuttgart (from €21.20, 40 minutes) along with frequent service to the railway hub of Mannheim (€4.90, 19 minutes), with connections throughout Germany.

The fastest way to get to Frankfurt airport (€23, one hour, every hour or two) is to take the eight-seat **Lufthansa Airport Shuttle** (☎06152-976 9099; www.transcontinental-group.com).

Baden-Baden

☎07221 / POP 54,500

'So nice that you have to name it twice', enthused Bill Clinton about Baden-Baden, whose air of old-world luxury and curative waters have attracted royals, the rich and celebrities over the years – Bismarck, Queen Victoria and Victoria Beckham included. 'Nice', however, does not really convey the amazing grace of this Black Forest town, with its grand colonnaded buildings and whimsically turreted art nouveau villas spread across the hillsides and framed by forested mountains. Add to that temple-like thermal baths – which put the *baden* (bathe) in Baden – and a palatial casino and you'll understand that the allure of this grand dame of German spa towns is as timeless as it is enduring.

Sights & Activities

Kurhaus & Casino LANDMARK
(www.kurhaus-baden-baden.de; Kaiserallee 1; guided tour €5; ⏲guided tour 9.30am-11.30am daily) The belle époque facade of the Kurhaus towers above well-groomed gardens and an alley of chestnut trees, flanked by boutiques, linking it with Kaiserallee. Inside is the sublime **casino** (www.casino-baden-baden.de; admission €5; ⏲2pm-2am Sun-Thu, 2pm-3am Fri & Sat), which seeks to emulate the gilded splendour of Versailles. Gents must wear a jacket and tie, rentable for €8 and €3 respectively. No need to dress up for the 25-minute guided tour.

TOP CHOICE **Friedrichsbad** SPA
(☎275 920; www.roemisch-irisches-bad.de; Römerplatz 1; 3hr ticket €23, incl soap-and-brush massage €33; ⏲9am-10pm, last admission 7pm) Abandon modesty (and clothing) to wallow in thermal waters at this sumptuous 19th-century spa as you slip into the regime of steaming, scrubbing, hot-cold bathing and dunking in the Roman-Irish bath. With its cupola, mosaics and Carrera marble pool, the bathhouse is the vision of a neo-Renaissance palace.

Caracalla Therme SPA
(www.caracalla.de; Römerplatz 11; 2/3/4hr €14/17/20; ⏲8am-10pm, last admission 8pm) Keep your bathing suit on at this glass-fronted spa as you make the most of the mineral-rich spring water in indoor and

outdoor pools, grottoes and surge channels. For those who dare to bare, saunas range from the rustic 'forest' to the roasting 95°C 'fire' variety.

Sleeping & Eating

Most restaurants huddle in the pedestrianised stretch around Leopoldsplatz. Nightlife is suited for people who've had the life boiled out of them.

Hotel Beek B&B €€
(☎367 60; www.hotel-beek.de; Gernsbacherstrasse 44-46; s €85-95, d €109-119; @) On a tree-fringed street in the heart of town, this pretty-in-pink hotel doubles as an excellent patisserie, going strong since 1885. Facing either a courtyard or the Neues Schloss, the bright rooms sport comfy beds; the best ones come with balconies.

Hotel am Markt HISTORIC HOTEL €
(☎270 40; www.hotel-am-markt-baden.de; Marktplatz 18; s €37-53, d €70-92; P@) Sitting pretty in front of the Stiftskirche, this 250-year-old hotel has 23 homely, well-kept rooms. It's quiet up here apart from your wake-up call of church bells, but you wouldn't want to miss out on the great breakfast.

Weinstube im Baldreit GERMAN €€€
(☎231 36; Küferstrasse 3; mains €12.50-19; 5-10pm Mon-Sat) Tucked down cobbled lanes, this wine cellar restaurant is tricky to find, but persevere. Baden-Alsatian fare such as *Flammkuchen* topped with Black Forest ham, Roquefort and pears is expertly matched with local wines. Eat in the ivy-swathed courtyard in summer, the vaulted interior in winter.

Café König CAFE €
(Lichtentaler Strasse 12; cake €3.50-5; 9.30am-6.30am Mon-Sat, 10.30am-6.30pm Sun) Liszt and Tolstoy once sipped coffee at this venerable cafe, which has been doing a brisk trade in top cakes, tortes, pralines and truffles for 250 years.

Rathausglöckel GERMAN €€
(☎906 10; Steinstrasse 7; mains €10-16; 6-11pm Mon-Sat, 11.30am-2pm & 6-11pm Sun, closed Wed;) Strong on old-school charm, this low-beamed tavern is cosily clad in dark wood and oil paintings and serves historic regional and German dishes.

Information

The **tourist office** (www.baden-baden.com; Kaiserallee 3; 10am-5pm Mon-Sat, 2-5pm Sun) is in the Trinkhalle.

Getting There & Around

Karlsruhe-Baden-Baden airport (Baden Airpark; www.badenairpark.de), 15km west of town, is linked to London and other European cities by Ryanair.

Buses to Black Forest destinations depart from the bus station, next to the Bahnhof.

Baden-Baden is close to the A5 (Frankfurt–Basel autobahn) and is the northern starting point of the zigzagging Schwarzwald-Hochstrasse, which follows the B500.

Baden-Baden is on a major north–south rail corridor. Twice-hourly destinations include Freiburg (€19.20 to €28, 45 to 90 minutes) and Karlsruhe (€10 to €15, 15 to 30 minutes).

Black Forest

The Black Forest (Schwarzwald) gets its name from its dark canopy of evergreens, which evoke mystery and allure. Although some parts heave with visitors, a 20-minute walk from even the most crowded spots will put you in quiet countryside interspersed with hulking traditional farmhouses and patrolled by amiable dairy cows. It's not nature wild and remote, but bucolic and picturesque. And, yes, there are many, many

BLACK FOREST SAVINGS

Check into almost any hotel in Baden-Württemberg, pay the nominal *Kurtaxe* (holiday tax) and you automatically receive the money-saving **Gästekarte** (Guest Card), entitling you to free or discounted entry to many attractions and activities plus hefty discounts on everything from bike hire and spas to ski lifts and boat trips. Versions with the Konus symbol mean free use of public transport.

Most tourist offices in the Black Forest sell the three-day **Schwarzwald-Card** for admission to around 150 attractions in the Black Forest. Details on both cards are available at www.blackforest-tourism.com.

Black Forest

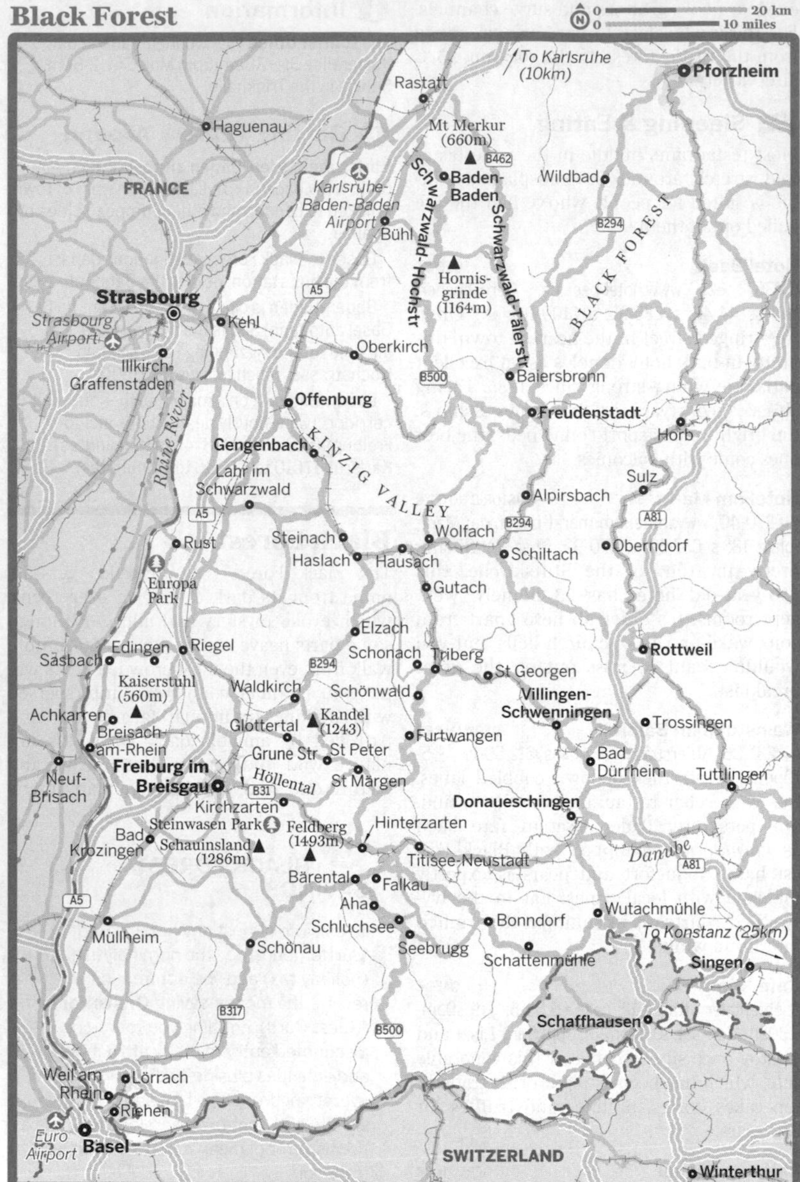

places to buy cuckoo clocks (you pay at least €150 for a good one).

Getting Around

With a car you'll find a visit especially rewarding, as you can explore the rolling hills and deep valleys at will. One of the main tourist roads is the scenic **Schwarzwald-Hochstrasse** (B500), which runs from Baden-Baden to Freudenstadt and from Triberg to Waldshut.

An hourly train line links Freudenstadt with Offenburg via Alpirsbach, Schiltach and other villages. From Hausach, trains run roughly hourly southeast to Triberg and Constance.

FREUDENSTADT

07441 / POP 23,550

Freudenstadt is a good base for exploring the northern Black Forest and hikes into the surrounding countryside. It's most notable feature is a vast cafe- and shop-lined **market square** that is the largest in the country. Stop by the **tourist office** (www.freudenstadt.de; Marktplatz 64; 9am-6pm Mon-Fri, 10am-2pm Sat & Sun May-Oct, shorter hours other times) for hiking suggestions.

The Gaiser family extend a warm welcome at **Hotel Adler** (915 20; www.adler-fds.de; Forststrasse 15-17; s €45-53, d €74-90, mains €12 to €17; P), a guesthouse with comfy, fusty rooms and a terrace. The bistro serves Swabian faves like *Spätzle*.

ALPIRSBACH

A small town, Alpirsbach, is worth a trip for its 12th-century Benedictine abbey, **Kloster Alpirsbach** (adult/concession €4/3.30; 10am-5.30pm Mon-Sat, 11am-5.30pm Sun), which conveys the simple, spiritual life in its flat-roofed church, spartan cells and Gothic cloister. The museum has a stash of 16th-century clothing, caricatures (of artistic scholars) and lines (of misbehaving ones).

Just across the old complex you'll find what's kept the monks busy all these years: the **Alpirsbacher Klosterbräu** (670; www.alpirsbacher.com; Marktplatz 1; tours €6.90; 2.30pm daily) brewery. Tours include a couple of glasses of the brew.

For more information, stop by the **tourist office** (951 6281; www.stadt-alpirsbach.de; Krähenbadstrasse 2; 10am-noon & 2-5pm Mon-Fri, closed Wed afternoon).

Alpirsbach is a stop for the hourly trains linking Schiltach and Freudenstadt.

SCHILTACH

07836 / POP 3875

A contender for the prettiest town in the Black Forest is Schiltach, where there is the always-underlying roar of the intersecting Kinzig and Schiltach Rivers. Half-timbered buildings lean at varying angles along the criss-crossing hillside lanes. Centred on a trickling fountain, the sloping, triangular **Marktplatz** is Schiltach at its picture-book best.

Don't miss the **Schüttesäge Museum** (Gerbegasse; 11am-5pm daily Apr-Oct, Sat & Sun only Nov-Mar), which illustrates Schiltach's rafting tradition with a reconstructed workshop, a functioning watermill and touchy-feely exhibits for kids.

Nineteen generations of the same family have run the 16th-century inn **Weysses Rössle** (387; www.weysses-roessle.de; Schenkenzeller Strasse 42; s/d €52/75; P), where countrified rooms feature snazzy bathrooms. The woodsy tavern uses locally sourced, organic fare.

The **tourist office** (www.schiltach.de; Hauptstrasse 5; 10am-5pm Mon-Fri, to 2pm Sat Apr-Oct) can help with accommodation and has a lot of English-language information.

TRIBERG

07722 / POP 5000

Heir to the Black Forest cake recipe, nesting ground of the world's biggest cuckoos and spring of Germany's highest waterfall – Triberg is a torrent of Schwarzwald superlatives and attracts gushes of guests.

Niagara they ain't, but Germany's highest **waterfalls** (adult/concession €3.50/3; Mar-early Nov, 25-30 Dec) do exude their own wild romanticism. The Gutach River feeds the seven-tiered falls, which drop a total of 163m. The trail starts near the tourist office, which also has a small museum.

Triberg is Germany's undisputed cuckoo-clock capital. Two timepieces claim the title of world's largest cuckoo clock, giving rise to the battle of the birds. To the casual observer, the biggest is undeniably the commercially savvy **Eble Uhren-Park** (www.uhren-park.de; Schonachbach 27; admission €2; 9am-6pm Mon-Sat, 10am-6pm Sun), listed in the Guinness World Records, on the B33 between Triberg and Hornberg. At the other end of town, in Schonach, is its underdog rival, the **1. Weltgrösste Kuckuckuhr** (07722-4689; Untertalstrasse

FOREST FOODIE FAVES

Black Forest specialities include *Schwarzwälder Schinken* (ham), which is smoked and served in a variety of ways. Rivalling those ubiquitous clocks in fame (but not price), *Schwarzwälder Kirschtorte* (Black Forest cake) is a chocolate and cherry concoction. A popular local beer is the crisp pilsener called Rothaus.

28; adult/concession €1.20/0.60; ⏲9am-6pm May-Oct, 10am-5pm Nov-Apr), nestled inside a snug chalet and complete with gear-driven innards. This giant timepiece – unable to compete in size alone – has taken to calling itself the world's oldest, largest cuckoo clock. It was built in the 1980s.

Above the shop of master woodcarver Gerald Burger is **Kukucksnest** (☎869 487; Wallfahrtstrasse 15; d €58), a beautiful nest he has carved for guests.

The kirsch-scented Black Forest cake at **Café Schäfer** (www.cafe-schaefer-triberg.de; Hauptstrasse 33; cake €3-4; ⏲9am-6pm Mon-Fri, 8am-6pm Sat, 11am-6pm Sun, closed Wed) is the real deal; it has the original recipe to prove it.

The hourly Schwarzwaldbahn train line loops southeast to Constance (€23.30, 1½ hours), and northwest to Offenburg (€11.10, 45 minutes). Bus 7150 travels north via Gutach to Offenburg; bus 7265 heads south to Villingen via St Georgen.

Triberg's train station is 1.7km from the centre; take any bus to the Markt.

Freiburg im Breisgau

☎0761 / POP 224,200

Sitting plump at the foot of the Black Forest's wooded slopes and vineyards, Freiburg is a sunny, cheerful university town; its medieval Altstadt a story-book tableau of gabled town houses, cobblestone lanes and cafe-rimmed plazas lorded over by a monumental 13th-century cathedral. Party-loving students spice up the local nightlife. Blessed with 2000 hours of annual sunshine, this is Germany's warmest city.

Sights & Activities

TOP CHOICE Münster CATHEDRAL

(Münsterplatz; tower adult/concession €1.50/1; ⏲10am-5pm Mon-Sat, 1-7.30pm Sun, tower 9.30am-5pm Mon-Sat, 1-5pm Sun) Freiburg's 13th-century minster is a red-sandstone pile whose punctured spires and gargoyles flush scarlet in the dusk light. Ascend the tower for an excellent view of the church's intricate construction; on clear days you can spy the Vosges Mountains in France.

Inside, the kaleidoscopic stained-glass windows dazzle. The **high altar** features a masterful triptych of the coronation of the Virgin Mary by Hans Baldung.

Rathausplatz SQUARE

(Town Hall Square) Freiburg locals hang out by the fountain in chestnut-shaded Rathausplatz. On its western side, note the red-sandstone, step-gabled **Neues Rathaus** (New City Hall; Rathausplatz).

Across the way is the mid-16th-century **Altes Rathaus** (Old City Hall; Universtitatstrasse), a flamboyant, ox-blood red edifice, embellished with gilt swirls and crowned by a clock and a fresco of the twin-headed Habsburg eagle.

On the square's northern side, the medieval **Martinskirche** demands attention with its covered cloister. Once part of a Franciscan monastery, the church was severely damaged in WWII, it was rebuilt in the ascetic style typical of this mendicant order.

Augustinermuseum MUSEUM

(☎201 2531; Salzstrasse 32; adult/child €6/4; ⏲10am-5pm Tue-Sun) This beautiful Augustinian monastery showcases prized medieval,

WORTH A TRIP

SOARING ABOVE THE FOREST

Freiburg seems tiny as you drift up above the city and a tapestry of meadows and forest on the **Schauinslandbahn** (adult/concession return €12/11, one-way €8.50/8; ⏲9am-5pm, to 6pm Jul-Sep) to the 1284m **Schauinsland peak** (www.bergwelt-schauinsland.de). The lift provides a speedy link between Freiburg and the Black Forest highlands.

Up top, enjoy commanding views to the Rhine Valley and Alps from the lookout tower, then hit a trail to capture the scenery from many different angles. You can also bounce downhill on the 8km off-road **scooter track** (www.rollerstrecke.de; €20; ⏲2pm & 5pm Sun May-Jun, Sat & Sun Jul & Sep-Oct, Wed-Sun Aug), one of Europe's longest; it takes around an hour from top to bottom station.

The Schauinslandbahn valley station is about 9km southeast of central Freiburg. Take tram 2 to Günterstal and then bus 21 to Talstation.

baroque and 19th-century art by such hot shots as Hans Baldung, Matthias Grünewald and Lucas Cranach. There's also lavish medieval stained glass.

Sleeping

TOP CHOICE Hotel Oberkirch HISTORIC HOTEL €€€
(☎202 6868; www.hotel-oberkirch.de; Münsterplatz 22; s €102-123, d €155-169, mains €13-23; P) Wake up to Münster views at this 250-year-old green shuttered hotel, whose country-style rooms feature floral wallpaper and half-canopied beds. The dark-wood **tavern** downstairs does a roaring trade in hearty local fare like venison ragout with *Knödel* (dumplings).

Hotel Schwarzwälder Hof HOTEL €€
(☎380 30; www.schwarzwaelder-hof.eu; Herrenstrasse 43; s/d/tr €65/99/120; @) This bijou hotel has an unrivalled style-for-euro ratio. A wrought-iron staircase sweeps up to snazzy rooms that are temples to chalk whites and chocolate browns. Some have Altstadt views.

Black Forest Hostel HOSTEL €
(☎881 7870; www.blackforest-hostel.de; Kartäuserstrasse 33; dm €14-23, s/d €30/50; @) Funky budget digs with chilled common areas, a shared kitchen, bike rental and spacey stainless-steel showers. It's a five-minute walk from the centre of town.

Eating & Drinking

Wolfshöhle MEDITERRANEAN €€€
(☎303 03; Konviktstrasse 8; mains €16-27; ⊙closed Mon lunch, Sun) With tables set up on a pretty square, Wolfshöhle is a summer-evening magnet. The menu whisks you off on a gastro tour of the Mediterranean, with well-executed dishes like Iberian pork with wild garlic puree and scampi with saffron-infused risotto.

Hausbrauerei Feierling BREWERY €€
(Gerberau 46; mains €6-12; ✎) Starring one of Freiburg's best beer gardens, this brewpub serves great vegetarian options and humungous schnitzels with *Brägele* (chipped potatoes).

Englers Weinkrügle GERMAN €€
(☎383 115; Konviktstrasse 12; mains €9-16; ⊙Tue-Sun) A warm, woody Baden-style *Weinstube* (wine tavern) with wisteria growing out front and regional flavours on the menu. The trout in various guises (for instance with riesling or almond-butter sauce) is delicious.

Schlappen PUB
(Löwenstrasse 2; ⊙11am-btwn 1am & 3am Mon-Sat, 3pm-1am Sun) With its jazz-themed back room and poster-plastered walls, this pub is a perennial favourite. Try one of 10 absinthe varieties and you'll be away with the green fairies. Punters spill onto the terrace in summer.

Information

Tourist office (☎388 1880; www.freiburg.de; Rathausplatz 2-4; ⊙8am-8pm Mon-Fri, 9.30am-5pm Sat, 11am-4pm Sun)

Getting There & Around

Freiburg shares **EuroAirport** (www.euroairport.com) with Basel (Switzerland) and Mulhouse (France). It buzzes with low-cost carriers. From Freiburg it is served hourly by the **Airport Bus** (☎500 500; www.freiburger-reisedienst.de; one-way/return €23/39; ⊙55 minutes).

The Frankfurt–Basel A5 passes just west of Freiburg. The scenic B31 leads east through the Höllental to Lake Constance. The B294 goes north into the Black Forest.

Fast trains connect Freiburg to Basel (from €16.40, 45 minutes) and Baden-Baden (from €19.20, 45 minutes). Freiburg is also the western terminus of the Höllentalbahn to Donaueschingen via Titisee-Neustadt (€5.10, 38 minutes, twice an hour).

LAKE CONSTANCE

Straddling Germany, Austria and Switzerland, Lake Constance (known locally as Bodensee) is Central Europe's third largest lake. Formed by the Rhine Glacier during the last ice age and fed and drained by that same sprightly river today, this whopper of a lake measures 63km long, 14km wide and up to 250m deep. Even if you never make contact with the water, this giant bulge in the sinewy course of the Rhine offers a delightful splash of refreshment. Historic towns line its vineyard-dappled periphery, which can be explored by boat or bicycle or on foot.

Getting There & Around

Trains link Lindau and Constance, and buses fill in the gaps to places like Meersburg. By car, the B31 hugs the northern shore of Lake Constance, but it can get rather busy.

TICKETS TO SAVINGS

EuregioBodensee Tageskarte (www.euregiokarte.com) All-day access to land transport around Lake Constance, including areas in Austria and Switzerland. It's sold at train stations and ferry docks and costs €16.50/22/29 for one/two/all zones.

Bodensee Erlebniskarte (adult/child €72/36, not incl ferries €40/21) This three-day card, available at local tourist and ferry offices from early April to mid-October, is good for unlimited travel on almost all boats and mountain cableways on and around Lake Constance (including its Austrian and Swiss shores) as well as free entry to around 180 tourist attractions and museums.

The most enjoyable, albeit slowest, way to get around is by ferry. Constance is the main hub, but Meersburg and Friedrichshafen also have plentiful ferry options. The most useful lines, run by **German BSB** (www.bsb-online.com) and **Austrian OBB** (www.bodenseeschifffahrt.at), link Constance with Meersburg (€5.30, 30 minutes), Friedrichshafen (€11.70, 1¾ hours), Lindau (€15.40, three hours) and Bregenz (€16.40, 3½ hours); children aged six to 15 years pay half-price. The websites list timetables.

Euregio Bodensee (www.euregiokarte.com), which groups all Lake Constance–area public transport, publishes a free *Fahrplan* with schedules for all train, bus and ferry services.

Constance

07531 / POP 84,700

Hugging the Swiss border, Constance (Konstanz) is a feelgood university town with a lively buzz and upbeat bar scene, particularly in the cobbled Altstadt and along the lively waterfront.

It achieved historical significance in 1414, when the Council of Constance convened to try to heal huge rifts in the Catholic Church. The consequent burning at the stake of the religious reformer Jan Hus as a heretic, and the scattering of his ashes over the lake, did nothing to block the Reformation.

Sights & Activities

TOP CHOICE Münster CATHEDRAL
(tower adult/child €2/1; 10am-6pm Mon-Sat, 10am-6pm Sun, tower 10am-5pm Mon-Sat, 12.30pm-5.30pm Sun) Crowned by a filigree spire and looking proudly back on 1000 years of history, the sandstone Münster is an architectural potpourri of Romanesque, Gothic, Renaissance and baroque styles. Standouts include the 15th-century **Schnegg**, an ornate spiral staircase, the 1000-year-old **crypt** and the sublime **Gothic cloister**. On cloudless days, it's worth ascending the **tower** for broad views over the city and lake.

Mainau GARDEN
(www.mainau.de; adult/concession €16.90/9.50; sunrise-sunset) Jutting out over the Lake Constance and bursting with flowers, the lusciously green islet of Mainau is a 45-hectare Mediterranean garden dreamed up by the Bernadotte family, relatives of the royal house of Sweden. Take bus 4 from Constance's train station or hop aboard a passenger ferry.

Sleeping & Eating

Münsterplatz and Markstätte are peppered with pizzerias and snack bars. Watch out for rip-offs around Stadtgarten.

Hotel Barbarossa HISTORIC HOTEL €€
(128 990; www.barbarossa-hotel.com; Obermarkt 8-12; s €55-75, d €95-130;) This 600-year-old patrician house harbours parquet-floored, individually decorated rooms, which are bright and appealing, if a tad on the small side. The terrace has views over Constance's rooftops and spires.

Riva BOUTIQUE HOTEL €€€
(363 090; www.hotel-riva.de; Seestrasse 25; s €110-150, d €200-240;) This ultrachic contender has crisp white spaces, glass walls and a snail-like stairwell. Zen-like rooms with hardwood floors feature perks including free minibars. The rooftop pool and Mediterranean-style restaurant (mains €18 to €25) overlook the lake.

Münsterhof GERMAN €€
(3638 427; Münsterplatz 3; mains €8.50-17;) Tables set up in front of the Münster, a slick bistro interior and a lunchtime buzz have earned Münsterhof a loyal local following. The two-course €6.90 lunch is a bargain.

Voglhaus CAFE €
(Wessenbergstrasse 8; light meals €2.50-6; 9am-6.30pm Mon-Sat, 11am-6pm Sun;) Locals flock to the 'bird house' for its chilled vibe and contemporary wood-and-stone interior,

warmed by an open fire in winter. Wood-oven bread with spreads, wholegrain bagels and cupcakes pair nicely with smoothies and speciality coffees like Hansel and Gretel (with gingerbread syrup).

Brauhaus Johann Albrecht BREWPUB
(Konradigasse 2; ⊙11.30am-1pm) This step-gabled microbrewery is a relaxed haunt for quaffing wheat beer or hoppy lager by the glass or metre, with a terrace for summer imbibing.

Information

The **tourist office** (☎133 030; www.konstanz-tourismus.de; Bahnhofplatz 43; ⊙9am-6.30pm Mon-Fri, 9am-4pm Sat, 10am-1pm Sun Apr-Oct, 9.30am-6pm Mon-Fri Nov-Mar) is in the train station.

Getting There & Away

Constance is Lake Constance's main ferry hub. By car, it's served by the B33, which links up with the A81 to and from Stuttgart near Singen. Or you can take the B31 to Meersburg and then catch a car ferry.

The town is also the southern terminus of the scenic Schwarzwaldbahn, which trundles hourly through the Black Forest. For northern shore towns, change in Radolfzell.

Meersburg

☎07532 / POP 5630

Tumbling down vine-streaked slopes to Lake Constance and crowned by a perkily turreted medieval castle, Meersburg lives up to all those clichéd knights-in-armour, damsel-in-distress fantasies. Its highlight is the **Altes Schloss** (adult/concession €8.50/6.50; ⊙9am-6.30pm Mar-Oct, 10am-6pm Nov-Feb), an archetypal medieval stronghold, complete with keep, drawbridge, knights' hall and dungeons.

The **tourist office** (☎440 400; www.meersburg.de; Kirchstrasse 4; ⊙9am-12.30pm & 2-6pm Mon-Fri, 10am-3pm Sat, 10am-1pm Sun, shorter hours in winter) is housed in a one time Dominican monastery.

Meersburg has no train station but is linked eight times daily by express bus 7394 to Constance (€3.25, 40 minutes) and Friedrichshafen (€3.10, 26 minutes).

Lindau

☎08382 / POP 24,800

Cradled in the southern crook of Lake Constance and almost dipping its toes into Austria, Lindau is a good-looking, car-free little town, with a candy-coloured postcard of an Altstadt, clear-day Alpine views and lakefront cafes. The town's biggest architectural stunner is the 15th-century, step-gabled **Altes Rathaus** (Old Town Hall; Bismarckplatz), a frescoed frenzy of cherubs, merry minstrels and galleons.

Spend at the night at the 18th-century **Hotel Garni-Brugger** (☎934 10; www.hotel-garni-brugger.de; Bei der Heidenmauer 11; s €56-78, d €92-106; @), where bright rooms are done up in floral fabrics and pine, and the owner-family bends over backwards to please. A good bet for regional fare is **Weinstube Frey** (☎947 9676; Maximilianstrasse 15; mains €13-22; ⊙closed Mon), a 500-year-old wine tavern oozing Bavarian charm. For a drink with a cool view, head to Seepromenade.

The **tourist office** (☎260 030; www.lindau.de; Ludwigstrasse 68; ⊙9am-6pm Mon-Fri, 2-6pm Sat & Sun May-Sep, 9am-5pm Mon-Fri Oct-Apr) is opposite the train station.

Lindau is on the B31 and is connected to Munich by the A96. The Deutsche Alpenstrasse (German Alpine Route), which winds eastward to Berchtesgaden, begins here. It is also at the eastern terminus of the rail line that goes along the northern lake shore as far as Radolfzell.

RHINELAND-PALATINATE

Rhineland-Palatinate (Rheinland-Pfalz) is deeply riven by rivers, and the two best known – the Rhine and the Moselle – are synonymous with the wines made from the grapes growing on their hillsides. Created after WWII from parts of the former Rhineland and Rhenish Palatinate regions, the area's turbulent history goes all the way back to the Romans, best demonstrated in Trier. In recent centuries it was hotly contested by the French and a variety of German states, which produced many of its charismatically crumbling medieval castles.

ROMANCING THE RHINE

Nearly every Rhine village has its own charms and is worth at least a quick spin on foot. Just pick one at random and make your own discoveries. Here are a few enticing teasers:

Boppard Roman walls and ruins and cable to Vierseenblick viewpoint. On the left bank.

Oberwesel Famous for its 3km-long partly walkable medieval town wall, punctuated by 16 guard towers. On the left bank.

Assmannhausen Relatively untouristed village known for its red wines, sweeping views and good hikes. On the right bank.

Rüdesheim Escape the day-tripper deluged *Drosselgasse* (alley) to soar above the vineyards to the mighty *Niederwalddenkmal* (memorial). On the right bank.

Romantic Rhine

A trip along the mighty Rhine is a highlight for most travellers to Germany. The section between Koblenz and Mainz is Unesco-protected and is called Romantic Rhine for good reason. This is Germany's landscape at its most dramatic – forested hillsides alternate with craggy cliffs and nearly-vertical terraced vineyards. Idyllic villages appear around each bend, their neat half-timbered houses and Gothic church steeples seemingly plucked from the world of fairy tales.

High above the river, which is busy with barge traffic, and the rail lines that run along each bank, are the famous medieval castles, some ruined, some restored, all shrouded in mystery.

Spring and autumn are the best times to visit; the area is overrun in summer and goes into hibernation in winter. Every river town brims with cute places to stay, eat and drink.

Although Koblenz and Mainz are the best starting points, the Rhine Valley is also easily accessible from Frankfurt on a (very long) day trip. Note that there are only car ferries (no bridges) along this stretch of river.

Getting There & Around

Each mode of transport on the Rhine has its own advantages and all are equally enjoyable. Try combining several. The **Köln-Düsseldorfer Line** (KD; ☎0221-2088 318; www.k-d.com) runs numerous boat services daily between Koblenz and Mainz (as well as the less-interesting stretch between Cologne and Koblenz) which stop at riverside towns along the way.

Villages on the Rhine's left bank (eg Bingen, Bacharach, Oberwesel and Boppard) are served hourly by local trains on the Koblenz–Mainz run. Right-bank villages such as Rüdesheim, Assmannshausen, Kaub, St Goarshausen and Braubach are linked hourly to Koblenz' Hauptbahnhof and Wiesbaden by the RheingauLinie, operated by Vias.

ST GOAR & ST GOARSHAUSEN

☎06741 / POP 3100

These twin towns face each other across the Rhine. On the left bank, St Goar is lorded over by **Burg Rheinfels** (www.st-goar.de; adult/child €4/2; ⌚9am-6pm mid-Mar–early Nov, 11am-5pm Sat & Sun in good weather early Nov–mid-Mar), one of the most impressive castles on the river. Its labyrinthine ruins reflect the greed and ambition of the local count who built the behemoth in 1245 to levy tolls on passing ships.

Across the river, just south of St Goarshausen, is the most fabled spot along the Romantic Rhine, the **Loreley Rock**. This vertical slab of slate owes its fame to a mythical maiden whose siren songs are said to have lured sailors to their death in the river's treacherous currents. Learn more at the multimedia visitor's centre **Loreley Besucherzentrum** (☎599 093; www.loreley-besucherzentrum.de; adult/student €2.50/1.50; ⌚10am-6pm Apr-Oct, 10am-5pm Mar, 11am-4pm Sat & Sun Nov-Feb). The outcrop can be reached by car, by shuttle bus from Goarshausen's Marktplatz (€2.65, hourly 10am to 5pm) and via the 400-step Treppenweg stairway, which begins about 2km upriver from St Goarshausen at the base of the breakwater.

St Goar's **Jugendherberge** (youth hostel; ☎388; www.djh.de; Bismarckweg 17; dm/s/d €18/30/50) is right below the castle, which also houses the upmarket **Romantik Hotel Schloss Rheinfels** (☎06741-8020; www.schloss-rheinfels.de; d €115-265, cheaper in winter; @🛜🏊) and its three restaurants.

BACHARACH

☎06743 / POP 2250

One of the prettiest of the Rhine villages, Bacharach conceals its considerable charms behind a 14th-century wall (you can stroll on top along most of it). Beyond the thick arched gateways awaits a beautiful medieval old town graced with half-timbered mansions such as the **Altes Haus**, the **Posthof** and the off-kilter **Alte Münze** along Oberstrasse. All house places to eat, drink and be merry.

The local youth hostel, **DJH Burg Stahleck** (☎1266; www.jugendherberge.de; Burg Stahleck; dm/d €20.50/52), has a dream location in a hillside medieval castle. Right on the medieval ramparts, the **Rhein Hotel** (☎1243; www.rhein-hotel-bacharach.de; Langstrasse 50; s €39-65, d €78-130; ❄📶) has 14 well-lit, soundproofed rooms with original artwork. The restaurant serves regional dishes.

MAINZ

☎06131 / POP 199,000

An easy day trip from Frankfurt, Mainz has an attractive old town anchored by its massive **Dom** (Marktplatz; ⏰9am-6.30pm Mon-Fri, 9am-4pm Sat, 12.45-6.30pm Sun & holidays, shorter hrs Nov-Feb), which has a blend of Romanesque, Gothic and baroque architecture.

Sampling local wines in a half-timbered Altstadt tavern is as much a part of any Mainz visit as viewing the ethereal Marc Chagall–designed windows in **St-Stephan-Kirche** (Kleine Weissgasse 12; ⏰10am-4.30pm) or the first printed Bible in the **Gutenberg Museum** (www.gutenberg-museum.de; Liebfrauenplatz 5; adult/child €5/3; ⏰9am-5pm Tue-Sat, 11am-5pm Sun), which honours local boy and moveable-type inventor Johannes Gutenberg.

For more information, visit the **tourist office** (☎286 210; www.touristik-mainz.de; Brückenturm am Rathaus; ⏰9am-6pm Mon-Fri, 10am-4pm Sat, 11am-3pm Sun).

In a 15th-century Carmelite nunnery near the cathedral, **Hotel Hof Ehrenfels** (☎971 2340; www.hof-ehrenfels.de; Grebenstrasse 5-7; s/d/tr €80/100/120, €10 less Fri-Sun) has Dom views that are hard to beat. For wine and sustenance, sit beneath the soaring Gothic vaults of a medieval hospital at **Heiliggeist** (www.heiliggeist-mainz.de; Mailandsgasse 11; mains €9.80-19.80; ⏰4pm-1am Mon-Fri, 9am-1am or 2am Sat, Sun & holidays).

Moselle Valley

Like a vine right before harvest, the Moselle hangs heavy with visitor fruit. Castles and half-timbered towns are built along the sinuous river below steep, rocky cliffs planted with vineyards. It's one of the country's most scenic regions, with a constant succession of views rewarding the intrepid hikers who brave the hilly trails. Unlike the Romantic Rhine, it's spanned by plenty of bridges. The region is busiest in May, on summer weekends and during the local wine harvest (mid-September to mid-October).

Getting There & Around

The most scenic part of the Moselle Valley runs 195km from Trier to Koblenz; it's most practical to begin your Moselle Valley trip from either town. Driving is the easiest way to explore this area. If you're coming from Koblenz, the B49 and then, after Bullay, the B53 follow the river all the way to Trier, crossing it several times.

Trains linking Koblenz with Trier (€19.20, 1½ to two hours, at least hourly) stop at river villages only as far as Bullay. From there, hourly shuttle trains head upriver to Traben-Trarbach. The villages between Traben-Trarbach and Trier, including Bernkastel-Kues, are served by bus 333, run by Moselbahn buses.

Frankfurt-Hahn Airport (www.hahn-airport.de), served by Ryanair, is 22km east of Traben-Trarbach and 17km east of Bernkastel-Kues. A shuttle bus links the airport with the railhead of Bullay (€6.80, 51 minutes).

KOBLENZ

☎0261 / POP 106,000

Founded by the Romans, Koblenz sits at the confluence of the Rhine and Moselle Rivers, a point known as **Deutsches Eck** (German 'Corner'), and is dominated by a bombastic 19th-century statue of Kaiser Wilhelm I on horseback. On the right Rhine bank high above the Deutsches Eck, the **Festung Ehrenbreitstein** (www.diefestungehrenbreitstein.de;

WORTH A TRIP

BURG ELTZ

South of Koblenz, at the head of the beautiful Eltz Valley, Burg Eltz is not to be missed. Towering over the surrounding hills, this superb medieval castle has frescoes, paintings, furniture and ornately decorated rooms.

By car, you can reach Burg Eltz via the village of Münstermaifeld; the castle is 800m from the car park (shuttle bus €1.50). Trains link Koblenz and Moselkern (also reachable by boat), where a 35-minute trail to the castle begins at the Ringelsteiner Mühle car park.

adult/child €6/3; ⏲10am-6pm Apr-Oct, to 5pm Nov-Mar)is one one of Europe's mightiest fortresses. Views are great and there's a regional museum inside. The castle is reached by an 850m-long **Seilbahn** (aerial cable car; www.seilbahn-koblenz.de; adult/6-14yr return €8/4, incl fortress €11.20/5.60, bicycle one-way €3; ⏲10am-6pm or 7pm Apr-Oct, to 5pm Nov-Mar).

The **tourist office** (☎313 04; Bahnhofplatz 17; ⏲9am-6pm Mon-Fri) is outside the Hauptbahnhof. Restaurants and pubs cluster around Münzplatz and Burgstrasse in the Altstadt and along the Rhine.

Several boat companies dock on the Rhine, south of the Deutsches Eck. Koblenz has two train stations, the main Hauptbahnhof on the Rhine's left bank about 1km south of the city centre, and Koblenz-Ehrenbreitstein on the right bank (right below the fortress).

BEILSTEIN

On the right bank of the Moselle, about 50km upriver from Koblenz, Beilstein is a pint-sized village right out of the world of fairy tales. Little more than a cluster of houses surrounded by steep vineyards, its historic highlights include the **Marktplatz** and **Burg Metternich**, a hilltop castle reached via a staircase.

The **Zehnthauskeller** (Marktplatz; ⏲11am-evening Tue-Sun) houses a romantically dark, vaulted wine tavern owned by the same family that also runs two local **hotels** (☎1850; www.hotel-lipmann.de).

TRABEN-TRARBACH

Full of fanciful art nouveau villas, the double town of Traben-Trarbach provides respite from the 'romantic half-timbered town' circuit. Pick up a map of the town at the **tourist office** (☎839 80; www.traben-trarbach.de; Am Bahnhof 5, Traben; ⏲10am-5pm Mon-Fri May-Aug, to 6pm Sep & Oct, to 4pm Nov-Apr, 11am-3pm Sat May-Oct; wi-fi). The ruined medieval **Grevenburg** castle sits high in the craggy hills above Trarbach and is reached via a steep footpath, the Sponheimer Weg, that begins a block north of the bridge.

Weingut Caspari (☎5778; www.weingut-caspari.de; Weiherstrasse 18, Trarbach; mains €6.50-16.90) is a rustic, old-time wine restaurant serving hearty local specialities; it's six short blocks inland from the bridge.

BERNKASTEL-KUES

The twin town of Bernkastel-Kues is at the heart of the middle Moselle region. On the right bank, Bernkastel has a charming **Markt**, a romantic ensemble of half-timbered houses with beautifully decorated gables. On Karlstrasse, the alley to the right as you face the Rathaus, the tiny **Spitzhäuschen** resembles a giant bird's house, its narrow base topped by a much larger, precariously leaning, upper floor.

Get your heart pumping by hoofing it from the Spitzhäuschen up to **Burg Landshut**, a ruined 13th-century castle – framed by vineyards and forests – on a bluff above town; allow 30 minutes. You'll be rewarded with glorious valley views and a cold drink at the **beer garden** (⏲10am-6pm mid-Feb–Nov).

Trier

☎0651 / POP 105,250

Founded by the Romans around 16 BC as Augusta Treverorum, Trier became the capital of Roman Gaul in the 3rd century and the residence of Constantine the Great in the 4th century. To this day, you'll find more – and better preserved – Roman ruins here than anywhere else north of the Alps. Trier's proximity to France can be tasted in its cuisine, while its large student population injects life among the ruins.

Sights

Porta Nigra ROMAN GATE
(adult/student €3/2.10, incl Stadtmuseum Simeonstift €7.20/5.80; ⏲9am-6pm Apr-Sep, to 5pm Mar & Oct, to 4pm Nov-Feb) Trier's chief landmark, the brooding 2nd-century city gate is held together by nothing but gravity and iron rods.

Amphitheater ROMAN SITE
(Olewiger Strasse; adult/child €3/2.10; ⏲9am-6pm Apr-Sep, to 5pm Mar & Oct, to 4pm Nov-Feb) This classic outdoor space once held 20,000 spectators during gladiator tournaments and animal fights – or when Constantine the Great crowned his battlefield victories by feeding his enemies to voracious animals.

Kaiserthermen ROMAN SITE
(Imperial Baths; Palastgarten; adult/student €3/2.10) This vast thermal bathing complex was created by Constantine.

Dom CHURCH
(www.dominformation.de; Liebfrauenstrasse 12; ⏲10am-5pm Mon-Sat, 12.30-5pm Sun, shorter hours Nov-Mar) Built above the palace of Constantine the Great's mother, Helena, this fortress-like cathedral is mostly Romanesque, with some

soaring Gothic and eye-popping baroque embellishments.

Konstantin Basilika CHURCH
(www.konstantin-basilika.de; Konstantinplatz; 10am-6pm Apr-Oct, 10am or 11am noon and 2 or 3pm-4pm Tue-Sat, noon-1pm Sun Nov-Mar) Constructed around AD 310 as Constantine's throne hall, the brick-built Konstantin Basilika (Aula Palatina) is now a typically austere Protestant church with mind-blowing dimensions.

Karl Marx Haus HISTORIC SITE
(www.fes.de/karl-marx-haus; Brückenstrasse 10; adult/child €3/2; 10am-6pm daily Apr-Oct, 2-5pm Tue-Sun Nov-Mar) The suitably modest birthplace of the author of *Das Kapital* is fast becoming a major pilgrimage stop for the growing numbers of mainland Chinese tourists to Europe.

Sleeping

Hotel Römischer Kaiser HOTEL €€
(977 00; www.friedrich-hotels.de; Porta-Nigra-Platz 6; s/d from €73.50/111;) Built in 1894, this hotel – convenient to the train station and the old centre – offers 43 bright, comfortable rooms with solid wood furnishings, parquet floors and spacious bathrooms.

Hille's Hostel HOSTEL €
(710 2785, outside office hrs 0171-329 1247; www.hilles-hostel-trier.de; Gartenfeldstrasse 7; dm from €14, s/d €40/50, breakfast €8; reception 9am-noon & 4-6pm or later; @) This laid-back indie hostel has a piano in the common kitchen and 12 attractive, spacious rooms, most with private bathrooms. Call ahead if arriving outside reception hours so they'll leave the door code and the key.

TOP CHOICE **Becker's Hotel** BOUTIQUE HOTEL €€
(938 080; www.beckers-trier.de; Olewiger Strasse 206; d €110-220; P@) This classy establishment pairs 31 supremely tasteful rooms – some ultramodern, others rustically traditional – with stellar dining. It's 3km southeast of the centre in the quiet wine district of Olewig, across the creek from the old monastery church. Served by buses 6, 16 and 81.

Eating

In the warm months, cafes fill Trier's public squares, including the Kornmarkt. The Olewig district, 3km southeast of the centre, is home to traditional wine taverns.

Zum Domstein ROMAN €€
(www.domstein.de; Hauptmarkt 5; mains €8.90-18.50, Roman dinner €17-35) A German-style bistro where you can either dine like an ancient Roman or feast on more conventional German and international fare.

Kartoffel Kiste POTATOES €€
(www.kiste-trier.de; Fahrstrasse 13-14; mains €7.20-17; 11am-midnight;) A local favourite, this place specialises in baked, breaded, gratineed, soupified and sauce-engulfed potatoes, as well as delicious schnitzel and steaks.

Information

Tourist Office (978 080; www.trier-info.de; just inside Porta Nigra; 9 or 10am-5 or 6pm Mon-Sat, 9 or 10am-1pm or later Sun).

Getting There & Away

Trier has at least hourly train connections to Koblenz (€20.80, 1½ to two hours) and frequent service to Luxembourg (same-day return €10.80, 50 minutes, at least hourly), with onward connections to Paris.

HESSE

About two-thirds of Hesse's population lives in the Rhine-Main region, a sprawling urban conglomeration – with excellent public transport – that stretches from Frankfurt am-Main in the north to Darmstadt in the south and Wiesbaden in the west. The attractive spa-city of Wiesbaden is the state capital, but it is Frankfurt, home of the European Central Bank, that wields the financial – and especially stock market – clout.

Frankfurt-am-Main

069 / POP 680,000

Unashamedly high-rise, Frankfurt-on-the-Main (pronounced 'mine') is unlike any other German city. Bristling with jagged skyscrapers, 'Mainhattan' is a true capital of finance and business, home base for one of the world's largest stock exchanges and the European Central Bank. It also hosts some of Europe's key trade fairs, including famous book and auto fairs.

Despite its business demeanour, Frankfurt consistently ranks high among Germany's most liveable cities thanks to its rich collection

Frankfurt-am-Main

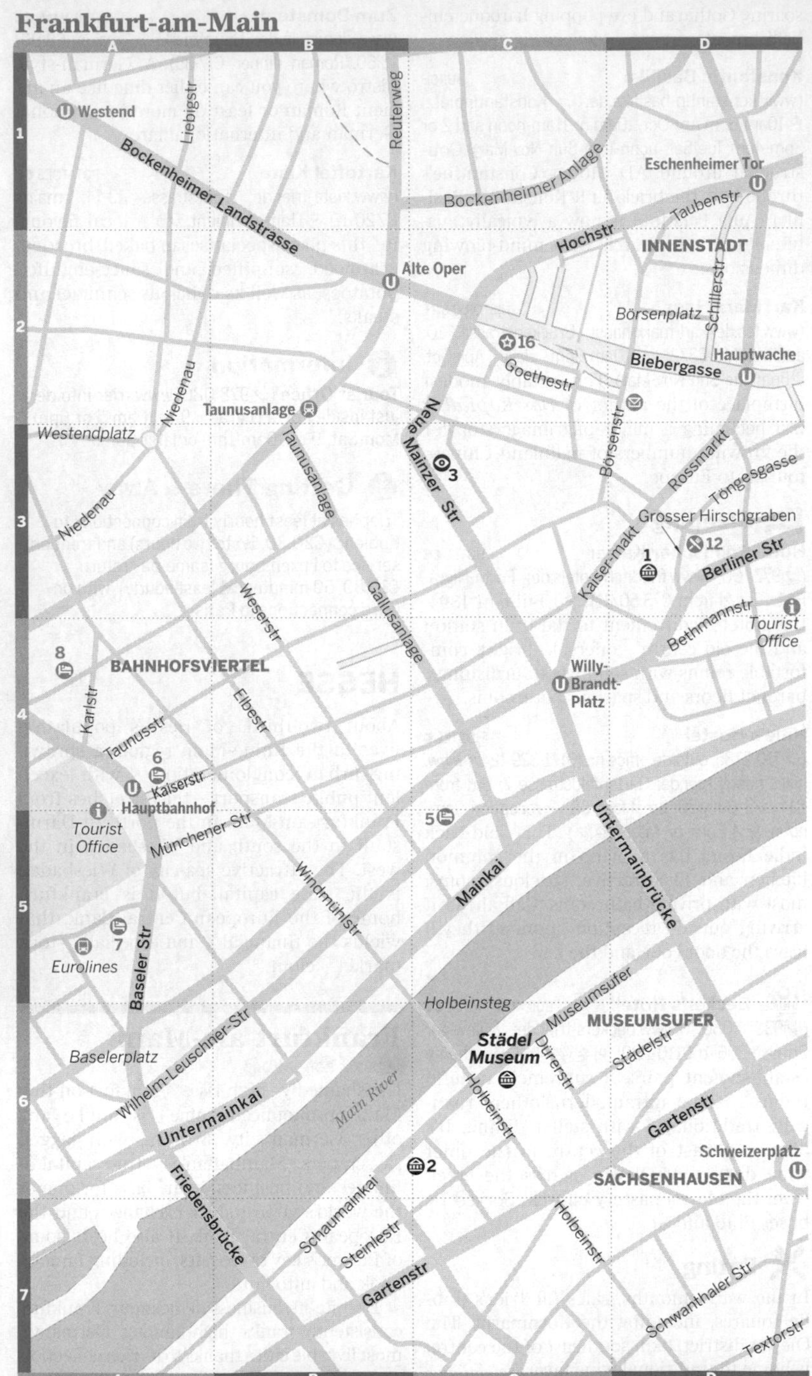

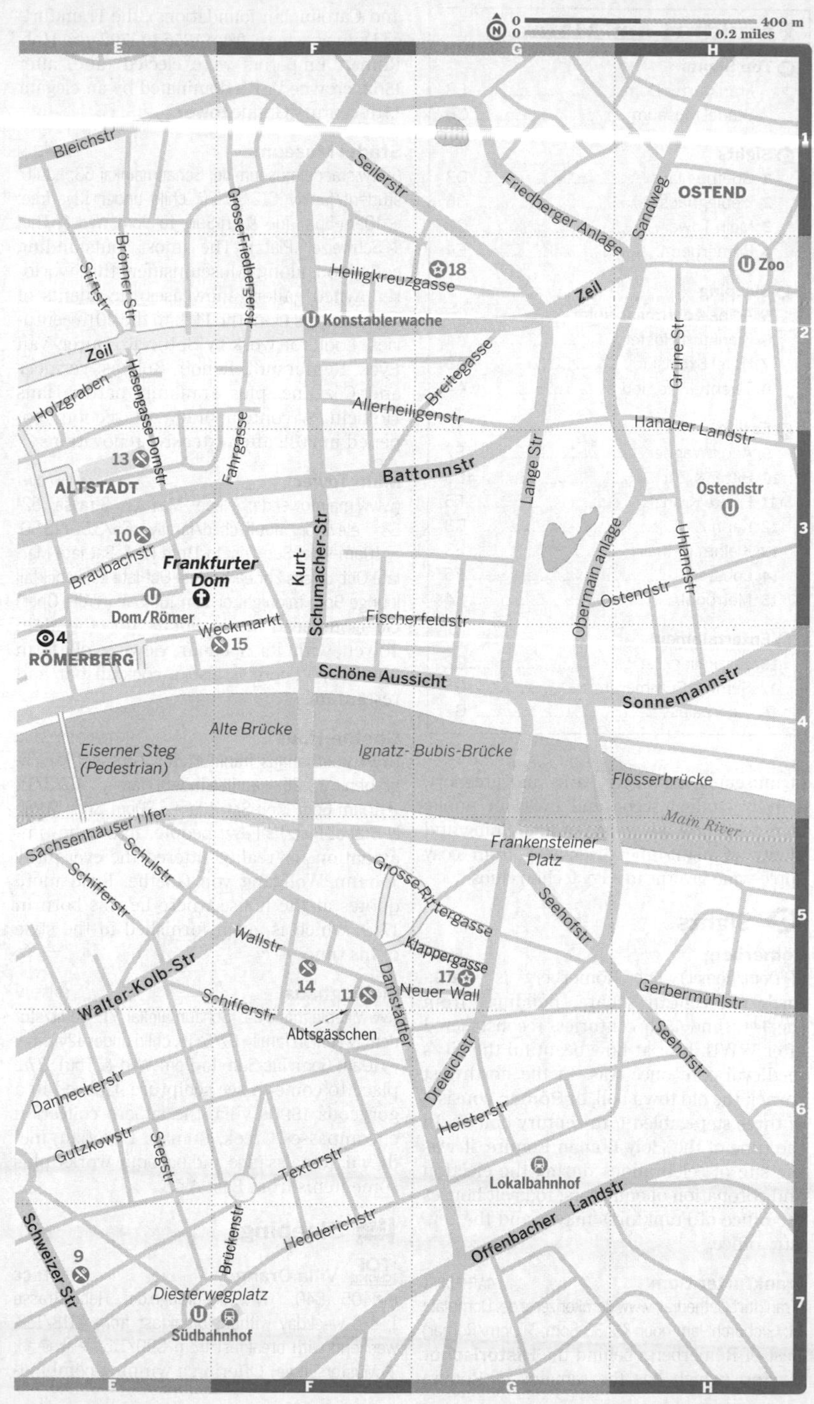

0 400 m
0 0.2 miles
E
F
G
H
1
2
3
4
5
6
7
Bleichstr
Seilerstr
Friedberger Anlage
Sandweg
OSTEND
Zoo
Grosse Friedbergerstr
Brönner Str
Stiftstr
Heiligkreuzgasse
18
Zeil
Konstablerwache
Zeil
Breitegasse
Grüne Str
Holzgraben
Hasengasse Domstr
Fahrgasse
Allerheiligenstr
Hanauer Landstr
13
ALTSTADT
Battonnstr
Lange Str
Ostendstr
10
Uhlandstr
Braubachstr
Frankfurter Dom
Kurt-Schumacher-Str
Obermain anlage
Ostendstr
Dom/Römer
Weckmarkt
Fischerfeldstr
4
RÖMERBERG
15
Schöne Aussicht
Sonnemannstr
Alte Brücke
Eiserner Steg (Pedestrian)
Ignatz-Bubis-Brücke
Flösserbrücke
Main River
Sachsenhäuser Ufer
Schulstr
Frankensteiner Platz
Schifferstr
Grosse Rittergasse
Seehofstr
Wallstr
Klappergasse
14
17
Walter-Kolb-Str
Schifferstr
11
Darmstädter
Neuer Wall
Gerbermühlstr
Abtsgässchen
Seehofstr
Danneckerstr
Dreieichstr
Heisterstr
Gutzkowstr
Stegstr
Textorstr
Lokalbahnhof
Schweizer Str
Brückenstr
Heddericshstr
Offenbacher Landstr
9
Diesterwegplatz
Südbahnhof

Frankfurt-am-Main

Top Sights

	Frankfurter Dom	E3
	Städel Museum	C6

Sights

1	Goethe-Haus	D3
2	Liebieghaus	C6
3	Main Tower	C3
4	Römerberg	E4

Sleeping

5	Adina Apartment Hotel	C5
6	Frankfurt Hostel	A4
7	Hotel Excelsior	A5
8	Twenty-Five Hours	A4

Eating

9	Adolf Wagner	E7
10	Bitter & Zart	E3
11	Fichte Kränzi	F5
12	Karin	D3
13	Kleinmarkthalle	E3
14	Lobster	F5
15	Metropol	F4

Entertainment

16	Jazzkeller	C2
17	Summa Summarum	G5
18	Tigerpalast	G2

of museums, expansive parks and greenery, a lively student scene and excellent public transport. Take advantage of fine dining and plenty of night-time diversions, from cosy apple-wine taverns to edgy techno clubs.

Sights

Römerberg PLAZA

(Dom/Römer) The Römerberg is Frankfurt's old central square. Buildings from the 14th and 15th centuries, reconstructed after WWII, hint at how beautiful the city's medieval core once was. In the northwest corner, the old town hall, or **Römer**, consists of three step-gabled 15th-century houses. In the time of the Holy Roman Empire, it was the site of celebrations during the election and coronation of emperors; today it houses the office of Frankfurt's mayor and the registry office.

Frankfurter Dom CATHEDRAL

(Frankfurt Cathedral; www.domkonzerte.de; Domplatz 14; church 9am-noon & 2.30-8pm; Dom/Römer) East of Römerberg, behind the **Historischer Garten** (which has the remains of Roman and Carolingian foundations), the Frankfurter Dom as where, from 1356 to 1792, the Holy Roman Emperors were elected (and, after 1562, crowned). It's dominated by an elegant 15th-century Gothic **tower**.

Städel Museum MUSEUM

(www.staedelmuseum.de; Schaumainkai 63; adult/student/family €12/10/20, child under 12yr free; 10am-5pm Tue & Fri-Sun, to 9pm Wed & Thu; Schweizer Platz) The most outstanding collection along Museumsufer, this world-renowned gallery showcases the talents of key painters from the 14th to the 20th centuries. Look for work by Botticelli, Dürer, Van Eyck, Rembrandt, Renoir, Rubens, Vermeer and Cézanne, plus Frankfurt native Hans Holbein. A contemporary art section reopened in 2012 after extensive renovations.

Main Tower VIEWPOINT

(www.maintower.de; Neue Mainzer Strasse 52-58; elevator adult/child/family €5/3.50/13.50; 10am-9pm Sun-Thu, to 11pm Fri & Sat late Mar-late Oct, closes 2hr earlier late Oct-late Mar, cocktail lounge 9pm-midnight or 1am Tue-Sat; Alte Oper) Get your head in the clouds atop the Main Tower, with its open-air viewing platform 200m up. There is also a cocktail bar and restaurant.

Goethe-Haus HISTORIC BUILDING

(www.goethehaus-frankfurt.de; Grosser Hirschgraben 23-25; adult/student/family €7/3/11; 10am-6pm Mon-Sat, 10am-5.30pm Sun; Willy-Brandt-Platz) 'Few people have the imagination for reality' uttered the ever-pithy Johann Wolfgang von Goethe. Read more quotes at the house where he was born in 1749, which is again furnished in the style of his time.

Liebieghaus MUSEUM

(www.liebieghaus.de; Schaumainkai 71; adult/student & senior/family €7/5/16, child under 12yr free; 10am-6pm Tue-Sun, to 9pm Wed & Thu) *The* place to come to see sculpture. Housed in a gorgeous 1890s villa, the superb collection encompasses Greek, Roman, Egyptian, medieval, Renaissance and baroque works, plus some items from East Asia.

Sleeping

TOP CHOICE **Villa Orange** HOTEL €€

(405 840; www.villa-orange.de; Hebelstrasse 1; s/d weekday without breakfast from €118/138, weekend with breakfast from €90/115; P; Musterschule) Offering a winning combina-

NAVIGATING FRANKFURT

The **airport** is 11 minutes by train southwest of the city centre. The **Hauptbahnhof** is on the western side of the city, within walking distance of the centre, best reached via **Kaiserstrasse**. This leads to Kaiserplatz and another square called **An der Hauptwache**. This is the retail hub, with stores stretching along in all directions, principally along the **Zeil**. The area between Hauptwache and the **Römerberg** contains vestiges of Frankfurt's **Altstadt** (Old Town).

The **Main River** flows just south of the Altstadt, with several bridges leading to charming **Sachsenhausen** whose northeastern corner, known as **Alt-Sachsenhausen**, has quaint old houses and wine taverns.

Numerous museums line the south bank of the Main River along the so-called **Museumsufer**. To sample them all, buy a 48 hour **Museumsufer ticket** (www.kultur-frankfurt.de; adult/concession/family €15/8/23).

Just northeast of the centre, Frankfurt's village roots are most strongly felt in **Bornheim**, whose spine – **Berger Strasse** – is lined with funky small shops, cafes and pubs.

tion of tranquillity, modern German design and small-hotel comforts (eg a quiet corner library), this century-old villa has 38 spacious rooms.

Twenty-Five Hours BOUTIQUE HOTEL €€
(25h; ☎256 6770; www.25hours-hotels.com; Niddastrasse 58; d without breakfast weekday/weekend from €107/77, during fairs up to €390; ❄@📶; 🚉Frankfurt Hauptbahnhof) Inspired by Levi's jeans, the 76 themed rooms are styled by decade from the 1940s (calm colours) through the 1980s (tiger-print walls). Guests can jam on the drums and guitars in the Gibson-designed basement music room or admire skyline views from the roof terrace.

TOP CHOICE **Frankfurt Hostel** HOSTEL €
(☎247 5130; www.frankfurt-hostel.com; Kaiserstrasse 74, 3rd fl; dm €19-25, s/d from €35/45, during fairs up to €80/100; @📶; 🚉Frankfurt Hauptbahnhof) This 200-bed hostel is reached via a marble-and-tile lobby and a mirrored lift. Kudos for the chill-out area, guest kitchen and the free spaghetti dinners! Dorms have three to 10 metal bunks and free lockers.

Adina Apartment Hotel HOTEL €€
(☎247 4740; www.adina.eu; Wilhelm-Leuschner-Strasse 6; d without breakfast from €84-135, during fairs up to €377; 📶🏊; 🚉Willy-Brandt-Platz) Self-caterers and families will appreciate these spacious studios and one- and two-bedroom apartments, all with kitchenettes.

Hotel Excelsior HOTEL €
(☎256 080; www.hotelexcelsior-frankfurt.de; Mannheimer Strasse 7-9; s/d from €61/75, during fairs €199/239; P@📶; 🚉Frankfurt Hauptbahnhof) Behind a light-green facade, this 197-room place offers excellent value and plenty of freebies: a business centre, landline phone calls within Germany, and coffee, tea, fruit and cakes in the lobby.

Eating & Drinking

The pedestrian strip linking the Alte Oper and the western end of the Zeil is also known as *Fressgass* thanks to its many eateries. Another cluster of places to drink and eat is in Alt-Sachsenhausen.

LOCAL KNOWLEDGE

APPLE-WINE TAVERNS

Apple-wine taverns are Frankfurt's great local tradition. They serve *Ebbelwei* (Frankfurt dialect for *Apfelwein*), an alcoholic apple cider, along with local specialities like *Handkäse mit Musik* (literally, 'hand-cheese with music'). This is a round cheese soaked in oil and vinegar and topped with onions; your bowel supplies the music. Anything with the sensational local sauce made from herbs, *Grüne Sosse*, is a winner. Some good *Ebbelwei* taverns are in Alt-Sachsenhausen, where **Fichtekränzi** (☎612 778; www.fichtekraenzi.de; Wallstrasse 5; mains €7.20-15.50; ⏰5-11pm; 🍴; 🚉Lokalbahnhof) and **Adolf Wagner** (☎612 565; www.apfelwein-wagner.com; Schweizer Strasse 71; mains €4.50-13.90; ⏰11am-midnight; 🍴; 🚉Südbahnhof) are recommended.

ALL ABOARD THE EBBELWEI-EXPRESS

The **Ebbelwei-Express** (Apple Wine Express; www.ebbelwei-express.com; adult/child under 14yr €7/3; half-hourly 1.30-5.30pm Sat, Sun & holidays Apr-Oct & Sat Nov-Mar, approx hourly 1.30-5pm Sun & holidays Nov-Mar) is a historic tram whose 70-minute circuit takes in both banks of the Main between the Zoo and the Messe. Jump on at any stop marked with the letters EE – including the Hauptbahnhof and Börneplatz. As you'd expect, the price includes *Ebbelwei* (apple wine) or juice, and pretzels.

Eckhaus GERMAN €€
(491 197; Bornheimer Landstrasse 45; mains €8-17.90; 5pm-midnight or 1am; Merianplatz) We love this place with its smoke-stained walls and ancient floorboards. The hallmark *Kartoffelrösti* (shredded potato pancake) has been served here for over 100 years.

TOP CHOICE **Kleinmarkthalle** MARKET €
(Hasengasse 5; 7.30am-6pm Mon-Fri, to 3pm Sat; ; Dom/Römer) This traditional covered food market has loads of fruit, vegetables and meats, as well as hot food.

Karin CAFE €€
(295 217; Grosser Hirschgraben 28; mains €8-14; 9am-midnight Mon-Sat, 10am-7pm Sun, 10am-midnight holidays; Willy-Brandt-Platz) This Frankfurt-style cafe serves German and international dishes and nine different breakfasts (until 6pm). Changing exhibits by local artists grace the walls. Cash only.

Bitter & Zart CAFE €
(www.bitterundzart.de; Braubachstrasse 14; 10am-8pm Mon-Sat, 10am-6pm Sun; Dom/Römer) Walk past the chocolate chair then turn left and you're in a delightful shop whose shelves are piled high with the finest chocolates; turn right and order espresso, light meals and breakfast (until noon) or yummy cakes.

Lobster BISTRO €€€
(612 920; www.lobster-weinbistrot.de; Wallstrasse 21; mains €15-20; 6pm-1am Mon-Sat, hot dishes until 10.30pm; Südbahnhof) In a 1950s grocery and milk shop, this cosy, friendly 'wine bistro' is renowned for mouth-watering meat and fish dishes that are 'a little bit French'. Serves three dozen wines by the glass. It's teensy, so book ahead.

Metropol BISTRO €€
(288 287; Weckmarkt 13-15; mains €9.50-14.50; 9am-1am or 2am Tue-Sat, 9am-midnight Sun; Dom/Römer) Serves dishes from a changing menu that ranges from bistro staples to the inspired. Has a lovely courtyard out the back where children can chill out. Cash only.

Wein-Dünker WINE CELLAR
(www.weinkellerei-duenker.de; Berger Strasse 265; 2pm-1am Mon-Thu, 2pm-3am Fri & Sat, 6pm-midnight Sun; Bornheim Mitte) Descend to this little wine cellar to try some of Germany's finest wines. It serves only snacks, but you can BYO and picnic atop an upturned barrel.

☆ Entertainment

FREE **Summa Summarum** LIVE MUSIC
(Klappergasse 3; 8pm-1am Tue-Sat) This vaulted stone cellar with just a half-dozen tables reverberates with traditional New Orleans jazz on Wednesday and Friday, and singer-songwriters (blues, rock etc) on Thursday and Saturday. Tuesday is open-mic night.

King Kamehameha CLUB
(4800 9610; www.king-kamehameha.de; Hanauer Landstrasse 192; admission Thu €8, Fri & Sat €10; 9pm-4am or later Thu, 10pm-4am or later Fri & Sat) 'KingKa' is legendary, with DJs on weekends and a house band on Thursdays. It's about 2km southeast of the zoo (tram 11).

Tigerpalast CABARET
(restaurant 9200 2225, tickets 920 0220; www.tigerpalast.com; Heiligkreuzgasse 16-20; adult €58.75-64.25, child halfprice; shows 7pm & 10pm Tue-Thu, 7.30pm & 10.30pm Fri & Sat, 4.30pm & 8pm Sun, closed mid-Jun–mid-Aug; Konstablerwache) Shows at this top-rated variety theatre often include acrobats and circus and magic performances. Hugely enjoyable even if you don't speak German. Book ahead.

Jazzkeller JAZZ
(www.jazzkeller.com; Kleine Bockenheimer Strasse 18a; admission €5-25; 8pm-2am Tue-Thu, 10pm-3am Fri, 9pm-2am Sat, 8pm-1am Sun; Alte Oper) A great jazz venue since 1952. Check out the walls for photos of jazz greats who've played here over the years. Concerts begin an hour after opening except on Friday, when there's dancing to Latin and funk. In a cellar across from Goethestrasse 27.

Information

Tourist Office (☎2123 8800; www.frankfurt-tourismus.de) Two branches: Hauptbahnhof (Hauptbahnhof; ⏰8am-9pm Mon-Fri, 9am-6pm Sat, Sun & holidays; 🚆Frankfurt Hauptbahnhof) and Römer (Römerberg 27; ⏰9.30am-5.30pm Mon-Fri, 9.30am-4pm Sat, Sun & holidays; 🚆Dom/Römer).

Getting There & Away

Air

Frankfurt Airport (FRA; www.frankfurt-airport.com), 12km southwest of the city centre, is Germany's busiest. Terminals 1 and 2 are linked by a driverless railway, the SkyLine.

The airport has two train stations accessible from Terminal 1. The *Regionalbahnhof* handles regional train and S-Bahn connections, while long-distance IC, EC and ICE trains stop at the *Fernbahnhof*. Coming from Terminal 2, use the yellow shuttle buses (rather than the SkyLine).

To get into town, take S-Bahn lines S8 and S9 from the Regionalbahnhof (€4.10, 15 minutes). A taxi costs about €27.

Note that **Frankfurt-Hahn airport** (HHN; www.hahn-airport.de) is 125km west of Frankfurt near the Moselle Valley.

Bus

Long-distance buses leave from the south side of the Hauptbahnhof, where you'll find **Eurolines** (☎790 3253; www.eurolines.eu; Mannheimer Strasse 15; ⏰7.30am-7.30pm Mon-Fri, 7.30am-2pm Sat, 7.30am-1pm Sun; 🚆Frankfurt Hauptbahnhof), with services to most European destinations. The Europabus (p504) headed to the Romantic Road also leaves from here.

Train

The Hauptbahnhof has train services to pretty much everywhere, including Berlin (€118, four hours).

Getting Around

Public Transport

Both single and day tickets for Frankfurt's excellent transport network called **traffiQ** (☎01801-069 960; www.traffiq.de) can be purchased from vending machines at most stops and stations. Single tickets cost €2.50 and a *Tageskarte* (24-hour ticket) costs €6.20 (€14.50 including the airport).

Taxi

Flagfall is €2.75 (€3.25 at night) and each kilometre is charged at €1.65 (€1.75 at night). There are taxi ranks throughout the city, or call a cab through **Taxi Frankfurt** (☎250 001, 230 001; www.taxi-frankfurt.de).

NORTH RHINE-WESTPHALIA

North Rhine-Westphalia harbours within its boundaries flat, windswept expanses and forested hills high enough to hold onto snow during winter. Villages sweetly lost in time contrast with frenzied metropolises habitually on fast-forward. Through it all carves the muscular Rhine, fed by tributaries such as the Ruhr that gives its name to an entire region.

Must sees include Cologne with its lofty Dom (cathedral), Bonn with its Beethoven legacy and fabulous museums, and Charlemagne's imperial capital of Aachen. There are historical cities like Münster, where the Thirty Years' War peace treaty was signed, and elegant ones like Düsseldorf, the state capital and art-world hub.

Cologne

☎0221 / POP 1 MILLION

Cologne (Köln) offers lots of attractions, led by its famous cathedral whose filigree twin spires dominate the skyline. The city's museum landscape is especially strong when it comes to art but it also has something in store for fans of chocolate, sports and Roman history. Its people are well known for their joie de vivre and it's easy to have a good time right along with them year-round in the beer halls of the Altstadt (Old Town).

Sights

Römisch-Germanisches Museum MUSEUM
(Roman Germanic Museum; ☎2212 2304; www.museenkoeln.de; Roncalliplatz 4; adult/child €8/4; ⏰10am-5pm Tue-Sun) Sculptures and ruins displayed outside are merely the overture

COLOGNE CARNIVAL

Ushering in Lent in late February or early March, Cologne's **Carnival** (Karneval) rivals Munich's Oktoberfest for exuberance, as people dress in creative costumes and party in the streets. Things kick off the Thursday before the seventh Sunday before Easter, culminate on Monday *(Rosenmontag)*, when there are televised street parades, and end on Ash Wednesday.

DON'T MISS

KÖLNER DOM

As easy as it is to get church fatigue in Germany, the huge **Kölner Dom** (Cologne Cathedral; ☎1794 0200; www.koelner-dom.de; ⊙6am-10pm May-Oct, to 7.30pm Nov-Apr, south tower 9am-6pm May-Sep, to 5pm Mar-Apr & Oct, to 4pm Nov-Feb) is one you shouldn't miss. Blackened with age, this gargoyle-festooned Gothic cathedral has a footprint of 12,470 sq metres, with twin spires soaring to 157m. Although its ground stone was laid in 1248, stop-start construction meant it wasn't finished until 1880, as a symbol of Prussia's drive for unification. Just over 60 years later it escaped WWII's heavy bombing largely intact.

Sunshine filtering softly through stained-glass windows and the weak glow of candles are the only illumination in the moody, high-ceilinged interior. Behind the altar lies the cathedral's most precious reliquary, the **Shrine of the Three Magi** (c 1150–1210), which reputedly contains the bones of the Three Wise Men. Brought to Cologne from Milan in the 12th century, it can just be glimpsed through the gates to the inner choir.

To see the shrine properly, you need to take a guided tour. For fine views, embark on the seriously strenuous climb of 509 steps of the Dom's south tower, passing the 24-tonne **Peter Bell**, the world's largest working clanger.

to a full symphony of Roman artefacts found along the Rhine. Highlights include the giant **Poblicius tomb** (AD 30–40), the magnificent 3rd-century **Dionysus mosaic** and astonishingly well-preserved glass items.

Museum Ludwig MUSEUM
(☎2212 6165; www.museenkoeln.de; Bischofsgartenstrasse 1; adult/child €10/7; ⊙10am-6pm Tue-Sun) This grand art museum gets extra big kudos for its collections of 1960s pop art (Warhol's *Brillo Boxes* are a highlight), German expressionism and Russian avant garde painting, as well as photography.

Kolumba MUSEUM
(☎933 1930; www.kolumba.de; Kolumbastrasse 4; adult/child €5/free; ⊙noon-5pm Wed-Mon, to 7pm Thu) Art, history, architecture and spirituality form a harmonious tapestry in this spectacular collection of religious treasures. Coptic textiles, Gothic reliquary and medieval painting are juxtaposed with works by Bauhaus legend Andor Weiniger and edgy room installations. Don't miss the 12th-century carved ivory crucifix.

NS Dokumentationszentrum MUSEUM
(☎2212 6332; www.museenkoeln.de; Appellhofplatz 23-25; adult/child €5/2; ⊙10am-6pm Tue-Fri, 11am-6pm Sat & Sun) An exhibit in the basement of the Gestapo (Nazi-era secret police) prison, where scores of people were interrogated, tortured and murdered, documents the history of Cologne during the Third Reich. Inscriptions on the cell walls offer a gut-wrenching record of the emotional and physical pain endured by prisoners.

Wallraf-Richartz-Museum & Fondation Corboud MUSEUM
(☎2212 1119; www.museenkoeln.de; Obenmarspforten; adult/child €9/6; ⊙10am-6pm Tue-Sun, to 9pm Thu) A famous collection of paintings from the 13th to the 19th centuries, this museum occupies a postmodern cube designed by the late OM Ungers. Standouts include brilliant examples from the Cologne School, known for its distinctive use of colour. Upstairs are Dutch and Flemish artists, including Rembrandt and Rubens, Italians such as Canaletto and Spaniards such as Murillo.

Chocolate Museum MUSEUM
(Schokoladen Museum; ☎931 8880; www.schokoladenmuseum.de; Am Schokoladenmuseum 1a; adult/concession €8.50/6; ⊙10am-6pm Tue-Fri, 11am-7pm Sat & Sun) At this hi-tech temple to the art of chocolate-making, exhibits on the origin of the 'elixir of the gods', as the Aztecs called it, and the cocoa-growing process are followed by a live-production factory tour and a stop at a chocolate fountain for a sample.

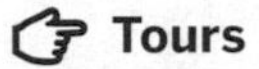

Tours

KD River Cruises BOAT TOUR
(☎258 3011; www.k-d.com; Frankenwerft 35; tour €10; ⊙10.30am-5pm) One of several companies offering one-hour spins taking in the splendid Altstadt panorama; other options include sunset cruises.

Sleeping

TOP CHOICE Hotel Hopper et cetera HOTEL €€
(☎924 400; www.hopper.de; Brüsseler Strasse 26; s €95-120, d €135-180; P@📶) A waxen monk welcomes you to this former monastery whose 49 rooms sport eucalyptus floors, cherry furniture and marble baths, along with such Zeitgeist-compatible touches as iPod docks. The sauna and bar, both in the vaulted cellars, are great for reliving the day's exploits.

Cerano Hotel HOTEL €€
(☎925 7300; www.cerano-hotels.de; Elisenstrasse 16; r €60-120; 📶) This unassuming five-storey hotel near the train station is peppered with extra touches: mineral water, juices and more apples than you'd find in an orchard. Staff are helpful and the breakfast is a delight.

Hotel Cristall HOTEL €€
(☎163 00; www.hotelcristall.de; Ursulaplatz 9-11; s €70-180, d €90-250; ❄@📶) This stylish boutique hotel makes excellent use of colour, customised furniture and light accents. Some rooms are rather compact; light sleepers should not get a street-facing one.

Lint Hotel HOTEL €€
(☎920 550; www.lint-hotel.de; Lintgasse 7; s €60-90, d €90-130; 📶) The 18 rooms of this cute, contemporary and ecoconscious (solar-panelled roof) hotel in the heart of the Altstadt are comfortable and sport hardwood floors. Partly organic breakfast buffet.

Station Hostel for Backpackers HOSTEL €
(☎912 5301; www.hostel-cologne.de; Marzellenstrasse 44-56; dm €17-20, s/d from €32/48; @📶) This is a hostel as hostels should be: central, convivial and economical. A lounge gives way to clean, colourful rooms sleeping one to six people. There's lots of free stuff, including linen, internet access, lockers, city maps and a guest kitchen.

Meininger City Hostel & Hotel HOSTEL €
(☎355 332 014; www.meininger-hostels.com; Engelbertstrasse 33-35; dm €18-24, s/d from €48/70; @📶) This charming hostel in the Zülpicher Viertel student quarter is loaded with retro appeal coupled with modern rooms featuring lockers, bunkside reading lamps, a small TV and private bathrooms. Freebies include linen, towels, and pasta that you can whip up in the small basement kitchen.

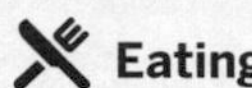

Eating

The largest variety and most happening restaurants are in the Zülpicher Viertel and Belgisches Viertel (Belgian Quarter) areas, both in the city centre.

Alcazar PUB €
(Bismarckstrasse 39; snacks €4-9, mains €10-16; 🖉) This is the kind of place that never goes out of fashion, thanks to its winning combination of freshly prepared international dishes, unpretentious ambience and chirpy service. No food service in the afternoon.

TOP CHOICE Salon Schmitz MODERN EUROPEAN €
(Aachener Strasse 28; snacks €4-8) No matter whether you prefer sidling up to the long bar or grabbing an ultracomfy sofa in the retro lounge, Schmitz is a perfect pit stop for relaxed chats over coffee, cocktails or its house-brand Kölsch beer. If hunger strikes, pop next door to the affiliated deli in a former butcher's shop.

Bei Oma Kleinmann GERMAN €€
(www.beiomakleinmann.de; Zülpicher Strasse 9; mains €12; ⏲5pm-1am Tue-Sun, kitchen to 11pm) Named for its long-time owner, who was still cooking almost to her last day at age 95 in 2009, this cosy trad restaurant has timeless dishes, including 14 kinds of schnitzel. Pull up a seat at the small wooden tables for a classic Cologne night out.

Feynsinn INTERNATIONAL €€
(☎240 9210; www.cafe-feynsinn.de; Rathenauplatz 7; mains €7-18) At this well-respected restaurant organic ingredients are woven into sharp-flavoured dishes. The owners raise their own meat. Get a table overlooking the park for a meal or just a drink.

Engelbät EUROPEAN €
(☎246 914; www.engelbaet.de; Engelbertstrasse 7; crepes €3-9; ⏲11am-1am) This cosy restaurant-pub is famous for its habit-forming crepes, which come as sweet, meat or vegetarian. The sidewalk tables are popular for drinks and there are many other choices nearby.

Drinking & Entertainment

As in Munich, beer in Cologne reigns supreme. Local breweries turn out a variety called *Kölsch,* which is relatively light and served in skinny 200mL glasses.

WORTH A TRIP

BONN

South of Cologne on the Rhine River, Bonn (population 312,000) became West Germany's capital in 1949. Now that Berlin has resumed this role, Bonn is doing just fine, sporting a healthy economy and lively urban vibe. For visitors, the birthplace of Ludwig van Beethoven has plenty in store, not least the great composer's birth house, a string of top-rated museums and a lovely riverside setting.

The **tourist office** (☎775 000; www.bonn.de; Windeckstrasse 1; ⏰10am-6pm Mon-Fri, to 4pm Sat, to 2pm Sun) is a three-minute walk along Poststrasse from the Hauptbahnhof, and can fill in the details.

Beethoven fans will head straight to the **Beethoven-Haus** (☎981 7525; www.beethoven-haus-bonn.de; Bonngasse 24-26; adult/child €5/4; ⏰10am-6pm Mon-Sat, 11am-6pm Sun Apr-Oct, to 5pm Nov-Mar), where the composer was born in 1770. The house contains memorabilia concerning his life and music, including his last piano, with an amplified sounding board to accommodate his deafness.

The **Haus der Geschichte der Bundesrepublik Deutschland** (FRG History Museum; ☎916 50; www.hdg.de; Willy-Brandt-Allee 14; ⏰9am-7pm Tue-Fri, 10am-6pm Sat & Sun) presents Germany's postwar history. It is part of the Museumsmeile, a row of museums in the old government quarter south of the city centre along the B9. It also includes the **Kunstmuseum Bonn** (☎776 260; www.kunstmuseum-bonn.de; Friedrich-Ebert-Allee 2; adult/concession €7/3.50; ⏰11am-6pm Tue & Thu-Sun, to 9pm Wed), which presents 20th-century art, especially by August Macke and other Rhenish expressionists.

The unfiltered ale is a must at **Brauhaus Bönnsch** (☎650 610; www.boennsch.de; Sterntorbrücke 4; mains €7-15; ⏰11am-1am), a congenial brew-pub adorned with photographs of famous politicians: Willy Brandt to, yes, Arnold Schwarzenegger. Schnitzel, spare ribs and sausages dominate the menu, but the *Flammkuchen* (Alsatian pizza) is also a winner.

Bonn is linked to Cologne many times hourly by U-Bahn lines U16 and U18 as well as by regional trains.

Früh am Dom BEER HALL

(☎258 0394; www.frueh.de; Am Hof 12-14; mains €5-12) This warren of a beer hall near the Dom epitomises Cologne earthiness. Sit inside amid loads of knick-knacks or on the flower-filled terrace next to a fountain. It's also known for great breakfasts.

TOP CHOICE **Päffgen** BEER HALL

(www.paeffgen-koelsch.de; Friesenstrasse 64-66) Busy, loud and boisterous, Päffgen has been pouring *Kölsch* since 1883 and hasn't lost a step since. In summer you can enjoy the refreshing brew and local specialities beneath starry skies in the beer garden.

Malzmühle BEER HALL

(☎210 117; www.muehlenkoelsch.de; Heumarkt 6; mains €6-15; ⏰10am-midnight) Expect plenty of local colour at this convivial beer hall off the beaten tourist track. It brews *Kölsch* with organic ingredients and is also known for its lighter *Malzbier* (malt beer, 2% alcohol).

Stadtgarten CLUB

(☎952 9940; www.stadtgarten.de; Venloer Strasse 40) In a small park, this Belgian Quarter favourite hosts vibrant dance parties and live jazz, soul and world music concerts in its cellar hall, but is also a great spot just for a drink (summer beer garden).

Papa Joe's Klimperkasten PIANO BAR

(☎258 2132; www.papajoes.de; Alter Markt 50) A piano player tickles the ivories nightly in this museumlike place where the smoky brown walls are strewn with yesteryear's photographs. There are Markt-facing outdoor tables in fine weather.

Alter Wartesaal CLUB

(☎912 8850; www.wartesaal.de; Johannisstrasse 11; ⏰Thu-Sat) In a former train station waiting hall, this is a stylish bar-disco-restaurant combo. Themed nights range from the erotic KitKatClub to SoulChannel. There are cafe tables out front in the shadow of the Dom where you can take a pause.

Information

Tourist Office (☎2213 0400; www.koelntourismus.de; Unter Fettenhennen 19; ⊙9am-8pm Mon-Sat, 10am-5pm Sun)

Getting There & Away

Air

About 18km southeast of the city centre, **Köln Bonn Airport** (CGN; ☎02203-404 001; www.airport-cgn.de) has direct flights to 130 cities and is served by numerous airlines,with destinations across Europe.The S13 train connects the airport and the Hauptbahnhof every 20 minutes (€2.80, 15 minutes). Taxis charge about €30.

Train

Cologne's Hauptbahnhof sits just a Frisbee toss away from the Dom. Services are fast and frequent in all directions. A sampling: Berlin (€113, 4¼ hours), Frankfurt (€67, 1¼ hours) and Munich (€134, 4½ hours). In addition there are fast trains to Brussels (for connecting to the Eurostar for London or Paris).

Getting Around

Cologne's comprehensive mix of buses, trams, and U-Bahn and S-Bahn trains is operated by **VRS** (☎01803-504 030; www.vrsinfo.de) in cooperation with Bonn's system. Short trips (up to four stops) cost €1.80, longer ones €2.60. Day passes are €7.50 for one person and €11.10 for up to five people travelling together. Buy your tickets from the orange ticket machines at stations and aboard trams; be sure to validate them.

Düsseldorf

☎0211 / POP 589,000

Düsseldorf dazzles with boundary-pushing architecture, zinging nightlife and an art scene to rival any other. It's a posh and modern city that seems all buttoned-up business at first: banking, advertising, fashion and telecommunications are among the fields that fuel the wealth of the state capital of North Rhine-Westphalia. Yet all it takes is a few hours of bar-hopping around the Altstadt, the historical quarter along the Rhine, to realise that locals have no problem letting their hair down once they slip out of those Boss jackets. The Altstadt may claim to be the 'longest bar in the world' but some attention has strayed a bit further south to Medienhafen, a redeveloped harbour area and a feast of international avant garde architecture.

Sights

Marktplatz SQUARE

Düsseldorf's historic Marktplatz is framed by the Renaissance **Rathaus** (town hall) and accented by an equestrian **statue of Jan Wellem**, an art-loving late 17th-century local ruler who's buried nearby in the early-baroque **Andreaskirche** (www.dominikaner-duesseldorf.de; Andreasstrasse 27; ⊙8am-6.30pm).

TOP CHOICE **Kunstsammlung Nordrhein-Westfalen** MUSEUM

(Art Collection of North Rhine Westphalia; www.kunstsammlung.de; combined ticket adult/child €20/5; ⊙10am-6pm Tue-Fri, 11am-6pm Sat & Sun) It's this modern art collection that gives Düsseldorf an edge in the art world. **K20 Grabbeplatz** (☎838 1130; Grabbeplatz 5; adult/child €12/9.50) has fabulous canvases by Paul Klee alongside other big-shots, including Pablo Picasso, Henri Matisse, and Düsseldorf's own Joseph Beuys. It is linked by shuttle to the **K21 Ständehaus** (☎838 1630; Ständehausstrasse 1; adult/child €10/2.50), a showcase of cutting-edge paintings, photographs, installations and video art created after 1980 by the likes of Nam June Paik and Bill Viola. A third gallery, the **Schmela Haus** (Mutter-Ey-Strasse 3), was being redeveloped at the time of research.

Rheinuferpromenade PROMENADE

(Rhine River Walk) **Burgplatz**, on the northern end of the Altstadt, marks the beginning of the Rhine promenade, whose cafes and benches fill with people in fine weather, creating an almost Mediterranean flair. Marking the south end of the Rhine promenade, the **Rheinturm** (Stromstrasse 20; adult/child €4/2.50; ⊙10am-11.30pm) has an observation deck at 168m with – yes indeed! – sweeping views on a clear day.

Medienhafen ARCHITECTURE

(Am Handelshafen) South of the Rheinturm, the old harbour area has been reborn as the Media Harbour, which is mostly an office quarter but noteworthy for its cutting-edge architecture by celebrated international architects. Frank Gehry's warped **Neuer Zollhof** is especially photogenic. A few cafes and restaurants let you give your feet a rest.

Sleeping

Stage 47 BOUTIQUE HOTEL €€
(☎388 030; www.stage47.de; Graf-Adolf-Strasse 47; s/d from €130/145; P❄@☜) Behind the drab exterior, movie glamour meets design chic at this urban boutique hotel. Rooms are named for famous people, who appear in enormous black-and-white prints framed on the wall, so let's hope you like who you sleep with...

Max Hotel Garni HOTEL €€
(☎386 800; www.max-hotelgarni.de; Adersstrasse 65; s/d from €70/85; @☜) Upbeat, contemporary and run with personal flair, this charmer is a Düsseldorf favourite. The 11 rooms are good-sized and decked out in bright hues and warm woods. Rates include coffee, tea, soft drinks and a regional public transport pass. Call ahead to arrange an arrival time.

Sir & Lady Astor HOTEL €€
(☎173 370; www.sir-astor.de; Kurfürstenstrasse 18 & 23; s €85-170, d €95-250; @☜) Never mind the ho-hum setting on a residential street near the Hauptbahnhof, this unique twin boutique hotel brims with class, originality and charm. Check-in is at Sir Astor, furnished in 'Scotland-meets-Africa' style, while Lady Astor across the street goes more for French floral sumptuousness. Book early.

Backpackers-Düsseldorf HOSTEL €
(☎302 0848; www.backpackers-duesseldorf.de; Fürstenwall 180; dm €15-23; @☜) Düsseldorf's adorable indie hostel sleeps 60 in clean four- to 10-bed dorms outfitted with individual backpack-sized lockers. It's a low-key place with a kitchen and a relaxed lounge where cultural and language barriers melt quickly. The reception is generally staffed from 8am to 9pm. Breakfast is included.

Eating & Drinking

On balmy nights, restaurants set up tables outside and the atmosphere – especially in the Altstadt – is electric and often raucous. The beverage of choice is *Altbier*, a dark and semisweet beer typical of Düsseldorf.

Brauerei im Füchschen GERMAN €€
(☎137 470; www.fuechschen.de; Ratinger Strasse 28; mains €5-15; ⊙9am-1am) Boisterous, packed and drenched with local colour – the 'Little Fox' in the Altstadt is all you expect a Rhenish beer hall to be. Mean *Schweinshaxe* (roast pork leg) and some of the best *Altbier* in town.

Weinhaus Tante Anna MODERN EUROPEAN €€€
(www.tanteanna.de; Andreasstrasse 2; mains/menus from €25/45) This is like your aunt's place (if she was a baroness); silver serving plates, subdued carved wood interior, wines decanted and poured properly – the details do go on. The constantly changing menu shows the range of the kitchen.

Libanon Express MIDDLE EASTERN €
(Berger Strasse 19-21; mains €3-20) Great kebabs, falafel and other Middle Eastern specialities.

TOP CHOICE **Zum Uerige** BEER HALL
(☎866 990; www.uerige.de; Berger Strasse 1) This cavernous beer hall is a superb place to soak up local colour along with your beer. The suds flow so quickly from giant copper vats that the waiters – called *Köbes* – simply carry huge trays of brew and plonk down a glass whenever they spy an empty.

Information

Altstadt Tourist Office (Marktstrasse/Ecke Rheinstrasse; ⊙10am-6pm)

Hauptbahnhof Tourist Office (Immermannstrasse 65b; ⊙9.30am-7pm Mon-Fri, to 5pm Sat)

Getting There & Away

Düsseldorf International Airport (DUS; www.dus-int.de) has three terminals and is served by a wide range of airlines. S-Bahns, regional RE and long-distance trains link it with Düsseldorf Hauptbahnhof, and cities beyond, every few minutes. A taxi into town costs about €16.

Düsseldorf is part of a dense S-Bahn and regional train network in the Rhine-Ruhr region, including Cologne (€12, 30 minutes). ICE/IC train links include Berlin (€107, 4¼ hours), Hamburg (€78, 3¾ hours) and Frankfurt (€78, 1¾ hours).

Getting Around

Rheinbahn (www.rheinbahn.de) operates an extensive network of U-Bahn trains, trams and buses throughout Düsseldorf. Most trips within the city cost €2.40. Day passes are €5.70.

Aachen

☎0241 / POP 258,700

A spa town founded by the Romans, with a hopping student population and tremendous amounts of character, Aachen has narrow cobbled streets, quirky fountains, shops full of delectable *Printen* (local biscuit, a bit

DON'T MISS

AACHENER DOM

It's impossible to overstate the significance of Aachen's magnificent **cathedral** (477 090; www.aachendom.de; Münsterplatz; 7am-7pm Apr-Dec, 7am-7pm Jan-Mar). The burial place of Charlemagne, it's where more than 30 German kings were crowned and where pilgrims have flocked since the 12th century.

Start your church visit at the new **Dom Visitors Centre** (4770 9127; Klosterplatz 2; 10am-1pm Mon, to 5pm Tue-Sun Jan-Mar, 10am-1pm Mon, to 6pm Tue-Sun Apr-Dec) for info and tickets for tours, and the **Domschatzkammer** (Cathedral Treasury; 4770 9127; adult/child €6.50/5.50; 10am-1pm Mon, to 5pm Tue-Sun Jan-Mar, 10am-1pm Mon, to 6pm Tue, Wed & Fri-Sun, to 9pm Thu Apr-Dec), an Aladdin's Cave of religious treasures.

The cathedral's oldest and most impressive section is the emperor's private palace chapel, the **Pfalzkapelle**, an outstanding example of Carolingian architecture. Completed in 800, the year of the Charlemagne's coronation, the octagonal structure boasts a colossal brass chandelier that was a gift from Emperor Friedrich Barbarossa during whose reign Charlemagne was canonised in 1165.

Pilgrims have poured into town ever since, drawn in as much by the cult surrounding Charlemagne as by several prized relics, including the loincloth said to have been worn by Jesus at his crucifixion. These days, they're only displayed once every seven years (next in 2014).

To accommodate the growing numbers of pilgrims, a Gothic choir was docked to the chapel in 1414 and fancifully decorated with a **pala d'oro**, a gold-plated altar-front depicting Christ's Passion, and the jewel-encrusted gilded copper **pulpit**, both fashioned in the 11th century. At the far end is the **gilded shrine of Charlemagne** that has held the emperor's remains since 1215. In front, the equally frilly shrine of St Mary shelters the cathedral's famous relics.

Unless you join a **guided tour** (adult/child €5/4; 11am-4.30pm Mon-Fri, 1-4pm Sat & Sun, tours in English 2pm), you'll barely catch a glimpse of Charlemagne's white marble imperial throne in the upstairs gallery. Reached via six steps – just like King Solomon's throne – it served as the coronation throne of 30 German kings between 936 and 1531.

like gingerbread), and – most famously – an ancient cathedral. It makes for an excellent day trip from Cologne or Düsseldorf or a worthy overnight stop.

Sights

Rathaus HISTORIC BUILDING
(Markt; adult/concession €5/3; 10am-6pm) Aachen's mighty Gothic town hall is festooned with 50 life-size statues of German rulers, including 30 German kings that were crowned in town. Inside, highlights are the **Kaisersaal** with its epic 19th-century **frescoes** by Alfred Rethel and the replicas of the **imperial insignia**: a crown, orb and sword (the originals are in Vienna).

Ludwig Forum für Internationale Kunst MUSEUM
(Ludwig Forum for International Art; 180 7104; www.ludwigforum.de; Jülicherstrasse 97-109; adult/child €5/3; noon-6pm Tue, Wed & Fri, noon-8pm Thu, 11am-6pm Sat & Sun) In a former umbrella factory, this art museum trains the spotlight on modern art (Warhol, Immendorf, Holzer, Penck, Haring etc) and also stages progressive changing exhibits.

Suermondt Ludwig Museum MUSEUM
(479 800; www.suermondt-ludwig-museum.de; Wilhelmstrasse 18; adult/child €5/3; noon-6pm Tue, Thu & Fri, noon-8pm Wed, 10am-6pm Sat & Sun) The Suermondt Ludwig is especially proud of its medieval sculpture but also has fine works by Cranach, Dürer, Macke, Dix and other masters.

Sleeping

Hotel Drei Könige HOTEL €€
(483 93; www.h3k-aachen.de; Büchel 5; s €90-130, d €120-180, apt €140-240;) The radiant Mediterranean decor is an instant mood enhancer at this family-run favourite with its doesn't-get-more-central location. Some

rooms are a tad twee but the two-room apartment sleeps up to four. Breakfast on the 4th floor comes with dreamy views over the rooftops and the cathedral.

DJH Hostel HOSTEL €
(☎0241 711 010; www.aachen.jugendherberge.de; Maria-Theresia-Allee 260; dm/s/d from €26/45/68) Aachen's modernised 180-bed hostel is nicely located in a park overlooking the city. About a third of the 55 rooms have private bathrooms. Take bus 2 (direction Preuswald) to the Ronheide stop.

Eating & Drinking

Aachen's students have their own 'Latin Quarter' along Pontstrasse, with dozens of bars and cheap eats. It runs for about 1km northeast of the Markt.

TOP CHOICE **Leo van den Daele** CAFE €
(www.van-den-daele.de; Büchel 18; treats from €3) Leather-covered walls, tiled stoves and antiques forge the yesteryear flair of this rambling cafe institution. Come for all-day breakfast, a light lunch or divine cakes.

Am Knipp GERMAN €€
(☎331 68; www.amknipp.de; Bergdriesch 3; mains €8-18; ⊙dinner Wed-Mon) Hungry grazers have stopped by this traditional inn since 1698, and you too will have a fine time enjoying hearty German cuisine served amid a flea market's worth of twee knick-knacks. A vast, lovely beer garden as well.

Apollo Kino & Bar BAR/CLUB
(☎900 8484; www.apollo-aachen.de; Pontstrasse 141-149) This cavernous basement joint does double duty as an art-house cinema and a sweaty dance club for the student brigade with a sound spectrum that covers all the bases.

Information

Tourist Office (☎0241 180 2961, 0241 180 2960; www.aachen-tourist.de; Friedrich-Wilhelm-Platz; ⊙9am-6pm Mon-Fri, to 2pm Sat, also 10am-2pm Sun Easter-Dec)

Getting There & Around

Regional trains to Cologne (€16, one hour) run twice hourly, with some proceeding beyond. Aachen is a stop for high-speed trains to/from Brussels and Paris.

Local bus tickets are €1.60; drivers sell tickets.

LOWER SAXONY

Lower Saxony (Niedersachsen) likes to make much of its half-timbered towns. Hamelin is certainly a true fairy-tale beauty, and lovely Lüneburg is quite unlike any other town you'll see. The state is also home to the global headquarters of Volkswagen and the business-minded capital, Hanover, as well as the western stretches of the pretty Harz mountains.

Hanover

☎0511 / POP 518,000

German comedians like to dismiss Hanover (Hannover in German) as 'the autobahn exit between Göttingen and Walsrode'. However, the capital of Lower Saxony is far livelier than its reputation assumes, and its residents are remarkably friendly and proud of their small city. While it's famous for hosting trade fairs, particularly the huge CEBIT computer show in March, it also boasts acres of greenery in the Versailles-like gardens, Herrenhäuser Gärten.

Less well-known but buried deep within its identity is a British connection – for over 100 years from the early 18th century, monarchs from the house of Hanover also ruled Great Britain and everything that belonged to the British Empire.

Sights & Activities

Neues Rathaus HISTORIC BUILDING
(Trammplatz 2; elevator adult/concession €3/2; ⊙9.30am-6.30pm Mon-Fri, 10am-6.30pm Sat & Sun, elevator closed mid-Nov–Mar) An excellent way to get your bearings in Hanover is to visit the Neues Rathaus (built in 1901–13) and travel 98m to the top in the **curved lift** inside its green dome. There are four viewing platforms here.

Die Nanas SCULPTURE
(Leibnizufer) Hanover's city fathers and mothers were inundated with nearly 20,000 letters of complaint when these three earth-mama sculptures were first installed beside the Leine River in 1974. Now, the voluptuous and fluorescent-coloured 'Sophie', 'Charlotte' and 'Caroline', by the late French artist Niki de Saint Phalle, are among the city's most recognisable, and most loved, landmarks.

TOP CHOICE Sprengel Museum MUSEUM

(www.sprengel-museum.de; Kurt-Schwitters-Platz; adult/concession €7/4, Fri free; ⊙10am-6pm Wed-Sun, to 8pm Tue) The Sprengel Museum is held in extremely high esteem, both for the design of the building as well as for the art it houses. Its cavernous interior is perfectly suited to showcase modern figurative, abstract and conceptual art, including a sprinkling of works by Nolde, Chagall and Picasso. A selection of scuptures by Niki de Saint Phalle is usually on show as well. Take bus 100 from Kröpcke to the Maschsee/Sprengel Museum stop.

TOP CHOICE Herrenhäuser Gärten GARDEN

(☎1684 7576; www.herrenhaeuser-gaerten.de; ⊙9am-sunset) Situated about 5km northwest of the centre, Herrenhäuser Gärten (Herrenhausen Gardens) is a remarkable ensemble of parks and gardens largely modelled on those at Versailles. The jewel in the crown, **Grosser Garten** (adult/concession incl Berggarten €5/4 Nov–mid-May, €8/5 mid-May-Oct) is grand both in format and history and peppered with statues, fountains and the colourfully tiled **Niki de Saint Phalle Grotto** (creator of the city's much-loved *Die Nanas* sculptures). The **Grosse Fontäne** (Great Fountain; the tallest in Europe) at the park's south end jets water up to 80m high. Popular summer attractions are the **Wasserspiele** (Fountain Display; ⊙11am-noon & 3-5pm Mon-Fri, 11am-noon & 2-5pm Sat & Sun Apr-Oct), water fountains that are synchronised to do some spectacular spurting, and the **Illuminations**, when the Grosser Garten is lit up for between one and two hours. Also part of the ensemble are two other gardens, the **Berggarten** (www.herrenhaeuser-gaerten.de; adult/concession late Mar-Oct €3.50/1.50, combination ticket with Grosser Garten adult/concession €5/4 Nov–mid-May, €8/5 mid-May–Oct), with its great assortment of flora from around the world, and the lake-dotted **Georgengarten** (admission free). Take tram/U-Bahn 4 or 5 from Kröpcke to Herrenhäuser Gärten.

Sleeping

City Hotel am Thielenplatz HOTEL €

(☎327 691; www.smartcityhotel.com; Thielenplatz 2; s/d from €59/69, breakfast €9.50; P ⓦ) This very central 'budget boutique' beauty has a reception and bar (open until 5am) styled with leather seating, black-and-white leaf-patterned wallpaper and lots of wood laminate. Rooms have been renovated, mostly in a minimalist style.

City Hotel Flamme HOTEL €€

(☎388 8004; www.city-hotel-flamme.de; Lammstrasse 3; s/d €70/125; P @ ⓦ) Most of the 24 rooms of this attractively mural painted hotel-pension open onto balconies facing a large atrium courtyard, which has a quirky eating area and glassed-in front wall.

DJH Hostel HOSTEL €

(☎131 7674; www.jugendherberge.de/jh/hannover; Ferdinand-Wilhelm-Fricke-Weg 1; 4-bed dm under/over 27yr from €21.80/25.80, s/d €38.50/57; P @ ⓦ; S3 or 7 to Bahnhof Linden/Fischerhof) This huge, space-lab-like structure houses a modern hostel with breakfast room and terrace bar overlooking the river. It's only a short walk from here to the Maschsee (lake).

GästeResidenz PelikanViertel APARTMENT €€

(☎399 90; www.gaesteresidenz-pelikanviertel.de; Pelikanstrasse 11; s €49-83, d €69-105, tr €100-125; P ⓦ; S3, 7 or 9 to Pelikanstrasse) Upmarket student residence meets budget hotel, this well-managed complex has a wide range of pleasant Ikea-ish rooms and apartments, some split over two levels. Use of kitchen utensils costs an additional €8 (plus €50 deposit) per apartment.

Eating & Drinking

TOP CHOICE Markthalle MARKET €

(www.hannover-markthalle.de; Kamarschstrasse 49; dishes €3.50-10; ⊙7am-8pm Mon-Wed, to 10pm Thu & Fri, to 4pm Sat; ☑) This huge covered market of food stalls and gourmet delicatessens is fantastic for a quick bite, both carnivorous and vegetarian.

Brauhaus Ernst August PUB

(www.brauhaus.net; Schmiedestrasse 13; ⊙8am-3am Mon-Thu, to 5am Fri & Sat, 9am-3pm Sun) A Hanover institution, this sprawling brewpub makes a refreshing unfiltered pilsner called Hannöversch. A party atmosphere reigns nightly, helped along by a varied roster of live bands and DJs.

Café Mezzo CAFE, BAR

(www.cafe-mezzo.de; Lister Meile 4; ⊙9am-2am Tue-Thu, to 3am Fri & Sat, to midnight Sun & Mon; ⓦ) This classic bar and cafe used to be a student hang-out, but today gets a balance of ages. It's popular any time of day (including for breakfast), but doubles well as a place to warm up in the evening before moving on to a club or performance.

Hiller VEGETARIAN €€
(www.hannover-vegetarisch.de; Blumenstrasse 3; mains €7.70-10.50, lunch menu €7.90-10.70; ⏲lunch & dinner Mon-Sat; 🅥) Germany's oldest vegetarian restaurant is a tad hushed and old-fashioned but the interior, with colourful draped cloth on the walls, is cheery. Food is well prepared and excellent value.

Georxx INTERNATIONAL €€
(www.georxx-hannover.de; Georgsplatz 3; pasta €8.50-13.50, mains €9.50-28.80; ⏲from 9am) Popular with businesspeople, office workers, shoppers, tired travellers and arty types, Georxx has pleasant outdoor seating in summer, a menu offering a taste for everyone (a bit of Asia, a bit of the Balkans etc) and good lunch specials (€6.50 to €9.50). Breakfast is served until 5pm.

ℹ Information

Hannover Tourismus (☎information 1234 5111, room reservations 1234 555; www.hannover.de; Ernst-August-Platz 8; ⏲9am-6pm Mon-Fri, to 2pm Sat, also 9am-2pm Sun Apr-Sep)

ℹ Getting There & Around

Hanover's **airport** (HAJ; www.hannover-airport.de) has many connections, including on Air Berlin.

Hanover is a major rail hub for European and national services, with frequent ICE trains to/from Hamburg Hauptbahnhof (€43, 1¼ hours), Bremen (€31, one hour), Munich (€125, 4¼ hours), Cologne (€68, 2¾ hours) and Berlin (€65, 1¾ hours), among others.

U-Bahn lines from the Hauptbahnhof are boarded in the station's north (follow signs towards Raschplatz), including the U8 to the Messe (fairgrounds). The U10 and U17 are overground trams leaving from south of the station near the tourist office.

Most visitors only travel in the central 'Hannover' zone. Single tickets are €2.30 and day passes €4.50.

Around Hanover

WOLFSBURG

Volkswagen *is* the Lower Saxon town of **Wolfsburg** – and the huge VW emblem adorning the company's global headquarters (and a factory the size of a small country) won't let you forget it.

Arriving in Wolfsburg, the first thing you see is the enormous Volkswagen emblem adorning the company's global headquarters. The top reason people come here is to experience the theme park called **Autostadt** (Car City; www.autostadt.de; Stadtbrücke; adult/concession €15/12, car tower discovery adult/concession €8/6; ⏲9am-6pm), where exhibitions run the gamut of automotive design and engineering, the history of the Beetle and the marketing of individual marques, including VW itself, Audi, Bentley and Lamborghini.

Nearby, **Phaeno** (www.phaeno.de; Willy Brandt-Platz 1; adult/child/concession/family €12/7.50/9/26.50; ⏲9am-5pm Tue-Fri, 10am-6pm Sat & Sun, last entry 1hr before closing) is a science centre housed in a sleek piece of futuristic architecture by celebrity architect Zaha Hadid. Serious car-ficionados might also want to check out the great collection of rare and unsual vehicles in the **AutoMuseum** (http://automuseum.volkswagen.de; Dieselstrasse 35; adult/concession/family €6/3/15; ⏲10am-6pm Tue-Sun).

Wolfsburg is about 90km east of Hanover via the A2 autobahn and is frequently served by direct train (from €17.50, 30 minutes).

CELLE

☎05141 / POP 70,250

With row upon row of ornate half-timbered houses, all decorated with scrolls and allegorical figures, Celle is graced with a picture-book town centre that is among the most attractive in the region. It's a pleasant place for a leisurely day trip from Hanover.

The tourist office (in the Altes Rathaus) has a good *Walk Through Celle* map in English that takes you from sight to sight.

👁 Sights

Schloss PALACE
(Ducal Palace; Schlossplatz; Residenzmuseum €5, combined Residenzmuseum, Bomann Museum & Kunstmuseum €8, Fri free, guided tours adult €6; ⏲10am-5pm Tue-Sun) Celle's wedding-cake Schloss was built in 1292 as a town fortification and in 1378 was expanded and turned into a residence. Today it houses administrative offices and the Palace Museum. One-hour **guided tours** take you the Renaissance **Schlosskapelle** (chapel), the 19th-century **Schlossküche** (kitchen) and – rehearsals permitting – the baroque **Schlosstheater** (☎tickets 127 14; www.schlosstheater-celle.de; Schlossplatz; ⏲closed Jul & Aug).

The frilly palace contrasts with the ultramodern **Kunstmuseum** (Art Museum; ☎123 55; www.kunst.celle.de; Schlossplatz 7; adult/concession incl Bomann Museum €5/3, free Fri; ⏲10am-

WORTH A TRIP

BERGEN-BELSEN

The Nazi-built concentration camp at **Bergen-Belsen** (www.bergenbelsen.de; Lohheide; ⌚10am-6pm) began its existence in 1940 as a POW camp, but was partly taken over by the SS from April 1943 to hold Jews as hostages in exchange for German POWs held abroad. In all, 70,000 Jews, Soviet soldiers, political hostages and other prisoners died here, most famously Anne Frank, whose posthumously published diary became a modern classic. The Documentation Centre today is one of the best of its kind and deals sensitively but very poignantly with the lives of the people who were imprisoned here – before, during and after incarceration.

Bergen-Belsen is about 25km northwest of Celle and 60km northeast of Hannover. It is difficult to reach by public transport. If you're driving, take the B3 to the town of Bergen and follow the signs to Belsen. A taxi from Celle costs about €35.

5pm Tue-Fri, to 6pm Sat & Sun) opposite, which presents contemporary German art and is illuminated at night into a '24-hour' museum.

Altes Rathaus HISTORIC BUILDING
Cellle's 16th-century town hall boasts a wonderful Weser Renaissance stepped gable, topped with the ducal coat of arms and a golden weather vane. At the tourist office door, on the building's south side, there are two **whipping posts**, used from 1786 to 1850 to punish minor offenders. Prisoners weren't in fact whipped but merely left here for 12 hours, to allow their neighbours to spit at them or throw insults and eggs.

Stadtkirche CHURCH
(www.stadtkirche-celle.de; An der Stadtkirche 8; tower adult/concession €1/0.50; ⌚church 10am-6pm Tue-Sat year-round, tower 10-11.45am & 2-4.45pm Tue-Sat Apr-Oct) The highlight of the 13th-century Stadtkirche is the 235 steps you can climb to the top of the church steeple for a view of the city. The city trumpeter climbs 220 steps to the white tower below the steeple for a trumpet fanfare in all four directions at 9.30am and 5.30pm daily.

Eating

Restaurant Bier Akademie GERMAN €€
(www.bier-akademie-celle.de; Weisser Wall 6; mains €11.10-22.50; ⌚lunch Mon-Thu, dinner Mon-Sat) This family-run restaurant serves an excellent range of beef, poultry and lamb as well as pork, but its speciality is a local roulade, which you can order as a starter or main course. It's just northeast of Schlossplatz.

Information

Tourist office (☎1212; www.region-celle.com; Markt 14-16; ⌚9am-6pm Mon-Fri, 10am-4pm Sat, 11am-2pm Sun)

Getting There & Away

Various train services run to Celle from Hanover (from €9.10, 45 minutes) and Lüneburg (€16.40, 1¼ hours). The Altstadt is about a 15-minute walk east of the Hauptbahnhof.

HAMELIN

☎05151 / POP 57,800

If you were to believe the 'Pied Piper of Hamelin' fairy tale, this quaint, ornate town on the Weser River ought to be devoid of both rats and children. According to legend, the Pied Piper *(Der Rattenfänger)* was employed by Hamelin's townsfolk to lure their pesky rodents into the river in the 13th century. When they refused to pay him, however, he picked up his flute again and led their kids away.

However, it is a bedtime story, after all. International tourism means the reality is very different. Everywhere you look along Hamelin's cobbled streets are – you guessed it – fake rats and happy young children.

Sights

Rattenfängerhaus HISTORIC BUILDING
(Rat Catcher's House; Osterstrasse 28) This is among the finest of the houses built in the ornamental Weser Renaissance style so prevalent throughout the Altstadt. Note the typically steep and richly decorated gable.

Hochzeitshaus HISTORIC BUILDING
(Wedding House; Osterstrasse 2) The Hochzeitshaus (1610–17) does double duty as city council offices and a police station. The **Rattenfänger Glockenspiel** at the far end of the building chimes daily at 9.35am and 11.35am, while a carousel of Pied Piper figures twirls at 1.05pm, 3.35pm and 5.35pm.

WORTH A TRIP

LÜNEBURG, THE WOBBLY TOWN

With an off-kilter church steeple, buildings leaning on each other and houses with swollen 'beer-belly' facades, it's as if charming Lüneburg has drunk too much of the pilsner lager it used to brew.

Of course, the city's wobbly angles and uneven pavements have a more prosaic cause. For centuries until 1980, Lüneburg was a salt-mining town, and as this 'white gold' was extracted from the earth, ground shifts and subsidence knocked many buildings sideways. Inadequate drying of the plaster in the now-swollen facades merely added to this asymmetry. But knowing the scientific explanation never detracts from the pleasure of being on Lüneburg's comic-book crooked streets.

Between Hanover (€26, one hour by train) and Hamburg (€12, 30 minutes), the city's an easy day trip from either. From the train station, head west into town towards the highly visible, 14th-century **St Johanniskirche** (☎435 94; Am Sande; admission €2; ⏰10am-5pm Sun-Wed, to 6pm Thu-Sat Apr-Oct, 9am-6pm Thu-Sat, to 4pm Sun Nov-Mar), the 106m-high spire of which leans 2.2m off true. Local legend has it that the architect tried to kill himself by jumping off it. (He fell into a hay cart and was saved, but celebrating his escape later in the pub he drank himself into a stupor, fell over, hit his head and died after all.)

The church stands at the eastern end of the city's oldest square, **Am Sande**, full of typically Hanseatic stepped gables. At the western end stands the beautiful black-and-white **Industrie und Handelskammer** (Chamber of Industry & Trade).

Continue one block past the Handelskammer and turn right into restaurant-lined Schröderstrasse, which leads to the Markt, where the ornate **Rathaus** (town hall) contains the **tourist office** (☎04131 207 6620; www.lueneburg.de; ⏰9am-6pm Mon-Fri, to 4pm Sat, 10am-4pm Sun May-Sep, 9am-5pm Mon-Fri, to 2pm Sat Oct-Apr).

Admire the square before continuing west along Waagestrasse and down our favourite Lüneburg street, **Auf dem Meere**, en route to the **St Michaeliskirche** (☎314 00; Johann-Sebastian-Bach-Platz; ⏰10am-5pm Mon-Sat, 2-5pm Sun May-Sep, to 4pm Oct-Apr). Here the wonky facades and wavy pavements are like something from a Tim Burton film.

It's too late now to regain your equilibrium, so head back along Am Flock for the pubs on **Am Stintmarkt** on the bank of the Ilmenau River.

Museum Hamelin MUSEUM
(Osterstrasse 8-9; adult/concession €5/4; ⏰11am-6pm Tue-Sun) Two gorgeous Weser Renaissance–style houses are home to the revamped regional history museum. The **Leisthaus** at No 9 was built for a patrician grain trader in 1585–89, whereas the **Stiftsherrenhaus** dates from 1558 and is the only surviving building in Hamelin decorated with figures, some of them planetary gods, others biblical figures.

Sleeping & Eating

TOP CHOICE **Hotel La Principessa** HOTEL €€
(☎956 920; www.laprincipessa.de; Kupferschmiedestrasse 2; s/d €78/99; P 📶) Cast-iron balustrades, tiled floors throughout and gentle Tuscan pastels and ochre shades make this Italian-themed hotel an unusual and distinguished option in Hamelin.

TOP CHOICE **Rattenfängerhaus** GERMAN €€
(Osterstrasse 28; mains €10-23; ⏰11am-10pm) Hamelin's traditional restaurants are unashamedly aimed at tourists, such as this cute half-timbered tavern with a speciality of 'rats' tails' flambéed at your table (fortunately, like most of the theme dishes here, it's based on pork). Schnitzels, herrings, vegie dishes and 'rat killer' herb liquor are also offered.

Information

Tourist office (☎957 823; www.hameln.de; Diesterallee 1; ⏰9am-6pm Mon-Fri, 9.30am-3pm Sat, 9.30am-1pm Sun)

Getting There & Away

By car, take the B217 to/from Hanover.

Frequent S-Bahn trains (S5) head to Hamelin from Hanover's Hauptbahnhof (€11.10, 45 minutes). The train station is about 800m east of the centre.

Bremen

☎0421 / POP 548,000

Bremen, the smallest of the German states, brings together culture and nightlife. It's a shame the donkey, dog, cat and rooster in Grimm's Town Musicians of Bremen never actually made it here – they would have fallen in love with the place. This little city is big on charm, from the fairy-tale character statue to a jaw-dropping art nouveau laneway and impressive town hall. On top of that, the Weser riverside promenade is a relaxing, cafe-lined refuge and the student district along Ostertorsteinweg knows it's got a good thing going.

Sights & Activities

Markt SQUARE

Bremen's Markt is striking, particularly because of its ornate, gabled **Rathaus**. In front stands a 13m-tall medieval statue of the knight **Roland**, Bremen's protector. On the building's western side, you'll find a sculpture of the **Town Musicians of Bremen** (1951). Local artist Gerhard Marcks has cast them in their most famous pose, scaring the robbers who invaded their house, with the rooster atop the cat, perched on the dog, on the shoulders of the donkey.

Dom St Petri CHURCH

(St Petri Cathedral; tower €1; ⌚10am 4.45pm Mon-Fri, to 1.30pm Sat, 2-4.45pm Sun, tower closed Nov-Easter) The 13th-century twin-towered Dom has great ribbed vaults and chapels, but its most intriguing – and certainly macabre – feature is the **Bleikeller** (Lead Cellar; adult/child €1.40/1; ⌚10am-5pm Mon-Fri, to 1.45pm Sat, noon-4.45pm Sun Apr-Oct) accessed via a separate entrance south of the main door. Eight bodies mummified in the incredibly dry air are displayed in open coffins, including a soldier with his mouth opened in a silent scream, and a student who died in a duel in 1705.

Böttcherstrasse STREET

This charming lane is a superb example of expressionist architecture and was largely designed by Bernhard Hoetger (1874–1959). Enter via the golden relief called the *Lichtbringer* (Bringer of Light), which shows a scene from the Apocalypse with the archangel Michael fighting a dragon. Hoetger's **Haus Atlantis** (now the Hilton Hotel) features a show-stopping, multicoloured, glass-walled spiral staircase. He also fused the 16th-century Roselius Haus with the adjoining Paula-Modersohn-Becker-Haus with its rounded edges and wall reliefs. Today these two are museums comprising the **Kunstsammlungen Böttcherstrasse** (Art Collection Böttcherstrasse; www.pmbm.de; Böttcherstrasse 6-10; combined ticket adult/concession €5/3; ⌚11am-6pm Tue-Sun).

Schnoor NEIGHBOURHOOD

The maze of narrow, winding alleys known as the Schnoorviertel was once the fishermen's quarter and then the red-light district. Now its doll's-house–sized cottages house souvenir shops and restaurants.

Beck's Brewery BREWERY

(☎01805-101 030; www.becks.de/besucherzentrum; Am Deich; tours €10.50; ⌚10am, 11.30am, 1pm, 3pm, 4.30pm & 6pm Thu-Sat May-Oct, less frequently Jan-Apr) You can see where the wares come from during a two-hour tour of the Beck's brewery, run in conjunction with the tourist office. Book online or by telephone and meet at the brewery by taking tram 1 or 8 to Am Brill. *Prost!*

Sleeping

Bremer Backpacker Hostel HOSTEL €

(☎223 8057; www.bremer-backpacker-hostel.de; Emil-Waldmann-Strasse 5-6; dm/s/d €18/29/48; P@📶) This private hostel is simply furnished but spotless, with a kitchen, communal room and a small courtyard out front for soaking up the sun.

TOP CHOICE **Hotel Bölts am Park** HOTEL €€

(☎346 110; www.hotel-boelts.de; Slevogtstrasse 23; s/d €65/85; P📶) This cosy family-run hotel in a leafy neighbourhood has real character, from the wonderfully old-fashioned breakfast hall to its well-proportioned doubles.

TOP CHOICE **Hotel Überfluss** BOUTIQUE HOTEL €€€

(☎322 860; www.hotel-ueberfluss.com; Langenstrasse 72/Schlachte 36; s €120-160, d €131-195, ste from €339; ❄📶🏊) Quite literally 7m above river level, this designer hotel has black bathrooms and stunning views from its more expensive rooms.

Hotel Lichtsinn HOTEL €€

(☎368 070; www.hotel-lichtsinn.com; Rembertistrasse 11; s/d €85/110; P@📶) Wooden floorboards, Persian carpets and vaguely Biedermeier-style furniture characterise most of this hotel's rooms, a favourite with the theatre world.

Eating & Drinking

The student quarter around Ostertorsteinweg brims with inexpensive restaurants and cafes. The waterfront promenade, Schlachte, is pricier and more mainstream. The Marktplatz is home to oodles of cheap snack stands.

TOP CHOICE Casa MEDITERRANEAN €€
(http://casa-bremen.com; Ostertorsteinweg 59; mains €8.40-19.60; from 10am;) Formerly known as Casa Blanca, Bremen's long-standing favourite now has a slightly more upmarket splash. It serves lava-grill fish and meat dishes alongside salads and pizza – often with a Mediterranean edge.

Piano INTERNATIONAL €
(www.cafepiano-bremen.de; Fehrfeld 64; mains €6.50-11.40; 9am-1am;) Enduringly popular, this bustling cafe place serves pizza, pasta, a few heartier dishes and vegie casseroles to all comers – from media types to young mums. On weekends, breakfast is served until the afternoon.

TOP CHOICE Engel Weincafe BAR, CAFE
(www.engelweincafe-bremen.de; Ostertorsteinweg 31; breakfast €4.90-8.60, Flammkuchen €6.70-9.50, cheeses & meats €4-13.30; 8am-1am Mon-Fri, 10am-1am Sat & Sun;) Housed in a former pharmacy, this popular hang-out recently morphed into a double act of cafe and wine bar that does good breakfasts and serves cheeses, cold cuts of meat and platters to accompany the fine wines.

Katzen Café INTERNATIONAL €€
(326 621; www.katzen-cafe.de; mains €15.50-24; lunch & dinner) This popular Moulin Rouge-style restaurant opens out into a rear sunken terrace bedecked with flowers. The menu runs the gamut from Alsatian to Norwegian, with seafood a strong theme.

TOP CHOICE Wohnzimmer BAR
(www.wohnzimmer-bremen.de; Ostertorsteinweg 99; from 4pm May-Aug, from 10am Sep-Apr) This bar and lounge mostly gets a relaxed 20s and early 30s crowd, who hang out on the sofas – which explains the name 'Living Room' – or lounge around on the mezzanine levels.

Information

Tourist Office (01805-101030; www.bremen-tourism.de) Two branches: Hauptbahnhof (www.bremen-tourism.de; main train station; 9am-7pm Mon-Fri, 9.30am-5pm Sat & Sun) and the branch office (Marktplatz, cnr Obernstrasse/Liebfraukirchhof; 10am-6.30pm Mon-Sat, to 4pm Sun).

Getting There & Around

Bremen's **airport** (BRE; www.airport-bremen.de) is about 3.5km south of the city centre and has flights to German and European destinations. Ryanair flies to Edinburgh and London-Stansted. Tram 6 travels between the Hauptbahnhof and the airport (€2.35, 15 minutes). A taxi from the airport costs about €15.

Frequent IC trains go to Hamburg (€26, one hour), Hanover (€31, one hour) and Cologne (€63, three hours).

HAMBURG

040 / POP 1.8 MILLION

'The gateway to the world' might be a bold claim, but Germany's second-largest city and biggest port has never been shy. Hamburg has engaged in business with the world ever since it joined the Hanseatic League trading bloc back in the Middle Ages, and this 'harbourpolis' is now the nation's premier media hub and among its wealthiest cities. It's also the site of Europe's largest urban-renewal project, the HafenCity, that is efficiently transforming the old docklands into a bold new city quarter.

Hamburg's maritime spirit infuses the entire city; from architecture to menus to the cry of gulls, you always know you're near the water. The city has given rise to vibrant neighbourhoods awash with multicultural eateries, as well as the gloriously seedy Reeperbahn red-light district.

Sights & Activities

Old Town HISTORIC AREA
Hamburg's medieval **Rathaus** (4283 120 10; tours adult/child €3/0.50; English-language tours hourly 10.15am-3.15pm Mon-Thu, to 1.15pm Fri, to 5.15pm Sat, to 4.15pm Sun; S Rathausmarkt or Jungfernstieg) is one of Europe's most opulent. North of here, you can wander through the **Alsterarkaden**, the Renaissance-style arcades sheltering shops and cafes alongside a canal or 'fleet'.

For many visitors, however, the city's most memorable building is south in the Merchants' District. The 1920s, brown-brick **Chile Haus** (cnr Burchardstrasse &

Johanniswall; S Mönckebergstrasse/Messberg) is shaped like an ocean liner, with remarkable curved walls meeting in the shape of a ship's bow and staggered balconies that look like decks.

TOP CHOICE **Speicherstadt & Harbour** HISTORIC AREA

The seven-storey red-brick warehouses lining the **Speicherstadt** archipelago are a well-recognised Hamburg symbol, stretching to Baumwall in the world's largest continuous warehouse complex. It's best appreciated by simply wandering through its streets or taking a boat up its canals.

The Speicherstadt merges into Europe's biggest inner-city urban development, the **HafenCity**. Here, a long-derelict port area of 155 hectares is being redeveloped with restaurants, shops, apartments and offices, all built to very strict sustainability standards. In the next 20 years, it's anticipated that some 40,000 people will work and 12,000 will live here. The main architectural highlight is the stunning concert hall called **Elbphilharmonie** (Elbe Philharmonic Hall; www.elbphilharmonie.de; S Messberg). For a project overview, head to the **HafenCity InfoCenter** (3690 1799; www.hafencity.com; Am Sandtorkai 30; 10am-6pm Tue-Sun; S Messberg).

Reeperbahn NEIGHBOURHOOD

(S Reeperbahn) No discussion of Hamburg is complete without mentioning St Pauli, home of the Reeperbahn, Europe's biggest red-light district. Sex shops, peep shows, dim bars and strip clubs line the streets, which generally start getting crowded with the masses after 8pm or 9pm. This is also where you find the notorious **Herbertstrasse** (a block-long street lined with brothels that's off-limits to men under 18 and to female visitors of all ages).

Fischmarkt MARKET

(5-10am Sun; Reeperbahn) Here's the perfect excuse to stay up all Saturday night. Every Sunday between 5am and 10am, curious tourists join locals of every age and walk of life at the famous Fischmarkt in St Pauli. The market has been running since 1703, and its undisputed stars are the boisterous *Marktschreier* (market criers) who hawk their wares at full volume. Live bands also entertainingly crank out cover versions of ancient German pop songs in the adjoining **Fischauktionshalle** (Fish Auction Hall).

Internationales Maritimes Museum MUSEUM

(3009 3300; www.internationales-maritimes-museum.de; Koreastrasse 1; adult/concession €12/8.50; 10am-6pm Tue, Wed & Fri-Sun, 10am-8pm Thu; S Messberg) Hamburg's maritime past – and future – is fully explored in this excellent private museum which sprawls over 10 floors of a rehabbed brick shipping warehouse. The vast collection includes 26,000 model ships.

Museum für Völkerkunde MUSEUM

(01805-308 888; www.voelkerkundemuseum.com; Rothenbaumchaussee 64; adult/child €7/free; 10am-6pm Tue, Wed & Fri-Sun, to 9pm Thu; S Hallerstrasse or Dammtor) The famous ethnology museum is packed with traditional and modern artefacts from Africa, Asia and the South Pacific, including masks, jewellery, costumes, musical instruments, carved wooden canoes and even a complete, intricately carved, Maori meeting hall.

Hamburger Kunsthalle MUSEUM

(428 131 200; www.hamburger-kunsthalle.de; Glockengiesserwall; adult/concession €8.50/5; 10am-6pm Tue, Wed & Fri-Sun, to 9pm Thu; Hauptbahnhof) Consists of two buildings, the old one housing old masters and 19th-century art, and a white concrete cube – the Galerie der Gegenwart – showcasing contemporary German artists, including Georg Baselitz and Gerhard Richter, alongside international stars such as David Hockney and Jeff Koons.

St Michaeliskirche CHURCH

(www.st-michaelis.de; tower adult/child €4/3, crypt €3/2, combo ticket €6/4; 10am-7.30pm May-Oct, to 5.30pm Nov-Apr; Stadthausbrücke) Northeast of the landing piers, the St Michaeliskirche, or 'Der Michel' as it's commonly called, is one of Hamburg's most recognisable landmarks and northern Germany's largest Protestant baroque church. Ascending the **tower** (by steps or lift) rewards with great panoramas across the canals.

Mahnmal St-Nikolai MEMORIAL

(Memorial St Nicholas; www.mahnmal-st-nikolai.de; Willy-Brandt-Strasse 60; adult/child €4/2; 10am-5pm; S Rödingsmarkt) Destroyed in WWII, this memorial now houses an unflinching

Hamburg

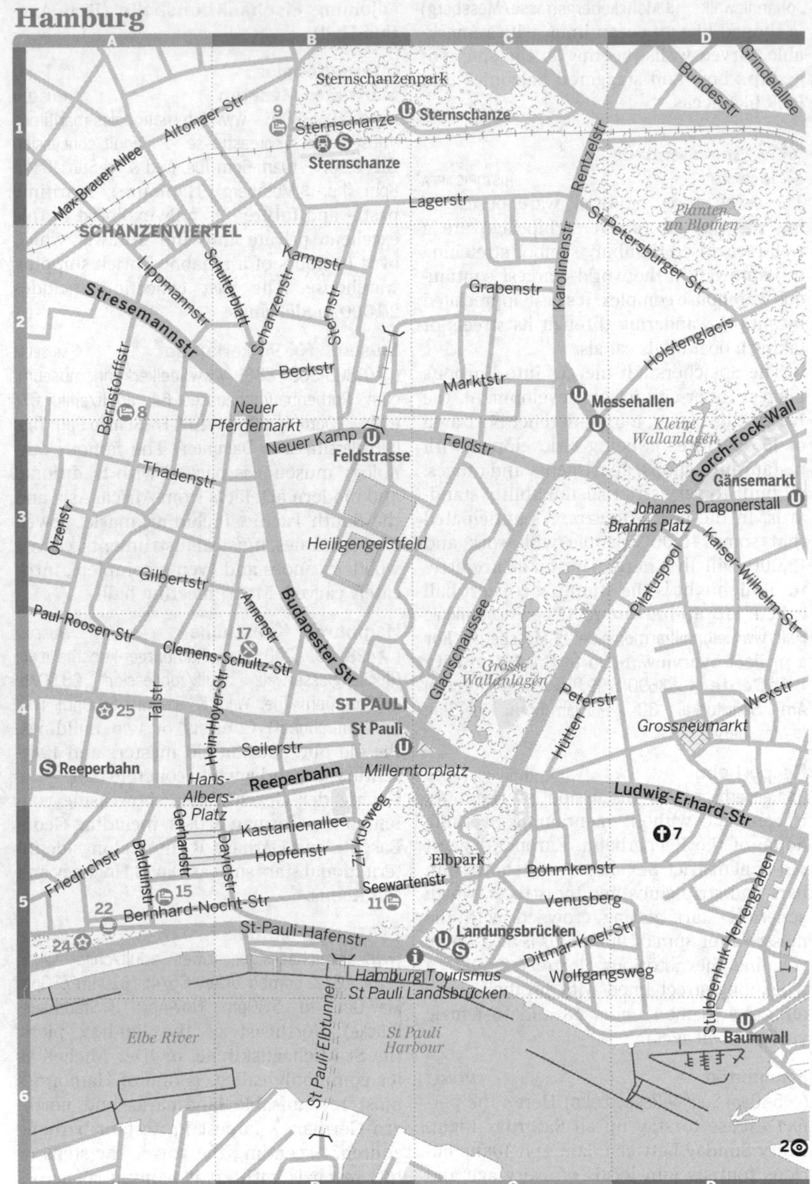

exhibit on the horrors of war focusing on three events in World War II: the German bombing of Coventry in 1940, the German destruction of Warsaw, and Operation Gomorrha, the combined British and American bombing of Hamburg over three days and nights in 1943 that killed 35,000 and incinerated much of the centre. Great views from the 76.3m-high viewing platform inside the surviving spire.

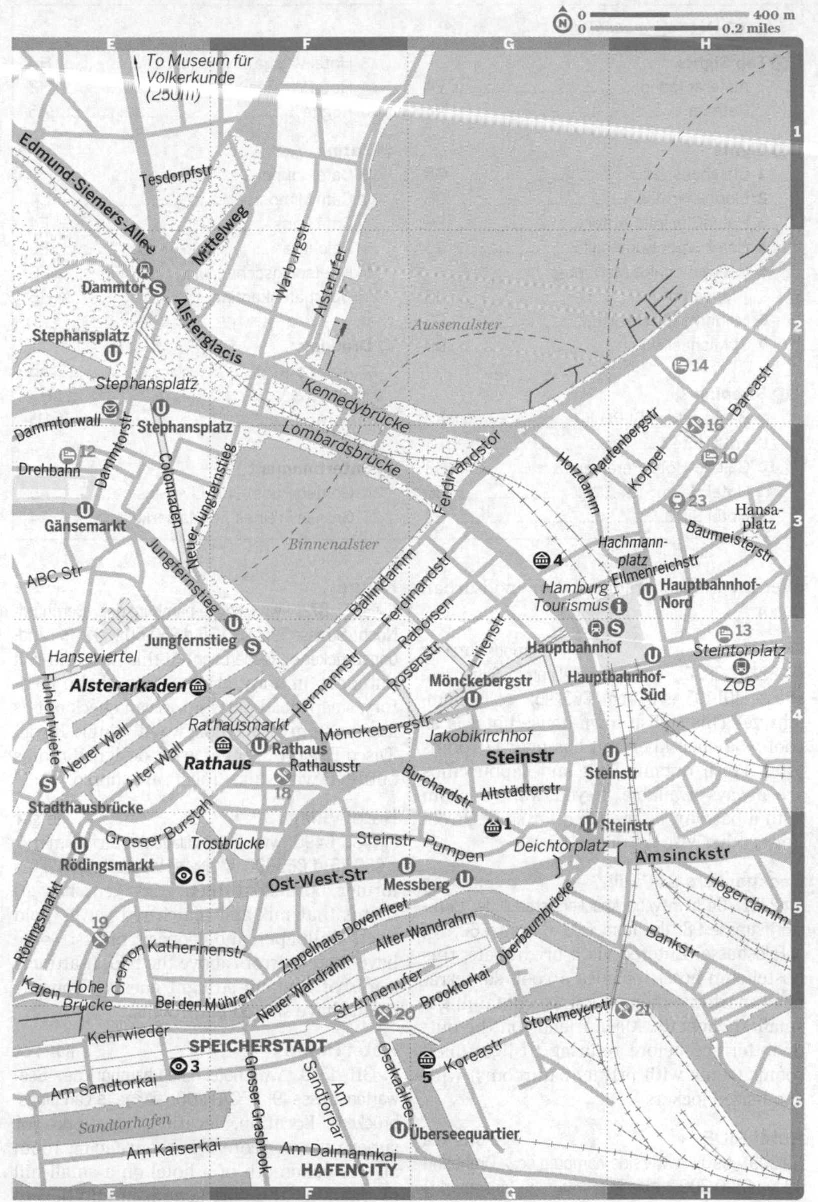

Sleeping

TOP CHOICE Hotel Wedina HOTEL €€
(☎280 8900; www.wedina.de; Gurlittstrasse 23; s €70-195, d €120-225; @; S Hauptbahnhof) You might find a novel instead of a chocolate on your pillow at this literary hotel, which has bedded Margaret Atwood, Jonathan Franzen, and JK Rowling among others. The 59 rooms spread over four colourful buildings

Hamburg

Top Sights
- Alsterarkaden ... E4
- Rathaus ... F4

Sights
- 1 Chilehaus ... G5
- 2 Elbphilharmonie ... D6
- 3 HafenCity InfoCenter ... E6
- 4 Hamburger Kunsthalle ... G3
- 5 Internationales Maritimes Museum ... G6
- 6 Mahnmal St-Nikolai ... E5
- 7 St Michaeliskirche ... D5

Sleeping
- 8 Backpackers St Pauli ... A2
- 9 Fritz Hotel ... B1
- 10 Galerie-Hotel Petersen ... H3
- 11 Hotel Hafen ... B5
- 12 Hotel SIDE ... E3
- 13 Hotel Village ... H4
- 14 Hotel Wedina ... H2
- 15 Kogge ... A5

Eating
- 16 Café Koppel ... H3
- 17 Café Mimosa ... B4
- 18 Café Paris ... F4
- 19 Deichgraf ... E5
- 20 Fleetschlösschen ... F6
- 21 Oberhafenkantine ... H6

Drinking
- 22 Amphore ... A5
- 23 Bar M & V ... H3
- Tower Bar ... (see 11)

Entertainment
- 24 Golden Pudel Club Live Music ... A5
- 25 Grosse Freiheit 36/Kaiserkeller ... A4

offer a choice of traditional or mod-urban decor.

Fritz Hotel BOUTIQUE HOTEL €€
(☎8222 2830; www.fritzhotel.com; Schanzenstrasse 101-103; s/d from €65/95; 🛜; Ⓢ Sternschanze) This stylish town-house hotel is as cool as a cucumber and has only 17 rooms total. Fresh organic fruit and cappuccinos are always available. If you want a room with a balcony, be prepared for some street noise, otherwise get one in back.

Backpackers St Pauli HOSTEL €
(☎2351 7043; www.backpackers-stpauli.de; Bernstorffstrasse 98; dm from €20, d from €60; 🛜; Ⓢ Feldstrasse) Entered via a bright cafe, this hostel-cum-hotel includes a cool, subterranean maritime-themed lounge containing a small kitchenette. Make friends on the outdoor terrace before returing to light-filled rooms (some with private bathrooms) with good-sized lockers.

Hotel SIDE HOTEL €€€
(☎309 990; www.side-hamburg.de; Drehbahn 49; r €120-300; P ❄ @ 🛜; Ⓢ Gänsemarkt) This Matteo Thun–designed stunner is built around a prism-shaped central atrium and has suites featuring vividly coloured free-standing bath-tubs. The 8th-floor chill-out lounge, strewn with 1950s-style saucers-from-outer-space sofas, opens to a panoramic sun deck.

Kogge HOTEL €
(☎312 872; www.kogge-hamburg.de; Bernhard-Nocht-Strasse 59; s €30-35, d €50-60; @🛜; Ⓢ Landungsbrücken or Reeperbahn) At this rock-and-roll pub deep in noisy, grungy Reeperbahn territory, sleepyhead party-goers can check out as late as 2pm from 'Bollywood', 'Punk Royal', 'Disco Dream' or other artist-designed rooms outfitted with sinks. Toilets are shared.

Hotel Village HOTEL €
(☎480 6490; www.hotel-village.de; Steindamm 4; s €50-75, d €65-100; @🛜; Ⓢ Hauptbahnhof) This former bordello turned edgy gem has 20 rooms that mix and match red velvet, gold flock wallpaper and leopard prints; some have huge mirrors above the bed. It attracts a mix of gay and straight guests. Economy rooms have shared bathrooms.

Hotel Hafen HOTEL €€
(☎311 1370; www.hotel-hafen-hamburg.de; Seewartenstrasse 9; r €70-200; @🛜; Ⓢ Landungsbrücken) Location, location, location. For superb views, score a harbour-facing room at this behemoth of a hotel on a small hill overlooking the port action. In addition to the refurbished, historic main building, a former seamen's home, there are newer modern wings.

Galerie-Hotel Petersen PENSION €€
(☎0173-200 0746, 249 826; www.ghsp.eu; Lange Reihe 50; s €60-100, d €70-170; ❄@🛜; Ⓢ Haupt-

bahnhof) This delightful B&B inside a historic 1790 town house is an extension of its welcoming artist-owner's personality. Furnishings include a mix of contemporary, antique and artdeco styles. Our pick of its five rooms is the top-floor studio, with a romantic terrace, kitchenette and separate living area.

Eating

The **Schanzenviertel** swarms with cheap eateries; try Schulterblatt for Portuguese outlets or Susanenstrasse for Asian and Turkish. Many fish restaurants around the Landungsbrücken are overrated and touristy. St Georg's **Lange Reihe** offers many characterful eating spots to suit every budget, and there is a seemingly endless selection of simple but quality, high-value sushi joints all over town.

TOP CHOICE **Oberhafenkantine** GERMAN €€
(www.oberhafenkantine-hamburg.de; Stockmeyerstrasse 39; mains €7-16; Steinstrasse) Serving traditional local fare since 1925, this is where you can order a 'Hamburger' and get the real thing: a patty made with various seasonings and onions. Fresh pollack, haddock and more conjure the days when the surrounding piers echoed to the shouts of seamen and the crash of cargo-laden nets.

Fleetschlösschen INTERNATIONAL €€
(Brooktorkai 17; snacks €7-10; 8am-8pm Mon-Fri, 11am-6pm Sat & Sun; S Messberg) One of the cutest cafes you ever saw, this former customs post overlooks a Speicherstadt canal and has brilliant outdoor seating areas. The owner's knick-knack collection includes centuries-old Dutch pottery unearthed during the construction of HafenCity.

TOP CHOICE **Café Paris** FRENCH €€
(www.cafeparis.net; Rathausstrasse 4; mains €10-20; 9am-11.30pm Mon-Fri, from 10am Sat & Sun; S Rathaus) Within a spectacularly tiled 1882 butchers' hall and adjoining art-deco salon, this elegant yet relaxed brasserie serves classical French cafe fare and a killer breakfast for two.

Deichgraf GERMAN €€€
(364 208; www.deichgraf-hamburg.de; Deichstrasse 23; mains €18-29; lunch Mon-Sat, dinner Sat; S Rödingsmarkt) In a prime setting, with the water on one side and long street-side tables on the other, Deichgraf excels in Hamburg specialties cooked to a high standard. Much of the food is sourced regionally.

Café Koppel VEGETARIAN €
(www.cafe-koppel.de; Lange Reihe 66; mains €5-10; ; S Hauptbahnhof) Set back from busy Lange Reihe, with a garden in summer, this vegie cafe is a refined oasis, where the menu could be an ad for the fertile fields of northern Germany. Salads, soups and much more are all made with fresh, seasonal ingredients.

Café Mimosa CAFE €
(www.cafemimosa.de; Clemens-Schultz-Strasse 87; mains €5-12; S St Pauli) Skip the greasy fast-food joints on the nearby Reeperbahn for this gem of a neighbourhood cafe and indulge in delicious pastas, salads and home-made cakes in a theatrical space or outside at a pavement table.

Drinking & Entertainment

Listings in **Szene** (www.szene-hamburg.de) are helpful for navigating the enormous bar scene. **Clubkombinat** (www.neu.clubkombinat.de) is the go-to source for club listings.

THE HISTORY OF THE HAMBURGER

A classic *Calvin and Hobbes* comic strip once asked if hamburgers were made out of people from Hamburg. And while Hamburg's citizens are, of course, known as Hamburgers, it was the city's role as an international port that gave rise to its most famous namesake.

The origins of the ubiquitous fast food date back to the 12th century. The Tartars (Mongolian and Turkish warriors) wedged pieces of beef between their saddles and the horses' backs, softening the meat as they rode until it was tender enough to be eaten raw. By the 17th century, Hamburg ships brought 'steak tartare' back to Germany, which visiting seafarers then referred to as 'steak in the Hamburg style'. These patties of salted minced beef – usually slightly smoked and mixed with breadcrumbs and onions – were highly durable, making them ideal for long sea voyages.

Hamburg emigrants to America continued making the patties, which they served in bread. As for who in America officially launched the burger remains a fanatical culinary debate.

Bar M & V
BAR

(www.mvbar.de; Lange Reihe 22; Hauptbahnhof) The drinks menu is like a designer catalogue at this grand old St Georg bar that's had a beautiful restoration. Settle into one of the wooden booths, smell the freesias and enjoy.

Amphore
CAFE

(www.cafe-amphore.de; Hafenstrasse 140; Reeperbahn) Beguiling in its trad beauty, non-fussy Amphore has terrace views out to the Elbe and pavement tables for neighbourhood gawking. An excellent St Pauli spot for a drink.

Strandperle
BAR

(www.strandperle-hamburg.de; Schulberg 2; almost year-round; 112) The mother of Hamburg's beach bars, Strandperle should not be missed. All ages and classes gather and mingle, especially at dusk as the sun sets while huge freighters glide past. From Altona station, take bus 112 west to Neumühlen/Övelgönne.

Tower Bar
LOUNGE

(www.hotel-hafen-hamburg.de; Seewartenstrasse 9; 6pm-1am Mon-Thu, 6pm-2.30am Fri-Sun; S Landungsbrücken) For a more elegant, mature evening, repair to this 14th-floor eyrie at the Hotel Hafen for unbeatable harbour views.

TOP CHOICE Hafenklang
CLUB

(www.hafenklang.org; Grosse Elbstrasse 84; Königstrasse) A collective of Hamburg industry insiders presents established and emerging DJs and bands, as well as clubbing events and parties. Look for the spray-painted name on the dark-brick harbour store above a blank metal door.

TOP CHOICE Golden Pudel Club Live Music
LIVE MUSIC

(3197 9930; www.pudel.com; St-Pauli-Fischmarkt 27; from 10pm; St Pauli) In a ramshackle wooden fisherman's hut, this bar-club was established by members of legendary Hamburg band Die Goldenen Zitronen and gets packed to the rafters for its quality electro, hip-hop, R&B and reggae gigs.

Grosse Freiheit 36/Kaiserkeller
LIVE MUSIC

(3177 7811; Grosse Freiheit 36; Reeperbahn) The Beatles once played in the basement Kaiserkeller at this now-mainstream venue mounting pop and rock concerts. It's the best reason today to detour up the Grosse Freiheit.

Information

Tourist Information

Hamburg Tourismus (3005 1200; www.hamburg-tourismus.de)

Hauptbahnhof (Kirchenallee exit; 8am-9pm Mon-Sat, 10am-6pm Sun)

Landungsbrücken (btwn piers 4 & 5; 8am-6pm Apr-Oct, 10am-6pm Nov-Mar; Landungsbrücken)

Airport (Airport Plaza btwn Terminals 1 & 2; 6am-11pm)

Getting There & Away

Air

Hamburg's **airport** (HAM; www.flughafen-hamburg.de) has frequent flights to domestic and European cities. The S1 S-Bahn travels to the city centre in 24 minutes (€2.85).

Bus

The **Zentral Omnibus Busbahnhof** (Busbahnhof, Central Bus Station; 247 576; www.zob-hamburg.de; Adenauerallee 78; ticket counters 5am-10pm Mon-Tue, Thu, Sat & Sun, to midnight Wed & Fri) is southeast of the Hauptbahnhof. **Eurolines** (www.eurolines.com) has buses to such eastern European destinations as Prague (€59) and Warsaw (€50).

Car & Motorcycle

The major A1 and A7 autobahns cross south of the Elbe River.

Train

Reading timetables, remember that Hamburg has four mainline train stations: the Hauptbahnhof, Dammtor, Altona and Harburg. Frequent trains serve Lübeck (€18.50, 40 minutes), Hanover (€40, 1¼ hours) and Bremen (from €20.80, 55 minutes). A direct service to Westerland on Sylt Island leaves every two hours (€44, 3¼ hours). Direct ICE trains depart frequently for Berlin-Hauptbahnhof (€68, 2¼ hours), Cologne (€79, four hours), Munich (€127, six hours), Frankfurt (€106, three hours) and Copenhagen (€78.80, five hours).

Getting Around

HVV (194 49; www.hvv.de) operates buses, ferries, and U-Bahn and S-Bahn trains. The city is divided into zones. **Ring A** covers the city centre, inner suburbs and airport. Single tickets are €2.85, day passes €6.95. Services run around the clock on weekends; between 12.30am and 4am Sunday to Thursday the night bus network takes over, converging on Rathausmarkt.

SCHLESWIG-HOLSTEIN

Sandwiched between the North and Baltic Seas, Schleswig-Holstein is Germany's answer to the Côte d'Azur. Of course, the weather here often makes it a pretty funny sort of answer, as dark clouds and strong winds whip in across the flat peninsula. Still, people flock to the beaches on the coasts, and the countryside in between has a stark beauty.

Lübeck

☎0451 / POP 210,300

Two pointed cylindrical towers of Lübeck's Holstentor (city gate) greet you upon arrival – if you think they're a tad crooked, you're not seeing things: they lean towards each other across the stepped gable that joins them. Right behind them, the streets are lined with medieval merchants' homes and spired churches forming the city's so-called 'crown'. It's hardly surprising that this 12th-century gem is on Unesco's World Heritage list.

Sights & Activities

TOP CHOICE Holstentor LANDMARK

Built in 1464, the impossibly cute city gate serves as Lübeck's museum as well as its symbol. The six gabled brick buildings east of the Holstentor are the Salzspeicher, once used to store the salt from Lüneburg that was pivotal to Lübeck's Hanseatic trade.

Marienkirche CHURCH

(Schüsselbuden 13; admission €1; ⊙10am-6pm Apr-Sep, to 5pm Oct, to 4pm Tue-Sun Nov-Mar) This 13th-century church is most famous for its shattered bells, left where they fell after a WWII bombing raid. Outside there's a little devil sculpture with an amusing folk tale (in German and English).

Petrikirche CHURCH

(☎397 730; www.st-petri-luebeck.de; Schüsselbuden 13; adult/child €3/2; ⊙9am-9pm Apr-Sep, 10am-7pm Oct-Mar) Panoramic city views unfold from the 50m-high viewing platform reached by lift.

Rathaus HISTORIC BUILDING

(☎122 1005; Breite Strasse 64; adult/concession €3/1.50; ⊙tours 11am, noon & 3pm Mon-Fri) Some described as a 'fairy tale in stone', Lübeck's medieval town hall is widely regarded as one of the most beautiful in Germany.

LOCAL KNOWLEDGE

BEHIND THE SCENES

In the Middle Ages, Lübeck was home to numerous craftspeople and artisans. In response to a housing shortage, tiny single-storey homes were built in courtyards – accessible via little walkways – behind existing rows of houses. Almost 90 such *Gänge* (walkways) and *Höfe* (courtyards) still exist, including the **Füchtingshof** (Glockengiesserstrasse 25) with its beautiful carvings and the 1612 **Glandorps Gang** (Glockengiesserstrasse 41-51), which you can peer into.

Quandt-Linie BOAT TOUR

(☎777 99; www.quandt-linie.de; Holstentorterrassen; adult/child from €12/6) The Trave River forms a moat around the Altstadt, and cruising it aboard a boat is a fine way to get a feel for Lübeck. One-hour tours leave every half-hour between 10am and 6pm (May to October) from just south of the Holstenbrücke bridge.

Sleeping

TOP CHOICE Klassik Altstadt Hotel BOUTIQUE HOTEL €€

(☎702 980; www.klassik-altstadt-hotel.de; Fischergrube 52; s €60-100, d €130-160; 📶) Rooms at this elegantly furnished boutique hotel are dedicated to a famous artist or writer such as Thomas Mann and Johann Sebastian Bach. Single rooms (some share baths) feature travelogues by famous authors.

Hotel an der Marienkirche HOTEL €

(☎799 410; www.hotel-an-der-marienkirche.de; Schüsselbuden 4; s €58-78, d €75-95; 📶) This small and bright budget hotel could not be better located; in fact, one of the 18 rooms has a view of the namesake church. The staff is as cheery as the Ikea-like furnishings. The breakfast buffet is especially healthy.

Hotel Lindenhof HOTEL €€

(☎872 100; www.lindenhof-luebeck.de; Lindenstrasse 1a; s €65-95, d €85-135; @📶) The 66 rooms at this family-run hotel in a quiet side street are small, but the breakfast buffet, friendly service and thoughtful touches such as free biscuits and newspapers give the Lindenhof an edge.

Rucksackhotel HOSTEL €
(☎706 892; www.rucksackhotel-luebeck.com; Kanalstrasse 70; dm €15-16, s €28, d €40; P @ ☎) This 30-bed hostel has a relaxed atmosphere, good facilities including a well-equipped kitchen, and colourful decor with the odd tropical touch.

Eating

TOP CHOICE **Schiffergesellschaft** GERMAN €€€
(☎767 76; www.schiffergesellschaft.com; Breite Strasse 2; mains €12-25) Opened in 1535, Lübeck's cutest – if not best – restaurant is stuffed with ships' lanterns, old model ships and orange Chinese-style lamps. As you sit on long benches resembling church pews, staff in long white aprons bring you Frisian specialities. On balmy nights, head up a flight of steps to the hidden garden out back. Book.

Brauberger GERMAN €€
(☎702 0606; Alfstrasse 36; mains €9-14; ⊙5pm-midnight Mon-Thu, 5pm-late Fri & Sat) The brewing kettles are right in the dining room and the humid air is redolent with hops at this traditional German brewer, which has been serving its own golden amber since 1225. Get a stein of the cloudy house brew and enjoy one of many excellent schnitzels or other trad fare.

Krützfeld DELI €
(☎728 32; Hüxstrasse 23; snacks from €2; ⊙8am-6pm Tue-Fri, 8am-2pm Sat) This classic deli has been serving all manner of fresh and smoked seafood for decades. There's no better place in town to assemble a picnic.

Shopping

TOP CHOICE **Niederegger** FOOD
(☎530 1126; www.niederegger.de; Breite Strasse 89; ⊙9am-7pm Mon-Fri, 9am-6pm Sat, 10am-6pm Sun) Niederegger is Lübeck's mecca for marzipan, which has been made locally for centuries. Even if you're not buying, the shop's elaborate seasonal displays are a feast for the eyes. At the back of the shop there's an elegant cafe.

Information

Lübeck Travemünde Tourismus (☎01805 882 233; www.luebeck-tourismus.de; Holstentorplatz 1; ⊙9.30am-7pm Mon-Fri, 10am-3pm Sat & 10am-2pm Sun Jun-Sep, 9.30am-6pm Mon-Fri &10am-3pm Sat Oct-May)

Getting There & Away

Ryanair and Wizzair serve **Lübeck airport** (LBC; www.flughafen-luebeck.de). Buses take passengers straight to Hamburg (€10, 55 minutes), while local bus 6 serves Lübeck's Hauptbahnhof and central bus station (€2.70).

Lübeck has hourly trains to Hamburg (€19, 40 minutes) and Rostock (€24, 2¼ hours, change in Bad Kleinen).

NORTH FRISIAN ISLANDS

With their grass-covered dunes, shifting sands, birds, seal colonies, lighthouses and rugged cliffs, you'd imagine Germany's North Frisian Islands to be the domain of intrepid nature lovers. Instead, these North Sea islands are a favourite of the German elite. On glamorous Sylt in particular, you'll find designer boutiques housed in quintessential reed-thatched cottages, gleaming Porches and Mercedes jamming the car parks, luxurious accommodation and some of the country's most extravagant restaurants. Those with less cash to splash can still enjoy the pure sea air, especially in Sylt's more remote corners. The islands of Amrum and Föhr are more peaceful still.

Sylt

☎04651 / POP 21,100

Sylt can't be labelled without scratching your head. **Westerland**, the largest town, is largely filled with high-rises that obscure views of the beach, although some of the world's best **windsurfing** can be found off its shore.

Further north, pretty **Kampen** teems with ritzy restaurants and celebrity guests who come to see and be seen along the main promenade, Stroenwai, aka Whiskey Alley. Its main natural attraction is the 52.5m-tall, **Uwe Dune**. Climb the wooden steps for stunning 360-degree views.

Historic reed-thatched houses strangled with ivy, lush gardens of colourful blooms, stone walls and the occasional garden gate made from two curving whalebones combine to create the island's prettiest village in **Keitum**.

Sleeping

Tourist offices have details about all accommodation options, including private rooms.

Village BOUTIQUE HOTEL €€€
(☎469 70; www.village-kampen.de; Alte Dorfstrasse 7, Kampen; r from €300; P🛜🏊) This flawless 10-room boutique hotel has service standards worthy of a palace. Discretion is the rule, whether at the indoor pool or out in the lovely gardens. Superb breakfasts.

Single Pension PENSION €
(☎920 70; www.singlepension.de; Trift 26, Westerland; s €38-70, d €55-80; P) Not only for singles, but certainly a social spot for solo travellers young and old, who can strike up a rapport over tea or lounging in the garden. The rooms are humble, but the location central and breakfast is served to 1pm.

DJH Hostel Dikjen Deel HOSTEL €
(☎835 7825; www.jugendherberge.de; Fischerweg 36-40, Westerland; dm under/over 26yr €23/28; ⏰closed mid-late Dec) Set amid the dunes, Westerland's hostel is a 45-minute walk from the Bahnhof. Alternatively, take bus 2 in the direction of Rantum/Hörnum to the Dikjen Deel stop. There are also DJH hostels in remote List-Mövenberg and Hörnum.

Eating

Kupferkanne CAFE €€
(☎410 10; www.kupferkanne-sylt.de; Stapelhooger Wai, Kampen; mains €6-15; ⏰8am-5pm) Enjoy coffee and yummy cake – or a full meal – surrounded by a maze of low bramble hedges in the enchanting gardens or in the knick-knack-filled thatched Frisian house.

TOP CHOICE **Gosch** SEAFOOD €€
(www.gosch.de; Hafenstrasse 16, List; mains €4-15) Coming to Sylt without visiting Gosch would be like coming to Germany without ordering a beer. A Sylt institution, it offers exceptionally fresh fish sandwiches, seafood pasta and smoked fish at its original kiosk in List harbour and at branches across the island.

Sansibar SEAFOOD, STEAK €€€
(☎964 646; www.sansibar.de; Hörnumer Strasse 80, Rantum; mains €14-35; ⏰11am-11pm, shorter hours in winter) Dining among the dunes in this large grass-roof beach pavilion is an unforgettable experience (book *well* ahead). Alternatively, stop by for a drink on its terrace at sunset.

Information

Tourist Information Desk (www.westerland.de; Bahnhofplatz, Westerland; ⏰9am-6pm) Inside the train station. A good first stop.

Getting There & Around

Sylt is connected to the mainland by a causeway used exclusively by trains. IC trains serve Hamburg Hauptbahnhof (€47, 3¼ hours), while regional trains have hourly direct services to Hamburg Altona (€34, 3½ hours).

Vehicles use the **car train** (www.syltshuttle.de; one-way/return €47/86 Fri-Mon, return €73 Tue-Thu) from Niebüll. There's at least one connection per hour in both directions; it doesn't take reservations. With loading and unloading, expect the journey to take about an hour.

WORTH A TRIP

AMRUM & FÖHR

Amrum is the smallest North Frisian Island; you can walk around it in a day. It's also the prettiest, with reed-thatched Frisian houses, a patchwork of dunes, woods, heath and marsh, and glorious Kniepsand – 12km of fine, white sand, sometimes up to 1km wide – that takes up half the island. Crowning the central village of **Wittdün** is northern Germany's tallest lighthouse, which stands 63m tall. The island's largest village is **Nebel**. The **tourist office** (☎04682 940 30; www.amrum.de; ferry landing, Wittdün; ⏰hours vary) can help find accommodation.

The 'green isle' of Föhr is interesting for its Frisian culture. Its main village, **Wyk**, boasts plenty of windmills; there are 16 northern hamlets tucked behind dikes up to 7m tall; and there's the large 12th-century church of **St Johannis** in Nieblum. The **tourist office** (☎04681-300; www.foehr.de; Poststraat 2, Nieblum; ⏰9am-5pm Mon-Fri, 9am-noon Sat, 10am-noon Sun) can help with more details. There is no camping here.

Ferries to Amrum and Föhr are operated by **WDR** (☎800; www.wdr-wyk.de) from Dagebüll Hafen.

UNDERSTAND GERMANY

History

Events on German soil have often dominated the European stage, but the country itself is a relatively recent invention: for most of its history Germany has been a patchwork of semi-independent principalities and city-states, occupied first by the Roman Empire, then the Holy Roman Empire and finally the Austrian Habsburgs. Perhaps because of this, many Germans retain a strong regional identity, despite the momentous events that have occurred since.

The most significant medieval events in Germany were pan-European in nature – Martin Luther brought on the Protestant Reformation with his criticism of the Catholic Church in Wittenberg in 1517, a movement that ultimately sparked the Thirty Years' War (1618–48). Germany became the battlefield of Europe, only regaining stability after the Napoleonic Wars with increasing industrialisation and the rise of the Kingdom of Prussia. In 1866 legendary Prussian 'Iron Chancellor' Otto von Bismarck brought the German states together, largely by force, and a united Germany emerged for the first time in 1871, under Kaiser Wilhelm I.

WWI & the Rise of Hitler

With the advent of the 20th century, Germany's rapid growth soon overtaxed the political talents of Kaiser Wilhelm II and led to mounting tensions with England, Russia and France. When war broke out in 1914, Germany's only ally was a weakened Austria-Hungary. Gruelling trench warfare on two fronts sapped the nation's resources, and by late 1918 Germany sued for peace. The Kaiser abdicated and escaped to the Netherlands. Amid widespread public anger and unrest, a new government – the Weimar Republic – was proclaimed.

The Treaty of Versailles in 1919 chopped huge areas off Germany and imposed heavy reparation payments. These were impossible to meet, and when France and Belgium occupied the Rhineland to ensure continued payments, the subsequent hyperinflation and miserable economic conditions provided fertile ground for political extremists. One party waiting in the wings was the Nationalsozialistische Deutsche Arbeiterpartei (National Socialist German Workers' Party, NSDAP, or Nazi Party), led by a failed Austrian artist and WWI German army veteran corporal named Adolf Hitler.

After the 1929 US stock market crash plunged the world in to economic depression, the Nazis increased their strength in general elections, and in 1933 replaced the Social Democrats as the largest party in the *Reichstag* (parliament). Hitler was appointed chancellor. Within one year, he consolidated absolute power with him as *Führer* and turned Germany into a one-party dictatorship.

WWII & Jewish Persecution

From 1935 Germany began to re-arm and build its way out of the economic depression with strategic public works such as the autobahns (freeways). Hitler reoccupied the Rhineland in 1936, and in 1938 annexed Austria and, following a compromise agreement with Britain and France, parts of Czechoslovakia.

All of this took place against a backdrop of growing racism at home. The Nuremberg Laws of 1935 deprived non-Aryans – mostly Jews and Roma (sometimes called Gypsies) – of their German citizenship and many other rights. On 9 November 1938 the horror escalated into *Kristallnacht* (Night of Broken Glass), in which synagogues and other Jewish institutions and businesses across Germany were desecrated, burned or demolished.

In September 1939, after signing a pact that allowed both Stalin and himself a free hand in the east of Europe, Hitler attacked Poland, which led to war with Britain and France. Germany quickly occupied large parts of Europe, but after 1942 began to suffer increasingly heavy losses. Massive bombing reduced Germany's cities to rubble, and the country lost 10% of its population. Germany surrendered unconditionally in May 1945, soon after Hitler's suicide.

After the war, the full scale of Nazi terror was exposed. 'Concentration camps' had exterminated some six million Jews and one million more Roma, communists, homosexuals and others in what has come to be known as the Holocaust.

The Two Germanies

At conferences in Yalta and Potsdam, the Allies (the Soviet Union, the USA, the UK and France) redrew the borders of Germany and divided it into four occupation zones.

In the Soviet zone of the country, the communist Socialist Unity Party (SED) won the 1946 elections and began a rapid nationalisation of industry. In September 1949 the Federal Republic of Germany (FRG) was created out of the three western zones; in response the German Democratic Republic (GDR) was founded in the Soviet zone the following month, with (East) Berlin as its capital.

As the West's bulwark against communism, the FRG received massive injections of US capital and experienced rapid economic growth (the *Wirtschaftswunder* or 'economic miracle') under the leadership of Konrad Adenauer. The GDR, on the other hand, had to pay massive war reparations to the Soviet Union and rebuild itself from scratch.

The widening economic gulf between the two Germanys prompted 3.6 million mostly young and well-educated East Germans to seek a future in the West, thus putting the GDR on the brink of economic and political collapse. To stop the exodus, the GDR government – with Soviet consent – built a wall around West Berlin in 1961 and fenced off the intra-German border.

The appointment of the more politically flexible Erich Honecker as government leader in 1971, combined with the *Ostpolitik* (East-friendly policy) of FRG chancellor Willy Brandt, eased the political relationship between the two Germanys. In the same year, all four Allies formally accepted the division of Berlin, and signed an accord that guaranteed West Berliners the right to visit East Berlin, whilst the GDR also granted GDR citizens the right to travel to West Germany in cases of family emergency.

Honecker's policies produced higher living standards in the GDR, yet East Germany barely managed to achieve a level of prosperity half that of the FRG. After Mikhail Gorbachev came to power in the Soviet Union in March 1985, the East German communists gradually lost Soviet backing.

Reunification

German reunification caught even the most insightful political observers by surprise. The fall of communism was a gradual development that ended in a big bang – the collapse of the Berlin Wall on 9 November 1989.

Once again, East Germans were leaving their country in droves, this time via Hungary, which had opened its borders with Austria. Some people sought refuge in the West German embassy in Prague. Meanwhile, mass demonstrations in Leipzig spread to other cities, including East Berlin.

As the situation escalated, Erich Honecker relinquished leadership to his security chief, Egon Krenz. Then suddenly on 9 November 1989, a decision to allow direct travel to the West was mistakenly interpreted as the immediate opening of all GDR borders with West Germany. That same night thousands of people streamed into the West past stunned border guards. Millions more followed in the next few days, and the dismantling of the Berlin Wall began soon thereafter.

Plans to reform the GDR were dismissed after East German citizens clearly voted in favour of the pro-reunification Christian Democratic Union (CDU) in the early 1990 elections. Unification was enacted on 3 October 1990. In the midst of national euphoria, the CDU-led coalition, led by Helmut Kohl, soundly defeated the Social Democrat opposition in elections on 2 December that year.

Since Reunification

Under Kohl's leadership East German assets were privatised; state industries were trimmed back, sold or closed; and infrastructure was modernised, all resulting in economic growth of about 10% each year until 1995. The trend slowed dramatically thereafter, however, creating an eastern Germany that consisted of unification winners and losers.

Amid allegations of widespread financial corruption, the Kohl government was replaced with a coalition government of SPD and Alliance 90/The Greens in 1998. This marked the first time an environmentalist party had governed nationally worldwide. The rise of the Greens and, more recently, the left, has changed the political landscape of Germany dramatically, making absolute majorities by the 'big two' all the more difficult to achieve. In 2005 the CDU/CSU and SPD formed a grand coalition and Angela Merkel became the first woman to hold the job of German chancellor. She won a second term in the 2009 election that also confirmed the trend towards a five-party political system in Germany.

Germany Today

Europe's Economic Engine

Germany seems to have weathered the recent financial crisis better than most industrial nations, in large part because it now bears the fruits of decade-old key reforms, especially the liberalisation of its labour laws. The German government launched a slew of proactive measures, such as allowing companies to put workers on shorter shifts without loss of pay and stimulating the economy by providing incentives for Germans to scrap older cars and buy new ones. The beginning of the millennium's second decade has seen the importance of Germany's stable economy grow, as the debt-driven crisis in the Eurozone has spread from Greece to threaten all of southern Europe. Germany is seen to have a key position in propping up the euro, the collapse of which could plunge economies across the globe back into recession. So far, so good.

Environmental Leadership

With a Green Party active in politics since the 1980s, Germany has long played a leading role in environmental and climate protection and is considered a pioneer in the development of renewable energies. In 2011, about 20% of total energy production came from alternative sources. The country has also reduced its greenhouse gas emissions by 24% since 1990, thus exceeding the 21% reduction called for by the 2005 Kyoto Protocol.

In 2011, following the nuclear disaster in Fukushima, Japan, Germany became the first industrial nation to completely opt out of nuclear power, immediately shutting down the eight oldest of its 17 reactors, with rest going off the grid by 2022.

Land of Immigration

Some 15 million people living in Germany have an immigrant background (foreign born or have at least one immigrant parent), accounting for about 18% of the total population. According to the United Nations, only the USA and Russia absorb a greater number of international migrants. The largest group are people of Turkish descent, a legacy of the post-WWII economic boom when 'guest workers' were recruited to shore up the war-depleted workforce. Many stayed. After reunification, the foreign population soared again as repatriates from the former USSR and refugees from war-ravaged Yugoslavia arrived by the millions.

Whether immigration enriches or endangers German culture has been the subject of much recent debate, but the fact is that – thanks to an ageing population and a low birth rate – the country needs newcomers to keep it, and its economy, running.

Arts

Germany's creative population has made major contributions to international culture, particularly during the 18th century when the courts at Weimar and Dresden attracted some of the greatest minds of Europe. With such rich traditions to fall back on, inspiration has seldom been in short supply for the new generations of German artists, despite the upheavals of the country's recent history.

Fine Arts

German art hit its first heyday in the Renaissance, which came late to Germany but flourished quickly. The heavyweight of the period is Albrecht Dürer, (1471–1528), who was the first to seriously compete with the Italian masters. Dürer influenced court painter Lucas Cranach the Elder (1472–1553) who worked in Wittenberg for more than 45 years.

Two centuries later, the baroque period brought great sculpture, including works by Andreas Schlüter in Berlin. Neoclassicism in the 19th century, meanwhile, ushered back interest in the human figure and an emphasis on Roman and Greek mythology. This segued into Romanticism, which drew heavily on dreamy idealism nicely captured in the paintings of Caspar David Friedrich and Otto Runge.

In 1905 Ernst Ludwig Kirchner, along with Erich Heckel and Karl Schmidt-Rottluff, founded the artist group *Die Brücke* (The Bridge) in Dresden that turned the art world on its head with ground-breaking visions that paved the way for German expressionism. By the 1920s art had become more radical and political, with artists such as George Grosz, Otto Dix and Max Ernst exploring the new concepts of Dada and surrealism. Käthe Kollwitz is one of the era's few major female artists, known for her social-realist drawings.

After 1945 abstract art became a mainstay of the West German scene, with key figures such as Joseph Beuys, Monica Bonvicini and Anselm Kiefer enjoying worldwide reputations. After reunification, the New Leipzig School achieved success at home and abroad with figurative painters such as Neo Rauch generating much acclaim.

Architecture

The scope of German architecture is such that it could easily be the focus of an entire visit. The first great wave of buildings in Germany came with the Romanesque period (800–1200), outstanding examples of which include the cathedrals at Worms, Speyer and Mainz. Gothic architecture brought such traits as ribbed vaults, pointed arches and flying buttresses nicely exemplified by Cologne's cathedral, Freiburg's Münster and Lübeck's Marienkirche.

For classic baroque, Balthasar Neumann's Residenz in Würzburg and the many classic buildings in Dresden are must-sees. The neoclassical period of the 19th century was dominated by Karl Friedrich Schinkel, who was especially prolific in Berlin and northern Germany.

No modern movement has had greater influence on design than Bauhaus, founded in 1919 by Walter Gropius. You can still visit the seminal school and private homes of Gropius and his fellow professors in Dresden-Rosslau. For an overview, drop by the Bauhaus Archive in Berlin. The Nazis shut down the Bauhaus in 1932 and reverted to the pompous and monumental. Berlin's Olympic Stadium and the Reichsparteitagsgelände (party rally grounds) in Nuremberg are among the few surviving buildings from that dark period.

Frankfurt shows Germany's take on the modern high-rise. For the boldest new architecture head to Berlin where such international starchitects as Daniel Libeskind, David Chipperfield and Lord Norman Foster have put their stamp on the city's post-reunification look.

Music

Forget brass bands and oompah music – few countries can claim the impressive musical heritage of Germany, which generated the greatness of Johann Sebastian Bach, Georg Friedrich Händel, Ludwig van Beethoven, Richard Strauss, Robert Schumann, Johannes Brahms and Richard Wagner, to name a few.

Germany has also made significant contributions to the contemporary-music scene. Internationally renowned artists include punk icon Nina Hagen, '80s balloon girl Nena, and rock bands from the Scorpions to Die Toten Hosen to Rammstein. Kraftwerk pioneered the original electronic sounds, which morphed into techno and became the seminal club music since the 1990s, especially in Berlin and Frankfurt. Today, Germany has the largest electronic-music scene in the world, and DJs such as Ellen Allien, Paul Kalkbrenner, Paul van Dyk and Sven Väth have become household names on the global party circuit.

Food & Drink

German Cuisine

Germany might not have the culinary kudos of its neighbours, but its robust, fresh flavours have made it a rising star in Europe's kitchen. Of course, if you crave traditional comfort food, you'll certainly find plenty of places to indulge in pork, potatoes and cabbage. These days, though, 'typical German' fare is lighter, healthier, creative and more likely to come from organic eateries, a UN worth of ethnic restaurants and gourmet kitchens. In fact, in 2012 Germany's Michelin skies twinkled brighter than ever before, with 208 one-star, 32 two-star and nine three-star restaurants.

When it comes to bread, Germany is a world-beater with over 300 tasty and textured varieties, often mixing wheat and

VEGETARIANS

Germany was slow in embracing vegetarianism – let alone veganism – but of late health-conscious cafes and restaurants serving meatless fare have been sprouting faster than alfalfa, at least in the cities. Even rural restaurants will have at least a couple of vegetarian dishes on the menu. Otherwise, Asian and Indian eateries are the usual good bet for vegie-based dishes. For a comprehensive list of vegan and vegetarian restaurants in Germany, see www.happycow.net/europe/germany.

DINING TIPS

Restaurants are often formal places with full menus, crisp white linen and high prices. Many are open all day as are cafes, which serve coffee and alcohol alongside light inexpensive meals. In cities, some eateries serve good-value 'business lunches' including a starter, main course and drink for under €10.

Handy speed-feed shops, called *Imbiss*, serve all sorts of savoury fodder, from sausage-in-a-bun to doner and pizza. Many bakeries serve sandwiches alongside pastries.

Rather than leaving money on the table, tip when you pay by stating a rounded-up figure or saying '*es stimmt so*' (that's the right amount). A tip of 10% is generally about right.

rye flour. *Brezeln* are traditional pretzels covered in rock salt. Seasonal specialities include *Bärlauch* (wild garlic), which starts showing up in salads and as pesto in early spring; white asparagus in May and June; fresh berries and cherries in summer and handpicked mushrooms such as *Steinpilze* (porcini) and loamy *Pfifferlinge* (chanterelles) in autumn.

Pastries and cakes such as the famous *Schwarzwälder Kirschtorte* (Black Forest cake) are often enjoyed during the traditional afternoon *Kaffee und Kuchen* (coffee and cake) break.

Beer

Beer, Germany's national beverage, is both excellent and inexpensive. Its 'secret' dates back to the *Reinheitsgebot* (purity law) – passed in 1516 – demanding breweries to use only malt, yeast, hops and water. Although no longer a legal requirement, most German brewers still conform to it. Here's a rundown of the most common beer types:

Pils (Pilsner) Full beer with pronounced hop flavour and a creamy head.

Weizenbier/Weissbier Fruity and a bit spicy, lovely on a hot day. *Hefeweizen* has a stronger shot of yeast, whereas *Kristallweizen* is clearer with more fizz.

Bockbier Strong, dark beer brewed seasonally (eg *Maibock* in May and *Weihnachtsbock* at Christmas).

Helles Bier Has strong malt aromas and is slightly sweet.

Dunkles Bier Dark and full-bodied.

Wine

The reputation of German wine was long sullied by the cloyingly sweet taste of Liebfraumilch and the naff image of Blue Nun. Now, thanks to rebranding campaigns, a new generation of wine growers and an overall rise in quality, German wine is winning critics' praise and international awards left and right.

There are 13 wine-growing regions, the Rhine and the Moselle being the internationally best known. Typical white wine varieties include riesling, Müller-Thurgau (aka Rivaner), Silvaner, Grauburgunder (Pinot gris) and Weissburgunder (Pinot blanc). Among the reds, Spätburgunder (Pinot noir), is the best of the bunch.

For a comprehensive rundown, visit www.winesofgermany.co.uk, www.germanwines.de or www.germanwineusa.org.

SURVIVAL GUIDE

Directory A–Z

Accommodation

Germany has all types of places to unpack your suitcase, from hostels, camping grounds and family hotels to chains, business hotels and luxury resorts.

» Reservations are a good idea, especially if you're travelling in the busy summer season (June to September). Local tourist offices will often go out of their way to find something in your price range.

» Camping grounds abound. Fees consist of charges per person (between €3 and €10), tent (€6 to €16, depending on size) and car (€3 to €8), plus additional fees for hot showers, resort tax, electricity and sewage disposal.

» **Deutsches Jugendherbergswerk** (DJH; www.jugendherberge.de) coordinates the official Hostelling International (HI) hostels in Germany. Rates in gender-segregated dorms, or in family rooms, range from €13 to €30 per person, including linen and breakfast. People over 27 are charged an extra €3 or €4. Indie hostels are more relaxed and can be found in most large cities.

PRICE RANGES

Unless noted in reviews, price ranges in this chapter refer to a double room with private bathroom and breakfast in high season.

€€€ more than €150

€€ €80 to €150

€ less than €80

Business Hours

We've listed business hours where they differ from the following standards. Where hours vary across the year, we've provided those applicable in high season.

Banks 9am to 4pm Monday to Friday, extended hours usually on Tuesday or Thursday

Bars 6pm to 1am

Cafes 8am to 8pm

Clubs 10pm to 4am

Post offices 9am to 6pm Monday to Friday, some Saturday mornings

Restaurants 11am to 10pm (varies widely, food service often stops at 9pm in rural areas)

Major stores & supermarkets 9.30am to 8pm Monday to Saturday (shorter hours in suburbs and rural areas, possible lunchtime break)

Customs Regulations

Duty-free shopping is only available if you're leaving the EU. Duty-free allowances (for anyone over 17) arriving from non-EU countries:

» 200 cigarettes or 100 cigarillos or 50 cigars or 250g of loose tobacco

» 1L of strong liquor or 2L of less than 22% alcohol by volume plus 4L of wine plus 16L of beer

» other goods up to the value of €300 if arriving by land or €430 if arriving by sea or air (€175 for under 15yr)

Discount Cards

Tourist offices in many cities sell 'Welcome Cards' entitling visitors to free or reduced admission on museums, sights and tours, plus unlimited local public transportation for the period of their validity (usually 24 or 48 hours). They can be good value if you want to fit a lot in.

Embassies & Consulates

All foreign embassies are in Berlin, but many countries have consular offices in such cities as Frankfurt, Munich, Hamburg and Düsseldorf.

Australia (☎030-880 0880; www.australian-embassy.de; Wallstrasse 76-79; ⓈMärkisches Museum)

Canada (☎030-203 120; www.kanada-info.de; Leipziger Platz 17; ⓈPotsdamer Platz, ⓇPotsdamer Platz)

New Zealand (☎030-206 210; www.nzembassy.com; Friedrichstrasse 60; ⓈStadtmitte)

UK (☎030-204 570; www.britischebotschaft.de; Wilhelmstrasse 70; ⓈBrandenburger Tor, ⓇBrandenburger Tor)

USA (☎030-830 50; www.germany.usembassy.gov; Clayallee 170; ⓈOskar-Helene-Heim)

Food

Price categories used in reviews in this chapter refer to the the cost of a main course.

€€€ more than €15

€€ €8 to €15

€ less than €8

Gay & Lesbian Travellers

» Germany is a magnet for *schwule* (gay) and *lesbische* (lesbian) travellers, with the rainbow flag flying especially proudly in Berlin and Cologne, with sizeable communities in Hamburg, Frankfurt and Munich.

» Generally speaking, attitudes towards homosexuality tend to be more conservative in the countryside, among older people and in the eastern states.

Legal Matters

» By law you must carry some form of photographic identification, such as your passport, national identity card or driving licence.

» The permissible blood alcohol limit is 0.05%; drivers caught exceeding this amount are subject to stiff fines, a confiscated licence and even jail time. Drinking in public is legal, but be discreet about it.

» There is no universal nationwide smoking law, with regulations left to each of the 16 German states. It's best to ask first before lighting up.

TIPPING

Restaurant bills always include a service charge *(Bedienung)* but most people add 5% or 10% unless the service was truly abhorrent.

Bartenders 5%

Hotel porters €1 to €1.50 per bag

Room cleaners €1 per night per person

Taxi drivers around 10%

Money

» Cash is king in Germany, so always carry some with you and plan to pay in cash almost everywhere.

» The easiest and quickest way to obtain cash is by using your debit (bank) card at an ATM (*Geldautomat*) linked to international networks such as Cirrus, Plus, Star and Maestro.

» Credit cards are becoming more widely accepted, but it's best not to assume that you'll be able to use one – enquire first.

» Change currency in foreign-exchange offices (*Wechselstuben*) at airports and train stations, particularly those of the Reisebank.

Public Holidays

Germany observes eight religious and three secular holidays nationwide. Shops, banks, government offices and post offices are closed on these days. States with predominantly Catholic populations, such as Bavaria and Baden-Württemberg, also celebrate Epiphany (6 January), Corpus Christi (10 days after Pentecost), Assumption Day (15 August) and All Saints' Day (1 November). Reformation Day (31 October) is only observed in eastern Germany.

The following are *gesetzliche Feiertage* (public holidays):

Neujahrstag (New Year's Day) 1 January

Ostern (Easter) Good Friday, Easter Sunday and Easter Monday

Christi Himmelfahrt (Ascension Day) Forty days after Easter

Maifeiertag/Tag der Arbeit (Labour Day) 1 May

Pfingsten (Whit/Pentecost Sunday & Monday) Fifty days after Easter.

Tag der Deutschen Einheit (Day of German Unity) 3 October

Weihnachtstag (Christmas Day) 25 December

Zweiter Weihnachtstag (Boxing Day) 26 December

Telephone

German phone numbers consist of an area code followed by the local number, which can be between three and nine digits long.

Country code ☎49

International access code ☎00

Directory inquiries ☎11837 for an English-speaking operator (charged at €1.99 per minute)

Travellers with Disabilities

Germany is fair at best (but better than much of Europe) for the needs of travellers with disabilities, with access ramps for wheelchairs and/or lifts in some public buildings. Resources include:

Deutsche Bahn Mobility Service Centre (☎ext 9 for English 0180-599 6633512; www.bahn.com; ⏲24hr) Train access information and route-planning assistance. The website has useful information in English (search for 'barrier-free travel').

German National Tourism Office (www.germany.travel) Your first port of call, with inspirational information in English.

Natko (www.natko.de) Central clearing house for inquiries about barrier-free travel in Germany.

Visas

» EU nationals only need their passport or national identity card to enter, stay and work in Germany, even for stays over six months.

» Citizens of Australia, Canada, Israel, Japan, New Zealand, Poland, Switzerland and the US need only a valid passport but no visa if entering Germany as tourists for up to three months within a six-month period. Passports must be valid for another three months beyond the intended departure date.

» Nationals from other countries need a Schengen Visa.

Getting There & Away

Most travellers arrive in Germany by air, or by rail and road connections from neighbouring countries. Flights, tours and rail tickets can be booked online at lonelyplanet.com/bookings.

Entering Germany

If you're arriving from any of the 24 other Schengen countries, such as the Netherlands, Poland, Austria or the Czech Republic, you no longer have to show your passport or go through customs in Germany, no matter which nationality you are.

Air

Budget carriers, **Lufthansa** (www.lufthansa.com) and international airlines serve numerous German airports from across Europe and the rest of the world. Frankfurt and Munich are the hubs, but there are also sizeable airports in Berlin, Hamburg, Cologne/Bonn and Stuttgart, and smaller ones in Bremen, Dresden, Hanover, Leipzig, Münster-Osnabrück and Nuremberg.

Lufthansa, Germany's national flagship carrier and Star Alliance member, operates a vast network of domestic and international flights and has one of the world's best safety records. Practically every other national carrier from around the world serves Germany, along with budget carriers **Air Berlin** (www.airberlin.com), **easyJet** (☎0900-1100 161; www.easyjet.com), **Flybe** (www.flybe.com), **airBaltic** (www.airbaltic.com), **Ryanair** (☎0900-116 0500; www.ryanair.com) and **germanwings** (www.germanwings.com).

Note that Ryanair usually flies to remote airports, which are often little more than recycled military airstrips. Frankfurt-Hahn, for instance, is actually near the Moselle River, about 125km west of Frankfurt proper.

Land

BUS

Travelling by bus between Germany and the rest of Europe is cheaper than by train or plane, but journeys will take a lot longer.

Eurolines (www.eurolines.com) is a consortium of national bus companies operating routes throughout the continent. The German affiliate is **Deutsche Touring** (www.touring.de). Sample one-way fares and travel times:

ROUTE	PRICE	DURATION (HR)
Budapest–Frankfurt	€96	14½–18
Florence–Munich	€78	8½
London–Cologne	€69	12
Paris–Munich	€61	13
Krakow–Berlin	€41	10

Children between the ages of four and 12 pay half price, while teens, students and seniors get 10% off regular fares. Tickets can be purchased online and at most train stations throughout Germany.

Backpacker-geared hop-on, hop-off **Busabout** (www.busabout.com) runs coaches along three interlocking European loops between May and October. Passes are sold online and through travel agents. Germany is part of the North Loop with buses stopping in Berlin, Dresden, Munich and Stuttgart.

CAR & MOTORCYCLE

When bringing your own vehicle to Germany, you need a valid driving licence, your car registration certificate and proof of insurance. Foreign cars must display a nationality sticker unless they have official European plates. You also need to carry a warning (hazard) triangle and a first-aid kit.

To decrease air pollution caused by fine particles, many German cities have introduced low-emissions Green Zones that may only be entered by cars displaying an *Umweltplakette* (emissions sticker). Check with your local automobile association or order a sticker online www.tuev-sued.de or www.tuev-nord.de (English instructions provided). The cost is €6.

TRAIN

A favourite way to get to Germany from elsewhere in Europe is by train. In Germany ticketing is handled by **Deutsche Bahn** (www.bahn.com). Long-distance trains connecting major German cities with those in other countries are called EuroCity (EC) trains. Seat reservations are essential during the peak summer season and around major holidays.

Germany is also linked by overnight train to many European cities; routes include Amsterdam to Munich, Zurich to Berlin and Paris to Hamburg.

SEA

Germany's main ferry ports are Kiel, Lübeck and Travemünde in Schleswig-Holstein, and Rostock and Sassnitz (on Rügen Island) in

Mecklenburg-Western Pomerania. All have services to Scandinavia and the Baltic states.

There are no longer any direct ferry services between Germany and the UK, but you can go via the Netherlands, Belgium or France and drive or train it from there. For fare details and to book tickets, check the ferry websites or go to www.ferrybooker.com or www.ferrysavers.com.

Getting Around

Germans are whizzes at moving people around, and the public-transport network is among the best in Europe. The best ways of getting around the country are by car and by train. Regional bus services fill the gaps in areas not well served by the rail network.

Air

There are lots of domestic flights, many with budget carriers such as **Air Berlin** (www.airberlin.com) and **germanwings** (www.germanwings.com), as well as **Lufthansa** (www.lufthansa.com). Unless you're flying from one end of the country to the other, say Berlin to Munich or Hamburg to Munich, planes are only marginally quicker than trains once you factor in the check-in and transit times.

Bicycle

» Cycling is allowed on all roads and highways but not on the autobahns (motorways). Cyclists must follow the same rules of the road as cars and motorcycles. Helmets are not compulsory (not even for children), but wearing one is common sense.

» Bicycles may be taken on most trains but require a separate ticket (*Fahrradkarte*). These cost €9 per trip on long-distance trains (IC and EC and City Night Line), or €10 per trip for international travel. You need to reserve a space at least one day ahead and leave your bike in the bike compartment usually at the beginning or end of the train. Bicycles are not allowed on high-speed ICE trains. The fee on local and regional trains (IRE, RB, RE, S-Bahn) is €5 per day.

» There is no charge at all on some local trains, which are listed in Deutsche Bahn's *Bahn & Bike* brochure (in German). The brochures also notes the almost 250 stations where you can rent bikes. It's available for download at www.bahn.de/bahnundbike.

» Otherwise, most towns and cities have private bicycle-hire stations, often at or near the train station. Hire costs range from €7 to €20 per day and from €35 to €85 per week, depending on the model of bicycle. A minimum deposit of €30 (more for fancier bikes) and/or ID are required.

» Hotels, especially in resort areas, sometimes keep a stable of bicycles for their guests, often at no charge.

Boat

With two seas and a lake- and river-filled interior, don't be surprised to find yourself in a boat at some point.

» Regular ferries serve the East Frisian Islands in Lower Saxony; the North Frisian Islands in Schleswig-Holstein; and the islands of Poel, Rügen and Hiddensee in Mecklenburg-Western Pomerania.

» Scheduled boat services also operate along sections of the Rhine, the Elbe and the Danube, and on major lakes such as the Chiemsee and Lake Starnberg in Bavaria and Lake Constance in Baden-Württemberg.

Bus

» In some rural areas buses may be your only option for getting around without your own vehicle. This is especially true of the Harz Mountains, sections of the Bavarian Forest and the Alpine foothills.

» The frequency of services varies from 'rarely' to 'constantly'. Commuter-geared routes offer limited or no service in the evenings and at weekends, so keep this in mind or risk finding yourself stuck in a remote place on a Saturday night.

» In cities, buses generally converge at the *Busbahnhof* or *Zentraler Omnibus Bahnhof* (ZOB; central bus station), which is often near the Hauptbahnhof (central train station).

» For long-distance travel between German cities, the main operators are **Deutsche Touring** (www.touring.de) and **Berlin Linien Bus** (www.berlinlinienbus.de). Discounts are available for children, students, seniors and groups.

Car & Motorcycle

» Germany's pride and joy is its 11,000km network of autobahns (motorways, freeways). Every 40km to 60km, you'll find elaborate service areas with petrol stations, toilet facilities and restaurants; many are open 24 hours. In between are rest stops (*Rastplatz*), which usually have picnic tables and toilet facilities. Orange emergency call boxes are spaced about 2km apart.

» Autobahns are supplemented by an extensive network of Bundesstrassen (secondary 'B' roads, highways) and smaller Landstrassen (country roads, 'L'). No tolls are charged on any public roads.

» If your car is not equipped with a navigational system, having a good map or road atlas is essential, especially in rural areas. Navigating is not done by the points of the compass. That is to say that you'll find no signs saying 'north' or 'west'. Rather, you'll see signs pointing you in the direction of a city, so you'd best have that map right in your lap to stay oriented. Maps are sold at every petrol station.

» Cars are impractical in urban areas. Leaving your car in a central *Parkhaus* (car park) can cost €20 per day or more.

AUTOMOBILE ASSOCIATIONS

ADAC (Allgemeiner Deutscher Automobil-Club; ☎0180-222 2222; www.adac.de) offers roadside assistance to members of its affiliates, including British AA, American AAA and Canadian CAA.

DRIVING LICENCES

Visitors do not need an international driving licence to drive in Germany; bring your licence from home.

HIRE

» To hire your own wheels, you'll need to be at least 25 years old and possess a valid driving licence and a major credit card. Some companies lease to drivers between the ages of 21 and 24 for an additional charge (about €12 to €20 per day). Younger people or those without a credit card are usually out of luck.

» For insurance reasons, driving into an eastern European country, such as the Czech Republic or Poland, is usually a no-no.

» All the main international companies maintain branches at airports, major train stations and towns.

» Rental cars with automatic transmission are rare in Germany and will usually need to be ordered well in advance.

INSURANCE

You must have third-party insurance to enter Germany with a vehicle.

ROAD RULES

Road rules are easy to understand, and standard international signs are in use. You drive on the right, and cars are left-hand drive. Right of way is usually signed, with major roads given priority, but at unmarked intersections traffic coming from the right always has right of way.

The blood-alcohol limit for drivers is 0.05%. Obey the road rules carefully: the German police are very efficient and issue heavy on-the-spot fines. Germany also has one of the highest concentrations of speed cameras in Europe.

Speed limits:

Towns & cities On bigger roads 50km/h, on residential streets 30km/h (or as posted).

Open road/country 100km/h

Autobahn Unlimited but many exceptions as posted.

Public Transport

» Public transport is excellent within big cities and small towns and may include buses, trams (Strassenbahn), S-Bahn (light rail) and U-Bahn (underground/subway trains).

» Tickets cover all forms of transit, and fares are determined by zones or time travelled, sometimes both. Multiticket strips and day passes are generally available, offering better value than single-ride tickets.

» Tickets must usually be bought from vending machines at the stations or stops. Only buses and some trams let you buy tickets from the driver.

» Normally, tickets must be stamped upon boarding in order to be valid. Inspections are random but fines (usually €40) are levied if you're caught without a valid ticket.

Train

» Operated almost entirely by **Deutsche Bahn** (www.bahn.com), the German train system is the finest in Europe and is generally the best way to get around the country.

» Several private operators provide train services on regional routes, such as the Ostdeutsche Eisenbahn in Saxony and the Bayerische Oberlandbahn in Bavaria.

» It's rarely worth buying a 1st-class ticket on German trains; 2nd class is usually quite comfortable. There's more difference between the train classifications – basically the faster a train travels, the plusher (and pricier) it is.

» Most train stations have coin-operated lockers costing from €1 to €4 per 24-hour period. Larger stations have staffed left-luggage offices (*Gepäckaufbewahrung*).

A PRIMER ON TRAIN TYPES

Here's the low-down on the alphabet soup of trains operated by Deutsche Bahn (DB):

InterCity Express (ICE) Long-distance, high-speed trains that stop at major cities only and run at one- or two-hour intervals.

InterCity (IC), EuroCity (EC) Long-distance trains that are fast but slower than the ICE; also run at one- and two-hour intervals and stop in major cities. EC trains run to major cities in neighbouring countries.

InterRegio-Express (IRE) Regional train connecting cities with few intermediary stops.

City Night Line (CNL) Night trains with sleeper cars and couchettes.

Regional Bahn (RB) Local trains, mostly in rural areas, with frequent stops; the slowest in the system.

Regional Express (RE) Local trains with limited stops that link rural areas with metropolitan centres and the S-Bahn.

S-Bahn Local trains operating within a city and its suburban area.

» Seat reservations (€4) for long-distance travel are highly recommended, especially on Friday or Sunday afternoons, during holiday periods or in summer. Reservations can be made online and at ticket counters up to 10 minutes before departure.

TICKETS

» Tickets may be bought online at www.bahn.de, using a credit card, at no surcharge. However, you will need to present a printout of your ticket, as well as the credit card used to buy it, to the conductor.

» Many train stations have a *Reisezentrum* (travel centre), where staff sell tickets (for a small fee) and can help you plan an itinerary (ask for an English-speaking agent).

» Smaller stations may only have a few ticket windows and the smallest ones aren't staffed at all. In this case, you must buy tickets from multilingual vending machines. These are also plentiful at staffed stations and convenient if you don't want to queue at a ticket counter. Both agents and machines accept major credit cards.

» Only conductors on long-distance trains sell tickets on board, at a surcharge; major credit cards are usually accepted. Not having a ticket carries a stiff penalty.

SPECIAL DEALS

Deutsche Bahn offers several permanent rail deals:

» **Schönes-Wochenende-Ticket** (Nice Weekend Ticket; €40 for up to five people travelling together) Valid for one day of unlimited 2nd-class travel on regional trains (IRE, RE, RB, S-Bahn), plus on local public transport. Available from midnight Saturday or Sunday until 3am the next day.

» **Quer-durchs-Land-Ticket** (Around Germany Ticket; €42 for the first person and €6 each for up to four additional persons) A weekday variation of the Schönes-Wochenende-Ticket.

» **Länder-Tickets** (Regional Tickets) One day of unlimited travel on regional trains and public transport within one of the German states (or, in some cases, also in bordering states). Tickets are generally valid for travel Monday to Friday from 9am to 3am the following day and on weekends from midnight until 3am the following day. Some passes are priced at a flat rate for up to five people travelling together (eg the Brandenburg-Berlin-Ticket costs €28); other have staggered pricing: the first person buys the main ticket and up to four people may join for a just few euros more per ticket (eg in Bavaria, the first person pays €22, additional tickets cost €4).

» On any of these schemes, children under 15 travel for free if accompanied by their parents or grandparents. See the website for details or check with a *Reisezentrum* if already in Germany.

» Tickets can be purchased online, from vending machines or, for a €2 surcharge, from station ticket offices.

GERMAN RAIL PASS

If your permanent residence is outside Europe, including Turkey and Russia, you qualify for the German Rail Pass. Tickets are sold through www.bahn.com, www.raileurope.com, or through agents in your home country.

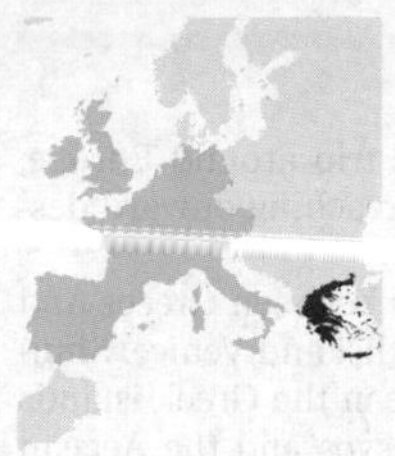

Greece Ελλάδα

Includes »

Best Places to Eat

» Marco Polo Café (p628)

» Alaloum (p592)

» Café Avyssinia (p581)

» Spondi (p583)

» Taverna Lava (p616)

Best Places to Stay

» 1700 (p603)

» Amfitriti Pension (p591)

» Francesco's (p614)

» Pension Sofi (p612)

» Hotel Afendoulis (p630)

Why Go?

Don't let headline-grabbing financial woes put you off going to Greece. The alluring combination of history and hedonism, which has made Greece one of the most popular destinations on the planet, continues to beckon, and now is as good a time as ever to turn up for some fun in the sun. Within easy reach of magnificent archaeological sites are breathtaking beaches and relaxed tavernas serving everything from ouzo to octopus. Wanderers can island-hop to their heart's content, while party types can enjoy pulsating nightlife in Greece's vibrant modern cities and on islands such as Mykonos, Ios and Santorini. Add welcoming locals with an enticing culture to the mix and it's easy to see why most visitors head home vowing to come back. Travellers to Greece inevitably end up with a favourite site they long to return to – get out there and find yours.

When to Go

Athens

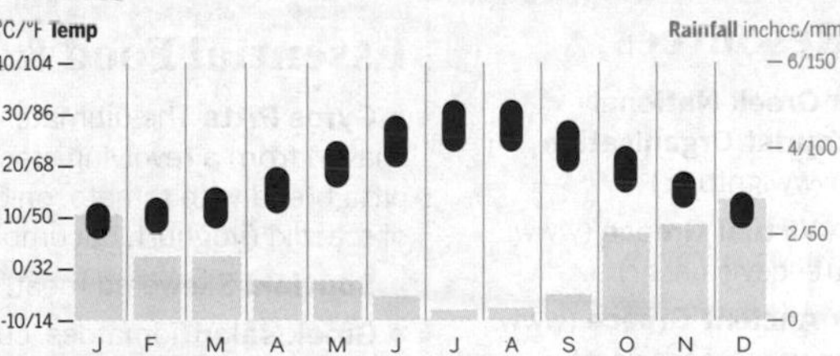

May & Jun Greece opens the shutters in time for Orthodox Easter; the best months to visit.

Jul & Aug Be prepared to battle summer crowds, high prices and soaring temperatures.

Sep & Oct The season winds down; a relaxing and pleasant time to head to Greece.

AT A GLANCE

- » **Currency** euro (€)
- » **Language** Greek
- » **Money** ATMs all over; banks open Mon-Fri
- » **Visas** Schengen rules apply

Fast Facts

- » **Area** 131,944 sq km
- » **Capital** Athens
- » **Country code** ☎30
- » **Emergency** ☎112

Exchange Rates

Australia	A$1	€0.82
Canada	C$1	€0.77
Japan	¥100	€0.83
New Zealand	NZ$1	€0.65
UK	UK£1	€1.18
USA	US$1	€0.78

Set Your Budget

- » **Budget hotel room** €50
- » **Two-course meal** €20
- » **Museum entrance** €5
- » **Beer** €2.50
- » **Athens metro ticket** €1.40

Resources

- » **Greek National Tourist Organisation** (www.gnto.gr)
- » **Virtual Greece** (www.greecevirtual.gr)
- » **Ancient Greece** (www.ancientgreece.com)
- » **Greek Ferries** (www.openseas.gr)

Connections

For those visiting Greece as part of a trip around Europe, there are various exciting options for reaching onward destinations overland or by sea.

There are regular ferry connections between Greece and the Italian ports of Ancona, Bari, Brindisi and Venice. Similarly, there are ferries operating between the Greek islands of Rhodes, Kos, Samos, Chios and Lesvos and the Aegean coast of Turkey. Island-hopping doesn't have to take you back to Athens.

Overland, it's possible to reach Albania, Bulgaria, the Former Yugoslav Republic of Macedonia (FYROM) and Turkey from Greece. If you've got your own wheels, you can drive through border crossings with these four countries. There are train and bus connections with Greece's neighbours, but check ahead, as these have been affected by the financial crisis. At the time of writing, no international train services from Greece were running.

ITINERARIES

One Week

Explore Athens' museums and ancient sites on day one before spending a couple of days in the Peloponnese visiting Nafplio, Mycenae and Olympia; ferry to the Cyclades and enjoy Mykonos and spectacular Santorini.

One Month

Give yourself some more time in Athens and the Peloponnese, then visit the Ionian Islands for a few days. Explore the villages of Zagorohoria before travelling back to Athens via Meteora and Delphi. Take a ferry from Piraeus south to Mykonos, then island-hop via Santorini to Crete. After exploring Crete, take the ferry east to Rhodes, then north to Symi, Kos and Samos. Carry on north to Chios, then head to Lesvos. Take the ferry back to Piraeus when you're out of time or money.

Essential Food & Drink

- » **Gyros Pitta** The ultimate in cheap eats. Pork or chicken shaved from a revolving stack of sizzling meat is wrapped in pitta bread with tomato, onion, fried potatoes and lashings of tzatziki (yoghurt, cucumber and garlic). Costs €2 to €3.
- » **Souvlaki** Skewered meat, usually pork.
- » **Greek salad** Tomatoes, cucumber, onion, feta and olives.
- » **Grilled octopus** All the better with a glass of ouzo.
- » **Ouzo** Sipped slowly, this legendary aniseed-flavoured tipple turns a cloudy white when ice and water are added.
- » **Raki** Cretan fire water produced from grape skins.
- » **Greek coffee** A legacy of Ottoman rule, Greek coffee should be tried at least once.

ATHENS ΑΘΗΝΑ

POP 3.8 MILLION

Ancient and modern, with equal measures of grunge and grace, bustling Athens is a heady mix of history and edginess. Iconic monuments mingle with first-rate museums, lively cafes and alfresco dining, and it's downright fun. With Greece's financial difficulties Athens has revealed its more restive aspect, but take the time to look beneath the surface and you'll discover a complex metropolis full of vibrant subcultures.

Greece Highlights

1 **Island-hop** (p656) at your own pace under the Aegean sun

2 In **Athens** (p571), trace the ancient to the modern from the Acropolis to booming nightclubs

3 Lose yourself within the medieval walls of **Rhodes Old Town** (p627)

4 Search for the oracle amidst the dazzling ruins of **Delphi** (p596)

5 Stare dumbfounded at the dramatic volcanic caldera of incomparable **Santorini** (p614)

6 Sip **ouzo** (p650) while munching on grilled octopus

7 Climb russet rock pinnacles to the exquisite monasteries of **Meteora** (p597)

8 Hike through Crete's stupendous **Samaria Gorge** (p622)

9 Let your cares float away from the pristine west-coast beaches of **Lefkada** (p642)

10 Use quaint **Nafplio** (p591) as a base for exploring the back roads and ruins of the Peloponnese

Central Athens

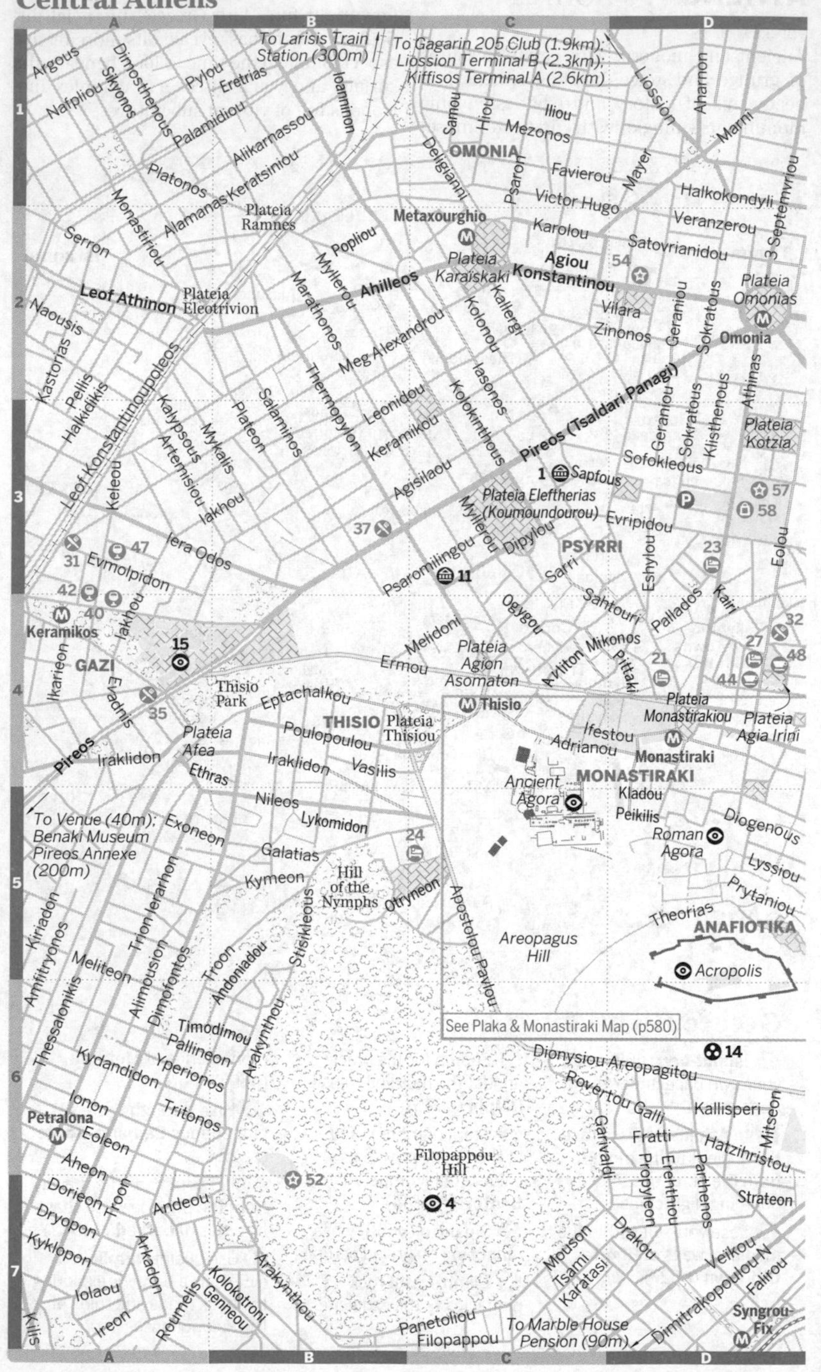

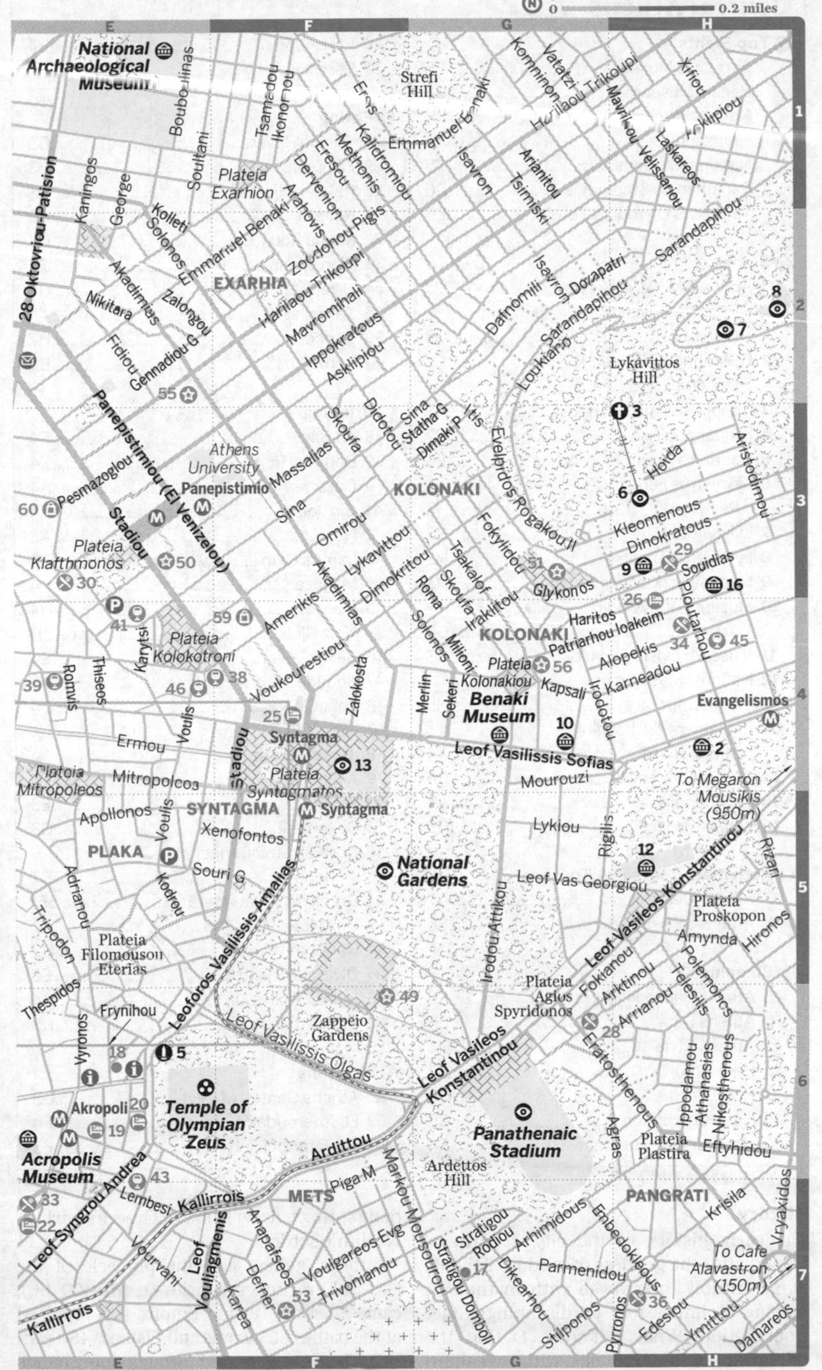

0 400 m
0 0.2 miles
National Archaeological Museum
Strefi Hill
Plateia Exarhion
EXARHIA
Lykavittos Hill
Athens University
Panepistimio
KOLONAKI
Plateia Klafthmonos
Plateia Kolokotroni
Plateia Kolonakiou
Benaki Museum
Leof Vasilissis Sofias
Evangelismos
Syntagma
Plateia Syntagmatos
To Megaron Mousikis (950m)
Plateia Mitropoleos
SYNTAGMA
PLAKA
National Gardens
Leof Vas Georgiou
Leof Vasileos Konstantinou
Plateia Proskopon
Plateia Filomousou Eterias
Leoforos Vasilissis Amalias
Plateia Agios Spyridonos
Zappeio Gardens
Leof Vasilissis Olgas
Temple of Olympian Zeus
Akropoli
Acropolis Museum
Panathenaic Stadium
Ardettos Hill
Plateia Plastira
METS
PANGRATI
Leof Syngrou Andrea
Leof Vouliagmenis
Kallirrois
To Cafe Alavastron (150m)
28 Oktovriou-Patision
Panepistimiou (El Venizelou)
Stadiou
Akadimias
Ermou
Mitropoleos
Apollonos
Xenofontos
Irodou Attikou
Ploutarhou
Patriarhou Ioakeim
Karneadou
Marko Mousourou
Arditou

Central Athens

Top Sights
Acropolis Museum ... E6
Benaki Museum ... G4
National Archaeological Museum ... E1
National Gardens ... F5
Panathenaic Stadium ... G6
Temple of Olympian Zeus ... E6

Sights
1 Andreas Melas & Helena Papadopoulos Gallery ... C3
2 Byzantine & Christian Museum ... H4
3 Chapel of Agios Giorgios ... H3
4 Filopappou Hill ... C7
5 Hadrian's Arch ... E6
6 Lykavittos Funicular Railway ... H3
7 Lykavittos Hill ... H2
8 Lykavittos Theatre ... H2
9 Medusa Art Gallery ... H3
10 Museum of Cycladic Art ... G4
11 Museum of Islamic Art ... C3
12 National Museum of Contemporary Art ... H5
13 Parliament & Changing of the Guard ... F4
14 Stoa of Eumenes ... D6
15 Technopolis ... A4
16 Xippas Gallery ... H3

Activities, Courses & Tours
17 Athens Centre ... G7
18 Athens Segway Tours ... E6

Sleeping
19 Athens Backpackers ... E6
20 Athens Gate ... E6
21 Athens Style ... D4
22 Hera Hotel ... E7
23 Hotel Cecil ... D3
24 Hotel Erechthion ... C5
25 Hotel Grande Bretagne ... F4
26 Periscope ... H4
27 Tempi Hotel ... D4

Eating
28 Cucina Povera ... G6
29 Filippou ... H3
30 Kalnterimi ... E3
31 Kanella ... A3
32 Mama Roux ... D4
33 Mani Mani ... E7
34 Oikeio ... H4
35 Sardelles ... A4
36 Spondi ... H7
37 Varoulko ... B3

Drinking
38 42 Bar ... F4
39 Baba Au Rum ... E4
40 Gazarte ... A4
41 Gin Joint ... E4
42 Hoxton ... A3
43 Lamda Club ... E6
44 Magaze ... D4
45 Mai Tai ... H4
Noiz Club ... (see 31)
46 Seven Jokers ... E4
47 Sodade ... A3
48 Tailor Made ... D4

Entertainment
49 Aigli Cinema ... F6
50 Astor ... E3
51 Dexameni ... G3
52 Dora Stratou Dance Theatre ... B7
Greek National Opera ... (see 55)
53 Half Note Jazz Club ... F7
54 National Theatre ... D2
55 Olympia Theatre ... E2
56 Rock'n'Roll ... G4
57 Stoa Athanaton ... D3

Shopping
58 Athens Central Market ... D3
59 Eleftheroudakis ... F4
60 To Pantopoleion ... E3

History

The early history of the city of Athens, named after the goddess of wisdom Athena, is inextricably interwoven with mythology, making it impossible to disentangle fact from fiction. What is known is that the hilltop site of the Acropolis, with two abundant springs, drew some of Greece's earliest Neolithic settlers.

Athens' golden age, the pinnacle of the classical era under Pericles (r 461–429 BC), came after the Persian Empire was repulsed at the battles of Salamis and Plataea (480–479 BC). The city has passed through many hands and cast off myriad invaders, from Sparta to Philip II of Macedon, the Roman and Byzantine Empires, and, most recently, the Ottoman Empire. In 1834 Athens superseded Nafplio as the capital of independent Greece.

Sights

TOP CHOICE Acropolis HISTORIC SITE
(Map p580; ☎210 321 0219; http://odysseus.culture.gr; adult/child €12/6; ⊙8am-8pm Mon-Fri, to 3pm Sat & Sun; MAkropoli) Arguably the most important ancient monument in the Western world, the Acropolis attracts multitudes of visitors, so head there in the early morning or late afternoon.

The site was inhabited in Neolithic times and the first temples were built during the Mycenaean era in homage to the goddess Athena. People lived on the Acropolis until the late 6th century BC, but in 510 BC the Delphic oracle declared that the Acropolis should be the province of the gods. When all of the buildings were reduced to ashes by the Persians on the eve of the Battle of Salamis (480 BC), Pericles set about rebuilding a city purely of temples.

Enter near the **Beule Gate**, a Roman arch added in the 3rd century AD. Beyond this lies the **Propylaea**, the enormous columned gate that was the city's entrance in ancient times. Damaged in the 17th century when lightning set off a Turkish gunpowder cache, it's since been restored. South of the Propylaea, the small, beautiful **Temple of Athena Nike** has been recently restored.

It's the **Parthenon**, however, that epitomises the glory of ancient Greece. Completed in 438 BC, it's unsurpassed in grace and harmony. To achieve the appearance of perfect form, columns become narrower towards the top and the bases curve upward slightly towards the ends – effects that make them look straight. The remains of its metopes, pediments and frieze can be seen at the Acropolis Museum.

The Parthenon was built to house the great statue of Athena commissioned by Pericles, and to serve as the new treasury. In AD 426 the gold-plated 12m-high statue was taken to Constantinople, where it disappeared.

To the north, lies the **Erechtheion** and its much-photographed caryatids, the six maidens who support its southern portico. These are plaster casts – the originals are in the Acropolis Museum (and one is in London).

ATHENS IN TWO DAYS

Walk the deserted morning streets of the charming Plaka district to reach the **Acropolis** and **Ancient Agora**, beating the crowds. Dig in to *mezedhes* at **Tzitzikas & Mermingas** before spending the afternoon at the **Acropolis Museum** and the **National Archaeological Museum**. Enjoy Parthenon views over dinner at **Café Avyssinia** or sup on gyros at **Thanasis**.

On day two, watch the changing of the guard at **Plateia Syntagmatos** (Syntagma Sq) before crossing the **National Gardens** to the **Panathenaic Stadium** and the **Temple of Olympian Zeus**. Visit the wonderful **Benaki Museum**, **Byzantine & Christian Museum** or the **Museum of Cycladic Art**, then rest up for a night out in **Gazi**.

On the southern slope of the Acropolis, the importance of theatre in the everyday lives of ancient Athenians is made manifest in the enormous **Theatre of Dionysos** (☎210 322 4625; Dionysiou Areopagitou; admission €2, free with Acropolis Pass; ⊙8am-8pm Mon-Fri, 8am-3pm Sat & Sun; underground rail Akropoli). Built between 340 and 330 BC on the site of an earlier theatre dating to the 6th century BC, it held 17,000 people. The **Stoa of Eumenes** (Map p572), built as a shelter and promenade for theatre audiences, runs west to the **Odeon of Herodes Atticus** (☎210 324 1807; www.hellenicfestival.gr; Dionysiou Areopagitou; underground rail Akropoli), built in Roman times (and open only for performances).

Acropolis Museum MUSEUM
(Map p572; ☎210 900 0901; www.theacropolismuseum.gr; Dionysiou Areopagitou 15, Makrygianni; admission €5; ⊙8am-8pm Tue-Sun, to 10pm Fri; MAkropoli) Don't miss this superb museum on the southern base of the hill, and magnificently reflecting the Parthenon on its glass facade; it houses the surviving treasures of the Acropolis.

Bathed in natural light, the 1st-floor **Archaic Gallery** is a forest of statues, including stunning examples of 6th-century *kore* (maidens). Finds from temples pre-dating the Parthenon include sculptures such as Heracles slaying the Lernaian Hydra, and a lioness devouring a bull.

UNCERTAIN TIMES

» Due to the financial difficulties in Greece, which became acute starting in 2010, opening hours, prices and even the existence of some establishments have fluctuated much more than usual.

» At the time of writing the government was running many archaeological sites on their shorter winter hours (closing around 3pm). This could change.

» If in doubt, call ahead.

The museum's crowning glory is the top-floor **Parthenon Gallery**, a glass hall built in alignment with the Parthenon, which is visible through the windows. It showcases the temple's metopes and 160m frieze shown in sequence for the first time in over 200 years. Interspersed between the golden-hued originals, white plaster replicates the controversial Parthenon Marbles removed by Lord Elgin in 1801 and later sold to the British Museum.

Other highlights include five **caryatids**, the maiden columns that held up the Erechtheion (the sixth is in the British Museum), a giant floral acroterion and a movie illustrating the history of the Acropolis.

The surprisingly good-value restaurant has superb views; there's also a fine museum shop.

Ancient Agora HISTORIC SITE

(Map p580; ☎210 321 0185; http://odysseus.culture.gr; Adrianou; adult/child €4/2, free with Acropolis pass; ⏰8am-3pm, museum closed 8-11am Mon; Ⓜ Monastiraki) The Ancient Agora was the marketplace of early Athens and the focal point of civic and social life; Socrates spent time here expounding his philosophy. The main monuments of the Agora are the well-preserved **Temple of Hephaestus** (Monastiraki), the 11th-century **Church of the Holy Apostles** (Monastiraki) and the reconstructed **Stoa of Attalos**, which houses the site's excellent **museum**.

Roman Agora HISTORIC SITE

(Map p580; ☎210 324 5220; cnr Pelopida & Eolou, Monastiraki; adult/child €2/1, free with Acropolis pass; ⏰8.30am-3pm; Ⓜ Monastiraki) The Romans built their agora just east of the ancient Athenian Agora. The wonderful **Tower of the Winds** was built in the 1st century BC by Syrian astronomer Andronicus. Each side represents a point of the compass and has a relief carving depicting the associated wind.

TOP CHOICE National Archaeological Museum MUSEUM

(Map p572; ☎210 821 7717; www.namuseum.gr; 28 Oktovriou-Patision 44, Exarhia; adult/child €7/free; ⏰1-8pm Mon, 8am-3pm Tue-Sun; Ⓜ Viktoria, 🚎2, 4, 5, 9 or 11 Polytechnio stop) One of the world's great museums, the National Archaeological Museum contains significant finds from major archaeological sites throughout Greece. The vast collections of Greek art masterpieces include exquisite **Mycenaean gold artefacts**, **Minoan frescos** from Santorini and stunning, enormous statues.

Temple of Olympian Zeus RUIN

(Map p572; ☎210 922 6330; adult/child €2/free, free with Acropolis pass; ⏰8am-3pm; Ⓜ Syntagma, Akropoli) Begun in the 6th century BC, Greece's largest temple is impressive for the sheer size of its Corinthian columns: 17m high with a base diameter of 1.7m. It took more than 700 years to build, with Emperor Hadrian overseeing its completion in AD 131, and sits behind **Hadrian's Arch** (Map p572; cnr Leoforos Vasilissis Olgas & Leoforos Vasilissis Amalias; Ⓜ Syntagma).

Panathenaic Stadium HISTORIC SITE

(Map p572; Leoforos Vasileos Konstantinou, Pangrati; adult/child €3/1.50; ⏰8am-7pm; Ⓜ Akropoli) The Panathenaic Stadium, built in the 4th century BC as a venue for the Panathenaic athletic contests, was restored (including seats of Pentelic marble for 70,000 spectators) and hosted the first modern Olympic Games in 1896, as well as some events of the 2004 Olympics.

Benaki Museum MUSEUM

(Map p572; ☎210 367 1000; www.benaki.gr; Koumbari 1, cnr Leoforos Vasilissis Sofias, Kolonaki; adult/child €7/free, free Thu; ⏰9am-5pm Wed, Fri & Sat, to midnight Thu, to 3pm Sun; Ⓜ Syntagma, Evangelismos) This superb museum houses an extravagant collection, including ancient sculpture, Persian, Byzantine and Coptic objects, Chinese ceramics, icons, El Greco paintings and fabulous traditional costumes. The museum's annexes around the city: **Museum of Islamic Art** (Map p572; ☎210 325 1311; Agion Asomaton 22 & Dipylou 12, Keramikos; adult/child €7/free; ⏰9am-5pm Thu-Sun; Ⓜ Thisio) and **Benaki Museum**

Pireos Annexe (☎210 345 3111; www.benaki.gr; Pireos 138, cnr Andronikou, Rouf; admission €5; ⊙10am-6pm Wed, Thu & Sun, to 10pm Fri & Sat, closed Aug; MKeramikos).

Museum of Cycladic Art MUSEUM
(Map p572; ☎210 722 8321; www.cycladic.gr; Neofytou Douka 4, cnr Leoforos Vasilissis Sofias, Kolonaki; adult/child €7/free; ⊙10am-5pm Mon, Wed, Fri & Sat, 10am-8pm Thu, 11am-5pm Sun; MEvangelismos) This wonderful private museum was custom-built to display its extraordinary collection of Cycladic art, with an emphasis on the early Bronze Age. It's easy to see how the graceful marble statues, some dating from 3000 BC to 2000 BC, influenced the art of Modigliani and Picasso.

TOP CHOICE **Byzantine & Christian Museum** MUSEUM
(Map p572; ☎210 721 1027; www.byzantinemuseum.gr; Leoforos Vasilissis Sofias 22, Kolonaki; adult/child €4/free; ⊙9am-4pm Tue-Sun; MEvangelismos) This outstanding museum presents a priceless collection of Christian art, dating from the 3rd to 20th centuries, exceptionally presented in expansive multilevel galleries in a restored villa. Artefacts include icons, frescoes, sculptures, textiles, manuscripts, vestments and mosaics.

FREE **Parliament & Changing of the Guard** CEREMONY
(Map p572; Plateia Syntagmatos; MSyntagma) In front of the parliament building on Plateia Syntagmatos, the traditionally costumed *evzones* (guards) of the **Tomb of the Unknown Soldier** change every hour on the hour. On Sunday at 11am, a whole platoon marches down Vasilissis Sofias to the tomb, accompanied by a band.

FREE **Filopappou Hill** LANDMARK, PARK
(Map p572; MAkropoli) Also called the Hill of the Muses, Filopappou is identifiable southwest of the Acropolis by the **Monument of Filopappos** at its summit. Built between AD 114 and 116, it honours Julius Antiochus Filopappos, a prominent Roman consul. The hill's pine-clad slopes offer superb views, with some of the best vantage points for photographing the Acropolis. Small paths weave all over the hill, but the paved path to the top starts near the *periptero* (kiosk) on Dionysiou Areopagitou. After 250m, the path passes the **Church of Agios Dimitrios Loumbardiaris**, which contains fine frescoes.

> **CHEAPER BY THE HALF-DOZEN**
>
> The €12 ticket at the Acropolis (valid for four days) includes entry to the other significant ancient sites: Ancient Agora, Roman Agora, Keramikos, Temple of Olympian Zeus and the Theatre of Dionysos.
>
> Enter the sites free on the first Sunday of the month (except for July, August and September) and on certain holidays. Anyone aged under 19 years or with an EU student card gets in free.

FREE **Lykavittos Hill** LANDMARK
(Map p572; MEvangelismos) Pine-covered Lykavittos is the highest of the eight hills dotting Athens. Climb to the summit for stunning views of the city, the Attic basin and the islands of Salamis and Aegina (pollution permitting). Little **Chapel of Agios Giorgios** is floodlit at night and open-air **Lykavittos Theatre** hosts concerts in summer.

The main path up starts at the top of Loukianou, or take the **funicular railway** from the top of Ploutarhou.

FREE **National Gardens** GARDENS
(Map p572; entrance on Leoforos Vasilissis Sofias & Leoforos Vasilissis Amalias, Syntagma; ⊙7am-dusk; MSyntagma) A delightful, shady refuge during summer, these gardens contain a large playground, a duck pond and a tranquil cafe.

Tours

The usual city tours exist like open bus **CitySightseeing Athens** (Map p580; ☎210 922 0604; www.city-sightseeing.com; Plateia Syntagmatos, Syntagma; adult/child €15/6.50; ⊙every 30min 9am-8pm; MSyntagma), **Athens Segway Tours** (Map p572; ☎210 322 2500; www.athenssegwaytours.com; Eschinou 9, Plaka; 2hr tour €59; MAkropoli) or the volunteer **This is My Athens** (www.thisisathens.org). Get out of town on the cheap with **Athens: Adventures** (☎210 922 4044; www.athensadventures.gr). Hike or kayak with **Trekking Hellas** (☎210 331 0323; www.trekking.gr; Saripolou 10, Exarhia; MViktoria).

CONTEMPORARY ART

Athens is not all about ancient art. For a taste of the contemporary, visit:

Taf (The Art Foundation; Map p580; www.theartfoundation.gr; Normanou 5, Monastiraki; ⏲1pm-midnight; Ⓜ Monastiraki) Eclectic art and music gallery.

Onassis Cultural Centre (www.sgt.gr; Leoforos Syngrou 109, Neos Kosmos; Ⓜ Syngrou-Fix) Multimillion-euro visual and performing arts centre.

National Museum of Contemporary Art (Map p572; www.emst.gr; Leoforos Vas Georgiou B 17-19, enter from Rigilis; adult/child €3/free; ⏲11am-7pm Tue, Wed & Fri-Sun, to 10pm Thu; Ⓜ Evangelismos) Will be moving to the old Fix brewery on Leoforos Syngrou.

Xippas Gallery (Map p572; Patriarhou Ioakeim 53, Kolonaki; ⏲Tue-Sat; Ⓜ Evangelismos)

Medusa Art Gallery (Map p572; www.medusaartgallery.com; Xenokratous 7, Kolonaki; Ⓜ Evangelismos)

Andreas Melas & Helena Papadopoulos Gallery (Map p572; http://melaspapadopoulos.com; Epikourou 26, cnr Korinis, Psyrri; ⏲noon-6pm Tue-Fri, noon-4pm Sat; Ⓜ Omonia)

Technopolis (Map p572; ☎210 346 7322; Pireos 100, Gazi; Ⓜ Keramikos) Former gasworks turned cultural centre.

Festivals include:

Art-Athina (www.art-athina.gr) International art in May.

Athens Biennial (www.athensbiennial.org) Every two years from June to October.

ReMap (www.remap.org) Parallel event to the Biennial, exhibiting in abandoned buildings.

Festivals

Hellenic Festival PERFORMING ARTS
(www.greekfestival.gr; ⏲late May-Oct) Top line-up of local and international music, dance and theatre in venues across Athens and Epidavros' ancient theatre.

Sleeping

Discounts apply in low season, for longer stays and online. Book well ahead for July and August.

Plaka

Central Hotel BOUTIQUE HOTEL €€
(Map p580; ☎210 323 4357; www.centralhotel.gr; Apollonos 21, Plaka; s/d incl breakfast from €80/100; ❄@; Ⓜ Syntagma) Pass through the sleek lobby and by the attentive staff to spacious white rooms hung with original art and decked out with all the mod cons. Some balconies have Acropolis views, as does the rooftop, where you can sunbake and relax in the Jacuzzi.

New BOUTIQUE HOTEL €€€
(Map p580; ☎210 628 4565; www.yeshotels.gr; Filellinon 16, Plaka; s/d incl breakfast from €170/185; P❄📶; Ⓜ Syntagma) Smart New is the latest entry on the high-end Athens scene. Whether you dig the groovy, designer furniture or the pillow menu (tell 'em how you like it!), you'll find some sort of decadent treat to tickle your fancy.

Hotel Adonis HOTEL €
(Map p580; ☎210 324 9737; www.hotel-adonis.gr; 3 Kodrou St, Plaka; s/d/tr incl breakfast €45/55/75; ❄@📶; Ⓜ Syntagma) Comfortable rooms, newly renovated bathrooms, conscientious staff and Acropolis views from the breakfast room/bar keep folks coming back.

Niki Hotel HOTEL €€
(Map p580; ☎210 322 0913; www.nikihotel.gr; Nikis 27, Syntagma; s/d/tr incl breakfast from €55/65/118; ❄@📶; Ⓜ Syntagma) This small hotel bordering Plaka with contemporary furnishings has well-appointed rooms and a two-level suite for families (€145), with Acropolis-view balconies.

Plaka Hotel HOTEL €€
(Map p580; ☎210 322 2096; www.plakahotel.gr; Kapnikareas 7, cnr Mitropoleos, Plaka; s/d/tr incl breakfast from €90/110/125; ❄📶; Ⓜ Monastiraki) Folks come here not for the tidy, bland rooms but for the excellent Acropolis views from the rooftop garden and top-floor digs.

Hotel Acropolis House PENSION €€
(Map p580; ☎210 322 2344; www.acropolishouse.gr; Kodrou 6-8, Plaka; s €65, d €65-82, tr from €113, q from €136, all incl breakfast; ❄📶; Ⓜ Syntagma) This well situated hotel in a 19th-century house feels more pension than hotel, with a comfy sitting room and hospitable management. Guests chat amicably over breakfast.

Student & Travellers' Inn HOSTEL €
(Map p580; ☎210 324 4808; www.studenttravellersinn.com; Kydathineon 16, Plaka; dm €20-22, s/d/tr €45/55/65, without bathroom €30/50/60; ❄@📶; Ⓜ Syntagma) The mixed-sex dorms may be spartan and houseekeeping a bit lean, but extras (laundry, left luggage) make up for it.

Monastiraki

TOP CHOICE **Magna Grecia** BOUTIQUE HOTEL €€
(Map p580; ☎210 324 0314; www.magnagreciahotel.com; Mitropoleos 54, Monastiraki; d incl breakfast €95-135; ❄📶; Ⓜ Monastiraki) Enjoy Acropolis views from the front rooms and rooftop terrace in a historic building opposite the cathedral. Imaginatve, luxe rooms sport comfortable mattresses.

Hotel Cecil HOTEL €€
(Map p572; ☎210 321 7079; www.cecil.gr; Athinas 39, Monastiraki; s/d/tr incl breakfast from €55/70/85; ❄@📶; Ⓜ Monastiraki) Aromatic spices waft into the lobby from nearby Asian markets, but double-pane windows keep the high-ceilinged rooms in this classical building quiet.

Tempi Hotel HOTEL €
(Map p572; ☎210 321 3175; www.tempihotel.gr; Eolou 29, Monastiraki; d/tr €57/67, s/d without bathroom €35/47; ❄📶; Ⓜ Monastiraki) No-frills rooms may be tiny, but some have balconies overlooking Plateia Agia Irini. A communal kitchen and nearby markets make it ideal for self-caterers.

Syntagma

Hotel Grande Bretagne LUXURY HOTEL €€€
(Map p572; ☎210 333 0000; www.grandebretagne.gr; Vasileos Georgiou 1, Syntagma; r/ste from €275/960; P❄@📶; Ⓜ Syntagma) Dripping with elegance and old-world charm, *the* place to stay in Athens has always has been these deluxe digs. Built in 1862 to accommodate visiting heads of state, it ranks among the great hotels of the world. From the decadent, chandeliered lobby, to the exquisite guestrooms, divine spa and rooftop restaurant, this place is built for pampering.

Makrygianni & Koukaki

TOP CHOICE **Athens Backpackers** HOSTEL, APARTMENT €
(Map p572; ☎210 922 4044; www.backpackers.gr; Makri 12, Makrygianni; dm incl breakfast €23-28, 2-/4-/6-person apt €90/120/150; ❄@📶; Ⓜ Akropoli) This excellent, popular hostel also has great apartments and boasts a rooftop party bar with Acropolis views, kitchen, daily movies, and the friendly Aussie management hosts (free!) barbecues. Breakfast and nonalcoholic drinks are included; long-term storage, laundry and airport pick-up available.

TOP CHOICE **Athens Gate** BUSINESS HOTEL €€
(Map p572; ☎210 923 8302; www.athensgate.gr; Leoforos Syngrou Andrea 10, Makrygianni; s/d incl breakfast from €120/130; ❄@📶; Ⓜ Akropoli) With stunning views over the Temple of Olympian Zeus from the spacious front rooms, and a central (if busy) location, this totally refurbished hotel is a great find. Stylish, immaculate rooms have all the mod cons, staff are friendly and breakfast is served on the superb rooftop terrace with 360-degree Athens views.

Hera Hotel BOUTIQUE HOTEL €€
(Map p572; ☎210 923 6682; www.herahotel.gr; Falirou 9, Makrygianni; s/d from €75/90, ste from €180; ❄@📶; Ⓜ Akropoli) The ornate interior complements the hotel's lovely neoclassical facade. The rooftop garden, restaurant and bar boast spectacular views and it is a short walk to the Acropolis and Plaka.

Marble House Pension PENSION €
(☎210 923 4058; www.marblehouse.gr; Zini 35a, Koukaki; s/d/tr €35/45/55, d/tr/q without bathroom €40/50/65; ❄📶; Ⓜ Syngrou-Fix) This long-standing Athens favourite is on a quiet cul-de-sac 10 minutes' walk from Plaka. Step through the garden to quiet, spotless rooms. For air-con add €9.

Psyrri & Thisio

Athens Style HOSTEL, APARTMENT €
(Map p572; ☎210 322 5010; www.athenstyle.com; Agias Theklas 10, Psyrri; dm €20-28, s/d/tr €51/80/96, apt from €90; ❄@; Ⓜ Monastiraki) This bright, arty hostel, the newest in town, has dorm beds and well-equipped apartments. The cool basement lounge holds art exhibitions, a pool table and home cinema; the rooftop bar has Acropolis views.

Plaka & Monastiraki

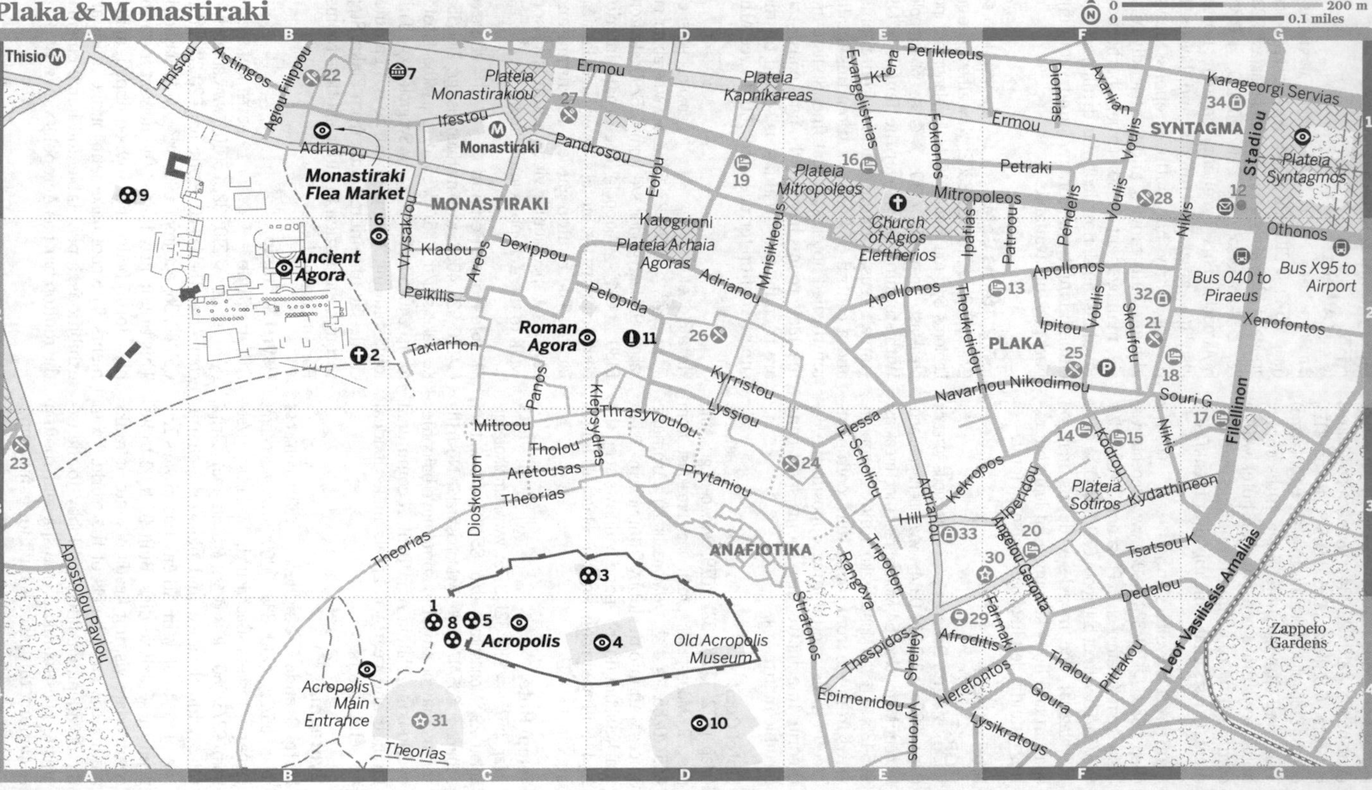

Plaka & Monastiraki

Top Sights
- Acropolis C4
- Ancient Agora B2
- Monastiraki Flea Market B1
- Roman Agora D2

Sights
- 1 Beule Gate C4
- 2 Church of the Holy Apostles B2
- 3 Erechtheion D3
- 4 Parthenon D4
- 5 Propylaea C4
- 6 Stoa of Attalos B2
- 7 Taf C1
- 8 Temple of Athena Nike C4
- 9 Temple of Hephaestus A1
- 10 Theatre of Dionysos D4
- 11 Tower of the Winds D2

Activities, Courses & Tours
- 12 CitySightseeing Athens G1

Sleeping
- 13 Central Hotel F2
- 14 Hotel Acropolis House F3
- 15 Hotel Adonis F3
- 16 Magna Grecia E1
- 17 New G3
- 18 Niki Hotel F2
- 19 Plaka Hotel D1
- 20 Student & Travellers' Inn F3

Eating
- 21 Avocado F2
- 22 Café Avyssinia B1
- 23 Filistron A3
- 24 Palia Taverna Tou Psara E3
- 25 Paradosiako F2
- 26 Platanos D2
- 27 Thanasis C1
- 28 Tzitzikas & Mermingas F1

Drinking
- 29 Brettos E4

Entertainment
- 30 Cine Paris F3
- 31 Odeon of Herodes Atticus C4

Shopping
- 32 Eleftheroudakis F2
- 33 Ioanna Kourbela E3
- 34 Public G1

Hotel Erechthion HOTEL €
(Map p572; ☎210 345 9606; www.hotelerechthion.gr; Flammarion 8, cnr Agias Marinas, Thisio; s/d/tr €40/60/70; ; MThisio) Simple, clean rooms with TVs, refrigerators, veneer furniture and basic bathrooms are not the highlights here. Much more impressive are the fantastic Acropolis views from the balconies, the low price and the homey neighbourhood.

Kolonaki

TOP CHOICE **Periscope** BOUTIQUE HOTEL €€
(Map p572; ☎210 729 7200; www.periscope.gr; Haritos 22, Kolonaki; d incl breakfast from €145; ; MEvangelismos) A hip hotel with a cool, edgy look, this place has comfortable minimalist rooms with all the mod cons and a quiet location.

Eating

In addition to mainstay tavernas, Athens has upscale eateries (wear your most stylish togs at night). Eat streets include Mitropoleos, Adrianou and Navarchou Apostoli in Monastiraki, the area around Plateia Psyrri, and Gazi, near Keramikos metro.

The fruit and vegetable **market** (Varvakios Agora; Map p572; Athinas, btwn Sofokleous & Evripidou; ⏲7am-3pm Mon-Sat; MMonastiraki, Panepistimio, Omonia) is opposite the meat market.

Syntagma & Monastiraki

TOP CHOICE **Café Avyssinia** MEZEDHES €
(Map p580; ☎210 321 7047; www.avissinia.gr; Kynetou 7, Monastiraki; mains €10-16; ⏲11am-1am Tue-Sat, to 7pm Sun; MMonastiraki) Hidden away on the edge of grungy Plateia Avyssinias in the middle of the flea market, this *mezedhopoleio* (*mezedhes* restaurant) gets top marks for atmosphere, and the food is not far behind. Often has live music on weekends.

TOP CHOICE **Tzitzikas & Mermingas** MEZEDHES €
(Map p580; ☎210 324 7607; Mitropoleos 12-14, Syntagma; mezedhes €6-11; MSyntagma) Greek merchandise lines the walls of this cheery, modern *mezedhopoleio*. The great range of delicious and creative *mezedhes* (appetisers) draws a bustling local crowd. Don't miss the decadent honey-coated fried cheese with ham…it's the kind of special dish that will haunt your future dreams.

Mama Roux INTERNATIONAL €
(Map p572; ☎213 004 8382; Eoulou 48-50, Monastiraki; mains €5-10; ⏰9am-midnight Tue-Sat, to 5pm Mon, noon-5pm Sun; 📶; Ⓜ Monastiraki) Downtown's hottest cheap-eats restaurant fills up with locals digging into a fresh, delicious mix of dishes: from real burritos and Cajun specials to whopping American-style burgers.

Kalnterimi TAVERNA €
(Map p572; ☎210 331 0049; www.kalnterimi.gr; Plateia Agion Theodoron, cnr Skouleniou; mains €5-8; ⏰lunch & dinner; Ⓜ Panepistimio) Find your way back behind the Church of Agii Theodori to this open-air taverna offering Greek food at its most authentic. Everything is fresh-cooked and delicious.

Thanasis SOUVLAKI €
(Map p580; ☎210 324 4705; Mitropoleos 69, Monastiraki; gyros €2.50; ⏰8.30am-2.30am; Ⓜ Monastiraki) In the heart of Athens' souvlaki hub, Thanasis is known for its kebabs on pitta with grilled tomato and onions. Live music, grill aromas and crowds give the area an almost permanently festive air.

Plaka & Makrygianni

TOP CHOICE Mani Mani REGIONAL CUISINE €
(Map p572; ☎210 921 8180; www.manimani.com.gr; Falirou 10, Makrygianni; mains €10-16; ⏰3pm-12.30am Tue-Thu, from 1pm Fri & Sat, 1-5.30pm Sun, closed Jul & Aug; Ⓜ Akropoli) Sample cuisine from Mani in the Peloponnese, such as tangy sausage with orange. Most dishes can be ordered as half-serves (at half-price), allowing you to try a wide range.

Paradosiako TAVERNA €
(Map p580; ☎210 321 4121; Voulis 44a, Plaka; mains €5-11; 📶; Ⓜ Syntagma) For great traditional fare, you can't beat this inconspicuous, no-frills taverna on the periphery of Plaka. Choose from daily specials such as delicious shrimp *saganaki* (fried Greek cheese).

Avocado VEGETARIAN €
(Map p580; ☎210 323 7878; www.avocadoathens.com; Nikis 30, Plaka; mains €6.50-9.50; ⏰11am-10pm Mon-Sat, to 7pm Sun; 📶🖉; Ⓜ Syntagma) A full array of vegan, gluten-free and organic treats (a rarity in Greece). Enjoy everything from fresh juices and sandwiches to quinoa with eggplant or mixed veg coconut curry.

Cucina Povera MEDITERRANEAN €
(Map p572; ☎210 756 6008; www.cucinapovera.gr; Efforionos 13, Pangrati; mains €9-14; ⏰dinner Tue-Sat, brunch Sun; Ⓜ Evangelismos) Dishes can be occasionally incandescent, like the salad with avocado, pear and goat cheese. The dining room embodies relaxed hipness, and the wine list rocks.

Platanos TAVERNA €
(Map p580; ☎210 322 0666; Diogenous 4, Plaka; mains €7-9; ⏰lunch & dinner; Ⓜ Monastiraki) Tasty, home-cooked-style Greek cuisine include delicious lamb dishes, and we love the leafy courtyard.

Palia Taverna Tou Psara TAVERNA €€
(Map p580; ☎210 321 8734; www.psaras-taverna.gr; Erehtheos 16, Plaka; mains €12-24; ⏰11am-12.30pm Wed-Mon; Ⓜ Akropoli) Situated on a path leading up towards the Acropolis, this gem of a taverna is one of Plaka's best, serving scrumptious *mezedhes* and excellent fish and meat classics on a tree-lined terrace.

Keramikos, Thisio & Gazi

Varoulko SEAFOOD €€€
(Map p572; ☎210 522 8400; www.varoulko.gr; Pireos 80, Keramikos; mains €35-60; ⏰from 8.30pm Mon-Sat; Ⓜ Thisio, Keramikos) For a magical Greek dining experience, you can't beat the winning combination of Acropolis views and delicious seafood by celebrated Michelin-starred chef Lefteris Lazarou. Athenian celebrities feast in an airy, glass-fronted dining room.

Kanella TAVERNA €
(Map p572; ☎210 347 6320; Leoforos Konstantinoupoleos 70, Gazi; dishes €7-10; ⏰1.30pm-late; Ⓜ Keramikos) Home-made village-style bread, mismatched retro crockery and brown-paper tablecloths set the tone for this trendy, modern taverna serving regional Greek cuisine.

Filistron MEZEDHES €€
(Map p580; ☎210 346 7554; Apostolou Pavlou 23, Thisio; mezedhes €8-14; ⏰lunch & dinner Tue-Sun; Ⓜ Thisio) Book a prized table on the rooftop terrace of this excellent *mezedhopoleio*, which enjoys breathtaking Acropolis- and Lykavittos-views.

Sardelles SEAFOOD €€
(Map p572; ☎210 347 8050; Persefonis 15, Gazi; fish dishes €10-17; Ⓜ Keramikos) As the name suggests (Sardelles means 'sardines'), , this modern fish taverna facing the illuminated gasworks specialises in seafood *mezedhes*.

Kolonaki & Pangrati

TOP CHOICE Spondi MEDITERRANEAN €€€

(Map p572; ☎210 752 0658; Pyrronos 5, Pangrati; mains €35-50; ⊙8pm-late) Dining in this superb restaurant's gorgeous vaulted cellar or in its bougainvillea-draped courtyard in summer is quite an understatedly elegant affair. Chef Arnaud Bignon has won two Michelin stars, creating extravagant seasonal menus adhering to French technique but embodying vibrant Greek flavours.

TOP CHOICE Oikeio TAVERNA €

(Map p572; ☎210 725 9216; Ploutarhou 15, Kolonaki; mains €7-13; ⊙1pm-2.30am Mon-Sat; MEvangelismos) With excellent home-style cooking, this modern taverna lives up to its name ('Homey'). The intimate bistro atmosphere spills out to tables on the pavement for glitterati-watching without the usual high Kolonaki bill. Reservations recommended.

Filippou TAVERNA €

(Map p572; ☎210 721 6390; Xenokratous 19, Kolonaki; mains €8-12; ⊙lunch & dinner, closed Sat night & Sun; MEvangelismos) Filippou has been dishing out yummy Greek dishes since 1923. Think soul cooking, with white linen, in the heart of chic Kolonaki.

Drinking

Athenians know how to party. Everyone has their favourite *steki* (hang-out), but expect people to show up after midnight. Head to Gazi (around Voutadon and the Keramikos metro station), Kolonaki (around Ploutarhou and Haritos, or Skoufa and Omirou) or Monastiraki (around Plateia Karytsi or Kolokotroni) and explore!

Omonia is best avoided late at night, and although Exarhia has a bohemian bar scene, the neighbourhood has been affected recently by street demonstrations.

Kolonaki has a mind-boggling array of cafes off Plateia Kolonakiou on Skoufa and Tsakalof. Another cafe-thick area is Adrianou, along the Ancient Agora.

Hoxton BAR

(Map p572; Voutadon 42, Gazi; MKeramikos) Kick back on overstuffed leather couches under modern art in this industrial space that fills up late with bohemians, ruggers and the occasional pop star.

Mai Tai BAR

(Map p572; Ploutarhou 18, Kolonaki; MEvangelismos) Jam-packed with well-heeled young Athenians, this is just one in a group of happening spots in Kolonaki.

WHAT'S ON

For comprehensive events listings, with links to online ticket sales points, try: www.breathtakingathens.gr, www.elculture.gr, www.tickethour.com, www.tickethouse.gr, www.ticketservices.gr. The *Kathimerini* supplement inside the *International Herald Tribune* contains event listings and a cinema guide.

Seven Jokers BAR

(Map p572; Voulis 7, Syntagma; MSyntagma) Lively and central Seven Jokers anchors the party block, also shared by spacious **42** (Kolokotroni 3, Syntagma) around the corner, for cocktails in wood-panelled splendour, with **Baba Au Rum** (Klitiou 6, Syntagma; MSyntagma) and **Gin Joint** (Lada 1, Syntagma; MSyntagma) nearby.

Gazarte BAR

(Map p572; ☎210 346 0347; www.gazarte.gr; Voutadon 32-34, Gazi; MKeramikos) Trendy crowd takes in mainstream music and rooftop city views including the Acropolis.

Brettos BAR

(Map p580; Kydathineon 41, Plaka; MAkropoli) This bar-distillery is back-lit by an eye-catching collection of coloured bottles.

Tailor Made CAFE, BAR

(Map p572; ☎213 004 9645; www.tailormade.gr; Plateia Agia Irini 2, Monastiraki; MMonastiraki) Cheerful Athenians spill from the mod art-festooned micro-roastery to tables alongside the flower market. At night it turns into a happening cocktail and wine bar.

Entertainment

Nightclubs

Athenians go clubbing after midnight and dress up. In summer try beachfront venues.

Rock'n'Roll CLUB, BAR

(Map p572; ☎210 721 7127; Plateia Kolonakiou, Kolonaki; MEvangelismos) Dependably fun, with a casual-cool Kolonaki crowd.

TOP CHOICE Venue CLUB

(☎210 341 1410; www.venue-club.com; Pireos 130, Rouf; ⊙Sep-May; MKeramikos) Arguably the city's biggest dance club: three-stage dance floor and an energetic crowd.

WANT MORE?

For in-depth information, reviews and recommendations at your fingertips, head to the Apple App Store to purchase Lonely Planet's *Athens City Guide* iPhone app.

Alternatively, head to **Lonely Planet** (www.lonelyplanet.com/greece/athens) for planning advice, author recommendations, traveller reviews and insider tips.

Akrotiri CLUB
(☎210 985 9147; www.akrotirilounge.gr; Vasileos Georgiou B5, Agios Kosmas) Beach-side in summer with a capacity for 3000 people, bars and lounges cover multiple levels.

Gay & Lesbian Venues

Gay bars cluster in Gazi near the railway line on Leoforos Konstantinoupoleos and Megalou Alexandrou, as well as Makrygianni, Psyrri, Metaxourghio and Exarhia. Check out www.athensinfoguide.com, www.gay.gr or a copy of the *Greek Gay Guide* booklet at newspaper kiosks.

Sodade GAY
(Map p572; ☎210 346 8657; www.sodade.gr; Triptolemou 10, Gazi; MKeramikos) Tiny, sleek and super-fun for dancing. It draws a great group.

Noiz Club LESBIAN
(Map p572; ☎210 342 4771; www.noizclub.gr; Evmolpidon 41, Gazi; MKeramikos) In Gazi's gay triangle, for a female crowd.

Lamda Club GAY
(Map p572; ☎210 942 4202; Lembesi 15, cnr Leoforos Syngrou, Makrygianni; MAkropoli) Busy, three levels and not for the faint of heart.

Magaze CAFE, BAR
(Map p572; ☎210 324 3740; Eolou 33, Monastiraki; MMonastiraki) All-day hang-out with Acropolis views from pavement tables; lively bar after sunset.

Live Music

In summer, concerts rock plazas and parks; some clubs shut down. Most authentic *rembetika* venues close during summer, but you can see a popularised version at some tavernas in Psyrri.

TOP CHOICE **Half Note Jazz Club** JAZZ
(Map p572; ☎210 921 3310; www.halfnote.gr; Trivonianou 17, Mets; MAkropoli) Dark, smoky venue for serious jazz.

Cafe Alavastron LIVE MUSIC
(☎210 756 0102; www.cafealavastron.gr; Damareos 78, Pangrati) Eclectic mix of modern jazz, ethnic and Greek music in a casual, intimate venue.

TOP CHOICE **Gagarin 205 Club** LIVE MUSIC
(www.gagarin205.gr; Liosion 205, Thymarakia; MAgios Nikolaos) Interesting international and local rock acts.

TOP CHOICE **Stoa Athanaton** REMBETIKA
(Map p572; ☎210 321 4362; Sofokleous 19, Central Market; ⊙3-6pm & midnight-6am Mon-Sat, closed Jun-Sep; MMonastiraki, Panepistimio, Omonia) Located above the meat market, this is still *the* place to listen to *rembetika*, often referred to as Greek blues.

Classical Music, Theatre & Dance

In summer, the excellent Hellenic Festival (p10) swings into action.

Megaron Mousikis PERFORMING ARTS
(Athens Concert Hall; ☎210 728 2333; www.megaron.gr; Kokkali 1, cnr Leoforos Vasilissis Sofias, Ilissia; ⊙box office 10am-6pm Mon-Fri, to 2pm Sat; MMegaro Mousikis) Superb concert venue hosting winter performances by local and international artists.

National Theatre THEATRE
(Map p572; ☎210 522 3243; www.n-t.gr; Agiou Konstantinou 22-24, Omonia; MOmonia) Contemporary plays and ancient theatre on the main stage and other venues.

Olympia Theatre PERFORMING ARTS
(Map p572; ☎210 361 2461; Akadimias 59, Exarhia; MPanepistimio) November to June: ballet, symphony and the **Greek National Opera** (Ethniki Lyriki Skini; Map p572; ☎210 360 0180; www.national opera.gr).

Dora Stratou Dance Theatre TRADITIONAL DANCE
(Map p572; ☎210 921 4650; www.grdance.org; Filopappou Hill; adult/child €15/5; ⊙performances 9.30pm Wed-Fri, 8.15pm Sat & Sun Jun-Sep; MPetralona) Traditional folk-dancing shows feature more than 75 musicians and dancers in an open-air amphitheatre.

Cinema

Most cinemas, like **Astor** (Map p572; ☎210 323 1297; Stadiou 28, Syntagma; Ⓜ Panepistimio), show recent releases in their original language; tickets cost around €8. In summer watch outdoors at **Aigli Cinema** (Map p572; ☎210 336 9369; Zappeio Gardens, Syntagma; Ⓜ Syntagma), **Dexameni** (Map p572; ☎210 362 3942; Plateia Dexameni, Kolonaki; Ⓜ Evangelismos) or **Cine Paris** (Map p580; ☎210 322 0721; Kydathineon 22, Plaka; Ⓜ Syntagma).

Shopping

Shop for cool jewellery, clothes, shoes and souvenirs such as backgammon sets, handwoven textiles, olive-oil beauty products, worry beads and ceramics. Find boutiques around Syntagma, from the Attica department store past Voukourestiou and on Ermou; designer brands and cool shops in Kolonaki; and souvenirs, folk art and leather in Plaka and Monastiraki.

Monastiraki Flea Market MARKET
(Map p580; Adrianou, Monastiraki; ⏱daily; Ⓜ Monastiraki) Enthralling; spreads daily from Plateia Monastirakiou.

To Pantopoleion FOOD, DRINK
(Map p572; ☎210 323 4612; Sofokleous 1, Omonia; Ⓜ Panepistimio) Expansive store selling traditional food products from all over Greece.

Ioanna Kourbela CLOTHING
(Map p580; ☎210 322 4591; www.ioannakourbela.com; Adrianou 109, Plaka; Ⓜ Sytnatgma) Classic, cool fashion by a young Greek designer.

Eleftheroudakis BOOKS
Syntagma (Map p572; ☎210 331 4180; Panepistimiou 17, Syntagma; Ⓜ Syntagma); **Plaka** (Map p580; ☎210 322 9388; Nikis 20, Plaka; Ⓜ Syntagma) English-language books.

Public BOOKS, ELECTRONICS
(Map p580; ☎210 324 6210; Plateia Syntagmatos, Syntagma; wi-fi; Ⓜ Syntagma) English language books on 3rd floor.

Information

Emergency

Visitor Emergency Assistance (☎112) Toll-free, 24 hours; in English.

Tourist Police (☎210 920 0724, 24hr 171; Veïkou 43-45, Koukaki; ⏱8am-10pm; Ⓜ Syngrou-Fix)

Police Station (☎210 725 7000; Plateia Syntagmatos; Ⓜ Syntagma) Phone ☎100 for the police.

SOS Doctors (☎1016, 210 821 1888; ⏱24hr) Pay service with English-speaking doctors.

Ambulance/First-aid Advice (☎166)

Internet Access

There are free wi-fi hot spots at Plateia Syntagmatos, Thisio, Gazi, the port of Piraeus, many cafes and on the 3rd floor of Public (see above).

DANGERS & ANNOYANCES

» Crime has heightened in Athens with the onset of the financial crisis. Though violent street crime remains relatively rare, travellers should be alert on the streets, especially at night, and beware the traps listed here.

» Streets surrounding Omonia have become markedly seedier, with an increase in prostitutes and junkies; avoid the area, especially at night.

» Watch for pickpockets on the metro and at the markets.

» When taking taxis, ask the driver to use the meter or negotiate a price in advance. Ignore stories that the hotel you've chosen is closed or full: they're angling for a commission from another hotel.

» Bar scams are commonplace, particularly in Plaka and Syntagma. They go something like this: friendly Greek approaches solo male traveller, discovers traveller is new to Athens, and reveals that he, too, is from out of town. However, friendly Greek knows a great bar where they order drinks and equally friendly owner offers another drink. Women appear and more drinks are served; at the end of the night the traveller is hit with an exorbitant bill.

» The recent financial reforms in Greece have caused strikes in Athens. If there is a strike while you are here (check http://livingingreece.gr/strikes), confirm that the sights you wish to see will be open and the transport you are planning to use will be running. Picketers tend to march in Plateia Syntagmatos.

Internet Resources

Official visitor site (www.breathtakingathens.gr)

Media

Kathimerini (www.ekathimerini.com) and **Athens News** (www.athensnews.gr) have English-language coverage.

Money

Banks suround Plateia Syntagmatos.

Eurochange (☎210 331 2462; Karageorgi Servias 2, Syntagma; ⏰8am-9pm; Ⓜ Syntagma)

Telephone

Kiosks sell phonecards for public phones and prepaid SIM cards for mobiles.

Tourist Information

EOT (Greek National Tourist Organisation; ☎210 331 0716, 210 331 0347; www.visitgreece.gr; Dionysiou Areopagitou 18-20, Makrygianni; ⏰8am-8pm Mon-Fri, 10am-4pm Sat & Sun May-Sep, 9am-7pm Mon-Fri Oct-Apr; Ⓜ Akropoli)

Athens Information Kiosk Acropolis (Acropolis; ⏰9am-9pm Jun-Aug; Ⓜ Akropoli)

Athens Information Kiosk Airport (☎210 353 0390; www.breathtakingathens.com; Airport; ⏰8am-8pm; Ⓜ Airport) Maps, transport information and all Athens info.

Getting There & Away

Air

Modern **Eleftherios Venizelos International Airport** (ATH; ☎210 353 0000; www.aia.gr), 27km east of Athens.

Boat

Most ferries, hydrofoils and high-speed catamarans leave from the massive port at Piraeus. Some depart from smaller ports at Rafina and Lavrio.

Bus

KTEL (☎14505; www.ktel.org) Athens has two main intercity bus stations, one 5km and one 7km to the north of Omonia. Tourist offices have timetables.

Mavromateon Terminal (☎210 822 5148, 210 880 8000; cnr Leoforos Alexandras & 28 Oktovriou-Patision, Pedion Areos; Ⓜ Viktoria) Buses for destinations in southern Attica leave from this terminal, about 250m north of the National Archaeological Museum.

Kifissos Terminal A (☎210 512 4910; Kifissou 100, Peristeri; Ⓜ Agios Antonios) Buses to the Peloponnese, Igoumenitsa, Ionian Islands, Florina, Ioannina, Kastoria, Edessa and Thessaloniki, among other destinations. Bus 051 goes to central Athens (junction of Zinonos and Menandrou, near Omonia) every 15 minutes from 5am to midnight. Taxis to Syntagma cost about €8.

Liossion Terminal B (☎210 831 7153; Liossion 260, Thymarakia; Ⓜ Agios Nikolaos) Buses to Trikala (for Meteora), Delphi, Larissa, Thiva, Volos and other destinations. To get here, take bus 024 from outside the main gate of the National Gardens on Amalias and ask to get off at Praktoria KTEL. Get off the bus at Liossion 260, turn right onto Gousiou and you'll see the terminal.

Car & Motorcycle

The airport has car rental, and Syngrou, just south of the Temple of Olympian Zeus, is dotted with car-hire firms, though driving in Athens is treacherous.

Avis (☎210 322 4951; Leoforos Vasilissis Amalias 48, Makrygianni; Ⓜ Akropoli)

Budget (☎210 922 4200; Leoforos Syngrou Andrea 23, Makrygianni; Ⓜ Akropoli)

Europcar (☎210 921 1444; Leoforos Syngrou Andrea 25, Makrygianni; Ⓜ Akropoli)

Train

Intercity trains to central and northern Greece depart from the central **Larisis train station**, about 1km northwest of Plateia Omonias. For the Peloponnese, take the suburban rail to Kiato and change for other OSE services, or check for available lines at the Larisis station. International trains have been discontinued.

OSE Office (☎210 529 7005, in English 1110; www.ose.gr; Karolou 1, Omonia; ⏰8am-3pm Mon-Fri; Ⓜ Metaxourghio)

Getting Around

To/From the Airport

BUS Tickets cost €5. Twenty-four-hour services:

Plateia Syntagmatos (Bus X95, 60 to 90 minutes, every 15 minutes) The Syntagma stop is on Othonos.

Piraeus Port (Bus X96, 1½ hrs, every 20 minutes)

Terminal A (Kifissos) Bus Station (Bus X93, 35 minutes, every 30 minutes)

METRO Blue line 3 links the airport to the city centre in around 40 minutes; it operates from Monastiraki from 5.50am to midnight, and from the airport from 5.30am to 11.30pm. Tickets (€8) are valid for all public transport for 90 minutes. Fare for two or more passengers is €14 total.

TAXI Fares vary according to the time of day and level of traffic; expect at least €35 from the airport to the centre, and €50 to Piraeus. Both trips can take up to an hour, more in heavy traffic.

Public Transport

The metro, tram and bus system makes getting around central Athens and to Piraeus easy. Athens' road traffic can be horrendous. Get maps and timetables at the tourist offices or **Athens Urban Transport Organisation** (OASA; ☎185; www.oasa.gr; ⏰6.30am-11.30pm Mon-Fri, 7.30am-10.30pm Sat & Sun).

BUS & TROLLEYBUS

Buses and electric trolleybuses operate every 15 minutes from 5am to midnight.

Piraeus From Syntagma and Filellinon to Akti Xaveriou catch Bus 040; from Omonia end of Athinas to Plateia Themistokleous, catch Bus 049.

METRO

Trains operate from 5am to midnight (Friday and Saturday to around 2am), every three to 10 minutes. Get timetables at www.ametro.gr.

TAXI

Flag fall is €1.16 with an additional surcharge of €1.05 from ports and train and bus stations, and €3.77 from the airport; then the day rate (tariff 1 on the meter) is €0.66 per kilometre. The night rate (tariff 2 on the meter, from midnight to 5am) is €1.16 per kilometre. Baggage costs €0.38 per item over 10kg. Minimum fare is €3.10. Booking a radio taxi costs €1.88 extra. Fixed rates are posted at the airport.

Taxibeat (https://taxibeat.gr) Mobile app for hailing available taxis by location and rating. Can book from abroad.

Athina 1 (☎210 921 2800)

Enotita (☎801 115 1000)

Ikaros (☎210 515 2800)

TRAIN

Fast **suburban rail** (☎1110; www.trainose.gr) links Athens with the airport, Piraeus, the outer regions and the northern Peloponnese. It connects to the metro at Larisis, Doukissis Plakentias and Nerantziotissa stations, and goes from the airport to Kiato.

TICKETS & PASSES

Tickets good for 90 minutes (€1.40), a 24-hour travel pass (€4) and a weekly ticket (€14) are valid for all forms of public transport except for airport services. Bus/trolleybus-only tickets (€1.20) cannot be used on the metro. Children under six travel free; people under 18 and over 65 pay half-fare. Buy tickets in metro stations, transport kiosks, or most *periptera* (street kiosks). Validate the ticket in the machine as you board your transport of choice.

AROUND ATHENS

Piraeus Πειραιάς

TRANSPORT HUB

POP 179,500

The highlights of Greece's main port and ferry hub are the otherworldly rows of ferries, ships and hydrofoils filling its seemingly endless quays. It takes around 40 minutes to get here (10km) from Athens' centre by metro, so there's no reason to stay in shabby Piraeus. The Mikrolimano (Small Harbour), with its cafes and fish restaurants, reveals the city's gentler side.

Sleeping

Piraeus Theoxenia LUXURY HOTEL €€

(☎210 411 2550; www.theoxeniapalace.com; Karaoli Dimitriou 23; s/d/tr incl breakfast €99/110/150; ❄@📶; ⓂPiraeus) Pireaus' most upmarket, central hotel, with plump bathrobes and satellite TV; get the best deals online.

Hotel Triton HOTEL €€

(☎210 417 3457; www.htriton.gr; Tsamadou 8; s/d/tr incl breakfast €45/70/80; ❄@; ⓂPiraeus) Refurbished hotel with simple executive-style rooms; a treat compared with Pireaus' usual run-down joints.

Eating

If you're killing time, take trolleybus 20 to Mikrolimano for harbourfront seafood.

Rakadiko TAVERNA €

(☎210 417 8470; Stoa Kouvelou, Karaoli Dimitriou 5; mains €12-20; ⏰lunch & dinner Tue-Sat) Under grapevines, dine quietly on *mezedhes* from all over Greece. Live *rembetika* on weekends.

Mandragoras DELI €

(☎210 417 2961; Gounari 14; ⏰7.30am-4pm Mon, Wed & Sat, to 8pm Tue, Thu & Fri) Fantastic array of fresh Greek products.

General Market MARKET €

(Dimosthenous; ⏰6am-4pm Mon-Fri)

Piraikon SUPERMARKET

(Makras Stoas 1; ⏰8am-8pm Mon-Fri, to 4pm Sat)

Piraeus

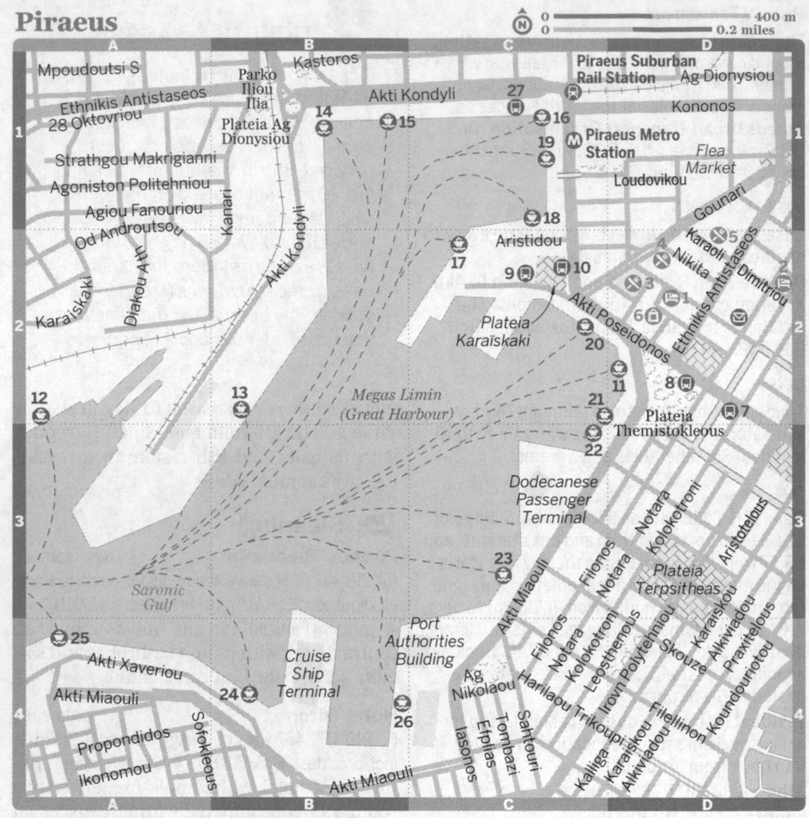

Piraeus

Sleeping

1 Hotel Triton D2
2 Piraeus Theoxenia D2

Eating

3 General Market D2
4 Mandragoras D2
5 Rakadiko D2

Shopping

6 Piraikon D2

Transport

7 Bus 040 to Syntagma D2
8 Bus 049 to Omonia D2
9 Bus Station C2
10 Bus X96 to Airport C2
11 Catamarans & Hydrofoils to the Peloponnese & Saronic Gulf D2
12 Gate E1 (for the Dodecanese) A2
13 Gate E2 (for Crete & Northeastern Aegean Islands) B2
14 Gate E3 .... B1
15 Gate E4 (for Crete) B1
16 Gate E5 .... C1
17 Gate E7 .... C2
18 Gate E7 (for the Cyclades) C1
19 Gate E7 (for the Western & Central Cyclades) C1
20 Gate E8 (for the Saronic Gulf Islands) C2
21 Gate E9 (for the Cyclades) C2
22 Gate E9 (for the Cyclades, Samos, Ikaria) C3
23 Gate E10 .... C3
24 Gate E11 .... B4
25 Gate E12 .... A4
26 International Ferries B4
27 Shuttle Bus to Gates E1 to E3 .... C1

Information

Internet Access Free wi-fi around the port.

Left Luggage At the metro station (€3 per 24 hours).

Getting There & Away

Boat

All ferry companies have online timetables and booths on the quays. EOT (p586) in Athens has a weekly schedule, or check www.openseas.gr. Schedules are reduced in April, May and October, and are radically cut in winter, especially to smaller islands. When buying tickets, confirm the departure point. For more details contact the **Piraeus Port Authority** (☎1441; www.olp.gr).

Hellenic Seaways (☎210 419 9000; www.hellenicseaways.gr; cnr Akti Kondyli & Elotikou) operates high-speed hydrofoils and catamarans to the Cyclades from early April to the end of October, and year-round services to the Saronic Gulf Islands. Other high-speed services include **Aegean Speedlines** (☎210 969 0950; www.aegeanspeedlines.gr).

Bus

The **X96** Piraeus–Athens Airport Express (€5) leaves from the southwestern corner of Plateia Karaïskaki. **Bus 040** goes to Syntagma in downtown Athens.

Metro

The fastest and most convenient link to Athens is the metro (€1.40, 40 minutes, every 10 minutes, 5am to midnight), near the ferries.

Train

Piraeus has a station for Athens' suburban rail.

Getting Around

Local bus 904 runs between the metro station and Zea Marina.

THE PELOPONNESE
ΠΕΛΟΠΟΝΝΗΣΟΣ

The Peloponnese encompasses a breathtaking array of landscapes, villages and ruins, where much of Greek history has played out. It's home to Olympia, birthplace of the Olympic Games; the ancient archaeological sites of magical Epidavros, Mycenae and Corinth; the fairy-tale Byzantine city of Mystras; and ancient Sparta.

Two of Greece's most memorable towns grace its shores: Venetian-style Nafplio and romantic Monemvasia. The isolated Mani Peninsula, best known for its wild landscape and people, bristles with fortified tower settlements and is blanketed with a colourful collection of spectacular wildflowers in spring.

Patra Πάτρα

POP 168,900

Greece's third-largest city, Patra is the principal ferry port for the Ionian Islands and Italy. Despite its 3000-year history, ancient sites and vibrant social life, few travellers linger here longer than necessary to transfer to their ferries.

Sights

FREE Archaeological Museum of Patras MUSEUM
(☎261 042 0645; cnr Amerikis & Patras-Athens National Rd; ⏲8.30am-3pm Tue-Sun) The country's second-largest museum features objects from prehistoric to Roman times.

FREE Kastro CASTLE
(⏲8.30am-3pm Tue-Sun) The Byzantine castle, originally Roman-built around AD 550, but rebuilt since, has excellent views to the Ionian Islands.

Festivals

Patras Carnival MARDI GRAS
(www.carnivalpatras.gr) Wild weekend of costume parades and floats in spring.

Sleeping

Pension Nikos HOTEL €
(☎261 062 3757; cnr Patreos 3 & Agiou Andreou 121; s/d/tr €30/40/55, s/d without bathroom €25/35; ❄) Marble stairs lead to spotlessly clean rooms smack in the city centre.

Olympic Star Hotel BUSINESS HOTEL €€
(☎261 062 2939; www.olympicstar.gr; Agiou Nikolau 46; s/d/tr incl breakfast €55/70/90; ❄📶) Business-style rooms feature hydro showers.

Eating & Drinking

Scores of stylish cafes and fast-food eateries lie between Kolokotroni and Ermou; drinking hot spots cluster on Agiou Nikolaou and near pedestrainised Riga Fereou. Pedestrianised Trion Navarhon is lined with tavernas.

Kouzina tis Kornilias BISTRO €
(☎261 027 2987; Plateia Kapodistrio 4; mains €8-14; ⏲dinner, lunch Sat & Sun) Dig in to Turkish braised beef with aubergine puree (€14) and

other delicate specialities in this cool bistro tucked in the corner of a quiet square.

Mythos TAVERNA €
(☎261 032 9984; cnr Trion Navarhon 181 & Riga Fereou; mains €8-14; ⏲dinner) Friendly waiters serve excellent home-cooked Greek classics in a chandelier-strewn town house.

Dia Discount Supermarket SUPERMARKET €
(Agiou Andreou 29; ⏲Mon-Sat)

Information

Tourist Office (☎261 046 1741; www.infocenterpatras.gr; Agiou Andreou 12-14, btwn Zaimi & Aratou; ⏲7.30am-9pm; 📶) Friendly multilingual staff with information on transport. A kiosk in central Plateia Trion Symahon operates from 7.30am to 9pm in summer.

Tourist Police (☎261 069 5191; Gounari 52; ⏲7.30am-9pm)

Getting There & Away

Boat

Schedules vary; the tourist office provides timetables. Ticket agencies line the waterfront.

Strintzis (☎261 024 0000; www.strintzisferries.gr) sails to:

Ithaki (€18.60, four hours, one daily)
Kefallonia (€18.20, 2¾ hours, one to two daily)

Minoan Lines (☎261 042 6000; www.minoan.gr), **ANEK Lines** (☎261 022 6053; www.anek.gr) and others sail to:

Igoumenitsa (€25, seven hours, one daily)
Italy (from €65/70 to Venice/Ancona)

WORTH A TRIP

DIAKOFTO–KALAVRYTA RAILWAY
ΔΙΑΚΟΦΤΟ–ΚΑΛΑΒΡΥΤΑ

This spectacular rack-and-pinion **train** (☎26910 43206), built in the 1890s, crawls up the deep **Vouraïkos river gorge** from the small coastal town of Diakofto, one hour east of Patra, to the mountain resort of Kalavryta, 22km away. It's a thrilling one-hour journey, with dramatic scenery best viewed from any forward-facing seat. They book up, so buy tickets (€10, five daily) in advance at any train station or online at **Trainose** (www.trainose.gr). Visit www.odontotos.com for more information.

Bus

Services from **KTEL Achaia bus station** (☎261 062 3886; cnr Zaimi 2 & Othonos Amalias):

Athens (€20, three hours, half-hourly, via Corinth)
Ioannina (€24, 4½ hours, two daily)
Kalamata (€23, four hours, two daily)
Kalavryta (€7, two hours, two daily)
Pyrgos (for Olympia; €10, two hours, 10 daily)
Thessaloniki (€44, seven hours, four daily)

Buses to the Ionian Islands, via the port of Kyllini, leave from the **KTEL Lefkada & Zakynthos bus station** (☎261 022 0993; www.ktel-zakynthos.gr; Othonos Amalias 48) or nearby **KTEL Kefallonia bus station** (☎261 027 4938; Othonos Amalias 58).

Train

At the time of research, train lines from **Patra train station** (☎261 063 9108; Othonos Amalias 27) were under construction and may reopen in 2013. Replacement buses serve Athens' Kiato station (connects to suburban rail), Diakofto, Kalamata and Pyrgos (for Olympia).

Corinth Κόρινθος

POP 26,400

Drab, modern Corinth (*ko*-rin-thoss), 6km west of the Corinth Canal, is an uninspiring town; it's better to stay in the village near Ancient Corinth if visiting the ruins.

Sleeping

Hotel Ephira HOTEL €
(☎27410 22434; www.ephirahotel.gr; Ethnikis Andistasis 52; d €50; ❄📶) Corinth's smartest hotel is comfortably furnished, but hides a few blemishes. Suites are a notch more upmarket.

Blue Dolphin Camping CAMPGROUND €
(☎27410 25766; www.camping-blue-dolphin.gr; campsites per tent/adult €5/6.50; ⏲Apr-Oct; 🏊) Has a beach, decent facilities and offers tours. It's at Lecheon, about 4km west of Corinth, just after the ancient Corinth turn-off. Offers pick-up from train or bus stations.

Getting There & Away

BUS Buses to Athens (€8, 1½ hours, half-hourly) and Ancient Corinth (€1.70, 20 minutes, hourly) leave from the **KTEL Korinthos bus station** (☎27410 75425; www.ktel-korinthias.gr; Dimocratias 4). Buses to the rest of the Peloponnese leave from the **Corinth Isthmus (Peloponnese) KTEL bus station** (☎27410 73987, 27410 83000) on the Peloponnese side of the Corinth Canal. All buses from Athens to the Peloponnese stop here. To get there from Corinth, catch one of the frequent local buses to Loutraki.

TRAIN At the time of research, train lines to Patra and Athens were closed for construction; they may reopen in 2013. The *proastiako* suburban train at nearby Kiato goes to Athens airport (€12, one hour, eight daily). Buses to/from the *proastiako* station go to/from Corinth's Plateia Kentriki (€1.50, 20 minutes).

Ancient Corinth & Acrocorinth
Αρχαία Κόρινθος & Ακροκόρινθος

Seven kilometres southwest of Corinth's modern city, the ruins of **Ancient Corinth** (☎27410 31207; site & museum €6; ⏰8.30am-8pm Apr-Oct, to 3pm Nov-Mar) and its lovely museum lie at the edge of a small village in the midst of fields sweeping to the sea. It was one of ancient Greece's wealthiest cities, but earthquakes and invasions have left only one Greek monument remaining: the imposing **Temple of Apollo**; the rest of the ruins are Roman. **Acrocorinth** (⏰8am-3pm), the remains of a citadel built on a massive outcrop of limestone, looms majestically over the site.

The great-value digs at **Tasos Taverna & Rooms** (☎27410 31225; s/d/tr €30/45/55; ❄), 200m from the museum, are spotlessly clean and above an excellent eatery serving Greek classics.

Nafplio Ναύπλιο

POP 14,000

Elegant Venetian houses and neoclassical mansions dripping with crimson bougainvillea cascade down Nafplio's hillside to the azure sea. Vibrant cafes, shops and restaurants fill winding pedestrian streets. Crenulated Palamidi Fortress perches above it all. What's not to love?

Sights

Palamidi Fortress FORTRESS

(☎27520 28036; admission €4; ⏰8am-7.30pm May–mid-Oct, to 4.30pm mid-Oct–Apr) Enjoy spectacular views of the town and surrounding coast from the magnificent hilltop fortress built by the Venetians between 1711 and 1714.

WORTH A TRIP

THE WINE ROAD

The Nemea region, in the rolling hills southwest of Corinth, is one of Greece's premier wine-producing areas, famous for its full-bodied reds from the local *agiorgitiko* grape and a white from *roditis* grapes. Some wineries offer tastings:

Skouras (☎27510 23688; www.skouras wines.com) Northwest of Argos.

Ktima (☎27460 24190; www.palivos.gr; Ancient Nemea) Palivou

Lafkioti (☎27460 31000; www.lafkiotis.gr; Ancient Kleonai) Located 3km east of Ancient Nemea.

Gaia Wines (☎27460 22057; www.gaia-wines.gr; Koutsi) North of Nemea.

Archaeological Museum MUSEUM

(☎27520 27502; Plateia Syntagmatos; admission €3; ⏰noon-4pm Mon, 9am-4pm Tue-Sun) Fine exhibits include fire middens from 32,000 BC and bronze armour from near Mycenae (12th to 13th centuries BC).

Peloponnese Folklore Foundation Museum MUSEUM

(☎27520 28379; www.pli.gr; Vas Alexandrou 1; admission €2; ⏰9am-2.30pm) One of Greece's best small museums, with displays of vibrant regional costumes and rotating exhibitions.

Sleeping

Exquisite hotels abound in Nafplio. The Old Town is *the* place to stay, but it has few budget options. Friday to Sunday the town fills and prices rise; book ahead. Cheaper spots dot the road to Argos and Tolo.

TOP CHOICE **Amfitriti Pension** PENSION €€

(☎27520 96250; www.amfitriti-pension.gr; Kapodistriou 24; d incl breakfast from €60; ❄📶) Quaint antiques fill these intimate rooms in a house in the Old Town. You can also enjoy stellar views at its nearby sister hotel, **Amfitriti Belvedere**, which is chock-full of brightly coloured tapestries and emits a feeling of cheery serenity.

Pension Marianna PENSION €€

(☎27520 24256; www.pensionmarianna.gr; Potamianou 9; s/d/tr incl breakfast €50/65/85;

P❄📶) Welcoming owners epitomise Greek *filoxenia* (hospitality) and serve delicious organic breakfasts. Up a steep set of stairs, and tucked under the fortress walls, a dizzying array of rooms intermix with sea-view terraces.

Adiandi BOUTIQUE HOTEL €€
(☎27520 22073; www.hotel-adiandi.com; Othonos 31; r incl breakfast €75-120; ❄📶) Rooms in this fun and upmarket place are quirkily decorated with artistic bedheads fashioned from doors and contemporary decor. Fantastic farm-fresh breakfasts.

Hotel Byron PENSION €
(☎27520 22351; www.byronhotel.gr; Platonos 2; d incl breakfast from €45; ❄) Tucked into two fine Venetian buildings, iron bedsteads, rich carpets and period furniture fill immaculate rooms.

Hotel Grande Bretagne LUXURY HOTEL €€
(☎27520 96200; www.grandebretagne.com.gr; Plateia Filellinon; d incl breakfast from €115; ❄📶) In the heart of Nafplio's cafe action and overlooking the sea, this splendidly restored hotel with high ceilings, antiques and chandeliers radiates plush opulence.

Kapodistrias PENSION €
(☎27520 29366; www.hotelkapodistrias.gr; Kokinou 20; d incl breakfast from €50; ⌚Mar–mid-Oct; ❄📶) Beautiful rooms, many with elegant canopy beds, come with sea or old-town views.

Pension Dimitris Bekas PENSION €
(☎27520 24594; Efthimiopoulou 26; s/d/tr €25/30/45) The only good, central budget option. Clean, homey rooms (some with shared bath) have a top-value location on the slopes of the Akronafplia, and the owner has a killer baseball cap collection.

Eating

Nafplio's Old Town streets are loaded with standard tavernas; those on Staïkopoulou or overlooking the port on Bouboulinas get jam-packed on weekends; Vasilissis Olgas is better, with tavernas like **Aeolos** (☎27520 26828; Vasilissis Olgas 30; mains €5-13) and **To Omorfo Tavernaki** (☎27520 25944; Vasilissis Olgas 1; mains €7-14).

TOP CHOICE **Alaloum** GREEK €€
(☎27520 29883; Papanikolaou 10; mains €10-18) Heaping creative interpretations of traditional dishes like rooster, veal or homemade pasta can be shared. Everything is made from scratch and salads are a meal in their own right.

TOP CHOICE **Antica Gelateria di Roma** ICE CREAM €
(☎27520 23520; cnr Farmakopoulou & Komninou) The best (yes, best) traditional gelati outside Italy.

To Kentrikon CAFE €
(☎27520 29933; Plateia Syntagmatos; mains €4-10) Relax under the shady trees on this pretty square during extensive breakfasts. Best coffees and teas.

Arapakos SEAFOOD €€
(☎27520 27675; www.arapakos.gr; Bouboulinas 81; mains €10-15) The best of the boardwalk catch for fresh seafood.

Shopping

Nafplio shopping is a delight, with jewellery workshops like **Metallagi** (☎27520 21267; Sofroni 3), boutiques and wonderful regional products, such as worry beads, honey, wine and handicrafts.

Odyssey BOOKS
(☎27520 23430; Plateia Syntagmatos) International papers, magazines and novels.

Drinking & Entertainment

Wander the Old Town to cafe- and bar-hop the lively scene. You could start at newcomer **O Mavros Gatos** (Sofroni 1), or creative stalwarts near Plateia Syntagmatos like **Cafe Rosso** (Komninou 5), where every table is different.

TOP CHOICE **Fougaro** CULTURAL CENTRE
(☎27520 96005; www.fougaro.gr; Asklipiou 98) Nafplio's marquee arts and cultural centre opened with fanfare in 2012 in an impeccably renovated factory that now houses an art shop, library, cafe and exhibition spaces, and holds performing arts programs.

Information

Emergency

Tourist Police (☎27520 28131; Kountouridou 16)

Tourist Information

Staikos Tours (☎27520 27950; Bouboulinas 50) Helpful; Avis rental cars; full travel services like occasional day-long boat trips (www.pegasus-cruises.gr) to Spetses, Hydra and Monemvasia.

WORTH A TRIP

GORGE YOURSELF

The picturesque prefecture of **Arkadia** occupies much of the central Peloponnese and is synonymous with grassy meadows, forested mountains and gurgling streams. West of Tripoli, a tangle of medieval villages and narrow winding roads weave into valleys of dense vegetation beneath the **Menalon Mountains**. These areas are best accessed by car.

Wonderful walks along the **Lousios Gorge** leave from **Dimitsana** (population 230), a delightful medieval village built amphitheatrically on two hills at the beginning of the gorge. It sits 11km north of **Stemnitsa** (population 412), another gorge gateway and a striking village of stone houses and Byzantine churches.

Trekking Hellas (☎697 445 9753, 27910 25978; www.trekkinghellas.gr) offers rafting (from €50) on the nearby Lousios and Alfios Rivers, gorge hikes (from €20) and multi-day tours (€275).

Leonidio (population 3224), 90km east of Sparta, is dramatically set at the mouth of the **Badron Gorge**. Some older residents still speak Tsakonika, a distinctive dialect from the time of ancient Sparta.

Getting There & Away

KTEL Argolis Bus Station (☎27520 27323; www.ktel-argolidas.gr; Syngrou 8) has the following services:

Argos (for Peloponnese connections; €1.60, 30 minutes, half-hourly)
Athens (via Corinth; €13.10, 2½ hours, hourly)
Epidavros (€2.90, 45 minutes, two Mon-Sat)
Mycenae (€2.90, one hour, three daily)

Epidavros Επίδαυρος

Spectacular World Heritage–listed **Epidavros** (☎27530 22009; admission €6; ⊙8am-6pm Apr-Oct, to 5pm Nov-Mar) was the sanctuary of Asclepius, god of medicine. Amid pine-covered hills, the magnificent **theatre** is still a venue during the Hellenic Festival, but don't miss the peaceful **Sanctuary of Asclepius**, an ancient spa and healing centre.

Go as a day trip from Nafplio (€2.90, 45 minutes, two daily buses Monday to Saturday).

For an early-morning visit to the site, stay at the **Hotel Avaton** (☎27530 22178; s/d €40/50; P❄), 1km away, at the junction of the road to Kranidi.

Mycenae Μυκήνες

Although settled as early as the 6th millennium BC, **Ancient Mycenae** (☎27510 76585; admission €8; ⊙8am-7pm Mon-Sat, to 4pm Sun Jun-Sep, 8am-6pm Mon-Sat, to 4pm Sun Oct-May), pronounced mih-*kee*-nes, was at its most powerful from 1600 to 1200 BC. Mycenae's grand entrance, the **Lion Gate**, is Europe's oldest monumental sculpture. Homer accurately described Mycenae as being 'rich in gold': excavations of **Grave Circle A** by Heinrich Schliemann in the 1870s uncovered magnificent gold treasures, such as the Mask of Agamemnon, now on display at Athens' National Archaeological Museum.

Most people visit on day trips from Nafplio, but the bare-bones **Belle Helene Hotel** (☎27510 76225; Christou Tsounta; d without bathroom, incl breakfast €35) is where Schliemann lived during excavations.

Three buses go daily to Mycenae from Argos (€1.60, 30 minutes) and Nafplio (€2.90, one hour).

Sparta Σπάρτη

POP 14,200

Cheerful, unpretentious modern Sparta (*spar*-tee) is at odds with its ancient Spartan image of discipline and deprivation. Although there's little to see, the town makes a convenient base from which to visit Mystras.

Modern **Hotel Lakonia** (☎27310 28951; www.lakoniahotel.gr; Palaeologou 89; s/d from €40/55; ❄📶) maintains comfy, welcoming rooms with spotless bathrooms. **Hotel Maniatis** (☎27310 22665; www.maniatishotel.gr; Paleologou 72-76; s/d incl breakfast €80/100; ❄📶) offers the sleekest digs in town.

The sweet smell of spices inundates **Restaurant Elysse** (☎27310 29896; Palaeologou 113; mains €6-12), which is run by a friendly

Greek-Canadian family. Locals chill out next door at **Café Ouzeri** (mains €4-6).

Sparta's **KTEL Lakonia bus station** (☎27310 26441; cnr Lykourgou & Thivronos), on the east edge of town, services Athens (€20, 3½ hours, eight daily) via Corinth, Gythio (€4.50, one hour, five daily), Monemvasia (€11, two hours, three daily) and Mystras (€2, 30 minutes, 11 daily).

Mystras Μυστράς

Magical **Mystras** (☎27310 83377; adult/child €5/3; ⏰8.30am-5.30pm Mon-Sat, to 3pm Sun, sometimes longer in summer) was once the effective capital of the Byzantine Empire. Ruins of palaces, monasteries and churches, most of them dating from between 1271 and 1460, nestle at the base of the Taÿgetos Mountains, and are surrounded by verdant olive and orange groves.

Allow half a day to explore the site. While only 7km from Sparta, staying in the village nearby allows you to get there early before it heats up. Enjoy exquisite views and a beautiful swimming pool at **Hotel Byzantion** (☎27310 83309; www.byzantionhotel.gr; s/d/tr €50/70/80; P❄@≋). Have a decadent escape at **Hotel Pyrgos Mystra** (☎27310 20870; www.pyrgosmystra.com; Manousaki 3; d incl breakfast €200; ❄), with its lovingly appointed rooms in a restored mansion.

Camp at **Castle View** (☎27310 83303; www.castleview.gr; campsites per adult/tent/car €6/4/4, 2-person bungalow €30; ⏰Apr-Oct; ≋), about 1km before Mystras village and set in olive trees, or **Camping Paleologio Mystras** (☎27310 22724; campsites per adult/tent/car €7/4/4; ⏰year-round; ≋), 2km west of Sparta and approximately 4km from Mystras. Buses will stop outside either if you ask.

Several tavernas serve traditional Greek meals.

Monemvasia & Gefyra Μονεμβάσια & Γέφυρα

POP 1320

Slip out along a narrow causeway, up around the edge of a towering rock rising dramatically from the sea and arrive at the exquisite walled village of Monemvasia. Enter the *kastro* (castle), which was separated from mainland Gefyra by an earthquake in AD 375, through a narrow tunnel on foot, and emerge into a stunning (carless) warren of cobblestone streets and stone houses. Beat the throngs of day trippers by staying over.

Signposted steps lead up to the ruins of a **fortress** built by the Venetians in the 16th century, and the Byzantine **Church of Agia Sophia**, perched precariously on the edge of the cliff. Views are spectacular, and wildflowers grow shoulder-high in spring.

Sleeping & Eating

Staying in a hotel in the *kastro* could be one of the most romantic things you ever do (ask for discounts in low season), but if you're on a tight budget stay in Gefyra.

Three traditional Greek tavernas sit cheek to cheek in Monemvasia's old town: **Matoula** (☎27320 61660; mains €8-13), **Marianthi** (☎27320 61371; mains €8-13) and **To Kanoni** (☎27320 61387; mains €8-13). You can't really go wrong with any of them.

TOP CHOICE **Hotel Malvasia** HISTORIC HOTEL €€
(☎27320 61160; malvasia@otenet.gr; d/apt from €60/100; ❄) A variety of cosy, traditionally decorated rooms and apartments (most with sea views) are scattered around the Old Town. Another branch, known as the **Malvasia Hotel** (http://malvasia-hotel.gr), has higher-end rooms.

Hotel Aktaion HOTEL €
(☎27320 61234; www.aktaion-monemvasia.gr; s/d €40/50) This clean, sunny hotel, on the Gefyra end of the causeway, has balconies with views of the sea and 'the rock'.

Taverna O Botsalo TAVERNA €
(☎27320 61486; mains €4-9) Just down the wharf on the mainland; serves savoury meals.

Getting There & Away

Buses stop in Gefyra at the friendly **Malvasia Travel** (☎27320 61752), where you can buy tickets. Four daily buses travel to Athens (€32, six hours) via Corinth and Sparta (€11, 2½ hours).

Gythio Γύθειο

POP 4490

Gythio (*yee*-thih-o) was once the port of ancient Sparta. Now it's an earthy fishing town on the Lakonian Gulf and gateway to the rugged, much more beautiful Mani Peninsula.

Peaceful **Marathonisi islet**, linked to the mainland by a causeway, is said to be ancient Cranae, where Paris (prince of Troy) and Helen (the wife of Menelaus of Sparta) consummated the love affair that sparked the Trojan War. You'll find the tiny **Museum of Mani History** (☎27330 24484; admission €2; ⊙8am-2.30pm) here in an 18th-century tower.

Sleeping & Eating

The waterfront is packed with fish taverna, like **I Gonia** (Vassilis Pavlou; mains €6-15), and cafes.

Hotel La Boheme BOUTIQUE HOTEL €
(☎27330 21992; www.labohemehotel.gr; Tzani Tzanitaki; s/d incl breakfast €45/60; P❄@) Sea views, upmarket rooms and a zippy downstairs bar-restaurant draw crowds.

Camping Meltemi CAMPGROUND €
(☎27330 23260; www.campingmeltemi.gr; campsites per tent/adult €5.50/6, bungalows €30-60; ⊙Apr-Oct; 🛜🏊) Birds chirp in these idyllic silver olive groves, 3km south of Gythio; private beach, swimming pool and summer beauty contests! The Areopoli bus stops here.

Xenia Karlaftis Rooms to Rent PENSION €
(☎27330 22719; opp Marathonisi islet; s/d €25/40) Friendly owner Voula keeps clean (if worn) rooms and offers kitchen access. Several nearby places are of similar quality if you can't get in here.

Getting There & Away

BUS The **KTEL Lakonia bus station** (☎27330 22228; http://ktel-lakonias.gr; cnr Vasileos Georgios & Evrikleos) is on the square near Hotel Aktion.

Areopoli (€2.80, 30 minutes, four daily)
Athens (€24, 4½ hours, six daily)
Geroliminas (€6, 1¼ hours, one daily)
Sparta (€4.50, one hour, four daily)

CAR & BOAT LANE Lines (www.lane.gr) has a weekly ferry to Crete (€23, seven hours) via Kythira (€11, 2½ hours) and Antikythira. Schedules change; check with **Rozakis Travel** (☎27330 22207; rosakigy@otenet.gr; Pavlou 5) which also rents cars.

The Mani Η Μάνη

The exquisite Mani completely lives up to its reputation for rugged beauty, with abundant wildflowers in spring and dramatic juxtapositions of sea and the Taÿgetos Mountains (threaded with wonderful walking trails). The Mani occupies the central peninsula of the southern Peloponnese and is divided into two regions: the arid Lakonian (inner) Mani in the south and the verdant Messinian (outer) Mani in the northwest near Kalamata. Explore the winding roads by car.

LAKONIAN MANI

For centuries the Maniots were a law unto themselves, renowned for their fierce independence and their spectacularly murderous internal feuds. To this day, bizarre tower settlements built as refuges during clan wars dot the rocky slopes of Lakonian Mani.

Areopoli (population 775), 30km southwest of Gythio and named after Ares, the god of war, is a warren of cobblestone and ancient towers. Stay in a tastefully decorated 200-year-old tower house at **Londas Pension** (☎27330 51360; www.londas.com; near Church of Taxiarhes; s/d/tr incl breakfast €65/75/103, s/d without bathroom €56/65). For a cushy boutique hotel experience, book in at **Areos Polis** (☎27330 51028; www.areospolis.gr; s/d/tr incl breakfast from €40/65/80; ❄🛜).

Step behind the counter to choose from the scrumptious specials at **Nicola's Corner Taverna** (☎27330 51366; Plateia Athanaton; mains €8-10), on the central square.

The **bus station** (☎27330 51229) services Athens (€28, four daily) via Gythio (€2.80, 30 minutes), Itilo (for the Messinian Mani, €2, 20 minutes, two daily Monday to Saturday), Gerolimenas (€3.40, 45 minutes, three daily) and the Diros Caves (€1.60, 15 minutes, one daily)

Eleven kilometres south, the extensive, though touristy **Diros Caves** (☎27330 52222; adult/child €12/7; ⊙8.30am-5.30pm Jun-Sep, to 3pm Oct-May) contain a subterranean river. In neighbouring **Pyrgos Dirou**, stay over at chic **Vlyhada** (☎27330 52469; www.vlyhada.gr; d incl breakfast €70; P❄).

Gerolimenas, a tranquil fishing village on a sheltered bay 20km further south, is home to the exceedingly popular boutique establishment **Kyrimai Hotel** (☎27330 54288; www.kyrimai.gr; d incl breakfast from €110; P❄🏊). Groovy music and mood lighting fill this exquisitely renovated castle with a seaside swimming pool and top-notch restaurant.

MESSINIAN MANI

Stone hamlets dot aquamarine swimming coves. Silver olive groves climb the foothills to the snow-capped Taÿgetos Mountains. Explore the splendid meandering roads and hiking trails from Itilo to Kalamata.

The people of the enchanting seaside village of **Kardamyli**, 37km south of Kalamata, know how good they've got it. Sir Patrick Leigh Fermor famously wrote about his rambles here in *Mani: Travels in the Southern Peloponnese*. Trekkers come for the magnificent **Vyros Gorge**. Walks are well organised and colour-coded.

Kardamyli has a good choice of small hotels and private rooms for all budgets; book ahead for summer.

Notos Hotel (☎27210 73730; www.notoshotel.gr; studio €110, apt €135-160; P❄) is really a boutique hamlet of individual stone houses with fully equipped kitchens, verandas and views overlooking the village, the mountains and the sea.

Olympia Koumounakou Rooms (☎27210 73623; s/d €30/40) is basic but clean and popular with backpackers, who like the communal kitchen and courtyard.

Beautiful **Elies** (☎27210 73140; mains €6-12; ⊙lunch), right by the beach 1km north of town, is worth a lunchtime stop.

Kardamyli is on the main bus route from Itilo to Kalamata (€4, one hour) and two to four buses stop daily at the central square.

Olympia Ολυμπία

POP 1000

Tucked alongside the Kladeos River, in fertile delta country, the modern town of Olympia supports the extensive ruins of the same name. The first Olympics were staged here in 776 BC, and every four years thereafter until AD 394, when Emperor Theodosius I banned them. During the competition the city-states were bound by a sacred truce to stop fighting and take part in athletic events and cultural exhibitions.

Ancient Olympia (☎26240 22517; adult/child €6/3, site & museum €9/5; ⊙8am-8pm Apr-Oct, 8.30am-3pm Nov-Mar) is dominated by the immense ruined **Temple of Zeus**, to whom the games were dedicated. Don't miss the statue of **Hermes of Praxiteles**, a classical sculpture masterpiece, at the exceptional **Archaeological Museum** (adult/child €6/3; ⊙1.30-8pm Mon, 8am-8pm Tue-Sun Apr-Oct, to 3pm Nov-Mar).

Sparkling-clean **Pension Posidon** (☎26240 22567; www.pensionposidon.gr; Stefanopoulou 9; s/d/tr €35/40/50; ❄) and quiet, spacious **Hotel Pelops** (☎26240 22543; www.hotelpelops.gr; Varela 2; s/d/tr incl breakfast €40/50/70; ❄@) offer the best value in the centre. Family-run **Best Western Europa** (☎26240 22650; www.hoteleuropa.gr; Drouva 1; s/d €80/100; P❄@) perches on a hill above town and has gorgeous sweeping vistas from room balconies and the wonderful swimming pool.

Pitch your tent in the leafy grove at **Camping Diana** (☎26240 22314; www.camping-diana.gr; campsites per tent/adult €6/8;), 250m west of town.

There are no outstanding favourites among Olympia's ho-hum restaurants. Take your pick, or head to outer villages. **O Thea** (☎26240 23264; mains €6-11; ⊙dinner year-round, lunch May-Oct), 1.5km north in Floka, offers hearty taverna fare and terrace views. Call to ensure it's open outside high season.

Olympia Municipal Tourist Office (☎26240 22262; Praxitelous Kondyli; ⊙9am-3pm Mon-Fri May-Sep) has transport schedules.

Catch buses at the stop on the north end of town. Northbound buses go via Pyrgos (€2, 30 minutes), where you connect to buses for Athens, Corinth and Patra. Two buses go east from Olympia to Tripoli (€12, 2½ hours) – you must reserve ahead at **KTEL Pyrgos** (☎26210 20600; www.ktelileias.gr). Local trains run daily to Pyrgos (€1, 30 minutes).

CENTRAL GREECE
ΚΕΝΤΡΙΚΗ ΕΛΛΑΔΑ

This dramatic landscape of deep gorges, rugged mountains and fertile valleys is home to the magical stone pinnacle-topping monasteries of Meteora and the iconic ruins of ancient Delphi, where Alexander the Great sought advice from the Delphic oracle. Established in 1938, **Parnassos National Park** (www.routes.gr), to the north of Delphi, attracts naturalists, hikers (it's part of the E4 European long-distance path) and skiers.

Delphi Δελφοί

POP 2800

Modern Delphi and its adjoining ruins hang stunningly on the slopes of Mt Parnassos overlooking the shimmering Gulf of Corinth.

According to mythology, Zeus released two eagles at opposite ends of the world and they met here, thus making Delphi the centre of the world. By the 6th century BC, **Ancient Delphi** (☎22650 82312; www.culture.gr; site or museum €6, combined adult/concession

€9/5; ⌚8am-3pm; sometimes varies) had become the Sanctuary of Apollo. Thousands of pilgrims flocked here to consult the middle-aged female oracle who sat at the mouth of a fume-emitting chasm. After sacrificing a sheep or goat, pilgrims would ask a question, and a priest would translate the oracle's response into verse. Wars, voyages and business transactions were undertaken on the strength of these prophecies. From the entrance, take the **Sacred Way** up to the **Temple of Apollo**, where the oracle sat. From here the path continues to the well-preserved **theatre** and **stadium**.

Opposite the main site and down the hill some 100m, don't miss the **Sanctuary of Athena** and the much-photographed **Tholos**, a 4th-century-BC columned rotunda of Pentelic marble.

In the town centre, the welcoming **Hotel Hermes** (☎22650 82318; www.hermeshotel.com.gr; Vasileon Pavlou & Friderikis 27; s/d incl breakfast €40/50; ❄) has spacious rooms sporting balconies with excellent valley views. **Hotel Appolonia** (☎22650 82919; www.hotelapollonia.gr; Ifeigenias 37-39; s/d/tr incl breakfast €60/80/100; ❄@📶) is a bit more upmarket.

Apollon Camping (☎22650 82762; www.apolloncamping.gr; campsites per person/tent €8.50/4; P@📶🏊), 2km west of town, has great facilities, including restaurant, pool and minimarket.

Specialities at **Taverna Vakhos** (☎22650 83186; Apollonos 31; mains €6-17) include stuffed zucchini flowers and rabbit stew. Locals pack **Taverna Gargadouas** (☎22650 82488; Vasileon Pavlou & Friderikis; mains €6-10) for grilled meats and slow-roasted lamb.

The **bus station** (☎22660 82317), post office and banks are all on modern Delphi's main street, Vasileon Pavlou. Six buses a day go to Athens (€15.50, three hours). Take a bus to Lamia (€9.20, two hours, two daily) or Trikala (€14, 4½ hours, two daily) to transfer for Meteora.

Meteora Μετέωρα

Meteora (meh-*teh*-o-rah) should be a certified Wonder of the World with its magnificent late-14th-century monasteries perched dramatically atop enormous rocky pinnacles. Try not to miss it. The tranquil village of **Kastraki**, 2km from Kalambaka, is the best base for visiting.

While there were once monasteries on all 24 pinnacles, only six are still occupied:

> WORTH A TRIP
>
> ### PELION PENINSULA
>
> The **Pelion Peninsula**, a dramatic mountain range whose highest peak is Pourianos Stavros (1624m), was inhabited, according to mythology, by half-man and half-horse *kentavri* (centaurs). Today it is a verdant destination for trekkers. The largely inaccessible eastern flank consists of high cliffs that plunge into the sea. The gentler western flank coils round the Pagasitikos Gulf.

Megalou Meteorou (Grand Meteoron; ☎24320 22278; ⌚9am-5pm Wed-Mon Apr-Oct, to 4pm Thu-Mon Nov-Mar), **Varlaam** (☎24320 22277; ⌚9am-4pm Sat-Thu Apr-Oct, to 3pm Sat-Wed Nov-Mar), **Agiou Stefanou** (☎24320 22279; ⌚9am-1.30pm & 3.30-5.30pm Tue-Sun Apr-Oct, 9.30am-1pm & 3-5pm Nov-Mar), **Agias Triados** (Holy Trinity; ☎24320 22220; ⌚9am-5pm Fri-Wed Apr-Oct, 10am-3pm Nov-Mar), **Agiou Nikolaou Anapafsa** (☎24320 22375; ⌚9am-3.30pm Sat-Thu) and **Agias Varvaras Rousanou** (⌚9am-6pm Thu-Tue Apr-Oct, to 4pm Nov-Mar). Admission is €2 for each monastery and strict dress codes apply (no bare shoulders or knees and women must wear skirts; borrow a long skirt at the door if you don't have one). Walk the footpaths between monasteries, drive the back asphalt road, or take the bus (€1.20, 20 minutes) that departs from Kalambaka and Kastraki at 9am, and returns at 1pm.

Meteora's stunning rocks are also a climbing paradise. Licensed mountain guide **Lazaros Botelis** (☎694 804 3655, 24320 79165; meteora.guide@gmail.gr; Kastraki) and mountaineering instructor **Kostas Liolios** (☎69725 67582; ksds_liolios@yahoo.com; Kalambaka) show the way.

Sleeping & Eating

TOP CHOICE **Doupiani House** PENSION €
(☎24320 75326; www.doupianihouse.com; s/d/tr incl breakfast €40/50/60; P❄@📶) Gregarious hosts Thanassis and Toula Nakis offer this comfy home from which to explore or simply enjoy the panoramic views. Request a balcony room.

Vrachos Camping CAMPGROUND €
(☎24320 22293; www.campingmeteora.gr; campsites per tent/adult €9/free; 🏊) Great views, excellent facilities and a good taverna; a short stroll from Kastraki.

Taverna Paradisos TAVERNA €
(☎24320 22723; mains €6.50-9) Look for outstanding traditional meals with spectacular views.

Taverna Gardenia TAVERNA, PENSION €
(☎24320 22504; Kastrakiou St; mains €6-9; s/d/tr incl breakfast €35/45/55) Freshest Greek food served with aplomb and more splendid views. The owners also have good-value, spacious rooms.

Getting There & Around

Local buses shuttle between Kalambaka and Kastraki (€1.90). Hourly buses go from Kalambaka's **KTEL bus station** (☎24320 22432; Ikonomou) to the transport hub of Trikala (€2, 30 minutes), from where buses go to Ioannina (€13.10, three hours, two daily) and Athens (€27, 4½ hours, seven daily).

From Kalambaka **train station** (☎24320 22451), trains run to Athens (regular/IC €15/25, 5½/4½ hours, both twice daily) and Thessaloniki (€13, four hours, three daily).

NORTHERN GREECE
ΒΟΡΕΙΑ ΕΛΛΑΔΑ

Northern Greece is graced with magnificent mountains, thick forests, tranquil lakes and archaeological sites. It's easy to get off the beaten track and experience aspects of Greece noticeably different to other mainland areas and the islands.

Thessaloniki
Θεσσαλονίκη

POP 342,200

Dodge cherry sellers in the street, smell spices in the air and enjoy waterfront breezes in Thessaloniki (thess-ah-lo-*nee*-kih), also known as Salonica. The second city of Byzantium and of modern Greece boasts countless Byzantine churches, a smattering of Roman ruins, engaging museums, shopping to rival Athens, fine restaurants and a lively cafe scene and nightlife.

Sights & Activites

Check out the seafront **White Tower** (Lefkos Pyrgos; ☎231 026 7832; www.lpth.gr; ⊙8.30am-3pm Tue-Sun) and wander *hammams* (Turkish baths), Ottoman and Roman sites, and churches such as the enormous, 5th-century **Church of Agios Dimitrios** (☎231 027 0008; Agiou Dimitriou 97; ⊙8am-10pm).

The award-winning **Museum of Byzantine Culture** (☎231 330 6400; www.mbp.gr; Leoforos Stratou 2; admission €4; ⊙9am-4pm) beautifully displays splendid sculptures, mosaics, icons and other intriguing artefacts. The **Archaeological Museum** (☎231 083 0538; www.amth.gr; Manoli Andronikou 6; admission €6; ⊙10am-6pm Mon, 9am-6pm Tue-Sat, 9am-4pm Sun) showcases prehistoric, ancient Macedonian and Hellenistic finds.

The compelling **Thessaloniki Centre of Contemporary Art** (☎231 059 3270; www.cact.gr; Warehouse B1; ⊙10am-6pm Tue-Sat, 11am-3pm Sun) and hip **Thessaloniki Museum of Photography** (☎231 056 6716; www.thmphoto.gr; Warehouse A, Thessaloniki Port; admission €2; ⊙11am-7pm Tue-Sun), beside the port, are worth an hour.

Wonderfully seen on foot, Thessaloniki can also be zigzagged by **bus tour** (ticket €3; ⊙hourly 8am-9pm Jun-Sep, 9am-4pm Oct-May) leaving from the White Tower. Get information at the tourist office.

Sleeping

Steep discounts abound during summer; prices rise during conventions (listed at www.helexpo.gr).

Electra Palace Hotel LUXURY HOTEL €€€
(☎231 029 4000; www.electrahotels.gr; Plateia Aristotelous 9; d from €150; ❄@🛜🏊) Dive into five-star seafront pampering: impeccable service, plush rooms, a rooftop bar, indoor and outdoor swimming pools and a *hammam*.

Rent Rooms Thessaloniki HOSTEL €
(☎231 020 4080; www.rentrooms-thessaloniki.com; Konstantinou Melenikou 9, near Kamara; dm/s/d/tr/q incl breakfast €19/38/49/67/82; ❄🛜) Cheery, clean and modern, with a back-garden cafe looking onto the Rotunda. Communal breakfast-cafe nook and cheap bike hire add to the appeal. Some dorms/rooms have minikitchens, and all have bathrooms. Book ahead.

Hotel Orestias Kastorias HOTEL €
(☎231 027 6517; www.okhotel.gr; Agnostou Stratiotou 14; s/d/tr €37/46/58; ❄@🛜) A friendly favourite with cosy, clean rooms, renovated in 2011.

Thessaloniki

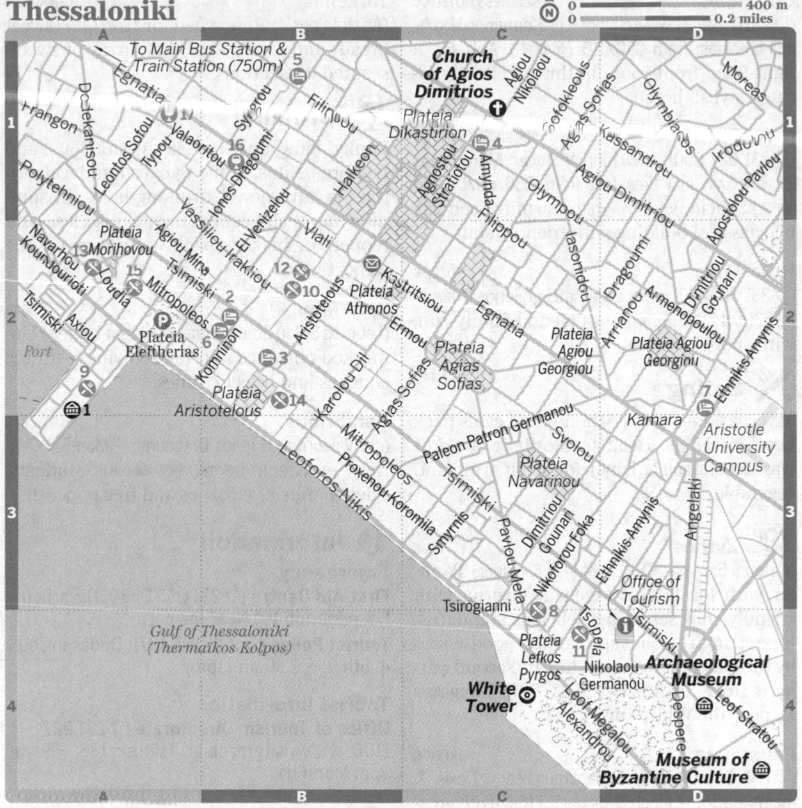

Thessaloniki

Top Sights
- Archaeological Museum D4
- Church of Agios Dimitrios C1
- Museum of Byzantine Culture D4
- White Tower C4

Sights
- 1 Thessaloniki Centre of Contemporary Art A2

Sleeping
- 2 City Hotel B2
- 3 Electra Palace Hotel B2
- 4 Hotel Orestias Kastorias C1
- 5 Hotel Pella B1
- 6 Hotel Tourist B2
- 7 Rent Rooms Thessaloniki D2

Eating
- 8 Dore Zythos C4
- 9 Kitchen Bar A2
- 10 Modiano Market B2
- 11 Myrsini C4
- 12 O Arhontis B2
- 13 Paparouna A2
- 14 Turkenlis B2
- 15 Zythos A2

Drinking
- 16 Gambrinus B1
- 17 Spiti Mou A1

City Hotel BUSINESS HOTEL €€
(☎2310269421; www.cityhotel.gr; Komninon 11; d/tr incl breakfast from €90/110; ❄@📶) Ask for a light-filled front room in this excellently located stylish hotel.

Hotel Tourist BUSINESS HOTEL €
(☎231 027 0501; www.touristhotel.gr; Mitropoleos 21; s/d/tr/q incl breakfast from €50/58/68/85; ❄@) Spacious rooms in a charming, central, neoclassical building with friendly staff.

Hotel Pella HOTEL €
(☎231 052 4221; www.pella-hotel.gr; Ionos Dragoumi 63; s/d €30/36; ❄📶) Quiet and family-run, with spotless rooms.

Eating

Tavernas dot Plateia Athonos and cafes pack Leoforos Nikis. Head to **Modiano Market** (Vassiliou Irakliou or Ermo) for fresh fruit and vegetables.

TOP CHOICE **Zythos** TAVERNA €
(Katouni 5; mains €8-12; ⏲lunch & dinner) Popular with locals, this excellent taverna with friendly staff serves up delicious standards, interesting regional specialities, good wines by the glass and beers on tap. Its second outlet is **Dore Zythos** (☎231 027 9010; Tsirogianni 7), near the White Tower.

Paparouna GREEK €
(☎231 051 0852; www.paparouna.com; Doxis 7; mains €8-16; ⏲lunch & dinner) This lively restaurant whips up inventive cuisine like chicken with peppermint and honey.

Myrsini CRETAN €
(☎231 022 8300; Tsopela 2; mains €8-12; ⏲Sep-Jun) Hearty portions of delicious Cretan dishes such as roast rabbit and *myzithropitakia* (flaky filo triangles with sweet sheep's-milk cheese).

Kitchen Bar INTERNATIONAL €
(☎231 050 2241; www.kitchenbar.com.gr; Warehouse B, Thessaloniki Port; mains €8-13; ⏲lunch & dinner) This perennial favourite offers both drinks and artfully prepared eclectic food, in a sumptuously decorated, renovated warehouse with waterfront tables.

O Arhontis STREET FOOD €
(Ermou 26; mains €5; ⏲11am-5pm) Eat delicious grilled sausages and potatoes off butcher's paper at this popular workers' eatery in Modiano Market.

Turkenlis BAKERY €
(Aristotelous 4) Renowned for *tzoureki* (sweet bread) and a mind-boggling array of sweet-scented confections.

Drinking

Funky bars line Plateia Aristotelous and Leoforos Nikis, while Syngrou and Valaoritou Sts have newer drinking holes. In summer many city-centre nightclubs close and reopen in bigger spaces outdoors, on the airport road.

Spiti Mou BAR
(Leontos Sofou 26, cnr Egnatia; ⏲1pm-late; 📶) Unmarked entrance and relaxed vibe, with big couches and eclectic tunes.

Gambrinus BAR
(cnr Valaoritou & Ionos Dragoumi; ⏲Mon-Sat) Variety of Czech beers, boisterous students, eclectic music, sausages and free popcorn.

Information

Emergency

First-Aid Centre (☎231 053 0530; Navarhou Koundourioti 10) Near the port.

Tourist Police (☎231 055 4871; Dodekanisou 4, 5th fl; ⏲7.30am-11pm)

Tourist Information

Office of Tourism Directorate (☎231 022 1100; www.visitgreece.gr; Tsimiski 136; ⏲9am-3pm Mon-Fri)

Getting There & Away

Air

Makedonia Airport (SKG; ☎231 047 3212; www.thessalonikiairport.com) is 16km southeast of the centre and served by local bus 78 (www.oasth.gr; €0.80, one hour, from 5am to 10pm). Taxis cost €12 (20 minutes).

Olympic Air, Aegean Airlines and **Astra Airlines** (☎231 048 9392; www.astra-airlines.gr) fly throughout Greece.

Boat

Weekly ferries go to, among others, Limnos (€22, eight hours), Lesvos (€32, 14 hours) and Chios (€35, 19 hours). **Karaharisis Travel & Shipping Agency** (☎231 052 4544; Navarhou Koundourioti 8) handles tickets.

Bus

The **main bus station** (☎231 059 5408; www.ktel-thes.gr; Monastiriou 319) services Athens (€42, 6¼ hours, 10 daily), Ioannina (€30, 4¾ hours, six daily) and other destinations. Buses to

WORTH A TRIP

HALKIDIKI ΧΑΛΚΙΔΙΚΗ

Beautiful pine-covered Halkidiki is a three-pronged peninsula that extends into the Aegean Sea, southeast of Thessaloniki. Splendid, if built-up, sandy beaches rim its 500km of coastline. The middle **Sithonian Peninsula** is most spectacular. With camping and rooms to rent, it is more suited to independent travellers than overdeveloped **Kassandra Peninsula**, although Kassandra has the summertime **Sani Jazz Festival** (www.sanifestival.gr). You'll need your own wheels to explore Halkidiki properly.

Halkidiki's third prong is occupied by the all-male Monastic Republic of **Mt Athos** (known in Greek as Agion Oros, the Holy Mountain), where 20 monasteries full of priceless treasures stand amid an impressive landscape of gorges, mountains and sea. Only men may visit, a permit is required and the summer waiting-list is long. Start months in advance by contacting the Thessaloniki-based **Mt Athos Pilgrims' Bureau** (☎231 025 2578; pilgrimsbureau@c-lab.gr; Egnatia 109; ⊙9am-1pm Mon-Fri, 10am-noon Sat).

the Halkidiki Peninsula leave from the **Halkidiki bus terminal** (☎231 031 6555; www.ktel-chalkidikis.gr; Karakasi 68).

At the time of writing, small bus companies, mostly across from the courthouse (Dikastirion), provided the only services to international destinations like Skopje, Sofia and Bucharest. Try **Simeonidis Tours** (☎231 054 0970; www.simeonidistours.gr; 26 Oktovriou 14). Train company OSE has run buses to Sofia and Tirana but service was in flux at the time of writing. Check at the office on the eastern side of the train station.

Train

The **train station** (☎231 059 9421; www.trainose.gr; Monastiriou) serves Athens (regular/IC €28/36, 6¾/5½ hours, seven/10 daily) but other lines like Alexandroupolis have been reduced, and all international trains were discontinued at the time of writing. Check schedules at the **train ticket office** (OSE; ☎231 059 8120; Aristotelous 18) or the station.

Alexandroupolis
Αλεξανδρούπολη

POP 59,900

Alexandroupolis (ah-lex-an-*dhroo*-po-lih) and nearby Komotini (ko-mo-tih-*nee*) enjoy lively student atmospheres that make for a satisfying stopover on the way to Turkey or Samothraki.

Waterfront **Hotel Bao Bab** (☎25510 34823; Alexandroupoli–Komotini Hwy; s/d/tr incl breakfast €40/50/60; P❄@), 1km west of town, has large, comfortable rooms and an excellent restaurant. Downtown, **Hotel Marianna** (☎25510 81456; Malgaron 11; s/d €40/50) has small, clean rooms.

Tuck into today's fresh catch at **Psarotaverna tis Kyra Dimitras** (☎25510 34434; cnr Kountourioti & Dikastirion; fish €6-11).

Alexandroupoli's cool nightspots change with the whims of its students. Leoforos Dimokratias has trendy bars; cafes line the waterfront.

The **municipal tourist office** (☎25510 64184; Leoforos Dimokratias 306; ⊙7.30am-3pm) is helpful.

ℹ Getting There & Away

AIR & BOAT Dimokritos Airport (☎25510 89300; www.alxd.gr), 7km east of town, is served by Olympic Air and Aegean Airlines. **Sever Travel** (☎25510 22555; sever1@otenet.gr; Megalou Alexandrou 24) handles ferry (to Samothraki and Limnos) and airline tickets.

BUS The **bus station** (☎25510 26479; Eleftheriou Venizelou 36) has departures to the following:

Athens (€64, 10 hours, one daily)

Thessaloniki (€30, 3¾ hours, nine daily)

İstanbul (Turkey; OSE bus €15, six hours, one daily Tue-Sun)

TRAIN At the time of writing, international trains were cancelled. Other schedules change. Check ahead at the **train station** (☎25510 26395; www.trainose.gr).

Athens (€50, 14 hours, one daily)

Thessaloniki (€9, seven hours, four daily)

Mt Olympus
Ολυμπος Ορος

Just as it did for the ancients, Greece's highest mountain, the cloud-covered lair of the Greek pantheon, fires the visitor's imagination today. The highest of Olympus' eight peaks is **Mytikas** (2917m), popular with trekkers, who use **Litohoro** (305m), 5km inland from the Athens–Thessaloniki highway, as their base. The main route up takes two days, with a stay overnight at one of the **refuges** (May-Oct). Good protective clothing is essential, even in summer. **EOS** (Greek Alpine Club; 23520 84544; Plateia Kentriki, Litohoro; Mon-Sat Jun-Sep) has information on treks.

From the **bus station** (23520 81271; Agiou Nikolaou, Litohoro) 13 buses daily go to Thessaloniki (€9, 1¼ hours) and three to Athens (€33, 5½ hours). Litohoro's **train station**, 9km away, gets 10 daily trains on the Athens–Volos–Thessaloniki line.

Xenonas Papanikolaou GUESTHOUSE €
(23520 81236; www.xenonas-papanikolaou.gr; Nikolaou Episkopou Kitrous 1; s/d incl breakfast €45/55; P❄@) This romantic guesthouse sits in a flowery garden up in the backstreets, a world away from tourist crowds.

Olympos Beach Camping CAMPGROUND €
(23520 22111; www.olympos-beach.gr; campsites per adult/tent €7/6, bungalows €45; Apr-Oct) Has a booming waterfront lounge and a pleasant beach.

TOP CHOICE **Gastrodromio En Olympio** GREEK €
(23520 21300; Plateia Eleftherias; mains €7-13; lunch & dinner) One of Greece's best country restaurants serves up specialities such as *soutzoukakia* (minced meat with cumin and mint) and delicious wild mushrooms with an impressive regional wine list and gorgeous Olympus views.

Ioannina Ιωάννινα

POP 64,500

Charming Ioannina (ih-o-*ah*-nih-nah) on the western shore of Lake Pamvotida at the foot of the Pindos Mountains, was a major intellectual centre during Ottoman rule. Today it's a thriving university town with a lively waterfront cafe scene.

Sights

Kastro NEIGHBOURHOOD
The narrow stone streets of the evocative old quarter sit on a small peninsula jutting into the lake. Within its impressive fortifications, **Its Kale**, an inner citadel with lovely grounds and lake views, is home to the splendid **Fetiye Cami** (Victory Mosque), built in 1611, and the gemlike **Byzantine Museum** (26510 25989; admission €3; 8am-5pm Tue-Sun).

Lake Pamvotida LAKE
The lake's serene *nisi* (island) shelters four **monasteries** among its trees. Frequent ferries (€2) leave from near Plateia Mavili.

Sleeping

TOP CHOICE **Filyra** BOUTIQUE HOTEL €
(26510 83560; http://hotelfilyra.gr; alley off Andronikou Paleologou 18; s/d €45/55; P❄) Five Old Town self-catering suites fill up fast. The affiliated **Traditional Hotel Dafni** (Ioustinianou 12; s/d/q €45/65/90) is built into the Kastro's outer walls.

Hotel Kastro PENSION €€
(26510 22866; www.hotelkastro.gr; Andronikou Paleologou 57; s/d incl breakfast €50/65; P❄) Ask for a high-ceilinged upstairs room at this quaint hotel, across from Its Kale.

Limnopoula Camping CAMPGROUND €
(26510 25265; Kanari 10; campsites per tent/adult €4/8; Apr-Oct) Tree-lined and splendidly set on the edge of the lake 2km northwest of town.

Eating & Drinking

Scores of cafes and restaurants line the waterfront. Enjoy a cold beer on a sunny day in Its Kale, at its exquisitely situated **cafe** (mains €4-8).

Sirios GREEK €
(26510 77070; www.seirioskouzina.gr; Patriarhou Evangelidi 1; mains €8-12; noon-11pm) An imaginative menu of decidedly delicious dishes, ranging from braised rooster to pork cutlets.

Taverna To Manteio TAVERNA €
(26510 25452; Plateia Georgiou 15; mains €7-8; lunch & dinner Tue-Sun) Join local families along the flower-filled Its Kale wall for deliciously simple *mezedhes*, salads and grills.

Ananta BAR
(cnr Anexartisias & Stoa Labei) Rock out in the shadows of the long bar.

Information

EOT (Tourist Office; 26510 41142; Dodonis 39; 7.30am-2.30pm Mon-Fri)

EOS (Greek Alpine Club; 26510 22138; Despotatou Ipirou 2; 7-9pm Mon-Fri)

Getting There & Away

AIR **Aegean Airlines** (☎26510 64444) and **Olympic Air** (☎26510 26518) fly to Athens. Slow buses ply the 2km road into town.

BUS The **station** (☎26510 26286; Georgiou Papandreou) is 300m north of Platela Dimokratias.

Athens (€40, 6½ hours, nine daily)
Igoumenitsa (€9.80, 1¼ hours, eight daily)
Thessaloniki (€32, 4¾ hours, six daily)
Trikala (€15.50, 2¼ hours, two daily)

Zagorohoria & Vikos Gorge
Τα Ζαγοροχώρια & Χαράδρα του Βικού

Do not miss the spectacular Zagori region, with its deep gorges, abundant wildlife, dense forests and snowcapped mountains. Some 46 charming villages, famous for their grey-slate architecture, and known collectively as the Zagorohoria, are sprinkled across a large expanse of the Pindos Mountains north of Ioannina. These beautifully restored gems were once only connected by stone paths and arching footbridges, but paved roads now wind between them. Get information on walks from Ioannina's EOT and EOS offices. Book ahead during high season (Christmas, Greek Easter and August); prices plummet in low season.

Tiny, carless **Dilofo** makes for a peaceful sojourn, especially if you lodge at excellent **Gaia** (☎26530 22570; www.gaia-dilofo.gr; s/d/tr incl breakfast from €60/70/80; 📶) or **Arhontiko Dilofo** (☎26530 22455; www.dilofo.com; d incl breakfast from €55; Ⓟ) and sup on the square at **Sopotseli** (☎26530 22629; mains €5-7).

Delightful **Monodendri**, known for its special pitta bread, is a popular departure point for treks through dramatic 12km-long, 900m-deep **Vikos Gorge**, with its sheer limestone walls. Get cosy at quaint **Archontiko Zarkada** (☎26530 71305; www.monodendri.com; s/d incl breakfast €40/60; Ⓟ), one of Greece's best-value small hotels.

Exquisite inns with attached tavernas abound in remote (but popular) twin villages **Megalo Papingo** and **Mikro Papingo**. Visit the **WWF Information Centre** (www.wwf.gr; Mikro Papingo; ⏰11am-5.30pm Fri-Wed) to learn about the area.

In Megalo Papingo, simple **Lakis** (☎26530 41087; d incl breakfast €35) is a *domatia* (B&B), taverna and store. Spectacular views and family-friendly studios add to the charms of **Papaevangelou** (☎26530 41135; www.hotelpapaevangelou.gr; d/studio incl breakfast from €75/120). Stylish **Tsoumani** (☎26530 41893; www.tsoumanisnikos.gr; d incl breakfast from €70; 📶) also serves some of the best food around. Two friendly brothers run charming **Xenonas tou Kouli** (☎26530 41115; d €60).

Hide away in Mikro Papingo's sweetly rustic **Xenonas Dias** (☎26530 41257; www.diaspapigo.gr; s/d incl breakfast €40/55) or fabulous, sumptuously minimalist **1700** (☎26530 41179; www.mikropapigo.gr; d from €80).

Infrequent buses run to Ioannina from Dilofo (€3.80, 40 minutes, three weekly), Monodendri (€3.60, one hour, three weekly) and the Papingos (€5.10, two hours, three weekly). It's best to explore by rental car from Ioannina; in a pinch take an (expensive) taxi.

Igoumenitsa
Ηγουμενίτσα

TRANSPORT HUB

POP 9160

Though tucked beneath verdant hills and lying on the sea, this characterless port is little more than a ferry hub: keep moving.

If you must stay over, look for *domatia* signs or opt for the most modern: **Angelika Pallas Hotel** (☎26650 26100; www.angelikapallas.gr; Agion Apostolon 145; s/d/tr incl breakfast from €60/70/90; ❄📶) across from the Corfu ferry terminal. It also has a restaurant.

The **bus station** (☎26650 22309) services Ioannina (€9.80, 2½ hours, nine daily) and Athens (€15, eight hours, five daily).

Several companies operate 90-minute **ferries to Corfu** (☎26650 99460; person/car €10/40; ⏰hourly) and hydrofoils in summer. International ferries go to the Italian ports of Ancona, Bari, Brindisi and Venice. Ticket agencies line the port. Book ahead for car tickets or sleeping cabins.

SARONIC GULF ISLANDS
ΝΗΣΙΑ ΤΟΥ ΣΑΡΩΝΙΚΟΥ

Scattered about the Saronic Gulf, these islands are within easy reach of Athens. The Saronics are named after the mythical King Saron of Argos, a keen hunter who drowned while chasing a deer that had swum into the gulf to escape.

You can either island-hop through the group then return to Piraeus, or carry on to the Peloponnese from any of the islands mentioned.

HELLENIC WILDLIFE HOSPITAL

While some Greeks may not appear too environmentally minded, others are making a sterling effort to face the country's ecological problems head-on. The **Hellenic Wildlife Hospital** (22970 28367; www.ekpaz.gr; by appointment) on the Saronic Gulf island of Aegina is one such place. As the oldest and largest wildlife rehabilitation centre in southern Europe, it tackles damage caused to wild birds and animals from hunting and pollution, and runs projects such as the release of raptors into the wilds of Crete and Northern Greece. You can visit the centre for free, though donations are appreciated. Better yet, the centre welcomes volunteers and accommodation is supplied.

Aegina Αίγινα

POP 14,500

Once a major player in the Hellenic world, thanks to its strategic position at the mouth of the gulf, Aegina (*eh*-yee-nah) now enjoys its position as Greece's premier producer of pistachios. Pick up a bag before you leave!

Bustling **Aegina Town**, on the west coast, is the island's capital and main port. There is no official tourist office, but information can be gleaned at www.aeginagreece.com.

The impressive **Temple of Aphaia** (adult/under 18yr €4/free; 8am-6.30pm) is a well-preserved Doric temple 12km east of Aegina Town. It's said to have served as a model for the construction of the Parthenon. Standing on a pine-clad hill with imposing views out over the gulf, it is well worth a visit. Buses from Aegina Town to the small resort of Agia Marina can drop you at the site.

In Aegina Town, **Hotel Rastoni** (22970 27039; www.rastoni.gr; d/tr incl breakfast €90/120; P ❄ @), a boutique hotel with excellent service, gets a big thumbs up for its quiet location, spacious rooms and lovely garden. **Electra Pension** (22970 26715; www.aegina-electra.gr; s/d €45/50; ❄) is in a quiet corner of town with rooms that are impeccable and comfy.

A flotilla of ferries (€9.50, 70 minutes) and hydrofoils (€13.50, 40 minutes) ply the waters between Aegina and Piraeus with great regularity. You can head back to Piraeus, carry on through the Saronic Gulf Islands or take a boat to Methana (€5.70, 40 minutes) on the Peloponnese. There is a good public bus service on the island.

Poros Πόρος

POP 5250

Only a few hundred metres from the village of Galatas on the shores of the mountainous Peloponnese, Poros is an attractive island with a friendly feel that is worth the effort. **Poros Town**, on the island's southern coast, is a haven for yachties, and with boats from all over tied up along the waterfront, there is a happy mood in the air.

Seven Brothers Hotel (22980 23412; www.7brothers.gr; s/d/tr €55/65/75; ❄) is conveniently close to the hydrofoil dock. This modern hotel has bright, comfy rooms with balconies and impressive bathrooms.

There is no tourist office, but also no shortage of businesses hoping to sell you your onward ticket. Hit www.poros.gr for extensive information.

There are ferry (€12.80, 2½ hours) and hydrofoil (€22.20, one hour) services daily between Poros and Piraeus. The ferries go via Aegina (€8.30, 1¼ hours), while the hydrofoils go direct. Many of the outbound boats head on to Hydra and Spetses. Small boats shuttle back and forth between Poros and Galatas (€1, five minutes) on the Peloponnese.

Hydra Υδρα

POP 2900

The catwalk queen of the Saronics, Hydra (*ee*-drah) is a delight. On the northern side of this sparsely populated island, **Hydra Town** has a picturesque horseshoe-shaped harbour with gracious white and pastel stone mansions stacked up the rocky hillsides that surround it. The island is known as a retreat for artists, writers and celebrities, and wears its celebrity with panache.

A major attraction is Hydra's tranquillity. Forget noisy motorbikes keeping you awake half the night! There are no motorised vehicles – apart from sanitation trucks – and the main forms of transport are foot and donkey.

Pension Erofili (22980 54049; www.pensionerofili.gr; Tombazi; s/d/tr €45/55/65; ❄), tucked away in the inner town, has clean, comfortable rooms, an attractive courtyard and breakfast features home-made preserves and jams. The owners add a friendly sparkle. **Hotel Miranda** (☎22980 52230; www.mirandahotel.gr; Miaouli; s/d incl breakfast €120/140; ❄) is worth a splurge. Originally built in 1810 as the mansion of a wealthy Hydriot sea captain, this stylish place retains much of its historical character and is a National Heritage building.

There is no tourist office, but check out www.hydra.com.gr for detailed information.

High-speed boat services (€25.50, 1½ hours) connect Hydra with Piraeus seven times daily. There are also services to Ermioni and Porto Heli on the Peloponnese mainland, inbound boats to Poros and outbound boats to Spetses.

Spetses Σπέτσες

POP 4400

Spetses is an appealing island that is packed with visitors in summer. Its attractiveness is largely thanks to Spetses-born philanthropist Sotirios Anargyrios, who made a fortune in the US after emigrating in 1848. Anargyrios returned in 1914, bought two-thirds of the then-barren island, planted Aleppo pines, financed the island's road system and commissioned many of the town's grandest buildings.

Spetses Town, the main port, sprawls along half the northeast coast of the island.

Opposite the small town beach to the east of the ferry quay, **Villa Marina** (☎22980 72646; www.villamarinaspetses.com; s/d €55/65; ❄) is a convenient, welcoming place with tidy rooms. Ask for a sea view.

There is no tourist office. See the website www.spetsesdirect.com for more information.

High-speed boats head regularly to Piraeus (€35, 2¼ hours). Another option is to carry on to the Peloponnese mainland on boats to Ermioni (€7.50, 30 minutes) or Porto Heli (€5.50, 15 minutes).

CYCLADES ΚΥΚΛΑΔΕΣ

The Cyclades (kih-*klah*-dez) are Greek islands to dream about. Named after the rough *kyklos* (circle) they form around the island of Delos, they are rugged outcrops of rock in the azure Aegean, speckled with white cubist buildings and blue-domed Byzantine churches. Throw in sun-blasted golden beaches, more than a dash of hedonism and a fascinating culture, and it's easy to see why many find the Cyclades irresistible.

Some of the islands, such as Mykonos, Ios and Santorini, have seized tourism with great enthusiasm. Prepare to battle the crowds if you turn up at the height of summer. Others are little more than clumps of rock, with a village, secluded coves and a few curious tourists. Ferry services rarely run in winter, while from July to September the Cyclades are vulnerable to the *meltemi,* a fierce northeasterly wind that can play havoc with ferry schedules.

History

Said to have been inhabited since at least 7000 BC, the Cyclades enjoyed a flourishing Bronze Age civilisation (3000–1100 BC), more or less concurrent with the Minoan civilisation. From the 4th century AD, the islands, like the rest of Greece, suffered a series of invasions and occupations. The Turks turned up in 1537 but neglected the Cyclades to the extent that they became backwaters prone to raids by pirates – hence the labyrinthine character of their towns, which was meant to confuse attackers. On some islands the whole population moved into the mountainous interior to escape the pirates, while on others they braved it out on the coast. Consequently, the *hora* (main town) is on the coast on some islands, while on others it is inland.

The Cyclades became part of independent Greece in 1827. During WWII they were occupied by the Italians. Before the revival of the islands' fortunes by the tourist boom that began in the 1970s, many islanders lived in poverty and many more headed for the mainland or emigrated to America or Australia in search of work.

Mykonos Μύκονος

POP 8000

Sophisticated Mykonos glitters happily under the Aegean sun, shamelessly surviving on tourism. The island has something for everyone, with marvellous beaches, romantic sunsets, chic boutiques, excellent restaurants and bars, and its long-held reputation as a mecca for gay travellers. The maze of white-walled streets in Mykonos Town was designed to confuse pirates, and it certainly manages to captivate and confuse the crowds that consume the island's capital in summer.

Mykonos

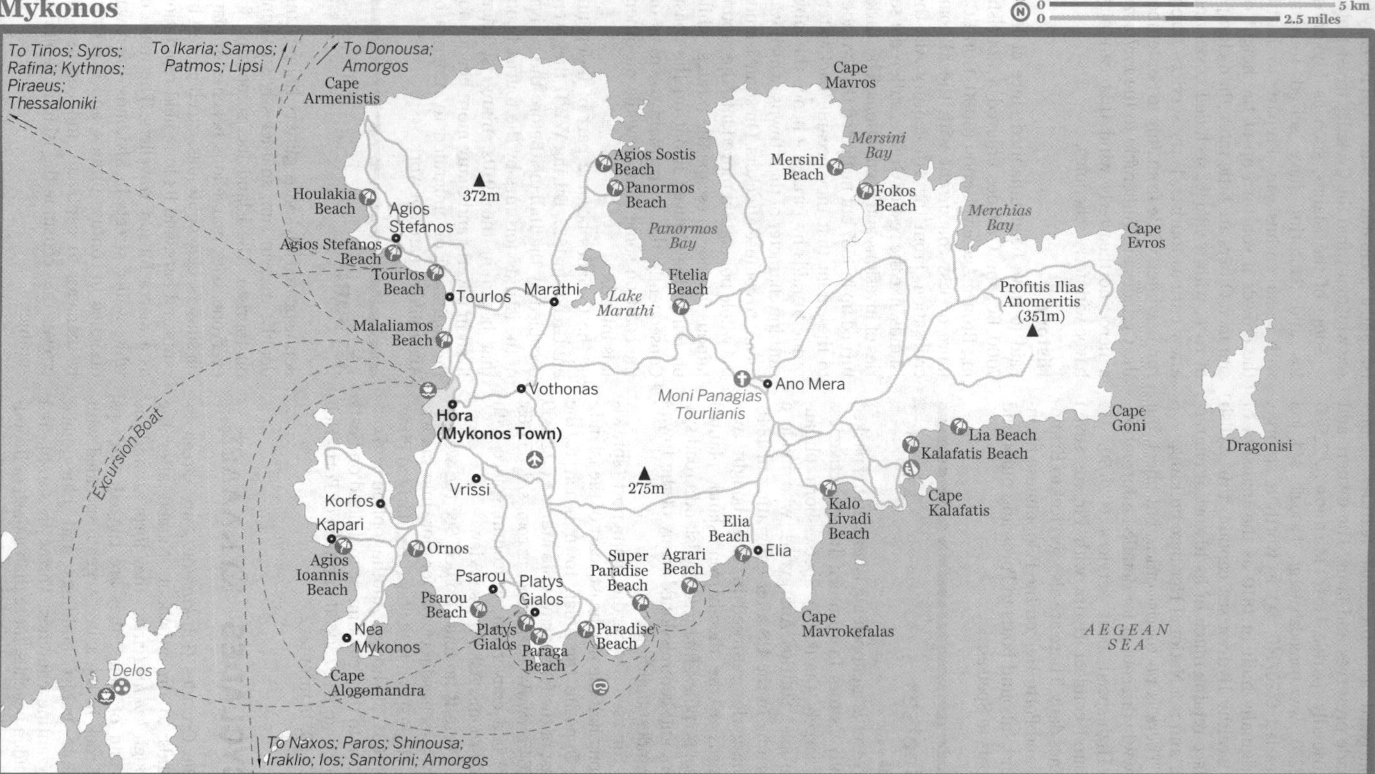
0 5 km
0 2.5 miles
To Tinos; Syros; Rafina; Kythnos; Piraeus; Thessaloniki
To Ikaria; Samos; Patmos; Lipsi
To Donousa; Amorgos
Cape Armenistis
Cape Mavros
Mersini Bay
Mersini Beach
Fokos Beach
Merchias Bay
Cape Evros
Agios Sostis Beach
Panormos Beach
Panormos Bay
Houlakia Beach
372m
Agios Stefanos
Agios Stefanos Beach
Tourlos Beach
Tourlos
Marathi
Lake Marathi
Ftelia Beach
Profitis Ilias Anomeritis (351m)
Malaliamos Beach
Vothonas
Moni Panagias Tourlianis
Ano Mera
Hora (Mykonos Town)
Excursion Boat
Cape Goni
Lia Beach
Kalafatis Beach
Dragonisi
Vrissi
275m
Cape Kalafatis
Korfos
Kapari
Kalo Livadi Beach
Elia Beach
Elia
Agios Ioannis Beach
Ornos
Super Paradise Beach
Agrari Beach
Psarou
Platys Gialos
Psarou Beach
Platys Gialos
Paradise Beach
Paraga Beach
Cape Mavrokefalas
Nea Mykonos
AEGEAN SEA
Delos
Cape Alogomandra
To Naxos; Paros; Shinousa; Iraklio; Ios; Santorini; Amorgos

Sights & Activities

Mykonos Town NEIGHBOURHOOD

A stroll around Mykonos Town, shuffling through snaking streets with blinding white walls and balconies of flowers is a must for any visitor. This is the centre of the action on the island. **Little Venice**, where the sea laps up to the edge of the restaurants and bars, and Mykonos' famous hilltop row of **windmills** should be included in the spots-to-see list. You're bound to run into one of Mykonos' famous resident pelicans on your walk.

Beaches

The island's most popular beaches are on the southern coast. **Platys Gialos** has wall-to-wall sun lounges, while nudity is not uncommon at **Paradise Beach**, **Super Paradise**, **Agrari** and gay-friendly **Elia**.

Sleeping

Rooms in Mykonos Town fill up quickly in high season; book ahead. Prices mentioned are for the peak season – they plummet further than on most islands outside of July and August.

Mykonos has two camping areas, both on the south coast. Minibuses from both meet the ferries, and buses go regularly into town.

TOP CHOICE **Carbonaki Hotel** BOUTIQUE HOTEL €€€

(www.carbonaki.gr; 23 Panahrantou; s/d/tr/q €140/168/210/240;) This family-run place on the edge of the old town has bright and comfortable rooms dotted around a sunny central courtyard. Throw in a Jacuzzi, sauna and delightful ambiance and this is a top place to stay.

Hotel Philippi HOTEL €€

(22890 22294; www.philippihotel.com; 25 Kalogera, Mykonos Town; s €60-90, d €75-120;) In the heart of the *hora*, Philippi, one of Mykonos' few affordable options, has spacious and clean rooms that open onto a railed veranda overlooking a lush garden. An extremely peaceful, pleasant place to stay. Free wi-fi.

Hotel Lefteris HOTEL €€

(22890 23128; www.lefterishotel.gr; 9 Apollonas, Mykonos Town; s/d €99/129, studios €239-279;) Tucked away just up from Plateia Taxi (Taxi Sq), Lefteris has bright, comfy rooms, and a relaxing sun terrace with superb views over town. A good international meeting place.

CYCLADIC CONNECTIONS

For planning purposes, it's worth noting that once the season kicks in, a batch of companies run daily catamarans and ferries up and down the Cyclades. You can start from Piraeus (for Athens), Iraklio on Crete, or just about anywhere in-between.

One boat heads south daily from Piraeus to Paros, Naxos, Ios and Santorini, returning along the same route. There's also a daily run from Piraeus to Syros, Tinos and Mykonos.

Heading north from Iraklio, another catamaran runs to Santorini, Ios, Paros, Mykonos and return.

If it all get a bits much to comprehend (the schedules are constantly changing!), check the online guide **Open Seas** (www.openseas.gr).

Island-hopping through the Cyclades from Piraeus to Crete (or vice-versa) is getting easier and easier – though ease of travel means there are more people out there doing it!

Paradise Beach Camping CAMPGROUND €

(22890 22852; www.paradisemykonos.com; campsites per tent/person €5/10;) There are lots of options here on the south coast of the island, including camping, beach cabins and apartments, as well as bars, a swimming pool, games etc. It is skin-to-skin mayhem in summer with a real party atmosphere. The website has it all.

Eating

There is no shortage of places to eat and drink in Mykonos Town. Cheap eateries are found around Plateia Taxi and the southern bus station. Restaurants offering abundant seafood abound in Little Venice and towards the Delos excursion boats. Mykonos' top touts are its two resident pelicans, who wander the restaurants looking for handouts, often with visitors following them.

Fato a Mano MEDITERRANEAN €

(Plateia Meletopoulou; mains €8-15) In the middle of the maze, this place is worth taking the effort to find. It serves up tasty Mediterranean and traditional Greek dishes with pride.

WORTH A TRIP

DELOS ΔΗΛΟΣ

Southwest of Mykonos, the island of **Delos** (sites & museum €5; ⏲8.30am-3pm Tue-Sun) is the Cyclades' archaeological jewel. The opportunity to clamber among the ruins shouldn't be missed.

According to mythology, Delos was the birthplace of Apollo – the god of light, poetry, music, healing and prophecy. The island flourished as an important religious and commercial centre from the 3rd millennium BC, reaching its apex of power in the 5th century BC.

Ruins include the **Sanctuary of Apollo**, containing temples dedicated to him, and the **Terrace of the Lions**. These proud beasts were carved in the early 6th century BC using marble from Naxos to guard the sacred area. The original lions are in the island's **museum**, with replicas on the original site. The **Sacred Lake** (dry since 1926) is where Leto supposedly gave birth to Apollo, while the **Theatre Quarter** is where private houses were built around the **Theatre of Delos**.

The climb up **Mt Kynthos** (113m), the island's highest point, is a highlight. The view of Delos and the surrounding islands is spectacular, and it's easy to see how the Cyclades got their name.

Take a sunhat, sunscreen and sturdy footwear. The island's cafeteria sells food and drinks. Staying overnight on Delos is forbidden.

Numerous boat companies offer trips from Mykonos to Delos (€18 return, 30 minutes) between 9am and 1pm. The return boats leave Delos between noon and 3pm. There is also a €5 per person entry fee on arrival at Delos.

Katerina's GREEK €€
(Agion Anargyron; mains €11-25) Long a legendary bar in Little Venice with breath-taking views out over the water, Katerina's has added an excellent restaurant offering up Greek dishes. The seafood is superb.

Drinking & Entertainment

The waterfront is perfect for sitting with a drink and watching an interesting array of passers-by, while Little Venice has bars with dreamy views and water lapping below your feet.

Long feted as a gay travel destination, there are many gay-centric clubs and hangouts. The waterfront area, between the Old Harbour and the Church of Paraportiani, is popular for late night gay interaction.

Cavo Paradiso CLUB
(☎22890 27205; www.cavoparadiso.gr) For those who want to go the whole hog, this place 300m above Paradise Beach picks up around 2am and boasts a pool the shape of Mykonos. A bus transports clubbers from town in summer.

Information

Mykonos Accommodation Centre (☎22890 23408; www.mykonos-accommodation.com; Enoplon Dynameon 10) This helpful place can do it all, from arranging hotels to tours.

Hoteliers Association of Mykonos (☎22890 24540; www.mha.gr; ⏲9.30am-4pm Apr-Oct) At the old port; can book accommodation. They also have a desk at the airport.

Island Mykonos Travel (☎22890 22232; www.discovergreece.org) On Plateia Taxi, where the port road meets the town; helpful for travel information, hotels, transfers and tickets.

Getting There & Around

Mykonos Town has two ferry quays. The old quay, where the smaller ferries and catamarans dock, is 400m north of the town waterfront. The new quay, where the bigger boats dock, is 2.5km north of town. Buses meet arriving ferries. When leaving Mykonos, double-check which quay your boat leaves from.

Air

There are daily flights connecting Mykonos airport (JMK) to Athens, plus a growing number of international flights winging in directly from May to September. Don't just assume you'll have to fly through Athens to get to Mykonos. The airport is 3km southeast of the town centre; €1.60 by bus from the southern bus station.

Boat

Daily ferries (€32, five hours) and catamarans (€50, three hours) arrive from Piraeus. From Mykonos, there are daily ferries and hydrofoils to most major Cycladic islands, daily services to Crete, and less-frequent services to the northeastern Aegean Islands and the Dodecanese.

Bus

The northern bus station is near the old port. It serves Agios Stefanos, Elia, Kalafatis and Ano Mera. The southern bus station, a 300m walk up from the windmills, serves the airport, Agios Ioannis, Psarou, Platys Gialos and Paradise Beach.

Local Boats

In summer, *caiques* (small fishing boats) from Mykonos Town and Platys Gialos putter to Paradise, Super Paradise, Agrari and Elia beaches.

Paros Πάρος

POP 13,000

Paros is an attractive, laid-back island with an enticing main town, good swimming beaches and terraced hills that build up to Mt Profitis Ilias (770m). It has long been prosperous, thanks to an abundance of pure white marble (from which the *Venus de Milo* and Napoleon's tomb were sculpted).

Paros' main town and port is **Parikia**, on the west coast. Opposite the ferry terminal, on the far side of Windmill roundabout, is Plateia Mavrogenous, the main square. Agora, also known as Market St, the main commercial thoroughfare, runs southwest from the far end of the square.

Sights

Panagia Ekatondapyliani CHURCH
(Parikia; ⌚7.30am-9.30pm) Dating from AD 326 and known for its beautiful ornate interior, this is one of the most impressive churches in the Cyclades. Within the church compound, the **Byzantine Museum** (admission €1.50; ⌚9.30am-2pm & 6-9pm) has an interesting collection of icons and artefacts.

Activities

A great option on Paros is to rent a scooter or car at one of the many outlets in Parikia and cruise around the island. There are sealed

Paros & Antiparos

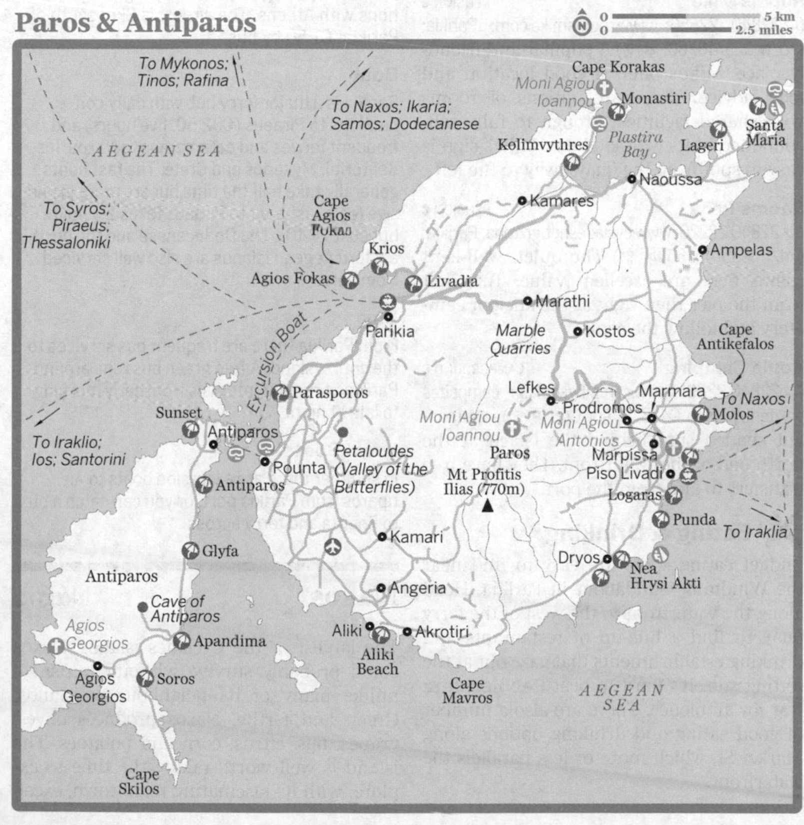

roads the whole way, and the opportunity to explore villages such as **Naoussa**, **Marpissa** and **Aliki**, and swim at beaches such as **Logaras**, **Punda** and **Golden Beach**. Naoussa is a cute little fishing village on the northeastern coast that is all geared up to welcome tourists.

Less than 2km from Paros, the small island of **Antiparos** has fantastic beaches, which have made it wildly popular. Another attraction is its **Cave of Antiparos** (admission €3.60; ⏲10.45am-3.45pm summer), considered to be one of Europe's best.

Sleeping

TOP CHOICE **Pension Sofia** PENSION €€
(☎22840 22085; www.sofiapension-paros.com; Parikia; d/tr €75/90; P ❄ @ ☜) If you don't mind a stroll to town, this place, with a beautifully tended garden and immaculate rooms, is a great option that won't be regretted. It's run with pride and passion.

Rooms Mike PENSION €
(☎22840 22856; www.roomsmike.com; Parikia; s/d/tr €25/40/60; ❄ ☜) A popular and friendly place, Mike's offers a good location and local advice. There are options of rooms with shared facilities through to fully self-contained units with kitchens. Mike's sign is easy to spot from the quay, away to the left.

Rooms Rena PENSION €
(☎22840 22220; www.cycladesnet.gr/rena; Parikia; s/d/tr €35/45/55; ❄ ☜) The quiet, well-kept rooms here are excellent value. Turn left from the pier then right at the ancient cemetery and follow the signs.

Koula Camping CAMPGROUND €
(☎22840 22801; www.campingkoula.gr; campsites per tent/person €4/8; ⏲Apr-Oct; P ☜) A pleasant shaded spot behind the beach at the north end of the waterfront. They have free transfers to and from the port.

Eating & Drinking

Budget eating spots are easy to find near the Windmill roundabout in Parikia. Head along the waterfront to the west of the ferry quay to find a line-up of restaurants and drinking establishments that gaze out at the setting sun. It's hard to beat **Pebbles Jazz Bar** for ambience. There are also a number of good eating and drinking options along Market St, which more or less parallels the waterfront.

Happy Green Cows VEGETARIAN €€
(dishes €12-18; ⏲dinner; ✎) Cheerful service goes with the quirky name of this little eatery, a vegetarian's delight at the back of the main square. It's a touch pricey, but worth it for the often saucily named dishes.

Levantis GREEK €€
(Kastro; dishes €11-19) A courtyard garden setting enhances the experience at this long-established restaurant at the heart of Kastro that serves excellent house wine.

Information

There is no tourist office. See www.parosweb.com for information.

Santorineos Travel (☎22840 24245; www.traveltoparos.gr) On the waterfront near the Windmill roundabout; good for ticketing, information and luggage storage.

Getting There & Around

Air

Paros' airport (PAS) has daily flight connections with Athens. The airport is 8km south of Parikia; €1.50 by bus.

Boat

Parikia is a major ferry hub with daily connections to Piraeus (€32.50, five hours) and frequent ferries and catamarans to Naxos, Ios, Santorini, Mykonos and Crete. The fast boats generally take half the time but are more expensive (eg a fast boat to Piraeus takes 2½ hours but costs €40). The Dodecanese and the northeastern Aegean Islands are also well serviced from here.

Bus

From Parikia there are frequent bus services to the entire island. A free green bus runs around Parikia at regular intervals from early morning to late at night.

Local Boats

In summer there are excursion boats to Antiparos from Parikia port, or you can catch a bus to Pounta and ferry across.

Naxos Νάξος

POP 12,000

The largest of the Cyclades islands, Naxos could probably survive without tourism – unlike many of its neighbouring islands. Green and fertile, Naxos produces olives, grapes, figs, citrus, corn and potatoes. The island is well worth taking the time to explore, with its fascinating main town, excel-

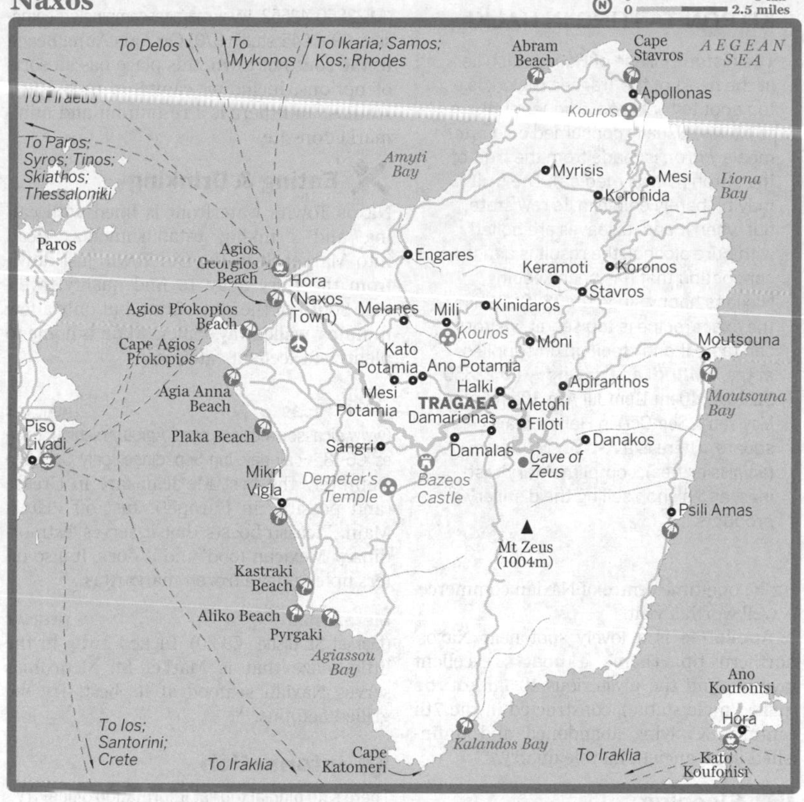

lent beaches, remote villages and striking interior.

Naxos Town, on the west coast, is the island's capital and port. The ferry quay is at the northern end of the waterfront, with the bus terminal out front. The island of Paros seems surprisingly close, directly to the west.

Sights & Activities

Kastro CASTLE

Behind the waterfront in Naxos Town, narrow alleyways scramble up to the spectacular hilltop 13th-century *kastro,* where the Venetian Catholics lived. The *kastro* looks out over the town, and has a well-stocked **archaeological museum** (admission €3; ⌚8.30am-3pm Tue-Sun).

Temple of Apollo ARCHAEOLOGICAL SITE

From the ferry quay it's a short stroll to the unfinished Temple of Apollo, Naxos' most famous landmark. Though there's not much to see other than two columns with a crowning lintel, people gather at sunset for views back to the whitewashed houses of town.

Beaches

The popular beach of **Agios Georgios** is just a 10-minute walk south from the main waterfront. Beyond it, wonderful sandy beaches stretch as far south as **Pyrgaki Beach. Agia Anna Beach**, 6km from town, and **Plaka Beach** are lined with accommodation and packed in summer.

Villages

A hire car or scooter will help reveal Naxos' dramatic and rugged landscape. The **Tragaea** region has tranquil villages, churches atop rocky crags and huge olive groves. **Filoti**, the largest inland settlement, perches on the slopes of **Mt Zeus** (1004m), the highest peak in the Cyclades. The historic village of

DON'T MISS

KITRON-TASTING IN HALKI

The historic village of Halki, which lies at the heart of the Tragaea region, is a top spot to try *kitron*, a liqueur unique to Naxos. Usually consumed cold after meals, *kitron* is made from the fruit of the citron *(Citrus medica)*. The fruit may be barely edible in its raw state, but when it and its leaves are boiled with pure alcohol, the result is a tasty concoction that has been keeping Naxians happy since the 1870s. While the exact recipe is top secret, visitors can taste it and stock up on supplies at the **Vallindras Distillery** (☎22850 31220; ⏰10am-11pm Jul-Aug, 10am-6pm May-Jun & Sep-Oct) in Halki's main square. There is a **Kitron Museum** (admission free), complimentary tastings, and a shop selling the distillery's products.

Halki, one-time centre of Naxian commerce, is well worth a visit.

Apollonas is a lovely spot near Naxos' northern tip. There's a **beach**, excellent taverna, and the mysterious 10.5m **kouros** (naked male statue), constructed in the 7th century BC, lying abandoned and unfinished in an ancient marble quarry.

Sleeping

TOP CHOICE **Pension Sofi** PENSION €

(☎22850 23077; www.pensionsofi.gr; r €30-90; ⏰year-round; ❄📶) Run by members of the Koufopoulos family, Pension Sofi is in Naxos Town, while their **Studios Panos** (☎22850 26078; www.studiospanos.com; Agios Georgios Beach; r €30-75; ❄📶) is a 10-minute walk away near Agios Georgios Beach. Guests are met with family-made wine, and immaculate rooms come with bathroom and kitchen. Rates at both places halve out of the high season. Call ahead for pick-up at the port.

Hotel Grotta HOTEL €€

(☎22850 22215; www.hotelgrotta.gr; s/d incl breakfast €70/85; P❄@📶🏊) Overlooking Grotta Beach at the northern end of town, this modern hotel has comfortable and immaculate rooms, a Jacuzzi and minipool, and offers great sea views.

Camping Maragas CAMPGROUND €

(☎22850 42552; www.maragascamping.gr; campsites €9, d €45, studio €70) On Agia Anna Beach to the south of town, this place has all sorts of options, including camping, rooms and studios, and there is a restaurant and minimarket on-site.

Eating & Drinking

Naxos Town's waterfront is lined with eating and drinking establishments. Head into Market St in the Old Town, just down from the ferry quay, to find quality tavernas. South of the waterfront, but only a few minutes' walk away, Plateia Main is home to plenty of excellent eateries.

TOP CHOICE **Picasso** MEXICAN €

(www.picassoismexican.com; Agiou Arseniou; dishes €6-18; ⏰all day Jun-Sep, dinner only Oct-May) Definitely the best Mexican fare in Greece (and possibly in Europe!). Just off Plateia Main, Picasso boasts that it serves 'extraordinary Mexican food' and it does. It also offers up exquisite frozen margaritas.

Metaximas TAVERNA €

(Market St; dishes €8-20) Tucked away in the little maze that is Market St, Metaximas serves Naxian seafood at its best. Try the grilled octopus.

Information

There's no official tourist information office. Try www.naxos-greece.net for more information.

Zas Travel (☎22850 23330; www.zastravel.com) Good for boat and air tickets, car rental, internet and luggage storage.

Getting There & Around

AIR Naxos airport (JNX) has daily flight connections with Athens. The airport is 3km south of town; no buses – a taxi costs €15.

BOAT There are daily ferries (€31, five hours) and catamarans (€48, 3¾ hours) from Naxos to Piraeus, and good ferry and hydrofoil connections to most Cycladic islands and Crete.

BUS Buses travel to most villages regularly from the bus terminal in front of the port.

CAR & MOTORCYCLE Having your own wheels is a good option on Naxos. Car and motorcycle rentals are readily available in Naxos Town.

Ios Ιος

POP 1900

Ios has long held a reputation as 'Party Island'. There are wall-to wall bars and nightclubs in 'the village' that thump all night, and fantastic fun facilities at Milopotas Beach that entertain all day. You won't leave disappointed if you're there to party.

But there's more to Ios than just hedonistic activities. British poet and novelist Lawrence Durrell thought highly of Ios as a place of poetry and beauty, and there is an enduring claim that Homer was buried here, with his alleged tomb in the north of the island.

Ios' three population centres are close together on the west coast. Ormos is the port, where ferries arrive. Two kilometres inland and up overlooking the port is 'the village', Hora, while 2km down from Hora to the southeast is Milopotas Beach.

Sights & Activities

The village has an intrinsic charm with its labyrinth of white-walled streets, and it's very easy to get lost, even if you haven't had one too many. Milopotas has everything a resort beach could ask for and parties hard. A rental car or scooter is a good option for exploring Ios.

Skarkos ARCHAEOLOGICAL SITE

('The Snail'; ⌚8.30am-3pm Tue-Sun) An award-winning archaeological triumph for Ios! This Bronze Age settlement crowns a low hill in the plain just to the north of Hora, and its excavations have been opened to the public. There are interpretation boards in Greek and English.

Manganari Beach BEACH

This isolated beach on the south coast is reached by rental vehicle, or by excursion boat or bus in summer. It's a beautiful spot

Ios

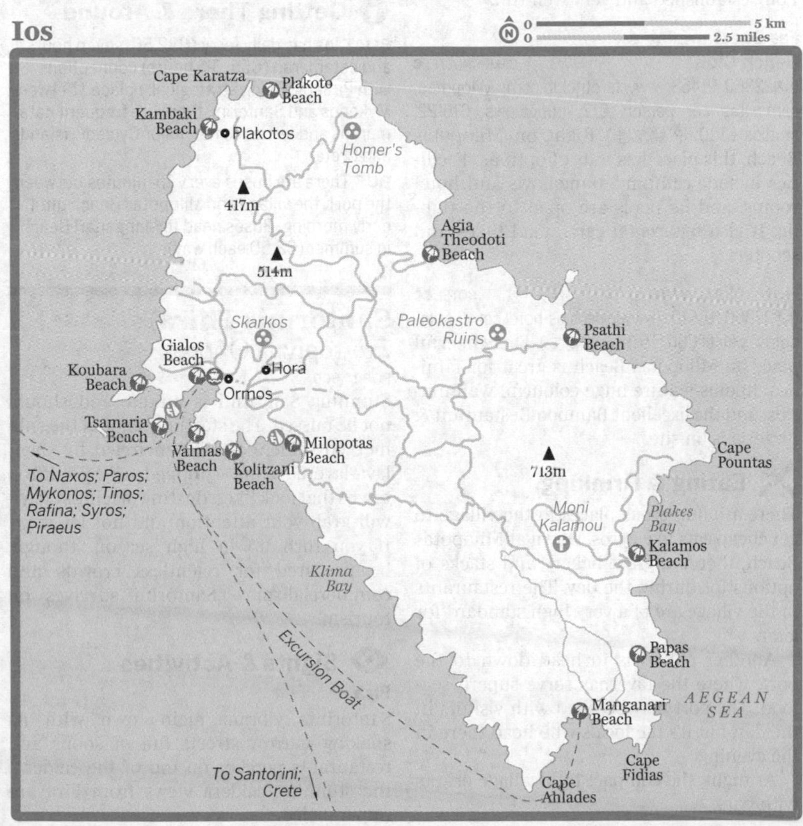

and the drive on Ios' newest sealed road is an experience in itself.

Homer's Tomb TOMB
You'll need your own wheels to get here, 12km north of Hora.

Meltemi Water Sports WATER SPORTS
(☎22860 91680; www.meltemiwatersports.com) This outfit at Milopotas Beach's far end has everything a beach could possibly provide, including rental windsurfers, sailboats and canoes.

Sleeping

TOP CHOICE **Francesco's** HOSTEL €
(☎22860 91223; www.francescos.net; s €40-45, d €50-60 ;) A lively meeting place in the village with superlative views from its terrace bar, legendary Francesco's is convenient for party-going, and rates halve out of high season. The party spirit rules here. Long established and very well run.

Far Out Camping & Beach Club CAMPGROUND €
(☎22860 91468; www.faroutclub.com; Milopotas; campsites per person €12, bungalows €15-22, studios €100;) Right on Milopotas Beach, this place has tons of options. Facilities include camping, bungalows and hotel rooms, and its pools are open to the public. It also has rental cars, quad bikes and scooters.

Hotel Nissos Ios HOTEL €€
(☎22860 91610; www.nissosios-hotel.com; Milopotas; s/d/tr €60/75/90;) This cheerful place on Milopotas Beach is great for families. Rooms feature huge colourful wall murals, and the excellent Bamboo Restaurant & Pizzeria is on-site.

Eating & Drinking

There are numerous places in the village to get cheap eats like gyros. Down at Milopotas Beach, there's a great bakery and stacks of options for during the day. The restaurants in the village are of a very high standard for later.

Another option is to head down to the port, where the tavernas serve superb seafood. The port may be filled with visitors in the day, but it's the locals who head there in the evening.

At night, the compact little village erupts with bars.

Ali Baba's THAI €
(Hora; dishes €7-12) This great Ios favourite is the place for tasty Thai dishes. The service is very upbeat and there's a garden courtyard. It's on the same street as the Emporiki bank.

Pithari GREEK €
(Hora; mains from €10) Behind the cathedral at the entrance to the Hora, Pithari offers an excellent array of tasty dishes; the seafood spaghetti is especially good.

Blue Note BAR
(Hora) A perennial village favourite, where happy hour continues all night long!

Information

There's no tourist office. See www.iosgreece.com for more information.

Acteon Travel (☎22860 91343; www.acteon.gr) Has offices in Ormos, the village and Milopotas and is extremely helpful.

Getting There & Around

BOAT Ios has daily ferry (€32.50, seven hours) and catamaran (€55, 3½ hours) connections with Piraeus. Being strategically placed between Mykonos and Santorini, there are frequent catamarans and ferries to the major Cycladic islands and Crete.

BUS There are buses every 15 minutes between the port, the village and Milopotas Beach until early morning. Buses head to Manganari Beach in summer (€3.50 each way).

Santorini (Thira)

Σαντορίνη (Θήρα)

POP 13,500

Stunning Santorini is unique and should not be missed. The startling sight of the submerged caldera almost encircled by sheer lava-layered cliffs – topped off by clifftop towns that look like a dusting of icing sugar – will grab your attention and not let it go. If you turn up in high season, though, be prepared for relentless crowds and commercialism – Santorini survives on tourism.

Sights & Activities

Fira

Santorini's vibrant main town with its snaking narrow streets full of shops and restaurants perches on top of the caldera; the stunning caldera views from Fira are unparalleled.

Santorini (Thira)

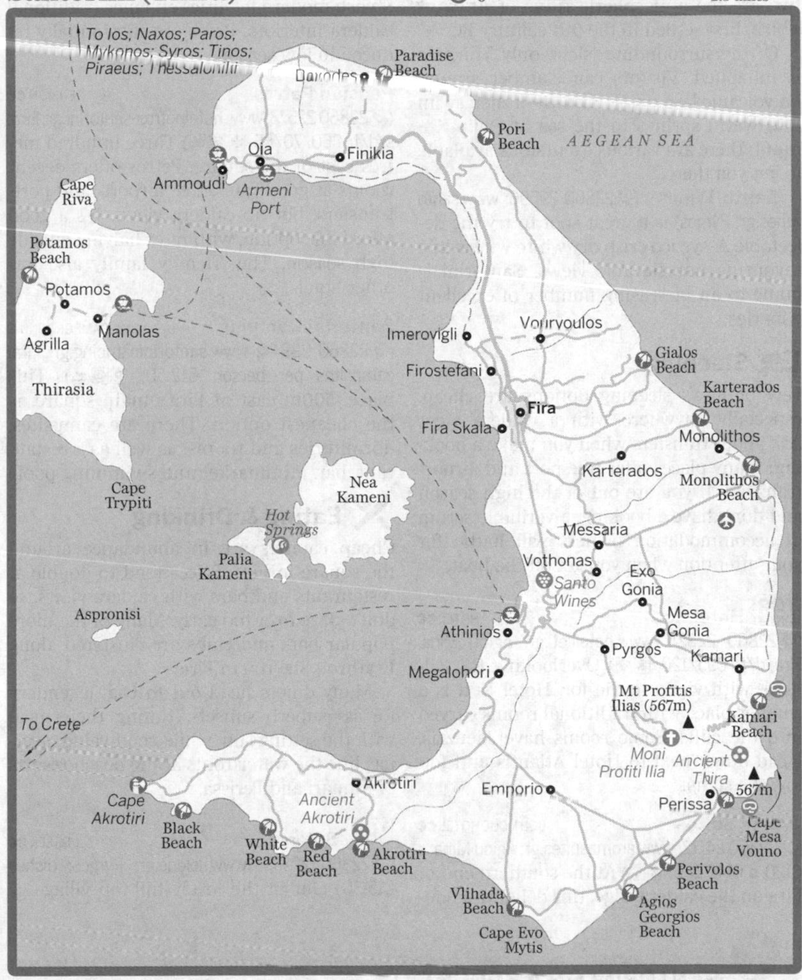

MUSEUMS

The exceptional **Museum of Prehistoric Thira** (admission €3; ⏲8.30am-8pm Tue-Sun), which has wonderful displays of artefacts predominantly from ancient Akrotiri, is two blocks south of the main square. **Megaron Gyzi Museum** (admission €3.50; ⏲10.30am-1.30pm & 5-8pm Mon-Sat, 10.30am-4.30pm Sun), behind the Catholic cathedral, houses local memorabilia, including photographs of Fira before and after the 1956 earthquake.

Around the Island

At the north of the island, the intriguing village of **Oia** (ee-ah), famed for its postcard sunsets, is less hectic than Fira and a must-visit. Its caldera-facing tavernas are superb spots for brunch. There's a path from Fira to Oia along the top of the caldera that takes three to four hours to walk; otherwise take a taxi or bus.

Excavations in 1967 uncovered the remarkably well-preserved Minoan settlement of **Akrotiri** at the south of the island, with its remains of two- and three-storey buildings. Akrotiri has recently reopened to the public after a seven-year hiatus.

Santorini's black-sand **beaches** of **Perissa** and **Kamari** sizzle – beach mats are essential. Sitting on a mountain between the two are the atmospheric ruins of **Ancient Thira**, first settled in the 9th century BC.

Of the surrounding islets, only **Thirasia** is inhabited. Visitors can clamber around on volcanic lava on **Nea Kameni** then swim into warm springs in the sea at **Palia Kameni**; there are various excursions available to get you there.

Santo Wines (22860 22596; www.santowines.gr; Pyrgos) is a great spot to try the delectable Assyrtico crisp dry white wine while savouring unbelievable views. Santorini is home to an increasing number of excellent wineries.

Sleeping

Few of Fira's sleeping options are cheap, especially anywhere with a caldera view. Ask about transfers when you make a booking; many places offer free port and airport transfers. If you are out of the high season and don't have a booking, a veritable scrum of accommodation owners will battle for your attention when you get off the boat.

TOP CHOICE Hotel Keti HOTEL €€
(22860 22324; www.hotelketi.gr; Agiou Mina, Fira; d/tr €95/120;) Overlooking the caldera, with views to die for, Hotel Keti is a smaller place with traditional rooms carved into the cliffs. Some rooms have Jacuzzis. Head down next to Hotel Atlantis and follow the signs.

Aroma Suites BOUTIQUE HOTEL €€
(22860 24112; www.aromasuites.gr; Agiou Mina; s €120, d €140-160;) At the southern end of Fira on the caldera edge, this delightful boutique hotel has charming owners to match. Stylish modern facilities enhance traditional caldera interiors. Rates are substantially reduced in low season.

Pension Petros PENSION €€
(22860 22573; www.hotelpetros-santorini.gr; Fira; s/d/tr €60/70/85;) Three hundred metres east of the square, Petros offers decent rooms at good rates, free airport- and port-transfers, but no caldera views. It's a good affordable option, with rates halving outside high season. The friendly family also has other hotels.

Santorini Camping CAMPGROUND €
(22860 22944; www.santorinicamping.gr; Fira; campsites per person €12.50;) This place, 500m east of Fira's main square, is the cheapest option. There are campsites, dormitories and rooms, as well as a restaurant, bar, minimarket and swimming pool.

Eating & Drinking

Cheap eateries are in abundance around the square in Fira. Prices tend to double at restaurants and bars with caldera views, so don't glaze over too early. Many of the more popular bars and clubs are clustered along Erythrou Stavrou in Fira.

Many diners head out to Oia, legendary for its superb sunsets, timing their meal with the setting sun, while good-value tavernas line the waterfronts at the beach resorts of Kamari and Perissa.

TOP CHOICE Selene GREEK €€
(22860 22249; www.selene.gr; Pyrgos; dishes €15-30) Out in the lovely hill-top village of

SANTORINI ON A BUDGET

Spectacular Santorini will take your breath away, and if you're on a tight budget, its prices might too. Expect to pay through the nose for caldera views at accommodation and eating establishments in and around Fira.

A budget alternative with the added bonus of a stunning black-sand beach is to head out to Perissa, on the southeast coast, and stay at **Stelios Place** (22860 81860; www.steliosplace.com; r €30-120;). Stelios is an excellent option one block back from the beach. There's a refreshing pool, very friendly service and free port- and airport-transfers. Rates halve out of high season.

All of your needs will be catered for in Perissa, which has bars and restaurants lining the waterfront. **Taverna Lava** (22860 81776), at the southern end of the waterfront, is an island-wide favourite that features a mouth-watering menu. Or just head back into the kitchen, see what Yiannis has conjured up for the day's meals and pick whatever looks good.

Public buses run regularly into Fira.

Pyrgos, Selene is in the heart of Santorinian farming and culinary culture, and specialises in creative cuisine based on Cycladic produce and unique local ingredients, such as small tomatoes and fava beans. The wine cellar houses some of Santorini's best.

Fanari GREEK €
(☎22860 25107; www.fanari-restaurant.gr; Fira; dishes €7-20) On the street leading down to the old port, Fanari serves up both tasty traditional dishes and superlative views.

Information

There is no tourist office. Try www.santorini.net for more information.

Dakoutros Travel (☎22860 22958; www.dakoutrostravel.gr; ⊙8.30am-10pm) Just down from the square and opposite the taxi station in Fira; extremely helpful and good for ticketing.

Getting There & Around

The bus station and taxi station are just south of Fira's main square, Plateia Theotokopoulou. The new port of Athinios, where most ferries dock, is 10km south of Fira by road. The old port of Fira Skala, used by cruise ships and excursion boats, is directly below Fira and accessed by cable car (adult/child €4/2 one way), donkey (€5, up only) or by foot (588 steps).

Air

Santorini airport (JTR) has daily flight connections with Athens, plus a growing number of domestic destinations and direct international flights from all over Europe. The airport is 5km southeast of Fira; frequent buses (€1.50) and taxis (€12).

Boat

There are daily ferries (€33.50, nine hours) and fast boats (€60, 5¼ hours) to Piraeus; daily connections in summer to Mykonos, Ios, Naxos, Paros and Iraklio; and ferries to the smaller islands in the Cyclades. Large ferries use Athinios port, where they are met by buses and taxis.

Bus

Buses go frequently to Oia, Kamari, Perissa and Akrotiri from Fira. Port buses usually leave Fira, Kamari and Perissa one to 1½ hours before ferry departures.

Car & Motorcycle

A car or scooter is a great option on Santorini. There are plenty of places to rent them (from €30 per day).

CRETE ΚΡΗΤΗ

POP 550,000

Crete is Greece's largest and most southerly island and its size and distance from the rest of Greece give it the feel of a different country. With its dramatic landscape and unique cultural identity, Crete is a delight to explore.

The island is split by a spectacular chain of mountains running east to west. Major towns are on the more hospitable northern coast, while most of the southern coast is too precipitous to support large settlements. The rugged mountainous interior, dotted with caves and sliced by dramatic gorges, offers rigorous hiking and climbing.

While Crete's proud, friendly and hospitable people have enthusiastically embraced tourism, they continue to fiercely protect their traditions and culture – and it is the people that remain a major part of the island's appeal.

For more detailed information, snap up a copy of Lonely Planet's *Crete*. Good websites on Crete include www.interkriti.org and www.explorecrete.com.

History

Crete was the birthplace of Minoan culture, Europe's first advanced civilisation, which flourished between 2800 and 1450 BC. Very little is known of Minoan civilisation, which came to an abrupt end, possibly destroyed by Santorini's volcanic eruption in around 1650 BC. Later, Crete passed from the warlike Dorians to the Romans, and then to the Genoese, who in turn sold it to the Venetians. Under the Venetians, Crete became a refuge for artists, writers and philosophers, who fled after it fell to the Turks. Their influence inspired the young Cretan painter Domenikos Theotokopoulos, who moved to Spain and there won immortality as the great El Greco.

The Turks conquered Crete in 1670. In 1898 Crete became a British protectorate after a series of insurrections and was united with independent Greece in 1913. There was fierce fighting during WWII when a German airborne invasion defeated Allied forces in the 10-day Battle of Crete. A fierce resistance movement drew heavy German reprisals, including the slaughter of whole villages.

Crete

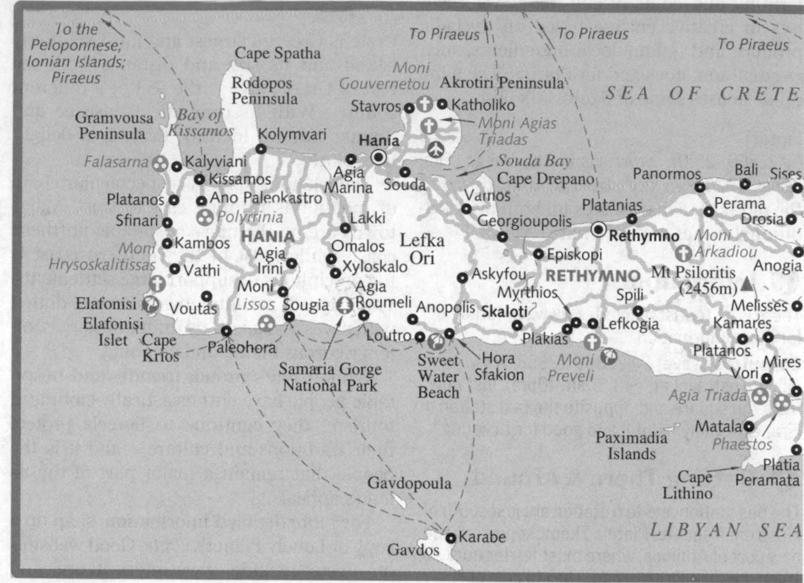

Iraklio Ηράκλειο

POP 138,000

Iraklio (ee-*rah*-klee-oh; often spelt Heraklion), Crete's capital and economic hub, is a bustling modern city and the fifth-largest in Greece. It has a lively city centre, an excellent archaeological museum and is close to Knossos, Crete's major visitor attraction.

Iraklio's harbours face north into the Sea of Crete. The old harbour is instantly recognisable, as it is protected by the old Venetian fortress. The new harbour is 400m east. Plateia Venizelou, known for its Lion Fountain, is the heart of the city, 400m south of the old harbour up 25 Avgoustou.

Sights & Activities

Archaeological Museum — MUSEUM

(www.odysseus.culture.gr; Xanthoudidou 2; adult/student €4/2; ⊙8.30am-3pm Nov-Mar) The outstanding Minoan collection here is second only to that of the national museum in Athens. The museum was under long-term reconstruction at the time of research, but its key exhibits are beautifully displayed in an annex.

Koules Venetian Fortress — FORTRESS

(admission €2; ⊙8.30am-7pm Tue-Sun May-Oct, to 3pm Nov-Apr) Protecting the old harbour, this impressive fortress is also known as Rocca al Mare, which, like the city walls, was built by the Venetians in the 16th century. It stopped the Turks for 21 years and later became a Turkish prison for Cretan rebels.

City Walls — FORTRESS

Iraklio burst out of its city walls long ago, but these massive Venetian fortifications, with seven bastions and four gates, are still very conspicuous, dwarfing the concrete structures of the 20th century.

Morosini Fountain — FOUNTAIN

(Plateia Venizelou) Iraklio's much loved 'lion fountain', built in 1628 by the Venetians, spurts water from four lions into eight ornate U-shaped marble troughs.

Cretan Adventures — OUTDOORS

(☎28103 32772; www.cretanadventures.gr; Evans 10, 3rd fl) Cretan Adventures is a well-regarded local company run by Fondas Spinthaikos that can organise hiking tours, mountain biking, and other specialist and extreme activities.

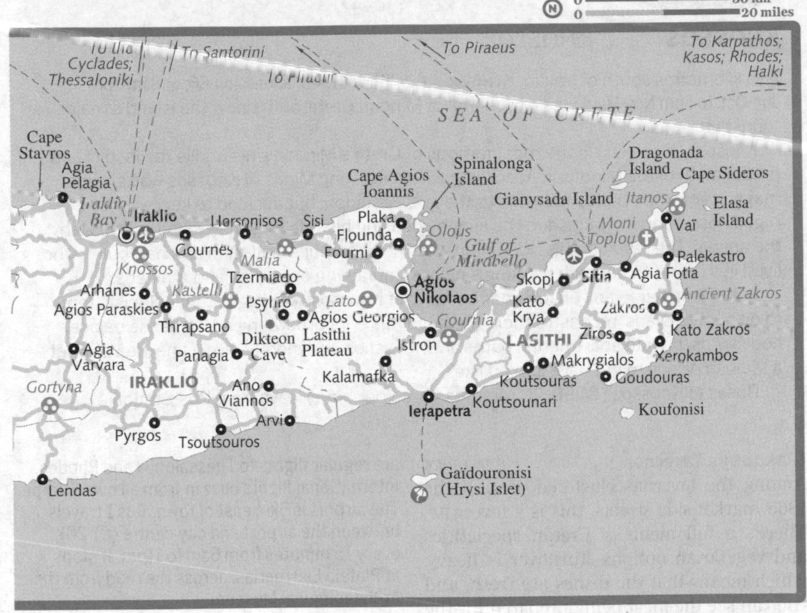

Sleeping

TOP CHOICE Lato Hotel BOUTIQUE HOTEL €€
(☎28102 28103; www.lato.gr; Epimenidou 15; d incl breakfast €90-120; P❄@📶) This stylish boutique hotel overlooking the waterfront is a top place to stay. Ask for a room with harbour views. The contemporary interior design extends to the bar, breakfast restaurant and **Brillant** (☎28102 28103; www.brillantrestaurant.gr; mains €10-25), the superb fine-dining restaurant on the ground floor. From May to October, the restaurant renames itself **Herb's Garden** and moves to the hotel rooftop for alfresco dining with harbour views.

Kronos Hotel HOTEL €
(☎28102 82240; www.kronoshotel.gr; Sofokli Venizelou 2; s/d €44/50; ❄@📶) After a thorough makeover, this waterfront hotel has pole-vaulted to the top of the budget hotel category. The comfortable rooms have double-glazed windows and balconies. Ask for one of the rooms with sea views.

Hotel Mirabello HOTEL €
(☎28102 85052; www.mirabello-hotel.gr; Theotokopoulou 20; s/d €42/48; ❄@📶) A pleasant, relaxed budget hotel on a quiet street in the centre of town, this place is run by an ex-sea captain who has travelled the world. A good-value option.

Eating & Drinking

There's a congregation of cheap eateries, bars and cafes in the Plateia Venizelou (Morosini Fountain) and El Greco Park area. The places around the park are packed at night. Head down towards the old harbour for plenty of seafood options.

DON'T MISS

MARKET ON 1866

Heading inland from Lion Fountain, cross the main street diagonally to the left and you'll be on Odos 1866 (1866 St). This bustling, colourful market street, perfect for people-watching, has everything on offer from fruit and vegetables to honey, herbs and succulent olives. Crete is known for its leather goods and this is a good spot to purchase them.

DON'T MISS

KNOSSOS ΚΝΩΣΣΟΣ

Five kilometres south of Iraklio, **Knossos** (☎28102 31940; admission €6; ⊙8am-7pm Jun-Oct, to 3pm Nov-May) was the capital of Minoan Crete, and is now the island's major tourist attraction.

Knossos (k-nos-*os*) is the most famous of Crete's Minoan sites and is the inspiration for the myth of the Minotaur. According to legend, King Minos of Knossos was given a magnificent white bull to sacrifice to the god Poseidon, but decided to keep it. This enraged Poseidon, who punished the king by causing his wife Pasiphae to fall in love with the animal. The result of this odd union was the Minotaur – half-man and half-bull – who lived in a labyrinth beneath the king's palace, munching on youths and maidens.

In 1900 Arthur Evans uncovered the ruins of Knossos. Although archaeologists tend to disparage Evans' reconstruction, the buildings – incorporating an immense palace, courtyards, private apartments, baths, lively frescos and more – give a fine idea of what a Minoan palace might have looked like.

Buses to Knossos (€1.50, 20 minutes, three per hour) leave from Bus Station A.

Giakoumis Taverna TAVERNA €
Among the tavernas clustered around the 1866 market side streets, this is a favourite. There's a full menu of Cretan specialities and vegetarian options. Turnover is heavy, which means that the dishes are fresh, and you can see the meat being prepared for the grill.

Ippokambos Ouzerie SEAFOOD €
Many locals come to this classic Iraklio haunt at the edge of the tourist-driven waterfront dining strip. Take a peek inside at the fresh trays and pots of *mayirefta* (ready-cooked meals) such as baked cuttlefish, and dine at one of the sidewalk tables or on the promenade across the road.

Veneto CAFE
(☎28102 23686; Epimenidou 9) This cafe has the best view of the harbour and fortress from its lovely terrace. It's in an historic building near Lato Hotel.

ℹ Information

Visit www.heraklion.gr for more information about the city.

Tourist Office (☎28102 46299; Xanthoudidou 1; ⊙8.30am-8.30pm Apr-Oct, to 3pm Nov-Mar)

Skoutelis Travel (☎28102 80808; www.skoutelisrentacar.gr; 25 Avgoustou 20) Between Lion Fountain and the old harbour, handles airline and ferry bookings, runs tours and rents cars.

ℹ Getting There & Around

Air

Flights depart daily from Iraklio's Nikos Kazantzakis airport (HER) for Athens and there are regular flights to Thessaloniki and Rhodes. International flights buzz in from all over Europe. The airport is 5km east of town. Bus 1 travels between the airport and city centre (€1.20) every 15 minutes from 6am to 11pm. It stops at Plateia Eleftherias, across the road from the Archaeological Museum.

Boat

Daily ferries service Piraeus (€37, seven hours), and catamarans head daily to Santorini and continue on to other Cycladic islands. Ferries sail east to Rhodes (€28, 12 hours) via Agios Nikolaos, Sitia, Kasos, Karpathos and Halki.

Bus

KTEL (Koino Tamio Eispraxeon Leoforion; http://www.bus-service-crete-ktel.com/) runs the buses on Crete and has useful tourist information inside Bus Station A.

Iraklio has two bus stations. The main **Bus Station A** is just inland from the new harbour and serves eastern Crete (Agios Nikolaos, Ierapetra, Sitia, Malia and the Lasithi Plateau), as well as Hania and Rethymno. **Bus Station B**, 50m beyond the Hania Gate, serves the southern route (Phaestos, Matala and Anogia).

Phaestos & Other Minoan Sites Φαιστός

Phaestos (☎29820 42315; admission €6; ⊙8am-7pm May-Oct, to 5pm Nov-Apr), 63km southwest of Iraklio, is Crete's second-most important Minoan site. While not as impressive as Knossos, Phaestos (fes-*tos*) is still worth a visit for its stunning views of the surrounding Mesara plain and Mt Psiloritis (2456m; also known as Mt Ida). The layout is similar to Knossos, with rooms arranged around a central courtyard. Eight buses a day head to Phaestos from Iraklio's Bus Station B (€6.30, 1½ hours).

Other important Minoan sites can be found at **Malia**, 34km east of Iraklio, where there's a palace complex and adjoining town, and **Zakros**, 40km southeast of Sitia, the last Minoan palace to have been discovered, in 1962.

Rethymno Ρέθυμνο

POP 28,000

Rethymno (*reth*-im-no) is Crete's third-largest town. It's also one of the island's architectural treasures, due to its stunning fortress and mix of Venetian and Turkish houses in the old quarter. Most spots of interest are within a small area around the old Venetian harbour.

The old quarter is on a peninsula that juts out into the Sea of Crete; the fortress sits at its head, while the Venetian harbour, ferry quay and beach are on its eastern side. El Venizelou is the main strip along the waterfront and beach.

Rethymno's 16th-century **Venetian fortezza** (Fortress; Paleokastro Hill; admission €4; ⊙8am-8pm May-Oct) is the site of the city's ancient acropolis and affords great views across the town and mountains. The main gate is on the eastern side of the fortress, opposite the interesting **archaeological museum** (☎28310 54668; admission €3; ⊙8.30am-3pm Tue-Sun), which was once a prison.

Happy Walker (☎28310 52920; www.happywalker.com; Tombazi 56) runs an excellent program of daily walks in the countryside and also longer walking tours.

Sea Front (☎28310 51981; www.rethymnoatcrete.com; Arkadiou 159; d €40-50; ❄📶) has all sorts of sleeping options and is ideally positioned with beach views and spacious rooms. **Hotel Fortezza** (☎28310 55551; www.fortezza.gr; Melissinou 16; s/d incl breakfast €75/88; P❄📶≋) is more upmarket; with a refreshing pool, it's in a refurbished old building in the heart of the Old Town. **Rethymno Youth Hostel** (☎28310 22848; www.yhrethymno.com; Tombazi 41; dm €11; 📶) is a well-run place with crowded dorms, free hot showers and no curfew.

The **municipal tourist office** (☎28310 29148; www.rethymno.gr; Eleftheriou Venizelou; ⊙9am-8.30pm), on the beach side of El Venizelou, is convenient and helpful. **Ellotia Tours** (☎28310 24533; www.rethymnoatcrete.com; Arkadiou 155) will answer all transport, accommodation and tour enquiries.

There are regular ferries between Piraeus and Rethymno (€30, nine hours), and a high-speed service in summer. Buses depart regularly to Iraklio (€7.60, 1½ hours) and Hania (€6.20, one hour).

Hania Χανιά

POP 54,000

Crete's most romantic, evocative and alluring town, Hania (hahn-*yah*; often spelt Chania) is the former capital and the island's second-largest city. There is a rich mosaic of Venetian and Ottoman architecture, particularly in the area of the old harbour, which lures tourists in droves. Modern Hania retains the exoticism of a city caught between East and West, and is an excellent base for exploring nearby idyllic beaches and a spectacular mountainous interior.

Sights & Activities

Old Harbour HISTORIC SITE

From Plateia 1866 in the middle of town, the old harbour is a short walk down Halidon. A stroll around here is a must for any visitor to Hania. It is worth the 1.5km walk around the sea wall to get to the Venetian **lighthouse** at the entrance to the harbour.

Venetian Fortifications FORTRESS

Part of a defensive system built by the Venetians from 1538, Hania's massive fortifications remain impressive. Best preserved is the western wall, running from the Firkas Fortress at the western entrance to the Old Harbour.

Archaeological Museum MUSEUM

(Halidon 30; admission €2; ⊙8.30am-3pm Tue-Sun) The museum is housed in a 16th-century Venetian church that the Turks made into a mosque. The building, 200m up Halidon from the Old Harbour, became a movie theatre in 1913 and then was a munitions depot for the Germans during WWII.

Food Market MARKET

Hania's covered food market, in a massive cross-shaped building 400m southeast of the Old Harbour, is definitely worth an inspection.

Sleeping

TOP CHOICE Pension Lena PENSION €

(☎28210 86860; www.lenachania.gr; Ritsou 5; s/d €35/55; ❄📶) For some real character in where you stay, Lena's pension (in an old Turkish building near the mouth of the old harbour) is the place to go. Help yourself to one of the appealing rooms if proprietor Lena isn't there – pick from the available ones on the list on the blackboard.

Amphora Hotel HOTEL €€

(☎28210 93224; www.amphora.gr; Parodos Theotokopoulou 20; s/d €95/120; ❄📶) Most easily found from the waterfront, this is Hania's most historically evocative hotel. Amphora is in an impressively restored Venetian mansion with elegantly decorated rooms around a courtyard. The hotel also runs the **waterfront restaurant**, which ranks as the best along that golden mile.

Vranas Studios APARTMENT €

(☎28210 58618; www.vranas.gr; Agion Deka 10; studio €40-70; ❄📶) This place is on a lively pedestrian street and has spacious, immaculately maintained studios with kitchenettes. All rooms have polished wooden floors, balconies, TVs and telephones.

Camping Hania CAMPGROUND €

(☎28210 31138; www.camping-chania.gr; Agii Apostoli; campsites per tent/person €4/7; P🏊) Take the Kalamaki Beach bus from the east corner of Plateia 1866 (every 15 minutes) to get to this camping ground, which is 3km west of town on the beach. There is a restaurant, bar and minimarket.

Eating & Drinking

The entire waterfront of the old harbour is lined with restaurants and tavernas, many of which qualify as tourist traps. Watch out for touts trying to reel you in. There are a number of good options one street back.

TOP CHOICE Michelas GREEK €

(☎28210 90026; mains €4-12; ⏲10am-4pm Mon-Sat) Serving up authentic Cretan specialities at reasonable prices for 75 years, this family-run place in the Food Market uses only local ingredients and cooks up a great selection each day that you can peruse, then choose from.

Taverna Tamam TAVERNA €€

(☎28210 58639; Zambeliou 49; mains €10-20; 🌶) A taverna in an old converted *hammam* (Turkish bathhouse) one street back from the Old Harbour, Tamam has tables that spill out onto the street. This place has tasty soups and a superb selection of vegetarian specialities.

Café Kriti BAR

(Kalergon 22; ⏲8pm-late) Near the eastern end of the Venetian harbour, Kriti is known for its down-to-earth atmosphere and live traditional Cretan music.

Information

For more information visit the **Hania website** (www.chania.gr).

Tellus Travel (☎28210 91500; www.tellustravel.gr; Halidon 108; ⏲8am-11pm) Has schedules and does ticketing, plus it rents out cars.

Tourist Information Office (☎28210 36155; Kydonias 29; ⏲8am-2.30pm) Under the town hall; helpful and provides practical information and maps.

Getting There & Away

Air

There are several flights a day between Hania airport (CHQ) and Athens, plus a number of flights to Thessaloniki each week. An increasing number of international flights are winging directly into Hania from around Europe. The airport is 14km east of town on the Akrotiri Peninsula. Taxis to town cost €20; buses cost €2.30.

Boat

Daily ferries sail between Piraeus (€35, nine hours) and the port of Souda, 9km southeast of Hania. Frequent buses (€1.65) and taxis (€10) connect town and Souda.

Bus

Frequent buses run along Crete's northern coast to Iraklio (€13.80, 2¾ hours, half-hourly) and Rethymno (€6.20, one hour, half hourly); buses run less frequently to Paleohora (€7.60, one hour 50 minutes, four daily), Omalos (€6.90, one hour, three daily) and Hora Sfakion (€7.60, 1½ hours, three daily) from the main bus station.

Hania's bus station is on Kydonias, two blocks southwest of Plateia 1866, one of the city's main squares. Buses for the beaches west of Hania leave from the eastern side of Plateia 1866.

Samaria Gorge

Φαράγγι της Σαμαριάς

The **Samaria Gorge** (☎28250 67179; admission €5; ⏲6am-3pm May–mid-Oct) is one of Europe's most spectacular gorges and a superb hike. Walkers should take rugged footwear,

BEAT THE CROWDS AT SAMARIA

The Samaria Gorge walk is extremely popular and can get quite crowded, especially in summer. Most walkers have given the gorge a day and are on a rushed trip from Hania or other northern-coast cities.

If you've got a bit of time on your hands, and decide to do things on your own, there are a couple of excellent options.

One is to take the afternoon bus from Hania and spend the night in the Cretan mountains at 1200m above sea level in **Omalos** (population 30) at the very pleasant **Neos Omalos Hotel** (28210 67269; www.neos-omalos.gr; s/d €25/35;). The hotel's restaurant serves excellent Cretan cuisine and local wine by the litre (€6); there's a shuttle to the start of the gorge track the next morning. Keen hikers may want to stay here a couple of nights and tackle Mt Gingilos (2080m; five hours return from Xyloskalo) before hiking the gorge.

Another option is to leave from Hania in the morning, but let the sprinters go and take your time hiking through this stupendous gorge. When you hit the coast at **Agia Roumeli** (population 125), down a cool beer and take a dip in the refreshing Libyan Sea. There are a number of restaurants and **Paralia Taverna & Rooms** (28250 91408; www.taverna-paralia.com; d €30;), right on the waterfront, is a good spot to stay the night. The next day you can take a ferry either west to Sougia or Paleohora, or east to Loutro or Hora Sfakion.

food, drinks and sun protection for this strenuous five- to six-hour trek.

You can do the walk as part of an excursion tour, or independently by taking the Omalos bus from the main bus station in Hania (€6.90, one hour) to the head of the gorge at Xyloskalo (1230m). It's a 16.7km walk (all downhill) to Agia Roumeli on the coast, from where you take a boat to Hora Sfakion (€10, 1¼ hours) and then a bus back to Hania (€7.60, 1½ hours). You are not allowed to spend the night in the gorge, so you need to complete the walk in a day.

Paleohora Παλαιόχωρα

POP 2200

Paleohora (pal-ee-o-*hor*-a) has a sleepy end-of-the-line feel about it. Isolated and a bit hard to get to, the village is on a peninsula with a sandy beach to the west and a pebbly beach to the east. On summer evenings the main street is closed to traffic and the tavernas move onto the road. If you're after a relaxing few days, Paleohora is a great spot to chill out.

Heading south from the bus stop, you'll find the main street, which is called Eleftheriou Venizelou.

The ruins of the 13th-century **Venetian castle** are worth clambering over, although there's not much left after the fortress was destroyed by the Turks, the pirate Barbarossa in the 16th-century and then the Germans during WWII.

Homestay Anonymous (28230 41509; www.cityofpaleochora.gr/cp; s/d/tr €23/28/32;) is a great option with its warm service and communal kitchen. Across the road from the sandy beach, the refurbished **Poseidon Hotel** (28230 41374; www.poseidon-paleohora.com; s/d/apt €35/40/50;) has a mix of tidy double rooms, studios and apartments. **Camping Paleohora** (28230 41120; campsites per tent/person €3/5) is 1.5km northeast of town, near the pebble beach. There's a taverna but no minimarket here.

There are plenty of eating options on the main street. Vegetarians rave about **Third Eye** (mains from €5;), just inland from the sandy beach.

There's a welcoming **tourist office** (28230 41507; 10am-1pm & 6-9pm Wed-Mon May-Oct) on the pebble beach road near the harbour and ferry quay. The opening hours listed here are indicative only! Back on the main street, **Notos Rentals/Tsiskakis Travel** (28230 42110; www.notoscar.com; 8am-10pm) handles almost everything, including tickets, rental cars/scooters and internet access.

There are four to six buses daily between Hania and Paleohora (€7.60, two hours). In summer, a bus for those hiking Samaria Gorge leaves for Omalos (€5.50, two hours) each morning at 6.15am. It also drops off hikers at the head of the Agia Irini Gorge.

WORTH A TRIP

SOUTHWEST COAST VILLAGES

Crete's southern coastline at its western end is dotted with remote, attractive little villages that are brilliant spots to take it easy for a few days.

Heading east from Paleohora are Sougia, Agia Roumeli, Loutro and Hora Sfakion. No road links the coastal resorts, but a daily boat from Paleohora to Sougia (€8.50, one hour), Agia Roumeli (€12.50, 1½ hours), Loutro (€14, 2½ hours) and Hora Sfakion (€16, three hours) connects the villages in summer. The ferry leaves Paleohora at 9.45am and returns along the same route from Hora Sfakion at 1pm. See www.sfakia-crete.com/sfakia-crete/ferries.html for up-to-date information.

If you're a keen hiker, keep in mind that it's also possible to walk right along this southern coast.

Sougia

At the mouth of the Agia Irini gorge, Sougia (soo-yah) is a laid-back and refreshingly undeveloped spot with a wide curve of sand-and-pebble beach. The 14.5km (six hours) walk from Paleohora is popular, as is the Agia Irini gorge walk which ends (or starts!) in Sougia. It's possible to get here by ferry, by car or on foot. Stay at **Santa Irene Hotel** (☎28230 51342; www.santa-irene.gr; d/tr €55/70; ❄📶), a smart beachside complex of apartments and studios that has its own cafe and bar.

Agia Roumeli

At the mouth of the Samaria Gorge, Agia Roumeli bristles with gorge-walkers from mid-afternoon until the ferry comes to take them away. Once they are gone, this pleasant little town goes into quiet mode until the first walkers turn up early afternoon the following day. Take your time to enjoy the village. Right on the waterfront, Paralia Taverna & Rooms (p623) offers everything you need; excellent views, tasty Cretan cuisine, cold beer and simple, clean rooms.

Loutro

This tiny village is a particularly picturesque spot, curled around the only natural harbour on the southern coast of Crete. With no vehicle access, the only way in is by boat or on foot. If you decide to walk, the track from Hora Sfakion comes via the stunning Sweetwater Beach. **Hotel Porto Loutro** (☎28250 91433; www.hotelportoloutro.com; s/d incl breakfast €50/60; ❄@) has tasteful rooms with balconies overlooking the harbour. The village beach, excellent walks, rental kayaks and boat transfers to Sweetwater Beach will help to fill in a peaceful few days. Take a book and chill out.

Hora Sfakion

Renowned in Cretan history for its rebellious streak, Hora Sfakion is an amiable town. WWII history buffs know this as the place where thousands of Allied troops were evacuated by sea after the Battle of Crete. To the visitor with a bit of time, Hora Sfakion offers a row of seafront tavernas serving fresh seafood, some intriguing and eccentric locals, and an opportunity to see 'the real Crete'. **Hotel Stavris** (☎28250 91220; http://www.hotel-stavris-chora-sfakion.com; s/d/tr €31/36/41; ❄📶) has simple rooms and breakfast outside in its courtyard.

Start or finish your southwest coast villages sojourn in Hora Sfakion. There are four buses daily both to and from Hania (€7.60, two hours).

Lasithi Plateau
Οροπέδιο Λασιθίου

The mountain-fringed Lasithi Plateau in eastern Crete is laid out like an immense patchwork quilt. At 900m above sea level, it is a vast flat expanse of orchards and fields, once dotted with thousands of stone windmills with white canvas sails. There are still plenty of windmills, but most are now of the rusted metal variety and don't work.

There are 20 villages around the periphery of the plain, the largest being **Tzermiado** (population 750), **Agios Georgios** (population 550) and **Psyhro** (population 210).

The **Dikteon Cave** (☎28440 31316; admission €4; ⏲8am-6pm Jun-Oct, to 2.30pm Nov-May) is where, according to mythology, Rhea hid the newborn Zeus from Cronos, his offspring-gobbling father. The cave, which covers 2200 sq metres and features numerous stalactites and stalagmites, is 1km from the village of Psyhro.

There are daily buses to the area from Iraklio and Agios Nikolaos, though having your own wheels would make life a lot easier.

Agios Nikolaos
Αγιος Νικόλαος

Agios Nikolaos (*ah*-yee-os nih-*ko*-laos) is an attractive former fishing village on Crete's northeast coast. The de facto town centre is around the picturesque **Voulismeni Lake**, which is ringed with cafes and tavernas, and is linked to the sea by a short canal. The ferry port is 150m past the canal.

The two nice little beaches in town, **Kytroplatia** and **Ammos**, get a bit crowded in summer. **Almyros Beach**, about 1km south, gets less so. Agios Nikolaos acts as a base for excursion tours to **Spinalonga Island**. The island's massive fortress was built by the Venetians in 1579 but taken by the Turks in 1715. It later became a leper colony. Nowadays it's a fascinating place to explore. Tours cost around €25.

Pergola Hotel (☎28410 28152; Sarolidi 20; s/d €35-40; ❄📶) is a friendly family-run place out near the ferry port, with clean rooms, balconies and sea views. **Du Lac Hotel** (☎28410 22711; www.dulachotel.gr; Oktovriou 17; s/d €40/60; ❄📶) is a refurbished hotel in a great location with views out over the lake.

Finding a place to eat will not be a problem; there are a lot of options around the lake. **Taverna Itanos** (☎28410 25340; Kyprou 1; mains €6-12), tucked away on a backstreet off the main square, is superb, has reasonable prices and offers the opportunity to wander into the kitchen and see what looks good.

The very helpful **municipal tourist office** (☎28410 22357; www.agiosnikolaos.gr; ⏲8am-9pm Apr-Nov) is on the north side of the bridge over the canal and does a good job of finding sleeping options.

Buses to Iraklio run every 30 minutes (€7.10, 1½ hours).

Sitia Σητεία

POP 9000

Sitia (si-*tee*-a) is a laid-back little town in the northeastern corner of Crete that has escaped much of the tourism frenzy along the north coast. It is on an attractive bay flanked by mountains, and is an easy place to unwind.

The main square, Plateia Iroon Plytehniou, is in the corner of the bay, and recognisable by its palm trees and statue of a dying soldier.

Porto Belis Travel (☎28430 22370; www.portobelis-crete.gr; Karamanli Aven 34), on the waterfront just before the start of the town beach, is a one-stop shop, handling ticketing, rental cars and scooters, and accommodation bookings in town. It also runs **Porto Belis House** (☎28430 22370; d/q €35/60; ❄📶) above the travel agency. These rooms are immaculate, have kitchens and look straight out onto the beach.

Itanos Hotel (☎28430 22900; www.itanoshotel.com; Karamanli 4; s/d incl breakfast €50/68; ❄@) is an upmarket establishment next to the square with its own excellent **Itanos Taverna** on the waterfront outside the front door.

The waterfront is lined with tavernas. **Balcony** (☎28430 25084; www.balcony-restaurant.com; Foundalidou 19; mains €12-19), a couple of streets back, is the finest dining in Sitia. It's in a charmingly decorated neoclassical building.

The helpful **tourist office** (☎28430 28300; Karamanli; ⏲9.30am-2.30pm & 5-8.30pm Mon-Fri, 9.30am-2pm Sat), on the waterfront, has town maps.

Sitia airport (JSH) has flights to Athens. There are buses daily to Iraklio (€14.70, 3½ hours) via Agios Nikolaos (€7.60, 1½ hours).

DODECANESE
ΔΩΔΕΚΑΝΗΣΑ

Strung out along the coast of western Turkey, the 12 main islands of the Dodecanese (*dodeca* means 12) have suffered a turbulent past of invasions and occupations that have endowed them with a fascinating diversity.

Conquered successively by the Romans, the Arabs, the Knights of St John, the Turks, the Italians, then liberated from the Germans by British and Greek commandos in

1944, the Dodecanese became part of Greece in 1947. These days, tourists rule.

The islands themselves range from the verdant and mountainous to the rocky and dry. While Rhodes and Kos host highly developed tourism, the more remote islands await those in search of traditional island life.

Rhodes Ρόδος

POP 98,000

Rhodes (Rodos in Greek) is the largest island in the Dodecanese. According to mythology, the sun god Helios chose Rhodes as his bride and bestowed light, warmth and vegetation upon her. The blessing seems to have paid off, for Rhodes produces more flowers and sunny days than most Greek islands. Throw in an east coast of virtually uninterrupted sandy beaches and it's easy to understand why sun-starved northern Europeans flock here.

Getting There & Away

Air

There are plenty of flights daily between Rhodes' **Diagoras airport** (RHO) and Athens, plus less-regular flights to Karpathos, Kastellorizo, Thessaloniki, Iraklio and Samos. Options are growing.

Rhodes

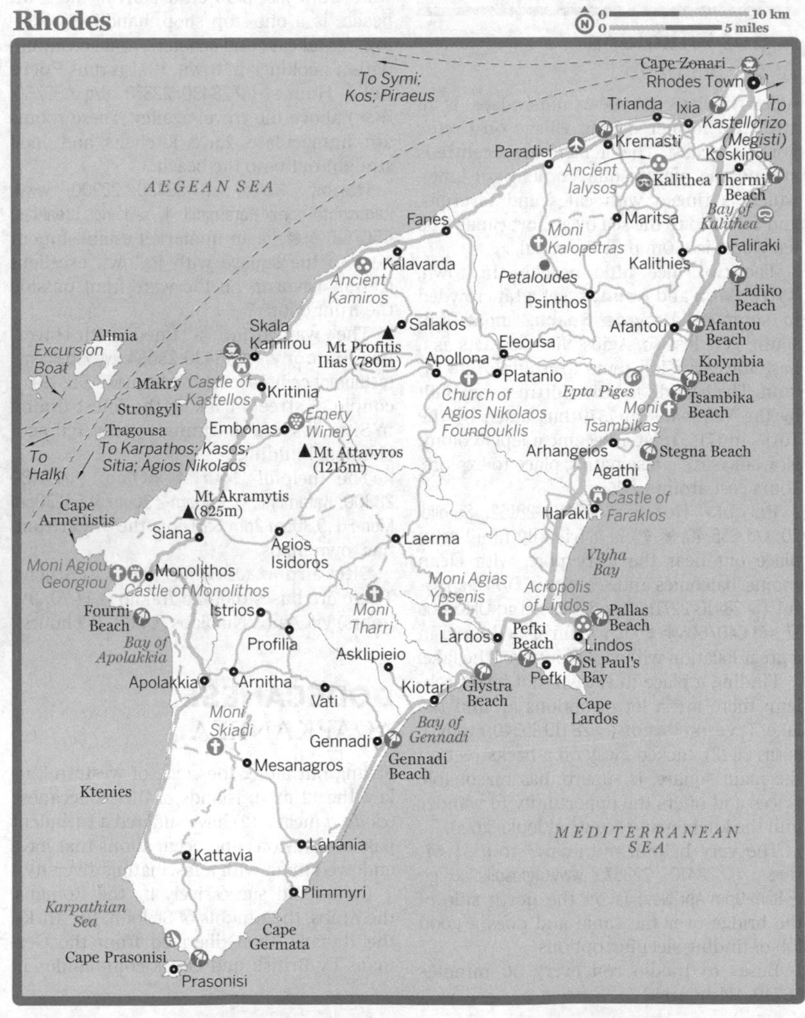

TALKING TURKEY

Turkey is so close that it looks like you could swim there from many of the Dodecanese and Northeastern Aegean islands. Here are the boat options:

Marmaris or Fethiye from Rhodes (p625)

Bodrum from Kos (p629)

Kuşadasi (near Ephesus) from Samos (p630)

Çeşme (near İzmir) from Chios (p633)

Dikili (near Ayvalık) from Lesvos (p633)

International charter flights swarm in summer, plus budget airlines fly in with scheduled flights. The airport is on the west coast, 16km southwest of Rhodes Town; 25 minutes and €2.20 by bus.

Boat

Rhodes is the main port of the Dodecanese and there is a complex array of departures. There are daily ferries from Rhodes to Piraeus (€59, 13 hours). Most sail via the Dodecanese north of Rhodes, but at least twice a week there is a service via Karpathos, Crete and the Cyclades.

In summer, catamaran services run up and down the Dodecanese daily from Rhodes to Symi, Kos, Kalymnos, Nisyros, Tilos, Patmos and Leros.

To Turkey

There are boats between Rhodes and Marmaris in Turkey (one-way/return including port taxes, €50/75, 50 minutes). Check www.marmarisinfo.com for up-to-date details.

You can also travel between Rhodes and Fethiye, Turkey (one way/return including port taxes €50/75, 90 minutes). See www.alaturkaturkey.com.

RHODES TOWN

POP 56,000

Rhodes' capital is Rhodes Town, on the northern tip of the island. Its **Old Town**, the largest inhabited medieval town in Europe, is enclosed within massive walls and is a joy to explore. To the north is **New Town**, the commercial centre. The **town beach**, which looks out at Turkey runs around the peninsula at the northern end of New Town.

The main port, **Commercial Harbour**, is east of the Old Town, and is where the big interisland ferries dock. Northwest of here is **Mandraki Harbour**, lined with excursion boats and smaller ferries, hydrofoils and catamarans. It was the supposed site of the Colossus of Rhodes, a 32m-high bronze statue of Apollo built over 12 years (294–282 BC). The statue stood for a mere 65 years before being toppled by an earthquake.

Sleeping

TOP CHOICE **Marco Polo Mansion** BOUTIQUE HOTEL €€

(☎22410 25562; www.marcopolomansion.gr; Agiou Fanouriou 40, Old Town; d incl breakfast from €90-180; ❄📶) In a 15th-century building in the Turkish quarter of the Old Town, this place is rich in Ottoman-era colours and features

DON'T MISS

OLD TOWN

A wander around Rhodes' World Heritage–listed Old Town is a must. It is reputedly the world's finest surviving example of medieval fortification, with 12m-thick walls. Throngs of visitors pack its busier streets and eating, sleeping and shopping options abound.

The Knights of St John lived in the Knights' Quarter in the northern end of the Old Town. The cobbled **Odos Ippoton** (Ave of the Knights) is lined with magnificent medieval buildings, the most imposing of which is the **Palace of the Grand Masters** (☎22410 23359; admission €6; ⊙8.30am-3pm Tue-Sun), which was restored, but never used, as a holiday home for Mussolini.

The 15th-century Knight's Hospital now houses the **Archaeological Museum** (☎22410 27657; Plateia Mousiou; admission €3; ⊙8am-4pm Tue-Sun). The splendid building was restored by the Italians and has an impressive collection that includes the ethereal marble statue *Aphrodite of Rhodes*.

The pink-domed **Mosque of Süleyman**, at the top of Sokratous, was built in 1522 to commemorate the Ottoman victory against the knights, then rebuilt in 1808.

You can take a pleasant walk around the imposing walls of the Old Town via the wide and pedestrianised moat walk.

DON'T MISS

MARCO POLO CAFÉ

A top spot to eat in Rhodes, **Marco Polo Café** (☎22410 25562; www.marcopolomansion.gr; Agiou Fanouriou 40, Old Town) is worth finding in the backstreets of the Old Town. Owner Efi is as tastefully colourful as her mansion and garden restaurant. This place serves its guests with a rare passion – and the desserts are exquisite!

in glossy European magazines. In the secluded garden is the highly recommended Marco Polo Café.

TOP CHOICE **Mango Rooms** PENSION €
(☎22410 24877; www.mango.gr; Plateia Dorieos 3, Old Town; s/d/tr €44/58/66; ❄@📶) A good-value, friendly one-stop shop near the back of the Old Town, Mango has an outdoor restaurant, bar and internet cafe down below, six well-kept rooms above, and a sunny terrace on top. Open year-round.

Hotel Andreas PENSION €€
(☎22410 34156; www.hotelandreas.com; Omirou 28d, Old Town; s/d/tr €45/70/85; ❄@📶) Tasteful Hotel Andreas has individually decorated rooms and terrific views from its terrace. Rates differ by room; check it all out online, and choose your room before you go.

Hotel International HOTEL €€
(☎22410 24595; www.international-hotel.gr; 12 Kazouli St, New Town; s/d/tr €45/60/75; ❄📶) In New Town, the International is a friendly family-run operation with immaculately clean and good-value rooms only a few minutes from Rhodes' main town beach. It's a 10-minute stroll to Old Town, and prices drop by a third out of high season.

Eating & Drinking

There's food and drink everywhere you look in Rhodes. Outside the city walls are many cheap places in the New Market, at the southern end of Mandraki Harbour. Head further north into New Town for countless restaurants and bars.

Inside the walls, Old Town has it all in terms of touts and over-priced tavernas trying to separate less-savvy tourists from their euro. The back alleys tend to throw up better-quality eateries and prices. Delve into the maze and see what you can come up with.

To Meltemi TAVERNA €
(Kountourioti 8; mains €10-15) At the northern end of Mandraki Harbour, To Meltemi is one place worth heading to. Gaze out on Turkey from this beachside taverna where the seafood is superb. Try the grilled calamari stuffed with tomato and feta, and inspect the old photos of Rhodes.

Information

For more information, visit the Rodos website (www.rodos.gr).

Tourist Information Office (EOT; ☎22410 35226; cnr Makariou & Papagou; ⏲8am-2.45pm Mon-Fri) Has brochures, maps and *Rodos News*, a free English-language newspaper.

Triton Holidays (☎22410 21690; www.tritondmc.gr; Plastira 9, Mandraki) In the New Town, this place is exceptionally helpful, handling accommodation bookings, ticketing and rental cars. The island-hopping experts, Triton can provide up-to-date advice in these times of constantly changing flight and boat schedules. Email ahead for advice.

Getting Around

BUS Rhodes Town has two bus stations a block apart next to the New Market. The west-side bus station serves the airport, Kamiros (€4.60, 55 minutes) and the west coast. The east-side bus station serves the east coast, Lindos (€5, 1½ hours) and the inland southern villages.

AROUND THE ISLAND

The **Acropolis of Lindos** (admission €6; ⏲8.30am-6pm Tue-Sun Jun-Aug, to 2.30pm Sep-May), 47km south from Rhodes Town, is an ancient city spectacularly perched atop a 116m-high rocky outcrop. Below is the town of **Lindos**, a tangle of streets with elaborately decorated 17th-century houses.

The extensive ruins of **Kamiros**, an ancient Doric city on the west coast, are well preserved, with the remains of houses, baths, a cemetery and a temple, but the site should be visited as much for its lovely setting on a gentle hillside overlooking the sea.

Karpathos Κάρπαθος

POP 6000

The elongated, mountainous island of Karpathos (*kar*-pah-thos), midway between Crete and Rhodes, is a scenic, hype-free place with a cosy port, numerous beaches and unspoilt villages. It is a wealthy island, reputedly receiving more money from emigrants living abroad than any other Greek island.

The main port and capital is **Pigadia**, on the southeast coast. The northern village of **Olymbos** is like a living museum. Locals wear traditional outfits and the facades of houses are decorated with bright plaster reliefs.

A great option on Karpathos is to hire a car and tour this rugged island on its excellent roads. The 19km stretch from Spoa to Olymbos may finally be sealed by the time you read this. Check before you go though!

Elias Rooms (22450 22446; www.eliasrooms.com; s/d €35/40;) is an excellent accommodation option. Owner Elias is a mine of information and his rooms have great views while being in a quiet part of town. Elias' website can tell you all you need to know about Karpathos and he is happy to provide information by email.

Possi Travel (22450 22235; www.possi-holidays.gr; 8am-1pm & 5.30-8.30pm), on pedestrianised Apodimon Karpathion, can suggest local tours and handles air and ferry tickets.

In summer, **Karpathos airport** (AOK), 13km southwest of Pigadia, has daily flights to Rhodes and Athens. With a huge new terminal, international charter flights also wing their way in. There are two ferries a week to Rhodes (€23, four hours) and two to Piraeus (€41, 17 hours) via Crete and the Cyclades.

There are also excursions from Pigadia to Diafani, at the north of the island, that include a bus trip to Olymbos.

Symi Σύμη

POP 2600

Simply superb, Symi is an inviting island to the north of Rhodes that should be on all island-hopper itineraries. The port town of **Gialos** is a Greek treasure, with pastel-coloured mansions heaped up the hills surrounding the protective little harbour. Symi is swamped by day trippers from Rhodes, and it's worth staying over to enjoy the island in cruise control. The town is divided into Gialos, the port and the tranquil *horio* (village) above it, accessible by taxi, bus or 360 steps from the harbour.

There is no tourist office. The best source of information is the free monthly English-language **Symi Visitor** (www.symivisitor.com), which includes maps of the town.

The **Monastery of Panormitis** (dawn-sunset) is a hugely popular complex at the southern end of the island. Its **museum** is impressive, but try to avoid the hordes of day trippers who arrive at around 10.30am on excursion boats from Rhodes.

WORTH A TRIP

CRYSTAL CLEAR

If you like mind-bogglingly clear water when you go to the beach, head to Karpathos for some of the clearest turquoise wet stuff to be seen anywhere. **Apella** and **Ahata** beaches, both north of Pigadia, are stunning; **Ammoöpi**, 8km south of the capital, will make you drool. Karpathos' top beaches are best accessed with your own wheels.

Budget accommodation is scarce. **Rooms Katerina** (69451 30112, 22460 71813; www.symigreece.com/sg/villakaterina; d €30;) is excellent, but get in quick as there are only three rooms. There is a communal kitchen with breathtaking views down over the port, and helpful Katerina is happy to answer all your questions.

On the waterfront next to the clock tower, **Hotel Nireus** (22460 72400; www.nireus-hotel.gr; s/d incl breakfast €80/115;) is bright, friendly, has free wi-fi and the bonus of being able to swim right out front.

Kalodoukas Holidays (22460 71077; www.kalodoukas.gr) handles accommodation bookings, ticketing and has a book of walking trails on the island.

There are frequent boats between Rhodes and Kos that stop at Symi, as well as daily excursion boats from Rhodes. **Symi Tours** (www.symitours.com) runs excursions on Saturdays to Datça in Turkey for €40.

Small taxi boats visit inaccessible east-coast beaches daily in summer, including spectacular Agios Georgious, backed by a 150m sheer cliff.

Kos Κως

POP 17,900

Captivating Kos, only 5km from the Turkish peninsula of Bodrum, is popular with history buffs as the birthplace of Hippocrates (460–377 BC), the father of medicine. The island also attracts an entirely different crowd – sun-worshipping beach lovers from northern Europe who flock here during summer. Tourism rules the roost, and whether you are there to explore the Castle of the Knights or to party till you drop, Kos should keep you happy for at least a few days.

Kos Town is based around a circular harbour, protected by the imposing Castle of the Knights, at the eastern end of the island. The ferry quay is just to the north of the castle.

Sights & Activities

Kos Town has recently developed a number of **bicycle paths** and renting a bike from one of the many places along the waterfront is a great option for getting around town and seeing the sights.

If the historical stuff is all too much, wander around and relax with the Scandinavians at the town beach past the northern end of the harbour.

Castle of the Knights CASTLE
(22420 27927; admission €4; 8am-2.30pm Tue-Sun) Built in the 14th century, this impressive castle protected the knights from the encroaching Ottomans, and was originally separated from town by a moat. That moat is now Finikon, a major street. Entrance to the castle is over the stone bridge behind the Hippocrates Plane Tree.

THE KNIGHTS OF ST JOHN

Do some island-hopping in the Dodecanese and you'll quickly realise that the Knights of St John left behind a whole lot of castles.

Originally formed as the Knights Hospitaller in Jerusalem in AD 1080 to provide care for poor and sick pilgrims, the knights relocated to Rhodes (via Cyprus) after the loss of Jerusalem in the First Crusade. They ousted the ruling Genoese in 1309, built a stack of castles in the Dodecanese to protect their new home, then set about irking the neighbours by committing acts of piracy against Ottoman shipping. Sultan Süleyman the Magnificent, not a man you'd want to irk, took offence and set about dislodging the knights from their strongholds. Rhodes finally capitulated in 1523 and the remaining knights relocated to Malta. They set up there as the Sovereign Military Hospitaller of Jerusalem, of Rhodes, and of Malta.

Asklipieion ARCHAEOLOGICAL SITE
(22420 28763; adult/student €4/3; 8am-7.30pm Tue-Sun) On a pine-clad hill 4km southwest of Kos Town stand the extensive ruins of the renowned healing centre where Hippocrates practised medicine. Groups of doctors come from all over the world to visit.

Ancient Agora RUIN
The ancient agora, with the ruins of the **Shrine of Aphrodite** and **Temple of Hercules**, is just off Plateia Eleftherias. North of the agora is the **Hippocrates Plane Tree**, under which the man himself is said to have taught his pupils.

Sleeping

TOP CHOICE **Hotel Afendoulis** HOTEL €
(22420 25321; www.afendoulishotel.com; Evripilou 1; s/d €30/50; Mar-Nov;) In a pleasant, quiet area about 500m south of the ferry quay, this well-kept hotel won't disappoint. Run by the charismatic English-speaking Alexis, this is a great place to relax and enjoy Kos. Port- and bus-station transfers are complimentary, and you can get your laundry done here.

Hotel Sonia HOTEL €
(22420 28798; www.hotelsonia.gr; Irodotou 9; s/d/tr €35/50/85;) Recently refurbished, Sonia's place has long been a popular spot to stay in Kos. It has large rooms and a relaxing veranda and garden. They'll pick you up at the port or bus station for free and there are laundry facilities on site. It's back behind the Dolphin roundabout.

Eating & Drinking

Restaurants line the central waterfront of the old harbour, but you might want to hit the backstreets for value. There are plenty of cheap places to eat on the beach to the north of the harbour, and a dozen discos and clubs around the streets of Diakon and Nafklirou, just north of the agora.

Stadium Restaurant SEAFOOD €
(22420 27880; mains €10-18) On the long waterfront 500m southeast of the castle, Stadium serves succulent seafood at good prices, along with excellent views of Turkey.

Information

Visit www.kosinfo.gr for more information.

Exas Travel (22420 28545; www.exas.gr) Near the Archaeological Museum, in the heart of town, to the southwest of the harbour; handles schedules, ticketing and excursions.

Municipal Tourist Office (☎22420 24460; www.kosinfo.gr; Vasileos Georgiou 1; ⊙8am-2.30pm & 3-10pm Mon-Fri, 9am-2pm Sat May-Oct) On the waterfront directly south of the port; provides maps and accommodation information.

 Getting There & Around

Air

There are daily flights to Athens from Kos' Ippokratis airport (KGS), which is 28km southwest of Kos Town. International charters and scheduled flights wing in throughout the summer from around Europe. Get to/from the airport by bus (€4) or taxi (€30).

Boat

There are frequent ferries from Rhodes to Kos that continue on to Piraeus (€53, 10 hours), as well as ferries heading the opposite way. Daily fast-boat connections head north to Patmos and Samos, and south to Symi and Rhodes.

To Turkey

In summer boats depart daily for Bodrum in Turkey (€20 return, one hour). Wander the waterfront and take your pick.

Bus

There is a good public bus system on Kos, with the bus station on Kleopatras, near the ruins at the back of town.

Mini-Train

Next to the tourist office is a blue mini-train for Asklipion (€5 return, hourly, Tuesday to Sunday) and a green mini-train that does city tours (€4, 20 minutes).

Patmos Πάτμος

POP 3050

Patmos has a sense of 'spirit of place', and with its great beaches and relaxed atmosphere, it's a superb place to unwind.

The main town and port of Skala is about halfway down the east coast of Patmos, with a protected harbour. Towering above Skala to the south is the *hora*, crowned by the immense Monastery of St John the Theologian.

Sights & Activities

Beaches BEACHES

Patmos' coastline provides secluded coves, mostly with pebble beaches. The best is **Psili Ammos**, in the south, reached by excursion boat from Skala port. **Lambi Beach**, on the north coast, is a pebble-beach-lover's dream come true.

> WORTH A TRIP
>
> **ST JOHN & THE APOCALYPSE**
>
> For the religiously motivated, Patmos is not to be missed. Orthodox and Western Christians have long made pilgrimages to Patmos, for it was here that John the Divine ensconced himself in a cave and wrote the Book of Revelation.
>
> The **Cave of the Apocalypse** (admission free, treasury €6; ⊙8am-1.30pm daily & 4-6pm Tue, Thu & Sun) is halfway between the port and Hora. Take a bus from the port or hike up the Byzantine path, which starts from a signposted spot on the Skala–Hora road.
>
> The **Monastery of St John the Theologian** (admission free; ⊙8am-1.30pm daily & 4-6pm Tue, Thu & Sun) looks more like a castle than a monastery and tops Patmos like a crown. It exhibits all kinds of monastic treasures, and attending a service here is unforgettable.

Sleeping

Pension Maria Pascalidis PENSION €

(☎22470 32152; s/d without bathroom €20/30) Maria has cosy rooms in a fragrant citrus-tree garden on the road heading up to the Hora and Monastery. A travellers' favourite, guests share a communal bathroom and kitchen.

Blue Bay Hotel BOUTIQUE HOTEL €€

(☎22470 31165; www.bluebaypatmos.gr; s/d/tr incl breakfast €65/90/108; ❄@📶) South of the harbour in Skala, this recommended waterfront hotel has superb rooms, internet access, and breakfast included in its rates (which tumble outside of high season).

Information

See the websites www.patmosweb.gr, and www.patmos-island.com for more information.

Apollon Travel (☎22470 31324; apollontravel@stratas.gr) On the waterfront; handles schedules and ticketing.

Tourist Office (☎22470 31666; ⊙8am-6pm Mon-Fri Jun-Sep) In the white building opposite the port in Skala, along with the post office and police station.

Getting There & Away

BOAT Patmos is well connected, with ferries to Piraeus (€37, seven hours) and south to Rhodes (€32, six hours). In summer, daily high-speed services head south to Kos and Rhodes, and north to Samos.

NORTHEASTERN AEGEAN ISLANDS
ΤΑ ΝΗΣΙΑ ΤΟΥ ΒΟΡΕΙΟ ΑΝΑΤΟΛΙΚΟ ΑΙΓΑΙΟΥ

One of Greece's best-kept secrets, these far-flung islands are strewn across the north-eastern corner of the Aegean Sea, closer to Turkey than mainland Greece. They harbour unspoilt scenery, welcoming locals, fascinating independent cultures and remain relatively calm even when other Greek islands are sagging with tourists at the height of summer.

Samos Σάμος

POP 32,800

A lush mountainous island only 3km from Turkey, Samos has a glorious history as the legendary birthplace of Hera, wife and sister of god-of-all-gods Zeus. Samos was an important centre of Hellenic culture, and the mathematician Pythagoras and storyteller Aesop are among its sons. The island has beaches that bake in summer, and a hinterland that is superb for hiking. Spring brings with it pink flamingos, wildflowers and orchids that the island grows for export, while summer brings throngs of package tourists.

Getting There & Around

Air

There are daily flights to Athens from **Samos airport** (SMI), 4km west of Pythagorio, plus less-regular flights to Iraklio, Rhodes, Chios and Thessaloniki. Charter flights wing in from Europe in summer.

Boat

Samos has two main ports: Vathy (Samos Town) in the northeast and Pythagorio on the south-east coast. Those coming from the south by boat generally arrive in Pythagorio. Big ferries use Vathy. Once you're on Samos and have onward tickets, double-check where your boat is leaving from. Buses between the two take 25 minutes.

A maritime hub, Samos offers daily ferries to Piraeus (€48, 10 hours), plus ferries heading north to Chios and west to the Cyclades. Once the season is up and going, fast speed services head south to Patmos and continue to Kos.

Bus

You can get to most of the island's villages and beaches by bus.

Car & Motorcycle

Rental cars and scooters are readily available around the island (cars/scooters from €60/30 per day).

To Turkey

There are daily ferries to Kuşadasi (for Ephesus) in Turkey (one-way/return €35/45, plus €10 port taxes). Day excursions are also available from April to October. Check with ITSA Travel in Vathy for up-to-date details.

VATHY (SAMOS TOWN) ΒΑΘΥ ΣΑΜΟΣ

POP 2030

Busy Vathy is an attractive working port town. Most of the action is along Themis-

Samos

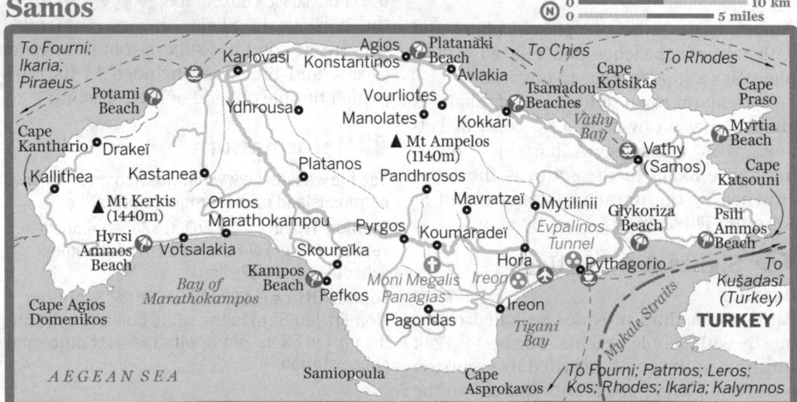

tokleous Sofouli, the main street that runs along the waterfront. The main square, Plateia Pythagorou, in the middle of the waterfront, is recognizable by its four palm trees and statue of a lion.

The **Archaeological Museum** (adult/student €3/2, free Sun; 8.30am-3pm Tue-Sun) by the municipal gardens, is first-rate and one of the best in the islands.

Pythagoras Hotel (22730 28601; www.pythagorashotel.com; Kallistratou 12, s/d/tr €20/35/45; Feb-Nov;) is a friendly, great-value place with a convivial atmosphere, run by English-speaking Stelio. There is a restaurant serving tasty home-cooked meals, a bar, satellite TV and internet access. Facing inland, the hotel is 400m to the left of the quay. Call ahead for free pick-up on arrival.

Ino Village Hotel (22730 23241; www.inovillagehotel.com; Kalami; s/d/tr incl breakfast €65/80/100;) is an impressive, elegant place in the hills north of the ferry quay. Its **Elea Restaurant** on the terrace serves up both invigorated Greek cuisine and views over town and the harbour.

ITSA Travel (22730 23605; www.itsatravelsamos.gr), opposite the quay, is helpful with travel enquiries, excursions, accommodation and luggage storage.

To get to Vathy's bus station, follow the waterfront south and turn left onto Lekati, 250m south of Plateia Pythagorou (just before the police station).

PYTHAGORIO ΠΥΘΑΓΟΡΕΙΟ

POP 1300

Pretty Pythagorio, 25 minutes south of Vathy by bus, is where you'll disembark if you've come by boat from Patmos. It is a small, enticing town with a yacht-lined harbour and a holiday atmosphere.

The 1034m-long **Evpalinos Tunnel** (adult/student €4/2; 8am-8pm Tue-Sun), built in the 6th century BC, was dug by political prisoners and used as an aqueduct to bring water from Mt Ampelos (1140m). In the Middle Ages, locals hid out in it during pirate raids. It's a 20-minute walk north of town.

Polyxeni Hotel (22730 61590; www.polyxenihotel.com; s/d/tr €40/45/55;) is a fun place to stay in the heart of the waterfront action. **Pension Despina** (22730 61677; www.samosrooms.gr/despina; A Nikolaou; d €35;), a block back from the water, offers simple studios and rooms, some with balconies and kitchenettes.

Tavernas and bars line the waterfront. **Poseidon Restaurant** (22730 62530; mains from €7), on the small town beach, past the jetty with the Pythagoras statue on it, offers superb seafood.

The cordial **municipal tourist office** (22730 61389; deap5@otenet.gr; 8am-9.30pm) is two blocks from the waterfront on the main street, Lykourgou Logotheti. The bus stop is two blocks further inland on the same street.

> **THAT TRIANGLE MAN**
>
> You don't need much of an imagination to figure out where the cute little town of Pythagorio got its name! The impressive statue of Pythagoras and his triangle on the town's waterfront should have you recalling his theorem from your high school maths days. If right-angled triangles weren't your thing, buy a T-shirt with the theorem emblazoned on it to remind you.

Around Samos

Ireon (adult/student €4/2; 8.30am-8pm Tue-Sun), the legendary birthplace of the goddess Hera, is 8km west of Pythagorio. The temple at this World Heritage site was enormous – four times the Parthenon – though only one column remains.

The captivating villages of **Vourliotes** and **Manolates**, on the slopes of imposing Mt Ampelos, northwest of Vathy, are excellent walking territory and have many marked pathways.

Choice beaches include **Tsamadou** on the north coast, **Votsalakia** in the southwest and **Psili Ammos** to the east of Pythagorio. The latter is sandy and stares straight out at Turkey, barely a couple of kilometres away.

Chios Χίος

POP 54,000

Due to its thriving shipping and mastic industries (mastic produces the resin used in chewing gum), Chios (*hee*-os) has never really bothered much with tourism. If you are an off-the-beaten-track type of Greek Islands traveller, you'll find Chios all the more appealing.

Chios Town, on the island's eastern coast, is a working port and home to half the island's inhabitants. A main street runs in a semicircle

THE ORIGINAL CHEWING GUM

Chios is home to the world's only gum-producing mastic trees and the southern *mastihohoria* (mastic villages) were wealthy for centuries. Not only were they wealthy, but the mastic trees are also said to have saved them when the Turks came and slaughtered the rest of the island's residents. The sultan's reputed fondness for mastic chewing gum – and the rumour that his harem girls used it for keeping their teeth clean and their breath fresh – meant that the *mastihohoria* were spared.

These days, **Masticulture Ecotourism Activities** (☎22710 76084; www.masticulture.com) in the southern village of Mesta, introduces visitors to the local history and culture, including mastic cultivation tours. In Chios Town, on the waterfront, **Mastihashop** (☎22710 81600; www.mastihashop.com; Leoforos Egeou 36) sells products such as mastic chewing gum, toothpaste and soaps, and **Mastic Spa** (☎22710 28643; www.masticspa.com; Leoforos Egeou 12) sells mastic-based cosmetics.

around the port, with most ferries docking at its northern end. The *kastro* (old Turkish quarter) is to the north of the ferry quay, and Plateia Vounakiou, the main square, is just south and inland from the quay.

Sights & Activities

In Chios Town, **Philip Argenti Museum** (Korais; admission €1.50; 8am-2pm Mon-Thu, to 2pm & 5-7.30pm Fri, 8am-12.30pm Sat) contains the treasures of the wealthy Argenti family.

World Heritage–listed **Nea Moni** (New Monastery; admission free; 8am-1pm & 4-8pm) is 14km west of Chios Town and reveals some fine Byzantine art, with mosaics dating from the 11th century. The mosaics survived, but the resident monks were massacred by the Turks in 1822. You can see their dented skulls in the chapel at the monastery's entrance.

Those in the ghost village of **Anavatos**, 10km from Nea Moni and built on a precipitous cliff, preferred a different fate, hurling themselves off the cliff rather than being taken captive by the Turks.

Pyrgi, 24km southwest of Chios Town, is one of Greece's most unusual villages. The facades of the town's dwellings are decorated with intricate grey-and-white geometric patterns and motifs. The tiny medieval town of **Mesta**, 10km from Pyrgi and nestled within fortified walls, features cobbled streets, overhead arches and a labyrinth of streets designed to confuse pirates.

Sleeping

TOP CHOICE **Chios Rooms** PENSION €
(☎22710 20198; www.chiosrooms.gr; Leoforos Egeou 110; s/d/tr €30/35/45; 📶) A top location to stay, this place is upstairs in a restored neoclassical house on the waterfront at the southern end of the harbour. It has bright, airy rooms, some with en suite bathrooms, and is being restored lovingly by its Kiwi owner, Don, who is a mine of information on Chios.

Hotel Kyma HOTEL €€
(☎22710 44500; kyma@chi.forthnet.gr; Evgenias Handris 1; s/d/tr incl breakfast €70/90/110; ❄📶) Just past the southern end of the waterfront, this place occupies a charismatic century-old mansion and is run by the enthusiastic multilingual Theodoris. Ask for a room overlooking the sea.

Eating

The waterfront has ample options in the way of eateries and bars, though for cheap eats, head one street back onto El Venizelou, which is lined with shops. The Plateia Vounakiou area, inland from where the ferries dock, also has up some good options.

TOP CHOICE **Hotzas Taverna** TAVERNA €
(☎22710 42787; Kondyli 3; mains from €6) Up the back of town, Hotzas is known by locals to provide the best Greek fare on the island. Get a local to mark it on a map, and enjoy the walk. It's worth the effort of finding.

Information

Check out the **Chios website** (www.chios.gr) for more information.

Agean Travel (☎22710 41277; www.aegeanspirit.gr; Leoforos Egeou 114)

Municipal Tourist Office (☎22710 44389; infochio@otenet.gr; Kanari 18; 7am-3pm & 6.30-10pm Apr-Oct, to 3pm Nov-Mar) Information on accommodation, car rental, bus and boat schedules.

Getting There & Around

Air

There are daily flights from Chios airport (JKH) to Athens and some to Rhodes, Samos, Lesvos and Thessaloniki. The airport is 4km south of Chios Town; there's no bus, a taxi costs €8.

Boat

Ferries sail daily to Piraeus (€32.50, six hours) and Lesvos (€19.50, three hours). Boats also head out less regularly to Thessaloniki and Samos.

Bus

Chios Town has two bus stations. Blue buses go regularly to local villages and Karfas Beach, and leave from the local bus station at the main square. Buses to Pyrgi (€2.70) and Mesta (€3.90) and other distant points leave from the long-distance bus station on the waterfront near the ferry quay.

To Turkey

Boats to Turkey run all year from Chios, with daily sailings from July to September to Çeşme (one-way/return €25/30), near İzmir. For details, check out **Miniotis Lines** (☎22710 24670; www.miniotis.gr; Neorion 24).

Lesvos (Mytilini) Λέσβος (Μυτιλήνη)

POP 93,500

Lesvos, or Mytilini as it is often called, tends to do things in a big way. The third-largest of the Greek Islands after Crete and Evia, Lesvos produces half the world's ouzo and is home to over 11 million olive trees. Mountainous yet fertile, the island presents excellent hiking and birdwatching opportunities, but remains relatively untouched in terms of tourism development.

Lesvos has always been a centre of philosophy and artistic achievement, and to this day is a spawning ground for innovative ideas in the arts and politics. An excellent source of information on the island is www.greeknet.com.

The two main towns on the island are the capital, **Mytilini**, on the southeast coast, and attractive **Mithymna** on the north coast.

Getting There & Away

Air

Written up on flight schedules as Mytilene, Lesvos' Odysseas airport (MJT) has daily connections with Athens, plus flights to Thessaloniki, Iraklio and a growing number of domestic destinations. The airport is 8km south of Mytilini town; a taxi costs €9 and a bus to town costs €1.50.

Boat

In summer there are daily fast/slow boats to Piraeus (€37/27, eight/13 hours) via Chios, and boats to Limnos, Thessaloniki and Samos.

To Turkey

There are regular ferries a week to Dikeli port (which serves Ayvalık) and to Fokias (which serves İzmir). Stop by Zoumboulis Tours in Mytilini for ticketing and schedules.

MYTILINI ΜΥΤΙΛΗΝΗ

POP 27,300

The capital and main port, Mytilini, is built between two harbours (north and south) with an imposing fortress on the promontory to the east. All ferries dock at the southern harbour, and most of the town's action is around this waterfront. With a large university campus, Mytilini is a lively place year-round.

Sights & Activities

Archaeological Museum MUSEUM
(8 Noemvriou; adult/child €3/2; ⏲8.30am-3pm Tue-Sun) Mytilini's excellent neoclassical Archaeological Museum has a fascinating collection from Neolithic to Roman times.

SAPPHO, LESBIANS & LESVOS

Sappho, one of Greece's great ancient poets, was born on Lesvos during the 7th century BC. Most of her work was devoted to love and desire, and the objects of her affection were often female. Because of this, Sappho's name and birthplace have come to be associated with female homosexuality.

These days, Lesvos is visited by many lesbians paying homage to Sappho. The whole island is very gay-friendly, in particular the southwestern beach resort of Skala Eresou, which is built over ancient Eresos, where Sappho was born. The village is well set up to cater to lesbian needs and has a 'Women Together' festival held annually in September. Check out www.sapphotravel.com for details.

There is an excellent statue of Sappho in the main square on the waterfront in Mytilini.

Teriade Museum MUSEUM
(☎22510 23372; admission €2; ⏰8.30am-2pm & 5-8pm Tue-Sun) Take a local bus 4km south of Mytilini to the village of Varia, where an unexpected treasure awaits: the Teriade Museum, with its astonishing collection of paintings by world-renowned artists like Picasso, Chagall, Miro, Le Corbusier and Matisse.

Theophilos Museum MUSEUM
(admission €2; ⏰9am-1pm & 5-8pm Tue-Sun) This shrine to the prolific folk painter and Lesvos native Theophilos is located 4km south of Mytilini in Varia village, next to the Teriade Museum.

Fortress FORTRESS
(adult/student €2/1; ⏰8am-2.30pm Tue-Sun) Mytilini's impressive fortress was built in early Byzantine times and enlarged by the Turks. The pine forest surrounding it is a superb place for a stroll or to have a picnic.

Sleeping

Porto Lesvos 1 Hotel HOTEL €€
(☎22510 41771; www.portolesvos.gr; Komninaki 21; s/d/tr incl breakfast €50/60/70; ❄📶) This hotel has attractive rooms and service – right down to robes and slippers – in a restored building one block back from the waterfront.

Pension Thalia PENSION €
(☎22510 24640; Kinikiou 1; s/d €25/30) This pension has clean, bright rooms in a large house. It is about a five-minute walk north of the main square, up Ermou, the road that links the south and north harbours. Follow the signs from the corner of Ermou and Adramytiou.

Eating & Drinking

Mytilini's top spots are a road or two back at the northern end of the harbour.

Stou Mihali GREEK €
(☎22510 43311; Ikarias 7, Plateia Sapphou; mains €4-10; ⏰9am-9pm) It's getting hard to find a free table at lunch at this tasty and inexpensive place. Everything is good; try the *soutzoukakia, imam baïldi* (roast eggplant) and Greek salad.

Mousiko Kafenio CAFE
(cnr Mitropoleos & Vernardaki; ⏰7.30am-2am) This relaxed, arty student cafe just in from the waterfront is full of colour, with eclectic paintings, mirrors and well-worn wooden fixtures.

Information

See www.lesvos.net for more information.

Tourist Office (EOT; ☎22510 42512; 6 Aristarhou; ⏰9am-1pm Mon-Fri) Located 50m up Aristarhou inland from the quay; offers brochures and maps, but its opening hours are limited.

Zoumboulis Tours (☎22510 37755; Kountourioti 69) On the waterfront; handles flights, boat schedules, ticketing and excursions to Turkey.

Getting Around

Mytilini has two bus stations. For local buses, head along the waterfront to the main square. For long-distance buses, walk 600m from the ferry along the waterfront to El Venizelou and turn right until you reach Agia Irinis park, which is next to the station. There are regular services in summer to Mithymna and Skala Eresou.

MITHYMNA ΜΗΘΥΜΝΑ

POP 1500

The gracious, preserved town of Mithymna (known by locals as Molyvos) is 62km north of Mytilini. Cobbled streets canopied by flowering vines wind up the hill below the impressive castle. The town is full of cosy tavernas and genteel stone cottages.

The noble **Genoese castle** (admission €2; ⏰8.30am-7pm Tue-Sun) perches above the town like a crown and affords tremendous views out to Turkey. Pebbly **Mithymna Beach** sits below the town and is good for swimming. Don't forget to stroll down to the harbour.

Eftalou hot springs (public/private bath per person €4/5; ⏰6am-9pm), 4km from town on the beach, is a superb bathhouse complex with a whitewashed dome and steaming, pebbled pool.

Nassos Guest House (☎22530 71432; www.nassosguesthouse.com; Arionis; d/tr without bathroom €20/35; 📶) is an airy, friendly place with shared facilities and a communal kitchen, in an old Turkish house oozing character. With rapturous views, it's highly recommended. It's the only blue house below the castle.

Betty's Restaurant (☎22530 71421; Agora; mains €3-12) has superb home-style Greek food, views and atmosphere in a building that was once a notorious bordello. Betty also has a couple of **cottages** (☎22530 71022; www.bettyscottages.molivos.net; cottages €50) with kitchens in her garden.

From the bus stop, walk straight ahead towards the town for 100m to the helpful **municipal tourist office** (www.mithymna.gr), which has good maps. Some 50m further on, the cobbled main thoroughfare of 17 Noemvriou heads up to the right. Go straight to get to the colourful fishing port.

Buses to Mithymna (€6.90) take 1¾ hours from Mytilini, though a rental car is a good option.

AROUND THE ISLAND

Southern Lesvos is dominated by **Mt Olympus** (968m) and the very pretty village of **Agiasos**, which has good artisan workshops making everything from handcrafted furniture to pottery.

Western Lesvos is known for its petrified forest, with petrified wood at least 500,000 years old, and for the gay-friendly town of **Skala Eresou**, the birthplace of Sappho, see boxed text p635.

SPORADES ΣΠΟΡΑΔΕΣ

Scattered to the southeast of the Pelion Peninsula, to which they were joined in prehistoric times, the 11 islands that make up the Sporades group have mountainous terrain, dense vegetation and are surrounded by scintillatingly clear seas.

The main ports for the Sporades are Volos and Agios Konstantinos on the mainland.

Skiathos Σκιάθος

POP 6150

Lush and green, Skiathos has a beach resort feel about it. Charter flights bring loads of package tourists, but the island still oozes enjoyment. Skiathos Town and some excellent beaches are on the hospitable south coast, while the north coast is precipitous and less accessible.

Skiathos Town's main thoroughfare is Papadiamanti, named after the 19th-century novelist Alexandros Papadiamanti, who was born here. It runs inland opposite the quay.

Sights & Activities

Beaches

Skiathos has superb beaches, particularly on the south coast. **Koukounaries** is popular with families. A stroll over the headland, **Big Banana Beach** is stunning, but if you want an all-over tan, head a tad further to **Little Banana Beach**, where bathing suits are a rarity.

MOVIES UNDER THE STARS

Greece has such great weather in summer that not only does it have a history of open air theatre, there is also an open-air cinema culture. **Cinema Attikon** (☎24720 22352; ticket €7), on Skiathos Town's main street of Papadiamanti, is a great example. You can catch current English-language movies under the stars, sip a beer and practise speed-reading Greek subtitles at the same time! Films are usually shown in their original language in Greece (ie not dubbed).

A number of other islands have similar outdoor cinemas.

Boat Trips

At the Old Harbour in Skiathos Town, there are all sorts of offerings in terms of **boat excursions** – trips to nearby beaches (€10), trips around Skiathos Island (€25) and full-day trips that take in Skopelos, Alonnisos and the Marine Park (€35).

Sleeping

TOP CHOICE **Hotel Bourtzi** BOUTIQUE HOTEL **€€**
(☎24270 21304; www.hotelbourtzi.gr; s/d/tr incl breakfast €80/115/140; P ❄ 📶 🏊) On upper Papadiamanti, the swanky Bourtzi escapes much of the downtown noise and features lovely rooms, along with an inviting garden and pool.

Pension Pandora PENSION **€**
(☎694 413 7377, 24270 24357; www.skiathosinfo.com/accomm/pension-pandora; r €30-70; P ❄ 📶) Run by the effervescent Georgina, this family-run place is 10 minutes' walk north of the quay and a great budget option. The spotless rooms have TV, kitchens and balconies. Georgina also has two exceptional apartments just off Papadiamanti.

Camping Koukounaries CAMPGROUND **€**
(☎24270 49250; campsites per tent/person €4/10; P) This place, 30 minutes from town by bus and at the southwestern end of the island, is at beautiful Koukounaries Beach. There are good facilities, a minimarket and a taverna.

ECOTOURISM ON THE RISE

In a country not noted for its ecological long-sightedness, locals (especially the fishermen) initially struggled with the idea of the **National Marine Park of Alonnisos** when it was established in 1992 to protect the highly endangered Mediterranean monk seal and to promote the recovery of fish stocks.

These days, though, the people of the Sporades have caught on to the advantages of having such a park on their doorstep. Ecotourism is on the rise, with daily excursions on licensed boats into the park from Skiathos, Skopelos and Alonnisos. Though your odds of seeing the shy monk seal aren't great – it's on the list of the 20 most endangered species worldwide – the chances of cruising among pods of dolphins (striped, bottlenose and common) are high.

Eating & Drinking

Skiathos Town is brimming with eateries. There are seafood options around the Old Harbour, and some excellent places up the stairs from there behind the small church.

TOP CHOICE **Piccolo** ITALIAN €
(☎24270 22780; www.firponet.com/piccolo; mains from €8) This Italian place behind the church up from the Old Harbour does exquisite pizzas and pastas in a lovely setting.

1901 GREEK €€
(☎69485 26701; www.skiathos1901.gr; mains from €15) A superb fine-dining restaurant with a glowing reputation, 1901 is up Grigoriou, above the church up from the Old Harbour.

Kentavros BAR
(☎24270 22980) A popular drinking spot just off Plateia Papadiamanti. Expect a mellow ambience and mixture of rock, jazz and blues.

Information

See the website www.skiathosinfo,com for more information.

Heliotropio Travel (☎24270 22430; www.heliotropio.gr) Opposite the ferry quay; handles ticketing and rents cars and scooters.

Tourist Information Booth (☎24270 23172) At the port, but it opens irregularly.

Getting There & Around

AIR Along with numerous charter flights from northern Europe, in summer there is a daily flight from Athens and one from Thessaloniki. Skiathos airport (JSI) is 2km northeast of Skiathos Town.

BOAT There are frequent daily hydrofoils to/from the mainland ports of Volos (€34, 1¼ hours) and Agios Konstantinos (€36, two hours), as well as cheaper ferries. The hydrofoils head to/from Skopelos (€12, 45 minutes) and Alonnisos (€18, one hour). In summer there is also a hydrofoil to Thessaloniki (€47, 4½ hours).

BUS Crowded buses ply the south-coast road between Skiathos Town and Koukounaries every 30 minutes between 7.30am and 11pm year-round, stopping at all the beaches along the way. The bus stop is at the eastern end of the harbour.

Skopelos Σκόπελος

POP 4700

A mountainous island, Skopelos is covered in pine forests, vineyards, olive groves and fruit orchards. While the northwest coast is exposed with high cliffs, the southeast is sheltered and harbours pleasant pebbled beaches. The island's main port and capital of **Skopelos Town**, on the east coast, skirts a semicircular bay and clambers in tiers up a hillside, culminating in a ruined fortress.

The island was used in the filming of *Mamma Mia*. The crew took over Skopelos Town's accommodation for a month and filmed at Agnontas and Kastani beaches on the western coast.

Pension Sotos (☎24240 22549; www.skopelos.net/sotos; s/d €30/45; ❄📶), in the middle of the waterfront, has big rooms in an enchanting old Skopelete building. Check out individual rooms and its different prices online before you go. **Hotel Regina** (☎24240 22138; www.skopelosweb.gr/regina; s/d incl breakfast €45/60; ❄📶) has bright and cheery rooms with balconies. The hotel's rooftop signage is easily spotted from the waterfront.

Top spot in town to chill out is under the huge plane tree at **Platanos Jazz Bar** (☎24240 23661) on the waterfront. It's open all day, plays wicked jazz and blues, and is the ideal place to recover from, or prepare for, a hangover.

In Skopelos Town, there is no tourist office, but **Thalpos Holidays** (☎24240 29036; www.holidayislands.com), on the waterfront, is handy for accommodation and tours. The bus station is next to the port. Excursion boats along the waterfront offer trips into the marine park.

Hydrofoils dash daily to Skiathos (€12, 45 minutes), Alonnisos (€9, 20 minutes), Volos (€44, 2¼ hours) and Agios Konstantinos (€44, three hours). Most hydrofoils also call in at Loutraki, the port below Glossa on the northwest coast of the island. There is also a daily ferry along the same route that costs less but takes longer. There are frequent buses from Skopelos Town to Glossa (€1.80, one hour) stopping at all beaches along the way.

Alonnisos Αλόννησος

POP 2700

Green, serene Alonnisos is at the end of the line and the least visited of the Sporades' main islands. The west coast is mostly precipitous cliffs, but the east coast is speckled with pebble-and-sand beaches. The island is well known as a walking destination.

The port village of Patitiri was slapped together in 1965 after an earthquake destroyed the hilltop capital of **Alonnisos Town**.

Pension Pleiades (☎24240 65235; www.pleiadeshotel.gr; s/d/tr from €25/35/50; ❄@) looks out over the harbour and is visible from the quay. The rooms are immaculate, balconied, bright and cheerful. There's also a good restaurant. **Liadromia Hotel** (☎24240 65521; www.liadromia.gr; d/tr/ste incl breakfast €50/70/95; P❄@📶) is an excellent-value place with tons of character, overlooking Patitiri's harbour. Follow the stairway opposite the National Bank. **Camping Rocks** (☎24240 65410; campsites per person €6) is a shady, basic camping ground. It is a steep hike about 1.5km from the port.

There is no tourist office, but on the waterfront, **Alonnisos Travel** (☎24240 66000; www.alonnisostravel.gr) handles boat scheduling and ticketing.

There are ferries with varying regularity connecting Alonnisos to Volos and Agios Konstantinos via Skopelos and Skiathos. Hydrofoils provide the most regular schedules between the islands. They travel several times a day to Skopelos Town (€9, 20 minutes), Skiathos (€16, 1½ hours), Volos (€44, three hours) and Agios Konstantinos (€44, four hours).

THE GREAT CHEESE PIE DEBATE

Tyropita (cheese pie), almost deified in its birthplace of the Sporades, is made with goat cheese rolled in delicate filo dough, coiled up, then fried quickly and served hot. The locals love it, but its origins are a source of hot debate.

Those from Alonnisos claim it evolved in the wood-fired oven kitchens of their island and was 'taken' to Skopelos in the 1950s, when farmers went to work on their neighbouring island. What smarts on Alonnisos is that the pie has become famous throughout Greece thanks to a popular TV host who credited Skopelos with its origin – and it is known as the 'Skopelos Cheese Pie'. Those on Alonnisos are cheesed off, to say the least!

IONIAN ISLANDS

ΤΑ ΕΠΤΑΝΗΣΑ

The idyllic cypress- and fir-covered Ionian Islands stretch down the western coast of Greece from Corfu in the north to Kythira, off the southern tip of the Peloponnese. Mountainous, with dramatic cliff-backed beaches, soft light and turquoise water, they're more Italian in feel, offering a contrasting experience to other Greek islands. Invest in a hire car to get to small villages tucked along quiet back roads. Prices drop in low season.

Corfu Κέρκυρα

POP 122,700

Many consider Corfu, or Kerkyra (*ker*-kihrah) in Greek, to be Greece's most beautiful island – the unfortunate consequence of which is that it's overbuilt and often overrun with crowds.

ℹ Getting There & Away

Air

Ioannis Kapodistrias Airport (CFU; ☎26610 30180) is 3km from Corfu Town. **Olympic Air** (☎801 801 0101) and **Aegean Airlines** (☎26610 27100) fly daily to Athens and a few times a week to Thessaloniki.

Sky Express (www.skyexpress.gr) operates seasonal routes to Preveza, Kefallonia, Zakynthos, Kythira and Crete. Charter planes and

Corfu

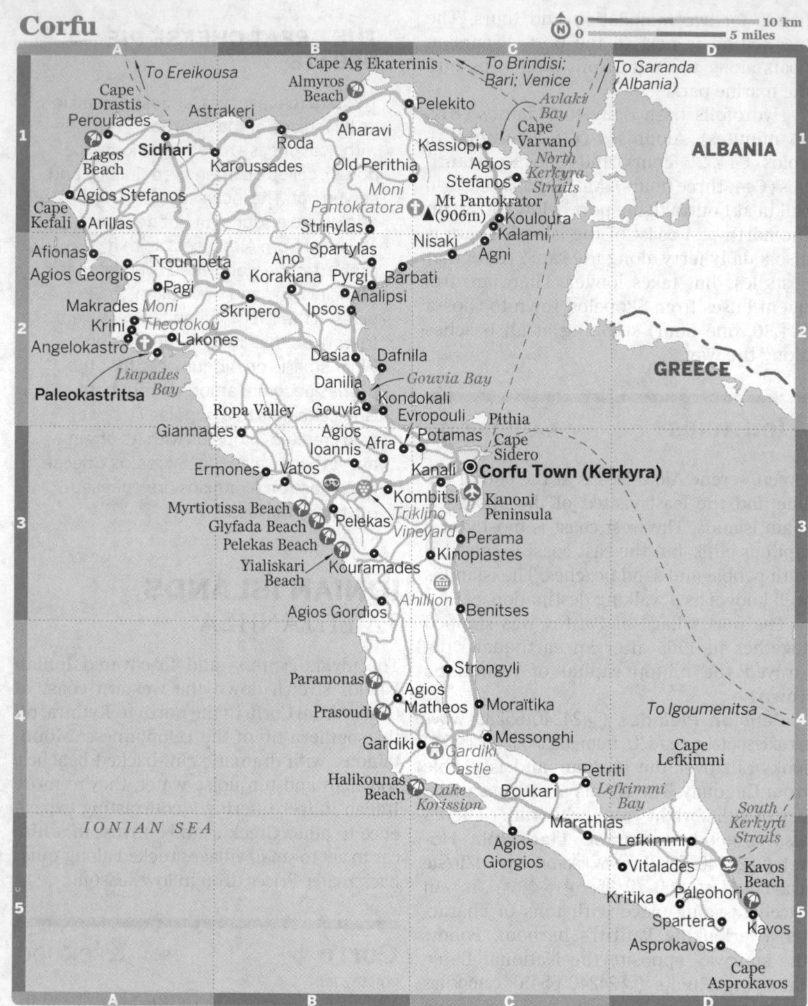

easyJet fly internationally in summer. A taxi from the airport to the centre costs around €12. Buses 6 and 10 stop 800m from the airport.

Boat

Ferries go to Igoumenitsa (€10, 1½ hours, hourly). In summer, daily ferries and hydrofoils go to Paxi, and international ferries (Italy, Albania) also stop in Patra (€35, six hours).

Bus

Daily **buses** (☎26610 28898; www.ktelkerkyras.gr) to Athens (€50, 8½ hours) and Thessaloniki (€45, eight hours) leave from Corfu's **long-distance bus station** (☎26610 28927; Ioannou Theotoki).

CORFU TOWN

POP 28,800

Built on a promontory and wedged between two fortresses, Corfu's Old Town is a tangle of narrow walking streets through gorgeous Venetian buildings. Explore the winding alleys and surprising plazas in the early morning or late afternoon to avoid the hordes of day trippers seeking souvenirs.

Sights

TOP CHOICE Museum of Asian Art MUSEUM
(☎26610 30443; adult/child €4/2; ⊙8.30am-8pm Tue-Sun Jun-Oct, 8.30am-2.30pm Tue-Sun Nov-May) Housed in the **Palace of St Michael & St George** this art collection is expertly curated with extensive English-language placards. Approximately 10,000 artefacts collected from China, Japan, India, Tibet and Thailand include priceless prehistoric bronzes, ceramics, jade figurines and coins.

TOP CHOICE Palaio Frourio FORTRESS
(☎26610 48310; adult/concession €4/2; ⊙8am-8pm May-Oct, 8.30am-3pm Nov-Mar) Constructed by the Venetians in the 15th century on the remains of a Byzantine castle and further altered by the British, the Palaio Frourio stands on an eastern promontory; the Neo Frourio (New Fortress) lies to the northwest.

Antivouniotissa Museum MUSEUM
(☎26610 38313; off Arseniou; admission €2; ⊙8am-2.30pm Tue-Sun) Exquisite basilica with an outstanding collection of Byzantine icons and artefacts dating from the 13th to the 17th centuries.

Mon Repos Estate PARK
(Kanoni Peninsula; ⊙8am-7pm May-Oct, to 5pm Nov-Apr) Sprawling gardens boast two Doric temples.

Church of Agios Spiridon CHURCH
(Agios Spiridonos) Richly decorated church displays the remains of St Spiridon.

Archaeological Museum MUSEUM
(☎26610 30680; P Vraila 5; admission €3; ⊙8.30am-3pm Tue-Sun) Houses a collection of finds from Mycenaean to classical times.

Sleeping

Accommodation prices fluctuate wildly depending on season; book ahead.

TOP CHOICE Bella Venezia BOUTIQUE HOTEL €€
(☎26610 46500; www.bellaveneziahotel.com; N Zambeli 4; s/d incl breakfast from €100/120; ⊜❄☜) Impeccable and understated; contemporary rooms are decked out in cream linens and marbles.

City Marina Hotel HOTEL €€
(☎26610 39505; www.citymarina.gr; Donzelot 15, Old Port; s/d €75/80; ❄☜) Recently renovated and with some sea views, light-filled rooms are managed by friendly staff.

Hermes Hotel HOTEL €
(☎26610 39268; www.hermes-hotel.gr; Markora 12; s/d/tr €50/60/75; ❄☜) Completely refurbished, pleasant, well-appointed rooms in the New Town.

Eating & Drinking

Corfu has excellent restaurants. Cafes and bars line the arcaded Liston. Try Corfu Beer.

La Cucina ITALIAN €€
(☎26610 45029; Guilford 17; mains €10-25) Every detail is cared for at this intimate bistro (and its annex down the street), from the hand-rolled tortelloni to the inventive pizzas and murals on the walls.

Rex MEDITERRANEAN €€
(☎26610 39649; Kapodistriou 66; mains €8-21) Set back from the Liston, this elegant restaurant elevates Greek home cooking to fine dining.

Chrisomalis TAVERNA €
(☎26610 30342; N Theotoki 6; mains €8-13) In the heart of the Old Town, this Ma and Pa operation dishes out the classics.

Rouvas TAVERNA €
(☎26610 31182; S Desilla 13; mains €5-8; ⊙9am-5pm) A favourite lunch stop for locals.

To Dimarchio ITALIAN, GREEK €€
(☎26610 39031; Plateia Dimarchio; mains €9-25) Relax in a luxuriant rose garden on a charming square.

Information

Tourist Police (☎26610 30265; Samartzi 4, 3rd fl)

Getting Around

Blue buses (€1.10 to €1.50) for villages near Corfu Town leave from Plateia San Rocco. Services to other destinations (around Corfu €1.60 to €4.40) leave from the long distance bus terminal.

AROUND THE ISLAND

To explore fully all regions of the island your own transport is best. Much of the coast just north of Corfu Town is overwhelmed with beach resorts, the south is quieter, and the west has beautiful, if popular, coastline. The **Corfu Trail** (www.thecorfutrail.com) traverses the island north to south.

In **Kassiopi**, **Manessis Apartments** (☎26610 34990; http://manessiskassiopi.com; 4-person apt €100; ❄☜) offers water-view apartments. In Sgombou, **Casa Lucia**

WORTH A TRIP

PAXI (ΠΑΞΟΙ)

Paxi lives up to its reputation as one of the Ionians' most idyllic and picturesque islands. At only 10km by 4km it's the smallest of the main holiday islands and makes a fine escape from Corfu's quicker-paced pleasures.

(☎26610 91419; www.casa-lucia-corfu.com; studios & cottages €70-120; P≋) is a garden complex of lovely cottages with a strong alternative ethos. Don't miss a dinner at one of the island's best tavernas, **Klimataria** (Bellos; ☎26610 71201; mains €8-14; ⊙dinner) in Benitses.

To gain an aerial view of the gorgeous cypress-backed bays around **Paleokastritsa**, the west coast's main resort, go to the quiet village of **Lakones**. Backpackers head to **Pelekas Beach** for low-key **Rolling Stone** (☎26610 94942; www.pelekasbeach.com; r/apt €35/98; @) or ramshackle **Sunrock** (☎26610 94637; www.sunrockcorfu.com; dm/r per person €18/24; @≋), a full-board hostel. Further south, good beaches surround tiny **Agios Gordios**.

Lefkada Λευκάδα

POP 22,500

Joined to the mainland by a narrow isthmus, fertile Lefkada with its mountainous interior and pine forests also boasts truly splendid beaches and one of the hottest windsurfing spots in Europe.

Getting There & Around

AIR Sky Express flies to Preveza-Aktio airport (PVK), 20km to the north.

BOAT West Ferry (www.westferry.gr) has an ever-changing schedule from Vasiliki to Kefallonia.

Ionian Pelagos (☎26450 31520) occasionally goes from Vasiliki via Piso Aetos (Ithaki) to Sami (Kefallonia).

Book with **Samba Tours** (☎26450 31520; www.sambatours.gr; Vasiliki) or **Borsalino Travel** (☎26450 92528; Nydri).

BUS & CAR KTEL Bus Station Lefkada Town (☎26450 22364; Ant Tzeveleki)

Athens (€32, 5½ hours, four daily)

Igoumenitsa (€12, two hours, daily)

Patra (€15, three hours, three weekly)

Preveza (€2.90, 30 minutes, six daily)

Thessaloniki (€41.50, eight hours, two weekly)

Rent cars in Lefkada Town, Nydri or Vasiliki.

LEFKADA TOWN

Most travellers' first port of call, Lefkada Town remains laid-back except for August high season. The town's unique earthquake-resistant corrugated-steel architecture somehow blends with its attractive marina, waterfront cafes and vibrant pedestrian thoroughfares.

Sleeping & Eating

Restaurants and cafes line the main street, **Dorpfeld**, central **Plateia Agiou Spyridonos** and the waterfront.

Boschetto Hotel BOUTIQUE HOTEL €€
(☎26450 24967; www.boschettohotel.com; Dorpfeld 1; d incl breakfast from €80; ❄@) Exquisite c 1900 building with four custom-designed rooms and one suite tricked out with all the chicest amenities.

Hotel Santa Maura HOTEL €
(☎26450 21308; Dorpfeld; s/d/tr incl breakfast €50/60/70; ❄) Think tropical Bahamas with sky-blue and shell-pink interiors and breezy balconies; best rooms on the top floor.

Pension Pirofani HOTEL €€
(☎26450 25844; Dorpfeld; r €60-80; ❄) Modern rooms have balconies for prime people-watching.

Ey Zhn INTERNATIONAL €
(☎69746 41160; Filarmonikis 8; mains €7-12; ⊙dinner Jan-Oct) Roadhouse meets artist's loft at this ambience-rich restaurant with excellent, eclectic food.

AROUND THE ISLAND

With its lovely bay, **Nydri** is unfortunately blighted by tacky souvenir shops and touristy tavernas. Lefkada's true gifts are its west-coast beaches. Cliffs drop to broad sweeps of white sand and turquoise waters. Explore! Tiny, bohemian **Agios Nikitas** village draws travellers, but gets very crowded in summer. Nearby, in Athani, get simple clean studios at **Aloni Studios** (☎26450 33604; www.alonistudios-lefkada.com; r €40; P❄).

Southernmost eucalyptus-scented **Vasiliki** is popular with windsurfers. Organise lessons through **Club Vass** (☎26450 31588; www.clubvass.com). Overlooking the port, **Pension Holidays** (☎26450 31426; s/d €45/50; ❄) has great-value rooms with kitchens.

Kefallonia Κεφαλλονιά

POP 37,000

Tranquil cypress- and fir-covered Kefallonia, the largest Ionian island, is breathtakingly beautiful with rugged mountain ranges, rich vineyards, soaring coastal cliffs and golden beaches. It has not succumbed to package tourism to the extent that some of the other Ionian Islands have and remains low-key outside resort areas. Due to the widespread destruction of an earthquake in 1953, much of the island's historic architecture was levelled; Assos and Fiskardo are exceptions.

 Getting There & Around

Air

Olympic Air (26710 41511) flies to Athens, and **Sky Express** serves the Ionians and Crete, from **Kefallonia Airport** (26710 41511), 9km south of Argostoli.

Boat

Ionian Ferries (www.ionianferries.gr) connects Poros and Argostoli to Kyllini (Peloponnese).

Ionian Pelagos (26450 31520) links Sami with Astakos (Peloponnese; sometimes via Piso Aetos in Ithaki).

Strintzis Lines (www.strintzisferries.gr) connects Sami with Patra (Peloponnese) and Vathy or Piso Aetos (Ithaki).

West Ferry (www.westferry.gr) loops from Fiskardo, and sometimes Sami, to Frikes (Ithaki) and Vasiliki.

In high season some ferries connect Sami with Bari, Italy. **Nautilus Travel** (26740 41440; Fiskardo) has information and tickets.

Bus

Three daily buses connect **KTEL Bus Station Argostoli** (26710 22276; Antoni Tritsi 5) with Athens (€47, seven hours) via Patra (€26, four hours). Buses also go to Athens from Sami (two daily), Poros (one daily) and Lixouri (one daily). Local buses don't run on Sunday.

Car

A car is best for exploring. **Pama Travel** (26740 41033; www.pamatravel.com; Fiskardo) rents cars and boats. **Karavomilos** (26740 22779; Sami) delivers cars.

FISKARDO

Pretty Fiskardo, with its pastel-coloured Venetian buildings set around a picturesque bay, is popular with European yachties but it's still peaceful enough to appeal to independent travellers. Take lovely walks to sheltered coves for swimming.

Sleeping

Archontiko PENSION €€
(26740 41342; r from €70;) Overlooking the harbour, people-watch from the balconies of luxurious rooms in a restored stone mansion.

Regina's Rooms PENSION €
(26740 41125; d/tr €40/50;) Some of its colourful, breezy rooms have bay views or kitchenettes.

Eating

Fiskardo has no shortage of excellent waterside restaurants.

TOP CHOICE **Tassia** MEDITERRANEAN €€
(26740 41205; mains €7-25) This unassuming but famous Fiskardo institution run by Tassia Dendrinou, celebrated chef and writer, serves up excellent seafood and Greek dishes.

Café Tselenti ITALIAN €€
(26740 41344; mains €10-23) Enjoy outstanding Italian classics served by friendly waiters; tucked back in a romantic plaza.

AROUND THE ISLAND

In **Argostoli**, the capital, stay over at **Vivian Villa** (26710 23396; www.kefalonia-vivianvilla.gr; Deladetsima 11; d/tr/apt €60/65/100;) with its big, bright rooms and friendly owners. Sample inventive Mediterranean cooking at

KEFALLONIA HIGH-SEASON FERRIES

FROM	TO	FARE (€)	DURATION (HR)
Argostoli	Kyllini (Peloponnese)	14	5
Pesada	Agios Nikolaos (Zakynthos)	8.50	1½
Poros	Kyllini	10	1½
Sami	Bari (Italy)	45	12
Sami	Patra (Peloponnese)	19	2¾
Sami	Piso Aetos & Vathy (Ithaki)	3/7	45min

Casa Grec (☎26710 24091; Metaxa 12; mains €12-22; ⊙dinner nightly, closed Sun & Mon Nov-Apr) or top Kefallonian cuisine at **Arhontiko** (☎26710 27213; 5 Risospaston; mains €7-17; ⊙breakfast, lunch & dinner).

Straddling a slender isthmus on the northwest coast, the petite pastel-coloured village of **Assos** watches over the ruins of a Venetian fortress perched upon a pine-covered peninsula. Eat at **Platanos** (☎69446 71804; mains €6-15; ⊙breakfast, lunch & dinner Easter-Oct) for home-cooked food at its best. Splendid **Myrtos Beach**, 13km south of Assos, is spellbinding from above, with postcard views from the precarious roadway.

Near **Sami**, eat at **Paradise Beach** (Dendrinos; ☎26740 61392; Agia Evfymia; mains €6-13; ⊙lunch & dinner mid-May–mid-Oct), a renowned Kefallonian taverna.

The interior **Omala Valley** is home to **Robola wines** (www.robola.gr). **Paliki Peninsula** is filled with under-explored beauty.

Ithaki Ιθάκη

POP 1550

Odysseus' long-lost home in Homer's *Odyssey*, Ithaki (ancient Ithaca) remains a pristine island blessed with cypress-covered hills and beautiful turquoise coves.

Getting There & Away

Strintzis Lines (www.strintzisferries.gr) has two ferries daily connecting Vathy or Piso Aetos with Patra (Peloponnese) via Sami (Kefallonia).

Ionian Pelagos (☎26450 31520) goes daily in high season between Piso Aetos, Sami and Astakos (mainland).

West Ferry (www.westferry.gr) has an ever-changing schedule from Frikes to Vasiliki (Lefkada); sometimes it goes to Fiskardo, but at the time of research was considering cutting the Frikes stop.

Check routes and schedules at **Delas Tours** (☎26740 32104; www.ithaca.com.gr) or **Polyctor Tours** (☎26740 33120; www.ithakiholidays.com) in Vathy.

KIONI

Tucked in a tiny, tranquil bay, Kioni is a wonderful place to chill for a few days.

Individuals rent rooms and **Captain's Apartments** (☎26740 31481; www.captains-apartments.gr; 2-/4-person apt €60/70; ❄) has shipshape, spacious apartments with kitchens, satellite TV and balconies overlooking the valley and village. **Mythos** (mains €6-10) taverna on the harbour has excellent *pastitsio* (a thick noodle and ground beef casserole). Comfy **Cafe Spavento** (per hr €2) has internet.

AROUND THE ISLAND

The dusty port of **Frikes**, where some ferries dock, is a funkier alternative to Kioni and has rooms to rent.

Vathy, Ithaki's small, bustling capital, is the spot for hiring cars and getting cash (no banks in Kioni). Elegant mansions rise from around its bay and **Hotel Perantzada** (☎26740 33496; www.arthotel.gr/perantzada; Odyssea Androutsou; s/d incl breakfast from €120/150; ⊙Easter–mid-Oct; ❄@🛜≋) occupies two with sensational rooms. **Odyssey Apartments** (☎26740 33400; www.ithaki-odyssey.com; d €60-80, studio €100, 1-/2-bedroom apt €120/150; P❄≋) overlooks town (500m up) and the sea with spotless studios and a pool.

> **FERRY BETWEEN ZAKYNTHOS & KEFALLONIA**
>
> From the northern port of Agios Nikolaos a ferry serves Pesada in southern Kefallonia twice daily from May to October (€8, 1½ hours). Get tickets at **Chlonis Tours** (☎26950 23894; Lomvardou 8, Zakynthos Town). *BUT*, in high season, there are only two buses a week from Zakynthos Town to Agios Nikolaos and two buses daily from Pesada to Argostoli (Kefallonia), making crossing without your own transport difficult. An alternative is to cross to Kyllini and catch another ferry to Kefallonia.

Zakynthos Ζάκυνθος

POP 41,000

The beautiful island of Zakynthos, or Zante, has stunning coves, dramatic cliffs and extensive beaches, but unfortunately is swamped by package-tour groups, so only a few special spots warrant your time.

Getting There & Around

AIR The **airport** (ZTH; ☎26950 28322) is 6km from Zakynthos Town. **Olympic Air** flies to Athens; **Sky Express** flies to Corfu via Kefallonia and Preveza, or to Crete; **easyJet** flies occasionally to Gatwick and Milan; **Air Berlin** flies to German cities.

BOAT **Ionian Ferries** (☎26950 22083/49500; www.ionianferries.gr; Lomvardou 40 & 72,

Zakynthos Town) travels from Zakynthos Town to Kyllini (Peloponnese; €8.50, one hour, four to seven daily).

Occasional ferries go to Brindisi, Italy (€75, 15½ hours), some via Igoumenitsa and Corfu (€32, 8¾hr, two weekly).

BUS The **KTEL bus station** (☎26950 22255; www.ktel-zakynthos.gr) is west of Zakynthos town. Budget an additional €8.50 for the ferry to Kyllini.

Athens (€26, six hours, four daily)
Patra (€8.50, 3½ hours, four daily)
Thessaloniki (€50, 10 hours, three weekly)

Local buses serve major resort towns.

CAR Europcar (☎26950 41541; Plateia Agiou Louka, Zakynthos Town) Delivers to the airport.

ZAKYNTHOS TOWN

The island's attractive Venetian capital and port were painstakingly reconstructed after the 1953 earthquake. The pine-tree-filled **Kastro** (☎26950 48099; admission €3; ⊙8.30am-2.30pm Tue-Sun), a ruined Venetian fortress high above town, makes for a peaceful outing. The **Byzantine Museum** (☎26950 42714; Plateia Solomou; admission €3; ⊙8.30am-3pm Tue-Sun) houses fabulous ecclesiastical art rescued from churches razed in the earthquake.

Sleeping & Eating

Restaurants abound but, as in most of the island, they tend to be overpriced and not overly inspiring. In Zakynthos Town, try **Mesathes** (☎26950 49315; Ethnikis Antistaseos; mains €9-11) for an elegant meal.

TOP CHOICE **Hotel Strada Marina** HOTEL €€
(☎26950 42761; www.stradamarina.gr; Lombardou 14; s/d incl breakfast from €60/70; ❄📶≋) Well-situated, portside rooms have balconies with sea views.

Hotel Diana HOTEL €€
(☎26950 28547; Plateia Agiou Markou; r incl breakfast from €60; ❄@📶) This comfortable and well-appointed hotel in a good, central location has a two-bedroom family suite (€100).

Camping Zante CAMPGROUND €
(☎26950 61710; www.zantecamping.gr; Ampula Beach; campsites per person/tent €6/5; @≋) Decent beachside camping 5km north of Zakynthos Town.

TOP CHOICE **Malanos** TAVERNA €
(☎26950 45936; www.malanos.gr; Agiou Athanasiou, Kiri area; mains €5-10; ⊙noon-4pm & 8pm-late) Serves up Zakynthos specialities like rooster, rabbit and wild boar. South, in the countryside; ask a local for directions.

AROUND THE ISLAND

Transport of your own is really necessary to unlock the charms of Zakynthos. The **Vasilikos Peninsula** is the pretty green region southeast of Zakynthos Town and fringing **Laganas Bay** with its long, lovely **Gerakas Beach**. The area has been declared **National Marine Park of Zakynthos** (NMPZ; www.nmp-zak.org) in order to protect the endangered loggerhead turtles that come ashore to lay their eggs in August, the peak of the tourist invasion. Inform yourself before exploring so as not to accidentally disrupt buried eggs.

Cape Keri, near the island's southernmost point, has spectacular views of sheer cliffs and beaches. **Villa Christina** (☎26950 49208; viganelichristina@hotmail.com; Limni Keriou; studio €50-55, apt €60-80, maisonette €150; ⊙May-Oct; P❄@≋) is tops for tidy apartments in lush gardens with a pool. **Tartaruga Camping** (☎26950 51967; www.tartaruga-camping.com; camp sites per adult/car/tent €5/3/3.60, r per person €15; ⊙Apr-Oct; P❄@📶), signed on the road from Laganas to Keri, sprawls through terraced olive groves and pines next to the sea.

Continue north and try to arrive early at remote **Limnionas** for swimming in crystal-clear turquoise coves, or explore lovely **Louha** tumbling down a central valley.

Many descend on famous **Shipwreck Beach**, magnificent photos of which grace every tourist brochure about Zakynthos. It is in Navagio Bay, at the northwest tip of the island. From above, a lookout platform gives

WORTH A TRIP

KYTHIRA ΚΥΘΗΡΑ

Kythira, despite its proximity to the Peloponnese, is considered a part of the Ionian Island group. Genuinely unspoilt, the population (3330) is spread among more than 40 villages with a white-cube Cycladic feel. Mythology suggests that Aphrodite was born in Kythira, but Cypriots claim otherwise. Tourism remains low-key except in July and August, when the island goes mad. Easiest way to get there: fly or get a ferry in Diakofti or Neapoli in the Peloponnese. **LANE Lines** (www.lane.gr) sometimes links Piraeus.

great views. For a (crowded in high season) sea-level look, take a boat from Cape Skinari near Agios Nikolaos, Porto Vromi or Alykes. Cape Skinari's **Windmill** (☎26950 31132; www.potamitisbros.gr; d €60; ❄) has quaint rooms, impressive views, cooking facilities and sea access.

UNDERSTAND GREECE

History

With its strategic position at the crossroads of Europe and Asia, Greece has endured a long and turbulent history. During the Bronze Age (3000–1200 BC in Greece), the advanced Cycladic, Minoan and Mycenaean civilisations flourished. The Mycenaeans were swept aside in the 12th century BC by the warrior-like Dorians, who introduced Greece to the Iron Age. The next 400 years are often referred to as the dark ages, a period about which little is known.

By 800 BC, when Homer's *Odyssey* and *Iliad* were first written down, Greece was undergoing a cultural and military revival with the evolution of the city states, the most powerful of which were Athens and Sparta. Greater Greece (Magna Graecia) was created, with southern Italy as an important component. The unified Greeks repelled the Persians twice, at Marathon (490 BC) and Salamis (480 BC). Victory over Persia was followed by unparalleled growth and prosperity known as the classical (or golden) age.

ORIGINAL OLYMPICS

The Olympic tradition emerged around the 11th century BC as a paean to the Greek gods, in the form of contests of athletic feats that were attended initially by notable men and women, who assembled before the sanctuary priests and swore to uphold solemn oaths. By the 8th century BC, the attendance had grown to include a wide confederacy of city states, and the festival morphed into a male-only major event lasting five days at the site of Olympia. A ceremonial truce was enforced for the duration of the games. Crowds of spectators lined the tracks, where competitors vied for victory in athletics, chariot races, wrestling and boxing. Three millennia later, while the scale and scope of the games may have expanded considerably, the basic format has remained essentially unchanged.

The Golden Age

During this period, Pericles commissioned the Parthenon, Sophocles wrote *Oedipus the King* and Socrates taught young Athenians to think. The golden age ended with the Peloponnesian War (431–404 BC), when the militaristic Spartans defeated the Athenians. They failed to notice the expansion of Macedonia under King Philip II, who easily conquered the war-weary city states.

Philip's ambitions were surpassed by those of his son, Alexander the Great, who marched triumphantly into Asia Minor, Egypt, Persia and what are now parts of Afghanistan and India. In 323 BC he met an untimely death at the age of 33, and his generals divided his empire between themselves.

Roman Rule & the Byzantine Empire

Roman incursions into Greece began in 205 BC. By 146 BC Greece and Macedonia had become Roman provinces. After the subdivision of the Roman Empire into eastern and western empires in AD 395, Greece became part of the Eastern (Byzantine) Empire, based at Constantinople.

In the centuries that followed, Venetians, Franks, Normans, Slavs, Persians, Arabs and, finally, Turks, took turns chipping away at the Byzantine Empire.

The Ottoman Empire & Independence

After the end of the Byzantine Empire in 1453, when Constantinople fell to the Turks, most of Greece became part of the Ottoman Empire. Crete was not captured until 1670, leaving Corfu as the only island not occupied by the Turks. By the 19th century the Ottoman Empire was in decline. The Greeks, seeing nationalism sweep through Europe, fought the War of Independence (1821–22). Greek independence was proclaimed on 13 January 1822, only for arguments among the leaders who had been united against the Turks to escalate into civil war. The Turks, with the help of the Egyptians, tried to retake Greece, but the great powers – Britain, France and Russia – intervened in 1827, and Ioannis Kapodistrias was elected the first Greek president.

Kapodistrias was assassinated in 1831 and the European powers stepped in once again, declaring that Greece should become a monarchy. In January 1833 Otho of Bavaria was installed as king. His ambition, called the Great Idea, was to unite all the lands of the Greek people to the Greek motherland. In 1862 he was peacefully ousted and the Greeks chose George I, a Danish prince, as king.

During WWI Prime Minister Venizelos allied Greece with France and Britain. King Constantine (George's son), who was married to the kaiser's sister Sophia, disputed this and left the country.

Smyrna & WWII

After the war Venizelos resurrected the Great Idea. Underestimating the new-found power of Turkey under the leadership of Atatürk (Mustafa Kemal), he sent forces to occupy Smyrna (the present-day Turkish port of İzmir), with its large Greek population. The army was heavily defeated and this led to a brutal population exchange between the two countries in 1923.

In 1930 George II, Constantine's son, was reinstated as king; he appointed the dictator General Metaxas as prime minister. Metaxas' grandiose ambition was to combine aspects of Greece's ancient and Byzantine past to create a Third Greek Civilisation. However, his chief claim to fame is his celebrated *ohi* (no) to Mussolini's request to allow Italian troops into Greece in 1940.

Greece fell to Germany in 1941 and resistance movements, polarised into royalist and communist factions, staged a bloody civil war lasting until 1949. The civil war was the trigger for a mass exodus that saw almost one million Greeks head off to countries such as Australia, Canada and the USA. Entire villages were abandoned as people gambled on a new start in cities such as Melbourne, Toronto, Chicago and New York.

The Colonels' Coup

Continuing political instability led to the colonels' coup d'état in 1967. The colonels' junta distinguished itself with its appalling brutality, repression and political incompetence. In 1974 it attempted to assassinate Cyprus' leader, Archbishop Makarios, and when he escaped the junta replaced him with the extremist Nikos Samson, prompting Turkey to occupy North Cyprus. The continued Turkish occupation of Cyprus remains one of the most contentious issues in Greek politics. The junta had little choice but to hand back power to the people. In November 1974 a plebiscite voted against restoration of the monarchy. Greece became a republic with the right-wing New Democracy (ND) party taking power.

The 1980s & 1990s

In 1981 Greece entered the European Community (now the EU) as its 10th, smallest and poorest member. Andreas Papandreou's Panhellenic Socialist Movement (Pasok) won the next election, giving Greece its first socialist government. Pasok, which ruled for most of the next two decades, promised the removal of US air bases and withdrawal from NATO, but delivered only rising unemployment and spiralling debt.

Elections in 1990 brought the ND party back to power, but tough economic reforms made the government unpopular and in 1993, Greeks again turned to Pasok and the ailing Papandreou. He had little option but to continue with the austerity program and became equally unpopular until he stood down in 1996 due to ill health. Pasok then abandoned its leftist policies, elected economist and lawyer Costas Simitis as leader, and romped to victory later that year.

The New Millennium

Simitis' government focused strongly on further integration with Europe and in January 2001 admission to the euro club was approved; Greece duly adopted the currency in 2002 and prices have been on the rise ever since.

Greece tilted to the right and in March 2004 elected the ND party led by Costas Karamanlis. This new broom was fortuitous, as the Olympic preparations were running late and suffering budget problems. While the Olympics were successful, Greece is still counting the cost.

During the long hot summer of 2007, forest fires threatened Athens and caused untold damage in the western Peloponnese, Epiros and Evia. Later that year, Karamanlis' government was returned to power for a second term, but amid growing discontent that included massive general strikes and riots, was turfed out in elections in October 2009 in favour of Pasok and George Papandreou, son and grandson of former prime ministers.

RECOGNISE THAT TWANG?

Don't be surprised if your hotel receptionist or waiter speaks perfect English with an Australian twang. A growing stream of young second- and third-generation Greeks are repatriating from the USA, Australia, Canada and other reaches of the Greek diaspora. A huge number of Greeks emigrated during their country's tumultuous history and it is said that over five million people of Greek descent live in 140 countries around the world. Strong sentimental attractions endure and many expat Greeks are involved in the political and cultural life of their ancestral islands, and many retire in Greece.

Greece Today

Textbooks are being written on Greece's 2010 financial crisis. Simply put, Greece almost fell over from years of over-borrowing, over-spending and breaking eurozone rules on deficit management. Financially crippled and looking likely to drag other failing eurozone economies down with it, Greece was on the receiving end of a succession of bail-out packages to help right the ship. Needless to say, austerity measures to help balance the budget were not popular, with citizens angry about cuts in spending, pensions and salaries, along with higher taxes.

Strikes and riots made world news and in May 2012 elections, no party or coalition of parties was able to form a government. New elections were called for June and in what was seen worldwide as a vote that would determine if Greece remained in the eurozone, a coalition of three parties formed a government with New Democracy's Antonis Samaris as prime minister.

Samaris hopes to keep both Greece's creditors and its populace happy, but without doubt, tough times are ahead.

People

Greece's population has topped 11.2 million, with around one-third of the people living in the Greater Athens area and more than two-thirds living in cities – confirming that Greece is now a primarily urban society. Less than 15% live on the islands, the most populous being Crete, Evia and Corfu. Greece has an ageing population and declining birth rate, with big families a thing of the past. Population growth over the last couple of decades is due to a flood of migrants, both legal and illegal.

About 95% of the Greek population belongs to the Greek Orthodox Church. The remainder is split between the Roman Catholic, Protestant, Evangelist, Jewish and Muslim faiths. While older Greeks and those in rural areas tend to be deeply religious, most young people are decidedly more secular.

The Greek year is centred on the saints' days and festivals of the church calendar. Name days (celebrating your namesake saint) are celebrated more than birthdays. Most people are named after a saint, as are boats, suburbs and train stations.

Orthodox Easter is usually at a different time than Easter celebrated by Western churches, though generally in April/May.

Arts

The arts have been integral to Greek life since ancient times, with architecture having had the most profound influence. Greek temples, seen throughout history as symbolic of democracy, were the inspiration for architectural movements such as the Italian Renaissance. Today masses of cheap concrete apartment blocks built in the 20th century in Greece's major cities belie this architectural legacy.

Thankfully, the great works of Greek literature are not as easily besmirched. The first and greatest Ancient Greek writer was Homer, author of *Iliad* and *Odyssey*, telling the story of the Trojan War and the subsequent wanderings of Odysseus.

Pindar (c 518–438 BC) is regarded as the pre-eminent lyric poet of ancient Greece and was commissioned to recite his odes at the Olympic Games. The great writers of love poetry were Sappho (6th century BC) and Alcaeus (5th century BC), both of whom lived on Lesvos. Sappho's poetic descriptions of her affections for women gave rise to the term 'lesbian'.

The Alexandrian Constantine Cavafy (1863–1933) revolutionised Greek poetry by introducing a personal, conversational style. Later, poet George Seferis (1900–71) won the Nobel Prize for literature in 1963, as did Odysseus Elytis (1911–96) in 1979. Nikos Kazantzakis, author of *Zorba the Greek* and numerous novels, plays and poems, is the most famous of 20th-century Greek novelists.

Greece's most famous painter was a young Cretan called Domenikos Theotokopoulos, who moved to Spain in 1577 and became known as the great El Greco. Famous painters of the 20th century include Konstantinos Parthenis and, later, George Bouzianis, whose work can be viewed at the National Art Gallery in Athens.

Music has been a facet of Greek life since ancient times. When visiting Greece today, your trip will inevitably be accompanied by the plucked-string sound of the ubiquitous bouzouki. The bouzouki is one of the main instruments of *rembetika* music – which is in many ways the Greek equivalent of the American blues and has its roots in the sufferings of refugees from Asia Minor in the 1920s.

Dance is also an integral part of Greek life. Whether at a wedding, nightclub or village celebration, traditional dance is widely practised.

Drama continues to feature in domestic arts, particularly in Athens and Thessaloniki. In summer, Greek dramas are staged in the ancient theatres where they were originally performed.

Greek film has for many years been associated with the work of film-maker Theo Angelopoulos, who won Cannes' Palme d'Or in 1998 with *An Eternity and One Day*. Yorgos Lanthimos was nominated for an Academy Award for Best Foreign Language Film for *Dogtooth* (Kynodonta) in 2011. However, the most internationally acclaimed film remains to be the 1964 classic, *Zorba the Greek*.

Greek TV is dominated by chat shows, sport and foreign movies, only to be interrupted by localised versions of the latest American 'reality TV' hit.

Environment

The Land

Greece sits at the southern tip of the Balkan Peninsula. Of its 1400 islands, only 169 are inhabited. The land mass is 131,944 sq km and Greek territorial waters cover a further 400,000 sq km. Nowhere in Greece is much more than 100km from the sea.

Around 80% of the land is mountainous, with less than a quarter of the country suitable for agriculture.

Greece sits in one of the most seismically active regions in the world – the eastern Mediterranean lies at the meeting point of three continental plates: the Eurasian, African and Arabian. Consequently, Greece has had more than 20,000 earthquakes in the last 40 years, most of them very minor.

Wildlife

The variety of flora in Greece is unrivalled in Europe, with a dazzling array of spectacular wildflowers best seen in the mountains of Crete and the southern Peloponnese.

You won't encounter many animals in the wild, mainly due to hunting. Wild boar, still found in the north, is a favourite target. Squirrels, rabbits, hares, foxes and weasels are all fairly common on the mainland. Reptiles are well represented by snakes, including several poisonous viper species.

Lake Mikri Prespa in Macedonia has the richest colony of fish-eating birds in Europe, while the Dadia Forest Reserve in Thrace counts such majestic birds as the golden eagle and the giant black vulture among its residents.

The brown bear, Europe's largest land mammal, still survives in very small numbers in the mountains of northern Greece, as does the grey wolf.

Europe's rarest mammal, the monk seal, once very common in the Mediterranean Sea, is now on the brink of extinction in Europe. There are about 400 left in Europe, half of which live in Greece. About 40 frequent the Ionian Sea and the rest are found in the Aegean.

The waters around Zakynthos are home to Europe's last large sea turtle colony, that of the loggerhead turtle *(Careta careta)*. The **Sea Turtle Protection Society of Greece** (☎21052 31342; www.archelon.gr) runs monitoring programs and is always on the look-out for volunteers.

National Parks

While facilities in Greek national parks aren't on par with many other countries, all have refuges and some have marked hiking trails. The most visited parks are Mt Parnitha, north of Athens, and the Samaria Gorge on Crete. The others are Vikos-Aoös and Prespa National Parks in Epiros; Mt Olympus on the border of Thessaly and Macedonia; and Parnassos and Iti National Parks in central Greece. There is also a national marine park off the coast of Alonnisos, and another around the Bay of Laganas area off Zakynthos.

Environmental Issues

Greece is belatedly becoming environmentally conscious but, regrettably, it's too late for some regions. Deforestation and soil erosion are problems that go back thousands of years, with olive cultivation and goats being the main culprits. Forest fires are also a major problem, with an estimated 250 sq km destroyed every year.

General environmental awareness remains at a depressingly low level, especially where litter is concerned. The problem is particularly bad in rural areas, where roadsides are strewn with aluminium cans and plastic packaging hurled from passing cars. It is somewhat surprising that the waters of the Aegean are as clear as they are considering how many cigarette butts are tossed off ferries.

Food & Drink

Snacks

Greece has a great range of fast-food options. Foremost among them are gyros and souvlaki. The gyros is a giant skewer laden with seasoned meat that grills slowly as it rotates, the meat being steadily trimmed from the outside. Souvlaki are small cubes of meat cooked on a skewer. Both are served wrapped in pitta bread with salad and lashings of tzatziki (a yogurt, cucumber and garlic dip). Other snacks are pretzel rings, spanakopita (spinach and cheese pie) and *tyropita* (cheese pie).

Starters

Greece is famous for its appetisers, known as *mezedhes* (literally, 'tastes'; meze for short). Standards include tzatziki, *melitzanosalata* (aubergine dip), taramasalata (fish-roe dip), dolmadhes (stuffed vine leaves; dolmas for short), *fasolia* (beans) and *oktapodi* (octopus). A selection of three or four starters represents a good meal and makes an excellent vegetarian option.

Mains

You'll find moussaka (layers of aubergine and mince, topped with béchamel sauce and baked) on every menu, alongside a number of other taverna staples. They include *moschari* (oven-baked veal and potatoes), *keftedes* (meatballs), *stifado* (meat stew), *pastitsio* (baked dish of macaroni with minced meat and béchamel sauce) and *yemista* (either tomatoes or green peppers stuffed with minced meat and rice).

Kalamaria (fried squid) is the most popular (and cheapest) seafood, while *barbouni* (red mullet) and *sifias* (swordfish) tend to be more expensive than meat dishes.

Fortunately for vegetarians, salad is a mainstay of the Greek diet. The most popular is *horiatiki salata,* normally listed on English-language menus as Greek salad. It's a delicious mixed salad comprising cucumbers, peppers, onions, olives, tomatoes and feta cheese. For the full scoop on Greece's legendary feta cheese, check out www.feta.gr.

Desserts

Most Greek desserts are Turkish in origin and are variations on pastry soaked in honey, such as baklava (thin layers of pastry filled with honey and nuts). Delicious Greek yogurt also makes a great dessert, especially with honey.

Drinks

Bottled mineral water is cheap and available everywhere, as are soft drinks and packaged juices.

Mythos, in its distinctive green bottle, and Alfa, are popular Greek beers.

Greece is traditionally a wine-drinking society. An increasingly good range of wines

THE ART OF OUZO

Ouzo is Greece's most famous but misunderstood tipple. While it can be drunk as an aperitif, for most Greeks ouzo has come to embody a way of socialising – best enjoyed during a lazy, extended summer afternoon of seafood *mezedhes* (appetisers) by the beach. Ouzo is sipped slowly and ritually to clean the palate between tastes. It is served in small bottles or *karafakia* (carafes) with water and a bowl of ice cubes – and is commonly drunk on the rocks, diluted with water (it turns a cloudy white). Mixing it with cola is a foreign abomination!

Made from distilled grapes, ouzo is also distilled with residuals from fruit, grains and potatoes, and flavoured with spices, primarily aniseed, giving it that liquorice flavour. The best ouzo is produced on Lesvos and there are more than 360 brands.

NO MORE SMOKE

Legislation that brought in anti-smoking laws similar to those throughout Europe in 2009 was not exactly popular with Greeks, the EU's biggest smokers. Smoking is now officially banned inside public places, with the penalty fines placed on the business owners.

made from traditional grape varieties is available. Wine enthusiasts should take a look at www.allaboutgreekwine.com. Retsina, wine flavoured with pine-tree resin, is a tasty alternative – though an acquired taste for some. Most tavernas will offer locally made house wines by the carafe.

Metaxa, Greece's dominant brandy, is sweet, while if you are offered some raki, make sure to take a small sip first!

'Greek' coffee should be tried at least once, but don't drink the mudlike grounds at the bottom!

Where to Eat & Drink

The most common variety of restaurant in Greece is the taverna, traditionally an extension of the Greek home table. *Estiatorio* is Greek for restaurant and often has the same dishes as a taverna but with higher prices. A *psistaria* specialises in charcoal-grilled dishes, while a *psarotaverna* specialises in fish. *Ouzeria* (ouzo bars) often have such a range of *mezedhes* that they can be regarded as eateries. Many restaurants are open for lunch and dinner daily during high season.

Kafeneia are the smoke-filled cafes where men gather to drink 'Greek' coffee, play backgammon and cards, and engage in heated political discussion. Every Greek town you'll visit now has at least one cafe-bar where Greece's youth while away hours over a frappé (frothy ice coffee).

Buying and preparing your own food is easy in Greece – every town of consequence has a supermarket, as well as fruit and vegetable shops.

To have a go at producing your own Greek culinary masterpieces, check out www.gourmed.gr. You'll also find information on the healthy Greek diet at www.mediterraneandiet.gr, while www.oliveoil.gr can tell you all about one of Greece's best-known products.

SURVIVAL GUIDE

Directory A–Z

Accommodation

Campgrounds Generally open from April to October; standard facilities include hot showers, kitchens, restaurants and minimarkets – and often a swimming pool; **Panhellenic Camping Association** (☎21036 21560; www.panhellenic-camping-union.gr).

Domatia Greek equivalent of a B&B, minus the breakfast; don't worry about finding them – owners will find you as they greet ferries and buses shouting 'room!'.

Hotels Classified as deluxe, or A, B, C, D or E class; ratings seldom seem to have much bearing on the price, which is determined more by season and location.

Mountain refuges Listed in *Greece Mountain Refuges & Ski Centres*, available free of charge at EOT and EOS (Ellinikos Orivatikos Syndesmos, the Greek Alpine Club) offices.

Youth hostels In most major towns and on some islands; **Greek Youth Hostel Organisation** (☎21075 19530; www.athens-yhostel.com).

SEASONAL PRICES

'High season' is usually in July and August. If you turn up in the 'middle' or 'shoulder seasons' (May and June; September and October) expect to pay significantly less. During 'low season' (late October to late April) prices can be up to 50% cheaper, but a lot of places, especially on the islands, virtually close their shutters for winter. Websites will usually display these differences in price.

Greek accommodation is subject to strict price controls, and by law a notice must be displayed in every room stating the category of the room and the seasonal price. It's usually on the back of the door. If you think there's something amiss, contact the Tourist Police.

PRICE RANGES

Prices quoted in listings are for high season (usually July and August) and include a private bathroom.

€€€ more than €150

€€ €60 to €150

€ less than €60

Business Hours

Banks 8am to 2.30pm Monday to Thursday, 8am to 2pm Friday (in cities, also: 3.30p 6.30pm Monday to Friday, 8am to 1.30pm Saturday)

Cafes 10am to midnight

Post offices 7.30am to 2pm Monday Friday (in cities 7.30am to 8pm Monday Friday, 7.30am- to 2pm Saturday)

Restaurants 11am to 3pm & 7pm to 1am (varies greatly)

Supermarkets 8am to 8pm Monday to Friday, 8am to 3pm Saturday

Street kiosks (*Periptera*) early to late Monday to Sunday

Children

It's safe and easy to travel with children in Greece, as Greeks tends to be very family-oriented. See www.greece4kids.com.

» Be very careful crossing roads with kids!

» Travel on ferries, buses and trains is free to age four; half-fare to age 10 (ferries) or 12 (buses and trains).

» Kids' menus abound.

HAPHAZARD OPENING HOURS

It's worth noting that with businesses associated with tourism, opening hours can be rather haphazard. In high season when there are plenty of visitors around, restaurants, cafes, nightclubs and souvenir shops are pretty much open whenever they think they can do good business. If there are few people around, some businesses will simply close early or won't bother opening at all. And in low season, some places, including some sleeping options, may close up for months at a time.

Customs Regulations

There are no longer duty-free restrictions within the EU.

It is strictly forbidden to export antiquities (anything over 100 years old) without an export permit.

Embassies & Consulates

Australian Embassy (210 870 4000; www.greece.embassy.gov.au; Ambelokipi, 6th fl, Thon Building, cnr Leoforos Alexandras & Leoforos Kifisias)

Canadian Embassy (210 727 3400; www.greece.gc.ca; Genadiou 4)

Japanese Embassy (210 670 9900; www.gr.emb-japan.go.jp; Ethnikís Antistáseos 46, Halandri)

New Zealand Embassy (210 687 4701; www.nzembassy.com; Kifisias 268, Halandri)

UK Embassy (210 723 6211; www.ukingreece.fco.gov.uk; Ploutarhou 1)

US Embassy (210 721 2951; http://athens.usembassy.gov; Leoforos Vasilissis Sofias 91)

Food

Price ranges for Eating are as follows:

€€€ more than €40

€€ €15 to €40

€ less than €15

Gay & Lesbian Travellers

The church plays a significant role in shaping society's views on issues such as sexuality, and homosexuality is generally frowned-upon.

It is wise to be discreet and to avoid open displays of togetherness. That said, Greece is a popular destination for gay travellers.

Athens has a busy gay scene that packs up and heads to the islands for summer, with Mykonos famous for its bars, beaches and hedonism, and Eresos on Lesvos something of a pilgrimage for lesbians.

Internet Access

Greece has embraced the internet big-time, but charges differ wildly (as does speed of access). Most midrange and top-end hotels will offer their guests some form of internet connection, and laptop-wielding visitors will often be able to connect to wi-fi at hotels and most internet cafes.

Language Courses

For intensive language courses check out the **Athens Centre** (Map p572; ☎210 701 2268; www.athenscentre.gr; Archimidous 48, Mets; Ⓜ Akropoli).

Money

ATMs Everywhere except the smallest villages.

Bargaining While souvenir shops will generally bargain, prices in other shops are normally clearly marked and non-negotiable; accommodation is nearly always negotiable outside peak season, especially for longer stays.

Cash Currency is king at street kiosks and small shops, and especially in the countryside.

Changing currency Banks, post offices and currency exchange offices are all over the places; exchange all major currencies.

Credit cards Generally accepted, but may not be on smaller islands or in small villages.

Tipping The service charge is included on the bill in restaurants, but it is the custom to 'round up the bill'; same for taxis.

Post

Tahydromia (post offices) are easily identified by the yellow sign outside.

Regular postboxes are yellow; red postboxes are for express mail.

The postal rate for postcards and airmail letters within the EU is €0.60; to other destinations it's €0.80.

Public Holidays

New Year's Day 1 January

Epiphany 6 January

First Sunday in Lent February

Greek Independence Day 25 March

Good Friday/Easter Sunday March/April

May Day (Protomagia) 1 May

Feast of the Assumption 15 August

Ohi Day 28 October

Christmas Day 25 December

St Stephen's Day 26 December

Safe Travel

Crime is traditionally low in Greece, but on the rise. Watch out for bar scams and *bombes* (spiked drinks), and be wary of pickpockets on the Athens metro, around Omonia and at the flea market. Generally speaking, thefts from tourists are often committed by other tourists.

Telephone

Maintained by Organismos Tilepikoinonion Ellados, known as OTE (o-*teh*). Public phones are everywhere, take all phonecards and are easy to use; pressing the 'i' button brings up the operating instructions in English.

For directory inquiries within Greece, call ☎131 or ☎132; for international directory enquiries, it's ☎161 or ☎162.

MOBILE PHONES

Mobile phones are a must-have in Greece. If you have a compatible GSM phone from a country with a global roaming agreement with Greece, you'll be able to use your phone there.

There are several mobile service providers in Greece; **CosmOTE** (www.cosmote.gr) has the best coverage. You can purchase a Greek SIM card for around €20.

The use of a mobile phone while driving in Greece is prohibited.

PHONE CODES

Telephone codes are part of the 10-digit number within Greece.

The landline prefix is 2 and for mobiles it's 6.

PHONECARDS

All public phones use OTE phonecards; sold at OTE offices and street kiosks. Phonecards come in €3, €5 and €10 versions; local calls cost €0.30 for three minutes. Discount-card schemes are available, offering much better value for money.

Time

There's one time zone throughout Greece, which is two hours ahead of GMT/UTC and three hours ahead on daylight-savings time (from the last Sunday in March to the last Sunday in October).

Toilets

Public toilets are rare, except at airports and bus and train stations.

Most places have Western-style toilets, but some public toilets may be Asian-style squat toilets.

Greek plumbing can't handle toilet paper: anything larger than a postage stamp will cause a blockage. Put your used toilet paper, sanitary napkins and tampons in the small bin provided next to every toilet.

Tourist Information

There's an EOT office or local tourist office In almost every town of consequence and on many of the islands, plus **Tourist Police** in popular destinations; they can also provide information. Head here if you think you've been ripped off.

Greek National Tourist Organisation (GNTO; www.gnto.gr) Known as EOT within Greece.

Travellers with Disabilities

Most hotels, museums and ancient sites are not wheelchair accessible; the uneven terrain is an issue even for able-bodied people. Few facilities exist for the visually or hearing impaired. Check out www.greecetravel.com/handicapped.

Visas

Visitors from most countries don't need a visa for Greece. Countries whose nationals can stay in Greece for up to three months include Australia, Canada, all EU countries, Iceland, Israel, Japan, New Zealand and the USA.

Getting There & Away

Air

Most visitors arrive by air, mostly into Athens. There are 17 international airports in Greece; most handle only summer charter flights to the islands.

There's a growing number of direct scheduled services into Greece by European budget airlines – Olympic Air (www. olympicair.com) and Aegean Airlines (www.aegeanair.com) also fly internationally.

Land

BORDER CROSSINGS

You can drive or ride through the following border crossings.

From Albania:

Kakavia (60km northwest of Ioannina)

Sagiada (28km north of Igoumenitsa)

Mertziani (17km west of Konitsa)

Krystallopigi (14km west of Kotas)

From Bulgaria:

Promahonas (109km northeast of Thessaloniki)

Ormenio (41km from Serres)

Exohi (50km north of Drama)

INTERNATIONAL AIRPORTS

CITY	AIRPORT	DESIGNATION
Aktion (for Lefkada)	Aktion National Airport	PVK
Athens	Eleftherios Venizelos Airport	ATH
Corfu	Corfu Intl Airport	CFU
Hania (Crete)	Hania Intl Airport	CHQ
Iraklio	Nikos Kazantzakis Airport	HER
Kalamata	Kalamata Intl Airport	KLX
Karpathos	Karpathos National Airport	AOK
Kavala	Alexander the Great Airport	KVA
Kefallonia	Kefallonia Intl Airport	EFL
Kos	Hippocrates Intl Airport	KGS
Mykonos	Mykonos National Airport	JMK
Rhodes	Diagoras Airport	RHO
Samos	Samos Intl Airport	SMI
Santorini (Thira)	Santorini National Airport	JTR
Skiathos	Skiathos National Airport	JSI
Thessaloniki	Macedonia Airport	SKG
Zakynthos	Zakynthos Intl Airport	ZTH

LONDON TO ATHENS OVERLAND

For overland enthusiasts, a trip from London to Athens can be accomplished in two days, taking in some gorgeous scenery along the way. A sample itinerary from London would see you catching the Eurostar to Paris and then an overnight sleeper train to Bologna in Italy. From there, a coastal train takes you to Bari, where there's an overnight boat to Patra on the Peloponnese. From Patra, it's a 4½-hour train journey to Athens.

From Macedonia:

Evzoni (68km north of Thessaloniki)

Niki (16km north of Florina)

Doïrani (31km north of Kilkis)

From Turkey:

Kipi (43km east of Alexandroupolis)

Kastanies (139km northeast of Alexandroupolis)

BUS

The **Hellenic Railways Organisation** (OSE; www.ose.gr) has been operating the following routes, but international buses are somewhat in limbo due to Greece's financial problems. Check the current status well in advance.

Albania Athens–Tirana overnight bus (16 hours, daily) via Ioannina and Gjirokastra

Bulgaria Athens–Sofia bus (15 hours, six weekly); Thessaloniki–Sofia (7½ hours, four daily)

Turkey Athens–İstanbul (22 hours, six weekly); stops at Thessaloniki (seven hours) and Alexandroupolis (13 hours)

TRAIN

Both international and domestic train routes have been severely curtailed due to the financial problems. Be sure to check the current situation well in advance. The following routes may or may not be in operation.

Bulgaria Sofia–Athens (18 hours, daily) via Thessaloniki

Macedonia Thessaloniki–Skopje (five hours, twice daily)

Turkey İstanbul–Thessaloniki (12 hours, daily)

Russia Thessaloniki–Moscow (70 hours, weekly, summer only)

Sea

Check out ferry routes, schedules and services online at www.greekferries.gr.

If you are travelling on a rail pass, check to see if ferry travel between Italy and Greece is included. Some ferries are free, others give a discount. On some routes you will need to make reservations.

ALBANIA

Saranda Petrakis Lines (☎26610 38690; www.ionian-cruises.com) has daily hydrofoils to Corfu (25 minutes).

ITALY

Ancona Patra (20 hours, three daily, summer)

Bari Patra (14½ hours, daily) via Corfu (eight hours) and Keffalonia (14 hours); also to Igoumenitsa (11½ hours, daily)

Brindisi Patra (15 hours, Apr–early Oct) via Igoumenitsa

Venice Patra (30 hours, up to 12 weekly, summer) via Corfu (25 hours)

TURKEY

Boat services operate between Turkey's Aegean coast and the Greek Islands.

Marmaris and Fethiye Rhodes (daily in summer, twice weekly in winter)

Bodrum Kos (one hour, daily in summer)

Kuşadasi Samos (one hour, daily in summer, weekly in winter)

Çeşme Chios (one hour, daily in summer)

Ayvalık Lesvos (one hour, four times weekly in summer)

MOVING ON?

For tips, recommendations and reviews beyond Greece, head to www.shop.lonelyplanet.com, where you can purchase downloadable PDFs of the Albania and Turkey chapters from Lonely Planet's *Mediterranean Europe* guide, or the Macedonia and Bulgaria chapters from *Eastern Europe*.

Getting Around

Greece has a comprehensive transport system and is easy to get around.

Air

Domestic air travel has been very price competitive of late, and it's sometimes cheaper to fly than take the ferry, especially if you book ahead online. A plan to merge Olympic Air and Aegean Airlines was prohibited by the European Commission in January 2011 due to its potential effect on competition and prices.

DOMESTIC AIRLINES

Aegean Airlines (A3; www.aegeanair.com) The big competition for Olympic Air offers newer aircraft and similar prices on popular routes.

Astra Airlines (A2; www.astra-airlines.gr) Based in Thessaloniki; a newcomer flying limited routes.

Athens Airways (☎210 669 6600, 801 801 4000; www.athensairways.com) New kid on the block, but growing steadily.

Olympic Air (OA; www.olympicair.com) Recently privatised; has the most extensive network.

Sky Express (☎281 022 3500; www.skyexpress.gr) Based in Iraklio, Crete; mainly flies routes that the big two don't.

Bicycle

Greece has very hilly terrain and the summer heat can be stifling. In addition, many drivers totally disregard the road rules.

See www.cyclegreece.gr for bicycle tour ideas. Bicycles are carried for free on ferries.

Rental bicycles are available at most tourist centres, but are generally for pedalling around town rather than for serious riding. Prices generally range from €10 to €20 per day.

Boat

FERRY

Ferries come in all shapes and sizes, from state-of-the-art 'superferries' that run on the major routes, to ageing open ferries that operate local services to outlying islands.

Newer high-speed ferries are slashing travel times, but cost much more.

'Classes' on ferries are largely a thing of the past; you have the option of 'deck class', which is the cheapest ticket, or 'cabin class' with air-con cabins and a decent lounge and restaurant.

When buying tickets you will automatically be given deck class.

Tickets can be bought at the last minute at the dock, but in high season, some boats may be full – plan ahead.

The Greek Ships app for smartphones can be used for real-time tracking to see if your ferry is going to turn up on time – seach for 'Greek Ships' in your app store.

ISLAND-HOPPING

For many, the idea of meandering from island to island by boat in the Greek Islands is the ultimate dream. It's still a lot of fun, but to some extent not what it used to be. Many of those slow, romantic old ferries you may have seen in the movies have disappeared, replaced by big modern people-movers. If you turn up in high season you might find it just as stressful as rush hour back home.

It's still possible to get away from it all, but it will require some thought – head to smaller islands off the beaten path before high season kicks in. Every island has a boat service of some sort!

Boat operations are highly seasonal and based on the tourist trade, so there's not a lot happening in winter. Services pick up from April, and during July and August Greece's seas are a mass of wake and wash.

Summer also brings the *meltemi,* a strong dry northerly wind that can blow for days and cause havoc to ferry schedules.

In any season, changes to schedules can take place at the last minute. Be prepared to be flexible. Boats seldom arrive early, but often arrive late! And some don't come at all. Think of it as part of the fun.

Check out www.openseas.gr for schedules, costs and links to individual boat company websites.

Main Ferry Routes

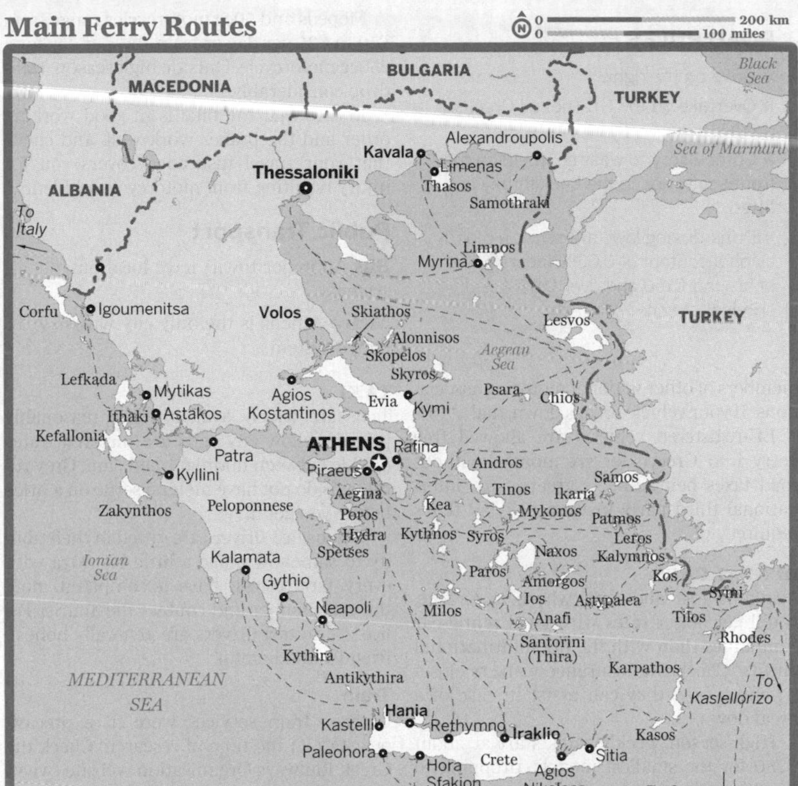

CATAMARAN

High-speed catamarans have become an important part of the island travel scene and are much less prone to cancellation in rough weather.

Catamaran fares are generally more expensive than ferries and about the same as hydrofoils.

HYDROFOIL

Hydrofoils are a faster alternative to ferries on some routes, take half the time, but cost twice as much. Most routes will operate only during the high season.

Tickets for hydrofoils must be bought in advance and they are often sold with seat allocation.

Bus

Long-distance buses are operated by **KTEL** (www.ktel.org). Fares are fixed by the government and service routes can be found on the company's website. Buses are comfortable, generally run on time, reasonably priced – eg Athens–Volos (€25, five hours) and Athens–Patra (€17, three hours) – and there are frequent services on all major routes. Tickets should be bought at least an hour in advance to ensure a seat. Buses don't have toilets and refreshments, but stop for a break every couple of hours.

Car & Motorcycle

Driving yourself is a great way to explore areas in Greece that are off the beaten track, but be careful – Greece has the highest road-fatality rate in Europe. The road network has improved dramatically in recent years, but freeway tolls are fairly hefty.

Almost all islands are served by car ferries, but they are expensive; costs vary by the size of the vehicle.

The Greek automobile club, **ELPA** (www.elpa.gr), generally offers reciprocal services to

ROAD RULES

» Drive on the right.

» Overtake on the left (not all Greeks do this!).

» Compulsory to wear seatbelts in the front seats, and in the back if they are fitted.

» Drink-driving laws are strict; a blood alcohol content of 0.05% incurs a fine of around €150 and over 0.08% is a criminal offence.

members of other national motoring associations. If your vehicle breaks down, dial ☎104.

EU-registered vehicles are allowed free entry into Greece for six months without road taxes being due; a green card (international third party insurance) is all that's required.

RENTAL CARS

Available just about anywhere in Greece, you'll get better rates with local rental-car companies than with the big multinational outfits. Check the insurance waivers closely; check how they can assist in case of a breakdown.

High-season weekly rates start at about €280 for the smallest models, dropping to €200 in winter – add tax and extras. Major companies will request a credit-card deposit.

Minimum driving age in Greece is 18, but most car-hire firms require a driver of 21 or over.

RENTAL MOPEDS & MOTORCYCLES

These are available for hire everywhere. Regulations stipulate that you need a valid motorcycle licence stating proficiency for the size of motorcycle you wish to rent – from 50cc upwards.

Mopeds and 50cc motorcycles range from €10 to €25 per day or from €25 per day for a 250cc motorcycle. Outside high season, rates drop considerably.

Ensure that the bike is in good working order and the brakes work well, and check that your travel insurance covers you for injury resulting from motorcycle accidents.

Public Transport

Bus All major towns have local bus systems.

Metro Athens is the only city with a metro system.

TAXI

Taxis are widely available and reasonably priced. Yellow city cabs are metered; rates double between midnight and 5am. Grey rural taxis do not have meters; settle on a price before you get in.

Athens taxi drivers are gifted in their ability to somehow make a little bit extra with every fare. If you have a complaint, note the cab number and contact the Tourist Police. Rural taxi drivers are generally honest, friendly and helpful.

Train

Greece's train services were in a precarious state at the time of research. Check the Greek Railways Organisation website (www.ose.gr) for the latest.

Greece has only two main lines: Athens north to Thessaloniki and Alexandroupolis, and Athens to the Peloponnese.

There are a number of branch lines, eg Pyrgos–Olympia line and the spectacular Diakofto–Kalavryta mountain railway.

InterRail and Eurail passes are valid; you still need to make a reservation.

In summer make reservations at least two days in advance.

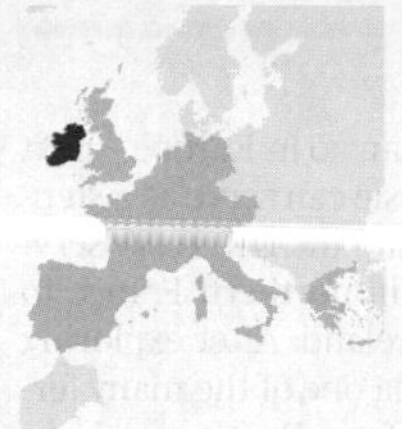

Ireland

Includes »

Best Places to Eat

» Farmgate Café (p679)
» Chapter One (p669)
» Fishy Fishy Cafe (p684)
» Ard Bia at Nimmo's (p697)
» Barking Dog (p709)

Best Places to Stay

» Isaacs Hostel (p667)
» Number 31 (p668)
» Garnish House (p679)
» Kinlay House (p669)
» Old Rectory (p708)

Why Go?

Few countries have an image so plagued by cliché. From shamrocks and shillelaghs (walking sticks) to leprechauns and lovable rogues, there's a plethora of platitudes to wade through before you reach the real Ireland.

But it's well worth looking beyond the tourist tat, for the Emerald Isle is one of Europe's gems, a scenic extravaganza of lakes, mountains, sea and sky. From wind-lashed Donegal to picture-postcard County Cork, there are countless opportunities to get outdoors and explore, whether surfing the beach breaks of Bundoran, cycling the coast of Antrim, or hiking the hills of Kerry and Connemara.

There are cultural pleasures too in the land of Joyce and Yeats, U2 and the Undertones. Dublin, Cork and Belfast all have party-on pubs and foot-stomping live-music scenes, while you can enjoy traditional music in the bars of Galway, Doolin and Killarney. So push aside the shamrocks and experience the real Ireland.

When to Go

Dublin

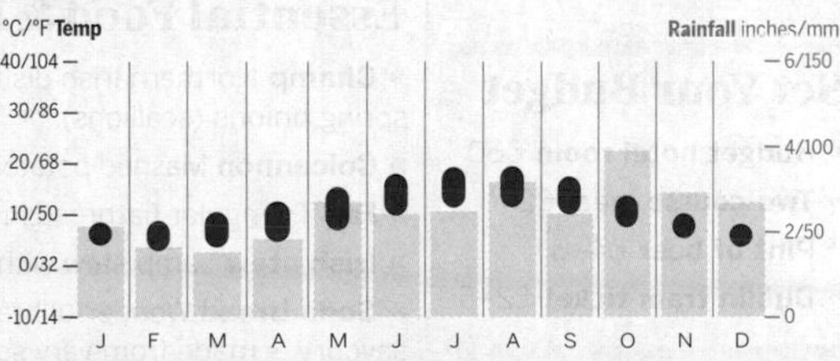

Late Mar Spring has sprung, landscape is greening, St Patrick's Day festivities beckon.

Jun Best chance of dry weather, long summer evenings; opera in Wexford, Bloomsday in Dublin.

Sep–Oct Summer crowds thin, autumn colours reign, surf's up on the west coast.

AT A GLANCE

» **Currency** euro (€) in Republic of Ireland, pound sterling (£) in Northern Ireland

» **Languages** English, Irish Gaelic

» **Money** ATMs widespread

» **Visas** Schengen rules do not apply.

Fast Facts

» **Area** 84,421 sq km

» **Capitals** Dublin (ROI)/ Belfast (NI)

» **Country code** ☎353 (ROI)/ ☎44 (NI)

» **Emergency** ☎112

Exchange Rates

Australia	A$1	€0.82/ UK£0.68
Canada	C$1	€0.77/ UK£0.64
Euro Zone	€1	UK£0.84
Japan	¥100	€0.83/ UK£0.70
New Zealand	NZ$1	€0.65/ UK£0.55
UK	UK£1	€1.18
USA	US$1	€0.78/ UK£0.65

Set Your Budget

» **Budget hotel room** €60

» **Two-course meal** €25

» **Pint of beer** €4–6

» **Dublin tram ticket** €2–5

Resources

» **Failte Ireland** (www.discoverireland.ie)

» **Northern Ireland Tourist Board** (www.nitb.com)

Connections

Ireland is just about as far west as you can go in Europe – next stop, North America. But the Emerald Isle can serve as a stepping stone between mainland Europe and the UK. Ferry services run from Roscoff and Cherbourg in northern France to Rosslare (near Wexford) in southeast Ireland. After exploring Ireland you can continue your travels via one of the many ferries linking Ireland with Great Britain: from Rosslare to Fishguard and Pembroke (both in Wales); from Cork to Swansea (Wales); from Dublin or Dun Laoghaire to Holyhead (Wales); from Dublin or Belfast to the Isle of Man and Liverpool (England); from Belfast to Cairnryan (Scotland); and from Larne to Troon (April to October only) or Cairnryan (both Scotland).

You can travel direct by coach (via a ferry crossing) from Dublin or Belfast to London and several other UK cities. Budget airlines fly direct from Dublin and Belfast to London, Cardiff, Edinburgh and other UK destinations.

ITINERARIES

One Week

Spend a couple of days in Dublin ambling through the excellent national museums, and gorging yourself on Guinness and good company in Temple Bar. Get medieval in Kilkenny before heading on to Cork and discovering why they call it 'The Real Capital'. Meander through lush, idyllic West Cork and take in the friendly spirit and melodious accents of its denizens.

Two Weeks

Follow the one-week itinerary, then make your way from West Cork up to touristy Killarney and the Ring of Kerry on your way to bohemian Galway. Using Galway as your base, explore the alluring Aran Islands and the hills of Connemara. Finally, head north to experience the newly optimistic vibe in fast-changing Belfast.

Essential Food & Drink

» **Champ** Northern Irish dish of mashed potatoes with spring onions (scallions).

» **Colcannon** Mashed potatoes with cabbage and fried onion.

» **Farl** Triangular flatbread in Northern Ireland and Donegal.

» **Irish stew** Lamb stew with potatoes, onions and thyme.

» **Soda bread** Wonderful bread – white or brown, sweet or savoury – made from very soft Irish flour and buttermilk.

» **Stout** Dark, almost black beer made with roasted barley; famous brands are Guinness in Dublin, and Murphy's and Beamish & Crawford in Cork.

» **Irish whiskey** Around 100 different types are produced by only four distilleries: Jameson, Bushmills, Cooley and recently reopened Kilbeggan.

Ireland Highlights

1. Meander through the museums, pubs and literary haunts of **Dublin** (p662), and ask a local, 'Where's the craic?'

2. Hang out in bohemian **Galway** (p693), with its hip cafes and live-music venues

3. Hike along the Causeway Coast and clamber across the **Giant's Causeway** (p713)

4. Take a boat trip to the 6th-century monastery perched atop the wild rocky islet of **Skellig Michael** (p689)

5. Sup a pint of Guinness while tapping your toes to a live music session in one of Dublin's **traditional Irish pubs** (p670)

6. Cycle through the spectacular lake and mountain scenery of the **Gap of Dunloe** (p686)

7. Discover the industrial history of the city that built the world's most famous ocean liner in Belfast's **Titanic Quarter** (p706)

8. Wander the wild, limestone shores of the remote and craggy **Aran Islands** (p697)

DUBLIN

01 / POP 1.1 MILLION

Form is temporary, but class is permanent: the good times may have gone, but Dublin still knows how to have a good time. From its music, art and literature to the legendary nightlife that has inspired those same musicians, artists and writers, Dublin has always known how to have fun and does it with deadly seriousness, as you'll soon find out.

There are world-class museums, superb restaurants and the best collection of entertainment in the country: from rock music to classical concerts there's almost always something on, and when there's not, you'll always have its thousand or so pubs to while away an evening in. Should you wish to get away from it all, the city has a handful of seaside towns at its edges that make for wonderful day trips.

Sights

Dublin is neatly divided by the River Liffey into the more affluent 'south side' and the less prosperous 'north side'. North of the river are O'Connell St, with its needle-shaped Monument of Light, and Gardiner St, with its B&Bs and guesthouses. Busáras, the main bus station, and Connolly station, one of the main train stations, are here too.

Immediately south of the river is the bustling Temple Bar district, Trinity College and, just below it, the lovely St Stephen's Green. Pedestrianised Grafton St and its surrounding streets and lanes are crammed with shops and restaurants. About 2km west is Heuston station, the city's other main train station.

Dublin's finest Georgian architecture, including its famed doorways, is found around **St Stephen's Green** and **Merrion Sq** just south of Trinity College; both are prime picnic spots when the sun shines.

TOP CHOICE **Trinity College & Book of Kells** MUSEUM

(www.bookofkells.ie; College Green; admission free to college grounds, Old Library adult/child €9/free, walking tours per person €10; 9.30am-5pm Mon-Sat year-round, 9.30am-4.30pm Sun May-Sep, noon-4.30pm Sun Oct-Apr, walking tours twice per hour 10.15am-3.40pm Mon-Sat & 10.15am-3pm Sun mid-May–Sep) Ireland's premier university was founded by Queen Elizabeth I in 1592. Its full name is technically the University of Dublin, but **Trinity College** is the institution's sole college. Until 1793 the students were all Protestant, but today most of them are Catholic. Women were first allowed to matriculate in 1903.

Student-guided **walking tours** depart from inside the main gate on College St. The tour is an especially good deal since it includes admission to the **Old Library** to see the **Book of Kells**, an elaborately illuminated gospel created by monks on the Scottish isle of Iona around AD 800, and the spectacular **Long Room**, an early-18th-century library lined with marble busts of writers and philosophers.

FREE **National Museum of Ireland – Archaeology** MUSEUM

(www.museum.ie; Kildare St; 10am-5pm Tue-Sat, 2-5pm Sun) Among the highlights of the National Museum's archaeology and history branch are its superb collection of **prehistoric gold objects**; the exquisite 12th-century **Ardagh Chalice**, the world's finest example of Celtic art; and ancient objects recovered from Ireland's bogs, including remarkably well-preserved human bodies. Other exhibits focus on early Christian art, the Viking period, and medieval Ireland.

O'Connell St HISTORIC AREA

Dublin's grandest avenue is dominated by the needle-like **Monument of Light**, better known as 'The Spire', which rises from the

DUBLIN IN TWO DAYS

Start by heading to **Trinity College**, where the tour takes in the famous **Book of Kells**. Afterwards, window-shop your way down **Grafton St** en route to **Fallon & Byrne** for lunch. Walk off the food and wine while marvelling at the Georgian architecture surrounding **St Stephen's Green** or wandering around the **Chester Beatty Library** before you party your arse off in **Temple Bar**. Then go sleep it off at the gorgeous **Grafton Guesthouse**. Begin your next day with a hearty Irish breakfast before venturing off to view the prehistoric gold at the **National Museum of Ireland – Archaeology**. Top off your visit by enjoying the best pint of your life at the **Guinness Storehouse**.

spot once occupied by a statue of Admiral Nelson – which disappeared in explosive fashion, thanks to the Irish Republican Army (IRA) in 1966. Soaring 120m into the sky, it is, apparently, the world's tallest sculpture.

Nearby is the 1815 **General Post Office** (www.anpost.ie; O'Connell St; ⌚8am-8pm Mon-Sat), an important landmark of the 1916 Easter Rising, when the Irish Volunteers used it as a base for attacks against the British army. After a fierce battle the GPO was burnt out. Upon surrendering, the leaders of the Irish rebellion and 13 others were taken to Kilmainham Gaol and executed.

WANT MORE?

For in-depth information, reviews and recommendations at your fingertips, head to the Apple App Store to purchase Lonely Planet's *Dublin City Guide* iPhone app.

Alternatively, head to **Lonely Planet** (www.lonelyplanet.com/ireland/dublin) for planning advice, author recommendations, traveller reviews and insider tips.

Guinness Storehouse — BREWERY, MUSEUM

(www.guinness-storehouse.com; St James's Gate, South Market St; adult/student/child €16.50/10.50/6.50, Conoisseur Experience €25, discounts apply for online bookings; ⌚9.30am-5pm Sep-Jun, to 7pm Jul-Aug; 21a, 51b, 78, 78a or 123 from Fleet St, St James's) The Guinness Storehouse sits in the malty fug of the mighty Guinness Brewery southwest of the city centre. The building is shaped like a pint of Ireland's favourite drink, with a bar in the 'head', and the best part of the tour is getting the finest-tasting Guinness of your life for free at the end. It has wheelchair access. Take bus 123 from O'Connell St or Dame St.

Kilmainham Gaol — MUSEUM

(www.heritageireland.com; Inchicore Rd; adult/child €6/2; ⌚9.30am-6pm Apr-Sep, 9.30am-5.30pm Mon-Sat, 10am-6pm Sun Oct-Mar) The threatening, grey Kilmainham Gaol, 2km west of the city centre, played a key role in Ireland's struggle for independence and was the site of mass executions following the 1916 Easter Rising. An excellent audiovisual introduction to the building is followed by a thought-provoking one-hour tour (last admission one hour before closing). Arrangements can be made for a wheelchair-accessible tour with advance booking. Buses 69 or 79 from Aston Quay and 13 or 40 from O'Connell St can all take you here.

National Gallery — MUSEUM

(www.nationalgallery.ie; West Merrion Sq; ⌚9.30am-5.30pm Mon-Wed, Fri & Sat, 9.30am-8.30pm Thu, noon-5.30pm Sun) A magnificent Caravaggio and a breathtaking collection of works by Jack B Yeats – William Butler's younger brother – are the main reasons to visit here. The Millennium wing has a small collection of contemporary Irish works. Free guided tours are held at 3pm on Saturday, and 2pm, 3pm and 4pm on Sunday.

Christ Church Cathedral — CHURCH

(Church of the Holy Trinity; www.cccdub.ie; Christ Church Pl; adult/child €6/2; ⌚9.30am-5pm Mon-Sat & 12.30-2.30pm Sun year-round, longer hrs Jun-Aug; 50, 50A or 56A from Aston Quay or 54 or 54A from Burgh Quay) Christ Church is the mother of all of Dublin's cathedrals, a simple wooden structure until 1169, when the present church was built. In the southern aisle is a monument to Strongbow, a 12th-century Norman warrior. Note the precariously leaning northern wall (it's been that way since 1562).

Across the street, connected to the cathedral by an arched walkway, is **Dublinia** (www.dublinia.ie; St Michael's Hill; adult/child €7.50/5; ⌚10am-5pm Apr-Sep, to 4.30pm Oct-Mar), a kitschy but lively attempt to bring Viking and medieval Dublin to life through models of the city at various stages in its history, streetscape tableaux and somewhat old-fashioned interactive displays.

St Patrick's Cathedral — CHURCH

(www.stpatrickscathedral.ie; St Patrick's Close; adult/child €5.50/free; ⌚9am-5pm Mon-Sat, 9-10.30am & 12.30-2.30pm Sun year-round, longer hrs Mar-Oct; 50, 50A or 56A from Aston Quay or 54 or 54A from Burgh Quay) There was a church on the site of St Patrick's Cathedral as early as the 5th century, but the present building dates from 1191. St Patrick's choir was part of the first group to perform Handel's *Messiah* in 1742, and you can hear their successors sing evensong at 5.45pm most weeknights.

Just around the corner is the antique **Marsh's Library** (www.marshlibrary.ie; St Patrick's Close; adult/child €2.50/free; ⌚9.30am-1pm & 2-5pm Mon & Wed-Fri, 10am-1pm Sat; 50, 50A or 56A from Aston Quay or 54 or 54A from Burgh Quay), the oldest public library in the country, with an atmosphere that has hardly changed since it opened its doors in 1707.

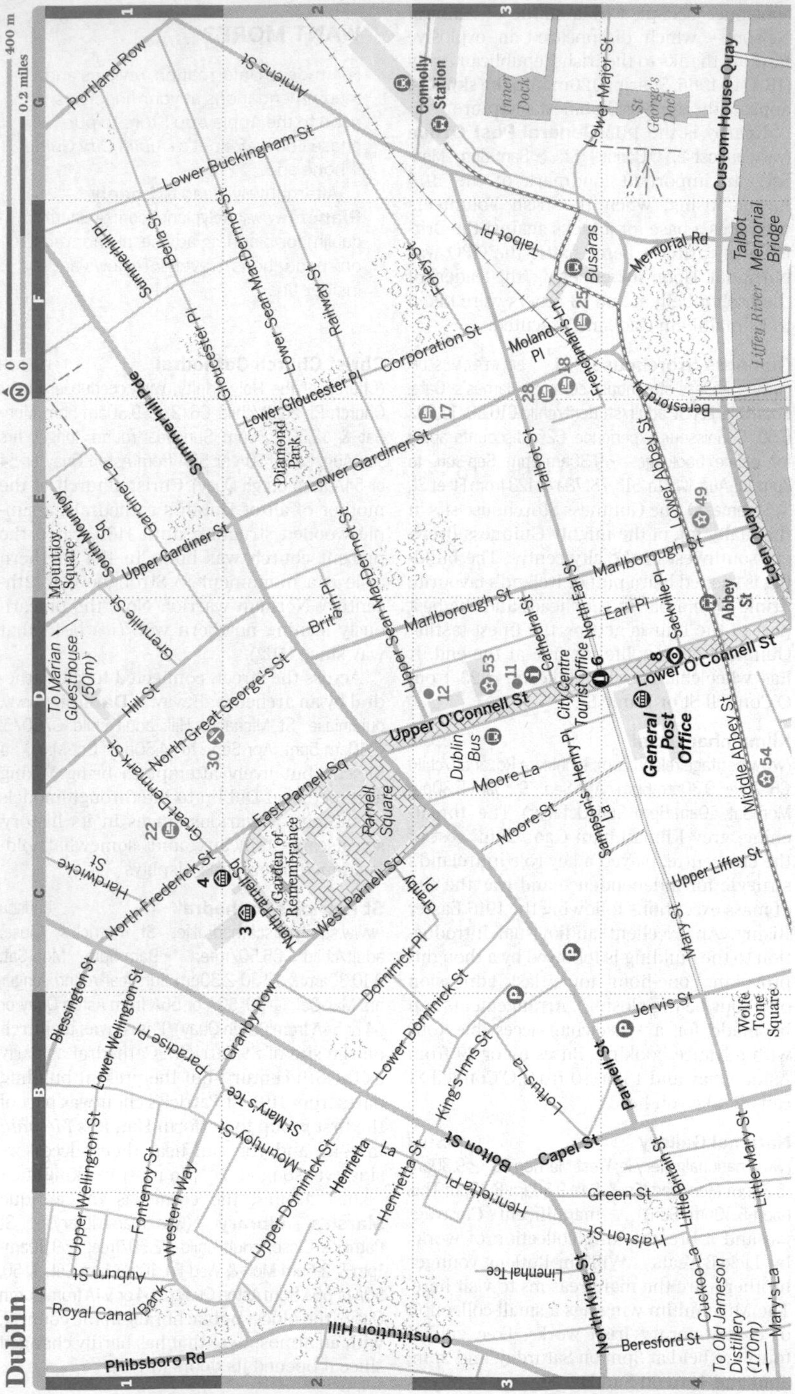

Dublin

0 — 400 m
0 — 0.2 miles

A B C D E F G
1 2 3 4

Phibsboro Rd
Royal Canal Bank
Auburn St
Upper Wellington St
Blessington St
Lower Wellington St
Fontenoy St
Western Way
Paradise Pl
Hardwicke St
North Frederick St
Great Denmark St
22
4
3
30
To Marian Guesthouse (50m)
Mountjoy Square
South Mountjoy Sq
Hill St
Grenville St
Upper Gardiner St
Gardiner La
North Great George's St
Summerhill Pde
Summerhill Pl
Bella St
Gloucester Pl
Portland Row
Lower Buckingham St
Lower Sean MacDermot St
Amiens St
Mountjoy St
St Mary's Tce
Granby Row
North Parnell Sq
Garden of Remembrance
East Parnell Sq
Upper Dominick St
Diamond Park
Lower Gloucester Pl
Railway St
Henrietta La
Henrietta St
Lower Dominick St
Dominick Pl
West Parnell Sq
Granby Pl
Parnell Square
Britain Pl
Upper Sean MacDermot St
Lower Gardiner St
Corporation St
Foley St
Connolly Station
17
12
Constitution Hill
Henrietta Pl
King's Inns St
Bolton St
Dublin Bus
Upper O'Connell St
53
11
Marlborough St
Linenhal Tce
Loftus La
Moore St
Moore La
Cathedral St
Talbot St
28
Moland Pl
Talbot Pl
Inner Dock
18
Frenchman's Ln
25
Busáras
Capel St
North King St
Sampson's La
Henry Pl
City Centre Tourist Office
6
North Earl St
Lower Major St
Parnell St
Halston St
Green St
Beresford St
Jervis St
General Post Office
8
Lower O'Connell St
Earl Pl
Sackville Pl
Beresford Pl
Memorial Rd
St George's Dock
Little Britain St
Cuckoo La
Mary St
Upper Liffey St
Lower Abbey St
49
Abbey St
To Old Jameson Distillery (170m)
Little Mary St
Mary's La
Wolfe Tone Square
Middle Abbey St
54
Eden Quay
Liffey River
Talbot Memorial Bridge
Custom House Quay

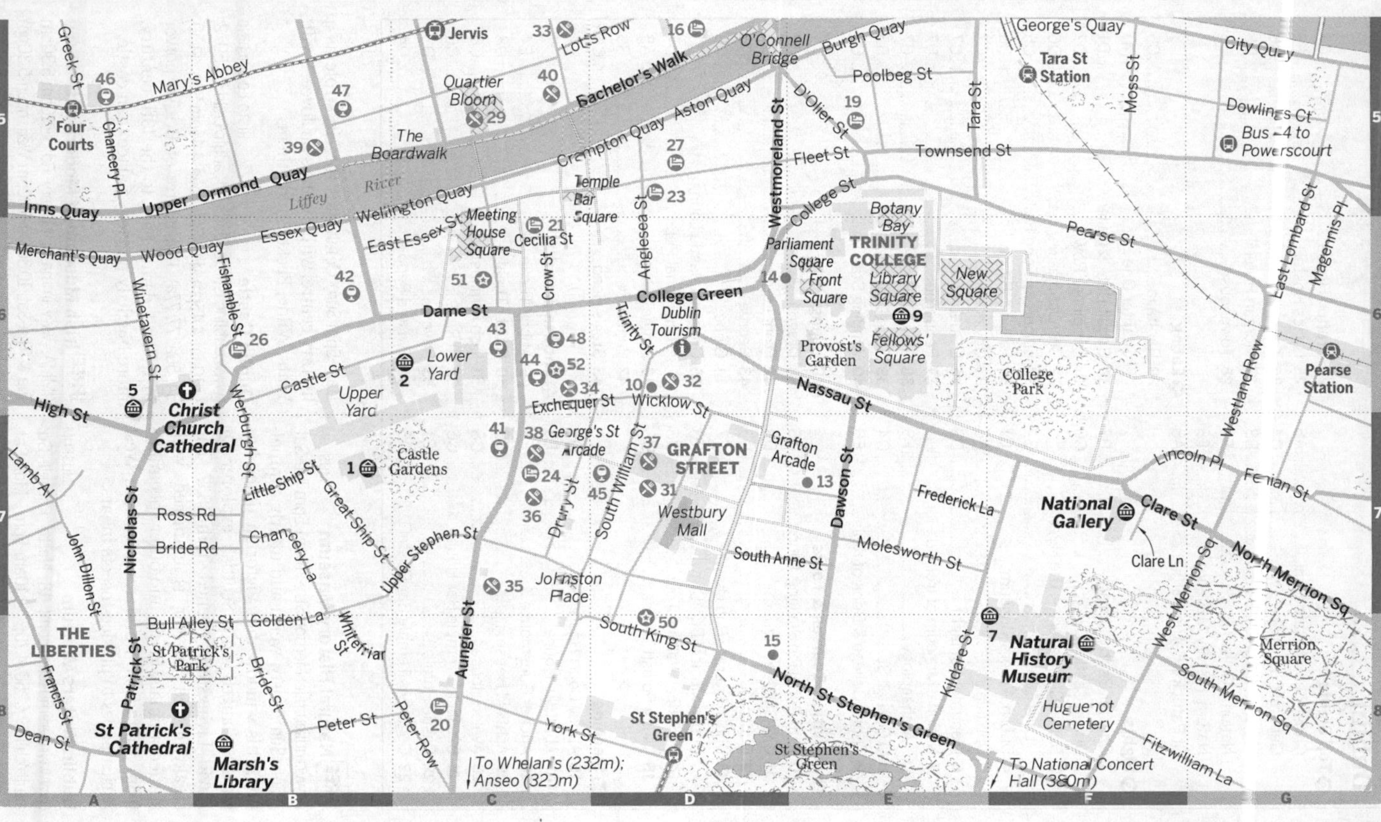
Jervis
Lots Row
O'Connell Bridge
Burgh Quay
George's Quay
Tara St Station
City Quay
Moss St
Greek St
Mary's Abbey
Four Courts
Chancery Pl
Quartier Bloom
Bachelor's Walk
Aston Quay
Poolbeg St
D'Olier St
Tara St
Dowlings Ct
Bus –4 to Powerscourt
The Boardwalk
Crampton Quay
Fleet St
Townsend St
Inns Quay
Upper Ormond Quay
River Liffey
Wellington Quay
Temple Bar Square
Westmoreland St
College St
Botany Bay
Pearse St
East Lombard St
Magennis Pl
Merchant's Quay
Wood Quay
Essex Quay
East Essex St
Meeting House Square
Cecilia St
Anglesea St
Parliament Square
TRINITY COLLEGE
Library Square
Front Square
New Square
Fishamble St
Crow St
College Green
Dublin Tourism
Dame St
Provost's Garden
Fellows' Square
Winetavern St
Castle St
Lower Yard
Trinity St
College Park
Pearse Station
Westland Row
High St
Christ Church Cathedral
Upper Yard
Exchequer St
Wicklow St
Nassau St
Werburgh St
George's St Arcade
GRAFTON STREET
Grafton Arcade
Dawson St
Lincoln Pl
Fenian St
Lamb Al
Castle Gardens
Little Ship St
Great Ship St
Drury St
South William St
Westbury Mall
Frederick La
National Gallery
Clare St
Nicholas St
Ross Rd
Bride Rd
Chancery La
Upper Stephen St
South Anne St
Molesworth St
Clare Ln
North Merrion Sq
John Dillon St
Johnston Place
West Merrion Sq
Bull Alley St
Golden La
South King St
THE LIBERTIES
St Patrick's Park
Whitefriar St
Aungier St
Kildare St
Natural History Museum
Merrion Square
Patrick St
Bride St
North St Stephen's Green
South Merrion Sq
Francis St
Peter St
Peter Row
York St
St Stephen's Green
Huguenot Cemetery
Dean St
St Patrick's Cathedral
Marsh's Library
To Whelan's (232m); Anseo (320m)
To National Concert Hall (380m)
Fitzwilliam La
A
B
C
D
E
F
G
5
6
7
8

Dublin

FREE Natural History Museum MUSEUM
(www.museum.ie; Merrion St; ⏲10am-5pm Tue-Sat, 2-5pm Sun) Dusty, weird and utterly compelling, this window into Victorian times has barely changed since Scottish explorer Dr David Livingstone opened it in 1857. The creaky-floored interior is crammed with stuffed animals, fossils and other specimens from around the world, ranging from West African apes to pickled insects in jars.

Dublin Writers Museum MUSEUM
(www.writersmuseum.com; 18 North Parnell Sq; adult/child €7.50/4.70; ⏲10am-5pm Mon-Sat, 11am-5pm Sun) Celebrates the city's role as a literary centre, with displays on Joyce, Swift, Yeats, Wilde, Beckett and others.

Dublin Castle HISTORIC BUILDING
(www.dublincastle.ie; Dame St; adult/child €4.50/2; ⏲10am-4.45pm Mon-Sat, noon-4.45pm Sun; 🚌50, 54, 56a, 77, 77a) The centre of British power in Ireland, dating back to the 13th century; more higgledy-piggledy palace than castle.

FREE Irish Museum of Modern Art MUSEUM
(IMMA; www.imma.ie; Military Rd; ⏲10am-5.30pm Tue & Thu-Sat, 10.30am-5.30pm Wed, noon-5.30pm

Sun, tours 2.30pm Tue-Sun, plus noon Sat; Heuston) Renowned for its conceptual installations and temporary exhibitions. Bus 51 or 79 from Aston Quay will get you there.

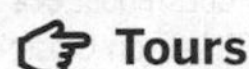
FREE Dublin City Gallery – The Hugh Lane GALLERY
(www.hughlane.ie; 22 North Parnell Sq; 10am-6pm Tue-Thu, 10am-5pm Fri & Sat, 11am-5pm Sun) Works by French Impressionists and 20th-century Irish artists, wheelchair accessible.

Old Jameson Distillery MUSEUM
(www.jamesonwhiskey.com; Bow St; adult/child €14/7.70; 9am-6pm Mon-Sat, 10am-6pm Sun) Guided tours (three or four daily) cover the entire whiskey-distilling process; tastings follow.

Tours

Bus

Hop-on, hop-off city tours are a good way of visiting several major sights in one day. You can board at any stop along the route.

City Sightseeing BUS TOUR
(www.citysightseeingdublin.ie; 14 Upper O'Connell St; adult/child €18/free; every 8-15min 9am-6pm) City Sightseeing's time-tested hop-on, hop-off open-top tours; tickets valid for two days.

Dublin Bus BUS TOUR
(www.dublinsightseeing.ie; Cathal Brugha St; adult/child €18/free; every 10-15min 9am-5.30pm, every 30min 5.30-6.30pm) Hop-on hop-off; tickets valid for two days.

Viking Splash Tours BUS TOUR
(01-707 6000; www.vikingsplash.ie; North St Stephen's Green; adult/child €20/10; every 30-90min 10am-3pm) It's hard not to feel a little cheesy with a plastic Viking helmet on your head, but the punters get a real kick out of these 1¼-hour amphibious vehicle tours that end up in the Grand Canal Dock.

Walking

Each tour lasts two to three hours and costs around €12. Book through Dublin Tourism, at hostels or by calling direct.

Dublin Literary Pub Crawl WALKING TOUR
(01-670 5602; www.dublinpubcrawl.com; 9 Duke St, Duke; adult/student €12/10; 7.30pm daily Apr-Oct, 7.30pm Thu-Sun Nov-Mar) Led by actors performing pieces from Irish literature; begins at the Duke pub.

DON'T MISS

CHESTER BEATTY LIBRARY

Bequeathed to the nation by mining engineer Sir Alfred Chester Beatty (1875–1968), this breathtaking collection of the **Chester Beatty Library** (www.cbl.ie; Dublin Castle; 10am-5pm Mon-Fri, 11am-5pm Sat, 1-5pm Sun year-round, closed Mon Oct-Apr, Reference Library by appointment only) includes more than 20,000 manuscripts, rare books, miniature paintings, clay tablets, costumes and other objects of artistic, historical and aesthetic importance. The library runs guided tours at 1pm on Wednesdays and at 3pm and 4pm on Sundays.

1916 Rebellion Walking Tour WALKING TOUR
(086 858 3847; www.1916rising.com; 23 Wicklow St; per person €12; 11.30am Mon-Sat, 1pm Sun Mar-Oct) Visits key sites of the rebellion; departs from the International Bar.

Dublin Musical Pub Crawl WALKING TOUR
(01-478 0193; www.discoverdublin.ie; Oliver St John Gogarty's, 58-59 Fleet St; adult/student €12/10; 7.30pm daily Apr-Oct, 7.30pm Thu-Sat Nov-Mar) Irish traditional music explained and demonstrated by two expert musicians in various Temple Bar pubs.

Historical Walking Tour WALKING TOUR
(01-878 0227; www.historicalinsights.ie; Trinity College Gate; adult/child €12/free; 11am & 3pm May-Sep, 11am Apr & Oct, 11am Fri-Sun Nov-Mar) 'Seminars on the street' conducted by history graduates of Trinity College Dublin.

Sleeping

Dublin is *always* bustling, so call ahead or book online, especially on weekends. Don't forget that Dublin Tourism Centres can find and book accommodation for €5, plus a 10% deposit for the first night's stay.

NORTH OF THE LIFFEY

TOP CHOICE **Isaacs Hostel** HOSTEL €€
(01-855 6215; www.isaacs.ie; 2-5 Frenchman's Lane; dm/tw €23/84;) This popular hostel set amid 200-year-old wine vaults has loads of character. The lounge area is where it all happens, from summer BBQs to live music, and the easygoing staff are on hand 24/7 for advice and help.

DUBLIN PASS

If you're planning some heavy-duty sightseeing, you'll save a packet by investing in the **Dublin Pass** (adult/child 1-day €35/19, 2-day €55/31, 3-day €65/39). Not only do you gain free entry to more than 30 attractions but you can skip whatever queue there is by presenting your card; it also includes free transfer to and from the airport on the Aircoach. Available from any of the Dublin Tourism offices.

Generator Hostel HOSTEL €€
(☎01-901 0222; www.generatorhostels.com/en/dublin; Smithfield Sq; dm/tw from €16/70; @ 📶) This European chain brings its own brand of funky, fun design to Dublin's hostel scene, with bright colours, comfortable dorms (including women-only) and a lively social scene. Good location on a pedestrian mall next to Old Jameson Distillery.

Townhouse INN €€
(☎01-878 8808; www.townhouseofdublin.com; 47-48 Lower Gardiner St; s/d/tr €129/149/169) Elegant but unpretentious, the Georgian Townhouse has beautiful, individually designed bedrooms named after plays by the famous 19th-century playwrights who once lived here (Dion Boucicault and Lafcadio Hearn), and a Japanese garden out back.

Abbey Court Hostel HOSTEL €€
(☎01-878 0700; www.abbey-court.com; 29 Bachelor's Walk; dm/d €18/79) What it lacks in physical charm is made up for in craic (fun) and central location. Many of its residents are long-termers, giving the joint a community feel, and its two large common rooms and fantastic staff make for a convivial atmosphere.

Castle Hotel HOTEL €€
(☎01-874 6949; www.castle-hotel.ie; 3-4 Great Denmark St; r from €89; P 📶) Established in 1809, this hotel claims to be Dublin's oldest, and while it's a bit frayed around the edges it's still one of the better hotels north of the Liffey. Many rooms are decent-sized, and retain their original Georgian cornicing.

Anchor Guesthouse B&B €€
(☎01-878 6913; www.anchorguesthouse.com; 49 Lower Gardiner St; s/d €139/149; P) This lovely Georgian guesthouse, with its delicious wholesome breakfasts and an elegance you won't find in many of the other B&Bs along this stretch, comes highly recommended.

Abraham House HOSTEL €
(☎01-855 0600; www.abraham-house.ie; 83 Lower Gardiner St; dm incl breakfast €10-18, d incl breakfast €48-60; @ 📶) Friendly is an understatement at this large and lively hostel; good rates if you book ahead online. It's close to Connolly Station.

Marian Guesthouse B&B €
(☎01-874 4129; www.marianguesthouse.ie; 21 Upper Gardiner St; per person €25-40; P @ 📶) Modest but reasonably priced option in the Upper Gardiner St area (north of the city centre).

SOUTH OF THE LIFFEY

TOP CHOICE **Number 31** GUESTHOUSE €€€
(☎01-676 5011; www.number31.ie; 31 Leeson Close; s/d/tr from €150/190/260; P 📶) The former dwelling of Modernist architect Sam Stephenson (1933–2006) still feels like a 1960s designer pad with sunken sitting room, leather sofas, mirrored bar and floor-to-ceiling windows. A hidden oasis of calm, five minutes' walk from St Stephen's Green.

Barnacles Temple Bar House HOSTEL €
(☎01-671 6277; www.barnacles.ie; 19 Lower Temple Lane; dm/d from €12/50; P 📶) Plenty bright and immaculately clean, Barnacles' location in the heart of the Temple Bar district makes it a great place to stay if you don't mind the sound of drunken revellers outside your window; rooms at the back are quieter.

Avalon House HOSTEL €
(☎01-475 0001; www.avalon-house.ie; 55 Aungier St; dm/tw €15/60; @ 📶) This grand old Victorian building near St Stephen's Green houses a megahostel with four-, 12- and 20-bed mixed dorms on two levels, offering some privacy. There's a large kitchen, several lounges and a poolroom.

Morgan Hotel BOUTIQUE HOTEL €€
(☎01-643 7000; www.themorgan.com; 10 Fleet St; r from €120; @ 📶) Falling somewhere between *Alice in Wonderland* and a cocaine-and-hooker-fuelled rock 'n' roll fantasy, the uber-cool Morgan sports a sexy colour scheme of white floors and walls, with dark blue and pink lighting that extends into the bar, the rooms and even the cigar patio.

Grafton House B&B €€
(☎01-648 0010; www.graftonguesthouse.com; 26-27 South Great George's St; s/d from €59/79; @ 📶)

This Gothic-style building has 16 bright and funky en suite rooms with contemporary fittings, stylish walnut furniture, retro wallpaper and terrific breakfasts; great value and location.

Staunton's on the Green HOTEL €€
(☎01-478 2300; www.stauntonsonthegreen.ie; 83 St Stephen's Green South; s/d from €89/99) This handsome Georgian house is smack on St Stephen's Green, but is priced like an upscale suburban townhouse; complete with floor-to-ceiling windows overlooking the green and a pleasant rear garden for summer breakfasts. For the price and location this is a pretty sweet deal.

Ashfield House HOSTEL €
(☎01-679 7734; www.ashfieldhouse.ie; 19-20 D'Olier St; dm incl breakfast €10-18, d incl breakfast €48-60; @) Housed in a converted church a stone's throw from Temple Bar and O'Connell Bridge, this hostel feels more like a small hotel, with a good range of private en suite rooms as well as four-, six- and eight-bed dorms.

Kinlay House HOSTEL €
(☎01-679 6644; www.kinlaydublin.ie; 2-12 Lord Edward St; dm/tw €18/60;) Big, bustling and always up for a party (earplugs available at reception!), this is not a place for shrinking violets.

Gogarty's Temple Bar Hostel HOSTEL €
(☎01-671 1822; www.gogartys.ie/hostel; 58-59 Fleet St; dm/tw €20/54; P) Lively, party-atmosphere hostel right in the middle of Temple Bar action.

Eating

Making a decent fist of the restaurant business is tough enough at the best of times, but since the crash it's become an exercise in blind optimism, as a bunch of the city's best-known restaurants have closed, with most others facing an uncertain future. We've done our best to include only those that stand a better-than-even shot of making it through these difficult times.

The most concentrated restaurant area is Temple Bar but, apart from a handful of good places, the bulk of eateries offer bland, unimaginative fodder and cheap set menus for tourists. Better food and service can usually be found on either side of Grafton St, while the top-end restaurants are clustered around Merrion Sq and Fitzwilliam Sq. Fast-food chains dominate the northside, though some fine cafes and eateries are finally appearing there too.

NORTH OF THE LIFFEY

TOP CHOICE **Chapter One** MODERN IRISH €€€
(☎01-873 2266; www.chapteronerestaurant.com; 18 North Parnell Sq; 2-course lunch €29, 4-course dinner €65; ⏲12.30-2pm Tue-Fri, 6-11pm Tue-Sat) One of the best restaurants in Dublin is this venerable old trooper in the vaulted basement of the Dublin Writers Museum. It sets its ambitions no further than modern Irish cuisine, which it has realised so brilliantly that those Michelin lads saw fit to throw one of their sought-after stars its way. Get there between 6pm and 7pm for the three-course Pre-Theatre Special (€36.50).

TOP CHOICE **Winding Stair** MODERN IRISH €€€
(☎01-873 7320; winding-stair.com; 40 Lower Ormond Quay; mains €23-27; ⏲noon-5pm & 5.30-10.30pm) This rustic dining room squeezed above a bookshop serves superb Irish grub, from Irish charcuterie with wheaten bread, to locally caught hake with celeriac mash, followed by sticky pear and ginger steam pud. Hugely popular, so book ahead.

Soup Dragon TAKEAWAY €
(www.soupdragon.com; 168 Capel St; soups €5-10; ⏲8am-5pm Mon-Fri, 10am-4pm Sat) Eat in or take away one of 12 tasty varieties of homemade soups, including Indian dahl or spicy vegetable gumbo. Bowls come in two different sizes, and prices include fresh bread and a piece of fruit.

Bar Italia ITALIAN €€
(28 Lower Ormond Quay; mains €10-24; ⏲10.30am-11pm Mon-Sat, 1-9pm Sun) One of a new generation of eateries that's showing the more established Italian restaurants how the Old Country really eats. Specialities include ever-changing pasta dishes, homemade risottos and excellent Palombini coffee; the early bird menu (3pm to 5pm weekdays) offers a main course and glass of wine for €12.50.

Cobalt Café & Gallery CAFE €
(☎01-873 0313; 16 North Great George's St; mains €6-10; ⏲10am-4.30pm Mon-Fri) This elegant and arty cafe in a bright and airy Georgian drawing room has a limited lunch menu (from noon to 2.30pm), but it's a great place to enjoy hearty soup by a roaring fire in winter, or a fresh sandwich in the garden on warmer days.

Epicurean Food Hall FOOD HALL €
(www.epicureanfoodhall.com; Lower Liffey St; mains €4-12; ⏲8am-8pm Mon-Wed, 8am-9pm Thu-Sat, 11am-7pm Sun) You'll be spoilt for choice in this bustling arcade that houses more than 20 food stalls. The quality can be hit-and-miss, but good choices include Viva Espana (tapas and excellent paella), Burdock's (for fish and chips), El Corte (for coffee) and Istanbul House (for kebabs).

SOUTH OF THE LIFFEY

TOP CHOICE L'Gueuleton FRENCH €€
(www.lgueuleton.com; 1 Fade St; mains €19-26; ⏲12.30-4pm & 6-10pm Mon-Sat, 1-4pm & 6-9pm Sun) Dubliners just can't get enough of this restaurant's take on French rustic cuisine, which ranges from regulars such as slow-roast pork belly with dauphinois potatoes, to specials such as braised venison with orange, juniper and roast root vegetables. No reservations – queue for a table, or leave your mobile number and they'll text when a table's ready.

Coppinger Row MEDITERRANEAN €€
(www.coppingerrow.com; Coppinger Row; mains €18-25; ⏲noon-5.30pm & 6-11pm Mon-Sat, 12.30-4pm & 6-9pm Sun) The chefs here add a Mediterranean touch to the best of Irish produce, which can be enjoyed as main courses or afternoon bar bites. Local crab and crayfish salad comes with basil and lemon, while lamb gets a spiced aubergine and apricot accompaniment.

Fallon & Byrne DELI €
(www.fallonandbyrne.com; Exchequer St; mains €5-10; ⏲8am-9pm Mon-Wed, 8am-10pm Thu & Fri, 9am-9pm Sat, 11am-7pm Sun) Queue for delicious salads and sandwiches at the deli counter in this trendy New York–style food hall, or try one of their hot lunch dishes (from Chinese chilli chicken to veggie burger with sweet and sour salsa). There's more formal dining upstairs at the chic, buzzy brasserie.

Simon's Place CAFE €
(George's St Arcade, South Great George's St; sandwiches €5; ⏲9am-5.30pm Mon-Sat) Simon hasn't had to change the menu of sandwiches made with thick-cut bread and wholesome vegetarian soups since he first opened shop two decades ago – and why should he? His grub is as heart-warming and legendary as he is.

Cornucopia VEGETARIAN €
(www.cornucopia.ie; 19 Wicklow St; mains €10-13; ⏲8.30am-9pm Mon & Tue, 8.30am-10.15pm Wed-Sat, noon-9pm Sun; 🖉) For those seeking escape from the Irish cholesterol habit, Cornucopia is a popular, mostly vegan cafe turning out scrumptious healthy goodies. There's even a vegetarian breakfast fry-up as an alternative to muesli.

Pepperpot CAFE €
(www.thepepperpot.ie; Powerscourt Townhouse; mains €5-9; ⏲10am-6pm Mon-Wed & Fri, to 8pm Thu, 9am-6pm Sat & noon-6pm Sun) Everything is baked and made daily at this lovely cafe on the 1st-floor balcony of the Powerscourt Townhouse. The salads with homemade brown bread are delicious but the real treat is the all-day breakfast menu that includes scrambled eggs with smoked salmon.

Queen of Tarts CAFE €
(www.queenoftarts.ie; 3-4 Cow's Lane; mains €5-10; ⏲8am-7pm Mon-Fri, 9am-7pm Sat, 10am-6pm Sun) Pocket-sized Queen of Tarts offers a mouth-watering array of savoury tarts and filled focaccias, fruit crumbles, healthy breakfasts and weekend brunch specials.

Govinda's VEGETARIAN €
(www.govindas.ie; 4 Aungier St; mains €7-10; ⏲noon-9pm Mon-Sat; 🖉) This place is totally vegetarian, with a wholesome mix of salads and Indian-influenced hot daily specials.

Drinking

Temple Bar, Dublin's 'party district', is almost always packed with raucous stag and hen parties, scantily clad girls, and loud guys from Ohio wearing Guinness T-shirts. If you're just looking to get smashed and hook up with someone from another country, there's no better place in Ireland. If that's not your style, there's plenty to enjoy beyond Temple Bar. In fact, most of the best old-fashioned pubs are outside the district.

TOP CHOICE Stag's Head PUB
(1 Dame Ct) Built in 1770, and remodelled in 1895, the Stag's Head is possibly the best traditional pub in Dublin (and therefore the world). You may find yourself philosophising in the ecclesiastical atmosphere, as James Joyce once did. Some of the fitters that worked on this pub probably also worked on churches in the area, so the

stained-wood-and-polished-brass similarities are no accident.

Grogan's Castle Lounge Traditional Pub PUB
(15 South William St) A city-centre institution, Grogan's has long been a favourite haunt of Dublin's writers and painters, as well as others from the bohemian, alternative set. Drinks are marginally cheaper in the stone-floored public bar than in the lounge.

Hughes' Bar PUB
(19 Chancery St) Directly behind the Four Courts, this bar has nightly, if impromptu, sessions that often result in a closed door – that is, they go on long past official closing time. The pub is also a popular lunchtime spot with barristers working nearby.

Dice Bar BAR
(79 Queen St) Co-owned by singer Huey from the band Fun Lovin' Criminals, the Dice Bar looks like something you'd find on New York's Lower East Side.

Anseo BAR
(28 Lower Camden St) Unpretentious, unaffected and incredibly popular hipster spot.

Globe BAR
(www.globe.ie; 11 South Great George's St; all city-centre) The granddaddy of Dublin's hipster bars.

☆ Entertainment

For events, reviews and club listings, pick up a copy of the fortnightly music review **Hot Press** (www.hotpress.com), or for free cultural events, check out the weekly e-zine **Dublin Event Guide** (www.dublineventguide.com). Friday's *Irish Times* has a pull-out section called 'The Ticket' that has reviews and listings of all things arty.

Cinemas

Irish Film Institute CINEMA
(01-679 5744; www.ifi.ie; 6 Eustace St) The fantastic IFI has two screens showing classic and art-house films. Wheelchair access available.

Savoy CINEMA
(01-874 6000; Upper O'Connell St; from 2pm) A traditional four-screen first-run cinema.

Clubs & Live Music

Twisted Pepper CLUB
(01-873 4800; www.bodytonicmusic.com/thetwistedpepper; 54 Middle Abbey St; bar 4pm-late, cafe 11am-6pm) Dublin's coolest new venue comes in four parts: the basement is where you can hear some of the best DJs in town, the stage is for live acts, the mezzanine is a secluded bar area above the stage and the cafe serves Irish breakfast all day. All run by the Bodytonic crew, one of the most exciting music and production crowds in town.

Rí Rá CLUB
(www.rira.ie; Dame Ct; Mon-Sat) One of the friendlier clubs in the city centre, Rí Rá is full nearly every night with a diverse crowd who come for the mostly funk music downstairs, or more laid-back lounge tunes and movies upstairs.

Whelan's LIVE MUSIC
(01-478 0766; www.whelanslive.com; 25 Wexford St) A Dublin institution, providing a showcase for Irish singer-songwriters and other lo-fi performers.

Gay & Lesbian Venues

Dublin's not a bad place to be gay. Most people in the city centre wouldn't bat an eyelid at public displays of affection between same-sex couples, but discretion is advised in the suburbs. Check out www.gcn.ie for the latest on Dublin's gay scene.

George GAY, BAR
(www.thegeorge.ie; 89 South Great George's St) The mother of Dublin's gay bars is a long-standing institution, having lived through the years when it was the only place in town where the gay crowd could, well, be gay. There are other places to go, but the George remains the best, if only for tradition's sake. Shirley's legendary Sunday night bingo is as popular as ever.

Dragon GAY, BAR
(64-65 South Great George's St) High-concept, high-octane and loaded with attitude, the Dragon is the slightly trendier alternative to the long-established George just along the street.

Front Lounge BAR
(33 Parliament St) The unofficially gay 'Flounge' is a sophisticated and friendly bar that is quieter and more demure than other gay joints, and popular with a mixed crowd.

Pantibar GAY, BAR
(www.pantibar.com; 7-8 Capel St) Pantibar is bold and brash, mostly because its owner, the eponymous Panti, is an outrageous entertainer who makes sure that a night in her bar is one to remember. The floor shows – both on

and off the stage –are fabulous. It's open late Friday and Saturday.

Theatre & Classical Music

Abbey Theatre THEATRE
(☎01-878 7222; www.abbeytheatre.ie; Lower Abbey St) The famous Abbey is Ireland's national theatre, putting on new Irish works as well as revivals of Irish classics. It's scheduled to move to a new location in the docklands by 2016.

National Concert Hall CONCERT VENUE
(☎01-417 0000; www.nch.ie; Earlsfort Tce) Just south of the city centre, Ireland's premier orchestral hall hosts a variety of concerts year-round, including a series of lunchtime concerts from 1.05pm to 2pm on Tuesday from June to August.

Gaiety Theatre THEATRE
(☎01-677 1717; www.gaietytheatre.com; South King St) This popular theatre – which famously staged the 1971 Eurovision Song Contest – hosts, among other things, a program of classical concerts, operas and musicals.

Information

Medical Services

Doctor on Duty (☎01-453 9333; www.mediserve.ie; ⏲24hr) Request a doctor to come to your accommodation.

Hickey's Pharmacy (☎01-873 0427; 55 Lower O'Connell St) Open until 10pm every night.

St James's Hospital (☎01-410 3000; www.stjames.ie; James's St) Dublin's main 24-hour accident and emergency department.

Well Woman Clinic (☎01-872 8051; www.wellwomancentre.ie; 35 Lower Liffey St; ⏲9.30am-7.30pm Mon, Thu & Fri, 8am-7.30pm Tue & Wed, 10am-4pm Sat) Handles women's health issues and can supply contraception.

Tourist Information

All Dublin tourist offices provide walk-in services only – no phone enquiries. For tourist information by phone, call ☎1850 230 330 from within the Republic.

Dublin Tourism (www.visitdublin.com; St Andrew's Church, 2 Suffolk St; ⏲9am-7pm Mon-Sat, 10.30am-3pm Sun Jul & Aug, 9am-5.30pm Mon-Sat Sep-Jun) Offers tourist information for all of Ireland, as well as accommodation bookings, car hire, maps, and tickets for tours, concerts and more. Ask about the **Dublin Pass** (www.dublinpass.ie), which allows you entrance into more than 30 of Dublin's attractions, as well as some tours and other special offers.

City Centre Tourist Office (14 O'Connell St; ⏲9am-5pm Mon-Sat)

Dun Laoghaire Tourist Office (Dun Laoghaire ferry port; ⏲10am-1pm & 2-6pm)

Northern Ireland Tourist Board (NITB; www.discovernorthernireland.com) Has a desk in the Dublin Tourism Centre; same hours.

Getting There & Away

Air

Dublin airport (☎01-814 1111; www.dublinairport.com), about 13km north of the city centre, is Ireland's major international gateway, with direct flights from Europe, North America and Asia. Budget airlines including Ryanair and Flybe land here.

Boat

There are direct ferries from Holyhead in Wales to Dublin Port, 3km northeast of the city centre, and to Dun Laoghaire, 13km southeast. Boats also sail direct to Dublin Port from Liverpool and from Douglas, on the Isle of Man.

Bus

Busáras (☎01-836 6111; www.buseireann.ie; Store St) (buh-*saw*-ras), Dublin's main bus station, is just north of the Liffey. Standard one-way fares from Dublin:

Belfast €17, 2½ hours, hourly
Cork €14, 4½ hours, six daily
Galway €14, 3¾ hours, hourly
Killarney €32, six hours, five daily
Rosslare Europort €19.50, 3½ hours, four daily

The private company **Citylink** (www.citylink.ie) has nonstop services from Dublin airport (picking up in the city centre at Bachelor's Walk, near O'Connell Bridge) to Galway (€16, three hours, hourly).

Train

Connolly station North of the Liffey; trains to Belfast, Derry, Sligo, other points north and Wexford.

Heuston station South of the Liffey and west of the city centre; trains for Cork, Galway, Killarney, Limerick, and most other points to the south and west.

Regular one-way fares from Dublin:

Belfast €35, 2¼ hours, up to eight daily
Cork €60, 2¾ hours, hourly
Galway €34, 2¾ hours, nine daily

Iarnród Éireann Travel Centre (☎1850-366 222; www.irishrail.ie; Connolly Station, Amiens St; ⏲9am-5pm Mon-Fri, to 1pm Sat) For general train information.

Getting Around

To & From the Airport

A taxi to the city centre should cost around €20 to €25. Some Dublin airport taxi drivers can be unscrupulous, so make sure the meter is on and mention up front that you'll need a meter receipt.

Aircoach (www.aircoach.ie; one-way/return €7/12) Serves various destinations in the city; departs every 10 to 20 minutes from 5am to midnight, hourly through the night (35 to 55 minutes, depending on traffic).

Airlink Express Coach (☎01-873 4222; www.dublinbus.ie; adult/child €6/3) Bus 747 runs every 10 to 20 minutes from 6am to midnight to Upper O'Connell St (35 minutes) and the central bus station (Busáras; 45 minutes).

Dublin Bus (☎01-873 4222, www.dublinbus.ie; 59 Upper O'Connell St; ⌚9am-5.30pm Mon-Fri, 9am-2pm Sat) A couple of buses serve the airport from various points in Dublin, including buses 16 (Rathfarnham), and 41 (Lower Abbey St and Gardiner St). Limited luggage capacity.

To & From the Ferry Terminals

There are dedicated ferry buses from Busáras to Dublin Port, timed to connect with Irish Ferries services to/from Holyhead (one-way €3). Also, bus 53 runs from Talbot St/Lower Gardiner St in the city centre to Dublin Port (one-way €3, 25 minutes, hourly).

Dun Laoghaire ferry terminal can be reached by DART (€2.50, 25 minutes, every 15 minutes), or bus 7 from O'Connell Bridge, Lower Grafton St and Merrion Sq, or bus 46A from O'Connel St, Kildare St and St Stephen's Green.

Bicycle

Rental rates begin at around €13/70 a day/week; you'll need a €50 to €200 cash deposit and photo ID.

Neill's Wheels (www.rentabikedublin.com; per day/week €12.50/70) Various outlets, including Kinlay House and Isaacs Hostel.

Car

Traffic in Dublin is a nightmare and parking is an expensive headache. There are no free spots to park anywhere in the city centre during business hours (7am to 7pm Monday to Saturday). Better to leave your vehicle at the Red Cow Park & Ride just off Exit 9 on the M50 ring road, and take the **Luas tram** into the city centre (€4.20 return, 30 minutes).

Public Transport

Various public transport passes are available; one day's unlimited bus travel costs €6.50 (including Airlink); bus and tram costs €7.80; and bus and DART costs €11.75.

BUS **Dublin Bus** (www.dublinbus.ie) local buses cost from €1.40 to €2.65 for a single journey. You must pay the exact fare when boarding; drivers don't give change. The Rambler 1 Day ticket (€6.50) allows one day's unlimited travel on buses including Airlink.

TRAIN **Dublin Area Rapid Transport** (DART; ☎01-836 6222; www.irishrail.ie) provides quick rail access as far north as Howth and south to Bray; Pearse station is handy for central Dublin.

TRAM **Luas** (www.luas.ie; ⌚5.30am-12.30am Mon-Fri, from 6.30am Sat, 7am-11.30pm Sun) runs on two (unconnected) lines; the green line runs from the eastern side of St Stephen's Green southeast to Sandyford, and the red line runs from Tallaght to Connolly station, with stops at Heuston station, the National Museum and Busáras. Single fares range from €1.60 to €2.90 depending on how many zones you travel through.

TAXI Taxis in Dublin are expensive; flag fall costs €4.10, plus €1.03 per kilometre. For taxi service, call **National Radio Cabs** (☎01-677 2222; www.radiocabs.ie).

AROUND DUBLIN

Dun Laoghaire

☎01 / POP 114,200

Dun Laoghaire (dun-*leary*), 13km south of central Dublin, is a seaside resort and busy harbour with ferry connections to Britain. The B&Bs are slightly cheaper here than in central Dublin, and the fast and frequent train connections make it a convenient stay.

At Sandycove, south of the harbour, is the Martello Tower, where James Joyce's epic novel *Ulysses* opens. It now houses the **James Joyce Museum** (☎01-280 9265; www.visitdublin.com; Joyce Tower; adult/child €6/4, combined ticket with Dublin Writers Museum €11.50/7.50; ⌚10am-1pm & 2-5pm Tue-Sat, 2-6pm Sun Apr-Aug, by appointment only Sep-Mar). If you fancy a cold saltwater dip, the nearby **Forty Foot Pool** (also mentioned in *Ulysses*) is the place.

Take the Dublin Area Rapid Transport (DART) rail service (€4.70 return, 25 minutes, every 10 to 20 minutes) from Dublin to Dun Laoghaire, then bus 59 to Sandycove Rd, or walk (1km).

Malahide Castle

☎01

Despite the vicissitudes of Irish history, the Talbot family managed to keep **Malahide Castle** (☎01-846 2184; www.malahidecastleandgardens.ie; Malahide; adult/child €12/6; ⌚9.30am-5.30pm, last tour of castle 4.30pm) from 1185 through to 1973. The castle is the usual hotchpotch of additions and renovations;

the oldest part is a three-storey 12th-century tower house. The facade is flanked by circular towers that were tacked on in 1765. The interior is packed with furniture and paintings, and Puck, the family ghost, is still in residence. The parkland around the castle is a good place for a picnic and, on a fine day, the best part of a visit.

Malahide is 13km northeast of Dublin; take the DART rail service from Dublin Connolly to Malahide station (€4.70, return, 22 minutes, every 10 to 20 minutes).

Brú na Bóinne

☎041

A thousand years older than Stonehenge, the extensive Neolithic necropolis known as Brú na Bóinne (Boyne Palace) is one of the most extraordinary prehistoric sites in Europe. Its tombs date from about 3200 BC, predating the great pyramids of Egypt by six centuries. The complex, including the Newgrange and Knowth passage tombs, can only be visited on a guided walk from the **Brú na Bóinne Visitor Centre** (☎041-988 0300; www.heritageireland.ie; Donore; adult/child €3/2; ⏲9am-5pm Nov-Jan, Feb-Apr 9.30am-5.30, May 9am-6.30pm, Jun-Sep 9am-7pm, Oct 9.30am-5.30pm). At 8.20am during the winter solstice, the rising sun's rays shine directly down Newgrange's long passage and illuminate the chamber for a magical 17 minutes. Arrive early in the summer months as tours tend to fill up.

The site is 50km north of Dublin, signposted off the M1. Take Bus Éireann's 100X or 101 service to Drogheda, then the 163 to Donore (total journey €18 return, 1½ to 2¼ hours, twice daily), which stops at the gates of the visitor centre. Or use the **Newgrange Shuttlebus** (☎1800-424 252; www.overthetop-tours.com; return €17; ⏲twice daily Apr-Sep, once daily Oct-Mar)

Guided day tours from Dublin by **Mary Gibbons** (☎086 355 1355; www.newgrangetours.com; tour per adult/student €35/25) are excellent.

THE SOUTHEAST

The southeast of Ireland is a hell of a lot sunnier and dryer than the rest of the country – it's probably why the Vikings settled here, and certainly a reason why people love to visit. But the weather isn't the only draw – the area is littered with early-Christian ruins such as Glendalough and impressive castles such as Powerscourt. There's also the Wicklow Way, one of many rugged hiking trails that allow you to explore the region's plentiful waterfalls, beaches and mountains. Combine this with artsy towns such as medieval Kilkenny and waterfront Wexford, and you have a region not only diverse, but also bathed in sunlight and warmth – well, by Irish standards at least.

County Wicklow

County Wicklow, situated immediately south of Dublin, has three contenders for the 'best in Ireland' label: best garden (at Powerscourt), best monastic site (at Glendalough) and best walk (the Wicklow Way). Pleasant seaside resorts and beaches – notably at Brittas Bay – straggle along the coast between Bray and Arklow. West towards Sally Gap and due south from here lie the sparsely populated Wicklow Mountains.

POWERSCOURT

In 1974, after major renovations, the 18th-century mansion at **Powerscourt Estate** (www.powerscourt.ie; near Enniskerry; admission to house free, gardens adult/child €6.50/3.50; ⏲9.30am-5.30pm Mar-Oct, to dusk Nov-Feb) burned to the ground when a bird's nest in a chimney caught fire. One wing of the Palladian building remains, with an exhibition room, luxury shops and a delightful terrace cafe, but people come mainly for the gorgeous, 19th-century formal gardens with views east to Great Sugarloaf (501m).

From the house, a scenic 6km trail leads to **Powerscourt Waterfall** (adult/child €5/3.50; ⏲9.30am-7pm May-Aug, 10.30am-5.30pm Mar-Apr & Sep-Oct, to 4.30pm Nov-Jan), at 121m it's the highest in Ireland. You can also reach the waterfall by road (5km), following signs from the estate entrance.

The entrance to Powerscourt is 500m south of Enniskerry's main square and about 22km south of Dublin, and is wheelchair accessible. Dublin Bus 44 runs regularly from O'Connell St in Dublin to Enniskerry (€4.10, 50 minutes, hourly).

GLENDALOUGH

☎0404 / POP 280

Nestled between two lakes, haunting Glendalough (Gleann dá Loch, meaning 'Valley of the Two Lakes') is one of the most significant monastic sites in Ireland and one of the

THE WICKLOW WAY

Running for 127km from Marlay Park, Rathfarnham, in southern County Dublin through to Clonegal, County Carlow, the **Wicklow Way** (www.wicklowway.com) is the oldest and most popular of Ireland's long-distance walks. The route is clearly signposted and documented in leaflets and guidebooks; one of the better ones is *The Complete Wicklow Way* by JB Malone. Much of the trail traverses countryside above 500m, so pack proper hiking boots and waterproofs.

The most attractive section of the walk is from Enniskerry to Glendalough (two days). Camping is possible along the route, with permission from local farmers. **Knockree Hostel** (☎01-276 7981; www.knockreeyouthhostel.com; dm/d €21/55; ⊙closed 10am-5pm; P@) is a luxury farm conversion with lovely views, right on the trail 7km west of Enniskerry. The village of **Roundwood**, a good stopover, has a camping ground and some B&Bs.

loveliest spots in the country, with a **round tower**, a **ruined cathedral** and the tiny **Church of St Kevin**.

It was founded in the late 6th century by St Kevin, a bishop who established a monastery on the Upper Lake's southern shore and about whom there is much folklore. During the Middle Ages, when Ireland was known as 'the island of saints and scholars', Glendalough became a monastic city catering to thousands of students and teachers. The site is entered through the only surviving **monastic gateway** in Ireland.

The **Glendalough Visitor Centre** (www.heritageireland.ie; adult/child €3/1; ⊙9.30am-6pm mid-Mar–mid-Oct, to 5pm mid-Oct–mid-Mar), near the Lower Lake car park, has historical displays and a good 20-minute **audiovisual show**. From the Upper Lake (1.5km west of the visitor centre), several good **hiking trails** head into the hills.

Visitors swarm to Glendalough in summer, so it's best to arrive early and/or stay late, preferably on a weekday, as the site is free and open 24 hours. The lower car park gates are locked when the visitor centre closes.

Sleeping

The Glendalough area also has plenty of moderately priced B&Bs.

Glendalough International Hostel HOSTEL € (☎0404-45342; www.anoige.ie; The Lodge; dm/d €24/50; @☎) Lying just 600m west of Glendalough visitor centre, close to the round tower, this modern hostel attracts outdoorsy types from all over the world, especially during summer. It has great wheelchair accessibility.

TOP CHOICE **Glendalough Hermitages** HERMITAGE €€ (☎0404-45140, for bookings 0404-45777; www.hermitage.dublindiocese.ie; St Kevin's Parish Church, Glendalough; s/d €50/75) Designed for contemplation, these modest, self-catering bungalows consist of a bedroom, a bathroom, a small kitchen area and an open fire. Visitors of all faiths are welcome, so long as their intentions are meditative; backpackers looking for a cheap bed are not. There is a minimum two-night stay.

Getting There & Away

St Kevin's Bus (☎01-281 8119; www.glendaloughbus.com) runs twice daily to Glendalough (1½ hours, twice daily) from outside the Mansion House on Dawson St in Dublin.

Wexford

☎053 / POP 9400

Wexford's claustrophobic maze of medieval streets is lined with a mixture of old-time pubs, posh boutiques and modern steel-and-glass buildings. The town's rich and bloody history includes being founded by the Vikings, and nearly obliterated by Oliver Cromwell.

Wexford is a convenient stopover for those travelling to France or Wales via the Rosslare ferry port, 21km southeast of town. Its main attraction, though, is the world-famous **Wexford Opera Festival** (www.wexfordopera.com), an 18-day extravaganza (held in October/November) that presents rarely performed works to packed audiences in the town's shiny modern **opera house** (www.wexfordoperahouse.ie; 27 High St). Running concurrently with the opera festival is the **Wexford Festival Fringe** (www.wexfordfringe.ie), with events ranging from drama and dance to jazz and historical tours.

About 4km northwest of Wexford, on the N11 Dublin–Rosslare road at Ferrycarrig, the **Irish National Heritage Park** (www.inhp.com;

Ferrycarrig; adult/child €9/4.50; ⏲9.30am-6.30pm May-Aug, to 5.30pm Sep-Apr) is a theme park that recreates dwellings and everyday life from the Stone Age to the early Norman period; last admission is 1½ hours before closing. A taxi from town will cost about €7.

Sleeping & Eating

TOP CHOICE Abbey B&B B&B €€
(☎053-912 4408; www.abbeyhouse.ie; 34-36 Abbey St; s/d €45/80; P📶) Dwarfed by the enormous Whites hotel across the street, this cute, black-and-white B&B blazes with window boxes trailing red blooms in summer. Its seven rooms all have private bathrooms and fresh floral decor. The owners are total charmers.

Blue Door B&B €€
(☎053-912 1047; www.bluedoor.ie; 18 Lower George St; s/d from €45/80; 📶) The breakfasts are a plus at this Georgian townhouse, with smoked salmon and vegetarian alternatives. It's central but quiet, and floor-to-ceiling (almost!) windows make the bedrooms bright and airy.

Stable Diet CAFE €
(100 South Main St; mains €8-10; ⏲9am-5.30pm Mon-Sat) This bright and busy cafe is famous for its home-baked breads, scones and cakes; the lunch menu consists of freshly made soups and sandwiches, while breakfast choices (€5) include French toast with bacon and maple syrup.

Yard Modern MODERN IRISH €€€
(www.theyard.ie; 3 Lower George St; lunch mains €9-12, dinner mains €17-29; ⏲cafe 9am-6pm, restaurant lunch & dinner) Wexford's top dining spot is a cool, intimate cafe and restaurant that opens to an elegant courtyard beneath a canopy of fairy lights, with a menu of adventurous contemporary cuisine. Early bird menu (6pm to 8pm Monday to Wednesday and 6pm to 7pm Thursday to Saturday) is €25 for three courses.

SkyView Cafe CAFE €
(Wexford Opera House, High St; dishes €5-10; ⏲10am-4pm Mon-Sat; 📶) The cafe on the top floor of Wexford's snazzy opera house offers breakfast and lunch accompanied by panoramic views.

Information

Tourist Office (www.visitwexford.ie; Quayfront; ⏲9am-6pm Mon-Sat Apr-Oct plus 11am-1pm & 2-5pm Sun Jul & Aug, 9.15am-1pm & 2-5pm Mon-Sat Nov-Mar; 📶)

Getting There & Away

BUS Buses depart from the train station.

Dublin €18, 2¾ hours, at least hourly

Rosslare Harbour €5.20, 30 minutes, at least hourly

TRAIN Wexford's O'Hanrahan train station is at the north end of the town centre.

Dublin Connolly €25, 2½ hours, three daily

Rosslare Harbour €5.50, 25 minutes, three daily

Kilkenny

☎056 / POP 26,500

Built from black limestone flecked with fossil seashells, Kilkenny is known as 'the marble city'. Its picturesque huddle of medieval lanes, strung between castle and cathedral along the bank of the Nore River, is one of the southeast's biggest tourist draws – the narrow streets are often clogged with tour coaches. But it's worth braving the crowds to soak up the atmosphere of one of Ireland's creative crucibles – Kilkenny is a centre for arts and crafts, and home to a host of fine restaurants, cafes, pubs and shops.

Sights

TOP CHOICE Kilkenny Castle HISTORIC BUILDING
(www.kilkennycastle.ie; adult/child €6/2.50, parkland admission free; ⏲9.30am-5pm Mar-Sep, 9.30am-4.30pm Oct-Feb, parkland daylight hours) Stronghold of the powerful Butler family, Kilkenny Castle has a history dating back to 1172, when the legendary Strongbow erected a wooden tower on the site, though much of its present look dates from the 19th century. Highlights of the guided tour include the painted roof beams of the Long Gallery, and the collection of Victorian antiques. There's an excellent tearoom in the former castle kitchens, all white marble and gleaming copper.

Craft Centres ARTS CENTRE
The former stables opposite Kilkenny Castle are home to the **National Craft Gallery** (www.nationalcraftgallery.ie; Castle Yard; admission free; ⏲10am-5.30pm Tue-Sat, 11am-5.30pm Sun) and the **Kilkenny Design Centre** (☎056-772 2118; www.kilkennydesign.com; Castle Yard; ⏲10am-7pm), showcases for contemporary Irish crafts. Pick up the **Kilkenny Craft Trail** (www.madeinkilkenny.ie) leaflet at the tourist office for a list of local crafts workshops.

St Canice's Cathedral CHURCH
(www.stcanicescathedral.ie; St Canice's Pl; adult/concession €4/3, round tower €3/2.50; ⌚9am-6pm Mon-Sat, 2-6pm Sun Jun-Aug, 10am-1pm & 2-5pm Mon-Sat, 2-5pm Sun Apr-May & Sep, until 4pm other times, round tower Apr-Oct) Ireland's second-largest cathedral is crammed with medieval monuments and tombs. Outside stands a 30m-tall **round tower** (open April to September), which you can climb – if you're over 12 years of age – for a grand view of the town.

Rothe House & Garden HISTORIC BUILDING, MUSEUM
(www.rothehouse.com; Parliament St; adult/child €5/4; ⌚10.30am-5pm Mon-Sat & 2-5pm Sun Apr-Oct, 10.30am-4.30pm Mon-Sat Nov-Mar) Dating from 1594 and now home to a fascinating museum, Rothe House is Ireland's finest example of a Tudor merchant's house, complete with restored medieval garden.

Festivals & Events

Kilkenny is rightly known as the festival capital of Ireland, with several world-class events throughout the year.

Kilkenny Arts Festival ARTS
(www.kilkennyarts.ie) In mid-August the city comes alive with theatre, cinema, music, literature, visual arts, children's events and street spectacles for 10 action-packed days.

Kilkenny Rhythm & Roots MUSIC
(www.kilkennyroots.com; ⌚early May) Over 30 pubs and other venues participate in hosting Ireland's biggest music festival, with an emphasis on country and 'old-timey' American roots music.

Sleeping

TOP CHOICE **Butler House** BOUTIQUE HOTEL €€
(☎056-772 2828; www.butler.ie; 16 Patrick St; s/d from €77/135; P@) You can't stay in Kilkenny Castle, but this historic mansion is surely the next best thing. Once the home of the earls of Ormonde, who built the castle, these days it houses a boutique hotel with aristocratic trappings including sweeping staircases, marble fireplaces, an art collection and impeccably trimmed gardens.

Celtic House B&B €€
(☎056-776 2249; www.celtic-house-bandb.com; 18 Michael St; r €80; P@) Artist Angela Byrne extends one of Ireland's warmest welcomes at her spick-and-span B&B. Some of the bright rooms have views of the castle, and Angela's landscapes adorn many of the walls. Guests return time and again – book ahead.

Kilkenny Tourist Hostel HOSTEL €
(☎056-776 3541; www.kilkennyhostel.ie; 35 Parliament St; dm/tw €17/42; @) Inside an ivy-covered 1770s Georgian town house, this cosy, 60-bed Independent Holiday Hostels (IHH) place has a sitting room warmed by an open fireplace, and a timber- and leadlight-panelled dining room adjoining the self-catering kitchen. Most pubs are within stumbling distance.

Eating

TOP CHOICE **Cafe Sol** MODERN IRISH €€
(☎056-776 4987; www.restaurantskilkenny.com; William St; mains lunch €8-13, dinner €17-25; ⌚11am-9.30pm Mon-Thu, 11am-10pm Fri-Sat, noon-9pm Sun) The seasonally changing menu at this funky little place lists local sources for most of the produce. The Irish-Mediterranean fusion cuisine, like the bold and edgy artwork on the walls, displays some unexpected combinations, but it works – the place is packed by 1pm, so get in early for lunch. Three-course early-bird menus (€27; 5.30pm to 9.30pm Sunday to Thursday, 5.30pm to 6.45pm Friday and Saturday) are great value.

TOP CHOICE **Cafe Blueberry** CAFE €
(Winston's, 8 Parliament St; main €7-10; ⌚9am-5pm Mon-Sat) On the top floor of Winston's department store there is a stunning cafe run by the long-established **Blueberry Deli** (2 Market Yard; ⌚8.30am-6pm Mon-Sat). Enjoy sandwiches, hot lunch specials, cakes and more out on the rooftop terrace. The original deli is still *the* place for picnic supplies.

Chez Pierre FRENCH €€
(17 Parliament St; mains €10-20; ⌚10am-5pm Mon-Sat, plus dinner Thu-Sat) This neat little bistro does great *tartines* (open sandwiches), soups and sweets during the day, plus classic French dishes for dinner.

Gourmet Store SANDWICHES €
(56 High St; sandwiches €3.50; ⌚9am-6pm Mon-Sat) This classy deli is a great place for takeaway sandwiches.

Drinking & Entertainment

TOP CHOICE Tynan's Bridge House PUB
(St John's Bridge) Looking like it might fall down at any moment, this wonky Georgian pub is the best traditional bar in town.

John Cleere PUB, LIVE MUSIC
(22 Parliament St) One of Kilkenny's finest venues for live music, this long bar has blues, jazz and rock, as well as traditional music sessions.

Watergate Theatre THEATRE
(www.watergatetheatre.com; Parliament St) Hosts musical and theatrical productions throughout the year.

Information

Tourist Office (www.kilkennytourism.ie; Rose Inn St; ⏲9.15am-5pm Mon-Sat)

Getting There & Away

BUS Buses depart from the train station.
Cork €19, three hours, two daily
Dublin €12, 2¼ hours, five daily
TRAIN Kilkenny train station (Dublin Rd) is east of the town centre along John St, next to the MacDonagh Junction shopping mall.
Dublin Heuston €24, 1¾ hours, eight daily
Galway €45, four hours, one daily (change at Kildare)

THE SOUTHWEST

The southwest comes closest to the misty-eyed vision of Ireland many visitors hold in their imagination – blue lakes and green mountains, blustery beaches, bird-haunted sea cliffs, picturesque hamlets, and welcoming towns where live music sparks up every night. Cork city buzzes with an energy that rivals Dublin's, while Killarney offers a gateway to some of the country's finest scenery.

Cork

☎021 / POP 120,000

There's a reason the locals call Cork (Corcaigh) 'Ireland's Real Capital' or 'The People's Republic of Cork'; something special is going on here. The city has long been dismissive of Dublin, and with a burgeoning arts, music and restaurant scene, it has a cultural reputation to rival the capital's. A flurry of urban renewal has seen new buildings, bars and arts centres spring up all over town, but the best of the city is still happily traditional – snug pubs with live music sessions most of the week, excellent local produce in an ever-expanding range of restaurants, and a genuinely proud welcome from the locals. The city's most entertaining quarters lie north and south of St Patrick's St: webs of narrow streets crammed with pubs, cafes, restaurants and shops.

Sights

TOP CHOICE Crawford Municipal Art Gallery GALLERY
(☎021-490 7855; www.crawfordartgallery.ie; Emmet Pl; admission free; ⏲10am-5pm Mon-Sat, to 8pm Thu) The 18th-century Cork Customs House is blended with 21st-century Dutch design in this intriguing gallery, a must-see for anyone who enjoys art and architecture. Pieces by Irish artists such as Jack Yeats and Cork's own James Barry sit among a fine permanent collection that includes artists from Continental Europe. The gallery has wheelchair access.

Cork City Gaol MUSEUM
(☎021-430 5022; www.corkcitygaol.com; Convent Ave, Sunday's Well; adult/child €8/4.50; ⏲9.30am-5pm Apr-Oct, 10am-4pm Nov-Mar) Closed down in 1923, this 19th-century prison is now a terrific museum about a terrifying subject. Restored cells, mannequins representing prisoners and guards, and a detailed audioguide bring home the horrors of Victorian prison life.

St Fin Barre's Cathedral CATHEDRAL
(☎021-496 3387; www.cathedral.cork.anglican.org; Bishop St; adult/child €5/3; ⏲9.30am-5.30pm Mon-Sat & 12.30-5pm Sun Apr-Oct, closed 12.45-2pm & Sun Nov-Mar) Just south of the city centre sits Cork's Protestant cathedral. Built in 1879, this beautiful Gothic Revival structure has a multitude of notable features, including a Golden Angel who sits on the eastern side of the cathedral, and whose job it is to blow her horn at the onset of the Apocalypse.

FREE Cork Public Museum MUSEUM
(www.corkcity.ie; Fitzgerald Park; ⏲11am-1pm & 2.15-5pm Mon-Fri, 11am-1pm & 2.15-4pm Sat year-round, 3-5pm Sun Apr-Sep) The city museum has a fine collection of artefacts that trace Cork's past from prehistory to the present, including the city's role in the fight for independence. Bus 8 goes to the University College Cork (UCC) main gates nearby.

Festivals & Events

Guinness Jazz Festival JAZZ
(www.corkjazzfestival.com) All-star line-up in venues across town for Cork's biggest festival, held in October

Cork Film Festival FILM
(www.corkfilmfest.org) Eclectic week-long program of international films held in October/November.

Sleeping

TOP CHOICE **Garnish House** B&B €€
(☎021-427 5111; www.garnish.ie; Western Rd; s/d from €75/88; P) With charming rooms (think flowers and fresh fruit), gourmet breakfasts and hosts who are eager to please, Garnish House is possibly the perfect B&B. From the moment you arrive and are greeted with tea and goodies, until the moment you leave, you will experience nothing short of absolute hospitality.

River Lee Hotel HOTEL €€
(☎021-425 2700; www.doylecollection.com; Western Rd; r from €125; P) This modern riverside hotel brings a touch of affordable luxury to the city centre. There are gorgeous public areas with huge sofas, a designer fireplace and a stunning five-storey glass-walled atrium, well-equipped bedrooms (nice and quiet at the back), and possibly the best breakfast buffet in Ireland.

Brú Bar & Hostel HOSTEL €
(☎021-455 9667; www.bruhostel.com; 57 MacCurtain St; dm €15-20, d & tr €48-60; @) Cork's funkiest hostel also has a popular bar and an internet cafe on the premises. This clean and friendly triple treat can be a rocking good time, especially on the weekends.

Kinlay House HOSTEL €
(☎021-450 8966; www.kinlayhousecork.ie; Bob & Joan's Walk; dm €15-18, d €48-70; @) This labyrinthine hostel is in a bucolic spot near St Anne's Church in Shandon. It has a fun, laid-back atmosphere; services include bureau de change, laundry and luggage storage. Guests can use the next-door gym at a discount.

Crawford House B&B €€
(☎021-427 9000; www.crawfordhouse.ie; Western Rd; r €60-90; P @) A top-notch B&B, Crawford House has spacious rooms with king-size beds, gracious furnishings and spa baths. The standard is that of a contemporary hotel, the atmosphere that of a family home.

Sheila's Hostel HOSTEL €
(☎021-450 5562; www.sheilashostel.ie; 4 Belgrave Pl, off Wellington Rd; dm €16-18, tw €46-52; P @) The sauna, cinema room, coffee shop and superfriendly staff make up for the occasionally cramped atmosphere in this always-heaving hostel.

Blue Dolphin B&B €€
(☎021-427 4908; www.blue-dolphin-cork.com; 3 College View, Western Rd; s/d from €40/70; P @) Bright and welcoming, one of several high-quality B&Bs on this strip.

Emerson House B&B €€
(☎021-450 3647; www.emersonhousecork.com; 2 Clarence Tce, North Summer Hill; s/d from €60/80; P) Upmarket, gay and lesbian guesthouse.

Eating

TOP CHOICE **Market Lane** IRISH, INTERNATIONAL €€
(☎021-427 4710; www.marketlane.ie; 5 Oliver Plunkett St; mains €13-22; noon-late Mon-Sat, 1-9pm Sun;) It's always hopping at this bright corner bistro with a walk-in policy (no reservations for fewer than six diners, sip a drink at the bar till a table is free). The menu is broad and hearty, changing to reflect what's fresh at the English Market: how about braised ox cheek stew, or smoked haddock with bacon and cabbage? Lots of wines by the glass.

TOP CHOICE **Farmgate Café** CAFE, BISTRO €€
(www.farmgate.ie; Princes St, English Market; mains €6-14; 8.30am-5pm Mon-Sat) An unmissable experience at the heart of the English Market, the Farmgate is perched on a balcony overlooking the market below, the source of all that fresh local produce on your plate. Up the stairs and turn left for table service, right for counter service.

DON'T MISS

ENGLISH MARKET

It could just as easily be called the Victorian Market for its ornate vaulted ceilings and columns, but the **English Market** (Princes St; 9am-5.30pm Mon-Sat) is a true gem, no matter what you name it. Scores of vendors sell some of the very best meat, fish, cheese and takeaway food in the region. On decent days, take your lunch to nearby Bishop Lucey Park, a popular al fresco eating spot.

Cork

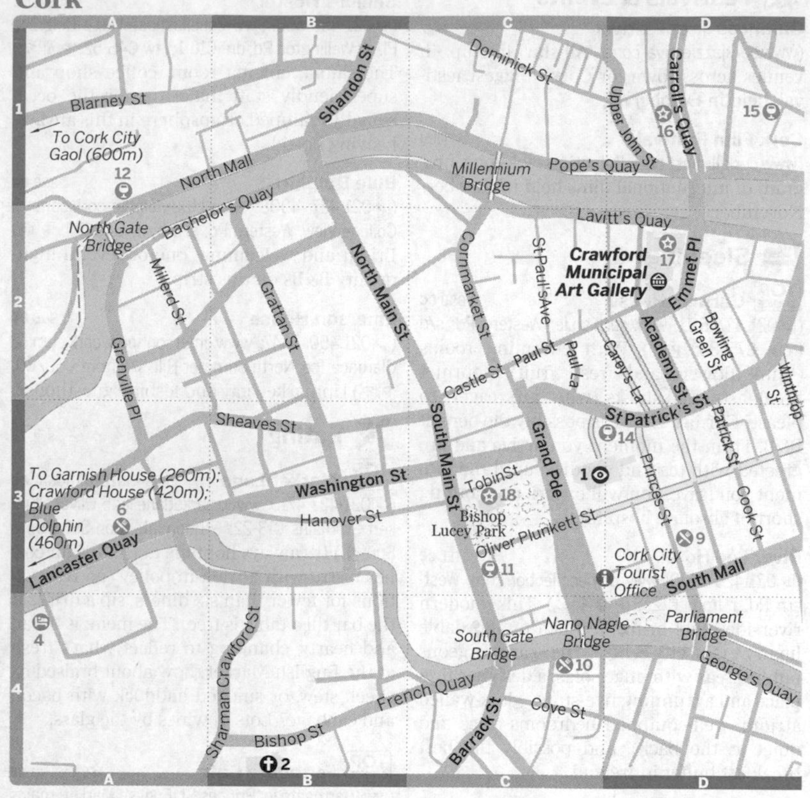

Nash 19 INTERNATIONAL €€
(☎021-427 0880; www.nash19.com; Princes St; mains €13-16; ⌚7.30am-5pm Mon-Fri, 8.30am-4pm Sat) A sensational bistro with its own market inside; local foods are honoured from breakfast to lunch and on to tea. Fresh scones draw in the crowds early; daily fresh specials (soups, salads, desserts etc) and an incredible burger keep them coming through the rest of the day.

Cafe Paradiso VEGETARIAN €€
(☎021-427 7939; www.cafeparadiso.ie; 16 Lancaster Quay; lunch mains €12-14, 2-/3-course dinner €33/40; ⌚noon-2.30pm Fri & Sat, 5.30-10pm Tue-Sat; ✎) Arguably the best vegetarian restaurant in Ireland, the inventive dishes on offer here will seduce even the most committed carnivore. The pre-theatre menu (5.30pm to 7pm Tuesday to Saturday) offers two/three courses for €23/29.

Idaho Café CAFE €
(☎021-427 6376; 19 Caroline St; mains €7-12; ⌚8.30am-5pm Mon-Thu, to 6pm Fri-Sat) It looks like a traditional old caff from the outside, but take a gander at the menu and you'll find all sorts of creative takes on Irish standards. The tea selection includes scads of herbal numbers and there's a good per-glass wine menu.

Quay Co-op CAFE €
(☎021-431 7026; www.quaycoop.com; 24 Sullivan's Quay; mains €9-11; ⌚9am-9pm Mon-Sat; ✎👪) Flying the flag for alternative Cork, this place offers a range of self-service vegie options, all organic, including big breakfasts and rib-sticking soups and casseroles. It also caters for gluten-, dairy- and wheat-free needs, and is amazingly child-friendly.

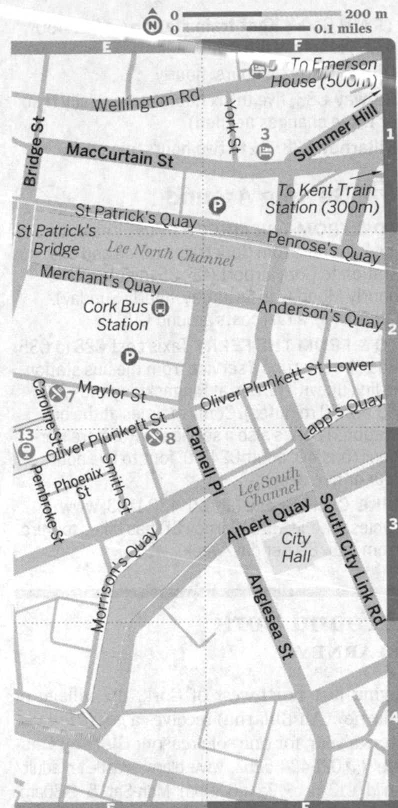

Cork

Top Sights
Crawford Municipal Art Gallery D2

Sights
1 English Market C3
2 St Fin Barre's Cathedral B4

Sleeping
3 Brú Bar & Hostel F1
4 River Lee Hotel A4
5 Sheila's Hostel F1

Eating
6 Cafe Paradiso A3
Farmgate Café .... (see 1)
7 Idaho Café E2
8 Market Lane E3
9 Nash 19 .... D3
10 Quay Co-op C4

Drinking
11 An Spailpín Fánac C3
12 Franciscan Well Brewery A1
13 Long Valley E3
14 Mutton Lane Inn D3
15 Sin É D1

Entertainment
16 Cork Arts Theatre D1
17 Cork Opera House D2
18 Triskel Arts Centre C3

Drinking

Cork's pub scene is cracking, easily rivalling Dublin's. Locally brewed Murphy's is the stout of choice here, not Guinness. Check www.corkgigs.com for pubs with live music.

Franciscan Well Brewery PUB
(www.franciscanwellbrewery.com; 14 North Mall; 3-11.30pm Mon-Thu, 3pm-12.30am Fri-Sat, 3-11pm Sun;) The copper vats gleaming behind the bar give the game away: the Franciscan Well brews its own beer. The best place to enjoy it is in the enormous beer garden at the back.

Mutton Lane Inn PUB
(Mutton Lane) With Victorian wallpaper, rock 'n' roll posters, and a covered outdoor area for drinking and smoking, Cork's oldest pub is the type of place that you'll wish you had in your home town.

Sin É PUB
(Coburg St) There are no frills or fuss here – just a comfy, sociable pub, long on atmosphere and short on pretension. There's music most nights, much of it traditional, but with the odd surprise.

An Spailpín Fánac PUB
(South Main St) The 'wandering labourer' hosts trad sessions almost nightly.

Long Valley PUB
(Winthrop St) This Cork institution has been going strong more or less since the mid-19th century.

Entertainment

Cork's cultural life is generally of a high calibre. To see what's happening grab **WhazOn?** (www.whazon.com), a free monthly booklet available from the tourist office, newsagencies, shops, hostels and B&Bs.

Cork Opera House OPERA
(021-427 0022; www.corkoperahouse.ie; Emmet Pl; box office 9am-8.30pm, to 5.30pm non-

performance nights) Cork's opera house and its Half Moon Theatre stage everything from opera and ballet to drama, comedy and live music. It has wheelchair access.

Cork Arts Theatre THEATRE
(021-450 5624; www.corkartstheatre.com; Camden Court, Carroll's Quay) An excellent theatre putting on thought-provoking drama and new works.

Triskel Arts Centre ARTS CENTRE
(021-472 2022; www.triskelart.com; Tobin St; tickets around €15) Hosts contemporary art, film, theatre, music and photography.

Information

Cork City Tourist Office (021-425 5100; www.cometocork.com; Grand Pde; 9am-6pm Mon-Sat, 10am-5pm Sun Jul & Aug, 9.15am-5pm Mon-Sat Sep-Jun)

Getting There & Away

AIR Cork airport (ORT; 021-431 3131; www.cork-airport.com) is 8km south of the city on the N27. Direct flights to Newcastle, Edinburgh, London, Manchester, Amsterdam, Barcelona, Munich, Paris, Warsaw and Rome.

BOAT Brittany Ferries (021-427 7801; www.brittanyferries.ie; 42 Grand Pde) has regular sailings from Cork to Roscoff (France). The ferry terminal is at Ringaskiddy, about 15 minutes by car southeast of the city centre along the N28.

BUS Aircoach (01-844 7118; www.aircoach.ie) provides a direct service to Dublin city and airport from St Patrick Quay (€18, four hours, eight daily). **Cork bus station** (cnr Merchants Quay & Parnell Pl) is east of the city centre.

Dublin €14, 4½ hours, six daily

Kilkenny €19, three hours, two daily

Killarney €18, 1¾ hours, hourly

TRAIN Cork's **Kent train station** (021-450 4777) is across the river.

Dublin €60, 2¾ hours, hourly

Galway €83, five to six hours, seven daily (two or three changes needed)

Killarney €28, 1½ to two hours, nine daily

Getting Around

TO & FROM THE AIRPORT Bus Éireann service 226 runs from Cork train station and bus station to Cork airport (€5, 35 minutes, twice hourly Monday to Saturday, hourly Sunday). Otherwise, a taxi costs around €15.

TO & FROM THE FERRY Taxis cost €28 to €35. Bus Éireann runs a service from the bus station to link up with ferries at Ringaskiddy (bus 223; €5.50, 50 minutes). Confirm times at the bus station. There's also a service to Rosslare Harbour (bus 40, adult €24.50, four to five hours, four or five daily).

BIKE Cycle Scene (021-430 1183; www.cyclescene.ie; 396 Blarney St) has bikes for hire from €15/80 per day/week.

Around Cork

BLARNEY

021 / POP 2150

Lying just northwest of Cork, the village of Blarney (An Bhlarna) receives a *gazillion* visitors a year, for one sole reason: **Blarney Castle** (021-438 5252; www.blarneycastle.ie; adult/child €12/5; 9am-6.30pm Mon-Sat & 9.30am-5.30pm Sun May-Sep, to 7pm Mon-Sat Jun-Aug, 9am-sundown Sun Oct-Apr). They come to kiss the castle's legendary **Blarney Stone** and get the 'gift of the gab' (Queen Elizabeth I, exasperated with Lord Blarney's ability to talk endlessly without agreeing to her demands, invented the term 'to talk Blarney' back in the 16th century). The stone is up on the battle-

WORTH A TRIP

ROCK OF CASHEL

The **Rock of Cashel** (www.heritageireland.com; adult/child €6/2; 9am-5.30pm mid-Mar–mid-Oct, to 7pm mid-Jun–Aug, to 4.30pm mid-Oct–mid-Mar) is one of Ireland's most spectacular archaeological sites. A prominent green hill, banded with limestone outcrops, it rises from a grassy plain on the outskirts of Cashel town and bristles with ancient fortifications. For more than 1000 years it was a symbol of power, and the seat of kings and churchmen who ruled over the region. Sturdy walls circle an enclosure that contains a complete **round tower**, a roofless **abbey** and the finest 12th-century **Romanesque chapel** in Ireland.

Cashel Lodge and Camping Park (062-61003; www.cashel-lodge.com; Dundrum Rd; campsite per person €8, dm/s/d €20/40/65; P) is a good place to stay, with terrific views of the Rock.

Bus Éireann (www.buseireann.ie) runs eight buses daily between Cashel and Cork (€14, 1½ hours).

mento, and bending over backwards to kiss it requires a head for heights, although there's someone there to hold you in position. It also helps if you're not germophobic – there's a greasy mark where millions of lips have been before. (The Blarney stain? Sorry.)

Bus 215 runs from Cork bus station to Blarney (€6.50 return, 30 minutes, every 30 minutes).

COBH

021 / POP 6800

In the wake of the Famine, 2.5 million people emigrated from the port of Cobh (pronounced cove) – go on a grey day and the sense of loss is still palpable. When the sun shines, though, you'll see another side to this pretty little town with its **brightly coloured houses** and **seaside promenade**. Be sure to visit the excellent **Cobh, The Queenstown Story** (021-481 3591; www.cobhheritage.com; Lower Rd; adult/child €7.50/4; 9.30am-6pm Mon-Sat, 11am-6pm Sun, last admission 1hr before closing) heritage centre in the old train station. It tells the story of the migrants who sailed from here, and of the town's links with the *Titanic* and the *Lusitania*.

Cobh is 24km southeast of Cork via the N25. Hourly trains (€7 return, 30 minutes) run here from Cork.

West Cork

The Irish coast begins the slow build of beauty that culminates in counties even further west and north, but what you find here in West Cork is already quite lovely. Kinsale is a superb little waterside town and there are many smaller ones almost as charming along the craggy coast to the Ring of Beara.

Travelling around West Cork by public transport can be tough. There are at least two daily bus services in summer connecting the main towns, but some routes are not serviced at all during the rest of the year. The trick is to plan ahead at Cork and be prepared to change buses and backtrack – use the online journey planner at www.buseireann.ie. If you're so inclined, hitchhiking is another way to get around West Cork (take the usual safety precautions).

KINSALE

021 / POP 2260

The picturesque yachting harbour of Kinsale (Cionn tSáile) is one of the many gems that dot the coastline of County Cork. Kinsale has been labelled the gourmet centre of Ireland and, for such a small place, it certainly contains more than its fair share of international-standard restaurants. It also has lots of craft galleries and shops.

Sights & Activities

Charles Fort FORTRESS

(021-477 2263; www.heritageireland.ie; adult/child €4/2; 10am-6pm mid-Mar–Oct, to 5pm Nov-mid-Mar, closed Mon mid-Dec–mid-Mar) Southeast of Kinsale, a scenic 2.5km walk from the town centre, stand the stout ruins of Charles Fort. Built in the 1670s, it is one of the best-preserved star forts in Europe and commands grand coastal views.

You can sail to Charles Fort and up the Bandon River aboard the **Spirit of Kinsale** (086 250 5456; www.kinsaleharbourcruises.com; adult/child €12.50/6). Departure times vary and are weather dependent – check the website or the tourist office for details.

Sleeping

Pier House B&B €€

(021-477 4475; www.pierhousekinsale.com; Pier Rd; r €100-140;) This superb guesthouse, set back from the road in a sheltered garden, is a lovely place to rest your head. Pristine rooms are decorated with shell-and-driftwood sculptures, and have black-granite bathrooms with power showers and underfloor heating. Four of the rooms also have balconies.

Olde Bakery B&B €€

(021-477 3012; www.theoldebakerykinsale.com; 56 Lower O'Connell St; r €80) A short walk southwest of Kinsale town centre is this very friendly place that once was the British garrison bakery. Rooms are a reasonable size, and terrific breakfasts around the kitchen table get everyone chatting.

Dempsey's HOSTEL €

(021-477 2124; www.hostelkinsale.com; Eastern Rd; dm/tw €15/40;) This basic hostel is nothing special, but it's the town's cheapest option, with separate male and female dorms, family rooms, a kitchen, and picnic tables in the front garden. It's the bright blue house by the petrol station on the road from Cork.

Eating

TOP CHOICE **Fishy Fishy Cafe** SEAFOOD €€€

(021-470 0415; www.fishyfishy.ie; Crowley's Quay; mains €14-35; noon-9pm Mar-Oct, noon-4pm Sun-Wed & noon-9pm Thu-Sat Nov-Feb) This seafood restaurant is beautifully understated, with stark white walls, local art and steel fish sculptures on the walls, and a decked terrace out front. All the fish is caught locally, from the lobster thermidor to the scallops with black pudding and parsnip purée.

Jim Edwards SEAFOOD €€
(021-477 2541; www.jimedwardskinsale.com; Market Quay; bar mains €14-18; food served noon-10pm) This is a pleasant and unassuming pub where a traditional ambience belies the high quality of the bar menu, which doffs a cap to meat-eaters but specialises mostly in all kinds of locally caught fish.

Fishy Fishy Shop & Chippie FISH & CHIPS €
(021-477 4453; Guardwell; meals €8-15; noon-4.30pm Tue-Sat) If the main restaurant is full (or too expensive), you can get a superb seafood lunch to take away at this chippy a few blocks away near Market Sq. The menu includes beer-battered haddock with chips and salad, and seafood chowder with tarragon and coriander.

Cucina CAFE €
(021-470 0707; www.cucina.ie; 9 Market St; mains €9-15; 8.30am-4.30pm Mon-Sat, 9.30am-2pm Sun, dinner Tue-Sat;) Laid-back jazz sets the mood at this friendly little cafe. Healthy bruschetta, salads and soups, and not-so-healthy but delicious cupcakes are served in a simple setting; great breakfasts include eggs Benedict, while the lunch and evening menus offers dishes such as crab and avocado salad and Thai chicken curry.

Information

Tourist Office (021-477 2234; www.kinsale.ie; cnr Pier Rd & Emmet Pl; 9.15am-5pm Tue-Sat Nov-Mar, Mon Apr-Jun, Sep & Oct, 10am-5pm Sun Jul & Aug) In the centre of town; opening hours vary, especially in the quieter months.

Getting There & Away

Kinsale is 25km south of Cork; to continue west by bus you have to return to Cork. Bus 249 from Cork (€13 return, 50 minutes, 14 daily Monday to Friday, 11 Saturday, five Sunday) stops near the tourist office.

BALTIMORE

028 / POP 400

Just 13km down the Ilen River from Skibbereen, sleepy Baltimore has a population of around 400 that swells enormously during summer. Its main attraction is the ferry to Sherkin and Clear Islands.

Baltimore has plenty of B&Bs, including the excellent **Rolf's Country House** (028-20289; www.rolfscountryhouse.com; Baltimore Hill; s/d €60/100; @).

The Skibbereen **tourist office** (028-21766; www.skibbereen.ie; 9am-7pm Jul & Aug, 9am-6pm Mon-Sat Jun & Sep, 9.15am-1pm & 2-5pm Mon-Fri Oct-May) can handle questions about the area.

CLEAR ISLAND

028 / POP 120

Clear Island, or Cape Clear as the locals call it, is the most southerly point of Ireland (apart from uninhabited Fastnet Rock, 6km to the southwest). It's a Gaeltacht (Irish-speaking) area, with about 120 Irish-speaking inhabitants, one shop, three pubs and its own website, **Oileán Chléire** (Cape Clear Island; www.oilean-chleire.ie). It's a place for quiet walks, birdwatching and hunting down standing stones. There's also a wonderful **storytelling festival** (www.capeclearstorytelling.com) held in early September.

An Óige's **Cape Clear Island Hostel** (028-41968; www.capeclearhostel.com; Old Coastguard Station; dm €17-20, tw €40-46; @) is in a large white building at the south harbour, or you can camp at **Chléire Haven** (028-39119; www.yurt-holidays-ireland.com; campsite per person €10; Jun-Sep).

Cluain Mara (028-39153; www.capeclearisland.com; North Harbour; r €54-70;) and **Ard Na Goithe** (028-39160; www.ardnagaoithe.ie; The Glen; r from €70) are both amazingly friendly places in typical island houses. They can be reached by taking the 'bus' (which is actually a silver minivan) from the pier.

The ferries **Cailín Óir** and **Dun Aengus** (028-41923; www.cailinoir.com; return adult/child €16/8) sail between Baltimore and Clear Island (weather permitting) three to four times daily in summer and twice daily in winter. The trip takes 45 minutes (bicycles go for free).

From June to September, the **Karycraft** (028-28278; www.capeclearferries.com; return adult/child €15/6; one to three per day) ferry connects Schull (on the Mizen Head Peninsula) with Clear Island, allowing you to use the island as a stepping stone to travel west.

MIZEN HEAD PENINSULA

028

The contorted sea cliffs of Mizen Head provide a foretaste of the spectacular coastal scenery that characterises southwest Ireland. The road west from the pretty village of **Schull** ends at the **Mizen Head Visitor Centre** (www.mizenhead.ie; adult/child €6/3.50; 10.30am-5pm Mar-Oct, to 6pm Jun-Aug, 11am-6pm Sat & Sun Nov-Feb), from which a short but spectacular walk leads to **Mizen Head**

Signal Station, on a small island connected to the mainland by a 45m-high bridge (you have to pay the visitor centre admission fee to get to the island). From here you can look down on the pounding sea, striking rock formations and maybe the odd seal.

Stanley House (☎028-28425; www.stanley-house.net; Colla Rd, Schull; s/d €50/76; ⊙Apr-Sep;), just outside of Schull, has sweeping views of the water from its front lawn, while **Glencairn** (☎028-28007; susanglencairn@yahoo.ie; Ardmanagh Dr, Schull; s/d €45/70), on a cul-de-sac just 100m off Main St, serves up a mighty Irish breakfast.

There's one direct bus a day from Cork to Schull (€18.50, 2½ hours), and two more changing at Skibbereen.

BEARA PENINSULA

☎027

The Beara Peninsula is a wild, handsome, rocky landscape that's ideal for exploring by foot or bike – lacking the constant stream of tour buses that infest its northern neighbour, it's a more peaceful but equally scenic alternative to the Ring of Kerry.

Beginning at the attractive Victorian resort of **Glengarriff**, it's possible to drive the 137km **Ring of Beara** in one day, although that would be missing the point. It's also possible to hitchhike around the Ring, which would definitely take more than a day. If you're driving or cycling (leg-power permitting), don't miss the beautiful **Healy Pass**.

Walkers might like to tackle the ruggedly beautiful **Hungry Hill**, made famous by Daphne du Maurier's book of the same name, just outside the pleasant fishing town of **Castletownbere**. Castletownbere is also home to **McCarthy's Bar**, which appears on the cover of the popular book (of the same name) by the late Pete McCarthy.

The village of **Allihies**, whose colourfully painted houses grace many a postcard and guidebook cover, lies at the centre of an old copper mining area. Its fascinating history is chronicled in the **Allihies Copper Mine Museum** (☎027-73218; adult/child €5/3; ⊙10am-5pm daily May-Sep, Sat & Sun Oct-Apr). Pick up a copy of the museum leaflet and follow the **Copper Mine Trail**, a waymarked hike among the remains of the old workings.

Tiny **Dursey Island**, at the end of the peninsula, is reached by Ireland's only **cable car** (adult/child return €4/1; ⊙9am-8pm Jun-Aug, 9-11am, 2.30-5pm & 7-8pm Mon-Sat, 9-10am, 1-2.30pm & 7-7.30pm Sun Sep-May), which sways 30m above Dursey Sound. In a perfect photo op, livestock take precedence over humans in the queue.

The island, just 6.6km long by 1.5km wide, is a bird and whale sanctuary, and dolphins can sometimes be seen swimming in the waters around it. There's no accommodation, but camping is legal, so long as you respect the common rules and clean up after yourself.

Sleeping

Murphy's Village Hostel HOSTEL €
(☎027-63555; www.murphyshostel.com; Main St; dm/d €15/40; ⊙Jun-Sep) Pleasantly informal hostel in the heart of Glengarriff.

Garranes Farmhouse Hostel HOSTEL €
(☎027-73032, 027-73147; www.dzogchenbeara.org; Garranes; dm/f €15/40) Between Castletownbere and Allihies, with a breathtaking location high above Bantry Bay. Owned by a Buddhist retreat centre.

Allihies Village Hostel HOSTEL €
(☎027-73107; www.allihieshostel.net; dm/d €18/50) Smart and gleaming hostel among the old copper mines.

Sea View Guesthouse GUESTHOUSE €€
(☎027-73004; www.seaviewallihies.com; Allihies; s/d €45/75; P) Ten cosy rooms in a tidy yellow building.

Getting There & Away

Bus Éireann's bus 236 runs from Cork to Castletownbere (€20.50, 3½ hours) via Bantry, Glengarriff and Adrigole, at least three times a week. Bus 282 runs from Castletownbere to Kenmare via Ardgroom (€11.80, 1½ hours, twice daily Monday to Saturday); the morning bus connects with bus 270 from Kenmare to Killarney. There is no public transport to Allihies.

Killarney

☎064 / POP 13,500

Killarney is a well-oiled tourism machine set in a sublime landscape of lakes, forests and 1000m peaks. Its manufactured tweeness is renowned, the streets filled with tour-bus visitors shopping for soft-toy shamrocks, and countless placards pointing to trad-music sessions. However, it has many charms beyond its proximity to waterfalls, woodlands, mountains and moors. In a town that's been practising the tourism game for more than 250 years, competition keeps standards high, and visitors on all budgets can expect to find superb restaurants, great pubs and good accommodation.

Sights & Activities

Most of Killarney's attractions are just outside the town, not actually in it. If you're not on two wheels, the traditional transport is the horse-drawn **jaunting car** (☎064-663 3358; www.killarneyjauntingcars.com), which comes with a driver/guide known as a jarvey. The pick-up point, nicknamed 'the Ha Ha' or 'the Block', is on Kenmare Pl. A one-hour tour of Ross Castle estate costs from €25 for two persons; cars can officially carry up to four people.

Killarney National Park NATIONAL PARK
(www.killarneynationalpark.ie) Any cynicism engendered by Killarney's shamrock-filled souvenir stores evaporates when you begin to explore the sublime Killarney National Park. Buses rumble up to Ross Castle and Muckross House, but it's possible to flee the rest of tourist-kind while taking in Ireland's largest area of ancient oak woods, panoramic views of its highest mountains, and the country's only wild herd of native red deer.

Lough Leane (the Lower Lake or 'Lake of Learning'), **Muckross Lake** and the **Upper Lake** make up about a quarter of the park. Their peaty waters are as rich in wildlife as the surrounding land: cormorants skim across the surface, deer swim out to graze on the islands, and salmon, trout and perch prosper in a pike-free environment.

Designated a Unesco Biosphere Reserve in 1982, the park extends to the southwest of town. There are pedestrian entrances opposite St Mary's Cathedral, with other entrances (for drivers) off the N71.

The restored 14th-century **Ross Castle** (☎064-663 5851; www.heritageireland.ie; Ross Rd; adult/child €4/2; ⏲9am-5.45pm Mar-Oct) is a 2.5km walk from St Mary's Cathedral. Hour-long **cruises on Lough Leane** (adult/child €10/5) leave the castle daily in summer; you can make bookings at the tourist office. From late September to May boats depart only on demand.

Inisfallen, Lough Leane's largest island, is where the 13th-century *Annals of Inisfallen* were written. The annals, now in the Bodleian Library at Oxford, remain a vital source of information about early Irish history. From Ross Castle you can hire a boat and row to the island to inspect the ruins of a 12th-century oratory. Alternatively, boatmen charge around €10 per person for the trip.

The core of Killarney National Park is **Muckross House** (☎064-667 0144; www.muckross-house.ie; adult/child €7/3, combined ticket with farms €12/6; ⏲9am-7pm Jul & Aug, to 5.30pm Sep-Jun) and its surrounding estate, donated to the government in 1932. You can pay to tour the house, or walk or cycle around the grounds for free. The house is 5km from central Killarney, set in beautiful gardens; you can walk, cycle, take a taxi or hire a jaunting car.

Gap of Dunloe SCENIC ROUTE
In summer the Gap of Dunloe, a scenic valley squeezed between Purple Mountain and Carrantuohil (at 1040m, Ireland's highest peak), is a tourist bottleneck crammed with coaches depositing crowds of day trippers for one-hour pony-and-trap rides through the pass. Rather than joining the hordes, think about hiring a bike and cycling the route.

Go anticlockwise (going clockwise means a very steep uphill climb), north around Lough Leane to **Kate Kearney's Cottage** (a restaurant), then up and through the Gap. An exhilarating downhill ride and a couple of left turns lead to **Lord Brandon's Cottage** (a cafe), where you can catch a boat (departure at 2pm) to Reen Pier near Ross Castle and a short ride back to town. This should cost about €30, including bike hire; **O'Connors Tours** (☎064-663 0200; www.gapofdunloetours.com; 7 High St, Killarney; ⏲Mar-Oct) can arrange bus transport to Kate Kearney's, bike hire and boat trip (boat must be booked in advance – if you miss it, it's a long way back to Killarney by road!). Please note that other tour operators do not take bikes from Lord Brandon's to Ross Castle.

It's also possible to walk through the Gap from Kate Kearney's to Lord Brandon's (12km; allow 2½ hours).

Sleeping

Wherever you stay, book ahead from June to August. Hostels often rent out bikes and offer discounted tours. Finding a room can be tricky during high season, so it may be worth the €5 fee to have the tourist office do the hunting.

TOP CHOICE **Crystal Springs** B&B €€
(☎064-663 3272; www.crystalspringsbb.com; Ballycasheen Cross; s/d from €55/86; P) You can cast a line from the timber deck of this relaxing riverside B&B, where rooms are richly furnished with patterned wallpapers and walnut timber, and en suite bathrooms (most with spa baths) are larger than many Irish hotel rooms. It's about a 15-minute stroll into town.

CLIMBING IRELAND'S HIGHEST HILL

Carrantuohil (1040m), the highest peak in Ireland, lies just 16km west of Killarney. Its summit, marked with a huge steel cross, makes a popular objective for visiting hikers.

The best approach is from **Cronin's Yard** (☎064-662 4044; www.croninsyard.com; Mealis, Beaufort), a farmhouse with a car park, a tearoom (packed lunches available on request), showers, toilets, and a public telephone. It's at the road's end (OS ref 836873), reached from the N72 via Beaufort, west of Killarney. You may be asked to pay a small fee for using the car park. A broad, easily followed path leads from the car park alongside the Gaddagh River for just over 3km to **Hag's Glen**, a spectacular valley with two small lakes (a worthwhile sight in itself).

From here the popular but hair-raising way to the summit of Carrantuohil lies directly ahead – the **Devil's Ladder**, a gruelling trudge up a badly eroded gully. The ground is loose in places (take great care not to dislodge stones), and in wet conditions the way becomes muddy. From its top, a steep but straightforward hike leads to the summit. The climb takes about six hours return from Cronin's Yard.

Climbing Carrantuohil should never be attempted without a map and compass (and the skills to use them), proper hillwalking boots, waterproofs and spare food and water.

Mountain guide **Con Moriarty** (☎087 2214 0002, 064-662 2681; www.hiddenireland-tours.com; €75 per person) leads guided ascents of Carrantuohil on Wednesday and Saturday (booking essential).

Súgán Hostel HOSTEL €
(☎064-663 3104; www.killarneysuganhostel.com; Lewis Rd; dm €12-15, tw €38;) Resembling a hobbit hole, this homely, alcohol-free hostel has a warm fire and equally warm hosts. The atmosphere is nothing short of familial, which makes leaving a hard task. Bicycle hire is €15 a day.

Neptune's Killarney Town Hostel HOSTEL €
(☎064-663 5255; www.neptuneshostel.com; Bishop's Lane, New St; dm €16-20, s/d €40/50; @) Neptune's mixed dorms can sleep over 150, but this central hostel feels much smaller thanks to the roaring fire in reception, free internet access, and the staff's unfailing helpfulness.

Kingfisher Lodge B&B €€
(☎064-663 7131; www.kingfisherlodgekillarney.com; Lewis Rd; s/d €65/100; P@) Lovely back gardens are a highlight at this immaculate B&B, located on a strip with others close to the centre. Walkers will be especially happy here as the owner is a certified guide with years of experience walking and hiking around the region.

Fairview B&B €€
(☎064-663 4164; www.fairviewkillarney.com; Lewis Rd; d from €90; P@) The Fairview tends towards the boutique end of the guesthouse spectrum, with a stylish interior enhanced by luxurious little touches such as plasma TVs and jacuzzis in most of the rooms; your host, James, is possibly the most attentive in Killarney. Rates are discounted in low season, and wheelchair access is available.

Rathmore House B&B €€
(☎064-663 2829; www.rathmorehousekillarney.com; Rock Rd; s/d €38/75; ⏰Mar-Nov; P) There's a real Irish welcome at this long-established, family-run B&B at the entrance to town.

Elyod House B&B €€
(☎064-663 6544; www.elyodhouse.ie; Ross Rd; r €60-80) This quietly located modern house is on the road to Ross Castle and a few minutes' walk from town. Rooms are fresh and clean, and the welcome is friendly.

Killarney Flesk Caravan & Camping Park CAMPGROUND €
(☎064-663 1704; www.killarneyfleskcamping.com; Muckross Rd; campsites per campervan plus 2 persons €26, hiker €10; ⏰Jun-Sep; P) About 1.5km south of the town centre on the N71 to Kenmare, this camping ground has great views of the mountains.

✕ Eating

Reservations are recommended for evening meals in high season.

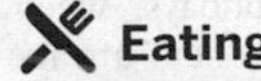
Chapter 40 MODERN IRISH €€€
(☎064-667 1833; www.chapter40.ie; Lower New St; mains €23-29; ⏰dinner Tue-Sat) Chic but unobtrusive decor of polished wood and cream

leather with walls of aubergine and silver sage provide the setting for a charming and witty menu that coaxes maximum flavour from local produce. The tasting plate of starters, served on a school slate, should not be missed, while the chef's inventive nature shines through in desserts such as mini jam doughnuts served with a coffee cup of cappuccino mousse.

The Smoke House BISTRO €€
(064-662 0801; www.thesmokehouse.ie; High St; mains lunch €7-14, dinner €15-26; 8am-11pm;) One of Killarney's newest and busiest ventures, this tiled bistro is the first establishment in Ireland to cook with a Josper (Spanish charcoal oven). Stylish salads include Dingle prawn, and roast fig and feta; its Kerry lamb burger, with mint, tomatoes and pickled onion, is delicious.

Treyvaud's IRISH €€€
(663 3062; www.treyvaudsrestaurant.com; 62 High St; mains €20-30; noon-10pm Tue-Sun, plus 5-10pm Mon May-Sep) A modish restaurant with a strong reputation for subtle dishes that merge trad Irish with seductive European influences, from fresh seafood chowder to rack of Kerry lamb with rosemary jus. Pre-6.45pm menu offers two courses for €25.

Bricín IRISH €€€
(www.bricin.com; 26 High St; mains €19-26; dinner Tue-Sat) This Celtic deco restaurant doubles as the town museum, with Jonathan Fisher's 18th-century views of the national park taking pride of place. Dishes include Kerry lamb, gourmet nut roast and house speciality *boxty* (potato pancake); the pre-6.30pm menu offers two/three courses for €19/29.

Jam CAFE €
(77 High St; mains €5-11; 8am-6pm Mon-Sat;) This funky little cafe is famed for superb and healthy soups, salads and sandwiches, and coffee and cake.

Drinking & Entertainment

Most pubs put on live music, and most nights are lively – even Mondays, when many of the town's hospitality staff are released to the fun side of the bar. Plunkett and College Sts are lined with pubs.

Killarney Grand BAR, CLUB
(www.killarneygrand.com; Main St) A great place for authentic music (if you can hear it over the boisterous crowd), the Grand has interesting takes on the traditional thing from 9pm. Wednesday night is *ceile* night (9pm to 11pm, €7 admission fee).

O'Connor's PUB
(High St) O'Connor's is a tiny but hugely popular pub that stages a mix of trad music, stand-up comedy, readings and pub theatre.

Courtney's PUB
(www.courtneysbar.com; Plunkett St) With a few nice fireplaces, barrels used as tables and nearly everything made from wood, Courtney's offers the ultimate Irish pub atmosphere.

Hussy's PUB
(High St) Escape the tourist mobs and muse over a pint in this small pub sporting a snug at the entrance and genial drinkers within.

Information

Tourist Office (064-663 1633; www.killarney.ie; Beech Rd; 9am-8pm Jun-Aug, 9.15am-5pm Sep-May) Busy but efficient; has a free map of the national park and details of bus services.

Getting There & Around

BIKE O'Sullivan's (www.killarneyrentabike.com; Beech Rd; per day/week €15/80) has bike rental; opposite the tourist office.

BUS Operating from the train station, Bus Éireann has regular services to:

Cork €18, 1¾ hours, hourly

Dingle (via Tralee) €15, 2½ hours, five daily

Dublin €27, six hours, six daily

Galway (via Limerick) €24.50, seven hours, six daily

Rosslare Harbour €29, seven hours, three daily

TAXI Taxis can be found at the taxi rank on College St. A cab from the edge of town (eg Flesk campsite) into the town centre costs around €9.

TRAIN Travelling by train to Cork (€28, 1½ to two hours, nine daily) or Dublin (€62, six hours, three daily) usually involves changing at Mallow.

Ring of Kerry

066

This 179km circuit of the Iveragh Peninsula pops up on every self-respecting tourist itinerary, and for good reason. The road winds past pristine beaches, medieval ruins, mountains and loughs (lakes) and the island-dotted Atlantic. Even locals stop their cars to gawk at the rugged coastline – particularly between Waterville and Caherdaniel in the

DON'T MISS

SKELLIG MICHAEL

The vertiginous climb up uninhabited **Skellig Michael** (www.heritageireland.ie) inspires an awe that monks could have clung to life in the meagre beehive-shaped stone huts that stand on the tiny strip of level land on top.

Calm seas permitting, boats run from spring to late summer from Portmagee (beside the bridge to Valentia Island) to Skellig Michael. The standard fare is around €45 return. Advance booking is essential; there are a dozen boat operators, including **Casey's** (☎066-947 2437; www.skelligislands.com; Portmagee) and **Sea Quest** (☎066-947 6214; www.skelligsrock.com).

The **Skellig Experience** (☎066-947 6306; www.skelligexperience.com; adult/child €5/3, incl cruise €27.50/14.50; ⏲10am-7pm Jul & Aug, to 6pm May, Jun & Sep, to 5pm Mar, Apr, Oct & Nov), on Valentia Island beside the bridge from Portmagee, has exhibits on the life and times of the monks who lived on Skellig Michael from the 7th to the 12th centuries. From April to September, a two-hour **cruise** around the Skelligs (without landing) departs from the centre daily at 2.45pm.

southwest of the peninsula, where the beauty dial is turned up to 11.

Although it can be 'done' in a day by car or bus, or three days by bicycle, the more time you take, the more you'll enjoy it. Tour buses travel the Ring in an anticlockwise direction. Getting stuck behind one is tedious, so driving in the opposite direction is preferred. Alternatively, you can detour from the main road – the **Ballaghbeama Pass** cuts across the peninsula's central highlands, and has spectacular views and little traffic.

The shorter **Ring of Skellig**, at the end of the peninsula, has fine views of the Skellig Rocks and its narrow roads are free of tourist coaches. You can forgo roads completely by walking the **Kerry Way**, which winds through the Macgillycuddy's Reeks mountains past **Carrantuohil**, Ireland's highest mountain.

Sights

Caherciveen TOWN

Daniel O'Connell (the Liberator) was born near Caherciveen (ca'ar-suh-*veen*), one of the Ring's larger towns. The excellent, wheelchair-accessible **Barracks Heritage Centre** (www.theoldbarracks.com; Bridge St; adult/student €4/2; ⏲10am-6pm Mon-Fri, 11am-4.30pm Sat, 10-3pm Sun May-Oct, reduced hrs mid-Mar–May, closed Nov–mid-Mar) occupies what was once an intimidating Royal Irish Constabulary (RIC) barracks. Exhibits focus on O'Connell and on the Famine's local impact.

Valentia Island ISLAND

South of Caherciveen the R565 branches west to Valentia Island, the 11km-long jumping-off point for an unforgettable experience: the **Skellig Rocks**, two tiny islands 12km off the coast.

Sleeping

There are plenty of hostels and B&Bs along the Ring. It's wise to book ahead, though, as some places are closed out of season and others fill up quickly.

CAHERCIVEEN

TOP CHOICE Mannix Point Camping & Caravan Park CAMPGROUND €

(☎066-947 2806; www.campinginkerry.com; Mannix Point; campsites per person €8.50; ⏲Mar-Oct; 📶) This place regularly wins awards as the best camping ground in Ireland. With a coastal location, sunset views, and a campers' lounge with peat fire, musical instruments and friendly resident cats, it's easy to see why.

Sive Hostel HOSTEL €

(☎066-947 2717; www.sivehostel.ie; East End, Caherciveen; dm/tw €15/44; 📶) Simple and sweet, this IHH affiliate is a good walking base. There's bike storage, a camping area, and it's close to several good pubs.

O'Shea's B&B B&B €€

(☎066-947 2402; www.osheasbnb.com; Church St, Caherciveen; s/d €45/70; Ⓟ) Right in the centre of town, across from the bus stop, O'Shea's is a friendly B&B with a nice view from the back of the house.

BALLINSKELLIGS

Ballinskelligs Inn B&B €€

(☎066-947 9106; www.ballinskelligsinn.com; Ballinskelligs; s/d €50/90; Ⓟ) A classic rural inn, this seaside spot is a comfortable place to spend the night after a long day of cycling, hiking or driving. The attached pub-restaurant is rip-roaring fun during summer.

Skellig Hostel HOSTEL €
(☎066-947 9942; www.skellighostel.com; Ballinskelligs; dm/d €15/52; P 📶) This modern building is a little characterless, but the rooms, lounge and dining room are comfortable, plus it's elevated, with sea views.

Getting Around

Bus Éireann runs a once-daily Ring of Kerry bus service (280) from late June to late August. Buses leave Killarney at 11.30am and stop at Killorglin, Glenbeigh, Caherciveen, Waterville, Caherdaniel and Molls Gap, arriving back at Killarney at 4.45pm (€19).

Travel agencies and hostels in Killarney offer daily tours of the Ring for about €20, year-round.

Dingle Peninsula

☎066

Remote and beautiful, the Dingle Peninsula ends in the Irish mainland's most westerly point. This is a Gaeltacht area – if you're driving, don't bother looking for road signs that say 'Dingle'; they all say 'An Daingean', the Irish equivalent.

Centred on pretty Dingle town, the peninsula has a high concentration of ring forts and other ancient ruins; activities on offer range from diving to playing the bodhrán (frame drum). There's an alternative way of life here in the craft workshops and cultural centres, traditional sessions and folkloric festivals.

DINGLE TOWN

POP 1800

The peninsula's capital is a special place whose charms have long drawn runaways from across the world, making the port town a surprisingly creative and cosmopolitan place. There are loads of cafes, bookshops and art and craft galleries, and a friendly dolphin called Fungie who has lived in the bay for 25 years.

Sights & Activities

Fungie the Dolphin BOAT TOUR
(☎066-915 2626; www.dingledolphin.com; The Pier; adult/child €16/8) The Dingle Boatmen's Association operates one-hour boat trips to visit Fungie the dolphin (free if Fungie doesn't show, but he usually does). There are also two-hour trips where you can swim with him (€25 per person, wetsuit hire €25 extra). Booking advisable.

Outdoor Activities OUTDOORS
Hike up **Mt Brandon** (951m), ride the peninsula with **Dingle Horse Riding** (☎066-915 2199; www.dinglehorseriding.com; The Stables, Baile na Buaile; per hr €35), or learn to surf or windsurf at Brandon Bay with **Jamie Knox Watersports** (☎066-713 9411; www.jamieknox.com; Maharees, Castlegregory); a two-hour taster session costs from €35 per person, including equipment.

Dingle Oceanworld AQUARIUM
(☎066-915 2111; www.dingle-oceanworld.ie; Dingle Harbour; adult/child/€13/7.50; ⏲10am-6pm Jul & Aug, to 5pm Sep-Jun; 👪) This state-of-the-art aquarium has a walk-through tunnel and touch pool, and is wheelchair accessible; look out for Molly the loggerhead turtle, found on a local beach in 2004 with injured flippers.

Dingle Bay Charters CRUISES
(☎066-915 1344; www.dinglebaycharters.com) Offers two-hour cruises from the marina to the Blasket Islands (adult/child €25/10) and one-hour trips around the bay (€10/5).

Sleeping

Pax House B&B €€
(☎066-915 1518; www.pax-house.com; Upper John St; s/d from €90/120; ⏲closed Dec-Feb; P @ 📶) From its highly individual decor (including contemporary paintings) to the outstanding views over the estuary from room balconies and the terrace, Pax House is a treat. Choose from cheaper hill-facing rooms, rooms that overlook the estuary, or two-room family suites opening to the terrace.

An Capall Dubh B&B €€
(☎066-915 1105; www.ancapalldubh.com; Green St; d €70-80; P 📶) Sitting on a cobbled courtyard and entered through a 19th-century stone-built coach entrance, this delightful B&B is a great place to relax after a long day in the outdoors – or a long night in the pub.

Hideout Hostel HOSTEL €
(☎066-915 0559; www.thehideouthostel.com; Dykegate Lane; dm €18, d €50; P @ 📶) Dingle's newest and best hostel has top-notch facilities including two lounges with groovy furnishings, bike storage and a well-equipped kitchen. Rates include light breakfast (tea, coffee, toast, cereal). Switched-on owner Mícheál is a fount of local info.

Eating

TOP CHOICE Garden Café CAFE €€
(www.thegardencafedingle.eu; Green St; mains €8-11; ⏲10am-4.30pm Mon & Wed-Sat, noon-4.30pm Sun) A cool little cafe with junk-shop furniture and outdoor tables at the back, the Garden focuses on fresh local produce with lunch dishes such as homemade lasagne, and the 'Dingle Dog' – gourmet sausages in a bun. Best coffee in town too.

Global Village Restaurant INTERNATIONAL €€€
(☎066-915 2325; www.globalvillagedingle.com; Upper Main St; mains €24-30; ⏲dinner Mar-Oct) With the sophisticated feel of a continental bistro, this restaurant offers a fusion of global recipes gathered by the well-travelled owner-chef. Fresh vegetables come from the restaurant's own organic garden.

Goat Street Cafe CAFE €
(Goat St; mains €6-13; ⏲10am-4pm Mon-Sat) This cheerful little cafe is a popular pit stop for breakfasts of scrambled egg with smoked salmon or pancakes with apple and cinnamon, or a lunch of soup, sandwiches or salad.

Drinking

Dick Mack's PUB
(http://dickmacks.homestead.com; Green St) Vestiges of its previous incarnation as a cobbler's workshop line the walls, while drunken revellers sing songs and slap each other's backs. Expect impromptu music sessions.

Small Bridge Bar PUB
(An Droichead Beag; Lower Main St) Now this is a pub! Filled with snugs, odd woodwork and a couple of bars, this cavernous place has trad music sessions nightly.

Foxy John's PUB
(Main St; 📶) Half hardware store, half old-school pub, Foxy John's is a great place to drop into for a pint, a bag of nails and some good craic.

Information

Tourist Office (☎066-915 1188; www.dingle-peninsula.ie; The Pier; ⏲9.15am-5pm Mon-Sat) At Dingle Town pier.

Getting There & Around

Buses stop outside the car park at the back of the Super Valu store in Dingle Town. Buses from Killarney to Dingle (change at Tralee) run five times daily Monday to Saturday (€15, 2½ hours).

Dingle has several bike-hire places. **Paddy Walsh** (Dykegate St), next to the Grapevine Hostel, rents bikes for €10 per day. Foxy John's also rents bikes (€10 a day)

NORTH & WEST OF DINGLE TOWN

From Dingle follow signs for the **Slea Head Drive**, a coastal road with views of the Blasket Islands that leads to **Dunmore Head**, mainland Ireland's most westerly point. The scenery here challenges the Ring of Kerry for finest in Ireland. Alternatively, you can head north across the **Connor Pass** (456m), the highest motor road in Ireland, with a spectacular descent on the north side.

Exhibits at Dunquin's excellent **Blasket Centre** (Ionad an Bhlascaoid Mhóir; ☎066-915 6444; www.heritageireland.ie; adult/child €4/2; ⏲10am-6pm Apr-Oct) celebrate the lives of the former islanders, many of them celebrated musicians, storytellers and writers.

Blasket Islands Tours (☎066-915 4864; www.blasketislands.ie) runs ferries from Dunquin to the bleak, uninhabited (since 1953) **Blasket Islands** (€20 return, 20 minutes, seven a day), and also offers 2½-hour **wildlife- and whale-watching cruises** around the islands (€25; depart from Ventry). Booking is essential.

Dún Chaion Hostel (☎066-915 6121; www.anoige.ie; Dunquin; dm €15-19, tw €44; ⏲Feb-Nov; P) has a terrific location with stunning views, near the Blasket Centre and not too far from Dunquin Pier, 15km west of Dingle Town. It's closed between 10am and 5pm.

Limerick

☎061 / POP 54,000

'There once was a city called Limerick...' Umm, no, can't think of anything that rhymes with Limerick. And no one is quite sure why those humorous five-line verses are named after this Irish city, though the name has been in use since the late 19th century.

Limerick (Luimneach) is still trying to shake off a reputation for violence and squalor that was vividly portrayed in Frank McCourt's novel *Angela's Ashes*. Redevelopment was stalled by the financial crisis, but a couple of interesting sights are worth a brief stop on the way to greener pastures.

Top of the list is the fascinating and unusual **Hunt Museum** (www.huntmuseum.com; Custom House, Rutland St; adult/child €5/2.50; ⏲10am-5pm Mon-Sat, 2-5pm Sun; 👪), which houses a superb collection of Bronze Age, Celtic and medieval artefacts, based on the private collection of antique dealers John and Gertrude Hunt. Half the fun is opening the drawers, where much of the collection is kept, to discover the random treasures hidden within. Look out for the tiny bronze horse by Leonardo da Vinci.

If you have time for lunch, **DuCarts** (Hunt Museum, Rutland St; mains €6-12; ⏲10am-5pm Mon-Sat, 2-5pm Sun) in the Hunt Museum offers a selection of freshly made salads, soups, sandwiches and hot dishes, all served with a smile.

The **tourist office** (☎061-317 522; Arthur's Quay; ⏲9.30am-1pm & 2-5.30pm Mon-Fri, 9.30am-1pm Sat) is near the Shannon River; ask here about *Angela's Ashes* tours.

Getting There & Away

AIR Shannon airport (SNN; www.shannonairport.com) is 24 kilometres west of Limerick. Hourly buses connect with Limerick bus and train station (€7.20, 45 minutes).

BUS Bus Éireann services operate from the train station.

Cork €15, two hours, hourly

Dublin €13, 3¼ hours, 12 daily

Galway €15, 1½ hours, hourly

TRAIN There are regular trains from **Limerick Railway Station** (☎061-315 555; Parnell St) to:

Cork €42, two hours, seven daily (change at Limerick Junction)

Dublin Heuston €50, 2½ hours, six daily

THE WEST COAST

The west coast is Ireland at its wildest and most remote, a storm-battered seaboard of soaring sea cliffs and broad surf beaches. Along its length you can explore the eerie lunar landscape of The Burren's limestone plateau, party on in the music pubs of bohemian Galway, and hike the heather-clad hills and bogs of Connemara. The weather is often just as wild as the landscape, but a bit of wind-torn mist and cloud just adds to the atmosphere.

The Burren

The Burren of northern County Clare is a harsh and haunting landscape of bare rock, softened with a sprinkling of rare wildflowers; *Boireann* is Irish for 'Rocky Country', and the name is no exaggeration. The rugged limestone plateau is littered with ancient dolmens, ring forts, round towers, high crosses and a surprisingly diverse range of flora, while rocky foreshores and splendid cliffs line its coast.

Tim Robinson's excellent *Burren Map & Guide* is available at bookshops or tourist offices. If you're stuck for transport, a number of bus tours leave the Galway tourist office every morning for The Burren and the Cliffs of Moher, including **O'Neachtain Tours** (☎091-553 188; www.irelandscenictours.ie). They all cost around €25.

A much better way to explore the Burren, however, is on foot: **Burren Hill Walks** (☎065-707 7168), based in Ballyvaughan, and **Burren Wild** (☎087 877 9565; www.burrenwalks.com), near Bellharbour, both offer half-day guided walks for €15 to €25 per person.

DOOLIN

☎065 / POP 200

Tiny Doolin – more a scatter of houses than a village proper – is famed for its **music pubs**, and makes a convenient base for exploring The Burren. It's also a gateway for boats to the Aran Islands. In summer it can be difficult to get a bed in Doolin, so book ahead. Some of the hostels rent out bikes for around €10 a day, plus deposit.

Doolin's reputation for top-notch traditional Irish music has spread like wildfire; summer nights find the local pubs packed with an appreciative cosmopolitan crowd.

Sleeping

TOP CHOICE **Cullinan's Guesthouse** INN €€
(☎065-707 4183; www.cullinansdoolin.com; s/d €70/96; P 📶) The eight rooms here are all of a high standard, with power showers and comfortable fittings. Right on the river (two rooms have balconies), it has a lovely back terrace for enjoying the views. The restaurant is one of the village's best.

Aille River Hostel HOSTEL €
(☎065-707 4260; www.ailleriverhosteldoolin.ie; dm €18-25, d from €55; ⏲Mar–Dec; P @ 📶) In a picturesque river spot near the village crossroads, this converted 17th-century farmhouse is the best budget choice. Has turf fires, hot showers, free laundry and good company.

Nagles Doolin Caravan & Camping Park CAMPGROUND €
(☎065-707 4458; www.doolincamping.com; campsites €17-19; ⏲Apr-Sep; 📶) Smooth grassy

pitches, sofas in the laundry, full-on views of the Cliffs of Moher, and Doolin pubs a short distance away – hard to beat!

Eating & Drinking

TOP CHOICE McGann's PUB

(Roadford) McGann's has all the classic touches of a full-on Irish music pub, and the food here is the best in the village. Inside you'll find locals playing darts in its warren of small rooms, some with turf fires. There's a small outside covered area.

O'Connor's PUB €€

(www.gusoconnorsdoolin.com; Fisher St; mains €11-25; food served 9.30am-10pm) The town's most popular pub makes a fine job of Irish standards – the seafood chowder, bacon and cabbage, and fish and chips are all excellent. Beware, however, of tour-bus crowds.

Doolin Cafe CAFE €€

(Roadford; mains €6-20; 10am-4pm & 6-10pm) There's a great atmosphere at this homely but elegant cafe, and great food too, from the full Irish breakfast to a dinner of sirloin steak or grilled sea bass.

Getting There & Away

There are direct buses to Doolin from Limerick, Ennis, Galway and even Dublin; the main Bus Éireann stop is across from Paddy Moloney's Doolin Hostel. For information on ferries to and from the islands.

CLIFFS OF MOHER

About 8km south of Doolin are the towering 200m-high Cliffs of Moher, one of Ireland's most famous natural features. In summer the cliffs are overrun with day trippers, so consider staying in Doolin and hiking or biking along The Burren's quiet country lanes, where the views are superb and crowds are never a problem. Either way, be careful along these sheer cliffs, especially in wet or windy weather.

The landscaped **Cliffs of Moher Visitor Centre** (www.cliffsofmoher.ie; adult/child €6/free; 8.30am-7.30pm Jun-Aug, 9am-6pm Mar-May, Sep & Oct, 9am-5pm Nov-Feb) has exhibitions about the cliffs and the environment called the 'Atlantic Edge'. Nearby is **O'Brien's Tower** (adult/child €2/1), which you can climb. You can avoid the crowds by visiting after the visitor centre closes, which is also the best time for photography (sun doesn't hit the cliffs till late in the day).

Galway

091 / POP 72,400

Arty and bohemian, Galway (Gaillimh) is legendary around the world for its entertainment scene. Students make up a quarter of the city's population, and brightly painted pubs heave with live music on any given night. Cafes spill out onto cobblestone streets filled with a frenzy of fiddles, banjos, guitars and bodhráns, and jugglers, painters, puppeteers and magicians in outlandish masks enchant passers-by.

Sights & Activities

Galway's city centre is tightly packed between the east bank of the Corrib River and Eyre Sq.

TOP CHOICE Hall of the Red Earl ARCHAEOLOGICAL SITE

(www.galwaycivictrust.ie; Druid Lane; admission free; 9.30am-4.45pm Mon-Fri) Back in the 13th century when the de Burgo family ran the show in Galway, Richard – the Red Earl – had a large hall built as a seat of power. Here locals would come looking for favours or to do a little grovelling as a sign of future fealty. After the 14 tribes took over, the hall fell into ruin and was lost. Lost that is until 1997 when expansion of the city's Custom House uncovered its foundations. Now after 10 years of archaeological research, the site is open for exploration. The custom house is built on stilts overhead, leaving the old foundations open. Artefacts and a plethora of fascinating displays give a sense of Galway life some 900 years ago.

FREE Galway City Museum MUSEUM

(www.galwaycitymuseum.ie; Spanish Pde; 10am-5pm Tue-Sat) Little remains of Galway's old city walls apart from the **Spanish Arch**, which is right beside the river. The nearby museum has exhibits on the city's history from 1800 to 1950, including an iconic Galway Hooker fishing boat, a collection of currachs (boats made from animal hides) and a much-loved statue of Galway-born writer and hell-raiser Pádraic O'Conaire (1883–1928).

Eyre Square PARK

The focal point of the city centre, Eyre Sq is a pleasant green space dotted with statues. In the centre of the square is Kennedy Park, honouring a visit by John F Kennedy

Galway City

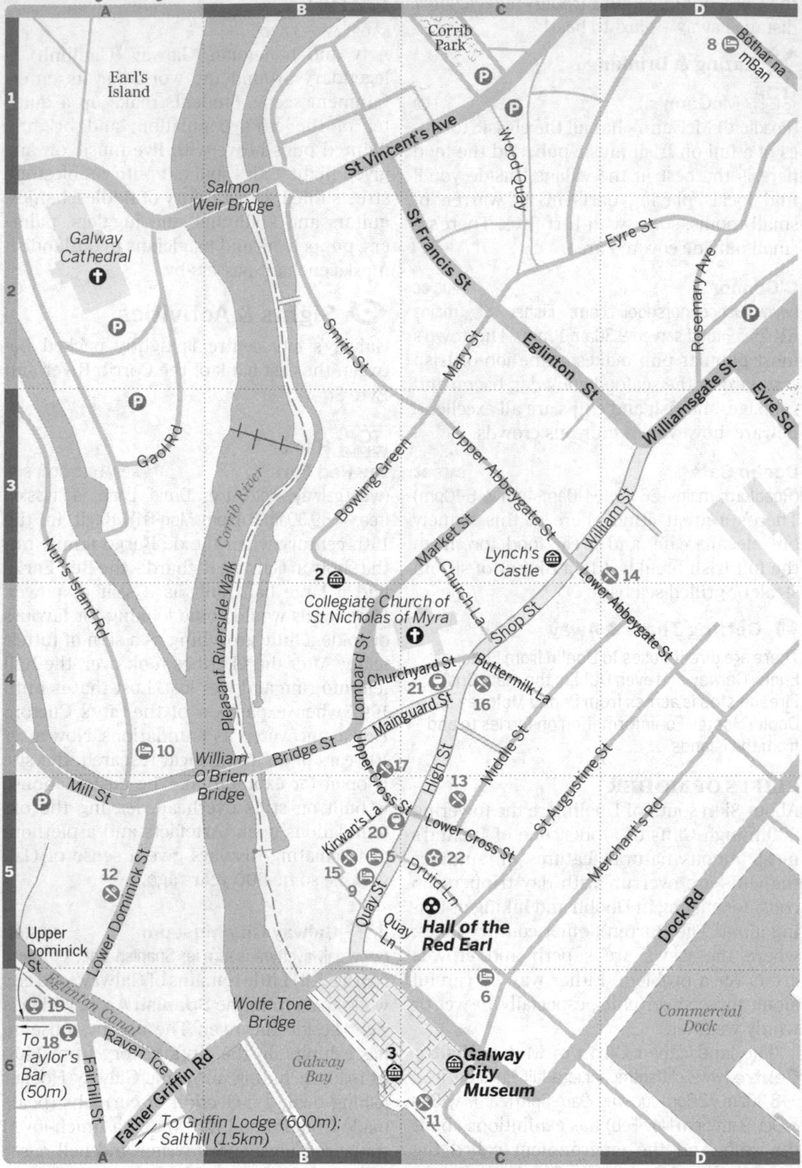

in 1963. A statue of local writer Pádraic O'Conaire was unveiled in Eyre Sq in 1935, and became a popular symbol of the city until it was vandalised in 1999; it is now in Galway City Museum (there are plans to place a replica in the square).

Shop Street HISTORIC AREA

Southwest of Eyre Sq, the **Collegiate Church of St Nicholas of Myra** dates from 1320 and has several tombs. Also on Shop St, parts of **Lynch Castle**, now a bank, date back to the 14th century. Lynch, so the story goes, was

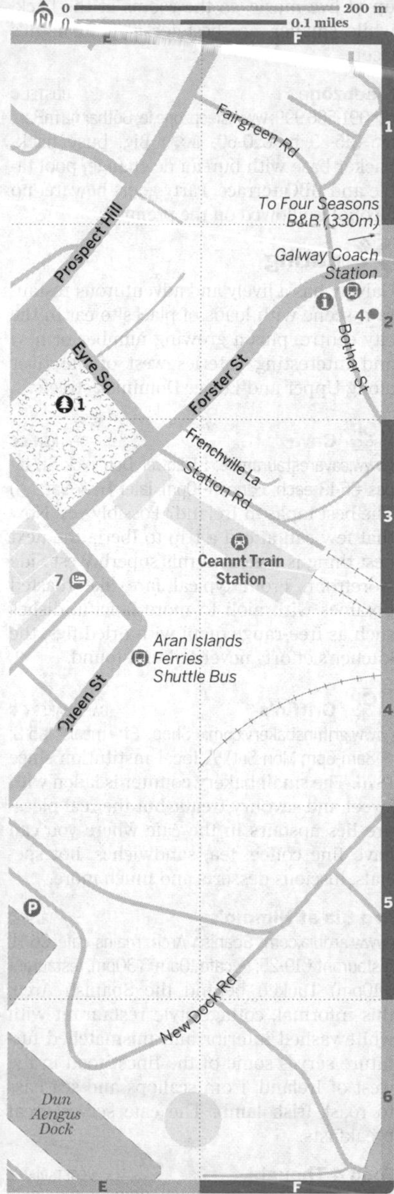

Galway City

Top Sights

Galway City Museum	C6
Hall of the Red Earl	C5

Sights

1 Eyre Square	E2
2 Nora Barnacle House	B3
3 Spanish Arch	B6

Activities, Courses & Tours

4 O'Neachtain Tours	F2

Sleeping

5 Barnacle's	B5
6 House Hotel	C6
7 Kinlay House	E3
8 Sleepzone	D1
9 Spanish Arch Hotel	B5
10 St Martins B&B	A4

Eating

11 Ard Bia at Nimmo's	C6
12 Cava	A5
13 Da Tang Noodle House	C5
14 Food 4 Thought	D3
15 Goya's	B5
16 Griffin's	C4
17 Kettle of Fish	B4

Drinking

18 Monroe's Tavern	A6
19 Róisín Dubh	A6
20 Góbán Ua Neáchtain	B5
21 Tig Cóilí	C4

Entertainment

22 Druid Theatre	C5
Taaffe's Bar	(see 16)

a mayor of Galway in the 15th century who, when his son was condemned for murder, personally acted as hangman. The stone facade that is the **Lynch Memorial Window** marks the spot of the deed.

Across the road, in the Bowling Green area, is the **Nora Barnacle House Museum** (☎091-564 743; 8 Bowling Green; adult/child €2.50/2; ⏲10am-1pm & 2-5pm, but hours vary), the former home of the wife and lifelong muse of James Joyce, which displays the couple's letters and photographs.

Festivals & Events

Galway Arts Festival ARTS
(www.galwayartsfestival.ie) Held in July, this is the main event on Galway's calendar

Galway Oyster Festival FOOD, DRINK
(www.galwayoysterfest.com) Going strong for more than 50 years now, this festival draws thousands of visitors in late September.

Sleeping

TOP CHOICE St Martins B&B B&B €€

(☎091-568 286; www.stmartins.ie; 2 Nun's Island Rd; s/d from €50/80; @📶) St Martin's is in a great location, with back-window views overlooking the William O'Brien Bridge and a simple garden on the banks of the Corrib. It's in a well-kept townhouse, and the home cooking, comfortable rooms, friendliness and central location make it an ideal choice.

TOP CHOICE Kinlay House HOSTEL €

(☎091-565 244; www.kinlayhouse.ie; Merchants Rd; dm €18-29, tw €58-70; @📶) Easygoing staff, a full range of facilities and a cream-in-the-doughnut location just off Eyre Sq make this a top choice. Spanning two huge, brightly lit floors, the recently revamped interior belies the slightly scruffy exterior. Amenities include two self-catering kitchens and two cosy TV lounges.

Four Seasons B&B B&B €€

(☎091-564 078; www.fourseasonsgalway.com; 23 College Rd; s/d from €50/80; P📶) 'If the Ritz is full there's always the Four Seasons.' Of course, this Four Seasons only has seven rooms and the nightly rates will leave you with enough loot for many a pint. One of the best choices on this strip, the Fitzgeralds offer up a large breakfast menu and simple, tidy rooms.

House Hotel HOTEL €€€

(☎091-538 900; www.thehousehotel.ie; Spanish Pde; r €139-209; P📶) It's a design odyssey at this boutique hotel. Public spaces contrast modern art with trad details and bold accents. The 40 rooms are plush, with beds having elaborately padded headboards (so you don't bonk your, er, well…) and a range of colour schemes. Bathrooms are commodious and ooze comfort.

Barnacle's HOSTEL €€

(☎091-568 644; www.barnacles.ie; 10 Quay St; dm €21-27, d €66-70; @📶) Set in a medieval townhouse with a modern extension, Barnacle's is at the heart of the action, surrounded by all the pubs, cafes and restaurants you came to Galway for.

Spanish Arch Hotel HOTEL €€

(☎091-569 600; www.spanisharchhotel.ie; Quay St; r €130-150; P📶) In a sensational spot on the main drag, this 20-room boutique hotel is housed in a 16th-century former Carmelite convent. Its solid-timber bar has a great line-up of live music, so the rooms at the back, while smaller, are best for a quiet night's sleep.

Sleepzone HOSTEL €

(☎091-566 999; www.sleepzone.ie; Bóthar na mBan; dm €15-25, tw €50-60; @📶) Big, busy backpacker base with bureau de change, pool table and BBQ terrace. Party-goers beware: no alcohol is allowed on the premises.

Eating

Galway has a lively and adventurous restaurant scene with loads of places to eat in the city centre, plus a growing number of new and interesting eateries west of the river along Upper and Lower Dominick streets.

TOP CHOICE Cava SPANISH €€

(www.cavarestaurant.ie; 51 Lower Dominick St; tapas €5-13 each; ⊙noon-10pm, later Fri & Sat; 🌿) The best tapas in Ireland? Possibly yes. Now that few can afford a trip to Iberia the next best thing is a meal at this superb West Side storefront. From typical fare like roasted potatoes with aioli to more fanciful dishes such as free-range quail with dried figs, the kitchen's efforts never fail to astound.

TOP CHOICE Griffin's CAFE, BAKERY €

(www.griffinsbakery.com; Shop St; meals €5-8; ⊙8am-6pm Mon-Sat) A local institution since 1876. The small bakery counter is laden with sweet and savoury treats, but the real pleasure lies upstairs in the cafe where you can have fine coffee, tea, sandwiches, hot specials, luscious desserts and much more.

Ard Bia at Nimmo's IRISH €

(www.ardbia.com; Spanish Arch; mains cafe €6-11, restaurant €19-25; ⊙cafe 10am-3.30pm, restaurant 6-10pm) Tucked behind the Spanish Arch, this informal, cottage-style restaurant with whitewashed interior and mismatched furniture serves some of the finest food in the west of Ireland, from scallops and sea bass to roast Irish lamb. The cafe serves great breakfasts.

Food 4 Thought VEGETARIAN €

(Lower Abbeygate St; mains €6-9; ⊙8am-6pm Mon-Sat, 11.30am-4pm Sun; 📶🌿) Head to this New Age cafe for organic and vegetarian sandwiches, savoury scones, and wholesome hot dishes such as cashew-nut roast, and moussaka made with textured vegetable protein. Excellent coffee too.

Goya's CAFE, DELI €
(www.goyas.ie; 2 Kirwan's Lane; mains €5-10; ⏲9.30am-6pm Mon-Sat) Goya's is a Galway treasure hidden down a narrow back alley, with cool pale-blue decor, Segafredo coffee, superb cakes, and hot lunchtime specials.

Da Tang Noodle House CHINESE €€
(www.datangnoodlehouse.com; 2 Middle St; mains €7-18; ⏲noon-10pm) This place serves up brilliant fresh fare bursting with flavour. Noodles are the start for soups, stir-fries, sizzling dishes and more. All are made to order and you can have dinner delivered to your hotel room.

Kettle of Fish FISH & CHIPS €
(The Square; mains €6-10; ⏲5pm-late) A New Age chipper that boasts of its line-caught fish, including salmon. Cash only.

Drinking & Entertainment

Most of Galway's pubs see musicians performing a few nights a week, whether playing informally or as headline acts, and many even have live music every night of the week. The free *Galway Advertiser* includes listings of what's on around the city; it's available on Thursday at the tourist office and newsstands around town.

Good spots to hear traditional music sessions include **Monroe's Tavern** (Upper Dominick St), which has Irish dancing on Tuesday, **Taaffe's Bar** (19 Shop St), **Taylor's Bar** (Upper Dominick St) and **Crane Bar** (2 Sea Rd).

TOP CHOICE **Tig Cóilí** PUB
(Mainguard St) Two ceilidh (live-music sessions) a day draw the crowds to this authentic fire-engine-red pub, just off High St. It's where musicians go to get drunk or drunks go to become musicians…or something like that.

Róisín Dubh PUB
(www.roisindubh.net; Upper Dominick St) A superpub complete with vast roof terrace, Róisín Dubh is the place to see emerging local indie bands before they hit the big time.

Séhán Ua Neáchtain PUB
(17 Upper Cross St) Known simply as Neáchtains (nock-tans), this dusty old pub has a fabulous atmosphere and attracts an eccentric, mixed crowd.

TOP CHOICE **Druid Theatre** THEATRE
(☎091-568 617; www.druid.ie; Druid Lane) The long-established Druid Theatre is famed for its experimental works by young Irish playwrights.

Information

Tourist Office (www.discoverireland.ie; Forster St; ⏲9am-5.45pm daily Easter-Sep, closed Sun Oct-Easter) In summer there can be a long wait to make accommodation bookings.

Getting There & Around

The bus and train stations are just east of Eyre Sq.

BIKE On Yer Bike (www.onyourbikecycles.com; 40 Prospect Hill; ⏲9am-5.30pm Mon-Sat) has bike hire from €10 per day.

BUS Bus Éireann buses depart from outside the train station. **Citylink** (www.citylink.ie) and **GoBus** (www.gobus.ie) use the **coach station** (Bothar St) a block northeast.

Clifden (Citylink) €12, 1½ hours, five daily

Doolin (Bus Éireann) €16.20, 1½ hours, five daily Monday to Saturday, four on Sunday

Dublin (Citylink) €10.50, 2½ hours, hourly

Killarney (Bus Éireann, via Limerick) €24.50, seven hours, six daily

TRAIN Trains run to and from Dublin (€33.50, three hours, five daily). You can connect with other trains at Athlone.

Aran Islands

The windswept Aran Islands are one of western Ireland's major attractions. As well as their rugged beauty – they are an extension of The Burren's limestone plateau – the Irish-speaking islands have some of the country's oldest Christian and pre-Christian ruins.

There are three main islands in the group, all inhabited year-round. Most visitors head for long and narrow (14.5km by a maximum 4km) **Inishmór** (or Inishmore). The land slopes up from the relatively sheltered northern shores of the island and plummets on the southern side into the raging Atlantic. **Inishmaan** and **Inisheer** are much smaller and receive far fewer visitors.

Though seemingly inhospitable, the islands were actually settled much earlier than the mainland, since agriculture was easier to pursue here than in the densely forested Ireland of the pre-Christian era.

JM Synge's *The Aran Islands* is the classic account of life on the islands and is readily available in paperback. A much less accessible (but more recent) tribute to the islands is map-maker Tim Robinson's

Stones of Aran. For detailed exploration, pick up a copy of his *The Aran Islands: A Map and Guide*.

The islands can get crowded during holiday times (St Patrick's Day, Easter) and in July and August, when accommodation is at a premium and advance reservations are advised.

INISHMÓR

The 'Big Island', as it's called, has four impressive **stone forts** thought to be 2000 years old. Halfway down the island and about 8km west of the village of Kilronan, semicircular **Dún Aengus** (Dún Aonghasa; www.heritageireland.ie; adult/child €3/1; ⌚9.45am-6pm Apr-Oct, 9.30am-4pm Nov-Mar, closed Mon & Tue Jan-Feb), perched on the edge of the sheer cliffs, is the best known of the four. It's an amazing place, but take great care near the cliff edge as there are no guard rails.

About 1.5km north is **Dún Eoghanachta**, while halfway back to Kilronan is **Dún Eochla**; both are smaller, perfectly circular ring forts. Directly south of Kilronan and dramatically perched on a promontory is **Dún Dúchathair**, surrounded on three sides by cliffs.

Kilronan Hostel (☎099-61255; www.kilronanhostel.com; Kilronan; dm €16-20, tw €45; @☎), perched above Tí Joe Mac's pub, is a friendly hostel just a two-minute walk away from the ferry; staff lend out fishing rods for free and can teach you to play hurling on the beach. **Mainistir House** (☎099-61169; www.aranislandshostel.com; Mainistir; dm/s/d €16/40/50; dinner €15; ⌚dinner served 8pm to closing summer, from 7pm winter; @☎) is a quirky and colourful 60-bed hostel on the main road north of Kilronan. It caters for both backpackers and families. Book ahead for the great-value organic, largely vegetarian buffet dinners.

Built for the 1930s film of the same name, **Man of Aran Cottage** (☎099-61301; www.manofarancottage.com; Kilmurvey; s/d €60/90; ⌚Mar-Oct) has authentic stone-and-wood interiors with a genuinely homely feel. It also has a **restaurant** (lunches/dinners from €6/35; ⌚lunch & dinner Jun-Sep, dinner Mar-May & Oct) that serves fresh local fish and organic vegies and herbs from the owners' garden (dinner bookings are essential).

INISHEER

The smallest of the Aran Islands, lying just 8km off the coast from Doolin, is Inisheer (Inis Oírr, or 'Eastern Island'; www.inisoirr-island.com). The 15th-century **O'Brien Castle** (Caislea'n Uí Bhriain) overlooks the beach and harbour, and a dense web of drystone walls – countless kilometres of them – subdivides every patch of rocky land.

Brú Radharc Na Mara (☎099-75024; www.bruhostelaran.com; dm €18-25, d €50; ⌚Mar-Oct; @☎) is an IHH hostel handily located next to a pub, while **South Aran House** (☎099-75073; www.southaran.com; Castle Village; s/d €49/78; ⌚Apr-Oct; ☎) is a sprightly B&B and cafe that's a mere five-minute walk from the pier.

INISHMAAN

The least visited of the three islands is peaceful Inishmaan (Inis Meáin, or 'Middle Island'), with a jagged coastline of startling cliffs and empty beaches. The main prehistoric site is **Dún Chonchúir**, a massive oval-shaped stone fort built on a high point and offering views of the island.

There are no hostels on Inishmaan; B&Bs cost about €25 to €50 per person sharing a double room; most do evening meals for €25 per person, or you can eat at the island pub.

Information

The **tourist office** (☎099-61263; Kilronan, Inishmór; ⌚11am-7pm Jun-Sep, 11am-1pm & 2-5pm Mon-Fri, 10am-1pm & 2-5pm Sat & Sun Oct-May) operates year-round at Kilronan, the arrival point and major village of Inishmór. You can leave your luggage and change money here. Around the corner is a Spar **supermarket** with an ATM (many places do not accept credit cards).

Getting There & Away

AIR Aer Arann (☎091-593 034; www.aerarannislands.ie) flights from Connemara regional airport at Minna, near Inverin, 38km west of Galway, cost €45 return. Flights serve Inishmór five times daily on weekdays (two or three daily at weekends) and two or three times daily to the other islands, and take less than 10 minutes. A connecting bus from outside Kinlay House in Galway costs €3 one-way.

FERRY All three islands are served year-round by **Aran Island Ferries** (www.aranislandferries.com; 37-39 Forster St, Galway); the trip takes around 40 minutes (adult/child €25/13 return). The boat leaves from Rossaveal, 37km west of Galway – it's an extra €7/4 return to catch an Island Ferries bus from near Kinlay House in Galway. Buses leave 1½ hours before ferry departure times and are scheduled to meet arriving ferries. If you have a car, you can go straight to Rossaveal and leave it in the car park for free.

From March to November, various companies run ferries from **Doolin** in County Clare to the islands (around half an hour to Inisheer, and at least 1½ hours to Inishmór). Rates vary as prices are very competitive, with each boat trying to undercut the others. Inisheer should cost about €15 to €25 return. Operators include **Doolin Ferries** (065-707 4455; www.doolinferries.com; Doolin, County Clare) and **O'Brien Line** (065-707 5555; www.obrienline.com).

Getting Around

Inter-island ferries only run from April to September.

Inisheer and Inishmaan are small enough to explore on foot, but on larger Inishmór bikes are definitely the way to go. **Aran Cycle Hire**, just up from Kilronan pier, is one of many bike shops that hire out bikes for €10 per day. The islands are tough on bikes, so check your cruiser carefully before hiring.

Plenty of small operators offer 2½-hour island bus tours for around €10.

Connemara

095

With its shimmering black lakes, pale mountains, lonely valleys and more than the occasional rainbow, Connemara in the northwestern corner of County Galway is one of the most gorgeous corners of Ireland. This is one of the most important Gaeltacht areas in the country; the lack of English signposting can be confusing at times.

The most scenic routes through Connemara are Oughterard–Recess (via the N59), Recess–Kylemore Abbey (via the R344) and the Leenane–Louisburgh route (via the R335). From Galway, **Lally Tours** (091-562 905; www.lallytours.com; bus tours adult/child €25/20, walking tours adult/child €10/8) and **O'Neachtain Tours** (www.irelandscenictours.ie) run day-long bus trips through Connemara for around €25 per person.

Sights & Activities

TOP CHOICE Connemara National Park — NATIONAL PARK

(www.connemaranationalpark.ie) Connemara is prime hillwalking country with plenty of wild terrain, none more so than the Twelve Bens, a ridge of rugged mountains that form part of Connemara National Park. The park's **visitor centre** (www.connemaranationalpark.ie; Letterfrack; 9am-6.30pm Jun-Aug, to 5.30pm Mon-Sat Mar-May & Sep-Oct) has some interesting displays on bog ecology and history, and is the starting point for short, waymarked hikes.

Lough Corrib — LAKE

(Aughnanure Castle adult/child €3/1; Aughnanure Castle 9.30am-6pm Apr-Oct) Much of eastern Connemara is occupied by the Republic's largest lake, famous for its trout and salmon fishing. On its western shore is **Aughnanure Castle** (www.heritageireland.com; adult/child €3/1; 9.30am-6pm Apr-Oct), a 16th-century tower house overlooking the lough 3km east of the pretty village of Oughterard. **Corrib Cruises** (092-46029; www.corribcruises.com; adult/child €28/14) run boat trips from Oughterard Pier to Inchagoill Island and Cong village (location of John Ford's 1951 classic Hollywood movie *The Quiet Man*).

Connemara Heritage & History Centre — MUSEUM

(www.connemaraheritage.com; Lettershea; adult/child €8/4; 10am-6pm Apr-Oct) The region's past comes to life at this cottage where farmer Dan O'Hara lived until his eviction and subsequent emigration to New York, where he ended up selling matches on the street. Its present owners have restored the property, turning it into a window onto lost traditional ways, with demonstrations of bog cutting, thatching, sheep shearing and so on. It's possible to stay at the **farmhouse B&B** (095-21246; Lettershea; per person €36-45; Apr-Oct) in more comfort than Dan ever enjoyed. The homestead is 7km east of Clifden on the N59.

Kylemore Abbey — HISTORIC BUILDING

(www.kylemoreabbeytourism.ie; Kylemore; adult/child €12.50/free; 9am-6pm Apr-Sep, shorter hrs Oct-Mar) Located on the national park's northern edge is this 19th-century neo-Gothic mansion set beside a lake. Admission also covers the abbey's Victorian walled gardens, while you can stroll around the lake and surrounding woods for free.

Sleeping

Letterfrack Lodge — HOSTEL €

(095-41222; www.letterfracklodge.com; Letterfrack; campsites from €12, dm €18-22, d €40-60; P@) Close to the Letterfrack crossroads, dorms come in a variety of sizes, but all are spacious. Doubles are like a basic B&B. Mike, the owner, is a great source of info on walks of all kinds through the region.

Canrawer House HOSTEL €
(☎091-552 388; www.oughterardhostel.com; Station Rd, Oughterard; dm €17-20, d €46; ⊙Feb-Oct; P@) This attractive modern house at the Clifden end of town is just over 1km down a signposted turning. It offers trout fishing trips for guests on Lough Corrib.

Clifden

☎095 / POP 1900

Connemara's 'capital', Clifden (An Clochán), is an appealing Victorian-era country town with an oval of streets offering evocative strolls. It presides over the head of the narrow bay where the Owenglin River tumbles down a series of waterfalls into the sea – you can see **salmon leaping the falls** here in season. There are craft shops and art galleries tucked among its pubs and restaurants, and the town hosts a popular **arts festival** (www.clifdenartsweek.ie) in September.

Monuments at **Derrygimla**, 5km south of town, record two momentous transatlantic events: a **Marconi** wireless station built here (its remains are still visible) sent the first wireless telegraph message across the ocean in 1907; and Alcock and Brown's first transatlantic flight crash-landed in a nearby bog in 1919.

Right in the centre of town, **Clifden Town Hostel** (☎095-21076; www.clifdentownhostel.com; Market St; dm €17-22, d from €50) is a cheery IHH hostel set in a cream-coloured house framed by big picture windows. Also in the centre, **Ben View House** (☎095-21256; www.benviewhouse.com; Bridge St; s/d €60/90; 📶) has an olde-worlde charm provided by timber beams, polished floorboards and old-fashioned hospitality.

There are plenty of good eateries to choose from. **Guy's Bar** (www.guysbarclifden.com; Main St; mains €8-20; ⊙10.30am-11pm; 📶👪) is a well-run pub that combines traditional charms with modern touches; the upmarket pub grub is good, especially dishes made with local seafood. For good coffee and hearty breakfasts, head for the **Steam Coffee House** (Clifden Station House; mains €6-9; ⊙8.30am-6pm Mon-Fri, 8.30am-5.30pm Sat, 9-5.30pm Sun; 👪), near the tourist office.

There are five express Citylink coaches daily between Clifden and Galway (€12, 1½ hours). Galway–Westport buses stop in Clifden, as well as at Oughterard, Maam Cross and Recess.

Westport

POP 5400

The lively resort town of Westport (Cathair na Mairt) is a popular stop on the way to/from Sligo or Donegal. It has a tree-lined mall running along the Carrowbeg River, handsome Georgian buildings, an attractive harbour and some good pubs.

Westport's major attraction, **Croagh Patrick**, 7km west of the town, is the hill from which St Patrick performed his snake expulsion (Ireland has been serpent-free ever since). Climbing the 765m peak is a ritual for thousands of pilgrims on the last Sunday of July.

Sleeping & Eating

Old Mill Holiday Hostel HOSTEL €
(☎098-27045; www.oldmillhostel.com; James St; dm/d €9/50; 📶) In a courtyard off James St sits an 18th-century former brewery that now houses the Old Mill Hostel. The relaxed atmosphere and comfortable beds make it a lovely place to stay.

St Anthony's B&B €€
(☎087-630 1550; www.st-anthonys.com; Distillery Rd; r per person €35-45; P📶) Simplicity is the theme at this cosy B&B, where breakfast is delicious and the hosts are gracious. All six rooms are simple and elegant, and two of them have jacuzzis.

An Port Mór SEAFOOD €€
(☎098-26730; www.anportmor.com; 1 Brewery Pl; mains €15-25; ⊙6-10pm Tue-Sun) Hidden down a lane off Bridge St, this wonderful little restaurant packs quite a punch. It's an intimate kind of place with a series of long narrow rooms and a menu that's understandably strong on seafood. Early bird menu (pre-7pm, or 6.30pm Saturday) offers two/three courses for €22/25.

Duo CAFE €
(James St; mains €5-6; ⊙10am-6pm Wed-Sat & Mon, noon-4pm Sun, closed Tue) Coolest cafe in town – has an art gallery, organic coffee and hot chocolate, and fresh homemade soup, sandwiches and bruschetta.

Information

Tourist Office (☎098-25711; www.discoverireland.ie; James St; ⊙9am-5.45pm Jul & Aug, 9am-5.45pm Mon-Fri, to 4.45pm Sat Mar-Jun & Sep & Oct)

Getting There & Away

BUS Buses depart from Mill St. Bus Éireann has a counter at the tourist office.

Dublin (change at Athlone) €21.50, five hours, twice daily

Galway €15, two hours, twice daily

Sligo €19.50, 2¾ hours, twice daily

TRAIN The **train station** (098-25253; Altamount St) is southeast of the town centre. Rail connections to Dublin (€37, 3½ hours, four daily) go via Athlone.

THE NORTHWEST

Ireland's northwest is a paradise for anyone seeking to get off the beaten path. WB Yeats' poetry still echoes through the sleepy towns and prehistoric sites of rustic County Sligo, while the wild and remote beaches of County Donegal offer some of the best surf spots in Europe.

Sligo

071/ POP 17,900

William Butler Yeats (1865–1939) was born in Dublin and educated in London, but his poetry is infused with the landscapes, history and folklore of his mother's native Sligo (Sligeach). He returned many times, and there are plentiful reminders of his presence in this sweet, sleepy town.

The island of **Innisfree**, immortalised in Yeats' poem *The Lake Isle of Innisfree*, is in Lough Gill, southeast of Sligo town.

Sights

FWB Yeats Exhibition MUSEUM

(www.yeats-sligo.com; Hyde Bridge; 10am-5pm Mon-Fri, tearoom 10am-5pm Mon-Sat) Prettily set near Hyde Bridge, the Yeats Building houses the WB Yeats Exhibition, featuring a video presentation and valuable draft manuscripts; the €2 exhibition catalogue makes a good souvenir of Sligo. The charming **tearoom** has outdoor tables overlooking the river.

Grave of WB Yeats CEMETERY

In the churchyard at Drumcliff, 8km north of Sligo, is Yeats' grave. In the 6th century, St Colmcille chose the same location for a monastery – you can still see the stumpy remains of the round tower on the main road nearby. In summer the church shows a 15-minute audiovisual on Yeats and St Colmcille.

The Model GALLERY

(www.themodel.ie; The Mall; 10am-5.30pm Tue-Sat, noon-5pm Sun) One of Ireland's leading contemporary arts centres, The Model houses an impressive collection of contemporary Irish art, including works by Jack B Yeats and Louis le Brocquy.

Sleeping & Eating

Pearse Lodge B&B €€

(071-916 1090; www.pearselodge.com; Pearse Rd; s/d €47/76; P@) Welcoming owners Mary and Kieron not only impeccably maintain the six stylish guest rooms at their cosy B&B but are also up on what's happening in town. A sunny sitting room opens to a beautifully landscaped garden.

White House Hostel HOSTEL €

(071-914 5160; Markievicz Rd; dm €15; P) There's not much choice of budget digs in Sligo – this basic hostel is at least conveniently located just north of the town centre.

TOP CHOICE **Source** IRISH €€

(071-914 7605; www.sourcesligo.ie; 1 John St; mains €9-22; 9.30am-9pm Mon-Sat;) Source is all about traceability in the food chain and the project champions local suppliers and food-stuffs. Large, arty photos of its favourite fishermen, farmers and cheese producers grace the walls of the ground-floor restaurant with its open kitchen and buzzy atmosphere, while upstairs in the **wine bar** things are more sedate, with wine from the owners' vineyard in France and plates of Irish-style tapas on offer.

Ósta CAFE €

(www.osta.ie; Hyde Bridge, Left Bank; mains €5-10; 8am-7.30pm Mon-Sat, 9am-6pm Sun;) Ósta is a superb cafe with a prime location overlooking the river, and outdoor tables in summer.

Information

Tourist Office (071-916 1201; O'Connell St; 9am-6pm Mon-Fri, 9am-5pm Sat, 10am-4pm Sun Jun-Aug, 9am-5pm Mon-Fri, 10am-4pm Sat Mar-May & Sep, 9am-5pm Mon-Fri Oct-Feb) Next door to the WB Yeats Exhibition.

Getting There & Away

The bus and train stations are next to each other, just west of the town centre and the N4 road on Knappagh Rd.

BUS Bus Éireann has services to:

Derry €20, 2½ hours, seven daily

Dublin €18, 3¾ hours, four daily

Galway €15, 2¾ hours, seven daily
Westport €19.50, two hours, four daily, change at Charlestown or Knock

TRAIN There are six to eight trains daily to Dublin Connolly station (€34, three hours).

Donegal

You could spend weeks losing yourself in wild and woolly Donegal. Ireland's second-largest county (only Cork is larger), severed from its traditional province when most of Ulster became Northern Ireland, is a land unto itself – a favourite with hikers, surfers and lovers of windswept mountain and coastal scenery.

BUNDORAN

☎071/ POP 1700

Surfers from all over the world come to Bundoran (Bun Dobhráin) to seek out some of Europe's best beach breaks. Pass by the tacky arcades, fast-food stalls and souvenir shops in the town centre and head for **Tullan Strand**, on the northern edge of town, the focal point of Bundoran's beach scene, or 3km-long **Rossnowlagh Strand**, 5km to the north.

Bundoran Surf Co (☎071-984 1968; www.bundoransurfco.com; Main St) and **Fin McCool** (☎071-985 9020; www.finmccoolsurfschool.com; gear rental per 3hr €29, 2hr lesson incl gear rental €35; ⏰10am-7pm Easter-Oct, 10am-7pm Sat & Sun mid-Mar–Easter & Nov-Christmas) both offer surfing lessons for beginners for €30 to €35 per person (three hours, including equipment). Surf and accommodation packages can also be arranged.

Bundoran is packed with budget accommodation, but music-themed **Homefield Rock Hostel** (☎071-982 9357; www.homefieldbackpackers.com; Bayview Ave; dm/d €20/50; ⏰Apr-Nov, bookings only Dec-Mar; P@☸), in a 300-year-old building that was once the holiday home of Viscount Enniskillen, is the pick of the bunch.

Main St has no shortage of greasy diners and pubs, but for a better bite head to **Maddens Ould Bridge Bar** (☎071-984 2050; www.maddensbridgebar.com; Main St; mains €10-20), a surfers' hangout that serves sensational pub grub.

Bus Éireann buses stop on Main St. There are direct daily services to Sligo (€10, 45 minutes), Derry (€18, 1¾ hours), Donegal (€8, 40 minutes) and more.

DONEGAL TOWN

☎074/ POP 2500

Donegal Town (Dún na nGall) is more of a gateway to the county than a destination. The Diamond (main square) is the centre of town; just south along the Eske River is the **tourist office** (☎074-972 1148; donegal@failteireland.ie; Quay St; ⏰9am-6pm Mon-Sat, noon-4pm Sun Jul-Aug, 9am-1pm & 2-5pm Mon-Sat Sep-Jun).

There are buses to Sligo (€14, 1¼ hours, five daily), Galway (€18.50, four hours, four daily), Derry (€15, 1½ hours), Ennsikillen (€12.30, one hour, four daily) and Dublin (€20, four hours, eight daily). The bus stop is on the Diamond, outside the Abbey Hotel.

GLENCOLUMBCILLE

'There's nothing feckin' here!', endearingly blunt locals warn visitors to Glencolumbcille (Gleann Cholm Cille). But, with some stunning walks fanning out from the three-pub village, scalloped beaches, an excellent **Irish language and culture centre** (www.oideas-gael.com; ⏰mid-Mar–Oct), and a fine little **folk museum** (www.glenfolkvillage.com; Doonalt; adult/child €3/2; ⏰10am-6pm Mon-Sat, noon-6pm Sun Easter-Sep), chances are you'll disagree.

Approaching Glencolumbcille via the scenic **Glen Gesh Pass** does, however, reinforce just how cut off this starkly beautiful coastal haven is from the rest of the world. You drive past miles and miles of hills and bogs before the ocean appears, followed by a narrow, green valley and the small Gaeltacht village within it.

This spot has been inhabited since 3000 BC and you'll find plenty of **Stone Age remains** throughout the collection of tiny settlements. It's believed that the 6th-century St Colmcille (Columba) founded a monastery here (hence the name, meaning 'Glen of Columba's Church'), and incorporated Stone Age standing stones called *turas* (after the Irish word for a pilgrimage, or journey) into Christian usage by inscribing them with a cross. At midnight on Colmcille's Feast Day (9 June) penitents walk around the *turas* and the remains of Colmcille's church before attending Mass at 3am in the local church.

Dooey Hostel (☎074-973 0130; campsites per person €8.50, dm/d €15/30; P) has character in spades. For one thing, it's owned by an elderly, wild-haired chain-smoker who calls herself 'Mad' Mary O'Donnell. For another, it's literally built into the hillside, with a corridor carved out of the plant-strewn rock face, and jaw-dropping views of the ocean and hills below. No credit cards. If you're driving, turn at the Glenhead Tavern for 1.5km; walkers can take a short cut beside the Folk Village.

Bus 490 runs from Donegal Town to Glencolumbcille (€9.20, 45 minutes) once daily Monday to Friday and Sunday (twice daily Saturday). In July and August an extra bus runs Monday to Saturday. In addition, bus 490/492 runs from Donegal Town as far as Killybegs (€8, 30 to 45 minutes) four times daily Monday to Saturday.

SLIEVE LEAGUE

The awe-inspiring cliffs at **Slieve League**, rising 300m above the Atlantic Ocean, are one of Donegal's top sights. To drive to the cliff-edge car park, take the Killybegs–Glencolumbcille road (R263) and, at Carrick, turn left (signposted 'Bunglas'), and then right (signposted 'The Cliffs'). From the parking area at the end of the steep, narrow road (continue through the farm gate), experienced hikers can spend a day walking along the top of the cliffs via the slightly terrifying One Man's Path to Malinbeg, near Glencolumbcille.

Derrylahan Hostel (074-973 8079; homepage.eircom.net/~derrylahan; campsites per person €8, dm/d €18/50; P), an IHH place on a farm 2km southeast of Carrick, is a convenient base for walkers; call for free pick-up from Kilcar or Carrick. Booking essential November to February.

Tí Linn (Teelin, Carrick; mains €7-9; 10.30am-5.30pm Easter-Sep, Fri-Tue Feb-Easter & Oct-Nov), at the start of 'The Cliffs' road, is a great lunch stop, serving dishes such as potato farl (potato bread) with smoked salmon and lemon butter.

Once-daily buses (twice daily in July and August) stop at Kilcar and Carrick on the route from Donegal to Glencolumbcille.

NORTHERN IRELAND

028/ POP 1.7 MILLION

When you cross from the Republic into Northern Ireland you notice a couple of changes: the accent is different, the road signs are in miles, and the prices are in pounds sterling or Northern Irish pounds. But there's no border checkpoint, no guards, not even a sign to mark the crossing point – the two countries are in a customs union, so there's no passport control and no customs declarations. All of a sudden and you're in the UK.

Dragged down for decades by the violence and uncertainty of the Troubles, Northern Ireland today is a nation rejuvenated. The 1998 Good Friday Agreement laid the groundwork for peace and raised hopes for the future, and since then this UK province has seen a huge influx of investment and redevelopment. Belfast has become a happening place with a famously wild nightlife, while Derry is coming into its own as a cool, artistic city, and the stunning Causeway Coast gets more and more visitors each year.

There are still plenty of reminders of the Troubles – notably the 'peace lines' that still divide Belfast – and the passions that have torn Northern Ireland apart over the decades still run deep. But despite occasional setbacks there is an atmosphere of determined optimism.

Belfast

028 / POP 277,000

Once lumped with Beirut, Baghdad and Bosnia as one of the four 'B's for travellers to avoid, Belfast has pulled off a remarkable transformation from bombs-and-bullets pariah to hip-hotels-and-hedonism party town. Despite the economic downturn, the city's skyline is in a constant state of flux as redevelopment continues. The old shipyards are giving way to the luxury waterfront apartments of the Titanic Quarter; and Victoria Sq, Europe's biggest urban regeneration project, has added a massive city-centre shopping mall to a list of tourist attractions that includes Victorian architecture, a glittering waterfront lined with modern art, foot-stomping music in packed-out pubs and the UK's second-biggest arts festival.

The city centre is compact, with the imposing City Hall in Donegall Sq as the central landmark. The principal shopping district is north of the square. North again, around Donegall St and St Anne's Cathedral, is the bohemian Cathedral Quarter.

South of the square, the so-called Golden Mile stretches for 1km along Great Victoria St, Shaftesbury Sq and Botanic Ave to Queen's University and the leafy suburbs of South Belfast; this area has dozens of restaurants and bars and most of the city's budget and midrange accommodation.

Belfast

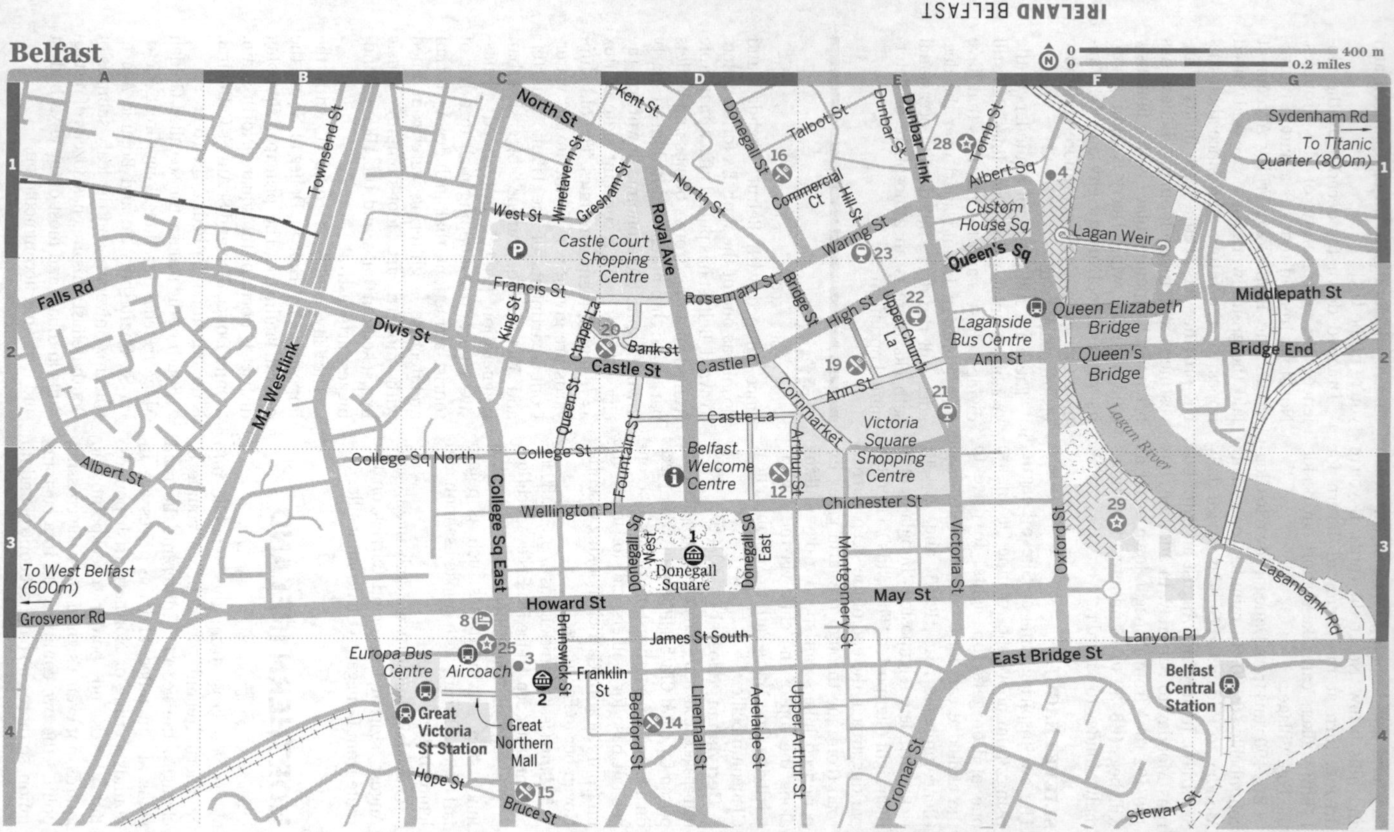
0 400 m
0 0.2 miles
A
B
C
D
E
F
G
1
2
3
4
North St
Kent St
Donegall St
Talbot St
Dunbar St
Dunbar Link
Tomb St
28
16
Commercial Ct
Hill St
Albert Sq
4
Custom House Sq
Lagan Weir
Sydenham Rd
To Titanic Quarter (800m)
Townsend St
West St
Winetavern St
Gresham St
Royal Ave
North St
Waring St
23
Queen's Sq
Castle Court Shopping Centre
P
Falls Rd
Francis St
Rosemary St
Bridge St
High St
Upper Church La
22
Laganside Bus Centre
Queen Elizabeth Bridge
Middlepath St
Divis St
King St
Chapel La
20
Bank St
Castle St
Castle Pl
19
Ann St
Queen's Bridge
Bridge End
M1 Westlink
Queen St
Cornmarket
21
Castle La
Lagan River
Victoria Square Shopping Centre
College Sq North
College St
Fountain St
Belfast Welcome Centre
Arthur St
12
Albert St
College Sq East
Wellington Pl
Chichester St
29
Donegall Sq West
1
Donegall Square
Donegall Sq East
Montgomery St
Victoria St
Oxford St
To West Belfast (600m)
Grosvenor Rd
Howard St
May St
Laganbank Rd
8
25
3
James St South
Lanyon Pl
Europa Bus Centre
Aircoach
Brunswick St
Franklin St
East Bridge St
Belfast Central Station
2
Great Victoria St Station
Great Northern Mall
Bedford St
14
Linenhall St
Adelaide St
Upper Arthur St
Cromac St
Hope St
15
Bruce St
Stewart St

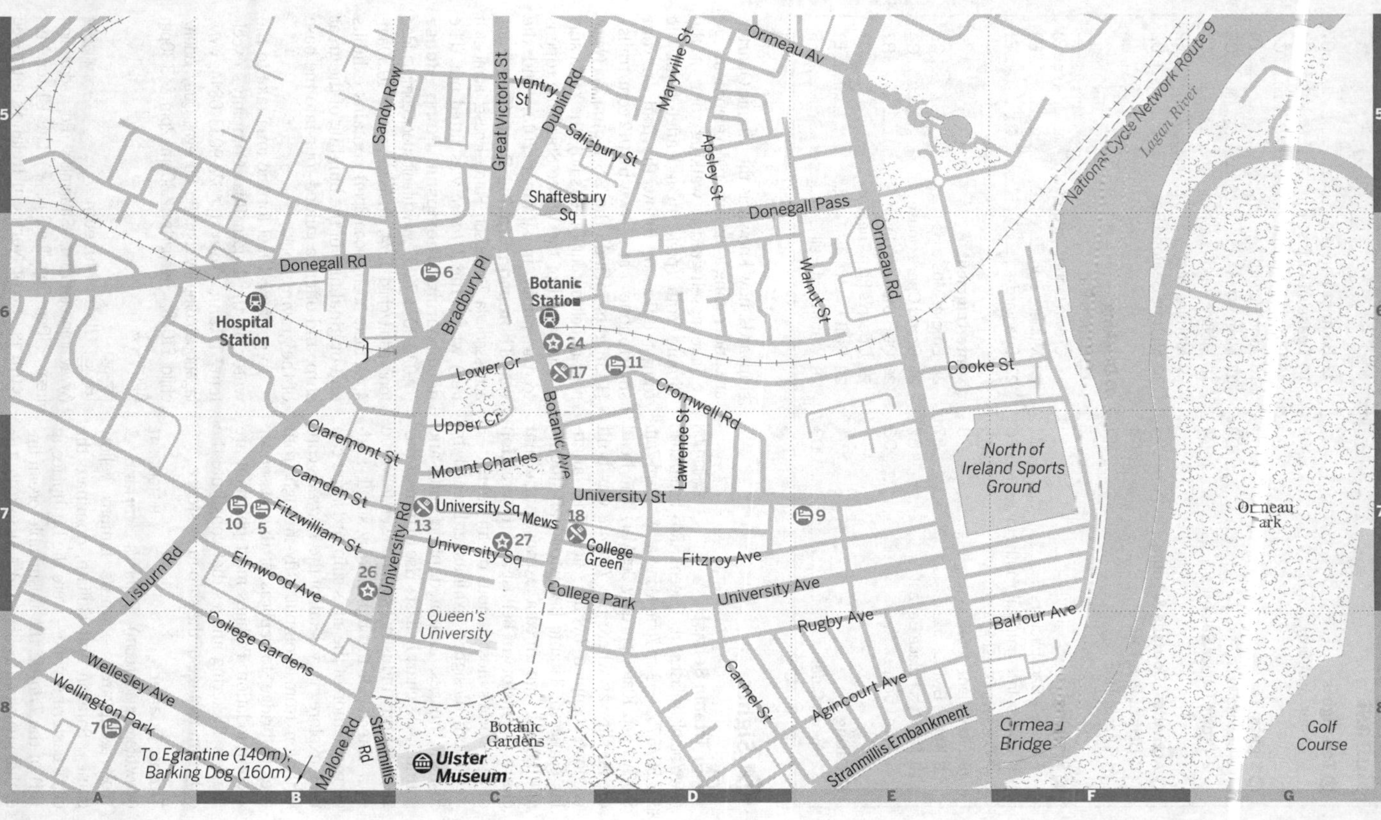

Ormeau Av
Ventry St
Dublin Rd
Maryville St
Salisbury St
Sandy Row
Great Victoria St
Apsley St
Shaftesbury Sq
Donegall Pass
Donegall Rd
Ormeau Rd
National Cycle Network Route 9
Lagan River
Walnut St
Hospital Station
Bradbury Pl
Botanic Station
Lower Cr
Cooke St
Cromwell Rd
Upper Cr
Claremont St
Mount Charles
Botanic Ave
Lawrence St
North of Ireland Sports Ground
Camden St
University St
University Sq Mews
Fitzwilliam St
University Rd
University Sq
College Green
Fitzroy Ave
Elmwood Ave
Lisburn Rd
College Park
University Ave
Queen's University
Rugby Ave
Balfour Ave
College Gardens
Wellesley Ave
Wellington Park
Carmel St
Agincourt Ave
Stranmillis Embankment
Ormeau Bridge
Ormeau Park
Golf Course
Botanic Gardens
Ulster Museum
Malone Rd
Stranmillis Rd
To Eglantine (140m); Barking Dog (160m)

Belfast

Top Sights
Ulster Museum ... C8

Sights
1 City Hall ... D3
2 Crown Liquor Saloon ... C4

Activities, Courses & Tours
3 Belfast Pub Tours ... C4
4 Titanic Tour ... F1

Sleeping
5 Arnie's Backpackers ... B7
6 Belfast International Youth Hostel ... C6
7 Camera Guest House ... A8
8 Fitzwilliam Hotel ... C3
9 Kate's B&B ... E7
10 Paddy's Palace Belfast ... B7
11 Tara Lodge ... D6

Eating
12 Avoca Cafe ... D3
13 Beatrice Kennedy ... C7
14 Deane's Deli Bistro ... D4
15 Ginger ... C4
16 John Hewitt ... D1
17 Maggie May's ... C6
18 Molly's Yard ... C7
19 Morning Star ... E2
20 Mourne Seafood Bar ... D2

Drinking
21 Bittle's Bar ... E2
Crown Liquor Saloon ... (see 2)
22 Muriel's Bar ... E2
23 Spaniard ... E1

Entertainment
24 Empire Music Hall ... C6
25 Grand Opera House ... C4
26 QUB Student Union ... B7
27 Queen's Film Theatre ... C7
28 Rain ... E1
29 Waterfront Hall ... F3

Sights

TOP CHOICE Titanic Belfast EXHIBITION
(www.titanicbelfast.com; Queen's Rd; adult/child £13.50/6.75; 9am-7pm Mon-Sat & 10am-7pm Sun Apr-Sep, 10am-5pm daily Oct-Mar) The head of the slipway where the *Titanic* was built is now occupied by the gleaming, angular edifice of Titanic Belfast, an all-singing all-dancing multimedia extravaganza that charts the history of Belfast and the creation of the world's most famous ocean liner.

Cleverly designed exhibits enlivened by historic images, animated projections and soundtracks chart Belfast's rise to turn-of-the-20th-century industrial superpower, followed by a hi-tech ride through a noisy, smells-and-all re-creation of the city's shipyards. You can then explore every detail of the *Titanic*'s construction, from a computer 'fly-through' from keel to bridge, to replicas of the passenger accommodation. Perhaps most poignant are the few flickering images that constitute the only film footage of the ship in existence.

Titanic Quarter HISTORIC SITE
(www.titanicquarter.com) Belfast's **Harland & Wolff** shipyards – whose famous yellow cranes, Samson and Goliath, dominate the city's eastern skyline – were the birthplace in 1911 of the *Titanic*, the 'unsinkable' ocean liner that struck an iceberg and sank in 1912. The shipyards, now known as the Titanic Quarter, are undergoing a massive redevelopment.

Take a self-guided walking tour of the Titanic Trail (pick up a leaflet from the tourist office, or follow the trail on your smartphone at www.ni2012.com/trails). Highlights include the **SS Nomadic** (www.nomadicbelfast.com; Queen's Rd), the only surviving vessel of the White Star Line (opens to the public in summer 2013), and the vast **Thompson Graving Dock** (Queen's Rd, accessed via Thompson Pump House; admission free) where the *Titanic* was fitted out. The neighbouring **Thompson Pump House** (028-9073 7813; www.titanicsdock.com; guided tour adult/child £7/4; visitor centre 10.30am-4pm, tours hourly noon-3pm) contains exhibits and original film of the building of the great ship, and offers a guided tour into the base of the graving dock.

To get a real feel for the area take to the water on the Lagan Boat Company's excellent **Titanic Tour** (028-9033 0844; www.laganboatcompany.com; 66 Donegall Quay; adult/child £10/8; departs 12.30pm, 2pm & 3.30pm Apr-Oct).

TOP CHOICE Ulster Museum MUSEUM
(www.nmni.com/um; Stranmillis Rd; admission free; 10am-5pm Tue-Sun;) The Ulster Museum is one of Northern Ireland's must-see

attractions. You could spend several hours browsing the beautifully designed displays, but if you're pressed for time don't miss the following: the Armada Room, with artefacts retrieved from the wreck of the Spanish galleon *Girona*; Takabuti, a 2500-year-old Egyptian mummy; the Bann Disc, a superb example of Celtic design dating from the Iron Age; the Malone Hoardof stone axe heads; and the Snapshot of an Ancient Sea Floor, a fossilised portion of a 200-million-year-old seabed.

West Belfast HISTORIC SITE

The Catholic **Falls Rd** and the Protestant **Shankill Rd** have been battlefronts in Belfast's sectarian conflict since the 1970s. Even so, these areas are now quite safe and well worth visiting, if only to see the famous **murals** expressing local political and religious passions, and the infamous **Peace Line** – a 4km-long barrier that divides Catholic and Protestant districts, and which has now been standing longer than the Berlin Wall.

If you don't fancy an organised taxi tour, pick up a **map of the murals** from the Belfast Welcome Centre and explore on foot.

Crown Liquor Saloon HISTORIC BUILDING

(www.crownbar.com; 46 Great Victoria St) There are not too many historical monuments that you can enjoy while savouring a pint of beer, but Belfast's most famous pub is one. It was built by Patrick Flanagan in 1885 and displays Victorian architecture at its most extravagant; the snugs are equipped with bells that were once connected to a board behind the bar, enabling customers to order drinks without leaving their seats.

Ulster Folk & Transport Museums MUSEUM

(www.nmni.com/uftm; Cultra, Holywood; adult/child £7/4.50, combined ticket to both museums £8.50/5; ⏲10am-5pm Tue-Sun Mar-Sep, 10am-4pm Tue-Fri & 11am-4pm Sat & Sun Oct-Feb) Farmhouses, forges, churches, mills and a complete village have been reconstructed at the **Folk Museum**, with human and animal extras combining to give a strong impression of Irish life over the past few hundred years. A bridge crosses the A2 highway to the **Transport Museum**, which contains various Ulster-related vehicles, including a prototype of the **De Lorean DMC sports car** (of *Back To The Future* fame), and a display on the *Titanic*. It's 11km northeast of the city centre on the A2 Bangor road near Holywood. From Belfast take Ulsterbus 1 or any Bangor-bound train that stops at Cultra station.

FREE **City Hall** HISTORIC BUILDING

(www.belfastcity.gov.uk; Donegall Sq; ⏲guided tours 11am, 2pm & 3pm Mon-Fri, 2pm & 3pm Sat) The Renaissance-style City Hall, completed in 1906, is a testament to the city's industrial prosperity. The highlights of the free guided tour include the sumptuous Italian marble and colourful stained glass of the entrance

WORTH A TRIP

MOURNE MOUNTAINS

The humpbacked hills of the Mourne Mountains form one of the most beautiful corners of Northern Ireland, a distinctive landscape of yellow gorse, grey granite and whitewashed cottages, the lower slopes of the hills latticed with a neat patchwork of dry-stone walls cobbled together from huge, rounded granite boulders. The hills were made famous in a popular song penned by Irish songwriter William Percy French in 1896, whose chorus, 'Where the Mountains of Mourne sweep down to the sea', captures perfectly their scenic blend of ocean, sky and hillside.

The Mournes offer some of the best hillwalking in Northern Ireland, detailed in the guidebook *The Mournes: Walks* by Paddy Dillon. You'll also need an Ordnance Survey map, either the 1:50,000 Discoverer Series (Sheet No 29: *The Mournes*) or the 1:25,000 Activity Series *(The Mournes)*.

The main base for exploring the Mournes is the holiday resort of Newcastle, where you'll find plenty of shops, pubs and restaurants. **Newcastle Youth Hostel** (☎028-4372 2133; www.hini.org.uk; 30 Downs Rd; dm £14; ⏲daily Mar-Oct, Fri & Sat nights only Nov & 1-22 Dec, closed 23 Dec-Feb), housed in an attractive 19th-century villa with sea views, is only a few minutes' walk from the bus station.

Ulsterbus service 20 runs to Newcastle from Belfast's Europa Bus Centre (£7, 1¼ hours, hourly Monday to Saturday, eight Sunday).

WANT MORE?

For in-depth information, reviews and recommendations at your fingertips, head to the Apple App Store to purchase Lonely Planet's *Belfast City Guide* iPhone app.

Alternatively, head to **Lonely Planet** (www.lonelyplanet.com/ireland/northern-ireland/belfast) for planning advice, author recommendations, traveller reviews and insider tips.

hall and rotunda; an opportunity to sit on the mayor's throne in the council chamber; and the idiosyncratic portraits of past lord mayors.

The building is fronted by an especially dour statue of Queen Victoria; her consort, Prince Albert, is commemorated nearby in the **Albert Memorial Clock Tower** (1867), which leans slightly to one side – Belfast's equivalent of Pisa's leaning tower.

Festivals & Events

Belfast Film Festival FILM
(www.belfastfilmfestival.org) Two-week celebration of Irish and international film held in early April.

Titanic Belfast Festival CULTURE
(www.belfastcity.gov.uk/titanic) A week-long celebration of the world's most famous ship, and the city that built it, with special exhibitions, tours, lectures and film screenings. First half of April.

Cathedral Quarter Arts Festival ARTS
(www.cqaf.com) This fantastic festival, in early May, attracts pioneering writers, comedians, musicians and artists, and presents theatre productions.

Féile An Phobail CULTURE
(www.feilebelfast.com) Said to be the largest community festival in Ireland; events include an opening carnival parade, street parties, theatre performances, concerts and historical tours. Ten days in early August.

Festival at Queen's ARTS
(www.belfastfestival.com) For three weeks in late October/early November, Belfast hosts the second-largest arts festival in the UK, in and around Queen's University.

Sleeping

Many B&Bs are concentrated in the pleasant university district of South Belfast, which is well stocked with restaurants and pubs.

TOP CHOICE **Old Rectory** B&B ££
(028-9066 7882; www.anoldrectory.co.uk; 148 Malone Rd; s/d £53/84; P@) This lovely red brick Victorian villa has four spacious bedrooms, a comfortable drawing room with a leather sofa, and fancy breakfasts (wild boar sausages, scrambled eggs with smoked salmon, freshly squeezed OJ). It's a 10-minute bus ride south of the city centre.

Tara Lodge B&B ££
(028-9059 0900; www.taralodge.com; 36 Cromwell Rd; s/d from £69/79; P@) This B&B is a cut above your average South Belfast guesthouse, with its stylish, minimalist decor; friendly, efficient staff; delicious breakfasts; and 18 bright and cheerful rooms. Great location too, on a quiet side street just a few paces from the buzz of Botanic Ave.

Arnie's Backpackers HOSTEL £
(028-9024 2867; www.arniesbackpackers.co.uk; 63 Fitzwilliam St; dm £10-14; @) More cosy than cramped, this small-scale hostel has a relaxed, down-home vibe, and Arnie manages to have a kindly disposition even when faced with an Estonian football fan club who've been drinking vodka for 12 hours straight.

Paddy's Palace Belfast HOSTEL ££
(028-9033 3367; www.paddyspalace.com; 68 Lisburn Rd; dm £10-15, d £40-50; P@) Paddy's offers clean and comfortable dorms, a big, well-equipped kitchen, a bright and homely common room (though the dorms are a bit gloomy) and friendly staff who are happy to point you to the best local pubs. There's no

BELFAST VISITOR PASS

The **Belfast Visitor Pass** (one/two/three days £6.50/10.50/14) allows unlimited travel on bus and train services in Belfast and around; it can be purchased at airports, main train and bus stations, the Metro kiosk on Donegall Sq, and the Belfast Welcome Centre.

sign outside, so it's easy to miss – bang on the door on Fitzwilliam St, near the corner of Lisburn Rd.

Camera Guest House B&B ££

(☎028-9066 0026; www.cameraguesthouse.com; 44 Wellington Park; s/d £48/62;) A cosy, welcoming Victorian B&B with an open fire in the drawing room, the Camera is set in yet another of South Belfast's peaceful, tree-lined terraced streets. The friendly young couple who own the place manage to create a family-friendly atmosphere, and are a fount of knowledge on what to see and do in town.

Kate's B&B B&B ££

(☎028-9028 2091; katesbb127@hotmail.com; 127 University St; r per person £25) Kate's is a homely kind of place, from the window boxes bursting with colourful flowers to the cute dining room crammed with bric-a-brac and a couple of resident cats. The bedrooms are basic but comfortable, and only a few minutes' walk from Botanic Ave.

Fitzwilliam Hotel HOTEL £££

(☎028-9044 2080; www.fitzwilliamhotelbelfast.com; 1-3 Great Victoria St; r from £120; @) A modern hotel in a truly central location, the Fitzwilliam pushes all the right style buttons with its use of designer fabrics, cool colours and mood lighting. Bedrooms have crisp linen sheets, fluffy bathrobes and powerful showers, and the staff are unstintingly helpful.

Belfast International Youth Hostel HOSTEL £

(☎028-9031 5435; www.hini.org.uk; 22-32 Donegall Rd; dm £11-16, s £22-32, tw £38-42; P@) Conveniently sited on the Golden Mile, which means it can be a bit noisy at night when the pubs and clubs empty.

Dundonald Touring Caravan Park CAMPGROUND £

(☎028-9080 9129; www.theicebowl.com; 111 Old Dundonald Rd; campsites per tent/caravan from £15/23; ⊙mid-Mar–Oct) Next to the Dundonald Icebowl, 7km east of the city centre (take bus 19 from Donegall Sq West); check in at the Icebowl reception desk.

Eating

There are lots of inexpensive eating places along Botanic Ave in South Belfast, and many pubs offer good-value meals.

DON'T MISS

BELFAST TOURS

Many operators, including **Official Black Taxi Tours** (☎028-9064 2264; www.belfasttours.com) and **Original Belfast Black Taxi Tours** (☎07751 565359; taxitours@live.co.uk) offer organised taxi tours of West Belfast, with an even-handed account of the Troubles. They run daily for £8 to £10 per person based on a group of three to six sharing (£25 for one or two), and pick-up can be arranged.

There are a number of walking tours available, including the two-hour **Belfast Pub Tour** (☎028-9268 3665; www.belfastpubtours.com; per person £6; ⊙7pm Thu & 4pm Sat May-Oct), taking in six of the city's historic pubs, beginning at the Crown Dining Rooms, above the Crown Liquor Saloon.

TOP CHOICE **Barking Dog** BISTRO ££

(☎028-9066 1885; www.barkingdogbelfast.com; 33-35 Malone Rd; mains £11-21; ⊙noon-10pm Mon-Sat, to 11pm Fri & Sat, to 9pm Sun) Chunky hardwood, bare brick, candlelight and quirky design create the atmosphere of a stylishly restored farmhouse, and the menu completes the feeling of cosiness and comfort with simple but sensational dishes such as crab and chilli salad, and a burger of meltingly tender beef shin wrapped in caramelised onion and horseradish cream. Superb service, too.

TOP CHOICE **Ginger** BISTRO £££

(☎028-9024 4421; www.gingerbistro.com; 7-8 Hope St; mains £13-23; ⊙noon-3pm Tue-Sat & 5-9pm Mon-Sat;) Ginger is a cosy and informal little bistro with an unassuming exterior, serving food that is anything but ordinary – top-quality Irish produce is turned into exquisite dishes such as roast pork belly with fennel, black pudding and apple sauce. The lunch and pre-theatre (from 5pm to 6.45pm Monday to Friday) menu offers main courses for £8 to £14.

Molly's Yard IRISH ££

(☎028-9032 2600; www.mollysyard.co.uk; 1 College Green Mews; bistro mains £8-11, restaurant £14-22; ⊙bistro noon-9pm Mon-Thu, to 6pm Fri & Sat, restaurant 6-9pm Mon-Sat) A restored Victorian stables courtyard is the setting for this cosy bar-bistro with outdoor tables in the yard, a more formal restaurant upstairs, and a seasonal menu focused on fresh local produce. Best to book for dinner.

Mourne Seafood Bar SEAFOOD ££

(028-9024 8544; www.mourneseafood.com; 34-36 Bank St; mains £10-20; noon-9.30pm Mon-Thu, noon-4pm & 5-10pm Fri & Sat, 1-6pm Sun) This informal, publike space, all red brick and dark wood with old oil lamps dangling from the ceiling, is tucked behind a fishmonger's shop, so the locally caught seafood is as fresh as it gets. Hugely popular, so book ahead.

Deane's Deli Bistro BISTRO ££

(www.michaeldeane.co.uk; 44 Bedford St; mains £7-20; noon-3pm Mon-Fri, 5.30-10pm Mon-Sat) Enjoy top-notch nosh at this relaxed and informal bistro, with gourmet burgers and posh fish and chips on the menu. Or just grab a sandwich at the next-door deli.

Avoca Cafe CAFE ££

(41 Arthur St; mains £9-14; 9.30am-5pm Mon-Fri, 9am-5pm Sat, 12.30-5pm Sun) Upstairs in the Avoca store, this cafe focuses on healthy rolls, wraps, salads and sandwiches to sit in or take away, as well as offering hot lunch specials such as grilled chicken with Mediterranean vegetables.

Maggie May's CAFE £

(www.maggiemaysbelfast.co.uk; 50 Botanic Ave; mains £3-7; 8am-10.30pm Mon-Sat, 10am-10.30pm Sun) This is a classic little cafe with cosy wooden booths, murals of old Belfast, and a host of hungover students wolfing down huge Ulster fries at lunchtime. The all-day breakfast menu runs from tea and toast to eggy bread and maple syrup, while lunch can be soup and a sandwich or steak-and-Guinness pie.

Beatrice Kennedy IRISH ££

(028-9020 2290; www.beatricekennedy.co.uk; 44 University Rd; mains £16-20; 5-10.30pm Tue-Sat, 12.30-2.30pm & 5-8.30pm Sun;) This is where Queen's students take their parents for a smart dinner. The candlelit Edwardian drawing-room decor sets off a simple menu of superb fusion cuisine, including homemade bread and ice cream; there's also a separate vegetarian menu. From 5pm to 7pm you can get a two-course dinner for just £15.

John Hewitt PUB £

(www.thejohnhewitt.com; 51 Donegall St; mains £7-9; food noon-3pm Mon-Sat) Named for the Belfast poet and socialist, this is a modern pub with a traditional atmosphere and a well-earned reputation for excellent food. The menu changes weekly.

Morning Star PUB ££

(www.themorningstarbar.com; 17 Pottinger's Entry; mains £8-22; food 11.45am-9pm Mon-Sat;) Morning Star is famed for its all-you-can-eat lunch buffet (£5.50; served 11.45am to 6pm Monday to Saturday).

Drinking

Belfast's pub scene is lively and friendly, with the older traditional pubs complemented – and increasingly threatened – by a rising tide of stylish designer bars.

Although the situation has improved in recent years, getting past the bouncers on the door can be a problem – the huge number of security staff employed in the city means that polite, well-trained door staff are a rarity. Some of the flashier bars have a dress code – usually no sneakers, no jeans, no baseball caps (so that the security cameras can get a clear shot of your face) and definitely no football colours. A few even specify 'No political tattoos'.

Club hours are generally 9pm to 3am, with no admittance after 1am; bouncers can be really picky about who they let in, especially if you're under 21.

Muriel's Bar BAR

(12-14 Church Lane) Hats meet harlotry (ask who Muriel was) in this delightfully snug and welcoming wee bar with retro-chic sofas and armchairs, heavy fabrics in shades of olive and dark red, gilt-framed mirrors and a cast-iron fireplace. Gin is Muriel's favourite tipple, and there's a range of exotic brands to mix with your tonic. The food menu is pretty good, too.

Bittle's Bar PUB

(103 Victoria St) A cramped and staunchly traditional bar, Bittle's is a 19th-century triangular red-brick building decorated with paintings of Ireland's literary heroes. Pride of place on the back wall is taken by a large canvas depicting Yeats, Joyce, Behan and Beckett at the bar with glasses of Guinness, and Wilde pulling the pints on the other side.

Spaniard BAR

(www.thespaniardbar.com; 3 Skipper St) Forget 'style': this narrow, crowded bar, which looks as if it's been squeezed into someone's flat, has more atmosphere in one battered sofa than most 'style bars' have in their shiny entirety. Friendly staff, good beer, an eclectic crowd and cool tunes played at a volume that still allows you to talk: bliss.

Crown Liquor Saloon PUB
(www.crownbar.com; 46 Great Victoria St) Despite being a tourist attraction the Crown still fills up with crowds of locals at lunchtime and in the early evening.

Eglantine PUB
(www.egbar.co.uk; 32 Malone Rd) The 'Eg' is a local institution, and widely reckoned to be the best of Belfast's student pubs.

☆ Entertainment

The Belfast Welcome Centre issues *Whatabout?*, a free monthly guide to Belfast events. Another useful guide is **The Big List** (www.thebiglist.co.uk).

QUB Student Union CLUB
(www.qubsu-ents.com; Queen's Students Union, University Rd) The student union has various bars and music venues hosting club nights, live bands and stand-up comedy.

Empire Music Hall LIVE MUSIC
(www.thebelfastempire.com; 42 Botanic Ave) Housed in a converted Victorian church, the Empire is a legendary live-music venue with three floors of entertainment, including a weekly stand-up comedy session on Tuesday nights.

Queen's Film Theatre CINEMA
(www.queensfilmtheatre.com; 20 University Sq) The QFT is a two-screen art-house cinema, close to the university, and a major venue for the Belfast Film Festival in March.

Rain CLUB
(www.rainnightclub.co.uk; 10-14 Tomb St; admission £5/10 Sun-Fri/Sat; ⊙9pm-3am) Set in a converted red-brick warehouse, Rain is an opulent and glamorous mainstream nightclub with DJs pumping out commercial music for a mixed, over-21s crowd.

Waterfront Hall CONCERT VENUE
(www.waterfront.co.uk; 2 Lanyon Pl) The impressive 2235-seat Waterfront is Belfast's flagship concert venue, hosting local, national and international performers from pop stars to symphony orchestras.

Lyric Theatre THEATRE
(www.lyrictheatre.co.uk; 55 Ridgeway St) The Lyric, south of the city, stages serious drama; Hollywood star Liam Neeson first trod the boards here. An award-winning new theatre building was opened in 2011.

Grand Opera House OPERA
(www.goh.co.uk; 2-4 Great Victoria St; ⊙box office 8.30am-9pm Mon-Fri, to 6pm Sat) This grand old venue plays host to a mixture of opera, popular musicals and comedy shows.

ℹ Information

Belfast Welcome Centre (☎028-9024 6609; www.gotobelfast.com; 47 Donegall Pl; ⊙9am-7pm Mon-Sat & 11am-4pm Sun Jun-Sep, 9am-5.30pm Mon-Sat & 11am-4pm Sun Oct-May) Tourist information for all of Ireland, accommodation bookings, left luggage, and internet access for £1 per 20 minutes.

ℹ Getting There & Away

Air

George Best Belfast City Airport (BHD; www.belfastcityairport.com; Airport Rd) Located 6km northeast of the city centre; flights from the UK, Cork and Paris.

Belfast International Airport (BFS; www.belfastairport.com) Located 30km northwest of the city; flights from Galway, UK, Europe and New York.

Boat

Ferries to Belfast from Cairnryan and Liverpool dock at **Victoria Terminal** (West Bank Rd), 5km north of the city centre; exit the M2 motorway at junction 1. Ferries from the Isle of Man arrive at **Albert Quay** (Serkeley Rd), 2km north of the centre.

Other car ferries to and from Scotland dock at Larne, 30km north of Belfast.

Bus

Europa Bus Centre (☎028-9066 6630; Great Victoria St) Reached via the Great Northern Mall beside the Europa Hotel. Main terminus for buses to Derry (£11, 1¾ hours, twice hourly), Dublin (£14.15, 2½ hours, hourly) and destinations in the west and south of Northern Ireland.

Laganside Bus Centre (☎028-9066 6630; Oxford St) Near the river. Mainly for buses to County Antrim and eastern County Down.

Aircoach (www.aircoach.ie) Leaves from Glengall St, near the Europa Bus Centre, Belfast, for Dublin airport (£13, 2½ hours, hourly) and Dublin city centre (£14).

Train

Belfast has two main train stations: **Great Victoria St** (Great Northern Mall), next to the Europa Bus Centre, and **Belfast Central** (East Bridge St), east of the city centre. If you arrive by train at Central Station, your rail ticket entitles you to a free bus ride into the city centre. A local train also connects with Great Victoria St.

Derry £11, 2¼ hours, seven or eight daily

Dublin £28, two hours, eight daily Monday to Saturday, five on Sunday

Larne Harbour £6.50, one hour, hourly

Getting Around

TO & FROM THE AIRPORTS Airport Express 300 buses link Belfast International Airport with the Europa Bus Centre every half-hour (£7, 30 minutes). Alternatively, a taxi costs about £25.

Airport Express 600 buses link George Best Belfast City Airport with the Europa Bus Centre (£2.20, 15 minutes) every 15 or 20 minutes between 6am and 10pm. The taxi fare to the city centre is about £7.

BIKE McConvey Cycles (028-9033 0322; www.rentabikebelfast.com; 183 Ormeau Rd; 9am-6pm Mon-Sat, to 8pm Thu) hires out bikes for £20/80 per day/week. Credit card deposit and photo ID required.

BUS A short trip on a city bus costs £1.40 to £2; a one-day ticket costs £3.50. Most local bus services depart from Donegall Sq, near the City Hall, where there's a ticket kiosk; otherwise, buy a ticket from the driver.

The Belfast-Derry Coastal Road

Ireland isn't short of scenic coastlines, but the **Causeway Coast** between Portstewart and Ballycastle – climaxing in the spectacular rock formations of the Giant's Causeway – and the Antrim Coast between Ballycastle and Belfast, are as magnificent as they come.

From April to September the **Ulsterbus** (028-9066 6630; www.translink.co.uk) Antrim Coaster (bus 252) links Belfast with Coleraine (£11, four hours, two daily Monday to Saturday) via Larne, the Glens of Antrim, Ballycastle, the Giant's Causeway, Bushmills, Portrush and Portstewart; a Sunday service operates from July to September only.

From June to September the Causeway Rambler (bus 402) links Coleraine and Carrick-a-Rede (£5.90, 40 minutes, seven daily) via Bushmills Distillery, the Giant's Causeway, White Park Bay and Ballintoy. The ticket allows unlimited travel in both directions for one day. Bus 172 runs year-round between Ballycastle and Portrush.

GLENS OF ANTRIM

Between Larne and Ballycastle, the Antrim Coast is characterised by a series of nine beautiful valleys knows as the Glens of Antrim, with lush green fields slung between black basalt crags, and picturesque harbour villages such as **Cushendall** and **Cushendun**. **Glenariff**, with its forest park and waterfalls, has been dubbed 'Queen of the Glens'.

Travelling between Cushendun and Ballycastle (with your own transport), leave the main A2 road for the narrower and more picturesque **Torr Head Scenic Road** (B92), with superb views across to the Scottish coast.

BALLYCASTLE

POP 4000

Ballycastle, where the Atlantic Ocean meets the Irish Sea, is a pleasant harbour town and a natural base for exploring the Antrim and Causeway Coasts.

The IHO **Ballycastle Backpackers** (028-2076 3612; www.ballycastlebackpackers.net; 4 North St; dm/tw from £15/40; P) is near the waterfront and the main bus stop.

CARRICK-A-REDE ROPE BRIDGE

The 20m-long **rope bridge** (028-2076 9839; nationaltrust.org.uk/carrick-a-rede; adult/child £5.60/3.10; 10am-7pm Jun-Aug, to 6pm Mar-May, Sep & Oct, 10.30am-3.30pm Nov & Dec) that connects Carrick-a-Rede Island to the mainland, swaying some 30m above the pounding waves, is a classic test of nerve. The island is the site of a salmon fishery and is a scenic 1.25km walk from the car park. Note that the bridge is closed in high winds.

Sheep Island View Hostel HOSTEL £
(028-2076 9391; www.sheepislandview.com; 42A Main St; campsites/dm/d £6/15/40; P@) This excellent independent hostel offers dorm beds, basic shared accommodation in the camping barn, or a place to pitch a tent. It's on the B15 coast road 1km west of Carrick-a-Rede, and makes an ideal overnight stop if you're hiking between Bushmills and Ballycastle.

GIANT'S CAUSEWAY

This spectacular rock formation – Northern Ireland's only Unesco World Heritage site – is one of Ireland's most impressive and atmospheric landscape features. When you first see it you'll understand why the ancients thought it wasn't a natural feature – the vast expanse of regular, closely packed, hexagonal stone columns looks for all the world like the handiwork of giants.

The more prosaic explanation is that the columns are simply contraction cracks caused by a cooling lava flow some 60 million years ago. The phenomenon is explained in the **Giant's Causeway Visitor Experience** (☎028-2073 1855; www.giantscausewaycentre.com; adult/child £8.50/4.25; ⌚9am-9pm Jul & Aug, to 7pm Apr-Jun & Sep, to 6pm Feb Mar & Oct, to 7pm Nov-Jan), a spectacular new ecofriendly building half-hidden in a hillside above the sea.

From the centre it's an easy 10- to 15-minute walk downhill to the Causeway itself, but a more interesting approach is to follow the clifftop path northeast for 2km to the **Chimney Tops** headland, then descend the **Shepherd's Steps** to the Causeway. For the less mobile, a minibus shuttles from the visitors centre to the Causeway (£2 return).

If you can, try to visit the Causeway out of season to avoid the crowds, and experience it at its most evocative.

BUSHMILLS

Bushmills, 4km southwest of the Giant's Causeway, makes a good base for visits to the Causeway Coast, but its real attraction is the **Bushmills Distillery** (www.bushmills.com; Distillery Rd; tour adult/child £7/3.50; ⌚9.15am-5pm Mon-Sat Jul-Oct, 10am-5pm Mon-Sat Nov-Jun, noon-5pm Sun year-round), the world's oldest legal distillery (King James I granted its licence in 1608). A tour of the industrial process is followed by a whiskey-tasting session; tours begin every half-hour or so.

The excellent Hostelling International Northern Ireland (HINI) **Mill Rest Hostel** (☎028-2073 1222, www.hini.org.uk; 49 Main St; dm/tw £18.50/41; ⌚closed 11am-2pm Jul & Aug, 11am-5pm Mar-Jun, Sep & Oct; @) has small dorms and one wheelchair-friendly twin room (reserve in advance).

Derry

☎028 / POP 83,700

Derry or Londonderry? The name you use for Northern Ireland's second-largest city can be a political statement, but today most people just call it Derry, whatever their politics. The 'London' prefix was added in 1613 in recognition of the Corporation of London's role in the 'plantation' of Ulster with Protestant settlers.

In 1968 resentment at the long-running Protestant domination of the city council boiled over into a series of (Catholic-dominated) civil rights marches. In August 1969 fighting between police and local youths in the poor Catholic Bogside district prompted the UK government to send British troops into Derry. In January 1972 'Bloody Sunday' resulted in the deaths of 13 unarmed Catholic civil rights marchers in Derry at the hands of the British army, an event that marked the beginning of the Troubles in earnest.

Today Derry is as safe to visit as anywhere else in Northern Ireland, while the Bogside and the inner city have been redeveloped. The city's long, dramatic history is still palpable – in the 17th-century city walls, in the captivating Bogside murals – but it's also a laid-back place with a well-founded reputation for musical excellence, from traditional to cutting-edge contemporary, and a lively arts scene that thrives in the city's many innovative venues.

In preparation for Derry's year in the limelight as **UK City of Culture 2013** (www.cityofculture2013.com), the city centre was given a makeover and an elegant new footbridge – the **Peace Bridge** – was built across the River Foyle. Among the many events planned, the city will host the presentation of the 2013 Turner Prize for contemporary art.

The centre of old Derry is the walled city on the western bank of the Foyle River. The bus station is just outside the walls at its north end; the modern city centre stretches north from here along Strand Rd. The train station is on the east bank of the Foyle, across Craigavon Bridge, in a district known as the Waterside. The Bogside lies to the west of the walled city.

Sights

FREE City Walls LANDMARK

Built between 1613 and 1618, Derry's city walls were the last to be constructed in Europe, and are the only ones in Ireland to survive almost intact. They're about 8m high, 9m thick and encircle the old city for 1.5km. The walls make for a fantastic walk, and provide a grandstand view of the Bogside (itself worth a closer look on foot) and the **People's Gallery**, a series of murals that decorate the gable ends of houses along Rossville St. Painted between 1997 and 2001 by the Bogside Artists, they commemorate key events in the Troubles, including the Battle of the Bogside, Bloody Sunday, and the 1981 hunger strike.

Tower Museum MUSEUM

(www.derrycity.gov.uk/Museums; Union Hall Pl; adult/child £4.20/2.65; ⌚10am-5pm Tue-Sat, plus

11am-3pm Sun Jul-Sep) O'Doherty's Tower, inside the northern corner of the city walls, is home to the Tower Museum, which traces the story of Derry from the days of St Columbcille to the present, and has an excellent exhibition telling the story of *La Trinidad Valenciera* – a ship of the Spanish Armada which was wrecked at Kinnagoe Bay in Donegal in 1588.

FREE Guildhall NOTABLE BUILDING
(www.derrycity.gov.uk/Guildhall; Guildhall Sq; 9am-5pm Mon-Fri) Reopened in 2013 after a major restoration, the fine neo-Gothic Guildhall was originally built in 1890 and is noted for its stained-glass windows. Guided tours are available in July and August.

Museum of Free Derry MUSEUM
(www.museumoffreederry.org; 55-61 Glenfada Park; adult/child £3/2; 9.30am-4.30pm Mon-Fri, plus 1-4pm Sat Apr-Sep, 1-4pm Sun Jul-Sep) Just off Rossville St, this museum chronicles the history of the Bogside, the civil rights movement and the events of Bloody Sunday.

St Columb's Cathedral CATHEDRAL
(www.stcolumbscathedral.org; London St; admission free, donation appreciated; 9am-5pm Mon-Sat year-round) Standing at the southern end of the walled city, off Bishop St Within, this austere cathedral dates from 1628.

Tours

City Tours GUIDED TOUR
(028-7127 1996; www.irishtourguides.com; Carlisle Stores, 11 Carlisle Rd; adult/child £4/2) Walking tours of the city walls.

Free Derry Tours GUIDED TOUR
(0779 328 5972; www.freederry.net; per person £5) Informative walking tours of the Bogside and the walled city.

Sleeping

TOP CHOICE Merchant's House B&B ££
(028-7126 9691; www.thesaddlershouse.com; 16 Queen St; s £40-60, d £55-70; @) This historic, Georgian-style townhouse has an elegant lounge and dining room with marble fireplaces and antique furniture, TV and coffee-making facilities in all rooms, and homemade marmalade at breakfast; there are even bathrobes in the rooms. Call at Saddler's House first to pick up a key.

Saddler's House B&B ££
(028-7126 9691; www.thesaddlershouse.com; 36 Great James St; s £40-55, d £50-65; @) Everything in this centrally located Victorian townhouse, from the sharp-witted hosts to their bulldog Bertie, is a joy; it's almost worth visiting Derry just to stay here or at its sister B&B, Merchant's House.

Derry City Independent Hostel HOSTEL £
(028-7128 0542; www.derry-hostel.co.uk; 44 Great James St; dm £12-15, d from £34; @) Run by experienced backpackers and decorated with souvenirs from their travels around the world, this small, friendly hostel is set in a Georgian town house, just a short walk northwest of the bus station.

Derry Palace Hostel HOSTEL £
(028-7130 9051; www.paddyspalace.com; Asylum Rd, 1 Woodleigh Tce; dm/tw from £13/36; P@) Part of the Ireland-wide Paddy's Palace chain, this hostel is central, comfortable and as friendly as they come. There's a sunny garden and a good party atmosphere, and the staff regularly organise nights out at local pubs with traditional music.

Eating

TOP CHOICE Café del Mondo CAFE, IRISH ££
(www.cafedelmondo.org; Craft Village, Shipquay St; mains cafe £5-9, dinner £13-23; 9am-6pm Mon-Sat, noon-5pm Sun, 6-11.30pm Tue-Sat) A bohemian cafe that serves excellent Fairtrade coffee and a range of healthy lunch dishes, including soups, stews and salads, served with homemade bread. The evening menu focuses on local produce, from wild mushroom risotto to Irish steak and seafood.

Encore Brasserie INTERNATIONAL ££
(028-7137 2492; Millennium Forum, Newmarket St; mains lunch £6, dinner £15-18; noon-3pm Mon-Sat, 5-9pm show nights;) Set in the lobby of the city's main cultural venue, the Encore is a stylish little place with friendly, efficient service and a crowd-pleasing menu of perennial favourites, from falafel wraps to steak with pepper sauce.

Café Blooms CAFE £
(www.verbalartscentre.co.uk/fac_cafe.htm; Verbal Arts Centre, Bishop St Within; mains £3-6; 8.30am-5pm Mon-Sat) This cool, literary-themed cafe is situated on top of the city walls, and serves delicious home-made soups, deli sandwiches, panini and excellent cappuccinos.

Drinking & Entertainment

Sandino's Cafe LIVE MUSIC
(www.sandinos.com; 1 Water St; live bands £5; ⊙11.30am-1am Mon-Sat, 1pm-midnight Sun) From the posters of Che to the Free Palestine flag, this relaxed cafe-bar exudes a liberal, left-wing vibe. There are live bands on Friday nights, DJ sessions on Saturdays, and occasional jazz, folk or comedy gigs; check the website for what's on.

Peadar O'Donnell's PUB
(peadars-gweedorebar.com; 63 Waterloo St) Peadar's goes for traditional music sessions nightly and often in the afternoon on weekends, too.

Playhouse THEATRE
(www.derryplayhouse.co.uk; 5-7 Artillery St; ⊙box office 10am-5pm Mon-Fri, Context Gallery 11am-5.30pm Tue-Sat) Housed in beautifully restored former school buildings with an award-winning modern extension at the rear, this community arts centre stages music, dance and theatre performances by local and international performers.

Millennium Forum THEATRE
(www.millenniumforum.co.uk; Newmarket St) Ireland's biggest theatre auditorium is a major venue for dance, drama, concerts, opera and musicals.

Nerve Centre ARTS CENTRE
(www.nerve-centre.org.uk; 7-8 Magazine St) A multimedia arts centre for young, local talent in the fields of music and film. It has a performance area, a theatre, an art-house cinema, a bar and a cafe.

Information

Derry Tourist Information Centre (☎028-7126 7284; www.derryvisitor.com; 44 Foyle St; ⊙9am-5pm Mon-Fri, 10am-5pm Sat, plus 10am-4pm Sun Mar-Oct) Tourist info for all of Northern Ireland and the Republic, as well as Derry. Also internet access (£1 per 20 minutes), currency exchange and accommodation-booking service.

Getting There & Away

AIR About 13km east of Derry along the A2, the **City of Derry airport** (☎028-7181 0784; www.cityofderryairport.com) has direct flights daily to London Stansted, Dublin, Glasgow Prestwick and Liverpool.

BUS The bus station is just northeast of the city walls, on Foyle St.

Ulsterbus (www.translink.co.uk) service 212, the Maiden City Flyer, is the fastest service between Belfast and Derry (£11, 1¾ hours, every half-hour, fewer on Sunday). Bus 234 goes to Coleraine (£6, one hour, five daily Monday to Friday, two Sunday), where you can connect with the 252 Antrim Coaster service. Bus 274 goes from Derry to Dublin (£18.35, 3½ hours, six daily).

Bus Éireann (www.buseireann.ie) service 64 runs from Derry to Galway (£26, 5½ hours, three daily, two on Sundays) via Donegal and Sligo; another four per day terminate at Sligo.

Lough Swilly Bus Company (www.loughswillybusco.com), with an office upstairs at the Ulsterbus station, serves County Donegal across the border.

Airporter (☎7126 9996; www.airporter.co.uk; Strand Rd, Quayside Shopping Centre) buses run direct from Derry's Quayside Shopping Centre to Belfast International Airport (one-way/return £18.50/29.50, 1½ hours) and George Best Belfast City Airport (same fare, two hours) every two hours Monday to Friday, five to seven daily at weekends.

TRAIN Derry's Waterside train station (always referred to as Londonderry in Northern Ireland timetables) lies across the Foyle River from the city centre, but is connected to it by a free Rail Link bus. Trains to Belfast (£11, two hours, five daily) run via Coleraine, where you can change for Portrush (£11, 1½ hours).

Enniskillen & Lough Erne

☎028

Enniskillen, the main town of County Fermanagh, perches amid the web of waterways that links Upper and Lower Lough Erne, one of Ireland's main centres for boating, canoeing and angling. The town centre is on an island in the Erne River.

Sights

Major sights around Enniskillen include the stately homes of **Castle Coole** (www.nationaltrust.org.uk; Dublin Rd; adult/child £5/2; ⊙house 11am-5pm daily Jul & Aug, Fri-Wed Jun, Sat, Sun & public hols mid-Mar–May & Sep, grounds 10am-7pm Mar-Oct, grounds adult/child £2.50/1.25 10am-4pm Nov-Feb) and **Florence Court** (www.nationaltrust.org.uk; Swanlinbar Rd; house tour adult/child £5/2, grounds £4/2; ⊙11am-5pm daily Jul & Aug, Wed-Mon May & Jun, Sat-Thu Sep, Sat & Sun Apr & Oct, grounds 10am-7pm Mar-Oct, 10am-4pm Nov-Feb), and the **Marble Arch Caves** (☎028-6634 8855; www.marblearchcaves.net; Marlbank Scenic Loop; adult/child £8.50/5.50; ⊙10am-5pm Jul & Aug, to 4.30pm Easter-Jun & Sep).

Lower Lough Erne has many interesting early Christian sites, including the remains of an **Augustinian monastery** and 12th-century **round tower** on **Devenish Island** (☎028-6862 1588; adult/child return £3/2; ⏲tours 10am, 1pm, 3pm & 5pm daily Apr-Sep), and a small 12th-century church on **White Island** (☎028-6862 1892; adult/child £4/2.50; ⏲11am-6pm daily Jul & Aug, to 5pm Sat & Sun Apr-Jun & Sep) with six extraordinary Celtic stone figures, thought to date from the 9th century, lined up along the wall like miniature Easter Island statues. Ferries to Devenish depart from Trory Point, 5km north of Enniskillen; boats for White Island leave from Castle Archdale Country Park, 16km northwest of Enniskillen.

Sleeping

TOP CHOICE **Westville Hotel** HOTEL ££
(☎028-6632 0333; www.westvillehotel.co.uk; 14-20 Tempo Rd; s/d from £75/90; P@) The Westville brings a dash of style to Enniskillen's rather staid accommodation scene with its designer fabrics, cool colour combinations, good food and welcoming staff.

Dromard House B&B B&B ££
(☎028-6638 7250; www.dromardhouse.com; Tamlaght; s/d from £40/60;) Roughly 3km along the A4 towards Florence Court sits this lovely traditional Ulster farmhouse on a working organic farm.

Bridges Youth Hostel HOSTEL £
(☎028-6634 0110; www.hini.org.uk; Belmore St; dm/s/tw £18/23/41; P@) A modern hostel with a great location overlooking a river in the centre of town.

Information

Tourist Office (☎028-6632 3110; www.fermanagh.gov.uk; Wellington Rd; ⏲9am-5.30pm Mon-Fri year-round, plus 10am-6pm Sat, 11am-5pm Sun Easter-Sep, 10am-2pm Sat & Sun Oct) About 100m south of the town centre; has internet access (£1 per 20 minutes).

Getting There & Away

Enniskillen's **bus station** (Shore Rd) is across from the tourist office.

Belfast £11, 2¼ hours, hourly Monday to Saturday, two on Sunday

Derry £11, three hours, six daily Monday to Saturday (change at Omagh)

Donegal £10, one hour, every two hours

Dublin £24, 2¾ hours, every two hours

UNDERSTAND IRELAND

History

Very Early Irish, Celts & Vikings

The tale of Irish history begins around 10,000 years ago, as the last ice caps melted and the rising sea level cut Ireland off from Britain. Hunter-gatherers may first have traversed the narrowing land bridge, but many more crossed the Irish Sea in small boats. Farming did not reach Ireland until around 4000 BC.

The Celtic warrior tribes who influenced Irish culture came from central Europe around 300 BC and were well ensconced by 100 BC. They had conquered large sections of southern Europe and plundered Rome in the 4th century BC. Known as 'Galli' (Gauls) by the Romans and 'Keltoi' by the Greeks, they were feared by both.

Christian monks, including St Patrick, arrived in Ireland around the 5th century AD, and as the Dark Ages enveloped Europe, Ireland became an outpost of European civilisation. In a land of saints, scholars and missionaries, thriving monasteries produced beautiful illuminated manuscripts, some of which, such as *The Book of Kells*, survive to this day.

From the end of the 8th century, the rich monasteries were targets of raids by Vikings. At the height of their power the Vikings ruled Dublin, Waterford and Limerick, but were eventually defeated by legendary Celtic hero Brian Ború, the king of Munster, at the Battle of Clontarf in 1014.

The British Arrive

The Norman conquest of England spread to Ireland in 1169, when Henry II, fearful of the Irish kingdoms' power, dispatched forces to the island.

Oppression of the Catholic Irish got seriously under way in the 1500s when Henry VIII and then Elizabeth I attempted to impose a new Protestant church. Land confiscated from Catholic nobles was given to Protestant settlers from Scotland and England, a policy known as 'the Plantation', sowing the seeds of today's divided Ireland.

In 1685 James II ascended the British throne, but was forced to flee the country because of his outspoken Catholicism. He sought unsuccessfully to regain his crown, which had been handed to the Protestant

ARCHAEOLOGY

Ireland is packed with archaeological sites that are reminders of its long and dramatic history. You may encounter the following terms:

Cashel A stone ring fort or *rath*.

Dolmen A portal tomb or Stone Age grave consisting of stone 'pillars' supporting a stone roof or capstone.

Passage tomb A megalithic mound-tomb with a narrow stone passage that leads to a burial chamber.

Ring fort/rath A circular fort, originally constructed of earth and timber, but later made of stone.

Round tower A tall tower or belfry built as a lookout and place of refuge from the Vikings.

William of Orange (a Dutchman). William's victory over James at the Battle of the Boyne on 12 July 1690 is commemorated to this day by northern Protestant Orange Parades.

By the 18th century, Ireland's Catholics held less than 15% of the land, and suffered brutal restrictions in employment, education and religion. The United Irishmen began agitating for Irish civil rights under the leadership of young Dublin Protestant and Republican Theobald Wolfe Tone (1763–98). The group was dissolved in 1798 with Wolfe Tone's capture by the British and subsequent suicide.

Ireland's Protestant gentry, alarmed by unrest, sought the security of closer ties with Britain. In 1800 the *Act of Union* was passed, joining Ireland politically with Britain. The Irish parliament voted itself out of existence, and around 100 Irish MPs moved to London's House of Commons.

In the first half of the 19th century, Daniel O'Connell (1775–1847) led Ireland towards greater independence by peaceful means, and won a seat in the British parliament in 1828. Rather than risk a rebellion, the British parliament passed the 1829 *Act of Catholic Emancipation,* allowing Catholics limited voting rights and the right to be elected as MPs.

O'Connell died as Ireland was suffering its greatest tragedy. Successive failures of the potato crop between 1845 and 1851 resulted in the mass starvation and emigration known as Ireland's Great Famine, or the Potato Famine.

Shamefully, during these years there were excellent harvests of crops, such as wheat and dairy produce. However, while millions starved, Ireland was forced to export its food to Britain and overseas. About one million died from disease or starvation – some were buried in mass graves, others left where they had dropped. Another million emigrated, and migration continued to reduce the population during the next 100 years.

At the turn of the century, the British parliament began to contemplate Irish home rule, but WWI interrupted the process. Ireland might still have moved, peacefully, towards some sort of home rule but for a bungled uprising in 1916. Though it is now celebrated as a glorious bid for freedom, the Easter Rising was heavy on rhetoric and light on planning on both sides. After the insurrection was put down, a series of trials and executions (15 in all) transformed the ringleaders into martyrs and roused international support for Irish independence.

The Road to Independence

In the 1918 election Irish republicans stood under the banner of Sinn Féin (Ourselves Alone) and won a majority of Irish seats. Ignoring London's parliament, where they were meant to sit, newly elected Sinn Féin deputies declared Ireland independent and formed the Dáil Éireann (Irish assembly), led by Eamon de Valera. The British had not conceded and confrontation was inevitable.

The Anglo-Irish War (1919–21) pitted Sinn Féin and its military wing, the Irish Republican Army (IRA), against the British. The brutal responses of Britain's Black and Tans infantry further roused anti-British sentiment. This was the period when Michael Collins, a charismatic and ruthless leader, masterminded the IRA's campaign of violence (while serving as finance minister in the new Dáil).

After months of negotiations in London, Collins and Arthur Griffith led the delegation that signed the Anglo-Irish Treaty on 6 December 1921. The treaty gave 26 of Ireland's 32 counties their independence, and allowed six largely Protestant counties in Ulster to remain a province of the UK.

The treaty was ratified by the Dáil in January 1922, but passions were so inflamed that within weeks civil war broke out. At issue was the fact that the British monarch remained the nominal head of the new Irish Free State and Irish MPs were required to swear allegiance. To many Irish Catholics, this was a betrayal of republican principles. In the ensuing violence Collins was assassinated in Cork by anti-Treaty forces, while the Free State government briefly imprisoned de Valera.

By 1923 the civil war had ground to a halt, and for nearly 50 years Ireland was relatively peaceful. After boycotting the Dáil for a number of years, de Valera founded Fianna Fáil (Warriors of Ireland), which won a majority in the 1932 election. De Valera introduced a new constitution in 1937 that abolished the oath of British allegiance and claimed sovereignty over the six counties of Ulster. In 1948 the Irish government declared the country a republic and, in 1949, left the British Commonwealth.

The Troubles

According to the Anglo-Irish Treaty, the six counties of Northern Ireland were to be governed by a Northern Irish parliament, which sat at Stormont, near Belfast, from 1920 until 1972.

The Protestant majority made its rule absolute by systematically excluding Catholics from power. This led to the formation of a nonsectarian civil rights movement in 1967 to campaign for fairer representation for Northern Irish Catholics. In January 1969 civil rights marchers walked from Belfast to Derry to demand a fairer division of jobs and housing. Just outside Derry, a Protestant mob attacked the mostly Catholic marchers. Further marches, protests and violence followed. Far from keeping the two sides apart, Northern Ireland's mainly Protestant police force, the Royal Ulster Constabulary (RUC), became part of the problem.

Finally, in August 1969, British troops were sent into Derry and Belfast to maintain law and order. Though Catholics initially welcomed the army, it was soon seen as a tool of the Protestant majority. The peaceful civil rights movement lost ground and the IRA, which had been hibernating, found new, willing recruits for an armed independence struggle.

Thus the so-called Troubles rolled back and forth throughout the 1970s and into the 1980s. Passions reached fever pitch in 1972, when 13 unarmed Catholics were shot dead by British troops in Derry on 'Bloody Sunday' (30 January). Then in 1981, IRA prisoners in Northern Ireland went on a hunger strike to demand the right to be recognised as political prisoners (rather than as terrorists). Ten of them fasted to death, the best known being an elected MP, Bobby Sands.

The waters were further muddied by the IRA splitting into 'official' and 'provisional' wings, from which sprang even more violent republican organisations. Protestant paramilitary organisations, such as the Ulster Volunteer Force (UVF), sprang up in opposition to the IRA and its splinter groups, and violence was met with violence.

Giving Peace a Chance

The 1985 Anglo-Irish Agreement gave the Dublin government an official consultative role in Northern Irish affairs for the first time. The Downing Street Declaration of December 1993, signed by Britain and the Republic, moved matters forward, with Britain declaring it had no 'selfish, economic or military interest' in preserving the division of Ireland.

In August 1994 a 'permanent cessation of violence' by the IRA, announced by Sinn Féin's leader Gerry Adams, offered the prospect of peace in Ulster. When Protestant paramilitary forces responded with their own ceasefire in October 1994, most British troops were withdrawn to barracks and roadblocks were removed.

In 1995 the British and Irish governments published two 'framework documents' to lay the groundwork for all-party peace talks. The subsequent negotiations stalled when Britain's Conservative prime minister, John Major, refused to allow all-party talks to start until the IRA decommissioned its weapons. An IRA bomb in the Docklands area of London shattered the negotiations in February 1996. In June, with the IRA's refusal to restore its ceasefire, 'all-party' talks on Ulster's future convened without Sinn Féin.

The peace process regained momentum with the landslide victory in May 1997 of

Tony Blair's Labour Party, its massive majority enabling it to act with a freer hand than the previous Conservative government. In June 1997 Britain's new Northern Ireland secretary, Dr Mo Mowlam, promised to admit Sinn Fein to all-party talks following any new ceasefire, which the IRA declared on 20 July 1997.

These talks produced the Good Friday Agreement on 10 April 1998. This agreement allowed the people of Northern Ireland to decide their political future by majority vote, and committed its signatories to 'democratic and peaceful means of resolving differences on political issues'. It established a new Northern Ireland Assembly and high-level political links between the Republic and Northern Ireland. In simultaneous referendums in May 1998 the agreement was approved by 71% of voters in the North and 94% in the South. However, despite these moves towards peace, later that year a bomb planted by the 'Real IRA' killed 29 people in Omagh.

The new assembly was beset by divisions from the outset, which resulted in no less than four suspensions, the latest from 2002 until 2007. After five years of direct rule from London, a deal hammered out between the Democratic Unionist Party and Sinn Féin saw the assembly members finally take their seats in Stormont on 8 May 2007.

Today a cautious optimism prevails and, despite economic recession, occasional flare-ups of sectarian violence, and a renewed campaign of violence by republican splinter groups in Northern Ireland, the vast majority of people north and south of the border are committed to a peaceful future.

People

The total population of Ireland is around six million: 4.3 million in the Republic and 1.7 million in Northern Ireland. Prior to the 1845–51 Great Famine, the population was around eight million; death and emigration reduced it to around six million, and emigration continued at high levels for the next 100 years. It wasn't until the 1960s that the population began to recover.

Thanks to the EU, Ireland has seen a modest influx of immigrants, mostly from Eastern Europe, within the past five years.

Arts

Literature

The Irish have made an enormous impact on world literature. Important writers include Jonathan Swift, Oscar Wilde, WB Yeats, George Bernard Shaw, James Joyce, Sean O'Casey, Samuel Beckett and Roddy Doyle, whose *Paddy Clarke Ha Ha Ha* won the Booker Prize in 1993. The Ulster-born poet Seamus Heaney was awarded the Nobel Prize for Literature in 1995. Earlier Irish Nobel laureates include Shaw (1925), Yeats (1938) and Beckett (1969). Frank McCourt became a world favourite with his autobiographical *Angela's Ashes* (1996), which won the Pulitzer Prize, and *'Tis* (1999). Edna O'Brien's debut novel *The Country Girls* (1960) revolutionised Irish writing with its frank portrayal of women's emotional and sexual lives; the book was considered so shocking that it was banned in many parts of Ireland.

Music

Traditional Irish music – played on instruments such as the bodhrán (a flat, goatskin drum), *uilleann* (or 'elbow') pipes, flute and fiddle – is an aspect of Irish culture impossible to miss. Of Irish groups, perhaps the best known are the Chieftains, the Dubliners and the Pogues. Popular Irish singers/musicians who have made it on the international stage include Van Morrison, Thin Lizzy, U2, Sinéad O'Connor, The Cranberries, The Corrs and Damien Rice.

Theatre

Ireland has a rich theatrical history. Dublin's first theatre was founded in Werburgh St in 1637. The literary revival of the late 19th century resulted in the establishment of Dublin's Abbey Theatre, now Ireland's national theatre, which presents works by former greats – WB Yeats, George Bernard Shaw and Sean O'Casey – and promotes modern Irish dramatists. One of the most outstanding playwrights of the last two decades is Frank McGuinness (born 1956), whose plays explore the consequences of 1972's Bloody Sunday on the people of Derry. Other playwrights to watch out for are Martin McDonagh, Brian Friel (of *Dancing at Lughnasa* fame), Conor McPherson, Donal O'Kelly and Enda Walsh.

RELIGION IN IRELAND

Religion has played a pivotal role in Irish history. About 90% of residents in the Republic are Roman Catholic, followed by 3% Protestant, 0.5% Muslim and the rest with no professed religious belief. In Northern Ireland, 53% are Protestant and 44% Catholic.

The Catholic Church has traditionally opposed attempts to liberalise laws governing contraception, divorce and abortion. Today condom machines can be found all over Ireland and divorce is legal, but abortion remains illegal in the Republic. Though still wielding considerable influence in the south, the Church has been weakened recently by drastically declining attendance at church services, by falling numbers of people entering religious life and by paedophile sex scandals. It's now treated with a curious mixture of respect and derision by various sections of the community.

Environment

Ireland is divided into 32 counties: 26 in the Republic and six in Northern Ireland. The island measures 84,421 sq km (about 83% is the Republic) and stretches 486km north to south and 275km east to west. The jagged coastline extends for 5631km. The midlands of Ireland are flat, rich farmland with huge swaths of peat (which is rapidly being depleted for fuel).

Carrauntuohil (1040m) on the Iveragh Peninsula, County Kerry, is the highest mountain on the island. The Shannon River, the longest in Ireland, flows for 259km before emptying into the Atlantic west of Limerick.

Ireland's rivers and lakes are well stocked with fish, and the island is home to some three-dozen mammal species. The Office of Public Works (OPW) maintains six national parks and 76 nature reserves in the Republic; the Department of the Environment owns or leases more than 40 nature reserves in Northern Ireland.

Food & Drink

In Irish B&B accommodation, breakfasts almost inevitably include 'a fry', a plate consisting of fried eggs, bacon, sausages, black pudding (blood sausage) and tomatoes. Traditional meals (such as Irish stew, often found in pubs) can be cheap and hearty. Potatoes are everywhere, colcannon and champ being two of the tastiest mashes. Seafood is often excellent, especially in the west, and there are some good vegetarian restaurants in cities and larger towns. The panini, an Italian type of sandwich, is so popular here you would think it was traditional.

In Ireland a drink means a beer, either lager or stout. Stout is usually Guinness, although in Cork it can mean a Murphy's or a Beamish. If you haven't developed a taste for stout, a wide variety of lagers are available, including Harp and Smithwicks (don't pronounce the 'w'!). Asking for a Guinness will get you a pint (568mL); if you want a half-pint, ask for a 'glass' or a 'half'.

If someone suggests visiting a pub for its good craic, it means a good time with convivial company. However, if you count cigarettes as an essential part of a good time, you're out of luck – smoking is banned in all public places throughout Ireland.

SURVIVAL GUIDE

Directory A–Z

Accommodation

Booking ahead is recommended in peak season (roughly April to October). See the following for booking services:

Fáilte Ireland (Irish Tourist Board; www.discoverireland.ie) Will book accommodation for a 10% room deposit and a fee of €5.

Northern Ireland Tourist Board (NITB; www.discovernorthernireland.com) Books accommodation at no cost but with a 10% deposit upfront.

Gulliver (www.gulliver.ie) Online booking service for both the Republic and Northern Ireland; deposit of 10% and a €5 fee is payable.

B&BS

Bed and breakfasts are as Irish as accommodation gets, with seemingly every other house a B&B, sometimes in the strangest locations. Typical costs are around €25 to €45 per person a night (sharing a double room), though more luxurious B&Bs can cost upwards of €55 per person. Most B&Bs are small, so in summer they quickly fill up.

CAMPING & HOSTELS

Commercial camping grounds typically charge €10 to €20 for a tent and two people. Unless otherwise indicated, prices quoted for 'campsites' are for a tent, car and two people.

Hostels in Ireland can be booked solid in summer. An Óige (meaning 'youth') and Hostelling International Northern Ireland (HINI) are branches of Hostelling International (HI); An Óige has 26 hostels in the Republic, while HINI has six in the North. Other hostel associations include Independent Holiday Hostels (IHH), a cooperative group with about 120 hostels throughout the island, and the Independent Hostels Owners (IHO) association, which has over 100 members around Ireland.

From June to September a dorm bed at most hostels costs €15 to €20, except for the more expensive hostels in Dublin, Belfast and a few other places.

An Óige (www.anoige.ie) Hostelling International (HI)-associated national organisation with 26 hostels scattered around the Republic.

Hostelling International Northern Ireland (www.hini.org.uk)

Independent Holiday Hostels of Ireland (IHH; www.hostels-ireland.com) Eighty tourist-board approved hostels throughout all of Ireland.

Independent Hostel Owners of Ireland (IHO; www.independenthostelsireland.com) Independent hostelling association.

PRICE RANGES

Prices are listed at high-season rates (low-season rates can be 15% to 20% less), based on two people sharing a double, and include a private bathroom unless otherwise stated.

In the Republic of Ireland:

€€€ more than €150

€€ €60 to €150

€ less than €60

In Northern Ireland:

£££ more than £100

££ £40 to £100

£ less than £40

Activities

Ireland is great for outdoor activities, and tourist offices have a wide selection of information covering birdwatching (County Donegal and County Wexford), surfing (great along the west coast), scuba-diving (West Cork), cycling, fishing, horse riding, sailing, canoeing and many other activities.

Walking is particularly popular, although you must come prepared for wet weather. There are now well over 20 waymarked trails throughout Ireland, one of the most popular being the 132km Wicklow Way.

Business Hours

Standard business hours are generally the same in both the Republic and Northern Ireland, as below:

Banks 9.30am-4.30pm Mon-Fri to 5pm Sat in Northern Ireland; 10am-4pm Mon-Fri, to 5pm Thu in the Republic.

Offices 9am-5pm Mon-Fri

Post offices 9am-5.30pm Mon-Fri & 9am-12.30pm Sat in Northern Ireland; 9am-6pm Mon-Fri & 9am-1pm Sat in the Republic. Smaller post offices may close at lunchtime and one day per week.

Pubs 11.30am-11pm Mon-Sat & 12.30-10pm Sun in Northern Ireland, pubs with late licences open until 1am Mon-Sat, and midnight Sun; 10.30am-11.30pm Mon-Thu, 10.30am-12.30am Fri & Sat, noon-11pm Sun in the Republic. All pubs close Christmas Day and Good Friday.

Restaurants noon-10.30pm, many close one day of the week.

Shops 9am-5.30pm or 6pm Mon-Sat (to 8pm Thu and sometimes Fri), noon-6pm Sun (in bigger towns); rural shops may close at lunchtime and one day per week.

Embassies & Consulates

Australian Embassy (☎01-664 5300; www.ireland.embassy.gov.au; Fitzwilton House, 7th fl, Wilton Tce, Dublin 2)

Canadian Embassy (☎01-234 4000; www.canada.ie; 7-8 Wilton Tce, Dublin 2)

UK Embassy (☎205 3700; www.britishembassy.ie; 29 Merrion Rd, Ballsbridge, Dublin 4)

USA Embassy (☎01-630 6200; dublin.usembassy.gov/; 42 Elgin Rd, Ballsbridge, Dublin) Consulate (☎028-9038 6100; Danesfort House, 223 Stranmillis Rd, Belfast) in Belfast (Northern Ireland).

Food

The following price indicators are used to indicate the cost of a main course at dinner.

In the Republic of Ireland:

€€€ more than €20

€€ €10 to €20

€ less than €10

In Northern Ireland

£££ more than £20

££ £10 to £20

£ less than £10

Gay & Lesbian Travellers

Despite the decriminalisation of homosexuality a couple of decades ago, gay life is generally neither acknowledged nor understood. Only Dublin and, to a lesser extent, Belfast, Cork, Galway and Limerick have open gay and lesbian communities.

Gay Community News (www.gcn.ie) Free monthly mag available at bars and cafes.

National Lesbian & Gay Federation (NLGF; ☎01-671 9076; www.nlgf.ie)

Outhouse (☎873 4932; www.outhouse.ie; 105 Capel St, Dublin) Drop-in centre for gay, lesbian and transgendered people.

Language

While Irish Gaelic is the official language of the Republic of Ireland, it is spoken only in a few rural areas (known as Gaeltacht) mainly in Cork, Donegal, Galway and Kerry. English is the everyday language in the Republic and in Northern Ireland.

Maps

Good-quality maps of Ireland include Michelin's *Ireland Motoring Map* No 923 (1:400,000) and Collins *Touring Map of Ireland*. The more detailed Ordnance Survey *Discovery* series (1:50,000) covers both Northern Ireland and the Republic in 89 sheets (around €9 each).

Money

The Irish Republic uses the euro (€), while Northern Ireland uses the British pound sterling (£) and the Northern Irish pound (£). Banks offer the best exchange rates; exchange bureaux, open longer, have worse rates and higher commissions. Post offices generally have exchange facilities and are open on Saturday morning.

In Northern Ireland several banks issue their own Northern Irish pound notes, which are equivalent to sterling but not readily accepted in mainland Britain. Many hotels, restaurants and shops in Northern Ireland accept euros.

Ireland is expensive, marginally more so than Britain, but prices vary around the island. Prices for sites and museums are usually 20% to 50% lower for children, students and senior citizens (OAPs); many state-run museums and galleries are free.

For budget travellers, €60 to €80 per day should cover hostel accommodation, getting around, a restaurant meal and a pint.

Fancy hotels and restaurants usually add a 10% or 15% service charge onto bills. Simpler places usually don't add a service charge; if you decide to tip, just round up the bill (or add 10% at most). Taxi drivers do not have to be tipped, but if you do, 10% is more than generous.

Public Holidays

Following is a list of the main public holidays in the Republic, Northern Ireland and both:

New Year's Day 1 January

St Patrick's Day 17 March

Easter (Good Friday to Easter Monday inclusive) March/April

May Holiday First Monday in May

Christmas Day 25 December

St Stephen's Day (Boxing Day) 26 December

NORTHERN IRELAND

Spring Bank Holiday Last Monday in May

Orangemen's Day 12 July (following Monday if 12th is at weekend)

August Bank Holiday Last Monday in August

REPUBLIC OF IRELAND

June Holiday First Monday in June

August Holiday First Monday in August

October Holiday Last Monday in October

Telephone

Local telephone calls from a public phone in the Republic cost a minimum of €0.50 for three minutes; in Northern Ireland a local call costs a minimum of £0.30. Some payphones in Northern Ireland accept euro coins. Prepaid phonecards by Eircom or private operators, available in newsagencies and post offices, work from all payphones and dispense with the need for coins.

To call Northern Ireland from the Republic, do not use ☎0044 as for the rest of the UK. Instead, dial ☎048 and then the local number. To dial the Republic from Northern Ireland, however, use the full international code ☎00-353, then the local number.

The mobile (cell-) phone network in Ireland runs on the GSM 900/1800 system compatible with the rest of Europe and Australia, but not the USA. Mobile numbers in the Republic begin with 085, 086 or 087. A local pay-as-you-go SIM for your mobile will cost from around €10, but may work out free after the standard phone-credit refund.

Tourist Information

The Irish tourist board, **Fáilte Ireland** (www.discoverireland.ie), and the **Northern Ireland Tourist Board** (NITB; ☎head office 028-9023 1221; www.discovernorthernireland.com) operate separately. Both are well organised and helpful, though Fáilte Ireland will not provide any information on places (such as B&Bs and camping grounds) that it has not approved. Every town big enough to have half-a-dozen pubs will have a tourist office, although smaller ones may close in winter. Most will find you a place to stay for a fee of €5.

Tourism Ireland (www.tourismireland.com) handles tourist information for both tourist boards overseas.

Travellers with Disabilities

Guesthouses, hotels and sights throughout Ireland are increasingly being adapted for people with disabilities, though facilities are still quite poor by European standards. Fáilte Ireland's various accommodation guides indicate which places are wheelchair accessible, and the NITB publishes *Accessible Accommodation in Northern Ireland*.

Citizens' Information Board (☎01-605 9000; www.citizensinformationboard.ie)

Disability Action (☎028-9066 1252; www.disabilityaction.org)

Visas

Citizens of the EU, Australia, Canada, New Zealand and the US don't need a visa to visit either the Republic or Northern Ireland. EU nationals are allowed to stay indefinitely, while other visitors can usually remain for three to six months. UK nationals born in Britain or Northern Ireland don't need a passport to visit the Republic, but should carry one anyway as identification.

Getting There & Away

Air

There are nonstop flights from Britain, Continental Europe and North America to Dublin, Shannon and Belfast International, and nonstop connections from Britain and Europe to Cork. International departure tax is normally included in the price of your ticket.

International airports in Ireland:

Belfast City (BHD; ☎028-9093 9093; www.belfastcityairport.com)

Belfast International Airport (BFS; ☎028-9448 4848; www.belfastairport.com)

Cork Airport (ORK; ☎021-431 3131; www.corkairport.com)

Derry Airport (LDY; ☎028-7181 0784; www.cityofderryairport.com)

Donegal Airport (CFN; ☎074-954 8284; www.donegalairport.ie)

Dublin Airport (DUB; ☎01-814 1111; www.dublinairport.com)

Kerry Airport (KIR; ☎066-976 4644; www.kerryairport.ie; Farranfore)

Ireland West Airport Knock (www.irelandwestairport.com)

Shannon Airport (SNN; ☎061-712 000; www.shannonairport.com)

Waterford Airport (WAT; ☎051-875 589; www.flywaterford.com)

Land

National Express and Bus Éireann's Eurolines operate services direct from London and other UK centres to Dublin, Belfast and other cities via various ferry crossings. From London to Dublin or Belfast by bus takes about 12½ hours and costs £46/67 one-way/return standard fare.

National Express (www.nationalexpress.com)

Bus Éireann (www.buseireann.ie)

Sea

There's a wide range of ferry services from Britain and France to Ireland. Prices vary depending on season, time of day, day of the week and length of stay. One-way fares for an adult foot passenger can be as little as £25, but can exceed £75 in summer. For a car plus driver and up to four adult passengers, prices can cost from £150 to £300.

Keep an eye out for special deals, discounted return fares and other money savers. And plan ahead – some services are booked up months in advance. **DirectFerries** (www.directferries.co.uk) lists all the available ferry routes and operators.

Ferry operators:

Brittany Ferries (www.brittany-ferries.com) Once weekly April to October.

Celtic Link Ferries (☎040-238 084, in France 02 33 43 23 87; www.celticlinkferries.com) Twice-weekly passenger-only service.

Irish Ferries (www.irishferries.com) Holyhead ferries up to four a day year-round, from France to Rosslare three times a week, mid-February to December.

P&O Irish Sea (www.poirishsea.com) Daily sailings year-round.

Steam Packet (☎1800-805 055, in the UK 0870 222 1333; www.steam-packet.com) Ferries operate daily Easter to September only.

Stena Line (www.stenaline.com)

DISCOUNTS & PASSES

Eurail Pass Holders get a 50% discount on Irish Ferries crossings to France.

InterRail Pass Holders get a 50% discount on Irish Ferries and Stena Line services.

Britrail Pass Has an option to add on Ireland for an extra fee, including ferry transit.

Getting Around

Travelling around Ireland looks simple, as the distances are short and there's a dense network of roads and railways. However, getting from A to B in Ireland seldom involves a straight line, and public transport can be expensive (particularly trains), infrequent or both. For these reasons having your own transport – either car or bicycle – can be a major advantage.

Air

There are flights within Ireland from Dublin to Derry and Donegal airports, and from Galway to the Aran Islands. Most domestic flights take 30 to 50 minutes.

Domestic carriers:

Aer Árann (www.aerarann.com)

FlyBe (www.flybe.com)

Bicycle

A bike is useful for exploring rural areas, but beware traffic on what are often narrow, potholed roads with no space to get out of the way. Note that there is no 'right to roam' as in the UK, and most off-road cycling is technically illegal without the landowner's permission.

Typical bike hire costs are from €20 to €25 per day or around €60 to €100 a week. Bags and other equipment can also be hired.

Bicycles can be transported by bus if there is enough room on board; the charge varies. On trains, the cost is €4 to €8 for a one-way journey, but bikes are not allowed on certain routes, including the Dublin Area Rapid Transit (DART).

Raleigh Rent-a-Bike (www.raleigh.ie) has a network of agencies all over Ireland; like many local bike shops, they offer one-way hire for an extra charge.

Bus

The Republic of Ireland's national bus line, **Bus Éireann** (☎01-836 6111; www.buseireann.ie), operates services all over the Republic and into Northern Ireland. Fares are much cheaper than train fares. Return trips are usually only slightly more expensive than one-way fares, and special deals (eg same-day returns) are often available. Most intercity buses in Northern Ireland are operated by **Ulsterbus** (☎028-9066 6600; www.ulsterbus.co.uk).

FERRY ROUTES: FRANCE TO IRELAND

ROUTE	OPERATOR	DURATION (HR)	ONE-WAY FARE (€)
Roscoff–Rosslare	Irish Ferries	17	64
Cherbourg–Rosslare	Irish Ferries, Celtic Link	20	64
Roscoff–Cork	Brittany Ferries	14	69

FERRY ROUTES: BRITAIN TO IRELAND

ROUTE	OPERATOR	DURATION (HR)	ONE-WAY FARE (£)
Fishguard–Rosslare	Stena Line	3½	29
Pembroke–Rosslare	Irish Ferries	2	29
Holyhead–Dublin	Stena Line, Irish Ferries	3	29
Holyhead–Dublin (fast boat)	Irish Ferries	1¾	34
Holyhead–Dun Laoghaire/ Dublin Port	Stena Line	1½	35
Douglas (Isle of Man)–Dublin	Steam Packet	2¾	45
Douglas (Isle of Man)–Belfast	Steam Packet	2¾	45
Cairnryan–Belfast	Stena Line	3	28
Cairnryan–Belfast (fast boat)	Stena Line	2	28
Cairnryan–Larne (fast boat)	P&O Irish Sea	1	26
Troon–Larne (fast boat)	P&O Irish Sea	2	26

DISCOUNTS & PASSES

Bus Éireann offers discounts to ISIC (International Student Identity Cards) holders.

Travel passes for buses in Ireland include:

Open Road Pass (www.buseireann.ie) For bus travel in the Republic. Three days' travel out of six consecutive days (€57); four out of eight days (€73); eight out of 16 days (€137); 15 out of 30 days (€249).

Irish Rover (www.buseireann.ie) Bus travel on Bus Éireann (Republic) and Ulsterbus (Northern Ireland). Three days' travel out of eight consecutive days (€88); eight out of 15 days (€200); 15 out of 30 days (€295).

Irish Explorer (www.buseireann.ie) Rail and bus travel in the Republic including DART. Eight days' travel out of 15 consecutive days (€245).

Zone 4 iLink Card (www.translink.co.uk/ilink) Replacement for the Freedom of Northern Ireland pass. Smartcard offering unlimited travel on bus and train in Northern Ireland; one day/one week costs £17/57 plus £1.50 on first purchase (can be topped up).

Car & Motorcycle

HIRE

Car hire in Ireland is expensive, so you're better off booking a package deal from home. In the high season it's wise to book ahead. Extra fees may apply if you cross the North–South border. Automatic cars are more expensive.

People aged under 21 years cannot hire a car; for most hire companies you must be at least 23 and have had a valid driving licence for one year. Some companies will not hire to those aged over 70 or 75. Your own local licence is usually sufficient to hire a car for up to three months.

In the Republic typical weekly high-season hire rates – with insurance, Value-Added Tax (VAT), unlimited distance and collision-damage waiver – cost from €170 for a small car. **Nova Car Hire** (www.novacarhire.com) acts as an agent for Alamo, Budget, European and National, and offers greatly discounted rates.

The international hire companies and major local operators have offices all over Ireland. Recommended firms in Dublin:

Argus Rent-A-Car (☎01-499 9611; www.argusrentals.com)

Dan Dooley Car Hire (☎01-677 2723; www.dan-dooley.ie)

Thrifty Car Rental (☎1800-515 800; www.thrifty.ie)

ROAD RULES

Driving is on the left-hand side and you should only overtake (pass) to the right of the vehicle ahead of you. The driver and passengers must wear safety belts, and children under 12 years of age cannot sit in the front. Motorcyclists and passengers must wear helmets; headlights should be dipped.

Minor roads can be potholed and narrow, but the traffic is rarely heavy, except

INTERCITY BUS SERVICES

ROUTE	COST	DURATION (HR)	FREQUENCY (DAILY MON-SAT)
Belfast–Dublin	£14.15	2½	10+
Derry–Belfast	£11	1¾	10+
Derry–Dublin	£8.35	3½	6
Dublin–Cork	€14	4½	6
Dublin–Donegal	€20	4	8
Dublin–Rosslare	€19.50	3½	4
Dublin–Killarney	€27	6	6
Killarney–Dingle	€15	2½	5
Killarney–Galway	€24.50	7	6

through tourist or commercial towns. Speed limits are posted in miles per hour in Northern Ireland and kilometres per hour in the Republic: 110km/h (70mph) on motorways, 100km/h (60mph) on main roads and 50km/h (30mph) or as signposted in towns. Beware of slow-moving tractors and livestock on narrow, winding rural roads. Ireland's blood-alcohol limit is 0.08% and strictly enforced.

Car parks and other specified areas in Ireland are regulated by 'pay and display' tickets or disc parking. Available from most newsagencies, discs are good for one hour. Double yellow lines by the roadside mean no parking at any time, while single yellow lines indicate restrictions (which will be signposted).

Train

The Republic of Ireland's railway system, **Iarnród Éireann** (Irish Rail; ☎1850-366 222; www.irishrail.ie), has routes radiating out from Dublin, but there is no direct north-south route along the west coast. Tickets can be twice as expensive as the bus, but travel times may be dramatically reduced. Special fares are often available, and a midweek return ticket sometimes costs just a bit more than the single fare; the flip side is that fares may be significantly higher on Friday and Sunday. **Rail Users Ireland** (www.railusers.ie) is more informative than the official website.

Northern Ireland Railways (NIR; ☎028-9089 9411; www.nirailways.co.uk; Belfast Central Station) has four lines from Belfast, one of which links up with the Republic's rail system.

DISCOUNTS & PASSES

Iarnród Éireann offers discounts to ISIC holders.

Travel passes for trains in Ireland include:

Eurail Pass Valid for train travel in the Republic of Ireland but not in Northern Ireland, 50% discount on Irish Ferries crossings to France.

InterRail Pass Discount of 50% on train travel within Ireland and on Irish Ferries and Stena Line services.

Britrail Pass Has an option to add on Ireland for an extra fee. The pass also covers ferry transit.

Irish Explorer Rail For train-only travel (five days' travel out of 15) for €160 within the Republic only.

Italy

Includes »

Best Places to Eat

- » Enoteca Provincia Romana (p751)
- » L'Osteria di Giovanni (p796)
- » Piccolo Napoli (p827)
- » Osteria de' Poeti (p785)
- » Cucina Casareccia (p823)

Best Places to Stay

- » Academy Hostel (p795)
- » Art Hotel Boston (p764)
- » Belludi37 (p772)
- » Novecento (p776)
- » Hostel of the Sun (p812)

Why Go?

Italians really do know how to live well. Ever since the Etruscans came, liked what they saw and decided to stay and party, the locals have embraced the finer things in life. Here, family, faith, friendship, food and wine reign supreme, contributing to the famous Italian *dolce vita* (sweet life).

Travellers have been falling under Italy's spell ever since the days of the 18th-century Grand Tour, enticed by its sun-kissed landscape, delectable cuisine and extraordinary art. This is the home of gently rolling Tuscan hills and postcard-perfect coastlines, and the place where simple dishes such as pizza and pasta regularly attain culinary perfection. It's where Michelangelo shocked the establishment with his assertively humanist sculptures and Caravaggio shocked everyone else with his criminal highjinks and darkly atmospheric paintings.

So make like Julius Caesar. Come and see – you're bound to be conquered.

When to Go

Rome

°C/°F **Temp** — **Rainfall** inches/mm

40/104 – 30/86 – 20/68 – 10/50 – 0/32 – -10/14

6/150 – 4/100 – 2/50 – 0

J F M A M J J A S O N D

Apr & May Perfect spring temperatures and blooming wildflowers make hikers happy.

Jul Summer means beach weather and a packed festival calendar.

Oct Enjoy mild temperatures, autumn cuisine and the *vendemmia* (grape harvest).

AT A GLANCE

- **Currency** euro (€)
- **Language** Italian
- **Money** ATMs widespread; credit cards widely accepted
- **Visas** Schengen rules apply

Fast Facts

- **Area** 301,230 sq km
- **Capital** Rome
- **Country code** ☎39
- **Emergency** ☎112

Exchange Rates

Australia	A$1	€0.82
Canada	C$1	€0.77
Japan	¥100	€0.83
New Zealand	NZ$1	€0.65
UK	UK£1	€1.18
USA	US$1	€0.78

Set Your Budget

- **Budget hotel room** €50–110
- **Two-course meal** €20–40 (pizza €10–15)
- **Museum entrance** €6.50–15
- **Beer** €2.50–5
- **Intercity train ticket** €12–80

Resources

- **Delicious Italy** (www.deliciousitaly.com) For foodies.
- **Italia** (www.italia.it) Official tourism site.
- **Lonely Planet** (www.lonelyplanet.com/italy) Destination information, hotel bookings, travellers forum and more.

Connections

Milan and Venice are northern Italy's two main transport hubs. From Milan, trains run to cities across Western Europe, including Paris, Geneva and Zürich. Venice is better placed for Eastern Europe, with rail connections to Ljubljana, Zagreb, Belgrade and Vienna. You can also pick up ferries in Venice for Croatia. Down the east coast, there are ferries from Bari to various Greek ports, as well as to Bar and Dubrovnik. Ferries to Barcelona leave from Genoa, and ferries to Tunis from both Genoa and Palermo.

ITINERARIES

One Week

A one-week whistle-stop tour of Italy is enough to take in the country's three most famous cities. After a couple of days exploring Venice's unique canal-scape, head south to Florence, Italy's great Renaissance city. Two days will whet your appetite for the artistic and architectural treasures waiting to be discovered on your final days in Rome.

Two Weeks

After the first week, continue south for some sea and southern passion. Spend a day dodging traffic in Naples, a day investigating the ruins at Pompeii and a day or two admiring the Amalfi Coast. Then backtrack to Naples for a ferry to Palermo and the gastronomic delights of Sicily, or to Cagliari and Sardinia's magical beaches.

Essential Food & Drink

- **Pizza** Two varieties: Roman, with a thin crispy base; and Neapolitan, with a higher, more doughy base. The best are always prepared in a *forno a legna* (wood-fired oven).
- **Gelato** Popular ice-cream flavours include *fragola* (strawberry), *nocciola* (hazelnut) and *stracciatella* (milk with chocolate shavings).
- **Wine** Ranges from big-name reds such as Piedmont's Barolo to light whites from Sardinia and sparkling *prosecco* from the Veneto.
- **Caffè** Join the locals for a morning cappuccino or post-lunch espresso, both taken standing at a bar.

Italy Highlights

1. Face up to iconic monuments in Italy's mesmerising capital, **Rome** (p730)
2. Take to the water and cruise past palaces, churches and piazzas in **Venice** (p772)
3. Explore the Renaissance time capsule of **Florence** (p788)
4. Feast on foodie delights and medieval architecture in hedonistic **Bologna** (p784)
5. Explore ancient rock dwellings in **Matera** (p820)
6. Taste the world's best pizza in **Naples** (p808)
7. Admire glorious Gothic architecture and Renaissance art in **Siena** (p801)
8. Visit regal palaces, magnificent museums and historic cafes in **Turin** (p764)
9. Take in an open-air opera in **Verona** (p770), one of Italy's most romantic cities.
10. Enjoy a bike ride and picnic atop the medieval city walls in **Lucca** (p803).

ROME

POP 2.76 MILLION

Even in this country of exquisite cities, Rome is special. Pulsating, seductive and utterly disarming, the Italian capital is an epic, monumental metropolis that will steal your heart and haunt your soul. They say a lifetime's not enough *(Roma, non basta una vita)*, but even on a short visit you'll be swept off your feet by its artistic and architectural masterpieces, its operatic piazzas, romantic corners and cobbled lanes. Yet while history reverberates all around, modern life is lived to the full – priests in designer shades walk through the Vatican talking into smartphones, scooters scream through medieval alleyways, fashionable drinkers sip *aperitivi* on baroque piazzas. It's this intoxicating mix of past and present, of style and urban grit, that makes Rome such a rich and compelling place.

History

According to legend Rome was founded by Romulus and Remus in 753 BC. Historians debate this, but archaeological evidence has confirmed the existence of a settlement on the Palatine Hill in that period.

The city was originally ruled by a king, but in 509 BC the Roman Republic was founded. Over the next five centuries the Republic flourished, growing to become the dominant force in the Western world. The end came in the 1st century BC when internal rivalries led to the murder of Julius Caesar in 44 BC and the outbreak of civil war between Octavian and Mark Antony. Octavian emerged victorious and was made Rome's first emperor with the title Augustus.

By AD 100 Rome had a population of 1.5 million and was the *caput mundi* (Capital of the World), but by the 5th century decline had set in. In 476 Romulus Augustulus, the last emperor of the Western Roman Empire, was deposed.

By this time Rome's Christian roots had taken hold. Christianity had been spreading since the 1st century AD, and under Constantine it received official recognition. Pope Gregory I (590–604) did much to strengthen the Church's grip over the city, laying the foundations for its later role as capital of the Catholic Church.

Under the Renaissance popes of the 15th and 16th centuries, Rome was given an extensive facelift. But trouble was never far away and in 1527 the city was sacked by Spanish forces under Charles V.

ROMA PASS

The **Roma Pass** (www.romapass.it; 3 days €30) provides free admission to two museums or sites (choose from a list of 45), as well as reduced entry to extra sites, unlimited city transport and discounted entry to other exhibitions and events. Valid for three days, it's available online or from tourist information points and participating museums.

By the 17th century Rome needed rebuilding, and turned to baroque masters Bernini and Borromini. With their exuberant churches, fountains and *palazzi* (palaces), these two bitter rivals changed the face of the city. A building boom following the declaration of Rome as the capital of a newly-unified Italy also profoundly influenced the look of the city, as did Mussolini and post-WWII expansion.

Sights

Most of Rome's sights are concentrated in the area between Stazione Termini and the Vatican. Halfway between the two, the Pantheon and Piazza Navona lie at the heart of the *centro storico* (historic centre), while to the southeast, the Colosseum lords it over the city's ancient core.

ANCIENT ROME

Colosseum AMPHITHEATRE

(Map p736; 06 399 67 700; www.coopculture.it; Piazza del Colosseo; adult/reduced/EU child incl Roman Forum & Palatino €12/7.50/free, audioguide €5.50; 8.30am-1hr before sunset; M Colosseo) Rome's great gladiatorial arena is the most thrilling of its ancient sights. Originally known as the Flavian Amphitheatre, the 50,000-seat Colosseum was started by Emperor Vespasian in AD 72 and finished by his son Titus in AD 80. It was clad in travertine and covered by a huge canvas awning that was held aloft by 240 masts. Inside, tiered seating encircled the sand-covered arena, itself built over underground chambers (known as the hypogeum) where animals were caged and elaborate stage sets prepared. Games involved gladiators fighting wild animals or each other, but, contrary to Hollywood folklore, bouts rarely ended in death.

The top tier and hypogeum can be visited on guided tours (€6 or €8 for both), which must be booked in advance, either at www.pierreci.it or by calling 06 399 67 700.

ROME IN...

Two Days

Get to grips with ancient Rome at the **Colosseum**, the **Roman Forum** and the **Palatino**. Spend the afternoon exploring the **Capitoline Museums** before an evening in **Trastevere**. On day two, hit the **Vatican**. Marvel at **St Peter's Basilica** and the **Sistine Chapel** in the **Vatican Museums**. Afterwards, ditch your guidebook and get happily lost in the animated streets around **Piazza Navona** and the **Pantheon**.

Four Days

With another couple of days, book a visit to the outstanding **Museo e Galleria Borghese** and check out **Piazza del Popolo**, the **Spanish Steps** and **Trevi Fountain**. Venture out to **Via Appia Antica** to explore the catacombs, and, if you can handle more art, take in the **Galleria Doria Pamphilj** and **Museo Nazionale Romano: Palazzo Massimo alle Terme**. In the evenings, sip in style in the bohemian **Monti** district or let your hair down with a concert at the **Auditorium Parco della Musica**.

West of the Colosseum, the **Arco di Costantino** (Map p736; MColosseo) was built to celebrate Constantine's victory over rival Maxentius at the battle of Milvian Bridge in AD 312.

Palatino RUINS

(Palatine Hill; Map p736; 06 399 67 700; www.coopculture.it; Via di San Gregorio 30; adult/reduced/EU child incl Colosseum & Roman Forum €12/7.50/free, audioguide €5; 8.30am-1hr before sunset; MColosseo) Rising above the Roman Forum, the Palatine Hill is where Romulus supposedly killed his twin Remus and founded the city in 753 BC. Archaeological evidence can't prove the legend, but it has dated human habitation here to the 8th century BC. Later, the Palatine was Rome's most exclusive neighbourhood and the emperor Augustus lived here all his life. After Rome's fall, it fell into disrepair, and in the Middle Ages churches and castles were built over the ruins and wealthy Renaissance families established gardens here.

Most of the area is covered by the ruins of Emperor Domitian's vast complex, which served as the main imperial palace for 300 years. Divided into the **Domus Flavia** (Imperial Palace), **Domus Augustana** (Emperor's Residence) and a **stadio** (Stadium), it was built in the 1st century AD.

Among the best-preserved buildings on the Palatine Hill is the **Casa di Livia**, home of Augustus' wife Livia, and, in front, Augustus' separate residence, the frescoed **Casa di Augusto** (11am-3.30pm Mon, Wed, Sat & Sun).

For grandstand views over the Roman Forum, head to the **Orti Farnesiani** gardens in the north of the complex.

Roman Forum RUINS

(Foro Romano; Map p736; 06 399 67 700; www.coopculture.it; Largo della Salara Vecchia; adult/reduced/EU child incl Colosseum & Palatino €12/7.50/free, audioguide €5; 8.30am-1hr before sunset) Now a collection of fascinating, if rather confusing, ruins, the Roman Forum was ancient Rome's showpiece centre, a grandiose district of temples, basilicas and vibrant public spaces. Originally an Etruscan burial ground, the area was first developed in the 7th century BC, and became the social, political and commercial heart of the Roman world. Its importance declined after the fall of the Roman Empire, until eventually the site was used as pasture land and plundered for marble.

As you enter from Largo della Salara Vecchia, ahead to your left is the **Tempio di Antonino e Faustina** (Map p736), built by the senate in AD 141 and transformed into a

COLOSSEUM TIPS

Follow these tips to beat the queues:

» Buy your ticket from the Palatine entrance (about 250m away at Via di San Gregorio 30) or the Roman Forum (Largo della Salara Vecchia).

» Get the Roma Pass, which is valid for three days and a whole host of sites.

» Book your ticket online at www.coopculture.it (plus booking fee of €1.50).

» Join an official English-language tour – €5 on top of the regular Colosseum ticket price.

Rome

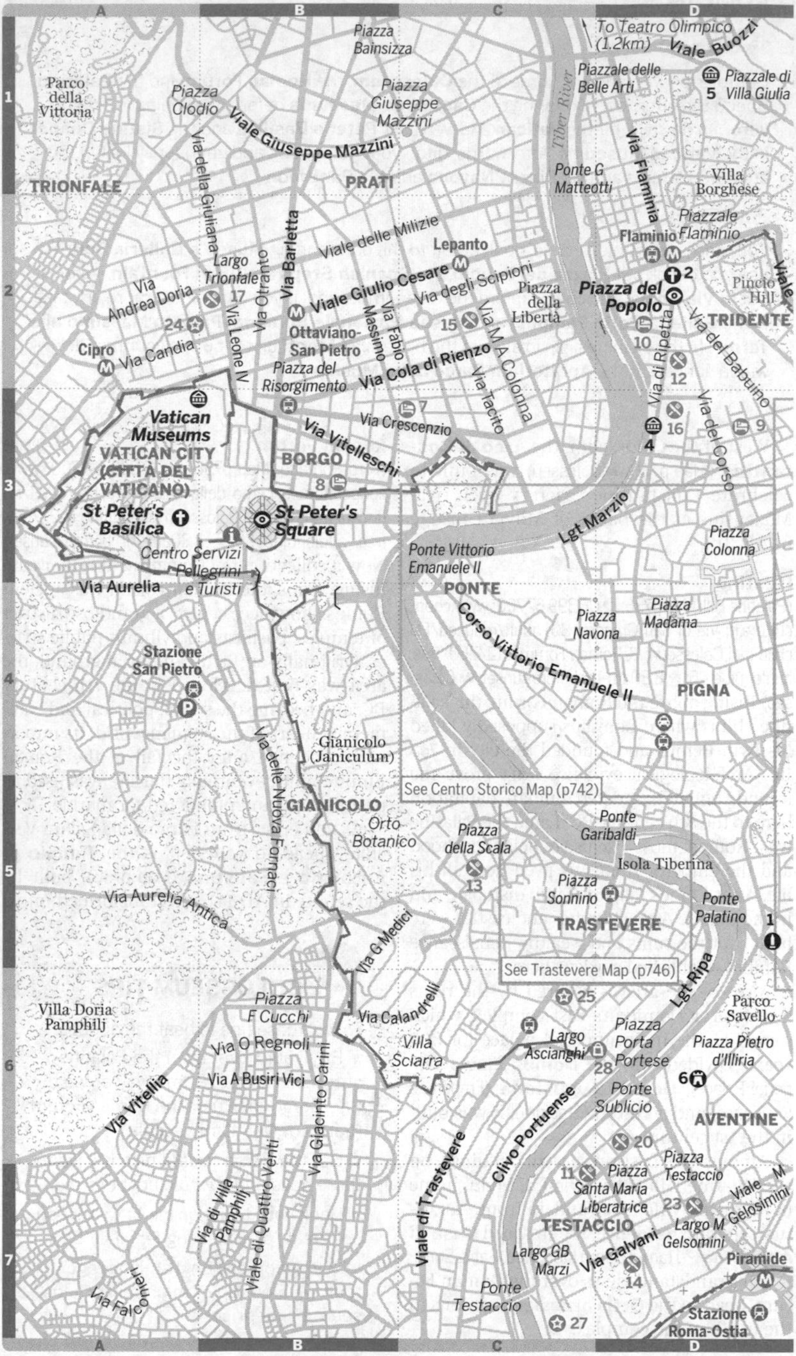

A B C D
1 2 3 4 5 6 7

Piazza Bainsizza
To Teatro Olimpico (1.2km)
Viale Buozzi
Parco della Vittoria
Piazza Clodio
Piazza Giuseppe Mazzini
Viale Giuseppe Mazzini
Piazzale delle Belle Arti
Tiber River
5 Piazzale di Villa Giulia
TRIONFALE
Via della Giuliana
PRATI
Via Flaminia
Ponte G Matteotti
Villa Borghese
Via Barletta
Viale delle Milizie
Piazzale Flaminio
Flaminio
Largo Trionfale
Via Otranto
Lepanto
Via Andrea Doria
17
Viale Giulio Cesare
Via degli Scipioni
2
Piazza della Libertà
Piazza del Popolo
Pincio Hill
Viale
24
Via Leone IV
Ottaviano-San Pietro
Via Fabio Massimo
15
Via M A Colonna
TRIDENTE
Cipro
Via Candia
Via Cola di Rienzo
10
Via di Ripetta
Via del Babuino
Piazza del Risorgimento
12
Via Tacito
Vatican Museums
7
Via Crescenzio
16
Via del Corso
9
4
VATICAN CITY (CITTÀ DEL VATICANO)
Via Vitelleschi
BORGO
8
St Peter's Basilica
St Peter's Square
Lgt Marzio
Piazza Colonna
Centro Servizi Pellegrini e Turisti
Ponte Vittorio Emanuele II
Via Aurelia
PONTE
Piazza Navona
Piazza Madama
Corso Vittorio Emanuele II
Stazione San Pietro
PIGNA
Via delle Nuova Fornaci
Gianicolo (Janiculum)
See Centro Storico Map (p742)
GIANICOLO
Orto Botanico
Piazza della Scala
Ponte Garibaldi
13
Isola Tiberina
Piazza Sonnino
Via Aurelia Antica
Ponte Palatino
TRASTEVERE
1
Via G Medici
See Trastevere Map (p746)
25
Lgt Ripa
Villa Doria Pamphilj
Piazza F Cucchi
Via Calandrelli
Parco Savello
Via O Regnoli
Villa Sciarra
Largo Ascianghi
Piazza Porta Portese
Piazza Pietro d'Illiria
28
Via A Busiri Vici
Via Giacinto Carini
6
Via Vitellia
Clivo Portuense
Ponte Sublicio
AVENTINE
Viale di Trastevere
20
Piazza Testaccio
11
Piazza Santa Maria Liberatrice
Via di Villa Pamphilj
Viale di Quattro Venti
23
Viale M Gelsomini
TESTACCIO
Largo M Gelsomini
Largo GB Marzi
Via Galvani
Piramide
14
Via Falconieri
Ponte Testaccio
27
Stazione Roma-Ostia

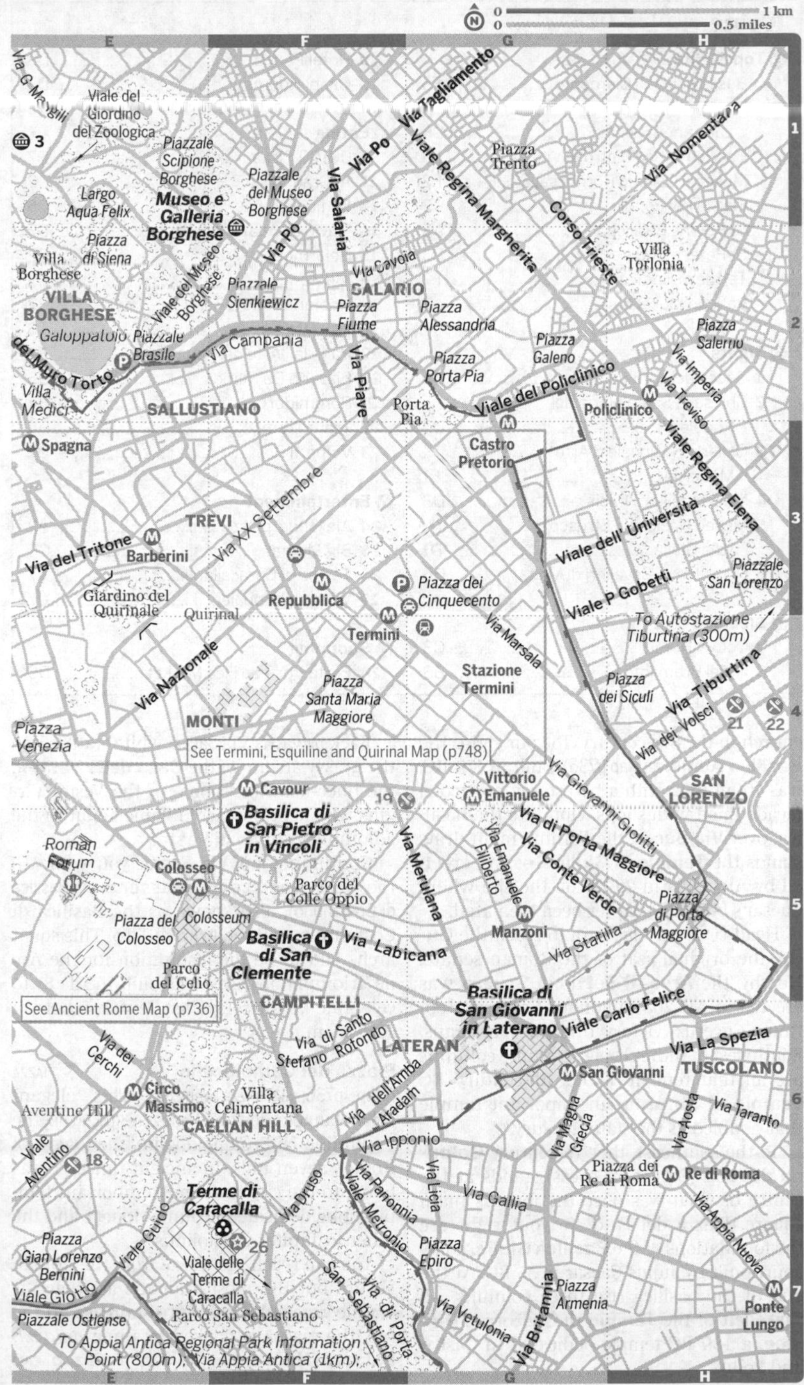
Museo e Galleria Borghese
Villa Borghese
Sallustiano
Trevi
Monti
Salario
Policlinico
Castro Pretorio
Stazione Termini
San Lorenzo
Basilica di San Pietro in Vincoli
Basilica di San Clemente
Basilica di San Giovanni in Laterano
Campitelli
Lateran
Tuscolano
Caelian Hill
Aventine Hill
Terme di Caracalla
Roman Forum
Colosseo
Colosseum
Repubblica
Termini
Barberini
Spagna
Cavour
Vittorio Emanuele
Manzoni
San Giovanni
Circo Massimo
Re di Roma
Ponte Lungo
Via Nomentana
Via Salaria
Via Po
Viale Regina Margherita
Corso Trieste
Viale del Policlinico
Viale Regina Elena
Viale dell' Università
Viale P Gobetti
Via Tiburtina
Via XX Settembre
Via del Tritone
Via Nazionale
Via Merulana
Via Labicana
Via di Porta Maggiore
Via Conte Verde
Via Giovanni Giolitti
Viale Carlo Felice
Via La Spezia
Via Appia Nuova
Via Ipponio
Via Gallia
Via Britannia
See Termini, Esquiline and Quirinal Map (p748)
See Ancient Rome Map (p736)
To Autostazione Tiburtina (300m)
To Appia Antica Regional Park Information Point (800m); Via Appia Antica (1km);
0 1 km
0 0.5 miles

Rome

Top Sights

Basilica di San Clemente F5
Basilica di San Giovanni in Laterano G6
Basilica di San Pietro in Vincoli F5
Museo e Galleria Borghese F2
Piazza del Popolo D2
St Peter's Basilica A3
St Peter's Square B3
Terme di Caracalla F7
Vatican Museums A3

Sights

1 Bocca della Verità D5
2 Chiesa di Santa Maria del Popolo D2
3 Galleria Nazionale d'Arte Moderna E1
4 Museo dell'Ara Pacis D3
5 Museo Nazionale Etrusco di Villa Giulia D1
6 Priorato dei Cavalieri di Malta D6

Sleeping

7 Colors Hotel C3
8 Hotel Bramante B3
9 Hotel Panda D3
10 Okapi Rooms D2

Eating

11 00100 Pizza C7
12 Al Gran Sasso D2
13 Da Lucia C5
14 Flavio al Velavevodetto D7
15 Gelarmony C2
16 'Gusto D3
17 Hostaria Dino & Tony B2
18 Il Gelato E6
19 Panella l'Arte del Pane F4
20 Pizzeria Da Remo D6
21 Pommidoro H4
22 Tram Tram H4
23 Volpetti Più D7

Entertainment

24 Alexanderplatz A2
25 Big Mama C6
26 Terme di Caracalla F7
27 Villaggio Globale C7

Shopping

28 Porta Portese Flea Market D6

church in the 8th century. To your right, the **Basilica Aemilia** (Map p736), built in 179 BC, was 100m long with a two-storey porticoed facade lined with shops. Opposite the basilica, over **Via Sacra**, the Forum's main drag, stands the **Tempio di Giulio Cesare**, erected by Augustus in 29 BC on the site where Caesar's body had earlier been cremated.

Head right up Via Sacra to reach the **Curia**, the original seat of the Roman senate. Nearby, the **Arco di Settimio Severo** was erected in AD 203 to honour Emperor Septimus Severus' victory over the Parthians. Southwest of the arch, eight granite columns are all that remain of the 5th-century BC **Tempio di Saturno**, an important temple that doubled as the state treasury.

To the southeast, the 7th-century **Colonna di Foca** (Column of Phocus) stands at the centre of what was once the forum's main square, Piazza del Foro. To your right are the foundations of the **Basilica Giulia**, a law court built by Julius Caesar in 55 BC. At the end of the basilica rise three columns, all that's left of the **Tempio di Castore e Polluce**, a 489 BC temple dedicated to Castor and Pollux.

Back towards Via Sacra, white statues line the grassy atrium of the **Casa delle Vestali**, the once-luxurious home of the Vestal Virgins who kept the sacred flame alight in the adjoining **Tempio di Vesta**.

Continuing up Via Sacra, you come to the vast **Basilica di Massenzio** (Basilica di Costantino), also known as the Basilica di Costantino, and the **Arco di Tito**. This squat arch, said to be the inspiration for the Arc de Triomphe in Paris, was built in AD 81 to celebrate victories against Jewish rebels in Jerusalem.

Piazza del Campidoglio PIAZZA

(Map p736; Piazza Venezia) This elegant Michelangelo-designed piazza sits atop the Capitoline Hill (Campidoglio), the lowest of Rome's seven hills. In ancient times, it was home to the city's two most important temples: one dedicated to Juno Moneta and the other to Jupiter Capitolinus.

You can reach the piazza from the Roman Forum but the most dramatic approach is via the graceful **Cordonata** staircase. At the top, the piazza is flanked by three *palazzi:* **Palazzo Nuovo** on the left, **Palazzo dei**

Conservatori on the right, and **Palazzo Senatorio**, seat of Rome's City Hall since 1143. In the centre, the bronze **statue of Marcus Aurelius** is a copy; the original is in the Capitoline Museums.

Capitoline Museums MUSEUM

(Musei Capitolini; Map p736; ☎06 06 08; www.museicapitolini.org; Piazza del Campidoglio 1; adult/reduced/child €9.50/7.50/free plus possible exhibition supplement, audioguide €5; ⊙9am-8pm Tue-Sun, last admission 7pm; 🚌Piazza Venezia) Housed in Palazzo dei Conservatori and Palazzo Nuovo on Piazza del Campidoglio, the Capitoline Museums are the world's oldest public museums, dating to 1471. Their collection of classical art is one of Italy's finest, including masterpieces such as the *Lupa Capitolina* (Capitoline Wolf), a sculpture of Romulus and Remus under a wolf, and the *Galata morente* (Dying Gaul), a moving depiction of a dying Gaul. The rich 2nd-floor **pinacoteca** (picture gallery) contains paintings by the likes of Titian, Tintoretto, Van Dyck, Rubens and Caravaggio.

Chiesa di Santa Maria in Aracoeli CHURCH

(Map p736; Piazza Santa Maria in Aracoeli; ⊙9am-12.30pm & 2.30-5.30pm; 🚌Piazza Venezia) Marking the highest point of the Campidoglio, this 6th-century church sits on the site of the Roman temple to Juno Moneta. According to legend it was here that the Tiburtine Sybil told Augustus of the coming birth of Christ, and the church still has a strong association with the nativity.

FREE **Il Vittoriano** MONUMENT

(Map p736; Piazza Venezia; ⊙9.30am-5.30pm summer, to 4.30pm winter; 🚌Piazza Venezia) Love it or loathe it as most locals do, you can't ignore Il Vittoriano (aka the *Altare della Patria;* Altar of the Fatherland), the massive mountain of marble that looms over Piazza Venezia. Begun in 1885 to honour Italy's first king, Vittorio Emanuele II, it incorporates the **Tomb of the Unknown Soldier** and the **Museo Centrale del Risorgimento** (Map p736; Via di San Pietro in Carcere; admission free; ⊙9.30am-6.30pm; 🚌Piazza Venezia), documenting Italian unification. At the back, a **panoramic lift** (Map p736; adult/reduced €7/3.50; ⊙9.30am-6.30pm Mon-Thu, to 7.30pm Fri-Sun) whisks you up to the top for Rome's best 360-degree views.

Over the square, the 15th-century **Palazzo Venezia** (Map p748; Piazza Venezia; 🚌Piazza Venezia) was the first of Rome's great Renaissance *palazzi*. Mussolini had his office here and there's now a museum of medieval and Renaissance art.

Mercati di Traiano Museo dei Fori Imperiali MUSEUM

(Map p748; ☎06 06 08; www.mercatiditraiano.it; Via IV Novembre 94; adult/reduced €9.50/7.50, plus possible exhibition supplement; ⊙9am-7pm Tue-Sun, last admission 6pm; 🚌Via IV Novembre) This striking museum brings to life the **Mercati di Traiano**, emperor Trajan's great 2nd-century market complex. From the main hallway, a lift whisks you up to the **Torre delle Milizie** (Militia Tower), a 13th-century red-brick tower, and the upper levels of the vast three-storey semi-circular construction that once housed hundreds of market traders.

Bocca della Verità MONUMENT

(Map p732; Piazza Bocca della Verità 18; donation €0.50; ⊙9.30am-4.50pm winter, to 5.50pm summer; 🚌Piazza Bocca della Verità) A mask-shaped round marble disc that was once part of an ancient fountain, or possibly an ancient manhole cover, the Mouth of Truth is one of Rome's great curiosities. According to legend, if you put your hand in the carved mouth and tell a lie, it will bite your hand off.

The mouth is in the portico of the **Chiesa di Santa Maria in Cosmedin**, one of Rome's most beautiful medieval churches.

THE VATICAN

The world's smallest sovereign state – it covers just 0.44 sq km – the Vatican is the modern vestige of the Papal States. This papal empire encompassed Rome and much of central Italy for more than a thousand years until it was forcibly incorporated into the Italian state during unification in 1861. Relations between Italy and the landless papacy remained strained until 1929 when Mussolini and Pope Pius XI signed the Lateran Treaty, formally establishing the Vatican State.

Ancient Rome

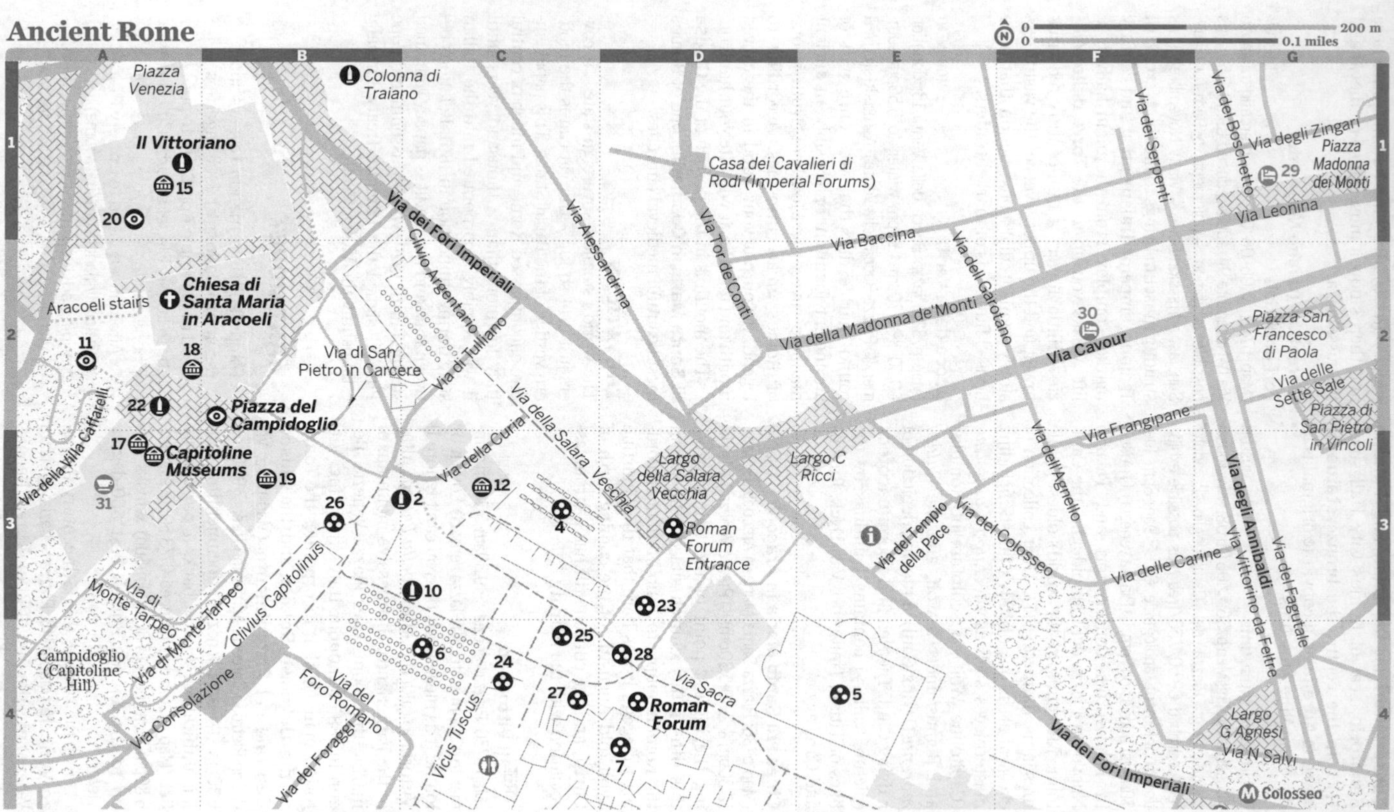

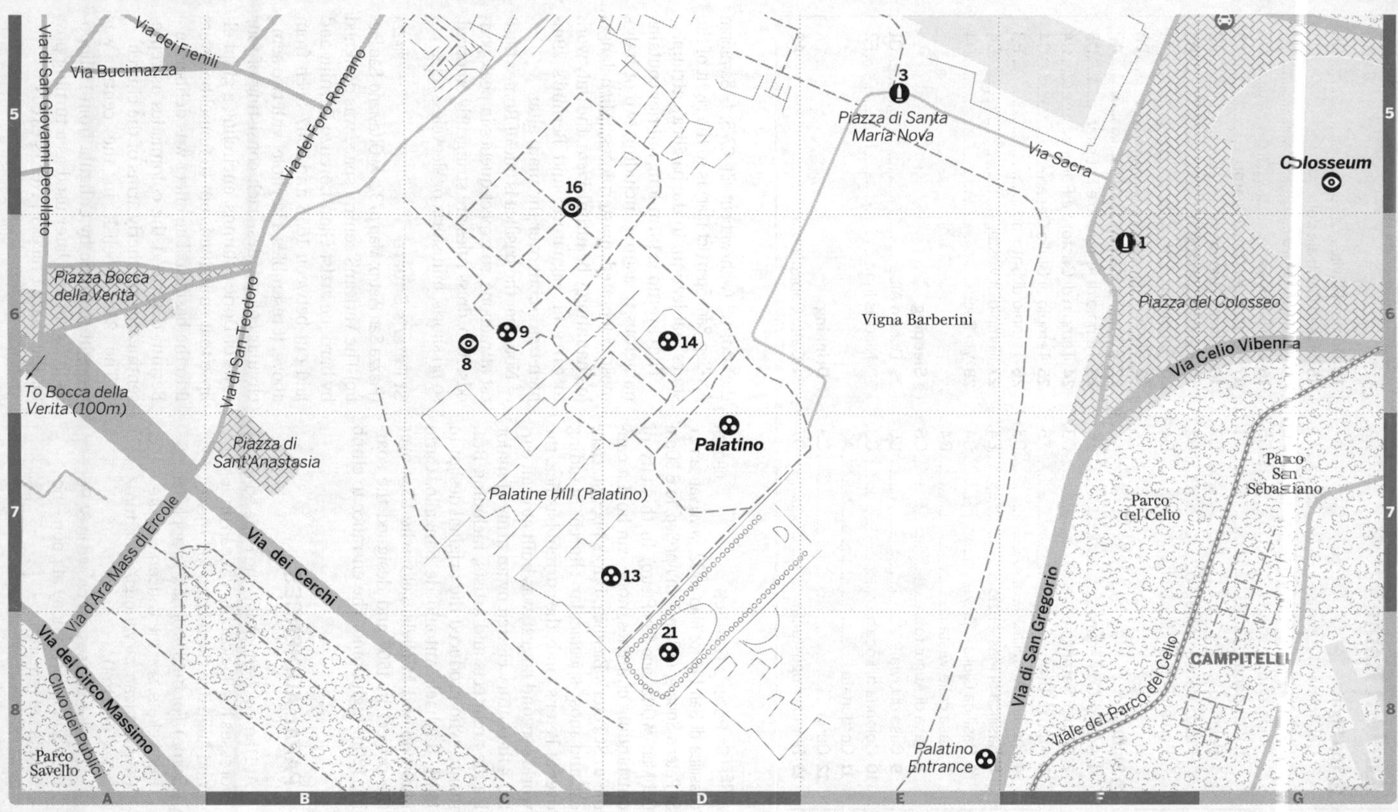

Via di San Giovanni Decollato
Via Bucimazza
Via dei Fienili
Via del Foro Romano
Piazza Bocca della Verità
To Bocca della Verita (100m)
Via di San Teodoro
Piazza di Sant'Anastasia
Via d Ara Mass di Ercole
Via dei Cerchi
Via del Circo Massimo
Clivo dei Publici
Parco Savello
16
9
8
14
Palatino
Palatine Hill (Palatino)
13
21
3
Piazza di Santa Maria Nova
Via Sacra
Vigna Barberini
Palatino Entrance
Via di San Gregorio
Colosseum
1
Piazza del Colosseo
Via Celio Vibenna
Parco del Celio
Parco San Sebastiano
CAMPITELLI
Viale del Parco del Celio

Ancient Rome

Top Sights

Capitoline Museums ... A3
Chiesa di Santa Maria in Aracoeli ... A2
Colosseum ... G5
Il Vittoriano ... A1
Palatino ... D7
Piazza del Campidoglio ... B2
Roman Forum ... D4

Sights

1 Arco di Costantino ... F6
2 Arco di Settimio Severo ... C3
3 Arco di Tito ... E5
4 Basilica Aemilia ... C3
5 Basilica di Massenzio ... E4
6 Basilica Giulia ... C4
7 Casa delle Vestali ... D4
8 Casa di Augusto ... C6
9 Casa di Livia ... C6
10 Colonna di Foca ... C3
11 Cordonata ... A2
12 Curia ... C3
13 Domus Augustana ... D7
14 Domus Flavia ... D6
15 Museo Centrale del Risorgimento ... A1
16 Orti Farnesiani ... C5
17 Palazzo dei Conservatori ... A3
18 Palazzo Nuovo ... A2
19 Palazzo Senatorio ... B3
20 Panoramic Lift ... A1
21 Stadio ... D8
22 Statue of Marcus Aurelius ... A2
23 Tempio di Antonino e Faustina ... D3
24 Tempio di Castore e Polluce ... C4
25 Tempio di Giulio Cesare ... C4
26 Tempio di Saturno ... B3
27 Tempio di Vesta ... C4
28 Via Sacra ... D4

Sleeping

29 Duca d'Alba ... G1
30 Nicolas Inn ... F2

Drinking

31 Caffè Capitolino ... A3

FREE St Peter's Basilica CHURCH

(Basilica di San Pietro; Map p732; www.vatican.va; St Peter's Square; 7am-7pm Apr-Sep, to 6.30pm Oct-Mar; M Ottaviano-San Pietro) In this city of outstanding churches, none can hold a candle to St Peter's Basilica, Italy's biggest, richest and most spectacular church. Standing over St Peter's tomb, the current basilica, the world's second largest, was built atop an earlier 4th-century church by an army of major league architects and artists, including Bramante, who produced the original design in 1506, Raphael, Antonio de Sangallo, Carlo Maderno and Michelangelo, who took over the project in 1507 and designed the soaring 120m-high dome. The entrance to climb the **dome** (with/without lift €7/5; 8am-6pm Apr-Sep, 8am-5pm Oct-Mar) is to the right of the stairs that lead up to the basilica's atrium.

The cavernous 187m-long interior contains numerous treasures, including two of Italy's most celebrated masterpieces: Michelangelo's hauntingly beautiful *Pietà,* the only work to carry his signature; and Bernini's 29m-high **baldachin** over the main altar.

Note that the basilica is one of Rome's busiest attractions, so expect queues in peak periods. Also, dress rules are stringently enforced, so no shorts, miniskirts or sleeveless tops.

PAPAL AUDIENCES

At 11am on Wednesday, the Pope addresses his flock at the Vatican (in July and August in Castel Gandolfo near Rome). For details of how to apply for free tickets, see the Vatican website (www.vatican.va/various/prefettura/index_en.html).

He also blesses the crowd in St Peter's Square on Sunday at noon – no tickets are required.

St Peter's Square PIAZZA

(Piazza San Pietro; Map p732; M Ottaviano-San Pietro) The Vatican's central space was designed by baroque artist Gian Lorenzo Bernini and laid out between 1656 and 1667. Seen from above, it resembles a keyhole with two semicircular colonnades, each consisting of four rows of Doric columns, encircling a giant ellipse that straightens out to funnel believers into the basilica. The effect was deliberate – Bernini described the colonnades as representing 'the motherly arms of the church'.

The 25m obelisk in the centre was brought to Rome by Caligula from Heliopolis in Egypt and later used as a turning post for the chariot races in Nero's circus.

Vatican Museums MUSEUM

(Musei Vaticani; Map p732; ☎06 698 84 676; http://mv.vatican.va; Viale Vaticano; adult/reduced/child €16/8/free, admission free last Sun of month; ⏰9am-6pm Mon-Sat, last admission 4pm, 9am-2pm last Sun of month, last admission 12.30pm; Ⓜ Ottaviano-San Pietro) Boasting one of the world's great art collections, the Vatican Museums are housed in the Palazzo Apostolico Vaticano, a vast 5.5-hectare complex comprising two palaces and three internal courtyards. You'll never cover it all in one day – there are about 7km of exhibits – so it pays to be selective.

For spectacular classical statuary, head to the **Museo Pio-Clementino**, home to the peerless *Apollo Belvedere* and the 1st-century *Laocoön,* both in the Cortile Ottagono (Octagonal Courtyard). Further on, beyond the magnificent **Galleria delle Carte Geografiche** (Map Gallery), are the **Stanze di Raffaello** (Raphael Rooms). These were once the private apartments of Pope Julius II, and are adorned with frescos by Raphael and his students, including Raphael's great masterpiece *La Scuola di Atene* (The School of Athens) in the Stanza della Segnatura.

From the Raphael Rooms, it's a short walk on to the **Sistine Chapel** (Cappella Sistina), the museums' grand finale. This soaring 15th-century chapel, where the papal conclave is locked to elect the pope, is home to two of the world's most celebrated works of art – Michelangelo's ceiling frescos and his *Giudizio Universale* (Last Judgment). The chapel was originally built in 1484 for Pope Sixtus IV, after whom it was named, but it was Julius II who commissioned Michelangelo to decorate it in 1508. Over the next four years, the artist painted the entire 800-sq-metre ceiling with episodes from the book of Genesis. Twenty-two years later he returned at the behest of Pope Clement VII to paint the *Last Judgment* on the 200-sq-metre west wall. The other walls of the chapel feature frescos produced by a crack team of Renaissance artists including Botticelli, Domenico Ghirlandaio, Pinturicchio and Luca Signorelli.

QUEUE JUMPING AT THE VATICAN MUSEUMS

To reduce waiting time:

» Book tickets at http://biglietteriamusei.vatican.va/musei/tickets (plus booking fee of €4).

» Time your visit: Wednesday mornings are good as everyone is at the Pope's weekly audience at St Peter's; on other days, afternoon is better than the morning; avoid Mondays, when many other museums are shut.

CENTRO STORICO

FREE **Pantheon** CHURCH

(Map p742; Piazza della Rotonda; audioguide €5; ⏰8.30am-7.30pm Mon-Sat, 9am-6pm Sun; 🚌Largo di Torre Argentina) A striking 2000-year-old temple, now church, the Pantheon is the best preserved of ancient Rome's great monuments. In its current form it dates to around AD 120 when the Emperor Hadrian built over Marcus Agrippa's original 27 BC temple (Agrippa's name remains inscribed on the pediment). The **dome**, considered the Romans' greatest architectural achievement, was the largest in the world until the 15th century and is still the largest unreinforced concrete dome ever built. It's a mind-boggling structure whose harmonious appearance is due to a precisely calibrated symmetry – its diameter is exactly equal to the Pantheon's interior height of 43.3m. Light (and rain, which drains away through 22 holes in the floor) enters through the **oculus**, an 8.7m opening that acts as a compression ring, absorbing and redistributing the dome's vast structural forces.

Inside, you'll find the tombs of Raphael and kings Vittorio Emanuele II and Umberto I.

Piazza Navona PIAZZA

(Map p742; 🚌Corso del Rinascimento) With its ornate fountains, baroque *palazzi,* pavement cafes and colourful cast of street artists, hawkers, tourists and pigeons, Piazza Navona is Rome's most celebrated square. Built over the ruins of the 1st-century Stadio di Domiziano (Domitian's Stadium), it was paved over in the 15th century and for almost 300 years hosted the city's main market.

Of the piazza's three fountains, the grand centrepiece is Gian Lorenzo Bernini's 1651 **Fontana dei Quattro Fiumi** (Fountain of the Four Rivers), a monumental ensemble representing the rivers Nile, Ganges, Danube and Plate.

Campo de' Fiori PIAZZA

(Map p742; 🚌Corso Vittorio Emanuele II) Noisy, colourful 'Il Campo' is a major focus of Roman life: by day it hosts a much-loved market, while at night it morphs into a raucous open-air pub. For centuries this was the site of public executions, and it was here that

VATICAN MUSEUMS ITINERARY

Follow this three-hour itinerary for the museums' greatest hits.

Cortile della Pigna First stop is this impressive courtyard, named after the huge Augustan-era bronze pine cone in the monumental niche. Cross the courtyard into the long corridor that is the Museo Chiaramonti and head left up the stairs.

Museo Pio-Clementino This stunning museum showcases some of the Vatican's finest classical statuary. Follow the flow of people through the Cortile Ottagono and push onto the Sala Croce Greca (Greek Cross Room) from where stairs lead up to the 1st floor of the Belvedere Palace.

Galleria dei Candelabri The Gallery of the Candelabra is the first of three galleries that run the length of the palace. It gets very crowded up here as you're funnelled through the Galleria degli Arazzi (Tapestry Gallery) and onto the striking Galleria delle Carte Geografiche (Map Gallery). At the end of the corridor, carry on through the Sala Sobieski to the Sala di Costantino, the first of the four Raphael Rooms.

Stanze di Raffaello (Raphael Rooms) Anywhere else these magnificent frescoed chambers would be the star attraction but here they're the warm-up for the grand finale, the Sistine Chapel. To get there, follow the one-way system past the modern art section and through the chapel's small and surprisingly discreet visitors' entrance.

Sistine Chapel Once in the chapel, head to the far wall for the best views of the frescos.

Castel Sant'Angelo (Map p742; ☎06 681 91 11; Lungotevere Castello 50; adult/reduced/EU child €8.50/6/free, plus possible exhibition supplement; ⏱9am-7.30pm Tue-Sun, last admission 6.30pm; 🚌Piazza Pia) An instantly recognisable landmark, this chunky round-keeped castle was built in the 2nd century AD as a mausoleum for the emperor Hadrian. It was converted into a papal fortress in the 6th century and now houses a museum with an assorted collection of sculptures, paintings, weapons and furniture. The terrace offers great views.

philosopher monk Giordano Bruno (the hooded figure in Ettore Ferrari's sinister statue) was burned at the stake for heresy in 1600.

Palazzo Farnese PALACE
(Map p742; www.inventerrome.com; Piazza Farnese; admission €5; ⏱guided tours 3pm, 4pm, 5pm Mon, Wed & Fri, advance booking obligatory; 🚌Corso Vittorio Emanuele II) One of Rome's most impressive Renaissance *palazzi,* now home to the French Embassy, this 16th-century palace was designed and built by a trio of top architects – Antonio da Sangallo the Younger, Michelangelo and Giacomo della Porta. Inside, the highlight is a series of frescos by Annibale Carracci, said by some to rival Michelangelo's in the Sistine Chapel. Visits are by guided tour only.

Galleria Doria Pamphilj MUSEUM
(Map p742; ☎06 679 73 23; www.dopart.it; Via del Corso 305; adult/reduced €11/7.50; ⏱9am-7pm, last admission 6pm; 🚌Piazza Venezia) Behind the grimy grey walls of Palazzo Doria Pamphilj is one of Rome's finest private art collections, with works by Raphael, Tintoretto, Brueghel, Titian, Caravaggio and Bernini. The undisputed highlight is the Velázquez portrait of Pope Innocent X, who grumbled that the portrait was 'too real'.

Trevi Fountain FOUNTAIN
(Fontana di Trevi; Map p748; Piazza di Trevi; Ⓜ Barberini) Immortalised by Anita Ekberg's sensual dip in Fellini's *La dolce vita,* the Trevi Fountain is Rome's largest and most famous fountain. The flamboyant ensemble was designed by Nicola Salvi in 1732 and depicts Neptune in a shell-shaped chariot being led by the Tritons and two sea horses representing the moods of the sea. The water comes from the *aqua virgo,* a 1st-century BC underground aqueduct, and the name 'Trevi' refers to the *tre vie* (three roads) that converge at the fountain.

The custom is to throw a coin into the fountain, thus ensuring your return to Rome. On average about €3000 is chucked away daily.

Galleria Nazionale d'Arte Antica: Palazzo Barberini GALLERY
(Map p748; ☎06 3 28 10; www.gebart.it; Via delle Quattro Fontane 13; adult/reduced €7/3.50, with Palazzo Corsini €9/4.50; ⏱8.30am-7pm Tue-Sun; Ⓜ Barberini) A must for anyone who's into Renaissance and baroque art, this sumpt

uous gallery is housed in Palazzo Barberini, one of Rome's most spectacular *palazzi*. Inside, you'll find works by Raphael, Caravaggio, Guido Reni, Bernini, Filippo Lippi and Holbein, as well as Pietro da Cortona's breathtaking *Trionfo della Divina Provvidenza* (Triumph of Divine Providence).

Spanish Steps ARCHITECTURE
(Map p748; Piazza di Spagna; MSpagna) Rising above Piazza di Spagna, the Spanish Steps, aka the Scalinata della Trinità dei Monti, have been a magnet for foreigners since the 18th century. The piazza was named after the Spanish embassy to the Holy See, although the staircase, which was built with French money in 1725, leads to the French church, **Chiesa della Trinità dei Monti** (Map p748; Piazza Trinità dei Monti; 6am-8pm Tue-Sun; MSpagna). At the foot of the steps, the fountain of a sinking boat, the **Barcaccia** (1627), is believed to be by Pietro Bernini, father of the more famous Gian Lorenzo. Opposite, Via dei Condotti is Rome's top shopping strip.

Piazza del Popolo PIAZZA
(Map p732; MFlaminio) This elegant landmark square was laid out in 1538 at the point of convergence of three roads – Via di Ripetta, Via del Corso and Via del Babuino – at what was then Rome's northern entrance. Guarding its southern approach are the twin 17th-century churches of **Santa Maria dei Miracoli** and **Santa Maria in Montesanto**, while on the northern flank is the **Porta del Popolo**, created by Bernini in 1655. The 36m-high obelisk in the centre was brought by Augustus from Heliopolis in ancient Egypt.

Chiesa di Santa Maria del Popolo CHURCH
(Map p732; Piazza del Popolo; 7.30am-noon & 4-7pm; MFlaminio) On the northern side of Piazza del Popolo stands one of Rome's earliest and richest Renaissance churches. The first chapel was built in 1099 to exorcise the ghost of Nero, who was buried on this spot and whose ghost was said to haunt the area, but its current form dates to 1472. Inside, the star attraction is the pair of Caravaggio masterpieces: the *Conversione di San Paolo* (Conversion of St Paul) and the *Crocifissione di San Pietro* (Crucifixion of St Peter).

TOP CHOICE **Museo dell'Ara Pacis** MUSEUM
(Map p732; 06 06 08; http://en.arapacis.it; Lungotevere in Augusta; adult/reduced €8.50/6.50; 9am-7pm Tue-Sun, last admission 6pm; MFlaminio) The first modern construction in Rome's historic centre since WWII, Richard Meier's white pavilion houses the **Ara Pacis Augustae** (Altar of Peace), one of the most important works of ancient Roman sculpture. The vast marble altar was completed in 13 BC as a monument to the peace that Augustus established both at home and abroad.

FREE THRILLS

Surprisingly, some of Rome's most famous sights are free:

- Trevi Fountain
- Spanish Steps
- Pantheon
- Bocca della Verità
- All churches, including St Peter's Basilica
- Vatican Museums on the last Sunday of the month

VILLA BORGHESE

Just north of the *centro storico*, Villa Borghese is Rome's best-known park. The grounds, which were created in the 17th century by Cardinal Scipione Borghese, are accessible from Piazzale Flaminio, Pincio Hill and the top of Via Vittorio Veneto. Bike hire is available at various points, typically costing €5 per hour.

TOP CHOICE **Museo e Galleria Borghese** MUSEUM
(Map p732; 06 3 28 10; www.galleriaborghese.it; Piazzale del Museo Borghese 5; adult/reduced €9/4.50, plus €2 booking fee and possible exhibition supplement; 9am-7pm Tue-Sun, pre-booking necessary; Via Pinciana) If you only have time, or inclination, for one art gallery in Rome, make it this one. Housing the 'queen of all private art collections', it boasts paintings by Caravaggio, Botticelli and Raphael, as well as some spectacular sculptures by Gian Lorenzo Bernini. There are highlights at every turn, but look out for Bernini's *Ratto di Proserpina* (Rape of Persephone) and *Apollo e Dafne;* Antonio Canova's *Venere vincitrice* (Conquering Venus); and the Caravaggios in room VIII.

Note that you'll need to pre-book your ticket and enter at an allotted time.

Museo Nazionale Etrusco di Villa Giulia MUSEUM
(Map p732; 06 322 65 71; www.villagiulia.beniculturali.it; Piazzale di Villa Giulia; adult/reduced/child €8/4/free; Villa Giulia 8.30am-7.30pm

Centro Storico

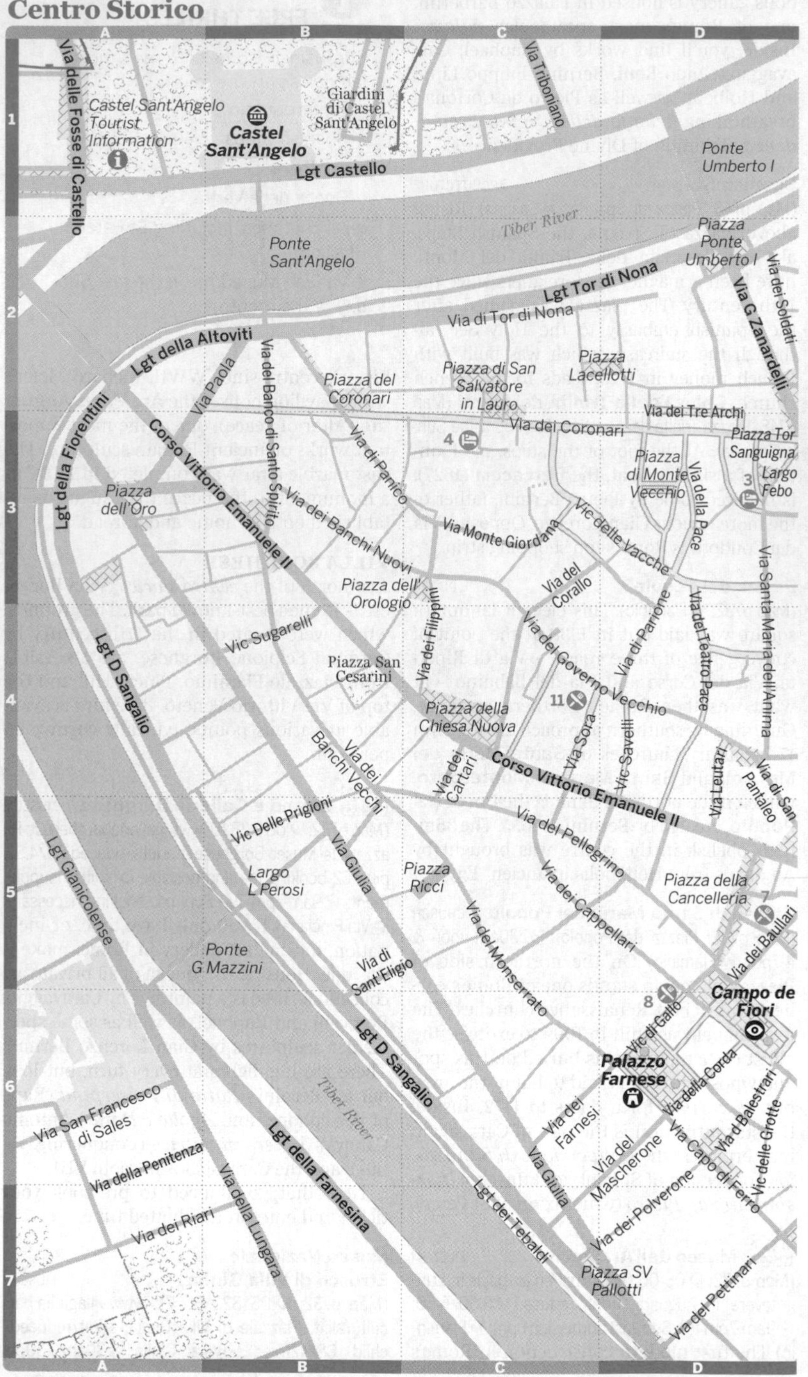

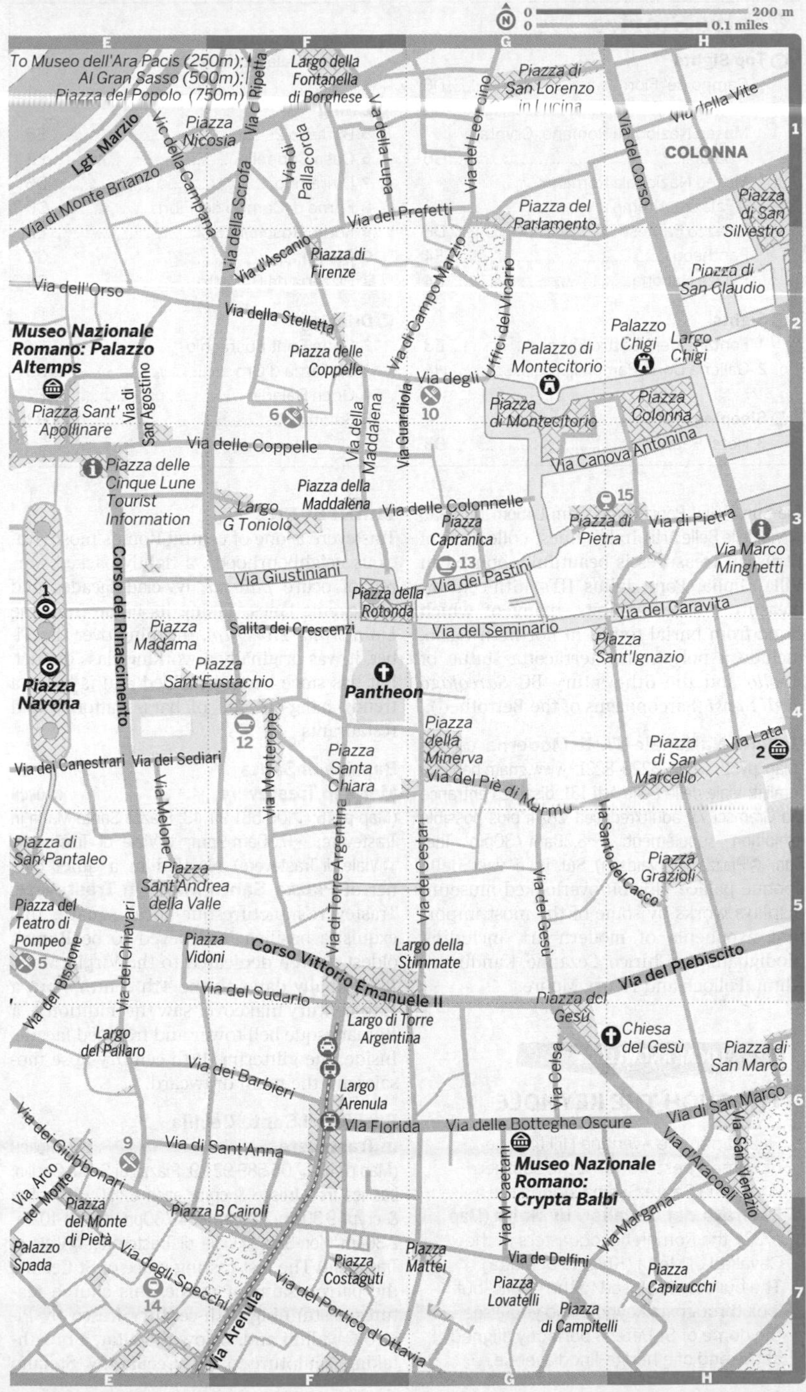

0 200 m
0 0.1 miles
E
F
G
H
To Museo dell'Ara Pacis (250m); Al Gran Sasso (500m); Piazza del Popolo (750m)
Largo della Fontanella di Borghese
Piazza di San Lorenzo in Lucina
Via della Vite
COLONNA
Lgt Marzio
Piazza Nicosia
Via di Ripetta
Vic della Campana
Via di Monte Brianzo
Via della Scrofa
Via di Pallacorda
V della Lupa
Via del Leoncino
Via del Corso
Piazza di San Silvestro
Via dei Prefetti
Piazza del Parlamento
Via d'Ascanio
Piazza di Firenze
Piazza di San Claudio
Via dell'Orso
Via di Campo Marzio
Uffici del Vicario
Via della Stelletta
Museo Nazionale Romano: Palazzo Altemps
Piazza delle Coppelle
Palazzo Chigi
Largo Chigi
Palazzo di Montecitorio
Via degli
10
Piazza di Montecitorio
Piazza Colonna
Piazza Sant' Apollinare
Via di San Agostino
6
Via della Maddalena
Via Guardiola
Via Canova Antonina
Via delle Coppelle
ITALY ROME
Piazza delle Cinque Lune Tourist Information
Piazza della Maddalena
Via delle Colonnelle
15
Largo G Toniolo
Piazza Capranica
Piazza di Pietra
Via di Pietra
Via Marco Minghetti
13
Via Giustiniani
Via dei Pastini
Piazza della Rotonda
Via del Caravita
1
Piazza Madama
Salita dei Crescenzi
Via del Seminario
Piazza Sant'Ignazio
Piazza Sant'Eustachio
Pantheon
Piazza Navona
Corso del Rinascimento
12
Via Monterone
Piazza della Minerva
Piazza di San Marcello
Via Lata
2
Via dei Canestrari
Via dei Sediari
Piazza Santa Chiara
Via del Piè di Marmo
Via Melone
Via di Torre Argentina
Via Santo del Cacco
Piazza di San Pantaleo
Via dei Cestari
Piazza Grazioli
Piazza Sant'Andrea della Valle
Via del Gesù
Piazza del Teatro di Pompeo
Via dei Chiavari
Piazza Vidoni
Largo della Stimmate
Corso Vittorio Emanuele II
Via del Plebiscito
5
Via del Biscione
Via del Sudario
Piazza del Gesù
Largo di Torre Argentina
Largo del Pallaro
Via Celsa
Chiesa del Gesù
Piazza di San Marco
Via dei Barbieri
Largo Arenula
Via di San Marco
Via dei Giubbonari
Via Florida
Via delle Botteghe Oscure
9
Via di Sant'Anna
Museo Nazionale Romano: Crypta Balbi
Via d'Aracoeli
Via San Venanzio
Via Arco del Monte
Piazza del Monte di Pietà
Piazza B Cairoli
Via M Caetani
Via Margana
Palazzo Spada
Via degli Specchi
Piazza Costaguti
Piazza Mattei
Via de Delfini
Piazza Capizucchi
14
Via Arenula
Via del Portico d'Ottavia
Piazza Lovatelli
Piazza di Campitelli

Centro Storico

Top Sights

Campo de' Fiori D6
Castel Sant'Angelo B1
Museo Nazionale Romano: Crypta Balbi G6
Museo Nazionale Romano: Palazzo Altemps E2
Palazzo Farnese D6
Pantheon F4
Piazza Navona E4

Sights

1 Fontana dei Quattro Fiumi E3
2 Galleria Doria Pamphilj H4

Sleeping

3 Hotel Raphaël D3
4 Relais Palazzo Taverna C3

Eating

5 Baffetto 2 ..... E5
6 Casa Coppelle F2
7 Ditirambo D5
8 Forno di Campo de' Fiori D6
9 Forno Roscioli E6
10 Giolitti G2
11 Pizzeria da Baffetto C4

Drinking

12 Caffè Sant'Eustachio F4
13 La Tazza d'Oro G3
14 Open Baladin E7
15 Salotto 42 ..... H3

Tue-Sun, Villa Poniatowski 9am-1.45pm Tue-Sat; Via delle Belle Arti) Italy's finest collection of Etruscan treasures is beautifully housed in Villa Giulia, Pope Julius III's 16th-century pleasure palace. Exhibits, many of which came from burial tombs in northern Lazio, include a polychrome terracotta statue of *Apollo* and the 6th-century BC *Sarcofago degli Sposi* (Sarcophagus of the Betrothed).

Galleria Nazionale d'Arte Moderna GALLERY
(Map p732; 06 3229 8221; www.gnam.beniculturali.it; Viale delle Belle Arti 131, disabled entrance Via Gramsci 71; adult/reduced €8/4, plus possible exhibition supplement; 8.30am-7.30pm Tue-Sun; Piazza Thorvaldsen) Set in a vast belle époque palace, this oft-overlooked museum displays works by some of the most important exponents of modern art, including Modigliani, De Chirico, Cezanne, Kandinsky, Klimt, Pollock and Henry Moore.

LOCAL KNOWLEDGE

THROUGH THE KEYHOLE

Head up to the Aventine Hill for one of Rome's best views. At the southern end of Via Santa Sabina stands the **Priorato dei Cavalieri di Malta** (Map p732), the Roman headquarters of the Cavalieri di Malta (Knights of Malta). The building is closed to the public, but look through its keyhole and you'll see the dome of St Peter's perfectly aligned at the end of a hedge-lined avenue.

TRASTEVERE

Trastevere is one of central Rome's most vivacious neighbourhoods, a tightly packed warren of ochre *palazzi,* ivy-clad facades and photogenic lanes. Taking its name from the Latin *trans Tiberium,* meaning over the Tiber, it was originally a working-class district, but has since been gentrified and is today a trendy hang-out full of bars, trattorias and restaurants.

Basilica di Santa Maria in Trastevere CHURCH
(Map p746; 06 581 94 43; Piazza Santa Maria in Trastevere; 7.30am-9pm; Viale di Trastevere, Viale di Trastevere) Nestled in a quiet corner of **Piazza Santa Maria in Trastevere**, Trastevere's picturesque focal square, this exquisite basilica is believed to be Rome's oldest church dedicated to the Virgin Mary. It originally dates to the 4th century, but a 12th-century makeover saw the addition of a Romanesque bell tower and frescoed facade. Inside, the glittering 12th-century apse mosaics are the main drawcard.

Basilica di Santa Cecilia in Trastevere CHURCH
(Map p746; 06 589 92 89; Piazza di Santa Cecilia; basilica free, fresco & crypt each €2.50; basilica & crypt 9.30am-2.30pm & 4-7.30pm, fresco 10am-2.30pm Mon-Sat; Viale di Trastevere, Viale di Trastevere) The last resting place of St Cecilia, the patron saint of music, this church features a stunning 13th-century fresco by Pietro Cavallini and, below the altar, a breathtaking sculpture of St Cecilia by Stefano

Moderno. Beneath the basilica, you can visit excavations of several Roman houses.

TERMINI & ESQUILINE

The largest of Rome's seven hills, the Esquiline (Esquilino) extends from the Colosseum up to Stazione Termini, Rome's main transport hub.

Basilica di San Pietro in Vincoli CHURCH

(Map p732; ☎06 978 44 950; Piazza di San Pietro in Vincoli 4a; ⏰8am-12.30pm & 3-7pm Apr-Sep, to 6pm Oct-Mar; Ⓜ Cavour) Pilgrims and art lovers flock to this church, just off Via Cavour, for two reasons: to see the chains worn by St Peter before his crucifixion (hence the church's name – St Peter in Chains), and to marvel at Michelangelo's *Moses*, the centrepiece of his unfinished tomb for Pope Julius II.

Basilica di Santa Maria Maggiore CHURCH

(Map p748; ☎06 698 86 800; Piazza Santa Maria Maggiore; basilica free, museum €3, loggia €2; ⏰7am-7pm, museum & loggia 9.30am-6.30pm; 🚌Piazza Santa Maria Maggiore) One of Rome's four patriarchal basilicas, this hulking church was built in AD 352 on the site of a miraculous snowfall. An architectural hybrid, it has a 14th-century Romanesque belfry (at 75m Rome's highest), an 18th-century baroque facade, a largely baroque interior and a series of glorious 5th-century mosaics.

SAN GIOVANNI & CAELIAN HILL

Basilica di San Giovanni in Laterano CATHEDRAL

(Map p732; Piazza di San Giovanni in Laterano 4; basilica free, cloister €3; ⏰7am-6.30pm, cloister 9am-6pm; Ⓜ San Giovanni) For a thousand years this monumental cathedral was the most important church in Christendom. Founded by Constantine in AD 324, it was the first Christian basilica built in the city and, until the late 14th century, was the pope's main place of worship. It is still Rome's official cathedral and the pope's seat as bishop of Rome. It has been revamped several times, most notably by baroque maestro Borromini in the run-up to the 1650 Jubilee, and by Alessandro Galilei who added the monumental facade in the 18th century.

Basilica di San Clemente CHURCH

(Map p732; www.basilicasanclemente.com; Via di San Giovanni in Laterano; church/excavations free/€5; ⏰9am-12.30pm & 3-6pm Mon-Sat, noon-6pm Sun; Ⓜ Colosseo) Nowhere better illustrates the various stages of Rome's turbulent history than this fascinating, multilayered church. The ground-level, 12th-century basilica sits atop a 4th-century church which, in turn, stands over a 2nd-century temple dedicated to the pagan god Mithras and a 1st-century Roman house. Beneath everything are foundations dating from the Roman Republic.

MUSEO NAZIONALE ROMANO

Spread over four sites, the Museo Nazionale Romano (National Roman Museum) houses one of the world's most important collections of classical art. A combined ticket including each of the sites costs adult/EU child €7/free (plus possible €3 exhibition supplement), and is valid for three days.

Palazzo Massimo alle Terme (Map p748; ☎06 399 67 700; www.coopculture.it; Largo di Villa Peretti 1; adult/reduced/EU child €7/3.50/free, audioguide €5; ⏰9am-7.45pm Tue-Sun; Ⓜ Termini) A fabulous museum with amazing frescos and wall paintings.

Terme di Diocleziano (Map p748; ☎06 399 67 700; www.coopculture.it; Viale Enrico de Nicola 78; adult/reduced/EU child €10/6.50/free 3-day integrated ticket includes Palazzo Massimo alle Terme & Aula Ottagona, audioguide €5; ⏰9am-7.30pm Tue-Sun; Ⓜ Termini) Ancient epigraphs and tomb artefacts in the Terme di Diocleziano (Diocletian's Baths), ancient Rome's largest baths complex.

Palazzo Altemps (Map p742; ☎06 399 67 700; http://archeoroma.beniculturali.it/en/museums/national-roman-museum-palazzo-altemps; Piazza Sant'Apollinare 44; adult/reduced/EU child €7/3.50/free plus possible €3 exhibition supplement; ⏰9am-7.45pm Tue-Sun; 🚌Corso del Rinascimento) Wonderful classical sculpture in an exquisite Renaissance *palazzo*.

Crypta Balbi (Map p742; ☎06 399 67 700; http://archeoroma.beniculturali.it/en/museums/national-roman-museum-crypta-balbi; Via delle Botteghe Oscure 31; adult/reduced/EU child €7/3.50/free plus possible €3 exhibition supplement; ⏰9am-7.45pm Tue-Sun ; 🚌Via delle Botteghe Oscure) Set atop an ancient Roman theatre, the Teatro di Balbus (13 BC).

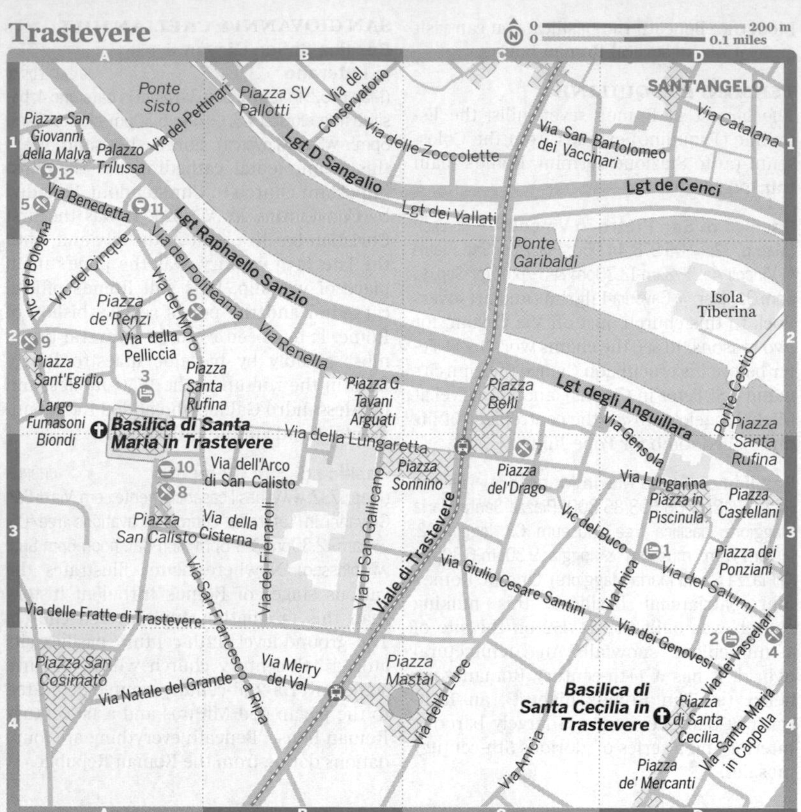

Terme di Caracalla RUINS

(Map p732; ☎06 399 67 700; www.coopculture.it; Viale delle Terme di Caracalla 52; adult/reduced/EU child €7/4/free, audioguide €5; ⏱9am-1hr before sunset Tue-Sun, 9am-2pm Mon year-round; 🚌Viale delle Terme di Caracalla) The vast ruins of the Terme di Caracalla are an awe-inspiring sight. Inaugurated in AD 217, the 10-hectare leisure complex could hold up to 1600 people and included richly decorated pools, gymnasiums, libraries, shops and gardens. The ruins are now used to stage summer opera.

Festivals & Events

Rome's year-round festival calendar ranges from the religious to the ribald, with traditional religious and historical celebrations, performing-arts festivals and an international film festival.

Easter RELIGIOUS

On Good Friday, the pope leads a candlelit procession around the Colosseum. At noon on Easter Sunday he blesses the crowds in St Peter's Square.

Settimana della Cultura CULTURAL

(www.beniculturali.it) During Culture Week admission is free to state-run museums, monuments, galleries and otherwise closed sites. Dates change annually but it's usually in April.

Natale di Roma CULTURAL

Rome celebrates its birthday on 21 April with music, historical recreations, fireworks and free entry to many museums.

Primo Maggio MUSIC

Rome's free May Day rock concert attracts huge crowds and top Italian performers to Piazza di San Giovanni in Laterano.

Estate Romana CULTURAL

(www.estateromana.comune.roma.it) From June to October Rome's big summer festival includes hundreds of cultural events and activities.

Trastevere

Top Sights

Basilica di Santa Cecilia in Trastevere........D4
Basilica di Santa Maria in Trastevere........A2

Sleeping

1 Arco del Lauro........D3
2 Maria-Rosa Guesthouse........D4
3 Villa Della Fonte........A2

Eating

4 Da Enzo........D4
5 Dar Poeta........A1
6 Forno la Renella........A2
7 Hostaria dar Buttero........C3
8 Paris........A3
9 Trattoria degli Amici........A2

Drinking

10 Bar San Calisto........A3
11 Freni e Frizioni........A1
12 Ma Che Siete Venuti a Fà........A1

Festa dei Santi Pietro e Paolo RELIGIOUS
Rome celebrates its patron saints Peter and Paul on 29 June. Festivities are centred on St Peter's Basilica and Via Ostiense.

Festa de'Noantri CULTURAL
Trastevere's annual party, held in the third week of July, involves plenty of food, wine, prayer and dancing.

RomaEuropa CULTURAL
(http://romaeuropa.net) From late September to November, top international artists take to the stage for Rome's premier dance and drama festival.

Festival Internazionale del Film di Roma FILM
(www.romacinemafest.org) Held at the Auditorium Parco della Musica in late October or early November, Rome's film festival rolls out the red carpet for Hollywood hotshots and Italian celebs.

Sleeping

Rome has plenty of accommodation, but rates are universally high. The best, most atmospheric places to stay are the *centro storico*, the Prati area near the Vatican and Trastevere. If you're on a tight budget, most hostels and cheap *pensioni* (guesthouses) are in the Termini area. You'll find a full list of accommodation options (with prices) at www.060608.it.

Always try to book ahead, even if it's just for the first night. But if you arrive without a booking, there's a **hotel reservation service** (Map p748; 06 699 10 00; booking fee €3; 7am-10pm) next to the tourist office at Stazione Termini.

ANCIENT ROME

Nicolas Inn B&B €€
(Map p736; 06 9761 8483; www.nicolasinn.com; Via Cavour 295, 1st fl; s €95-160, d €100-180; ; MCavour) This sunny B&B offers a warm welcome and a convenient location, a stone's throw from the Roman Forum. Run by a friendly couple, it has four big guest rooms, each with homely furnishings, colourful pictures and large en suite bathrooms.

Duca d'Alba HOTEL €€
(Map p736; 06 48 44 71; www.hotelducadalba.com; Via Leonina 14; r €70-200; ; MCavour) This refined four-star sits amid the boutiques and wine bars of the hip Monti district. It's a tight squeeze, but the individually decorated guest rooms are sleek and stylish with parquet floors and modern grey-white colour schemes.

THE VATICAN

Hotel Bramante HOTEL €€€
(Map p732; 06 6880 6426; www.hotelbramante.com; Vicolo delle Palline 24-25; s €100-160, d €140-240, tr €170-250, q €175-260; ; Piazza del Risorgimento) Tucked away in an alley under the Vatican walls, the Hotel Bramante exudes country-house charm with its quietly elegant rooms and cosy internal courtyard. It's housed in the 16th-century building where architect Domenico Fontana lived before Pope Sixtus V banished him from Rome.

Colors Hotel HOTEL €
(Map p732; 06 687 40 30; www.colorshotel.com; Via Boezio 31; s €35-90, d €45-125; ; Via Cola di Rienzo) Popular with young travellers, this is a bright budget hotel with smart, vibrantly coloured rooms spread over three floors (no lift, though). There are also cheaper rooms with shared bathrooms and, from June to August, dorms (€12 to €35 per person) for guests under 38 years of age.

CENTRO STORICO

TOP CHOICE **Daphne Inn** BOUTIQUE HOTEL €€
(Map p748; 06 8745 0086; www.daphne-rome.com; Via di San Basilio 55 ; s €110-180, d €140-230, without bathroom s€70-130, d €90-160; ;

Termini, Esquiline and Quirinal

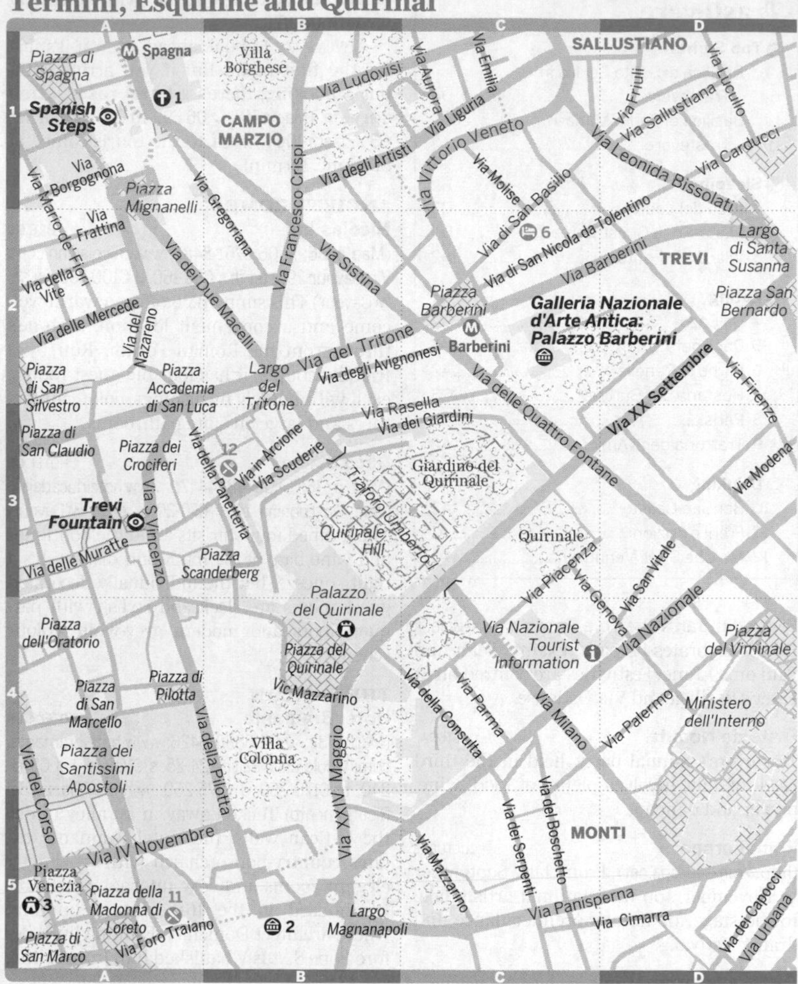

Ⓜ Barberini) Daphne is a gem. Spread over two sites (Daphne Veneto and Daphne Trevi) near Piazza Barberini, it offers value for money, exceptional service and chic modern rooms. The English-speaking staff go that extra mile, even lending guests a cell phone during their stay.

TOP CHOICE **Hotel Panda** PENSION €
(Map p732; ☎06 678 01 79; www.hotelpanda.it; Via della Croce 35; s €65-80, d €85-108, tr €120-140, q €180; 📶; Ⓜ Spagna) A great position near the Spanish Steps, small, simply furnished rooms, and honest rates ensure a year-round stream of travellers to this budget stalwart. Cheaper rooms are also available with shared bathrooms. Breakfast, which is optional, costs €5 and is served in a nearby bar.

Okapi Rooms HOTEL €
(Map p732; ☎06 3260 9815; www.okapirooms.it; Via della Penna 57; s €65-80, d €85-120, tr €110-140, q €120-180; ❄📶; Ⓜ Flaminio) Occupying a tall townhouse near Piazza del Popolo, the Okapi is a bargain low-midrange option. Rooms, spread over six floors, are small and simple with cream walls, terracotta-tiled floors and tiny en suite bathrooms. Several also have small terraces.

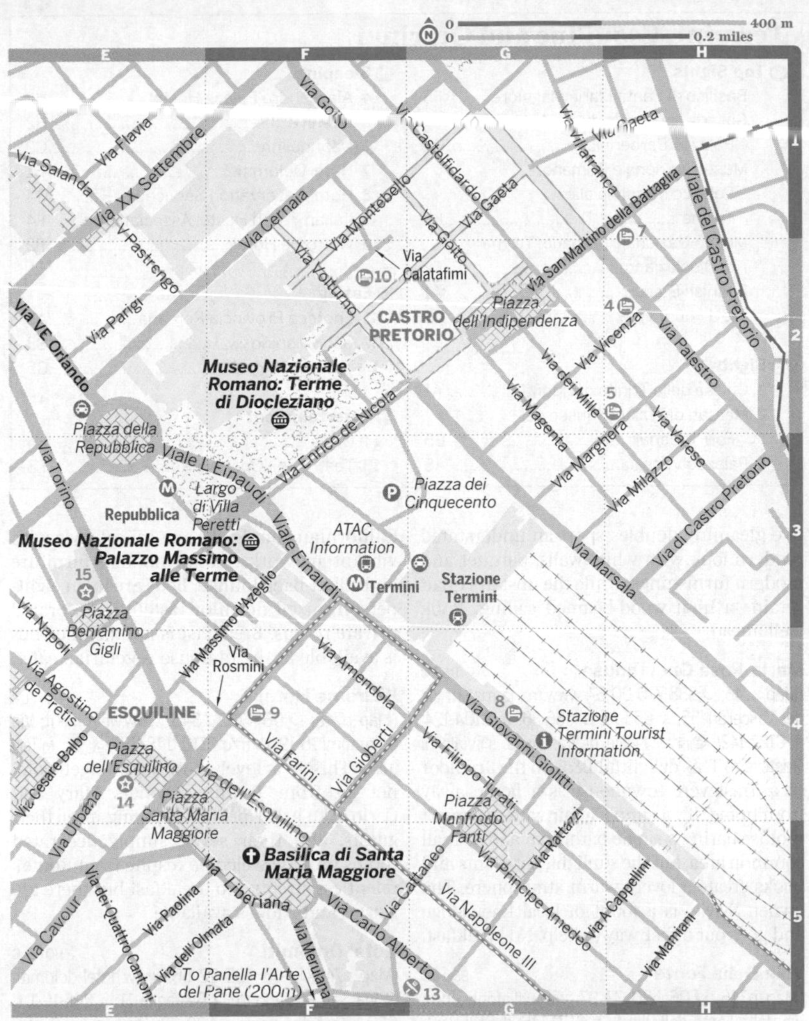

Relais Palazzo Taverna BOUTIQUE HOTEL €€

(Map p742; ☎06 2039 8064; www.relaispalazzotaverna.com; Via dei Gabrielli 92; s €80-140, d €80-150, tr €120-240; ❄📶; 🚌Corso del Rinascimento) Housed in a 15th-century *palazzo,* this boutique hotel is superbly located in the heart of the *centro storico*. Its six rooms cut a stylish dash with white wood-beamed ceilings, funky wallpaper and dark parquet. Tea- and coffee-making facilities add a homey touch.

Hotel Raphaël HISTORIC HOTEL €€€

(Map p742; ☎06 68 28 31; www.raphaelhotel.com; Largo Febo 2; d from €280; ❄📶; 🚌Corso del Rinascimento) An ivy-clad landmark just off Piazza Navona, the Raphaël boasts a serious art collection – Picasso ceramics and lithographs by Miró – as well as minimalist Richard Meier–designed rooms and a panoramic rooftop restaurant.

TRASTEVERE

TOP CHOICE **Arco del Lauro** B&B €

(Map p746; ☎9am-2pm 06 9784 0350, mobile 346 2443212; www.arcodellauro.it; Via Arco de' Tolomei 27; s €75-125, d €95-145; ❄@📶; 🚌Viale di Trastevere, 🚋Viale di Trastevere) This friendly B&B is in a medieval *palazzo* on a narrow cobbled street in Trastevere's quieter eastern half. Its

Termini, Esquiline and Quirinal

Top Sights

Basilica di Santa Maria Maggiore F5
Galleria Nazionale d'Arte Antica: Palazzo Barberini C2
Museo Nazionale Romano: Palazzo Massimo alle Terme F3
Museo Nazionale Romano: Terme di Diocleziano F2
Spanish Steps A1
Trevi Fountain A3

Sights

1 Chiesa della Trinità dei Monti A1
2 Mercati di Traiano Museo dei Fori Imperiali B5
3 Palazzo Venezia A5

Sleeping

4 Alessandro Palace Hostel H2
5 Beehive H2
6 Daphne Inn C2
7 Hotel Dolomiti H1
8 Hotel Reservation Service G4
9 Italian Youth Hostel Association F4
10 Welrome Hotel F2

Eating

11 Enoteca Provincia Romana A5
12 San Crispino B3
13 Trattoria Monti G5

Entertainment

14 Orbis E4
15 Teatro dell'Opera di Roma E3

five gleaming doubles sport an understated modern look with white walls, parquet and modern furnishings, while the upstairs quad retains a high wood-beamed ceiling. Book well ahead.

Maria-Rosa Guesthouse B&B €

(Map p746; ☎338 770 00 67; www.maria-rosa.it; Via dei Vascellari 55; s €53-73, d €66-86, tr €104-124, q €122-142; @📶; 🚌Viale di Trastevere, 🚊Viale di Trastevere) This delightful B&B on the 3rd floor of a Trastevere townhouse is a home away from home. It's a simple affair with two guest rooms sharing a single bathroom and a small common area, but the sunlight, pot plants and books create a lovely, warm atmosphere. The owner, Sylvie, is a fount of local knowledge and goes out of her way to help. No breakfast.

Villa Della Fonte B&B €€

(Map p746; ☎06 580 37 97; www.villafonte.com; Via della Fonte dell'Olio 8; s €110-145, d €135-180; ❄📶; 🚌Viale di Trastevere, 🚊Viale di Trastevere) Near Piazza Santa Maria in Trastevere, this charming B&B occupies an ivy-clad, 17th-century *palazzo*.The five rooms are small but tastefully decorated and there's a sunny garden terrace for alfresco breakfasts.

TERMINI & ESQUILINE

TOP CHOICE **Beehive** HOSTEL €

(Map p748; ☎06 4470 4553; www.the-beehive.com; Via Marghera 8; dm €25-30, s €50-60, d €90-100, without bathroom s €40-50, d €80-90, tr €95-105; ❄📶; Ⓜ Termini) More boutique chic than backpacker crashpad, the Beehive is one of the best hostels in town. Run by a southern Californian couple, it's an oasis of style with vibrant art works, funky modular furniture and a laid-back lounge. Beds are in an eight-person mixed dorm or tastefully decorated private rooms. Breakfast is not included but is available at the in-house vegetarian cafe.

Welrome Hotel HOTEL €

(Map p748; ☎06 4782 4343; www.welrome.it; Via Calatafimi 15-19; d/tr/q €110/148/187; ❄📶; Ⓜ Termini) This is a lovely, low-key budget hotel not far from Termini. Owners Mary and Carlo take great pride in looking after their guests, and their seven simply decorated rooms provide welcome respite from Rome's relentless streets. No breakfast but there are kettles and fridges available.

Hotel Dolomiti HOTEL €

(Map p748; ☎06 495 72 56; www.hotel-dolomiti.it; Via San Martino della Battaglia 11; s €45-100, d €60-160, extra person €20-35; ❄@📶; Ⓜ Castro Pretorio) A warm, family-run hotel, the Dolomiti is a reliable option. Rooms, which come with cream walls, cherry-wood furniture and prints of chubby-cheeked cherubs, are spread over three floors of a big apartment block not far from Termini.

Alessandro Palace Hostel HOSTEL €

(Map p748; ☎06 446 19 58; www.hostelsalessandro.com; Via Vicenza 42; dm €19-35, d €70-120, tr €95-120; ❄@📶; Ⓜ Castro Pretorio) A long-standing favourite in the Termini area, this slick hostel offers spick-and-span hotel-style rooms, as well as dorms sleeping from four to eight. It's managed by an efficient inter-

WORTH A TRIP

VIA APPIA ANTICA

Completed in 190 BC, ancient Rome's *regina viarum* (queen of roads) connected the capital with Brindisi on Italy's southern Adriatic coast. Nowadays, Via Appia Antica (The Appian Way) is one of Rome's most exclusive addresses, a beautiful cobbled thoroughfare flanked by grassy fields, ancient ruins and towering pine trees. But it has a dark history – it was here that Spartacus and 6000 of his slave rebels were crucified in 71 BC, and it was here that the early Christians buried their dead in underground catacombs.

The two main catacombs are the **Catacombe di San Sebastiano** (☎06 785 03 50; www.catacombe.org; Via Appia Antica 136; adult/reduced/child €8/5/free; ⏲10am-5pm Mon-Sat, closed mid-Nov–mid-Dec; 🚌Via Appia Antica), which extends beneath the **Basilica di San Sebastiano**, and the **Catacombe di San Callisto** (☎06 513 01 51; www.catacombe.roma.it; Via Appia Antica 110 & 126; adult/reduced €8/5; ⏲9am-noon & 2-5pm, closed Wed mid-Jan–mid-Feb; 🚌Via Appia Antica), where the remains of thousands of Christians have been unearthed.

To get to Via Appia Antica, take bus 660 from Colli Albani metro station (line A) or bus 118 from Piramide (line B).

For information on the area, stop off at the **Appia Antica Regional Park Information Point** (☎06 513 53 16; www.parcoappiaantica.org; Via Appia Antica 58-60; ⏲9.30am-1.30pm & 2-5.30pm Mon-Sat, to 4.30pm winter, 9.30am-6.30pm Sun).

national crew, has 24-hour reception, and serves cut-price beer in the hostel bar.

Eating

Eating out is one of the great joys of visiting Rome and everywhere you go you'll find trattorias, pizzerias, *gelaterie* (ice-cream shops) and restaurants. Traditional Roman cooking holds sway but *cucina creativa* (creative cooking) has taken off in recent years and there are plenty of exciting, contemporary restaurants to try.

The best areas are the *centro storico* and Trastevere, but there are also excellent choices in San Lorenzo east of Termini and Testaccio. Watch out for overpriced tourist traps around Termini and the Vatican.

Roman specialities include *cacio e pepe* (pasta with pecorino cheese, black pepper and olive oil), *pasta all'amatriciana* (with tomato, pancetta and chilli), *fiori di zucca* (fried courgette flowers) and *carciofi alla romana* (artichokes with garlic, mint and parsley).

ANCIENT ROME

TOP CHOICE Enoteca Provincia Romana TRADITIONAL ITALIAN €€
(Map p748; ☎06 699 40 273; Via Foro Traiano 82-4; mains €17, aperitif from €5; ⏲11am-11pm Mon-Sat; 🚌Via dei Fori Imperiali) Specialising in regional food and wine, this stylish wine bar-cum-restaurant offers a daily menu of pastas and mains, wine by the glass, finger foods and an evening aperitif. Service is friendly and with an enviable location overlooking the Colonna di Traiano, it's a top choice. Lunchtimes are busy but it quietens in the evening.

THE VATICAN

Hostaria Dino & Tony TRATTORIA €€
(Map p732; ☎06 397 33 284; Via Leone IV 60; mains €12; ⏲Mon-Sat, closed Aug; Ⓜ Ottaviano-San Pietro) An authentic trattoria in the Vatican area. Kick off with the monumental antipasto before plunging into its signature dish, *rigatoni all' amatriciana*. Finish up with a *granita di caffè* (a crushed ice coffee served with a full inch of whipped cream). No credit cards.

CENTRO STORICO

TOP CHOICE Casa Coppelle MEDITERRANEAN €€
(Map p742; ☎06 688 91 707; www.casacoppelle.it; Piazza delle Coppelle 49; meals €35; 🚌Corso del Rinascimento) Exposed brick walls, books, flowers and subdued lighting set the stage for wonderful French-inspired food at this intimate, romantic restaurant. There's a full range of starters and pastas but the real *tour de force* is the steak served with crisp, thinly sliced potato crisps. Book ahead.

Al Gran Sasso TRATTORIA €€
(Map p732; ☎06 321 48 83; www.trattoriaalgransasso.com; Via di Ripetta 32; mains €13; ⏲lunch & dinner Sun-Fri; Ⓜ Flaminio) The perfect lunchtime spot, this is a classic, dyed-in-the-wool trattoria. It's a relaxed place with a welcoming vibe, garish murals on the walls (strangely, often a good sign) and tasty country food.

HOW TO EAT & DRINK FOR LESS

» Lunch on *pizza al taglio* (pizza by the slice) and ice cream; dine on bar snacks over an *aperitivo* (aperitif).

» Take advantage of the fixed-price lunch menus that some restaurants offer.

» Fill up on the bread they bring you when you sit down – you'll pay for it whether you eat it or not.

» Drink standing at the bar rather than sitting at a table.

Forno di Campo de' Fiori BAKERY €

(Map p742; Campo de' Fiori 22; pizza slices about €3; ⊙7.30am-2.30pm & 4.45-8pm Mon-Sat; ⊡Corso Vittorio Emanuele II) This is one of Rome's best bakeries, serving bread, panini and delicious straight-from-the-oven *pizza al taglio* (by the slice). Aficionados swear by the *pizza bianca* (white pizza), but the panini and *pizza rossa* (with tomato) are just as good.

Pizzeria da Baffetto PIZZERIA €

(Map p742; ☎06 686 16 17; www.pizzeriabaffetto.it; Via del Governo Vecchio 114; pizzas €6-9; ⊙6.30pm-1am; ⊡Corso Vittorio Emanuele II) For the full-on Roman pizza experience, get down to this local institution. Meals are raucous, chaotic and fast, but the thin-crust pizzas are spot on and the vibe is fun. To partake, join the queue and wait to be squeezed in wherever there's room. There's also **Baffetto 2** (Map p742; Piazza del Teatro di Pompeo 18; ⊙6.30pm-12.30am Mon & Wed-Fri, 12.30-3.30pm & 6.30pm-12.30am Sat & Sun; ⊡Corso Vittorio Emanuele II) near Campo de' Fiori.

Ditirambo MODERN ITALIAN €€

(Map p742; ☎06 687 16 26; www.ristoranteditirambo.it; Piazza della Cancelleria 72; meals €40; ⊙closed lunch Mon; ⊡Corso Vittorio Emanuele II) This popular new-wave trattoria dishes up a laid-back atmosphere and innovative, organic cooking. The menu changes regularly, but there's always a good choice of vegetarian dishes such as ricotta ravioli with cherry tomatoes and capers. Book ahead.

TOP CHOICE **Forno Roscioli** PIZZA, BAKERY €

(Map p742; Via dei Chiavari 34; pizza slices from €2, snacks from €1.50; ⊙7.30am-8pm Mon-Fri, 7.30am-2.30pm Sat; ⊡Via Arenula) Join the lunchtime crowds at this revered bakery for a slice of *pizza bianca* or a freshly baked pastry. There's also a counter serving hot pastas and vegetable side dishes.

'Gusto RISTORANTE €

(Map p732; ☎06 322 62 73; Piazza Augusto Imperatore 9; pizzas €7-10; ⊡Via del Corso) All exposed brickwork and industrial chic, this '90s-style warehouse operation is a lunchtime favourite with office workers, serving everything from thick-crust pizza to cheese platters, salads and overpriced fusion food. At lunch the buffet is a bargain.

TRASTEVERE

Trattoria degli Amici TRATTORIA €€

(Map p746; ☎06 580 60 33; www.trattoriadegliamici.org; Piazza Sant'Egidio 6; mains €15; ⊡Viale di Trastevere, ⊡Viale di Trastevere) Boasting a prime piazza location, this cheerful trattoria is run by a local charity and staffed by volunteers and people with disabilities who welcome guests with a warmth not always apparent in this touristy neck of the woods. With its outside tables, it's a lovely place to dig into well-prepared Italian classics and enjoy the neighbourhood vibe.

Da Lucia TRATTORIA €€

(Map p732; ☎06 580 36 01; Vicolo del Mattinato 2; mains €12.50; ⊙Tue-Sun; ⊡Viale di Trastevere, ⊡Viale di Trastevere) For a real Trastevere experience, search out this terrific neighbourhood trattoria on a hidden cobbled backstreet. It's popular with locals and tourists alike for its authentic Roman soul food, including a fine *spaghetti alla gricia* (with pancetta and cheese). Cash only.

Paris RISTORANTE €€€

(Map p746; ☎06 581 53 78; www.ristoranteparis.it; Piazza San Calisto 7a; meals €55; ⊙Tue-Sat, lunch only Sun; ⊡Viale di Trastevere, ⊡Viale di Trastevere) An elegant, old-fashioned restaurant set in a 17th-century building, Paris is a great place to experience traditional Roman-Jewish cuisine. Signature dishes include *fritto misto con baccalà* (deep-fried vegetables with salt cod) and *carciofi alla giudia* (Jewish-style fried artichokes).

Dar Poeta PIZZERIA €

(Map p746; ☎06 588 05 16; Vicolo del Bologna 46; pizzas from €6; ⊙lunch & dinner; ⊡Piazza Trilussa) Loud and always busy, this much-loved pizzeria guarantees a bustling, cheery atmosphere and hearty wood-fired pizzas that fall somewhere between wafer-thin Roman pizzas and the softer, doughier Neapolitan version. Expect queues.

Forno la Renella BAKERY €
(Map p746; ☎06 581 72 65; Via del Moro 15-16; pizza slices from €2.50; ⏰7am-2am Tue-Sat, to 10pm Sun & Mon; 🚌Piazza Trilussa) The wood-fired ovens at this historic Trastevere bakery have been firing for decades, producing a delicious daily batch of pizza, bread and biscuits.

Hostaria dar Buttero TRATTORIA €€
(Map p746; ☎06 580 05 17; Via della Lungaretta; mains €13; ⏰Mon-Sat; 🚌Viale di Trastevere, 🚊Viale di Trastevere) On Trastevere's quieter eastern side, this is a typical old-school trattoria, attracting a mixed crowd of tourists and Romans. The menu lists all the usual pastas, grilled meats and pizzas (evenings only), but the food is well cooked, the atmosphere is convivial and the prices are right for the area.

Da Enzo TRATTORIA €€
(Map p746; ☎06 581 83 55; www.daenzoal29.com; Via dei Vascellari 29; meals €35; ⏰Mon-Sat; 🚌Viale di Trastevere, 🚊Viale di Trastevere) This rough-around-the-edges Trastevere institution is as authentic as it gets. Don't expect silver service; just traditional Roman food dished up to crowds of hungry diners. Menu stalwarts include *cacio e pepe* and *polpette al sugo* (meat balls in tomato sauce).

TESTACCIO

TOP CHOICE **Flavio al Velavevodetto** TRATTORIA €€
(Map p732; ☎06 574 41 94; www.flavioalvelavevodetto.it; Via di Monte Testaccio 97-99; meals €30-35; ⏰closed Sat lunch & Sun summer; 🚌Via Marmorata) This welcoming Testaccio eatery is the sort of place that gives Roman trattorias a good name. Housed in a rustic Pompeian-red villa, complete with intimate covered courtyard and an open-air terrace, it specialises in earthy, no-nonsense Italian food prepared with skill and served in mountainous portions.

TOP CHOICE **00100 Pizza** PIZZA €
(Map p732; www.00100pizza.com; Via Branca 88; pizza slices from €3, trapizzini from €3.50; ⏰noon-11pm; 🚌Via Marmorata) A pocket-size pizza pusher, this is one of a select group of Roman takeaways with culinary ambitions. As well as pizzas topped with unusual combos – cream of chickpea; mozzarella, gorgonzola and port – the trademark here is the *trapizzini,* small cones of pizza base stuffed with fillers like *polpette al sugo*.

Pizzeria Da Remo PIZZERIA €
(Map p732; ☎06 574 62 70; Piazza Santa Maria Liberatrice 44; pizzas from €5.50; ⏰7pm-1am Mon-Sat; 🚌Via Marmorata) Remo is one of Rome's most popular pizzerias, its spartan interior always full of noisy young Romans. Tick your order on a sheet of paper slapped down by an overstretched waiter and wait for your huge, sizzling, charred disc. Queues are the norm after 8.30pm.

Volpetti Più CAFETERIA €
(Map p732; Via Volta 8; mains €8; ⏰10.30am-3.30pm & 5.30-9.30pm Mon-Sat; 🚌Via Marmorata) One of the few places in town where you can sit down and eat well for less than €20. Volpetti Più is a sumptuous *tavola calda* ('hot table') offering an opulent choice of pizza, pasta, soup, meat, vegetables and fried nibbles.

GELATO GALORE

To get the best out of Rome's *gelaterie* (ice-cream shops) look for the words *'produzione proprio'*, meaning 'own production'. As a rough guide, expect to pay from €1.50 for a *cono* (cone) or *coppa* (tub). Our choice of the city's finest:

San Crispino (Map p748; ☎06 679 39 24; Via della Panetteria 42; ice cream from €2.30; ⏰noon-12.30am Mon, Wed, Thu & Sun, 11am-1.30am Fri & Sat; Ⓜ Barberini) Near the Trevi Fountain, it serves natural, seasonal flavours – think *fichi secci* (dried figs) and *miele* (honey) – in tubs only.

Gelarmony (Map p732; Via Marcantonio Colonna 34; ice cream from €1.50; ⏰10am-late; Ⓜ Lepanto) A Sicilian *gelateria* serving 60 flavours and heavenly *cannoli* (pastry tubes filled with ricotta and candied fruit).

Il Gelato (Map p732; Viale Aventino 59; ⏰11am-9pm Tue-Sun, to 10.30pm daily summer; Ⓜ Circo Massimo) Creative, preservative-free combos from Rome's *gelato* king Claudio Torcè.

Gelateria Giolitti (Map p742; ☎06 699 12 43; www.giolitti.it; Via degli Uffici del Vicario 40; ⏰7am-1am; 🚌Via del Corso) Rome's most famous *gelateria,* near the Pantheon.

TERMINI & ESQUILINE

Trattoria Monti RISTORANTE €€

(Map p748; ☎06 446 65 73; Via di San Vito 13a; meals €45; ⊙lunch & dinner Tue-Sat, lunch Sun, closed Aug; MVittorio Emanuele) Loved by locals and visitors alike, this intimate, arched restaurant – it's a trattoria in name only – serves top-notch regional cooking from Le Marche (a hilly region on Italy's Adriatic coast). Expect exemplary game stews and pungent truffles, as well as wonderful fried starters like *olive ascolane* (fried meat-stuffed olives). Book for dinner.

Panella l'Arte del Pane BAKERY, CAFE €

(Map p732; ☎06 487 24 35; Via Merulana 54; pizza slices around €3; ⊙noon-midnight Mon-Sat, 10am-4pm Sun Mar-Oct; MVittorio Emanuele) A devilishly tempting bakery-cum-cafe-cum-deli with a sumptuous array of *pizza al taglio*, *supplì* (fried rice balls), focaccia and fried croquettes. You can sit outside – perfect for a leisurely breakfast or chilled drink – or perch on a high stool and eye the shelves of gourmet delicacies.

Pommidoro TRATTORIA €€

(Map p732; ☎06 445 26 92; Piazza dei Sanniti 44; meals €35; ⊙Mon-Sat, closed Aug; 🚌Via Tiburtina) Unchanged throughout San Lorenzo's metamorphosis from working-class district to bohemian enclave, century-old Pommidoro is a much-loved local institution. It was a favourite of film director Pier Paolo Pasolini, and contemporary celebs still stop by, but it's an unpretentious place with traditional food and magnificent grilled meats.

Tram Tram OSTERIA €€

(Map p732; ☎06 49 04 16; www.tramtram.it; Via dei Reti 44; meals around €40; ⊙12.30-3.30pm & 7.30-11.30pm Tue-Sun; 🚌Via Tiburtina) This cosy San Lorenzo *osteria* (tavern) takes its name from the trams that rattle past outside. Very popular locally, it offers tasty traditional dishes and wonderful Sicilian-inspired seafood such as *alici frittodorate* (fried anchovies) and *involtini di pesce spada* (swordfish rolls). Book ahead.

Drinking

Rome has plenty of drinking venues, ranging from neighbourhood hang-outs to elegant streetside cafes, dressy lounge bars and Irish-theme pubs. During the day, bars are generally visited for a quick coffee while early evening sees the city's hipsters descend on the fashionable watering holes for *aperitivi* (aperitifs).

Much of the action is in the *centro storico* – Campo de' Fiori fills with young, rowdy drinkers, while the lanes around Piazza Navona host a more calm, dressier scene. Over the river, Trastevere is another popular spot with dozens of bars and pubs, while to the east of Termini, San Lorenzo and Pigneto attract students and bohemian uptowners.

TOP CHOICE **Caffè Sant'Eustachio** CAFE

(Map p742; Piazza Sant'Eustachio 82; ⊙8.30am-1am Sun-Thu, to 1.30am Fri, to 2am Sat; 🚌Corso del Rinascimento) This small, unassuming cafe, generally three-deep at the bar, is famous for its *gran caffè*, said by many to be the best coffee in town. Created by beating the first drops of espresso and several teaspoons of sugar into a frothy paste, then adding the rest of the coffee, it's guaranteed to put some zing into your sightseeing.

Open Baladin BAR

(Map p742; www.openbaladinroma.it; Via degli Specchi 6; ⊙12pm-2am; 🚌Via Arenula) This designer bar is a leading light on Rome's burgeoning beer scene. It's a slick, stylish place with more than 40 beers on tap and up to 100 bottled beers, many produced by Italian artisanal breweries.

La Tazza d'Oro CAFE

(Map p742; Via degli Orfani 84-86; ⊙7am-8pm Mon-Sat, 10.30am-7.30pm Sun; 🚌Via del Corso) A busy, burnished cafe, this is one of Rome's best coffee houses. Its espresso hits the mark perfectly and there's a range of delicious coffee concoctions, including *a* refreshing *granita di caffè*.

Salotto 42 BAR

(Map p742; www.salotto42.it; Piazza di Pietra 42; ⊙10am-2am Tue-Sat, to midnight Sun & Mon; 🚌Via del Corso) On a picturesque piazza facing a 2nd-century Roman temple, this is a hip lounge bar, complete with vintage armchairs, suede sofas and heavy-as-houses designer tomes. Come for the daily lunch buffet or to hang out with the beautiful people over an aperitif.

Ma Che Siete Venuti a Fà PUB

(Map p746; Via Benedetta 25; ⊙11am-2am; 🚌Piazza Trilussa) This pint-sized pub – whose name, a football chant, translates politely as 'What did you come here for?' – is a beer-buff's paradise, packing a huge number of artisanal beers into its tiny interior.

Freni e Frizioni BAR

(Map p746; www.freniefrizioni.com; Via del Politeama 4-6; ⊙6.30pm-2am; 🚌Piazza Trilussa) Housed in a former garage – hence its name meaning 'breaks' and 'clutches' – this designer-grunge bar draws a spritz-loving crowd that flocks here to slurp on mojitos and fill up at the popular 7pm *aperitivo*.

Caffè Capitolino CAFE
(Map p736; Piazzale Caffarelli 4; ⌚9am-7.30pm Tue-Sun; 🚌Piazza Venezia) The stylish rooftop cafe of the Musei Capitolini is a good place for a timeout over a coffee, cool drink or light snack. And you don't need a museum ticket to drink here – it's accessible via an independent entrance on Piazza Caffarelli.

Bar San Calisto CAFE
(Map p746; Piazza San Calisto 3-5; ⌚6am-2am Mon-Sat; 🚌Viale di Trastevere, 🚊Viale di Trastevere) Down-at-heel 'Sanca' is a perennial Trastevere favourite. A motley crew of students, punks, alcoholics, affected bohemians and card-playing *nonni* (grandpas) congregate here for dirt-cheap drinks and the bar's legendary chocolate – drunk hot in winter, eaten as ice cream in summer.

☆ Entertainment

Rome has a thriving cultural scene, with a year-round calendar of concerts, performances and festivals. In summer, the Estate Romana (p746) festival sponsors hundreds of cultural events, many staged in atmospheric parks, piazzas and churches. Autumn is another good time, with festivals dedicated to dance, drama and jazz.

A useful listings guide is *Trova Roma*, a free insert which comes with *La Repubblica* newspaper every Thursday. Upcoming events are also listed on www.turismoroma.it, www.060608.it and www.auditorium.com.

For tickets, try **Orbis** (Map p748; ☎06 474 4776; Piazza dell'Esquilino 37), which accepts cash payment only, or the online agency **Hellò Ticket** (☎800 90 70 80; www.helloticket.it).

Classical Music & Opera

TOP CHOICE **Auditorium Parco della Musica** CONCERT VENUE
(☎06 802 41 281; www.auditorium.com; Viale Pietro de Coubertin 30; 🚌shuttle bus M from Stazione Termini, 🚊Viale Tiziano) This Renzo Piano-designed modernist complex is Rome's cultural hub and premier concert venue. Its three concert halls and 3000-seat open-air arena stage everything from classical music concerts to tango exhibitions, book readings and film screenings. The auditorium is also home to Rome's top orchestra, the world-class Orchestra dell'Accademia Nazionale di Santa Cecilia (www.santacecilia.it).

Teatro Olimpico THEATRE
(☎06 326 59 91; www.teatroolimpico.it; Piazza Gentile da Fabriano 17; 🚌Piazza Mancini, 🚊Piazza Mancini) The Accademia Filarmonica Romana (www.filarmonicaromana.org), one of Rome's major classical music organisations, stages a varied program of classical and chamber music here as well as opera, ballet and contemporary multimedia events.

Teatro dell'Opera di Roma OPERA
(Map p748; ☎06 4817 003; www.operaroma.it; Piazza Beniamino Gigli; ballet €12-80; opera €17-150; ⌚box office 9am-5pm Mon-Sat, 9am-1.30pm Sun; Ⓜ Repubblica) Rome's premier opera house also stages the city's ballet company. The opera season runs from December to June, with summer performances staged at the **Terme di Caracalla** (Map p732; Viale delle Terme di Caracalla 52; 🚌Viale delle Terme di Caracalla).

Nightclubs & Live Music

Clubbing action caters to most tastes, with DJs spinning everything from lounge and jazz to house, dancehall and hip hop. The scene is centred on Testaccio and the Ostiense area, although you'll also find places in Trastevere and the *centro storico*. Out from the centre, San Lorenzo and Pigneto are happening areas.

You'll need to dress the part for the big clubs, which can be tricky to get into, especially for groups of men. Gigs are often listed for 10pm but don't kick off until around 11pm, while clubs rarely hot up much before midnight or 1am. Admission is often free but drinks are expensive, typically €10 to €16. Note also that many clubs shut between mid-June and mid-September.

TOP CHOICE **Circolo degli Artisti** CLUB
(www.circoloartisti.it; Via Casilina Vecchia 42; ⌚7pm-2am Tue-Thu, to 4.30am Fri-Sun; 🚌Ponte Casilino) East of the Pigneto district, this kicking club offers one of Rome's best nights out with top live music from Italian and international bands, cracking DJ turns, and a large garden area for outdoor beer. Admission is either free or a bargain.

Alexanderplatz JAZZ
(Map p732; www.alexanderplatz.it; Via Ostia 9; ⌚concerts 9.45pm Sun-Thu, 10.30pm Sat & Sun;

Ⓜ Ottaviano-San Pietro) Rome's top jazz joint attracts international performers – regulars include George Coleman and Lionel Hampton – and a passionate, knowledgeable crowd. In July and August the club goes alfresco at the under-the-stars Villa Celimontana Jazz Festival.

Big Mama BLUES
(Map p732; www.bigmama.it; Vicolo di San Francesco a Ripa 18; ⊙9pm-1.30am, show 10.30pm Thu-Sat, closed Jun-Sep; Viale di Trastevere, Viale di Trastevere) To wallow in the Eternal City blues, there's only one place to go – this cramped Trastevere basement. There are weekly residences from well-known Italian musicians and regular blues, jazz, funk, soul and R&B concerts by international acts.

Goa NIGHTCLUB
(www.goaclub.com; Via Libetta 13; ⊙11.30pm-4.30am Thu-Sat; Ⓜ Garbatella) Goa is Rome's serious super-club, with international names, a fashion-forward crowd, podium dancers and heavies on the door. Thursday is always a big night with top European DJs.

Villaggio Globale CLUB, LIVE MUSIC
(Map p732; www.ecn.org/villaggioglobale/joomla; Via Monte del Cocci 22; Via Marmorata) For a warehouse-party vibe, head to Testaccio and Rome's best-known *centro sociale* (an ex-squat turned cultural centre) in the city's graffiti-sprayed former slaughterhouse. Entrance is cheap, the beer flows and the sound systems serve a steady supply of dancehall, reggae, dubstep and drum'n'bass.

Shopping

Rome boasts the usual cast of flagship chain stores and glitzy designer outlets, but what makes shopping here fun is its legion of small, independent shops – historic, family-owned delis, small-label fashion boutiques, artists' studios, neighbourhood markets. For designer clothes head to Via dei Condotti and the area around Piazza di Spagna, while for something more left-field check out the vintage shops and boutiques on Via del Governo Vecchio, around Campo de' Fiori, and in the Monti neighbourhood.

Rome's markets are great places for bargain hunting. The most famous, **Porta Portese** (Map p732; Piazza Porta Portese; ⊙7am-1pm Sun; Viale di Trastevere), is held every Sunday morning near Trastevere, and sells everything from antiques to clothes, bikes, bags and furniture.

For the best bargains, time your visit to coincide with the *saldi* (sales). Winter sales run from early January to mid-February and summer sales from July to early September.

Information

Dangers & Annoyances

Rome is not a dangerous city but petty theft can be a problem. Watch out for pickpockets around the big tourist sites, at Stazione Termini and on crowded public transport – the 64 Vatican bus is notorious.

Emergency

Ambulance (☎118)
Fire (☎115)
Police (☎113, 112)
Main Police Station (Questura; ☎06 4 68 61; http://questure.poliziadistato.it; Via San Vitale 15; ⊙8.30am-11.30pm Mon-Fri, 3-5pm Tue & Thu)

Internet Access

Free wi-fi is widely available in hostels, B&Bs and hotels. Some places also provide laptops/computers for guests' use. Internet cafes are fairly thin on the ground, with costs usually between €4 and €6 per hour.

Medical Services

For problems that don't require hospital treatment call the **Guardia Medica Turistica** (☎06 7730 6650; Via Emilio Morosini 30). For emergency treatment, go to the *pronto soccorso* (casualty) section of an *ospedale* (hospital). Pharmacists will serve prescriptions and can provide basic medical advice.

Pharmacy (☎06 488 00 19; Piazza Cinquecento 51; ⊙7.30am-10pm daily) There's also a pharmacy in Stazione Termini, next to platform 1, open 7.30am to 10pm.

Ospedale Santo Spirito (☎06 6 83 51; Lungotevere in Sassia 1) Near the Vatican; multilingual staff.

Policlinico Umberto I (☎06 4 99 71; www.policlinicoumberto1.it; Viale del Policlinico 155) East of Stazione Termini.

Money

ATMs are liberally scattered around the city.

Most midrange and top-end hotels accept credit cards, as do most restaurants and large shops. Some cheaper *pensioni*, trattorias and pizzerias only accept cash. Don't rely on credit cards at museums or galleries.

There are money-exchange booths at Stazione Termini and Fiumicino and Ciampino airports.

Tourist Information

For phone enquiries, the Comune di Roma runs a multilingual **tourist information line** (☎060608; www.060608.it; ⏲9am-9pm).

There are tourist information points at **Fiumicino** (Terminal 3, International Arrivals; ⏲8am-7.30pm) and **Ciampino** (International Arrivals, baggage reclaim area; ⏲9am-6.30pm) airports. Also at the following locations across the city, open 9.30am to 7pm (except at Stazione Termini):

Castel Sant'Angelo Tourist Information (Map p742; Piazza Pia; ⏲9.30am-7pm)

Fori Imperiali Tourist Information (Map p736; Via dei Fori Imperiali; ⏲9.30am-7pm; 🚌Via dei Fori Imperiali)

Piazza delle Cinque Lune Tourist Information (Map p742; ⏲9.30am-7pm) Near Piazza Navona.

Stazione Termini Tourist Information (Map p748; ⏲8am-8.30pm) In the hall that runs parallel to platform 24.

Via Marco Minghetti Tourist Information (Map p742; ⏲9.30am-7pm) Near the Trevi Fountain.

Via Nazionale Tourist Information (Map p748; ⏲9.30am-7pm)

For information about the Vatican, contact the **Centro Servizi Pellegrini e Turisti** (Map p732; ☎06 6988 1662; St Peter's Square; ⏲8.30am-6pm Mon-Sat).

Websites

060608 (www.060608.it) Provides information on sites, shows, transport etc.

Coop Culture (www.coopculture.it) Information and ticketing for Rome's monuments, museums and galleries.

Turismo Roma (www.turismoroma.it) Rome's official tourist website.

Vatican (www.vatican.va) The Vatican's official website.

ℹ Getting There & Away

Air

Rome's main international airport, Leonardo da Vinci (p845), better known as Fiumicino, is on the coast 30km west of the city. The much smaller Ciampino airport (p846), 15km southeast of the city centre, is the hub for low-cost carrier **Ryanair** (www.ryanair.com).

Boat

Rome's port is at Civitavecchia, about 80km north of Rome.

Ferry bookings can be made at the Termini-based **Agenzia 365** (☎06 474 09 23; www.agenzie365.it; ⏲8am-9pm), at travel agents or online at www.traghettionline.net. You can also buy directly at the port.

Half-hourly trains depart from Roma Termini to Civitavecchia (€5 to €14.50, 40 minutes to one hour). On arrival, it's about 700m to the port (to your right) as you exit the station.

The main ferry companies:

Grimaldi Lines (☎081 49 64 44; www.grimaldi-lines.com) To/from Trapani (Sicily), Porto Torres (Sardinia), Barcelona (Spain) and Tunis (Tunisia).

Tirrenia (☎89 21 23; www.tirrenia.it) To/from Arbatax, Cagliari and Olbia (all Sardinia).

Bus

Long-distance national and international buses use the Autostazione Tiburtina in front of Stazione Tiburtina. Take metro line B to Tiburtina.

You can get tickets from the offices next to the bus terminus or at travel agencies. Bus operators:

Interbus (☎091 34 25 25; www.interbus.it) To/from Sicily.

Marozzi (☎080 579 01 11; www.marozzivt.it) To/from Sorrento, Bari, Matera and Lecce.

SENA (☎0861 199 19 00; www.sena.it) To/from Siena, Bologna and Milan.

Sulga (☎800 09 96 61; www.sulga.it) To/from Perugia, Assisi and Ravenna.

Car & Motorcycle

Driving into central Rome is a challenge, involving traffic restrictions, one-way systems, a shortage of street parking and aggressive drivers.

The city is circled by the Grande Raccordo Anulare (GRA), to which all autostradas (motorways) connect, including the main A1 north–south artery (the Autostrada del Sole), and the A12, which runs to Civitavecchia and Fiumicino airport.

CAR HIRE

Rental cars are available at the airport and Stazione Termini. As well as international companies, try **Maggiore National** (www.maggiore.it)

Near Termini, **Bici & Baci** (☎06 482 84 43; www.bicibaci.com; Via del Viminale 5; ⏲8am-7pm) is one of many agencies renting out scooters. Bank on from €19 per day.

Train

Almost all trains arrive at and depart from Stazione Termini. There are regular connections to other European countries, all major Italian cities, and many smaller towns.

Train information is available from the customer service area on the main concourse to the left of the ticket desks. Alternatively, check www.trenitalia.com, or phone the **Trenitalia Call Centre** (☎89 20 21; ⏲24hr).

Left luggage (1st 5hr €5, 6-12hr per hr €0.70, 13hr & over per hr €0.30; ⏲6am-11pm) is on the lower ground floor under platform 24.

Rome's second train station is Stazione Tiburtina, a short ride away on metro line B.

 Getting Around

To/From the Airport

FIUMICINO

The easiest way to get to/from the airport is by train but there are also bus services. The set taxi fare to the city centre is €48 (valid for up to four people with luggage).

Cotral Bus (www.cotralspa.it; one-way €5, €7 if bought on bus) Runs to/from Stazione Tiburtina via Stazione Termini. Eight daily departures including night services from the airport at 1.15am, 2.15am, 3.30am and 5am, and from Tiburtina at 12.30am, 1.15am, 2.30am and 3.45am. Journey time is one hour.

FR1 Train (€8) Connects the airport to Trastevere, Ostiense and Tiburtina stations, but not Termini. Departures from the airport every 15 minutes (hourly on Sunday and public holidays) between 5.58am and 11.28pm; from Ostiense between 5.18am and 10.48pm.

Leonardo Express Train (adult/child €14/free) Runs to/from platform 24 at Stazione Termini. Departures from the airport every 30 minutes between 6.38am and 11.38pm, from Termini between 5.52am and 10.52pm. Journey time is 30 minutes.

SIT Bus (☎06 591 68 26; www.sitbusshuttle.it; Fiumicino one-way €6 or €5 online, €4/6 from/to Ciampino) From the airport regular departures between 8.30am and 12.30am to Via Marsala outside Stazione Termini; from Termini between 9.30am and 1.10am. Tickets are available on the bus. Journey time is one hour.

CIAMPINO

The best option is to take one of the regular bus services into the city centre. Alternatively, you can take a bus to Ciampino train station and then pick up a train to Stazione Termini. The set taxi fare is €30.

Cotral Bus (www.cotralspa.it; one-way €3.90) Runs 15 daily services to/from Via Giolitti near Stazione Termini. Also buses to/from Anagnina metro station (€1.20) and Ciampino train station (€1.20), where you can get a train to Stazione Termini (€1.30).

SIT Bus (www.sitbusshuttle.com; from airport €4, to airport €6) Regular departures from the airport to Via Marsala outside Stazione Termini between 7.45am and 11.15pm, and from Termini between 4.30am and 9.30pm. Get tickets on the bus. Journey time is 45 minutes.

Terravision Bus (www.terravision.eu; one-way €4) Twice hourly departures to/from Via Marsala outside Stazione Termini. From the airport, services are between 8.15am and 12.15am; from Via Marsala between 4.30am and 9.20pm. Buy tickets at Terracafé in front of the Via Marsala bus stop. Journey time is 40 minutes.

Car & Motorcycle

Most of the *centro storico* is closed to normal traffic from 6.30am to 6pm Monday to Friday, from 2pm to 6pm Saturday, and from 11pm to 3am Friday to Sunday – see http://muovi.roma.it for details of the capital's limited traffic zones (*zone a traffico limitato;* ZTL).

PARKING

Blue lines denote pay-and-display parking spaces with tickets available from meters (coins only) and *tabacchi* (tobacconists). Expect to pay up to €1.20 per hour between 8am and 8pm (11pm in some places). After 8pm (or 11pm) parking is generally free until 8am the next morning. If your car gets towed away, check with the **traffic police** (☎06 676 92 303).

Car parks:

Piazzale dei Partigiani (per hr/day €0.77/5; ⊙6am-11pm)

Stazione Termini (Piazza dei Cinquecento; per hr/day €2/18; ⊙6am-1am)

Villa Borghese (Viale del Galoppatoio 33; per hr/day €2.20/20; ⊙24hr)

Public Transport

Rome's public transport system includes buses, trams, metro and a suburban train network.

TICKETS

Tickets are valid for all forms of transport and come in various forms:

Single (BIT; €1.50) Valid for 100 minutes, during which time you can use as many buses or trams as you like but can only go once on the metro.

Daily (BIG; €6) Unlimited travel until midnight of the day of purchase.

Three-day (BTI; €16.50) Unlimited travel for three days.

Weekly (CIS; €24) Unlimited travel for seven days.

Buy tickets at *tabacchi,* newsstands and from vending machines at main bus stops and metro stations. They must be purchased before you start your journey and validated in the machines on buses, at the entrance gates to the metro or at train stations. Ticketless riders risk an on-the-spot €50 fine.

Children under 10 travel free.

BUS

Buses and trams are run by **ATAC** (☎06 57 003; www.atac.roma.it). The main bus station is in front of Stazione Termini on Piazza dei Cinquecento, where there's an **information booth** (Map p748; ⊙7.30am-8pm). Other important hubs are at Largo di Torre Argentina and Piazza Venezia.

Buses generally run from about 5.30am until midnight, with limited services throughout the night.

METRO

Rome's two main metro lines, A (orange) and B (blue), cross at Termini, the only point at which you can change from one line to the other. There is a third line 'B1', which serves the northern suburbs, but you're unlikely to need it.

Take line A for the Trevi Fountain (Barberini), Spanish Steps (Spagna) and Vatican (Ottaviano-San Pietro); line B for the Colosseum (Colosseo).

Trains run between 5.30am and 11.30pm (to 1.30am on Friday and Saturday).

Taxi

Official licensed taxis are white with the symbol of Rome on the doors. Always go with the metered fare, never an arranged price (the set fares to and from the airports are exceptions). Official rates are posted in taxis.

You can hail a taxi, but it's often easier to wait at a rank or phone for one. There are major taxi ranks at the airports, **Stazione Termini**, **Largo di Torre Argentina**, **Piazza della Repubblica** and the **Colosseum**. You can book a taxi by phoning the Comune di Roma's automated **taxi line** (☎06 06 09) or calling a taxi company direct:

La Capitale (☎06 49 94)
Radio Taxi (☎06 35 70)
Samarcanda (☎06 55 51)

AROUND ROME

Ostia Antica

An easy day trip from Rome, the well-preserved ruins of Ostia Antica, ancient Rome's main seaport, form one of Italy's most compelling and under-appreciated archaeological sites. The city was founded in the 4th century BC at the mouth of the Tiber and developed into a major port with a population of around 100,000. Decline came in the 5th century when barbarian invasions and an outbreak of malaria led to its abandonment and slow burial in river silt, thanks to which it has survived so well.

The ruins, the **Scavi Archeologici di Ostia Antica** (☎06 563 52 830; www.ostiantica.info; adult/reduced/EU child €6.50/3.25/free, plus possible exhibition supplement; ⏲8.30am-6pm Tue-Sun Apr-Oct, to 5pm Mar, to 4pm Nov-Dec & Jan-Feb), are spread out and you'll need a few hours to do them justice. The main thoroughfare, the **Decumanus Maximus** leads from the city's entrance, **Porta Romana**, to highlights such as the **Terme di Nettuno** (Baths of Neptune) and the steeply stacked **amphitheatre**. Behind the theatre, the **Piazzale delle Corporazioni** (Forum of the Corporations) housed Ostia's merchant guilds and is decorated with well-preserved mosaics. Further towards Porta Marina, the **Thermopolium** is an ancient cafe complete with a bar and fresco advertising the bill of fare.

To get to Ostia Antica take the Ostia Lido train (25 minutes, half-hourly) from Stazione Porta San Paolo next to Piramide metro station. The journey is covered by standard public-transport tickets. By car, take Via del Mare or Via Ostiense and follow signs for the *scavi*.

Tivoli

POP 56,530

An ancient resort town and playground for the Renaissance rich, hilltop Tivoli is home to two Unesco-listed sites: Villa Adriana, Emperor Hadrian's sprawling summer residence, and Villa d'Este, a Renaissance villa famous for its garden fountains. You can cover both in a day trip from Rome, but you'll have to start early.

Sights

TOP CHOICE **Villa Adriana** ARCHAEOLOGICAL SITE

(☎06 399 67 900; www.villaadriana.beniculturali.it; adult/reduced/EU child €8/4/free, plus possible exhibition supplement, car park €3; ⏲9am-1hr before sunset) Emperor Hadrian's sprawling 1st-century summer residence, 5km outside Tivoli proper, was one of the largest and most sumptuous villas in the Roman Empire. Hadrian personally designed much of it, taking inspiration from buildings he'd seen around the world. The **pecile**, a large porticoed pool, was a reproduction of a building in Athens, and the **canopo** is a copy of the sanctuary of Serapis near Alexandria. To the east of the *pecile* is Hadrian's private retreat, the **Teatro Marittimo**.

Allow several hours to explore the site.

Villa d'Este GARDENS

(☎0774 331 20 70; www.villadestetivoli.info; Piazza Trento; adult/reduced/EU child €8.50/4/free, plus possible exhibition supplement; ⏲8.30am-1hr before sunset Tue-Sun) In Tivoli's hilltop centre, the Renaissance Villa d'Este was originally a Benedictine convent before Lucrezia Borgia's son, Cardinal Ippolito d'Este, transformed into a pleasure palace in 1550. Later, in the 19th century, the composer Franz Liszt lived and worked here.

More than the villa itself, it's the elaborate gardens and fountains that are the main attraction. Highlights include the **Fountain of the Organ**, an extravagant baroque ensemble that uses water pressure to play music through a concealed organ, and the 130m-long **Avenue of the Hundred Fountains**.

Information

Information is available at the **tourist information point** (☎0774 31 35 36; Piazzale delle Nazione Unite; ⏲9.30am-5.30pm Tue-Sun) near the bus stop in the *centro storico*.

Getting There & Away

Tivoli is 30km east of Rome and accessible by Cotral bus (€1.30, 50 minutes, every 10 minutes) from Ponte Mammolo metro station. The fastest route by car is on the Rome–L'Aquila autostrada (A24).

To get to Villa Adriana from Tivoli town centre, take CAT bus 4 or 4X (€1, 10 minutes, half-hourly) from Largo Garibaldi.

NORTHERN ITALY

Italy's well-heeled north is a fascinating area of historical wealth and natural diversity. Bordered by the northern Alps and boasting some of the country's most spectacular coastline, it also encompasses Italy's largest lowland area, the fertile Po valley plain. Of the cities, it's Venice that hogs the limelight, but in their own way Turin, Genoa and Bologna offer plenty to the open-minded traveller. Verona is justifiably considered one of Italy's most beautiful cities, while Padua and Ravenna harbour celebrated artistic treasures.

Genoa

POP 607,900

One of the Mediterranean's great ports, Genoa (Genova) is an absorbing city of aristocratic *palazzi,* dark, malodorous alleyways, Gothic architecture and industrial sprawl. Its shadowy, sometimes seedy, *centro storico* teems with life while its grand palaces house artistic treasures amassed during its heyday as a powerful maritime republic known as La Superba. The city's main draw – apart from its cosmopolitan air and sense of history (Christopher Columbus was born here in 1451) – is its aquarium, Europe's second largest.

Sights

Most sights are in the *centro storico* and Porto Antico (Old Port) between the city's two main train stations: Stazione Brignole and Stazione Principe.

For assiduous museum-goers, the **museum card** (24/48hr €12/16) gives free admission to 22 museums and discounted entry to the aquarium and other sights. Buy it at tourist offices or participating museums.

Piazza de Ferrari PIAZZA

Genoa's main piazza is a good place to start exploring the city. Grandiose and impressive, it's centred on an exuberant fountain and ringed by imposing *palazzi* – **Palazzo della Borsa**, Italy's former stock exchange, **Teatro Carlo Felice**, the city's neoclassical opera house, and the huge **Palazzo Ducale** (www.palazzoducale.genova.it; Piazza Giacomo Matteotti 9; admission depends on exhibition; ⏲exhibitions 9am-9pm), once the seat of the city's rulers but now used to host major art exhibitions.

Musei di Strada Nuova MUSEUM

(www.museidigenova.it; combined ticket adult/concession €8/6; ⏲9am-7pm Tue-Fri, 10am-7pm Sat & Sun) Genoa's main museums are in a series of *palazzi* on Via Garibaldi, where the city's richest families once lived. The three most important, known collectively as the Musei di Strada Nuova, are housed in **Palazzo Bianco** (Via Garibaldi 11), **Palazzo Rosso** (Via Garibaldi 18) and **Palazzo Doria-Tursi** (www.museidigenova.it; Via Garibaldi 9). The first two feature works by Flemish, Dutch, Spanish and Italian masters, while the third displays the personal effects of Genoa's legendary violinist Niccolò Paganini. Tickets, valid for all three museums, are available from the bookshop in Palazzo Doria-Tursi.

Cattedrale di San Lorenzo CHURCH

(Piazza San Lorenzo; ⏲8am-noon & 3-7pm) Genoa's Gothic-Romanesque cathedral is notable for its striking black-and-white-striped facade. Fronted by twisting columns and crouching lions, it was first consecrated in 1118 but the two bell towers and cupola were added in the 16th century.

Acquario di Genova AQUARIUM

(☎010 2 34 51; www.acquariodigenova.it; Ponte Spinola; adult/child €19/13; ⏲8.30am-10pm daily

Jul & Aug, varied hrs rest of year) The main attraction in Genoa's **Porto Antico** is Europe's second-largest aquarium. Designed by Italian architect Renzo Piano, it houses 5000 animals in six million litres of water.

Renzo Piano was also responsible for two of the port's other landmarks: the **Biosfere** (Ponte Spinola; adult/child €5/3.50; ⌚10am-7pm mid-Mar–mid-Nov, 10am-5pm rest of year), a giant glass ball housing a tropical ecosystem, and the **Bigo** (Calata Cattaneo; adult/child €4/3; ⌚10am-11pm Jun-Aug, 2-6pm Mon, 10am-6pm Tue-Sun Mar-May, Sep & Oct, 10am-5pm Sat & Sun Nov-Feb), an eye-catching panoramic lift.

Sleeping

TOP CHOICE Hotel Cairoli HOTEL €€
(☎010 246 14 54; www.hotelcairoligenova.com; Via Cairoli 14/4; r €60-160; ❄@📶) Colourful, friendly and central, the Cairoli makes quite an impression. Rooms are themed on works by celebrated modern artists and the public spaces, which include a communal library, chill-out area, internet room and fully equipped gym, create a bright, welcoming vibe.

Locanda di Palazzo Cicala BOUTIQUE HOTEL €€
(☎010 251 88 24; www.palazzocicala.it; Piazza San Lorenzo 16; r €109-129, ste €159-219; ❄@📶) Housed in a grand 16th-century *palazzo* opposite the cathedral, this welcoming boutique hotel has huge high-ceilinged rooms replete with parquet and slick designer furniture. There are also several apartments available in nearby buildings.

Albergo Carola PENSION €
(☎010 839 13 40; www.pensionecarola.com; 3rd fl, Via Groppallo 4; d €60-90, without bathroom s €23-50, d €40-90; 📶) This is a classic family-run *pensione* with nine simple, well-kept rooms on the 3rd floor of a lovely old building near Stazione Brignole. Rates don't include breakfast.

Ostello Genova HOSTEL €
(☎010 242 24 57; www.ostellogenova.it; Via Costanzi 120; dm €17, s/d €28/50, without bathroom s/d €24/44; ⌚reception 9am-3.30pm & midnight-7am Feb–mid-Dec; P📶) A steep bus ride from the centre, Genoa's hillside hostel is a functional, institutional affair with basic facilities and sweeping city views. Hostelling International (HI) cards, which are available at check-in, are mandatory. Catch bus 40 from Stazione Brignole or Via Napoli.

Eating

Ligurian specialities include pesto (a sauce of basil, garlic, pine nuts and Parmesan cheese) served with *trofie* (pasta curls), and focaccia (flat bread made with olive oil).

Trattoria della Raibetta TRATTORIA €€
(www.trattoriadellaraibetta.it; Vico Caprettari 10-12; mains €14; ⌚Tue-Sun) For a taste of authentic Genoese cooking, search out this inviting trattoria near the Porto Antico. It's a snug place with a low, brick-vaulted ceiling, pale yellow walls, and a thoughtful menu featuring minestrone and pesto alongside steaks and fresh seafood.

Regina Margherita RISTORANTE €€
(☎010 595 57 53; Piazza della Vittoria 89-103; mains from €15, pizzas from €6) A bright, modern set-up with a two-floor interior and a small outdoor terrace. It's not in a particularly enticing location – on Piazza della Vittoria – but it's very popular and the food is excellent. Speciality of the house is the wood-fired Neapolitan pizza.

La Cremeria delle Erbe GELATERIA €
(Piazza delle Erbe 15-17; cones from €2; ⌚11am-1am Mon-Thu & Sun, to 2am Fri & Sat) On humming cafe-clad Piazza delle Erbe, this fab *gelateria* is perfectly placed for a quick ice-cream fix. The cream-based flavours are especially good, including a blissful *millefoglie*.

Osteria San Matteo OSTERIA €€
(☎010 247 32 82; Piazza San Matteo 4r; mains €13) With its wood beams and exposed-brick walls, this is an inviting *osteria* in the heart of the *centro storico*. It serves a full menu but the reasonably priced seafood is the thing to go for.

Drinking & Entertainment

Action centres on the *centro storico*, with a number of good bars clustered around Piazza delle Erbe.

Mcafé CAFE
(Piazza Giacomo Matteotti 5; ⌚8am-9.30pm Tue-Fri, 10am-9.30pm Sat & Sun) This swish cafe in the atrium of Palazzo Ducale is good any-time of the day – for a morning cappuccino, a quick lunchtime bite or an evening *aperitivo*. Upstairs, a restaurant serves set lunch menus (€12) on weekdays and brunch (€16) at weekends.

Storico Lounge Café CAFE
(Piazza de Ferrari 34/36r; ⏰6am-3am) The daily *aperitivo* (5pm to 10.30pm) draws a mixed crowd to this popular cafe overlooking Piazza de Ferrari. Grab a square-side table and join the locals over a cool, well-mixed cocktail and snacks from the abundant buffet.

Teatro Carlo Felice THEATRE
(☎010 538 12 24; www.carlofelice.it; Passo Eugenio Montale 4) Genoa's historic four-stage opera house stages a full program of opera, ballet and classical music. Tickets generally start at around €23 for ballet and €25 for opera.

Information

There are tourist offices at: **Airport** (☎010 601 52 47; Airport; ⏰10am-1pm & 1.30-6.30pm); **De Ferrari** (☎010 860 61 22; www.visitgenoa.it; Largo Pertini 13; ⏰10am-1pm & 3-6pm Mon-Sat); **Via Garibaldi** (☎010 557 29 03; Via Garibaldi 12r; ⏰9am-6.30pm); **Antico Porto.** (010 557 42 00; Piazza Caricamento; ⏰9am-6.30pm summer, to 6pm winter)

Getting There & Around

Air

Genoa's **Cristoforo Colombo airport** (☎010 6 01 51; www.airport.genova.it) is 6km west of the city. To get to/from it, the Volabus shuttle connects with Stazione Brignole and Stazione Principe (€6, 30 minutes, hourly 5.20am to 10.10pm to airport, 6am to 11.30pm from airport). Buy tickets on board or at tourist offices.

A taxi costs €7 per person (minimum three peole) from Stazione Principe and €8 from Brignole. For fewer than three people the minimum rate is €15.

Boat

Ferries sail to/from Spain, Sicily, Sardinia, Corsica and Tunisia from **Terminal Traghetti** (Ferry Terminal; www.porto.genova.it; Via Milano 51), west of the city centre. Ferry companies:

Grandi Navi Veloci (GNV; ☎010 209 45 91; www.gnv.it) To/from Sicily (Palermo from €58, 20½ hours), Barcelona (€95, 19½ hours) and Tunis (€99, 23½ hours).

Moby Lines (☎199 30 30 40; www.mobylines.it) To/from Sardinia (Olbia from €80.85, 11 hours).

Tirrenia (☎89 21 23; www.tirrenia.it) To/from Sardinia (Porto Torres €54, 10 hours), Olbia (€54, 9¾ hours) and Arbatax (€55, 14½ hours).

Bus

Buses to international and regional destinations depart from Piazza della Vittoria, south of Stazione Brignole. Book tickets at **Geotravels** (Piazza della Vittoria 57).

Local buses are run by **AMT** (www.amt.genova.it). Tickets cost €1.50 and are valid for 100 minutes. Bus 20 runs from Via Luigi Cadorna near Stazione Brignole up to Piazza de Ferrari and Via Andrea Doria, stopping near Stazione Principe.

AMT tickets are also valid on Genoa's small metro system.

Train

There are direct trains to Turin (€18, two hours, up to 15 daily), Milan (€18.50, 1½ hours, hourly), Pisa (€18, two to three hours, up to 14 daily) and Rome (€44 to €58.50, 4½ to 5½ hours, nine daily). Regional trains to La Spezia serve the Cinque Terre (€7.30, two hours, hourly).

It generally makes little difference whether you leave from Brignole or Principe.

Cinque Terre

Liguria's eastern Riviera boasts some of Italy's most dramatic coastline, the highlight of which is the Unesco-listed **Parco Nazionale delle Cinque Terre** (Cinque Terre National Park) just north of La Spezia. Running for 18km, this awesome stretch of plunging cliffs and vine-covered hills is named after its five tiny villages: Riomaggiore, Manarola, Corniglia, Vernazza and Monterosso.

The area's beauty masks its vulnerability; in autumn 2011 heavy rainfall caused severe flooding and mudslides, leaving four people dead. Further problems arose a year later when four Australian tourists were injured by rockfalls on the coast's most popular trail. The villages are now up and running again but several paths remain closed.

It gets very crowded in summer, so try to come in spring or autumn. You can either visit on a day trip from Genoa or La Spezia, or stay overnight in one of the five villages.

Sights & Activities

The Cinque Terre villages are linked by the 9km **Sentiero Azzurro** (Blue Trail; admission with Cinque Terre Card), a magnificent, mildly challenging five-hour trail. The path, which is marked No 2 on maps, is in four stages, the easiest of which is the first from Riomaggiore to Manarola (Via dell'Amore; 20 minutes) and the second from Manarola to Corniglia (one hour). For the final two stages, you'll need to be fit and wearing proper walking shoes. The stretch from Corniglia to Vernazza takes approximately 1½ hours and from Vernazza to Monterosso it's two hours. Make sure you bring a hat, sunscreen and plenty of water if walking in hot weather. At the time of writing, the Sentiero was closed for reconstruction work after the floods in 2011 and rockfalls in 2012. For the latest information check www.parconazionale5terre.it.

The Sentiero Azzurro is just one of a network of footpaths and cycle trails that criss-cross the park – details are available from the park offices. If water sports are more your thing, you can hire snorkelling gear (€10 per day) and kayaks (double €10 per hour) at the **Diving Center 5 Terre** (www.5terrediving.com; Via San Giacomo) in Riomaggiore. It also offers a snorkelling boat tour for €20.

CINQUE TERRE CARD

To walk the Sentiero Azzurro or any other of the Cinque Terre paths, you'll need a Cinque Terre Card. This comes in two forms:

Cinque Terre Card (adult/child 1 day €5/2.50, 2 days €8/4, family card 1/2 days €12.50/20) Available at all park offices.

Cinque Terre Treno Card (adult/child 1 day €10/6, 2 days €19) As for the Cinque Terre Card plus unlimited train travel between La Spezia and the five villages.

Sleeping & Eating

L'Eremo sul Mare B&B €
(346 019 58 80; www.eremosulmare.com; d €80-110;) On the Sentiero Azzurro, about a 15-minute steep walk from Vernazza, this charming B&B is set in an idyllic cliffside position. With only three rooms and stunning sea views, it's a wonderful spot for a romantic escape. Cash only.

Hotel Ca' d'Andrean HOTEL €
(0187 92 00 40; www.cadandrean.it; Via Doscovolo 101, Manarola; s €55-75, d €70-105;) An excellent family-run hotel offering comfortable rooms and value-for-money in the upper part of Manarola. Rooms are big and cool with tiled floors and unobtrusive furniture; some also have private terraces. Breakfast (€6) is served in the garden. No credit cards.

Ostello 5 Terre HOSTEL €
(0187 92 00 39; www.hostel5terre.com; Via Riccobaldi 21, Manarola; dm €20-23, d €55-65, q €88-100;) In Manarola, this is a decent private-run hostel with bright single-sex dorms and private rooms with en suite bathrooms. Extras include breakfast (€5) and dinner (€10), laundry facilities and a book exchange. Book at least a week ahead in summer.

Dau Cila MODERN ITALIAN €€
(0187 76 00 32; www.ristorantedaucila.com; Via San Giacomo 65, Riomaggiore; mains €18; 8am-2am Mar-Oct) Perched within pebble-lobbing distance of Riomaggiore's snug harbour, Dau Cila is a smart restaurant-cum-*enoteca* (wine bar) specialising in excellent local wine and classy seafood such as *paccheri* (large pasta rings) with cuttlefish and red cabbage.

Marina Piccola SEAFOOD €
(0187 76 20 65; www.hotelmarinapiccola.com; Via Lo Scalo 16, Manarola; mains €16, s/d €90/120, half-/full-board per person €90/105;) Dine on fresh-off-the-boat seafood and house speciality *zuppa di datteri* (date soup) at this popular harbour-side restaurant in Manarola. If you want to stay, the adjoining hotel has small, comfortable rooms.

Information

The most convenient **information office** (0187 92 06 33; 8am-7pm) is at Riomaggiore train station. There are also offices in the stations at Manarola, Corniglia, Vernazza, Monterosso and La Spezia (most open 8am to 7pm).

Online information is available at www.parconazionale5terre.it and www.cinqueterre.com

Getting There & Away

Boat

Between July and September, **Golfo Paradiso** (0185 77 20 91; www.golfoparadiso.it) operates excursions from Genoa's Porto Antico to Vernazza and Monterosso. These cost €18 one-way, €33 return.

From late March to October, **Consorzio Marittimo Turistico 5 Terre** (0187 73 29 87; www.navigazionegolfodeipoeti.it) runs daily ferries between La Spezia and four of the villages (not Corniglia), costing €18 one-way. Return trips are covered by a daily ticket (weekdays/weekends €25/27).

Train

From Genoa Principe (€7.30) and Brignole (€6.60) direct trains run to Riomaggiore (1½ to two hours, 18 daily), stopping at each of the Cinque Terre villages.

Between 4.30am and 11.10pm, one to three trains an hour crawl up the coast from La Spezia to Levanto (€3.30, 30 minutes), stopping at all of the villages en route.

Turin

POP 907,600

First-time visitors are often surprised by Turin (Torino). Expecting a bleak, industrial sprawl dominated by Fiat factories, they are instead confronted with a dynamic and attractive city full of regal *palazzi,* historic cafes, baroque piazzas and world-class museums. Thc city was the seat of the royal Savoy family for centuries, and between 1861 and 1864 was Italy's first post-unification capital. More recently, it hosted the 2006 Winter Olympics and was European Capital of Design in 2008.

Sights

Serious sightseers should consider the **Torino & Piedmont Card** (2/3/5/7 days €25/29/34/37, junior 2 days €12), available at tourist offices, which gives free entry to 180 museums, monuments and castles, as well as discounts on tourist attractions and car rental.

Mole Antonelliana MUSEUM

(Via Montebello 20) The symbol of Turin, this 167m tower with its distinctive aluminium spire appears on the Italian two-cent coin. It was originally intended as a synagogue but now houses the enjoyable **Museo Nazionale del Cinema** (www.museonazionaledelcinema.org; adult/reduced €9/7, incl panoramic lift €12/9; ⏲9am-8pm Tue-Fri & Sun, to 11pm Sat) and its comprehensive collection of film memorabilia. Don't miss the glass **panoramic lift** (Mole Antonelliana Tower; adult/reduced €6/4, incl museum €12/9; ⏲10am-8pm Tue-Fri & Sun, to 11pm Sat), which whisks you up 85m to the Mole's roof terrace in 59 seconds.

Museo Egizio MUSEUM

(Egyptian Museum; www.museoegizio.org; Via Accademia delle Scienze 6; adult/reduced €8/6; ⏲8.30am-7.30pm Tue-Sun) Opened in 1824, this legendary museum houses the most important collection of Egyptian treasure outside of Cairo. Two of many highlights are a statue of Ramesses II (one of the world's most important pieces of Egyptian art) and over 500 items found in the tomb of Kha and Merit (from 1400 BC).

Piazza Castello PIAZZA

Turin's grandest square is bordered by porticoed promenades and regal palaces. Dominating the piazza, the part-medieval, part-baroque **Palazzo Madama**, the original seat of the Italian parliament, is home to the **Museo Civico d'Arte Antica** (www.palazzomadamatorino.it; Piazza Castello; adult/reduced €10/8; ⏲10am-6pm Tue-Sat, to 7pm Sun), whose impressive collection includes Gothic and Renaissance paintings and some interesting majolica work. To the north, statues of Castor and Pollux guard the entrance to the **Palazzo Reale** (Piazza Castello; adult/reduced €10/5; ⏲8.30am-7.30pm Tue-Sun), built for Carlo Emanuele II around 1646. The palace's **Giardino Reale** (Royal Garden; admission free; ⏲9am-1hr before sunset) was designed by André le Nôtre, who also created the gardens at Versailles.

A short walk away, **Piazza San Carlo**, known as Turin's drawing room, is famous for its cafes and twin baroque churches **San Carlo** and **Santa Cristina**.

Cattedrale di San Giovanni Battista CHURCH

(Piazza San Giovanni; ⏲8am-noon & 3-7pm) Turin's 15th-century cathedral houses the famous **Shroud of Turin** *(Sindone),* supposedly the cloth used to wrap the crucified Christ. A copy is on permanent display in front of the altar, while the real thing is kept in a vacuum-sealed box and rarely revealed.

Pinacoteca Giovanni e Marella Agnelli GALLERY

(www.pinacoteca-agnelli.it; Via Nizza 230; adult/reduced €4/2.50; ⏲10:30am-7pm Tue-Sun) This Renzo Piano–designed modern art gallery displays masterpieces by Canaletto, Renoir, Manet, Matisse and Picasso in the Lingotto, Fiat's former car factory.

Sleeping

TOP CHOICE **Art Hotel Boston** BOUTIQUE HOTEL €€€

(☎011 50 03 59; www.hotelbostontorino.it; Via Massena 70; s €80-120, d €110-400; ❄@📶) The Boston's austere facade gives no inkling of the explosion of modern art inside. Public areas are filled with original works by Warhol, Lichtenstein and Aldo Mondino, while individually styled guest rooms are themed on subjects as diverse as Lavazza coffee, the Diabolik comic character, Ayrton Senna and Pablo Picasso.

Hotel Montevecchio HOTEL €€

(☎011 562 00 23; www.hotelmontevecchio.com; Via Montevecchio 13; s €40-90, d €55-140; @📶) In a quiet residential area 300m from Stazione Porta Nuova, this two-star offers a friendly welcome and bright, good-sized rooms. Useful extras include a laundry service and wi-fi (€1 for 30 minutes).

HISTORIC CAFES

Turin is home to an impressive array of historic cafes:

Baratti & Milano (☎011 561 30 60; Piazza Castello 27; mains about €10-15; ⏰8am-9pm Tue-Sun) Serving coffee and confectionary since 1875.

Caffè San Carlo (Piazza San Carlo 156; ⏰8am-midnight Tue-Fri, to 1am Sat, to 9pm Mon) Dates from 1822.

Caffè Torino (Piazza San Carlo 204; ⏰7.30am-1am) A relative newcomer, this art nouveau gem opened in 1903.

Neuv Caval'd Brôns (Piazza San Carlo 155; ⏰7.30am-1am) A 20th-century imposter named after the equestrian statue of Emanuele Filiberto on Piazza San Carlo.

San Tommaso 10 (Via San Tommaso 10; ⏰8am-midnight Mon-Sat) This is where Lavazza started. It now serves an unorthodox array of flavoured coffees as well as all the classics.

L'Orso Poeta B&B **€€**
(☎011 517 89 96; www.orsopoeta-bed-and-beakfast.it; Corso Vittorio Emanuele II 10; s/d €70/110; ❄📶) A welcoming B&B in a historic apartment building by the Po River. Its two small, pastel-shaded rooms have bathrooms and lots of character. Note that it's closed in August, December and January.

Alpi Resort Hotel BUSINESS HOTEL **€**
(☎011 812 96 77; www.hotelalpiresort.it; Via A Bonafous 5; s €54-65, d €69-85; ❄📶) A businesslike three-star in an excellent location just off Piazza Vittorio Veneto. Its impeccably clean, carpeted rooms are quiet and comfortable, if rather characterless.

Eating & Drinking

Turin has a reputation for magnificent gelato, which you can sample at outlets of **Grom** (www.grom.it; Piazza Pietro Paleocapa; ⏰11am-midnight Sun-Thu, to 1am Fri & Sat) at Piazza Paleocapa 1d, Via Accademia delle Scienze 4 and Via Garibaldi 11, or the critically acclaimed newcomer **+ Di Un Gelato** (www.piudiungelato.it; Galleria Subalpina 32, entrance on Piazza Carlo Alberto; small cone or tub €2; ⏰12.30am-8pm Mon-Fri, to 10pm Sat & Sun).

Early evening is the time to make for one of the city's cafes and enjoy an *aperitivo* (about €8) accompanied by a sumptuous buffet (included in the price). Popular *aperitivo* precincts include Piazza Emanuele Filiberto and environs, and Piazza Vittorio Veneto: try **I Tre Galli** (www.3galli.com; Via Sant'Agostino 25; ⏰12.30am-2.30pm & 6.30pm-midnight Mon-Wed, to 2am Thu-Sat) or **La Drogheria** (www.la-drogheria.it; Piazza Vittorio Veneto 18; ⏰10am-2am).

L'Hamburgheria di Eataly BURGERS **€**
(Piazza Solferino 16a; burgers from €5.50; ⏰11am-11pm Mon-Thu & Sun, to 1am Sat) Run by the Slow Food–backed Eataly chain, this cool burger bar takes fast food upmarket with a smart brick-and-steel interior and select menu. Choose your gourmet burger, made from locally sourced Piedmontese beef, and sit back with a bottle of artisanal beer as you wait.

Sfashion PIZZERIA **€**
(☎011 516 00 85; Via Cesare Battisti 13; pizzas from €5.80, mains from €8.50) Overlooking Piazza Carlo Alberto, Sfashion is currently the hottest pizza ticket in town. The Neapolitan-style pizzas fly like hot bullets from the ovens of this kooky cafe-cum-pizzeria owned by local TV celebrity Piero Chiambretti.

Otto Etre Quarti PIZZERIA, RISTORANTE **€€**
(☎011 517 63 67; Piazza Solferino 8c; pizzas from €5, mains from €15) Claim a table in one of 8¾'s high-ceilinged dining rooms or on the square-side terrace and feast on fab pizzas or tasty pastas such as *cavatelli con salsiccia e zafferano* (small fingers of pasta with sausage and saffron).

Information

The city's efficient **tourist office** (☎010 53 51 81; www.turismotorino.org) has branches at **Porta Nuova station** (⏰9am-6pm Mon-Sat, to 3pm Sun), **Piazza Castello** (⏰9am-7pm) and **Via Giuseppe Verdi** (⏰9am-7pm) near the Mole Antonelliana.

Getting There & Around

In Caselle, 16km northwest of the city centre, **Turin airport** (www.turin-airport.com) serves flights to/from European and national destinations.

Sadem (www.sadem.it) runs an airport shuttle (€5.50 or €6 on board, 40 minutes, half-hourly) between the airport and Porta Nuova train station. A taxi costs approximately €35 to €40.

Direct trains connect with Milan (€11 to €30, one to two hours, up to 30 daily), Florence (€65, three hours, seven daily), Genoa (€18, two hours, up to 15 daily) and Rome (€90, 4¼ hours, nine daily).

Milan

POP 1.32 MILLION

Few Italian cities polarise opinion like Milan, Italy's financial and fashion capital. Some people love the cosmopolitan, can-do atmosphere, the vibrant cultural scene and the sophisticated shopping; others grumble that the city's dirty, ugly and expensive. Certainly, it lacks the picture-postcard beauty of many Italian towns, but in among the urban hustle are some truly great sights – Leonardo da Vinci's *Last Supper*, the immense Duomo and the world-famous La Scala opera house.

Originally founded by Celtic tribes in the 7th century BC, Milan was conquered by the Romans in 222 BC and developed into a major trading and transport centre. From the 13th century it flourished under the rule of two powerful families, the Visconti and Sforza.

Sights

Milan's main attractions are concentrated in the area between Piazza del Duomo and Castello Sforzesco. To get to the piazza from Stazione Centrale, take the yellow MM3 underground line.

Duomo CHURCH

(www.duomomilano.it; Piazza del Duomo; roof stairs/lift €7/12; 7am-6.45pm, roof stairs 9am-6.30pm, lift 9am-8.30pm; MDuomo) With a capacity of 40,000 people, this is the world's largest Gothic cathedral and the third-largest church in Europe. Commissioned in 1386 to a florid French-Gothic design and finished nearly 600 years later, it's a fairy-tale ensemble of 3200 statues, 135 spires and 146 stained-glass windows. Climb to the roof for memorable city views with tickets bought at the nearby **Duomo Information Point** (02 720 23 375; www.duomomilano.it; Via dell'Arcivescovado 1; 9am-8.30pm).

Galleria Vittorio Emanuele II ARCHITECTURE

(Piazza del Duomo; MDuomo) Opening onto Piazza Duomo, the neoclassical Galleria Vittorio Emanuele is a soaring iron-and-glass shopping arcade known locally as *il salotto bueno,* the city's fine drawing room. Long-standing Milanese tradition claims you can ward off bad luck by grinding your heel into the testicles of the mosaic bull on the floor.

Teatro alla Scala OPERA HOUSE

(La Scala; www.teatroallascala.org; Via Filodrammatici 2) Milan's legendary opera house hides its sumptuous six-tiered interior behind a surprisingly severe exterior. You can peek inside as part of a visit to the theatre's **Museo Teatrale alla Scala** (La Scala Museum; 02 433 53 521; Largo Ghiringhelli 1; adult/child €6/4; 9am-12.30pm & 1.30-5.30pm) providing there are no performances or rehearsals in progress.

The Last Supper MURAL

(Il Cenacolo Vinciano; 02 928 00 360; www.cenacolovinciano.net; Piazza Santa Maria delle Grazie 2; adult/reduced/EU child €6.50/3.25/free, plus booking fee €1.50; 8.15am-6.45pm Tue-Sun; MCadorna) Milan's most famous tourist attraction – Leonardo da Vinci's mural of *The Last Supper* – is in the Cenacolo Vinciano, the refectory of the **Chiesa di Santa Maria delle Grazie**, west of the city centre. To see it you need to book ahead or take a city tour.

Castello Sforzesco CASTLE

(02 884 63 700; www.milanocastello.it; Piazza Castello; 7am-7pm summer, to 6pm winter; MCairoli) Originally a Visconti fortress, this immense red-brick castle was later home to the Sforza dynasty that ruled Renaissance Milan. Today, it shelters the **Musei del Castello** (www.milanocastello.it; Piazza Castello 3; adult/EU child €3/free; 9am-5.30pm Tue-Sun), a series of museums dedicated to art, sculpture, archaeology and music. Entry is free on Friday between 2pm and 5.30pm and on Tuesday, Wednesday, Thursday, Saturday and Sunday between 4.30pm and 5.30pm.

Pinacoteca di Brera GALLERY

(02 722 63 264; www.brera.beniculturali.it; Via Brera 28; adult/concession/EU child €6/3/free; 8.30am-7.15pm Tue-Sun; MLanza) Above the prestigious Brera Academy, this gallery houses Milan's most impressive collection of old masters, including works by Rembrandt, Goya, van Dyck, Titian, Tintoretto and Caravaggio. A highlight is Andrea Mantegna's brutal masterpiece *Cristo morto nel Sepolcro e tre Dolenti* (Lamentation over the Dead Christ).

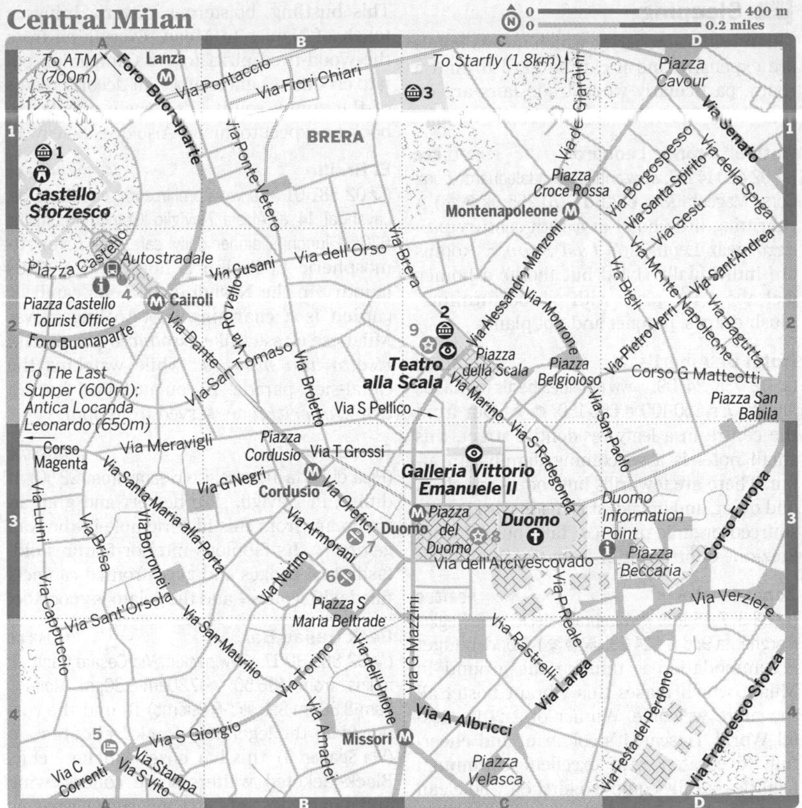

Central Milan

Top Sights

Castello Sforzesco	A1
Duomo	C3
Galleria Vittorio Emanuele II	C3
Teatro alla Scala	C2

Sights

1 Musei del Castello	A1
2 Museo Teatrale alla Scala	C2
3 Pinacoteca di Brera	C1

Activities, Courses & Tours

4 Autostradale	A2

Sleeping

5 Ariston Hotel	A4

Eating

6 Peck Delicatessen	B3
7 Peck Italian Bar	B3

Entertainment

8 Box Office	C3
9 Teatro alla Scala	C2

Tours

Autostradale (☎02 720 01 304; www.autostradale.it; Piazza Castello 1) runs walking tours (€20) and three-hour multilingual bus tours (€60) that take in the main sights and include entry to *The Last Supper*. Book tickets online or at the Autostradale office.

Sleeping

Milan is a business city, which means hotels are expensive and it can be hard to find a room, particularly when trade fairs are on (which is often). Booking is essential.

Antica Locanda Leonardo HOTEL €€€
(☎02 480 14 197; www.anticalocandaleonardo.com; Corso Magenta 78; s €120, d €170-265; ❄@📶) A charming little hotel in a 19th-century *palazzo* near Leonardo's *Last Supper*. Rooms are individually styled but there's a homey feel about the place with period furniture, plush drapes, parquet and pot plants.

Hotel De Albertis HOTEL €€
(☎02 738 34 09; www.hoteldealbertis.it; Via De Albertis 7; s €50-100, d €50-160; @📶) Out from the centre in a leafy residential street, this small hotel is a welcoming, family-run affair. There are few frills but rooms are clean and quiet, and breakfast is made with locally sourced organic produce. Take bus 92 from Stazione Centrale or 27 from the Duomo.

Zebra Hostel HOSTEL €
(☎02 367 05 185; www.zebrahostel.it; Viale Regina Margherita 9; dm €24-29; ❄@📶) Good budget accommodation is thin on the ground in Milan, which makes this vibrant hostel all the more welcome. Winner of a 2012 Hostel World 'Hoscar', it's colourful and cheerfully decorated with excellent communal facilities, a fully equipped kitchen, and clean mixed and same-sex dorms.

Ariston Hotel HOTEL €€€
(☎02 720 00 556; www.aristonhotel.com; Largo Carrobbio 2; s €66-280, d €80-400; ❄@📶) A business-style hotel offering decent three-star rooms about 10 minutes' walk from Piazza del Duomo. Check the website for low-season deals.

Eating & Drinking

Local specialities include *risotto alla milanese* (saffron-infused risotto cooked in bone-marrow stock) and *cotoletta alla milanese* (breaded veal cutlet).

There are hundreds of bars and restaurants in Milan but as a general rule, the area around the Duomo is full of smart business-oriented restaurants, Brera is a fashionable bar haunt and the lively Navigli canal district caters to all tastes.

Piccola Ischia PIZZERIA €
(☎02 204 76 13; Via Morgagni 7; pizzas €3-8; ⏲lunch & dinner Mon, Tue, Thu & Fri, dinner only Sat & Sun) This bustling, boisterous pizzeria brings a touch of Naples to Milan. Everything from the wood-fired pizza to the Campanian potato croquettes and exuberant decor screams of the sunny south. It's hugely popular so book or expect to queue. Also does takeaway.

El Brellin RISTORANTE €€€
(☎02 581 01 351; www.brellin.com; cnr Vicolo dei Lavandai 14 & Alzaia Naviglio Grande 14; mains €20; ⏲lunch & dinner daily, cafe from 6pm) Atmospheric El Brellin is housed in a 1700s laundry in the Navigli district. Its candlelit garden is a charming spot to linger over Milanese classics like *ossobucco* (oxtail) *con risotto alla milanese* while watching the canal-side parade. If you just just fancy a drink, *aperitivi* are served from 6pm.

Rinomata GELATERIA €
(Ripa di Porta Ticinese; ice creams from €2.50) If dining in Navigli, skip dessert and grab an ice cream from this historic hole-in-the-wall *gelateria*. Its fabulous interior features old-fashioned fridges and glass-fronted cabinets filled with cones – and the gelato is good, too.

Peck Italian Bar ITALIAN €€
(☎02 869 30 17; www.peck.it; Via Cesare Cantù 3; mains from €16.50; ⏲7.30am-8.30pm Mon-Fri, 9am-8.30pm Sat; ❄; ⓂDuomo) Round the corner from the legendary **Peck Delicatessen** (Via Spadari 9), this bar oozes Milanese chic. Black-jacketed waiters serve coffees, wine and a daily dose of pasta to a stylish, sharply dressed crowd.

BQ Navigli BAR
(Birra Artigianale di Qualità; Via Alzaia Naviglio Grande 44; ⏲6pm-2am) In recent years Italy has been rediscovering the joys of beer and this canal-front bar has a fine selection of local brews ranging from light lagers to dark, hardcore bitters. Panini and *piadine* (pitta bread-style rolls) provide the solids.

Entertainment

Milan offers a rich and vibrant cultural scene, ranging from opera at La Scala to world-class football and cutting-edge club nights. September is a good time for classical-music fans, as the city co-hosts the **Torino Milano Festival Internazionale della Musica** (www.mitosettembremusica.it).

The opera season at **Teatro alla Scala** (☎02 8 87 91; www.teatroallascala.org; Piazza della Scala; ⓂDuomo) runs from November to July, but you can see theatre, ballet and concerts year-round, with the exception of August.

FOOTBALL IN MILAN

Milan is home to Italy's two most successful *calcio* (football) teams: the Berlusconi-owned AC Milan and Internazionale, aka Inter. During the season (September to May), the two clubs play on alternate Sundays at the **Stadio Giuseppe Meazza** (Via Piccolomini 5; Ⓜ Lotto), aka the San Siro. Match tickets (from €18) are available from branches of Banca Intesa (AC Milan) and Banca Popolare di Milano (Inter). To get to the stadium on match days, take the free shuttle bus from the Lotto (MM1) metro station.

Tickets are available online or from the **box office** (Galleria del Sagrato; ⏲noon-6pm) beneath Piazza del Duomo. Bank on €12 to €187 for opera and €10 to €115 for ballet performances.

For jazz, **Blue Note** (☎02 690 16 888; www.bluenotemilano.com; Via Borsieri 37; tickets €20-35; ⏲Tue-Sun Sep-Jul; Ⓜ Zara, Garibaldi) stages top international and Italian performers.

Shopping

For designer clobber head to the so-called Golden Quad, the area around Via della Spiga, Via Sant'Andrea, Via Monte Napoleone and Via Alessandro Manzoni. Street markets are held around the canals, notably on Viale Papiniano on Tuesday mornings and Saturdays.

Information

There are tourist offices at **Piazza Castello** (☎02 774 04 343; Piazza Castello 1; ⏲9am-6pm Mon-Fri, 9am-1.30pm & 2-6pm Sat, to 5pm Sun) and **Stazione Centrale** (☎02 774 04 318; opposite platform 13, Stazione Centrale; ⏲9am-6pm Mon-Fri, 9am-1.30pm & 2-6pm Sat, to 5pm Sun).

Useful websites include www.visitamilano.it and www.hellomilano.it.

Pharmacy (☎02 669 07 35; Stazione Centrale; ⏲24hr)

Police Station (☎02 6 22 61; Via Fatebenefratelli 11)

Getting There & Away

Air

Most international flights fly into Malpensa Airport (p846), about 50km northwest of Milan. Domestic and some European flights use **Linate airport** (LIN; ☎flight information 02 23 23 23; www.milanolinate.eu/it), about 7km east of the city. Low-cost airlines often use **Orio al Serio airport** (BG; ☎035 32 63 23; www.sacbo.it), near Bergamo.

Train

Regular daily trains depart Stazione Centrale for Venice (€36, 2½ hours), Bologna (€40, one hour), Florence (€50, 1¾ hours), Rome (€86, three to 3½ hours) and other Italian and European cities. Note that these prices are for the fast Frecce services.

Most regional trains also stop at Stazione Nord in Piazzale Cadorna.

Getting Around

To/From the Airport

MALPENSA

Malpensa Shuttle (☎02 585 83 185; www.malpensashuttle.it; adult/child €10/5) Buses run to/from Piazza Luigi di Savoia next to Stazione Centrale every 20 minutes between 4.15am and 12.30pm. Buy tickets at Stazione Centrale or the airport. Journey time is 50 minutes.

Malpensa Bus Express (☎02 805 81 354; www.autostradale.it; adult/child €10/5) To/from Piazza Luigi di Savoia half-hourly between 4am and 12.40am.The trip takes 50 minutes.

Malpensa Express (☎800 50 00 05; www.malpensaexpress.it) Trains depart every 30 minutes to Terminal 1 from Stazione Centrale (adult/child €10/5, 45 minutes) and Stazione Nord (adult/child €11/5, 40 minutes).

LINATE

ATM (☎800 80 81 81; www.atm-mi.it) Local bus 73 runs from Piazza San Babila every 10 to 15 minutes between 5.30am and 12.30am. Use a regular bus ticket (€1.50).

Starfly (☎02 585 87 237; www.starfly.net; €5) Buses to/from Piazza Luigi di Savoia half-hourly between 5.30am and 10.45pm. Journey time is 30 minutes. Buy tickets at newsstands or on board.

ORIO AL SERIO

Autostradale (☎02 720 01 304; www.autostradale.it; €5) Half-hourly buses to/from Piazza Luigi di Savoia between 4am and 11.30pm. Journey time is one hour.

Orio Shuttle (☎035 33 07 06; www.orioshuttle.com; adult/child €8/3, one hour) Runs half-hourly to/from outside Stazione Centrale (one hour) between 3am and 12.15am.

Bus & Metro

Milan's excellent public transport system is run by ATM (p769). Tickets (€1.50) are valid for one underground ride or up to 90 minutes' travel on city buses and trams. A day ticket costs €4.50. Buy them at metro stations, *tabacchi* and newsstands.

Verona

POP 263,700

Wander Verona's atmospheric streets and you'll understand why Shakespeare set *Romeo and Juliet* here – this is one of Italy's most beautiful and romantic cities. Known as *piccola Roma* (little Rome) for its importance in imperial days, its heyday came in the 13th and 14th centuries when it was ruled by the Della Scala (aka Scaligeri) family, who built *palazzi* and bridges, sponsored Giotto, Dante and Petrarch, oppressed their subjects and feuded with everyone else.

Sights

The **Verona Card** (www.veronacard.it; 2/5 days €15/20), available from tourist offices, sites and *tabacchi*, covers city transport and the city's main monuments and churches.

Arena di Verona AMPHITHEATRE
(www.arena.it; Piazza Brà; adult/reduced/child €6/4.50/free; ⊙1.30am-7.30pm Mon plus 8.30am-7.30pm Tue-Sun, to 4.30pm on performance days) In the corner of Piazza Brà, the 1st-century pink marble Arena is the third-largest Roman amphitheatre in Italy. And although it can no longer seat 30,000, it still draws sizeable crowds to its summer opera performances.

Casa di Giulietta MUSEUM
(Juliet's House; ☎045 803 43 03; Via Cappello 23; adult/reduced €6/4.50 or with VeronaCard; ⊙8.30am-7.30pm Tue-Sun, 1.30-7.30pm Mon) Juliet and her lover Romeo were entirely fictional characters but that doesn't stop visitors flocking to this 14th-century *palazzo* to act out their romantic fantasies and add their lovelorn words to the graffiti on the arched gateway.

Piazzas PIAZZA
Set over the city's Roman forum, **Piazza delle Erbe** is lined with sumptuous *palazzi* and filled with touristy market stalls. Through the **Arco della Costa**, the quieter **Piazza dei Signori** is flanked by the early Renaissance **Loggia del Consiglio**, aka the Loggia Fra Gioconda, and the **Palazzo del Podestà**, the 14th-century residence of Cangrande I, the most celebrated of the Della Scala rulers. Nearby, the **Arche Scaligere** are the Della Scala family's elaborate Gothic tombs.

Basilica di San Zeno Maggiore CHURCH
(www.chieseverona.it; Piazza San Zeno; adult/child €2.50/free, incl Verona church €6 or with VeronaCard; ⊙8.30am-6pm Tue-Sat, 12.30-6pm Sun Mar-Oct, 10am-1pm & 1.30-5pm Tue-Sat, 12.30-5pm Sun Nov-Feb) This masterpiece of Romanesque architecture honours the city's patron saint. Note Mantegna's 1457–59 altarpiece, *Maesta della Vergine* (Majesty of the Virgin), and the 12th-century bronze doors.

Sleeping

High-season prices apply during the opera season and it is absolutely essential to book for this period. If you arrive without a booking, the tourist office has a hotel reservation service.

Hotel Aurora HOTEL €€€
(☎045 59 47 17; www.hotelaurora.biz; Piazza delle Erbe; s €100-160, d €110-240; ❄📶) Gleaming after a recent makeover, this friendly three-star is right in the heart of the action on central Piazza delle Erbe. Rooms, some of which have piazza views, are smart with laminated parquet, polished wood and modern mosaic-tiled bathrooms. Breakfast can be enjoyed on a lovely terrace overlooking the piazza.

Appartamenti L'Ospite APARTMENT €€
(☎045 803 69 94; www.lospite.com; Via XX Settembre 3; apt 1 or 2 people €35-105, apt 2-4 people €40-180; ❄📶) Over the river from the *centro storico*, L'Ospite has six self-contained apartments for up to four people. Simple and bright with fully equipped kitchens, they come with wi-fi and are ideal for families.

Villa Francescatti HOSTEL €
(☎045 59 03 60; www.ostelloverona.it; Salita Fontana del Ferro 15; dm €18-20; ⊙7am-midnight) This HI youth hostel is in a 16th-century villa a 20-minute walk from central Verona. Dinners cost €9 (reservations required); there are no cooking facilities. Rooms are off limits 9am to 5pm, but you can use the common rooms. Catch bus 73 (weekdays) or bus 90 (Sunday and holidays) from the train station. There's a strict 11.30pm curfew.

Eating

Boiled meats are a Veronese speciality, as is crisp Soave white wine.

Al Pompiere TRATTORIA €€
(☎045 803 05 37; www.alpompiere.com; Vicolo Regina d'Ungheria 5; mains €16; ⊙Tue-Sat) Near the

Casa di Giulietta, this handsome trattoria – think low wooden ceiling, hanging sausages and framed photos – is famed for its vast cheese selection and house-cured *salumi.* Make a meal of the starters with wine by the glass, or fill up on robust meaty mains. Reservations recommended.

Trattoria Al Bersagliere TRATTORIA **€€**
(☎045 800 48 24; www.trattoriaalbersagliere.it; Via Dietro Pallone 1; mains €11-15; ⏱Tue-Sat) With its wood-beamed ceilings and internal courtyard, this much-loved trattoria is a lovely place to dine on rustic Veronese cooking such as *pasta c fasoi* (Veneto-style bean soup) and *patissada de Caval con polenta* (stewed horse meat with polenta), a local speciality since the 15th century.

Café Noir CAFE **€**
(☎045 803 05 00; Via Pellicciai 12; mains €7; ⏱7.30am-9pm Mon-Sat) This popular cafe is a favourite with local shoppers who stop by for fresh lunchtime salads, daily pastas and simple risottos. No dinner.

☆ Entertainment

Tickets for the opera season at the **Arena** (☎045 800 51 51; www.arena.it; Piazza Brà; tickets €23-200; ⏱opera season mid-Jun–early Sep) are available online or at various places across town, including the tourist office; see the website for details.

ℹ Information

Information, opera tickets and hotel reservations are available at the central **tourist office** (☎045 806 86 80; www.tourism.verona.it; Via degli Alpini 9; ⏱9am-7pm Mon-Sat, 10am-4pm Sun) just off Piazza Brà. There's a second **office** (☎045 861 91 63; Verona-Villafranca airport; ⏱10am-4pm Mon & Tue, to 5pm Wed-Sat) in the airport arrivals hall.

ℹ Getting There & Around

The **Aeroporto di Verona** (Valerio Catullo airport; ☎045 809 56 66; www.aeroportidelgarda.it), 12km outside the city, is accessible by bus from the train station (€6, 20 minutes, every 20 minutes between 5.15am and 11.10pm).

From stand A outside the train station, buses 90, 92, 93, 98 and 510 run to Piazza Brà. Tickets cost €1.30 or €1.50 if bought on board.

Direct trains connect with Milan (€11.30 to €19, one hour 20 minutes to two hours, three hourly), Venice (€7.40 to €19, 50 minutes to 2¼ hours, half-hourly) and Bologna (€8.90 to €19, 50 minutes to 1½ hours, 20 daily).

Padua

POP 214,200

The elegant city of Padua (Padova) sees only a fraction of the visitors who pile into nearby Venice. Yet, it's a fascinating place, a handsome medieval city with a long and cultured past (Galileo taught astronomy at the city university), one of the world's oldest (Shakespeare set parts of *The Taming of the Shrew* here), and Giotto painted one of Italy's greatest works of art in the city's Cappella degli Scrovegni.

Sights

The **PadovaCard** (www.padovacard.it; per 48/72hr €16/21) provides free parking, public transport and entry to many sights, including the Cappella degli Scrovegni (plus €1 booking fee). Get it at tourist offices or participating sites.

Cappella degli Scrovegni CHURCH
(☎049 201 00 20; www.cappelladegliscrovegni.it; Piazza Eremitani 8; adult/reduced €13/8; ⏱9am-7pm Mon, to 10pm Tue-Sun Mar-Oct, 9am-7pm Nov-Dec, by reservation only) Giotto's frescos in the Scrovegni chapel – named after the banker Enrico Scrovegni who originally commissioned it – are among the defining works of early Renaissance art. Painted between 1303 and 1305, the 38 colourful panels cover the chapel from floor to ceiling, depicting events from the life of Christ and the Virgin Mary.

Visits, which must be booked online or by phone at least 24 hours beforehand, last only 15 minutes and are preceded by a mandatory, 15-minute video introduction.

The picture galleries in the nearby **Musei Civici agli Eremitani** (☎049 8204 5450; Piazza Eremitani 8; adult/reduced €10/8; ⏱9am-7pm Tue-Sun) are home to an impressive collection of paintings and sculptures, including two Giottos.

FREE **Basilica di Sant'Antonio** CHURCH
(Il Santo; www.basilicadelsanto.org; Piazza del Santo; ⏱6.20am-7.45pm Apr-Oct, to 7pm Nov-Mar) On the other side of the *centro storico* from the Cappella degli Scrovegni is this domed basilica, a major pilgrimage site. Thousands come to pay homage to the town's patron saint, St Anthony (1193–1231), whose gaudy tomb is covered with requests and thanks for miracle cures and the recovery of lost objects.

Outside, Donatello's 1453 equestrian statue, which commemorates a 15th-century

Venetian mercenary called Gattamelata ('Honeyed Cat'), is considered the first great Italian Renaissance bronze.

Sleeping

TOP CHOICE Belludi37 BOUTIQUE HOTEL €€
(☎049 66 56 33; www.belludi37.it; Via Luca Belludi 37; s €97, d €120-145;) This sleek boutique hotel ticks all the boxes, providing excellent value for money, a central location near the Basilica di Sant'Antonio, a chic, contemporary look, and friendly, helpful staff. Parking is also available for €15 per night. Highly recommended.

Albergo Verdi HOTEL €
(☎049 836 41 63; www.albergoverdipadova.it; Via Dondi dall'Orologio 7; s €70, d €100;) A modern three star offering spruce, bright rooms and mod cons such as wi-fi (€2 per three hours) and satellite TV. The guest rooms are not the biggest but it's a friendly place and the central location near Piazza dei Signori is handy for the sights.

Ostello Città di Padova HOSTEL €
(☎049 875 22 19; www.ostellopadova.it; Via Aleardi 30; dm €19-23, d €76; ⊙reception 7.15-9.30am & 3.30-11.30pm;) On a quiet side street in the *centro storico*, Padua's rather drab youth hostel has functional dorms with bunk beds for four to six people. Take bus 8 or 12 or the tram from the train station to Via Cavalletto, then follow on foot.

Eating & Drinking

TOP CHOICE Godenda MODERN ITALIAN €€
(☎049 877 41 92; www.godenda.it; Via Squarcione 4/6; meals €25-40; ⊙10am-3pm & 6pm-2am Mon-Sat) Hidden under an ancient portico, this foodie favourite sets a fashionable, contemporary stage for creative modern dishes such as *crema di patate al curry con sauté di cozze* (curried mashed potato with sautéed mussels) as well as traditional cheese platters and tasty vegetable pastas. Reservations recommended.

L'Anfora OSTERIA €€
(☎049 65 66 29; Via dei Soncin 13; meals €25-30; ⊙9am-11pm Mon-Sat) At this laid-back *osteria* with bare wooden tables and racked wine bottles, the menu changes daily, with the emphasis on regional, local dishes. It can get pretty busy, particularly on Saturday nights, so book ahead.

Antica Osteria dal Capo OSTERIA €€
(☎049 66 31 05; www.osteriadalcapo.it; Via degli Obizzi 2; mains €10-16; ⊙Tue-Sat) A cosy *osteria* serving earthy Veneto cuisine. Seafood features strongly on the seasonal menu alongside hearty vegetable soups and old-school meat dishes like *fegato alla veneziana con polenta* (Venetian-style liver and onions with polenta). Reservations recommended.

Information

There are tourist offices: at the **train station** (☎049 875 20 77; www.turismopadova.it; ⊙9.15am-7pm Mon-Sat, 9am-noon Sun), **Galleria Pedrocchi** (☎049 876 79 27; www.turismopadova.it; Vicolo Pedrochhi; ⊙9am-1.30pm & 3-7pm Mon-Sat) and **Piazza del Santo** (☎049 875 30 87; www.turismopadova.it; ⊙10.30am-1.30pm & 3-6pm Tue-Sun).

Getting There & Away

Busitalia (☎049 820 68 44; www.fsbusitalia.it) buses leave from the bus station outside the train station for Venice's Marco Polo airport (€8 or €10 on board, one hour, hourly between 6.25am and 8.25pm), stopping off at Venice en route.

Regional trains serve Venice (€3.50, one hour, every 20 minutes), Verona (€5.95, 1½ hours, hourly) and Bologna (€9, 1½ hours, hourly).

Venice

POP 270,900

Venice (Venezia) is a hauntingly beautiful city. At every turn you're assailed by unforgettable images – tiny bridges crossing limpid canals, delivery barges jostling chintzy gondolas, excited tourists posing on Piazza San Marco. Its celebrated sights are legion and its labyrinthine backstreets exude a unique, almost eerie, atmosphere, redolent of dark passions and dangerous secrets. Parts of the Cannaregio, Dorsoduro and Castello *sestieri* (districts) rarely see many tourists, and you can lose yourself for hours in the lanes between the Accademia and train station.

Despite its romantic reputation, the reality of modern Venice is a city besieged by rising tides and up to 20 million visitors a year. This and the sky-high property prices mean that most locals live over the lagoon in Mestre.

History

Venice's origins date to the 5th and 6th centuries when barbarian invasions forced the

Greater Venice

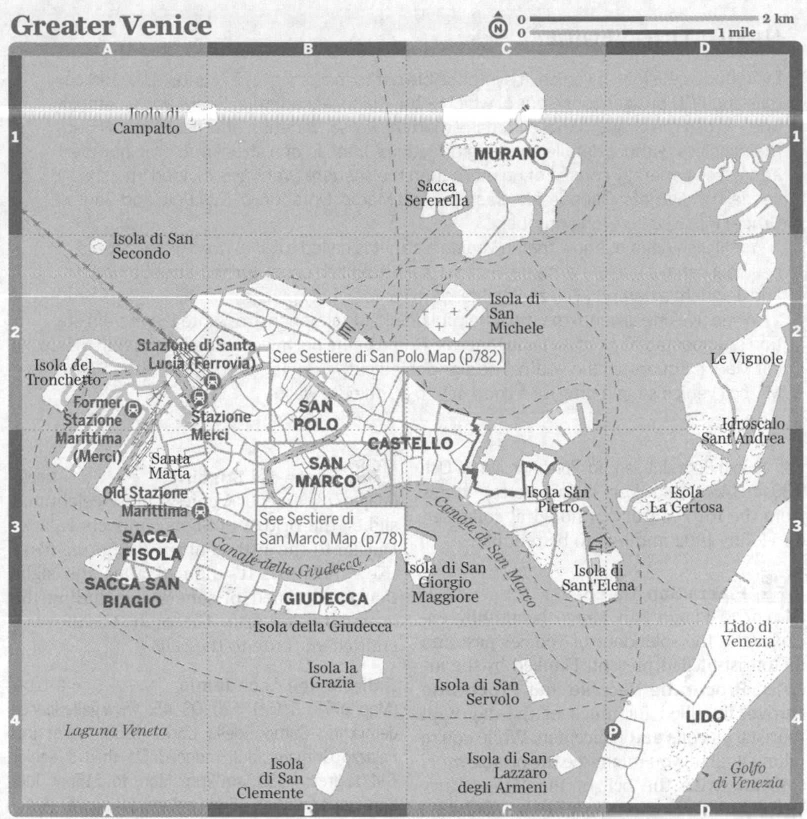

Veneto's inhabitants to seek refuge on the lagoon's islands. Initially the city was ruled by the Byzantines from Ravenna, but in 726 the Venetians went it alone and elected their first doge (duke). Over successive centuries, the Venetian Republic grew into a great merchant power, dominating half the Mediterranean and the trade routes to the Levant – it was from Venice that Marco Polo set out for China in 1271. Decline began in the 16th century and in 1797 the city authorities opened the gates to Napoleon, who, in turn, handed the city over to the Austrians. In 1866, Venice was incorporated into the Kingdom of Italy.

Sights

Whet your sightseeing appetite by taking *vaporetto* (small passenger ferry) No 1 along the **Grand Canal** lined with rococo, Gothic, Moorish and Renaissance palaces. Alight at Piazza San Marco, Venice's main square.

TOP CHOICE **Basilica di San Marco** CHURCH

(St Mark's Basilica; Map p778; 041 270 83 11; www.basilicasanmarco.it; Piazza San Marco; 9.45am-4.45pm Mon-Sat, 2-4pm Sun & holidays, baggage storage 9.30am-5.30pm; San Marco) With its spangled spires, Byzantine domes, luminous mosaics and lavish marble work, Venice's signature church is an unforgettable sight. It was first built to house the corpse of St Mark, but the original chapel was destroyed by fire in 932 and a new basilica was built over it in 1094. For the next 500 years it was a work in progress as successive doges added mosaics and embellishments looted from the East.

Inside, behind the main altar, check out the **Pala d'Oro** (admission €2; 9.45am-5pm Mon-Sat, 2-4.30pm Sun, to 4pm winter), a stunning gold altarpiece decorated with priceless jewels.

Outside in the piazza, the basilica's 99m freestanding **campanile** (Bell Tower; www.basilicasanmarco.it; Piazza San Marco; admission

NAVIGATING VENICE

Everybody gets lost in Venice. It's impossible not to in a city of 117 islands, 150-odd canals and 400 bridges (only four of which – the Rialto, Accademia, Scalzi and Costituzione – cross the Grand Canal). To make matters worse, Venetian addresses are all but meaningless without detailed walking directions. Instead of a street and civic number, addresses generally consist of no more than the *sestiere* (Venice is divided into six *sestieri* or districts: Cannaregio, Castello, San Marco, Dorsoduro, San Polo and Santa Croce) followed by a long number.

You'll also need to know that in Venice a street is called a *calle, ruga* or *salizada;* beside a canal it's a *fondamenta*. A canal is a *rio*, a filled canal-turned-street a *rio terrà*, and a square a *campo* (Piazza San Marco is Venice's only piazza).

When walking around, the most helpful points of reference are Santa Lucia train station (signposted as *ferrovia*) and Piazzale Roma in the northwest, and Piazza San Marco (St Mark's Square) in the south. The signposted path from the station to Piazza San Marco (Venice's main drag) is a good 40- to 50-minute walk.

€8; 9am-9pm Jul-Sep, to 7pm Apr-Jun & Oct, 9.30am-3.45pm Nov-Mar; San Marco) dates from the 10th century, although it collapsed on 14 July 1902 and had to be rebuilt.

TOP CHOICE Piazza San Marco PIAZZA

(Map p778) Piazza San Marco beautifully encapsulates the splendour of Venice's past and its tourist-fuelled present. Flanked by the arcaded **Procuratie Vecchie** and **Procuratie Nuove**, it's filled for much of the day with tourists, pigeons and policemen. While you're taking it all in, you might see the bronze *mori* (Moors) strike the bell of the 15th-century **Torre dell'Orologio** (Clock Tower; 041 4273 0892; www.museicivicivenezianі.it; Piazza San Marco; adult/reduced with Museum Pass €12/7; tours in English 10am & 11am Mon-Wed, 2pm & 3pm Thu-Sun, in Italian noon & 4pm daily, in French 2pm & 3pm Mon-Wed, 10am & 11am Thu-Sun; San Marco).

TOP CHOICE Palazzo Ducale MUSEUM

(Ducal Palace; Map p778; 848 08 20 00; www.palazzoducale.visitmuve.it; Piazzetta San Marco 52; adult/reduced/child incl Museo Correr €16/8/free or with Museum Pass; 8.30am-7pm Apr-Oct, to 5.30pm Nov-Mar; San Zaccaria) The official residence of the doges from the 9th century and the seat of the Republic's government, Palazzo Ducale also housed Venice's prisons. The doges' apartments on the 1st floor are suitably lavish, but it's the vast **Sala del Maggiore Consiglio** on the 2nd floor that will really take your breath away. Measuring 53m by 25m, this echoing hall is dominated by Tintoretto's *Paradiso* (Paradise), one of the world's largest oil paintings.

TOP CHOICE Ponte dei Sospiri BRIDGE

(Map p778) One of Venice's most celebrated sights, the Bridge of Sighs connects Palazzo Ducale to the 16th-century *Priggione Nove* (New Prisons). It's named after the sighs that condemned prisoners – including the legendary lothario Giacomo Casanova – emitted en route to the cells.

Gallerie dell'Accademia GALLERY

(Map p778; 041 520 03 45; www.gallerieaccademia.org; Campo della Carità 1050; ticket incl Palazzo Grimani adult/reduced/EU child & senior €14/11/free; 8.15am-2pm Mon, to 7.15pm Tue-Sun, last admission 45min before closing; P; Accademia) This grand old gallery traces the development of Venetian art from the 14th to the 18th century. You'll find works by Bellini, Titian, Carpaccio, Tintoretto, Giorgione and Veronese, whose controversial *Feast in the House of Levi* was condemned by the church Inquisition for its depiction of dogs, drunks and dwarfs cavorting with the apostles.

TOP CHOICE Collezione Peggy Guggenheim GALLERY

(Map p778; 041 240 54 11; www.guggenheim-venice.it; Dorsoduro 701, Palazzo Venier dei Leoni; adult/reduced/child €12/7/free; 10am-6pm Wed-Mon) The American heiress Peggy Guggenheim was one of the great art collectors of the 20th century. Her spellbinding collection, displayed here in her former home, runs the gamut of modern art with works by Picasso, Pollock, Braque, Kandinsky, Klee and many more. In the sculpture garden you'll find the graves of Peggy and her dogs.

Palazzo Grassi MUSEUM

(Map p778; ☎box office 199 13 91 39, 041 523 16 80; www.palazzograssi.it; Campo San Samuele 3231; adult/reduced/child €15/10/free, 72hr ticket incl Punta della Dogana €20/15/free; ⊙10am-7pm Wed-Mon; ⛴San Samuele) One of the most impressive buildings on the Grand Canal, the 18th-century Palazzo Grassi provides the dramatic setting for exhibitions and installations by big-name contemporary artists like Jeff Koons and Richard Prince. In 2009, the museum opened a second exhibition space, the **Punta della Dogana** (Map p778; ☎041 271 90 39; www.palazzograssi.it; adult/reduced/child €15/10/free, incl Palazzo Grassi €20/15/free; ⊙10am-7pm Wed-Mon; ⛴Salute).

Churches CHURCH

As in much of Italy, Venice's churches harbour innumerable treasures; unusually, though, you have to pay to get into many of them. The Chorus Pass (p776) gives admission to 16 of the city's most important churches, which otherwise charge adult/reduced €3/1.50.

Scene of the annual Festa del Redentore (Feast of the Redeemer), the **Chiesa del Santissimo Redentore** (Church of the Redeemer; Campo del SS Redentore 194; adult/reduced/child €3/1.50/free or with Chorus Pass; ⊙10am-5pm Mon-Sat; ⛴Redentore) was built by Palladio on the island of Giudecca to commemorate the end of the Great Plague in 1577.

At the entrance to the Grand Canal, the 17th-century **Chiesa di Santa Maria della Salute** (La Salute; Map p778; ☎041 241 10 18; www.seminariovenezia.it; Campo della Salute 1b; admission free, sacristy adult/reduced €3/1.50; ⊙9am-noon & 3-5.30pm; ⛴Salute) contains works by Tintoretto and Titian. Arguably the greatest of Venetian artists, Titian is buried in the **Basilica di Santa Maria Gloriosa dei Frari** (www.basilicadeifrari.it; Campo dei Frari, San Polo; adult/reduced/child €3/1.50/free or Chorus Pass; ⊙9am-6pm Mon-Sat, 1-6pm Sun), near his celebrated *Assunta* (Assumption; 1518).

The Lido ISLAND

Unless you're on the Lido for the Venice Film Festival, the main reason to visit is to head to the beach. One of the best is **Alberoni**, in the south of the island.

The Lido is accessible by various *vaporetti*, including Nos 1 and 2 from San Zaccaria.

Islands ISLAND

The island of **Murano** is the home of Venetian glass. Tour a factory for a behind-the-scenes look at production or visit the **Museo del Vetro** (Glass Museum; ☎041 73 95 86, www.museovetro.visitmuve.it; Fondamenta Giustinian 8; adult/reduced €8/5.50; ⊙10am-6pm Apr-Oct, to 5pm Nov-Mar; ⛴Museo) near the Museo *vaporetto* stop. **Burano**, with its cheery pastel-coloured houses, is renowned for its lace. **Torcello**, the republic's original island settlement, was largely abandoned due to malaria and now counts no more than 80 residents. Its not-to-be-missed Byzantine cathedral, the **Basilica di Santa Maria Assunta** (Piazza Torcello; adult/reduced €5/4, incl museum €8/6; ⊙10.30am-6pm Mar-Oct, 10am-5pm Nov-Feb; ⛴Torcello), is Venice's oldest.

To get to Murano take *vaporetto* 4.1, 4.2 from San Zaccaria or Fondamente Nove. For Burano take No 12 from Fondamente Nove. Torcello is linked to Burano by *vaporetto* 9.

TOILETS

Don't get caught short. You'll find public toilets at the train station, Piazzale Roma, Ponte dell'Accademia, Campo San Bartolomeo, and by the Giardini ex Reali near Piazza San Marco. To use them you'll need €1.50 in change.

Activities

Be prepared to pay through the nose for that quintessential Venetian experience, a **gondola ride**. Official rates start at €80 or €100 from 7pm to 8am – these prices are per gondola (maximum six people). Additional time is charged in 20-minute increments (day/night €40/50). Haggling is unlikely to get you a reduction but you can save money by taking a gondola tour with the tourist office or a reliable tour operator.

Tours

Between April and October, Venice's tourist offices offer a range of tours, including a 35-minute gondola ride (€28 per person), a 40-minute gondola serenade (€40), a 1½-hour city walking tour (€21) and a four-hour trip to Murano, Burano and Torcello (€20).

There are also private outfits running tours, including **TU.RI.VE** (☎041 241 34 22; www.turive.it), which organises itineraries exploring the city's Byzantine heritage (€36) and legends (€20).

ADMISSION DISCOUNTS

Venice Card (041 24 24; www.venicecard.com; adult/junior €39.90/29.90; call centre 8am-7.30pm), valid for seven days, gives free entry to Palazzo Ducale, 10 civic museums, the 16 churches covered by the Chorus Pass, as well as discounts on exhibitions, concerts and parking. Buy it at tourist offices and HelloVenezia booths.

Venice Card San Marco (041 24 24; www.venicecard.com; €24.90) provides free admission to Palazzo Ducale, three civic museums and three Chorus churches, plus discounts on exhibitions, concerts and parking. Available at tourist offices and HelloVenezia booths.

Rolling Venice Card (041 24 24; www.hellovenezia.com; 14-29yr €4) offers discounts on food, accommodation, shopping, transport and museums. Get it at tourist offices and HelloVenezia booths. You'll need ID.

Museum Pass (Musei Civici Pass; www.visitmuve.it; adult/reduced €20/14) is valid for single entry to 10 civic museums, or just the four museums around Piazza San Marco (adult/concession €16/8). Buy it at participating museums or online at www.visitmuve.it or www.veniceconnected.com.

Chorus Pass (041 275 04 62; www.chorusvenezia.org; adult/reduced/child €10/7/free) covers admission to 16 of Venice's major churches and is available online or at the churches.

Festivals & Events

Carnevale CARNIVAL
(www.carnevale.venezia.it) Venice's carnival celebrations take over town in the two-week run-up to Ash Wednesday. Costume parties are held in every *campo* (square) until a Grand Canal flotilla marks the end of festivities.

Palio delle Quattro Antiche Repubbliche Marinare BOAT RACE
(Regatta of the Four Ancient Maritime Republics) Venice, Amalfi, Genoa and Pisa take turns to host this historic regatta in early June. It will be in Venice in 2015.

Venice Biennale ART
(www.labiennale.org) An important exhibition of international visual arts. It's held every odd-numbered year from June to November.

Festa del Redentore RELIGIOUS
(Feast of the Redeemer; www.turismovenezia.it) Held on the third weekend in July; celebrations climax with a spectacular fireworks display.

Venice Architecture Biennale ARCHITECTURE
(www.labiennale.org) This major architecture shindig is held every even-numbered year from late August to November.

Venice Film Festival FILM
(Mostra del Cinema di Venezia; www.labiennale.org/en/cinema) Italy's top film fest comes to town in late August or early September at the Lido's Palazzo del Cinema.

Regata Storica BOAT RACE
(www.comune.venezia.it) Costumed parades precede gondola races on the Grand Canal; held on the first Sunday in September.

Sleeping

Venice is Italy's most expensive city. It's always advisable to book ahead, especially at weekends, in May and September, and during Carnevale and other holidays.

SAN MARCO

TOP CHOICE **Novecento** BOUTIQUE HOTEL €€
(Map p778; 041 241 37 65; www.novecento.biz; Calle del Dose 2683/84; d €140-300; ; Santa Maria del Giglio) Sporting a bohemian-chic oriental look, the Novecento is a real charmer. Its nine individually decorated rooms feature Turkish kilim pillows, Fortuny draperies, carved bedsteads and immaculate designer bathrooms, while its garden is a gorgeous spot for a leisurely breakfast.

PalazzinaG BOUTIQUE HOTEL €€€
(Map p778; 041 528 46 44; www.palazzinag.com; San Marco 3247; r from €288;) Luxury goes hand in hand with a fashionable Philippe Stark design at this Grand Canal boutique hotel. Common areas are lavishly decorated while the light-drenched rooms cleverly use mirrors and white furnishings to maximise space.

DORSODURO

Pensione La Calcina HOTEL €€

(041 520 64 66; www.lacalcina.com; Fondamenta Zattere ai Gesuati 780, Dorsoduro 780; s €90-170, d €110-310;) A historic landmark on the Giudecca canalfront, this centuries-old hotel exudes character. Author John Ruskin stayed here in 1877 (in room 2) and there's an air of quiet gentility about the sunny antique-clad rooms. Out front, the elegant bar/restaurant is a prime spot for a relaxed waterfront meal.

SAN POLO & SANTA CROCE

TOP CHOICE **Oltre il Giardino** BOUTIQUE HOTEL €€

(Map p782; 041 275 00 15; www.oltreilgiardino-venezia.com; Fondamenta Contarini, San Polo 2542; d incl breakfast €180-250; ; San Tomà) Once home to Alma Mahler, the composer's widow, this gorgeous hotel is hidden behind a walled garden full of pomegranate, olive and magnolia trees. Inside, six sharply designed rooms combine mod cons and deftly chosen antiques to stylish effect.

Ca' Angeli BOUTIQUE HOTEL €€

(041 523 24 80; www.caangeli.it; Calle del Traghetto de la Madonnetta 1434, San Polo; d incl breakfast €70-215; ; San Silvestro) An elegant choice overlooking the Grand Canal, Ca' Angeli offers tastefully decorated rooms and suites with canal views. Staff are friendly, the organic breakfast is excellent, and wi-fi is free if you book through the hotel's website.

Pensione Guerrato INN €€

(Map p782; 041 528 59 27; www.pensioneguerrato.it; Calle Drio la Scimia 240a, San Polo; d/tr/q incl breakfast €145/165/185; ; Rialto Mercato) Housed in a 13th-century tower near the Rialto market, this hospitable *pensione* has comfortable, good-sized rooms on several floors (no lift) and friendly, helpful owners. Check the website for low-season offers.

Hotel Alex PENSION €

(Map p782; 041 523 13 41; www.hotelalexinvenice.com; Rio Terà, San Polo 2606; d €60-124, tr €80-150, q €100-190, without bathroom s €35-60, d €40-94, tr €60-120, q €80-144; ; San Tomà) In a quiet spot near Campo dei Frari, no-frills Alex offers 11 simple but decent-sized rooms, some of which come with a balcony overlooking two canals.

L'Imbarcadero HOSTEL €

(392 584 06 00; www.hostelvenice.net; cnr Imbarcadero Riva de Biasio & Calle Zen, Santa Croce; dm from €27, r per person €32-40;) This is a popular hostel with decent mixed and female-only dorms and private rooms with shared bathrooms. It's not the easiest place to find, although only about five minutes' walk from the train station.

CANNAREGIO

Giardino dei Melograni GUESTHOUSE €€

(041 822 61 31; www.pardesrimonim.net; Ghetto Nuovo, Cannaregio 2873/c; s €70-100, d €80-160, tr €110-190, q €140-220;) Run by Venice's Jewish community, the 'Garden of Pomegranates' is a sparkling new kosher residence. It's wonderfully located on the tranquil Campo Ghetto Nuovo and offers 14 modern white-grey rooms and a courtyard restaurant serving Jewish and Venetian cuisine (€25 for a meal or €30 on Friday night and Saturday lunch).

Hotel Bernardi HOTEL €

(Map p782; 041 522 72 57; www.hotelbernardi.com; SS Apostoli Calle dell'Oca 4366; s €48-72, d €57-90, f €75-130, without bathroom s €25-32, d €45-62;) Just off Venice's main drag, this excellent budget option has rooms spread over two sites – this, the main hotel, and a nearby annexe. Rooms come in various shapes and sizes but the general look is classic Venetian with chandeliers, wooden beams, rugs and antiques.

CASTELLO

Foresteria Valdese HOSTEL €

(Palazzo Cavagnis; 041 528 67 97; www.foresteriavenezia.it; Castello 5170; dm €30-35, d €70-140, q €95-190; Ospedale, San Zaccaria) One of the cheapest sleeps in the *centro storico*, this hostel is run by the Waldensian church and housed in a rambling old palace with 18th-century frescos, canal views and a range of rooms. Adding to the deal are free music concerts, usually held at 6pm on Wednesdays.

Ca' Valeri B&B €€

(041 241 15 30; www.locandacavaleri.com; Ramo Corazzieri 3845; r €69-280, ste €79-280;) To escape the teeming hordes, search out this far-flung retreat whose classically decorated rooms provide a lovely base for exploring the nearby Arsenale.

Sestiere di San Marco

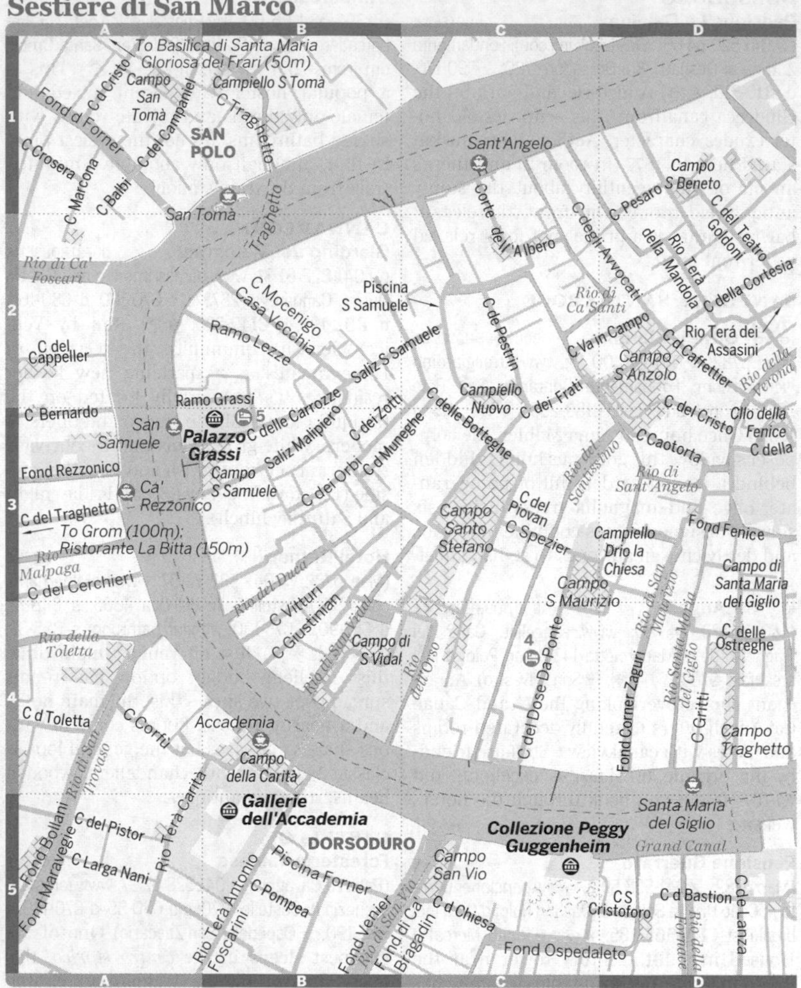

Sestiere di San Marco

Top Sights

Basilica di San Marco H2
Collezione Peggy Guggenheim C5
Gallerie dell'Accademia B5
Palazzo Ducale H3
Palazzo Grassi B3
Piazza San Marco G3
Ponte dei Sospiri H3
Punta della Dogana F5

Sights

1 Basilica di Santa Maria della Salute E5
2 Campanile G3
3 Torre dell'Orologio G2

Sleeping

4 Novecento C4
5 PalazzinaG B3

Drinking

6 Caffè Florian G3
7 Harry's Bar F4

Entertainment

8 Teatro La Fenice E3

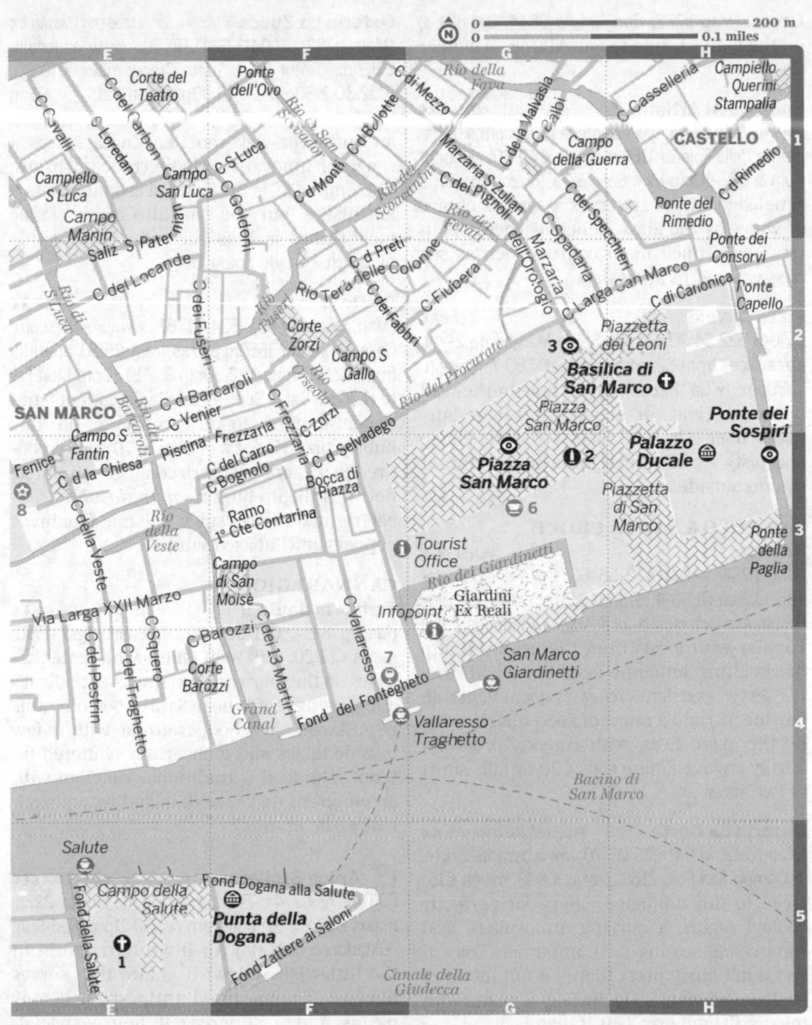

Eating

Venetian specialities include *risi e bisi* (pea soup thickened with rice) and *sarde in saor* (fried sardines marinated in vinegar and onions).

DORSODURO

Ristorante La Bitta RISTORANTE €€

(☎041 523 05 31; Calle Lunga San Barnaba 2753a; meals €30-40; ⊙dinner Mon-Sat; Ca' Rezzonico) With its woody bottle-lined interior and attractive internal courtyard, this is a lovely place to enjoy rustic dishes such as *tagliolini con verdure e zenzero* (thin pasta ribbons with vegetables and ginger) and *galletto al peperone* (chicken with peppers). Cash only.

Grom GELATERIA €

(☎041 099 17 51; www.grom.it; Campo San Barnaba 2461; gelati €2.50-4; ⊙11am-midnight Sun-Thu, to 1am Fri & Sat; ; Ca' Rezzonico) An ice cream from this Slow Food–rated *galeteria* is the perfect pick-me-up. Seasonal flavours are made with top ingredients from around the world – lemons and almonds from Sicily, chocolate from South America, cinnamon from Sri Lanka. There's a second

Grom (Map p782; Cannaregio 3844, Ca' d'Oro) on the main station to San Marco strip near Ca' d'Oro.

Enoteca Ai Artisti RISTORANTE €€€
(041 523 89 44; www.enotecaartisti.com; Fondamenta della Toletta 1169a; meals €40-50; noon-4pm & 6.30-10pm Mon-Sat; Ca' Rezzonico) This canal-side wine bar serves a serious choice of wines by the glass, delicious cheese platters and refined main courses such as sea bass with herbs and salad.

Pizza Al Volo PIZZERIA €
(041 522 54 30; Campo Santa Margherita 2944; pizza slices from €2, small pizzas €4.50-7; noon-11.30pm; Ca' Rezzonico) A hole-in-the-wall takeaway great for a quick lunch or late-night filler. Grab a slice – they're cheap and tasty – and munch away on the vibrant square outside.

SAN POLO & SANTA CROCE

All'Arco VENETIAN €
(Map p782; 041 520 56 66; Calle dell'Ochialer 436; cicheti €1.50-4; 8am-3.30pm Mon-Sat, plus 6-9pm Apr-Oct, closed Jul & Aug; Rialto Mercato) Popular with locals from the nearby Rialto market, this authentic neighbourhood *osteria* serves excellent *cicheti* (typical Venetian bar snacks) and a range of good-quality wine by the glass. Even with copious *prosecco,* hardly any meal here tops €20 or falls short of five stars.

Birraria La Corte PIZZERIA, RISTORANTE €€
(Map p782; 041 275 05 70; www.birrarialacorte.it; Campo San Polo 2168; pizzas €8-13, mains €15) Head to this animated eatery for perfectly cooked pizzas, a buzzing atmosphere and square-side seating on Campo San Polo. If you don't fancy pizza there's a full menu of pastas and mains, including a mammoth meat grill, and excellent Italian beers.

Vecio Fritolin VENETIAN €€€
(Map p782; 041 522 28 81; www.veciofritolin.it; Calle della Regina 2262, Santa Croce; mains €25, tasting menu €55; noon-2.30pm & 7-10.30pm Wed-Sun, 7-10.30pm Tue; San Stae) Traditionally a *fritolin* was an eatery where diners sat at a communal table and tucked into fried fish. This is the modern equivalent, if considerably smarter and more sophisticated. The menu includes meat and vegetable dishes, but the headline act is the top-quality seafood, sourced daily from the nearby Rialto market.

Osteria La Zucca MODERN ITALIAN €€
(Map p782; 041 524 15 70; www.lazucca.it; Calle del Tintor 1762, Santa Croce; mains €10-20; 12.30-2.30pm & 7-10.30pm Mon-Sat; ; San Stae) A snug wood-panelled restaurant in an out-of-the-way spot, La Zucca serves a range of innovative Mediterranean dishes. The emphasis is on fresh, seasonal vegetarian dishes, but you can also order classic meat dishes such as duck with green apple or English-style roast beef.

Ae Oche PIZZERIA €
(Map p782; 041 524 11 61; www.aeoche.com; Calle del Tentor 1552a; pizzas from €5.50, aperitifs from €2.50; noon-2.30pm & 7-10.30pm Mon-Fri, to 11.30pm Sat & Sun; San Stae) Students and budget-minded foodies converge on this bubbly pizzeria for a choice of 70-plus wood-fired pizzas and well-priced ale. Keep things hot with the lip-buzzing *mangiafuoco* (fire-eater) made with spicy salami, Calabrese peppers and Tabasco sauce.

CANNAREGIO

Trattoria da Bepi VENETIAN €€
(Map p782; 041 528 50 31; Cannaregio 4550; mains €10-20; Fri-Wed) One of the better eateries on the touristy main drag – actually it's a few metres off it near Santi Apostoli – this is a classic old-school trattoria with a few outside tables and a cheerfully cluttered interior. The food is traditional Venetian with an emphasis on seafood, including an excellent *sarde in saor*.

Anice Stellato VENETIAN €€€
(041 72 07 44; Fondamenta della Sensa 3272; mains €18-23; noon-2pm & 7.30-11pm Wed-Sun; Madonna dell'Orto) An inviting trattoria in the little-visited Jewish ghetto that serves huge plates of seafood antipasti, delicious pastas and a super-sized house speciality of fried fish with polenta. Book a table outside by the boats or share a communal table inside.

Fiaschetteria Toscana RISTORANTE €€€
(Map p782; 041 528 52 81; Salizada San Giovanni Grisostomo 5719; mains €22-40, tasting menu €48; lunch & dinner Thu-Mon, dinner Wed; Ca' d'Oro) This formal, old-fashioned restaurant specialises in classic local cuisine and fresh lagoon seafood, but varies the formula with a few Tuscan triumphs, including delectable Chianina-beef steaks. Tuscan wines also feature on the mighty 600-label wine list.

Da Marisa TRATTORIA €€

(☎041 72 02 11; Fondamenta di San Giobbe 652b; lunch set price €15, dinner €35-40; ⊙lunch daily, dinner Tue & Thu-Sat) Search out this modest family-run trattoria for a taste of authentic Venetian home cooking and sunset views over the lagoon. Expect brusque service and a fixed daily menu, which is mostly meat but sometimes seafood. Reservations recommended. Cash only.

Drinking

Al Mercà WINE BAR

(Map p782; ☎393 992 47 81; Campo Cesare Battisti 213; ⊙9.30am-2.30pm & 6-9pm Mon-Sat; Rialto-Mercato) This hole-in-the-wall bar draws daily crowds for its excellent snacks (meatballs and mini-panini from €1.50) and keenly priced drinks, including top-notch *prosecco* and DOC wines by the glass (from €2).

TOP CHOICE **Cantina Do Spade** PUB

(Map p782; ☎041 521 05 83; www.cantinadospade.it; Calle delle Do Spade 860; ⊙10am-3pm & 6-10pm) A warm, woody neighbourhood *osteria* great for a relaxed glass of local wine or a double-malt beer. Keep hunger at bay by snacking on *cicheti* (from €1) such as *sarde fritte* (fried sardines), anchovies and meatballs.

Muro Venezia BAR

(Map p782; www.murovinoecucina.it; Campo Cesare Battisti, San Polo 222; ⊙9am-3pm & 4pm-2am Mon-Sat, 4pm-2am Sun) The centre of a happening nightlife scene in the market squares of the Rialto, Muro is the watering hole of choice for young locals, who spill out into the square with their drinks. Come at Saturday lunch to enjoy a plate of fried fish and glass of Chardonnay for €8.

Il Caffè Rosso CAFF, BAR

(☎041 528 79 98; Campo Santa Margherita 2963; ⊙7am-1am Mon-Sat; Ca' Rezzonico) The most popular of the bars and cafes on vibrant Campo Santa Margherita. Its sunny piazza seating fills quickly with students drawn by the laid-back buzz and 6pm Spritz cocktails.

Harry's Bar BAR

(Map p778; ☎041 528 57 77; Calle Vallaresso 1323; cocktails €12-22; ⊙10.30am-11pm; San Marco) To try a Bellini (white peach pulp and *prosecco*) at the bar that invented them is to follow in prestigious footsteps – Ernest Hemingway, Charlie Chaplin and Orson Welles have all drunk here, and Woody Allen likes to pop in when in town.

Ancorà WINE BAR

(Map p782; ☎041 520 70 66; www.ancoravenezia.it; San Polo 120, Fabbriche Vecchie; ⊙10am-2am; Rialto) Jazz, Grand Canal views, *prosecco*, raw oysters and modern romance are house specialities at this chic cocktail bar tucked under the porticos of the Rialto's waterfront warehouses.

TOP CHOICE **Caffè Florian** CAFE

(Map p778; ☎041 520 56 41; www.caffeflorian.com; Piazza San Marco 56/59; drinks €6.50-16; ⊙10am-midnight Thu-Tue; San Marco) With its historic pedigree (it opened in 1720), house orchestra and eye-watering prices (a cappuccino costs €9), Venice's most celebrated cafe is everything you'd expect it be. Byron, Goethe and Rousseau are among the luminaries who have sipped here.

Entertainment

Upcoming events are listed in the free *Shows & Events* guide, available at tourist offices, and at www.veneziadavivere.com. Tickets for most events are sold at **HelloVenezia ticket outlets** (☎041 24 24; www.hellovenezia.it) in front of the train station, at Piazzale Roma and near key *vaporetto* stops.

Teatro La Fenice OPERA

(Map p778; ☎041 78 65 11; www.teatrolafenice.it; Campo San Fantin 1965; adult/reduced €8.50/6, opera tickets from €40; ⊙tours 9.30am-6pm) One of Italy's top opera houses, La Fenice hosts a year-round program of opera, ballet and classical music. You can also visit on a guided tour between 9.30am and 6pm most days – check www.festfenice.com for details.

Information

Emergency

Police Station (☎041 270 55 11; Castello 5053, Fondamenta di San Lorenzo)

Medical Services

Ospedale Civile (☎041 529 41 11; Campo SS Giovanni e Paolo 6777)

Tourist Information

Pick up the free *Shows & Events* guide at tourist offices. It contains comprehensive city listings and up-to-date details of exhibitions and events. The tourist offices also sell a handy map of the city (€2.50).

Tourist Office (Azienda di Promozione Turistica; ☎041 529 87 11; www.turismovenezia.it) Marco Polo (Marco Polo airport, arrivals hall; ⊙9am-8pm); Piazzale Roma (Piazzale Roma, ground fl, multistorey car park; ⊙9.30am-

Sestiere di San Polo

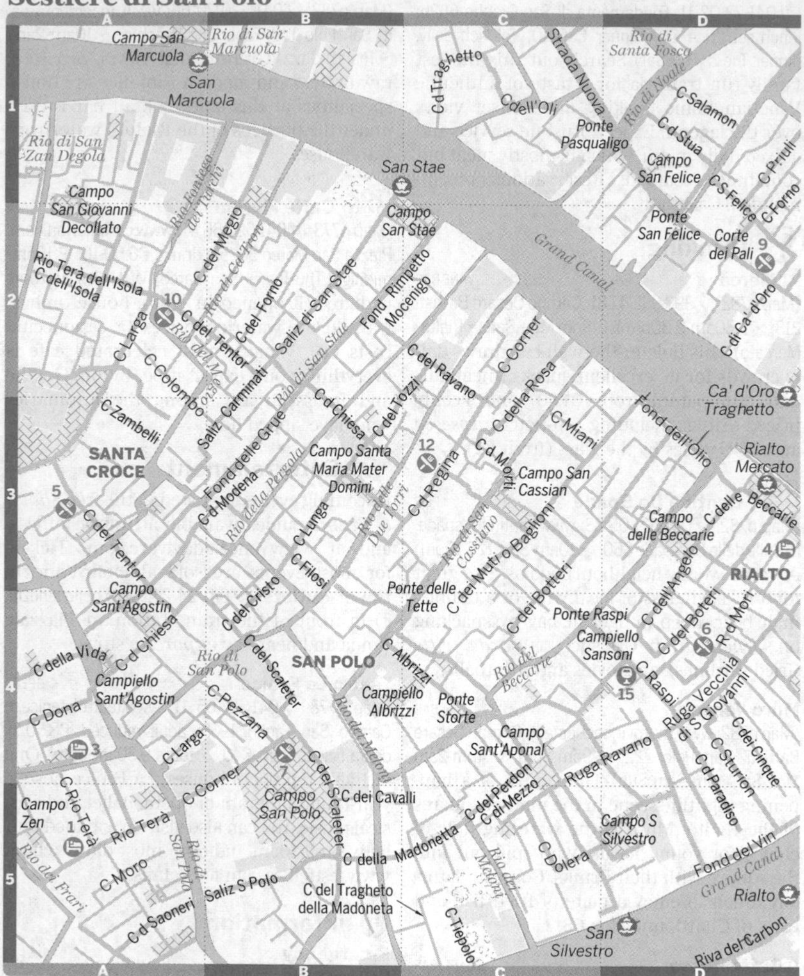

Sestiere di San Polo

Sleeping

1	Hotel Alex	A5
2	Hotel Bernardi	E2
3	Oltre il Giardino	A4
4	Pensione Guerrato	D3

Eating

5	Ae Oche	A3
6	All'Arco	D4
7	Birraria La Corte	B4
8	Fiaschetteria Toscana	F3
9	Grom	D2
10	Osteria La Zucca	A2
11	Trattoria da Bepi	F2
12	Vecio Fritolin	C3

Drinking

13	Al Mercà	E4
14	Ancorà	E4
15	Cantina Do Spade	D4
16	Muro Venezia	E3

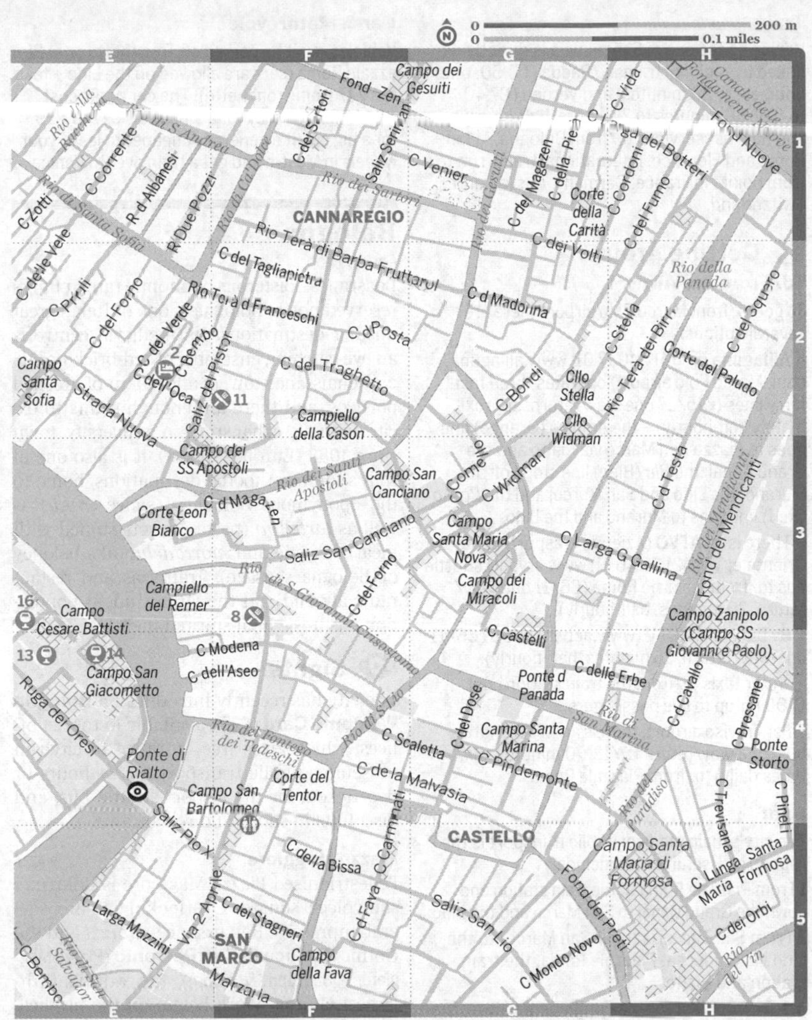

2.30pm; Santa Chiara); Piazza San Marco (Piazza San Marco 71f; 9am-7pm; San Marco); Stazione di Santa Lucia (Stazione di Santa Lucia; 9am-7pm Nov-Mar, 1.30-7pm Apr-Oct; Ferrovia Santa Lucia); Venice Pavilion (041 529 87 11; fax 041 523 03 99; Venice Pavilion, next to the Giardini Ex Reali, near St Mark's Square; 9am-6pm)

Getting There & Away

Air

Most flights land at **Marco Polo airport** (041 260 92 60; www.veniceairport.it), 12km outside Venice. Ryanair flies to **Treviso airport** (0422 31 51 11; www.trevisoairport.it; Via Noalese 63), about 30km away.

Boat

Venezia Lines (041 882 11 01; www.venezia-lines.com) operates high-speed boats to/from several ports in Croatia between mid-April and early October, including Pola (€69 to €74).

Bus

ACTV (Azienda del Consorzio Trasporti Veneziano; 041 24 24; www.actv.it) buses service surrounding areas, including Mestre, Padua and Treviso. Tickets and information are available at the bus station in Piazzale Roma.

Train

Venice's Stazione di Santa Lucia is directly linked by regional trains to Padua (€3.50, one hour, every 20 minutes) and Verona (€7.40 to €19, 50 minutes to 2¼ hours, half-hourly), and has fast services to/from Bologna, Milan, Rome and Florence. International trains run to/from points in France, Germany, Austria and Switzerland.

Getting Around

To/From the Airport

To get to/from Marco Polo airport there are several options.

Alilaguna (041 240 17 01; www.alilaguna.com; Marco Polo airport) operates three fast-ferry lines (€15/27 one-way/return, approximately half-hourly) – the *Arancio* (Orange) line goes to Piazza San Marco via Rialto and the Grand Canal; the *Blu* (Blue) line stops off at Murano, the Lido and San Marco; and the *Rosso* (Red) line runs to Murano and the Lido.

There is an **ATVO** (Azienda Trasporti Veneto Orientale; 0421 59 46 71; www.atvo.it) shuttle bus to/from Piazzale Roma (€6/11 one-way/return, 20 minutes, half-hourly).

By bus, take **ACTV** (www.actv.it) bus 5 (€6/11 one-way/return, 25 minutes, half-hourly).

Water taxis to/from the train station cost €100 for up to five passengers.

For Treviso airport, there's an ATVO shuttle bus (one-way/return €7/13, 70 minutes, six times daily) to/from Piazzale Roma.

Boat

The city's main mode of public transport is the *vaporetto*. Useful routes include:

1 From Piazzale Roma to the train station and down the Grand Canal to San Marco and the Lido.

2 From San Zaccaria (near San Marco) to the Lido via Giudecca, Piazzale Roma, the train station and Rialto.

4.1 To/from Murano via Fondamente Nove, the train station, Piazzale Roma, Giudecca and San Zaccaria.

9 From Burano to Torcello and vice versa.

Tickets, available from ACTV and HelloVenezia booths at the major *vaporetti* stops, are expensive: €7 for a single trip; €18 for 12 hours; €20 for 24 hours; €25 for 36 hours; €30 for two days; €35 for three days; €50 for seven days.

There are significant discounts for holders of the Rolling Venice Card and all tickets are cheaper if you purchase them online at www.veniceconnected.com.

The poor man's gondola, *traghetti* (€2 per crossing), are used to cross the Grand Canal where there's no nearby bridge.

Car & Motorcycle

Vehicles must be parked on Tronchetto or at Piazzale Roma (cars are allowed on the Lido – take ferry 17 from Tronchetto). The car parks cost €24 to €26 per day for a small car, €27 to €29 for a big car. It's generally cheaper to leave your wheels in Mestre and get a train over to Venice.

Bologna

POP 380,200

Boasting a boisterous bonhomie rare in Italy's reserved north, Bologna is one of Italy's great unsung destinations. Its medieval centre is an eye-catching ensemble of red-brick *palazzi*, Renaissance towers and 40km of arcaded porticos, and there are enough sights to excite without exhausting. A university town since 1088 (Europe's oldest), it is also one of Italy's foremost foodie destinations, home to the eponymous bolognese sauce *(ragù)* as well as *tortellini* (pasta pockets stuffed with meat), lasagne and *mortadella* (aka baloney or Bologna sausage). Trattorias and restaurants abound and the large student population ensures a high-spirited nightlife.

Sights

The city has recently introduced a **Bologna Welcome Card** (€20), available in tourist offices, which gives free entrance to city-run museums, public transport for 24 hours or two tickets for the airport shuttle bus, and discounts in shops and restaurants.

Piazza Maggiore PIAZZA

Pedestrianised Piazza Maggiore is Bologna's showpiece square. Overlooking it are several impressive Renaissance *palazzi* and the Gothic **Basilica di San Petronio** (Piazza Maggiore; 8am-1pm & 3-6pm), the world's fifth-largest church. Work began on the basilica, which is dedicated to Petronius, the city's patron saint, in 1390, but it was never finished and still today the facade is incomplete.

To the basilica's west, **Palazzo Comunale** (Bologna's Town Hall) is home to the city's art collection, the **Collezioni Comunali d'Arte** (051 20 36 29; Palazzo Comunale; adult/reduced/child €5/3/free; 9am-6.30pm Tue-Fri, 10am-6.30pm Sat & Sun), and the **Museo Morandi** (tel, info 051 20 36 29; www.mambo-bologna.org/museomorandi; Palazzo Comunale; adult/reduced €6/4; 11am-6pm Tue-Fri, 11am-8pm Sat & Sun) dedicated to the work of Giorgio Morandi. At the time of research the Museo Morandi was about to be temporarily transferred to the MAMbo to allow for repair work.

Adjacent to the square, Piazza del Nettuno is named after the 16th-century **Fontana del Nettuno** (Neptune's Fountain), featuring an impressively muscled Neptune.

Le Due Torri TOWER

(Torre degli Asinelli admission €3; Torre degli Asinelli 9am-6pm, to 5pm Oct-May) Standing sentinel over Piazza di Porta Ravegnana are Bologna's two leaning towers. You can climb the taller of the two, the 97.6m-high **Torre degli Asinelli**, which was built between 1109 and 1119. The neighbouring 48m-high **Torre Garisenda** is sensibly out of bounds given its drunken 3.2m tilt.

Basilica di San Domenico CHURCH

(Piazza San Domenico 13; 9.30am-12.30pm & 3.30-6.30pm Mon-Fri, to 5.30pm Sat & Sun) This 13th-century church is noteworthy for the elaborate sarcophagus of San Domenico, founder of the Dominican order. The tomb stands in the **Cappella di San Domenico**, which was designed by Nicola Pisano and later added to by Michelangelo.

Museo Civico Archeologico MUSEUM

(Via dell'Archiginnasio 2; adult/reduced/child €5/3/free; 9am-3pm Tue-Fri, 10am-6.30pm Sat & Sun) Impressive in its breadth of historical coverage, this museum displays well-documented Egyptian and Roman artefacts along with one of Italy's best Etruscan collections.

MAMbo MUSEUM

(Museo d'Arte Moderna di Bologna; www.mambo-bologna-org; Via Don Minzoni 14; adult/reduced/child €6/4/free; noon-6pm Tue, Wed & Fri, to 10pm Thu, to 8pm Sat & Sun) An excellent modern-art museum in a converted bakery.

Sleeping

Accommodation is largely geared to the business market so there are few budget options. Avoid the busy spring and autumn trade fairs when prices skyrocket and reservations are essential.

Il Convento dei Fiori di Seta BOUTIQUE HOTEL €€€

(051 27 20 39; www.silkflowersnunnery.com; Via Orfeo 34; r €140-420, ste €250-520;) This seductive boutique hotel is a model of sophisticated design. Housed in a 15th-century convent, it features contemporary furniture juxtaposed against exposed brick walls and religious frescos, Mapplethorpe-inspired flower motives and mosaic-tiled bathrooms.

Albergo delle Drapperie HOTEL €

(051 22 39 55; www.albergodrapperie.com; Via delle Drapperie 5; s €60-70, d €75-85;) Bed down in the heart of the atmospheric Quadrilatero district at this welcoming three-star. Rooms, which all differ slightly, are attractive with wood-beamed ceilings, wrought-iron beds and the occasional brick arch. Breakfast costs €5 extra and wi-fi €2. At a second site, the **Residence delle Drapperie** (051 22 39 55; www.residencedrapperie.com; Via Galliera 48; apt from €55) has 10 mini-apartments for stays of two nights or more.

Hotel University Bologna HOTEL €€

(051 22 97 13; www.hoteluniversitybologna.com; Via Mentana 7; d €70-250;) A low-key three-star offering value for money and an excellent location in the orange-hued university district. There are few frills but the functionally furnished rooms are comfortable and it's great to be in such a lively neighbourhood.

Albergo Panorama PENSION €

(051 22 18 02; www.hotelpanoramabologna.it; Via Livraghi 1, 4th fl; d €65-90, without bathroom s €40-60, d €55-70, tr €70-90, q €90-120;) A budget bolthole within easy walking distance of Piazza Maggiore, this is a cheerful old-school *pensione* with simple, spacious rooms, lovely rooftop views, and flowers in the hallway. Note that air-con is only in rooms overlooking the street. Cash only.

Eating

Foodie hot spots include the university district northeast of Via Rizzoli and the Quadrilatero district east of Piazza Maggiore.

Osteria de' Poeti RISTORANTE €€

(www.osteriadepoeti.com; Via de' Poeti 1b; mains €12; closed dinner Mon & Sun) In the wine cellar of a 14th-century *palazzo*, this historic eatery is a bastion of old-style service and classic local cuisine. Take a table by the stone fireplace and enjoy warming regional staples such as *tortellini in brodo di carne* (in a meat broth). Evenings feature frequent live music.

Il Saraceno RISTORANTE €€

(051 23 66 28; www.ristorantesaracenobologna.com; Via Calcavinazzi 2; pizzas from €5, mains €12-20) Popular with lunching locals, this is a good all-purpose eatery just off central Via Ugo Basso. Tables are on a small outdoor terrace or in a smart white-grey interior, and the menu covers all bases, from steak to seafood, pasta to pizza.

Trattoria del Rosso TRATTORIA €
(☎051 23 67 30; www.trattoriadelrosso.com; Via A Righi 30; daily menu €10, mains €7.50-10) The oldest trattoria in town is the perfect place for a cheap lunchtime fill-up. Sit down to filling pastas and honest journeyman's fare, cooked simply and served fast.

La Sorbetteria Castiglione GELATERIA €
(www.lasorbetteria.it; Via Castiglione 44; ⌚8.30am-midnight Tue-Sat, 9am-11.30pm Sun) A walk out of the centre, this much-vaunted *gelateria* produces superb ice cream, as well as *granite* (crushed ice drinks), *frappè* (milk shakes) and smoothies.

Drinking & Entertainment

Bologna's nightlife is one of the most vibrant in the country, with a huge number of bars, cafes and clubs. Thirsty students congregate on and around Piazza Verdi, while the fashionable Quadrilatero district hosts a dressier, more upmarket scene.

Café de Paris BAR
(Piazza del Francia 1c; ⌚7.30am-3am Mon-Sat, 4pm-3am Sun) Modish bar with daily aperitifs between 7.30pm and 9.30pm.

La Scuderia BAR, CAFE
(www.lascuderia.bo.it; Piazza Verdi 2; ⌚8am-2.30am; 📶) A popular student hang-out housed in medieval stables. *Aperitivi* and regular live music.

Caffè degli Orefici CAFE
(Via Orefici 6; ⌚Mon-Sat) A modern cafe next to a historic coffee shop.

Cantina Bentivoglio JAZZ
(www.cantinabentivoglio.it; Via Mascarella 4b; ⌚8pm-2am) Bologna's top jazz joint is part wine bar (choose from over 500 labels), part restaurant (the set-price menu costs €30) and part concert venue (there's live music nightly).

Cassero CLUB
(www.cassero.it; Via Don Minzoni 18) Saturday and Wednesday are the big nights at this legendary gay and lesbian (but not only) club, home of Italy's Arcigay organisation.

Information

HOSPITAL Ospedale Maggiore (☎051 647 81 11; Largo Nigrisoli 2)

TOURIST INFORMATION Bologna (www.bolognawelcome.com), Airport (☎051 647 21 13; ⌚9am-7pm Mon-Sat, to 4pm Sun); Piazza Maggiore (☎051 23 96 60; Piazza Maggiore 1/e; ⌚9am-7pm Mon-Sat, 10am-5pm Sun)

Getting There & Around

Air

European and domestic flights serve **Guglielmo Marconi airport** (☎051 647 96 15; www.bologna-airport.it), 6km northwest of the city. From the airport, an Aerobus shuttle (€6, 30 minutes, every 15 to 30 minutes) connects with the main train station; tickets can be bought on board.

Bus

National and international coaches depart from the bus station on Piazza XX Settembre. However, for most destinations the train is a better bet.

Bologna's efficient bus system is run by **ATC** (www.atc.bo.it). To get to the centre from the train station take bus A, 25 or 30 (€1.20).

Train

Bologna is a major rail hub. From the central train station on Piazza delle Medaglie d'Oro, fast trains run to Venice (€30, 1½ hours, hourly), Florence (€24 to €36, 40 minutes, half-hourly), Rome (€56 to €81, 2½ hours, half-hourly) and Milan (€32 to €40, one to two hours, hourly).

Ravenna

POP 158,700

Easily accessible from Bologna, and worth a day trip at the very least, the refined town of Ravenna is famous for its remarkable Early Christian mosaics. These Unesco-listed treasures, relics of the town's golden age as capital of the Western Roman and Byzantine Empires, have been impressing visitors ever since the 13th century when Dante described them in his *Divine Comedy* (much of which was written here).

Adding to the town's cultural credentials is the **Ravenna Festival** (www.ravennafestival.org), which sees classical music concerts staged across town in June and July.

Sights

Mosaics MOSAICS
Ravenna's mosaics are spread over several sites in and around town. The five main ones – Basilica di San Vitale, Mausoleo di Galla Placida, Basilica di Sant'Appollinare Nuovo, Museo Arcivescovile and Battistero Neoniano – are covered by a single ticket (adult/reduced/child €9.50/8.50/free) which is available at any of the five locations.

On the northern edge of the *centro storico,* the sombre exterior of the 6th-century **Basilica di San Vitale** (Via Fiandrini, entrance on Via San Vitale; ⌚9am-7pm Apr-Sep, to 5.30pm Mar & Oct, 9.30am-5pm Nov-Feb) hides a dazzling interior with mosaics depicting Old Testament scenes. In the same complex, the small **Mausoleo di Galla Placidia** (Via Fiandrini; ⌚9am-7pm Apr-Sep, to 5.30pm Mar & Oct, 9.30am-5pm Nov-Feb) contains the city's oldest mosaics, dating to around AD 430. Note that between March and mid-September there's a €2 booking fee for the Mausoleo.

Adjoining Ravenna's unremarkable cathedral, the **Museo Arcivescovile** (Piazza Arcivescovado; ⌚9am-7pm Apr-Sep, 9.30am-5.30pm Oct & Mar, 10am-5pm Nov-Feb) boasts an exquisite 6th-century ivory throne, while next door in the **Battistero Neoniano** (Piazza del Duomo; ⌚9am-7pm Apr-Sep, 9.30am-5.30pm Mar & Oct, 10am-5pm Nov-Feb) the baptism of Christ and the apostles is represented in the domed roof mosaics. To the east, the **Basilica di Sant'Apollinare Nuovo** (Via di Roma; ⌚9am-7pm Apr-Sep, 9.30am-5.30pm Mar & Oct, 10am-5pm Nov-Feb) boasts, among other things, a superb mosaic depicting a procession of martyrs headed towards Christ and his apostles.

Five kilometres southeast of town, the apse mosaic of the **Basilica di Sant'Apollinare in Classe** (Via Romea Sud; adult/reduced/child €5/2.50/free; ⌚8.30am-7.30pm Mon-Sat, 1-7.30pm Sun) is a must-see. Take bus 4 (€1.20) from Piazza Caduti per la Libertà.

FREE Dante's Tomb MAUSOLEUM
(Via Dante Alighieri 9; admission free; ⌚9.30am-6.30pm) Italy's greatest literary hero, Dante Alighieri (1265–1321), spent the last 20 years of his life in Ravenna after he was expelled from his hometown, Florence, in 1302. As a perpetual act of penance, Florence still supplies the oil for the lamp that burns continuously in his tomb.

Sleeping & Eating

Ostello Galletti Abbiosi HOSTEL €
(☎0544 3 13 13; www.galletti.ra.it; Via Roma 140; s €50, d €70-140; P ❄ @ 📶) More hotel than hostel, this excellent budget option occupies an aristocratic 18th-century *palazzo*. As a result, rooms are spacious and high-ceilinged, there's a monumental staircase, a handsome internal courtyard and even an on-site chapel.

Hotel Sant'Andrea HOTEL €€
(☎0544 21 55 64; www.santandreahotel.com; Via Cattaneo 33; s €50-100, d €80-180; ❄ @ 📶) In the *centro storico*, this charming three-star provides elegant accommodation in a converted convent. A grand wooden staircase leads up to smart, carpeted rooms overlooking a lawned garden where breakfast is served in spring and summer.

La Gardela TRATTORIA €
(☎0544 21 71 47; Via Ponte Marino 3; mains €8-16, fixed-price menu €15/25; ⌚closed Thu) A cheerful, unpretentious place that gives you exactly what you want from an Italian trattoria – large helpings of hearty home-cooked food, a jovial, warm atmosphere, and efficient service. Particularly good value is the €15 set menu, ideal for lunch.

Ca' de Vèn RISTORANTE €€
(☎0544 3 01 63; Via Corrado Ricci 24; mains €12-18; ⌚Tue-Sun) Yes, it's touristy, but this cavernous *enoteca*-cum-restaurant is still a memorable spot for a meal and glass of wine. Housed in a 15th-century *palazzo* with frescoed domes and vaulted brick ceilings, it offers a full menu of regional specialities, cheese and *piadine* (sandwiches made with a local flatbread), alongside an encyclopaedic wine list.

Information

Information is available online at www.turismo.ravenna.it and at three tourist offices – the **main office** (☎0544 3 54 04; Via Salara 8; ⌚8.30am-7pm Mon-Sat, 10am-6pm Sun) and branches at **Teodorico** (☎0544 45 15 39; Via delle Industrie 14; ⌚9.30am-12.30pm & 3.30-6.30pm) and **Classe** (☎0544 47 36 61; Via Romea Sud 266, Classe; ⌚9.30am-12.30pm & 3.30-6.30pm).

Getting There & Around

Regional trains run to/from Bologna (€6.80, 1½ hours, 14 daily) and destinations on the east coast.

In town, cycling is popular. The main tourist office runs a free bike-hire service to visitors aged 18 or over (take ID).

TUSCANY

Tuscany is one of those places that well and truly lives up to its hype. The fabled landscape of rolling, vine-covered hills dotted with cypress trees and stone villas has long been considered the embodiment of rural chic, and its historically intact cities are home to a significant portfolio of the world's medieval and Renaissance art. Some people never venture beyond Florence, but those who do are inevitably enchanted by their visits to hilltop towns, medieval monasteries, picturesque wine estates and some of Italy's best restaurants.

WORTH A TRIP

THE DOLOMITES

A Unesco Natural Heritage site since 2009, the Dolomites stretch across the northern regions of **Trentino-Alto Adige** and the **Veneto**. Their stabbing sawtooth peaks and vertiginous walls provide thrilling scenery and superb sport.

Ski resorts abound, offering downhill and cross-country skiing as well as snowboarding and other winter sports. Facilities are generally excellent and accommodation is widely available. Ski passes cover either single resorts or a combination of slopes – the most comprehensive is the **Dolomiti Superski pass** (www.dolomitisuperski.com; high season 3-/6-day pass €144/254) which accesses 1220km of runs in 12 valleys. Popular ski destinations include **Cortina d'Ampezzo**, one of Italy's most fashionable, expensive and well-equipped resorts; **Canazei** in the **Val di Fassa**; and **Ortisei**, **Santa Cristina** and **Selva Gardena** in the **Val Gardena**.

Hiking opportunities run the gamut from kid-friendly strolls to hard-core mountain treks. Trails are well marked with numbers on red-and-white bands or inside coloured triangles on the *Alte Vie* (High Routes). Recommended areas include the **Alpe di Siusi**, a vast plateau above the Val Gardena; the area around Cortina; and the **Pale di San Martino**, a highland plateau accessible by cable car from **San Martino di Castrozza**.

Tourist offices in individual resorts can provide local advice, but for area-wide information contact the offices in **Trento** (0461 21 60 00; www.apt.trento.it; Via Manci 2; 9am-7pm) and **Bolzano** (0471 30 70 00; www.bolzano-bozen.it; Piazza Walther 8; 9am-7pm Mon-Fri, 9.30am-6pm Sat). The best online resource is www.dolomiti.org.

Most places are accessible by bus, with services run by **Trentino Trasporti** (0461 82 10 00; www.ttesercizio.it) in Trento; **SAD** (0471 45 01 11; www.sad.it) in Alto Adige; and **Dolomiti Bus** (0437 21 71 11; www.dolomitibus.it) in the Veneto. During winter, most resorts also offer 'ski bus' services.

Florence

POP 371,300

Visitors have rhapsodised about the beauty of Florence (Firenze) for centuries, and once here you'll appreciate why. An essential stop on every Italian itinerary, this Renaissance time capsule is busy year-round, but even the enormous and inevitable crowds of tourists fail to diminish its lustre. A list of the city's famous sons reads like a Renaissance who's who – under 'M' alone you'll find Medici, Machiavelli and Michelangelo – and its treasure trove of galleries, museums and churches showcases a magnificent array of Renaissance artworks.

History

Many hold that Florentia was founded by Julius Caesar around 59 BC, but archaeological evidence suggests an earlier village, possibly founded by the Etruscans around 200 BC. Though it was a rich merchant city by the 12th century, Florence's golden age took a bit longer to arrive, and did so under the auspices of the Medici family. They ruled the city between the 14th and 17th centuries and their visionary patronage of writers, artists and thinkers culminated in the Renaissance.

The Medicis were succeeded in the 18th century by the French House of Lorraine, which ruled until 1860, when the city was incorporated into the kingdom of Italy. From 1865 to 1870, Florence was capital of the fledgling kingdom.

During WWII, parts of the city were destroyed by bombing and in 1966 a devastating flood destroyed or damaged many important works of art. Recent decades have been blessedly free of such events, and the city is undergoing a modern Renaissance spearheaded by the opening of cultural institutions such as the Palazzo Strozzi and the long-overdue restoration and expansion of the Uffizi Gallery.

Sights

From the main train station, Stazione Santa Maria Novella, it's a 550m walk along Via de' Panzani and Via de' Cerretani to the Duomo. From Piazza di San Giovanni, next to the Duomo, Via Roma leads down to Piazza della Repubblica and continues as Via Calimala and Via Por Santa Maria to the Ponte Vecchio.

There are seven major neighbourhoods in Florence's *centro storico*: Duomo and

Piazza della Signoria, Santa Maria Novella, San Lorenzo, San Marco, Santa Croce, Oltrarno and Boboli/San Miniato al Monte. Most of these owe their names to the significant basilicas located within their borders, which make excellent navigational landmarks.

Piazza del Duomo & Around PIAZZA

Photographs don't do justice to the exterior of Florence's Gothic **Duomo** (Cattedrale di Santa Maria del Fiore, St Mary of the Flower; www.duomofirenze.it; dome admission €10, crypt admission €3, campanile adult/child €7/free; ⏲10am-5pm Mon-Wed & Fri, to 3.30pm Thu, to 4.45pm Sat, to 3.30pm 1st Sat of month, 1.30-4.45pm Sun, Mass in English 5pm Sat, dome 8.30am-7pm Mon-Fri, to 5.40pm Sat, crypt 10am-5pm Mon-Wed & Fri, to 4.45pm Sat, campanile 8.30am-7.30pm). While they reproduce the startling colours of the tiered red, green and white marble facade and the beautiful symmetry of the dome, they fail to give any real sense of its monumental size and its importance as the city's major landmark. Officially known as the Cattedrale di Santa Maria del Fiore, the building's construction began in 1294 but the cathedral itself wasn't consecrated until 1436. Construction of its most famous feature, the enormous octagonal **Cupola** (admission €10), was overseen by Brunelleschi after his design won a public competition in 1420. There's a magnificent view from the top of the cupola, but the climb is steep (463 steps) and also extremely cramped in places, so it's best avoided if you are unfit or claustrophobic.

The cathedral's interior is decorated with frescos by Vasari and Zuccari, and the stained-glass windows are by Donatello, Paolo Uccello and Lorenzo Ghiberti. The facade is a 19th-century replacement of the unfinished original, pulled down in the 16th century.

The design of the 82m **Campanile** (bell tower; www.operaduomo.firenze.it; adult €7; ⏲9am-6pm) was begun by Giotto in 1334 and completed after his death by Andrea Pisano and Francesco Talenti. The views from the top make the 414-step climb worthwhile.

The stunning Romanesque **Battistero** (Baptistry; Piazza di San Giovanni; admission €6; ⏲11.15am-6.30pm Mon-Sat, 8.30am-2pm 1st Sat of every month, till 11pm Thu-Sat Jun-22 Sep, 8.30am-2pm Sun) is one of the oldest buildings in Florence. Built on the site of a Roman temple between the 5th and 11th centuries, it's famous for its gilded-bronze doors, particularly Lorenzo Ghiberti's *Gate of Paradise*.

Surprisingly overlooked by the crowds, the **Museo dell'Opera di Santa Maria del Fiore** (Cathedral Museum; www.operaduomo.firenze.it; Piazza del Duomo 9; admission €7; ⏲9am-6pm Mon-Sat, 9am-1pm Sun) safeguards treasures that once adorned the Duomo, Battistero and Campanile and is one of the city's most impressive museums. Its collection includes Ghiberti's *Gate of Paradise* panels (those on the Baptistry doors are copies) and a Pietà by Michelangelo.

Three cumulative tickets are available: €13 for entrance to the Cupola and the Museo dell'Opera di Santa Maria del Fiore; €17 for the Campanile, Battistero and Museo; and €26.50 for every Duomo sight (valid four days). All can be purchased at the ticket desk at the Museo.

Galleria degli Uffizi MUSEUM

(Uffizi Gallery; www.uffizi.firenze.it; Piazzale degli Uffizi 6; adult/reduced €6.50/3.25, incl temporary exhibition €11/5.50; ⏲8.15am-6.05pm Tue-Sun) This magnificent gallery safeguards the Medici family's private art collection, which was bequeathed to the city in 1743 on the condition that it never leaves Florence. It occupies the Palazzo degli Uffizi, a handsome structure built between 1560 and 1580 to house government offices.

A major refurbishment and redevelopment of the gallery was under way as this book went to print. The completion date was uncertain, although nine new exhibition rooms opened in mid-2012 and remaining works are progressing.

The gallery is home to the world's greatest collection of Italian Renaissance art. Highlights include Simone Martini's shimmering *Annunciation* (room 3); Piero della Francesca's famous profile portraits of the Duke and Duchess of Urbino (room 7); Botticelli's *Birth of Venus* and *Allegory of Spring* (Primavera; rooms 10 to 14); Leonardo da Vinci's *Annunciation* (room 15); and Michelangelo's *Holy Family* (room 25). Allow at least four hours for your visit.

For a break, head to the gallery's rooftop cafe. Members of the Medici family once congregated here to watch events in the Piazza della Signoria.

Piazza della Signoria PIAZZA

(cnr Via Calimaruzza & Via de' Calzaiuoli) The city's most splendid piazza was created in the 13th century and has been the hub of Florentine

Florence

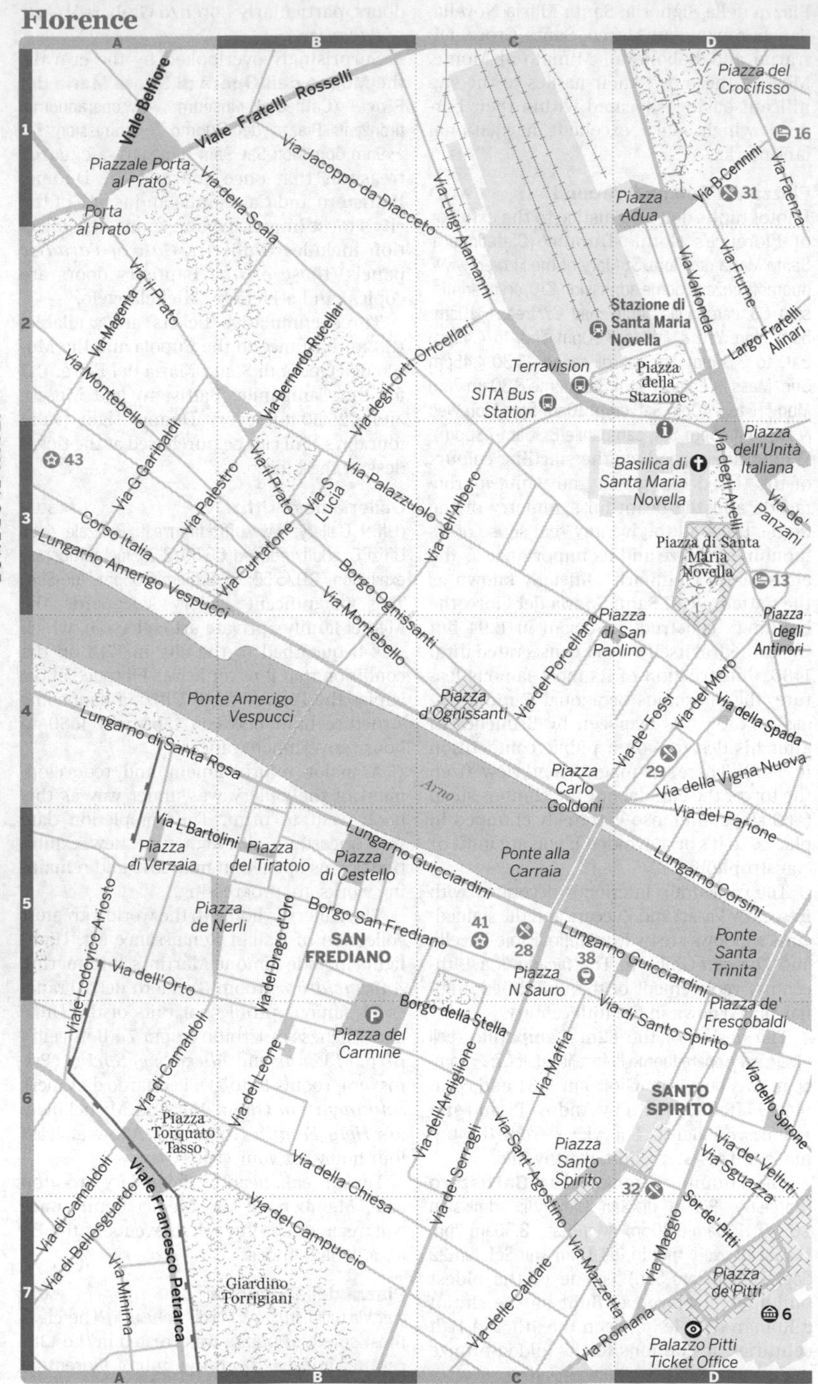

Viale Belfiore
Viale Fratelli Rosselli
Piazzale Porta al Prato
Porta al Prato
Via della Scala
Via Jacopo da Diacceto
Via Luigi Alamanni
Piazza del Crocifisso
16
Via B Cennini
31
Via Faenza
Piazza Adua
Via Fiume
Via Valfonda
Stazione di Santa Maria Novella
Largo Fratelli Alinari
Terravision
SITA Bus Station
Piazza della Stazione
Via il Prato
Via Magenta
Via Montebello
Via Bernardo Rucellai
Via degli Orti Oricellari
43
Via G Garibaldi
Via Palestro
Via il Prato
Via S Lucia
Via Palazzuolo
Via dell'Albero
Piazza dell'Unità Italiana
Basilica di Santa Maria Novella
Via degli Avelli
Via de' Panzani
Piazza di Santa Maria Novella
13
Corso Italia
Lungarno Amerigo Vespucci
Via Curtatone
Borgo Ognissanti
Via Montebello
Piazza di San Paolino
Piazza degli Antinori
Via del Porcellana
Piazza d'Ognissanti
Via del Moro
Via de' Fossi
Via della Spada
Ponte Amerigo Vespucci
Lungarno di Santa Rosa
Arno
29
Via della Vigna Nuova
Piazza Carlo Goldoni
Via del Parione
Via L Bartolini
Piazza di Verzaia
Piazza del Tiratoio
Piazza di Cestello
Lungarno Guicciardini
Ponte alla Carraia
Lungarno Corsini
Viale Lodovico Ariosto
Piazza de Nerli
Via del Drago d'Oro
Borgo San Frediano
SAN FREDIANO
41
28
38
Lungarno Guicciardini
Ponte Santa Trinita
Via dell'Orto
Piazza N Sauro
Piazza de' Frescobaldi
Borgo della Stella
Via di Santo Spirito
Via di Camaldoli
Via del Leone
Piazza del Carmine
Via Maffia
Via dell'Ardiglione
Via dello Sprone
SANTO SPIRITO
Piazza Torquato Tasso
Via de Serragli
Via Sant' Agostino
Via de' Velluti
Via Sguazza
Viale Francesco Petrarca
Via della Chiesa
Piazza Santo Spirito
32
Via di Camaldoli
Via di Bellosguardo
Via del Campuccio
Sdr de' Pitti
Via Maggio
Via Mazzetta
Via Minima
Giardino Torrigiani
Via delle Caldaie
Piazza de' Pitti
6
Via Romana
Palazzo Pitti Ticket Office
A
B
C
D
1
2
3
4
5
6
7

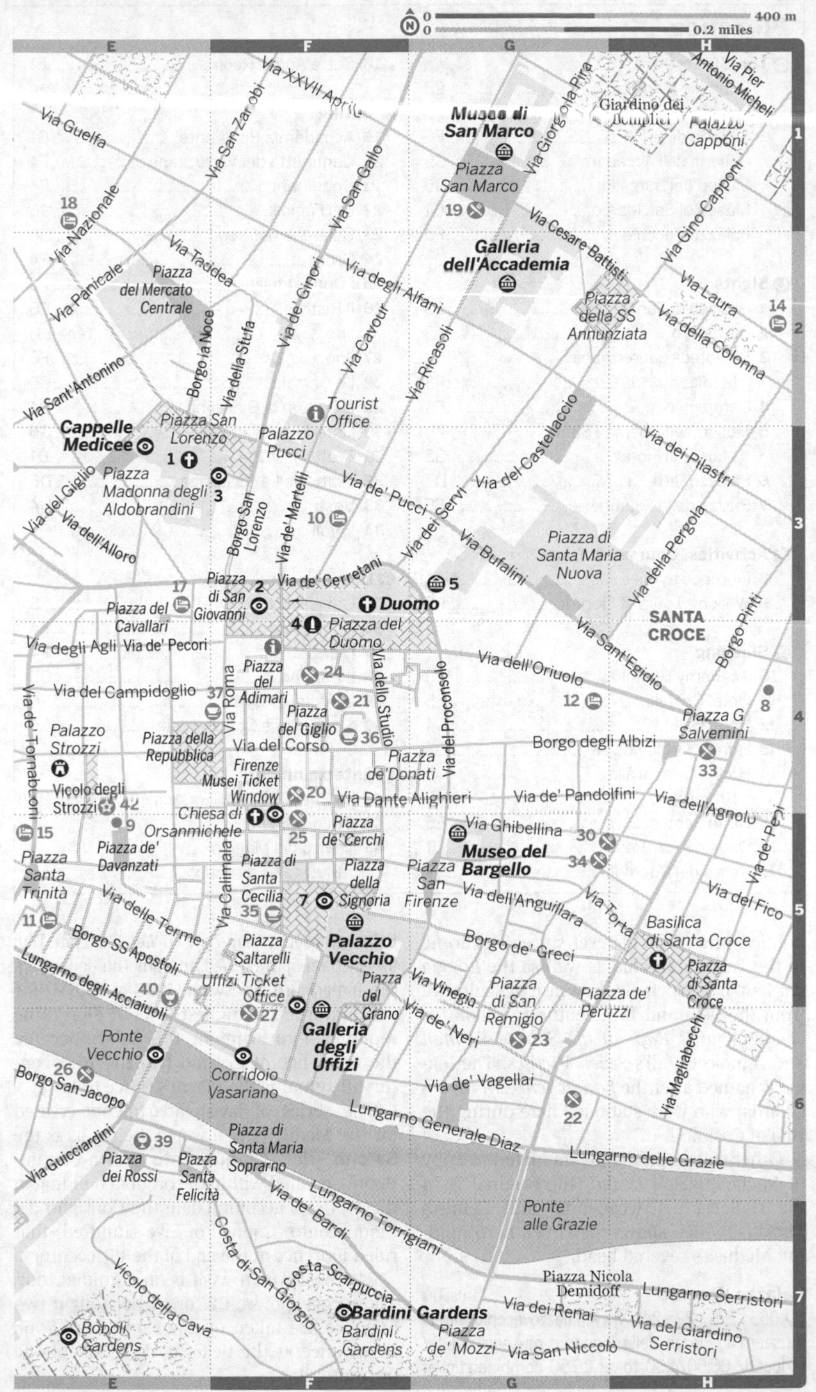

0
400 m
0
0.2 miles
E
F
G
H
1
2
3
4
5
6
7
Via Guelfa
Via XXVII Aprile
Via San Zanobi
Via San Gallo
Museo di San Marco
Piazza San Marco
19
Via Giorgio La Pira
Giardino dei Semplici
Palazzo Capponi
Via Pier Antonio Micheli
Via Gino Capponi
18
Via Nazionale
Via Taddea
Via Panicale
Piazza del Mercato Centrale
Via de' Ginori
Via degli Alfani
Galleria dell'Accademia
Via Cesare Battisti
Piazza della SS Annunziata
Via Laura
14
Via della Colonna
Borgo la Noce
Via della Stufa
Via Cavour
Via Ricasoli
Via Sant'Antonino
Tourist Office
Piazza San Lorenzo
Cappelle Medicee
Palazzo Pucci
1
3
Piazza Madonna degli Aldobrandini
Via del Giglio
Via dell'Alloro
Borgo San Lorenzo
Via de' Martelli
10
Via de' Pucci
Via dei Servi
Via del Castellaccio
Via dei Pilastri
Via Bufalini
Piazza di Santa Maria Nuova
Via della Pergola
17
Piazza di San Giovanni
2
Via de' Cerretani
5
Duomo
Piazza del Cavallari
4
Piazza del Duomo
SANTA CROCE
Via degli Agli
Via de' Pecori
Via Sant'Egidio
Borgo Pinti
Piazza del Adimari
24
Via dello Studio
Via dell'Oriuolo
Via del Proconsolo
Via del Campidoglio
37
Via Roma
21
Piazza del Giglio
12
8
Piazza G Salvemini
Via de' Tornabuoni
Palazzo Strozzi
Piazza della Repubblica
Via del Corso
36
Borgo degli Albizi
33
Piazza de'Donati
Firenze Musei Ticket Window
20
Via Dante Alighieri
Via de' Pandolfini
Via dell'Agnolo
Vicolo degli Strozzi
42
Chiesa di Orsanmichele
Via Ghibellina
30
34
9
15
25
Piazza de' Cerchi
Piazza de' Davanzati
Museo del Bargello
Via de' Pepi
Piazza Santa Trinità
Piazza di Santa Cecilia
Piazza della Signoria
7
Piazza San Firenze
Via dell'Anguillara
Via del Fico
Via Calimala
35
Via delle Terme
Via Torta
Basilica di Santa Croce
11
Borgo SS Apostoli
Piazza Saltarelli
Palazzo Vecchio
Borgo de' Greci
Piazza di Santa Croce
Lungarno degli Acciaiuoli
Uffizi Ticket Office
40
Piazza del Grano
Via Vinegia
Piazza di San Remigio
Piazza de' Peruzzi
27
Via de' Neri
Galleria degli Uffizi
23
Via Magliabecchi
Ponte Vecchio
Corridoio Vasariano
26
Borgo San Jacopo
Via de' Vagellai
22
Lungarno Generale Diaz
Lungarno delle Grazie
39
Via Guicciardini
Piazza dei Rossi
Piazza Santa Felicità
Piazza di Santa Maria Soprarno
Via de' Bardi
Lungarno Torrigiani
Ponte alle Grazie
Costa di San Giorgio
Costa Scarpuccia
Vicolo della Cava
Piazza Nicola Demidoff
Lungarno Serristori
Via dei Renai
Bardini Gardens
Via del Giardino Serristori
Boboli Gardens
Piazza de' Mozzi
Via San Niccolò

Florence

Top Sights

Cappelle Medicee E3
Duomo F3
Galleria degli Uffizi F6
Galleria dell'Accademia G2
Museo del Bargello G5
Museo di San Marco G1
Palazzo Vecchio F5

Sights

1 Basilica di San Lorenzo E3
2 Battistero F3
3 Biblioteca Laurenziana Medicea F3
4 Campanile F4
5 Museo dell'Opera di Santa Maria del Fiore G3
6 Palazzo Pitti D7
7 Piazza della Signoria F5

Activities, Courses & Tours

8 Florence by Bike H4
9 Walking Tours of Florence E5

Sleeping

10 Academy Hostel F3
11 Hotel Cestelli E5
12 Hotel Dalí G4
13 Hotel L'Orologio D3
14 Hotel Morandi alla Crocetta H2
15 Hotel Scoti E5
16 Ostello Archi Rossi D1
17 Relais del Duomo E3
18 Sette Angeli Rooms E1

Eating

19 Accademia Ristorante G1
20 Cantinetta dei Verrazzano F4
21 Coquinarius F4
22 Del Fagioli G6
23 Gelateria dei Neri G6
24 Grom F4
25 I Due Fratellini F5
26 Il Ristoro E6
'Ino .... (see 13)
27 'Ino F6
28 La Carraia C5
29 L'Osteria di Giovanni D4
30 Osteria del Caffè Italiano G5
31 Trattoria I Due G D1
32 Trattoria La Casalinga D6
33 Vestri H4
34 Vivoli G5

Drinking

35 Caffè Rivoire F5
36 Chiaroscuro F4
37 Gilli F4
38 Il Santino C5
39 Le Volpi e l'Uva E6
40 Sky Lounge Continentale E5

Entertainment

41 La Cité C5
42 Odeon Cinehall E4
43 Teatro del Maggio Musicale Fiorentino A3

political and social life ever since. It is home to the Palazzo Vecchio as well as the Loggia dei Lanzi, an open-air showcase of sculpture from the 14th and 16th centuries – look for Giambologna's *Rape of the Sabine Women* and Agnolo Gaddi's *Seven Virtues*. The loggia is named after the *Lanzichenecchi* (Swiss Guards) who were stationed here during the rule of Cosimo I.

Other statues in the piazza include a copy of Michelangelo's *David* (the original is in the Galleria dell'Accademia) and Cellini's *Perseus*, which shows the Greek hero holding Medusa's severed head.

Palazzo Vecchio MUSEUM

(055 276 82 24; www.palazzovecchio-familymuseum.it; Piazza della Signoria; museum adult/reduced/ €6.50/4.50, tower €6.50, combined ticket €10; museum 9am-7pm Fri-Wed, to 2pm Thu; tower 10am-5pm Fri-Wed, to 2pm Thu, longer hrs in summer) Built between 1298 and 1340 for the Signoria, the highest level of Florentine republican government, this palace became the residence of Cosimo I in the 16th century. It remains the mayor's office today.

The series of lavish apartments created for the Medici is well worth seeing, as is the **Salone dei Cinquecento** (16th-Century Room), created within the original building in the 1490s to accommodate the Consiglio dei Cinquecento (Council of Five Hundred) that ruled Florence at the end of the 15th century.

The best way to visit is on a guided tour. These cost a mere €2 (or €1 per tour if two or more are taken on the same day). Book in advance at the ticket desk, by telephone or by email.

Museo del Bargello MUSEUM
(☎055 294 883; www.polomuseale.firenze.it; Via del Proconsolo 4; adult/EU 18-25/EU child & senior €4/2/free, incl temporary exhibition €6/3/free; ⏰8.15am-4.20pm Tue-Sun & 1st & 3rd Mon of month) Home to Italy's most comprehensive collection of Tuscan Renaissance sculpture, the Bargello features Donatello's two versions of *David* (one in marble and the other in bronze) plus a number of important early works by Michelangelo.

Palazzo Pitti MUSEUM
(☎055 294 883; www.polomuseale.firenze.it; Piazza Pitti; ticket one adult/EU 18-25/EU child & senior €8.50/4.25/free, ticket two €7/3.50/free, ticket three €11.50/5.75/free; ⏰8.15am-4.30pm Tue-Sun, longer hours high season, closed 1st & last Mon of month) Originally commissioned by the Pitti family, great rivals of the Medici, this vast 15th-century palace was acquired by Cosimo I and Eleonoradi Toledo in 1549 and became the Medici family residence. It remained the official residence of Florence's rulers until 1919, when the Savoys gave it to the state.

Today it houses four museums, of which the **Galleria Palatina** is the most important. Works by Raphael, Botticelli, Caravaggio, Filippo Lippi, Titian and Rubens adorn its lavishly decorated rooms, culminating in the **Appartamenti Reali** (Royal Apartments), which retain their late-19th-century decoration. Three other museums – the **Museo degli Argenti** (Medici Treasury), **Galleria d'Arte Moderna** (Gallery of Modern Art) and **Galleria del Costume** (Costume Gallery) – are located within the palace buildings.

Behind the palace are the **Boboli Gardens** (Giardino di Boboli) and the adjacent **Bardini Gardens** (Giardino di Bardini).

Ticketing can be confusing: ticket one gives entrance to the Galleria Palatina, Appartamenti Reali and Galleria d'Arte Moderna; ticket two gives entrance to the Museo degli Argenti and Galleria del Costume, plus the Boboli and Bardini Gardens; and ticket three gives entrance to all museums and gardens and is valid for three days.

Galleria dell'Accademia MUSEUM
(☎055 29 48 83; Via Ricasoli 60; adult/EU 18-25/EU child & senior €6.50/3.25/free; ⏰8.15am-6.20pm Tue-Sun) Expect a lengthy queue when visiting the home of Michelangelo's *David*. Fortunately, the most famous statue in the world is well worth the wait. Carved from a single block of marble, the nude warrior assumed his pedestal in the Piazza della Signoria in 1504, providing Florentines with a powerful emblem of power, liberty and civic pride. The statue was moved here in 1873.

Adjacent rooms contain paintings by Andrea Orcagna, Taddeo Gaddi, Domenico Ghirlandaio, Filippino Lippi and Sandro Botticelli.

Basilica di San Lorenzo CHURCH
(Piazza San Lorenzo; adult/child €3.50/free; ⏰10am-5pm Mon-Sat year-round, 1.30-5pm Sun Mar-Oct) One of the city's finest examples of Renaissance architecture, this basilica was designed by Brunelleschi in the 15th century and includes his austerely beautiful **Sagrestia Vecchia** (Old Sacristry), which features sculptural decoration by Donatello. Michelangelo was commissioned to design the building's facade in 1518 but his design in white Carrara marble was never executed, hence its rough, unfinished appearance. He also designed the attached **Biblioteca Medicea Laurenziana** (Medici Library; www.bml.firenze.sbn.it; Piazza San Lorenzo 9; admission €3, incl basilica €6; ⏰9.30am-1.30pm Mon-Fri), with its sensuously curvaceous staircase.

Cappelle Medicee MAUSOLEUM
(☎055 294 883; www.polomuseale.firenze.it; Piazza Madonna degli Aldobrandini; adult/EU 18-25/EU child & senior €6/3/free; ⏰8.15am-1.20pm, till 4.20pm late Mar-early Nov, closed 2nd & 4th Sun & 1st, 3rd & 5th Mon of month) Principal burial place of the Medici rulers, this mausoleum is home to the stark but graceful **Sagrestia Nuova** (New Sacristy), Michelangelo's first architectural work and the showcase for three of his most haunting sculptures: *Dawn and Dusk*, *Night and Day* and *Madonna and Child*.

TOP CHOICE **Museo di San Marco** MUSEUM
(☎055 294 883; www.polomuseale.firenze.it; Piazza San Marco 1; adult/EU 18-25/EU child & senior €4/2/free; ⏰8.15am-1.20pm Mon-Fri, 8.15am-4.20pm Sat & Sun, closed 1st, 3rd & 5th Sun & 2nd & 4th Mon of month) Housed in a Dominican monastery, this spiritually uplifting museum is a showcase of the work of Fra Angelico, who decorated the cells with deeply devotional frescos to guide the meditation of his fellow friars. His most famous work, *Annunciation* (c 1450), is at the top of the stairs that lead to the cells.

CUTTING THE QUEUES

Sightseeing in Florence can entail hours spent in queues. Fortunately, there are two ways of saving time – one of which can also save you money.

For €4 extra per museum you can book tickets for the Uffizi and Galleria dell'Accademia (the museums with the longest queues) through **Firenze Musei** (Florence Museums; 055 29 48 83; www.firenzemusei.it; telephone booking line 8.30am-6.30pm Mon-Fri, 8.30am-12.30pm Sat). Book online in advance, or purchase tickets in person before your visit from the ticket desks at the Palazzo Pitti, Museo di San Marco or at the rear of the Chiesa di Orsanmichele.

If you are planning to visit most of the major museums, consider purchasing a **Firenze Card** (www.firenzecard.it; €50). These are valid for 72 hours, allow the holder to bypass both advance booking and queues, and also give free entry to one accompanying child under 18 (EU citizens only). Cards can be purchased online, at the tourist information offices opposite Stazione Santa Maria Novella and in Via Cavour, and at the ticket desks at the Palazzo Pitti, Palazzi Vecchio and Galleria degli Uffizi (door 2).

Tours

Cycling

A number of Florence-based companies offer cycling tours of Chianti, sometimes leaving by minibus and getting on bikes in Chianti and at other times doing the full tour by bike. Most include lunch and a wine-tasting, and are offered from March to October.

Florence by Bike CYCLING
(055 48 89 92; www.florencebybike.it; Via San Zanobi 120r) This shop hires mountain, hybrid and race bikes (€22 to €37 per day) and provides self-guided itineraries and maps of tours through Chianti. It also offers a 32km-long day tour of northern Chianti (adult/under 26 €79/71).

I Bike Italy CYCLING
(055 012 39 94; www.ibikeitaly.com) One-day guided tours in Chianti (€80) and a two-hour guided ride around Florence (including gelato; €25). 10% student discount.

I Bike Tuscany CYCLING
(335 812 07 69; www.ibiketuscany.com) One-day rides in the Florentine Hills, in Chianti and from Chianti to Siena (with bus transfers from Florence), led by former bike racer Marco Vignoli, cost €95 to €145.

Walking

Freya's Florence WALKING
(349 074 89 07; www.freyasflorence.com; per hr €70) A knowledgeable and enthusiastic Australian-born, Florence-based private tour guide; you'll pay admission fees on top of the guiding fee.

Walking Tours of Florence WALKING
(055 264 50 33; www.italy.artviva.com; Via de' Sassetti 1; tours per person from €25) The Artviva outfit offers a range of city tours, all led by English-speaking guides.

Festivals & Events

Scoppio del Carro EASTER
A cart of fireworks is exploded in front of the cathedral at 11am on Easter Sunday – get there at least two hours early to grab a good position.

Maggio Musicale Fiorentino ARTS
(www.maggiofiorentino.com) Italy's oldest arts festival is held in the Teatro del Maggio Musicale Fiorentino and stages performances of theatre, classical music, jazz and dance; April to June.

Festa di San Giovanni MIDSUMMER
Florence celebrates its patron saint, John, with a *calcio storico* (historical football) match on Piazza di Santa Croce and fireworks over Piazzale Michelangelo; 24 June.

Sleeping

Although there are hundreds of hotels in Florence, it's still prudent to book ahead. Look out for low-season website deals – prices often drop by up to 50%.

DUOMO & PIAZZA DELLA SIGNORIA

Hotel Dalí HOTEL €
(055 234 07 06; www.hoteldali.com; Via dell'Oriuolo 17; d/tr €85/110, apt from €95, with shared bathroom s/d €40/70; P@) This overwhelmingly friendly hotel offers 10 light and airy rooms with double-glazed windows, tea- and coffee-making facilities and ceiling fans; the best

overlook the rear garden. Parking is included in the room cost, but breakfast isn't. The owners also offer three nearby self-catering apartments sleeping between two and six.

Relais del Duomo B&B €
(055 21 01 47; www.relaisdelduomo.it; Piazza dell'Olio 2; s €40-90, d €70-130) The location is the prime selling point of this B&B on a quiet traffic-free street around the corner from the Duomo. The four pastel-coloured rooms are simple, but comfortable, and manager Elisabetta is extremely helpful.

Hotel Cestelli PENSION €
(055 21 42 13; www.hotelcestelli.com; Borgo SS Apostoli 25; d €50-100, ste €80-115, without bathroom s €40-60, d €50-80; closed Jan-Feb, Aug) Run by Florentine photographer Alessio and his Japanese wife Asumi, this eight-room hotel on the 1st floor of a 12th-century *palazzo* is wonderfully located. Though dark, rooms are attractively furnished, clean, quiet and cool. No breakfast.

SANTA MARIA NOVELLA

TOP CHOICE **Hotel L'Orologio** BOUTIQUE HOTEL €€€
(055 27 73 80; www.hotelorologioflorence.com; Piazza di Santa Maria Novella 24; r €160-550; P) This design-driven hotel has four stars, five floors and 54 well-equipped and extremely comfortable rooms. The magnificent top-floor breakfast area commands views over Piazza Santa Maria Novella, and the elegant ground floor offers lounges and a popular wine bar.

Ostello Archi Rossi HOSTEL €
(055 29 08 04; www.hostelarchirossi.com; Via Faenza 94r; dm €18-27, s €30-60, d €55-80; closed 2 weeks Dec; @) Guests' paintings and graffiti pattern the walls at this ever-busy hostel near Stazione di Santa Maria Novella. Rooms and dorms are simple but very clean, and there's a pleasant garden area. Bonuses include free breakfast, computers in some rooms, free guided walking tours and free pasta-and-salad meals six nights per week in the low season.

TOP CHOICE **Hotel Scoti** PENSION €
(055 29 21 28; www.hotelscoti.com; Via de' Tornabuoni 7; s €29-75, d €45-125, tr €75-150;) Wedged between Prada and McQueen, this *pensione* on Florence's most famous and glamorous shopping strip is a splendid mix of old-fashioned charm and value for money. Run with smiling aplomb by Australian Doreen and Italian Carmello, it offers 16 clean and comfortable rooms and a magnificent frescoed living room. Breakfast costs €5.

SAN LORENZO

TOP CHOICE **Academy Hostel** HOSTEL €
(055 239 86 65; www.academyhostel.eu; Via Ricasoli 9; dm €32-34, d with shared bathroom €76, s/d €42/86; @) The philosophy of this truly excellent small hostel close to the Duomo is that cheap accommodation shouldn't compromise comfort. Its immaculately maintained dorms sleep between four and six, and come with night lights, lockers and one shower and toilet for every four beds. Rates include breakfast.

Johlea & Johanna B&B €€
(055 462 72 96, 055 463 32 92; www.johanna.it; d €60-165; @) This highly regarded, professionally run operation has two elegant suite apartments and more than a dozen beautifully decorated and well-equipped ensuite B&B rooms housed in five historic residences in the quiet San Marco and San Lorenzo districts. One (Johanna 2) has parking, another (Antica Dimora Johlea) has a terrace with wonderful views and all offer a delicious breakfast and all-day tea, coffee (Nespresso) and cake. The pick of the bunch is Antica Dimora Johlea.

Sette Angeli Rooms B&B €
(393 949 08 10; www.setteangelirooms.com; Via Nazionale 31; s €45-60, d €85-110, tr €95-135;) Tucked behind the central market on a mainstream shopping street, Seven Angels is a tantalising mix of great value and recent renovation. Its rooms are perfectly comfortable and guests can pay an extra €10 to use the self-catering kitchen corner.

SAN MARCO

Hotel Morandi alla Crocetta HOTEL €€
(055 234 47 47; www.hotelmorandi.it; Via Laura 50; s €70-140, d €93-220, tr €130-195, q €150-370; P) This medieval convent-turned-hotel away from the madding crowd is a stunner. Rooms have traditional furnishings and an old-fashioned ambience; a couple have handkerchief-sized gardens to laze in and one (No 29) is the frescoed former chapel.

SAN MINIATO AL MONTE

Campeggio Michelangelo CAMPGROUND €
(055 681 19 77; www.ecvacanze.it; Viale Michelangelo 80; campsite adult €9.50-11.70, child 3-11 free-€6.90, car & tent €12.50-15.30; P@) Just off Piazzale Michelangelo, this large and comparatively leafy site has lovely city views.

Take bus 13 from Stazione di Santa Maria Novella or walk – steeply uphill!

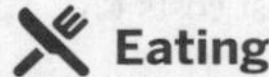

Eating

Classic Tuscan dishes include *ribollita* (a heavy vegetable soup) and *bistecca alla fiorentina* (Florentine steak served rare). Chianti is the local tipple.

DUOMO & PIAZZA DELLA SIGNORIA

'Ino SANDWICHES €

(Via dei Georgofili 3r-7r; panini €8, tasting platter €12; 11am-8pm Mon-Sat, noon-5pm Sun) Artisan ingredients are sourced locally and utilised creatively at this stylish address near the Uffizi. Create your own combination or pick a house special and scoff on the spot with a glass of wine. There's another **branch** in the Hotel l'Orologio on piazza Santa Maria Novella.

Cantinetta dei Verrazzano BAKERY €

(Via dei Tavolini 18-20; focaccias €3-3.50; noon-9pm Mon-Sat) Together, a *forno* (baker's oven) and *cantinetta* (small cellar) equal a match made in heaven. Head here for a foccacia straight from the oven and a glass of wine from the Verrazzano estate in Chianti.

I Due Fratellini SANDWICHES €

(www.iduefratellini.com; Via dei Cimatori 38r; panini €3; 9am-8pm Mon-Sat, closed Fri & Sat 2nd half of Jun & all Aug) This hole-in-the-wall has been in business since 1875. Locals flock here to order panini filled to order and eaten standing in the street.

Coquinarius WINE BAR

(www.coquinarius.com; Via delle Oche 11r; crostini & carpacci €4; noon-10.30pm) Nestled within the shadow of the Duomo, this *enoteca* is extremely popular with tourists – try the justly famous ravioli with cheese and pear. Note: at the time of research, a move to a nearby location was on the cards; telephone ahead for an update.

SANTA MARIA NOVELLA

L'Osteria di Giovanni TUSCAN €€€

(055 28 48 97; www.osteriadigiovanni.it; Via del Moro 22; mains €20-27; dinner Mon-Fri, lunch & dinner Sat & Sun) The house antipasto is a great way to sample Tuscan specialities such as *crostini* (small toasts with toppings) and *lardo* (pork fat), and both the pasta dishes and the *bistecca alla fiorentina* are sensational. Everything a perfect neighbourhood eatery should be, and then some.

SAN LORENZO

Trattoria I Due G TRATTORIA €€

(055 21 86 23; www.trattoriai2g.com; Via B Cennini 6r; mains €10-17; lunch & dinner Mon-Sat) There isn't a tourist in sight at this old-fashioned trattoria near the train station (well, there wasn't before we published this review). Huge servings of tasty salads, pastas and mains tempt every palate, but the sentimental favourite is undoubdtedly the delicious *pollo fritto* (fried chicken).

SAN MARCO

Accademia Ristorante TRATTORIA €€

(055 21 73 43; www.ristoranteaccademia.it; Piazza San Marco 7r; mains €12-22, pizzas €6-18; lunch & dinner) There aren't too many decent eateries in this area, which is one of the reasons why this family-run restaurant is perennially packed. Factors such as friendly staff, cheerful decor and consistently tasty food help, too.

SANTA CROCE

Trattoria Cibrèo TRATTORIA €€

(Via dei Macci 122r; meals €30; lunch & dinner Tue-Sat Sep-Jul) The small casual dining annexe of Florence's most famous (and considerably more expensive) restaurant is a gem. *Primi* include a justly famous fish soup and *secondi* comprise a small main dish matched with a side of seasonal vegetables; everything is exceptionally well priced considering its quality. No reservations and no credit cards.

Del Fagioli TRATTORIA €

(055 24 42 85; Corso Tintori 47r; mains €8.50-10; lunch & dinner Mon-Fri, closed Aug) This Slow Food favourite near the Basilica di Santa Croce is the archetypical Tuscan trattoria. It opened in 1966 and has been serving well-priced bean dishes, soups and roasted meats to throngs of appreciative local workers and residents ever since. No credit cards.

Osteria del Caffè Italiano TUSCAN €€€

(055 28 90 20; www.caffeitaliano.it; Via dell'Isola delle Stinche 11-13r; meals €45; lunch & dinner Tue-Sun) This old-fashioned *osteria* occupies the ground floor of a 14th-century *palazzo* and is an excellent spot to try the city's famous *bistecca alla fiorentina* (per kg €60). The adjoining **pizzeria** (pizzas €7 to €8) offers a choice of three pizza types – margherita, napoli and marinara – which are best enjoyed with an icy-cold beer (€6). No credit cards at the pizzeria.

TOP FIVE GELATERIE

There are plenty of places offering *gelato artiginale* (traditional, usually homemade, ice cream and sorbet). Flavours change according to what fruit is in season, and a small cone or tub can cost anywhere from €2 to €3.

La Carraia (Piazza Nazario Sauro 25r; tubs €1.50-6,cones €1.50-3; ⊙9am-11pm summer, to 10pm winter) Look for the ever-present queue next to the Ponte Carraia, and you will find this fantastic *gelateria*.

Gelateria dei Neri (Via de' Neri 22r; ⊙9am-midnight) Semifreddo-style gelato that is cheaper than its competitors; known for its Giotto (almond, hazelnut and coconut) flavour.

Gelateria Vivoli (Via dell'Isola delle Stinche 7; ⊙7.30am-midnight Tue-Sat, 9am-midnight Sun Apr-Oct, to 9pm Nov-Mar) Choose a flavour from the huge choice on offer (the chocolate with orange is a perennial favourite) and scoff it in the pretty piazza opposite; tubs only.

Grom (www.grom.it; cnr Via del Campanile & Via delle Oche; ⊙10.30am-midnight Apr-Sep, to 11pm Oct-Mar) Delectable flavours and often-organic ingredients.

Vestri (www.vestri.it; Borgo degli Albizi 11r; ⊙10.30am-8pm Mon-Sat) Specialises in chocolate; go for the decadent white chocolate with wild strawberries or the chocolate with pepper.

OLTRANO

La Casalinga TRATTORIA €

(☎055 21 86 24; Via de' Michelozzi 9r; mains €10; ⊙lunch & dinner Mon-Sat) Family run and locally loved, this busy place is one of Florence's cheapest trattorias. You'll be relegated behind locals in the queue – it's a fact of life and not worth protesting – with the eventual reward being hearty peasant dishes such as *bollito misto con salsa verde* (mixed boiled meats with green sauce).

Il Ristoro TUSCAN €

(☎055 264 55 69; Borgo San Jacopo 48r; mains €10; ⊙noon-4pm Mon, noon-10pm Tue-Sun) A disarmingly simple address not to be missed; this two-room restaurant with deli counter is a great budget choice. Pick from classics like *pappa al pomodoro* (tomato and bread soup) or a plate of cold cuts and swoon over views of the Arno swirling beneath your feet.

Drinking

TOP CHOICE Le Volpi e l'Uva WINE BAR

(www.levolpieluva.com; Piazza dei Rossi 1; crostini €6.50, cheese and meat platter €8; ⊙11am-9pm Mon-Sat) This intimate *enoteca con degustazione* (wine bar with tasting) offers an impressive list of wines by the glass (€4 to €8). To attain true bliss indulge in *crostini* topped with honeyed speck or *lardo*, or a platter of boutique Tuscan cheese and meat.

Caffè Rivoire CAFE

(Piazza della Signoria 4; ⊙Tue-Sun) Rivoire's terrace has the best view in the city. Settle in for a long *aperitivo* or coffee break – it's worth the high prices.

Gilli CAFE, BAR

(www.gilli.it; Piazza della Repubblica 39r; ⊙Wed-Mon) The city's grandest cafe, Gilli has been serving excellent coffee and delicious cakes since 1733. Claiming a table on the piazza is *molto* expensive – we prefer standing at the spacious Liberty-style bar.

Chiaroscuro CAFE, BAR

(www.chiaroscuro.it; Via del Corso 36r; ⊙7.30am-9pm Mon-Sat, noon-9pm Sun, closed 1 week mid-Aug) This casual cafe roasts its own beans and serves what may well be the best coffee in Florence. Its *aperitivo* buffet (6pm to 8pm) is justly popular.

Sky Lounge Continentale BAR

(www.continentale.it; Vicolo dell Oro 6r; ⊙2.30-11.30pm daily Apr-Sep) Accessible from the 5th floor of the Ferragamo-owned Hotel Continentale, this chic bar has amazing views over the Arno. Dress the part or feel out of place.

TOP CHOICE Il Santino WINE BAR

(Via Santo Spirito 34; soup €5, antipasti €6-10, panini €5.50; ⊙daily) This pocket-sized wine bar is the much-loved sibling of Il Santo Bevitore, one of the city's most fashionable eateries. Go early to claim a stool, graze on antipasti and choose from a list of quality wines by the glass; later in the evening drinkers spill out onto the street.

✩ Entertainment

Florence's definitive monthly listings guide, *Firenze Spettacolo* (€2), is sold at newsstands and has a small English-language section on the final pages.

Concerts, opera and dance are performed year-round at the **Teatro Comunale** (☎055 28 72 22; www.maggiofiorentino.com; Corso Italia 16), also the venue for events organised by the Maggio Musicale Fiorentino.

English-language films are screened at the **Odeon Cinehall** (☎055 29 50 51; www.cinehall.it; Piazza Strozzi 2; ⊙Oct-Jun).

La Cité LIVE MUSIC
(www.lacitelibreria.info; Borgo San Frediano 20r; ⊙3pm-1am Mon-Thu, 5pm-2am Fri & Sat;) By day it's a cafe-bookshop, but by night this intimate space morphs into a vibrant live-music space: think swing, fusion, jam-session jazz.

ℹ Information

Emergency

Police Station (Questura; ☎055 4 97 71; http://questure.poliziadistato.it; Via Zara 2; ⊙24hr)

Medical Services

Dr Stephen Kerr: Medical Service (☎335 836 16 82, 055 28 80 55; www.dr-kerr.com; Piazza Mercato Nuovo 1; ⊙3-5pm Mon-Fri, or by appointment) Resident British doctor.

Emergency Doctor (Guardia Medica; ☎north of the Arno 055 233 94 56, south of the Arno 055 21 56 16) For a doctor at night, weekends or on public holidays.

Tourist Information

Tourist Offices (www.firenzeturismo.it) Located at Via Cavour (☎055 29 08 33, 055 29 08 32; www.firenzeturismo.it; Via Cavour 1r; ⊙8:30am-6:30pm Mon-Sat); the airport (☎055 31 58 74; ⊙8.30am-6.30pm); Piazza della Stazione (☎055 21 22 45; www.commune.fi.it; Piazza della Stazione 4; ⊙8.30am-7pm Mon-Sat, to 2pm Sun) and the Bigallo (☎055 28 84 96; www.comune.fi.it; Loggia del Bigallo, Piazza San Giovanni 1; ⊙9am-7pm Mon-Sat, 9am-2pm Sun).

ℹ Getting There & Away

Air

The main airport serving Florence is Pisa international airport (p846). There's also the small, city **Florence airport** (www.aeroporto.firenze.it), 5km northwest of Florence.

Bus

The **SITA bus station** (www.sitabus.it; Via Santa Caterina da Siena 17r; ⊙information office 8.30am-12.30pm & 3-6pm Mon-Fri, 8.30am-12.30pm Sat) is just south of the train station. Buses leave for Siena (€7.80, 1¼ hours, every 30 to 60 minutes) and San Gimignano via Poggibonsi (€6.80, 1¼ hours, 14 daily).

Car & Motorcycle

Florence is connected by the A1 autostrada to Bologna and Milan in the north and Rome and Naples to the south. The A11 links Florence with Pisa and the coast, and a *superstrada* (expressway) joins the city to Siena.

Train

Florence is well connected by train. There are regular services to/from Pisa (Regionale €7.80, one hour, every 30 minutes), Rome (Freccia Rossa; €29, 90 minutes, hourly), Venice (Freccia Argento; €29 to €45, 2¼ hours, 12 daily) and Milan (Freccia Rossa; €39 to €49, 1¾ hours, hourly).

ℹ Getting Around

To/From the Airport

ATAF (☎800 42 45 00; www.ataf.net) runs a shuttle bus (€5, 25 minutes, half-hourly from 5.30am to 11pm) connecting Florence airport with the SITA bus station.

Taxis charge a fixed rate of €20 plus €1 per bag (€23.30 at night) for the trip between Florence airport and the *centro storico*.

Terravision (www.terravision.eu) runs a bus service between Pisa (Galileo Galilei) airport and the paved bus park in front of Stazione Santa Maria Novella (one-way/return €6/10, 70 minutes, 12 daily). In Florence, buy your tickets at the Terravision desk inside Deanna Café, opposite the station.

Autostradale also runs a bus service between Pisa airport (one-way/return €6/10) and Stazione Santa Maria Novella. In Florence, tickets are available from the newsstand at the tram stop next to the station.

A limited number of trains run from Pisa airport directly to Florence each day (€7.80, one hour); regular services run to Pisa Centrale from where you can change to a Florence train.

Bus

ATAF buses service the city centre and Fiesole, a picturesque small town in the hills 8km northeast of Florence. Take bus 7 from Piazza San Marco for Fiesole, and bus 12 or 13 from Stazione Santa Maria Novella for Piazzale Michelangelo. Tickets (90 minutes €1.20) are sold at *tabacchi* and newsstands – you can also buy a 90-minute ticket on board the bus (€2).

Car & Motorcycle

Note that there is a strict Limited Traffic Zone (ZTL) in the *centro storico* from 7.30am to 7.30pm Monday to Friday and 7.30am to 6pm on Saturday. Fines are hefty if you enter the centre during these times without a special permit having been organised by your hotel in advance. For information about the ZTL go to www.comune.fi.it.

The ZTL means that the best option is to leave your car in a car park and use public transport to access the centre. Porta al Prato is a good choice as it's only one tram stop away from Santa Maria Novella. It charges €1 for the first hour, €2 per hour for the second or subsequent hour, or €20 per 24 hours. Buy tickets for the tram (No 1 to/from Villa Costanza; €1.20) from the machines at the tram stop. Details of other car parks are available from **Firenze Parcheggi** (☎055 500 19 94; www.firenzeparcheggi.it).

Pisa

POP 88,300

Most people know Pisa as the home of an architectural project gone terribly wrong, but the Leaning Tower is just one of a number of noteworthy sights in this compact and compelling university city.

Pisa's golden age came in the 12th and 13th centuries when it was a maritime power rivalling Genoa and Venice. It was eventually defeated by the Genoese in 1284, and in 1406 it fell to Florence. Under the Medici, the arts and sciences flourished and Galileo Galilei (1564–1642) taught at the university.

Sights & Activities

The Piazza dei Miracoli is a straightforward 1.5km walk from the bus and train stations – follow Viale F Crispi north, cross the Ponte Solferino over the Arno and continue straight up Via Roma to Campo dei Miracoli.

Piazza dei Miracoli PIAZZA
(Campo dei Miracoli; www.opapisa.it; ⏲10am-5pm Jan-Feb & Nov-Dec, 9am-6pm Mar, 8am-8pm Apr-Sep, 9am-7pm Oct) Pisans claim that the Piazza dei Miracoli is among the most beautiful urban spaces in the world. Certainly, the immaculate walled lawns provide a gorgeous setting for the architecturally harmonious Romanesque architectural trio of cathedral, baptistry and tower.

The centrepiece is the **Duomo** (Piazza dei Miracoli; adult/reduced €2/1, admission free Nov-Feb; ⏲10am-8pm Apr-Sep, 10am-7pm Oct, 10am-12.45pm & 2-5pm Nov-Feb, 10am-6pm Mar), the construction of which began in 1064. It has a graceful tiered facade and a cavernous interior featuring a carved marble pulpit by Giovanni Pisano. The transcept's bronze doors are by Bonanno Pisano.

Construction of the cupcake-like **Battistero** (Piazza dei Miracoli; ⏲8.30am-8pm Apr-Sep, 9am-7pm Oct, 10am-5pm Nov-Feb, 9am-6pm Mar) to the west of the Duomo started in 1153 and was completed under the supervision of Nicola and Giovanni Pisano in 1260. Inside, note Nicola Pisano's beautiful pulpit.

But it's to the campanile, better known as the **Leaning Tower** (Torre Pendente; €15 at ticket office, €17 when booked online; ⏲8.30am-8pm Apr-May & Sep, 8.30am-11pm Jun-Aug, 9am-7pm Oct, 9.30am-5.30pm Nov & Feb, 10am-4.30pm Dec-Jan, 9am-5.30pm Mar), that all eyes are drawn. Construction began in 1173 under the supervision of Bonanno Pisano, but his plans came a cropper almost immediately. Only three of the tower's seven tiers were completed before it started tilting – continuing at a rate of about 1mm per year. By 1990 the lean had reached 5.5 degrees – a tenth of a degree beyond the critical point established by computer models. Stability was finally ensured in 1998 when a combination of biased weighting and soil drilling forced the tower into a safer position. Today it's almost 4.1m off the perpendicular.

PIAZZA DEI MIRACOLI TICKETING

Ticket pricing for Piazza dei Miracoli sights is complicated. Tickets to the Leaning Tower and Duomo are sold individually, but for the remaining sights combined tickets are available. These cost €5/6/8/10 for one/two/four/five sights and cover the Duomo, Baptistry, Camposanto cemetery, Museo dell'Opera del Duomo and Museo delle Sinópie. Entry for children aged under 10 years is free for all sights except the Tower. Any ticket will also give access to the multimedia and information areas located in the Museo Dell'Opera del Duomo and Museo delle Sinópie.

Tickets are sold at two **ticket offices** (www.opapisa.it; Piazza dei Miracoli; ⏲8am-7.30pm Apr-Sep, 8.30am-7pm Oct, 9am-5pm Nov & Feb, 9.30am-4.30pm Dec-Jan, 8.30am-6pm Mar) on the piazza: the central ticket office is behind the tower and a second office is in the entrance foyer of the Museo delle Sinópie. To ensure your visit to the tower, book tickets via the website at least 15 days in advance.

Visits to the tower are limited to groups of 40, and children under eight years are not allowed entrance; entry times are staggered and queuing is inevitable. It is wise to book ahead.

Flanking the Campo, the beautiful **Camposanto cemetery** (Piazza dei Miracoli; ⌚8.30am-8pm Apr-Sep, 9am-7pm Oct, 10am-5pm Nov-Feb, 9am-6pm Mar) is said to contain soil shipped from Calvary during the crusades. Look out for the 14th-century fresco *The Triumph of Death* on the southern cloister wall.

A free audioguide to the sight is available in podcast format at www.opapisa.it. Guided tours of the piazza are conducted by **Pisa Guide** (☎333 614 49 24; www.pisaguide.com; adult/child 10-18yr/child under 10yr €8/6/free; ⌚11am-noon Fri-Sun Oct-May).

Sleeping

Many people visit Pisa on a day trip from Florence, but if you're keen to sample the lively bar scene at night there are a few decent overnight options.

Hostel Pisa Tower HOSTEL €
(☎329 701 73 87, 050 520 24 54; www.hostelpisatower.it; Via Piave 4; dm €18-22, apt €49-69; @) This extremely friendly place near the Piazza dei Miracoli opened in 2011. Occupying a villa with a rear garden, it is cheerful, clean and comfortable but suffers from a lack of communal kitchen and bathroom facilities (only two showers and two toilets for 22 beds). The apartment sleeps two or three and has a small kitchen and private car park; wi-fi is free but internet access costs €4 per hour.

Hostel Pisa HOSTEL
(☎050 520 18 41; www.hostelpisa.it; Via Corridoni 29; dm €15, d/t €40/56, d with shared bathroom €35; @) Opened in 2011, this hostel is close to the train station (expect noise) and offers characterless, but cheap and clean, accommodation. There's a communal kitchen, a concrete courtyard with ping-pong table, and a lounge with TV and pool table. Breakfast costs €5.50 and bike rental (24 hour) costs €10. Rooms are hot in summer.

Royal Victoria Hotel HOTEL €€
(☎050 94 01 11; www.royalvictoria.it; Lungarno Pacinotti 12; d €65-150, ste €150-190, without bathroom r €30-80;) This doyen of Pisan hotels has been run with pride by the Piegaja family since 1837. Rooms vary, but most are a perfect shabby-chic mix of antique ambience and modern-day comfort. The flowery 4th-floor terrace is a highlight.

Eating & Drinking

The best restaurants and bars are in the streets around Piazza Dante Alighieri, Piazza Vettovaglie and along the riverbank.

Il Montino PIZZERIA €
(Vicolo del Monte 1; pizza slices €1.50; ⌚10.30am-3pm & 5-10pm Mon-Sat) Students and sophisticates alike adore the *cecina* (chickpea pizza) and *spuma* (sweet, nonalcoholic drink) that are the specialities of this local institution. Order to go or claim one of the outdoor tables.

biOsteria 050 ORGANIC €
(☎050 54 31 06; www.zerocinquanta.com; Via San Francesco 36; burgers €6.50-8.50, mains €9.50-13; ⌚lunch Mon-Sun, dinner Tue-Sun;) The chef here uses produce that is strictly local and organic to create his tasty dishes. There are ample choices for vegetarians and coeliac sufferers, and excellent-value daily lunch specials are chalked on the board outside.

Bar Pasticceria Salza CAFE, PASTICCERIA €
(Borgo Stretto 44; ⌚8am-8.30pm Apr-Oct, shorter hours Tue-Sun Nov-Mar) This old-fashioned cafe and cake shop has been tempting Pisans off Borgo Stretto and into sugar-induced indulgence since the 1920s.

Sottobosco CAFE
(www.sottoboscocafe.it; Piazza San Paolo all'Orto; ⌚10am-midnight Tue-Fri, noon-1am Sat, 7pm-midnight Sun) What a tourist-free breath of fresh air this bohemian cafe is! Enjoy coffee, herbal teas, pastries and light lunches during the day, or head here on Friday, Saturday and Sunday nights for live music (often jazz).

Information

For city information, check www.pisaunicaterra.it or pop into the tourist office at the airport or in the city centre.

Getting There & Around

Pisa international airport (p846) is linked to the city centre by train (€1.40, five minutes, 15 daily), or by the **CPT** (www.cpt.pisa.it) LAM Rossa bus (€1.10, 10 minutes, every 10 minutes). Buy bus tickets at the newsstand at the train station or any *tabacchi*.

A taxi between the airport and the city centre costs €15 (€20 at night).

Terravision buses depart from the airport to Florence (one-way/return €6/10, 70 minutes, 12 daily). **Train Spa** (www.trainspa.it) shuttle buses go to Siena via Poggibonsi (€14, one daily).

Regular trains run to Lucca (Regionale €3.30, 30 minutes, every 30 to 60 minutes), Florence (Regionale €7.80, 1¼ hours, every 30 minutes), Rome (Freccia Bianca €19 to €44.50, three hours, five daily) and Genoa (InterCity €9 to €18, 2½ hours, eight daily).

Siena

POP 54,600

Siena is one of Italy's most enchanting medieval towns. Its walled centre, a beautifully preserved warren of dark lanes punctuated with Gothic *palazzi,* has at its centre Piazza del Campo (known as Il Campo), the sloping square that is the venue for the city's famous annual horse race, Il Palio.

According to legend, Siena was founded by the sons of Remus (one of the founders of Rome). In the Middle Ages its dramatic rise caused political and cultural friction with nearby Florence and the two cities strove to outdo each other with their artistic and architectural achievements. Painters of the Sienese School (most notably in the 13th to 15th centuries) produced significant works of art, many of which are on show in the city's impressive museums and churches.

Sights

From the train station take bus 8 or 9 (€1.10) to Piazza Gramsci, from where Piazza del Campo is a short, signposted walk away. Buy your ticket from the *tabacchi* at the station.

From the bus station it's a 10-minute walk up Via La Lizza and Via delle Terme. The centre's main streets – the Banchi di Sopra, Via di Città and Banchi di Sotto – curve around Il Campo.

Piazza del Campo — PIAZZA

Il Campo has been Siena's civic and social centre for nearly 600 years. Near the top of the slope is a copy of the **Fonte Gaia** (Happy Fountain), decorated in 1419 by Sienese sculptor Jacopo della Quercia. The recently restored originals are on show in the Complesso Museale Santa Maria della Scala. Down the slope from the fountain is the **Palazzo Comunale** (aka Palazzo Pubblico), a striking example of Sienese Gothic architecture that is home to the splendid Museo Civico.

TOP CHOICE Museo Civico — MUSEUM

(www.comune.siena.it; Palazzo Comunale; adult/EU reduced €8/4.50; ⏲10am-6.15pm mid-Mar–Oct, to 5.15pm Nov–mid-Mar) The collection here includes Simone Martini's famous *Maestà* (Virgin Mary in Majesty; 1315–16) and his oft-reproduced fresco (1328–30) of Guidoriccio da Fogliano, a captain of the Sienese army.

Also here is the most important secular painting of the Renaissance, Ambrogio Lorenzetti's fresco cycle known as the *Allegories of Good and Bad Government* (c 1337–40).

The museum is on the 1st floor of the *palazzo;* from the ground floor it is possible to access the **Torre del Mangia** (admission €8; ⏲10am-7pm Mar–mid-Oct, to 4pm mid-Oct–Feb), a 102m-high bell tower offering great views over the city. A combined ticket to the museum and tower costs €13.

Duomo — CHURCH

(www.operaduomo.siena.it; Piazza del Duomo; admission Mar-Oct €3, Nov-Feb free; ⏲10.30am-7pm Mon-Sat, 1.30-6pm Sun Mar-Oct, 10.30am-5.30pm Mon-Sat, 1.30-5.30pm Sun Nov-Feb) Siena's cathedral is one of Italy's greatest Gothic churches. Begun in 1196, it was opened in 1215, although work continued on features such as the apse and dome well into the 13th century. The magnificent facade of white, green and red polychrome marble was finished towards the end of the 14th century and the mosaics in the gables are 19th-century additions. Notable features include the carved pulpit by Giovanni and Nicola Pisano, Donatello's bronze of St John the Baptist and the inlaid marble floor, decorated with 56 panels depicting historical and biblical subjects. The most valuable panels are kept covered and are revealed only from 21 August through 27 October each year (admission is €7 during this period).

Through a door from the north aisle is the **Libreria Piccolomini** (Piccolomini Library; Piazza Jacopo della Quercia, Duomo Nuovo), which is decorated with vivid narrative frescos by Pinturicchio.

Battistero di San Giovanni — BAPTISTRY

(Piazza San Giovanni; admission €4; ⏲10.30am-7pm Mon-Sat & 1.30-6pm Sun Mar-Oct, 10.30am-5.30pm Mon-Sat & 1.30-5.30pm Sun Nov-Feb) While this baptistry's Gothic facade has remained unfinished, the interior is richly decorated with frescos. The centrepiece is a marble font by Jacopo della Quercia, decorated with bronze panels in relief and depicting the life of St John the Baptist. Artists include Lorenzo

Ghiberti (*Baptism of Christ* and *St John in Prison*) and Donatello (*Herod's Feast*).

Museo Opera del Duomo MUSEUM
(Piazza del Duomo; admission €7; ⌚10.30am-7pm Mon-Sat & 1.30-6pm Sun Mar-Oct, 10.30am-5.30pm Mon-Sat & 1.30-5.30pm Sun Nov-Feb) This museum is home to a large collection of Sienese painting and sculpture, including an entire room dedicated to the work of Duccio di Buoninsegna, the most significant painter of the Sienese School. The ticket also includes access to a panoramic terrace.

Complesso Museale Santa Maria della Scala CULTURAL BUILDING
(www.santamariadellascala.com; Piazza del Duomo 1; adult/reduced/child under 11 €6/3.50/free; ⌚10.30am-4pm, till 6.30pm in high season) This former hospital, parts of which date to the 13th century, is directly opposite the Duomo and houses three museums – the Archaeological Museum, Art Museum for Children, and Center of Contemporary Art (SMS Contemporanea) – as well as a variety of historic halls, chapels and temporary exhibition spaces. Though the atmospheric **Archaeological Museum** housed in the basement tunnels is impressive, the complex's undoubted highlight is the upstairs **Pellegrinaio** (Pilgrim's Hall), with its vivid 15th-century frescos.

COMBINATION PASSES

There are a number of money-saving passes to Siena's churches and museums on offer:

Siena Itinerari d'Arte (SIA) Museo Civico, Complesso Museale Santa Maria della Scala, Museo Opera del Duomo and Battistero (€17 mid-March to October, €14 November to mid-March, valid seven days).

Musei Comunali Ticket Museo Civico and Complesso Museale Santa Maria della Scala (€11, valid two days).

OPA Si Pass Duomo, Libraria Piccolomini, Battistero, Museo Opera del Duomo and Panoramic Terrace (€12, valid three days).

All three passes can be purchased at the Duomo ticket office. The Siena Itinerari d'Arte and Musei Comunali Ticket are also available at the ticket offices at the Museo Civico and Complesso Museale Santa Maria della Scala.

Festivals & Events

Siena's great annual event is the **Palio** (⌚2 Jul & 16 Aug), a pageant culminating in a bareback horse race round Il Campo. The city is divided into 17 *contrade* (districts), of which 10 are chosen annually to compete for the *palio* (silk banner).

Sleeping

It's always advisable to book in advance, but for August and the Palio, it's essential.

TOP CHOICE **Campo Regio Relais** BOUTIQUE HOTEL €€€
(☎0577 22 20 73; www.camporegio.com; Via della Sapienza 25; s €150-300, d €190-300, ste €250-600; ❄@📶) Siena's most charming hotel occupies a 16th-century *palazzo* and has only six rooms, all of which are individually decorated and luxuriously equipped. Breakfast is served in the sumptuous lounge or on the terrace, which has a sensational view of the Duomo and Torre del Mangia.

TOP CHOICE **Hotel Alma Domus** HOTEL €
(☎0577 4 41 77; www.hotelalmadomus.it; Via Camporegio 37; s €40-48, d €60-85, tr €80-110; ❄@📶) Owned by the Catholic diocese and still home to six Dominican nuns who act as guardians at the Casa Santuario di Santa Caterina (in the same complex), this convent is now privately operated as a budget hotel. Many of the spotlessly clean rooms have views over the narrow green Fontebranda valley across to the Duomo. There's a 1am curfew.

Antica Residenza Cicogna B&B €
(☎0577 28 56 13; www.anticaresidenzacicogna.it; Via dei Termini 67; s €70-90, d €85-110, ste €120-150; ❄@📶) Charming host Elisa supervised the recent restoration of this 13th-century building and will happily recount its history (it's been owned by her family for generations). The seven rooms are clean and well maintained, with comfortable beds, painted ceilings and tiled floors.

Eating & Drinking

Traditional Sienese dishes include *panzanella* (summer salad of soaked bread, basil, onion and tomatoes), *pappardelle con la lepre* (ribbon pasta with hare) and panforte (a rich cake of almonds, honey and candied fruit).

TOP CHOICE **Enoteca I Terzi** MODERN ITALIAN €€
(☎0577 4 43 29; www.enotecaiterzi.it; Via dei Termini 7; mains €18; ⌚11am-1am Mon-Sat) Close to the

Campo but off the well-beaten tourist trail, this classy, modern *enoteca* is a favourite with bankers from the nearby headquarters of the Monte dei Paschi di Siena bank, who love to linger over their working lunches of handmade pasta, flavoursome risotto and succulent grilled meats.

Morbidi DELI €

(Via Banchi di Sopra 75; ⏲9am-8pm Mon-Sat, lunch buffet 12.30-2.30pm) Local gastronomes shop here, as the range of cheese, cured meats and imported delicacies is the best in Siena. If you are self-catering you can join them, but make sure you also investigate the downstairs lunch buffet (€12), which offers fantastic value.

Kopa Kabana GELATERIA €

(www.gelateriakopakabana.it; Via dei Rossi 52-55; gelati €1.70-2.30; ⏲11am-midnight mid-Feb–mid-Nov) Come here for fresh gelato made by self-proclaimed ice-cream master, Fabio (we're pleased to concur).

Caffè Fiorella CAFE

(www.torrefazionefiorella.it; Via di Città 13; ⏲7am-8pm Mon-Sat) Squeeze into this tiny space behind the Campo to enjoy Siena's best coffee. In summer, the coffee granita with a dollop of cream is a wonderful indulgence.

Information

Tourist Office (☎0577 28 05 51; www.terresiena.it; Piazza del Campo 56; ⏲9am-7pm)

Getting There & Away

Siena is not on a main train line, so it's easier to arrive by bus. From the bus station on Piazza Gramsci, SITA/Siena Mobilità buses run to Florence (€7.80, 1½ hours, every 30 to 60 minutes) and San Gimignano (€6, 1¼ hours, hourly), either direct or via Poggibonsi. A Train SPA bus travels to Pisa airport (€14, two hours, one daily).

Sena (☎861 199 19 00; www.sena.it) operates services to/from Rome Tiburtina and Fiumicino Airport (€23, 3½/4 hours, 11 daily weekdays, fewer on weekends), Milan (€36, 4½ hours, five daily), Perugia (€12, 1½ hours, one daily) and Naples (€32, 6½ hours, one daily). Services to Naples depart from outside the railway station.

Both Train Siena Mobilità and Sena have ticket offices underneath the piazza.

There's a ZTL in the *centro storico*, although visitors can drop off luggage at their hotel, then leave (make sure the hotel reception reports your licence number or you will be fined). The paid car parks at San Francesco and Santa Caterina (aka Fontebranda) each charge €1.60 per hour and have a *scala mobile* (escalator) to take you into the centre. For details, check www.sienaparcheggi.com (in Italian).

Lucca

POP 85,000

Lucca is a love-at-first-sight type of place. Hidden behind monumental Renaissance walls, its *historic centre* is chock-full of handsome churches, excellent restaurants and tempting *pasticcerie*. Founded by the Etruscans, it became a city state in the 12th century and stayed that way for 600 years. Most of its streets and monuments date from this period.

From the train station walk across Piazza Ricasoli, cross Viale Regina Margherita, and then follow the path across the grass and through the wall to reach the centre.

Sights & Activities

A two-hour guided walking tour of the historical centre (adult/child under 15yr €10/free) leaves from the Città di Lucca tourist office at 2pm every day between April and September.

Opera buffs should visit in July and August, when the **Puccini Festival** (www.puccinifestival.it) is held in a purpose-built outdoor theatre in the nearby settlement of Torre del Lago. For other festivals and events, check www.luccaitinera.it.

City Walls FORTRESS

Lucca's massive *mura* (walls), built around the old city in the 16th and 17th centuries and defended by 126 cannons, remain in almost perfect condition. Twelve metres high and 4km in length, the ramparts are crowned with a tree-lined footpath that looks down on the old town and out towards the Apuane Alps – it's the perfect spot to stroll, cycle, run and get a feel for local Lucchesi life.

Cattedrale di San Martino CHURCH

(Piazza San Martino; sacristy adult/reduced €2/1.50; ⏲7am-6pm Apr-Sep, to 5pm Oct-Mar) Lucca's predominantly Romanesque cathedral dates to the start of the 11th century. Its exquisite facade was constructed in the prevailing Lucca-Pisan style and designed to accommodate the pre-existing campanile. Inside, there's a simply fashioned image of a dark-skinned, life-sized Christ on a wooden crucifix, known as the *Volto Santo,* and a magnificent *Last Supper* by Tintoretto. The **sacristy** features Domenico Ghirlandaio's 1479 *Madonna Enthroned with Saints* and a marble memorial carved by Jacopo della Quercia in 1407.

Chiesa e Battistero dei SS Giovanni e Reparata ARCHAEOLOGICAL SITE
(☎0583 49 05 30; Piazza San Giovanni; adult/concession €2.50/1.50) The 12th-century interior of this deconsecrated church is a hauntingly atmospheric setting for one-hour opera recitals staged by **Puccini e la sua Lucca** (☎340 810 60 42; www.puccinielasualucca.com; adult/reduced €17/13; ⏲7pm daily mid-Mar–Oct, 7pm Fri-Wed Nov–mid-Mar) every evening from mid-March to November. Professional singers present a one-hour program of arias and duets dominated by the music of Puccini. Tickets are available from the church between 10am and 6pm.

Casa Natale Giacomo Puccini MUSEUM
(☎0583 58 40 28; www.puccinimuseum.it; Corte San Lorenzo 9; adult/reduced €7/5; ⏲10am-6pm Wed-Mon Apr-Oct, 11am-5pm Wed-Mon Nov-Mar) The great composer was born in this modest house in 1858. It's now a somewhat dull showcase of everyday objects telling the tale of the composer's life. For afficionados only.

Sleeping

2italia APARTMENT €€
(☎3355 20 82 51; www.2italia.com; Via della Anfiteatro 74; apt for 2 adults & up to 4 children €150-170; 📶) This clutch of family-friendly self-catering apartments overlooks Piazza Anfiteatro, one of the city's major landmarks. Available on a nightly basis (minimum two nights), they sleep up to six, have fully equipped kitchen and washing machine, and come with sheets and towels. The owners also organise cycling tours, cooking courses, wine tastings and olive pickings.

Ostello San Frediano HOSTEL €
(☎0583 46 99 57; www.ostellolucca.it; Via della Cavallerizza 12; dm/s/d/tr €22/45/65/80, without bathroom dm €20; P@📶) Comfort and service levels are high at this HI-affiliated hostel set in a lovely garden. There are 149 beds in private rooms and segregated dorms, a courtyard and a grandiose dining room (breakfast €3 to €5, dinner €11). Wi-fi and parking are free; internet access costs €1 per hour.

Piccolo Hotel Puccini HOTEL €
(☎0583 5 54 21; www.hotelpuccini.com; Via di Poggio 9; s €50-73, d €70-97; ❄📶) Close to the Casa Natale Giacomo Puccini, this well-run, small hotel has rooms with old-fashioned decor, satellite TV and small clean bathrooms. Breakfast costs €3.

Eating

La Pecora Nera TRATTORIA €
(☎0583 46 97 38; www.lapecoraneralucca.it; Piazza San Francesco 4; pizzas €5-9, mains €8.50-13; ⏲lunch Sat, dinner Wed-Sun) The Black Sheep is the only Lucchesi restaurant recommended by the Slow Food Movement. It also scores extra brownie points for social responsibility (its profits fund workshops for young people with Down syndrome). The menu features pizzas (dinner only), Tuscan favourites and daily specials.

Taddeucci PASTICCERIA €
(www.taddeucci.com; Piazza San Michele 34; 300/600/900g loaf €4.50/9/13.50; ⏲8.30am-7.45pm, closed Thu winter) This *pasticceria* is where the traditional Lucchesi treat of *buccellato* was created in 1881. These ring-shaped loaves made with flour, sultanas, sugar and aniseed seeds are the perfect accompaniment to a mid-morning or afternoon espresso.

Forno Giusti BAKERY €
(Via Santa Lucia 20; pizzas & filled focaccias per kg €8-16; ⏲7am-1pm & 4-7.30pm Mon, Tue & Thu-Sat, 7am-1.30pm Wed, 4-7.30pm Sun) The best way to enjoy a Lucchese lunch is to picnic on the walls, particularly if you buy delectable provisions from this excellent bakery.

Da Felice PIZZERIA €
(www.pizzeriadafelice.com; Via Buia 12; focaccias €1-3.50, pizza slices €1.30; ⏲10am-8.30pm Mon-Sat) This buzzing local favourite behind Piazza San Michele serves *cecina* and *castagnacci* (chestnut cakes).

Information

The **Città di Lucca tourist office** (☎0583 58 31 50; www.luccaitinera.it; Piazzale Verdi; ⏲9am-7pm Apr-Oct, to 5pm Nov-Mar) holds luggage (€7.50 per day), offers toilet facilities (€0.50), hires bicyles (€2.50 per hour), operates an internet point (€1 per 30 minutes), sells concert tickets, and supplies free maps and information. In the high season there's another tourist office near **Porta Elisa** (☎0583 355 51 00; www.luccatourist.it; Piazza Napoleone; ⏲10am-1pm & 2-6pm Mon-Sat).

Getting There & Around

The bus station is on Piazzale Giuseppe Verdi, near Porta Vittorio Emanuele Santa Anna. From the bus station **VaiBus** (www.vaibus.it; ⏲hourly Mon-Sat, every 2 hours Sun) buses run to/from Pisa airport (€3, one hour).

Lucca is on the Florence–Pisa–Viareggio train line. Regional trains run to/from Florence (€7,

WORTH A TRIP

SAN GIMIGNANO

This tiny hilltop town deep in the Tuscan countryside is a mecca for day-trippers from Florence and Siena. Its nickname is 'The Medieval Manhattan' courtesy of the 11th-century towers that soar above its pristine *centro storico*. Originally 72 were built as monuments to the town's wealth but only 14 remain.

The **tourist office** (☎0577 94 00 08; www.sangimignano.com; Piazza del Duomo 1; ⊙10am-1pm & 3-7pm Mar-Oct, 10am-1pm & 2-6pm Nov-Feb) is a short walk from Piazza dei Martiri di Montemaggio, the nearest San Gimignano has to a bus terminal. Next door, the **Palazzo Comunale** (Piazza del Duomo; gallery & tower admission adult/reduced €5/4; ⊙9.30am-7pm Apr-Sep, 11am-5.30pm Oct-Mar) houses San Gimignano's art gallery (the **Pinacoteca**) and tallest tower, the Torre Grossa.

Nearby, the Romanesque cathedral, known as the **Collegiata** (Piazza del Duomo; adult/child €3.50/1.50; ⊙10am-7.10pm Mon-Fri, to 5.10pm Sat, 12.30-7.10pm Sun Apr-Oct, shorter hours rest of year, closed 2nd half Nov & Jan), boasts an interior covered with 14th-century frescos by Bartolo di Fredi, Lippo Memmi and Tadeo di Bartolo. The small **Cappella di Santa Fina** off the south aisle features frescos by Domenico Ghirlandaio.

While in town, be sure to sample the local wine, Vernaccia, while marvelling at the spectacular view from the terrace of the **Museo del Vino** (Wine Museum; Parco della Rocca; admission free; ⊙11.30am-6.30pm mid-Mar–Oct), which is located next to the Rocca (fortress).

For lunch, head to **Dal Bertelli** (Via Capassi 30; panini €3-5, glasses of wine €1.50; ⊙1-7pm Mar-early Jan) for a panino made with local artisan ingredients, followed by an icy delight from the justly famous **Gelateria di Piazza** (www.gelateriadipiazza.com; Piazza della Cisterna 4; gelati €1.80- 2.50; ⊙8.30am-11pm Mar–mid-Nov).

Regular buses link San Gimignano with Florence (€6.80, 1¼ hours, 14 daily), travelling via Poggibonsi. There are also services to/from Siena (€6, 1¼ hours, hourly).

1½ hours, every 30 to 90 minutes) and Pisa (€3.30, 30 minutes, every 30 to 60 minutes).

There are plenty of car parks around the walls. Most charge €1.50 per hour between 8am and 6.30pm.

Cicli Bizzarri (☎0583 49 66 82; www.ciclibizzarri.net; Piazza Santa Maria 32; ⊙9am-7pm) and **Biciclette Poli** (☎0583 49 37 87; www.biciclettepoli.com; Piazza Santa Maria 42; ⊙9am-7pm) on Piazza Santa Maria rent bikes for €3 per hour (€8 for an electric bike).

UMBRIA

Dubbed the 'green heart of Italy', this predominantly rural region harbours some of Italy's best-preserved historic *borghi* (villages) and many important artistic, religious and architectural treasures. The regional capital, Perugia, provides a convenient base, with Assisi and Orvieto easy day trips away.

Perugia

POP 168,200

With its hilltop medieval centre and international student population, Perugia is Umbria's largest and most cosmopolitan city. There's not a lot to see here, but the presence of the University for Foreigners ensures a buzz that's not always apparent in the region's sleepy hinterland. In July, music fans inundate the city for the prestigious **Umbria Jazz Festival** (www.umbriajazz.com) and in the third week of October the **Eurochocolate** (☎075 502 58 80; www.eurochocolate.com) festival lures chocoholics from across the globe.

Perugia has a bloody and lively past. In the Middle Ages, the Baglioni and Oddi families fought for control of the city, while later, as a papal satellite, the city fought with its neighbours. All the while art and culture thrived: painter Perugino and Raphael, his student, both worked here.

The *centro storico* is on top of the hill, the train station is at the bottom and the regional bus station, Piazza dei Partigiani, is halfway between the two. From Piazza Partigiani there are *scale mobili* (escalators) going up to Piazza Italia, where local buses terminate. From Piazza Italia, pedestrianised Corso Vannucci runs up to Piazza IV Novembre, the city's focal point.

Sights

The **Perugia Città Museo Card** (adult/student €10/6) gives one adult and one child aged under 18 years access to five city museums and is valid for 48 hours.

Piazza IV Novembre PIAZZA
This meeting point for Etruscans and Romans and former medieval political centre is now a popular gathering place for students and tourists. The 14th-century **Cattedrale di San Lorenzo** (☎075 572 38 32; Piazza IV Novembre; ⏱8am-noon & 4-6.30pm) forms an impressive backdrop and the 13th-century **Fontana Maggiore** (Great Fountain) carved by Nicola and Giovanni Pisano provides a stolid centrepoint.

Palazzo dei Priori MUSEUM
Constructed between the 13th and 14th centuries and formerly the headquarters of the city's magistrature, this *palazzo* now houses some of the best museums in Perugia, including Umbria's foremost art gallery, the stunning **Galleria Nazionale dell'Umbria** (☎800 69 76 16; Corso Vannucci 19; adult/EU 18-25/EU under 18 & over 65 €6.50/3.25/free; ⏱8.30am-6.30pm Tue-Sun). An art historian's dream, it showcases 30 rooms of works featuring everything from Byzantine art to the 16th-century creations of home town heroes Pinturicchio and Perugino.

The same building also holds what some consider the most beautiful bank in the world, the **Nobile Collegio del Cambio** (Exchange Hall; ☎075 572 85 99; Corso Vannucci 25; adult/reduced €4.50/2.60; ⏱9am-12.30pm & 2.30-5.30pm Mon-Sat, 9am-1pm Sun, closed Mon afternoon Nov–mid-Mar). Its walls are adorned with frescos by Perugino – look for his self-portrait in the painted frame.

COURSES

The **Università per Stranieri** (☎075 5 74 61; www.unistrapg.it; Piazza Fortebraccio 4, Palazzo Gallenga) runs hundreds of courses in language, art, history, music and architecture.

Sleeping

Primavera Minihotel PENSION €
(☎075 572 16 57; www.primaveraminihotel.it; Via Vincioli 8; s €45-65, d €70-100, tr €95-120; ❄@📶) On the top floor of a 16th-century *palazzo*, this well-run two-star *pensione* has eight modern rooms that are as clean as they are comfortable (ask for the top-floor room with terrace). Only a few rooms have air-con; breakfast costs an extra €5 to €8.

Ostello di Perugia HOSTEL €
(☎075 572 28 80; www.ostello.perugia.it; Via Bontempi 13; dm €16, sheet supplement €2; ⏱mid-Jan–mid-Dec) If the 10am to 4pm lockout doesn't scare you off, you're sure to appreciate the sweeping countryside view and wafting sounds of church bells from the hostel's terrace, where guests often gather after making dinner. Enjoy the 16th-century frescoed ceilings and tidy four- to six-person rooms.

Eating

TOP CHOICE **Sandri** CAFE, PASTICCERIA €
(☎075 572 41 12; Corso Vannucci 32; ⏱8am-8pm Tue-Sun) Sandri has been serving sweet temptations and the best coffee in town since 1860. Sit at a table on the *corso* or stand at the bar and eye off the decadent cakes, pastries and chocolates on offer.

Civico 25 UMBRIAN €€
(☎075 571 63 76; Via della Viola 25; mains €13.50-14; ⏱dinner Mon-Sat) There's lots to like about this *enoteca* – great jazz on the sound system, friendly staff, delicious food and an excellent range of wine by the glass.

Pizzeria Mediterranea PIZZERIA €
(☎075 572 13 22; Piazza Piccinino 11/12; pizzas €5-12; ⏱lunch & dinner) Perugians know to come here for the best pizza in town. The wood-fired brick oven cooks margherita and other choices that can be topped with *mozzarella di bufala* (fresh buffalo-milk mozzarella) for a small surcharge.

Information

City maps and printed mini-guides are available at the **tourist office** (☎075 573 64 58; www.perugia.umbria2000.it; Piazza Matteotti 18; ⏱8.30am-6.30pm). For information about what's on in town, buy a copy of *Viva Perugia* (€1) from a local newsstand.

Getting There & Away

From the intercity bus station on Piazza dei Partigiani, **Sulga** (☎800 09 96 61; www.sulga.it) buses depart for Florence (€10.10, two hours, twice weekly), Rome's Tiburtina bus station (€16, 2½ hours, five daily), Fiumicino airport (€23, 3¾ hours, three daily Monday to Saturday, two Sunday), Naples (€23, 4½ hours, two daily), Assisi (€3.20, 50 minutes, five daily) and Orvieto (€6.90, two hours, once daily). Sena buses go to Siena (€12, 1½ hours, once daily).

Regional trains connect with Rome (€11.20, 2¾ hours, six daily) and Florence (€12.35, two hours, seven daily).

Getting Around

From the train station, take the *minimetrò* (€1.50) to the Pincetto stop just below Piazza Matteotti, or bus G to Piazza Italia, bus C to Piazza Cavallini behind the Cattedrale di San Lorenzo or bus R to Via XIV Settembre near Piazza Matteotti (tickets all €1.50, €2 if purchased on bus). From the intercity bus station on Piazza dei Partigiani, take the free *scala mobila*.

The centre is mostly closed to traffic, so it's best to park in the free car park at Pian di Massiano and take the *minimetrò* into the centre. Otherwise, the supervised car park at Piazza dei Partigiani charges €16 per 24 hours.

Assisi

POP 28,200

St Francis was born here in 1182, making this medieval town a major destination for millions of pilgrims. Its major sight is the Basilica di San Francesco, a treasure trove of Renaissance frescos.

Sights

Dress rules are applied rigidly at the main religious sights, so no shorts, miniskirts, low-cut dresses or tops. To book guided tours (in English) of the Basilica di San Francesco, telephone or email its **information office** (075 819 00 84; www.sanfrancescoassisi.org; 9.15am-noon & 2.15-5.30pm Mon-Sat).

Churches CHURCH

The **Basilica di San Francesco** (075 81 90 01; Piazza di San Francesco; Reliquary Chapel 9am-6pm daily, 1-4.30pm holidays) comprises two churches. The **upper church** (8.30am-6.45pm Easter-Oct, to 6pm Nov-Easter) was damaged during a severe earthquake in 1997, but has since been restored to its former glory. Built between 1230 and 1253 in the Italian Gothic style, it features a huge fresco cycle by Giottoi.

Downstairs in the dimly lit **lower church** (6am-6.45pm Easter-Oct, to 6pm Nov-Easter), constructed between 1228 and 1230, you'll find a series of colourful frescos by Simone Martini, Cimabue and Pietro Lorenzetti. The **crypt** where St Francis lies buried is below the church.

The 13th-century **Basilica di Santa Chiara** (075 81 22 82; Piazza Santa Chiara; 6.30am-noon & 2-7pm Apr-Oct, to 6pm Nov-Mar) contains the remains of St Clare, friend of St Francis and founder of the Order of Poor Clares.

Sleeping & Eating

You'll need to book ahead during peak times: Easter, August and September, and the Feast of St Francis (3 and 4 October). The tourist office can supply a list of convents and monasteries offering accommodation to pilgrims.

WORTH A TRIP

ORVIETO

Strategically located on the major train line and autostrada between Rome and Florence, this spectacularly sited hilltop town has one major drawcard: its simply extraordinary Gothic-style **Cattedrale** (0763 34 11 67; www.opsm.it; Piazza Duomo; admission €3; 9.30am-7pm Mon-Sat Apr-Oct, to 6pm Sat Mar & Oct, 9.30am-1pm & 2.30-5pm Mon-Sat Nov-Feb, 1-6.30pm Sun Jun-Sep, to 5.30pm Sun Mar-May & Oct, 2.30-5.30pm Sun Nov-Feb). Construction of the cathedral commenced in 1290 and took three centuries to complete. Its facade is perhaps the most beautiful to grace any Italian church. The cathedral has a stark but ethereally beautiful interior and its two chapels are decorated with major works of art including Luca Signorelli's *The Last Judgment* fresco cycle.

The **tourist office** (0763 34 17 72; info@iat.orvieto.tr.it; Piazza Duomo 24; 8.15am-1.50pm & 4-7pm Mon-Fri, 10am-1pm & 3-6pm Sat & Sun) is opposite the cathedral, and one of Umbria's best restaurants, **I Sette Consoli** (0763 34 39 11; www.isetteconsoli.it; Piazza Sant'Angelo 1/a; mains €19-20, 6-course degustation menu €42; lunch & dinner Thu-Tue), is nearby.

If you arrive by train, you'll need to take a **cable car** (€1 each way, €0.80 with train ticket; every 10min 7.05am-8.25pm Mon-Fri, every 15min 8.15am-8pm Sat & Sun) up to the town centre. Tickets are available from the *tabacchi* at the station.

Trains run to/from Florence (Intercity; €9 to €20, 1¾ hours, hourly) and Rome (Regionale €7.50, 80 minutes, hourly). To get here from Perugia (€7.10, 1¾ hours), you'll need to change trains at Terontola-Cortona.

Hotel Alexander B&B €€
(☎075 81 61 90; http://hotelalexanderassisi.it; Piazza Chiesa Nuova 6; s €60-80, d €80-140;) Smack-bang in the centre of town, this safe choice offers nine rooms that vary in size – try to get the one on the top floor, which is huge and has great countryside views. The decor is modern and breakfast in served in your room.

Ostello della Pace HOSTEL €
(☎075 81 67 67; www.assisihostel.com; Via Valecchie 177; dm incl breakfast €17-19, r from €40; 1 Mar-8 Nov & 27 Dec-6 Jan; P@) Student groups, couples appreciating the handful of private rooms, backpackers and pilgrims are all welcome at Assisi's HI hostel. Thrifty travellers will appreciate the dinners (€10.50), hikers will appreciate the boxed lunches (€7) and everyone will appreciate the idyllic setting. You'll find it just off the road coming in from Santa Maria degli Angeli.

Trattoria da Erminio TRATTORIA €
(☎075 81 25 06; www.trattoriadaerminio.it; Via Montecavallo 19; mains €7-11, set menus €16; lunch & dinner Fri-Wed, closed Feb & 1st half of Jul) Da Erminio is known for its grilled meats, which are prepared on a huge fireplace in the main dining area. In summer, tables on the pretty cobbled street are hot property. You'll find it in the upper town near Piazza Matteotti.

Trattoria Pallotta TRATTORIA €€
(☎075 81 26 49; www.pallottaassisi.it; Vicolo della Volta Pinta; mains €12-18, set menus €18-27; lunch & dinner Wed-Mon) Head through the Volta Pinta (Painted Vault) off Piazza del Comune into this old-fashioned eatery. They offer all the Umbrian classics here – rabbit, homemade *strangozzi* (pasta) and pigeon – as well as an excellent *antipasto della casa* (house antipasto; €9). Vegetarians are well catered for.

Mangiar di Vino RISTORANTE €€
(☎0758 15 51 32; www.mangiardivino.it; Via Francalancia 2; mains €10-18, pizzas €7-8) This modern *enoteca* on the *passaggiata* (evening walk) route between Piazza del Comune and Piazza Santa Chiara serves pastas, simple mains and pizzas. It's a good choice for *aperitivo*, and the two-course *menu del giorno* (menu of the day) is excellent value at only €16.

ℹ Information

Tourist Office (☎075 813 86 80; www.assisi.regioneumbria.eu; Piazza del Comune 22; 8am-2pm & 3-6pm Mon-Fri, 9.30am-5pm Sat & Sun, later in summer) Supplies maps, brochures and practical information.

ℹ Getting There & Away

It is better to travel to Assisi by bus rather than train, as the train station is 4km from Assisi proper, in Santa Maria degli Angeli. Buses arrive at and depart from Piazza Matteotti, stopping at Piazza Unita d'Italia below the basilica en route.

Sulga buses connect Assisi with Perugia (€3.20, 50 minutes, five daily), Rome (€18, three hours, one daily) and Florence (€12.50, 2½ hours, twice weekly).

If you arrive by train, a bus (Linea C; €1, half-hourly) runs between Piazza Matteotti and the station. Regional trains run to Perugia (€2.40, 20 minutes, hourly).

SOUTHERN ITALY

Southern Italy is a robust contrast to the genteel north. Its beaches, baroque towns and classical ruins exist alongside ugly urban sprawl and scruffy coastal development (sometimes in the space of a few kilometres) and its residents are a raucous lot who are often wary of interlopers, be they from other countries or the regions north of Rome.

Yet for all its flaws – organised crime, corrupt officialdom, unchecked and outrageous property development – *il mezzogiorno* (the midday sun, as southern Italy is known) is an essential part of every Italian itinerary, offering cheeky charm, culinary masterpieces and architectural treasures galore.

Naples

POP 959,600

Naples (Napoli) is dirty, noisy, dishevelled and totally exhilarating. Founded by Greek colonists, it became a thriving Roman city and was later the Bourbon capital of the Kingdom of the Two Sicilies. In the 18th century it was one of Europe's great cities, something you'll readily believe as you marvel at its profusion of baroque *palazzi*.

The city fronts the waterfront and is divided into *quartieri* (districts). A convenient point of reference is Stazione Centrale, which forms the eastern flank of Piazza Garibaldi, Naples' ugly transport hub. From Piazza Garibaldi, Corso Umberto I skirts the *centro storico*, which is centred on two parallel roads: Via San Biagio dei Librai and its continuation Via Benedetto Croce (together known as Spaccanapoli); and Via dei Tribunali. West of the *centro storico*, Via Toledo, Naples' main shopping strip, leads down to Piazza del Plebiscito. South of here lies the seafront Santa Lucia district; to the west is Chiaia, an upmarket and extremely fashionable area. Above it all, Vomero is a natural balcony with grand views.

Sights

TOP CHOICE Museo Archeologico Nazionale MUSEUM
(081 44 01 66; Piazza Museo Nazionale 19; admission €6.50; 9am-7.30pm Wed-Mon; M Museo, Piazza Cavour) If you visit only one museum in southern Italy, make it this one. Boasting priceless classical sculptures as well as mosaics and frescos from Pompeii and Herculaneum, its collection is mind-bogglingly impressive.

Many of the exhibits once belonged to the Farnese family, including the mighty *Toro Farnese* (Farnese Bull) in Room XVI and the muscle-bound *Ercole* (Hercules) in Room XI. The mezzanine floor is home to an exquisite collection of Pompeian mosaics, including *La battaglia di Alessandro contro Dario* (The Battle of Alexander against Darius) in Room LXI and the amusing *Scene di commedia: musici ambulanti* (Comedy Scene: Street Musicians) in room LIX.

Beyond the mosaics, the **Gabinetto Segreto** (Secret Chamber) contains a small but much-studied collection of ancient erotica.

Cappella Sansevero CHAPEL
(081 551 84 70; www.museosansevero.it; Via Francesco de Sanctis 19; adult/EU student/child under 10 €7/5/free; 10am-5.40pm Mon & Wed-Sat, to 1.10pm Sun; M Dante) This chapel sports a sumptuous baroque interior and is home to the *Cristo velato* (Veiled Christ), Giuseppe Sanmartino's incredibly lifelike sculpture of a recumbent dead Christ covered by a veil.

Basilica di Santa Chiara CHURCH
(081 195 75 915; www.monasterodisantachiara.eu; Via Benedetto Croce; cloisters adult/reduced €5/3.50; basilica 7.30am-1pm & 4.30-8pm, cloisters 9.30am-5pm Mon-Sat, 10am-2pm Sun; M Dante) This huge basilica is actually a 20th-century recreation of Gagliardo Primario's 14th-century original, which was severely damaged in World War II. The pièce de résistance, however, is the basilica's adjoining **Chiostro Maiolicato** (Nuns' Cloister), encrusted with colourful 17th-century majolica tiles and frescos.

Palazzo Reale MUSEUM
(Royal Palace; 081 40 04 54; Piazza del Plebiscito; adult/reduced/EU under 18 & over 65 €4/3/free; 9am-7pm Thu-Tue) This former residence of the Bourbon and Savoy kings now houses a museum showcasing baroque and neoclassical furnishings, statues and paintings. Among the many highlights is the **Teatrino di Corte**, a lavish private theatre built in 1768 to celebrate the marriage of Ferdinand IV and Marie Caroline of Austria.

DISCOUNT CARDS

Campania ArteCards (0639 96 76 50, 800 60 06 01; www.campaniaartecard.it) offer discounted admission to museums in Naples and Campania. Choose the version that suits you best; some include free public transport. The Tutti la Regione three-day card (adult/EU 18-25 €27/20) includes free Unicocampania public transport (including the Alibus from Napoli airport) and free entrance to your choice of two museums and sights, including Pompeii and the Museo Archeologico Nazionale di Napoli. The seven-day card (€30) includes free entrance to five museums or sights and a 50% discount to all others (no transport, though). The cards are available at participating museums, at Capodichino airport, at Stazione Centrale in Naples, online or through the call centre.

Certosa e Museo di San Martino MUSEUM
(848 80 02 88; Largo San Martino 5; adult/reduced €6/3; 8.30am-6.30pm Thu-Tue) Originally built by Charles of Anjou in 1325, this former Carthusian monastery houses a superb collection of Neapolitan art. Highlights include the main church and sacristy, the 16th-century Chiostro Grande (Great Cloister), the 'Images and Memories of Naples' exhibition in the Quarto del Priore (Priors Quarters) and the Sezione Presepiale, which houses a whimsical collection of rare Neapolitan *presepi* (nativity scenes) carved in the 18th and 19th centuries.

The easiest way to get up to Vomero is to take the Funiculore Centrale (€1.20) from Stazione Cumana di Montesanto, near Via Toledo.

Catacomba di San Gennaro ARCHAEOLOGICAL SITE
(081 744 37 14; www.catacombedinapoli.it; Via Tondo di Capodimonte 13; adult/reduced €8/5; 1hr tours every hour 10am-5pm Mon-Sat, to 1pm Sun) Naples' oldest catacomb became a Christian pilgrimage site when the body of the city's patron saint, Gennaro, was interred

Central Naples

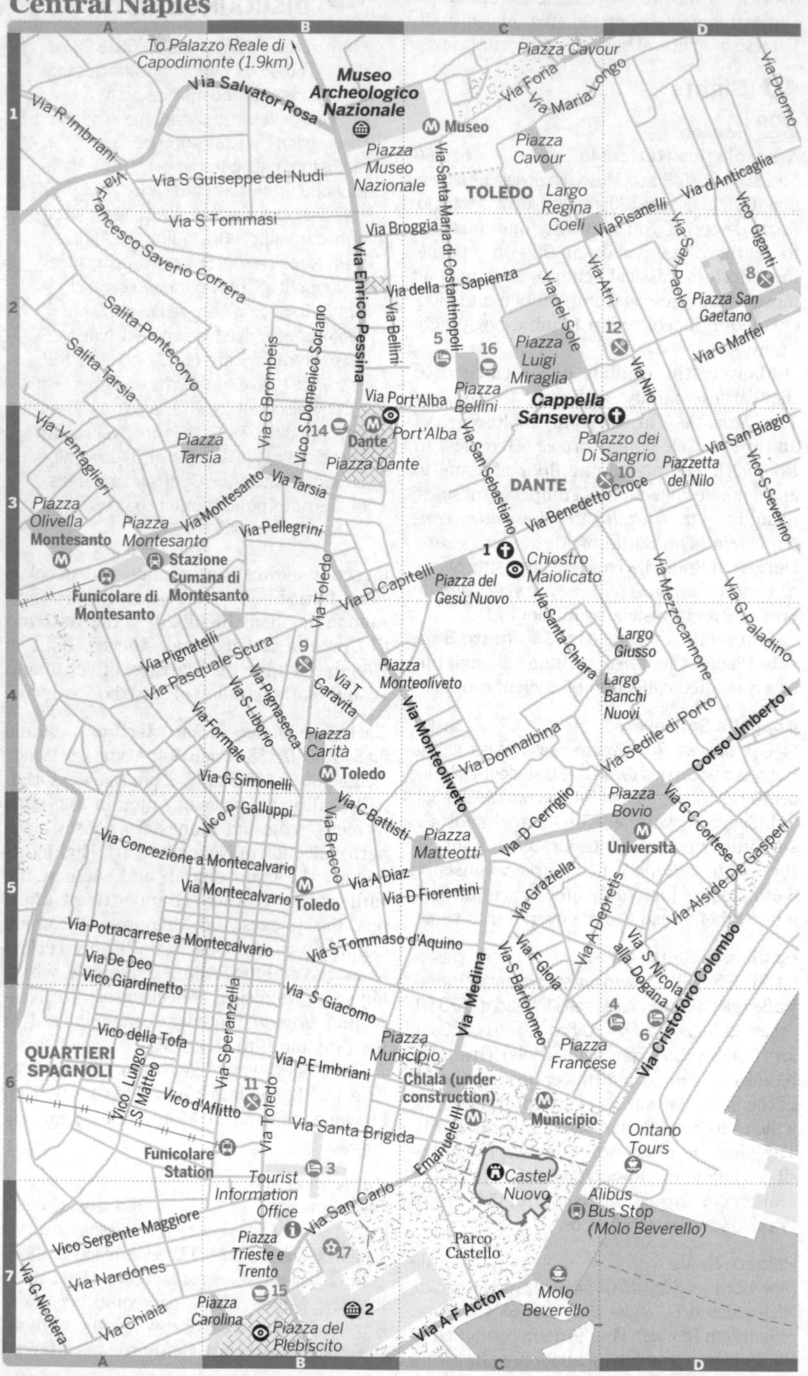

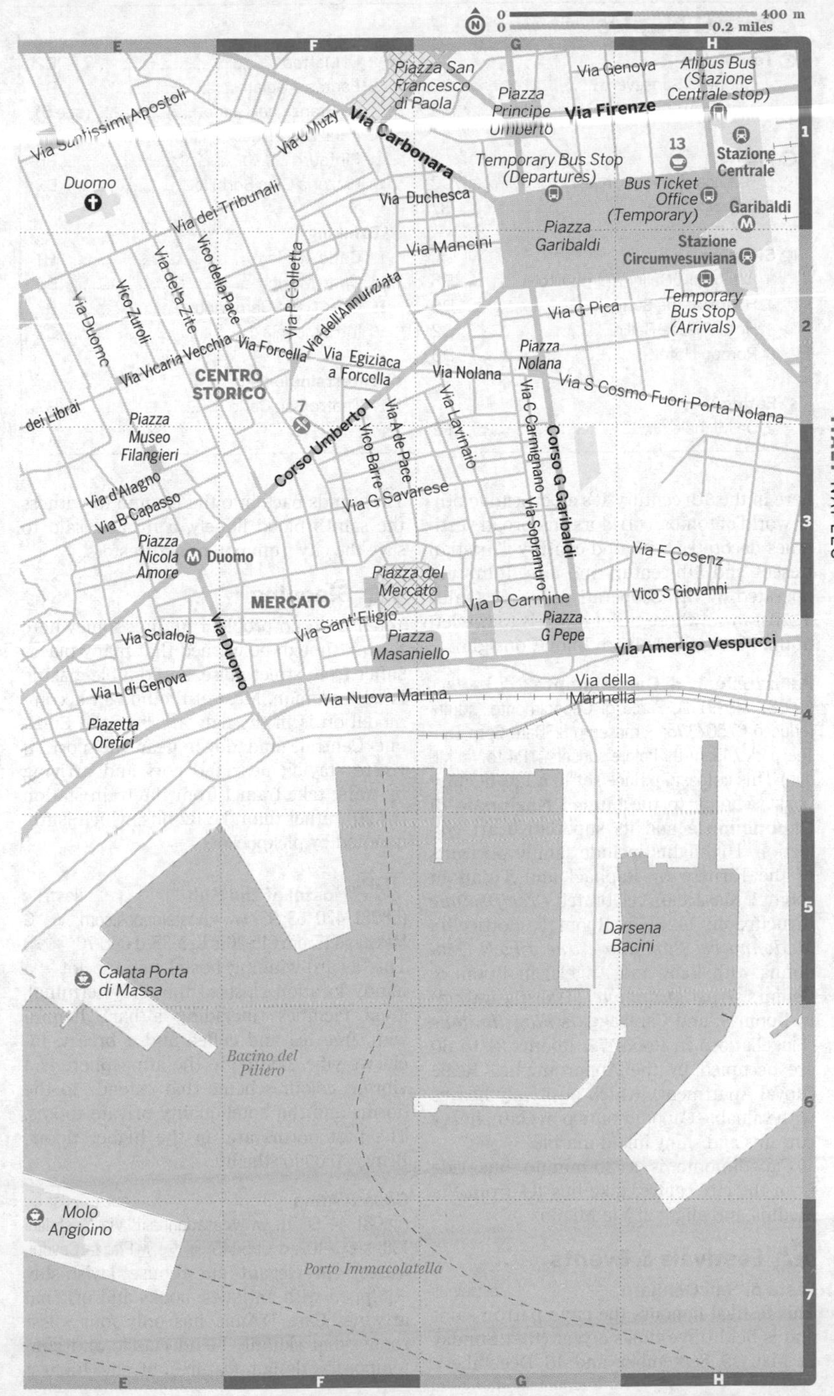

400 m
0.2 miles
Piazza San Francesco di Paola
Via Genova
Alibus Bus (Stazione Centrale stop)
Piazza Principe Umberto
Via Firenze
Via Carbonara
Via Santissimi Apostoli
Via C Muzy
13
Stazione Centrale
Temporary Bus Stop (Departures)
Bus Ticket Office (Temporary)
Garibaldi
Duomo
Via dei Tribunali
Via Duchesca
Piazza Garibaldi
Via Mancini
Stazione Circumvesuviana
Vico della Pace
Via della Zite
Via P Colletta
Via dell'Annunziata
Vico Zuroli
Via Duomo
Via G Pica
Temporary Bus Stop (Arrivals)
Via Vicaria Vecchia
Via Forcella
Via Egiziaca a Forcella
Piazza Nolana
Via Nolana
CENTRO STORICO
Via S Cosmo Fuori Porta Nolana
dei Librai
7
Corso Umberto I
Via A de Pace
Via Lavinaio
Via C Carmignano
Corso G Garibaldi
Piazza Museo Filangieri
Vico Barre
Via d'Alagno
Via B Capasso
Via G Savarese
Via Sopramuro
Piazza Nicola Amore
Duomo
Via E Cosenz
Piazza del Mercato
Vico S Giovanni
MERCATO
Via D Carmine
Via Sant'Eligio
Piazza G Pepe
Via Scialoia
Piazza Masaniello
Via Amerigo Vespucci
Via L di Genova
Via della Marinella
Via Nuova Marina
Piazetta Orefici
Darsena Bacini
Calata Porta di Massa
Bacino del Piliero
Molo Angioino
Porto Immacolatella

Central Naples

Top Sights
Cappella Sansevero D3
Museo Archeologico Nazionale B1

Sights
1 Basilica di Santa Chiara C3
2 Palazzo Reale B7

Sleeping
3 Art Resort Galleria Umberto B6
4 Hostel of the Sun D6
5 Hotel Piazza Bellini C2
6 Romeo Hotel D6

Eating
7 Da Michele F2
8 Di Matteo D2
9 Fantasia Gelati B4
La Stanza del Gusto .... (see 5)
10 Palazzo Petrucci D3
11 Pintauro B6
12 Pizzeria Gino Sorbillo D2

Drinking
13 Caffè Mexico H1
14 Caffè Mexico B3
15 Gran Caffè Gambrinus B7
16 Intra Moenia C2

Entertainment
17 Teatro San Carlo B7

here in the 5th century. It's an evocative other world of tombs, corridors and broad vestibules decorated with 2nd-century Christian frescos and 5th-century mosaics. Tours are operated by the Cooperativa Sociale Onlus 'La Paranza', whose ticket office is to the left of the Chiesa di Madre di Buon Consiglio.

Palazzo Reale di Capodimonte PALACE
(☎081 749 91 11; Parco di Capodimonte; adult/reduced €7.50/3.75; ⊙museum 8.30am-6pm Thu-Tue, park 7.45am-1hr before sunset; 🚌R4 to Via Miano) This colossal palace set in a 130-hectare park is home to the **Museo Nazionale di Capodimonte** and its superlative art collection. Highlights include family portraits of the Farnese by Raphael and Titian in room 2, Masaccio's celebrated *Crocifissione* (Crucifixion; 1426) in Room 3, Botticelli's *Madonna col Bambino e due angeli* (Madonna with Baby and Angels) in Room 6, Bellini's *Trasfigurazione* (Transfiguration) in Room 8, and Caravaggio's *Flagellazione* (Flagellation) in Room 78. Rooms 31 to 60 are occupied by the Appartamento Reale (Royal Apartment), which positively heaves with valuable Capodimonte porcelain, heavy curtains and shiny inlaid marble.

Capodimonte is a 30-minute bus ride from the city centre; take bus R4 from Via Medina and alight at Via Miano.

Festivals & Events

Festa di San Gennaro RELIGIOUS
This festival honours the city's patron saint and is held three times a year (first Sunday in May, 19 September and 16 December). Thousands pack into the Duomo to witness the saint's blood liquefy, a miracle said to save the city from potential disasters.

Sleeping

You'll have no problem finding somewhere to stay, though be warned that many places suffer from street noise, and double-glazing is not common. Most of the budget accommodation is in the ugly area around Stazione Centrale and down near the port; if you're staying near the port and arriving by train, take tram 1 from the train station (€1.20) rather than the R2 bus, which is frequented by pickpockets.

TOP CHOICE **Hostel of the Sun** HOSTEL €
(☎081 420 63 93; www.hostelnapoli.com; Via G Melisurgo 15; dm €15-20, s €25-35, d €60-70; ❄📶) This award-winning hostel has the lot – a handy location close to the ferry terminal, great facilities (including a bar), helpful staff, free tea and coffee and a breezy, inclusive vibe. Adding to the atmosphere is a vibrant colour scheme that extends to the dorms and the hotel-quality private rooms. The best dorms are on the higher floors. Bring €0.05 for the lift.

Casa D'Anna GUESTHOUSE €€
(☎081 44 66 11; www.casadanna.it; Via Cristallini 138; s €67-102, d €95-145; ❄📶; Ⓜ Piazza Cavour, Museo) An elegant guesthouse lavishishly equipped with antiques, books and original artwork, Casa D'Anna has only four guest rooms that skilfully blend classic and contemporary design features of the highest

quality. Breakfast includes homemade baked treats and jams. Two-night minimum stay.

Hotel Piazza Bellini BOUTIQUE HOTEL €€
(☎081 45 17 32; www.hotelpiazzabellini.com; Via Costantinopoli 101; s €70-140, d €80-165; ❄@📶; Ⓜ Dante) Only steps away from buzzing nightspot Piazza Bellini, this sleek hotel inhabits a 16th-century *palazzo* and its cool white spaces are adorned with original majolica tiles and the work of emerging artists. Rooms offer pared-back chic, with comfortable beds and small bathrooms.

B&B Cappella Vecchia B&B €
(☎081 240 51 17; www.cappellavecchia11.it; Vico Santa Maria a Cappella Vecchia 11; s €50-80, d €75-120; ❄@📶; 🚌C24 to Piazza dei Martiri) Run by a super-helpful young couple, this B&B is a first-rate choice. There are six simple, comfy rooms and a spacious communal area for breakfast. Check the website for monthly packages.

UNA Napoli BUSINESS HOTEL €€
(☎081 563 69 01; www.unahotels.it/en/una_hotel_napoli/napoli_hotels.htm; Piazza Garibaldi 10; r €84-151; ❄@📶) A convenient location opposite the train station and excellent online specials mean that it's well worth considering this well-run business hotel. Rooms are blessedly quiet due to double-glazed windows and have every amenity you will need.

Art Resort Galleria Umberto BOUTIQUE HOTEL €€
(☎081 497 62 81; www.artresortgalleriaumberto.it; Galleria Umberto I 83, 4th fl, Via Toledo, Quartieri Spagnoli; r €94-193; ❄@📶) For a taste of Neapolitan glitz and grandeur, book into this boutique hotel secreted on an upper floor of the magnificent Galleria Umberto I. The price includes a delicious buffet breakfast and evening *aperitivo*. You'll need €0.10 for the lift.

Romeo Hotel LUXURY HOTEL €€€
(☎081 017 50 01; www.romeohotel.it; Via Cristoforo Colombo 45; r €150-330, ste €240-400; ❄@📶) A quick walk from the ferries takes you to this relatively new hotel and design buff's dream. Designed by Paul Tange (son of Japanese starchitect Kenzo Tange), it features luxe rooms, A-list art and furniture, a glam sushi bar, a rooftop restaurant and a truly jaw-dropping spa centre.

Eating

Neapolitans are justifiably proud of their food. The pizza was created here – there are any number of toppings but locals favour margherita (tomato, mozzarella and basil) or marinara (tomato, garlic, oregano and olive oil), cooked in a wood-fired oven. Pizzerias serving the 'real thing' have a sign on their door – *la vera pizza napoletana* (the real Neapolitan pizza).

For something sweet try a *sfogliatella*, a flaky pastry filled with sweet orange-flavoured ricotta that is ideally served warm.

Pizza

TOP CHOICE Pizzeria Gino Sorbillo PIZZERIA €
(☎081 44 66 43; www.accademiadellapizza.it; Via dei Tribunali 32; pizzas from €2.50; ⏲Mon-Sat; Ⓜ Dante) The clamouring crowds say it all: Gino Sorbillo is the city's pizza king. Be sure to go to Gino – there are two other Sorbillo pizzerias on the same block, all from one family of 21 pizza-making siblings.

Da Michele PIZZERIA €
(☎081 553 92 04; www.damichele.net; Via Cesare Sersale 1; small/medium/large pizzas €4/5/6; ⏲Mon-Sat) Da Michele has been serving since 1870, and its popularity shows no sign of waning. Things are plain and simple here: unadorned marble tabletops, brisk service and two types of pizza – margherita or marinara. Just show up, take a ticket and wait your turn.

Di Matteo PIZZERIA €
(☎081 45 52 62; Via dei Tribunali 94; snacks €0.50, pizzas from €2.50; ⏲9am-midnight Mon-Sat; Ⓟ; 🚌C55 to Via Duomo) The little street stall at this no-frills pizzeria sells some of the city's best fried snacks, from golden *crocchè* (potato croquettes) to nourishing *arancini* (fried rice balls). Head inside for low lighting, surly waiters and lip-smacking pizzas.

Not Pizza

La Stanza del Gusto OSTERIA €€
(☎081 40 15 78; www.lastanzadelgusto.com; Via Costantinopoli 100; soup €10, platters €13-20, filled panini €5-8; ⏲11am-midnight Tue-Sat, till 4pm Sun; Ⓜ Dante) There's a restaurant serving modern twists on local favourites upstairs, but we prefer the atmospheric *osteria* on the ground floor, where it's possible to enjoy a glass of wine accompanied by a cheese or *salumi* (cured meat) platter, panino (lunch only) or bowl of soup.

Palazzo Petrucci MODERN ITALIAN €€€
(☎081 552 40 68; www.palazzopetrucci.it; Piazza San Domenico Maggiore 4; mains €16-25, degustation menu €55; ⏲lunch Tue-Sun, dinner Mon-Sat; Ⓜ Dante) Progressive Petrucci is a breath of fresh air, exciting palates with mostly

successful new-school creations that balance technique and flavour well. The fine-dining air may be a bit stuffy for some.

 **Pintauro** PASTICCERIA €
(☎348 778 16 45; Via Toledo 275; sfogliatelle €2; ⏲8am-2pm & 2.30-8pm Mon-Sat, 9am-2pm Sun Sep-May) This cinnamon-scented local institution sells warm *sfogliatelle* dusted with icing sugar to shoppers on Via Toleda. Delicious!

Fantasia Gelati GELATERIA €
(☎081 551 12 12; Via Toledo 381; gelato from €2; ⏲7.30am-midnight; Ⓜ Toledo) Head here for the city's finest gelato. The heavenly, made-on-site flavours include a dangerously dense chocolate *'cuore nero'* (dark heart). There's another branch in Vomero.

Drinking

Caffè Mexico CAFE
(Piazza Dante 86; ⏲7am-8.30pm Mon-Sat) This retro gem makes the best coffee in the city. The espresso is served *zuccherato* (sweetened), so request it *amaro* if you drink it unadorned. In summer, the *caffè freddo con panna* (iced coffee with cream) is a treat. There's another **branch** at Piazza Garibaldi 70.

Gran Caffè Gambrinus CAFE
(www.caffegambrinus.com; Via Chiaia 1-2; ⏲7am-2am) Naples' most venerable cafe features a showy art nouveau interior and a cast of self-conscious drinkers served by smart, waistcoated waiters. It's great value when you stand at the bar.

Intra Moenia CAFE
(☎081 29 07 20; Piazza Bellini 70; ⏲10am-2am; 📶; Ⓜ Dante) This arty cafe-bookshop-bar on Piazza Bellini attracts a bohemian crowd who adore its laid-back, literary ambience.

Entertainment

Opera fans will enjoy an evening at **Teatro San Carlo** (☎081 797 23 31; www.teatrosancarlo.it; Via San Carlo 98; ⏲box office 10am-7pm Tue-Sat, 10am-3.30pm Sun), the oldest opera house in Italy. The opera season runs from December to May and performances of music and ballet are held at other times of the year.

In May, the **Maggio dei Monumenti** festival stages concerts and cultural activities in museums and monuments around town. Entry to most of these is free; check details with a tourist office.

Information

Dangers & Annoyances

Despite Naples' notoriety as a Mafia hot spot, the city is pretty safe. That said, travellers should be careful about walking alone late at night near Stazione Centrale and Piazza Dante. Petty crime is also widespread – be vigilant for pickpockets (especially on the city's public transport) and be on guard against moped bandits.

Emergency

Police Station (Questura; ☎081 794 11 11; Via Medina 75)

Medical Services

Ospedale Loreto-Mare (Hospital; ☎081 254 27 93; Via Amerigo Vespucci 26) On the waterfront, near the train station.

Tourist Information

There are several **tourist information points** (www.inaples.it) around town: Piazza del **Gesù Nuovo** (Piazza del Gesù Nuovo 7; ⏲9.30am-1.30pm & 2.30-6.30pm Mon-Sat, 9.30am-1.30pm Sun), Via **Santa Lucia** (☎081 240 09 14; Via Santa Lucia; ⏲9am-7pm daily) and Via **San Carlo** (☎081 40 23 94; Via San Carlo; ⏲9.30am-1.30pm & 2.30-6.30pm Mon-Sat, 9.30am-1.30pm Sun).

Getting There & Away

Air

Capodichino airport (p846), 7km northeast of the city centre, is southern Italy's main airport. Flights operate to most Italian cities and up to 30 European destinations, as well as New York.

Boat

A fleet of *traghetti* (ferries), *aliscafi* (hydrofoils) and *navi veloci* (fast ships) connect Naples with Sorrento, the bay islands, the Amalfi Coast, Salerno, Sicily and Sardinia. Most fast ferries and hydrofoils leave from Molo Beverello; a few services to Capri, Ischia and Procida also leave from Molo Mergellina. Ferries for Sicily and Sardinia sail from Molo Angioino, next to Molo Beverello, and also from the neighbouring Calata Porta di Massa.

Tickets for shorter journeys can be bought at Molo Beverello or Molo Mergellina. For longer journeys try **Ontano Tours** (☎081 551 71 64; www.ontanotour.it; Molo Angioino; ⏲8.30am-8pm Mon-Sat), in the car park in front of Molo Angioino. You can also purchase tickets online.

Note that ferry services are pared back in winter and adverse sea conditions may affect sailing schedules.

The major companies servicing Naples:

Alilauro (☎081 497 22 38; www.alilauro.it) To/from Sorrento (€11, bags €2 each, 35 minutes, five daily).

Caremar (☎199 11 66 55; www.caremar.it) Runs services from Naples to Capri (ferry/hydrofoil €11.50/18.80, 80/50 minutes, frequent in summer).

Gescab (☎081 807 18 12; www.gescab.it) Runs hydrofoils to Sorrento (€11, 35 minutes, six daily).

Metrò del Mare (☎199 60 07 00; www.metrodelmare.net) Usually runs services between Naples and Sorrento, Positano and Amalfi over the summer months, but had suspended services when this book went to print.

NLG (☎081 552 07 63; www.navlib.it) To/from Capri (€20.20, nine daily) and Sorrento (€12.10, nine daily).

Siremar (☎199 11 88 66; www.siremar.it) Operates boats to the Aeolian Islands and Milazzo (seat from €70.20, six times weekly in summer, twice weekly in the low season).

SNAV (☎091 428 55 55; www.snav.it) Runs hydrofoils to Capri (€19.80, seven daily) and Sorrento (€13.10, five daily) as well as ferries to Palermo (from €48, 10 hours, one daily). In summer there are daily services to the Aeolian Islands.

Tirrenia (☎081 720 11 11; www.tirrenia.it) Twice-weekly service to and from Cagliari (from €45, 11¼ hours) and a daily service to Palermo (from €34).

TTT Lines (☎081 580 27 44; www.tttlines.it) To/from Catania (from €38, 11 hours, one daily).

Bus

Most long-distance buses leave from the temporary bus stop in Piazza Garibaldi, opposite the Hotel Cavour. **Miccolis** (☎081 20 03 80; www.miccolis-spa.it) runs buses to Bari (€19, three hours, three daily) and Lecce (€32, three hours, three daily) via Brindisi (€29, five hours). **Marino** (☎080 311 23 35; www.marinobus.it) operates services to Matera (€19, 4¼ hours, two daily). Buy tickets and catch buses from the temporary ticket booth in front of Stazione Centrale.

Car & Motorcycle

The city is easily accessible from Rome on the A1 autostrada. The Naples–Pompeii–Salerno motorway (A3) connects with the coastal road to Sorrento and the Amalfi Coast. If you value your sanity, skip driving in Naples itself.

Train

Most trains stop at Stazione Centrale, which incorporates Stazione Garibaldi. There are up to 30 trains daily to Rome (Intercity €19, 2¼ hours) and a few to Palermo (Intercity €29, nine hours).

The **Circumvesuviana** (☎081 772 24 44; www.vesuviana.it), accessible through Stazione Centrale, operates a service to Sorrento (€4, 65 minutes) via Ercolano for Herculaneum (€2.10, 10 minutes), Pompeii (€2.10, 35 minutes) and other towns along the coast. There are about 40 trains daily running between 5am and 10.40pm, with reduced services on Sunday.

ℹ Getting Around

To/From the Airport

By public transport you can either take the regular **ANM** (☎800 63 95 25; www.unicocampania.it) bus 3S (€1.10, 20 minutes, half-hourly) from Piazza Garibaldi, or the Alibus airport shuttle (€3, 45 minutes) from Piazza del Municipio or Stazione Centrale. This operates every 30 minutes between 6am and midnight.

Taxi fares are set at €16 to/from the *centro storico* and €19 to/from the port.

Public Transport

You can travel around Naples by bus, metro and funicular. Journeys are covered by the **Unico Napoli ticket** (www.unicocampania.it), which comes in various forms: the standard ticket, valid for 90 minutes, costs €1.20; a daily pass is €3.60 and a weekend daily ticket is €3. Note that these tickets are not valid on the Circumvesuviana line.

Taxi

Taxi fares are set at €6 between the *centro storico* and Piazza Garibaldi and from the centre to the port. A trip from Piazza Garibaldi to the port costs €11. There's a €3 surcharge after 10pm (€5.50 on Sunday).

Be warned that there are a number of unlicensed taxi drivers operating from outside the train station; only use official white taxis.

Capri

POP 14,200

The most visited of the islands in the Bay of Naples, Capri deserves more than a quick day trip. Beyond the glamorous veneer of chichi cafes and designer boutiques is an island of rugged seascapes, desolate Roman ruins and a surprisingly unspoiled rural inland.

Emperor Augustus made Capri his private playground and Tiberius retired there in AD 27. Its modern incarnation as a tourist destination dates to the early 20th century when it was invaded by an army of European artists, writers and Russian revolutionaries, drawn as much by the beauty of the local boys as by the thrilling landscape.

The island is easily reached from Naples and Sorrento. Hydrofoils and ferries dock at Marina Grande, from where it's a short funicular ride up to Capri, the main town. A further bus ride takes you up to the island's second settlement, Anacapri.

WORTH A TRIP

POMPEII & HERCULANEUM

On 24 August AD 79 Mt Vesuvius erupted, submerging the town of Pompeii in lapilli (burning fragments of pumice stone) and the town of Herculaneum in mud. As a result, both towns were destroyed and over 2000 residents died. The Unesco-listed ruins of both provide remarkable models of working Roman cities, complete with streets, temples, houses, baths, forums, taverns, shops and even a brothel. Exploring both gives a fascinating glimpse into ancient Roman life.

Visitors can choose to visit one site, or can purchase a combination ticket that covers both and is valid for three days.

To visit **Herculaneum** (081 732 43 38; www.pompeiisites.org; Corso Resina 6, Ercolano; adult/EU 18-24/EU under 18 & over 65 €11/5.50, combined ticket incl Pompeii; 8.30am-6pm Apr-Oct, to 3.30pm Nov-Mar; Ercolano-Scavi), take the Circumvesuviana train from Naples (€2.10, 10 minutes), alight at the Ercolano stop and walk straight down the main street to reach the archaeological site. Highlights include the Sede degli Augustali, the Casa del Salone Nero and the Casa Sannitica.

For **Pompeii** (081 857 53 47; www.pompeiisites.org; entrances at Porta Marina & Piazza Anfiteatro; adult/EU 18-24/EU under 18 & over 65 €11/5.50/free, combined ticket incl Herculaneum €20/10; 8.30am-6pm Apr-Oct, 8.30am-3.30pm Nov-Mar), take the Circumvesuviana to the Pompeii Scavi-Villa dei Misteri stop (€2.10, 35 minutes), located right next to the Porta Marina entrance to the ruins. There's a huge amount to see here, but be sure not to miss the Lupanare (Brothel), the Casa del Menandro, the *anfiteatro* (ampitheatre) and the Villa dei Misteri with its extraordinary frescos.

For the best views on the island, take the **seggiovia** (chairlift; one-way/return €7/10; 9am-5pm Mar-Oct, 9am-3pm Nov-Feb) up from Piazza Vittoria to the summit of **Mt Solaro** (589m), Capri's highest point.

Sights & Activities

Grotta Azzura CAVE

(Blue Grotto; admission €12.50; 9am–3pm) This stunning sea cave illuminated by an otherworldly blue light is Capri's major attraction and is best visited in the morning. Boats leave from Marina Grande (return incl Grotto entrance €24.50); allow a good hour or so. Alternatively, take a bus from Viale Tommaso de Tommaso in Anacapri (€1.80, 15 minutes) or take a bus to Piazza Vittoria and then follow the pedestrian-only path down Via G Orlandi, Via Pagliaro and Via Grotta Azzura (35 minutes). Note that the grotto is not visitable when seas are rough or tides are high.

Giardini di Augusto GARDENS

(Gardens of Augustus; admission €1; 9am-1hr before sunset) Once you've explored Capri Town's picture-perfect streets, head to this garden to enjoy breaktaking views. From here Via Krupp zigzags down to Marina Piccola.

Villa Jovis RUIN

(Jupiter's Villa; 081 837 06 34; Via Amaiuri; adult/reduced €2/1; 9am-1hr before sunset) This was the largest and most sumptuous of the island's 12 Roman villas and was Tiberius' main Capri residence. Although not in great shape today, it gives a good idea of the scale on which the emperor liked to live.

Sleeping

Capri has plenty of top-end hotels, but few genuinely budget options. Always book ahead, as hotel space is at a premium during summer and many places close between November and Easter.

Hotel Villa Eva HOTEL €€

(081 837 15 49; www.villaeva.com; Via La Fabbrica 8, Anacapri; r €100-120; Mar-Oct; P@) Hidden among fruit and olive trees, Villa Eva has rooms with lashings of character, a swimming pool and treetop views down to the sea. To get here take a taxi (€30) or the Grotta Azzura bus from Anacapri and ask the driver where to get off.

Hotel La Tosca PENSION €€

(081 837 09 89; www.latoscahotel.com; Via Dalmazio Birago 5, Capri Town; s €50-100, d €75-160; Apr-Oct;) This charming one-star *pensione* is hidden down a quiet back lane overlooking the mountains and away from the glitz of the centre. Plain but comfortable rooms have large bathrooms and several have private terraces.

Capri Palace LUXURY HOTEL €€€

(☎081 978 01 11; www.capripalace.com; Via Capodimonte 2b, Anacapri; s/d/ste from €195/295/620; ⏲Apr-Oct; ❄📶🏊) This ultra-fashionable retreat has a stylish Mediterranean-style decor and is full of contemporary art. Guests rarely leave the hotel grounds, taking full advantage of the huge pool, on-site health spa and top-notch L'Olivo restaurant. There's a three-night minimum stay in high season.

Eating & Drinking

Be warned that restaurants on Capri are overpriced and underwhelming. Many close between November and Easter.

La Taverna di Pulcinella PIZZERIA €

(☎081 837 64 85; Via Tiberio 7; pizzas from €7; ⏲Apr-Oct) If you can bear being served by waiters in Punchinello (Pulcinella) costumes, you'll be rewarded by what are generally acknowledged to be the best pizzas on Capri.

Salemeria da Aldo DELI €

(Via Cristoforo Colombo 26; panini from €3.50) Ignore the restaurant touts and head straight to this honest portside deli, where bespectacled Aldo will make you his legendary *panino alla Caprese* (crusty bread stuffed with silky mozzarella and tomatoes from his own garden).

Lo Sfizietto GELATERIA €

(☎081 837 00 91; Via Longano 6) Located just off La Piazzetta, this *gelateria* uses only organic ingredients with choices that include *cremolate* with 60% fresh fruit and the namesake choice *sfizietto* (caramel with pine nuts).

Pulalli WINE BAR

(Piazza Umberto I 4; mains €25; ⏲Wed-Mon) Climb the clock-tower steps to the right of Capri Town's tourist office and your reward is this laid-back local hang-out, where fabulous vino meets a discerning selection of cheeses, *salumi* and pastas.

Information

Information is available online at www.capritourism.com or from one of the three tourist offices: **Marina Grande** (☎081 837 06 34; ⏲8.30am-2.30pm Mon-Sat Nov-Mar, 9.15am-1.15pm & 3.15-6.15pm daily Apr-Jun & Sep-Oct, 9am-1pm & 3.30-6.45pm daily Jul & Aug), **Capri Town** (☎081 837 06 86; Piazza Umberto 1; ⏲9.15am-1.15pm & 3-6.15pm Mon-Sat Nov-Mar, 8.30am-8.30pm Mon-Sat Apr-Oct) and **Anacapri** (☎081 837 15 24; Via G Orlando 59; ⏲9am-3pm Mon-Sat Mar-Oct).

Getting There & Around

There are year-round hydrofoils and ferries to Capri from Naples. Timetables and fare details are available online at www.capritourism.com; look under 'Shipping timetable'.

From Naples, ferries depart from Calata Porta di Massa and hydrofoils from Molo Beverello and Mergellina. Services are regular and tickets cost €19 to €21 (hydrofoil), €17.80 (fast ferry) and €11.50 (ferry).

There are services to/from Sorrento (hydrofoil €17 to €18, fast ferry €15 to €16.20, 20 minutes, 11 daily) and from Easter to November there are also services to Positano (€15.50, 45 minutes, four daily).

On the island, buses run from Capri Town to/from Marina Grande, Anacapri and Marina Piccola. There are also buses from Marina Grande to Anacapri. Single tickets cost €1.80 on all routes, as does the funicular (€1.80) that links Marina Grande with Capri Town in a four-minute trip.

Taxis between Marina Grande and Capri Town cost €15 (€20 to Anacapri) and can carry up to six people.

A private tour around the island by motorboat (stopping for a swim and at the Grotta Azzurra on the way) costs between €150 and €200 per group; a couple of companies based at Marina Grande offer one-hour public tours (€15).

Sorrento

POP 16,600

A stunning location overlooking the Bay of Naples and Mt Vesuvius makes Sorrento a popular package-holiday destination despite the fact that it has no decent beach. Its profusion of sweet-smelling citrus trees and laid-back local lifestyle are certainly attractive, and its relative proximity to the Amalfi Coast, Pompeii and Capri make it a good base for those who don't wish to deal with the chaos and cacophany of Naples.

The centre of town is Piazza Tasso, a short distance northwest of the train and bus station. From Marina Piccola, where ferries and hydrofoils dock, walk south along Via Marina Piccola then climb the steps or take the *ascensore* (lift; €1) to reach the piazza.

Sights & Activities

You'll probably spend most of your time in the *centro storico,* which is full of narrow streets lined with shops, cafes, churches and restaurants. To the north, the **Villa Comunale Park** (⏲8am-midnight) commands grand views over the sea to Mt Vesuvius.

The two main swimming spots are **Marina Piccola** and **Marina Grande**, although neither is especially appealing. Nicer by far is **Bagni Regina Giovanna**, a rocky beach set among the ruins of a Roman villa, 2km west of town.

Sleeping

Casa Astarita B&B €

(081 877 49 06; www.casastarita.com; Corso Italia 67, Sorrento; s €50-100, d €70-120, tr €85-145;) Housed in a 16th-century building on the town's major *passaggiata* strip, this family-run place offers six quiet rooms combining rustic charm with modern comforts (iPod docks, Apple TV, kettle, fridge). The colourful decor is extremely attractive, and all rooms are freshly painted and immaculately maintained.

Ulisse Deluxe Hostel HOSTEL €

(081 877 47 53; www.ulissedeluxe.com; Via del Mare 22; dm €18-28, s €45-75, d €50-100;) Resembling a three-star hotel, the Ulisse offers quiet modern rooms and single-sex dorms (all with bathroom). The decor is a bit sterile and the ambience impersonal, but the efficient staff, excellent amenities and clean, comfortable rooms certainly compensate. Breakfast costs an extra €7, use of the pool in the attached wellness centre €5 and parking €10. To find it, walk west along Via Corso and then down the stairway next to the hospital.

Eating & Drinking

Aurora Light CAMPANIAN €€

(081 877 26 31; www.auroralight.it; Piazza Tasso 3-4; mains €15) Close examination of its seasonally driven menu shows that Aurora Light's enthusiastic young owner enjoys giving traditional Campanian dishes an innovative twist. There are plenty of vegetarian options on offer.

Garden CAMPANIAN €€

(081 878 11 95; Corso Italia 50-52; mains €15; closed Jan-Mar) Enjoy local and Italian wines by the glass accompanied by slices of prosciutto and cheese in the sophisticated downstairs wine bar, or head to the upstairs terrace garden where the menu includes all the mainstay pasta dishes and plenty of seafood.

Information

The main **tourist office** (081 807 40 33; Via Luigi De Maio 35; 8.30am-4.10pm Mon-Sat) is near Piazza San Antonino, but there are also information points at **Marina Piccola** (8am-1pm) and on **Corso Italia** (9am-1pm & 3-10pm) near Piazza Tasso. Note that their opening hours can be erratic, especially in the low season.

Getting There & Away

Circumvesuviana trains run half-hourly between Sorrento and Naples (€4, 65 minutes) via Pompeii (€2.10, 30 minutes) and Ercolano (€2.10, 45 minutes). A daily ticket covering all stops on the route costs €12 (€6.30 on weekends) and a daily ticket covering stops at Ercolano, Pompeii and Sorrento costs €6.30 (€3.40 on weekends).

Curreri (081 801 54 20; www.curreriviaggi.it) buses travel between Naples' Capodichino airport and the front of Sorrento train station (€10, 90 minutes, six daily). Buy tickets on the bus.

Regular SITA buses leave from the train station for the Amalfi Coast, stopping in Positano (40 minutes) and then continuing to Amalfi (90 minutes). See the boxed text for ticket prices. When travelling from Sorrento to Amalfi, sit on the left-hand side of the bus for the best views; from Amalfi to Sorrento, sit on the right.

There are boat services to Capri (€17 to €18 hydrofoil, €15 to €16.20 fast ferry, 20 minutes, 11 daily) and Naples (return hydrofoil €22, 35 minutes, six daily).

Amalfi Coast

Stretching 50km along the southern side of the Sorrentine Peninsula, the Amalfi Coast (Costiera Amalfitana) is a postcard-perfect vision of shimmering blue water fringed by vertiginous cliffs to which whitewashed villages with terraced lemon groves cling. This Unesco-protected area is one of Italy's top tourist destinations, attracting hundreds of thousands of visitors each year (70% of them between June and September).

Getting There & Away

There are two main entry points to the Amalfi Coast: Sorrento and Salerno. Both can be accessed by train from Naples (Sorrento on the Circumvesuviana and Salerno on Treitalia).

Regular SITA buses run from Sorrento to Positano (40 minutes) and Amalfi (90 minutes), and from Salerno to Amalfi (75 minutes). All trips are covered by a 90-minute or greater Unico Costiera travel card.

Boat services are generally limited to the period between April and October. Gescab-**Alicost** (089 87 14 83; www.alicost.it) operates one daily ferry/hydrofoil from Salerno to Amalfi (€7/9), Positano (€11/13) and Capri (€18.50/20). It also runs daily ferries from Sorrento to Positano (€13) and Amalfi (€14). **TraVelMar** (089 87 29 50; www.travelmar.it) and

Mètro del Mare also run services over summer; check their websites for details.

By car, take the SS163 coastal road at Vietri sul Mare.

POSITANO

pop 4000

Approaching Positano by boat, you will be greeted by an unforgettable view of colourful, steeply stacked houses clinging to near-vertical green slopes. This is a destination where people come to see and be seen – the main activities are hanging out on the small beach, drinking and dining on flower-laden terraces, and browsing the expensive boutiques that are scattered around town. Be warned that all of this activity occurs only in summer – there's absolutely no good reason to come here in the low season.

The **tourist office** (☎089 87 50 67; Via del Saracino 4; ⏱8am-2pm & 3.30-8pm Mon-Sat Apr-Oct, 9am-3pm Mon-Fri Nov-Mar) can provide information on walking in the densely wooded Lattari Mountains, including details of the spectacular 12km **Sentiero degli Dei** (Path of the Gods) between Positano and Praiano, and the **Via degli Incanti** (Trail of Charms) between Positano and Amalfi.

Sleeping

Pensione Maria Luisa PENSION €
(☎089 87 50 23; www.pensionemarialuisa.com; Via Fornillo 42; r €70-85; ⏱Apr-Oct; @📶) The best budget choice in town is run by Carlo, a larger-than-life character who will go out of his way to assist and advise. Rooms are attractive and have modern bathrooms; those with private terraces are well worth the extra €10 to €15 for the view of the bay. Breakfast costs an additional €5.

Albergo Miramare HOTEL €€€
(☎089 87 50 02; www.miramarepositano.it; Via Trara Genoino 29; s €150-175, d €195-480; ⏱Apr-Oct; ❄@📶) Every room at this gorgeous hotel has a terrace with sea view, just one of the features that makes it a dream holiday destination. Rooms are extremely comfortable, sporting all mod cons, and the common areas include a comfortable lounge and breakfast room with spectacular views.

Hostel Brikette HOSTEL €
(☎089 87 58 57; www.brikette.com; Via Marconi 358; dm from €22, d from €75, without bathroom d from €65; ⏱late Mar-Nov; ❄📶) Close to the Bar Internazionale bus stop on the coastal road, this bright and cheerful hostel offers the cheapest accommodation in town. There are various options: six- to eight-person dorms (single sex and mixed), double rooms, and apartments for two to five people.

UNICO COSTIERA

If you are travelling in Sorrento and along the Amalfi Coast on a SITA bus, you can save money and time by investing in a Unico Costiera travel card, available for durations of 45 minutes (€2.40), 90 minutes (€3.60), 24 hours (€7.20) and 72 hours (€18). The 24-hour and 72-hour tickets also cover one trip on the city sightseeing bus that travels between Amalfi and Ravello and Amalfi and Maiori. Buy the cards from bars, *tabacchi* and SITA or Circumvesuviana ticket offices.

Eating & Drinking

Next 2 NEAPOLITAN €€
(☎089 812 35 16; www.next2.it; Viale Pasitea 242; mains €18; ⏱7-11pm) We're not sure which is the more enticing: Next 2's outside terrace with oversized white parasols and wicker seating, or its menu, which showcases organic ingredients as much as possible and includes interesting takes on classic Neapolitan dishes.

Da Vincenzo TRATTORIA €€
(☎089 87 51 28; Viale Pasitea 172-178; mains €18; ⏱Apr-Nov, closed lunch Tue Jul & Aug) The emphasis at this old-fashioned place is on fish dishes. Listen to the sound of Neapolitan guitarists during the summer months and be sure to try co-owner Marcella's legendary desserts, which are widely considered to be the best in town.

Da Costantino TRATTORIA €
(☎089 87 57 38; Via Montepertuso; mains €12, pizzas from €4; ⏱closed Wed) One of the few authentic trattorias in Positano, this place high up the hill serves honest, down-to-earth Italian grub. Expect amazing views, good pastas and pizzas and a selection of fail-safe grilled meats.

La Zagara CAFE
(☎089 812 28 92; Via dei Mulini 4; panini €5, cakes €3) A terrace draped with foliage and flowers is but one of the attractions of this cafe, bar and *pasticceria,* alongside decadent cakes, live music and plenty of Positano poseur-watching potential.

AMALFI

POP 5400

Amalfi is a popular summer holiday destination for no good reason. The beach is unappealing, there's a surfeit of souvenir shops and crowds can be oppressive. Outside the high season, its tangle of narrow alleyways, whitewashed houses and sun-drenched piazzas make it worthy of a day trip but little more.

The **tourist office** (☎089 87 11 07; www.amalfituristoffice.it; Corso delle Repubbliche Marinare 33; ⏲8.30am-1.30pm & 3-7.15pm Mon-Fri, 8.30am-noon Sat) can provide information about sights, activities and transport.

Sights & Activities

Cattedrale di Sant'Andrea CHURCH
(☎089 87 10 59; Piazza del Duomo; ⏲9am-7pm)

Looming over the central piazza is the town's landmark Duomo, one of the few relics of Amalfi's past as an 11th-century maritime superpower. In high season, entrance between 10am and 5pm is through the adjacent **Chiostro del Paradiso** (☎089 87 13 24; Piazza del Duomo; adult/reduced €2.50/1; ⏲9am-7pm).

Grotta dello Smeraldo CAVE
(admission €6; ⏲9am-4pm; 👪) The local version of Capri's famous sea cave can be visited on one-hour boat trips from Amalfi's harbour (€14 return, 9.20am to 3pm daily May to October).

Sleeping & Eating

Hotel Lidomare HOTEL €€
(☎089 87 13 32; www.lidomare.it; Largo Duchi Piccolomini 9; s €55-65, d €103-145; ⏲year-round; ❄@📶) The spacious rooms at this old-fashioned, family-run favourite have an endearing air of gentility; the best have sea views.

A'Scalinatella Hostel HOSTEL €
(☎089 87 14 92; www.hostelscalinatella.com; Piazza Umberto I; dm €30, d €70-140) This bare-bones operation, just around the headland in Atrani, has dorms, rooms and apartments scattered across the village. Breakfast is included in the price.

Marina Grande SEAFOOD €€€
(☎089 87 11 29; www.ristorantemarinagrande.com; Viale Delle Regioni 4; mains €16-26, tasting menu lunch €22, dinner €48; ⏲Tue-Sun Mar-Oct) Run by the third generation of the same family and patronised primarily by locals, this classy restaurant fronting the beach serves food made with seasonal ingredients. It's known for its fresh fish dishes.

Dolcería dell' Antíco Portico PASTICCERIA €
(☎089 87 11 43; Via Supportico Rua 10; cakes from €3) Named for its location under the arches, this celebrated cake shop and small cafe gives a contemporary twist to traditional sweet treats such as *sfogliatella*.

Matera

POP 60,900

Set atop two rocky gorges, Matera is one of Italy's most remarkable towns and is the most compelling reason to visit the region of Basilicata. Dotting the ravines are the famous *sassi* (cave dwellings), where up to half the town's population lived until the late 1950s. These *sassi* now underpin Matera's economy, attracting visitors from all over the world.

The geographical centre of the town is handsome Piazza Vittorio Veneto, from where you can access the *sassi*.

Sights & Activities

Sassi CAVES
Within Matera there are two *sassi* areas: the largely restored **Barisano** and more impoverished and run-down **Caveoso**. Both feature serpentine alleyways and staircases, Byzantine-era cave churches and hidden piazzas. With a map you can explore them on your own, although you might find an audioguide (€8) from **Viaggi Lionetti** (☎0835 33 40 33; www.viaggilionetti.com; Via XX Settembre 9; ⏲9am-1pm & 4-8pm Mon-Fri, 9am-1pm Sat) helpful. It and **Ferula Viaggi** (www.ferulaviaggi.it) also offer guided tours.

Inhabited since the Paleolithic Age, the *sassi* were brought to public attention with the publication of Carlo Levi's book *Cristo si é fermato a Eboli* (Christ Stopped at Eboli; 1945). His description of children begging for quinine to stave off endemic malaria shamed the authorities into action and about 15,000 people were forcibly relocated in the late 1950s. In 1993 the *sassi* were declared a Unesco World Heritage site.

Accessible from Via Ridola, Sasso Caveoso is older and more evocative than Sasso Barisano. Its highlights include the *chiese rupestre* (rock churches) of **Santa Maria d'Idris** (Piazza San Pietro Caveoso; adult/reduced €3/2; ⏲10am-1pm & 2.30-7pm Tue-Sun Apr-Oct, 10.30am-1.30pm Tue-Sun Nov-Mar) and **Santa Lucia alle Malve** (Via la Vista; adult/reduced €3/2; ⏲10am-1pm & 2.30-7pm Apr-Oct, 10.30am-1.30pm Tue-Sun Nov-Mar) with their well-preserved 13th-century frescos.

The countryside outside of Matera, the **Murgia Plateau**, is littered with dozens of Paleolithic caves and monastic developments. It's best explored with a guide.

Sleeping

TOP CHOICE Hotel in Pietra BOUTIQUE HOTEL €€
(☎0835 34 40 40; www.hotelinpietra.it; Via San Giovanni Vecchio 22; s €55-100, d €95-150, ste €180-220; ❄@🛜) Housed in a 13th-century rock-hewn church in the Sasso Barisano, this boutique hotel features butter-yellow stone walls, a chic minimalist decor and stylish bathrooms set in rocky embrasures. A light gourmet breakfast provides the final touch of class.

La Dolce Vita B&B B&B €
(☎0835 31 03 24; www.ladolcevitamatera.it; Rione Malve 51; s €40-60, d €60-80; 🛜) This delightful ecofriendly B&B in Sasso Caveoso offers cool, comfortable and homey rooms. Owner Vincenzo is passionate about Matera and is a mine of information on the *sassi*.

Le Monacelle HOSTEL €
(☎0839 34 40 97; www.lemonacelle.it; Via Riscatto 9-10; dm €18, s/d €55/86; ❄🛜) Behind the Duomo and incorporating the delightful chapel of the Chiesa di San Franceso d'Assisi, this HI-run hostel is set in a 15th-century monastery (look for the 'Casa del Pellegrino Le Monacelle' signs). It offers large, mixed-sex dorms with bathrooms as well as plainly furnished private rooms. Its best feature is an atmospheric cobbled terrace, which has stunning *sassi* views. Breakfast costs an extra €4.

Eating

TOP CHOICE Il Cantuccio RISTORANTE €€
(☎0835 33 20 90; Via delle Beccherie 33; antipasto €15, mains €10-15; ⌚Tue-Sun) Family-run Il Cantuccio is a Slow Food–recommended restaurant serving creative regional fare. The speciality of the house is a lavish, seven-dish antipasto, which includes delights such as a deliciously creamy ricotta with fig syrup and a tasty *caponata* (sweet-and-sour aubergine ratatouille).

Le Botteghe TRATTORIA €€
(☎0835 34 40 72; Piazza San Pietro; mains €11.50-16; ⌚lunch & dinner daily Apr-Sep, closed lunch Tue-Thu Oct-Mar) This endearingly old-fashioned place offers a menu featuring local specialities that utilise products celebrated by the Presidio Slow Food. The freshly made pasta dishes and *salsiccia di maiale pezzente* (local 'beggar style' pork sausages) are particularly tasty.

Information

The **Agenzia di Promozione Territoriale Basilicata** (APT; ☎0835 33 19 83; www.aptbasilicata.it; 1st fl, Via De Viti De Marco 9; ⌚9am-1.30pm Mon-Fri, 4-6.30pm Mon & Tue) has a Matera office near the train station that can supply maps and brochures. In summer, tourist information booths operate next to the Convento Santa Lucia next to Sasso Barisano, and opposite the Palazzo della Provincia next to Sasso Caveoso. Online information is available at the APT's website and at www.sassiweb.it.

Getting There & Away

You can reach Matera by bus from Rome, Tuscany and Naples, or by train from Bari. The train station is close to the *sassi*, but the long-distance bus station is at Villa Longo on the edge of town, from where it's a 40-minute walk up Via Nazionale and Via Annunziatella to get to Piazza Vittorio Veneto.

Marozzi (☎06 225 21 47; www.marozzivt.it) runs two or three daily buses to/from Rome's Stazione Tiburtina (€34.50, 6½ hours) and one service per day to Siena (€46, 8¼ hours), Florence (€51, 9½ hours) and Pisa (€57.50, 12 hours). **Marino** (www.marinobus.it, ☎080 311 23 35) runs two daily services (one on Sunday) to/from Naples (€19, 4¼ hours).

By train, the **Ferrovie Appulo Lucano** (☎080 572 52 29; www.fal-srl.it) runs services to/from Bari (€4.50, 1¼ hour, 14 daily). Note that these do not run on Sundays.

Bari

TRANSPORT HUB

Most travellers visit Puglia's main town to take the Ferrovie Appulo Lucano to Matera or catch a ferry to Greece, Croatia or Montenegro. While it has no sights that in themselves demand a visit, the Old City (Bari Vecchia) has some architecturally notable Norman buildings that are worth exploring if you have a few hours to while away before your ferry leaves.

Bari Vecchia isn't particularly safe at night. Be aware of your personal safety and watch your bags and wallets.

Sleeping & Eating

B&B Casa Pimpolini B&B €
(☎080 521 99 38; www.casapimpolini.com; Via Calefati 249; s €45-60, d €70-80; ❄@) This lovely B&B in the new town is within easy walking distance of shops, restaurants and Bari Vecchia. Its two guest rooms are warm and welcoming, and the homemade breakfast is a treat.

Hotel Adria HOTEL €€
(☎080 524 66 99; www.adriahotelbari.com; Via Zuppetta 10; s/d €70/110; P❄@) This safe option near the train station offers comfortable, bright and modern rooms.

TOP CHOICE **Alberosole** MODERN ITALIAN €€
(☎080 523 54 46; www.alberosole.com; Corso Vittorio Emanuele II 13; mains €13-21; ⊙lunch & dinner Tue-Sun; ☜) Brioni-suited bankers and a loyal coterie of ladies-who-lunch are regulars at this elegant restaurant, drawn by its refined and perfectly executed modern Italian cuisine. Fantastic value considering the quality of the food on offer.

Drinking

Bar Savoia CAFE
(cnr Via Sparano da Bari & Via Celefati; ⊙7am-midnight) The *passaggiata* crowds head towards this ever-fashionable cafe on the new town's main pedestrian mall for coffee and liberal doses of people-watching.

Information

There's a helpful **tourist information point** (☎080 990 93 41; www.infopointbari.com; Piazza Aldo Moro; ⊙9am-7pm Mon-Sat, 9am-1pm Sun) in front of the train station, and another at the port which is only open May to October and whose hours are dependent on ferry arrivals.

Getting There & Away

Air

Bari is served by **Karol Wojtyla airport** (BRI; ☎080 580 03 58; www.seap-puglia.it), 15km northwest of town in Palese. **Tempesta** (www.autoservizitempesta.it) runs an hourly shuttle bus (€4.15, 30 minutes) between the airport and the train station. Alternatively, take local bus 16 (€0.90, 40 minutes).

Boat

Ferries run from Bari to Greece (Igoumenitsa and Patra), Croatia (Dubrovnik) and Montenegro (Bar). Ferries to Corfu and Kefallonia (also Patra) in Greece leave from Brindisi, approximately 115km south of Bari and easily accessed by train.

Ferry companies have offices at Bari's port, accessible by bus 20/ (€0.90) from the train station. Note: only board a bus with / after the 20.

Train

Bari is on the main east-coast rail line and there are trains to/from Rome (Freccia Argento from €54, 4½ hours), Brindisi (Regionale €7.70, one hour 20 minutes) and Lecce (Regionale €9.70, 1½ to two hours).

Lecce

POP 95,600

Its profusion of opulent *barocco leccese* (Lecce baroque) architecture has earned this sophisticated city a reputation as the 'Florence of the South'. The presence of a highly regarded university means that there is a vibrant bar scene, and the elegant *centro storico* is easily explored on foot.

Sights

Basilica di Santa Croce CHURCH
(☎0832 24 19 57; www.basilicasantacroce.eu; Via Umberto I; ⊙9am-noon & 5-8pm) This basilica is the city's most celebrated example of *barocco leccese*. It took a team of 16th- and 17th-century craftsmen more than a century to create the carved facade that you see today, which features a magnificent allegorical feast of writhing sheep, dodos, cherubs and beasties.

Piazza del Duomo PIAZZA
During times of invasion the inhabitants of Lecce would barricade themselves in this bombastically baroque square, which has conveniently narrow entrances. The 12th-century **cathedral** (⊙8.30am-12.30pm & 4-6.30pm) is unusual in that it has two facades, one on the western end and the other, more ornate, facing the piazza. It's framed by the 15th-century **Palazzo Vescovile** (Episcopal Palace) and the 18th-century Seminario, which now houses the **Museo Diocesano** (Piazza del Duomo; admission museum €4, cloisters €1; ⊙9.30am-12.30pm & 4-7pm Mon-Sat).

Sleeping

There are no youth hostels in Lecce, and no budget options worth recommending. The following boutique hotels are well worth an extra slice of your daily budget, though.

TOP CHOICE **Suite 68** BOUTIQUE HOTEL €
(☎0832 30 35 06; www.kalekora.it; Via Prato 7-9; s €70-80, d €80-120; ❄@☜) Vaulted ceilings, contemporary art and colourful rugs give the comfortable, well-sized rooms here loads of character. There's also a communal terrace on the roof, an attractive breakfast room downstairs and free use of bicycles. Prices are a steal for what's on offer.

Palazzo Rollo BOUTIQUE HOTEL, APARTMENT €
(☎0832 30 71 52; www.palazzorollo.it; Via Vittorio Emanuele II 14; s €50-60, d €70-90, ste €100-120,

apt €70-90; P❄@) Stay in a 17th-century palace – the family seat for over 200 years. Six gorgeous upstairs suites are furnished with antiques and some have painted ceilings. Downstairs, small self-catering apartments sleeping two or three people open onto an ivy-hung courtyard. The rooftop garden has a wonderful view of the Duomo. Parking costs €7 per day.

Eating

The main eating and drinking strip is on Via Umberto I, north of the Basilica di Santa Croce.

TOP CHOICE **Cucina Casareccia** TRATTORIA €€
(☎0832 24 51 78; Viale Costadura 19; mains €12; ⏲lunch Tue-Sun, dinner Tue-Sat) Ring the bell to gain entry into a place that feels like a private home and is run with great warmth by Anna Carmela Perrone. In fact, it's known locally as *Trattoria le Zie* (The Aunts' Trattoria). Here you'll taste true Puglian cuisine, including an outstanding stuffed calamari. Booking is essential.

Alle due Corti TRATTORIA €€
(☎0832 24 22 23; www.alleduecorti.com; Via Prato 42; mains €12; ⏲lunch & dinner daily, closed winter) For a taste of sunny Salento, check out this no-frills, fiercely traditional restaurant. The seasonal menu is classic Pugliese, written in a dialect that even some Italians struggle with. Celebrated chef Rosalba De Carla also runs cooking classes.

Trattoria di Nonna Tetti TRATTORIA €
(☎0832 24 60 36; Piazzetta Regina Maria 28; mains €8-12; ⏲lunch & dinner daily) A warmly inviting restaurant that is popular with all ages and budgets, and serves a wide choice of tasty and traditional dishes.

Information

Tourist Office (☎0832 24 80 92; Corso Vittorio Emanuele 24; ⏲9am-1pm & 4-8.30pm Mon-Sat Apr-Sep, to 6pm Nov-Mar) The tourist information office is of little use, as staff speak no languages other than Italian. It's best to ask your hotel for advice instead.

Ufficio Informazioni Duomo (☎0832 52 18 77; www.infolecce.it; Piazza del Duomo 2; ⏲9.30am-1.30pm & 3.30-7.30pm Mon-Fri Sep-Jul, from 10am Sat, 9.30am-7.30pm daily Aug) Rents out bikes (per hour/day €4/18) and runs guided tours (€40 for two hours). There's a second office at Via G Palmieiri 47.

Getting There & Away

Lecce is the end of the main southeastern rail line and there are frequent direct trains to/from Brindisi (Regionale €2.60, 30 minutes, hourly), Bari (Regionale €9.70, 1½ to two hours) and Rome (Freccia Argento; €66, 5½ hours, three daily). The train station is in the centre of town, an easy 15-minute walk from the Duomo.

Long-distance buses arrive at and leave from the **STP bus station** (☎800 43 03 46; Viale Porta D'Europa) opposite Grand Hotel Tiziano, past Porta Napoli. Miccolis has services to Naples (€32, six hours, three daily) and STP services travel to Brindisi airport (€6, 35 minutes, nine daily).

By car, take the SS16 to Bari via Monopoli and Brindisi. For Taranto take the SS7.

SICILY

Everything about the Mediterranean's largest island is extreme – the beauty of the rugged landscape, the robust flavours of the regional cuisine, the relentless summer sun and the all-powerful influence of its criminal underbelly.

Over the centuries, the strategic location and agricultural riches of Sicily have lured foreign invaders ranging from the Phoenicians and ancient Greeks to the Spanish Bourbons. All have contributed to the island's cultural landscape, leaving in turn Greek temples, Arab domes, Byzantine mosaics, Norman castles, Angevin churches and baroque facades.

This cultural complexity is complemented by Sicily's volcanic geography. Dominating the east coast, Mt Etna (3350m) is Sicily's most famous volcano, although not its most active; Stromboli usually claims that accolade. All round the island aquamarine seas lap at the craggy coastline, while inland, hilltop towns are strewn across the countryside.

Getting There & Away

Air

Flights from Italy's mainland cities, Tunisia (Tunis) and some European destinations land at Sicily's two main air hubs: Palermo's **Falcone-Borsellino airport** (PMO; ☎091 702 01 11; www.gesap.it) and Catania's Fontanarossa airport (p846).

Boat

Regular car and passenger ferries cross to Sicily (Messina) from Villa San Giovanni in Calabria. The island is also accessible by ferry from Genoa, Livorno, Civitavecchia (near Rome),

Naples, Salerno (on the Amalfi Coast) and Cagliari, as well as Tunisia. The main ports are Palermo, Milazzo, Catania, Trapani, Termini Imerese (near Palermo) and the Aeolian Islands.

Timetables are seasonal, so get up-to-date information and book your tickets at www.traghettiweb.it. Note that you should book well in advance during summer, particularly if you have a car.

The major routes and the companies that operate them:

PORT	TO/FROM	COMPANY
Aeolian Islands	Naples	SNAV, Siremar
Catania	Naples	TTT Lines
Milazzo	Naples	Siremar
Palermo	Cagliari	Tirrenia
Palermo	Civitavecchia	Grandi Navi Veloci, SNAV
Palermo	Genoa	Grandi Navi Veloci
Palermo	Livorno	Grandi Navi Veloci
Palermo	Naples	SNAV, Tirrenia
Palermo	Tunis	Grandi Navi Veloci, Grimaldi
Termini Imerese	Livorno	Grandi Navi Veloci
Termini Imerese	Salerno	Caronte & Tourist
Trapani	Cagliari	Tirrenia
Trapani	Civitavecchia	Grimaldi Lines
Trapani	Naples	Ustica Lines
Trapani	Tunis	Grimaldi Lines

Bus

Bus services between Rome and Sicily are operated by **SAIS** (☎800 21 10 20; www.saisautolinee.it), **Interbus** (☎0935 2 24 60; www.interbus.it) and **Segesta** (☎091 616 79 19; www.segesta.it), departing from Rome's Piazza Tiburtina. There are daily buses to Messina, Catania, Palermo and Syracuse.

Train

Direct trains run from Milan, Florence, Rome, Naples and Reggio di Calabria to Palermo and Catania. For further information go to the **Trenitalia** (☎89 20 21; www.trenitalia.com) website.

Getting Around

Generally the best way to get around Sicily is by bus. Trains tend to be cheaper on the major routes, but once you're off the coast, they can be painfully slow.

Roads are generally good and autostradas connect major cities.

Palermo

POP 655,875

Exploring this chaotic yet compelling city can be exhausting, but once you've acclimatised to the congested and noisy streets you'll be rewarded with some of southern Italy's most imposing architecture, impressive art galleries, vibrant street markets and an array of tempting restaurants and cafes.

Palermo's centre is large but it's relatively easy to explore on foot. The main street is Via Maqueda, which runs parallel to Via Roma, the busy road running north from the train station. Corso Vittorio Emanuele crosses Via Maqueda at a junction known as the Quattro Canti (Four Corners). You'll find that most sights and hotels are within easy walking distance of this intersection.

Sights

At the time of research the city's famous Archeological Museum on Piazza Olivella was closed for restoration and the date of its reopening was unknown.

Churches — CHURCH

Around the corner from Piazza Pretoria, Piazza Bellini is home to three churches: the **Chiesa di Santa Caterina** (☎338 722 87 75; Piazza Bellini; admission €2; ⊙9.30am-1pm & 3-7pm Mon-Sat, to 1.30pm Sun Apr-Nov, to 1.30pm daily Dec-Mar & 25 Nov), one of the city's most impressive baroque churches; **La Martorana** (Chiesa di Santa Maria dell'Ammiraglio; Piazza Bellini 3; donation requested; ⊙8.30am-1pm & 3.30-5.30pm Mon-Sat, 8.30am-1pm Sun), Palermo's most famous medieval church; and the red-domed **Chiesa Capitolare di San Cataldo** (Piazza Bellini 3; admission €2; ⊙9.30am-1.30pm & 3.30-5.30pm Mon-Sat, 9.30am-1.30pm Sun), of interest more for its Arab-Norman exterior than its surprisingly bare interior.

A short walk west up Corso Vittorio Emanuele II brings you to the **Cattedrale di Palermo** (www.cattedrale.palermo.it; Corso Vittorio Emanuele; admission free; ⊙7am-7pm), a visual riot of arches, cupolas and crenellations. Modified many times over the centuries, it's a stunning example of Sicily's unique Arab-Norman architectural style. Its impressive **Museo Diocesano** (☎tel, info 091 60 77 215; www.museodiocesanopa.it; Via Matteo Bonello 2; adult/6-17 & over 65/child under 6 €4.50/3/free; ⊙9.30am-1.30pm Tue-Fri & Sun, 10am-6pm Sat) is in a building on the opposite side of Via Matteo Bonello, on the western side of the cathedral.

Central Palermo

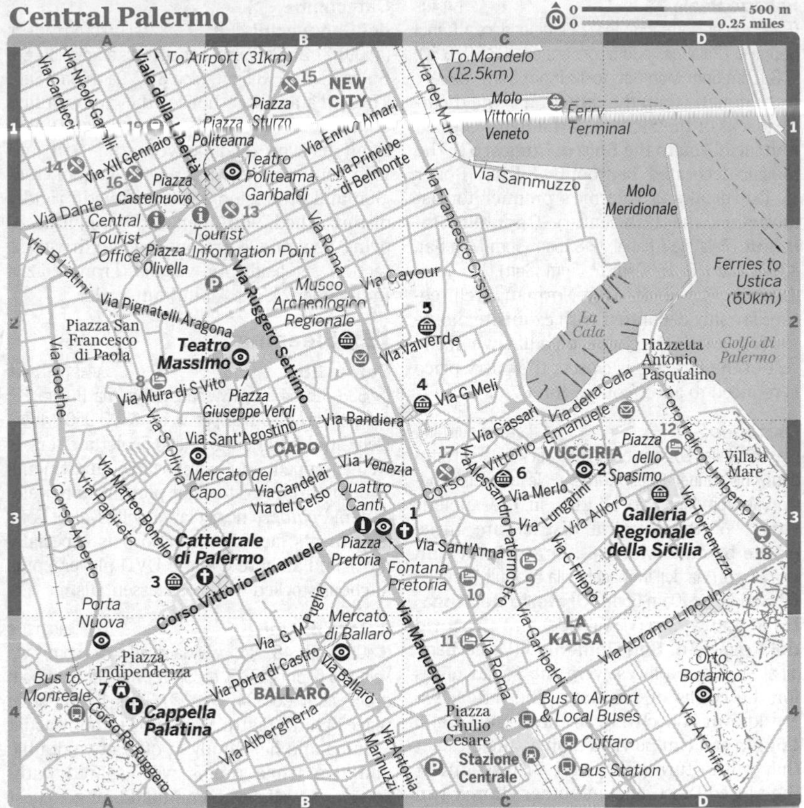

Central Palermo

Top Sights

Cappella Palatina A4
Cattedrale di Palermo A3
Galleria Regionale della Sicilia D3
Teatro Massimo B2

Sights

Chiesa Capitolare di San Cataldo .... (see 1)
1 Chiesa di Santa Caterina C3
2 Giardino Garibaldi C3
La Martorana .... (see 1)
3 Museo Diocesano A3
4 Oratorio del Rosario di San Domenico C2
5 Oratorio del Rosario di Santa Zita C2
6 Oratorio di San Lorenzo C3
7 Palazzo Reale A4

Sleeping

8 A Casa di Amici A2
9 Al Giardino dell'Alloro C3
10 Ambasciatori Hotel C3
11 B&B Panormus C4
12 Butera 28 .... D3

Eating

13 Antico Caffè Spinnato B1
14 Cappello Pasticceria A1
15 Piccolo Napoli B1
16 Pizzeria Biondo A1
17 Trattoria Il Maestro del Brodo C3

Drinking

18 Kursaal Kalhesa D3
19 Pizzo & Pizzo A1

Palazzo Reale PALACE

(Palazzo dei Normanni; Piazza Indipendenza 1; incl Cappella Palatina adult/concession €8.50/6.50; ⏲8.15am-5pm Mon-Sat, to 12.15pm Sun) Barely less dramatic than the cathedral is the theatrical seat of the Sicilian parliament. Guided tours lead you to the **Sala di Ruggero II**, the mosaic-decorated bedroom of King Roger II. Downstairs is Palermo's premier tourist attraction, the 12th-century **Cappella Palatina** (Palatine Chapel; ⏲8.15am-5pm Mon-Sat, 8.15-9.30am & 11.30am-12.15pm Sun), a jaw-dropping jewel of Arab-Norman architecture lavishly decorated with exquisite mosaics. If you visit the chapel on a day when the rest of the *palazzo* is closed, the entry price is reduced to adult/concession €7/5.

Oratories HISTORIC BUILDING

(Tesori della Loggia combined ticket adult/student/child under 6 €5/4/free; ⏲Tesori della Loggia 9am-1pm Mon-Sat) Hidden in the ancient streets of the Vucciria district are three ornate baroque oratories: **Oratorio di San Lorenzo** (Via dell'Immacolatella 5; adult/reduced €2.50/1.50; ⏲10am-6pm), **Oratorio del Rosario di Santa Zita** (Via Valverde) and **Oratorio del Rosario di San Domenico** (Via dei Bambinai 2). These places were the social clubs for the celebs of the time. The latter two are known collectively as the **Tesori della Loggia** and can be visited on a single ticket that will in turn give you a €1 discount at the Museo Diocesano and other church-run museums in the city.

Galleria Regionale della Sicilia MUSEUM

(Palazzo Abatellis; ☎091 623 00 11; www.regione.sicilia.it/beniculturali/palazzoabatellis/; Via Alloro 4; adult/EU 18-25/EU under 18 & over 65 €8/4/free; ⏲9am-6pm Tue-Fri, to 1pm Sat & Sun) Tucked down a side street in the stately 15th-century Palazzo Abatellis, this splendid museum has a wide-ranging collection featuring works by Sicilian artists from the Middle Ages to the 18th century.

Teatro Massimo CULTURAL BUILDING

(☎tour reservations 091 605 32 67; www.teatromassimo.it; Piazza Giuseppe Verdi; guided tours adult/reduced €8/5; ⏲10am-2.30pm Tue-Sun) A Palermo landmark, this grand neoclassical opera house took more than 20 years to complete and has become a symbol of the triumph and tragedy of the city. Appropriately, the closing scene of *The Godfather: Part III,* with its visually stunning juxtaposition of high culture, low crime, drama and death, was filmed here.

Catacombe dei Cappuccini ARCHAEOLOGICAL SITE

(☎091 21 21 17; Piazza Cappuccini; admission €3; ⏲9am-1pm & 3-5pm Mon-Sat, 9am-1pm Sun) These catacombs house the mummified bodies and skeletons of some 8000 Palermitans who died between the 17th and 19th centuries. Earthly power, gender, religion and professional status are still rigidly distinguished, with men and women occupying separate corridors, and a first-class section set aside for virgins. From Piazza Indipendenza, it's a 15-minute walk.

Sleeping

Butera 28 APARTMENT €€

(☎333 316 54 32; www.butera28.it; Via Butera 28; apt per day €50-170, per week €300-950; ❄📶) Delightful bilingual owner Nicoletta offers 11 well-equipped and comfortable apartments sleeping from two to eight persons in her elegant old *palazzo* near Piazza della Kalsa. Four apartments face the sea (No 9 is especially nice), and all have CD and DVD players, plus kitchens stocked with basic essentials.

A Casa di Amici HOSTEL €

(☎091 58 48 84; www.acasadiamici.com; Via Volturno 6; dm €17-23, d €56-72, without bathroom d €40-75, tr €60-84; ❄@📶) This hostel-style place behind Teatro Massimo is run by artist Claudia and her family. It offers two double and two triple rooms with shared bathrooms, as well as a communal lounge, guest kitchen and laundry. The annexe across the street has four additional rooms, including one with private bathroom and terrace. Internet costs €1 per 30 minutes; wi-fi is free – neither is available in the annexe.

B&B Panormus B&B €

(☎091 617 58 26; www.bbpanormus.com; Via Roma 72; s €43-65, d €55-85, tr €75-110; ❄📶) Keen prices, charming host Giovanni and five attractive and extremely comfortable rooms make this one of the city's most popular B&Bs. Each room has its own small private bathroom down the passageway (bathrobes are supplied).

Al Giardino dell'Alloro B&B €

(☎091 617 69 04; www.giardinodellalloro.it; Vicolo San Carlo 8; s €40-45, d €80-90, tr €120) This bijou B&B with flat-screen TVs, free wi-fi and walls hung with artwork from the nearby academy is a very pleasant retreat. The rooms are painted in vivid colours and there's a communal fridge for guests' use.

It's tucked down a slender alley opposite a wisteria-draped wall.

Ambasciatori Hotel HOTEL €
(info 091 616 68 81; www.ambasciatorihotelpalermo.com; Via Roma 111, 5; s €50-75, d €60-95, tr €75-110,) A decent option occupying the 5th floor of an old *palazzo;* the Ambasciatori has clean, reasonably comfortable rooms and a marvellous rooftop terrace where you can eat your breakfast in the morning and sip cocktails in the evening. Request a quiet room with a view (there are eight of these).

Eating

Like its architecture, Palermo's food is a unique mix of influences. Traditional yet spicy, it marries the island's superb produce – praised by Homer in *The Odyssey* – with recipes imported by the Arab Saracens in the 9th century. The street food is also superb. Three specialities to try are *arancini, panelle* (chickpea fritters) and cannoli (pastry tubes filled with sweetened ricotta and candied fruit).

For an adrenalin-charged food experience, head to one of Palermo's legendary markets: Capo on Via Sant'Agostino or Il Ballarò in the Albergheria quarter, off Via Maqueda. Both are open 7am to 8pm Monday to Saturday (to 1pm on Wednesday). The Capo is also open on Sunday mornings.

TOP CHOICE **Piccolo Napoli** SEAFOOD €€
(091 32 04 31; Piazzetta Mulino a Vento 4; antipasti €4-8, mains from €8; lunch Mon-Sat, dinner Thu-Sat) Known throughout the city for its spectacularly fresh seafood, delectable antipasti (try the *caponata* and the green olives) and fried morsels including *panelle,* this is a destination that serious foodies should not miss. The atmosphere is bustling and the genial owner greets most customers by name – a clear sign that once sampled, the food here exerts a true siren's call. Booking is advisable.

Pizzeria Biondo PIZZERIA €
(091 58 36 62; Via Nicolò Garzilli 27; pizzas €5-14; dinner Thu-Tue) Made with super-fresh *mozzarella di bufala,* Biondo's pizzas are often described as the best in Palermo. An animated crowd fills the sidewalk tables and inside rooms every night.

Trattoria Il Maestro del Brodo TRATTORIA €€
(Via Pannieri 7; mains €8-16; lunch Tue-Sun, dinner Fri & Sat) A Slow Food–recommended eatery, this no-frills place in the Vucciria offers a sensational antipasto buffet with loads of vegetarian choices (€8), delicious pastas and soups, and an array of ultra-fresh seafood.

Cappello Pasticceria PASTICCERIA €
(Via Niccolò Garzilli 10; 7am-9.30pm Thu-Tue) The chocolates and cakes here are true works of art, as beautiful to look at as they are delicious to eat. There's a boudoir-style salon at the back of the shop.

Antico Caffè Spinnato CAFE €
(091 32 92 20; Via Principe di Belmonte 107-15; snacks €4-8) Join Palermo's snappily dressed shoppers for a daytime coffee or an early evening drink at this sophisticated cafe, which dates to 1860.

Drinking

Pizzo & Pizzo WINE BAR
(www.pizzoepizzo.com; Via XII Gennaio 5; closed Sun) Patrons here are enticed by an extensive and excellent list of wines by the glass, a buzzing atmosphere and a tempting array of cheeses, cured meats and smoked fish.

Kursaal Kalhesa BAR
(www.kursaalkalhesa.it; Foro Umberto I 21; noon-3pm & 6pm-1am Tue-Sun) A lively, unpretentious crowd is attracted by Kursaal Kalhesa's program of music and literary events. Meals (mains €16) are served upstairs on a leafy patio flanked by 15th-century walls.

Information

Emergency

Police Station (Questura; 091 23 90 00; Piazza della Vittoria)

Medical Services

Presidio Ospedaliero Villa Sofia (091 780 40 33; www.ospedaliriunitipalermo.it/presidio_villa_sofia.html; Piazza Salerno; 24hr emergency) In the New City, near Parco della Favorita.

Tourist information

The **central tourist office** (091 58 38 47; www.palermotourism.com; Piazza Castelnuovo 34; 8.30am-2pm & 2.30-6pm Mon-Fri) is operated by the Provincia Regionale di Palermo, as is the **tourist information point** (091 59 16 98; in downstairs hall, Falcone-Borsellino airport; 8.30am-7.30pm Mon-Fri, to 2pm Sat) at Falcone-Borsellino airport. The Città di Palermo (City of Palermo) operates tourist information booths at Piazza Bellini, Piazza Castelnuovo (corner Via R Settimo), Piazza Marina, Piazza della Vittoria, the port and the train station. All of these are open from 9am to 1pm Monday to Friday; in

WORTH A TRIP

CATTEDRALE DI MONREALE

Just 8km southwest of Palermo, the 12th-century **Cattedrale di Monreale** (☎091 640 44 03; Piazza del Duomo; admission to cathedral free, north transept €2, terrace €2; ⌚8am-6pm) is the finest example of Norman architecture in Sicily. The entire 6400-sq-metre ceiling is covered in mosaics depicting 42 Old Testament stories, including the Creation, Adam and Eve, and Noah and his Ark. Try to visit in the morning, when there is enough light in the building to see the mosaics properly. Afterwards, pop into the cathedral's tranquil **cloisters** (adult/EU 18-25/EU under 18 & over 65 €6/3/free; ⌚9am-1.30pm & 2-7pm).

To get here from Palermo, take bus 389 (€1.30 from *tabacchi*, €1.70 on bus, every 25 minutes Monday to Saturday, hourly Sunday) from Piazza Indipendenza. A taxi costs €15 to €20.

high season those at Piazza Bellini and Piazza Castelnuovo are also open from 3pm to 7pm.

ℹ Getting There & Away

National and international flights arrive at Falcone-Borsellino airport, 35km west of Palermo.

The ferry terminal is northeast of the *centro storico*, off Via Francesco Crispi. Ferries for Cagliari and Naples leave from Molo Vittorio Veneto; for Genoa they leave from Molo Santa Lucia.

The new intercity bus station is in Piazza Cairoli, behind the train station. Sicily's buses are privatised and different routes are serviced by various companies, most of which have ticket offices here. The main companies:

Cuffaro (☎091 616 15 10; www.cuffaro.info; Via Paolo Balsamo 13) Services to Agrigento (€8.70, two hours, three to nine daily).

Interbus (☎0935 56 51 11; www.interbus.it) To/from Syracuse (€12, 3¼ hours, three daily Monday to Saturday, two on Sunday).

SAIS Autolinee (☎091 616 60 28; www.saisautolinee.it) To/from Catania (€14.90, 2½ hours, every 30 minutes Monday to Saturday, eight services Sunday).

Regular trains leave from the Stazione Centrale for Messina (Regionale €11.80, 3¼ hours, hourly) via Milazzo (Regionale €10.40, 2½ hours), the jumping-off point for the Aeolian Islands. There are also slow services to Catania, Syracuse and Agrigento, as well as to nearby towns such as Cefalù. Long-distance trains go to Naples (Intercity €56.50, 9¼ hours, three daily) and Rome (Intercity €69, 11½ hours, four daily).

ℹ Getting Around

To/From the Airport

A half-hourly bus service run by **Prestia e Comandé** (☎091 58 63 51; www.prestiaecomande.it) connects the airport with the train station via Piazza Politeama and operates between 5am and 10.30pm. Tickets for the 50-minute journey cost €6.10 and are available on the bus.

A taxi from the airport to the centre costs €45 (set fare).

Bus

Walking is the best way to get around Palermo's centre but if you want to take a bus, most stop outside or near the train station. Tickets cost €1.30 (€1.70 on bus) and are valid for 90 minutes. There are two small lines – Gialla and Rossa – that operate in the *centro storico*.

Aeolian Islands

Rising out of the cobalt-blue seas off Sicily's northeastern coast, the Unesco-protected Aeolian Islands (Isole Eolie) have been seducing visitors since Odysseus' time. Their wild, windswept mountains, hissing volcanoes and rich waters attract divers, sun seekers and adrenalin junkies.

Part of a huge volcanic ridge, the seven islands (Lipari, Salina, Vulcano, Stromboli, Alicudi, Filicudi and Panarea) represent the very pinnacle of a 3000m-high outcrop that was formed one million years ago. Lipari is the biggest and busiest of the seven, and the main transport hub. From there you can pick up connections to all the other islands, including Vulcano, famous for its therapeutic mud, and Stromboli, whose permanently active volcano supplies spectacular fire shows.

Sights & Activities

Lipari ISLAND

On Lipari you can explore the volcanic history of the islands and – even more interestingly – an impressive collection of classical-era artefacts at the **Museo Archeologico Regionale Eoliano** (☎090 988 01 74; www.regione.sicilia.it/beniculturali/museolipari; Castello di Lipari; adult/18-25/EU under 18 & over 65 €6/3/free; ⌚9am-1pm & 3-6pm Mon-Sat, 9am-1pm Sun) located in the Spanish-built **citadel**. For sunbathing, head to Canneto and the Spiaggia Bianca or to Porticello for Spiaggia Papesca. Snorkelling and diving are popular – contact **Diving Center**

La Gorgonia (☎090 981 26 16; www.lagorgoniadiving.it; Salita San Giuseppe, Marina Corta; dive/night dive/beginner course €30/40/55) for equipment and guided dives. For tours of the islands, **Da Massimo Dolce Vita Group** (☎090 981 30 86; www.damassimo.it; Via Maurolico 2) offers various packages, ranging from a €15 tour of Lipari and Vulcano to a €80 summit climb of Stromboli.

Vulcano ISLAND

From Lipari, it's a short boat ride to Vulcano, a malodorous and largely unspoilt island. Most people come here to make the hour-long trek up the **Fossa di Vulcano**, the island's active volcano (€3 for crater entrance in summer), or to wallow in the sulphurous **Fanghi di Vulcano** thermal mud baths (€2, plus €1 for shower). To get to the volcano, follow the signs from the port along Strada Provinciale and then turn left onto the gravel track.

Stromboli ISLAND

Famous for its spectacular fireworks, Stromboli's **volcano** is the most active in the region, last exploding in April 2009. To make the tough six- to seven-hour ascent to the 920m summit you are legally required to hire a guide. At the top you're rewarded with incredible views of the Sciara del Fuoco (Trail of Fire) and constantly exploding crater. **Magmatrek** (☎090 986 57 68; www.magmatrek.it; Via Vittorio Emanuele) organises afternoon climbs for €28 per person (minimum 10 people).

Sleeping & Eating

Most accommodation is on Lipari. Always try to book ahead, as summer is busy and many places close over winter. Prices fall considerably outside of high season.

Villa Diana HOTEL €€

(☎090 981 14 03; www.villadiana.com; Via Edwin Hunziker 1; s €43-80, d €67-145; closed Nov-Mar; P ❄ wi-fi) Swiss artist Edwin Hunziker converted this Aeolian house into a bohemian-spirited hotel in the 1950s. It stands above Lipari town in a garden of citrus trees and olives and offers panoramic views from the terrace. Amenities include free wi-fi (in the reception area only) and use of the tennis court.

Diana Brown B&B €

(☎090 981 25 84; www.dianabrown.it; Vico Himera 3; s €30-90, d €40-100, tr €50-130; ❄ wi-fi) South African–born Diana runs this excellent-value B&B, which is tucked down a narrow alley off the main drag. Rooms have abundant hot water, cheerful decor and welcome extras such as kettles, fridges, clothes-drying racks and satellite TV. Some downstairs rooms have kitchenettes, but these are a bit dark. Breakfast costs €5 extra.

E Pulera SICILIAN €€

(☎090 981 11 58; Via Isabella Vainicher Conti; mains from €17; dinner May-Oct) Its serene garden setting and exquisite food make this an upscale but relaxed choice for dinner. Choose from a vast array of Aeolian and Sicilian meat and fish dishes, then finish off with biscotti and sweet Malvasia wine.

Kasbah SICILIAN €€

(☎090 981 10 75; Via Maurolico 25, Lipari; pizzas €6-9, mains from €15; dinner, closed Wed Oct-Mar) Choose the environment that suits you best: the sleek, contemporary interior dining room or the vine-covered, candlelit garden out back. Menu choices include delicious pizzas and seafood delicacies.

Bar Pasticceria Subba PASTICCERIA €

(☎090 981 13 52; Corso Vittorio Emanuele 92, Lipari; pastries from €1; 7am-10pm) Subba has been supplying indulgent cakes, pastries and gelato to locals since 1930.

Drinking

Bar Chicco Tosto CAFE

(Corso Vittorio Emanuele II 281; 6am-7pm Mon-Sat) The name says it all – Chicco Tosto roasts its own beans and makes the best coffee on the islands. It's opposite the port and opens at 6am, which is convenient for those leaving or arriving early.

Eden Bar BAR

(Corso Vittorio Emanuele II 133; daily year-round) The bar of choice for locals of every age, plus almost every tourist in town. It hops on a Saturday evening when its tables and crowd spill onto the street, which is closed to traffic.

Information

The islands' only **tourist office** (☎090 988 00 95; www.aasteolie.191.it; Corso Vittorio Emanuele 202; 8.30am-1.30pm & 4.30-7.30pm Mon-Fri, 8.30am-1.30pm Sat & Sun Jul & Aug) is on Lipari.

Getting There & Away

The main departure point for the islands is Milazzo. If arriving in Milazzo by train, you'll need to catch a bus (€1) or taxi (€15) to the port, 4km from the station. At the port you'll find ticket offices lined up on Corso dei Mille.

Ustica Lines (www.usticalines.it) runs hydrofoils from the islands to/from Messina (€22.70, 1¾ hours) and Milazzo (€23.70, one hour). Siremar ferries travel to/from Milazzo (€16.20) but take longer than the hydrofoils. Frequency of service varies wildly according to the season.

Siremar also runs ferries from Naples to Lipari, the other islands and Milazzo (seat from €70.20).

Getting Around

Lipari is the main transport hub. Ustica Lines runs regular services to Vulcano (€7, 10 minutes), Stromboli (€18.30, 1¾ hours) and the other islands. You can get full timetable information and buy tickets at Lipari's port.

Lipari's Guglielmo Urso Bus service travels around the island (€7 for six trips). Its terminus is at the port.

Taormina

POP 11,100

Crowning a clifftop terrace overlooking the Ionian Sea and Mt Etna, this sophisticated town has attracted socialites, artists and writers ever since Greek times. Its pristine medieval core, proximity to beaches, grandstand coastal views and chic social scene make it a hugely popular summer holiday destination, meaning that crowds can be oppressive in July and August.

Sights & Activities

The principal pastime in Taormina is wandering the pretty hilltop streets, browsing the shops and eyeing up fellow holidaymakers.

For a swim you'll need to take the **funivia** (cable car; one-way/return €2/3.50; ⏲9am-8.15pm, to 1am Apr-Sep) down to Taormina's beach, **Lido Mazzarò**, and **Isola Bella**, a tiny island set in its own picturesque cove.

SAT (☎0942 2 46 53; www.satgroup.it; Corso Umberto I 73) is one of a number of agencies that organises day trips to Mt Etna (€40), as well as to Syracuse (€45), Palermo and Cefalù (€55), and Agrigento (€50).

Teatro Greco AMPHITHEATRE

(☎0942 2 32 20; Via Teatro Greco; adult/reduced/EU under 18 & over 65 €8/4/free; ⏲9am-1hr before sunset) Suspended between sea and sky, and with Mt Etna looming on the southern horizon, this horseshoe-shaped theatre is Taormina's premier attraction. Built in the 3rd century BC, it's the most dramatically situated Greek theatre in the world and the second largest in Sicily (after Syracuse). In summer the theatre is used as a venue for international arts and film festivals. In peak season, explore early in the morning to avoid the crowds.

Corso Umberto STREET

One of the chief delights of Taormina is wandering along its pedestrianised main street, which is lined with antique and jewellery shops, delis and designer boutiques. Midway down, pause to revel in the stunning panoramic views of Mt Etna and the sea coast from **Piazza IX Aprile**. A few blocks further along is **Piazza del Duomo**, where teenagers congregate around an ornate baroque fountain dating from 1635. On the eastern side of this piazza is the 13th-century **cathedral** (Piazza del Duomo; ⏲9am-8pm).

Sleeping & Eating

TOP CHOICE **Hotel Villa Belvedere** HOTEL €€€

(☎094 22 37 91; www.villabelvedere.it; Via Bagnoli Croce 79; s €70-190, d €80-280, ste €120-450; ⏲Mar–late-Nov; ❄@🛜≋) Built in 1902, the jaw-droppingly pretty Villa Belvedere is in a quiet but central pocket and has fabulous views, luxuriant gardens and a swimming pool. Rooms are small but comfortable and most have terraces overlooking the sea – the best are on the 3rd floor. Suites have large dining/lounge areas, excellent kitchens and private terraces; they're perfect for families. Internet and wi-fi cost an extra €3 for the duration of your stay.

Hostel Taormina HOSTEL €

(☎094 262 55 05, mobile 349 102 61 61; www.hosteltaormina.com; Via Circonvallazione 13; dm €18-25, d €58-80; ❄@🛜) The town's only hostel opened for business in 2011 and operates year-round. It's small (only 23 beds in three dorms and one private room) and the facilities are basic, but it has a roof terrace commanding panoramic sea views, comfortable beds and a communal kitchen. No breakfast.

Tiramisù PIZZERIA, SICILIAN €€

(☎0942 2 48 03; Via Cappuccini 1; pizzas €7-14, mains €13-20; ⏲closed Tue) Known for its excellent pizzas and trademark *tiramisù,* this casual place close to Porta Messina offers indoor and outdoor eating areas and is a good choice for a casual meal.

Al Duomo SICILIAN €€€

(☎0942 62 56 56; Vico Ebrei 11; mains €20-22; ⏲lunch & dinner, closed Mon Nov-Mar) A romantic terrace overlooking the cathedral and a menu of classic Sicilian dishes are the attractions here. The chef's six-course tasting menu (€60) is a great introduction to the best that the island has to offer.

Information

Tourist Office (☎0942 2 32 43; www.gate2taormina.com; Piazza Santa Caterina, off Corso Umberto I; ⊙8.30am-2.30pm & 3.30-7pm Mon-Fri year-round, 9am-1pm & 4-6.30pm Sat Apr-Oct) Has helpful multilingual staff, plenty of practical information and tour bookings.

Getting There & Away

Taormina is best reached by bus. From the bus terminus on Via Pirandello, Interbus serves Messina (€3.90, 1½ hours, seven daily Monday to Saturday, one on Sunday) and **Etna Trasporti** (☎095 53 27 16; www.etnatrasporti.it) connects with Catania airport (€7, 1½ hours, five daily Monday to Saturday, three on Sunday).

Taormina's train station is some 2km downhill from the main town, making the train a last resort. If you do arrive by train, catch the Interbus service (€1.80) up to town. Buses run roughly every 30 to 90 minutes, less often on Sunday.

Mt Etna

The dark silhouette of Mt Etna (3350m) broods ominously over the east coast, more or less halfway between Taormina and Catania. One of Europe's highest and most volatile volcanoes, it erupts frequently, most recently in April 2012.

By public transport the best way to get to the mountain is to take the daily AST bus from Catania. This departs from in front of the main train station at 8.15am daily (returning at 4.30pm; €5.60 return) and drops you at the Rifugio Sapienza (1923m), where you can pick up the **Funivia dell'Etna** (☎095 91 41 41; www.funiviaetna.com; cable car one-way/return €14.50/27, incl bus & guide €51; ⊙9am-4.30pm) to 2500m. From June to September there is another departure at 11.20am. From Rifugio Sapienza buses courier you up to the official crater zone (2920m). If you want to walk, allow up to four hours for the round trip.

Gruppo Guide Alpine Etna Sud (☎095 791 47 55; www.etnaguide.com) is one of hundreds of outfits offering guided tours, typically involving 4WD transport and a guided trek. These cost from €45 per person for a half-day tour (usually morning or sunset) and about €60 for a full-day tour.

Armchair excursionists can enjoy Etna views by hopping on a **Ferrovia Circumetnea train** (www.circumetnea.it; single/return €7.25/11.60). Catch the metro from Catania's main train station to the FCE station at Via Caronda (metro stop Borgo). Note that the service doesn't operate on Sundays from mid-September to March.

Further Etna information is available from the **municipal tourist office** (☎095 742 55 73; www.comune.catania.it; Via Vittorio Emanuele II 172; ⊙8.15am-7.15pm Mon-Fri, to 12.15pm Sat) in Catania.

Syracuse

POP 123,900

Syracuse (Siracusa) has a fascinating past. Founded in 734 BC by Corinthian settlers, it became the dominant Greek city state on the Mediterranean and was known as the most beautiful city in the ancient world. After falling to the Romans in 212 BC its power waned, and Palermo took over as the island's most important city. A devastating earthquake in 1693 destroyed most of the Syracuse's buildings; their replacements, built in the fashionable Sicilian baroque style, remain largely intact and visually resplendent in the streets of Ortigia, the *centro storico*.

Sights

Ortygia HISTORIC AREA

Connected to the town centre by a bridge, the island of Ortygia is an atmospheric warren of baroque *palazzi*, lively piazzas and busy trattorias. Just off Via Roma, the 7th-century **Duomo** (Piazza del Duomo; ⊙8am-7pm) was built over a pre-existing 5th-century BC Greek temple, incorporating most of the original columns in its three-aisled structure. Its sumptuous baroque facade was added in the 18th century.

Parco Archaeologico della Neapolis ARCHAEOLOGICAL SITE

(☎0931 6 50 68; Viale Paradis; adult/18-25/under 18 & EU over 65 €10/5/free; ⊙9am-6pm Apr-Oct, to 4pm Nov-Mar) For the classicist, Syracuse's real attraction is this archaeological park with its 5th-century BC **Teatro Greco** hewn out of the rock above the city. This theatre staged the last tragedies of Aeschylus, which were first performed here in his presence. In summer it is brought to life again with an annual season of classical theatre.

Just beside the theatre is the mysterious **Latomia del Paradiso**. The stone for the ancient city was extracted from these deep, precipitous limestone quarries.

Back outside this area you'll find the entrance to the 2nd-century AD **Anfiteatro Romano**, which was used originally for gladiatorial combats and horse races. The Spaniards largely destroyed the site in the 16th century, and used it as a quarry to build Ortigia's city walls.

To reach the park, take bus 1, 3 or 12 (€1) from in front of the post office on Piazza Poste in Ortigia and get off at the corner of Corso Gelone and Viale Teocrito. Buy bus tickets from a *tabacchi*. Alternatively, the walk from Ortigia will take about 30 minutes. If driving, you can park along Viale Augusto (tickets available at the nearby souvenir kiosks).

Museo Archeologico Paolo Orsi MUSEUM
(Viale Teocrito; adult/reduced €8/4; ⌚9am-6pm Tue-Sat, 9am-1pm Sun) Head to the grounds of Villa Landolina, about 500m east of the archaeological park, to find this huge, well-organised and incredibly impressive archaeological museum. Allow plenty of time to get through the four distinct sectors; serious archaeology buffs may even want to consider splitting their visit into two days. A tip: don't miss the coin collection – it's quite extraordinary. A combined ticket is available for the museum and the archaeological park (adult/EU student 18-25/ EU under 18 & over 65 €13.50/7/free).

Sleeping

TOP CHOICE **Palazzo del Sale** B&B €
(☎0931 6 59 58; www.palazzodelsale.com; Via Santa Teresa 25, Ortigia; s €75-95, d €90-115, d with terrace €100-125; ❄@📶) This is as stylish as Syracuse gets: the six rooms at this designer B&B are well sized, with high ceilings and good beds. Extra touches include free coffee and tea in the comfortable communal lounge. The owners also operate a second property right on the beach near Porto Piccolo (www.giuggiulena.it).

B&B dei Viaggiatori, Viandanti e Sognatori B&B €
(☎0931 2 47 81; www.bedandbreakfastsicily.it; Via Roma 156, Ortigia; s €35-50, d €55-70, tr €75-80; ❄📶) On the 4th floor of an old *palazzo* at the end of Via Roma, this welcoming B&B is run by a young couple and their toddler, who live on site. It offers simple, colourfully decorated rooms and a sunny roof terrace with sweeping sea views. No lift.

Lol Hostel HOSTEL €
(☎0931 46 50 88; www.lolhostel.com; Via Francesco Crispi 94; dm €20-27, d €56-65; ❄@📶) This modern, well-kept hostel is located in a scruffy street near the bus and train stations. It has six mixed dorms (sleeping eight, 10 and 20) and two doubles. The pleasant common spaces include an open, airy guest kitchen, an outdoor patio and a sprawling lounge with computers (€1 per 30 minutes) and bar (April to September only). It's 10 minutes on foot to Ortigia, or five minutes with one of the hostel's rental bikes.

Eating & Drinking

The two best bars in Ortigia are **Il Blu** (Via Nizza) and **Biblios Cafe** (Via del Consiglio Regionale 11; ⌚10am-1.30pm & 5-9pm, closed Wed).

Sicilia in Tavola SICILIAN €
(☎392 461 08 89; Via Cavour 28; pasta €7-12; ⌚closed Mon) There are only a dozen tables available at this popular local eatery specialising in seafood antipasti and homemade pasta dishes, so arrive early or be prepared to queue.

Ristorante Regina Lucia SICILIAN €€
(☎0931 2 25 09; www.reginalucia.it; Piazza Duomo 6, Ortigia; mains €13-18, degustation menus €45-65; ⌚lunch & dinner Wed-Mon) Romantics will adore this atmospheric place with its ancient-meets-arty decor featuring Kartell chairs, vaulted stone ceilings, candelabras and contemporary art. This complements a menu of modern Sicilian dishes dictated by the season.

Gelati Bianca GELATERIA €
(Via Pompeo Picherali 2; cone/cup from €1.80; ⌚daily) It's not just the location off Piazza Duomo that's the attraction here – the house-made gelati is pretty good, too.

Information

The most useful **tourist information office** (☎0800 05 55 00; infoturismo@provsr.it; Via Roma 31; ⌚8am-8pm Mon-Sat, 9.15am-6.45pm Sun) is operated by the municipality.

Getting There & Around

It's quickest and most convenient to get here by bus rather than train. Buses use the terminus close to the train station. Interbus runs services to/from Catania airport (€6, one hour, hourly Monday to Saturday, six Sunday) and Catania (€6, 1¼ hours). It also operates a service to Palermo (€12, 3¼ hours, three daily Monday to Saturday, two Sunday).

Regional trains service Taormina (€8.30, two hours, five daily), Catania (€6.35, 1¼ hours, seven daily) and Messina (€9.70, 2¾ hours, five daily).

A free shuttle bus (No 20) runs between the bus station and Ortigia every 30 minutes from 6.30am to 9.30pm, stopping at Parcheggio Talete, Piazza Archimede and Via Maestranza.

Note that there's a ZTL in Ortigia – the car park at Talete, just inside the bridge, charges €6 per day.

Agrigento

POP 59,200

Agrigento was founded around 581 BC by Greek settlers and became an important trading centre under the Romans and Byzantines. These days, the only trading that occurs is around the souvenir stands surrounding one of Italy's most wonderful ancient sights, the Valley of the Temples (Valle dei Templi).

Up in the main town, the tourist information desk in the office of the **Provincia Regionale di Agrigento** (☎0922 59 32 27; www.provincia.agrigento.it; Piazza Vittorio Emanuele; ⊙8.30am-1pm & 2.30-7pm Mon-Fri, 8.30am-2pm Sat) can supply maps but little else.

Sights

Valley of the Temples ARCHAEOLOGICAL SITE
(Valle dei Templi) One of the most magnificent archaeological sites in Southern Europe, this Unesco-listed complex of temples and old city walls from the ancient city of Akragas dates from 581 BC. The five Doric temples actually stand along a ridge, not a valley, and were designed to be visible from all around and a beacon for homecoming sailors.

Though in varying states of ruin, the temples give a tantalising glimpse of what must truly have been one of the most luxurious cities in Magna Graecia. You'll need a full day to do justice to the **Archaeological Park** (☎0922 49 72 26; adult/EU reduced/child €10/5/free; ⊙8.30am-7pm, later in summer), which is divided into eastern and western zones. The most spectacular temples are in the eastern zone. First up is the oldest, the **Tempio di Ercole**, built at the end of the 6th century BC and equivalent in size to the Parthenon. Continuing east, the intact **Tempio della Concordia** was transformed into a Christian church in the 6th century, and the **Tempio di Giunone** boasts an impressive sacrificial altar.

Over the road in the western zone, the remains of the 5th-century BC **Tempio di Giove** suggest just how big the original must have been. In fact, it covered an area of 112m by 56m with 20m-high columns interspersed with *telamoni* (giant male statues), one of which now stands in the valley's **Museo Archeologico** (☎0922 4 01 11; Contrada San Nicola; incl Archaeological Park adult/EU reduced €13.50/7; ⊙9am-7pm Tue-Sat, 9am-1pm Sun & Mon), north of the temples.

If you are planning to visit both the park and the museum, purchase a combined ticket (adult/EU reduced €13.50/7).

The most scenic time to visit is in February and March when the valley is awash with almond blossoms.

Sleeping & Eating

TOP CHOICE **Villa Athena** LUXURY HOTEL €€€
(☎0922 59 62 88; www.hotelvillaathena.it; Via Passeggiata Archeologica 33; s €130-190, d €150-350, ste €240-890; P❄@🛜≋) Close proximity to the Valley of the Temples (a five-minute walk), views of the Tempio della Concordia, a landscaped garden with swimming pool and a recently refurbished and extremely classy interior fitout make this five-star hotel an irresistably indulgent choice.

Atenea 191 B&B €
(☎349 59 55 94; www.atenea191.com; Via Atenea 191; s €45-60, d €65-85) Though musty and worn, this B&B on Agrigento's main shopping thoroughfare is open all year and has a breakfast terrace with sweeping views over the valley.

Kalòs MODERN SICILIAN €€
(Piazzetta San Calogero; mains €15; ⊙closed Mon) This stylish eatery compensates for bland decor by focusing full attention on its well-prepared fish, meat and pasta.

Drinking

Mojo Wine Bar WINE BAR
(☎0922 46 30 13; Piazza San Francesco 11-13; ⊙Mon-Sat) A trendy *enoteca* in a pretty piazza. Enjoy a cool white Inzolia and munch on olives and spicy salami as you listen to some laid-back jazz.

Getting There & Away

Bus is generally the easiest way to get to Agrigento. Intercity buses arrive on Piazzale F Rosselli, from where it's a short walk downhill to the train station on Piazza Guglielmo Marconi, to catch local bus 1, 2 or 3 to the Valley of the Temples (€1.10). Buy tickets at the station *tabacchi*.

A taxi from the bus station to the Valley of the Temples costs €10.

Cuffaro runs buses to/from Palermo (€8.70, two hours, nine daily Monday to Saturday, three Sunday) and SAIS services go to Catania (€13, three hours, hourly).

SARDINIA

The Mediterranean's second-largest island, Sardinia, is a rugged and beautiful place. Tourist interest is largely focused on the coast, which is one of Italy's most impressive, with stunning sandy beaches, crystalline waters and idyllic coves; but venture inland and you'll discover an altogether different island, of untamed nature and proud tradition, dark granite peaks, dizzying valleys and silent cork forests. Adding a sense of mystery are the 7000 *nuraghi* (circular stone towers) that pepper the landscape, all that's left of Sardinia's mysterious prehistoric past.

Sardinia's top coastal resorts, including the celeb-studded Costa Smeralda (Emerald Coast), are among the most expensive holiday destinations on the Med and get extremely busy in peak season. Visit out of high summer, though, and you'll find that space is not a problem and prices compare very favourably with the mainland (or 'continent' as Sardinians refer to it).

You can get around Sardinia on public transport but you'll discover much more with your own wheels.

Getting There & Away

Air

Flights from Italian and European cities serve Sardinia's three airports: Elmas (p836) in Cagliari; Alghero's **Fertilia** (☎079 93 52 82; www.aeroportodialghero.it); and **Olbia Costa Smeralda** (OLB; ☎0789 56 34 44; www.geasar.it).

Boat

Car and passenger ferries sail year-round from various Italian ports, including Genoa, Livorno, Piombino, Civitavecchia, Naples and Palermo. Several companies ply these routes and services are at their most frequent between June and September. There are also summer-only routes from Fiumicino. The major routes and the companies that operate them are:

Civitavecchia To/from Olbia (Moby Lines, SNAV, Tirrenia); Cagliari (Tirrenia); Golfo Aranci (Sardinia Ferries); Arbatax (Tirrenia).

Genoa To/from Porto (Grandi Navi Veloci, Tirrenia); Torres (Grandi Navi Veloci, Tirrenia); Olbia (Grandi Navi Veloci, Moby Lines, Tirrenia).

Livorno To/from Olbia (Moby Lines); Golfo Aranci (Sardinia Ferries).

Naples To/from Cagliari (Tirrenia)

Palermo To/from Cagliari (Tirrenia)

Piombion To/from Olbia (moby Lines); Golfo Aranci (Sardinia Ferries).

Get up-to-date information and book tickets at www.traghettiweb.it.

Getting Around

Getting round Sardinia by public transport is time-consuming but not impossible. In most cases buses are preferable to trains. The main transport provider, **ARST** (☎800 86 50 42; www.arst.sardegna.it), operates bus services across the island, as well as the **Trenino Verde** (☎070 58 02 46; www.treninoverde.com), a tiny tourist train that trundles through Sardinia's most inaccessible countryside.

Cagliari

POP 156,500

Sardinia's capital and most cosmopolitan city, Cagliari rises from the sea in a helter-skelter of golden-hued *palazzi*, domes and facades. Yet for all its splendour, it remains what it always has been – a busy working port with a gritty, down-to-earth atmosphere and a vibrant buzz. With its landmark citadel, great restaurants and popular, sandy beach, Cagliari is very much its own city.

Sights & Activities

Cagliari's sights are concentrated in four central districts: Castello, the medieval citadel that towers over the city; Marina, the bustling seafront area; Stampace, which extends westwards of Largo Carlo Felice, modern Cagliari's showpiece street; and Villanova, east of Castello.

Museo Archeologico Nazionale MUSEUM
(☎070 68 40 00; Piazza dell'Arsenale; adult/reduced €3/1.50; ⏰9am-8pm Tue-Sun) Housed in what was once Cagliari's arsenal, the **Citadella dei Musei** is the city's main museum complex. Of its four museums, the most impressive is the Museo Archeologico Nazionale whose collection of archaeological artefacts includes a number of pint-sized bronze figurines. In the absence of any written records, these provide vital clues to the island's mysterious *nuraghic* culture.

Torre di San Pancrazio TOWER
(Piazza Indipendenza; adult/reduced €4/2.50; ⏰10.30am-7pm Tue-Sun summer, to 4.30pm winter) Guarding the entrance to the Citadella dei Musei, this 36m-high tower was completed in 1305 on the city's highest point.

Climb to the top for grandstand views of the Golfo di Cagliari.

Cattedrale di Santa Maria CHURCH
(Piazza Palazzo 4; 7.30am-8pm Mon-Sat, 8am-1pm & 4.30-8.30pm Sun) Cagliari's graceful, 13th-century cathedral sits aloft in the hilltop Castello district. Apart from its bell tower, little remains of the original Gothic structure, but it's still an impressive sight with an imitation Pisan-Romanesque facade and a baroque interior. Inside, note the imposing Romanesque pulpits.

Bastione San Remy LOOKOUT
This monumental terrace, formerly a strong point in the defensive walls, affords sweeping views over Cagliari's higgledy-piggledy rooftops and distant lagoons.

Anfiteatro Romano AMPHITHEATRE
(www.anfiteatroromano.it; Viale Sant'Ignazio) This 2nd-century amphitheatre is the most important Roman monument in Sardinia. Summer concerts are staged here; at the time of research the amphitheatre was closed for restoration.

Spiaggia di Poetto BEACH
A short bus ride from the centre, Cagliari's vibrant beach boasts inviting blue waters and a happening summer bar scene. Take bus PQ or PF.

Festivals & Events

Cagliari's annual bonanza, the **Festa di Sant'Efisio**, involves four days of costumed processions from 1 May.

Sleeping

Il Cagliarese B&B €
(339 654 40 83; www.ilcagliarese.it; Via Vittorio Porcile 19; s €45-70, d €60-90;) In the heart of the lively Marina district, this snug B&B gets everything right – the location is central, its three guest rooms are clean, comfortable and quiet, there's free wi-fi, and a great breakfast spread. Overseeing it all, the friendly owners are a mine of local information.

Hotel A&R Bundes Jack HOTEL €
(070 65 79 70; www.hotelbjvittoria.it; Via Roma 75; s €52-72, d €80-92;) An excellent seafront option is this old-fashioned family-run *pensione*. Run by a garrulous old gent, it has spacious, high-ceilinged rooms decorated with solid antique furniture and sparkling chandeliers. Breakfast is not included but is available for €7.

Hostel Marina HOSTEL €
(070 67 08 18; www.hostelmarinacagliari.it; Scalette S Sepolcro; dm/s/d/q €22/40/60/100;) This central hostel, housed in a beautifully converted 800-year-old former monastery, has oodles of historic charm and a wide range of accommodation, from single-sex six-person dorms to private rooms with en suite bathrooms.

Eating & Drinking

Monica e Ahmed SEAFOOD €€
(070 640 20 45; Corso Vittorio Emanuele 119; mains €20, fixed-price menus €15/25/30; closed dinner Sun) Search out this colourful, laid-back restaurant for fresh seafood served with a smile. Kick off with a lavish antipasto spread of swordfish, mussels, fried calamari, cuttlefish and tuna, before diving into spaghetti with *ricci* (sea urchins) and grilled catch of the day.

Il Fantasma PIZZERIA €
(070 65 67 49; Via San Domenico 94; pizzas €6.50-10; Mon-Sat) A five-minute walk east of Piazza Martiri d'Italia, this unpretentious pizzeria prepares some of the best pizza in town. Grab a table in the barrel-vaulted interior and bite into classic pizzas served blisteringly hot from the wood-fired oven. Bookings recommended.

Sa Schironada TRATTORIA €
(070 451 07 71; Via Baylle 39; set menus €13-38, pizza & drink €10) A big, barnlike trattoria that's good for a cheap, tasty fill-up. There are several menu options but take it easy when you order – the portions are huge and the antipasto is a minor meal in itself.

Antico Caffè CAFE
(www.anticocaffe1855.it; Piazza Costituzione 10; 7am-2am) Authors DH Lawrence and Grazia Deledda once frequented this grand old cafe, Cagliari's most famous. Join the locals to chat over leisurely coffees, cocktails and snacks.

Information

Tourist Information Points (070 677 71 87; www.infopointcagliari.it; 8am-8pm) The most useful information points are at Piazza Indipendenza, near the Torre di San Pancrazio, and at Piazza Costituzione, under Bastione San Remy.

WORTH A TRIP

CALA GONONE

Cala Gonone is a popular resort on the eastern **Gulf of Orosei**. It sits at the heart of one of Italy's most beautiful coastlines where the rocky mountains of the **Parco Nazionale del Golfo di Orosei e del Gennargentu** abruptly meet the sea, forming a curtain of plunging white cliffs riven by hidden coves and lapped by crystalline waters. The swimming is sublime and, inland, the rugged terrain is ideal for hiking and climbing.

In town, there's a small beach but the best swimming spots, including **Cala Fuili** and **Cala Luna**, lie to the south. Also to the south is the **Grotta del Bue Marino** (adult/reduced €8/4; guided tours hourly 9am-noon & 3-5pm Aug, 10am-noon & 3pm Jul, 10am, 11am & 3pm Sep, 11am & 3pm Oct-Nov & Mar-Jun), a complex of stalactite- and stalagmite-filled caves where monk seals used to pup. The easiest way to reach these places is to take a boat trip from Cala Gonone's small port. The **Nuovo Consorzio Trasporti Marittimi** (0784 9 33 05; www.calagononecrociere.it; Porto Cala Gonone) is one of several operators that sails to Cala Luna (€15 to €23) and the Grotta del Bue Marino (€19 to €22, including Cala Luna €26 to €35) between March and October.

For accommodation lists and information on tour operators offering excursions and guided hikes, contact the helpful **tourist office** (0784 9 36 96; www.dorgali.it; Viale Bue Marino 1a; 9am-7pm Jul & Aug, 9am-1pm & 3-7pm Easter-Jun & Sep-Oct, to noon rest of year).

If travelling by public transport, Cala Gonone is accessible by ARST bus from Nuoro (€3.50, 70 minutes, up to six daily).

Getting There & Away

Air

Flights from mainland Italy and European cities arrive at **Elmas airport** (070 21 12 11; www.cagliariairport.it), 6km northwest of the city. Half-hourly **ARST** (www.arst.sardegna.it) buses connect the airport with the bus station on Piazza Matteotti; the 10-minute journey costs €4.

Boat

Cagliari's ferry port is just off Via Roma. **Tirrenia** (892 123; www.tirrenia.it; Via dei Ponente 1) is the main ferry operator, with year-round services to Civitavecchia (from €58, 16½ hours), Naples (from €47, 16¼ hours) and Palermo (from €45, 14½ hours).

Bus

From the bus station on Piazza Matteotti, daily **ARST** (800 865 042; www.arst.sardegna.it) buses serve Oristano (€7, 1½ hours, two daily) and Nuoro (€15.50, 3½ hours, two daily), as well as destinations on the Costa del Sud and Costa Rei. Get tickets from the McDonald's on the square.

Turmo Travel (0789 2 14 87; www.gruppoturmotravel.com) runs a daily bus to Olbia (€19, 4¼ hours).

Car & Motorcycle

Down by the port, you can rent cars, bikes and scooters at **CIA Rent a Car** (070 65 65 03; www.rentcagliari.com; Via S Agostino 13). Bank on from €38 per day for a small car.

Train

From the station on Piazza Matteotti direct trains run to Oristano (€5.95, one to 1½ hours, hourly) and Sassari (€15.75, 3¾ hours, two daily).

Alghero

POP 40,700

Alghero, a picturesque medieval town, is the main resort on Sardinia's northwest coast. Interest is centred on the *centro storico,* a small tangle of tight-knit lanes and busy piazzas enclosed by robust honey-coloured sea walls.

The town was founded in the 11th century by the Genovese and later became an important outpost of the Aragonese Catalans. Still today the local dialect is a form of Catalan and the town retains something of a Spanish atmosphere.

Sights & Activities

If you're in town for a few days, consider the **A-ticket** (1 adult & child €20, 2 adults & children

€40), a discount card that covers admission to the Grotta di Nettuno, Nuraghe di Palmavera and various museums. It's available at the tourist office and participating sites.

Centro Storico NEIGHBOURHOOD

Alghero's medieval core is a charming mesh of narrow cobbled alleys hemmed in by Spanish Gothic *palazzi*. Of the various churches, the most interesting is the **Chiesa di San Francesco** (Via Carlo Alberto), with its mix of Romanesque and Gothic styles. A short walk away, the **campanile** (bell tower; ☎079 973 30 41; Via Principe Umberto; adult/child €2/free; ⊙10.30am-12.30pm Mon-Fri & 7-9pm Mon & Fri Jun-Aug, 10.30am-12.30pm Mon, Tue, Thu, Fri & 4-6pm Mon & Fri Sep-Oct, on request Nov-May) of the **Cattedrale di Santa Maria** (Piazza Duomo; ⊙7am-noon & 5-7.30pm) is a fine example of Gothic-Catalan architecture.

For lovely sea views, walk the town's honey-coloured **ramparts** from Piazza Sulis to the **Bastioni della Maddalena**, the only remnant of the town's former land battlements.

Grotta di Nettuno CAVE

(☎079 94 65 40; adult/child €13/7; ⊙9am-7pm May-Sep, to 6pm Apr-Oct, to 3pm Nov-Mar) From the port you can take a boat trip along the impressive northern coast to the grandiose Grotta di Nettuno cave complex. The cheapest boat is the Navisarda ferry (adult/child return €15/8), which departs hourly between 9.30am and 5.30pm from June to September, and twice daily between March and May and in October. Cheaper still, you can get a bus to the caves from Via Catalogna (€4.50 return, 50 minutes, three times daily summer, once winter).

Nuraghe di Palmavera RUIN

(admission €3; ⊙9am-7pm May-Sep, to 6pm Apr & Oct, 10am-2pm Nov-Mar) Ten kilometres west of Alghero, this 3500-year-old *nuraghe* village is well worth a visit.

Sleeping

There's plenty of accommodation in Alghero but you'll need to book between June and September.

TOP CHOICE **Angedras Hotel** HOTEL €€

(☎079 973 50 34; www.angedras.it; Via Frank 2; s €60-130, d €65-150; ❄📶) A model of white-washed Mediterranean style, the Angedras (Sardegna backwards) has cool white-tiled rooms with big French doors opening onto sunny patios. Note that it's a good 15-minute walk from the *centro storico*.

Hotel San Francesco HOTEL €

(☎079 98 03 30; www.sanfrancescohotel.com; Via Ambrogio Machin 2; s €52-63, d €82-101, tr €110-135; ❄@📶) This welcoming three-star is the only hotel in Alghero's *centro storico*. Housed in an ex-convent – monks still live on the 3rd floor – it has modest, comfortable rooms set around an attractive 14th-century cloister where summer concerts are sometimes staged.

Eating

Angedras Restaurant SARDINIAN €€

(☎079 973 50 78; www.angedrasrestaurant.it; Bastioni Marco Polo 41; mains €14, lunch menu €16) Alghero's sea-facing ramparts set a memorable stage for alfresco dining. This is one of the better restaurants on the walls, serving a largely regional menu of pasta, meat and elegantly presented seafood.

Gelateria I Bastioni GELATERIA €

(Bastioni Marco Polo 5; cones €1-3, milkshakes €3.50, granite €2.50; ⊙Apr-Oct) Homemade ice creams, creamy milkshakes, lush smoothies and cooling *granite* – this hole-in-the-wall gem does the lot. Particularly fab are the fresh fruit flavours, ideally topped by a generous squirt of whipped cream.

Il Ghiotto FAST FOOD €

(☎079 97 48 20; Piazza Civica 23; mains €8) Part bar, part canteen, part shop, the Ghiotto is ideal for a cheap and cheerful fill-up. Grab a tray and stock up from the tantalising spread of panini, pastas, salads and main courses. There's seating in a dining area behind the main hall or outside on a busy wooden terrace.

Information

On the eastern fringe of the *centro storico*, the superhelpful **tourist office** (☎079 97 90 54; www.comune.alghero.ss.it; Piazza Porta Terra 9; ⊙8am-8pm, closed Sun winter) can answer every imaginable question.

Getting There & Around

Alghero's **Fertilia airport** (☎079 93 52 82; www.aeroportodialghero.it) is used by a number of low-cost carriers, with connections to mainland Italy and destinations across Europe. To get into town take the hourly bus (€1, on board €1.50, 20 minutes) to the bus terminus on Via Cagliari.

In town you can walk most places, but for the beach, local bus AF runs along the seafront to/from Via Cagliari.

UNDERSTAND ITALY

History

Despite having an ancient history, Italy is actually a very young country. It only came into being with Italian unification in 1861; until then the Italian peninsula had been a complex patchwork of often warring empires, city states and maritime republics.

The Etruscans & Greeks

Of the many Italic tribes that emerged from the Stone Age, the Etruscans left the most enduring mark. By the 7th century BC their city states – places such as Caere (modern-day Cerveteri) and Tarquinii (Tarquinia) – were the dominant forces in central Italy, important Mediterranean powers rivalled only by the Greeks on the south coast. Greek traders had been settling in Italy since the 8th century BC and over the centuries had founded a number of independent city states, collectively known as Magna Graecia. Despite Etruscan attempts to conquer the Greeks, both groups thrived until the 3rd century BC, when legionnaires from the emerging city of Rome began to expand their territory and power.

Rise & Fall of Rome

Rome's origins are mired in myth. Romantics hold that the city was founded by Romulus in 753 BC on the site where he and his twin brother Remus had been suckled by a she-wolf. Few historians accept this as fact, although they acknowledge the existence of a settlement on Palatine Hill dating to the 8th century BC and it is generally accepted that Romulus was the first of Rome's seven kings. The last king, the Etruscan Tarquinius Superbus, was ousted in 509 BC, paving the way for the creation of the Roman Republic.

The fledgling republic got off to a shaky start but soon found its feet and by the 2nd century BC had seen off all its main rivals – the Etruscans, Greeks and Carthaginians – to become the undisputed master of the Western world. The republic's most famous leader was Julius Caesar, a gifted general and ambitious politician whose lust for power eventually proved his, and the republic's, undoing. His assassination on the Ides of March (15 March) in 44 BC sparked a power struggle between his chosen successor and great-nephew Octavian and Mark Antony, talented soldier and the lover of Egyptian queen, Cleopatra. Octavian prevailed and in 27 BC became Augustus, Rome's first emperor.

Augustus ruled well and Rome flourished, reaching its zenith in the 2nd century AD. Unfortunately, the same can't be said for his crazy successors Caligula and Nero. By the 3rd century, economic decline and the spread of Christianity were fuelling discontent. Diocletian tried to stop the rot by splitting the empire into eastern and western halves, but when his successor, Constantine (the first Christian emperor), moved his court to Constantinople, Rome's days were numbered. Sacked by the Goths in 410 and plundered by the Vandals in 455, the Western Empire finally fell in 476.

From the Renaissance to the Risorgimento

The Middle Ages in Italy was a period of almost constant warfare. While the Papal States fought the Holy Roman Empire for control over Europe's Catholics, the French and Spanish battled over southern Italy, and Italy's prosperous northern city states struggled for territorial gain. Eventually Milan, Venice and Florence (the latter under the powerful Medici family) emerged as regional powers. Against this fractious background, art and culture thrived. In the latter half of the 15th century, the Renaissance emerged in Florence. A sweeping intellectual and artistic movement, it soon spread south to Rome before snowballing into a Europe-wide phenomenon.

By the end of the 16th century most of Italy was in foreign hands – the Spanish in the south and the Austrians in the north. Three centuries later, Napoleon's brief Italian interlude gave rise to the Risorgimento (unification movement). With Count Cavour providing the political vision and Garibaldi the military muscle, the movement culminated in the 1861 unification of Italy under King Vittorio Emanuele. In 1870 Rome was wrested from the papacy and became Italy's capital.

Fascism, WWII & the Italian Republic

Following a meteoric rise to power, Benito Mussolini became Italy's leader in 1925, six years after he had founded his Fascist Party. Invoking Rome's imperial past, Mussolini embarked on a disastrous invasion of Abyssinia (modern-day Ethiopia) and in 1940 entered WWII on Germany's side. Three years later, after the Allies invaded Sicily, his nation rebelled: King Vittorio Emanuele III had Mussolini arrested and Italy surrendered soon after. Mussolini was killed by Italian partisans in April 1945.

In the aftermath of the war Italy voted to abolish the monarchy, declaring itself a constitutional republic in 1946.

A founding member of the European Economic Community, Italy enjoyed a largely successful postwar period. Consistent economic growth survived domestic terrorism in the 1970s and continued well into the 1980s.

The Berlusconi Era

The 1990s heralded a period of crisis. In 1992 a minor bribery investigation ballooned into a nationwide corruption scandal known as Tangentopoli ('kickback city'). Top business figures were imprisoned and the main political parties were reduced to tatters, creating a power vacuum into which billionaire media mogul Silvio Berlusconi deftly stepped. A controversial and deeply divisive figure, Berlusconi dominated Italian public life from his first foray into government in 1994 until he was forced out of office in 2011 amid a severe national economic downturn. Economist Mario Monti took over as prime minister and committed to an agenda of economic reform, but his tenure was built on an unstable alliance with Berlusconi's People of Freedom party. Elections in February 2013 saw Berlusconi's bid to regain overall power fail, but the outcome was far from decisive, with the centre-left Democratic Party (PD) gaining a majority in the lower house, the PDL gaining a majority in the upper house, and the maverick Five Star Movement led by satirist Beppe Grillo gaining the highest overall vote (25.5%). After a two-month stalemate, the PD and PDL formed an uneasy parliamentary alliance, installing the PD's Enrico Letta as prime minister and Angelino Alfano from the PDL as deputy prime minister.

People

With a population of 60.62 million, Italy is Europe's fourth-most populous country after Germany, France and the UK. Almost half of all Italians live in the industrialised north and one in five is aged over 65 years. At the other end of the age scale, Italy is dragging its heels. The country has one of the world's lowest birth rates (0.38%, or an average of 1.4 children for every mother) and, were it not for immigration, the Italian population would be in decline. Foreign residents now constitute 7.5% of Italy's population.

Traditionally, Italians are very conscious of their regional identity and very family oriented. Times are changing, but it is still common for Italian children to remain at home until they marry.

For a fascinating portrait of Italy's people and its national character, read Luigi Barzini's 1964 book *The Italians*.

Religion

Up to 80% of Italians consider themselves Catholic, although only about one in three regularly attends church. Similarly, the Vatican remains a powerful voice in national debate, but can't find enough priests for its parish churches. Still, first Communions, church weddings and regular feast days remain an integral part of Italian life.

There are no official figures but it's estimated that there are up to 1.5 million Muslims in Italy, making Islam Italy's second and fastest-growing religion. Italy also has small but well-established Orthodox, Protestant and Jewish communities.

Arts

Literature

Italian literature runs the gamut from Virgil's *Aeneid* to the chilling WWII stories of Primo Levi, the fantastical writings of Italo Calvino and the powerful contemporary writing of Niccolò Ammaniti, author of *Io non ho paura* (I'm Not Scared; 2001).

Dante, whose *Divina commedia* (Divine Comedy) dates to the early 1300s, was one of three 14th-century greats alongside Petrarch and Giovanni Boccaccio. The latter is considered the first Italian novelist.

Italy's southern regions provide rich literary pickings. Giuseppe Tomasi di Lampedusa depicts Sicily's melancholic resignation in *Il gattopardo* (The Leopard; 1958), a theme that Leonardo Sciascia later returns to in *Il giorno della civetta* (The Day of the Owl; 1961). Carlo Levi denounces southern poverty in *Cristo si é fermato a Eboli* (Christ Stopped at Eboli; 1945), an account of his internal exile under the Fascists, and more recently, Andrea Camilleri's Sicilian-based Montalbano detective stories have enjoyed great success. *The Shape of Water* (1994) is the first title in the series.

ITALY ON SCREEN

A few films that are sure to whet your appetite for an Italian vacation:

» *Il Postino* (1994) – spectacular Aeolian Island scenery sets the stage for this heart-breaking tale of thwarted dreams.

» *Room with a View* (1985) – dreamy shots of Florence and some great performances in a Merchant Ivory treatment of EM Forster's novel of the same name.

» *Cinema Paradiso* (1988) – bittersweet tale about a successful film director who returns to his home village in Sicily for a funeral, triggering memories of his early years.

» *Roman Holiday* (1953) – Gregory Peck and Audrey Hepburn give great performances, but director William Wyler hands the starring role to the Eternal City itself.

» *Pane e Tulipani* (2000) – an eccentric, feel-good romance set in Venice.

Cinema

The influence of Italian cinema goes well beyond its success at the box office. In creating the spaghetti western Sergio Leone inspired generations of film-makers, as did horror master Dario Argento and art-house genius Michelangelo Antonioni.

Italy has won more Academy Awards for Best Foreign-Language Film than any other country. Many of the winning films were made during the post-WWII period, when the neo-realists Vittorio de Sica and Roberto Rossellini created masterpieces such as *Ladri di biciclette* (Bicycle Thieves; 1948) and *Roma città aperta* (Rome Open City; 1945).

Taking a decidedly different turn, Federico Fellini created his own highly visual style and won an international audience with films such as *La dolce vita* (The Sweet Life; 1959). His contemporary Lucino Visconti made films melding extraordinary visual beauty and powerful narrative; these include *Morte a Venezia* (Death in Venice; 1961) and his masterpiece, *Il Gattopardo* (The Leopard; 1963).

Of Italy's notable contemporary directors, Roberto Benigni won an Oscar for *La vita è bella* (Life is Beautiful; 1997), Nanni Moretti won Cannes' Palme D'Or for *La stanza del figlio* (The Son's Room; 2001) and brothers Paolo and Vittorio Taviani won the Palme D'Or for *Padre padrone* (Father and Master; 1971) and the Golden Bear at Berlin for *Cesare deve morire* (Ceasar Must Die; 2012).

Music

Emotional and highly theatrical, opera has always appealed to Italians. Performances of Verdi and Puccini are regularly staged at legendary theatres such as Milan's Teatro alla Scala and Naples' Teatro San Carlo.

On the classical front, Antonio Vivaldi (1675–1741) created the concerto in its present form and wrote *Le quattro stagione* (The Four Seasons). In more recent times, pop singer Eros Ramazzotti and operatic tenor Andrea Bocelli have enjoyed considerable international success.

Architecture & Visual Arts

Italy is littered with architectural and artistic reminders of the country's convoluted history. Etruscan tombs at Tarquinia and Greek temples at Agrigento tell of glories long past, while Pompeii's skeletal ruins offer insights into the day-to-day life of ancient Romans, and Byzantine mosaics in Ravenna, Venice and Palermo reveal influences sweeping in from the East.

The Renaissance left an indelible mark, particularly in Florence and Rome. This was the period when Filippo Brunelleschi designed and oversaw construction of the Duomo's huge dome and Michelangelo swept aside all convention in his Sistine Chapel decoration. Contemporaries Leonardo da Vinci and Raphael further enriched the scene.

Controversial and highly influential, Michelangelo Merisi da Caravaggio dominated the late 16th century with his revolutionary use of light. He painted in Rome and in the south of the country; both destinations where the baroque style of art and architecture became prominent in the 17th-century.

Signalling a return to sober classical lines, neoclassicism majored in the late 18th and early 19th centuries. Its most famous Italian exponent was Canova, who carved a name for himself with his smooth, sensual style.

In sharp contrast to backward-looking neoclassicism, Italian futurism provided a rallying cry for modernism, with Giacomo Balla proving hugely influential.

Continuing in this modernist tradition are Italy's two superstar architects: Renzo

Piano, the visionary behind Rome's Auditorium, and Rome-born Massimiliano Fuksas.

Environment

Bound on three sides by four seas (the Adriatic, Ligurian, Tyrrhenian and Ionian), Italy has more than 8000km of coastline. Inland, about 75% of the peninsula is mountainous – the Alps curve around the northern border and the Apennines extend down the boot.

The peninsula and its surrounding seas harbour a rich fauna. You're unlikely to spot them but there are bears, wolves and wildcats in the national parks of central Italy, as well as over 150 types of bird. Swordfish, tuna and dolphins are common along the coastline, and although white sharks are known to exist, attacks are rare.

Italy has 24 national parks, covering about 5% of the country, and more than 400 nature reserves, natural parks and wetlands. It also boasts 47 Unesco World Heritage sites, more than any other country in the world.

EARTHQUAKES & VOLCANOES

Italy is one of the world's most earthquake-prone countries. A fault line runs through the entire peninsula – from eastern Sicily, up the Apennines and into the northeastern Alps. The country is usually hit by minor quakes several times a year and devastating earthquakes are not uncommon in central and southern Italy. The most recent, measuring 6.3 on the Richter scale, struck the central region of Abruzzo on 6 April 2009, killing 295 people and leaving up to 55,000 homeless.

Italy also has six active volcanoes: Stromboli and Vulcano in the Aeolian Islands; Vesuvius, the Campi Flegrei and the island of Ischia near Naples; and Etna on Sicily. Stromboli and Etna are among the world's most active volcanoes, while Vesuvius has not erupted since 1944.

Environmental Issues

The three most insidious environmental issues affecting Italy are air pollution, waste disposal and coastal development. Heavy industry and high levels of car ownership have combined to produce dense smog and poor air quality. This affects many Italian cities but is especially widespread in the industrialised north.

Inadequate waste disposal is another major cause of pollution, particularly in Naples, where the sight of rubbish rotting on the streets has become sadly familiar. At the heart of the problem lies a chronic lack of facilities – there are insufficient incinerators to burn the refuse and the landfill sites that do exist are generally full, often with waste dumped illegally by organised crime outfits.

Italy's coast has been subject to almost continuous development since the boom in beach tourism in the 1960s. While this has undoubtedly brought short-term advantages, it has also put a great strain on natural resources.

Food & Drink

Despite the ubiquity of pasta and pizza, Italian cuisine is highly regional. Local specialities abound and regional traditions are proudly maintained, so expect pesto in Genoa, pizza in Naples and *ragù* (bolognese sauce) in Bologna. It's the same with wine – Piedmont produces Italy's great reds, Barolo, Barbaresco and Dolcetto, while Tuscany is famous for its Chianti, Vino Nobile di Montepulciano, Brunello di Montalcino and Vernaccia di San Gimignano.

Vegetarians will find delicious fruit and veg in the hundreds of daily markets, and although few restaurants cater specifically to vegetarians, most serve vegetable-based antipasti (starters), pastas, *contorni* (side dishes) and salads.

Where to Eat & Drink

The most basic sit-down eatery is a *tavola calda* (literally 'hot table'), which offers canteen-style food. Pizzerias, the best of which have a *forno a legna* (wood-fired oven), often serve a full menu as well as pizzas. For takeaway, a *rosticceria* sells cooked meats and a *pizza al taglio* joint sells pizza by the slice.

For wine, make for an *enoteca* (wine bar), many of which also serve light snacks and a few hot dishes. Alternatively, most bars and cafes serve *tramezzini* (sandwiches) and panini (bread rolls). A cheaper option is to go to an *alimentari* (delicatessen) and ask them to make a panino with the filling of your choice. At a *pasticceria* you can buy pastries, cakes and biscuits. *Forni* (bakeries) are another good choice for a cheap snack.

For a full meal you'll want a trattoria or a *ristorante*. Traditionally, trattorias were family-run places that served a basic menu of local dishes at affordable prices and thankfully, a few still are. *Ristoranti* offer more choice and smarter service.

Restaurants, all of which are nonsmoking, usually open for lunch from noon to 3pm and for dinner from 7.30pm (earlier in tourist areas).

On the bill expect to be charged for *pane e coperto* (bread and a cover charge). This is standard and is added even if you don't ask for or eat the bread. Typically it ranges from €1 to €4. *Servizio* (service charge) of 10% to 15% might or might not be included; if it's not, tourists are expected to leave around 10% tip.

Habits & Customs

A full Italian meal consists of an antipasto, a *primo* (first course; pasta or rice dish), *secondo* (second/main course; usually meat or fish), an *insalata* (salad) or *contorno* (vegetable side dish), *dolci* (dessert) and coffee, though most Italians will only eat a meal this large at Sunday lunch or for special occasions. When eating out it's perfectly acceptable to mix and match any combination and order, say, a *primo* followed by an *insalata* or *contorno*.

Italians don't tend to eat a sit-down *colazione* (breakfast), preferring instead a cappuccino and *cornetto* (pastry filled with custard, chocolate or jam) at a bar. *Pranzo* (lunch) was traditionally the main meal of the day, although many people now have a light lunch and bigger *cena* (dinner). Italians are late diners, often not eating until after 9pm.

SURVIVAL GUIDE

Directory A–Z

Accommodation

The bulk of Italy's accommodation is made up of *alberghi* (hotels) and *pensioni* – often housed in converted apartments. Other options are youth hostels, camping grounds, B&Bs, *agriturismi* (farm-stays), mountain *rifugi* (Alpine refuges), monasteries and villa/apartment rentals.

Prices fluctuate enormously between the high, shoulder and low seasons. High-season rates apply at Easter, in summer (mid-June to August), and over the Christmas to New Year period.

The north of Italy is generally more expensive than the south.

Many city-centre hotels offer discounts in August to lure clients from the crowded coast. Check hotel websites for last-minute offers.

Most hotels in coastal resorts shut for winter, typically from November to March. The same applies to *agriturismi* and villa rentals in rural areas.

PRICE RANGES

In this chapter prices quoted are the minimum-maximum for rooms with a private bathroom, and unless otherwise stated include breakfast. The following price indicators apply (for a high-season double room):

€€€ more than €200

€€ €110 to €200

€ less than €110

HOTEL TAX

Since early 2011 a number of Italian cities, including Rome, Florence and Venice, have introduced a hotel occupancy tax *(tassa di soggiorno)*. This is charged on top of your regular hotel bill and must sometimes be paid in cash. The exact amount, which varies from city to city, depends on your type of accommodation, but as a rough guide expect to pay €1 per night in a one-star hotel or hostel, €2 in a B&B, €2 to €3 in a three-star hotel etc.

Note that prices quoted in this book do not include the tax.

B&BS

There's a huge number of bed and breakfasts (B&Bs) across the country. Quality varies, but the best offer comfort greater than you'd get in a similarly priced hotel room.

Prices are typically €70 to €180 for a double room.

CAMPING

Campers are well catered for in Italy.

Lists of camping grounds are available from local tourist offices or online at www.campeggi.com, www.camping.it and www.italcamping.it.

In high season expect to pay up to €20 per person and a further €25 for a tent pitch.

Independent camping is not permitted in many places.

CONVENTS & MONASTERIES

Basic accommodation is often available in convents and monasteries. See www.monasterystays.com, a specialist online booking service.

FARM-STAYS

An *agriturismo* (farm-stay) is a good option for a country stay, although you will usually need your own transport to access these.

Accommodation varies from spartan billets on working farms to palatial suites at luxurious rural retreats.

For information and lists check out www.agriturist.it or www.agriturismo.com.

HOSTELS

Official HI-affiliated *ostelli per la gioventù* (youth hostels) are run by the **Italian Youth Hostel Association** (Associazione Italiana Alberghi per la Gioventù; Map p748; ☎06 487 11 52; www.aighostels.com; Via Cavour 44). A valid HI card is required for these; you can get one in your home country or directly at hostels.

There are many privately run hostels offering dorms and private rooms.

Dorm rates are typically between €15 and €30, with breakfast usually included.

REFUGES

Italy boasts an extensive network of mountain *rifugi*.

Open from July to September, refuges offer basic dorm-style accommodation, although some larger ones have double rooms.

Reckon on €20 to €30 per person per night with breakfast included.

Further information is available from the **Club Alpino Italiano** (CAI; www.cai.it), which owns and runs many of the refuges.

Activities

Cycling Tourist offices can provide details on trails and guided rides. The best time is spring. Lonely Planet's *Cycling in Italy* offers practical tips and several detailed itineraries.

Diving There are hundreds of schools offering courses and guided dives for all levels.

Hiking & Walking Thousands of kilometres of *sentieri* (marked trails) criss-cross Italy; the hiking season is June to September. Useful websites include www.cai.it and www.parks.it. Lonely Planet's *Hiking in Italy* includes descriptions of 59 hikes.

Skiing Italy's ski season runs from December to March. Prices are generally high, particularly in the top Alpine resorts; the Apennines are cheaper. The best way to save money is to buy a *settimana bianca* (literally 'white week') package deal, covering seven days' accommodation, food and ski passes.

Business Hours

In this chapter, opening hours are provided in Information, Eating, Drinking, Entertainment and Shopping sections when they differ from the following standard hours:

Banks 8.30am-1.30pm & 3-4.30pm Mon-Fri

Bars & Cafes 7.30am-8pm; many open earlier and some stay open until the small hours; pubs often open noon-2am

Discos & Clubs 10pm-4am

Pharmacies 9am-1pm & 4-7.30pm Mon-Fri, to 1pm Sat; outside of these hours, pharmacies open on a rotation basis – all are required to post a list of places open in the vicinity

Post offices Major offices 8am-7pm Mon-Fri, to 1.15pm Sat; branch offices 8.30am-2pm Mon-Fri, to 1pm Sat

Restaurants noon-3pm & 7.30-11pm or midnight; most restaurants close one day a week

Shops 9am-1pm & 3.30-7.30pm, or 4-8pm Mon-Sat; in larger cities many chain stores and supermarkets open from 9am to 7.30pm Mon-Sat; some also open Sun morning, typically 9am -1pm; food shops are generally closed Thu afternoon; some other shops are closed Mon morning

Many museums, galleries and archaeological sites operate summer and winter opening hours. Typically, winter hours will apply between November and late March or early April.

Embassies

The following embassies are based in Rome.

Australian Embassy (☎06 85 27 21; www.italy.embassy.gov.au; Via Antonio Bosio 5)

New Zealand Embassy (☎06 853 75 01; rome@nzembassy.it; Via Clitunno 44)

UK Embassy (☎06 422 00 001; http://ukinitaly.fco.gov.uk/en/; Via XX Settembre 80a)

US Embassy (☎06 4 67 41; italy.usembassy.gov; Via Vittorio Veneto 121)

Food

Throughout this chapter, the following price indicators have been used (prices refer to the cost of a main course):

€€€ more than €18

€€ €10 to €18

€ less than €10

Gay & Lesbian Travellers

Homosexuality is legal in Italy, but same-sex couples have no shared rights to property, social security and inheritance. There is a push to legalise gay marriage, but this seems unlikely in the near future.

Homosexuality is well tolerated in major cities but overt displays of affection could attract a negative response, particularly in small towns and in the more conservative south.

Italy's main gay and lesbian organisation is **Arcigay** (www.arcigay.it), based in Bologna.

Internet Access

Most hotels, hostels, B&Bs and *pensioni* offer wi-fi, either free or for a daily charge.

The icon in accommodation reviews means wi-fi is available. An @ icon denotes availability of a computer for guest use.

Access is also available in internet cafes throughout the country, although many have closed in recent years. Charges are typically around €5 per hour.

To use internet points in Italy you must present photo ID.

Money

Italy's currency is the euro.

ATMs, known in Italy as *bancomat,* are widespread and will accept cards displaying the appropriate sign. Visa and MasterCard are widely recognised, as are Cirrus and Maestro; American Express is less common. If you don't have a PIN, some, but not all, banks will advance cash over the counter.

Credit cards are widely accepted, although many small trattorias, pizzerias and *pensioni* only take cash. Don't assume museums, galleries and the like accept credit cards.

If your credit/debit card is lost, stolen or swallowed by an ATM, telephone toll-free to block it: **Amex** (06 729 00 347); **MasterCard** (800 870866); and **Visa** (800 819014).

ADMISSION PRICES

EU citizens aged between 18 and 25 years and students from countries with reciprocal arrangements generally qualify for a discount (usually half-price) at galleries and museums. EU citizens who are under 18 and over 65 often get in free. In all cases you'll need proof of your age, ideally a passport or ID card.

Post

Italy's postal system, **Poste Italiane** (803 160; www.poste.it), is reasonably reliable.

The standard service is *posta prioritaria.* Registered mail is known as *posta raccomandata,* insured mail as *posta assicurato.*

Francobolli (stamps) are available at post offices and *tabacchi* (tobacconists) – look for a big white 'T' against a blue/black background. Tobacconists keep regular shop hours.

Public Holidays

Most Italians take their annual holiday in August. This means that many businesses and shops close down for at least a part of the month, usually around Ferragosto (15 August). Easter is another busy holiday.

Public holidays:

New Year's Day (Capodanno) 1 January

Epiphany (Epifania) 6 January

Anniversary of the Unification of Italy (Anniversario dell'Unità d'Italia) 17 March

Easter Monday (Pasquetta) March/April

Liberation Day (Giorno delle Liberazione) 25 April

Labour Day (Festa del Lavoro) 1 May

Republic Day (Festa della Repubblica) 2 June

Feast of the Assumption (Ferragosto) 15 August

All Saints' Day (Ognisanti) 1 November

Day of National Unity and the Armed Forces (Giornata dell'Unità Nazionale e delle Forze Armate) 4 November

Feast of the Immaculate Conception (Immacolata Concezione) 8 December

Christmas Day (Natale) 25 December

Boxing Day (Festa di Santo Stefano) 26 December

Individual towns also have holidays to celebrate their patron saints:

St Mark (Venice) 25 April

St John the Baptist (Florence, Genoa and Turin) 24 June

Sts Peter and Paul (Rome) 29 June

St Rosalia (Palermo) 15 July

St Janarius (Naples) First Sunday in May, 19 September and 16 December

St Ambrose (Milan) 7 December

Safe Travel

Petty theft is prevalent in Italy. Be on your guard against pickpockets and moped thieves in popular tourist centres such as Rome, Florence and Venice, and especially in Naples.

Don't take it for granted that cars will stop at red lights.

Telephone

Area codes are an integral part of all Italian phone numbers and must be dialled even when calling locally. The area codes have been listed in telephone numbers throughout this chapter.

To call Italy from abroad, dial ☎0039 and then the area code, including the first zero.

To call abroad from Italy, dial ☎00, then the relevant country code followed by the telephone number.

To make a reverse-charge (collect) international call, dial ☎170. All operators speak English.

You'll find cut-price call centres in all of the main cities. For international calls, their rates are often cheaper than at payphones.

Skype is available in many internet cafes and on hostel computers.

MOBILE PHONES

Italy uses the GSM 900/1800 network, which is compatible with the rest of Europe and Australia, but not with the North American GSM 1900 or the Japanese system (although some GSM 1900/900 phones do work here).

If you have a GSM dual- or tri-band cellular phone that you can unlock (check with your service provider), you can buy a *prepagato* (prepaid) SIM card in Italy.

Companies offering SIM cards include **TIM** (Telecom Italia Mobile; www.tim.it), **Wind** (www.wind.it) and **Vodafone** (www.vodafone.it). You'll need ID to open an account.

PHONE CODES

Italy's country code is ☎39.

Mobile phone numbers begin with a three-digit prefix starting with a 3.

Toll-free (free-phone) numbers are known as *numeri verdi* and start with 800. These are not always available if calling from a mobile phone.

PHONECARDS

To phone from a public payphone you'll need a *scheda telefonica* (telephone card; €3, €5). Buy these at post offices, *tabacchi* and newsstands.

Tourist Information

For pre-trip information, check out the website of the **Ministro del Turismo** (www.italia.it). The ministry also runs a multilingual telephone information service, **Easy Italy** (☎039 039 039; ⊙9am-10pm).

Tourist offices in Italy are listed throughout this chapter.

Travellers with Disabilities

Italy is not an easy country for travellers with disabilities. Cobbled streets, blocked pavements and tiny lifts all make life difficult. Rome-based **Consorzio Cooperative Integrate** (COIN; ☎06 712 90 11; www.coinsociale.it) is the best point of reference for travellers with disabilities.

If you're travelling by train, **Trenitalia** (www.trenitalia.com) runs a telephone info line (☎199 30 30 60) with details of assistance available at stations.

Visas

Schengen visa rules apply for entry to Italy.

Unless staying in a hotel/B&B/hostel etc, all foreign visitors are supposed to register with the police within eight days of arrival.

Non-EU citizens who want to study in Italy must obtain a study visa from their nearest Italian embassy or consulate.

A *permesso di soggiorno* (permit to stay) is required by all non-EU nationals who stay in Italy longer than three months. You must apply within eight days of arriving in Italy. Check the exact documentary requirements on www.poliziadistato.it.

EU citizens do not require a *permesso di soggiorno*.

Getting There & Away

Getting to Italy is straightforward. It is well served by Europe's low-cost carriers and there are plenty of bus, train and ferry routes into the country. Flights, tours and rail tickets can be booked online at lonelyplanet.com/bookings.

Air

There are direct intercontinental flights to/from Rome and Milan. European flights also serve regional airports.

Italy's main international airports:

Rome Leonardo da Vinci (☎06 6 59 51; www.adr.it/fiumicino) Italy's main airport, also known as Fiumicino.

Milan Malpensa (☎02 23 23 23; www.milanomalpensa1.eu/it) Milan's principal airport.

Rome Ciampino (☎06 6 59 51; www.adr.it/ciampino) Rome's second airport. Hub for Ryanair flights.

Pisa International Airport Galileo Galilei (☎050 84 93 00; www.pisa-airport.com) Main gateway for Florence and Tuscany.

Venice Marco Polo (☎041 260 92 60; www.veniceairport.i

Cagliari Elmas (☎070 21 12 11; www.cagliariairport.it) Sardinia's main airport.

Naples Capodichino (☎081 789 61 11; www.gesac.it)

Catania Fontanarossa (☎095 723 91 11; www.aeroporto.catania.it) Sicily's busiest airport.

Italy's national carrier is **Alitalia** (☎89 20 10; www.alitalia.com).

Land

BORDER CROSSINGS

Italy borders France, Switzerland, Austria and Slovenia. The main points of entry:

From France The coast road from Nice; the Mont Blanc tunnel from Chamonix.

From Switzerland The Grand St Bernard tunnel; the Simplon tunnel; the Lötschberg Base tunnel.

From Austria The Brenner Pass.

BUS

Eurolines (www.eurolines.com) operates buses from European destinations to many Italian cities.

CAR & MOTORCYCLE

If traversing the Alps, note that border crossings from the Brenner Pass, Grand St Bernard tunnel, Simplon tunnel and Lötschberg Base tunnel are open year-round. Other mountain passes are often closed in winter and sometimes even in spring and autumn. Make sure you have snow chains in your car.

TRAIN

Direct international trains connect with various cities:

Milan To/from Paris, Basel, Lugano, Geneva and Zürich.

Rome To/from Munich

Venice To/from Paris, Munich, Geneva, Innsbruck.

There are also international trains from Verona, Padua, Bologna and Florence. Get details at www.trenitalia.com.

In the UK, the **Rail Europe Travel Centre** (☎0844 848 40 78; www.raileurope.co.uk) can provide fare information on journeys to/from Italy, most of which require a change at Paris. Another excellent resource is www.seat61.com.

Eurail and Inter-Rail passes are both valid in Italy.

Sea

Dozens of ferry companies connect Italy with other Mediterranean countries. Timetables are seasonal, so always check ahead – you'll find details of routes, companies and online booking at www.traghettiweb.it.

MAIN INTERNATIONAL FERRY ROUTES

FROM	TO	COMPANY	MIN-MAX FARE (€)	DURATION (HR)
Ancona	Igoumenitsa	Minoan, Superfast	75-111	16
Ancona	Patra	Minoan, Superfast	75-111	15½-22
Ancona	Split	Jadrolinija, SNAV	46-63	4½-11
Bari	Igoumenitsa	Superfast	78-93	8-12
Bari	Patra	Superfast	78-93	16
Bari	Dubrovnik	Jadrolinija	46-63	10-12
Bari	Bar	Montenegro	50-55	9
Brindisi	Igoumenitsa	Endeavor, Agoudimos	48-83	8
Brindisi	Patra	Endeavor	56-94	14
Brindisi	Corfu	Endeavor, Agoudimos	48-83	6½-11½
Brindisi	Kefallonia	Endeavor	56-94	12½
Genoa	Barcelona	GNV, SNAV	95	19½
Genoa	Tunis	GNV, SNAV	99	23½

Prices quoted here are for a one-way *poltrona* (reclinable seat). Holders of Eurail and InterRail passes should check with the ferry company if they are entitled to a discount or free passage.

Major ferry companies:

Agoudimos (www.agoudimos-lines.com)

Endeavor Lines (www.endeavor-lines.com)

Grandi Navi Veloci (www.gnv.it)

Jadrolinija (www.jadrolinija.hr)

Minoan Lines (www.minoanlines.it)

Montenegro (www.montenegrolines.com)

SNAV (www.snav.it)

Superfast (www.superfast.com)

Tirrenia (www.tirrenia.it)

Getting Around

Air

Domestic flights serve most major Italian cities and the main islands (Sardinia and Sicily), but are expensive. Airlines serving national routes include:

Alitalia (☎89 20 10; www.alitalia.com)

Air One (☎89 24 44; www.flyairone.it)

Blu-Express (☎06 989 56 666; www.blu-express.com)

Meridiana (☎89 29 28; www.meridiana.it)

easyJet (☎199 20 18 40; www.easyjet.com)

Ryanair (☎899 55 25 89; www.ryanair.com)

Bicycle

» Tourist offices can generally provide details of designated bike trails and bike hire (at least €10 per day).

» Bikes can be taken on regional and international trains carrying the bike logo, but you'll need to pay a supplement (€3.50 on regional trains, €12 on international trains). Bikes can be carried free if dismantled and stored in a bike bag.

» Bikes generally incur a small supplement on ferries, typically €10 to €15.

Boat

Navi (large ferries) service Sicily and Sardinia; *traghetti* (smaller ferries) and *aliscafi* (hydrofoils) cover the smaller islands.

The main embarkation points for Sardinia are Genoa, Piombino, Livorno, Civitavecchia and Naples; for Sicily, it's Naples and Villa San Giovanni in Calabria.

The major domestic ferry companies:

Grandi Navi Veloci (☎010 209 45 91; www.gnv.it) To/from Sardinia and Sicily.

Moby (☎199 30 30 40; www.mobylines.it) To/from Sardinia and Sicily.

Sardinia Ferries (☎199 40 05 00; www.corsica-ferries.it) To/from Golfo Aranci (Sardinia).

SNAV (☎Ancona 071 207 61, Naples 081 428 55 55; www.snav.it) To/from Sardinia, Sicily, Aeolian Islands, Capri.

Tirrenia (☎89 21 23; www.tirrenia.it) To/from Sardinia and Sicily.

Bus

» Italy boasts an extensive and largely reliable bus network.

» Buses are not necessarily cheaper than trains, but in mountainous areas they are often the only choice.

» In larger cities, companies have ticket offices or operate through agencies but in most villages and small towns tickets are sold in bars or on the bus.

» Reservations are only necessary for high-season long-haul trips.

Car & Motorcycle

» Roads are generally good and there's an excellent system of autostradas (motorways).

» There's a toll to use most autostradas, payable in cash or by credit card at exit barriers.

» Autostradas are indicated by an A with a number (eg A1) on a green background; *strade statali* (main roads) are shown by an S or SS and number (eg SS7) against a blue background.

» Italy's motoring organisation **Automobile Club d'Italia** (ACI; www.aci.it; Via Colombo 261) provides 24-hour roadside assistance – call ☎803 116 from a landline or Italian mobile, ☎800 116 800 from a foreign mobile.

» Cars use unleaded petrol *(benzina senza piombo)* and diesel *(gasolio)*; both are expensive but diesel is slightly cheaper.

DRIVING LICENCES

All EU driving licences are recognised in Italy. Holders of non-EU licences must get an International Driving Permit (IDP) to accompany their national licence.

HIRE

To hire a car you must:

» have a valid driving licence (plus IDP if required)

» have had your licence for at least a year

» be 21 or over. Under-25s will often have to pay a young-driver's supplement on top of the usual rates

» have a credit card

Make sure you understand what is included in the price (unlimited kilometres, tax, insurance, collision damage waiver etc) and what your liabilities are. For the best rental rates, book your car before leaving home. Note also that most cars have manual gear transmission.

The most competitive agencies:

Avis (☎199 10 01 33; www.avis.com)

Budget (☎800 472 33 25; www.budget.com)

Europcar (☎199 30 70 30; www.europcar.com)

Hertz (☎199 11 22 11; www.hertz.com)

Italy by Car (☎091 639 31 20; www.italybycar.it)

Maggiore (☎199 15 11 20; www.maggiore.it)

You'll have no trouble hiring a scooter or motorcycle (provided you're over 18); there are agencies in all Italian cities. Rates start at about €30 a day for a 50cc scooter.

INSURANCE

If you're driving your own car, you'll need an international insurance certificate, known as a Carta Verde (Green Card), available from your insurance company.

ROAD RULES

» Drive on the right, overtake on the left and give way to cars coming from the right.

» It's obligatory to wear seatbelts, to drive with your headlights on when outside built-up areas, and to carry a warning triangle and fluorescent waistcoat in case of breakdown.

» Wearing a helmet is compulsory on all two-wheeled vehicles.

» The blood alcohol limit is 0.05% or zero for drivers who have had their licence for less than three years.

Unless otherwise indicated, speed limits are as follows:

» 130km/h (in rain 110km/h) on autostradas

» 110km/h (in rain 90km/h) on all main, non-urban roads

» 90km/h on secondary, non-urban roads

» 50km/h in built-up areas

Most major Italian cities operate a Limited Traffic Zone in their *centro storico*. You can enter a ZTL *(Zona a Traffico Limitato)* on a *motorino* (moped/scooter) but not in private or hire cars.

Train

Italy has an extensive rail network. Trains are relatively cheap, and many are fast and comfortable. Most services are run by **Trenitalia** (☎89 20 21; www.trenitalia.com) but as of April 2012 **Italo Treno** (☎06 07 08; www.italotreno.it) high-speed trains also connect Salerno, Naples, Rome, Florence, Bologna, Milan, Turin, Padua and Venice.

There are several types of train:

Frecciarossa Italy's fastest trains capable of 360km/h.

Frecciargento Slightly quicker than the Frecciabianca with a top speed of 250km/h.

Frecciabianca High-speed trains that run up to 200km/h.

Eurostar Italia (ES) Similar to InterCity but faster.

InterCity (IC) Trains between major cities.

Regionale or interregionale (R) Slow local services.

TICKETS

» Train prices quoted here are for the most common trains on any given route – that might be a slow Regionale train or a fast Frecciarossa.

» Regional trains are the cheapest.

» InterCity trains require a supplement, which is incorporated in the ticket price. If you have a standard ticket and board an InterCity you'll have to pay the difference on board.

» Eurostar and the Freccia trains require prior reservation.

» Generally, it's cheaper to buy all local train tickets in Italy.

» If your ticket doesn't include a reservation with an assigned seat, you must validate it before boarding by inserting it into one of the machines dotted around stations.

» Some services offer 'ticketless' travel – book and pay for your seat on www.trenitalia.com and then communicate your booking code to the controller on board.

» Children under four travel free; kids between four and 12 are entitled to discounts of between 30% and 50%.

The Netherlands

Includes »

Best Places to Eat

- » Blauw (p878)
- » De Dames Proeverij (p867)
- » De Ballentent (p875)
- » Gadjah Mas (p882)
- » Van Dobben (p859)

Best Places to Stay

- » Cocomama (p858)
- » Hotel de Emauspoort (p870)
- » Hotel New York (p874)
- » Kruisherenhotel (p881)
- » Stempels (p865)

Why Go?

Great Dutch artists Rembrandt, Vermeer and Van Gogh have spanned the centuries, and touring the Netherlands you'll see why. Discover clichés such as tulips and windmills, or stroll canals in the midst of 17th-century splendour in beautiful small towns such as Leiden and Delft. Of course, enticing Amsterdam's phenomenal and diverse nightlife is world-famous, from its throbbing clubs to quaint brown cafes.

The locals live on bicycles and you can too. Almost every train station has a shop to rent a bike – you'll soon be off on the ubiquitous bike paths, wherever your mood takes you.

Finally there's the Dutch themselves. Warm, friendly and funny, you'll have a hard time being alone in a cafe as someone will soon strike up a conversation, and usually in English. Revel in Amsterdam, don't miss exquisite Maastricht or pulsing Rotterdam, and pick a passel of small towns to add contrast. It's a very big small country.

When to Go

Amsterdam

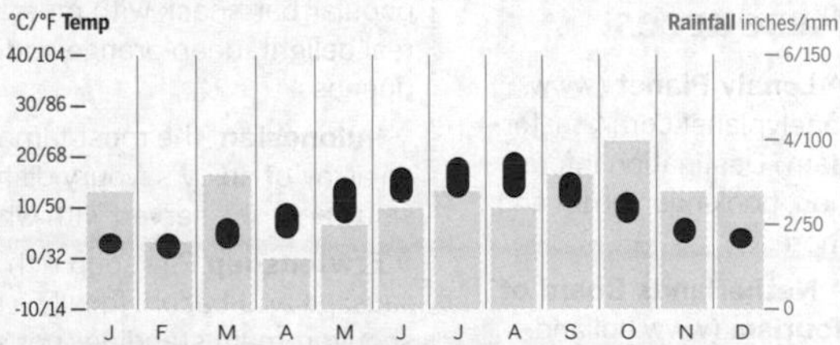

Mar–May Holland explodes in colour as billions of bulbs bloom.

Jul Mild summer temps and lots of daylight keep you outside cycling and drinking.

Dec–Feb The Dutch passion for ice skating is on display on canals nationwide.

AT A GLANCE

» **Currency** euro (€)

» **Language** Dutch, English widespread

» **Money** ATMs common, cash preferred for small purchases

» **Visas** Schengen rules apply

Fast Facts

» **Area** 41,526 sq km

» **Capital** Amsterdam

» **Country code** ☎31

» **Emergency** ☎112

Exchange Rates

Australia	A$1	€0.82
Canada	C$1	€0.77
Japan	¥100	€0.83
New Zealand	NZ$1	€0.65
UK	UK£1	€1.18
USA	US$1	€0.78

Set Your Budget

» **Double room** €80–150

» **Two-course meal** €15

» **Heineken** €3

» **Bicycle hire** €10 per day

Resources

» **Lonely Planet** (www.lonelyplanet.com/amsterdam) Destination information, bookings, forum and more.

» **Netherlands Board of Tourism** (www.holland.com) Comprehensive tourist information.

» **Windmill Database** (www.molendatabase.nl) Get the spin on windmills across the Netherlands.

Connections

Train connections to neighbouring countries are good. Amsterdam is linked to Cologne (2½ hours) and Brussels (two hours on the Thalys/Fyra high-speed line), where you can connect with Eurostar to London. Maastricht is right on the Belgian and German borders; connections to Cologne and Brussels take 1½ hours. It would be easy to put together a circle itinerary that includes the wines of the Moselle Valley in Germany and the beers of Belgium.

ITINERARIES

One Week

Spend three days canal exploring, museum hopping and cafe swooping in Amsterdam. Work your way through the ancient towns of the Randstad and the modern vibe of Rotterdam, and save a day for the grandeur of Maastricht.

Two Weeks

Allow four days for Amsterdam's many delights, plus a day trip to the old towns of the north, such as Edam, and a day or two exploring some of the region's smaller towns. Then add a day each at beautiful Delft, regal Hague, cute Utrecht, Rotterdam, and the monumental Delta Project. Finish off with two days in Maastricht.

Essential Food & Drink

» **Vlaamse frites** The iconic French fries smothered in mayonnaise or myriad other gooey sauces.

» **Beer** While the big names like Heineken are ubiquitous, small brewers like Gulpen, Haarlem's Jopen, Bavaria, Drie Ringen, Leeuw and Utrecht are the best.

» **Gouda** The tastiest varieties have strong, complex flavours and are best enjoyed with a bottle of wine or two. Try some *oud* (old) Gouda, hard and rich in flavour and a popular bar snack with mustard. *Oud Amsterdammer* is a real delight, deep orange and crumbly with white crystals of ripeness.

» **Indonesian** The most famous dish is *rijsttafel* (rice table): an array of spicy savoury dishes such as braised beef, pork satay and ribs served with white rice.

» **Erwtensoep** Pea soup rich with onions, carrots, smoked sausage and bacon. Ideally a spoon stuck upright in the pot should remain standing (not served in summer).

» **Kroketten** Croquettes are dough balls with various fillings that are crumbed and deep-fried; the variety called *bitterballen* are a popular brown cafe snack served with mustard.

Netherlands Highlights

1. Stroll canals and soak up one of Europe's most beautiful, vibrant and offbeat old cities, **Amsterdam** (p852)
2. Immerse yourself in the urban vibe and architecture of **Rotterdam** (p871)
3. Lose yourself amid the ancient walls and cosmopolitan shops of **Maastricht** (p880)
4. Take a day trip to evocative **Delft** (p870), where Vermeer found his inspiration
5. Wander the beautiful tree-lined boulevards and classy museums of **Den Haag** (p867)
6. Find inspiration at **Leiden**, home of Rembrandt, and in the explosion of tulips at nearby **Keukenhof Gardens** (p866)
7. Go **bike crazy** (p887) across the Netherlands, following dikes along shimmering canals on the world's best network of bike lanes and long-distance routes
8. Lose a few hours drinking beer in the atmospheric confines of a convivial, uniquely Dutch **brown cafe**

AMSTERDAM

020 / POP 781,000

If Amsterdam were a staid place it would still be one of Europe's most beautiful and historic cities, right up there with Venice and Paris. But add in the qualities that make it Amsterdam – the funky and mellow bars, brown cafes full of characters, pervasive irreverence, whiffs of pot and an open air marketplace for sleaze and sex – and you have a literally intoxicating mix.

Amsterdam's been a liberal place ever since the Netherlands' Golden Age, when it led European art and trade. Centuries later, in the 1960s, it again led the pack – this time in the principles of tolerance, with broad-minded views on drugs and same-sex relationships taking centre stage.

Wander the 17th-century streets, tour the iconic canals, stop off to enjoy a masterpiece, discover a funky shop and choose from food around the world. Walk or ride a bike around the concentric rings of the centre then explore the historic lanes of the Jordaan district or the Plantage, and bask in the many worlds-within-worlds, where nothing ever seems the same twice.

Sights & Activities

Amsterdam is compact, and you can roam the city on foot. Hop on the occasional tram to rest your feet – or stop off in a cafe.

CITY CENTRE

The not-overly-impressive **Royal Palace** (Koninklijk Paleis; Map p854; 620 40 60; www.paleisamsterdam.nl; Dam; adult/child €7.50/3.75; 11am-5pm daily Jul & Aug, noon-5pm Tue-Sun Sep-Jun) and the square that puts the 'Dam' in Amsterdam anchor Amsterdam's oldest quarter. This is the busiest part of town for tourists: many leave the train station and head straight for the coffee shops and the Red Light District.

Nieuwe Kerk CHURCH

(New Church; Map p854; 638 69 09; www.nieuwekerk.nl; Dam; adult/child €8/free; 10am-5pm; 1/2/5/13/14/17 Raadhuisstraat) The Nieuwe Kerk is a historical stage for Dutch coronations. The 15th-century late-Gothic basilica is only 'new' in relation to the Oude Kerk. A few monumental items dominate the otherwise spartan interior – a magnificent carved oak chancel and enormous stained-glass windows. The building is now used for exhibitions and organ concerts.

Oude Kerk CHURCH

(Old Church; Map p854; 625 82 84; www.oudekerk.nl; Oudekerksplein 23; adult/child €8/6; 11am-5pm Mon-Sat, 1-5pm Sun; 4/9/16/24/25 Dam) Amsterdam's oldest building, the 14th-century Oude Kerk, was built to honour the city's patron saint, St Nicholas. Inside there's a dramatic Müller organ, gilded oak vaults and impressive stained-glass 929 windows. Watch for the **World Press Photo show** (www.worldpressphoto.org) in late April.

Red Light District NEIGHBOURHOOD

The Red Light District retains the power to make your jaw go limp, even if near-naked prostitutes propositioning passers-by from black-lit windows is the oldest Amsterdam cliché. Note that even in the dark heart of the district there are charming shops and cafes where the only thing that vibrates is your mobile phone. Despite the neon-lit sleaze, the district is tightly regulated and reasonably safe for strolling. The city government has been steadfastly reducing the number of licensed windows.

Amsterdam Museum MUSEUM

(Map p854; 523 18 22; www.amsterdammuseum.nl; Kalverstraat 92; adult/child €10/5; 10am-5pm; 1/2/5 Spui) Housed in the old civic orphanage, the Amsterdams Historisch Museum takes you through all the fascinating twists and turns of Amsterdam's convoluted history. Look for a recreation of the original Cafe het Mandje, a touchstone in the gay-rights movement.

FREE **Begijnhof** HISTORIC BUILDING

(Map p854; 622 19 18; www.begijnhofamsterdam.nl; main entrance off Gedempte Begijnensloot; 8am-5pm; 1/2/5 Spui) To escape Amsterdam's buzz, duck into the Begijnhof, an en-

FREE THRILLS

Much of the allure of Amsterdam can be experienced on foot and for free.

» The Red Light District can cost you an arm and a leg (or more) but voyeurism is free.

» Regain your inner virtue walking through the Begijnhof.

» Find natural peace in the green expanses of Vondelpark (p855).

» Walk the canals and decide which old gabled house leans the most.

Amsterdam

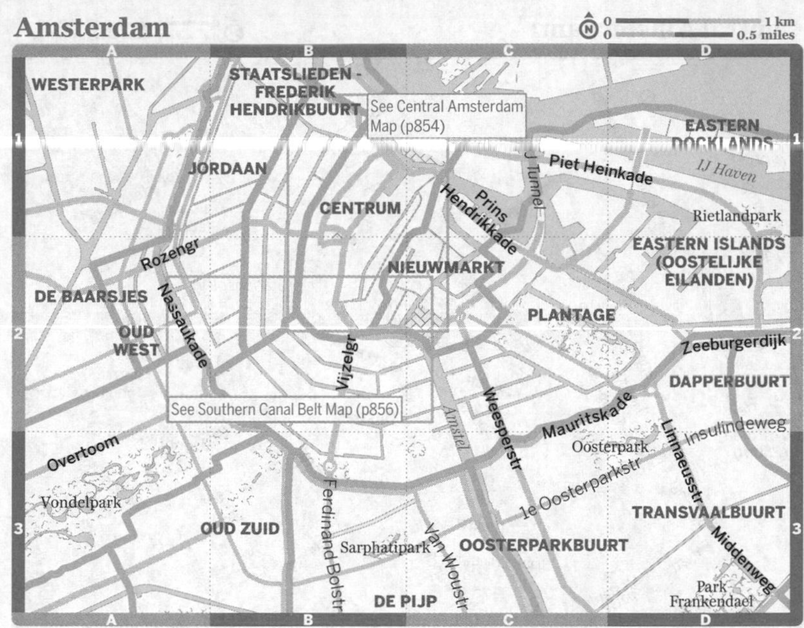

closed former convent from the early 14th century. It's a surreal oasis of peace, with tiny houses and postage-stamp gardens around a well-kept courtyard. The Beguines were a Catholic order of unmarried or widowed women who cared for the elderly and lived a religious life without taking monastic vows. The last died in the 1970s.

CANAL BELT

Created in the 17th century as an upscale neighbourhood, the Canal Belt, especially in the west and south, remains Amsterdam's top district. Wandering here amid architectural treasures and their reflections on the narrow waters of the Prinsengracht, Keizersgracht and Herengracht can cause days to vanish quicker than some of Amsterdam's more lurid pursuits. No two buildings are alike, yet they combine in ever-changing, ever-pleasing harmony.

Anne Frank Huis MUSEUM

(Anne Frank House; ☎556 71 05; www.annefrank.org; Prinsengracht 276; adult/child €9/free; ⏲9am-7pm daily, later Sat & mid-Mar–mid-Sep; 🚋13/14/17 Westermarkt) The Anne Frank Huis, where Anne wrote her famous diary, lures almost a million visitors annually with its secret annexe, reconstruction of Anne's melancholy bedroom, and her actual diary, with its sunnily optimistic writing tempered by quiet despair. Look for the photo of Peter Schiff, her 'one true love'. Try going in the early morning or evening when crowds are lightest; book online to avoid long queues.

FOAM GALLERY

(Fotografie Museum Amsterdam; Map p856; www.foam.nl; Keizersgracht 609; adult/child €8.50/free; ⏲10am-6pm Sat-Wed, to 9pm Thu & Fri; 🚋16/24/25 Keizersgracht) FOAM is an airy gallery devoted to painting with light. Two storeys of changing exhibitions feature world-renowned photographers such as Sir Cecil Beaton, Annie Leibovitz and Henri Cartier-Bresson.

MUSEUMPLEIN

The genteel streets here are a bit bland but what you'll find inside Amsterdam's big three museums will knock your wooden shoes off.

WANT MORE?

For in-depth information, reviews and recommendations at your fingertips, head to the Apple App Store to purchase Lonely Planet's *Amsterdam City Guide* iPhone app.

Central Amsterdam

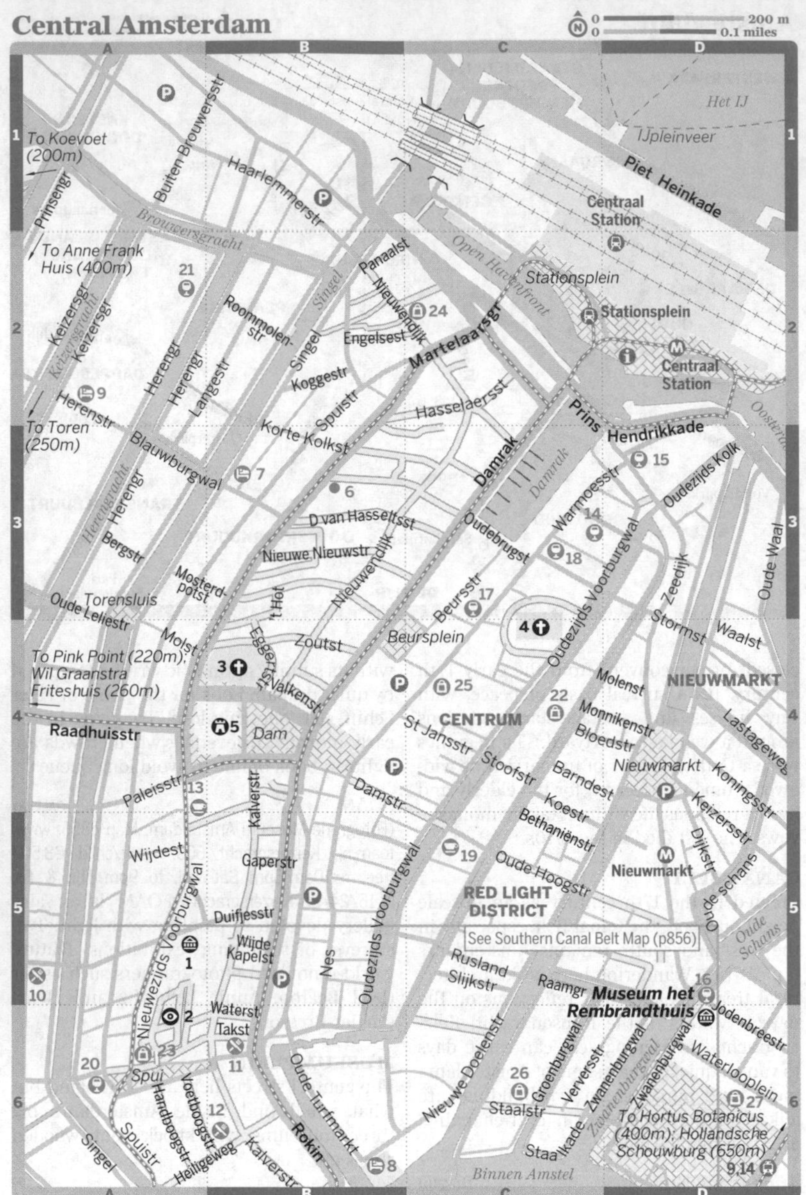

TOP CHOICE **Van Gogh Museum** MUSEUM

(☎570 52 00; www.vangoghmuseum.nl; Paulus Potterstraat 7; adult/child €14/free, audioguide €5; ⊙10am-6pm Sat-Thu, to 10pm Fri; 👪; 🚋2/3/5/12 Van Baerlestraat) This outstanding museum houses the world's largest Van Gogh collection. Trace the artist's life from his tentative start though to his Japanese phase, and on to the black cloud that descended over him and his work. There's also works by contemporaries Gauguin, Toulouse-Lautrec, Monet and Bernard.

Central Amsterdam

Top Sights

Museum het Rembrandthuis D6

Sights

1 Amsterdam Museum A5
2 Begijnhof A6
3 Nieuwe Kerk B4
4 Oude Kerk C4
5 Royal Palace B4

Activities, Courses & Tours

6 Yellow Bike B3

Sleeping

7 Hotel Brouwer B3
8 Hotel de L'Europe B6
9 Maes B&B A2

Eating

10 Buffet van Odette A5
11 Gartine B6
12 Vleminckx B6

Drinking

13 Abraxas A4
14 Brouwerij De Prael C3
15 Café In 't Aepjen D3
16 De Sluyswacht D5
17 FUXXX C3
18 Getto C3
19 Greenhouse C5
20 Hoppe A6
21 't Arendsnest A2

Shopping

22 Absolute Danny C4
23 American Book Center A6
24 Chills & Thrills C2
25 Condomerie Het Gulden Vlies C4
26 Droog C6
27 Waterlooplein Flea Market D6

Rijksmuseum MUSEUM

(National Museum; ☎674 70 00; www.rijksmuseum.nl; Stadhouderskade 42; adult/child €15/free; ⌚9am-5pm; 🚻; 🚋2/5 Hobbemastraat) The Rijksmuseum is the Netherlands' premier art trove. After a 10-year renovation, it reopened in its entirety in April 2013, splashing Rembrandts, Vermeers and 7500 other masterpieces over 1.5km of galleries.

The Golden Age works are the highlight. Feast your eyes on meaty still lifes, gentlemen in ruffed collars and landscapes bathed in pale yellow light. Rembrandt's *Night Watch* (1642) takes pride of place. Other must-sees are the Delftware (blue-and-white pottery), dollhouses (insanely detailed) and the brand-new Asian Pavilion. The sculpture-studded gardens around the exterior are free to visit.

To avoid the biggest crowds, come after 3pm or pre-book tickets online, which provides fast-track entry.

Stedelijk Museum MUSEUM

(☎573 29 11; www.stedelijk.nl; Museumplein 10; adult/child €15/free; ⌚11am-5pm Tue & Wed, 11am-10pm Thu, 10am-6pm Fri-Sun; 🚻; 🚋2/3/5/12 Van Baerlestraat) Amsterdam's weighty modern art museum is among the world's best. It struts Matisse cut-outs, Kandinsky abstracts, Picasso drawings, Rodin sculptures and a vivid collection of paintings by Dutch homeboys Piet Mondrian, Willem de Kooning, Charlie Toorop and Karel Appel. After a nine-year renovation, the Stedelijk reopened in September 2012 with a huge new wing (dubbed 'the Bathtub').

Vondelpark PARK

(www.vondelpark.nl; Stadhouderskade; ⌚24hr; 🚋2/5 Hobbemastraat) Vondelpark is an English-style park with free concerts, ponds, lawns, thickets, winding footpaths and three outdoor cafes. It was named after the poet and playwright Joost van den Vondel, the 'Dutch Shakespeare', and is popular with joggers, skaters, buskers and lovers.

JORDAAN

Originally a stronghold of the working class, the Jordaan is now one of the most desirable areas to live in Amsterdam. It's a pastiche of modest 17th- and 18th-century merchants' houses, humble workers' homes and a few modern carbuncles, squashed in a grid of tiny lanes peppered with bite-sized cafes and shops. Its intimacy is contagious, and now the average Jordaan dweller is more likely to be a gallery owner than a labourer.

DE PIJP

Heineken Experience BREWERY

(☎523 9435; www.heinekenexperience.com; Stadhouderskade 78; adult/child €17/13; ⌚10.30am-7pm Jun-Aug, 11am-5.30pm Sep-May; 🚋16/24 Stadhouderskade) The Heineken Experience is the much-gussied-up reincarnation of the brewer's old brewery tour featuring multimedia displays, rides and plenty of gift shops. At Amsterdam's most popular attraction, acolytes enjoy samples of the beer, which (like Stella Artois et al) is dismissed as

Southern Canal Belt

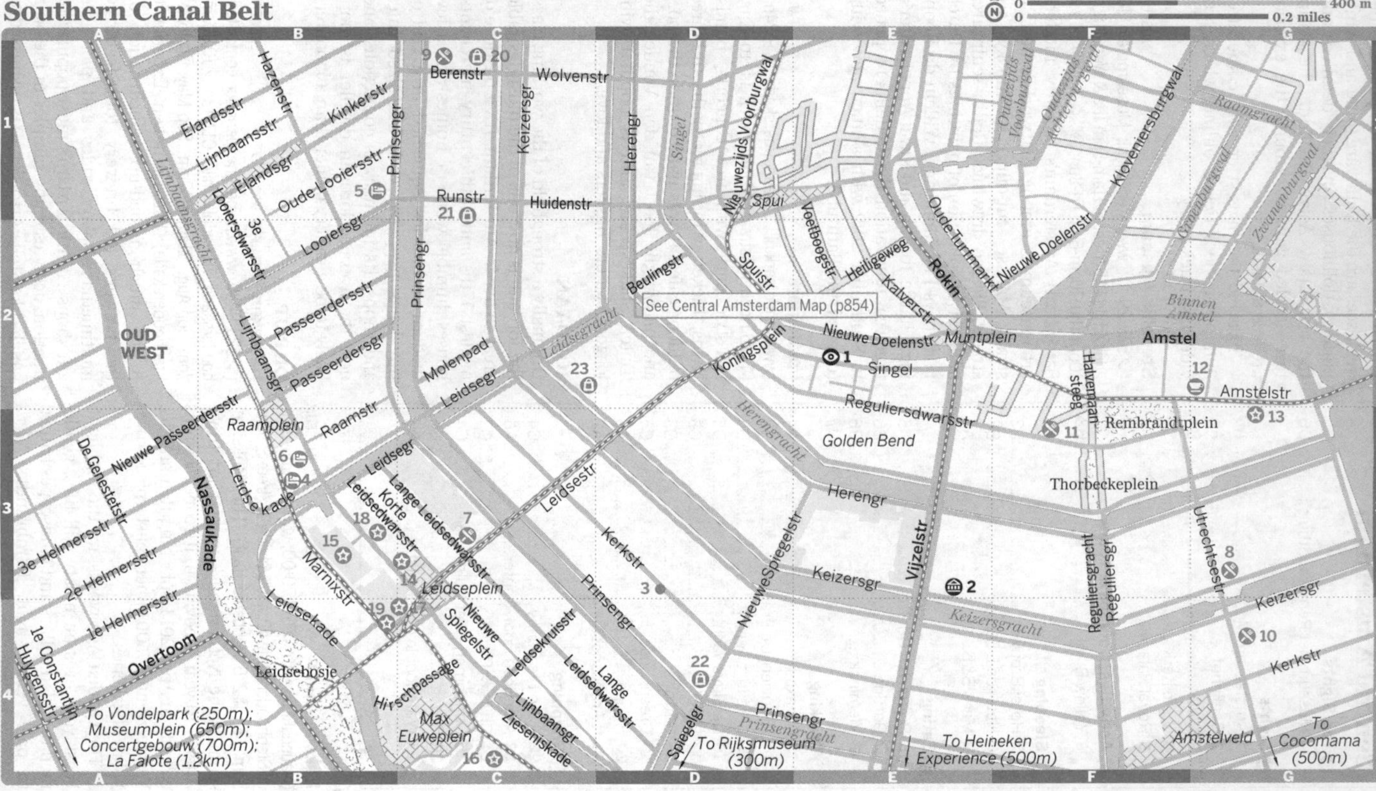

an 'old man's beer' domestically and sold at a premium abroad.

NIEUWMARKT & PLANTAGE

The streets around the Rembrandt House are prime wandering territory, offering a vibrant mix of old Amsterdam, canals and quirky shops and cafes.

TOP CHOICE **Museum het Rembrandthuis** MUSEUM
(Rembrandt House Museum; Map p854; ☎520 04 00; www.rembrandthuis.nl; Jodenbreestraat 4-6; adult/child €10/3; ⏲10am-5pm; 🚋9/14 Waterlooplein) You almost expect to find the master himself at the Museum het Rembrandthuis, the house where Rembrandt van Rijn ran his painting studio, only to lose the lot when profligacy set in, enemies swooped, and bankruptcy came knocking. The museum has scores of etchings and sketches.

Joods Historisch Museum MUSEUM
(Jewish Historical Museum; ☎626 99 45; www.jhm.nl; Nieuwe Amstelstraat 1; adult/child €12/3; ⏲11am-5pm; 👪; 🚋9/14 Mr Visserplein) A beautifully restored complex of four Ashkenazic synagogues from the 17th and 18th centuries shows the history of Jews in the Netherlands. It vividly captures the vibrant Jewish community snuffed out by WWII.

Hollandsche Schouwburg MEMORIAL
(Holland Theatre; ☎626 99 45; www.hollandscheschouwburg.nl; Plantage Middenlaan 24; suggested donation €2.50; ⏲11am-4pm; 🚋9/14 Plantage Kerklaan) After 1942 this theatre became a detention centre for Jews awaiting deportation. Up to 80,000 people passed through here on their way to the death camps. Among the displays, the tale of Bram and Eva Beem is heart-breaking (the Nazis paid a 750 guilder reward for people who betrayed Jews in hiding – equivalent to about €15,000 today).

DON'T MISS

HORTUS BOTANICUS

Established in 1638, the **Hortus Botanicus** (Botanical Garden; www.dehortus.nl; Plantage Middenlaan 2a; adult/child €7.50/3.50; ⏲10am-5pm; 🚋9/14 Mr Visserplein) became a repository for tropical seeds and plants brought by Dutch ships from the East and West Indies. The 4000-plus species are kept in wonderful structures and in compact grounds. Look for Amsterdam's oldest tree plus the alien-like Victoria water lily.

☞ Tours

There are many companies offering bike tours of the city, as well as canal boat tours that let you hop on and hop off (see p863).

TOP CHOICE **St Nicolaas Boat Club** BOAT TOUR
(Map p856; www.amsterdamboatclub.com; Kerkstraat 134) By far the best boat tour in the city. The open-air, 10-seat boats can manoeuvre into the narrowest canals. Patrons are allowed to smoke dope and drink beer on

Southern Canal Belt

Sights

1 Bloemenmarkt ... E2
2 FOAM ... E3

Activities, Courses & Tours

3 St Nicolaas Boat Club ... D3

Sleeping

4 Backstage Hotel ... B3
5 Hotel Amsterdam Wiechmann ... B1
6 International Budget Hostel ... B3

Eating

7 FEBO ... C3
8 Loekie ... G3
9 Pancakes! ... C1
10 Tempo Doeloe ... G4
11 Van Dobben ... F3

Drinking

12 Vivelavie ... G2

Entertainment

13 Air ... G3
14 Boom Chicago & Chicago Social Club ... C3
15 Melkweg ... B3
16 Paradiso ... C4
17 Stadsschouwburg ... C4
18 Sugar Factory ... B3
19 Uitburo ... B4

Shopping

20 Boekie Woekie ... C1
21 De Kaaskamer ... C1
22 Eduard Kramer ... D4
23 Young Designers United ... C2

board, while the captains tell stories about alternative Amsterdam. Rides last 60 to 90 minutes. There is no set fee, just a suggested donation of €10. Departure is from Mike's Bikes; times vary according to numbers.

Sleeping

Book ahead for weekends and in summer. Many cheaper places cater specifically to party animals with booze flowing, pot smoking and general mayhem around the clock. Others exude refined old-world charm. Wi-fi is near universal but elevators are not.

TOP CHOICE All Inn the Family B&B B&B €€
(☎776 36 36; www.allinnthefamily.nl; 2e Egelantiersdwarsstraat 10; r €95-140;) This new B&B, in a charming old Amsterdam canal house, gets rave reviews for embodying the very qualities of the inimitable Jordaan itself. Spirited hosts who speak five languages, a bountiful organic Dutch breakfast, and a quiet location in the heart of the neighbourhood.

TOP CHOICE Cocomama HOSTEL €
(☎627 24 54; www.cocomama.nl; Westeinde 18; dm/r from €37/108; @) Rather than hide its tawdry past (the building was once home to a high-end brothel), Amsterdam's first self-proclaimed 'boutique hostel' plays it up with wink-wink humour – from the high-ceilinged, brothel-themed bunk rooms (with red curtains and 1970s porn) to the brothel shrine in the lobby.

Toren BOUTIQUE HOTEL €€
(☎622 60 33; www.toren.nl; Keizersgracht 164; r €130-210, ste from €300 ; @) A title-holder for price, room size and personal service, the Toren's communal areas mix 17th-century decadence – gilded mirrors, fireplaces and magnificent chandeliers – with a sensual, decadent flair that screams (or, rather, whispers) Parisian boudoir. Guest rooms are elegantly furnished with modern facilities (including Nespresso coffee machines).

Hotel de L'Europe LUXURY HOTEL €€€
(Map p854; ☎531 17 77; www.leurope.nl; Nieuwe Doelenstraat 2-8; r from €340; @) Oozing Victorian elegance, L'Europe welcomes you with a glam chandelier, a marble lobby, 100 gloriously large rooms (some have terraces and all have handsome marble bathrooms) and smart extras like a shoeshine service and boats for canal cruises.

Hotel Brouwer HOTEL €€
(Map p854; ☎624 63 58; www.hotelbrouwer.nl; Singel 83; r €60-100; @) Our favourite hotel in this price range, it has just eight rooms in a house dating back to 1652. Its rooms, named for Dutch painters, are furnished with simplicity, but all have canal views. There's – get this – a tiny lift.

Backstage Hotel HOTEL €€
(Map p856; ☎624 40 44; www.backstagehotel.com; Leidsegracht 114; r €125-205, r without bathroom €85-155; @) We wanna rock all night at the Backstage. This seriously fun music-themed hotel is a favourite among musicians jamming at nearby Melkweg and Paradiso, as evidenced by the lobby bar's band-signature-covered piano and pool table.

Hotel Fita HOTEL €€
(☎679 09 76; www.hotelfita.com; Jan Luijkenstraat 37; r €109-169; @) This tiny, family-owned hotel, on a quiet street off Museumplein and PC Hooftstraat, is one of the best in the Old South. It has 15 handsome rooms with nicely appointed bathrooms; a bountiful breakfast of eggs, pancakes, cheeses and breads; and an elevator.

Maes B&B B&B €€
(Map p854; ☎427 51 65; www.bedandbreakfastamsterdam.com; Herenstraat 26hs; s €95-115, d €115-135, apt €135-260; @) If you were designing a traditional home in the western canals, it would probably turn out a lot like this property: oriental carpets, wood floors and exposed brick. It's actually fairly spacious for such an old building.

Hotel Amsterdam Wiechmann HOTEL €€
(Map p856; ☎626 33 21; www.hotelwiechmann.nl; Prinsengracht 328; r €90-210; @) This family-run hotel occupies three houses in a marvellous canalside location. The cosy, lovingly cared-for rooms are furnished like an antique shop, with country quilts and chintz, and the lobby *tchotchkes* (knick-knacks) have been here for some 60 years.

International Budget Hostel HOSTEL €
(Map p856; ☎624 27 84; www.internationalbudgethostel.com; Leidsegracht 76; dm €18-40, r €65-80; @) Reasons to stay: canalside location in a former warehouse; really close to nightlife; four-person limit in rooms; cool mix of backpackers from around the world; clean rooms with lockers; printer access and bike rental.

Eating

Amsterdam abounds in food choices. Happy streets for hunting include Utrechtsesraat, Spuistraat and any of the little streets lining and connecting the west canals, such as Berenstraat.

TOP CHOICE Van Dobben SANDWICHES €
(Map p856; ☎624 42 00; www.eetsalonvandobben.nl; Korte Reguliersdwarsstraat 5; items €2.75-6.50; ⏱10am 9pm Mon-Thu, to 2am Fri & Sat, 11.30am-9pm Sun; 🚋4/9/14 Rembrandtplein) Open since the 1940s, the venerable Van Dobben has white-tile walls and white-coated counter men who specialise in snappy banter. Traditional meaty Dutch fare is its forte: try the *pekelvlees* (something close to corned beef). The *kroketten* (croquettes) are the best in town.

TOP CHOICE Gartine CAFE €
(Map p854; ☎320 41 32; www.gartine.nl; Taksteeg 7; mains €6-12, high tea €12-21; ⏱10am-6pm Wed-Sun; 🥕; 🚋4/9/14/16/24/25 Spui) Gartine makes delectable breakfast pastries, sandwiches and salads from produce grown in its own garden plot. Throw in Slow Food credentials and gorgeous antique plates and it's a winner.

Tempo Doeloe INDONESIAN €€€
(Map p856; ☎625 67 18; www.tempodoeloerestaurant.nl; Utrechtsestraat 75; mains €20-25, rijsttafel & set menus €28-40; ⏱dinner Mon-Sat; 🥕; 🚋4 Keizersgracht) Tempo Doeloe's setting and service are pleasant and decorous without being overdone. The same applies to the *rijsttafel* (rice table): a ridiculously overblown affair at many places, here it's a fine sampling of the range of flavours found in the country. Warning: dishes marked 'very hot' are indeed like napalm.

Koevoet ITALIAN €€
(☎624 08 46; Lindenstraat 17; mains €12-23; ⏱dinner Tue-Sun; 🥕; 🚋3 Nieuwe Willemsstraat) The congenial Italian owners of Koevoet took over a former cafe on a quiet side street, left the decor untouched and started cooking up their home-country staples. Don't miss its signature, drinkable dessert, *sgroppino limone* (€7): sorbet, vodka and prosecco.

Pancakes! DUTCH €
(Map p856; www.pancakesamsterdam.com; Berenstraat 38; pancakes €6-10; ⏱10am-7pm; 👪; 🚋13/14/17 Westermarkt) Just as many locals as tourists grace the blue-tile tables at snug little Pancakes!, carving into all the usual options, plus daily creations like ham, chicory and cheese or chicken curry pancakes. The batter is made with flour sourced from a local mill.

Moeders DUTCH €€
(☎626 79 57; www.moeders.com; Rozengracht 251; mains €15-19, 3-course menus €25-30; ⏱5pm-midnight Mon-Fri, noon-midnight Sat & Sun; 🥕; 🚋10/13/14/17 Marnixstraat) Mum's the word at 'Mothers'. When this friendly place opened over 20 years ago, staff asked customers to bring their own plates and photos of their mums as donations, and the result is still a delightful hotchpotch. Book ahead.

La Falote DUTCH €€
(☎622 54 54; www.lafalote.nl; Roelof Hartstraat 26; mains €13-19; ⏱dinner Mon-Sat; 🚋3/5/12/24 Roelof Hartplein) Wee chequered-tablecloth La Falote is about Dutch home-style cooking, such as calf liver, meatballs with endives, and stewed fish with beets and mustard sauce.

Vleminckx FAST FOOD €
(Map p854; Voetboogstraat 31; small/large €2.20/2.70, sauces €0.80; ⏱11am-6pm Tue-Sat, to 7pm Thu, noon-6pm Sun & Mon; 🚋1/2/5 Koningsplein) This hole-in-the-wall takeaway has drawn the hordes for its monumental *frites* since 1887. The standard is smothered in mayonnaise.

Wil Graanstra Friteshuis FAST FOOD €
(☎624 40 71; Westermarkt 11; frites €2-3.75; ⏱11am-6pm Mon-Sat) This little stall near Anne Frank Huis has been serving up crispy fries with delectable mayo since 1956. Legions of Amsterdammers swear by them.

DON'T MISS

FEAST FOR A COIN

FEBO (Map p856; ☎620 86 15; Leidsestraat 94; mains €3-6; ⏱11am-3am Sun-Thu, 11am-4am Fri & Sat; 🚋1/2/5 Prinsengracht) We don't exactly recommend this Dutch fast-food icon. The *bami* rolls are hot as napalm, the *frikadel* frightening and the *kaassoufflé* utterly unsoufflé-like. But plucking a treat from the yellow automat windows is a drunken Dutch tradition.

Winkel CAFE €
(www.winkel43.nl; Noordermarkt 43; mains €4-14; breakfast, lunch & dinner; ; 3 Nieuwe Willemsstraat) This sprawling, indoor-outdoor space is great for people-watching, popular for coffees and small meals, and out-of-the-park for its tall, cakey apple pie.

Buffet van Odette CAFE €
(Map p854; www.buffet-amsterdam.nl; Herengracht 309; mains €8-16; 10am-8.30pm Wed-Sat, to 5pm Sun & Mon; ; 1/2/5 Spui) This is not a buffet but a sit-down cafe, where Odette and Yvette show how good simple cooking can taste when you start with great ingredients and a dash of creativity. Sit by the window for one of the city's loveliest canal views.

Loekie SANDWICHES €
(Map p856; www.loekie.net; Utrechtsestraat 57; sandwiches €5-9; 9am-6pm Mon-Sat, to 1pm Wed; 4 Keizersgracht) This delicatessen piles fresh, delicious ingredients into its takeaway sandwiches, such as smoked beef with egg and salt, or warm goat's cheese with pine nuts and honey.

Drinking

A particular Amsterdam joy is discovering your own brown cafe. They are found everywhere, often tucked into the most atmospheric of locations. Many serve food.

TOP CHOICE **Hoppe** BROWN CAFE
(Map p854; www.cafehoppe.nl; Spui 18-20; 1/2/5 Spui) Go on. Do your bit to ensure Hoppe maintains one of the highest beer turnovers in the city. The gritty brown cafe has been filling glasses for more than 300 years. Journalists, bums, socialites and raconteurs toss back brews amid the ancient wood panelling.

> **GET UIT & ABOUT**
>
> Not sure how to spend your evening? Head to the last-minute ticket desk at the **Uitburo** (Map p856; 621 13 11; www.amsterdamsuitburo.nl; Leidseplein 26; 10am-7pm Mon-Fri, 10am-6pm Sat, noon-6pm Sun; 1/2/5/7/10 Leidseplein), in the corner of the Stadsschouwburg on the Leidseplein. Tickets for comedy, dance, concerts, even club nights are often available at a significant discount – and handily marked 'LNP' (language no problem) if understanding Dutch isn't vital.

TOP CHOICE **Café 't Smalle** BROWN CAFE
(www.t-smalle.nl; Egelantiersgracht 12; from 10am; 13/14/17 Westermarkt) Take your boat and dock right on 't Smalle's pretty stone terrace – there's hardly a more convivial setting in the daytime or a more romantic one at night. It's equally charming inside, dating back to 1786 as a *jenever* (Dutch gin) distillery and tasting house.

Café In 't Aepjen BROWN CAFE
(Map p854; www.cafeintaepjen.nl; Zeedijk 1; 4/9/16/24/25 Centraal Station) Candles burn even during the day at this bar based in a mid-16th-century house, one of two remaining wooden buildings in the city.

De Sluyswacht BROWN CAFE
(Map p854; www.sluyswacht.nl; Jodenbreestraat 1; from 11.30am; 9/14 Waterlooplein) Listing like a ship in a high wind, this tiny black building was once a lock-keeper's house on the Oude Schans. Today the canalside terrace is one of the nicest spots we know in town to relax and down a beer.

't Arendsnest BAR, CAFE
(Map p854; www.arendsnest.nl; Herengracht 90; from 4pm Mon-Fri, from 2pm Sat & Sun; 1/2/5/13/17 Nieuwezijds Kolk) This gorgeous, restyled brown cafe, with its glowing copper *jenever* (Dutch gin) boilers behind the bar, only serves Dutch beer.

Brouwerij De Prael BAR, CAFE
(Map p854; 408 44 69; www.deprael.nl; Oudezijds Armsteeg 26; 11am-11pm Tue-Sun; 4/9/16/24/25 Centraal Station) Sample organic beers named after classic Dutch singers at this spacious, wood-panelled tasting room decorated with old radios and album covers.

Entertainment

Find out what's on in **I Amsterdam** (www.iamsterdam.com/events).

Coffee Shops

Cafes have coffee, 'coffee shops' are where one buys pot.

Abraxas COFFEE SHOP
(Map p854; www.abraxas.tv; Jonge Roelensteeg 12; from 10am;) Hands down the most beautiful coffee shop in town. Choose from southwest USA, Middle Eastern and other styles of decor, spread over three floors.

Greenhouse COFFEE SHOP
(Map p854; Oudezijds Voorburgwal 191; from 9am; ; 4/9/16/24/25 Dam) One of the

GAY & LESBIAN AMSTERDAM

Information

Gay Amsterdam (www.gayamsterdam.com) Lists hotels, shops, restaurants and clubs, and provides maps.

Pink Point (www.pinkpoint.org; ⌚noon-6pm Mar-Aug, limited hours Sep-Feb) On the Keizersgracht, behind the Westerkerk. Part information kiosk, part souvenir shop, with details on myriad gay and lesbian hangouts, and copies of the candid *Bent Guide*.

Entertainment

Amsterdam's gay scene is among the world's largest. Some hubs: Warmoesstraat in the Red Light District hosts the infamous, kink-filled leather and fetish bars. Nearby on the upper end of the Zeedijk, bright crowds spill onto laid-back bar terraces. In the Southern Canal Ring, the area around Rembrandtplein (aka the 'Amstel area') has traditional pubs and brown cafes, some with a campy bent.

Some places to start:

Getto (Map p854; www.getto.nl; Warmoesstraat 51; ⌚Tue-Sun; 🚋4/9/16/24/25 Centraal Station) A younger crowd piles in to this groovy, welcoming bar-restaurant for cheap food and fun people-watching.

Vivelavie (Map p856; www.vivelavie.net; Amstelstraat 7; ⌚from 4pm; 📶) Just off Rembrandtplein, this lively place is probably Amsterdam's most popular lesbian cafe, with flirty girls, loud music and a buzzy outdoor terrace.

FUXXX (Map p854; www.clubfuxxx.com; Warmoesstraat 96; ⌚from 11pm Thu-Sun) Lots of action here. It's men only for hardcore dancing and cruising Thursday through Saturday. Women join the ranks on Sundays.

most popular coffee shops in town. Smokers love the funky music, multicoloured mosaics, psychedelic stained-glass windows, and high-quality weed and hash.

COFFEE SHOP DO'S & DON'TS

Keep in mind the following at coffee shops in the Netherlands:

» Ask at the bar for the menu of cannibis-related goods on offer, usually packaged in small bags. You can also buy ready-made joints (€3 to €7). Most shops offer rolling papers, pipes or even bongs to use.

» Don't light up anywhere besides a coffee shop without checking that it's OK to do so.

» Alcohol and tobacco products are not permitted in coffee shops.

Nightclubs

Sugar Factory CLUB

(Map p856; www.sugarfactory.nl; Lijnbaansgracht 238; 🚋1/2/5/7/10 Leidseplein) A cool vibe, an excellent location and a varied line-up are the hallmarks here. But this ain't your average club – most nights start with music, cinema, or a dance or spoken-word performance, followed by late-night DJs and dancing.

Air CLUB

(Map p856; ☎820 06 70; www.air.nl; Amstelstraat 16; ⌚Thu-Sun; 🚋4/9/14 Rembrandtplein) One of Amsterdam's It clubs, Air has an environmentally friendly design and a unique tiered dance floor.

Live Music

TOP CHOICE **Concertgebouw** CLASSICAL MUSIC

(☎671 83 45; www.concertgebouw.nl; Concertgebouwplein 2-6; ⌚box office 1-7pm Mon-Fri, 10am-7pm Sat & Sun; 🚋3/5/12/16/24 Museumplein) One of the world's great concert halls, the Concertgebouw has near-perfect acoustics that flatter the already esteemed Royal Concertgebouw Orchestra. Every Wednesday at 12.30pm from September till the end of June, the Concertgebouw holds free half-hour concerts, traditionally of chamber music or public rehearsals of an evening event.

Paradiso LIVE MUSIC

(Map p856; www.paradiso.nl; Weteringschans 6; 🚋7/10 Spiegelgracht) Worship rock 'n' roll in a gorgeous old church where the Beatles once played. Opened in 1968 as 'Cosmic Relaxation Center Paradiso', this historic, multi-storeyed club exudes an anything-goes, relaxed vibe.

Melkweg LIVE MUSIC

(Map p856; www.melkweg.nl; Lijnbaansgracht 234a; 1/2/5/7/10 Leidseplein) The 'Milky Way' is a dazzling galaxy of diverse music. One night it's reggae or punk, the next night heavy-metal legend Zach Wilde lures in the leather-jacketed biker crowd.

Theatre

Boom Chicago & Chicago Social Club COMEDY, CLUB

(Map p856; 423 01 01; www.boomchicago.nl; Leidseplein 12; box office 4-8.30pm Wed-Fri, 3-11pm Sat; 1/2/5/7/10 Leidseplein) Enjoy Amsterdam's leading English-language improv comedy show over a few drinks at this late night bar and nightclub, At the time of writing the improv troop were due to move to new premises at the **Rosentheater** (Rozengracht 117); check the website for updates.

Stadsschouwburg THEATRE

(Map p856; www.stadsschouwburgamsterdam.nl; Leidseplein 26) Amsterdam's most beautiful theatre was built in 1894. It features large-scale productions, operettas, dance and summer English-language productions and performances.

Sport

Four-time European champion Ajax is the Netherlands' most famous football team. Ajax plays in the **Amsterdam Arena** (www.ajax.nl; Arena Blvd 1), usually on Saturday evenings and Sunday afternoons August to May. Enjoy a 'World of Ajax' tour.

Shopping

The real pleasure of shopping in Amsterdam is finding some tiny shop selling something you'd find nowhere else.

MEDIEVAL CENTRE & RED LIGHT DISTRICT

The big department stores cluster around the Dam; chains line the pedestrian (in more ways than one) Kalverstraat. The Red Light District buzzes with vibrating latex creations.

TOP CHOICE **Condomerie Het Gulden Vlies** SPECIALITY SHOP

(Map p854; www.condomerie.nl; Warmoesstraat 141; 4/9/16/24/25 Dam) This is where the well-dressed Johnson shops for variety. Perfectly positioned near the Red Light District, this boutique stocks hundreds of types of condoms.

American Book Center BOOKS

(ABC; Map p854; www.abc.nl; Spui 12; 11am-8pm Mon, from 10am Tue-Sat, 11am-6.30pm Sun; 1/2/5 Spui) This excellent three-storey shop is the biggest source of English-language books in Amsterdam.

Absolute Danny EROTICA

(Map p854; www.absolutedanny.com; Oudezijds Achterburgwal 78; 11am-9pm Mon-Sat, from noon Sun; 4/9/16/24/25 Dam) Named by Dutch *Playboy* as Amsterdam's classiest sex shop, Absolute Danny specialises in fetish clothing, lingerie and leather, along with hard-core videos and dildos just for fun.

Chills & Thrills SPECIALITY SHOP

(Map p854; www.chillsandthrills.com; Nieuwendijk 17; 10am-10pm) This rather busy shop sells truffles, herbal trips, E-testing kits, psychoactive cacti, amino-acid and vitamin drinks, novelty bongs and life-sized alien sculptures.

MARKETS

Markets of just about every description are scattered across the city. Amsterdam's largest and busiest market, **Albert Cuypmarkt** (www.albertcuypmarkt.nl; Albert Cuypstraat, btwn Ferdinand Bolstraat & Van Woustraat; 10am-5pm Mon-Sat; 16/24 Albert Cuypstraat) is 100 years old. Food of every description, flowers, souvenirs, clothing, hardware and household goods can be found here.

Bloemenmarkt (Flower Market; Map p856; Singel, btwn Muntplein & Koningsplein; 9am-5.30pm Mon-Sat, 11am-5.30pm Sun; 1/2/5 Koningsplein) is a touristy 'floating' flower market that's actually on pilings. Still, at the stalls that actually stock flowers (as opposed to plastic clogs), the vibrant colours burst forth.

Waterlooplein Flea Market (Map p854; www.waterloopleinmarkt.nl; 9am-5pm Mon-Sat) is Amsterdam's most famous flea market: curios, secondhand clothing, music, used footwear, ageing electronic gear, New Age gifts, cheap bicycle parts.

NIEUWMARKT

Several good streets for typically eccentric local stores stripe the neighbourhood, including Oude Hoogstraat.

Droog HOMEWARES

(Map p854; www.droog.nl; Staalstraat 7b; ⌚Tue-Sun; 🚋4/9/14/16/24/25 Muntplein) This slick Amsterdam-based firm is a market leader, with inventions such as the 85-lamp chandelier, the cow chair, and curtains with dress patterns.

JORDAAN & WESTERN CANAL BELT

Several streets along the Western Canals are dotted with surprising little shops: try Reesstraat and Hartenstraat and the blocks south to Runstraat and Huidenstraat.

Boekie Woekie BOOKS

(Map p856; Berenstraat 16; ⌚noon-6pm; 🚋13/14/17 Westermarkt) While other shops handle art books, this artist-run bookstore sells books *as* art, created by artists specifically for this medium.

De Kaaskamer FOOD, DRINK

(Map p856; www.kaaskamer.nl; Runstraat 7; ⌚noon-6pm Mon, 9am-6pm Tue-Fri, 9am-5pm Sat, noon-5pm Sun; 🚋1/2/5 Spui) The name means 'cheese room' and it is indeed stacked to the rafters with Dutch and organic varieties, as well as olives, tapenades, salads and other picnic ingredients.

SOUTHERN CANAL BELT & DE PIJP

The Spiegel Quarter, along Spiegelgracht and Nieuwe Spiegelstraat, is ground zero for quality antiques and art.

Young Designers United CLOTHING

(Map p856; www.ydu.nl; Keizersgracht 447; ⌚Mon-Sat; 🚋1/2/5 Keizersgracht) Angelika Groenendijk Wasylewski's boutique is a showcase for young designers (mainly Dutch).

Eduard Kramer ANTIQUES

(Map p856; www.antique-tileshop.nl; Nieuwe Spiegelstraat 64; ⌚Tue-Sun; 🚋16/24/25 Keizersgracht) Specialising in antique Dutch tiles, this tiny store is also crammed with lots of other interesting stuff – silver candlesticks, crystal decanters, jewellery and pocket watches.

ℹ Information

GWK Travelex (☎0900 05 66; www.gwk.nl; Centraal Station; ⌚8am-10pm Mon-Sat, 9am-10pm Sun; 🚋Centraal Station) Exchanges travellers cheques and makes hotel reservations; also at Schiphol airport.

I Amsterdam Card (www.iamsterdam.com; per 24/48/72hr €40/50/60) Available at VVV offices and some hotels. Provides admission to many museums, canal boat trips, and discounts and freebies at shops, attractions and restaurants. Also includes a GVB transit pass.

Tourist office (Map p854; www.iamsterdam.nl; Stationsplein 10; ⌚9am-7pm Mon-Fri, 10am-6pm Sat & Sun) Maps, guides and transit passes.

ℹ Getting There & Away

Air

Most major airlines serve **Schiphol** (AMS; www.schiphol.nl) airport, 18km southwest of the city centre.

Bus

Eurolines connects with all major European capitals. Buses arrive at Amstelstation, south of the centre, which has an easy metro link to Centraal Station (about a 15-minute trip).

Eurolines Ticket office (Rokin 38a) is near the Dam.

Train

Amsterdam's main train station is fabled **Centraal Station** (⌚8am-10pm Mon-Sat, 9am-10pm Sun), with services to the rest of the country and major European cities.

ℹ Getting Around

To/From the Airport

A **taxi** into Amsterdam from Schiphol airport takes 25 to 45 minutes and costs about €45. **Trains** to Centraal Station leave every few minutes, take 15 to 20 minutes, and cost €4/7 per single/return.

Bicycle

Amsterdam is cycling nirvana: flat, beautiful, with dedicated bike paths. About 150,000 bicycles are stolen each year in Amsterdam, so always lock up. Rental agencies include the following:

Bike City (☎626 37 21; www.bikecity.nl; Bloemgracht 68-70; bikes from €14 per day) There's no advertising on the bikes, so you can pretend you're a local.

Yellow Bike (Map p854; ☎620 69 40; www.yellowbike.nl; Nieuwezijds Kolk 29; city/countryside tours €19.50/29.50) Choose from city tours or the longer countryside tour through the pretty Waterland district to the north. Also rents bikes.

Boat

Amsterdam's **canal boats** are a popular way to tour the town but most are actually a bit claustrophobic, with steamed-up glass windows surrounding passengers. Look for a boat with an open seating area.

There are also free **ferries** from behind Centraal Station to destinations around the IJ, notably Amsterdam Noord.

Canal Bus (www.canal.nl; day pass adult/child €22/11) Offers a unique hop-on, hop-off service; has 17 docks around the city near the big museums.

Car & Motorcycle

Amsterdam is horrendous for parking, with charges averaging €5 per hour. Your best bet is to ditch the car at an outlying train station and ride in.

Public Transport

Services – including Amsterdam's iconic **trams** – are run by the local transit authority, GVB. Its highly useful **GVB information office** (www.gvb.nl; Stationsplein 10; ⏲7am-9pm Mon-Fri, 10am-6pm Sat & Sun) is located across the tram tracks from the Centraal Station main entrance. You can avoid the often-long lines by buying day passes at the adjoining VVV office instead.

Public transport in Amsterdam uses the *OV-chipkaart*. Rides cost €2.70 when bought on the tram or bus. Unlimited-ride passes are available for between one to seven days (€7.50–31), valid on trams, most buses and the metro are good value.

Night buses take over shortly after midnight, which is when the trams and regular buses stop running.

Taxi

Amsterdam taxis are expensive, even over short journeys. Try **Taxicentrale Amsterdam** (TCA; ☎777 77 77; www.tcataxi.nl).

AROUND AMSTERDAM

Zaanse Schans

People come for an hour and stay for several at this open-air museum on the Zaan river, which is *the* place to see **windmills** operating. It's got a touristy element, but the six operating mills are completely authentic and are operated with enthusiasm and love. Visitors can explore the windmills at their leisure, seeing firsthand the vast moving parts that make these devices a combination of sailing ship and Rube Goldberg. As a bonus, the river-bank setting is lovely.

The site is free; entrance fees to the individual windmills average €3/1.50 per adult/child. At least a couple are open on any given day; hours tend to be 10am to 4pm. There are several cafes and restaurants on-site.

From Amsterdam Centraal Station (€3, 17 minutes, four times hourly) take the train towards Alkmaar and get off at Koog Zaandijk – it's a well-signposted 1km walk to Zaanse Schans.

Alkmaar

☎072 / POP 94,000

This picturesque town stages its famous **cheese market** (Waagplein; ⏲10am-noon Fri Apr-early Sep) in the historic main square. The market dates from the 17th century. Dealers in officious white smocks insert a hollow rod to extract cheese samples, sniffing and crumbling for fat and moisture content. Then the porters, wearing colourful hats to signify their cheese guild, heft the cheeses on wooden sledges to a large scale. An average 30 tonnes of cheese is on display at the Alkmaar market at any one time.

Arrive early for more than fleeting glimpses. There are four trains per hour from Amsterdam Centraal Station (€7, 30 to 40 minutes).

THE RANDSTAD

When people think of the Netherlands outside of Amsterdam, they are often really thinking about the Randstad. One of the most densely populated places on the planet, it stretches from Amsterdam to Rotterdam and features the classically Dutch towns and cities of Den Haag, Utrecht, Haarlem, Leiden, Delft and Gouda. Most people focus their visit to the Netherlands here, enjoying the peerless cycling network that links the towns amid tulip fields.

Haarlem

☎023 / POP 152,000

Haarlem is the Netherlands in microcosm, with canals, gabled buildings and cobblestone streets. Its historic buildings, grand churches, museums, cosy bars, good restaurants and antique shops draw scores of day trippers – it's only 15 minutes by train from Amsterdam.

The Randstad

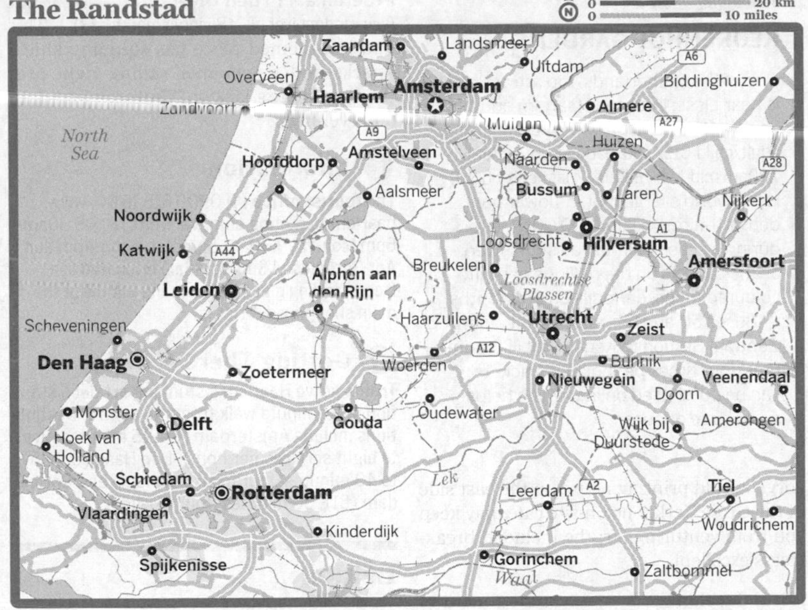

Sights

A couple of hour's stroll – with stops for refreshments – will cover Haarlem's tidy centre, which radiates out from the **Grote Markt**, where there are markets on many days.

Town Hall HISTORIC BUILDING

At the western end of the Grote Markt stands the florid, 14th-century town hall, which sprouted many extensions including a balcony where judgements from the high court were pronounced.

Grote Kerk van St Bavo CHURCH

(www.bavo.nl; Oude Groenmarkt 23; adult/child €2.50/free; ⏲10am-5pm Mon-Sat) This Gothic cathedral with a towering 50m-high steeple contains some fine Renaissance artworks, but the star attraction is its stunning Müller organ – one of the most magnificent in the world, standing 30m high with about 5000 pipes. It was played by Handel and Mozart, the latter when he was just 10.

Frans Hals Museum GALLERY

(www.franshalsmuseum.nl; Groot Heiligland 62; adult/child €7.50/free; ⏲11am-5pm Tue-Sat, noon-5pm Sun) A short stroll south of Grote Markt, the Frans Hals Museum is a must for anyone interested in the Dutch Masters. Kept in a poorhouse where Hals spent his final years, the collection focuses on the 17th-century Haarlem School; its pride and joy are eight group portraits of the Civic Guard that reveal Hals' exceptional attention to mood and psychological tone.

FREE **Corrie ten Boom House** HISTORIC BUILDING

(www.corrietenboom.com; Barteljorisstraat 19; ⏲10am-4pm Tue-Sat Apr-Oct, 11am-3pm Tue-Sat Nov-Mar) Also known as 'the hiding place', the Corrie Ten Boom House is named for the matriarch of a family that lived in the house during WWII. Using a secret compartment in her bedroom, she hid hundreds of Jews and Dutch resistors until they could be spirited to safety. In 1944 the family was betrayed and sent to concentration camps, where three died. Tours are in English.

Sleeping

Looking for a mellow alternative to Amsterdam? Haarlem is peace personified at night.

TOP CHOICE **Stempels** HOTEL €€

(☎512 39 10; www.stempelsinhaarlem.nl; Klokhuisplein 9; r €95-160; @☎) Haarlem's most interesting lodging has 17 spacious rooms (with high ceilings and stark, artful decor) in a

DON'T MISS

KEUKENHOF GARDENS

One of the Netherlands' top attractions is near Lisse, between Haarlem and Leiden. **Keukenhof** (www.keukenhof.nl; adult/child €15/7.50, parking €6; 8am-7.30pm mid-Mar–mid-May, last entry 6pm) is the world's largest bulb-flower garden, attracting nearly 800,000 visitors during a season almost as short-lived as the blooms on the millions of multicoloured tulips, daffodils and hyacinths.

Buses 50 and 54 travel from Leiden Centraal Station to Keukenhof (30 minutes, four times per hour). All tickets can be purchased online, which helps avoid huge queues.

gorgeous old printing house on the east side of the Grote Kerk. The on-site cafe may keep you from venturing far; the included breakfast is excellent.

Hotel Carillon HOTEL €€
(531 05 91; www.hotelcarillon.com; Grote Markt 27; s/d from €60/80;) Small but tidy white rooms in the shadow of the Grote Kerk are the hallmark here. A couple share bathrooms and cost from €40. Breakfast (included) can be taken in wicker chairs on the sidewalk cafe.

Eating & Drinking

Lange Veerstraat has a bounty of cafes, while Schagchelstraat is lined with restaurants. The Saturday morning market on Grote Markt is one of Holland's best; try the fresh *Stroopwafels* (small caramel-filled waffles).

TOP CHOICE **De Haerlemsche Vlaamse** FAST FOOD €
(Spekstraat 3; frites €2.10) Practically on the doorstep of the Grote Kerk, this *frites* joint, not much bigger than a telephone box, is a local institution. Line up for its crispy, golden fries made from fresh potatoes.

Jacobus Pieck INTERNATIONAL €€
(www.jacobuspieck.nl; Warmoesstraat 18; mains lunch €6-10, dinner €10-20; lunch & dinner Tue-Sat) Touches such as freshly squeezed OJ put this tidy bistro on a higher plane. The menu bursts with fresh dishes, from salads and sandwiches at lunch to more complex pasta and seafood choices at dinner. Snag a sunny table on the back patio.

Proeflokaal in den Uiver BROWN CAFE
(www.indenuiver.nl; Riviervismarkt 13) This nautical-themed place has shipping knick-knacks and a schooner sailing right over the bar. There's jazz on Thursday and Sunday evenings.

Information

The **tourist office** (0900 616 16 00; www.haarlemmarketing.com; Verwulft 11; 9.30am-6pm Mon-Fri, 9.30am-5pm Sat, noon-4pm Sun Apr-Sep, closed Sun Oct-Mar) is located in a free-standing glass house in the middle of the main shopping district.

Getting There & Away

Trains serve Haarlem's stunning art deco station, a 10-minute walk from the centre. Destinations include Amsterdam (€4, 15 minutes, five to eight services per hour), Den Haag (€8, 35 to 40 minutes, four to six per hour) and Rotterdam (€11, 50 minutes, four per hour).

Leiden

071 / POP 118,700

Leiden is a busy, vibrant town that is another popular day trip from Amsterdam. Claims to fame: it's Rembrandt's birthplace, it's home to the Netherlands' oldest university (and 20,000 students) and it's where America's pilgrims raised money to lease the leaky Mayflower that took them to the New World in 1620. Large, dignified 17th-century buildings with tall, almost regal windows line the canals.

Sights & Activities

The best way to experience Leiden is by strolling the historic centre, especially along the Rapenburg canal.

Follow the huge steeple of **Pieterskerk** (Pieterskerkhof; 10am-4pm Mon-Fri, 1.30-4pm Sat & Sun May-Sep, 1.30-4pm daily Oct-Apr), which shines after a grand restoration (a good thing as it's been prone to collapse since it was built in the 14th century). The precinct here is as old-Leiden as you'll get and includes the gabled old **Latin School** (Schoolstraat), which – before it became a commercial building – was graced by a pupil named Rembrandt from 1616 to 1620. Across the plaza, look for the **Gravensteen**, which dates to the 13th century and once was a prison. The gallery facing the plaza was where judges watched executions.

Head east to the 15th-century **St Pancraskerk** (Nieuwstraat), which is surrounded by tiny buildings unchanged since the pilgrims were here in 1620.

TOP CHOICE Lakenhal MUSEUM
(www.lakenhal.nl; Oude Singel 28-32; adult/child €7.50/free; ⏲10am-5pm Tue-Fri, noon-5pm Sat & Sun) Get your Rembrandt fix at the 17th-century Lakenhal, which houses the Municipal Museum, with an assortment of works by Old Masters, as well as period rooms and temporary exhibits.

Rijksmuseum van Oudheden MUSEUM
(National Museum of Antiquities; www.rmo.nl; Rapenburg 28; adult/child €9/free; ⏲10am-5pm Tue-Sun) This museum has a world-class collection of Greek, Roman and Egyptian artefacts, the pride of which is the extraordinary Temple of Taffeh.

De Valk MUSEUM
(The Falcon; ☎071-516 53 53; 2e Binnenvestgracht 1; adult/child €3/2; ⏲10am-5pm Tue-Sat, 1-5pm Sun) Leiden's landmark windmill museum, De Valk receives loving care (another restoration commenced in 2012), and many consider it the best example of its kind.

Sleeping

TOP CHOICE Hotel Nieuw Minerva HOTEL €€
(☎512 63 58; www.hotelleiden.com; Boommarkt 23; s/d from €75/80; @📶) Located in six 16th-century canalside houses, this central hotel has a mix of 40 regular (ie nothing special) and some very fun themed rooms, including a room with a bed in which King Lodewijk Bonaparte (aka Louis Bonaparte) slept. We prefer the thematic 'room of angels', a luminous vision of white.

Hotel de Doelen HOTEL €€
(☎512 05 27; www.dedoelen.com; Rapenburg 2; s/d from €85/105; @📶) It has a slightly faded air of classical elegance; some canalside rooms in this regal building are larger and better appointed than others. There are 128 rooms overall, some on the ground floor.

Eating & Drinking

The city-centre canals and narrow old streets abound with choices, although there's little of interest on the walking route in from the station. The sprawling Saturday **market** along Nieuwe Rijn abounds with fresh fare and flowers.

TOP CHOICE De Dames Proeverij CAFE €€
(www.proeverijdedames.nl; Nieuwe Rijn 37; mains €12-20) Run by two women who have excellent taste, this cafe seems to have just what you want at any time of day. There is an excellent range of coffee drinks as well as dozens of top wines by the glass. Enjoy your sips at the tables out front overlooking the canal.

Mangerie De Jonge Koekop BISTRO €€
(Lange Mare 60; mains €20-25; ⏲dinner Mon-Sat) Always popular, this bistro has fresh and inventive fare. Dine under the stars at outside tables in summer. Look for the sculpted cow's head on the front. Dishes change seasonally.

Fresh 'n Fast CAFE €
(www.freshnfast.nl; Kloksteeg 7; mains €8-12; ⏲5pm-midnight) A fabulous find near Pieterskerk, everything here is sourced from the best local and organic producers. The cheeses are from famous nearby dairies. Get a bench at a table out front.

TOP CHOICE Café L'Esperance BROWN CAFE
(www.lesperance.nl; Kaiserstraat 1) Long, dark and handsome, all decked out in nostalgic wood panelling *and* overlooking an evocative bend in the canal. Tables abound outside in summer; good meals too.

Information

The **tourist office** (☎516 60 00; www.vvvleiden.nl; Stationsweg 41; ⏲8am-6pm Mon-Fri, 10am-4pm Sat, 11am-5pm Sun), across from the train station, has good maps and info on local history.

Getting There & Away

Buses leave from directly in front of Centraal Station. **Train** destinations, all with six departures per hour, include Amsterdam (€8, 34 minutes), Den Haag (€3.50, 10 minutes) and Schiphol Airport (€6, 15 minutes).

Den Haag

☎070 / POP 501,000

Den Haag (The Hague), officially known as 's-Gravenhage (Count's Hedge), is the Dutch seat of government (although Amsterdam is the capital). Wide, tree-lined boulevards like Lange Voorhout give Den Haag a suitably regal air: it's the kind of place where the musky aftershave of suave men wearing pink cravats mingles with the frilly scents of sachets sold in pricey boutiques. The many embassies here plus various international courts of justice – which keep Den Haag in the news – give the city a worldly air. Nightlife thrives with fun seekers on international assignment and its museums include one exquisite star.

Sights & Activities

TOP CHOICE **Mauritshuis** MUSEUM
(www.mauritshuis.nl; Korte Vijverberg 8; adult/child €13.50/free; ⏲11am-5pm Tue-Sun) For a painless introduction to Dutch and Flemish Art 101, visit the Mauritshuis, a small museum in a jewel-box of an old palace. Highlights include the Dutch *Mona Lisa:* Vermeer's *Girl with a Pearl Earring*. Rembrandts include a wistful self-portrait from the year of his death, 1669, and *The Anatomy Lesson of Dr Nicolaes Tulp*.

Even if you're just passing Den Haag on the train, it's well worth hopping off to visit.

Binnenhof PALACE
(⏲10am-4pm Mon-Sat) The Binnenhof is surrounded by parliamentary buildings that have long been at the heart of Dutch politics, though parliament now meets in a modern building on the south side.

The central courtyard looks sterile today but was once used for executions. A highlight of the complex is the 13th-century **Ridderzaal** (Knights' Hall). The Gothic dining hall has been carefully restored.

To see the Binnenhof's buildings you will need to join a tour. **ProDemos** (www.prodemos.nl; Hofweg 1; Ridderzaal tours €4, government tours €6; ⏲10am-5pm Mon-Sat, 11am-4pm Sun) is the visitor organisation to the government centre that is also charged with promoting democracy. It leads the **Ridderzaal tour** (admission €4; ⏲10am-4pm Mon-Sat) as well as various **government tours** (tours from €6; ⏲schedule varies, usually Mon-Sat mornings) that take in the two chambers of parliament.

Grote Kerk CHURCH
(Rond de Grote Kerk 12) The Grote Kerk, dating from 1450, has a fine pulpit that was constructed 100 years later. The neighbouring 1565 **old town hall** (*oude raadhuis*) is a splendid example of Dutch Renaissance architecture.

Gemeentemuseum MUSEUM
(Municipal Museum; www.gemeentemuseum.nl; Stadhouderslaan 41; adult/child €13.50/free; ⏲11am-5pm Tue-Sun) Admirers of De Stijl, and in particular of Piet Mondrian, mustn't miss the Berlage-designed Gemeentemuseum. It houses a large collection of works by neoplasticist artists and others from the late 19th century, as well as extensive exhibits of applied arts, costumes and musical instruments.

Take tram 17 from CS and HS.

Madurodam AMUSEMENT PARK
(www.madurodam.nl; George Maduroplein 1; adult/child €15/11; ⏲9am-7pm) Complete with 1:25 scale versions of Schiphol, Amsterdam, windmills and tulips, Rotterdam harbour and the Delta dykes, Madurodam is a miniaturised Netherlands. It's an enlightening example of the Dutch tendency to put their world under a microscope. It reopened in 2012 after a large expansion added many more tiny things. Take tram 9 from CS and HS.

Scheveningen BEACH
(www.scheveningen.com) The long beach at Scheveningen, pronounced – if possible – as s'CHay-fuh-ninger, attracts nine million visitors per year. It's tacky, but you might just find pleasure in the carnival atmosphere. Better yet, you can escape to wide-open beaches and nature with just a bit of effort, especially to the south where the hype tapers off as you pass the harbour.

Sleeping

Discreet and subtly elegant hotels are scattered throughout the centre.

Hotel Sebel BOUTIQUE HOTEL €€
(☎385 92 00; www.hotelsebel.nl; Prins Hendrikplein 20; r €80-150; 📶) This 33-room boutique hotel is in a proud art nouveau corner building. Everything has been tastefully updated and the lobby is downright minimalist. The cheapest rooms let you touch the walls – all at once. It's on tram line 17 from CS and HS.

Hotel La Ville HOTEL €€
(☎346 36 57; www.hotellaville.nl; Veenkade 5-6; r €50-120; 📶) The 21 rooms here are the best deal close to the centre. The decor is a minimalist white, grey and maroon; some rooms share bathrooms. Apartments have basic cooking facilities and there's a small cafe. Book ahead.

Stayokay Den Haag HOSTEL €
(☎315 78 88; www.stayokay.com; Scheepmakerstraat 27; dm from €25, r from €66; @📶) This branch of the Stayokay hostel chain has all the usual facilities, including a bar, a restaurant, internet and games. It's around 15 minutes' walk from HS station.

DON'T MISS

GOUDA

Its association with cheesy comestibles has made Gouda famous – the town's namesake fermented curd is among the Netherlands' best known exports. But Gouda, the town, has a bit more to it than that. It enjoyed economic success and decline in the same manner as the rest of Holland from the 16th century onwards.

The central **Markt** is one of the largest such squares in the Netherlands. Right in the middle is the mid-15th-century **town hall** (Markt; admission €1.50; ⏲10am-4pm Mon-Fri, 11am-3pm Sat). Constructed from shimmering sandstone, this regal Gothic structure bespeaks the wealth Gouda enjoyed from the cloth trade when it was built.

On the north side of the Markt, you can't miss the **Waag**, a former cheese-weighing house built in 1668. If you have any doubt about its use, check out the reliefs carved into the side showing the cheese being weighed. The **cheese market** (www.goudakaas.nl; ⏲10am-12.30pm Thu late-Jun–Aug) is a touristy spectacle.

Just south of the Markt is **Sint Janskerk** (Achter de Kerk; adult/child €4.50/2; ⏲10am-5pm). The church itself had chequered beginnings: it burned down with ungodly regularity every 100 years or so from 1361 until the mid-16th century, when what you see today was completed. The stained-glass windows are renowned.

Gouda is on the busy train line between Utrecht (€6, 20 minutes) and Rotterdam (€5, 20 minutes).

Eating & Drinking

All those expats on expense accounts support a diverse and thriving cafe culture. The cobbled streets and canals off Denneweg are an excellent place to stroll hungry.

TOP CHOICE **Bloem** CAFE €
(www.bloemdenhaag.nl; Korte Houtstraat 6; mains €5-8; ⏲10am-6pm Mon-Sat) A cute little cafe across the Plein from the Binnenhof. There are white tables, chairs and flowers out front. Housemade tarts are superb and sandwiches include a tasty club. Smoothies will give you a dose of healthy goodness. Stop by for afternoon high tea.

It Rains Fishes SEAFOOD €€
(☎365 25 98; www.itrainsfishes.nl; Noordeinde 123; mains from €22; ⏲noon-2.30pm Mon-Fri, 6-11pm Mon-Sat) It's the 'restaurant on the sunny side of the street', a multi-award-winning seafood place serving grilled, fried and poached fish, mussels and scallops. The menu reflects what's fresh.

De Zwarte Ruiter CAFE
(The Black Rider; Grote Markt 27; snacks from €4) The Rider faces off with the competing Botерwaag across the Markt like rival kings of cool. We call this one the winner, with its terrace and art deco mezzanine – light-filled, split-level and cavernous – and boisterous crowds of commoners, diplomats and, no doubt, the odd international jewel thief.

Entertainment

Nederlands Dans Theater DANCE
(www.ndt.nl; Schedeldoekshaven 60) This world-famous dance company has two main components: NDT1, the main troupe of 32 dancers, and NDT2, a small group of 12 dancers under 21.

Shopping

Grote Markstraat is fittingly the street for large stores. Interesting shops and oddball boutiques line Hoogstraat, Noordeinde and Heulstraat; the real treats are along Prinsestraat. **Stanley & Livingstone** (☎365 73 06; Schoolstraat 21) is an excellent travel bookshop.

Information

The **tourist office** (VVV; www.scheveningendenhaag.com; Spui 68; ⏲10am-8pm Mon-Fri, to 5pm Sat, noon-5pm Sun; 📶) sells tickets for local events and has internet access.

Getting There & Around

Most **trains** start/stop their journeys from **Den Haag Centraal Station** (CS). But some through trains only stop at **Den Haag HS** (Holland Spoor) station just south of the centre. Sample destinations, with about four services per hour, include Amsterdam (€11, 50 minutes), Rotterdam (€5, 25 minutes) and Schiphol Airport (€8, 30 minutes).

A useful **day pass** for local trams costs €7.50 but you have to wait in often-long ticket queues at CS and HS.

Delft

015 / POP 98,700

Compact, charming and relaxed, Delft may be the perfect Dutch day trip. Founded around 1100, it maintains tangible links to its romantic past despite the pressures of modernisation and tourist hordes. Many of the canalside vistas could be scenes from the *Girl with a Pearl Earring*, the novel about Golden Age painter Johannes Vermeer, which was made into a movie (and partially shot here) in 2003. His *View of Delft* is an enigmatic vision of the town (it hangs in the Mauritshuis in Den Haag). Delft is also famous for its 'delftware', the distinctive blue-and-white pottery originally duplicated from Chinese porcelain by 17th-century artisans.

Sights

The 14th-century **Nieuwe Kerk** (www.nieuwekerk-delft.nl; Markt; adult/child incl Oude Kerk €3.50/1.50, ; 9am-6pm Apr-Oct, 11am-4pm Nov-Mar, closed Sun) houses the crypt of the Dutch royal family and the mausoleum of Willem the Silent. The fee includes entrance to the **Oude Kerk** (www.oudekerk-delft.nl; Heilige Geestkerkhof 25; adult/child incl Nieuwe Kerk €3.50/1.50). The latter, 800 years old, is a surreal sight: its tower leans 2m from the vertical. Among the tombs inside is Vermeer's. The **town hall** and the **Waag** on the **Grote Markt** are right out of the 17th century.

TOP CHOICE Vermeer Centrum Delft MUSEUM
(www.vermeerdelft.nl; Voldersgracht 21; adult/child €7/3; 10am-5pm) As the place where Vermeer was born, lived, and worked, Delft is 'Vermeer Central' to many art-history and Old Masters enthusiasts. Along with viewing life-sized images of Vermeer's oeuvre, you can tour a replica of Vermeer's studio, which gives insight into the way the artist approached the use of light and colour in his craft.

Municipal Museum het Prinsenhof MUSEUM
(www.prinsenhof-delft.nl; St Agathaplein 1; adult/child €7.50/free; 10am-5pm Tue-Sat, 1-5pm Sun) The former convent where Willem the Silent was assassinated in 1584 (the bullet hole in the wall is preserved) is now a museum displaying various objects telling the story of the Eighty Years War with Spain, as well as 17th-century paintings.

De Candelaer PORCELAIN STUDIO
(www.candelaer.nl; Kerkstraat 13; 9am-5.30pm Mon-Fri, to 5pm Sat year-round, 9am-5pm Sun Mar-May) The most central and modest Delftware outfit is de Candelaer, just off the Markt. It has five artists, a few of whom work most days.

De Koninklijke Porceleyne Fles PORCELAIN FACTORY
(Royal Delft; www.royaldelft.com; Rotterdamseweg 196; adult/child €12/free; 9am-5pm, closed Sun Nov-Mar) Pottery fans, and even those new to the iconic blue-and-white earthenware, will enjoy this factory-meets-gallery-meets-shopping experience. Royal Delft is a 15-minute walk from the train station.

Sleeping

Compact in size and oh-so-charming, Delft makes a good base for exploring much of the Netherlands, with frequent and fast train services putting towns from Leiden to Rotterdam less than 20 minutes away.

TOP CHOICE Hotel de Emauspoort HOTEL €€
(219 02 19; www.emauspoort.nl; Vrouwenregt 9-11; s/d from €90/100;) Couples, singles, and business travellers alike rave about this sweet, well-priced little hotel near the Markt. Spacious rooms strike a nice balance of old-world antique and totally modern comfort.

Hotel Coen HOTEL €€
(214 59 14; www.hotelcoendelft.nl; Coenderstraat 47; s/d from €72/90;) Just behind the train station construction site, this family-run hotel has 55 beds in a variety of rooms, from budget singles as thin as your wallet to grander doubles.

Eating & Drinking

Spijshuis de Dis DUTCH €€
(www.spijshuisdedis.com; Beestenmarkt 36; lunch €5-15, dinner €16-25; noon-2pm & 5-9.30pm Tue-Sun;) Foodies, romantics and oenophiles flock to this cosily elegant restaurant, where fresh fish and amazing soups served in bread bowls take centre stage.

De Visbanken SEAFOOD €
(Camaretten 2; snacks from €3; 10am-6pm) People have been selling fish on this spot since 1342. The present vendors line the display cases in the old open-air pavilion with all manner of things fishy.

Stadys Koffyhuis CAFE €
(www.stads-koffyhuis.nl; Oude Delft 133; mains €7-12) Savour Delft from seats on a terrace barge moored out the front. Savour drinks, sandwiches and pancakes while admiring possibly the best view in Delft – the Oude Kerk.

TOP CHOICE **Locus Publicus** BROWN CAFE

(Brabantse Turfmarkt 67) Glowing from within, this beer cafe has more than 200 beers. It's charming and filled with cheery locals who are quaffing their way through the list. Good people watching from the front-terrace tables.

Information

The **tourist office** (VVV; ☎215 40 51; www.delft.nl; Hippolytusbuurt 4; ⏰10am-4pm Sun & Mon, 9am-6pm Tue-Fri, 10am-5pm Sat) has free internet; the thematic walking guides are excellent.

Getting There & Away

The area around the **train station** will be a vast construction site for years to come as the lines are moved underground. Train services include Amsterdam (€12, one hour, two per hour), Den Haag (€3, 12 minutes, four per hour) and Rotterdam (€3.50, 12 minutes, four per hour).

Rotterdam

☎010 / POP 616,000

Rotterdam bursts with energy. Vibrant nightlife, a diverse, multi-ethnic community, an intensely interesting maritime tradition and a wealth of top-class museums all make it a must-see part of any visit to Holland, especially if you are passing by on the high-speed trains.

The Netherlands' 'second city', central Rotterdam was bombed flat during WWII and spent the following decades rebuilding. You won't find the classic Dutch medieval centre here – it was swept away along with the other rubble and detritus of war. In its place is an architectural aesthetic that's unique in Europe, a progressive, perpetual motion approach to architecture that's clearly a result of the city's postwar, postmodern, anything-goes philosophy (a fine example of this is the Paul McCarthy statue titled **Santa with Butt Plug** that the city placed in the main shopping district).

Sights & Activities

Rotterdam is split by the vast Nieuwe Maas shipping channel, which is crossed by a series of tunnels and bridges, notably the fabulously postmodern Erasmusbrug. The centre is on the north side of the water and is easily strolled. The historic neighbourhood of Delfshaven is 3km west.

TOP CHOICE **Museum Boijmans van Beuningen** MUSEUM

(www.boijmans.nl; Museumpark 18-20; adult/child €12.50/free, Wed free; ⏰11am-5pm Tue-Sun) Museum Boijmans van Beuningen is among Europe's very finest museums and has a permanent collection taking in Dutch and European art (Bosch, Van Eyck, Rembrandt, Tintoretto, Titian and Bruegel's *Tower of Babel*). The surrealist wing features ephemera, paraphernalia and famous works from Dalí, Duchamp, Magritte, Man Ray and more.

MARITIME ROTTERDAM

Rotterdam has embraced the sea, shipping and trade since the 16th century. Harbour tours of Europe's busiest port are fascinating, while museums and exhibits on the water bring this heritage to life.

Maritiem Museum Rotterdam (Maritime Museum; www.maritiemmuseum.nl; Leuvehaven 1; adult/child €7.50/4; ⏰10am-5pm Tue-Sat, 11am-5pm Sun year-round, plus 10am-5pm Mon Jul & Aug) This engaging museum looks at the Netherlands' rich maritime traditions. There's an array of models that any youngster would love to take into the tub, plus more interesting and explanatory displays.

Haven Museum (Leuvehaven 50; admission free; ⏰visitor centre 10am-5pm Tue-Sun) All manner of old and historic ships moored in the basin just south of the Maritiem Museum. You can wander the quays around the clock.

Oude Haven (Oude Haven) Near the Overblaak Development and the Blaak train, metro and tram station, the oldest part of the harbour dates from the 14th century. Historic boats are moored here and you can often see restorations in progress.

Spido (www.spido.nl; Willemsplein 85; adult/child €11/7; ⏰9.30am-5pm Jun-Sep, shorter hours Oct-May) Offers daily harbour tours.

Rotterdam

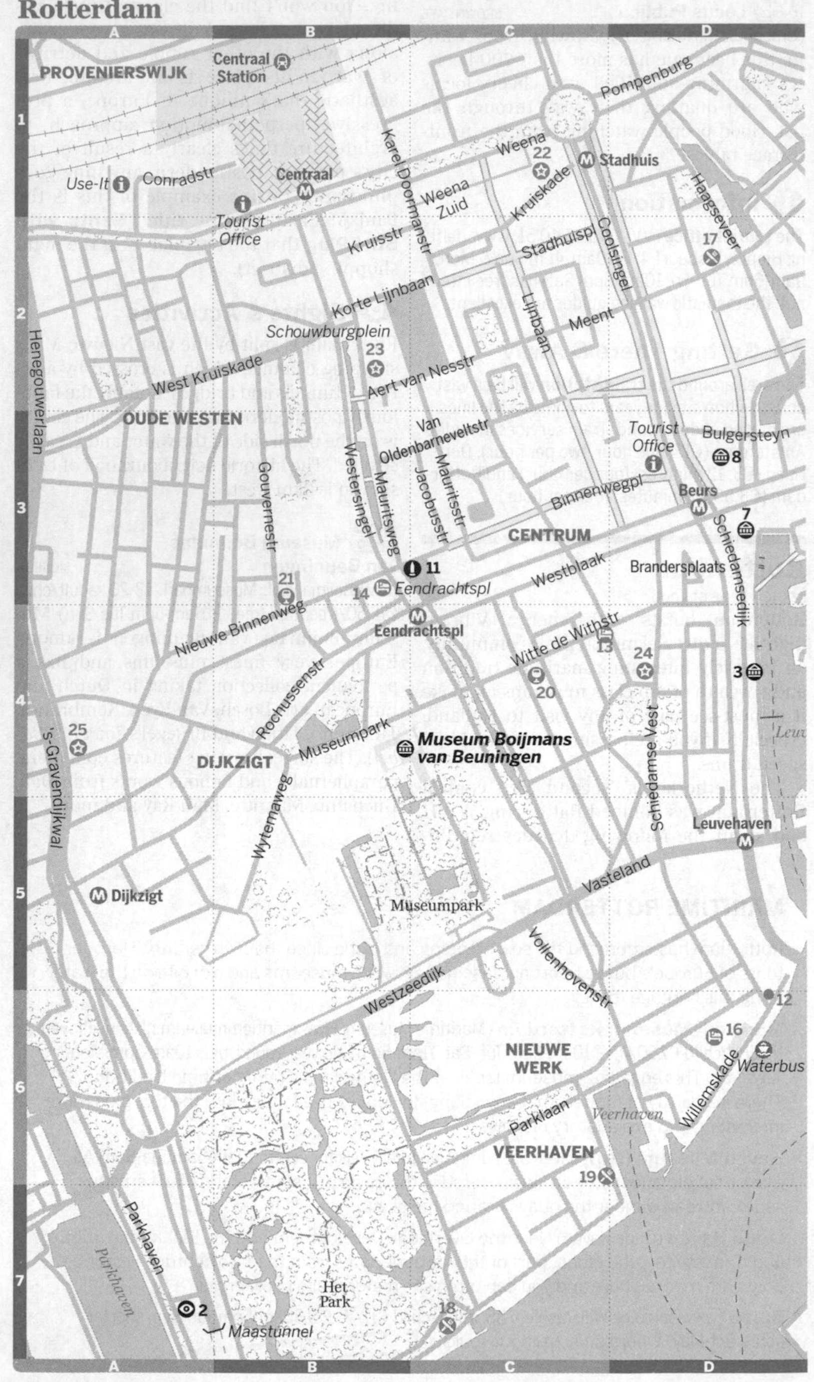

THE NETHERLANDS ROTTERDAM

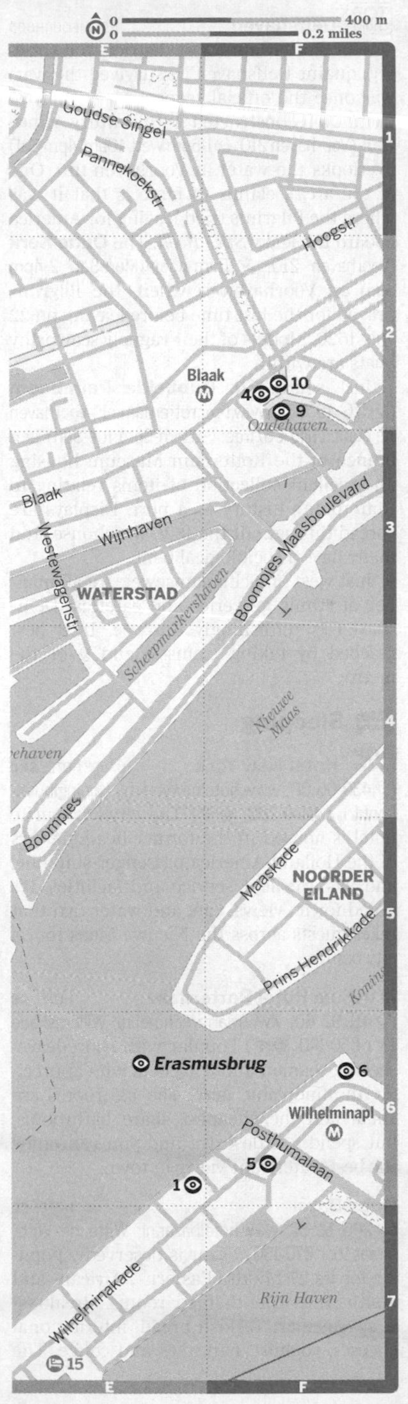

Rotterdam

Top Sights

Erasmusbrug ... E6
Museum Boijmans van Beuningen ... B4

Sights

1 De Rotterdam ... E6
2 Euromast ... A7
3 Haven Museum ... D4
4 Kijk-Kubus Museum-House ... F2
5 KPN Telecom Headquarters ... F6
6 MaasToren ... F6
7 Maritiem Museum Rotterdam ... D3
8 Museum Rotterdam ... D3
9 Oude Haven ... F2
10 Overblaak Development ... F2
11 Santa with Butt Plug Statue ... C3

Activities, Courses & Tours

12 Spido ... D6

Sleeping

13 Hotel Bazar ... C4
14 Hotel Emma ... B3
15 Hotel New York ... E7
16 Maritime Hotel Rotterdam ... D6
Stayokay Rotterdam ... (see 10)

Eating

Bazar ... (see 13)
17 Burger Trut ... D2
18 De Ballentent ... C7
19 Z&M ... C6

Drinking

20 De Witte Aap ... C4
21 Rotown ... B3

Entertainment

22 Corso ... C1
23 De Unie ... B2
24 Gay Palace ... D4
25 Nemo ... A4

Architecture NOTABLE BUILDING

Like those mod visions of the future that never seem to come to pass, Rotterdam's architecture is both fanciful and arresting.

The **Overblaak Development** (1978–84), designed by Piet Blom, is marked by its pencil-shaped tower and arresting upended, cube-shaped apartments. One unit, the **Kijk-Kubus Museum-House** (www.kubuswoning.nl; adult/child €2.50/1.50; 11am-5pm), lets you see what it's like to live at odd angles.

DON'T MISS

BLOWING IN THE WIND

In 1740 a series of windmills were built to drain a polder about 12km southeast of Rotterdam. Today 19 of the Dutch icons survive at **Kinderdijk** (www.kinderdijk.nl; admission free), which is a Unesco monument. You can wander the dikes for over 3km amid the spinning sails and visit inside one of the windmills. It's a good bicycle ride; you can rent bikes once there or travel from Rotterdam (16km); get a map from the tourist office.

A fantastic day trip is by the **Waterbus** (www.waterbus.nl; Willemskade; day pass adult/child €12.50/9). The fast ferries leave from Rotterdam every 30 minutes and a connection puts you at Kinderdijk, 1km from the first mill. After the visit, continue by ferry to utterly charming **Dordrecht** and then return to Rotterdam by train.

Designed by Ben van Berkel, the 1996 800m-long **Erasmusbrug** bridge is a city icon. Nearby, on the south bank, look for **KPN Telecom headquarters**, built in 2000 and designed by Renzo Piano, who also designed Paris' Pompidou Centre. The building leans at a sharp angle, seemingly resting on a long pole. There's also the 165m-tall **Maastoren** and **De Rotterdam**, which will be the largest building in the country when completed in 2014.

Museum Rotterdam MUSEUM
(www.hmr.rotterdam.nl; Korte Hoogstraat 31; adult/child €6/free; ⌚11am-5pm Tue-Sun) The city's history is preserved at one of the centre's few surviving 17th-century buildings. Exhibits focus on everyday life through the ages, such as the (purportedly) oldest surviving wooden shoe. It has a branch at the De Dubbelde Palmboom in Delftshaven.

Euromast VIEWPOINT
(www.euromast.com; Parkhaven 20; adult/child from €9/6; ⌚10am-11pm) A shimmy up the 185m Euromast offers unparalleled 360-degree views of Rotterdam from the 100m-high observation deck. There are all manner of extra diversions here and a bevy of combo tickets with other attractions around town.

TOP CHOICE **Delfshaven** NEIGHBOURHOOD
One of Rotterdam's best districts for strolling, quaint Delfshaven (it survived the war) was once the official seaport for the city of Delft. A reconstructed 18th-century **windmill** (Voorhaven 210; ⌚1-5pm Wed, 10am-4pm Sat) overlooks the water at Voorhaven 210. One of the area's claims to fame is that it was where the Pilgrims tried leaving for America aboard the leaky *Speedwell*. The **Oude Kerk** (Voorhaven 210; ⌚10am-noon Mon-Sat, 2-4pm Sun) on Voorhaven is where the Pilgrims prayed for the last time before leaving on 22 July 1620. Models of their vaguely seaworthy boats are within.

Just south, **De Dubbelde Palmboom** (☎476 15 33; www.hmr.rotterdam.nl; Voorhaven 12; adult/child €6/free; ⌚11am-5pm Tue-Sun) is a branch of the Rotterdam Museum housing an excellent collection of items relating to Rotterdam's history as a port. Displays are spread throughout the 1826 warehouse, and many have a sociological bent.

Just west on Schiedamseweg are all manner of ethnic groceries and eateries; Delftshaven is refreshingly un-twee. It is best reached by taking trams 4 and 9 or the metro.

Sleeping

TOP CHOICE **Hotel New York** LUXURY HOTEL €€€
(☎439 05 00; www.hotelnewyork.nl; Koninginnenhoofd 1; r €110-280; @📶) The city's favourite hotel is housed in the former headquarters of the Holland-America passenger-ship line, and has excellent service and facilities. It's noted for its views, cafe and water taxi that takes guests across the Nieuwe Maas to the city centre.

Maritime Hotel Rotterdam HOTEL €€
(☎411 92 60; www.maritimehotel.nl; Willemskade 13; r €50-140; @📶) Popular with shore-leave-seeking seamen and travellers who appreciate the fine value here. The 135 rooms are small and the cheapest share bathrooms, but spend a little extra and you can enjoy the best waterfront views in town.

Hotel Bazar HOTEL €€
(☎206 51 51; www.hotelbazar.nl; Witte de Withstraat 16; r €70-130) Bazar is deservedly popular for its 27 Middle Eastern–, African- and South American–themed rooms. Breakfast is spectacular: Turkish bread, international cheeses, yoghurt, pancakes and coffee. The

ground-floor bar and restaurant is justifiably popular.

Stayokay Rotterdam HOSTEL €
(☎436 57 63; www.stayokay.com; Overblaak 85-87; dm from €20, r from €55; @) Those odd angles you see at this hostel may not be to do with what you just smoked; this hostel is in the landmark Overblaak development. There are 245 beds in oddly shaped rooms that sleep two to eight.

Hotel Emma HOTEL €€
(☎436 55 33; www.hotelemma.nl; Nieuwe Binnenweg 6; r €60-150; @) Nicely refurbished, the Emma is a modern place with 24 rooms close to the city centre. Touches include posh bathrooms and double-glazed windows. The free breakfast includes fresh-baked goods.

Eating

CENTRAL ROTTERDAM

Look for myriad eating choices in Veerhaven, Witte de Single, Nieuwe Binnenweg and Oude Haven.

TOP CHOICE **De Ballentent** CAFE €
(www.deballentent.nl; Parkkade 1; meals from €6; 9am-11pm) Rotterdam's best waterfront pub-cafe is also a great spot for a meal. Dine on one of two terraces or inside. Mussels, schnitzels and more line the menu, but the real speciality here are *bals*, huge home-made meatloafy meatballs. Waiters and customers alike enjoy a good laugh.

Z&M BISTRO €€
(☎436 65 79; www.zenmdelicatessen.nl; Veerhaven 13; lunch mains from €7, dinner mains from €20; noon-10pm Tue-Sun) A cosy, chic French/Mediterranean bistro revered for using only organic produce from small farms, a rarity in the factory-farm-laden Netherlands. Open through the day, you can get snacks between meals and linger over a drink.

Bazar MIDDLE EASTERN €€
(Witte de Withstraat 16; mains €7-15) On the ground floor of the creative Hotel Bazar, this vast and popular eatery comes up with creative Middle Eastern fusion fare that compliments the stylised decor. The outside tables are *the* neighbourhood meeting spot day and night.

Burger Trut CAFE €
(Meent 129; mains from €6; 5-10pm Tue, 11.30am-10pm Wed-Sat, 2-8pm Sun;) Support the arts by enjoying a meal at this uniquely hybrid cafe that mixes vegetarian sensibilities with both meatless and meaty burgers. The menu is mostly Mediterranean (except for the burgers).

DELFSHAVEN

Historic and appealing, Delfshaven is a vibrant, multi-ethnic neighbourhood with many cafes and bars, especially along the canal near the Oude Kerk.

Het Eethuisje DUTCH €
(Mathenesserdijk 436; mains €8-10; 4-9pm Mon-Sat) Traditional meaty, filling Dutch food is served from this little storefront near a canal. Utterly tourist free.

Stadsbrouwerij De Pelgrim DUTCH €€
(www.pelgrimbier.nl; Aelbrechtkolk 12; mains €12-22) It's named for the religious folk who passed through on their way to America, and you can take your own voyage through the various beers brewed in the vintage surrounds. Meals range from casual lunches to more ambitious multicourse dinners.

Drinking

TOP CHOICE **Rotown** BAR
(www.rotown.nl; Nieuwe Binnenweg 17-19) A smooth bar, a dependable live rock venue, an agreeable restaurant and a popular meeting place. The musical program features new local talent, established international acts and crossover experiments.

De Witte Aap BROWN CAFE
(Witte de Withstraat 78) Fine corner boozer that's always crowded with locals from this artist-filled 'hood. The front opens right up and a huge awning keeps inclement weather at bay.

Entertainment

Rotterdam draws clubgoers from across Europe.

TOP CHOICE **Corso** CLUB
(www.corsorotterdam.nl; Kruiskade 22) This is where it's at: bleeding-edge local and international DJs mashing up a high-fibre electronic diet of bleeps 'n' beats. Art displays provide diversions at this prototypical Rotterdam club.

TOP CHOICE **De Unie** CONCERT VENUE
(www.deunie.nu; Mauritsweg 35) Truly cultural, this venue is a vision in white, which provides a blank slate for events from cabaret to forums about taxation and the middle class to acoustic folk. The cafe has excellent food.

Gay Palace CLUB
(www.gay-palace.nl; Schiedamsesingel 139) And here we have Rotterdam's only weekly gay nightclub, with four floors of throbbing gay action – with different scenes on each floor – to work you into a lather and get you sweaty.

Nemo COFFEE SHOP
(www.coffeeshop-nemo.nl; Nieuwe Binnenweg 181) Disney would not approve of the logo at this slick yet cheery shop. Browse the 15 kinds of weed on offer before you visit.

Information

The Rotterdam Welcome Card (from adult/child €10/7) offers discounts for sights, hotels and restaurants and free public transport. Buy it from the tourist office.

Tourist Office (VVV; ☎790 01 40; www.rotterdam.info; 📶) Free internet. The main (city) branch is located in the City Information Centre (Coolsingel 197; ⏱9am-6pm Mon-Fri, to 5pm Sat & Sun), with a good display on architecture since the war and a huge town model. A second location is near the train station in the landmark Groothandelsgebouw (Weena; ⏱9am-5.30pm Mon-Sat, 10am-5pm Sun). There are excellent walking guides.

Use-It (www.use-it.nl; Schaatsbaan 41-45; ⏱9am-6pm Tue-Sun mid-May–mid-Sep, to 5pm Tue-Sat mid-Sep–mid-May; 📶) Offbeat independent tourist organisation just west of the station. Books cheap accommodation and publishes the invaluable *Simply the Best* local guide.

Getting There & Away

Rotterdam Centraal Station is a new architectural stunner that will be fully open in 2014.

DESTINATION	PRICE (€)	DURATION (MIN)	FREQUENCY (PER HR)
Amsterdam via Leiden	14	65	5
Amsterdam (high speed)	16-21	43	2
Brussels	22-62	70-76	1-2
Schiphol	11-14	25-50	4-5
Utrecht	10	40	4

Getting Around

Rotterdam's trams, buses and metro are provided by **RET** (www.ret.nl). Most converge in front of CS, where there is an **information booth** (⏱7am-7pm) that also sells tickets. Day passes are sold for varying durations: 1/2/3 days costs €7/10.50/14. A single-ride ticket purchased from a bus driver or tram conductor costs €3.

Utrecht

☎030 / POP 317,000

Utrecht is one of the Netherlands' oldest cities and boasts a beautiful, vibrant, old-world city centre, ringed by striking 13th-century canal wharves. The wharves, well below street level, are unique to Utrecht. Canalside streets alongside brim with shops, restaurants and cafes.

DUTCH TOWNS WORTH A VISIT

Some cities and towns in the Netherlands you may wish to consider for day trips or longer visits.

Arnhem While the town itself is missable, nearby museums and memorials to WWII fighting are moving.

Dordrecht A good day trip by fast ferry from Rotterdam for its medieval canals.

Edam A tiny gem of an old town that's an easy day trip by bus north from Amsterdam.

Enkhuizen Home to the fascinating open-air Zuiderzeemuseum, one hour by train from Amsterdam.

Nijmegen With a relaxed riverside setting, it has the soaring 14th-century Sint Stevenskerk.

Texel Largest of the Frisian Islands, it boasts endless walks along dune-backed beaches and excellent local seafood.

Zwolle A compact centre packed with 14th-century buildings from Hanseatic times.

Initial impressions may be less auspicious. When you step off the train you'll find yourself lost in the maze that is the Hoog Catharijne shopping centre. The Hoog is huge...and it's attached to the station...and it seemingly goes on forever...and ever. It's really a nightmare but a vast construction project (www.nieuwhc.nl) is transforming the entire area.

The city's student community of 40,000 is the largest in the country. Saturdays are mad with shoppers and day trippers in from every polder in the region. In contrast, Sunday mornings are a fab time to immerse yourself in the moody charms of empty streets echoing with church bells.

Sights

Focus your wanderings on the **Domplein** and south along the tree-lined **Oudegracht**. The tourist office has a good booklet that covers Utrecht's myriad small museums, which feature everything from waste water to old trains.

TOP CHOICE Domtoren HISTORIC BUILDING
(Cathedral Tower; www.domtoren.nl; Domplein; adult/child €9/5; ⌚11am-4pm) The Domtoren is 112m high, with 465 steps and 50 bells. It's a tough haul to the top but well worth the exertion, given that the tower gives unbeatable city views; on a clear day you can see Amsterdam. The guided tour, in Dutch and English, is detailed and gives privileged insight into this beautiful structure.

Finished in the 14th century, the cathedral and its tower are the most striking medieval landmarks in a city that once had 40 cathedrals. Appreciate the craft: it took almost 300 years to complete. In 1674 the North Sea winds reached hurricane force and blew down the cathedral's nave, leaving the tower and transept behind.

Centraal Museum MUSEUM
(www.centraalmuseum.nl; Nicolaaskerkhof 10; adult/child €9/4; ⌚11am-5pm Tue-Sun) The Centraal Museum has a wide-ranging collection. It displays applied arts dating back to the 17th century, as well as paintings by some of the Utrecht School artists and a bit of De Stijl to boot – including the world's most extensive Gerrit Rietveld collection. Admission here includes Dick Bruna House and Rietveld-Schröderhuis.

Dick Bruna House

One of Utrecht's favourite sons, author and illustrator Dick Bruna is the creator of beloved cartoon rabbit Miffy and she naturally takes pride of place at his **studio** (www.dickbrunahuis.nl; Nicolaaskerkhof 10; ⌚11am-5pm Tue-Sun) across from the museum.

Rietveld-Schröderhuis

This Unesco-recognised landmark **house** (☎reservations 236 23 10; Prins Hendriklaan 50; admission surcharge €3; ⌚11am-5pm Wed-Sun) is just outside the city centre. Built in 1924 by Utrecht architect Gerrit Rietveld, it is a stark example of 'form follows function'. Visits are by mandatory tour, which should be booked in advance at Centraal Museum (see website for details); the museum will give you a map for the pleasant 25-minute stroll to the house or loan you a free bike.

Museum Catharijneconvent MUSEUM
(www.catharijneconvent.nl; Lange Nieuwegracht 38; adult/child €12/7; ⌚10am-5pm Tue-Fri, 11am-5pm Sat & Sun) The Museum Catharijneconvent has the finest collection of medieval religious art in the Netherlands – virtually the history of Christianity. It's housed in a Gothic former convent and a 18th-century canalside house.

Sleeping

TOP CHOICE B&B Utrecht GUESTHOUSE €
(☎06 5043 4884; www.hostelutrecht.nl; Lucas Bolwerk 4; dm/r from €21/60; @📶) Straddling the border between hostel and hotel, this spotless inn located in an elegant old building has an internal Ikea vibe. Breakfast, lunch and dinner ingredients are free! Internet access (in a computer room with scanners, printers etc) is also free, as is use of a huge range of musical instruments and DVDs.

Mary K Hotel HOTEL €€
(☎230 48 88; www.marykhotel.com; Oudegracht 25; r €120-180; 📶) A bevy of Utrecht artists decorated the rooms at this creative new Utrecht hotel in an ideal location. Rooms come in three basic sizes (small, medium and large) but no two are alike.

Strowis Budget Hostel HOSTEL €
(☎238 02 80; www.strowis.nl; Boothstraat 8; dm from €18, r €65; @📶) This 17th-century building is near the town centre and has been

DON'T MISS

HOGE VELUWE NATIONAL PARK

Hoge Veluwe (www.hogeveluwe.nl; adult/child/car €8.20/4.10/6; ⏲8am-10pm Jun & Jul, 9am-6pm Dec-Mar) is the Netherlands' largest national park, featuring a mix of forests and woods, shifting sands and heathery moors, along with red deer, wild boar and mouflon (wild sheep).

It features the world-class **Kröller-Müller Museum** (☎0318-59 12 41; www.kmm.nl; Houtkampweg 6; park admission plus adult/child €8.20/4.10; ⏲10am-5pm Tue-Sun), which has a superb collection of works by Van Gogh, as well as other pieces by Picasso, Renoir and Manet.

From Arnhem train station (Utrecht to Arnhem by train: €10, 37 minutes, four per hour), take bus 21 (20 minutes, every 30 minutes) to the Schaarsbergen park entrance (stop: Museum 40 45). Various buses run inside the park to the museum or you can ride one of the famous free white bikes.

lovingly restored and converted into a hostel (four- to 14-bed rooms). Housed in a beautiful old 17th-century building it has a fine rear garden. It also rents bikes.

Eating

When Utrecht groans with visiting mobs, you can escape down to the waterside canal piers with a picnic.

TOP CHOICE Blauw INDONESIAN €€
(www.restaurantblauw.nl; Springweg 64; set menu from €25; ⏲dinner) Blauw is *the* place for stylish Indonesian food in Utrecht. Young and old alike enjoy superb *rijsttafels* amid the red decor that mixes vintage art with hip minimalism.

Deeg FUSION €€€
(☎233 11 04; www.restaurantdeeg.nl; Lange Nieuwstraat 71; set menus from €35; ⏲dinner) A charming corner location in the museum quarter is but the first draw at this casual bistro, which has nightly set menus that change regularly. Fresh local produce gets a Mediterranean accent and many items – such as the cheeses – are organic.

Florin BROWN CAFE €
(www.florinutrecht.nl; Nobelstraat 2-4; mains €9-15) Battered benches and scarred wooden tables are the hallmarks of a good brown cafe and Florin nicely fits the bill. There's more emphasis on food here than at some brown cafes, but the burgers, salads and more on the menu appeal to scores of students nightly.

Drinking & Entertainment

TOP CHOICE 't Oude Pothuys BROWN CAFE
(Oudegracht 279) Small and dark, this basement pub has nightly music – jam sessions with locals trying their hand at rock and jazz. Enjoy drinks on the canalside pier.

TOP CHOICE ACU BAR
(www.acu.nl; Voorstraat 71) Billing itself as a 'political cultural centre', ACU is a classic student dive. It combines bar, venue, lecture hall and more. Argue about whether Trotsky was too conservative while downing organic vegan food.

Café Ledig Erf BAR
(Tolsteegbrug 3) This classy pub overlooks a confluence of canals (and other cafes) at the southern tip of town. The terrace vies with the beer list in offering the most joy. The autumn bock beer fest is a winner.

Information

The **tourist office** (VVV; ☎0900 128 87 32; www.utrechtyourway.nl; Domplein 9; ⏲noon-5pm Sun & Mon, 10am-5pm Tue-Sat) sells maps and tours of the nearby Domtoren.

Getting There & Away

Utrecht is easily walked (once you escape the shopping mall). The **train station**, which is in the process of being replaced, is a major connection point and is Holland's busiest. It is on the line linking Amsterdam to Cologne. Sample fares include Amsterdam (€7, 30 minutes, four per hour), Maastricht (€24, two hours, two per hour) and Rotterdam (€10, 40 minutes, four per hour).

THE DELTA REGION

The province of Zeeland (Sea Land) is three slivers of land nestling in the middle of a vast delta through which many of Europe's rivers drain; it dominates this peaceful corner of the Netherlands. As you survey the calm, flat landscape, consider that the region was home to two massive waterborne tragedies.

In 1421 the St Elizabeth's Day flood killed more than 100,000 people; and in 1953, yet another flood laid waste to 2000 lives and 800km of dikes, leaving 500,000 homeless and leading to the Delta Project, among the world's greatest engineering feats.

Middelburg

☎0118 / POP 48,000

Middelburg, Zeeland's sleepy medieval capital, is a friendly, low-key settlement: not exactly flush with nightlife, but perfect for exploring a region that is quintessentially Dutch.

Sights

This pretty, airy little town is eminently suitable for walking, with cobblestones and snaking alleyways leading in and away from the town square, which hosts a famous **market** on Thursday.

The sizable **Abdij** complex dates from the 12th century and houses the regional government as well as three churches and two museums. **Wandelkerk** (admission free, tower €4; ⏲10.30am-5pm Mon-Fri, 1.30-5pm Sat & Sun mid-Apr–Oct, tower 10am-5pm) features **Lange Jan**, a climbable 91m-high tower dating from the 14th century. The revamped **Zeeuws Museum** (www.zeeuwsmuseum.nl; adult/child €8.50/free; ⏲11am-5pm Tue-Sun), in the former monks' dormitories, features traditional garb, which must have been an expensive burden for people barely eking out a living farming.

The **town hall** (☎675 452; adult/child €4.25/3.75; ⏲tours 11.30am & 3.15pm Mar-Oct) grabs the eye: it's staggeringly beautiful. The Gothic side facing the Markt is from the 1400s, while the classical Noordstraat segment dates from the 1600s.

Sleeping & Eating

TOP CHOICE **Hotel Auberge Provençal** HOTEL €€
(☎627 659; www.auberge-provencal.nl; Koepoortstraat 10; s/d from €60/100; @📶) Dating from 1530, this building has eight comfortable rooms that are recently remodelled with stylish colours that accent the historic room details. It's a small, family-run establishment; there's a nice garden and a good breakfast buffet.

Het Princenjagt HOTEL €
(☎613 416; www.hotelhetprincenjagt.nl; Nederstraat 2; r €40-85; 📶) This eight-room B&B has a kitchen for guests to use and a jaunty location by the marina. Touches include a little toaster on each table at breakfast and nice chairs for slouching in the rooms. Four rooms share bathrooms.

TOP CHOICE **De Mug** PUB €€
(www.demug.nl; Vlasmarkt 54-56; mains €16-21; ⏲dinner Tue-Sat) Don't be fooled by the Heineken signs; the beer list is long and boasts many rare Trappist varieties. Also try the Mug Bitter, heavy on the hops. The menu goes well with the brews: hearty seafood and meat plus more simple fare for snacking.

WORTH A TRIP

THE DUTCH VS THE SEA

The disastrous 1953 flood was the impetus for the country's enormous Delta Project, which began shortly after and was finished decades later. The southwest river deltas were blocked using a network of dams, dikes and a remarkable 3.2km storm-surge barrier, which is lowered in rough conditions.

The **Waterland Neeltje Jans** (www.neeltjejans.nl; admission Nov-Mar €17, Apr-Oct €22; ⏲mostly 10am-5.30pm Sat & Sun Nov-Mar) is located near the main surge barrier. You can still explore the absorbing exhibits about floods, dams and plucky Dutch courage in battling the sea, but now the complex also includes other amusements, such as seals, a water park, a fake beach and the worrisomely named thrill ride: the Moby Dick. For a big blow, try the hurricane simulator.

The entire sandy, wind-blown, wave-tossed region has coastal sections that are part of the **National Park Oosterschelde** (www.npoosterschelde.nl; Neeltje Jans; visitor centre admission free; ⏲10am-5pm, to 9pm Jun-Aug); there's interesting displays in the visitors centre across the N57 from Waterland. Bus 133 stops at the Waterland Neeltje Jans on its run from Middelburg station (30 minutes, every 30 to 120 minutes).

De Gouden Bock DUTCH €€
(www.degoudenbock.nl; Damplein 17; mains €12-25; ⏲11am-9.30pm Tue-Sat) The colours of the coastal dunes add warmth to one of the town's most attractive restaurants. The food is from the region and the menu changes regularly; seafood is a speciality.

Getting There & Away

Middelburg is near the end of a long train line from Rotterdam (€19, 1½ hours) via Roosendaal.

THE NORTH & EAST

This region includes **Friesland**, which, once upon a time, incorporated regions of the Netherlands, northern Germany and Denmark, until it became part of the united Netherlands. The land is spongy and green, dotted with cows, lakes and centuries-old churches in little villages like **Hindeloopen**. Though the Frisian language is similar to Dutch, pronunciation is entirely different.

You can access the Unesco-recognised **Waddenzee** coastal area and sandy offshore **Frisian Islands** like **Ameland** from small ports. The capital, **Leeuwarden**, has good museums while the nearby city of **Groningen** bustles with students.

Deventer

Deventer was already a bustling mercantile port as far back as AD 800, and it maintained its prosperous trading ties for centuries, evidence of which you'll see everywhere in its sumptuously detailed old buildings.

The **Brink** is the main square and Deventer's commercial heart. The town's famous **Waag** (☎69 37 80; Brink; museum adult/child €5/2; ⏲museum 10am-5pm Tue-Sat, 1-5pm Sun), the 1528 weigh house in the middle of the square, was restored in 2003. Look for the cauldron on the north side – a gruesome and well-supported legend tells of a 16th-century clerk boiled alive in it, after he was discovered substituting cheap metals for precious ones in the local money supply.

The **Grote of Lebuïnuskerk** (admission €3; ⏲11am-5pm Mon-Sat) is the city's main church. It stands on a site where other churches were razed by flames and other catastrophes time and again, before the present Gothic structure was built between 1450 and 1530 during the Hanseatic League era.

Deventer is so well preserved that most streets will have something to see. On **Assenstraat** and **Polstraat** there are wall carvings and window decorations created over several centuries.

The **tourist office** (VVV; ☎71 01 20; www.vvvdeventer.nl; Brink 56; ⏲10am-5pm Tue-Sat, 1-5pm Sun & Mon) sells excellent walking guides and shares space with a small museum inside the Waag.

Deventer is at the junction of several minor train lines, including one to Utrecht (€13, one hour).

THE SOUTHEAST

The Dutch Southeast includes Noord Brabant, the country's largest province, primarily a land of agriculture and industry peppered with a few historic towns, including Den Bosch. The long and narrow Limburg province is home to Maastricht, contender for the title of finest Dutch city, as well as the presence of – wait for it – hills.

Maastricht

☎043 / POP 121,000

The Netherlands' other great old city couldn't be further from Amsterdam and the pearls of the Randstad and still be in the country. Granted, Maastricht sits on a little geographic appendage dangling down like an appendix but it is well worth the time to journey here from the northwest (and you can easily continue on to Belgium and Germany).

Among the 1650 listed historic buildings, look for Spanish and Roman ruins, French and Belgian twists in the architecture, splendid food and the small-town cosmopolitan flair that made Maastricht a natural location for the signing of the namesake treaty, which created the modern EU in 1992.

Sights & Activities

Maastricht's delights are scattered along both banks of the Maas. The best approach is to just start strolling. The city's ruins, old fortifications, museums and cafes (and the odd surprise) reward walkers. **Onze Lieve Vrouweplein** is an intimate cafe-filled square named after its church, which still attracts pilgrims. The busy pedestrian **Sint Servaasbrug** dates from the 13th-century and links Maastricht's centre with the Wyck district.

TOP CHOICE Bonnefantenmuseum MUSEUM
(www.bonnefantenmuseum.nl; Ave Cèramique 250; adult/child €9/free; 11am-5pm Tue-Sun) The Bonnefantenmuseum features a 28m tower that's a local landmark. Old Masters and medieval sculpture are on one floor, contemporary art by Limburg artists on the next. Make time for the world-class Neuteling collection of medieval art.

Vrijthof SQUARE
This large square, a focal point of Maastricht, is surrounded by grand cafes, museums and churches.

Sint Servaasbasiliek CHURCH
(www.sintservaas.nl; adult/child €4/free; 10am-4.30pm) Sint Servaasbasiliek, a pastiche of architecture dating from 1000, dominates the Vrijthof. The **Treasury** is filled with gold artwork from the 12th century.

Museum Aan Het Vrijthof MUSEUM
(321 13 27; www.museumspaansgouvernement.nl; Vrijthof 18; adult/child €8/2; 10am-6pm Tue-Sun) Newly opened in 2012 on the south side of the Vrijthof, this museum combines local art, history and crafts to tell a compelling story tracing Maastricht's history and creativity.

Festivals & Events

Carnaval is celebrated with greater vigour in Maastricht than anywhere else in Europe, save Venice (Italy) and Sitges (Spain). The orgy of partying and carousing begins the Friday before Shrove Tuesday and lasts until the last person collapses some time on the following Wednesday.

Sleeping

TOP CHOICE Kruisherenhotel BOUTIQUE HOTEL €€€
(329 20 20; www.chateauhotels.nl; Kruisherengang 19-23; r from €190;) This superb option is housed inside the former Crutched Friar monastery complex, dating from 1483. Where there are modern touches, such as moulded furniture and padded walls, they accent the historical surrounds. Breakfast is suitably heavenly.

TOP CHOICE Eden Designhotel Maastricht HOTEL €€
(328 25 25; www.edendesignhotel.com; Stationsstraat 40; r €80-160;) On the main drag from the train station to the centre, this regal old hotel has been given a shot of youth and tarted up for a sprightly future. The 105

WORTH A TRIP

DEN BOSCH

This sweet old town has a top-notch church, outstanding cafes, cave-like canals and atmospheric streets. The official name is 's-Hertogenbosch (Duke's Forest), but everyone calls it Den Bosch (den boss). It's also the birthplace of 15th-century painter Hieronymous Bosch, who took his name from the town. It's ideal for a day trip.

St Janskathedraal (www.sint-jan.nl; Choorstraat 1; tower €4; 8am-5pm), one of the finest Gothic churches in the Netherlands; took from 1380 to 1530 to complete. Look for the menagerie of oddball characters carved in stone above the flying buttresses.

You can find traces of Bosch in his city today. There's a **statue** of him in front of the town hall. Much more interestingly, the unmissable **Jheronimus Bosch Art Center** (www.jheronimusbosch-artcenter.nl; Jeroen Boschplein 2; adult/child €6/3; 10am-5pm Tue-Sun) re-creates all of his works and uses interactive exhibits to explore his work and life.

Canals in Den Bosch are different from the others you've been seeing: many have long stretches where they pass under buildings, plazas and roads. These tunnels add spice to the usual canal tours and have inspired more than one tunnel-of-love moment. **Binnendieze** (www.binnendieze.nl; Molenstraat 15a; adult/child €7/3.50; tickets 9.30am-5pm Apr-Oct) runs various 50-minute tours of the centre's canals.

For a respite, you can't beat **Artisan** (Verwerstraat 24; lunch menus from €29, dinner menu from €43; noon-10pm Tue-Sun), which serves fresh fare sourced locally. Lunches feature imaginative sandwiches, salads and specials. Or try the local speciality, the *Bossche bol* (Den Bosch ball), a chocolate-coated cake the size of a softball, filled with sweetened cream. They're best at **Jan de Groot** (Stationsweg 24; treats from €2; 8am-6pm Mon-Fri, to 5pm Sat) near the station.

Den Bosch is easily reached by train. Destinations include Masstricht (€19, 85 minutes) and Utrecht (€8, 30 minutes).

rooms have stark style with bold colours and details set against hardwood floors. Breakfast is included.

Hotel Holla HOTEL €
(☎321 35 23; www.hotelholla.nl; Boschstraat 104-106; r €65-100; @📶) In an elegant 1855 building, the 24 rooms here are smartly decorated and feature stylish linens. Adding to the fine value is the ground-floor cafe, which serves excellent coffee in stylish surrounds.

Stayokay Maastricht HOSTEL €
(☎750 17 90; www.stayokay.com/maastricht; Maasboulevard 101; dm from €22, r from €60; @📶) A stunner of a hostel with a large terrace right on the Maas. Choose from one of the 199 beds in dorms and private rooms. It's just south of the centre in a park.

Eating

Excellent restaurants are even more common than old fortifications in Maastricht.

TOP CHOICE **Gadjah Mas** INDONESIAN €€
(www.gadjahmas.nl; Rechtstraat 42; mains €17-25; ⏲5-10pm) The Rechtstraat, east of the river, is one of the best streets for dining in Maastricht. This small, lovely Indonesian bistro has *rijsttafels* that break with the clichéd norm.

TOP CHOICE **Bisschopsmolen** BAKERY, CAFE €
(www.bisschopsmolen.nl; Stenebrug 1-3; meals €5-12; ⏲9.30am-6pm Tue-Sun) A working 7th-century water wheel powers a vintage flour mill that supplies an adjoining bakery. The loaves come in many forms and are joined by other tasty treats (direct from the ovens that are on view out the back). Tour the mill and see how flour's been made for eons.

Sjieke DUTCH €€
(www.cafesjiek.nl; St Pieterstraat 13; meals €12-25; ⏲5pm-2am Mon-Fri, noon-11pm Sat & Sun, kitchen closes at 11pm; 📶) This cosy corner spot turns out traditional Dutch fare, including hearty stews, roasts, fresh fish and more, with colour and flair. In summer there's a bevy of tables in the park across the street. Have a red beer and pick out the stars through the trees. Glorious.

Reitz FAST FOOD €
(Markt 75; frites €2; ⏲11am-6pm Tue-Sun) Join the queue for this iconic French-fries counter, which has been serving perfectly scrumptious *frites* under the classic neon sign for decades.

Drinking

TOP CHOICE **Take One** BROWN CAFE
(www.takeonebiercafe.nl; Rechtstraat 28) Cramped and narrow from the outside, this 1930s' tavern has well over 100 beers from the most obscure parts of the Benelux. It's run by a husband-and-wife team who help you select the beer most appropriate to your taste.

EDD's GRAND CAFE
(www.edds-cafe.nl; Heggenstraat 3; mains €12-25; ⏲11am-2am) The acronym says it all: Eat, Drink and Dance. Match your mood to that of this humble-looking side street cafe with a striking post-industrial interior.

Information

Tourist Office (VVV; ☎043 325 21 21; www.vvvmaastricht.nl; Kleine Straat 1; ⏲9am-6pm Mon-Fri, to 5pm Sat year-round, 11am-3pm Sun May-Oct) In the 15th-century Dinghuis; offers excellent walking-tour brochures.

Getting There & Away

Regular **trains** link Maastricht to Brussels (€30, 1½ hours) via Liege; with connections, Cologne (€25) is two hours away. Other routes include Amsterdam (€24, 2½ hours, two per hour) and Utrecht (€23, two hours, two per hour).

UNDERSTAND THE NETHERLANDS

History

Although the Netherlands is geographically tiny, it has been a major player in world affairs throughout the ages – often unwittingly. While the nation's borders have been repeatedly sliced and diced, the Dutch themselves have blitzed distant lands. Away from conflict, the Netherlands has made a stellar contribution to the visual arts and has initiated many world firsts in 'social engineering'.

The Early Years

The Netherlands' early history is bound with that of Belgium and Luxembourg – the three were known as the Low Countries until the 16th century. In 1579 provinces in the northern Low Countries formed the United Provinces, which was the basis for the Netherlands today. They were opposed to the Spanish rule that was in place, while the southern regions, which eventually became Belgium, were open to compromise. The United Provinces fought the Spanish in the 80-year-long Revolt of the Netherlands, which ended in 1648 with a treaty that recognised them as an independent republic.

The Golden Age & the United Kingdom

The Netherlands' Golden Age lasted from about 1580 to 1740. The era's wealth was generated by the Dutch East India Company, which sent ships to the Far East for spices and other exotic goods, while colonising the Cape of Good Hope and Indonesia, and establishing trading posts throughout Asia. Later the West Indies Company sailed to West Africa and the Americas. A number of Caribbean islands were also captured in a bid to thwart the Spanish. One unfortunate by-product of Dutch colonisation was the extinction of the dodo in Mauritius, largely due to introduced species.

The wealthy merchant class supported scores of artists, including Vermeer, Steen, Hals and Rembrandt. The sciences thrived: Christiaan Huygens, for example, discovered Saturn's rings and invented the pendulum clock.

In 1795 the French invaded. When occupation ended in 1815, the United Kingdom of the Netherlands – incorporating Belgium and Luxembourg – was born. Earlier that year prostitution was legalised in the Netherlands by Napoleon (who wanted to control STDs), though it took until 1988 for the Dutch to define it as a legal profession and to allow prostitutes to join trade unions.

In 1830 the Belgians rebelled and became independent, and Luxembourg was split between Belgium and the Netherlands. Nine years later the Dutch part gained independence and officially became Luxembourg.

World Wars & Beyond

The Netherlands stayed neutral in WWI and tried to repeat the feat in WWII, only to be invaded by the Germans. Rotterdam was levelled, Dutch industry was commandeered for war purposes, and thousands of Dutch men were sent to work in Nazi factories in Germany.

Before WWII the Netherlands was home to 140,000 Jews. During the war, the occupying Nazis brought about the almost complete annihilation of the Dutch Jewish community. Less than 30,000 survived the war (25,000 in hiding and 5000 in the camps), and Amsterdam's Jewish quarter was left a ghost town.

Indonesia won independence from the Netherlands in 1949, despite Dutch military opposition. Suriname followed, peacefully, in 1975. The Antilles has close ties with the Netherlands but is self-ruled.

In 1953 a high spring tide and severe storm breached Zeeland's dikes, drowning 2000 people. Under the Delta Project a massive engineering project was created to prevent the tragedy from repeating.

In the 1960s Amsterdam became Europe's radical heart, giving rise to the riotous squatters' movement and the promiscuity that lingers today.

Maastricht Treaty to Present Day

Perhaps because of the devastating Nazi occupation, the Dutch have largely embraced European integration. In 1992 European Community members met in Maastricht to sign the treaty that created the EU.

In 1993 the Netherlands became the first country to regulate doctor-assisted euthanasia, and in 2000 the practice was legalised under stringent guidelines. That year the Netherlands also became the first nation in the world to legalise same-sex marriages.

As the Netherlands has become ever more crowded, immigration has become a topic of debate. In 2002 right-wing politician Pim Fortuyn, an advocate of zero immigration, was shot dead a few days before the Dutch general election.

In 2004 there was another high-profile assassination. Theo van Gogh, an inflammatory right-wing film-maker and columnist was killed in Amsterdam by a Moroccan Muslim, which further inflamed anti-immigrant sentiment.

The famously tolerant Dutch have moved to the right somewhat in recent years, although the centre again was dominant in 2012 elections. Questions about the Dutch commitment to the EU were quieted by a strong showing by pro-EU politicians.

Legal efforts to close and restrict the nation's famous coffee shops and their sale of pot all but ended after initial efforts in Maastricht and other southern areas caused numerous problems (open street dealing of drugs returned etc). Polls showed that the Dutch public (barely 5% of which use pot) largely disliked the laws and that the requirement for locals to register to enter the surviving coffee shops was particularly hated because of privacy concerns.

The big royal news in 2013 was the abdication after 33 years of Queen Beatrix, in favour of her son Willem-Alexander. The official handover was on 30 April and thus the often raucous celebrations of Queen's Day became King's Day.

Arts

The Netherlands claims a superb artistic heritage: many non-Dutch would be able to name at least one famous Dutch painter.

From the 15th century, Hieronymus Bosch's nightmarish works can be seen as an antecedent of surrealism. During the Golden Age, Rembrandt (1606–69) emerged with the brightest glow of all, creating shimmering religious scenes, in-demand portraits and contemplative landscapes. Frans Hals (1582–1666) captured his subjects in unguarded moments, and Jan Vermeer (1632–75) concentrated on everyday occurrences in middle-class homes, giving a proto-cinematographic quality to his compositions.

Vincent van Gogh's (1853–90) revolutionary use of colour, coarse brushwork and layered contours established him on a higher plane than his contemporaries, yet he only sold one work while alive. A bit later, Piet Mondrian (1872–1944), along with Theo van Doesburg, founded the De Stijl movement; his style of abstract rectangular compositions came to be known as neoplasticism.

MC Escher's (1902–72) graphic art still has uncanny power: a waterfall simultaneously flows up and down; a building folds in on itself. It's popular with mathematicians and stoners alike.

Environment

The Netherlands' land mass now encompasses 41,526 sq km, roughly half the size of Scotland, and half of it lies at or below sea level in the form of polders (stretches of land reclaimed from the sea). If the Netherlands lost its 2400km of dikes and dunes the large cities would be inundated, so pumping stations run around the clock to drain off excess water. Rising water levels due to climate change is a huge concern.

The Netherlands' highest point, the Vaalserberg, is in the province of Limburg, at a grand elevation of 321m.

Food & Drink

Dutch Dishes

Dutch food is hearty and designed to line the stomach; dishes include *stamppot* (mashed pot) – potatoes mashed with kale, endive or sauerkraut and served with smoked sausage or pork strips. *Hutspot* (hotchpotch) is similar, but with potatoes, carrots, onions and braised meat.

The Dutch consume almost 17kg of cheese per person per year (nearly two-thirds of it is Gouda). Look for aged varieties, often sold in brown cafes as snacks and at street markets.

Seafood is found at street stalls, including raw, slightly salted herring cut into bite-sized pieces and served with onion and pickles. Smoked eel and *kibbeling* (deep-fried cod parings) are also popular.

Drinks

Lager beer is the staple drink, served cool and topped by a big head of froth. Some places serve half-litre mugs to please tourists. More bars are serving interesting beers from a growing number of small Dutch and Belgian brewers. Look for hoppy Jopen from Haarlem.

Dutch *jenever,* or gin, is made from juniper berries and drunk chilled from a shot glass filled to the brim. Most people prefer *jonge* (young) *jenever,* which is smoother; the strong juniper flavour of *oude* (old) *jenever* can be an acquired taste.

Where to Eat & Drink

As well as restaurants, there are *eetcafes,* which are affordable, small and popular pub-like eateries. Eating venues are smokefree.

'Cafe' means a pub, also known as a *kroeg.* They generally serve food, and many have outdoor terraces. The most famous type is the cosy *bruin cafe* (brown cafe) – the name comes from smoke stains on the walls, although pretenders make do with brown paint. The best ooze the uniquely Dutch con-

EAT EARLY

The Dutch eat dinner early – popular places fill up by 7pm and most kitchens close by 10pm (9pm outside of Amsterdam and Rotterdam). Lunch tends to be more of a snack, and just a half-hour break is common. Coffee breaks are frequent.

cept of *gezelligheid,* which is one of those words that defies easy translation but which combines cosy, fun and quaint with an overlay of familiarity and good cheer.

Grand cafes are more spacious, have comfortable furniture and are very popular. Munchies are squelched around the clock at fast-food joints such as Febo, where deep-fried snacks sing their siren song from behind coin-operated doors.

SURVIVAL GUIDE

Directory A–Z

Accommodation

Always book accommodation ahead, especially during high season; note that many visitors choose to stay in Amsterdam even if travelling elsewhere. The tourist offices operate booking services; when booking for two, make it clear whether you want two single (twin) beds or a double bed.

Many Dutch hotels have steep, perilous stairs but no lifts, although most top-end and some midrange hotels are exceptions.

Lists of camping grounds are available from the tourist offices. Expect to pay roughly €10 to €20 for two people and a tent overnight, plus €3 to €6 for a car. The camping grounds have plenty of caravan hook-ups.

Stayokay (www.stayokay.com) is the Dutch hostelling association. A youth-hostel card costs €15 at the hostels; nonmembers pay an extra €2.50 per night and after six nights you become a member. The usual HI discounts apply.

PRICE RANGES

Prices quoted here include private bathrooms unless otherwise stated and are high-season rates. Breakfast is not included unless specified. Most rooms are nonsmoking.

€€€ more than €160

€€ €80 to €160

€ less than €80

Business Hours

Banks & government offices 9.30am-4pm Mon-Fri

Bars & cafes 11am-1am

Clubs Mostly 10pm-4am

Museums Most closed Monday

Post offices 9am-6pm Mon-Fri

Restaurants 10am-10pm or 11am-10pm, with a 3-6pm break

Shops Noon-6pm Mon, 9am-6pm Tue-Sat (also Sun in large cities), to 9pm Thu; supermarkets to 8pm

Discount Cards

Museumkaart (Museum Card; www.museumkaart.nl; adult/child €45/22.50, plus €5 for first-time registrants) Free and discounted entry to some 400 museums all over the country for one year. Purchase at museum ticket counters or at Uitburo ticket shops.

Embassies & Consulates

Australia (☎070-310 82 00; www.netherlands.embassy.gov.au; Carnegielaan 4, Den Haag)

Canada (☎070-311 16 00; www.netherlands.gc.ca; Sophialaan 7, Den Haag)

New Zealand (☎070-346 93 24; www.nzembassy.com; Eisenhowerlaan 77, Den Haag)

UK (☎070-427 04 27; www.britain.nl; Lange Voorhout 10, Den Haag) Amsterdam (☎020-676 43 43; www.britain.nl; Koningslaan 44)

USA (☎070-310 22 09; http://thehague.usembassy.gov; Lange Voorhout 102, Den Haag) Amsterdam (☎020-575 53 09; http://amsterdam.usconsulate.gov; Museumplein 19)

Food

The following price categories are for the cost of a main course.

€€€ more than €25

€€ €12 to €25

€ less than €12

Legal Matters

Drugs are actually illegal in the Netherlands. Possession of soft drugs up to 5g is tolerated but larger amounts can get you jailed. Hard drugs are treated as a serious crime.

Smoking is banned in all public places, including most bars (except for tiny family-run pubs). In a uniquely Dutch solution, you can still smoke pot in coffee shops as long as there's no tobacco mixed in.

Money

TIPPING

Tipping is not essential as restaurants, hotels, bars etc include a service charge on their bills. A little extra is always welcomed though, and it's an excellent way to compliment the service (if you feel it needs complimenting). The tip can be anything from rounding up to the nearest euro, to 10% of the bill.

ATMS

Automatic teller machines can be found outside banks and at train stations.

CREDIT CARDS

All major international cards are recognised, and you will find that most hotels, restaurants and major stores accept them (although *not* the Dutch railway). But always check first to avoid, as they say, disappointment.

Public Holidays

Public holidays in the Netherlands:

Nieuwjaarsdag New Year's Day

Goede Vrijdag Good Friday

Eerste Paasdag Easter Sunday

Tweede Paasdag Easter Monday

Koningsdag (King's Day) 30 April

Bevrijdingsdag (Liberation Day) 5 May

Hemelvaartsdag Ascension Day

Eerste Pinksterdag Whit Sunday (Pentecost)

Tweede Pinksterdag Whit Monday

Eerste Kerstdag (Christmas Day) 25 December

Tweede Kerstdag (Boxing Day) 26 December

Safe Travel

The Netherlands is a safe country, but be sensible all the same and *always* lock your bike. Never buy drugs on the street: you'll get ripped off or mugged, and it's illegal. And don't light up joints just anywhere – stick to coffee shops.

Telephone

Most public phones will accept credit cards as well as various phonecards.

Country code ☎31

Collect call (gesprek) domestic ☎0800 01 01; international ☎0800 04 10

International access code ☎00

International directory inquiries ☎0900 84 18

National directory inquiries ☎1888

Operator assistance ☎0800 04 10

Getting There & Away

Air

Huge **Schiphol Airport** (AMS; www.schiphol.nl) is the Netherlands' main international airport. **Rotterdam Airport** (RTM; www.rotterdamthehagueairport.nl) and **Eindhoven Airport** (EIN; www.eindhovenairport.nl) are small.

Land

BUS

The most extensive European bus network is maintained by **Eurolines** (www.eurolines.com). It offers a variety of passes with prices that vary by time of year.

CAR & MOTORCYCLE

You'll need the vehicle's registration papers, third-party insurance and an international driver's permit in addition to your domestic licence. The national auto club, **ANWB** (Dutch automobile association; www.anwb.nl), has offices across the country and will provide info if you can show an auto-club card from your home country (eg AAA in the US or AA in the UK).

TRAIN

The Netherlands has good train links to Germany, Belgium and France. All Eurail, Inter-Rail, Europass and Flexipass tickets are valid on the Dutch national train service, **Nederlandse Spoorwegen** (Netherlands Railway | NS; www.ns.nl). Many international services, including those on the high-speed line to Belgium, are operated under the **Hispeed** (www.nshispeed.nl) and **Fyra** (www.fyra.com) brands. In addition, **Thalys** (www.thalys.com) fast trains serve Brussels (where you can connect to Eurostar) and Paris. Major Dutch train stations have international ticket offices and, in peak periods, it's wise to reserve seats in advance.

Finally open (years late and far over budget), the high-speed line from Amsterdam (via Schipol and Rotterdam) speeds travel times to Antwerp (70 minutes), Brussels (two hours) and Paris (3¼ hours).

German ICE high-speed trains run six times a day between Amsterdam and Cologne (2½ hours) via Utrecht. Many continue on to Frankfurt (four hours) via Frankfurt Airport.

Sea

There are several companies operating car/passenger ferries between the Netherlands and the UK:

DFDS Seaways (www.dfds.co.uk) Sails between Newcastle and IJmuiden (15 hours), which is close to Amsterdam.

P&O Ferries (www.poferries.com) Operates an overnight ferry every evening (11 hours) between Hull and Europoort (near Rotterdam).

Stena Line (www.stenaline.co.uk) Sails between Harwich and Hoek van Holland (3¾ to 6¼ hours).

Getting Around

Boat

Ferries connect the mainland with the five Frisian Islands, including Texel. Other ferries span the Westerschelde in the south of Zeeland, providing road links to the bit of the Netherlands south of here as well as to Belgium. These are popular with people using the Zeebrugge ferry terminal and run frequently year-round.

Car & Motorcycle

HIRE

Outside Amsterdam, car-hire companies can be in inconvenient locations if you're arriving by train. You must be at least 23 years of age to hire a car in the Netherlands. Some car-hire firms levy a small surcharge for drivers under 25.

ROAD RULES

Traffic travels on the right and the minimum driving age is 18 for vehicles and 16 for motorcycles. Seat belts are required and children under 12 must ride in the back if there's room. Trams always have the right of way and, if turning right, bikes have priority.

Speed limits are 50km/h in built-up areas, 80km/h in the country, 100km/h on major through-roads, and 120km/h on freeways (sometimes 100km/h, clearly indicated). Hidden speeding cameras are everywhere and they will find you through your rental car company.

THE NETHERLANDS BY BIKE

The Netherlands has more than 20,000km of dedicated **bike paths** *(fietspaden)*, which makes it the most bike-friendly place on the planet. You can criss-cross the country on the motorways of cycling: the **LF routes**. Standing for *landelijke fietsroutes* (long-distance routes), but virtually always simply called LF, there are more than 25 routes comprising close to 7000km. All are well marked by distinctive green-and-white signs.

The best overall maps are the widely available Falk/VVV *Fietskaart met Knooppuntennetwerk* (cycling network) maps, a series of 20 that blanket the country in 1:50,000 scale, and cost €8. The keys are in English and they are highly detailed and very easy to use. Every bike lane, path and other route is shown, along with distances.

Web Resources

There are many online resources. Here are some excellent starting points (go to translate.google.com to instantly translate Dutch sites into English):

Cycling in the Netherlands (holland.cyclingaroundtheworld.nl) Superb English-language site with a vast amount of useful and inspiring information.

Cycling Homepage (fiets.startpagina.nl) Dutch site that lists every conceivable website associated with cycling in the Netherlands.

Bike Rentals

Independent rental shops are available in abundance. Many day trippers avail themselves of the train-station bicycle shops, called **Rijwiel shops** (www.ov-fiets.nl), which are found in more than 100 stations. Operating long hours (6am to midnight is common), the shops hire out bikes from €3 to €12 per day, with discounts by the week. You'll have to show an ID and leave a deposit (usually €25 to €100). The shops also usually offer repairs, sell new bikes and have cheap, secure bike parking.

On Trains

You may bring your bicycle onto any train as long as there is room; a day pass is required for bicycles (*dagkaart fiets*, €6).

TRAINS & TRIBULATIONS

Buying a train ticket is the hardest part of riding Dutch trains. Among the challenges:

» Only some ticket machines accept cash, and those are coins-only, so you need a pocketful of change.

» Ticket machines that accept plastic will not work with credit and ATM cards without embedded chips. The exceptions are a limited number of machines at Schiphol airport and Amsterdam Centraal.

» Ticket windows do not accept credit or ATM cards, although they will accept paper euros. Lines are often quite long and there is a surcharge for the often-unavoidable need to use a ticket window.

» Discounted tickets for Hispeed and Fyra trains sold on the web require a Dutch credit card. The cheap fares can't be bought at ticket windows.

» The much-hyped *Voordeelurenabonnement* (Off-Peak Discount Pass) yields good discounts but only if you have a Dutch bank account.

Public Transport

National public transport info is available in English by phone (☎0900 9292) and on the web (www.9292ov.nl). There is also an excellent smartphone app.

The universal form of transport payment in the Netherlands, the **OV-chipkaart** (www.ov-chipkaart.nl; €2.70, good for one hour) is a smartcard that you use in place of cash. Visitors can buy one from vending machines in stations or at ticket windows. Each card stores the value of your payment and deducts the cost of trips as you use it. Refill from machines or ticket windows (although the latter are often thronged).

When you enter and exit a bus, tram or train, you hold the card against a reader at the doors or station gates. The system then calculates your fare and deducts it from the card. Fares for the chip cards are much lower than a ticket bought from the driver or conductor. You can also buy OV-chipkaarts good for unlimited use for one or more days and this is often the most convenient option.

Train

The train network is run by **NS** (www.ns.nl). First-class sections are barely different from 2nd-class areas, but they are less crowded. Trains are fast and frequent and serve most places of interest. Distances are short. Most train stations have lockers operated by credit cards (average cost €5).

TICKETS

Enkele reis One way; you can break your journey along the direct route.

Dagretour Day return; 10% to 15% cheaper than two one-way tickets.

Weekendretour Weekend return; costs the same as a normal return and is valid from 7pm Friday to 4am Monday.

Dagkaart Day pass; allows unlimited train travel throughout the country. Only good value if you're planning to spend the day on the train.

Portugal

Includes »

Best Places to Eat

» The Decadente (p902)

» Bistro 'oPorto' (p912)

» A Forja (p912)

» Botequim da Mouraria (p915)

» DOP (p925)

Best Places to Stay

» Lisbon Story Guesthouse (p897)

» Albergaria Calvario (p915)

» Casa das Marés (p917)

» Casa das Obras (p921)

» Guest House Douro (p924)

Why Go?

With medieval castles, frozen-in-time villages, captivating cities and golden-sand beaches, the Portuguese experience can mean many things. History, great food and wine, idyllic scenery and blazing nightlife are just the beginning...

Portugal's capital, Lisbon, and its northern rival, Porto, are gems among the urban streetscapes of Europe. Both are magical places for the wanderer, with picturesque views over the river, rattling trams and atmospheric lanes that hide boutiques and old-school record shops, stylish lounges and a vibrant mix of restaurants, fado clubs and open-air cafes.

Outside the cities, Portugal's landscape unfolds in all its variegated beauty. Here you can stay overnight in converted hilltop fortresses fronting age-old vineyards, hike amid granite peaks or explore historic villages of the little-visited hinterland. More than 800km of coast offers more outdoor enticements. You can gaze out over dramatic end-of-the-world cliffs, surf stellar breaks off dune-covered beaches or laze peacefully on sandy islands fronting calm blue seas.

When to Go

Lisbon

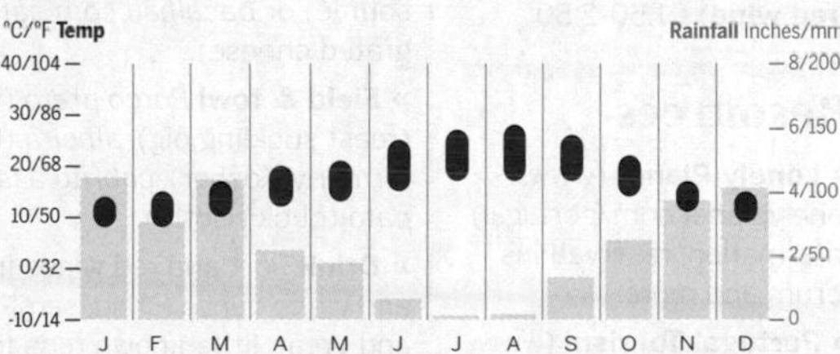

Apr & May Sunny days and wildflowers set the stage for hiking and outdoor activities.

Jun–Aug Lovely and lively, with a packed festival calendar and steamy beach days.

Late Sep & Oct Crisp mornings and sunny days; prices dip, crowds disperse.

AT A GLANCE

» **Currency** euro (€)

» **Language** Portuguese

» **Money** ATMs widespread; banks open Mon-Fri

» **Visas** Schengen rules apply

Fast Facts

» **Area** 91,470 sq km

» **Capital** Lisbon

» **Country code** ☎351

» **Emergency** ☎112

Exchange Rates

Australia	A$1	€0.82
Canada	C$1	€0.77
Japan	¥100	€0.83
New Zealand	NZ$1	€0.65
UK	UK£1	€1.18
USA	US$1	€0.78

Set Your Budget

» **Budget hotel room** €40

» **Two-course meal** €10–18

» **Museum entrance** €4–6

» **Glass of vinho tinto (red wine)** €1.50-2.50

Resources

» **Lonely Planet** (www.lonelyplanet.com/portugal) Information, reservations, forum and more

» **Portugal Tourism** (www.visitportugal.com) Official tourism site

Connections

Travelling overland from Portugal entails a trip through Spain. Good places to cross the (invisible) border include ferry crossing from Vila Real de Santo António in The Algarve, with onward connections to Seville. There are also links from Elvas (going across to Badajoz) and rail links from Valença do Minho in the north (heading up to Santiago de Compostela in Galicia).

ITINERARIES

One Week

Devote three days to Lisbon, including a night of fado in the Alfama, bar-hopping in Bairro Alto and Unesco-gazing and pastry-eating in Belém. Spend a day taking in the wooded wonderland of Sintra, before continuing to Coimbra, Portugal's own Cambridge. End your week in Porto, gateway to the magical wine-growing region of the Douro Valley.

Two Weeks

On week two, stroll the historic lanes of Évora and visit the nearby megaliths. Take in the picturesque castle towns of Monsaraz and Estremoz before hitting the beaches of the Algarve. Travel along the coast, visiting the pretty riverfront town of Tavira and the dramatic cliffs of Sagres. End the grand tour back in sunny Lisbon.

Essential Food & Drink

» **Seafood** Char-grilled *lulas* (squid), *polvo* (octopus) or *sardinhas* (sardines). Other treats: *cataplana* (seafood and sausage cooked in a copper pot), *caldeirada* (hearty fish stew) and *açorda de mariscos* (bread stew with shrimp).

» **Cod for all seasons** Portuguese have dozens of ways to prepare *bacalhau* (salted cod). Try *bacalhau a brás* (grated cod fried with potatoes and eggs), *bacalhau espiritual* (cod soufflé) or *bacalhau com natas* (baked cod with cream and grated cheese).

» **Field & fowl** *Porco preto* (sweet 'black' pork), *leitão* (roast suckling pig), *alheira* (bread and meat sausage – formerly Kosher), *cabrito assado* (roast kid) and *arroz de pato* (duck risotto).

» **Drink** Port and red wines from the Douro valley, *alvarinho* and *vinho verde* (crisp, semi-sparkling wine) from the Minho and great, little-known reds from the Alentejo and the Beiras (particularly the Dão region).

» **Pastries** The *pastel de nata* (custard tart) is legendary, especially in Belém. Other delicacies: *travesseiros* (almond and egg pastries) and *queijadas* (mini-cheese pastries).

Portugal Highlights

1. Follow the sound of fado spilling from the lamplit lanes of the **Alfama** (p892), an enchanting old-world neighbourhood in the heart of Lisbon

2. Take in the laid-back charms of **Tavira** (p911), before hitting some of The Algarve's prettiest beaches

3. Catch live music in a backstreet bar in **Coimbra** (p919), a festive university town with a stunning medieval centre

4. Explore the wooded hills of **Sintra** (p907), studded with fairy-tale-like palaces, villas and gardens

5. Conquer the trails of the ruggedly scenic **Parque Nacional da Peneda-Gerês** (p929)

6. Enjoy heady beach days in **Lagos** (p912), a surf-loving town with a vibrant drinking and dining scene

7. Explore the Unesco World Heritage–listed centre of **Porto** (p921), sampling velvety ports at riverside wine lodges

LISBON

POP 550,000

Spread across steep hillsides overlooking the Rio Tejo, Lisbon has captivated visitors for centuries. Windswept vistas at breathtaking heights reveal the city in all its beauty: Roman and Moorish ruins, white-domed cathedrals and grand plazas lined with sun-drenched cafes. The real delight of discovery, though, is delving into the narrow cobblestone lanes.

As bright-yellow trams clatter through curvy tree-lined streets, Lisboetas (residents of Lisbon) stroll through lamplit old quarters, much as they've done for centuries. Village-life gossip is exchanged over fresh bread and wine at tiny patio restaurants as fado singers perform in the background. In other parts of town, Lisbon reveals her youthful alter ego at stylish dining rooms and lounges, late-night street parties, riverside nightspots and boutiques selling all things, classic and cutting-edge.

Just outside Lisbon, there's more to explore: enchanting woodlands, gorgeous beaches and seaside villages – all ripe for discovery.

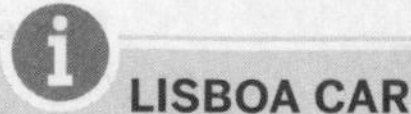

LISBOA CARD

If you're planning on doing a lot of sightseeing, you might consider this discount card. It offers free or discounted entry to key museums and attractions, plus unlimited use of public transport. The 24-/48-/72hr versions cost €19/32/39; it's available at tourist offices.

Sights

At the riverfront is the grand Praça do Comércio. Behind it march the pedestrian-filled streets of Baixa (lower) district, up to Praça da Figueira and Praça Dom Pedro IV (aka Rossio). From Baixa, it's a steep climb west, through swanky shopping district Chiado, into the narrow streets of nightlife haven Bairro Alto. Eastward from Baixa it's another climb to Castelo de São Jorge and the labyrinthine Alfama below it. The Unesco World Heritage sites of Belém lie further west along the river, an easy tram-ride from Praça do Comércio.

BAIXA & ALFAMA

Alfama is Lisbon's Moorish time capsule: a medina-like district of tangled alleys, hidden palm-shaded squares and narrow terracotta-roofed houses that tumble down to the glittering Tejo. The terrace at **Largo das Portas do Sol** provides a splendid view over the neighbourhood.

Elevador de Santa Justa ELEVATOR
(Map p898; cnr Rua de Santa Justa & Largo do Carmo; admission €5; ⏲7am-10pm) Lisbon's only vertical street lift, this lanky neo-Gothic marvel provides sweeping views over the city's skyline. From the top, it's a short stroll to the fasci-

LISBON IN...

Two Days

Take a roller-coaster ride on tram 28, hopping off to scale the ramparts of **Castelo de São Jorge**. Sample Portugal's finest at **Wine Bar do Castelo**, then stroll the picturesque lanes of **Alfama**, pausing for a pick-me-up in arty **Pois Café**. Glimpse the fortress-like **Sé** cathedral en route to shopping in pedestrianised **Baixa**. By night, return to lantern-lit Alfama for first-rate fado at **Mesa de Frades**.

On day two, breakfast on cinnamon-dusted pastries in **Belém**, then explore the fantastical Manueline cloisters of **Mosteiro dos Jerónimos**. River-gaze from the **Torre de Belém** and see cutting-edge art at the **Museu Colecção Berardo**. Head back for sundowners and magical views at **Noobai Café**, dinner at **100 Maneiras** and bar crawling in **Bairro Alto**.

Four Days

Go window-shopping and cafe-hopping in well-heeled **Chiado**, then head to futuristic **Parque das Nações** for riverfront gardens and the head-spinning **Oceanário**. That night, dine at **Mezzaluna** or **The Decadente** then go dancing in clubbing temple **Lux**.

On day four, catch the train to **Sintra**, for walks through boulder-speckled woodlands to fairy-tale palaces. Back in **Rossio**, toast your trip with cherry liqueur at **A Ginjinha** and alfresco dining at **Chapitô**.

HEAVENLY VIEWS

Lisbon's *miradouros* (viewpoints) provide memorable settings to take in the panorama. Some have outdoor cafes attached.

Largo das Portas do Sol (Map p898) With a stylish bar and cafe.

Miradouro da Graça (Map p894; ⏲10:30am-3am) A pine-fringed square that's perfect for sundowners.

Miradouro da Senhora do Monte (Map p894) The highest lookout, with memorable castle views.

Miradouro de São Pedro de Alcântara (Map p898; Rua São Pedro de Alcântara; underground rail Restauradores) Drinks and sweeping views on the edge of Bairro Alto.

Miradouro de Santa Catarina (Map p894; Rua de Santa Catarina; ⏲24hr; 🚊Elevador da Bica) Youthful spot with guitar-playing rebels, artful graffiti and a first-rate eating/drinking spot (Noobai Café) attached.

nating ruins of **Convento do Carmo**, mostly destroyed in an earthquake in 1755 (and today housing an archaeological museum).

Castelo de São Jorge CASTLE, RUINS
(Map p898; admission €7.50; ⏲9am-9pm) Dating from Visigothic times, St George's Castle sits high above town with stunning views of the city and river. Inside the Ulysses Tower, a **camera obscura** offers a unique 360-degree angle on Lisbon, with demos every half-hour. If you'd rather not walk, take scenic tram 28 from Largo Martim Moniz.

Museu do Fado MUSEUM
(Map p894; www.museudofado.pt; Largo do Chafariz de Dentro; admission €5; ⏲10am-6pm Tue-Sun) This engaging museum provides vibrant audiovisual coverage of the history of fado from its working-class roots to international stardom.

BELÉM

This quarter, 6km west of Rossio, reflects Portugal's golden age and is home to several iconic sights. In addition to heritage architecture, Belém spreads some of the country's best *pastéis de nata* (custard tarts).

To reach Belém, hop aboard tram 15 from Praça da Figueira or Praça do Comércio.

Mosteiro dos Jerónimos MONASTERY
(Praça do Império; admission €7; ⏲10am-6pm Tue-Sun) Dating from 1496, this Unesco World Heritage site is one of Lisbon's icons, and is a soaring extravaganza of Manueline architecture with stunning carvings and ceramic tiles.

FREE **Museu Colecção Berardo** MUSEUM
(www.museuberardo.pt; Praça do Império; admission free; ⏲10am-7pm) Houses an impressive collection of abstract, surrealist and pop art, along with some of the city's best temporary exhibits. There's also a great indoor-outdoor cafe.

Torre de Belém TOWER
(admission €5; ⏲10am-6pm Tue-Sun) Another of Belém's Unesco World Heritage–listed wonders, the Tower of Belém symbolises the voyages that made Portugal powerful. Brave the cramped winding staircase to the turret for fantastic river views.

SALDANHA

Museu Calouste Gulbenkian MUSEUM
(Map p894; Avenida de Berna 45; admission €4; ⏲10am-6pm Tue-Sun) This celebrated museum showcases an epic collection of Eastern and Western art: Egyptian mummy masks, Mesopotamian urns, Qing porcelain and paintings by Rembrandt, Renoir and Monet.

Centro de Arte Moderna MUSEUM
(Modern Art Centre; Map p894; Rua Dr Nicaulau de Bettencourt; admission €5; ⏲10am-6pm Tue-Sun) In a sculpture-dotted garden alongside Museu Calouste Gulbenkian, the modern art museum contains a stellar collection of 20th-century Portuguese art.

SANTA APOLÓNIA & LAPA

The museums listed here are west and east of the city centre, but are well worth visiting.

Museu Nacional do Azulejo MUSEUM
(Map p894; Rua Madre de Deus 4; admission €5; ⏲10am-6pm Tue-Sun) Languishing in a sumptuous 17th-century convent, this museum showcases Portugal's artful *azulejos* (ceramic tiles), as well as a fascinating 36m-long panel depicting pre-earthquake Lisbon.

Greater Lisbon

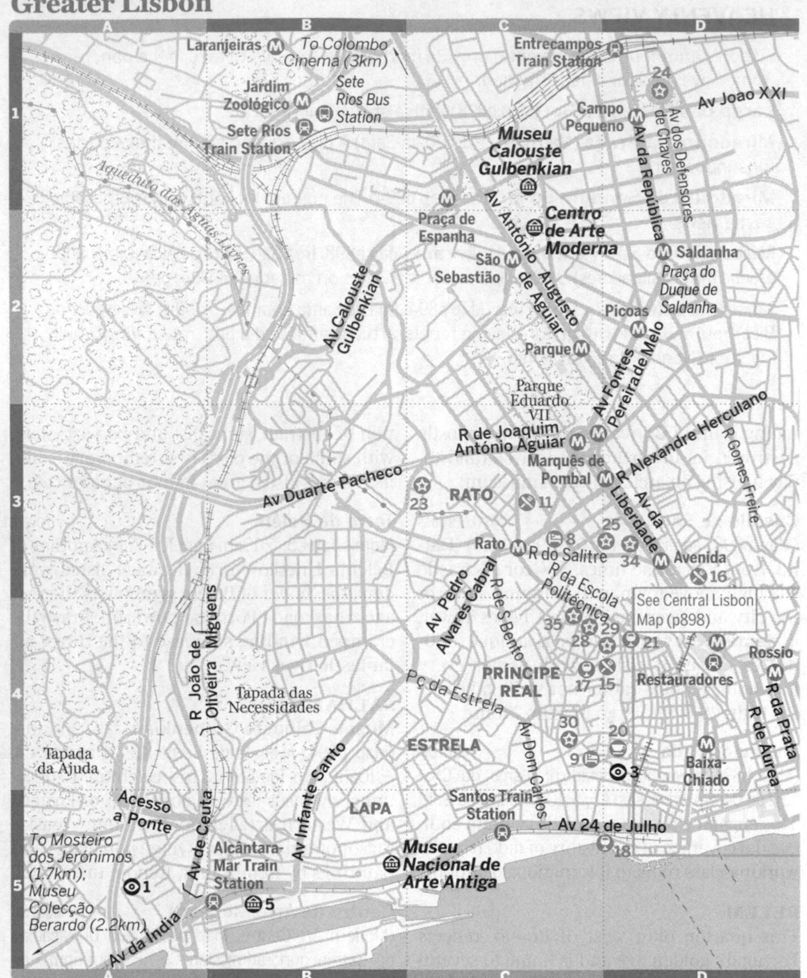

Museu Nacional de Arte Antiga MUSEUM
(Ancient Art Museum; Map p894; Rua das Janelas Verdes; admission €5; ⏲10am-6pm Tue-Sun) Set in a lemon-fronted, 17th-century palace, this museum presents a star-studded collection of European and Asian paintings and decorative arts.

PARQUE DAS NAÇÕES

The former Expo '98 site, a revitalised 2km-long waterfront area in the northeast, equals a family fun day out. There's weird and wonderful public art on display, gardens and casual riverfront cafes. Other highlights include the epic **Oceanário** (www.oceanario.pt; Doca dos Olivais; adult/child €13/9; ⏲10am-8pm), Europe's second-largest oceanarium, and **Pavilhão do Conhecimento,** (Living Science Centre; adult/child €7/4; ⏲10am-6pm Tue-Fri, 11am-7pm Sat & Sun) with over 300 interactive exhibits for kids of all ages. Take the metro to Oriente station – a stunner designed by star Spanish architect Santiago Calatrava.

Greater Lisbon

Top Sights

Centro de Arte Moderna........C2
Museu Calouste Gulbenkian........C1
Museu Nacional de Arte Antiga........B5

Sights

1 LX Factory........A5
2 Miradouro da Senhora do Monte........E3
3 Miradouro de Santa Catarina........D4
4 Museu do Fado........E4
5 Museu do Oriente........B5
6 Museu Nacional do Azulejo........F3

Sleeping

7 Alfama Patio Hostel........E4
8 Lisbon Dreams........C3
9 Oasis Lisboa........C4
10 Pensão São João da Praça........E4

Eating

11 Mezzaluna........C3
12 Páteo 13........E4
13 Pois Café........E4
14 Santo António de Alfama........E4
15 Terra........D4
16 Zé Varunca........D3

Drinking

17 Cinco Lounge........C4
18 Meninos do Rio........D5
19 Miradouro da Graça........E4
20 Noobai Café........D4
21 Pavilhão Chinês........D4

Entertainment

22 A Baîuca........E4
23 Amoreiras Cinema........C3
24 Campo Pequeno........D1
25 Cinemateca Portuguesa........D3
26 Clube de Fado........E4
27 Clube Ferroviário........F3
28 Construction........C4
29 Finalmente........D4
30 Incógnito........C4
31 Lux........F4
32 Mesa de Frades........E4
33 Onda Jazz Bar........E4
34 São Jorge........D3
35 Trumps........C4

Shopping

36 Feira da Ladra........E4

ALCÂNTARA

Today, these former wharves house a sleek and modern strip of bars and restaurants with tables spilling onto the long promenade. It's an intriguing place for a waterfront stroll, a bite or a drink, though the metallic drone of traffic across the bridge can be rather grating.

FREE Museu do Oriente MUSEUM
(Map p894; ☎213 585 200; www.museudooriente.pt; Doca de Alcântara; adult/child €5/2, 6-10pm Fri;

FREE LISBOA

Aside from the Castelo de São Jorge, many sights in Lisbon have free entrance on Sundays from 10am to 2pm. For a free cultural fix on other days, make for Belém's **Museu Colecção Berardo** for great art exhibits, **Museu do Teatro Romano** (Roman Theatre Museum; Map p898; Pátio do Aljube 5; ⏲10am-1pm & 2-6pm Tue-Sun) for Roman theatre ruins, and the fortresslike **Sé** (Cathedral; Map p898; ☎218 866 752; admission free; ⏲9am-7pm Tue-Sat, 9am-5pm Mon & Sun), built in 1150 on the site of a mosque. For more Roman ruins, take a free tour of the **Núcleo Arqueológico** (Map p898; Rua dos Correeiros 9; ⏲10am-5pm Mon-Sat), which contains a web of tunnels hidden under the Baixa. The new **Museu de Design e da Moda** (Map p898; Rua Augusta 24; ⏲10am-8pm Tue-Sun) exhibits eye-catching furniture, industrial design and couture dating to the 1930s.

⏲10am-6pm Tue-Thu, Sat & Sun, 10am-10pm Fri) Set in a revamped 1940s *bacalhau* (salted cod) warehouse, the Museu do Oriente explores Portugal's ties with Asia with a fascinating collection of art and relics from China, Japan and East Timor.

LX Factory ART CENTRE
(Map p894; www.lxfactory.com; Rua Rodrigues de Faria 103, Alcântara) Lisbon's new hub of creativity hosts a dynamic menu of events from live concerts and film screenings to fashion shows and art exhibitions. You'll find restaurants, a bookshop and design-minded shops.

Tours

We Hate Tourism Tours DRIVING TOUR
(☎913 776 598; www.wehatetourismtours.com; tours from €25 per person) Offers unique perspectives of Lisbon. Popular outings include the three-hour 'King of the Hills' open-topped jeep tour, dinner outings and Sintra trips.

Lisbon Walker WALKING
(Map p898; ☎218 861 840; www.lisbonwalker.com; Rua dos Remédios 84; 3hr walk €15; ⏲10am & 2.30pm) Well-informed, English-speaking guides lead fascinating themed walking tours through Lisbon. They depart from the northwest corner of Praça do Comércio.

Lisbon Explorer WALKING
(☎213 629 263; www.lisbonexplorer.com; tours adult/child from €34/free) Peel back the many layers of Lisbon's history during three-hour walking tours (admission to sights and transport included). It also hosts a nightly Taste of Portugal: sample (and learn about) Portuguese wines, cheeses and cured meats.

Transtejo BOAT TOUR
(Map p898; ☎210 422 417; www.transtejo.pt; Terreiro do Paço ferry terminal; adult/child €20/10; ⏲May-Oct) These 2½-hour river cruises are a laid-back way to enjoy Lisbon's sights with multilingual commentary.

Festivals & Events

The **Festa de Santo António** (Festival of Saint Anthony), from 12 June to 13 June, culminates the three-week **Festas de Lisboa**, with processions and dozens of street parties; it's liveliest in the Alfama.

Sleeping

Lisbon has a good mix of boutique hotels, stylish hostels and old-fashioned pensions that won't break the bank. Book well ahead during high season (July to mid-September).

BAIXA, ROSSIO & CAIS DO SODRÉ

Lavra Guest House GUESTHOUSE **€€**
(Map p898; ☎218 820 000; www.lavra.pt; Calçada de Santano 198, Rossio; d from €59; wifi) Set in a former convent, the Lavra Guest House has a range of rooms, from basic quarters facing onto an inner courtyard, to brighter rooms with wood floors and tiny balconies.

CYCLING THE TEJO

A **cycling/jogging path** courses along the Tejo for 7km, between Cais do Sodré and Belém. Complete with artful touches – including the poetry of Pessoa printed along parts of it – the path takes in ageing warehouses, weathered docks and open-air restaurants and nightspots.

A handy place to rent bikes is a short stroll from Cais do Sodré: **Bike Iberia** (Map p898; www.bikeiberia.com; Largo Corpo Santo 5; bike hire per hr/day €4/14; ⏲9.30am-7.30pm).

Lisbon Story Guesthouse GUESTHOUSE €€
(Map p898; ☎211 529 313; www.lisbonstoryguesthouse.com; Largo de São Domingos 18, Rossio; d €90-110, without bathroom €40-80 ; @☎) Overlooking the Praça São Domingos is a small, welcoming guesthouse with small, well-maintained rooms and a shoe-free lounge with throw pillows and low tables.

Lisbon Destination Hostel HOSTEL €
(Map p898; ☎213 466 457; www.rossiopatio.com; top floor, Rossio Train Station; dm/d/tr €22/60/75; @☎) Despite its location inside a train station, this hostel has loads of style, with a glass ceiling flooding the spacious plant-filled common area with light. Rooms are crisp and and well-maintained, and there are loads of activities (bar crawls, beach day trips, etc), plus excellent multi-course meals available (€8 per person including wine).

Beach Destination Hostel HOSTEL €
(Map p898; ☎210 997 735; Cais do Sodré Train Station; dm/d €22/60; @☎) New in 2012, this beautifully designed hostel has comfy rooms, a swanky dining room, a top-notch kitchen and a roof terrace with impressive river views.

Goodnight Hostel HOSTEL €
(Map p898; ☎213 430 139; www.goodnighthostel.com; Rua dos Correiros 113, Baixa; dm/d €20/50; @☎) Set in a converted 18th-century townhouse, this glam hostel rocks with its fab location and retro design. The high-ceilinged dorms offer vertigo-inducing views over Baixa.

Lounge Hostel HOSTEL €
(Map p898; ☎213 462 061; www.lisbonloungehostel.com; Rua de São Nicolau 41, Baixa; dm/d incl breakfast €25/64; @☎) These ultrahip Baixa digs have a party vibe. Bed down in immaculate dorms and meet like-minded travellers in the funky lounge watched over by a wacky moose head.

Travellers House HOSTEL €
(Map p898; ☎210 115 922; www.travellershouse.com; Rua Augusta 89, Baixa; dm from €22; @☎) This superfriendly hostel is set in a converted 250-year-old house and offers cosy dorms, a retro lounge with beanbags, an internet corner and a communal kitchen.

Residencial Florescente GUESTHOUSE €€
(Map p898; ☎213 426 609; www.residencialflorescente.com; Rua das Portas de Santo Antão 99, Rossio; s/d from €45/65; ❄@☎) On a vibrant street lined with alfresco restaurants, lemon-fronted Florescente has comfy rooms in muted tones with shiny modern bathrooms. It's a two-minute walk from Rossio.

Pensão Imperial GUESTHOUSE €
(Map p898; ☎213 420 166; Praça dos Restauradores 78, Rossio; s/d €25/40) Above Praça dos Restauradores, four flights up, this simple pensión has high-ceilinged rooms with basic wooden furniture; it's nothing flash, but some rooms have balconies overlooking the plaza.

ALFAMA

Alfama Patio Hostel HOSTEL €
(Map p894; ☎218 883 127; http://alfamapatio.com; Rua das Escolas Gerais 3; dm/d from €20/60; @☎) Located in the heart of the Alfama, this place attracts a cool, laid-back crowd. There are loads of activities (pub crawls, day trips to the beach), plus barbecues on the garden-like patio.

Solar dos Mouros BOUTIQUE HOTEL €€€
(Map p898; ☎218 854 940; www.solardosmouros.pt; Rua do Milagre de Santo António 4; d €87-187; ❄) Affording river or castle views, the 12 rooms at this boutique charmer bear the imprint of artist Luís Lemos and offer high-end trappings, plus a tiny water garden.

Pensão Ninho das Águias GUESTHOUSE €
(Map p898; ☎218 854 070; Costa do Castelo 74; s/d/tr without bathroom €30/40/60) It isn't called 'eagle's nest' for nothing: this guest-house has a Rapunzel-esque turret affording magical 360-degree views over Lisbon. Book ahead.

Pensão São João da Praça GUESTHOUSE €
(Map p894; ☎218 862 591; 218 862 591@sapo.pt; Rua de São João da Praça 97, 2nd fl; s/d without bathroom €30/40, d €45-55; ☎) So close to the Sé you can almost touch the gargoyles, this 19th-century guesthouse has a pick-and-mix of clean, sunny rooms; the best has a river-facing veranda.

CHIADO, BAIRRO ALTO & PRÍNCIPE REAL

Oasis Lisboa HOSTEL €
(Map p894; ☎213 478 044; www.oasislisboa.com; Rua de Santa Catarina 24, Principe Real; dm incl breakfast €17-21; @☎) Behind yellow wonder

WANT MORE?

For in-depth information, reviews and recommendations at your fingertips, head to the Apple App Store to purchase Lonely Planet's *Lisbon City Guide* iPhone app.

Central Lisbon

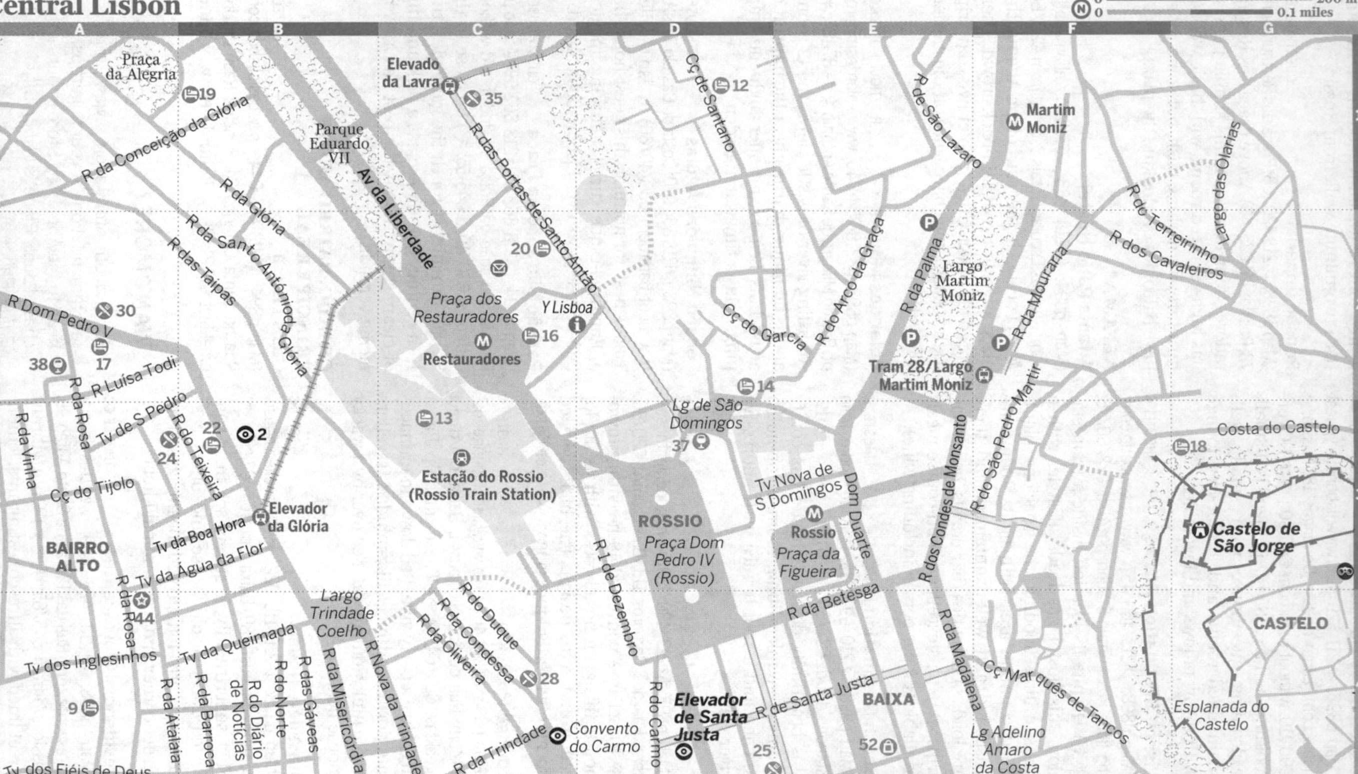

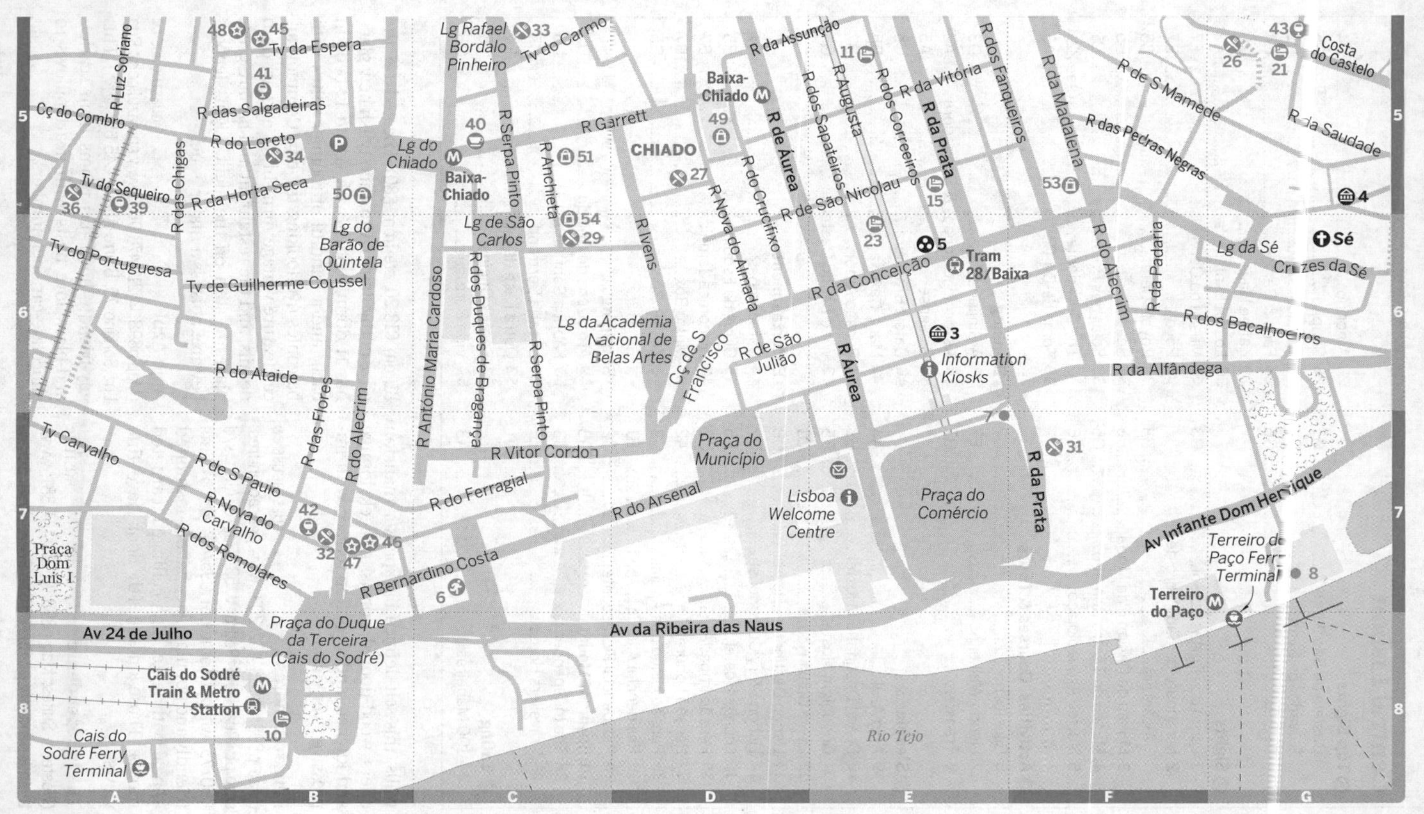
Costa do Castelo
R de S Mamede
R da Saudade
R das Pedras Negras
Sé
Lg da Sé
Cruzes da Sé
R da Padaria
R dos Bacalhoeiros
R da Alfândega
Av Infante Dom Henrique
Terreiro do Paço Ferry Terminal
Terreiro do Paço
R da Madalena
R do Alecrim
R dos Fanqueiros
R da Prata
R da Vitória
R dos Correeiros
R Augusta
R dos Sapateiros
R de São Nicolau
R da Assunção
R de Áurea
Baixa-Chiado
R do Crucifixo
R Nova do Almada
R da Conceição
Tram 28/Baixa
Information Kiosks
R Áurea
R de São Julião
Praça do Comércio
Lisboa Welcome Centre
Praça do Município
Cç de S Francisco
Lg da Academia Nacional de Belas Artes
R Ivens
CHIADO
R Garrett
R Anchieta
R Serpa Pinto
Lg de São Carlos
Lg Rafael Bordalo Pinheiro
Tv do Carmo
Lg do Chiado
R dos Duques de Bragança
R António Maria Cardoso
R Vitor Cordon
R do Ferragial
R do Arsenal
R Bernardino Costa
Av da Ribeira das Naus
Rio Tejo
Tv da Espera
R Luz Soriano
R das Salgadeiras
Cç do Combro
R do Loreto
R das Chigas
Tv do Sequeiro
R da Horta Seca
Lg do Barão de Quintela
Tv do Portuguesa
Tv de Guilherme Coussel
R do Ataide
R das Flores
R do Alecrim
Tv Carvalho
R de S Paulo
R Nova do Carvalho
R dos Remolares
Praça Dom Luís I
Praça do Duque da Terceira (Cais do Sodré)
Av 24 de Julho
Cais do Sodré Train & Metro Station
Cais do Sodré Ferry Terminal

Central Lisbon

Top Sights

Castelo de São Jorge ... G3
Elevador de Santa Justa ... D4
Sé ... G6

Sights

1 Largo das Portas do Sol ... G3
2 Miradouro de São Pedro de Alcântara ... B3
3 Museu de Design e da Moda ... E6
4 Museu do Teatro Romano ... G5
5 Núcleo Arqueológico ... E6

Activities, Courses & Tours

6 Bike Iberia ... C7
7 Lisbon Walker ... E7
8 Transtejo ... G7

Sleeping

9 Anjo Azul ... A4
10 Beach Destination Hostel ... B8
11 Goodnight Hostel ... E5
12 Lavra Guest House ... D1
13 Lisbon Destination Hostel ... C3
14 Lisbon Story Guesthouse ... D2
15 Lounge Hostel ... E5
16 Pensão Imperial ... C2
17 Pensão Londres ... A2
18 Pensão Ninho das Águias ... G3
19 Residencial Alegria ... B1
20 Residencial Florescente ... C2
21 Solar dos Mouros ... G5
22 The Independente ... B3
23 Travellers House ... E6

Eating

24 100 Maneiras ... A3
25 Amorino ... D4
26 Chapitô ... G5
27 Fábulas ... D5
28 Faca & Garfo ... C4
29 Kaffee Haus ... C6
30 Lost in Esplanada ... A2
31 Museu da Cerveja ... F7
32 Povo ... B7
33 Royale Café ... C5
34 Sea Me ... B5
35 Solar dos Presuntos ... C1
The Decadente ... (see 22)
36 Toma Lá-Dá-Cá ... A5

Drinking

37 A Ginjinha ... D3
38 Associação Loucos & Sonhadores ... A2
39 Bicaense ... A5
40 Café a Brasileira ... C5
41 Maria Caxuxa ... B5
42 Pensão Amor ... B7
43 Wine Bar do Castelo ... G5

Entertainment

44 Catacumbas ... A4
45 Clube da Esquina ... B5
46 Discoteca Jamaica ... B7
47 Music Box ... B7
48 Zé dos Bois ... B5

Shopping

49 Armazéns do Chiado ... D5
50 Fábrica Sant'Ana ... B5
51 Livraria Bertrand ... C5
52 Outra Face da Lua ... E4
53 Santos Oficios ... F5
54 Vida Portuguesa ... C6

walls, this self-defined backpacker mansion offers wood-floored dorms, a sleek lounge and kitchen, and a rooftop terrace with impressive river views.

Pensão Londres GUESTHOUSE €€
(Map p898; ☎213 462 203; www.pensaolondres.com.pt; Rua Dom Pedro V 53, Bairro Alto; s/d €50/75, without bathroom €35/45; @☞) This friendly and popular place has old-fashioned appeal with large, high-ceilinged, carpeted rooms. Those on the 4th floor have fine views.

The Independente HOSTEL €
(Hostel & Suites; Map p898; ☎213 461 381; www.theindependente.pt; Rua de São Pedro de Alcântara 81; dm €18-20, ste from €80) Located on the edge of the Bairro Alto, this stylish new place has 11 dorm rooms (with six- to 12-beds in each) and a handful of roomier suites with balconies overlooking the city. Common areas feature vintage furnishings and art deco details, and the restaurant and bar are great places to start off the night. Light sleepers beware: noise is a major issue.

Anjo Azul GUESTHOUSE €€
(Map p898; ☎213 478 069; www.anjoazul.com; Rua Luz Soriano 75, Bairro Alto; r €45-65; @☞) This gay-friendly hotel has rooms from scarlet-and-black love nests with heart pillows to chocolate-caramel numbers.

AVENIDA DE LIBERDADE, RATO & MARQUÊS DE POMBAL

Lisbon Dreams GUESTHOUSE €€
(Map p894; ☎213 072 393; www.lisbondreamsguesthouse.com; Rua Rodrigo da Fonseca 29, Rato; s/d without bathroom incl breakfast €50/60; @📶) On a quiet street lined with jacaranda trees, Lisbon Dreams offers excellent value with its bright modern rooms with tall ceilings and high-end mattresses. Bathrooms are shared, but spotlessly clean.

Residencial Alegria GUESTHOUSE €€
(Map p898; ☎213 220 670; www.alegrianet.com; Praça da Alegria 12; d €60-83; ❄) Overlooking a palm-dotted plaza, this lemon-fronted belle époque gem has airy and peaceful rooms, with antique-filled corridors.

New-generation chefs, first-rate ingredients and a generous pinch of old-world spice have helped put Lisbon on the gastronomic map. In addition to creative newcomers, you'll find inexpensive, traditional dining rooms home to classic Portuguese fare.

BAIXA, ROSSIO & CAIS DO SODRÉ

Solar dos Presuntos PORTUGUESE €€€
(Map p898; ☎213 424 253; Rua das Portas de Santo Antão 150, Rossio; mains €15-26; ⏲lunch & dinner Mon-Sat) Renowned for its excellent seafood as well as its smoked and grilled meats, this buzzing restaurant serves up memorable lobster and prawn curry, salt-baked sea bass and delectable seafood paella, among other great picks.

Povo PORTUGUESE €
(Map p898; Rua Nova do Carvalho 32; small plates €4-8; ⏲noon-2am Tue-Sat, 6pm-1am Sun & Mon) On bar-lined Rua Nova do Carvalho, Povo serves up tasty Portuguese comfort food in the form of *petiscos* (small plates). Try the *favinhas e chouriço* (fava beans with chorizo), *salada de polvo* (octopus salad) or *camarão ao alhinho* (garlic prawns). There's also outdoor seating and live fado nights (Thursdays are best).

Museu da Cerveja PORTUGUESE €€
(Map p898; Praça do Comerçio 62; mains €10-16; ⏲9am-2am) One of a number of new eating and drinking spaces lining the east and west sides of the Praça do Comerçio, this sprawling restaurant serves up grilled meats and seafood as well as microbrews and beers from Angola. The outdoor tables are great for people watching.

Amorino ICE CREAM €
(Map p898; Rua Augusta 209; small/large ice cream €3.50/5.50; ⏲11am-9pm) Amorino serves the city's best gelato – creamy, rich decadence made from organic, high-quality ingredients.

ALFAMA

Santo António de Alfama PORTUGUESE €€€
(Map p894; ☎218 881 328; Beco de Saõ Miguel 7; mains €14-20; ⏲lunch & dinner) With a lovely front courtyard and atmospheric interior, this bistro is one of the Alfama's stars, with tasty appetisers (try gorgonzola-stuffed mushrooms or roasted aubergines with yoghurt), as well as more filling traditional Portuguese dishes.

Páteo 13 PORTUGUESE €€
(Map p894; Calçadinha de Santo Estêvão 13; mains €8-12) Follow the scent of chargrilled fish to this local favourite, tucked away on a small, festively decorated plaza in the Alfama. Join buzzing crowds hunkered over picnic tables as they feast on barbecued seafood and meats, washed down with ever-flowing Alentejan reds.

Chapitô CONTEMPORARY €€€
(Map p898; ☎218 867 334; Costa do Castelo 7; mains €17-20; ⏲lunch & dinner) This creative spot (which shares space with a circus school) has a gardenlike courtyard and a top-floor restaurant, affording mesmerising views over Lisbon. The small menu leans toward grilled meats and fish and the bar onsite often features live music, film screenings and other events.

Pois Café CAFE €€
(Map p894; Rua de São João da Praça 93; mains €5-12; ⏲11am-10pm Tue-Sun) Boasting a laid-back vibe, Pois Café has creative salads, sandwiches and fresh juices, plus daily specials (soup and main for €9.50). Its sofas invite lazy afternoons reading novels and sipping coffee.

AVENIDA DE LIBERDADE, RATO & MARQUÊS DE POMBAL

Mezzaluna ITALIAN €€€
(Map p894; ☎213 879 944; Rua Artilharia Um 16; mains €16-20; ⏲lunch Mon-Fri, dinner Mon-Sat) Run by a Neopolitan chef who grew up in New York, Mezzaluna prepares beautifully turned out dishes that blend classic Italian recipes with mouthwateringly fresh Portuguese ingredients. Start off with tender carpaccio or endive leaves wrapped in prosciutto, parmesan and *ginjinha* (cherry brandy) reduction, before moving on to linguine with octopus or pan-seared duck breast with prune sauce.

Zé Varunca PORTUGUESE €€

(Map p894; Rua de São José 54; mains €10-14; ⌚lunch & dinner Mon-Sat) This charming, rustically decorated restaurant specialises in Alentejo cooking, with a changing menu of regional favourites such as oven-roasted duck and *migas de bacalhau* (a bread-based dish cooked with cod).

CHIADO, BAIRRO ALTO & PRÍNCIPE REAL

The Decadente PORTUGUESE €€

(Map p898; ☎913 069 345; Rua de São Pedro de Alcântara 81, The Independente; mains €10-14) This beautifully designed restaurant, with touches of industrial chic, geometric artwork and an enticing back patio, attracts a mix of hip Lisboetas and foreign guests staying at the Independente. All come for inventive dishes showcasing high-end Portuguese ingredients at excellent prices. The changing three-course lunch menu (€10) is first-rate. Start off with creative cocktails in the front bar.

100 Maneiras FUSION €€€

(Map p898; ☎210 990 475; Rua do Teixeira 35, Bairro Alta; tasting menus €45; ⌚dinner) One of Lisbon's best-rated restaurants, 100 Maneiras has no menu, just a 10-course tasting menu that changes daily and features creative, delicately prepared dishes. There's a lively buzz to the small space. Reservations essential.

Sea Me SEAFOOD €€€

(Map p898; ☎213 461 564; Rua do Lareto 21; mains €17-28; ⌚lunch & dinner) One of Lisbon's best seafood restaurants serves up magnificent grilled fish by the kilo (check out the tempting fresh selection in back), as well as flavourful plates with international accents – risotto with shrimp, Thai green curry with grilled salmon, seared scallops with mango relish and fish ceviche among other standouts.

Lost in Esplanada INTERNATIONAL €€

(Map p898; Rua Dom Pedro V 56; mains €11-15; ⌚4pm-midnight Mon, 12.30pm-midnight Tue-Sat) Hidden behind an Indian textile shop, this well-concealed terrace is set with painted whicker chairs, a gurgling fountain, and a Krishna mural, though the view over the city is the real star. Vegie burgers, prawn curry, Portuguese sharing plates and the like make up the menu. Live jazz on Thursdays (from 9 to 11pm).

Fábulas CAFE €€

(Map p898; Calçada Nova de São Francisco 14, Chiado; mains €9-13; ⌚10am-midnight Mon-Sat, noon-10pm Sun; 📶) Stone walls, low lighting and twisting corridors that open onto cosy nooks and crannies do indeed conjure a storybook *fábula* (fable). Sink into a comfy couch with coffee or wine, or have a bite to eat from the menu of creative salads, curries, burritos and daily specials.

Faca & Garfo PORTUGUESE €

(Map p898; Rua da Condessa 2, Chiado; mains €7-9; ⌚lunch & dinner Mon-Sat) The sweet *azulejo*-filled Faca & Garfo ('knife and fork') serves carefully prepared Portuguese recipes at reasonable prices. Try the authentic *alheira de Mirandela* (chicken sausage) or the *bife à casa* (steak with cream and port wine sauce).

Terra VEGETARIAN €€

(Map p894; ☎213 421 407; Rua da Palmeira 15, Principe Real; buffet €13-16; ⌚lunch & dinner Tue-Sun; 🖉) Terra is famed for its superb vegetarian buffet (including vegan options) of salads, kebabs and curries, plus organic wines and juices. A fountain gurgles in the tree-shaded courtyard, lit by twinkling lights after dark.

Toma Lá-Dá-Cá PORTUGUESE €

(Map p898; ☎213 479 243; Travessa do Sequeiro 38; mains €7-12; ⌚lunch & dinner) Get your tongue in a twist pronouncing the name of this Santa Catarina gem, where there's often an anaconda of a queue. The inviting space rolls out perfectly grilled fish, along with superb desserts.

Kaffee Haus CAFE €€

(Map p898; Rua Anchieta 3, Chiado; mains €9-13; ⌚11am-midnight Tue-Thu, 11am-2am Fri & Sat, 11am-8pm Sun) Overlooking a peaceful corner of Chiado, this cool but unpretentious cafe has daily chalkboard specials – big salads, tasty schnitzels, vegetarian risotto, strudels, cakes and more.

Royale Café CAFE €

(Map p898; ☎213 469 125; Largo Rafael Bordalo Pinheiro 29, Chiado; mains around €10; ⌚10am-midnight Mon-Sat, to 8pm Sun) This chichi cafe has a pleasant vine-clad courtyard that's ideal for drinks, create-your-own sandwiches, salads and Portuguese fusion fare.

BELÉM

Antiga Confeitaria de Belém BAKERY €

(☎213 637 423; Rua de Belém 86-88; ⌚8am-11pm) Since 1837, this patisserie has been transporting locals to sugar-coated nirvana with heavenly *pastéis de belém*: crispy crusted pastry nests filled with custard cream.

Nosolo Italia ITALIAN €€
(Av de Brasília 202; mains €10-14; ⏲noon-10pm) This bustling eatery with outdoor tables perched over the water has a big menu of tasty thin-crust pizzas, pastas, salads and crepes; there's also a popular ice cream counter.

Drinking

All-night street parties in Bairro Alto, sunset drinks from high-up terraces, and sumptuous art deco cafes scattered about Chiado – Lisbon has many enticing options for imbibers.

Pensão Amor BAR
(Map p898; Rua Nova do Carvalho 36; ⏲noon-2am Mon-Wed, to 4am Thu & Fri, 6pm-4am Sat) Set inside a former brothel, this cheeky bar pays homage to its passion-filled past with colourful wall murals, a library of erotic-tinged works and a boutique selling amorous accoutrements. Numerous other bars line the street (including O Bar da Velha Senhora where you can sometimes catch burlesque shows); expect huge crowds on weekends.

Pavilhão Chinês LOUNGE
(Map p894; Rua Dom Pedro V 89-91, Principe Real) An old curiosity shop of a bar with oil paintings and model spitfires dangling from the ceiling, and cabinets brimming with glittering Venetian masks and Action Men. Play pool or bag a comfy armchair with a port or beer in hand.

Bicaense BAR
(Map p898; Rua da Bica de Duarte Belo 42a, Bica) Indie kids have a soft spot for this chilled Santa Catarina haunt, kitted out with retro radios, projectors and squishy beanbags. DJs spin house to the pre-clubbing crowd and the back room stages occasional gigs.

Wine Bar do Castelo WINE BAR
(Map p898; Rua Bartolomeu de Gusmão 13, Castelo; ⏲noon-10pm) Near the entrance to the Castelo de São Jorge, this welcoming place serves more than 150 Portuguese wines by the glass, along with gourmet smoked meats, cheeses, olives and other tasty accompaniments.

Associação Loucos & Sonhadores BAR
(Map p898; Travessa do Conde de Soure 2) Though it's in Bairro Alto, this bohemian drinking den feels secreted away from the heaving masses on nearby streets. Kitschy decor, free (salty) popcorn and eclectic tunes – it's a great place for conversation rather than pounding shots.

Cinco Lounge LOUNGE
(Map p894; Rua Ruben António Leitão 17, Principe Real; ⏲9pm-2am) Take an award-winning London-born mixologist, add a candlelit, gold-kissed setting and give it a funky twist and you have Cinco Lounge. Come for the laid-back scene and legendary cocktails.

Meninos do Rio BAR
(Map p894; Rua da Cintura do Porto de Lisboa, Armação 255, Santos; ⏲12.30pm-1am Sun-Thu, to 4am Fri & Sat) Perched on the river's edge, Meninos do Rio has palm trees, wooden decks, DJs and tropical cocktails, giving it a vibe that's more Caribbean than Iberian.

Maria Caxuxa BAR
(Map p898; Rua Barroca 6, Bairro Alto; ⏲8am-2am) Maria Caxuxa has effortless style, its several rooms decked with giant mixers, *azulejo*-lined walls and 1950s armchairs and sofas, as funk-laden jazz plays overhead.

Café a Brasileira CAFE, BAR
(Map p898; ☎213 469 547; Rua Garrett 120, Chiado; ⏲8am-2am) An historic watering hole for Lisbon's 19th-century greats, with warm wooden innards and a busy counter serving daytime coffees and pints at night.

Noobai Café CAFE, BAR
(Map p894; Miradouro de Santa Catarina, Santa Catarina; ⏲noon-midnight) Lisbon's best-kept secret is next to Miradouro de Santa Catarina, with a laid-back vibe, jazzy beats and magnificent views from the terrace.

A Ginjinha BAR
(Map p898; Largo de Saõ Domingos 8, Rossio; ⏲9am-10pm) Join a wide swath of society for a refreshingly potent quaff of *ginjinha* at this tiny bar/stand-up counter near Rossio.

Entertainment

For the latest goings-on, pick up the weekly *Time Out Lisboa* (www.timeout.pt) from bookstores, or the free monthly *Follow me Lisboa* or *Agenda Cultural Lisboa* from the tourist office.

Live Music

Zé dos Bois LIVE MUSIC
(Map p898; ☎213 430 205; www.zedosbois.org; Rua da Barroca 59, Bairro Alta) Focusing on tomorrow's performing arts and music trends, Zé dos Bois is an experimental venue with a laid-back courtyard. Come for concerts, DJs and changing exhibitions.

PORTUGUESE SOUL

Infused by Moorish song and the ditties of homesick sailors, bluesy, bittersweet **fado** encapsulates the Lisbon psyche like nothing else. The uniquely Portuguese style was born in the Alfama, still the best place in Lisbon to hear it live. Minimum consumption charges range from €15 to €25 per person.

A Baîuca (Map p894; Rua de São Miguel 20; ⏲dinner Thu-Mon) On a good night, walking into A Baîuca is like gatecrashing a family party. It's a special place with *fado vadio*, where locals take a turn and spectators hiss if anyone dares to chat during the singing.

Clube de Fado (Map p894; ☎218 852 704; www.clube-de-fado.com; Rua de São João da Praça; ⏲9pm-2.30am Mon-Sat) Hosts the cream of the fado crop in vaulted, dimly lit surrounds. Big-name *fadistas* perform here alongside celebrated guitarists.

Mesa de Frades (Map p894; ☎917 029 436; www.mesadefrades.com; Rua dos Remédios 139a; admission from €15; ⏲dinner Wed-Mon) A magical place to hear fado, tiny Mesa de Frades used to be a chapel. It's tiled with exquisite *azulejos* and has just a handful of tables. Reserve ahead.

Onda Jazz Bar JAZZ
(Map p894; www.ondajazz.com; Arco de Jesus 7, Alfama) This vaulted cellar features a menu of mainstream jazz, plus more-eclectic beats from bands hailing from Brazil and Africa.

Catacumbas JAZZ
(Map p898; Travessa da Água da Flor 43, Bairro Alta) Moodily lit and festooned with portraits of legends such as Miles Davis, this den is jampacked when it hosts live jazz on Thursday nights.

Nightclubs

Cover charges for nightclubs typically run from €5 to €12.

Lux CLUB
(Map p894; www.luxfragil.com; Avenida Infante Dom Henrique, Santo Apolónia) Still Lisbon's best club, this beautifully conceived two-storey club attracts a mixed crowd who come for an eclectic lineup of concerts, along with big-name DJs. The rooftop terrace has fine views over the Tejo.

Music Box CLUB
(Map p898; www.musicboxlisboa.com; Rua Nova do Carvalho 24, Cais do Sodré) Under the brick arches on Rua Nova do Carvalho lies one of Lisbon's hottest clubs. Music Box hosts loud and bouncy club nights with music shifting from electro to rock, as well as ear-splitting gigs by rising bands.

Incógnito CLUB
(Map p894; Rua dos Polais de São Bento 37, Santa Catarina) No-sign, pint-sized Incógnito offers an alternative vibe and DJs thrashing out indie rock and electro-pop. Sweat it out with a fun crowd on the tiny basement dance floor, or breathe more easily in the loft bar upstairs.

Discoteca Jamaica CLUB
(Map p898; Rua Nova do Carvalho, Cais do Sodré; ⏲11pm-4am) Gay and straight, black and white, young and old – everyone has a soft spot for this long-running club. It gets going around 2am at weekends with DJs pumping out reggae, hip hop and retro.

Clube Ferroviário CLUB
(Map p894; Rua de Santa Apolónia 59) Above Santa Apolónia Train Station, this former social club of Lisbon's railworkers has been transformed into an intriguing nightspot with DJs and occasional concerts; the best feature is the roof terrace with Tejo views.

Gay & Lesbian Venues

Lisbon's small gay scene is headquarted in Príncipe Real, though you'll also find a few gay bars in Bairro Alto. Lux draws both a gay and straight crowd.

Construction GAY, CLUB
(Map p894; Rua Cecílio de Sousa 84; ⏲midnight-6am Fri & Sat) New in 2012, Construction is the hot club of the moment, with pumping house music and a dark room. Popular with bears.

Finalmente GAY, CLUB
(Map p894; Rua da Palmeira 38) This popular club has a tiny dance floor, nightly drag shows and wall-to-wall crowds.

Trumps GAY, CLUB
(Map p894; www.trumps.pt; Rua da Imprensa Nacional 104b) Lisbon's hottest gay club, with

cruisy corners, a sizeable dance floor and events from live music to drag.

Clube da Esquina GAY, BAR
(Map p898; Rua da Barroca 30; ⏲10pm-4am; underground Fall Baixa-Chiado) DJs playing hip hop and house to an eye-candy crowd. Several other gay bars are nearby.

Cinemas

Lisbon's cinematic standouts are the grand **São Jorge** (Map p894; Avenida da Liberdade 175) and, just around the corner, **Cinemateca Portuguesa** (Map p894; www.cinemateca.pt; Rua Barata Salgueiro 39); both screen offbeat, art-house, world and old films. For Hollywood fare, visit multiscreen **Amoreiras Cinema** (Map p894; Avenida Eng Duarte Pacheco, Amoreiras Shopping Centre) or **Colombo Cinema.** (Centro Colombo, Avenida Lusíada)

Sport

Lisbon's football teams are Benfica, Belenenses and Sporting. Euro 2004 led to the upgrading of the 65,000-seat **Estádio da Luz** and the construction of the 54,000-seat **Estádio Nacional**. Bullfights are staged on Thursday from May to October at **Campo Pequeno** (Map p894; Avenida da República; tickets €10-75). Tickets are available at **ABEP ticket kiosk** (Praça dos Restauradores). State-of-the-art stadium **Estádio José de Alvalade** (Rua Prof Fernando da Fonseca) seats 54,000 and is just north of the university. Take the metro to Campo Grande.

 Shopping

Shops in Lisbon are a mix of the classic and the wild, with antiques, frozen-in-time button and tinned-fish shops, and edgy boutiques all sprinkled across the hilly landscape. Rua Garrett and nearby Largo do Chiado, across Rua da Misericórdia, are home to some of Lisbon's oldest and most upmarket boutiques. Meanwhile, Bairro Alto attracts vinyl lovers and vintage fans to its cluster of late-opening boutiques.

Feira da Ladra MARKET
(Map p894; Campo de Santa Clara, Alfama; ⏲7am-5pm Sat) You'll find old records, coins, jewellery, vintage postcards, dog-eared poetry books and other attic treasure/trash at this lively Saturday market.

Vida Portuguesa PORTUGUESE
(Map p898; Rua Anchieta 11, Chiado) With high ceilings and polished cabinets, this store lures nostalgics with all-Portuguese products, from retro-wrapped Tricona sardines to lime-oil soap and Bordallo Pinheiro porcelain swallows.

Santos Oficios HANDICRAFTS
(Map p898; Rua da Madalena 87, Baixa) Touristy but fine selection of Portuguese folk art.

Armazéns do Chiado MALL
(Map p898; Rua do Carmo 2, Chiado) A convenient, well-concealed shopping complex. The Fnac store here is good for books, music and booking concert tickets.

Outra Face da Lua VINTAGE
(Map p898; Rua da Assunção 22, Baixa) A fun-to-explore vintage shop in Baixa, with a cafe inside.

Fábrica Sant'Ana HANDICRAFTS
(Map p898; Rua do Alecrim 95, Chiado) Great spot for purchasing fabulous new and old *azulejos*.

Livraria Bertrand BOOKS
(Map p898; ☎213 421 941; Rua Garrett 73, Chiado) Bertrand has both Portuguese and foreign-language books sold amid 18th-century charm.

Information

Emergency

Police, Fire & Ambulance (☎119)

Police Station (☎217 654 242; Rua Capelo 13)

Tourist Police (☎213 421 634; Palácio Foz, Praça dos Restauradores; ⏲24hr)

Internet Access

Most hostels and mid-range guesthouses offer wireless (usually free). Loads of cafes and restaurants also offer wi-fi – just ask for the *codigo* (access code).

Portugal Telecom (Praça Rossio 68; ⏲9am-10pm) Handy place to get online next to Praça Rossio. Also has rows of telephone booths.

Internet Resources

Time Out (www.timeout.pt) Details on upcoming gigs, cultural events and interesting commentary, in Portuguese.

Go Lisbon (www.golisbon.com) Up-to-date info on sightseeing, eating, nightlife and events.

Visit Lisboa (www.visitlisboa.com) Lisbon's comprehensive tourism website, with the low-down on sightseeing, transport and accommodation.

Medical Services

Farmácia Estácio (Rossio 62) A central pharmacy.

British Hospital (☎217 213 400; Rua Tomás da Fonseca) English-speaking staff and doctors.

Money

Cota Câmbios (Rossio 41) One of the best exchange rates in town.

Post

Main Post Office (Praça do Comércio)

Post Office (Praça dos Restauradores)

Tourist Information

Ask Me Lisboa (www.askmelisboa.com; Praça dos Restauradores; ⏲9am-8pm) The largest and most helpful tourist office. Can book accommodation or reserve rental cars.

Y Lisboa (www.askmelisboa.com; Rua Jardim do Regedor 50; ⏲9am-8pm)

Lisboa Welcome Centre (www.visitlisboa.com; Praça do Comércio; ⏲9am-6pm)

Information Kiosks (near Rua Conceição; ⏲10am-1pm & 2-6pm) Santa Apolónia (door 47, inside train station, Santa Apolónia; ⏲8am-1pm Tue-Sat) ;Belém (Largo dos Jernónimos, Belém; ⏲10am-1pm & 2-6pm Tue-Sat) ;Airport (Airport; ⏲7am-midnight).

Getting There & Away

Air

Around 6km north of the centre, **Aeroporto de Lisboa** (Lisbon Airport; www.ana.pt) operates direct flights to many European cities.

Bus

Lisbon's long-distance bus terminal is **Sete Rios** (Rua das Laranjeiras), conveniently linked to both Jardim Zoológico metro station and Sete Rios train station. The big carriers, **Rede Expressos** (☎213 581 460; www.rede-expressos.pt) and **Eva** (☎213 581 466; www.eva-bus.com), run frequent services to almost every major town.

The other major terminal is Gare do Oriente (at Oriente metro and train station), concentrating on services to the north and to Spain. The biggest companies operating from here are **Renex** (☎218 956 836; www.renex.pt)and the Spanish operator **Avanza** (☎218 940 250; www.avanzabus.com).

Train

Santa Apolónia station is the terminus for northern and central Portugal. You can catch trains from Santa Apolónia to Gare do Oriente train station, which has departures to The Algarve and international destinations. Cais do Sodré station is for Belém, Cascais and Estoril. Rossio station is the terminal for trains to Sintra via Queluz.

The overnight Lusitânia Comboio Hotel train (one-way seat/berth €61/84) departs Lisbon daily at 9.18pm, passing through Coimbra and Salamanca (Spain) before reaching Madrid the next morning at 8.20am.

For fares and schedules, visit www.cp.pt.

Getting Around

To/From the Airport

The **AeroBus** runs every 20 minutes from 7am to 11pm, taking 30 to 45 minutes between the airport and Cais do Sodré; buy your ticket (€3.50) on the bus.

The red line of the **metro** (€1.40) goes from the airport into town. Change at Alameda (green line) to reach Rossio and Baixa. A **taxi** into town is about €10 to €15.

Car & Motorcycle

On the outskirts of the city there are cheap **car parks** near Parque das Nações and Belém. The most central underground car park is at Praça dos Restauradores, costing around €2 per hour. On Saturday afternoons and Sunday, parking is normally free in the pay-and-display areas in the centre.

Public Transport

A 24-hour **Bilhete Carris/Metro** (€5) gives unlimited travel on all buses, trams, metros and funiculars. Pick it up from Carris kiosks and metro stations.

BUS, TRAM & FUNICULAR Buses and trams run from 6am to 1am, with a few all-night services. Pick up a transport map from tourist offices or Carris kiosks. A single ticket costs more if you buy it on board (€2.85/1.75/3.50 for tram/bus/funicular), and much less (€1.25 per ride) if you buy a refillable *Viva Viagem* card (€0.50), available at Carris offices and in metro stations.

There are three funiculars: Elevador da Bica; Elevador da Glória; Elevador do Lavra.

Don't leave the city without riding tram 28 from Largo Martim Moniz through the narrow streets of the Alfama; tram 12 goes from Praça da Figueira out to Belém.

FERRY Car, bicycle and passenger ferries leave frequently from the Cais do Sodré ferry terminal to Cacilhas (€1.15, 10 minutes). From Terreiro do Paço terminal catamarans zip across to Montijo (€2.70, every 30 minutes) and Seixal (€2.30, every 30 minutes).

METRO The **metro** (www.metrolisboa.pt; 1-/2-zone single €0.85/1.15; ⏲6.30am-1am) is useful for hops across town and to the Parque das Nações. Buy tickets from metro ticket machines, which have English-language menus.

Taxi

Lisbon's taxis are metered and best hired from taxi ranks. Beware of rip-offs from the airport. From Rossio to Belém is around €8 and to the castle about €6. To call one, try **Rádio Táxis** (☎214 942 527) or **Autocoope** (☎217 932 756).

WORTH A TRIP

COSTA DA CAPARICA

Located 10km southwest of Lisbon, Costa da Caparica's seemingly never-ending beach attracts sun-worshipping Lisboetas craving all-over tans, surfer dudes keen to ride Atlantic waves, and day-tripping families seeking clean sea and soft sand. It hasn't escaped development, but head south and the high-rises soon give way to pine forests and mellow beach-shack cafes.

During the summer, a **narrow-gauge railway** runs the length of the beach for 20 stops. The nearer beaches, including **Praia do Norte** and **Praia do São Sebastião**, are great for families, while the further ones are younger and trendier, including **Praia da Sereia** (stop 15), with its cool beachfront bar, Bar Waikiki. **Praia do Castelo** (stop 11) and **Praia da Bela Vista** (stop 17) are more-secluded gay and nudist havens.

The **main beach** (called Praia do CDS, or Centro Desportivo de Surf) is lined with cafes, bars and surfing clubs along its promenade.

The best way to get here is by ferry (€1.20, 12 minutes) to Cacilhas from Lisbon's Cais do Sodré, where buses 135 (express) and 124 (local) run to Costa da Caparica town (€3.50, 30 to 45 minutes, every 20 minutes).

Sport-minded folk can also get there by bike and ferry, by riding along the **Tejo bike path** 7km from Cais do Sodré to Belém, taking the ferry from there to Trafaria, then continuing on another new bike path (also separate from traffic) that runs for another 6km down to Costa da Caparica.

AROUND LISBON

Sintra

POP 26,200

Lord Byron called this hilltop town a 'glorious Eden' and, although best appreciated at dusk when the coach tours have left, it *is* a magnificent place. Less than an hour west of Lisbon, Sintra was the traditional summer retreat of Portugal's kings. Today it's a fairy-tale setting of stunning palaces and manors surrounded by rolling green countryside.

Sights & Activities

Although the whole town resembles a historical theme park, there are several compulsory eye-catching sights. Multi-sight admission tickets, available at the tourist office, will save you a few euros.

TOP CHOICE Quinta da Regaleira NOTABLE BUILDING, GARDENS
(www.regaleira.pt; Rua Barbosa du Bocage; adult/child €6/3; ⌚10am-8pm) Exploring this neo-Manueline manor and gardens is like delving into another world. The villa has ferociously carved fireplaces, frescos and Venetian glass mosaics with wild mythological and Knights Templar symbols. The playful gardens hide fountains, grottoes, lakes and underground caverns. All routes seem to lead to the 30m-deep initiation well, **Poço Iniciáto**, with mysterious hollowed-out underground galleries lit by fairy lights.

Palácio Nacional de Sintra PALACE
(Largo Rainha Dona Amélia; admission €7; ⌚10am-5.30pm Thu-Tue) The whimsical interior of Sintra's iconic twin-chimney palace is a mix of Moorish and Manueline styles, with arabesque courtyards, barley-twist columns and stunning 15th- and 16th-century geometric *azulejos*.

Castelo dos Mouros CASTLE
(adult/child €7/6; ⌚10am-8pm) An energetic, 3km greenery-flanked hike from the centre, the 8th-century ruined ramparts of this castle provide fine views.

Palácio Nacional da Pena PALACE
(adult/child €13.50/11; ⌚10am-7pm) This exuberantly kitsch palace is 800m from the Castelo dos Mouros, and is an architectural extravaganza crammed with treasures.

Convento dos Capuchos RELIGIOUS, SPIRITUAL
(Capuchin Monastery; ☎219 237 300; adult/child €6/5; ⌚9.30am-8pm) Hidden in the woods is this bewitchingly hobbit-hole-like convent, built in 1560 to house 12 monks who lived in incredibly cramped conditions, their tiny cells having low, narrow doors. The warren of cells, chapels, kitchen and cavern make for fascinating exploring.

WORTH A TRIP

PARQUE NATURAL DA ARRÁBIDA

Thickly green, hilly and edged by gleamingly clean, golden beaches and chiselled cliffs, the Arrábida Natural Park stretches along the southeastern coast of the Setúbal Peninsula, some 40km south of Lisbon. Highlights here are the long, golden beaches of windsurfer hot-spot **Figueirinha** and the sheltered bay of **Galapo**. Most stunning of all is **Portinho da Arrábida**, with fine sand, azure waters and a small 17th-century fort built to protect the monks from Barbary pirates.

Further west lies the former fishing village turned resort town of **Sesimbra**, with a fine beach, a hilltop castle and good seafood restaurants. Keep heading west to reach the haunting **Cabo Espichel**, home to a desolate church and striking ocean views over the cliffs.

Your best option for getting here and exploring the area is to rent a car. Be warned: parking is tricky near the beaches.

Monserrate Park GARDENS, PALACE
(www.parquesdesintra.pt; adult/child €7/6; ⌚9.30am-8pm) This wild, rambling 30-hectare wooded garden 3.5km west of Sintra bristles with exotic foliage. A manicured lawn sweeps up to the whimsical, 19th-century Moorish-inspired **palácio** (palace).

Sleeping

Hotel Sintra Jardim GUESTHOUSE €€
(☎219 230 738; hotelsintrajardim@gmail.com; Travessa dos Avelares 12; d incl breakfast €65-80; @📶🏊) This stately 1850s manor overlooks rambling gardens and an inviting pool, and offers captivating views of the castle. The bright, high-ceilinged rooms are decorated in crisp hues with shiny wood floors.

Almaa HOSTEL €€
(☎219 240 008; www.almaasintrahostel.com; Caminho dos Frades; dm/d/tr €26/64/84) Sustainably-minded Almaa is an idyllic spot to recharge for a few days, with a quirky design scheme (featuring recycled furniture) and a beautiful setting – some rooms have views to the sea. The surrounding 3.5 hectares of lush grounds is set with walking paths and an old spring-fed reservoir for swimming. It's a 10-minute walk from the village centre.

Casa de Hóspedes Dona Maria da Parreirinha GUESTHOUSE €
(☎219 232 490; Rua João de Deus 12-14; d €45-55) A short walk from the train station, this small, homely guesthouse has old-fashioned but spotless rooms, with dark-wood furnishings and floral fabrics.

Eating & Drinking

Sintra is famous for its pastries, including *queijadas* (crisp pastry shells filled with marzipan-like cheese, sugar, flour and cinnamon) and *travesseiros* (light rolled and folded puff pastries filled with almond-and-egg yolk cream). Sample the goods at **Fábrica das Verdadeiras Queijadas da Sapa** (Alameda Volta do Duche 12; ⌚closed Mon) and **Casa Piriquita** (Rua das Padarias 1-5; ⌚closed Wed).

Tulhas PORTUGUESE €€
(Rua Gil Vicente 4; mains €10-14; ⌚closed Wed) This converted grain warehouse is dark, tiled and quaint, with twisted chandeliers and a relaxed, cosy atmosphere. It's renowned for its *bacalhau com natas* (baked cod with cream and grated cheese).

Saudade CAFE €
(Avenida Dr Miguel Bombardo 8; snacks €2-4; ⌚8.30am-midnight Mon-Tue & Thu-Sat, 9am-8pm Sun; 📶) This former bakery with changing art exhibitions has cherub-covered ceilings and a rambling interior. It's a charming spot for pastries or lighter fare, plus daily specials.

Dom Pipas PORTUGUESE €€
(Rua João de Deus 62; mains €7-12; ⌚9am-midnight Tue-Sun) A local favourite, Dom Pipas serves up excellent Portuguese dishes, amid *azulejos* and rustic country decor. It's behind the train station (left out of the station, first left, then left again to the end).

Information

Tourist Office (www.cm-sintra.pt; Praça da República 23; ⌚9am-7pm) Has useful maps and can help with accommodation.

Getting There & Away

The **Lisbon–Sintra railway** terminates in Sintra, a 1km scenic walk northeast of the town's historic centre. Sintra's **bus station**, and another train station, are a further 1km east in the new town Portela de Sintra. Frequent **shuttle buses** link the historic centre with the bus station.

Train services (€2.05, 40 minutes, every 15 minutes) run between Sintra and Lisbon's Rossio station. Buses run regularly from Sintra to Cascais (€4, 60 minutes), Estoril (€4, 40 minutes) and Mafra (45 minutes).

Getting Around

A handy bus for accessing the castle is the hop-on, hop-off Scotturb bus 434 (€5), which runs from the train station via Sintra-Vila to Castelo dos Mouros (10 minutes), Palácio da Pena (15 minutes) and back.

A **taxi** to Pena or Monserrate costs around €6 one-way.

Cascais

POP 34,000

Cascais is a handsome seaside resort with elegant buildings, an atmospheric old town and a happy abundance of restaurants and bars.

Sights & Activities

Coast & Beaches BEACH

Cascais' three sandy bays – **Praia da Conceição**, **Praia da Rainha** and **Praia da Ribeira** – are great for a sunbake or a tingly Atlantic dip, but attract crowds in summer.

Estoril is a somewhat faded resort 2km east of Cascais with a popular sandy beach and Europe's largest **casino**.

The sea roars into the coast at **Boca do Inferno** (Hell's Mouth), 2km west of Cascais. Spectacular **Cabo da Roca**, Europe's westernmost point, is 16km from Cascais and Sintra and is served by buses from both towns.

FREE **Casa das Histórias Paula Rego** GALLERY

(www.casadashistoriaspaularego.com; Avenida da República 300; ⏲10am-7pm) A boon to Sintra's cultural cache, this small museum showcases the disturbing, fairy-tale-like paintings of Paula Rego, one of Portugal's finest living artists.

Museu Condes de Castro Guimarães MUSEUM

(⏲10am-5pm Tue-Sun) The picturesque gardens of **Parque Marechal Carmona** (Avenida Rei Humberto II) house this museum in a whimsical early-19th-century mansion, complete with castle turrets and Arabic cloister.

Sleeping & Eating

Residencial Solar Dom Carlos GUESTHOUSE €€

(☎214 828 115; www.solardomcarlos.pt; Rua Latino Coelho 104; s/d €50/70; P@) Hidden down a sleepy alley, this 16th-century former royal residence turned guest house retains lots of original features, from chandeliers to wood beams, *azulejos* and a frescoed breakfast room.

Confraria Sushi JAPANESE €€

(Rua Luís Xavier Palmeirim 16; mains €8-13; ⏲noon-midnight Tue-Sun) This art-slung cafe, jazzed up with technicolour glass chandeliers, is a fun spot for sushi and tasty salads. Patio seating.

Viriato PORTUGUESE €€

(Av Vasco da Gama 34; mains €8-12; ⏲lunch daily, dinner Wed-Mon) Amid rustic country decor, Viriato is a local favourite for its chargrilled fish and Portuguese classics.

Information

Tourist Office (www.visiteestoril.com; Rua Visconde de Luz 14) Can provide accommodation lists and bus timetables.

Getting There & Around

Trains run frequently to Cascais via Estoril (€2.05, 40 minutes) from Cais do Sodré station in Lisbon.

BIKE TO THE BEACH

Free bikes are available from 8am to 7pm from a kiosk on Largo da Estação near the train station (bring ID). There's a bicycle path that runs the entire 9km stretch from Cascais to wild **Guincho beach**, a popular surf spot.

THE ALGARVE

Love it or loathe it, it's easy to see the allure of The Algarve: breathtaking cliffs, golden sands, scalloped bays and long sandy islands. Although overdevelopment has blighted parts of the coast, head inland and you'll land solidly in lovely Portuguese countryside once again. Algarve highlights include the forested slopes of Monchique, the pretty riverside town of Tavira and windswept, historic Sagres. Underrated Faro is the regional capital.

The Algarve

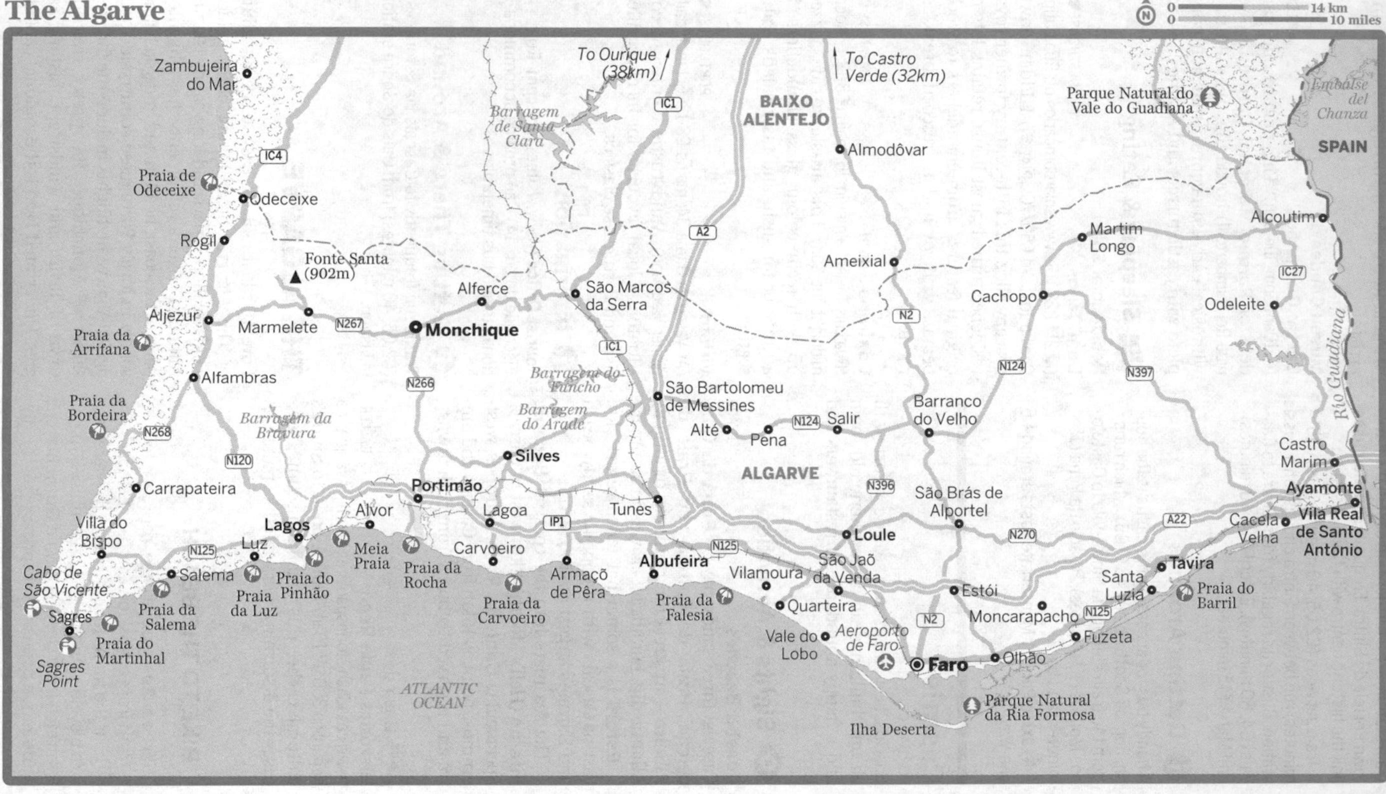
0 14 km
0 10 miles
Zambujeira do Mar
Praia de Odeceixe
Odeceixe
Rogil
Fonte Santa (902m)
Aljezur
Praia da Arrifana
Marmelete
Monchique
Alferce
Alfambras
Praia da Bordeira
Barragem da Bravura
Carrapateira
Villa do Bispo
Cabo de São Vicente
Sagres
Sagres Point
Praia do Martinhal
Salema
Praia da Salema
Luz
Praia da Luz
Praia do Pinhão
Lagos
Meia Praia
Alvor
Praia da Rocha
Portimão
Lagoa
Carvoeiro
Praia da Carvoeiro
Silves
Barragem do Arade
Barragem do Funcho
Barragem de Santa Clara
To Ourique (38km)
São Marcos da Serra
São Bartolomeu de Messines
Alté
Pena
Salir
Tunes
Armação de Pêra
Albufeira
Praia da Falesia
Vilamoura
Quarteira
São Jaõ da Venda
Vale do Lobo
Aeroporto de Faro
Faro
Ilha Deserta
Parque Natural da Ria Formosa
Olhão
Loule
Estói
Moncarapacho
Fuzeta
São Brás de Alportel
Barranco do Velho
BAIXO ALENTEJO
ALGARVE
To Castro Verde (32km)
Almodôvar
Ameixial
Cachopo
Martim Longo
Parque Natural do Vale do Guadiana
Alcoutim
Odeleite
Rio Guadiana
Embalse del Chanza
SPAIN
Castro Marim
Ayamonte
Vila Real de Santo António
Cacela Velha
Tavira
Santa Luzia
Praia do Barril
ATLANTIC OCEAN
IC4
N268
N120
N125
N267
N266
IC1
A2
IP1
N124
N2
N396
N270
N397
A22
IC27

Faro

POP 65,000

Faro is an attractive town with a palm-clad waterfront, well-maintained plazas and a small pedestrianised centre sprinkled with outdoor cafes. There are no beaches in Faro itself, though it's an easy jaunt by ferry to picturesque beaches nearby. A boat trip through the Ria Formosa Natural Park is another highlight.

Sights & Activities

Ilha Deserta ISLAND

Around six ferries per day make the 35-minute trip (€10 return) out to Ilha da Barreta (aka Ilha Deserta), a long narrow-strip of sand just off the mainland. There's a good seafood restaurant there, but little other development. Boats depart from the west side of Cidade Velha; exiting the tourist office, turn left and follow the edge of the old walls. Other depatures from here go to **Praia de Faro** (bus 14 and 16 also go here) and **Praia de Farol.**

Parque Natural da Ria Formosa PARK

For visits to the Ria Formosa Natural Park, sign up for a boating or birdwatching tour with the environmentally friendly outfits of **Ria Formosa** (918 720 002; www.formosamar.pt) and **Lands** (289 817 466; www.lands.pt), both in the Clube Naval in Faro's marina.

Sleeping & Eating

Residencial Oceano GUESTHOUSE €

(289 823 349; Rua Ivens 21; s/d €40/50; @) Up a tile-lined stairway, you'll find this simple and friendly option with tidy rooms (some of which lack windows).

Residencial Dandy GUESTHOUSE €€

(289 824 791; Rua Filipe Alistão 62; d from €40;) Plastic flowers, African masks and museum-style paraphernalia are features of this rambling place. The best rooms have antique furniture, high ceilings and wrought-iron balconies.

Pousada da Juventude HOSTEL €

(289 826 521; www.pousadasjuventude.pt; Rua da Polícia de Segurança Pública 1; dm/d from €15/34;) Adjoining a small park, this hostel offers basic, clean rooms with no frills but is a good ultrabudget option.

Adega Nova PORTUGUESE €€

(Rua Francisco Barreto 24; mains €7-13) This much-loved place serves tasty meat and fish dishes amid country charm. The daily specials are superb value.

Restaurante A Taska PORTUGUESE €€

(289 824 739; Rua do Alportel 38; mains €7-14; lunch & dinner Mon-Sat) Popular with locals, this cosy, busy trattoria-style restaurant serves delicious regional food such as *xarém* (corn meal), and has daily specials on a blackboard.

Information

Tourist Office (www.visitalgarve.pt; Rua da Misericórdia 8) A helpful, multilingual office.

Getting There & Away

Faro airport has both domestic and international flights.

From the **bus station**, just west of the centre, there are at least six daily express coaches to Lisbon (€20, four hours), plus several slower services, and frequent buses to other coastal towns.

The **train station** is a few minutes' walk west of the bus station. Five trains run daily to Lisbon (€22, four hours).

Getting Around

The **airport** is 6km from the centre. **Buses** 14 and 16 (€1.90) run into town until 9pm. A **taxi** from the airport to the town centre costs about €12.

Tavira

POP 25,400

Set on either side of the meandering Rio Gilão, Tavira is a charming town with a hilltop castle, an old Roman bridge and a smattering of Gothic churches. The pretty sands of Ilha da Tavira are a short boat ride away.

Sights & Activities

FREE **Castle** CASTLE

(Rua da Liberdade; 10am-5pm) Tavira's ruined castle dominates the town. Nearby, the 16th-century **Palácio da Galeria** (281 320 540; Calçada da Galeria; admission €2; 10am-12.30pm & 3-6.30pm Tue-Sat) holds occasional exhibitions.

Igreja da Misericórdia CHURCH

(Rua da Galeria) One of the town's 30-plus churches, the 16th-century Igreja da Misericórdia is among the most striking in The Algarve.

Ilha da Tavira ISLAND, BEACH
You can reach this island beach by a ferry at Quatro Águas (€1.40 return) or Tavira (summer only, €1.90 return). It's a 2km walk to Quatro Águas (from the south bank of the river, follow the road south-southwest).

Casa Abilio BICYCLE RENTAL
(Rua João Vaz Corte Real 23; per day around €7) Enjoy pedal power with a rented bike.

Sport Nautica KAYAKING
(Rua Jacques Pessoa 26; per half-/full day €15/25) Rent kayaks for a paddle along the river.

Sleeping & Eating

Pensão Residencial Lagôas GUESTHOUSE €
(281 328 243; Rua Almirante Cândido dos Reis 24; s/d from €20/30) A long-standing favourite, friendly Lagôas has small (some cramped), well-maintained rooms. There's a sunny terrace with views.

Residencial Princesa do Gilão GUESTHOUSE €€
(281 325 171; www.residencial-gilao.com; Rua Borda d'Água de Aguiar 10; s/d €52/58;) This '80s-style place on the river has tight but neat rooms with identical decor. Go for a room with a river view.

Restaurante Bica SEAFOOD €€
(Rua Almirante Cândido dos Reis 24; mains €8-14) Deservedly popular, Bica serves splendid food, such as fresh grilled fish and *cataplana* (seafood and sausage cooked in a copper pot), which diners enjoy with good-value Borba wine.

Bistro 'oPorto' INTERNATIONAL €€
(Rua Dr José Pires Padinha 180; mains €10-15; lunch & dinner Tue-Sun) Head to this artfully decorated French-owned restaurant with a relaxed riverside setting for octopus rice, codfish cakes, coconut curry and other flavourful bites.

Information

Câmara Municipal (Praça da Republica; 9am-8pm Mon-Fri, 10am-1pm Sat) Free internet access.

Tourist Office (Praça da República) Can help with accommodation.

Getting There & Away

Some 15 **trains** and six express **buses** run daily between Faro and Tavira (€3.50, one hour).

Lagos

POP 29,700

In summer, the pretty fishing port of Lagos has a party vibe; its picturesque cobbled streets and pretty nearby beaches are packed with revellers and sun-seekers.

Sights & Activities

Museu Municipal MUSEUM
(Rua General Alberto da Silveira; admission €3; 10am-5.30pm Tue-Sun) The municipal museum houses an eclectic mix of archaeological and ecclesiastical treasures (and oddities). Admission includes the adjacent **Igreja de Santo António**, one of the best baroque churches in Portugal.

Beaches BEACH
The beach scene includes **Meia Praia**, a vast strip to the east; **Praia da Luz** to the west; and the smaller **Praia do Pinhão**.

Blue Ocean OUTDOORS
(964 665 667; www.blue-ocean-divers.de) Organises diving trips. Along the promenade, fishermen can offer motorboat jaunts to nearby grottoes.

Kayak Adventures KAYAKING
(913 262 200; www.kayakadventures-lagos.com) Offers kayaking trips from Batata Beach.

Sleeping

Pensão Marazul GUESTHOUSE €€
(282 770 230; www.pensaomarazul.com; Rua 25 de Abril 13; s/d €45/55;) Draws a good mix of foreign travellers to its small but cheerfully painted rooms – the best of which offer sea views.

Sol a Sol HOTEL €€
(282 761 290; www.residencialsolasol.com; Rua Lançarote de Freitas 22; r €55-65) This central, small hotel has neat rooms with tiny balconies and views over the town.

Caza de São Gonçalo GUESTHOUSE €€
(919 841 622; Rua Candido dos Reis 73; dm/d €25/60) New in 2012, this beautifully restored mansion has a handful of attractive dorm rooms and roomier doubles, all with en-suite bathrooms. There's also a jacuzzi and a lounge area.

Eating

oA Forja PORTUGUESE €€
(Rua dos Ferreiros 17; mains €8-15; lunch & dinner Sun-Fri) This buzzing place pulls in the

crowds for its hearty, top-quality traditional food. Plates of the day are always reliable, as are the fish dishes.

Casinha do Petisco PORTUGUESE SEAFOOD €€
(Rua da Oliveira 51; mains €7-13; Mon-Sat) This tiny traditional gem comes highly recommended by locals for its seafood grills and shellfish dishes. Come early to beat the lines.

Information

Tourist Office (www.visitalgarve.pt; Praça Gil Eanes) In the centre of town.

Getting There & Away

Bus and **train** services depart frequently for other Algarve towns, and around eight times daily to Lisbon (€21, 4¼ hours).

Getting Around

A **bus service** (tickets €1-2; 7am-8pm Mon-Sat) provides useful connections to the beaches of Meia Praia and Luz. Rent bicycles and motorbikes from **Motorent** (282 769 716; www.motorent.pt; Rua Victor Costa e Silva; bike/motorcycle per 3 days from €21/60).

Monchique

POP 5900

High above the coast, in cooler mountainous woodlands, the picturesque hamlet of Monchique makes a lovely base for exploring, with some excellent options for walking, cycling and canoeing.

Sights & Activities

Caldas de Monchique, 6km south, is a peaceful hamlet with a **spa resort** (www.monchiquetermas.com). Some 8km west is The Algarve's 'rooftop', the 902m **Fóia** peak atop the Serra de Monchique, with breezy views through a tangle of radio masts.

Igreja Matriz CHURCH
(Rua da Igreja) This church features a stunning Manueline portal, with its stone seemingly tied in knots. Keep climbing to reach the ruins of the 17th-century Franciscan monastery, **Nossa Senhora do Desterro**, which overlooks the town from its wooded hilltop. From there, it's another 5km along a marked trail to the lookout at **Fóia**.

Outdoor Tours OUTDOORS
(282 969 520; www.outdoor-tours.com; Mexilhoeira Grande; trips from €20) Offers cycling, kayaking and walking trips.

Sleeping & Eating

Residencial Miradouro GUESTHOUSE €
(282 912 163; Rua dos Combatentes do Ultramar; s/d from €25/40) This 1970s hilltop place offers sweeping views and neat rooms, some with balcony.

A Charrete PORTUGUESE €€
(Rua Dr Samora Gil 30-34; mains €11-15; lunch & dinner Thu-Tue) Touted as the town's best eatery for its regional specialities, this place serves reliably good cuisine amid country rustic charm.

Information

Tourist Office (Largo de São Sebastião; 9.30am-1pm & 2-5.30pm Mon-Fri) Uphill from the bus stop.

Getting There & Away

There are five to nine **buses** daily from Portimão (€4.20, 45 minutes) to Monchique.

Silves

POP 11,000

The one-time capital of Moorish Algarve, Silves is a pretty town of jumbling orange rooftops scattered above the banks of the Rio Arade. Clamber around the ramparts of its fairy-tale **castle** for superb views.

Sleeping & Eating

Residencial Ponte Romana GUESTHOUSE €
(282 443 275; Horta da Cruz; s/d €20/35) Floral-themed rooms beside the Roman bridge, with castle views and a cavernous bar-restaurant full of old-timers and Portuguese families.

Quinta da Figueirinha INN €€
(282 440 700; www.qdf.pt; 2-/4 /6-person apt from €54/94/135;) Four kilometres outside of Silves, this 36-hectare organic farm offers simple apartments in idyllic, farmlike surroundings.

Café Ingles INTERNATIONAL €€
(282 442 585; mains €10-23;) Situated at the castle entrance, this funky English-owned place with romantic rooftop terrace has wood-fired pizzas, prawn curry, lamb cutlets with rosemary and other global dishes. In summer, there's live music on weekends.

Getting There & Away

Silves **train station** is 2km from town; trains from Lagos (€2.85, 35 minutes) stop eight times daily (from Faro, change at Tunes), to be met by local buses. Four to seven **buses** run daily connecting Silves and Albufeira (€4.20, 50 minutes).

Sagres

POP 2100

The small, elongated village of Sagres has an end-of-the-world feel with its sea-carved cliffs and empty, wind-whipped fortress high above the ocean.

Sights & Activities

Coast & Beaches BEACH

Visit Europe's southwestern-most point, the **Cabo de São Vicente** (Cape St Vincent), 6km to the west. A solitary lighthouse stands on this barren cape.

This coast is ideal for surfing; hire windsurfing gear at sand-dune fringed **Praia do Martinhal**. Rental shops on the main street hire out bikes, surfboards and wetsuits. You can sign up for surfing lessons with **Sagres Natura** (282 624 072; www.sagresnatura.com; Rua São Vicente). **DiversCape** (965 559 073; www.diverscape.com; Porto da Balereira) organises diving trips.

Fortaleza de Sagres FORTRESS

(adult/child €3/1.50, free 10am-2pm Sun ; 10am-8.30pm) Sagres' fort offers breathtaking views over the seaside cliffs. According to legend, this is where Henry the Navigator established his navigation school and primed the early Portuguese explorers.

Mar Ilimitado BOAT TOUR

(916 832 625; www.marilimitado.com; Porto da Baleeira) **Mar Ilimitado** offers dolphin-spotting boat trips (€32) from the marina.

Sleeping & Eating

Casa do Cabo de Santa Maria GUESTHOUSE €€

(282 624 722; www.casadocabodesantamaria.com; Rua Patrão António Faústino; r/apt from €50/80;) These squeaky-clean rooms and apartments might not have sweeping views, but they are handsomely furnished.

A Tasca SEAFOOD €€

(Porto da Baleeira; mains €12-17; lunch & dinner Thu-Tue) Overlooking the marina, this cosy place whips up tasty *cataplana* and other seafood dishes, best enjoyed on the sunny terrace.

Information

Tourist Office (Rua Comandante Matoso; Tue-Sat) Central to town.

Getting There & Away

Frequent **buses** run daily to Sagres from Lagos (€3.80, one hour), with fewer on Sunday. One continues to Cabo de São Vicente on weekdays.

CENTRAL PORTUGAL

The vast centre of Portugal is a rugged swath of rolling hillsides, whitewashed villages and olive groves and cork trees. Richly historic, it is scattered with prehistoric remains and medieval castles. It's also home to one of Portugal's most architecturally rich towns, Évora, as well as several spectacular walled villages. There are fine local wines and, for the more energetic, plenty of outdoor exploring in the dramatic Beiras region.

Évora

POP 54,300

Évora is an enchanting place to delve into the past. Inside the 14th-century walls, Évora's narrow, winding lanes lead to a striking medieval cathedral, a Roman temple and a picturesque town square. These old-fashioned good looks are the backdrop to a lively student town surrounded by wineries and dramatic countryside.

Sights & Activities

Sé CHURCH

(Largo do Marquês de Marialva; admission €2-5; 9am-noon & 2-5pm) Évora's cathedral has fabulous cloisters and a museum jam-packed with ecclesiastical treasures.

Templo Romano RUINS

(Temple of Diana; Largo do Conde de Vila Flor) Once part of the Roman Forum; it's a heady slice of drama right in town.

Capela dos Ossos CHAPEL

(Praça 1 de Maio; admission €2; 9am-1pm & 2.30-6pm) Built from the skeletons of several thousand people, the ghoulish Chapel of Bones in the Igreja de São Francisco provides a real *Addams Family* day out.

MEGALITHS

Ancient Greek for 'big stones', **megaliths** are found all over the ancient landscape that surrounds Évora. Such prehistoric structures, built around 5000 to 6000 years ago, dot the European Atlantic coast, but here in Alentejo there is an astounding number of Neolithic remains.

The star attraction is the **Cromeleque dos Almendres**, the Iberian peninsula's most important megalithic group. The site consists of a huge oval of some 95 rounded granite monoliths – some of which are engraved with symbolic markings. They were erected over different periods it seems, with geometric and astral consideration, probably for social gatherings or sacred rituals. It lies 15km west of Évora.

Two and a half kilometres before Cromeleque dos Almendres stands **Menhir dos Almendres**, a single stone about 4m high, with some faint carvings near the top.

A bit further out (25km west of Évora) is the recently reopened **Gruta do Escoural** (266 857 000; admission €2; 11am & 2.30pm Wed-Sat), a cave containing Neolithic rock art.

To get to this area, your best option is to rent a car or bike (note that about 5km of the route is rough and remote). Stop by the tourist office for exact driving directions.

Sleeping

TOP CHOICE Albergaria Calvario BOUTIQUE HOTEL €€€
(266 745 930; www.albergariadocalvario.com; Travessa dos Lagares 3; d/studio incl breakfast €108/125) Elegant, friendly and comfortable, this place has an ambience that travellers adore. Pleasant lounge areas, a terrace, books and classical music, plus comfortable beds, ensure a homely stay.

Hostel Namaste HOSTEL €
(266 743 014; www.hostelnamasteevora.pt; Largo Doutor Manuel Alves Branco 12; dm/s/d €17/30/40;) New in 2012, this welcoming guesthouse has two attractively decorated four-bed dorm rooms and two private rooms (one with ensuite). The young, well-travelled owners create a familial ambience, and you can join them for dinner (€7 per person).

Casa dos Teles GUESTHOUSE €
(266 702 453; casadosteles.planetaclix.pt; Rua Romão Ramalho 27; s/d €30/35, with shared bathroom €20/25;) These nine rooms – mostly light and airy – are good value; quieter rooms at the back overlook a pretty courtyard.

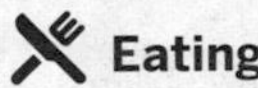

Eating

TOP CHOICE Botequim da Mouraria PORTUGUESE €€
(266 746 775; Rua da Mouraria 16a; mains €13-16.50; lunch & dinner Mon-Fri, lunch Sat) Poke around the old Moorish quarter to find this cosy spot serving some of Évora's finest food and wine. There are no reservations, just 12 stools at a counter.

Dom Joaquim PORTUGUESE €€
(266 731 105; Rua dos Penedos 6; mains €12-15; lunch Tue-Sun, dinner Tue-Sat) Amid stone walls and modern artwork, Dom Joaquim serves excellent traditional cuisine including meats (game and succulent, fall-off-the bone oven lamb) and seafood dishes.

Vinho e Noz PORTUGUESE €€
(Ramalho Orgigão 12; mains €11-12; lunch & dinner Mon-Sat) This family-run place has a warmly lit, brick-walled interior, a large wine list and good-quality cuisine.

Um Quarto Para as Nove PORTUGUESE €€
(Rua Pedro Simões 9; mains €12-19; lunch & dinner Thu-Tue) Serves up some of Évora's best seafood, including a tasty *açorda de mariscos* (a shrimp, clam and bread stew).

Pastelaria Conventual Pão de Rala BAKERY €
(Rua do Cicioso 47; pastries from €2; 7.30am-8pm) Specialises in heavenly pastries, all made on the premises.

Drinking

Bar do Teatro BAR
(Praça Joaquim António de Aguiar; 8pm-2am) This small, inviting bar with its high ceilings and old-world decor draws a friendly mixed crowd. Come early for an outdoor table overlooking the park.

Spettus CAFE, BAR
(Praça de Sertório 3; noon-2am) On a peaceful plaza near the town hall, laid-back Spettus

has outdoor tables that fill with a student crowd by night.

Terrazza BAR
(Jardim do Paço; Palácio das Cinco Quinas) A few steps from the Templo Romano, this plant-filled garden courtyard attracts a slightly more sophisticated crowd.

Information

Câmara Municipal (9am-12.30pm & 2-5pm Mon-Fri) Free internet inside; free 24-hour wi-fi out front.

Tourist Office (www.cm-evora.pt; Praça do Giraldo 73) Has an excellent city map.

Getting There & Away

Évora has six to 12 **buses** daily to Lisbon (€12, two hours) and three to Faro (€16.20, five hours), departing from the station off Avenida São Sebastião (700m southwest of the centre). Regular **trains** go direct to Lisbon (€12-16, 90 minutes) and indirectly, via Pinhal Novo, to Faro (€28, 4¼ hours) and Lagos (€31, five hours). The train station is 600m south of the Jardim Público.

Monsaraz

POP 970

In a dizzy setting high above the plain, this walled village has a moody medieval feel and magnificent views. The biennial **Monsaraz Museu Aberto** held in July on even-numbered years, features exhibitions and concerts.

The **Museu do Fresco** (Plaça Dom Nuno Álvares; admission €1.80; 10am-12.30pm & 2-6pm) has a superb 15th-century fresco. Situated 3km north of town is **Menhir of Outeiro**, one of the tallest megalithic monuments ever discovered.

There are several places to stay in town, including the friendly **Casa St Condestável** (266 557 181; www.condestavel-monsaraz.com; Rua Direita 4; r/ste €55/80) with wooden trimmings, whitewashed walls and heavy wooden furniture.

Casa do Forno (Travessa da Sanabrosa; 266 557 190; mains €8-10; lunch & dinner Wed-Mon) is a small local favourite for its classic Alentejan cooking. There's a terrace with views.

The **tourist office** (266 557 136; Rua Direita 2) can offer advice on accommodation.

Up to four daily **buses** connect Monsaraz with Reguengos de Monsaraz (€3, 35 minutes, Monday to Friday), with connections to Évora.

Estremoz

POP 9000

One of three marble towns in these parts, Estremoz has an attractive centre set with peaceful plazas, orange-tree-lined lanes and a hilltop castle and convent. In its prime, the town was one of the most strongly fortified in Portugal, with its very own palace (now a luxurious *pousada;* upmarket inn).

Sights

Museu Municipal MUSEUM
(268 339 219; Rua D Dinis; adult €1.55; 9am-12.30pm & 2-5.30pm Tue-Sun) In a beautiful 17th-century almshouse, the municipal museum specialises in fascinating pottery figurines, including an entire Easter parade.

Sleeping & Eating

Hotel O Gadanha HOTEL €
(268 339 110; www.hotelogadanha.com; Largo General Graça 56; s/d/tr €23/38/50 ;) This whitewashed house offers excellent value for its bright, fresh and clean rooms overlooking the square.

Adega do Isaías PORTUGUESE €€
(Rua do Almeida 21; mains €11-13; lunch & dinner Mon-Sat;) This award-winning, rustic *tasca* (tavern) serves tender fish, meat and Alentejan specialities inside a wine cellar crammed with tables and huge wine jars.

Information

Tourist Office (www.cm-estremoz.pt; Rossio Marquês de Pombal) On the south side of Rossio, the huge main square.

Getting There & Away

Estremoz is linked to Évora by three local **buses** (€4, 1¼ hours), Monday to Friday.

WORTH A TRIP

PALÁCIO DUCAL

Located in another marble town 17km from Estremoz, the **Palácio Ducal** (Terreiro do Paça, Vila Viçosa; admission €6, armoury/coach collection/Chinese Porcelain/treasury €3/2/2.50/2.50; 2.30-5.30pm Tue, 10am-1pm & 2.30-5.30pm Wed-Sun) is the magnificent ancestral home of the dukes of Bragança, and is rich with *azulejos*, frescoed ceilings and elaborate tapestries.

Peniche

POP 16,000

Popular for its nearby surfing beaches and also as a jumping-off point for the beautiful Ilhas Berlengas nature reserve, the coastal city of Peniche remains a working port, giving it a slightly grittier and more 'lived-in' feel than its beach-resort neighbours. It has a walled historic centre and lovely beaches east of town.

From the bus station, it's a 10-minute walk west to the historic centre.

Sights

FREE Fortress FORTRESS
(admission free, museum admission €1.50; ⌚9am-12.30pm & 2-5.30pm Tue-Fri, from 10am Sat & Sun) Peniche's imposing 16th-century fortress served as one of dictator Salazar's infamous jails for political prisoners and was later a temporary home for African refugees. The on-site **museum** houses the chilling interrogation chambers and cells on the top floor.

Islands ISLAND
About 5km to the northeast of Peniche is the scenic island-village of **Baleal**, connected to the mainland village of Casais do Baleal by a causeway. The fantastic sweep of sandy beach here offers some fine surfing. Surf schools dot the sands, as do several bar-restaurants.

Sitting about 10km offshore from Peniche, **Berlenga Grande** is a spectacular, rocky and remote island, with twisting, shocked-rock formations and gaping caverns. It's the only island of the Berlenga archipelago you can visit; the group consists of three tiny islands surrounded by clear, calm, dark-blue waters full of shipwrecks – great for snorkelling and diving. Several outfits make the 40-minute trip to the island, including **Viamar** (☎262 785 646; www.viamar-berlenga.com; return adult/child €18/10).

Activities

Surfing

Surf camps offer week-long instruction (from €250 to 500 per week including lodging) as well as two-hour classes (€35 to 50), plus board and wetsuit hire. Well-established names include **Baleal Surfcamp** (www.balealsurfcamp.com), **Maximum Surfcamp** (www.maximumsurfcamp.com) and **Peniche Surfcamp** (www.penichesurfcamp.com).

Diving

There are good diving opportunities around Peniche, and especially around Berlenga Grande. Expect to pay about €65 to €75 for two dives (less around Peniche) with **Acuasuboeste** (www.acuasuboeste.com; Porto de Pesca) or **Haliotis** (www.haliotis.pt; Avenida Monsenhor Bastos).

Sleeping

TOP CHOICE Casa das Marés B&B €€
(☎262 769 371, 262 769 200, 262 769 255; www.casadasmares2.com; Praia do Baleal; d €80; 📶) At the picturesque, windswept tip of Baleal, this unique place is loaded with character and all rooms have great sea views.

Peniche Hostel HOSTEL €
(☎969 008 689; www.penichehostel.com; Rua Arquitecto Paulino Montês 6; dm/d €20/50; @📶) This cosy, welcoming hostel has a colourfully decorated lounge and very clean rooms. Surfboards and bikes are available for hire, and there's an attached surf school.

Eating & Drinking

Restaurante A Sardinha SEAFOOD €€
(Rua Vasco da Gama 81; mains €6-12; ⌚lunch & dinner) This simple place on a narrow street parallel to Largo da Ribeira does a roaring trade with locals and tourists alike.

Bar da Praia BAR
(Praia do Baleal; ⌚noon-2am) One of several lively bars right on Baleal beach, with an outdoor terrace and DJs most nights.

Getting There & Away

Peniche's **bus station** (☎968 903 861) is located 400m northeast of the tourist office (cross the Ponte Velha connecting the town to the isthmus). Buses go to Lisbon (€9, 1½ hours, every one to two hours), Coimbra (€14.50, 2¾ hours, three daily) and Óbidos (€3.15, 40 minutes, five to 13 daily).

Óbidos

POP 3100

This exquisite walled village was a wedding gift from Dom Dinis to his wife Dona Isabel (beats a fondue set), and its historic centre is a delightful place to wander. Highlights include the **Igreja de Santa Maria** (Rua Direita), with fine *azulejos*, and views from the town walls.

From mid-July to mid-August, Óbidos hosts the **Mercado Medieval** (www.mercadomedievalobidos.pt), featuring jousting matches, wandering minstrels and abundant medieval mayhem.

Sleeping & Eating

Hostel Argonauta HOSTEL €
(262 958 088; http://hostel-argonauta.blogspot.com; Rua Adelaide Ribeirete 14; dm/d incl breakfast from €20/40;) The friendly and welcoming Señora Rozas runs this cosy place with spacious, handsomely furnished rooms, a short stroll (uphill) to the heart of the medieval centre.

Casal da Eira Branca GUESTHOUSE €€
(966 629 868; www.casaldaeirabranca.com; Travessa do Facho 45; d/apt €65/105) Offers character-filled rooms with beamed ceilings and decorative balconies, one block from the main street (Rua Direita).

Petrarum Domus PORTUGUESE €€
(Rua Direita; mains €9-18; lunch & dinner) Amid age-old stone walls, Petrarum serves up hearty dishes like pork with mushrooms, mixed seafood sautes and several *bacalhau* plates. The multilevel dining room is one of Óbidos' most atmsopheric settings.

Information

Espaço Internet (Rua Direita 107) Free internet access.

Tourist Office (Rua Direita) This helpful tourist office is just outside Porta da Vila, the town's main entrance gate.

Getting There & Away

Rodotejo (www.rodotejo.pt), runs frequent buses (every 45 minutes weekdays, eight daily weekends) between Obidos and Lisbon (€8, 70 minutes).

Nazaré

POP 16,000

Nazaré has a bustling coastal setting with narrow cobbled lanes running down to a wide, cliff-backed beach. The town centre is jammed with seafood restaurants and bars; expect huge crowds in July and August.

Sights & Activities

The **beaches** here are superb, although swimmers should be aware of dangerous currents. Climb or take the funicular to the clifftop **Sítio**, with its cluster of fishermen's cottages and great view.

Historic Monasteries ARCHITECTURE
Two of Portugal's big-time architectural masterpieces are close by. Follow the signs to Alcobaça where, right in the centre of town, is the immense **Mosteiro de Santa Maria de Alcobaça** (admission €6; 9am-7pm) dating from 1178; don't miss the colossal former kitchen.

Batalha's massive **Mosteiro de Santa Maria de Vitória** (admission €6; 9am-6.30pm), dating from 1388, is among the supreme achievements of Manueline architecture.

Sleeping & Eating

Many townspeople rent out rooms; doubles start at €35. Ask around near the seafront Av da República.

Vila Conde Fidalgo GUESTHOUSE €
(262 552 361; http://condefidalgo.planetaclix.pt; Avenida da Independência Nacional 21a; d/apt from €40/80) This pretty little complex uphill a few blocks from the beach is built around a series of flower-filled courtyards. Rooms all have kitchenettes.

Adega Oceano HOTEL €
(262 561 161; www.adegaoceano.com; Avenida da República 51; d €60;) This little oceanfront place offers pleasantly set rooms – renovated modern rooms in back, beach-view quarters in front.

A Tasquinha SEAFOOD €€
(Rua Adrião Batalha 54; mains €7-11; lunch & dinner Tue-Sun) This enormously popular family-run tavern serves high-quality seafood at reasonable prices. Expect queues on summer nights.

Information

Tourist Office (www.cm-nazare.pt; Av Manuel Remígio) On the beachfront (south of the main centre).

Getting There & Away

Nazaré has numerous **bus** connections to Lisbon (€10.50, two hours).

Tomar

POP 16,000

A charming town straddling a river, Tomar has the notoriety of being home to the Knights Templar; check out their headquarters, the outstanding monastery **Convento**

de Cristo (admission €6; ⌚9am-6.30pm), a steep climb above town. Other rarities include a medieval **synagogue** (Rua Dr Joaquim Jacinto 73; admission free; ⌚10am-7pm Tue-Sun). The town is backed by the dense greenery of the **Mata Nacional dos Sete Montes** (Seven Hills National Forest).

Sleeping & Eating

Residencial União GUESTHOUSE €
(☎249 323 161; www.hotel-ami.com/hotel/uniao; Rua Serpa Pinto 94; s/d €30/40; 📶) Tomar's most atmospheric budget choice, this once-grand townhouse features large and sprucely maintained rooms with antique furniture and fixtures.

Estalagem de Santa Iria INN €€
(☎249 313 326; www.estalagemsantairia.com; Mouchão Parque; s/d/ste €65/85/125; 📶) Centrally located on an island in Tomar's lovely riverside park, this '40s-style inn has large comfortable rooms, most with balconies overlooking the leafy grounds or the river.

Calça Perra INTERNATIONAL €€
(Rua Pedro Dias 59; mains €12-15; ⌚lunch & dinner Tue-Sun) A charming restaurant specializing in delicious grilled fish; eat in the elegant dining room or in the bougainvillea-draped courtyard below.

Restaurante Tabuleiro PORTUGUESE €
(☎249 312 771; Rua Serpa Pinto 140; mains €7.50; ⌚lunch & dinner Mon-Sat) This family-friendly local eatery with outdoor seating has attentive service and great food served up in ample portions. It's located just off Tomar's main square.

Information

Tourist Office (Rua Serpa Pinto) Can provide town and forest maps.

Getting There & Away

Frequent **trains** run to Lisbon (€9.50, two hours).

Coimbra

POP 107,000

Coimbra is a dynamic, fashionable, yet comfortably lived-in city, with a student life centred on the magnificent 13th-century university. Aesthetically eclectic, there are elegant shopping streets, ancient stone walls and backstreet alleys with hidden *tascas* and fado bars. Coimbra was the birth and burial place of Portugal's first king, and was

WORTH A TRIP

ROMAN RUINS

Conimbriga, 16km south of Coimbra, is the site of the well-preserved ruins of a **Roman town** (⌚10am-7pm) including mosaic floors, elaborate baths and trickling fountains. It's a fascinating place to explore, with a good **museum** (www.conimbriga.pt; admission €4, free Sun before 2pm; ⌚10am-7pm) that describes the once-flourishing and later abandoned town. There's a sunny cafe serving good lunch buffets. Frequent buses run to Condeixa, 2km from the site; there are also two direct buses (€2.50) from Coimbra.

the country's most important city when the Moors captured Lisbon.

Sights & Activities

Sé Velha CATHEDRAL
(Old Cathedral; ☎239 825 273; Largo da Sé Velha; admission €2; ⌚10am-6pm Mon-Sat) Coimbra's stunning **old cathedral**, dating from the late 12th century, is one of the finest examples of Romanesque architecture in all of Portugal.

Velha Universidade UNIVERSITY
(Old University; admission €7; ⌚10am-noon & 2-5pm) The old university is unmissable in its grandeur. You can visit various buildings, including the library with its gorgeous book-lined hallways and the Manueline chapel dating back to 1517.

O Pioneiro do Mondego KAYAKING
(☎239 478 385; www.opioneirodomondego.com; per person €23) Offers daily kayak excursions along the Rio Mondego up to Penacova. The 18km trip departs at 10am from Torres de Mondego, 7km southwest of Coimbra's Largo da Portagem.

Festivals & Events

Coimbra's annual highlight is **Queima das Fitas**, a boozy week of fado and revelry that begins on the first Thursday in May when students celebrate the end of the academic year.

Sleeping

TOP CHOICE **Casa Pombal Guest House** GUESTHOUSE €€
(☎239 835 175; www.casapombal.com; Rua das Flores 18; d €45-68, without bathroom €35-52;

@) This winning, Dutch-run guesthouse squeezes tons of charm into a small space. Also has an ample morning buffet.

Pensão-Restaurante Flôr de Coimbra GUESTHOUSE €€
(239 823 865; flordecoimbrahr.com.sapo.pt; Rua do Poço 5; s/d/tr €50/60/70, without bathroom €20/35/45;) This once-grand 19th-century home with its own (recommended) restaurant offers loads of character in a great location.

Grande Hostel de Coimbra HOSTEL €
(239 108 212; www.grandehostelcoimbra.com; Rua Antero Quental 196; dm/d €18/40; @) You won't find a hostel more laid-back than this and it's hard to beat the location in a grand, century-old townhouse near the nightlife of Coimbra's university campus.

Eating & Drinking

Self-caterers should stop by the modern **Mercado Municipal Dom Pedro V** (Rua Olímpio Nicolau Rui Fernandes; Mon-Sat) for fruit, vegetables and more.

Restaurante Zé Manel PORTUGUESE €€
(Beco do Forno 12; mains €8-10; lunch & dinner Mon-Fri, lunch Sat) Great food, huge servings and a zany atmosphere, with walls papered with diners' comments, cartoons and poems.

Restaurante Zé Neto PORTUGUESE €€
(Rua das Azeiteiras 8; mains €6-10; lunch & dinner Mon-Sat) This marvellous family-run place specialises in homemade Portuguese standards, including *cabrito* (kid).

Italia ITALIAN €€
(Parque Dr Manuel de Braga; mains €8-15; noon-midnight) Expand your midriff at this excellent Italian restaurant on the riverfront, with laden dishes of excellent pizza and pasta.

Cafetaria do Museu CAFE
(Sé Nova; 8am-7pm Sun-Thu to 4am Fri & Sat) This stylish cafe attracts a hip crowd who come for gourmet burgers, crepes, coffees and cocktails, with fine views from the breezy terrace. It's located near the Sé Nova (the 'New Cathedral', although it's facade dates to the 17th century).

Café Santa Cruz CAFE
(Praça 8 de Maio; Mon-Sat) An atmospheric cafe inside a former chapel. Outdoor seating and occasional fado nights.

Café Tropical BAR
(Praça da República 35; 10am-2am Mon-Sat) One of several indoor-outdoor bars overlooking Praça da República, Café Tropical is a favourite place to start out the night.

Entertainment

Coimbra-style fado is more cerebral than the Lisbon variety, and its adherents are staunchly protective.

oÁ Capella LIVE MUSIC
(918 113 307; www.acapella.com.pt; Rua Corpo de Deus; admission incl 1 drink €10; 9pm-2am) Housed in a fabulous 14th-century former chapel, Á Capella regularly hosts the city's most renowned fado musicians.

Information

Ciberespaço (Loja 4, Av Sá da Bandeira; per hr €2.20; 10am-11pm Mon-Sat, 1-9pm Sun) Paid access on the ground floor of the shopping centre.

Tourist Office (Praça da Porta Férrea) Located near the bridge (Ponte de Santa Clara).

Getting There & Away

There are at least a dozen buses to Lisbon (€13.30, 2½ hours) and Porto (€12, 1½ hours), and regular service to Faro and Évora via Lisbon. There are also frequent trains to Lisbon (€19 to €25, 2 to 3 hours) and Porto (€9 to 17, 1¼ to 2 hours). The main train stations are **Coimbra B**, 2km northwest of the centre, and the central **Coimbra A**. Most long-distance trains call at Coimbra B. The **bus station** (Avenida Fernão Magalhães) is about 400m northeast of the centre.

Luso & the Buçaco Forest

POP 2000

This sylvan region harbours a lush forest of century-old trees surrounded by countryside that's dappled with heather, wildflowers and leafy ferns. There's even a fairy-tale **palace** (231 937 970; www.almeidahotels.com; Mata Nacional do Buçaco; 7–8-course meal €35/40; lunch & dinner;) here, a 1907 neo-Manueline extravagance, where deep-pocketed visitors can dine or stay overnight. The palace lies amid the Mata Nacional do Buçaco, a forest criss-crossed with trails, dotted with crumbling chapels and graced with ponds, fountains and exotic trees. Buçaco was chosen as a retreat by 16th-century monks, and it surrounds the lovely spa town of Luso. From the centre, it's a 2km walk through forest up to the palace.

The **Maloclinic Spa** (www.maloclinicspa.com; Rua Álvaro Castelões; 10am-6pm Mon-Fri, 9am-6pm Sat & Sun, extended hours summer) offers a range of treatments.

Sleeping & Eating

Alegre Hotel BOUTIQUE HOTEL €€
(231 930 256; www.alegrehotels.com; Rua Emídio Navarro 2; s €45-55, d €60-86; P) This grand, peach-coloured 19th-century townhouse has polished period furniture and other appealing touches. There's a formal parlour and a vine-draped garden with pool.

Information

Tourist Office (Avenida Emídio Navarro 136; Mon-Sat) Has maps and leaflets about the forest and trails.

Getting There & Away

Buses to/from Coimbra (€3.50, 45 minutes) run four times daily each weekday and twice daily on Saturdays. **Trains** to/from Coimbra B station (€2.55, 35 minutes) run several times daily; it's a 15-minute walk to town from the station.

Serra da Estrela

The forested Serra da Estrela has a raw natural beauty and offers some of the country's best hiking. This is Portugal's highest mainland mountain range (1993m), and the source of its two great rivers: Rio Mondego and Rio Zêzere. The town of **Manteigas** makes a great base for hiking and exploring the area (plus skiing in winter). The **main park office** (275 980 060; pnse@icn.pt; Rua 1 de Maio 2, Manteigas; Mon-Fri) provides details of popular walks in the Parque Natural da Serra da Estrela – some of which leave from town or just outside it; additional offices are at Seia, Gouveia and Guarda.

Sleeping

Casa das Obras B&B €€
(275 981 155; www.casadasobras.pt; Rua Teles de Vasconcelos, Manteigas; r summer/winter €68/80; P) This lovely 18th-century townhouse has antique-filled rooms, and a pool in a grassy courtyard across the street.

Albergaria Berne HOTEL €€
(275 981 351; www.albergariaberne.com; Quinta de Santo António, Manteigas; s/d from €35/55; P@) At the base of town, Albergaria Berne has wood-accented rooms, some with balconies and views of Manteigas and the mountains above. Also has an excellent restaurant.

Pensão Serradalto GUESTHOUSE €
(tel/fax 275 981 151; Rua 1 de Maio 15; s/d/ste winter €35/45/60, summer€25/35/50) In the heart of town, the Serradalto has clean simple, wood-floored rooms, most with fine valley views.

Getting There & Around

Two regular weekday **buses** connect Manteigas with Guarda, from where there are onward services to Coimbra and Lisbon.

THE NORTH

Beneath the edge of Spanish Galicia, northern Portugal is a land of lush river valleys, sparkling coastline, granite peaks and virgin forests. This region is also gluttony for wine lovers: it's the home of the sprightly *vinho verde* wine and ancient vineyards along the dramatic Rio Douro. Gateway to the north is Porto, a beguiling riverside city blending both medieval and modern attractions. Smaller towns and villages also offer cultural allure, from majestic Braga, the country's religious heart, to the seaside beauty Viana do Castelo.

Porto

POP 208,000

At the mouth of the Rio Douro, the hilly city of Porto presents a jumble of styles, eras and attitudes: narrow medieval alleyways, extravagant baroque churches, prim little squares, and wide boulevards lined with beaux-arts edifices. A lively walkable city with chatter in the air and a tangible sense of history, Porto's old-world riverfront district is a Unesco World Heritage site. Across the water twinkle the neon signs of Vila Nova de Gaia, the headquarters of the major port manufacturers.

Sights & Activities

Head for the riverfront Ribeira district for an atmospheric stroll around, checking out the gritty local bars, sunny restaurants and river cruises.

A few kilometres west of the city centre, the seaside suburb of **Foz do Douro** is a prime destination on hot summer weekends. It has a long beach promenade and a smattering of oceanfront bars and restaurants.

Porto

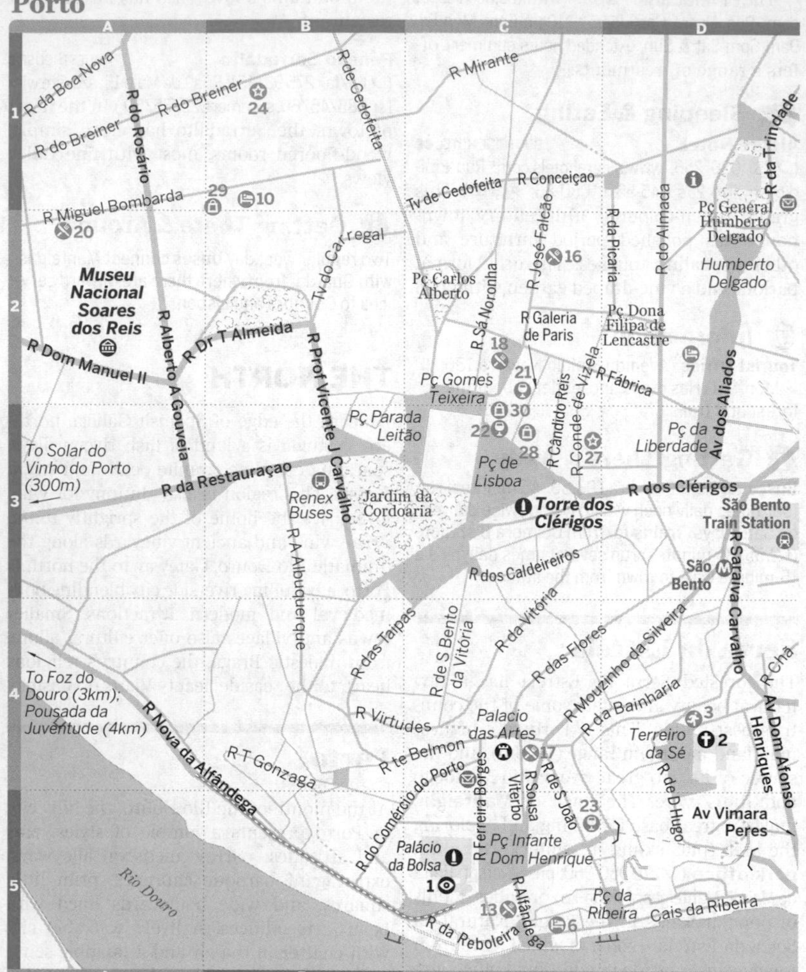

Museums MUSEUM

Within the verdant gardens 4km west of the city, the arrestingly minimalist **Museu de Arte Contemporânea** (www.serralves.pt; Rua Dom João de Castro 210; admission €7; ⏲10am-5pm Tue-Fri, to 8pm Sat & Sun) features works by contemporary Portuguese artists. Take bus 201 from SaPraça Dom João I.

Porto's best art museum, the **Museu Nacional Soares dos Reis** (Rua Dom Manuel II 44; admission €5, free Sun 10am-2pm; ⏲10am-6pm Wed-Sun, 2-6pm Tue), exhibits Portuguese painting and sculpture masterpieces from the 19th and 20th centuries.

Torre dos Clérigos TOWER

(Rua dos Clérigos; admission €2; ⏲9am-7pm) This tower rewards those who ascend the 225 steps to the top with an excellent view over the city.

Sé CHURCH

(Terreiro da Sé; cloisters €3; ⏲9am-12.15pm & 2.30-6.30pm; 👪) Dominating Porto, the cathedral is worth a visit for its mixture of architectural styles and vast ornate interior.

Igreja de São Francisco ARCHITECTURE

(☎222 062 100; Rua Infante Dom Henrique; admission €3.50; ⏲9am-6pm) Near the water-

front, this Gothic church – austere from the outside – hides one of Portugal's most dazzling displays of gilded baroque finery.

Port-Wine Lodges TOUR

Many of the port-wine lodges in Vila Nova de Gaia offer daily tours and tastings, including **Taylor's** (www.taylor.pt; Rua do Choupelo 250; admission €3; ⊙10am-6pm Mon-Fri, to 5pm Sat & Sun), **Croft** (www.croftport.com; free; ⊙10am-6pm) and **Graham's** (www.grahamsportlodge.com; Rua Rei Ramiro 514; per person €3; ⊙9.30am-6pm Mon-Sat).

Porto

Top Sights

- Museu Nacional Soares dos Reis....... A2
- Torre dos Clérigos....... C3

Sights

- 1 Igreja de São Francisco....... C5
- 2 Sé....... D4

Activities, Courses & Tours

- 3 Porto Tours....... D4

Sleeping

- 4 6 Only....... F3
- 5 B&B Hotel Porto....... E3
- 6 Guest House Douro....... C5
- 7 Hotel Aliados....... D2
- 8 Magnólia Hostel....... F3
- 9 Pensão Astória....... E4
- 10 Pensão Favorita....... B1
- 11 Residencial Belo Sonho....... F3
- 12 Tattva Design Hostel....... E4

Eating

- 13 A Grade....... C5
- 14 Café Majestic....... F2
- 15 Cafe Santiago....... F3
- 16 Café Vitória....... C2
- 17 DOP....... C4
- 18 Leitaria Quinta Do Paço....... C2
- 19 Mercado do Bolhão....... E1
- 20 Rota do Chá....... A2

Drinking

- 21 Casa do Livro....... C2
- 22 Era Uma Vez no Porto....... C3
- 23 Vinologia....... C5

Entertainment

- 24 Breyner 85....... B1
- 25 Hot Five Jazz & Blues Club....... E4
- 26 Maus Hábitos....... F3
- 27 Plano B....... C3

Shopping

- 28 A Vida Portuguesa....... C3
- 29 CC Bombarda....... B1
- 30 Livraria Lello....... C3
- 31 Via Catarina Shopping Centre....... F2

Teleférico de Gaia CABLE CAR

(one-way/return €5/8; ⊙10am-8pm) In Vila Nova de Gaia, this new aerial gondola provides fine views over the Douro and Porto on its short, five-minute jaunt. It runs 562m between the south end of the Ponte Dom Luis I and the riverside.

PORT WINE PRIMER

With its intense flavours, silky textures and appealing sweetness, port wine is easy to love, especially when taken with its proper accompaniments: cheese, nuts and dried fruit.

It was probably Roman soldiers who first planted grapes in the Douro valley some 2000 years ago, but tradition credits the discovery of port itself to 17th-century British merchants. With their country at war with France, they turned to their old ally Portugal to meet their wine habit. According to legend, the British threw in some brandy with grape juice, both to take off the wine's bite and preserve it for shipment back to England – port wine was the result.

Festivals & Events

Festa de São João FESTIVAL
(St John's Festival) From 20 to 24 June; Porto's biggest festival, with processions, live music and merry-making all across town.

Noites Ritual Rock MUSIC FESTIVAL
Late August; music festival.

Serralves Em Festa CULTURAL FESTIVAL
(http://serralvesemfesta.com) Concerts, exhibitions, theatre and loads of events at this fest in early June.

Sleeping

TOP CHOICE **Guest House Douro** BOUTIQUE HOTEL €€€
(☎222 015 135; www.guesthousedouro.com; Rua de Fonte Taurina 99-101; r €140-180; ❄@📶) In a restored relic overlooking the Douro, this friendly guesthouse has excellent service and beautifully designed rooms; the best have river views. There's a 1am curfew.

6 Only GUESTHOUSE €€
(☎222 013 971; www.6only.pt; Rua Duque de Loulé 97; d €70-80; @📶) True to name, 6 Only has just six rooms, all with simple but stylish details. There's a lounge, a Zen-like courtyard and friendly staff.

Pensão Favorita GUESTHOUSE €€
(☎220 134 157; www.pensaofavorita.pt; Rua Miguel Bombarda 267; s/d from €60/80; 📶) An artful addition to Porto, Pensão Favorita has inviting rooms of ample size with big windows, mid-century furnishings and wide plank floors. The rooms in back overlook the garden; there's also a lounge and restaurant with outdoor seating.

Tattva Design Hostel HOSTEL €
(☎220 944 622; www.tattvadesignhostel.com; Rua do Cativo 26; dm/d from €15/44; @📶) One of Portugal's best hostels, Tattva has excellent facilities and attractive rooms with thoughtful touches – big lockers, good lighting, privacy curtains around every bed, and a bathroom in every room. The open-air rooftop lounge is a great place for a sundowner.

Magnólia Hostel HOSTEL €
(☎222 014 150; magnoliahostel.com; Av Rodrigues de Freitas 387; dm €17-22; 📶) You'll find excellent ambience at this attractive, well-maintained hostel with a range of rooms spread over three floors of a converted townhouse. There's a lounge with a spooky out-of-tune piano, and an outdoor space that sometimes hosts concerts.

Residencial Belo Sonho GUESTHOUSE €
(☎222 003 389; Rua Passos Manuel 186; s/d €25/35; 📶) Belo Sonho has simple but comfy rooms with parquet floors and small, tidy bathrooms. Management doesn't speak much English but is warm and friendly.

B&B Hotel Porto HOTEL €
(☎222 407 000; www.hotelbb.pt; Praça da Batalha 32; d €46; 📶) Set in a restored art deco building, this place offers a dash of style at low prices. Rooms are trim and modern, and there's a grassy if rather minimalist courtyard out back. Good location on Praça da Batalha.

Pensão Astória GUESTHOUSE €
(☎222 008 175; Rua Arnaldo Gama 56; r €25-35) In an aging town house above the Rio Douro, Astória has old-world charm; several rooms have superb views.

Hotel Aliados GUESTHOUSE €€
(☎222 004 853; www.hotelaliados.com; Rua Elísio de Melo 27; r €55-80; ❄📶) Set in one of Porto's marvellous beaux-arts buildings, offering comfortable rooms with wooden floors and dark-wood furnishings.

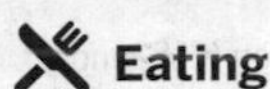

Eating

A Grade PORTUGUESE €€€
(☎223 321 130; Rua da São Nicolau 9; mains €12-20; ⏲lunch & dinner Mon-Sat) Both a humble operation and a masterwork of traditional fare, with standouts such as baked octopus in butter and wine, roast goat, and lime tart for dessert. Reservations recommended.

DOP PORTUGUESE €€€
(☎222 014 313; www.ruipaula.com; Largo S Domingos 18; mains €30-60; ⏲lunch & dinner) Sit at the 'long table' and watch the chef prepare tapas tableside, or find a romantic corner and linger over duck risotto and a bottle of Douro red. This is one of Porto's finest dining rooms.

Café Vitória INTERNATIONAL €€
(Rua José Falcão 156; mains €6-14; ⏲noon-1am Mon, Wed, Thu, 2pm-2am Fri & Sat) This little-known gem serves lighter fare in the bar downstairs (noodles with shitake mushrooms, smoked salmon sandwiches, good-value daily specials) and heartier Portuguese fare in the elegant upstairs dining room. There's a pleasant garden in back, and a festive cocktail-sipping scene on weekends.

Café Majestic CAFE €
(Rua Santa Catarina 112; snacks €2-3; ⏲9.30am-midnight Mon-Sat) An art-nouveau extravagance where old souls linger over afternoon tea.

Cafe Santiago PORTUGUESE €€
(Rua Passos Manuel 226; mains €8-12; ⏲lunch & dinner) One of the best places to try Porto's classic belly-filling treat, the *francesinha:* a thick open-faced sandwich, piled with cheese, sausage, egg and/or assorted other meats, plus a tasty rich sauce.

Leitaria Quinta Do Paço CAFE €
(Praça Guilherme Gomes Fernandes 47; sandwiches €4; ⏲9am-8pm Sun-Thu, to 1am Fri & Sat) The Leitaria is famed for its heavenly eclairs. You can dine al fresco at tables on the plaza.

Rota do Chá CAFE €
(Rua Miguel Bombarda 457; 2-course lunch €7.50; ⏲noon-8pm Sun-Thu, noon-midnight Fri & Sat; 🖉) This proudly bohemian cafe has a verdant but rustic back garden and a magnificent tea selection.

Mercado do Bolhão MARKET €
(Rua Formosa; ⏲8am-5pm Mon-Fri, to 1pm Sat) Fruit, vegies, cheese and deli goodies in a 19th-century wrought-iron building.

Tattva CAFE
(Rua do Cativo 26; 3-course lunch €7; ⏲lunch Mon-Fri, dinner Fri & Sat) This hostel serves excellent set lunches, and there's always a vegetarian option. Come on Friday nights for Portuguese cuisine and on Saturday nights for superb Indian cooking.

Drinking

The bar-lined Rua Galeira de Paris and nearby streets are packed with revellers most nights. Down by the water, the open-air bar scene on Praça da Ribeira is a pleasant but touristy option on warm nights.

Era Uma Vez no Porto BAR
(Rua das Carmelitas 162) Artwork lines the walls of this cosy, lowlit Baixa bar, and there's a mellow buzz to the place, making it a fine retreat from the mayhem of nearby Rua Galeria de Paris. Step onto the tiny balcony for views of the Torre dos Clérigos across the way.

Casa do Livro LOUNGE
(Rua Galeria de Paris 85; ⏲9pm-3am Mon-Sat) Vintage wallpaper, gilded mirrors and walls of books give a discreet charm to this perfectly lit bar. On weekends, DJs spin funk, soul and retro sounds in the back room for pretty people.

Vinologia WINE BAR
(Rua de São João 46; ⏲4pm-midnight) This oaky French-owned wine bar is an excellent place to sample Porto's fine quaffs.

Solar do Vinho do Porto WINE BAR
(Rua Entre Quintas 220; ⏲4pm-midnight Mon-Sat) In a 19th-century house near the Palácio de Cristal, this upmarket spot has a manicured garden with picturesque views of the Douro and hundreds of ports by the glass.

☆ Entertainment

Plano B GALLERY
(Rua Cândido dos Reis 30; ⏲closed Aug) This creative space has an art gallery and cafe, with a cosy downstairs space where DJs and live bands hold court.

Maus Hábitos CLUB
(www.maushabitos.com; Rua Passos Manuel 178, 4th fl) This bohemian, multiroom space hosts art exhibits, while live bands and DJs work the back stage.

Breyner 85 LIVE MUSIC
(www.breyner85.com; Rua do Breyner 85; ⌚3-9pm Mon, to 2am Tue-Sun) This creative space with a grassy terrace features an eclectic line-up of bands covering rock, jazz and blues. Sunday night's jam sessions are particularly popular.

Hot Five Jazz & Blues Club JAZZ
(www.hotfive.eu; Largo Actor Dias 51; ⌚10pm-3am Wed-Sun) Hosts live jazz and blues as well as acoustic, folk and all-out jam sessions.

Shopping

Major shopping areas are eastward around the Bolhão market and Rua Santa Catarina.

A Vida Portuguesa SOUVENIRS
(Rua Galeria de Paris 20) This lovely shop showcases a medley of vintage Portuguese products – classic toys, old-fashioned soaps and retro journals, plus those emblematic ceramic *andorinhas* (swallows).

CC Bombarda GALLERIA
(Rua Miguel Bombarda) For something a little edgier, visit this gallery of stores selling urban wear, stylish home knick-knacks, Portuguese indie rock and other hipster-pleasing delights.

Livraria Lello BOOKS
(Rua das Carmelitas 144) Even if you're not after books, don't miss this beautiful 1906 neo-Gothic confection.

Via Catarina Shopping Centre MALL
(Rua Santa Catarina) The best central shopping mall.

Information

Santo António Hospital (☎222 077 500; Largo Prof Abel Salazar) Has English-speaking staff.

Main Post Office (Praça General Humberto Delgado) Across from the main tourist office.

Main Tourist Office (www.portoturismo.pt; Rua Clube dos Fenianos 25) Opposite the *câmara municipal*.

Getting There & Away

Air

Porto is connected by daily flights from Lisbon and London, and direct links from other European cities, particularly with easyJet and Ryanair.

Bus

Porto has many private bus companies leaving from different terminals; the main tourist office can help. In general, for Lisbon (€18) and The Algarve (€30), the choice is **Renex** (www.renex.pt; Campo Mártires de Pátria 37) or **Rede Expressos.** (www.rede-expressos.pt; Rua Alexandre Herculano 370).

Three companies operate from or near Praceto Régulo Magauanha, off Rua Dr Alfredo Magalhães: Transdev-Norte goes to Braga (€6); and AV Minho goes to Viana do Castelo (€8).

Train

Porto is a northern Portugal rail hub with three stations. Most international trains, and all intercity links, start at **Campanhã**, 2km east of the centre. Inter-regional and regional services depart from Campanhã or the central **São Bento station** (Praça Almeida Garrett). Frequent local trains connect these two.

At **São Bento station** you can book tickets to any other destination.

Getting Around

To/From the Airport

The **metro's 'violet' line** provides handy service to the airport. A one-way ride to the centre costs €1.80 and takes about 45 minutes. A daytime **taxi** costs €20 to €25 to/from the centre.

Public Transport

Save money on transport by purchasing a refillable **Andante Card** (€0.50), valid for transport on buses, metro, funicular and tram. You can buy them from STCP kiosks or newsagents.

Metro Porto's metro currently comprises four metropolitan lines that all converge at the Trinidade stop. Tickets cost €1.15 with an Andante Card. There are also various day passes (€4 to €7) available.

Tram Porto has three antique trams that trundle around town. The most useful line, 1E, travels along the Douro towards the Foz district.

Bus Central hubs of Porto's extensive bus system include Jardim da Cordoaria, Praça da Liberdade and São Bento station. Tickets purchased on the bus are €1.80 one-way, or €1.15 with the Andante Card.

Funicular A panoramic funicular shuttles up and down a steep incline from Avenida Gustavo Eiffel to Rua Augusto Rosa (€1.80, from 8am to 8pm).

Taxi

To cross town, expect to pay between €5 and €8. There's a 20% surcharge at night, and an additional charge to leave city limits, which includes Vila Nova de Gaia. There are taxi ranks throughout the centre or you can call a **radio taxi** (☎225 076 400).

Along the Douro

Portugal's best-known river flows through the country's rural heartland. In the upper reaches, port-wine grapes are grown on steep terraced hills, punctuated by remote stone villages and, in spring, splashes of dazzling white almond blossom.

The Rio Douro is navigable right across Portugal. Highly recommended is the train journey from Porto to Pinhão (€11, 2½ hours, five trains daily), the last 70km clinging to the river's edge; trains continue to Pocinho (from Porto €13, 3½ hours). **Porto Tours** (☎222 000 045; www.portotours.com; Calçada Pedro Pitões 15, Torre Medieval), situated next to Porto's cathedral, can arrange tours, including idyllic Douro cruises. Cyclists and drivers can choose river-hugging roads along either bank, and visit wineries along the way (check out www.rvp.pt for an extensive list of wineries open to visitors). You can also stay overnight in scenic wine lodges among the vineyards.

Viana do Castelo

POP 38,000

The jewel of the Costa Verde (Green Coast), Viana do Castelo has both an appealing medieval centre and lovely beaches just outside the city. In addition to its natural beauty, Viana do Castelo whips up some excellent seafood and hosts some magnificent traditional festivals, including the spectacular **Festa de Nossa Senhora da Agonia** in August.

Sights

The stately heart of town is **Praça da República**, with its delicate fountain and grandiose buildings, including the 16th-century **Misericórdia**, a former almshouse.

FREE Templo do Sagrado Coração de Jesus CHURCH

(Temple of the Sacred Heart of Jesus; ⌚10am-5pm Sep-Jun, 9am-8pm Jul & Aug) Atop Santa Luzia Hill, the Temple of the Sacred Heart of Jesus offers a grand panorama across the river. It's a steep 2km climb; you can also catch a ride on a funicular railway (one-way/return €2/3).

Praia do Cabedelo BEACH

Viana's enormous arcing beach is one of the Minho's best, with little development to spoil its charm. It's across the river from town, best reached by **ferry** (adult/child €1.30/0.70; ⌚hourly 9am to 8pm Mon-Fri, from 10am Sat & Sun) from the pier south of Largo 5 de Outubro.

Gil Eannes SHIP

(☎258 809 710; www.fundacaogileannes.pt; Doca Comercial; admission €2; ⌚9am-7pm) On the waterfront near Largo 5 de Outubro, this pioneering naval hospital ship once provided on-the-job care for those fishing off the coast of Newfoundland. You can clamber around the decks and cabins, or even overnight in a spooky youth hostel.

Sleeping

Margarida da Praça BOUTIQUE HOTEL €€

(☎258 809 630; www.margaridadapraca.com; Largo 5 Outubre 58; r €50-75; @☎) Fantastically whimsical, this friendly boutique inn offers colourful rooms accented by candelabra lanterns and lush duvets.

Hospedaria Senhora do Carmo GUESTHOUSE €

(☎258 825 118; batistaesilva@sapo.pt; Rua Grande 72; r €35, without bathroom €20) Well-located in the historic centre, this friendly, family-run guesthouse is excellent value with its clean, freshly painted rooms with parquet floors. The best have views over the rooftops of Viana.

Pousada da Juventude Gil Eannes HOSTEL €

(☎258 847 169; www.pousadasjuventude.pt; Gil Eannes; dm/d €12/26; ☎) Sleep in the bowels of a huge, creaky hospital ship where men were stitched up and underwent emergency dentistry. This floating hostel scores well for novelty, but has few amenities.

Eating

Taberna do Valentim SEAFOOD €€

(Campo do Castelo; mains €12-15; ⌚lunch & dinner Mon-Sat) This popular seafood restaurant serves grilled fish by the kilogram, and rich seafood stews – *arroz de tamboril* (monkfish rice) and *caldeirada* (fish stew). It's on the main road facing Castelo de São Thiago, 400m west of the centre.

Os 3 Potes PORTUGUESE €€€

(☎258 829 928; Rua Beco dos Fornos 7; mains €14-17; ⌚lunch & dinner) Set in the former public kiln, this cosy restaurant serves traditional Minho delicacies.

Dolce Vianna ITALIAN €
(☎258 824 860; Rua do Poço 44; pizzas €6-7) In the centre, this pleasant local favourite cooks up thin-crust, cheese-heavy pizzas in a wood-burning oven.

Freguez CAFE €
(Rua do Poço 42; snacks €2-3) A charming cafe with a fado soundtrack and outdoor tables on the pedestrian lane.

Information

Tourist Office (Rua Hospital Velho) Handily located in the old centre.

Getting There & Away

Five to 10 **trains** go daily to Porto (€7 to €8, 1½ to 2¼ hours), as well as express **buses** (€8, 1 to 1½ hours).

Braga

POP 135,000

Portugal's third-largest city boasts a fine array of churches, their splendid baroque facades looming above the old plazas and narrow lanes of the historic centre. Lively cafes, trim little boutiques, and some good restaurants add to the appeal.

Sights

It's an easy day trip to **Guimarães** with its medieval town centre and a palace of the dukes of Bragança. It's also a short jaunt to **Barcelos**, a town famed for its sprawling Thursday market.

Sé CHURCH
(Rua Dom Paio Mendes; admission free, treasury €3, choir €2; ⏲8am-6.30pm) In the centre of Braga, this is one of Portugal's most extraordinary cathedrals, with roots dating back a thousand years. Within the cathedral you can also visit the **treasury** and **choir**.

Escadaria do Bom Jesus RELIGIOUS
At Bom Jesus do Monte, a hilltop pilgrimage site 5km from Braga, there is an extraordinary stairway with allegorical fountains, chapels and a superb view. City bus 2 runs frequently from Braga to the site, where you can climb the steps (pilgrims sometimes do this on their knees) or ascend by funicular railway (€1.50).

Sleeping

Pop Hostel HOSTEL €
(☎253 058 806; dm/d from €16/45; @📶) New in 2011, the small cosy Pop Hostel is a great addition to Braga, with a colourfully decorated lounge and a friendly owner who knows all the best eating and drinking spots in town. Bike hire and tours available.

Casa Santa Zita GUESTHOUSE €
(☎253 618 331; Rua São João 20; s/d from €22/35) This impeccably kept pilgrims' lodge has bright, spotless rooms (some with ensuite) and an air of palpable serenity. Midnight curfew.

Residencial Dos Terceiros GUESTHOUSE €
(☎253 270 466; www.terceiros.com; Rua dos Capelistas 85; s/d €30/43) On a quiet pedestrianised street near Praça da República, Terceiros offers simple rooms; some with small balconies.

Eating

Anjo Verde VEGETARIAN €
(☎253 264 010; Largo da Praça Velha 21; mains €8-9; ⏲lunch & dinner Mon-Sat; 🖉) Braga's best vegetarian restaurant serves up elegantly presented plates in a lovely, airy dining room or on the peaceful lane in front. Several other attractive indoor-outdoor restaurants are on the same street.

Domus Vinum TAPAS €
(www.domus-vinum.com; Largo da Nossa Senhora da Boa Luz 12; tapas €4-6; ⏲6pm-2am Tue-Sun) With Brazilian beats, a lantern-lit front patio and excellent wines by the glass, Domus Vinum draws a stylish crowd. The Portuguese and Spanish tapas is excellent. It's just west of the old town entrance portal, Arco da Porta Nova.

Manjar Bacalhau PORTUGUESE €€
(Campo das Hortas; mains €8-12; ⏲closed Mon) True to name, this place serves superb *bacalhau* dishes, as well as regional favourites.

Livraria Café CAFE €
(Avenida Central 118; mains €4-5; ⏲9am-7.30pm Mon-Sat) Tucked inside the bookshop Centésima Página, this cafe with rustic garden serves tasty sandwiches, salads and desserts.

Information

Tourist Office (www.cm-braga.pt; Praça da República 1) Can help with accommodation and maps.

Getting There & Away

Trains arrive regularly from Lisbon (€33, 3½ to 4½ hours), Coimbra (€20, 2½ hours) and Porto (€3, 1¼ hours), and there are daily connections north to Viana do Castelo. Daily **bus** services link Braga to Porto (€6, one hour) and Lisbon (€19, 4½ hours). **Car hire** is available at **AVIC** (253 203 910; Rua Gabriel Pereira de Castro 28; Mon-Fri), with prices starting at €35 per day.

Parque Nacional da Peneda-Gerês

Spread across four impressive granite massifs, this vast park encompasses boulder-strewn peaks, precipitous valleys, gorse-clad moorlands and forests of oak and pine. It also shelters more than 100 granite villages that, in many ways, have changed little since Portugal's founding in the 12th century. For nature lovers, the stunning scenery here is unmatched in Portugal for camping, hiking and other outdoor adventures. The park's main centre is at Vila do Gerês, a sleepy, hot-springs village.

Activities

Hiking

There are trails and footpaths through the park, some between villages with accommodation. Leaflets detailing these are available from the park offices.

Day hikes around Vila do Gerês are popular. An adventurous option is the **old Roman road** from Mata do Albergaria (10km up-valley from Vila do Gerês), past the **Vilarinho das Furnas** reservoir to Campo do Gerês. More distant destinations include **Ermida** and **Cabril**, both with simple accommodation.

Cycling & Horse Riding

Mountain bikes can be hired in Campo do Gerês (15km northeast of Vila do Gerês) from **Equi Campo** (253 161 405; www.equicampo.com; per hr/day €5/18; 10am-7pm). Guides here also lead horse-riding trips, hikes and combination hiking/climbing/abseiling excursions.

Water Sports

Rio Caldo, 8km south of Vila do Gerês, is the base for water sports on the Caniçada Reservoir. English-run **AML** (Água Montanha e Lazer; 253 391 779; www.aguamontanha.com; Lugar de Paredes) rents kayaks, pedal boats, rowing boats and small motorboats. It also organises kayaking trips along the Albufeira de Salamonde.

Sleeping & Eating

Vila do Gerês has plenty of *pensões* (guesthouses), but you may find vacancies are limited; many are block-booked by spa patients in summer.

Hotel de Peneda BOUTIQUE HOTEL €€
(251 460 040; www.hotelpeneda.com; Lugar da Peneda; r €50-75; P) Set in the Serra da Peneda, in the northern reaches of the park, this mountain lodge has a waterfall backdrop and attractive rooms with picturesque views. Also has a good restaurant.

Beleza da Serra GUESTHOUSE €€
(253 391 457; www.bserra.com; Lugar do Bairro 25, Vilar da Veiga; d/tr €59/79) This friendly waterfront guesthouse overlooks the Caniçada Reservoir, 4.5km south of Vila do Gerês. It has simple, clean, comfortable rooms and a decent on-site restaurant.

Pousada da Juventude de Vilarinho das Furnas HOSTEL €
(253 351 339; www.pousadasjuventude.pt; dm/bungalow €15/52; P@) Campo's woodland hostel offers spartan dormitories, simply furnished doubles (with bathrooms) and roomier bungalows with kitchen units.

Parque Campismo de Cerdeira CAMPGROUND €
(253 351 005; www.parquecerdeira.com; camping per person/tent/car €5.50/5/5, bungalows €50-68; year-round; P) In Campo do Gerês, this place has oak-shaded sites, laundry, pool, minimarket and a particularly good restaurant. The ecofriendly bungalows open onto unrivalled mountain views.

Information

The head park office is **Adere-PG** (258 452 250; www.adere-pg.pt; Mon-Fri) in Ponte de Barca. Obtain park information and reserve cottages and other park accommodation through here. Other Adere-PG stations are at Mezio and Lamas de Mouro.

Getting There & Away

Because of the lack of transport within the park, it's good to have your own wheels. You can rent cars in Braga.

UNDERSTAND PORTUGAL

History

Portugal has an early history of occupation, stretching back to 700 BC when the Celts arrived on the Iberian peninsula, followed by the Phoenicians, Greeks, Romans, Visigoths, Moors and Christians.

Life Under the Moors

The Moors ruled southern Portugal for more than 400 years, and some scholars describe that time as a golden age. The Arabs introduced irrigation, previously unknown in Europe. Two Egyptian agronomists came to Iberia in the 10th century and wrote manuals on land management, animal husbandry, plant and crop cultivation and irrigation designs. They also introduced bananas, rice, coconuts, maize and sugar cane, and also encouraged small-scale, cooperatively run communities, specialising in olive oil and wine production, and food markets – still embraced in many parts of Portugal.

The Moors opened schools and set about campaigns to achieve mass literacy (in Arabic of course), as well as the teaching of maths, geography and history. Medicine reached new levels of sophistication. There was also a degree of religious tolerance that evaporated when the Christian crusaders came to power. Much to the chagrin of Christian slave owners, slavery was not permitted in the Islamic kingdom – making it a refuge for runaway slaves. Muslims, Christians and Jews all peacefully coexisted, at times even collaborating together, creating the most scientifically and artistically advanced society the world had, until that time, ever known.

Age of Discovery

The 15th century marked a golden era in Portuguese history, when Portuguese explorers helped transform the small kingdom into a great imperial power.

The third son of King João I, Henrique 'O Navegador' (Henry the Navigator, 1394–1460) played a pivotal role in establishing Portugal's maritime dominance. As governor of The Algarve, he assembled the very best sailors, map-makers, shipbuilders, instrument-makers and astronomers.

By 1431, Portuguese explorers discovered the islands of Madeira and the Azores, followed by Gil Eanes' 1534 voyage beyond Cape Bojador in West Africa, breaking a maritime superstition that this was the end of the world. More achievements followed over the next century. In 1488, Portuguese sailors, under navigator Bartolomeu Dias, were the first Europeans to sail around Africa's southern tip and into the Indian Ocean. This was followed by the epic voyage in 1497–98 when Vasco da Gama reached southern India, and in 1500 when Cabral discovered Brazil. With gold and slaves from Africa and spices from the East, Portugal was soon rolling in riches. As its explorers reached Timor, China and eventually Japan, Portugal cemented its power with garrison ports and trading posts. The monarchy, taking its 'royal fifth' of profits, became the wealthiest in Europe, and the lavish Manueline architectural style symbolised the exuberance of the age.

The Salazar Years

In 1908, King Carlos and his eldest son were assassinated in Lisbon. Two years later Portugal became a republic, which set the stage for an enormous power struggle. Over the next 16 years, chaos ruled, with an astounding 45 different governments coming to power, often the result of military intervention. Another coup in 1926 brought forth new names and faces, most significantly António de Oliveira Salazar, a finance minister who would rise up through the ranks to become prime minister – a post he would hold for 36 years.

Salazar hastily enforced his 'New State' – a republic that was nationalistic, Catholic, authoritarian and essentially repressive. All political parties were banned except for the loyalist National Union, which ran the show, and the National Assembly. Strikes were banned and propaganda, censorship and brute force kept society in order. The new secret police, Polícia Internacional e de Defesa do Estado (PIDE), inspired terror and suppressed opposition by imprisonment and torture. Various attempted coups during Salazar's rule came to nothing. The only good news was a dramatic economic turnaround, with surging industrial growth through the 1950s and 1960s.

Decolonisation finally brought the Salazarist era to a close. Independence movements in Portugal's African colonies led to costly and unpopular military interventions. In 1974, military officers reluctant to continue fighting bloody colonial wars staged a nearly bloodless coup – later nicknamed the Revolution of the Carnations (after victorious soldiers stuck carnations in their rifle barrels). Carnations are still a national symbol of freedom.

Portugal Today

After the revolution, Portugal faced enormous challenges as it modernized its economy and embraced a left-leaning democracy. Joining the EEC (European Economic Community) in 1986 and adopting the euro in 1999 gave the economy a boost, though the 2007 Global Financial Crisis hit the country hard. Portugal continues to struggle with a shrinking economy and EU-mandated austerity measures that have left many citizens disgruntled. The country has had more success in the realm of renewable energy (harvesting solar, wind and hydroelectric power). Today more than half of Portugal's energy comes from renewable sources, making it one of the world leaders in sustainability.

Arts

Music

The best-known form of Portuguese music is the melancholy, nostalgic songs called fado (literally 'fate'), said to have originated from troubadour and African slave songs. The late Amália Rodrigues was the Edith Piaf of Portuguese fado. Today it is Mariza who has captured the public's imagination with her extraordinary voice and fresh contemporary image. Lisbon's Alfama district has plenty of fado houses, ranging from the grandiose and tourist-conscious to small family affairs.

Architecture

Unique to Portugal is Manueline architecture, named after its patron, King Manuel I (1495–1521). It symbolises the zest for discovery of that era and is hugely flamboyant, characterised by fantastic spiralling columns and elaborate carving and ornamentation.

Visual Arts

Portugal's stunning painted *azulejo* tiles coat contemporary life, covering everything from houses to churches. The art form dates from Moorish times and reached a peak in the late 19th century when the art nouveau and art deco movements provided fantastic facades and interiors. Lisbon has its very own *azulejo* museum.

Environment

Portugal has made an astounding transformation from a nation powered largely by fossil fuels to one powered by solar, wind and hydropower. In 2005, only 17% of electricity in Portugal's grid came from green energy. By 2012, the figure had risen to over 50% – a gain unprecedented elsewhere in Europe. In 2008 one of the world's largest solar farms opened in the Alentejo, powering 30,000 homes. Portugal also has numerous wind farms as well as cutting edge 'wave farms' to harness the ocean's power, located just north of Porto.

Food & Drink

Freshly baked bread, olives, cheese, red wine or crisp *vinho verde*, chargrilled fish, *cataplana* (seafood stew), smoked meats – the Portuguese have perfected the art of cooking (and eating) simple, delicious meals. Sitting down to table means experiencing the richness of Portugal's bountiful coastline and fertile countryside. Of course, you don't have to sit, you can take your piping-hot *pastel de nata* (custard tart) standing up, or wander through scenic vineyards, sipping the velvety ports of the Douro Valley – the oldest demarcated wine region on earth. For local specialties see p890.

SURVIVAL GUIDE

Directory A–Z

Accommodation

There's an excellent range of good-value accommodation in Portugal. Budget places offer some of Western Europe's cheapest rooms, while you'll find atmospheric accommodation in converted castles and farmhouses.

PRICE RANGES

We list high-season rates for a double room; breakfast is generally not included.

€€€ more than €100

€€ €50 to €100

€ less than €50

ECOTOURISM & FARMSTAYS

Turismo de Habitação (www.turihab.pt) is a private network of historic, heritage or rustic properties, ranging from 17th-century mansions

SEASONS

High season mid-June to mid-September.

Mid-season May to mid-June and mid-September to October.

Low season November to April.

to quaint farmhouses or self-catering cottages. Doubles run from about €60 to €120.

POUSADAS

These are government-run former castles, monasteries or palaces, often in spectacular locations. For details, contact tourist offices or **Pousadas de Portugal** (www.pousadas.pt).

GUESTHOUSES

The most common types are the *residencial* and the *pensão:* usually simple, family-owned operations. Some have cheaper rooms with shared bathrooms. Double rooms with private bathroom typically run €40 to 60.

HOSTELS

Portugal has a growing number of hostels, particularly in Lisbon. Nationwide, Portugal has over 30 *pousadas da juventude* (youth hostels; www.pousadasjuventude.pt) within the Hostelling International (HI) system. The average price for a dorm room is about €20.

CAMPING

For detailed listings of campsites nationwide, pick up the **Roteiro Campista** (www.roteiro-campista.pt; €7), updated annually and sold at bookshops. The swishest places are run by **Orbitur** (www.orbitur.pt) and **Inatel** (www.inatel.pt).

Activities

The best **hiking** is found in Parque Nacional da Peneda-Gerês and Serra da Estrela. The ambitious can follow the 240km walking trail Via Algarviana across southern Portugal.

Popular **water sports** include surfing, windsurfing, canoeing, rafting and water skiing. For local specialists, see Lagos, Sagres, Tavira, Coimbra and Parque Nacional da Peneda-Gerês.

Good starting points for **cycling** trips are Tavira in The Algarve, Sintra in central Portugal and Parque Nacional da Peneda-Gerês in the north.

Modest alpine **skiing** is possible at Torre in the Serra da Estrela, usually from January through to March.

Business Hours

Standard hours are as follows:

Banks 8.30am to 3pm Monday to Friday

Bars 7pm to 2am

Cafes 9am to 7pm

Malls 10am to 10pm

Nightclubs 11pm to 4am Thursday to Saturday

Post offices 8.30am to 4pm Monday to Friday

Restaurants noon to 3pm & 7pm to 10pm

Shops 9.30am to noon & 2pm to 7pm Monday to Friday, 10am to 1pm Saturday

Sights 10am to 12.30pm & 2-5pm Tuesday to Sunday

Discount Cards

If you plan to do a lot of sightseeing in Portugal's main cities, the **Lisboa Card** and **Porto Card** are sensible investments. Sold at tourist offices, these cards offer discounts or free admission to many attractions, and free travel on public transport.

Embassies & Consulates

Australian Embassy (☎213 101 500; www.portugal.embassy.gov.au; 2nd fl, Av da Liberdade 200, Lisbon)

Canadian Embassy (☎213 164 600; Avenida da Liberdade 196, Edifício Victoria)

New Zealand Embassy (☎39 06 853 7501; www.nzembassy.com) The New Zealand embassy in Rome represents travellers.

UK Embassy (☎213 924 000; http://ukinportugal.fco.gov.uk; Rua de São Bernardo 33) Also in Portimaõ.

US Embassy (☎217 273 300; http://portugal.usembassy.gov; Av das Forças Armadas, Lisbon)

Food

The following price indicators (per main course) are used here:

€€€ more than €15

€€ €8 to €15

€ less than €8

Money

There are numerous banks with ATMs located throughout Portugal. Credit cards are accepted in midrange and top-end hotels, restaurants and shops.

Public Holidays

New Year's Day 1 January

Carnaval Tuesday February/March – the day before Ash Wednesday

Good Friday March/April

Liberty Day 25 April – celebrating the 1974 revolution

Labour Day 1 May

Corpus Christi May/June – 9th Thursday after Easter

Portugal Day 10 June – also known as Camões and Communities Day

Feast of the Assumption 15 August

Republic Day 5 October – commemorating the 1910 declaration of the Portuguese Republic

All Saints' Day 1 November

Independence Day 1 December – commemorating the 1640 restoration of independence from Spain

Feast of the Immaculate Conception 8 December

Christmas Day 25 December

Telephone

Portugal's country code is ☎351. There are no regional area codes. Mobile phone numbers have nine digits and begin with 9.

All Portuguese phone numbers consist of nine digits. These include area codes, which always need to be dialled. For general information dial ☎118, and for reverse-charge (collect) calls dial ☎120.

Phonecards are the most reliable and cheapest way of making a phone call from a telephone booth. They are sold at post offices, newsagents and tobacconists in denominations of €5 and €10.

Visas

Schengen visa rules apply.

Getting There & Away

Air

TAP (www.tap.pt) is Portugal's international flag carrier as well as its main domestic airline. Portugal's main airports:

Lisbon (LIS; ☎218 413 500; www.ana-aeroportos.pt)

Porto Airport (OPO; ☎229 432 400; www.ana-aeroportos.pt)

Faro (☎289 800 800; www.ana-aeroportos.pt)

Land

BUS

UK–Portugal and France–Portugal Eurolines services cross to Portugal via northwest Spain. Buses from London (£169) take approximately 35 hours to reach Lisbon. Daily buses to Lisbon take 26 hours from Paris (€92-125) and 8 hours from Madrid (€40-50 euros). Operators include the following:

Alsa (www.alsa.es)

Avanza (www.avanzabus.com)

Damas (www.damas-sa.es)

Eurolines (www.eurolines.com)

Eva (www.eva-bus.com)

CAR & MOTORCYCLE

There is no border control in Portugal.

TRAIN

The most popular train link from Spain is on the Sud Express, operated by **Renfe** (www.renfe.com; one-way tickets from €59), which has a nightly sleeper service between Madrid and Lisbon (one-way from €61, 11 hours). Badajoz (Spain)–Elvas–Lisbon is slow and there is only one regional service daily, but the scenery is stunning. Coming from Galicia, in the northwest of Spain, travellers can go from Vigo to Valença do Minho (Portugal) (€9.25, 40 minutes) and continue on to Porto (€15, 2 hours).

SPAIN TO PORTUGAL BUS SERVICES

FROM	TO	VIA	COST (€)	DURATION (HRS)	COMPANY
Madrid	Porto	Guarda	47	8½	Eurolines
Madrid	Lisbon	Évora	39	8	Eurolines, Avanza, Alsa
Barcelona	Lisbon	Évora	70	19	Eurolines
Santiago de Compostela	Porto	Braga	31	4	Eurolines
Sevilla	Lisbon	Évora	38	7	Eurolines, Alsa
Sevilla	Faro	Huelva	21	3½	Eurolines, Eva, Damas

Getting Around

Air

TAP Portugal (TAP; www.flytap.com) has daily Lisbon–Faro flights (under an hour) year-round.

Bicycle

Mountain biking is a fine way to explore the country, although given the Portuguese penchant for overtaking on blind corners, it can be dangerous on lesser roads. Bicycle lanes are rare: veteran cyclists recommend the Parque Nacional da Peneda-Gerês. A handful of towns have bike-hire outfits (from €10 to €20 a day). If you're bringing your own, pack plenty of spare inner tubes. Bicycles can be taken free on all regional and inter-regional trains as accompanied baggage. They can also go on a few suburban services on weekends. Most domestic bus lines won't accept bikes.

Boat

Portugal is not big on water-borne transport as a rule; however, there are river cruises along the Rio Douro from Porto, Lisbon's river trips and commuter ferries.

Bus

A host of small bus operators, most amalgamated into regional companies, run a dense network of services across the country. Among the largest companies are **Rede Expressos** (www.rede-expressos.pt), **Rodonorte** (www.rodonorte.pt) and The Algarve line **Eva** (www.eva-bus.com).

Most bus-station ticket desks will give you a computer printout of fares, and services and schedules are usually posted at major stations.

CLASSES

Expressos Comfortable, fast buses between major cities

Rápidas Quick regional buses

Carreiras Marked CR, slow, stopping at every crossroad

COSTS

Travelling by bus in Portugal is fairly inexpensive. A Lisbon–Faro express bus costs €19; Lisbon–Porto costs about €18. Both take four hours. An under-26 card should get you a small discount on long-distance services.

Car & Motorcycle

AUTOMOBILE ASSOCIATIONS

Automóvel Clube de Portugal (ACP; ☎213 180 100; www.acp.pt) has a reciprocal arrangement with foreign automobile clubs, including AA and RAC. It provides medical, legal and breakdown assistance. The 24-hour emergency help number is ☎707 509 510.

HIRE

To hire a car in Portugal you must be at least 25 years old and have held your home licence for over a year (some companies allow younger drivers at higher rates). To hire a scooter of up to 50cc you must be over 18 years old and have a valid driving licence. For more powerful scooters and motorbikes you must have a valid driving licence covering these vehicles from your home country.

INSURANCE

Although most car-insurance companies within the EU will cover taking your car to Portugal, it is prudent to consider extra cover for assistance in case your car breaks down. The minimum insurance required is third party.

ROAD RULES

The various speed limits for cars and motorcycles are 50km/h within cities and public centres, 90km/h on normal roads and 120km/h on motorways (but 50km/h, 70km/h and 100km/h for motorcycles with sidecars).

Driving is on the right side of the road. Drivers and front passengers in cars must wear seatbelts. Motorcyclists and passengers must wear helmets, and motorcycles must have headlights on day and night. Using a mobile phone while driving could result in a fine.

Drink-driving laws are strict in Portugal, with a maximum legal blood-alcohol level of 0.05%.

Train

Caminhos de Ferro Portugueses (www.cp.pt) is the statewide train network and is generally efficient.

There are four main types of long-distance service. Note that international services are marked IN on timetables.

Regional (marked R on timetables) Slow trains that stop everywhere

Interregional (IR) Reasonably fast trains

Intercidade (IC) or **Rápido** Express trains

Alfa Pendular Deluxe, marginally faster and much pricier service.

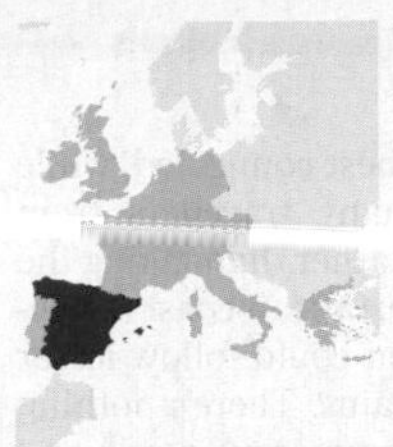

Spain

Includes »

Best Places to Eat

» La Cuchara de San Telmo (p993)
» Arzak (p993)
» Simply Fosh (p1008)
» Tickets (p982)
» La Pepica (p1003)

Best Places to Stay

» Hostal de San Marcos (p965)
» Hotel Meninas (p945)
» Hospedería Alma Andalusí (p1021)
» Sabinas (p990)
» Casa Morisca Hotel (p1023)

Why Go?

Passionate, sophisticated and devoted to living the good life, Spain is at once a stereotype come to life and a country more diverse than you ever imagined.

Spanish landscapes stir the soul, from the jagged Pyrenees and wildly beautiful cliffs of the Atlantic northwest to charming Mediterranean coves, while astonishing architecture spans the ages at seemingly every turn. Spain's cities march to a beguiling beat, rushing headlong into the 21st century even as timeless villages serve as beautiful signposts to Old Spain. And then there's one of Europe's most celebrated (and varied) gastronomic scenes.

But, above all, Spain lives very much in the present. Perhaps you'll sense it along a crowded after-midnight street when it seems all the world has come out to play. Or maybe that moment will come when a flamenco performer touches something deep in your soul. Whenever it happens, you'll find yourself nodding in recognition: *this* is Spain.

When to Go

Madrid

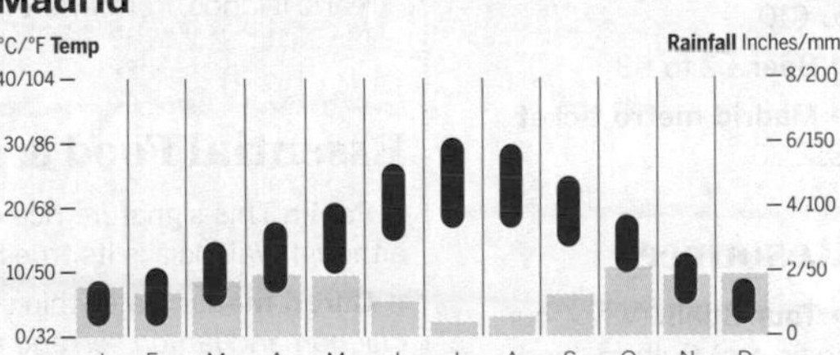

Mar–Apr Spring wildflowers, Semana Santa processions and mild southern temps.

May & Sep Mild and often balmy weather but without the crowds of high summer.

Jun–Aug Spaniards hit the coast in warm weather, but quiet corners still abound.

AT A GLANCE

» **Currency** euro

» **Language** Spanish (Castilian), Catalan, Basque, Galician (Gallego)

» **Money** ATMs everywhere

» **Visas** Schengen rules apply

Fast Facts

» **Area** 505,370 sq km

» **Capital** Madrid

» **Country code** ☎34

» **Emergency** ☎112

Exchange Rates

Australia	A$1	€0.82
Canada	C$1	€0.77
Japan	¥100	€0.83
New Zealand	NZ$1	€0.65
UK	UK£1	€1.18
USA	US$1	€0.78

Set Your Budget

» **Budget hotel room** €60

» **Two-course meal** €35 to €40

» **Museum entrance** €8 to €10

» **Beer** €2 to €3

» **Madrid metro ticket** €12.20

Resources

» **Tour Spain** (www.tourspain.org) Culture, food, hotels and transport links

» **Turespaña** (www.spain.info) Official tourism site

» **Lonely Planet** (www.lonelyplanet.com/spain)

Connections

Spanish airports are among Europe's best connected, while the typical overland route leads many travellers from France over the Pyrenees into Spain. Rather than taking the main road/rail route along the Mediterranean coast (or between Biarritz and San Sebastián), you could follow lesser known, pretty routes over the mountains. There's nothing to stop you carrying on to Portugal: numerous roads and the Madrid–Lisbon rail line connect the two countries.

The most obvious sea journeys lead across the Strait of Gibraltar to Morocco. The most common routes connect Algeciras or Tarifa with Tangier, from where there's plenty of transport deeper into Morocco. Car ferries also connect Barcelona with Italian ports.

There is a high-speed rail service between Paris and Barcelona (7½ hours), but at the time of writing it still required a change of trains in Figueres Vilafant. The Madrid–Paris line is also being upgraded to become a high-speed service.

ITINERARIES

One Week

Marvel at Barcelona's art nouveau–influenced Modernista architecture and seaside style before taking the train to San Sebastián, with a stop in Zaragoza on the way. Head on to Bilbao for the Guggenheim Museum and end the trip living it up in Madrid's legendary night scene.

One Month

Fly into Seville and embark on a route exploring the town and picture-perfect Ronda, Granada and Córdoba. Take the train to Madrid, from where you can check out Toledo, Salamanca and Segovia. Make east for the coast and Valencia, detour northwest into the postcard-perfect villages of Aragón and the Pyrenees, then travel east into Catalonia, spending time in Tarragona before reaching Barcelona. Take a plane or boat for the Balearic Islands, from where you can get a flight home.

Essential Food & Drink

» **Paella** This signature rice dish comes in infinite varieties, although Valencia is its true home.

» **Cured meats** Wafer-thin slices of *chorizo, lomo, salchichón* and *jamón serrano* appear on most Spanish tables.

» **Tapas** These bite-sized morsels range from uncomplicated Spanish staples to pure gastronomic innovation.

» **Olive oil** Spain is the world's largest producer of olive oil.

» **Wine** Spain has the largest area of wine cultivation in the world. La Rioja and Ribera del Duero are the best-known wine-growing regions.

MADRID

POP 3.26 MILLION

No city on earth is more alive than Madrid, a beguiling place whose sheer energy carries a simple message: *madrileños* know how to live. Explore the old streets of the centre, relax in the plazas, soak up the culture in Madrid's excellent art museums, and spend at least one night exploring the city's legendary nightlife scene.

History

Established as a Moorish garrison in 854, Madrid was little more than a muddy provincial village when King Felipe II declared it Spain's capital in 1561. That began to change when it became the permanent home of the previously roaming Spanish court. Despite being home to generations of nobles, the city was a squalid grid of unpaved alleys and dirty buildings until the 18th century, when King Carlos III turned his attention to public works. With 175,000 inhabitants under Carlos' rule, Madrid had become Europe's fifth largest capital.

The postcivil war 1940s and '50s were trying times for the capital, with rampant poverty. When Spain's dictator, General Franco, died in 1975, the city exploded with creativity and life, giving *madrileños* the party-hard reputation they still cherish.

Terrorist bombs rocked Madrid in March 2004, just before national elections, and killed 191 commuters on four trains. In 2007 two people died in a Basque terrorist bomb attack at the city's airport. With remarkable aplomb, the city quickly returned to business as usual on both occasions.

Sights

Get under the city's skin by walking its streets, sipping coffee and beer in its plazas and relaxing in its parks. Madrid de los Austrias, the maze of mostly 15th- and 16th-century streets that surround Plaza Mayor, is the city's oldest district. Tapas-crazy La Latina, alternative Chueca, bar-riddled Huertas and Malasaña, and chic Salamanca are other districts that reward pedestrian exploration.

TOP CHOICE Museo del Prado MUSEUM

(Map p946; www.museodelprado.es; Paseo del Prado; adult/child €12/free, free 6-8pm Mon-Sat & 5-7pm Sun, audioguides €3.50; ⏲10am-8pm Mon-Sat, to 7pm Sun; Ⓜ Banco de España) Spain's premier art museum, the Prado is a seemingly endless parade of priceless works from Spain and beyond. The 1785 neoclassical Palacio de Villanueva opened as a museum in 1819.

The collection is roughly divided into eight major collections: Spanish paintings (1100–1850), Flemish paintings (1430–1700), Italian paintings (1300–1800), French paintings (1600–1800), German paintings (1450–1800), sculptures, decorative arts, and drawings and prints. There is generous coverage of Spanish greats including Goya, Velázquez and El Greco. In addition to these Spanish masterpieces, don't miss *El Jardín de las Delicias* (The Garden of Earthly Delights; Room 56A), a three-panelled painting by Hieronymus Bosch of the creation of man, the pleasures of the world, and hell, or the works by Peter Paul Rubens, Pieter Bruegel, Rembrandt, Anton Van Dyck, Albrecht Dürer, Raphael, Titian, Tintoretto, Joaquín Sorolla, Thomas Gainsborough, Fra Angelico and Tiepolo.

From the 1st floor of the Palacio de Villanueva, passageways lead to the Edificio Jerónimos, the Prado's modern extension. The main hall contains information counters, a bookshop and a cafe. Rooms A and B (and Room C on the 1st floor) host temporary exhibitions.

TOP CHOICE Museo Thyssen-Bornemisza MUSEUM

(Map p946; ☎902 760 511; www.museothyssen.org; Paseo del Prado 8; adult/child €9/free; ⏲10am-7pm Tue-Sun; Ⓜ Banco de España) Opposite Museo del Prado, the Museo Thyssen-Bornemisza is an outstanding collection of international masterpieces. Begin your visit on the 2nd floor, where you'll start with medieval art, and make your way down to modern works on the ground level, passing paintings by Titian, El Greco, Rubens, Rembrandt, Anton van Dyck, Canaletto, Cézanne, Monet, Sisley, Renoir, Pissarro, Degas, Constable, Van Gogh, Miró, Modigliani, Matisse, Picasso, Gris, Pollock, Dalí, Kandinsky, Toulouse-Lautrec, Lichtenstein and many others on the way.

TOP CHOICE Centro de Arte Reina Sofía MUSEUM

(Map p940; ☎91 774 10 00; www.museoreinasofia.es; Calle de Santa Isabel 52; adult/concession €6/free, free Sun, 7-9pm Mon-Fri & 2.30-9pm Sat; ⏲10am-9pm Mon-Sat, to 2.30pm Sun; Ⓜ Atocha) If modern art is your thing, the Reina Sofía is your museum. A stunning collection of mainly Spanish modern art, the Centro de Arte Reina Sofía is home to Picasso's *Guernica* – his protest against the German bombing of the Basque town of Guernica

Spain Highlights

❶ Explore the **Alhambra** (p1022), an exquisite Islamic palace complex in Granada

❷ Visit Gaudí's singular work in progress, Barcelona's **La Sagrada Família** (p976), a cathedral that truly defies imagination

❸ Wander amid the horseshoe arches of Córdoba's **Mezquita** (p1019), close to perfection wrought in stone

❹ Eat your way through **San Sebastián** (p992), a gourmand's paradise with an idyllic setting

❺ Join the pilgrims making their way to magnificent **Santiago de Compostela** (p998)

❻ Soak up the scent of orange blossom, admire the architecture and surrender to the party atmosphere in sunny **Seville** (p1013)

❼ Discover the impossibly beautiful Mediterranean beaches and coves of **Menorca** (p1012)

❽ Spend your days in some of Europe's best art galleries then revel amid the best nightlife in **Madrid** (p937)

❾ Be carried away by the soulful strains of live **flamenco** (p1039)

Bordeaux
FRANCE
Avignon
Nîmes
Montpellier
Toulouse
BASQUE COUNTRY
San Sebastián
San Sebastián Airport
Bilbao
Irún
NAVARRA
Golfe de Beauduc
CANTABRIA
Vitoria
PYRENEES
Perpignan
Pamplona
Andorra la Vella
ANDORRA
Miranda de Ebro
Logroño
Jaca
Figueres
AP1
Burgos
Calahorra
Huesca
CATALONIA
Girona
Fornells
Girona-Costa Brava Airport
AP68
Costa Brava
Aranda de Duero
Soria
Lleida
Manresa
Tossa de Mar
Monestir de Monserrat
A9
Zaragoza
AP2
Barcelona
CASTILLA Y LEÓN
El Prat de Llobregat Airport
Sitges
Tarragona
A1
ARAGÓN
A23
AP7
Guadalajara
Alcalá de Henares
Barajas Airport
Teruel
Ciutadella de Menorca
Menorca
Maó
Chinchón
Aranjuez
Cuenca
A3
Inca
Artà
Mallorca
Sagunto
Manacor
Alcázar de San Juan
Valencia
Palma de Mallorca
VALENCIA
Alginet
Manzanares
Albacete
Airport
Balearic Islands
AP7
Ibiza
Denia
Valdepeñas
Benidorm
A4
Alicante
Elche
Cieza
Murcia
MURCIA
A7
Costa Blanca
MEDITERRANEAN SEA
A91
Cartagena
Guadix
Granada
Mojácar
Costa Cálida
Almería
Adra
Almería Airport
Salobreña
Costa De Almería
ALGERIA
0 200 km
0 100 miles

Madrid

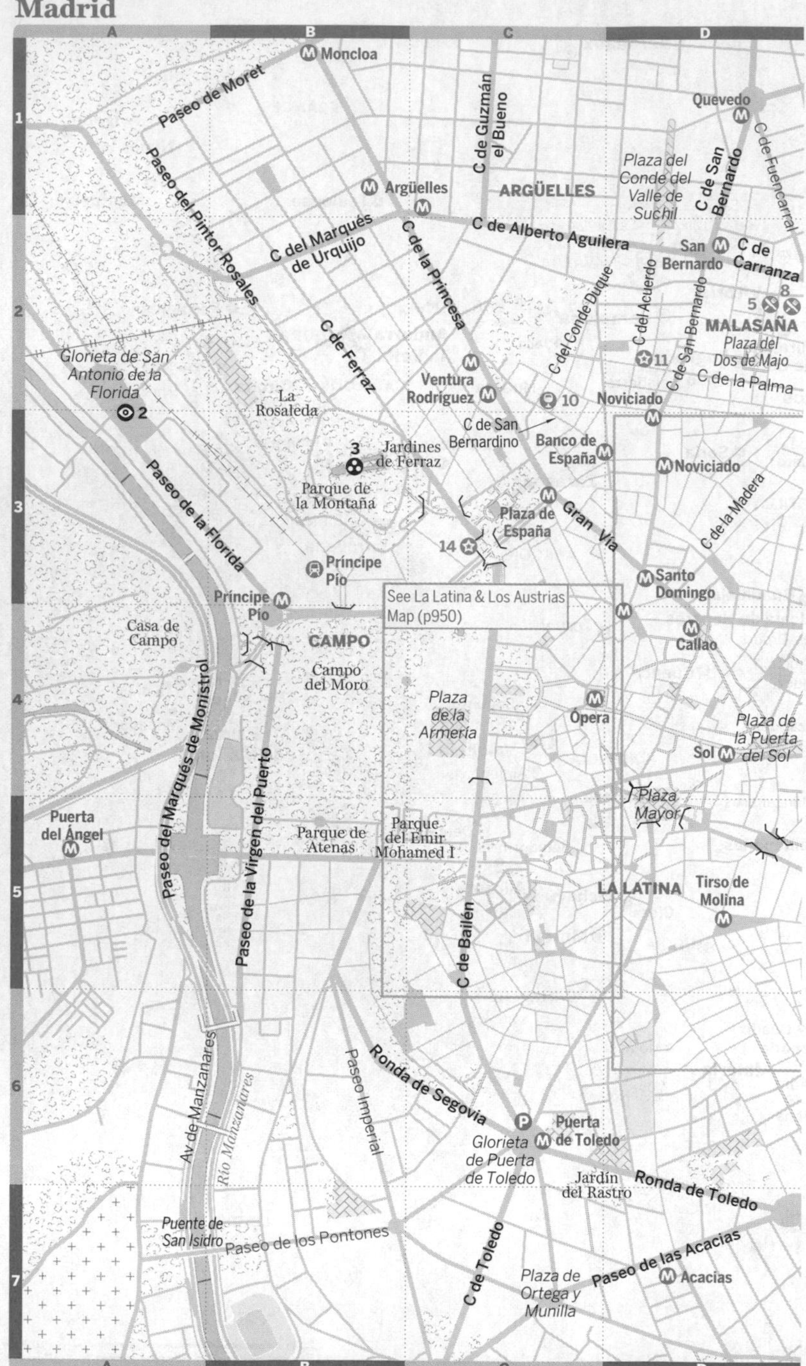
Moncloa
Paseo de Moret
Paseo del Pintor Rosales
C de Guzmán el Bueno
Argüelles
ARGÜELLES
Quevedo
C de Fuencarral
Plaza del Conde del Valle de Suchil
C de San Bernardo
C del Marqués de Urquijo
C de la Princesa
C de Alberto Aguilera
San Bernardo
C de Carranza
C del Conde Duque
C del Acuerdo
MALASAÑA
Plaza del Dos de Majo
C de la Palma
C de Ferraz
Glorieta de San Antonio de la Florida
La Rosaleda
Ventura Rodríguez
Noviciado
C de San Bernardino
Banco de España
Jardines de Ferraz
Parque de la Montaña
Plaza de España
Gran Vía
C de la Madera
Paseo de la Florida
Príncipe Pío
Santo Domingo
See La Latina & Los Austrias Map (p950)
Callao
Casa de Campo
CAMPO
Campo del Moro
Plaza de la Armería
Ópera
Plaza de la Puerta del Sol
Sol
Paseo del Marqués de Monistrol
Paseo de la Virgen del Puerto
Plaza Mayor
Puerta del Ángel
Parque de Atenas
Parque del Emir Mohamed I
LA LATINA
Tirso de Molina
C de Bailén
Av de Manzanares
Río Manzanares
Paseo Imperial
Ronda de Segovia
Glorieta de Puerta de Toledo
Puerta de Toledo
Jardín del Rastro
Ronda de Toledo
Puente de San Isidro
Paseo de los Pontones
C de Toledo
Plaza de Ortega y Munilla
Paseo de las Acacias
Acacias

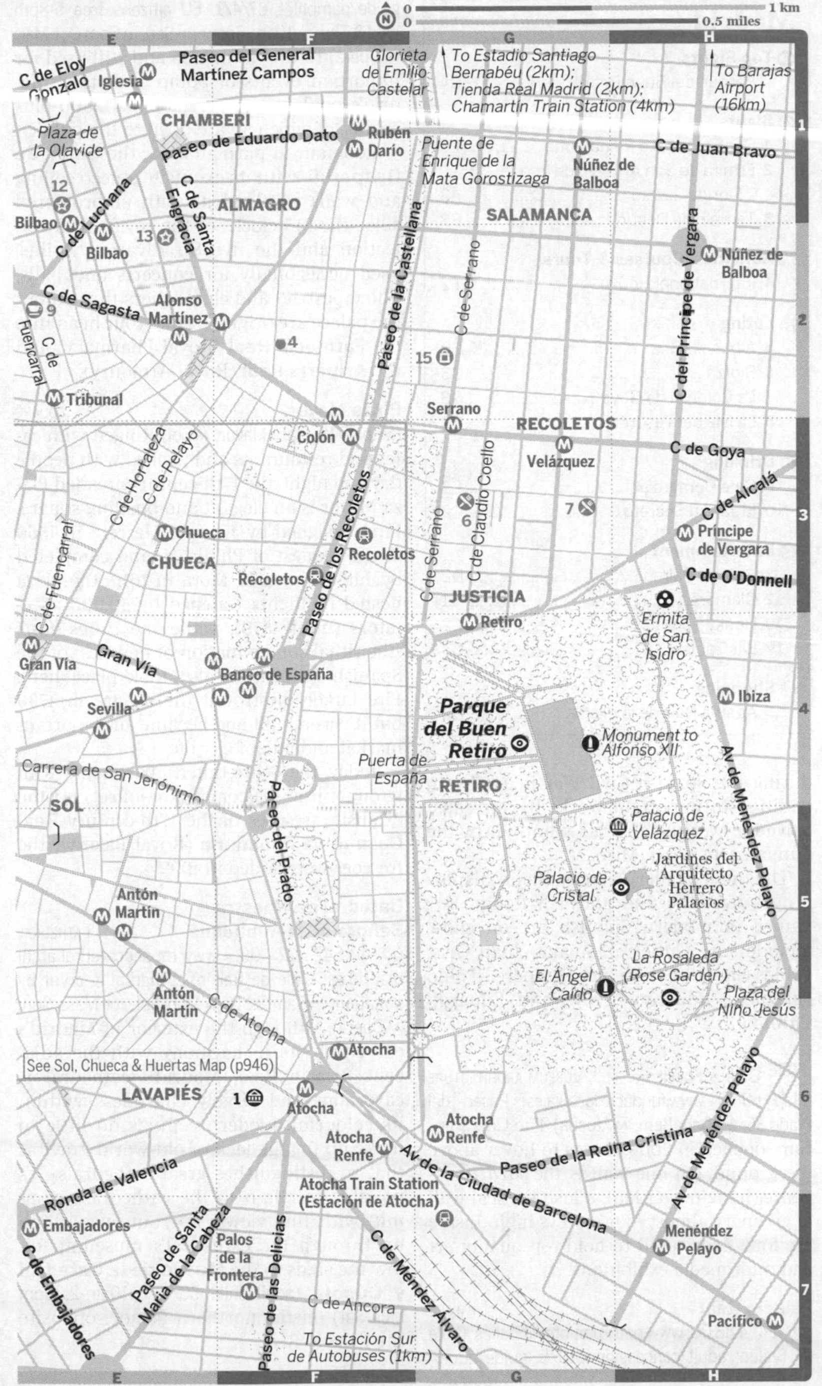

0 1 km
0 0.5 miles
Paseo del General Martínez Campos
C de Eloy Gonzalo
Iglesia
Glorieta de Emilio Castelar
To Estadio Santiago Bernabéu (2km); Tienda Real Madrid (2km); Chamartín Train Station (4km)
To Barajas Airport (16km)
CHAMBERI
Plaza de la Olavide
Paseo de Eduardo Dato
Rubén Darío
Puente de Enrique de la Mata Gorostizaga
Núñez de Balboa
C de Juan Bravo
ALMAGRO
SALAMANCA
C de Luchana
C de Santa Engracia
Bilbao
C de Sagasta
Alonso Martínez
Paseo de la Castellana
C de Serrano
C del Príncipe de Vergara
C de Fuencarral
Tribunal
Serrano
RECOLETOS
Colón
Velázquez
C de Goya
C de Hortaleza
C de Pelayo
C de Claudio Coello
C de Alcalá
Chueca
Paseo de los Recoletos
Príncipe de Vergara
CHUECA
Recoletos
C de O'Donnell
JUSTICIA
Retiro
Ermita de San Isidro
Gran Vía
Banco de España
Sevilla
Ibiza
Parque del Buen Retiro
Monument to Alfonso XII
Puerta de España
Carrera de San Jerónimo
RETIRO
SOL
Paseo del Prado
Palacio de Velázquez
Av de Menéndez Pelayo
Antón Martín
Palacio de Cristal
Jardines del Arquitecto Herrero Palacios
La Rosaleda (Rose Garden)
El Ángel Caído
Plaza del Niño Jesús
C de Atocha
Atocha
See Sol, Chueca & Huertas Map (p946)
LAVAPIÉS
Atocha Renfe
Paseo de la Reina Cristina
Ronda de Valencia
Av de la Ciudad de Barcelona
Atocha Train Station (Estación de Atocha)
Embajadores
Paseo de Santa María de la Cabeza
Palos de la Frontera
Paseo de las Delicias
C de Méndez Álvaro
Menéndez Pelayo
C de Embajadores
C de Ancora
To Estación Sur de Autobuses (1km)
Pacífico
SPAIN MADRID

Madrid

Top Sights

	Parque del Buen Retiro	G4

Sights

1	Centro de Arte Reina Sofía	F6
2	Ermita de San Antonio de la Florida	A3
3	Templo de Debod	B3

Activities, Courses & Tours

4	International House	F2

Eating

5	Albur	D2
6	Biotza	G3
7	La Colonial de Goya	G3
8	La Isla del Tesoro	D2

Drinking

9	Café Comercial	E2
10	El Jardín Secreto	C2

Entertainment

11	Café La Palma	D2
12	Clamores	E1
13	Honky Tonk	E2
14	Las Tablas	C3

Shopping

15	Agatha Ruiz de la Prada	G2

during the Spanish Civil War in 1937 – in addition to important works by surrealist Salvador Dalí and abstract paintings by the Catalan artist Joan Miró.

The main gallery's permanent display ranges over the 2nd and 4th floors. Key names in modern Spanish art on show include José Gutiérrez Solana, Juan Gris, Pablo Gargallo, Eusebio Sempere, Pablo Palazuelo, Eduardo Arroyo and Eduardo Chillida.

FREE Caixa Forum MUSEUM, ARCHITECTURE

(Map p946; www.fundacio.lacaixa.es; Paseo del Prado 36; 10am-8pm; M Atocha) The Caixa Forum, opened in 2008, seems to hover above the ground. On one wall is the *jardín colgante* (hanging garden), a lush vertical wall of greenery almost four storeys high. Inside are four floors used to hold top quality art and multimedia exhibitions.

Palacio Real PALACE

(91 454 88 00; www.patrimonionacional.es; Calle de Bailén; adult/concession €10/5, guide/audioguide/pamphlet €7/4/1, EU citizens free 5-8pm Wed & Thu; 10am-8pm Apr-Sep, to 6pm Oct-Mar; M Ópera) Dating from 1755 and still used for important events of pomp and state, Madrid's opulent royal palace has 2800-plus rooms, of which 50 are open to the public.

Look out in particular for the **Salón de Gasparini**, with its exquisite stucco ceiling and walls resplendent with embroidered silks, the 215 clocks of the royal clock collection and the five Stradivarius violins, used occasionally for concerts and balls. The tapestries and chandeliers throughout the palace are original. Poke your head into the **Farmacia Real** (Royal Pharmacy) and the **Armería Real** (Royal Armoury).

Plaza Mayor SQUARE

(Map p946; Plaza Mayor; M Sol) Ringed with cafes and restaurants and packed with people day and night, the 17th-century arcaded Plaza Mayor is an elegant and bustling square. First designed by Juan de Herrera in 1560 at the request of Phillip II, and completed by Juan Gómez de Mora in 1619, the plaza hosted bullfights watched by 50,000 spectators (until 1878), while the *autos-da-fé* (the ritual condemnation of heretics) of the Spanish Inquisition also took place here. Fire largely destroyed the square in 1790 but it was rebuilt and became an important market and hub of city life.

Today, the ochre-tinted apartments with wrought-iron balconies are offset by the exquisite frescoes of the 17th-century **Real Casa de la Panadería** (Royal Bakery); the frescoes were added in 1992.

Catedral de Nuestra Señora de la Almudena CATHEDRAL

(91 542 22 00; www.museocatedral.archimadrid.es; Calle de Bailén; cathedral & crypt by donation; 9am-8.30pm Mon-Sat, for Mass Sun; M Ópera) Although the exterior of Madrid's cathedral sits in harmony with the adjacent Palacio Real, Madrid's cathedral is cavernous and largely charmless within; its colourful, modern ceilings do little to make up for the lack of old-world gravitas that so distinguishes great cathedrals. It's possible to climb to the cathedral's summit, with fine views. En route you climb up through the cathedral's museum; follow the signs to the **Museo de la Catedral y Cúpola** (adult/child €6/4; 10am-2.30pm Mon-Sat) on the northern facade, opposite the Palacio Real.

Basílica de San Francisco El Grande CHURCH

(Plaza de San Francisco 1; adult/concession €3/2; ⌚Mass 8am-10.30am Mon-Sat, museum 10.30am-12.30pm & 4-6pm Tue-Sun; Ⓜ La Latina, Puerta de Toledo) Lording it over the southwestern corner of La Latina, this imposing and recently restored baroque basilica is one of Madrid's grandest old churches. Its extravagantly frescoed dome is, by some estimates, the largest in Spain and the fourth largest in the world, with a height of 56m and diameter of 33m. The fresco in the neo-plateresque Capilla de San Bernardino was painted by Goya.

Iglesia de San Ginés CHURCH

(Map p946; Calle del Arenal 13; ⌚8.45am-1pm & 6-9pm Mon-Sat, 9.45am-2pm & 6-9pm Sun; Ⓜ Sol, Ópera) Due north of Plaza Mayor, San Ginés is one of Madrid's oldest churches: it has been here in one form or another since at least the 14th century. The church houses some fine paintings, including El Greco's *Expulsion of the Moneychangers from the Temple* (1614).

Convento de las Descalzas Reales CONVENT

(Convent of the Barefoot Royals; Map p946; www.patrimonionacional.es; Plaza de las Descalzas 3; adult/child €7/4, incl Convento de la Encarnación €10/5, EU citizens free Wed & Thu afternoon; ⌚10.30am-2pm & 4-6.30pm Tue-Sat, 10am-3pm Sun; Ⓜ Ópera, Sol) Opulent inside, though with a rather plain plateresque exterior, the Convento de las Descalzas Reales was founded in 1559 by Juana of Austria. Daughter of Spain's King Carlos I and Isabel of Portugal, Juana transformed one of her mother's palaces into the noblewomen's convent of choice. On the obligatory guided tour you'll see a gaudily frescoed Renaissance stairway and a number of extraordinary tapestries based on works by Rubens. Some 33 nuns still live here and there are 33 chapels dotted around the convent.

Parque del Buen Retiro GARDENS

(Map p940; ⌚6am-midnight May-Sep, to 11pm Oct-Apr; Ⓜ Retiro, Príncipe de Vergara, Ibiza, Atocha) The splendid gardens of El Retiro are littered with marble monuments, landscaped lawns, the occasional elegant building and abundant greenery. It's quiet and contemplative during the week, but comes to life on weekends.

The focal point for so much of El Retiro's life is the artificial *estanque* (lake), which is watched over by the massive ornamental structure of the **Monument to Alfonso XII** on the east side of the lake, complete with marble lions. Hidden among the trees south of the lake, the late-19th-century **Palacio de Cristal**, a magnificent metal and glass structure that is arguably El Retiro's most beautiful architectural monument, is now used for temporary exhibitions.

At the southern end of the park, near **La Rosaleda** (Rose Garden) with its more-than-4000 roses, is a statue of **El Ángel Caído** (the Fallen Angel, aka Lucifer), one of the few statues to the devil anywhere in the world. It sits 666m above sea level...

In the northeastern corner of the park is the ruined **Ermita de San Isidro**, a small country chapel noteworthy as one of the few, albeit modest, examples of Romanesque architecture in Madrid.

FREE **Ermita de San Antonio de la Florida** CHURCH

(Map p940; Glorieta de San Antonio de la Florida 5; ⌚9.30am-8pm Tue-Fri, 10am-2pm Sat & Sun, hours vary Jul & Aug; Ⓜ Príncipe Pío) The frescoed ceilings of the hermitage are one of Madrid's most surprising secrets. In the southern of the two small chapels you can see Goya's work in its original setting, rendered in 1798. The painter is buried in front of the altar.

FREE **Templo de Debod** RUIN

(Map p940; www.munimadrid.es/templodebod; Paseo del Pintor Rosales; ⌚10am-2pm & 6-8pm Tue-Fri, 10am-2pm Sat & Sun Apr-Sep, 9.45am-1.45pm & 4.15-6.15pm Tue-Fri & 10am-2pm Sat & Sun Oct-Mar; Ⓜ Ventura Rodríguez) This authentically ancient Egyptian Temple was transferred here stone by stone from Egypt in 1972 as a gesture of thanks to Spanish archaeologists who helped save Egyptian monuments from the rising waters of the Aswan Dam.

MADRID'S BEST PLAZAS

Madrid also has some lovely public squares, among the best are:

Plaza de Oriente (Ⓜ Ópera)

Plaza de la Villa (Ⓜ Ópera)

Plaza de la Paja

Plaza de Santa Ana (Map p946; Ⓜ Sevilla, Sol, Antón Martín)

MUSEO DEL PRADO ITINERARY: ICONS OF SPANISH ART

The Museo del Prado's collection can be overwhelming in scope, but, if your time is limited, zero in on the museum's peerless collection of Spanish art.

Goya is displayed on all three floors of the Prado, but begin at the southern end of the ground or lower level. In rooms 64 and 65, Goya's *El Dos de Mayo* and *El Tres de Mayo* rank among Madrid's most emblematic paintings. In rooms 66 and 67, Goya's disturbing *Pinturas Negras* (Black Paintings) are so named for the distorted animalesque appearance of their characters. Of Goya's remarkable royal portraits, *La Família de Carlos V* (Room 32), on the 1st floor, is especially worth seeking out. Also on the 1st floor, in Room 36, are two more of Goya's best-known and most intriguing oils: *La Maja Vestida* and *La Maja Desnuda*. These portraits of an unknown woman, commonly believed to be the Duquesa de Alba (who some think may have been Goya's lover).

Having studied the works of Goya, turn your attention to Velázquez, beginning with *Las Meninas* (Room 12). Completed in 1656, it is more properly known as *La Família de Felipe IV* (The Family of Felipe IV). His mastery of light and colour is never more apparent than here. In the neighbouring rooms 14 and 15, watch also for his paintings of various members of royalty who seem to spring off the canvas – Felipe II, Felipe IV, Margarita de Austria (a younger version of whom features in *Las Meninas*), El Príncipe Baltasar Carlos and Isabel de Francia. In Room 9a, seek out his masterful *La Rendición de Breda* (The Surrender of Breda).

Further, Bartolomé Esteban Murillo (Room 17), José de Ribera (Room 9), the stark figures of Francisco de Zurbarán (Room 10a) and the vivid, almost surreal works of El Greco (Room 8b) should all be on your itinerary.

Real Academia de Bellas Artes de San Fernando MUSEUM
(Map p946; ☎91 524 08 64; http://rabasf.insde.es; Calle de Alcalá 13; adult/child €5/free, free Wed; ⏲9am-3pm Tue-Sat, to 2.30pm Sun Sep-Jun, hours vary Jul & Aug; MSol, Sevilla) The somewhat fusty Real Academia de Bellas Artes de San Fernando offers a broad collection of old and modern masters, including works by Zurbarán, El Greco, Rubens, Tintoretto, Goya, Sorolla and Juan Gris.

Courses

International House LANGUAGE SCHOOL
(Map p940; ☎902 141517; www.ihmadrid.es; Calle de Zurbano 8; MAlonso Martínez) Some of the best and cheapest classes in town.

Academia Inhispania LANGUAGE SCHOOL
(Map p946; ☎91 521 22 31; www.inhispania.com; Calle de la Montera 10-12; MSol) Language school.

Academia Madrid Plus LANGUAGE SCHOOL
(☎91 548 11 16; www.madridplus.es, Calle del Arenal 21, 6th fl; MÓpera) Language school.

Kitchen Club COOKING SCHOOL
(Map p946; ☎91 522 62 63; www.kitchenclub.es; Calle de Ballesta 8; MGran Vía, Callao) Run by one of Madrid's most celebrated chefs, Andrés Madrigal, Kitchen Club spans the globe with a range of courses operating just off Gran Vía in the city centre. For further information about food and drink in Spain see p1040.

Tours

Visitas Guiadas Oficiales GUIDED TOUR
(Official Guided Tours; ☎902 221424; www.esmadrid.com/guidedtours; Plaza Mayor 27; adult/child €3.90/free; MSol) Twenty highly recommended guided tours conducted in Spanish and English. Organised by the Centro de Turismo de Madrid (p958).

Madrid City Tour BUS TOUR
(☎902 024758; http://www.esmadrid.com/en/tourist-bus; 1-day ticket adult €21, child free-€9; ⏲9am-10pm Mar-Oct, 10am-6pm Nov-Feb) Hop-on, hop-off, open-topped buses that run every 10 to 20 minutes along two routes: Historical Madrid and Modern Madrid. Information, including maps, is available at tourist offices, most travel agencies and some hotels, or you can get tickets on the bus.

Festivals & Events

Fiesta de San Isidro CULTURAL
(www.esmadrid.com/sanisidro) Around 15 May, Madrid's patron saint is honoured with a week of nonstop processions, parties, bullfights and free concerts.

Suma Flamenca FLAMENCO
(www.madrid.org/sumaflamenca) A soul-filled flamenco festival that draws some of the biggest names in the genre in June.

Veranos de la Villa SUMMER FESTIVAL
(www.veranosdelavilla.esmadrid.com) Madrid's town hall stages a series of cultural events, shows and exhibitions throughout July and August, known as Summers in the City.

Sleeping

Madrid has a plethora of high-quality accommodation across all price ranges. Where you decide to stay will play an important role in your experience of Madrid. Los Austrias, Sol and Centro put you in the heart of the busy downtown area, while La Latina (the best *barrio* – neighbourhood – for tapas), Lavapiés and Huertas (good for nightlife) are ideal for those who love Madrid nights and don't want to stagger too far to get back to their hotel. You don't have to be gay to stay in Chueca, but you'll love it if you are, while Malasaña is another inner-city *barrio* with great restaurants and bars.

LOS AUSTRIAS, SOL & CENTRO

TOP CHOICE **Hotel Meninas** BOUTIQUE HOTEL €€
(91 541 28 05; www.hotelmeninas.com; Calle de Campomanes 7; s/d from €99/119; ; MÓpera) Inside a refurbished 19th-century mansion, the Meninas combines old-world comfort with modern, minimalist style. The colour scheme is blacks, whites and greys, with dark-wood floors and splashes of fuchsia and lime-green.

Praktik Metropol BOUTIQUE HOTEL €€
(Map p946; 91 521 29 35; www.hotelpraktikmetropol.com; Calle de la Montera 47; s/d from €65/79; ; MGran Vía) The rooms here have a fresh, contemporary look with white wood furnishings and some (especially the corner rooms) have brilliant views down to Gran Vía and out over the city.

Posada del Dragón BOUTIQUE HOTEL €€
(Map p946; 91 119 14 24; www.posadadeldragon.com; Calle de la Cava Baja 14 ; r from €91; ; MLa Latina) This restored 19th-century inn sits on one of our favourite streets in Madrid and rooms either look out over the street or over the pretty internal patio. Bold, brassy colour schemes and designer everything dominates the rooms.

Cat's Hostel HOSTEL €
(Map p946; 91 369 28 07; www.catshostel.com; Calle de Cañizares 6; dm €15-20; ; MAntón Martín) Forming part of a 17th-century palace, the internal courtyard here is one of Madrid's finest, with lavish Andalucian tilework, a fountain, a spectacular glass ceiling and stunning Islamic decoration. There's a supercool basement bar with free internet and fiestas.

Hostal Madrid HOSTAL, APARTMENT €
(Map p946; 91 522 00 60; www.hostal-madrid.info; Calle de Esparteros 6; s €35-55, d €45-75, d apt per night €55-150, per month €1200-2500; ; MSol) The 24 rooms at this well-run *hostal* have been wonderfully renovated with exposed brickwork, brand-new bathrooms and a look that puts many three-star hotels to shame. It also has terrific apartments (www.apartamentosmayorcentro.com).

Hotel Plaza Mayor HOTEL €€
(Map p946; 91 360 06 06; www.h-plazamayor.com; Calle de Atocha 2; s/d from €55/85; ; MSol, Tirso de Molina) Stylish decor, charming original elements of a 150-year-old building and helpful staff are selling points here. The rooms are attractive, some with a light colour scheme and wrought-iron furniture. The attic rooms have great views.

Hostal Acapulco HOSTAL €
(Map p946; 91 531 19 45; www.hostalacapulco.com; Calle de la Salud 13, 4th fl; s/d €55/65; ; MGran Vía, Callao) This immaculate little *hostal* has marble floors, renovated bathrooms, double-glazed windows and comfortable beds. Street-facing rooms have balconies overlooking sunny Plaza del Carmen.

Hotel de Las Letras HOTEL €€
(Map p946; 91 523 79 80; www.hoteldelasletras.com; Gran Vía 11; d from €100; ; MGran Vía) Hotel de las Letras started the rooftop hotel-bar trend in Madrid. The bar's wonderful, but the whole hotel is excellent with individually styled rooms, each with literary quotes scribbled on the walls.

HUERTAS & ATOCHA

Hotel Alicia BOUTIQUE HOTEL €€
(Map p946; 91 389 60 95; www.room-matehoteles.com; Calle del Prado 2; d €100-175, ste from €200; ; MSol, Sevilla, Antón Martín) With beautiful, spacious rooms, Alicia overlooks Plaza de Santa Ana. It has an ultra-modern look and the downstairs bar is oh-so-cool.

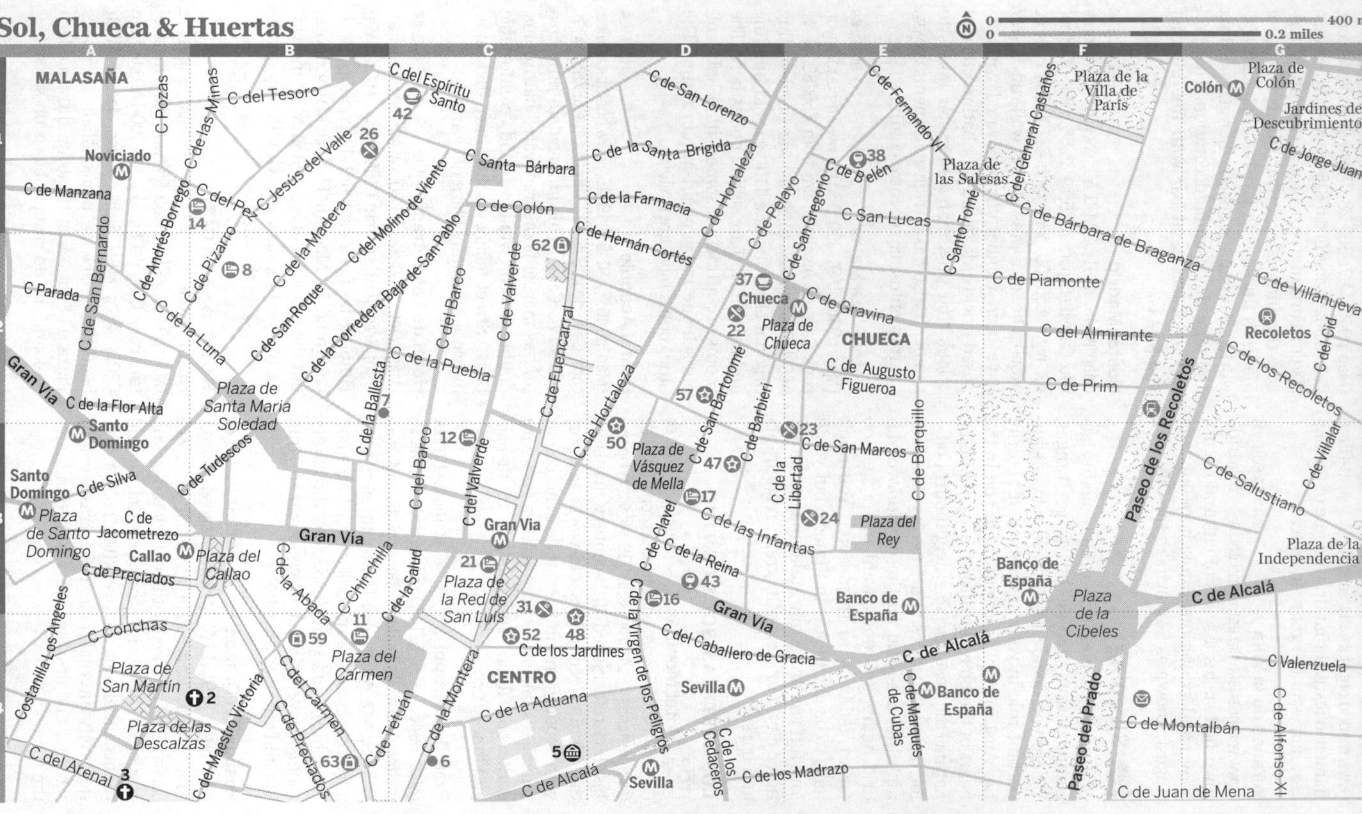
Sol, Chueca & Huertas
400 m
0.2 miles
MALASAÑA
CHUECA
CENTRO
Plaza de Colón
Colón
Jardines de Descubrimiento
Plaza de la Villa de París
Plaza de las Salesas
Plaza de Chueca
Chueca
Plaza de Vásquez de Mella
Plaza del Rey
Plaza de la Independencia
Plaza de la Cibeles
Banco de España
Sevilla
Gran Vía
Plaza de la Red de San Luis
Plaza del Carmen
Plaza del Callao
Callao
Plaza de Santo Domingo
Santo Domingo
Plaza de Santa María Soledad
Plaza de San Martín
Plaza de las Descalzas
Noviciado
Recoletos
Paseo de los Recoletos
Paseo del Prado
C de Alcalá
C de Jorge Juan
C del Cid
C de Villanueva
C de los Recoletos
C de Villalar
C de Salustiano
C Valenzuela
C de Alfonso XI
C de Montalbán
C de Juan de Mena
C de Bárbara de Braganza
C del Almirante
C de Piamonte
C de Prim
C del General Castaños
C Santo Tomé
C de Fernando VI
C San Lucas
C de Belén
C de Gravina
C de Augusto Figueroa
C de Barquillo
C de San Marcos
C de la Libertad
C de las Infantas
C de Marqués de Cubas
C de San Gregorio
C de Pelayo
C de Hortaleza
C de Barbieri
C de San Bartolomé
C de San Lorenzo
C de la Santa Brígida
C de la Farmacia
C de Hernán Cortés
C de Fuencarral
C de Clavel
C de la Reina
C del Caballero de Gracia
C de los Madrazo
C de los Cedaceros
C de la Virgen de los Peligros
C de los Jardines
C de la Aduana
C Santa Bárbara
C de Colón
C de Valverde
C del Valverde
C del Espíritu Santo
C del Barco
C de la Puebla
C de la Montera
C de la Salud
C de Tetuán
C del Molino de Viento
C de la Corredera Baja de San Pablo
C de la Ballesta
C Chinchilla
C de la Abada
C del Carmen
C de Preciados
C del Tesoro
C de la Madera
C de San Roque
C Jesús del Valle
C del Pez
C de las Minas
C de Pizarro
C de la Luna
C de Tudescos
C del Maestro Victoria
C Pozas
C de Andrés Borrego
C de San Bernardo
C de la Flor Alta
C de Silva
C de Jacometrezo
C Conchas
Costanilla Los Ángeles
C del Arenal
C de Manzana
C Parada

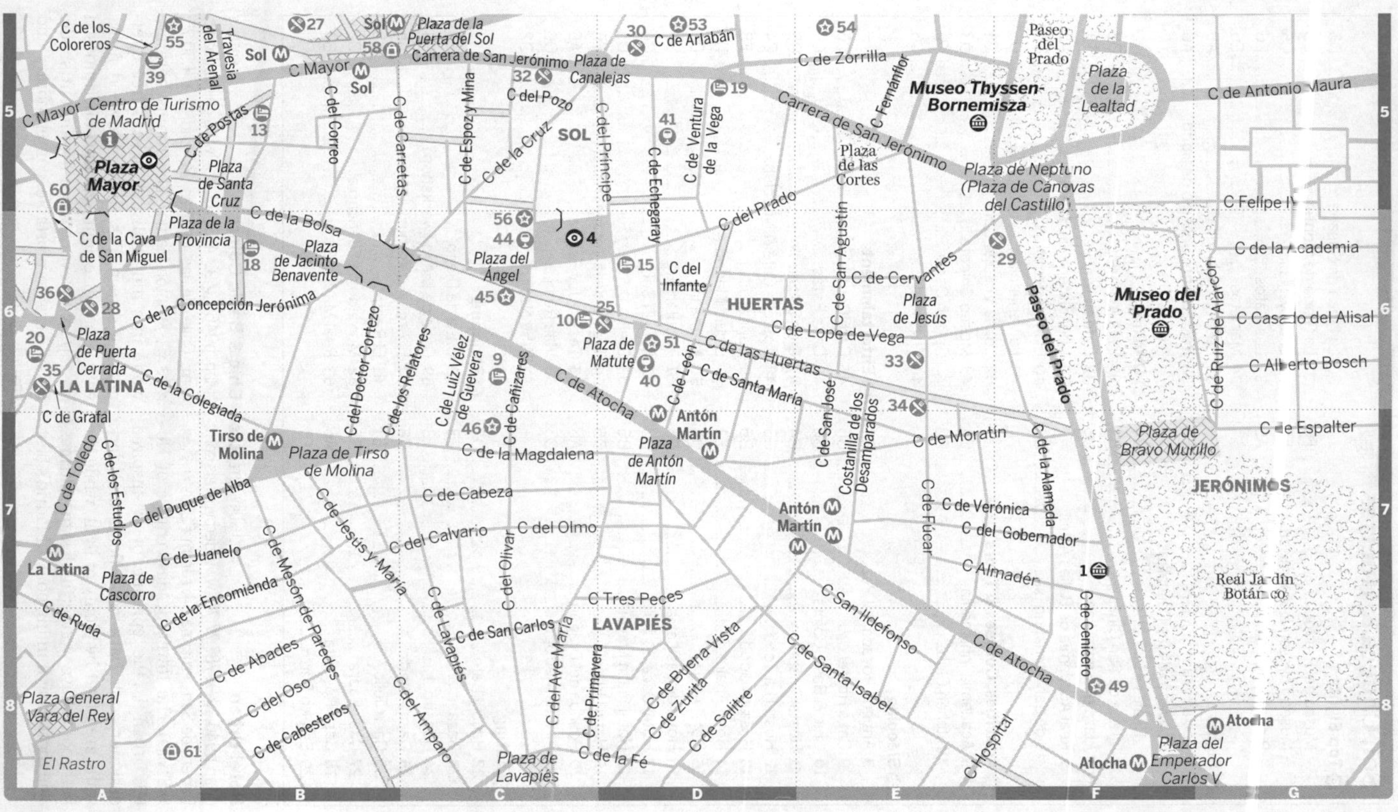
C de los Coloreros
Plaza de la Puerta del Sol
Carrera de San Jerónimo
Plaza de Canalejas
C de Arlabán
C de Zorrilla
Museo Thyssen-Bornemisza
Paseo del Prado
Plaza de la Lealtad
C de Antonio Maura
C Mayor
Centro de Turismo de Madrid
Travesia del Arenal
Sol
C de Postas
C del Correo
C de Carretas
C de Espoz y Mina
C del Pozo
C de la Cruz
SOL
C del Príncipe
C de Echegaray
C de Ventura de la Vega
C Fernanflor
Plaza de las Cortes
Plaza de Neptuno (Plaza de Cánovas del Castillo)
C Felipe IV
Plaza Mayor
Plaza de Santa Cruz
Plaza de la Provincia
C de la Cava de San Miguel
C de la Bolsa
Plaza de Jacinto Benavente
Plaza del Ángel
C del Prado
C del Infante
C de San Agustín
C de Cervantes
C de la Academia
HUERTAS
Plaza de Jesús
Museo del Prado
C Casado del Alisal
C de Ruiz de Alarcón
C de la Concepción Jerónima
Plaza de Puerta Cerrada
LA LATINA
C de Grafal
C de la Colegiada
C del Doctor Cortezo
C de los Relatores
C de Luiz Vélez de Guevara
C de Cañizares
Plaza de Matute
C de León
C de las Huertas
C de Lope de Vega
C de Santa María
Paseo del Prado
C Alberto Bosch
C de Atocha
Antón Martín
Plaza de Antón Martín
C de San José
Costanilla de los Desamparados
C de Moratín
Plaza de Bravo Murillo
C de Espalter
C de Toledo
C de los Estudios
Tirso de Molina
Plaza de Tirso de Molina
C de la Magdalena
C de la Alameda
JERÓNIMOS
C del Duque de Alba
C de Cabeza
C de Jesús y María
C de Fúcar
C de Verónica
C del Gobernador
La Latina
C de Juanelo
C del Calvario
C del Olmo
C de Mesón de Paredes
C Almadén
Real Jardín Botánico
Plaza de Cascorro
C de la Encomienda
C del Olivar
C Tres Peces
C de Ruda
C de Lavapiés
C de San Carlos
LAVAPIÉS
C San Ildefonso
C de Cenicero
C de Abades
C de Buena Vista
C de Santa Isabel
Plaza General Vara del Rey
C del Oso
C del Amparo
C del Ave María
C de Primavera
C de Zurita
C de Salitre
Atocha
C de Cabesteros
C Hospital
Plaza del Emperador Carlos V
El Rastro
Plaza de Lavapiés
C de la Fé

Sol, Chueca & Huertas

Top Sights
Museo del Prado ... F6
Museo Thyssen-Bornemisza ... E5
Plaza Mayor ... A5

Sights
1 Caixa Forum ... F7
2 Convento de las Descalzas Reales ... B4
3 Iglesia de San Ginés ... A4
4 Plaza de Santa Ana ... C6
5 Real Academia de Bellas Artes de San Fernando ... C4

Activities, Courses & Tours
6 Academia Inhispania ... C4
7 Kitchen Club ... B2

Sleeping
8 Antigua Posada del Pez ... B2
9 Cat's Hostel ... C6
10 Chic & Basic Colors ... C6
11 Hostal Acapulco ... B4
12 Hostal La Zona ... C3
13 Hostal Madrid ... B5
14 Hotel Abalú ... B1
15 Hotel Alicia ... D6
16 Hotel de Las Letras ... D3
17 Hotel Óscar ... D3
18 Hotel Plaza Mayor ... B6
19 Hotel Urban ... D5
20 Posada del Dragón ... A6
21 Praktik Metropol ... C3

Eating
22 Baco y Beto ... D2
23 Bazaar ... E3
24 Bocaito ... E3
25 Casa Alberto ... D6
26 Casa Julio ... B1
27 Casa Labra ... B5
28 Casa Revuelta ... A6
29 Estado Puro ... F6
30 La Finca de Susana ... D5
31 La Gloria de Montera ... C3
32 Lhardy ... C5
33 Los Gatos ... E6
34 Maceiras ... E6
35 Posada de la Villa ... A6
36 Restaurante Sobrino de Botín ... A6

Drinking
37 Café Acuarela ... D2
38 Café Belén ... E1
39 Chocolatería de San Ginés ... A5
40 El Imperfecto ... D6
41 La Venencia ... D5
42 Lolina Vintage Café ... C1
43 Museo Chicote ... D3
Splash Óscar ... (see 17)
44 The Roof ... C6

Entertainment
45 Café Central ... C6
46 Casa Patas ... C7
47 Club 54 Studio ... D3
48 Costello Café & Niteclub ... C4
49 Kapital ... F8
Liquid Madrid ... (see 47)
50 Mamá Inés ... D3
51 Populart ... D6
52 Sala El Sol ... C4
53 Stella ... D5
54 Teatro de la Zarzuela ... E5
55 Teatro Joy Eslava ... A5
56 Villa Rosa ... C6
57 Why Not? ... D2

Shopping
58 Casa de Diego ... B5
59 Casa de Diego (workshop) ... B4
60 El Arco Artesanía ... A5
61 El Rastro ... A8
62 Mercado de Fuencarral ... C2
63 Real Madrid Store ... B4

Hotel Urban LUXURY HOTEL €€€
(Map p946; ☎91 787 77 70; www.derbyhotels.com; Carrera de San Jerónimo 34; r from €225; ❄☜☒; ⓂSevilla) The towering glass edifice of Hotel Urban is the epitome of art-inspired designer cool. Dark-wood floors and dark walls are offset by plenty of light, while the bathrooms have wonderful designer fittings. The rooftop swimming pool is Madrid's best.

Chic & Basic Colors HOTEL €
(Map p946; ☎91 429 69 35; www.chicandbasic.com; Calle de las Huertas 14, 2nd fl; r €50-75; ❄☜☒; ⓂAntón Martín) The rooms here are white in a minimalist style with free internet, flat-screen TVs, dark hardwood floors with a bright colour scheme superimposed on top, with every room a different shade. It's all very comfortable, contemporary and casual.

MALASAÑA & CHUECA

TOP CHOICE **Hotel Óscar** BOUTIQUE HOTEL €€
(Map p946; ☎91 701 11 73; www.room-matehoteles.com; Plaza de Vázquez de Mella 12; d €90-200, ste €150-280; ; Gran Via) Hotel Óscar's designer rooms ooze style and sophistication. Some have floor-to-ceiling murals, the lighting is always funky and the colour scheme is awash with pinks, lime-greens, oranges or a more minimalist black-and-white.

TOP CHOICE **Hotel Abalú** BOUTIQUE HOTEL €€
(Map p946; ☎91 531 47 44; www.hotelabalu.com; Calle del Pez 19; d/apt from €84/110; ; Noviciado) Malasaña's very own boutique hotel is an oasis of style amid the *barrio*'s timeworn feel. Suitably located on cool Calle del Pez, each room here has its own design, from retro chintz to Zen, baroque and pure white and most aesthetics in between. You're close to Gran Vía, but away from the tourist scrum.

Antigua Posada del Pez HOTEL €€
(Map p946; ☎91 531 42 96; www.antiguaposadadelpez.com; Calle de Pizarro 16; r €60-110; ; Noviciado) This place inhabits the shell of an historic Malasaña building, but the rooms are slick and contemporary with designer bathrooms. You're also just a few steps up the hill from Calle del Pez, one of Malasaña's most happening streets.

Hostal La Zona HOSTAL €
(Map p946; ☎91 521 99 04; www.hostallazona.com; Calle de Valverde 7, 1st fl; s/d incl breakfast €50/70; ; Gran Vía) Catering primarily to a gay clientele, the stylish Hostal La Zona has exposed brickwork, wooden pillars and a subtle colour scheme. Other highlights include free internet, helpful staff and air-conditioning/heating in every room.

Eating

It's possible to find just about any kind of cuisine and eatery in Madrid, from traditional to trendy fusion. Madrid is a magnet for cuisines from around the country and is particularly associated with seafood; despite not having a sea, Madrid has the world's second-largest fish market (after Tokyo).

From the chaotic tapas bars of La Latina to countless neighbourhood favourites, you'll have no trouble tracking down specialities like *cochinillo asado* (roast suckling pig) or *cocido madrileño* (a hearty stew made of chickpeas and various meats).

LOS AUSTRIAS, SOL & CENTRO

TOP CHOICE **Mercado de San Miguel** TAPAS, MARKET €
(www.mercadodesanmiguel.es; Plaza de San Miguel; tapas from €1; 10am-midnight Sun-Wed, to 2am Thu-Sat; Sol) One of Madrid's oldest and most beautiful markets, the Mercado de San Miguel has undergone a stunning major renovation and bills itself as a 'culinary cultural centre'. Within the early 20th-century glass walls, the market has become an inviting space strewn with tables (difficult to nab) where you can enjoy the freshest food or a drink. You can order tapas at most of the counter-bars.

TOP CHOICE **Restaurante Sobrino de Botín** CASTILIAN €€€
(Map p946; ☎91 366 42 17; www.botin.es; Calle de los Cuchilleros 17; mains €18.50-28; La Latina, Sol) It's not every day that you can eat in the oldest restaurant in the world (1725), which also appears in many novels about Madrid, most notably Hemingway's *The Sun Also Rises*. The secret of its staying power is fine *cochinillo* (suckling pig) and *cordero asado* (roast lamb) cooked in wood-fired ovens. Eating in the vaulted cellar is a treat.

Restaurante Sandó CONTEMPORARY SPANISH €€€
(☎91 547 99 11; www.restaurantesando.es; Calle de Isabel la Católica 2; mains €18-26, menú degustación €49; lunch & dinner Tue-Sat, lunch Sun; Santo Domingo) Juan Mari Arzak, one of Spain's most famous chefs, and his increasingly celebrated daughter Elena, have finally set up shop in Madrid. Bringing Basque innovation to bear upon local tradition, their cooking is assured with dishes such as bites of beef with fresh garlic and pineapple. If you can't decide, try the *menú degustación* (tasting menu).

La Gloria de Montera SPANISH €
(Map p946; www.lagloriademontera.com; Calle del Caballero de Gracia 10; mains €7-10; Gran Vía) Minimalist style, tasty Mediterranean dishes and great prices mean that you'll probably have to wait in line (no reservations taken) to eat here.

Taberna La Bola MADRILEÑO €€
(☎91 547 69 30; www.labola.es; Calle de la Bola 5; mains €16-24; lunch & dinner Mon-Sat, lunch Sun, closed Aug; Santo Domingo) Taberna La Bola (going strong since 1870 and run by the sixth generation of the Verdasco family) is known for its traditional local cuisine. If you're going to try *cocido madrileño* while in Madrid, this is a good place to do so.

La Latina & Los Austrias

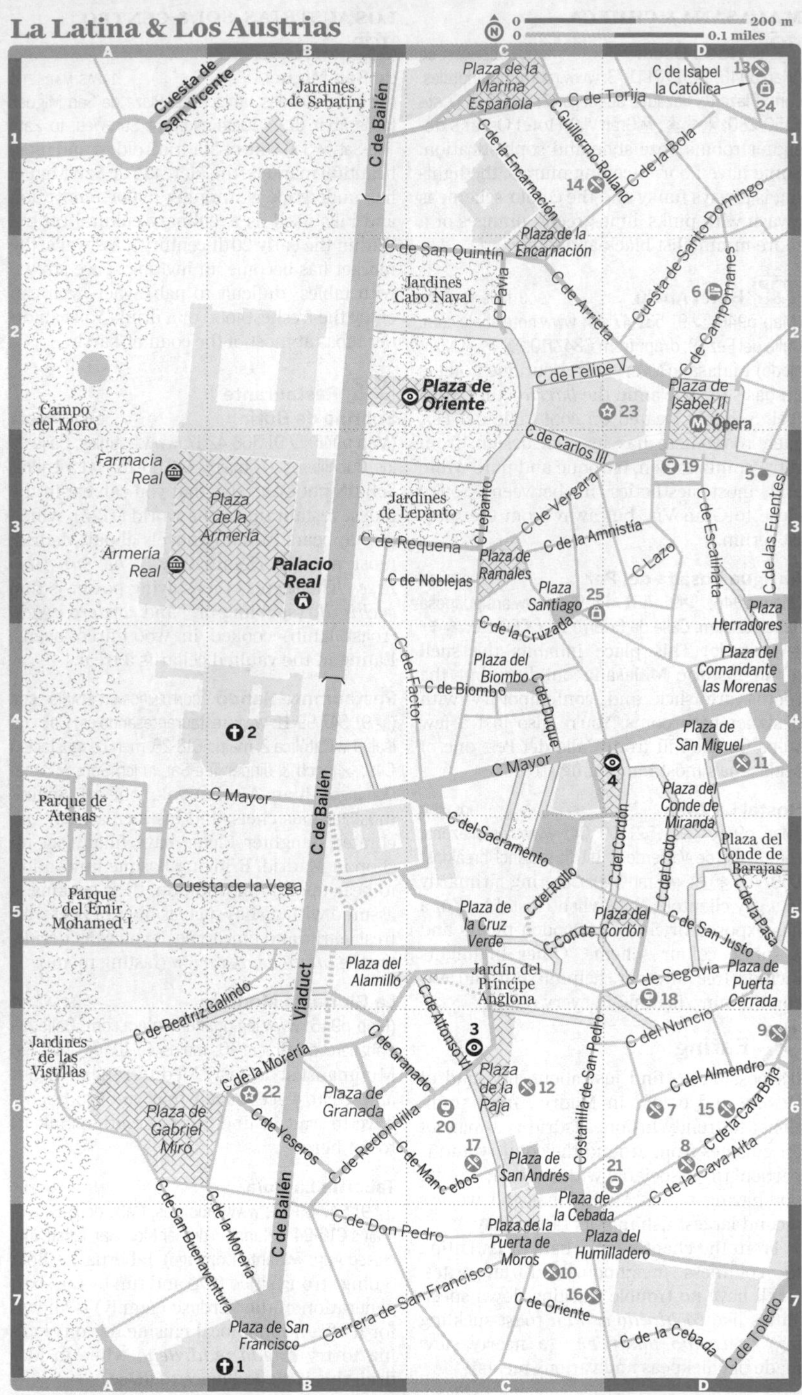

La Latina & Los Austrias

Top Sights
Palacio Real ... B3
Plaza de Oriente ... C2

Sights
1 Basílica de San Francisco El Grande ... B7
2 Catedral de Nuestra Señora de la Almudena ... B4
3 Plaza de la Paja ... C6
4 Plaza de la Villa ... D4

Activities, Courses & Tours
5 Academia Madrid Plus ... D3

Sleeping
6 Hotel Meninas ... D2

Eating
7 Almendro 13 ... D6
8 Casa Lucio ... D6
9 Enotaberna del León de Oro ... D6
10 Juana La Loca ... C7
11 Mercado de San Miguel ... D4
12 Naïa Restaurante ... C6
13 Restaurante Sandó ... D1
14 Taberna La Bola ... C1
15 Txacolina ... D6
16 Txirimiri ... C7
17 Viva La Vida ... C6

Drinking
18 Café del Nuncio ... D5
19 Café del Real ... D3
20 Delic ... C6
21 Taberna Tempranillo ... D6

Entertainment
22 Corral de la Morería ... B6
23 Teatro Real ... D2

Shopping
24 Antigua Casa Talavera ... D1
25 El Flamenco Vive ... C3

LA LATINA & LAVAPIÉS

Naïa Restaurante FUSION €€
(☎91 366 27 83; Plaza de la Paja 3; mains €12-19; ⊙lunch & dinner Tue-Sun; ⓂLa Latina) On the lovely Plaza de la Paja, Naïa has a real buzz about it, with modern Spanish cuisine, a chill-out lounge downstairs and a cooking laboratory overseen by Carlos López Reyes.

Enotaberna del León de Oro SPANISH €€
(☎91 119 14 94; www.posadadelleondeoro.com; Calle de la Cava Baja 12; mains €13-15; ⊙lunch & dinner; ⓂLa Latina) At this fine, new bar–restaurant the emphasis is on matching carefully chosen wines with creative dishes in a casual atmosphere. It's a winning combination.

Viva La Vida VEGETARIAN €
(www.vivalavida.com.es; Costanilla de San Andrés 16; buffet 500g plus drink €10; ⊙noon-midnight Mon-Wed, 11am-2am Thu-Sun; ; ⓂLa Latina) This organic food shop has as its centrepiece an appealing vegetarian buffet with hot and cold food that's always filled with flavour. On the cusp of Plaza de la Paja, it's a great place at any time of the day, especially outside normal Spanish eating hours.

Casa Lucio SPANISH €€
(☎91 365 32 52; www.casalucio.es; Calle de la Cava Baja 35; mains €12-25; ⊙lunch & dinner Sun-Fri, dinner Sat, closed Aug; ⓂLa Latina) Lucio has been wowing *madrileños* with his light touch, quality ingredients and home-style local cooking for ages – think seafood, roasted meats and eggs (a Lucio speciality) in abundance.

Posada de la Villa MADRILEÑO €€€
(Map p946; ☎91 366 18 80; www.posadadelavilla.com; Calle de la Cava Baja 9; mains €20-28; ⊙lunch & dinner Mon-Sat, lunch Sun, closed Aug; ⓂLa Latina) This wonderfully restored 17th-century *posada* (inn) is something of a local landmark. The atmosphere is formal, the decoration sombre and traditional (heavy timber and brickwork), and the cuisine decidedly local.

HUERTAS & ATOCHA

Casa Alberto SPANISH, TAPAS €€
(Map p946; ☎91 429 93 56; www.casaalberto.es; Calle de las Huertas 18; mains €16-20; ⊙lunch & dinner Tue-Sat, lunch Sun; ⓂAntón Martín) One of the most atmospheric old *tabernas* (taverns) of Madrid, Casa Alberto has been around since 1827. The secret to its staying power is vermouth on tap, excellent tapas at the bar and fine sit-down meals; Casa Alberto's *rabo de toro* (bull's tail) is famous among aficionados. The *raciones* have none of the frilly innovations that have come to characterise Spanish tapas. *Jamón,* Manchego cheese and *croquetas* are recurring themes.

A TAPAS TOUR OF MADRID

Madrid's home of tapas is La Latina, especially along Calle de la Cava Baja and the surrounding streets. **Almendro 13** (☎91 365 42 52; Calle del Almendro 13; mains €7-15; ⏰12.30-4pm & 7.30pm-midnight Sun-Thu, 12.30-5pm & 8pm-1am Fri & Sat; Ⓜ La Latina) is famous for quality rather than frilly elaborations, with cured meats, cheeses, tortillas and *huevos rotos* (literally, 'broken eggs') the house specialities. Down on Calle de la Cava Baja, **Txacolina** (☎91 366 48 77; Calle de la Cava Baja 26; tapas from €3; ⏰dinner Mon & Wed-Fri, lunch & dinner Sat, lunch Sun; Ⓜ La Latina) does some of the biggest *pintxos* (Basque tapas) you'll find. Not far away, **Juana La Loca** (☎91 364 05 25; Plaza de la Puerta de Moros 4; tapas from €4, mains €8-19; ⏰lunch & dinner Tue-Sun, dinner Mon; Ⓜ La Latina) does a magnificent *tortilla de patatas* (potato and onion omelette). **Txirimiri** (☎91 364 11 96; www.txirimiri.es; Calle del Humilladero 6; tapas from €4; ⏰lunch & dinner Mon-Sat, closed Aug; Ⓜ La Latina) is also outstanding.

In the centre, for *bacalao* (cod) the historic **Casa Labra** (Map p946; ☎91 532 14 05; www.casalabra.es; Calle de Tetuán 11; tapas from €1; ⏰9.30am-3.30pm & 5.30-11pm; Ⓜ Sol) and **Casa Revuelta** (Map p946; ☎91 366 33 32; Calle de Latoneros 3; tapas from €2.60; ⏰10.30am-4pm & 7-11pm Tue-Sat, 10.30am-4pm Sun, closed Aug; Ⓜ Sol, La Latina) have no peers.

Down the bottom of the Huertas hill, **Los Gatos** (Map p946; ☎91 429 30 67; Calle de Jesús 2; tapas from €3.50; ⏰noon-1am Sun-Thu, to 2am Fri & Sat; Ⓜ Antón Martín) has eclectic decor and terrific canapés. Nearby, along the Paseo del Prado, there's supercool **Estado Puro** (Map p946; ☎91 330 24 00; www.tapasenestadopuro.com; Plaza de Cánovas del Castillo 4; tapas €5-12.50; ⏰11am-1am Tue-Sat, to 4pm Sun; Ⓜ Banco de España, Atocha) with gourmet tapas inspired by Catalonia's world-famous (but now closed) El Bulli restaurant. In Salamanca, **Biotza** (Map p940; www.biotzarestaurante.com; Calle de Claudio Coello 27; tapas €2.50-3.50; ⏰9am-midnight Mon-Thu, to 1am Fri & Sat; Ⓜ Serrano) offers creative Basque *pintxos* in stylish surrounds.

Chueca is another stellar tapas *barrio*. Don't miss **Bocaito** (Map p946; ☎91 532 12 19; www.bocaito.com; Calle de la Libertad 4-6; tapas from €3.50, mains €12-20; ⏰lunch & dinner Mon-Fri, dinner Sat; Ⓜ Chueca, Sevilla), another purveyor of Andalucian *jamón* (ham) and seafood. **Casa Julio** (Map p946; ☎91 522 72 74; Calle de la Madera 37; 6/12 croquetas €5/10; ⏰lunch & dinner Mon-Sat; Ⓜ Tribunal) is widely touted as the home of Madrid's best *croquetas* (croquettes). Another brilliant choice is **Baco y Beto** (Map p946; ☎91 522 84 81; Calle de Pelayo 24; tapas from €4; ⏰dinner Mon-Fri, lunch & dinner Sat; Ⓜ Chueca).

Maceiras GALICIAN €€
(Map p946; ☎91 429 15 84; Calle de las Huertas 66; mains €7-14; Ⓜ Antón Martín) Galician tapas (think octopus, green peppers etc) never tasted so good as in this agreeably rustic bar down the bottom of the Huertas hill, especially when washed down with a crisp white Ribeiro. The simple wooden tables, loyal customers and handy location make this a fine place to rest after (or en route to) the museums along the Paseo del Prado.

Lhardy MADRILEÑO €€€
(Map p946; ☎91 521 33 85; www.lhardy.com; Carrera de San Jerónimo 8; mains €18.50-39; ⏰lunch & dinner Mon-Sat, lunch Sun, closed Aug; Ⓜ Sol, Sevilla) This Madrid landmark (since 1839) is an elegant treasure-trove of takeaway gourmet tapas. Upstairs is the upscale preserve of house specialities. It's expensive, but the quality and service are unimpeachable.

La Finca de Susana SPANISH €€
(Map p946; www.lafinca-restaurant.com; Calle de Arlabán 4; mains €7-12; Ⓜ Sevilla) It's difficult to find a better combination of price, quality cooking and classy atmosphere anywhere in the centre. The softly lit dining area is bathed in greenery and the sometimes innovative, sometimes traditional food draws a hip, young crowd. It doesn't take reservations.

MALASAÑA & CHUECA

Bazaar CONTEMPORARY SPANISH €
(Map p946; www.restaurantbazaar.com; Calle de la Libertad 21; mains €6.50-10; ⏰lunch & dinner; Ⓜ Chueca) Bazaar's popularity among the well-heeled and often-famous shows no sign of abating. Its pristine white interior design with theatre lighting may draw a crowd that looks like it stepped out of the pages of *Hola!* magazine, but the food is extremely well priced and innovative. It doesn't take

reservations so be prepared to wait whether you're famous or not.

TOP CHOICE **Albur** TAPAS, SPANISH €€
(Map p940; ☎01 594 27 33; www.restaurantealbur.com; Calle de Manuela Malasaña 15; mains €13-18; ⊙noon-1am Sun-Thu, to 2am Fri & Sat; MBilbao) One of Malasaña's best deals, this place has a wildly popular tapas bar and a classy but casual restaurant out the back. Albur is known for terrific rice dishes and tapas, and has a well-chosen wine list.

La Isla del Tesoro VEGETARIAN €€
(Map p940; ☎91 593 14 40; www.isladeltesoro.net; Calle de Manuela Malasaña 3; mains €12.50-14.50; ⊙lunch & dinner; ☑; MBilbao) La Isla del Tesoro is loaded with quirky charm – the dining area is like someone's fantasy of a secret garden come to life. The cooking here is assured and wide-ranging in its influences and the menu is full of surprises.

SALAMANCA

La Colonial de Goya TAPAS €
(Map p940; www.restauranterincondegoya.es; Calle de Jorge Juan 34; tapas €3-4.50; ⊙8am-midnight Mon-Fri, noon-1am Sat & Sun; MVelázquez) A mere 63 varieties of canapé should be sufficient for most, but La Colonial de Goya also serve a range of carpaccios, *croquetas* and main dishes at this engaging little tapas bar.

Drinking

The essence of Madrid lives in its streets and plazas, and bar-hopping is a pastime enjoyed by young and old alike. If you're after the more traditional, with tiled walls and flamenco tunes, head to Huertas. For gay-friendly drinking holes, Chueca is the place. Malasaña caters to a grungy, funky crowd, while La Latina has friendly bars that guarantee atmosphere most nights of the week. In summer, the terrace bars that pop up all over the city are unbeatable.

The bulk of Madrid bars open to 2am Sunday to Thursday, and to 3am or 3.30am Friday and Saturday.

LOS AUSTRIAS & CENTRO

TOP CHOICE **Museo Chicote** COCKTAIL BAR
(Map p946; www.museo-chicote.com; Gran Vía 12; ⊙6pm-3am Mon-Thu, to 4am Fri & Sat; MGran Vía) The founder of this Madrid landmark is said to have invented more than a hundred cocktails, which the likes of Hemingway, Ava Gardner, Grace Kelly, Sophia Loren and Frank Sinatra all enjoyed at one time or another. It's at its best after midnight when a lounge atmosphere takes over, couples cuddle on the curved benches and some of the city's best DJs do their stuff.

> **MADRID'S FAVOURITE POST-CLUBBING MUNCHIES**
>
> Join the sugar-searching throngs who end the night at **Chocolatería de San Ginés** (Map p946; Pasadizo de San Ginés 5; ⊙9.30am-7am; MSol), a legendary bar, famous for its freshly fried *churros* (fried sticks of dough) and syrupy hot chocolate.

Café del Real BAR, CAFE
(Plaza de Isabel II 2; ⊙9am-1am Mon-Thu, to 3am Fri & Sat; MÓpera) A cafe and cocktail bar in equal parts, this intimate little place serves up creative coffees and a few cocktails to the soundtrack of chill-out music. The best seats are upstairs, where the low ceilings, wooden beams and leather chairs are a great place to pass an afternoon with friends.

LA LATINA & LAVAPIÉS

Delic BAR, CAFE
(www.delic.es; Costanilla de San Andrés 14; ⊙11am-2am Fri-Sun & Tue-Thu, 7pm-2am Mon; MLa Latina) We could go on for hours about this long-standing cafe-bar, but we'll reduce it to this most basic element: nursing an exceptionally good mojito (€8) or three on a warm summer's evening at Delic's outdoor tables on one of Madrid's prettiest plazas is one of life's great pleasures.

Taberna Tempranillo WINE BAR
(Calle de la Cava Baja 38; ⊙1-3.30pm & 8pm-midnight Tue-Sun, 8pm-midnight Mon; MLa Latina) You could come here for the tapas, but we recommend Taberna Tempranillo primarily for its wines, of which it has a selection that puts many Spanish bars to shame, and many are sold by the glass.

Café del Nuncio BAR, CAFE
(Calle de Segovia 9; ⊙noon-2am Sun-Thu, to 3am Fri & Sat; MLa Latina) Café del Nuncio straggles down a stairway passage to Calle de Segovia. You can drink on one of several cosy levels inside or, better still in summer, enjoy the outdoor seating that one local reviewer likened to a slice of Rome.

HUERTAS & ATOCHA

The Roof COCKTAIL BAR

(Map p946; www.memadrid.com/the-roof; Plaza de Santa Ana 14; admission €25; 9pm-3am Wed & Thu, to 3.30am Fri & Sat; M Antón Martín, Sol) High above the Plaza de Santa Ana, this sybaritic open-air (7th floor) cocktail bar has terrific views over Madrid's rooftops. The high admission price announces straight away that riff-raff are not welcome and it's a place for sophisticates, with chill-out areas strewn with cushions, funky DJs and a dress policy designed to sort out the classy from the wannabes.

La Venencia BAR

(Map p946; Calle de Echegaray 7; 1-3.30pm & 7.30pm-1.30am; M Sol, Sevilla) La Venencia is a *barrio* classic, with fine sherry from Sanlúcar and manzanilla from Jeréz poured straight from the dusty barrel, accompanied by a small selection of tapas with an Andalucian bent.

El Imperfecto COCKTAIL BAR

(Map p946; Plaza de Matute 2; 3pm-2am Mon-Thu, to 2.30am Fri & Sat; M Antón Martín) Its name notwithstanding, the 'Imperfect One' is our ideal Huertas bar, with live jazz most Tuesdays at 9pm and a drinks menu as long as a saxophone, ranging from cocktails (€7) and spirits to milkshakes, teas and creative coffees.

MALASAÑA & CHUECA

TOP CHOICE **Café Comercial** CAFE

(Map p940; Glorieta de Bilbao 7; 7.30am-midnight Mon-Thu, 7.30am-2am Fri, 8.30am-2am Sat, 9am-midnight Sun; M Bilbao) This glorious old Madrid cafe proudly fights a rearguard action against progress with heavy leather seats, abundant marble and old-style waiters. As close as Madrid came to the intellectual cafes of Paris' Left Bank, Café Comercial now has a clientele that has broadened to include just about anyone.

Splash Óscar LOUNGE BAR

(Map p946; Plaza de Vázquez de Mella 12; 5pm-2am Mon-Thu, 4pm-3am Fri-Sun; M Gran Vía) On of Madrid's stunning rooftop terraces (although this one has a small swimming pool), atop Hotel Óscar (p949), this chilled space with gorgeous skyline views has become a cause célèbre among A-list celebrities.

El Jardín Secreto BAR, CAFE

(Map p940; Calle del Conde Duque 2; 5.30pm-12.30am Sun-Thu, 6.30pm-2.30am Fri & Sat; M Plaza de España) 'The Secret Garden' is all about intimacy and romance in a *barrio* that's one of Madrid's best-kept secrets. Lit by Spanish designer candles, draped in organza from India and serving up chocolates from the Caribbean, it never misses a beat.

Café Belén BAR

(Map p946; Calle de Belén 5; 3.30pm-3am; M Chueca) Café Belén is cool in all the right places – lounge and chill-out music, dim lighting, a great range of drinks (the mojitos are especially good) and a low-key crowd that's the height of casual sophistication.

Lolina Vintage Café CAFE

(Map p946; www.lolinacafe.com; Calle del Espíritu Santo 9; 9am-2.30am Mon-Fri, 10am-2.30am Sat, 11am-2.30am Sun; M Tribunal) Lolina Vintage Café seems to have captured the essence of the *barrio* in one small space. With a studied retro look (comfy old-style chairs and sofas, gilded mirrors and 1970s-era wallpaper), it confirms that the new Malasaña is not unlike the old. It's low-key, full from the first breakfast to closing time and it caters to every taste with salads and cocktails.

☆ Entertainment

The **Guía del Ocio** (www.guiadelocio.com) is the city's classic weekly listings magazine. Also good are **Metropoli** (www.elmundo.es/metropoli) and **On Madrid** (www.elpais.com), respectively *ABC's* and *El País'* Friday listings supplements.

Nightclubs

No *barrio* is without a decent club or disco, but the most popular dance spots are in the centre. Don't expect dance clubs or *discotecas* (nightclubs) to get going until after 1am at the earliest. Standard entry fee is €12, which usually includes the first drink, although megaclubs and swankier places charge a few euros more.

Teatro Joy Eslava CLUB

(Joy Madrid; Map p946; 91 366 37 33; www.joy-eslava.com; Calle del Arenal 11; 11.30pm-6am; M Sol) The only things guaranteed at this grand old Madrid dance club (housed in a 19th-century theatre) are a crowd and the fact that it will be open; the club claims to have opened every single day for the past 30 years. Every night's a little different. Loco Monday kicks off the week in spectacular fashion, Thursday is student night and Friday's 'Fabulush' is all about glamour. Throw in occasional live acts and cabaret-style per-

GAY & LESBIAN MADRID

The heartbeat of gay Madrid is the inner-city *barrio* of Chueca, where Madrid didn't just come out of the closet, but ripped the doors off in the process.

A good place to get the low-down is the laid-back **Mamá Inés** (Map p946; www.mamaines.com; Calle de Hortaleza 22; ⏰10am-2pm Sun-Thu, to 3am Fri & Sat; Ⓜ Gran Vía, Chueca). **Café Acuarela** (Map p946; www.cafeacuarela.es; Calle de Gravina 10; ⏰11am-2am Sun-Thu, to 3am Fri & Sat; Ⓜ Chueca) is another dimly lit centrepiece of gay Madrid.

Two of the most popular Chueca nightspots are **Club 54 Studio** (Map p946; www.studio54madrid.com; Calle de Barbieri 7; ⏰11.30am-3.30am Wed-Sat; Ⓜ Chueca), modelled on the famous New York club Studio 54, and **Liquid Madrid** (Map p946; www.liquid.es; Calle de Barbieri 7; ⏰9pm-3am Mon-Thu, to 3.30am Fri & Sat; Ⓜ Chueca). **Why Not?** (Map p946; www.whynotmadrid.com; Calle de San Bartolomé 7; admission €10; ⏰10.30pm-6am; Ⓜ Chueca) is the sort of place where nothing's left to the imagination.

formances on stage and it's a point of reference for Madrid's professional party crowd.

Kapital CLUB
(Map p946; ☎91 420 29 06; www.grupo-kapital.com; Calle de Atocha 125; ⏰5.30-10.30pm & midnight-6am Fri & Sat, midnight-6am Thu & Sun; Ⓜ Atocha) One of the most famous mega-clubs in Madrid, this massive seven-storey nightclub has something for everyone: from cocktail bars and dance music to karaoke, salsa, hip hop and more chilled spaces for R&B and soul, as well as an area devoted to 'Made in Spain' music. It's such a big place that a cross-section of Madrid society (VIPs and the Real Madrid set love this place) all hang out here without ever getting in each other's way.

Stella CLUB
(Map p946; ☎91 531 63 78; www.web-mondo.com; Calle de Arlabán 7; ⏰12.30am-6am Thu-Sat; Ⓜ Sevilla) One of Madrid's enduring success stories, Stella is one of the city's best nightclubs. If you arrive here after 3am, there simply won't be room and those inside have no intention of leaving until dawn. The DJs here are some of Madrid's best and the great visuals will leave you cross-eyed – that's if you weren't already from the music in this heady place. Thursday and Saturday nights ('Mondo', for electronica) rely on resident and invited DJs, while Friday nights are more house-oriented.

Theatre

Teatro de la Zarzuela THEATRE
(Map p946; ☎91 524 54 00; http://teatrodelazarzuela.mcu.es; Calle de Jovellanos 4; tickets €5-42; ⏰box office noon-6pm Mon-Fri, 3-6pm Sat & Sun; Ⓜ Banco de España, Sevilla) This theatre, built in 1856, is the premier place to see *zarzuela*, the uniquely Spanish combination of theatre and music. It also hosts a smattering of classical music and opera, as well as the cutting edge Compañía Nacional de Danza.

Teatro Real OPERA
(☎902 24 48 48; www.teatro-real.com; Plaza de Oriente; Ⓜ Ópera) After spending €100 million-plus on a long rebuilding project, the Teatro Real is the city's grandest stage for elaborate operas, ballets and classical music. You'll pay as little as €6 for distant seats and as much as €125 for the best seats in the house.

Live Music

FLAMENCO

Corral de la Morería FLAMENCO
(☎91 365 84 46; www.corraldelamoreria.com; Calle de la Morería 17; admission incl drink €42-45, meals from €43; ⏰8.30pm-2.30am, shows 9.30pm & 11.30pm Sun-Fri, 7pm, 10pm & midnight Sat; Ⓜ Ópera) This is one of the most prestigious flamenco stages in Madrid, with 50 years' experience as a leading flamenco venue and top performers most nights. The stage area has a rustic feel, and tables are pushed up close. We'd steer clear of the restaurant, which is overpriced, but the performances have a far better price-quality ratio.

Las Tablas FLAMENCO
(Map p940; ☎91 542 05 20; www.lastablasmadrid.com; Plaza de España 9; admission €27; ⏰shows 10.30pm Sun-Thu, 8pm & 10pm Fri & Sat; Ⓜ Plaza de España) Las Tablas has a reputation for quality flamenco and reasonable prices; it could just be the best choice in town. Antonia Moya and Marisol Navarro, leading lights in the flamenco world, are regular performers here.

Casa Patas FLAMENCO
(Map p946; ☎91 369 04 96; www.casapatas.com; Calle de Cañizares 10; admission €32; ⊙shows 10.30pm Mon-Thu, 9pm & midnight Fri & Sat; Ⓜ Antón Martín, Tirso de Molina) One of the top flamenco stages in Madrid, this *tablao* (flamenco venue) always offers flawless quality that serves as a good introduction to the art. It's not the friendliest place in town, especially if you're only here for the show, and you're likely to be crammed in a little, but no one complains about the standard of the performances.

Villa Rosa FLAMENCO
(Map p946; ☎91 521 36 89; www.villa-rosa.es; Plaza de Santa Ana 15; admission €17; ⊙shows 8.30pm & 10.45pm Sun-Thu, 8.30pm, 10.45pm & 12.15am Fri & Sat, 11pm-6am Mon-Sat; Ⓜ Sol) The extraordinary tiled facade appeared in the Pedro Almodóvar film *Tacones Lejanos* (High Heels; 1991). It's been going strong since 1914 and has seen many manifestations – it has recently returned to its flamenco roots with well-priced shows and meals that won't break the bank.

JAZZ

TOP CHOICE **Café Central** JAZZ
(Map p946; ☎91 369 41 43; www.cafecentralmadrid.com; Plaza del Ángel 10; admission €10-15; ⊙1.30pm-2.30am Sun-Thu, to 3.30am Fri & Sat; Ⓜ Antón Martín, Sol) In 2011, the respected jazz magazine *DownBeat* included this art-deco bar on the list of the world's best jazz clubs (said by some to be the jazz equivalent of earning a Michelin star) and with well over 9000 gigs under its belt, it rarely misses a beat. Performers usually play here for a week and then move on, so getting tickets shouldn't be a problem, except on weekends; shows start at 10pm and tickets go on sale an hour before the set starts.

FREE **Populart** JAZZ
(Map p946; ☎91 429 84 07; www.populart.es; Calle de las Huertas 22; ⊙6pm-2.30am Sun-Thu, to 3.30am Fri & Sat; Ⓜ Antón Martín, Sol) One of Madrid's classic jazz clubs, this place offers a low-key atmosphere and top-quality music, which is mostly jazz with occasional blues, swing and even flamenco thrown into the mix. Shows start at 10.45pm but, if you want a seat, get here early.

OTHER LIVE MUSIC

TOP CHOICE **Sala El Sol** ROCK, SOUL
(Map p946; ☎91 532 64 90; www.elsolmad.com; Calle de los Jardines 3; admission €8-25; ⊙11pm-5.30am Tue-Sat Jul-Sep; Ⓜ Gran Vía) Sala El Sol opened in 1979, just in time for *la movida madrileña,* and quickly established itself as a leading stage for all the icons of the era. *La movida* may have faded into history, but it lives on at El Sol, where the music rocks and rolls and usually resurrects the '70s and '80s, while soul and funk also get a run. It's a terrific venue and although most concerts start at 11pm and despite the official opening hours, some acts take to the stage as early as 10pm. After the show, DJs spin rock, fusion and electronica from the awesome sound system.

Costello Café & Niteclub POP, ROCK
(Map p946; www.costelloclub.com; Calle del Caballero de Gracia 10; admission €5-10; ⊙6pm-1am Sun-Wed, to 2.30am Thu-Sat; Ⓜ Gran Vía) Costello Café & Niteclub is smooth-as-silk ambience wedded to an innovative mix of pop, rock and fusion in Warholesque surrounds. There's live music at 9.30pm every night of the week except Sundays, with resident and visiting DJs keeping you on your feet until closing time from Thursday to Saturday.

Café La Palma ROCK
(Map p940; ☎91 522 50 31; www.cafelapalma.com; Calle de la Palma 62; admission free-€12; ⊙4.30pm-3am; Ⓜ Noviciado) It's amazing how much variety Café La Palma has packed into its labyrinth of rooms. Live shows featuring hot local bands are held at the back, while DJs mix it up at the front. You might find live music other nights as well, but there are always two shows at 10pm and midnight from Thursday to Saturday.

Clamores LIVE MUSIC
(Map p940; ☎91 445 79 38; www.clamores.es; Calle de Alburquerque 14; admission €5-15; ⊙6pm-3am; Ⓜ Bilbao) Clamores is one of the most diverse live music stages in Madrid. Jazz is a staple, but world music, flamenco, soul fusion, singer-songwriter, pop and rock all make regular appearances. Live shows can begin as early as 7pm on weekends but sometimes really only get going after 1am!

FREE **Honky Tonk** ROCK
(Map p940; ☎91 445 61 91; www.clubhonky.com; Calle de Covarrubias 24; ⊙9pm-5am; Ⓜ Alonso Martínez) Despite the name, this is a great place to see blues or local rock 'n' roll, though many acts have a little country, jazz or R&B thrown into the mix too. It's a fun vibe in a smallish club that's been around since the heady 1980s and opens 365 days a year.

Sport

Estadio Santiago Bernabéu FOOTBALL

(☎902 301709, 91 398 43 00; www.realmadrid.com; Calle Concha Espina 1; ⏲10am-7.30pm Mon-Sat, 10.30am-6.30pm Sun, except match days; ⓂSantiago Bernabéu) El Estadio Santiago Bernabéu is one of the world's great football arenas; watching a game here is akin to a pilgrimage for sports fans and doing so alongside 80,000 passionate *Madridistas* (Real Madrid supporters) in attendance will send chills down your spine. Those who can't come to a game can at least stop by for a **tour** (adult/child €19/13), a peek at the trophies or to buy some Real Madrid memorabilia in the **club shop** (Gate 57, Estadio Santiago Bernabéu, ⏲10am-8.30pm). There is another **shop** (Tienda Real Madrid; Map p946; ☎91 521 79 50; Calle del Carmen 3; ⏲10am-8.45pm Mon-Sat, 10am-6.45pm Sun; ⓂSol) in the centre of town.

The Spanish football season runs from September (or the last weekend in August) until May, with a two-week break just before Christmas until early in the New Year. Tickets for football matches in Madrid start at around €40 and run up to the rafters for major matches; you pay in inverse proportion to your distance from the pitch.

To buy tickets, turn up at the Estadio Santiago Bernabéu ticket office at Gate 42 on Calle de Conche de Espina early in the week before a scheduled game (eg Monday morning for a Sunday game). The all-important telephone number for booking tickets (which you later pick up at Gate 42) is ☎902 324 324, which only works if you're calling from within Spain. Tickets can also be bought on the website – click on 'Entradas'.

Shopping

The key to shopping Madrid-style is knowing where to look. Salamanca is the home of upmarket fashions, with chic boutiques lining up to showcase the best that Spanish and international designers have to offer. Some of it spills over into Chueca, but Malasaña is Salamanca's true alter ego, home to fashion that's as funky as it is offbeat and ideal for that studied underground look that will fit right in with Madrid's hedonistic after-dark crowd. Central Madrid – Sol, Huertas or La Latina – offers plenty of individual surprises.

During *las rebajas*, the annual winter and summer sales, prices are slashed on just about everything. The winter sales begin around 7 January and last well into February. Summer sales begin in early July and last into August.

Shops may (and many do) open on the first Sunday of every month and throughout December.

TOP CHOICE El Rastro MARKET

(Map p946; Calle de la Ribera de Curtidores; ⏲8am-3pm Sun; ⓂLa Latina, Puerta de Toledo, Tirso de Molina) A Sunday morning at El Rastro, Europe's largest flea market, is a Madrid institution. You could easily spend an entire morning inching your way down the Calle de la Ribera de Curtidores and through the maze of streets that hosts El Rastro every Sunday morning. For every 10 pieces of junk, there's a real gem (a lost masterpiece, an Underwood typewriter) waiting to be found. A word of warning: pickpockets love El Rastro as much as everyone else.

Antigua Casa Talavera CERAMICS

(Calle de Isabel la Católica 2; ⏲10am-1.30pm & 5-8pm Mon-Fri, 10am-1.30pm Sat; ⓂSanto Domingo) The extraordinary tiled facade of this wonderful old shop conceals an Aladdin's cave of ceramics from all over Spain. This is not the mass-produced stuff aimed at a tourist market, but comes from the small family potters of Andalucía and Toledo.

El Arco Artesanía HANDICRAFTS

(Map p946; www.artesaniaelarco.com; Plaza Mayor 9; ⏲11am-9pm; ⓂSol, La Latina) This original shop in the southwestern corner of Plaza Mayor sells an outstanding array of home-made designer souvenirs, from stone and glass work to jewellery and home fittings. The papier mâché figures are gorgeous, but there's so much else here to turn your head.

El Flamenco Vive FLAMENCO

(www.elflamencovive.es; Calle Conde de Lemos 7; ⏲10.30am-2pm & 5-9pm Mon-Sat; ⓂÓpera) This temple to flamenco has it all, from guitars and songbooks to well-priced CDs, polka-dotted dancing costumes, shoes, colourful plastic jewellery and literature about flamenco. It's the sort of place that will appeal as much to curious first-timers as to serious students of the art.

Casa de Diego ACCESSORIES

(Map p946; www.casadediego.com; Plaza de la Puerta del Sol 12; ⏲9.30am-8pm Mon-Sat; ⓂSol) This classic shop has been around since 1858, making, selling and repairing Spanish fans, shawls, umbrellas and canes. Service is old style and occasionally grumpy, but the fans are works of antique art. It has another **shop and workshop** (Map p946; ☎91 531 02 23; www.casadediego.com; Calle del los Mesoneros Romanos 4; ⏲9.30am-1.30pm & 4.45-8pm Mon-Sat; Ⓜ Callao, Sol) nearby.

Agatha Ruiz de la Prada FASHION
(Map p940; www.agatharuizdelaprada.com; Calle de Serrano 27; ⏲10am-8.30pm Mon-Sat; Ⓜ Serrano) This boutique has to be seen to be believed, with pinks, yellows and oranges everywhere you turn. It's fun and exuberant, but not just for kids. It also has serious and highly original fashion; Agatha Ruiz de la Prada is one of the enduring icons of Madrid's 1980s outpouring of creativity known as *la movida madrileña*.

Mercado de Fuencarral CLOTHING
(Map p946; www.mdf.es; Calle de Fuencarral 45; ⏲11am-9pm Mon-Sat; Ⓜ Tribunal) Madrid's home of alternative club cool is still going strong, revelling in its reverse snobbery. With shops like Fuck, Ugly Shop and Black Kiss, it's funky, grungy and filled to the rafters with torn T-shirts and more black leather and silver studs than you'll ever need.

Information

Dangers & Annoyances

Madrid is a generally safe city, although, as in most European cities, you should be wary of pickpockets in the city centre, on the metro and around major tourist sights.

Prostitution along Calle de la Montera means that you need to exercise extra caution along this street.

Discount Cards

The **Madrid Card** (☎91 360 47 72; www.madridcard.com; 1-/2-/3-days adult €39/49/59, child age 6-12 €20/28/34) includes free entry to more than 40 museums in and around Madrid and discounts on public transport.

Emergency

Emergency (☎112)

Policía Nacional (☎091)

Servicio de Atención al Turista Extranjero (Foreign Tourist Assistance Service; ☎902 102112, 91 548 85 37, 91 548 80 08; www.esmadrid.com/satemadrid; Calle de Leganitos 19; ⏲9am-10pm; Ⓜ Plaza de España, Santo Domingo) To report thefts or other crime-related matters, cancel your credit cards, contact your embassy and other related matters, this is your best bet.

Internet Access

Café Comercial (Glorieta de Bilbao 7; per 50min €1; ⏲7.30am-midnight Mon-Thu, 7.30am-2am Fri, 8.30am-2am Sat, 9am-midnight Sun; Ⓜ Bilbao) One of Madrid's grandest old cafes, with internet upstairs.

Centro de Turismo de Madrid (www.esmadrid.com) Free 15-minute internet access, with more generous time limits (depending on demand) at the other tourist office underneath Plaza de Colón.

Left Luggage

At Madrid's Barajas airport, there are three *consignas* (left-luggage offices; ⏲24hr). In either, you pay €4.95 for the first 24-hour period (or fraction thereof). Thereafter, it costs €4.33/5.56 per day per small/large bag. Similar services operate for similar prices at Atocha and Chamartín train stations (⏲7am to 11pm).

Medical Services

Unidad Medica (Anglo American; ☎91 435 18 23; www.unidadmedica.com; Calle del Conde de Aranda 1; ⏲9am-8pm Mon-Fri, 10am-1pm Sat; Ⓜ Retiro) A private clinic with a wide range of specialisations and where all doctors speak Spanish and English, with some also speaking French and German. Each consultation costs around €125.

Farmacia Mayor (☎91 366 46 16; Calle Mayor 13; ⏲24hr; Ⓜ Sol)

Post

Main Post Office (Map p946; www.correos.es; Plaza de la Cibeles; ⏲8.30am-9.30pm Mon-Fri, to 2pm Sat; Ⓜ Banco de España)

Tourist Information

Centro de Turismo de Madrid (Map p946; ☎91 588 16 36; www.esmadrid.com; Plaza Mayor 27; ⏲9.30am-8.30pm; Ⓜ Sol) Excellent city tourist office with a smaller office underneath Plaza de Colón and information points at Plaza de la Cibeles, Plaza de Callao, outside the Centro de Arte Reina Sofía and at the T4 terminal at Barajas airport.

Comunidad de Madrid (www.turismomadrid.es) The regional Madrid government maintains this useful site for the entire Madrid region.

Getting There & Away

Air

Madrid's international Barajas airport (MAD), 15km northeast of the city, is Europe's fourth- or fifth-busiest airport (depending on the year), with flights coming in from all over Europe and beyond.

Bus

Estación Sur de Autobuses (☎91 468 42 00; www.estaciondeautobuses.com; Calle de Méndez Álvaro 83; Ⓜ Méndez Álvaro) just south of the M-30 ring road, is the city's principal bus station. It serves most destinations to the south and many in other parts of the country. Major bus companies:

ALSA (902 422242; www.alsa.es) One of the largest Spanish companies with many services throughout Spain. Most depart from Estación Sur but some buses headed north (including to Bilbao and Zaragoza, and some services to Barcelona) leave from the Intercambiador de Avenida de América with occasional services from T4 of Madrid's Barajas airport.

Avanzabus (902 020052; www.avanzabus.com) Services to Extremadura (eg Cáceres), Castilla y León (eg Salamanca and Zamora) and Valencia via Cuenca, as well as Lisbon, Portugal. All leave from the Estación Sur.

Car & Motorcycle

The city is surrounded by two main ring roads, the outermost M-40 and the inner M-30; there are also two additional partial ring roads, the M-45 and the more-distant M-50.

Train

Madrid is served by two main train stations. The bigger of the two is **Puerta de Atocha** (M Atocha Renfe), at the southern end of the city centre. **Chamartín train station** (M Chamartín) lies in the north of the city. The bulk of trains for Spanish destinations depart from Atocha, especially those going south. International services arrive at and leave from Chamartín. For bookings, contact **Renfe** (902 240202; www.renfe.es) at either station.

High-speed Tren de Alta Velocidad Española (AVE) services connect Madrid with Seville (via Córdoba), Valladolid (via Segovia), Toledo, Valencia, Málaga and Barcelona (via Zaragoza and Tarragona).

Getting Around

To/From the Airport

BUS The **Exprés Aeropuerto** (Airport Express; www.emtmadrid.es; €5; 24hr;) bus runs between Puerta de Atocha train station and the airport. Buses run every 13 to 23 minutes from 6am to 11.30pm, and every 35 minutes throughout the rest of the night. The trip takes 40 minutes. From 11.55pm until 5.35am, departures are from the Plaza de Cibeles, not the train station.

The excellent, privately run **AeroCITY** (91 747 75 70; www.aerocity.com; per person from €20, express service from €35 per minibus) operates a door-to-door service from the airport.

METRO Line 8 of the metro (entrances in T2 and T4) runs to the Nuevos Ministerios transport interchange, which connects with lines 10 and 6. It operates from 6.05am to 2am. A one-way ticket to/from the airport costs €4.50. The journey from the airport to Nuevos Ministerios takes around 15 minutes, around 25 minutes from T4.

> **WANT MORE?**
>
> For in-depth information, reviews and recommendations at your fingertips, head to the Apple App Store to purchase Lonely Planet's *Madrid City Guide* iPhone app.
>
> Alternatively, head to **Lonely Planet** (www.lonelyplanet.com/madrid) for planning advice, author recommendations, traveller reviews and insider tips.

TAXI A taxi to the city centre will cost you around €25 in total (up to €35 from T4), depending on traffic and where you're going; in addition to what the meter reads, you pay a €5.50 airport supplement.

Public Transport

METRO Madrid's **metro** (www.metromadrid.es) is extensive and well maintained. A single ride costs €1.50 and a 10-ride ticket is €12.20. The metro is quick, clean, relatively safe and runs from 6.05am until 2am.

BUS The bus system is also good; contact **EMT** (www.emtmadrid.es) for more information. Twenty-six night-bus *búhos* (owls) operate from midnight to 6am, with all routes originating in Plaza de la Cibeles.

Taxi

You can pick up a taxi at ranks throughout town or simply flag one down. Flag fall is €2.15 from 6am to 10pm daily, €2.20 from 10pm to 6am Sunday to Friday and €3.10 from 10pm Saturday to 6am Sunday. Several supplementary charges, usually posted inside the taxi, apply; these include €5.50 to/from the airport and €2.95 from taxi ranks at train and bus stations.

Radio-Teléfono Taxi (91 547 82 00; www.radiotelefono-taxi.com)

Tele-Taxi (91 371 21 31; www.tele-taxi.es)

Around Madrid

The Comunidad de Madrid, the province surrounding the capital, has some of Spain's finest royal palaces and gardens that make for easy day trips from the city.

Places worth exploring include the royal palace complex at **San Lorenzo de El Escorial** (91 890 78 18; www.patrimonionacional.es; adult/concession €10/5, guide/audioguide €7/4, EU citizens free 5-8pm Wed & Thu; 10am-8pm Apr-Sep, 10am-6pm Oct-Mar, closed Mon) Check also at www.sanlorenzoturismo.org.

Other worthwhile excursions include **Aranjuez** (www.aranjuez.es) and its **royal palace** (www.patrimonionacional.es; adult/child €5/2.50, EU citizens free Wed; ⏲palace 10am-6.15pm Tue-Sun, gardens 8am-8.30pm); the traditional village of **Chinchón** (www.ciudad-chinchon.com); and the university town (and birthplace of Miguel de Cervantes), **Alcalá de Henares** (www.turismoalcala.com). All of these places can be reached on the suburban rail network.

CASTILLA Y LEÓN

Spain's Castilian heartland, Castilla y León is scattered with hilltop towns sporting magnificent Gothic cathedrals, monumental city walls and mouth-watering restaurants.

Ávila

POP 59,010

Ávila's old city, surrounded by imposing city walls comprising eight monumental gates, 88 watchtowers and more than 2500 turrets, is one of the best-preserved medieval bastions in all of Spain. It's a perfect place to spend a day strolling narrow laneways and soaking up history. The city is known as the birthplace of Santa Teresa, a mystical writer and reformer of the Carmelite order.

Sights

Murallas WALLS
(adult/child €4/2.50; ⏲10am-8pm Tue-Sun) Ávila's splendid 12th-century walls rank among the world's best-preserved medieval defensive perimeters. Raised to a height of 12m between the 11th and 12th centuries, the walls stretch for 2.5km atop the remains of earlier Roman and Muslim battlements.

Two sections of the walls can be climbed – a 300m stretch that can be accessed from just inside the **Puerta del Alcázar**, and a longer 1300m stretch that runs the length of the old town's northern perimeter, in the process connecting the two access points at **Puerta de los Leales** and **Puerta del Puente Adaja**. The regional tourist office runs free guided tours.

Cathedral CHURCH
(Plaza de la Catedral; admission €4; ⏲10am-7pm Mon-Fri, to 8pm Sat, noon-6pm Sun) Embedded into the eastern city walls, this splendid 12th-century cathedral was the first Gothic-style church built in Spain. It boasts rich walnut choir stalls and a long, narrow central nave that makes the soaring ceilings seem all the more majestic.

FREE **Convento de Santa Teresa** MUSEUM
(Plaza de la Santa; ⏲8.45am-1.30pm & 3.30-9pm Tue-Sun) Built in 1636 over the saint's birthplace, this is the epicentre of the cult surrounding Teresa. In addition to the gilded main chapel, it's home to relics, including a piece of the saint's ring finger, as well as a small museum about her life.

Sleeping

TOP CHOICE **Hotel El Rastro** HISTORIC HOTEL €
(☎920 35 22 25; www.elrastroavila.com; Calle Cepedas; s/d €35/55; ❄📶) This superb choice occupies a former 16th-century palace with original natural stone, exposed brickwork and a warm colour scheme of earth tones exuding a calming understated elegance.

Hotel Las Leyendas HISTORIC HOTEL €€
(☎920 35 20 42; www.lasleyendas.es; Calle de Francisco Gallego 3; s/d €56/79; ❄📶) Occupying the house of 16th-century Ávila nobility, this intimate hotel overflows with period touches wedded to modern amenities. Some rooms have original wooden beams, exposed brick and stonework, others are more modern with muted tones.

Hostal Arco San Vicente HOSTAL €€
(☎920 22 24 98; www.arcosanvicente.com; Calle de López Núñez 6; s/d €40/65; ❄📶) This gleaming *hostal* has small, blue-carpeted rooms with pale paintwork and wrought-iron bed heads. Rooms on the 2nd floor have attic windows and air-con, some on the 1st floor look out at the Puerta de San Vicente.

Eating & Drinking

Ávila is famous for its *chuleton de Ávila* (T-bone steak) and *judías del barco de Ávila* (white beans, often with chorizo, in a thick sauce).

TOP CHOICE **Hostería Las Cancelas** CASTILIAN €€
(☎920 21 22 49; www.lascancelas.com; Calle de la Cruz Vieja 6; mains €16-25; ⏲Feb-Dec) This courtyard restaurant occupies a delightful interior patio dating back to the 15th century. Renowned for being a mainstay of Ávila cuisine, its traditional meals are prepared with a salutary attention to detail. Reservations recommended.

Restaurante Reyes Católicos CASTILIAN €€
(www.restaurante-reyescatolicos.com; Calle de los Reyes Católicos 6; mains €16-24, menú del día €16) Fronted by a popular tapas bar, this place has bright decor and an accomplished kitchen that churns out traditional dishes that benefit from a creative tweak. Its set menus include the *menú degustacion cocina tradicional de Ávila* (tasting menu of traditional Ávila cooking; €12).

TOP CHOICE **La Bodeguita de San Segundo** WINE BAR
(www.vinoavila.com; Calle de San Segundo 19; ⏲11am-midnight Thu-Tue) Situated in the 16th-century Casa de la Misericordia, this superb wine bar is standing-room only most nights and more tranquil in the quieter afternoon hours. There's over 1000 wines to choose from, with tapas-sized servings of cheeses and cured meats the perfect accompaniment.

Information

Centro de Recepción de Visitantes (☎920 35 40 00, ext 790; www.avilaturismo.com; Avenida de Madrid 39; ⏲9am-8pm) Municipal tourist office.

Regional Tourist Office (☎920 21 13 87; www.turismocastillayleon.com; Casa de las Carnicerías, Calle de San Segundo 17; ⏲9am-8pm)

Getting There & Away

BUS From Ávila's bus station, there are frequent services to Segovia (€5, one hour) and Salamanca (€6.08, 1½ hours).

TRAIN More than 30 trains run daily to Madrid (from €6.80, 1¼ to two hours) and to Salamanca (€8.55, one to 1½ hours, nine daily).

Salamanca

POP 153,470

Whether floodlit by night or bathed in the midday sun, Salamanca is a dream destination. This is a city of rare architectural splendour, awash with golden sandstone overlaid with Latin inscriptions in ochre, and with an extraordinary virtuosity of plateresque and Renaissance styles. The monumental highlights are many but this is also Castilla's liveliest city, home to a massive Spanish and international student population who throng the streets at night and provide the city with youth and vitality.

DON'T MISS

CASTILLA Y LEÓN'S BEST CASTLES

While Segovia's Disneyesque Alcázar may get all the attention, lonely hilltop castles are something of a regional specialty. Our favourites include the following:

Pedraza de la Sierra (Pedraza de la Sierra; admission €5; ⏲11am-2pm & 5-8pm Wed-Sun) Has an unusually intact outer wall; northeast of Segovia.

Coca (guided tours €2.50; ⏲tours 10am-1.30pm & 4.30-7pm Mon-Fri, 11am 1pm & 4-7pm Sat & Sun) An all-brick, virtuouso piece of Gothic-Mudéjar architecture 50km northwest of Segovia.

Ponferrada (adult/concession €4/2; ⏲10am-2pm & 4.30-8.30pm Tue-Sun) A fortress-monastery built by the Knights Templar in the 13th century, west of León.

Peñafiel (Museo Provincial del Vino; Peñafiel; admission castle €3, incl museum €6, audioguides €2; ⏲11am-2.30pm & 4.30-8.30pm Tue-Sun) One of the longest castles in Spain and now a wine museum.

Sights & Activities

Plaza Mayor SQUARE
Built between 1729 and 1755, Salamanca's exceptional grand square is widely considered to be Spain's most beautiful central plaza. The square is particularly memorable at night when illuminated (until midnight) to magical effect.

Catedral Nueva & Catedral Vieja CHURCHES
(www.catedralsalamanca.org) Curiously, Salamanca is home to two cathedrals: the newer and larger cathedral was built beside the old Romanesque one instead of on top of it, as was the norm. The **Catedral Nueva** (Plaza de Anaya; ⏲9am-8pm), completed in 1733, is a late-Gothic masterpiece that took 220 years to build. Its magnificent Renaissance doorways stand out. For fine views over Salamanca, head to the southwestern corner of the cathedral facade and the **Puerta de la Torre** (Jeronimus; Plaza de Juan XXIII; admission €3.75; ⏲10am-7.15pm), from where stairs lead up through the tower.

FIND THE FROG

The Universidad Civil's facade is an ornate mass of sculptures and carvings, and hidden among this 16th-century plateresque creation is a tiny stone frog. Legend says that those who find the frog will have good luck in studies, life and love. If you don't want any help, look away now... It's sitting on a skull on the pillar that runs up the right-hand side of the facade.

The largely Romanesque **Catedral Vieja** (Plaza de Anaya; admission €4.75; ⏲10am-7.30pm) is a 12th-century temple with a stunning 15th-century altarpiece, which has 53 panels depicting scenes from the life of Christ and Mary, topped by a representation of the Final Judgement. The entrance is inside the Catedral Nueva.

Universidad Civil HISTORIC BUILDING
(Calle de los Libreros; adult/child €4/2, Mon morning free; ⏲9.30am-1.30pm & 4-6.30pm Mon-Fri, 10am-1.30pm Sun) Founded initially as the Estudio Generál in 1218, Salamanca's university came into being in 1254 and reached the peak of its renown in the 15th and 16th centuries. Its facade is a tapestry in sandstone, bursting with images of mythical heroes, religious scenes and coats of arms. You can visit the old classrooms and the oldest university library in Europe. The latter is reached via the **Escalera de la Universidad** (University Staircase), which has symbols carved into the balustrade – to decode them was seen as symbolic of the quest for knowledge.

FREE **Casa de las Conchas** HISTORICAL BUILDING
(Calle de la Compañia 2; ⏲9am-9pm Mon-Fri, 10am-2pm & 4-7pm Sat & Sun) This glorious building has been a city symbol since it was built in the 15th century.

Convento de San Esteban CONVENT
(Plaza del Concilio de Trento; adult/concession €3/2; ⏲10am-1.30pm & 4-7.30pm) The church here has an extraordinary altar-like facade, with the stoning of San Esteban (St Stephen) as its central motif.

Sleeping

TOP CHOICE **Microtel Placentinos** BOUTIQUE HOTEL €€
(☎923 28 15 31; www.microtelplacentinos.com; Calle de Placentinos 9; s/d incl breakfast Sun-Thu €56/72, Fri & Sat €86/99; ❄📶) One of Salamanca's most charming boutique hotels, Microtel Placentinos is tucked away on a quiet street and has rooms with exposed stone walls and wooden beams. The service is faultless, and the overall atmosphere is one of intimacy and discretion.

Aparthotel El Toboso APARTMENT €
(☎923 27 14 62; www.hoteltoboso.com; Calle del Clavel 7; s/d €30/45, 3-/4-/5-person apt €75/85/95; ❄📶) These rooms have a homey spare-room feel and are super value, especially the enormous apartments, which come with kitchens (including washing machines) and renovated bathrooms. It's ideal for families.

Hostal Concejo HOSTAL €
(☎923 21 47 37; www.hconcejo.com; Plaza de la Libertad 1; s/d €45/60; P❄📶) A cut above the average *hostal*, the stylish Concejo has polished-wood floors, tasteful furnishings, light-filled rooms and a superb central location. Try and snag one of the corner rooms (like number 104) with its traditional glassed-in balcony.

Hostal Catedral HOSTAL €
(☎923 27 06 14; www.hostalcatedralsalamanca.com; Rúa Mayor 46; s/d €30/48; ❄📶) Just across from the cathedrals, this pleasing *hostal* with an attentive, motherly owner, has just six extremely pretty, impeccable, bright bedrooms with showers. All look out onto the street or cathedral, which is a real bonus.

Eating & Drinking

TOP CHOICE **La Cocina de Toño** TAPAS €€
(www.lacocinadetoño.es; Calle Gran Via 20; menú del día €17, tapas €1.30-3.80, mains €6.90-23; ⏲lunch & dinner Tue-Sat, lunch Sun) We're yet to hear a bad word about this place and its loyal following owes everything to its creative *pinchos* (tapas) and half-servings of exotic dishes. The restaurant serves more traditional fare as befits the decor, but the bar is one of Salamanca's gastronomic stars.

Mesón Las Conchas CASTILIAN €€
(Rúa Mayor 16; menú del día €12, mains €10-21; ⏲noon-midnight) Enjoy a choice of outdoor

tables (in summer), an atmospheric bar or the upstairs, wood-beamed dining area. The bar caters mainly to locals who know their *embutidos* (cured meats). For sit-down meals, there's a good mix of roasts, *platos combinados* and *raciones*.

Mesón Cervantes CASTILIAN **€€**
(www.mesoncervantes.com; Plaza Mayor 15; menú del día €13.50, mains €10-22; ⏲10am-midnight) Although there are outdoor tables on the plaza, the dark wooden beams and atmospheric buzz of the Spanish crowd on the 1st floor should be experienced at least once; if you snaffle a window table in the evening, you've hit the jackpot. The food's a mix of *platos combinados,* salads and *raciones*.

El Pecado MODERN SPANISH **€€**
(☎923 26 65 58; www.elpecadorestaurante.es; Plaza de Poeta Iglesias 12; menú del día €15, mains €15-33) A trendy place that regularly attracts Spanish celebrities (eg Pedro Almodóvar and Ferran Adrià), El Pecado (The Sin) has an intimate dining room and a quirky, creative menu; it's a reasonably priced place to sample high-quality, innovative Spanish cooking.

TOP CHOICE **Tío Vivo** MUSIC BAR
(www.tiovivosalamanca.com; Calle del Clavel 3-5; ⏲4pm-late) Sip drinks by flickering candlelight to a background of '80s music, enjoying the whimsical decor of carousel horses and oddball antiquities. There is live music Tuesdays to Thursdays from midnight, sometimes with a €5 cover charge.

ℹ Information

Municipal Tourist Office (☎923 21 83 42; www.turismodesalamanca.com; Plaza Mayor 14; ⏲9am-2pm & 4.30-8pm Mon-Fri, 10am-8pm Sat, 10am-2pm Sun)

Regional Tourist Office (☎923 26 85 71; www.turismocastillayleon.com; Casa de las Conchas, Rúa Mayor; ⏲9am-8pm)

ℹ Getting There & Away

BUS Services depart from the **bus station** (Avenida de Filiberto Villalobos 71-85) to Madrid (regular/express €12.88/20.30, three/2½ hours, hourly), Ávila (€6.08, 1½ hours, one to four daily) and Segovia (€11.08, 2¾ hours, two daily).

TRAIN Up to eight trains depart daily for Madrid's Chamartín station (€19.85, 2½ hours) via Ávila (€10.05, one hour). The train station is about 1km beyond Plaza de España.

Segovia

POP 55,220

Unesco World Heritage–listed Segovia has a stunning monument to Roman grandeur and a castle said to have inspired Walt Disney, and is otherwise a city of warm terracotta and sandstone hues set amid the rolling hills of Castilla.

👁 Sights

Acueducto ROMAN AQUEDUCT
El Acueducto, an 894m-long engineering wonder that looks like an enormous comb of stone blocks plunged into the lower end of old Segovia, is the obvious starting point of a tour of town. This Roman aqueduct is 28m high and was built without a drop of mortar – just good old Roman know-how.

Alcázar CASTLE
(www.alcazardesegovia.com; Plaza de la Reina Victoria Eugenia; adult/child €4/3, tower €2, EU citizens free 3rd Tue of month; ⏲10am-7pm Apr-Sep) The fortified and fairy-tale Alcázar is perched dramatically on the edge of Segovia. Roman foundations are buried somewhere underneath the splendour, but what we see today is a 13th-century structure that burned down in 1862 and was subsequently rebuilt. Inside is a collection of armour and military gear, but even better are the ornate interiors of the reception rooms and the 360-degree views from the Torre de Juan II. Walt Disney reportedly used the Alcázar as inspiration for Sleeping Beauty's castle.

Catedral CHURCH
(Plaza Mayor; adult/child €3/2, free 9.30am-1.15pm Sun; ⏲9.30am-6.30pm) In the heart of town, the resplendent late-Gothic Catedral was started in 1525 and completed a mere 200 years later. The Cristo del Consuelo **chapel** houses a magnificent Romanesque doorway preserved from the original church that burned down.

Iglesia de Vera Cruz CHURCH
(Carretera de Zamarramala; admission €1.75; ⏲10.30am-1.30pm & 4-7pm Tue-Sun, closed Nov) The most interesting of Segovia's numerous churches, and one of the best preserved of its kind in Europe, is the 12-sided Iglesia de la Vera Cruz. Built in the 13th century by the Knights Templar and based on the Church of the Holy Sepulchre in Jerusalem, it long housed what was said to be a piece of the Vera Cruz (True Cross).

Sleeping

TOP CHOICE Hospedería La Gran Casa Mudéjar HISTORIC HOTEL €€
(☎921 46 62 50; www.lacasamudejar.com; Calle de Isabel la Católica 8; r €90; ❄@📶) Spread over two buildings, this place has been magnificently renovated, blending genuine, 15th-century carved wooden ceilings in some rooms with modern amenities. In the newer wing, where the building dates from the 19th century, the rooms on the top floors have fine mountain views.

Hotel Alcázar BOUTIQUE HOTEL €€€
(☎921 43 85 68; www.alcazar-hotel.com; Calle de San Marcos 5; s/d incl breakfast €135/163; ❄📶) Sitting by the riverbank in the valley beneath the Alcázar, this charming, tranquil little hotel has lavish rooms beautifully styled to suit those who love old-world luxury. Breakfast on the back terrace is a lovely way to pass the morning, and there's an intimacy and graciousness about the whole experience.

Hostal Fornos HOSTAL €
(☎921 46 01 98; www.hostalfornos.com; Calle de la Infanta Isabel 13; s/d €41/55; ❄) This tidy little *hostal* is a cut above most other places in this price category. It has a lovely, cheerful air and rooms with a fresh white-linen-and-wicker-chair look. Some rooms are larger than others, but the value is unbeatable.

Natura – La Hostería HOTEL €
(☎921 46 67 10; www.naturadesegovia.com; Calle de Colón 5-7; r €60; ❄📶) An eclectic choice a few streets back from Plaza Mayor. The owner obviously has a penchant for Dalí prints and the rooms have plenty of character, with chunky wooden furnishings and bright paintwork.

Eating

Just about every restaurant proudly boasts its *horno de asar* (roasts) and the main speciality is *cochinillo asado* (roast suckling pig). Reservations are always recommended.

TOP CHOICE Restaurante El Fogón Sefardí SEPHARDIC €€€
(☎921 46 62 50; www.lacasamudejar.com; Calle de Isabel la Católica 8; meals €30-40) Located within the Hospedería La Gran Casa Mudéjar, this is one of the most original places in town. Sephardic cuisine is served in either the intimate patio or splendid dining hall with original, 15th-century flourishes. The theme in the bar is equally diverse with dishes from all the continents.

TOP CHOICE Casa Duque GRILL €€€
(☎921 46 24 87; www.restauranteduque.es; Calle de Cervantes 12; meals €25-35, menús del día €21-40) Casa Duque has been serving *cochinillo asado* here since the 1890s. For the uninitiated, try the *menú segoviano* (€30), which includes *cochinillo,* or the *menú gastronómico* (€43.50). Downstairs is the informal *cueva* (cave), where you can get tapas and full-bodied *cazuelas* (stews).

Mesón de Cándido GRILL €€
(☎921 42 81 03; www.mesondecandido.es; Plaza del Azoguejo 5; meals €30-40) Set in a delightful 18th-century building in the shadow of the aqueduct, Mesón de Cándido is another place famous throughout Spain for its suckling pig and the more unusual roast boar with apple.

Information

Centro de Recepción de Visitantes (Tourist Office; www.turismodesegovia.com; Plaza del Azoguejo 1; ⏲10am-7pm Sun-Fri, 10am-8pm Sat) Guided city tours are available, departing daily at 11.15 for a minimum of four people.

Regional Tourist Office (www.segoviaturismo.es; Plaza Mayor 10; ⏲9am-8pm Sun-Thu, 9am-9pm Fri & Sat)

Getting There & Away

BUS Buses run half-hourly to Segovia from Madrid's Paseo de la Florida bus stop (€6.70, 1½ hours). Buses also run to/from Ávila (€5, 1¼ hours, five daily) and Salamanca (€11.08, 2¾ hours, two daily).

TRAIN Up to nine normal trains run daily from Madrid to Segovia (€6.75 one way, two hours), leaving you at the main train station, 2.5km from the aqueduct. The faster option is the high-speed Avant (€10.60, 35 minutes), which deposits you at the newer Segovia-Guiomar station, 5km from the aqueduct.

León

POP 132,740

León's stand-out attraction is the cathedral, one of the most beautiful in Spain. By day, this pretty city rewards long exploratory strolls. By night, the city's large student population floods into the narrow streets and plazas of the city's picturesque old quarter, the Barrio Húmedo.

Sights

Catedral CATHEDRAL
(www.catedraldeleon.org; adult/concession/child €5/4/free; ⌚8.30am-1.30pm & 4-8pm Mon-Sat, 8.30am-2.30pm & 5-8pm Sun) León's 13th-century cathedral, with its soaring towers, flying buttresses and truly breathtaking interior, is the city's spiritual heart. The extraordinary facade has a radiant rose window, three richly sculpted doorways and two muscular towers. After going through the main entrance, lorded over by the scene of *The Last Supper*, an extraordinary gallery of *vidrieras* (stained-glass windows) awaits. French in inspiration and mostly executed from the 13th to the 16th centuries, the windows evoke an atmosphere unlike that of any other cathedral in Spain; the kaleidoscope of coloured light is offset by the otherwise gloomy interior. There are 128 windows with a surface of 1800 sq metres in all, but mere numbers cannot convey the ethereal quality of light permeating this cathedral.

Real Basílica de San Isidoro CHURCH
Older even than León's cathedral, the Real Basílica de San Isidoro provides a stunning Romanesque counterpoint to the former's Gothic strains. The church remains open night and day by historical royal edict. The attached **Panteón Real** (admission €4, free Thu afternoon; ⌚10am-1.30pm & 4-6.30pm Mon-Sat, 10am-1.30pm Sun) houses sarcophagi beneath a canopy of some of the finest Romanesque frescoes in Spain.

FREE **Museo de Arte Contemporáneo** MUSEUM
(Musac; www.musac.org.es; Avenida de los Reyes Leóneses 24; ⌚11am-8pm Tue-Thu, to 9pm Fri, 10am-9pm Sat & Sun) León's showpiece Museo de Arte Contemporáneo belongs to the new wave of innovative Spanish architecture. A pleasing square-and-rhombus edifice of colourful glass and steel, it has been acclaimed for the 37 shades of coloured glass that adorn the facade; they were gleaned from the pixelisation of a fragment of one of the cathedral's stained-glass windows.

Although the museum has a growing permanent collection, it mostly houses temporary displays of cutting-edge Spanish and international photography, video installations and other similar forms.

Convento de San Marcos CONVENT
More than 100m long and blessed with a glorious facade, the plateresque exterior of this former pilgrims' hospital is sectioned off by slender columns and decorated with delicate medallions and friezes; most of it dates to 1513, by which time the edifice had become a monastery of the Knights of Santiago. Much of the former convent is now a supremely elegant *parador* (luxury hotel).

Barrio Gótico NEIGHBOURHOOD
On the fringes of León's Barrio Gótico (also known as the old town), Plaza de San Marcelo is home to the **ayuntamiento** (town hall), which occupies a charmingly compact Renaissance-era palace. The Renaissance theme continues in the form of the splendid **Palacio de los Guzmanes** (1560). Next door is Antoni Gaudí's sober contribution to León's skyline, the castle-like, neo-Gothic **Casa de Botines** (1893).

Down the hill, the delightful **Plaza de Santa María del Camino** (also known as Plaza del Grano) feels like a cobblestone Castilian village square. At the northeastern end of the old town is the beautiful and time-worn 17th-century **Plaza Mayor**.

Sleeping & Eating

TOP CHOICE **La Posada Regia** HISTORIC HOTEL €€
(☎987 21 31 73; www.regialeon.com; Calle de Regidores 9-11; s/d €65/120; ❄📶) You won't find many places better than this in northern Spain. The secret is a 14th-century building, magnificently restored (wooden beams, exposed brick and understated antique furniture), with individually styled rooms, character that overflows into the public areas and supremely comfortable beds and bathrooms.

Hostal de San Marcos HISTORIC HOTEL €€€
(☎987 23 73 00; www.parador.es; Plaza de San Marcos 7; d from €198; ❄@📶) León's sumptuous *parador* is one of the finest hotels in Spain. With palatial rooms fit for royalty and filled with old-world luxury and decor, this is one of the Parador chain's flagship properties.

Hostal San Martín HOTEL €
(☎987 87 51 87; www.sanmartinhostales.com; Plaza de Torres de Omaña 1, 2nd fl; s/d/tr €31/43/55, s without bathroom €20) In a splendid central position, this recently overhauled 18th-century building has light, airy rooms painted in candy colours with small terraces.

El Llar TAPAS €€
(Plaza de San Martín 9; meals €25-30; 🖉) This old León *taberna* is a great place to *tapear*

WORTH A TRIP

BURGOS

The northern Castilian city of Burgos is home to a Unesco World Heritage–listed cathedral. A 13th-century French-Gothic creation, it has two extraordinary doors, the **Puerta del Sarmental**, the main entrance for visitors, and the **Puerta de la Coronería**.

Inside the main sanctuary, note the light and airy **Capilla de la Presentación** and the **Capilla de la Concepción** with its impossibly gilded, 15th-century **altar**. The main altar is a typically overwhelming piece of gold-encrusted extravagance, while directly beneath the star-vaulted central dome lies the **tomb of El Cid**. The **Capilla del Condestable**, behind the main altar, is a remarkable late-15th-century production.

If you're staying overnight, the **Hotel Norte y Londres** (947 26 41 25; www.hotelnorteylondres.com; Plaza de Alonso Martínez 10; s/d €66/100; P@), **Hotel La Puebla** (947 20 00 11; www.hotellapuebla.com; Calle de la Puebla 20; s/d €50/65; @) and **Hotel Mesón del Cid** (947 20 87 15; www.mesondelcid.es; Plaza de Santa María 8; s/d €70/100; P) are all excellent. For superb food, try **Cervecería Morito** (Calle de la Sombrerería 27; tapas €3, raciones €5-7).

The **tourist office** (www.aytoburgos.es; Plaza del Rey Fernando 2; 10am-2pm & 4.30-7.30pm Mon-Fri, 10am-1.30pm & 4-7.30pm Sat & Sun) is in the town centre, and the city is well connected by train and bus to Madrid, León and Bilbao.

(eat tapas) with its innovative selection of *raciones*. The upstairs restaurant has a fine, classic look and the menu includes vegetarian options.

El Picoteo de la Jouja TAPAS €
(Plaza de Torres de Omaña) This intimate little bar has earned a loyal following for its concentration on traditional local tapas (try the six tapas for €13.50) and local wines, including some from the nearby Bierzo region. The tapas include cured meats, snails and all manner of León specialties.

Drinking

The Barrio Húmedo's night-time epicentre is Plaza de San Martín – prise open the door of any bar here or in the surrounding streets (especially Calle de Juan de Arfe and Calle de la Misericordia), inch your way to the bar and you're unlikely to want to leave until closing time.

TOP CHOICE **Camarote Madrid** WINE BAR
(www.camarotemadrid.com; Calle Cervantes 8) We could equally recommend this fantastic and enduringly popular bar for its tapas (the little ceramic cup of *salmorejo* – a cold, tomato-based soup – is rightly famous), but the extensive wine list wins the day amid the buzz of a happy crowd swirling around the central bar. Recent renovations have thrust this sophisticated place into the 21st century.

Rebote BAR
(Plaza de San Martín 9; 8pm-1am Mon-Sat) A reliably popular bar at the lower end of Plaza de San Martín, Rebote is a good place for first drinks; the *croquetas* here are rightly famous.

Information

Tourist Office (www.turismocastillayleon.com; Calle el Cid 2; 9am-8pm)

Getting There & Away

BUS From the **bus station** (Paseo del Ingeniero Sáez de Miera), there are numerous daily buses to Madrid (€22.60, 3½ hours) and Burgos (€14.50, two hours).

TRAIN Regular daily trains travel to Burgos (from €20.80, two hours), Oviedo (from €8.20, two hours), Madrid (from €34.75, 4½ hours) and Barcelona (from €70.70, nine hours).

CASTILLA-LA MANCHA

Known as the stomping ground of Don Quijote and Sancho Panza, Castilla-La Mancha conjures up images of lonely windmills, medieval castles and bleak, treeless plains. The characters of Miguel de Cevantes provide the literary context, but the richly historic cities of Toledo and Cuenca are the most compelling reasons to visit.

Toledo

POP 83,110

Toledo is Spain's equivalent of a downsized Rome. Commanding a hill rising above the Tajo River, it's crammed with monuments that attest to the waves of conquerors and communities – Roman, Visigoth, Jewish, Muslim and Christian – who have called the city home during its turbulent history. It's one of the country's major tourist attractions.

Sights

TOP CHOICE Catedral CATHEDRAL
(Plaza del Ayuntamiento; adult/child €7/free; ⌚10.30am-6.30pm Mon-Sat, 2-6.30pm Sun) Toledo's cathedral dominates the skyline, reflecting the city's historical significance as the heart of Catholic Spain. Within its hefty stone walls there are stained-glass windows, tombs of kings and art in the sacristy by the likes of El Greco, Zurbarán, Crespi, Titian, Rubens and Velázquez. Behind the main altar lies a mesmerising piece of 18th-century Churrigueresque baroque, the **Transparente**. Look out for the **Custodia de Arfe**, by the celebrated 16th-century goldsmith Enrique de Arfe. With 18kg of pure gold and 183kg of silver, this 16th-century conceit bristles with some 260 statuettes.

Alcázar FORTRESS, MUSEUM
(Museo del Ejército; Calle Alférecès Provisionales; adult/child €5/free; ⌚10am-9pm Thu-Tue Jun-Sep, to 7pm Oct-May) At the highest point in the city looms the foreboding Alcázar. Abd ar-Rahman III raised an *al-qasr* (fortress) here in the 10th century, which was thereafter altered by the Christians. The Alcázar was heavily damaged during the siege of the garrison by loyalist militias at the start of the Spanish Civil War in 1936. The soldiers' dogged resistance, and the commander, Moscardó's, famous refusal to give it up in exchange for his son's life, made it a powerful nationalist symbol.

Rebuilt under Franco, the Alcázar has recently been reopened as an absolutely enormous military museum, with strict staff barking orders adding to the martial experience. The usual displays of uniforms and medals are here, but the best part is the exhaustive historical section, with an in-depth overview of the nation's history in Spanish and English.

Sinagoga del Tránsito SYNAGOGUE
(http://museosefardi.mcu.es; Calle Samuel Leví; adult/child €3/1.50; ⌚9.30am-8pm Tue-Sat Apr-Sep, to 6.30pm Oct-Mar, 10am-3pm Sun) Toledo's former *judería* (Jewish quarter) was once home to 11 synagogues. The bulk of Toledo's Jews were expelled in 1492. This magnificent synagogue was built in 1355 by special permission of Pedro I (construction of synagogues was prohibited in Christian Spain). The synagogue now houses the **Museo Sefardi**.

Sinagoga de Santa María La Blanca SYNAGOGUE
(Calle de los Reyes Católicos 4; admission €2.50; ⌚10am-6.45pm) This modest synagogue is characterised by the horseshoe arches that delineate the five naves – classic Almohad architecture.

Monasterio San Juan de los Reyes MONASTERY
(Calle San Juan de los Reyes 2; admission €2.50; ⌚10am-6.45pm) This early 17th-century Franciscan monastery and church of San Juan de los Reyes is notable for its delightful cloisters. Provocatively built in the heart of the Jewish quarter, the monastery was founded by Isabel and Fernando to demonstrate the supremacy of the Catholic faith. The rulers had planned to be buried here but, when they took the greater prize of Granada in 1492, opted for the purpose-built Capilla Real. Throughout the church and cloister the coat of arms of Isabel and Fernando dominates, and the chains of Christian prisoners liberated in Granada dangle from the outside walls. The prevalent late-Flemish Gothic style is enhanced with lavish Isabelline ornament, counterbalanced by Mudéjar decoration.

FREE Museo de Santa Cruz MUSEUM
(Calle Cervantes 3; ⌚10am-6.30pm Mon-Sat, to 2pm Sun) Just off the Plaza de Zocodover, the 16th-century Museo de Santa Cruz is a beguiling combination of Gothic and Spanish Renaissance styles. The cloisters and carved wooden ceilings are superb, as are the upstairs displays of Spanish ceramics. The ground-level gallery contains a number of El Grecos, a painting attributed to Goya (*Cristo Crucificado*), and the wonderful 15th-century *Tapestry of the Astrolabes*.

Iglesia de Santo Tomé CHURCH
(www.santotome.org; Plaza del Conde; admission €2.50; ⏲10am-6pm, to 7pm mid-Mar–mid-Oct) This otherwise modest church contains El Greco's masterpiece, *El Entierro del Conde de Orgaz* (The Burial of the Count of Orgaz). When the count was buried in 1322, Saints Augustine and Stephen supposedly descended from heaven to attend the funeral. El Greco's work depicts the event, complete with miracle guests including himself, his son and Cervantes.

Mezquita del Cristo de la Luz MOSQUE
(Calle Cristo de la Luz; admission €2.50; ⏲10am-2pm & 3.30-6.45pm Mon-Fri, 10am-6.45pm Sat & Sun) On the northern slopes of town you'll find this modest, yet beautiful mosque where architectural traces of Toledo's medieval Muslim conquerors are still in evidence. Built around AD 1000, it suffered the usual fate of being converted to a church (hence the religious frescoes), but the original vaulting and arches survived.

Sleeping

Accommodation is often full, especially from Easter to September. Many visitors choose to come on a day trip from Madrid.

TOP CHOICE **Casa de Cisneros** BOUTIQUE HOTEL €€
(☎925 22 88 28; www.hostal-casa-de-cisneros.com; Calle Cardenal Cisneros; s/d incl breakfast €55/75; ❄🛜) Right by Toledo's cathedral, this lovely 16th-century house was once the home of the cardinal and Grand Inquisitor Cisneros (often known as Ximénes). It's a superb choice, with cosy, seductive rooms with original wooden beams and walls and voguish bathrooms.

Casa de los Mozárabes APARTMENT €€
(☎925 21 17 01; www.casadelosmozarabes.com; Callejón de Menores 10; apt €96-170; ❄🛜) Occupying an historic Toledo house on a quiet central lane, these excellent apartments have modern furnishings that combine well with the exposed brick and historic features of the building. There's a common lounge area with a pool table and a few weights.

Hostal del Cardenal HISTORIC HOTEL €€
(☎925 22 49 00; www.hostaldelcardenal.com; Paseo de Recaredo 24; s/d incl breakfast €90/120; ❄🛜) This wonderful 18th-century mansion has soft ochre-coloured walls, arches and columns. The rooms are grand, yet welcoming, with dark furniture, plush fabrics and parquet floors. Several rooms overlook the glorious terraced gardens.

La Posada de Manolo BOUTIQUE HOTEL €€
(☎925 28 22 50; www.laposadademanolo.com; Calle de Sixto Ramón Parro 8; s/d incl breakfast €46/76; ❄🛜) This memorable hotel has themed each floor with furnishings and decor reflecting one of the three cultures of Toledo: Christian, Islamic and Jewish. There are stunning views of the old town and cathedral from the terrace.

Eating

TOP CHOICE **Alfileritos 24** MODERN SPANISH €€
(www.alfileritos24.com; Calle de los Alfileritos 24; mains €15-21, bar food €6-11; ⏲9.30am-midnight, to 1am Fri & Sat) The 14th-century surroundings of columns, beams and barrel-vault ceilings are snazzily coupled with modern artwork and bright dining rooms in an atrium space spread over four floors. The menu demonstrates an innovative flourish in the kitchen. The ground-floor bar offers good-value tapas and cheaper fare designed for sharing.

La Abadía TAPAS €
(www.abadiatoledo.com; Plaza de San Nicolás 3; raciones €4-15) In a former 16th-century palace, arches, niches and subtle lighting are spread over a warren of brick-and-stone-clad rooms. The menu includes lightweight dishes and tapas portions – perfect for small appetites.

Taberna El Embrujo TAPAS €
(www.tabernaembrujo.com; Calle Santa Leocadia 6; raciones €8-22) Near the top of the escalator up to the old town, this friendly bar has an appealing stone-clad dining area and an outdoor terrace across the street. It does a great line in high-quality deli-style tapas, with tasty tomato salads, delicious foie gras and seafood options, all served with a smile.

Information

Main Tourist Office (☎925 25 40 30; www.toledo-turismo.com; Plaza del Ayuntamiento; ⏲10am-6pm)

Provincial Tourist Office (www.diputoledo.es; Subida de la Granja; ⏲10am-5pm Mon-Sat, to 3pm Sun)

Getting There & Away

For most major destinations, you'll need to backtrack to Madrid.

WORTH A TRIP

CUENCA

A World Heritage site, Cuenca is one of Spain's most memorable small cities, its old centre a stage set of evocative medieval buildings. Most emblematic are the 14th-century *casas colgadas*, the hanging houses that jut out precariously over the steep defile of Río Huécar. Inside one of the houses is the **Museo de Arte Abstracto Español** (Museum of Abstract Art; www.march.es/arte/cuenca; adult/child €3/free; 11am-2pm & 4-6pm Tue-Fri, 11am-2pm & 4-8pm Sat, 11am-2.30pm Sun). Cuenca is also famous for its Semana Santa (Holy Week) processions; stop by the **Museo de la Semana Santa** (www.msscuenca.org; Calle Andrés de Cabrera 13; adult/child €3/free; 11am-2pm & 4.30-7.30pm Thu-Sat, 11am-2pm Sun) to see why.

If you're staying overnight, the **Hostal Tabanqueta** (969 21 12 90; www.hostaltabanqueta.com; Calle Trabuco 13; d €60;), **Posada de San José** (969 21 13 00; www.posadasanjose.com; Ronda de Julián Romero 4; d from €82, s/d without bathroom €30/43) and **Parador de Cuenca** (969 23 23 20; www.parador.es; Calle de Hoz de Huécar; s/d €138/173; P) are all excellent. For a meal, try **La Bodeguilla de Basilio** (Calle Fray Luis de León 3; raciones €10-13; lunch & dinner Mon-Sat, lunch Sun).

There's a **tourist office** (http://turismo.cuenca.es; Calle Alfonso VIII 2; 9am-9pm Mon-Sat, to 2.30pm Sun), and Cuenca is most easily reached along the Madrid–Valencia rail line.

BUS From Toledo's **bus station** (Avenida de Castilla La Mancha), buses depart for Madrid (from €5.25,one to 1½ hours) every half-hour from 6am to 10pm daily (less often on Sunday). There are also services on weekdays and Sunday to Cuenca (€12.80, 2¼ hours).

TRAIN The high-speed AVE service runs every hour or so to Madrid (€10.60, 30 minutes).

CATALONIA

Home to stylish Barcelona, ancient Tarragona, romantic Girona and countless alluring destinations along the coast, in the Pyrenees and in the rural interior, Catalonia (Catalunya in Catalan, Cataluña in Castilian) is a treasure box waiting to be opened.

Barcelona

POP 1.62 MILLION

Barcelona is one of Europe's coolest cities. Despite two millennia of history, it's a forward-thinking place, always on the cutting edge of art, design and cuisine. Whether you explore its medieval palaces and plazas, admire the Modernista masterpieces, shop for designer fashions along its bustling boulevards, sample its exciting nightlife or just soak up the sun on the beaches, you'll find it hard not to fall in love with this vibrant city.

As much as Barcelona is a visual feast, it will also lead you into culinary temptation. Anything from traditional Catalan cooking to the latest in avant-garde new Spanish cuisine will have your appetite in overdrive.

Sights

LA RAMBLA

La Rambla is Spain's most talked-about boulevard. It certainly packs a lot of colour into a short walk, with flower stands, historic buildings, a sensory-rich produce market, overpriced beers and tourist tat, and a ceaselessly changing parade of people from all corners of the globe.

TOP CHOICE **Mercat de la Boqueria** MARKET
(Map p974; 93 412 13 15; www.boqueria.info; La Rambla 91; 8am-8.30pm Mon-Sat, closed Sun; M Liceu) One of the greatest sound, smell and colour sensations in Europe is Barcelona's most central produce market, the Mercat de la Boqueria. It spills over with all the rich and varied colour of plentiful fruit and vegetable stands, seemingly limitless varieties of sea critters, sausages, cheeses, meat (including the finest Jabugo ham) and sweets. Note also its Modernista-influenced design.

Gran Teatre del Liceu ARTS CENTRE
(Map p974; 93 485 99 14; www.liceubarcelona.com; La Rambla dels Caputxins 51-59; admission with/without guide €10/5; guided tour 10am, unguided visits 11.30am, noon, 12.30pm & 1pm; M Liceu) If you can't catch a night at the opera, you can still have a look around one of Europe's greatest opera houses, known to locals as the Liceu. Smaller than Milan's La

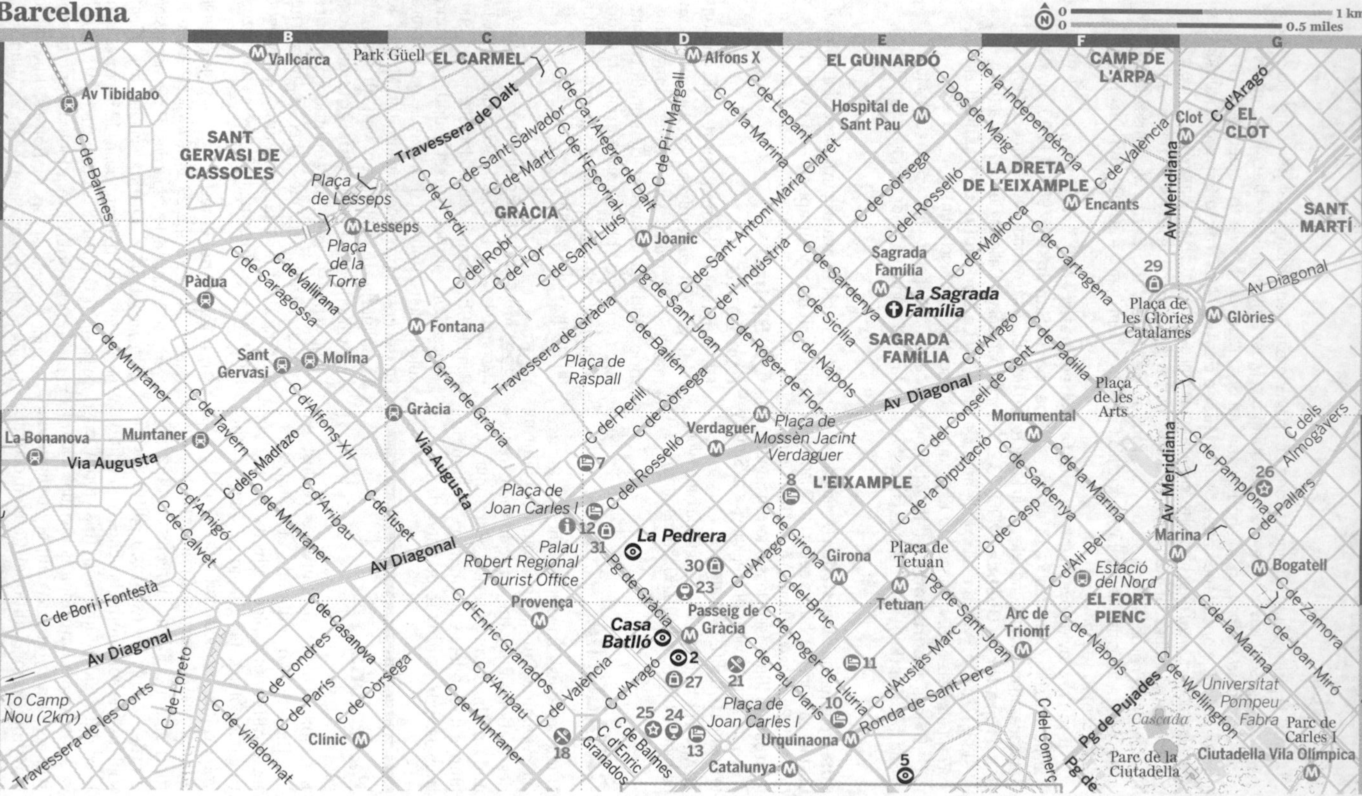
Barcelona
0
1 km
0
0.5 miles
Vallcarca
Park Güell
EL CARMEL
Alfons X
EL GUINARDÓ
CAMP DE L'ARPA
Av Tibidabo
C de Balmes
SANT GERVASI DE CASSOLES
Travessera de Dalt
Plaça de Lesseps
Lesseps
Plaça de la Torre
C de Sant Salvador
C de Martí
C de Ca l'Alegre de Dalt
C de l'Escorial
C de Pi i Margall
C de Verdi
GRÀCIA
C de la Marina
C de Lepant
Hospital de Sant Pau
C Dos de Maig
C de la Independència
LA DRETA DE L'EIXAMPLE
C de València
Clot
C d'Aragó
EL CLOT
Encants
Av Meridiana
SANT MARTÍ
Pàdua
C de Saragossa
C de Vallirana
C del Robí
C de l'Or
C de Sant Lluís
Joanic
C de Sant Antoni Maria Claret
C de Còrsega
C del Rosselló
C de Mallorca
C de Cartagena
Sagrada Família
La Sagrada Família
29
Plaça de les Glòries Catalanes
Glòries
Av Diagonal
C de Muntaner
Fontana
Pg de Sant Joan
C de l'Indústria
C de Sardenya
C de Sicília
SAGRADA FAMÍLIA
Sant Gervasi
Molina
Travessera de Gràcia
Plaça de Raspall
C de Bailèn
C de Roger de Flor
C de Nàpols
C de Padilla
Plaça de les Arts
C Gran de Gràcia
Gràcia
C d'Alfons XII
C del Perill
C de Còrsega
Verdaguer
Plaça de Mossèn Jacint Verdaguer
C del Consell de Cent
Monumental
C dels Almogàvers
La Bonanova
Muntaner
Via Augusta
C de Tavern
C dels Madrazo
7
8
L'EIXAMPLE
C de la Diputació
C de la Marina
C de Pamplona
26
C de Pallars
C d'Amigó
C de Calvet
C d'Aribau
C de Tuset
Plaça de Joan Carles I
12
La Pedrera
C de Girona
C de Casp
Marina
Palau Robert Regional Tourist Office
31
30
Girona
Plaça de Tetuan
C d'Alí Bei
Estació del Nord
Bogatell
C de Bori i Fontestà
Provença
23
Pg de Gràcia
C del Bruc
Tetuan
EL FORT PIENC
C de Zamora
C d'Enric Granados
Casa Batlló
Passeig de Gràcia
C de Roger de Llúria
Arc de Triomf
C de Casanova
2
11
C d'Ausiàs Marc
C de la Marina
C de Joan Miró
C de Londres
27
21
C de Pau Claris
Ronda de Sant Pere
To Camp Nou (2km)
C de Loreto
C de París
Plaça de Joan Carles I
10
Pg de Pujades
C de Wellington
Universitat Pompeu Fabra
Travessera de les Corts
C de Viladomat
Clínic
25
24
13
18
C de Balmes
C d'Enric Granados
Urquinaona
Catalunya
5
C del Comerç
Cascada
Parc de Carles I
Parc de la Ciutadella
Ciutadella Vila Olímpica
Pg de

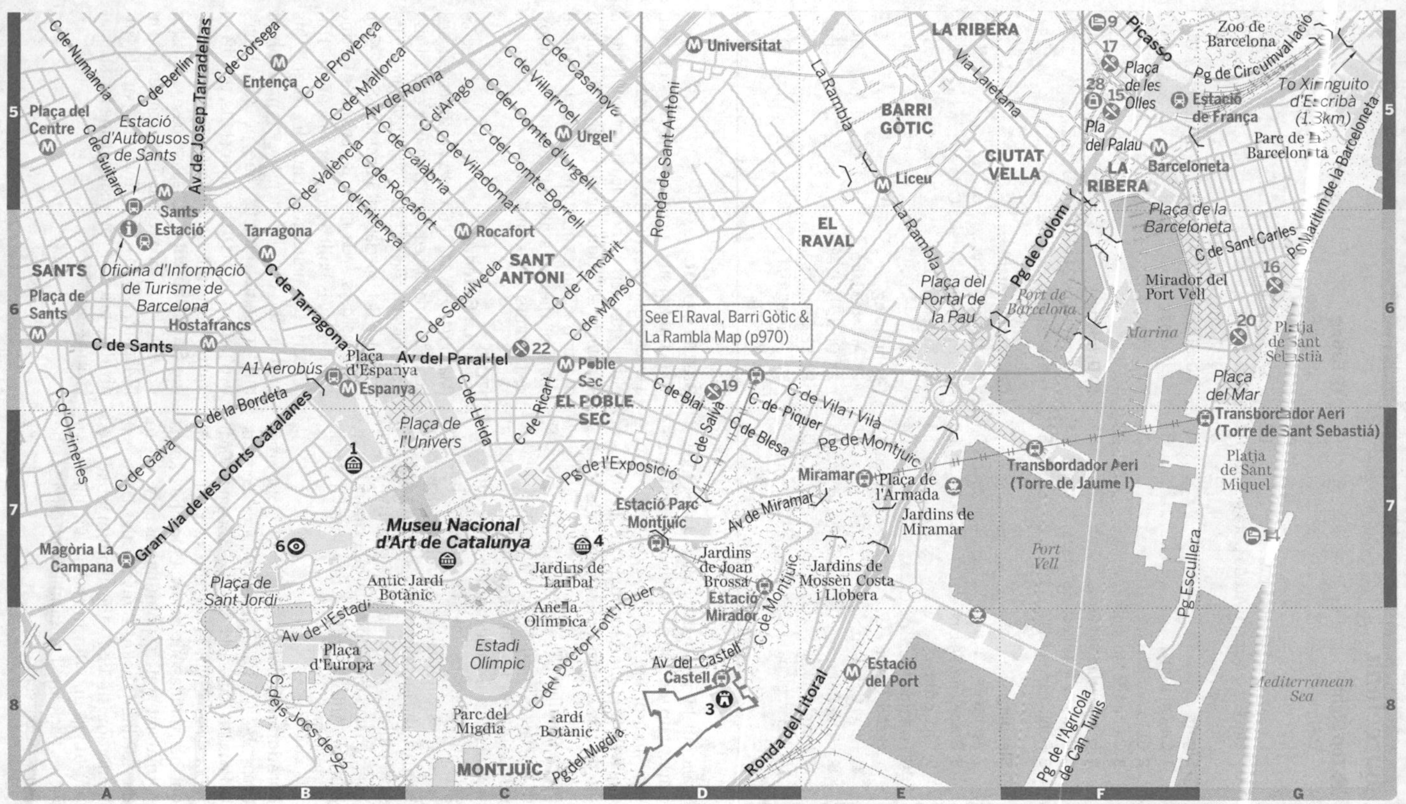
C de Numància
C de Berlín
Av de Josep Tarradellas
C de Còrsega
Entença
C de Provença
C de Mallorca
Av de Roma
C d'Aragó
C de Villarroel
C de Casanova
C del Comte d'Urgell
Urgell
C del Comte Borrell
C de Viladomat
C de Calàbria
C de Rocafort
C de València
C d'Entença
Plaça del Centre
C de Guitard
Estació d'Autobusos de Sants
Sants Estació
Tarragona
Rocafort
SANTS
Oficina d'Informació de Turisme de Barcelona
C de Tarragona
SANT ANTONI
C de Tamarit
C de Sepúlveda
C de Mansó
Plaça de Sants
Hostafrancs
C de Sants
Plaça d'Espanya
Av del Paral·lel
22
Poble Sec
A1 Aerobús
Espanya
C de la Bordeta
C d'Olzinelles
C de Lleida
C de Ricart
EL POBLE SEC
Plaça de l'Univers
Gran Via de les Corts Catalanes
C de Gavà
1
Pg de l'Exposició
Museu Nacional d'Art de Catalunya
Magòria La Campana
6
4
Estació Parc Montjuïc
Plaça de Sant Jordi
Antic Jardí Botànic
Jardins de Laribal
Av de l'Estadi
Anella Olímpica
Plaça d'Europa
Estadi Olímpic
C del Doctor Font i Quer
C dels Jocs de 92
Parc del Migdia
Jardí Botànic
Pg del Migdia
MONTJUÏC
Universitat
Ronda de Sant Antoni
La Rambla
LA RIBERA
Via Laietana
BARRI GÒTIC
CIUTAT VELLA
Liceu
EL RAVAL
Plaça del Portal de la Pau
Pg de Colom
Port de Barcelona
See El Raval, Barri Gòtic & La Rambla Map (p970)
C de Blai
19
C de Salvà
C de Piquer
C de Vila i Vilà
C de Blesa
Pg de Montjuïc
Miramar
Plaça de l'Armada
Av de Miramar
Jardins de Miramar
Jardins de Joan Brossa
Estació Mirador
C de Montjuïc
Jardins de Mossèn Costa i Llobera
Av del Castell
Castell
3
Ronda del Litoral
Estació del Port
Transbordador Aeri (Torre de Jaume I)
Port Vell
Pg de l'Agrícola de Can Tunis
9
Picasso
17
Plaça de les Olles
28
15
Pla del Palau
LA RIBERA
Zoo de Barcelona
Pg de Circumval·lació
Estació de França
To Xiringuito d'Escribà (1.3km)
Parc de la Barceloneta
Barceloneta
Pg Marítim de la Barceloneta
Plaça de la Barceloneta
C de Sant Carles
16
Mirador del Port Vell
Marina
20
Platja de Sant Sebastià
Plaça del Mar
Transbordador Aeri (Torre de Sant Sebastià)
Platja de Sant Miquel
Pg Escullera
14
Mediterranean Sea
SPAIN BARCELONA

Barcelona

Top Sights

Casa Batlló D4
La Pedrera D3
La Sagrada Família E2
Museu Nacional d'Art de Catalunya C7

Sights

1 CaixaForum B7
2 Casa Amatller D4
3 Castell de Montjuïc D8
4 Fundació Joan Miró C7
5 Palau de la Música Catalana E4
6 Poble Espanyol B7

Sleeping

7 Aparteasy D3
8 Barcelona On Line E3
9 Chic & Basic F5
10 Five Rooms E4
Hostal Goya ..... (see 10)
11 Hotel Constanza E4
12 Hotel Omm D3
13 Hotel Praktik D4
14 W Barcelona G7

Eating

15 Cal Pep F5
16 Can Majó G6
17 Casa Delfín F5
18 Cinc Sentits C4
19 Quimet i Quimet D6
20 Suquet De L'Almirall G6
21 Tapaç 24 ..... D4
22 Tickets C6

Drinking

23 Les Gens Que J'Aime D3
24 Monvínic D4

Entertainment

25 Arena Madre D4
Palau de la Música Catalana ..... (see 5)
26 Razzmatazz G3

Shopping

27 Antonio Miró D4
28 Custo Barcelona F5
29 Els Encants Vells F2
30 Joan Murrià D3
31 Vinçon D3

Scala but bigger than Venice's La Fenice, it can seat up to 2300 people in its grand horseshoe auditorium. You can take a 20-minute quick turn around the main public areas of the theatre or join a one-hour guided tour.

Plaça Reial SQUARE

(Map p974; Ⓜ Liceu) One of the most photogenic squares in Barcelona, the Plaça Reial is a delightful retreat from the traffic and pedestrian mobs on the nearby Rambla. Numerous eateries, bars and nightspots lie beneath the arcades of 19th-century neoclassical buildings, with a buzz of activity at all hours. The lamp posts by the central fountain are Antoni Gaudí's first known works in the city.

Mirador de Colom VIEWPOINT

(Map p974; ☎93 302 52 24; Plaça del Portal de la Pau; lift adult/child €4/3; ⏲8.30am-8.30pm; Ⓜ Drassanes) High above the swirl of traffic on the roundabout below, Columbus keeps permanent watch, pointing vaguely out to the Mediterranean. Built for the Universal Exhibition in 1888, the monument allows you to zip up 60m in the lift for bird's-eye views back up La Rambla and across the ports of Barcelona.

BARRI GÒTIC

You could easily spend several days or even a week exploring the Barri Gòtic, Barcelona's oldest quarter, without leaving the medieval streets. In addition to major sights, its tangle of narrow lanes and tranquil plazas conceal some of the city's most atmospheric shops, restaurants, cafes and bars.

TOP CHOICE **La Catedral** CHURCH

(Map p974; ☎93 342 82 60; www.website.es/catedralbcn; Plaça de la Seu; admission free, special visit €5, choir admission €2.20; ⏲8am-12.45pm & 5.15-8pm Mon-Sat, special visit 1-5pm Mon-Sat, 2-5pm Sun & holidays; Ⓜ Jaume I) Barcelona's Gothic Catedral was built atop the ruins of an 11th-century Romanesque church. Highlights include the cool cloister, the crypt tomb of martyr Santa Eulàlia (one of Barcelona's two patron saints), the choir stalls, the lift to the rooftop and the modest art collection in the **Sala Capitular** (Chapter House; admission €2; ⏲10am-12.15pm & 5.15-7pm Mon-Sat, 10am-12.45pm & 5.15-7pm Sun). You only pay the individual prices if you visit outside the special visiting hours.

TOP CHOICE Museu d'Història de Barcelona MUSEUM

(Map p974; ☎93 256 21 00; www.museuhistoria.bcn.cat; Plaça del Rei; adult/child €7/free, from 4pm 1st Sat of month and from 3pm Sun free; ⏲10am-7pm Tue-Sat, 10am-8pm Sun; MJaume I) Not far from the Barcelona Catedral is pretty Plaça del Rei and the fascinating Museu d'Història de Barcelona, where you can visit a 4000-sq-metre excavated site of Roman Barcelona under the plaza. The museum encompasses historic buildings, including the **Palau Reial Major** (Main Royal Palace), once a residence of the kings of Catalonia and Aragón, and its **Saló del Tinell** (Great Hall).

Sinagoga Major SYNAGOGUE

(Map p974; ☎93 317 07 90; www.calldebarcelona.org; Carrer de Marlet 5; admission by suggested donation €2.50; ⏲10.30am-6.30pm Mon-Fri, to 2.30pm Sat & Sun; MLiceu) When an Argentine investor bought a run-down electrician's store with an eye to converting it into central Barcelona's umpteenth bar, he could hardly have known he had stumbled onto the remains of what could be the city's main medieval synagogue. A guide will explain what is thought to be the significance of the site in various languages.

EL RAVAL

To the west of La Rambla is El Raval district, a once-seedy, now-funky area overflowing with cool bars and shops.

MACBA MUSEUM

(Museu d'Art Contemporani de Barcelona; Map p974; ☎93 412 08 10; www.macba.cat; Plaça dels Àngels 1; adult/concession €7.50/6; ⏲11am-8pm Mon & Wed, to midnight Thu-Fri, 10am-8pm Sat, 10am-3pm Sun & holidays; MUniversitat) Designed by Richard Meier and opened in 1995, MACBA has become the city's foremost contemporary art centre, with captivating exhibitions for the serious art lover. The permanent collection is on the ground floor and dedicates itself to Spanish and Catalan art from the second half of the 20th century, with works by Antoni Tàpies, Joan Brossa and Miquel Barceló, among others, though international artists, such as Paul Klee, Bruce Nauman and John Cage are also represented.

Església de Sant Pau CHURCH

(Map p974; Carrer de Sant Pau 101; ⏲cloister 10am-1pm & 4-7pm Mon-Sat; MParal·lel) The best example of Romanesque architecture in the city is the dainty little cloister of this church. Set in a somewhat dusty garden, the 12th-century church also boasts some Visigothic sculptural detail on the main entrance.

LA RIBERA

In medieval days, La Ribera was a stone's throw from the Mediterranean and the heart of Barcelona's foreign trade, with homes belonging to numerous wealthy merchants. Now it's a trendy district full of boutiques, restaurants and bars.

TOP CHOICE Museu Picasso MUSEUM

(Map p974; ☎93 256 30 00; www.museupicasso.bcn.es; Carrer de Montcada 15-23; adult/senior & child under 16yr/student €11/free/6, temporary exhibitions adult/senior & child under 16yr/student €6/free/2.90, 3-8pm Sun & 1st Sun of month free; ⏲10am-8pm Tue-Sun & holidays; MJaume I) The setting alone, in five contiguous medieval stone mansions, makes the Museu Picasso unique (and worth the probable queues). The pretty courtyards, galleries and staircases preserved in the first three of these buildings are as delightful as the collection inside.

While the collection concentrates on the artist's formative years – sometimes disappointing for those hoping for a feast of his better-known later works (they had better head for Paris) – there is enough material from subsequent periods to give you a thorough impression of the man's versatility and genius.

Església de Santa Maria del Mar CHURCH

(Map p974; ☎93 319 05 16; Plaça de Santa Maria del Mar; ⏲9am-1.30pm & 4.30-8pm; MJaume I) At the southwest end of Passeig del Born stands Barcelona's finest Catalan Gothic church, Santa Maria del Mar (Our Lady of the Sea). Built in the 14th century with record-breaking alacrity for the time (it took just 54 years), the church is remarkable for its architectural harmony and simplicity.

Palau de la Música Catalana ARCHITECTURE

(Map p970; ☎902 475 485; www.palaumusica.org; Carrer de Sant Francesc de Paula 2; adult/child/student & EU senior €15/free/€7.50; ⏲50min tours every 30 minutes 10am-6pm Easter week & Aug, 10am-3.30pm Sep-Jul; MUrquinaona) The opulent Palau de la Música Catalana is one of the city's most delightful Modernista works. Designed by Lluís Domènech i Montaner in 1905, it hosts concerts regularly. It is well worth joining the guided tours to get a look inside if you don't make a concert.

El Raval, Barri Gòtic & La Rambla

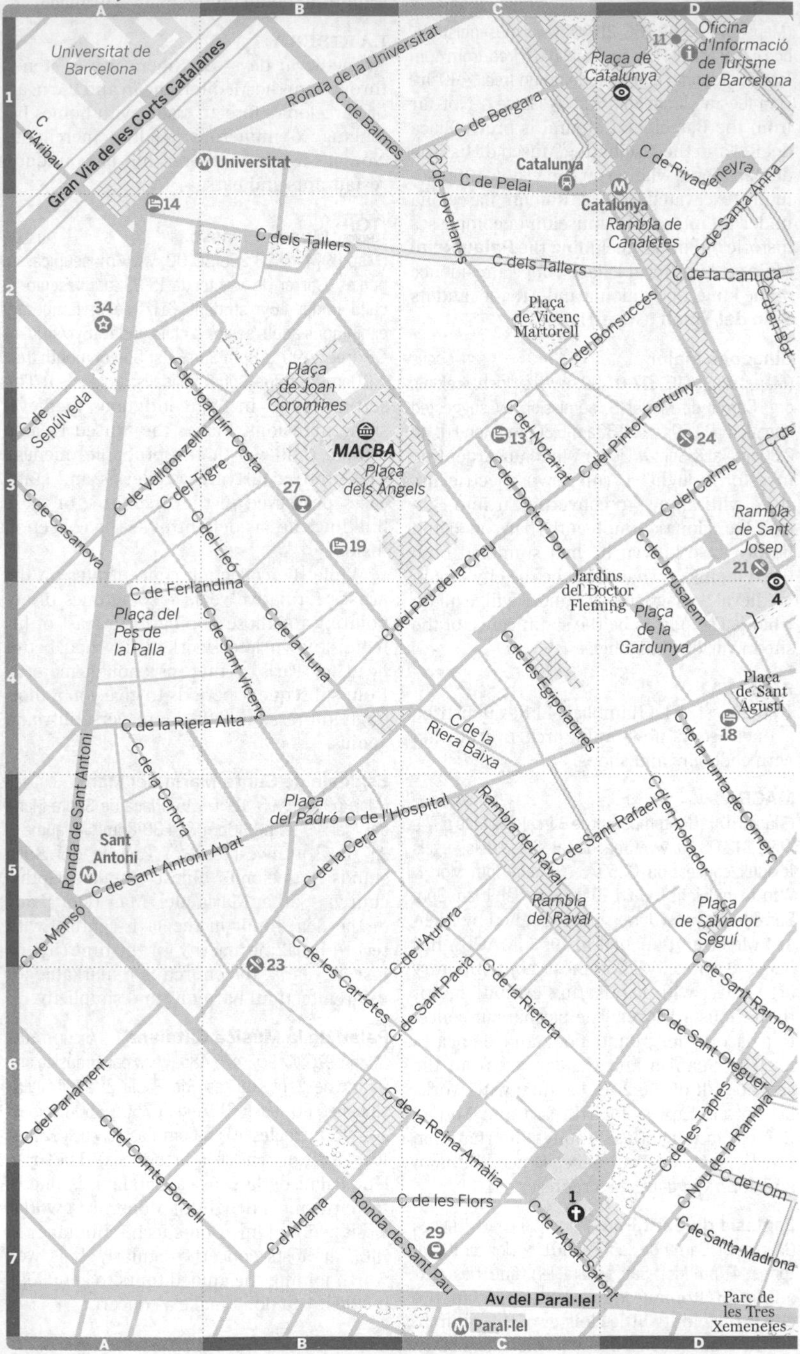

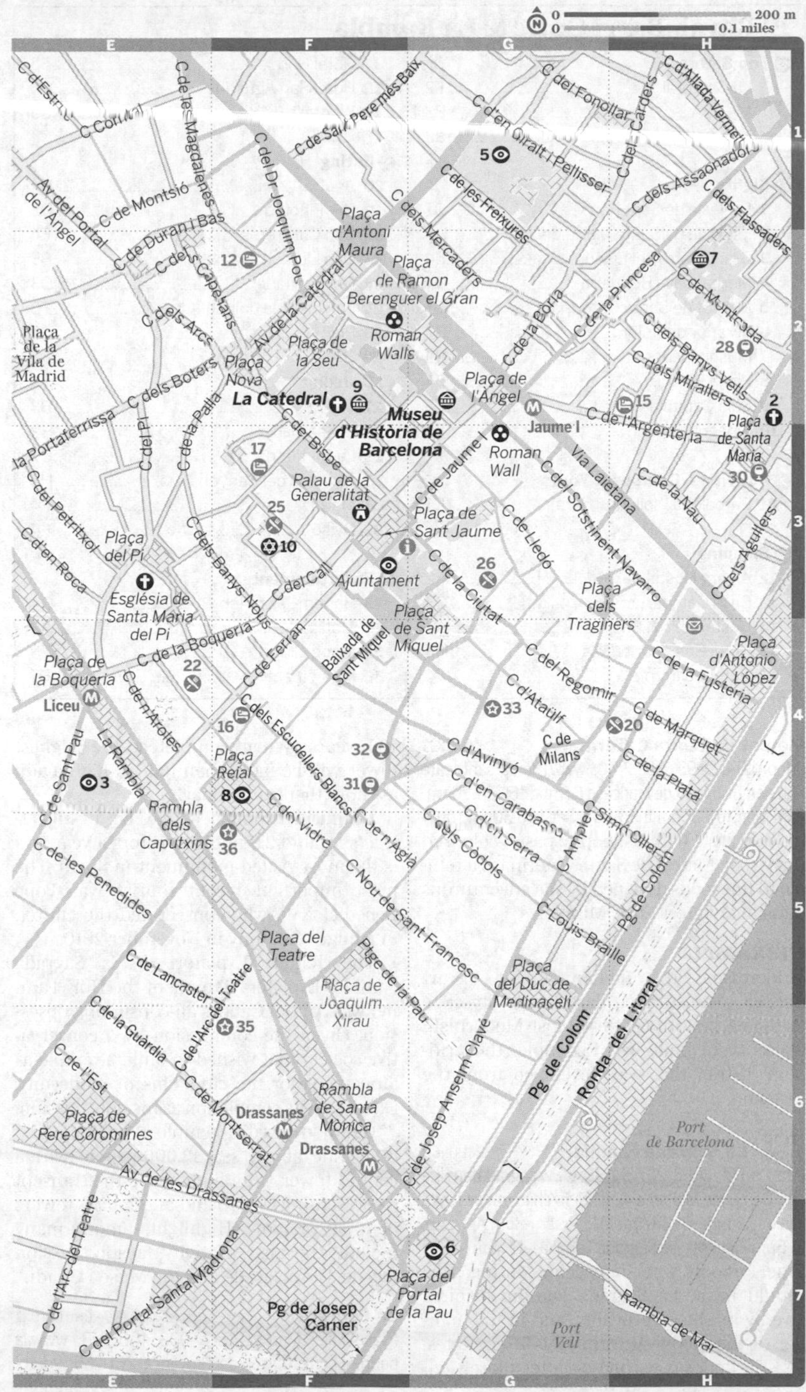
0 200 m
0 0.1 miles
C d'Estruc
C Comtal
C de les Magdalenes
C de Sant Pere més Baix
C del Fonollar
C dels Carders
C d'Allada Vermell
C d'en Giralt i Pellisser
C dels Assaonadors
C dels Flassaders
C de les Freixures
C dels Mercaders
C del Dr Joaquim Pou
Av del Portal de l'Àngel
C de Montsió
C de Duran i Bas
C dels Capellans
Plaça d'Antoni Maura
Plaça de Ramon Berenguer el Gran
Roman Walls
Av de la Catedral
C de la Princesa
C de Montcada
C dels Banys Vells
C dels Miralls
C de la Bòria
Plaça de la Vila de Madrid
C dels Arcs
Plaça de la Seu
Plaça Nova
C dels Boters
La Catedral
Museu d'Història de Barcelona
Plaça de l'Àngel
Jaume I
C de l'Argenteria
Plaça de Santa Maria
la Portaferrissa
C del Pi
C de la Palla
C del Bisbe
Roman Wall
C de Jaume I
Via Laietana
C de la Nau
C del Sotstinent Navarro
C dels Agullers
C del Petritxol
Palau de la Generalitat
Plaça de Sant Jaume
C de Lledó
C d'en Roca
Plaça del Pi
C dels Banys Nous
C del Call
Ajuntament
C de la Ciutat
Plaça dels Traginers
Església de Santa Maria del Pi
C de la Boqueria
C de Ferran
Baixada de Sant Miquel
Plaça de Sant Miquel
Plaça d'Antonio López
Plaça de la Boqueria
C d'en Arolès
C del Regomir
C de la Fusteria
Liceu
C d'Ataülf
C de Marquet
C dels Escudellers Blancs
C de Milans
C de Sant Pau
La Rambla
Plaça Reial
C d'Avinyó
C de la Plata
C d'en Carabassa
Rambla dels Caputxins
C del Vidre
C d'en Serra
C Simó Oller
C Ample
C dels Còdols
C de les Penedides
C Nou de Sant Francesc
C d'en Aglà
C Louis Braille
Pg de Colom
Plaça del Teatre
Ptge de la Pau
Plaça del Duc de Medinaceli
C de Lancaster
C de l'Arc del Teatre
Plaça de Joaquim Xirau
C de Josep Anselm Clavé
Ronda del Litoral
C de la Guàrdia
C de l'Est
C de Montserrat
Rambla de Santa Mònica
Drassanes
Port de Barcelona
Plaça de Pere Coromines
Av de les Drassanes
C de l'Arc del Teatre
C del Portal Santa Madrona
Plaça del Portal de la Pau
Pg de Josep Carner
Port Vell
Rambla de Mar
E
F
G
H
1
2
3
4
5
6
7
2
3
5
6
7
8
9
10
12
15
16
17
20
22
25
26
28
30
31
32
33
35
36

El Raval, Barri Gòtic & La Rambla

Mercat de Santa Caterina MARKET
(Map p974; ☎93 319 17 40; www.mercatsantacaterina.net; Avinguda de Francesc Cambó 16; ⏰7.30am-2pm Mon, to 3.30pm Tue, Wed & Sat, to 8.30pm Thu & Fri; Ⓜ Jaume I) With its loopily pastel-coloured wavy roof, Mercat de Santa Caterina is a temple to fine foods designed by the adventurous Catalan architect Enric Miralles.

L'EIXAMPLE

Modernisme, the Catalan version of art nouveau, transformed Barcelona's cityscape in the early 20th century. Most Modernista works were built in L'Eixample, the grid-plan district that was developed from the 1870s on.

TOP CHOICE **La Sagrada Família** CHURCH
(Map p970; ☎93 207 30 31; www.sagradafamilia.org; Carrer de Mallorca 401; adult/child under 10yr/senior & student €13/free/11; ⏰9am-8pm Apr-Sep, to 6pm Oct-Mar; Ⓜ Sagrada Família) If you have time for only one sightseeing outing, this should be it. La Sagrada Família inspires awe by its sheer verticality, and in the manner of the medieval cathedrals it emulates, it's still under construction after more than 100 years. When completed, the highest tower will be more than half as high again as those that stand today.

Unfinished though it may be, it still attracts around 2.8 million visitors a year and is the most visited monument in Spain. The most important recent tourist was Pope Benedict XVI, who consecrated the church in a huge ceremony in November 2010.

The Temple Expiatori de la Sagrada Família (Expiatory Temple of the Holy Family) was Antoni Gaudí's all-consuming obsession. Given the commission by a conservative society that wished to build a temple as atonement for the city's sins of modernity, Gaudí saw its completion as his holy mission.

Gaudí devised a temple 95m long and 60m wide, able to seat 13,000 people, with a central tower 170m high above the transept (representing Christ) and another 17 towers of 100m or more. Highlights among many include the apse, Nativity façade, Passion façade, Glory façade and the Museu Gaudí.

La Pedrera ARCHITECTURE
(Casa Milà; Map p970; ☎902 400 973; www.lapedrera.com; Carrer de Provença 261-265; adult/

student/child €15/13.50/7.50; ⌚9am-8pm Mar-Oct, to 6.30pm Nov-Feb; Ⓜ Diagonal) This undulating beast is another madcap Gaudí masterpiece, built in 1905–10 as a combined apartment and office block. Formally called Casa Milà, after the businessman who commissioned it, it is better known as La Pedrera (the Quarry) because of its uneven grey stone facade, which ripples around the corner of Carrer de Provença.

The Fundació Caixa Catalunya has opened the top-floor apartment, attic and roof, together called the Espai Gaudí (Gaudí Space), to visitors. The roof is the most extraordinary element, with its giant chimney pots looking like multicoloured medieval knights.

One floor below the roof, where you can appreciate Gaudí's taste for parabolic arches, is a modest museum dedicated to his work.

Casa Batlló ARCHITECTURE

(Map p970; ☎93 216 03 06; www.casabatllo.es; Passeig de Gràcia 43; adult/child under 7yr/ €18.15/free; ⌚9am-8pm; Ⓜ Passeig de Gràcia) One of the strangest residential buildings in Europe, this is Gaudí at his hallucinogenic best. The facade, sprinkled with bits of blue, mauve and green tiles and studded with wave-shaped window frames and balconies, rises to an uneven blue-tiled roof with a solitary tower.

FREE **Casa Amatller** ARCHITECTURE

(Map p970; ☎93 487 72 17; www.amatller.org; Passeig de Gràcia 41; ⌚10am-8pm Mon-Sat, to 3pm Sun, guided tour in English noon Fri, in Catalan & Spanish noon Wed; Ⓜ Passeig de Gràcia) One of Puig i Cadafalch's most striking bits of Modernista fantasy, Casa Amatller combines Gothic window frames with a stepped gable borrowed from Dutch urban architecture. But the busts and reliefs of dragons, knights and other characters dripping off the main facade are pure caprice.

MONTJUÏC

Southwest of the city centre and with views out to sea and over the city, Montjuïc serves as a Central Park of sorts and is a great place for a jog or stroll.

TOP CHOICE **Museu Nacional d'Art de Catalunya** MUSEUM

(MNAC; Map p970; ☎93 622 03 76; www.mnac.es; Mirador del Palau Nacional; adult/senior & child under 15yr €10/free, 1st Sun of month free; ⌚10am-7pm Tue-Sat, to 2.30pm Sun & holidays, library 10am-6pm Mon-Fri, to 2.30pm Sat; Ⓜ Espanya) From across the city, the bombastic neobaroque silhouette of the Palau Nacional can be seen on the slopes of Montjuïc. Built for the 1929 World Exhibition and restored in 2005, it houses a vast collection of mostly Catalan art spanning the early Middle Ages to the early 20th century. The high point is the collection of extraordinary Romanesque frescoes.

Fundació Joan Miró MUSEUM

(Map p970; www.bcn.fjmiro.es; Plaça de Neptu; adult/senior & child €10/7; ⌚10am-8pm Tue, Wed, Fri & Sat, to 9.30pm Thu, to 2.30pm Sun & holidays; 🚌50, 55, 193, funicular Paral·lel) Joan Miró, the city's best-known 20th-century artistic progeny, bequeathed this art foundation to his hometown in 1971. Its light-filled buildings

DON'T MISS

PARK GÜELL

North of Gràcia and about 4km from Plaça de Catalunya, **Park Güell** (☎93 413 24 00; Carrer d'Olot 7; ⌚10am-9pm Jun-Sep, to 8pm Apr, May & Oct, to 7pm Mar & Nov, to 6pm Dec-Feb; 🚌24, Ⓜ Lesseps, Vallcarca) is where Gaudí turned his hand to landscape gardening. It's a strange, enchanting place where his passion for natural forms really took flight – to the point where the artificial almost seems more natural than the natural.

Park Güell originated in 1900, when Count Eusebi Güell bought a tree-covered hillside (then outside Barcelona) and hired Gaudí to create a miniature city of houses for the wealthy in landscaped grounds. The project was a commercial flop and was abandoned in 1914 – but not before Gaudí had created 3km of roads and walks, steps, a plaza and two gatehouses in his inimitable manner. In 1922 the city bought the estate for use as a public park. The park is extremely popular (it gets an estimated 4 million visitors a year, about 86% of them tourists) and there is talk of limiting access to keep a lid on damage done by the overkill. Its quaint nooks and crannies are irresistible to photographers – who on busy days have trouble keeping out of each other's pictures.

are crammed with seminal works, from Miró's earliest timid sketches to paintings from his last years.

FREE **Castell de Montjuïc** FORTRESS, GARDENS
(Map p970; 9am-9pm Tue-Sun Apr-Sep, to 7pm Tue-Sun Oct-Mar; 193, Telefèric de Montjuïc) The forbidding Castell (castle or fort) de Montjuïc dominates the southeastern heights of Montjuïc and enjoys commanding views over the Mediterranean. It dates, in its present form, from the late 17th and 18th centuries.

Poble Espanyol CULTURAL CENTRE
(Map p970; www.poble-espanyol.com; Avinguda de Francesc Ferrer i Guàrdia; adult/child €9.50/5.60; 9am-8pm Mon, to 2am Tue-Thu, to 4am Fri, to 5am Sat, to midnight Sun; 50, 61 or 193, M Espanya) A showcase of typical Spanish architecture from around the country, Poble Espanyol has craft shops, restaurants and nightlife.

CaixaForum GALLERY
(Map p970; www.fundacio.lacaixa.es; Avinguda de Francesc Ferrer i Guàrdia 6-8; adult/student & child €3/2, first Sun of the month free; 10am-8pm Tue-Fri & Sun, to 10pm Sat; P; M Espanya) CaixaForum is housed in a remarkable former Modernista factory designed by Puig i Cadafalch and puts on major art exhibitions.

BARCELONA'S WATERFRONT

Barcelona has two major ports: **Port Vell** (Old Port), at the base of La Rambla, and **Port Olímpic** (Olympic Port), 1.5km up the coast. Shops, restaurants and nightlife options are plentiful around both marinas, particularly Port Olímpic. Barcelona boasts 4km of city *platjas* (beaches), beginning with the gritty **Platja de la Barceloneta** and continuing northeast, beyond Port Olímpic, with a series of cleaner, more attractive strands. All get packed in summer.

Tours

Barcelona Walking Tours WALKING TOUR
(Map p974; 93 285 38 34; www.barcelonaturisme.com; Plaça de Catalunya 17-S; M Catalunya) The Oficina d'Informació de Turisme de Barcelona organises guided walking tours. One explores the **Barri Gòtic** (adult/child €14/5; in English 9.30am daily, in Spanish & Catalan 11.30am Sat); another follows in the footsteps of **Picasso** (adult/child €20/7; in English 3pm Tue, Thu & Sun) and winds up at the Museu Picasso, entry to which is included in the price; and a third takes in the main jewels of **Modernisme** (adult/child €14/5; in English 4pm Fri & Sat Oct-May, 6pm Fri & Sat Jun-Sep). Also offered is a **gourmet tour** (adult/child €20/7; in English 10am Fri & Sat, in Spanish & Catalan 10.30am Sat) of traditional purveyors of fine foodstuffs across the old city. All tours last two hours and start at the tourist office. All tours are also available in both English and Spanish at 6pm from June to September.

Bus Turístic BUS TOUR
(93 285 38 32; www.barcelonaturisme.com; day ticket adult/child €24/14; 9am-8pm) This hop-on, hop-off service covers three circuits (44 stops) linking virtually all the major tourist sights. Tourist offices, TMB transport authority offices and many hotels have leaflets explaining the system.

Festivals & Events

The **Festes de la Mercè** (www.bcn.cat/merce), held around 24 September, is the city's biggest party, with four days of concerts, dancing, *castellers* (human castle-builders), fireworks and *correfocs* – a spectacular parade of firework-spitting dragons and devils.

The evening before the **Dia de Sant Joan** (24 June) is a colourful midsummer celebration with bonfires and fireworks. The beaches are crowded with revellers to the wee hours.

Sleeping

There's no shortage of hotels in Barcelona. Those looking for cheaper accommodation close to the action should check out the Barri Gòtic and El Raval. Some good lower-end *pensiones* are scattered about L'Eixample, as well as a broad range of midrange and top-end places, most in easy striking distance of the old town. A growing range of options now makes it easier to stay in La Ribera and near the beaches at La Barceloneta.

Numerous private apartment-rental companies operate in Barcelona. These can often be a better deal than staying in a hotel. Start your search at **Aparteasy** (Map p970; 93 451 67 66; www.aparteasy.com; Carrer de Santa Tecla 3; M Diagnoal), **Barcelona On Line** (Map p970; 902 887017, 93 343 79 93; www.barcelona-on-line.es; Carrer de València 352) and **Rent a Flat in Barcelona** (93 342 73 00; www.rentaflatinbarcelona.com; Ronda del Guinardó 2).

LA RAMBLA & BARRI GÒTIC

TOP CHOICE **Hotel Neri** DESIGN HOTEL €€€
(Map p974; 93 304 06 55; www.hotelneri.com; Carrer de Sant Sever 5; d from €270; ;

(MLiceu) This tranquil hotel occupies a beautifully adapted, centuries-old building backing on Plaça de Sant Felip Neri. The sandstone walls and timber furnishings lend a sense of history, while the rooms feature cutting-edge technology, including plasma-screen TVs and infrared lights in the stone-clad designer bathrooms.

Alberg Hostel Itaca HOSTEL €

(Map p974; 93 301 97 51; www.itacahostel.com; Carrer de Ripoll 21; dm €11-26, d €60; @; MJaume I) A bright, quiet hostel near Barcelona's Catedral, Itaca has spacious dorms (sleeping six, eight or 12 people) with parquet floors and spring colours, and two doubles. It also features two nearby apartments for six people (€120 per night).

Hotel California HOTEL €€

(Map p974; 93 317 77 66; www.hotelcaliforniabcn.com; Carrer d'en Rauric 14; s/d €70/120; @; MLiceu) This (gay) friendly and central hotel has 31 straightforward but fastidiously sparkling-clean rooms, with light, neutral colours, satellite plasma TV and good-sized beds. Double glazing helps ensure a good night's sleep.

EL RAVAL

TOP CHOICE Casa Camper DESIGN HOTEL €€€

(Map p974; 93 342 62 80; www.casacamper.com; Carrer d'Elisabets 11; s/d €240/270; @; MLiceu) The massive foyer looks like a contemporary-art museum, but the rooms are the real surprise. Decorated in red, black and white, each room has a sleeping and bathroom area, where you can put on your Camper slippers, enjoy the Vinçon furniture and contemplate the hanging gardens outside your window. Across the corridor is a separate, private sitting room with balcony, TV and hammock.

Whotells APARTMENT €€

(Map p974; 93 443 08 34; www.whotells.com; Carrer de Joaquín Costa 28; apt from €180; @; MUniversitat) These comfortable home-away-from-home apartments, decked out with Muji furniture, can sleep four to six people. Cook up a storm in the kitchen with products bought in the nearby La Boqueria market, or flop in front of the LCD TV.

Hostal Chic & Basic HOSTAL €€

(Map p974; 93 302 51 83; www.chicandbasic.com; Carrer de Tallers 82; s €80, d €103-124; @; MUniversitat) The colour scheme here is predominantly white, with exceptions like the screaming orange fridge in the communal kitchen and chill-out area. Rooms are also themed lily white, from the floors to the sheets. Finishing touches include the plasma-screen TVs and the option of plugging your iPod into your room's sound system. The street can get noisy.

Hotel San Agustín HOTEL €€

(Map p974; 93 318 16 58; www.hotelsa.com; Plaça de Sant Agustí 3; r from €80-180; @; MLiceu) This former 18th-century monastery opened as a hotel in 1840, making it the city's oldest. The location is perfect – a quick stroll off La Rambla on a curious square. Rooms sparkle, and are mostly spacious and light-filled.

LA RIBERA & LA BARCELONETA

TOP CHOICE Hotel Banys Orientals BOUTIQUE HOTEL €€

(Map p974; 93 268 84 60; www.hotelbanysorientals.com; Carrer de l'Argenteria 37; s/d €88/105, ste €130; @; MJaume I) Book well ahead to get into this magnetically popular designer haunt. Cool blues and aquamarines combine with dark-hued floors to lend this clean-lined, boutique hotel a quiet charm. All rooms, on the small side, look onto the street or back lanes.

Chic & Basic DESIGN HOTEL €€

(Map p970; 93 295 46 52; www.chicandbasic.com; Carrer de la Princesa 50; s €96, d €132-192; @; MJaume I) This is a very cool hotel indeed, with its 31 spotlessly white rooms and fairy-lights curtains that change colour, adding an entirely new atmosphere to the space. The ceilings are high and the beds enormous.

W Barcelona LUXURY HOTEL €€€

(Map p970; 93 295 28 00; www.w-barcelona.com; Plaça de la Rosa del Vents 1; r from €310; P@; 17, 39, 57 or 64, MBarceloneta) This spinnaker-shaped, beach-adjacent tower of glass contains 473 rooms and suites that are the last word in contemporary hotel chic. Self-indulgence is a byword and guests can flit between gym, infinity pool (with bar) and spa.

L'EIXAMPLE

TOP CHOICE Hotel Praktik BOUTIQUE HOTEL €€

(Map p970; 93 343 66 90; www.hotelpraktikrambla.com; Rambla de Catalunya 27; r from €80-170; @; MPasseig de Gràcia) This Modernista gem hides a gorgeous little boutique experience. While the high ceilings and the bulk of the original tile floors have been maintained, the 43 rooms have daring ceramic touches, spot lighting and contemporary art.

Five Rooms BOUTIQUE HOTEL €€
(Map p970; ☎93 342 78 80; www.thefiverooms.com; Carrer de Pau Claris 72; s/d from €115/135, apt from €175; ❄@📶; Ⓜ Urquinaona) Like they say, there are five rooms (standard rooms and suites) in this 1st-floor flat virtually on the border between L'Eixample and the old centre of town. Each room is different; features include broad, firm beds, stretches of exposed brick wall, restored mosaic tiles and minimalist decor. There are also two apartments.

Hotel Omm DESIGN HOTEL €€€
(Map p970; ☎93 445 40 00; www.hotelomm.es; Carrer de Rosselló 265; d from €360; P❄@≋; Ⓜ Diagonal) Design meets plain zany here, where the balconies look like strips of skin peeled back from the shiny hotel surface. The idea would no doubt have appealed to Dalí. In the foyer, a sprawling, minimalist and popular bar opens before you. Light, clear tones dominate in the ultramodern rooms, of which there are several categories.

Hotel Constanza BOUTIQUE HOTEL €€
(Map p970; ☎93 270 19 10; www.hotelconstanza.com; Carrer del Bruc 33; s/d €130/150; ❄@; Ⓜ Girona, Urquinaona) This boutique beauty has stolen the hearts of many a visitor to Barcelona. Design touches abound, and little details like flowers in the bathroom add charm. Suites and studios are further options.

Hostal Goya HOSTAL €€
(Map p970; ☎93 302 25 65; www.hostalgoya.com; Carrer de Pau Claris 74; s €70, d €96-113; ❄; Ⓜ Passeig de Gràcia, Urquinaona) The Goya is a modestly priced gem on the chichi side of L'Eixample. Rooms have a light colour scheme that varies from room to room. In the bathrooms, the original mosaic floors have largely been retained, combined with contemporary design features.

Eating

Barcelona is foodie heaven. The city has firmly established itself as one of Europe's gourmet capitals, and innovative, cutting-edge restaurants abound. Some of the most creative chefs are one-time students of world-renowned chef Ferran Adrià, whose influence on the city's cuisine is strong.

Although Barcelona has a reputation as a hot spot of 'new Spanish cuisine', you'll still find local eateries serving up time-honoured local grub, from squid-ink *fideuà* (a satisfying paella-like noodle dish) to pigs' trotters, rabbit with snails, and *butifarra* (a tasty local sausage).

LA RAMBLA & BARRI GÒTIC

Skip the overpriced traps along La Rambla and get into the winding lanes of the Barri Gòtic.

TOP CHOICE Pla FUSION €€
(Map p974; ☎93 412 65 52; www.elpla.cat; Carrer de la Bellafila 5; mains €18-24; ⏲dinner; 🖉; Ⓜ Jaume I) One of Gòtic's long-standing favourites, Pla is a stylish, romantically lit medieval den (with a huge stone arch) where the cooks churn out such temptations as oxtail braised in red wine, seared tuna with roasted aubergine, and 'Thai-style' monkfish with prawns, lemongrass and apple foam. It has a tasting menu for €36 Sunday to Thursday.

La Vinateria dell Call SPANISH €€
(Map p974; ☎93 302 60 92; www.lavinateriadelcall.com; Carrer de Sant Domènec del Call 9; small plates €7-11; ⏲dinner; Ⓜ Jaume I) In a magical setting in the former Jewish quarter, this tiny jewel-box of a restaurant serves up tasty Iberian dishes, including Galician octopus, cider-cooked chorizo and the Catalan *escalivada* (roasted peppers, aubergine and onions) with anchovies.

Can Culleretes CATALAN €€
(Map p974; ☎93 317 30 22; www.culleretes.com; Carrer Quintana 5; mains €8-14; ⏲lunch & dinner Tue-Sat, lunch Sun; Ⓜ Liceu) Founded in 1786, Barcelona's oldest restaurant is still going strong, with tourists and locals flocking to enjoy its rambling interior, old-fashioned tile-filled decor and enormous helpings of traditional Catalan food. The multicourse lunch specials are good value.

Agut CATALAN €€
(Map p974; www.restaurantagut.com; Carrer d'en Gignàs 16; mains €16-25; ⏲lunch & dinner Tue-Sat, lunch Sun; Ⓜ Jaume I) Deep in the Gothic labyrinth lies this classic eatery. A series of cosy dining areas is connected by broad arches while, high up, the walls are tightly lined by artworks. There's art in what the kitchen serves up too, from the oak-grilled meat to a succulent variety of seafood offerings.

EL RAVAL

TOP CHOICE Bar Pinotxo TAPAS €€
(Map p974; www.pinotxobar.com; Mercat de la Boqueria; meals €20; ⏲6am-5pm Mon-Sat Sep-Jul; Ⓜ Liceu) Bar Pinotxo is arguably Barcelona's best tapas bar. It sits among the half-dozen or so informal eateries within Mercat de la Boqueria (p969), and the popular owner, Juanito, might serve up chickpeas with a sweet sauce of pine nuts and raisins, baby soft baby squid with cannellini beans, or a quivering cube of caramel sweet pork belly.

Can Lluís CATALAN €€€
(Map p974; Carrer de la Cera 49; meals €30-35; ⏲Mon-Sat, closed Aug; ⓂSant Antoni) Three generations have kept this spick and span old-time classic in business since 1929. Beneath the olive-green beams in the back dining room you can see the spot where an anarchist's bomb went off in 1946, killing the then owner. Expect fresh fish and seafood.

Granja Viader CAFE €
(Map p974; ☎93 318 34 86; www.granjaviader.cat; Carrer d'en Xuclà 4; ⏲9am-1.45pm & 5-8.45pm Tue-Sat, 5-8.45pm Mon; ⓂLiceu) For more than a century, people have flocked down this alley to get to the cups of homemade hot chocolate and whipped cream (ask for a *suís*) ladled out in this classic Catalan-style milk bar cum deli.

LA RIBERA & WATERFRONT

La Barceloneta is the place to go for seafood; Passeig Joan de Borbó is lined with eateries but locals head for the back lanes.

TOP CHOICE Cal Pep TAPAS €€
(Map p970; ☎93 310 79 61; www.calpep.com; Plaça de les Olles 8; mains €8-18; ⏲lunch Tue-Sat, dinner Mon-Fri, closed Aug; ⓂBarceloneta) It's getting a foot in the door here that's the problem. Elbowing your way to the bar for some of the tastiest gourmet seafood tapas in town. Pep recommends *cloïsses amb pernil* (clams and ham) or the *trifàsic* (combo of calamari, whitebait and prawns). Its other pièce de résistance is a super smooth *tortilla de patatas* (Spanish omelette).

Casa Delfín SPANISH €
(Map p970; Passeig del Born 36; mains €4-12; ⏲noon-1am; ⓂBarceloneta) One of Barcelona's culinary delights, Casa Delfín is everything you dream of when you think of Catalan (and Mediterranean) cooking. Start with the tangy and sweet *calçots* (a cross between a leek and an onion; February and March only) or salt-strewn *padron* peppers, moving on to grilled sardines specked with parsley, then tackle the meaty monkfish roasted in white wine and garlic.

Can Majó SEAFOOD €€
(Map p970; ☎93 221 54 55; www.canmajo.es; Carrer del Almirall Aixada 23; mains €18-24; ⏲lunch & dinner Tue-Sat, lunch Sun; 🚌45, 57, 59, 64, 157, ⓂBarceloneta) Virtually on the beach (with tables outside in summer), Can Majó has a long and steady reputation for fine seafood, particularly its rice dishes and bountiful *suquets* (fish stews). The *bollabessa de peix i marisc* (fish and seafood bouillabaisse) is succulent. Or try a big *graellada* (mixed seafood grill).

Suquet De L'Almirall SEAFOOD €€€
(Map p970; ☎93 221 62 33; www.suquetdelalmirall.com; Passeig de Joan de Borbó 65; meals €45-50; ⏲lunch & dinner Tue-Sat, lunch Sun; 🚌17, 39, 57, 64, ⓂBarceloneta) A family business run by an alumnus of Ferran Adrià's El Bulli, the order of the day is top-class seafood with the occasional unexpected twist. The house specialty is *suquet*. A good option is the *pica pica marinera* (a seafood mix) or you could opt for the tasting menu (€44). Grab one of the few outdoor tables.

L'EIXAMPLE & GRÀCIA

Tapaç 24 TAPAS €€
(Map p970; www.carlesabellan.com; Carrer de la Diputació 269; mains €10-20; ⏲9am-midnight Mon-Sat; ⓂPasseig de Gràcia) Carles Abellán runs this basement tapas haven known for its gourmet versions of old faves. Specials include the *bikini* (toasted ham and cheese sandwich – here the ham is cured and the truffle makes all the difference) and a thick black *arròs negre de sípia* (squid-ink black rice).

Cinc Sentits INTERNATIONAL €€
(Map p970; ☎93 323 94 90; www.cincsentits.com; Carrer d'Aribau 58; mains €10-20; ⏲lunch & dinner Tue-Sat; ⓂPasseig de Gràcia) Enter this somewhat overlit realm of the 'Five Senses' to indulge in a tasting menu (from €49 to €69), consisting of a series of small, experimental dishes. A key is the use of fresh local produce, such as fish landed on the Costa Brava and top-quality suckling pig from Extremadura. Less ambitious, but cheaper, is the set lunch at €30.

Montjuïc, Sants & Poble Sec

TOP CHOICE Tickets SPANISH €€

(Map p970; www.ticketsbar.es; Avinguda del Paral·lel 164; tapas €4-12; lunch & dinner; M Paral·lel) This is, literally, one of the sizzling tickets in the restaurant world. It's the new tapas bar opened by Ferran Adrià, of the legendary (now closed) El Bulli, and his brother Albert. And unlike El Bulli, it's an affordable venture – if you can book a table, that is (you can only book online, and two months in advance).

Quimet i Quimet TAPAS €€

(Map p970; Carrer del Poeta Cabanyes 25; tapas €3-11; lunch & dinner Mon-Fri, noon-6pm Sat; M Paral·lel) Quimet i Quimet is a family-run business that has been passed down from generation to generation. There's barely space to swing a calamari in this bottle-lined, standing-room-only place, but it is a tapas treat for the palate.

Drinking

Barcelona abounds with day-time cafes, laid-back lounges and lively night-time bars. Closing time is generally 2am from Sunday to Thursday, and 3am Friday and Saturday.

BARRI GÒTIC

Oviso BAR

(Map p974; Carrer d'Arai 5; 10am-2am; M Liceu) Oviso is a popular, budget-friendly restaurant with outdoor tables on the plaza, but shows its true bohemian colours by night, with a wildly mixed crowd, a rock-and-roll vibe and a two-room fin-de-siècle interior plastered with curious murals.

Marula Cafè BAR

(Map p974; www.marulacafe.com; Carrer dels Escudellers 49; 11pm-5am; M Liceu) A fantastic funk find in the heart of the Barri Gòtic, Marula will transport you to the 1970s and the best in funk and soul. James Brown fans will think they've died and gone to heaven.

EL RAVAL

TOP CHOICE La Confiteria BAR

(Map p974; Carrer de Sant Pau 128; 11am-2am; M Paral·lel) This is a trip into the 19th century. Until the 1980s it was a confectioner's shop and, although the original cabinets are now lined with booze, the look of the place has barely changed in its conversion into a laid-back bar.

33|45 BAR

(Map p974; Carrer Joaquín Costa 4; 10am-1:30am Mon-Thu, to 3am Fri & Sat, to midnight Sun; M Universitat) A supertrendy cocktail bar on the nightlife-laden Joaquín Costa street, this place has excellent mojitos – even pink, strawberry ones! – and a fashionable crowd. The main area has DJ music and lots of excited noise making, while the back room is scattered with sofas and armchairs for a post-dancing slump.

LA RIBERA

TOP CHOICE El Xampanyet WINE BAR

(Map p974; Carrer de Montcada 22; noon-4pm & 7-11pm Tue-Sat, noon-4pm Sun; M Jaume I) Nothing has changed for decades at El Xampanyet, one of the city's best-known *cava* (Catalan version of champagne) bars. Plant yourself at the bar or seek out a table against the decoratively tiled walls for a glass or three of *cava* and an assortment of tapas.

La Vinya del Senyor WINE BAR

(Map p974; www.lavinyadelsenyor.com; Plaça de Santa Maria del Mar 5; noon-1am Tue-Sun; M Jaume I) Relax on the *terrassa*, which lies in the shadow of Església de Santa Maria del Mar, or crowd inside at the tiny bar. The wine list is as long as *War and Peace* and there's a table upstairs for those who opt to sample by the bottle rather than the glass.

L'EIXAMPLE & GRÀCIA

TOP CHOICE Monvínic WINE BAR

(Map p970; 932 72 61 87; www.monvinic.com; Carrer de la Diputació 249 ; wine bar 1.30-11.30pm, restaurant 1.30-3.30pm & 8.30-10.30pm; M Passeig de Gracia) Proclaimed as 'possibly the best wine bar in the world' by the *Wall Street Journal*, and apparently considered unmissable by El Bulli's former sommelier, Monvínic is an ode, a rhapsody even, to wine loving. The interactive wine list sits on the bar for you to browse on a digital tablet and boasts more than 3000 varieties.

But that's not to say that it's for connoisseurs only; you can also come here to taste wine by the glass – there are 60 selections.

Les Gens Que J'Aime BAR

(Map p970; www.lesgensquejaime.com; Carrer de València 286; 6pm-2.30am Sun-Thu, to 3am Fri & Sat; M Passeig de Gràcia) This intimate basement relic of the 1960s follows a deceptively simple formula: chilled jazz music in the background, minimal lighting from an assortment of flea-market lamps and a cosy, cramped scattering of red velvet-backed lounges around tiny dark tables.

Entertainment

To keep up with what's on, pick up a copy of the weekly listings magazine, *Guía del Ocio* (€1) from news-stands.

Nightclubs

Barcelona clubs are spread a little more thinly than bars across the city. They tend to open from around midnight until 6am. Entry can cost from nothing to €20 (one drink usually included).

Elephant CLUB
(☎93 334 02 58; www.elephantbcn.com; Passeig dels Til·lers 1; ⏲11.30pm-4am Thu, to 5am Fri & Sat; MPalau Reial) Getting in here is like being invited to a private fantasy party in Beverly Hills. Models and wannabes mix with immaculately groomed lads who most certainly didn't come by taxi. A big tentlike dance space is the main game here, but smooth customers slink their way around a series of garden bars in summer too.

Moog CLUB
(Map p974; www.masimas.com/moog; Carrer de l'Arc del Teatre 3; admission €10; ⏲midnight-5am; MDrassanes) This fun and minuscule club is a standing favourite with the downtown crowd. In the main dance area, DJs dish out house, techno and electro, while upstairs you can groove to a nice blend of indie and occasional classic-pop throwbacks.

Razzmatazz CLUB
(Map p970; ☎93 320 82 00; www.salarazzmatazz.com; Carrer de Pamplona 88; admission €15-30; ⏲midnight-3.30am Thu, to 5.30am Fri & Sat; MMarina, Bogatell) Bands from far and wide occasionally create scenes of near hysteria in this, one of the city's classic live-music and clubbing venues. Five different clubs in one huge postindustrial space attract people of all dance persuasions and ages.

Gay & Lesbian Venues

Barcelona's gay and lesbian scene is concentrated in the blocks around Carrers de Muntaner and Consell de Cent (dubbed Gayxample). Here you'll find ambience every night of the week in the bars, discos and drag clubs.

Party hard at classic gay discos such as **Arena Madre** (Map p970; ☎93 487 83 42; www.arenadisco.com; Carrer de Balmes 32; admission €6-12; ⏲12.30am-5.30am; MPasseig de Gràcia) and **Metro** (Map p974; ☎93 323 52 27; www.metrodiscobcn.com; Carrer de Sepúlveda 185; ⏲1am-5am Mon, midnight-5am Sun & Tue-Thu, midnight-6am Fri & Sat; MUniversitat).

Live Music

TOP CHOICE **Palau de la Música Catalana** CLASSICAL MUSIC
(☎902 442882; www.palaumusica.org; Carrer de Sant Francesc de Paula 2; ⏲box office 10am-9pm Mon-Sat; MUrquinaona) A feast for the eyes, this Modernista confection is also the city's traditional venue for classical and choral music. Just being here for a performance is an experience. Sip a preconcert tipple in the foyer, its tiled pillars all a-glitter. Head up the grand stairway to the main auditorium, a whirlpool of Modernista whimsy. The *palau* has a wide-ranging programme.

Harlem Jazz Club JAZZ
(Map p974; ☎93 310 07 55; www.harlemjazzclub.es; Carrer de la Comtessa de Sobradiel 8; admission €6-15; ⏲8pm-4am Tue-Thu & Sun, to 5am Fri & Sat; MDrassanes) This narrow, old-town dive is one of the best spots in town for jazz. Every now and then it mixes it up with a little Latin, blues or African rhythms. It attracts a mixed crowd who maintain a respectful silence during the acts. Usually there are two sessions with different musos each night.

Sala Tarantos FLAMENCO
(Map p974; ☎93 319 17 89; www.masimas.net; Plaça Reial 17; admission from €7; ⏲shows 8.30pm, 9.30pm & 10.30pm; MLiceu) Since 1963, this basement locale has been the stage for up-and-coming flamenco groups performing in Barcelona. These days Tarantos has become a mostly tourist-centric affair, with half-hour shows held three times a night. Still, it's a good introduction to flamenco, and not a bad setting for a drink.

Sport

FC Barcelona (Barça for aficionados) has one of the best stadiums in Europe – the 99,000-capacity **Camp Nou** (☎93 496 36 00; www.fcbarcelona.com; Carrer d'Aristides Maillol; adult/child €23/17; ⏲10am-8pm Mon-Sat, to 2.30pm Sun; MPalau Reial) in the west of the city. Tickets for national-league games are available at the stadium, by phone or online. For the latter two options, non-members must book 15 days before the match.

Shopping

Most mainstream fashion stores are along a shopping 'axis' that runs from Plaça de Catalunya along Passeig de Gràcia, then left (west) along Avinguda Diagonal.

The El Born area in La Ribera is awash with tiny boutiques, especially those purveying young, fun fashion. There are plenty of shops scattered throughout the Barri Gòtic (stroll Carrer d'Avinyò and Carrer de Portaferrissa). For secondhand stuff, head for El Raval, especially Carrer de la Riera Baixa.

Joan Murrià FOOD
(Map p970; 93 215 57 89; www.murria.cat; Carrer de Roger de Llúria 85; Passeig de Gràcia) Note the century-old Modernista shop-front advertisements featured at this culinary temple. For a century the gluttonous have trembled here at this altar of speciality food goods from around Catalonia and beyond.

Els Encants Vells MARKET
(Fira de Bellcaire; Map p970; 93 246 30 30; www.encantsbcn.com; Plaça de les Glòries Catalanes; 7am-6pm Mon, Wed, Fri & Sat; Glòries) The 'Old Charms' flea market is the biggest of its kind in Barcelona. It's all here, from antique furniture through to secondhand clothes. A lot of it is junk, but occasionally you'll stumble across a *ganga* (bargain). The most interesting time to be here is from 7am to 9am on Monday, Wednesday and Friday, when the public auctions take place.

Vinçon HOMEWARES
(Map p970; 93 215 60 50; www.vincon.com; Passeig de Gràcia 96; 10am-8.30pm Mon-Sat; Diagonal) An icon of the Barcelona design scene, Vinçon has the slickest furniture and household goods (particularly lighting), both local and imported. Not surprising, really, since the building, raised in 1899, belonged to the Modernista artist Ramon Casas.

> **WANT MORE?**
>
> For in-depth information, reviews and recommendations at your fingertips, head to the Apple App Store to purchase Lonely Planet's *Barcelona City Guide* iPhone app.
>
> Alternatively, head to **Lonely Planet** (www.lonelyplanet.com/Spain/Barcelona) for planning advice, author recommendations, traveller reviews and insider tips.

Antonio Miró FASHION
(Map p970; 93 487 06 70; www.antoniomiro.es; Carrer del Consell de Cent 349; 10am-8pm Mon-Sat; Passeig de Gràcia) Antonio Miró is one of Barcelona's haute couture kings. The entrance to the airy store, with dark hardwood floor, seems more like a hip hotel reception. Miró concentrates on light, natural fibres to produce smart, unpretentious men's and women's fashion.

Custo Barcelona FASHION
(Map p970; 93 268 78 93; www.custo-barcelona.com; Plaça de les Olles 7; Jaume I) The psychedelic decor and casual atmosphere lend this avant-garde Barcelona fashion store a youthful edge. The dazzling colours and cut of anything from dinner jackets to hot pants are for the uninhibited. It has five other stores around town.

Information

Dangers & Annoyances

Purse snatching and pickpocketing are major problems, especially around Plaça de Catalunya, La Rambla and Plaça Reial.

Emergency

Tourists who want to report thefts need to go to the Catalan police, known as the **Mossos d'Esquadra** (088; Carrer Nou de la Rambla 80; Paral.lel), or the **Guàrdia Urbana** (Local Police; 092; La Rambla 43; Liceu)

In an emergency, call 112.

Internet Access

Bornet (Carrer de Barra Ferro 3; per hr/10hr €2.80/20; 10am-11pm Mon-Fri, 2-11pm Sat, Sun & holidays; Jaume I) A cool little internet centre and art gallery.

Medical Services

Call 010 to find the nearest late-opening duty pharmacy.

Farmàcia Clapés (La Rambla 98; Liceu)

Hospital Clínic i Provincial (Carrer de Villarroel 170; Hospital Clínic)

Tourist Information

Oficina d'Informació de Turisme de Barcelona (Map p974, 93 285 38 34; www.barcelonaturisme.com; underground at Plaça de Catalunya 17-S; 8.30am-8.30pm; Catalunya) also has branches at Aeroport del Prat (Aeroport del Prat, terminals 1, 2B & 2A; 9am-9pm), Estació Sants (Estació Sants; 8am-8pm; Estació Sants) and Town hall (Plaça Sant Jaume; 93 285 38 32; Carrer de la Ciutat 2; 8.30am-8.30pm

WORTH A TRIP

ANDORRA

This mini-country wedged between France and Spain offers by far the best ski slopes and resort facilities in all the Pyrenees. Once the snow melts, there's an abundance of great walking, ranging from easy strolls to demanding day hikes in the principality's higher, more remote reaches. Strike out above the tight valleys and you can walk for hours, almost alone.

The only way to reach Andorra is by road from Spain or France. If driving, fill up in Andorra; fuel is substantially cheaper there. There are bus services to/from Lleida, Barcelona's Estació del Nord, Barcelona's airport El Prat de Llobregat, and Toulouse (France). All bus services arrive at and leave from Andorra la Vella. **Andorra Direct Bus** (www.andorradirectbus.es) is one of a number of companies offering direct services to/from Barcelona (three hours) and Barcelona's Prat Airport (3½ hours).

Mon-Fri, 9am-7pm Sat, 9am-2pm Sun & holidays; MJaume I).

There is also a **Regional Tourist Office** (www.gencat.net/probert; Passeig de Gràcia 107; ⌚10am-7pm Mon-Sat, to 2.30pm Sun; MDiagonal).

Getting There & Away

Air

Barcelona's airport, **El Prat de Llobregat** (☎902 404704; www.aena.es), is 12km southwest of the city centre. Barcelona is a big international and domestic destination, with direct flights from North America as well as many European cities.

Boat

Regular passenger and vehicular ferries to/from the Balearic Islands, operated by **Acciona Trasmediterránea** (☎902 454645; www.trasmediterranea.es), dock along both sides of the Moll de Barcelona wharf in Port Vell.

The Grimaldi group's **Grandi Navi Veloci** (www1.gnv.it) runs high-speed, thrice-weekly luxury ferries between Barcelona and Genoa, while **Grimaldi Ferries** (☎902 531333, www.grimaldi-lines.com) operates similar services to Civitavecchia (near Rome), Livorno (Tuscany) and Porto Torres (northwest Sardinia).

Bus

The main terminal for most domestic and international buses is the **Estació del Nord** (☎902 260606; www.barcelonanord.com; Carrer d'Ali Bei 80; MArc de Triomf). ALSA goes to Madrid (€30, eight hours, up to 16 daily), Valencia (€27, 4½ to 6½ hours, up to 14 daily) and many other destinations.

Eurolines (www.eurolines.es) also offers international services from Estació del Nord and **Estació d'Autobusos de Sants** (Map p970; Carrer de Viriat; MEstació Sants).

Train

Virtually all trains travelling to and from destinations within Spain stop at **Estació Sants** (Plaça dels Països Catalans; MEstació Sants). High-speed trains to Madrid via Lleida and Zaragoza take as little as two hours and 40 minutes; prices vary wildly. Other trains run to Valencia (€36 to €45, three to 4½ hours, 15 daily) and Burgos (from €66, six to seven hours, four daily).

There are also international connections with French cities from the same station.

Getting Around

To/From the Airport

The **A1 Aerobús** (☎93 415 60 20; one way €5.65) runs from Terminal 1 to Plaça de Catalunya from 6.05am to 1.05am, taking 30 to 40 minutes. A2 Aerobús does the same run from Terminal 2, from 6am to 12.30am. Buy tickets on the bus.

Renfe's R2 Nord train line runs between the airport and Passeig de Gràcia (via Estació Sants) in central Barcelona (about 35 minutes). Tickets cost €3.60, unless you have a T-10 multitrip public-transport ticket.

A taxi to/from the centre, about a half-hour ride depending on traffic, costs around €25 to €30.

Public Transport

Barcelona's metro system spreads its tentacles around the city in such a way that most places of interest are within a 10-minute walk of a station. Buses and suburban trains are needed only for a few destinations. A single metro, bus or suburban train ride costs €2, but a T-1 ticket, valid for 10 rides, costs €9.25.

Taxi

Barcelona's black-and-yellow taxis are plentiful and reasonably priced. The flag fall is €2.05. If you can't find a street taxi, call ☎93 303 30 33.

Monestir de Montserrat

The monks who built the Monestir de Montserrat (Monastery of the Serrated Mountain), 50km northwest of Barcelona, chose a spectacular spot. The Benedictine **monastery** (www.abadiamontserrat.net; ⏲9am-6pm) sits on the side of a 1236m-high mountain of weird, bulbous peaks. The monastery was founded in 1025 and pilgrims still come from all over Christendom to kiss the Black Virgin (La Moreneta), the 12th-century wooden sculpture of the Virgin Mary.

The **Museu de Montserrat** (www.museudemontserrat.com; Plaça de Santa Maria; adult/student €6.50/5.50; ⏲10am-6pm) has an excellent collection, ranging from an Egyptian mummy to art by El Greco, Monet, Degas and Picasso.

If you're around the basilica at the right time, you'll catch a brief performance by the **Montserrat Boys' Choir** (www.escolania.cat; ⏲performances 1pm & Mon-Thu, 1pm Fri, noon Sun late Aug–late Jun)

You can explore the mountain above the monastery on a web of paths leading to some of the peaks and to 13 empty and rather dilapidated hermitages. Running every 20 minutes, the **Funicular de Sant Joan** (one way/return €5.05/8; ⏲every 20min 10am-6.50pm, closed Jan & Feb) will carry you up the first 250m from the monastery.

Getting There & Away

Montserrat is an easy day trip from Barcelona. The R5 line trains operated by FGC run from Plaça d'Espanya station in Barcelona to Monistrol de Montserrat up to 18 times daily starting at 5.16am. They connect with the rack-and-pinion train, or **cremallera** (☎902 312020; www.cremalleerademontserrat.com; one way/return €6/9), which takes 17 minutes to make the upwards journey.

Girona

POP 96,120

A tight huddle of ancient arcaded houses, grand churches, climbing cobbled streets and medieval baths, all enclosed by defensive walls and a lazy river, constitute a powerful reason for visiting north Catalonia's largest city, Girona (Castilian: Gerona).

Sights

Catedral CATHEDRAL
(www.catedraldegirona.org; Plaça de la Catedral; museum adult/child €5/1.20, Sun free; ⏲10am-8pm) The billowing baroque facade of the cathedral stands at the head of a majestic flight of steps rising from Plaça de la Catedral. Repeatedly rebuilt and altered down the centuries, it has Europe's widest Gothic nave (23m). The cathedral's **museum**, through the door marked 'Claustre Tresor', contains the masterly Romanesque *Tapís de la Creació* (Tapestry of the Creation) and a Mozarabic illuminated *Beatus* manuscript, dating from 975. The fee for the museum also admits you to the beautiful 12th-century Romanesque cloister.

TOP CHOICE **Passeig Arqueològic** RUINS
Across the street from the Banys Àrabs, steps lead up into some heavenly gardens where town and plants merge into one organic masterpiece. The gardens follow the city walls up to the 18th-century Portal de Sant Cristòfol gate, from where you can walk back down to Girona's cathedral.

DALÍ'S CATALONIA

A short train ride north of Girona, Figueres is home to the zany **Teatre-Museu Dalí** (www.salvador-dali.org; Plaça de Gala i Salvador Dalí 5; admission incl Dalí Joies & Museu de l'Empordá adult/child €12/free; ⏲9am-8pm Jul-Sep, 9.30am-6pm Mar-Jun & Oct, shorter hr rest of yr), housed in a 19th-century theatre converted by Salvador Dalí (who was born here). 'Theatre-museum' is an apt label for this multidimensional trip through one of the most fertile (or disturbed) imaginations of the 20th century. It's full of surprises, tricks and illusions, and contains a substantial portion of Dalí's life's work.

Dalí fans will want to travel south to visit the equally kooky **Castell de Púbol** (www.salvador-dali.org; Plaça de Gala Dalí; adult/student & senior €8/5; ⏲10am-8pm daily mid-Jun–mid-Sep, shorter hr rest of yr) at La Pera, 22km northwest of Palafrugell, and the **Casa Museu Dalí** (☎972 25 10 15; www.salvador-dali.org; adult/child €11/free) at his summer getaway in Port Lligat (1.25km from Cadaqués), where entry is by advance reservation only.

The Call HISTORIC DISTRICT

Until 1492 Girona was home to Catalonia's second-most important medieval Jewish community (after Barcelona), and its Jewish quarter, the Call, centred on Carrer de la Força. For an idea of medieval Jewish life and culture, visit the **Museu d'Història dels Jueus de Girona** (Carrer de la Força 8; adult/child €2/free; ⏲10am-8pm Mon-Sat, to 2pm Sun Jul & Aug, shorter hr rest of yr).

Sleeping & Eating

Bed & Breakfast Bells Oficis B&B **€€**

(☎972 22 81 70; www.bellsoficis.com; Carrer dels Germans Busquels 2; r incl breakfast €40-85; ❄📶) Up the wobbly-winding staircase of a 19th-century building right in the heart of Girona you'll discover six very desirable rooms, lovingly restored by knowledgeable Javi and his wife. Some have unusual pebble art in the bathrooms, while others have views over the street.

Casa Cúndaro BOUTIQUE HOTEL **€€**

(☎972 22 35 83; www.casacundaro.com; Pujada de la Catedral 9; d €60-80; 📶) The understated exterior of this medieval Jewish house, run by a friendly family, hides five sumptuous rooms and four self-catering apartments – all combining original exposed stone walls with modern luxuries, such as satellite TV.

Hotel Llegendes de Girona HOTEL **€€€**

(☎972 22 09 05; www.llegendeshotel.com; Portal de la Barca 4; d from €123, 'Fountain of Lovers' room €288; P❄📶) The rooms at this restored 18th-century building are supremely comfortable, with all manner of high-tech gadgets, and the all-glass bathrooms have huge rain showers. This incongruous blend of modernity and antiquity includes a guide to tantric sex positions in each room; three of the rooms even have an 'Eros' sofa to try them out on.

TOP CHOICE **Restaurant Txalaka** BASQUE **€€**

(☎972 22 59 75; www.restauranttxalaka.com; Carrer Bonastruc de Porta 4; mains €17-23, pintxos €2.50-4; ⏲closed Sun) For sensational Basque cooking and *pintxos* washed down with *txakoli* (the fizzy white wine from the Basque coast) poured from a great height, don't miss this popular local spot.

L'Alqueria CATALAN **€€**

(☎972 22 18 82; www.restaurantalqueria.com; Carrer de la Ginesta 8; mains €18-22; ⏲lunch & dinner Wed-Sat, lunch only Tue & Sun) This smart minimalist *arrocería* serves the finest *arrós negre* (rice cooked in cuttlefish ink) and *arrós a la Catalan* in the city, as well as around 20 other superbly executed rice dishes, including paellas. Book ahead for dinner.

Information

Tourist Office (www.girona.cat; Joan Maragall 2; ⏲8am-8pm Mon-Fri, 8am-2pm & 4-8pm Sat, 9am-2pm Sun)

Getting There & Away

AIR Girona-Costa Brava airport, 11km south of the centre and just off the AP7 and A2, is Ryanair's Spanish hub.

TRAIN There are more than 20 trains per day to Figueres (€4.80 to €14.10, 30 to 40 minutes) and Barcelona (from €9.70, 1½ hours).

The Costa Brava

The Costa Brava (Rugged Coast) was Catalonia's first tourist centre, and after you visit its rocky coastline, romantic coves, turquoise waters and former fishing villages, you'll see why. Overdevelopment has ruined some stretches but much of the coast retains its spectacular beauty.

Sights & Activities

The Costa Brava is all about picturesque inlets and coves – and there are many. Although buses run along much of the coast, the best way to uncover some of these gems is with your own wheels.

The first truly pretty stop on the Costa Brava when heading northeast from Barcelona is **Tossa de Mar**, with its golden beach, ochre medieval village core and nearby coves. The coast road on to **Sant Feliu de Guíxols** is spectacular.

Further north are three gorgeous beach towns near Palafrugell: **Tamariu** (the smallest, least crowded and most exclusive), **Llafranc** (the biggest and busiest) and **Calella de Palafrugell**. There are further fine beaches and coves on the coast near Begur, a little further north.

North of the Costa Brava's main dive centre, **L'Estartit**, are the ruins of the Greek and Roman town of **Empúries** (☎972 77 02 08; www.mac.cat; adult/child €3/free; ⏲10am-8pm Jun-Sep, to 6pm Oct-May), 2km outside **L'Escala**.

Cadaqués, at the end of an agonising series of hairpin bends one hour from Figueres, is postcard perfect. Beaches are of the pebbly variety, so people spend a lot of time sitting at waterfront cafes or strolling. It's a pleasant 2km walk from central Cadaqués to Port Lligat, where you'll find Dalí's summer residence. Some 10km northeast of Cadaqués is **Cap de Creus**, an impressive cape that is Spain's easternmost point.

Of the many historic towns inland from the Costa Brava, the pretty walled town of **Pals**, 6km inland from Begur, and the nearby impeccably preserved medieval hamlet of **Peratallada** are the most charming.

Sleeping & Eating

TOSSA DE MAR

TOP CHOICE **Hostal Cap d'Or** HOSTAL €€
(☎972 34 00 81; www.hotelcapdor.com; Passeig de la Vila Vella 1; s/d incl breakfast €63/103; ❄☎) Rub up against the town's history in this family-run spot right in front of the town walls. Rooms are lovingly decorated in sea-blues and whites, and the best of them look straight onto the beach.

Hotel Diana HOTEL €€€
(☎972 34 18 86; www.hotelesdante.com; Plaça d'Espanya 6; d incl breakfast €145, with sea views €170-180; ⊙Apr-Nov; P❄☎) Fronting Platja Gran, this artistic 1920s hotel has a Gaudí-built fireplace in the lounge and oozes Modernista decor and has stained glass in the central covered courtyard. Half of the spacious, tiled rooms have beach views.

TOP CHOICE **La Cuina de Can Simon** CATALAN €€€
(☎972 34 12 69; www.lacuinadecansimon.com; Carrer del Portal 24; mains €30-50, taster menus €68-98; ⊙lunch & dinner Wed-Sat & Mon, lunch Sun) Tossa's culinary star nestles by the old walls in a former fisherman's stone house and distinguishes itself by the most imaginative creations in town. Taking the *mar i muntanya* theme to its logical extreme, it presents you with pig trotters with sea cucumber as well as the more mainstream *fideuá* with rock fish.

CADAQUÉS

Hostal Vehí PENSION €€
(☎972 25 84 70; www.hostalvehi.com; Carrer de l'Església 5; s/d without bathroom €30/55, d with bathroom €77; ❄☎) Near the church in the heart of the old town, this simple *pensión* with clean-as-a-whistle rooms, run by a friendly family, tends to be booked up for July and August. It's a pain to get to if you have a lot of luggage, but it's easily the cheapest deal in town, and also about the best. Breakfast is €6 extra.

Information

There are tourist offices in **Palafrugell** (☎972 61 44 75; Carrer de les Voltes 6; ⊙10am-8pm Jul-Aug, shorter hr rest of year) and other towns on the coast and inland.

Getting There & Away

Sarfa (☎902 30 20 25; www.sarfa.com) runs buses from Barcelona, Girona and Figueres to most towns along the Costa Brava.

Tarragona

POP 133,223

Barcelona's senior in Roman times (when the city was called Tarraco) and a lesser medieval city, Tarragona is a provincial sort of place with some outstanding attractions: Catalonia's finest Roman ruins, a magnificent medieval cathedral in a pretty old town and some decent beaches.

Sights

Museu d'Història de Tarragona RUINS
(MHT; www.museutgn.com; adult/child per site €3/free, all MHT sites €10/free; ⊙9am-9pm daily Easter-Sep, shorter hr rest of yr) The 'museum' title is somewhat misleading, as they are in fact four separate Roman sites (which, since 2000, together have constituted a Unesco World Heritage site).

Start exploring with the **Pretori i Circ Romans** (Plaça del Rei), which includes part of the vaults of the Roman circus, where chariot races were once held, ending at the Pretori tower on Plaça de Rei. Near the beach is the crown jewel of Tarragona's Roman sites, the well-preserved **Amfiteatre Romá** (Plaça d'Arce Ochotorena; ⊙9am-9pm Tue-Sat, to 3pm Sun Easter-Sep, to 5pm Tue-Sat, 10am-3pm Sun & holidays Oct-Easter), where gladiators battled either each other or wild animals to the death. Much of the amphitheatre was picked to bits and the stone used to build the port, so what you see now is partial reconstruction. The northwest half of **Fórum Romá** (Carrer del Cardenal Cervantes) was occupied by a judicial basilica (where legal disputes were settled), from where the rest of the forum stretched downhill to the southwest. Linked to the site by a footbridge is another excavated area which includes a stretch of Roman street. The **Passeig Arqueològic** (admission €3; ⊙9am-9pm Tue-Sat,

9am-3pm Sun Easter-Oct, shorter hr rest of yr) is a peaceful walk around part of the perimeter of the old town.

Museu Nacional Arqueològic de Tarragona MUSEUM
(www.mnat.es; Plaça del Rei 5; adult/child €3.50/free; ⌚10am-8pm Tue-Sat, to 2pm Sun & holidays Jun-Sep, shorter hr rest of yr) This carefully presented museum gives further insight into Roman Tarraco. Exhibits include part of the Roman city walls, mosaics, frescoes, sculpture and pottery.

Catedral CATHEDRAL
(Pla de la Seu; adult/child €4/1.40; ⌚10am-7pm Mon-Sat Jun–mid-Oct, shorter hr rest of yr) Sitting grandly at the top of the old town, Tarragona's cathedral demands a solid chunk of your time. Built between 1171 and 1331 on the site of a Roman temple, it combines Romanesque and Gothic features, as typified by the main facade on Pla de la Seu. The entrance is by the cloister on the northwest flank of the building. The cloister and its perfectly presented gardens have Gothic vaulting and Romanesque carved capitals.

Sleeping & Eating

Look for tapas bars and inexpensive cafes on the Plaça de la Font. The Moll de Pescadors (Fishermen's Wharf) is the place to go for seafood restaurants.

Hotel Plaça de la Font HOTEL €€
(☎977 24 61 34; www.hotelpdelafont.com; Plaça de la Font 26; s/d €55/70; ❄) Simple, spic-and-span rooms overlooking a bustling terrace in a you-can't-get-more-central-than-this location, right on the popular Plaça de la Font.

Hotel Lauria HOTEL €€
(☎977 23 67 12; www.hotel-lauria.com; Rambla Nova 20; s/d from €49/69; P❄📶🏊) In the newer part of town, a five-minute walk from the medieval part, this smart hotel offers modern rooms with welcome splashes of colour, large bathrooms and a small swimming pool.

Arcs Restaurant MEDITERRANEAN €€
(☎977 21 80 40; www.restaurantarcs.com; Carrer Misser Sitges 13; menu €23; ⌚lunch & dinner Tue-Sat) Inside a medieval cavern with bright splashes of colour in the form of contemporary art, you are served some wonderful takes on Mediterranean dishes, including the most intense *salmorejo* (a cold, tomato-based soup) outside Andalucía.

Aq CATALAN €€
(☎977 21 59 54; www.aq-restaurant.com; Carrer de les Coques 7; menus from €18; ⌚lunch & dinner Tue-Sat) This is a bubbly designer haunt with stark colour contrasts (black, lemon and cream linen), slick lines and intriguing plays on traditional cooking.

Information

Regional Tourist Office (Carrer de Fortuny 4; ⌚9am-2pm & 4-6.30pm Mon-Fri, 9am-2pm Sat)

Tourist Office (www.tarragonaturisme.cat; Carrer Major 39; ⌚10am-8pm Mon-Sat, to 2pm Sun Jul-Oct, 10am-2pm & 4-7pm Mon-Sat)

Getting There & Away

BUS Services run to Barcelona, Valencia, Zaragoza, Madrid, Alicante, Pamplona, the main Andalucian cities, Andorra and the north coast. The bus station is around 1.5km northwest of the old town.

TRAIN At least 16 regional trains per day run to/from Barcelona's Passeig de Gràcia via Sants. Fares start at €15.90 and go up to €35.10; the journey takes one to 1½ hours.

ARAGÓN, BASQUE COUNTRY & NAVARRA

This northeastern area of Spain is brimming with fascinating destinations: the arid hills and proud history of Aragón; the lush coastline and gourmet delights of the Basque Country (País Vasco); and the wine country and famous festivals of Navarra.

Aragón

Zaragoza is the capital of the expansive Aragón region, though by no means is the city its only attraction. The national parks and pretty towns of the Pyrenees are well worth exploring too.

ZARAGOZA

POP 674,725

Sitting on the banks of the mighty Ebro River, Zaragoza (a contraction of Caesaraugusta, the name the Romans gave to this city when they founded it in 14 BC) is a busy regional capital with a seemingly voracious appetite for eating out and late-night revelry. The historic old centre, crowned by the majestic Basílica del Pilar, throws up echoes of its Roman and Muslim past. The old town is also home to El Tubo (The Tube), a maze of streets with countless tapas bars and cafes.

Sights

FREE Basílica de Nuestra Señora del Pilar CHURCH
(Plaza del Pilar; lift admission €2; ⏲7am-8.30pm, lift 10am-1.30pm & 4-6.30pm Tue-Sun) Brace yourself for the saintly and the solemn in this great baroque cavern of Catholicism. It was here on 2 January AD 40, that Santiago (St James the Apostle) is believed by the faithful to have seen the Virgin Mary descend atop a marble *pilar* (pillar). A chapel was built around the remaining pillar, followed by a series of ever-more-grandiose churches, culminating in the enormous basilica that you see today. Originally designed in 1681, it was greatly modified in the 18th century and the towers were not finished until the early 20th century. The exterior, with its splendid main dome lording over a flurry of 10 mini-domes, each encased in chunky blue, green, yellow and white tiles, creates a kind of rugged Byzantine effect. A **lift** whisks you most of the way up the north tower (Torre Pilar) for fine views.

Aljafería PALACE
(Calle de los Diputados; adult/under 12yr €3/free, free Sun; ⏲10am-2pm Sat-Wed, 4.30-8pm Mon-Wed, Fri & Sat Jul & Aug, shorter hr rest of year) La Aljafería is Spain's finest Islamic-era edifice outside Andalucía. It's not in the league of Granada's Alhambra or Córdoba's Mezquita, but it's nonetheless a glorious monument. The Aljafería was built as a pleasure palace for Zaragoza's Islamic rulers, chiefly in the 11th century. After the city passed into Christian hands in 1118, Zaragoza's Christian rulers made alterations.

Inside the main gate, cross the rather dull introductory courtyard into a second, the Patio de Santa Isabel, once the central courtyard of the Islamic palace. Here you're confronted by the delicate interwoven arches typical of the geometric mastery of Islamic architecture.

La Seo CHURCH
(Catedral de San Salvador; Plaza de la Seo; admission €4; ⏲10am-6pm Tue-Fri, 10am-2pm & 3-6pm Sat, 10-11.30am & 2.30-6pm Sun Jun-Sep) La Seo may lack the fame of the Basílica de Nuestra Señora del Pilar, but its interior is easily its architectural superior. Built between the 12th and 17th centuries, it displays a fabulous spread of architectural styles from Romanesque to baroque.

FREE Museo Camón Aznar MUSEUM
(Museo Ibercaja; Calle de Espoz y Mina 23; ⏲10am-1.45pm & 5-8.45pm Tue-Sat, 10am-1.45pm Sun) This collection of Spanish art through the ages is dominated by an extraordinary series of etchings by Goya (on the 2nd floor), one of the premier such collections in existence. You'll also find paintings by other luminaries (including Ribera and Zurbarán), which spread over the three storeys of the Palacio de los Pardo, a Renaissance mansion.

Museo del Foro de Caesaraugusta MUSEUM
(Plaza de la Seo 2; admission €2.50; ⏲9am-8.30pm Tue-Sat, 10am-2pm Sun Jun-Sep, shorter hr rest of year) The trapezoid building on Plaza de la Seo is the entrance to an excellent reconstruction of part of Roman Caesaraugusta's forum, now well below ground level.

Museo del Teatro de Caesaraugusta RUIN, MUSEUM
(Calle de San Jorge 12; admission €3.50; ⏲9am-8.30pm Tue-Sat, to 1.30pm Sun) Discovered during the excavation of a building site in 1972, the ruins of Zaragoza's Roman theatre are the focus of this interesting museum; the theatre once seated 6000 spectators.

Sleeping

TOP CHOICE Sabinas APARTMENT €
(☎976 20 47 10; www.sabinas.es; Calle de Alfonso I 43; d/apt €50/75; ❄📶) Apartments with a kitchen and sitting room styled with a contemporary look and a location a few steps off Plaza del Pilar make this a terrific option. The bathrooms are lovely and the price is extraordinarily good considering the location and size of the rooms. Reception is at **Hotel Sauce** (☎976 20 50 50; www.hotelsauce.com; Calle de Espoz y Mina 33), around the corner.

Hotel Las Torres HOTEL €€
(☎976 39 42 50; www.hotellastorres.com; Plaza del Pilar 11; s/d incl breakfast from €75/85; ❄📶) The rooms are designer cool with dazzling white furnishings and daring wallpaper in the public spaces. The bathrooms have hydromassage showers, and the views of the square and basilica from the balconies in most rooms are simply stunning. Our only complaint? Two years after it opened, the fittings are already showing considerable wear and tear.

Hostal el Descanso HOSTAL €
(☎976 29 17 41; www.hostaleldescanso.es; Calle de San Lorenzo 2; s/d without bathroom €18/30;) This welcoming family-run place combines a terrific location overlooking a pretty plaza near the Roman theatre with simple, bright rooms with comfortable mattresses. It adds up to one of the best budget choices in town.

Eating & Drinking

Zaragoza has some terrific tapas bars, with dozens of places on or close to Plaza de Santa Marta. Otherwise the narrow streets of El Tubo, north of Plaza de España, are tapas central.

Calle del Temple, southwest of Plaza del Pilar, is the spiritual home of Zaragoza's roaring nightlife. This is where the city's students head out to drink. There are more bars lined up along this street than anywhere else in Aragón.

Casa Pascualillo TAPAS €
(Calle de la Libertad 5; mains €5-14; lunch & dinner Tue-Sat, lunch Sun) This celebrated bar groans under the weight of enticing tapas varieties; the house speciality is El Pascualillo, a 'small' *bocadillo* (filled roll) of *jamón,* mushrooms and onion. There's also a more formal restaurant attached.

Mery Limón Gastrobar INTERNATIONAL €€
(www.merylimon.com; Calle de Santiago 30; mains €6-14, menú del día €15) This terrific little bar has an unusual menu divided into three parts – Italian, New York and Mediterranean. But what really stands out is the *menú del día* (daily set menu), which combines seven small dishes from the cutting-edge of Spanish gastronomy, and wines to go with them.

El Rincón de Aragón ARAGONESE €€
(☎976 20 11 63; Calle de Santiago 3-5; mains €10-20) The decor here is basic and the food stripped down to its essence, but the eating is top-notch and ideal for finding out why people get excited about Aragonese cooking. If you're feeling hungry, numerous local dishes appear on the four-course *menú Aragonés.* The restaurant is in the covered lane between Calle de Santiago and Plaza del Pilar.

Information

Main Tourist Office (☎976 39 35 37; www.zaragozaturismo.com; Plaza del Pilar; 9am-9pm Easter-Oct, 10am-8pm Nov-Easter) The city information office.

Oficina de Turismo de Aragón (www.turismodearagon.com; Avenida de César Augusto 25; 9am-2pm & 5-8pm Mon-Fri, from 10am Sat & Sun) Covers all of Aragón region.

Getting There & Away

AIR Zaragoza-Sanjurjo airport (☎976 71 23 00) has domestic and international flights.

BUS Services from the bus station attached to the Estación Intermodal Delicias train station include Madrid (from €15.29, 3¾ hours) and Barcelona (€14.49, 3¾ hours).

TRAIN Zaragoza's **Estación Intermodal Delicias** (Calle Rioja 33) is connected by almost hourly high-speed AVE services to Madrid (€60.10, 1½ hours, 10 daily) and Barcelona (€65.80, from 1½ hours). There are also trains to Valencia (€29.80, 4½ hours, three daily) and Teruel (€16.55, 2¼ hours, four daily).

Around Aragón

In Aragón's south, little visited **Teruel** is home to some stunning Mudéjar architecture. Nearby, **Albarracín** is one of Spain's most beautiful villages.

In the north, the Pyrenees dominate and the **Parque Nacional de Ordesa y Monte Perdido** is excellent for hiking; the pretty village of **Torla** is the gateway. South of the hamlet of **La Besurta** is the great Maladeta massif, a superb challenge for experienced climbers. This forbidding line of icy peaks, with glaciers suspended from the higher crests, culminates in **Aneto** (3404m), the highest peak in the Pyrenees. There are plenty of hiking and climbing options for all levels in these mountain parks bordering France. Another enchanting base for exploration in the region is **Aínsa**, a hilltop village of stone houses.

In Aragón's northwest, **Sos del Rey Católico** is another gorgeous stone village draped along a ridge.

Basque Country

The Basques, whose language is believed to be among the world's oldest, claim two of Spain's most interesting cities – San Sebastián and Bilbao – as their own. Stately San Sebastián offers a slick seaside position and some of the best food Spain has to offer. Bilbao has the extraordinary Guggenheim Bilbao museum as its centrepiece.

SAN SEBASTIÁN

POP 185,500

Stylish San Sebastián (Donostia in Basque) has the air of an upscale resort, complete with an idyllic location on the shell-shaped Bahía de la Concha. The natural setting – crystalline waters, a flawless beach, green hills on all sides – is captivating. But this is one of Spain's true culinary capitals, with more Michelin stars (14) per capita here than anywhere else on earth.

Sights & Activities

Beaches & Isla de Santa Clara BEACH

Fulfilling almost every idea of how a perfect city beach should be formed, **Playa de la Concha** and its westerly extension, **Playa de Ondarreta**, are easily among the best city beaches in Europe. The **Isla de Santa Clara**, about 700m from the beach, is accessible by **glass-bottom boats** (to the island €3.80, tour the bay €6) that run every half-hour from June to September from the fishing port. Less popular, but just as showy, **Playa de Gros** (Playa de la Zurriola), east of Río Urumea, is the city's main surf beach.

Museo Chillida Leku MUSEUM, PARK

(www.museochillidaleku.com; adult/child €8.50/free; ⏲10.30am-8pm Mon-Sat, to 3pm Sun Jul & Aug, shorter hr rest of year) This open-air museum is the most engaging one in rural Basque Country. Amid the beech, oak and magnolia trees, you'll find 40 sculptures of granite and iron created by the renowned Basque sculptor Eduardo Chillida. Many more of Chillida's works appear inside the renovated 16th-century farmhouse.

To get here, take the G2 bus (€1.35) for Hernani from Calle de Okendo in San Sebastián and get off at Zabalaga.

Aquarium AQUARIUM

(www.aquariumss.com; Paseo del Muelle 34; adult/4-12yr €12/6; ⏲10am-8pm Mon-Fri, to 9pm Sat & Sun Apr-Jun & Sep, shorter hr rest of year) In San Sebastián's excellent aquarium, huge sharks bear down on you, and you'll be tripped out by fancy fluoro jellyfish. The highlights of a visit are the cinema-screen-sized deep-ocean and coral-reef exhibits and the long tunnel, around which swim monsters of the deep.

Monte Igueldo VIEWPOINT

The views from the summit of Monte Igueldo, just west of town, will make you feel like a circling hawk staring over the vast panorama of the Bahía de la Concha and the surrounding coastline and mountains. The best way to get there is via the old-world **funicular railway** (return adult/child €2.80/2.10; ⏲10am-10pm).

San Telmo Museoa MUSEUM

(☎943 48 15 80; www.santelmomuseoa.com; Plaza Zuloaga 1; adult/child €5/free, free Tue; ⏲10am-8pm Tue-Sun) This museum of Basque culture and society has displays that range from historical artefacts to the squiggly lines of modern art, and all the pieces are supposed to reflect Basque culture and society in some way or another.

Monte Urgull CASTLE, MUSEUM

You can walk to the top of Monte Urgull, topped by low castle walls and a grand statue of Christ, by taking a path from Plaza de Zuloaga or from behind San Sebastián's aquarium. The views are breathtaking. The castle houses the well-presented **Mirando a San Sebastián** (admission free; ⏲10am-2pm & 3-5.30pm), a small museum focusing on the city's history.

Sleeping

Pensión Bellas Artes BOUTIQUE HOTEL €€

(☎943 47 49 05; www.pension-bellasartes.com; Calle de Urbieta 64; s €69-89, d €89-109; 📶) To call this magnificent place a mere *pensión* is to do it something of a disservice. Its rooms (some with glassed-in balconies), with their exposed stone walls and excellent bathrooms, should be the envy of many a more-expensive hotel. It also has to be the friendliest hotel in town.

Pensión Aida BOUTIQUE HOTEL €€

(☎943 32 78 00; www.pensionesconencanto.com; Calle de Iztueta 9; s €60, d €82-88, studios €130-150; ❄@📶) The rooms here are bright and bold, full of exposed stone and everything smells fresh and clean. The communal area, stuffed with soft sofas and mountains of information, is a big plus. For our money, we'd say this one is very hard to beat.

Pensión Amaiur Ostatua BOUTIQUE HOTEL €

(☎943 42 96 54; www.pensionamaiur.com; Calle de 31 de Agosto 44; s €45, d €54-65; @📶) This old town classic has always been one of the city's stand out accommodation options. At the time of research it was closed for major renovations that promise to make it even better than before. It will have re-opened by the time this book hits the shelves.

Pensión Altair PENSION €€
(☎943 29 31 33; www.pension-altair.com; Calle Padre Larroca 3; s/d €60/86; ❄@📶) This *pensión* is in a beautifully restored town house, with unusual church-worthy arched windows and modern, minimalist rooms that are a world away from the fusty decor of the old-town *pensiones*. Reception is closed between 1.30pm and 5pm.

Eating

San Sebastián is paradise for food lovers. Considered the birthplace of *nueva cocina española* (Spanish nouvelle cuisine), this area is home to some of the country's top chefs. Yet not all the good food is pricey. Head to the Parte Vieja for San Sebastián's *pintxos,* Basque-style tapas.

Do what the locals do – go on crawls of the city centre's bars. *Pintxo* etiquette is simple. Ask for a plate and point out what *pintxos* (bar snacks – more like tasty mounds of food on little slices of baguette) you want. Keep the toothpicks and go back for as many as you'd like. Accompany with *txakoli,* a cloudy white wine poured like cider to create a little fizz. When you're ready to pay, hand over the plate with all the toothpicks and tell the bar staff how many drinks you've had. It's an honour system that has stood the test of time. Expect to pay €2.50 to €3.50 for a *pintxo* and *txakoli.*

TOP CHOICE **La Cuchara de San Telmo** BASQUE €€
(www.lacucharadesantelmo.com; Calle de 31 de Agosto 28) This unfussy, hidden-away (and hard to find) bar offers miniature *nueva cocina vasca* from a supremely creative kitchen. Chefs Alex Montiel and Iñaki Gulin conjure up delights and a percentage of profits goes to the Fundación Vicente Ferrer charity.

Arzak BASQUE €€€
(☎943 27 84 65; www.arzak.info; Avenida Alcalde Jose Elosegui 273; meals €175; ⌚closed Sun-Mon & Nov & late Jun) With three shining Michelin stars, acclaimed chef Juan Mari Arzak takes some beating when it comes to *nueva cocina vasca* and his restaurant is, not surprisingly, considered one of the best places to eat in Spain. Arzak is now assisted by his daughter Elena and they never cease to innovate. Reservations, well in advance, are obligatory. The restaurant is about 1.5km east of San Sebastián.

Astelena BASQUE €€
(Calle de Iñigo 1) The *pintxos* draped across the counter in this bar, tucked into the corner of Plaza de la Constitución, stand out as some of the best in the city. Many of them are a fusion of Basque and Asian inspirations, but the best of all are perhaps the foie-gras-based treats.

Restaurante Alberto SEAFOOD €
(☎943 42 88 84; Calle de 31 de Agosto 19; menus €15; ⌚closed Tue) A charming old seafood restaurant with a fishmonger-style window display of the day's catch. It's small and friendly and the pocket-sized dining room feels like it was once someone's living room. The food is earthy and good and the service swift.

La Mejillonera BASQUE €€
(Calle del Puerto 15, mussels from €3) If you thought mussels only came with garlic sauce, come here to discover mussels by the thousand in all their glorious forms. Mussels not for you? Opt for the calamari and *patatas bravas* (fried potatoes with a spicy tomato and mayo sauce). We promise you won't regret it.

Information

Street signs are in Basque and Spanish.

Oficina de Turismo (☎943 48 11 66; www.sansebastianturismo.com; Alameda del Boulevard 8; ⌚9.30am-1.30pm & 3.30-7pm Mon-Thu, 10am-7pm Fri & Sat, 10am-2pm Sun)

Getting There & Away

AIR The city's **airport** (☎902 404704; www.aena.es) is 22km out of town, near Hondarribia. There are regular flights to Madrid and occasional charters to European cities.

BUS Daily bus services leave for Bilbao (€10.10 to €14, one hour), Bilbao Airport (€15.70, 1¼ hours), Biarritz (France; €6.60, 1¼ hours), Madrid (from €33.60, five hours) and Pamplona (€7.29, one hour).

TRAIN The main **Renfe train station** (Paseo de Francia) is just across Río Urumea. There are regular services to Madrid (from €54.20, five hours) and Barcelona (from €63.30, eight hours). There's only one direct train to Paris, but there are plenty more from the Spanish/French border town of Irun (or sometimes Hendaye) (€2.20, 25 minutes), which is also served by **Eusko Tren/Ferrocarril Vasco** (www.euskotren.es). Trains depart every half-hour from Amara train station, about 1km south of the city centre.

BILBAO

POP 351,300

The commercial hub of the Basque Country, Bilbao (Bilbo in Basque) is best known for the magnificent Guggenheim Museum. An architectural masterpiece by Frank Gehry, the museum was the catalyst of a turnaround that saw Bilbao transformed from an industrial port city into a vibrant cultural centre. After visiting this must-see temple to modern art, spend time exploring Bilbao's Casco Viejo (Old Quarter), a grid of elegant streets dotted with shops, cafes, *pintxos* bars and several small but worthy museums.

Sights

Museo Guggenheim MUSEUM

(www.guggenheim-bilbao.es; Avenida Abandoibarra 2; adult/child €13/free; ⏲10am-8pm, closed Mon Sep-Jun) Opened in 1997, Bilbao's Museo Guggenheim lifted modern architecture and Bilbao into the 21st century – with sensation. Some might say, probably quite rightly, that structure overwhelms function here and that the Guggenheim is more famous for its architecture than its content. But Canadian architect Frank Gehry's inspired use of flowing canopies, cliffs, promontories, ship shapes, towers and flying fins is irresistible. The interior of the Guggenheim is purposefully vast. The cathedral-like atrium is more than 45m high. Light pours in through the glass cliffs. Permanent exhibits fill the ground floor and include such wonders as mazes of metal and phrases of light reaching for the skies. For most people, though, it is the temporary exhibitions that are the main attraction (check the Guggenheim's website for a full program of upcoming exhibitions).

Museo de Bellas Artes MUSEUM

(Fine Arts Museum; www.museobilbao.com; Plaza del Museo 2; adult/child €6/free, free Wed; ⏲10am-8pm Tue-Sun) A mere five minutes from Museo Guggenheim is Bilbao's Museo de Bellas Artes. There are three main subcollections: Classical Art, with works by Murillo, Zurbarán, El Greco, Goya and van Dyck; Contemporary Art, featuring works by Gauguin, Francis Bacon and Anthony Caro; and Basque Art, with the works of the great sculptors Jorge de Oteiza and Eduardo Chillida, and also strong paintings by the likes of Ignacio Zuloago and Juan de Echevarria.

Casco Viejo OLD TOWN

The compact Casco Viejo, Bilbao's atmospheric old quarter, is full of charming streets, boisterous bars, and plenty of quirky and independent shops. At the heart of the Casco are Bilbao's original 'seven streets', Las Siete Calles, which date from the 1400s. The 14th-century Gothic **Catedral de Santiago** (Plaza de Santiago; ⏲10am-1pm & 4-7pm Tue-Sat, 10.30am-1.30pm Sun) has a splendid Renaissance portico and pretty little cloister. Further north, the 19th-century arcaded Plaza Nueva is a rewarding *pintxo* haunt.

Euskal Museoa MUSEUM

(Museo Vasco; Plaza Miguel Unamuno 4; adult/child €3/free, free Thu; ⏲11am-5pm Tue-Sat, to 2pm Sun) This is probably the most complete museum of Basque culture and history in all the Basque regions. The story kicks off back in the days of prehistory and from this murky period the displays bound rapidly through to the modern age. The museum is housed in a fine old building, at the centre of which is a peaceful cloister that was part of an original 17th-century Jesuit College.

Sleeping

The Bilbao tourism authority has a useful **reservations department** (☎902 877298; www.bilbaoreservas.com) for accommodation.

Pensión Iturrienea Ostatua BOUTIQUE HOTEL €

(☎944 16 15 00; www.iturrieneaostatua.com; Calle de Santa María 14; r €50-70; 📶) Easily the most eccentric hotel in Bilbao, it's part farmyard, part old-fashioned toyshop, and a work of art in its own right. The nine rooms here are so full of character that there'll be barely enough room for your own! There's a lovely breakfast area and, with baby beds and chairs and lots of toys, it's family friendly.

Hostal Begoña BOUTIQUE HOTEL €

(☎944 23 01 34; www.hostalbegona.com; Calle de la Amistad 2; s/d from €50/55; @📶) Begoña speaks for itself with colourful rooms decorated with modern artworks, all with funky tiled bathrooms and wrought-iron beds. It's probably the best hotel in the city in which to meet other travellers. There's a car park nearby.

Gran Hotel Domine DESIGN HOTEL €€€

(☎944 25 33 00; www.granhoteldominebilbao.com; Alameda Mazarredo 61; r from €132; P❄@📶) Designer chic all the way, from the Javier Mariscal interiors to the Phillipe Starck and Arne Jacobsen fittings – and that's just in the toilets. This stellar showpiece of the Silken chain has views of the Guggenheim from some of its pricier rooms, a giant column of rounded beach stones reaching for the heavens and a water feature filled with plates and glasses.

Eating

Rio-Oja BASQUE €
(☎944 15 08 71; Calle de Perro 4; mains €8-11) An institution that shouldn't be missed. It specialises in light Basque seafood and heavy inland fare, but to most foreigners the snails, sheep brains or squid floating in pools of its own ink are the makings of a culinary adventure story they'll be recounting for years.

Mina Restaurante BASQUE €€€
(☎944 79 59 38; www.restaurantemina.es; Muelle Marzana; tasting menu from €61) Offering unexpected sophistication and fine dining in an otherwise fairly grimy neighbourhood, this riverside, and appropriately fish-based, restaurant has been making waves in the Bilbao culinary world, with some critics citing it as the new *número uno* of Basque cooking. Reservations are essential.

Nerua BASQUE €€€
(☎944 00 04 30; www.nerua.com; tasting menu €80; ⊙closed Mon & Jan–mid-Feb) The Guggenheim's modernist, chic restaurant, Nerua, is under the direction of super chef Josean Martínez Alija. Needless to say, the *nueva cocina vasca* (Basque nouvelle cuisine) is breathtaking – even the olives come from 1000-year-old olive trees! Reservations are essential. If the gourmet restaurant is too extravagant for you try El Goog's bistro, which has set menus from €18.

Information

Tourist Office (www.bilbao.net/bilbaoturismo; Plaza del Ensanche 11; ⊙9am-2pm & 4-7.30pm Mon-Fri) Other branches at the Teatro Arriaga, Museo Guggenheim and airport.

Getting There & Away

AIR Bilbao's **airport** (BIO; ☎902 404704; www.aena.es), with domestic and a handful of international flights, is near Sondika, 12km northeast of the city. The airport bus Bizkaibus A3247 (€1.30, 30 minutes) runs to/from Termibus (bus station), where there is a tram stop and a metro station.

BUS Regular services operate to/from Madrid (€28.45, 4¾ hours), Barcelona (€43.81, seven hours), Pamplona (€13.75, two hours) and Santander (from €7.02, 1¼ hours).

TRAIN Two Renfe trains runs daily to Madrid (from €50.50, six hours) and Barcelona (€64.80, six hours) from the Abando train station. Slow **FEVE** (www.feve.es) trains run from Concordia station, heading west into Cantabria and Asturias.

Navarra

Navarra, historically and culturally linked to the Basque Country, is known for its fine wines and for the Sanfermines festival in Pamplona.

PAMPLONA

POP 195,800

Immortalised by Ernest Hemingway in *The Sun Also Rises,* the pre-Pyrenean city of Pamplona (Iruña in Basque) is home of the wild Sanfermines (aka Encierro or Running of the Bulls) festival, but is also an extremely walkable city that's managed to mix the charm of old plazas and buildings with modern shops and a lively nightlife.

Sights

Catedral CHURCH
(Calle Dormitalería; guided tours adult/child €4.40/2.60; ⊙10am-7pm Mon-Fri, to 2pm Sat mid-Jul–mid-Sep) Pamplona's main cathedral stands on a rise just inside the city ramparts amid a dark thicket of narrow streets. It's a late-medieval Gothic gem spoiled only by its rather dull neoclassical facade, an 18th-century appendage. The real joys are the vast interior and the Gothic cloister, where there is marvellous delicacy in the stonework.

Ciudadela & Parks FORTRESS, PARK
(Avenida del Ejército) The walls and bulwarks of the grand fortified citadel, the star-shaped Ciudadela, lurk amid the verdant grass and trees in what is now a charming park, the portal to three more parks that unfold to the north and lend Pamplona a beautiful green escape.

Museo de Navarra MUSEUM
(www.cfnavarra.es/cultura/museo; Calle Cuesta de Santo Domingo 47; adult €2, free Sat afternoon & Sun; ⊙9.30am-2pm & 5-7pm Tue-Sat, 11am-2pm Sun) Housed in a former medieval hospital, this superb museum has an eclectic collection of archaeological finds (including a number of fantastic Roman mosaics unearthed mainly in southern Navarra), as well as a selection of art including Goya's *Marqués de San Adrián*.

Museo Oteiza MUSEUM
(www.museooteiza.org; Calle de la Cuesta 7, Alzuza; adult €4, free Fri; ⊙11am-7pm Tue-Sat, to 3pm

SANFERMINES

The Sanfermines festival is held from 6 to 14 July, when Pamplona is overrun with thrill-seekers, curious onlookers and, yes, bulls. The *encierro* (Running of the Bulls) begins at 8am daily, when bulls are let loose from the Coralillos Santo Domingo. The 825m race lasts just three minutes.

Since records began in 1924, 16 people have died during Pamplona's bull-run. Many of those who run are full of bravado (and/or drink) and have little idea of what they're doing. For dedicated *encierro* news, check out www.sanfermin.com.

Animal-rights groups oppose bull-running as a cruel tradition, and the participating bulls will almost certainly all be killed in the afternoon bullfight. The PETA-organised anti-bullfighting demonstration, the Running of the Nudes, takes place two days before the first bull-run.

Sun) Around 9km northeast of Pamplona in the town of Alzuza, this impressive museum contains almost 3000 pieces by the renowned Navarran sculptor Jorge Oteiza. Three buses a day run to Alzuza from Pamplona's bus station. If you're driving, Alzuza is signposted north off the NA150, just east of Huarte.

Sleeping

Accommodation is hard to come by during Sanfermines – book months in advance. Our prices don't reflect the huge (up to fivefold) mark-up you'll find in mid-July.

TOP CHOICE **Palacio Guendulain** HISTORIC HOTEL €€
(☎948 22 55 22; www.palacioguendulain.com; Calle Zapatería 53; d incl breakfast from €134; P❄📶) To call this stunning hotel, inside the converted former home of the Viceroy of New Granada, sumptuous is an understatement. The rooms contain *Princess and the Pea*–soft beds, enormous showers and regal armchairs.

Hostel Hemingway HOSTEL €
(☎948 98 38 84; www.hostelhemingway.com; Calle Amaya 26; dm €19-22, s/d from €22/42; @) Bright, funky colours predominate at this well-run hostel a few minutes' walk from the old town. The dorms have four to six beds and share three bathrooms. There's a TV lounge and a kitchen for guest use. It's just off Avenida de Carlos III.

Hotel Puerta del Camino BOUTIQUE HOTEL €€
(☎948 22 66 88; www.hotelpuertadelcamino.com; Calle Dos de Mayo 4; s/d from €89/95; P❄📶) A very stylish hotel inside a converted convent beside the northern gates to the old city. The functional rooms have clean, modern lines and it's positioned in one of the prettier, and quieter, parts of town. Some rooms have Pyrenean views.

Eating & Drinking

Central streets such as Calle de San Nicolás and Calle de la Estafeta are lined with tapas bars, many of which morph into nightspots on weekends.

Baserri BASQUE €
(☎948 22 20 21; Calle de San Nicolás 32; menú del día €14) This place has won enough *pintxo* awards that we could fill this entire book listing them. In fact, it's staggering to know that so many food awards actually exist! As you'd expect from such a certificate-studded bar, the *pintxos* and full meals are superb.

Casa Otaño BASQUE €€
(☎948 22 50 95; Calle de San Nicolás 5; mains €15-18) A little pricier than many on this street but worth the extra. Its formal atmosphere is eased by the dazzling array of pink and red flowers spilling off the balcony. Great dishes range from the locally caught trout to heavenly duck dishes. The *menú del día* is good value.

Café Iruña CAFE
(www.cafeiruna.com; Plaza del Castillo 44) Opened on the eve of Sanfermines in 1888, Café Iruña's dominant position, powerful sense of history and frilly belle-époque decor make this by far the most famous and popular watering hole in the city.

Information

Tourist Office (www.turismo.navarra.es; Calle de Esclava 1; ⏲9am-8pm Mon-Sat, to 2pm Sun)

Getting There & Away

AIR Pamplona's **airport** (☎948 16 87 00), about 7km south of the city, has regular flights to Madrid and Barcelona. Bus 16 (€1.20) travels between the city (from the bus station) and the airport.

BUS From the **main bus station** (Calle Conde Oliveto 8), buses leave for Bilbao (€14.15, two hours) and San Sebastián (€7.29, one hour).

TRAIN Pamplona's train station is linked to the city centre by bus 9 from Paseo de Sarasate every 15 minutes. Trains run to/from Madrid (€57.90, three hours, four daily) and San Sebastián (from €21.20, two hours, two daily).

CANTABRIA, ASTURIAS & GALICIA

With a landscape reminiscent of parts of the British Isles, 'Green Spain' offers great walks in national parks, seafood feasts in sophisticated towns and oodles of opportunities to plunge into the ice-cold waters of the Bay of Biscay.

Cantabria

Cantabria may be small, but it is one of Spain's more varied regions. Here you'll find green hills and jagged peaks shadowing a coastline that's home to some of Spain's prettiest villages.

SANTILLANA DEL MAR

POP 4,200

Some 34km west of the regional capital, Santander, **Santillana del Mar** (www.santillanadelmar.com) is a bijou medieval village and the obvious overnight base for visiting the nearby Cueva de Altamira.

The country's finest prehistoric art, in the Cueva de Altamira, 2km southwest of Santillana del Mar, is off-limits to all but the scientific community. Since 2002, however, the **Museo Altamira** (www.museodealtamira.mcu.es; adult/child, EU senior or student €3/free, Sun & from 2.30pm Sat free; ⌚9.30am-8pm Tue-Sat, to 3pm Sun & holidays; P) has allowed all comers to view the inspired, 14,500-year-old depictions of bison, horses and other beasts (or rather, their replicas) in this full-size, dazzling re-creation of the cave's most interesting chamber, the Sala de Polícromos (Polychrome Hall).

Buses run three to four times a day from Santander to Santilla del Mar.

Asturias

If you ask Spaniards their favourite region of the country, many will nominate Asturias. With a gorgeous coast, the spectacular Picos de Europa and a food culture all its own, it's not difficult to see why.

WORTH A TRIP

PICOS DE EUROPA

These jagged mountains straddling Asturias, Cantabria and northeast Castilla y León amount to some of the finest walking country in Spain.

They comprise three limestone massifs (whose highest peak rises 2648m). The 647-sq-km **Parque Nacional de los Picos de Europa** (www.picosdeeuropa.com) covers all three massifs and is Spain's second-biggest national park.

There are numerous places to stay and eat all over the mountains. Getting here and around by bus can be slow going but the Picos are accessible from Santander and Oviedo (the latter is easier) by bus.

OVIEDO

POP 225,000

The elegant parks and modern shopping streets of Asturias' capital are agreeably offset by what remains of the *casco antiguo* (old town).

Just outside the city (within 3km) is a scattering of 9th-century, pre-Romanesque buildings, including the **Iglesia de San Julián de los Prados** (Iglesia de Santullano; adult/child €1.20/0.60, Mon free; ⌚10am-12.30pm Mon, 10am-12.30pm & 4-5.30pm Tue-Fri, 9.30am-noon & 3.30-5pm Sat, closed afternoons Oct-Apr), **Palacio de Santa María del Naranco** (adult/child incl Iglesia de San Miguel de Lillo €3/2, free Mon; ⌚9.30am-1pm & 3.30-7pm Tue-Sat, 9.30am-1pm Sun & Mon, shorter hours Oct-Mar) and the **Iglesia de San Miguel de Lillo** (⌚9.30am-1pm & 3.30-7pm Tue-Sat, 9.30am-1pm Sun & Mon, shorter hours Oct-Mar). Get information from the tourist offices in town.

Sights

Catedral de San Salvador CATHEDRAL

(⌚10am-7pm Mon-Sat mid-May–Sep, 10am-1pm & 4-7pm Mon-Fri, 10am-1pm & 4-6pm Sat Sep–mid-May) In a sense, the mainly Gothic edifice you see today forms the outer casing of a many-layered history in stone of Spanish Christianity. Its origins lie in the **Cámara Santa**, a chapel built by Alfonso II to house holy relics. The chapel is now the inner sanctuary of the cathedral, which was chiefly built between the 14th and 16th centuries. The **cloister** is pure 14th-century Gothic, rare enough in Asturias, and just off it the *sala capitular* (chapter house) contains some well-restored Flemish Gothic choir stalls.

Old Town HISTORIC AREA

The old town's nooks and crannies include **Plaza de la Constitución**, capped at one end by the Iglesia de San Isidoro and fronted by an eclectic collection of old shops, cafes and the 17th-century *ayuntamiento*. To the south, past the **Mercado El Fontán** food market, arcaded **Plaza Fontán** is equipped with a couple of *sidrerías* (cider houses). Other little squares include Plaza de Trascorrales, Plaza de Riego and Plaza del Paraguas.

Sleeping & Eating

Oviedo's *sidrería* rules include getting good food at reasonable prices. Calle de la Gascona is a particularly happy hunting ground.

Hotel de la Reconquista HOTEL €€

(☎985 24 11 00; www.hoteldelareconquista.com; Calle de Gil de Jaz 16; r €119-163; P❄@📶) The city's fanciest lodgings, two blocks northwest of the central Campo de San Francisco, started life as an 18th-century hospice. Built around several patios, the somewhat formal rooms come in different shapes and sizes, with timber furniture, floor-to-ceiling windows and gentle ochre-and-white colour schemes.

Hotel Fruela HOTEL €€

(☎985 20 81 20; www.hotelfruela.com; Calle de Fruela 3; r €72-79; P❄📶) With a pleasing contemporary style and a touch of original art, plus professional yet friendly service, the 28-room Fruela achieves a cosy, almost intimate feel and is easily the top midrange option in central Oviedo.

Tierra Astur SIDRERÍA €€

(☎985 20 25 02; www.tierra-astur.com; Calle de la Gascona 1; mains €9-21; ⊙lunch & dinner) A particularly atmospheric *sidrería*/restaurant, Tierra Astur is famed for its grilled meats and prize-winning cider. People queue for tables, or give up and settle for tapas at the bar. Platters of Asturian sausage, cheese or ham are a good starter option.

La Corrada del Obispo ASTURIAN €€

(☎985 22 00 48; www.lacorradadelobispo.com; Calle de la Canóniga 18; mains €16-24; ⊙closed Sun dinner, Mon) Modern decor combines with the exposed stone walls of this 18th-century house to provide a welcoming setting for fine local cooking. It offers a tempting variety of fish and meat dishes, including game such as wild boar and venison when they're in season. Woody Allen shot some scenes for *Vicky Cristina Barcelona* here.

Information

Oficina Municipal de Turismo (☎984 08 60 60; www.turismo.ayto-oviedo.es; Plaza de la Constitución 4 ; ⊙9.30am-7.30pm)

Oficina de Turismo de Asturias (☎902 300202; www.infoasturias.com; Calle de Cimadevilla 4; ⊙10am-7pm Mon-Sat year-round, to 5pm Sun Jul & Aug)

Getting There & Away

AIR The **Aeropuerto de Asturias** (☎902 404704) is at Santiago del Monte, 47km northwest of Oviedo and 40km west of Gijón. There are flights to European cities and around Spain. Buses run hourly to/from Oviedo's ALSA bus station (€7.50, 45 minutes).

BUS From the **ALSA bus station** (☎902 422242; www.alsa.es; Calle de Magnus Blikstad), 300m northeast of the train station, direct services head to Gijón (€2.25, 30 minutes) every 10 or 15 minutes. Other daily buses head to Asturian towns, Galicia, Cantabria and elsewhere.

TRAIN One **station** (Avenida de Santander; 📶) serves both train companies, Renfe and FEVE (for buses to Santander and Bilbao), the latter located on the upper level. **Renfe** (www.renfe.com) runs trains to León, Madrid and Barcelona at least once daily. For Gijón, Renfe *cercanías* (local area trains; €2.85, 35 minutes) go once or twice an hour.

Galicia

Utterly unlike anywhere else in Spain, green Galicia has Spain's most beautiful coastline, fabulous food and Santiago de Compostela, one of Europe's most sacred pilgrimage destinations.

SANTIAGO DE COMPOSTELA

POP 95,400

The supposed burial place of St James (Santiago), Santiago de Compostela is a bewitching city. Christian pilgrims journeying along the Camino de Santiago often end up mute with wonder on entering its medieval centre. Fortunately, they usually regain their verbal capacities over a celebratory late-night foray into the city's lively bar scene.

Sights

TOP CHOICE **Catedral de Santiago de Compostela** CATHEDRAL

(www.catedraldesantiago.es; Praza do Obradoiro; ⊙7am-9pm) The grand heart of Santiago, the cathedral soars above the city centre in a splendid jumble of moss-covered spires and statues. Though Galicia's grandest monument was built piecemeal through the centuries, its beauty is only enhanced by the mix of Romanesque, baroque and Gothic flourishes. What you see today is actually the fourth church to stand on this spot. The bulk of it was built between 1075 and 1211, in Romanesque style with a traditional Latin-cross layout and three naves.

The main entrance is via the lavish staircase and facade on the Praza do Obradoiro, or through the south door on Praza de Praterías. The baroque **Obradoiro facade** was erected in the 18th century partly to protect the cathedral's original entrance, which is now just inside it – the artistically unparalleled Pórtico de la Gloria (Galician: Porta da Gloria), with its 200 Romanesque sculptures by Maestro Mateo.

Towards the far (west) end of the cathedral's main nave, to the right of the Churrigueresque **Altar Mayor** (main altar), a small staircase leads up above the altar to a 13th-century statue of Santiago, which the faithful queue up to embrace.

A special pilgrims' Mass is usually celebrated at noon daily, with other Masses usually at 9.30am or 10am daily, 1.15pm Sunday, 6pm Saturday and Sunday, and 7.30pm daily. Touristic visits are not allowed during these services.

For an unforgettable bird's-eye view of the city, take the **cathedral rooftop tour** (981 55 29 85; per person €10; 10am-2pm & 4-8pm).

Museo da Catedral MUSEUM

(www.catedraldesantiago.es; Praza do Obradoiro; adult/student & pilgrim/child €5/3/free; 10am-2pm & 4-8pm, closed Sun afternoon) The Cathedral Museum, entered to the right of the cathedral's Obradoiro facade, spreads over four floors and includes the cathedral's large, 16th-century, Gothic/plateresque cloister. You'll see a sizeable section of Maestro Mateo's original carved stone choir (destroyed in 1603 but recently pieced back together), an impressive collection of religious art (including the *botafumeiros*, in the 2nd-floor library), the lavishly decorated 18th-century *sala capitular* (chapter house) and, off the cloister, the Panteón de Reyes, which contains tombs of kings of medieval León.

FREE **Museo das Peregrinacións** MUSEUM

(www.mdperegrinacions.com; Rúa de San Miguel 4; 10am-8pm Tue-Fri, 10.30am-1.30pm & 5-8pm Sat, 10.30am-1.30pm Sun) Explore the eight rooms investigating the Camino de Santiago phenomenon over the centuries.

Cidade da Cultura de Galicia CULTURAL CENTRE

(City of Culture of Galicia; www.cidadedacultura.org; 8am-11pm, building interiors 10am-2pm & 4-8pm, museum closed Mon; P) This vast prestige project is taking shape atop Monte Gaiás, a hill about 1.5km southeast of the old town, to the designs of American Peter Eisenman. The first sections, the Library and Archive of Galicia, opened in 2011. The overall shape resembles a giant stone wave sliced into sections and is intended to be vaguely similar to a conch shell (symbol of the Camino de Santiago), while the passageways between the buildings are meant to recall the streets trodden by pilgrims arriving in Santiago.

A walk around the existing buildings and spaces is worth an hour or two of your time. Free guided visits in Spanish are given at 12.30pm and 6.30pm daily except Monday. You can reach the City of Culture on bus 9 (hourly Monday to Friday until 10.35pm and Saturday until 1.35pm) or bus C11 (5.35pm and 8.05pm Saturday and four times on Sunday), northbound from a stop opposite the market on Rúa da Virxe da Cerca.

AROUND THE CATHEDRAL

Catedral de Santiago de Compostela is surrounded by handsome plazas that invite you to wander through them. The grand **Praza do Obradoiro** (Workshop Plaza), to which most arriving Camino pilgrims instinctively find their way, earned its name from the stonemasons' workshops set up here while the cathedral was being built. At its northern end, the Renaissance **Hostal dos Reis Católicos** (admission €3; noon-2pm & 4-6pm Sun-Fri) was built in the early 16th century. Today it shelters well-off travellers instead, as a luxurious *parador*. Along the western side of the square is the elegant 18th-century **Pazo de Raxoi** (Praza do Obradoiro), now the city hall.

Around the corner, **Praza das Praterías** (Silversmiths' Square) is marked with the Fuente de los Caballos (1829) fountain, with the cathedral's south facade at the top of the steps. Curiously, the Casa do Cabildo, facing it on the lower side of the square, is no more than a 3m-deep facade, erected in 1758 to embellish the plaza.

Sleeping

Hotel Costa Vella BOUTIQUE HOTEL €€

(981 56 95 30; www.costavella.com; Rúa da Porta da Pena 17; s €59, d €81-97;) The tranquil,

thoughtfully designed rooms (some with glassed-in galleries), friendly welcome and lovely garden cafe make this a wonderful option. Even if you don't stay, it's an ideal spot for breakfast or coffee.

Hotel Casas Reais BOUTIQUE HOTEL €€
(☎981 55 57 09; www.casasreais.es; Rúa das Casas Reais 29; d incl breakfast €90; ❄📶) The 11 bright, contemporary rooms here are originally and discreetly themed after different real or pop-culture monarchs. White linen, mirrors and galleries all help to maximise light – this is undoubtedly one of the most attractive of Santiago's recent wave of new hotels in old buildings.

Casa-Hotel As Artes BOUTIQUE HOTEL €€
(☎981 55 52 54; www.asartes.com; Travesía de Dos Puertas 2; r €95-105; @📶) On a quiet street close to the cathedral, As Artes' seven lovely stone-walled rooms exude a romantic rustic air. Breakfast (€10.80) is served in a homey dining room overlooking the street.

Parador Hostal dos Reis Católicos HISTORIC HOTEL €€€
(☎981 58 22 00; www.parador.es; Praza do Obradoiro 1; s/d incl breakfast from €224/280; P❄📶) Opened in 1509 as a pilgrims' hostel, and with a claim to be the world's oldest hotel, this palatial *parador* is Santiago's top hotel, with regal (if rather staid) rooms. If you're not staying, stop in for a look round and coffee and cakes at the elegant cafe, or a meal in one of the restaurants (mains €20 to €35).

Eating

O Curro da Parra GALICIAN €€
(www.ocurrodaparra.com; Rúa do Curro da Parra 7; mains €14-20, tapas €5-8; ⊙closed Mon) With a neat little stone-walled dining room upstairs and a narrow tapas and wine bar below, this relative newcomer serves up a broad range of thoughtfully created, market-fresh fare. On weekday lunchtimes it serves a great-value *menú mercado* (market menu).

Bierzo de Enxebre LEONESE €€
(www.bierzoenxebre.es; Rúa da Troia 10; raciones €8-14; ⊙closed Tue) The cuisine at this busy and atmospheric spot is that of El Bierzo, a rural area of northwest Castilla y León, meaning excellent grilled and cured meats, but also cheeses, pies and vegetables. There are two small, stone-walled, wood-beamed dining rooms and the outside tables are highly popular.

Mesón Ó 42 GALICIAN €€
(www.restauranteo42.com; Rúa do Franco 42; raciones €6-14, mains €16-19; ⊙closed Sun evening) With a solid list of favourite local *raciones* like *empanadas* (pies), shellfish, octopus and tortillas, as well as fish, meat and rice dishes, this popular place stands out from the crowd with well-prepared food and good service.

Drinking

If you're after tapas and wine, graze along Rúa do Franco and Rúa da Raíña. For people-watching, hit the cafes along Praza da Quinatana and Rúa do Vilar. The liveliest area lies east of Praza da Quintana, especially along Rúa de San Paio de Antealtares, known as a hot spot for live music.

Information

Turismo de Santiago (☎981 55 51 29; www.santiagoturismo.com; Rúa do Vilar 63; ⊙9am-9pm, to 7pm Nov-Mar) Efficient main municipal tourist office.

Oficina de Acogida de Peregrinos (Pilgrims' Reception Office; ☎981 56 88 46; www.peregrinossantiago.es; Rúa do Vilar 3; ⊙9am-9pm) People who have covered at least the last 100km of the Camino de Santiago on foot or horseback, or the last 200km by bicycle, with spiritual or religious motives, can obtain their 'Compostela' certificate to prove it here.

Oficina de Turismo de Galicia (www.turgalicia.es; Rúa do Vilar 30-32; ⊙10am-8pm Mon-Fri, 11am-2pm & 5-7pm Sat, 11am-2pm Sun) The scoop on all things Galicia as well as on the Camino de Santiago.

Getting There & Away

AIR Flights from various Spanish and European destinations land at **Lavacolla airport** (☎981 54 75 00; www.aena.es). Up to 36 Empresa Freire buses (€3) run daily between Lavacolla airport and Rúa do Doutor Teixeiro, in the new town southwest of Praza de Galicia.

BUS The **bus station** (☎981 54 24 16; www.tussa.org; Praza de Camilo Díaz Baliño; 📶) is about a 20-minute walk northeast of the centre. Castromil-Monbus runs to destinations throughout Galicia. ALSA has services to Oviedo (€28, 5¼ to 8¾ hours), León (€28, six hours) and Madrid (€44 to €63, 7¾ to 10 hours). ALSA also has direct daily services to Porto (€30, 4¼ hours) and Lisbon (€50, 9¾ hours).

TRAIN From the **train station** (☎981 59 18 59; Rúa do Hórreo), regional trains run up and down the coast, while a daytime Talgo and an overnight Trenhotel head to Madrid (from €50.60, 6¼ to 9½ hours).

Around Galicia

Galicia's dramatic Atlantic coastline is one of Spain's best-kept secrets, with wild and precipitous cliffs and isolated fishing villages. The lively port city of **A Coruña** has a lovely city beach and fabulous seafood (a recurring Galician theme). It's also the gateway to the stirring landscapes of the **Costa da Morte** and **Rías Altas**; the latter's highlight among many is probably **Cabo Ortegal**. Inland Galicia is also worth exploring, especially the old town of **Lugo**, surrounded by what many consider to be the world's best preserved Roman walls.

VALENCIA & MURCIA

A warm climate, an abundance of seaside resorts and interesting cities make this area of Spain a popular destination. The beaches of the Costa Blanca (White Coast) draw most of the visitors, but venture beyond the shore to get a real feel for the region.

Valencia

POP 815,000

Valencia, where paella first simmered over a wood fire, is a vibrant, friendly, slightly chaotic place. It has two outstanding fine-arts museums, an accessible old quarter, Europe's newest cultural and scientific complex, and one of Spain's most exciting nightlife scenes.

Sights & Activities

TOP CHOICE **Ciudad de las Artes y las Ciencias** SCIENCE CENTRE

(City of Arts & Sciences; 902 100031; www.cac.es; combined ticket adult/child €31.50/24) The aesthetically stunning City of Arts & Sciences occupies a massive 350,000-sq-metre swath of the old Turia riverbed. It's mostly the work of stellar local architect, the world-renowned Santiago Calatrava. The complex includes the **Oceanogràfic** (adult/child €24.90/18.80; 10am-6pm or 8pm), a stunning aquarium; **Hemisfèric** (adult/child €7.85/6.10), a planetarium and IMAX cinema; **Museo de las Ciencias Príncipe Felipe** (adult/child €7.85/6.10; 10am-7pm or 9pm), an interactive science museum; and the extraordinary **Palau de les Arts Reina Sofía** (www.lesarts.com) concert hall. Take bus 35 from Plaza del Ayuntamiento or bus 95 from Torres de Serranos or Plaza de América.

Barrio del Carmen HISTORIC AREA

You'll see Valencia's best face by simply wandering around the Barrio del Carmen. Valencia's Romanesque-Gothic-baroque-Renaissance **catedral** (Plaza de la Virgen; adult/child incl audioguide €4.50/3; 10am-4.45pm or 5.45pm Mon-Sat, 2-4.45pm Sun) is a compendium of centuries of architectural history and home to the **Capilla del Santo Cáliz**, a chapel said to contain the Holy Grail (the chalice Christ supposedly used in the last supper). Climb the 207 stairs of the **Micalet bell tower** (adult/child €2/1; 10am-7pm or 7.30pm) for sweeping city views.

Plaza del Mercado HISTORIC PLAZA

Over on Plaza del Mercado, two emblematic buildings, each a masterpiece of its era, face each other. Valencia's Modernista covered market, the **Mercado Central** (www.mercadocentralvalencia.es; 7.30am-3pm Mon-Sat) recently scrubbed and glowing as new, was constructed in 1928. With over 900 stalls, it's a swirl of smells, movement and colour. **La Lonja** (adult/child €2/1; 10am-7pm Tue-Sat, to 3pm Sun) is a splendid late-15th-century building, a Unesco World Heritage site and was originally Valencia's silk and commodity exchange.

FREE **Museo de Bellas Artes** MUSEUM

(www.museobellasartesvalencia.gva.es; Calle San Pío V 9; 10am-7pm Tue-Sun, 11am-5pm Mon) Bright and spacious, the Museo de Bellas Artes ranks among Spain's best. Highlights include the grandiose Roman *Mosaic of the Nine Muses*, a collection of magnificent late-medieval altarpieces and works by El Greco, Goya, Velázquez, Murillo and Ribalta, plus artists such as Sorolla and Pinazo of the Valencian impressionist school.

Instituto Valenciano de Arte Moderno (IVAM) GALLERY

(www.ivam.es; Calle Guillem de Castro 118; adult/child €2/1; 10am-8pm Tue-Sun) IVAM (pronounced '*ee*-bam') hosts excellent temporary exhibitions and houses an impressive permanent collection of 20th-century Spanish art.

Beaches

Playa de la Malvarrosa runs into **Playa de las Arenas**. Each is bordered by the **Paseo Marítimo** promenade and a string of restaurants. **Playa El Salér**, 10km south, is backed

Valencia City

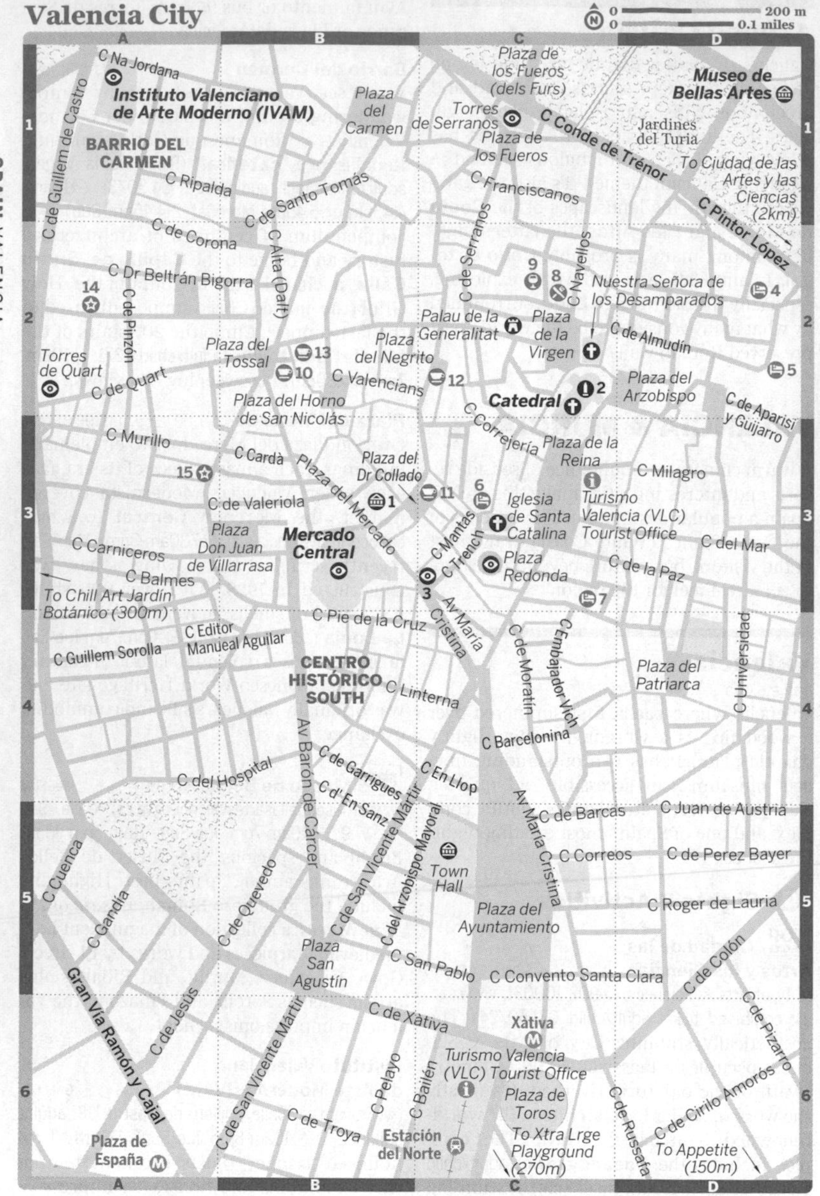

by shady pine woods. **Autocares Herca** (☎96 349 12 50; www.autocaresherca.com) buses run between Valencia and Perelló hourly (half-hourly in summer), calling by El Salér village. The beaches lie east and southeast of the city centre.

Sleeping

Caro Hotel HOTEL €€€
(☎96 305 90 00; www.carohotel.com; Calle Almirante 14; r €140-200; ❄📶) This spanking new hotel, housed in a sumptuous 19th-century mansion, sits atop some 2000 years of Va-

Valencia City

Top Sights
- Catedral.......C2
- Instituto Valenciano de Arte Moderno (IVAM).......A1
- Mercado Central.......B3
- Museo de Bellas Artes.......D1

Sights
1. La Lonja.......B3
2. Miguelete Bell Tower.......C2
3. Plaza del Mercado.......C3

Sleeping

4. Ad Hoc Monumental.......D2
5. Caro Hotel.......D2
6. Hostal Antigua Morellana.......C3
7. Petit Palace Bristol.......C3

Eating

8. Delicat.......C2
- Seu-Xerea.......(see 8)

Drinking

9. Café de las Horas.......C2
10. Café Infanta.......B2
11. Café Lisboa.......C3
12. Cafe Bar Negrito.......C2
13. Sant Jaume.......B2

Entertainment

14. Music Box.......A2
15. Radio City.......A3

lencian history. Its recent restoration has revealed a hefty hunk of the Arab wall, Roman column bases and Gothic arches. Each room is furnished in soothing dark shades and is unique in design.

Chill Art Jardín Botánico BOUTIQUE HOTEL €€
(☎96 315 40 12; www.hoteljardinbotanico.com; Calle Doctor Peset Cervera 6; s/d from €85/90; ❄📶) Welcoming and megacool, this intimate – only 16 rooms – hotel is furnished with great flair. Candles flicker in the lounge and each bedroom has original artwork.

Ad Hoc Monumental HOTEL €€
(☎96 391 91 40; www.adhochoteles.com; Calle Boix 4; s €65-101, d €76-125; ❄📶) Friendly Ad Hoc offers comfort and charm deep within the old quarter and also runs a splendid small restaurant (⏰dinner Monday to Saturday). The late-19th-century building has been restored to its former splendour with great sensitivity, revealing original ceilings, mellow brickwork and solid wooden beams.

Petit Palace Bristol BOUTIQUE HOTEL €€
(☎96 394 51 00; www.hthoteles.com; Calle Abadía San Martín 3; r €60-130; ❄@📶) Hip and minimalist, this boutique hotel, a comprehensively made-over 19th-century mansion, retains the best of its past and does a particularly scrumptious buffet breakfast. Invest €15 extra for one of the superior top-floor doubles, with a broad wooden terrace giving panoramic views over the city. Free bikes for guests.

Hostal Antigua Morellana HOSTAL €
(☎96 391 57 73; www.hostalam.com; Calle En Bou 2; s €45-55, d €55-65; ❄) The friendly, family-run 18-room Hostal Antigua Morellana is tucked away near the central market. It occupies a renovated 18th-century *posada* (where wealthier merchants bringing their produce to the nearby food market would spend the night) and has cosy, good-sized rooms, most with balconies.

Eating

At weekends, locals in their hundreds head for Las Arenas, just north of the port, where a long line of restaurants overlooking the beach all serve up authentic paella in a three-course meal costing around €15.

La Pepica SEAFOOD €€€
(☎96 371 03 66; www.lapepica.com; Paseo de Neptuno 6-8; meals around €25; ⏰lunch & dinner Mon-Sat, lunch Sun) More expensive than its many beachside competitors, La Pepica, run by the same family for more than a century, is renowned for its rice dishes and seafood. Here, Ernest Hemingway, among other luminaries, once strutted. Between courses, browse through the photos and tributes that plaster the walls.

Delicat TAPAS, FUSION €
(☎96 392 33 57; seudelicat@hotmail.es; Calle Conde Almodóvar 4; mains €4-11, menus €12; ⏰Tue-Sun) At this particularly friendly, intimate option (there are only nine tables, plus the terrace in summer), Catina, working up front, and her partner, Paco, on full view in the kitchen, offer an unbeatable

value five-course menu of samplers for lunch and a range of truly innovative tapas anytime.

TOP CHOICE **A Tu Gusto** MEDITERRANEAN €€
(☎96 322 70 26; www.atugusto.com; cnr Avenida Instituto Obrero & Calle Escritor Rafael Ferreres; mains €14-20, menus €10-36; ⊙lunch & dinner Wed-Sat, lunch Sun & Tue) At this strictly contemporary place, the decor is sleek, all pistachio and pitch black but for the gleaming white bar. Salvador Furió, the powerhouse in the kitchen, has worked with some of Spain's finest chefs. His cuisine is modern, creative and attractively presented, and portions are generous.

Tridente FUSION €€
(☎96 356 77 77; Paseo de Neptuno 2; mains €16, menus €29-49; ⊙lunch & dinner Mon-Sat, lunch Sun) Begin with an aperitif on the broad beachfront terrace of Tridente, restaurant of Neptuno hotel, then move inside, where filtered sunlight bathes its soothing cream decor. There's an ample à la carte selection but you won't find details of the day's *menús* in front of you – they're delivered verbally by the maître d', who speaks good English.

Appetite INTERNATIONAL, FUSION €€€
(☎96 110 56 60; www.appetite.es; Calle Salvador Abril 7; 6-/8-course menu €26/32; ⊙dinner Thu-Mon, lunch Sat & Sun) 'Multicultural cuisine' is how Bonnie from Australia and her partner, Arantxa, as Valencian as they come, describe Appetite's fusion delights with an Asian slant, reflecting Bonnie's Singaporean origins. Sit back and let her compose your menu for you.

Seu-Xerea FUSION, MEDITERRANEAN €€€
(☎96 392 40 00; www.seuxerea.com; Calle Conde Almodóvar 4; mains around €20, menus €19-45; ⊙Tue-Sat) Recently made over, this welcoming restaurant is favourably quoted in almost every English-language press article about Valencia city. The creative, regularly changing, rock-reliable à la carte menu features dishes both international and deep rooted in Spain. Wines, selected by the owner, a qualified sommelier, are uniformly excellent.

Drinking

The Barrio del Carmen, the university area (around Avenidas de Aragón and Blasco Ibáñez), the area around the Mercado de Abastos and, in summer, the new port area and Malvarrosa are all jumping with bars and clubs.

Sant Jaume CAFE, BAR
(Plaza del Tossal) At this converted pharmacy, you can still see the old potion bottles and jars ranged behind the counter. Its 1st floor is all quiet crannies and poky passageways.

Cafe-Bar Negrito CAFE, BAR
(www.cafenegrito.com; Plaza del Negrito) El Negrito's large terrace trumps the cramped interior. It occupies the whole of the square and traditionally attracts a more left-wing, intellectual clientele.

Café Lisboa CAFE, BAR
(Plaza del Doctor Collado 9) This lively, student-oriented bar has a large, street-side terrace. The bulletin board is a palimpsest of small ads for things like apartment shares and language tuition.

Café Infanta CAFE, BAR
(Plaza del Tossal) The interior is a clutter of cinema memorabilia, while its external terrace, beside the busy Plaza del Tossal, is great for people-watching.

Café de las Horas COCKTAIL BAR
(www.cafedelashoras.com; Calle Conde de Almodóvar 1) Offers high baroque, tapestries, music of all genres, candelabras, bouquets of fresh flowers and a long list of exotic cocktails.

☆ Entertainment

Terraza Umbracle LOUNGE BAR
(www.umbracleterraza.com; ⊙midnight-8am Thu-Sat May–mid-Oct) At the southern end of the Umbracle walkway within the Ciudad de las Artes y las Ciencias, this is a cool, sophisticated spot to spend a hot summer night. Catch the evening breeze under the stars on the terrace, then drop below to **Mya** (Autopista del Saler; ⊙1-7.30am Fri & Sat year round), a top-of-the-line club with an awesome sound system. Admission (around €20 including first drink) covers both venues.

Radio City CLUB
(www.radiocityvalencia.es; Calle de Santa Teresa 19; ⊙11pm-3.30am) Almost as much mini-cultural centre as club, Radio City, always seething, pulls in the punters with activities including cinema, flamenco and dancing to an eclectic mix.

Music Box CLUB
(Calle del Pintor Zariñena 16; ⊙midnight-7am Tue-Sat) The music here is eclectic with some-

LAS FALLAS

In mid-March, Valencia hosts one of Europe's wildest street parties: **Las Fallas de San José** (www.fallas.es). For one week (12 to 19 March), the city is engulfed by an anarchic swirl of fireworks, music, festive bonfires and all-night partying. On the final night, giant *ninots* (effigies), many of political and social personages, are torched in the main plaza.

If you're not in Valencia then, see the *ninots* saved from the flames by popular vote at the **Museo Fallero** (Plaza Monteolivete 4; adult/child €2/1; ⌚10am-7pm Tue-Sat, to 3pm Sun).

thing for everyone. Entry is free except after 3am on Friday and Saturday, when there's a €10 admission.

Xtra Lrge Playground BAR, CLUB
(cnr Gran Vía de las Germanias & Calle de Cádiz; ⌚midnight-4am Thu-Sat) Spread over 600 sq metres, this recently opened venue merits its outsize name. All soft pastel colours on brute metal and concrete, it offers live DJs, and is already popular with Valencia's movers and shakers. Sip something special at the Spanglishly named Gintonería-Coktelería, then dance away until late.

Black Note JAZZ
(www.blacknoteclub.com; Calle Polo y Peyrolón 15; ⌚from 11.30pm; Ⓜ Aragón) Valencia city's most active jazz venue, Black Note has live music daily except Sunday and good canned jazz. Admission, including first drink, ranges from free to €15, depending on who's grooving.

Information

Regional Tourist Office (☎96 398 64 22; www.comunitatvalenciana.com; Calle de la Paz 48; ⌚9am-8pm Mon-Sat, 10am-2pm Sun)

Turismo Valencia (VLC) Tourist Office (☎96 315 39 31; www.turisvalencia.es; Plaza de la Reina 19; ⌚9am-7pm Mon-Sat, 10am-2pm Sun) Has several other branches around town, including the train station and airport arrivals area.

Getting There & Away

AIR Valencia's **Aeropuerto de Manises** (☎96 159 85 00) is 10km west of the city centre. It's served by metro lines 3 and 5. Budget flights serve major European destinations.

BOAT **Acciona Trasmediterránea** (www.acciona-trasmediterranea.es) operates car and passenger ferries to Ibiza, Mallorca and Menorca.

BUS Valencia's **bus station** (☎96 346 62 66) is beside the riverbed on Avenida Menéndez Pidal. **Avanza** (www.avanzabus.com) operates hourly bus services to/from Madrid (€27.50 to €34.50, four hours). **ALSA** (www.alsa.es) has numerous buses to/from Barcelona (€27 to €32, 4½ hours) and Alicante (€19, 2½ hours), most passing by Benidorm (€15.20, 1¾ hours).

TRAIN From Valencia's Estación del Norte, major destinations include Alicante (€17 to €29, 1¾ hours, eight daily) and Barcelona (€40 to €44, three to 3½ hours, at least 12 daily). The AVE, the high-speed train, now links Madrid and Valencia, with up to 15 high-speed services daily and a journey time of around 1¾ hours.

Getting Around

Metro line 5 connects the airport, city centre and port. The high-speed tram leaves from the FGV tram station, 500m north of the cathedral, at the Pont de Fusta. This is a pleasant way to get to the beach, the paella restaurants of Las Arenas and the port.

Alicante

TRANSPORT HUB

Although it's an attractive seaside city with palm-lined boulevards and lively nightlife, Alicante (Alacant in Valenciano) is primarily a gateway town for the Mediterranean – its airport is one of Spain's busiest in summer and the city is otherwise well-connected to the rest of Spain by train and bus.

Sleeping & Eating

The old quarter (known as El Barrio) around Catedral de San Nicolás is wall-to-wall bars of the tapas and drinking variety. Down by the harbour, the Paseo del Puerto, tranquil by day, is a double-decker line of bars, cafes and night-time discos.

Hostal Les Monges Palace HOSTAL €
(☎96 521 50 46; www.lesmonges.es; Calle San Agustín 4; s €37-45, d €53-60; ❄@☎) This agreeably quirky place is a treasure with its winding corridors, tiles, mosaics and antique furniture. Each room is individually decorated and reception couldn't be more welcoming.

Guest House Antonio BOUTIQUE HOTEL €
(☎650 718353; www.guesthousealicante.com; Calle Segura 20; s €35-40, d €45-50; ❄☎) Each of the eight large, tastefully decorated rooms

here has a safe, a full-sized fridge and free beverage-making facilities.

Piripi VALENCIAN €€
(☎96 522 79 40; Avenida Oscar Esplá 30; mains €12-26) This highly regarded restaurant is strong on rice, seafood and fish, and there's a huge variety of tapas.

 Getting There & Away

AIR Alicante's **El Altet airport**, gateway to the Costa Blanca, is around 12km southwest of the centre. It's served by budget airlines, charters and scheduled flights from all over Europe.

BUS Destinations include Murcia (€5.63, one hour, at least seven daily) and Valencia (€19, 2½ hours, 10 daily).

TRAIN Destinations from the main **Renfe Estación de Madrid** (Avenida de Salamanca) include Barcelona (€55, five hours, eight daily), Madrid (€60, 3¼ hours, seven daily), Murcia (from €8, 1¼ hours, hourly) and Valencia (€14 to €30, 1¾ to two hours, eight daily).

Costa Blanca

Clean white beaches, bright sunshine and a rockin' nightlife have made the **Costa Blanca** (www.costablanca.org) one of Europe's favourite summer playgrounds. Many resorts are shamefully overbuilt, but it is still possible to discover charming towns and unspoilt coastline. Some of the best towns to explore include **Benidorm**, a highrise nightlife hot spot in summer (but otherwise home to pensioners the rest of the year); **Altea**, famed for its church with a pretty blue-tiled dome; and **Calpe**, known for the Gibraltar-like **Peñon de Ifach** (332m). All are accessible by train from Alicante.

BALEARIC ISLANDS

POP 1.1 MILLION

The Balearic Islands (Illes Balears in Catalan) adorn the glittering Mediterranean waters off Spain's eastern coastline. Beach tourism destinations *par excellence*, each of the islands has a quite distinct identity and they have managed to retain much of their individual character and beauty. All boast beaches second to none in the Med but each offers reasons for exploring inland too.

Check out websites like www.illesbalears.es and www.platgesdebalears.com.

Getting There & Away

AIR In summer, charter and regular flights converge on Palma de Mallorca and Ibiza from all over Europe. Major operators from the Spanish mainland include **Iberia** (www.iberia.es), **Air Europa** (www.aireuropa.com), **Spanair** (www.spanair.com), **Air Berlin** (www.airberlin.com) and **Vueling** (www.vueling.com).

BOAT Compare prices and look for deals at **Direct Ferries** (www.directferries.es). Ferry companies include:

Acciona Trasmediterránea (☎902 454 645; www.trasmediterranea.es)

Baleària (☎902 160 180; www.balearia.com)

Iscomar (☎902 119 128; www.iscomar.com)

The main ferry routes to the mainland are:

Ibiza (Ibiza City) To/from Barcelona (Acciona Trasmediterránea, Baleària), Valencia (Acciona Trasmediterránea)

Ibiza (Sant Antoni) To/from Denia, Barcelona and Valencia (Baleària)

Mallorca (Palma de Mallorca) To/from Barcelona and Valencia (Acciona Trasmediterránea, Baleària), Denia (Baleària)

Menorca (Maó) To/from Barcelona and Valencia (Acciona Trasmediterránea, Baleària)

The main interisland ferry routes:

Ibiza (Ibiza City) To/from Palma de Mallorca (Acciona Trasmediterránea and Baleària)

Mallorca (Palma de Mallorca) To/from Ibiza City (Acciona Trasmediterránea and Baleària) and Maó (Acciona Trasmediterránea and Baleària)

Mallorca (Port d'Alcúdia) To/from Ciutadella (Iscomar and Baleària)

Menorca (Ciutadella) To/from Port d'Alcúdia (Iscomar and Baleària)

Menorca (Maó) To/from Palma de Mallorca (Acciona Trasmediterránea and Baleària)

Mallorca

POP 402,000

The sunny, warm hues of the medieval heart of Palma de Mallorca, the archipelago's capital, make a great introduction to the islands. The northwest coast, dominated by the Serra de Tramuntana mountain range, is a beautiful region of olive groves, pine forests and ochre villages, with a spectacularly rugged coastline. Most of Mallorca's best beaches are on the north and east coasts, and although many have been swallowed up by tourist developments, you can still find the occasional exception. There is also a scattering of fine beaches along the south coast.

Getting Around

BUS Most of the island is accessible by bus from Palma. All buses depart from or near the **bus station** (Carrer d'Eusebi Estada).

TRAIN Two train lines run from Plaça d'Espanya in Palma de Mallorca. The popular, old train runs to Sóller, a pretty ride. A standard train line runs inland to Inca, where the line splits with a branch to Sa Pobla and another to Manacor.

PALMA DE MALLORCA

Sights

Catedral CATHEDRAL
(La Seu; ☎902 022445, 971 723 130; www.catedraldemallorca.org; Carrer del Palau Reial 9; adult/child €6/free; ⏰10am-6.15pm Mon-Fri, to 2.15pm Sat) This awesome structure, completed in 1601, is predominantly Gothic, apart from the main facade (replaced after an earthquake in 1851) and parts of the interior. The cathedral's interior is stunning, with ranks of slender columns supporting the soaring ceiling and framing three levels of elaborate stained-glass windows. The front altar's centrepiece, a light, twisting wrought-iron sculpture suspended from the ceiling, is one of Gaudí's more eccentric creations. For once, Gaudí is upstaged by the island's top contemporary artist, Miquel Barceló, who reworked the Capella del Santíssim i Sant Pere, at the head of the south aisle, in a dream-fantasy, swirling ceramic rendition of the miracle of the loaves and fishes.

Palau de l'Almudaina PALACE
(Carrer del Palau Reial; adult/child €9/4, audioguide €4, guided tour €6; ⏰10am-5.45pm Mon-Fri, to 1.15pm Sat) Originally an Islamic fort, this mighty construction was converted into a residence for the Mallorcan monarchs at the end of the 13th century. It is still occasionally used for official functions when King Juan Carlos is in town. At other times, you can wander through a series of cavernous and austere stone-walled rooms, a chapel with a rare Romanesque entrance, and upstairs royal apartments adorned with Flemish tapestries and period furniture.

Es Baluard MUSEUM
(Museu d'Art Modern i Contemporani; www.esbaluard.org; Porta de Santa Catalina 10; adult/child €6/free, temporary exhibitions €4, free entry Tue; ⏰10am-8pm Tue-Sat, to 3pm Sun) This 21st-century concrete complex nests within Palma's grand Renaissance-era seaward fortifications. A playful game of light, surfaces and perspective, it makes the perfect framework for the creations within; these include works by Joan Miró, Miquel Barceló and Picasso.

Palau March MUSEUM
(Carrer de Palau Reial 18; adult/child €4.50/free; ⏰10am-6.30pm Mon-Fri, to 2pm Sat) This house, palatial by any definition, contains sculptures by such 20th-century greats as Henry Moore, Auguste Rodin, Barbara Hepworth and Eduardo Chillidan, which grace the outdoor terrace. Within is a set of Salvador Dalí prints.

FREE **Museu d'Art Espanyol Contemporani** MUSEUM
(Museu Fundació Juan March; www.march.es/arte/palma; Carrer de Sant Miquel 11; ⏰10am-6.30pm Mon-Fri, 10.30am-2pm Sat) On permanent display within this 18th-century mansion are some 70 pieces held by the Fundación Juan March. Together they constitute a veritable who's who of mostly 20th-century artists, including Picasso, Miró, Juan Gris (of cubism fame), Dalí and the sculptor Julio González.

Sleeping

TOP CHOICE **Hotel Dalt Murada** HISTORIC HOTEL €€€
(☎971 425 300; www.daltmurada.com; Carrer de l'Almudaina 6A; s/d incl breakfast €177/210; ❄📶; 🚌2) Gathered around a medieval courtyard, this carefully restored old townhouse, which dates from 1500, has 14 rooms and is a gorgeous option, with antique furnishings (including chandeliers and canopied beds) and art work, much of which belongs to the friendly family who still own and run the place.

Hotel Santa Clara BOUTIQUE HOTEL €€€
(☎971 72 92 31; www.santaclarahotel.es; Carrer de Sant Alonso 16; s/d from €122/168; ❄@📶) Boutique meets antique in this historic mansion, converted with respect, where subdued greys, steely silvers and cream blend harmoniously with the warm stone walls, ample spaces and high ceilings of the original structure.

Misión de San Miguel BOUTIQUE HOTEL €€€
(☎971 214 848; www.urhotels.com; Carrer de Can Maçanet 1; r from €139; 🚭❄@📶) This 32-room boutique hotel is an astounding deal, with excellent prices and stylish designer rooms; it does the little things well with firm mattresses and rain showers, although some rooms open onto public areas and can be a little noisy.

Mallorca

Eating

TOP CHOICE Simply Fosh INTERNATIONAL €€
(☎971 72 01 14; www.simplyfosh.com; Carrer de la Missió 7A; mains €18-26, dinner menús €48; ⏰Mon-Sat) Lovingly prepared Mediterranean grub with a special touch is the order of the day in the convent refectory, one of the home kitchens of Michelin-starred chef Marc Fosh. The range of set menus is a wonderful way to sample high-quality cooking at a reasonable price, but there are also à la carte choices.

Misa Braseria BRASSERIE, RESTAURANT €€
(☎971 595 301; www.misabraseria.com; Carrer de Can Maçanet 1; mains €16-20, menús from €17; ⏰1-3.30pm & 7.30-10.30pm Mon-Sat) The latest addition to Marc Fosh's ever-expanding restaurant empire, this attractive place consists of a basement restaurant adorned with famous restaurant menus on the walls, or offers lunchtime dining upstairs in its modern patio. The food is slickly presented and tastes are typically fresh with dishes that change weekly and with the seasons.

La Bodeguilla SPANISH €€
(☎971 71 82 74; www.la-bodeguilla.com; Carrer de Sant Jaume 3; mains €17.50-19.50; ⏰Mon-Sat) This gourmet restaurant does creative interpretations of dishes from across Spain; try the *cochinillo* (suckling pig) from Segovia or the *lechazo* (young lamb, baked Córdoba-style in rosemary). Also on offer is an enticing range of tapas.

13% TAPAS €€
(www.13porciento.com; Carrer Sant Feliu 13A; meals around €15; 🌶) At the quieter end of the old town, this L-shaped barn of a place is at once a wine and tapas bar, bistro and delicatessen. Most items are organic and there's plenty of choice for vegetarians. Wines are displayed on racks (both bar and takeaway prices are quoted, so you know the exact mark-up).

Drinking & Entertainment

The old quarter is the city's most vibrant nightlife zone. Particularly along the narrow streets between Plaça de la Reina and Plaça de la Drassana, you'll find an enormous selection of bars, pubs and bodegas. According to a much flouted law, bars should shut by 1am Sunday to Thursday (3am Friday and Saturday).

TOP CHOICE Puro Beach BAR
(www.purobeach.com; 11am-2am Apr-Oct) This uber-laid-back, sunset chill lounge has a tapering outdoor promontory with an all-white bar that's perfect for sunset cocktails, DJ sessions and fusion food escapes. It is just a two-minute walk east of Cala Estancia (itself just east of Ca'n Pastilla). It's southeast of Palma de Mallorca along the coast.

Ca'n Joan de S'Aigo CAFE
(Carrer de Can Sanç 10; 8am-9pm Wed-Mon) Dating from 1700, this is *the* place for a hot chocolate (€1.40) in what can only be described as an antique-filled milk bar. The house speciality is *quart,* a feather-soft sponge cake that children love, with almond-flavoured ice cream.

Abaco BAR
(Carrer de Sant Joan 1; from 8pm) Inhabiting the restored patio of an old Mallorcan house, Abaco is filled with ornate candelabra, elaborate floral arrangements, cascading towers of fresh fruit and bizarre artworks. It hovers between extravagant and kitsch, but the effect is overwhelming, whatever your opinion. Paying this much for a cocktail is an outrage, but one might just be worth it here.

Information

Consell de Mallorca Tourist Office (971 17 39 90; www.infomallorca.net; Plaça de la Reina 2; 8am-8pm Mon-Fri, 9am-2pm Sat) Covers the whole island. For cultural and sporting events, consult *On Anar,* its free quarterly 'what's happening' guide with a version in English.

Municipal Tourist Office (902 102365; 9am-8pm Mon-Sat) In one of the railway buildings off Plaça d'Espanya.

AROUND MALLORCA

Mallorca's northwestern coast is a world away from the high-rise tourism on the other side of the island. Dominated by the Serra de Tramuntana, it's a beautiful region of olive groves, pine forests and small villages with shuttered stone buildings. There are a couple of highlights for drivers: the hair-raising road down to the small port of **Sa Calobra**, and the amazing trip along the peninsula leading to the island's northern tip, **Cap de Formentor**.

Sóller is a good place to base yourself for hiking and the nearby village of **Fornalutx** is one of the prettiest on Mallorca.

From Sóller, it's a 10km walk to the beautiful hilltop village of **Deià** (www.deia.info), where Robert Graves, poet and author of *I Claudius,* lived for most of his life. From the village, you can scramble down to the small shingle beach of **Cala de Deià**. Boasting a fine monastery and pretty streets, **Valldemossa** (www.valldemossa.com) is further southwest down the coast.

Further east, **Pollença** and **Artà** are attractive inland towns. Nice beaches include those at **Cala Sant Vicenç**, **Cala Mondragó** and around **Cala Llombards.**

Sleeping & Eating

The **Consell de Mallorca tourist office** (971 71 22 16; www.infomallorca.net; Plaça de la Reina 2; 8am-8pm Mon-Fri, 9am-2pm Sat) in Palma can supply information on rural and other types of accommodation around the island.

DEIÀ

TOP CHOICE S'Hotel des Puig HISTORIC HOTEL €€€
(971 639 409; www.hoteldespuig.com; Carrer des Puig 4; s €95, d €150-160; Feb-Nov;) The eight rooms of this gem in the middle of the old town reflect a muted modern taste within ancient stone walls. Out the back are secrets impossible to divine from the street, such as the pool and lovely terrace.

Hostal Miramar HOTEL €€
(971 63 90 84; www.pensionmiramar.com; Carrer de Ca'n Oliver; r incl breakfast €91, without bathroom €75; Mar–mid-Nov; P) Hidden within the lush vegetation above the main road and with views across to Deià's hillside church and the sea beyond, this 19th-century stone house with gardens is a shady retreat with nine rooms. The rooms with shared bathrooms have the best views; others look onto the garden.

Restaurant Juame MALLORCAN €€€
(971 63 90 29; www.restaurantejuame-deia.com; Avinguda del Arxiduc Lluís Salvador 22; mains €20-25; closed Mon) This is the kind of restuarant we like. Family-run and exceptionally friendly, with a relaxed, easy going vibe but

simply superb gourmet Mallorcan dishes incorporating the very best local produce. It's a little more expensive than some of the other options in the village but it's worth every euro.

SÓLLER

The Sóller area has plenty of boutique hotels in historic buildings or country houses; many are listed on www.sollernet.com.

Ca'n Isabel HOTEL €€
(☎971 638 097; www.canisabel.com; Carrer de d'Isabel II 13; s €99.50-131.50, d €124.50-156.50; ⏲mid-Feb–mid-Nov; ❄@☎) With just six rooms, this 19th-century house is a gracefully decorated hideaway, with a fine garden out the back. The decor won't be to everyone's taste, but the owners have retained the period style impeccably. The best (and dearest) of the rooms come with their own delightful terrace.

Ca's Carreter MALLORCAN €€
(☎971 63 51 33; www.cascarreter.net; Carrer del Cetre 9; mains €13-17; ⏲lunch & dinner Tue-Sat, lunch Sun) In an atmospheric former cart workshop, Ca's Carreter is a welcoming spot that serves unpretentious Mallorcan cooking, including fresh local fish and other mainly regional ingredients.

Ibiza

Ibiza (Eivissa in Catalan) is an island of extremes. Its formidable party reputation is completely justified, with some of the world's greatest clubs attracting hedonists from the world over. The interior and northeast of the island, however, are another world. Peaceful country drives, hilly green territory, a sprinkling of mostly laid-back beaches and coves, and some wonderful inland accommodation and eateries, are light years from the ecstasy-fuelled madness of the clubs that dominate the west.

IBIZA CITY

Sights & Activities

Ibiza City's port area of **Sa Penya** is crammed with funky and trashy clothing boutiques and arty-crafty market stalls. From here, you can wander up into **D'Alt Vila**, the atmospheric old walled town.

Ramparts HISTORIC SITE
A ramp leads from Plaça de Sa Font in Sa Penya up to the **Portal de ses Taules** gateway, the main entrance. Completed in 1585, the fortifications include seven artillery bastions joined by thick protective walls up to 22m in height. You can walk the entire perimeter of these impressive Renaissance-era walls, designed to withstand heavy artillery, and enjoy great views along the way.

Catedral CATHEDRAL
(⏲9.30am-1.30pm & 5-8pm) Ibiza's cathedral elegantly combines several styles: the original 14th-century structure is Catalan Gothic but the sacristy was added in 1592 and a major baroque renovation took place in the 18th century.

Centre d'Interpretació Madina Yasiba MUSEUM
(Carrer Major 2; adult/child €2/1.50; ⏲10am-2pm & 6-9pm Tue-Sat, 10am-2pm Sun) This small display replicates the medieval Muslim city of Madina Yabisa (Ibiza City) prior to the island's fall to Christian forces in 1235. Artefacts, audiovisuals and maps help transport you to those times.

Sleeping

Many of Ibiza City's hotels and *hostales* are closed in the low season and heavily booked between April and October. Make reservations well in advance.

Hotel La Ventana HISTORIC HOTEL €€€
(☎971 30 35 37; www.laventanaibiza.com; Carrer de Sa Carossa 13; d from €165; ❄☎) This charming 15th-century mansion is set on a little tree-shaded square in the old town. Some rooms come with stylish four-poster beds and mosquito nets. The rooftop terrace, trim gardens and restaurant are welcome extras. Prices drop massively out of season.

Hostal Parque HOTEL €€€
(☎971 30 13 58; www.hostalparque.com; Carrer de Vicent Cuervo 3; s €70-90, d €130-190; ❄☎) The rooms here are small, but otherwise what you get are the basics done very well indeed, and it manages to be modern and cool without being over the top. Rarely for central Ibiza City, there's decent double glazing so noise shouldn't be too much of an issue. The best doubles overlook pleasant Plaça des Parc and the downstairs cafe is a very popular place for a drink or a meal.

Hostal La Marina HOTEL €€
(☎971 31 01 72; www.hostal-lamarina.com; Carrer de Barcelona 7; r €75-170; ❄) Looking onto both the waterfront and bar-lined Carrer de Barcelona, this mid-19th-century building has

rooms that are as flamboyant and colourful as an Ibizan club night. A handful of singles and some doubles look onto the street (with the predictable noise problem), but you can opt for pricier doubles and attics with terraces and panoramic port and/or town views.

Eating

TOP CHOICE Comidas Bar San Juan MEDITERRANEAN €
(Carrer de Guillem de Montgrí 8; mains from €6; Mon-Sat) This family-run operation, with two small dining rooms, harks back to the days before Ibiza became a by-word for glam. It offers outstanding value, with fish dishes for around €10 and many small mains for €6 or less. It doesn't take reservations, so arrive early and expect to have other people sat at the same table as you.

Restaurant of Hotel Mirador de Dalt Vila MEDITERRANEAN €€€
(971 30 30 45; Plaça d'Espanya 4; menú €45, mains €26-30; Easter-Dec) At this intimate – do reserve – restaurant with its painted barrel ceiling and original canvases around the walls, you'll dine magnificently. Service is discreet yet friendly, and dishes are creative, colourful and delightfully presented.

Drinking

Sa Penya is the nightlife centre. Dozens of bars keep the port area jumping. Alternatively, various bars at Platja d'en Bossa combine sounds, sand, sea and sangria.

Discobus BUS
(www.discobus.es; per person €3; midnight-6am Jun-Sep) Discobus runs around the major clubs, bars and hotels in Ibiza City, Platja d'en Bossa, Sant Rafel, Es Canar, Santa Eulària and Sant Antoni.

Teatro Pereira MUSIC BAR
(www.teatropereyra.com; Carrer del Comte de Rosselló 3; 8am-4am) Away from the waterfront hubbub, this hugely atmospheric time warp of a place, which is all stained wood and iron girders, was once the foyer of the long-abandoned 1893 theatre at its rear. It's packed most nights with a more eclectic crowd than the standard preclubbing bunch, and offers nightly live music sessions.

Bora Bora Beach Club BEACH BAR
(noon-4am May-Sep) At Platja d'en Bossa, about 2km from the old town, this is *the* place – a long beachside bar where sun and fun worshippers work off hangovers and prepare new ones. Entry's free and

CLUBBING IN IBIZA

In summer (late May to the end of September), the west of the island is a continuous party from sunset to sunrise and back again. In 2011 the International Dance Music Awards ranked four Ibiza clubs (see below) among their worldwide top eight.

The clubs operate nightly from around 1am to 6am and each has something different. Theme nights, fancy-dress parties and foam parties (where you are half-drowned in the stuff) are regular features. Admission can cost anything from €25 to €60.

Space (www.space-ibiza.es; admission €29-60; Jun–mid-Oct) In Platja d'en Bossa, aptly named Space, which can pack in as many as 40 DJs and up to 12,000 clubbers, is considered one of the world's best nightclubs. Action here starts mid-afternoon and regular daytime boats make the trip between Platja d'en Bossa and Ibiza City (€6 return).

Pacha (www.pacha.com; admission €23-57; nightly Jun-Sep, Fri & Sat Oct-May) In business on the northern side of Ibiza City's port since 1973, Pacha has 15 bars (!) and various dance spaces that can hold 3000 people. The main dance floor, a sea of colour, mirror balls and veils draped from the ceiling, heaves to deep techno. On the terrace, sounds are more gentle and relaxing.

Amnesia (www.amnesia.es; admission €40-65; early Jun–Sep) Four kilometres out on the road to Sant Rafel, Amnesia has a sound system that seems to give your body a massage. A huge glasshouse-like internal terrace, filled with palms and bars, surrounds the central dance area with a seething mass of mostly tireless 20-something dancers.

Privilege (www.privilegeibiza.com; admission around €40) Five kilometres along the road to Sant Rafel, this club, with its 20 bars, interior pool and capacity for 10,000 clubbers, claims to be one of the world's largest. The main domed dance temple is an enormous, pulsating area, where the DJ's cabin is suspended above the pool.

the ambience is chilled, with low-key club sounds wafting over the sand. From midnight, everyone crowds inside. It's off Carrer del Fumarell.

Information

Tourist Office (☎971 39 92 32; www.eivissa.es; Plaça de la Catedral; ⏰10am-2pm & 6-9pm Mon-Sat, 10am-2pm Sun) Can provide audioguides to the city; bring your passport or identity document. Other branches around the city.

AROUND IBIZA

Ibiza has numerous unspoiled and relatively undeveloped beaches. **Cala de Boix**, on the northeastern coast, is the only black-sand beach on the island, while further north are the lovely beaches of **S'Aigua Blanca**.

On the north coast near Portinatx, **Cala Xarraca** is in a picturesque, secluded bay, and near Port de Sant Miquel is the attractive **Cala Benirrás**.

In the southwest, **Cala d'Hort** has a spectacular setting overlooking two rugged rock islets, Es Verda and Es Verdranell.

The best thing about rowdy **Sant Antoni**, the island's second biggest town and north of Ibiza City, is heading to the small rock-and-sand strip on the north shore to join hundreds of others for sunset drinks at a string of chilled bars. The best known remains **Café del Mar** (⏰4pm-1am), our favourite, but it's further north along the pedestrian walkway.

Local **buses** (www.ibizabus.com) run to most destinations between May and October.

Sleeping & Eating

Check out rural accommodation at www.ibizaruralvillas.com. For more standard accommodation, start at www.ibizahotelsguide.com.

Hostal Cala Boix HOSTAL €€
(☎971 33 52 24; www.hostalcalaboix.com; Cala Boix; d €60-80; ⏰May-Oct; ❄) Set uphill and back from Cala Boix, this option couldn't be further from the Ibiza madness. All rooms have a balcony and many have sea views. At S'Arribiada, its hearty resturant, Thursday is barbeque day, while each Tuesday fresh sardines sizzle on the grill.

Hostal Restaurante Es Alocs HOTEL €€
(☎971 33 50 79; www.hostalalocs.com; Platja Es Figueral; s/d €40/65; ⏰May-Oct; ❄📶) This very friendly choice sits right on the beach at Platja Es Figueral. Rooms occupy two floors and most have a small fridge and balcony. The bar-restaurant has a wonderful terrace, deeply shaded with tangled juniper and chaste trees.

Bar Anita TAVERN €
(Sant Carles de Peralta; mains €8-16) A timeless tavern opposite the village church of Sant Carles de Peralta, this restaurant and bar has been attracting all sorts from around the island for decades. They come to enjoy pizza, pasta and a hearty meal – or simply to drink and chat.

Menorca

Renowned for its pristine beaches and archaeological sites, tranquil Menorca was declared a Biosphere Reserve by Unesco in 1993. The capital, Maó, is known as Mahón in Castilian.

Getting Around

TO/FROM THE AIRPORT Bus 10 (€1.80) runs between Menorca's airport, 7km southwest of Maó, and the city's bus station every half-hour. A taxi costs around €15.

Sights & Activities

Maó absorbs most of the tourist traffic. North of Maó, a drive across a lunar landscape leads to the lighthouse at **Cap de Faváritx**. South of the cape stretch some fine sandy bays and beaches, including **Cala Presili** and **Platja d'en Tortuga**, reachable on foot.

Ciutadella, with its smaller harbour and historic buildings, has a more distinctly Spanish feel to it and is the more attractive of the two. A narrow country road leads south of Ciutadella (follow the 'Platges' sign from the *ronda*, or ring road) and then forks twice to reach some of the island's loveliest beaches: from west to east **Arenal de Son Saura**, **Cala en Turqueta**, **Es Talaier**, **Cala Macarelleta** and **Cala Macarella**. As with most beaches, you'll need your own transport.

In the centre of the island, the 357m-high **Monte Toro** has great views; on a clear day you can see Mallorca.

On the northern coast, the picturesque town of **Fornells** is on a large bay popular with windsurfers.

Sleeping

Many accommodation options on the island are closed between November and April.

MAÓ

TOP CHOICE Casa Alberti HISTORIC HOTEL €€€

(☎971 35 42 10; www.casalberti.com; Carrer d'Isabel II 9; s/d incl breakfast €130/160; ⊙Easter-Oct) Climb the central stairs with striking wrought-iron banisters to your vast room with white walls and whitest-of-white sheets. Each of the six bedrooms within this 18th-century mansion is furnished with traditional items, while bathrooms are designer cool and contemporary.

CIUTADELLA

Hotel Géminis HOTEL €

(☎971 38 46 44; www.hotelgeminismenorca.com; Carrer de Josepa Rossinyol 4; s incl breakfast €31-56, d incl breakfast €45-92; ⊙April–mid-October; ❄📶🏊) A friendly, stylish two-star place, this graceful, three-storey, rose-and-white lodging offers comfortable if somewhat neutral rooms just a short walk away from the city centre. The best rooms have a sizeable balcony.

Hostal-Residencia Oasis PENSION €

(☎971 38 21 97; www.hostaloasismenorca.es; Carrer de Sant Isidre 33; r €34-64) Run by a delightful elderly couple, this quiet place is close to the heart of the old quarter. Rooms, mostly with bathroom, are set beside a spacious garden courtyard. Furnishings, though still trim, are from deep into the last century.

Eating & Drinking

The ports in both Maó and Ciutadella are lined with bars and restaurants.

MAÓ

El Varadero SPANISH €€

(☎971 35 20 74; Moll de Llevant 4; mains €13-17; ⊙Easter-Nov) With such a splendid vista from the harbourside terrace, El Varadero offers tempting rice dishes and a short, select choice of fish and meat mains. If a full meal is too much, drop by for a tapa or two with a glass of wine and savour the view.

CIUTADELLA

Cas Ferrer de sa Font MENORCAN €€

(☎971 48 07 84; www.casferrer.com; Carrer del Portal de sa Font 16; mains €15-20; ⊙Tue-Sun) Nowhere on the island will you find more authentic Menorcan cuisine – here you'll enjoy meats and vegetables from the owner's organic farm. Dine on the delightful interior patio of this charming 18th-century building or inside, below beams and soft curves, in what was once a blacksmith's forge.

Es Molí CAFE, BAR

(Plaça de ses Palmeres) Sit among the arches, pillars and mellow stonework of the interior, where the core of the old *molí* (windmill) still juts from its heart. Or, if you don't mind the traffic, plant yourself on the terrace for a fine prospect of the little square.

FORNELLS

Es Port SEAFOOD €€

(☎971 37 64 03; Passeig Marítim 5; menú €15.50, mains €10-21; ⊙Sat-Thu Easter-Oct) The fish and other seafood are of the freshest here – unsurprisingly since Es Port has its own boat and lobster pots. Like most of its neighbours, it does *caldereta de llagosta* (lobster stew; €65), but less financial outlay goes into a sizzling *paella de llomanto* (lobster paella; €35).

Information

Tourist Office (Plaça de la Catedral 5, Ciutadella; ⊙8.30am-3pm & 5-9pm)

ANDALUCÍA

Images of Andalucía are so potent, so quintessentially Spanish that it's sometimes difficult not to feel a sense of déjà vu. It's almost as if you've already been there in your dreams: a solemn Easter parade, an ebullient spring festival, exotic nights in the Alhambra. In the stark light of day the picture is no less compelling.

Seville

POP 703,000

A sexy, gutsy and gorgeous city, Seville is home to two of Spain's most colourful festivals, fascinating and distinctive *barrios*, and a local population that lives life to the fullest. A fiery place (as you'll soon see in its packed and noisy tapas bars), it is also hot climatewise – avoid July and August!

Sights

Cathedral & Giralda CHURCH

(www.catedraldesevilla.es; adult/child €8/free; ⊙11am-5.30pm Mon-Sat, 2.30-6.30pm Sun Sep-Jun, 9.30am-4.30pm Mon-Sat, 2.30-6.30pm Sun Jul & Aug) After Seville fell to the Christians in 1248 its main mosque was used as a church until 1401 when it was knocked down to make way for what would become one of the world's largest cathedrals and an icon of Gothic architecture. The building wasn't completed until 1507. Over 90m high, the perfectly proportioned and exquisitely decorated **La Giralda** was the minaret of the mosque that stood on the site before the cathedral. The views from the summit are exceptional.

Inside, the **Capilla de San Antonio** contains Murillo's large 1666 canvas depicting the vision of St Anthony of Padua. Inside the cathedral's southern door stands the elaborate **tomb of Christopher Columbus**, dating from 1902. Towards the east end of the main nave is the **Capilla Mayor**; its Gothic altarpiece is the jewel of the cathedral and reckoned to be the biggest altarpiece in the world with more than 1000 carved biblical figures. The **Sacristía de los Cálices** (Sacristy of the Chalices) contains Goya's 1817 painting of the Seville martyrs *Santas Justa y Rufina*. The room's centrepiece is the **Custodia de Juan de Arfe**, a huge 475kg silver monstrance made in the 1580s by Renaissance metalsmith Juan de Arfe. Displayed in a glass case are the city keys handed to the conquering Fernando III in 1248.

Alcázar CASTLE
(adult/child €7.50/free; ⏲9.30am-7pm Apr-Sep, to 6pm Oct-Mar) Seville's Alcázar, a royal residence for many centuries, was founded in 913 as a Muslim fortress. The Alcázar has been expanded and rebuilt many times in its 11 centuries of existence. The Catholic Monarchs, Fernando and Isabel, set up court here in the 1480s as they prepared for the conquest of Granada. Later rulers created the Alcázar's lovely gardens. The highlights include exquisitely adorned patios and the showpiece **Palacio de Don Pedro**.

FREE **Archivo de Indias** MUSEUM
(Calle Santo Tomás; ⏲10am-4pm Mon-Sat, to 2pm Sun & holidays) On the western side of Plaza del Triunfo, the Archivo de Indias is the main archive of Spain's American empire, with 80 million pages of documents dating from 1492 through to the end of the empire in the 19th century: a most effective statement of Spain's power and influence during its Golden Age.

Barrio de Santa Cruz HISTORIC DISTRICT
Seville's medieval *judería* (Jewish quarter), east of the cathedral and Alcázar, is today a tangle of atmospheric, winding streets and lovely plant-decked plazas perfumed with orange blossom. Among its most characteristic plazas is **Plaza de Santa Cruz**, which gives the *barrio* its name. **Plaza de Doña Elvira** is another romantic perch, especially in the evening.

Metropol Parasol LANDMARK
(www.metropolsevilla.com; Plaza de la Encarnación) The opinion-dividing Metropol Parasol which opened in March 2011 in the Plaza de la Encarnación claims to be the largest wooden building in the world. Its undulating honeycombed roof is held up by five giant mushroom-like pillars.

Six years in the making, the construction covers a former dead zone in Seville's central district. Roman ruins discovered during the building's conception have been cleverly incorporated into the foundations at the Museo Antiquarium, while upstairs on level 2 you can pay €1.20 to stroll along a surreal panoramic walkway with killer city views. The Metropol also houses the plaza's former market, a restaurant and a concert space.

Museo del Baile Flamenco MUSEUM
(www.museoflamenco.com; Calle Manuel Rojas Marcos 3; adult/child €10/6; ⏲9.30am-7pm) The brainchild of Sevillana flamenco dancer, Cristina Hoyos, this museum is spread over three floors of an 18th-century palace, although at €10 a pop it's a little overpriced. Exhibits include sketches, paintings, photos of erstwhile (and contemporary) flamenco greats, plus a collection of dresses and shawls.

Parque de María Luisa & Plaza de España PARK
(⏲8am-10pm) This is a large area transformed for Seville's 1929 international fair, the Exposición Iberoamericana. Architects adorned it with fantastical buildings, many of them harking back to Seville's past glory or imitating the native styles of Spain's former colonies. In its midst is the large Parque de María Luisa, a living expression of Seville's Moorish and Christian past.

Festivals & Events

The first of Seville's two great festivals is **Semana Santa** (www.semana-santa.org), the week leading up to Easter Sunday. Throughout the week, thousands of members of religious brotherhoods parade in penitents' garb with tall, pointed *capirotes* (hoods) accompanying sacred images through the city, while huge crowds look on.

The **Feria de Abril**, a week in late April, is a welcome release after this solemnity: the festivities involve six days of music, dancing, horse riding and traditional dress, plus daily bullfights.

The city also stages Spain's largest flamenco festival, the month-long **Bienal de Flamenco** (www.labienal.com). It's held in September in even-numbered years.

Sleeping

There's plenty of accommodation in the Barrio de Santa Cruz (close to the Alcázar), El Arenal and El Centro.

Prices over Semana Santa and the Feria de Abril can be up to double the high-season prices cited here. Accommodation is often full on weekends and is always booked solid during festivals, so make reservations well in advance.

TOP CHOICE **Hotel Casa 1800** LUXURY HOTEL €€€
(954 56 18 00; www.hotelcasa1800sevilla.com; Calle Rodrigo Caro 6; d €145-198;) Straight in at number one as Seville's favourite hotel is this newly revived Santa Cruz jewel. This really is your home away from home (albeit a posh one!), with charming staff catering for your every need. Highlights include a sweet afternoon tea buffet, plus a quartet of penthouse garden suites with Giralda views.

Un Patio en Santa Cruz HOTEL €€
(954 53 94 13; www.patiosantacruz.com; Calle Doncellas 15; s €65-85, d €65-125;) Feeling more like an art gallery than a hotel, this place has starched white walls coated in loud works of art, and strange sculptures and preserved plants. The rooms are immensely comfortable, staff are friendly and there's a cool rooftop terrace with mosaic Moroccan tables.

Hotel Amadeus HOTEL €€
(954 50 14 43; www.hotelamadeussevilla.com; Calle Farnesio 6; s/d €85/95; P) Just when you thought you could never find hotels with pianos in the rooms anymore, along came Hotel Amadeus. Run by an engaging musical family in the old Judería, several of the astutely decorated rooms come complete with soundproofed walls and upright pianos ensuring you don't miss out on your daily practice.

Hotel Puerta de Sevilla HOTEL €€
(954 98 72 70; www.hotelpuertadesevilla.com; Calle Puerta de la Carne 2; s/d €66/86; P@) This superfriendly – and super-positioned – hotel is a great mix of the chintz and the stylish. The lobby, lined with superb Seville tile work, has an indoor water feature. The rooms are all flower-pattern textiles, wrought-iron beds and pastel wallpaper. It also features an unbeatable people-watching rooftop terrace.

Hotel Simón HOTEL €€
(954 22 66 60; www.hotelsimonsevilla.com; Calle García de Vinuesa 19; s €60-70, d €95-110; @) A typically grand 18th-century Sevillan house, with an ornate patio and spotless and comfortable rooms, this place gleams way above its two-star rating. Some of the rooms are embellished with rich *azulejos* tile work.

Oasis Backpackers' Hostel HOSTEL €
(954 29 37 77; www.oasissevilla.com; Plaza de la Encarnación 29; dm/d incl breakfast €15/50; @) Seville's offbeat, buzzing backpacker central offers 24-hour free internet access. The new location is in Plaza Encarnación, a narrow street behind the Church of the Anunciación. Each dorm bed has a personal safe, and there is a small rooftop pool. There's no curfew: this is Spain!

Hotel Goya HOTEL €€
(954 21 11 70; www.hotelgoyasevilla.com; Calle Mateos Gago 31; s €39-60, d €65-95; @) The gleaming Goya is more popular than ever. Pets are welcome. Book ahead.

Eating

TOP CHOICE **Vinería San Telmo** TAPAS, FUSION €€
(954 41 06 00; www.vineriasantelmo.com; Paseo Catalina de Ribera 4; tapas €3.50, media raciones €10) San Telmo invented the *rascocielo* (skyscraper) tapa, an 'Empire State' of tomatoes, aubergine, goat's cheese and smoked salmon. If this and other creative nougats don't make you drool with expectation then there's something wrong.

Catalina TAPAS €€
(Paseo Catalina de Ribera 4; raciones €10) If your view of tapas is 'glorified bar snacks', then your ideas could be blown out of the water here with a creative mix of just about every ingredient known to Iberian cooking. Start with the cheese, aubergine and paprika special.

Seville

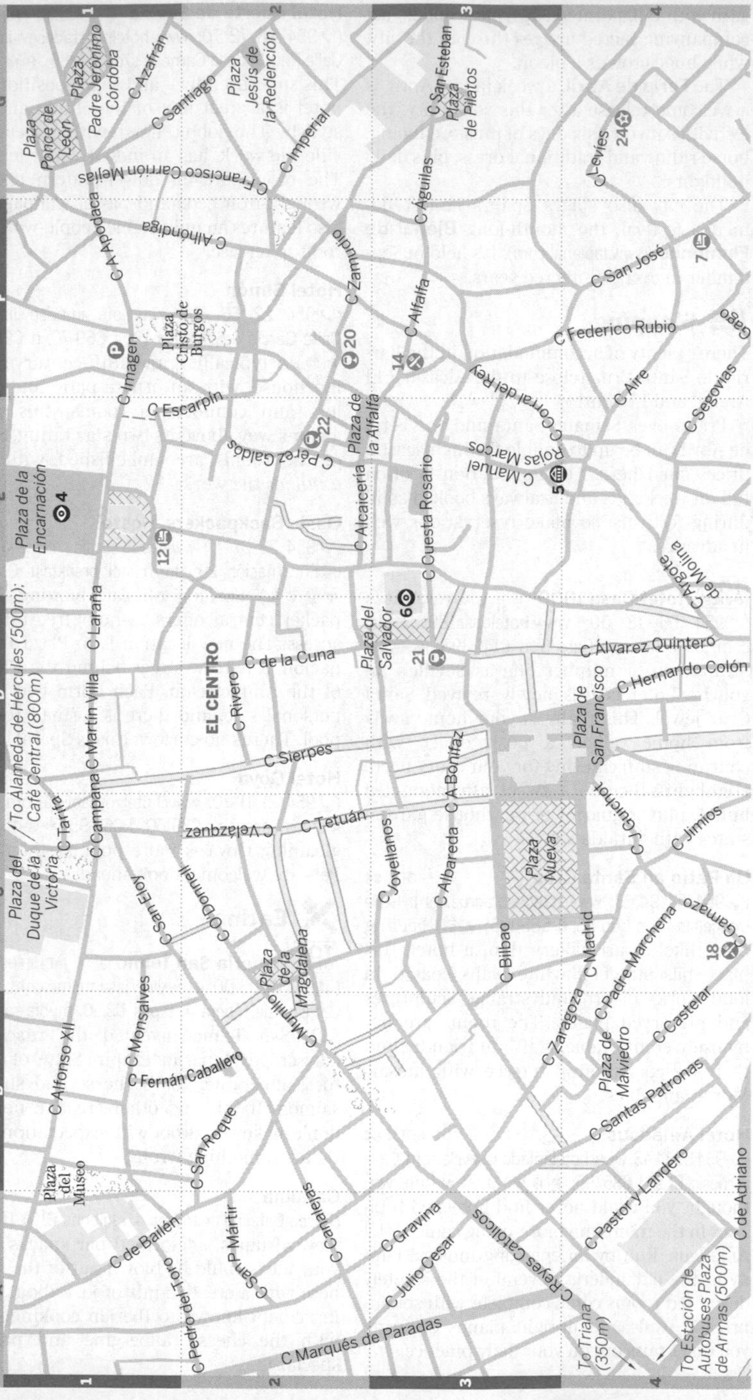

0 200 m
0 0.1 miles
A
B
C
D
E
F
G
1
2
3
4
Plaza del Duque de la Victoria
To Alameda de Hércules (500m); Café Central (800m)
Plaza de la Encarnación
4
Plaza Ponce de León
Plaza Padre Jerónimo Córdoba
Plaza del Museo
C Alfonso XII
C Tarifa
C Campana
C Martín Villa
C Laraña
C A Apodaca
C Imagen
C de Bailén
C Monsalves
C San Eloy
12
C Escarpín
Plaza Cristo de Burgos
C Alhóndiga
C Francisco Carrión Mejías
C Azafrán
C Santiago
C Pedro del Toro
C San Roque
C Fernán Caballero
C O'Donnell
C Velázquez
EL CENTRO
C Rivero
C Pérez Galdós
Plaza Jesús de la Redención
C San P Mártir
C Murillo
Plaza de la Magdalena
C Sierpes
C de la Cuna
C Imperial
C Marqués de Paradas
C Canalejas
C Tetuán
22
20
C Zamudio
C Alcaicería
Plaza de la Alfalfa
Plaza del Salvador
C Jovellanos
C Julio César
C Gravina
6
14
C Alfalfa
C Águilas
21
C Cuesta Rosario
C San Esteban
Plaza de Pilatos
C Albareda
C A Bonifaz
C Reyes Católicos
C Bilbao
C Manuel Rojas Marcos
C Corral del Rey
Plaza Nueva
C Zaragoza
5
C Madrid
Plaza de San Francisco
C Federico Rubio
To Triana (350m)
C Pastor y Landero
C Santas Patronas
Plaza de Malviedro
C Padre Marchena
C J Guichot
C Álvarez Quintero
C Hernando Colón
C Aire
C San José
C Levíes
24
To Estación de Autobuses Plaza de Armas (500m)
C Castelar
18
C Gamazo
C Jimios
C Argote de Molina
C Segovias
Gago
7
C de Adriano

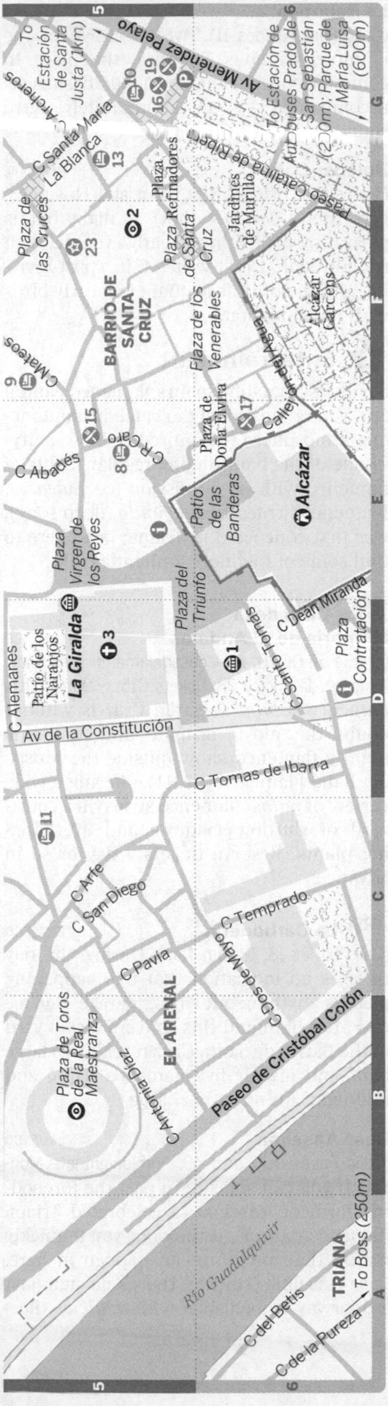

Seville

Top Sights

	Alcázar	E6
	La Giralda	D5

Sights

1	Archivo de Indias	D6
2	Barrio de Santa Cruz	F5
3	Cathedral & Giralda	D5
4	Metropol Parasol	E1
5	Museo del Baile Flamenco	E3
6	Plaza del Salvador	D3

Sleeping

7	Hotel Amadeus	F4
8	Hotel Casa 1800	E5
9	Hotel Goya	F5
10	Hotel Puerta de Sevilla	G5
11	Hotel Simón	C5
12	Oasis Backpackers' Hostel	E1
13	Un Patio en Santa Cruz	G5

Eating

14	Bar Alfalfa	F3
15	Bodega Santa Cruz	E5
16	Catalina	G5
17	Extraverde	E6
18	Mesón Cinco Jotas	C4
19	Vinería San Telmo	G5

Drinking

20	El Garlochi	F2
21	La Antigua Bodeguita	D3
22	La Rebótica	E2

Entertainment

23	Casa de la Memoria de Al-Andalus	F5
24	La Carbonería	G4

Bodega Santa Cruz TAPAS €

(Calle Mateos Gago; tapas €2) Forever crowded and with a mountain of paper on the floor, this place is usually standing room only, with tapas and drinks enjoyed alfresco as you dodge the marching army of tourists squeezing through Santa Cruz's narrow streets.

Extraverde TAPAS €

(www.extraverde.es; Plaza de Doña Elvira 8; tapas €2.50-4; 10.30am-11.30pm) Recent to the Santa Cruz scene, Extraverde is a unique bar-shop specialising in Andalucian products, such as olive oil, cheese and wine. You can taste free samples standing up, or sit down inside and order a full tapa.

Mesón Cinco Jotas TAPAS €€
(www.mesoncincojotas.com; Calle Castelar 1; tapas €3.80, media raciones €10) In the world of *jamón*-making, if you are awarded 'Cinco Jotas' (Five Js) for your *jamón,* it's like getting an Oscar. The owner of this place, Sánchez Romero Carvajal, is the biggest producer of Jabugo ham, and has a great selection on offer.

Bar Alfalfa TAPAS €
(cnr Calles Alfalfa & Candilejo; tapas €3) It's amazing how many people, hams, wine bottles and other knick-knacks you can stuff into such a small space. No matter, order through the window when the going gets crowded. You won't forget the tomato-tinged magnificence of the Italy-meets-Iberia *salmorejo* bruschetta.

Drinking

Bars usually open 6pm to 2am weekdays and 8pm till 3am at the weekend. Drinking and partying really get going around midnight on Friday and Saturday (daily when it's hot). In summer, dozens of open-air late-night bars *(terrazas de verano)* spring up along both banks of the river.

Plaza del Salvador is brimful of drinkers from mid-evening to 1am. Grab a drink from **La Antigua Bodeguita** next door and sit on the steps of the Parroquia del Salvador.

El Garlochi BAR
(Calle Boteros 4) Dedicated entirely to the iconography, smells and sounds of Semana Santa, the ubercamp El Garlochi is a true marvel. A cloud of church incense hits you as you go up the stairs, and the faces of baby Jesus and the Virgin welcome you into the velvet-walled bar, decked out with more Virgins and Jesuses. Taste the rather revolting sounding cocktails Sangre de Cristo (Blood of Christ) or Agua de Sevilla, both heavily laced with vodka, whisky and grenadine, and pray they open more bars like this.

WANT MORE?

For in-depth information, reviews and recommendations at your fingertips, head to the Apple App Store to purchase Lonely Planet's *Seville City Guide* iPhone app.

La Rebótica BAR
(Calle Pérez Galdós 11) Two's a crowd in the cramped, sinuous Rebótica, the place to come for cheap shots and 1980s flashbacks accompanied by an appropriately retro soundtrack.

Bulebar Café BAR, CAFE
(Alameda de Hércules 83; ⏰4pm-late) This place gets pretty *caliente* (hot) at night but is pleasantly chilled in the early evening, with friendly staff. Don't write off its spirit-reviving alfresco breakfasts that pitch early-birds with up-all-nighters.

Entertainment

Seville is arguably Spain's flamenco capital and you're most likely to catch a spontaneous atmosphere (of unpredictable quality) in one of the bars staging regular nights of flamenco with no admission fee. *Soleares,* Flamenco's truest *cante jondo* (deep song), was first concocted in Triana; head here to find some of the more authentic clubs.

TOP CHOICE **Casa de la Memoria de Al-Andalus** FLAMENCO
(☎954 56 06 70; www.casadelamemoria.es; Calle Ximénez de Enciso 28; tickets €15; ⏰9pm) This flamenco *tablao* in Santa Cruz is without doubt the most intimate and authentic nightly flamenco show outside the Museo del Baile Flamenco (p1014), offering a wide variety of *palos* (flamenco styles) in a courtyard of shifting shadows and overhanging plants. Reserve tickets a day or so in advance.

FREE **La Carbonería** FLAMENCO
(Calle Levíes 18; ⏰8pm-4am) During the day there is no indication that this happening place is anything but a large garage. But, arrive after 8pm and this converted coal yard in the Barrio de Santa Cruz reveals two large bars, and nightly live flamenco (11pm and midnight) for no extra charge.

Casa Anselma FLAMENCO
(Calle Pagés del Corro 49; ⏰midnight-late Mon-Sat) If you can squeeze in past the foreboding form of Anselma (a celebrated Triana flamenco dancer) at the door you'll quickly realise that anything can happen in here. Casa Anselma (beware: there's no sign, just a doorway embellished with *azulejos* tiles)

is the antithesis of a tourist flamenco *tablao,* with cheek-to-jowl crowds, thick cigarette smoke, zero amplification and spontaneous outbreaks of dexterous dancing. Pure magic. To get here, cross the Puente de Isabel II, then turn right on Calle Pagés del Corro - Casa Anselma is around 100m along on your right.

Information

There are branches of the regional tourist office at **Avenida de la Constitución** (9am-8pm Mon-Fri, 10am-2pm Sat & Sun, closed holidays) and **Estación de Santa Justa.** (954 53 76 26; Estación Santa Justa; 9am-8pm Mon-Fri, 10am-2pm Sat & Sun, closed holidays)

Discover Sevilla (www.discoversevilla.com) An excellent, comprehensive site.

Explore Seville (www.exploreseville.com) A good, informative site.

Seville Tourism (www.turismo.sevilla.org) The city's official tourism site; its 'Accessible Guide' is especially useful for travellers with a disability.

Turismo Sevilla (www.turismosevilla.org; Plaza del Triunfo 1; 10.30am-7pm Mon-Fri) Information on all Sevilla province.

Getting There & Away

Air

A range of domestic and international flights land in Seville's **Aeropuerto San Pablo** (SVQ; www.sevilla-airport.com; 24hr), 7km from the city centre.

Bus

From the **Estación de Autobuses Prado de San Sebastián** (Plaza San Sebastián), there are 12 or more buses daily to/from Cádiz, Córdoba, Granada, Ronda and Málaga. From the **Estación de Autobuses Plaza de Armas** (www.autobusesplazadearmas.es; Avenida del Cristo de la Expiración), destinations include Madrid, Mérida, Cáceres and Portugal.

Train

The modern, efficient **Estación de Santa Justa** (902 43 23 43; Avenida Kansas City) is 1.5km northeast of the city centre. There's also a city-centre **Renfe ticket office** (Calle Zaragoza 29).

Twenty or more superfast AVE trains, reaching speeds of 280km/h, whiz daily to/from Madrid (€83.80, 2½ hours). Other services include Cádiz (€13.25, 1¾ hours, 13 daily), Córdoba (€17 to €33.20, 40 minutes to 1½ hours, 21 or more daily), Granada (€24.80, three hours, four daily) and Málaga (€38.70, two hours, 11 daily).

Getting Around

Los Amarillos (www.losamarillos.es) runs buses between the airport and the Avenida del Cid near the bus station (€2.40, at 15 and 45 minutes past the hour). A taxi costs about €22.

Tussam's **Tranvía** (www.tussam.es) the city's sleek tram service, was launched in 2007. Individual rides cost €1.30, or you can buy a *Bono* (travel pass offering five rides for €5) from many newspaper stands and tobacconists.

Córdoba

POP 328,000

Córdoba was once one of the most enlightened Islamic cities on earth, and enough remains to place it in the contemporary top three Andalucian draws. The centrepiece is the gigantic and exquisitely rendered Mezquita. Surrounding it is an intricate web of winding streets, geranium-sprouting flower boxes and cool intimate patios that are at their most beguiling in late spring.

Sights & Activities

TOP CHOICE Mezquita MOSQUE

(Mosque; 957 47 05 12; www.mezquitadecordoba.org; Calle Cardenal Herrero; adult/child €8/4, 8.30-10am Mon-Sat free; 10am-7pm Mon-Sat, 8.30-10am & 2-7pm Sun Mar-Oct, 8.30am-6pm Mon-Sat, 8.30-10am & 2-6pm Sun Nov-Feb) Founded in 785, Córdoba's gigantic mosque is a wonderful architectural hybrid with delicate horseshoe arches making this unlike anywhere else in Spain. The main entrance is the **Puerta del Perdón**, a 14th-century Mudéjar gateway, with the ticket office immediately inside. Within the gateway is the aptly named **Patio de los Naranjos** (Courtyard of the Orange Trees). Once inside, you can see straight ahead to the mihrab, the prayer niche in a mosque's qibla (the wall indicating the direction of Mecca) that was the focus of prayer. The first 12 transverse aisles inside the entrance, a forest of pillars and arches, comprise the original 8th-century mosque.

Judería NEIGHBOURHOOD

The medieval *judería*, extending northwest from the Mezquita almost to Avenida del Gran Capitán, is today a maze of narrow streets and whitewashed buildings with flowery window boxes. The beautiful little 14th-century **Sinagoga** (Calle de los Judíos 20; admission €0.30; 9.30am-2pm & 3.30-5.30pm Tue-Sat, 9.30am-1.30pm Sun & holidays) is one of

Córdoba

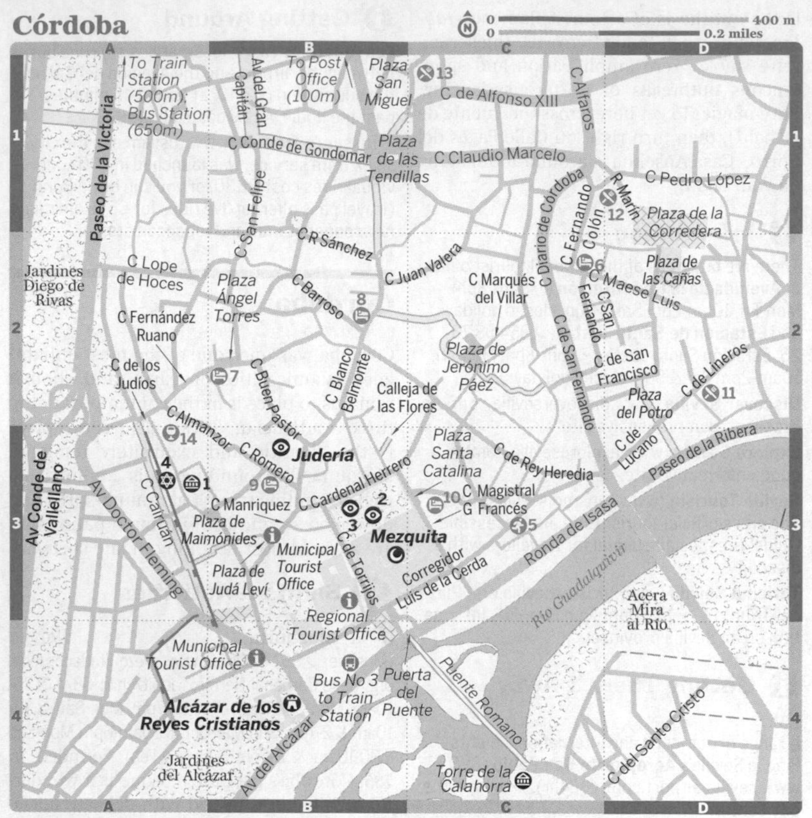

Córdoba

Top Sights

Alcázar de los Reyes Cristianos B4
Judería B3
Mezquita B3

Sights

1 Casa de Sefarad A3
2 Patio de los Naranjos & Minaret B3
3 Puerta del Perdón B3
4 Sinagoga A3

Activities, Courses & Tours

5 Hammam Baños Árabes C3

Sleeping

6 Casa de los Azulejos C2
7 Hospedería Alma Andalusí B2
8 Hospedería Añil B2
9 Hotel Lola B3
10 Hotel Mezquita C3

Eating

11 Bodegas Campos D2
12 Taberna Salinas D1
13 Taberna San Miguel El Pisto C1

Drinking

14 Bodega Guzmán A3

only three surviving medieval synagogues in Spain and the only one in Andalucía. In the heart of the *judería*, and once connected by an underground tunnel to the Sinagoga, is the 14th-century **Casa de Sefarad** (www.casadesefarad.es; cnr Calle de los Judíos & Averroes; admission €4; 10am-6pm Mon-Sat, 11am-2pm Sun). This small, beautiful museum is devoted to reviving interest in the Sephardic-Judaic-Spanish tradition.

Alcázar de los Reyes Cristianos CASTLE
(Castle of the Christian Monarchs; Campo Santo de Los Mártires; admission €4, Fri free; ⏲10am-2pm & 5.30-7.30pm Tue-Sat, 9.30am-2.30pm Sun & holidays) Just southwest of the Mezquita, the Alcázar began as a palace and fort for Alfonso X in the 13th century. From 1490 to 1821 the Inquisition operated from here. Today its gardens are among the most beautiful in Andalucía.

Medina Azahara RUINS
(Madinat al-Zahra; adult/EU citizen €1.50/free; ⏲10am-6.30pm Tue-Sat, to 8.30pm May–mid-Sep, to 2pm Sun) Even in the cicada-shrill heat and stillness of a summer afternoon, the Medina Azahara whispers of the power and vision of its founder, Abd ar-Rahman III. The self-proclaimed caliph began the construction of a magnificent new capital 8km west of Córdoba around 936, and took up full residence around 945. It was destroyed in the 11th century and just 10% of the site has been excavated. A taxi from Córdoba costs €37 for the return trip, with one hour to view the site, or you can book a three-hour coach tour for €6.50 to €10 through many Córdoba hotels.

Hammam Baños Árabes BATHHOUSE
(☎957 48 47 46; www.hammamspain.com/cordoba; Calle del Corregidor Luis de la Cerda 51; bath/bath & massage €26/33; ⏲2hr sessions 10am, noon, 2pm, 4pm, 6pm, 8pm & 10pm) Follow the lead of the medieval Cordobans and dip your toe in these beautifully renovated Arab baths, where you can enjoy an aromatherapy massage, with tea, hookah and Arabic sweets in the cafe afterwards.

Sleeping

Hospedería Alma Andalusí BOUTIQUE HOTEL €€
(☎957 76 08 88; www.almaandalusi.com; Calle Fernández Ruano 5; s/d €45/100; ❄📶) The builders of this guesthouse in a quiet section of the *judería* have brilliantly converted an ancient structure into a stylish, modern establishment while keeping the rates down. Thoughtfully chosen furnishings, polished wood floors and solid colours make for a comfortable base.

Casa de los Azulejos HOTEL €€
(☎957 47 00 00; www.casadelosazulejos.com; Calle Fernando Colón 5; s/d incl breakfast from €85/107; ❄@📶) Mexican and Andalucian styles converge in this chic hotel, where the patio is all banana trees, ferns and potted palms bathed in sunlight. Colonial-style rooms feature tall antique doors, massive beds, walls in lilac and sky blues, and floors adorned with the beautiful old *azulejos* tiles that give the place its name.

Hotel Mezquita HOTEL €€
(☎957 47 55 85; www.hotelmezquita.com; Plaza Santa Catalina 1; s/d €42/74; ❄) One of the best deals in town, Hotel Mezquita stands right opposite its namesake monument, amid the bric-a-brac of the tourism zone. The 16th-century mansion has large, elegant rooms with marble floors, tall doors and balconies, some affording views of the great mosque.

Hospedería Añil HOSTEL €
(☎957 49 15 44; www.sensesandcolours.com; Calle Barroso 4; dm/s/d from €12/30/42; 📶) This vibrant, superfriendly establishment is aimed at the backpacker set, though it cuts no corners in the style and comfort departments. Primary colours and fanciful murals maintain an upbeat vibe. It's a skip and a jump to either the Mezquita or Plaza de las Tendillas.

Hotel Lola HOTEL €€
(☎957 20 03 05; www.hotellola.es; Calle Romero 3; r incl breakfast €129; ❄@📶) Individualism and a quirky style are the prime ingredients here. Each room, named after an Arab princess, is decorated with large antique beds and covetable items that you will wish you could take home with you. What's more, you can eat your breakfast on the roof terrace overlooking the Mezquita's bell tower.

Eating & Drinking

Córdoba's liveliest bars are mostly scattered around the newer parts of town and start buzzing at about 11pm or midnight on weekends. Most bars in the medieval centre close around midnight.

TOP CHOICE **Taberna San Miguel El Pisto** TAPAS €
(www.casaelpisto.com/en; Plaza San Miguel 1; tapas €3, media raciones €5-10; ⏲closed Sun & Aug) Brimming with local character, El Pisto is one of Córdoba's best *tabernas*, both in terms of atmosphere and food. Traditional tapas and *media-raciones* are done perfectly, and inexpensive Moriles wine is ready in jugs on the bar.

Bodegas Campos ANDALUCIAN €€
(☎957 49 75 00; www.bodegascampos.com; Calle de Lineros 32; tapas €5, mains €13-21) One of Córdoba's most atmospheric and famous wine cellar/restaurants, this sprawling hall

features dozens of rooms and patios, with oak barrels signed by local and international celebrities stacked up alongside. The bodega produces its own house Montilla wine.

Taberna Salinas TAPAS €
(www.tabernasalinas.com; Calle Tundidores 3; tapas/raciones €2.50/8; ⊙closed Sun & Aug) A historic *taberna* that dates back to 1879, with a reputation that ensures the tables are always busy.

Bodega Guzmán BAR
(Calle de los Judíos 7; ⊙noon to 4pm & 8pm-midnight, closed Thu) Close to the Sinagoga, this atmospheric drinking spot bedecked with bullfighting memorabilia is frequented by both locals and tourists. Montilla wine is dispensed from three giant barrels behind the bar: don't leave without trying some *amargoso* (bitter).

Information

Municipal Tourist Office (Plaza de Judá Levi; ⊙8.30am-2.30pm Mon-Fri)

Regional Tourist Office (Calle de Torrijos 10; ⊙9am-7.30pm Mon-Fri, 9.30am-3pm Sat, Sun & holidays) Inside the Palacio Episcopal.

Getting There & Away

BUS The **bus station** (☎957 40 40 40; www.estacionautobusescordoba.es; Glorieta de las Tres Culturas) is 1km northwest of Plaza de las Tendillas. Destinations include Seville (€10.50, 1¾ hours, six daily), Granada (€12.50, 2½ hours, seven daily) and Málaga (€13, 2¾ hours, five daily).

TRAIN From Córdoba's **train station** (☎957 40 02 02; Glorieta de las Tres Culturas), destinations include Seville (€11 to €33, 40 to 90 minutes, hourly), Madrid (€53 to €68, 1¾ to 6¼ hours, hourly), Málaga (€22 to €45, one to 2½ hours, nine daily) and Barcelona (€138, 4½ hours, four daily).

Granada

POP 258,000 / ELEV 685M

Granada's eight centuries as a Muslim capital are symbolised in its keynote emblem, the remarkable Alhambra, one of the most graceful architectural achievements in the Muslim world. Islam was never completely expunged here, and today it seems more present than ever in the shops, restaurants, tearooms and the mosque of a growing North African community in and around the maze of the Albayzín. The tapas bars fill to bursting with hungry and thirsty revellers, while flamenco bars resound to the heart-wrenching tones of the south.

Sights & Activities

TOP CHOICE **Alhambra** PALACE
(☎902 44 12 21; www.alhambra-tickets.es; adult/under 8yr €13/free, Generalife only €6; ⊙8.30am-8pm 16 Mar-31 Oct, to 6pm 1 Nov-14 Mar, night visits 10-11.30pm Tue-Sat Mar-Oct, 8-9.30pm Fri & Sat Nov-Feb) The mighty Alhambra is breathtaking. Much has been written about its fortress, palace, patios and gardens, but nothing can really prepare you for seeing the real thing.

The **Alcazaba**, the Alhambra's fortress, dates from the 11th to the 13th centuries. There are spectacular views from the tops of its towers. The **Palacio Nazaríes** (Nasrid Palace), built for Granada's Muslim rulers in their 13th- to 15th-century heyday, is the centrepiece of the Alhambra. The beauty of

ALHAMBRA TICKETS

Up to 6600 tickets to the Alhambra are available for each day. About one-third of these are sold at the ticket office on the day, but they sell out early and you need to start queuing by 7am to be reasonably sure of getting one. It's highly advisable to book in advance (you pay €1 extra per ticket). You can book up to three months ahead in two ways:

Alhambra Advance Booking (☎international calls 0034 934 92 37 50, national calls 902 888001; www.alhambra-tickets.es; ⊙8am-9pm)

Servicaixa (www.servicaixa.com) Online booking in Spanish and English. You can also buy tickets in advance from Servicaixa cash machines (⊙8am to 7pm March to October, 8am to 5pm November to February), but only in the Alhambra grounds

For internet or phone bookings you need a Visa card, MasterCard or Eurocard. You receive a reference number, which you must show, along with your passport, national identity card or credit card, at the Alhambra ticket office when you pick up the ticket on the day of your visit.

its patios and intricacy of its stuccoes and woodwork, epitomised by the **Patio de los Leones** (Patio of the Lions) and **Sala de las Dos Hermanas** (Hall of the Two Sisters), are stunning. The **Generalife** (Palace Gardens) is a great spot to relax and contemplate the complex from a little distance.

Albayzín NEIGHBOURHOOD

Exploring the narrow, hilly streets of the Albayzín, the old Moorish quarter across the river from the Alhambra, is the perfect complement to the Alhambra. The cobblestone streets are lined with gorgeous *cármenes* (large mansions with walled gardens, from the Arabic *karm* for garden). It survived as the Muslim quarter for several decades after the Christian conquest in 1492. Head uphill to reach the **Mirador de San Nicolás** – a viewpoint with breathtaking vistas and a relaxed scene.

Capilla Real HISTORIC BUILDING

(www.capillarealgranada.com; Calle Oficios; admission €3.50; 10.30am-1.30pm & 4-7.30pm Mon-Sat, 11am-1.30pm & 4-7pm Sun Apr-Oct) The **Royal Chapel**, adjoins Granada's cathedral, and is an outstanding Christian building. Catholic monarchs Isabella and Ferdinand commissioned this elaborate Isabelline-Gothic-style mausoleum. It was not completed until 1521 and the monarchs lie in simple lead coffins in the crypt beneath their marble monuments in the chancel, enclosed by a stunning gilded wrought-iron screen.

Sleeping

Casa Morisca Hotel HISTORIC HOTEL €€

(958 22 11 00; www.hotelcasamorisca.com; Cuesta de la Victoria 9; d €118-148;) This late-15th-century mansion perfectly captures the spirit of the Albayzín. A heavy wooden door shuts out city noise, and rooms are soothing, with lofty ceilings, fluffy white beds and flatweave rugs over brick floors.

Carmen de la Alcubilla HISTORIC HOTEL €€

(958 21 55 51; www.alcubilladelcaracol.com; Calle del Aire Alta 12; s/d €100/120;) This exquisitely decorated place is located on the slopes of the Alhambra. Rooms are washed in pale pastel colours contrasting with cool cream and antiques. There are fabulous views and a pretty terraced garden.

Parador de Granada HISTORIC HOTEL €€€

(958 22 14 40; www.parador.es; Calle Real de la Alhambra; r €315; P) It would be remiss not to mention this hotel, the most luxurious of Spain's *paradors*. If you're looking for romance and history (it's in a converted 15th-century convent in the Alhambra grounds) and money is no object, then book well ahead.

Hotel Zaguán del Darro HISTORIC HOTEL €€

(958 21 57 30; www.hotelzaguan.com; Carrera del Darro 23; s/d €55/70;) This place offers excellent value for the Albayzín. The 16th-century house has been tastefully restored, with sparing use of antiques. Its 13 rooms are all different; some look out over the Río Darro. There's a good bar-restaurant below.

Hostal Arteaga HOSTAL €

(958 20 88 41; www.hostalarteaga.com; Calle Arteaga 3; s/d €40/49;) A charming bargain option just off the Gran Vía de Colón, inching into the Albayzín. The rooms are spruced up with lavender walls, striped bedspreads and chequered blue bathroom tiles for a tidy, modern feel.

Eating

Granada is one of the last bastions of that fantastic practice of free tapas with every drink, and some have an international flavour. The labyrinthine Albayzín holds a wealth of eateries tucked away in the narrow streets. Calle Caldereria Nueva is a fascinating muddle of *teterías* (tearooms) and Arabic-influenced takeaways.

Arrayanes MOROCCAN €€

(958 22 84 01; www.rest-arrayanes.com; Cuesta Marañas 4; mains €8-15; from 8pm;) The best Moroccan food in a city that is well known for its Moorish throwbacks? Recline on lavish patterned seating, try the rich, fruity tagine casseroles and make your decision. Note that Restaurante Arrayanes does not serve alcohol.

El Ají SPANISH €€

(Plaza San Miguel Bajo 9; mains €12-20;) Up in the Albayzín, this chic but cosy neighbourhood restaurant is no bigger than a shoebox but serves from breakfast right through to the evening. Chatty staff at the tiny marble bar can point out some of the highlights of the creative menu.

Ruta del Azafrán FUSION €€

(www.rutadelazafran.es; Paseo del Padre Manjón 1; mains €13-20) One of the few high-concept restaurants in Granada, this sleek spot with its steely-modern interior has an eclectic menu which ranges from Asian-inspired

Granada

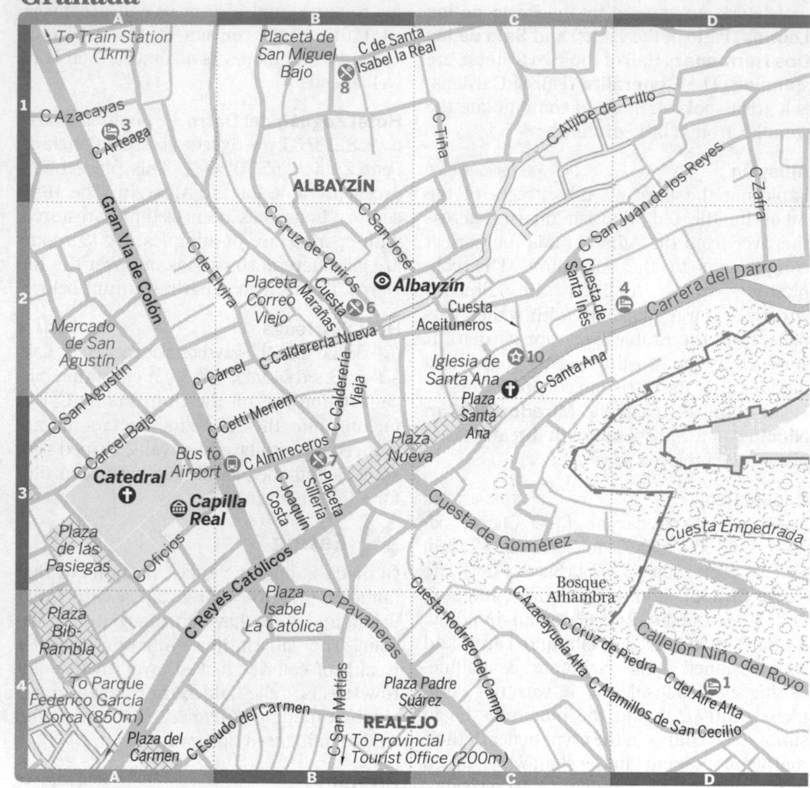

temporas to broccoli-based pesto, lamb couscous and roasted pork. The terrace outside on the Río Darro is a great place for a snack, but you'll get better service inside.

Bodegas Castañeda BAR €
(Calle Almireceros; tapas €2-3, raciónes €6-8) An institution among locals and tourists alike, this buzzing bar doles out hearty portions of food (try a hot or cold *tabla,* or platter; a half order is ample for two) and dispenses drinks from big casks mounted in the walls.

☆ Entertainment

The excellent monthly *Guía de Granada* (€1), available from kiosks, lists entertainment venues and tapas bars.

Peña de la Platería FLAMENCO
(www.laplateria.org.es; Placeta de Toqueros 7) Buried in the Albayzín warren, Peña La Platería claims to be the oldest flamenco aficionados' club in Spain. It's a private affair, though, and not always open to nonmembers. Performances are usually Thursday and Saturday at 10.30pm – look presentable, and speak a little Spanish at the door, if you can.

Le Chien Andalou FLAMENCO
(www.lechienandalou.com; Carrera del Darro 7; admission €8; ⌚shows 9pm) This is one of Granada's most atmospheric venues to enjoy some vigorous castanet-clicking flamenco, with a varied and professional line up of musicians and dancers throughout the week. The cave-like surroundings of a renovated *aljibe* (well) create a fittingly moody setting.

ℹ Information

Provincial Tourist Office (www.turismodegranada.org; Plaza de Mariana Pineda 10; ⌚9am-10pm Mon-Fri, 10am-7pm Sat) Information on the whole Granada region; a short walk east of Puerta Real.

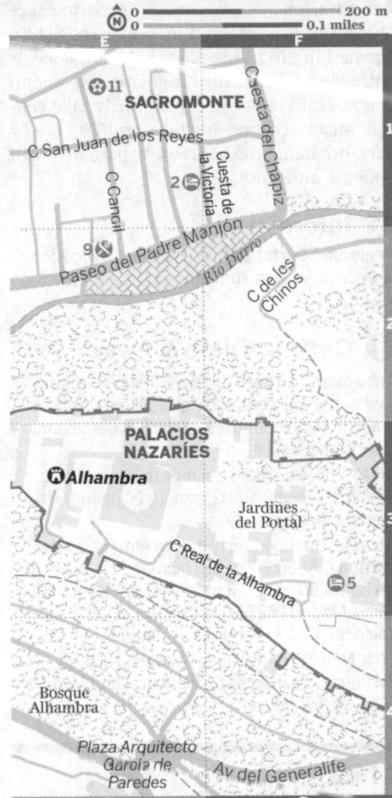

Granada

Top Sights
- Albayzín ... B2
- Alhambra ... E3
- Capilla Real ... A3
- Catedral ... A3

Sleeping
1. Carmen de la Alcubilla ... D4
2. Casa Morisca Hotel ... E1
3. Hostal Arteaga ... A1
4. Hotel Zaguán del Darro ... D2
5. Parador de Granada ... F3

Eating

6. Arrayanes ... B2
7. Bodegas Castañeda ... B3
8. El Ají ... B1
9. Ruta del Azafrán ... E2

Entertainment

10. Le Chien Andalou ... C2
11. Peña de la Platería ... E1

Municipal Tourist Office (www.granadatur.com; Calle Almona del Campillo, 2; ⌚9am-7pm Mon-Fri, to 6pm Sat, 10am-2pm Sun) Opposite the city's Parque Federico García Lorca.

Getting There & Away

AIR Destinations from Granada's airport include Madrid, Barcelona, Milan and Bologna. **Autocares J González** (www.autocaresjosegonzalez.com) runs buses between the airport and the city centre (€3, five daily) on Gran Vía de Colón.

BUS Granada's **bus station** (Carretera de Jaén) is 3km northwest of the city centre. Destinations include Córdoba (€13.50, 2¾ hours direct, nine daily), Seville (€20.50, three hours, ten daily), Málaga (€10.50, 1½ hours direct, 18 daily) and an overnight service to Madrid's Barajas Airport (€24.50, six hours).

TRAIN The **train station** (☎958 24 02 02; Avenida de Andaluces) is 1.5km west of the centre. Trains run to/from Seville (€24, three hours, four daily), Almería (€16.50, 2¼ hours, four daily), Ronda (€15, three hours, three daily), Algeciras (€25, 4½ hours, three daily), Madrid (€68, four to five hours, one or two daily), Valencia (€52.50, 7½ to eight hours, one daily) and Barcelona (€58, 12 hours, one daily).

Costa de Almería

The coast east of Almería in eastern Andalucía is perhaps the last section of Spain's Mediterranean coast where you can have a beach to yourself. This is Spain's sunniest region – even in late March it can be warm enough to strip off and take in the rays.

Sights & Activities

The **Alcazaba** (Calle Almanzor; adult/EU citizen €1.50/free; ⌚9am-8.30pm Tue-Sun Apr-Oct, to 6.30pm Tue-Sun Nov-Mar), an enormous 10th-century Muslim fortress, is the highlight of Almería City.

The best thing about the region is the wonderful coastline and semidesert scenery of the Cabo de Gata promontory. All along the 50km coast from El Cabo de Gata village to Agua Amarga, some of the most beautiful and empty beaches on the Mediterranean alternate with precipitous cliffs and scattered villages. The main village is laid-back San José, with excellent beaches nearby, such as **Playa de los Genoveses** and **Playa de Mónsul**.

Sleeping & Eating

ALMERÍA CITY

Hotel Catedral HOTEL €€
(950 27 81 78; www.hotelcatedral.net; Plaza de la Catedral 8; r €70;) Cosied up to the Almería Cathedral and built with the same warm honey-coloured stone, the hotel building dates from 1850 and has been sensitively restored. Rooms are large, with luxury touches, and the sun terrace has heady cathedral views.

Plaza Vieja Alejandro HOTEL €€
(950 28 20 96; www.plazaviejahl.com; Plaza de la Constitución 5; r €80-110;) This is, arguably, the most stylish accommodation in the city. Part of the stunning Hammam Aire de Almería, the rooms are spacious and modern with high ceilings, lots of glass and shiny wood, soft natural colours and vast photo-friezes of local sights like the Cabo de Gato.

TOP CHOICE **Tetería Almedina** TEAHOUSE €€
(www.restauranteteteriaalmedina.com; Calle Paz 2, off Calle de la Almedina; teas €3, mains €7-12; 11am-11pm Tue-Sun;) This lovely little cafe in the old city serves a fascinating range of teas, delectable sweets and good couscous. It's run by a group dedicated to restoring and revitalising the old city, and functions as a sort of casual Islamic cultural centre. There's usually live music on Sundays, in addition to art shows and similar.

CABO DE GATA

Atalaya Hotel HOTEL €
(950 38 00 85; www.atalayahotel.net; Avenida de San José, San José; r incl breakfast €75;) This central hotel, situated over a bustling restaurant and bar, has rooms set around small terraces. At the time of research, the owners were in the throes of giving the rooms a Moroccan-style update with warm burgundy-painted walls, low beds and sparkling slate grey bathrooms.

Hostal Aloha HOSTAL €
(950 38 04 61; www.hostalaloha.com; Calle Cala Higuera, San José; r €55;) White walls, firm beds and gleaming bathrooms make this an appealing budget hotel to start with. Then throw in the enormous pool on the back terrace, and it's one of the best deals in San José. It's a few blocks back from the beach; to reach it, turn left off the main street at the tourist office.

Acá Charles INTERNATIONAL €€
(Avenida de San José 51, San José; mains €14-19) Opened in 2012, this place has all the locals enthusing about the sophisticated menu where seafood doesn't necessarily take central stage. Dishes include truffles, crispy Serrano ham, fresh green asparagus with polenta, and similar.

Information

Regional Tourist Office (Parque de Nicolás Salmerón; 9am-7pm Mon-Fri, 10am-2pm Sat & Sun)

Getting There & Away

AIR Almería **airport** (950 21 37 00), 10km east of the city centre, receives flights from several European countries, as well as Barcelona, Madrid and Melilla.

BOAT There are daily sailings to/from Melilla, Nador (Morocco) and Ghazaouet (Algeria). The tourist office has details.

BUS Destinations served from Almería's **bus station** (950 26 20 98) include Granada (€13, 2¼ hours, 10 daily), Málaga (€17, 3¼ hours, 8 daily), Madrid (€27, 10 hours, three daily) and Valencia (€37, 8½ hours, five daily).

TRAIN Daily trains run to Granada (€16.50, 2¼ hours), Seville (€40, 5½ hours) and Madrid (€45.50, 6¾ hours).

Málaga

POP 558,000

The exuberant port city of Málaga may be uncomfortably close to the overdeveloped Costa del Sol, but it's a wonderful amalgam of old Andalucian town and modern metropolis. The centre presents the visitor with narrow, old streets and wide, leafy boulevards, beautiful gardens and impressive monuments, fashionable shops and a burgeoning cultural life. The city's terrific bars and nightlife, the last word in Málaga *joie de vivre,* stay open very late.

Sights & Activities

TOP CHOICE **Museo Picasso Málaga** MUSEUM
(902 44 33 77; www.museopicassomalaga.org; Calle San Agustín 8; permanent/temporary collection €6/4.50, combined ticket €8; 10am-8pm Tue-Thu & Sun, to 9pm Fri & Sat) The hottest attraction on Málaga's tourist scene is tucked away on a pedestrian street in what was medieval Málaga's *judería.* The Museo Picasso Málaga has 204 Picasso works and also

stages high-quality temporary exhibitions on Picasso themes. The Picasso paintings, drawings, engravings, sculptures and ceramics on show (many never previously on public display) span almost every phase and influence of the artist's colourful career. Picasso was born in Málaga in 1881 but moved to northern Spain with his family when he was nine.

Casa Natal de Picasso MUSEUM
(Plaza de la Merced 15; admission €1; ⏲9.30am-8pm) The house where Picasso was born in 1881 has a replica 19th-century artist's studio and small quarterly exhibitions of Picasso's work. Personal memorabilia of Picasso and his family make up part of the display.

Catedral CATHEDRAL
(☎952 21 59 17; Calle Molina Lario; cathedral & museum €3.50; ⏲10am-6pm Mon-Sat, closed holidays) Preserved rather magnificently, like an unfinished Beethoven symphony, Málaga's cathedral was begun in the 16th century on the former site of the main mosque and never properly completed. Consequently the building exhibits a mishmash of architectural styles absorbed during over two centuries of construction.

Alcazaba CASTLE
(Calle Alcazabilla; admission €2.10, incl Castillo de Gibralfaro €3.40; ⏲9.30am-8pm Tue-Sun Apr-Oct) At the lower, western end of the Gibralfaro hill, the wheelchair-accessible Alcazaba was the palace-fortress of Málaga's Muslim governors, dating from 1057. The brick path winds uphill, interspersed with arches and stone walls and refreshingly cool in summer. Roman artefacts and fleeting views of the harbour and city enliven the walk, while honeysuckle, roses and jasmine perfume the air.

Castillo de Gibralfaro CASTLE
(admission €2.10; ⏲9am-9pm Apr-Sep, to 6pm Oct-Mar) Above the Alcazaba rises the Castillo de Gibralfaro, built by Abd ar-Rahman I, the 8th-century Cordoban emir, and rebuilt in the 14th and 15th centuries. Nothing much remains of the castle's interior, but the walkway around the ramparts affords exhilarating views, and there's a tiny museum with a military focus.

There are plans to build a funicular railway up the hill to the Castillo but no completion date was available at research time.

Beaches BEACHES
Sandy city beaches stretch several kilometres in each direction from the port. **Playa de la Malagueta**, handy to the city centre, has some excellent bars and restaurants close by. **Playa de Pedregalejo** and **Playa del Palo**, about 4km east of the centre, are popular and reachable by bus 11 from Paseo del Parque.

Sleeping

El Riad Andaluz GUESTHOUSE €€
(☎952 21 36 40; www.elriadandaluz.com; Calle Hinestrosa 24; s/d €70/86; ❄@📶) This French-run guesthouse, near the **Teatro Cervantes** (www.teatrocervantes.com; Calle Ramos Marín; ⏲closed mid-Jul–Aug), has eight rooms set around an atmospheric patio. The decoration is Moroccan but each room is different, including colourfully tiled bathrooms. Breakfast is available.

El Hotel del Pintor HOTEL €€
(☎952 06 09 81; www.hoteldelpintor.com; Calle Álamos 27; r from €75; ❄@📶) The red, black and white colour scheme of this friendly small hotel echoes the abstract artwork of *malagueño* (person from Málaga) artist Pepe Bornov, whose paintings are on permanent display throughout the public areas and rooms. The rooms in the front can be noisy, especially on a Saturday night.

Room Mate Larios HOTEL €€
(☎952 22 22 00; www.room-matehotels.com; Calle Marqués de Larios 2; s/d €80/100; ❄@📶) Located on the central Plaza de la Constitución, this hotel is housed in a 19th-century building that has been elegantly restored. Rooms are luxuriously furnished with king-size beds and carpeting throughout; several rooms have balconies overlooking Calle Marqués de Larios.

Parador Málaga Gibralfaro HISTORIC HOTEL €€€
(☎952 22 19 02; www.parador.es; Castillo de Gibralfaro; r €160-171; P❄📶≋) With an unbeatable location perched on the pine-forested Gibralfaro, Málaga's stone-built *parador* is a popular choice, although the rooms are fairly standard. Most have spectacular views from their terraces, however, and you can dine at the excellent terrace restaurant even if you are not a guest at the hotel.

Eating

Most of the best eating places are sandwiched in the narrow streets between Calle Marqués de Larios and the cathedral.

TOP CHOICE **Vino Mio** INTERNATIONAL €€
(www.restaurantevinomio.com/en; Plaza Jeronimo Cuervo 2; mains €10-15) This Dutch-owned restaurant has a diverse and interesting menu that includes dishes like kangaroo steaks, vegetable stir fries, duck breast with sweet chilli, pasta and several innovative salads.

La Moraga Antonio Martín ANDALUCÍAN €€€
(☎952 22 41 53; www.lamoraga.com; Plaza Malagueta 4; tapas from €5, mains from €20) This is Michelin-star chef Dani Garcia's second Málaga-based La Moraga (the first is on Calle Fresca in the centre). The concept is based on traditional tapas given the nouvelle treatment.

Tapeo de Cervantes TAPAS €
(www.eltapeodecervantes.com; Calle Cárcer 8; tapas €4-6; ⊙Tue-Sun) This place has caught on big time which, given its squeeze-in space, can mean a wait. Choose from traditional or more innovative tapas and *raciones* with delicious combinations and stylish presentation. Portions are generous.

Drinking & Entertainment

On weekend nights, the web of narrow old streets north of Plaza de la Constitución comes alive. Look for bars around Plaza de la Merced, Plaza Mitjana and Plaza de Uncibay.

Málaga's substantial flamenco heritage has its nexus to the northwest of Plaza de la Merced. Venues here include **Kelipe** (☎692 82 98 85; www.kelipe.net; Calle Pena 11), a flamenco centre which puts on *muy puro* (authentic) performances Thursday to Saturday at 9.30pm; entry of €15 includes one drink and tapa; reserve ahead. Intensive weekend courses in guitar and dance are also held. **Amargo** (Calle R Franquillo 3) offers Friday and Saturday night gigs, while **Vino Mio** (www.restaurantevinomio.com; Calle Alamos) is a small restaurant with an international menu where musicians and dancers fill the wait for the food.

TOP CHOICE **Bodegas El Pimpi** BAR
(www.bodegabarelpimpi.com; Calle Granada 62; ⊙11am-2am) This rambling bar is an institution in this town. The cavernous interior encompasses a warren of rooms with a central courtyard and large open terrace overlooking the recently renovated Roman amphitheatre. Walls are decorated with historic *feria* (bullfighting) posters and photos of celeb-style visitors.

Information

Municipal Tourist Office (Plaza de la Marina, www.malagaturismo.com) also has a branch at Casita del Jardinero (Avenida de Cervantes 1; ⊙9am-8pm Mar-Sep, to 6pm Oct-Feb)

Regional Tourist Office (www.andalucia.org; Pasaje de Chinitas 4; ⊙9am-7.30pm Mon-Fri, 10am-7pm Sat, 10am-2pm Sun) There is another branch at the airport; these offices cover the whole of Málaga and all of Andalucía.

Getting There & Away

AIR Málaga's busy **airport** (☎952 04 88 38), the main international gateway to Andalucía, receives flights by dozens of airlines from around Europe. The Aeropuerto train station on the Málaga–Fuengirola line is a five-minute walk from the airport. Trains run about every half-hour to Málaga-Renfe station (€2.20, 11 minutes) and Málaga-Centro station.

BUS Málaga's **bus station** (☎952 35 00 61; www.estabus.emtsam.es; Paseo de los Tilos) is 1km southwest of the city centre. Frequent buses go to Seville (€30, 2½ hours), Granada (€10.50, 1½ to two hours), Córdoba (€13.50, 3½ hours) and Ronda (€9.50, 2½ hours).

TRAIN The main station, **Málaga-Renfe** (www.renfe.es; Explanada de la Estación), is around the corner from the bus station. The superfast AVE service runs to Madrid (€87, 2½ hours, 10 daily). Trains also go to Córdoba (from €26, 2½ hours, 10 daily) and Seville (from €18.50, 2¾ hours, 11 daily).

Ronda

POP 37,000 / ELEV 744M

Perched on an inland plateau riven by the 100m fissure of El Tajo gorge and surrounded by the beautiful Serranía de Ronda, Ronda is the most dramatically sited of Andalucía's *pueblos blancos* (white villages).

Sights

The **Plaza de Toros** (built 1785), considered the national home of bullfighting, is a mecca for aficionados; inside is the small but fascinating **Museo Taurino** (Calle Virgen de la Paz; admission €6; ⊙10am-8pm Apr-Sep, to 6pm Oct-Mar).

The amazing 18th-century **Puente Nuevo** (New Bridge) is an incredible engineering feat crossing the gorge to the originally Muslim La Ciudad (Old Town). At the **Casa del Rey Moro** (House of the Moorish King; Calle Santo Domingo 17), a romantically crumbling 18th-century house, supposedly built over the remains of an Islamic palace, you can visit the cliff-top gardens and climb down La Mina, a Muslim-era stairway cut inside the rock, right to the bottom of the gorge.

Also well worth a visit are the beautiful 13th-century **Baños Arabes** (Arab Baths; Hoyo San Miguel; admission €3, free on Sun; ⏲10am-7pm Mon-Fri, to 3pm Sat & Sun). Nearby, the amusing **Museo del Bandolero** (www.museobandolero.com; Calle de Armiñán 65; admission €3; ⏲10.30am-8pm Apr-Sep, to 6pm Oct-Mar) is dedicated to the banditry for which central Andalucía was renowned in the 19th century.

Sleeping & Eating

Hotel Alavera de los Baños HOTEL **€€**
(☎952 87 91 43; www.alaveradelosbanos.com; Hoyo San Miguel; s/d incl breakfast €70/95; ❄≋) Taking its cue from the Arab baths next door, the Alavera de los Baños continues the Hispano-Islamic theme throughout, with oriental decor and tasty North African-inspired cuisine using predominantly organic foods.

Jardín de la Muralla HISTORIC HOTEL **€€**
(☎952 87 27 64; www.jardindelamuralla.com; Calle Espiritu Santo 13, Ronda; s/d incl breakfast €80/91; ❄@≋) José María has ensured that his historic family home retains plenty of evocative atmosphere with antiques, chandeliers, ancestral portraits and wonderful claw-foot bath-tubs. The terraced gardens lead to the 15th-century city walls. Pets allowed.

Parador de Ronda HOTEL **€€€**
(☎952 87 75 00; www.parador.es; Plaza de España; r €160-171; P❄@≋) Acres of shining marble and deep-cushioned furniture give this modern *parador* a certain appeal. The terrace is a wonderful place to drink in views of the gorge with your coffee or wine, especially at night.

TOP CHOICE **Bodega San Francisco** TAPAS **€**
(www.bodegasanfrancisco.com; Calle Ruedo Alameda; raciones €6-10) With three dining rooms and tables spilling out onto the narrow pedestrian street, this may well be Ronda's top tapas bar. The menu is vast and should suit the fussiest of families, even vegetarians, with nine-plus salad choices.

Information

Municipal Tourist Office (www.turismoderonda.es; Paseo de Blas Infante; ⏲10am-7.30pm Mon-Fri, 10.15am-2pm & 3.30-6.30pm Sat, Sun & holidays)

Regional Tourist Office (www.andalucia.org; Plaza de España 1; ⏲9am-7.30pm Mon-Fri May-Sep, to 6pm Oct-Apr, 10am-2pm Sat year-round)

Getting There & Away

Trains and buses run to/from Algeciras, Granada, Córdoba and Málaga.

Algeciras

TRANSPORT HUB

A gritty industrial and fishing town between Tarifa and Gibraltar, Algeciras is the major port linking Spain with Morocco and, as such, is an important way station en route between the two countries. Otherwise, we can't think of a single reason to come here. Keep your wits about you around the port area.

Sleeping & Eating

Hostal Marrakech HOTEL **€**
(☎956 57 34 74; Calle Juan de la Cierva 5; s/d €25/40) The Moroccan family who run this place have a handful of bold and tarty rooms with communal bathrooms only.

Hotel Reina Cristina HOTEL **€€€**
(☎956 60 26 22; www.hotelesglobales.com; Paseo de la Conferencia s/n; s/d €89/149) For old-world ambience head south to this colonial-style hotel with two swimming pools.

Restaurante Montes ANDALUCIAN **€€**
(☎956 65 42 07; Calle Juan Morrison 27; menú €9.50, mains €15) The Montes has a hugely fishy lunch *menú* consisting of three courses, bread and wine. There is also a long list of tempting à la carte seafood.

Getting There & Away

BOAT The fastest ferry services, **FRS** (☎956 68 18 30; www.frs.es), run from Algeciras to Tangier (passenger/car €23/84, 70 minutes, eight daily).

BUS The bus station is on Calle San Bernardo. Buses arrive regularly from for La Línea (for Gibraltar; 30 minutes), Tarifa (30 minutes), Cádiz (2½ hours) and Seville (2½ hours).

TRAIN The **train station** (☎956 63 10 05) runs services to/from Madrid (€70.90, five hours 20 minutes, two daily) and Granada (€24.80, 4¼ hours, three daily).

Cádiz

POP 125,000

Cádiz, widely considered the oldest continuously inhabited settlement in Europe, is crammed onto the head of a promontory like an overcrowded ocean liner. Columbus sailed from here on his second and fourth voyages, and after his success in the Americas, the town grew into Spain's richest and most cosmopolitan city in the 18th century. The best time to visit is during the February *carnaval* (carnival).

Sights & Activities

Catedral CHURCH
(Plaza de la Catedral; adult/student €5/3, free 7-8pm Tue-Fri, 11am-1pm Sun; ⏲10am-6.30pm Mon-Sat, 1.30-6.30pm Sun) Cádiz' yellow-domed cathedral is an impressively proportioned baroque–neoclassical construction. It fronts a broad, traffic-free plaza where the cathedral's ground-plan is picked out in the paving stones. From a separate entrance on Plaza de la Catedral, climb to the top of the **Torre de Poniente** (Western Tower; adult/child €4/3; ⏲10am-6pm, to 8pm mid-Jun–mid-Sep) for marvellous views.

Museo de Cádiz MUSEUM
(Plaza de Mina; admission €1.50; ⏲2.30-8.30pm Tue, 9am-8.30pm Wed-Sat, 9.30am-2.30pm Sun) The Museo de Cádiz, on one of Cádiz' leafiest squares, is outstanding with fine Phoenician and Roman artefacts on the ground floor and fine arts upstairs; in the latter look especially for the 18 superb canvases of saints, angels and monks by Francisco de Zurbarán.

Playa de la Victoria BEACH
This lovely, wide strip of fine Atlantic sand stretches about 4km along the peninsula from its beginning at the Puertas de Tierra. At weekends in summer almost the whole city seems to be out here.

Sleeping & Eating

Hotel Argantonio HOTEL €€
(☎956 21 16 40; www.hotelargantonio.com; Calle Argantonio 3; s/d incl breakfast €90/107; ❄@📶) At this small-is-beautiful hotel in Cádiz' old quarter, the stand-out features are the hand-painted doors, beautifully tiled floors that adorn both bedrooms and bathrooms, and the intricate Moorish arch in the lobby.

Hotel Patagonia Sur HOTEL €€
(☎856 17 46 47; www.hotelpatagoniasur.es; Calle Cobos 11; d €80-130; ❄@📶) This sleek gem opened in Cádiz' old town in 2009 and offers clean-lined modernity just steps from the 18th-century cathedral. Bonuses include its sun-filled attic rooms on the 5th floor with cathedral views.

Casa Caracol HOSTEL €
(☎956 26 11 66; www.caracolcasa.com; Calle Suárez de Salazar 4; dm/hammock incl breakfast €16/10; @📶) Casa Caracol is the only backpacker hostel in the old town. Friendly, as only Cádiz can be, it has bunk dorms for four and eight, a communal kitchen and a roof terrace with hammocks.

TOP CHOICE **El Aljibe** TAPAS €€
(www.pablogrosso.com; Calle Plocia 25; tapas €2-3.50, mains €10-15) Refined restaurant upstairs and supercool tapas bar downstairs, El Aljibe on its own is almost reason enough to come to Cádiz. The cuisine developed by *gaditano* chef Pablo Grosso is a delicious combination of the traditional and the adventurous.

Arrocería La Pepa SPANISH €€
(☎956 26 38 21; www.restaurantelapepa.es; Paseo Maritimo 14; paella per person €12-17) To get a decent paella you have to leave the old town behind and head for a few kilometres southeast along Playa de la Victoria – a pleasant, appetite-inducing ocean-side walk or a quick ride on the No 1 bus. Either method is worth it.

Information

Municipal Tourist Office (Paseo de Canalejas; ⏲8.30am-6pm Mon-Fri, 9am-5pm Sat & Sun)

Regional Tourist Office (Avenida Ramón de Carranza; ⏲9am-7.30pm Mon-Fri, 10am-2pm Sat, Sun & holidays)

Getting There & Away

BUS Destinations include Seville (€9, one hour), Tarifa (€7, 1½ hours), Málaga (€25, four hours) and Granada (€33, 5½ hours).

TRAIN From the **train station** (☎902 240202) trains run daily to Seville (€13.50, 1¾) and Madrid (€72.50, 4½ hours). High-speed AVE services to Madrid are due to commence in 2015.

Tarifa

POP 17,900

Windy, laid-back Tarifa is so close to Africa that you can almost hear the call to prayer issuing from Morocco's minarets. The town is a bohemian haven of cafes and crumbling Moorish ruins. There's also a lively windsurfing and kitesurfing scene.

Stretching west are the long, sandy (and largely deserted) beaches of the Costa de la Luz (Coast of Light), backed by cool pine forests and green hills.

Sights

A wander round the old town's narrow streets, of mainly Islamic origin, is an appetiser for Morocco. The Mudéjar **Puerta de Jerez** was built after the Reconquista. Wind your way to the mainly 15th-century **Iglesia de San Mateo** (Calle Sancho IV El Bravo; 9am-1pm & 5.30-8.30pm). South of the church, the **Mirador El Estrecho**, atop part of the castle walls, has spectacular views across to Africa, only 14km away. The 10th-century **Castillo de Guzmán** (Calle Guzmán El Bueno; admission €2; 11am-4pm) is also worth a wander; tickets for the latter must be bought at the tourist office.

Activities

Beaches

On the isthmus leading out to Isla de las Palomas, tiny **Playa Chica** lives up to its name. Spectacular **Playa de los Lances** is a different matter, stretching northwest for 10km to the huge sand dune at **Ensenada de Valdevaqueros**.

Kitesurfing & Windsurfing

Tarifa now has around 30 kitesurf and windsurf schools, many of them with offices or shops along Calle Batalla del Salado or Calle Mar Adriático. Most rent equipment and run classes. Most of the action occurs along the coast between Tarifa and Punta Paloma.

Horse Riding

Located on Playa de los Lances, **Aventura Ecuestre** (956 23 66 32; www.aventuraecuestre.com; N340 Km79.5, Hotel Dos Mares) and **Hurricane Hípica** (646 964279; N340 Km78, Hurricane Hotel) both rent well-kept horses with excellent guides. An hour's beach ride costs €30. Three- or four-hour inland rides cost €70.

Whale-watching

The Strait of Gibraltar is a top site for viewing whales and dolphins. Killer whales visit in July and August, huge sperm and fin whales lurk here from spring to autumn, and pilot whales and three types of dolphin stay all year. Several organisations in Tarifa run daily two- to 2½-hour boat trips to observe these marine mammals, and most offer a free second trip if you don't at least see dolphins. **Firmm** (956 62 70 08; www.firmm.org; Calle Pedro Cortés 4; Mar-Oct) is the best and uses every trip to record data.

Sleeping & Eating

Posada La Sacristía BOUTIQUE HOTEL €€

(956 68 17 59; www.lasacristia.net; Calle San Donato 8; r incl breakfast €115-135;) Tarifa's most elegant boutique accommodation is in a beautifully renovated 17th-century town house. Attention to detail is impeccable with 10 stylish rooms, tasteful colour schemes, large comfortable beds and rooms on several levels around a central courtyard.

Hostal Africa HOSTAL €

(956 68 02 20; www.hostalafrica.com; Calle María Antonia Toledo 12, Tarifa; s/d €50/65, with shared bathroom €35/50;) This revamped 19th-century house close to the Puerta de Jerez is one of the best *hostales* along the coast. The owners are hospitable and the rooms sparkle with bright colours and plenty of space. There's a lovely, expansive roof terrace with an exotic cabana and views of Africa.

Mandrágora MOROCCAN €€

(956 68 12 91; www.mandragoratarifa.com; Calle Independencia 3; mains €12-18; from 8pm Mon-Sat) Behind Iglesia de San Mateo, this intimate place serves Andalucían-Arabic food and does so terrifically well.

Information

Tourist Office (956 68 09 93; www.aytotarifa.com; Paseo de la Alameda; 10am-2pm daily, 6-8pm Mon-Fri Jun-Sep) Near the top end of the palm-lined Paseo de la Alameda.

Getting There & Away

BUS Daily services are offered by **Comes** (956 68 40 38; www.tgcomes.es; Calle Batalla del Salado 13) to Cádiz (€9, 1½ hours), Algeciras (€2.50, 30 minutes), La Línea de la Concepción (for Gibraltar; €4.50, 45 minutes), Seville (€18.50, three hours) and Málaga (€13.50, two hours).

BOAT Fast ferries are operated by **FRS** (956 68 18 30; www.frs.es; Avenida Andalucía 16) between Tarifa and Tangier (passenger/car/motorcycle €37/93/31, 35 minutes, eight daily).

WORTH A TRIP

MOROCCO

At once African and Arab, visible from numerous points along Spain's Andalucían coast, Morocco is an exciting detour from your Western European journey. The country's attractions are endless, from the fascinating souqs and medieval architecture of Marrakesh and Fes to the Atlantic charms of Asilah and Essaouira, from the High Atlas and Rif Mountains to the soulful sand dunes of Sahara. For further information, head to www.shop.lonelyplanet.com to purchase Lonely Planet's *Morocco* guide.

Casablanca and Marrakesh in particular are well-connected by air to numerous European cities, while car-and-passenger ferry services connect Tangier with Algeciras, Barcelona, Gibraltar and Tarifa, with an additional service between Nador and Almería.

GIBRALTAR

POP 30,000

The British colony of Gibraltar is like 1960s Britain on a sunny day, with Bobbies, double-decker buses and fried-egg-and-chip-style eateries. In British hands since 1713, the island was the starting point for the Muslim conquest of Iberia a thousand years earlier. Spain has never fully accepted UK control of the island but, for the moment at least, talk of joint sovereignty seems to have gone cold. Inhabitants speak English and Spanish, and signs are in English.

Sights & Activities

In town, the **Gibraltar Museum** (www.gibmuseum.gi; Bomb House Lane; adult/child £2/1; 10am-6pm Mon-Fri, to 2pm Sat), with its interesting historical collection and Muslim-era bathhouse, is worth a peek.

The large **Upper Rock Nature Reserve** (adult/child incl attractions £10/5, vehicle £2, pedestrian excl attractions £0.50; 9am-6.15pm, last entry 5.45pm), covering most of the upper rock, has spectacular views. The rock's most famous inhabitants are its colony of Barbary macaques, the only wild primates in Europe. Some of these hang around the **Apes' Den** near the middle cable-car station; others can often be seen at the top station or Great Siege Tunnels. Other attractions include **St Michael's Cave**, a large natural grotto renowned for its stalagmites and stalactites, and the **Great Siege Tunnels** (adult/child £8/4, price given is for admission by road - pedestrians pay less; 9.30am-7pm; walking downhill from top cable-car station), a series of galleries hewn from the rock by the British during the Great Siege by the Spaniards (1779–83) to provide new gun emplacements.

Dolphin-watching is an option from April to September. Most boats go from Watergardens Quay or adjacent Marina Bay. The trips last about 1½ hours and cost around £20 per adult. Tourist offices have full details.

Sleeping & Eating

Compared with Spain, expect to pay through the nose for accommodation and food.

Bristol Hotel HOTEL ££
(20 07 68 00; www.bristolhotel.gi; 10 Cathedral Sq; s/d/tr £63/81/93;) Veterans of bucket-and-spade British seaside holidays can wax nostalgic at the stuck-in-the-70s Bristol with its creaking floorboards, red patterned carpets and Hi-de-Hi reception staff.

Caleta Hotel HOTEL £££
(20 07 65 01; www.caletahotel.gi; Sir Herbert Miles Rd; d without/with sea view £110/150) This has a wonderful location overlooking Catalan Bay, on the east side of the Rock, five minutes from town. Its cascading terraces have panoramic sea views, and there's a host of gym and spa facilities. Bedrooms are large and luxurious.

TOP CHOICE **Bistro Madeleine** CAFE, BISTRO £
(256 Main St; cakes from £3; 9am-11pm;) If you've just polished off a steak and ale pie in the local pub, have your dessert here, a refined, smoke-free bistro that serves Illy coffee with big chunks of English-inspired cake.

Information

Money

The currency is the Gibraltar pound. You can also use euros or pounds sterling.

Telephone

To dial Gibraltar from Spain, you precede the five-digit local number with the code 00350; from other countries, dial the international access code, then the Gibraltar country code

(☎350) and local number. To phone Spain from Gibraltar, just dial the nine-digit Spanish number.

Tourist Information

Gibraltar Tourist Board (www.gibraltar.gov.uk; Duke of Kent House, Cathedral Sq; ⏲9am-5.30pm Mon-Thu, to 5.15pm Fri)

Tourist Office (Grand Casemates Sq; ⏲9am-5.30pm Mon-Fri, 10am-3pm Sat, to 1pm Sun & holidays)

Visas

To enter Gibraltar, you need a passport or EU national identity card. EU, USA, Canadian, Australian, New Zealand and South African passport-holders are among those who do not need visas for Gibraltar.

Getting There & Away

AIR Budget airline **easyJet** (www.easyjet.com) flies daily to/from London-Gatwick and three times a week from Liverpool, **British Airways** (www.ba.com) operate seven weekly flights from London Heathrow, and **Monarch Airlines** (www.flymonarch.com) flies daily to/from London Luton and Manchester.

BUS There are no regular buses to Gibraltar, but La Línea de la Concepción bus station is only a five-minute walk from the border.

CAR & MOTORCYCLE Snaking vehicle queues at the 24-hour border and congested traffic in Gibraltar often make it easier to park in La Línea and walk across the border. To take a car into Gibraltar (free) you need an insurance certificate, registration document, nationality plate and driving licence, which will be more trouble than it's worth for most.

FERRY One ferry (www.frs.es) a week sails between Gibraltar and Tangier in Morocco (€46/30 per adult/child one way, 70 minutes).

EXTREMADURA

A sparsely populated stretch of vast skies and open plains, Extremadura is far enough from most beaten tourist trails to give you a genuine sense of exploration.

Trujillo

POP 9690

With its medieval architecture, leafy courtyards, fruit gardens, churches and convents, Trujillo truly is one of the most captivating small towns in Spain. It can't be much bigger now than it was in 1529, when its most famous son, Francisco Pizarro, set off with his three brothers and a few buddies for an expedition that culminated in the bloody conquest of the Incan empire.

Sights

Plaza Mayor SQUARE

On the south side of the spectacular Plaza Mayor, carved images of Pizarro and his lover Inés Yupanqui (sister of the Inca emperor Atahualpa) decorate the corner of the 16th-century **Palacio de la Conquista**. Through a twisting alley above the Palacio de la Conquista is the **Palacio Juan Pizarro de Orellana** (admission free; ⏲10am-1pm & 4.30-6.30pm Mon-Sat, 10am-12.30pm Sun), converted from miniature fortress to Renaissance mansion by one of the Pizarro cousin conquistadors. Overlooking the Plaza Mayor from the northeast corner is the 16th-century **Iglesia de San Martín** (adult/child €1.40/free; ⏲10am-2pm & 4-7pm) with delicate Gothic ceiling tracing, stunning stained-glass windows and a grand organ (climb up to the choir loft for the best view).

Upper Town HISTORIC AREA

The 900m of walls circling the upper town date from Muslim times and it was here that the newly settled noble families built their mansions and churches after the Reconquista.

The 13th-century **Iglesia de Santa María la Mayor** (adult/child €1.40/free; ⏲10am-2pm & 4-7pm) has a mainly Gothic nave and a Romanesque tower that you can ascend (all 106 steps) for fabulous views.

At the top of the hill, Trujillo's impressive **castle** (adult/under 12yr €1.40/free; ⏲10am-2pm & 4-7pm) has 10th-century Muslim origins (evident by the horseshoe-arch gateway just inside the main entrance) and was later strengthened by the Christians. Patrol the battlements for magnificent 360-degree sweeping views.

Sleeping & Eating

TOP CHOICE **Posada dos Orillas** HISTORIC HOTEL €€

(☎927 65 90 79; www.dosorillas.com; Calle de Cambrones 6; d €70-90 Sun-Thu, €80-107 Fri & Sat; ❄📶) This tastefully renovated 16th-century mansion is in a great location in the walled town. Rooms replicate Spanish colonial taste, and are named for the countries in which towns called Trujillo are found. Personal service from the owners is excellent.

El Mirador de las Monjas HOTEL €
(☎927 65 92 23; www.elmiradordelasmonjas.com; Plaza de Santiago 2; s/d incl breakfast €50/60 Mon-Thu, €60/70 Fri-Sun; ❄) High in the old town, this six-room *hostería* attached to a quality restaurant has spotless, light, modern rooms decorated in minimalist style. The upstairs ones with sloping ceilings and pleasant vistas are slightly better than the ones below.

Restaurante La Troya SPANISH €€
(Plaza Mayor 10; menus €15) Famed for its copious servings of no-frills *comida casera* (home-style cooking), Troya enjoys a prime location on the main town square. On entering, you'll be directed to one of several dining areas, to be presented with plates of tortilla and chorizo, followed by a three-course *menú*. It's all about quantity, and queues stretch out the door on weekends.

Mesón Alberca SPANISH €€
(Calle de Cambrones 8; mains €11-17; ⏲Thu-Sun) A pretty ivy-clad terrace or dark-timber tables laid with gingham tablecloths create a choice of warm atmospheres for sampling classic *extremeño* cooking. The specialities here are oven roasts and local cheeses. The regional set menu is excellent value at €24.50.

Information

Tourist Office (www.trujillo.es; Plaza Mayor; ⏲10am-2pm & 4-7pm Oct-May, 10am-2pm & 5-8pm Jun-Sep)

Getting There & Away

The **bus station** (☎927 32 12 02; Avenida de Miajadas) is 500m south of Plaza Mayor. There are services to/from Madrid (€18 to €30, three to 4¼ hours, five daily), Cáceres (€3.50, 40 minutes, eight daily) and Mérida (€8.25, 1½ hours, three daily).

Cáceres

POP 95,030

Cáceres' *ciudad monumental* (old town), built in the 15th and 16th centuries, is perfectly preserved. The town's action centres on Plaza Mayor, at the foot of the old town, and busy Avenida de España, a short distance south.

Sights

Plaza de Santa María SQUARE
Enter the old town from Plaza Mayor through the 18th-century **Arco de la Estrella**, built with a wide span for the passage of carriages. The 15th-century Gothic cathedral, **Concatedral de Santa María** (Plaza de Santa María; admission €1; ⏲9.30am-2pm & 5.30-8.30pm Mon-Sat, 9.30-11.50am & 5.30-7.15pm Sun May-Sep), creates an impressive opening scene. Climb the **bell tower** (€1) for stunning views.

Also on the plaza are the **Palacio Episcopal** (Bishop's Palace), the **Palacio de Mayoralgo** and the **Palacio de Ovando**, all in 16th-century Renaissance style. Heading back through Arco de la Estrella, you can climb the 12th-century **Torre de Bujaco** (Plaza Mayor; adult/child €2/free; ⏲10am-2pm & 5.30-8.30pm Mon-Sat, 10am-2pm Sun Apr-Sep, 10am-2pm & 4.30-7.30pm Mon-Sat, 10am-2pm Sun Oct-Mar) for good stork's-eye views of the Plaza Mayor.

Plaza de San Mateo & Plaza de las Veletas SQUARE
From Plaza de San Jorge, Cuesta de la Compañía climbs to Plaza de San Mateo and the **Iglesia de San Mateo**, traditionally the church of the land-owning nobility and built on the site of the town's mosque.

Below the square is the excellent **Museo de Cáceres** (Plaza de las Veletas 1; non-EU/EU citizens €1.20/free; ⏲9am-2.30pm & 5-8.15pm Tue-Sat, 10.15am-2.30pm Sun) in a 16th-century mansion built over an evocative 12th-century *aljibe* (cistern), the only surviving element of Cáceres' Muslim castle. It has an impressive archaeological section and an excellent fine-arts display (open only in the mornings), with works by Picasso, Miró, Tapiès and others.

Sleeping & Eating

TOP CHOICE **Hotel Casa Don Fernando** BOUTIQUE HOTEL €€
(☎927 21 42 79; www.casadonfernando.com; Plaza Mayor 30; d €60-140; ❄📶) The classiest midrange choice in Cáceres, this boutique hotel sits on Plaza Mayor directly opposite the Arco de la Estrella. Spread over four floors, the designer rooms and bathrooms are tastefully chic; superior rooms have the best plaza views and come with free minibar (€30 more than the standards).

Parador de Cáceres HOTEL €€€
(☎927 21 17 59; www.parador.es; Calle Ancha 6; s/d €139/173; P❄@📶) A substantial makeover has given this 14th-century Gothic palace in the old town a swish modern look to its

interiors, with bedrooms and bathrooms exhibiting a distinctively nonmedieval level of style and comfort. If you're driving here, pay close attention to the directions you're given when booking.

TOP CHOICE **Atrio** SPANISH €€€
(☎927 24 29 28; www.restauranteatrio.com; Plaza de San Mateo 1; menus €99-119; ⏰lunch & dinner) With a stunning location in the heart of old Cáceres, the city's fine-dining highlight seems to be going from strength to strength. The focus is on local produce of highest quality; there's a tasting menu chosen by the chef or you can pick from a selection of daily specials to make up your own menu.

Restaurante Torre de Sande FUSION €€
(☎927 21 11 47; www.torredesande.com; Calle Condes 3; mains €12-20; ⏰lunch & dinner Tue-Sat, lunch Sun) Dine in the pretty courtyard at this elegant gourmet restaurant in the heart of the Ciudad Monumental. More modestly, stop for a drink and a tapa at the interconnecting *tapería* (tapas bar), which has appealing streetside tables.

Information

Main Tourist Office (www.turismoextremadura.com; Plaza Mayor 3; ⏰8.30am-2.30pm & 4-6pm or 5-7pm Mon-Fri, 10am-2pm Sat & Sun) At the entrance to the Ciudad Monumental. Opens later in the afternoon in summer.

Municipal Tourist Office (Calle de los Olmos 3; ⏰10am-2pm & 4.30-7.30pm or 5.30-8.30pm)

Getting There & Away

BUS The **bus station** (Carretera de Sevilla; ☎927 23 25 50) has services to Trujillo (€4.40, 40 minutes) and Mérida (€5.60, one hour).

TRAIN Up to five trains per day run to/from Madrid (€27, four hours) and Mérida (€6.10, one hour).

Mérida

POP 57,000

Once the biggest city in Roman Spain, Mérida is home to more ruins of that age than anywhere else in the country and is a wonderful spot to spend a few archaeologically inclined days.

Sights

Roman Remains RUINS
The **Teatro Romano** (Calle Álvarez de Buruaga; ⏰9.30am-7.30pm Jun-Sep, 9.30am-1.45pm & 4-6.15pm Oct-May), built around 15 BC to seat 6000 spectators and set in lovely gardens, has a dramatic and well-preserved two-tier backdrop of Corinthian stone columns; the stage's *scaenae frons* (facade) was inaugurated in AD 105. The theatre hosts performances during the Festival del Teatro Clásico in summer. The adjoining **Anfiteatro**, opened in 8 BC for gladiatorial contests, had a capacity of 14,000.

Los Columbarios (Calle del Ensanche; ⏰9.30am-1.45pm & 5-7.15pm Jun-Sep, 9.30am-1.45pm & 4-6.15pm Oct-May) is a Roman funeral site. A footpath connects it with the **Casa del Mitreo** (Calle Oviedo; adult/child €4/free; ⏰9.30am-1.45pm & 5-7.15pm Jun-Sep, 9.30am-1.45pm & 4-6.15pm Oct-May), a 2nd-century Roman house with several intricate mosaics and a well-preserved fresco.

Don't miss the extraordinarily powerful spectacle of the **Puente Romano** over the Río Guadiana, which at 792m in length with 60 granite arches, is one of the longest bridges built by the Romans.

The **Templo de Diana** (Calle de Sagasta) stood in the municipal forum, where the city government was based. The restored **Pórtico del Foro**, the municipal forum's portico, is just along the road.

Museo Nacional de Arte Romano MUSEUM
(http://museoarteromano.mcu.es; Calle de José Ramón Mélida; adult/child €3/free, EU seniors & students free; ⏰9.30am-3.30pm & 5.30-8.30pm Tue-Sun Jul-Sep, shorter hr rest of year) On no account miss this fabulous museum, which has a superb collection of statues, mosaics, frescoes, coins and other Roman artefacts, all beautifully displayed. Designed by the architect Rafael Moneo, the soaring brick structure makes a remarkable home for the collection.

Alcazaba FORTRESS
(Calle Graciano; ⏰9.30am-1.45pm & 5-7.15pm Jun-Sep, 9.30am-1.45pm & 4-6.15pm Oct-May) This large Muslim fort was built in the 9th century on a site already occupied by the Romans and Visigoths. Down below, its pretty, goldfish-populated *aljibe* (cistern) reuses Visigothic marble and stone slabs, while the ramparts look out over the Guadiana.

Sleeping & Eating

TOP CHOICE **La Flor de al-Andalus** HOSTAL €
(☎924 31 33 56; www.laflordeal-andalus.es; Avenida de Extremadura 6; s/d €33/45; ❄📶) If only all

hostales were this good. Describing itself as a 'boutique *hostal*', La Flor de al-Andalus has beautifully decorated rooms in an Andalucían style, with friendly service and a good location within walking distance of all of the main sights. This is hotel standard at a great price. Try to avoid the rooms on the ground floor by reception.

Hotel Adealba HOTEL €€
(☎924 38 83 08; www.hoteladealba.com; Calle Romero Leal 18; d incl breakfast from €96; P ❄ 📶) This chic but cordial hotel occupies a 19th-century town house close to the Templo de Diana and does so with a classy, contemporary look. The designer rooms have big windows, some with balcony, a minimalist feel, and there's a compact on-site spa complex. It's cheaper midweek. Valet parking available.

TOP CHOICE **Casa Benito** SPANISH €€
(Calle San Francisco 3; tapas €3.30, mains €14-22) Squeeze onto a tiny stool in the wood-panelled dining room, prop up the bar or relax on the sunny terrace for tapas at this bullfighting enthusiasts' hang-out; its walls plastered with photos, posters and memorabilia from the ring. The tapas are original and supertasty, while the upstairs restaurant specialises in roasts and is also a fine choice.

Tábula Calda SPANISH €€€
(www.tabulacalda.com; Calle Romero Leal 11; meals €20-25; ⏲lunch & dinner Mon-Sat, lunch Sun) This inviting space, with tilework and abundant greenery, serves up well-priced meals (including set menus from €12 to €24.50) that cover most Spanish staples. It effortlessly combines traditional home cooking, thoughtful presentation and subtle innovations.

ℹ Information

Municipal Tourist Office (www.merida.es; Paseo de José Álvarez Sáenz de Buruaga; ⏲9.30am-2pm & 5-7.30pm)

ℹ Getting There & Away

BUS From the **bus station** (☎924 37 14 04; Avenida de la Libertad), destinations include Seville (€13.50, 2½ hours), Cáceres (€5.50, 50 minutes), Trujillo (€8.50, 1¼ hours) and Madrid (from €26.50, four to five hours).

TRAIN Services to Madrid (from €33, 4½ to 6½ hours), Cáceres (from €5.50, 50 minutes) and Seville (€17, four hours).

UNDERSTAND SPAIN

History

Ancient Civilisations

Spain's story is one of European history's grand epics, and it's a story that begins further back than most – the oldest pieces of human bone in Europe (dating back a mere 780,000 years) have been found in Spain, in the Sierra de Atapuerca near Burgos.

The point at which Spanish history really gets interesting, however, is when the great civilisations of the Ancient Mediterranean began to colonise what we now know as the Iberian Peninsula, from around 1000 BC. The sea-going Phoenicians founded a great seafaring empire which depended on the establishment of ports around the Mediterranean rim. One of these ports, Cádiz, is widely believed to Europe's oldest continuously inhabited settlement.

The Romans arrived in the 3rd century BC and while they took 200 years to subdue the peninsula, they would hold it for six centuries. Called Hispania, Roman Spain became an integral part of the Roman Empire, with its impact upon language, architecture and religion lasting to this day. Reminders of Roman times include Segovia's aqueduct, the ancient theatres and other monuments of Mérida, Tarragona and Zaragoza.

Muslim Spain & the Reconquista

In 711 Muslim armies invaded the peninsula, most of which they would end up occupying. Muslim dominion would last almost 800 years in parts of Spain. In Islamic Spain (known as al-Andalus), arts and sciences prospered, new crops and agricultural techniques were introduced, and palaces, mosques, schools, public baths and gardens were built. The spirit of these times lives on most powerfully in Andalucía.

In 1085 Alfonso VI, king of Castile, took Toledo, the first definitive victory of the Reconquista (the struggle to wrestle Spain into Christian hands). By the mid-13th century, the Christians had taken most of the peninsula, except for the emirate of Granada.

The kingdoms of Castile and Aragón emerged as Christian Spain's two main powers, and in 1469 they were united by the marriage of Isabel, princess of Castile, and Fernando, heir to Aragón's throne. Known as the Catholic Monarchs, they laid the foundations for the Spanish Golden Age, but were also responsible for one of the darkest hours in Spain's history – the Spanish Inquisition: a witch-hunt to expel or execute Jews and other non-Christians. In 1492 the last Muslim ruler of Granada surrendered to them, marking the end of the Reconquista. In the same year, Jews were expelled from Spain, with Muslims sent into exile eight years later.

The Golden Age

In the same year that marked the end of the Reconquista, Christopher Columbus (Colón in Castilian) landed in the Bahamas and later Cuba. His voyages sparked a period of exploration and exploitation that was to yield Spain enormous wealth, while destroying the ancient American empires. Over the centuries that followed, Spain's growing confidence was reflected in an extravagant cultural outpouring, producing towering figures such as Velázquez and Cervantes. For three centuries, gold and silver from the New World were used to finance the rapid expansion of the Spanish empire but were not enough to prevent its slow decline. By the 18th century, the mighty Spanish empire was on its way out, the life sucked out of it by a series of unwise kings, a self-seeking noble class and ceaseless warfare.

Struggle for the Soul of Spain

By the early 19th century, Spain's royal court had descended into internecine squabbles over succession to the Spanish throne. The consequences for the rest of the country were profound.

In 1807–08 Napoleon's forces occupied a weakened Spain, and King Carlos IV abdicated without a fight. In his place Napoleon installed his own brother, Joseph Bonaparte. The Spaniards retaliated with a five-year war of independence. The French were expelled in 1813 after defeat at Vitoria. A Bourbon, Fernando VII, was restored to the Spanish throne – despite periods of interruption to their rule, the Bourbon royal family rule Spain to this day.

Independence may have been restored, but Spain spent much of the next century embroiled in wars at home and abroad. The Spanish-American War of 1898 marked the end of the Spanish empire. The USA crushed Spanish forces and took over its last overseas possessions – Cuba, Puerto Rico, Guam and the Philippines. Spain was in a dire state.

Franco's Spain

Begun in the 19th century, the battle between conservatives and liberals, and between monarchists and republicans came to a head in July 1936 when Nationalist plotters in the army rose against the Republican government, launching a civil war (1936–39) that would create bitter wounds that are still healing today. The Nationalists, led by General Francisco Franco (who stood at the head of an alliance of the army, Church and the Fascist-style Falange Party), received military support from Nazi Germany and Fascist Italy, while the elected Republican government received support from the Soviet Union and other foreign leftists.

The war ended in 1939, with Franco the victor. Some 350,000 Spaniards died in the war, most of them on the battlefield but many others in executions, prison camps or simply from disease and starvation. After the war, thousands of Republicans were executed, jailed or forced into exile, and Franco's 36-year dictatorship began with Spain isolated internationally and crippled by recession. It wasn't until the 1950s and '60s, when the rise in tourism and a treaty with the USA combined to provide much-needed funds, that the country began to recover, although Franco retained an iron grip over the country.

The New Spain

Franco died in 1975, having named Juan Carlos, the grandson of Alfonso XIII, as his successor. Despite Franco's careful grooming, King Juan Carlos opted for the creation of a constitutional monarchy and a democratic government. The first elections were held in 1977 and a new constitution was drafted in 1978. It was a dramatic shift and although deep schisms remain to this day, the country's democratic transition has been an extraordinary success.

Post-Franco Spain bore little resemblance to what went before and the country revelled in its new-found freedoms. Seemingly everything – from political parties to drugs – was legalised and the 1980s, despite the spectre of killings by the Basque terrorist group ETA, was a period of great cultural innovation, and Spain's reputation as Europe's party capital was born. Spain joined the European Community (EC) in 1986 and celebrated its return to the world stage in style in 1992, with Expo '92 in Seville and the Olympic Games in Barcelona.

At a political level, Spain was ruled from 1982 until 1996 by the Partido Socialista Obrero Español (Spanish Socialist Party; PSOE) of Felipe González. By 1996 the PSOE government stood accused of corruption and was swept from power by the centre-right Partido Popular (Popular Party; PP), led by José María Aznar. The PP went on to establish programs of economic decentralisation and liberalisation.

Long accustomed to terrorist attacks by ETA (which has killed more than 800 people in the past four decades), Spain was nonetheless shaken to its core by the largest-ever terrorist attack on Spanish soil (later claimed by al-Qaeda), in Madrid on 11 March 2004. In national elections held three days later, the PP lost the presidential election to the PSOE. Among his first actions as president, José Luís Rodríguez Zapatero withdrew Spanish troops from Iraq.

The Socialists embarked on something of a social revolution, legalising gay marriage, regularising the status of hundreds of thousands of illegal immigrants, removing the Church's role in religious education in schools, making abortions easier to obtain, and pushing through a law aimed at investigating the crimes and executions of the Franco years; the latter broke the 'pact of silence' that had prevailed throughout the transition to democracy in the late 1970s.

Within months of the Socialists' reelection in 2008, years of economic boom came shuddering to an end amid the global financial crisis; unemployment jumped from around 7% in 2007 to above 20% in 2010. With the economy deep in recession, the Socialists' popularity plummeted.

Spain Today

Prime Minister Zapatero's delay in acknowledging the crisis sealed the government's fate, and it was defeated by the PP of Prime Minister Mariano Rajoy in a landslide on 20 November 2011. By late 2012, unemployment was stuck at around 25%, youth unemployment was close to 50% and the government was forced to seek billions of euros of assistance from the EU. The government's deeply unpopular austerity program slashed public services and ushered in regular protests in Madrid and across the country. Many of Spain's regions were also forced to seek bailouts from the central government in Madrid.

Against this backdrop of economic meltdown, Spain's restive regions of Catalonia and the Basque Country began demanding greater autonomy, with plans also underway in both regions for de facto referenda on independence.

Good news may be hard to come by, but the announcement of a ceasefire by a much-weakened ETA in September 2010, followed a year later by what ETA announced was a 'definitive cessation of its armed activity'.

Religion

Only about 20% of Spaniards are regular churchgoers, but Catholicism is deeply ingrained in the culture and an estimated 94% of Spaniards identify themselves as Catholics. As the writer Unamuno said, 'Here in Spain we are all Catholics, even the atheists'.

However, many Spaniards have a deep-seated scepticism about the Church. During the civil war and the four decades of Franco's rule, the Catholic Church was, for the most part, a strong supporter of his policies. The Church retains a powerful public voice in national debates.

Spain's most significant (and growing) religious community after the Catholics are Muslims.

Arts

Literature

Miguel de Cervantes' novel *Don Quijote* is the masterpiece of the literary flowering of the 16th and 17th centuries, not to mention one of the world's great works of fiction. Centuries later, the towering figure of the early 20th century was poet and playwright Federico García Lorca, who won international acclaim before he was murdered in the civil war for his Republican sympathies.

Popular contemporary authors include Arturo Pérez Reverte, Almudena Grandes and Javier Marías.

Cinema

Modern Spanish cinema's best-known director is Pedro Almodóvar, whose humorous, cutting-edge films are often set amid the great explosion of drugs and creativity that occurred in Madrid in the 1980s. His *Todo Sobre Mi Madre* (All About My Mother;

1999) and *Habla Con Ella* (Talk to Her; 2002) are both Oscar winners, while *Volver* (2006) is his most acclaimed recent work.

Alejandro Amenábar, the young Chilean-born director of *Abre los Ojos* (Open Your Eyes; 1997), *The Others* (2001) and the Oscar-winning *Mar Adentro* (The Sea Inside; 2004), is Almodóvar's main competition for Spain's 'best director' title. That latter film's star, Javier Bardem, won the Oscar for Best Supporting Actor in the Coen brothers' disturbing *No Country for Old Men* in 2008. The Madrid-born actress Penélope Cruz won an Oscar for Best Supporting Actress for her role in Woody Allen's *Vicky Cristina Barcelona* (2008).

Architecture

The Muslims left behind some of the most splendid buildings in the Islamic world, particularly in Andalucía. Examples include Granada's Alhambra, Córdoba's Mezquita and Seville's Alcázar – the latter is an example of Mudéjar architecture, the name given to Islamic artistry built in Christian-held territory. Outside of Andalucía, Zaragoza's Aljafería captures the same spirit, albeit on a smaller scale.

The first main Christian architectural movement was Romanesque, best seen in churches and monasteries across the north of the country. Later came the great Gothic cathedrals, such as those in Toledo, Burgos, León, Ávila, Salamanca and Seville of the 12th to 16th centuries. Spain then followed the usual path to baroque (17th and 18th centuries) and neoclassicism (19th century).

Around the turn of the 20th century, Catalonia produced its startling Modernista movement and many buildings in this style adorn Barcelona's streets; Antoni Gaudí's La Sagrada Família is the most stunning example.

Of the daring contemporary structures appearing all over Spain, Valencia's Ciudad de las Artes y las Ciencias and Bilbao's Guggenheim are the most eye-catching.

Painting

The giants of Spain's Golden Age (around 1550 to 1650) were Toledo-based El Greco (originally from Crete) and Diego Velázquez, considered Spain's best painter by greats including Picasso and Dalí. El Greco and Velázquez are well represented in Madrid's Museo del Prado, as is the genius of the 18th and 19th centuries, Francisco Goya. Goya's versatility ranged from unflattering royal portraits and anguished war scenes to bullfight etchings and tapestry designs.

Catalonia was the powerhouse of early-20th-century Spanish art, claiming the hugely prolific Pablo Picasso (although born in Málaga, Andalucía), the colourful symbolist Joan Miró and surrealist Salvador Dalí. To get inside the latter's world, head for Figueres or the Castell de Púbol. The two major museums dedicated to Picasso's work are the Museu Picasso in Barcelona and the Museo Picasso Málaga, while his signature *Guernica* and other works are found in Madrid's Centro de Arte Reina Sofía. The Reina Sofía also has works by Joan Miró, as does the Fundació Joan Miró.

Important artists of the late 20th century include the Basque sculptor Eduardo Chillida; his Museo Chillida Leku is south of San Sebastián.

Flamenco

Most musical historians speculate that flamenco probably dates back to a fusion of songs brought to Spain by the Roma people, with music and verses from North Africa crossing into medieval Muslim Andalucía.

FLAMENCO – THE ESSENTIAL ELEMENTS

A flamenco singer is known as a *cantaor* (male) or *cantaora* (female); a dancer is a *bailaora*. Most of the songs and dances are performed to a blood-rush of guitar from the *tocaora* (flamenco guitarist). Percussion is provided by tapping feet, clapping hands and sometimes castanets. Flamenco *coplas* (songs) come in many different types, from the anguished *soleá* or the intensely despairing *siguiriya* to the livelier *alegría* or the upbeat *bulería*. The first flamenco was *cante jondo* (deep song), an anguished instrument of expression for a group on the margins of society. *Jondura* (depth) is still the essence of pure flamenco.

The traditional flamenco costume – shawl, fan and long, frilly *bata de cola* (tail gown) for women, flat Cordoban hats and tight black trousers for men – dates from Andalucian fashions in the late 19th century.

Flamenco as we now know it first took recognisable form in the 18th and early 19th centuries among Roma people in western Andalucía. Suitably, for a place considered the cradle of the genre, the Seville–Jerez de la Frontera–Cádiz axis is still considered the flamenco heartland and it's here, purists believe, that you must go for the most authentic flamenco experience.

Environment

The Land

Spain is a geographically diverse country, with landscapes ranging from the near-deserts of Almería to the emerald green countryside of Asturias and deep coastal inlets of Galicia, from the rolling sunbaked plains of Castilla-La Mancha to the rugged Pyrenees. The country covers 84% of the Iberian Peninsula and spreads over 505,370 sq km, about 40% of which is high *meseta* (tableland).

Wildlife

The brown bear, wolf, Iberian lynx (the world's most endangered cat species, although it's making a hesitant and much-assisted comeback) and wild boar all survive in Spain, although only the boar exists in abundance. Spain's high mountains harbour the chamois and Spanish ibex, and big birds of prey such as eagles, vultures and lammergeier. The marshy Ebro Delta and Guadalquivir estuary are important for waterbirds, among them the spectacular greater flamingo.

Environmental Issues

Spain faces some of the most pressing environmental issues of our time. Drought, massive overdevelopment of its coastlines, overexploitation of scarce water resources by tourism projects and intensive agriculture, and spiralling emissions of greenhouse gases are all major concerns. It's a slightly more nuanced picture than first appears – Spain is a leading player in the wind-power industry, it has locked away around 40,000 sq km of protected areas, including 14 national parks, and its system of public transport is outstanding – but the apparent absence of any meaningful political will to tackle these issues is storing up problems for future generations.

Food & Drink

Reset your stomach's clock in Spain unless you want to eat alone, with other tourists or, in some cases, not at all.

Most Spaniards start the day with a light *desayuno* (breakfast), perhaps coffee with a *tostada* (piece of toast) or *pastel/bollo* (pastry), although they might stop in a bar later for a mid-morning *bocadillo* (baguette). *La comida* (lunch) is usually the main meal of the day, eaten between about 2pm and 4pm. The *cena* (evening meal) is usually lighter and most locals won't sit down for it before 9pm. The further south you go, the later start times tend to be – anything from 10pm to midnight!

At lunchtime from Monday to Friday, most places offer a *menú del día* – a fixed-price lunch menu and the traveller's best friend. For €10 to €14 you typically get three courses, bread and a drink. The *plato combinado* (combined plate) is a cousin of the *menú* and usually includes a meat dish with some vegetables.

JAMÓN – A PRIMER

Unlike Italian prosciutto, Spanish *jamón* is a bold, deep red and well marbled with buttery fat. Like wines and olive oil, Spanish *jamón* is subject to a strict series of classifications. *Jamón serrano* refers to *jamón* made from white-coated pigs introduced to Spain in the 1950s. Once salted and semidried by the cold, dry winds of the Spanish sierra, most now go through a similar process of curing and drying in a climate-controlled shed for around a year. *Jamón serrano* accounts for approximately 90% of cured ham in Spain.

Jamón ibérico – more expensive and generally regarded as the elite of Spanish hams – comes from a black-coated pig indigenous to the Iberian Peninsula and a descendant of the wild boar. If the pig gains at least 50% of its body weight during the acorn-eating season, it can be classified as *jamón ibérico de bellota*, the most sought-after designation for *jamón*.

Staples & Specialities

The variety in Spanish cuisines is quite extraordinary, and each region has its own styles and specialities. One of the most characteristic dishes, from the Valencia region, is paella – rice, seafood, the odd vegetable and often chicken or meat, all simmered together and traditionally coloured yellow with saffron. *Jamón serrano* (cured ham) is a delicacy available in many different qualities.

Many would argue that tapas are Spain's greatest culinary gift to the world, not least because the possibilities are endless. You can also order *raciones*, a large-sized serving of tapas. Anything can be a tapa, from a handful of olives or a piece of *tortilla de patatas* (potato and onion omelette) to more elaborate and often intensely surprising combinations of tastes. For tapas, the cities of Andalucía are usually (but not always) bastions of tradition, while the undoubted king of tapas destinations is San Sebastián, in Basque country, where they call tapas '*pintxos*'. It all comes together in Madrid.

Drinks

Start the day with a strong coffee, either as a *cafe con leche* (half-coffee, half-milk), *cafe solo* (short black, espresso-like) or *cafe cortado* (short black with a little milk).

The most common way to order a *cerveza* (beer) is to ask for a *caña* (small draught beer). In Basque Country this is a *zurrito*. A larger beer (about 300mL) is often called a *tubo*. All these words apply to *cerveza de barril* (draught beer) – if you just ask for a *cerveza* you're likely to get bottled beer, which is a little more expensive.

Vino (wine) comes *blanco* (white), *tinto* (red) or *rosado* (rosé). Exciting wine regions include Penedès, Priorat, Ribera del Duero and La Rioja. There are also many regional specialities, such as *jerez* (sherry) in Jerez de la Frontera and *cava* (a sparkling wine) in Catalonia. Sangria, a sweet punch made of red wine, fruit and spirits, is a summer drink and especially popular with tourists.

Agua del grifo (tap water) is usually safe to drink.

Vegetarians & Vegans

Vegetarians may have to be creative in Spain. You'll find dedicated vegetarian restaurants in larger cities. Otherwise, most traditional restaurants will offer salads and egg tortillas, but little else for non-carnivores. Even salads may come laden with sausages or tuna. Pasta and pizza are readily available, as is seafood for those who eat it. Vegans will have an especially hard time away from the big cities (and not an easy time in them).

SURVIVAL GUIDE

Directory A–Z

Accommodation

Budget options include everything from dorm-style youth hostels to family-style *pensiones* and slightly better-heeled *hostales*. At the upper end of this category you'll find rooms with air-conditioning and private bathrooms. Midrange *hostales* and hotels are more comfortable and most offer standard hotel services. Business hotels, trendy boutique hotels and luxury hotels are usually in the top-end category.

Virtually all accommodation prices are subject to IVA *(impuesto sobre el valor añadido)*, the Spanish version of value-added tax, which is 10%. This may or may not be included in the quoted price. To check, ask: *Está incluido el IVA?* (Is IVA included?)

PRICE RANGES

Our reviews refer to double rooms with a private bathroom, except in hostels or where otherwise specified. Quoted rates are for high season, which is generally May to September (though this varies greatly from region to region).

€ less than €65 (less than €75 for Madrid/Barcelona)

€€ €65 to €140 (€75 to €200 for Madrid/Barcelona)

€€€ more than €140 (more than €200 for Madrid/Barcelona)

CAMPING

Spain has around 1000 officially graded *campings* (camping grounds) and they vary greatly in service, cleanliness and style. They're officially rated as 1st class (1ªC), 2nd class (2ªC) or 3rd class (3ªC). Camping grounds usually charge per person, per tent and per vehicle – typically €5 to €10 for each. Many camping grounds close from around October to Easter.

The following are useful websites:

Campings Online (www.campingsonline.com/espana) Booking service.

Campinguía (www.campinguia.com) Contains comments (mostly in Spanish) and links.

Guía Camping (www.guiacampingfecc.com) Online version of the annual *Guía Camping* (€13.60), which is available in bookshops around the country.

HOTELS, HOSTALES & PENSIONES

Most options fall into the categories of hotels (one to five stars, full amenities), *hostales* (high-end guesthouses with private bathroom; one to three stars) or *pensiones* (guesthouses, usually with shared bathroom; one to three stars). A gem of Spain's accommodation scene, **paradores** (☎902 547979; www.parador.es) are luxury, but well-priced state-run hotels, often inhabiting beautiful old castles, monasteries and former palaces.

YOUTH HOSTELS

Albergues juveniles (youth hostels) are cheap places to stay, especially for lone travellers. Expect to pay from €15 to €28 per night, depending on location, age and season. Spain's Hostelling International (HI) organisation, **Red Española de Albergues Juveniles** (REAJ, Spanish Youth Hostel Network; www.reaj.com), has around 250 youth hostels throughout Spain. Official hostels require HI membership (you can buy a membership card at virtually all hostels) and some have curfews.

Activities

HIKING

» Lonely Planet's *Walking in Spain* – read more about some of the best treks in the country.

» Maps by Editorial Alpina –useful for hiking, especially in the Pyrenees. Buy at bookshops, sports shops and sometimes petrol stations near hiking areas.

» GR (*Grandes Recorridos,* or long distance) trails – indicated with red-and-white markers.

SKIING

» Cheaper, less varied than much of rest of Europe.

» Season: December to mid-April.

SURFING, WINDSURFING & KITESURFING

The Basque Country has good surf spots, including San Sebastián, Zarautz and the legendary left at Mundaka. Tarifa, with its long beaches and ceaseless wind, is generally considered to be the windsurfing capital of Europe. It's also a top spot for kitesurfing.

Business Hours

Reviews in this guidebook won't list business hours unless they differ from the following standards:

Banks 8.30am to 2pm Monday to Friday; some also open 4pm to 7pm Thursday and 9am to 1pm Saturday

Central post offices 8.30am to 9.30pm Monday to Friday, 8.30am to 2pm Saturday

Nightclubs midnight or 1am to 5am or 6am

Restaurants lunch 1pm to 4pm, dinner 8.30pm to midnight or later

Shops 10am to 2pm and 4.30pm to 7.30pm or 5pm to 8pm; big supermarkets and department stores generally open from 10am to 10pm Monday to Saturday

Embassies & Consulates

Australia Embassy (☎91 353 66 00; www.spain.embassy.gov.au; Paseo de la Castellana 259D, 24th fl, Madrid)

Canada Embassy (☎91 382 84 00; www.espana.gc.ca; Paseo de la Castellana 259D, Torre Espacio, Madrid)

New Zealand Embassy (☎91 523 02 26; www.nzembassy.com/spain; Calle de Pinar 7, 3rd Fl, Madrid)

UK Embassy (☎91 714 62 00; www.ukinspain.fco.gov.uk; Paseo de la Castellana 259D, Torre Espacio, Madrid)

USA Embassy (☎91 587 22 00; http://spanish.madrid.usembassy.gov/; Calle de Serrano 75, Madrid)

Food

The following price categories for the cost of a main course are used in the listings in this chapter.

€€€ more than €20

€€ €10 to €20

€ less than €10

Gay & Lesbian Travellers

Homosexuality is legal in Spain. In 2005 the Socialists gave the country's conservative Catholic foundations a shake with the legalisation of same-sex marriages in Spain.

Lesbians and gay men generally keep a fairly low profile, but are quite open in the cities. Madrid, Barcelona, Sitges, Torremolinos and Ibiza have particularly lively scenes.

Internet Access

» Wi-fi increasingly available at most hotels and some cafes, restaurants and airports; generally (but not always) free.

» Good cybercafes are increasingly hard to find; ask at the local tourist office. Prices per hour range from €1.50 to €3.

Language Courses

» Popular places to learn Spanish: Barcelona, Granada, Madrid, Salamanca and Seville

» **Escuela Oficial de Idiomas** (EOI; www.eeooiinct.com) is a nationwide institution teaching Spanish and other local languages. On the website's opening page, hit 'Centros' under 'Comunidad' and then 'Centros en la Red' to get to a list of schools.

Legal Matters

Drugs Cannabis is legal but only for personal use and in very small quantities. Public consumption of any drug is illegal.

Smoking Not permitted in any enclosed public space, including bars, restaurants and nightclubs.

Money

ATMs Many credit and debit cards can be used for withdrawing money from *cajeros automáticos* (automatic teller machines) that display the relevant symbols such as Visa, MasterCard, Cirrus etc.

Cash Most banks will exchange major foreign currencies and offer the best rates. Ask about commissions and take your passport.

Credit & Debit Cards Can be used to pay for most purchases. You'll often be asked to show your passport or some other form of identification, or to type in your pin. The most widely accepted cards are Visa and MasterCard.

Moneychangers Exchange offices, indicated by the word *cambio* (exchange), offer longer opening hours than banks, but worse exchange rates and higher commissions.

Taxes & Refunds In Spain, value-added tax (VAT) is known as IVA (*ee*-ba; *impuesto sobre el valor añadido*). Visitors are entitled to a refund of the 18% IVA on purchases costing more than €90.16 from any shop if they are taking them out of the EU within three months.

Tipping Menu prices include a service charge. Most people leave some small change. Taxi drivers don't have to be tipped but a little rounding up won't go amiss.

Travellers Cheques Can be changed (for a commission) at most banks and exchange offices.

Public Holidays

The two main periods when Spaniards go on holiday are Semana Santa (the week leading up to Easter Sunday) and July or August. At these times accommodation can be scarce and transport heavily booked.

There are at least 14 official holidays a year – some observed nationwide, some locally. National holidays:

Año Nuevo (New Year's Day) 1 January

Viernes Santo (Good Friday) March/April

Fiesta del Trabajo (Labour Day) 1 May

La Asunción (Feast of the Assumption) 15 August

Fiesta Nacional de España (National Day) 12 October

La Inmaculada Concepción (Feast of the Immaculate Conception) 8 December

Navidad (Christmas) 25 December

Regional governments set five holidays and local councils two more. Common dates include the following:

Epifanía (Epiphany) or **Día de los Reyes Magos** (Three Kings' Day) 6 January

Día de San José (St Joseph's Day) 19 March

Jueves Santo (Good Thursday) March/April. Not observed in Catalonia and Valencia.

Corpus Christi June; the Thursday after the eighth Sunday after Easter Sunday.

Día de San Juan Bautista (Feast of St John the Baptist) 24 June

Día de Santiago Apóstol (Feast of St James the Apostle) 25 July

Día de Todos los Santos (All Saints Day) 1 November

Día de la Constitución (Constitution Day) 6 December

Safe Travel

Most visitors to Spain never feel remotely threatened, but a sufficient number have unpleasant experiences to warrant an alert. The main thing to be wary of is petty theft (which may of course not seem so petty if your passport, cash, travellers cheques, credit card and camera go missing). Stay alert and you can avoid most thievery techniques. Algeciras, Barcelona, Madrid and Seville are the worst offenders, as are popular beaches in summer (never leave belongings unattended). Common scams include the following:

» Kids crowding around you asking for directions or help.

» A person pointing out bird droppings on your shoulder (some substance their friend has sprinkled on you) – as they help clean it off they are probably emptying your pockets.

» The guys who tell you that you have a flat tyre. While your new friend and you check the tyre, his pal is emptying the car.

» The classic snatch-and-run. Never leave your belongings unattended.

» An old classic: the ladies offering flowers for good luck. We don't know how they do it, but your pockets always wind up empty.

Telephone

Blue public payphones are common and fairly easy to use. They accept coins, phonecards and, in some cases, credit cards. Phonecards come in €6 and €12 denominations and, like postage stamps, are sold at post offices and tobacconists.

International reverse-charge (collect) calls are simple to make: dial ☎900 99 followed by the appropriate code. For example: ☎900 99 00 61 for Australia, ☎900 99 00 44 for the UK, ☎900 99 00 11 (AT&T) for the USA etc.

To speak to an English-speaking Spanish international operator, dial ☎1008 (for calls within Europe) or ☎1005 (rest of the world).

MOBILE PHONES

All Spanish mobile phone companies (Telefónica's MoviStar, Orange and Vodafone) offer *prepagado* (prepaid) accounts for mobiles. The SIM card costs from €50, which includes some prepaid phone time.

Mobile phone numbers in Spain start with the number 6.

PHONE CODES

Area codes in Spain are an integral part of the phone number. All numbers are nine digits and you just dial that nine-digit number.

Numbers starting with 900 are national toll-free numbers, while those starting 901 to 905 come with varying costs; most can only be dialled from within Spain. In a similar category are numbers starting with 800, 803, 806 and 807.

Tourist Information

All cities and many smaller towns have an *oficina de turismo*. In the country's provincial capitals you'll sometimes find more than one tourist office – one specialising in information on the city alone, the other carrying mostly provincial or regional information. National and natural parks also often have visitor centres offering useful information. Spain's official tourism site is *Turespaña* (www.spain.info).

Visas

Spain is one of 26 member countries of the Schengen Convention and Schengen visa rules apply.

Citizens/residents of EU & Schengen countries No visa required.

Citizens/ residents of Australia, Canada, Israel, Japan, NZ and the USA No visa required for tourist visits of up to 90 days.

Other countries Check with a Spanish embassy or consulate.

To work or study in Spain A special visa may be required – contact a Spanish embassy or consulate before travel.

Work

Norwegian, Swiss, Icelandic and EU nationals may work in Spain without a visa. Everyone else must obtain a work permit (from a Spanish consulate in their country of residence) and, if they plan to stay more than 90 days, a residence visa.

Teaching English is an obvious option; a TEFL (Teaching English as a Foreign Language) certificate will be a big help. Other possibilities include summer bar and restaurant work, as well as getting work on yachts in major ports.

Getting There & Away

Entering the Country

Immigration and customs checks usually involve a minimum of fuss, although there are exceptions. Your vehicle could be searched on arrival from Morocco; they're looking for controlled substances. Expect long delays at these borders, especially in summer.

The tiny principality of Andorra is not in the EU, so border controls (and rigorous customs checks for contraband) remain in place.

Air

Flights from all over Europe, including numerous budget airlines, serve main Spanish airports. All of Spain's airports share the user-friendly website and flight information telephone number of **Aena** (☎902 404 704; www.aena.es), the national airports authority. For more information on each airport on Aena's website, choose English and click on the drop-down menu of airports. Each airport's page has details on practical information (such as parking and public transport) and a full list of (and links to) airlines using that airport.

Madrid's Aeropuerto de Barajas is Spain's busiest (and Europe's fifth-busiest) airport.

Land

Spain shares land borders with France, Portugal and Andorra.

Apart from shorter cross-border services, **Eurolines** (www.eurolines.com) is the main operator of international bus services to Spain from most of Western Europe and Morocco.

In addition to the rail services connecting Spain with France and Portugal, there are direct trains between Zürich and Barcelona (via Bern, Geneva, Perpignan and Girona), and between Milan and Barcelona (via Turin, Perpignan and Girona). For these and other services, visit the website of **Renfe** (☎902 24 34 02; www.renfe.com), the Spanish national railway company.

Regular buses connect Andorra with Barcelona (including winter ski buses and direct services to the airport) and other destinations in Spain (including Madrid) and France.

TRANSPORT FROM FRANCE

Bus

DESTINATION	COMPANY	DURATION	FREQUENCY
Paris to Madrid	Eurolines	17¾ hr	daily
Paris to Barcelona	Eurolines	14¾ hr	daily

Car & Motorcycle

The main road crossing into Spain from France is the highway that links up with Spain's AP7 tollway, which runs down to Barcelona and follows the Spanish coast south (with a branch, the AP2, going to Madrid via Zaragoza). A series of links cut across the Pyrenees from France and Andorra into Spain, as does a coastal route that runs from Biarritz in France into the Spanish Basque Country.

Train

The main rail lines into Spain cross the Franco–Spanish frontier along the Mediterranean coast and via the Basque Country. Another minor route runs inland across the Pyrenees from Latour-de-Carol to Barcelona.

TGV (high-speed) trains connect Paris Montparnasse with Irún, where you change to a normal train for the Basque Country and on towards Madrid. Up to three TGVs also put you on track to Barcelona (leaving from Paris Gare de Lyon), with a change at Montpellier or Narbonne.

There are plans for direct high-speed rail links from Paris to Madrid and Barcelona.

DESTINATION	COMPANY	PRICE	DURATION	FREQUENCY
Paris Austerlitz to Madrid Chamartín	*Trenhotel Francisco de Goya*	chair/sleeper class €162.30/177.80	13½ hours	one daily
Paris Austerlitz to Barcelona Estacio de Franca	*Trenhotel Joan Miró*	chair/sleeper class €153.10/166.50	12 hours	one daily
Montpellier to Lorca	Talgo	€105	12½ hours	daily

FERRIES TO SPAIN

Ferries run to mainland Spain regularly from the Canary Islands, Italy, North Africa (Algeria, Morocco and the Spanish enclaves of Ceuta and Melilla) and the UK. Most services are run by the Spanish national ferry company, **Acciona Trasmediterránea** (☎902 454645; www.trasmediterranea.es). You can take vehicles on the following routes.

Algeria

DESTINATION	COMPANY	DURATION	FREQUENCY
Almería–Ghazaouet	Acciona Trasmediterránea	eight hours	four weekly (late June–mid Sep)
Almería–Oran	Acciona Trasmediterránea	eight hours	two weekly (May–Sep)

France

DESTINATION	COMPANY	DURATION	FREQUENCY
Gijón-Saint–Nazaire	LD Lines (www.ldlines.com)	14 hours	three weekly

Italy

DESTINATION	DURATION	FREQUENCY
Barcelona–Genoa	18 hours	three weekly
Barcelona–Civitavecchia (near Rome)	20½ hours	six to seven weekly
Barcelona–Livorno (Tuscany)	19½ hours	three weekly
Barcelona–Porto Torres (Sardinia)	12 hours	one daily

Morocco

In addition to the following services, there are also ferries to the Spanish enclaves of Melilla (from Almería and Málaga) and Ceuta (from Algeciras).

DESTINATION	DURATION	FREQUENCY
Tangier–Algeciras	90 minutes	up to eight daily
Tangier–Barcelona	24-35 hours	weekly
Tangier–Tarifa	35 minutes	up to eight daily
Nador–Almería	five to eight hours	up to three daily

UK

From mid-March to mid-November, **Brittany Ferries** (www.brittanyferries.com) runs the following services:

DESTINATION	DURATION	FREQUENCY
Plymouth–Santander	20 hours	weekly
Portsmouth–Santander	24 hours	weekly
Portsmouth-Bilbao	24 hours	twice weekly

Getting Around

Students and seniors are eligible for discounts of 30% to 50% on most types of transport within Spain.

Air

Domestic Spanish routes are operated by the following airlines:

Air Berlin (www.airberlin.com) Madrid to Valencia, Palma de Mallorca, Ibiza, Seville,

TRANSPORT FROM PORTUGAL

Bus

DESTINATION	COMPANY	PRICE	DURATION	FREQUENCY
Lisbon–Madrid	Avanza (www.avanzabus.com)	€37.50	7½ to 9hr	two daily

Other bus services run north via Porto to Tui, Santiago de Compostela and A Coruña. Local buses cross the border from towns such as Huelva, Badajoz and Ourense.

Car & Motorcycle

The A5 freeway linking Madrid with Badajoz crosses the Portuguese frontier and continues on to Lisbon, and there are many other road connections up and down the length of the Hispano–Portuguese frontier.

Train

From Portugal, the main line runs from Lisbon across Extremadura to Madrid.

DESTINATION	PRICE	DURATION	FREQUENCY
Lisbon–Madrid	chair/sleeper class €63.20/91.40	10½ hours	one daily
Lisbon–Irún	chair/sleeper class €73.80/103.50	14½ hours	one daily

Jerez de la Frontera, Alicante, Bilbao and Santiago de Compostela.

Air Europa (www.aireuropa.com) Madrid to Ibiza, Palma de Mallorca, Vigo and Santiago de Compostela.

easyJet (www.easyjet.com) Madrid to Ibiza, Menorca, Asturias (Gijón) and Santiago de Compostela.

Iberia (www.iberia.es) Spain's national airline and its subsidiary, Iberia Regional-Air Nostrum, have an extensive domestic network.

Ryanair (www.ryanair.com) Numerous domestic Spanish routes.

Volotea (www.volotea.com) New budget airline; domestic and international flights.

Vueling (www.vueling.com) Spanish low-cost company with loads of domestic flights.

Bicycle

Regional trains have space for carrying bikes, and they're also permitted on most *cercanías* (local trains in cities like Madrid and Barcelona); long-distance trains have more restrictions. As a rule, you have to be travelling overnight in a sleeper or couchette for (dismantled) bikes to be accepted as normal luggage.

Boat

Regular ferries connect the Spanish mainland with the Balearic Islands.

Bus

Spain's bus network is operated by countless independent companies, and reaches into the most remote towns and villages. Many towns and cities have one main station for arrivals and departures, which usually has an information desk. Tourist offices can also help with information on bus services.

Local services can get you nearly anywhere, but most buses connecting rural towns aren't geared to tourist needs. Frequent weekday services drop off to a trickle on weekends. It's not necessary, and often not possible, to make reservations for local bus journeys. It is, however, a good idea to turn up at least 30 minutes before the bus leaves to guarantee a seat.

Generally, bus fares are cheaper than on the faster, long-distance trains. For longer trips, you should buy your ticket in advance.

Among the hundreds of bus companies operating in Spain, the following have the largest networks:

ALSA (☎902 422242; www.alsa.es)

Avanza (☎902 020999; www.avanzabus.com)

Car & Motorcycle

Spain's roads vary enormously but are generally good. Fastest are the *autopistas;* on some, you have to pay hefty tolls.

Every vehicle should display a nationality plate of its country of registration and you must always carry proof of ownership of a private vehicle, as well as a warning triangle and a reflective jacket (to be used in case of breakdown). Third-party insurance is required throughout Europe.

AUTOMOBILE ASSOCIATIONS

The **Real Automóvil Club de España** (RACE; 902 404 545; www.race.es) is the national automobile club. They may well come to assist you in case of a breakdown, but you should obtain an emergency telephone number for Spain from your own insurer.

DRIVING LICENCES

All EU driving licences are recognised. Other foreign licences should be accompanied by an International Driving Permit (although in practice local licences are usually accepted).

HIRE

To rent a car in Spain you have to have a licence, be aged 21 or over and have a credit or debit card. Rates vary widely: the best deals tend to be in major tourist areas, including airports. Prices are especially competitive in the Balearic Islands. Expect a compact car to cost from €30 and up per day.

INSURANCE

Third-party motor insurance is a minimum requirement and it is compulsory to have an internationally recognised proof of insurance, which can be obtained from your insurer. Also ask your insurer for a European Accident Statement form, which can simplify matters in the event of an accident.

ROAD RULES

Blood-alcohol limit 0.05%.

Legal driving age for cars 18.

Legal driving age for motorcycles & scooters 16 (80cc and over) or 14 (50cc and under). A licence is required.

Motorcyclists Must use headlights at all times and wear a helmet if riding a bike of 125cc or more.

Side of the road Drive on the right.

Speed limits In built-up areas 50km/h (and in some cases, such as inner-city Barcelona, 30km/h), which increases to 100km/h on major roads and up to 120km/h on *autovías* and *autopistas* (toll-free and tolled dual-lane highways). Cars towing caravans are restricted to 80km/h.

Train

Renfe (902 240 202; www.renfe.es) is the national railway company. Trains are mostly modern and comfortable, and late arrivals are the exception rather than the rule. The high-speed network is in constant expansion.

Passes are valid for all long-distance Renfe trains; Inter-Rail users pay supplements on Talgo, InterCity and AVE trains. All passholders making reservations pay a small fee.

Among Spain's numerous types of trains:

Alaris, Altaria, Alvia, Arco and Avant Long-distance intermediate-speed services.

Cercanías For short hops and services to outlying suburbs and satellite towns in Madrid, Barcelona and 11 other cities.

Euromed Similar to the AVE trains, they connect Barcelona with Valencia and Alicante.

Regionales Trains operating within one region, usually stopping at all stations.

Talgo and Intercity Slower long-distance trains.

Tren de Alta Velocidad Española (AVE) High-speed trains that link Madrid with Barcelona, Burgos, Córdoba, Cuenca, Huesca, Lerida, Málaga, Seville, Valencia, Valladolid and Zaragoza. There are also Barcelona–Seville and Barcelona–Málaga services. In coming years Madrid–Cádiz and Madrid–Bilbao should come on line.

Trenhotel Overnight trains with sleeper berths.

CLASSES & COSTS

All long-distance trains have 2nd and 1st classes, known as *turista* and *preferente*. The latter is 20% to 40% more expensive.

Fares vary enormously depending on the service (faster trains cost considerably more) and, in the case of some high-speed services such as the AVE, on the time and day of travel.

Children aged between four and 12 years are entitled to a 40% discount; those aged under four travel for free (except on high-speed trains, for which they pay the same as those aged four to 12). Buying a return ticket often gives you a 10% to 20% discount on the return trip. Students and people up to 25 years of age with a Euro<26 Card (Carnet Joven in Spain) are entitled to 20% to 25% off most ticket prices.

RESERVATIONS

Reservations are recommended for long-distance trips; you can make them in train stations, Renfe offices, travel agencies and online. A growing number of stations let you pick up prebooked tickets from machines scattered about the station concourse.

Switzerland

Includes »

Best Places to Eat

» Bottegone del Vino (p1090)
» Wirtshaus Galliker (p1072)
» Alpenrose (p1082)
» Lötschberg AOC (p1068)
» Whymper Stube (p1066)

Best Places to Stay

» Hotel Bahnhof (p1066)
» Hôtel Beau-Rivage Palace (p1061)
» Hotel du Thèâtre (p1081)
» Hotel Landhaus (p1068)
» Palace Luzern (p1072)

Why Go?

What giddy romance Zermatt, St Moritz and other glitterati-encrusted names evoke. This is *Sonderfall Schweiz* ('special case Switzerland'), a privileged neutral country, proudly idiosyncratic, insular and unique. Blessed with gargantuan cultural diversity, its four official languages alone say it all.

The Swiss don't do half-measures: Zürich, their most gregarious urban centre, has cutting-edge art, legendary nightlife and one of the world's highest living standards. The national passion for sweat, stamina and clingy Lycra takes 65 year olds across 2500m-high mountain passes for Sunday strolls, sees giggly three year olds skiing rings around grown-ups, prompts locals done with 'ordinary' marathons to sprint backwards up mountains – all in the name of good old-fashioned fun.

So don't depend just on your postcard images of Bern's chocolate-box architecture, the majestic Matterhorn or the thundering Rheinfall – Switzerland is a place that's so outrageously beautiful, it simply must be seen to be believed.

When to Go

Geneva

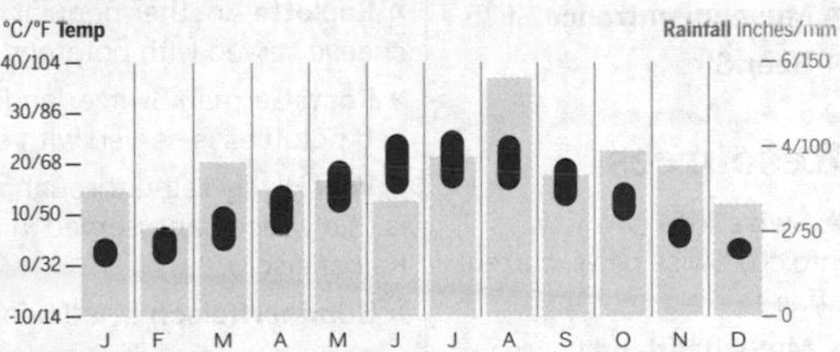

Dec–early Apr Carve through powder and drink gluhwein at an alpine resort.

May–Sep Hike in the shadow of the Matterhorn and be wowed by its mesmerising stance.

Aug Celebrate Swiss National Day on 1 August and witness Swiss national pride in full force.

AT A GLANCE

» **Currency** Swiss franc (Sfr)

» **Languages** French, German, Italian, Romansch

» **Money** ATMs readily available

» **Visas** Schengen rules apply

Fast Facts

» **Area** 41,285 sq km

» **Capital** Bern

» **Country code** ☎41

» **Emergency** police ☎117; fire ☎118; ambulance ☎144

Exchange Rates

Australia	A$1	Sfr0.99
Canada	C$1	Sfr0.93
Euro	€1	Sfr1.22
Japan	¥100	Sfr1.01
New Zealand	NZ$1	Sfr0.79
UK	UK£1	Sfr1.44
USA	US$1	Sfr0.95

Set Your Budget

» **Budget hotel** Sfr80-100

» **Two-course meal** Sfr30

» **Museum entrance** Sfr15

» **Beer** Sfr5

Resources

» **Swiss Info** (www.swissinfo.ch) Swiss news, current affairs.

» **MySwitzerland** (www.myswitzerland.com) Swiss tourism.

Connections

Landlocked between France, Germany, Austria, Liechtenstein and Italy, Switzerland is well-linked. Geneva city buses run as far as the French border (a couple cross into France, continuing along the southern shore of Lake Geneva). Fast and frequent French TGV trains link Geneva and Lausanne with Paris. In the north, newly completed high-speed lines in France mean that Zürich is only four hours from Paris while Basel is but three. Basel also has fast ICE trains that serve major German cities, while Zürich is well linked to Stuttgart, Munich and Austria. Regular trains serve Milan from Zürich, Lucerne and Lugano.

ITINERARIES

One Week

Starting in vibrant Zürich, shop famous Bahnhofstrasse and find the medieval corners. Next, head to the Jungfrau region to explore some kick-ass alpine scenery (think James Bond racing an avalanche down a sheer snowy rock face). Take a pit stop in beautiful Lucerne before finishing up in country capital Bern.

Two Weeks

As above, then head west for French-immersion lessons in Geneva or lakeside Lausanne. Stop in Gruyères to dip into a cheesy fondue and overdose on meringues drowned in thick double cream. Zip to Zermatt or across to St Moritz to frolic in snow or green meadows, then loop east to taste the Italian side of Switzerland at lakeside Lugano.

Essential Food & Drink

» **Fondue** Switzerland's best-known dish, in which melted Emmental and Gruyère cheese are combined with white wine in a large pot and eaten with bread cubes.

» **Raclette** Another popular artery-hardener of melted cheese served with potatoes.

» **Rösti** German Switzerland's national dish of fried shredded potatoes is served with everything.

» **Veal** Highly rated throughout the country; in Zürich, veal is thinly sliced and served in a cream sauce *(Gschnetzeltes Kalbsfleisch)*.

» **Bündnerfleisch** Dried beef, smoked and thinly sliced.

» **Chocolate** Good at any time of day and available in dozens of luscious flavours.

GENEVA

POP 192,400

Slick and cosmopolitan, Geneva (Genève in French, Genf in German) is a rare breed of city. It's one of Europe's priciest. Its people chatter in every language under the sun (184 nationalities comprise 45% of the city's population) and it's constantly thought of as the Swiss capital – which it isn't. This business-like city strung around the sparkling shores of Europe's largest alpine lake is, in fact, only Switzerland's second-largest city.

Yet the whole world is here: the UN, International Red Cross, International Labour Organization, World Health Organization – 200-odd governmental and nongovernmental international organisations fill the city's plush hotels with big-name guests, feast on an incredulous choice of cuisine and help prop up the overload of banks, jewellers and chocolate shops for which Geneva is known. Strolling manicured city parks, lake sailing and skiing next door in the Alps are weekend pursuits.

GENEVA IN TWO DAYS

Explore the left-bank parks, gardens and **Jet d'Eau**, then hit the **Old Town** for lunch and a stroll. Tummy full, take in a museum, followed by a dip in the water and an aperitif at **Bains des Pâquis**. On day two, plan a tour of **CERN** or **Palais des Nations**, followed by another stroll along the lake.

Sights

The city centre is so compact it's easy to see many of the main sights on foot.

Lake Geneva LAKE

Begin your exploration of Europe's largest alpine lake by having a coffee on **Île Rousseau**, where a statue honours the celebrated freethinker. Cross to the southern side of the lake and walk west to the **Horloge Fleurie** (Flower Clock; Quai du Général-Guisan) in the Jardin Anglais. Geneva's most photographed clock, crafted from 6500 flowers, can be oddly disappointing after all the hype.

Far more rewarding is the iconic 140m-tall **Jet d'Eau** (Lake Geneva, Jetée des Eaux-Vives; admission free; 9.30am-11.15pm Mar-Oct) on the lake's southern shore. When the fountain climaxes there are seven tonnes of water in the air, shooting up to create its sky-high plume, kissed by a rainbow on sunny days.

TOP CHOICE **Old Town** HISTORIC AREA

The main street of the Vieille Ville (Old Town), Grand-Rue, shelters the **Espace Rousseau** (022 310 10 28; www.espace-rousseau.ch; Grand-Rue 40; adult/child Sfr5/3; 11am-5.30pm Tue-Sun), where the 18th-century philosopher was born. It's Geneva's best area for walking; the Place du Bourg-de-Four is timeless and ringed by good cafes.

Nearby, the part-Romanesque, part-Gothic **Cathédrale de St-Pierre** (St Peter's Cathedral; Cour St-Pierre; admission free; 9.30am-6.30pm Mon-Sat, noon-6.30pm Sun Jun-Sep, 10am-5.50pm Mon-Sat, noon-5.30pm Sun Oct-May) is where Protestant John Calvin preached from 1536 to 1564. Revel in the flamboyant **Chapel of the Maccabees**. Beneath the cathedral is the **site archéologique** (022 311 75 74; www.site-archeologique.ch; Cour St-Pierre 6; adult/child Sfr8/4; 10am-5pm Tue-Sun), an interactive space safeguarding fine 4th-century mosaics and a 5th-century baptismal font.

You can trace Calvin's life in the neighbouring **Musée Internationale de la Réforme** (International Museum of the Reformation; 022 310 24 31; www.musee-reforme.ch; Rue du Clootre 4; adult/student/child Sfr8/3/2; 10am-5pm Tue-Sun).

Palais des Nations LANDMARK

(022 907 48 96; www.unog.ch; Av de la Paix 14; adult/child Sfr12/7; 10am-noon & 2-4pm Mon-Fri Sep-Mar, 10am-noon & 2-4pm daily Apr-Jun, 10am-5pm daily Jul & Aug) The art deco Palais des Nations is the European arm of the UN and the home of 3000 international civil servants. You can see where decisions about world affairs are made on the hour-long tour. Afterwards check out the extensive gardens – don't miss the towering grey monument coated with heat-resistant titanium donated by the USSR to commemorate the conquest of space. An ID or passport is obligatory for admission. Tram 15 stops here.

International Red Cross & Red Crescent Museum MUSEUM

(Musée Internationale de la Croix Rouge et du Croissant-Rouge; 022 748 95 25; www.micr.org; Av de la Paix 17) Closed at the time of research, the museum was set to reopen in 2013 after a massive rethink. Visitors engage with displays along three themes: 'Defending

(Continued on page 1056)

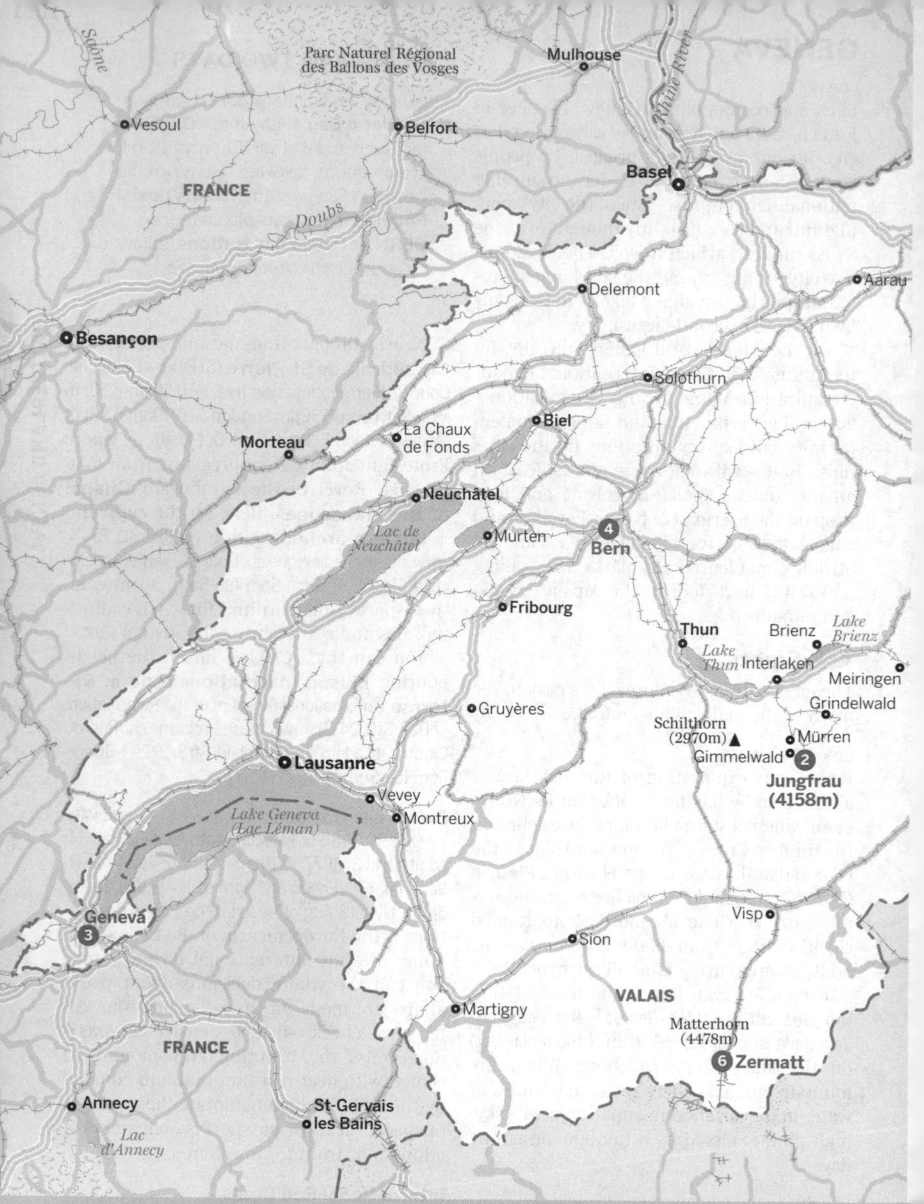

Switzerland Highlights

1 Discover the zest of **Zürich** (p1078) with a daytime stroll along the city's sublime lake followed by a rollicking night out

2 Be wowed by the Eiger's monstrous north face on a ride to the 'top of Europe', 3471m **Jungfraujoch** (p1077)

3 Board a boat in **Geneva** (p1051) for a serene lake cruise to Nyon or medieval Lausanne

4 Be surprised by Swiss capital **Bern** (p1066): think medieval charm, folkloric fountains and a cafe and dining culture

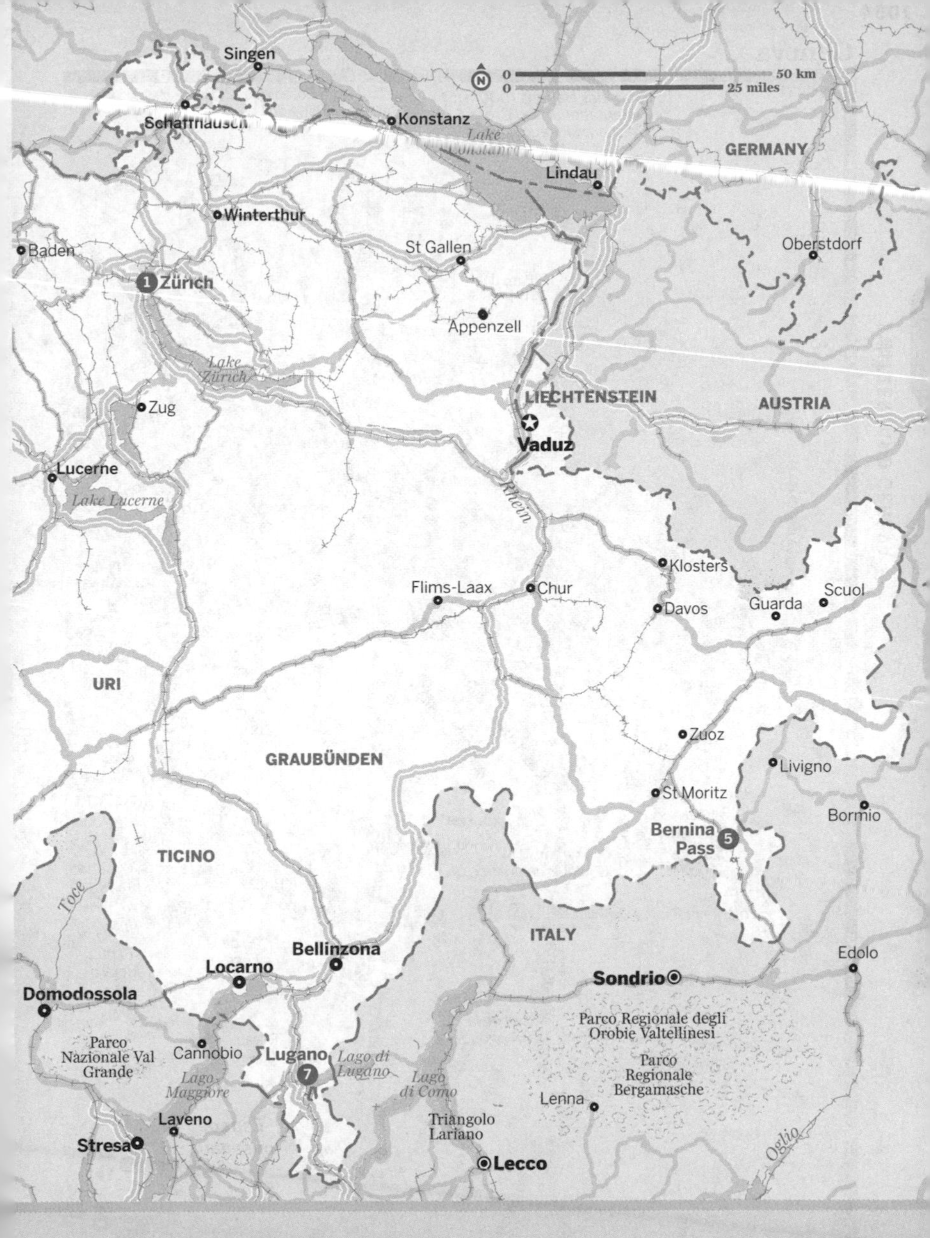

5 Ride one of Switzerland's iconic scenic trains, such as one over the **Bernina Pass** (p1091)

6 Gape at the iconic Matterhorn and wander around the car-free alpine village of **Zermatt** (p1065)

7 Try out your Italian accent at **Lugano** (p1089), which has a lovely, temperate lake setting

Geneva

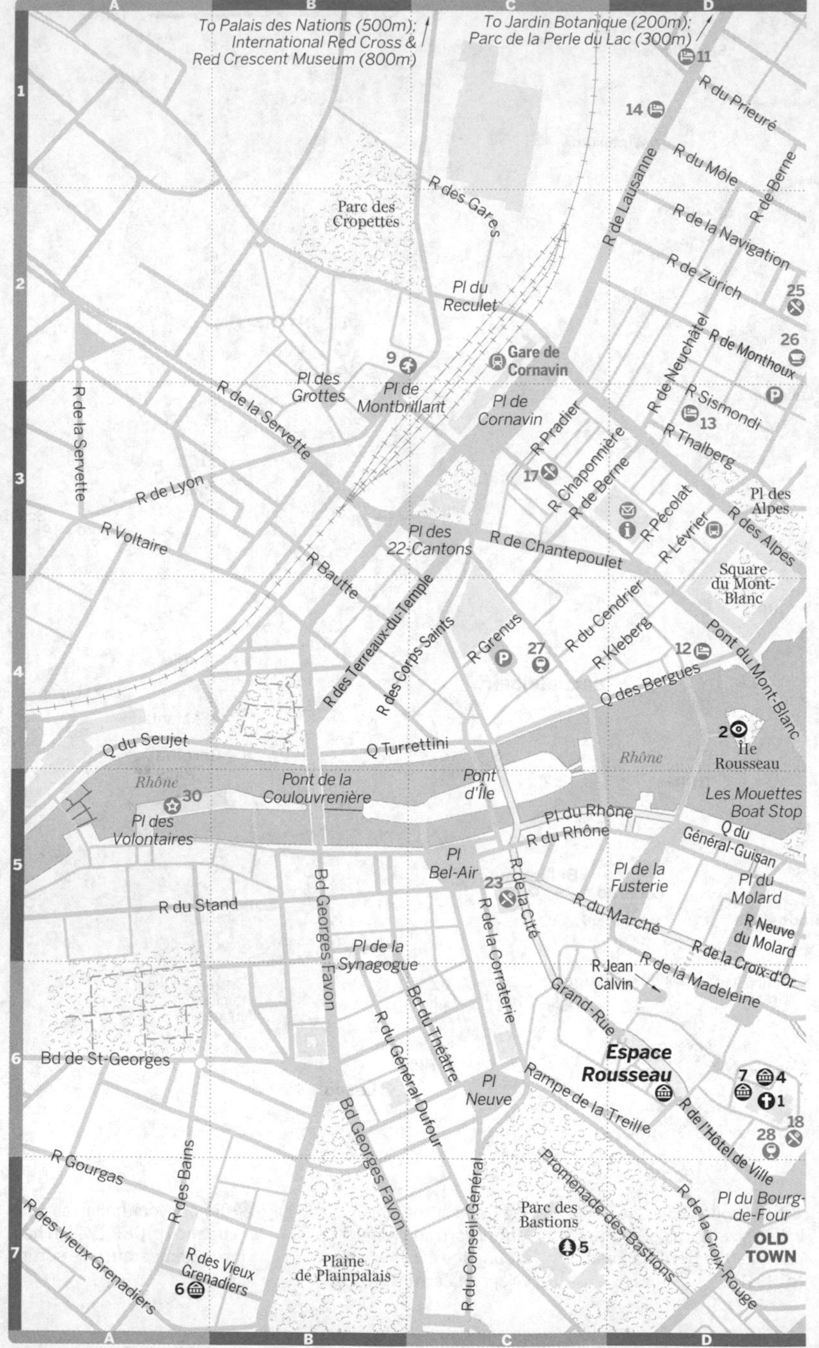

To Palais des Nations (500m); International Red Cross & Red Crescent Museum (800m)
To Jardin Botanique (200m); Parc de la Perle du Lac (300m)
Parc des Cropettes
R des Gares
R du Prieuré
R du Môle
R de Berne
R de Lausanne
R de la Navigation
R de Zürich
Pl du Reculet
R de Neuchâtel
R de Monthoux
Gare de Cornavin
Pl des Grottes
Pl de Montbrillant
Pl de Cornavin
R Sismondi
R Thalberg
R de la Servette
R Pradier
R Chaponnière
R de Berne
R de Lyon
R Voltaire
Pl des 22-Cantons
R de Chantepoulet
R Pécolat
R Lévrier
Pl des Alpes
R des Alpes
Square du Mont-Blanc
R Bautte
R des Terreaux-du-Temple
R des Corps Saints
R Grenus
R du Cendrier
R Kleberg
Pont du Mont-Blanc
Q des Bergues
Q du Seujet
Q Turrettini
Île Rousseau
Rhône
Pont de la Coulouvrenière
Pont d'Île
Les Mouettes Boat Stop
Pl des Volontaires
Pl du Rhône
R du Rhône
Q du Général-Guisan
Pl Bel-Air
Pl de la Fusterie
Pl du Molard
R de la Cité
R du Stand
R du Marché
R Neuve du Molard
Bd Georges Favon
R de la Corraterie
R de la Croix-d'Or
Pl de la Synagogue
R Jean Calvin
R de la Madeleine
Grand-Rue
Bd du Théâtre
R du Général Dufour
Espace Rousseau
Bd de St-Georges
Pl Neuve
Rampe de la Treille
R de l'Hôtel de Ville
R Gourgas
R du Conseil-Général
Promenade des Bastions
Pl du Bourg-de-Four
R des Bains
Parc des Bastions
R de la Croix-Rouge
OLD TOWN
R des Vieux Grenadiers
Plaine de Plainpalais

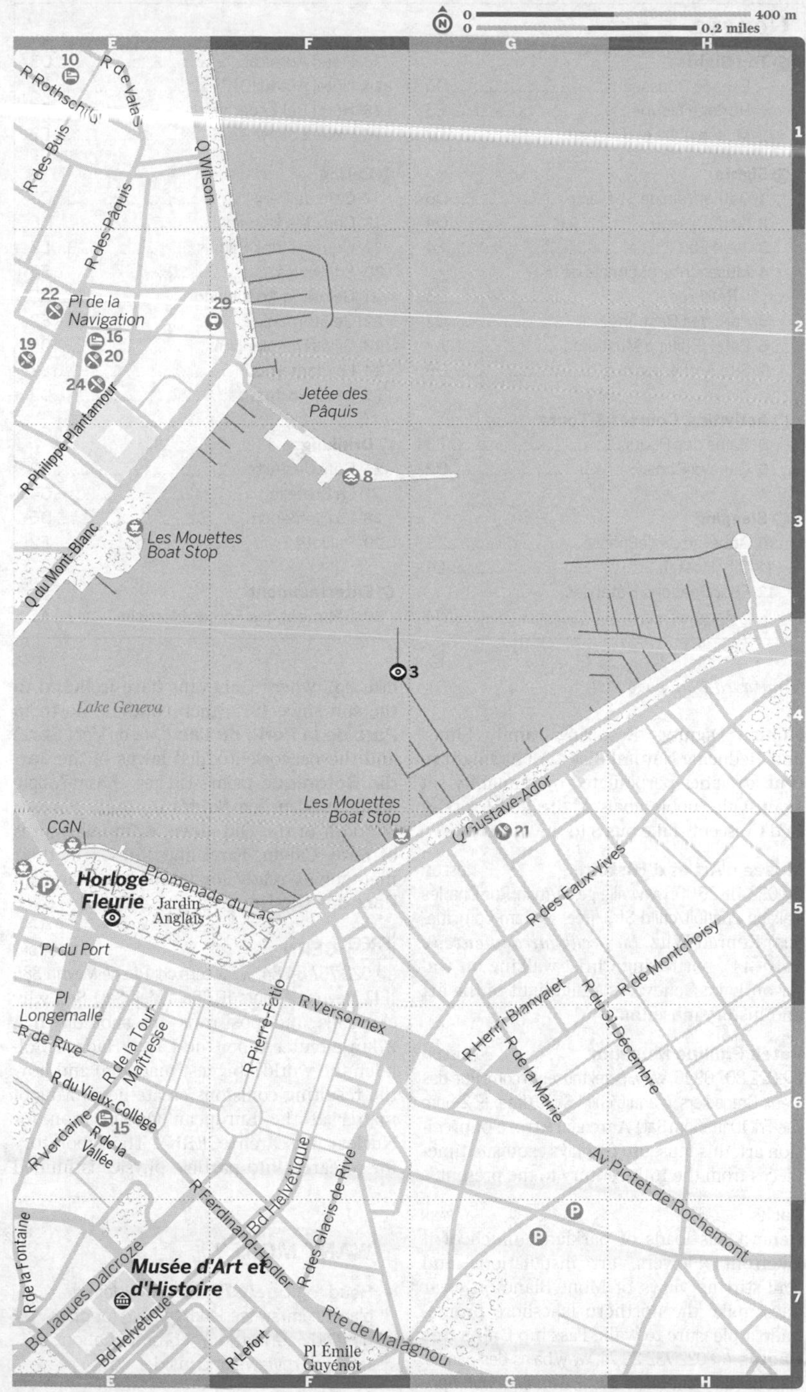

0
400 m
0
0.2 miles
E
F
G
H
1
2
3
4
5
6
7
R Rothschild
R de Valais
R des Buis
Q Wilson
R des Pâquis
Pl de la Navigation
R Philippe Plantamour
Jetée des Pâquis
Les Mouettes Boat Stop
Q du Mont-Blanc
Lake Geneva
Les Mouettes Boat Stop
Q Gustave-Ador
CGN
Horloge Fleurie
Jardin Anglais
Promenade du Lac
R des Eaux-Vives
Pl du Port
R de Montchoisy
Pl Longemalle
R Versonnex
R Pierre-Fatio
R Henri Blanvalet
R du 31 Décembre
R de Rive
R de la Tour-Maîtresse
R de la Mairie
R du Vieux-Collège
R Verdaine
R de la Vallée
Av Pictet de Rochemont
Bd Helvétique
R des Glacis de Rive
R Ferdinand-Hodler
R de la Fontaine
Bd Jaques Dalcroze
Musée d'Art et d'Histoire
Bd Helvétique
R Lefort
Pl Émile Guyénot
Rte de Malagnou
10
22
29
19
16
20
24
8
3
21
15

Geneva

Top Sights

Espace Rousseau ... D6
Horloge Fleurie ... E5
Musée d'Art et d'Histoire ... E7

Sights

1 Cathédrale de St-Pierre ... D6
2 Île Rousseau ... D4
3 Jet d'Eau ... F4
4 Musée Internationale de la Réforme ... D6
5 Parc des Bastions ... C7
6 Patek Phillipe Museum ... A7
7 Site Archéologique ... D6

Activities, Courses & Tours

8 Bains des Pâquis ... F3
9 Genève Roule ... B2

Sleeping

10 Auberge de Jeunesse ... E1
11 City Hostel ... D1
12 Four Seasons Hôtel des Bergues ... D4
13 Hotel Admiral ... D3
14 Hôtel Auteuil ... D1
15 Hôtel Bel'Esperance ... E6
16 Hotel Edelweiss ... E2

Eating

17 Café de Paris ... C3
18 Chez Ma Cousine ... D6
19 Crêperie des Pâquis ... E2
20 Edelweiss ... E2
21 Gelateria Arlecchino ... G5
22 Gelatomania ... E2
23 Gilles Desplanches ... C5
24 Le Plantamour ... E2
25 Les 5 Portes ... D2

Drinking

26 Café des Arts ... D2
27 La Bretelle ... C4
28 La Clémence ... D6
29 Paillote ... F2

Entertainment

30 Bâtiment des Forces Motrices ... A5

(Continued from page 1051)

Human Dignity', 'Restoring Family Links' and 'Reducing Natural Risks'. All highlight recent atrocities perpetuated by humanity set against the noble goals of the Red Cross & Red Crescent. Take bus 8 to the Appia stop.

Musée d'Art et d'Histoire MUSEUM
(☎022 418 26 00; www.ville-ge.ch/mah; Rue Charles Galland 2; adult/child Sfr3/free; ⊙11am-6pm Tue-Sun) Konrad Witz' *La pêche miraculeuse* (c 1440–44), portraying Christ walking on water on Lake Geneva, is a highlight of the art and history museum.

Patek Phillipe Museum MUSEUM
(☎022 807 09 10; www.patekmuseum.com; Rue des Vieux Grenadiers 7; adult/child Sfr10/free; ⊙2-6pm Tue-Fri, 10am-6pm Sat) A treasure trove of precision art, this museum displays exquisite timepieces from the 16th century to the present.

Parks PARK
Geneva has loads of parkland, much of it lakefront. Flowers, art installations and soul-stirring views of Mont Blanc on clear days make the northern lakeshore promenade a pleasure to walk. Pass hip **Bains des Pâquis** (☎022 732 29 74; www.bains-des-paquis.ch; Quai du Mont-Blanc 30; ⊙9am-8pm mid-Apr–mid-Sep), where Genevans have frolicked in the sun since 1872, then continue north to **Parc de la Perle du Lac** (Quai du Mont-Blanc) and the peacock-studded lawns of the **Jardin Botanique** (admission free; ⊙8am-7.30pm Apr-Oct, 9.30am-5pm Nov-Mar).

South of the Old Town, 4.5m-tall figures of Bèze, Calvin, Farel and Knox – in their nightgowns ready for bed – loom large in **Parc des Bastions**.

FREE **CERN** LABORATORY
(☎022 767 84 84; www.cern.ch; Rte de Meyrin 385 1217, Meyrin; ⊙tours 10.30am Mon-Sat) See why electrons and positrons are shot down a 27km circular tube (the Large Hadron Collider, the world's biggest machine) and how the resulting collisions create new forms of matter at the European Organisation for Nuclear Research (CERN). The laboratory for research into particle physics is funded

WANT MORE?

Head to **Lonely Planet** (www.lonelyplanet.com/switzerland/geneva) for planning advice, author recommendations, traveller reviews and insider tips.

FREE THRILLS

Bags of fabulous things to see and do in Geneva don't cost a cent. Our favourite freebies:

» Dashing like mad under the iconic Jet d'Eau (p1051).

» Getting lost in the Old Town (p1051).

» Hobnobbing with big-bang scientists at CERN (p1056).

» Going green in the Jardin Botanique (p1056).

» Flopping on the beach on the Bains des Pâquis (p1056) jetty.

» Pedalling along the lake into France or towards Lausanne.

by 20 nations and can be visited on free tours (book at least one month in advance). Otherwise, enjoy **Microcosm** (☎022 767 84 84; admission free; ⊙8.30am-5.30pm Mon-Fri, 9am-5pm Sat), the on-site multimedia and interactive visitors centre. CERN is 8km west of Geneva; take tram 14.

Festivals & Events

August's two-week **Fêtes de Genève** (www.fetes-de-geneve.ch) ushers in parades, open-air concerts, lakeside merry-go-rounds and fireworks. On 11 December, the **Escalade** celebrates the foiling of an invasion by the Duke of Savoy in 1602 with a costumed parade, the smashing and eating of chocolate cauldrons, and a day of running races around the Old Town.

Sleeping

When checking in, ask for your free public transport ticket covering unlimited bus travel for the duration of your hotel stay.

There are loads of cheap hotels southeast of the train station on and off the Rue des Alpes; although the neighbourhood can look gritty, the hotels are usually fine, albeit, at times, worn. Ask to see rooms.

Hôtel Bel'Esperance HOTEL €€
(☎022 818 37 37; www.hotel-bel-esperance.ch; Rue de la Vallée 1; s/d from Sfr105/160; @☁) This two-star hotel is a two-second flit to the Old Town and offers extraordinary value for a pricey city like Geneva. Rooms are quiet and cared for, and those on the 1st floor share a kitchen. Ride the lift to the 5th floor to flop in a chair on its wonderful flower-filled rooftop terrace.

Hotel Edelweiss HOTEL €€
(☎022 544 51 51; www.manotel.com; Place de la Navigation 2; r from Sfr160; ❄@☁) Plunge yourself into the heart of the Swiss Alps at this Heidi-style hideout, with its fireplace, wildflower-painted pine bedheads and big, cuddly St Bernard lolling over the banister.

Four Seasons Hôtel des Bergues LUXURY HOTEL €€€
(☎022 908 70 00; www.fourseasons.com/geneva; Quai des Bergues 33; r from Sfr625; ❄@☁) Geneva's oldest hotel continues to live up to its magnificent heritage. Chandelier-lit moulded ceilings, grandiose flower arrangements, original oil paintings in heavy gold frames and diamonds glittering behind glass is what this lakeside neoclassical gem from 1834 is all about.

La Cour des Augustins HOTEL €€
(☎022 322 21 00; www.lacourdesaugustins.com; Rue Jean-Violette 15; s/d from Sfr190/250; P❄@☁) 'Boutique gallery design hotel' is how this slick, contemporary space in Carouge markets itself. Disguised by a 19th-century facade, its crisp white interior screams cutting edge.

Hotel Admiral HOTEL €
(☎022 906 97 00; www.hoteladmiral.ch; Rue Pellegrino Rossi 8; s/d from Sfr90/100; ❄@☁) Excellent-value modest hotel between the train station and the lake. The street is slightly sleazy but the rooms are clean if small. There's an elevator, lavish complimentary buffet-breakfast and the staff are quite helpful.

Hôtel Auteuil HOTEL €€€
(☎022 544 22 22; www.manotel.com; Rue de Lausanne 33; r from Sfr320; P⊖❄@☁) The star of this crisp, design-driven hotel near the station is its enviable collection of black-and-white photos of 1950s film stars in Geneva. Borrow the book from reception to find out precisely who's who and where.

Auberge de Jeunesse HOSTEL €
(☎022 732 62 60; www.yh-geneva.ch; Rue Rothschild 28-30; dm from Sfr29, d/q Sfr95/135; @☁) At this well-equipped, HI-affiliated apartment block, rates include breakfast and bunk-bed dorms max out at 12 beds. Non HI-card holders pay Sfr6 more a night.

City Hostel HOSTEL €
(☎022 901 15 00; www.cityhostel.ch; Rue de Ferrier 2; dm from Sfr32, s/d from Sfr61/77; P@☁)

Spanking clean is the trademark of this well-organised hostel, where two-bed dorms give travellers a chance to double up cheaply. Rates include sheets, towels and use of the kitchen. Reception is closed from noon to 1pm.

Eating

Geneva flaunts ethnic cuisines galore. If it's local and traditional you're after, dip into a cheese fondue or platter of pan-fried *filets de perche* (perch fillets). But beware: not all those cooked up are fresh from the lake. Many come frozen from Eastern Europe, so it's imperative to pick the right place to sample this simple Lake Geneva speciality.

Eateries crowd Place du Bourg-de-Four, Geneva's oldest square, in the lovely Old Town. Otherwise, head down the hill towards the river and Place du Molard, packed with tables and chairs for much of the year.

In Pâquis, there's a tasty line-up of more affordable restaurants on Place de la Navigation.

TOP CHOICE Les 5 Portes BISTRO €

(☎022 731 84 38; Rue de Zürich 5; mains Sfr16-24; ⏰11am-11pm) The Five Doors is a fashionable Pâquis port of call that embraces every mood and moment. It has a rich, retro bistro feel yet works fine for just a glass of wine. The menu changes nightly and reflects what's fresh. Service is excellent and there is a long – and reasonable – wine list. Tables outside are good for a stylish pause.

Edelweiss FONDUE €€

(☎022 544 51 51; Place de la Navigation 2; mains from Sfr35; ⏰6-10pm Mon-Sat) This chalet-style restaurant in the namesake hotel is a key address among Genevans for traditional cheese fondue. Choose from cheesy variations as well as other hearty old-time Swiss dishes.

Le Plantamour DELI €

(www.leplantamour.ch; Rue Philippe Plantamour 37; mains Sfr8-15; ⏰7am-8pm Mon-Sat) No place cooks up a tastier, healthier lunch for an affordable Sfr15, than this modern delicatessen with a great terrace in a former baker's shop. Grab a pre-packaged salad or hot dish at the counter and take a seat outside.

Crêperie des Pâquis FRENCH €

(www.creperie-paquis.com; Rue de Zürich 6; mains Sfr15-20; ⏰6pm-2am Mon, from 9am Tue-Fri, from 5pm Sat, from 11am Sun) Sweet and savoury, this laid-back address with seating both in and out to suit every taste cooks up fabulous crêpes with a mindboggling choice of fillings. Don't miss the daily specials chalked on the board.

Café de Paris FRENCH €€

(www.cafe-de-paris.ch; Rue du Mont-Blanc 26; mains Sfr42; ⏰11am-11pm) A memorable dining experience since 1930. Everyone goes for the same thing here: green salad, beef steak with a killer herb-and-butter sauce, and as many *frites* (fries) as you can handle. A quick walk from the train station.

Chez Ma Cousine CHICKEN €

(☎022 310 96 96; www.chezmacousine.ch; Place du Bourg-de-Four; mains Sfr15-17) *'On y mange du poulet'* (we eat chicken) is the tagline of this institution near the cathedral, which appeals for one good reason – generously handsome and homely portions of chicken, potatoes and salad at a price that can't possibly break the bank.

Gilles Desplanches CAFE €

(☎022 810 30 28; www.gillesdesplanches.com; Rue de la Confédération 2; mains Sfr12-20; ⏰7am-7pm Mon-Wed & Fri, 7am-8pm Thu, 8am-7pm Sat, 10am-6pm Sun) One for serious chocolate fanatics. With its shocking-pink facade and exquisitely crafted cakes and chocolates alongside imaginative savoury tarts, this is one address that bursts at the seams at lunchtime. Good sandwiches, quiches, salads and more.

Drinking & Entertainment

Pâquis, the district in between the train station and lake, is particularly well endowed with bars. In summer the **paillote** (Quai du Mont-Blanc 30; ⏰to midnight), with wooden tables inches from the water, gets crammed.

For a dose of Bohemia, head to Carouge on tram 12. This shady quarter of 17th-century houses and narrow streets has galleries, hip bars and funky shops.

TOP CHOICE La Clémence BAR

(☎022 312 24 98; www.laclemence.ch; Place du Bourg-de-Four 20; ⏰7am-1am Mon-Thu & Sun, to 2am Fri & Sat) Indulge in a glass of local wine or an artisanal beer at this venerable cafe-bar located on Geneva's loveliest square.

Café des Arts CAFE

(☎022 321 58 85; Rue des Pâquis 15; ⏰11am-2am Mon-Fri, 8am-2am Sat & Sun) As much a place to drink as a daytime cafe, this Pâquis hang-out lures a local crowd with its Parisian-style

TOP TWO GELATO SHOPS

Gelateria Arlecchino (☎022 736 70 60; Rue du 31 Décembre 1; per scoop Sfr3.50, milkshakes Sfr7) Left-bank choice a stone's throw from the Jet d'Eau. Chocolate and ginger, honey, peanut cream and mango are among the 40 flavours at this lip-licking parlour.

Gelatomania (☎022 741 41 44; Rue des Pâquis 25; per scoop Sfr3.50) Right-bank choice. A constant queue loiters outside this shop where ice-cream maniacs wrap their tongues around a plethora of exotic flavours and old faves.

terrace and artsy interior. Foodwise, think meal-sized salads, designer sandwiches and burgers (Sfr15 to Sfr20).

Le Cheval Blanc BAR
(☎022 343 61 61; www.lechevalblanc.ch; Place de l'Octroi 15; ⊙11.30am-1am or 2am Tue-Sat, 10.30am-1am Sun) The White Horse is a real Carouge favourite. Quaff cocktails and eat tapas – some of Geneva's best – at the pink neon-lit bar upstairs, then head downstairs to its club and concert space, Le Box.

La Bretelle BAR
(☎022 732 75 96; Rue des Étuves 17; ⊙6pm-2am) Little has changed since the 1970s, when this legendary bar opened. Live accordion accompanies French chansons most nights.

La Plage BAR
(☎022 342 20 98; Rue Vautier 19; ⊙11am-1am Mon-Thu, 10am-2am Fri & Sat, 5pm-1am Sun) With bare-wood tables, checked lino floor, green wooden shutters and tables outside, the Beach in Carouge is a timeless drinking hole.

Bar du Nord BAR
(☎022 342 38 20; Rue Ancienne 66; ⊙5pm-2am Thu-Fri, 9am-2am Sat) Bar du Nord, one of Carouge's oldest, is a stylish bar with Bauhaus-inspired furniture, the best whisky selection in town and a small courtyard terrace out back. The best nights are Thursday and Friday with good music (lots of electro) and DJs.

Le Chat Noir LIVE MUSIC
(☎022 343 49 98; www.chatnoir.ch; Rue Vautier 13; ⊙Tue-Sat) A hot address in Carouge packed most nights, the Black Cat is a lovely spot for an after-work aperitif and, come dark, live music. There's also a small selection of tapas to nibble on.

Le Déclic CLUB
(☎022 320 59 40; www.ledeclic.ch; Blvd du Pont d'Arve 28; ⊙5pm-2am Mon-Fri, 9pm-2am Sat) A gay nightclub with numerous theme nights.

Bâtiment des Forces Motrices PERFORMING ARTS
(☎022 322 12 20; www.bfm.ch; Place des Volontaires 4) Geneva's one-time riverside pumping station (1886) is now a striking space for classical music concerts, dance, ballet and other cultural events. Its Sunday morning Musique sur Rhône concerts are particularly delightful.

Shopping

Designer shopping is wedged between Rue du Rhône and Rue de Rive; the latter has lots of chain stores. Grand-Rue in the Old Town and Carouge boast artsy boutiques.

Information

Post Office (Rue du Mont-Blanc 18; ⊙7.30am-6pm Mon-Fri, 9am-4pm Sat)

Tourist Office (☎022 909 70 00; www.geneve-tourisme.ch; Rue du Mont-Blanc 18; ⊙9am-6pm Mon-Sat, 10am-4pm Sun) Offers good walking-tour information. The Geneva Pass (from Sfr25) offers free admissions and discounts.

Getting There & Away

AIR Aéroport International de Genève (p1102), 5km from town, has connections to major European cities and many others worldwide.

BOAT CGN (Compagnie Générale de Navigation; ☎084 881 18 48; www.cgn.ch) operates a web of scenic steamer-services from its Jardin Anglais jetty to other villages on Lake Geneva. Many only sail May to September, including those to/from Lausanne (Sfr43, 3½ hours). Eurail and Swiss Pass holders are valid on CGN boats or there is a one-day CGN boat pass (Sfr56).

BUS International buses depart from the **bus station** (☎022 732 02 30, 0900 320 320; www.coach-station.com; Place Dorcière).

TRAIN Trains run to major Swiss towns including at least every 30 minutes to/from Lausanne (Sfr22, 33 to 48 minutes), Bern (Sfr49, 1¾ hours) and Zürich (Sfr84, 2¾ hours).

International daily rail connections from Geneva include Paris by TGV (3¼ hours) and Milan (four hours).

Getting Around

TO/FROM THE AIRPORT Getting from the airport is easy with regular trains into Gare de Cornavin (Sfr3, eight minutes). Slower bus 10 (Sfr3) does the same 5km trip. A metered taxi costs from Sfr30 to Sfr50.

BICYCLE Pick up a bike at **Genève Roule** (022 740 13 43; www.geneveroule.ch; Place de Montbrillant 17; 8am-6pm Mon-Sat) or its seasonal Jetée des Pâquis pick-up point for Sfr12/20 per day/weekend. May to October, borrow a bike (with advertisements on it) for free.

PUBLIC TRANSPORT Buses, trams, trains and boats service the city, and ticket dispensers are found at all stops. Most services are operated by **TPG** (www.tpg.ch; 7am-7pm Mon-Fri, 7am-6pm Sat). Typical tickets cost Sfr3.50 (one hour); a day pass is Sfr8 when purchased after 9am. The same tickets are also valid on the yellow shuttle boats known as Les Mouettes (the seagulls) that criss-cross the lake every 10 minutes between 7.30am and 6pm.

LAKE GENEVA REGION

East of Geneva, Western Europe's biggest lake stretches like a giant liquid mirror between French-speaking Switzerland on its northern shore and France to the south. Known as Lake Geneva by many and Lac Léman to Francophones, the Swiss side of the lake cossets the elegant city of Lausanne, the pretty palm-tree-studded Riviera resort of Montreux, and the marvellous emerald spectacle of vines marching up steep hillsides in strict unison.

Nyon

POP 18,800

Of Roman origin but with a partly Celtic name (the 'on' comes from *dunon,* which means fortified enclosure), Nyon is a pretty lake town pierced at its hilltop-heart by the gleaming white turrets of a fairy-tale chateau and a tasty lunch address.

Nyon's castle was started in the 12th century, modified 400 years later and now houses the town's **Musée Historique et des Porcelaines** (www.chateaudenyon.ch; Place du Château; adult/child Sfr8/free; 10am-5pm Tue-Sun).

Nyon is a perfect break on a boat trip between Geneva and Lausanne.

Eating & Drinking

Good eating and drinking are a reward for a chateau visit, otherwise stick near the harbour for sensational gelato.

TOP CHOICE L'Auberge du Château ITALIAN €€
(022 361 00 32; www.aubergeduchateau.ch; Place du Château 8; mains Sfr30-50; 8am-midnight, closed Sun Oct-Apr) No restaurant and cafe terrace has such a stunning view as this. Filling the pretty pedestrian square in front of Nyon's lovely chateau, tables look out on the Sleeping Beauty towers and lake beyond. The cuisine is Italian and creative – *taglierini* (pasta) with figs, simple homemade gnocchi and authentic pizza cooked in a wood-fired oven.

Caveau des Vignerons CAFE €
(Place du Château; samples from Sfr20; 2-9pm Fri & Sat, 11am-8pm Sun) In the chateau's old stone cellars, the Caveau des Vignerons is where you can taste different Nyon wines by local producers. Pay Sfr20 to sample two reds and two whites with a plate of charcuterie.

TOP CHOICE Gelateria Venezia GELATO €
(Rue de Rive 44; ice cream Sfr3-7; 11am-7pm) Slip your tongue into the extraordinary Italian-style ice cream here. From Nyon's CGN boat jetty on the lakefront, walk one block inland and look for the line outside the door.

Getting There & Away

Nyon is served by several trains per hour running between Geneva and Lausanne. There are year-round **CGN** (Compagnie Générale de Navigation; www.cgn.ch) boats to/from Geneva (Sfr22, 75 minutes); boats to Lausanne (Sfr33, two hours) run early April to mid-September.

Lausanne

POP 128,200

In a fabulous location overlooking Lake Geneva, Lausanne is an enchanting beauty with several distinct personalities: the former fishing village of Ouchy, with its summer beach-resort feel; Place St-François, with stylish, cobblestone shopping streets; and Flon, a warehouse district of bars, galleries and boutiques. It's also got a few good sights. One of the country's grandest Gothic cathedrals dominates its medieval centre.

Sights & Activities

Downhill by the water in **Ouchy**, Lake Geneva is the source of many a sporting opportunity, including sailing, windsurfing, waterskiing and swimming; the tourist offices have details. Seasonal stands in front of Chateau d'Ouchy rent pedalos and kayaks, and cycling and rollerblading are big on the silky-smooth waterfront promenades. West of Ouchy, **Vidy Beach**, backed by thick woods and parklands, is one of Lake Geneva's few sandy beaches.

In the heart of the **Vieille Ville** (Old Town), the 9th-century medieval market square **Place de la Palud** – pretty as a picture – was originally bogland. For five centuries it has been home to the city government, now housed in the 17th-century **Hôtel de Ville** (town hall). A fountain pierces one end of the square, presided over by a brightly painted column topped by the allegorical figure of Justice, clutching scales and dressed in blue.

Cathédrale de Notre Dame CHURCH

(⏲7am-7pm Mon-Fri, 8am-7pm Sat & Sun, to 5.30pm Sep-Mar) Lausanne's Gothic cathedral, Switzerland's finest, stands proudly at the heart of the Old Town. Raised in the 12th and 13th centuries on the site of earlier, humbler churches, it lacks the lightness of French Gothic buildings but is remarkable nonetheless.

Musée de l'Art Brut MUSEUM

(☎021 315 25 70; www.artbrut.ch; Av des Bergières 11-13; adult/child Sfr10/free; ⏲11am-6pm Tue-Sun) This alluring museum showcases a fascinating amalgam of 15,000 works of art created by untrained artists – psychiatric patients, eccentrics and incarcerated criminals. The works offer a striking variety, at times a surprising technical capacity and in some cases an inspirational world view. The museum is about 600m northwest of Place St François; take bus 2 or 3 to the Beaulieu stop.

Musée Olympique MUSEUM

(☎021 621 65 11; www.museum.olympic.org; Quai d'Ouchy 1) Lausanne is home to the International Olympic Committee and the Musée Olympique is easily the city's most lavish museum and a real must for sports buffs (and kids). Under renovation until late 2013, its usual home is a gorgeous building atop a tiered landscaped garden in the Parc Olympique.

Sleeping

Hotel guests get a Lausanne Transport Card covering unlimited use of public transport for the duration of their stay.

TOP CHOICE **Hôtel Beau-Rivage Palace** HISTORIC HOTEL €€€

(☎021 613 33 33; www.beau-rivage-palace.ch; Place du Port 17-19; r from Sfr550; ❄@🛜≋) Easily the most stunningly located hotel in town and one of only two five-star options, this luxury lakeside address is suitably sumptuous. A beautifully maintained early-19th-century mansion set in immaculate grounds, it tempts with magnificent lake- and Alpviews and famous bars and restaurants.

Lausanne Guest House GUESTHOUSE €

(☎021 601 80 00; www.lausanne-guesthouse.ch; Chemin des Épinettes 4; dm from Sfr39, r from Sfr100, without bathroom from Sfr90; P⊖@🛜) An attractive mansion converted into quality backpacking accommodation near the train station. Many rooms have lake views and you can hang out in the garden or on the terrace.

Hôtel du Port HOTEL €€

(☎021 612 04 44; www.hotel-du-port.ch; Place du Port 5; s/d from Sfr165/195; ⊖🛜) A perfect location in Ouchy, just back from the lake, makes this a good choice. The best doubles peep at the lake and suites slumber on the 3rd floor.

Hôtel du Marché HOTEL €

(☎021 647 99 00; www.hoteldumarche-lausanne.ch; Rue Pré du Marché 42; s/d from Sfr115/145, without bathroom Sfr80/135) A five-minute walk from the Old Town, the no-frills rooms here are clean and spacious, and the kettle and complimentary tea and coffee in each room is a great touch.

Eating

TOP CHOICE **Café St-Pierre** MODERN EUROPEAN €€

(☎021 326 36 36; www.cafesaintpierre.ch; Place Benjamin Constant 1; meals Sfr12-30; ⏲7.30am-midnight Tue & Wed, to 1am Thu, to 2am Fri, 11am-2am Sat, 11am-6pm Sun) The fact that every table is snapped up by noon while waiters buzz between tables and a constantly ringing telephone says it all – this hip cafe-bar rocks! Its interior is retro, trendy and relaxed, and the cuisine is contemporary European. Besides dinner there is tapas and weekend brunch. Reserve in advance.

Café Romand SWISS €

(☎021 312 63 75; Place St François 2; mains Sfr20-30; ⌚11am-11pm Mon-Sat) Hidden in an unpromising-looking arcade, this Lausanne legend dating to 1951 is a welcome blast from the past. Everyone from bankers to punks pours into the broad, somewhat sombre dining area littered with timber tables to gorge on fondue, *pied de porc* (pork trotters) and other traditional dishes.

Café de Grancy MODERN EUROPEAN €

(☎021 616 86 66; www.cafédegrancy.ch; Ave du Rond Point 1; mains Sfr20-35; ⌚8am-midnight; 📶) An old-time bar resurrected with colour and flair by young entrepreneurs, this spot is a hip hang-out with comfy lounges, weekend brunch and a tempting restaurant out back.

Café du Vieil Ouchy SWISS €€

(☎021 616 21 94; Place du Port 3; mains Sfr20-40; ⌚9am-11pm Thu-Mon) A simple but charming location near the lake and metro for fondue, rösti and other classics. Follow up with a meringue smothered in thick double Gruyère cream.

🍷 Drinking & Entertainment

Lausanne is one of Switzerland's busier night-time cities. Look for the handy free listings booklet **What's Up** (www.whats upmag.ch) in bars.

Bleu Lézard BAR

(☎021 321 38 30; www.bleu-lezard.ch; Rue Enning 10; ⌚7am-late; 📶) This corner bar and bistro with royal-blue paintwork and wicker chairs to match is an old favourite that never loses its appeal – day or night (or at weekends for brunch). Lunch (mains from Sfr25), including some great veggie options, is served until 3pm and when your feet wanna jive to a live band, there's the basement music club, La Cave.

Great Escape PUB

(☎021 312 31 94; www.the-great.ch; Rue de la Madeleine 18; ⌚11am-late) Beneath the whopping beams that hold up the roof of what could be a country house is a noisy pub with plenty of beers and ales on tap. Good burgers too.

Le Bourg LIVE MUSIC

(☎021 625 07 07; www.lebourg.ch; Rue de Bourg 51; ⌚7pm-1am Wed-Thu, to 2am Fri-Sat) What was once an old cinema is now one of central Lausanne's happening drink dens and live music stages. Squeeze upstairs past the bar for a good view down to the stage area.

Le D! Club CLUB

(☎021 351 51 40; www.dclub.ch; Place de Centrale 1; admission Sfr10-25; ⌚11pm-5am Wed-Sat) DJs spin funk to house at this heaving club. Take the stairs down from Rue du Grand Pont, turn right and descend to Place de Centrale.

ℹ Information

The **tourist office** (☎021 613 73 21; www.lausanne-tourisme.ch; Place de la Navigation 4; ⌚9am-6pm Oct-Mar, to 7pm Apr-Sep) neighbours Ouchy metro station; there is also a branch at the train station (Place de la Gare 9; ⌚9am-7pm).

ℹ Getting There & Around

Lausanne spans several steep hillsides, so prepare for some good walks.

BOAT The **CGN steamer service** (www.cgn.ch) runs early April to mid-September to/from Geneva (Sfr43, 3½ hours) via Nyon. Other services lace the lake.

PUBLIC TRANSPORT Buses and trolley buses service most destinations; the vital M2 metro line (single trip/day pass Sfr1.90/8.80) connects the lake (Ouchy) with the train station (Gare), cathedral area and Flon district.

TRAIN There are frequent trains to/from Geneva (Sfr22, 33 to 48 minutes) and Bern (Sfr32, 66 minutes).

Montreux

POP 24,600

In 1971 Frank Zappa was doing his thing in the Montreux casino when the building caught fire, casting a pall of smoke over Lake Geneva and inspiring the members of Deep Purple to pen their classic rock number 'Smoke on the Water'.

The showpiece of the Swiss Riviera has been a usually flame-free inspiration to writers, artists and musicians for centuries. Famous one-time residents include Lord Byron, Ernest Hemingway and the Shelleys. It's easy to see why: Montreux boasts stunning Alp views, tidy rows of pastel buildings and Switzerland's most extraordinary castle.

Crowds throng to the legendary (and not all-jazz) **Montreux Jazz Festival** (www.montreuxjazz.com) for a fortnight in early July. Free concerts take place every day, but big-name gigs cost Sfr75 to Sfr240.

WORTH A TRIP

GRYON & LEYSIN

Trek off the beaten track to lap up Swiss alpine charm in untouched **Gryon** (1130m), with great meadow hiking trails and **Chalet Martin** (☎024 498 33 21; www.gryon.com; dm from Sfr25, r Sfr70-90; P@), a Swiss-Australian–run hostel that travellers give rave reviews. The vibe is strictly laid-back and the place organises dozens of activities – paragliding, skiing and chocolate-tasting included. Take a train from Lausanne to Bex (Sfr19, 40 minutes, hourly), then the cogwheel train to Gryon (Sfr7, 30 minutes, hourly). The hostel is a five-minute signposted walk from the train stop.

Equally chilled is **Leysin**, a hub for skiers, boarders and hikers who throng to **Hiking Sheep** (☎024 494 35 35; www.hikingsheep.com, dm/r from Sfr30/80; P❄@). The tall, art deco house has a kitchen, great communal facilities, a pine-forested backyard and breathtaking views from its balconies. Find it a two-minute walk from Leysin-Grand Hôtel train station. Ride the cogwheel train from Aigle (Sfr12, 30 minutes, hourly), in turn linked by train with Lausanne (Sfr16, 30 minutes, hourly).

Sights

TOP CHOICE Château de Chillon CASTLE
(☎021 966 89 10; www.chillon.ch; Ave de Chillon 21; adult/child Sfr12/6; ⊙9am-7pm Apr-Sep, 9.30am-6pm Mar & Oct, 10am-5pm Nov-Feb, last entry 1hr before close) Originally constructed on the shores of Lake Geneva in the 11th century, Château de Chillon was brought to the world's attention by Lord Byron and the world has been filing past ever since. Spend at least a couple of hours exploring its numerous courtyards, towers, dungeons and halls filled with arms, period furniture and artwork.

The castle is a lovely 45-minute lakefront walk from Montreux. Otherwise trolley bus 1 (Sfr2.50) passes every 10 minutes; better still, come on a CGN steamer from Montreux (Sfr10, 15 minutes).

Sleeping & Eating

TOP CHOICE Tralala Hôtel BOUTIQUE HOTEL €€
(☎021 963 49 73; www.tralalahotel.ch; Rue du Temple 2; r Sfr130-300; ❄) A boutique hotel designed around Montreux' extraordinary musical heritage just had to open – and it has, perched up high from the lake in the old part of Montreux. Rooms come in three sizes – S ('Small & Sexy'), L or XL – and each one pays homage to a different artist.

Hôtel La Rouvenaz HOTEL €€
(☎021 963 27 36; www.rouvenaz.ch; Rue du Marché 1; r Sfr90-200; @) A stylish family-run spot with its own tasty Italian restaurant downstairs and wine bar next door. You cannot get any closer to the lake or the heart of the action. Its 15 rooms are lovely and mostly have views, plus there's a nice terrace.

Hôtel Masson HISTORIC HOTEL €€
(☎021 966 00 44; www.hotelmasson.ch; Rue Bonivard 5; r from Sfr200; P) In 1829, this vintner's mansion was converted into a hotel. Its old charm has remained intact and the hotel, set in magnificent grounds, is on the Swiss Heritage list of most beautiful hotels in the country. It lies back in the hills southeast of Montreux, best reached by taxi.

Café du Grütli SWISS €€
(☎021 963 42 65; Rue du Grand Chêne 8; mains Sfr18-30; ⊙Wed-Mon) This cheerful little eatery is hidden in the old part of town and provides good home cooking. Think rösti with ham, hearty meat dishes, salads and the inevitable fondue. It's a small hike uphill.

Getting There & Away

There are frequent trains to Lausanne (Sfr13, 25 minutes) and other lakeside points. Make the scenic journey to Interlaken via the **GoldenPass Line** (www.goldenpass.ch), with a change at Zweisimmen and a stop at the fabled ski resort of Gstaad (Sfr57, three hours, daily; rail passes valid).

Gruyères

POP 1800

Cheese and featherweight meringues drowned in thick cream are what this dreamy village is all about. Named after the emblematic *gru* (crane) brandished by the medieval Counts of Gruyères, it is a riot of 15th- to 17th-century houses tumbling down a hillock. Its heart is cobbled, a castle is its crowning glory and hard AOC Gruyère (the village is Gruyères but the 's' is dropped for the cheese) has been made for centuries in its surrounding Alpine pastures.

Sights & Activities

TOP CHOICE Château de Gruyères CASTLE
(☎026 921 21 02; www.chateau-gruyeres.ch; adult/child Sfr10/3; ⏰9am-6pm Apr-Oct, 10am-4.30pm Nov-Feb) This turreted castle is Gruyères' crowning glory. Inside, view period furniture, tapestries and modern 'fantasy art'. Don't miss the short footpath that weaves its way around the castle.

Musée HR Giger MUSEUM
(☎026 921 22 00; adult/child Sfr12.50/4; ⏰10am-6pm Apr-Oct, 1-5pm Tue-Fri, 10am-6pm Sat & Sun Nov-Mar) Fans of the *Alien* movies will relish this shrine to film designer HR Giger's expansive imagination. Just hope you don't feel any stomach cramps in the *Alien*-styled bar across the way...

TOP CHOICE Maison du Gruyère CHEESE FACTORY
(☎026 921 84 00; www.lamaisondugruyere.ch; adult/under 12yr Sfr7/6; ⏰9am-7pm Apr-Sep, to 6pm Oct-Mar) The secrets behind Gruyères' famous cheese are revealed here at this slick visitors centre right across from the train station and at the base of the path up to the village. Cheese-making takes place several times daily and can be watched through windows. There's a cafe and a picnic-happy deli, which, besides cheese, sells myriad forms of Swiss chocolate.

Fromagerie d'Alpage de Moléson CHEESE FACTORY
(☎026 921 10 44; www.fromagerie-alpage.ch; adult/child Sfr5/2; ⏰9.30am-10pm May-Sep) At this 17th-century mountain chalet, 5km southwest of Gruyères in Moléson-sur-Gruyères, cheese is made a couple of times a day in summer using old-fashioned methods.

Sentier des Fromageries WALKING
Cheese is still produced in a couple of traditional mountain chalets along the Sentier des Fromageries, a trail that takes walkers through green Gruyères pastures. Ask at the Maison du Gruyère for the brochure outlining the two-hour walk (7km to 8km).

Cailler CHOCOLATE FACTORY
(www.cailler.ch; Rue Jules Bellet 7; adult/child Sfr10/free; ⏰10am-6pm Apr-Oct, to 5pm Nov-Mar) Cailler has been making chocolate since 1825. Tours of its factory offer anecdotes, samples, demonstrations and a sort of sensory overload (no doubt exacerbated by the chance to buy factory seconds a mere 80m up the road). It gets packed on weekends and during holidays – and rightly so. Find the factory 2km north of Gruyères, in Broc, by following the signs to Nestlé.

Eating

Browse a variety of cheese-themed restaurants that face onto the centre of Gruyères. There are several small inns here as well.

Chalet de Gruyères SWISS €€
(☎026 921 21 54; www.chalet-gruyeres.ch; Rue du Château 53; fondues & raclettes from Sfr30; ⏰lunch & dinner) A quintessential Gruyères address, this cosy wooden chalet strung with cow bells oozes Alpine charm – and fodder (fondue, raclette, grilled meats). There's a flower-bedecked terrace in the warmer months too.

Information

There's a small **tourist office** (☎026 921 10 30; www.gruyeres.ch; Rue du Bourg 1; ⏰10.30am-noon & 1.30-4.30pm Mon-Fri, plus 9am-5pm Sat & Sun Jul-Sep) near the entrance to town. It has an ATM and loads of regional info.

Getting There & Away

Gruyères can be reached by train (Sfr17, 40 minutes, twice hourly) from Fribourg to Bulle, then another hourly train (Sfr5, 9 minutes). The village is a 10-minute walk uphill from the train station or you can take a free bus that meets trains.

Unusually for a Swiss train station, there are no lockers but you can leave your bags at the Maison du Gruyère across from the station.

VALAIS

This is Matterhorn country, an intoxicating land that seduces the toughest of critics with its endless panoramic vistas and breathtaking views. It's an earthy part of southern Switzerland where farmers were so poor a century ago they didn't have two francs to rub together, yet today it's a jet-set land where celebrities sip Sfr10,000 champagne cocktails from ice-carved goblets.

An area of extraordinary natural beauty, the outdoors here is so great it never goes out of fashion. Switzerland's 10 highest mountains – all over 4000m – rise to the sky here, while snow-fiends ski and board in one of Europe's top resorts, Zermatt. When snows melt and valleys turn lush green, hiking opportunities are boundless.

The main train line from Lake Geneva to Brig runs along the Rhône River at the base of the beautiful valley. Centuries-old vineyards climb the surrounding hillsides. At towns like Sion, you can stop for walks among the grapes, which take in wineries and hillside bistros. Tourist offices have maps of myriad routes.

Zermatt

POP 5850

Since the mid-19th century, Zermatt has starred among Switzerland's glitziest resorts. Today it attracts intrepid mountaineers and hikers, skiers who cruise at a snail's pace, spellbound by the scenery, and style-conscious darlings flashing designer togs in the lounge bars. But all are smitten with the **Matterhorn** (4478m), the Alps' most famous peak and an unfathomable monolith synonymous with Switzerland that you simply can't quite stop looking at.

Sights

TOP CHOICE Matterhorn Glacier Paradise CABLE CAR
(www.matterhornparadise.ch; adult/child from Sfr72/40; ⏲7am-4.20pm Jul & Aug, 8.30am-3.35pm mid-Oct–Dec, 8.30am-4.20pm rest of year) Views from Zermatt's cable cars and gondolas are all pretty remarkable, but the Matterhorn Glacier Paradise is the icing on the cake. Ride Europe's highest-altitude cable car up to 3883m and gawp at a top-of-the-beanstalk panorama of 14 glaciers and 38 mountain peaks over 4000m from the **Panoramic Platform**. Don't miss the **Glacier Palace**, an ice palace complete with glittering ice sculptures, a glacier crevasse to walk through and – one for the kids – an ice slide to swoosh down.

Gornergratbahn RAILWAY
(www.gornergrat.ch; Bahnhofplatz 7; adult/child from Sfr40/20; ⏲2-3 departures hourly 7am-6pm May & mid-Oct–Nov, 7am-10pm Jun-Sep, every 20 min 7am-5.15pm Dec-Apr) This splendid cogwheel railway – Europe's highest – climbs through picture-postcard scenery to Gornergrat (3089m). Tickets allow you to get on and off en route; Matterhorn views abound.

Matterhorn Museum MUSEUM
(☎027 967 41 00; www.matterhornmuseum.ch; Kirchplatz; adult/child Sfr10/5; ⏲11am-6pm Dec-Oct) This crystalline, state-of-the-art museum provides a fascinating insight into Valaisian village life, mountaineering, the dawn of tourism in Zermatt and the lives Matterhorn has claimed.

Activities

Zermatt is **skiing** heaven, with mostly long, scenic red runs, plus a smattering of blues for ski virgins and knuckle-whitening blacks for experts. The main skiing areas in winter are **Rothorn**, **Stockhorn** and **Klein Matterhorn**; 350km of ski runs in all with a link from Klein Matterhorn to the Italian resort of Cervinia and a freestyle park with halfpipe for snowboarders. A day pass covering all ski lifts in Zermatt (excluding Cervinia) costs Sfr67/57/34 per adult/student/child (Sfr75/64/38 including Cervinia).

Summer skiing (20km of runs, May to mid-October) and boarding (gravity park at Plateau Rosa on the Theodul glacier) are the most extensive in Europe.

Alpin Center SKIING, HIKING
(☎027 966 24 60; www.alpincenter-zermatt.ch; Bahnhofstrasse 58; ⏲9am-noon & 3-7pm mid-Nov–Apr & Jul-Sep) This activities centre houses the ski school and mountain guides office. Climbs led by mountain guides can be arranged to major 4000ers, including Breithorn (Sfr165), Riffelhorn (Sfr257) and, for experts willing to acclimatise for a week, Matterhorn (Sfr998). The program also covers multiday hikes, glacier hikes to Gorner (Sfr120), snowshoeing (Sfr140) and ice-climbing (Sfr175).

Klein Matterhorn SKIING
Klein Matterhorn is topped by Europe's highest cable-car station (3820m), providing access to Europe's highest skiing, Switzerland's most extensive summer skiing (25km of runs) and deep powder at the Italian resort of **Cervinia**. Broad and exhilarating, the No 7 run down from the border is a must-ski. Don't forget your passport.

If the weather is fine, take the lift up to the summit of Klein Matterhorn (3883m) for sweeping views over the Swiss Alps (from Mont Blanc to Aletschhorn) and deep into Italy.

Sleeping

Most places close May to mid-June and again from October to mid-November.

TOP CHOICE Hotel Bahnhof HOTEL €

(☎027 967 24 06; www.hotelbahnhof.com; Bahnhofstrasse; dm Sfr40-60, r Sfr80-220;) Opposite the train station, these five-star budget digs have proper beds and spotless bathrooms that are a godsend after scaling or schussing down mountains all day. Rooms for four are fabulous for families. There's a kitchen for preparing your own breakfast.

Berggasthaus Trift GUESTHOUSE €

(☎079 408 70 20; www.zermatt.net/trift; dm/d with half-board from Sfr66/156; ⊙Jul-Sep) Run by Hugo (a whizz on the alpenhorn) and Fabienne at the foot of the Triftgletscher. A stiff two-hour hike from Zermatt, it has simple rooms, mesmerising views of its glacial 4000m surrounds and a great terrace to kick back on over home-cured beef and oven-warm apple tart. Call in advance to ensure a bed.

Matterhorn Hostel HOSTEL €

(☎027 968 19 19; Schluhmattstrasse 32; dm Sfr36-56, r Sfr92-142; ⊙reception 7.30-10am or 11am & 4-9pm or 10pm;) Tucked in a 1960s wooden chalet, a two-minute walk from the lifts, this hostel is first-rate. Rooms are modern and its busy ground-floor bar cooks up a great vibe and great food.

Eating & Drinking

TOP CHOICE Whymper Stube SWISS €€

(☎027 967 22 96; www.whymper-stube.ch; Bahnhofstrasse 80; mains Sfr22-44) An advance reservation is essential at this legendary address, known for its excellent raclette and fondues, both cheese and meat. Service is relaxed and friendly, tables are packed tightly together, and the place has a real buzz.

Bayard Metzgerei SWISS €

(☎027 967 22 66; Bahnhofstrasse 9; sausages from Sfr6; ⊙noon-6.30pm Jul-Sep, 4-6.30pm Dec-Mar) Join the line in the street for a sausage (pork, veal or beef) and chunk of bread to down with a beer on the hop – or at a bar stool with the sparrows in the alley by this butcher's shop.

Hennu Stall BAR

(☎027 966 35 10; Klein Matterhorn; ⊙2-7pm) Last one down to this snow-bound 'chicken run' is a rotten egg. Hennu is the wildest après-ski shack on Klein Matterhorn. A metre-long 'ski' of shots will make you cluck all the way down to Zermatt.

Z'alt Hischi BAR

(☎027 967 42 62; www.hischibar.ch; Hinterdorfstrasse 44; ⊙9pm-2am) Hidden on what must be Zermatt's most charming street, this busy watering hole comes packaged in an ancient, 'I've-seen-it-all' wooden chalet.

Information

The **tourist office** (☎027 966 81 00; www.zermatt.ch; Bahnhofplatz 5; ⊙8.30am-6pm mid-Jun–Sep, 8.30am-noon & 1-6pm Mon-Fri, 8.30am-6pm Sat, 9.30am-noon & 4-6pm Sun rest of year) has all the bumph.

Getting There & Around

CAR Zermatt is car-free. Motorists have to park in Täsch (www.matterhornterminal.ch; per day Sfr14.50), load luggage onto a trolley (Sfr5) and ride the Zermatt Shuttle (adult/child Sfr8/4, 12 minutes, every 20 minutes from 6am to 9.40pm) train the last 5km to Zermatt.

TRAIN Trains depart regularly from Brig (Sfr37, 1½ hours) – a major rail hub – stopping at Visp en route. Zermatt is also the starting point of the popular *Glacier Express* to Graubünden.

BERN

POP 125,700

One of the planet's most underrated capitals, Bern is a fabulous find. With the genteel old soul of a Renaissance man and the heart of a high-flying 21st-century gal, the riverside city is both medieval and modern. The 15th-century Old Town is gorgeous enough to sweep you off your feet and make you forget the century (it's definitely worthy of its 1983 Unesco World Heritage site status). But the edgy vintage boutiques, artsy-intellectual bars and Renzo Piano's futuristic art museum crammed with Paul Klee pieces bring you firmly back into the present.

Sights

TOP CHOICE Old Town HISTORIC AREA

Bern's flag-bedecked medieval centre is an attraction in its own right, with 6km of covered arcades and cellar shops/bars descending from the streets. After a devastating fire in 1405, the wooden city was rebuilt in today's sandstone. Unique to Bern are

WORTH A TRIP

GLACIER EXPRESS

Like a glacier faced with climate change, you'll have a hard time avoiding the hype for the **Glacier Express** (www.glacierexpress.ch), the train that links Zermatt with the eastern towns and resorts of Chur (1st-/2nd-class Sfr254/145, 5¾ hours), Davos (Sfr235/134, 7½ hours) and St Moritz (Sfr198/113, eight hours).

Although there is some stunning scenery of glacier-cleaved valleys and soaring peaks along the route, much of the run is down in valleys, so don't expect non-stop scenic thrills. Also eight hours on a train may test your endurance. You can shorten the duration by starting at the rail hub of Brig instead of Zermatt or just doing the leg between St Moritz and Chur (another rail hub).

Swiss Cards cover the entire route, while Eurail and InterRail are good for about 50% of the fare. See also the boxed text on p1104.

the beautiful and deeply arcaded streets totalling some 6km in length and lined with shops, cafes and more.

Bern's **Zytglogge** (clock tower) is a focal point; crowds congregate around to watch its figures twirl rather somnolently at four minutes before the hour, after which the actual chimes begin.

Equally enchanting are the 11 decorative **fountains** (1545) depicting historical and folkloric characters. Most are along Marktgasse as it becomes Kramgasse and Gerechtigkeitsgasse, but the most famous lies in Kornhausplatz: the **Kindlifresserbrunnen** (Ogre Fountain) of a giant snacking on children.

Inside the 15th-century Gothic **Münster** (Cathedral; www.bernermuenster.ch; tower admission adult/child Sfr5/2; ⏲10am-5pm Tue-Sat, 11.30am-5pm Sun Easter-Nov, noon-4pm Tue-Fri, to 5pm Sat, 11.30am-4pm Sun rest of year, tower closes 30min earlier), a 344-step hike up the lofty spire – Switzerland's tallest – is worth the climb. Outside, pause on the **Münster Plattform**, a gem of a park overlooking the Aare.

TOP CHOICE Paul Klee Centre — MUSEUM

(☎031 359 01 01; www.zpk.org; Monument im Fruchtland 3; adult/child Sfr20/7; ⏲10am-5pm Tue-Sun) The architecturally bold Paul Klee Centre is an eye-catching 150m-long building filled with modern art, with a huge emphasis on its namesake. Renzo Piano's curvaceous building swoops up and down like waves to create a trio of 'hills' that blend into the landscape east of town.

The middle hill houses the main exhibition space, showcasing 4000 rotating works from Klee's prodigious career. His works span mediums and are at times graphically precise, utterly playful and heart-tuggingly poignant. In the basement of another 'hill' is the fun-packed **Kindermuseum Creaviva**, an inspired children's art centre.

Take bus 12 from Bubenbergplatz to Zentrum Paul Klee (Sfr4.20, 15 minutes). By car the museum is right next to the Bern-Ostring exit off the A6.

Einstein Museum — MUSEUM

(☎031 312 00 91; www.einstein-bern.ch; Kramgasse 49; adult/student Sfr6/4.50; ⏲10am-5pm Feb-Dec) The world's most famous scientist developed his special theory of relativity in Bern in 1905. Find out more at the small museum inside the humble apartment where Einstein lived with his young family between 1903 and 1905 while working in the Bern patent office.

FREE Houses of Parliament — HISTORIC SITE

(Bundeshäuser; ☎031 332 85 22; www.parliament.ch; Bundesplatz; ⏲hourly tours 9am-4pm Mon-Sat) The 1902 home of the Swiss Federal Assembly is impressively ornate, with statues of the nation's founding fathers and a stained-glass dome adorned with cantonal emblems. Tours are offered when parliament is in recess; otherwise watch from the public gallery. Bring your passport to get in.

Bärengraben — BEAR PARK

(www.baerenpark-bern.ch; ⏲9.30am-5pm) After decades of living in a cramped concrete pit (and lots of protests from animal-rights advocates), Bern's iconic bears got a new spacious 6000-sq-metre open-air riverside park dotted with trees and terraces in 2009, in which a number of bears roam (although they still have access to the old pit). The bear park is at the eastern end of the Nydeggbrücke.

Kunstmuseum MUSEUM
(031 328 09 44; www.kunstmuseumbern.ch; Hodlerstrasse 8-12; adult/child Sfr7/free; 10am-9pm Tue, to 5pm Wed-Sun) The permanent collection at the workmanlike Museum of Fine Arts includes works by Italian artists such as Fra Angelico and Swiss artists such as Ferdinand Hodler, alongside Picasso and Dalí pieces.

Sleeping

The tourist office books rooms and offers hotel deals.

TOP CHOICE **Hotel Landhaus** HOTEL €
(031 331 41 66; www.albertfrida.ch; Altenbergstrasse 4; dm from Sfr33, r from Sfr160, without bathroom from Sfr120; P) Backed by the grassy slope of a city park and fronted by the river and Old Town spires, this historic hotel oozes character. Its soulful ground-floor restaurant, a tad Bohemian, draws a staunchly local crowd.

Hotel National HOTEL €
(031 381 19 88; www.nationalbern.ch; Hirschengraben 24; s/d Sfr100/150, without bathroom from Sfr65/130; @) A quaint, endearing hotel, the National charms with its wrought-iron lift and Persian rugs over wooden floors. All 58 rooms are unique. Breakfast at the in-house restaurant is included. It adheres to slow-food principles and is a local favourite.

Marthahaus Garni HOTEL €
(031 332 41 35; www.marthahaus.ch; Wyttenbachstrasse 22a; s/d from Sfr115/145, without bathroom from Sfr70/105; @) Plum in a leafy residential location, this five-storey elevator building feels like a friendly boarding house. Clean, simple rooms are very white with a smattering of modern art, plus there's a kitchen.

Hotel City am Bahnhof HOTEL €€
(031 311 53 77; www.fassbindhotels.com; Bubenbergplatz 7; r Sfr110-200;) Close to the train station, the 58 rooms here are business-standard and have decent desks. Ask for one of the rooms with a small terrace overlooking the action far below.

Hotel Belle Epoque HOTEL €€
(031 311 43 36; www.belle-epoque.ch; Gerechtigkeitsgasse 18; s/d from Sfr170/240; @) A romantic Old Town hotel with opulent art-nouveau furnishings, the Belle Epoque's design ethos sees TVs tucked away into steamer-trunk-style cupboards so as not to spoil the look. It's a small operation, with a popular cafe.

SYHA Hostel HOSTEL €
(031 326 11 11; www.youthhostel.ch/bern; Weihergasse 4; dm from Sfr36; reception 7am-noon & 2pm-midnight; @) Prettily set along the river, this well-organised hostel sports spotless dorms and a leafy terrace, plus a good-value eatery. To get there, follow the paths downhill from the parliament building or ride the funicular.

Hotel Glocke Backpackers Bern HOSTEL €
(031 311 37 71; www.bernbackpackers.com; Rathausgasse 75; dm incl breakfast Sfr35-47, d Sfr142, s/d without bathroom Sfr74/110 ; reception 8-11am & 3-10pm; @) Its Old Town location makes this many backpacker's first choice, although street noise might irritate light sleepers.

Eating

Look for interesting cafes and bistros scattered amid the arcades on Old Town streets including Zeughausgasse, Rathausgasse, Marktgasse and Kramgasse.

TOP CHOICE **Lötschberg AOC** SWISS €
(031 311 34 55; www.loetschberg-aoc.ch; Zeughausgasse 16; mains Sfr14-30; 9am-11pm) Take an all-Swiss wine and beer list, add cheese specialities from the Valais (including fondue and raclette, of course), toss in some salads, decorate the cheerful yellow walls with circular, wooden wine racks and you have one of the most dynamic Swiss restaurants in the country. This popular, casual spot serves exceptional Swiss fare without kitsch. Book for dinner.

Altes Tramdepot SWISS €
(031 368 14 15; www.altestramdepot.ch; Am Bärengraben; mains Sfr16-20; 11am-12.30am) Even locals recommend this cavernous microbrewery by the bear pits. Swiss specialities snuggle up to wok-cooked stir-fries, pasta and international dishes on its bistro-styled menu. Sample some of the 20 seasonal beers brewed through the year.

Terrasse & Casa ITALIAN €€
(031 350 50 01; www.schwellenmaetteli.ch; Damaziquai 11; mains Sfr25-45; Terrasse 9am-midnight Mon-Sat, to 11pm Sun, Casa lunch & dinner Tue-Fri & Sun, dinner Sat) Dubbed 'Bern's Riviera', this twinset of classy hang-outs on the Aare is an experience. Terrasse is a glass shoebox with wooden decking over the

TOP QUICK EATS

Munch between meals on a *brezel* (pretzel; around Sfr3) smothered in salt crystals or sunflower, pumpkin or sesame seeds from kiosks, or a bag of piping-hot chestnuts crunched to the tune of the astronomical clock striking.

Sous le Pont Grab fries, falafel or a schnitzel from the graffiti-covered hole-in-the wall next to the eponymous cafe-bar and dine at the graffiti-covered table in the graffiti-covered courtyard. Beer costs Sfr3.80/5.20 per 300/500mL glass.

Tibits (031 312 91 11; Bahnhofplatz 10; 6.30am-11.30pm Mon-Wed, to midnight Thu-Sat, 8am-11pm Sun;) This vegetarian buffet restaurant inside the train station is just the ticket for a quick healthy meal, any size, any time of day. Serve yourself, get it weighed and pay accordingly.

Markets (8am-4pm Tue & Sat year-round, plus Thu Apr-Oct) Peruse choice produce and prepared goods at the markets held on Bundesplatz.

water and sun-loungers overlooking a weir, while Casa serves Italian food in a country-styled timber-framed house.

Kornhauskeller MODERN EUROPEAN €€€
(031 327 72 72; Kornhausplatz 18; mains Sfr25-50; noon-11pm Mon-Sat, from 5pm Sun) Fine dining takes place beneath vaulted frescoed arches at Bern's surprisingly ornate former granary, now a stunning cellar restaurant serving Mediterranean cuisine. In its neighbouring cafe, punters lunch in the sun on the busy pavement terrace. The buzzy bar is open late.

Markthalle INTERNATIONAL €
(Bubenbergplatz 9; meals Sfr12-35; 6.30am-11.30pm Mon-Wed, to 12.30am Thu & Fri, 7.30am-12.30am Sat;) Buzzing in atmosphere and quick-snack action, this covered market arcade near the train station is jam-packed with cheap eateries from around the world. You name it, it's here, to be eaten standing at bars or around plastic tables. More formal eateries offer table service.

Drinking & Entertainment

Bern has a healthy drinking scene. Several spaces, such as Kornhauskeller and Altes Tramdepot, are as much drinking as dining spots. A few bright and busy after-work aperitif-bars stud Gurtengasse near the Bundeshäuser and Rathäustrasse.

TOP CHOICE **Café des Pyrénées** BAR
(031 311 30 63; Kornhausplatz 17; Mon-Sat) With its mix of wine-quaffing trendies and beer-loving students, this Bohemian joint feels like a Parisian cafe-bar. It's dimly lit and not over-adorned.

Sous le Pont BAR
(031 306 69 55; www.souslepont.ch; Neubrückstrasse 8; 7pm-2am Tue-Sat) Delve into the grungy underground scene around the station in the bar of the semichaotic, alternative-arts centre, Reitschule. Find it in an old stone, graffiti-covered building – an old riding school built in 1897 – by the railway bridge.

Silo Bar BAR
(031 311 54 12; www.silobar.ch; Mühlenplatz 11; 10pm-3.30am Thu-Sat) By the water in the hip Matte quarter, Bern's monumental 19th-century corn house throbs with mainstream hits and a lively, predominantly student set.

Stadttheater Bern PERFORMING ARTS
(031 329 51 51; www.stadttheaterbern.ch; Kornhausplatz 20) Opera, dance, classical music and plays (in German).

Information

Bern Tourismus (031 328 12 12; www.berninfo.com; Bahnhoftplatz; 9am-8.30pm Jun-Sep, to 6.30pm Mon-Sat, 10am-5pm Sun Oct-May) Street-level floor of the train station. City tours, free hotel bookings, internet access (per hour Sfr12). There is a second office (031 328 12 12; Bärengraben; 9am-6pm Jun-Sep,10am-4pm Mar-May & Oct, 11am-4pm Nov-Feb) in the Altes Tram depot by the bear pits.

Post Office (Schanzenstrasse 4; 7.30am-9pm Mon-Fri, 8am-4pm Sat, 9am-4pm Sun)

Getting There & Around

AIR **Bern-Belp airport** (BRN; 031 960 21 21; www.alpar.ch), 9km southeast of the city centre, is a small airport with direct flights to/from Amsterdam, Barcelona, London, Munich and other cities. Most services are with the small regional carrier **SkyWork** (www.flyskywork.com). Bus 334 links with flights.

BICYCLE Bern Rollt (☎079 277 28 57; www.bernrollt.ch; 1st 4hr free, then per hr Sfr1; ⏲7.30am-9.30pm May-Oct) Pedal around with a bike, microscooter or skateboard, with kiosks inside the train station, at the western end of Zeughausgasse and just off Bubenbergplatz on Hirschengrasse.

PUBLIC TRANSPORT Buses and trams are operated by BernMobil (www.bernmobil.ch). Tickets are available from ticket machines and cost Sfr2.30 for up to six stops, or Sfr4.20 for a single journey within zones 1 & 2. Day passes cost Sfr12.

TRAINS Frequent trains connect to most Swiss towns, including Geneva (Sfr49, 1¾ hours), Basel (Sfr39, one hour) and Zürich (Sfr49, one hour).

Murten

POP 6100

Like something you'd build on the beach, this walled medieval village on the eastern shore of *Murten See* (Lac de Morat) isn't called Murten (Morat) – derived from the Celtic word *moriduno*, meaning 'fortress on the lake' – for nothing. In May 1476 the Burgundy duke Charles the Bold set off from Lausanne to besiege Murten, only to have 8000 of his men butchered or drowned in Murten Lake during the Battle of Murten (the Duke managed to run away). Even today, this German-speaking town marks the border with French-speaking Switzerland.

Murten is a cobblestone three-street town crammed with arcaded houses that make it feel like a mini-Bern. A string of hotel-restaurants, culminating in a 13th-century **castle** (closed to visitors), line Rathausgasse; shops and eateries stud parallel Hauptgasse, capped by the medieval **Berntor city gate** at its eastern end.

The real highlights here are the nearly intact town **ramparts** (admission free; ⏲8am-9pm) – some of the best in Europe. Scale the wooden **Aufstieg auf die Ringmauer** (rampart stairs) behind the **Deutsche Kirche** (German Church) to reach the covered walkway traversing part of the sturdy medieval walls. Alternate your views of the architecturally harmonious old town with views out to where the battle ended French-speaking Charles' dreams of dominance.

The **Hotel Murtenhof & Krone** (☎026 672 90 30; www.murtenhof.ch; Rathausgasse 1-5; s/d from Sfr120/160, mains Sfr15-40; ⏲restaurant 11am-10pm; 📶), in a 16th-century patrician's house, mixes old and new to create a spacious 58-room place to eat and sleep. Its terrace restaurant cooks up first-class lake views and a traditional cuisine with a worldly hint of fusion. Book for terrace tables with views.

ℹ Getting There & Away

The train station is 300m south of the city walls. Murten is a hub of hourly train services, including Bern (Sfr14, 35 minutes), Fribourg (Sfr12, 30 minutes) and Neuchâtel (Sfr13, 25 minutes).

Murten train station rents bicycles (per day Sfr33; ⏲9am to 4pm).

Navigation Lacs de Neuchâtel et Morat (☎032 729 96 00; www.navig.ch; adult/child Sfr25/12.50; ⏲Apr–mid-Oct) runs seasonal boats to/from Neuchâtel (1¾ hours).

Neuchâtel

POP 32,800

Its Old Town sandstone elegance, the airy Gallic nonchalance of its cafe life and the gay lakeside air that imbues the shoreline of its lake make Neuchâtel disarmingly charming.

The attractive Old Town streets are lined by fine, shuttered 18th-century mansions and studded with fanciful gold-leaf fountains. The 15th-century **Chateau de Neuchâtel** (☎032 889 60 00; ⏲guided tours 10am-noon & 2-4pm Mon-Sat, 2-4pm Sun Apr-Sep) and the adjoining **Collegiate Church** are the centrepieces of the Old Town. The striking cenotaph of 15 statues dates from 1372. Scale the nearby **prison tower** (☎032 717 71 02; Rue Jehanne de Hochberg 5; admission Sfr2; ⏲8am-6pm Apr-Sep) for broad views of town and lake.

Visit the **Musée d'Art et d'Histoire** (☎032 717 79 25; www.mahn.ch; Esplanade Léopold Robert 1; adult/under 16yr Sfr8/free, Wed free; ⏲11am-6pm Tue-Sun) to see beloved 18th-century clockwork figures.

Sample regional flavours such as *tripes à la Neuchâteloise* (Neuchâtel-style tripe) and roast pork and Neuchâtel blue-cheese sausage at **Le Jura Brasserie** (☎032 725 14 10; www.brasserielejura.ch; Rue de la Treille 7; meals Sfr20-50; ⏲cafe 9am-11pm Mon-Sat). The long menu changes daily.

The pedestrian zone and Place Pury (the local bus hub) are about 1km from the train station; walk down the hill along Ave de la Gare.

Trains serve Geneva (Sfr40, 65 minutes, hourly) and Bern (Sfr20, 35 minutes, hourly).

CENTRAL SWITZERLAND & BERNESE OBERLAND

The Bernese Oberland should come with a health warning – caution: may cause trembling in the north face of Eiger, uncontrollable bouts of euphoria at the foot of Jungfrau and 007 delusions at Schilthorn. Mark Twain wrote that no opiate compared to walking through this landscape – and he should know – and even when sober, the electric-green spruce forests, mountains so big they'll swallow you up, surreal china-blue skies, swirling glaciers and turquoise lakes seem hallucinatory. Up at Europe's highest train station, Jungfraujoch, husky-yapping mingles with a cacophony of 'oohs' and 'ahhs'. Just paces away, the serpentine Aletsch Glacier flicks out its tongue and you're surrounded by 4000m turrets and frosty stillness.

Lucerne

POP 76,200

Recipe for a gorgeous Swiss city: take a cobalt lake ringed by mountains of myth, add a medieval Old Town and sprinkle with covered bridges, sunny plazas, candy-coloured houses and waterfront promenades. Lucerne is bright, beautiful and has been Little Miss Popular since the likes of Goethe, Queen Victoria and Wagner savoured her views in the 19th century. Legend has it that an angel with a light showed the first settlers where to build a chapel in Lucerne, and today it still has amazing grace.

Sights

Your first port of call should be the medieval Old Town, with its ancient rampart walls and towers. Wander the cobblestoned lanes and squares, pondering 15th-century buildings with painted facades and the two much-photographed covered bridges over the Reuss. **Kapellbrücke** (Chapel Bridge), dating from 1333, is Lucerne's best-known landmark. It's famous for its distinctive water tower and the spectacular 1993 fire that nearly destroyed it. Though it has been rebuilt, fire damage is still obvious on the 17th-century pictorial panels under the roof. In contrast are the spooky and dark *Dance of Death* panels under the roofline of **Spreuerbrücke** (Spreuer Bridge, 1408). Sinners repent!

Further explorations should include walks along – and boat rides across – the lake.

TOP CHOICE **Museum**

Sammlung Rosengart MUSEUM

(041 220 16 60; www.rosengart.ch; Pilatusstrasse 10; adult/student Sfr18/16; 10am-6pm Apr-Oct, 11am-5pm Nov-Mar) Lucerne's blockbuster cultural attraction is the Rosengart Collection, occupying a graceful neoclassical pile. It showcases the outstanding stash of Angela Rosengart, a Swiss art dealer and close friend of Picasso. Alongside works by the great Spanish master are paintings and sketches by Cézanne, Kandinsky, Miró (including the stunning 1925 *Dancer II*), Matisse and Monet.

The basement has over 100 works of Paul Klee, which show the full range of his prodigious talents. The works are at times playful and introspective. Look for *Memory of a November Night's Adventure* (1922) among many great works.

Complementing the collection are some 200 photographs by David Douglas Duncan of the last 17 years of Picasso's life with his family in their home on the French Riviera. It's a portrait of the artist as an impish craftsman, lover and father.

Lion Monument MONUMENT

(Löwendenkmal; Denkmalstrasse) Victorian attractions from the earliest days of mass tourism lure nostalgia buffs just north of the Old Town. By far the most touching is this 1820 10m-long monument carved on a limestone cliff face in a cute park. Lukas Ahorn's sculpture of a dying lion commemorates Swiss soldiers who died defending King Louis XVI during the French Revolution. Mark Twain once called it the 'saddest and most moving piece of rock in the world'.

Verkehrshaus MUSEUM

(041 370 44 44; www.verkehrshaus.ch; Lidostrasse 5; adult/child Sfr30/15; 10am-6pm Apr-Oct, to 5pm Nov-Mar) Planes, trains and automobiles are the name of the game in the huge, family-oriented Transport Museum, east of the city centre, which is devoted to Switzerland's proud transport history. Switzerland's most popular museum, the sprawling complex has a fascinating railway hall that shows how the plucky Swiss scaled their mountains with iron. Take bus 6, 8 or 24 from Bahnhofplatz, or, better, enjoy the 2km walk along the lake.

Activities

Check out the cycling routes circumnavigating the lake; an easygoing and scenic option is the 16km pedal to Winkel via Kastanienbaum. You can rent bikes from **Next Bike** (041 508 08 00; www.nextbike.net; Lucerne Bahnhof; bikes per hour/day Sfr2/20) at the train station; register online or call and you're good to go.

Strandbad Lido SWIMMING
(041 370 38 06; www.lido-luzern.ch; Lidostrasse 6a; adult/child Sfr7/free; 9am-8pm mid-May–Sep) Perfect for a splash or sunbathe, this lakefront beach has a playground, volleyball court and heated outdoor pool. Or swim for free on the other bank of the lake by Seepark, off Alpenquai.

Festivals & Events

Lucerne's six-day **Fasnacht** celebrations are more boisterous and fun than Basel's carnival. The party kicks off on 'Dirty Thursday' with the emergence of the character 'Fritschi' from a window in the town hall, when bands of musicians and revellers take to the streets. The carnival moves through raucous celebrations climaxing on Mardi Gras (Fat Tuesday), and is over on Ash Wednesday.

June's **Jodler Fest Luzern** (www.jodlerfestluzern.ch) is a classic alpine shindig: think 12,000 Swiss yodellers, alphorn players and flag throwers.

Sleeping

TOP CHOICE **Palace Luzern** HOTEL €€€
(041 416 16 16; www.palace-luzern.ch; Haldenstrasse 10; r from Sfr400;) This luxury belle époque hotel on the lakefront is a favourite with those looking for trad splendour. Inside it's all gleaming marble, chandeliers and turn-of-the-century grandeur. Go for a room with a view across the lake to the Alps beyond. Look for online deals for the smaller rooms in the eaves.

Backpackers Lucerne HOSTEL €
(041 360 04 20; www.backpackerslucerne.ch; Alpenquai 42; dm/d from Sfr32/74; reception 7-10am & 4-11pm; @) Right on the lake, this is a soulful place to crash with art-slung walls, bubbly staff, a well-equipped kitchen and immaculate dorms with balconies. It's a 15-minute walk southeast of the station.

Hotel De La Paix HOTEL €
(041 418 80 00; www.ambassador.ch; Museggstrasse 2; r Sfr110-200; @) Centrally located on the edge of the Old Town, this 31-room hotel is an excellent modest option. The lobby is minute but the rooms – especially corner ones – are very large and there are elevators. The included breakfast buffet is a good one.

Tourist Hotel HOTEL €€
(041 410 24 74; www.touristhotel.ch; St-Karli-Quai 12; r Sfr90-170; P@) Don't be put off by the uninspired name and institutional-green facade of this central, riverfront cheapie. Rooms are cheerily modern – the cheaper ones have shared bathrooms – and there's a guest laundry.

Hotel Alpha HOTEL €
(041 240 42 80; www.hotelalpha.ch; Zähringerstrasse 24; r Sfr75-140; @) Easy on the eyes and wallet, this hotel is in a quiet residential area 10 minutes' walk from the Old Town. Rooms are simple, light and spotlessly clean; there are cheaper rooms with shared bathrooms.

The Hotel HOTEL €€€
(041 226 86 86; www.the-hotel.ch; Sempacherstrasse 14; ste from Sfr430; @) This shamelessly hip hotel, bearing the imprint of architect Jean Nouvel, is all streamlined chic, with refined suites featuring stills from movie classics on the ceilings.

Eating & Drinking

Local specialities include fish from Lake Lucerne and *chögalipaschtetli* (vol-au-vents stuffed with meat and mushrooms).

There is an excellent **market** (8am-3pm Sat) that runs along both sides of the Reuss.

TOP CHOICE **Wirtshaus Galliker** SWISS €€
(041 240 10 01; Schützenstrasse 1; mains Sfr22-50; 11.30am-2pm & 5-10pm Tue-Sat, closed Jul–mid-Aug) This old-style tavern has been passionately run by the Galliker family over four generations since 1856. Motherly waiters dish up Lucerne soul food (rösti, *chögalipaschtetli* and the like) that is batten-the-hatches filling. Book ahead for dinner.

Restaurant Schiff SWISS €€
(041 418 52 52; Unter den Egg 8; mains Sfr20-45) Under the waterfront arcades and lit by tea lights at night, this restaurant has bags of charm. Try fish from Lake Lucerne and some of the city's most celebrated *chögalipaschtetli*.

Heini CAFE €
(☎041 412 20 20; www.heini.ch; Falkenplatz; snacks from Sfr5) The original outlet for this lavish local chain of bakery-cafes is by the Lion Monument, but we prefer this modern version on a key square in the Old Town. Sandwiches and salads satisfy lunch needs but the real action here is in the display cases where the cakes, tortes and more will have you drooling. Find a table, then browse.

La Terraza ITALIAN €€
(☎041 410 36 31; www.ristorante-laterrazza.ch; Metzgerrainle 9; mains Sfr18-45) Set in a 12th-century building that has housed fish sellers, dukes and scribes over the years, La Terraza oozes atmosphere. Think *bella* Italia with an urban edge. When the sun's out, sit on the riverfront terrace.

Rathaus Bräuerei BREWERY €
(☎041 410 52 57; www.rathausbrauerei.ch; Unter den Egg 2; mains from Sfr15; ⏲8am-midnight) Sip house-brewed beer (try the bock) under the vaulted arches of this buzzy tavern, or nab a pavement table and watch the river flow. There are seasonal brews as well as excellent traditional German-Swiss fare. Nightly specials reflect the seasons.

La Madeleine BAR
(www.lamadeleine.ch; Baselstrasse 15) This is a lovely little spot for a low-key gig, with two performance areas and a cosy-glam bar. Jazz, blues, pop, funk and more are played.

Information

Lucerne Card (24/48/72hr Sfr19/27/33) Offers 50% discount on museum admissions, unlimited use of public transport and other reductions.

Luzern Tourism (☎041 227 17 17; www.luzern.com; Zentralstrasse 5; ⏲8.30am-7pm Mon-Sat, 9am-5pm Sun May-Oct, 8.30am-5.30pm Mon-Fri, 9am-5pm Sat & Sun Nov-Apr) Accessed from platform 3 of the train station.

Getting There & Around

Frequent trains serve Bern (Sfr37, one hour), Geneva (Sfr76, 2¾ hours), Lugano (Sfr58, 2½ hours) and Zürich (Sfr24, one hour).

Trains also connect Lucerne and Interlaken East on the stunning GoldenPass Line via Meiringen (Sfr31, two hours).

SGV (www.lakelucerne.ch) operates boats (sometimes paddle-steamers) on Lake Lucerne daily. Services are extensive. Rail passes are good for free or discounted travel.

City buses leave from outside the Hauptbahnhof at Bahnhofplatz. Tickets cost Sfr2.40 for a journey around town; day passes are Sfr6.40.

Interlaken

POP 5300

Once Interlaken made the Victorians swoon with its dreamy mountain vistas, viewed from the chandelier-lit confines of its grand hotels. Today it makes daredevils scream with its adrenalin-loaded adventures. Straddling the glittering Lakes Thun and Brienz (thus the name), and dazzled by the pearly whites of Eiger, Mönch and Jungfrau, the scenery here is exceptional.

In fact you may want to stay closer to the amazing sights. Many tour groups use Interlaken as a base and the streets are lined with kitsch by day and rollicking bars by night. You may want to just stop off here as you head into the hills or avail yourself of the adventure operators here.

Sights

Interlaken's central park, **Höhe-Matte**, has a few strategically placed cows munching on the grass. Their greatest interruption are the regular landings of paragliders.

Interlaken also has a small old town, **Unterseen**, across the Aare River.

Activities

Tempted to hurl yourself off a bridge, down a cliff or along a raging river? You're in the right place. Switzerland is the world's second-biggest adventure-sports centre and Interlaken is its busiest hub.

Almost every heart-stopping pursuit you can think of is offered here. You can white-water raft on the Lütschine, Simme and Saane Rivers, go canyoning in the Saxetet, Grimsel or Chli Schliere gorges, and canyon jump at the Gletscherschlucht near Grindelwald. If that doesn't grab you, there's paragliding, glacier bungee jumping, skydiving, ice climbing, hydrospeeding and, phew, much more.

Sample prices are around Sfr110 for rafting or canyoning, Sfr130 for bungee or canyon jumping, Sfr160 for tandem paragliding, Sfr180 for ice climbing, Sfr225 for hang-gliding and Sfr430 for sky-diving. A half-day mountain-bike tour will set you back around Sfr25.

WORTH A TRIP

MOUNTAIN DAY TRIPS FROM LUCERNE

There are three classic day-trips to Alpine peaks from Lucerne, and all are marketed heavily. The summits offer a variety of walks and activities but the real appeal are the jaw-dropping views and the actual journeys themselves. Don't bother with these trips on cloudy days.

Mount Pilatus

Rearing above Lucerne from the southwest, Mt Pilatus (www.pilatus.com) is 2132m high. From May to October, you can reach Mt Pilatus on a classic 'golden round-trip'. Board the lake steamer from Lucerne to Alpnachstad, then rise with the world's steepest cog railway to Mt Pilatus. From the summit, cable cars bring you down to Kriens via Fräkmüntegg and Krienseregg, where bus 1 takes you back to Lucerne. The return trip costs Sfr91 (less with valid Swiss, Eurail or InterRail passes).

Mount Rigi

The Jungfrau peaks dominate the horizon from 1797m-high Rigi (www.rigi.ch). Two rival railways carry passengers to the top. One runs from Arth-Goldau (one-way/return Sfr40/64), the other from Vitznau (one-way/return Sfr45/72). Holders of Swiss, Eurail and InterRail passes receive a 50% discount on fares.

Mount Titlis

Central Switzerland's tallest mountain, Titlis (www.titlis.ch), has its only glacier and is reached on a breathtaking four-stage journey; the final link is on a revolving cable car. At Titlis station (3020m) the oohs and aahs come when you step out onto the terrace, where the panorama of glacier-capped peaks stretches to Eiger, Mönch and Jungfrau in the Bernese Oberland. The return trip to Titlis (45 minutes each way) costs Sfr90 from Engelberg. There are reductions of 50% for Swiss, Eurail and InterRail pass holders. Engelberg is at the end of a train line, about an hour from Lucerne (Sfr17). If on a day trip, check the Lucerne tourist office's Mt Titlis excursion tickets.

The major operators able to arrange most sports from May to September include the following. Advance bookings are essential.

Alpinraft (☎033 823 41 00; www.alpinraft.ch; Hauptstrasse 7)

Outdoor Interlaken (☎033 826 77 19; www.outdoor-interlaken.ch; Hauptstrasse 15)

Swissraft (☎033 821 66 55; www.swissraft-activity.ch; Obere Jungfraustrasse 72)

Sleeping

TOP CHOICE Hotel Rugenpark B&B €
(☎033 822 36 61; www.rugenpark.ch; Rugenparkstrasse 19; s/d from Sfr87/130, without bathroom from Sfr62/105; closed Nov–mid-Dec; P ⊖ @) Chris and Ursula have worked magic to transform this place into a sweet B&B. Rooms are humble, but the place is spotless and has been enlivened with colourful butterflies, beads and travel trinkets. Quiz your knowledgeable hosts for help and local tips.

Victoria-Jungfrau Grand Hotel & Spa HOTEL €€€
(☎033 828 28 28; www.victoria-jungfrau.ch; Höheweg 41; s/d from Sfr560/680; P ⊖ @ 🛜 🏊) The reverent hush and impeccable service evoke an era when only royalty and the seriously wealthy travelled. It's a perfect melding of well-preserved Victorian features and modern luxury.

Backpackers Villa Sonnenhof HOSTEL €
(☎033 826 71 71; www.villa.ch; Alpenstrasse 16; dm Sfr39-45, s Sfr69-79, d Sfr118-138; reception 7am-11pm; @ 🛜) Sonnenhof is a slick combination of ultramodern chalet and elegant art nouveau villa. Dorms are immaculate, and some have balconies with Jungfrau views. There's also a relaxed lounge, a well-equipped kitchen and a leafy garden for kicking back and enjoying the Jungfrau views.

Hôtel du Lac HOTEL €€
(☎033 822 29 22; www.dulac-interlaken.ch; Höheweg 225; s/d Sfr160/280) Smiley old-

fashioned service and a riverfront location near Interlaken Ost make this 19th-century hotel a solid choice. It has been in the same family for generations.

Walter's B&B B&B €

(☎033 822 76 88; www.walters.ch; Oelestrasse 35; s/d without bathroom from Sfr50/66;) Walter is a real star with his quick smile, culinary skills and invaluable tips. Sure, the rooms are a blast from the 1970s (and have shared bathrooms), but they are super clean and you'd be hard pushed to find better value in Interlaken.

Balmer's Herberge HOSTEL €

(☎033 822 19 61; www.balmers.ch; Hauptstrasse 23; dm from Sfr31, s/d from Sfr47/81; P@) Adrenalin junkies hail Balmer's for its fun frat-house vibe. These party-mad digs offer beer-garden happy hours, a pumping bar with DJs and chill-out hammocks for nursing your hangover.

Eating & Drinking

Am Marktplatz is scattered with bakeries and bistros with alfresco seating. Höheweg, east of the park, is lined with ethnic eateries with reasonable prices.

The bars at Balmer's and Funny Farm are easily the liveliest drinking holes for revved-up party people.

Benacus SWISS €€

(☎033 821 20 20; www.benacus.ch; Stadthausplatz; mains Sfr20-33; closed Sun) Supercool Benacus is a breath of urban air with its glass walls, slick wine-red sofas, lounge music and street-facing terrace. The German TV show *Funky Kitchen Club* is filmed here. The menu stars creative, seasonal flavours.

Sandwich Bar SWISS €

(☎033 821 63 25; Rosenstrasse 5; snacks Sfr4-9; 7.30am-7pm Mon-Fri, 8am-5pm Sat) This crimson-walled, zebra-striped cafe is a great snack spot. Choose your bread and get creative with fillings. Or try the soups, salads, toasties and locally made ice cream.

Schuh CAFE €€

(☎033 822 94 41; www.schuh-interlaken.ch; Höheweg 56; meals from Sfr20; 9am-11.30pm) A Viennese-style coffee house famous for its pastries, pralines and park-facing terrace. The menu covers all the bases, from rösti to Asian accents. The chocolate-making show (Sfr15) is touristy but fun; it runs at 5pm most days in the high season.

Goldener Anker INTERNATIONAL €€

(☎033 822 16 72; www.anker.ch; Marktgasse 57; mains Sfr18-42; dinner;) This beamed restaurant covers a lot of bases with its menu, which runs from Switzerland to Asia with a brief stop in Mexico. Besides meaty mains, there are good salads and numerous veggie options. It has live music many nights with an equally polyglot line-up.

Information

Tourist Office (☎033 826 53 00; www.interlakentourism.ch; Höheweg 37; 8am-7pm Mon-Fri, to 5pm Sat, 10am-noon & 5-7pm Sun Jul & Aug, 8am-noon & 1.30-6pm Mon-Fri, 9am-noon Sat rest of year) Halfway between the stations. There's also a hotel booking board outside the office and at both train stations.

Getting There & Away

The only way south for vehicles without a detour around the mountains is the car-carrying train from Kandersteg, south of Spiez.

There are two train stations. Interlaken West is slightly closer to the centre and is a stop for trains to Bern (Sfr27, one hour). Interlaken East is the rail hub for all lines, including the scenic ones up into the Jungfrau region and the lovely GoldenPass Line to Lucerne (Sfr31, two hours).

Jungfrau Region

If the Bernese Oberland is Switzerland's Alpine heart, the Jungfrau region is where yours will skip a beat. Presided over by glacier-encrusted monoliths Eiger, Mönch and Jungfrau (Ogre, Monk and Virgin), the scenery stirs the soul and strains the neck muscles. It's a magnet for skiers and snowboarders with its 214km of pistes, 44 lifts and much more; a one-day ski pass for Kleine Scheidegg–Männlichen, Grindelwald-First or Mürren-Schilthorn costs Sfr71.

Come summer, hundreds of kilometres of walking trails allow you to capture the landscape from many angles, but it never looks less than astonishing.

The Lauterbrunnen Valley branches out from Interlaken with sheer rock faces and towering mountains on either side, attracting an army of hikers and mountain bikers.

The main villages of Grindelwald, Wengen and Mürren, as well as the rail hub of Lauterbrunnen, all have ATMs. The first two are the only viable choices for staying during the off-season months of April and November.

JUNGFRAU ONLINE

The Jungfrau region's website, www.jungfrau.ch, is an excellent resource. It has 3D and downloadable maps of all the winter skiing areas and summer hiking trails, along with the complex thicket of train, cable car, bus and lift schedules.

It also has live cams from the peaks so you can do a final weather check before deciding to make the sizeable investment in time and money to ascend the summits.

Getting There & Around

Hourly trains (www.jungfrau.ch) depart for the Jungfrau region from Interlaken Ost station. Sit in the front half of the train for Lauterbrunnen (Sfr7.20) or the back half for Grindelwald (Sfr10.40).

From Grindelwald, trains ascend to Kleine Scheidegg (Sfr32), where you can transfer for Jungfraujoch. From Lauterbrunnen, trains ascend to Wengen (Sfr6.40) and continue to Kleine Scheidegg (Sfr24) for Jungfraujoch.

You can reach Mürren two ways from Lauterbrunnen: with a bus and cable car via Stechelberg (Sfr14.20) or with a cable car and train via Grütschalp (Sfr10.40). Do a circle trip for the full experience. Gimmelwald is reached by cable car from Stechelberg and Mürren. Many cable cars close for servicing in April and November.

Regional passes can save you money. The **Berner Oberland Regional Pass** (www.regiopass-berneroberland.ch; 7 days Sfr233) gives you three days' unlimited free travel and four days' discounted travel. The **Jungfraubahnen Pass** (www.jungfrau.ch; 6 days unlimited travel Sfr210, with Swiss Pass, Swiss Card or Half-Fare Card Sfr160) gives you six days unlimited travel though you still have to pay Sfr55 to Jungfraujoch.

GRINDELWALD

POP 3900

Grindelwald's charms were discovered by skiers and hikers in the late 19th century, making it one of Switzerland's oldest resorts and the Jungfrau's largest. It has lost none of its appeal over the decades, with archetypal alpine chalets and verdant pastures set against the chiselled features of the Eiger north face.

Grindelwald tourist office (☎033 854 12 12; www.grindelwald.ch; Dorfstrasse 110; ⏱8am-noon & 1.30-6pm Mon-Fri, 9am-noon & 1.30-5pm Sat & Sun) is at the Sportzentrum, 200m from the train station.

Sights & Activities

The **Grindelwald-First** skiing area has runs stretching from Oberjoch at 2486m to the village at 1050m. In the summer it caters to hikers with 90km of trails at about 1200m, 48km of which are open year-round.

Gletscherschlucht GLACIER
(Glacier Gorge; adult/child Sfr7/4; ⏱10am-5pm May-Oct, to 6pm Jul & Aug) Turbulent waters carve a path through the craggy Gletscherschlucht, a 30-minute walk south of the centre. A footpath weaves through tunnels hacked into cliffs – a popular spot for canyon- and bungee-jumping expeditions.

Grindelwald Sports ADVENTURE SPORTS
(☎033 854 12 80; www.grindelwaldsports.ch; Dorfstrasse 110; ⏱8am-noon & 1.30-6pm, closed Sat & Sun in low season) In the tourist office, this outfit arranges mountain climbing, ski and snowboard instruction, canyon jumping and glacier bungee jumping at the Gletscherschlucht.

Sleeping & Eating

TOP CHOICE **Gletschergarten** HOTEL €€
(☎033 853 17 21; www.hotel-gletschergarten.ch; Dorfstrasse; s Sfr120-150, d Sfr230-300; @) The sweet Breitenstein family make you feel at home in their rustic timber chalet, brimming with heirlooms from landscape paintings to family snapshots. Decked out in pine and flowery fabrics, the rooms have balconies facing Unterer Gletscher at the front and Wetterhorn (best for sunset) at the back.

Mountain Hostel HOSTEL €
(☎033 854 38 38; www.mountainhostel.ch; dm Sfr37-44, r Sfr94-108; P@) Near the Männlichen cable-car station, this is a good base for sports junkies. There's a beer garden, ski and bike room and TV lounge.

Hotel Tschuggen HOTEL €€
(☎033 853 17 81; www.tschuggen-grindelwald.ch; Dorfstrasse 134; s Sfr70-95, d Sfr160-190;) Monika and Robert extend a warm welcome at this dark-wood chalet in the centre of town. The light, simple rooms are spotlessly clean; opt for a south-facing double for terrific Eiger views.

Memory SWISS €€
(☎033 854 31 31; Dorfstrasse; mains Sfr21-30; ⏱11.30am-10.30pm) Always packed, the Eiger Hotel's unpretentious restaurant rolls out tasty Swiss grub such as rösti and fon-

due. Try to bag a table on the street-facing terrace.

C & M SWISS €€
(☎033 853 07 10; mains Sfr20-36; ⏰8.30am-11pm Wed-Mon) Just as appetising as the wide-ranging menu are the stupendous views to Unterer Gletscher from this gallery-style cafe's sunny terrace.

WENGEN

POP 1300

Photogenically poised on a mountain ledge, Wengen's celestial views include the silent majesty of the glacier-capped giant peaks as well as the shimmering ribbons of waterfalls spilling into the Lauterbrunnen Valley below.

The village is car-free and can only be reached by train. It's a fabulous hub for **hiking** for much of the year as well as **skiing** in winter. The **tourist office** (☎033 856 85 85; www.wengen.ch; ⏰9am-6pm Mon-Sat, 9am-noon & 1-6pm Sun, closed Sat & Sun Nov, Mar & Apr) has the usual bounty of maps and can help with the myriad rental chalets and rooms in addition to hotels.

Hotel Bären (☎033 855 14 19; www.baeren-wengen.ch; s Sfr90-150, d Sfr190-280; 📶) is close to the station. Loop back under the tracks and head down the hill to this snug log chalet with bright, if compact, rooms. The affable Brunner family serves a hearty breakfast.

For an excellent meal with ingredients sourced both organically and locally, try **Restaurant Eiger** (☎033 856 05 05; www.restaurant-eiger.ch; mains Sfr10-40; ⏰8am-11pm), which is right by the train station. It has casual meals during the day, including excellent fondue, which you can enjoy on the terrace. At night the seasonal menu is a creative treat. The **Coop Supermarket** by the train station is the best in the region.

JUNGFRAUJOCH

Sure, the world wants to see Jungfraujoch (3471m) and yes, tickets are expensive, but don't let that stop you. It's a once-in-a-lifetime trip and there's a reason why two million people a year visit Europe's highest train station. The icy wilderness of swirling glaciers and 4000m turrets that unfolds is truly enchanting.

Clear good weather is essential for the trip; check www.jungfrau.ch or call ☎033 828 79 31, and don't forget warm clothing, sunglasses and sunscreen. Up top, when you tire of the view (is this possible?), dash downhill on a snow disc (free) or on myriad other icy options.

From Interlaken Ost, the journey time is 2½ hours each way (return Sfr191; discounts with rail passes). The last train back is at 5.50pm in summer, and 4.40pm in winter. There are cheaper 'good morning' and 'good afternoon' tickets (Sfr140) with time restrictions.

JUNGFRAU REGION HIKING 101

There are hundreds of hikes along the hundreds of kilometres of trails in the Jungfrau Region. All include some of the world's most stunning scenery. Every skill and fortitude level is accommodated and options abound. Here are three to get you started.

Grütschalp to Mürren

Ride the cable car up from Lauterbrunnen and follow the trail along the railway tracks. The walk to Mürren takes about an hour and is mostly level. There are unbeatable views, Alpine woods and babbling glacier-fed streams.

Männlichen to Kleine Scheidegg

Reach the Männlichen lift station by cable cars from Wengen and Grindelwald. Now follow the well-marked, spectacular path down to Kleine Scheidegg. It takes about 90 minutes and you have nothing but Alps in front of you.

Kleine Scheidegg to Wengen

This downhill hike takes about three or more hours and gives you good views all the way. Parts are utterly silent while many stretches are quite steep. The odd mountain hut and cafe offer ample reasons to pause.

GIMMELWALD

POP 120

Decades ago some anonymous backpacker scribbled these words in the guestbook at the Mountain Hostel: 'If heaven isn't what it's cracked up to be, send me back to Gimmelwald.' Enough said. When the sun is out in Gimmelwald, this pipsqueak of a village will simply take your breath away. Sit outside and listen to the distant roar of avalanches on the sheer mountain faces arrayed before you.

The surrounding **hiking trails** include an easy one down from Mürren (30 to 40 minutes) and a steep one up from Stechelberg.

The rustic **Mountain Hostel** (☎033 855 17 04; www.mountainhostel.com; dm from Sfr28; ⊙reception 8.30am-noon & 6-11pm Apr–mid-Nov; @) is a backpacker's legend. A soak in its outdoor whirlpool with stunning views hits the spot every time. (And don't forget to sign the guestbook!) **Esther's Guest House** (☎033 855 54 88; www.esthersguesthouse.ch; s/d Sfr55/130, apt Sfr160-230; @ 🛜) is a sweet B&B with a tiny shop inside, where you can stock up on local goodies like Gimmelwald salami and Stechelberg honey.

MÜRREN

POP 500

Arrive on a clear evening when the sun hangs low on the horizon, and you'll think you've died and gone to heaven. Car-free Mürren *is* storybook Switzerland.

In summer, the **Allmendhubel funicular** (www.schilthorn.ch; return Sfr12.60; ⊙9am-5pm) takes you above Mürren to a panoramic restaurant. From here, you can set out on many walks, including the famous **Northface Trail** (1½ hours) via Schiltalp to the west, with spellbinding views of the Lauterbrunnen Valley and monstrous Eiger north face – bring binoculars to spy intrepid climbers.

The **tourist office** (☎033 856 86 86; www.mymuerren.ch; ⊙8.30am-7pm Mon-Sat, to 8pm Thu, to 6pm Sun, reduced hours in low season) is in the sports centre.

Sleeping options include **Eiger Guesthouse** (☎033 856 54 60; www.eigerguesthouse.com; r Sfr120-200; @ 🛜), by the train station, with the downstairs pub serving tasty food; and **Hotel Jungfrau** (☎033 856 64 64; www.hoteljungfrau.ch; s Sfr80-140, d Sfr160-280; @ 🛜), overlooking the nursery slopes from its perch above Mürren. It dates to 1894 and has a beamed lounge with open fire. Ten out of 10 to much-lauded chalet **Hotel Alpenruh** (☎033 856 88 00; www.alpenruh-muerren.ch; s Sfr140-180, d Sfr200-280; 🛜), for service, food and unbeatable views to Jungfrau massif.

WANT MORE?

Head to **Lonely Planet** (www.lonelyplanet.com/switzerland/zurich) for planning advice, author recommendations, traveller reviews and insider tips.

SCHILTHORN

There's a tremendous 360-degree panorama available from the 2970m **Schilthorn** (www.schilthorn.ch). On a clear day, you can see over 200 peaks, from Titlis to Mont Blanc and across to the German Black Forest. Note that this was the site of Blofeld's HQ in the under-appreciated 1969 James Bond film *On Her Majesty's Secret Service* (as the hype endlessly reminds you).

From Interlaken East a combined ticket to the summit costs Sfr125. From Mürren it's Sfr77 for the two long cable-car rides. There are discounts with rail passes.

ZÜRICH

POP 376,000

Zürich is an enigma. A savvy financial centre with possibly the densest public transport system in the world, it also has a gritty, post-industrial edge that always surprises. The nation's largest city has an evocative old town and lovely lakeside location. Its museums, shops and myriad restaurants can easily keep you busy for a couple of days, while its hip quarters will fill your nights.

Sights

Old Town HISTORIC AREA

Explore the cobbled streets of the pedestrian Old Town lining both sides of the river.

The bank vaults beneath **Bahnhofstrasse**, the city's most elegant street, are said to be crammed with gold and silver. Indulge in affluent Züricher-watching and ogle at the luxury shops selling watches, clocks, chocolates, furs, porcelain and fashion labels galore.

Walk up to the **Lindenhof**, a large shady square that perches above the Old Town, for views down over the city and Limmat River.

As you walk, see how many of the city's 1221 fountains you can spot – each with a spout of drinkable glacier-fed water.

On Sundays all of Zürich strolls around its namesake lake. Take one short meander and you'll understand why: it's relaxing and simply sublime. On a clear day you'll glimpse the Alps in the distance.

Fraumünster CHURCH

(www.fraumuenster.ch; Münsterplatz; 9am-6pm Apr-Oct, 10am-4pm Nov-Mar) The 13th-century cathedral is renowned for its stained-glass windows, designed by the Russian-Jewish master Marc Chagall (1887–1985).

Grossmünster CHURCH

(www.grossmuenster.ch; Grossmünsterplatz; 10am-6pm Mar-Oct, to 5pm Nov-Feb) On the north bank of the river, the dual-towered Grossmünster was where, in the 16th century, the Protestant preacher Huldrych Zwingli first spread his message of 'pray and work' during the Reformation. The figure glowering from the south tower of the cathedral is Charlemagne, who ordered the original church built in the spot in the 10th century.

St Peterskirche CHURCH

(St Peter's Church; St Peterhofstatt; 8am-6pm Mon-Fri, to 4pm Sat, 11am-5pm Sun) From any position in the city, it's impossible to overlook the 13th-century tower of St Peterskirche. Its prominent clock face, 8.7m in diameter, is Europe's largest.

Kunsthaus MUSEUM

(044 253 84 84; www.kunsthaus.ch; Heimplatz 1; adult/child Sfr15/free, Wed free; 10am-8pm Wed-Fri, to 6pm Tue, Sat & Sun) Zürich's Fine Arts Museum boasts a rich collection of Alberto Giacometti stick-figure sculptures, Monets, Van Goghs, Rodin sculptures and other 19th- and 20th-century art. A large new addition is in the works for 2017; in the meantime the collection can feel chaotic.

Schweizerisches Landesmuseum MUSEUM

(Swiss National Museum; www.musee-suisse.ch; Museumstrasse 2; adult/child Sfr10/free; 10am-5pm Tue-Sun, to 7pm Thu) Inside a purpose-built cross between a mansion and a castle sprawls an eclectic and imaginatively presented tour through Swiss history. Collections range from ancient arms to a series of rooms recreating the interiors of everything from a 15th-century convent to contemporary pads crammed with designer furniture. You can dart in from the train station between trains.

DON'T MISS

TOASTING FROSTY

Sechseläuten (www.sechselaeuten.ch) is a spring festival on the third Monday of April that features guild members parading down the streets in historical costume. In one of Europe's more spectacular – and odd – traditions, a fireworks-filled 'snowman' (the *Böögg*) is ignited atop a huge pyre on Bellevueplatz to celebrate the end of winter. The entire country watches the spectacle on live TV and how long it takes for the snowman's head to explode is said to determine whether summer will be warm and sunny, or wet and dreary (six minutes is *very* good).

Activities

Zürich comes into its own in summer when its green lakeshore parks buzz with bathers, sun-seekers, in-line skaters, footballers, lovers, picnickers, party animals, preeners and police patrolling on rollerblades!

Swimming Areas SWIMMING

(admission Sfr6; 9am-7pm May & Sep, to 8pm Jun-Aug) From mid-May to mid-September, outdoor swimming areas – think a rectangular wooden pier partly covered by a pavilion – open around the lake and up the Limmat River. Many offer massages, yoga and saunas, as well as snacks and rollicking bars. Our favourites include **Seebad Enge** (044 201 38 89; www.seebadenge.ch; Mythenquai 95; admission Sfr7), a trendy bar that opens until midnight in fine weather (it's about 700m southwest of Bürkliplatz); and **Letten** (044 362 92 00; Lettensteg 10; admission free), a hipster hangout where people swim, barbecue, play volleyball or just drink and loll on the grass and concrete.

Festivals & Events

Street Parade FESTIVAL

(www.street-parade.ch) This techno celebration in the middle of August is one of Europe's largest street parties.

Zürich

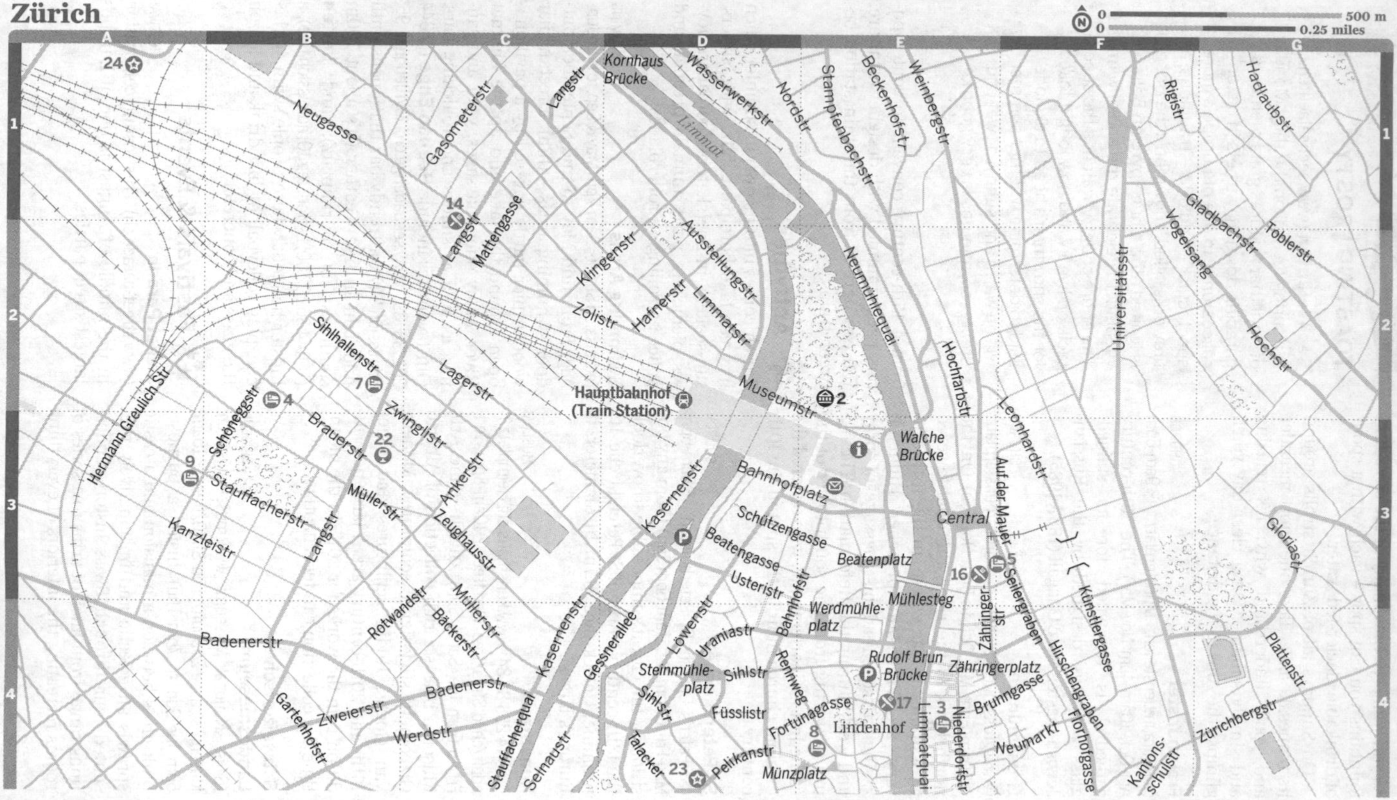

500 m
0.25 miles

Hadlaubstr
Toblerstr
Hochstr
Gladbachstr
Vogelsang
Rigistr
Universitätstr
Gloriastr
Plattenstr
Zürichbergstr
Kantonsschulstr
Künstlergasse
Hirschengraben
Florhofgasse
Leonhardstr
Seilergraben
Auf der Mauer
Zähringerstr
Zähringerplatz
Brunngasse
Neumarkt
Niederdorfstr
Limmatquai
Central
Hochfarbstr
Weinbergstr
Beckenhofstr
Stampfenbachstr
Neumühlequai
Walche Brücke
Mühlesteg
Werdmühle-platz
Beatenplatz
Rudolf Brun Brücke
Lindenhof
Rennweg
Fortunagasse
Münzplatz
Nordstr
Wasserwerkstr
Limmat
Museumstr
Bahnhofplatz
Schützengasse
Bahnhofstr
Uraniastr
Sihlstr
Füsslistr
Pelikanstr
Ausstellungsstr
Limmatstr
Beatengasse
Usteristr
Löwenstr
Steinmühleplatz
Talacker
Kornhaus Brücke
Hauptbahnhof (Train Station)
Kasernenstr
Gessnerallee
Selnaustr
Stauffacherquai
Hafnerstr
Klingenstr
Zollstr
Langstr
Mattengasse
Gasometerstr
Lagerstr
Zeughausstr
Müllerstr
Bäckerstr
Badenerstr
Werdstr
Ankerstr
Zwinglistr
Sihlhallenstr
Brauerstr
Rotwandstr
Zweierstr
Gartenhofstr
Neugasse
Schöneggstr
Stauffacherstr
Kanzleistr
Hermann Greulich Str

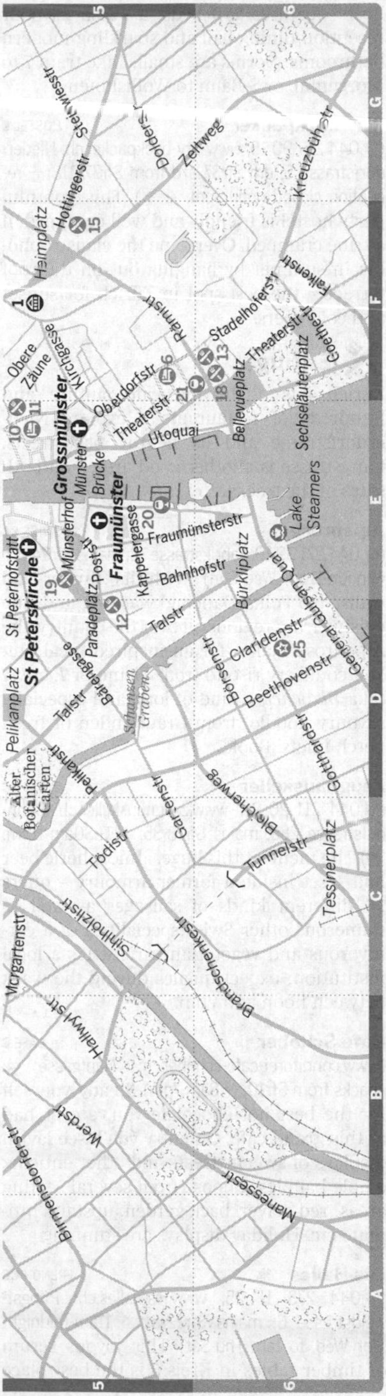

Zürich

Top Sights

Fraumünster E5
Grossmünster E5
St Peterskirche E5

Sights

1 Kunsthaus F5
2 Schweizerisches Landesmuseum E2

Sleeping

3 City Backpacker E4
4 Dakini B2
5 Hotel du Théâtre F3
6 Hotel Otter F5
7 Hotel Rothaus B2
8 Hotel Widder E4
9 Pension für Dich A3
10 SYHA Hostel E5

Eating

11 Café Schober E5
12 Café Sprüngli D5
13 Kronenhalle F6
14 Lily's C1
15 My Place F5
16 Restaurant Brasserie Johanniter E3
17 Schipfe 16 .... E4
18 Sternen Grill F6
19 Zeughauskeller E5

Drinking

20 Barfussbar E5
21 Café Odeon F6
22 Longstreet Bar B3

Entertainment

23 Kaufleuten D4
24 Supermarket A1
25 Tonhalle D6

Sleeping

Zürich accommodation prices are fittingly high for the main city of expensive Switzerland. You might consider options such as www.airbnb.com here.

TOP CHOICE **Hotel du Théâtre** HOTEL **€€**
(044-2672670; www.hotel-du-theatre.ch; Seilergraben 69; s/d from Sfr155/205;) Located in the lively Niederdorf and within walking distance to the train station, this boutique hotel is decorated with designer furniture and old film stills (an ode to the hotel's past – in the 1950s it was a combined theatre and hotel).

Pension für Dich PENSION €

(☎044 317 91 60; www.fuerdich.ch; Stauffacherstrasse 141; s/d without bathroom from Sfr100/110;) These simple but fabulous apartments have been converted into comfy rooms – think retro furnishings meets Ikea. A number of rooms have balconies. There's a good cafe downstairs, plus you're smack in the centre of the Kreis 4 nightlife action.

Hotel Widder HOTEL €€€

(☎044 224 25 26; www.widderhotel.ch; Rennweg 7; d from Sfr500;) A stylish hotel in the equally grand Augustiner district, the Widder is a pleasing fusion of modernity and traditional charm. Rooms and public areas across the eight town houses here boast art and designer furniture.

Dakini B&B €

(☎044 291 42 20; www.dakini.ch; Brauerstrasse 87; s/d from Sfr90/150;) This relaxed B&B attracts a Bohemian crowd of artists and performers, academics and trendy tourists who don't bat an eyelid at its location near the red-light district. There's a communal kitchen. Take tram 8 to Bäckeranlange.

Hotel Rothaus HOTEL €

(☎043 322 10 58; www.hotelrothaus.ch; Sihlhallenstrasse 1; s/d from Sfr100/140;) Smack in the middle of the Langstrasse action, this cheerful red-brick building is a real find. A variety of fresh, airy rooms are complemented by a busy little eatery-bar downstairs. Guests can rent bikes cheaply.

Hotel Otter HOTEL €€

(☎044 251 22 07; www.wueste.ch; Oberdorfstrasse 7; s/d/apt from Sfr125/155/200;) The Otter has 17 rooms with a variety of colour schemes ranging from white and blue stripes to olive green. You might get pink satin duvet covers. Studio apartment-style rooms with kitchens are another option. A popular bar, Wüste, is downstairs.

Hotel Seegarten HOTEL €€

(☎0443883737; www.hotel-seegarten.ch; Seegartenstrasse 14; s/d from Sfr195/295;) Rattan furniture and vintage tourist posters give this place a rustic Mediterranean atmosphere, which is reinforced by the proximity to the lake and the on-site Restaurant-Bar Latino. Take tram 2 or 4 to Kreuzstrasse.

SYHA Hostel HOSTEL €

(☎043 399 78 00; www.youthhostel.ch; Mütschellenstrasse 114, Wollishofen; dm from Sfr42, s/d from Sfr118/138;) This bulbous, purple-red hostel features 290 beds, a swish 24-hour reception/dining hall and sparkling modern bathrooms. Dorms are small. Take tram 7 to Morgental, or S-Bahn to Wollishofen.

City Backpacker HOSTEL €

(☎044 251 90 15; www.city-backpacker.ch; Niederdorfstrasse 5; dm Sfr37, s/d from Sfr77/118; reception closed noon-3pm;) This youthful party hostel is friendly and well equipped, if a trifle cramped. Overcome the claustrophobia in summer by hanging out on the roof terrace – the best spot in Zürich for sunset and cold beers.

Eating

Zürich has a thriving cafe culture and hundreds of restaurants – explore Niederdorfstrasse and its nearby backstreets. Langstrasse is another good area – on both sides of the tracks.

Alpenrose SWISS €€

(☎044 271 39 19; Fabrikstrasse 12; mains Sfr24-42; noon-11pm Wed-Sun) With its timber-clad walls, 'No Polka Dancing' warning and fine cuisine from regions all over the country, the Alpenrose makes for an inspired meal out. You could try risotto from Ticino or *Pizokel* (aka *Bizochel,* a kind of long and especially savoury noodle) from Graubünden or fresh perch fillets. Book.

Zeughauskeller SWISS €€

(☎044 211 26 90; www.zeughauskeller.ch; Bahnhofstrasse 28a; mains Sfr18-35; 11.30am-11pm;) The menu at this huge, atmospheric beer hall – set inside a former armoury – offers 20 different kinds of sausages as well as numerous other Swiss specialities of a carnivorous and vegetarian variety. It's a local institution; expect queues during the week between noon and 2pm.

Café Schober CAFE €

(www.conditorei-cafe-schober.ch; Napfgasse 4; snacks from Sfr10; 8am-7pm) Steady yourself for the best hot chocolate you've ever had at this grand cafe. On entry you'll see lavish displays of sweets, treats and other enticing edible baubles. Choose from several seating areas: red velvet, back garden, upstairs intimate etc. Holiday displays are stunning.

Les Halles FRENCH €€

(☎044 273 11 25; www.les-halles.ch; Pfingstweidstrasse 6; mains Sfr22-31; 11am-midnight Mon-Wed, to 1am Thu-Sat) This joyous scrum of timber tables in Kreis 5 is the best place in town to sit down to *Moules mit Frites* (mussels and fries). Hang at the bustling bar and shop at the market. It is one of several chirpy bar-restaurants in formerly derelict factory buildings in the area.

Schipfe 16 INTERNATIONAL €
(044 211 21 22; Schipfe 16; menus Sfr17-20; 11am-2pm Mon-Fri) Overlooking the Limmat River from the historic Schipfe area, Schipfe 16 is a good-natured canteen-style spot in an unbeatable location on the river. Enjoy one of three daily menus (made with seasonal locally sourced ingredients) at outdoor tables.

Restaurant Brasserie Johanniter SWISS €
(www.johanniter.com; Niederdorfstrasse 70; mains Sfr14-35; 10am-midnight) In the very heart of the old town, this century-old traditional beer hall serves up Swiss standards (think lots of pork, veal and potatoes). There is a long list of daily specials and you can expect a hearty meal no matter what you order. Modestly sized, there is a suitably excellent selection of fresh beers available by the stein.

Kronenhalle BRASSERIE €€€
(044 251 66 69; Rämistrasse 4; mains Sfr32-87; noon-11pm) A haunt of city movers-and-shakers in suits, the Crown Hall is a brasserie-style establishment with an old-world feel, white tablecloths and lots of dark wood. Impeccably mannered waiters move discreetly below Chagall, Miró, Matisse and Picasso originals.

Café Sprüngli SWISS €
(044 224 47 31; www.spruengli.ch; Bahnhofstrasse 21; mains Sfr9-15; 8am-5pm) Indulge in cakes, chocolate and coffee at this epicentre of sweet Switzerland, in business since 1836. You can have a light lunch too but, whatever you do, don't fail to check out the chocolate shop heaven around the corner on Paradeplatz.

Lily's ASIAN €€
(044 440 18 85; www.lilys.ch; Langstrasse 197; 11am-midnight) This trendy noodle-bar's convenient location and casual, upbeat atmosphere are fun, while the menu of Asian stir-fries and other classics is excellent. Dine at long tables and expect waits at prime times.

My Place CAFE €
(www.myplacedesign.ch; Hottingerstrasse 4; meals from Sfr9; 8am-10pm;) Ideally located close to the Kunsthaus, this sprightly cafe has excellent coffees and fresh fruit juices. It also has daily lunch specials that are healthy and seasonal.

Sternen Grill SWISS €
(Theatrestrasse 22; snacks from Sfr7; 11.30am-midnight) This is the city's most famous – and busiest – sausage stand, just follow the crowds streaming in. The classic *Kalbsbratwurst mit Gold Bürli* (veal sausage with bread roll) costs Sfr7. There are a few vegetarian options too.

Drinking & Entertainment

Options abound across town, but the bulk of the more animated drinking dens are in Züri-West, especially along Langstrasse in Kreis 4 and Hardstrasse in Kreis 5.

Züritipp (www.zueritipp.ch) comes out on Thursdays with the *TagesAnzeiger* newspaper, which is jammed with info about what's on.

Café Odeon BAR
(044 251 16 50; www.odeon.ch; Am Bellevueplatz; 9am-late) This one-time haunt of Lenin and the Dadaists is still a prime people-watching spot for gays and straights alike. Come for the art-nouveau interior, the OTT chandeliers and a whiff of another century. It serves food too.

Longstreet Bar BAR
(044 241 21 72; www.longstreetbar.ch; Langstrasse 92; 8pm-late Tue-Sat) The Longstreet is a music bar with a varied roll call of DJs coming in and out. Try to count the thousands of light bulbs in this purple-felt-lined one-time cabaret.

Café des Amis CAFE
(www.desamis.ch; Nordstrasse 88; 8am-late Tue-Fri, 9am-1am Sat, to 6pm Sun) A good weekend brunch stop (until 4pm), this is above all a popular new place to hang out and drink anything from coffee to cocktails. In summer, spread out in the generous, cobbled terrace area.

Barfussbar BAR
(Barefoot Bar; 044 251 33 31; www.barfussbar.ch; Stadthausquai 12; 11.30am-late Mon-Fri, 2pm-2am Sat, 3.30-11.30pm Sun) One of the first gay bars in the country and still going strong, Barfussbar now incorporates a sushi bar and has mellowed over the years – gays and straights feel equally at home.

Supermarket CLUB
(044 440 20 05; www.supermarket.li; Geroldstrasse 17; 11pm-late Thu-Sat) Looking like an

DON'T MISS

ZÜRI-WEST

The reborn part of the city, known as Züri-West and stretching west of the Hauptbahnhof, is primarily made up of two former working-class districts: Kreis 4 and Kreis 5. At night, it becomes a hedonists' playground.

Kreis 4, still a red-light district and centred on Langstrasse south of the tracks, is lined with eateries, bars and tawdry shops.

Langstrasse continues north over the railway lines into Kreis 5, where it quietens down a little but still offers plenty of options. The main focus of Kreis 5 action is along what promoters have dubbed the **Kulturmeile** (Culture Mile; www.kulturmeile.ch), Hardstrasse.

innocent little house, Supermarket boasts three cosy lounge bars around the dance floor, a covered back courtyard and an interesting roster of DJs playing house and techno. The crowd tends to be mid-20s. Take a train from Hauptbahnhof to Hardbrücke.

Kaufleuten CLUB
(☎044 225 33 22; Pelikanplatz 18; ⏰11pm-late Thu-Sat) An opulent art-deco theatre with a stage, mezzanine floor and bars arranged around the dance floor, Zürich's 'establishment' club plays house, hip hop and Latin rhythms to a slightly older crowd.

Moods BLUES, JAZZ
(☎044 276 80 00; www.moods.ch; Schiffbaustrasse 6; ⏰7.30pm-midnight Mon-Thu, to late Fri & Sat, 6-10pm Sun) One of the city's top jazz spots, although other musical genres such as Latin and world music grab the occasional spot on its calendar.

Tonhalle CLASSICAL MUSIC
(☎044 206 34 34; www.tonhalle-orchester.ch; Claridenstrasse 7) An opulent venue used by Zürich's orchestra and chamber orchestra.

Shopping

For high fashion, head for Bahnhofstrasse and surrounding streets. Across the river, funkier boutiques are dotted about the lanes of Niederdorf. For grunge, preloved gear and some none-too-serious fun young stuff, have a stroll along Langstrasse in Kreis 4.

Information

Post Office (⏰7am-9pm) Located inside the train station.

Zürich Tourism (☎044 215 40 00, hotel reservations 044 215 40 40; www.zuerich.com; ⏰8am-8.30pm Mon-Sat, 8.30am-6.30pm Sun) Offers walking tours (Sfr25) most mornings at 11am. Located inside the train station.

ZürichCard (adult/child 24hr Sfr20/14, 72hr Sfr40/28) Excellent-value discount card available from the tourist office and airport train station. Provides free public transport, free museum admission and more.

Getting There & Away

AIR Zürich airport (ZRH; ☎043 816 22 11; www.zurich-airport.com), 10km north of the centre, is Switzerland's main airport.

TRAIN Zürich has services to all neighbouring countries. Destinations include Milan (4¼ hours), Munich (four hours), Paris (four hours) and Vienna (eight hours).

There are regular direct departures to most major Swiss towns, such as Basel (Sfr32, one hour), Bern (Sfr49, one hour), Geneva (Sfr84, 2¾ hours), Lucerne (Sfr24, one hour) and Lugano (Sfr62, 2¾ hours).

Getting Around

TO/FROM THE AIRPORT Up to nine trains an hour run each direction between the airport and the main train station (Sfr7, nine to 13 minutes). Most continue on to cities such as Lucerne and Geneva.

BICYCLE City bikes (www.zuerirollt.ch) can be picked up from the station at **Velogate** (⏰8am-9.30pm) for free day use; if you keep it overnight it costs Sfr10.

BOAT Lake steamers (☎044 487 13 33; www.zsg.ch) run between April and October. They leave from Bürkliplatz. A small circular tour (Kleine Rundfahrt) takes 1½ hours (adult/child Sfr8.20/4.10) and departs every 30 minutes between 11am and 7.30pm. There are longer tours too.

PUBLIC TRANSPORT The comprehensive, unified bus, tram and S-Bahn **public transit system** (ZVV; www.zvv.ch) includes boats plying the Limmat River. Short trips under five stops are Sfr2.40; typical trips are Sfr4.20. A 24-hour pass for the city centre is Sfr8.40.

NORTHERN SWITZERLAND

This region is left off most people's Switzerland itineraries – which is precisely why you should visit! Sure, it is known for industry and commerce, but it also has some great attractions. Breathe in the sweet (OK slightly stinky) odours of black-and-white cows as you roll through the bucolic countryside. Take time to explore the tiny rural towns set among green rolling hills, and on Lake Constance (Bodensee) and the Rhine (Rhein) River on the German border.

Basel

POP 170,600

Basel is the closest Switzerland comes to having a seaport; the Rhine is navigable for decent-sized ships from this point until it reaches the North Sea in the Netherlands. Basel's year-round attractions, including the engaging Old Town, are mostly concentrated in Grossbasel (Greater Basel) on the south bank of the Rhine.

Sights & Activities

TOP CHOICE Old Town HISTORIC AREA

The medieval Old Town in the heart of Basel is a delight. Start in **Marktplatz**, which is dominated by the astonishingly vivid red facade of the 16th century **Rathaus** (town hall). Just north, the Fischmarktplatz features the Gothic **Fischmarktbrunnen**, a splendid medieval fountain.

A walk about 400m west of Marktplatz through the former artisans' district along Spalenberg leads uphill to the 600-year-old **Spalentor** city gate, one of only three to survive the wall's demolition in 1866.

The narrow lanes that riddle the hillside between Marktplatz and the Spalentor form the most captivating part of old Basel. Lined by impeccably maintained, centuries-old houses, lanes like Spalenberg, Heuberg and Leonhardsberg are worth a gentle stroll.

TOP CHOICE Fondation Beyeler GALLERY

(☎061 645 97 00; www.fondationbeyeler.ch; Baselstrasse 101, Riehen; adult/child Sfr25/6; ⏰10am-6pm, to 8pm Wed) The art space to really knock your socks off is the Fondation Beyeler, housed in an open-plan building by Italian architect Renzo Piano. The quality of its 19th- and 20th-century paintings is matched only by the way Miró and Max Ernst sculptures are juxtaposed with similar tribal figures. Take tram 6 to Riehen.

Historisches Museum Basel MUSEUM

(Basel History Museum; ☎061 205 86 00; www.hmb.ch; Barfüsserplatz; adult/child Sfr12/free; ⏰10am-5pm Tue-Sun) Housed in the former Barfüsserkirche (the Barefooted Ones Church, after the barefoot Franciscan friars who founded it in the 14th century), the collections of the history museum include pre-Christian-era archaeological finds, a collection of religious objects from the cathedral and plenty of material documenting the city's development.

Kunstmuseum GALLERY

(Museum of Fine Arts; ☎061 206 62 62; www.kunstmuseumbasel.ch; St Alban-Graben 16; adult/child Sfr15/free; ⏰10am-5pm Tue-Sun) Art lovers can ogle at Switzerland's largest art collection, including works by Klee and Picasso.

Sleeping

Hotels are often full during Basel's trade fairs and conventions, so book ahead. Guests receive a pass for free travel on public transport.

TOP CHOICE Au Violon HOTEL €

(☎061 269 87 11; www.au-violon.com; Im Lohnhof 4; s/d from Sfr125/150; ⊜📶) The doors are one of the few hints that quaint, atmospheric Au Violon was a prison from 1835 to 1995. Most of the rooms are two cells rolled into one and either look onto a delightful cobblestone courtyard or have views of the Münster. Sitting on a leafy hilltop, it also has a well-respected restaurant.

Hotel Stadthof HOTEL €

(☎061 261 87 11; www.stadthof.ch; Gerbergasse 84; s/d from Sfr80/130; ⊜) Book ahead to snag one of nine rooms at this spartan but decent central hotel, located above a pizzeria on an Old Town square. The cheaper rooms share toilet and shower.

Der Teufelhof BOUTIQUE HOTEL €€

(☎061 261 10 10; www.teufelhof.com; Leonhardsgraben 49; r from Sfr160) 'The Devil's Court' fuses two hotels into one. The Kunsthotel's nine rooms are each decorated by a different artist. The larger Galerie hotel annexe, a former convent, is more about stylish everyday design.

5 Signori GUESTHOUSE €

(☎061 361 87 73; www.restaurantsignori.ch; Güterstrasse 183; r without bathroom from Sfr90; 📶) Just a 10-minute walk southeast of the train station, this simple but stylish guesthouse is located above an excellent restaurant, known for its freshly sourced ingredients. The rooms share bathrooms and there is a small, private terrace for guests to use.

WORTH A TRIP

THE JURA

The grandest towns in this clover-shaped canton are little more than enchanting villages. Deep, mysterious forests and impossible green clearings succeed one another across the low mountains of the Jura, and some 1200km of marked paths across the canton give hikers plenty of scope. This is the place for an escape.

The highlight is **St Ursanne**, a drop-dead-gorgeous medieval village with a 12th-century Gothic church, 16th-century town gate, clusters of ancient houses and a lovely stone bridge crossing the Doubs River right into the ramparts. Feast on thin crisp *tartes flambées* and apple cake to die for at **Hôtel-Restaurant de la Demi Lune** (☎032 461 35 31; www.demi-lune.ch; Rue Basse 2; r Sfr60-130).

The unexciting canton capital of Delémont (which is on the Basel–Geneva train line) has trains to St Ursanne (Sfr8, 15 minutes, hourly).

Hotel Krafft HOTEL €
(☎061 690 91 30; www.hotelkrafft.ch; Rheingasse 12; s/d from Sfr75/125; 📶) Design-savvy urbanites adore this place. Sculptural chandeliers dangle in the creaky-floored dining room (for fine food) overlooking the Rhine, and stainless-steel ornaments adorn each landing of the spiral staircase.

Basel Backpack HOSTEL €
(☎061 333 00 37; www.baselbackpack.ch; Dornacherstrasse 192; dm Sfr32, s/d from Sfr80/100; 🚭@📶) Converted from a factory, this independent 81-bed hostel south of the main train station has cheerful, colour-coded eight-bed dorms and more sedate doubles and family rooms.

Eating & Drinking

Head to the Marktplatz for a daily market and several stands selling excellent quick bites, such as local sausages and sandwiches.

St Alban Stübli SWISS €€€
(☎061 272 54 15; www.st-alban-stuebli.ch; St Alban Vorstadt 74; mains Sfr40-60; ⏰11.30am-2pm & 6-10pm Mon-Fri) Set in a lovely quiet street, this is your quintessential cosy local tavern with dim yellow lighting, plenty of timber and fine linen. Food fuses local with French.

Acqua ITALIAN €€
(☎061 564 66 66; www.acquabasilea.ch; Binningerstrasse 14; mains Sfr17-42; ⏰lunch & dinner Tue-Fri, dinner Sat) For a special experience, head to these converted waterworks beside a quiet stream. The atmosphere is glam post-industrial; the food is Tuscan. Basel's beautiful people drink in the attached lounge-bar.

Zum Roten Engel CAFE
(☎061 261 20 08; Andreasplatz 15; mains from Sfr15; ⏰9am-midnight) This student-filled venue, spilling onto an irresistible, tiny cobblestone square, is great for a latte and snacks by day and a glass of wine or three in the evening. It's a temperate way to start the night. Sunday brunch is a treat.

Charon FRENCH €€€
(☎061 261 99 80; www.restaurant-charon.ch; Schützengraben 62; mains Sfr40-50; ⏰11.30am-2pm & 5-10pm Mon-Fri May-Sep, Tue-Sun Oct-Apr) In what looks like someone's home, this understated restaurant with art-nouveau decorative touches offers carefully prepared dishes leaning slightly to French tastes. Look for hearty country dishes sourced from the region.

Confiserie Schiesser CAFE €
(www.confiserie-schiesser.ch; Marktplatz 19; snacks from Sfr5; ⏰8am-6pm) Since 1870, this gem-like bakery and cafe has been creating sweet treats from bonbons to tortes to elaborate cakes. Browse the display cases and then head upstairs to the cafe for light meals and excellent coffee.

Entertainment

Steinenvorstadt and Barfüsserplatz teem with teens and 20-somethings on the weekends. A faint whiff of grunge floats around Kleinbasel, the area around Rheingasse and Utengasse, with a few watering holes and something of a red-light zone to lend it edge.

Bird's Eye Jazz Club JAZZ
(☎061 263 33 41; www.birdseye.ch; Kohlenberg 20; ⏰8pm-midnight Tue-Sat Sep-May, Wed-Sat Jun-Aug) This is among Europe's top jazz dens, attracting local and headline foreign acts. Concerts start most evenings at 8.30pm.

Die Kuppel CLUB
(☎061 270 99 39; www.kuppel.ch; Binningerstrasse 14; ⏰9pm-late Tue, 10pm-late Thu-Sat) This is an

atmospheric wooden dome with a dance floor and cocktail bar located in a secluded park. Salsa, soul, house and '70s and '80s music are regularly on the bill. The closing time is late and flexible.

Shopping

The area around Marktplatz and Barfüsserplatz teems with shops, selling everything from fashion to fine foods. Long, pedestrian-only Freie Strasse, which runs southeast from Marktplatz, is lined with stores of all persuasions.

Spalenberg, a lovely climbing lane to explore in its own right, is home to a line-up of intriguing boutiques.

Läckerli Huus FOOD
(www.laeckerli-huus.ch; Gerbergasse 57) Basel has a signature treat, *Leckerli*, which dates back to the Middle Ages. An oddly crunchy yet chewy biscuit, it combines honey, nuts and citrus flavours. You can buy it all over town but this is the original location of a company that makes the best example.

Information

Tourist Office (☎061 268 68 68; www.basel.com) The tourist office has branches at SBB Bahnhof (Bahnhof; ⊙8.30am-6pm Mon-Fri, 9am-5pm Sat, to 3pm Sun & holidays) and Stadtcasino (Steinenberg 14; ⊙9am-6.30pm Mon-Fri, to 5pm Sat, 10am-3pm Sun & holidays). The Stadtcasino branch organises two-hour English-language walking tours of the city centre (adult/child Sfr15/7.50), usually starting at 2.30pm Monday to Saturday, May through October, and on Saturdays the rest of the year.

Getting There & Away

AIR The **EuroAirport** (BSL or MLH; ☎061 325 31 11; www.euroairport.com), 5km northwest of town in France, is the main airport for Basel. It is a hub for easyJet and there are flights to major European cities.

TRAIN Basel is a major European rail hub. The main station, Basel SBB, has TGVs to France (Paris, three hours) and fast ICEs to major cities in Germany. There are frequent services to Freiburg (45 minutes), gateway to the Black Forest.

Services within Switzerland include frequent trains to Bern (Sfr39, one hour) and Zürich (Sfr32, one hour).

Getting Around

Bus 50 links the airport and Basel SBB (Sfr3.40, 20 minutes). Trams 8 and 11 link the station to Marktplatz (Sfr3.40, day pass Sfr9).

Schaffhausen & the Rhine

Schaffhausen is the kind of quaint medieval town one more readily associates with Germany (perhaps no coincidence given how close the border is). Ornate frescos and oriel windows adorn pastel-coloured houses in the pedestrian-only Altstadt (Old Town).

Prime views preen their feathers atop the 16th-century **Munot fortress** (admission free; ⊙8am-8pm May-Sep, 9am-5pm Oct-Apr), a 15-minute uphill walk through vineyards from town.

Westward along the river on foot (40 minutes) or aboard bus 1 or 6 to Neuhausen is **Rheinfall** (Rhine Falls; www.rhinefalls.ch; 1, 6 or 9 to Neuhausen), waterfalls that, though only 23m tall, are deemed Europe's largest. The amount of water thundering down is extraordinary. Get off one stop after Migross in the centre, then follow signs leading to north bank of river.

The 45km **boat trip** (Untersee und Rhein; ☎052 634 08 88; www.urh.ch; Freier Platz; single Sfr47; ⊙Apr-Oct) from Schaffhausen to Constance (which is an excellent entry point

DON'T MISS

ST GALLEN'S TREASURE

St Gallen's 16th-century **Stiftsbibliothek** (abbey library; ☎071 227 34 16; www.stiftsbibliothek.ch; Klosterhof 6d; adult/child Sfr10/7; ⊙10am-5pm Mon-Sat, to 4pm Sun, closed late Nov) is one of the world's oldest and the finest example of rococo architecture. Along with the rest of the monastery complex surrounding it, the library forms a Unesco World Heritage site.

Filled with priceless books and manuscripts painstakingly handwritten by monks during the Middle Ages, it's a dimly lit confection of ceiling frescos, stucco, cherubs and parquetry. Only 30,000 of the total 150,000 volumes are in the library at any one time, and only a handful in display cases, arranged into special exhibitions. If there's a tour guide in the library at the time, you might see the monks' filing system, hidden in the wall panels.

There are regular trains from St Gallen to Bregenz in Austria (Sfr19, 35 minutes) and Zürich (Sfr29, 65 minutes via Winterthur).

into Germany; see p524) sails past one of the Rhine's more beautiful stretches. It passes meadows, castles and ancient villages, including **Stein am Rhein**, 20km to the east, where you could easily wear out your camera snapping pictures of the buildings in the picture-perfect Rathausplatz.

Direct hourly trains run to/from Schaffhausen and Zürich (Sfr27, 40 minutes to one hour).

Appenzellerland

Appenzellers are firmly rooted in tradition: the village Innerrhoden continues to hold a yearly open-air parliament and didn't permit women to vote until 1991.

Such devotion to rural tradition has an upside: locals go to great lengths to preserve their heritage. This area of impossibly green valleys, thick forests and mighty mountains is dotted with timeless villages and criss-crossed by endless **hiking** and **cycling** paths.

The pastel-hued village of **Appenzell** is a feast for the eyes and the stomach. Behind the gaily decorative coloured facades of its traditional buildings lie cafes, cake shops, cheese shops, delicatessens, butchers and restaurants all offering local specialities.

Hotel Appenzell (☎071 788 15 15; www.hotel-appenzell.ch; Landsgemeindeplatz; s/d from Sfr130/220;) sits in a brightly decorated, typical Appenzeller building and is a solid choice to both sleep and sample seasonal cuisine, including vegetarian dishes and the local strong-smelling Appenzell cheese.

APPENZELL WALKS

Hiking trails abound around Appenzell. One more unusual one is the **Barefoot Path** from Gonten, 5km west of Appenzell, to Gontenbad (one hour), for which you really don't need shoes – think lush green moors and meadows. In Gontenbad, dip in mud-laden water from the moors at **Natur-Moorbad** (☎071 795 31 23; www.naturmoorbad.ch; Gontenbad; admission Sfr30; ⏲closed Tue), a moor bath dating to 1740, whose wholly natural products relieve stress or skin conditions (adding in nettles, ferns and other plants) or simply serve to luxuriate with sweet rose baths (Sfr86 for two).

The train station, 400m from the town centre, is also home to the **tourist office** (☎071 788 96 41; www.appenzell.ch; Hauptgasse 4; ⏲9am-noon & 1.30-6pm Mon-Fri, 10am-noon & 2-5pm Sat & Sun Apr-Oct, 9am-noon & 2-5pm Mon-Fri, 2-5pm Sat & Sun Nov-Mar). There is a train to St Gallen (Sfr7.20, 50 minutes, twice hourly).

TICINO

Switzerland meets Italy: the summer air is rich and hot, and the peacock-proud posers propel their scooters in and out of traffic. Italian weather, Italian style. And that's not to mention the Italian ice cream, Italian pizza, Italian architecture and Italian language.

South of the Alps, Ticino (Tessin in German and French) has a distinct look. The canton manages to perfectly fuse Swiss cool with Italian passion, as evidenced by a lusty love for Italian comfort food and full-bodied wines that's balanced by a healthy respect for rules and regulations.

Getting There & Around

TRAIN Ticino is connected by a web of integrated trains (www.arcobaleno.ch; day pass Sfr20.40) that travel to Lugano, Locarno and Bellinzona, and reach into Italy. From Cadenazzo on the Locarno line there are trains to Milan's Malpensa airport (route S30; two hours, every two hours).

For an amazing scenic journey, take the **Centovalli Express** (www.centovalli.ch) from Locarno to Domodossola in Italy (two hours, hourly), where you can connect to Brig and points north in Switzerland. The views of gorges and rivers are incredible.

Locarno

POP 15,200

The rambling red enclave of Italianate town houses, piazzas and arcades ending at the northern end of Lake Maggiore, coupled with more hours of sunshine than anywhere else in Switzerland, give this laid-back town a summer resort atmosphere.

The lowest town in Switzerland, Locarno seemed like a soothing spot to host the 1925 peace conference that was intended to bring stability to Europe after WWI. It didn't work.

Locarno is on the northeast corner of Lago Maggiore, which mostly lies in Italy's Lombardy region. **Navigazione Lago Maggiore** (www.navigazionelaghi.it) operates boats across the entire lake.

WORTH A TRIP

BELLINZONA'S UNESCO CASTLES

Ticino's capital is a quiet stunner. Strategically placed at the conversion point of several valleys leading down from the Alps, Bellinzona is visually unique. Inhabited since Neolithic times, it is dominated by three grey-stone, fairy-tale medieval castles that have attracted everyone from Swiss invaders to painters such as JMW Turner. Turner may have liked the place, but Bellinzona has a surprisingly low tourist profile, in spite of its castles together forming a Unesco World Heritage site.

The main event is the medieval **Castelgrande** (www.bellinzonaunesco.ch; Mont San Michele; 9am-6pm, later in summer), which is a 10-minute walk from the train station and is reached by an elevator. Skip the dull museum inside and focus on explorations of the ramparts where you can appreciate how these castles formed a strategic barrier to marauders heading up the pass north into Switzerland.

You can also roam the ramparts of the two larger castles; the **Castello di Montebello** (Salita ai Castelli; 091 825 13 42; castle admission free, museum adult/concession Sfr5/2; castle 8am-8pm mid-Mar–Oct, museum 10am-6pm mid-Mar–Oct) is a further 3.5km-hike on. Both castles are in great condition and offer panoramic views of the town and countryside.

The **tourist office** (091 825 21 31; www.bellinzonaturismo.ch; Piazza Nosetto; 9am-6pm Mon-Fri, to noon Sat, reduced hours in winter) is in the restored Renaissance town hall in the centre of town.

Bellinzona is on the main train route connecting Zürich to Lugano (Sfr10.20, 22 to 30 minutes) and Italy. Trains also serve Locarno (Sfr8.20, 20 to 25 minutes).

Sights

Locarno's Italianate Old Town fans out from **Piazza Grande**, a photogenic ensemble of arcades and Lombard-style houses. A craft-and-produce market takes over the square every Thursday.

Santuario della Madonna del Sasso SANCTUARY

Don't miss the formidable Madonna del Sasso, located up on the hill, with panoramic views of the lake and town. The sanctuary was built after the Virgin Mary allegedly appeared in a vision in 1480. It features a church with 15th-century paintings, a small museum and several distinctive statues.

There is a funicular from the town centre, but the 20-minute climb is not demanding (take Via al Sasso off Via Cappuccini) and you pass some shrines on the way.

Sleeping & Eating

Lake Maggiore has a great variety of fresh and tasty fish, including *persico* (perch) and *corigone* (whitefish).

Vecchia Locarno HOTEL €

(091 751 65 02; www.hotel-vecchia-locarno.ch; Via della Motta 10; s Sfr55-90, d Sfr100-140;) A sunny inner courtyard forms the centrepiece of this laid-back guesthouse. Rooms are bright and simple; the best have views over the Old Town and hills.

Osteria Chiara ITALIAN €€

(091 743 32 96; www.osteriachiara.ch; Vicolo della Chiara 1; mains Sfr16-30; Tue-Sat; ; Cannobio) Tucked away on a cobbled lane, this has the cosy feel of a grotto. Sit at granite tables beneath the pergola or at timber tables by the fireplace for homemade pasta. From the lake follow the signs up Vicolo dei Nessi.

Getting There & Away

Locarno is well-linked to Ticino and the rest of Switzerland via Bellinzona. The scenic **Centovalli Express** (www.centovalli.ch) runs to Brig via Domodossola in Italy. The train station is five minutes away from Piazza Grande.

Lugano

POP 54,500

There is a distinct vibrant snappiness in the air in Lugano, Switzerland's southernmost tourist town, where visitors unravel the spaghetti maze of cobblestone streets while locals toil queitly in cash-stuffed banks – this is the country's third-most important banking centre.

A sophisticated slice of Italian life with colourful markets, upmarket shops, interlocking *piazze* and lakeside parks, lucky Lugano lounges on the northern shore of Lake Lugano, at the feet of Mts San Salvatore and Bré. It's a superb base for lake trips, water sports and hillside hikes.

Sights & Activities

The **Centro Storico** (Old Town) is a 10-minute walk downhill from the train station; take the stairs or the fun funicular (Sfr1.10).

Wander through the mostly porticoed lanes woven around the busy main square, **Piazza della Riforma** – which is even more lively when the Tuesday- and Friday-morning markets are held. Via Nassa is the main shopping street and boasts a *Vogue*-worthy line-up of high-end stores.

Chiesa di Santa Maria degli Angioli CHURCH
(St Mary of the Angel; Piazza Luini; 7am-6pm) This simple Romanesque church contains two frescos by Bernardino Luini dating from 1529. Covering the entire wall that divides the church in two is a grand didactic illustration of the crucifixion of Christ. The closer you look, the more scenes of Christ's Passion are revealed. The power and vivacity of the colours are astounding.

Museo del Cioccolato Alprose MUSEUM
(091 611 88 88; www.alprose.ch; Via Rompada 36, Caslano; adult/child Sfr3/1; 9am-5.30pm Mon-Fri, to 4.30pm Sat & Sun) Chomp on a chocolate-coated history lesson: watch the sweet substance being made and taste it for free. Get there by the Ferrovia Ponte Tresa train (Sfr7).

Lago Lugano BOAT TOUR
(www.lakelugano.ch; tours from Sfr25; Apr-Oct) Take a boat trip to one of the photogenic villages hugging the gorgeous shoreline – car-free **Gandria** is popular – and feast on traditional Ticinese dishes in your pick of quintessential Ticinese grottos.

Sleeping

Many hotels close for part of the winter.

TOP CHOICE **Hotel & Hostel Montarina** HOTEL, HOSTEL €
(091 966 72 72; www.montarina.ch; Via Montarina 1; dm from Sfr27, s Sfr80-90, d Sfr110-130;) Occupying a bubblegum-pink villa dating to 1860, this hotel and hostel behind the train station has lingering traces of old-world grandeur. Choose between the dorms in the vaulted basement, wood-floored antique rooms and contemporary rooms with private bathrooms. There's a shared kitchen-lounge, toys to amuse the kids, a swimming pool set in palm-dotted gardens and even a tiny vineyard.

Hotel International au Lac HOTEL €€
(091 922 75 41; www.hotel-international.ch; Via Nassa 88; s Sfr120-185, dSfr195-330; Apr-Oct;) Choose a front room to gaze out across Lago Lugano at this century-old hotel on the lakefront. Rooms are comfortable, with a smattering of antique furniture, and the garden-fringed pool invites relaxation.

Acquarello HOTEL €€
(091 911 68 68; www.acquarello.ch; Piazza Cioccaro 9; r Sfr90-190;) You can't get more central than this modest yet rambling hotel right at the base of the funicular from the train station. Basic rooms may get some noise, but the better ones are bright and some ('superior') have sweeping lake views.

Eating

For pizza or pasta, any of the places around Piazza della Riforma are pleasant and lively. For a salad bar and vegetarian joy, try **Manora** (Piazza Dante Alighieri; 7.30am-9pm;) restaurant in the Manor department store.

TOP CHOICE **Bottegone del Vino** ITALIAN €€
(091 922 76 89; Via Magatti 3; mains Sfr20-45; 11am-11pm Mon-Sat) This is a great place to taste fine local wines over an excellent meal. The menu changes daily and features fresh ingredients sourced locally. Knowledgeable waiters fuss around the tables, only too happy to suggest the perfect Ticino tipple (the basic house red is superb). Try the sublime acacia honey with cheese.

Grand Café Al Porto INTERNATIONAL €€€
(091 910 51 30; Via Pessina 3; mains Sfr31-48; 8am-6.30pm Mon-Sat) This cafe, which began life way back in 1803, has several fine rooms for dining inside. Be sure to head upstairs to take a peek into the frescoed Cenacolo Fiorentino, once a monastery dining hall.

Gabbani CAFE, RESTAURANT €
(091 921 34 70; www.gabbani.com; Piazza Cioccaro 1; meals from Sfr15; deli 8am-6pm, restaurant until late) This sprawling empire at the base

of the funicular has been serving up the best in local food and drink since 1937. There's a bakery, deli (picnics!), food-to-go, cafe, bar and a fine restaurant. Have a morning coffee under the arches with a perfect little pastry. On the high floors there are stylish hotel rooms (from Sfr190).

L'Antica Osteria del Porto SWISS €€
(☎091 971 42 00; Via Foce 9; mains Sfr25-40; ⏰9am-11pm Wed-Mon) Set back from Lugano's sailing club, this is the place for local fish and Ticinese dishes like polenta crostini with porcini. The terrace overlooking the Cassarate stream is pleasant, as are the lake views.

Drinking & Entertainment

Soho Café COCKTAIL BAR
(☎091 922 60 80; Corso Pestalozzi 3; ⏰7am-1am Mon-Fri, 7pm-1am Sat) All those good-looking Lugano townies crowd in to this long, orange-lit bar for cocktails. Chilled DJ music creates a pleasant buzz.

New Orleans Club CLUB
(☎091 921 44 77; www.neworleansclublugano.com; Piazza Indipendenza 1; ⏰5pm-1am Mon-Sat) A lively spot Thursday to Saturday nights with Latin, hip-hop and disco nights. A good cocktail bar other times.

Information

The **tourist office** (☎091 913 32 32; www.lugano-tourism.ch; Riva Giocondo Albertolli; ⏰9am-7pm Mon-Fri, 10am-5pm Sat & Sun) also runs a seasonal booth at the train station.

Getting There & Away

Lugano is on the main line between Milan (60 to 90 minutes) and Zürich (Sfr62, 2¾ hours) and Lucerne (Sfr58, 2½ hours).

GRAUBÜNDEN

Don't be fooled by Graubünden's diminutive size on a map. This is topographic origami at its finest. Unfold the rippled landscape to find an outdoor adventurer's paradise riddled with more than 11,000km of walking trails, 600-plus lakes and 1500km of downhill ski slopes – including super swanky St Moritz and backpacker mecca Flims-Laax. You'll hear Italian, German and Romansch (the commonly used *crap* actually means peak).

WORTH A TRIP

BERNINA EXPRESS

The popular **Bernina Express** (www.berninaexpress.ch; ⏰mid-May–early Dec) route runs from Lugano to St Moritz (Sfr72, six hours), Davos and the rail hub of Chur (Sfr101, 6½ hours). Fares include obligatory reservations. From Lugano to Tirano (in Italy) a bus is used for the scenic run along Italy's Lake Como.

The train route over the Bernina Pass between Tirano and St Moritz is one of Switzerland's most spectacular and is Unesco-recognised. Some trains feature open-top cars.

Flims-Laax

They say if the snow ain't falling anywhere else, you'll surely find some around Flims-Laax. These towns, along with tiny Falera, 20km west of Chur, form a single ski area known as the **Weisses Arena** (White Arena; www.alpenarena.ch), with 220km of slopes (most above 2000m) catering for all levels. Laax in particular is a mecca for snowboarders, who spice up the local nightlife too. The resort is barely two hours by train and bus from Zürich airport.

Activities

Ask clued-up snowboarders to rattle off their top Swiss resorts and Laax will invariably make the grade. The riders' mecca boasts both Europe's smallest and largest half-pipe, excellent free-style parks and many off-piste opportunities. Skiers are equally content to bash the pistes in the interlinked resorts. A day pass costs from Sfr70.

The **hiking** network spans 250km. The **Naturlehrpfad circuit** at the summit of Cassons is brilliant for spotting wild Alpine flowers and critters.

Try **river rafting** on a turbulent 17km stretch of the Vorderrhein between Ilanz and Reichenau with **Swissraft** (☎081 911 52 50; www.swissraft.ch; half-/full-day trips from Sfr110/160).

Sleeping & Eating

Riders Palace HOSTEL €
(☎081 927 97 00; www.riderspalace.ch; Laax Murschetg; dm Sfr30-60, d Sfr120-280; 📶) This design-focused boutique hostel draws a party-mad

LIECHTENSTEIN

If Liechtenstein (pop 36,400) didn't exist, someone would have invented it. A tiny German-speaking mountain principality (160 sq km) governed by an iron-willed monarch in the heart of 21st-century Europe, it certainly has novelty value. Only 25km long by 12km wide (at its broadest point) – just larger than Manhattan – Liechtenstein is mostly visited by people who want a glimpse of the castle and a spurious passport stamp. Stay a little longer and you can escape into its pint-sized Alpine wilderness.

History

Austrian prince Johann Adam Von Liechtenstein purchased the counties of Schellenberg (1699) and Vaduz (1712) from impoverished German nobles and gave them his name. Long a principality under the Holy Roman Empire, Liechtenstein gained independence in 1866. In 1923, it formed a customs union with Switzerland (today it uses the Swiss franc). Prince Hans Adam II ascended the throne in 1989. In 2003, he won sweeping powers to dismiss the elected government, appoint judges and reject proposed laws. The following year, he handed the day-to-day running of the country to his son Alois.

Vaduz

Vaduz is a postage-stamp-sized city with a postcard-perfect backdrop. Crouching at the foot of forested mountains, hugging the banks of the Rhine and crowned by a turreted castle, its location is visually stunning.

The centre itself is curiously modern and sterile, with its mix of tax-free luxury-goods stores and cube-shaped concrete buildings. Yet just a few minutes' walk brings you to traces of the quaint village that existed just 50 years ago and quiet vineyards where the Alps seem that bit closer.

Vaduz Castle is closed to the public, but is worth the climb for the vistas. Trails climb the hill from the end of Egertastrasse. To see how Vaduz once looked, amble northeast to Mitteldorf. This and the surrounding streets form a charming quarter of traditional houses and rose-strewn gardens.

crowd of young riders to its strikingly lit, bare concrete spaces. Choose between basic five-bed dorms, slick rooms with Philippe Starck tubs, and hi-tech suites complete with PlayStation and Dolby surround sound. It's 200m from the Laax lifts.

Posta Veglia HISTORIC HOTEL **€€**
(☎081 921 44 66; www.postaveglia.ch; Via Principala 54, Laax; s/d from Sfr150/250; 📶) Today this 19th-century post office delivers discreet service and rustic flavour. The seven country-cottage-style rooms and suites are filled with beams, antiques and mod cons like DVD players. The restaurant has creative takes on fusion cuisine.

ℹ Information

The main **tourist office** (☎081 920 92 00; www.alpenarena.ch; Via Nova; ⊙8am-6pm Mon-Fri, 8am-noon Sat mid-Jun–mid-Aug, 8am-5pm Mon-Sat mid-Dec–mid-Apr) is in Flims.

ℹ Getting There & Away

Postal buses run to Flims and the other villages in the White Arena area hourly from the rail hub of Chur (to Flims-Dorf Sfr13.20, 35 minutes). A free local shuttle bus connects the various villages.

St Moritz

POP 5200

Switzerland's original winter wonderland and the cradle of Alpine tourism, St Moritz (San Murezzan in Romansch) has been luring royals, celebrities and moneyed wannabes since 1864. With its shimmering aquamarine lake, emerald forests and aloof mountains, the town looks a million dollars.

Yet despite the string of big-name designer boutiques on Via Serlas and celebs bashing the pistes, this resort isn't all show. The real riches lie outdoors with superb carving on Corviglia, hairy black runs on Diavolezza and miles of hiking trails when the snow melts.

Historic and creakily elegant, the six-century-old **Gasthof Löwen** (238 11 41; www.hotel-loewen.li; Herrengasse 35; s/d from Sfr200/300; P) has eight spacious rooms with antique furniture and modern bathrooms. There's a cosy bar, fine-dining restaurant and outdoor terrace overlooking grapevines.

Creaking wood floors and lilac walls create a rustic-chic backdrop for Swiss classics and Vaduz wines at the **Adler Vaduz** (232 21 31; www.adler.li; Herrengasse 2; mains Sfr18-50; lunch & dinner Mon-Fri).

Around Vaduz

Outside Vaduz the air is crisp and clear with a pungent, sweet aroma of cow dung and flowers. The countryside is dotted with tranquil villages and enticing churches set to a craggy Alps backdrop.

Triesenberg, on a terrace above Vaduz, commands excellent views over the Rhine valley. It has a pretty, onion-domed church. Take bus 21 from Vaduz.

There are loads of well-marked **cycling** routes throughout Liechtenstein (look for signs with a cycle symbol; distances and directions will also be included), as well as 400km of **hiking trails**; see www.wanderwege-llv.li. The most famous is the **Fürstensteig trail**, a rite of passage for nearly every Liechtensteiner. Falling away to a sheer drop in parts, the four-hour hike begins at the Berggasthaus Gaflei (take bus 22 from Triesenberg).

Information

Liechtenstein's international phone prefix is 423. The **Liechtenstein Center** (239 63 00; www.tourismus.li; Städtle 37, Vaduz; 9am-5pm) offers brochures and souvenir passport stamps (Sfr3), as well as housing the **Philatelie Liechtenstein**, which will interest stamp collectors. The post office is nearby.

The nearest train stations are in the Swiss border towns of Buchs and Sargans. From each of these towns there are frequent buses to Vaduz (from Buchs/Sargans Sfr3.40/5.80; Swiss Pass valid). Buses run every 30 minutes from the Austrian border town of Feldkirch.

Activities

Skiers and snowboarders will revel in the 350km of runs in three key areas. Avid cross-country skiers can glide through snow-dusted woodlands and plains on 160km of groomed trails.

You can also hike or try your hand at golf (including on the frozen lake in winter), tennis, in-line skating, fishing, horse riding, sailing, windsurfing and river rafting, to mention just a few available activities.

See www.engadin.stmoritz.ch for year-round activities information.

Corviglia & Signal SKIING
(day pass adult/child from Sfr73/24) For groomed slopes with big mountain vistas, head to Corviglia (2486m), accessible by funicular from Dorf. From Bad a cable car goes to Signal (shorter queues), giving access to the slopes of Piz Nair.

Diavolezza SKIING
(day pass adult/child from Sfr62/20) Silhouetted by glaciated 4000ers, Diavolezza (2978m) is a must-ski for free-riders and fans of jaw-dropping descents.

Sleeping & Eating

Hotel Eden HOTEL €€
(081 830 81 00; www.edenstmoritz.ch; Via Veglia 12; s Sfr160-190, d Sfr270-320;) Right in the heart of town, the Eden centres on an attractive central atrium and antique-strewn lounge where a fire crackles in winter. The old-style, pine-panelled rooms are cosy, and those on the top floor afford terrific lake- and mountain-views.

The Piz HOTEL, B&B €€
(081 832 11 11; www.piz-stmoritz.ch; Via dal Bagn 6; s/d/apt Sfr120/210/500;) Splashes of crimson, hardwood floors and clean lines define this contemporary B&B in St Moritz Bad. Fitted with rain showers and mod gizmos, the rooms are sleek and comfy, though street noise may disturb light sleepers. The breakfast buffet is good.

WORTH A TRIP

SWISS NATIONAL PARK

The road west from Müstair stretches 34km over the Ofenpass (Pass dal Fuorn, 2149m), through the thick woods of Switzerland's only national park (Jun-Oct) and on to Zernez and the hands-on **Swiss National Park Centre** (081 851 41 41; www.nationalpark.ch; adult/child Sfr7/3; 8.30am-6pm Jun-Oct, 9am-noon & 2-5pm Nov-May). Look for dolomite peaks, shimmering glaciers, larch woodlands, gentian-flecked pastures, clear waterfalls and high moors strung with topaz lakes.

Trains run regularly from Zernez to St Moritz (Sfr18.40, 45 minutes), stopping in scenic S-chanf, Zuoz and Celerina.

Jugendherberge St Moritz HOSTEL €
(081 836 61 11; www.youthhostel.ch/st.moritz; Stille Via Surpunt 60; dm/d Sfr60/150; @) Budget beds are gold-dust rare in St Moritz, but you'll find one at this hostel edging the forest. The four-bed dorms and doubles are quiet and clean. There's a kiosk, games room and laundrette.

Hatecke SWISS €€
(081 864 11 75; www.hatecke.ch; snacks & mains Sfr15-30; 9am-6.30pm Mon-Fri, to 6pm Sat) Organic, locally sourced *Bündnerfleisch* (smoked, air-dried beef) and melt-in-your-mouth venison ham are carved into wafer-thin slices on a century-old machine in this speciality shop. Take a seat on a sheepskin stool in the next-door cafe for a casual lunch.

Engiadina SWISS €€
(081 833 32 65; www.restaurant-engiadina.ch; Plazza da Scuola 2; fondue Sfr28-48; 11am-11pm Tue-Sun, closed May) A proper locals' place, Engiadina is famous for fondue, and that's the best thing to eat here. Champagne gives the melted cheese a kick. The pizza and polenta are also good.

Drinking

Around 20 bars and clubs pulsate in winter. While you shuffle to the beat, your wallet might also waltz itself wafer-thin: nights out with the glitterati in St Moritz can be expensive.

Bobby's Pub PUB
(081 834 42 83; Via dal Bagn 50a; 9.30am-1.30am) This laid-back and friendly English-style watering hole serves 30 different brews and attracts young snowboarders in season. It's among the few places open year-round.

Information

Tourist Office (081 837 33 33; www.stmoritz.ch; Via Maistra 12; 9am-6.30pm Mon-Fri, 9am-12.30pm & 1.30-6.30pm Sat, 4-6pm Sun, shorter hours rest of year) Uphill from the train station.

Getting There & Away

TRAIN Regular hourly trains (Sfr40, two hours) make the scenic run to/from the rail hub of Chur.

St Moritz is also an end point on the much-hyped *Glacier Express* (p1067).

The *Bernina Express* (p1091) provides seasonal links to Lugano, which include the stunning Unesco-recognised train line over the Bernina Pass to Tirano in Italy.

UNDERSTAND SWITZERLAND

History

The region's first inhabitants were a Celtic tribe, the Helvetii. The Romans arrived in 107 BC via the Great St Bernard Pass, but were gradually driven back by the Germanic Alemanni tribe, which settled in the region in the 5th century AD. Burgundians and Franks also came to the area, and Christianity was gradually introduced.

The territory was united under the Holy Roman Empire in 1032, but central control was never tight, and neighbouring nobles fought each other for local influence. Rudolph I spearheaded the Germanic Habsburg expansion and gradually brought the squabbling nobles to heel.

The Swiss Confederation

Upon Rudolph's death in 1291, local leaders saw a chance to gain independence. The forest communities of Uri, Schwyz and Nidwalden formed an alliance on 1 August 1291, which is seen as the origin of the Swiss Confederation (their struggles against the Habsburgs are idealised in the legend of William Tell). This union's success prompted other communities to join: Lucerne (1332), followed by Zürich (1351), Glarus and Zug (1352), and Bern (1353).

Encouraged by successes against the Habsburgs, the Swiss acquired a taste for territorial expansion and more land was seized. Fribourg, Solothurn, Basel, Schaffhausen and Appenzell joined the confederation, and the Swiss gained independence from the Holy Roman Emperor Maximilian I after their victory at Dornach in 1499.

Eventually, the Swiss over-extended themselves when they took on a superior force of French and Venetians at Marignano in 1515 and lost. Realising they could no longer compete against better-equipped larger powers, they declared their neutrality. Even so, Swiss mercenaries continued to serve in other armies for centuries, and earned an unrivalled reputation for skill and courage.

The Reformation during the 16th century caused upheaval throughout Europe. The Protestant teachings of Luther, Zwingli and Calvin spread quickly, although the inaugural cantons remained Catholic. This caused internal unrest that dragged on for centuries.

The French Republic invaded Switzerland in 1798 and established the Helvetic Republic. The Swiss vehemently resisted such centralised control, causing Napoleon to restore the former confederation of cantons in 1803. Yet France still retained overall jurisdiction. Following Napoleon's defeat by the British and Prussians at Waterloo, Switzerland finally gained independence.

The Modern State

Throughout the gradual move towards one nation, each canton remained fiercely independent, to the extent of controlling coinage and postal services. The cantons lost these powers in 1848, when a new federal constitution was agreed upon, with Bern as the capital. The Federal Assembly was set up to take care of national issues, but the cantons retained legislative and executive powers to deal with local matters.

Having achieved political stability, Switzerland could concentrate on economic and social matters. Poor in mineral resources, it developed industries dependent on highly skilled labour. A network of railways and roads was built, opening up previously inaccessible regions of the Alps and helping the development of tourism.

The Swiss carefully guarded their neutrality in the 20th century. Their only involvement in WWI was organising units of the Red Cross (founded in Geneva in 1863 by Henri Dunant). Switzerland did join the League of Nations after peace was won, but only on the condition that its involvement was financial and economic rather than military. Apart from some accidental bombing, WWII left Switzerland largely unscathed.

IT ALL HAPPENED IN SWITZERLAND

» Albert Einstein came up with his theories of relativity and the famous formula $E=MC^2$ in Bern in 1905.

» Switzerland gave birth to the World Wide Web at the acclaimed CERN (European Organisation for Nuclear Research) institute outside Geneva.

» The first acid trip took place in Switzerland. In 1943 chemist Albert Hofmann was conducting tests for a migraine cure in Basel when he accidentally absorbed the lysergic acid diethylamide, or LSD compound through his fingertips.

» Of the 800 or so films produced by India's huge movie-making industry each year, more are shot in Switzerland than in any other foreign country. 'For the Indian public, Switzerland is the land of their dreams', film star Raj Mukherjee has said. Favourite destination shoots include the Bernese Oberland, Central Switzerland and Geneva.

» Switzerland's central Alpine region possesses one of Europe's richest traditions of myth and legend. Pontius Pilate is said to rise out of the lake on Mt Pilatus, near Lucerne, every Good Friday (the day he condemned Jesus Christ) to wash blood from his hands – and anybody who witnesses this event will allegedly die within the year. Tiny 'wild folk' with supernatural powers, called Chlyni Lüüt, were once reputed to inhabit Mt Rigi, also near Lucerne. Their children's spleens were removed at birth, giving them the ability to leap around mountain slopes.

Forever Neutral: A Nation Apart

Since the end of WWII, Switzerland has enjoyed an uninterrupted period of economic, social and political stability – thanks, in predictable Swiss fashion, to the neutrality that saw it forge ahead from an already powerful commercial, financial and industrial base while the rest of Europe was still picking up and rebuilding the broken pieces from the war. Zürich developed as an international banking and insurance centre, and the World Health Organization and a stash of other international bodies set up headquarters in Geneva. To preserve its much-vaunted neutrality, however, Switzerland opted to remain outside the UN (although Geneva has hosted its second-largest seat after the main New York headquarters from the outset) and, more recently, the European Union.

Then, in the late 1990s, a series of scandals forced Switzerland to begin reforming its famously secretive banking industry. In 1995, after pressure from Jewish groups, Swiss banks announced that they had discovered millions of dollars lying in dormant pre-1945 accounts, belonging to Holocaust victims and survivors. Three years later, amid allegations they'd been sitting on the money without seriously trying to trace its owners, the two largest banks, UBS and Credit Suisse, agreed to pay US$1.25 billion in compensation to Holocaust survivors and their families.

New Millennium

A hefty swing to the conservative right in the 2003 parliamentary elections served to further enhance Switzerland's standing as a nation staunchly apart. In 2006, the anti-EU, anti-immigration Swiss People's Party (SVP) called for the toughening up of immigration and political asylum laws; the policies were passed with an overwhelming majority at national referendum. Then there was the rumpus over its bid to ban building new minarets for Muslim calls to prayer – an idea that aroused much anger internationally, but was approved by the constitution after 57.7% of voters said 'yes' to the ban in a national referendum.

Isolationism aside, there have been concrete signs that Switzerland is opening up to the wider world. The country became the 190th member of the UN in 2002 (a referendum on the issue had last been defeated in 1986), and three years later it voted to join Europe's passport-free travel zone, Schengen (finally completing the process at the end of 2008). In another referendum the same year, the Swiss narrowly voted in favour of legalising civil unions for same-sex couples (but not marriage).

Yet few expect Switzerland to even consider joining either the EU or the euro single-currency zone any time soon (if ever). Traditionally, the western, French-speaking cantons have long desired both, while the German-speaking cantons (and Ticino) have generally been opposed.

Switzerland Today

Peaceful and prosperous, safe and sound, a magnet for the rich and a safe haven for wealth: this privileged land of quality living and global finance, of outdoor magnificence and Alpine aesthetic, found itself the victim of its own success in 2011 and 2012.

The Swiss franc, long recognised as one of the world's most stable currencies, had become so overvalued it was threatening the traditionally robust Swiss economy. So strong was the franc that Swiss exports were falling along with the number of incoming tourists as price-conscious visitors from abroad suddenly realised just how much a cup of coffee in Switzerland was going to cost them.

Even the Swiss were abandoning their local shops and hopping across the borders into cheaper France, Germany and Italy to do their weekly shop. So in 2011 the Swiss National Bank, in an unprecedented move, made the value of the Swiss franc tumble in an instant (by 9% in 15 minutes!) by pegging it at 1.20 to the euro. In the following year, the franc held at this new level, although visitors still reacted with shock at the price of a cup of coffee.

Meanwhile the normally staid world of Swiss banking was roiled by charges of vast scams involving international interest-rate rigging, a leaked list of accounts held by purported Greek tax dodgers and efforts by the German government to investigate similar actions by its citizens.

People

Switzerland's name may stand for everything from knives to watches, but don't expect this nation to take a stand for anyone other than itself. Militarily neutral for centuries, and armed to the teeth to make sure it stays that way, in Switzerland it's the Swiss Way or the highway.

With a population of almost 7.8 million, the country averages 176 people per sq km. Zürich is the largest city, followed by Geneva, Basel and Bern. Most people are of Germanic origin, as reflected in the breakdown of the four national languages. Around 20% of residents in Switzerland are not Swiss citizens.

The Swiss are polite, law-abiding people who usually see no good reason to break the rules. Living quietly with your neighbours is a national obsession. Good manners infuse the national psyche, and politeness is the cornerstone of all social intercourse. Always shake hands when being introduced to a Swiss, and kiss on both cheeks to greet and say goodbye to friends. Don't forget to greet shopkeepers when entering shops. When drinking with the Swiss, always wait until everyone has their drink and toast each of your companions, looking them in the eye and clinking glasses. Drinking before the toast is unforgivable, and will lead to seven years of bad sex…or so the superstition goes. Don't say you weren't warned.

In a few mountain regions such as Valais, people still wear traditional rural costumes, but dressing up is usually reserved for festivals. Yodelling, playing the alphorn and Swiss wrestling are also part of the alpine tradition.

Religion

The split between Roman Catholicism (42%) and Protestantism (35%) roughly follows cantonal lines. Strong Protestant areas include Zürich, Geneva, Vaud, Bern and Neuchâtel; Valais, Ticino, Fribourg, Lucerne and the Jura are predominantly Catholic.

Just over 4% of the population is Muslim.

Arts

Many foreign writers and artists, including Voltaire, Byron, Shelley and Turner, have visited and settled in Switzerland. Local and international artists pouring into Zürich during WWI spawned its Dadaist movement.

Paul Klee (1879–1940) is the best-known native painter. He created bold, hard-lined abstract works, which you can see in Bern and Lausanne. The writings of Genevan philosopher Jean-Jacques Rousseau (1712–78) played an important part in the development of democracy. Critically acclaimed postwar dramatists and novelists Max Frisch (1911–91) and Friedrich Dürrenmatt (1921–90) entertained readers with their dark satire, tragi-comedies and morality plays. On the musical front, Arthur Honegger (1892–1955) is Switzerland's most recognised composer.

The Swiss have made important contributions to graphic design and commercial art. Anyone who's ever used a computer will have interacted with their fonts, from Helvetica to Frutiger to Univers.

The father of modern architecture, Le Corbusier (1887–1965), who designed Notre Dame du Haut chapel at Ronchamps in France, Chandigarh in India and the UN headquarters in New York, was Swiss. One of the most acclaimed contemporary architectural teams on earth, Jacques Herzog and Pierre de Meuron, live and work in Basel. Winners of the prestigious Pritzker Prize in 2001, this pair created London's acclaimed Tate Modern museum building.

Gothic and Renaissance architecture are prevalent in urban areas, especially Bern. Rural Swiss houses vary according to region, but are generally characterised by ridged roofs with wide, overhanging eaves, and balconies and verandahs enlivened by colourful floral displays, especially geraniums.

Environment

Mountains make up 70% of Switzerland's 41,285 sq km. Farming is intensive and cows graze on the upper slopes as soon as the retreating snow line permits.

Europe's highest elevations smugly sit here. The Dufourspitze (4634m) of Monte Rosa in the Alps is Switzerland's highest point, but the Matterhorn (4478m), with its Toblerone-shaped cap is better known. Then of course there's Mont Blanc (4807m), a hulk of a mountain – Europe's highest – shared with France and Italy.

Switzerland's 1800 glaciers cover a 2000-sq-km area, but global warming means they're melting rapidly. The country's most famous mass of ice, rock and snow – the 23km-long Aletsch Glacier – shrunk 114.6m in 2006 alone and could shrink 80% by 2100 if things don't change, say experts. Six hundred people posed nude on the glacier in 2007 for a photo by New Yorker Spencer Tunick as part of a Greenpeace campaign calling for governments worldwide to act quickly.

The St Gotthard Mountains in Central Switzerland are the source of many lakes and rivers, including the Rhine and the Rhône. The Jura Mountains straddle the border with France, and peak at around 1700m. Between the two is the Mittelland, a region of hills also known as the Swiss Plateau, criss-crossed by rivers, ravines and winding valleys.

The ibex, with its huge, curved, ridged horns is the most distinctive alpine animal. In all, some 12,000 of this type of mountain goat roam Switzerland and prime ibex-spotting terrain is the country's only national park (169 sq km), unimaginatively called the Swiss National Park.

Switzerland is extremely environmentally friendly: its citizens produce less than 400kg of waste each per year (half the figure for the USA), are diligent recyclers and are actively encouraged to use public transport. Moreover, pioneering green travel-networks integrate the country's nonmotorised traffic routes: **SwitzerlandMobility** (www.switzerlandmobility.ch) maps out 169 routes for walkers (6300km), cyclists (8500km), mountain bikers (3300km), roller-bladers or -skaters (1000km) and canoeists (250km) countrywide, all perfectly signposted and easy to follow.

SWISS CHOCOLATE

The Spanish conquistador Hernando Cortez brought the first load of cocoa to Europe in 1528. He could not have anticipated the subsequent demand for his cargo – especially among visitors! The Spaniards, and soon other Europeans, developed an insatiable thirst for the sweetened beverage produced from it. The solid stuff came later.

Swiss chocolate built its reputation in the 19th century, thanks to pioneering with familiar names such as François-Louis Cailler (1796–1852), Philippe Suchard (1797–1884), Henri Nestlé (1814–90), Jean Tobler (1830–1905), Daniel Peter (1836–1919) and Rodolphe Lindt (1855–1909).

Swiss supermarkets have shelves laden with myriad forms of chocolate at truly reasonable prices. Sample as many as you can.

Food & Drink

There is far more to Swiss cuisine than chocolate, cheese and Swiss-German rösti. But the very best of Swiss dining in this essentially rural country is all about the nation's own foods. And you'd be nuts to miss it. While the chic city crowd feasts on international fare, the Swiss kitchen is extraordinarily rich thanks to French, German and Italian influences on the local dishes.

Cheese

First things first: not all Swiss cheese has holes. Emmental, the hard cheese from the Emme Valley east of Bern, does – as does the not dissimilar Tilsiter from the same valley. But, contrary to common perception, most of Switzerland's 450 different types of cheese (*käse* in German, *fromage* in French, *formaggio* in Italian) are hole-less.

Take the well-known hard cheese Gruyère made in the town of Gruyères near Fribourg, or the overwhelmingly stinky Appenzeller used in a rash of tasty, equally strong-smelling dishes in the same-name town in northeastern Switzerland, or *Sbrinz,* Switzerland's oldest hard cheese and transalpine ancestor to Italian parmesan, ripened for 24 months to create its distinct taste.

Fondue & Raclette

It is hard to leave Switzerland without dipping into a fondue (from the French verb *fondre*, meaning 'to melt'). And you shouldn't! The main French contribution to the Swiss table, a pot of gooey melted cheese is placed in the centre of the table and kept on a slow burn while diners dip in cubes of crusty bread using slender two-pronged fondue forks. Just the sight of the creamy cheese languidly glistening on the bread is enough to make some diners swoon.

The classic fondue mix in Switzerland is equal amounts of Emmental and Gruyère cheese, grated and melted with white wine and a shot of kirsch (cherry-flavoured brandy); order a side platter of cold meats and tiny gherkins to accompany it.

Switzerland's other signature alpine cheese dish is raclette. Unlike fondue, raclette – both the name of the dish and the cheese at its gooey heart – is eaten year-round with boiled potatoes, cold meats and pickled onions or gherkins.

Other Dishes

Be sure not to miss rösti (fried, shredded potatoes). Baked to a perfect crisp, the shredded potato is mixed with seasonal mushrooms and bacon bits to create a perfect lunch, paired with nothing more than a simple green salad.

For a quintessential Swiss lunch, nothing beats an alfresco platter of air-dried beef, a truly sweet and exquisitely tender delicacy from Graubünden that is smoked, thinly sliced and served as *Bündnerfleisch*.

Veal is highly rated and is tasty when thinly sliced and smothered in a cream sauce such as *geschnetzeltes Kalbsfleisch* in Zürich.

Wine & Beer

Wine is considered an essential part of a meal and savouring local wine in Switzerland is an exquisite, gastronomic joy.

The bulk of Swiss wine production takes place in the French-speaking part of the country where vineyards line the shores of Lake Geneva, from where they stagger sharply up hillsides in tightly-packed terraces knitted together by ancient dry-stone walls.

Most of Lake Geneva's winemaking estates are found on either side of Lausanne in the canton of Vaud. Whites from the pea-green terraced vineyards of the Lavaux wine region between Lausanne and Montreux are so outstanding that the area has been designated a Unesco World Heritage site.

Drenched in an extra bonanza of sunshine and light from above the southern Alps, much of the land north of the Rhône River in western Valais is planted with vines – and this is where some of Switzerland's best wines are produced. Dryish white Fendant, the perfect accompaniment to fondue and raclette, and best served crisp cold, is the region's best-known wine. Dôle, made from Pinot noir and Gamay grapes, is the principal red blend and is as full bodied as an opera singer with its firm fruit flavour.

For beer, there are several bland lagers but there is a growing number of microbreweries. Ueli, Rappi, BFM, Felsenau and Trois Dames brew some excellent beers, many seasonal.

SURVIVAL GUIDE

Directory A–Z

Accommodation

From opulent palaces and castles to mountain refuges, nuclear bunkers, icy igloos or simple hay lofts, Switzerland sports traditional and creative accommodation in every price range.

The prices may seem steep – even the most inexpensive places are pricey compared with other parts of Europe. The upside is that standards are usually quite high.

In Switzerland, many budget hotels have cheaper rooms with shared toilet and shower facilities. From there the sky is truly the limit. Breakfast buffets can be extensive and tasty but are not always included in room rates.

When online looking for specials, besides the usual booking websites, take a gander at city and regional tourist authority websites where you can, at times, find excellent special deals.

Rates in cities and towns stay constant most of the year. In mountain resorts prices are seasonal (and can fall by 50% or more outside high season):

Low season mid-September to mid-December, mid-April to mid-June

Mid-season January to mid-February, mid-June to early July, September

High season July to August, Christmas, mid-February to Easter

PRICE RANGES

The following price ranges refer to a double room with a private bathroom, except in hostels or where otherwise specified. Quoted rates are for the high season and don't include breakfast unless otherwise noted.

€ less than Sfr150

€€ Sfr150 to Sfr350

€€€ more than Sfr350

HAY BARNS

If you're looking for a way to experience life on a Swiss farm, **Aventure sur la Paille/Schlaf im Stroh** (☎041 678 12 86; www.schlaf-im-stroh.ch) offers the ultimate adventure. When their cows are out to pasture in summer, or indeed even after they've been brought in for the winter come early October, farmers charge travellers Sfr20 to Sfr30 per adult and Sfr10 to Sfr20 per child to sleep on straw in their hay barns or lofts. Cotton undersheets and woolly blankets are provided, but guests need their own sleeping bags and pocket torch. Nightly rates include a farmhouse breakfast; showers and evening meals are extras.

HOSTELS

Switzerland has two types of hostels: **Swiss Youth Hostels** (SYHA; www.youthhostel.ch), affiliated with Hostelling International (HI), where nonmembers pay an additional 'guest fee' of Sfr6, and independent hostels which can be more charismatic. Prices listed for SYHA hostels may not include the guest fee. On average a dorm bed in either type costs Sfr31 to Sfr40, including sheets.

Backpacker hostels tend to be more flexible in their regulations, reception times and opening hours, and are usually free of school or youth groups. Membership is not required; over 30 such hostels are loosely affiliated under **Swiss Backpackers** (☎033 823 46 46; www.swissbackpackers.ch).

There are another 80 hostels in the shape of alpine chalets or rural farmhouses that offer hostel-style accommodation under the green umbrella group **Naturfreundehaus** (Friends of Nature; www.nfhouse.org).

Activities

There are dozens of ski resorts throughout the Alps, pre-Alps and Jura, and 200-odd different ski schools. Equipment hire is available at resorts, and ski passes allow unlimited use of mountain transport.

There is simply no better way to enjoy Switzerland's spectacular scenery than to walk through it. There are 50,000km of designated paths, often with a convenient inn or cafe located en route. Yellow signs marking the trail make it difficult to get lost, and each provides an average walking time to the next destination. Slightly more strenuous mountain paths have white-red-white markers. The **Schweizer Alpen-Club** (SAC; ☎031 370 18 18; www.sac-cas.ch; Monbijoustrasse 61, Bern) maintains huts for overnight stays at altitude and can also help with extra information.

Business Hours

The reviews in this chapter don't list hours unless they differ from the hours listed here. Hours are given for the high season (April through October) and tend to decrease in the low season.

Banks 8.30am-4.30pm Mon-Fri, usually with late opening hours one day a week.

Offices 8am-noon & 2-5pm Mon-Fri.

Post Offices 7.30am-noon & 2-6.30pm Mon-Fri, to 11am Sat (typically; however, opening times vary).

Restaurants noon-2pm & 6-10pm.

Shops 9am-7pm Mon-Fri (sometimes with a one- to two-hour break for lunch at noon in small towns), 9am-6pm Sat. In cities, there's often shopping until 9pm on Thursday or Friday. Sunday sees some souvenir shops and supermarkets at some train stations open.

Discount Cards

Regular or long-term visitors to Switzerland may want to buy the **Swiss Museum Pass** (www.museumspass.ch; adult/family Sfr144/255), which covers entry to the permanent collection (only) of 450 museums.

In many resorts and cities there's a **visitors' card** (*Gästekarte*), which provides various benefits such as reduced prices for museums, swimming pools, public transport or cable cars. Cards are issued by your accommodation.

Electricity

The electricity current is 220V, 50Hz. Swiss sockets are recessed, three-holed, hexagonally shaped and incompatible with many plugs from abroad. They sometimes, however, take the standard European two-pronged plug.

Embassies & Consulates

For a list of embassies and consulates in Switzerland, go to www.eda.admin.ch. Embassies are in Bern but cities such as Zürich and Geneva have consulates.

Food

The following price ranges refer to a two-course meal.

€ less than Sfr25

€€ Sfr25 to Sfr45

€€€ more than Sfr45

THREE LANGUAGES

Located in the corner of Europe where Germany, France and Italy meet, Switzerland is a linguistic melting pot with three official federal languages: German (spoken by 64% of the population), French (19%) and Italian (8%). Swiss 'German' speakers write standard or 'high' German, but speak their own language: Schwyzertutsch has no official written form and is mostly unintelligible to outsiders.

A fourth language, Romansch, is spoken by less than 1% of the population, mainly in the canton of Graubünden. Derived from Latin, it's a linguistic relic that has survived in the isolation of mountain valleys. Romansch was recognised as a national language by referendum in 1938 and given federal protection in 1996.

English-speakers will have few problems being understood in the German-speaking parts. However, it is simple courtesy to greet people with the Swiss-German *grüezi* and to enquire *Sprechen Sie Englisch?* (Do you speak English?) before launching into English. In French Switzerland you shouldn't have too many problems either; in Italian-speaking Switzerland, people are more monolingual but you'll still encounter plenty of English-speakers.

Language Areas

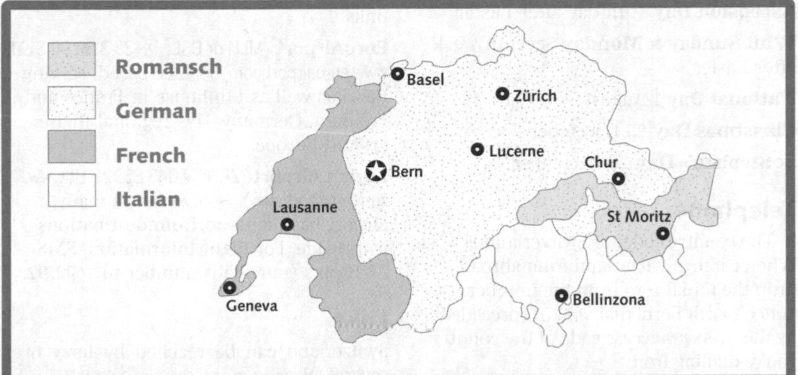

Gay & Lesbian Travellers

Attitudes towards homosexuality are reasonably tolerant in Switzerland. Zürich and Geneva have particularly lively gay scenes.

Online resources:

Cruiser Magazine (www.cruiser.ch)

Pink Cross (www.pinkcross.ch)

Internet Access

Internet access in Switzerland – like most things – is expensive. Public wi-fi can easily cost Sfr5 for 30 minutes. Free hotspots are comparatively rare, even at cafes.

Maps

There's one great deal in Switzerland: maps. They are copious, beautifully detailed, lavishly rendered and given away for free at tourist offices.

Money

ATMs Automated teller machines (ATMs) – called Bancomats in banks and Postomats in post offices – are common.

Cash Swiss francs are divided into 100 centimes (*Rappen* in German-speaking Switzerland). There are notes for 10, 20, 50, 100, 200 and 1000 francs, and coins for 5, 10, 20 and 50 centimes, as well as for one, two and five francs. Euros are accepted by many tourism businesses.

Credit Cards The use of credit cards is slightly less widespread than in the UK or

USA and not all shops, hotels or restaurants accept them.

Moneychangers Exchange money at large train stations.

Tipping Not necessary, given that hotels, restaurants, bars and even some taxis are legally required to include a 15% service charge in bills. You can round up the bill after a meal for good service, as locals do.

Post

Postcards and letters sent to Europe cost Sfr1.30/1.20 priority/economy; to elsewhere they cost Sfr1.80/1.40.

Public Holidays

New Year's Day 1 January

Easter March/April (Good Friday, Easter Sunday and Monday)

Ascension Day 40th day after Easter

Whit Sunday & Monday Seventh week after Easter

National Day 1 August

Christmas Day 25 December

St Stephen's Day 26 December

Telephone

» The country code for Switzerland is ☎41. When calling Switzerland from abroad, drop the initial zero from the number; hence to call Bern, dial ☎41 31 (preceded by the overseas access code of the country you're dialling from).

» The international access code from Switzerland is ☎00. To call Britain (country code ☎44), start by dialling ☎00 44

» Telephone numbers with the code ☎0800 are toll-free; those with ☎0848 are charged at the local rate. Numbers beginning with 156 or 157 are charged at the premium rate.

» Mobile phone numbers start with the code ☎076, ☎078 or ☎079.

» SIM cards are widely available from train station ticket counters, exchange bureaus and mobile telephone shops. Several providers offer the same good deal: €20 for a SIM card that comes with €20 credit.

Tourist Information

Make the Swiss tourist board **Switzerland Tourism** (www.myswitzerland.com) your first port of call. Local tourist offices are extremely helpful and have reams of literature to give out, including maps (nearly always free).

Visas

For up-to-date details on visa requirements, go to the **Swiss Federal Office for Migration** (www.eda.admin.ch) and click 'Services'.

Visas are not required for passport holders from the UK, EU, Ireland, the USA, Canada, Australia, New Zealand, South Africa, Norway and Iceland.

Getting There & Away

Air

The main international airports:

Aéroport International de Genève (GVA; ☎0900 571 500; www.gva.ch) The country's second airport has decent international links.

EuroAirport (MLH or BSL; ☎+33 3 89 90 31 11; www.euroairport.com) France-based, serving Basel as well as Mulhouse in France and Freiburg, Germany. Has regional flights around Europe.

Zürich Airport (ZRH; ☎043 816 22 11; www.zurich-airport.com) Switzerland's main airport has flights to/from destinations worldwide. For flight information, SMS ZHR plus your flight number to ☎92 92.

Lake

Switzerland can be reached by ferry over several lakes.

Lake Constance (☎071 466 78 88; www.sbsag.ch) Austria (☎05574 42868; www.bodenseeschifffahrt.at; Austria); Germany (☎07531 3640 389; www.bsb-online.com; Germany)

Lake Geneva (☎0848 811 848; www.cgn.ch) From France.

Lago Maggiore (☎091 751 61 40; www.navigazionelaghi.it) From Italy.

Land

BUS

Eurolines (www.eurolines.com) has buses with connections across Western Europe.

CAR & MOTORCYCLE

There are fast, well-maintained highways to Switzerland through all bordering countries. The Alps present a natural barrier to entering Switzerland, so main roads gener-

PASSES & DISCOUNTS

Convenient discount passes make the Swiss transport system even more appealing. On extensive travel within Switzerland the following national travel passes generally offer better savings than Eurail or InterRail passes.

Swiss Pass The Swiss Pass entitles the holder to unlimited travel on almost every train, boat and bus service in the country, and on trams and buses in 41 towns, plus free entry to 400-odd museums. Reductions of 50% apply on funiculars, cable cars and private railways. Different passes are available, valid between four days (1st/2nd class US$460/288) and one month.

Swiss Flexi Pass This pass allows you to nominate a certain number of days (anywhere from three to six) during a month when you can enjoy unlimited travel.

Half-Fare Card Almost every Swiss owns one of these. As the name suggests, you pay only half the fare on trains with this card, plus you get some discounts on local-network buses, trams and cable cars. An adult one-year Half-Fare Card costs Sfr175 (photo necessary).

Swiss Card A variation on the Half-Fare Card that includes a round-trip ticket to/from a border area and is good for 30 days. It is sold abroad for US$300/200 1st/2nd class.

Junior Card The Sfr30 card gets free travel (on trains, buses and boats, even on some cable cars) for those aged six to 16 years when travelling with at least one of their parents. Children within that age bracket travelling with an adult who is not a relative get 50% off.

Regional Passes Network passes valid only within a particular region are available in several parts of the country. Such passes are available from train stations in the region.

ally head through tunnels. Smaller roads are more scenically interesting, but special care is needed when negotiating mountain passes.

TRAIN

Located in the heart of Europe, Switzerland is a hub of train connections to the rest of the continent. Zürich is the busiest international terminus, with service to all neighbouring countries. Destinations include Milan (4¼ hours), Munich (four hours) and Vienna (eight hours).

There are numerous TGV trains daily from Paris to several cities, including Geneva (three hours), Lausanne (3¾ hours), Basel (three hours) and Zürich (four hours). Basel is a hub for services to Germany: fast ICE trains serve most major German cities. An easy way into Germany from Zürich is via medieval Constance (Sfr31, 1¼ hours).

Getting Around

Swiss public transport is an efficient, fully integrated and comprehensive system, which incorporates trains, buses, boats and funiculars.

Marketed as the **Swiss Travel System** (www.swisstravelsystem.com), the network has a useful website and there are excellent free maps covering the country available at train stations and tourist offices.

Bicycle

You can hire bikes from most train stations for about Sfr10 per day. Local tourist offices often have good cycling information.

Boat

Ferries and steamers link towns and cities on many lakes, including Constance, Geneva, Lucerne, Lugano, Murten and Zürich.

Bus

Yellow postal buses are a supplement to the rail network, following postal routes and linking towns to the more inaccessible regions in the mountains. In all, routes cover some 8000km of terrain. Services are regular, and departures link to train schedules. Postbus stations are next to train stations and offer destination and timetable information.

SWITZERLAND'S SCENIC TRAINS

Swiss trains, buses and boats are more than a means of getting from A to B. Stunning views invariably make the journey itself the destination. Switzerland boasts the following routes among its classic sightseeing journeys.

Bear in mind that you can choose just one leg of the trip, and that scheduled services often ply the same routes for standard fares; these are cheaper than the named trains, which often have cars with extra-large windows and require reservations.

Bernina Express A spectacular bus and train journey between Lugano and St Mortiz/Davos/Chur. See p1091.

Glacier Express A fabled journey between Zermatt and St Moritz, Chur or Davos. See p1067.

Jungfrau Region You can spend days ogling stunning Alpine scenery from the trains, cable cars and more here. See p1076.

GoldenPass Line (www.goldenpass.ch) Travels between Lucerne and Montreux in three sections; the Lucerne to Interlaken East leg is especially scenic.

Centovalli Express (www.centovalli.ch) An underappreciated gem of a line (two hours) that snakes along fantastic river gorges in Switzerland and Italy, travelling from Locarno to Domodossola. Trains run through the day and it is easy to connect to Brig and beyond from Domodossola in Italy.

Mont Blanc/St Bernard Expresses (www.tmrsa.ch) From Martigny to Chamonix, France, or over the St Bernard Pass.

Wilhelm Tell Express (www.williamtellexpress.ch; ⌚May-Oct) Begins with a placid 2½-hour cruise from Lucerne to Flüelen, where you get a train for the somewhat scenic run to Locarno and Lugano. This route is easily done with regular services.

Car

The **Swiss Touring Club** (Touring Club der Schweiz; ☎022 417 24 24; www.tcs.ch), Switzerland's largest motoring organisation, has reciprocal agreements with motoring organisations worldwide.

» You do not need an International Driving Permit to operate a vehicle in Switzerland. A licence from your home country is sufficient.

» Be prepared for winding roads, high passes and long tunnels.

» Normal speed limits are 50km/h in towns, 120km/h on motorways, 100km/h on semimotorways (designated by roadside rectangular pictograms showing a white car on a green background) and 80km/h on other roads.

» Mountain roads are well maintained. Some minor Alpine passes are closed from November to May – check with the local tourist offices before setting off.

Train

The Swiss rail network combines state-run and private operations. The **Swiss Federal Railway** (www.rail.ch) is abbreviated to SBB in German, CFF in French and FFS in Italian.

» All major train stations are connected to each other by hourly departures, at least between 6am and midnight, and most long-distance trains have a dining car.

» Second-class seats are perfectly acceptable, but cars are often close to full. First-class carriages are more comfortable, spacious and have fewer passengers.

» Powerpoints for laptops let you work aboard and some seats are in wi-fi hotspots – look for the insignia on the carriage.

» Ticket vending machines accept most major credit cards from around the world.

» Most stations have ticket counters.

» The SBB smartphone app is an excellent resource and can be used to store your tickets electronically.

» Check the SBB website for cheap Supersaver tickets on major routes.

» Most stations have 24-hour lockers (small/large locker Sfr6/9), usually accessible from 6am to midnight.

» Seat reservations (Sfr5) are advisable for longer journeys, particularly in the high season.

Survival Guide

Directory A–Z

Accommodation

Where you stay in Western Europe may be one of the highlights of your trip. Quirky family-run inns, manic city hostels and low-key beach resorts are just some of the places where you'll make both new memories and, more than likely, new friends.

The cheapest places to stay in Western Europe are camping grounds, followed by hostels and accommodation in student dormitories. Cheap chain hotels are popping up across the region, but pensions, private rooms and B&Bs have much more character and are often good value. Self-catering apartments and cottages are worth considering when travelling with a group, especially if you plan to stay somewhere for a while. During peak holiday periods, accommodation can be hard to find, and it's advisable to book ahead. Even camping grounds can fill up, especially in or around big cities.

B&Bs & Guest Houses

There's a huge range of accommodation above the hostel level. In the UK and Ireland, B&Bs – where you get bed and breakfast in a private home – are real bargains. In some areas every second house will have a B&B sign out the front.

In other countries, similar private accommodation (though often without breakfast) may go under the name of pension, guesthouse, *gasthaus, Zimmerfrei, chambre d'hôte* (B&B) and so on. Although the majority of guesthouses are simple affairs and not the potpourri-scented luxuries North Americans may be used to, there are more expensive ones around.

With this type of accommodation especially, make certain that the place is centrally located and not in some dull and distant suburb.

Camping

Camping is immensely popular in Western Europe and provides the cheapest form of accommodation. There's usually a charge per tent or site, per person and per vehicle. National tourist offices often provide booklets or brochures listing camping grounds throughout their countries.

In large cities, most camping grounds will be some distance from the centre of town. For this reason camping is most popular with people who have their own transport. If you're on foot, the money you save by camping can quickly be eaten up by the cost of commuting to and from a town centre. Many camping grounds rent bungalows or cottages accommodating from two to eight people.

Camping other than at designated camping grounds is difficult; there are few places in Western Europe where you can pitch a tent away from prying eyes, and you usually need permission from the local authorities (the police or local council office) or from the owner of the land.

In some countries, such as Austria, the UK, France and Germany, free camping is illegal on all but private land; in Greece it's illegal altogether.

Hostels

Hostels offer the cheapest (secure) roof over your head in Western Europe, and you don't have to be a youngster to use them.

HOSTELLING INTERNATIONAL

Most hostels are part of the national Youth Hostel Association (YHA), which is affiliated with **Hostelling International** (HI; www.hihostels.com). The HI website has links to all the national organisations and you can use it to book beds or rooms in advance. You can join YHA or HI in advance or at the hostels. Members usually pay about 10% less on rates.

At a hostel, you get a bed in a dorm or a private room plus the use of communal facilities, which often include a kitchen where you can prepare your own meals.

Hostels vary widely in character, but increased competition from other forms of accommodation – particularly the emergence of privately owned hostels –

have prompted many places to improve their facilities and cut back on rules and regulations.

The trend is moving toward smaller dormitories with just four to six beds. Single and double rooms with private bathrooms are common and it's not unusual to find entire families at hostels.

PRIVATE HOSTELS

There are many private hostelling organisations in Western Europe and hundreds of unaffiliated backpacker hostels. Private hostels have fewer rules (eg no curfew, no daytime lockout), more self-catering kitchens and a much lower number of large, noisy school groups. They often also have a much more party-friendly vibe.

However, whereas HI hostels must meet minimum safety and cleanliness standards, private hostels do not, which means that facilities vary greatly (although some, such as Germany's Meininger chain, are slickly run and have luxe trappings). Dorms in some private hostels, especially in Germanic countries, can be mixed gender. Most private hostels now have small dorm rooms of three to eight beds, and private singles and doubles.

The following websites are recommended as resources for hostellers; all of them have booking engines, helpful advice from fellow travellers and excellent tips for novices.

Europe's Famous Hostels (www.famoushostels.com)

Hostel World (www.hostelworld.com)

Hostelling International (HI; www.hihostels.com)

Hostels.com (www.hostels.com)

Hostelz (www.hostelz.com)

Hotels

From fabulous five-star icons to workaday cheapies, the range of hotels in Western Europe is immense. You'll often find inexpensive hotels clustered around bus and train station areas, which are always good places to start hunting; but these can be charmless and scruffy. Look for moderately priced places closer to the interesting parts of town.

Check your hotel room and bathroom before you agree to stay, and make sure you know what it's going to cost – discounts are often available for groups or for longer stays. Ask about breakfast; sometimes it's included, sometimes it's not.

If you think a room is too expensive, ask if there's anything cheaper; hotel owners often try to steer you towards more expensive options, and you can sometimes find affordable rooms in some of Western Europe's famous old hotels simply by asking. They may be in the attic or have a weird shape but can be great value. In southern Europe in particular, hotel owners may be open to a little bargaining if times are slack.

Besides big booking sites such as **Hotels.com** (www.hotels.com), we've had good luck with the following discount booking sites:

Booking.com (www.booking.com)

Direct Rooms (www.directrooms.com)

Hotel Club (www.hotelclub.net)

Hotel Info (www.hotel.info)

HRS (www.hrs.com)

LateRooms (www.laterooms.com)

Rental Accommodation

Rentals can be both advantageous and fun for families travelling together or for those staying in one place for a few nights. You can have your own chic Left Bank apartment in Paris or a villa in Tuscany with a pool – and often at cheaper rates than for hotels.

You'll have the freedom of coming and going whenever you like without worrying about curfews and strict checkout times, plus a feeling of coming 'home' after a hard day of sightseeing. All rentals should be equipped with kitchens (or at least a kitchenette), which can save on the food bill and allow you to peruse the neighbourhood markets and shops, eating like the locals do. Some are a little more upmarket with laundry facilities, parking and even daily maid services.

For leads, try the following websites:

AirBnB (www.airbnb.com) Now with thousands of locations in all price ranges across Western Europe. Rentals (which may be an entire apartment, a room in someone else's apartment or just a sofa) may be offered for one night, one week or even longer.

Holiday Havens (www.holidayhavens.co.uk)

Homelidays (www.homelidays.com)

Vacations-Abroad (www.vacations-abroad.com)

Vacation Rentals By Owner (www.vrbo.com)

Resorts

From foreboding Irish mansions to grand Swiss hotels, Western Europe has many fabled resorts, where travellers try to avoid ever checking out. Ask about deals and rooms that are cheaper than the average.

BOOK YOUR STAY ONLINE

For more accommodation reviews by Lonely Planet authors, check out http://hotels.lonelyplanet.com. You'll find independent reviews, as well as recommendations on the best places to stay. Best of all, you can book online.

Activities

Europe offers countless opportunities to indulge in more active pursuits than simply snapping photos and posting them to your blog. The varied geography and climate supports the full range of outdoor activities: boating, windsurfing, skiing, fishing, hiking, cycling and mountaineering.

Boating

Europe's many lakes, rivers and diverse coastlines offer a variety of boating options unmatched anywhere in the world. You can houseboat in France, kayak in Switzerland, charter a yacht in Greece, row on a peaceful Alpine lake, join a Danube River cruise from Amsterdam to Vienna, rent a sailing boat on the Côte d'Azur or dream away on a canal boat along the extraordinary canal network of Britain (or Ireland, or France) – the possibilities are endless.

Cycling

Along with hiking, cycling is the best way to really get close to the scenery and the people, keeping yourself fit in the process. It's also a good way to get around many cities and towns.

Popular cycling areas include the Belgian Ardennes, the west of Ireland, much of the Netherlands (the world's most bike-friendly nation), the coasts of Sardinia and Puglia, anywhere in the Alps (for those fit enough), and the south of France.

Usually your bike can fly with you, albeit in the cargo hold. Check with your airline. Alternatively, places to hire a bicycle are myriad.

Hiking

Keen hikers can spend a lifetime exploring Western Europe's many exciting trails. Popular routes feature places to stay, often far up on some breathtakingly gorgeous peak.

Highlights include:

The Alps Spanning Switzerland, Austria, Germany and Italy, with echoes of Heidi, bell-ringing dairy cows and trails organised with Swiss precision.

Italian Dolomites Like the Alps but less crowded and with better food.

Pyrenees Follow the trails of partisans through hills with Gallic-Iberian flavours.

Corsica & Sardinia Sun-drenched rugged beauty, with a Mediterranean view around every corner.

Northern Portugal A glass of port awaits after a day on the trail.

Scotland's West Highland Way Brambles, moors and locations from *Monty Python and the Holy Grail.*

Ramblers (www.ramblers.org.uk) is a non-profit organisation that promotes long-distance walking in the UK and can help you with maps and information. The British-based **Ramblers Holidays** (www.ramblersholidays.co.uk) offers hiking-oriented trips in Europe and elsewhere. For shorter day hikes, local tourist offices are usually excellent resources. Just ask.

Every country in Western Europe has national parks and other interesting areas or attractions that may qualify as a hiker's paradise, depending on your preferences. Guided hikes are often available for those who prefer expert leadership.

Skiing

In winter, Europeans take to the pistes, flocking to hundreds of resorts located in the Alps and Pyrenees for downhill skiing and snowboarding. Cross-country skiing is also very popular in some areas.

Equipment hire (or even purchase) can be relatively cheap if you follow the tips in this guide, and the hassle of bringing your own skis may not be worth it. As a rule, a skiing holiday in Europe will work out to be about twice as expensive as a summer holiday of the same length.

The skiing season generally lasts from early December to late March, though at higher altitudes it may extend an extra month either side. Snow conditions can vary greatly from one year to the next and from region to region, but January and February tend to be the best (and busiest) months.

Ski resorts in the French and Swiss Alps offer legendary skiing and facilities but are also the most expensive. Expect high prices in the German Alps too. Austria is generally slightly cheaper than France and Switzerland (especially in Carinthia). Prices in the Italian Alps are similar to Austria (with some upmarket exceptions such as Cortina d'Ampezzo) and can be relatively cheap given the right package.

For comprehensive reports on ski conditions, try www.onthesnow.com.

Windsurfing

Windsurfing is a European passion, practised most places there's water and sand (which is also a commentary on the breezy nature of Western European beaches). It's easy to rent sailboards in many tourist centres, and courses are usually available for beginners.

Business Hours

Standard business hours vary hugely in Western Europe, where dinner means 10pm in Madrid and 7pm in Holland. Some countries have embraced Sunday shopping and others haven't. Check individual country chapters for more specific information.

Children

Europe is the home of *Little Red Riding Hood, Cinderella, King Arthur, Tintin* et al, and is a great place to travel with kids. Successful travel with young children requires some careful planning and effort. Don't try to overdo things; even for adults, packing too much sightseeing into the time available can cause problems.

Most car-hire firms in Western Europe have children's safety seats for hire at a nominal cost, but it's essential that you book them in advance. The same goes for high chairs and cots (cribs); they're standard in most restaurants and hotels but numbers are limited (although they can be hard to find in Greece).

Customs Regulations

Duty-free goods are not sold to those travelling from one EU country to another. For goods purchased at airports or on ferries *outside* the EU, the usual allowances apply for tobacco (200 cigarettes, 50 cigars or 250g of loose tobacco) – although some countries have reduced this to curb smoking – and alcohol (1L of spirits or 2L of liquor with less than 22% alcohol by volume; 4L of wine). The total value of these goods cannot exceed €300.

Discount Cards

Camping Card International

The **Camping Card International** (CCI; www.campingcardinternational.com) is a camping ground ID that can be used instead of a passport when checking into a camping ground and includes third-party insurance. As a result, many camping grounds offer a small discount (usually 5% to 10%) if you sign in with one.

Senior Cards

Museums and various other sights and attractions (including public swimming pools and spas), as well as transport companies, frequently offer discounts to retired people, old-age pensioners and/or those aged over 60.

Make sure you bring proof of age; that suave signor in Italy or that polite Parisian mademoiselle is not going to believe you're a day over 39.

Student & Youth Cards

The **International Student Travel Confederation** (ISTC; www.istc.org) issues three cards for students, teachers and under-26s, offering thousands of worldwide discounts on transport, museum entry, youth hostels and even some restaurants. These cards are: the ISIC (International Student Identity Card), the ITIC (International Teacher Identity Card) and the IYTC (International Youth Travel Card). You can check the full list of discounts and where to apply for the cards on the ISTC website. Issuing offices include **STA Travel** (www.statravel.com). Most places, however, will also accept regular student identity cards.

For people aged under 30, there's also the **European Youth Card** (www.euro26.org), which has scores of discounts.

Electricity

Most of Europe runs on 220V/50Hz AC (as opposed to, say, North America, where the electricity is 120V/60Hz AC). Chargers for phones, iPods and laptops *usually* can handle any type of electricity. If in doubt, read the tiny print.

CONTINENTAL EUROPE

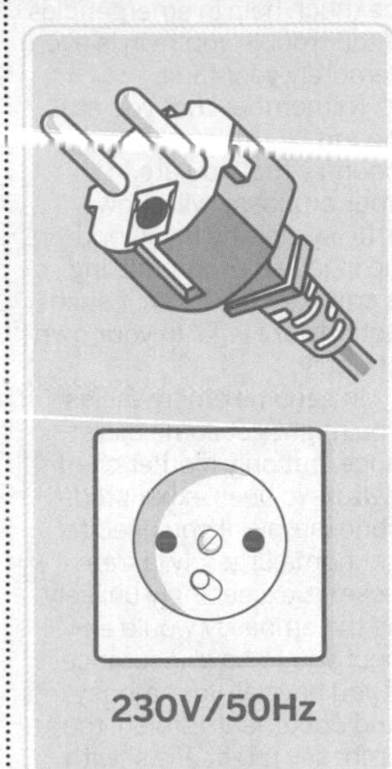

BRITAIN & IRELAND

Embassies & Consulates

As a tourist, it is vitally important that you understand what your own embassy (the embassy of the country of which you are a citizen) can and cannot do. Generally speaking, embassies won't be much help in emergencies if the trouble you're in is even remotely your fault.

Remember that you are bound by the laws of the country that you are in. Your embassy will show little sympathy if you end up in jail after committing a crime locally, even if such actions are legal in your own country.

In genuine emergencies you might get some assistance, but only if other channels have been exhausted. For example, if you need to get home urgently, a free ticket is exceedingly unlikely as the embassy would expect you to have insurance. If you have all your money and documents stolen, the embassy might assist with getting a new passport, but a loan for onward travel is almost always out of the question.

Locations

Nations such as Australia, Canada, New Zealand and the US have embassies and consulates across Western Europe in capitals and major cities.

You can find locations using these websites:

Australia (www.dfat.gov.au)

Canada (www.international.gc.ca)

New Zealand (www.mfat.govt.nz)

United Kingdom (www.gov.uk/fco)

United States (www.travel.state.gov)

Gay & Lesbian Travellers

In cosmopolitan centres in Western Europe you'll find very liberal attitudes toward homosexuality. Belgium, the Netherlands and Spain have legalised same-sex marriages. Many other countries allow civil partnerships that grant all or most of the rights of marriage.

London, Paris, Berlin, Madrid, Lisbon and Amsterdam have thriving gay communities and pride events. The Greek islands of Mykonos and Lesvos are popular gay beach destinations.

The following websites are useful:

Damron (www.damron.com) The USA's leading gay publisher offers guides to world cities.

International Lesbian and Gay Association (www.ilga.org) Campaigning group with some country-specific information on homosexual issues (not always up to date) and a conference calendar.

Spartacus International Gay Guide (www.spartacus-world.com) A male-only directory of gay entertainment venues in Europe and the rest of the world.

Health

It is unlikely that you will encounter unusual health problems in Western Europe, and if you do, standards of care are world-class. It's also important to have health insurance for your trip.

A few travelling tips:

» Bring medications in their original, clearly labelled containers.

» Bring a list of your prescriptions (photocopies of the containers are good) including generic names, so you can get replacements if your bags go on holiday – carry this info separately.

» If you have health problems that may need treatment, bring a signed and dated letter from your physician describing your medical conditions and medications.

» If carrying syringes or needles, have a physician's letter documenting their medical necessity.

» If you need vision correction, carry a spare pair of contact lenses or glasses, and/or take your optical prescription with you.

Recommended Vaccinations

No jabs are necessary for Western Europe. However, the World Health Organization (WHO) recommends that all travellers should be covered for diphtheria, tetanus, measles, mumps, rubella and polio, regardless of their destination.

Insurance

It's foolhardy to travel without insurance to cover theft, loss and medical problems. Start by seeing what your own insurance covers, be it medical, home owner's or renter's. You may find that many aspects of travel in Western Europe are covered. You may also find gaping holes. If you need to purchase coverage, there's a wide variety of policies, so check the small print.

Some policies pay doctors or hospitals directly, but most require you to pay upfront, save the documentation and then claim later. Some policies also ask you to call back (reverse charges) to a centre in your home country, where an immediate assessment of your problem is made. Check that the policy covers ambulances or an emergency flight home.

If you're an EU citizen, the European Health Insurance Card (EHIC) covers you for most medical care. If you do need health insurance, strongly consider a policy that covers you for the worst possible scenario. Find out in advance if your insurance plan will make payments directly to providers or reimburse you later for overseas health expenditures. The former option is generally preferable, as it doesn't require you to pay out-of-pocket costs in a foreign country.

The policies handled by **STA Travel** (www.statravel.

com) and other student travel agencies are usually good value. In the UK, the website **Money Supermarket** (www.moneysupermarket.com) does an automated comparison of 450 partner policies and comes up with the best for your needs.

Worldwide travel insurance is available at lonelyplanet.com/travel_services. You can buy, extend and claim online anytime – even if you're already on the road.

Internet Access

The number of internet cafes is plummeting. You'll still find them in tourist areas and around big train stations. Otherwise you may end up at online gaming parlours where you can compose an email asking for money from home or bragging about the cute local you met in a pub while boys blast aliens all around you. When in doubt, ask at a tourist office.

» Hostels, hotels and other accommodation usually have wi-fi (WLAN in Germany).

» Wi-fi access is best the further north in Western Europe you go (Greece and Portugal are laggards) while in Switzerland it's rare to find free wi-fi.

» Wi-fi is often free in hostels and midrange places, while costing €20 or more at top-end hotels.

» Internet access places may add a surcharge of €1 to €5 per hour for using Skype.

Legal Matters

Most Western European police are friendly and helpful, especially if you have been a victim of a crime. You are required by law to prove your identity if asked by police, so always carry your passport, or an identity card if you're an EU citizen.

Illegal Drugs

Narcotics are sometimes openly available in Europe, but that doesn't mean they're legal. The Netherlands is famed for its liberal attitudes, with 'coffee shops' openly selling cannabis. However, even there it's a case of the police turning a blind eye. Possession of cannabis is decriminalised but not legalised (except for medicinal use). Don't take this relaxed attitude as an invitation to buy harder drugs; if you get caught, you'll be punished. In Belgium, the possession of up to 5g of cannabis is legal but selling the drug isn't, so if you get caught at the point of sale you could be in trouble. In Portugal, the possession of *all* drugs has been decriminalised. Once again, however, selling is illegal.

Smoking

Cigarette-smoking bans have been progressively introduced across Europe. Although outdoor seating has long been a tradition at European cafes, it's gained new popularity given that most Western European countries have banned smoking in public places, including restaurants and bars. Some hotels still allow smoking in rooms in a few countries, so if you're a non-smoker it's worth asking if you can get a no-smoking room when reserving. If you're a smoker, the easiest strategy is to assume you can't and then light up with relish if you see locals puffing away.

Money

For security and flexibility, diversify your source of funds. Carry an ATM card, credit card and cash.

ATMs

Most countries in Western Europe have international ATMs allowing you to withdraw cash directly from your home account, and this is the most common way European travellers access their money. You should always have a back-up option, however, as some travellers have reported glitches with ATMs in various countries, even when their card worked elsewhere across Western Europe. In some remote villages, ATMs might be scarce too.

When you withdraw money from an ATM the amounts are converted and dispensed in local currency but there will be fees. If you're uncertain, ask your bank.

Finally, don't forgot your normal security procedures: cover the keypad when entering your PIN and make sure there are no unusual devices (which might copy

EURO

The euro is the official currency used in 16 of the 27 EU states: Austria, Belgium, Cyprus, Finland, France, Germany, Greece, the Republic of Ireland, Italy, Luxembourg, Malta, the Netherlands, Portugal, Slovakia, Slovenia and Spain. Denmark, Britain, Switzerland and Sweden have held out against adopting the euro for political reasons.

The euro is divided into 100 cents and has the same value in all EU member countries. There are seven euro notes (5, 10, 20, 50, 100, 200 and 500 euros) and eight euro coins (1 and 2 euros, then 1, 2, 5, 10, 20 and 50 cents). One side is standard for all euro coins and the other side bears a national emblem of participating countries.

your card's information) attached to the machine. If your card disappears and the screen goes blank before you've even entered your PIN, don't enter it – especially if a 'helpful' bystander tells you to do so. If you can't retrieve your card, call your bank's emergency number as soon as possible.

Cash

Nothing beats cash for convenience...or risk. If you lose it, it's gone forever and very few travel insurers will come to your rescue. Those that do will limit the amount to somewhere around €300 or £200.

If flying into Western Europe from elsewhere, you'll find ATMs and currency exchanges in the arrivals area of the airport. There is no reason to get local currency before arriving in Western Europe, especially as exchange rates in your home country are likely to be abysmal.

Credit Cards

Credit cards are handy for major purchases such as air or rail tickets, and offer a lifeline in certain emergencies.

Visa and MasterCard/Eurocard are more widely accepted in Europe than Amex and Diners Club. There are, however, regional differences in the general acceptability of credit cards. In the UK, for example, you can usually flash your plastic in the most humble of budget restaurants; in Germany some restaurants don't take credit cards. Cards are not widely accepted off the beaten track.

As with ATM cards, banks have loaded up credit cards with hidden charges for foreign purchases. Cash withdrawals on a credit card are almost always a much worse idea than using an ATM card due to the fees and high interest rates. Plus, purchases in different currencies are likely to draw various conversion surcharges that are simply there to add to the bank's profit. These can run up to 5% or more. Your best bet is to check these things before leaving.

International Transfers

International bank transfers are good for secure one-off movements of large amounts of money, but they might take three to five days and there will be a fee (about £25 in the UK, for example).

In an emergency, it's quicker and easier to have money wired via **Western Union** (www.westernunion.com) or **MoneyGram** (www.moneygram.com). All are quite costly.

Money Exchange

In general, US dollars and UK pounds are the easiest currencies to exchange in Western Europe. Get rid of Scottish and Northern Ireland banknotes before leaving the UK; nobody outside Britain will touch them.

Most airports, central train stations, big hotels and many border posts have banking facilities outside regular business hours, at times on a 24-hour basis. Post offices in Western Europe often perform banking tasks, tend to be open longer hours and outnumber banks in remote places.

The best exchange rates are usually at banks. *Bureaux de change* usually – but not always – offer worse rates or charge higher commissions. Hotels are almost always the worst places to change money.

Taxes & Refunds

Sales tax applies to many goods and services in Western Europe (although the amount – 10% to 20% – is already built into the price of the item). Luckily, when non-EU residents spend more than a certain amount (about €75) they can usually reclaim that tax when leaving the country.

Making a tax-back claim is straightforward. First, make sure the shop offers duty-free sales (often a sign will be displayed reading 'Tax-Free Shopping'). When making your purchase ask the shop attendant for a tax-refund voucher, filled in with the correct amount and the date. This can be used to claim a refund

MINIMISING ATM CHARGES

When you withdraw cash from an ATM overseas there are several ways you can get hit. Firstly, most banks add a hidden 2.75% loading to what's called the 'Visa/Mastercard wholesale' or 'interbank' exchange rate. In short, they're giving you a worse exchange rate than strictly necessary. Additionally, some banks charge their customers a cash withdrawal fee (usually 2% with a minimum €2 or more). If you're really unlucky, the bank at the foreign end might charge you as well. Triple whammy. If you use a credit card in ATMs you'll also pay interest – usually quite high – on the cash withdrawn.

Most experts agree that having the right bankcard is still cheaper than exchanging cash directly. If your bank levies fees, then making larger, less frequent withdrawals is better. It's also worth seeing if your bank has reciprocal agreements with banks where you are going that minimise ATM fees.

directly at international airports (beware, however, of very long lines), or be stamped at ferry ports or border crossings and mailed back for a refund.

None of this applies to EU residents. Even an American citizen living in London is not entitled to a rebate on items bought in Paris. Conversely, an EU-passport holder living in New York is.

Tipping

Adding another 5% to 10% to a bill at a restaurant or cafe for good service is common across Western Europe, although tipping is never expected.

Travellers Cheques

Travellers cheques are rarely used.

Travel Money Cards

In recent years prepaid cards – also called travel money cards, prepaid currency cards or cash passport cards – have become a popular way of carrying money.

These enable you to load a card with as much foreign currency as you want to spend. You then use it to withdraw cash at ATMs – the money comes off the card and not out of your account – or to make direct purchases in the same way you would with a Visa or MasterCard. You can reload it via telephone or online.

Advantages of a prepaid card:

» You avoid foreign exchange fees as the money you put on your card is converted into foreign currency at the moment you load it.

» You can control your outlay by only loading as much as you want to spend.

» Security: if it's stolen your losses are limited to the balance on the card as it's not directly linked to your bank account.

» Lower ATM withdrawal fees.

» Americans and others who carry credit cards without embedded chips can use these cards (which have chips and PINs) for the many European purchases that require a card with a chip. Train ticket vending machines in the Netherlands are an example.

Against this you'll need to weigh the costs. Fees are charged for buying the card and then every time you load it. ATM withdrawal fees also apply. You might also be charged a fee if you don't use the card for a certain period of time or to redeem any unused currency. Note also that if the card has an expiry date, you'll forfeit any money loaded onto the card after that date.

One source of travel money cards is Travelex (www.travelex.com).

Safe Travel

On the whole, you should experience few problems travelling in Western Europe – even alone – as the region is well developed and relatively safe. But do exercise common sense. Whatever you do, don't leave friends and relatives back home worrying about how to get in touch with you in case of an emergency. Work out a list of places where they can contact you or, best of all, phone home now and then or email.

Also, leave a record (ie a photocopy) of your passport, credit and ATM cards and other important documents in a safe place. You can scan your documents and credit cards and post the file somewhere safe online, perhaps by emailing it to yourself. This gives you access from anywhere and saves you from having both the originals and copies lost. If things are stolen or lost, replacement is much easier when you have the vital details available.

> **EMERGENCY NUMBERS**
>
> The EU-wide general emergency number is 112 (but 999 in the UK).

Drugs

Always treat drugs with caution. There are a lot of drugs available in Western Europe, sometimes quite openly (particularly in the Netherlands), but that doesn't mean they're legal. Even a little hashish can cause a great deal of trouble in some places.

Scams

Generally, be aware of shopkeepers in touristy places who may short-change you.

Theft

Theft happens in Western Europe; be wary of theft by other travellers, too. The most important things to secure are your passport, papers, tickets and money, in that order.

You can lessen the risks further by being careful of 'snatch thieves' who go for cameras and shoulder bags. They sometimes operate from motorcycles or scooters and expertly slash the strap before you have a chance to react. A small day pack is better, but watch your rear. Be very careful at cafes and bars; loop the strap of your bag around your leg while seated.

Pickpockets are most active in dense crowds, especially in busy train stations and on public transport during peak hours. A common ploy is for one person to distract you while another zips through your pockets. Beware of gangs of kids – who can look either dishevelled or well dressed – madly waving newspapers and demanding attention. In the blink of an eye, a wallet or camera can go missing. And a jacket or purse left on the back of a chair is an invitation for theft.

Telephone

Treat your hotel phone and its often hidden and outrageous rates the same way you'd treat a thief. Using wi-fi in the room for Skype is the most common way to connect.

Mobile Phones

Travellers can easily purchase prepaid mobile phones (from £20/€30) or SIM cards (from £5/€10). GSM phones can be used throughout all countries in Western Europe. Mobile shops are everywhere. Shops in large train stations are especially adept at getting visitors set up.

You can bring your mobile phone from home and buy a local SIM card to enjoy cheap local calling rates if it is A) unlocked and B) compatible with European GSM networks. Check first.

If you bring your mobile phone from home:

» Check international roaming rates in advance; often they are very expensive.

» Check roaming fees for data usage for email and web connections; users of smart phones (eg iPhones) can get socked with huge fees. You may be able to buy a data package to limit your costs.

Time

Greenwich Mean Time (GMT)/UTC Britain, Ireland

Central European Time (GMT/UTC + one hour) Andorra, Austria, Belgium, France, Germany, Greece, Italy, Liechtenstein, Luxembourg, the Netherlands, Portugal, Spain, Switzerland

East European Time (GMT/UTC + two hours) Greece

Daylight Saving Time/ Summer Time Last Sunday in March to the last Sunday in October

Tourist Information

Tourist offices in Western Europe are common and almost universally helpful. They can find accommodation, maps, advise on sights and activities and help with more obscure queries such as, 'Where can I wash my clothes?'.

Visas

Most travellers will have very little to do with visas. While border procedures between EU and non-EU countries can still be thorough, citizens of Australia, Canada, Japan, New Zealand and the USA don't need visas for tourist visits to the UK or any Schengen country. With a valid passport you should be able to visit Western European countries for up to 90 days in a six-month period, provided you have some sort of onward or return ticket and/or 'sufficient means of support' (ie money).

For those who do require visas, it's important to remember that these will have a 'use-by' date, and you'll be refused entry after that period has elapsed. It may not be checked when entering these countries overland, but major problems can arise if it is requested during your stay or on departure and you can't produce it.

Schengen Visa Rules

As per the Schengen Agreement, there are no passport controls at borders between the following countries:

» Austria
» Belgium
» Czech Republic
» Denmark
» Estonia
» Finland
» France
» Germany
» Greece
» Hungary
» Iceland
» Italy
» Latvia
» Liechtenstein
» Lithuania
» Luxembourg
» Malta
» The Netherlands
» Norway
» Poland
» Portugal
» Slovakia
» Slovenia
» Spain
» Sweden
» Switzerland

Think of this zone as one country in terms of your three-month stay. It won't work to try to stay in each of the countries for three months.

If you are planning to stay in Western Europe for longer than three months, remember that you are only permitted to remain in the Schengen zone for up to 90 days within a six month period (so you can't do a 'visa run' to a country outside the zone, unless you remain there for 90 days).

Weights & Measures

The metric system is used throughout Western Europe. In Britain, however, nonmetric equivalents are common (distances continue to be given in miles and beer is sold in pints, not litres).

Transport

GETTING THERE & AWAY

Part of the adventure is figuring out how to get to Western Europe, and in these days of cut-throat competition among airlines there are plenty of opportunities to find cheap tickets to a variety of gateway cities.

Flights, cars and tours can be booked online at lonelyplanet.com.

Air

Western Europe is well served by just about every major airline in the world. Once in Europe you can take advantage of cheap fares for getting around at a good price, although trains will be better for two environments: yours and the planet's.

Land

You can easily get to Western Europe from the rest of Europe by road, bus or train. Things become more complicated, however, the further away you're coming from.

Train

It *is* possible to get to Western Europe by train from central and eastern Asia, but count on spending at least eight days doing it. Four different train lines wind their way to Moscow: the Trans-Siberian (9297km from Vladivostok), the Trans-Mongolian (7860km from Beijing) and the Trans-Manchurian (9001km from Beijing) all use the same tracks across Siberia but have different routes east of Lake Baikal, while the Trans-Kazakhstan (another Trans-Siberian line) runs between Moscow and Urumqi in northwestern China. Prices vary enormously depending on where you buy the ticket and what's included – advertised 2nd-class fares cost about £600 from Beijing to Moscow.

There are many travel options between Western Europe and Moscow as well as other Eastern European countries and the Baltic countries. Poland, the Czech Republic and Hungary all have myriad rail links.

Sea

Ferries

There are many ferries crossing the Mediterranean between Africa and Western Europe. The ferry you take will depend on your travels in Africa, but the options include Spain–Morocco, France–Morocco, France–Tunisia and Italy–Tunisia. There are also ferries between Greece and Israel via Cyprus. Ferries also serve Germany from all the Scandinavian countries.

Passenger Ships

Cunard's **Queen Mary 2** (www.cunard.com) sails between New York and Southampton (England) several times a year; the trip takes six nights each way and costs

CLIMATE CHANGE & TRAVEL

Every form of transport that relies on carbon-based fuel generates CO_2, the main cause of human-induced climate change. Modern travel is dependent on aeroplanes, which might use less fuel per kilometre per person than most cars but travel much greater distances. The altitude at which aircraft emit gases (including CO_2) and particles also contributes to their climate change impact. Many websites offer 'carbon calculators' that allow people to estimate the carbon emissions generated by their journey and, for those who wish to do so, to offset the impact of the greenhouse gases emitted with contributions to portfolios of climate-friendly initiatives throughout the world. Lonely Planet offsets the carbon footprint of all staff and author travel.

under US$3000 for two people in a standard double cabin. Deals abound. Other cruise lines have occasional crossings as well.

GETTING AROUND

Discount airlines are revolutionising the way people cover long distances within Europe. However, hopping on a plane deprives you the fun of travelling by train and the cultural experiences of navigating train stations, and there are important concerns about carbon emissions.

Air

Getting around Western Europe by air is very popular thanks to the proliferation of discount airlines and cheap fares. It's possible to go from London to Berlin at times for less than €30; fares around Europe for less than €100 are common. More interestingly, dozens of tiny airports across Europe now boast airline services, so a trip to Italy doesn't mean choosing between Milan and Rome, but rather scores of airports up and down the 'boot'.

It's possible to put together a practical itinerary that might bounce from London to the south of Spain to Italy to Amsterdam in a two-week period, all at an affordable price and avoiding endless train rides.

Airlines in Western Europe

Although many people first think of budget airlines when they consider a cheap ticket in Western Europe, you should compare all carriers, including established ones like British Airways and Lufthansa, which serve major airports close to main destinations. Deals crop up in the darndest places.

Major budget airlines in Western Europe are listed following. There are also scores of smaller airlines with more limited services.

Air Berlin (www.airberlin.com) Hubs in Germany; service across Europe.

easyJet (www.easyjet.com) Flies to major airports across Europe.

Germanwings (www.germanwings.com) Hubs in Germany; service across Europe.

Ryanair (www.ryanair.com) Flies to scores of destinations across Europe, but confirm your destination airport is not a deserted airfield out in the sticks.

Vueling (www.vueling.com) Serves a broad swath of Europe from its Spanish hubs.

The best place to buy cheap airline tickets is on the internet. In fact, many airlines only sell their cheapest tickets online. Various websites compare fares across a range of airlines within Europe, including the following:

- www.cheapoair.com
- www.kayak.com
- www.skyscanner.net

DISCOUNT AIRLINES

With cheap fares come many caveats. Some of the barebones airlines are just that – expect nonreclining seats, nonexistent legroom and nonexistent window shades. At some far-flung airports, customer service may also be nonexistent – the same goes for convenience. If you really want to go to Carcassonne in the south of France, then getting a €20 ticket from London will be a dream come true. But if you want to go to Frankfurt in Germany and end up buying a ticket to 'Frankfurt-Hahn', you will find yourself at a small airport 120km west of Frankfurt and two hours away by bus. Also beware of discount airline websites such as those of Air Berlin which show nonstop flights that are actually connections.

Bicycle

A tour of Western Europe by bike may seem like a daunting prospect but help is at hand. The **Cyclists' Touring Club** (www.ctc.org.uk) is based in the UK and offers members an information service on all matters associated with cycling, including cycling conditions, detailed routes, itineraries and maps.

The key to a successful cycling trip is to travel light. What you carry should be determined by your destination and the type of trip you're taking. Even for the most basic trip, it's worth carrying the tools necessary for repairing a puncture. Bicycle shops are found everywhere, but you still might want to pack the following if you don't want to rely on others:

- Allen keys
- spanners
- spare brake and gear cables
- spare spokes
- strong adhesive tape

Wearing a helmet is not always compulsory but is advised. A seasoned cyclist can average about 80km a day, but this depends on the terrain and how much you are carrying.

Hire

It's easy to hire bicycles in Western Europe and you can often negotiate good deals. Rental periods vary. Local tourist offices, hostels and hotels will have information on rental outlets. Occasionally you can drop off the bicycle at a different location so you don't have to double back on your route.

Urban bike-hire schemes, where you check out a bike from one stand and return it to another after brief use, have taken off in cities as huge as London and Paris.

Purchase

For major cycling tours it's best to have a bike you're familiar with, so consider bringing your own rather than buying one on arrival. If you can't be bothered with the hassle of transporting your own, there are plenty of places to buy bikes in Western Europe (shops sell them new and secondhand).

Transporting a Bicycle

If you want to use your own bicycle in Western Europe, you should be able to take it with you on the plane. Check with the airline for details before you buy your ticket as each one has a different policy.

Within Western Europe, bikes can sometimes be taken onto a train with you, subject to a small supplementary fee.

Boat

Multiple ferry companies compete on the main ferry routes, and the resulting service is comprehensive but complicated. The same ferry company can have a host of different prices for the same route, depending on the time of day or year, the validity of the ticket or the length of your vehicle. It's worth planning (and booking) ahead where possible as there may be special reductions on off-peak crossings and advance-purchase tickets. Most ferry companies adjust prices according to the level of demand (so-called 'fluid' or 'dynamic' pricing), so it may pay to offer alternative travel dates. Vehicle tickets usually include the driver and a full complement of passengers.

The main areas of ferry service for Western Europe travellers are between Ireland and the UK; Ireland and France; the UK and Continental Europe (especially France, but also Belgium, the Netherlands and Spain); and Italy and Greece.

Compare fares and routes using **ferrysavers.com** (www.ferrysavers.com).

Rail-pass holders are entitled to discounts or free travel on some lines. If you take your vehicle on board, you are usually denied access to it during the voyage.

Bus

Buses sometimes have the edge in terms of costs, but are generally slower and much less comfortable than trains and not as quick or sometimes as cheap as airlines.

Eurolines

Europe's largest network of international buses is provided by a consortium of bus companies that operates under the name **Eurolines** (www.eurolines.com). There are many services and it's possible to travel very far for less than €100. Eurolines' various affiliates offer many national and regional bus passes.

Campervan

A popular way to tour Europe is for three or four people to band together to buy or rent a campervan. London is the usual embarkation point. Some good British publications and websites to check out for campervan purchases and rentals include the following:

» **Loot** (www.loot.com)

» **Auto Trader** (www.autotrader.co.uk)

» **Worldwide Motorhome Hire** (www.worldwide-motorhome-hire.com)

Campervans usually feature a fixed high-top or elevating roof and two to five bunk beds. Apart from the essential gas cooker, professional conversions may include a sink, a fridge and built-in cupboards. Prices and facilities vary considerably and it's certainly worth getting advice from a mechanic to see if you are being offered a fair price. Getting a mechanical check (costing from £40) is also a good idea.

Car

Travelling with your own vehicle allows increased flexibility and the option to get off the beaten track. Unfortunately, cars can be the proverbial ball-and-chain in city centres when you have to negotiate one-way streets or find somewhere to park amid a confusing concrete jungle and a welter of insanely expensive parking options.

Automobile Associations

Perish the thought of ever breaking down in some remote rural village in the Pyrenees or the isolated Irish countryside. But it happens. Should you find yourself in a predicament, you can contact the local automobile association for emergency assistance if it has an agreement with the auto club in your home country (and if you're a member!). These associations can provide a variety of roadside services such as petrol refills, flat-tyre repair and towing, plus predeparture information such as maps and itineraries and even an accommodation reservation service. Check with the main automobile association in your home country for coverage options.

Driving Licences

Proof of ownership of a private vehicle should always be carried (a Vehicle Registration Document for British-registered cars) when touring Europe. An EU driving licence is acceptable for driving throughout Europe.

Many non-European driving licences are valid in Europe. Some travel websites and auto clubs advise carrying an International Driving Permit (IDP), but this costly multilingual document sold by national auto clubs is not necessary in Western Europe – especially not to rent a car.

Fuel

Fuel prices can vary enormously from country to country (though it's always more expensive than in North America or Australia) and may bear little relation to the general cost of living. For fuel prices across the EU, surf over to the **AA Ireland** (www.aaroadwatch.ie/eupetrolprices) website.

Unleaded petrol and diesel are available across Western Europe.

Hire

The big international rental companies will give you reliable service and a good standard of vehicle. Usually you will have the option of returning the car to a different outlet at the end of the rental period. Rates vary widely, but expect to pay somewhere between €25 and €70 per day. Prebook for the lowest rates – if you walk into an office and ask for a car on the spot, you're likely to pay much more. For really good deals, prepay for your rental. Fly/drive combinations and other programs are worth looking into. All major firms operate in Western Europe.

Rental brokers can be a lot cheaper than the major rental firms. Good companies to try include the following:

Auto Europe (www.autoeurope.com)

AutosAbroad (www.autosabroad.com)

Holiday Autos Car Hire (www.holidayautos.com)

Kemwel (www.kemwel.com)

No matter where you rent from, it is imperative to understand exactly what is included in your rental agreement (collision waiver, unlimited mileage etc). Make sure you are covered with an adequate insurance policy. And take note: less than 4% of European cars have automatic transmissions, so if you're afraid of a stick, you'll pay more than double for your car.

The minimum age to rent a vehicle is usually 21 or even 23, and you'll need a credit card. If you get a ticket from one of Europe's thousands of hidden speeding cameras, they will track you down through your rental company.

Insurance

Third-party motor insurance is compulsory in Europe if you are driving your own car (rental cars usually come with insurance). Most UK motor-insurance policies automatically provide this for EU countries. Get your insurer to issue a Green Card (which may cost extra), which is an internationally recognised proof of insurance, and check that it lists all the countries you intend to visit.

It's a good investment to take out a European motoring-assistance policy, such as the AA Five Star Service or the RAC European Motoring Assistance. Expect to pay about £50 for 14 days' cover, with a 10% discount for association members. Non-Europeans might find it cheaper to arrange international coverage with their national motoring organisation before leaving home. Ask your motoring organisation for details about free services offered by affiliated organisations around Western Europe.

Every vehicle travelling across an international border should display a sticker showing its country of registration. Car rental/hire agencies usually ensure cars are properly equipped; when in doubt, ask. UK drivers should contact the following for more information.

AA (www.theaa.com)

RAC (www.rac.co.uk)

Purchase

Britain is probably the best place to buy a vehicle as secondhand prices are good and, whether buying privately or from a dealer, if you're an English-speaker the absence of language difficulties will help you establish what you are getting and what guarantees you can expect in the event of a breakdown.

Some good British papers to check out for vehicle purchases are **Loot** (www.loot.com) and **AutoTrader** (www.autotrader.co.uk).

Bear in mind that you will be getting a car with the steering wheel on the right-hand side in Britain. If you want left-hand drive and can afford to buy new, prices are usually reasonable in Greece, France, Germany, Belgium, Luxembourg and the Netherlands.

For a real adventure, consider buying a new car at the source. European car companies such as BMW, Mercedes and Volvo will sell the same model of car you'd buy in your home country but let you pick it up at the factory in Europe and drive it while on holiday. The company then has it shipped to your hometown.

Road Conditions

Conditions and types of roads vary across Western Europe, but it is possible to make some generalisations. The fastest routes are four- or six-lane dual carriageways/highways, ie two or three lanes either side (motorway, autobahn, autoroute, autostrada etc). These roads are great for speed and comfort but driving can be dull, with little or no interesting scenery. Some of these roads incur expensive tolls (eg in Italy, France and Spain) or have a general tax for usage (Switzerland and Austria), but there will usually be an alternative route you can take. Motorways and other primary routes are almost always in good condition.

Road surfaces on minor routes are not perfect in some countries (eg Greece), although normally they will be more than adequate. These roads are narrower and progress is generally much slower. To compensate, you can expect much better scenery and plenty of interesting villages along the way.

Road Rules

Automobile associations can supply members with country-by-country information about motoring regulations, or they may produce motoring guidebooks for general sale.

With the exception of Britain and Ireland, driving is on the right-hand side of the road.

Take care with speed limits, as they vary from country to country. You may be surprised at the apparent disregard of traffic regulations in some places (particularly in Italy and Greece), but as a visitor it is always best to be cautious. In many countries, driving infringements are subject to an on-the-spot fine; always ask for a receipt.

European drink-driving laws are particularly strict. The blood-alcohol concentration (BAC) limit when driving is between 0.05% and 0.08%, but in certain areas it can be 0%.

Hitching

Hitching is never entirely safe in any country and we don't recommend it. Travellers who decide to hitch should understand they are taking a small but potentially serious risk. Key points to remember:

» Hitch in pairs; it will be safer.

» Solo women should never hitch.

» Don't hitch from city centres; take public transport to suburban exit routes.

» Hitching is usually illegal on motorways – stand on the slip roads or approach drivers at petrol stations and truck stops.

» Look presentable and cheerful, and make a cardboard sign indicating your intended destination in the local language.

» Never hitch where drivers can't stop in good time or without causing an obstruction. At dusk, give up and think about finding somewhere to stay.

» It is sometimes possible to arrange a lift in advance: scan student noticeboards in colleges or contact car-sharing agencies. Such agencies are particularly popular in Germany where they're called *Mitfahrzentrale*.

Motorcycle

With its good-quality winding roads, stunning scenery and an active motorcycling scene, Western Europe is made for motorcycle touring. The weather is not always reliable, though, so make sure your wet-weather gear is up to scratch. The wearing of helmets for rider and passenger is compulsory everywhere in Western Europe.

On ferries, motorcyclists can sometimes be squeezed on board without a reservation, although booking ahead is certainly advisable during peak travelling periods.

Take note of local customs about parking motorcycles on footpaths. Although this is illegal in some countries, the police usually turn a blind eye as long as the vehicle doesn't obstruct pedestrians. Don't try this in Britain – your feeble excuses to traffic wardens will fall on deaf ears.

If you are thinking of touring Europe on a motorcycle, contact the **British Motorcyclists Federation** (☎0116-284 5380; www.bmf.co.uk) for help and advice.

Motorcycle and moped rental is easy in countries such as Italy, Spain, Greece and in the south of France. In tourist areas just ask around for nearby rental agencies.

Public Transport

Most Western European cities have excellent public transport systems, which comprise some combination of metros (subways), trains, trams and buses. Service is usually comprehensive. Major airports generally have fast-train or metro links to the city centre.

Taxi

Taxis in Western Europe are metered and rates are generally high. There might also be supplements (depending on the country) for things such as luggage, the time of day, the location at which you boarded and for extra passengers. Good public transport networks make the use of taxis almost unnecessary, but if you need one in a hurry they can usually be found idling near train stations or outside big hotels. Spain, Greece and Portugal have lower fares, which makes taking a taxi more viable.

Don't underestimate the local knowledge that can be gleaned from taxi drivers. They can often tell you about the liveliest places in town and know all about events happening during your stay.

Tours

Package tours, whether tailor-made or bog-standard, cater for all tastes, interests and ages. The internet is an excellent resource for finding unusual tours that might not receive media or trade attention. Many people have had memorable trips on tours organised by cultural institutions such as the **US**

Smithsonian Institution (www.smithsonian.com), which run tours lead by experts in fields such as art. Try searching for your own interest (eg walking) with 'Europe tour' and see what you get.

Train

Trains are a popular way of getting around: they are comfortable, frequent and generally on time. The Channel Tunnel makes it possible to get from Britain to Continental Europe using **Eurostar** (www.eurostar.com). For many people, travel in Europe would not be travel in Europe without trains. But note that the traditional image of compartments with little wine-bottle holders and various colourful characters roaming the corridor has been completely replaced by fast, modern trains that are more like much-more-comfortable versions of airliners. Diners have mostly been replaced by snack bars or trolleys, although most people buy their food before boarding.

Information

Every national railway has a website with a vast amount of schedule and fare information. Other recommended websites include the following:

DB Bahn (www.bahn.de) Excellent schedule and fare information in English for trains across Europe.

Man In Seat Sixty-One (www.seat61.com) Invaluable train descriptions and details of journeys to the far reaches of the continent.

If you plan to travel extensively by train, you might enjoy the Thomas Cook *European Rail Timetable*, which gives a cleverly condensed listing of train schedules that indicate where extra fees apply or where reservations are necessary. The timetable is updated monthly and is available from **Thomas Cook** (www.thomascookpublishing.com) outlets and bookshops in the UK (order online elsewhere in the world).

Most of the major national railway companies in Europe also offer apps for smartphones. These are excellent ways to check schedules and many can be used to store tickets bought online or through the phone.

Instead of having to print that cheap ticket you bought online, the conductor can scan a screen on your phone.

Tickets

Normal international tickets are valid for two months and you can make as many stops as you like en route. Used this way, a ticket from Paris to Vienna can serve as a mini railpass, as long as you stay on the route shown on the ticket.

High-Speed Trains

Western European trains (outside of Greece and Portugal) are often fast, frequent and usually comfortable. High-speed networks (300km/h or more) continue to expand and have given the airlines major competition on many routes.

Some sample travel times include the following:

ROUTE	DURATION
Amsterdam–Paris	3hr
Barcelona–Madrid	3hr
Brussels–Cologne	2¼hr
London–Paris	2¼hr
Milan–Rome	4hr
Nuremberg–Munich	1hr
Paris–Frankfurt	3¾hr
Paris–Marseille	3hr
Zürich–Milan	3¾hr

Major high-speed trains that cross borders include the following:

Eurostar (www.eurostar.com) Links beautiful St Pancras station in London to Brussels and Paris in about two hours.

ICE (www.bahn.de) The fast trains of the German railways span the country and extend to Paris, Brussels, Amsterdam, Vienna and Switzerland.

TGV (www.sncf.com) The legendary fast trains of France reach Belgium, Luxembourg, Germany, Switzerland and Italy.

Thalys (www.thalys.com) Links Paris with Brussels, Amsterdam and Cologne.

Other Trains

It does bear reiterating: you'll have a splendid holiday in Western Europe if you rely entirely on the convenient, comfortable trains.

NIGHT TRAINS

The romantic image of the European night train is becoming a lot less common with the popularity of budget airlines; however, you can still find a good network of routes from the north to Italy. Besides the national railways, you can try:

Caledonian Sleeper (www.scotrail.co.uk) Links London overnight with Scotland (as far north as Inverness and Aberdeen).

City Night Line (www.citynightline.de) Operates night trains from Germany and the Netherlands south through Switzerland and Austria into Italy as well as France.

Thello (www.thello.com) Runs services between Paris and Rome and points in between.

On the trains, look for these types of accommodation:

Couchette Bunks that are comfortable enough, if lacking a bit in privacy. There are four per compartment in 1st class or six in 2nd class. A bunk costs about €15 for most international trains, irrespective of the length of the journey.

Sleepers (wagon-lits) The most comfortable option, offering beds for one or two passengers in 1st class, and two or three passengers in 2nd class. Charges vary depending on the journey, but they are significantly more expensive than couchettes. Expect to pay at least €100 per person.

EXPRESS TRAINS

Slower but still reasonably fast trains that cross borders are often called **EuroCity** (EC) or **InterCity** (IC). Reaching speeds of up to 200km/h or more, they are comfortable and frequent. A good example is Austria's **Railjet** service, which reaches Munich and Zürich.

Reservations

At weekends and during holidays and the summer, it's a good idea to reserve seats on trains (which costs about €3 to €5). Standing at the end of the car for five hours is not what holiday dreams are made of. Some heavily discounted tickets bought online may include an assigned seat on a train, but most regular tickets are good for any train on the route.

You can usually reserve ahead of time using a ticket machine in stations or at a ticket window. On many high-speed trains – such as France's TGVs – reservations are mandatory.

Pass-holders should note that reservations are a good idea for the same reasons. Just because your pricey pass lets you hop-on/hop-off at will, there's no guarantee that you'll have a seat.

Train Passes

Think carefully about purchasing a rail pass. In particular, prices for the multitude of Eurail passes have become quite expensive. Spend a little time online checking the national railways' websites and determine what it would cost to do your trip by buying the tickets separately. More often than not, you'll find that you'll spend less than if you buy a Eurail pass.

Shop around as pass prices can vary between different outlets. Once purchased, take care of your pass as it cannot be replaced or refunded if lost or stolen. Passes get reductions on the Eurostar through the Channel Tunnel and on certain ferry routes (eg between France and Ireland). In the USA, **Rail Europe** (www.raileurope.com) sells a variety of rail passes; note that its individual train tickets tend to be more expensive than what you'll pay buying from railways online or in stations.

EURAIL

There are so many different **Eurail** (www.eurail.com) passes to choose from and such a wide variety of areas and time periods covered that you need to have a good idea of your itinerary before purchasing one. These passes can only be bought by residents of non-European countries and are supposed to be purchased before arriving in Europe. There are two flavours: one for adults and one for people aged under 26.

Eurail passes are valid for unlimited travel on national railways and some private lines in the Western European countries of Austria, Belgium, France, Germany, Greece, Ireland, Italy, Luxembourg, the Netherlands, Portugal, Spain and Switzerland (including Liechtenstein), plus several more neighbouring ones. They are also valid on some ferries between Italy and Greece. Reductions are given on some other ferry routes and on river/lake steamer services in various countries and on the Eurostar to/from the UK. The UK is *not* covered by Eurail – it has its own Britrail pass.

Pass types include the following:

Eurail Global All the European countries (despite the much grander-sounding name) for a set number of consecutive days.

DISCOUNT TRAIN TICKETS ONLINE

Many railways offer cheap ticket deals through their websites. It's always worth checking online for the same kinds of sales we now expect from budget airlines, including advance-purchase reductions, one-off promotions and special circular-route tickets.

How you actually receive the discount train tickets you've purchased online varies. Common methods include the following:

» Reservation number issued with the reservation which you use at a station ticket-vending machine (some UK lines).

» Credit card you used to purchase the tickets at a station ticket-vending machine (France, but non-French credit card holders must retrieve their tickets at a ticket window).

» Ticket is emailed to buyer who then prints it out (Germany).

» The ticket is sent to the passenger's cell phone either as an email or as a stored graphic on an app from the train company.

» Nonlocal credit cards aren't accepted online and you can't buy the discounted fares at the station (the Netherlands).

RAIL PASS RATES

Eurail Passes

AGE	CLASS	VALID FOR	PRICE (€)
12-25	2nd	1 month	586
12-25	2nd	15 days	369
over 26	1st	1 month	899
over 26	1st	15 days	567
12-25	2nd	10 days in 2 months	435
12-25	2nd	15 days in 2 months	571
over 26	1st	10 days in 2 months	668
over 26	1st	15 days in 2 months	876

InterRail Passes

AGE	CLASS	VALID FOR	PRICE (€)
12-25	2nd	5 days in 10 days	181
12-25	2nd	10 days in 22 days	265
12-25	2nd	1 month	435
over 26	1st	5 days in 10 days	434
over 26	1st	10 days in 22 days	618
over 26	1st	1 month	1034

Eurail Saver Two to five people travelling together as a group for the entire trip can save about 15% on various pass types.

Eurail Selectpass Buyers choose which neighbouring countries it covers and for how long. Options are myriad and can offer significant savings over the other passes if, for example, you are only going to three or four countries. Use the Eurail website to calculate these.

EXTRA FEES

Eurail likes to promote the hop-on/hop-off any train aspect of their passes. But when it comes to the most desirable high-speed trains this is not always the case. While German ICE trains may be used at will, French TGVs require a seat reservation and the catch is that these are not always available to pass holders on all trains. In addition, some of the high-speed services like Thalys trains require a fairly hefty surcharge from pass users (1st class/2nd class €41/€26).

INTERRAIL

The **InterRail** (www.interrailnet.com) pass is available to European residents of more than six months' standing (passport identification is required). Terms and conditions vary slightly from country to country, but in the country of origin there is a discount of around 50% on the normal fares. The pass covers up to 30 countries.

InterRail passes are generally cheaper than Eurail, but most high-speed trains require that you also buy a seat reservation and pay a supplement of €3 to €40 depending on the route.

InterRail passes are also available for individual countries. Compare these to passes offered by the national railways.

NATIONAL RAIL PASSES

If you're intending to travel extensively within one country, check what national rail passes are available as these can sometimes save you a lot of money. In a large country such as Germany where you might be covering long distances, a pass can make sense, whereas in a small country such as the Netherlands it won't.